AMG's COMPREHENSIVE DICTIONARY *of* NEW TESTAMENT WORDS

E. RICHARD PIGEON, Ph.D.
with Gretchen S. Lebrun

God's Word to you is our highest calling.

AMG's Comprehensive Dictionary of New Testament Words

Published by AMG Publishers
6815 Shallowford Road
Chattanooga, TN 37421-1755

Based on and adapted from *Dictionnaire du Nouveau Testament* by E. Richard Pigeon.

Unless otherwise noted Scripture "quotations" are either English translations of the author's paraphrased renderings in the original French edition of the work or simply paraphrases in English.

ISBN 13: 978-0-89957-740-1
ISBN 10: 0-89957-740-7
EPUB ISBN: 978-1-61715-301-3
MOBI ISBN: 978-1-61715-302-0

Edited by Dr. Warren Baker, Richard Wright, and Ken Campbell.
Cover design by Michael Largent of InView Graphics.
Interior design by Adept Content Solutions.

Printed in Canada
19 18 17 16 15 14 –M– 6 5 4 3 2 1

Table of Contents

Preface

AMG's Comprehensive Dictionary of New Testament Words covers all the common words (nouns, verbs, adjectives, etc.) and all the proper names (both people and places) found in the New Testament (N.T.). It was written to serve as a primary multifunctional reference tool for students of the N.T., those who teach the Word of God, and all those who read it, with or without knowledge of the Greek language. Those who use this tool will develop an appreciation for the richness of the Greek words and expressions used in the books of the N.T. They will also cultivate a deeper knowledge and understanding of the mind of God through comprehension of the terms used by the authors of the 27 books of the N.T. who wrote them under the direction of the Holy Spirit.

The idea of a dictionary of all the words of the N.T. came to me after consulting, at the beginning of my Christian life, the excellent work in the English language by W. E. Vine, *An Expository Dictionary of New Testament Words*. Some years ago I wanted to make available to French-language readers a similar dictionary of N.T. terms with their meanings, Greek etymologies, and biblical references. The resulting *Dictionnaire du Nouveau Testament* was published in France by Éditions Bibles et Publications Chrétiennes in 2008. In recent years we have translated and adapted that work into English. *AMG's Comprehensive Dictionary of New Testament Words* takes into consideration terms used by seven different translations of the Bible, all excellent and trustworthy: English Standard Version®, J. N. Darby, King James Version, New American Standard Bible®, New International Version® (1984, 2011), and New King James Version®.

In Part I of *AMG's Comprehensive Dictionary of New Testament Words*, I have indicated, in the vast majority of cases, all the Biblical references for the entries of the terms listed, thus allowing the work to serve as a concordance also. It contains definitions for all N.T. Greek terms listed in *Strong's Exhaustive Concordance of the Bible* and other terms (identified by the closest Strong's number followed by an "a"). Part II of this comprehensive dictionary is a lexicon of Greek terms that relates each one to the entries of the corresponding English terms. Part I of the dictionary comprises common words as well as the names of people and places in alphabetical order; Part II comprises the Greek words in Strong's coding order.

For each English term listed, the reader will find the corresponding Greek term or terms. As a general rule, each entry or subentry includes the transliteration of the Greek word, the part of speech of the word, the Greek word, the Strong's number, as well as the etymology of the word and the meaning of the name of the person or place. It includes as well a definition of the term, paraphrased verses enabling the reader to understand the context in which the term is used, other N.T. references, and, if occasions arise, different Greek words found in other manuscripts. Different English terms used in other versions of the N.T. are provided in braces "{}". The present work contains more than 8,000 English terms that are defined or presented as cross-references, and approximately 5,600 Greek terms.

I am grateful to the Lord who, during the years of research, writing, and editing these dictionaries in French and English, sustained me and gave me the courage to persevere. I wish to express my gratitude to those who have collaborated in the work of translation, adaptation, correction, and revision of the French and Greek of the original work. In a special way I note the thoroughness and dedication of Gretchen S. Lebrun, the person mainly responsible for the translation and adaptation of this work into English. She has sought through much research to better understand the Greek terms of the N.T. and to translate my French definitions of these terms as well as possible, on occasions with increased precision. Guy-Bernard Roy and André Mathez have also participated in the revision of this dictionary, each with exemplary dedication and conviction. I thank the three of you for sharing my vision to produce a tool for understanding the Scriptures that is within the reach of everyone.

I especially thank my wife Géraldine, who from the beginning believed in the project of a N.T. dictionary and whose unwavering support allowed me to devote thousands of hours of work to realize it. Likewise, I thank my sons Antoine, Marc, and Benjamin for their interest and their practical involvement in the work of the dictionary on many occasions.

Finally, I thank my editor, AMG Publishers, and Dr. Warren Baker especially, who also believed in the project and collaborated in the production of this work. I am indebted to AMG for their authorization to use their definitions of *The Complete Word Study Dictionary New Testament* for some 200 Greek words. Nevertheless, of course, I assume full responsibility for any errors or omissions in the dictionary.

Dear reader, the last Greek word in the Greek-English lexicon of this work is ὠφέλιμος (*ōphelimos*), which means "profitable," "useful," "having value." It is my sincere desire that you will find this dictionary useful when studying the word of God, teaching it, or serving the Lord. Please do not hesitate to write to me or the editor to share your comments and your suggestions for a future edition, if the Lord permits. We are currently working on a translation and adaptation of this work into Spanish. Thank you for your interest, and now I welcome you to begin exploring the pages of *AMG's Comprehensive Dictionary of New Testament Words!*

E. Richard Pigeon
Gatineau (Quebec)
Canada
erpigeon@videotron.ca
April 2014

Abbreviations and Symbols

acc.	→	accusative
adj.	→	adjective
adv.	→	adverb
approx.	→	approximately
Aram.	→	Aramaic
art.	→	article
card.	→	cardinal
comp.	→	compare
compar.	→	comparative
cond.	→	conditional
conj.	→	conjunction
defin.	→	definition
dimin.	→	diminutive
Engl.	→	English
e.g.	→	for example (*exempli gratia*)
et al.	→	and others (*et alii*)
expr(s).	→	expression(s)
fem.	→	feminine
figur.	→	figurative, figuratively
Heb.	→	Hebrew, Hebraic
i.e.	→	that is (*id est*)
imper.	→	imperative
indef.	→	indefinite
indic.	→	indicative
intens.	→	intensive
interj.	→	interjection
KJV	→	King James Version
Lat.	→	Latin
lit.	→	literal, literally
masc.	→	masculine
mss.	→	manuscript(s)
N.T.	→	New Testament
neg.	→	negative (privative)
neut.	→	neuter
num.	→	number, numeral
ord.	→	ordinal
O.T.	→	Old Testament
other ref(s).	→	other reference(s) where the Greek word is found
pass.	→	passive
perf.	→	perfect
plur.	→	plural
poss.	→	possibly
prep.	→	preposition
pres.	→	present
prob.	→	probably
pron.	→	pronoun
ptcp.	→	participle, participial
ref(s).	→	reference(s) where the Greek word is found
sing.	→	singular
superl.	→	superlative
syn.	→	synonym
transl.	→	translated, translation(s)
v.	→	verse
vv.	→	verses
var.	→	variant of
¶	→	indication of the completeness of references provided
*	→	not all N.T. references provided in the Dictionary
{text…}	→	translated word or phrase in one or more N.T. versions
‡	→	definition borrowed from *The Complete Word Study Dictionary: New Testament*

Books of the Bible

Old Testament Books

Gen.	→	Genesis
Ex.	→	Exodus
Lev.	→	Leviticus
Num.	→	Numbers
Deut.	→	Deuteronomy
Josh.	→	Joshua
Judg.	→	Judges
Ruth	→	Ruth
1 Sam.	→	1 Samuel
2 Sam.	→	2 Samuel
1 Kgs.	→	1 Kings
2 Kgs.	→	2 Kings
1 Chr.	→	1 Chronicles
2 Chr.	→	2 Chronicles
Ezra	→	Ezra
Neh.	→	Nehemiah
Esther	→	Esther
Job	→	Job
Ps.	→	Psalms
Prov.	→	Proverbs
Eccl.	→	Ecclesiastes
Song	→	Song of Solomon
Is.	→	Isaiah
Jer.	→	Jeremiah
Lam.	→	Lamentations
Ezek.	→	Ezekiel
Dan.	→	Daniel
Hos.	→	Hosea
Joel	→	Joel
Amos	→	Amos
Obad.	→	Obadiah
Jon.	→	Jonah
Mic.	→	Micah
Nah.	→	Nahum
Hab.	→	Habakkuk
Zeph.	→	Zephaniah
Hag.	→	Haggai
Zech.	→	Zechariah
Mal.	→	Malachi

New Testament Books

Matt.	→	Matthew
Mark	→	Mark
Luke	→	Luke
John	→	John
Acts	→	Acts
Rom.	→	Romans
1 Cor.	→	1 Corinthians
2 Cor.	→	2 Corinthians
Gal.	→	Galatians
Eph.	→	Ephesians
Phil.	→	Philippians
Col.	→	Colossians
1 Thes.	→	1 Thessalonians
2 Thes.	→	2 Thessalonians
1 Tim.	→	1 Timothy
2 Tim.	→	2 Timothy
Titus	→	Titus
Phm.	→	Philemon
Heb.	→	Hebrews
Jas.	→	James
1 Pet.	→	1 Peter
2 Pet.	→	2 Peter
1 John	→	1 John
2 John	→	2 John
3 John	→	3 John
Jude	→	Jude
Rev.	→	Revelation

Guide to the Transliteration and Erasmian Pronunciation of the Greek Alphabet

Capital Letter	Small Letter	Greek Name	Transliteration	Phonetic Sound	Example
Α	α	alpha	*a*	a	f**a**ther
Β	β	bēta	*b*	b	a**b**ove
Γ	γ	gamma	*g*	g	**g**ame
Δ	δ	delta	*d*	d	**d**ebt
Ε	ε	epsilon	*e*	e	m**e**t (short)
Ζ	ζ	zēta	*z*	z	**z**ebra
Η	η	ēta	*ē*	ee	s**ee** (long)
Θ	θ	thēta	*th*	th	**th**in
Ι	ι	iōta	*i*	i	mach**i**ne or f**i**t
Κ	κ	kappa	*k*	k	**k**ill
Λ	λ	lambda	*l*	l	**l**and
Μ	μ	mu	*m*	m	**m**other
Ν	ν	nu	*n*	n	**n**ow
Ξ	ξ	xi	*x*	x	wa**x**
Ο	ο	omicron	*o*	o	h**o**t (short)
Π	π	pi	*p*	p	**p**et
Ρ	ρ	rho	*r, rh*	r	**r**un
Σ	σ, ς	sigma	*s*	s	**s**it
Τ	τ	tau	*t*	t	**t**ell (soft accent)
Υ	υ	upsilon	*u*	u	**u**nity
Φ	φ	phi	*ph*	ph	gra**ph**ic
Χ	χ	chi	*ch*	ch	lo**ch**
Ψ	ψ	psi	*ps*	ps	ti**ps**
Ω	ω	omega	*ō*	o	n**o**te (long)

Combinations of Consonants

Small Letter	Greek Names	Transliteration	Phonetic Sound	Example
γγ	gamma + gamma	*ng*	ng	a**ng**le
γκ	gamma + kappa	*nk*	nk	ma**nk**ind
γξ	gamma + xi	*nx*	nx	lary**nx**
γχ	gamma + chi	*nch*	nch	i**nch**

Diphthongs (double vowels)

Small Letter	Greek Names	Transliteration	Phonetic Sound	Example
αι	alpha + iōta	*ai*	ai	**ai**sle
αυ	alpha + upsilon	*au*	ou	h**ou**se
ει	epsilon + iōta	*ei*	ai	n**ai**l
ευ	epsilon + upsilon	*eu*	eu	f**eu**d
υι	upsilon + iōta	*ui*	we	**we**ek
ηυ	ēta + upsilon	*ēu*	eu	f**eu**d
οι	omicron + iōta	*oi*	oi	t**oi**l
ου	omicron + upsilon	*ou*	oo	f**oo**d

Breathings (only with initial vowels)

(’) Smooth, not transliterated or pronounced.
When words begin with vowels, it may occur at the beginning of words with every vowel or double vowel. For instance, ἔργον (*ergon*: work); εὐχή (*euchē*: vow).

(‘) Rough = h.
When words begin with vowels, it may occur at the beginning of words with every vowel or double vowel. There is no distinction in pronunciation from the smooth breathing. To indicate the rough breathing, the “h” is used in the transliteration. For instance, ἥλιος (*hēlios*: sun).

Explanations of Entries

Part I – Entry for a Common Word

For each entry of an English N.T. word being defined in this Comprehensive Dictionary, information is provided about the Greek word translated: its English transliteration, the part of speech of the word (noun, verb, etc.), the Greek word with the corresponding Strong's number, as well as information on the etymology of the word. A definition of the Greek word and its corresponding English word follows. Verses where the word is found in the N.T. are paraphrased and/or references are provided. In a large number of entries, all references are given (indicated by the sign ¶). In a few entries, an * indicates that all references are not given. Numerous cross references of terms used in other versions of the N.T. are provided and linked to definitions of common words and names of people and places.

① English word
② Transliteration of Greek word
③ Part of speech of the word in Greek
④ Greek word
⑤ Strong's Number
⑥ Etymology
⑦ Definition
⑧ Paraphrased verse(s)
⑨ Biblical reference for each verse
⑩ Cross-references for same Greek word
⑪ Indication of the completeness of references provided
⑫ Cross-reference(s) for the English word leading to another entry

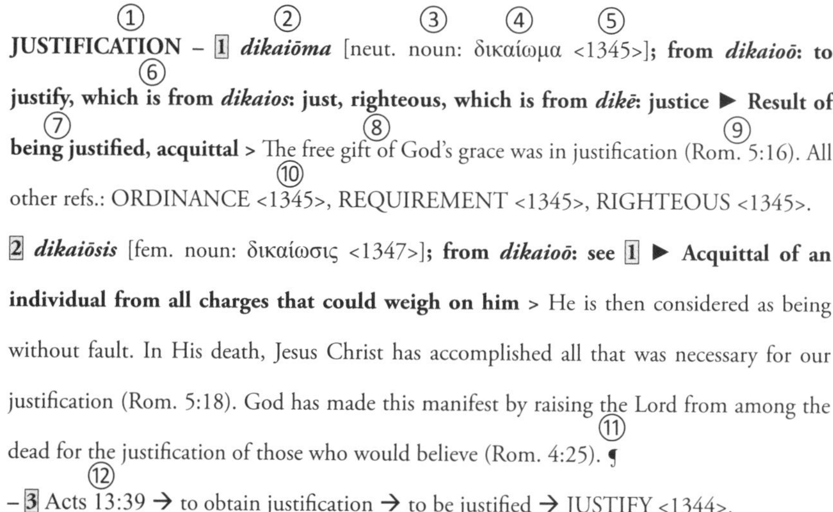

JUSTIFICATION – [1] ***dikaiōma*** [neut. noun: δικαίωμα <1345>]; **from *dikaioō*: to justify, which is from *dikaios*: just, righteous, which is from *dikē*: justice ► Result of being justified, acquittal** > The free gift of God's grace was in justification (Rom. 5:16). All other refs.: ORDINANCE <1345>, REQUIREMENT <1345>, RIGHTEOUS <1345>.

[2] ***dikaiōsis*** [fem. noun: δικαίωσις <1347>]; **from *dikaioō*: see [1] ► Acquittal of an individual from all charges that could weigh on him** > He is then considered as being without fault. In His death, Jesus Christ has accomplished all that was necessary for our justification (Rom. 5:18). God has made this manifest by raising the Lord from among the dead for the justification of those who would believe (Rom. 4:25). ¶

– [3] Acts 13:39 → to obtain justification → to be justified → JUSTIFY <1344>.

Part I – Entry for a Name of Person or Place

For each entry of an English name of person or place used in the N.T., information is provided about the Greek name translated: its English transliteration, the gender of the name or place in Greek, the Greek name with the corresponding Strong's number, as well as the etymology and/or meaning of the name when known. Information on the person or place is then provided. Verses where the word is found in the N.T. are paraphrased and/or references are provided. All references are given, unless indicated by an asterisk.

① English name
② Transliteration of Greek name
③ Part of speech of the word in Greek
④ Greek name
⑤ Strong's Number
⑥ Etymology and/or meaning
⑦ Definition
⑧ Paraphrased verse(s)
⑨ Reference for each verse
⑩ Indication of the completeness of references provided

① **DEMETRIUS** – ② ***Dēmētrios*** [③ masc. name: ④ Δημήτριος ⑤ <1216>]; **from Demeter,** ⑥ **agrarian divinity ▶ a. Ephesian** ⑦ **who made silver shrines of the goddess Diana** > This ⑧ Demetrius stirred up the other artisans against Paul, fearing that the temple of Diana (or: Artemis) would lose its prestige, which would have reduced their business (Acts ⑨ 19:24, 38). **b. Believing man of the N.T.** > The apostle John wrote concerning a Demetrius who had a good report of all, and of the truth itself (3 John 12). ⑩ ¶

Part I – Entry for Cross-References

Numerous cross-references of terms are provided and linked to definitions of common words and names of people and places. It is possible that you may not find an English word of interest in Part I. However, if you know the Greek term, you can find the cross-reference by consulting the Greek-English Lexicon in Part II.

① English term
② Reference
③ Target Entry
④ Corresponding Strong's number

①   ②   ③   ④

DISCOURSE (noun) – 1 Luke 7:1 → SAYING <4487> 2 Acts 1:1 → ACCOUNT (noun) <3056> 3 Acts 20:7 → MESSAGE <3056> 4 1 Tim. 1:6 → vain discourse → VAIN <3150>.

Part II – GREEK-ENGLISH LEXICON

Part II of this Comprehensive Dictionary provides a list of all N.T. terms and, for each one, its corresponding English common word or name of person or place. The Strong's number, the English transliteration, and the frequency is also given for each Greek term. Frequencies of some terms may vary from those indicated by other authors, given that different manuscripts may have been considered.

① Strong's number
② Greek term
③ Transliteration of Greek term
④ Target entries
⑤ Frequency of Greek term in the N.T.

①   ②   ③   ④   ⑤

<20> ἀγαλλίασις ***agalliasis*** [GLADNESS 1, JOY (noun) 1] 5x

<21> ἀγαλλιάω ***agalliaō*** [EXULT 1, to exult: EXULTATION 1, REJOICE 1] 11x

<22> ἄγαμος ***agamos*** [UNMARRIED 1] 4x

<23> ἀγανακτέω ***aganakteō*** [to be indignant: INDIGNANT 1] 7x

Part I

Dictionary of New Testament Words

 **A** 

AARON – ***Aarōn*** [masc. name: Ἀαρών <2>] **▶ Older brother of Moses (see Ex. 4:14; 6:20)** > Elizabeth was a descendant of Aaron (Luke 1:5). The sons of Israel told Aaron to make them gods in the absence of Moses (Acts 7:40; see vv. 37–41). Despite his failures, as head of the priestly line in Israel, Aaron represents Christ in His office of high priest (Heb. 5:4; see v. 5). His holy clothes (see Exodus 28) speak figur. of the glories of the Lord exercising His present priesthood of intercession for Christians (Heb. 7:11; see 7:26–28 and 9:24). Aaron's rod that had budded was kept in the ark of the covenant (Heb. 9:4). ¶

ABADDON – ***Abaddōn*** [masc. name: Ἀβαδδών <3>]**: destruction ▶ Hebrew term found in the O.T. (Job 26:6; 28:22; 31:12; Ps. 88:11; Prov. 15:11; 27:20)** > In Rev. 9:11, the name Abaddon (i.e., destruction) is symbolically given to the king of the locusts, the angel of the bottomless pit, a Satanic agent performing the first woe on unbelievers. In the same verse, the Greek name *Apolluōn* (Apollyon in Engl., i.e., destroyer) is given to him. ¶

ABANDON – [1] Acts 2:27 → LEAVE (verb) <1459> [2] Acts 2:31 → LEAVE (verb) <2641> [3] Acts 15:38; 1 Tim. 4:1 → DEPART <868> [4] Acts 27:20 → to be gradually abandoned → to be taken away → TAKE <4014> [5] 2 Cor. 4:9 → FORSAKE <1459> [6] 1 Tim. 5:12 → REJECT <114> [7] Jude 6 → LEAVE (verb) <620> [8] Jude 11 → to abandon oneself → to give oneself up → GIVE <1632> [9] Rev. 2:4 → LEAVE (verb) <863>.

ABANDONED – 2 Pet. 2:7 → LEWDNESS <766>.

ABASE – ***tapeinoō*** [verb: ταπεινόω <5013>]**; from *tapeinos*: humble ▶ To cause to become humble, to make low; pass.: to be in need** > Paul asks the Corinthians if he had committed a sin, abasing {humbling, lowering} himself in order that they might be exalted (2 Cor. 11:7). He knew both how to be abased {get along with humble means} and how to abound (Phil. 4:12). All other refs.: HUMBLE (verb) <5013>, LOW <5013>.

ABBA – ***Abba*** [Ἀββά <5>]**: Father ▶ Term in Aram. meaning "father" in the familiar sense of the word** > The name "abba" is not simply a mark of respect. It expresses also the affection and the confidence that a child has in his relationship with his father. Among the Jews, slaves were forbidden to address the head of the household by this name. In the N.T., we find the expr. "Abba, Father" three times in relation to God. First, when Jesus addresses Himself to His Father at Gethsemane, expressing then a most intimate relationship (Mark 14:36). Second, it is said of the Christian believers that they have received the Spirit of adoption whereby they cry: "Abba, Father" (Rom. 8:15). Finally, in Gal. 4:6, it is the Spirit crying in the hearts of Christians: "Abba, Father." ¶

ABEL – ***Abel*** [masc. name: Ἄβελ <6>]**: vapor, vanity, in Heb.; also written: Ἄβελ (*Habel*) ▶ Second son of Adam and Eve** > Jesus calls him "righteous Abel" (Matt. 23:35). He was killed by his brother Cain, who was jealous of the fact that God had respect for Abel's offering but not for his (Matt. 23:35; Luke 11:51; see Gen. 4:3–6). Abel offered to God a more excellent sacrifice than Cain (Heb. 11:4), because it spoke in advance of the sacrifice of Jesus Christ at the cross. The offering of Cain symbolizes man's deeds, which cannot redeem them. The blood of Jesus speaks better things than the blood of Abel (Heb. 12:24). ¶

ABHOR – [1] ***apostugeō*** [verb: ἀποστυγέω <655>]**; from *apo*: from (intens.), and *stugeō*: to hate ▶ To utterly detest, to flee with dread** > Christians are to abhor {hate} evil (Rom. 12:9). ¶

[2] ***bdelussomai*** [verb: βδελύσσομαι <948>]**; from *bdeō*: to stink ▶ To have in abomination, in horror; to detest** > Paul asks the one who abhors idols if he commits sacrilege (or: robs temples) (Rom. 2:22). This verb yields the adj. "abominable"

(*ebdelugmenos*) {vile} (Rev. 21:8); see ABOMINABLE <948>. ¶

ABIA – ***Abia*** [masc. name: Ἀβιά <7>]**: Jehovah is my father, in Heb. ▶ a. Name of a king of Judah, grandson of Solomon >** Abia is mentioned in the genealogy of Jesus Christ (Matt. 1:7). He is called Abijam in 1 Kgs. 15:1, 7a, b and Abijah in 2 Chr. 13:1, 2. **b. Family of priests >** Zacharias, the father of John the Baptist, was a member of that family (Luke 1:5). ¶

ABIATHAR – ***Abiathar*** [masc. name: Ἀβιαθάρ or Ἀβιάθαρ <8>]**: the great one is father, in Heb. ▶ A priest in Israel >** Abiathar escaped from Saul, who had commanded the murder of other priests, and he found refuge with David, whose lot he shared when David fled from Saul (see 1 Sam. 22:11–23). Jesus mentions Abiathar the high priest in Mark 2:26. ¶

ABIDE – [1] Matt. 10:11; Mark 6:10; 14:34; Luke 1:56; 8:27; 9:4; 10:7; 19:5; 24:29a, b; John 1:32, 33, 38, 39a, b; 2:12; 3:36; 4:40a, b; 5:38; 6:27, 56; 7:9; 8:35a, b; 10:40; 11:6; 12:24, 34, 46; 14:10, 16, 17, 25; 15:4a–c, 5, 6, 7a, b, 9, 10a, b, 16; 21:22, 23; Acts 16:15; 18:3; 21:7, 8; 27:31; Rom. 9:11; 1 Cor. 3:14; 7:8, 20, 24, 40; 13:13; 2 Cor. 3:11; Phil. 1:25; 2 Tim. 2:13; 3:14; 4:20; Heb. 7:3; 13:1; 1 John 2:6, 10, 14, 17, 24a–c, 27a, b, 28; 3:6, 9, 14, 15, 17, 24a, b; 4:12, 13, 15, 16a, b; 2 John 2, 9a, b → REMAIN <3306> [2] Luke 2:8 → to abide in the field, to abide without → FIELD <63> [3] Luke 21:37 → to stay at night → STAY (verb) <835> [4] John 3:22; Acts 12:19; 14:3, 28; 16:12; 20:6 → STAY (verb) <1304> [5] John 8:31 → CONTINUE <3306> [6] John 8:44 → STAND (verb) <2476> [7] Acts 1:13 → STAY (verb) <2650> [8] Acts 11:23 → CONTINUE <4357> [9] Acts 14:22; Gal. 3:10 → CONTINUE <1696> [10] Acts 15:34 → REMAIN <1961> [11] Acts 17:14 → REMAIN <5278> [12] Acts 20:23 → AWAIT <3306> [13] Rom. 11:22, 23; Col. 1:23 → CONTINUE <1961> [14] 1 Cor. 16:6 → STAY (verb) <3887> [15] Gal. 1:18; Phil. 1:24 → STAY (verb) <1961> [16] Phil. 1:25 → to abide with → to continue with → CONTINUE <4839> [17] 1 Tim. 1:3 → to abide still → REMAIN <4357> [18] Jas. 1:25 → CONTINUE <3887> [19] 1 Pet. 1:23 → which abides forever → LASTING <3306>.

ABIDING – Heb. 10:34; 13:14 → LASTING <3306>.

ABIHUD – ***Abioud*** [masc. name: Ἀβιούδ <10>]**: father of renown, in Heb. ▶ Man in the O.T., son of Zorobabel; also spelled: Abiud >** Abihud is mentioned in the genealogy of Jesus Christ (Matt. 1:13a, b). ¶

ABILENE – ***Abilēnē*** [fem. name: Ἀβιληνή <9>] **▶ Region in the north of Palestine (in Syria, northwest of Damascus) of which the capital was Abila >** Lysanias was the tetrarch of Abilene under the reign of Tiberius Caesar (Luke 3:1). ¶

ABILITY – [1] ***dunamis*** [fem. noun: δύναμις <1411>]**; from *dunamai*: to be able ▶ Means, possibility, capacity of doing something; also transl.: power >** In a parable, a man gave talents to his servants according to the particular ability of each one (Matt. 25:15). The churches of Macedonia had acted spontaneously according to their ability and beyond their ability (2 Cor. 8:3a, b), in contributing to the needs of the saints. All other refs.: MEANING <1411>, MIRACLE <1411>, POWER[1] <1411>, POWER[3] <1411>, STRENGTH <1411>.

– [2] Acts 8:19 → AUTHORITY <1849> [3] Acts 11:29 → according to his ability → as he had means → to have means → MEANS <2141> [4] Rom. 7:18 → "the ability" added in Engl. [5] 1 Cor. 10:13 → beyond your ability → beyond what you are able → ABLE <1410> [6] 1 Cor. 12:10 → ability to distinguish → DISCERNING <1253> [7] 1 Pet. 4:11 → STRENGTH <2479>.

ABIUD – See ABIHUD <10>.

ABLAZE – [1] Jas. 3:5 → to set ablaze → KINDLE <381> [2] Rev. 8:8 → all ablaze → burning → BURN <2545>.

ABLE – [1] ***dunatos*** [adj.: δυνατός <1415>]; **from *dunamai*: see [2] ▶ Apt, capable, powerful** > A king going to war considers first whether he is able to meet him who comes against him (Luke 14:31). Paul was not able to stand in God's way (Acts 11:17). He said that he was persuaded that Jesus Christ was able to keep the deposit he had entrusted to Him (2 Tim. 1:12). An overseer must be able to encourage with sound doctrine and refute those who contradict (Titus 1:9). Abraham considered that God was able to raise the dead (Heb. 11:19). A perfect man does not offend in words, but is able to bridle the whole body (Jas. 3:2). All other refs.: see entries in Lexicon at <1415>.

[2] **to be able: *dunamai*** [verb: δύναμαι <1410>] **▶ To be capable, to have the power to do something** > The word of God is able to build up Christians (Acts 20:32) and to save their souls (Jas. 1:21). The Christians in Rome were able {were competent} to admonish one another (Rom. 15:14). God was able to establish the Christians of Rome according to the glad tidings of Paul and the preaching of Jesus Christ (Rom. 16:25). Paul asks if there was no one among the Corinthians who would be able {be wise enough} to decide between his brothers (1 Cor. 6:5). Being encouraged by God, he would be able to {could} encourage others (2 Cor. 1:4). If a law had been able to {could} quicken, then righteousness would be on the principle of law (Gal. 3:21a, b). The Lord Jesus is able {has the power} to subdue all things to Himself (Phil. 3:21). He is able to aid those who are being tempted (Heb. 2:18). The high priest is able to {can} deal gently with those who are ignorant and erring (Heb. 5:2). God the Savior is able to keep Christians without stumbling (Jude 24). This Greek verb is most often transl. by "can." Other refs.: Matt. 3:9; 5:14, 36; 6:24, 27; 7:18; 8:2; 9:15, 28; 10:28a, b; 12:29, 34; 16:3; 17:16, 19; 19:12, 25; 20:22a, b; 22:46; 26:9, 42, 53, 61; 27:42; Mark 1:40, 45; 2:4, 7, 19a, b; 3:20, 23–27; 4:32, 33; 5:3; 6:5, 19; 7:15, 18, 24; 8:4; 9:3, 22, 23, 28, 29, 39; 10:26, 38, 39; 14:5, 7; 15:31; Luke 1:20, 22; 3:8; 5:12, 21, 34; 6:39, 42; 8:19; 9:40; 11:7; 12:25, 26; 13:11; 14:20, 26, 27, 33; 16:2, 13a, b, 26; 18:26; 19:3; 20:36; 21:15; John 1:46; 3:2, 3, 4a, b, 5, 9, 27; 5:19, 30, 44; 6:44, 52, 60, 65; 7:7, 34, 36; 8:21, 22, 43; 9:4, 16, 33; 10:21, 29, 35; 11:37; 12:39; 13:33, 36, 37; 14:5, 17; 15:4, 5; 16:12; Acts 4:16, 20; 5:39; 8:31; 10:47; 13:39; 15:1; 17:19; 19:40; 20:32; 21:34; 24:8, 11, 13; 25:11; 26:32; 27:12, 15, 31, 39, 43; Rom. 8:7, 8, 39; 1 Cor. 2:14; 3:1, 2a, b, 11; 7:21; 10:13a, b, 21a, b; 12:3, 21; 14:31; 15:50; 2 Cor. 3:7; 13:8; Eph. 3:4, 20; 6:11, 13, 16; 1 Thes. 2:6; 3:9; 1 Tim. 5:25; 6:7, 16; 2 Tim. 2:13; 3:7, 15; Heb. 3:19; 4:15; 5:7; 7:25; 9:9; 10:1, 11; Jas. 2:14; 3:8, 12; 4:2, 12; 1 John 3:9; 4:20; Rev. 2:2; 3:8; 5:3; 6:17; 7:9; 9:20; 13:4, 17; 14:3; 15:8. ¶

[3] ***hikanos*** [adj.: ἱκανός <2425>]; **from *hikneomai*: to come, to occur ▶ Competent, capable** > Paul was not able of {adequate in, sufficient of} himself to think anything as of himself, but his competency was of God (2 Cor. 3:5). Faithful men were to be able {qualified} to teach others (2 Tim. 2:2). Other refs.: see entries in Lexicon at <2425>.

[4] **to be able: *ischuō*** [verb: ἰσχύω <2480>]; **from *ischus*: capacity, strength ▶ To be capable, to have strength, to be strong >** Simon Peter was not able to watch one hour with Jesus (Mark 14:37), nor were the other apostles (Matt. 26:40). Paul was able to do all things in Him who gave him power (Phil. 4:13). The fervent supplication of the righteous man has much power (lit.: is very strong) (Jas. 5:16). Other refs.: Matt. 8:28; Mark 5:4; 9:18; Luke 6:48; 8:43; 13:24; 14:6, 29, 30; 16:3; 20:26; John 21:6; Acts 6:10; 15:10; 25:7; 27:16; Gal. 6:15 in some mss. All other refs.: see entries in Lexicon at <2480>.

[5] **to be able, to be fully able: *exischuō*** [verb: ἐξισχύω <1840>]; **from *ek*: intens., and *ischuō*: see [4]; lit.: to be strong enough ▶ To have the full capacity, to be entirely capable >** Paul was praying that the Ephesians would be fully able {might have

power} to understand the love of Christ (Eph. 3:18). ¶
– 6 Luke 21:36 → to be able → lit.: to count worthy → WORTHY <2661> 7 Acts 11:29 → as each one was able → lit.: according as he had means → MEANS <2141> 8 2 Cor. 3:6 → to make able → to make competent → COMPETENT <2427> 9 2 Cor. 8:3a → as much as they were able → lit.: according to their ability → ABILITY <1411> 10 1 Tim. 3:2; 2 Tim. 2:24 → able to teach → TEACH <1317> 11 Heb. 4:12 → able to judge → DISCERNER <2924>.

ABNORMAL – Luke 14:2 → suffering from abnormal swelling of the body → DROPSICAL <5203>.

ABOARD – Acts 21:2, 6 → to go aboard → BOARD (verb) <1910>.

ABODE – John 14:2, 23 → MANSION <3438>.

ABOLISH – 1 ***katargeō*** [verb: καταργέω <2673>]; **from *kata*: intens., and *argeō*: to be inactive, which is from *a*: neg. and *ergon*: work ▶ To abrogate, to make disappear, to destroy; also transl.: to annul** > Christ has abolished the enmity, which is the law of commandments in ordinances (Eph. 2:15). The Savior Jesus Christ has abolished death (2 Tim. 1:10). All other refs.: see entries in Lexicon at <2673>.
– 2 Matt. 5:17a, b → DESTROY <2647>.

ABOMINABLE – 1 ***athemitos*** [adj.: ἀθέμιτος <111>]; **from *a*: neg., and *themitos*: lawful, legal, which is from *themis*: law, prerogative, rights ▶ Illegal, criminal, but also profane, impious** > Before their conversion, Christians had walked in abominable {detestable, unhallowed} idolatries (1 Pet. 4:3). Other ref.: Acts 10:28; see UNLAWFUL <111>. ¶
2 ***bdeluktos*** [adj.: βδελυκτός <947>]; **from *bdelussō*: to abhor, to detest ▶ Which provokes disgust, repulsion; detestable** > The term "abominable" characterizes those who profess to know God, but deny Him in their works; they are also disobedient and found unfit for any good work (Titus 1:16). ¶
3 ***ebdelugmenos*; perf. pass. ptcp. of *bdelussomai*** [verb: βδελύσσομαι <948>]: **to abhor, to detest ▶ Someone who is an object of horror, a depraved person** > Those who make themselves abominable {detestable, vile} will have their part in the lake of fire and brimstone (Rev. 21:8). Other ref.: Rom. 2:22; see ABHOR <948>. ¶
– 4 Rev. 17:4 → abominable thing → ABOMINATION <946>.

ABOMINATION – ***bdelugma*** [neut. noun: βδέλυγμα <946>]; **from *bdelussō*: to abhor, to detest ▶ A detestable, repulsive object in the eyes of God and true Christian believers; what takes the place of God in the life of a person** > In the O.T., an abomination is an idol (see 2 Kgs. 23:13; Is. 44:19; Ezek. 16:36) which is repulsive in the eyes of God. Matt. 24:15 and Mark 13:14 make reference to the abomination of desolation mentioned by Daniel the prophet (see Dan. 9:24–27) which will be established in the temple rebuilt in Jerusalem. It will bring a great desolation on the Jews and Jerusalem. The golden cup full of abominations {abominable things} (Rev. 17:4) refers to moral corruptions Babylon offers the world; she is the mother of the abominations of the earth (v. 5). Anyone that makes an abomination {does what is shameful} will not enter into the new Jerusalem (Rev. 21:27). In Luke 16:15, what is highly thought of among men (i.e., love of money; see v. 14) is an abomination {detestable} before God. ¶

ABOUND – 1 ***perisseuō*** [verb: περισσεύω <4052>]; **from *perissos*: abundant, which is from *peri*: above, beyond ▶ To surpass the measure, to exceed; also transl.: to be abundant, to be more abundant, to excel, to increase, to overflow** > Someone may say that his lie makes the truth of God to abound more to the glory of God, but he will still be judged for it (Rom. 3:7). The grace of God and the free gift of grace of Jesus Christ have abounded to many (Rom. 5:15). Christians can abound in hope by the power of the Holy Spirit (Rom. 15:13) and in the faith with thanksgiving (Col. 2:7). As the sufferings of the Christ abounded in the life of Paul and Timothy, so their encouragement also abounded through the Christ (2 Cor. 1:5a {to flow over}, v. 5b {to be in abundance}). The abundance of the joy and the deep poverty of the Macedonian churches abounded {welled up} in the riches of their liberality (2 Cor. 8:2). Paul asks the Corinthians, who abounded in every way, to see that they may abound also in the grace of giving to other saints (2 Cor. 8:7a, b). God is able to make every gracious gift abound (2 Cor. 9:8a). Christians should abound always {give themselves fully} in the work of the Lord (1 Cor. 15:58); they should also abound in every good work (2 Cor. 9:8b), in love (Phil. 1:9; 1 Thes. 4:10 {to do so more and more}), and in a walk pleasing to God (1 Thes. 4:1 {to do so more and more}). Christians are to increase and abound {overflow} in love toward one another (1 Thes. 3:12). The grace abounding (*pleonazō*) through the many may cause thanksgiving to abound {redound} (*perisseuō*) to the glory of God (2 Cor. 4:15). Paul's service was abounding by many thanksgivings to God (2 Cor. 9:12). God has caused the riches of His grace to abound toward {has lavished on, upon} the Christians (Eph. 1:8; see v. 7). By Paul's presence again with the Philippians, their boasting in Christ Jesus would abound (Phil. 1:26). Paul knew both how to abound {have abundance, have plenty, live in plenty, live in prosperity} and how to suffer deprivation (Phil. 4:12a, b); he had all things in full supply and abounded {had in abundance, even more}, having received the gift from the Philippians (v. 18). The verb is transl. "to be the better" in 1 Cor. 8:8. All other refs.: see entries in Lexicon at <4052>.

2 to abound much more, to abound all the more: *huperperisseuō* [verb: ὑπερπερισσεύω <5248>]; **from *huper*: beyond, and *perisseuō*: see 1 ▶ To abound excessively, to overflow excessively; also transl.: to increase all the more, to overabound, to overflow** > Where sin abounded (*pleonazō*), grace has overabounded (*huperperisseuō*) (Rom. 5:20). Paul overabounded in joy in all his affliction (2 Cor. 7:4). ¶

3 *pleonazō* [verb: πλεονάζω <4121>]; **from *pleon*: more ▶ To surpass in quantity, to exceed; also transl.: to increase** > The law came in, in order that the offense might abound (*pleonazō*), but where sin abounded (*pleonazō*), grace has overabounded (*huperperisseuō*) (Rom. 5:20a, b). We cannot continue in sin that grace may abound (Rom. 6:1). The abounding (*pleonazō*) grace {abundant grace, grace which is spreading the more} through the many may cause thanksgiving to abound (*perisseuō*) to the glory of God (2 Cor. 4:15). Paul was seeking fruit abounding {what may be credited} to the account of the Philippians (Phil. 4:17). The Thessalonians were to increase and abound in love for one another and for all (1 Thes. 3:12). The love of the Thessalonians for one another was abounding {growing greater} (2 Thes. 1:3). If various qualities (virtue, knowledge, godliness, etc.) exist and abound {exist in increasing measure} in Christians, they will be kept from being barren and unfruitful (2 Pet. 1:8). Other ref.: 2 Cor. 8:15 {to have much}, in relation to the manna. ¶

4 *plēthunō* [verb: πληθύνω <4129>]; **from *plēthos*: company, multitude; lit.: to make full ▶ To increase, to prevail** > During the tribulation, lawlessness will abound (Matt. 24:12). All other refs.: MULTIPLY <4129>.

ABOUNDING – 1 Acts 9:36 → FULL <4134> 2 2 Cor. 4:15 → ABOUND <4121> 3 Jas. 1:21 → OVERFLOW (noun) <4050>.

ABOUT – **1 *pou*** [indef. adv.: πού <4225>] ▶ **Close to, almost** > Abraham was about one hundred years old when God made him the promise that Sarah would conceive (Rom. 4:19). The word is transl. "somewhere" in Heb. 2:6; 4:4. ¶

2 about them, around them: *peri auton*; *peri* [prep.: περί <4012>]; ***autos*** [pron.: αὐτός <846>] ▶ **In the vicinity** > Sodom and Gomorrah, and the cities around them

{surrounding}, had given themselves over to sexual immorality (Jude 7).
[3] ***hōs*** [rel. adv.: ὡς <5613>]; **from *hos*: who ▶ Approximately, close to** > The herd of swine, that drowned in the sea, was about two thousand (Mark 5:13). Those who had eaten were about four thousand when Jesus multiplied the seven loaves and a few small fish (Mark 8:9). Anna was a widow of about (until: *eōs*, in some mss.) eighty-four years (Luke 2:37). The daughter of Jairus was about twelve years of age (Luke 8:42). Other refs.: John 1:39; 6:19 {near, nigh}; 11:18; 21:8 {as it were}; Acts 1:15; 5:7; 13:18, 20; Rev. 8:1. *
[4] ***hōsei*** [cond. adv.: ὡσεί <5616>]; **from *hōs*: see [3], and *ei*: if ▶ Almost, approximately** > Those who had eaten were about five thousand men, besides women and children, when Jesus multiplied the five loaves and the two fish (Matt. 14:21; Luke 9:14; John 6:10). Mary stayed with Elizabeth about three months (Luke 1:56). Jesus began His ministry at about thirty years of age (Luke 3:23). On the Mount of Olives, Jesus was withdrawn from His disciples about a stone's throw (Luke 22:41). During the crucifixion, it was about the sixth hour (i.e., about noon) when darkness came over the whole land (Luke 23:44). Other refs.: Matt. 3:16; 9:36; 28:3, 4; Mark 1:10; 6:44; 9:26; Luke 3:22; 9:28; 22:44, 59; 24:11; John 1:32; 4:6; 19:14, 39; Acts 2:3, 41; 4:4; 5:36; 6:15; 9:18; 10:3; 19:7; Heb. 1:12; 11:12; Rev. 1:14. ¶
– [5] Luke 13:1; John 3:25; et al. → CONCERNING <4012> [6] John 10:24 → to come round about → SURROUND <2944>.

ABOVE – [1] **from above: *anōthen*** [adv.: ἄνωθεν <509>]; **from *anō*: above, and suffix *then*: from ▶ From the highest place** > He who is from above is above all (John 3:31a). Other refs.: John 19:11; Jas. 1:17; 3:15, 17. All other refs.: AGAIN <509>, BEGINNING <509>, FIRST <509>, TOP <509>.
[2] ***epanō*** [adv.: ἐπάνω <1883>]; **from *epi*: upon, and *anō*: above, up ▶ Up, up above** > The word is used as an adv. of place and number (Matt. 2:9; Mark 14:5; Luke 11:44; 1 Cor. 15:6) and as a prep. (Matt. 5:14; 21:7; 23:18, 20, 22; 27:37; 28:2; Luke 4:39; 10:19; Rev. 6:8; 20:3). It is also used when speaking of authority and dignity: over (Luke 19:17, 19; John 3:31). ¶ ‡
– [3] John 8:23; Acts 2:19, Gal. 4:26; Col. 3:1, 2 → on high → HIGH (ON) <507> [4] Heb. 10:8 → HIGHER <511>.

ABOVE (UP, HIGH, FAR) – ***huperanō*** [adv.: ὑπεράνω <5231>]; **from *huper*: above (intens.), and *anō*: up ▶ The word indicates an advantage** > Refs.: Eph. 1:21; 4:10; Heb. 9:5. ¶

ABRAHAM – ***Abraam*** [masc. name: Ἀβραάμ <11>]: **father of a multitude, in Heb. ▶ Patriarch from whom the Israelites originate** > God had told Abraham to leave his country and his family, and that He would make him a great nation (see Gen. 12:1–3). His name is mentioned in the genealogy of Jesus Christ (Matt. 1:1, 2; Luke 3:34). Abraham believed God, and it was counted to him for righteousness (Rom. 4:3). Because of his exemplary faith, he is the father of those who walk in the steps of that faith (Rom. 4:12). He is named as a man of faith (Heb. 11:8, 17). His faith worked together with his actions, and by them his faith was made perfect (Jas. 2:21, 23; see v. 22). He was called a friend of God (Jas. 2:23). *

ABROAD – [1] Mark 1:45 → to blaze abroad → to spread abroad → SPREAD <1310> [2] Mark 4:22; Luke 8:17 → to light → LIGHT (noun) <1519> <5318> [3] Luke 2:17 → to make known abroad → KNOW <1107> <1232> [4] Rom. 16:19 → to come abroad → to become known → KNOWN <864> [5] Jas. 1:1 → to be scattered abroad → DISPERSION <1290>.

ABSENCE – [1] ***apousia*** [fem. noun: ἀπουσία <666>]; **from *apeimi*: to be absent, to be away, which is from: *apo*: from, and *eimi*: to be ▶ State of not being present in a place or being away** > In the absence of Paul, the Philippians had to

work out their own salvation with fear and trembling (Phil. 2:12). ¶
– [2] Luke 22:6 → in the absence of → WITHOUT <817> [3] 1 Cor. 16:17 → LACK (noun) <5303> [4] Phil. 1:27 → in my absence → lit.: being absent → ABSENT (BE) <548>.

ABSENT (BE) – [1] ***apeimi*** [verb: ἄπειμι <548>]; **from *apo*: from, and *eimi*: to be ► Not to be present in a place; to be away >** Even though Paul was absent in body {was not physically present}, he was present with the Corinthians in spirit (1 Cor. 5:3). He was bold toward the Corinthians when absent from among them {when away} (2 Cor. 10:1); as he was in word by letters when absent, so also he was in deed when present (v. 11). While absent, Paul repeats a warning concerning those who had sinned before (2 Cor. 13:2, 10). He uses this same verb with the Philippians (Phil. 1:27) and the Colossians (Col. 2:5). ¶
[2] ***ekdēmeō*** [verb: ἐκδημέω <1553>]; **from *ekdēmos*: away from home, which is from *ek*: out of, and *dēmos*: area of living, people; lit.: to be away from one's country ► To be away, to live far from home >** Christians are absent from the Lord, while present in the body (2 Cor. 5:6); they would be pleased to be absent from the body and present with the Lord (vv. 8, 9). ¶

ABSTAIN – [1] ***apechomai*** [verb: ἀπέχομαι <567>]; **middle voice of *apechō*: to be absent, which is from *apo*: from, away, and *echō*: to have, to keep ► To stay at a distance, to avoid >** James wrote to the Christians among the Gentiles to abstain from things contaminated by idols, sexual immorality, what is strangled, and blood (Acts 15:20); the other apostles agreed with him (v. 29). The will of God, for the sanctification of the Thessalonians, was that they should abstain from sexual immorality (1 Thes. 4:3). They were to abstain from every form of wickedness (1 Thes. 5:22). Paul said that, in later times, some would abandon the faith and order people to abstain from foods created by God (1 Tim. 4:3). Peter exhorts Christians to abstain from fleshly lusts, which war against the soul (1 Pet. 2:11). ¶
– [2] Acts 21:25 → GUARD (verb) <5442> [3] Rom. 14:3a, b → the one who abstains → lit: the one not eating [4] 2 Tim. 2:19 → DEPART <868>.

ABSTINENCE – [1] ***asitia*** [fem. noun: ἀσιτία <776>]; **from *a*: neg., and *sitos*: food; lit.: without food ► Voluntary deprivation of food or drink, fasting >** After long abstinence from food {After having gone a long time without food} (lit.: And much abstinence being) on board the ship, Paul stood up and addressed the other passengers (Acts 27:21). ¶
– [2] 1 Tim. 4:3 → who require abstinence → ordering people to abstain → ABSTAIN <567>.

ABSURD – Acts 25:27 → UNREASONABLE <249>.

ABUNDANCE – [1] ***hadrotēs*** [fem. noun: ἁδρότης <100>]; **from *hadros*: abundant, dense; lit.: strength, vigor ► Great amount, generous gift; also transl.: lavish gift, liberal gift >** Paul wanted to avoid being blamed concerning the way he administered the abundance of the churches (most likely: a great sum of money) (2 Cor. 8:20). ¶
[2] ***perisseia*** [fem. noun: περισσεία <4050>]; **from *perisseuō*: see [4] ► Overabundance, extraordinary measure >** Those who receive the abundance {abundant provision} of grace will reign in life through Jesus Christ (Rom. 5:17). Paul speaks of the abundance of {overflowing} joy of the churches in Macedonia despite much affliction (2 Cor. 8:2). Other refs.: 2 Cor. 10:15 {*eis perisseian*: more abundantly}; Jas. 1:21 {abounding, overflow}. ¶
[3] ***perisseuma*** [neut. noun: περίσσευμα <4051>]; **from *perisseuō*: see [4] ► Overflow, surplus >** A good man speaks out of the abundance of {That which fills} the heart (Matt. 12:34; Luke 6:45). The abundance {plenty} of the Corinthians would supply what the other churches needed, and their abundance would also supply what the Corinthians needed, so that

there might be equality (2 Cor. 8:14a, b). Other ref.: Mark 8:8 (that remained); see REST (noun)[2] <4051>. ¶

[4] **to be in abundance, to consist in the abundance, to have an abundance, to have in abundance: *perisseuō*** [verb: περισσεύω <4052>]; **from *perissos*: abundant, i.e., great in quantity or quality, which is from *peri*: above, beyond ▶ To surpass the measure, to have more than enough, to be rich >** In two parables, Jesus said that whoever has, to him will be given, and he will have an abundance (Matt. 13:12; 25:29). A man's life does not consist in the abundance of his possessions (Luke 12:15). In a parable, the hired servants had bread in abundance {had enough and to spare, had more than enough, had to spare} (Luke 15:17). All other refs.: see entries in Lexicon at <4052>.

– [5] 2 Cor. 7:15 → to abound all the more → more abundant → ABUNDANT <4056> [6] 2 Cor. 12:7 → exceeding greatness → GREATNESS <5236> [7] 1 Pet. 1:2; 2 Pet. 1:2; Jude 2 → to be in abundance → MULTIPLY <4129>.

ABUNDANT – [1] exceedingly abundant, more abundant: *perissoterōs* [adv.: περισσοτέρως <4056>]; **from *perissos*: abundant, i.e., great in quantity or quality, which is from *peri*: above, beyond ▶ Much more, excessively; also transl.: far more, more frequent, more frequently >** The affections of Titus were more abundant {were more abundantly towards, were greater for, abounded all the more for} the Corinthians (2 Cor. 7:15). Paul uses this term regarding his service for Christ in labors and in prisons (2 Cor. 11:23a, b). Other refs.: ABUNDANTLY <4056>, EXCEEDINGLY <4056>, MORE <4056>.

[2] **to be more than abundant, to be exceeding abundant, to be exceedingly abundant: *huperpleonazō*** [verb: ὑπερπλεονάζω <5250>]; **from *huper*: above (intens.), and *pleonazō*: to have more than enough ▶ To abound excessively, to overflow >** The grace of the Lord Jesus Christ was more than abundant {poured out abundantly, surpassingly over-abounded} with faith and love which is in Christ Jesus (1 Tim. 1:14). ¶

– [3] Luke 12:16 → to yield an abundant harvest → to bring forth abundantly → BRING <2164> [4] Rom. 5:17 → abundant provision → ABUNDANCE <4050> [5] 2 Cor. 1:5a; 9:12; Phil. 1:26 → to be abundant, to be more abundant → ABOUND <4052> [6] 2 Cor. 4:15 → the abundant grace → lit.: the abounding grace → ABOUND <4121> [7] 2 Cor. 9:10 → to make abundant → MULTIPLY <4129>.

ABUNDANTLY – [1] overabundance: *perisseia* [fem. noun: περισσεία <4050>]; **from *perissos*: abundant, i.e., great in quantity or quality, which is from *peri*: above, beyond ▶ Measure greater than normal, surplus >** Paul had hope that his activity would expand abundantly {greatly, even more} (lit.: until overabundance) among the Corinthians (2 Cor. 10:15). The word is transl. "abundance" in Rom. 5:17; 2 Cor. 8:2; Jas. 1:21. ¶

[2] ***perisson*; from *perissos*** [adj. used as adv.: περισσός <4053>]; **from *peri*: above, beyond ▶ Which exceeds the measure, surpassingly >** Jesus has come that His sheep might have life and have it abundantly {more abundantly, to the full} (John 10:10). All other refs.: ADVANTAGE (noun) <4053>, HIGHLY (VERY) <4053>, SUPERFLUOUS <4053>.

[3] **more abundantly: *perissoteron*** [adj. and adj. used as adv.: περισσότερον <4054>]; **from *perissos*: see [1] ▶ Much more, in a much greater way >** God was willing to show more abundantly {show more convincingly, show even more, make very clear} to the heirs of the promise the unchangeableness of His purpose (Heb. 6:17). Other refs.: Mark 7:36 {the more}; 1 Cor. 15:10; Heb. 7:15. ¶

[4] **very abundantly: *perissoterōs*** [adv.: περισσοτέρως <4056>]; **from *perissos*: see [1] ▶ To a greater degree, excessively >** Paul had written to the Corinthians that they might know the love he had very abundantly {more abundantly, so abundantly, especially} {the depth of his love} for them (2 Cor. 2:4; 12:15). Other ref.: 2 Cor. 1:12 {supremely}.

Other refs.: ABUNDANT <4056>, EXCEEDINGLY <4056>, MORE <4056>.

[5] **exceeding, exceedingly, far more abundantly: *huperekperissou*** [adv.: ὑπερεκπερισσοῦ <5238a>]; **from *huper*: above, *ek*: out of, and *perissos*: see [1] ▶ Extremely more, immeasurably more** > God can do far more abundantly {far exceedingly above} all that we ask or think (Eph. 3:20). Other refs.: 1 Thes. 3:10; 5:13; see EXCEEDINGLY <5238a>. ¶

– [6] 2 Cor. 1:5 → we share abundantly in the sufferings → lit.: the sufferings abound in us → ABOUND <4052> [7] 2 Cor. 9:8 → God is able to bless you abundantly → lit.: God is able to make all grace abound toward you [8] 2 Thes. 1:3 → to grow abundantly → GROW <5232> [9] Titus 3:6; 2 Pet. 1:11 → RICHLY <4146>.

ABUSE (noun) – [1] Matt. 27:39; Mark 15:29; Luke 23:39; 1 Pet. 4:4; 2 Pet. 2:10; Jude 8 → to hurl abuse, to heap abuse → REVILE <987> [2] Acts 13:45 → to heap abuse → BLASPHEME <987> [3] 2 Pet. 2:11 → to heap abuse when bringing judgment → lit.: to bring a reviling judgment → BRING <5342>, REVILING <989>, JUDGMENT <2920>.

ABUSE (verb) – [1] Luke 6:28 → to falsely accuse → ACCUSE <1908> [2] Acts 14:5 → MISTREAT <5195> [3] 1 Cor. 7:31; 9:18 → USE (verb) <2710>.

ABUSER – 1 Cor. 6:9 → abuser {one who abuses} of oneself with men → HOMOSEXUAL <733>.

ABUSIVE – [1] ***loidoros*** [adj. used as masc. noun: λοίδορος <3060>] ▶ **One who uses insulting language, humiliates others** > Christians should not mix with any so-called brother who is abusive {reviler, slanderer} (1 Cor. 5:11). Abusive people will not inherit the kingdom of God (1 Cor. 6:10). ¶

– [2] Acts 18:6 → to become abusive → BLASPHEME <987> [3] Col. 3:8 → abusive speech → filthy language → FILTHY <148> [4] 1 Tim. 6:4 → abusive language → injurious word → INJURIOUS <988> [5] 2 Tim. 3:2 → BLASPHEMER <989>.

ABUSIVELY – Acts 13:45 → to talk abusively → BLASPHEME <987>.

ABYSS – Luke 8:31; Rom. 10:7; Rev. 9:1, 2, 11; 11:7; 17:8; 20:1, 3 → BOTTOMLESS <12>.

ACCEDE – [1] Acts 18:20 → CONSENT (verb) <1962> [2] 1 Tim. 6:3 → CONSENT (verb) <4334>.

ACCENT – Matt. 26:73 → SPEECH <2981>.

ACCEPT – [1] ***apodechomai*** [verb: ἀποδέχομαι <588>]; **from *apo*: intens., and *dechomai*: to accept, to receive ▶ To recognize, to agree willfully** > Tertullus accepted {acknowledged} the great peace and the excellent measures for the Jewish nation by the forethought of Felix (Acts 24:3). All other refs.: RECEIVE <588>.

[2] ***prosdechomai*** [verb: προσδέχομαι <4327>]; **from *pros*: for, and *dechomai*: to accept, to receive ▶ To agree to, to assent to** > O.T. people of faith were tortured, not accepting {refusing} deliverance, that they might get a better resurrection (Heb. 11:35). All other refs.: LOOK (verb) <4327>, RECEIVE <4327>, TAKE <4327>, WAIT (verb) <4327>.

– [3] Mark 4:20; Acts 16:21; 22:18; Heb. 12:6 → RECEIVE <3858> [4] John 5:43a, b, 44; 2 Cor. 11:4, 8 → RECEIVE <2983> [5] Acts 10:35 → God accepts men → lit.: men are accepted → ACCEPTED <1184> [6] Acts 18:14 → to accept your complaint → lit.: to suffer you → SUFFER <430> [7] Rom. 10:16 → OBEY <5219> [8] Rom. 14:1, 3; 15:7a, b; Phm. 17 → RECEIVE <4355> [9] Rom. 15:31 → accepted → ACCEPTABLE <2144> [10] 1 Cor. 16:11 → to refuse to accept → DESPISE <1848> [11] 2 Cor. 5:9 → accepted → ACCEPTABLE <2101> [12] 2 Cor. 11:16; 1 Thes. 1:6; 2:13; Jas. 1:21 → RECEIVE <1209> [13] Gal. 5:2, 3 → to accept circumcision → to be circumcised → CIRCUMCISE

<4059> [14] Heb. 11:4 → "accepting" added in Engl. [15] 1 John 5:10 → to accept the witness → to have the witness → HAVE <2192> [16] 3 John 9 → RECEIVE <1926>.

ACCEPTABLE – [1] ***dektos*** [verbal adj.: δεκτός <1184>]; **from *dechomai*: to accept, to receive, to welcome ► Worthy to be received, agreeable, favorable** > Jesus had been sent to preach the acceptable {favorable} year of the Lord (Luke 4:19). The things sent from the Philippians were an acceptable sacrifice to Paul (Phil. 4:18). Other refs.: Luke 4:24; Acts 10:35; 2 Cor. 6:2a; see ACCEPTED <1184>. ¶

[2] ***apodektos*** [adj.: ἀπόδεκτος <587>]; **from *apo*: intens., and *dektos*: see [1] ► Approved, very acceptable; also transl.: pleasing** > It is good and acceptable before the Savior God to pray for all men, in particular for all who are in authority (1 Tim. 2:3). It is also acceptable in the sight of God that children learn first to be pious in regard to their own home, i.e., their parents or grandparents who are widows (1 Tim. 5:4). ¶

[3] ***euprosdektos*** [adj.: εὐπρόσδεκτος <2144>]; **from *eu*: well, and *prosdechomai*: to accept, to receive, which is from *pros*: close to, and *dechomai*: see [1]; lit.: well-accepted ► Approved, becoming, well received; also transl.: accepted** > Paul wanted the offering up of the Gentiles to be acceptable (Rom. 15:16), and that his service might be acceptable to the saints (v. 31). Quoting Isaiah, he speaks of the acceptable time for God {the time of God's favor} to listen to His servants (2 Cor. 6:2b). The readiness to give is acceptable according to what one may have, not according to what one does not have (2 Cor. 8:12). Christians can offer spiritual sacrifices acceptable to God by Jesus Christ (1 Pet. 2:5). ¶

[4] ***euarestos*** [adj.: εὐάρεστος <2101>]; **from *eu*: well, and *arestos*: pleasing, or *areskō*: to please ► Fully agreeable; also transl.: pleasing, well pleasing** > Paul urges Christians to present their bodies as a living sacrifice, holy, acceptable to God (Rom. 12:1); they must prove what is the acceptable will of God (v. 2). He who serves Christ in respecting his brother is acceptable to God (Rom. 14:18). Christians are zealous to be acceptable {agreeable, accepted} to {to please} the Lord (2 Cor. 5:9); they find out what is acceptable to {is agreeable to, pleases} Him (Eph. 5:10). Other refs.: Phil. 4:18; Col. 3:20; Titus 2:9; Heb. 13:21; see well-pleasing under PLEASING <2101> and WELL PLEASING <2101>. ¶

[5] **grace: *charis*** [fem. noun: χάρις <5485>]; **from *chairō*: to rejoice ► Something pleasing, agreeable (e.g., to God)** > This is acceptable {a favor, commendable, thankworthy} (lit.: This is a grace), if one, for conscience sake toward God, suffers (1 Pet. 2:19, 20). Other refs.: see entries in Lexicon at <5485>.

– [6] Heb. 11:4 → more acceptable → more excellent → EXCELLENT <4119> [7] Heb. 12:28 → ACCEPTABLY <2102>.

ACCEPTABLY – ***euarestōs*** [adv.: εὐαρέστως <2102>]; **from *euarestos*: well-pleasing, which is from *eu*: well, and *arestos*: pleasing, or *areskō*: to please ► In a way which is agreeable, pleasing** > Christians must serve (or: worship) God acceptably {offer to God an acceptable service} with reverence and fear (Heb. 12:28). ¶

ACCEPTANCE – [1] ***proslēpsis*** [fem. noun: πρόσληψις <4356>]; **from *proslambanō*: to receive unto oneself, which is from *pros*: to, and *lambanō*: to receive, to take; also written: *proslēmpsis* ► Admission, integration; also transl.: receiving, reception** > The acceptance of Israel will be life from among the dead (Rom. 11:15). ¶

– [2] Rom. 2:11; Eph. 6:9; Col. 3:25; Jas. 2:1 → acceptance of persons → RESPECT OF PERSONS <4382> [3] 1 Tim. 1:15; 4:9 → ACCEPTATION <594>.

ACCEPTATION – ***apodochē*** [fem. noun: ἀποδοχή <594>]; **from *apodechomai*: to accept, which is from *apo*: intens., and *dechomai*: to accept, to receive ► Approbation, agreement; also transl.: acceptance** > It is a faithful word, and worthy of all acceptation, that Christ Jesus came into the world to save sinners (1 Tim. 1:15); also, that Christians hope in a living God (4:9; see v. 10). ¶

ACCEPTED – [1] ***dektos*** [verbal adj.: δεκτός <1184>]; **from *dechomai*: to accept, to receive, to welcome ▶ Worthy to be received, agreeable, approved; also transl.: acceptable, welcome** > No prophet is accepted in his own country (Luke 4:24), i.e., he is not appreciated. He who fears God and works righteousness is accepted by Him (Acts 10:35). Paul says that God has listened in an accepted time {in the time of His favor} (2 Cor. 6:2a). Other refs.: Luke 4:19; Phil. 4:18; see ACCEPTABLE <1184>. ¶
[2] **to make accepted: *charitoō*** [verb: χαριτόω <5487>]; **from *charis*: grace, which is from *chairō*: to rejoice ▶ To make acceptable, to fill with divine grace** > God the Father has made accepted {has blessed, has freely bestowed His grace on, has given His grace to} the Christians in the Beloved (Eph. 1:6). Other ref.: Luke 1:28; see FAVOR (verb) <5487>. ¶
– [3] Rom. 15:31; 2 Cor. 8:12 → ACCEPTABLE <2144> [4] 2 Cor. 5:9 → ACCEPTABLE <2101>.

ACCESS – ***prosagōgē*** [fem. noun: προσαγωγή <4318>]; **from *pros*: to, and *agōgē*: manner of life, which is from *agō*: to bring, to lead; or from *prosagō*: to bring to, to bring near ▶ Ability to approach someone, to benefit from something** > Christians have access {introduction} by faith into the favor in which they stand (Rom. 5:2). They have access to the Father through Christ by one Spirit (Eph. 2:18); in Jesus, they have access to {may approach} God with confidence (3:12). ¶

ACCLAIM – Mark 15:18 → GREET <782>.

ACCOMPANY – [1] ***propempō*** [verb: προπέμπω <4311>]; **from *pro*: before, and *pempō*: to send ▶ To go with, to provide (for a journey); to help one in view of his journey** > The elders of the church in Ephesus accompanied Paul to the ship (Acts 20:38), knowing they would no more see his face. All other refs.: JOURNEY (noun) <4311>, SET (verb) <4311>, WAY <4311>.
[2] ***sunepomai*** [verb: συνέπομαι <4902>]; **from *sun*: together, and *hepomai*: to follow; lit.: to follow with ▶ To travel with someone as a companion** > Sopater and others accompanied Paul when returning through Macedonia (Acts 20:4). ¶
[3] ***sunerchomai*** [verb: συνέρχομαι <4905>]; **from *sun*: with, together, and *erchomai*: to come ▶ To assemble with, to come together; also transl.: to company, to be with** > Men had assembled with the apostles during the life of Jesus on earth (Acts 1:21). Six brothers from Joppa accompanied {went along with, went with} Peter to meet Cornelius (Acts 10:23; 11:12). All other refs.: COME <4905>, FOLLOW <4905>, GO <4905>.
– [4] Mark 5:37; Luke 23:49 → FOLLOW <4870> [5] Mark 16:17 → FOLLOW <3877> [6] Mark 16:20 → FOLLOW <1872> [7] Luke 14:25 → to go with → GO <4848> [8] Acts 16:3 → to go forth with him → GO <1831> [9] 2 Cor. 8:19 → FELLOW TRAVELER <4898>.

ACCOMPLISH – [1] ***exartizō*** [verb: ἐξαρτίζω <1822>]; **from *ek*: intens., and *artizō*: to develop, to perfect ▶ To complete entirely; also transl.: to fully accomplish** > When he had accomplished {come to the end of, completed, ended} his days {When his time was up} in Tyre, Paul departed and went on his way (Acts 21:5). All Scripture is given that the man (lit.: the human being) of God may be fully accomplished {equipped, thoroughly equipped, thoroughly furnished, fully fitted} (2 Tim. 3:17). ¶
[2] ***katergazomai*** [verb: κατεργάζομαι <2716>]; **from *kata*: intens., and *ergazomai*: to work ▶ To achieve, to complete** > The Christian is to take the whole armor of God, so that he may be able to withstand in the evil day and, having accomplished {having done} all things, to stand (Eph. 6:13). Other refs.: Rom. 15:18; Jas. 1:20. All other refs.: see entries in Lexicon at <2716>.

3 ***plēthō*** [verb: πλήθω <4130>] ▶ **To fill; also transl.: to complete, to end** > The days of service of Zacharias were accomplished (Luke 1:23). The days were accomplished {The time came} that Mary should give birth (Luke 2:6). Eight days were accomplished {It was time on the eighth day} for the circumcision of the child Jesus (Luke 2:21). The days of purification of Joseph and Mary were accomplished (Luke 2:22). All other refs.: FILL (verb) <4130>.

4 ***poieō*** [verb: ποιέω <4160>] ▶ **To make, to realize** > God has accomplished {carried out} His eternal purpose in Christ Jesus (Eph. 3:11). Other refs.: see entries in Lexicon at <4160>.

5 ***teleō*** [verb: τελέω <5055>]; **from *telos*: completion, goal** ▶ **To execute completely, to terminate something by attaining one's goal** > Jesus was distressed until His baptism (i.e., His crucifixion and going into death) was accomplished {completed} (Luke 12:50). All things written about the Son of Man by the prophets would be accomplished {fulfilled} (Luke 18:31); what was written had to be accomplished {fulfilled} in the Lord (22:37). On the cross, Jesus knew that all things were now accomplished {completed, finished} (John 19:28). All other refs.: see entries in Lexicon at <5055>.

6 ***epiteleō*** [verb: ἐπιτελέω <2005>]; **from *epi*: upon (intens.), and *teleō*: see 5; lit.: to finish completely** ▶ **a. To carry out, to perform completely (a service)** > The priests went always into the first tabernacle, accomplishing {carrying on} the service of God (Heb. 9:6). **b. To undergo (sufferings)** > The same afflictions were accomplished in {experienced by, undergone by} the brothers of those to whom Peter addressed his letter (1 Pet. 5:9). All other refs.: see entries in Lexicon at <2005>.

– 7 Matt. 5:18; Luke 21:32 → FULFILL <1096> 8 Matt. 27:24; John 12:19 → PREVAIL <5623> 9 Mark 13:4 → FULFILL <4931> 10 Luke 1:1 → to believe most surely → BELIEVE <4135> 11 Luke 1:45 → lit.: to be a performance → PERFORMANCE <5050> 12 Luke 9:31; 21:22; Acts 14:26; 19:21 → FULFILL <4137> 13 John 4:34; 5:36; 17:4 → FINISH <5048> 14 Acts 2:1 → to fully come → COME <4845> 15 2 Tim. 4:17 → to fully accomplish → to preach fully → PREACH <4135> 16 Jas. 1:15 → FINISH <658> 17 2 John 8 → WORK (verb) <2038>.

ACCOMPLISHED – 2 Cor. 10:16 → made ready → READY <2092>.

ACCOMPLISHMENT – 1 ***ekplērōsis*** [fem. noun: ἐκπλήρωσις <1604>]; **from *ekplēroō*: to fulfill, which is from *ek*: intens., and *plēroō*: to fulfill** ▶ **Fulfillment, ending** > Paul signified the accomplishment {expiration, completion} of the days of purification {when it would end} (Acts 21:26). ¶

– 2 2 Cor. 10:16 → made ready → READY <2092>.

ACCORD (noun) – 1 **of one's own accord, willing of one's own accord: *authairetos*** [adj.: αὐθαίρετος <830>]; **from *autos*: himself, and *haireō*: to choose** ▶ **Voluntary, acting by free choice; spontaneous** > The churches of Macedonia had acted willingly of their own accord {entirely on their own, freely willing} in sharing their substance (2 Cor. 8:3). Titus went of his own accord to the Corinthians (2 Cor. 8:17). ¶

2 **with one accord: *homothumadon*** [adv.: ὁμοθυμαδόν <3661>]; **from *homothumos*: unanimous, which is from *homos*: common, similar, and *thumos*: the soul as the seat of feelings, heart, mind** ▶ **Unanimously, together; also transl.: with one mind, with one heart** > The word is used concerning Christians (Acts 1:14; 2:1 in some mss., 46; 4:24; 5:12; 15:25), those who had listened to Stephen (Acts 7:57 {with one impulse, all, together}), the crowds who were listening to Philip (Acts 8:6), the people of Tyre and Sidon (Acts 12:20), the Jews against Paul (Acts 18:12), and the citizens of Ephesus (Acts 19:29 {as one man}). Christians are called to glorify the God and Father of the Lord Jesus Christ

with one accord and one mouth (Rom. 15:6). ¶

– 3 John 5:19; 7:28; 8:42; 11:51; 18:34 → of one's own accord → lit.: of oneself 4 Rom. 15:5 → in accord with → according to → ACCORDING <2596> 5 2 Cor. 6:15 → CONCORD <4857> 6 Phil. 2:2 → being of one accord → joined in soul → SOUL <4861> 7 Titus 2:1 → to be in accord with → FITTING (BE) <4241> 8 Phm. 14 → of one's own accord → VOLUNTARY <1595>.

ACCORD (verb) – Titus 2:1 → to accord with → FITTING (BE) <4241>.

ACCORDANCE – 1 Rom. 12:6; 16:25; 1 Cor. 15:3, 4 → in accordance with → lit.: according (*kata*) to 2 Eph. 4:22b → in accordance → CONCERNING <2596>.

ACCORDING – 1 ***kata*** [prep.: κατά <2596>] ▶ **Depending on, in conformity to** > Paul speaks of what is opposed to sound teaching, according to the gospel of the glory of God (1 Tim. 1:11). Other refs.: CONCERNING <2596>.

2 **according, according to what: *katho*** [adv.: καθό <2526>]; **from *kata*: according as, and *ho*: that which; also transl.: inasmuch as** ▶ **In like manner** > Refs.: Rom. 8:26; 2 Cor. 8:12; 1 Pet. 4:13. ¶ ‡

– 3 2 Tim. 2:5 → according to the rules → LAWFULLY <3545>.

ACCORDING AS – 1 ***katha*** [adv.: καθά <2505>]; **from *kata*: according to, and *hos*: which, who** ▶ **Just as** > Ref.: Matt. 27:10. ¶ ‡

2 ***kathoti*** [adv.: καθότι <2530>]; **from *kata*: according to, and *hoti*: that** ▶ **So far as** > Refs.: Acts 2:45; 4:35. All other refs.: FORASMUCH <2530>. ‡

3 ***kathōs*** [adv.: καθώς <2531>]; **from *kata*: according to, and *hōs*: as** ▶ **Just as** > Equivalent to the simple *hōs*. ‡

ACCORDINGLY – 2 Cor. 8:6 → lit.: for (*eis*).

ACCOUNT (noun) – 1 ***logos*** [masc. noun: λόγος <3056>]; **from *legō*: to say, to speak** ▶ **a. Explanation, report** > Men will give an account for every idle word in the judgment day (Matt. 12:36). In one parable, the lord of the servants came and settled accounts {reckoned} with them (Matt. 25:19). In another, a rich man asked his steward to give an account {reckoning} of his stewardship (Luke 16:2). Each individual will give an account concerning himself to God (Rom. 14:12). Those who rule over Christians watch over their souls, as those who will give account (Heb. 13:17). Evil men will render account to Him who is ready to judge the living and the dead (1 Pet. 4:5). **b. Advantage, benefit** > Paul was seeking fruit abounding to the account {credit} of the Philippians (Phil. 4:17). Other ref.: Heb. 4:13 {with whom we have to do; lit.: to whom we must give account}. **c. Written document, record; also transl.: book, discourse, treatise** > Luke had composed the first account (the Gospel which bears his name) about all the things which Jesus began to do and teach (Acts 1:1). Other refs.: WORD <3056>.

2 **to take account, to settle accounts: *sunairō logon*; to take: *sunairō*** [verb: συναίρω <4868>]; **from *sun*: together with, and *airō*: to take; account: *logos*** [masc. noun: λόγος <3056>]; **from *legō*: see** 1 ▶ **To count, to resolve a financial matter** > A king wanted to settle accounts with {to reckon with} his servants (Matt. 18:23: *sunarai logon*); when he had begun to settle accounts {to reckon} (lit.: to settle), one was brought to him who owed him ten thousand talents (v. 24: *sunarein*). Other ref. (*sunairō*): Matt. 25:19; see RECKON <4868>. ¶

3 ***diēgēsis*** [fem. noun: διήγησις <1335>]; **from *diēgeomai*: to relate in detail, to relate completely, which is from *dia*: through (intens.), and *hēgeomai*: to lead** ▶ **Record, history** > Many had undertaken to draw up an account {a declaration, a narrative, a relation} of the life of Jesus (Luke 1:1); Luke wrote these various things in an orderly fashion (see v. 3). ¶

[4] **on account of what: *charin tinos*; *charin*** [prep.: χάριν <5484>]**; acc. of *charis*: grace; *tis*** [pron.: τίς <5101>]**; lit.: because of what ▶ For what reason, therefore >** John uses this expr. in 1 John 3:12. Other refs.: Luke 7:47; Gal. 3:19; Eph. 3:1, 14; 1 Tim. 5:14; Titus 1:5, 11; Jude 16. ¶

– [5] Luke 1:3 → orderly account → in order → ORDER (noun) <2517> [6] Luke 9:10 → to give an account → RELATE <1334> [7] John 11:50 → to take into account → CONSIDER <1260> [8] Acts 19:40; 1 Pet. 3:15 → REASON (noun) <3056> [9] Rom. 4:8 → to take into account → COUNT <3049> [10] Rom. 5:13; Phm. 18 → to put to, to put on, to take into, to charge the account → to put on the account → IMPUTE <1677> [11] 1 Cor. 6:4 → to be of no account, to be of little account → to esteem least → ESTEEM (verb) <1848> [12] 1 Cor. 13:5 → to take into account → IMPUTE <3049> [13] 2 Cor. 4:11 → on account of → SAKE OF (FOR THE) <1223> [14] 2 Cor. 10:10 → of no account → CONTEMPTIBLE <1848>.

ACCOUNT (verb) – [1] Matt. 18:23 → to settle accounts → ACCOUNT (noun) <4868> <3056> [2] Mark 10:42 → REGARD (verb) <1380> [3] Luke 20:35; 21:36 → to count worthy → WORTHY <2661> [4] Luke 22:24 → CONSIDER <1380> [5] Acts 19:40 → lit.: to give an account, a reason → REASON (noun) <3056> [6] Rom. 4:3, 5, 9, 10, 22; Gal. 3:6; Jas. 2:23 → COUNT <3049> [7] Rom. 8:36; Heb. 11:19 → CONSIDER <3049> [8] 1 Cor. 4:1 → THINK <3049> [9] 1 Tim. 1:12; 2 Pet. 2:13 → COUNT <2233> [10] 2 Pet. 1:13 → THINK <2233> [11] 2 Pet. 3:15 → CONSIDER <2233>.

ACCOUNT (ON) – See BECAUSE <1360>.

ACCOUNT? (ON WHAT) – See WHEREFORE? <1302>.

ACCOUNTABLE – [1] Rom. 3:19 → GUILTY <5267> [2] Jas. 2:10 → GUILTY <1777>.

ACCREDIT – [1] Acts 2:22 → APPROVE <584> [2] 1 Cor. 16:3 → APPROVE <1381>.

ACCUMULATE – 2 Tim. 4:3 → HEAP <2002>.

ACCURATE – Acts 23:15, 20; 24:22 → more accurate → more accurately → ACCURATELY <197>.

ACCURATELY – [1] ***akribōs*** [adv.: ἀκριβῶς <199>]**; from *akron*: extremity, or *akribēs*: accurate, exact ▶ Precisely, exactly, carefully >** Apollos was speaking and teaching accurately {diligently} the things of the Lord (Acts 18:25). Other refs.: Matt. 2:8; Luke 1:3; Eph. 5:15; 1 Thes. 5:2; see CAREFULLY <199>, PERFECTLY <199>. ¶

[2] **more accurately: *akribesteron*** [adv.: ἀκριβέστερον <197>]**; acc. compar. of *akribōs*: see** [1] **▶ More precisely, more exactly, more carefully >** Aquila and Priscilla were explaining to Apollos the way of God more accurately {more adequately} (Acts 18:26). Other refs.: Acts 23:15 {more accurate, more thorough, further}, 20 {more accurate, more fully, more precise, more thoroughly}; 24:22 {more perfect, more accurate, more exact, well}. ¶

– [3] Matt. 2:7, 16 → to accurately inquire → DETERMINE <198> [4] 2 Tim. 2:15 → to handle accurately → to divide rightly → DIVIDE <3718>.

ACCURSED – [1] **curse: *anathema*** [neut. noun: ἀνάθεμα <331>]**; from *anatithēmi*; *ana*: above, up (intens.), and *tithēmi*: to put, to place; lit.: to place up ▶ The word denotes the fact of being given over to God's condemnation >** Some Jews had bound themselves under a great curse (*anathema*) {a solemn oath} (lit.: by curse); they had committed themselves by curse (*anathematizō*) until they should have killed Paul (Acts 23:14). Paul could wish to be accursed {cursed} (lit.: a curse) from the Christ for his Jewish brothers (Rom. 9:3). No man speaking by the Spirit of God calls Jesus accursed (lit.: says: Curse on Jesus) (1 Cor. 12:3). If any man love not the Lord

Jesus Christ, Paul says that a curse be on him {to let him be accursed, to let him be Anathema} (1 Cor. 16:22). About a man preaching a different gospel than his, Paul says to let him be accursed (lit.: be curse) (Gal. 1:8, 9). ¶

– [2] Matt. 25:41 → to curse → CURSED <2672> [3] John 7:49 → CURSED <1944> [4] 2 Pet. 2:14 → CURSE (noun) <2671> [5] Rev. 22:3 → anything accursed → lit.: every curse → CURSE (noun) <2652>.

ACCUSATION – [1] ***aitia*** [fem. noun: αἰτία <156>]; **from *aiteō*: to ask, or *aitios*: responsible ▶ Charge, crime, reason for condemnation** > The soldiers placed the written accusation {the charge} against Jesus above His head (Matt. 27:37; Mark 15:26). The accusers of Paul brought no accusation against him (Acts 25:18); it was unreasonable not to specify the accusations against him (v. 27). All other refs.: CASE <156>, CAUSE (noun) <156>, FAULT <156>, REASON (noun) <156>.

[2] ***katēgoria*** [fem. noun: κατηγορία <2724>]; **from *katēgoreō*: to speak against, to accuse; which is from *kata*: against, and *agoreuō*: to speak in front of an assembly (*agora*) ▶ Charge, reason for condemnation** > The scribes and the Pharisees were watching to see if Jesus would heal on the Sabbath, that they might find an accusation against Him (other mss.: something with which to accuse Him) (Luke 6:7). Pilate asked what accusation was being brought against this man Jesus (John 18:29). An accusation must not be received against an elder, unless there are two or three witnesses (1 Tim. 5:19). The word is used also in Titus 1:6 (see accusation under ACCUSE <2724>). ¶

[3] **to bring an accusation: *enkaleō*** [verb: ἐγκαλέω <1458>]; **from *en*: in, and *kaleō*: to call ▶ To accuse, to call to account** > Paul asks who will bring an accusation against {bring a charge against, lay anything to the charge of} God's elect (Rom. 8:33). All other refs.: ACCUSE <1458>, CALL (verb) <1458>.

– [4] Luke 3:14; 19:8 → false accusation → to accuse falsely → ACCUSE <4811> [5] Acts 23:29 → CHARGE (noun)[1] <1462> [6] Acts 24:2; 24:19; 28:19 → ACCUSE <2723> [7] Col. 1:22 → free from accusation → above reproach → REPROACH (noun) <410>.

ACCUSE – [1] ***diaballō*** [verb: διαβάλλω <1225>]; **from *dia*: through, and *ballō*: to cast, to throw ▶ To attack by words; the verb could also mean: to accuse falsely** > The steward of a rich man was accused of {was reported as} wasting his goods (Luke 16:1). ¶

[2] ***enkaleō*** [verb: ἐγκαλέω <1458>]; **from *en*: in, and *kaleō*: to call; lit.: to call to give account ▶ To press charges, to prosecute at law, to reproach** > The courts were open for Demetrius and the craftsmen to accuse {bring charges against, press charges against, implead} Paul (Acts 19:38). Paul was accused by the Jews who were about to kill him (Acts 23:28); Claudius Lysias found him to be accused over {the accusation had to do with} questions about the Jewish law (v. 29). Paul made his defense concerning all the things of which he was accused {all the accusations} by the Jews in front of Agrippa (Acts 26:2); he was accused by the Jews because of his hope of the promise made by God to the Jewish fathers (v. 7). All other refs.: ACCUSATION <1458>, CALL (verb) <1458>.

[3] ***katēgoreō*** [verb: κατηγορέω <2723>]; **from *kata*: against, and *agoreuō*: to speak in front of an assembly (*agora*) ▶ To make a complaint, to press charges, to bring charges** > Jesus was constantly questioned by the Jews that they might accuse Him (Matt. 12:10; 27:12; Mark 3:2; 15:3; Luke 6:7; 11:54 in some mss.; 23:2, 10, 14 {to make charges}; John 8:6). Jesus would not accuse the Jews before the Father; Moses was accusing them (John 5:45a, b). The Jews accused Paul (Acts 22:30; 24:2, 8, 13, 19 {to make accusations, to object}). The Jewish leaders had the opportunity to accuse {prosecute} Paul (Acts 25:5); if the things they accused him of were not true, then he could not be given up to them (v. 11). It was not the custom of the Romans to give up any man before the accused (*ho katēgoroumenos*) had faced his accusers (*tous katēgorous*)

(Acts 25:16). Paul had nothing to accuse his nation of {no accusation against his nation} (Acts 28:19). The thoughts of the Gentiles accuse them (Rom. 2:15). Satan accuses the brothers before God day and night (Rev. 12:10). ¶

[4] **to falsely accuse: *epēreazō*** [verb: ἐπηρεάζω <1908>]; **from *epi*: against, and *epēreia*: threat, insult ► To slander, to decry** > Peter speaks of those who falsely accuse {calumniate, revile, speak maliciously against} the good conduct of Christians in Christ (1 Pet. 3:16). Other refs.: Matt. 5:44; Luke 6:28 (to use despitefully); see USE (verb) <1908>. ¶

[5] **to accuse falsely: *sukophanteō*** [verb: συκοφαντέω <4811>]; **from *sukon*: fig, and *phainō*: to show, to declare, which is from *phōs*: light; lit.: to denounce the robbers or exporters of consecrated figs ► To bring false charges against someone** > Jesus told soldiers not to accuse falsely (Luke 3:14). If Zacchaeus had accused falsely {cheated, defrauded, taken something by false accusation from} someone, he would return four times the amount (Luke 19:8). ¶

[6] **accusation: *katēgoria*** [fem. noun: κατηγορία <2724>]; **from *katēgoreō*: see [3] ► Charge, reason for public condemnation** > The children of an elder should not be accused (lit.: under the accusation) of misconduct or being disobedient (Titus 1:6). Other refs.: Luke 6:7; John 18:29; 1 Tim. 5:19. ¶

– [7] Mark 15:4 → to testify against → TESTIFY <2649> [8] Mark 15:26 → what He was accused of → ACCUSATION <156> [9] 1 Pet. 2:12 → to speak against → SPEAK <2635> [10] 3 John 10 → to unjustly accuse → PRATE <5396>.

ACCUSED – Acts 25:16 → lit.: the one being accused → ACCUSE <2723>.

ACCUSER – [1] ***katēgoros*** [masc. noun: κατήγορος <2725>]; **from *katēgoreō*: to speak against, to accuse; which is from *kata*: against, and *agoreuō*: to speak in front of an assembly (*agora*) ► One who charges another with an offense, who declares him guilty** > The etymology of the word suggests an accuser speaking against someone in front of a group of persons (see Zech. 3:1, 2). The term is used concerning the accusers of Paul in Acts (23:30, 35; 24:8; 25:16, 18). It is a name that characterizes the devil: Satan is the accuser of the brothers before God (Rev. 12:10; other mss.: *katēgōr*). Other ref.: John 8:10 in some mss. ¶

[2] **false accuser: *diabolos*** [masc. noun: διάβολος <1228>]; **from *diaballō*: to accuse, which is from *dia*: through, and *ballō*: to cast, to throw ► One who utters accusing words (true or false) with the purpose of making people enemies; also transl.: malicious gossip, malicious talker, slanderer, slanderous** > Women who serve the Lord (1 Tim. 3:11) and older women (Titus 2:3) should not be false accusers. In the last days, men will be false accusers (2 Tim. 3:3). All other refs.: DEVIL <1228>.

– [3] Matt. 5:25a, b; Luke 12:58 → ADVERSARY <476> [4] John 5:45b → lit.: the accusing → ACCUSE <2723>.

ACCUSTOMED – [1] 1 Cor. 8:7 → accustomed to idols → lit.: by habit of the idol → CUSTOM[1] <4914> [2] Heb. 5:13 → not accustomed → UNSKILLED <552>.

ACCUSTOMED (BE) – [1] ***eiōtha*** [verb: εἴωθα]; perf. tense of an obsolete pres. of ***ethō*** [verb: ἔθω <1486>] **► To have the habitual practice, to act in a usual way in particular circumstances** > At the feast, the governor was accustomed {it was his custom} to release one prisoner to the crowd (Matt. 27:15). Jesus taught the crowds as He was accustomed {according to His custom, as He was wont} (Mark 10:1). He entered into the synagogue on a Sabbath day, as His custom was (Luke 4:16). According to His custom, Paul went in the synagogue in Thessalonica (Acts 17:2). ¶

– [2] Mark 15:8 → as he had been accustomed to do → lit.: as he had always done → ALWAYS <104> [3] Luke 22:39 → CUSTOM[1] <1485>.

ACELDAMA – ***Hakeldama*** [name: Ἀκελδαμά <184>]: **field of blood in the dialect of the people of Jerusalem; also written:**

Hakeldamach ► **Place known as the "potter's field"; also spelled: Akel Dama, Akeldama, Hakeldama >** The chief priests bought this field with the thirty pieces of silver that Judas returned to the temple after having delivered up Jesus; it was bought as a burial place for strangers (Acts 1:19; see Matt. 27:1–10). ¶

ACHAIA – ***Achaia*** [fem. name: Ἀχαΐα <882>]: **trouble ► Region of Ancient Greece in which Corinth was the capital; in the N.T., the two provinces of Achaia and Macedonia represented the part of Greece over which the Romans ruled >** Paul visited Achaia more than once (Acts 18:12, 27; 19:21). Christians from Achaia made a contribution for the poor Christians in Jerusalem (Rom. 15:26). Stephanas was most likely one of the first converts in Achaia (1 Cor. 16:15). Other refs.: Rom. 16:5 in some mss.; 2 Cor. 1:1; 9:2; 11:10; 1 Thes. 1:7, 8. ¶

ACHAICUS – ***Achaikos*** [masc. name: Ἀχαϊκός <883>]: **belonging to Achaia ► Christian who came to Corinth to visit Paul >** The coming of Achaicus rejoiced the apostle Paul (1 Cor. 16:17). ¶

ACHAZ – See AHAZ <881>.

ACHIEVE – [1] 2 Cor. 4:17 → WORK (verb) <2716> [2] Jas. 1:20 → ACCOMPLISH <2716>.

ACHIM – ***Achim*** [masc. name: Ἀχίμ <885>]: **Jehovah will establish, in Heb.; also *Acheim* in Greek ► Man in the O.T. >** Achim is mentioned in the genealogy of Jesus Christ (Matt. 1:14a, b). This name corresponds to Jachin in the O.T. (1 Kgs. 7:21). ¶

ACKNOWLEDGE – [1] Matt. 10:32a, b; Luke 12:8a, b; John 9:22; 12:42; Acts 23:8; Heb. 11:13; 13:15; 1 John 2:23; 4:2, 3, 15; 2 John 7 → to acknowledge, to openly acknowledge → CONFESS <3670> [2] Luke 7:29 → JUSTIFY <1344> [3] Acts 24:3 → ACCEPT <588> [4] Rom. 1:28 → lit.: to keep in the knowledge → KNOWLEDGE <1922> [5] Rom. 14:11; Phil. 2:11; Rev. 3:5 → CONFESS <1843> [6] 1 Cor. 14:37; 16:18; 2 Cor. 1:13a, b, 14 → RECOGNIZE <1921> [7] 1 Thes. 5:12 → KNOW <1492> [8] 2 Tim. 3:7 → lit.: to come to the knowledge → COME <2064>, KNOWLEDGE <1922> [9] Heb. 3:1 → whom we acknowledge → lit.: of our confession → CONFESSION <3671> [10] 3 John 9 → does not acknowledge our authority → does not receive us → RECEIVE <1926>.

ACKNOWLEDGING, ACKNOWLEDGMENT – 2 Tim. 2:25; Titus 1:1; Phm. 6 → KNOWLEDGE <1922>.

ACQUAINT – Luke 1:3 → to be acquainted with → INVESTIGATE <3877>.

ACQUAINTANCE – [1] ***gnōstos*** [adj. used as noun: γνωστός <1110>]; **from *ginōskō*: to know; lit.: known ► Person who is well known, but not necessarily a close friend >** The parents of Jesus sought Him among their relatives and acquaintances {friends} (Luke 2:44). All the acquaintances of {Those who knew} Jesus were standing at a distance when He was on the cross (Luke 23:49). All other refs.: EVIDENT <1110>, KNOWN <1110>.
[2] **to make acquaintance: *historeō*** [verb: ἱστορέω <2477>]; **from *histōr*: one who knows ► To find out about, to visit >** Paul went up to Jerusalem to make acquaintance with {become acquainted with, to see} Peter (Gal. 1:18). ¶

ACQUAINTED – [1] Acts 26:3 → well acquainted → EXPERT <1109> [2] Gal. 1:18 → to become, to get acquainted → to make acquaintance → ACQUAINTANCE <2477>.

ACQUAINTED (BE) – [1] Acts 19:15 → KNOW <1987> [2] 2 Tim. 3:15 → KNOW <1492>.

ACQUIRE – [1] ***katatithēmi*** [verb: κατατίθημι <2698>]; **from *kata*: down (intens.),**

and *tithēmi*: to put ▶ To do something in order to obtain; also transl.: to do, to grant, to show > Festus wanted to acquire the favor of the Jews (Acts 24:27; 25:9). Certain mss. have this verb in Mark 15:46 {to lay, to place} with the sense of: to lay down. ¶
– [2] Matt. 10:9 → PROVIDE <2932> [3] Acts 1:18 → PURCHASE (verb) <2932> [4] Acts 22:28 → OBTAIN <2932> [5] Eph. 1:14 → to acquire possession → redemption of the possession → REDEMPTION <629>.

ACQUIRED – Eph. 1:14 → acquired possession → POSSESSION <4047>.

ACQUIT – 1 Cor. 4:4 → JUSTIFY <1344>.

ACROSS – Luke 8:26 → OPPOSITE <495>.

ACT (noun) – [1] **in the very act: *epautophōrō*** [adv.: ἐπαυτοφώρῳ <1888>]; **from *epi*: in, and *autophōros*: caught in the act of stealing (or committing another crime), which is from *autos*: same, and *phōra*: theft; also written in some mss.: *ep' autophōrō* ▶ While engaged in a reprehensible activity** > A woman had been caught in the very act, committing adultery (John 8:4). ¶
– [2] Acts 9:36 → acts of charity → ALMS <1654> [3] Rom. 12:8 → to do acts of mercy → lit.: to show mercy [4] 2 Cor. 8:7, 19 → "act of" added in Engl. [5] Heb. 11:17 → was in the act of offering up → lit.: was offering up.

ACT (verb) – [1] **to act as if: *prospoieō*** [verb: προσποιέω <4364>]; **from *pros*: alongside, toward, and *poieō*: to make ▶ To behave as though, to conduct oneself so as to suggest a particular intent** > Jesus acted as if He would have gone farther when in the company of the two disciples of Emmaus (Luke 24:28). ¶
– [2] Matt. 7:24, 26; Luke 6:47, 49 → to put in practice → PRACTICE (noun) <4160> [3] Acts 17:7 → to act contrary → CONTRARY <4238> <561> [4] Rom. 14:15; 1 Cor. 3:3; 2 Cor. 12:18; Col. 4:5 → WALK <4043> [5] 1 Cor. 7:36; 13:5 → to act unbecomingly → to behave uncomely, unseemly → BEHAVE <807> [6] 2 Cor. 7:4; Heb. 5:1 → "to act," "I am acting with" added in Engl. [7] 1 Tim. 1:13; Jas. 2:12 → DO <4160> [8] Heb. 13:18 → to conduct oneself → CONDUCT (verb)[1] <390> [9] Jas. 1:25 → a doer who acts → lit.: a doer of the work → WORK (noun) <2041> [10] Rev. 13:5 → CONTINUE <4160> [11] Rev. 17:17b → EXECUTE <4160>.

ACTION – [1] ***ergon*** [neut. noun: ἔργον <2041>]; **from *ergō*: to work ▶ Deed, result of work** > What he was in word in his letters, Paul was also in his actions (2 Cor. 10:11). All other refs.: DEED <2041>, WORK (noun) <2041>.
– [2] Luke 12:35 → stay dressed for action → lit.: let your loins be girded about → GIRD <4024> [3] Luke 23:51 → DEED <4234> [4] Rom. 7:15 → my own actions → lit.: what I do (*katergazomai*) [5] 1 Pet. 1:13 → to prepare for action → to gird up → GIRD <328>.

ACTIVE – [1] Phm. 6 → EFFECTIVE <1756> [2] Heb. 4:12 → OPERATIVE <1756> [3] Jas. 2:22 → to be active along with → to work with → WORK (verb) <4903>.

ACTIVITY – [1] 1 Cor. 12:6 → OPERATION <1755> [2] 2 Cor. 10:15 → area of activity → RULE (noun) <2583> [3] 2 Thes. 2:9 → WORKING (noun) <1753>.

ACTUALLY – [1] ***holōs*** [adv.: ὅλως <3654>]; **from *holos*: all, whole ▶ Entirely, completely** > It was actually {universally, commonly} reported that there was immorality among the Corinthians (1 Cor. 5:1). Other refs.: Matt. 5:34 (at all); 1 Cor. 6:7 (already); 15:29 (at all). ¶
– [2] 1 Thes. 2:13 → TRULY <230>.

ADAM – ***Adam*** [masc. name: Ἀδάμ <76>]: **ruddy, in Heb. ▶ Name of the first man** > God created Adam from dust (see 1 Cor. 15:47). By his disobedience, sin entered into the world and affected all of his posterity, all of mankind; all die because of sin (1 Cor. 15:22), but those who believe in the Son of God have eternal life (see John 5:24). Jesus Christ, called the "last Adam" (1 Cor. 15:45b), is the head of a new line of descendants (Rom. 5:14a, b; see vv. 14–21), the believers in Him justified by faith. The name of Adam is mentioned in the genealogy of Jesus (Luke 3:38). Other refs.: 1 Cor. 15:45a; 1 Tim. 2:13, 14; Jude 14. ¶

ADAPTED – Acts 27:12 → ill adapted → not suitable → SUITABLE <428>.

ADD – [1] ***epidiatassomai*** [verb: ἐπιδιατάσσομαι <1928>]; **from *epi*: upon, besides, and *diatassō*: to arrange in order, which is from *dia*: through, and *tassō*: to order ▶ To join something, to ordain besides** > No one adds other dispositions to a confirmed covenant (Gal. 3:15). ¶
[2] ***epitithēmi*** [verb: ἐπιτίθημι <2007>]; **from *epi*: upon, and *tithēmi*: to put ▶ To say or write more; to inflict** > If anyone adds to the things in Revelation, God will add to him the plagues which are written in this book (Rev. 22:18a, b). All other refs.: see entries in Lexicon at <2007>.
[3] ***epichorēgeō*** [verb: ἐπιχορηγέω <2023>]; **from *epi*: to, and *chorēgeō*: see SUPPLY** (verb) <5524> **▶ To provide more, to supplement** > Christians are to add {to supply} virtue to their faith (2 Pet. 1:5). All other refs.: NOURISH <2023>, SUPPLY (verb) <2023>.
[4] ***prosanatithēmi*** [verb: προσανατίθημι <4323>]; **from *pros*: beside, meaning in addition to, and *anatithēmi*: to communicate, which is from *ana*: intens., and *tithēmi*: to put ▶ To give, to impart something else** > Those who seemed to be important added {communicated, contributed} nothing to Paul (Gal. 2:6). Other ref.: Gal. 1:16; see CONFER <4323>. ¶
[5] ***prostithēmi*** [verb: προστίθημι <4369>]; **from *pros*: to, besides, and *tithēmi*: to put; lit.: to put more ▶ a. To increase, to augment** > No one by worrying can add one cubit to his stature (Matt. 6:27; Luke 12:25). To those who seek first the kingdom of God and His righteousness, various things will be added {will be given as well} (Matt. 6:33; Luke 12:31). Herod added to all his other evil deeds shutting up John the Baptist in prison (Luke 3:20). Jesus added and spoke {went on to tell} a parable (Luke 19:11). About three thousand souls were added to the church in one day (Acts 2:41); the Lord added daily to the church those who were to be saved (v. 47). A large crowd of people were added {were brought} to the Lord in Antioch (Acts 11:24). The law was added because of transgressions (Gal. 3:19). **b. To unite, to gather** > Christians were more than ever added to the Lord (Acts 5:14). David was added to {was laid unto, was laid among, was buried with} his fathers (Acts 13:36). Other refs.: Mark 4:24; Luke 17:5; 20:11, 12; Acts 12:3; Heb. 12:19. ¶
– [6] Acts 1:26 → NUMBER (verb) <4785> [7] Phil. 1:16 → STIR (verb) <2018> [8] Heb. 10:9 → SAY <2046>.

ADDI – ***Addi*** [masc. name: Ἀδδί <78>] ▶ **Man of the O.T.** > Addi is mentioned in the genealogy of Jesus (Luke 3:28). ¶

ADDICT – 1 Cor. 16:15 → to addict oneself → to devote oneself → DEVOTE <5021>.

ADDICTED (BE) – [1] 1 Tim. 3:3; Titus 1:7 → addicted to wine → given to wine → GIVE <3943> [2] 1 Tim. 3:8 → to be addicted → to be given → GIVE <4337> [3] Titus 2:3 → to be under bondage → BONDAGE <1402>.

ADDRESS (noun) – Acts 12:21 → to deliver an address, to deliver a public address → to make a public oration → ORATION <1215>.

ADDRESS (verb) – [1] ***prosphōneō*** [verb: προσφωνέω <4377>]; **from *pros*: to, and *phōneō*: to speak ▶ To speak to, to deliver a speech to someone** > Pilate addressed {called out, appealed} again to the crowd, wishing to release Jesus (Luke 23:20). Paul addressed the people in the Hebrew tongue (Acts 21:40; 22:2). Other refs.: Matt. 11:16;

Luke 6:13; 7:32; 13:12; see CALL (verb) <4377>. ¶
– [2] Acts 3:12; Rev. 7:13 → ANSWER (verb) <611> [3] 1 Tim. 4:5 → PRAYER <1783> [4] Heb. 5:10 → DESIGNATE <4316> [5] Heb. 12:5 → SPEAK <1256> [6] Heb. 12:19 → SPEAK <4369> [7] 1 Pet. 1:17 → CALL (verb) <1941>.

ADEQUACY – 2 Cor. 3:5 → SUFFICIENCY <2426>.

ADEQUATE – [1] 2 Cor. 2:16 → SUFFICIENT <2425> [2] 2 Cor. 3:5 → ABLE <2425> [3] 2 Cor. 3:6 → to make adequate → to make competent → COMPETENT <2427> [4] 2 Tim. 3:17 → COMPLETE (adj.) <739>.

ADEQUATELY – Acts 18:26 → more adequately → more accurately → ACCURATELY <197>.

ADHERENT – Rom. 4:14, 16 → "adherent" added in Engl.

ADIEU – [1] Luke 9:61 → to bid adieu → to bid farewell → FAREWELL <657> [2] 2 Cor. 2:13 → to bid adieu → to take leave → LEAVE (noun) <657>.

ADJOINED (BE) – **to be adjoined to:** ***sunomoreō*** [verb: συνομορέω <4927>]**; from *sun*: together, and *homoros*: bordering, which is from *homos*: common, joint, and *horos*: border ▶ To be contiguous with, to share a common wall with** > The house of Justus, who worshipped God, was adjoined to {joined hard to, was next to, was next door to} the synagogue (Acts 18:7). ¶

ADJOURN – ***anaballō*** [verb: ἀναβάλλω <306>]**; from *ana*: back, and *ballō*: to send, to throw ▶ To postpone, to put off until a future time** > Felix adjourned {deferred, put off} hearing Paul and his accusers (Acts 24:22). ¶

ADJUDGE – Luke 23:24 → to give sentence → SENTENCE <1948>.

ADJURE – [1] ***horkizō*** [verb: ὁρκίζω <3726>]**; from *horkos*: pledge, oath; lit.: to make to swear ▶ a. To ask, to request earnestly** > A man with an evil spirit, i.e., the spirit himself, adjured {implored} Jesus by God that He would not torment him (Mark 5:7). Paul adjured {charged} the Thessalonians that his epistle be read to all the holy brothers (1 Thes. 5:27; other mss.: *enorkizō*). **b. To command** > Some exorcists were adjuring {exorcising} evil spirits to come out by invoking the name of Jesus, whom Paul preached (Acts 19:13; other mss.: *exorkizō*). ¶
[2] ***exorkizō*** [verb: ἐξορκίζω <1844>]**; from *ek*: intens., and *horkizō*: see [1] ▶ To ask someone to testify, to command** > The high priest adjured {charged under oath, put under oath} Jesus to tell him and others if He was the Christ, the Son of God (Matt. 26:63). ¶

ADMIN – Luke 3:33 in some mss. → ARAM <689>.

ADMINISTER – [1] ***diakoneō*** [verb: διακονέω <1247>]**; from *diakonos*: servant, deacon, poss. from *diakō*: to hasten ▶ To assume a service, to manage; also transl.: to serve, to minister** > Paul was carrying a gift (most likely an important sum) which he administered to the glory of the Lord (2 Cor. 8:19); he wanted to avoid being blamed concerning the way he administered {in the administration of} this gift (v. 20). All other refs.: MINISTER (verb) <1247>, SERVE <1247>.
– [2] Heb. 11:33 → WROUGHT (HAVE) <2038>.

ADMINISTRATING – 1 Cor. 12:28 → ADMINISTRATION <2941>.

ADMINISTRATION – [1] ***diakonia*** [fem. noun: διακονία <1248>]**; from *diakonos*: servant, deacon, poss. from *diakō*: to hasten ▶ What a servant has to do, ministry** > The administration of their service by the Corinthians {The service they performed, Their ministration} was supplying the needs of God's people (2 Cor.

9:12). All other refs.: MINISTRY <1248>, SERVE <1248>, SERVICE <1248>.
[2] ***kubernēsis*** [fem. noun: κυβέρνησις <2941>]; **from *kubernaō*: to govern, to direct ▶ Spiritual gift that relates to the direction given to a local church** > God has given administrations {administrating, governments} as a gift of grace (1 Cor. 12:28). Thus he who exercises leadership in a local church is called to do so with diligence (see Rom. 12:8). ¶
– [3] 1 Cor. 9:17; Eph. 1:10; 3:2, 9; 1 Tim. 1:4 → DISPENSATION <3622> [4] 2 Cor. 8:20 → ADMINISTER <1247> [5] 1 Tim. 1:4 → EDIFYING <3622>.

ADMIRABLE – Phil. 4:8 → of good report → REPORT (noun) <2163>.

ADMIRATION – [1] **to have in admiration: *thaumazō*** [verb: θαυμάζω <2296>]; **from *thauma*: object of amazement, wonder; lit.: to be surprised ▶ To regard with approval, to show amazement** > Jude speaks of those who have men's persons in admiration {who are flattering people, who are admiring persons} because of benefits (Jude 16). All other refs.: ADMIRE <2296>, MARVEL (verb) <2296>, WONDER (verb) <2296>.
– [2] Rev. 17:6 → AMAZEMENT <2295>.

ADMIRE – ***thaumazō*** [verb: θαυμάζω <2296>]; **from *thauma*: object of amazement, wonder; lit.: to be surprised ▶ To marvel, to regard with wonder** > Jesus will come to be admired among all those who have believed (2 Thes. 1:10). All other refs.: ADMIRATION <2296>, MARVEL (verb) <2296>, WONDER (verb) <2296>.

ADMIT – [1] Acts 24:14; Heb. 11:13 → CONFESS <3670> [2] 1 Tim. 5:19 → to admit a charge → to receive an accusation → RECEIVE <3858>.

ADMONISH – [1] ***noutheteō*** [verb: νουθετέω <3560>]; **from *nous*: mind, intelligence, and *tithēmi*: to put, to set ▶ To remind, to caution, to exhort in view of helping others** > Paul was persuaded that the Christians of Rome were able to admonish {instruct} one another (Rom. 15:14). He himself admonished {warned} every man to the end that he might present every man perfect in Christ (Col. 1:28). He urged the Colossians to admonish one another, in psalms, hymns, and spiritual songs (Col. 3:16). The Thessalonians were to know those who were admonishing them {giving them instructions} (1 Thes. 5:12), and to esteem them very highly (see v. 13). They were to admonish {warn} a brother who did not obey the word of God (2 Thes. 3:15). Other refs.: Acts 20:31; 1 Cor. 4:14; 1 Thes. 5:14; see WARN <3560>. ¶
[2] ***paraineō*** [verb: παραινέω <3867>]; **from *para*: near, unto, and *aineō*: to recommend, to order ▶ To exhort, to warn** > Paul admonished {advised, counselled} the passengers that the sailing would be dangerous (Acts 27:9). Other refs.: Luke 3:18 in some mss.; Acts 27:22; see EXHORT <3867>. ¶
[3] ***sōphronizō*** [verb: σωφρονίζω <4994>]; **from *sōphrōn*: sound, moderate, prudent ▶ To teach, to train (by encouraging sound judgment)** > The older women are to admonish {to encourage, to urge} the young women to love their husbands and their children (Titus 2:4). ¶

ADMONITION – ***nouthesia*** [fem. noun: νουθεσία <3559>]; **from *noutheteō*: to admonish; which is from *nous*: mind, intelligence, and *tithēmi*: to put, to set ▶ Advice, instruction; also: warning, reprimand** > The things that have happened to Israel have been written for our admonition (1 Cor. 10:11). Fathers must bring up their children in the discipline and admonition of the Lord (Eph. 6:4). Titus was to reject a heretical man after a first and a second admonition (Titus 3:10). ¶

ADO – Mark 5:39 → to make an ado → to make a tumult → TUMULT <2350>.

ADOPT – [1] Acts 7:21 → lit.: to take up, to take away [2] Eph. 1:5 → to be adopted → lit.: for adoption → ADOPTION <5206>.

ADOPTION – ***huiothesia*** [fem. noun: υἱοθεσία <5206>]; **from *huios*: son, and *tithēmi*: to place, to designate; lit.: sonship ▶ Act of taking legally as a son into one's family; also transl.: adoption as sons, adoption to sonship** > Christians have received a spirit of adoption {sonship} by whom they cry: Abba, Father (Rom. 8:15). They wait for the adoption, i.e., the redemption of their body (Rom. 8:23), when the Lord will return. The adoption also belongs to the Israelites as an earthly people (Rom. 9:4). The adoption {full rights of sons} was made possible for those under the law by the redemption accomplished by the Son of God (Gal. 4:5). God has predestined Christians for adoption {to be adopted} as sons by Jesus Christ to Himself (Eph. 1:5). ¶

ADORN – ***kosmeō*** [verb: κοσμέω <2885>]; **from *kosmos*: harmonious arrangement, world ▶ a. To arrange, to set in order, to embellish; also transl.: to decorate, to garnish** > An unclean spirit finds his previous house unoccupied, swept, and adorned {put in order, garnished} (Matt. 12:44; Luke 11:25). The scribes and the Pharisees adorned the tombs of the just (Matt. 23:29). The temple was adorned with beautiful stones and consecrated offerings (Luke 21:5). The foundations of the wall of the city were adorned with every precious stone (Rev. 21:19). **b. To honor** > Christian bondservants are to adorn {make attractive} the teaching of their Savior God in all things (Titus 2:10). **c. To clothe oneself with elegance** > Believing women are to adorn {to dress} themselves with modest dress (1 Tim. 2:9). Peter speaks of the fashion in which holy women adorned themselves {made themselves beautiful} in former times (1 Pet. 3:5). **d. Figur.: to deck out, to dress** > The new Jerusalem was prepared as a bride adorned {beautifully dressed} for her husband (Rev. 21:2). Other ref.: Matt. 25:7; see TRIM <2885>. ¶

ADORNING – 1 Pet. 3:3; v. 4 in some mss. → ADORNMENT <2889>.

ADORNMENT – ***kosmos*** [masc. noun: κόσμος <2889>]; **comp. *komeō*: to take care of ▶ Harmonious, attractive arrangement** > In 1 Pet. 3:3, the adornment {adorning, beauty} of a believing woman is not to be an outward one, but rather one of the heart and spirit (see v. 4). Other refs.: WORLD <2889>.

ADRAMYTTIAN – Acts 27:2 → of Adramyttium → ADRAMYTTIUM <98>.

ADRAMYTTIUM – **of Adramyttium: *Adramuttēnos*** [adj.: Ἀδραμυττηνός <98>] **▶ Port of Asia Minor on the Aegean Sea** > During their journey to Rome, Paul and other prisoners boarded a ship returning to its home port of Adramyttium (Acts 27:2). ¶

ADRIATIC SEA – ***Adrias*** [masc. name: Ἀδρίας <99>] **▶ Part of the Mediterranean Sea situated between Italy and the Balkan peninsula** > On its journey to Rome, the ship which Paul and other prisoners had boarded faced a fierce storm on the Adriatic Sea (Acts 27:27). ¶

ADRIFT – 2 Cor. 11:25 → adrift at sea → lit.: in the deep; see DEEP (noun) <1037>.

ADULT – 1 Cor. 14:20 → mature man → MATURE <5046>.

ADULTERATE – 2 Cor. 4:2 → FALSIFY <1389>.

ADULTERER – ***moichos*** [masc. noun: μοιχός <3432>] **▶ Person guilty of conjugal unfaithfulness** > God will judge adulterers {the adulterous} (Heb. 13:4). Other refs.: Luke 18:11; 1 Cor. 6:9; Jas. 4:4a, b (in some mss.). ¶

ADULTEROUS (adj.) – ***moichalis*** [fem. noun and noun used as adj.: μοιχαλίς <3428>] **▶ Term applied to a generation or a person to characterize its unfaithfulness** > Jesus uses the expr. "adulterous generation" to stigmatize the unfaithfulness of the Jewish people in relation to the covenant God had contracted with them (Matt. 12:39). Other refs.: Matt. 16:4; Mark 8:38; Rom. 7:3a, b; Jas. 4:4 (in some mss.); 2 Pet. 2:14 {of adultery}. ¶

ADULTEROUS (noun) – Heb. 13:4 → the adulterous → ADULTERER <3432>.

ADULTERY – [1] ***moicheia*** [fem. noun: μοιχεία <3430>]; **from *moicheuō*: to commit adultery ▶ Sexual intercourse outside marriage of which a married person is guilty >** Adultery comes forth out of the heart (Matt. 15:19; Mark 7:21 or 22); it is one of the works of the flesh (Gal. 5:19 in some mss.). A woman caught in adultery was brought to Jesus (John 8:3). ¶
[2] **to commit adultery: *moichaō*** [verb: μοιχάω <3429>] **or *moicheuō*** [verb: μοιχεύω <3431>]; **from *moichos*: adulterer ▶ To have sexual intercourse outside marriage >** Jesus said that whoever looks at a woman to lust for her has already committed adultery with her in his heart (Matt. 5:28). A woman was caught in adultery (lit.: caught committing adultery) (John 8:4). The expr. "to commit adultery" has the meaning of being guilty of unfaithfulness in Rev. 2:22. Other refs.: Matt. 5:27, 32a, b; 19:9, 18; Mark 10:11, 12, 19; Luke 16:18a, b; 18:20; Rom. 2:22a, b; 13:9; Jas. 2:11a, b. ¶
– [3] 2 Pet. 2:14 → of adultery → ADULTEROUS (adj.) <3428>.

ADVANCE – [1] **to be well advanced: *probainō*** [verb: προβαίνω <4260>]; **from *pro*: before, forward, and *bainō*: to go, to walk ▶ The verb is used to describe the state of older persons >** Zacharias and Elizabeth were both well advanced {stricken} in years (Luke 1:7, 18). Anna was far advanced in years {of a great age, well advanced in age, advanced in years} (Luke 2:36). Other refs. (to go, to go on): Matt. 4:21; Mark 1:19. ¶
– [2] Luke 2:52; Gal. 1:14; 2 Tim. 2:16 → INCREASE (verb) <4298> [3] Phil. 1:12 → lit.: for the furtherance → FURTHERANCE <4297> [4] 1 Tim. 1:4 → advancing God's work → godly edifying → EDIFYING <3622> [5] 2 Tim. 3:9 → PROCEED <4298> [6] 2 Tim. 3:13 → GROW <4298>.

ADVANTAGE (noun) – [1] ***perisson*; from *perissos*** [adj. used as noun: περισσός <4053>]; **from *peri*: above, beyond ▶ More beneficial state, superiority >** Paul asks what is the advantage of the Jew (Rom. 3:1). All other refs.: ABUNDANTLY <4053>, HIGHLY (VERY) <4053>, SUPERFLUOUS <4053>.
[2] **to take advantage: *pleonekteō*** [verb: πλεονεκτέω <4122>]; **from *pleion*: more, and *echō*: to have ▶ To get the better of someone, to use fraudulent means >** Satan could take advantage of {outwit} the Christians, but they are not ignorant of his schemes (2 Cor. 2:11). All other refs.: CHEAT <4122>, WRONG (verb) <4122>.
[3] **to take advantage: *huperbainō*** [verb: ὑπερβαίνω <5233>]; **from *huper*: above, beyond, and *bainō*: to go, to walk ▶ To act to the detriment of someone, e.g., by going over the limits of chastity >** No one should take advantage of {overstep the rights of, transgress} and wrong his brother by committing adultery with his wife (1 Thes. 4:6); one transl. inverts the verbs: to wrong and to take advantage. ¶
– [4] Mark 5:26 → to find advantage → HELPED (BE) <5623> [5] John 16:7; 2 Cor. 8:10 → to be to the advantage → to be profitable → PROFITABLE <4851> [6] Acts 7:19 → to take shrewd advantage → to deal subtly → DEAL <2686> [7] Rom. 3:1 → PROFIT (noun) <5622> [8] Rom. 3:9 → do we have any advantage → lit.: are we better → BETTER <4284> [9] 1 Cor. 10:33 → PROFIT (noun) <4852a> [10] 1 Cor. 15:32 → PROFIT (verb) <3786> [11] Gal. 5:2 → to be of advantage → PROFIT (noun) <5623> [12] Phil. 2:6 → something to be used to His own advantage → ROBBERY <725> [13] Heb. 13:17 → of no advantage → UNPROFITABLE <255>.

ADVANTAGE (verb) – 1 Cor. 15:32 → lit.: to be the profit → PROFIT (noun) <3786>.

ADVANTAGED (BE) – Luke 9:25 → PROFIT (verb) <5623>.

ADVENTURE – **to adventure oneself: *didōmi heauton*; to give: *didōmi*** [verb:

δίδωμι <1325>]; **oneself: *heautou*** [pron.: ἑαυτοῦ <1438>]; **lit.: to give oneself, i.e., to expose oneself ▶ To venture, to take the risk to go** > Paul's friends urged him not to adventure {to throw} himself in the theatre in Ephesus (Acts 19:31). Other refs. (*didōmi*): GIVE <1325>.

ADVERSARY – [1] ***antidikos*** [masc. noun: ἀντίδικος <476>]; **from *anti*: against, and *dikē*: judgment, trial ▶ Opponent in a lawsuit; also transl.: adverse party, opponent** > Jesus says to make friends quickly with an adversary, otherwise there is a risk of being thrown into prison (Matt. 5:25a, b; Luke 12:58). In a parable, a widow wanted to be avenged from her adversary (Luke 18:3). The devil is the adversary {enemy} of the Christians (1 Pet. 5:8; see Job 1:7–12). ¶

[2] ***hupenantios*** [adj. and adj. used as noun: ὑπεναντίος <5227>]; **from *hupo*: under, and *enantios*: who is in front, contrary, which is from: *en*: in, and *antios*: set against ▶ Opponent, rebel** > The adversaries {enemies} of God are about to be devoured by the heat of a fire (Heb. 10:27). Other ref.: Col. 2:14; see CONTRARY <5227>. ¶

[3] **to be the adversary: *antikeimai*** [verb: ἀντίκειμαι <480>]; **from *anti*: against, and *keimai*: to lie, to find oneself ▶ To be the opponent** > The lit. expr. "those who are the adversaries" is also transl. "the adversaries" {the opposers, the opponents, those who oppose} in the following refs. The adversaries of Jesus were ashamed (Luke 13:17). The adversaries of the disciples would not be able to reply to or resist their words and wisdom (Luke 21:15). Paul was saying that there were many adversaries (1 Cor. 16:9). The Philippians should not be frightened in anything by their adversaries (Phil. 1:28). The younger women should not give occasion to the adversary {enemy} concerning reproach (1 Tim. 5:14). Other refs.: Gal. 5:17; 2 Thes. 2:4; 1 Tim. 1:10; see OPPOSE <480>. ¶

ADVERSE – Matt. 5:25a, b; Luke 12:58; 18:3 → adverse party → ADVERSARY <476>.

ADVERSITY – Heb. 13:3 → to suffer adversity → TORMENTED (BE) <2558>.

ADVICE – [1] ***gnōmē*** [fem. noun: γνώμη <1106>]; **from *ginōskō*: to learn, to understand, to discern ▶ Thought, decision based on the capacity of discerning** > Paul gave his advice {opinion} to the Corinthians to share what they had (2 Cor. 8:10). All other refs.: JUDGMENT <1106>, MIND (noun) <1106>, OPINION <1106>, PURPOSE (verb) <1106>.
– [2] Acts 27:12 → ADVISE <1014> [3] Acts 27:21 → to follow, to take the advice → LISTEN <3980>.

ADVISABLE – 1 Cor. 16:4 → MEET (adj.) <514>.

ADVISE – [1] ***boulomai*** [verb: βούλομαι <1014>]; **advice: *boulē*** [fem. noun: βουλή <1012>] **▶ To want, to decide** > Most people on board Paul's ship advised {counselled} to attain Phoenix (Acts 27:12); some mss. have: gave the advice (*boulē*). Other refs. (*boulomai*): PLEASE <1014>, PURPOSE (verb) <1014>, WANT (verb) <1014>, WILL (verb) <1014>.
– [2] John 18:14 → CONSULT <4823> [3] Acts 27:9 → ADMONISH <3867> [4] Rev. 3:18 → COUNSEL (verb) <4823>.

ADVOCATE (noun) – ***Paraklētos*** [masc. noun: Παράκλητος <3875>]; **from *parakaleō*: to encourage, to comfort, which is from *para*: near, to the side of, and *kaleō*: to call ▶ One who defends the cause of someone else, who intercedes on his behalf; this includes the notions of helping, comforting, and encouraging** > This word is a title of Jesus Christ the righteous: He is the Advocate {one who speaks in the defense} of the Christians with the Father (1 John 2:1), prob. emphasizing the Lord's role as intercessor. "Advocate" also designates the Holy Spirit and is transl. by "Comforter" {Counselor, Helper} in John

14:16, 26; 15:26; 16:7. The Father would give another Comforter to be with Christians forever (John 14:16). This Comforter, the Holy Spirit sent by the Father in the name of Jesus, would teach all things and bring to remembrance all things said by Jesus (John 14:26). He would bear witness concerning Jesus (John 15:26). Jesus had to go away before He could send the Comforter (John 16:7). Thus, the Lord Jesus in heaven and the Holy Spirit on earth look after the interests of Christians by interceding for them. ¶

ADVOCATE (verb) – 1 Acts 16:21 → PREACH <2605> 2 1 Tim. 6:3 → to advocate a different doctrine → to teach other doctrine → DOCTRINE <2085>.

ADVOCATING – Acts 17:18 → PROCLAIMER <2604>.

AENEAS – ***Aineas*** [masc. name: Αἰνέας <132>] ▶ **Paralyzed man of Lydda** > Aeneas was healed by Peter in the name of Jesus (Acts 9:33, 34). His healing resulted in turning those who lived in his region to the Lord (see Acts 9:35). ¶

AENON – ***Ainōn*** [fem. name: Αἰνών <137>] ▶ **Place in Palestine near Salim** > John baptized in Aenon because there was much water there (John 3:23); this site is near the Jordan river. ¶

AFAR OFF – 1 ***porrōthen*** [adv.: πόρρωθεν <4207>]; **from *porrō*: far off, and suffix *then*: from, at a place** ▶ **At a distance** > Ten lepers met Jesus and stood afar off (Luke 17:12). Other ref.: Heb. 11:13 {from a distance}. ¶

– 2 Luke 23:49; Rev. 18:10, 15, 17 → at a distance → DISTANCE <575> <3113>.

AFFAIR – 1 ***pragmateia*** [fem. noun: πραγματεία <4230>]; **from *pragmateuomai*: to do business, which is from *pragma*: matter, business** ▶ **Business, transaction; in classical Greek, the word means "occupation," "business," and "troubles" in the plur.** > No one serving as a soldier entangles himself with the affairs of life (2 Tim. 2:4). ¶

2 ***ta***; **fem. of *ho*** [art.: ὁ <3588>] ▶ **Lit.: the (matters), the (things)** > Paul speaks of "our affairs" {how we are} (Eph. 6:22), "your affairs" {your state, how you get on, news about you} (Phil. 2:19), "my affairs" {how it goes with me} (Phil. 2:23), "your affairs" {your circumstances, your state, your estate} (Col. 4:8). *

AFFECTION – 1 **affection, inward affection: *splanchnon*** [neut. noun: σπλάγχνον <4698>]; **comp. *splēn*: spleen; lit.: entrails; the word is always plur. in the N.T.; in Classical Greek, *splanchna* are the viscera (mainly heart, liver, lung)** ▶ **Tenderness, kind feelings; figur.: heart** > Paul said that the inward affection {the affections} of Titus was {were} more abundantly toward the Corinthians (2 Cor. 7:15). All other refs.: ENTRAILS <4698>, TENDERNESS <4698>.

2 **inordinate affection: *pathos*** [neut. noun: πάθος <3806>]; **from *paschō*: to suffer** ▶ **The word is used concerning passions and evil desires, lust** > The Christian must abstain from inordinate affection {passion, vile passions} (Col. 3:5). Other refs.: Rom. 1:26; 1 Thes. 4:5; see PASSION <3806>. ¶

3 **without natural affection: *astorgos*** [adj.: ἄστοργος <794>]; **from *a*: neg., and *storgē*: tenderness, in particular between parents and children** ▶ **Without feelings proper to family relationships** > Paul speaks of men without natural affection {heartless, unloving, without love} (Rom. 1:31; 2 Tim. 3:3). ¶

– 4 Rom. 12:10 → brotherly affection → brotherly love → LOVE (noun) <5360> 5 1 Cor. 7:3 → GOOD WILL <2133> 6 Gal. 5:24 → PASSION <3804> 7 Col. 3:2 → to set the affection → lit.: to be of the same mind → MIND (noun) <5426> 8 1 Thes. 2:8 → to have a fond affection → to be affectionately desirous → AFFECTIONATELY <2442>.

AFFECTIONATE – **kindly affectionate: *philostorgos*** [adj.: φιλόστοργος <5387>]; **from *philos*: friend, and *storgē*: affection,**

tenderness, in particular between parents and children ▶ Showing kindness, tenderness > Christians should be kindly affectionate {kindly affectioned, devoted} toward one another as to brotherly love (Rom. 12:10). ¶

AFFECTIONATELY – to be affectionately desirous: *himeiromai* [verb: ἱμείρομαι <2442>]; **from *himeros*: strong desire, yearning ▶ To desire with much affection, to love >** Paul and his companions were affectionately desirous of {were affectionately longing for, were yearning over, had a fond affection for} the Thessalonians (1 Thes. 2:8), i.e., they were full of affection for them; *homeiromai* in other mss.: to long for. ¶

AFFECTIONED – Rom. 12:10 → kindly affectioned → kindly affectionate → AFFECTIONATE <5387>.

AFFIRM – 1 to affirm; to affirm constantly, confidently, strenuously: *diabebaioomai* [verb: διαβεβαιόομαι <1226>]; **from *dia*: intens., and *bebaioō*: to confirm, to assure ▶ To strongly affirm, to stress >** Some men do not understand what they so strenuously affirm {the matters about which they do make confident assertions} (1 Tim. 1:7). Paul wanted Titus to affirm constantly {to insist strenuously, to speak confidently} on certain things (Titus 3:8). ¶

2 to confidently affirm, to constantly affirm: *diischurizomai* [verb: διϊσχυρίζομαι <1340>]; **from *dia*: intens., and *ischurizomai*: to affirm, which is from *ischuros*: strong, vigorous ▶ To insist, to affirm with strength >** A man confidently affirmed {asserted, stoutly maintained} that Peter had been with Jesus (Luke 22:59). Rhoda constantly affirmed {kept insisting, maintained} that Peter was standing before the gate (Acts 12:15). Other ref.: Acts 15:2 in some mss. ¶

3 *phēmi* [verb: φημί <5346>]; **from *phaō*: to give light ▶ To bring to light by speech, i.e., to say, to claim >** Some affirmed that Paul and his friends said to practice evil things that good ones might come (Rom. 3:8). Other refs.: SAY <5346>.

– 4 Acts 24:9; 25:19 → SAY <5335> 5 Eph. 4:17 → TESTIFY <3143>.

AFFIRM (I) – *nē* [particle: νή <3513>] **▶ Yes indeed, I swear >** The word is used in swearing or affirming an oath; ref.: 1 Cor. 15:31. ¶ ‡

AFFLICTED (BE) – 1 *thlibō* [verb: θλίβω <2346>]; **similar to Lat. *fligere*: to strike ▶ To be oppressed, to be weighed down; also transl.: to be hard pressed, to be in distress, to be in tribulation, to be distressed, to be harassed, to be persecuted, to be troubled, to suffer affliction, to suffer tribulation >** If Paul and Timothy were afflicted, it was for the encouragement and salvation of the Corinthians (2 Cor. 1:6). Paul was afflicted in every way, but not distressed (2 Cor. 4:8). When Paul and Timothy came into Macedonia, they were afflicted on every side (2 Cor. 7:5). Paul had said beforehand that he was going to suffer affliction (1 Thes. 3:4). O.T. people of faith were afflicted (Heb. 11:37). Other refs.: Matt. 7:14 {to be narrow}; Mark 3:9 {to crowd}; 2 Thes. 1:6, 7; 1 Tim. 5:10. ¶

– 2 Matt. 4:24 → TAKE <4912> 3 Matt. 24:9 → AFFLICTION <2347> 4 John 5:4 → HAVE <2722> 5 Acts 5:16 → TORMENT (verb) <3791> 6 Acts 7:6 → OPPRESS <2559> 7 Acts 28:8 → SUFFER <4912> 8 Jas. 4:9 → to be afflicted → LAMENT <5003> 9 Jas. 5:13 → SUFFER <2553>.

AFFLICTION – 1 *thlipsis* [fem. noun: θλῖψις <2347>]; **from *thlibō*: to compress, to oppress ▶ Oppression, suffering; also transl.: distress, tribulation, trouble >** Before Jesus returns, the disciples will be delivered up to affliction {will be afflicted, will be handed over to be persecuted} (Matt. 24:9). God delivered Joseph out of all his afflictions in Egypt (Acts 7:10). Paul was writing to the Corinthians with much affliction and distress of heart {out of a great distress and anguish of heart} (2 Cor. 2:4). The Philippians took part in Paul's affliction (Phil. 4:14). Paul was filling up in his flesh what was lacking in the afflictions of Christ for His body, the church (Col. 1:24). The Hebrews were made a spectacle both in reproaches and afflictions {persecutions} (Heb. 10:33). Pure and undefiled religion is to visit orphans and widows in their affliction (Jas. 1:27). All other refs.: ANGUISH <2347>, DISTRESS <2347>, TRIBULATION <2347>, TROUBLE (noun) <2347>.

[2] ***mastix*** [fem. noun: μάστιξ <3148>]; **comp. *maiomai*: to seek, to pursue with zeal ► Very distressing illness or evil; also transl.: disease, plague, scourge, sickness, suffering** > All those who were afflicted with any affliction pressed on Jesus to be healed (Mark 3:10). A woman was healed of her affliction when she touched Jesus (Mark 5:29, 34). Jesus healed many people of diseases and afflictions (Luke 7:21). Other refs.: Acts 22:24; Heb. 11:36; see SCOURGING <3148>. ¶

[3] **to suffer affliction with: *sunkakoucheomai*** [verb: συγκακουχέομαι <4778>]; **from *sun*: with, and *kakoucheō*: to mistreat, to torment ► To be mistreated with, to be persecuted with** > Moses chose rather to suffer affliction along with {to endure ill-treatment with, to be mistreated along with} the people of God than to have the temporary pleasure of sin (Heb. 11:25). ¶

– [4] Matt. 4:23; 9:35; 10:1 → DISEASE <3119> [5] Acts 7:34 → OPPRESSION <2561> [6] 1 Thes. 3:4 → to suffer affliction → to be afflicted → AFFLICTED (BE) <2346> [7] 2 Tim. 1:8 → to be partaker of the afflictions → to join in suffering → SUFFERING <4777> [8] 2 Tim. 3:11; Heb. 10:32; 1 Pet. 5:9 → SUFFERING <3804> [9] 2 Tim. 4:5 → to endure afflictions → to endure hardship → HARDSHIP <2553>, SUFFER <2553>.

AFFORD – [1] 1 Tim. 6:17 → GIVE <3930> [2] Titus 2:7 → to afford to be → SHOW (verb) <3930>.

AFFRIGHT – Mark 16:5, 6 → ALARM (verb) <1568>.

AFFRIGHTED – [1] Luke 24:37 → FRIGHTENED <1719> [2] Rev. 11:13 → AFRAID <1719>.

AFLAME (SET) – Jas. 3:5 → KINDLE <381>.

AFOOT – [1] Mark 6:33 → on foot → FOOT[1] <3979> [2] Acts 20:13 → to go afoot → to go on foot → FOOT[1] <3978>.

AFOREHAND – Mark 14:8 → to come aforehand → COME <4301>.

AFORETIME – ***pote*** [adv.: ποτέ <4218>] ► **Once, formerly** > One who had aforetime been blind was brought to the Pharisees (John 9:13). Other refs.: FORMERLY <4218>, PAST <4218>.

AFRAID – [1] **exceedingly afraid, greatly afraid: *ekphobos*** [adj.: ἔκφοβος <1630>]; **from *ekphobeō*: to greatly fear, which is from *ek*: intens., and *phobeō*: to fear, which is from *phobos*: fear ► Scared, terrified** > The disciples on the mountain were greatly afraid {sore afraid, filled with fear} (Mark 9:6). Moses said he was exceedingly afraid on the mountain (Heb. 12:21 {to exceedingly fear, to be exceedingly afraid, to be full of fear}). ¶

[2] ***emphobos*** [adj.: ἔμφοβος <1719>]; **from *en*: in, and *phobos*: fear ► Scared, terrified** > The women were afraid {were filled with fear, were in fright} at the tomb of Jesus (Luke 24:5). Cornelius became afraid {full of fear, in terror} when he saw an angel of God coming to him in a vision (Acts 10:4). Felix was afraid {trembled, was filled with fear, was much alarmed} after hearing Paul speak about faith in Christ (Acts 24:25). The remnant who were not killed in the earthquake were afraid {affrighted, filled with fear, terrified} (Rev. 11:13). Other refs.: Luke 24:37 {frightened}; Acts 22:9 (to be afraid; lit.: to become frightened): see FRIGHTENED <1719>. ¶

[3] **to be afraid, to fear: *phobeō*** [verb: φοβέω <5399>]; **from *phobos*: fear ► To dread, to be anxious, to be scared** > Individuals were told not to be afraid: Joseph (Matt.

1:20), Zacharias (Luke 1:13), Mary (Luke 1:30), and Paul (Acts 27:24). Jesus told His disciples not to fear (Matt. 10:26, 28a, 31; Luke 12:4, 7). He told the ruler of the synagogue not to be afraid (Mark 5:36; Luke 8:50), as well as Simon (Luke 5:10), the little flock (Luke 12:32), Paul (Acts 18:9), and John (Rev. 1:17; 2:10). Those suffering for righteousness' sake should not be afraid (1 Pet. 3:14). Other refs.: Matt. 2:22; 9:8 {to marvel, to be filled with awe; some mss. have *thaumazō*}; 14:5, 27, 30; 17:6, 7; 21:26, 46; 25:25; 27:54; 28:5, 10; Mark 4:41; 5:15, 33 {to be frightened}; 6:20, 50; 9:32; 10:32 {to be fearful}; 11:18, 32; 12:12; 16:8; Luke 1:30, 50; 2:9, 10; 8:25 {to be fearful}, 35; 9:34, 45; 18:2, 4; 19:21; 20:19; 22:2; 23:40; John 6:19, 20; 9:22; 12:15; 19:8; Acts 5:26; 9:26; 10:2, 22, 35; 13:16, 26; 16:38; 27:17, 29; Rom. 11:20; 13:3 {to be unafraid, to have no fear}, 4; 2 Cor. 11:3; 12:20; Gal. 2:12; 4:11; Eph. 5:33 {to respect}; Col. 3:22; Heb. 4:1; 11:23, 27; 13:6; 1 Pet. 2:17; 3:6 {to be frightened}; 1 John 4:18; Rev. 11:18; 14:7; 15:4; 19:5; see FEAR (verb) <5399> for many of these other refs. ¶

[4] **to be afraid: *deiliaō*** [verb: δειλιάω <1168>]**; from *deilos*: fearful, timid ▶ To be timid, to be characterized by fear** > Jesus told His disciples to not let their heart be troubled, neither let it be afraid {let it fear, let it be fearful} (John 14:27). ¶

– [5] Matt. 8:26; Mark 4:40 → FEARFUL <1169> [6] Matt. 9:8 → WONDER (verb) <2296> [7] Matt. 28:8 → FEAR (noun) <5401> [8] 1 Cor. 16:10 → without cause to be afraid → without fear → FEAR (noun) <870> [9] 2 Pet. 2:10 → to be afraid → TREMBLE <5141>.

AFTER – [1] **to contain: *periechō*** [verb: περιέχω <4023>]**; from *peri*: about, and *echō*: to have, to hold ▶ To include** > The commander wrote a letter after {as follows} (lit.: containing; other mss. have "having": *echō*) a specific form (Acts 23:25). All other refs.: CONTAIN <4023>, SEIZE <4023>.

– [2] Matt. 15:23; Luke 23:26 → BEHIND <3693> [3] Acts 24:27 → after two years → lit.: two years being fulfilled → FULFILL <4137>.

AFTERNOON – [1] Matt. 20:5; 27:45, 46; Mark 15:33, 34; Luke 23:44 → three in the afternoon → lit.: the ninth hour [2] Matt. 20:6, 9 → five in the afternoon → lit.: the eleventh hour [3] Luke 9:12 → late in the afternoon → lit.: the day began to wear away → to wear away → WEAR <2827> [4] John 1:39; 4:52 → four in the afternoon → lit.: the tenth hour.

AFTERWARD – [1] ***hexēs*** [adv.: ἑξῆς <1836>]**; from *echō*: to have ▶ Following, next** > The word is found in exprs. such as "day after," "next day," and "following day." See Luke 7:11; 9:37; Acts 21:1; 25:17; 27:18. ¶

[2] ***metepeita*** [adv.: μετέπειτα <3347>]**; from *meta*: after, and *epeita*: then ▶ Thereafter, subsequently** > Afterward, desiring to inherit the blessing, Esau was rejected (Heb. 12:17). ¶

[3] ***husteron*** [adv.: ὕστερον <5305>]**; from *husteros*: a later one ▶ Finally, lastly; also transl.: later** > Afterward, on the day of His resurrection, Jesus appeared to the eleven (Mark 16:14). Simon Peter would follow Jesus afterward (John 13:36). Afterward, discipline yields the peaceful fruit of righteousness to those who are exercised by it (Heb. 12:11). Other refs.: Matt. 4:2; 21:29, 32, 37; 22:27; 25:11; 26:60; Luke 4:2; 20:32. ¶

– [4] Matt. 21:37; Luke 20:32 → at last, but last → LAST (adv. and noun) <5305> <1161> [5] Mark 9:39 → soon afterward → LIGHTLY <5035> [6] Jude 5 → SECOND <1208>.

AFTERWARDS – See AFTERWARD; see also THEREUPON <1899>.

AGABUS – ***Hagabos*** [masc. name: Ἄγαβος <13>] **▶ Christian prophet, poss. from Judea** > Agabus foretold a great famine by the Holy Spirit (Acts 11:28). He predicted also that Paul would be made prisoner in Jerusalem (21:10; see v. 11). ¶

AGAIN – [1] ***anōthen*** [adv.: ἄνωθεν <509>]**; from *anō*: above, and suffix *then*: from ▶ From above, from the beginning; also**

transl.: anew > Unless someone is born again, he cannot see the kingdom of God (John 3:3); we must be born again (v. 7). The Galatians should not have wanted to be enslaved all over again (Gal. 4:9). All other refs.: ABOVE <509>, BEGINNING <509>, FIRST <509>, TOP <509>.

[2] ***palin*** [adv.: πάλιν <3825>] ▶ **Anew, once more** > This word is used in Matt. 26:42–44, 72; Mark 2:1; 3:20; 7:14, 31; 8:13; 10:32; 14:39, 40, 70; Luke 23:20; John 4:13; 6:15; 12:28; 16:28; 18:7; 19:9; 20:26; Acts 11:10; Rom. 11:23; 1 Cor. 7:5; 2 Cor. 1:16; 3:1; 5:12; 10:7; 11:16; 12:21; Gal. 1:17; 2:1; 4:9, 19; 5:1, 3; Phil. 4:4; Heb. 4:7; 5:12; 6:1; Jas. 5:18; 2 Pet. 2:20; 1 John 2:8; Rev. 10:8, 11. *

– [3] Matt. 26:29 → from now on → NOW <737> [4] Mark 5:10 → again and again → EARNESTLY <4183> [5] Acts 10:16 → IMMEDIATELY <2117> [6] 2 Cor. 12:19 → long ago → LONG (adj.) <3819> [7] 1 Pet. 2:23 → to revile again → REVILE <486>.

AGAINST – [1] Matt. 14:24; Mark 6:48; Acts 26:9; 27:4; 28:17 → CONTRARY <1727> [2] Acts 20:15 → OPPOSITE <481> [3] Col. 2:14 → CONTRARY <5227> [4] 1 Thes. 2:15 → he who is against → he who is opposed → OPPOSED <1727>.

AGAR – See HAGAR <28>.

AGATE – Rev. 21:19 → CHALCEDONY <5472>.

AGE – [1] ***aiōn*** [masc. noun: αἰών <165>] ▶ **Period of time of undetermined duration; also transl.: world** > The term has this meaning, e.g., in Matt. 12:32; Luke 16:8. **a. "Before the ages of time"**: before creation (2 Tim. 1:9 and Titus 1:2 [*aiōnios*: αἰώνιος <166>]). Same meaning for "before the ages" (1 Cor. 2:7), "throughout the ages" (Eph. 3:9), "from ages" (Col. 1:26), and "from before the whole age" (Jude 25). **b. "The ages"** (Heb. 9:26) are those times prior to the first coming of the Lord. **c. "The present age"** began when man rejected and crucified Jesus Christ, the Son of God (1 Tim. 6:17). It is called evil (Gal. 1:4); it is characterized by vanity and corruption, and its alienation from God under the influence of the devil, the god of this age (Matt. 13:39, 40; Rom. 12:2; 1 Cor. 1:20; 2:6a, b, 8; 3:18; 2 Cor. 4:4; 2 Tim. 4:10; Titus 2:12). During this period, the Lord preserves His own (Matt. 28:20). **d. "The coming age"** then follows; it is characterized by the full power and dominion of the Lord Jesus (Mark 10:30; Luke 18:30; 20:35; Eph. 1:21; 2:7; Heb. 6:5). **e. "The ages of ages"** correspond to eternity, beyond time (Gal. 1:5; Eph. 3:21; Phil. 4:20; 1 Tim. 1:17; 2 Tim. 4:18; Heb. 1:8; 13:21; 1 Pet. 4:11; 5:11; Rev. 1:6, 18; 4:9, 10; 5:13; 7:12; 10:6; 11:15; 14:11; 15:7; 19:3; 20:10; 22:5). Other refs.: Matt. 13:22, 49; 24:3; Mark 4:19; Luke 20:34; 1 Cor. 10:11; Eph. 3:11; et al. Other refs.: COURSE <165>, FOREVER <165>, TROUBLE (noun) <165>, WORLD <165>.

[2] ***hēlikia*** [fem. noun: ἡλικία <2244>]; **from *hēlikos*: how great or from *hēlix*: comrade, of the same age** ▶ **Maturity, state of full development** > The blind man healed by Jesus was of age (i.e., full aged, adult), and thus could be interrogated (John 9:21, 23). Sarah was past age {past the age, beyond a seasonable age, beyond the proper time of life} to conceive (Heb. 11:11), lit.: despite the time of the age. Other refs.: Matt. 6:27; Luke 2:52; 12:25; 19:3; Eph. 4:13; see STATURE <2244>. ¶

[3] ***hēmera*** [fem. noun: ἡμέρα <2250>] ▶ **Day** > The prophetess Anna was of a great age {very old, advanced in years, far advanced in years} (lit.: advanced in many days) (Luke 2:36). Other refs.: DAY <2250>, TIME <2250>, YEAR <2250>.

[4] **who has passed the flower of age: *huperakmos*** [adj.: ὑπέρακμος <5230>]; **from *huper*: beyond, and *akmē*: point, tip** ▶ **Who has become older, having passed the high point of one's years** > Paul speaks of a person who has passed the flower of her age {of youth; who is getting along in years} and is not married yet (1 Cor. 7:36); some translate *huperakmos* by "whose passions are strong." ¶

– [5] Rom. 16:25 → the times of the ages, long ages past → eternal times →

ETERNAL <166> 6 Gal. 1:14 → of one's own age → EQUAL <4915> 7 Gal. 1:14 → many Jews of my own age → lit.: many contemporaries of my nation → NATION <1085> 8 1 Tim. 5:9 → "of age" added in Engl. 9 1 Tim. 6:19 → coming age → time to come → TIME <3195> 10 Heb. 5:14 → one of full age → mature man → MATURE <5046> 11 Heb. 9:9 → TIME <2540>.

AGED – 1 Phm. 9 → OLD MAN <4246> 2 Heb. 8:13 → to grow old → OLD <1095>.

AGED WOMAN – ***presbutis*** [fem. noun: πρεσβῦτις <4247>]; **from *presbus*: older ▶ Older, elder woman** > Older women are to be reverent in their behavior (Titus 2:3). ¶

AGENT – Rom. 13:4 → agent of wrath to bring punishment → lit.: an avenger who brings wrath → AVENGER <1558>.

AGGRESSOR – 1 Tim. 1:13 → violent aggressor → insolent man → INSOLENT <5197>.

AGING – Heb. 8:13 → to grow old → OLD <1095>.

AGITATED (BE) – John 6:18 → ARISE <1326>.

AGITATOR – Gal. 5:12 → those agitators → lit.: those who were troubling → TROUBLE (verb) <387>.

AGONY – 1 ***agōnia*** [fem. noun: ἀγωνία <74>]; **from *agōn*: struggle, fight ▶ Trouble of the soul, extremely great moral suffering** > In Gethsemane, being in an agony {anguish, conflict}, Jesus prayed more earnestly (Luke 22:44). ¶

– 2 Luke 16:24, 25 → to be in agony → to be tormented → TORMENT (verb) <3600> 3 Acts 2:24 → pain, labor pain → PAIN (noun) <5604> 4 Rev. 9:5 → TORMENT (noun) <929> 5 Rev. 12:2 → PAIN (noun) <928> 6 Rev. 16:10 → PAIN (noun) <4192>.

AGREE – 1 ***eunoeō*** [verb: εὐνοέω <2132>]; **from *eunoos*: benevolent, well-disposed, which is from *eu*: well, and *nous*: mind, understanding; lit.: to be conciliatory ▶ To concur, to settle problems** > Reconciliation is compared to the fact of agreeing {making friends, settling matters} quickly with one's adversary on the way before standing in front of the judge (Matt. 5:25). ¶

2 ***homoiazō*** [verb: ὁμοιάζω <3662>]; **from *homoios*: similar ▶ To resemble, to show** > The speech of Peter conformed to the Galilean dialect (Mark 14:70). Other ref.: Matt. 23:27 in some mss. ¶

3 ***peithō*** [verb: πείθω <3982>] **▶ To convince, to persuade; pass.: to be persuaded** > The Jews agreed with {took, listened to} Gamaliel's advice {were persuaded by his speech} to release the apostles (Acts 5:40). All other refs.: see entries in Lexicon at <3982>.

4 ***sumphōneō*** [verb: συμφωνέω <4856>]; **from *sumphonos*: symphonious, which is from *sun*: together, and *phonē*: sound, voice; lit.: to be in harmony ▶ a. To concur, to be of one accord** > If two Christians agree concerning any matter they may ask, it will be done for them by the Father (Matt. 18:19). In a parable, a landowner agreed to pay the workmen a denarius a day (Matt. 20:2), and they also agreed with him (v. 13). Ananias and Sapphira had agreed together {had conspired} to test the Spirit of the Lord (Acts 5:9). The words of the prophets agree {are in agreement} with the fact that God has taken from the Gentiles a people for His name (Acts 15:15; see v. 14). **b. To be in harmony, to fit together** > A patch from a new garment will not agree with {suit, match} an old garment (Luke 5:36). ¶

5 ***suntithēmi*** [verb: συντίθημι <4934>]; **from *sun*: together, and *tithēmi*: to put ▶ To be in accord, to consent** > The chief priests and captains agreed {covenanted} to give Judas money to betray Jesus (Luke 22:5). The Jews had agreed {had decided} to exclude from the synagogue anyone who confessed that Jesus was the Christ (John 9:22). The Jews had agreed to make a request that Paul be brought down to the

council (Acts 23:20). Other ref.: Acts 24:9 (to join in a matter); see JOIN <4934>. ¶

6 **to not agree: *isos ouk eimi*; equal: *isos*** [adj.: ἴσος <2470>]; **not: *ouk*** [neg. particle: οὐκ <3756>]; **to be: *eimi*** [verb: εἰμί <1510>]; **lit.: to not be equal ▶ To disagree, to be inconsistent** > The false witnesses of many against Jesus did not agree (Mark 14:56, 59). All other refs. (*isos*): EQUAL <2470>, LIKE (adj., adv., noun) <2470>, SAME <2470>.

7 **who does not agree: *asumphōnos*** [adj.: ἀσύμφωνος <800>]; **from *a*: neg., and *sumphōnos*: in agreement, which is from *sumphoneō*: to agree, which is from *sun*: together, and *phonē*: sound, voice; lit.: discordant, not harmonious ▶ Who has a different opinion, who disagrees** > Not agreeing among themselves on what Paul was saying, the leaders of the Jews began to leave (Acts 28:25). ¶

– 8 Acts 15:25 → to seem good → THINK <1380> 9 Rom. 7:16 → CONSENT (verb) <4852> 10 2 Cor. 13:11 → to agree with one another → lit.: to think the same thing → THINK <5426> 11 Phil. 4:2 → to agree with each other → to mind the same thing → MIND (verb) <5426> 12 1 Tim. 6:3 → CONSENT (verb) <4334> 13 Rev. 17:17 → lit.: to act with one mind → EXECUTE <4160> 14 Rev. 17:17b → lit.: to act with one mind → MIND (noun) <1106>.

AGREEABLE – Phil. 4:18 → WELL PLEASING <2101>.

AGREEMENT – 1 ***sunkatathesis*** [fem. noun: συγκατάθεσις <4783>]; **from *sunkatatithēmi*: to consent, which is from *sun*: together, *kata*: down, and *tithēmi*: to put ▶ Accord, compatibility** > Paul asks what agreement has the temple of God with idols (2 Cor. 6:16). ¶

– 2 Luke 22:6 → to come to an agreement → PROMISE (verb) <1843> 3 Acts 8:1 → to be in hearty agreement → CONSENT (verb) <4909> 4 Acts 15:15 → to be in agreement → AGREE <4856> 5 1 Cor. 7:5 → CONSENT (noun) <4859>.

AGRIPPA – ***Agrippas*** [masc. name: Ἀγρίππας <67>] **▶ This name refers to Herod Agrippa II, great-grandson of Herod the Great** > Paul made his defense before Agrippa (Acts 26). He had been found innocent, but having appealed to Caesar, he had to appear before Agrippa in Rome. Refs.: Acts 25:13, 22–24, 26; 26:1, 2, 7 in some mss., 19, 27, 28, 32. ¶

AGROUND – 1 Acts 27:29 → to run aground → RUN <1601> 2 Acts 27:41 → to run aground → RUN <2027>.

AH! – Mark 15:29 → HA! <3758>.

AHA! – Mark 15:29 → HA! <3758>.

AHAZ – ***Achaz*** [masc. name: Ἀχάζ <881>]: **he has grasped, possessor, in Heb. ▶ King of Judah; also spelled: Achaz** > Ahaz is mentioned in the genealogy of Jesus Christ (Matt. 1:9a, b). He committed abominations and gave himself up to idolatry (see 2 Kgs. 16:1–4). ¶

AHEAD – 1 **to go ahead: *proagō*** [verb: προάγω <4254>]; **from *pro*: before, and *agō*: to lead ▶ To precede** > Jesus compelled the disciples to go ahead of {to go before} Him to the other shore (Matt. 14:22). All other refs.: see entries in Lexicon at <4254>.

– 2 Mark 1:2; Luke 7:27; 10:1 → ahead of → lit.: before the face → FACE (noun) <4383>.

AID (noun) – 1 Acts 20:35 → to come in aid → HELP (verb) <482> 2 Acts 21:28; Heb. 2:18 → to come to the aid → HELP (verb) <997> 3 Rom. 15:25 → to bring aid → MINISTER (verb) <1247> 4 Heb. 2:16a, b → to give aid → to take hold → TAKE <1949>.

AID (verb) – Heb. 2:18 → HELP (verb) <997>.

AIDE – Acts 12:20 → personal aide → CHAMBERLAIN <2846>.

AILMENT – [1] Gal. 4:13 → WEAKNESS <769> [2] 1 Tim. 5:23 → ILLNESS <769>.

AIM (noun) – [1] Acts 20:24 → my only aim is to finish the race → lit.: so as I may finish the race [2] Rom. 15:20 → to make it one's aim → STRIVE <5389> [3] 1 Cor. 9:26 → UNCERTAINLY <84> [4] 2 Cor. 5:9 → to make it one's aim → LABOR (verb) <5389> [5] 2 Cor. 8:21 → PROVIDE <4306> [6] 1 Tim. 1:5 → END (noun) <5056> [7] 2 Tim. 2:4 → since his aim is to please → lit.: that he may please [8] 2 Tim. 3:10 → aim in life → PURPOSE (noun) <4286>.

AIM (verb) – Rom. 15:20 → STRIVE <5389>.

AIMLESS – 1 Pet. 1:18 → VAIN <3152>.

AIMLESSLY – 1 Cor. 9:26 → UNCERTAINLY <84>.

AIR – [1] ***aēr*** [masc. noun: ἀήρ <109>]; **from *aō*: to blow ▶ Atmosphere where living beings breathe** > The Jews were throwing dust into the air (Acts 22:23). Paul was fighting, not as one beating the air (1 Cor. 9:26). If they would not speak intelligibly, the Corinthians would speak into the air (1 Cor. 14:9). Satan is the ruler of the authority of the air (Eph. 2:2); the air, in this instance, could be regions higher than the atmosphere. Believers in the Lord Jesus who are alive will be caught up, together with the dead in Christ, to meet Him in the air (1 Thes. 4:17). The sun and the air {sky} were darkened with the smoke of the pit (Rev. 9:2). The seventh angel poured out his bowl into the air (Rev. 16:17). ¶
– [2] Matt. 6:26; et al. → HEAVEN <3772> [3] 2 Cor. 11:20 → to put on airs → to exalt oneself → EXALT <1869>.

AKEL DAMA, AKELDAMA – See ACELDAMA <184>.

ALABASTER – alabaster box: *alabastron* [neut. noun: ἀλάβαστρον <211>] **▶ Alabaster is a variety of gypsum which is translucent and whitish; it was commonly used to make boxes or flasks to contain perfume or ointment; also transl.: alabaster flask, jar, vial** > A woman had an alabaster box of very precious ointment and poured it out on the head of Jesus (Matt. 26:7; Mark 14:3a, b). Luke writes about a woman who brought an alabaster box of myrrh (Luke 7:37) and anointed the feet of Jesus with the myrrh (see v. 38). In Mark 14:3, "to break the alabaster flask of ointment" meant most likely to open the flask by breaking its seals. ¶

ALARM (noun) – 2 Cor. 7:11 → FEAR (noun) <5401>.

ALARM (verb) – [1] ***ekthambeō*** [verb: ἐκθαμβέω <1568>]; **from *ekthambos*: astonished, greatly amazed, which is from *ek*: intens., and *thambos*: admiration, astonishment, fear ▶ To greatly astonish, to terrorize** > At the tomb of Jesus, the women were alarmed {affrighted, amazed} (Mark 16:5, 6). Other refs.: Mark 9:15 {to be amazed}; 14:33 {to be distressed}. ¶
– [2] Matt. 24:6; Mark 13:7; 2 Thes. 2:2 → to be alarmed → to be troubled → TROUBLE (verb) <2360> [3] Phil. 1:28 → TERRIFY <4426>.

ALARMED – [1] Acts 16:38; 22:29 → to be alarmed → FEAR (verb) <5399> [2] Acts 24:25 → AFRAID <1719>.

ALAS – Matt. 24:19; Mark 13:17; Luke 21:23 → WOE! <3759>.

ALERT – [1] Matt. 24:42, 43; 25:13; Mark 13:34, 35, 37; Luke 12:37; Acts 20:31; 1 Cor. 16:13; Col. 4:2; 1 Pet. 5:8 → to be alert, to be on the alert, to keep alert, to stay on the alert → WATCH (verb) <1127> [2] Mark 13:33; Luke 21:36; Eph. 6:18 → to be alert, to be on the alert, to keep on the alert → WATCH (verb) <69> [3] Heb. 4:12 → LIVING (adj.) <2198> [4] 1 Pet. 1:13 → with minds that are alert → lit.: girding up the loins of your mind → GIRD <328>, LOINS <3751> [5] 1 Pet. 4:7 → SELF-CONTROLLED <4993>.

ALEXANDER – ***Alexandros*** [masc. name: Ἀλέξανδρος <223>]: **defender of men; from *alexō*: to defend, to protect, and *anēr*: man ▶ a. Son of Simon of Cyrene >** His father was compelled to carry the cross of Jesus (Mark 15:21). **b. Name of a priest >** He served in the Sanhedrin (Acts 4:6). **c. Jew from Ephesus >** The Jews had put this Alexander forward; he was intending to make a defense to the people (Acts 19:33a, b). **d. Worker in copper >** This other Alexander had done many evil things against the apostle Paul (2 Tim. 4:14) and had greatly withstood his words (see v. 15). He could be the same one who had to learn by discipline not to blaspheme (1 Tim. 1:20). ¶

ALEXANDRIA – Acts 27:6; 28:11 → of Alexandria → ALEXANDRIAN <222>.

ALEXANDRIAN – [1] ***Alexandreus*** [adj. used as name: Ἀλεξανδρεύς <221>]; **from the name Alexander: see Alexander** <223> **▶ Native or resident of Alexandria, a city and a port in Egypt >** The Alexandrians had their own synagogue in Jerusalem. People rose up against Stephen (Acts 6:9) and took part in his stoning (see 7:58). Apollos was an Alexandrian by birth (Acts 18:24). ¶

[2] ***Alexandrinos*** [adj.: Ἀλεξανδρῖνος <222>]; **from the name Alexander: see Alexander** <223> **▶ Belonging to Alexandria, which is a port city on the Mediterranean, situated in northern Egypt; it was founded by Alexander the Great in 332 B.C.; also transl.: of Alexandria >** Paul boarded an Alexandrian ship sailing to Italy (Acts 27:6). After being shipwrecked, he boarded another Alexandrian ship sailing to Rome (Acts 28:11). ¶

ALIEN – [1] Acts 7:29 → DWELLER <3941> [2] Eph. 2:12 → to be alien → ALIENATED (BE) <526> [3] Eph. 2:19; 1 Pet. 2:11 → FOREIGNER <3941> [4] Heb. 11:34 → STRANGER <245> [5] 1 Pet. 1:1 → DISPERSION <1290> [6] 1 Pet. 1:1 → one who resides as alien → STRANGER <3927>.

ALIENATE – Gal. 4:17 → EXCLUDE <1576>.

ALIENATED (BE) – [1] ***apallotrioō*** [verb: ἀπαλλοτριόω <526>]; **from *apo*: from (intens.), and *allotrioō*: to alienate, which is from *allotrios*: other; lit.: to estrange, to alienate completely ▶ To be so far that one is a stranger and cannot enjoy fellowship >** The Ephesians were once alienated {were aliens, were excluded} from the citizenship of Israel (Eph. 2:12). Unbelievers are alienated {estranged, excluded, separated} from the life of God (Eph. 4:18). The Colossians were once alienated and enemies in mind by wicked works (Col. 1:21). ¶

– [2] Gal. 5:4 → to make of no effect → EFFECT (noun) <2673>.

ALIVE – [1] **to make alive: *zōopoieō*** [verb: ζῳοποιέω <2227>]; **from *zōos*: alive, and *poieō*: to make ▶ To vivify, to revive >** In Christ, all will be made alive (1 Cor. 15:22). All other refs.: LIFE <2227>.

[2] **to make alive with: *suzōopoieō*** [συζωοποιέω <4806>]; **from *sun*: together, and *zōopoieō*: see [1] ▶ To give life together with >** God has made alive {has quickened} the repentant sinner together with Christ (Eph. 2:5; Col. 2:13). ¶

– [3] Matt. 27:63, Rom. 7:2, 9; Col. 2:20; Heb. 9:17; et al. → to be alive → LIVE <2198> [4] Mark 16:11; Acts 20:12; Rom. 6:11, 13; Rev. 19:20 → LIVING <2198> [5] Acts 7:19 → to be kept alive → LIVE <2225> [6] Rom. 7:9 → to become alive → REVIVE <326> [7] 1 Cor. 15:6 → to be alive → REMAIN <3306> [8] Rev. 2:8 → to be alive → to come to life → LIFE <2198>.

ALL – [1] **at all: *holōs*** [adv.: ὅλως <3654>]; **from *holos*: whole ▶ Entirely, altogether >** Paul asks what those baptized for the dead will do if the dead do not rise (1 Cor. 15:29). All other refs.: ACTUALLY <3654>, UTTERLY <3654>.

[2] ***pas*** [adj.: πᾶς <3956>] **▶ Complete, whole, entire >** James says to count it all {pure} joy when Christians fall into various trials (Jas. 1:2). *

[3] ***hapas*** [adj.: ἅπας <537>]; **from *hama*: together, and *pas*: see [2] ▶ The whole, universally** > Refs.: Matt. 6:32; 24:39; Mark 16:15; Luke 9:15; 17:27, 29; 21:4; 23:1; Acts 2:1, 4. Spoken also of a large number without necessarily including every individual of that number (Mark 8:25; 11:32; Luke 3:21; 8:37; 19:48); see also Matt. 28:11; Mark 5:40; 16:15; Luke 2:39; 3:16; 4:6; 5:11, 26, 28; 7:16; 15:13; 17:27, 29; 19:7, 48; 21:12; Acts 2:14, 44; 4:31, 32; 5:12, 16; 6:15; 10:8; 13:29. * ‡

– [4] Luke 13:11 → at all → to the uttermost → UTTERMOST <3838> [5] Acts 23:8 → BOTH <297>.

ALL-SURPASSING – 2 Cor. 4:7 → EXCELLENCE <5236>.

ALL TOGETHER – ***pamplēthei*** [adv.: παμπληθεί <3826>]; **from *pas*: all, every, and *plēthos*: multitude ▶ All in a mass** > Ref.: Luke 23:18. ¶ ‡

ALL-VARIOUS – Eph. 3:10 → MANIFOLD <4182>.

ALLEGE – Acts 17:3 → to lay down → LAY <3908>.

ALLEGEDLY – 2 Thes. 2:2 → allegedly from us → lit.: as through us.

ALLEGIANCE – Rom. 6:17 → that has claimed your allegiance → lit.: into which you were instructed → INSTRUCT <3860>.

ALLEGORIC, ALLEGORICAL, ALLEGORICALLY – Gal. 4:24 → to be allegoric, to have an allegorical sense, to be allegorically speaking → to be an allegory → ALLEGORY <238>.

ALLEGORY – [1] ***paroimia*** [fem. noun: παροιμία <3942>]; **from *para*: beside, and *oimos*: way, or *oimē*: story, poem ▶ Briefer account than a parable, but also setting forth a spiritual teaching; also transl.: figurative language, figure of speech, illustration, parable, proverb** > Jesus used a figure of speech regarding a shepherd who calls his own sheep by name and leads them out of the sheepfold (John 10:6; see vv. 1–6). He had spoken things in figures of speech to His apostles, but the hour was coming that He would no longer speak to them in figures of speech (John 16:25a, b); when He told them clearly that He was going to the Father, His disciples told Him that He was speaking no figure of speech (v. 29). Other ref.: 2 Pet. 2:22; see PROVERB <3942>. ¶

[2] **to be an allegory: *allēgoreō*** [verb: ἀλληγορέω <238>]; **from *allos*: another, and *agoreuō*: to speak in a public place, which is from *agora*: marketplace ▶ To use a concrete reality to help understand another reality which is more abstract; to symbolize** > In Gal. 4:24, Paul related the events which happened concerning the two sons of Abraham and used those events as an allegory to describe two covenants. We read lit.: "These (things) are being an allegory (or: are being allegorized)." Other transl.: these are being allegoric; these are being symbolic; these have an allegorical sense; this is allegorically speaking; these may be taken figuratively. ¶

ALLELUIA – ***hallēlouia*** [interj.: ἀλληλουϊά <239>] **▶ Heb. term which signifies "Praise Jah" (or "Jehovah," i.e., the Lord)** > In the N.T., the term "Alleluia" {Hallelujah} is found only in Revelation 19 (vv. 1, 3, 4, 6). It is borrowed as is from the Heb. This word of praise is used both in heaven and on earth. ¶

ALLEY – Luke 14:21 → LANE <4505>.

ALLOT – [1] Acts 1:17 → to be allotted a share in → to receive a part in → RECEIVE <2975> [2] Acts 17:26 → allotted periods → ordained times → ORDAIN <4367> [3] Rom. 12:3 → DISTRIBUTE <3307> [4] 1 Cor. 9:15 → to allow anyone to deprive → to make void → VOID <2758> [5] 1 Pet. 5:3 → ENTRUST <2819>.

ALLOW – [1] ***eaō*** [verb: ἐάω <1439>] **▶ To let happen, to not restrain; also transl.: to suffer, to permit** > The master of the house would have watched and not allowed {suffered} his house to be broken into (Matt. 24:43). Jesus did not allow the demons to speak (Luke 4:41). The Spirit did not allow Paul to go to Bithynia (Acts 16:7). The disciples did not allow Paul to go in to the people (Acts 19:30). God will not allow Christians to be tempted above what they are able to bear (1 Cor. 10:13). The verb is transl. "to leave" in Acts 14:16; 23:32. Other refs.: Luke 22:51 {to suffer, to permit, to stop}; Acts 5:38; 27:32, 40 {to leave}; 28:4; Rev. 2:20 {to suffer, to tolerate}. ¶

– 2 Matt. 3:15; 7:4; 8:22; 13:30; 23:13; Mark 1:34; 5:37; 11:16; Luke 6:42; 8:51; 9:60; 12:39; Rev. 11:9 → LET <863> 3 Matt. 19:8; Mark 10:4; Luke 9:59, 61; John 19:38; Acts 21:39, 40; 27:3; 28:16; 1 Cor. 14:34; 1 Tim. 2:12 → PERMIT <2010> 4 Luke 11:48 → APPROVE <4909> 5 Acts 2:27; 13:35 → LET <1325> 6 Acts 22:22 → to be allowed → FITTING (BE) <2520> 7 Acts 24:15 → RECEIVE <4327> 8 Acts 27:7 → to allow to hold the course → to permit to proceed → PROCEED <4330> 9 Rom. 7:15 → RECOGNIZE <1097> 10 Rom. 14:22; 1 Thes. 2:4 → APPROVE <1381> 11 Rev. 9:5; 13:5, 7, 14, 15; 16:8 → GIVE <1325>.

ALLOWED – Matt. 20:15; Acts 2:29; 21:37; 2 Cor. 12:4 → to be allowed → to be lawful → LAWFUL <1832>.

ALLURE – 2 Pet. 2:14, 18 → ENTICE <1185>.

ALMIGHTY – 1 ***Pantokratōr*** [masc. name: Παντοκράτωρ <3841>]; **from *pas*: all, and *kratos*: power ▶ Name of the Lord God** > This name is found in 2 Cor. 6:18 and Rev. 1:8; 4:8; 11:17; 15:3; 16:7, 14; 19:6, 15; 21:22. ¶

– 2 Rom. 9:29; Jas. 5:4 → of Sabaoth → SABAOTH <4519>.

ALMOST – 1 ***en oligō*; in: *en*** [prep.: ἐν <1722>]; **little: *oligos*** [adj. used as adv.: ὀλίγος <3641>]; **lit.: in little ▶ Nearly, in a short time** > Agrippa told Paul that he would almost {in a little} persuade him to become a Christian (Acts 26:28).

2 ***schedon*** [adv.: σχεδόν <4975>]; **from *eschon*: aorist tense of *echō* (to have) ▶ Approximately, about; also transl.: nearly, practically** > The word is used of the city of Antioch (Acts 13:44), Asia (Acts 19:26), and of things in general (Heb. 9:22). ¶

ALMOST GONE – Rom. 13:12 → to be far spent → SPEND <4298>.

ALMS – 1 ***dikaiosunē*** [fem. noun: δικαιοσύνη <1343>]; **from *dikaios*: just, righteous, which is from *dikē*: justice, judgment ▶ Justice, practice of justice, acts of charity** > Jesus says to take heed not to do our alms {acts of righteousness, charitable deeds, righteousness} before men, to be seen by them (Matt. 6:1); some mss. have *eleēmosunē* (see 2). All other refs.: RIGHTEOUSNESS <1343>.

2 **alms, alms-deeds: *eleēmosunē*** [fem. noun: ἐλεημοσύνη <1654>]; **from *eleēmōn*: compassionate, merciful, which is from *eleos*: compassion, mercy ▶ Charitable gift made to the poor; also transl.: charitable deeds, charity, giving, money** > Jesus says to give alms of what we have and even sell what we possess (Luke 11:41; 12:33), and to do it with discretion (Matt. 6:2–4). A lame man was asking alms of those who were going in the temple (Acts 3:2, 3, 10). Dorcas was full of alms-deeds (Acts 9:36). Cornelius gave much alms to the people (Acts 10:2, 4, 31). Paul had come to bring alms to his nation and to present offerings (Acts 24:17). ¶

ALOES – ***aloē*** [fem. noun: ἀλόη <250>] ▶ **Resinous plant which is very aromatic with bitter juice** > The wood of aloes was used for fumigation and embalming. Nicodemus brought a mixture of myrrh and aloes to embalm the body of Jesus (John 19:39). ¶

ALONE – 1 ***monos*** [adj.: μόνος <3441>]; **poss. from *manos*: sparse ▶ Unique, solitary** > The term is used in Matt. 4:4;

Luke 4:4; Gal. 6:4. Other refs.: Rom. 16:27; 1 Tim. 1:17; 6:16; see ONLY <3441>.

2 ***katamonas*** [adv.: καταμόνας <2651>]; **from *kata*: in, at, and *monos*: see** 1 ▶ **Apart from anyone else, privately** > When Jesus was alone, those around Him with the twelve asked Him about the parables (Mark 4:10). Jesus was praying alone {in private} (Luke 9:18). ¶

– 3 Mark 1:24; Luke 4:34 → Let us alone! → EH! <1436> 4 Mark 4:34 → when alone → PRIVATELY <2398> 5 John 17:20; Acts 11:19; 19:26; Rom. 4:23; Phil. 2:27; Jas. 2:24; 1 John 2:2 → ONLY <3440> 6 1 Tim. 5:5 → to be left alone, to be left all alone → to be desolate → DESOLATE <3443>.

ALONG – ***kata*** [prep.: κατά <2596>] ▶ **Down, against** > Paul's ship was about to sail along the coasts of Asia (Acts 27:2). Other refs.: CONCERNING <2596>.

ALOOF – Gal. 2:12 → to hold oneself aloof → SEPARATE <873>.

ALOUD – 1 Matt. 9:27 → to cry aloud → to cry, to cry out → CRY (verb) <2896> 2 Matt. 12:19 → to cry aloud → to cry, to cry out → CRY (verb) <2905> 3 Rev. 1:3 → to read aloud → sense of: to read publicly → READ <314> 4 Rev. 18:15 → to mourn aloud → MOURN <3996>.

ALPHA – ***alpha*** [neut. noun: ἄλφα <1>] ▶ **First letter of the Greek alphabet written "α"** > The letter "alpha" is used with the letter "omega," the last letter of the Greek alphabet. The expr. "the Alpha and the Omega" is a name of God and of Christ found only in the book of Revelation (1:8, 11 in some mss.; 21:6; 22:13). It underlines their eternal existence. ¶

ALPHAEUS – ***Halphaios*** [masc. name: Ἁλφαῖος <256>]; **also spelled *Alphaios*** (Ἀλφαῖος) ▶ **a. Father of James, who was an apostle of the Lord** > Alphaeus is mentioned in Matt. 10:3; Mark 3:18; Luke 6:15; Acts 1:13. **b. Father of Levi also called Matthew** > This Alphaeus is mentioned in Mark 2:14. ¶

ALREADY – Col. 1:5 → to hear already → HEAR <4257>.

ALTAR – 1 ***bōmos*** [masc. noun: βωμός <1041>]; **from *bainō*: to go, to step** ▶ **Idolatrous table on which to offer sacrifices** > Paul had found in Athens an altar to the unknown God (Acts 17:23). ¶

2 ***thusiastērion*** [neut. noun: θυσιαστήριον <2379>]; **from *thusiazō*: to sacrifice** ▶ **Structure made according to divine instructions on which were offered sacrifices or incense to God** > The word is used in Matt. 5:23, 24; 23:18, 19, 20a, b, 35; Luke 1:11; 11:51; Rom. 11:3; 1 Cor. 9:13a, b; 10:18; Heb. 7:13; Jas. 2:21. In Heb. 13:10, the Christian altar symbolizes Jesus Christ offered in sacrifice, by whom the Christian can offer a sacrifice of praise to God (see vv. 8–10). The word is also found in Revelation in relation to the testimony (6:9), the prayers of the saints (8:3a, b), the angelic activity (8:5; 9:13), and the temple (11:1; 14:18); in Rev. 16:7, the altar speaks to God. ¶

– 3 Heb. 9:4 → altar of incense → CENSER <2369>.

ALTER – Acts 6:14 → CHANGE (verb) <236>.

ALTHOUGH – ***kaitoige*** [particle: καίτοιγε <2544>]; **from *katoi*: though, and *ge*: indeed** ▶ **Despite the fact that, even though** > It was said that Jesus baptized more disciples than John, although {however, though} Jesus Himself did not baptize, but His disciples did (John 4:2). Other refs.: Acts 14:17; 17:27. ¶

ALTOGETHER – 1 ***pantōs*** [adv.: πάντως <3843>]; **from *pas*: all** ▶ **Absolutely, in all cases, necessarily** > The Corinthians were not to mix with sexually immoral people, not altogether {necessarily, at all} meaning the fornicators or other immoral people of this world (1 Cor. 5:10). Paul asks if God says it altogether {entirely} for us when He

speaks about the plowman who should plow in hope (1 Cor. 9:10). Other refs.: DOUBT (adv.) <3843>, SURELY <3843>.
– 2 John 8:25 → lit.: from the beginning → BEGINNING <746> 3 John 9:34 → COMPLETELY <3650>.

ALWAY – See ALWAYS.

ALWAYS – 1 ***aei*** [adv.: ἀεί <104>] ▶ **Constantly, continuously** > The crowd asked Pilate to do as he had always done for them (Mark 15:8 {ever, usually}), in releasing a prisoner. The Jews were always resisting the Holy Spirit (Acts 7:51). Paul was always being delivered over to death on account of Jesus (2 Cor. 4:11); He was as sorrowful, yet always rejoicing (6:10). Christians are to always be prepared to give an answer, but with meekness and respect, to everyone who asks them to give a reason for the hope that is in them (1 Pet. 3:15). Other refs.: Titus 1:12; Heb. 3:10; 2 Pet. 1:12. ¶
2 ***dia pantos*; lit.: through all; through: *dia*** [prep.: διά <1223>]; **all: *pas*** [adj. used as adv.: πᾶς <3956>] ▶ **Constantly, continually** > The angels of the little ones always see the face of the Father (Matt. 18:10).
3 ***diapantos*** [adv.: διαπαντός <1275>]; **from *dia*: through, and *pas*: all** ▶ **Constantly, continually; also transl.: at all times, regularly** > A man with an unclean spirit was always night and day in the mountains and in the tombs (Mark 5:5). After the ascension of Jesus, the disciples were always in the temple praising and blessing God (Luke 24:53). Cornelius prayed to God always (Acts 10:2). Paul exercised himself to have always {in everything} a conscience blameless before God and men (Acts 24:16). David asked God to bend the backs of his enemies always {forever} (Rom. 11:10). The priests always went into the first part of the tabernacle, performing the service (Heb. 9:6). Other ref.: Heb. 13:15 {continually}. ¶
4 ***pantote*** [adv.: πάντοτε <3842>]; **from *pas*: all, and *tote*: then** ▶ **At all times, continually; also transl.: ever, evermore, forever** > Jesus always did the things that pleased the Father (John 8:29). The Father always heard Him (John 11:42). The disciples had the poor with them always, but they would not always have Jesus with them (Matt. 26:11a, b; Mark 14:7a, b; John 12:8a, b). The Greek term is used in regard to the older son in the parable of the prodigal son in Luke 15 (v. 31). The disciples were always to pray and not to give up (Luke 18:1). Paul always thanked his God for the Corinthians (1 Cor. 1:4). The Corinthians were always to abound in the work of the Lord (1 Cor. 15:58). Paul thanked God who always leads His people in triumph in Christ (2 Cor. 2:14). He always carried about in the body the dying of Jesus (2 Cor. 4:10). It is good to be always zealous in what is right (Gal. 4:18). Christians are to always give thanks for all things, in the name of the Lord Jesus Christ, to God the Father (Eph. 5:20). Paul always made supplication for all the Philippians, with joy (Phil. 1:4); he always gave thanks for the Colossians (Col. 1:3); he always thanked God for all the Thessalonians (1 Thes. 1:2; 2 Thes. 1:3; 2:13) and prayed for them (2 Thes. 1:11); he always made mention of Philemon in his prayers (Phm. 4). The Philippians were always to rejoice in the Lord (Phil. 4:4). The word of the Colossians was to be always in a spirit of grace (Col. 4:6). Epaphras was always combating for the Colossians in prayers (Col. 4:12). At the rapture, Christians will be always with the Lord (1 Thes. 4:17). The Thessalonians were always to pursue that which is good (1 Thes. 5:15) and to rejoice always (v. 16). Jesus always lives to intercede for us (Heb. 7:25). Other refs.: John 6:34; 7:6; 18:20; Rom. 1:9; 2 Cor. 5:6; 9:8; Phil. 1:20; 2:12; 1 Thes. 2:16; 3:6; 2 Tim. 3:7. ¶
– 5 Eph. 6:18 → lit.: with all perseverance → PERSEVERANCE <4343> 6 2 Pet. 1:15 → at any time → TIME <1539>.

AMAZED – **greatly amazed: *ekthambos*** [adj.: ἔκθαμβος <1569>]; **from *ek*: out (intens.), and *thambos*: amazement, astonishment** ▶ **Astonished, much surprised** > As the lame man was healed, the people were greatly amazed {greatly wondering, full of amazement} (Acts 3:11). ¶

AMAZED (BE) – [1] ***existēmi*** [verb: ἐξίστημι <1839>]; **from *ek*: out, and *histēmi*: to stand ► To be astonished, to be much surprised, to wonder** > The crowds were amazed that Jesus had healed a demon-possessed man who was blind and mute (Matt. 12:23). Simon was amazed, seeing the miracles and signs done by Philip (Acts 8:13). All who heard Paul were amazed (Acts 9:21). Other refs.: Mark 2:12; Luke 8:56; Acts 2:7, 12 {to continue in amazement}; 12:16. All other refs.: ASTONISHED (BE) <1839>, MIND (noun) <1839>.

[2] ***ekplēssō*** [verb: ἐκπλήσσω <1605>]; **from *ek*: intens., and *plēssō*: to strike ► To astonish, to stupefy** > The proconsul was amazed at the teaching of the Lord (i.e., about the Lord) (Acts 13:12). All other refs.: ASTONISHED (BE) <1605>.

[3] ***thambeō*** [verb: θαμβέω <2284>]; **from *thambos*: see [5] ► To wonder, to be astonished** > The crowd was amazed that Jesus had healed a possessed man (Mark 1:27). The disciples were amazed at the words of Jesus (Mark 10:24). They were amazed and were afraid as they followed Him (Mark 10:32). Other ref.: Acts 9:6 {to be astonished}. ¶

[4] ***ekthambeō*** [verb: ἐκθαμβέω <1568>]; **from *ek*: intens., and *thambeō*: see [3] ► To wonder greatly, to be astonished greatly** > When the crowd saw Jesus, they were amazed {greatly amazed, overwhelmed with wonder} (Mark 9:15). Other refs.: Mark 14:33 {to be sore amazed, to be troubled}; 16:5 and 6 {to be alarmed}. ¶

[5] **amazement, wonder: *thambos*** [neut. noun: θάμβος <2285>] **► Astonishment from admiration** > All were amazed (lit.: There was an amazement {astonishment} on all) that Jesus had healed a possessed man (Luke 4:36). Other refs.: Luke 5:9; Acts 3:10; see ASTONISHMENT <2285>. ¶

– [6] Matt. 8:10; 27:14; Mark 6:51; 12:17; 15:5; Luke 2:33; 8:25; 9:43; John 5:20; 7:21; Gal. 1:6 → MARVEL (verb) <2296> [7] Matt. 8:27; 15:31; 21:20; 22:22; Gal. 1:6; Rev. 13:3; et al. → WONDER (verb) <2296> [8] Mark 16:8 → they were amazed → lit.: amazement had gripped them → ASTONISHMENT <1611>, GRIP <2192> [9] Luke 1:65 → they were amazed → lit.: amazement came upon them → to come upon → COME <1096> [10] Luke 5:26 → all were amazed → lit.: amazement seized all → AMAZEMENT <1611>, SEIZE <2983>.

AMAZEMENT – [1] ***ekstasis*** [fem. noun: ἔκστασις <1611>]; **from *existēmi*: to remove from its normal place, which is from *ek*: out, and *histēmi*: to stand ► Astonishment, wonder** > The crowd was filled with wonder (*thambos*) and amazement (*ekstasis*) at what had happened to the lame man (Acts 3:10). People were all amazed (lit.: An amazement {astonishment} took all the people) when they saw Jesus heal a man who was paralyzed (Luke 5:26). Other refs.: Acts 10:10; 11:5 and 22:17 {ecstasy, trance}. Other refs.: Mark 5:42; 16:8; see ASTONISHMENT <1611>. ¶

[2] ***thauma*** [neut. noun: θαῦμα <2295>]; **from *thaomai*: to wonder ► Admiration, astonishment, wonder** > Along with the verb *thaumazō*, John marveled with great amazement {wondered greatly, was greatly astonished} when he saw the woman drunk with the blood of the saints and the witnesses of Jesus (Rev. 17:6). Other ref.: 2 Cor. 11:14 in some mss.; see WONDER (adj. and noun) <2298>. ¶

– [3] Mark 7:37 → to be overwhelmed with amazement → ASTONISHED (BE) <1605> [4] Luke 5:9 → ASTONISHMENT <2285> [5] Acts 2:12 → to continue in amazement → AMAZED (BE) <1839> [6] Acts 3:11 → full of amazement → greatly amazed → AMAZED <1569> [7] 1 Pet. 3:6 → FEAR (noun) <4423>.

AMAZING – John 9:30; Rev. 15:1, 3 → MARVELOUS <2298>.

AMBASSADOR (BE) – ***presbeuō*** [verb: πρεσβεύω <4243>]; **from *presbus*: older person, ambassador ► To be a person with experience chosen to represent the interests of another person or a country** > The Christians are ambassadors for Christ in this world (2 Cor. 5:20). Paul speaks of himself as being an ambassador in chains (Eph. 6:20). ¶

AMBASSAGE – Luke 14:32 → DELEGATION <4242>.

AMBITION – [1] Rom. 15:20 → to have the ambition → STRIVE <5389> [2] 2 Cor. 5:9 → to have as one's ambition → LABOR (verb) <5389> [3] 2 Cor. 12:20; Gal. 5:20 → selfish ambition → CONTENTION <2052> [4] 1 Thes. 4:11 → to make one's ambition → STUDY <5389> [5] Jas. 3:14, 16 → selfish ambition → STRIFE <2052>.

AMBITIOUS – Rom. 2:8 → one who is selfishly ambitious → SELF-SEEKING <2052>.

AMBUSH – [1] ***enedra*** [fem. noun: ἐνέδρα <1747>]; **from *en*: in, and *hedra*: seat, sitting ► Surprise attack by people in hiding** > The high priest and the chief men of the Jews laid in ambush {set an ambush, laid in wait} to kill Paul (Acts 25:3). Other possible ref. according to reading of the Greek: Acts 23:16 (*tēn enedran*); see [3]. ¶

[2] **to wait in ambush: *enedreuō*** [verb: ἐνεδρεύω <1748>]; **from *enedra*: see [1] ► To wait for someone at a place to wound or kill him; also transl.: to lie in wait, to plot** > The scribes and the Pharisees were plotting against Jesus to catch Him in something He might say (Luke 11:54 {to wait, to watch}). Jews were waiting in ambush for Paul in order to kill him (Acts 23:21). ¶

[3] ***enedron*** [neut. noun: ἔνεδρον <1749>]; **from *enedra*: see [1] ► Action of persons hiding with the intention to wound or kill; also transl.: lying in wait, plot** > The son of Paul's sister had heard of an ambush against Paul (Acts 23:16; *to enedron*); other reading: see [1]. ¶

AMEN – [1] ***Amēn*** [adv. used as name: Ἀμήν <281>]: **verily, surely, in Heb. ► Name of Christ** > He is the Amen, the faithful and true Witness, the Beginning of the creation of God (Rev. 3:14).

[2] ***amēn*** [adv.: ἀμήν <281>]; **word borrowed from the Heb. ► In truth, verily, may it be so!** > The word "Amen" refers to what is sure and worthy of trust (2 Cor. 1:20; Rev. 1:7). It is a name of God Himself in Heb. (in Is. 65:16, the God of truth is lit.: "Elohim Amen"), and in Revelation it is a name of Christ (3:14). "Amen" indicates our agreement with the words uttered by someone else, e.g., when giving thanks (1 Cor. 14:16). The word is used with exprs. of blessings (Rom. 1:25; 9:5), glory to God and Jesus Christ (Rom. 11:36; 16:27; Gal. 1:5; Eph. 3:21; Phil. 4:20; 1 Tim. 1:17; 2 Tim. 4:18; Heb. 13:21; 1 Pet. 4:11; 5:11; 2 Pet. 3:18; Jude 25; Rev. 1:6; 7:12a, b), honor and strength to God (1 Tim. 6:16), and praises {wishes or greetings} (Rom. 15:33; 16:24; 1 Cor. 16:24; Gal. 6:18; Phil. 4:23; Heb. 13:25, Rev. 5:14; 19:4). In response to the Lord's promise to come quickly, the church responds: "Amen. Even so, come, Lord Jesus!" (Rev. 22:20). Other refs. (in some mss.): Matt. 28:20; Mark 6:11; 16:20; Luke 13:35; 24:53; John 21:25; 2 Cor. 13:14; Eph. 6:24; Col. 4:18; 1 Thes. 5:28; 2 Thes. 3:18; 1 Tim. 6:21; 2 Tim. 4:22; Titus 3:15; Phm. 25; 1 Pet. 5:14; 1 John 5:21; 2 John 13; Rev. 22:21. All other refs.: VERILY <281>.

AMEND – John 4:52 → to begin to amend → to get better → BETTER <2866>.

AMETHYST – ***amethustos*** [fem. noun: ἀμέθυστος <271>]; **from *a*: neg., and *methuō*: to get drunk; lit.: not drunken ► Variety of quartz, a precious stone of purple or violet color; the name was given apparently because the color of this stone resembles wine diluted with water, which cannot lead to drunkenness** > The twelfth foundation of the wall of the heavenly Jerusalem is adorned with amethyst (Rev. 21:20). ¶

AMIABLE – Phil. 4:8 → LOVELY <4375>.

AMINADAB – See AMMINADAB <284>.

AMISS – [1] Luke 23:41 → WRONG (adj.) <824> [2] Jas. 4:3 → SICK (adv. and noun) <2560>.

AMMINADAB – ***Aminadab*** [masc. name: Ἀμιναδάβ <284>]: **people of liberality, i.e., willing to give generously, in Heb.; also spelled: Aminadab ▶ Man from the O.T.** > Amminadab is mentioned in the genealogy of Jesus Christ (Matt. 1:4a, b; Luke 3:33). ¶

AMON – ***Amōn*** [masc. name: Ἀμών <300>] ▶ **King of Judah** > Amon gave himself up to idolatry and did not walk in the way of the Lord; his servants conspired against him and killed him (2 Kgs. 21:19–25); he was the father of Josiah (v. 26). His name is mentioned in the genealogy of Jesus Christ (Matt. 1:10a, b). ¶

AMONG – [1] **from, from among:** ***apo*** [prep.: ἀπό <575>] ▶ **Within** > This word is found, for instance, in Luke 19:39; Eph. 4:31. Other refs.: DISTANCE <575>.
[2] ***en*** [prep.: ἐν <1722>] ▶ **Within** > This word is also transl. "in," "with," "over," "by," "through." Some refs.: Matt. 11:21, 23; Luke 9:46; 10:13; John 1:14; Acts 2:29; 20:28; 24:21; 26:4; Rom. 1:12; 11:17; 1 Cor. 1:6; 2 Cor. 1:19; 6:16; 10:1, 15; 12:12; 13:3; Gal. 3:5; 2 Thes. 3:7; 1 Pet. 4:12; Jude 14; Rev. 8:13; 14:6. *
– [3] Matt. 13:49; 18:20; Luke 8:7; 10:3; 22:27; 22:55b; John 1:26; Acts 17:33; 23:10; 1 Cor. 5:2; 2 Cor. 6:17; 1 Thes. 2:7 → in the midst → MIDST <3319> [4] John 7:35 → TO <4314> [5] 1 Cor. 5:13 → from among → FROM <1537>.

AMOS – [1] ***Amōs*** [masc. name: Ἀμώς <301>]: **strong, in Heb. ▶ Man in the O.T.** > Amos is mentioned in the genealogy of Jesus (Luke 3:25). ¶
– [2] Matt. 1:10a, b → AMON <300>.

AMOUNT (noun) – [1] Matt. 13:33; Luke 13:21 → large amount → lit.: three measures → MEASURE (noun) <4568> [2] Luke 6:34 → the same amount → the like → LIKE (adj., adv., noun) <2470>.

AMOUNT (verb) – 2 Cor. 10:10 → to amount to nothing → to treat with contempt → CONTEMPTIBLE <1848>.

AMPHIPOLIS – ***Amphipolis*** [fem. name: Ἀμφίπολις <295>]: **city surrounded (by a river) ▶ City of Macedonia, founded by the Greeks during the 5th century B.C.** > Paul travelled through Amphipolis before arriving at Thessalonica during his second missionary journey (Acts 17:1). ¶

AMPLE – [1] Luke 12:19 → ample goods → much goods → MUCH <4183> [2] Phil. 1:26 → to have ample cause → ABOUND <4052>.

AMPLIAS – See AMPLIATUS <291>.

AMPLIATUS – ***Amplias*** [masc. name: Ἀμπλίας <291>]; **from *amplus*, in Lat.: enlarged, distinguished; also written: *Ampliatos* ▶ Christian from Rome** > Paul salutes Ampliatus, his beloved in the Lord (Rom. 16:8). ¶

AMPLY – Phil. 4:18 → to be amply supplied → to fill up → FILL (verb) <4137>.

ANALYZE – Luke 12:56a, b → DISCERN <1381>.

ANANIAS – ***Hananias*** [masc. name: Ἀνανίας <367>]: **Jehovah has dealt graciously, in Heb.; also written: Ἀνανίας (*Ananias*) ▶ a. Christian of Jerusalem** > Ananias was married to Sapphira (Acts 5:1); he lied to the Holy Spirit (v. 3), which brought divine judgment upon him and his wife, who also lied. Both fell down and died (Acts 5:5; see vv. 5–10). **b. Disciple of Damascus** > Ananias was sent so that Paul might recover his sight after his conversion (Acts 9:10, 12, 13, 17); he was a devout man according to the law, having a good witness of all the Jews in Damascus (Acts 22:12). **c. High priest** > This Ananias gave commandment to strike Paul on the mouth (Acts 23:2). He was one of those who lodged a complaint against Paul (Acts 24:1). ¶

ANATHEMA – 1 Cor. 16:22 → ACCURSED <331>.

ANCESTOR – [1] Matt. 23:30, 32; Luke 1:55, 72; Acts 5:30; 7:11; et al. → FATHER <3962> [2] Acts 22:3; 24:14 → of the fathers → FATHER <3971> [3] 2 Tim. 1:3 → FOREFATHER <4269> [4] 1 Pet. 1:18 → handed down from the ancestors → received by tradition from the fathers → FATHER <3970>.

ANCHOR (noun) – [1] ***ankura*** [fem. noun: ἄγκυρα <45>]**; from *ankōn*: curvature, act or result of bending ▶ Iron instrument, with a curved shape, used to keep a vessel from drifting >** Four anchors were dropped from the stern of the ship on which Paul was aboard (Acts 27:29, 30, 40). In Heb. 6:19, the Christian hope is compared to an anchor of the soul, both secure and firm. ¶
– [2] Acts 27:13 → to weigh anchor → WEIGH <142> [3] Acts 27:17 → sea anchor → SAIL (noun) <4632>.

ANCHOR (verb) – Mark 6:53 → to draw to the shore → SHORE <4358>.

ANCIENT – [1] ***archaios*** [adj.: ἀρχαῖος <744>]**; from *archē*: beginning ▶ Person of another era, ancestor >** It was said to the ancients {them of old, them of old time} in Israel not to kill and swear falsely (Matt. 5:21, 33). All other refs.: OLD <744>.
– [2] Heb. 11:2 → ELDER <4245>.

AND – [1] ***kai*** [conj.: καί <2532>] **▶ Indicates a connection between a word or words and the following one(s).** *
[2] ***te*** [conj.: τέ <5037>] **▶ Similar, but not as strong as [1].** *

AND FROM THERE, AND FROM THAT TIME – ***kakeithen*** [contraction of two words.: κἀκεῖθεν <2547>]**; from *kai*: and, and *ekeithen*: from there ▶** Refs.: Mark 10:1; Acts 7:4; 13:21; 14:26; 20:15; 21:1; 27:4, 12; 28:15. ¶ ‡

AND HE, AND SHE, AND IT – ***kakeinos*** [contraction of two words: κἀκεῖνος <2548>]**; from *kai*: and, and *ekeinos*: that one ▶ That one also >** Refs.: Matt. 15:18; 20:4; 23:23; Mark 12:4; Luke 20:11; 22:12; John 7:29; 14:12. * ‡

AND THERE – ***kakei*** [contraction of two words.: κἀκεῖ <2546>]**; from *kai*: and, and *ekei*: there ▶** Refs.: Matt. 5:23; 10:11; 28:10; Mark 1:35, 38; John 11:54; Acts 14:7; 17:13; 22:10; 25:20; 27:6. ¶ ‡

ANDREW – ***Andreas*** [masc. name: Ἀνδρέας <406>]**; from *anēr*: man ▶ One of the twelve apostles of the Lord Jesus >** Andrew was the brother of Simon Peter (Matt. 4:18; 10:2; Mark 1:16; 3:18; Luke 6:14). He led his brother Peter to the Lord Jesus (John 1:40; see v. 42). We know that he was a fisherman (Matt. 4:18) from the town of Bethsaida (John 1:44) and a disciple of John the Baptist (see John 1:35–42). According to tradition, he suffered martyrdom in Achaia and was crucified on an X-shaped cross. Other refs.: Mark 1:29; 13:3; John 6:8; 12:22a, b; Acts 1:13. ¶

ANDRONICUS – ***Andronikos*** [masc. name: Ἀνδρόνικος <408>]**: man of victory; from *anēr*: man, and *nikos*: victory ▶ Christian, Paul's kinsman and fellow-captive >** Paul salutes Andronicus in his Epistle to the Romans (Rom. 16:7). ¶

ANGEL – [1] ***angelos*** [masc. noun: ἄγγελος <32>]**; of unknown origin, but may be related to *angareuō*: to compel; *angelos* has given *angelia*: a message delivered ▶ Celestial being created by God >** Angels are spirits created by God to praise Him (e.g., Ps. 148:2) and His Son (e.g., Heb. 1:6), and to serve Him (e.g., Ps. 91:11). They can take a human form (e.g., Luke 1:19; John 20:12). There is mention of angels who have sinned (2 Pet. 2:4) and those who did not keep their first estate (Jude 6). According to Heb. 1:14, angels are ministering spirits sent forth to serve for those who will inherit salvation. See CHERUBIM and SERAPHIM. Other refs.: Matt. 1:20, 24; 2:13, 19; 4:6, 11; 13:39, 41, 49; 16:27; 18:10; 22:30; 24:31, 36; 25:31, 41; 26:53; 28:2, 5; Mark 1:13; 8:38; 12:25;

13:27, 32; Luke 1:11, 13, 18, 26, 28, 30, 34, 35, 38; 2:9, 10, 13, 15, 21; 4:10; 9:26; 12:8, 9; 15:10; 16:22; 22:43; 24:23; John 1:52; 5:4; 12:29; Acts 5:19; 6:15; 7:30, 35, 38, 53; 8:26; 10:3, 7, 22; 11:13; 12:7–11, 15, 23; 23:8, 9; 27:23; Rom. 8:38; 1 Cor. 4:9; 6:3; 11:10; 13:1; 2 Cor. 11:14; 12:7; Gal. 1:8; 3:19; 4:14; Col. 2:18; 2 Thes. 1:7; 1 Tim. 3:16; 5:21; Heb. 1:4, 5, 7a, b, 13; 2:2, 5, 7, 9, 16; 12:22; 13:2; 1 Pet. 1:12; 3:22; 2 Pet. 2:11; Rev. 1:1, 20; 2:1, 8, 12, 18; 3:1, 5, 7, 14; 5:2, 11; 7:1, 2a, b, 11; 8:2–6, 8, 10, 12, 13; 9:1, 11, 13, 14a, b, 15; 10:1, 5, 7–10; 11:15; 12:7–9; 14:6, 8–10, 15, 17–19; 15:1, 6–8; 16:1, 5; 17:1, 7; 18:1, 21; 19:17; 20:1; 21:9, 12, 17; 22:6, 8, 16. All other refs.: MESSENGER <32>.

[2] **equal unto angels, like angels: *isangelos*** [adj.: ἰσάγγελος <2465>]**; from *isos*: equal, and *angelos*: see [1] ► Similar to angels, the celestial beings created by God >** Those who are resurrected from the dead are equal to angels (Luke 20:36). ¶

– [3] 1 Cor. 10:10 → destroying angel → DESTROYER <3644>.

ANGELIC – 2 Pet. 2:10; Jude 8 → angelic majesty → DIGNITARY <1391>.

ANGER (noun) – [1] Matt. 18:34; Luke 14:21 → to be moved with anger, in anger → to be angry, to become angry → ANGRY <3710> [2] Mark 3:5; Eph. 4:31; Col. 3:8; 1 Tim. 2:8; Heb. 3:11; Jas. 1:19, 20 → WRATH <3709> [3] Rom. 2:8 → INDIGNATION <2372> [4] Rom. 10:19; Eph. 6:4 → to move to anger, to provoke to anger → ANGER (verb) <3949> [5] 2 Cor. 12:20; Gal. 5:20; Eph. 4:31; Heb. 11:27 → anger, outburst of anger → WRATH <2372> [6] Eph. 4:26 → WRATH <3950>.

ANGER (verb) – ***parorgizō*** [verb: παροργίζω <3949>]**; from *para*: toward, and *orgizō*: to make angry, which is from *orgē*: anger, wrath ► To irritate, to provoke to deep resentment, to enrage >** Moses says to Israel that God would anger them {move them to anger, make them angry} by a nation without understanding (Rom. 10:19). Fathers are told not to provoke to anger {to provoke to wrath, to exasperate} (lit.: to anger) their children, but bring them up in the discipline and instruction of the Lord (Eph. 6:4). Other ref.: Col. 3:21 in some mss. ¶

ANGERED (BE) – 1 Cor. 13:5 → to be easily angered → to be quickly provoked → PROVOKE <3947>.

ANGRY – [1] **soon angry: *orgilos*** [adj.: ὀργίλος <3711>]**; from *orgē*: anger, wrath ► Easily angered, irascible, irritable >** An overseer must not be soon angry {quick-tempered, passionate} (Titus 1:7). ¶

[2] **to be angry, to become angry: *orgizō*** [verb: ὀργίζω <3710>]**; from *orgē*: see [1] ► To feel irascible, vexed against someone >** Whoever is angry with his brother without a cause will be subject to the judgment (Matt. 5:22). In a parable, the master was angry {was moved with anger, was wroth} against his servant and delivered him to the torturers (Matt. 18:34). In another parable, the master of the house became angry because there were guests who had refused his invitation to his great supper (Luke 14:21). In the parable of the prodigal son, the older brother became angry and would not go in the house (Luke 15:28). Paul says to be angry and not sin (Eph. 4:26). All other refs.: ENRAGED (BE) <3710>.

[3] **to be very angry: *thumomacheō*** [verb: θυμομαχέω <2371>]**; from *thumos*: anger, indignation, and *machomai*: to struggle ► To be enraged; also transl.: to be highly displeased, to be in bitter hostility, to be quarrelling >** Herod was very angry against the Tyrians and the Sidonians (Acts 12:20). ¶

[4] **to be angry: *thumoō*** [verb: θυμόω <2373>]**; from *thumos*: indignation, wrath ► To be infuriated, to be enraged >** Herod was exceedingly angry {very enraged, furious, infuriated, exceedingly wroth} after having been deceived by the wise men (Matt. 2:16). ¶

[5] **to be angry: *prosochthizō*** [verb: προσοχθίζω <4360>]**; from *pros*: against, toward, and *ochtheō*: to be afflicted, to be indignant ► To be irritated, to**

be exacerbated, to be outraged by the behavior of someone else > God was angry with the Israelites who came out of Egypt (Heb. 3:10, 17 {to be grieved, to be wroth}). ¶

[6] **to be angry:** ***cholaō*** [verb: χολάω <5520>]; **from** ***cholē*: bile, gall ► To be upset, to be bitterly enraged** > Jesus asked the Jews if they were angry with Him because He healed a man on the Sabbath (John 7:23). ¶

– [7] Matt. 22:7 → ENRAGED (BE) <3710> [8] Rom. 10:19 → to make angry → ANGER (verb) <3949> [9] 2 Cor. 12:20 → angry temper → WRATH <2372> [10] Eph. 4:26 → while you are still angry → lit.: on your anger → WRATH <3950> [11] Jas. 1:19 → slow to become angry → lit.: slow to wrath → WRATH <3709>.

ANGUISH – [1] ***thlipsis*** [fem. noun: θλῖψις <2347>]; **from** ***thlibō*: to compress, to oppress ► Suffering, distress** > When she has given birth, a woman no longer remembers her anguish (John 16:21). All other refs.: AFFLICTION <2347>, DISTRESS <2347>, TRIBULATION <2347>, TROUBLE (noun) <2347>.

[2] ***stenochōria*** [fem. noun: στενοχωρία <4730>]; **from** ***stenos*: narrow, and** ***chora*: space; lit.: narrow space ► Great distress, great trouble arising from within** > Paul says there will be tribulation and anguish {distress} on every soul of man who does evil (Rom. 2:9). Other refs.: Rom. 8:35; 2 Cor. 6:4; 12:10; see DISTRESS <4730>. ¶

[3] ***sunochē*** [fem. noun: συνοχή <4928>]; **from** ***sunechō*: to hold together, which is from** ***sun*: together, and** ***echō*: to hold, to have; lit.: a holding together ► Dismay, consternation; figur.: anxiety, distress** > Paul had written to the Corinthians in much affliction and anguish of heart (2 Cor. 2:4). Other ref.: Luke 21:25; see DISTRESS <4928>. ¶

– [4] Luke 16:24, 25 → to be in anguish → to be tormented → TORMENT (verb) <3600> [5] Luke 22:44 → AGONY <74> [6] Gal. 4:19 → to be in the anguish of childbirth → LABOR (verb) <5605> [7] Rev. 16:10 → PAIN (noun) <4192>.

ANIMAL – [1] Mark 1:13; Acts 11:6; Heb. 12:20; Jas. 3:7; Rev. 18:2 in some mss. → BEAST <2342> [2] Luke 10:34; 1 Cor. 15:39 → BEAST <2934> [3] Acts 7:42 → slain beast → BEAST <4968> [4] Heb. 13:11; 2 Pet. 2:12; Jude 10 → BEAST <2226> [5] Jas. 3:7 → sea animal → SEA <1724> [6] 2 Pet. 2:16 → "an animal" added in Engl.

ANISE – ***anēthon*** [neut. noun: ἄνηθον <432>] **► Plant with fragrant seeds used as condiment; also transl.: dill** > The Pharisees were paying tithes of mint, anise, and cumin, but were leaving aside the weightier matters of the law (Matt. 23:23). Other ref.: Luke 11:42 in some mss. ¶

ANKLE – ***sphuron*** [neut. noun: σφυρόν <4974>]; **from** ***sphura*: hammer; some mss.:** ***sphudron*** **► Part of the body between the foot and the leg** > Peter and John healed the lame man, and his feet and ankles {ankle bones} were made strong (Acts 3:7). ¶

ANNA – ***Hanna*** [fem. name: Ἄννα <451>]**: grace, in Heb. ► A prophetess far advanced in age who served God in the temple** > Anna is mentioned at the time Jesus was presented in the temple (Luke 2:36); read 2:36–38. ¶

ANNAS – ***Hannas*** [masc. name: Ἄννας <452>]**: grace, in Heb. ► Father-in-law to Caiaphas** > Annas was high priest at the same time as Caiaphas (Luke 3:2). Jesus was first led away to him bound (John 18:13); Annas later sent him to Caiaphas (v. 24). Annas inquired of Peter and John after their arrest (Acts 4:6). ¶

ANNOUNCE – [1] ***anangellō*** [verb: ἀναγγέλλω <312>]; **from** ***ana*: upon (intens.), and** ***angellō*: to serve as a messenger, to announce, which is from** ***angelos*: messenger ► To preach, to proclaim** > Paul had already announced {shown} and taught publicly and in every house (Acts 20:20). All other refs.: see entries in Lexicon at <312>.

[2] **to announce beforehand, to announce previously: *prokatangellō*** [verb: προκαταγγέλλω <4293>]; **from *pro*: before, and *katangellō*: to declare openly, which is from *kata*: intens., and *angelō*: to tell ► To report in advance, to declare in advance >** God had announced beforehand {shown before, foretold} by the mouth of the prophets that His Christ would suffer (Acts 3:18). Stephen reminded the Jews that their fathers had killed the prophets who had announced beforehand the coming of the Just One (Acts 7:52). Other refs. in some mss.: Acts 3:24 (FORETELL <4293>); 2 Cor. 9:5 (NOTICE [verb] <4293>). ¶

– [3] Luke 3:18; 4:43; 8:1; 9:6; 20:1; Acts 5:42; 8:4, 12, 25, 35, 40; 10:36; 14:7, 21; 15:35; 16:10; 17:18; Rom. 1:15; 10:15a, b; 1 Cor. 15:1, 2; Gal. 1:11, 16, 23; Eph. 2:17; 3:8; 1 Pet. 1:12, 25; Rev. 14:6; et al. → to announce the glad tidings → PREACH <2097> [4] Luke 9:60 → PREACH <1229> [5] John 20:18; Acts 12:14 → REPORT (verb) <518> [6] Acts 13:5; 15:36; 16:17, 21; 17:3, 13, 23; 26:23; 1 Cor. 9:14; 11:26; Phil. 1:18; Col. 1:28 → PREACH <2605> [7] Acts 21:26 → SIGNIFY <1229> [8] Acts 26:20 → SHOW (verb) <518> [9] Gal. 3:8 → to announce beforehand the glad tidings → to preach before the gospel → PREACH <4283> [10] Heb. 2:3 → SPEAK <2980>.

ANNOUNCER – Acts 17:18 → PROCLAIMER <2604>.

ANNOY – [1] Luke 18:5 → TROUBLE (verb) <3930> <2873> [2] Acts 16:18 → to annoy, to annoy greatly → GRIEVE <1278>.

ANNOYED – Acts 4:2 → greatly annoyed → DISTURBED (BE) <1278>.

ANNUL – [1] ***luō*** [verb: λύω <3089>]; **lit.: to unbind ► To abrogate, to put an end to; to make void, to cancel >** Jesus spoke of the consequences of annulling {breaking, doing away with} one of the least commandments of the divine law (Matt. 5:19). All other refs.: BREAK <3089>, DESTROY <3089>, DISSOLVE <3089>, LOOSE <3089>, RELEASE (verb) <3089>.

– [2] Rom. 6:6; 1 Cor. 1:28 → to make of no effect → EFFECT (noun) <2673> [3] 1 Cor. 15:24, 26; 2 Thes. 2:8 → DESTROY <2673> [4] 2 Cor. 3:7, 11, 13, 14 → to do away → AWAY <2673> [5] Gal. 3:15 → REJECT <114> [6] Gal. 3:17 → to make of no effect → EFFECT (noun) <208> [7] Eph. 2:15; 2 Tim. 1:10 → ABOLISH <2673> [8] Heb. 2:14 → to render powerless → POWERLESS <2673>.

ANNULLING – Heb. 7:18 → putting away → PUTTING <115>.

ANOINT – [1] ***aleiphō*** [verb: ἀλείφω <218>]; **akin to *lipos*: oil ► a. To cover a part of the body with a liquid substance, in general a perfumed oil; also transl.: to put oil, to pour >** Jesus said to anoint one's head when one fasts (Matt. 6:17). The disciples anointed many infirm people with oil and healed them (Mark 6:13). A woman anointed the feet of Jesus with perfume (Luke 7:38 {to pour a perfume}, 46a, b); perhaps this woman was Mary of Bethany (John 11:2). Later this same Mary anointed the feet of Jesus with a perfume of pure nard of great price (John 12:3). The elders of the church may pray over one who is sick, anointing this person with oil in the name of the Lord (Jas. 5:14). **b. To rub a dead body with ointment, to embalm >** On the first day of the week, some women bought aromatic spices to anoint {embalm} the body of Jesus (Mark 16:1). ¶

[2] ***murizō*** [verb: μυρίζω <3462>]; **from *muron*: ointment, perfume, fragrant oil ► To anoint for burial >** A woman had beforehand anointed {poured perfume on} the body of Jesus for His burial (Mark 14:8). ¶

[3] ***chriō*** [verb: χρίω <5548>]; **similar to *chrainō*: to touch lightly, and later: to coat, to anoint ► To consecrate, or set apart, for God and His service >** Jesus had been anointed to preach the gospel (Luke 4:18). God has anointed His holy servant Jesus (Acts 4:27; also Heb. 1:9; comp. Ps. 2:2, 6); He anointed Him with the Holy

Spirit (Acts 10:38). God has also anointed Christians (2 Cor. 1:21). ¶

4 ***enchriō*** [verb: ἐγχρίω <1472>]; **from *en*: in, and *chriō*: see 3 ▶ To apply a substance, to rub it in** > The angel of Laodicea is advised to anoint his eyes with an eye salve (Rev. 3:18 {to put on}). ¶

5 ***epichriō*** [verb: ἐπιχρίω <2025>]; **from *epi*: upon, and *chriō*: see 3 ▶ To apply a substance, to smear it over** > Jesus anointed the eyes of a blind man (John 9:6 {to put as ointment, to apply}, 11). ¶

– 6 1 John 2:20 → to be anointed → to have an unction → UNCTION <5545>.

ANOINTING – 1 John 2:20, 27a, b → UNCTION <5545>.

ANON – Matt. 13:20; Mark 1:31 → IMMEDIATELY <2112> <2117>.

ANOTHER – 1 **another, another man, other man, other: *allotrios*** [adj.: ἀλλότριος <245>]; **from *allos*: other ▶ Which belongs to someone else, which concerns another** > Jesus talked about being faithful with what belongs to another {someone's else property} (Luke 16:12). Paul wrote about not judging the servant of another (Rom. 14:4). He did not want to build upon another's foundation (Rom. 15:20). He did not boast of other men's labors (2 Cor. 10:15) or another's sphere (v. 16). He exhorted Timothy not to partake in other's sins (1 Tim. 5:22). All other refs.: FOREIGN <245>, STRANGER <245>.

2 ***heteros*** [pron.: ἕτερος <2087>]; **also transl.: other ▶ Someone else, something else, different** > Paul spoke about a man judging another (Rom. 2:1). We should seek the advantage of the other {each one the other's well-being, every man another's wealth, the good of his neighbor} (1 Cor. 10:24). The liberty of Paul was not judged by another's conscience (1 Cor. 10:29). The glory of the celestial bodies is one (lit.: another, different), and the glory of the terrestrial is another (1 Cor. 15:40a, b). In examining his own work, a man rejoices in respect to himself alone, and not in what belongs to another (Gal. 6:4). The word is used in relation to teaching another (Rom. 2:21). Other refs.: DIFFERENT <2087>, OTHER <2087>.

– 3 Acts 10:28 → one of another nation → NATION <246> 4 Rom. 14:19 → ONE ANOTHER <240>.

ANSWER (noun) – 1 ***apokrisis*** [fem. noun: ἀπόκρισις <612>]; **from *apokrinomai*: to give a response, to reply, which is from *apo*: from, and *krinō*: to judge; lit.: to conclude for oneself ▶ Verbal response to one who poses a question** > Those who heard Jesus at twelve years of age in the temple were astonished at His answers (Luke 2:47). The chief priests and scribes wondered at the answer of Jesus in the matter of paying tribute to Caesar (Luke 20:26). Priests and Levites asked John the Baptist who he was, so that they might give an answer to those who had sent them (John 1:22). Jesus gave no answer to Pilate's question: "Where do you come from?" (John 19:9). ¶

2 ***apologia*** [fem. noun: ἀπολογία <627>]; **from *apologeomai*: to respond in defense of oneself, which is from *apo*: from, and *logos*: word, speech ▶ Apology, i.e., a verbal defense or justification of a belief, a doctrine, or something else** > In 1 Pet. 3:15, Christians are always to be prepared to give an answer {a defense} to everyone who asks them to give an account of the hope that is in them. All other refs.: ANSWER (verb) <627>, DEFENSE <627>, EXCUSING <627>.

3 ***eperōtēma*** [neut. noun: ἐπερώτημα <1906>]; **from *eperōtaō*: to question, to make a request, which is from *epi*: upon (intens.), and *erōtaō*: to ask, to pray ▶ Commitment, profession, testimony** > Baptism is the answer {engagement, pledge, response} of a good conscience toward God {an appeal to God of a good conscience} (1 Pet. 3:21). ¶

4 **divine answer, answer of God: *chrēmatismos*** [masc. noun: χρηματισμός <5538>]; **from *chrēmatizō*: to speak as an oracle, which is from *chrēma*: matter, business ▶ Special response, revelation coming from God** > In His divine answer {divine response}, God addressed Elijah

and told him about seven thousand men who had not bowed the knee to Baal (Rom. 11:4). ¶
– [5] Matt. 26:62; 27:14 → to give an answer → ANSWER (verb) <611>.

ANSWER (verb) – [1] **to answer back:** ***antilegō*** [verb: ἀντιλέγω <483>]; **from** ***anti*****: against, and** ***legō*****: to talk; lit.: to talk against ▶ To contradict, to contest >** Titus was to exhort bondservants to not answer back {answer again, be gainsaying, be argumentative, talk back} (Titus 2:9). All other refs.: DENY <483>, SPEAK <483>.
[2] ***apokrinomai*** [verb: ἀποκρίνομαι <611>]; **from** ***apo*****: from, and** ***krinō*****: to discern, to judge; lit.: to conclude for oneself ▶ To give a response, to begin speaking >** The chiliarch answered {said}: "I, for a great sum, bought this citizenship." (Acts 22:28). This verb is used very frequently in the N.T., especially in the Gospels (e.g., Matt. 3:15; Luke 4:4; John 2:18, 19). *
[3] ***antapokrinomai*** [verb: ἀνταποκρίνομαι <470>]; **from** ***anti*****: against, and** ***apokrinomai*****: see** [2] **▶ To reply by opposing >** The Pharisees were not able to answer {could make no reply} to the things which Jesus said concerning the Sabbath (Luke 14:6). Other ref.: Rom. 9:20 (to reply against); see REPLY (verb) <470>. ¶
[4] ***apologeomai*** [verb: ἀπολογέομαι <626>]; **from** ***apo*****: from, and** ***logos*****: word, speech; lit.: to respond for oneself ▶ To defend, to justify oneself against an accusation, to make an apology >** The disciples were not to worry about how or what they would answer {would speak, defend themselves} before the synagogues and the magistrates (Luke 12:11). They did not have to meditate on what they would answer {would prepare to defend themselves} (Luke 21:14). Paul answered for himself {said in his own defense, made his defense} that he did not offend in anything against the law of the Jews, the temple, nor Caesar (Acts 25:8). All other refs.: DEFEND <626>, DEFENSE <626>, EXCUSE (verb) <626>.
[5] ***hupakouō*** [verb: ὑπακούω <5219>]; **from** ***hupo*****: under, and** ***akouō*****: to hear ▶ To listen attentively with the intention of responding >** While Peter was knocking at the door of the gate, a maid called Rhoda came to answer {listen, hearken} (Acts 12:13). All other refs.: OBEY <5219>.
[6] **to answer for oneself; lit.: defense:** ***apologia*** [fem. noun: ἀπολογία <627>]; **from** ***apologeomai*****: see** [4] **▶ Verbal response to an accusation, apology in relation to legal matters >** It was the custom of the Romans to give the accused the opportunity to answer for himself {to make his defense} (lit.: to receive a defense) concerning the charge against him (Acts 25:16); some mss.: *apōleia*. All other refs.: ANSWER (noun) <627>, DEFENSE <627>, EXCUSING <627>.
– [7] Luke 10:30 → REPLY <5274> [8] 1 Cor. 4:13 → to answer kindly → PLEAD <3870> [9] Gal. 4:25 → CORRESPOND <4960>.

ANSWERABLE – Matt. 5:22 → SUBJECT (noun)[1] <1777>.

ANTICHRIST – ***antichristos*** [masc. noun: ἀντίχριστος <500>]; **lit.: who is against Christ, who is instead of Christ ▶ a. One who opposes Christ, His adversary >** The antichrist is coming and his spirit is already in the world (1 John 2:18a; 4:3). He will perform miracles and will seduce people, but he will receive his power from Satan. He will be cast alive in the lake of fire when the Lord Jesus will introduce His reign. Other names of the antichrist are: the false prophet, the other beast, the man of sin, the son of perdition, and the wicked one. Read Dan. 11:36–39; 2 Thes. 2:1–12; Rev. 13:11–18; 19:19–21. **b. Other person who opposes Christ, who is His adversary >** The apostle John speaks of many antichrists who went out from among the Christians and who deny the Father and the Son as well as that Jesus is the Christ, and who do not confess that Jesus Christ has come in flesh (1 John 2:18b, 22; 2 John 7). ¶

ANTICIPATE – [1] ***prophthanō*** [verb: προφθάνω <4399>]; **from** ***pro*****: before, and** ***phthanō*****: to arrive first, to be ahead of ▶ To speak first, to take the lead; also transl.: to prevent >** Jesus anticipated Peter

by asking him a question about collecting tribute (Matt. 17:25). ¶
– [2] Acts 12:11 → EXPECTATION <4329> [3] 1 Thes. 4:15 → PRECEDE <5348>.

ANTIOCH – [1] ***Antiocheia*** [fem. name: Ἀντιόχεια <490>]; **from Antiochus, a Syrian king ► a. Capital of Syria founded around 300 B.C. by Seleucus Nicator, a general of Alexander the Great** > It was in Antioch that the disciples of the Lord Jesus were first called Christians (Acts 11:26b). Paul visited this city on many occasions (see Acts 11:26a; 13:1; 14:26; 15:30, 35; 18:22). Other refs.: Acts 11:19, 20, 22, 27; 15:22, 23; Gal. 2:11. **b. Roman colony of Pisidia in Asia Minor** > Paul preached the gospel in the synagogue of Antioch of Pisidia (Acts 13:14). Certain Jews of this town stoned him at Lystra (Acts 14:19); he suffered persecutions at Antioch (2 Tim. 3:11). He strengthened the souls of the disciples at Antioch (Acts 14:21). ¶
[2] **from Antioch: *Antiocheus*** [masc. name: Ἀντιοχεύς <491>]; **from *Antiocheia*: see** [1] **► Native of Antioch** > Nicolas was a proselyte from Antioch (Acts 6:5). ¶

ANTIPAS – ***Antipas*** [masc. name: Ἀντιπᾶς <493>]: **against all; or contracted form of Antipater, i.e., like his father ► Christian who suffered martyrdom at Pergamum** > We know only that Antipas was a faithful witness (Rev. 2:13). ¶

ANTIPATRIS – ***Antipatris*** [fem. name: Ἀντιπατρίς <494>]: **like his father ► City located northeast of Jerusalem; it was the O.T. city of Aphek (1 Sam. 4:1; 29:1)** > Paul was brought as a prisoner by night to Antipatris, on his way from Jerusalem to Caesarea (Acts 23:31). ¶

ANTITYPE – 1 Pet. 3:21 → FIGURE <499>.

ANXIETY – [1] **to be in anxiety: *meteōrizō*** [verb: μετεωρίζω <3349>]; **from *meteoros*: high, which is from *meta*: in the midst of, and *aēr*: air, atmosphere; originally: to be suspended in doubt ► To be troubled, to worry, to torment oneself about certain things** > Jesus said not to be in anxiety {be of doubtful mind, have an anxious mind, keep worrying, worry} about food and drink (Luke 12:29). ¶
– [2] Matt. 28:14 → from all anxiety → out of trouble → TROUBLE (noun) <275> [3] Luke 21:34; 2 Cor. 11:28; 1 Pet. 5:7 → CARE (noun) <3308> [4] 1 Cor. 7:32 → free from anxieties → free from concern → CONCERN (noun) <275> [5] Phil. 2:28 → to have less anxiety → to be less sorrowful → SORROWFUL <253>.

ANXIOUS – [1] Matt. 13:22 → anxious care → CARE (noun) <3308> [2] Luke 12:29 → to have an anxious mind → to be in anxiety → ANXIETY <3349> [3] Rom. 8:19 → anxious longing, anxious looking out → earnest expectation → EXPECTATION <603> [4] Phil. 2:28 → SORROWFUL <253>.

ANXIOUS (BE) – [1] ***merimnaō*** [verb: μεριμνάω <3309>]; **from *merimna*: concern, care, which is from *meris*: part ► To be troubled, to worry about certain things; older versions: to be careful** > The Christian is to be anxious for nothing, but to make known his requests to God (Phil. 4:6). All other refs.: CARE (noun) <3309>, CARE (verb) <3309>, WORRY (verb) <3309>.
– [2] Mark 13:11 → to be anxious beforehand → to worry beforehand → WORRY (verb) <4305>.

ANXIOUSLY – [1] Luke 2:48 → to be distressed → DISTRESSED <3600> [2] Jude 21 → to wait anxiously for → to look for → LOOK (verb) <4327>.

ANY TIME (AT) – ***pōpote*** [adv.: πώποτε <4455>]; **from *pō*: even, and *pote*: never ► At no time, ever** > No one has seen God at any time (John 1:18; 1 John 4:12). The disciples had neither heard the Father's voice at any time, nor seen His form (John 5:37). He who comes to Jesus shall never hunger, and he who believes in Him shall never thirst at any time (John 6:35). Other refs.: Luke 19:30; John 8:33. ¶

ANYONE – ***hostis*** [pron.: ὅστις <3748>]; **from *hos*: he who, and *tis*: anyone, someone ▶ Anyone who, someone who, whoever, whatever.** Refs.: Matt. 7:24, 26; 13:52; Luke 2:10; 7:37; 12:1; Acts 16:16; 24:1; Rom. 16:6, 12; 1 Cor. 7:13; Phil. 2:20. * ‡

APART – [1] **apart from: *chōris*** [adv.: χωρίς <5565>]; **from *chōra*: region ▶ At a distance, separately, without** > Apart from the Lord, Christians can do nothing (John 15:5). Other refs.: BESIDES <5565>.
– [2] Matt. 14:13, 23; 17:1, 19; Mark 6:31, 32; 7:33; 9:2; Luke 9:10 → PRIVATELY <2596> <2398> [3] John 10:36; 1 Pet. 3:15 → to set apart → SANCTIFY <37> [4] Rom. 1:1; Acts 13:2; Gal. 1:15 → to set apart → SEPARATE <873> [5] Heb. 7:26 → to set apart → SEPARATE <5563> [6] Jude 19 → to set oneself apart → to separate oneself → SEPARATE <592>.

APELLES – ***Apellēs*** [masc. name: Ἀπελλῆς <559>] ▶ **Christian of Rome** > Paul salutes Apelles in his Epistle to the Romans; he considers him as "approved (*dokimos*) in Christ" (Rom. 16:10). ¶

APOLLONIA – ***Apollōnia*** [fem. name: Ἀπολλωνία <624>]: **belonging to Apollo, a god of the Greek mythology ▶ City of Macedonia** > Paul passed through this city before arriving at Thessalonica, during his second missionary journey (Acts 17:1). ¶

APOLLOS – ***Apollōs*** [masc. name: Ἀπολλῶς <625>]: **prob. from Apollo, the god of light ▶ A Jew from Alexandria; he became a Christian and served the Lord** > Apollos was an eloquent man and mighty in the Scriptures (Acts 18:24). After his preaching in the synagogue of Ephesus, Aquila and Priscilla unfolded to him the way of God more exactly (see Acts 18:26). Soon afterwards, Apollos contributed much to those who believed and showed by the Scriptures that Jesus was the Christ (see Acts 18:27, 28). Apollos had worked with the Corinthians (Acts 19:1; 1 Cor. 1:12; 3:4–6, 22; 4:6), but he was not ready to return to Corinth when Paul wrote his letter (1 Cor. 16:12). Paul asked Titus to set diligently on their way Apollos and Zenas so that nothing might be lacking to them (Titus 3:13). ¶

APOLLYON – ***Apolluōn*** [masc. name: Ἀπολλύων <623>]: **Destroyer; from *apollumi*: to destroy, to corrupt ▶** For this name in Rev. 9:11, see ABADDON <3>. ¶

APOLOGIZE – Acts 16:39 → BESEECH <3870>.

APOSTASY – ***apostasia*** [fem. noun: ἀποστασία <646>]; **from *aphistēmi*: to separate oneself, to go away, which is from *apo*: from, and *histēmi*: to stand; lit.: defection, giving up of a doctrine ▶ Giving up of the truth, leaving of the faith** > Paul was accused of teaching all the Jews among the Gentiles apostasy from {to forsake, to turn away from} Moses (Acts 21:21). There will be an apostasy {falling away, rebellion} first before the revelation of the man of sin (2 Thes. 2:3). Before the return of Christ, apostasy will be widespread; it will be characterized by the public and general disowning of the Christian doctrine. ¶

APOSTATIZE – 1 Tim. 4:1 → DEPART <868>.

APOSTLE – ***apostolos*** [masc. noun: ἀπόστολος <652>]; **from *apostellō*: to send away, which is from *apo*: away, and *stellō*: to send; lit.: missionary ▶ One who is sent on a mission, delegate; also transl.: messenger** > Jesus chose twelve apostles among His disciples (Luke 6:13), to be with Him during His ministry on earth (see Mark 3:14). The apostles were eyewitnesses of the events of His ministry (see 2 Pet. 1:16). Jesus gave them power against unclean spirits and to heal all kinds of sickness and disease (see Matt. 10:1). He ate the Passover with them before suffering (Luke 22:14; see v. 15), and He instituted the Lord's Supper on this occasion (see vv. 19, 20). Judas was replaced by Matthias (Acts 1:26). The apostles witnessed the resurrection of the Lord (see Acts 1:22). Paul is also an apostle, having seen the Lord in glory after His ascent into heaven (1 Cor. 9:1). He uses the title "called to be an apostle" to designate himself (e.g., 1 Cor. 1:1). The term "apostle" is also used to designate other servants (Acts 14:4, 14; 1 Cor. 15:7). Christ Jesus is called the "Apostle and High Priest of our confession {profession}" (Heb. 3:1). Other refs.: Matt. 10:2; Mark 6:30; Luke 9:10; 11:49; 17:5; 24:10; John 13:16 {he who is sent}; Acts 1:2, 12 (added in Engl.); 2:37, 42, 43; 4:33, 35–37; 5:2, 12, 18, 29, 34, 40; 6:6; 8:1, 14, 18; 9:27; 11:1; 15:2, 4, 6, 22, 23, 33; 16:4; Rom. 1:1; 11:13; 16:7; 1 Cor. 4:9; 9:2, 5; 12:28, 29; 15:9a, b; 2 Cor. 1:1; 8:23; 11:5, 13b; 12:11, 12; Gal. 1:1, 17, 19; Eph. 1:1; 2:20; 3:5; 4:11; Phil. 2:25; Col. 1:1; 1 Thes. 2:6; 1 Tim. 1:1; 2:7; 2 Tim. 1:1, 11; Titus 1:1; 1 Pet. 1:1; 2 Pet. 1:1; 3:2; Jude 17; Rev. 2:2; 18:20; 21:14. ¶

APOSTLESHIP – ***apostolē*** [fem. noun: ἀποστολή <651>]; **from *apostellō*: to send away, which is from *apo*: away, and *stellō*: to send; lit.: mission ▶ Activity of an apostle, one sent to accomplish a mission** > The word "apostleship" is used concerning three apostles: Matthias (Acts 1:25), Paul (Rom. 1:5; 1 Cor. 9:2), and Peter (Gal. 2:8 {ministry}). ¶

APOSTOLIC – Gal. 2:8 → apostolic ministry → APOSTLESHIP <651>.

APPAREL – [1] ***esthēs*** [fem. noun: ἐσθής <2066>]; **from *ennumi*: to clothe, to dress ▶ Clothing, garment** > Herod, clothed in royal apparel {robes}, made a public oration to the people (Acts 12:21). All other refs.: CLOTHES <2066>.

[2] **modest apparel; apparel: *katastolē*** [fem. noun: καταστολή <2689>]; **from *katastellō*: to put down, to appease, which is from *kata*: down, and *stellō*: to repress; modest: *kosmios*** [adj.: κόσμιος <2887>]; **from *kosmos*: orderly arrangement ▶ Clothes which are modest and of good taste** > Paul exhorts women to adorn themselves in modest apparel {decent deportment and dress, proper clothing} {to dress properly} (1 Tim. 2:9); some mss. have the adv. *kosmiōs*: respectably. Other ref. (*kosmios*): 1 Tim. 3:2; see RESPECTABLE <2887>. ¶

– [3] Luke 24:4 → CLOTHES <2067> [4] Acts 20:33 → CLOTHING <2441> [5] 1 Pet. 3:3 → CLOTHES <2440>.

APPARENT – Acts 4:16 → MANIFEST (adj.) <5318>.

APPARITION – Matt. 14:26; Mark 6:49 → GHOST <5326>.

APPEAL – [1] ***epikaleō*** [verb: ἐπικαλέω <1941>]; **from *epi*: upon, and *kaleō*: to call ▶ Verb designating the right of a Roman citizen to stand before the emperor and to be judged by him; also transl.: to make an appeal** > The apostle Paul appealed to Caesar (Acts 25:11, 12, 21, 25; 26:32; 28:19). All other refs.: CALL (verb) <1941>, INVOKE <1941>, PRAY <1941>, SURNAME (verb) <1941>.

– [2] Matt. 8:5 → to appeal to → to plead with → PLEAD <3870> [3] Matt. 26:53; Acts 16:9, 39; Phm. 9, 10 → BESEECH <3870> [4] Luke 4:38 → ASK <2065> [5] Luke 23:20 → ADDRESS (verb) <4377> [6] Acts 25:24 → PETITION (verb) <1793> [7] Rom. 11:2 → PLEAD <1793> [8] Rom. 12:1; 15:30; 16:17; 1 Cor. 1:10; 2 Cor. 5:20; 6:1; 10:1; 1 Tim. 5:1; Heb. 13:22; 1 Pet. 5:1; Jude 3 → EXHORT <3870> [9] 2 Cor. 5:20 → to make an appeal → SUPPLICATE <1189> [10] 2 Cor. 8:17; 1 Thes. 2:3 → EXHORTATION <3874> [11] 2 Cor. 13:11 → listen to my appeal → lit.: be encouraged → ENCOURAGE <3870> [12] 1 Pet. 3:21 → ANSWER (noun) <1906>.

APPEAR – [1] ***phainō*** [verb: φαίνω <5316>] **▶ a. To become evident, to be manifest; from *phōs*: light** > Hypocrites disfigure their faces so that they may appear to men to be fasting (Matt. 6:16); when fasting, one should anoint his head and wash his face, in order not to appear to be fasting (v. 18). The scribes and the Pharisees were like whitewashed tombs which appear beautiful outwardly (Matt. 23:27); they appeared righteous to men (v. 28). The sign of the Son of Man will appear in heaven (Matt. 24:30). In Rom. 7:13, sin, that it might appear sin, worked death. Paul did not want to appear approved (2 Cor. 13:7). That which is seen has not taken its origin from things which appear (Heb. 11:3). Our life is but a vapor appearing for a little while and then disappearing (Jas. 4:14). Peter asks where the impious and the sinner will appear if it is hard for the righteous to be saved (1 Pet. 4:18). In Rev. 8:12, the verb has the sense of "to shine." **b. To show oneself** > An angel of the Lord appeared three times to Joseph in a dream (Matt. 1:20; 2:13, 19). Herod enquired from the wise men the time of the star that was appearing (Matt. 2:7). Some were saying that Elijah had appeared (Luke 9:8). After His resurrection, Jesus appeared first to Mary of Magdala (Mark 16:9). The coming of the Son of Man will be like the lightning coming out of the east and appearing {shining, flashing, being visible} to the west (Matt. 24:27). Other refs.: Matt. 6:5; 9:33; 13:26; Mark 14:64; Luke 24:11 {to seem}; John 1:5; 5:35; Phil. 2:15; 2 Pet. 1:19; 1 John 2:8; Rev. 1:16; 18:23; 21:23. ¶

[2] ***emphanizō*** [verb: ἐμφανίζω <1718>]; **from *emphanēs*: manifest, which is from *en*: intens., and *phainō*: see [1] ▶ To be manifested, to show oneself, to become visible** > When Jesus died, many bodies of the saints were raised and they appeared to many (Matt. 27:53). Christ now appears before the face of God for Christians (Heb. 9:24). All other refs.: CHARGE (noun)[1] <1718>, MANIFEST (verb) <1718>, PLAINLY <1718>, REVEAL <1718>, SIGNIFY <1718>.

[3] ***epiphainō*** [verb: ἐπιφαίνω <2014>]; **from *epi*: over, on, and *phainō*: see [1] ▶ To shine, to show oneself, to manifest oneself** > Neither sun nor stars appeared for many days when Paul's ship was beaten by the storm (Acts 27:20). The grace of God, which brings with it salvation, has appeared to all men (Titus 2:11). The kindness and love of the Savior God toward man has also appeared (Titus 3:4). Other ref.: Luke 1:79 (to give light); see LIGHT (noun) <2014>. ¶

[4] ***phaneroō*** [verb: φανερόω <5319>]; **from *phaneros*: manifest, visible, which is from *phainō*: see [1] ▶ To manifest oneself** > After His resurrection, Jesus appeared to two disciples (Mark 16:12) and to the eleven disciples (v. 14). All other refs.: MANIFEST (verb) <5319>, SHOW (verb) <5319>.

[5] ***optomai*** [verb: ὀπτομαι <3700>]; **a form of *horaō*: to see ▶ To allow oneself to be seen** > Moses appeared to {shewed himself to, came upon} two Israelites as they were fighting (Acts 7:26). *

[6] ***horaō*** [verb: ὁράω <3708>] **and a form of *horaō*: *optanomai*** [verb: ὀπτάνομαι <3700>] **▶ To see, to have been seen** > Moses and Elijah appeared at the transfiguration of Jesus (Matt. 17:3; Mark 9:4; Luke 9:31). An angel of the Lord appeared to Zacharias (Luke 1:11). An angel appeared to Jesus in Gethsemane (Luke 22:43). The risen Lord had appeared to Simon (Luke 24:34). At Pentecost, divided tongues, like fire, appeared to the disciples who were all in one place (Acts 2:3). The God of glory had appeared to Abraham (Acts 7:2). An angel of the Lord appeared to Moses (Acts 7:30, 35). The Lord Jesus had appeared to Saul on the road (Acts 9:17; 26:16a) and would appear to him later (26:16b {to show, to reveal}). Christ will appear a second time, apart from sin, for salvation (Heb. 9:28). The ark of the covenant of God appeared in His temple (Rev. 11:19). A great sign appeared in the heaven (Rev. 12:1), followed by another one (v. 3). Other refs.: BEWARE <3708>, LOOK (verb) <3708>, SEE <3708>.

[7] ***phantazō*** [verb: φαντάζω <5324>] **▶ To be exposed, to be visible; from *phainō*: see [1].** > The verb is used in Heb. 12:21: the sight (lit.: the thing appearing) was fearful. ¶

[8] **which appear not: *adēlos*** [adj.: ἄδηλος <82>]; **from *a*: neg., and *dēlos*: evident ▶ Indistinct, not recognizable** > The Pharisees were like graves which appear not {unmarked graves, concealed tombs} (Luke 11:44). Other ref.: 1 Cor. 14:8; see UNCERTAIN <82>. ¶

– [9] Matt. 24:11, 24; Mark 13:22 → to rise up → RISE (verb) <1453> [10] Luke

1:80 → until he appeared publicly → lit.: until the day of his manifestation → MANIFESTATION <323> [11] Luke 2:9; Acts 10:17; 11:11 → STAND (verb) <2186> [12] John 7:27, 31 → COME <2064> [13] Acts 5:27 → to make appear → SET (verb) <2476> [14] Acts 5:37 → to rise up → RISE (verb) <450> [15] Acts 10:40 → made Him to appear → lit.: has given Him to become manifest → MANIFEST (adj.) <1717> [16] Acts 22:30 → to come together → COME <4905> [17] 2 Cor. 10:9 → SEEM <1380> [18] 1 Tim. 4:15 → may appear → lit.: may be evident → EVIDENT <5318> [19] 1 Tim. 5:24 → to appear later → to follow after → FOLLOW <1872> [20] Rev. 15:2 → what appeared to be a sea → lit.: as (*hōs* <5613>) a sea.

APPEARANCE – [1] ***logos*** [masc. noun: λόγος <3056>]; **from *legō*: to say, to talk intelligently ▶ Word (in the sense of spoken report), reputation** > The commandments and teachings of men have an appearance of {a shew of} (lit.: are having a reputation of) wisdom (Col. 2:23). Other refs.: WORD <3056>.
[2] ***opsis*** [fem. noun: ὄψις <3799>]; **from *optomai*: to see ▶ What is seen, sight** > Jesus says not to judge according to the appearance, but with righteous judgment (John 7:24). Other refs.: John 11:44; Rev. 1:16; see FACE (noun) <3799>. ¶
[3] ***prosōpon*** [neut. noun: πρόσωπον <4383>]; **from *pros*: toward, and *ōps*: eye, face ▶ a. Facade, face** > Paul speaks of those who boast in appearance {in what is seen} and not about in what is in the heart (2 Cor. 5:12). **b. Outward appearance of an inanimate thing** > The beauty of the appearance {fashion, look} of the flower is destroyed (Jas. 1:11). All other refs.: FACE (noun) <4383>, PERSON <4383>, PRESENCE <4383>.
[4] ***schēma*** [neut. noun: σχῆμα <4976>]; **from a form of *echō*: to have ▶ Appearance, outward manner of being; also transl.: fashion, figure, form** > The form of this world is passing away (1 Cor. 7:31). This word refers also to what man could perceive of the Lord Jesus on earth: who was found in appearance as a man (Phil. 2:8), but without sin in Him (see 1 John 3:5). ¶
– [5] Matt. 28:3 → COUNTENANCE <2397> [6] Mark 12:40; Luke 20:47 → PRETEXT <4392> [7] Luke 1:80 → public appearance → MANIFESTATION <323> [8] Luke 9:29 → FASHION <1491> [9] Gal. 6:12 → to have a fair appearance → to make a good showing → SHOWING <2146> [10] 1 Thes. 5:22 → FORM (noun) <1491> [11] 2 Thes. 2:8 → APPEARING <2015> [12] 2 Tim. 3:5 → FORM (noun) <3446> [13] Rev. 4:3 → VISION <3706> [14] Rev. 9:7 → LIKENESS <3667>.

APPEARING – [1] ***epiphaneia*** [fem. noun: ἐπιφάνεια <2015>]; **from *epiphainō*: to appear, which is from *epi*: upon, and *phainō*: to shine, which is from *phōs*: light ▶ Manifestation of Jesus Christ to the world when He will come to establish His reign of glory** > The term "appearing" is found in 1 Tim. 6:14 and 2 Tim. 4:1, 8. The Lord Jesus will put an end to the activity of the antichrist by the appearing {appearance, brightness, splendor} of His coming (2 Thes. 2:8). In 2 Tim. 1:10, the "appearing" of Jesus Christ on earth refers to His first coming as Savior. Other ref.: Titus 2:13. ¶
– [2] Acts 2:20 → gloriously appearing → AWESOME <2016> [3] 1 Pet. 1:7 → REVELATION <602>.

APPEASE – [1] ***katastellō*** [verb: καταστέλλω <2687>]; **from *kata*: down, and *stellō*: to repress; lit.: to put in order ▶ To calm down; pass.: to be quiet** > The town clerk of Ephesus appeased {quieted} the crowd (Acts 19:35); the crowd had to be quiet {to keep calm} (v. 36). ¶
– [2] Matt. 28:14 → PERSUADE <3982> [3] Acts 16:39 → BESEECH <3870>.

APPETITE – Rom. 16:18; Phil. 3:19 → appetites, appetite → lit.: belly → WOMB <2836>.

APPHIA – ***Apphia*** [fem. name: Ἀπφία <682>] ▶ **Christian woman from Colossae** > Apphia was prob. the wife of Philemon (Phm. 2). ¶

APPII FORUM – See MARKET OF APPIUS <675> <5410>.

APPLICATION – Heb. 11:28 → application of blood → sprinkling of blood → SPRINKLING <4378>.

APPLY – **1 to apply, to figuratively apply:** ***metaschēmatizō*** [verb: μετασχηματίζω <3345>]; **from *meta*: indicates a change, and *schēmatizō*: to form, which is from *schēma*: appearance, outward form ▶ To present in another form; also transl.: to transfer, to transfer in its application** > Paul had figuratively applied certain things to himself and Apollos (1 Cor. 4:6). Other refs.: 2 Cor. 11:13–15; Phil. 3:21; see TRANSFORM <3345>. ¶
– 2 Matt. 3:10; Luke 3:9 → LAY <2749> 3 John 9:6 → ANOINT <2025> 4 John 9:15 → LAY <2007> 5 Acts 25:24 → PETITION (verb) <1793> 6 Titus 3:14 → to apply oneself → MAINTAIN <4291> 7 Heb. 9:10 → IMPOSE <1945> 8 2 Pet. 1:5 → GIVE <3923>.

APPOINT – 1 ***anadeiknumi*** [verb: ἀναδείκνυμι <322>]; **from *ana*: intens., and *deiknumi*: to show ▶ To choose, to designate** > The Lord appointed seventy messengers to preach the kingdom of God (Luke 10:1). Other ref.: Acts 1:24; see SHOW (verb) <322>. ¶
2 ***histēmi*** [verb: ἵστημι <2476>] ▶ **To determine, to establish** > Two disciples were appointed {proposed, put forward} so that the Lord would show which one was to replace Judas (Acts 1:23). God has appointed {has set, has fixed} a day on which He will judge the world in righteousness (Acts 17:31). Other refs.: SET (verb) <2476>, STAND (verb) <2476>.
3 ***kathistēmi*** [verb: καθίστημι <2525>]; **from *kata*: down (intens.), and *histēmi*: see 2 ▶ To designate, to establish; also transl.: to ordain, to make, to constitute** > Titus was to appoint elders in every city (Titus 1:5). God has appointed {has set} Jesus over the works of His hands (Heb. 2:7 in some mss.). Other refs.: Acts 6:3 {to put in charge, to turn the responsibility to}; 7:27; Heb. 5:1; 7:28; 8:3. All other refs.: CONDUCT (verb)[2] <2525>, MAKE <2525>, RENDER <2525>.
4 ***keimai*** [verb: κεῖμαι <2749>] ▶ **To be there, to be designated** > Paul had been appointed {put, set} for the defense of the gospel (Phil. 1:17 or v. 16 in some mss.). Paul and the Thessalonians were appointed {destined, set} for afflictions (1 Thes. 3:3). Other refs.: LAID OUT (BE) <2749>, LAY <2749>, LIE (verb)[1] <2749>, SITUATE <2749>, STAND (verb) <2749>.
5 ***apokeimai*** [verb: ἀπόκειμαι <606>]; **from *apo*: from, away, and *keimai*: see 4; lit.: to set away ▶ To reserve** > It is appointed {is destined, is the portion} for men to die once, and after this comes judgment (Heb. 9:27). All other refs.: LAY <606>, PUT <606>.
6 ***poieō*** [verb: ποιέω <4160>] ▶ **To designate, to name** > Jesus appointed {ordained} twelve that they might be with Him (Mark 3:14). Jesus was faithful to God who appointed {constituted} Him (Heb. 3:2). Other refs.: see entries in Lexicon at <4160>.
7 ***tassō*** [verb: τάσσω <5021>]; **lit.: to put in a fixed or determined place ▶ a. To determine, to decide** > A day was appointed {was arranged, was set} for Paul to expound the truth to many Jews in Rome (Acts 28:23). **b. To designate, to establish** > The eleven disciples went to the mountain which Jesus had appointed {designated, told them to go to} (Matt. 28:16). Paul was to be told of all the things which it was appointed {assigned} him to do (Acts 22:10). The authorities are appointed {set up, ordained} by God (Rom. 13:1). **c. To be designated** > Those who had been appointed {ordained} to eternal life believed (Acts 13:48). Other refs.: Luke 7:8 {to place}; Acts 15:2 {to appoint, to determine}; 1 Cor. 16:15 {to devote}. ¶
8 ***tithēmi*** [verb: τίθημι <5087>]; **from *theō*: to place ▶ To set, to designate, to assign; also transl.: to destine, to establish, to make, to name, to ordain, to place, to put, to set** > The portion of the evil servant will be appointed with the hypocrites (Matt. 24:51; Luke 12:46). Jesus had chosen and appointed His disciples

that they should go and bear fruit (John 15:16). Paul and Barnabas spoke of Him who had been appointed as a light to the Gentiles (Acts 13:47). The Holy Spirit had appointed the elders as overseers in Ephesus (Acts 20:28). God has appointed Abraham a father of many nations (Rom. 4:17). Jesus had appointed Paul to the ministry (1 Tim. 1:12). God has not appointed the Christians for wrath, but for obtaining salvation through the Lord Jesus Christ (1 Thes. 5:9). Paul had been appointed a preacher and an apostle (1 Tim. 2:7; 2 Tim. 1:11). God has appointed His Son heir of all things (Heb. 1:2). Those who are disobedient to the word are appointed to stumble (1 Pet. 2:8). God had appointed Sodom and Gomorrah an example to those who afterward would live ungodly lives (2 Pet. 2:6). All other refs.: see entries in Lexicon at <5087>.

9 ***diatithemai*** [verb: διατίθεμαι <1303>]; **from *dia*: intens., and *tithēmi*: see 8 ▶ To confer, to give in virtue of an authority** > Jesus was appointing a kingdom to His disciples as His Father had appointed {granted, bestowed} one to Him (Luke 22:29a, b). All other refs.: MAKE <1303>, TESTATOR <1303>.

– 10 Matt. 26:15 → to count out to → COUNT <2476> 11 Matt. 26:19; 27:10 → DIRECT <4929> 12 Luke 3:13; Acts 7:44; 20:13; Gal. 3:19; Titus 1:5 → ORDAIN <1299> 13 Acts 3:20 → FOREORDAIN <4400> 14 Acts 10:42; 17:31 → to appoint, to determinately appoint → ORDAIN <3724> 15 Acts 14:23; 2 Cor. 8:19 → ORDAIN <5500> 16 Acts 22:14 → CHOOSE <4400> 17 Acts 26:16 → MAKE <4400> 18 Rom. 1:4; Heb. 4:7 → DETERMINE <3724> 19 Rom. 13:2 → what God has appointed → lit.: the ordinance of God → ORDINANCE <1296> 20 1 Cor. 6:4 → to appoint to judge, as judge → JUDGE (verb) <2523> 21 2 Cor. 10:13 → DISTRIBUTE <3307> 22 Heb. 5:5 → "was appointed by" added in Engl. 23 Rev. 11:3 → lit.: to give authority → lit.: to give → GIVE <1325>.

APPOINTED – 1 Luke 1:20 → appointed time → lit.: at the time of them 2 Luke 2:34 → LAY <2749> 3 Acts 12:21 → SET (adj.) <5002> 4 Acts 17:26 → appointed, before appointed → ORDAIN <4367> 5 1 Cor. 4:9 → appointed to death → condemned to death → DEATH <1935> 6 1 Cor. 7:29 → "appointed" added in Engl. 7 Gal. 4:2 → time appointed → TIME <4287>.

APPORTION – 1 1 Cor. 12:11 → DISTRIBUTE <1244> 2 2 Cor. 10:13 → DISTRIBUTE <3307> 3 Eph. 4:7 → as Christ apportioned it → lit.: according to the measure of the gift of Christ → MEASURE (noun) <3358> 4 Heb. 7:2 → GIVE <3307>.

APPRAISE – 1 Cor. 2:14, 15a, b → DISCERN <350>.

APPREHEND – 1 Matt. 15:17; Rom. 1:20; Heb. 11:3 → UNDERSTAND <3539> 2 John 1:5; Eph. 3:18 → COMPREHEND <2638> 3 Acts 12:4 → TAKE <4084> 4 2 Cor. 11:32 → SEIZE <4084> 5 Phil. 3:12a, b, 13 → to lay hold, to take hold → HOLD (noun) <2638>.

APPREHENSIVE – Luke 21:26 → EXPECTATION <4329>.

APPROACH – 1 Matt. 21:1, 34; Mark 11:1; Luke 7:12; 15:25; 19:29, 37; 22:1, 47; 24:15, 28; Acts 7:17; 10:9 → to draw near → DRAW <1448> 2 Luke 8:19 → to come at → COME <4940> 3 Luke 9:51 → to fully come → COME <4845> 4 Luke 12:33; 19:29; Acts 9:3; 22:6 → to come near → COME <1448> 5 Luke 18:35 → to come into the neighborhood → NEIGHBORHOOD <1448> 6 Luke 19:41 → to draw near → NEAR (adv.) <1448> 7 John 6:19 → to draw near → DRAW <1096> <1451> 8 Acts 7:23 → FULFILL <4137> 9 Acts 7:31; Heb. 10:22 → to draw near → DRAW <4334> 10 Acts 27:27 → to draw near → DRAW <4317> 11 Eph. 3:12 → lit.: to have access → ACCESS <4318> 12 1 Tim. 6:16 → which no man can approach → UNAPPROACHABLE <676> 13 Heb. 4:16 → COME <4334> 14 Heb. 10:25 → to be at hand → HAND <1448>.

APPROPRIATE – 1 Acts 26:20 → MEET (adj.) <514> 2 1 Tim. 2:10 → to be appropriate → to be proper → PROPER <4241> 3 Titus 2:1 → to be appropriate → FITTING (BE) <4241>.

APPROVAL – 1 Acts 6:5 → to find approval → PLEASE <700> 2 Acts 8:1; 22:20 → to give approval → CONSENT (verb) <4909> 3 Acts 12:3 → met with approval → was pleasing → PLEASING <701> 4 Rom. 1:32 → to give hearty approval → APPROVE <4909> 5 Rom. 13:3 → to receive approval → lit.: to have praise → HAVE <2192>, PRAISE (noun) <1868> 6 Rom. 14:18; 1 Cor. 11:19 → to receive human approval, one who has God's approval → lit.: to be approved by men, the approved → APPROVE <1384> 7 2 Cor. 9:13 → approval of the service → experience of the ministry → EXPERIENCE (noun) <1382> 8 Gal. 1:10 → to try to win the approval → PERSUADE <3982>.

APPROVE – 1 ***apodeiknumi*** [verb: ἀπο-δείκνυμι <584>]; **from *apo*: intens., and *deiknumi*: to show ▶ To designate, to recognize, to accredit** > Peter speaks of Jesus as a man approved of {attested of, borne witness to by} God (Acts 2:22). All other refs.: PROVE <584>, SET (verb) <584>, SHOW (verb) <584>.

2 ***dokimazō*** [verb: δοκιμάζω <1381>]; **from *dokimos*: see 3 ▶ To accept, to decide; also transl.: to allow** > Blessed is he who does not judge himself in what he approves (Rom. 14:22). Paul would send to Jerusalem whomsoever the Corinthians would approve (1 Cor. 16:3). He was approved by God to have the gospel entrusted to him (1 Thes. 2:4). All other refs.: DISCERN <1381>, LIKE (verb) <1381>, TEST (noun and verb) <1381>.

3 **approved: *dokimos*** [adj.: δόκιμος <1384>]; **comp. *dechomai*: to accept, to receive ▶ Accepted, proven; also transl.: having stood the test** > Paul speaks of one approved by men (Rom. 14:18). He asked the Christians in Rome to greet Apelles who was approved in Christ (Rom. 16:10). Those approved among the Corinthians would be made manifest (1 Cor. 11:19). He whom the Lord commends is approved (2 Cor. 10:18). Paul did not want to appear approved (2 Cor. 13:7). Timothy had to strive diligently to present himself approved to God (2 Tim. 2:15). When the man who endures temptation (or: trial) is approved {tried, proved}, he will receive the crown of life (Jas. 1:12). ¶

4 ***suneudokeō*** [verb: συνευδοκέω <4909>]; **from *sun*: with, together, and *eudokeō*: to please, which is from *eu*: well, and *dokeō*: to think, to appear ▶ To consent, to agree** > The Jews approved {allowed} the works of their fathers (Luke 11:48). Some approve {have fellow delight in, have pleasure in, give hearty approval to} those who do wicked things (Rom. 1:32). All other refs.: CONSENT (verb) <4909>, WILL (verb) <4909>.

– 5 2 Cor. 6:4 → COMMEND <4921> 6 2 Cor. 7:11 → PROVE <4921>.

APPROVED – Rom. 14:18; 16:10; 1 Cor. 11:19; 2 Cor. 10:18; 13:7; 2 Tim. 2:15; Jas. 1:12 → APPROVE <1384>.

APRON – ***simikinthion*** [neut. noun: σιμι-κίνθιον <4612>]; **Lat.: *semicinctium* (half girding or narrow covering) ▶ Narrow garment of cloth worn over the front part of the body by workers and servants** > Handkerchiefs and aprons were brought from the body of Paul and put upon the sick; the diseases left them and the wicked spirits went out (Acts 19:12). ¶

APT – 1 Tim. 3:2; 2 Tim. 2:24 → apt to teach → able to teach → TEACH <1317>.

AQUILA – ***Akulas*** [masc. name: Ἀκύλας <207>]; **from Lat. *aquila*: eagle ▶ Christian of Jewish origin** > Aquila came from Italy with his wife Priscilla (Acts 18:2). Paul stayed and worked with them, because they were of the same trade, for they were tent-makers (see v. 3). Aquila and his wife Priscilla accompanied Paul (Acts 18:18) to Ephesus (see v. 19). This couple unfolded to Apollos the Christian doctrine more exactly (Acts 18:26). Paul greets them as his fellow workers in his Epistle to the Romans (16:3; see v. 4) and in his Second Epistle to Timothy (2 Tim. 4:19. He conveys to the Corinthians the couple's greetings and those of the church gathered in their house (1 Cor. 16:19). ¶

ARAB – ***Araps*** [masc. name: Ἄραψ <690>] ▶ **Person from Arabia** > On the Day of Pentecost, Arabs heard the gospel in their own tongue (Acts 2:11). ¶

ARABIA – ***Arabia*** [fem. name: Ἀραβία <688>]: **sterility, dry country, in Heb.** ▶ **Region located east and south of Israel** > Paul went to Arabia, and from there to Damascus (Gal. 1:17). Mount Sinai is located in Arabia (Gal. 4:25). ¶

ARABIAN – See ARAB <690>.

ARAM – ***Aram*** [masc. name: Ἀράμ <689>]: **elevated, in Heb.** ▶ **Man in the O.T.; also written: *Admin* and *Ram* in Luke** > Aram is mentioned in the genealogy of Jesus Christ (Matt. 1:3, 4; Luke 3:33). ¶

ARBITER – Luke 12:14 → DIVIDER <3312>.

ARBITRATOR – Luke 12:14 → DIVIDER <3312>.

ARCHANGEL – ***archangelos*** [masc. noun: ἀρχάγγελος <743>]; **from *archō*: to lead, to command, which is from *archē*: beginning, and *angelos*: messenger, angel** ▶ **Angel of a superior rank** > The archangel's voice will be heard when the Christians will be caught up to meet the Lord in the air (1 Thes. 4:16). The only archangel specifically mentioned is Michael (Jude 9). ¶

ARCHELAUS – ***Archelaos*** [masc. name.: Ἀρχέλαος <745>]: **leader of the people; from *archō*: to rule, which is from *archē*: beginning, and *laos*: people** ▶ **King of the Jews, son of Herod the Great** > Archelaus reigned in Judea in his father's place (Matt. 2:22). He was the son of a Samaritan woman. ¶

ARCHIPPUS – ***Archippos*** [masc. name: Ἄρχιππος <751>]: **master of the horse; from *archō*: to rule, which is from *archē*: beginning, and *hippos*: horse** ▶ **Christian from Colossae** > The apostle Paul told Archippus to take heed to the ministry he had received in the Lord, that he might fulfill it (Col. 4:17). Paul referred to him in his Epistle to Philemon as his fellow soldier (v. 2). ¶

ARCHITECT – 1 Cor. 3:10 → MASTER BUILDER <753>.

ARDENT – [1] 2 Cor. 7:7, 11 → ardent desire → DESIRE (noun) <1972> [2] 2 Cor. 7:7 → ardent concern → fervent mind → MIND (noun) <2205>.

ARDENTLY – 2 Tim. 1:4 → to ardently desire → DESIRE (verb) <1971>.

ARE (THEY) – ***eisi*** [verb: εἰσί <1526>] ▶ Third person plur. of *eimi*, the pres. indic. of the verb "to be." * ‡

ARE (WE) – ***esmen*** [verb: ἐσμέν <2070> ▶ First person plur. of the pres. indic. of the verb "to be."* ‡

ARE (YOU) – [1] ***ei*** [verb: εἶ <1488>] ▶ Second person sing. of the pres. indic. of the verb "to be." * ‡

[2] ***este*** [verb: ἐστέ <2075> ▶ Second person plur. of the verb "to be." * ‡

AREA – [1] Matt. 4:13 → REGION <3725> [2] Mark 5:10 → COUNTRY <5561> [3] Luke 4:37 → surrounding area → COUNTRY <4066> [4] Acts 20:2 → PART (noun) <3313> [5] 2 Cor. 10:13 → area of influence → measure of rule → MEASURE (noun) <3358> [6] 2 Cor. 10:15, 16 → "area" added in Engl.

AREOPAGITE – ***Areopagitēs*** [masc. name: Ἀρεοπαγίτης <698>]: **from Ares, the god of war among the Greeks** ▶ **Judge serving as a member of the court of the Areopagus, which convened on the Hill of Ares (called**

Mars by the Romans) > Dionysius was one of these judges (Acts 17:34). ¶

AREOPAGUS – ***Areios Pagos*** [masc. name: Ἄρειος Πάγος <697>]: **rocky height of Ares; from *Arēs*: the Greek god of war, and *pagos*: what is fixed ▶ Hill situated to the west of the Acropolis, the citadel of Athens** > Paul was brought to the Areopagus by philosophers who wanted to hear the new doctrine he preached concerning Jesus and the resurrection (Acts 17:19, 22). This hill was dedicated to Ares, the god of war (known under the name of Mars by the Romans); the supreme court of Athens (the Council of the Areopagus) rendered its decisions at this location. ¶

ARETAS – ***Aretas*** [masc. name: Ἀρέτας <702>]: **a name common to many of the kings of Arabia ▶ King of Arabian descent** > The ethnarch of Aretas the king wanted to apprehend Paul (2 Cor. 11:32). ¶

ARGUE – [1] Mark 8:11; 9:14, 16; 12:28; Acts 6:9; 9:29 → to argue with → DISPUTE (verb) <4802> [2] Mark 9:33 → REASON (verb) <1260> [3] Mark 9:34; Acts 24:12 → DISPUTE (verb) <1256> [4] John 6:52 → to argue, to argue sharply → QUARREL (verb) <3164> [5] Acts 23:9 → to argue heatedly, vigorously → STRIVE <1264> [6] Acts 25:8 → to argue in one's defense → to answer for oneself → ANSWER (verb) <626>.

ARGUING – Phil. 2:14 → REASONING <1261>.

ARGUMENT – [1] **argument over words:** ***logomachia*** [fem. noun: λογομαχία <3055>]; **from *logomacheō*: to strive about words, which is from *logos*: word, and *machē*: fight ▶ Quarrelsome exchange of words** > Some may be obsessed with arguments over words {strifes, disputes, quarrels of words} (1 Tim. 6:4). ¶
– [2] Luke 9:46 → REASONING <1261> [3] John 3:25 → DISPUTE (noun) <2214> [4] 2 Cor. 10:5 → REASONING <3053> [5] Col. 2:4 → persuasive argument, fine-sounding argument → persuasive word → WORD <4086> [6] 1 Tim. 6:20 → OPPOSITION <477> [7] Heb. 6:16 → DISPUTE (noun) <485>.

ARGUMENTATIVE – Titus 2:9 → to be argumentative → to answer back → ANSWER (verb) <483>.

ARID – Matt. 12:43; Luke 11:24 → DRY (noun) <504>.

ARIMATHAEA – See ARIMATHEA <707>.

ARIMATHEA – ***Arimathaia*** [fem. name: Ἀριμαθαία <707>]: **heights, in Heb. ▶ Native town of Joseph, the one who took upon himself the burial of Jesus; also spelled: Arimathaea** > Arimathea is mentioned in Matt. 27:57; Mark 15:43; Luke 23:51; John 19:38. We do not know precisely where Arimathea was situated, but it was a city of the Jews (see Luke 23:51). In Mark 15:43 and Luke 23:51, this name is written Ἁριμαθαία (*Harimathaia*) in some mss. ¶

ARISE – [1] ***anistēmi*** [verb: ἀνίστημι <450>]; **from *ana*: above, again, and *histēmi*: to stand ▶ To get up, to stand up; to leave; also transl.: to arise up, to rise, to rise up, to lift up, to stand up** > The verb is used concerning Jesus (Mark 1:35; 7:24; 10:1; Luke 4:16, 38; 22:45). It is also used concerning Matthew (Matt. 9:9; Mark 2:14; Luke 5:28), men of Nineveh (Matt. 12:41; Luke 11:32), the high priest (Matt. 26:62; Mark 14:60; Acts 5:17), a young girl who was dead (Mark 5:42; Luke 8:55), a child who was possessed (Mark 9:27), Bartimaeus (Mark 10:50), Mary (Luke 1:39), the Jews (Luke 4:29; 23:1), Peter's mother-in-law (Luke 4:39), a paralytic (Luke 5:25), a man who had a withered hand (Luke 6:8), a certain lawyer (Luke 10:25), a man in bed (Luke 11:7, 8a), the prodigal son (Luke 15:18, 20), a leper (Luke 17:19), the disciples (Luke 22:46), Peter (Luke 24:12; Acts 1:15; 9:39, 41; 10:13, 20; 11:7; 12:7; 15:7), two disciples (Luke 24:33), Mary of Bethany (John 11:31), young men (Acts

5:6), Gamaliel (Acts 5:34), Theudas (Acts 5:36), men of a synagogue (Acts 6:9), a king from Egypt (Acts 7:18), Philip (Acts 8:26, 27), Saul (Acts 9:6, 11, 18), Aeneas (Acts 9:34a, b), Dorcas (Acts 9:40), Cornelius (Acts 10:26), Agabus (Acts 11:28), Paul (Acts 13:16; 14:20; 22:10, 16; 26:16), a man without strength in his feet (Acts 14:10), men speaking perverse things (Acts 20:30), scribes (Acts 23:9), Agrippa (Acts 26:30), Israel (1 Cor. 10:7), and another high priest (Heb. 7:11, 15). Paul, quoting Isaiah, says to one who is spiritually asleep to wake up and to arise up {to rise} from among the dead (Eph. 5:14). Other refs.: RAISE <450>, RISE (verb) <450>.

[2] ***ballō*** [verb: βάλλω <906>]; **lit.: to cast, to throw ▶ To come down violently, to rage furiously** > A hurricane arose {came down, rushed down, swept down} on the island of Crete (Acts 27:14). All other refs.: CAST (verb) <906>, IMPOSE <906>, LIE (verb)[1] <906>, POUR <906>, PUT <906>, THROW (verb) <906>.

[3] ***ginomai*** [verb: γίνομαι <1096>] **▶ To take place, to occur, to come, to come up** > A great windstorm arose (Matt. 8:24; Mark 4:37). Jesus speaks of one who is offended when tribulation or persecution arises because of the word of God (Matt. 13:21; Mark 4:17). A murmuring of the Hellenists arose against the Hebrews (Acts 6:1). The verb is transl. "to have," "to take place" in Acts 15:2. The law, which came four hundred and thirty years after the promise to Abraham, does not invalidate a covenant confirmed beforehand by God (Gal. 3:17). The verb is also used in regard to a flood (Luke 6:48) and a famine (Luke 15:14). Other refs.: Acts 11:19; 19:23; 23:7, 9, 10.

[4] ***egeirō*** [verb: ἐγείρω <1453>] **▶ To wake up, to stand up; also transl.: to arise, to lift up, to rise, to rise up, to stand forth, to step forward, to raise** > This verb is used concerning Jesus (Matt. 8:26; 9:19; Luke 8:24; John 13:4). It is also used concerning Joseph, the father of Jesus (Matt. 2:13, 14, 20, 21), the mother-in-law of Peter (Matt. 8:15; Mark 1:31), a paralytic (Matt. 9:5–7; Mark 2:9, 11, 12; Luke 5:23, 24), a little girl who was dead (Matt. 9:25; Mark 5:41; Luke 8:54), the queen of the South (Matt. 12:42; Luke 11:31), three disciples (Matt. 17:7), the ten virgins (Matt. 25:7), the disciples (Matt. 26:46; Mark 14:42; John 14:31), a man who had a withered hand (Mark 3:3; Luke 6:8), a man who scattered seed on the ground (Mark 4:27), a blind man (Mark 10:49), a young man who was dead (Luke 7:14), a man who was in bed (Luke 11:8b), a master of a house (Luke 13:25), a man with an infirmity (John 5:8), Mary of Bethany (John 11:29), a lame man (Acts 3:6, 7), Saul (Acts 9:8), and John (Rev. 11:1). All other refs.: ARISE <1453>, LIFT <1453>, RAISE <1453>, RISE (verb) <1453>, WAKE <1453>.

[5] ***diegeirō*** [verb: διεγείρω <1326>]; **from *dia*: intens., and *egeirō*: see [4] ▶ To become agitated** > The sea arose {began to be stirred up, grew rough} by a strong wind blowing (John 6:18). All other refs.: WAKE <1326>.

[6] ***eiserchomai*** [verb: εἰσέρχομαι <1525>]; **from *eis*: in, and *erchomai*: to come; lit.: to enter ▶ To take place, to occur** > A dispute arose {started, came} among the disciples as to which of them should be the greatest (Luke 9:46). All other refs.: ENTER <1525>.

– [7] Matt. 27:24 → RISE (verb) <1096> [8] Mark 4:6; 2 Pet. 1:19 → RISE (verb) <393> [9] Luke 24:38; Rev. 9:2 → to go up → GO <305> [10] Heb. 7:14 → SPRING (verb) <393>.

ARISING – Matt. 27:53 → RESURRECTION <1454>.

ARISTARCHUS – ***Aristarchos*** [masc. name: Ἀρίσταρχος <708>]: **best ruler; from *aristos*: best, and *archō*: to rule, which is from *archē*: beginning ▶ Macedonian Christian from Thessalonica** > Aristarchus was a travelling companion of the apostle Paul (Acts 19:29; 20:4; 27:2). Paul sent the greetings of Aristarchus to the Colossians (4:10) and to Philemon (Phm. 24). ¶

ARISTOBULUS – ***Aristoboulos*** [masc. name: Ἀριστόβουλος <711>]: **best counselor; from *aristos*: best, and *boulē*:**

advice ▶ Christian of Rome > The apostle Paul salutes those who are of Aristobulus's household (Rom. 16:10). ¶

ARK – ***kibōtos*** [fem. noun: κιβωτός <2787>]; **lit.: coffer, chest ▶ a. Huge floating vessel built by Noah with God's specifications >** By faith, Noah prepared an ark for the saving of his household through the flood (Heb. 11:7; 1 Pet. 3:20). He entered into the ark with his family and the animals before the flood (Matt. 24:38; Luke 17:27). This ark was made of gopher wood, had rooms in it, and was covered inside and outside with pitch; it had three decks; its length was three hundred cubits, its width fifty cubits, and its height thirty cubits; its door was on the side and the only window was on top (see Gen. 6:14–16). **b. Principal object in the holy place of the tabernacle >** The ark of the covenant (Heb. 9:4) was in the tabernacle when Israel was in the desert, and later in the temple of Jerusalem. The ark was a coffer made of acacia wood and covered with pure gold; its cover, the mercy seat, was made entirely of pure gold. See Ex. 25:10–22. The ark represents the perfect humanity of the person of the Lord Jesus, the mercy seat represents His atoning work on the cross for the redemption of sinners. The ark is not mentioned after the destruction of the temple (see 2 Kgs. 25:9) or among the objects carried to Babylon. There was no ark in the temple rebuilt after the return from captivity or during the time of the Lord on earth. The ark appears symbolically in Rev. 11:19 where it is seen in the temple of God in heaven. ¶

ARM (noun)[1] – **1** ***ankalē*** [fem. noun: ἀγκάλη <43>]; ***onkos*** **is a bend, a curvature; lit.: bent object, bent arm ▶ Upper limb of the human body joined to the shoulder >** Simeon took Jesus in his arms and blessed God (Luke 2:28). ¶

2 **to take in one's arms:** ***enankalizomai*** [verb: ἐναγκαλίζομαι <1723>]; **from** ***en*****: in, into, and** ***ankalizomai*****: to take in the arms, which is from** ***ankalē*****: see** **1** **▶ To hold in one's arms, to hug >** Jesus took in His arms a little child (Mark 9:36) and little children (10:16). ¶

3 ***brachiōn*** [masc. noun: βραχίων <1023>]; **poss. the compar. of** ***brachus*****: short, e.g., the shorter part of the arm ▶ Term always related in the N.T. to the power of God >** God has shown strength with His arm (Luke 1:51). Isaiah asks to whom the arm of the Lord has been revealed (John 12:38). God brought Israel out of Egypt with a high arm {with mighty power} (Acts 13:17). ¶

– **4** Luke 15:20 → to throw the arms around → lit.: to fall on the neck → FALL (verb) <1968>, NECK <5137> **5** Acts 20:10 → to put one's arms around → EMBRACE <4843> **6** Heb. 12:12 → lit.: hand → HAND (noun) <5495>.

ARM (noun)[2] – 2 Cor. 6:7; 10:4 → WEAPON <3696>.

ARM (verb) – ***hoplizō*** [verb: ὁπλίζω <3695>]; **from** ***hoplon*****: weapon, armor ▶ To equip oneself, to take something as a weapon >** Christians must arm themselves with the thought that they should no longer live for men's lusts, but for God's will (1 Pet. 4:1). ¶

ARMAGEDDON – ***Harmaged(d)ōn*** [Heb. name: Ἁρμαγεδ(δ)ών <717>]**: mountain of Megiddo or of appointment ▶ Plain in Palestine, north of Jerusalem, which is about 35 kilometers in length by 25 kilometers in width; also spelled: Armagedon, Har-Magedon >** Megiddo was known in the history of Israel for being an important strategic military location; many battles were fought near this city. In a coming day, many armies of the earth will be gathered at Armageddon (Rev. 16:16) to make war against the Lord (see Rev. 19:11–19). The beast and the false prophet will then be taken and cast into the lake of fire; the rest shall be killed by divine power, and the birds shall be filled with their flesh (see Rev. 19:20, 21). ¶

ARMAGEDON – See ARMAGEDDON <717>.

ARMED – to be armed, to be fully armed: ***kathoplizō*** [verb: καθοπλίζω <2528>]; **from *kata*: intens., and *hoplizō*: to equip oneself with weapons, which is from *hoplon*: weapon, armor ► To be armed well, to fully equip oneself with weapons >** The strong man fully armed (Luke 11:21) is an image of Satan and his great power, but someone stronger, the Lord Jesus, attacks and overcomes him (see v. 22). ¶

ARMOR – [1] armor, whole armor, full armor: ***panoplia*** [fem. noun: πανοπλία <3833>]; **from *pas*: all, and *hoplon*: weapon, armor ► Combination of protective parts worn by a warrior; Greek and Roman infantry soldiers were each equipped with a whole set of armor; also transl.: panoply >** The strong man who confides in his armor illustrates Satan who is overcome by one stronger than he, i.e., Christ, who takes from him all his armor and divides his spoil (Luke 11:22). The whole armor of God (Eph. 6:11, 13) corresponds to the resources made available by God to the Christian to stand against the wiles of the devil (see Eph. 6:10–20). The seven parts of the armor are defensive: the loins girded with truth, the breastplate of righteousness, the feet shod with the preparation of the gospel of peace, the shield of faith, the helmet of salvation, the sword (to defend oneself) of the Spirit, which is the word of God, and praying always. Against the temptation of the world (see 1 Thes. 5:8), the apostle Paul mentions the breastplate of faith and love, and the helmet of the hope of salvation. ¶

– [2] Rom. 13:12; 2 Cor. 6:7 → WEAPON <3696>.

ARMOUR – See ARMOR <3833>.

ARMY – [1] ***parembolē*** [fem. noun: παρεμβολή <3925>]; **from *paremballō*: to surround, which is from *para*: alongside, and *emballō*: to throw (*ballō*) in (*en*) ► Military troops gathered in an encampment >** By faith, O.T. believers made foreign armies give way (Heb. 11:34). All other refs.: CAMP <3925>, FORTRESS <3925>.

[2] ***strateuma*** [neut. noun: στράτευμα <4753>]; **from *strateuomai*: to be a soldier, which is from *stratos*: army; lit.: army in campaign, armed forces ► Troops of variable size gathered for fighting >** During the judgment of the sixth trumpet, the number of the armies {hosts, troops} of the horsemen was two hundred millions (Rev. 9:16). The armies in heaven followed the One who is called the Word of God upon white horses (Rev. 19:14); the beast, the kings of the earth, and their armies were gathered together to make war against Him and His armies (v. 19). Other refs.: Matt. 22:7; Luke 23:11; Acts 23:10, 27; see TROOPS <4753>. ¶

[3] ***stratopedon*** [neut. noun: στρατόπεδον <4760>]; **from *stratos*: army, and *pedon*: ground, plain ► Military troops gathered in an encampment >** Jesus spoke of Jerusalem surrounded by armies (Luke 21:20). ¶

– [4] Heb. 11:30 → "the army" added in Engl.

AROMA – [1] ***osmē*** [fem. noun: ὀσμή <3744>]; **from *ozō*: to smell, to emit an odor ► Fragrance; agreeable odor in the N.T. >** Christ delivered Himself up for us, for a sweet-smelling aroma {KJV: savour} (Eph. 5:2). The gift of the Philippians had been an aroma {KJV: odour} of sweet savor for Paul (Phil. 4:18). Other refs.: John 12:3; 2 Cor. 2:14, 16a, b; see ODOR <3744>. ¶

– [2] 2 Cor. 2:15; Eph. 5:2; Phil. 4:18 → fragrant aroma, sweet-smelling aroma → sweet odor → ODOR <2175>.

AROMATIC – Mark 16:1; Luke 23:56; 24:1 → sweet spice → SPICE <759>.

AROUND – [1] ***kuklothen*** [adv.: κυκλόθεν <2943>]; **from *kuklos*: circle, and suffix *then*: from or at a place ► All around; also transl.: round >** John uses this word in Rev. 4:3, 4, 8; 5:11. ¶

[2] ***kuklō*** [adv.: κύκλῳ <2945>]; **from *kuklos*: circle ► All around; also transl.: round about >** John saw in the midst and around

the throne four living creatures full of eyes (Rev. 4:6); he heard the voice of many angels around the throne (5:11); he saw all the angels standing around the throne, as well as the elders and the four living creatures (7:11). All other refs.: CIRCUIT <2945>, ROUND <2945>.
– [3] Matt. 3:5; Luke 3:3 → region around → REGION <4066> [4] Matt. 21:33; Mark 12:1 → to set around → SET (verb) <4060> [5] Mark 14:51 → to throw around → WEAR <4016> [6] John 20:14 → BACK (adv. and noun) <3694> [7] Acts 5:16 → round about → ROUND <4038> [8] Acts 14:20 → to gather around → SURROUND <2944>.

AROUSE – [1] Acts 13:50 → EXCITE <3951> [2] Acts 21:30 → DISTURB <2795> [3] Phil. 1:16 or 17 → STIR (verb) <2018>.

ARPHAXAD – ***Arphaxad*** [masc. name: Ἀρφαξάδ <742>] ▶ **Man in the O.T.** > Arphaxad, grandson of Noah, is mentioned in the genealogy of Jesus (Luke 3:36). ¶

ARRANGE – [1] Acts 15:2 → DETERMINE <5021> [2] Acts 20:13 → ORDAIN <1299> [3] Acts 28:23 → APPOINT <5021> [4] 1 Cor. 11:34 → to set in order → ORDER (noun) <1299> [5] 1 Cor. 12:18 → SET (verb) <5087> [6] 2 Cor. 9:5 → to arrange beforehand → to make up beforehand → MAKE <4294> [7] Heb. 9:6 → PREPARE <2680>.

ARRANGEMENT – [1] Luke 9:52 → to make arrangements → PREPARE <2090> [2] Acts 20:13 → to make the arrangement → ORDAIN <1299> [3] Heb. 9:9 → "arrangement" added in Engl.

ARRANGING – 1 Pet. 3:3 → BRAIDING <1708>.

ARRAY (noun) – 1 Tim. 2:9 → CLOTHING <2441>.

ARRAY (verb) – [1] Matt. 6:29; Luke 12:27; 23:11; John 19:2; Rev. 17:4 → CLOTHE <4016> [2] Acts 12:21; Rev. 19:14 → CLOTHE <1746>.

ARREST – [1] Matt. 4:12; Mark 1:14 → to be arrested → to be betrayed → BETRAY <3860> [2] Matt. 14:3; Mark 6:17 → to lay hold, to take hold → TAKE <2902> [3] Matt. 21:46; 26:4, 48, 50, 55, 57; Mark 12:12; 14:1, 44, 46, 49; Acts 24:6 → SEIZE <2902> [4] Matt. 26:55; Mark 14:48; Acts 1:16; 12:3 → TAKE <4815> [5] Mark 13:11 → LEAD (verb) <71> [6] Luke 20:19; Acts 4:3; 5:18 → lit.: to lay hands on → HAND (noun) <5495> [7] Luke 22:54; John 18:12; Acts 23:27 → SEIZE <4815> [8] John 7:30, 32, 44; 8:20; 10:39; 11:57; Acts 12:4 → TAKE <4084> [9] Acts 9:14 → BIND <1210> [10] Acts 21:33 → SEIZE <1949> [11] Acts 22:4 → BIND <1195> [12] 2 Cor. 11:32 → SEIZE <4084>.

ARRIVE – [1] ***katantaō*** [verb: καταντάω <2658>]**; from *kata*: intens., and *antaō*: to meet, which is from *anta*: face to face ▶ To reach, to attain, to come** > The twelve tribes hoped to arrive at {to see fulfilled} the hope of the promise (Acts 26:7). Paul asked the Corinthians if the word of God had come to them only (1 Cor. 14:36). The various gifts of the Spirit have been given until all Christians arrive at the unity of the faith and of the knowledge of the Son of God (Eph. 4:13). Paul desired to arrive at {attain to} the resurrection from among the dead (Phil. 3:11). The verb is also used in Acts 18:24; 25:13. All other refs.: ATTAIN <2658>, COME <2658>.
[2] ***katapleō*** [verb: καταπλέω <2668>]**; from *kata*: down, and *pleō*: to sail ▶ To navigate, to come by water to some place >** Jesus and His disciples arrived in {sailed to} the country of the Gadarenes (Luke 8:26). ¶
[3] ***paraballō*** [verb: παραβάλλω <3846>]**; from *para*: near, and *ballō*: to throw ▶ To bring a ship near, to reach** > Paul's ship arrived at Samos (Acts 20:15 {to put in, to cross over}). Other ref.: Mark 4:30; see COMPARE <3846>. ¶
– [4] Matt. 2:1; Luke 11:6; Acts 13:14; 14:27; 15:4; 17:10; 18:27; 23:35; 25:7 → COME <3854> [5] Mark 6:33 → to arrive before → OUTGO <4281> [6] Luke 19:15 → to arrive back again → RETURN (verb) <1880> [7] Acts 2:1 → to fully come → COME

<4845> [8] Acts 11:11 → STAND (verb) <2186> [9] Acts 18:5 → to come down → COME <2718> [10] Acts 25:1 → COME <1910> [11] Acts 27:3 → TOUCH <2609> [12] Rom. 9:31; Phil. 3:16 → COME <5348> [13] Phil. 3:12 → to arrive at the goal → to be perfected → PERFECT (verb) <5048> [14] 2 Tim. 3:7 → COME <2064>.

ARROGANCE – [1] ***alazoneia*** [fem. noun: ἀλαζονεία <212>]; **from *alazōn*: boaster ▶ Empty boasting to impress others, ostentation** > Certain people were boasting in their arrogance (lit.: arrogances) {arrogant schemes, boastings, vauntings} (*alazoneia*); all such boasting (*kauchēsis*) was evil (Jas. 4:16). Other ref.: 1 John 2:16; see PRIDE <212>. ¶

– [2] Mark 7:22 → PRIDE <5243> [3] 2 Cor. 12:20 → PUFFING UP <5450>.

ARROGANT – [1] Rom. 1:30; 2 Tim. 3:2 → PROUD <5244> [2] Rom. 11:18a, b; Jas. 3:14 → to be arrogant → GLORIFY <2620> [3] Rom. 11:20; 1 Tim. 6:17 → to be arrogant → to be conceited → CONCEITED <5309> [4] 1 Cor. 4:6, 18, 19; 5:2; 8:1; 13:4 → to be, become, make arrogant → PUFF UP <5448> [5] Titus 1:7; 2 Pet. 2:10 → SELF-WILLED <829> [6] 2 Pet. 2:18 → arrogant words → swelling words → WORD <5246>.

ARROGANT SCHEME – Jas. 4:16 → your arrogant schemes → lit.: your arrogances → ARROGANCE <212>.

ARROGANTLY – Jude 16 → swelling words → WORD <5246>.

ARROW – Eph. 6:16 → DART <956>.

ART – [1] ***technē*** [fem. noun: τέχνη <5078>]; **from *tiktō*: to bring forth ▶ Creative human activity, craft, skill** > What is divine is not like gold or silver or stone, a graven form of man's art and imagination {design and skill} (Acts 17:29). Other refs.: Acts 18:3; Rev. 18:22; see OCCUPATION <5078>. ¶

– [2] Acts 8:9 → to use magic arts → to practice sorcery → SORCERY <3096> [3] Acts 8:11 → magic arts → SORCERY <3095> [4] Rev. 18:22 → OCCUPATION <5078>.

ARTEMAS – ***Artemas*** [masc. name: Ἀρτεμᾶς <734>]; **poss. from Artemis, goddess of hunting ▶ Companion of Paul** > Paul speaks of sending Artemas to Titus (Titus 3:12). ¶

ARTEMIS – Acts 19:24, 27, 28, 34, 35 → DIANA <735>.

ARTICLE – ***skeuos*** [neut. noun: σκεῦος <4632>] **▶ Object, item** > Babylon the great was buying articles {vessels} of ivory and most precious wood (Rev. 18:12a, b). All other refs.: GOOD (adj. and noun) <4632>, SAIL (noun) <4632>, VESSEL[1] <4632>.

ARTIFICE – Eph. 6:11 → WILE <3180>.

ARTIFICER – Rev. 18:22 → CRAFTSMAN <5079>.

ARTISAN – Acts 19:24, 38 → CRAFTSMAN <5079>.

AS – [1] 2 Tim. 3:8 → MANNER <5158> [2] Rev. 9:3 → LIKE (adj., adv., noun) <5613>.

AS, EVEN AS, AS WELL AS – ***kathaper*** [adv.: καθάπερ <2509>]; **from *katha*: according as, and *per*: very ▶** Refs.: Rom. 4:6; 12:4; 1 Cor. 12:12; 2 Cor. 1:14; 3:13, 18; 8:11; 1 Thes. 2:11; 3:6, 12; 4:5; Heb. 4:2; 5:4. ¶ ‡

AS INDEED, AS NOW – ***epeidē*** [conj.: ἐπειδή <1894>]; **from *epei*: as, because, and *dē*: indeed, a particle of affirmation or emphasis ▶ Since indeed, since now, because now** > Refs.: Matt. 21:46; Luke 11:6; Acts 13:46; 14:12; 15:24; 1 Cor. 1:21, 22; 14:16; 15:21; 2 Cor. 5:4; Phil. 2:26. ¶ ‡

AS IT WERE – ***hōsperei*** [adv.: ὡσπερεί <5619>] ▶ Ref.: 1 Cor. 15:8. ¶

ASA – ***Asa*** [masc. name: Ἀσά <760>]: **physician, in Heb.; also written:** Ἀσάφ **(*Asaph*)** ▶ **King of Judah** > Asa did what was right in the sight of the Lord (see 1 Kgs. 15:11). His name is mentioned in the genealogy of Jesus Christ (Matt. 1:7, 8). ¶

ASAPH – Matt. 1:7, 8 → ASA <760>.

ASCEND – [1] Luke 19:28; John 1:51; 3:13; 6:62; 20:17a, b; Acts 2:34; 25:1; Rom. 10:6; Eph. 4:8–10; Rev. 7:2; 8:4; 11:7, 12; 14:11; 17:8 → to go up → GO <305> [2] Heb. 4:14 → who has ascended into heaven → lit.: having passed through the heavens → PASS <1330>.

ASCENSION – The term "ascension" describes the elevation of Christ into heaven from the midst of His own disciples. The word is used by some while others use "receiving up" {taken up} in Luke 9:51: see RECEIVE <354>. Mark and Luke relate the ascension of the Lord in their Gospels: He was carried up into heaven (see Mark 16:19; Luke 24:51). We read also in Acts 1:9 that the Lord was taken up from the earth and a cloud received Him.

ASCERTAIN – [1] Matt. 2:7, 16 → DETERMINE <198> [2] Acts 21:34; 24:11 → KNOW <1097> [3] Acts 22:29 → KNOW <1921> [4] Acts 24:8 → to take knowledge → KNOWLEDGE <1921>.

ASCETICISM – Col. 2:18, 23 → HUMILITY <5012>.

ASER – See ASHER <768>.

ASH – [1] ***spodos*** [fem. noun: σποδός <4700>] ▶ **What is left from the combustion of some organic matter** > "Sitting in sackcloth and ashes" is an expr. of sorrow, humiliation, and repentance (Matt. 11:21; Luke 10:13). The ashes of a red heifer (Heb. 9:13) were used for the purification of the Israelites (see Num. 19). ¶

[2] **to reduce, to burn to ashes:** ***tephroō*** [verb: τεφρόω <5077>]; **from *tephra*: ashes** ▶ **To consume by fire** > The cities of Sodom and Gomorrah were reduced to ashes (2 Pet. 2:6 {to turn, to burn to ashes}; *katapimprēmi* in some mss.), i.e., they were destroyed by the fire. ¶

ASHAMED – [1] **to make ashamed:** ***kataischunō*** [verb: καταισχύνω <2617>]; **from *kata*: intens., and *aischunō*: to be ashamed, to be disappointed, which is from *aischos*: shame, infamy, ugliness** ▶ **To dishonor, to humiliate** > Hope does not make ashamed (Rom. 5:5). All other refs.: ASHAMED (BE) <2617>, DISHONOR (verb) <2617>, SHAME (noun) <2617>.

[2] **who does not need to be ashamed:** ***anepaischuntos*** [adj.: ἀνεπαίσχυντος <422>]; **from *a*: neg., and *epaischunomai*: to dishonor, to humiliate, which is from *epi*: upon (intens.), and *aischunō*: see** [1] ▶ **Who does not have cause to blush, to be confused** > Timothy was to be a worker who did not need to be ashamed (2 Tim. 2:15). ¶ – [3] 1 Cor. 4:14 → to make ashamed → SHAME (verb) <1788>.

ASHAMED (BE) – [1] ***aischunō*** [verb: αἰσχύνω <153>]; **from *aischos*: shame, infamy, ugliness** ▶ **a. To be dishonored, to be humiliated** > The unjust manager was ashamed to beg (Luke 16:3). He who suffers as a Christian is not to be ashamed (1 Pet. 4:16). We must abide in the Son so that we may not be ashamed {may not be put to shame, may not shrink away in shame, may be unashamed} at His coming (1 John 2:28). **b. To be confused, to be disappointed; also transl.: to put to shame** > Paul would not be ashamed if he should boast about the authority the Lord had given him for edification (2 Cor. 10:8). He should be ashamed in nothing according to his earnest expectation and hope (Phil. 1:20). ¶

[2] ***epaischunomai*** [verb: ἐπαισχύνομαι <1870>]; **from *epi*: about, on account of (intens.), and *aischunō*: see** [1] ▶ **To be dishonored, to be humiliated** > The Son of Man will be ashamed of whoever will be ashamed of Him and His words when He

comes in His glory (Mark 8:38a, b; Luke 9:26a, b). Paul was not ashamed of the gospel (Rom. 1:16). The Christians of Rome were ashamed of the things they had done before their conversion (Rom. 6:21). Timothy was not to be ashamed of the testimony of the Lord (2 Tim. 1:8). Paul was not ashamed, for he knew whom he had believed (2 Tim. 1:12 {to be a cause for shame}). Onesiphorus had not been ashamed of Paul's chain (2 Tim. 1:16). Jesus is not ashamed to call brothers those who are sanctified (Heb. 2:11). God is not ashamed of those who have died in faith (Heb. 11:16). ¶

[3] ***kataischunō*** [verb: καταισχύνω <2617>]; **from *kata*: down (intens.), and *aischunō*: see [1] ▶ To be confused, to be disappointed; also transl.: to put to shame, to be confounded** > He who believes on the Lord Jesus will not be ashamed (Rom. 9:33; 10:11; 1 Pet. 2:6). If Paul had boasted anything to Titus about the Corinthians, he was not ashamed {embarrassed} (2 Cor. 7:14); he did not want to be ashamed of his confident boasting concerning their service for the saints (9:4). Those who defame Christians will be ashamed when they find out about their good conduct in Christ (1 Pet. 3:16). All other refs.: ASHAMED <2617>, DISHONOR (verb) <2617>, SHAME (noun) <2617>.

– [4] 2 Thes. 3:14; Titus 2:8 → to shame (someone), to be ashamed → SHAME (verb) <1788> [5] 2 Tim. 2:15 → who does not need to be ashamed → ASHAMED <422>.

ASHEN – Rev. 6:8 → GREEN <5515>.

ASHER – ***Asēr*** [masc. name: Ἀσήρ <768>]: **blessed, in Heb. ▶ Son of Jacob as well as one of the twelve tribes named after him; also transl.: Aser** > The prophetess Anna was from the tribe of Asher (Luke 2:36). Twelve thousand from the tribe of Asher shall be sealed (Rev. 7:6). ¶

ASHORE – [1] Matt. 13:48 → lit.: onto the shore (*epi ton aigialon*) → SHORE <123> [2] Acts 27:26 → to cast ashore → to run aground → RUN <1601>.

ASIA – [1] ***Asia*** [fem. name: Ἀσία <773>] ▶ **In the N.T., a name indicating Asia Minor (present-day Turkey), which corresponds roughly to the Roman province bearing the same name; it is situated to the east of Europe and north of the Mediterranean** > Paul visited Asia on various occasions and founded many Christian churches in the regions thereof (Acts 19:10, 22, 26; 20:4a, b, 16, 18; 1 Cor. 16:19; 2 Cor. 1:8). The seven churches of Revelation 3 and 4 are situated in Asia Minor (Rev. 1:4; see v. 11). Peter sent his First Epistle to the Christians of Asia (1 Pet. 1:1). Other refs.: Acts 2:9; 6:9; 16:6; 19:27; 21:27; 24:18; 27:2; Rom. 16:5; 2 Tim. 1:15. ¶

– [2] Acts 19:31 → chief of Asia, official of Asia → ASIARCH <775> [3] Acts 20:4 → of Asia → ASIAN <774>.

ASIAN – [1] ***Asianos*** [adj. used as noun: Ἀσιανός <774>] ▶ **Native of Asia** > The Asians Tychicus and Trophimus accompanied Paul on a journey (Acts 20:4). ¶

– [2] Acts 20:4 → the Asians → of Asia → ASIA <773>.

ASIARCH – ***Asiarchēs*** [masc. name: Ἀσιάρχης <775>]; **from *Asia*: Asia, and *archē*: authority, rule ▶ An elected ruler in the Roman province of Asia; also transl.: chief of Asia, official of Asia, official of the province** > The Asiarchs presided annually over the religious ceremonies and public games in that province, Ephesus being the capital. Paul had friends who were Asiarchs in Ephesus (Acts 19:31). ¶

ASIDE – [1] Mark 7:8 → to lay aside → LAY <863> [2] Mark 7:9; Gal. 2:21; 3:15; 1 Tim. 5:12 → to set aside → REJECT <114> [3] Luke 9:10 → to go aside → WITHDRAW <5298> [4] John 11:28 → SECRETLY <2977> [5] John 13:4 → to lay aside → LAY <5087> [6] Rom. 3:12 → to turn aside → TURN (verb) <1578> [7] Rom. 13:12; Heb. 12:1; Jas. 1:21; 1 Pet. 2:1 → to lay aside, to put aside → to cast away → CAST (verb) <659> [8] 1 Tim. 1:6; 5:15 → to turn aside → TURN (verb) <1624> [9] Heb. 10:9 → to set aside → to take away → TAKE

<337> [10] Heb. 12:13 → to turn aside → DISLOCATE <1624>.

ASK – [1] ***aiteō*** [verb: αἰτέω <154>] ► **To solicit, to make a request; also transl.: to desire, to require, to pray, etc.** > The Father gives good things to those who ask Him (Matt. 7:11). The Father will do anything that two ask if they agree on earth (Matt. 18:19). Of everyone to whom much has been committed (or: entrusted), much will be asked (Luke 12:48). Jesus said to His disciples that if they ask anything in His name, He would do it (John 14:14). Whatever they would ask the Father in His name, He would give them (John 16:23b). Those who were dwelling in Jerusalem asked {begged, desired} Pilate to put Jesus to death (Acts 13:28). Paul asked {besought, desired} the Ephesians not to lose courage because of his afflictions (Eph. 3:13). If we ask anything according to the will of the Son of God, He hears us; whatever we ask, we know that we have the petitions we have asked of Him (1 John 5:14, 15a, b). We do not have because we do not ask (Jas. 4:2); we ask and we do not receive, because we ask wrongly (v. 3a, b). Other refs.: Matt. 5:42; 6:8, 25; 7:7–10; 14:7; 20:20, 22; 21:22; 27:20, 58; Mark 6:22–24; 10:35, 38; 11:24; 15:6, 8, 43; Luke 1:63; 6:30; 11:9–13; 23:23, 25, 52; John 4:9, 10; 11:22; 14:13; 15:7, 16; 16:24a, b, 26; Acts 3:2, 14; 7:46; 9:2; 12:20; 13:21; 16:29; 25:3, 15 {to require}; 1 Cor. 1:22; Eph. 3:20; Col. 1:9; Jas. 1:5, 6; 1 Pet. 3:15; 1 John 3:22; 5:16. ¶

[2] **to ask for: *exaiteō*** [verb: ἐξαιτέω <1809>]; **from *ek*: out, and *aiteō*: see [1] ► To claim, to demand for one's own purpose** > Satan had asked for {had desired to have, had demanded to have} the disciples, that he might sift them as wheat (Luke 22:31). ¶

[3] **to ask questions: *anakrinō*** [verb: ἀνακρίνω <350>]; **from *ana*: intens, and *krinō*: to judge; lit.: to examine ► To enquire, to find out, to request information** > The Christian is to eat whatever is sold in the meat market, not asking questions {not raising questions, making no inquiry} for conscience's sake (1 Cor. 10:25, 27). All other refs.: DISCERN <350>, EXAMINE <350>, JUDGE (verb) <350>, SEARCH (verb) <350>.

[4] ***exetazō*** [verb: ἐξετάζω <1833>]; **from *ek*: out (intens.), and *etazō*: to examine ► To find out, to inquire, to question** > None of the disciples dared ask Jesus who He was, knowing that it was the Lord (John 21:12). All other refs.: INQUIRE <1833>, SEARCH (verb) <1833>.

[5] ***erōtaō*** [verb: ἐρωτάω <2065>]; **from *eromai*: to ask, to question, to consult ► a. To make a request, to pray; also transl.: to demand, to question, etc.** > Jesus spoke of the day when His disciples will ask Him nothing (John 16:23a). We can directly ask (*aiteō*) the Father in the name of Jesus; accordingly Jesus did not say that He will ask (*erōtaō*) the Father for us (John 16:26b). The disciples knew that Jesus had no need that anyone should ask Him (John 16:30). Jesus was asking for those the Father had given Him, and not for the world (John 17:9a, b). He was not asking that the Father would take His own out of the world (John 17:15). He did not ask for His disciples alone, but also for those who believe in Him through their word (John 17:20). The Jews asked Pilate that the legs of the ones crucified be broken and that they be taken off the cross (John 19:31). Joseph of Arimathea asked Pilate to take away the body of Jesus (John 19:38). The verb is also used in regard to the disciples (Matt. 15:23), a Greek woman (Mark 7:26), the mother-in-law of Peter (Luke 4:38), Jesus (Luke 5:3; John 14:16), a centurion (Luke 7:3), Pharisees (Luke 7:36; 11:37), a multitude (Luke 8:37), men who had bought different things (Luke 14:18, 19), a rich man (Luke 16:27), the disciples (John 4:31), the Samaritans (John 4:40), a royal official (John 4:47), Greeks (John 12:21), those who were baptized (Acts 10:48), the Jews of Ephesus (Acts 18:20), Paul's nephew (Acts 23:18), conspirators (Acts 23:20), one of Paul's fellow workmen (Phil. 4:3), the Thessalonians (1 Thes. 4:1; 5:12; 2 Thes. 2:1), and the elect lady (2 John 5). **b. To demand, to question** > Jesus asked His disciples a question concerning who the Son of Man was (Matt. 16:13). Many people asked Jesus questions on various occasions

(Matt. 19:17, in some mss.: to call (*legō*); John 8:7; 18:19); they wanted to ask Him what He meant (John 16:19). The disciples asked Jesus various questions (Mark 4:10; John 9:2); they feared to ask Him about His statement concerning the Son of Man (Luke 9:45). Jesus spoke of a king who sends an embassy to another king to ask for {to desire} conditions of peace (Luke 14:32). He considered it useless to ask the members of the Sanhedrin a question (Luke 22:68). John the Baptist was asked why he was baptizing (John 1:25). The parents of a man who was born blind were asked how he could now see (John 9:19). The parents answered, telling the Jews to ask their son (John 9:21, 23). Other refs.: Matt. 21:24; Luke 19:31; 20:3; John 1:19, 21; 5:12; 9:15, 19, 21, 23; 16:5; Acts 3:3; 16:39; 1 John 5:16. ¶

[6] ***eperōtaō*** [verb: ἐπερωτάω <1905>]**; from *epi*: upon (intens.), and *erōtaō*: see [5] ▶ To interrogate, to inquire; also transl.: to question >** Jesus asked an unclean spirit what was his name (Mark 5:9; Luke 8:30). He asked a question about the baptism of John (Mark 11:29). He asked if it was lawful on the Sabbath to do good or to do evil (Luke 6:9). The Lord was made manifest to those who did not ask for {inquire after} Him (Rom. 10:20). People asked Jesus questions on various occasions (Matt. 12:10; 22:23, 35, 46; 27:11; Mark 7:5; 12:18, 34; 14:60, 61; 15:2, 4; Luke 17:20; 18:18; 20:21, 27 or 28, 40; 21:7; 22:64; 23:3, 9). Jesus asked the teachers questions (Luke 2:46), as likewise His disciples (Mark 8:27; 9:16; Luke 9:18), the Pharisees (Matt. 22:41), and a blind man (Luke 18:40). He answered the high priest, questioning why he asked Him, and told him to rather ask those who had heard Him (John 18:21a in some mss., b). The disciples asked Jesus about various matters (Matt. 17:10; Mark 7:17; 9:11; 10:10; 13:3; Luke 8:9; Acts 1:6) or feared to ask Him about a certain teaching (Mark 9:32). The high priest asked Peter and the other apostles a question (Acts 5:27). If the women wish to learn anything, they are to ask their own husbands at home (1 Cor. 14:35). Other refs.: Matt. 16:1 {to desire}; Mark 8:5, 23; 9:21, 28, 33; 10:2, 17; 12:28; 15:44; Luke 3:10, 14; 23:6; John 18:7; Acts 23:34. ¶

[7] ***legō*** [verb: λέγω <3004>] ▶ **To say >** Festus asked Paul whether he was willing to go to Jerusalem and be judged there (Acts 25:9). Other refs.: SPEAK <3004>.

[8] ***punthanomai*** [verb: πυνθάνομαι <4441>] ▶ **To obtain information, to find out; also transl.: to inquire >** Peter asked for what reason Cornelius had sent for him (Acts 10:29). Other refs.: Luke 15:26; 18:36; John 13:24; Acts 4:7; 10:18; 21:33 {to demand}; 23:19. Other refs.: Matt. 2:4; John 4:52; Acts 23:20, 34; see INQUIRE <4441>, UNDERSTAND <4441>. ¶

– [9] Matt. 8:5 → PLEAD <3870> [10] Matt. 9:38; Luke 10:2; 2 Cor. 10:2 → SUPPLICATE <1189> [11] Matt. 12:39; Mark 8:12; Luke 11:29 → SEEK <1934> [12] Matt. 12:46 → SEEK <2212> [13] Mark 1:27 → to ask each other → to question together → QUESTION (verb) <4802> [14] Luke 6:30 → to ask back → to demand back → DEMAND (verb) <523> [15] John 9:10; 20:15 → SAY <3004> [16] John 16:19 → to ask one another → INQUIRE <2212> [17] Acts 3:10 → the one who sat asking for alms → lit.: the one sitting for alms [18] Acts 8:31 → BESEECH <3870> [19] Acts 8:34 → PRAY <1189> [20] Acts 10:17 → to ask directions → to make inquiry → INQUIRY <1331> [21] Acts 10:22 → to ask to come → to send for → SEND <3343> [22] Acts 28:20 → to call for → CALL (verb) <3870> [23] Rom. 1:10 → to make request → REQUEST (noun) <1189> [24] 1 Cor. 6:4 → to ask for a ruling → to set to judge → JUDGE (verb) <2523> [25] Gal. 3:2 → let me ask → I (Paul) want to learn → WANT (verb) <2309>, LEARN <3129> [26] Gal. 3:5 →"so again I ask" added in Engl.

ASLEEP – [1] Acts 20:9b → to be sound asleep → to be overcome by sleep → SLEEP (noun) <5258> [2] 2 Pet. 2:3 → to be asleep → SLUMBER (verb) <3573>.

ASLEEP (BE, FALL) – See SLEEP (verb).

ASP – ***aspis*** [fem. noun: ἀσπίς <785>] ▶ **Serpent found in brushwood, small and**

venomous > As an illustration, Paul writes that the poison of asps {vipers} is under the lips of unbelievers (Rom. 3:13, citing Ps. 140:3). ¶

ASPIRE – [1] Rom. 15:20 → STRIVE <5389> [2] 1 Thes. 4:11 → STUDY <5389> [3] 1 Tim. 3:1 → DESIRE (verb) <3713> [4] 1 Tim. 6:10 → COVET <3713>.

ASS – [1] Matt. 21:2, 5a, 7; Luke 13:15; 14:5; John 12:15 → DONKEY <3688> [2] Matt. 21:5b; 2 Pet. 2:16 → DONKEY <5268> [3] John 12:14 → DONKEY <3678>.

ASSAIL – [1] Luke 11:53 → PRESS <1758> [2] Acts 27:20 → BEAT <1945>.

ASSARIA – Luke 12:6 → plur. of "assarion" → PENNY <787>.

ASSASSIN – Acts 21:38 → MURDERER <4607>.

ASSAULT (noun) – Acts 14:5 → ATTEMPT (noun) <3730>.

ASSAULT (verb) – ***ephistēmi*** [verb: ἐφίστημι <2186>]; **from *epi*: against, and *histēmi*: to stand; lit.: to stand against ▶ To attack, to beset** > The Jews assaulted {came upon, rushed to} the house of Jason in search of Paul and Silas (Acts 17:5). All other refs.: COME <2186>, FALL (verb) <2186>, HAND (noun) <2186>, READY <2186>, STAND (verb) <2186>.

ASSAY – [1] Acts 9:26; 16:7 → TRY[1] <3985> [2] Heb. 11:29 → ATTEMPT (verb) <3984>.

ASSEMBLE – [1] **to be assembled together: *sunalizō*** [verb: συναλίζω <4871>]; **from *sun*: together, and *halizō*: to gather, to assemble ▶ To be with, to be gathered together** > Being assembled together with His disciples after the resurrection, Jesus commanded them not to depart from Jerusalem, but to wait for the coming of the Holy Spirit (Acts 1:4). Some translate *sunalizō* by "to eat with" (lit.: to share the salt together). ¶

– [2] Matt. 2:4; 26:3 {to assemble together}, 57; 27:17 {to assemble together}; 28:12; Luke 22:66; John 20:19 in some mss.; Acts 4:31; 11:26; 13:44; 20:7, 8; 1 Cor. 5:4; Rev. 16:14, 16; 19:17, 19 → GATHER <4863> [3] Mark 14:53 → to assemble with → to come together → COME <4905> [4] Luke 23:48 → to come together → COME <4836> [5] Luke 24:33 → to assemble together → to gather together → GATHER <4867>.

ASSEMBLING – [1] ***episunagōgē*** [fem. noun: ἐπισυναγωγή <1997>]; **from *episunagō*: to bring together, which is from *epi*: upon, and *sunagō*: to gather, which is from *sun*: together, and *agō*: to lead ▶ a. Gathering of believers in the Lord Jesus in heaven at His coming** > Paul speaks of the coming of the Lord Jesus Christ and the gathering together (or: assembling) of Christians to Him (2 Thes. 2:1). **b. Gathering of Christian believers during the time of the church on the earth, particularly for the meetings of the local church** > The author of the Epistle to the Hebrews exhorts Christians not to forsake the assembling of themselves {meeting} together (Heb. 10:25). ¶

– [2] 1 Thes. 4:16 → assembling shout → SHOUT (noun) <2752>.

ASSEMBLY – [1] ***panēguris*** [fem. noun: πανήγυρις <3831>]; **from *pas*: all, and *aguris*: gathering, crowd, which is from *agora*: place of meeting ▶ Gathering of all the Greek people to celebrate a religious ceremony or games; also transl.: general assembly** > Some apply the word to the church of the Firstborn in Heb. 12:23. Others believe it should be related to the angels and be part of v. 22. ¶

– [2] Luke 1:10; Acts 15:12; 23:7 → MULTITUDE <4128> [3] Luke 22:66 → assembly of the elders → council of elders, elderhood → ELDER <4244> [4] Acts 5:21 → full assembly of the elders → SENATE <1087> [5] Acts 19:30, 33 → PEOPLE <1218> [6] Acts 19:32, 39, 41; et al. → CHURCH <1577>.

ASSENT – [1] Luke 23:51 → CONSENT (verb) <4784> [2] Acts 24:9 → to join in the attack → JOIN <4934>.

ASSERT – [1] Luke 22:59 → AFFIRM <1340> [2] Acts 24:9; 25:19 → SAY <5335> [3] 1 Thes. 2:6 → to assert authority → lit.: to be a burden → BURDEN (noun) <922> [4] 2 Thes. 2:2 → "by the teaching asserting" added in Engl.

ASSERTION – 1 Tim. 1:7 → to make confident assertions → AFFIRM <1226>.

ASSIGN – [1] Matt. 24:51; Luke 12:46 → APPOINT <5087> [2] Luke 22:29a, b → APPOINT <1303> [3] Acts 22:10 → APPOINT <5021> [4] Rom. 12:3; 1 Cor. 7:17; 2 Cor. 10:13 → DISTRIBUTE <3307>.

ASSIMILATE – Heb. 7:3 → to make like → LIKE (adj., adv., noun) <871>.

ASSIST – [1] ***paristēmi*** [verb: παρίστημι <3936>]; **from *para*: near, and *histēmi*: to stand ▶ To help, to attend to someone's needs** > Paul commended Phoebe to the Christians in Rome to assist {help} her in whatever she had need (Rom. 16:2). Other refs.: see entries in Lexicon at <3936>.

– [2] Acts 13:5 → to assist them → as their servant → SERVANT <5257> [3] Phil. 4:3 → HELP (verb) <4815> [4] 1 Tim. 5:10, 16a, b → RELIEVE <1884>.

ASSISTANT – Acts 13:5 → SERVANT <5257>.

ASSOCIATE (noun) – Acts 22:5 → their associates → lit.: their brothers → BROTHER <80>.

ASSOCIATE (verb) – [1] ***sunapagō*** [verb: συναπάγω <4879>]; **from *sun*: together, and *apagō*: to take along, which is from *apo*: from, and *agō*: to lead; lit.: to let oneself be taken along with ▶ To go along, to join together** > Christians in Rome were to associate with {condescend to} men of low position (Rom. 12:16). Other refs.: Gal. 2:13; 2 Pet. 3:17; see CARRY <4879>. ¶

– [2] John 4:9 → to have dealings → DEALINGS <4798> [3] Acts 5:13; 9:26 → JOIN <2853> [4] Acts 10:28 → to keep company → COMPANY (noun) <2853> [5] 1 Cor. 5:9, 11; 2 Thes. 3:14 → to keep company, to have company → COMPANY (noun) <4874>.

ASSOCIATION – 1 Cor. 8:7 → through former association with idols → lit.: by habit of the idol → CUSTOM[1] <4914>.

ASSOS – ***Assos*** [fem. name: Ἄσσος <789>] ▶ **City of Mysia in Asia Minor and port of the Aegean Sea** > On his third missionary journey, Paul sailed to Assos, as he was going to Jerusalem, stopping on his way at Miletus, near Ephesus (Acts 20:13, 14). ¶

ASSUME – [1] Acts 21:29 → SUPPOSE <3543> [2] 1 Tim. 2:12 → to assume authority → AUTHORITY <831>.

ASSURANCE – [1] ***pistis*** [fem. noun: πίστις <4102>]; **from *peithō*: to convince, to persuade ▶ Sure proof, certitude** > The resurrection of Jesus is the assurance {proof} that He will judge the world in righteousness (Acts 17:31). See FAITH <4102>.

[2] **full assurance, much assurance: *plērophoria*** [fem. noun: πληροφορία <4136>]; **from *plērophoreō*: to fulfill, which is from *plērēs*: complete, full, and *phoreō*: to fill, which is from *pherō*: to carry, to bear ▶ Entire certainty, complete conviction** > Paul wanted the Colossians to have full assurance of {the complete} understanding to know fully the mysteries of God (Col. 2:2). The glad tidings of Paul had been preached to the Thessalonians in much assurance {deep conviction, full conviction} (1 Thes. 1:5). Christians are to show the same diligence to the full assurance of hope {to make their hope sure} unto the end (Heb. 6:11). They can approach God in full assurance of faith (Heb. 10:22). ¶

– [3] 1 Tim. 3:13 → BOLDNESS <3954> [4] Heb. 3:14 → CONFIDENCE <5287> [5] Heb. 11:1 → SUBSTANCE <5287>.

ASSURE – [1] ***peithō*** [verb: πείθω <3982>] ▶ **To convince, to persuade** > Christians assure {set at rest} their hearts before God, knowing that God knows all things (1 John 3:19). The verb is also used concerning O.T. people of faith in Heb. 11:13 in some mss. Other refs.: see entries in Lexicon at <3982>.
– [2] Acts 7:17 → PROMISE (verb) <3660> [3] Rom. 4:21 → to be fully assured → to be fully persuaded → PERSUADE <4135> [4] 2 Cor. 2:8 → REAFFIRM <2964> [5] Col. 2:7 → ESTABLISH <950>.

ASSURED – Col. 4:12 → fully assured → to be complete → COMPLETE (adj.) <4135>.

ASSURED (BE) – [1] ***pistoō*** [verb: πιστόω <4104>]; **from *pistos*: faithful, or *peithō*: to convince** ▶ **To be fully convinced, to be fully persuaded** > Timothy had to continue in the things which he had learned and been assured {became convinced} (2 Tim. 3:14). ¶
– [2] Acts 2:36 → lit.: to know assuredly → ASSUREDLY <806>.

ASSUREDLY – [1] ***asphalōs*** [adv.: ἀσφαλῶς <806>]; **from *asphalēs*: safe, which is from *a*: neg., and *sphallō*: to make to fall, to make to vacillate** ▶ **Certainly, firmly** > The house of Israel was to know assuredly {know for certain, be assured} that God had made Jesus both Lord and Christ (Acts 2:36). Other refs.: Mark 14:44; Acts 16:23; see SECURELY <806>. ¶
– [2] Matt. 5:18, 26; Mark 11:23; Luke 12:37; et al. → VERILY <281> [3] Acts 16:10 → to assuredly gather → CONCLUDE[1] <4822> [4] Heb. 2:16 → VERILY <1222>.

ASTONISH – [1] See ASTONISHED (BE).
– [2] Luke 5:9 → they were astonished → lit.: amazement had seized them → ASTONISHMENT <2285>, SEIZE <4023> [3] Acts 13:12 → AMAZE <1605> [4] Rev. 17:7 → to be greatly astonished → lit.: to wonder with great wonder (v. 6) → WONDER (verb) <2296>.

ASTONISHED – Acts 3:11 → greatly amazed → AMAZED <1569>.

ASTONISHED (BE) – [1] ***ekplēssō*** [verb: ἐκπλήσσω <1605>]; **from *ek*: intens., and *plessō*: to strike** ▶ **To admire, to be amazed** > The crowds were astonished at the teaching of Jesus (Matt. 7:28; 13:54; 22:33; Mark 1:22; Luke 4:32). The disciples were exceedingly astonished at the words of Jesus (Matt. 19:25; Mark 10:26). Many hearing Jesus were astonished (Mark 6:2); later all the people were astonished at His teaching (11:18). People were astonished beyond measure {were overwhelmed with amazement} at the miracles of Jesus (Mark 7:37). When they found Jesus in the temple, His parents were astonished (Luke 2:48). People were all astonished at the greatness of God after Jesus healed the possessed child (Luke 9:43). Other ref.: Acts 13:12 (to be amazed); see AMAZED (BE) <1605>. ¶
[2] **to astonish, to be astonished: *existēmi*** [verb: ἐξίστημι <1839>]; **from *ek*: out, and *histēmi*: to stand** ▶ **To amaze, to be amazed, to be much surprised** > People were astonished with great astonishment {were overcome with great amazement, were completely astounded, were completely astonished} after the resurrection of the young girl by Jesus (Mark 5:42). The disciples were exceedingly astonished (Mark 6:51). All who heard Jesus in the temple, when He was twelve years old, were astonished (Luke 2:47). Certain believing women astonished {amazed} other believers by reporting what they had seen the morning of the resurrection of the Lord (Luke 24:22). Simon astonished {amazed, bewitched} the people of Samaria with his magic arts (Acts 8:9, 11), i.e., his sorcery. The Jews who had believed were astonished that the gift of the Holy Spirit had been poured out on the Gentiles also (Acts 10:45). All other refs.: AMAZED (BE) <1839>, MIND (noun) <1839>.
– [3] Matt. 8:10; 9:33; Mark 6:6, 51; Luke 1:63; 8:25; 11:14; Acts 3:12 →

MARVEL (verb) <2296> 4 Mark 5:42 → to be completely astonished → lit.: to be astonished with great astonishment → ASTONISHMENT <1611> 5 Mark 10:24, 32 → AMAZED (BE) <2284> 6 Luke 5:9 → lit.: to be seized by astonishment → ASTONISHMENT <2285> 7 Rev. 13:3; et al. → WONDER (verb) <2296> 8 Rev. 17:6 → to be greatly astonished → AMAZEMENT <2295>.

ASTONISHMENT – 1 ***ekstasis*** [fem. noun: ἔκστασις <1611>]; **from *existēmi*: to remove from its normal place, which is from *ek*: out, and *histēmi*: to stand ▶ Amazement, stupor, wonder** > The witnesses of the resurrection of a little girl were astonished with great astonishment {overcome with great amazement, completely astonished, completely astounded} (Mark 5:42). Trembling and astonishment {excessive amazement} had gripped the women at the tomb of Jesus (Mark 16:8). Other refs.: Luke 5:26; Acts 3:10; 10:10; 11:5; 22:17; see AMAZEMENT <1611>, ECSTASY <1611>. ¶

2 ***thambos*** [neut. noun: θάμβος <2285>] ▶ **Amazement, dread** > All were amazed (lit.: There was amazement {astonishment} on all) that Jesus had healed a possessed man (Luke 4:36). Astonishment laid hold on Peter and on all those who were with him (Luke 5:9). The word is transl. "wonder" in Acts 3:10. ¶

ASTOUNDED – Acts 3:11 → utterly astounded → greatly amazed → AMAZED <1569>.

ASTOUNDED (BE) – 1 Mark 5:42 → to be completely astounded → lit.: to be astonished with great astonishment → ASTONISHED (BE) <1839>, ASTONISHMENT <1611> 2 Mark 6:51 → ASTONISHED (BE) <1839> 3 Luke 11:38 → MARVEL (verb) <2296> 4 Acts 13:41 → WONDER (verb) <2296>.

ASTRAY – 1 **to go astray: *planaō*** [verb: πλανάω <4105>]; **from *planē*: error, illusion ▶ To wander, to err, to go out of the way** > The high priest can have compassion on those who are ignorant and going astray {misguided} (Heb. 5:2: *planōmenos*). Before their conversion, Christians were like sheep going astray {straying} (1 Pet. 2:25: *planōmenos*). All other refs.: DECEIVE <4105>, MISTAKEN (BE) <4105>, STRAY <4105>, WANDER <4105>.

– 2 Mark 13:22 → to lead astray → DECEIVE <635> 3 John 16:1 → to go astray → OFFEND <4624> 4 Acts 19:26 → to lead astray → to turn away → TURN (verb) <3179> 5 2 Cor. 11:3 → to lead astray → CORRUPT (verb) <5351> 6 1 Tim. 6:21; 2 Tim. 2:18 → to go astray → STRAY <795> 7 2 Tim. 3:6 → to lead astray → LEAD (verb) <71>.

ASUNDER – 1 Matt. 19:6; Mark 10:9 → to put asunder → SEPARATE <5563> 2 Matt. 24:51 → to cut asunder → to cut in two → CUT <1371> 3 Acts 1:18 → to burst asunder → BURST <2997>.

ASYNCRITUS – ***Asunkritos*** [masc. name: Ἀσύγκριτος <799>]: **incomparable; from *a*: neg., and *sunkritos*: comparable ▶ A Christian from Rome** > Paul salutes Asyncritus in his Epistle to the Romans (Rom. 16:14). ¶

AT ALL – ***katholou*** [adv.: καθόλου <2527>]; **from *kata*: of, and *holos*: all, whole ▶ Wholly, entirely** > Peter and John were commanded not to speak at all nor to teach in the name of Jesus (Acts 4:18). ¶

ATHENIAN – ***Athēnaios*** [adj. used as noun: Ἀθηναῖος <117>]: **from Athena, goddess of wisdom ▶ Resident of the city of Athens** > Athenians spent their time telling and hearing the latest news (Acts 17:21); in the midst of the Areopagus Paul preached the gospel to them (v. 22). ¶

ATHENS – ***Athēnai*** [fem. name: Ἀθῆναι <116>]: **name given in honor of Athena, the goddess of wisdom who, according to mythology, founded the city ▶ The capital of Greece in the plain of Attica, which became the metropolis of culture and arts in antiquity; it fell to the Romans**

in 86 B.C. > Paul came to Athens and preached at the Areopagus before educated but pagan men (Acts 17:15, 16). He was left alone in Athens (1 Thess. 3:1), from whence he later departed for Corinth (Acts 18:1). ¶

ATHIRST (BE) – Rev. 21:6; 22:17 → THIRST (verb) <1372>.

ATHLETE – 1 Cor. 9:25 → lit.: everyone striving → STRIVE <75>.

ATHLETICS – 2 Tim. 2:5a, b → to compete in athletics → STRIVE <118>.

ATONEMENT – 1 Rom. 3:25; Heb. 9:5 → sacrifice of atonement, atonement cover → MERCY SEAT <2435> 2 Heb. 2:17 → to make atonement → to make propitiation → PROPITIATION <2433>.

ATONEMENT COVER – Heb. 9:5 → MERCY SEAT <2435>.

ATONING – 1 John 2:2; 4:10 → atoning sacrifice → PROPITIATION <2434>.

ATTACHED (BE) – 1 Titus 2:4 → attached to one's husband → loving one's husband → HUSBAND <5362> 2 Titus 2:4 → being attached to one's children → loving one's children → CHILD <5388>.

ATTACK (noun) – 1 Acts 16:22 → to join in the attack → to rise up together → RISE (verb) <4911> 2 Acts 18:12 → to make a united attack → to rise up against → RISE (verb) <2721> 3 Rom. 7:8, 11 → point of attack → OCCASION <874>.

ATTACK (verb) – 1 ***eperchomai*** [verb: ἐπέρχομαι <1904>]; **from *epi*: upon, and *erchomai*: to come ▶ To appear, to arrive; also transl. lit.: to come upon** > Jesus spoke of someone who attacks and who is stronger than the strong man (speaking of Himself and His victory over Satan) (Luke 11:22). All other refs.: COME <1904>.

– 2 Matt. 7:6 → to tear to pieces → TEAR (verb) <4486> 3 Luke 10:30 → to be attacked by robbers → to fall among robbers → FALL (verb) <4045> 4 Luke 18:5 → to completely harass → HARASS <5299> 5 John 10:12 → SEIZE <726> 6 Acts 16:22 → joined in attacking → to rise up together → RISE (verb) <4911> 7 Acts 17:5 → ASSAULT (verb) <2186> 8 Acts 18:10 → to lay on → LAY <2007>.

ATTAIN – 1 ***katalambanō*** [verb: καταλαμβάνω <2638>]; **from *kata*: intens., and *lambanō*: to take ▶ To find, to seize; also transl.: to obtain** > Paul asks if Gentiles, who did not pursue righteousness, attained righteousness (Rom. 9:30). All other refs.: see entries in Lexicon at <2638>.

2 ***katantaō*** [verb: καταντάω <2658>]; **from *kata*: intens., and *antaō*: to meet, from *anta*: face to face ▶ To arrive, to reach** > In Acts 27:12, the majority wanted to attain Phoenix, a harbor in Crete. All other refs.: ARRIVE <2658>, COME <2658>.

3 ***tunchanō*** [verb: τυγχάνω <5177>] **▶ To obtain, to take part; also transl.: to have part** > There are those who are counted worthy to take part in that world {to attain in that age} to come (Luke 20:35). All other refs.: COMMON <5177>, ENJOY <5177>, OBTAIN <5177>, ORDINARY <5177>, PERHAPS <5177>.

– 4 Rom. 9:31; Phil. 3:16 → COME <5348> 5 Gal. 3:3 → to try to attain one's goal → to make perfect → PERFECT (adj.) <2005> 6 1 Tim. 4:6 → FOLLOW <3877>.

ATTAINABLE – Heb. 7:11 → "attainable" added in Engl.

ATTALIA – ***Attaleia*** [fem. name: Ἀττάλεια <825>]: **from Attalos, a king of Pergamum ▶ Seaport in Pamphylia** > Paul passed through Attalia on his way to Antioch during his first missionary journey (Acts 14:25). ¶

ATTEMPT (noun) – 1 ***hormē*** [fem. noun: ὁρμή <3730>]; **from *ornumi*: to excite, to make to rise ▶ Effort to repel, hostile movement** > An attempt {assault, plot, violent attempt} was made to mistreat and

stone Paul and Barnabas (Acts 14:5). Other ref.: Jas. 3:4; see INCLINATION <3730>. ¶
– 2 1 Thes. 2:3 → attempt to deceive → SUBTLETY <1388>.

ATTEMPT (verb) – 1 **attempt:** ***peira*** [fem. noun: πεῖρα <3984>]; **from *peirō*: to pass through, to pierce ▶ Trial, effort** > Attempting {Assaying, Trying} (lit.: Having made an attempt} to cross the Red Sea, the Egyptians were drowned (Heb. 11:29). Other ref.: Heb. 11:36; see TRIAL <3984>. ¶
– 2 Acts 9:26; 26:21 → TRY[1] <3987> 3 Acts 9:29 → SEEK <2021> 4 Acts 16:7; 24:6 → TRY[1] <3985> 5 Acts 19:13 → to take in hand → TAKE <2021>.

ATTEND – 1 **to attend continually: *proskartereō*** [verb: προσκαρτερέω <4342>]; **from *pros*: to, and *kartereō*: to be strong ▶ To persevere, to apply oneself, which is from *karteros*: strength** > Those to whom taxes are paid attend continually {devote themselves, give their full time} to being God's officers (Rom. 13:6). All other refs.: CONTINUE <4342>, PERSEVERING <4342>, READY <4342>.
– 2 Matt. 4:11 → SERVE <1247> 3 Acts 16:14 → to give heed → HEED (noun) <4337> 4 Acts 24:23 → MINISTER (verb) <5256> 5 1 Cor. 7:35 → to attend upon → DEVOTION <2137a> 6 1 Cor. 9:13 → to attend at, to attend to → SERVE <4332>.

ATTENDANCE – **to give attendance: *prosechō*** [verb: προσέχω <4337>]; **from *pros*: to, and *echō*: to have, to hold ▶ To give heed, to give attention** > Timothy was to give attendance {give himself, devote himself} to reading, exhortation, and teaching (1 Tim. 4:13). No man of Judah's tribe gave attendance {has officiated, has been attached to the service} at the altar (Heb. 7:13). All other refs.: BEWARE <4337>, GIVE <4337>, HEED (noun) <4337>.

ATTENDANT – 1 ***hupēretēs*** [masc. noun: ὑπηρέτης <5257>]; **from *hupo*: under, and *eretēs*: rower ▶ Servant particularly charged with executing the commands of the Sanhedrin or the synagogue** > Jesus gave the book back to the attendant (Luke 4:20). All other refs.: MINISTER (noun) <5257>, OFFICER <5257>, SERVANT <5257>.
– 2 Matt. 14:2 → SERVANT <3816> 3 Matt. 22:13 → SERVANT <1249> 4 Acts 10:7 → to be an attendant → CONTINUE <4342>.

ATTENTION – 1 **to give attention: *epechō*** [verb: ἐπέχω <1907>]; **from *epi*: upon, and *echō*: to have ▶ To observe, to give heed** > The lame man gave attention {fixed his attention, gave heed} to Peter and John (Acts 3:5). All other refs.: HEED (noun) <1907>, HOLD (verb) <1907>, REMARK <1907>, STAY (verb) <1907>.
– 2 Matt. 6:28 → to observe with attention → CONSIDER <2648> 3 Matt. 7:3; Luke 6:41 → to pay attention → CONSIDER <2657> 4 Matt. 22:5 → to pay no attention → to make light → LIGHT (adj.) <272> 5 Matt. 22:16; Mark 12:14 → to pay attention → REGARD (verb) <991> 6 Matt. 24:1 → to call the attention → SHOW (verb) <1925> 7 Mark 4:24 → to pay attention → SEE <991> 8 Luke 17:3; Acts 8:6, 10, 11; 16:14; 20:28; 1 Tim. 1:4; 4:1; Titus 1:14; Heb. 2:1; 2 Pet. 1:19 → to give attention, to pay attention, to pay close attention → to give heed → HEED (noun) <4337> 9 Acts 6:4 → to give one's attention → CONTINUE <4342> 10 Acts 18:17 → to pay attention to → to care about → CARE <3199> 11 Acts 26:26 → to escape the attention, to escape the notice → HIDDEN (BE) <2990> 12 Acts 27:11 → to pay attention → PERSUADED (BE) <3982> 13 1 Tim. 4:13 → to give attention → ATTENDANCE <4337> 14 Titus 3:8 → to pay diligent attention → MAINTAIN <4291> 15 Jas. 2:3 → to pay attention, to pay special attention, to show attention → to look upon → LOOK (verb) <1914> 16 3 John 10 → to call attention → REMIND <5279>.

ATTENTIVE – Luke 19:48 → to be very attentive → to hang on → HANG <1582>.

ATTEST – [1] Acts 2:22 → APPROVE <584> [2] Heb. 2:3 → CONFIRM <950>.

ATTIRE – 1 Tim. 2:9 → CLOTHING <2441>.

ATTITUDE – [1] Rom. 15:5; Phil. 3:15 → to have the attitude → THINK <5426> [2] Phil. 2:5 → to have the attitude, to let the attitude be → MIND (verb) <5426> [3] Heb. 4:12 → INTENT <1771> [4] 1 Pet. 4:1 → MIND (noun) <1771>.

ATTORNEY – Acts 24:1 → ORATOR <4489>.

ATTRACTIVE – Titus 2:10 → to make attractive → ADORN <2885>.

AUDACITY – Luke 11:8 → shameless audacity → PERSISTENCE <335>.

AUDIENCE – [1] Acts 13:16; 15:12; 22:22 → to give audience → HEAR <191> [2] Acts 25:23 → hall of audience, audience room → place of hearing → HEARING <201>.

AUDITORIUM – Acts 25:23 → place of hearing → HEARING <201>.

AUGUSTAN – Acts 27:1 → see AUGUSTUS <4575>.

AUGUSTUS – [1] ***Augoustos*** [masc. name: Αὔγουστος <828>]: **venerable ▶ Title given to the Roman emperors** > The first emperor of Rome was Octavius, great-nephew of Gaius Julius Caesar; he was the first one to take up this title, having himself called Caesar Augustus (Luke 2:1). ¶

[2] ***Sebastos*** [adj. used as masc. name and adj.: Σεβαστός <4575>]; **from *sebazomai*: to venerate ▶ Title of Roman emperors** > Nero was called Augustus (venerable, in Lat.) (Acts 25:21, 25). A company was named after Augustus (or Augustan cohort) (Acts 27:1). ¶

AUSTERE – Luke 19:21, 22 → HARSH <840>.

AUTHOR – [1] ***aitios*** [adj. used as noun: αἴτιος <159>] **▶ Who is the cause, the active source** > Christ became the author {source} of eternal salvation to all who obey Him (Heb. 5:9). ¶

[2] ***archēgos*** [masc. noun: ἀρχηγός <747>]; **from *archē*: beginning, rule, and *agō*: to lead ▶ Chief, initiator** > Jesus is the author {leader} and completer of the faith of Christians (Heb. 12:2). All other refs.: CAPTAIN <747>, PRINCE <747>.

AUTHORITY – [1] ***exousia*** [fem. noun: ἐξουσία <1849>]; **from *exesti*: it is permissible, which is from *ek*: out, and *eimi*: to be ▶ Liberty, capacity, power to act; also transl.: power, right** > The Son of Man had authority on earth to forgive sins (Matt. 9:6; Mark 2:10; Luke 5:24). Seeing a man healed and his sins forgiven by Jesus, the crowds glorified God who gave such authority to men (Matt. 9:8). God has authority to cast into hell (Luke 12:5). The chief priests and the scribes wanted to deliver Jesus up to the power (*archē*) and authority (*exousia*) of the governor (Luke 20:20). At Gethsemane, the authority of darkness was present (Luke 22:53). Jesus had the authority to lay down His life and the authority to take it again (John 10:18a, b). Pilate said he had the authority to release Jesus and the authority to crucify Him (John 19:10a, b); Jesus answered that he would have had no authority over Him, if it had not been given to him from above (v. 11). Simon the magician wanted to obtain the authority {ability} to transmit the Holy Spirit (Acts 8:19). Before his conversion, Paul had the authority to bind those who called on the name of Jesus (Acts 9:14) and to shut them up in prison (Acts 26:10, 12). He had been sent so that the nations might turn from the authority {dominion} of Satan to God (Acts 26:18). The potter has authority {a right} over the clay (Rom. 9:21). The Father has delivered Christians from the authority {domain, dominion} of darkness (Col. 1:13). Jude uses this word in his closing doxology (Jude 25). Authority was given to Death over one-fourth of the earth (Rev. 6:8). Authority was also given to the locusts (Rev.

9:3a, b, 10). The two witnesses have power to shut the heaven and to turn the waters into blood (Rev. 11:6a, b). A great voice said that the power (*dunamis*), the kingdom of God, and the authority (*exousia*) of Christ had come (Rev. 12:10). The dragon gave the beast his power (*dunamis*), his throne, and great authority (*exousia*) (Rev. 13:2, 4, 5, 7). The second beast exercises all the authority of the first beast (Rev. 13:12). An angel, having authority over {charge of} fire, came out of the altar (Rev. 14:18); another angel will descend out of heaven, having great authority (18:1). God has authority {control} over the plagues that He will send (Rev. 16:9). Ten kings will receive authority with the beast (Rev. 17:12); they will give their power (*dunamis*) and authority (*exousia*) to the beast (v. 13). The second death has no authority over him who has part in the first resurrection (Rev. 20:6). The term designates also the authority of the Father (Acts 1:7), the authority of the Lord Jesus (Matt. 7:29; 21:23a, b, 24, 27; 28:18; Mark 1:22, 27; 11:28a, b, 29, 33; Luke 4:32, 36; 20:2a, b, 8; John 5:27; 17:2), the authority given to the apostles (Matt. 10:1; Mark 3:15; 6:7; Luke 9:1; 10:19; 2 Cor. 10:8; 13:10), Satan's authority (Luke 4:6; Eph. 2:2), and the authority of the one who overcomes (Rev. 2:26). The centurion was under the authority of someone else (Matt. 8:9; Luke 7:8). In a parable, the servants received authority (Mark 13:34). The word applies also to men or angels in a position of authority (Luke 12:11; Rom. 13:1a, b, 2, 3; 1 Cor. 15:24; Eph. 1:21; 3:10; 6:12; Col. 1:16; 2:10, 15; Titus 3:1; 1 Pet. 3:22 {authorities}). A slave in a parable received authority over ten cities (Luke 19:17). The woman must have authority, i.e., a symbol of authority, on her head because of the angels (1 Cor. 11:10; see vv. 3, 4). In 1 Cor. 7:37, "who has power over his own will" is lit.: who has authority over his own will. Other refs.: Luke 23:7 {jurisdiction}; John 1:12 {right}; Acts 5:4 {control, disposal}; 1 Cor. 8:9 {liberty}; 9:4–6, 12, 18 {right}; 2 Thes. 3:9 {right}; Heb. 13:10 {right}; Rev. 9:19 {power}; 22:14 {right}. ¶

2 to exercise authority, to have authority: *exousiazō* [verb: ἐξουσιάζω <1850>]**; from *exousia*: see 1 ► a. To dominate** > Those who exercise authority over the nations are called benefactors (Luke 22:25). **b. To have power, to have liberty** > The wife has not authority over her own body, but the husband; in like manner also, the husband does not have authority over his own body, but the wife (1 Cor. 7:4a, b). Other ref.: 1 Cor. 6:12; see POWER[2] <1850>. ¶

3 to exercise authority: *katexousiazō* [verb: κατεξουσιάζω <2715>]**; from *kata*: against (intens.), and *exousiazō*: see 2 ► To dominate, to rule** > Great men exercise authority over the Gentiles (Matt. 20:25; Mark 10:42). ¶

4 of authority, who has authority: *dunatos* [adj.: δυνατός <1415>]**; from *dunamai*: to be able, i.e., to be capable ► Which has certain capabilities, qualified; also transl.: influential, leader, who is able** > Festus wanted men of authority to come down with him to Jerusalem to accuse Paul if he had done anything wrong (Acts 25:5). Other refs.: see entries in Lexicon at <1415>.

5 *epitagē* [fem. noun: ἐπιταγή <2003>]**; from *epitassō*: to command, which is from *epi*: upon, over, and *tassō*: to give orders, to command ► Power, right to command** > Titus could rebuke with all authority (Titus 2:15). All other refs.: see COMMANDMENT <2003>.

6 to usurp authority: *authenteō* [verb: αὐθεντέω <831>]**; from *authentēs*: one who acts of himself, absolute master, murderer, which is from *autos*: himself, and *entea*: arms, armor ► To dominate** > Paul does not permit a woman to usurp authority {have authority, exercise authority} over the man (1 Tim. 2:12). ¶

7 in authority: pres. ptcp. of *huperechō* [verb: ὑπερέχω <5242>]**: to surpass, which is from *huper*: over, above, and *echō*: to have ► Which is above** > Christians should submit themselves for the Lord's sake to every human institution, e.g., to a king as the one in authority {as supreme; lit.: as being supreme} (1 Pet. 2:13). All other refs.: EXCELLENCE <5242>, GOVERNING

<5242>, IMPORTANT <5242>, SURPASS <5242>.

8 ***huperochē*** [fem. noun: ὑπεροχή <5247>]; **from *huperechō*: see 7 ▶ Preeminence, the fact of holding authority** > We should pray for all who are in authority {dignity} (1 Tim. 2:2). Other ref.: 1 Cor. 2:1; see EXCELLENCE <5247>. ¶

– 9 Luke 22:25; Rom. 7:1 → to have authority, to exercise authority → to have dominion → DOMINION <2961> 10 John 7:17, 18, 28; 8:28 → on one's own authority → lit.: of oneself 11 John 7:26, 48; 12:42 → RULER <758> 12 Acts 8:27 → of great authority → court official → OFFICIAL <1413> 13 Acts 16:19 → MAGISTRATE <758> 14 Acts 17:6, 8 → city authority → ruler of the city → RULER <4173> 15 Rom. 13:4 → the one in authority → lit.: he 16 Rom. 13:6 → MINISTER (noun) <3011> 17 1 Cor. 9:8 → on human authority → lit.: according to man 18 2 Cor. 11:17 → with the Lord's authority → lit.: according (*kata*) to the Lord 19 1 Thes. 2:6 → to assert authority → to be a burden → BURDEN (noun) <922> 20 1 Pet. 2:13 → INSTITUTION <2937> 21 2 Pet. 2:10; Jude 8 → DOMINION <2963> 22 2 Pet. 2:10 → DIGNITARY <1391> 23 3 John 9 → does not acknowledge our authority → does not receive us → RECEIVE <1926>.

AUTHORIZATION – Acts 15:24 → without our authorization → lit.: we have not given a commandment → COMMANDMENT <1291>.

AUTHORIZE – Luke 3:13 → ORDAIN <1299>.

AUTUMN – 1 Jas. 5:7 → EARLY <4406> 2 Jude 12 → late autumn → AUTUMNAL <5352>.

AUTUMNAL – ***phthinopōrinos*** [adj.: φθινοπωρινός <5352>]; **from *phthinō*: to decline, to arrive at its term, and *opōra*: autumn ▶ Of the end of the season, of late autumn** > Jude speaks of certain men who have crept in unnoticed among the faithful and who are like autumnal {late autumn} trees without fruit, twice dead (Jude 12). ¶

AVAIL – 1 Matt. 27:24 → PREVAIL <5623> 2 Gal. 5:6 → to have value → VALUE (noun) <2480>.

AVARICIOUS – 1 Cor. 5:10, 11 → COVETOUS (noun) <4123>.

AVENGE – 1 ***ekdikeō*** [verb: ἐκδικέω <1556>]; **from *ekdikos*: avenger, which is from *ek*: from, out, and *dikē*: justice ▶ To obtain justice, to punish** > A widow asked a judge to avenge her of {to get justice for her from, to grant her justice against, to give her legal protection from} her adversary (Luke 18:3, 5). Christians are not to avenge themselves {to take their own revenge} (Rom. 12:19). The souls of those who had been slain for the word of God asked the Lord to avenge their blood on those who dwell on the earth (Rev. 6:10). God will avenge the blood of His servants, calling the great prostitute to account for it (Rev. 19:2). Other ref.: 2 Cor. 10:6; see PUNISH <1556>. ¶

– 2 Luke 18:7, 8 → lit.: to bring about justice → JUSTICE <1557> 3 Luke 21:22; Acts 7:24; Rom. 12:19; Heb. 10:30 → VENGEANCE <1557> 4 Rev. 18:20 → God has avenged; lit.: God has judged the cause → JUDGE (verb) <2919>, CAUSE <2917>.

AVENGER – ***ekdikos*** [masc. noun: ἔκδικος <1558>]; **from *ek*: from, out, and *dikē*: justice ▶ He who does justice, who punishes** > The one in authority is God's servant, an avenger {revenger} who brings wrath on the one who practices evil (Rom. 13:4). The Lord is the avenger in matters of one who wrongs his brother (1 Thes. 4:6). ¶

AVENGING – Luke 21:22; 2 Cor. 7:11 → avenging, avenging of wrong → VENGEANCE <1557>.

AVOID – 1 ***ekklinō*** [verb: ἐκκλίνω <1578>]; **from *ek*: out, and *klinō*: to fold, to incline ▶ To move away, to turn away**

from someone > Christians must avoid {keep away from} those who cause divisions and occasions of falling (Rom. 16:17). Other refs.: Rom. 3:12; 1 Pet. 3:11; see TURN (verb) <1578>. ¶

2 ***ektrepō*** [verb: ἐκτρέπω <1624>]; **from *ek*: from, and *trepō*: to turn ▶ To shun, to turn away from** > Timothy was to avoid profane and empty chatter (1 Tim. 6:20). All other refs.: DISLOCATE <1624>, TURN (verb) <1624>.

3 ***paraiteomai*** [verb: παραιτέομαι <3868>]; **from *para*: aside, and *aiteō*: to ask ▶ To reject, to refuse; also transl.: to have nothing to do with** > Timothy was to avoid profane fables (1 Tim. 4:7). He had also to avoid foolish and senseless questionings (2 Tim. 2:23). Titus was to avoid {to be done with, to reject} a heretical man (Titus 3:10). All other refs.: BEG <3868>, EXCUSE (verb) <3868>, REFUSE (verb) <3868>.

4 ***stellō*** [verb: στέλλω <4724>] ▶ **To stay at a distance, to shun, to withdraw** > Paul was avoiding {taking precaution} that anyone should blame him concerning the gift he was administering (2 Cor. 8:20). He exhorted the Thessalonians to withdraw from {to keep away from} every brother walking disorderly (2 Thes. 3:6). ¶

– 5 Acts 15:29 → KEEP (verb) <1301> 6 Rom. 13:4 → to avoid → lit.: because of (*dia*) 7 1 Thes. 4:3; 5:22 → ABSTAIN <567> 8 2 Tim. 2:16; Titus 3:9 → SHUN <4026> 9 2 Tim. 3:5 → to turn away → TURN (verb) <665>.

AVOW – 1 Matt. 7:23 → DECLARE <3670> 2 Acts 24:14 → CONFESS <3670>.

AWAIT – 1 ***menō*** [verb: μένω <3306>] ▶ **To remain for someone, to be in store** > Bonds and afflictions were awaiting {were abiding} Paul (Acts 20:23). All other refs.: CONTINUE <3306>, LASTING <3306>, REMAIN <3306>, STAY (verb) <3306>, TARRY <3306>.

– 2 Mark 15:43; Luke 2:25 → to wait for → WAIT (verb) <4327> 3 Luke 1:21 → to wait for → WAIT (verb) <4328> 4 Acts 1:4 → to wait for → WAIT (verb) <4037> 5 Rom. 8:23; 1 Cor. 1:7; Gal. 5:5; Phil. 3:20 → to wait eagerly → WAIT (verb) <553>

6 1 Thes. 1:10 → to wait for → WAIT (verb) <362> 7 Titus 2:13; Jude 21 → to look for → LOOK (verb) <4327> 8 Jas. 5:7 → WAIT (verb) <1551>.

AWAKE (adj.) – 1 Matt. 24:43; Mark 13:34, 35, 37; Luke 12:37; 1 Thes. 5:6, 10; Rev. 16:15 → to be, keep, stay awake → WATCH (verb) <1127> 2 Mark 13:33; Luke 21:36 → to keep awake, to stay awake → WATCH (verb) <69> 3 Luke 12:38 → lit.: so (*outō*) 4 1 Cor. 4:4 → to be aware → KNOW <4894>.

AWAKE (verb) – 1 **to awake up: *ananēphō*** [verb: ἀνανήφω <366>]; **from *ana*: again, and *nēphō*: to be sober; lit.: to remain sober ▶ To come to one's senses** > Those who oppose a servant of the Lord may awake up {wake up, recover themselves} out of the snare of the devil (2 Tim. 2:26). ¶

2 ***eknēphō*** [verb: ἐκνήφω <1594>]; **from *ek*: out of, and *nēphō*: to be sober; lit.: to sober up ▶ To come back to reason, to become sober-minded** > The Corinthians were to awake to righteousness (lit.: to awake righteously) {to become sober-minded, to come back to their senses} so they might live righteously (1 Cor. 15:34). ¶

– 3 Matt. 1:24; 8:25; Rom. 13:11; et al. → to wake up → WAKE <1453> 4 Mark 4:39; Luke 8:24 → to wake up → WAKE <1326> 5 John 11:11 → to awake out of sleep → WAKE UP <1852>.

AWAKE (BE) – **to be fully awake: *diagrēgoreō*** [verb: διαγρηγορέω <1235>]; **from *dia*: through (intens.), and *grēgoreō*: to awake ▶ To be fully alert** > Being fully awake, Peter, James, and John saw the glory of Jesus with Moses and Elijah (Luke 9:32). ¶

AWAKENED – Acts 16:27 → awakened out of sleep → SLEEP (noun) <1853>.

AWAKING – Acts 16:27 → awaking from sleep, awaking out of sleep → SLEEP (noun) <1853>.

AWARD – 2 Tim. 4:8 → GIVE <591>.

AWARE – 1 **to be aware, to become aware: *suneidō*** [verb: συνείδω <4894>]**; from *sun*: together, and *eidō*: to know; also transl.: to find out, to be ware ▶ To know, to be conscious, to find out** > Paul and Barnabas became aware that people wanted to mistreat them (Acts 14:6). All other refs.: CONSCIOUS <4894>, CONSIDER <4894>, KNOW <4894>, PRIVY <4894>.
– 2 Matt. 12:15; 16:8; 22:18; 24:50; 26:10; Mark 8:17; 15:10; Luke 8:46; 9:11; 12:46 → to be aware → KNOW <1097> 3 Mark 5:33; Luke 11:44; John 6:61; Acts 23:5; 1 Thes. 5:2; 2 Tim. 1:15 → to be aware → KNOW <1492> 4 Acts 10:28 → to be aware → KNOW <1987>.

AWAY – 1 **to do away: *katargeō*** [verb: καταργέω <2673>]**; from *kata*: intens., and *argeō*: to be inactive, which is from *argos*: idle, useless, which is from *a*: neg., and *ergon*: work ▶ To be abolished by becoming of no effect; also transl.: to annul, to disappear, to fade, to pass away, to remove** > Prophecies, says Paul, shall be done away, and knowledge shall be done away (1 Cor. 13:8a, b), for when that which is perfect has come, that which is in part shall be done away (v. 10). The glory of the face of Moses was to be done away {to fade away, to pass away} (2 Cor. 3:7). Other refs.: 2 Cor. 3:11, 13, 14. All other refs.: see entries in Lexicon at <2673>.
2 ***apo*** [prep.: ἀπό <575>] ▶ **At a distance of** > Bethany was near Jerusalem, about two miles (fifteen stadia in Greek) away {off} (John 11:18). Other refs.: DISTANCE <575>.
3 For the preposition *apo* used with a verb (to carry, to depart, to go, to move, to turn, etc.), see the verb of interest.
– 4 Matt. 7:23 → away from me → lit.: depart from me → DEPART <672> 5 Matt. 9:31, 32 → to go away → GO <1831> 6 Matt. 13:53 → to go away → DEPART <3332> 7 Matt. 19:15 → to go away → DEPART <4198> 8 Luke 13:27 → away from me → lit.: depart from me → DEPART <868> 9 2 Cor. 5:6, 8, 9 → to be away → ABSENT (BE) <1553> 10 2 Cor. 10:1; 13:10 → to be away → ABSENT (BE) <548> 11 2 Thes. 3:6 → to keep away → WITHDRAW <4724> 12 Heb. 10:9 → to do away → to take away → TAKE <337>.

AWE – 1 Matt. 9:8 → to be filled with awe → to be afraid → AFRAID <5399> 2 Matt. 27:54 → to be filled with awe → FEAR (verb) <5399> 3 Luke 1:65; 5:26; 7:16; Acts 2:43 → FEAR (noun) <5401> 4 Heb. 12:28 → godly fear → FEAR (noun) <1189a>.

AWESOME – ***epiphanēs*** [adj.: ἐπιφανής <2016>]**; from *epiphainō*: to shine upon, which is from *epi*: upon, and *phainō*: to shine, which is from *phōs*: light ▶ Illustrious, glorious, splendid** > The sun will be changed to darkness and the moon to blood before the coming of the great and awesome {gloriously appearing, notable} day of the Lord (Acts 2:20). ¶

AX – Matt. 3:10; Luke 3:9 → AXE.

AXE – ***axinē*** [fem. noun: ἀξίνη <513>]**; prob. from *agnumi*: to break ▶ Tool for chopping trees and splitting wood** > The axe is applied to the root of the trees (poss. an illustration of the Jews in the time of the Lord) not producing good fruit for God (Matt. 3:10; Luke 3:9); other ref.: Luke 13:7 in some mss. ¶

AZOR – ***Azōr*** [masc. name: Ἀζώρ <107>]**: helper, in Heb. ▶ Man in the O.T.** > Azor is mentioned in the genealogy of Jesus Christ (Matt. 1:13, 14). ¶

AZOTUS – ***Azōtos*** [fem. name: Ἄζωτος <108>]**: ravager, in Heb. ▶ City located between Gaza and Joppa, a few kilometers from the Mediterranean; in the O.T., it is called Ashdod** > Philip was found in Azotus after the Ethiopian's conversion and baptism (Acts 8:40). ¶

 B 

BAAL – ***Baal*** [masc. name: Βάαλ <896>]: **lord, owner, in Heb. ▶ Main deity of the Phoenicians and the Canaanites** > Many Israelites had worshipped Baal, a pagan deity (Rom. 11:4); this deity symbolizes idolatry. ¶

BABBLE (noun) – 1 Tim. 6:20; 2 Tim. 2:16 → BABBLING <2757>.

BABBLE (verb) – Matt. 6:7 → to keep on babbling → to use vain repetitions → REPETITION <945>.

BABBLER – ***spermologos*** [masc. noun: σπερμολόγος <4691>]; **from *sperma*: seed, and *legō*: to gather; lit.: gatherer of seeds ▶ One who collects and communicates pieces of information** > Paul was accused by the philosophers in Athens of being a babbler {chatterer} (Acts 17:18). ¶

BABBLING – **idle babbling: *kenophōnia*** [fem. noun: κενοφωνία <2757>]; **from *kenos*: empty, vain, and *phonē*: sound, voice ▶ Discussion without interest, foolish talk** > Timothy was to avoid profane and idle babblings {vain babblings, empty chatter, godless chatter} (1 Tim. 6:20) and shun them (2 Tim. 2:16). ¶

BABE – 1 ***brephos*** [neut. noun: βρέφος <1025>] **▶ Baby, infant; also infant in the womb of the mother or older infant; also transl.: young child** > The babe John the Baptist leaped in Elizabeth's womb (Luke 1:41, 44). The shepherds found the babe Jesus lying in the manger (Luke 2:12, 16). Christians must desire the pure milk of the word as newborn babes (1 Pet. 2:2). Other refs.: Luke 18:15; Acts 7:19; 2 Tim. 3:15 {childhood}. ¶
2 ***nēpios*** [adj. and adj. used as noun: νήπιος <3516>]; **from *nē*: neg., and *epos*: word; lit.: who does not speak ▶ Infant, baby, child** > The Father has revealed things to babes (Matt. 11:25; Luke 10:21). God has perfected praise through the mouths of babes (*nēpios*) and nursing infants (*thēlazōntos*) {of infants and nursing babes} (Matt. 21:16). Paul speaks of a Jew who is a teacher of babes {the immature} (Rom. 2:20). He had spoken to the Corinthians as babes in Christ (1 Cor. 3:1). Christians should no longer be babes tossed and carried about by every wind of teaching (Eph. 4:14). Everyone who partakes of milk is unskilled in the word of righteousness, for he is a babe (Heb. 5:13). The word "babe" {child, childish} is found five times in 1 Cor. 13:11. Other refs.: Gal. 4:1, 3; 1 Thes. 2:7; see CHILD <3516>. ¶
– 3 1 Cor. 14:20 → to be babes → to be children → CHILD <3515>.

BABY – Luke 1:41, 44; 2:12, 16; 18:15; Acts 7:19; 1 Pet. 2:2 → BABE <1025>.

BABYLON – ***Babulōn*** [fem. name: Βαβυλών <897>]; **from Babel: confusion, in Heb.; see Gen. 11:1–9 ▶ a. Capital of Babylonia (or Chaldea), country of western Asia, east of Palestine. The Jews were deported to Babylon by Nebuchadnezzar in 606 B.C.** > A remnant of Jews came back from Babylon to Jerusalem after a captivity lasting 70 years to reconstruct the Temple (Matt. 1:11, 12, 17a, b; Acts 7:43). **b. City where a church might have existed** > A Christian sister from Babylon sent greetings to the Christians of the dispersion (1 Pet. 5:13). **c. Mystical name of heathen Rome** > Babylon will be destroyed by the Beast, i.e., the head of the restored Roman Empire (Rev. 14:8; 16:19; 17:5; 18:2, 10, 21). ¶

BACK (adv. and noun) – 1 **on the back: *opisthen*** [adv.: ὄπισθεν <3693>]; **from *opis*: a looking back, and suffix *then*: from or at a place ▶ On the reverse, on the outside** > John saw in the right hand of Him who sat on the throne a book, written inside and on the back {on the backside} (Rev. 5:1). All other refs.: BEHIND <3693>.
2 ***opisō*** [adv.: ὀπίσω <3694>]; **from *opis*: a looking back ▶ To the rear, in the back** > During the great tribulation, he who is in the field should not turn back to get his clothes (Matt. 24:18; Mark 13:16; Luke 17:31). A man who has put his hand to the plow and looks back is not fit for the kingdom of

God (Luke 9:62). Mary of Magdala turned herself back {turned around} and saw Jesus (John 20:14). *

[3] **to draw back: *aperchomai*** [verb: ἀπέρχομαι <565>]; **from *apo*: from, and *erchomai*: to go to; backward: *opisō*** [adv.: ὀπίσω <3694>]; **from *opis*: a looking back (lit.: to go away backward); to go away ▶ To move to the rear** > When Jesus had said to those who accompanied Judas that it was He whom they were seeking, they drew back (lit.: they went away backward) and fell to the ground (John 18:6). All other refs. (*aperchomai*): see entries in Lexicon at <565>.

– [4] Acts 20:20 → to keep back → KEEP (verb) <5288> [5] Phm. 15 → to have back → POSSESS <568>.

BACK (noun) – ***nōtos*** [masc. noun: νῶτος <3577>] ▶ **Part of the body opposite to the front, between the shoulders and the end of the spine** > David asked God to always bend the back of his enemies (Rom. 11:10). ¶

BACKBITER – ***katalalos*** [adj. used as noun: κατάλαλος <2637>]; **from *katalaleō*: to speak against, which is from *kata*: against, and *laleō*: to speak ▶ One who speaks against another; also transl.: slanderer** > In Rom. 1:30, the Greek word has the meaning of a "calumniator." ¶

BACKBITING – ***katalalia*** [fem. noun: καταλαλιά <2636>]; **from *katalaleō*: to speak against, which is from *kata*: against, and *laleō*: to speak ▶ The action of speaking evil of someone, instead of passing over a matter in silence** > Paul feared he would find backbitings {evil speaking, slanders} among the Corinthians (2 Cor. 12:20). In 1 Pet. 2:1, the Greek word is transl. "evil speaking" {slander}: Christians must reject all evil speakings. ¶

BACKSIDE – Rev. 5:1 → on the backside → on the back → BACK (adv. and noun) <3693>.

BACKWARD – John 18:6 → to go away backward → to draw back → BACK (adv. and noun) <565>.

BAD – [1] ***atopos*** [adj.: ἄτοπος <824>]; **from *a*: out of, and *topos*: place; lit.: which is out of place ▶ Wicked, perverse** > Paul requested prayer that he might be delivered from bad (*atopos*) and evil (*ponēros*) {perverse and evil, unreasonable and wicked, wicked and evil} men (2 Thes. 3:2). Other refs.: Luke 23:41 {amiss, wrong}; Acts 25:5 {improper}; 28:6 {harm, unusual}. ¶

[2] ***sapros*** [adj.: σαπρός <4550>]; **from *sēpō*: to cause to rot ▶ Corrupted, rotten; of bad quality** > The Greek word is generally transl. "bad," but also "corrupt." It is used in relation to trees (Matt. 7:17a, 18b; 12:33a; Luke 6:43b), fruit (Matt. 12:33b; Luke 6:43a), and fish (Matt. 13:48). No corrupt {unwholesome} word should proceed out of the mouth of Christians (Eph. 4:29). ¶

– [3] Matt. 6:23; 7:17b, 18a; 22:10; Luke 11:34 → EVIL (adj.) <4190> [4] Luke 16:25; 2 Cor. 5:10 → EVIL (noun) <2556> [5] Acts 28:21 → EVIL (noun) <4190> [6] Rom. 9:11; Titus 2:8 → EVIL (adj.) <5337> [7] Rom. 13:3; 1 Cor. 15:33 → EVIL (adj.) <2556>.

BAFFLE – Acts 9:22 → CONFOUND <4797>.

BAG – [1] ***glōssokomon*** [neut. noun: γλωσσόκομον <1101>]; **from *glōssa*: tongue, and *komeō*: to take care; lit.: case for the tongues of a flute ▶ Case to put money** > Judas had the bag {money box, money bag} in which was put the money for food and the poor (John 12:6; 13:29); some mss. add: and used to take what was put in it. ¶

[2] ***pēra*** [fem. noun: πήρα <4082>] ▶ **Sack for provisions, usually of leather** > Carrying such a sack {scrip} is associated with undertaking a journey (Matt. 10:10; Mark 6:8; Luke 9:3; 10:4; 22:35, 36). ¶

– [3] Matt. 18:24; 25:15a, 16a, b, 20a, b, 22a, b, 24, 28a, b → bag, bag of gold → lit.: talent → TALENT <5007> [4] Matt. 25:15b, c, 17, 18 → two bags, one bag →

lit.: two, one 5 Luke 10:4; 12:33; 22:35, 36 → money bag → PURSE <905>.

BALAAM – ***Balaam*** [masc. name: Βαλαάμ <903>]: **not of the people, i.e., foreigner, in Heb. ▶ A soothsayer in the O.T. >** Balaam taught Balak to entice the Israelites to sin; the doctrine of Balaam is associated with idolatry and sexual immorality (Rev. 2:14; see Num. 31:16). He was killed by the children of Israel (see Josh. 13:22). Other refs.: 2 Pet. 2:15; Jude 11. ¶

BALAC – Rev. 2:14 → BALAK <904>.

BALAK – ***Balak*** [masc. name: Βαλάκ <904>]: **spoiler, devastator, in Heb. ▶ King of Moab >** Balak convinced Balaam to curse Israel (Rev. 2:14; see Num. 22:5, 6). ¶

BALANCE – ***zugos*** [masc. noun: ζυγός <2218>]; **from *zeugnumi*: to harness; first meaning: yoke ▶ Instrument with two pans to weigh objects >** In John's vision, he who sat on the black horse had a balance {pair of balances, pair of scales} in his hand (Rev. 6:5). Other refs.: Matt. 11:29, 30; Acts 15:10; Gal. 5:1; 1 Tim. 6:1; see YOKE <2218>. ¶

BAND (noun)[1] – 1 ***zeuktēria*** [fem. noun: ζευκτηρία <2202>]; **from *zeugnumi*: to put under the yoke, to join ▶ Rope, chain >** Loosing the rudder bands on Paul's boat, those on board hoisted the mainsail and made for shore (Acts 27:40). ¶
– 2 Mark 7:35; Luke 8:29; Acts 16:26 → CHAIN (noun) <1199> 3 Col. 2:19 → BOND[1] <4886> 4 Rev. 1:13; 15:6 → BELT <2223>.

BAND (noun)[2] – Matt. 27:27; Mark 15:16; John 18:3, 12; Acts 10:1; 21:31; 27:1 → COHORT <4686>.

BAND (verb) – 1 Acts 4:26 → to band together → to gather together → GATHER <4863> 2 Acts 23:12 → to band together → lit.: to form a conspiracy → CONSPIRACY <4963>.

BANDAGE – Luke 10:34 → BIND <2611>.

BANDIT – 2 Cor. 11:26 → ROBBER <3027>.

BANISH – Rom. 11:26 → to turn away → TURN (verb) <654>.

BANK[1] – 1 ***trapeza*** [fem. noun: τράπεζα <5132>]; **from *tessares* or *tetra*: four, and *pous* or *peza*: foot ▶ Table (as having four legs), in particular to exchange money; a place to deposit money >** In the parable, the master told his servant he should have put his money in the bank {on deposit} (Luke 19:23). All other refs.: TABLE[1] <5132>.
– 2 Matt. 25:27 → EXCHANGER <5133>.

BANK[2] – 1 Matt. 8:32; Mark 5:13; Luke 8:33 → steep bank → steep place → PLACE (noun) <2911> 2 Luke 19:43 → to throw up a bank → to build around → BUILD <4016>.

BANKER – Matt. 25:27 → EXCHANGER <5133>.

BANQUET – 1 Matt. 22:2; et al. → wedding banquet → WEDDING <1062> 2 Matt. 23:6; Mark 6:21; 12:39; Luke 14:12, 16, 17, 24; 20:46 → SUPPER <1173> 3 Luke 5:29; 14:13 → FEAST (noun) <1403> 4 John 2:8, 9a, b → master of the banquet → master of the feast → FEAST (noun) <755>.

BANQUETING – 1 Pet. 4:3 → DRINKING <4224>.

BAPTISM – 1 ***baptisma*** [neut. noun: βάπτισμα <908>]; **to baptize: *baptizō*** [verb: βαπτίζω <907>]; **from *baptō*: to dip, to immerse ▶ a. Christians who have been baptized with Christ Jesus have been baptized for His death; they have been buried with Him through baptism into death to walk in newness of life (read Col. 2:12; Rom. 6:4; Gal. 3:27). >** Jesus told the eleven apostles to make disciples of all the nations, baptizing them in the name of the

Father and of the Son and of the Holy Spirit (Matt. 28:19; Mark 16:16). Peter exhorts in Acts 2 to repent and be baptized in the name of Jesus Christ (v. 38); about three thousand souls received his word and were baptized at that time (v. 41). There are many references to the baptism of Christians (Acts 8:12, 13, 16, 36, 38; 9:18; 10:47, 48; 16:15, 33; 18:8; 19:5; 22:16; Rom. 6:3a, b; 1 Cor. 1:13–15; Eph. 4:5). Paul had baptized the household of Stephanas (1 Cor. 1:16a, b); however, Christ had not sent him to baptize, but to preach the gospel (v. 17). The answer of a good conscience toward God goes along with the baptism (1 Pet. 3:21). In addition to this baptism for the death of the Lord Jesus (the Christian baptism), the word of God mentions six other baptisms. **b. Baptism of fire** > In Matt. 3:11b, this baptism corresponds to the judgment of God to be exercised in condemnation (see v. 7) against the one who refuses the proposed salvation. John said that Jesus would baptize with the Holy Spirit (which happened at Pentecost) and with fire (in a future day before His return). **c. Baptism of John** > John was baptizing with water in the Jordan (Matt. 3:6; Mark 1:4; Luke 3:3; John 1:26, 31; Acts 13:24). This baptism was to prepare the Jews to receive a living Christ and to be introduced in His kingdom (Acts 19:4). Jesus Himself was baptized by John the Baptist (Matt. 3:13, 14, 16; Mark 1:9; Luke 3:21a, b), identifying himself by doing so with the repenting remnant of Israel. Jesus baptized in Judea (John 3:22; 4:1), or rather His disciples baptized (4:2). Other refs.: Matt. 21:25; Mark 6:14 (lit.: the baptizing); 11:30; Luke 3:7, 12; 7:29, 30; 20:4; John 3:23a, b, 26; 10:40; Acts 1:5a, 22; 10:37; 11:16a; 18:25; 19:3a, b. **d. Baptism of the death of Jesus** > This baptism corresponds to the sufferings endured on the cross by the Lord Jesus and to His atoning death (Mark 10:38, 39; Luke 12:50). **e. Baptism of the Holy Spirit** > The baptism of the Holy Spirit happened at Pentecost (see Acts 2:1–4) in view of the formation of the church of God in one body, the body of Christ (Matt. 3:11b; Mark 1:8b; Luke 3:16b; John 1:33b). According to the word of the Lord, this baptism occurred a few days after His ascension (Acts 1:5b; 11:16b). By this baptism of the Holy Spirit, all Christians were baptized into one body (1 Cor. 12:13). **f. Baptism for the dead** > This expression is found in 1 Cor. 15:29a, b. **g. Baptism for Moses** > The sons of Israel who crossed the Red Sea (see Ex. 14) were baptized for Moses in the sea (1 Cor. 10:2); they recognized the authority of Moses, leader of the people established by God, to deliver them of Egypt and bring them into the promised land. ¶

[2] ***baptismos*** [masc. noun: βαπτισμός <909>]; **from *baptizō*: see [1] ► The action of washing in relation to Judaic rites of purification** > The term "baptism" {washing, ceremonial washing} is found in Heb. 6:2; 9:10. The Greek word is also transl. "washing" in Mark 7:4, 8 in some mss. ¶

BAPTIST – [1] ***baptistēs*** [masc. name: βαπτιστής <910>]; **from *baptizō*: to baptize, which is from *baptō*: to dip, to immerse ► Surname of John, precursor of Jesus** > This title "Baptist" is used 14 times: Matt. 3:1; 11:11, 12; 14:2, 8; 16:14; 17:13; Mark 6:24, 25; 8:28; Luke 7:20, 28, 33; 9:19. See BAPTISM [1] **c.** ¶

– [2] Mark 6:14 → lit.: the baptizing (*ho baptizōn*) → BAPTISM [1] **c.** <908>.

BAPTIZE – See BAPTISM <907>.

BAPTIZER – See BAPTIST <910>.

BAR-JESUS – ***Bariēsous*** [masc. name: Βαριησοῦς <919>]: **son of Jesus (or: Joshua), in Aram. ► Magician and Jewish false prophet** > Bar-Jesus sought to turn away the proconsul Sergius Paulus from the faith (Acts 13:6); he was struck blind for a time (see v. 11). ¶

BARABBAS – ***Barabbas*** [masc. name: Βαραββᾶς <912>]: **son of the father, in Aram. ► A man imprisoned for murder in the days of the Lord** > The crowd chose to have Barabbas released instead of Jesus (Matt. 27:16, 17, 20, 21, 26; Mark 15:7, 11, 15; Luke 23:18; John 18:40). Some mss.

have Jesus Barabbas as his full name in Matt. 27:16, 17. Barabbas was a robber (John 18:40); he had been imprisoned for murder (see Acts 3:14). ¶

BARACHIAH – Matt. 23:35 → BARACHIAS <914>.

BARACHIAS – ***Barachias*** [masc. name: Βαραχίας <914>]**: blessing of Jehovah, in Heb. ▶ Father of Zechariah, a priest >** His son Zechariah was put to death by his fellow Jews (Matt. 23:35; see 2 Chr. 24:22). ¶

BARAK – ***Barak*** [masc. name: Βαράκ <913>]**: lightning, lightning flash, in Heb. ▶ A man in the O.T. >** Barak is mentioned among the persons of faith in Hebrews 11 (v. 32). Upon the order of Deborah, the prophetess who judged Israel, Barak gathered 10,000 men to go to war against the captain of the army of the king of Canaan. He conquered him and defeated the enemy's army (see Judges 4). ¶

BARBARIAN – ***barbaros*** [adj. and masc. noun: βάρβαρος <915>]**; this Greek word does not have the same pejorative connotation as in Engl. ▶ a. Stranger to the Greek and Roman cultures >** The terms "barbarous people" and "barbarian" are used in Acts 28:2 and 4 {native, islander}; Rom. 1:14 {non-Greek}; Col. 3:11. **b. Person speaking a language which is not understood >** The term "barbarian" {foreigner} is used in 1 Cor. 14:11a, b. ¶

BARBAROUS – Acts 28:2, 4 → barbarous people → BARBARIAN <915>.

BARE – **1** ***gumnos*** [adj.: γυμνός <1131>]; **lit.: naked ▶ Sole, mere >** Paul speaks of a bare grain of wheat (1 Cor. 15:37). All other refs.: NAKED <1131>.

– **2** 1 Cor. 14:25 → laid bare → REVEALED <5318> **3** Heb. 4:13 → to lay bare → OPEN (verb) <5136>.

BARELY – **1** Matt. 13:15; Acts 28:27 → to barely hear → to be hard of hearing → HARD <917> **2** 2 Pet. 2:18 → JUST (adv.) <3643a>.

BARJONAS – ***Bariōnas*** [masc. name: Βαριωνᾶς <920>]**: son of Jonas (or: Jonah), a dove, in Aram. ▶ Surname of Simon, the apostle Peter >** Jesus referred to Peter with this name after Peter declared that He was the Christ, the Son of the Living God (Matt. 16:17). ¶

BARLEY (adj.) – ***krithinos*** [adj.: κρίθινος <2916>]**; from *krithē*: barley ▶ Made of barley, a cereal used to make bread >** Jesus multiplied the five barley loaves of a little boy to feed a great crowd (John 6:9); twelve hand-baskets full of fragments were filled with the five barley loaves which were over and above those who had been eaten (v. 13). ¶

BARLEY (noun) – ***krithē*** [fem. noun: κριθή <2915>] **▶ Cereal used to make bread >** Three measures of barley will be worth a denarius at the time of the apocalyptic judgments (Rev. 6:6). ¶

BARN – ***apothēkē*** [fem. noun: ἀποθήκη <596>]**; from *apotithēmi*: to lay aside, which is from *apo*: beside, and *tithēmi*: to put ▶ Storage area, farm building >** He who was coming after John the Baptist would gather His wheat into the barn (Matt. 3:12; 13:30; Luke 3:17). The birds of heaven do not gather into barns (Matt. 6:26; Luke 12:24). A man said he would build larger barns to store all his grain and his goods (Luke 12:18). ¶

BARNABAS – ***Barnabas*** [masc. name: Βαρναβᾶς <921>]**: son of prophet or son of consolation, in Aram. ▶ Jewish Christian from Cyprus whose name was Joseph (or Joses) >** The apostles gave the name Barnabas to this Joseph (Acts 4:36). He sold some land and brought the resultant sum to the apostles (see Acts 4:37). He led Saul to the apostles (Acts 9:27). At Antioch, Barnabas, together with Paul later on, taught the Christians (Acts 11:22; see v. 23 and v. 26). He accompanied Paul during a missionary journey (see Acts 13, 14). They both went up to Jerusalem to resolve the issue of circumcision (see Acts 15). They went their separate ways following a sharp contention regarding Mark, Barnabas's nephew. The latter took Mark and sailed away to Cyprus, to continue the gospel work on this island; Paul left accompanied by Silas (Acts 15:37, 39). Barnabas was carried away by the hypocrisy of the Jews in conduct compelling the Gentiles to yield to Jewish practices (Gal. 2:13). Other refs.: Acts 11:30; 12:25; 13:1, 2, 7, 43, 46, 50; 14:12, 14, 20; 15:2, 12, 22, 25, 35, 36; 1 Cor. 9:6; Gal. 2:1, 9; Col. 4:10. ¶

BARRACKS – Acts 21:34, 37; 22:24; 23:10, 16, 32 → FORTRESS <3925>.

BARREN – [1] ***steiros*** [adj. and adj. used as fem. noun (*steira*): στεῖρος <4723>]; **poss. from *stereos*: firm, solid; other Greek word: *steriphos* and Lat. word: *sterilis* ▶ Sterile, who cannot conceive a child** > Elizabeth was barren (Luke 1:7, 36). In a coming day the barren will be called blessed (Luke 23:29). Paul uses this term in regard to the Jerusalem above (Gal. 4:27). ¶
– [2] 2 Pet. 1:8 → UNFRUITFUL <175> [3] 2 Pet. 1:8 → IDLE <692>.

BARRENNESS – Rom. 4:19 → DEADNESS <3500>.

BARRICADE – Luke 19:43 → EMBANKMENT <5482>.

BARRIER – [1] Eph. 2:14 → SEPARATION <5418> [2] Eph. 2:14 → middle wall → WALL <3320>.

BARSABBAS – ***Barsabbas*** [masc. name: Βαρσαββᾶς <923>]: **son of Saba, i.e., son of rest, in Aram.; Saba, in Heb.: to summon; also written in some mss.: *Barsabas* ▶ a. Another name for Joseph, one of the two men proposed to replace Judas Iscariot** > Barsabbas was surnamed Justus (Acts 1:23). **b. Surname of a man, Judas, who accompanied Paul and Barnabas to Antioch** > This Barsabbas was one of the leading men among the brothers (Acts 15:22); he exhorted the brothers with many words and strengthened them (see v. 32). ¶

BARTHOLOMEW – ***Bartholomaios*** [masc. name: Βαρθολομαῖος <918>]: **son (in Aram.) of Tolmai (in Heb.), Tolmai meaning ridged ▶ One of the twelve apostles** > Bartholomew is mentioned in Acts 1:13. The fact that his name is associated with the name of Philip (Matt. 10:3; Mark 3:18; Luke 6:14) may suggest that this is the surname of Nathanael, whom Philip led to Jesus (see John 1:46–50). ¶

BARTIMAEUS – ***Bartimaios*** [masc. name: Βαρτιμαῖος <924>]: **son (in Aram.) of Timaeus: honorable (in Greek), poss. from *timē*: honor, respect ▶ Blind beggar** > Jesus healed Bartimaeus as He was going out from Jericho (Mark 10:46); then Bartimaeus followed Jesus (see v. 52). ¶

BASE (adj.) – [1] ***agenēs*** [adj.: ἀγενής <36>]; **from *a*: neg., and *genos*: family, race ▶ Of no reputation, of low degree** > God has chosen the base {lowly, ignoble} things of this world, those that are despised, and those that are not to nullify the things that are (1 Cor. 1:28). ¶
– [2] 2 Cor. 10:1 → LOWLY <5011> [3] Titus 1:11 → DISHONEST <150>.

BASE (noun) – 1 Tim. 3:15 → FOUNDATION <1477>.

BASE (verb) – Rom. 9:32; 11:6 → the verb is added in Engl.

BASER – Acts 17:5 → of the baser sort → from the market place → MARKETPLACE <60>.

BASIC – Col. 2:8, 20; Heb. 5:12 → basic principle → ELEMENT <4747>.

BASIN – ***niptēr*** [masc. noun: νιπτήρ <3537>]; **from *niptō*: to wash ▶ Bowl for washing the feet** > Jesus poured water into a basin {bason} and began to wash the disciples' feet (John 13:5). ¶

BASIS – 1 **on the basis of:** ***epi*** [prep.: ἐπί <1909>]; **lit.: on, upon ▶ In relation to >** The people of Israel received their law on the basis of {in connection with} the Levitical priesthood (Heb. 7:11).
– 2 Luke 23:4, 14 → basis for a charge → FAULT <158> 3 John 18:38; 19:4, 6 → basis for a charge → FAULT <156>.

BASKET – 1 ***kophinos*** [masc. noun: κόφινος <2894>] ▶ **Hamper somewhat smaller than the one in 2** > After the crowds had eaten the five loaves which the Lord had multiplied, the disciples took up twelve baskets full of the fragments that remained (Matt. 14:20; Mark 6:43; Luke 9:17; John 6:13; also Matt. 16:9 and Mark 8:19). ¶
2 ***spuris*** [fem. noun: σπυρίς <4711>]; **from *speira*: something that is coiled; *spira*, in Lat.: spiral, plait; *sparton* is a braided rope ▶ Container for food, relatively big and circular, made of intertwined reeds or straw** > After the multiplication of the loaves and the fish, there were seven large baskets full of the fragments that were left (Matt. 15:37; 16:10; Mark 8:8, 20). The disciples took Paul by night and let him down through the wall in a large basket to escape the king Aretas (Acts 9:25; see 2 Cor. 11:32, 33). ¶
3 ***sarganē*** [fem. noun: σαργάνη <4553>]; **from a Heb. word meaning: to intertwine ▶ Hamper prob. made of ropes** > In telling the preceding story of Acts 9:25, Paul uses this Greek word (2 Cor. 11:33). ¶
– 4 Matt. 5:15; Mark 4:21; Luke 11:33 → BUSHEL <3426> 5 Matt. 13:48 → VESSEL[1] <30>.

BASKETFUL – 1 Matt. 14:20; Mark 6:43; 8:19; Luke 9:17; John 6:13 → lit.: full baskets → BASKET <2894> FULL <4134> 2 Matt. 15:37; 16:10; Mark 8:8, 20 → lit.: basket full of → BASKET <4711>, FULL <4134> 3 Mark 8:20 → lit.: full baskets → BASKET <4711>, FULL <4138>.

BASON – John 13:5 → BASIN <3537>.

BASTARD – Heb. 12:8 → ILLEGITIMATE <3541>.

BATCH – 1 Cor. 5:6, 7; Gal. 5:9 → batch of dough → LUMP <5445>.

BATH (noun)[1] – Luke 16:6 → MEASURE (noun) <943>.

BATH (noun)[2] – John 13:10 → to have a bath → WASH <3068>.

BATH, BATHE (verb) – John 13:10 → WASH <3068>.

BATTALION – Matt. 27:27; Mark 15:16 → COHORT <4686>.

BATTERED (BE) – Matt. 14:24 → TOSS <928>.

BATTERING – Acts 27:18 → to take a violent battering from the storm → to be tossed with a tempest → TEMPEST <5492>.

BATTLE (noun) – 1 ***polemos*** [masc. noun: πόλεμος <4171>]; **from which: *polemeō*: to make war, to fight ▶ Fight, conflict; also transl.: war** > If the trumpet makes an uncertain sound, who will prepare for battle? (1 Cor. 14:8). The locusts were like horses prepared for the battle (Rev. 9:7, 9). John saw a battle in heaven: Michael and his angels fighting with the dragon (Rev. 12:7). The kings of the world will be gathered by spirits of demons to the battle of the great day of God Almighty (Rev. 16:14; 19:19). At the end of the millennium, Satan will gather the nations together for battle (Rev. 20:8). All other refs.: FIGHT (noun) <4171>, WAR (noun) <4171>.
– 2 1 Tim. 1:18 → WARFARE <4752>.

BATTLE (verb) – Jas. 4:1 → WAR (verb) <4754>.

BAY – ***kolpos*** [masc. noun: κόλπος <2859>]; **first meaning: chest, breast;**

derived meaning: coastal inlet ▶ Small gulf, cove > Those on board Paul's boat decided to run the ship ashore into a certain bay {creek} (Acts 27:39). All other refs.: BOSOM <2859>.

BE – 1 ***eimi*** [verb: εἰμί <1510>] ▶ **Verb expressing existence, as in Engl.** > In the beginning was the Word, and the Word was with God, and the Word was God (John 1:1a–c). This verse speaks of the eternal existence, coexistence, and divinity of the Son of God. The verb is found more than 2,600 times in the N.T. *

2 ***einai*** [verb: εἶναι <1511>] ▶ Pres. infinitive of the verb "to be," "to exist." * ‡

3 ***ginomai*** [verb: γίνομαι <1096>] ▶ **To take place, to happen** > A few refs.: Matt. 24:20; 26:54; Mark 13:18; Luke 1:8; 2:6; 12:54, 55; 17:26; 22:24; Acts 15:7. The verb is found more than 650 times in the N.T. *

4 **it must be, it can be: *endechomai*** [verb: ἐνδέχομαι <1735>]; **from *en*: in, and *dechomai*: to receive ▶ It is acceptable, it is permitted** > It must not be that a prophet perish out of Jerusalem (Luke 13:33). ¶

5 **I shall be: *esomai*** [verb: ἔσομαι <2071>]; **from *esti*: to be ▶** Future first person sing. of "to be," "to exist." *

6 **it shall be: *estai*** [verb: ἔσται <2074a>] ▶ **It shall happen** > Ref.: Matt. 16:22; Luke 1:34; 22:49 {what would follow; what was going to happen}.

7 **he (she, it) is: *esti*** [verb: εστι <2076>] ▶ Third person sing. of "to be," "to exist." *

8 ***huparchō*** [verb: ὑπάρχω <5225>]; **from *hupo*: under, and *archō*: to begin, which is from *archē*: beginning ▶ To put forward (as a pretext)** > There was no cause {No cause existed} whereby the Ephesians could give an account for their disorderly gathering (Acts 19:40). Other refs.: see entries in Lexicon at <5225>.

– 9 Acts 21:35 → to be, to have to be → HAPPEN <4819>.

BE THOU – 1 ***estō*** [verb: ἔστω <2077> ▶ Third person sing. imper. of *eimi*: to be.

2 ***isthi*** [verb: ἴσθι <2468>] ▶ Pres. imper. second person sing. of *eimi*: to be > Refs.: Matt. 2:13; 5:25; Mark 5:34; Luke 19:17; 1 Tim. 4:15. ¶ ‡

BE UP – Matt. 13:6; Mark 4:6 → RISE (verb) <393>.

BE WITH – ***suneimi*** [verb: σύνειμι <4895>]; **from *sun*: together, and *eimi*: to be ▶** Refs.: Luke 9:18; Acts 22:11. ¶

BEACH – 1 ***aigialos*** [masc. noun: αἰγιαλός <123>]; **from *aissō*: to surge, and *hals* (fem. noun): sea ▶ Bank, strand** > Paul's boat made for the beach (Acts 27:39, 40). Other refs.: Matt. 13:2, 48; John 21:4; Acts 21:5; see SHORE <123>. ¶

– 2 Acts 27:40 → to head for the beach, to make for the beach → to make for the shore → SHORE <2722>.

BEAM – ***dokos*** [fem. noun: δοκός <1385>]; **perhaps from *dechomai*: to receive ▶ Piece of wood; also transl.: plank, log** > The word is used by the Lord as an image of a great offense in speaking of "the beam that is in your eye" (Matt. 7:3–5; Luke 6:41, 42a, b). ¶

BEAR (noun) – ***arkos*** [masc. and fem. noun: ἄρκος <715>]; **also written in some mss.: ἄρκτος (*arktos*) ▶ Large, heavy carnivorous mammal; its paws have retractile claws** > The beast which John saw at Patmos had feet like those of a bear (Rev. 13:2). ¶

BEAR (verb) – 1 ***airō*** [verb: αἴρω <142>] ▶ **To lift, to carry** > The verb is used in regard to the Lord Jesus (Matt. 4:6; Luke 4:11), His cross (Matt. 27:32; Mark 15:21), and a paralytic (Mark 2:3). All other refs.: see entries in Lexicon at <142>.

2 ***anapherō*** [verb: ἀναφέρω <399>]; **from *ana*: up, and *pherō*: to carry, to bring ▶ To take upon oneself** > Christ bore {took away} the sins of many (Heb. 9:28). He bore our sins in His body on the tree (1 Pet. 2:24). All other refs.: CARRY <399>, LEAD (verb) <399>, OFFER <399>.

3 ***bastazō*** [verb: βαστάζω <941>]; **from *basis*: basis, which is from *bainō*: to go; *bastagma* is a load, a burden in Greek ▶**

a. To take, to lift, to carry, to carry off, to support > The verb is used in regard to the Lord Jesus (Luke 11:27 {to give birth}), His cross (John 19:17), His name (Acts 9:15), and His marks which Paul bore in his body (Gal. 6:17). It is also used in regard to sandals (Matt. 3:11), diseases (Matt. 8:17), the burden of the day and the heat (Matt. 20:12), a pitcher of water (Mark 14:13; Luke 22:10), a young man who had died (Luke 7:14 {the bearers; lit.: those who bore}), purse, knapsack, and sandals (Luke 10:4), our cross (Luke 14:27), that which was put into the bag of Judas (John 12:6 {to pilfer, to help oneself}), a man who was lame (Acts 3:2), a yoke (Acts 15:10), Paul (Acts 21:35), a root (Rom. 11:18 {to support}), the infirmities of the weak (Rom. 15:1), judgment (Gal. 5:10 {to pay}), burdens (Gal. 6:2), a burden (Gal. 6:5), and the beast (Rev. 17:7 {to ride}). **b. To accept, to take upon oneself >** The apostles were not able to bear at the time many things that Jesus had to say to them (John 16:12). **c. To endure, to have patience, to tolerate >** The church at Ephesus could not bear evil men (Rev. 2:2) and endured (i.e., bore afflictions) for the name of the Lord (v. 3). Other refs.: John 10:31 {to take up, to pick}; 20:15 {to carry away}. ¶

4 ***gennaō*** [verb: γεννάω <1080>]; **from *genna*: birth, race ► To beget, to give birth >** Elizabeth would bear Zacharias a son (Luke 1:13), i.e., John the Baptist. Jesus said that days were coming in which the wombs that have not borne would be called blessed (Luke 23:29). The covenant of Mount Sinai bears {genders to} bondage (Gal. 4:24). All other refs.: see entries in Lexicon at <1080>.

5 **to bear about: *peripherō*** [verb: περιφέρω <4064>]; **from *peri*: around, and *pherō*: to carry ► To carry around with oneself >** Paul always bore about {carried about} in the body the death of Jesus (2 Cor. 4:10). All other refs.: CARRY <4064>.

6 ***poieō*** [verb: ποιέω <4160>]; **lit.: to make ► To produce, to yield >** The verb is used in regard to fruit (Luke 13:9; Rev. 22:2). Other refs.: Matt. 3:8, 10; 7:17a, b, 18a, b, 19; 13:23b, 26; 21:43; Luke 3:8, 9; 6:43a, b; 8:8; Jas. 3:12 → PRODUCE <4160>. Other refs.: see entries in Lexicon at <4160>.

7 ***stegō*** [verb: στέγω <4722>]; **akin to *tegere*, in Lat.: to cover, to keep to oneself; from which *stegē*: roof of a house ► To endure, to make proof of patience >** Paul bore all things, that he might put no hindrance in the way of the gospel of Christ (1 Cor. 9:12 {to suffer}). Love bears all things, believes all things, hopes all things, endures all things (1 Cor. 13:7 {to protect}). Paul uses this verb also in 1 Thes. 3:1, 5. ¶

– **8** Matt. 1:23; Gal. 4:27; Rev. 12:4b → to give birth → BIRTH <5088> **9** Matt. 10:18; Mark 13:9; Luke 21:13; Heb. 3:5 → to bear testimony, to bear witness → lit.: for a witness → WITNESS (noun)[1] <3142> **10** Matt. 17:17; Mark 9:19; Luke 9:41; Acts 18:14; 2 Cor. 11:1a, b, 4, 19, 20; Eph. 4:2; Col. 3:13; 2 Tim. 4:3; Heb. 13:22 → to bear, to bear with → SUFFER <430> **11** Matt. 21:19 → lit.: to become (*ginomai*) **12** Matt. 23:4; Luke 11:46 → hard to bear → HARD <1419> **13** Luke 18:7 → to bear long → to have patience → PATIENCE <3114> **14** Luke 23:26; John 2:8a, b; 12:24; 15:2a–c, 4, 5, 8, 16; Heb. 13:13 → BRING <5342> **15** John 2:25; 3:26, 32 → to bear witness → WITNESS (verb) <3140> **16** John 8:43 → to be able → ABLE <1410> **17** Acts 2:40 → to bear witness → TESTIFY <1263> **18** Acts 15:17 → INVOKE <1941> **19** Acts 27:15 → to bear up into → to head into → HEAD (verb) <503> **20** Rom. 2:17 → to bear the name → NAME (verb) <2028> **21** Rom. 9:22; Heb. 12:20 → ENDURE <5342> **22** Rom. 13:4; 1 Cor. 15:49a, b → WEAR <5409> **23** 1 Cor. 10:13 → ENDURE <5297> **24** 1 Cor. 13:7; 1 Pet. 2:20a, b → ENDURE <5278> **25** 1 Cor. 16:3 → CARRY <667> **26** 1 Tim. 5:14 → to bear children → CHILD <5041> **27** 2 Tim. 2:19 → bearing this seal → having (*echō*) this seal **28** Heb. 6:7 → PRODUCE <5088> **29** Heb. 6:8 → to bring forth → BRING <1627> **30** Heb. 11:11 → to bear children → CONCEIVE <2602> **31** Jas. 5:18 → PRODUCE <985> **32** 2 Pet. 1:17, 18 → the voice was borne to Him → the voice came to Him → COME <5342> **33** 2 Pet. 3:15 → to bear in mind → CONSIDER

<2233> 34 1 John 1:2 → to bear witness → WITNESS (noun)[1] <3140> 35 Rev. 2:3 → lit.: to have patience → PATIENCE <5281> 36 Rev. 6:9 → "borne" added in Engl. 37 Rev. 16:2 → to bear the mark → lit.: to have (*echō*) the mark.

BEARABLE – Matt. 10:15; 11:22, 24; Luke 10:12, 14 → more bearable → more tolerable → TOLERABLE <414>.

BEARER – Luke 7:14 → the bearers → lit.: those carrying → BEAR (verb) <941>.

BEARING – 1 Tim. 2:15 → bearing of children → CHILDBEARING <5042>.

BEAST – 1 ***zōon*** [neut. noun: ζῷον <2226>]; **from *zōos*: alive ▶ a. Living being; also transl.: living creature** > In Revelation, the beasts {living creatures} are symbolical creatures who stand before the throne and give glory, honor, and thanksgiving to God (4:6, 7a–d, 8, 9; 5:6, 8, 11, 14; 6:1, 3, 5–7; 7:11; 14:3; 15:7; 19:4). **b. Animal creature** > In Heb. 13:11, the beasts {animals} are offered in sacrifice. Those who walk according to the flesh in the lust of uncleanness and despising authority are like brute and irrational beasts {animals} (2 Pet. 2:12; Jude 10). ¶

2 **beast, wild beast: *thērion*** [neut. noun: θηρίον <2342>]; **dimin. of *ther*: wild animal ▶ a. Wild animal** > The word "beast" {animal} is used in Mark 1:13 {wild beasts}; Acts 11:6; 28:4, 5 {creature, snake}; Heb. 12:20; Jas. 3:7; Rev. 6:8. **b. Term used figur. to describe people** > One of their prophets had described the Cretans as evil beasts {brutes} (Titus 1:12). **c. Term used figur. to describe the antichrist** > According to one view, there are two separate beasts in Revelation, who will manage the political and religious matters, respectively, after the rapture of the church (Rev. 11:7; 13:1–3, 4a–c, 11, 12a, b, 14a, b, 15a–c, 17, 18; 14:9, 11; 15:2; 16:2, 10, 13; 17:3, 7, 8a, b, 11–13, 16, 17; 18:2 in some mss.; 19:19, 20a, b; 20:4, 10). ¶

3 ***ktēnos*** [neut. noun: κτῆνος <2934>]; **from *ktaomai*: to acquire, to possess ▶ Animal used to carry heavy loads; animal in general** > The Samaritan put the wounded man on his own beast {donkey} (Luke 10:34). The word designates a beast in general, a quadruped animal in 1 Cor. 15:39. Other refs.: Acts 23:24; Rev. 18:13; see CATTLE <2934>, MOUNT (noun)[1] <2934>. ¶

4 **slain beast: *sphagion*** [neut. noun: σφάγιον <4968>]; **from *sphazō*: to slay, to sacrifice ▶ Victim for a sacrifice, slaughtered offering** > God asks the house of Israel if they had offered Him slain beasts {slaughtered animals, victims} and sacrifices {sacrifices and offerings} in the wilderness (Acts 7:42). ¶

5 **to fight with beasts, to fight wild beasts: *thēriomacheō*** [verb: θηριομαχέω <2341>]; **from *thērion*: see 2, and *machomai*: to fight ▶ To contend, to struggle with wild animals** > Paul had fought with beasts at Ephesus (1 Cor. 15:32). This verb is most likely used in a figur. sense to describe Paul's adversaries; see Acts 19:29. ¶

– 6 Matt. 22:4 → fatted beast → FATLING <4619> 7 2 Pet. 2:16 → DONKEY <5268>.

BEAT – 1 ***derō*** [verb: δέρω <1194>]; **from the root *der* which has given *derma*: skin ▶ a. To strike, to severely mistreat; also transl.: to hit, to slap, to smite** > In a parable, the husbandmen beat the servants of the landowner (Matt. 21:35; Mark 12:3, 5; Luke 20:10, 11). Jesus told His disciples that they would be beaten {flogged} in the synagogues (Mark 13:9). According to their knowledge or not of their master's will, servants will be beaten with many or few stripes {will receive many lashes, will be flogged} (Luke 12:47, 48). The men who held Jesus beat Him (Luke 22:63). During the high priest's interrogation, Jesus asked, "Why do you strike me?" (John 18:23). After having been beaten {flogged}, the apostles were enjoined not to speak in the name of Jesus (Acts 5:40). Paul had been beaten publicly without trial (Acts 16:37). Before his conversion, he was in every synagogue beating those who believed in Jesus (Acts 22:19). **b. To hit** > Paul was not combating as one who beats the air (1 Cor. 9:26). The

Corinthians put up with it if anyone beat them on the face (2 Cor. 11:20). ¶
2 ***epiballō*** [verb: ἐπιβάλλω <1911>]; **from *epi*: upon, and *ballō*: to throw ▶ To throw oneself upon, to fall upon** > The waves beat into {broke over} the ship (Mark 4:37). All other refs.: FALL (verb) <1911>, LAY <1911>, PUT <1911>, THINK <1911>.
3 ***epikeimai*** [verb: ἐπίκειμαι <1945>]; **from *epi*: on, and *keimai*: to lay; lit.: to be upon, to press ▶ To threaten, to act with violence** > A great storm beat on Paul and the other passengers on board the ship (Acts 27:20); also transl.: to assail, to continue raging, to lay, to lie. All other refs.: IMPOSE <1945>, INSISTENT <1945>, LAY <1945>, PRESS <1945>.
4 **to beat, to beat with the fists: *kolaphizō*** [verb: κολαφίζω <2852>]; **from *kolaphos*: blow, slap ▶ To mistreat, to treat with violence; also transl.: to buffet, to strike with the fists, to torment, to treat brutally, to treat harshly, to treat roughly** > People spat in the face of Jesus and beat Him with their fists (Matt. 26:67; Mark 14:65). Paul was beaten (1 Cor. 4:11). A messenger of Satan had been given to Paul to torment him, to keep him from exalting himself concerning the exceeding greatness of the revelations made to him (2 Cor. 12:7). There is no glory if one endures being beaten for sinning (1 Pet. 2:20). ¶
5 **to beat upon, to beat against: *proskoptō*** [verb: προσκόπτω <4350>]; **from *pros*: against, and *koptō*: to hit repeatedly ▶ To knock against** > The winds blew and beat upon {burst against} the house, and it fell (Matt. 7:27). All other refs.: STRIKE <4350>, STUMBLE <4350>.
6 **to beat upon: *prospiptō*** [verb: προσπίπτω <4363>]; **from *pros*: against, and *piptō*: to fall ▶ To burst against, to fall upon** > The winds blew and beat upon the house built on the rock, and it did not fall (Matt. 7:25). All other refs.: FALL (verb) <4363>.
7 ***tuptō*** [verb: τύπτω <5180>] **▶ To hit, to wound** > In a parable, a servant began to beat his fellow-servants (Matt. 24:49 {to smite}; Luke 12:45). The Greeks beat Sosthenes before the judgment seat (Acts 18:17). When they saw the chiliarch and the soldiers, the Jews ceased beating Paul (Acts 21:32). All other refs.: STRIKE <5180>, WOUND (verb) <5180>.
– 8 Matt. 14:24 → TOSS <928> 9 Luke 6:48, 49 → to beat vehemently against → to break upon → BREAK <4366> 10 Luke 10:30 → lit.: to cover with wounds → WOUND (verb) <2007> <4127> 11 Luke 18:5 → to beat down → to completely harass → HARASS <5299> 12 Acts 16:22; 2 Cor. 11:25 → to beat, to beat with rods → ROD <4463> 13 1 Cor. 9:27 → DISCIPLINE (verb) <5299> 14 2 Cor. 6:9 → CHASTEN <3811> 15 2 Cor. 11:23 → lit.: in stripes → STRIPE <4127> 16 Rev. 7:16 → to beat down → STRIKE <4098>.

BEATER – Acts 19:24 → silver beater → SILVERSMITH <695>.

BEATING – 1 Luke 12:47, 48b → to receive a severe beating, light beating → lit.: to be beaten with many stripes, few stripes → BEAT <1194> 2 Luke 12:48a; 2 Cor. 6:5; 11:23 → STRIPE <4127> 3 Acts 19:16 → to give a beating → WOUND (verb) <5135> 4 Acts 19:16 → to give a beating → OVERPOWER <2480>.

BEAUTIFUL – 1 ***asteios*** [adj.: ἀστεῖος <791>]; **from *astu*: city; lit.: from the city, of good taste ▶ Agreeable, gracious** > The parents of Moses saw that he was a beautiful {no ordinary, proper} child (Heb. 11:23). For the lit. expr. "beautiful to God" (Acts 7:20), see "well pleasing to God" under PLEASING <791> <2316>. ¶
2 ***kalos*** [adj.: καλός <2570>] **▶ Good, nice; worthy, precious** > The kingdom of heaven is like a merchant seeking beautiful {goodly, fine} pearls (Matt. 13:45). The temple was adorned with beautiful {goodly} stones (Luke 21:5). Other refs.: see entries in Lexicon at <2570>.
3 ***hōraios*** [adj.: ὡραῖος <5611>]; **from *hōra*: hour, time, season; lit.: which is of the season ▶ Good-looking, nice** > The scribes and the Pharisees were like whitewashed tombs appearing beautiful outwardly (Matt. 23:27). A gate of the temple was called Beautiful (Acts 3:2, 10);

there was a lame man there whom Peter healed. The feet of those who preach the gospel of peace are beautiful (Rom. 10:15). ¶
– [4] 1 Pet. 3:5 → to make oneself beautiful → to adorn oneself → ADORN <2885>.

BEAUTIFULLY – Rev. 21:2 → to be beautifully dressed → to be adorned → ADORN <2885>.

BEAUTY – [1] Jas. 1:11 → GRACE <2143> [2] 1 Pet. 3:3 → ADORNMENT <2889>.

BECAUSE – [1] ***dioti*** [conj.: διότι <1360>]; **from *dia*: for, and *hoti*: that ► Also transl.: on account of this or that, for this reason, that, simply because, for** > Refs.: Luke 1:13; 2:7; 21:28; Acts 10:20; 17:31; 18:10; 22:18; Rom. 1:19, 21; 3:20; 8:7; 1 Cor. 15:9; Gal. 2:16; Phil. 2:26; 1 Thes. 2:8; 4:6; Heb. 11:5, 23; Jas. 4:3; 1 Pet. 1:16, 24. ¶ ‡
[2] ***hoti*** [conj.: ὅτι <3754>] ► Refs.: Matt. 13:13; John 8:47; 10:17; 12:39; 1 John 3:1. *
– [3] Matt. 10:41, 42 → in the name of → NAME (noun) <1519> <3686> [4] Acts 20:16 → SO THAT <3704>.

BECKON – [1] Luke 1:22 → to make signs → SIGN <1269> [2] Luke 5:7 → SIGNAL (verb) <2656> [3] John 13:24; Acts 24:10 → to make a sign → SIGN <3506> [4] Acts 12:17; 13:16; 19:33; 21:40 → to make a sign → SIGN <2678>.

BECOME – [1] ***ginomai*** [verb: γίνομαι <1096>] ► **To pass from one state to another, to happen; also transl.: to make, to be** > The Word, the Son of God, became flesh (John 1:14). Christ has become a curse for us (Gal. 3:13). He humbled Himself and became obedient to the point of death (Phil. 2:8). Jesus has become high priest forever (Heb. 6:20). Other refs.: Matt. 4:3; 9:16; 13:32; 18:3; 20:26; 21:42; 23:15; 28:4; Mark 1:17; 2:21; 4:32; 6:14; 9:3, 26, 50 (lit.: if salt becomes not salted); 10:43, 44; 12:10; Luke 4:3; 6:16; 8:17; 9:29; 13:19; 18:23, 24; 20:17; 22:44; 23:12; 24:31 (lit.: he became invisible); John 2:9; 9:27; Acts 4:11; 5:24; 7:32 (lit.: became trembling), 40; 12:18; 26:29; Rom. 2:25; 4:18; 7:13; 9:29; 11:9, 17; 1 Cor. 3:18; 4:13; 7:21, 23; 8:9; 9:20, 22a, b; 10:32 {to give}; 13:11; 15:45; 2 Cor. 5:21; 12:11; Gal. 4:16; Eph. 3:7; Phil. 1:13; Col. 1:23, 25; 1 Thes. 1:6, 7; 2:8, 14; Titus 3:7; Heb. 1:4; 3:14; 5:9, 11, 12 {to come}; 6:4, 12; 7:21; 11:7, 24, 34; Jas. 2:4, 11; 1 Pet. 2:7; 3:6, 13; Rev. 6:12; 8:8, 11; 16:3, 4, 10; 18:2. Other refs.: see entries in Lexicon at <1096>.
– [2] Matt. 3:15; Eph. 5:3; Titus 2:1; Heb. 2:10; 7:26 → FITTING (BE) <4241> [3] Rom. 7:13 → MAKE <2716> [4] Rom. 16:2 → as becometh → WORTHY <516> [5] 1 Tim. 2:10 → to be proper → PROPER <4241> [6] Titus 2:3 → as becometh holiness → REVERENT <2412> [7] Jas. 4:4 → MAKE <2525>.

BECOMING – 1 Tim. 5:13 → OUGHT <1163>.

BECOMINGLY – Rom. 13:13 → HONESTLY <2156>.

BED – [1] ***klinē*** [fem. noun: κλίνη <2825>]; **from *klinō*: to incline, to recline ► Device for carrying a sick person or for reclining; also transl.: couch, mat** > A paralytic lying on a bed was brought to Jesus (Matt. 9:2, 6). The lamp should not be put under the bed (Mark 4:21; Luke 8:16). The Jews hold the tradition of washing beds {tables} (Mark 7:4 in some mss.). A woman found her daughter lying on a bed, the demon having gone out of her (Mark 7:30). Men brought on a bed a man who was paralyzed (Luke 5:18), and Jesus healed him. When Christ returns after the tribulation on earth to establish His millennial reign, two will be in one bed; one will be taken (for judgment) and one will be left (to enjoy millennial blessings) (Luke 17:34). The woman Jezebel will be cast upon a bed {sickbed} (Rev. 2:22). ¶
[2] **little bed: *klinarion*** [neut. noun: κλινάριον <2824a>]; **dimin. of *klinē*: bed; see [1] ► Little couch, pallet** > The sick were brought out into the street and laid on beds {cots} and couches {mats} so that Peter might heal them (Acts 5:15). ¶

3 **little bed: *klinidion*** [neut. noun: κλινίδιον <2826>]**; dimin. of *klinē*: bed; see** 1 **▶ Little couch, cot >** Some men let down a paralyzed man on his little bed {couch, mat, stretcher} through the tiles of the housetop (Luke 5:19, 24). ¶

4 ***koitē*** [fem. noun: κοίτη <2845>]**; from *keimai*: to lie down ▶ Bed for sleeping, conjugal bed >** A man did not want to be troubled, because his children and him were in bed (Luke 11:7). Marriage must be held every way in honor, and the bed {marriage bed} must be undefiled (Heb. 13:4). Other refs.: Rom. 9:10 (lit.: having had the conjugal bed); 13:13 {sexual immorality, sexual promiscuity}. ¶

5 ***krabattos*** [masc. noun: κράβαττος <2895>]**; *grabatus*, in Lat.: low bed, pallet ▶ Small bed used by the poor, cot, stretcher; also transl.: couch, mat, pallet >** Four men let down the bed on which a paralytic was lying (Mark 2:4, 9, 11, 12). People carried about on beds those who were sick to where they heard that Jesus was (Mark 6:55). Jesus healed a sick man lying on a bed (John 5:8–12). Aeneas was lying on a bed {was bedridden} (Acts 9:33); Peter healed him (see v. 34). Other ref.: Acts 5:15; see COUCH <2895>. ¶

6 **to make one's bed: *strōnnuō*** [verb: στρωννύω <4766>] **▶ To arrange, to spread >** Peter told Aeneas to make his own bed {couch, mat} (Acts 9:34). Other refs.: Matt. 21:8; Mark 11:8; see SPREAD <4766>. ¶

BEDRIDDEN (BE) – to be lying: *katakeimai* [verb: κατάκειμαι <2621>]**; from *kata*: down, and *keimai*: to be lying ▶ To be confined to bed, to lay because of sickness >** Peter healed Aeneas who had been bedridden {had kept his bed} (lit.: had been lying on a bed) (Acts 9:33; see v. 34). All other refs.: LAY <2621>, LIE (verb)[1] <2621>, SIT <2621>, TABLE[1] <2621>.

BEELZEBUB – See BEELZEBUL <954>.

BEELZEBUL – *Beelzeboul* [masc. name: Βεελζεβούλ <954>]**: lord of the flies, in Heb.; also transl.: Beelzebub ▶ Name given to Satan, the chief of the demons >** The Jews called Satan Beelzebul (Matt. 10:25). The Pharisees accused Jesus of casting out demons by Beelzebul (Matt. 12:24, 27; Mark 3:22; Luke 11:15, 18, 19). Comp. 2 Kgs. 1:2. ¶

BEFALL – 1 ***ginomai*** [verb: γίνομαι <1096>] **▶ To become, to happen >** The verb "to befall" is found in Mark 5:16. Other refs.: see entries in Lexicon at <1096>.

2 ***sunantaō*** [verb: συναντάω <4876>]**; from *sun*: together, and *antaō*: to meet ▶ To encounter, to happen to >** Paul was going bound in the spirit to Jerusalem, not knowing the things that would befall him (Acts 20:22). All other refs.: MEET (verb) <4876>.

– 3 Matt. 8:33 → what was befallen to the possessed → lit.: the (things) of the possessed 4 Acts 20:19 → HAPPEN <4819>.

BEFORE – 1 ***enanti*** [adv.: ἔναντι <1725>]**; from *en*: in, into, and *anti*: against, opposite ▶ Over against, in the presence of >** Ref.: Luke 1:8. ¶ ‡

2 ***enantion*** [adv.: ἐναντίον <1726>]**; neuter of *enantios*: contrary, which is from *en*: in, into, and *anti*: against, opposite ▶ In front of >** Refs.: Mark 2:12; Luke 20:26; 24:19; Acts 7:10; 8:32. ¶ ‡

3 ***pro*** [prep.: πρό <4253>] **▶** Used both of place and time. Refs.: Acts 5:23; 12:6; 1 Cor. 2:7; 4:5. *

4 ***proteron*** [adj. used as adv.: πρότερον <4386>]**; from *proteros*: first, previous, which is from *pro*: before ▶ Previously, formerly >** The Son of Man would ascend where He was before (John 6:62). Some had seen the blind man before his healing, when he was a beggar (John 9:8). Paul had intended to come to the Corinthians before {at first} (2 Cor. 1:15). He had been before {once} a blasphemer (1 Tim. 1:13). Other ref.: John 7:51. All other refs.: EARLIER <4386>, FIRST <4386>, FORMER <4386>.

5 ***prin*** [adv.: πρίν <4250>]**; from *pro*: before ▶ Prior to, previously >** The word is used in Luke 2:26; 22:34 {until}. *

[6] **to be before: *prouparchō*** [verb: προϋπάρχω <4391>]; **from *pro*: before, and *huparchō*: to begin underneath, to exist, which is from *hupo*: under, and *archō*: to begin ▶ To be previously, to be formerly >** After seeing Jesus, Pilate and Herod became friends, for they had been at enmity with each other before (Luke 23:12). A man named Simon had been practicing magic before (Acts 8:9). ¶

– [7] Matt. 14:22 → to go before → to go ahead → AHEAD <4254> [8] Matt. 14:25 → shortly before dawn → lit.: in the fourth watch of the night → WATCH (noun) <5438> [9] Mark 2:12 → in the presence of → PRESENCE <1715> [10] Luke 22:47 → to go before → PRECEDE <4281> [11] John 8:9 → standing before Him → lit.: standing in the midst [12] Acts 21:29 → to see before → SEE <4308> [13] Col. 1:5 → to hear before → HEAR <4257> [14] 2 Tim. 2:6 → FIRST <4413> [15] Heb. 7:18 → to go before → FORMER <4254>.

BEFOREHAND – [1] Matt. 24:25; Gal. 5:21a → to tell beforehand → TELL <4302> [2] Mark 13:11 → to worry, to be anxious, to be careful beforehand → PREMEDITATE <3191> [3] Mark 14:8 → to come beforehand → COME <4301> [4] 2 Cor. 9:5 → to make up, to prepare beforehand → MAKE <4294> [5] 1 Tim. 5:24, 25 → open, manifest beforehand → clearly evident → CLEARLY <4271>.

BEG – [1] ***epaiteō*** [verb: ἐπαιτέω <1871>]; **from *epi*: upon (intens.), and *aiteō*: to ask ▶ To ask alms in order to live, to ask for as charity >** The unjust steward was ashamed to beg (Luke 16:3). Other ref.: Luke 18:35 in some mss.; see [4]. ¶

[2] ***paraiteomai*** [verb: παραιτέομαι <3868>]; **from *para*: aside, and *aiteō*: see [1] ▶ To decline, to refuse >** The verb is used in Heb. 12:19: some begged {intreated} that the word of God might not be addressed to them. All other refs.: AVOID <3868>, EXCUSE (verb) <3868>, REFUSE (verb) <3868>.

[3] ***parakaleō*** [verb: παρακαλέω <3870>]; **from *para*: beside, and *kaleō*: to call ▶ To invite, to request earnestly, to solicit >** The Gentiles of Antioch in Pisidia begged {besought} that the gospel might be preached to them the next Sabbath (Acts 13:42). All other refs.: see entries in Lexicon at <3870>.

[4] ***prosaiteō*** [verb: προσαιτέω <4319>]; **from *pros*: to (intens.), and *aiteō*: see [1] ▶ To ask for as charity without relent, to implore alms >** Bartimaeus, the blind man, was begging as Jesus was leaving Jericho (Mark 10:46; Luke 18:35); *prosaitēs* in some mss.: beggar. A blind man who was begging was healed by Jesus (John 9:8). ¶

– [5] Matt. 5:42; 27:58; Luke 6:30; 23:52; Acts 13:28 → ASK <154> [6] Matt. 15:23; Mark 7:26; Luke 7:3, 36; 16:27; John 4:47; 14:16; Acts 10:48; 1 Thes. 4:1; 5:12; 2 Thes. 2:1 → ASK <2065> [7] Luke 5:12; 8:28, 38; 9:38, 40; 2 Cor. 10:2 → SUPPLICATE <1189> [8] Luke 23:24 → REQUEST (verb) <155> [9] Acts 3:2, 10 → lit.: to ask for alms → ALMS <1654> [10] 2 Cor. 8:4 → IMPLORE <1189>.

BEGET – [1] ***gennaō*** [verb: γεννάω <1080>]; **from *genna*: birth, race ▶ To give birth, to be the father, to become the father; also transl.: to be born >** In the genealogy of Jesus (Matt. 1:2–16), the verb "to beget" is found 39 times. Abraham begat {became the father of} Isaac (Acts 7:8). Moses begat {had} two sons in the land of Midian (Acts 7:29). God had said to Jesus: "You are My Son, this day I have begotten You" (Acts 13:33; Heb. 1:5; 5:5), in relation to His resurrection. Paul had begotten the Corinthians in Christ Jesus through the gospel (1 Cor. 4:15). He had begotten Onesimus while in his chains (Phm. 10). Everyone who believes that Jesus is the Christ is begotten of God, and everyone who loves Him who has begotten loves also Him who is begotten of Him (1 John 5:1a–c). All other refs.: see entries in Lexicon at <1080>.

– [2] Jas. 1:18 → to bring forth → BRING <616> [3] 1 Pet. 1:3 → to beget again → BORN AGAIN (BE) <313>.

BEGGAR – [1] **to beg: *prosaiteō*** [verb: προσαιτέω <4319>]; **from *pros*: to (intens.), and *aiteō*: to ask, to beg ▶**

To ask for alms in order to live; to ask earnestly, repeatedly > A beggar (lit.: One who begs) was healed by Jesus (John 9:8); some mss. say that he was blind. Other refs.: Mark 10:46; Luke 18:35; see BEG <4319>. ¶
– 2 Luke 16:20, 22 → POOR (noun) <4434>.

BEGGARLY – ***ptōchos*** [adj.: πτωχός <4434>]; **from *ptōssō*: to crouch down, to huddle up like a beggar ▶ Poor; also transl.: miserable, worthless** > In Gal. 4:9, the expr. "beggarly principles (or: worthless elements)" refers to the ordinances of the Mosaic law which can only reduce to bondage. All other refs.: POOR (adj.) <4434>, POOR (noun) <4434>.

BEGIN – 1 ***archomai*** [verb: ἄρχομαι <756>]; **middle voice of *archō*: to begin, which is from *archē*: beginning ▶ To start, to commence** > Jesus began to preach (Matt. 4:17), to teach (Mark 4:1). He began to rebuke cities (Matt. 11:20). He began to show to His disciples that He had to go to Jerusalem and to suffer much (Matt. 16:21; Mark 8:31). In Gethsemane, He began to be sorrowful and deeply distressed (Matt. 26:37; Mark 14:33). He had begun His ministry at about thirty years (Luke 3:23). At Pentecost, believers in the Lord began to speak with other tongues (Acts 2:4). Paul asked if he began again to commend himself (2 Cor. 3:1). The time has come for judgment to begin at the house of God (1 Pet. 4:17). Other refs.: Matt. 11:7; 12:1; 14:30; 16:22; 18:24; 20:8; 26:22; Mark 1:45; 2:23; 5:17, 20; 6:2, 7, 34, 55; 8:11, 32; 10:28, 32, 41, 47; 11:15; 12:1; 13:5; 14:19, 65, 69, 71; 15:8, 18; Luke 3:8; 4:21; 5:21; 7:15, 24, 38, 49; 9:12; 11:29, 53; 12:1, 45; 13:25, 26; 14:9, 18, 29, 30; 15:14, 24; 19:37, 45; 20:9; 21:28; 22:23; 23:2, 5, 30; 24:27, 47; John 8:9; 13:5; Acts 1:1, 22; 8:35; 10:37; 11:4, 15; 18:26; 24:2; 27:35. ¶
2 **to begin in: *enarchomai*** [verb: ἐνάρχομαι <1728>]; **from *en*: in, by, and *archomai*: see 1 ▶ To start, to commence** > The Galatians had begun in the Spirit and could not be made perfect in the flesh (Gal. 3:3). He who has begun a good work in Christians will complete it until the day of Jesus Christ (Phil. 1:6). ¶
3 ***proenarchomai*** [verb: προενάρχομαι <4278>]; **from *pro*: before, and *enarchomai*: see 2 ▶ To start, to commence before** > Titus had begun {had previously made a beginning} in a service for the Corinthians (2 Cor. 8:6); they had begun {were the first} to give and to want to give their goods (v. 10). ¶
4 ***ginomai*** [verb: γίνομαι <1096>] ▶ **To originate, to appear (in history)** > The ministry of death began {came} with glory (2 Cor. 3:7). Other ref.: Matt. 27:24; see RISE (verb) <1096>. Other refs.: see entries in Lexicon at <1096>.
– 5 Matt. 28:1; Luke 23:54 → to begin, to be about to begin, to begin to dawn → DAWN (verb) <2020> 6 John 4:52 → to begin to amend → to get better → BETTER <2866> 7 Rom. 3:2 → to begin with → FIRST <4412> 8 Rom. 16:25 → since the world began → since eternal times → ETERNAL <166>, TIME <5550> 9 1 Cor. 4:8a, b → "begun" added twice in Engl. 10 Heb. 2:3 → began → lit.: having taken the beginning (*archē*) → BEGINNING <746>.

BEGINNING – 1 ***archē*** [fem. noun: ἀρχή <746>] ▶ **Commencement, start** > Mark 10:6 and Heb. 1:10 refer to the beginning of the creation. In contrast, "In the beginning was the Word" (John 1:1) indicates an absolute, before the course of time. This verse attests to the eternal existence of the Son of God; He was in the beginning with God (John 1:2). Having neither beginning of days nor end of life, Melchizedek typifies the Son of God (Heb. 7:3) in His everlasting priesthood. The name of "beginning" given to the Son of God (Col. 1:18; Rev. 3:14; 21:6; 22:13) relates to His preeminence; He is at the origin of the new creation as well as the present creation. The author of the Epistle to the Hebrews speaks of a so great salvation which at the first began (lit.: having taken beginning) to be spoken by the Lord (Heb. 2:3). Other refs.: Matt. 19:4, 8; 24:8, 21; Mark 1:1; 13:8, 19; Luke 1:2; John 2:11; 6:64; 8:44; 15:27; 16:4; Acts 11:15; 26:4;

Phil. 4:15; 2 Thes. 2:13; Heb. 3:14; 6:1 {principle} (lit.: the word of the beginning); 2 Pet. 3:4; 1 John 1:1; 2:7, 13, 14, 24a, b; 3:8, 11; 2 John 5, 6. See [2] for John 8:25. Other refs.: Luke 12:11; 20:20; Acts 10:11; 11:5; Rom. 8:38; 1 Cor. 15:24; Eph. 1:21; 3:10; 6:12; Col. 1:16; 2:10, 15; Titus 3:1; Heb. 5:12; Jude 6; Rev. 1:8 in some mss. ¶

[2] **from the beginning: *tēn archēn*; *archē*** [fem. noun: ἀρχή <746>] **▶ From the start, before everything, all that time >** Jesus was what He had been saying to the Jews from the beginning {all along, altogether} (John 8:25). All other refs. (*archē*): see [1].

[3] **from the beginning: *anōthen*** [adv.: ἄνωθεν <509>]; **from *anō*: above, and suffix *then*: from ▶ From the start, from the commencement >** The Jews knew Paul from the beginning {from the outset, for a long time} (Acts 26:5). All other refs.: ABOVE <509>, AGAIN <509>, FIRST <509>, TOP <509>.

– [4] Luke 11:50 → FOUNDATION <2602> [5] John 2:10 → at the beginning → FIRST <4412> [6] 2 Cor. 8:6 → to make a beginning previously → BEGIN <4278> [7] Heb. 5:12 → the first {elementary} principles → lit.: the principles of the beginning (*tēs archēs*).

BEGOTTEN (BE) – 1 John 2:29; 3:9a, b; 4:7; 5:1a, b, 4, 18a, b → BORN (BE) <1080>.

BEGRUDGE – Matt. 20:15 → lit.: one's eye to be evil → EYE <3788>, EVIL (adj.) <4190>.

BEGUILE – [1] 2 Cor. 11:3 → DECEIVE <1818> [2] Col. 2:4; Jas. 1:22 → DECEIVE <3884> [3] 2 Pet. 2:14 → ENTICE <1185>.

BEHAVE – [1] ***ginomai*** [verb: γίνομαι <1096>] **▶ To be, to live >** Paul told the Thessalonians they were witnesses how he devoutly and justly and blamelessly behaved himself {conducted himself, was} among them (1 Thes. 2:10). Other refs.: see entries in Lexicon at <1096>.

[2] **to behave uncomely, unseemly: *aschēmoneō*** [verb: ἀσχημονέω <807>]; **from *aschēmōn*: indecent, shameful, which is from *a*: neg., and *schēma*: manner of being ▶ To conduct oneself in an improper way >** A man may think that he behaves unseemly {behave improperly, act unbecomingly} toward his virgin (1 Cor. 7:36). Love does not behave unseemly {does not behave rudely, does not act unbecomingly, is not rude} (1 Cor. 13:5); *euschēmoneō* in some mss. ¶

– [3] Rom. 13:13; 1 Cor. 3:3 → WALK <4043> [4] 2 Cor. 1:12; 1 Tim. 3:15 → CONDUCT (verb)[1] <390>.

BEHAVIOR – [1] ***katastēma*** [neut. noun: κατάστημα <2688>]; **from *kathistēmi*: to conduct, to organize, which is from *kata*: down, and *histēmi*: to stand ▶ Conduct, manner of living >** The older women should be reverent in their behavior {their deportment, the way they live} (Titus 2:3). ¶

– [2] 1 Tim. 3:2 → of good behavior → RESPECTABLE <2887> [3] Jas. 3:13; 1 Pet. 1:15; 2:12; 3:1, 2, 16 → CONDUCT (noun) <391>.

BEHEAD – [1] ***apokephalizō*** [verb: ἀποκεφαλίζω <607>]; **from *apo*: away, and *kephalē*: head ▶ To cut off the head, to decapitate >** Herod had John beheaded in the prison (Matt. 14:10; Mark 6:16, 27; Luke 9:9). ¶

[2] ***pelekizō*** [verb: πελεκίζω <3990>]; **from *pelekus*: axe ▶ To cut off with an axe, especially to decapitate >** John saw the souls of those who had been beheaded on account of the testimony of Jesus and the word of God (Rev. 20:4). ¶

BEHIND – [1] ***opisō*** [adv.: ὀπίσω <3694>]; **from *opis*: a looking back ▶ From the side opposite to the face, in the back >** Jesus told Peter to get behind Him (Matt. 16:23; Mark 8:33). A woman who was a sinner stood at the feet of Jesus behind Him and was weeping (Luke 7:38). Paul was forgetting the things behind and reaching forward to the things ahead (Phil. 3:13). John heard behind him a great voice on the Lord's day (Rev. 1:10). *

[2] **behind, from behind: *opisthen*** [adv.: ὄπισθεν <3693>]; **from *opis*: a looking**

back, and suffix *then*: from or at a place ▶ From the side opposite to the face, in the back > A woman came behind and touched the hem of Jesus's garment (Matt. 9:20; Mark 5:27; Luke 8:44). The word is transl. "after" in Matt. 15:23; Luke 23:26. It is transl. "in back" in Rev. 4:6: the four living creatures were full of eyes in front and in back {before and behind}. Other ref.: Rev. 5:1; see BACK (adv. and noun) <3693>. ¶

– [3] 1 Cor. 1:7 → to come behind → LACK (verb) <5302> [4] 2 Cor. 11:5; 12:11 → to be behind → INFERIOR (BE) <5302> [5] Col. 1:24 → that which is behind → that which is lacking → LACKING <5303> [6] Heb. 6:19 → INNER <2082>.

BEHOLD (interj.) – ***ide*** [particle used as an interj.: ἴδε <2396>]; **from *eidō*: to see, calling attention to what may be seen or heard or mentally apprehended in any way ▶ Observe, consider** > A particle of exclamation and calling attention to something present (Matt. 25:20, 22, 25; Mark 11:21; John 1:47; 19:5: "Behold the man," 14). Addressed apparently to several, but directed to one (Mark 3:34; John 1:29; 7:26; 11:36; 19:4). With the meaning of observe, consider (Mark 15:4; John 1:36; 5:14; Rom. 2:17; Gal. 5:2). * ‡

BEHOLD (verb) – [1] ***anatheōreō*** [verb: ἀναθεωρέω <333>]; **from *ana*: intens., and *theōreō*: to look, to consider ▶ To consider attentively, to contemplate** > Paul had beheld {considered, examined, looked carefully at} the objects of the worship of the Athenians (Acts 17:23); *diistoreō* in some mss.: to examine with great attention. Other ref.: Heb. 13:7; see CONSIDER <333>. ¶

[2] **to behold earnestly, steadfastly: *atenizō*** [verb: ἀτενίζω <816>]; **from *atenēs*: attentive, intent, which is from *a*: intens., and *teinō*: to stretch ▶ To fix with the eyes; also transl.: to look earnestly, intently, straight, steadily** > Paul was earnestly beholding the council (Acts 23:1). The sons of Israel could not behold steadfastly the face of Moses (2 Cor. 3:7, 13). All other refs.: FASTEN <816>, FIX <816>, LOOK (verb) <816>.

[3] ***blepō*** [verb: βλέπω <991>] **▶ To look, to consider** > Paul told the Corinthians to behold {consider, observe, see} Israel after the flesh (1 Cor. 10:18). Other refs.: SEE <991>.

[4] ***eidō*** [verb: εἴδω <1492>]; **lit.: to see ▶ To understand, to consider** > Paul exhorts his readers to behold the goodness and severity of God (Rom. 11:22).

[5] **to behold as in a mirror: *katoptrizō*** [verb: κατοπτρίζω <2734>]; **from *katoptron*: mirror, which is from *kata*: down, and *ōps*: eye ▶ To reflect as a mirror** > Christians, with unveiled face, reflecting {beholding as in a mirror, looking on, beholding as in a glass} the glory of the Lord, are being transformed into the same image from glory to glory, just as by the Spirit of the Lord (2 Cor. 3:18). ¶

– [6] Matt. 6:26; 19:26; Mark 10:21; Luke 20:17; John 1:42 → to look at → LOOK (verb) <1689> [7] Matt. 22:11 → SEE <1492> [8] Matt. 27:55; Mark 3:11; 12:41; 15:47; Luke 21:6; 23:35; John 2:23; 6:40; Rev. 11:11, 12 → SEE <2334> [9] Mark 6:38; 13:1; Luke 23:49; John 20:27 → LOOK (verb) <3708> [10] Luke 23:55; John 1:14, 32 → SEE <2300> [11] John 4:35; 1 John 1:1 → to look at, to look upon → LOOK (verb) <2300> [12] Acts 2:25 → FORESEE <4308> [13] Acts 4:29 → to look upon → LOOK (verb) <1896> [14] Acts 7:31, 32; Jas. 1:23, 24 → CONSIDER <2657> [15] 1 Pet. 2:12; 3:2 → WITNESS (verb) <2029>.

BEING (noun) – [1] Matt. 24:22 → human being → FLESH <4561> [2] Acts 17:29 → divine being → divine nature → DIVINE <2304> [3] Rom. 7:22; 2 Cor. 4:16; Eph. 3:16 → inner being → inner man → MAN <2080>, <444> [4] Phil. 1:26 → COMING <3952> [5] Heb. 1:3 → SUBSTANCE <5287> [6] Jude 8 → celestial being → DIGNITARY <1391>.

BEING (verb) – ***ōn*** [pres. ptcp.: ὤν <5607>] **▶ Pres. ptcp. of *eimi*.** *

BEING TAKEN – Heb. 11:5c → TRANSLATION <3331>.

BELIAL – ***Belial*** [masc. name: Βελίαλ <955>] **or** ***Beliar*** [masc. name: Βελιάρ <955>]**: worthless, wickedness, in Heb. ▶ This O.T. name is symbolic of that which is evil, that which is wicked (e.g., see Prov. 6:12)** > The name Belial applies to Satan, the adversary of Christ; there is no agreement between Christ and Belial (2 Cor. 6:15). In the O.T. (e.g., Deut. 13:13; Judg. 19:22; 1 Kgs. 21:10), this name symbolizes iniquity, wickedness. ¶

BELIAR – See BELIAL <955>.

BELIEVE – [1] ***pisteuō*** [verb: πιστεύω <4100>]; **from** ***pistis*****: belief, assurance, which is from** ***peithō*****: to persuade, to convince ▶ To have faith, i.e., to be persuaded, to put one's trust in someone or something** > Everyone who believes in the Son of God will not perish, but have eternal life (John 3:15, 16, 36; 6:47); he who believes in Him is not condemned, but he who does not believe is condemned already, because he has not believed in the name of the only begotten Son of God (John 3:18a–c). Whoever believes in Jesus receives remission of sins (Acts 10:43). Everyone who believes in Jesus is justified (Acts 13:39). Having believed, Christians were sealed with the Holy Spirit of promise (Eph. 1:13). Whoever believes that Jesus is the Christ is born of God (1 John 5:1); he who believes that Jesus is the Son of God overcomes the world (v. 5). The Lord will come to be glorified in His saints and to be admired among all those who believe (2 Thes. 1:10). Other refs.: Matt. 8:13; 9:28; 18:6; 21:22, 25, 32a–c; 24:23, 26; 27:42; Mark 1:15; 5:36; 9:23a, b, 42; 11:23, 24, 31; 13:21; 15:32; 16:13, 14, 16, 17; Luke 1:20, 45; 8:12, 13, 50; 20:5; 22:67; 24:25; John 1:7, 12, 50; 2:11, 22–24; 3:12a, b; 4:21, 39, 41, 42, 48, 50, 53; 5:24, 38, 44, 46a, b, 47a, b; 6:29, 30, 35, 36, 40, 64a, b, 69; 7:5, 31, 38, 39, 48; 8:24, 30, 31, 45, 46; 9:18, 35, 36, 38; 10:25, 26, 37, 38a–c, 42; 11:15, 25, 26a, b, 27, 40, 42, 45, 48; 12:11, 36–39, 42, 44a, b, 46; 13:19; 14:1a, b, 10, 11a, b, 12, 29; 16:9, 27, 30, 31; 17:8, 20, 21; 19:35; 20:8, 25, 29a, b, 31a, b; Acts 2:44; 4:4, 32; 5:14; 8:12, 13, 37; 9:26, 42; 11:17, 21; 13:12, 41, 48; 14:1, 23; 15:5, 7, 11; 16:31, 34; 17:12, 34; 18:8a, b, 27; 19:2, 4, 18; 21:20, 25; 22:19; 24:14; 26:27a, b; 27:25; Rom. 1:16; 3:22; 4:3, 5, 11, 17, 18, 24; 6:8; 9:33; 10:4, 9–11, 14a, b, 16; 13:11; 14:2; 15:13; 1 Cor. 1:21; 3:5; 11:18; 13:7; 14:22a, b; 15:2, 11; 2 Cor. 4:13a, b; Gal. 2:16; 3:6, 22; Eph. 1:19; Phil. 1:29; 1 Thes. 1:7; 2:10, 13; 4:14; 2 Thes. 1:10a, b; 2:11, 12; 1 Tim. 1:11, 16; 3:16; 2 Tim. 1:12; Titus 1:3; 3:8; Heb. 4:3; 11:6; Jas. 2:19a, b, 23; 1 Pet. 1:8, 21; 2:6, 7; 1 John 3:23; 4:1, 16; 5:10a–c, 13; Jude 5. Some particular refs. among the previous ones: see BELIEVER <4100>, COMMIT <4100>, ENTRUST <4100>. ¶

[2] **to not believe:** ***apisteō*** [verb: ἀπιστέω <569>]; **from** ***apistos*****: untrustworthy, faithless, which is from** ***a*****: neg., and** ***pistis*****: faith ▶ To not have faith, i.e., to not be persuaded, to not put one's trust in someone or something; also transl.: to refuse to believe, to disbelieve** > Those who had been with Jesus did not believe He was alive (Mark 16:11 {to refuse to believe}; Luke 24:11). He who does not believe will be condemned (Mark 16:16). The disciples still did not believe because of their joy that Jesus was risen (Luke 24:41). The Jews did not believe concerning Jesus (John 9:18). Some did not believe what Paul was saying about Jesus (Acts 28:24). If some did not believe, their unbelief will not make the faithfulness of God without effect (Rom. 3:3). If we are faithless (or: we do not believe), God remains faithful (2 Tim. 2:13). ¶

[3] **to not believe:** ***apeitheō*** [verb: ἀπειθέω <544>]**; from** ***apeithēs*****: disobedient, which is from** ***a*****: neg., and** ***peithō*****: to persuade ▶ To refuse to be persuaded, to obey; to disbelieve** > He who does not believe {is not subject to, does not obey, rejects} the Son will not see life, but the wrath of God abides on him (John 3:36). The unbelieving Jews (lit.: The Jews not believing) stirred up the Gentiles against the brothers (Acts 14:2). Some were hardened and did not believe {became disobedient to} what Paul was saying (Acts 19:9). God will judge those who do not believe {do not obey, are disobedient to}

the truth (Rom. 2:8). Paul solicited prayers that he might be delivered from those who did not believe {the unbelievers, those who were disobedient} in Judea (Rom. 15:31). God swore to those who did not believe {did not obey, were disobedient} that they would not enter His rest (Heb. 3:18). Rahab did not perish with those who did not believe {who were disobedient} (Heb. 11:31). Other ref.: Acts 17:5 in some mss. All other refs.: DISBELIEVE <544>, DISOBEDIENT <544>, OBEY <544>, UNBELIEVING <544>.

4 **faith:** ***pistis*** [fem. noun: πίστις <4102>]; **from** ***peithō*****: to have confidence, to be persuaded ▶ Belief, confidence, trust in someone or something** > The author of the Epistle to the Hebrews was of those who believe (lit.: those of faith) to the saving of the soul (Heb. 10:39). Other refs.: see entries in Lexicon at <4102>.

5 **to believe most surely:** ***plērophoreō*** [verb: πληροφορέω <4135>]; **from** ***plērēs*****: full, and** ***phoreō*****: to fill, which is from** ***pherō*****: to carry, to bear; lit.: to accomplish fully ▶ To believe fully; to be fulfilled** > Many had taken in hand to set in order a narrative of the matters which were most surely believed {fully believed, had been fulfilled, accomplished} among the Christians (Luke 1:1). All other refs.: COMPLETE (adj.) <4135>, PERSUADE <4135>, PREACH <4135>, PROOF <4135>.

– 6 John 11:26 → to live by believing → lit.: to live and believe 7 John 20:27; 2 Cor. 6:15 → BELIEVING <4103> 8 Acts 17:4; 28:24 → PERSUADE <3982> 9 Acts 23:8 → CONFESS <3670> 10 Acts 27:11 → PERSUADED (BE) <3982> 11 1 Cor. 7:12, 13; 10:27; 14:22a, b, 24; 2 Cor. 4:4; Titus 1:15 → who does not believe → UNBELIEVING <571> 12 1 Tim. 4:10, 12; 5:16; 6:2 → one who believes → FAITHFUL <4103> 13 2 Tim. 2:13 → to not believe → to be faithless → FAITHLESS <569> 14 2 Tim. 3:14 → to believe firmly → ASSURED (BE) <4104>.

BELIEVER – 1 **to believe:** ***pisteuō*** [verb: πιστεύω <4100>]; **from** ***pistis*****: belief, assurance, faith, which is from** ***peithō*****: to persuade, to convince ▶ To have faith, i.e., to be persuaded, to put one's trust in someone (e.g., the Lord Jesus) or something (e.g., salvation through faith in the person and the work of the Lord)** > Believers (lit.: Those who believe) were increasingly added to the Lord (Acts 5:14). All other refs.: BELIEVE <4100>.

– 2 John 21:23; Acts 1:15; 9:30; 2 Thes. 3:6; Jas. 1:9; 3 John 3, 10; et al. → lit.: the brothers 3 Acts 16:1; 2 Cor. 6:15; Gal. 3:9; 1 Tim. 6:2 → BELIEVING <4103> 4 1 Cor. 7:12, 13 → who is not a believer → UNBELIEVING <571> 5 1 Cor. 7:17 → to live as a believer → WALK <4043>.

BELIEVING – 1 ***pistos*** [adj.: πιστός <4103>]; **from** ***peithō*****: to trust, to obey ▶ Trusting God, having faith, having confidence in God** > Believers through the ages have trusted God according to His testimonies. Since Pentecost, believers who have heard the gospel have believed in the person and the work of Jesus Christ. They are blessed with believing {faithful, the believer} Abraham (Gal. 3:9). The Lord told Thomas to believe (lit.: to be believing) (John 20:27). Timothy was the son of a certain Jewish woman who believed {who was a believer} (lit.: believing) (Acts 16:1). The believer {The believing, He who believes} has no part with the unbeliever (2 Cor. 6:15). Those who have believing masters should not despise them, but serve them because they are believing {believers, faithful} (1 Tim. 6:2). Other refs.: FAITHFUL <4103>.

– 2 1 Cor. 7:15; 9:5 → SISTER <79> 3 Gal. 3:5 → by believing what you heard → by hearing of faith → FAITH <4102>.

BELLY – 1 Matt. 12:40; 15:17; Mark 7:19; John 7:38; Rom. 16:18; Phil. 3:19; Rev. 10:9, 10 → WOMB <2836> 2 Luke 15:16 → to fill one's belly → to fill one's stomach → STOMACH <5526> 3 1 Cor. 6:13a, b → STOMACH <2836> 4 Titus 1:12 → GLUTTON <1064>.

BELONG – 1 ***huparchō*** [verb: ὑπάρχω <5225>]; **from** ***hupo*****: under, and** ***archō*****: to begin, which is from** ***archē*****: beginning ▶**

To be in the possession of, to be found > In the country surrounding the place where Paul had shaken the viper from his hand were the lands belonging to Publius (Acts 28:7). Other refs.: see entries in Lexicon at <5225>.

– 2 Matt. 20:14, 15; Rom. 9:4–6; Heb. 10:39 → the verb is added in Engl. 3 Acts 2:10 → belonging to → lit.: over against (*kata*) 4 Acts 5:4a, b → REMAIN <3306> 5 Acts 7:6 → belonging to others → FOREIGN <245> 6 1 Cor. 7:4a, b → to have authority → AUTHORITY <1850> 7 Heb. 7:13 → PERTAIN <3348> 8 Jas. 2:7 → CALL (verb) <1941>.

BELONGING – 1 Acts 4:32 → anything belonging to him → lit.: his possessions → POSSESSIONS <5224> 2 1 Pet. 2:9 → belonging → acquired possession → POSSESSION <4047>.

BELONGINGS – Acts 2:45 → GOOD (adj. and noun) <5223>.

BELOVED – 1 ***agapētos*** [adj.: ἀγαπητός <27>]**; from *agapaō*: to love ► Who is loved with deep affection; also transl.: wellbeloved, dear, dear friend >** Jesus is the beloved of the Father (Matt. 3:17; 12:18; 17:5; Mark 1:11; 9:7; Luke 3:22; 9:35; 2 Pet. 1:17). In a parable, the master of the vineyard sent his beloved son to receive of the fruit of the vineyard (Mark 12:6; Luke 20:13). The adj. "beloved" {dear friends} is used to describe Barnabas and Paul (Acts 15:25), and Paul {dear} (2 Pet. 3:15). Paul uses the adj. "beloved" {friend} when addressing believers in a church (Rom. 1:7; 12:19; 1 Cor. 4:14; 10:14; 15:58; 2 Cor. 7:1; 12:19; Eph. 5:1; Phil. 2:12; 4:1a, b; 1 Thes. 2:8; Heb. 6:9), as also do James (Jas. 1:16, 19; 2:5), Peter (1 Pet. 2:11; 4:12; 2 Pet. 3:1, 8, 14, 15, 17), John (1 John 2:7; 3:2, 21; 4:1, 7, 11), and Jude (Jude 3, 17, 20). The adj. "beloved" also qualifies Persis (Rom. 16:12) and other Christians: Epaenetus (Rom. 16:5), Amplias (v. 8), Stachys (v. 9), Timothy (1 Cor. 4:17; 2 Tim. 1:2), Tychicus (Eph. 6:21; Col. 4:7), Epaphras (Col. 1:7), Onesimus (Col. 4:9), Luke (Col. 4:14), Philemon (Phm. 1, 16), and Gaius (3 John 1, 2, 5, 11). The Jews are beloved for the sake of the fathers (Rom. 11:28). The believing masters of the servants are beloved (1 Tim. 6:2). ¶

2 **from the verb *agapaō*** [verb: ἀγαπάω <25>]**: to love ► To have affection for someone, to find one's joy in something or someone >** In the following verses, the Greek word can be transl. lit.: having been loved. God will call Israel beloved {loved one} who was not beloved {loved one} (Rom. 9:25a, b). God has made the Christians accepted in His Son, the Beloved {the One He loves} (Eph. 1:6). Paul addresses himself to the Colossians as beloved {loved; lit.: being dearly loved} (Col. 3:12). Jude addresses himself to the beloved {those who are loved} in God the Father (v. 1 in some mss.). Jerusalem is called the beloved city {the city God loves} (Rev. 20:9). All other refs.: LOVE (verb) <25>.

– 3 Phm. 2 → SISTER <79>.

BELOW – See DOWNWARDS <2736>.

BELT – ***zōnē*** [fem. noun: ζώνη <2223>]**; from *zōnnumi*: to wrap around ► Band of material or leather around the waist to gird on clothing; money could be put in it; also transl.: band, girdle >** John had a leather belt around his loins (Matt. 3:4; Mark 1:6). Jesus told His disciples to provide neither gold, nor silver, nor brass in their belts {money belts, purses} (Matt. 10:9; Mark 6:8). Agabus took Paul's belt and bound his own hands and feet (Acts 21:11a, b). The Son of Man was girded about the chest with a golden band {sash} (Rev. 1:13), and so were the seven angels of Rev. 15:6 as well. ¶

BENCH – Matt. 21:12; Mark 11:15 → SEAT (noun) <2515>.

BEND – 1 **to bend over: *sunkuptō*** [verb: συγκύπτω <4794>]**; from *sun*: together, and *kuptō*: to bend, to bow ► To lean forward >** Jesus healed a woman who was bent over {bent together, bent double} and could not raise herself up (Luke 13:11). ¶

– [2] Luke 4:39 → to bend over → to stand over → STAND (verb) <2186> [3] John 8:6, 8 → STOOP <2955> [4] John 20:5, 11 → to bend over → STOOP <3879> [5] Acts 20:10 → to bend over → to fall upon → FALL (verb) <1968> [6] Rom. 11:10 → BOW (verb) <4781>.

BENEFACTOR – [1] ***euergetēs*** [masc. noun: εὐεργέτης <2110>]; **from *eu*: well, and *ergon*: action, work ► One who does good to others >** Jesus says that those who exercise authority over the nations are called benefactors (Luke 22:25). ¶

– [2] Rom. 16:2 → HELPER <4368>.

BENEFICIAL – 1 Cor. 6:12; 10:23 → to be beneficial → to be profitable → PROFITABLE <4851>.

BENEFIT (noun) – [1] Luke 6:32, 33 → CREDIT (noun) <5485> [2] Acts 4:9 → DEED <2108> [3] Rom. 3:1 → PROFIT (noun) <5622> [4] 1 Cor. 7:35 → PROFIT (noun) <4852a> [5] 2 Cor. 8:23 → for your benefit → lit.: for you [6] Gal. 5:2; Heb. 13:9 → to be of benefit → PROFIT (verb) <5623> [7] 1 Tim. 6:2 → SERVICE <2108> [8] Phm. 14 → GOOD (adj. and noun) <18> [9] Phm. 20 → to have benefit → BENEFIT <3685> [10] Heb. 13:17 → of no benefit → UNPROFITABLE <255>.

BENEFIT (verb) – [1] ***oninēmi*** [verb: ὀνίνημι <3685>] **► To profit, to obtain an advantage >** Paul wrote to Philemon saying he would like to benefit {have profit, have some benefit, have joy} from him in the Lord (Phm. 20). In this epistle, the name *Onēsimos* (Onesimus), the servant of Philemon, means "useful," "profitable one"; there is most likely a wordplay on the verb *oninēmi* and the name *Onēsimos*. ¶

– [2] 1 Cor. 14:6; Heb. 4:2 → PROFIT (verb) <5623> [3] 2 Cor. 8:10 → to be profitable → PROFITABLE <4851> [4] Eph. 4:29 → lit.: to minister grace → MINISTER (verb) <1325> [5] 1 Tim. 6:2 → PROFIT (verb) <482>.

BENEVOLENCE – 1 Cor. 7:3 → GOOD WILL <2133>.

BENJAMIN – ***Beniamin*** [masc. name: Βενιαμίν <958>]**: son of the right hand, in Heb. ► Youngest of Jacob's twelve sons and name of a tribe descended from him >** King Saul was of the tribe of Benjamin (Acts 13:21), as well as the apostle Paul (Rom. 11:1; Phil. 3:5). Twelve thousand out of the tribe of Benjamin will be sealed (Rev. 7:8). ¶

BEOR – See BOSOR <1007>.

BEREA – [1] ***Beroia*** [fem. name: Βέροια <960>] **► City of Macedonia, near Thessalonica, which Paul visited during his second missionary journey >** Many Jews in Berea believed the preaching of Paul and Silas, as well as Greek women of the upper classes and a great number of men (Acts 17:10, 13). ¶

[2] **of Berea: *Beroiaios*** [adj.: Βεροιαῖος <961>] **► Inhabitant of the city of Berea; see [1] >** Sopater, a traveling companion of Paul, was originally from Berea (Acts 20:4). ¶

BERECHIAH – See BARACHIAS <914>.

BERNICE – ***Bernikē*** [fem. name: Βερνίκη <959>]**: victorious ► Sister of King Agrippa II >** Bernice and Agrippa visited Festus at Caesarea; Paul made his defense before them (Acts 25:13, 23; 26:30). ¶

BERRY – Jas. 3:12 → olive berries → lit.: olives → OLIVE <1636>.

BERYL – ***bērullos*** [masc. and fem. noun: βήρυλλος <969>] **► Precious stone of a green or blue color >** The eighth foundation of the wall of the heavenly Jerusalem is adorned with beryl (Rev. 21:20). ¶

BESEECH – [1] ***parakaleō*** [verb: παρακαλέω <3870>]; **from *para*: beside, and *kaleō*: to call ► To ask insistently, to supplicate; also transl.: to appeal, to ask, to beg, to desire, to entreat, to implore,**

to intreat, to invite, to petition, to plead, to present charges, to request, to urge > The verb is used in regard to demons (Matt. 8:31; Mark 5:10, 12; Luke 8:31, 32), a city (Matt. 8:34; Mark 5:17), those who were ill (Matt. 14:36), Jesus (Matt. 26:53), a man who had been possessed by demons (Mark 5:18), people who laid the sick in the marketplaces (Mark 6:56), those who brought a deaf man (Mark 7:32), those who brought a blind man (Mark 8:22), the elders of the Jews (Luke 7:4), the father of the prodigal son (Luke 15:28), a eunuch (Acts 8:31), two men sent to Peter (Acts 9:38), a Macedonian man (Acts 16:9), Lydia (Acts 16:15), praetors (Acts 16:39 {to appease}), Asiarchs (Acts 19:31), Tertullus (Acts 24:4), the Jews who accused Paul (Acts 25:2), the brothers of Puteoli (Acts 28:14), Paul (1 Cor. 16:12; 2 Cor. 9:5; 12:18), Timothy (1 Tim. 1:3), Philemon (Phm. 9, 10), and the readers of the Epistle to the Hebrews (Heb. 13:19). All other refs.: see entries in Lexicon at <3870>.

– 2 Matt. 9:38; Luke 5:12; 8:28, 38; 9:38, 40; 10:2; 2 Cor. 5:20; 10:2 → SUPPLICATE <1189> 3 Matt. 15:23; Mark 7:26; Luke 4:38; 7:3; 8:37; 11:37; 16:27; John 4:40, 47; 19:31; 1 Thes. 4:1; 5:12; 2 Thes. 2:1; 2 John 5 → ASK <2065> 4 Luke 22:32; Acts 21:39; 26:3; Gal. 4:12; 1 Thes. 3:10 → PRAY <1189> 5 Rom. 1:10 → to make request → REQUEST (noun) <1189> 6 Eph. 3:13 → ASK <154>.

BESET – 1 Mark 3:10 → to fall upon → FALL (verb) <1968> 2 Luke 6:18; Acts 5:16 → TORMENT (verb) <3791> 3 Acts 17:5 → ASSAULT (verb) <2186> 4 Heb. 5:2 → to be subject → SUBJECT (verb) <4029> 5 Heb. 12:1 → which besets so easily, which ensnares so easily → ENSNARE <2139>.

BESIDE – 1 Matt. 14:21; 15:38; 2 Cor. 11:28 → BESIDES <5565> 2 2 Cor. 5:13 → to be beside oneself → to be out of one's mind → MIND (noun) <1839>.

BESIDES – ***chōris*** [prep.: χωρίς <5565>] ▶ **Aside from, without counting >** Jesus fed a crowd of about five thousand men, besides women and children (Matt. 14:21). On another occasion, he fed four thousand men, besides women and children (Matt. 15:38). Besides {Apart from} those things which were without, the solicitude for all the churches pressed upon Paul daily (2 Cor. 11:28). *

BESIEGE – Luke 11:53 → to make to speak → SPEAK <653>.

BEST – 1 ***prōtos*** [adj.: πρῶτος <4413>]**; superl. of *pro*: before, in front ▶ First, nicest >** In the parable, the father had the best robe brought out for his son who had returned home (Luke 15:22). All other refs.: CHIEF <4413>, FIRST <4413>, PROMINENT <4413>.

– 2 Acts 24:16 → to do one's best → EXERCISE (verb) <778> 3 2 Cor. 8:10 → to be best → to be profitable → PROFITABLE <4851> 4 2 Tim. 1:18 → very well → WELL (adv.) <957> 5 2 Tim. 2:15 → to do one's best → to be diligent → DILIGENT <4704> 6 2 Tim. 4:9, 21; Titus 3:12 → to do one's best → to make every effort → EFFORT <4704>.

BESTOW – 1 ***didōmi*** [verb: δίδωμι <1325>] ▶ **To give, to offer as a gift >** The Father has bestowed {has lavished} such love on the Christians, that they are called children of God (1 John 3:1). Other refs.: see entries in Lexicon at <1325>.

2 ***peritithēmi*** [verb: περιτίθημι <4060>]**; from *peri*: around, and *tithēmi*: to put; lit.: to surround ▶ To give, to dress >** The less honorable members of the body are bestowed {clothed with, treated with} greater honor (1 Cor. 12:23). All other refs.: PUT <4060>, SET (verb) <4060>.

– 3 Luke 7:21; Phil. 2:9 → to freely give, to give → GIVE <5483> 4 Luke 12:17, 18 → GATHER <4863> 5 Luke 22:29a, b → APPOINT <1303> 6 Rom. 10:12 → "bestowing" added in Engl. 7 1 Cor. 13:3 → to give to feed → FEED <5595> 8 Eph. 1:6 → to bestow one's grace freely → to make accepted → ACCEPTED <5487>.

BETHABARA – John 1:28 → BETHANY <962>.

BETHANY – [1] ***Bēthania*** [fem. name: Βηθανία <963>]**: house of depression or misery, in Heb. ▶ a. Village of Palestine >** Jesus visited Bethany (Matt. 21:17; Mark 11:11; John 11:1), which was near Jerusalem (Mark 11:1; Luke 19:29; John 11:18). He stayed there sometimes, when Martha, Mary, and Lazarus received Him in their home. A few days before His death, they made Him a supper there (John 12:1, see v. 2). Matt. 26:6 and Mark 14:3 speak of Jesus being at Bethany in the house of Simon the leper. It was when He had gone out of Bethany that Jesus cursed the fig tree which had leaves, but no fruit (Mark 11:12). The ascension of the Lord took place at Bethany (Luke 24:50). **b. Name of a place beyond the Jordan >** John baptized at Bethany (John 1:28; see [2]). ¶
[2] ***Bēthabara*** [fem. name: Βηθαβαρά <962>]**: house of the crossing, in Heb. ▶** Certain mss. have the name Bethabara in John 1:28 instead of Bethany. ¶

BETHESDA – ***Bēthesda*** [fem. name: Βηθεσδά <964>]**: house of mercy, in Heb.; other name: *Bēthzatha*: house of olive (oil) ▶ Pool in Jerusalem >** The pool of Bethesda had five porches in which lay a multitude of people who were sick, blind, lame, and paralyzed (John 5:2; see v. 3). Jesus healed a man who had an infirmity for 38 years at this place (see John 5:5–9). ¶

BETHLEHEM – ***Bēthleem*** [fem. name: Βηθλέεμ <965>]**: house of bread, in Heb. ▶ Small city of Judea >** Jesus was born in Bethlehem (Matt. 2:1, 5, 6; Luke 2:4; John 7:42). Shepherds went there to render homage to the newborn Jesus (Luke 2:15). Later, wise men came to Bethlehem to bring offerings to Jesus (see Matt. 2:1, 2); when he knew this, Herod (Matt. 2:8) put to death the male children from two years old and under at Bethlehem in an attempt to slay Jesus (v. 16). ¶

BETHPHAGE – ***Bēthphagē*** [fem. name: Βηθφαγή <967>]**: house of figs, in Heb. ▶ Village near the Mount of Olives in Jerusalem >** Jesus sent two of His disciples to Bethphage to look for a colt, on which He sat for His entry into Jerusalem several days before His crucifixion (Matt. 21:1; Mark 11:1; Luke 19:29). ¶

BETHSAIDA – ***Bēthsaida*** [fem. name: Βηθσαϊδά <966>]**: house of fishing or hunting, in Heb. ▶ City north of the Sea of Galilee near Capernaum >** Jesus visited Bethsaida (Mark 6:45; Luke 9:10). He rebuked the city for unbelief despite the miracles witnessed there (Matt. 11:21; Luke 10:13). Philip, Andrew, and Peter were from Bethsaida (John 1:44; 12:21). Jesus healed a blind man there (Mark 8:22; see vv. 22–26). ¶

BETRAY – [1] ***paradidōmi*** [verb: παραδίδωμι <3860>]**; from *para*: over to, and *didōmi*: to give ▶ To remit to another to be judged, condemned; to be a traitor >** The verb is also transl.: "betrayer" (lit.: the one betraying) and often: to deliver. It is sometimes transl.: to give, to give up, to give over, to cast in prison, to put in prison, to commit, to hand over. The verb is used regarding the Lord Jesus (Matt. 10:4; 17:22; 20:18, 19; 26:2, 15, 16, 21, 23–25, 45, 46, 48; 27:2–4, 18, 26; Mark 3:19; 9:31; 10:33a, b; 14:10, 11, 18, 21, 41, 42, 44; 15:1, 10, 15; Luke 9:44; 18:32; 20:20; 22:4, 6, 21, 22, 48; 23:25; 24:7, 20; John 6:64, 71; 12:4; 13:2, 11, 21; 18:2, 5, 30, 35, 36; 19:11, 16; 21:20; Acts 3:13; Rom. 4:25; 8:32; Gal. 2:20; Eph. 5:2, 25). It is also used regarding John the Baptist (Matt. 4:12; Mark 1:14), the disciples (Matt. 10:17, 19; 24:9; Mark 13:9, 11; Luke 21:12, 16), Paul (Acts 21:11; 28:17), and Peter (Acts 12:4). God delivered wicked men to uncleanliness, vile passions, and a debased mind (Rom. 1:24, 26, 28). Other refs.: Matt. 5:25a, b; 10:21; 18:34; 24:10; Mark 13:12; Acts 7:42; 8:3; 22:4; 28:16; 1 Cor. 5:5; 11:23; 13:3; 2 Cor. 4:11; 1 Tim. 1:20; 2 Pet. 2:4. All other refs.: see entries in Lexicon at <3860>.

– [2] Matt. 26:73 → to make manifest → MANIFEST (adj.) <1212>.

BETRAYER – [1] ***prodotēs*** [masc. noun: προδότης <4273>]; **from *prodidōmi*: to deliver, to give into enemy hands, which is from *pro*: before, and *didōmi*: to give ▶ One who delivers to an enemy, traitor** > The Jews became betrayers {deliverers up} and murderers of the Just One (Acts 7:52). Other refs.: Luke 6:16; 2 Tim. 3:4; see TRAITOR <4273>. ¶
– [2] Matt. 26:46, 48; 27:3; Mark 14:42, 44; Luke 22:21 → lit.: the one betraying → BETRAY <3860>.

BETROTH – 2 Cor. 11:2 → PROMISE (verb) <718>.

BETROTHED – 1 Cor. 7:25, 28, 34, 36–38 in some mss. → the betrothed, betrothed woman → VIRGIN <3933>.

BETROTHED (BE) – Matt. 1:18; Luke 1:27; 2:5 → to be betrothed → to be pledged to be married → MARRIED (BE) <3423>.

BETTER – [1] ***kalon*; from *kalos*** [adj.: καλός <2570>]; **neuter of *kalos*: beautiful, good ▶ Of an advantageous or favorable manner** > It is better {good} to have certain disadvantages in life than to be cast into the everlasting fire (Matt. 18:8, 9; Mark 9:43, 45, 47). Other ref.: Mark 9:42. Other refs.: see entries in Lexicon at <2570>.
[2] ***kreisson*** [adj. used as an adv.: κρεῖσσον <2908>]; **from *kratus*: strong ▶ Excellently, advantageously** > It is better to marry than to burn with passion (1 Cor. 7:9). He who gives in marriage {some versions: He who marries himself} does well, and he who does not give in marriage {some versions: marry} does better (1 Cor. 7:38). The Corinthians came together, not for the better (1 Cor. 11:17). It was much better for Paul to depart and to be with Christ (Phil. 1:23). God had provided some better thing (or: something better) for Christians (Heb. 11:40). The blood of sprinkling speaks of better things than that of Abel (Heb. 12:24). It would be better not to have known the way of righteousness than, having known it, to turn back from the holy commandment (2 Pet. 2:21). Other ref.: 1 Cor. 12:31 in some mss. ¶
[3] ***kreissōn*** [adj. and adv.: κρείσσων <2909>]; **compar. of *kratus*: strong ▶ More advantageous, more excellent; also transl.: superior** > Christians are to earnestly desire the better gifts (1 Cor. 12:31 in some mss.). Jesus has taken a place so much better than the angels (Heb. 1:4). The inferior is blessed by the better {greater} (Heb. 7:7). In the Epistle to the Hebrews, the word is used in regard to those things which are connected with salvation (6:9), hope by which we draw near to God (7:19), a covenant of which Jesus has become the surety (7:22; 8:6a), promises (8:6b), sacrifices (9:23), an enduring possession (10:34), a heavenly country (11:16), and resurrection (11:35). It is better to suffer for doing good than for doing evil (1 Pet. 3:17). ¶
[4] ***kompsoteron*** [adv.: κομψότερον <2866>]; **compar. neut. of *kompsos*: nice, well ▶ In an improved condition (as: convalescent)** > The nobleman inquired of his servants at what hour his son got better {began to amend} (John 4:52). ¶
[5] ***chrēstos*** [adj.: χρηστός <5543>]; **from *chraomai*: to use; lit.: which can be used ▶ Good, pleasant** > The old wine is better (Luke 5:39). All other refs.: EASY <5543>, GOOD (adj.) <5543>, GOODNESS <5543>.
[6] **to be better: *lusiteleō*** [verb: λυσιτελέω <3081>]; **from *lusitelēs*: profitable, which is from *luō*: to unloose, and *telos*: toll, tribute ▶ To be more useful, more advantageous** > It would be better {more profitable} to be thrown into the sea than to offend a little one who believes in Jesus (Luke 17:2). ¶
[7] **to be better: *proechō*** [verb: προέχω <4284>]; **from *pro*: before, and *echō*: to have, to be ▶ To be superior, to have superiority** > The Jews are not better than the Greeks (Rom. 3:9); *prokatechō* in some mss. ¶
– [8] Matt. 5:29, 30; 18:6; 19:10; John 11:50 → to be better → to be profitable

→ PROFITABLE <4851> [9] Matt. 6:26; 10:31; 12:12; Luke 12:7, 24 → to be better → to be of more value → VALUE (noun) <1308> [10] Mark 5:26 → to be better, to become better → HELPED (BE) <5623> [11] Rom. 14:5 → as better → lit.: above (*para*) [12] 1 Cor. 8:8 → to be the better → ABOUND <4052> [13] 2 Cor. 12:16 → to get the better → TAKE <2983> [14] Phil. 2:3 → more important → IMPORTANT <5242> [15] Heb. 11:4 → more excellent → EXCELLENT <4119>.

BETTERED (BE) – Mark 5:26 → HELPED (BE) <5623>.

BEWAIL – [1] ***pentheō*** [verb: πενθέω <3996>]; **from *penthos*: sadness, bereavement ▶ To grieve, to be bereaved** > Paul feared that he would bewail {mourn for, grieve over, be grieved over} many who had sinned before and had not repented (2 Cor. 12:21). All other refs.: MOURN <3996>.
– [2] Luke 8:52 → LAMENT <2875> [3] Luke 23:27 → MOURN <2875> [4] Rev. 18:9 → WEEP <2799>.

BEWARE – [1] ***blepō*** [verb: βλέπω <991>]; **lit.: to look ▶ To watch out, to pay attention** > Jesus said to beware of the scribes (Mark 12:38). Other refs.: SEE <991>.
[2] ***tēreō*** [verb: τηρέω <5083>]; **from *tēros*: warden, guard ▶ To watch, to hold** > Paul had kept himself from being a burden to the Corinthians, and so would continue to keep himself (2 Cor. 11:9a, b). All other refs.: see entries in Lexicon at <5083>.
[3] ***diatēreō*** [verb: διατηρέω <1301>]; **from *dia*: intens., and *tēreō*: see [2] ▶ To carefully avoid** > Christians are to avoid {keep themselves from} things sacrificed to idols, from blood, from what is strangled, and from sexual immorality (Acts 15:29). Other ref.: Luke 2:51; see KEEP (verb) <1301>. ¶
[4] ***horaō*** [verb: ὁράω <3708>]; **lit.: to look ▶ To pay attention, to look out, to see** > Jesus told His disciples to beware of the leaven of the Pharisees and of the leaven of Herod (Mark 8:15). An angel told John to see that he not do homage to himself (Rev. 19:10; 22:9). Other refs.: APPEAR <3708>, LOOK (verb) <3708>, SEE <3708>.
[5] ***prosechō*** [verb: προσέχω <4337>]; **from *pros*: to, and *echō*: to have ▶ To pay attention, to take heed; also transl.: to be on guard, to be careful, to consider carefully, to keep watch, to take care, to watch out** > Jesus says to beware not to do our charitable deeds before men to be seen by them (Matt. 6:1). He says to beware of false prophets (Matt. 7:15). He tells His disciples to beware of men, for they will deliver them up to the courts (Matt. 10:17). He also tells them to beware of the leaven of the Pharisees and Sadducees (Matt. 16:6, 11, 12); He tells them to beware of the leaven of the Pharisees, which is hypocrisy (Luke 12:1). He tells His disciples to beware of the scribes (Luke 20:46). Gamaliel told the Israelites to take heed to themselves in regard to what they proposed to do to the apostles (Acts 5:35). All other refs.: ATTENDANCE <4337>, GIVE <4337>, HEED (noun) <4337>.
– [6] Luke 12:15; 2 Tim. 4:15; 2 Pet. 3:17 → to be on one's guard → GUARD (noun) <5442>.

BEWILDERED (BE) – [1] Mark 16:8 → lit.: to be gripped by astonishment → ASTONISHMENT <1611> [2] Acts 2:6 → to be confounded → CONFOUND <4797>.

BEWILDERMENT – Acts 2:6 → to come in bewilderment → to be confounded → CONFOUND <4797>.

BEWITCH – [1] ***baskainō*** [verb: βασκαίνω <940>]; **from *baskanos*: who looks with suspicion, jealous ▶ To use witchcraft or magic to influence, to cast a spell** > The Galatians had been bewitched, in the sense of being induced into error, to believe they were saved on the principle of the works of the law rather than by the grace of God (Gal. 3:1). ¶
– [2] Acts 8:9, 11 → to astonish → ASTONISHED (BE) <1839>.

BEWRAY – Matt. 26:73 → to make manifest → MANIFEST (adj.) <1212>.

BEYOND – 1 ***epekeina*** [adv.: ἐπέκεινα <1900>]; **from *epi*: upon, and *ekeinos*: that one ▶ Adv. of time and order; also transl.: afterwards, next, then** > The word is found in Acts 7:43. ¶ ‡
– 2 John 6:1 → OVER <4008> 3 Acts 19:39 → FURTHER (adv.) <4007a> 4 2 Cor. 10:16 → region beyond → REGION <5238>.

BEZER – 2 Pet. 2:15 → BOSOR <1007>.

BIAS – 1 Tim. 5:21 → PREJUDICE <4299>.

BID – 1 Matt. 1:24 → ORDAIN <4367> 2 Matt. 14:28 → COMMAND (verb) <2753> 3 Matt. 22:3b, 4, 8; Luke 14:7, 17 → INVITE <2564> 4 Luke 14:12 → to bid again → to invite back → INVITE <479> 5 Acts 18:21; 2 Cor. 2:13 → to bid farewell, to bid adieu → to take leave → LEAVE (noun) <657>.

BIER – ***soros*** [fem. noun: σορός <4673>] ▶ **Funeral bed on which a dead person was carried** > Jesus touched the bier {coffin, open coffin} of the only son of a mother (Luke 7:14). ¶

BIGGER – Luke 7:43 → lit.: the more → MORE <4119>.

BILL – 1 ***gramma*** [neut. noun: γράμμα <1121>]; **from *graphō*: to write; lit.: writing ▶ Accounting book** > The unjust steward told the debtors to take their bill and write different amounts than what they owed (Luke 16:6, 7). All other refs.: LEARNING <1121>, LETTER <1121>, WRITING <1121>.
– 2 Mark 10:4 → CERTIFICATE <975>.

BILLOW – Acts 2:19 → VAPOR <822>.

BIND – 1 ***desmeuō*** [verb: δεσμεύω <1195>]; **from *desmos*: band, bond ▶ To fasten with a bond, to chain** > The scribes and Pharisees bound {tied} heavy burdens and laid them on the shoulders of men (Matt. 23:4). A possessed man was being bound, kept with chains and fetters (Luke 8:29); some mss. have *desmeō* [δεσμέω <1196>]. Saul bound {arrested} and delivered up to prison Christian men and women (Acts 22:4). ¶
2 ***deō*** [verb: δέω <1210>] ▶ **To fasten with a bond or to tie; to deprive of liberty by shutting up in a prison** > One must first bind the strong man before plundering his house (Matt. 12:29; Mark 3:27). The tares must be bound in bundles (Matt. 13:30). Herod had bound John (Matt. 14:3; Mark 6:17). Whatever Peter might bind on earth would be bound in heaven (Matt. 16:19a, b), likewise for the disciples (18:18a, b). The king told his servants to bind the hands and feet of the man who did not have on a wedding garment (Matt. 22:13). Jesus was bound (Matt. 27:2; Mark 15:1; John 18:12, 24). No one could bind a possessed man, for he had often broken his chains (Mark 5:3, 4). Jesus loosed from her bond a woman whom Satan had bound with an infirmity (Luke 13:16). Lazarus came forth from the tomb bound {wrapped} hand and foot (John 11:44). Nicodemus and Joseph bound {wound, wrapped} the body of Jesus in strips of linen with spices before His burial (John 19:40). Saul wanted to bring Christians bound to Jerusalem {take them as prisoners, arrest them} (Acts 9:2, 14, 21; 22:5 {in chains}). Peter saw an object like a great sheet bound {knit} at the four corners (Acts 10:11). He was sleeping, bound with two chains (Acts 12:6). Paul was bound in his spirit {compelled by the Spirit} (Acts 20:22). Agabus bound his own hands and feet with Paul's belt, to show him that he would be bound in this manner and delivered to the Gentiles (Acts 21:11a, b); Paul was ready to be bound (v. 13). He was bound with two chains (Acts 21:33; 22:29 {in chains}). Felix left Paul bound {imprisoned, in prison} (Acts 24:27). Paul uses the verb in regard to the married man and woman (Rom. 7:2; 1 Cor. 7:27a, 39). He was bound {in chains} for the mystery of Christ (Col. 4:3). The word of God is not bound {chained}

(2 Tim. 2:9). The four angels bound at the Euphrates were to be released (Rev. 9:14). Satan will be bound for one thousand years (Rev. 20:2). Other refs.: Matt. 21:2; Mark 11:2, 4; 15:7; Luke 19:30; see TIE <1210>, CHAIN (verb) <1210>. ¶

3 **to bind up: *katadeō*** [verb: καταδέω <2611>]; **from *kata*: down (intens.), and *deō*: see 2 ▶ To bandage, to dress the wounds** > The Samaritan bound up the wounds of the man in a half-dead state (Luke 10:34). ¶

4 **to bind with: *sundeō*** [verb: συνδέω <4887>]; **from *sun*: together, together, and *deō*: see 2 ▶ To tie with, to imprison with** > We should remember prisoners as if bound {chained, in prison} with them {as if fellow prisoners} (Heb. 13:3). ¶

5 **to be bound with: *perikeimai*** [verb: περίκειμαι <4029>]; **from *peri*: about, around, and *keimai*: to lie ▶ To be compassed (with fetters)** > Paul was bound with {had, was wearing} a chain for the hope of Israel (Acts 28:20). All other refs.: HANG <4029>, SUBJECT (verb) <4029>, SURROUND <4029>.

6 ***proteinō*** [verb: προτείνω <4385>]; **from *pro*: forth, and *teinō*: to extend ▶ To stretch out and tie a person before scourging** > Paul was bound {stretched forward, stretched out} with thongs (Acts 22:25). ¶

– 7 Matt. 23:16, 18 → to bind by an oath → lit.: to be a debtor → DEBTOR <3784> 8 Mark 15:17 → to put on → PUT <4060> 9 Luke 13:16 → what bound her → lit.: her bound → CHAIN (noun) <1199> 10 John 11:44 → to bind about → WRAP <4019> 11 Acts 8:23; Col. 3:14 → BOND[1] <4886> 12 Acts 12:8 → to bind on → SHOD <5265> 13 Acts 23:14 → ACCURSED <331> 14 Rom. 7:1 → to be binding → to have dominion → DOMINION <2961> 15 Rom. 7:2 → the law that binds her to him → lit.: the law of the husband 16 1 Cor. 7:15 → to be bound → to be under bondage → BONDAGE <1402>.

BINDING – Heb. 2:2 → FIRM <949>.

BIRD – 1 ***orneon*** [neut. noun: ὄρνεον <3732>]; **dimin. of *ornis*: hen ▶ Animal covered with feathers capable of flying; also transl.: fowl** > Babylon will become the habitation of every unclean and hateful bird (Rev. 18:2). An angel told all the birds to gather together to the great supper of God (Rev. 19:17). The birds were filled with the flesh of those who were slain (Rev. 19:21). ¶

2 ***peteinon*** [neut. noun: πετεινόν <4071>]; **from *petomai*: to fly ▶ See defin. in 1** > The Lord spoke of birds on many occasions (Matt. 6:26; 8:20; 13:4, 32; Mark 4:4, 32; Luke 8:5; 9:58; 12:24; 13:19). Peter saw in a vision the birds of the heaven (Acts 10:12; 11:6). Men changed the glory of the incorruptible God into the likeness of birds (Rom. 1:23). Every species of birds can be tamed (Jas. 3:7). ¶

3 ***ptēnon*** [neut. noun: πτηνόν <4421>]; **contraction of 2; the word is used in the plur.: *ta ptēna* ▶ See defin. in 1** > The flesh of birds differs from other flesh (1 Cor. 15:39). ¶

BIRTH – 1 ***genetē*** [fem. noun: γενετή <1079>]; **from *genea*: generation, or *ginomai*: to become ▶ Origin, arrival in the world** > Jesus saw a man blind from birth (John 9:1). ¶

2 ***gennēsis*** [fem. noun: γέννησις <1083>]; **from *gennaō*: to engender, which is from *genna*: birth, race ▶ Arrival in the world** > The word is used in regard to Jesus Christ (Matt. 1:18) and John the Baptist (Luke 1:14). Other ref.: 1 John 5:18 in some mss. ¶

3 ***genos*** [neut. noun: γένος <1085>]; **from *ginomai*: to become ▶ Race, descent** > Barnabas was a Cyprian by birth {of the country of Cyprus} (Acts 4:36). All other refs.: see entries in Lexicon at <1085>.

4 **to have by birth; lit.: to be free born: *gennaō*** [verb: γεννάω <1080>]; **from *genna*: birth, race ▶ To be at birth** > Paul was free born {was born a citizen} (Acts 22:28), i.e., he had his Roman citizenship by birth. All other refs.: see entries in Lexicon at <1080>.

5 **to give birth: *tiktō*** [verb: τίκτω <5088>] **▶ To beget, to bring forth; also**

transl.: to bear, to be in travail, to be in labor, to be born, to be delivered > Mary gave birth to Jesus (Matt. 1:21, 23, 25; Luke 1:31; 2:6, 7, 11). The wise men sought Jesus who had been born King of the Jews (Matt. 2:2). Elizabeth gave birth to John (Luke 1:57). When she gives birth, a woman has sorrow because her hour has come (John 16:21). It is written: Rejoice, you who does not give birth {who bears no children} (Gal. 4:27). Having conceived, lust gives birth to sin (Jas. 1:15). John saw a woman crying out, being in travail, and in pain to give birth (Rev. 12:2, 4a, b, 5); the dragon persecuted the woman who had given birth to the male child (v. 13). Other refs.: Heb. 6:7 {to produce}; 11:11 {to conceive} in some mss. ¶
– [6] Matt. 19:12 → to have been thus from birth → lit: to have been born thus from the womb → BORN (BE) <1080>, WOMB <2836> [7] Matt. 24:8; Mark 13:8; 1 Thes. 5:3 → birth pang, birth pain → pain, labor pain → PAIN (noun) <5604> [8] Luke 11:27 → to give birth → BEAR (verb) <941> [9] Luke 19:12; 1 Cor. 1:26 → noble birth → lit.: noble → NOBLE <2104> [10] Gal. 2:15 → NATURE <5449> [11] Gal. 4:19; Rev. 12:2 → to travail in birth → LABOR (verb) <5605> [12] Jas. 1:15b, 18 → to give birth → to bring forth → BRING <616> [13] 1 Pet. 1:3 → to give new birth → BORN AGAIN (BE) <313>.

BIRTHDAY – ***genesia*** [neut. noun: γενέσια <1077>]; **from *genesis*: birth, generation ▶ Day commemorating the birth of a person** > The daughter of Herodias danced before Herod on his birthday, and pleased him (Matt. 14:6; Mark 6:21). ¶

BIRTHRIGHT – ***prōtotokia*** [neut. noun: πρωτοτόκια <4415>]; **from *prōtos*: first, and *tiktō*: to give birth ▶ Right (or title) conferring advantage to the eldest in the line of succession** > Esau sold his birthright {inheritance rights} to Jacob for one meal (Heb. 12:16). ¶

BISHOP – [1] Phil. 1:1; 1 Tim. 3:2; Titus 1:7; 1 Pet. 2:25 → OVERSEER <1985> [2] 1 Tim. 3:1 → the office of a bishop, the position of a bishop → OVERSIGHT <1984>.

BISHOPRICK – Acts 1:20 → OFFICE <1984>.

BIT – ***chalinos*** [masc. noun: χαλινός <5469>] ▶ **Loop on a halter-cord passed through the mouths of horses in order to direct them** > Bits are put in horses' mouths so that they may obey us (Jas. 3:3). Blood came out of the winepress of the wrath of God up to the horses' bits {bridles} (Rev. 14:20). ¶

BITE – ***daknō*** [verb: δάκνω <1143>] ▶ **To wound by reproaches (figur. sense)** > Biting and devouring one another may lead to being consumed by one another (Gal. 5:15). ¶

BITHYNIA – ***Bithunia*** [fem. name: Βιθυνία <978>] ▶ **Mountainous Roman province in northern Asia Minor** > The Spirit did not allow Paul to go to Bithynia (Acts 16:7). The gospel was nevertheless preached there later, because Peter speaks of Christians of Bithynia (1 Pet. 1:1). ¶

BITTER – [1] ***pikros*** [adj.: πικρός <4089>] ▶ **Acrid, disagreeable to the taste** > James asks if a fountain (or: spring) sends forth fresh and bitter {salt} water from the same opening (Jas. 3:11); he speaks of bitter envying (v. 14), i.e., envying characterized by sadness and resentment. ¶
[2] **to be bitter, to make bitter: *pikrainō*** [verb: πικραίνω <4087>]; **from *pikros*: see [1] ▶ To become bitter, to be irritated; to become acrid, disagreeable to the taste** > Husbands must not be bitter toward {embittered against, harsh with} their wives (Col. 3:19). The water had been made bitter (Rev. 8:11). The little book made bitter {turned sour} John's stomach (Rev. 10:9, 10). ¶
– [3] Heb. 12:15 → bitter root → lit.: root of bitterness → BITTERNESS <4088> [4] Rev. 8:11 → turned bitter → lit.: became wormwood → WORMWOOD <894>.

BITTERLY – ***pikrōs*** [adv.: πικρῶς <4090>]; **from *pikros*: bitter ▶ With bitterness, with great sorrow** > After having denied Jesus, Peter wept bitterly (Matt. 26:75; Luke 22:62). ¶

BITTERNESS – ***pikria*** [fem. noun: πικρία <4088>]; **from *pikros*: bitter ▶ State of soul characterized by sorrow and resentment** > Simon, who previously practiced sorcery, was in the gall of bitterness, i.e., full of bitterness (Acts 8:23). The mouth of the evil ones is full of cursing and bitterness (Rom. 3:14). All bitterness must be removed from the Christians (Eph. 4:31). A root of bitterness {bitter root} could spring up and trouble them (Heb. 12:15). ¶

BLACK – [1] ***melas*** [adj.: μέλας <3189>] ▶ **Of a very dark color** > One cannot make a hair white or black (Matt. 5:36). John saw a black horse, and he who sat on it had a balance in his hand (Rev. 6:5). When the sixth seal was opened, the sun became black (Rev. 6:12). ¶
– [2] Jude 13 → BLACKNESS <2217>.

BLACKEST – 2 Pet. 2:17; Jude 13 → BLACKNESS <2217>.

BLACKNESS – [1] ***zophos*** [masc. noun: ζόφος <2217>] ▶ **Thick darkness; also transl.: black, gloom** > Peter speaks of the godless, men without reason, to whom the blackness of {blackest} darkness is reserved forever (2 Pet. 2:17). Jude speaks of dreamers who defile the flesh and reject authority: the blackness of {blackest} darkness has been reserved for them (Jude 13). The word is transl. "darkness" in Heb. 12:18; 2 Pet. 2:4; Jude 6. ¶
– [2] Heb. 12:18 → OBSCURITY <1105>.

BLADE – ***chortos*** [masc. noun: χόρτος <5528>] ▶ **Grass growing in fields, hay; also transl.: grain, wheat** > In a parable, the blade sprouted and produced fruit, then the tares also appeared (Matt. 13:26). All other refs.: GRASS <5528>, HAY <5528>.

BLAME (noun) – [1] Eph. 1:4 → without blame → BLAMELESS <299> [2] 1 Thes. 3:13 → without blame → BLAMELESS <273> [3] 1 Thes. 5:23 → without blame → BLAMELESSLY <274> [4] 1 Tim. 5:7; 6:14 → not open to blame, without blame → above reproach → REPROACH (noun) <423>.

BLAME (verb) – [1] ***mōmaomai*** [verb: μωμάομαι <3469>]; **from *mōmos*: fault, defect ▶ To criticize; also transl.: to discredit** > Paul was giving no offense in anything, that his ministry might not be blamed (2 Cor. 6:3). He did not want anyone to blame him {any criticism} for the abundance which he administered (2 Cor. 8:20). ¶
– [2] Rom. 9:19 → to find fault → FAULT <3201> [3] Gal. 2:11 → CONDEMN <2607>.

BLAMELESS – [1] ***amemptos*** [adj.: ἄμεμπτος <273>]; **from *a*: neg., and *memphomai*: to reproach ▶ Without defect, without reproach** > Zacharias and Elizabeth were both blameless (Luke 1:6). Paul desired that the Philippians might be blameless and pure (Phil. 2:15). Before his conversion, Paul himself was blameless {faultless} as to righteousness (Phil. 3:6). He prayed that the Lord might confirm the hearts of the Thessalonians blameless {unblamable, unblameable, without blame} in holiness (1 Thes. 3:13). The word is transl. "faultless" in Heb. 8:7. ¶
[2] ***amōmos*** [adj.: ἄμωμος <299>]; **from *a*: neg., and *mōmos*: defect, spot ▶ Concerning whom one cannot make any reproach; also transl.: faultless, unblamable, unblameable, without blame, without blemish, without fault** > Christians are seen in the eyes of God as blameless (Eph. 1:4; Col. 1:22). Christ will present the church to Himself blameless (Eph. 5:27). God is able to make Christians stand blameless before His glory (Jude 24). Those who follow the Lamb are blameless (Rev. 14:5). All other refs.: BLEMISH <299>, SPOT <299>.

[3] ***anaitios*** [adj.: ἀναίτιος <338>]; **from *a*: neg., and *aitia*: accusation, crime ▶ Not guilty; also transl.: innocent** > On the Sabbath, the priests in the temple profane the Sabbath and are blameless (Matt. 12:5). In some mss.: Acts 16:37. Other ref.: Matt. 12:7; see GUILTLESS <338>. ¶

[4] ***anenklētos*** [adj.: ἀνέγκλητος <410>]; **from *a*: neg., and *enkaleō*: to accuse, which is from *en*: in, and *kaleō*: to call ▶ Which one cannot criticize or blame, free from all charge; also transl.: above reproach, without charge** > God will confirm Christians to be blameless {unimpeachable} in the day of the Lord Jesus Christ (1 Cor. 1:8). Servants are to be without charge against themselves (1 Tim. 3:10), as well as elders (Titus 1:6) and the overseer (v. 7). All other refs.: REPROACH (noun) <410>.

– [5] Luke 1:6; Phil. 2:15; 3:6; 1 Thes. 3:13 → BLAMELESS <273> [6] Acts 24:16; Phil. 1:10 → without offense → OFFENSE <677> [7] 1 Thes. 2:10; 5:23 → BLAMELESSLY <274> [8] 1 Tim. 3:2; 5:7; 6:14 → above reproach → REPROACH (noun) <423> [9] Heb. 7:26 → INNOCENT <172> [10] 2 Pet. 3:14 → IRREPROACHABLE <298>.

BLAMELESSLY – [1] ***amemptōs*** [adv.: ἀμέμπτως <274>]; **from *amemptos*: blameless, which is from *a*: neg., and *memphomai*: to reproach ▶ Without blame, without reproach; also transl.: blameless** > Paul had conducted himself righteously and blamelessly toward Christians in Thessalonica (1 Thes. 2:10). He prayed that the Thessalonians might be preserved blamelessly {blameless} at the coming of the Lord (1 Thes. 5:23). ¶

– [2] Luke 1:6 → BLAMELESS <273>.

BLASPHEME – [1] ***blasphēmeō*** [verb: βλασφημέω <987>]; **from *blasphēmos*: blasphemer; which is poss. from *blaptō*: to harm, and *phēmē*: reputation ▶ To speak slanderously, in a defaming way, more specifically against God; to curse** > Jesus was accused of blaspheming (Matt. 9:3; 26:65 {to speak blasphemy}; Mark 2:7; John 10:36 {to speak blasphemy}). Jesus speaks of the sons of men blaspheming {speaking injuriously, uttering blasphemies} (Mark 3:28). The Jews were blaspheming {talking abusively, becoming abusive} (Acts 13:45; 18:6). Paul and his companions were not blasphemers of (lit.: ones blaspheming) the goddess Diana (Acts 19:37). Saul had been compelling the saints to blaspheme (Acts 26:11). The name of God is blasphemed {being slandered} among the Gentiles because of the Jews (Rom. 2:24). Hymenaeus and Alexander had to learn not to blaspheme (1 Tim. 1:20). Bondservants had to honor their masters, so that the name of God and His doctrine would not be blasphemed {slandered} (1 Tim. 6:1). Older Christians must conduct themselves in a godly way, that the word of God may not be blasphemed {evil spoken of, dishonored, maligned} (Titus 2:5). James speaks of rich men who blaspheme the name of Jesus (Jas. 2:7). The way of truth will be blasphemed {brought in disrepute} because of false teachers (2 Pet. 2:2). The beast, as well as men being judged by God (Rev. 16:9, 11, 21), blasphemed the name of God (13:6). Other ref.: 1 Pet. 4:14 in some mss. All other refs.: see entries in Lexicon at <987>.

– [2] Rev. 13:6 → lit.: for blasphemies → BLASPHEMY <988>.

BLASPHEMER – [1] ***blasphēmos*** [adj. used as noun: βλάσφημος <989>]; **poss. from *blaptō*: to harm, and *phēmē*: reputation ▶ One who speaks slanderously, in a defaming way, more specifically against God** > Paul says that he was before a blasphemer (1 Tim. 1:13). He wrote that, in the last days, men will be blasphemers {abusive, evil speakers, revilers} (2 Tim. 3:2). All other refs.: BLASPHEMOUS <989>, REVILING <989>.

[2] **to blaspheme: *blasphēmeō*** [verb: βλασφημέω <987>]; **from *blasphēmos*; see [1] ▶ To speak slanderously, to insult** > Paul and his companions were not blasphemers of (lit.: ones blaspheming) the goddess Diana (Acts 19:37). All other refs.: see entries in Lexicon at <987>.

BLASPHEMING – Luke 22:65 → injurious → INJURE <987>.

BLASPHEMOUS – [1] ***blasphēmos*** [adj.: βλάσφημος <989>]; **poss. from *blaptō*: to harm, and *phēmē*: reputation ▶ Which constitutes a slanderous, defaming speech, more specifically against God** > Some men said they had heard Stephen speaking blasphemous words {words of blasphemy} against Moses and God (Acts 6:11; v. 13 in some mss.). All other refs.: BLASPHEMER <989>, REVILING <989>.

– [2] Luke 22:65 → injurious → INJURE <987> [3] Jude 9; Rev. 13:1, 5; 17:3 → lit.: of blasphemy → BLASPHEMY <988>.

BLASPHEMY – [1] ***blasphēmia*** [fem. noun: βλασφημία <988>]; **from *blasphēmos*: blasphemer; which is poss. from *blaptō*: to harm, and *phēmē*: reputation ▶ a. Slanderous speech, more specifically against God** > The blasphemy against the Holy Spirit (Matt. 12:31a, b), according to the context (see vv. 22–32), was to attribute to Satan the power of the Holy Spirit manifested in Jesus (see also Mark 3:28, 29; Luke 12:10). Jesus was accused of speaking blasphemies by confirming He was the Christ, the Son of God (Matt. 26:65; Mark 14:64), by forgiving sin (Luke 5:21), and by making Himself God (John 10:33). The beast had upon his heads names of blasphemy {a blasphemous name, blasphemous names} (Rev. 13:1); it was full of names of blasphemy {blasphemous names} (17:3); he spoke blasphemies against God (13:5, 6). **b. Calumny, insult; also transl.: evil speaking, injurious language, slander** > Out of the heart come forth blasphemies (Matt. 15:19; Mark 7:22). All injurious language is to be removed from the midst of Christians (Eph. 4:31). We are to renounce blasphemy (Col. 3:8). Michael the archangel did not dare to bring a railing judgment {railing accusation, reviling accusation} (lit.: judgment of blasphemy) against Satan (Jude 9). Other ref.: Mark 2:7 in some mss. All other refs.: INJURIOUS <988>, RAILING <988>.

– [2] Matt. 26:65; John 10:36 → to speak blasphemy → BLASPHEME <987> [3] Acts 6:11 → of blasphemy → lit.: blasphemous → BLASPHEMOUS <989>.

BLAST – Heb. 12:19 → SOUND (noun) <2279>.

BLASTUS – ***Blastos*** [masc. name: Βλάστος <986>]: **sprout, what germinates ▶ Chamberlain of King Herod Agrippa I; as such, he was responsible for the service of the sovereign's chamber** > The people of Tyre and Sidon gained the support of Blastus for their cause (Acts 12:20). ¶

BLAZE – [1] Mark 1:45 → to blaze abroad → to spread abroad → SPREAD <1310> [2] Acts 26:13 → to blaze around → to shine around → SHINE <4034>.

BLAZING – [1] Matt. 13:42, 50 → blazing furnace → lit.: furnace of fire → FIRE <4442> [2] 2 Thes. 1:8; Rev. 1:14; 2:18; 19:12 → FLAME <5395> [3] Heb. 12:18; Rev. 4:5; 8:10 → BURN <2545>.

BLEACH – Mark 9:3 → WHITE (verb) <3021>.

BLEEDING – [1] Matt. 9:20 → to be subject to bleeding → to have a flow of blood → FLOW (noun) <131> [2] Mark 5:25; Luke 8:43, 44 → lit.: a flow of blood → FLOW (noun) <4511>, BLOOD <129> [3] Mark 5:29 → lit.: the flow of blood → FLOW (noun) <4077>.

BLEMISH – [1] ***mōmos*** [masc. noun: μῶμος <3470>]; **perhaps from *memphomai*: to blame ▶ Disgrace, spot, stain** > Peter speaks of unbelievers who are spots and blemishes, reveling in the pleasures of their own deceits (2 Pet. 2:13). ¶

[2] **without blemish: *amōmos*** [adj.: ἄμωμος <299>]; **from *a*: neg., and *mōmos*: defect, imperfection ▶ Without imperfection, without defect** > Christians have been redeemed by the precious blood of Christ, as of a lamb without blemish {unblemished}

and without spot (1 Pet. 1:19). All other refs.: BLAMELESS <299>, SPOT <299>.
– [3] Phil. 2:15; 2 Pet. 3:14 → without blemish → IRREPROACHABLE <298> [4] Jude 12 → SPOT <4694>.

BLESS – [1] ***eulogeō*** [verb: εὐλογέω <2127>]; **from *eu*: well, and *logos*: word ► To say good things, to give thanks, to praise; to do good to someone** > Christians must bless those who curse them (Matt. 5:44 in some mss.; Luke 6:28) and those who persecute them (Rom. 12:14). Jesus looked up to heaven and blessed before breaking the loaves of bread (Matt. 14:19; Mark 6:41; Luke 9:16). He was acclaimed by the words: Blessed is He who comes in the name of the Lord (Matt. 21:9; Mark 11:9; Luke 13:35; 19:38; John 12:13). The Jews would say: Blessed is he who comes in the name of the Lord (Matt. 23:39). The blessed (lit.: Those who are blessed) of the Father will inherit the kingdom prepared for them (Matt. 25:34). At the last supper before His death, Jesus took bread, blessed and broke it, and gave it to His disciples (Matt. 26:26; Mark 14:22); He did the same with the disciples at Emmaus the evening of His resurrection (Luke 24:30). He blessed the few small fish and had his disciples distribute them to the multitude (Mark 8:7). He blessed the little children (Mark 10:16; other mss.: *kateulogeō*). The verb "to bless" is also used to celebrate the coming of the kingdom of David (Mark 11:10). Mary, the mother of Jesus, was blessed among many women (Luke 1:28 in some mss.), as well as the fruit of her womb (v. 42). Zacharias blessed God (Luke 1:64). Simeon took the child Jesus in his arms and blessed God (Luke 2:28); he also blessed His parents (v. 34). Before His ascension into heaven, Jesus blessed His disciples (Luke 24:50); while He blessed them, He was parted from them (v. 51). The disciples were blessing God in the temple (Luke 24:53). God has sent Jesus to bless first the Israelites (Acts 3:26). Even though he was reviled, Paul blessed (1 Cor. 4:12). The cup of blessing which we bless is the communion of the blood of Christ (1 Cor. 10:16). Paul says to bless with the spirit in an intelligible way (1 Cor. 14:16). Those who are of faith are blessed with believing Abraham (Gal. 3:9). God the Father has blessed Christians with every spiritual blessing in the heavenly places in Christ (Eph. 1:3b). God said to Abraham that He would bless him (Heb. 6:14). The lesser (Abraham) is blessed by the greater (Melchizedek) (Heb. 7:1, 6, 7). By faith, Isaac blessed Jacob and Esau (Heb. 11:20); by faith, Jacob, when he was dying, blessed the sons of Joseph (v. 21). James says that, with the tongue, we bless God the Father and we curse men (Jas. 3:9); it should not be so (see v. 10). Christians must bless others (1 Pet. 3:9). ¶

[2] ***eneulogeō*** [verb: ἐνευλογέω <1757>]; **from *en*: in, and *eulogeō*: see [1] ► To bless in; pass.: to receive favors** > All the families of the earth would be blessed in the seed of Abraham (Acts 3:25) and in Abraham himself (Gal. 3:8). ¶

– [3] 2 Cor. 9:8 → God is able to bless you abundantly → lit.: God is able to make all grace abound (*perisseuō* <4052>) toward you [4] Eph. 1:6 → to make accepted → ACCEPTED <5487>.

BLESSED – [1] ***eulogētos*** [adj.: εὐλογητός <2128>]; **from *eulogeō*: to say good things, to bless ► Who is worthy of praise; this term is used concerning God alone; also transl.: Praise** > See BLESSED ONE <2128>.

[2] ***makarios*** [adj.: μακάριος <3107>]; **from *makar*: blessed one ► Who is the object of a blessing, the blessing itself; happy** > Jesus used the term "blessed" in the Beatitudes during a sermon on a mountain (Matt. 5:3–11; Luke 6:20, 21a, b, 22) and on various other occasions (Matt. 11:6; 13:16; 16:17; 24:46; Luke 7:23; 10:23; 11:27, 28; 12:37, 38, 43; 14:14, 15; 23:29; John 13:17; 20:29; also transl. "it will be good" in some of these refs.). It is more blessed to give than to receive (Acts 20:35). Paul considered himself happy to make his defense before Agrippa (Acts 26:2). In Paul's opinion, a widow is happier if she remains unmarried (1 Cor. 7:40). The term "blessed" is used concerning God (1 Tim. 1:11) and

the Lord Jesus (1 Tim. 6:15). “Blessed” is found seven times in Revelation (1:3; 14:13; 16:15; 19:9; 20:6; 22:7, 14) and seven times in the epistles (Rom. 4:7, 8; 14:22; Jas. 1:12, 25; 1 Pet. 3:14; 4:14). Elizabeth used the word “blessed” (Luke 1:45). Christians are awaiting the blessed hope (Titus 2:13). ¶

[3] **to call blessed, to count blessed: *makarizō*** [verb: μακαρίζω <3106>]; **from *makar*: blessed one ▶ To say that one is favored, happy** > All generations would call Mary blessed (Luke 1:48). James says that we call blessed {call happy} those who persevere (Jas. 5:11). ¶

– [4] Matt. 25:34 → the blessed → lit.: those who are blessed → BLESS <2127>.

BLESSED ONE – ***Eulogētos*** [adj. used as a personal name: Εὐλογητός <2128>]: **worthy of praise; from *eulogeō*: to say good things, to bless, which is from *eu*: well, and *logos*: word ▶ Name of God; also transl.: Blessed** > The high priest asked Jesus if He was the Christ, the Son of the Blessed One (Mark 14:61), i.e., the Son of God. Zacharias said: “Blessed is the Lord God of Israel” (Luke 1:68). The term is used in relation to God the Creator, who is blessed (Rom. 1:25); Christ, who is over all blessed eternally (Rom. 9:5); and the God and Father of the Lord Jesus Christ, who is also blessed (2 Cor. 1:3; 11:31; Eph. 1:3a; 1 Pet. 1:3). ¶

BLESSEDNESS – ***makarismos*** [masc. noun: μακαρισμός <3108>]; **from *makarizō*: to count blessed, or *makarios*: blessed ▶ Happiness, state of favor; also transl.: blessing** > David describes the blessedness of the man to whom God imputes righteousness without works (Rom. 4:6); this blessedness was that of Abraham even before his circumcision (v. 9). Paul asks the Galatians what was their blessedness {all their joy} (Gal. 4:15). ¶

BLESSING – [1] ***eulogia*** [fem. noun: εὐλογία <2129>]; **from *eulogeō*: to bless, which is from *eu*: well, and *logos*: word ▶ Favor, privilege granted to someone; praise** > Paul would come to the Romans in the fullness of the blessing of the gospel of Christ (Rom. 15:29). The cup of blessing {thanksgiving} which the Christians bless is the communion of the blood of the Christ (1 Cor. 10:16). The blessing of Abraham has come to the Gentiles in Christ Jesus (Gal. 3:14). God the Father has blessed Christians with every spiritual blessing in the heavenly places in Christ (Eph. 1:3). The earth partakes of blessing from God (Heb. 6:7). Esau desired to inherit the blessing but was rejected, for he found no place for repentance (Heb. 12:17). Out of the same mouth goes forth blessing and cursing (sing. verb in Greek); it should not be so (Jas. 3:10). Christians have been called to inherit blessing (1 Pet. 3:9). In Revelation, blessing is ascribed to the Lamb (5:12), to Him who sits on the throne and the Lamb (5:13), and to God (7:12). All other refs.: BOUNTIFULLY <2129>, GIFT <2129>, SPEECH <2129>.

– [2] Matt. 14:19; Mark 6:41; Luke 9:16; Heb. 11:20 → to say a blessing, to invoke blessings on → BLESS <2127> [3] Rom. 4:6, 9; Gal. 4:15 → BLESSEDNESS <3108> [4] 2 Cor. 1:11 → GIFT <5486>.

BLIND (adj.) – ***tuphlos*** [adj.: τυφλός <5185>]; **from *tuphō*: to fill with smoke, to deprive of vision ▶ Unable to see** > Jesus healed one who was possessed by a demon and blind (Matt. 12:22). He told the scribes and the Pharisees that they were blind guides (Matt. 23:16, 24, 26). In John 9, Jesus healed a man blind from his birth (vv. 1, 2, 13, 18–20, 24, 25). He has come into this world so that those who do not see may see, and that those who see may become blind (John 9:39–41). Elymas would be blind (Acts 13:11). Peter speaks of those who are spiritually blind (2 Pet. 1:9). The church of Laodicea is blind (Rev. 3:17). Other refs.: BLIND (noun) <5185>. ¶

BLIND (noun) – ***tuphlos*** [masc. noun: τυφλός <5185>]; **from *tuphō*: to fill with smoke ▶ Person who is unable to see; also transl.: blind man, blind person, etc.** > Jesus healed two blind men following Him (Matt. 9:27, 28). He said to two of

John's disciples to go and tell John that the blind were seeing (Matt. 11:5; Luke 7:21, 22). He healed the blind brought by the multitudes (Matt. 15:30, 31). He healed two blind men sitting by the way side (Matt. 20:30) and two others who came to Him in the temple (21:14). He told the scribes and the Pharisees that they were blind (Matt. 23:17, 19), blind leaders of the blind (Matt. 15:14a–d; Luke 6:39a, b). He healed a blind man out of Bethsaida (Mark 8:22, 23), as well as Bartimaeus (Mark 10:46, 49, 51; Luke 18:35). He had been sent to preach the recovering of sight to the blind (Luke 4:18). He says to invite the blind when giving a feast (Luke 14:13), which the master of the house did in a parable (v. 21). A multitude of blind persons were waiting for the moving of the water (John 5:3). Jesus healed a man who was born blind (John 9:17, 32; 11:37). Some were saying: Can a devil open the eyes of the blind? (John 10:21). Paul addresses himself to a Jew who knows the law and is confident that he is a leader of the blind (Rom. 2:19). Other refs.: BLIND (adj.) <5185>. ¶

BLIND (verb) – [1] ***tuphloō*** [verb: τυφλόω <5186>]; **from *tuphlos*: blind, unable to see, which is from *tuphō*: to fill with smoke ▶ To render incapable of seeing >** God has blinded the eyes of the Jews (John 12:40). The god of this world has blinded the thoughts of the unbelievers (2 Cor. 4:4). The darkness has blinded the eyes of one who hates his brother (1 John 2:11). ¶
– [2] Acts 22:11 → the light had blinded me → lit.: I (Paul) could not see because of the light → SEE <991> [3] Rom. 11:7; 2 Cor. 3:14 → HARDEN <4456>.

BLINDFOLD – Mark 14:65; Luke 22:64 → COVER <4028>.

BLINDNESS – Rom. 11:25; Eph. 4:18 → HARDNESS <4457>.

BLOCK (noun) – Rom. 14:13; 1 Cor. 8:9 → STUMBLING BLOCK <4348>.

BLOCK (verb) – 1 Thes. 2:18 → HINDER (verb) <1465>.

BLOOD – [1] ***haima*** [neut. noun: αἷμα <129>] **▶ Fluid that circulates in our veins and arteries >** The word is used concerning Jesus (Matt. 26:28; 27:4, 6, 8, 24, 25; Mark 14:24; Luke 22:20, 44; John 6:53–56; 19:34; Acts 1:19; 5:28; 20:28; Rom. 3:25; 5:9; 1 Cor. 10:16; 11:25, 27; Eph. 1:7; 2:13; Col. 1:14 (in some mss.), 20; Heb. 9:12b, 14; 10:19, 29; 12:24; 13:12, 20; 1 Pet. 1:2, 19; 1 John 1:7; 5:6 a, b, 8; Rev. 1:5 or 6; 5:9; 7:14 or 15; 12:11), prophets (Matt. 23:30; Luke 11:50), murders (Matt. 23:35a), Abel (Matt. 23:35b; Luke 11:51a), Zechariah (Matt. 23:35c; Luke 11:51b), a woman (Mark 5:25, 29; Luke 8:43, 44), Galileans (Luke 13:1), Christians (John 1:13), the last days (Acts 2:19, 20), the human race (Acts 17:26 in some mss.), the Jews (Acts 18:6), Paul's listeners (Acts 20:26), Stephen (Acts 22:20), animal sacrifices in the O.T. (Heb. 9:7, 12a, 13, 18–21, 22a; 10:4; 11:28; 13:11), martyrs (Rev. 6:10), saints and prophets (Rev. 16:6a; 18:24), saints (Rev. 17:6a), witnesses of Jesus (Rev. 17:6b), servants of God (Rev. 19:2), and a robe (Rev. 19:13). Gentile Christians are to abstain from eating blood (Acts 15:20, 29; 21:25). The expr. "flesh and blood" is used to designate a human being (Matt. 16:17; 1 Cor. 15:50; Gal. 1:16; Eph. 6:12; Heb. 2:14). Other refs.: Rom. 3:15; Heb. 9:25; 12:4; Rev. 6:12; 8:7, 8; 11:6; 14:20; 16:3, 4, 6b. ¶
– [2] Matt. 9:20 → to be diseased with an issue of blood → to have a flow of blood → FLOW (noun) <131> [3] Heb. 9:22 → SHEDDING OF BLOOD <130>.

BLOODSHED – Heb. 12:4 → to bloodshed → lit.: to blood, i.e., to shedding blood → BLOOD <129>.

BLOODY FLUX – Matt. 9:20 → to have a bloody flux → to have a flow of blood → FLOW (noun) <131>.

BLOT (noun) – 2 Pet. 2:13 → SPOT <4696>.

BLOT (verb) – **to blot out: *exaleiphō*** [verb: ἐξαλείφω <1813>]; **from *ek*: out (intens.), and *aleiphō*: to rub, to wipe ▶ To wipe out completely, to remove completely** > Peter tells the Jews to repent and be converted that their sins may be blotted out {wiped away, wiped out} (Acts 3:19). God has blotted out {canceled, canceled out, effaced, wiped out} the handwriting of requirements which stood against Christians (Col. 2:14). Jesus will not blot out {erase} from the book of life the name of the overcomer in Sardis (Rev. 3:5). Other refs.: Rev. 7:17; 21:4; see WIPE <1813>. ¶

BLOW (noun) – 1 **blow on the face: *rhapisma*** [neut. noun: ῥάπισμα <4475>]; **from *rhapizō*: to strike the face ▶ Slap, hard stroke with the hand or the fist** > One of the officers gave a blow on the face to Jesus {struck Jesus, struck Jesus with the palm of his hand, struck Jesus in the face} (John 18:22), as likewise did the soldiers (19:3 {to give slaps in the face, to smite with the hand, to strike in the face}). Other ref.: Mark 14:65; see SLAP (noun) <4475>. ¶

– 2 Acts 16:23 → STRIPE <4127> 3 1 Cor. 9:27 → to strike a blow to the body → to discipline the body → DISCIPLINE (verb) <5299>.

BLOW (verb) – 1 ***epiginomai*** [verb: ἐπιγίνομαι <1920>]; **from *epi*: upon, and *ginomai*: to come, to occur ▶ To take place, to happen** > The south wind blew {came up, sprang up} (Acts 28:13). Other ref.: Acts 27:27 in some mss. ¶

2 ***pneō*** [verb: πνέω <4154>] ▶ **To displace air, as does the wind** > Jesus speaks of winds that blew and beat on a house (Matt. 7:25, 27). Seeing the south wind blow, one says there will be hot weather (Luke 12:55). The wind blows where it wills, and one hears the sound of it; but one does not know where it comes from and where it is going: so is everyone who is born of the Spirit (John 3:8). The sea arose by reason of a great wind that blew (John 6:18). Four angels held back the four winds of the earth, so that no wind might blow on the earth, nor on the sea, nor on any tree (Rev. 7:1). In Acts 27:40, some mss. have lit. "to the blowing" (*tē pneousē*), i.e., the blowing wind; other mss. have *pnoē*, i.e., the wind. ¶

3 **to blow gently, to blow softly: *hupopneō*** [verb: ὑποπνέω <5285>]; **from *hupo*: under, and *pneō*: see 2 ▶ To displace air moderately** > The south wind blew gently (Acts 27:13). ¶

– 4 Eph. 4:14; Jude 12 → to blow here and there, to blow along → to carry about → CARRY <4064> 5 Jas. 1:6 → to blow by the wind → to drive by the wind → WIND (noun) <416> 6 Rev. 8:6–8, 10, 12, 13; 9:1, 13; 11:15 → to sound a trumpet → TRUMPET <4537>.

BLOWING – 1 Acts 2:2 → WIND (noun) <4157> 2 Acts 2:2 → RUSHING <5342>.

BOANERGES – ***Boanērges*** [masc. name: Βοανηργές <993>]: **sons of thunder, in Aram. ▶ Surname of James and John** > Jesus gave the surname Boanerges to these two disciples (Mark 3:17), most likely because of their impetuosity (see Luke 9:54). ¶

BOARD (noun) – 1 ***sanis*** [fem. noun: σανίς <4548>] ▶ **Piece of wood, plank** > Certain passengers who traveled with Paul managed to reach dry land from the grounded ship on planks (Acts 27:44). ¶

2 **to take on board: *airō*** [verb: αἴρω <142>] ▶ **To bring up, to hoist, to take up** > The skiff was taken on board (Acts 27:17). All other refs.: see entries in Lexicon at <142>.

3 **to take on board: *analambanō*** [verb: ἀναλαμβάνω <353>]; **from *ana*: up, and *lambanō*: to take ▶ To embark (e.g., on a boat)** > Paul was taken on board of {taken aboard, taken in} the ship (Acts 20:13, 14). All other refs.: RECEIVE <353>, TAKE <353>.

– 4 Mark 8:13 → to go on board → ENTER <1684> 5 Acts 21:2, 6; 27:2 → to go on board → BOARD (verb) <1910> 6 Acts 28:10 → to put on board → SUPPLY (verb) <2007>.

BOARD (verb) – ***epibainō*** [verb: ἐπιβαίνω <1910>]; **from *epi*: upon, and *bainō*: to go ► To get on (a ship); also transl.: to go aboard, to go on board, to take (ship), to enter, to embark >** Paul and his companions boarded a ship (Acts 21:2). Other refs.: Acts 21:6; 27:2. All other refs.: COME <1910>, SIT <1910>.

BOAST (noun) – 1 ***kauchēma*** [neut. noun: καύχημα <2745>]; **from *kauchaomai*: to boast ► Reason to be proud; also transl.: boasting, joy, proud confidence, rejoicing >** Paul was the boast {reason to be proud, rejoicing} of the Corinthians (2 Cor. 1:14). The boasting of the Philippians was to abound in Christ Jesus (Phil. 1:26). All other refs.: BOASTING <2745>, GLORIFY <2745>.

– 2 Rom. 2:17; 5:11; 2 Cor. 7:14; 2 Thes. 1:4; et al. → to make one's boast → GLORIFY <2744> 3 2 Cor. 1:12 → reason to boast → GLORIFY <2746> 4 Jas. 3:5 → to make great boasts → lit.: to boast great things → BOAST (verb) <3166> 5 2 Pet. 2:18 → loud boasts → swelling words → WORD <5246>.

BOAST (verb) – 1 **to boast great things: *megalaucheō*** [verb: μεγαλαυχέω <3166>]; **from *megala*: great things, and *aucheō*: to boast ► To brag greatly, to vaunt oneself of grandiose things in speech or action >** The tongue is a little member and boasts great things (Jas. 3:5; other mss.: *aucheō*). ¶

2 ***perpereuomai*** [verb: περπερεύομαι <4068>]; **from *perperos*: boastful, pretentious ► To give prominence to oneself; also transl.: to brag, to parade, to vaunt >** Love does not boast (1 Cor. 13:4). ¶

– 3 1 Cor. 13:3; Jas. 1:9 → GLORIFY <2744> 4 1 Cor. 15:31 → BOASTING <2746> 5 2 Cor. 1:14 → lit.: to be the boast → BOAST (noun) <2745> 6 2 Thes. 1:4 → GLORIFY <2744> 7 Jas. 4:16 → you boast and brag → lit.: you boast in your arrogance → GLORIFY <2744>, ARROGANCE <212> 8 Jude 16 → boastful words → WORD <5246>.

BOASTED – 2 Cor. 11:12 → in their boasted mission → lit.: in that which they glorify → GLORIFY <2744>.

BOASTER – 1 ***alazōn*** [masc. noun: ἀλαζών <213>]; **from *alē*: wandering ► Arrogant, braggart; also transl.: boastful >** Paul uses this word in Rom. 1:30 and 2 Tim. 3:2. ¶

– 2 Jude 16 → loud-mouthed boasters → lit.: their mouth speaks boastful words → WORD <5246>.

BOASTFUL – 1 Rom. 1:30; 2 Tim. 3:2 → BOASTER <213> 2 2 Cor. 11:17 → BOASTING <2746> 3 Gal. 5:26 → CONCEITED <2755> 4 1 John 2:16 → boastful pride → PRIDE <212> 5 Jude 16 → boastful words → WORD <5246>.

BOASTING – 1 ***kauchēma*** [neut. noun: καύχημα <2745>]; **from *kauchaomai*: to boast ► Reason for glorifying oneself, for being proud >** Paul tells the Corinthians that their boasting {glorying} is not good (1 Cor. 5:6). All other refs.: BOAST (noun) <2745>, GLORIFY <2745>.

2 ***kauchēsis*** [fem. noun: καύχησις <2746>]; **from *kauchaomai*: to boast ► Act of glorifying oneself; glory, pride >** Boasting has been excluded by the law of faith (Rom. 3:27). Paul speaks of the boasting {rejoicing} in the Corinthians which he had in Christ Jesus his Lord (1 Cor. 15:31). He spoke in a confidence of boasting {a boastful confidence} (2 Cor. 11:17). Those whom James addressed gloried in their arrogance; such boasting {glorying, rejoicing} was evil (Jas. 4:16). Other ref.: 2 Cor. 9:4 in some mss. All other refs.: "reason to glorify" under GLORIFY <2746>.

– 3 2 Cor. 11:16 → to do boasting → GLORIFY <2744> 4 Jas. 4:16a → ARROGANCE <212> 5 1 John 2:16 → PRIDE <212>.

BOAT – 1 ***skaphē*** [fem. noun: σκάφη <4627>]; **from *skaptō*: to dig; lit.: something dug out ► Small boat propelled by oars and kept on board of a ship, skiff, lifeboat >** On Paul's ship, the boat

was secured with difficulty; then, since the sailors had let it down to escape with it, the soldiers cut away the ropes of the boat and let it fall in the sea (Acts 27:16, 30, 32). ¶
– 2 Matt. 4:21, 22; 8:23, 24; et al. → SHIP <4143> 3 Mark 3:9; 4:36b; John 6:22a, 23; 21:8 → small boat, etc. → small ship, etc. → SHIP <4142> 4 John 21:11 → climbed back into the boat → lit.: went up; i.e., went aboard.

BOAZ – ***Booz*** [masc. name: Boόζ <1003>]**: in him is strength, in Heb. (see 1 Kgs. 7:21); in some mss.: *Boos* ▶ Man of Bethlehem, husband of Ruth the Moabitess** > Booz (or Boaz) used his right as kinsman-redeemer to marry Ruth (see Ruth 4:13). He is mentioned in the genealogy of Jesus Christ (Matt. 1:5a, b; Luke 3:32). He was the great-grandfather of David. ¶

BODILY (adj.) – 1 ***sōmatikos*** [adj.: σωματικός <4984>]**; from *sōma*: body ▶ Which relates to the body, physical** > The Holy Spirit descended in bodily form as a dove upon Jesus (Luke 3:22). Bodily exercise {Physical training} is profitable for a little, but godliness is profitable for everything (1 Tim. 4:8). ¶
– 2 Col. 2:9 → in bodily form → BODILY (adv.) <4985> 3 Heb. 7:16 → concerning bodily descent → CARNAL <4559>.

BODILY (adv.) – 1 ***sōmatikōs*** [adv.: σωματικῶς <4985>]**; from *sōma*: body ▶ In the form of a body** > In Christ dwells all the fullness of the Godhead bodily {in bodily form} (Col. 2:9). ¶
– 2 2 Cor. 10:10 → bodily presence → lit.: presence in the body → BODY <4983>.

BODY – 1 ***sōma*** [neut. noun: σῶμα <4983>] ▶ **Physical substance and structure of a human being, an animal, a plant** > It may be the body of a living human being (e.g., Matt. 6:22), of a dead one (Matt. 27:52) or of a resurrected (spiritual) one (1 Cor. 15:44b, d). It can also refer to bodies of animals (Heb. 13:11), the body of a grain of wheat (1 Cor. 15:37, 38a, b). There are celestial bodies and terrestrial bodies (1 Cor. 15:40a, b). Sometimes, the word refers to the entire human being (Matt. 5:29; 6:22; Rom. 12:1, 4; Jas. 3:6; Rev. 18:13 {slaves}). It may correspond to a person (Acts 9:40); this is the case also of the Lord Jesus (John 19:40). The body is not the human being, because the human being can exist apart from the body (2 Cor. 12:2a, b, 3a, b). The body is an essential part of a person, and, consequently, the redeemed person is not made perfect before the resurrection (see Heb. 11:40); every person will have his body in the final state (see John 5:28, 29; Rev. 20:13). The word *sōma* is used for the physical nature, which is distinct from the *pneuma*, the spiritual nature (e.g., 1 Cor. 5:3), and the *psuchē*, the soul (1 Thes. 5:23). The body also designates metaphorically the mystical body of Christ, the universal church of God (e.g., Eph. 1:23; Col. 1:18, 22, 24) or a local church (e.g., 1 Cor. 12:27). Pilate gave the body of Jesus to Joseph of Arimathea (Mark 15:45). The lowly body of the Christian will be transformed by the Lord Jesus Christ that it may be conformed to His glorious body (Phil. 3:21a, b). *
2 **same body: *sussōmos*** [adj.: σύσσωμος <4954>]**; from *sun*: together, and *sōma*: see 1 ▶ Being united in one body, belonging to the same body** > The Gentiles are of the same body {fellow members of the body, members together of one body}, i.e., members of the body of Christ (Eph. 3:6). ¶
3 ***chrōs*** [masc. noun: χρώς <5559>] ▶ **Surface of the body, skin** > Handkerchiefs or aprons were brought from Paul's body and put upon the sick, and they were healed physically and from evil spirits (Acts 19:12). ¶
– 4 Matt. 15:17; Mark 7:19 → to go out of the body → to go into the draught → DRAUGHT <856> 5 Matt. 24:29; Mark 13:25; Luke 21:26 → heavenly bodies → lit.: powers of the heavens → POWER[3] <1411> 6 Mark 6:29; Rev. 11:8, 9a, b → body, dead body → CORPSE <4430> 7 Luke 14:2 → suffering from abnormal swelling of the body → DROPSICAL <5203> 8 John 7:23 → man's whole body → lit.: whole man 9 Acts 7:42 → HOST[1] <4756> 10 1 Cor.

15:53a, b; Eph. 4:15 → "body" added Engl. 11 Eph. 2:3 → FLESH <4561> 12 1 Thes. 4:4 → VESSEL[1] <4632> 13 Heb. 3:17 → CORPSE <2966> 14 Heb. 9:10 → for the body → CARNAL <4559> 15 2 Pet. 1:14 → lit.: tent → TENT <4638>.

BODY COAT – Matt. 5:40; 10:10; Mark 6:9; Luke 3:11; 6:29; 9:3; John 19:23a, b; Acts 9:39 → TUNIC <5509>.

BOISTEROUS – Matt. 14:30 → STRONG <2478>.

BOLD – 1 **to be bold: *tharreō*** [verb: θαρρέω <2292>]; **from *tharsos*: boldness, courage ▶ To be confident, to exercise courage** > Absent from the Corinthians, Paul was bold toward them (2 Cor. 10:1); he did not want to be bold when he would be present (v. 2). All other refs.: BOLDLY <2292>, CONFIDENT <2292>.

2 **to grow bold: *parrēsiazomai*** [verb: παρρησιάζομαι <3955>]; **from *parrēsia*: freedom to speak, which is from *pas*: all, and *rhēsis*: act of speaking ▶ To be full of assurance in expressing oneself** > Paul and Barnabas grew bold {spoke boldly, waxed bold} and said to the Jews that they would turn to the Gentiles (Acts 13:46). All other refs.: BOLDLY <3955>.

3 **to be bold: *tolmaō*** [verb: τολμάω <5111>]; **from *tolma*: boldness, courage, which is from *tlaō*: to sustain, to endure ▶ To dare, to display audacity, to act with courage** > Paul did not want to be bold (*tharreō*) when he was present among the Corinthians with that confidence by which he intended to be bold (*tolmaō*) {be daring, be courageous} against some (2 Cor. 10:2). Most of the brothers were more bold {dared all the more, had far more courage} to speak the word of God fearlessly (Phil. 1:14). All other refs.: BOLDLY <5111>, DARE <5111>.

4 **to be very bold: *apotolmaō*** [verb: ἀποτολμάω <662>]; **from *apo*: intens., and *tolmaō*: see 3 ▶ To act with great boldness, assurance, courage** > Isaiah is very bold when he says that God has been found by those not seeking Him (Rom. 10:20). ¶

– 5 2 Cor. 3:12; Phm. 8 → BOLDNESS <3954> 6 2 Cor. 10:2 → to be bold → to act with confidence → CONFIDENCE <4006> 7 2 Pet. 2:10 → PRESUMPTUOUS <5113>.

BOLDLY – 1 **to have confidence: *tharreō*** [verb: θαρρέω <2292>]; **from *tharsos*: boldness, courage ▶ To show courage, to have assurance** > Christians may boldly {confidently} say (lit.: may say having confidence): The Lord is my helper (Heb. 13:6). All other refs.: BOLD <2292>, CONFIDENT <2292>.

2 **boldness: *parrēsia*** [fem. noun: παρρησία <3954>]; **from *pas*: all, and *rhēsis*: act of speaking; lit.: freedom to speak ▶ Absence of reserve, assurance, openness** > Jesus spoke boldly {publicly} (lit.: with boldness) (John 7:26). All other refs.: BOLDNESS <3954>, CONFIDENCE <3954>, OPENLY <3954>, PUBLIC <3954>.

3 **to speak boldly: *parrēsiazomai*** [verb: παρρησιάζομαι <3955>]; **from *parrēsia*: see 2 ▶ To speak with assurance, audacity, without reservation; also transl.: to speak freely, with confidence, with all freedom; to be bold** > Paul had spoken boldly {had preached fearlessly} in the name of Jesus (Acts 9:27) in Damascus, and he did the same at Jerusalem (v. 28 or v. 29). Paul and Barnabas spoke boldly in Iconium (Acts 14:3). Apollos began to speak boldly in the synagogue (Acts 18:26). Paul spoke boldly in the synagogue (Acts 19:8). He spoke freely before Agrippa (Acts 26:26). He solicited prayer that he might make known with boldness the mystery of the gospel, that he might speak boldly (Eph. 6:20). He had been bold in his God to speak the gospel (1 Thes. 2:2). Other ref.: Acts 13:46; see BOLD <3955>. ¶

4 **to go boldly: *tolmaō*** [verb: τολμάω <5111>]; **from *tolma*: boldness, courage, which is from *tlaō*: to sustain, to endure ▶ To be bold, to embolden oneself, to gather one's courage** > Joseph of Arimathea went boldly to Pilate and asked him for the body

of Jesus (Mark 15:43). All other refs.: BOLD <5111>, DARE <5111>.

5 more, quite, very boldly: *tolmēroteron* [adv.: τολμηρότερον <5112>]; **compar. of *tolmēros*: bold ► With more audacity, with greater freedom** > Paul had written in some sort more (or: rather) boldly (Rom. 15:15); *tolmēroterōs* in some mss. ¶

– 6 Rom. 10:20 → to say boldly → lit.: to be very bold in saying → to be very bold → BOLD <662>.

BOLDNESS – **1** ***parrēsia*** [fem. noun: παρρησία <3954>]; **from *pas*: all, and *rhēsis*: act of speaking; lit.: freedom to speak ► a. Assertiveness, lack of reserve; also transl.: assurance, confidence, courage, freedom, openness, boldly (i.e., with boldness)** > Peter spoke with boldness {confidently, freely, with freedom} about the things concerning David to his Jewish brothers (Acts 2:29). The Jews saw the boldness of Peter and John (Acts 4:13). The early Christians asked the Lord to give them boldness (Acts 4:29), and so they proclaimed the word of God with boldness (v. 31). Paul preached and taught with all boldness (Acts 28:31). He used much boldness {used plainness, was very bold} when speaking (2 Cor. 3:12). We have boldness and confident access to God by Jesus Christ (Eph. 3:12). Paul wanted to make known with boldness {fearlessly} the mystery of the gospel (Eph. 6:19). He hoped that in all boldness Christ would be magnified in his body (Phil. 1:20). Those who have served well obtain for themselves much boldness in the faith (1 Tim. 3:13). Paul might have much boldness {have much confidence, have been very bold, be bold, be much bold} in Christ to command Philemon what was fitting (Phm. 8). Christians have boldness {confidence} for entering into the Holiest by the blood of Jesus (Heb. 10:19). **b. Freedom of speech; used as an adv.: openly** > The Jews wanted Jesus to tell them openly {plainly} (lit.: with boldness) if He was the Christ (John 10:24). Paul's boldness {confidence, frankness} was great toward the Corinthians (2 Cor. 7:4). All other refs.: BOLDLY <3954>, CONFIDENCE <3954>, OPENLY <3954>, PUBLIC <3954>.

– 2 2 Cor. 10:2 → to show boldness → to be bold → BOLD <2292>.

BOND[1] – **1** ***sundesmos*** [masc. noun: σύνδεσμος <4886>]; **from *sundeō*: to join together, which is from *sun*: together, and *deō*: to join ► That which holds together; band, ligament** > Simon the magician was in the bond of {in the bondage of, bound by, captive to} iniquity (Acts 8:23). Christians are to use diligence to keep the unity of the Spirit in the bond of peace (Eph. 4:3). The body of Christ (i.e., His church) is knit together by joints and bonds {sinews} (Col. 2:19). Love is the bond of perfection (Col. 3:14). ¶

– 2 Luke 13:16; Acts 16:26; 20:23; 23:29; 26:29, 31; Phil. 1:13, 14, 16; Col. 4:18; 2 Tim. 2:9; Phm. 10, 13; Heb. 11:36; Jude 6 → CHAIN (noun) <1199> 3 Acts 22:5 → in bonds → bound → BIND <1210> 4 Acts 25:14 → in bonds → lit.: a prisoner → PRISONER <1198> 5 Eph. 6:20 → CHAIN (noun) <254>.

BOND[2] – Acts 17:9 → SECURITY <2425>.

BONDAGE – **1** ***douleia*** [fem. noun: δουλεία <1397>]; **from *douleuō*: see 2 ► Servitude, slavery** > Christians have not received a spirit of bondage (Rom. 8:15). The creation will be set free from the bondage of corruption (Rom. 8:21). Sinai (representing the law) is a covenant which bears children to bondage (Gal. 4:24). Paul tells the Galatians not to be held again in a yoke of bondage (Gal. 5:1). Jesus has set free all those who, through fear of death, were through the whole of their life subject to bondage (Heb. 2:15). ¶

2 to be in bondage, to be under bondage: *douleuō* [verb: δουλεύω <1398>]; **from *doulos*: servant, slave ► To do the service of a slave, to submit to a master** > The Jews told Jesus that they had never been in bondage to anyone (John 8:33 {to be slaves, to be enslaved}). God would judge the nation to whom the Israelites would be in bondage {serve as slaves} (Acts 7:7). Before their conversion, the Galatians were in bondage {did service, did serve, were slaves, were enslaved} to them which by nature are not gods and may have desired again to be in bondage (Gal. 4:8, 9). Jerusalem is in bondage with her children (Gal. 4:25 {to be in slavery}). All other refs.: SERVE <1398>, SERVICE <1398>.

[3] **to bring into bondage:** ***douloō*** [verb: δουλόω <1402>]; **from *doulos*: servant, slave ▶ To make a servant, to reduce to slavery; also transl.: to be under (in) bondage, to be bound, to become servant, to make oneself a servant, to be the servant, to become slave, to be the slave, to be given, to enslave, to be enslaved, to be in slavery** > God had foretold that the descendants of Abraham would be brought into bondage (Acts 7:6). The Christians have become the servants {slaves, bondmen} of righteousness (Rom. 6:18) and of God (v. 22). If the unbelieving husband or wife departs, a brother or a sister is not under bondage in such cases (1 Cor. 7:15). Paul had made himself servant to all (1 Cor. 9:19). Before their conversion, the Christians were in bondage under the principles of this world (Gal. 4:3). The older women must not be given {be addicted} to much wine (Titus 2:3). Some promise liberty to others, but are themselves the servants of corruption (2 Pet. 2:19). ¶

[4] **to bring into bondage:** ***katadouloō*** [verb: καταδουλόω <2615>]; **from *kata*: intens., and *douloō*: see [3] ▶ To make entirely a servant, to reduce entirely to slavery** > The Corinthians were bearing with being brought into bondage {being enslaved} (2 Cor. 11:20). False brothers wanted to bring Paul into bondage (Gal. 2:4). ¶

– [5] Acts 8:23 → BOND[1] <4886> [6] Rom. 6:19a, b → SLAVE (noun) <1400>.

BONDMAID – [1] Luke 1:38, 48 → HANDMAID <1399> [2] Gal. 4:22 → SERVANT GIRL <3814>.

BONDMAN – Acts 2:18 → SERVANT <1401>.

BONDSERVANT – See SERVANT <1401>.

BONDSLAVE – [1] Luke 1:38, 48; Acts 2:18 → HANDMAID <1399> [2] Acts 2:18 → bondslave man → SERVANT <1401> [3] Acts 2:18 → bondslave woman → BONDWOMAN <1399>.

BONDWOMAN – [1] ***doulē*** [fem. noun: δούλη <1399>]; **fem. of *doulos*: slave, servant ▶ Female servant totally devoted to the service of a master** > God would pour out of His Spirit on His bondmen and on His bondwomen {handmaiden, maidservants} (Acts 2:18); other transl.: My servants {bondslaves}, both men and women. Other refs.: Luke 1:38, 48; see HANDMAID <1399>. ¶

– [2] Gal. 4:22, 23, 30a, b, 31 → SERVANT GIRL <3814>.

BONE – [1] ***osteon*** [neut. noun: ὀστέον <3747>] ▶ **a. Hard substance which forms the skeleton of the human body and of vertebrate animals** > A spirit does not have flesh and bones (Luke 24:39). Like the lamb sacrificed at the Jewish Passover, not a bone of Jesus was broken (John 19:36; see Ex. 12:46). Christians are members of the spiritual body of Christ, the church, of His flesh and of His bones (Eph. 5:30 in some mss.). Joseph gave commandment concerning his bones (Heb. 11:22), instructing the sons of Israel to carry them when they would leave Egypt (see Gen. 50:25). **b. Dried out, emaciated bone** > Jesus called the scribes and Pharisees whitewashed tombs, which are full of dead men's bones (Matt. 23:27). ¶

– [2] Acts 3:7 → ankle bone → ANKLE <4974>.

BOOK – [1] ***biblos*** [fem. noun: βίβλος <976>]; **whence Bible, the Book by excellence ▶ Volume, scroll, roll** > At its origin, the Greek word for "book" designated the medium for writing used most frequently in antiquity: the inner bark of Egyptian papyrus plant cross-layered and glued together to make "paper." It was also customary to write on carefully tanned thin hides (*membrana*), called "parchments" due to the reputation of hides prepared at Pergamum. Ancient books were scrolls; "volume" comes from the Lat. word meaning: to roll, to unroll (see Ps. 40:7; Heb. 10:7 {scroll}: see Jer. 36:2, 4, 6). In contrast, modern books are "codices," i.e., rectangles glued or bound together at one side, which the reader leafs through. As a general rule, scrolls were written on the side which was rolled up, hence hidden (see Is. 29:11); Rev. 5:1 describes a scroll (see 2) with writing on the inside and on the back (comp. Ezek. 2:9). By extension, "book" signifies a lengthy written work that forms a whole: the Gospel of Matthew which is presented as the book {record, scroll} of the genealogy of Jesus Christ (Matt. 1:1); the Gospel of John (John 20:30: see 2); the book of Moses (Mark 12:26), i.e., Exodus, one of the five books forming the Pentateuch (in Greek: ensemble of five books); the book of Psalms (Luke 20:42; Acts 1:20) grouped in five sections; the book of the prophets (Acts 7:42); the book of the prophet Isaiah (Luke 3:4); Revelation (Rev. 22:19a). The book of life (Phil. 4:3; Rev. 3:5; 20:15) contains the names of all those who have eternal life (comp. Ex. 32:32; Luke 10:20; Heb. 12:23); it corresponds to the book of life of the Lamb (Rev. 13:8). The books {scrolls} burned by the converts of Acts 19:19 were most likely books of magic. ¶

2 ***biblion*** [neut. noun: βιβλίον <975>]; **dimin. of 1 ► Small volume; also transl.: scroll** > Jesus was handed the book of the prophet Isaiah to read (Luke 4:17a, b, 20). Many other miracles of Jesus are not written in the book, i.e., the Gospel, of John (John 20:30); the world could not contain the books that would be written of those many other things which Jesus did (21:25). Paul told Timothy to bring the books (2 Tim. 4:13). In the roll of the book it is written of Jesus that He had come to do the will of God (Heb. 10:7). John saw in the right hand of Him who sat on the throne a book written inside and on the back (Rev. 5:1–5, 7–9). The word is transl. "certificate" in Matt. 19:7; Mark 10:4; see CERTIFICATE <975>. Other refs.: Gal. 3:10; Heb. 9:19; Rev. 1:11; 6:14; 17:8; 20:12a–c; 21:27; 22:7, 9, 10, 18a, b, 19a, c. ¶

3 **little book: *biblaridion*** [neut. noun: βιβλαρίδιον <974>]; **dimin. of 1; some mss.: *biblarion*, *biblidarion* ► Small volume, booklet** > John took the little book {scroll} from the angel and ate it (Rev. 10:2, 8–10). ¶

– 4 Acts 1:1 → ACCOUNT (noun) <3056>.

BOOTHS (FEAST OF) – John 7:2 → TABERNACLES (FEAST OF) <4634>.

BOOZ – See BOAZ <1003>.

BORDER – 1 ***horion*** [neut. noun: ὅριον <3725>]; **dimin. of *horos*: limit ► Limit of a territory; region along the boundary line of another** > Jesus went away into the borders {region, vicinity} of Tyre and Sidon (Mark 7:24). All other refs.: COAST (noun) <3725>, REGION <3725>.

2 ***methorion*; neuter of *methorios*** [adj. used as noun: μεθόριος <3181>]; **from *meta*: with, and *horos*: limit ► See 1.** > Certain mss. have this term in Mark 7:24 (see 1). ¶

– 3 Matt. 23:5; Mark 6:56; Luke 8:44 → FRINGE <2899>.

BORN – 1 ***gennētos*** [adj.: γεννητός <1084>]; **from *gennaō*: to be born, which is from *genna*: birth, race ► Engendered, procreated** > The word is used in the expr. "born of women" (Matt. 11:11; Luke 7:28). ¶

2 **born out of due time, untimely born, one abnormally born: *ektrōma*** [neut. noun: ἔκτρωμα <1626>]; **from *ektitrōskō*: to miscarry, which is from *ek*: out, and *titrōskō*: to wound ► Fetus born prematurely** > Paul applies this Greek term (transl.: born out of due time) to himself (1 Cor. 15:8), maybe as one not deserving to be an apostle. He indicates his inferiority in relation to the other apostles in v. 9. ¶

– 3 Matt. 1:23; 2:2; Rev. 12:2, 4a, b, 5 → to be born → to give birth → BIRTH <5088> 4 Mark 7:26; Acts 18:2, 24 → RACE[1] <1085> 5 Luke 1:15; Gal. 1:15 → before one is born → from the womb of one's mother → WOMB <2836> 6 2 Pet. 2:12 → born as creature of instinct → NATURAL <5446>.

BORN (BE) – 1 **to beget:** ***gennaō*** [verb: γεννάω <1080>]; **from** ***genna*****: birth, race ▶ Used in the pass. in Greek: to come into the world, to be brought forth, to be engendered; also transl.: to be begotten** > The verb is used in regard to Jesus Christ, the Son of God (Matt. 1:16; 2:1, 4; Luke 1:35; John 18:37). It is also used in regard to eunuchs (Matt. 19:12), Judas (Matt. 26:24; Mark 14:21), the children of God (John 1:13; 1 John 2:29; 3:9a, b; 4:7; 5:1a, b; 5:4, 18a, b), man in general (John 3:4a, b; 16:21a, b), the Jews (John 8:41; Heb. 11:12), a blind man (John 9:2, 19, 20, 32, 34), Moses (Acts 7:20; Heb. 11:23), Paul (Acts 22:3), and Ishmael (Gal. 4:23, 29). Other refs.: John 3:3, 5, 6a, b, 7, 8; Acts 2:8; Rom. 9:11; 2 Pet. 2:12 {to be made}. All other refs.: see entries in Lexicon at <1080>.
2 ***ginomai*** [verb: γίνομαι <1096>] ▶ **To be born, to be made, to come** > Jesus was born of David's seed {was a descendant of David} (Rom. 1:3). He was born of woman, born under the law (Gal. 4:4a, b). The verb is used regarding the fruit of a fig-tree in Matt. 21:19 where the Greek word is transl.: let there be {may you bear}.
3 ***tiktō*** [verb: τίκτω <5088>]; **lit.: to bring forth, to produce ▶ Used in the pass. in Greek: to come into the world, to be brought forth** > A Savior was born who is Christ the Lord (Luke 2:11). All other refs.: BIRTH <5088>.

BORN AGAIN (BE) – 1 **to beget:** ***gennaō*** [verb: γεννάω <1080>]; **from** ***genna*****: birth, race; again, from above:** ***anōthen*** [adv.: ἄνωθεν <509>], **and suffix** ***then*****: from ▶ Used in the pass. in Greek: to receive by the Holy Spirit a new nature which comes from above, i.e., from God; also transl.: to be born anew** > Because of the introduction of sin into the world by the first man, the nature of every human being is a sinful nature. Jesus explained to Nicodemus that no one can enter the kingdom of God unless he is born again (John 3:3, 7). Such a one is born of water and of the Spirit (lit.: of water and Spirit; see John 3:5). Water washes and purifies; it is a figure of the word of God (see Eph. 5:26) applied to the soul in the power of the Holy Spirit; it brings life while subjecting to death all that pertains to the first Adam. The Holy Spirit communicates to the believer in the Lord a new nature which comes from God (see 1 John 3:9). All other refs. (*gennaō*): see entries in Lexicon at <1080>.
2 ***anagennaō*** [verb: ἀναγεννάω <313>]; **from** ***ana*****: again, and** ***gennaō*****: see** 1 ▶ **To cause to be born anew** > God has given believers in the Lord to be born again {has given them new birth, has begotten them again} into a living hope (1 Pet. 1:3). They have been born again by the word of God (v. 23). See REGENERATION <3824>. ¶

BORN ANEW (BE) – John 3:3, 7 → BORN AGAIN (BE) <509>.

BORROW – ***daneizō*** [verb: δανείζω <1155>]; **from** ***daneion*****: loan, debt, which is from** ***danos*****: gift, interest loan; also spelled:** ***danizō*** ▶ **To obtain as a loan** > Jesus says to not turn away from the one who desires to borrow (Matt. 5:42). Other refs.: Luke 6:34a, b, 35; see LEND <1155>. ¶

BOSOM – 1 ***kolpos*** [masc. noun: κόλπος <2859>]; **lit.: the front of the body between the arms ▶ a. The "bosom of the Father" speaks of affections which are eternal and continued in time between the Father and the Son** > The Son, who is in the bosom of the Father {at the Father's side}, has made God known to us (John 1:18). **b. The "bosom of Jesus" speaks of proximity** > John was reclining on the bosom of {next to} Jesus (John 13:23). **c. The "bosom of Abraham" is a metaphorical expr. used by the Jews; it evokes the blessed place of Christians after death, like that of Abraham, while waiting for the resurrection** > Lazarus died and was carried away into the bosom of Abraham (Luke 16:22, 23). **d. Lap** > The measure given back to us will be given into

our bosom (Luke 6:38). Other ref.: Acts 27:39; see BAY <2859>. ¶
– [2] John 13:25; 21:20 → BREAST <4738>.

BOSOR – ***Bosor*** [masc. name: Βοσόρ <1007>]**: lamp, in Heb.; also spelled: *Beor*, *Bezer* ▶ Moabite man** > He was the father of Balaam (2 Pet. 2:15). ¶

BOTH – ***amphoteros*** [adj.: ἀμφότερος <297>]**; from *amphō*: the two ▶ One and the other** > The word is used about wine and new skins (Matt. 9:17; Luke 5:38 in some mss.), tares and wheat (Matt. 13:30), blind guides of the blind (Matt. 15:14; Luke 6:39), Zacharias and Elizabeth (Luke 1:6, 7), boats (Luke 5:7), debtors (Luke 7:42), Philip and the eunuch (Acts 8:38), resurrection, as well as an angel and a spirit (Acts 23:8 {all}), circumcision and uncircumcision (Eph. 2:14 {the two}, 16), and Jews and Gentiles (Eph. 2:18). Other ref.: Acts 19:16 in some mss. ¶

BOTHER – [1] Matt. 26:10; Mark 14:6; Luke 18:5 → to give trouble → TROUBLE (verb) <2873> [2] Mark 5:35; Luke 8:49 → TROUBLE (verb) <4660> [3] Luke 10:41 → to be bothered → to be troubled → TROUBLE (verb) <5182> [4] Luke 11:7 → lit.: to cause trouble → TROUBLE (noun) <2873>.

BOTTLE – Matt. 9:17a–d; Mark 2:22a–d; Luke 5:37a–c, 38 → WINESKIN <779>.

BOTTOMLESS – **abyss: *abussos*** [fem. noun: ἄβυσσος <12>]**; from *a*: intens., and *buthos*: deep, bottom, bottom of the sea ▶ Profound depth, chasm; it also symbolizes the source of Satanic evil and misery** > Demons begged Jesus that He would not command them to go away into the abyss {bottomless pit, deep} (Luke 8:31). A star fallen from heaven to earth will be given the key of the bottomless pit (lit.: the pit of the abyss) and will open it (Rev. 9:1, 2). Satan is the angel of the bottomless pit (lit.: of the abyss) (Rev. 9:11). The beast will ascend out of the bottomless pit (lit.: of the abyss) (Rev. 11:7; 17:8). The bottomless pit {deep abyss} is reserved for some fallen angels (see Luke 8:31), and later for the devil (Rev. 20:1, 3; lit.: the abyss). After their judgment, the devil and his angels will be cast in the eternal fire prepared for them (see Matt. 25:41). Paul asks who will descend into the abyss {deep} to bring up Christ again from the dead (Rom. 10:7). ¶

BOUND – [1] Acts 17:26 → BOUNDARY <3734> [2] 2 Cor. 7:4 → my joy knows no bounds → lit.: I (Paul) overabound in joy → ABOUND <5248>.

BOUND (BE) – [1] Luke 17:1 → certain things are bound to come → lit.: it is impossible that certain things do not come → IMPOSSIBLE <418> [2] 2 Cor. 6:14 → to be bound together → to be unequally yoked → YOKED (BE) <2086>.

BOUNDARY – ***horothesia*** [fem. noun: ὁροθεσία <3734>]**; from *horos*: boundary, and *tithēmi*: to put ▶ Limit, border** > God has determined the boundaries {bounds, exact places} of the dwelling of men (Acts 17:26). ¶

BOUNDLESS – Eph. 3:8 → UNSEARCHABLE <421>.

BOUNTIFUL – 2 Cor. 9:5 → bountiful gift → generous gift → GIFT <2129>.

BOUNTIFULLY – **blessing: *eulogia*** [fem. noun: εὐλογία <2129>]**; from *eulogeō*: to bless, to praise, which is from *eu*: well, and *logos*: word ▶ Abundance, liberality** > He who sows bountifully {generously} (lit.: in blessing) will also reap bountifully {generously} (lit.: in blessing) (2 Cor. 9:6a, b). All other refs.: BLESSING <2129>, GIFT <2129>, SPEECH <2129>.

BOUNTIFULNESS – 2 Cor. 9:11 → LIBERALITY <572>.

BOUNTY – [1] 1 Cor. 16:3 → GIFT <5485> [2] 2 Cor. 9:5 → generous gift → GIFT <2129>.

BOW (noun) – 1 ***toxon*** [neut. noun: τόξον <5115>] ▶ **Curved device for shooting arrows** > He who sat on the white horse had a bow (Rev. 6:2). ¶
– 2 Acts 27:30, 41 → PROW <4408>.

BOW (verb) – 1 ***kamptō*** [verb: κάμπτω <2578>] ▶ **To bend, to incline in homage** > God had reserved for Himself seven thousand men who had not bowed the knee before Baal (Rom. 11:4). Every knee will bow to the Lord (Rom. 14:11). Paul bowed his knees {kneeled} before the Father of the Lord Jesus Christ (Eph. 3:14). At the name of Jesus every knee will bow of heavenly and earthly and infernal beings (Phil. 2:10). ¶
2 **to bow down: *sunkamptō*** [verb: συγκάμπτω <4781>]; **from *sun*: together, and *kamptō*: see** 1 ▶ **To bend under pressure** > David tells God to bow down {bend} the backs of his enemies always (Rom. 11:10). ¶
3 **to bow, to bow down: *klinō*** [verb: κλίνω <2827>] ▶ **To incline, to tilt** > At the tomb of Jesus, the women bowed down their faces to the ground (Luke 24:5). Jesus bowed His head and gave up His spirit (John 19:30). All other refs.: FLIGHT <2827>, LAY <2827>, WEAR <2827>.
– 4 Matt. 2:11; 4:9 → to bow down → to fall down → FALL (verb) <4098> 5 Matt. 8:2; 9:18; 15:25; 20:20; Mark 5:6; 15:19; Heb. 11:21; Rev. 3:9 → to bow before, to bow down, to bow in worship → WORSHIP (verb) <4352> 6 Mark 15:19 → to bow (the knee; lit. to place the knee) → LAY <5087>.

BOWEL – Phil. 2:1 → TENDERNESS <4698>.

BOWELS – Luke 1:78; Acts 1:18; 2 Cor. 6:12; Phil. 1:8; Col. 3:12; Phm. 7, 12, 20; 1 John 3:17 → ENTRAILS <4698>.

BOWL – 1 ***phialē*** [fem. noun: φιάλη <5357>] ▶ **Deep container open at the top; also transl.: vial** > In Rev. 5:8, the golden bowls full of incense are the prayers of the saints. Other bowls are full of the wrath of God (Rev. 15:7; 16:1–4, 8, 10, 12, 17; 17:1; 21:9). ¶
– 2 Matt. 5:15; Mark 4:21; Luke 11:33 → BUSHEL <3426> 3 Matt. 26:23; Mark 14:20 → DISH <5165>.

BOX (noun) – 1 Matt. 26:7; Mark 14:3a, b → ALABASTER BOX <211> 2 Mark 12:41, 43; Luke 21:1 → offering box → temple treasury → TREASURE (noun) <1049> 3 John 12:6; 13:29 → money box → BAG <1101>.

BOX (verb) – 1 Cor. 9:26 → FIGHT (verb) <4438>.

BOXER – 1 Cor. 9:26 → to fight like a boxer → FIGHT (verb) <4438>.

BOY – 1 ***pais*** [masc. or fem. noun: παῖς <3816>] ▶ **Child, young man** > Jesus healed a boy possessed by a demon (Matt. 17:18). The boy Eutychus was brought away alive (Acts 20:12). All other refs.: CHILD <3816>, DAUGHTER <3816>, SERVANT <3816>, SON <3816>.
2 ***paidarion*** [neut. noun: παιδάριον <3808>]; **dimin. of *pais*: see** 1 ▶ **Young child** > A boy {lad, little boy} had five barley loaves and two small fish (John 6:9). Certain mss. have this term in Matt. 11:16 where it is transl. "children," "little children." ¶
– 3 Mark 10:20; Luke 18:21 → since he was a boy → since his youth → YOUTH <3503> 4 John 7:22, 23 → a boy → lit.: a human → MAN <444>.

BRAG – 1 Cor. 13:4 → BOAST (verb) <4068>.

BRAIDED – 1 Pet. 3:3 → BRAIDING <1708>.

BRAIDED HAIR – ***plegma*** [neut. noun: πλέγμα <4117>]; **from *plekō*: to plait, to weave** ▶ **Interwoven strands of hair** > Believing women are to adorn themselves with modesty and discretion in decent dress, not with braided hair {broided hair, plaited hair} (most likely an extravagant hairstyle) and gold, or pearls, or costly clothing (1 Tim. 2:9). ¶

BRAIDING – ***emplokē*** [fem. noun: ἐμπλοκή <1708>]; **from *emplekō*: to braid in, which is from *en*: in, and *plekō*: to plait, to weave ▶ Interlacing in an elaborate manner as ornament** > The adornment of a Christian woman is not to be an outward one of braiding the {arranging the, braided, plaiting the, tressing of} hair (most likely an extravagant hairstyle) and of wearing gold and putting on fine clothes (1 Pet. 3:3); *plokē* in some mss. ¶

BRAKE (obsolete past tense of "break") – [1] Mark 14:3 → BREAK <4937> [2] Luke 8:29 → BREAK <1284>.

BRAMBLE – Mark 12:26; Luke 20:37 → bramble, bramble bush → BUSH <942>.

BRANCH – [1] ***baion*** [neut. noun: βαΐον <902>]; **from *bais*: palm branch ▶ Bough of a tree** > A great crowd took branches of palms and went out to meet Jesus as He came to Jerusalem (John 12:13). ¶

[2] ***klados*** [masc. noun: κλάδος <2798>]; **from *klaō*: to break, to prune ▶ Growing extension of a tree or shrub** > In a parable, a grain of mustard becomes a tree, so that the birds nest in its branches (Matt. 13:32; Luke 13:19); the branches are great (Mark 4:32). People cut down branches from the trees and strew them on the pathway of Jesus (Matt. 21:8); note that Mark and John use different words: see [1] and [4]. Jesus told a parable about the branch {twigs} of the fig-tree (Matt. 24:32; Mark 13:28). Paul speaks of the branches of the olive tree which represents Israel (Rom. 11:16–19, 21). ¶

[3] ***klēma*** [neut. noun: κλῆμα <2814>]; **from *klaō*: to break ▶ Shoot, young twig of the vine** > The branches represent those who belong to the Lord. They must be pruned to bear more fruit (John 15:2), to the Father's glory (see v. 8). The branch cannot bear fruit of itself, unless it remains in the vine (v. 4). The Lord is the vine and those who believe in Him are the branches (v. 5). The withered branches (which do not have the life of Christ) are burned (v. 6). ¶

[4] ***stibas*** [fem. noun: στιβάς <4741a>] **or *stoibas*:** [fem. noun: στοιβάς <4746>]; **from *steibō*: to walk on ▶ Foliage which might be spread as a layer** > People cut down branches {leafy branches} from trees and laid them on the pathway of Jesus as He came to Jerusalem (Mark 11:8). ¶

BRAND – Gal. 6:17 → MARK (noun) <4742>.

BRANDING – 1 Tim. 4:2 → to sear with a branding iron → IRON <2743>.

BRANDMARK – Gal. 6:17 → MARK (noun) <4742>.

BRASEN VESSEL – Mark 7:4 → BRAZEN VESSEL <5473>.

BRASS – [1] ***chalkos*** [masc. noun: χαλκός <5475>] **▶ Copper, an alloy of copper (70%) and zinc (30%), or bronze (an alloy of copper and tin)** > Money (Matt. 10:9 {copper}), musical instruments (1 Cor. 13:1 {gong}), and various articles (Rev. 18:12 {bronze}) were made of brass. Other refs.: Mark 6:8; 12:41; see MONEY <5475>. ¶

[2] **of brass: *chalkeos*** [adj.: χάλκεος <5470>]; **from *chalkos*: see [1]; also written: *chalkous* ▶ Made of copper or brass** > Men will worship idols of brass {brazen idols, bronze idols} (Rev. 9:20). ¶

[3] **fine brass: *chalkolibanon*** [neut. noun: χαλκολίβανον <5474>]; **from *chalkos*: see [1], and *libanos*: frankincense-tree ▶ High quality brass; also transl.: bronze, burnished bronze** > In John's vision, the Son of Man had feet like fine brass (Rev. 1:15; 2:18). ¶

BRAVE – 1 Cor. 16:13 → to be brave → to act like a man → MAN <407>.

BRAWLER – 1 Tim. 3:3; Titus 3:2 → not a brawler → not quarrelsome → QUARRELSOME <269>.

BRAWLING – Eph. 4:31 → CLAMOR <2906>.

BRAZEN – [1] Mark 7:4 → brazen utensil, brazen vessel → BRAZEN VESSEL <5473> [2] Rev. 9:20 → of brass → BRASS <5470>.

BRAZEN VESSEL – ***chalkion*** [neut. noun: χαλκίον <5473>]; **from *chalkos*: brass, copper ► Plate, container made of brass or copper** > Traditionally, the Jews were washing brazen vessels {brazen utensils, copper pots, copper vessels, kettles} (Mark 7:4). ¶

BREACH – Luke 6:49 → RUIN (noun) <4485>.

BREAD – [1] ***artos*** [masc. noun: ἄρτος <740>] **► Food composed of flour mingled with water and baked; bread was broken rather than cut; also transl.: loaf** > Jesus said that man will not live by bread alone, but by every word that goes out through the mouth of God (Matt. 4:4; Luke 4:4). Jesus said that He was the bread of life which has come down from heaven (John 6:35, 41, 48, 50, 51a–c, 58a, b). Early Christians devoted themselves to the breaking of bread (Acts 2:42); they broke bread in their houses (v. 46). Paul was assembled with other Christians on the first day of the week to break bread (Acts 20:7, 11). The bread that we break when remembering the Lord's death is the communion of the body of Christ (1 Cor. 10:16). Christians are one bread, one body, for they all partake of that one bread (1 Cor. 10:17a, b). As often as Christians eat the bread and drink the cup (at the Lord's remembrance supper), they announce the death of the Lord until He comes (1 Cor. 11:26). Other refs.: Matt. 4:3; 6:11; 7:9; 12:4; 14:17, 19a, b; 15:2, 26, 33, 34, 36; 16:5, 7–12; 26:26; Mark 2:26; 3:20; 6:8, 36–38, 41a, b, 44, 52; 7:2, 5, 27; 8:4–6, 14a, b, 16, 17, 19; 14:22; Luke 4:3; 7:33; 9:3, 13, 16; 11:3, 5, 11; 14:1, 15; 15:17; 22:19; 24:30, 35; John 6:5, 7, 9, 11, 13, 23, 26, 31, 32a, b, 33, 34; 13:18; 21:9, 13; Acts 27:35; 1 Cor. 11:23, 27, 28; 2 Cor. 9:10; 2 Thes. 3:8, 12; Heb. 9:2. ¶

[2] See EXPOSITION OF THE LOAVES <4286> <740>, UNLEAVENED <106>, UNLEAVENED BREAD <106>.

– [3] John 13:26a, b, 27, 30 → piece of bread → PIECE <5596>.

BREADTH – ***platos*** [neut. noun: πλάτος <4114>]; **from *platus*: wide, spacious ► a. Dimension of a thing, in the sense opposed to its length; also transl.: width** > Paul wanted Christians to be fully able to understand the breadth (he is not specifying of what), and to know the love of Christ (Eph. 3:18). The length and breadth and height of the new Jerusalem are equal (Rev. 21:16a, b). **b. Expanse** > At the end of one thousand years, the nations will come up on the breadth {broad plain} of the land and surround the camp of the saints at Jerusalem (Rev. 20:9). ¶

BREAK – [1] **to break in, into, through: *diorussō*** [verb: διορύσσω <1358>]; **from *dia*: through, and *orussō*: to dig ► To make an opening in order to penetrate (by burglary) into a house** > Thieves break in {dig through} and steal on earth (Matt. 6:19), but not in heaven (v. 20). If the master of the house had known at what time the thief was coming, he would have watched and not have suffered his house to be broken into {dug through} (Matt. 24:43; Luke 12:39). ¶

[2] ***klaō*** [verb: κλάω <2806>] **► To separate, to split** > Jesus broke the five loaves of bread to feed the crowds (Matt. 14:19; Mark 8:19). On another occasion, He broke seven loaves of bread to feed a crowd (Matt. 15:36; Mark 8:6). On the evening before His death, He broke bread and gave it to His disciples to eat (Matt. 26:26; Mark 14:22; Luke 22:19; 1 Cor. 11:24: *thruptō* in some mss.). On the evening of His resurrection, He broke bread in the house of two disciples of Emmaus (Luke 24:30). Early Christians broke bread in their homes (Acts 2:46). We read that Paul broke bread in memory of the Lord (Acts 20:7, 11) and broke bread at a meal (Acts 27:35). The bread which Christians break at the Lord's supper is the communion

of the body of Christ (1 Cor. 10:16). See BREAK BREAD <2806> <740>. ¶

3 **to break off:** ***ekklaō*** [verb: ἐκκλάω <1575>]; **from** ***ek*****: out (intens.), and** ***klaō*****: see** 2 **► To remove by breaking out, to prune** > Paul speaks of the Jews as branches broken off because of their unbelief, allowing the Gentiles to be grafted in among them (Rom. 11:17, 19, 20). ¶

4 ***kataklaō*** [verb: κατακλάω <2622>]; **from** ***kata*****: intens., and** ***klaō*****: see** 2 **► To break in pieces, to divide** > Jesus broke five loaves of bread to feed the crowd (Mark 6:41; Luke 9:16). ¶

5 ***katagnumi*** [verb: κατάγνυμι <2608>]; **from** ***kata*****: intens., and** ***agnumi*****: to break ► To rend in pieces, to crack** > Jesus would not break a bruised reed (Matt. 12:20). The Jews asked Pilate that the legs of those who were crucified might be broken (John 19:31), which the soldiers did to the two malefactors (v. 32), but not to Jesus who was already dead (v. 33). Breaking the legs resulted in hastening the death of those who were crucified. ¶

6 ***luō*** [verb: λύω <3089>]; **lit.: to untie, to loose ► a. To abolish, to destroy** > The Scripture cannot be broken (John 10:35). **b. To break up, i.e., to dissolve, to disperse** > After the congregation had broken up {was dismissed}, many of the Jews and proselytes followed Paul and Barnabas (Acts 13:43). **c. To loose, to go to pieces** > The stern of the grounded ship was broken by the force of the waves (Acts 27:41). An angel proclaims: Who is worthy to open the book and to break its seals? (Rev. 5:2). **d. To fail to comply with, to contravene; also transl.: to violate** > Jesus was accused of having violated the Sabbath (John 5:18). Since a man received circumcision on a Sabbath day, that the law of Moses might not be violated, Jesus asked the Jews if they were angry with Him because He had completely healed a man on such a day (John 7:23). All other refs.: ANNUL <3089>, DESTROY <3089>, DISSOLVE <3089>, LOOSE <3089>, RELEASE (verb) <3089>.

7 **to break forth:** ***rhēgnumi*** [verb: ῥήγνυμι <4486>]; **lit.: to break ► To show a joyful emotion, to rejoice** > The barren woman was to break forth {break out} and shout (Gal. 4:27). All other refs.: BURST <4486>, TEAR (verb) <4486>.

8 ***diarrēgnumi*** [verb: διαρρήγνυμι <1284>]; **from** ***dia*****: intens., and** ***rhēgnumi*****: see** 7 **► To break completely** > The net of the fishermen broke because of the great number of fish (Luke 5:6). Other ref.: Luke 8:29; see 9. ¶

9 ***diarrēssō*** [verb: διαρρήσσω <1284>]; **from** ***dia*****: denoting separation, and** ***rhēgnumi*****: see** 7 **► To smash, to rend in pieces** > A possessed man was breaking {bursting} his bonds (Luke 8:29). Other ref.: Luke 5:6; see 8. ¶

10 **to break upon:** ***prosrēgnumi*** [verb: προσρήγνυμι <4366>]; **from** ***pros*****: against, and** ***rhēgnumi*****: see** 7 **► To beat violently against, to dash against; also transl.: to beat vehemently, to burst against, to strike** > The stream broke upon a house (Luke 6:48, 49). ¶

11 ***sunthlaō*** [verb: συνθλάω <4917>]; **from** ***sun*****: together, and** ***thlaō*****: to crush ► To crush together, to shatter** > Whoever will fall on the rejected stone (Jesus Christ) will be broken (Matt. 21:44; Luke 20:18). ¶

12 ***sunthruptō*** [verb: συνθρύπτω <4919>]; **from** ***sun*****: intens., and** ***thruptō*****: to break, to crush, to soften ► To discourage, to weaken** > The heart of Paul was broken by those pleading with him not to go up to Jerusalem (Acts 21:13). ¶

13 **to break, to break in pieces, to break to pieces, to break to shivers, to dash to pieces:** ***suntribō*** [verb: συντρίβω <4937>]; **from** ***sun*****: together (intens.), and** ***tribō*****: to break, to rub; lit.: to break by rubbing ► To crush together, to smash, to shatter** > A woman broke an alabaster flask of spikenard and poured it on the head of Jesus (Mark 14:3). Not a bone of Jesus was to be broken (John 19:36). The overcomer in Thyatira will rule the nations with a rod of iron, and the nations will be broken in pieces like the potter's vessels (Rev. 2:27). Other ref.: Luke 4:18 {to be brokenhearted}. All other refs.: BRUISE <4937>, PIECE <4937>.

14 ***schizō*** [verb: σχίζω <4977>] **► To split, to tear** > The net of Simon Peter was not broken {rent, torn}, although there were one

hundred and fifty-three large fish in it (John 21:11). All other refs.: DIVIDE <4977>, SPLIT <4977>, TEAR (verb) <4977>.

– [15] Matt. 12:5 → PROFANE (verb) <953> [16] Matt. 15:2, 3 → TRANSGRESS <3845> [17] Mark 2:4 → to break up, to break through → to dig up → DIG <1846> [18] Mark 4:37 → BEAT <1911> [19] Mark 6:26 → to break one's word → REFUSE (verb) <114> [20] Luke 24:35 → lit.: in the breaking → BREAKING <2800> [21] Acts 11:19 → to break out → lit.: to occur (*ginomai*) [22] Rom. 1:16; 11:15; 15:18; 16:26 → the verb is added in Engl. [23] Acts 23:3 → to break the law → CONTRARY <3891> [24] Rom. 2:25, 27 → lit.: breaker, one who breaks the law → TRANSGRESSOR <3848> [25] Rom. 5:14 → by breaking a command → lit.: in the likeness of the transgression → LIKENESS <3667> [26] Rom. 6:6 → to bring to nothing → to make of no effect → EFFECT (noun) <2673> [27] Rom. 7:13 → to bring about my death → to work death in me → WORK (verb) <2716> [28] 1 Tim. 5:12 → REJECT <114> [29] Heb. 2:14 → to render powerless → POWERLESS <2673>.

BREAK BREAD – **to break:** ***klaō*** [verb: κλάω <2806>]; **bread:** ***artos*** [masc. noun: ἄρτος <740>] ► **The act of breaking bread (or: the breaking of bread) is part of the Lord's supper** > The Lord Jesus broke bread on the night He was betrayed (1 Cor. 11:24). He broke bread and gave it to His disciples, saying: Take and eat; this is My body (speaking figur.) (Matt. 26:26; Mark 14:22). The bread which Christians break is the communion of the body of Christ (1 Cor. 10:16), for they are one bread, one body, and all partake of one bread (see v. 17). The early Christians devoted themselves to the breaking (*klasis*) of bread (Acts 2:42); they broke bread in their homes (v. 46). Paul broke bread on the first day of the week at Troas (Acts 20:7, 11). On another occasion, he broke bread (Acts 27:35), but this act was not related to the Lord's supper: it was rather a matter of taking food.

BREAK OF DAY – ***augē*** [fem. noun: αὐγή <827>] ► **Rising of the sun, dawn** > Paul talked a long while, until break of day {daybreak, daylight} (Acts 20:11). ¶

BREAKER – Rom. 2:25 → TRANSGRESSOR <3848>.

BREAKFAST – John 21:12, 15 → to eat breakfast → DINE <709>.

BREAKING – [1] ***klasis*** [fem. noun: κλάσις <2800>]; **from *klaō*: to break** ► **Action of dividing into parts** > Jesus made Himself known to the two disciples of Emmaus in the breaking of bread (Luke 24:35), i.e., in breaking bread during a meal (see v. 30). The early Christians devoted themselves to the breaking of bread (Acts 2:42). ¶

– [2] Rom. 2:23; 5:14 → breaking, breaking a command → TRANSGRESSION <3847>.

BREAST – [1] ***mastos*** [masc. noun: μαστός <3149>] ► **a. The female organ which secretes milk, mammary gland; also transl.: pap** > The term is used in the plur. (Luke 11:27; 23:29). **b. Chest** > John saw one like the Son of Man girded at the chest (lit.: breasts) with a golden sash (Rev. 1:13). ¶

[2] ***stēthos*** [neut. noun: στῆθος <4738>]; **from *histēmi*: to stand** ► **Part of the body which stands out and contains the heart and the lungs** > A tax collector was beating his breast, asking God to have mercy on him (Luke 18:13). Returning from the crucifixion of Jesus, all the people beat their breasts (Luke 23:48). John leaned on the breast {bosom} of Jesus (John 13:25; 21:20). Seven angels were girded about the breasts {around the chests} with golden girdles (Rev. 15:6). ¶

BREASTPLATE – ***thōrax*** [masc. noun: θώραξ <2382>]; **lit.: thorax** ► **Defensive weapon made of two parts to protect the front and the back of the body, from the neck to the waist** > Paul speaks of the Christian putting on the breastplate of righteousness (Eph. 6:14) and the breastplate of faith and love (1 Thes. 5:8). John saw locusts who had breastplates like breastplates of iron (Rev. 9:9a, b); those who sat on the horses had breastplates of fiery red, hyacinth blue, and sulfur yellow (v. 17). ¶

BREATH – [1] ***pneuma*** [neut. noun: πνεῦμα <4151>]**; from *pneō*: to breathe ▶ Respiration, spirit** > The Lord Jesus will consume the lawless one with the breath {spirit} of His mouth and will annul him by the appearance of His coming (2 Thes. 2:8). It will be given to the second beast to give breath {life} to the image of the first beast (Rev. 13:15). Other refs.: SPIRIT <4151>, WIND (noun) <4151>.
[2] ***pnoē*** [fem. noun: πνοή <4157>]**; from *pneō*: to breathe ▶ Blowing, wind** > God gives to all life and breath (Acts 17:25). Other refs.: Acts 2:2; 27:40; see WIND (noun) <4157>. ¶

BREATHE – [1] **to breathe, to breathe out: *empneō*** [verb: ἐμπνέω <1709>]**; from *en*: in, and *pneō*: to breathe ▶ To inhale, to be animated by** > Paul was still breathing out threatenings and slaughter against the disciples of the Lord when He appeared to him (Acts 9:1). ¶
[2] **to breathe on: *emphusaō*** [verb: ἐμφυσάω <1720>]**; from *en*: in, and *phusao*: to blow ▶ To blow in, to respire into** > Jesus breathed on {breathed into} His apostles, and said to them: Receive the Holy Spirit (John 20:22). ¶
– [3] Mark 15:37, 39; Luke 23:46 → to breathe one's last → EXPIRE <1606> [4] Acts 5:5, 10; 12:23 → to breathe his last → EXPIRE <1634> [5] 2 Tim. 3:16 → breathed by God → DIVINELY INSPIRED <2315>.

BREED – 2 Tim. 2:23 → GENERATE <1080>.

BRETHREN – Archaic plur. of "brother." See BROTHER <80>.

BRIAR – [1] ***tribolos*** [masc. noun: τρίβολος <5146>]**; from *treis*: three, and *belos*: point, dart ▶ Prickly, injurious shrub; also transl.: brier, thistle** > False prophets are known by their fruits; they are like briars on which figs cannot be gathered (Matt. 7:16). If the earth bears thorns and briars, it is rejected and near to being cursed (Heb. 6:8). ¶
– [2] Mark 12:26 → briar bush → BUSH <942>.

BRIBE – Acts 24:26 → MONEY <5536>.

BRIDE – ***numphē*** [fem. noun: νύμφη <3565>] ▶ **Woman united to a man by marriage** > The word with this usual meaning is found in Rev. 18:23. It designates the church of God, the bride of Christ (John 3:29; Rev. 21:2, 9; 22:17). The word also means "daughter-in-law" and is transl. as such in Matt. 10:35 and Luke 12:53a, b. Other ref.: Matt. 25:1 in some mss. ¶

BRIDECHAMBER – ***numphōn*** [masc. noun: νυμφών <3567>]**; from *numphē*: bride ▶ Room in which was the nuptial bed; the sons of the bridechamber were the friends of the bridegroom and were providing what was required for the wedding** > The sons of the bridechamber {friends, attendants, guests of the bridegroom} cannot mourn while the bridegroom is with them (Matt. 9:15); they cannot fast (Mark 2:19; Luke 5:34). Other ref.: Matt. 22:10 in some mss. ¶

BRIDEGROOM – [1] ***numphios*** [masc. noun: νυμφίος <3566>]**; from *numphē*: bride ▶ Man newly united to a woman by marriage** > The word with this usual meaning is found in John 2:9 and Rev. 18:23. During His passage in Israel, Jesus was like the bridegroom with the friends of the bridegroom (Matt. 9:15b; Mark 2:19a, b, 20; Luke 5:34b, 35; John 3:29a–c). The word also refers to Christ and His bride, the church: in Matt. 25 (vv. 1, 5, 6, 10), Jesus speaks of Himself as the bridegroom. ¶
– [2] Matt. 9:15; Mark 2:19; Luke 5:34 → attend, friend, guest of the bridegroom → son of the bridechamber → SON OF THE BRIDECHAMBER <5207> <3567>.

BRIDLE (noun) – Rev. 14:20 → BIT <5469>.

BRIDLE (verb) – ***chalinagōgeō*** [verb: χαλιναγωγέω <5468>]; **from *chalinos*: bit, bridle, and *agō*: to lead, to govern; lit.: to guide with the bit ► To prevent from acting, to hold back** > The religion of a man is vain if he does not bridle {keep a tight rein on} his tongue (Jas. 1:26). A perfect man is able also to bridle {keep in check} the whole body (Jas. 3:2). ¶

BRIEFLY – [1] ***di' oligōn*; formed from *dia*** [prep.: διά <1223>] **and *oligos*** [adj. used as noun: ὀλίγος <3641>]; **lit.: by few ► In a few words** > Peter had written briefly with Silvanus's help (1 Pet. 5:12). Other ref.: Eph. 3:3 → in few words → FEW <3641>.
– [2] Acts 24:4 → a few words → WORD <4935>.

BRIER – [1] Matt. 7:16; Heb. 6:8 → BRIAR <5146> [2] Luke 6:44 → BUSH <942>.

BRIGHT – [1] ***lampros*** [adj.: λαμπρός <2986>]; **from *lampō*: to shine ► a. Which gives light, shining** > Jesus is the bright morning star (Rev. 22:16). **b. Magnificent, splendid** > Herod and his men arrayed Jesus in a bright {elegant, gorgeous} robe (Luke 23:11). A man stood before Cornelius in bright {shining} clothing (Acts 10:30). James speaks of those who make a difference between a man in bright {fine, goodly, gay} clothes and a poor man in filthy clothes (Jas. 2:2, 3). The word is used in Revelation about the clothes of seven angels (15:6 {white}), the things for Babylon the great (18:14 {the splendors, goodly}), the clothes of the wife of the Lamb (19:8 {white}). **c. Pure, clear** > John was shown a bright river of water of life (Rev. 22:1). ¶
[2] ***phōteinos*** [adj.: φωτεινός <5460>]; **from *phōs*: light, luminousness ► Radiant, full of light** > A bright cloud overshadowed Jesus and those who were with Him at the transfiguration (Matt. 17:5). Other refs.: Matt. 6:22; Luke 11:34, 36a, b; see LIGHT (noun) <5460>. ¶
– [3] Luke 11:36 → bright shining → SHINING <796> [4] Acts 26:13 → brighter than the sun → lit.: greater (*huper*) than the splendor (*lamprotēs*) of the sun → BRIGHTNESS <2987> [5] Rev. 6:4 → bright red → RED <4450> [6] Rev. 18:1 → to make bright → ILLUMINATE <5461>.

BRIGHTER – Acts 26:13 → brighter than → lit.: above the brightness of → BRIGHTNESS <2987>.

BRIGHTNESS – [1] ***lamprotēs*** [fem. noun: λαμπρότης <2987>]; **from *lampros*: bright ► Radiancy, splendor** > Paul saw a light above the brightness of {brighter than} the sun (Acts 26:13). ¶
– [2] Luke 11:36 → bright shining → SHINING <796> [3] 2 Thes. 2:8 → APPEARING <2015> [4] Heb. 1:3 → RADIANCE <541>.

BRILLIANCE – [1] Rev. 1:16 → STRENGTH <1411> [2] Rev. 21:11 → LIGHT (noun) <5458>.

BRIM – John 2:7 → up to the brim → on high → HIGH (ON) <507>.

BRIMSTONE – [1] Luke 17:29; Rev. 9:17b, 18; 14:10; 19:20; 20:10; 21:8 → SULFUR <2303> [2] Rev. 9:17a → as sulfur → SULFUR <2306>.

BRING – [1] ***agō*** [verb: ἄγω <71>] **► To lead, to take** > The disciples were to be brought before governors and kings for the sake of Jesus (Matt. 10:18; Luke 21:12). Jesus said to bring the donkey and the colt to Him (Matt. 21:2; Luke 19:30), and the disciples did that (Matt. 21:7; Luke 19:35). Sick people with various diseases were brought to Jesus (Luke 4:40). A Samaritan brought a wounded man to the inn (Luke 10:34). Jesus commanded that a blind man be brought to Him (Luke 18:40). In a parable, a king ordered that his enemies be brought before him (Luke 19:27). Andrew brought Simon Peter to Jesus (John 1:42). Officers were asked why they had not brought Jesus (John 7:45). A woman taken in adultery was brought to Jesus (John 8:3). The one who had been blind was brought to the Pharisees (John 9:13). Jesus must bring other sheep (John 10:16). Pilate brought out

Jesus to the crowd (John 19:4, 13). Barnabas brought Saul to the apostles (Acts 9:27); he brought him later to Antioch (Acts 11:26). Paul was brought to Athens (Acts 17:15), and then to the Areopagus (v. 19). He was brought by night to Antipatris (Acts 23:31). Other refs.: Acts 5:21, 26, 27; 6:12; 9:2, 21; 13:23 {to raise}; 18:12; 19:37; 20:12; 21:16; 22:5; 23:10, 18a, b; 25:6, 17, 23; 1 Thes. 4:14; 2 Tim. 4:11; Heb. 2:10. All other refs.: GO <71>, LEAD (verb) <71>.

[2] **to bring, to bring up: *anagō*** [verb: ἀνάγω <321>]**; from *ana*: up, and *agō*: see** [1] ► **a. To lead up, to carry >** The parents of Jesus brought {took} him to Jerusalem (Luke 2:22). **b. To lead, to cause to appear, to produce >** Herod wanted to bring Peter out to the people (Acts 12:4). **c. To bring forth, to lead up >** The God of peace brought again from among the dead the Lord Jesus (Heb. 13:20). **d. To lead to a higher place >** The jailer brought Paul and Barnabas up into his house (Acts 16:34). Paul asked who would descend into the abyss to bring up Christ from the dead (Rom. 10:7). All other refs.: see entries in Lexicon at <321>.

[3] ***apagō*** [verb: ἀπάγω <520>]**; from *apo*: from, and *agō*: see** [1] ► **To take >** Paul told a centurion to bring {lead} his nephew to the commander (Acts 23:17). Other ref.: John 18:13 in some mss. All other refs.: CARRY <520>, DEATH <520>, LEAD (verb) <520>, TAKE <520>.

[4] **to bring, to bring in, into: *eisagō*** [verb: εἰσάγω <1521>]**; from *eis*: in, and *agō*: see** [1] ► **To have someone enter, to introduce; also transl.: to lead into, to take into >** The parents brought the child Jesus into the temple (Luke 2:27). The master of the house had the poor and various disabled people brought to the great supper (Luke 14:21). Jesus was brought into the high priest's house (Luke 22:54). John brought Peter into the courtyard of the high priest (John 18:16). The Israelites brought the tabernacle of the testimony with Joshua into the promised land (Acts 7:45). Paul was accused of having brought Greeks into the temple (Acts 21:28, 29). He was about to be brought into the barracks (Acts 21:37). He was brought into the fortress (Acts 22:24). God speaks when He brings the Firstborn into the habitable world (Heb. 1:6). All other refs.: LEAD (verb) <1521>.

[5] **to bring out, to bring forth: *exagō*** [verb: ἐξάγω <1806>]**; from *ek*: out, and *agō*: see** [1] ► **To lead, to lead out, to take out >** An angel of the Lord opened the prison doors and brought out the apostles (Acts 5:19). Moses brought the Israelites out of Egypt (Acts 7:36, 40). The Lord had brought Peter out of the prison (Acts 12:17a). God brought Israel out of Egypt with a high arm (Acts 13:17). All other refs.: LEAD (verb) <1806>.

[6] **to bring upon, to bring in upon: *epagō*** [verb: ἐπάγω <1863>]**; from *epi*: upon, and *agō*: see** [1] ► **To inflict on something, to cause to fall >** The verb is used in Acts 5:28; 2 Pet. 2:1, 5. Other ref.: Acts 14:2 (to stir up) in some mss. ¶

[7] **to bring, to bring down: *katagō*** [verb: κατάγω <2609>]; **from *kata*: down (intens.), and *agō*: see** [1] ► **a. To bring below >** The verb is used concerning Christ (Rom. 10:6), and Paul appearing before the council (Acts 22:30; 23:15, 20, 28). **b. To bring back, to land, to dock >** The disciples brought {pulled, ran} their boats to land (Luke 5:11). The brothers brought {took} Paul down to Caesarea (Acts 9:30). All other refs.: LAND (verb) <2609>, TOUCH <2609>.

[8] **to bring out, forth, before, etc.: *proagō*** [verb: προάγω <4254>]**; from *pro*: before, forth, and *agō*: see** [1] ► **To take before >** Herod was going to bring Peter forth to the people (Acts 12:6); in some mss.: *prosagō*. The jailer brought out {led out} Paul and Silas (Acts 16:30). The Jews sought to bring out Paul and Silas to the people (Acts 17:5). Paul was brought forth before Agrippa (Acts 25:26). All other refs.: see entries in Lexicon at <4254>.

[9] ***prosagō*** [verb: προσάγω <4317>]**; from *pros*: to, and *agō*: see** [1] ► **To bring toward, to lead to >** Jesus told a man to bring his son who was possessed by an unclean spirit (Luke 9:41). Paul and Silas were brought up to the magistrates (Acts 16:20). Christ has suffered for sins to bring us to God (1 Pet.

3:18). Other refs.: Acts 12:6: see 8; Acts 27:27; see DRAW <4317>. ¶

10 **to bring, to bring against, to bring forth:** ***pherō*** [verb: φέρω <5342>] ▶ **To bear, to carry, to lay, to take** > Those who were suffering and those who were possessed by demons (Mark 1:32), a paralytic (2:3), a deaf man with an impediment in his speech (7:32), a blind man (8:22), a son who had a dumb spirit (9:17, 20) were brought to Jesus. Jesus was brought to a place called Golgotha (Mark 15:22). The father of the prodigal son said to bring the fatted calf (Luke 15:23). The chief priest of Jupiter brought oxen and garlands in honor of Paul and Barnabas (Acts 14:13). Grace will be brought {given} at the revelation of Jesus Christ (1 Pet. 1:13). We should not receive anyone not bringing the doctrine of Christ (2 John 10). The verb is also used in regard to the head of John the Baptist (Matt. 14:11), a paralyzed man (Luke 5:18), the cross of Jesus (Luke 23:26), water which had been made wine (John 2:8a, b), fruit (John 12:24; 15:2a–c, 4, 5, 8, 16), an accusation (John 18:29), accusations (Acts 25:7), the reproach of Christ (Heb. 13:13), and an injurious charge (2 Pet. 2:11). Other refs.: Matt. 14:11, 18; 17:17; Mark 4:8; 6:27, 28; 9:19; 12:15, 16; Luke 24:1; John 4:33; 19:39; 21:10; Acts 4:34, 37; 5:2, 16; 25:18 (some mss.: *epipherō*); 2 Tim. 4:13; Heb. 9:16; Rev. 21:24, 26. All other refs.: see entries in Lexicon at <5342>.

11 ***apopherō*** [verb: ἀποφέρω <667>]; **from *apo*: from, and *pherō*: see 10** ▶ **To place, to apply** > Handkerchiefs or aprons were brought {were carried, were taken} from Paul's body to the sick (Acts 19:12); other mss. have *epipherō*. All other refs.: CARRY <667>.

12 **to bring in:** ***eispherō*** [verb: εἰσφέρω <1533>]; **from *eis*: in, and *pherō*: see 10** ▶ **To introduce, to carry** > Men sought to bring in a paralyzed man and lay him before Jesus (Luke 5:18); they could not find how they might bring him in (v. 19). Paul was bringing (lit.: bringing in) strange things to the ears of the people in Athens, according to them (Acts 17:20). We have brought nothing into the world (1 Tim. 6:7). All other refs.: CARRY <1533>, LEAD (verb) <1533>.

13 **to bring out, to bring forth:** ***ekpherō*** [verb: ἐκφέρω <1627>]; **from *ek*: out, and *pherō*: see 10** ▶ **To bring outside; also transl.: to bear, to yield** > The father said to bring out the best robe for his son who was back (Luke 15:22). The sick were brought out {carried} into the streets to be healed by Peter (Acts 5:15). The verb is used in regard to thorns and briars (Heb. 6:8). All other refs.: CARRY <1627>.

14 ***epipherō*** [verb: ἐπιφέρω <2018>]; **from *epi*: upon, and *pherō*: see 10; lit.: to adduce against** ▶ **To invoke, to accuse** > Michael the archangel did not dare to bring {to pronounce} a railing judgment against the devil (Jude 9). All other refs.: INFLICT <2018>, STIR (verb) <2018>.

15 ***prospherō*** [verb: προσφέρω <4374>]; **from *pros*: to, and *pherō*: see 10** ▶ **To present, to take along** > Various sick people were brought to Jesus (Matt. 4:24). A dumb man possessed by a demon was brought to Him (Matt. 9:32), and one possessed by a demon, blind and dumb (12:22). See also: Matt. 8:16; 9:2; 14:35; 17:16; 19:13; Mark 10:13; Luke 18:15. In a parable, a servant who owed ten thousand talents to his king was brought to him (Matt. 18:24); in another one, a servant who had received five talents came and brought five other talents (Matt. 25:20). Some Pharisees and Herodians brought Jesus a denarius as He requested (Matt. 22:19). The disciples were to be brought before the synagogues and the rulers and the authorities (Luke 12:11). Jesus was brought to Pilate as one leading away the people (Luke 23:14). All other refs.: DEAL <4374>, OFFER <4374>.

16 **to bring, to bring forth:** ***propherō*** [verb: προφέρω <4393>]; **from *pro*: before, and *pherō*: see 10** ▶ **To produce, to draw forth** > Good or wicked things are brought forth out of the good or wicked treasure of a good or wicked man, respectively (Luke 6:45a, b). ¶

17 **to bring together:** ***sumpherō*** [verb: συμφέρω <4851>]; **from *sun*: together, and *pherō*: see 10** ▶ **To carry together** > Many brought together their books of magic and

burned them (Acts 19:19). All other refs.: PROFIT (noun) <4851>, PROFITABLE <4851>.

18 **to bring up: *trephō*** [verb: τρέφω <5142>]; **lit.: to feed; has given *trophē*: food ▶ To educate, to train** > Jesus had been brought up in Nazareth (Luke 4:16); some mss.: *anatrephō*. All other refs.: NOURISH <5142>.

19 **to bring up: *anatrephō*** [verb: ἀνατρέφω <397>]; **from *ana*: intens., and *trephō*: see 18 ▶ To educate, to train** > Moses was brought up {nourished, nurtured} by Pharaoh's daughter (Acts 7:20, 21). Paul had been brought up in Jerusalem (Acts 22:3). Other ref.: Luke 4:16 in some mss. ¶

20 **to bring up: *ektrephō*** [verb: ἐκτρέφω <1625>]; **from *ek*: out (intens.), and *trephō*: see 18 ▶ To educate, to train** > Fathers must bring up their children in the discipline and admonition of the Lord (Eph. 6:4). Other ref.: Eph. 5:29; see NOURISH <1625>. ¶

21 **to bring up children: *teknotropheō*** [verb: τεκνοτροφέω <5044>]; **from *teknon*: child, and *trephō*: see 18 ▶ To educate, to train children** > Paul speaks of the widow who has brought up children (1 Tim. 5:10). ¶

22 **brought up with: *suntrophos*** [adj. or masc. noun: σύντροφος <4939>]; **from *sun*: together, and *trephō*: see 18; lit.: nourished with ▶ Fellow nursling, one who is brought up with another; companion of one's youth** > Manaen had been brought up with {was the foster-brother of} Herod the tetrarch (Acts 13:1). ¶

23 **to bring forth: *apokueō*** [verb: ἀποκυέω <616>]; **from *apo*: far from, away from, and *kueō*: to be pregnant ▶ To engender, to give birth** > Sin, fully completed, brings forth {gives birth to} death (Jas. 1:15). In a spiritual sense, God has brought forth {begat, has given birth to} Christians by the word of truth (Jas. 1:18). ¶

24 **to bring forth: *gennaō*** [verb: γεννάω <1080>]; **from *genna*: birth, race ▶ To bear** > Elizabeth brought forth {gave birth to} a son (Luke 1:57). All other refs.: see entries in Lexicon at <1080>.

25 **to bring near; to become: *ginomai*** [verb: γίνομαι <1096>]; **near: *engus*** [adv.: ἐγγύς <1451>] **▶ To become close** > Those who once were far away have been brought near {made nigh, become nigh} by the blood of Christ (Eph. 2:13). Other refs. (*ginomai*): see entries in Lexicon at <1096>; other refs. (*engus*): see NEAR (adv.) <1451>.

26 **to bring, to bring forth, to bring out: *ekballō*** [verb: ἐκβάλλω <1544>]; **from *ek*: out, and *ballō*: to throw ▶ To produce, to extract, to draw out** > Jesus was going to bring forth {to send forth, to lead} judgment unto victory (Matt. 12:20). Good or wicked things are brought forth from the good or wicked treasure of a good or wicked man, respectively (Matt. 12:35a, b). A householder brings out of his treasure things new and old (Matt. 13:52). All other refs.: see entries in Lexicon at <1544>.

27 **to bring back: *epistrephō*** [verb: ἐπιστρέφω <1994>]; **from *epi*: toward, and *strephō*: to turn ▶ To cause to return; also transl.: to convert, to turn, to turn back** > Someone who brings back one who has erred from the truth will have brought back a sinner from the error of his way, and will save a soul from death and will cover a multitude of sins (Jas. 5:19, 20). All other refs.: CONVERT (verb) <1994>, RETURN (verb) <1994>, TURN (verb) <1994>.

28 **to bring good news, to bring good tidings: *euangelizō*** [verb: εὐαγγελίζω <2097>]; **from *euangelos*: bringing good news, which is from *eu*: well, and *angellō*: to proclaim, which is from *angelos*: messenger ▶ To announce good news** > Timothy had brought good news to Paul of the faith and love of the Thessalonians (1 Thes. 3:6). All other refs.: PREACH <2097>.

29 **to bring forth abundantly, plentifully: *euphoreō*** [verb: εὐφορέω <2164>]; **from *eu*: well, and *phoreō*: to bear, to fill, which is from *pherō*: to carry, to bear ▶ To produce much** > The land of a certain rich man brought forth abundantly {yielded plentifully, was very productive, produced a good crop} (Luke 12:16). ¶

30 **to bring before: *histēmi*** [verb: ἵστημι <2476>] **▶ To remit someone to another**

person so that he may be judged > Jesus told His disciples that they would be brought before {stand before} governors and kings for His sake, as a testimony to them (Mark 13:9). Other refs.: see entries in Lexicon at <2476>.

31 ***komizō*** [verb: κομίζω <2865>]; **from *komidē*: what is brought, or *komeō*: to take care ▶ To carry, to bear** > A woman had brought {had taken} an alabaster box of myrrh to anoint Jesus (Luke 7:37). All other refs.: RECEIVE <2865>.

32 ***lambanō*** [verb: λαμβάνω <2983>] ▶ **To receive, to cause to come** > The verb is used in Rom. 13:2 concerning bringing judgment on oneself. Other refs.: see entries in Lexicon at <2983>.

33 ***parechō*** [verb: παρέχω <3930>]; **from *para*: next to, and *echō*: to have ▶ To furnish, to procure** > A possessed female slave brought much profit to {earned a great deal of money for} her masters (Acts 16:16). Demetrius brought no small gain to the artisans of Ephesus (Acts 19:24). All other refs.: see entries in Lexicon at <3930>.

34 **to bring forth: *tiktō*** [verb: τίκτω <5088>] ▶ **To give birth, to bear; to be born** > Mary brought forth {gave birth to} her firstborn Son (Luke 2:7). Other refs.: Matt. 1:21, 23, 25; Jas. 1:15; Rev. 12:2, 4a, b, 5, 13. All other refs.: BIRTH <5088>.

– 35 Matt. 3:8, 10; 7:17a, b, 18a, b, 19; 13:23b, 26; 21:43; Luke 3:8, 9; 6:43a, b; 8:8 → to bring forth → PRODUCE <4160> 36 Matt. 10:34a, b → PUT <906> 37 Matt. 12:10; John 8:6; Acts 24:13; 25:5 → to bring charges against, to bring up against → ACCUSE <2723> 38 Matt. 12:45; Mark 9:2; Luke 11:26 → to bring with → to take along with → TAKE <3880> 39 Matt. 13:8 → to bring forth → PRODUCE <1325> 40 Matt. 17:1 → to bring up → LEAD (verb) <399> 41 Matt. 22:10; John 11:52; Acts 14:27 → to bring together → to gather together → GATHER <4863> 42 Matt. 27:3 → to bring again, to bring back → RETURN (verb) <4762> 43 Matt. 28:8, 9, 10; Mark 16:10, 13 → to bring word, to take word → TELL <518> 44 Mark 4:29 → to bring forth → PRODUCE <3860> 45 Mark 15:4 → to bring against → to testify against → TESTIFY <2649> 46 Luke 1:52 → to bring down → to put down → PUT <2507> 47 John 2:10 → to bring out → SERVE <5087> 48 John 16:8 → to bring demonstration → CONVINCE <1651> 49 Acts 5:31 → to bring to repentance → to give repentance → GIVE <1325> 50 Acts 7:16 → to bring back → to carry back → CARRY <3346> 51 Acts 7:20 → to bring up → NOURISH <397> 52 Acts 11:24 → ADD <4369> 53 Acts 12:25 → bringing with → taking along with → TAKE <4838> 54 Acts 15:3 → CAUSE (verb) <4160> 55 Acts 17:20 → to bring strange things → STRANGE <3579> 56 Acts 19:25 → to bring together → to gather together → GATHER <4867> 57 Acts 23:24 → to bring safe, safely → SAFELY <1295> 58 Acts 25:7 → CAST (verb) <2702> 59 Acts 27:24 → to bring before → STAND (verb) <3936> 60 Rom. 3:5a → to bring out → COMMEND <4921> 61 Rom. 4:15; 5:3; 7:8 → to bring, to bring about → PRODUCE <2716> 62 Rom. 5:20 → to bring in, to be brought in → COME <3922> 63 Rom. 9:28 → to bring to an end → FINISH <4931> 64 Rom. 10:7 → to bring up → GO UP <305> 65 1 Cor. 1:19 → to bring to nothing → REJECT <114> 66 1 Cor. 4:5 → to bring to light → LIGHT (noun) <5461> 67 1 Cor. 6:12 → to bring under the power → POWER[2] <1850> 68 1 Cor. 6:13; 2 Thes. 2:8 → to bring to nothing, to bring to an end → DESTROY <2673> 69 1 Cor. 8:8 → to bring near → COMMEND <3936> 70 1 Cor. 9:27 → to bring into subjection → SUBJECTION <1396> 71 2 Cor. 2:16a, b → an aroma that brings death, an aroma that brings life → lit.: an aroma of death to death, an aroma of life to life 72 2 Cor. 3:9a, b → ministry that brought condemnation, ministry that brings righteousness → lit.: ministry of condemnation, ministry of righteousness 73 2 Cor. 4:14 → to bring into His presence → PRESENT (verb) <3936> 74 2 Cor. 7:1 → to bring to completion → PERFECT (verb) <2005> 75 2 Cor. 8:6 → to bring to completion → FINISH <2005> 76 2 Cor. 10:5 → to bring into captivity → CAPTIVE (adj.) <163> 77 2 Cor. 11:20 → to bring into bondage → BONDAGE <2615> 78 Eph. 1:10 → to bring together → to gather together → GATHER <346> 79 Phil. 1:6 → to bring to completion → PERFORM <2005> 80 Col. 1:13 → TRANSFER <3179> 81 1 Tim. 4:6 → to bring up → NOURISH <1789> 82 Titus 2:11 → that brings salvation → SALVATION <4992> 83 Heb. 6:6 → to bring back → RENEW <340> 84 Jas. 5:18 → to bring forth → PRODUCE <985> 85 2 Pet. 2:1 → to bring in by the bye → to secretly introduce → SECRETLY <3919> 86 Rev. 16:5 → to bring judgments → JUDGE (verb) <2919> 87 Rev. 22:12 → "bringing" added in Engl.

BRINGING IN – Heb. 7:19 → INTRODUCTION <1898>.

BROAD – 1 ***euruchōros*** [adj.: εὐρύχωρος <2149>]; **from *eurus*: wide, and *chōros*: space ► Wide, spacious** > As for the salvation of his soul, a man must enter in by the narrow gate for wide is the gate and broad is the way that leads to destruction (Matt. 7:13). ¶

– 2 Matt. 23:5 → to make broad → EXPAND <4115> 3 Rev. 20:9 → broad plain → BREADTH <4114>.

BROADEN – Matt. 23:5 → EXPAND <4115>.

BROIDED HAIR – 1 Tim. 2:9 → BRAIDED HAIR <4117>.

BROILED – ***optos*** [adj.: ὀπτός <3702>]; **from *optaō*: to cook, to roast ► Cooked, roasted** > The disciples gave Jesus a piece of a broiled fish (Luke 24:42). ¶

BROKEN – Matt. 14:20; 15:37; Mark 6:43; 8:8, 19; Luke 9:17 → broken piece, broken meat → FRAGMENT <2801>.

BROKENHEARTED – Luke 4:18 → BREAK <4937>.

BRONZE – 1 Rev. 1:15; 2:18 → burnished bronze → fine brass → BRASS <5474> 2 Rev. 9:20 → of brass → BRASS <5470> 3 Rev. 18:12 → BRASS <5475>.

BROOD – 1 ***gennēma*** [neut. noun: γέννημα <1081>]; **from *gennaō*: to conceive, to engender, which is from *genna*: birth, race ► Descent, posterity; also transl.: generation, offspring** > John the Baptist called the Pharisees and the Sadducees, and the crowds coming out to be baptized by him, "brood of vipers" (Matt. 3:7; Luke 3:7). Jesus also called the scribes and Pharisees "offspring of vipers" (Matt. 12:34; 23:33). ¶

2 ***nossia*** [fem. noun: νοσσιά <3555>]; **from *neossos*: young bird ► Group of young birds hatched at one time and cared for together** > Jesus would have gathered the children of Jerusalem together, as a hen gathers her brood {chicks} under her wings (Luke 13:34). ¶

– 3 Matt. 23:37 → chickens → CHICKEN <3556>.

BROTHER – ***adelphos*** [masc. noun: ἀδελφός <80>]; **from *a*: particle of union, and *delphus*: womb; lit.: of the same womb ► Relative born of the same mother; Christian believer** > This term may refer to a brother according to the flesh, having the same parents; e.g., Andrew was the brother of Peter (Matt. 4:18). The term may also be used in regard to the Jews (e.g., Acts 3:17 when Peter addressed those of his nation) or Christians (e.g., Acts 10:23 when the brothers from Joppa accompanied Peter). The term is used on various occasions to indicate a Christian (e.g., the brother Quartus in Rom. 16:23). It may also designate any man (Matt. 5:22; 7:3), in the sense of neighbor. *

BROTHERHOOD – ***adelphotēs*** [fem. noun: ἀδελφότης <81>]; **from *adelphos*: brother ► Brotherly relationship** > Peter uses this term, which is similar to *adelphos*, in 1 Pet. 2:17; 5:9; it is also transl.: brothers, family of believers. ¶

BROTHERLY – [1] **brotherly, full of brotherly love:** ***philadelphos*** [adj.: φιλάδελφος <5361>]; **from *philos*: friend, and *adelphos*: brother, which is from *a*: particle of union, and *delphus*: womb ▶ Affectionate toward brothers and sisters in the faith >** Christians are to be brotherly (1 Pet. 3:8). ¶
– [2] Rom. 12:10; 1 Thes. 4:9; Heb. 13:1; 2 Pet. 1:7 → brotherly love, brotherly kindness → LOVE (noun) <5360>.

BROW – ***ophrus*** [fem. noun: ὀφρῦς <3790>]; **lit.: eyebrow ▶ Steep slope, escarpment >** Jesus was led up to the brow of a mountain because some wanted to throw Him down the precipice (Luke 4:29). ¶

BRUISE – [1] ***suntribō*** [verb: συντρίβω <4937>]; **from *sun*: together (intens.), and *tribō*: to rub ▶ To break, to crush, to maul >** Jesus would not break a bruised reed (Matt. 12:20). An evil spirit departed from a child after bruising {destroying} him (Luke 9:39). The God of peace will bruise Satan under the feet of the Christians shortly (Rom. 16:20). All other refs.: BREAK <4937>, PIECE <4937>.
– [2] Luke 4:18 → to oppress → OPPRESSED (BE) <2352>.

BRUSHWOOD – Acts 28:3 → STICK (noun) <5434>.

BRUTAL – ***anēmeros*** [adj.: ἀνήμερος <434>]; **from *a*: neg., and *ēmeros*: mild, gentle; lit.: not tame, wild ▶ Cruel, barbarian >** Paul says that, in the last days, men will be brutal {fierce, implacable} (2 Tim. 3:3). ¶

BRUTE – [1] Titus 1:12 → BEAST <2342> [2] 2 Pet. 2:12; Jude 10 → without reason → REASON (noun) <249>.

BUCKLE – Eph. 6:14 → GIRD <4024>.

BUD – [1] ***blastanō*** [verb: βλαστάνω <985>]; **from *blastos*: bud, germ ▶ To produce buds, to germinate >** Aaron's rod had budded {sprouted} and was placed in the ark of the covenant (Heb. 9:4). All other refs.: PRODUCE <985>, SPROUT <985>.
– [2] Luke 21:30 → to shoot forth → SPROUT <4261>.

BUFFET – [1] Matt. 14:24 → TOSS <928> [2] 1 Cor. 4:11; 2 Cor. 12:7; 1 Pet. 2:20 → BEAT <2852> [3] 1 Cor. 9:27 → DISCIPLINE (verb) <5299>.

BUGLE – 1 Cor. 14:8 → TRUMPET <4536>.

BUILD – [1] ***kataskeuazō*** [verb: κατασκευάζω <2680>]; **from *kata*: intens., and *skeuazō*: to fix, to prepare, which is from *skeuē*: equipment, which is from *skeuos*: vessel, instrument ▶ To construct (and fully furnish) by assembling materials >** God is the One who has built {the builder of: *ho kataskeuasas*} all things (Heb. 3:3, 4b); every house is built by someone (v. 4a). All other refs.: MAKE <2680>, PREPARE <2680>.
[2] ***oikodomeō*** [verb: οἰκοδομέω <3618>]; **from *oikodomos*: builder, building a house, which is from *oikos*: house, building, and *demō*: to build ▶ To construct (a building in particular), to erect >** A wise man built his house on a rock (Matt. 7:24; Luke 6:48); a foolish man built his house on the sand (Matt. 7:26; Luke 6:49). According to the revelation made to Peter, Jesus would build His church (Matt. 16:18). In a parable, a householder built a tower (Matt. 21:33; Mark 12:1). Jesus was the stone which was rejected by the builders (lit.: by the building ones) (Matt. 21:42; Mark 12:10; Luke 20:17; Acts 4:11 {other mss.: *oikodomos*}; 1 Pet. 2:7). The scribes and the Pharisees were building the tombs of the prophets (Matt. 23:29; Luke 11:47, 48). False witnesses declared that Jesus had said He would build the temple of God in three days (Matt. 26:61 {to rebuild}; Mark 14:58). Those who passed by blasphemed Jesus on the cross saying that He was destroying the temple and building it in three days (Matt. 27:40; Mark 15:29). Nazareth was built on the brow of a mountain (Luke 4:29). A Roman centurion had built a synagogue

for the Jews in Capernaum (Luke 7:5). In a parable, a rich man was going to build greater barns (Luke 12:18). The one intending to build a tower normally sits down first and counts the cost (Luke 14:28, 30). In the days of Lot, people were building (Luke 17:28). The temple of the Jews had taken forty-six years to build (John 2:20). Solomon built a house to God (Acts 7:47); but the Lord asks what house will be built to Him because His hand has made all these things (v. 49; see v. 50). If Paul were to build again {to rebuild} the things concerning the law which he had thrown down, he would constitute himself a transgressor (Gal. 2:18). All other refs.: EDIFY <3618>, EMBOLDENED (BE) <3618>.

[3] **to build up, to build upon: *epoikodomeō*** [verb: ἐποικοδομέω <2026>]; **from *epi*: upon, and *oikodomeō*: see [2] ► To construct (in a spiritual sense), to edify** > God is able to build up the Christians (Acts 20:32; some mss.: *oikodomeō*). Paul speaks of building in relation to the Christian ministry (1 Cor. 3:10a, b, 12, 14). Christians are built upon the foundation of the apostles and prophets (Eph. 2:20). They must walk in the Lord, rooted and built up in Him (Col. 2:7). Christians build themselves up on their most holy faith (Jude 20). ¶

[4] **to build together: *sunoikodomeō*** [verb: συνοικοδομέω <4925>]; **from *sun*: with, and *oikodomeō*: see [2] ► To edify spiritually together** > Christians are built together for a habitation of God in the Spirit (Eph. 2:22). ¶

[5] **to build around: *periballō*** [verb: περιβάλλω <4016>]; **from *peri*: around, and *ballō*: to throw ► To construct around, to raise up (entrenchments) around** > Jesus had spoken of days when the enemies of Jerusalem would build an embankment around {cast a trench about, make a palisaded mound about, throw up a bank before} Jerusalem (Luke 19:43); some mss. have *paremballō*. All other refs.: CLOTHE <4016>, WEAR <4016>, WRAP <4016>.

– [6] Matt. 5:14 → SITUATE <2749> [7] Luke 6:48 → lit.: to be founded on the rock → FOUND <2311> [8] Acts 15:16a, b → to build again → REBUILD <456> [9] Rom. 14:19; 15:2; 1 Cor. 14:5, 12, 26; 2 Cor. 10:8; 12:19; 13:10; Eph. 4:12, 16, 29 → to build up, building up → lit.: for edification → EDIFICATION <3619> [10] Heb. 8:5a → MAKE <2005> [11] Rev. 21:18 → the wall was built → lit.: the building of the wall was → BUILDING <1739>.

BUILDER – [1] ***technitēs*** [masc. noun: τεχνίτης <5079>]; **from *technē*: art, trade ► Craftsman, tradesman, artist** > Abraham was waiting for the city whose builder {architect} and constructor is God (Heb. 11:10). Other refs.: Acts 19:24, 38; Rev. 18:22; see CRAFTSMAN <5079>. ¶

– [2] Matt. 21:42; Mark 12:10; Acts 4:11; 1 Pet. 2:7 → BUILD <3618> [3] 1 Cor. 3:10 → MASTERBUILDER <753> [4] 1 Cor. 3:15 → the builder will receive a reward → lit.: he will receive a reward [5] Heb. 3:3, 4b → lit.: the one building → BUILD <2680> [6] Heb. 11:10 → MAKER <1217>.

BUILDING – [1] ***endōmēsis*** [fem. noun: ἐνδώμησις <1739>]; **from *en*: in, and *dōmaō*: to build ► That which is built, structure** > The building {material} of the wall of the holy city was of jasper (Rev. 21:18). ¶

[2] ***oikodomē*** [fem. noun: οἰκοδομή <3619>]; **from *oikos*: house, building, and *demō*: to build ► Construction, structure; act of constructing** > The disciples came to Jesus to point out to Him the buildings of the temple (Matt. 24:1; Mark 13:1, 2). Christians are God's building (1 Cor. 3:9). They have a building from God in the heavens (2 Cor. 5:1). The building constituted by the Christians increases to a holy temple in the Lord (Eph. 2:21). All other refs.: EDIFICATION <3619>.

– [3] Heb. 9:11 → CREATION <2937>.

BUILDING UP – Rom. 14:19; 2 Cor. 10:8; 13:10; Eph. 4:12, 16 → EDIFICATION <3619>.

BUILT – Acts 17:24 → built by hands → HAND (noun) <5499>.

BULL – ***tauros*** [masc. noun: ταῦρος <5022>] ► **Bullock, male bovine; also transl.: oxen, in the plur.** > A king had killed his oxen for the wedding feast of his son (Matt. 22:4). The priest of Jupiter, having brought bulls and garlands, would have done sacrifice along with the crowds in honor of Barnabas and Paul (Acts 14:13). In the O.T., the blood of goats and bulls sanctified for the purity of the flesh (Heb. 9:13), but it is impossible that the blood of bulls and goats should take away sins (10:4). ¶

BUNCH – Rev. 14:18 → CLUSTER <1009>.

BUNDLE – [1] ***desmē*** [fem. noun: δέσμη <1197>]; **from *desmos*: bond, or *deō*: to bind** ► **Sheaf of vegetation (e.g., wheat) bound together** > The owner will say to the reapers to gather first the tares and bind them in bundles to burn them (Matt. 13:30). ¶
– [2] Acts 28:3 → QUANTITY <4128>.

BURDEN (noun) – [1] ***baros*** [neuter noun: βάρος <922>] ► **Load, weight** > The workers in the parable murmured against the master of the house, saying they had borne the burden and heat of the day (Matt. 20:12). It had seemed good to the Holy Spirit to lay no other burden on Christians than to abstain from things sacrificed to idols, from blood, from what is strangled, and from sexual immorality (Acts 15:28; see v. 29). Christians must bear one another's burdens (Gal. 6:2). Paul, Silvanus, and Timothy could have been a burden {been burdensome, made demands, been a charge, asserted their authority} as Christ's apostles (1 Thes. 2:6). The Lord puts no other burden on the Christians of Thyatira (Rev. 2:24). Other ref.: 2 Cor. 4:17; see WEIGHT <922>. ¶
[2] **to be a burden: *epibareō*** [verb: ἐπιβαρέω <1912>]; **from *epi*: upon (intens.), and *bareō*: to burden, which is from *baros*: see [1]** ► **To overload, to put an excessive weight on someone** > Paul had labored night and day that he might not be a burden {be chargeable} to the Thessalonians (1 Thes. 2:9; 2 Thes. 3:8). Other ref.: 2 Cor. 2:5; see OVERCHARGE <1912>. ¶
[3] ***phortion*** [neut. noun: φορτίον <5413>]; **from *phortos*: load, which is from *pherō*: to carry** ► **Something which one carries, physical or spiritual** > The yoke of Jesus is easy and His burden is light (Matt. 11:30). The scribes and the Pharisees were binding burdens heavy and hard to bear, which they laid on the shoulders of men (Matt. 23:4 {load}; Luke 11:46a), but they themselves did not touch these burdens (Luke 11:46b). Each one shall carry his own burden {load} (Gal. 6:5). For a similar word in Acts 27:10 (*phortos*), see LADING <5414>. ¶
[4] ***gomos*** [masc. noun: γόμος <1117>]; **from *gemō*: to be full, to be loaded** ► **Load of commodities carried by a ship** > The ship on which Paul was sailing was to discharge its burden {cargo} at Tyre (Acts 21:3). Other refs.: Rev. 18:11, 12; see MERCHANDISE <1117>. ¶
– [5] 2 Cor. 11:9 → not being a burden → not burdensome → BURDENSOME <4> [6] 2 Cor. 11:28 → CARE (noun) <3308> [7] 2 Cor. 12:16 → to be a burden → BURDEN (verb) <2599> [8] Heb. 13:17 → a burden → lit.: groaning → GROAN (verb) <4727>.

BURDEN (verb) – [1] ***bareō*** [verb: βαρέω <916>]; **from *baros*: weight, burden** ► **To overwhelm, to oppress** > Paul had been burdened beyond measure {pressed out of measure, pressed beyond measure, under great pressure} in Asia (2 Cor. 1:8). He was groaning, being burdened (2 Cor. 5:4). The local church should not be burdened {charged} with widows who have family to assist them (1 Tim. 5:16). All other refs.: HEAVY <916>.
[2] ***katabareō*** [verb: καταβαρέω <2599>]; **from *kata*: down (intens.), and *bareō*: see [1]** ► **To overwhelm, to weigh down** > Paul did not burden {had not been a burden to} the church in Corinth (2 Cor. 12:16). ¶
– [3] Matt. 11:28 → to be burdened → to be heavy laden → LOAD (verb) <5412> [4] Acts 15:28 → lit.: to lay a burden → LAY <2007>, BURDEN (noun) <922>

[5] 2 Cor. 11:9; 12:13, 14 → to lazily burden, to be a burden → to be burdensome → BURDENSOME <2655> [6] 2 Cor. 11:9 → not a burden, not burdening → not burdensome → BURDENSOME <4> [7] 2 Tim. 3:6 → LOAD (verb) <4987>.

BURDENED – 2 Cor. 8:13 → lit.: in distress → DISTRESS <2347>.

BURDENED (BE) – Gal. 5:1 → ENTANGLED (BE) <1758>.

BURDENSOME – [1] ***barus*** [adj.: βαρύς <926>] ▶ **Heavy, crushing** > The commandments of God are not burdensome {grievous} (1 John 5:3). All other refs.: HEAVY <926>, SAVAGE <926>, SERIOUS <926>, WEIGHTIER <926>.

[2] **not burdensome: *abarēs*** [adj.: ἀβαρής <4>]**; from *a*: neg., and *baros*: burden; lit.: not heavy** ▶ **Who does not rely on others to satisfy his needs** > Paul had kept himself from being burdensome {from being a burden} (lit.: had kept himself not burdensome) to the Corinthians (2 Cor. 11:9). ¶

[3] **to be burdensome: *katanarkaō*** [verb: καταναρκάω <2655>]**; from *kata*: against, and *narkaō*: to be numb, which is from *narkē*: numbness, torpor** ▶ **To be a burden to others, e.g., financially** > Paul had not been burdensome {been a burden, been in laziness a charge} to {lazily burdened} the church in Corinth (2 Cor. 11:9; 12:13, 14). ¶

– [4] 1 Thes. 2:6 → BURDEN (noun) <922>.

BURIAL – [1] ***entaphiasmos*** [masc. noun: ἐνταφιασμός <1780>]**; from *entaphiazō*: see [3]** ▶ **Embalming, internment** > A woman had anticipated the moment to anoint the body of the Lord Jesus for His burial (Mark 14:8; John 12:7). ¶

[2] **burial place: *taphē*** [fem. noun: ταφή <5027>]**; from *thaptō*: to bury, to lay in the grave, from which *taphos*: burial, funeral, tomb** ▶ **Place of interment, burying ground** > The chief priests bought with Judas's silver the field of the potter as a burial place for strangers (Matt. 27:7). ¶

[3] **to bury: *entaphiazō*** [verb: ἐνταφιάζω <1779>]**; from *entaphios*: funeral, funerary, which is from *en*: in, and *taphos*: burial, funeral, tomb, which is from *thaptō*: to bury, to lay in the grave** ▶ **To prepare a body for interment** > A woman poured out an ointment on the body of the Lord to prepare Him for His burial (lit.: for His burying) (Matt. 26:12). Other ref.: John 19:40; see BURY <1779>. ¶

– [4] Acts 8:2 → to carry to one's burial → CARRY <4792> [5] Heb. 11:22 → "the burial of" added in Engl. [6] Rev. 11:9 → TOMB <3418>.

BURN – [1] ***kaiō*** [verb: καίω <2545>] ▶ **To be alight or consume with fire** > The lamps of the Christians should be burning {alighted} (Luke 12:35). The hearts of the disciples of Emmaus were burning in them as Jesus opened the Scriptures to them (Luke 24:32). John the Baptist was the burning and shining light (John 5:35). The branches which do not bear fruit are burned (John 15:6). Though one gives his body to be burned {to the flames}, but does not have love, it profits him nothing (1 Cor. 13:3); *kauchēsōmai* (boast) in some mss. The Hebrews had not come to the mount that could be touched and burned with fire {and to a blazing fire} (Heb. 12:18; see Deut. 4:11). There were seven lamps of fire burning {blazing} before the throne (Rev. 4:5). A great mountain burning with fire was cast into the sea (Rev. 8:8). A great star fell from heaven, burning {blazing} as a torch (Rev. 8:10). The beast and the false prophet will be cast alive into the lake of fire which burns with brimstone (Rev. 19:20). Many will have their part in the lake which burns with fire and brimstone (Rev. 21:8). Other ref.: Matt. 5:15; see LIGHT (verb) <2545>. ¶

[2] ***ekkaiō*** [verb: ἐκκαίω <1572>]**; from *ek*: out (intens.), and *kaiō*: see [1]; lit.: to burn out** ▶ **To be consumed (with sensual desire)** > Some men burned {were inflamed} in their lust toward one another (Rom. 1:27). ¶

[3] ***katakaiō*** [verb: κατακαίω <2618>]; **from *kata*: down (intens.), and *kaiō*: see [1]; lit.: to burn down ▶ To burn completely, to consume entirely** > The One who would come after John the Baptist would burn the chaff with unquenchable fire (Matt. 3:12; Luke 3:17). At the end of this world, the weeds will be gathered and burned in the fire (Matt. 13:30, 40). Many in Ephesus burned their books of magic before all (Acts 19:19). If anyone's work is burned {consumed}, he will suffer loss (1 Cor. 3:15). The bodies of the beasts, whose blood was carried in the sanctuary, were burned outside the camp (Heb. 13:11). In the day of the Lord, the earth and its works will be burned up (2 Pet. 3:10 in some mss.). When the first trumpet was sounded, a third of the earth was burned up, as well as a third of the trees and all green grass (Rev. 8:7a–c). The prostitute, Babylon, will be burned with fire (Rev. 17:16; 18:8 {to consume}). ¶

[4] **burning: *kausis*** [fem. noun: καῦσις <2740>]; **from *kaiō*: see [1] ▶ Action of burning, combustion** > The end of the earth, which bears thorns and briars, is to be burned (lit.: for burning) (Heb. 6:8). ¶

[5] ***emprēthō*** [verb: ἐμπρήθω <1714>]; **from *en*: in, and *prēthō*: to blow a flame, to burn ▶ To set on fire** > In a parable, the king burned the city of the murderers of his servants (Matt. 22:7); *empiprēmi* in some mss. ¶

[6] ***puroō*** [verb: πυρόω <4448>]; **from *pur*: fire ▶ To be set on fire, to be consumed (by passions)** > It is better to marry than to burn {burn with passion} (1 Cor. 7:9). Paul asked who was offended, and he burned not {and he did not inwardly burn, without his intense concern} (2 Cor. 11:29), i.e., being affected deeply by the scandal. All other refs.: FIERY <4448>, FIRE <4448>, PURIFY <4448>, REFINE <4448>.

– [7] Matt. 13:6; Mark 4:6; Rev. 16:8, 9 → to burn, to burn up → SCORCH <2739> [8] Luke 1:9 → to burn incense → INCENSE <2370> [9] 2 Pet. 2:6 → to burn to ashes → ASH <5077> [10] 2 Pet. 3:12 → lit.: burning with fervent heat → HEAT <2741>.

BURNING – [1] ***purōsis*** [fem. noun: πύρωσις <4451>]; **from *puroō*: to burn, which is from *pur*: fire ▶ Fire, conflagration** > The smoke of the burning of Babylon the great will be seen (Rev. 18:9, 18). Other ref.: 1 Pet. 4:12; see FIERY <4451>. ¶

– [2] Matt. 20:12; Jas. 1:11 → burning heat → HEAT <2742> [3] Luke 20:37 → burning bush → BUSH <942> [4] John 5:35 → to burn → BURN <2545> [5] Rev. 7:16 → burning heat → HEAT <2738>.

BURNISHED – Rev. 1:15; 2:18 → burnished bronze → fine brass → BRASS <5474>.

BURNT OFFERING – ***holokautōma*** [neut. noun: ὁλοκαύτωμα <3646>]; **from *holokautoō*: to burn completely, which is from *holos*: all, whole, and *kaiō*: to consume, to burn ▶ Sacrifice offered to God under the law, in virtue of which the worshipper was accepted** > The burnt offering (see Lev. 1:1–17; 6:1–6) symbolizes the offering of Jesus Christ to God on the cross. To love God and one's neighbor is more than to offer burnt offerings and sacrifices in a ritual manner (Mark 12:33; see Hos. 6:6). God did not take pleasure in burnt offerings and sacrifices for sin; this is why Christ came (Heb. 10:6, 8). ¶

BURST – [1] ***laschō*** [verb: λάσχω <2997>] ▶ **To open, to tear** > Having fallen headlong, Judas burst {burst open, burst asunder} in the middle (Acts 1:18); some mss. have *lakaō*. ¶

[2] ***rhēgnumi*** [verb: ῥήγνυμι <4486>] ▶ **To separate into two or several pieces, to break** > New wine bursts old wineskins (Matt. 9:17; Mark 2:22; Luke 5:37). All other refs.: BREAK <4486>, TEAR (verb) <4486>.

– [3] Matt. 7:25 → to burst against → to beat upon → BEAT <4363> [4] Matt. 7:27 → to burst against → to beat upon → BEAT <4350> [5] Luke 6:48, 49 → to burst against → to break upon → BREAK <4366> [6] Luke 8:29 → BREAK <1284>.

BURY – [1] ***thaptō*** [verb: θάπτω <2290>]; **from which *taphos*: burial, funeral, tomb ▶ To put a dead person in a tomb >** Various people were buried: David (Acts 2:29), John the Baptist (Matt. 14:12), a rich man in a parable (Luke 16:22), Christ (1 Cor. 15:4), and Ananias (Acts 5:6, 9) and Sapphira (Acts 5:10). Jesus told a disciple to let the dead bury their own dead (Matt. 8:21, 22; Luke 9:59, 60). ¶
[2] **to bury with: *sunthaptō*** [verb: συνθάπτω <4916>]; **from *sun*: together, and *thaptō*: see [1] ▶ To inter a dead person with someone else >** Christians were buried with Christ through and in baptism into death (Rom. 6:4; Col. 2:12). ¶
[3] ***entaphiazō*** [verb: ἐνταφιάζω <1779>]; **from *entaphios*: funeral, funerary, which is from *en*: in, and *taphos*: burial, funeral, tomb ▶ To prepare the body of a dead person for burial, to embalm >** Joseph of Arimathea and Nicodemus bound the body of Jesus in linen with spices, as was the custom of the Jews to bury {prepare for burial} their dead (John 19:40). Other ref.: Matt. 26:12; see BURIAL <1779>. ¶
– [4] Matt. 27:7 → lit.: as a burying place → burial place → BURIAL <5027> [5] Acts 8:2 → to carry to one's burial → CARRY <4792> [6] Acts 13:36 → ADD <4369>.

BURYING – [1] Matt. 26:12 → lit.: to bury → BURIAL <1779> [2] Matt. 27:7 → burying ground → burial place → BURIAL <5027>.

BUSH – ***batos*** [fem. noun: βάτος <942>] ▶ **Prickly shrub; also transl.: bramble, bramble bush, burning bush, briar bush, brier, thorn >** Grapes are not gathered from a bush (Luke 6:44). God spoke to Moses in the account of the bush (Mark 12:26; Luke 20:37), i.e., the burning bush in the desert. The Lord appeared to Moses in a flame of fire in a bush {thorn bush} (Acts 7:30, 35). ¶

BUSHEL – [1] ***modios*** [masc. noun: μόδιος <3426>]; **from the Lat. *modius* ▶ Roman unit of dry measure equivalent to approx. 9 liters; it relates also to a container >** A lighted lamp is not put under the bushel {basket, corn-measure, peck-measure, bowl} (Matt. 5:15; Mark 4:21; Luke 11:33). ¶
– [2] Luke 16:6 → MEASURE (noun) <943>.

BUSINESS – [1] ***emporia*** [fem. noun: ἐμπορία <1711>]; **from *emporos*: one who travels for his commerce, merchant, which is from *en*: in, and *poros*: way ▶ Commercial activity, merchandise >** Guests who were invited to a wedding feast paid no attention and went their way, one to his farm, another to his business (Matt. 22:5). ¶
[2] ***emporion*** [neut. noun: ἐμπόριον <1712>]; **from *emporos*: see [1] ▶ Place where commerce occurs, marketplace, emporium >** Jesus told those who were selling doves in the temple to take them away and not to make His Father's house a place of business {house of merchandise, market} (John 2:16). ¶
[3] ***ergasia*** [fem. noun: ἐργασία <2039>]; **from *ergazomai*: to work, which is from *ergon*: action, task, work ▶ Enterprise, industry >** The wealth of the Ephesians came from the business {craft, trade, work} of making silver temples of Artemis (Acts 19:25). All other refs.: EFFORT <2039>, GAIN (noun) <2039>, WORKING (noun) <2039>.
[4] ***pragma*** [neut. noun: πρᾶγμα <4229>]; **from *prassō*: to do, to make ▶ Matter, affair >** Christians in Rome were to assist Phoebe in whatever business she had need of them (Rom. 16:2). All other refs.: MATTER <4229>, THING <4229>, WORK (noun) <4229>.
[5] **to do business, to engage in business: *pragmateuomai*** [verb: πραγματεύομαι <4231>]; **from *pragma*: see [4] ▶ To conduct banking or another commercial activity >** Having called ten of his servants, a nobleman gave them ten minas and told them to do business {to occupy, to put money to work, to trade} until he should come (Luke 19:13). ¶
[6] ***chreia*** [fem. noun: χρεία <5532>]; **from *chraomai*: to use, or *chreos*: debt ▶**

Service, function > Seven men were to be established over the business {responsibility, task} of the widows being neglected in the daily distribution (Acts 6:3). All other refs.: NECESSITY <5532>, NEED (noun) <5532>.

7 ***ta*; neut. plur. of *ho*** [art.: ὁ <3588>] ► **Lit.: the *matters*** > Jesus had to be about His Father's business (Luke 2:49). Paul exhorts the Thessalonians to do their own business (lit.: their own) (1 Thes. 4:11).

– **8** Luke 19:15 → to do business → to gain by trading → GAIN (verb) <1281> **9** Acts 19:27 → PART (noun) <3313> **10** Rom. 12:11 → diligent zealousness → ZEALOUSNESS <4710> **11** Jas. 1:11 → PURSUIT <4197> **12** Jas. 4:13 → to carry on business, to engage in business → EXPLOIT <1710>.

BUSYBODY – **1** **to be a busybody, to act like a busybody: *periergazomai*** [verb: περιεργάζομαι <4020>]; **from *peri*: around, about, and *ergazomai*: to work, which is from *ergon*: work, business; lit.: to work all about** ► **To be occupied with things that are without importance or to bustle about in the affairs of other people** > There were some among the Thessalonians who were busybodies (2 Thes. 3:11). ¶

2 ***periergos*** [adj. used as noun: περίεργος <4021>]; **from *peri*: around (intens.), and *ergon*: work, business** ► **Occupying oneself with things of no importance or interfering in the affairs of others; also transl.: meddler** > Paul uses this word in regard to young widows (1 Tim. 5:13). Other ref.: Acts 19:19; see MAGIC <4021>. ¶

3 **busybody in other people's matters: *allotriepiskopos*** [masc. noun: ἀλλοτριεπίσκοπος <244>]; **from *allotrios*: which concerns others, and *episkopos*: overseer, which is from *epi*: over, and *skopos*: watchman** ► **One who mixes in other people's affairs, who is indiscrete or supervisor of foreign matters that do not concern him** > None should act as a busybody in other people's matters {an overseer of other people's matter, a meddler, a troublesome meddler} (1 Pet. 4:15); some mss. have *allotrioepiskopos*. ¶

BUT – **1** ***alla*** [conj.: ἀλλά <235>]; **from *allos*: other** ► **However, on the contrary** > In regard to drinking the cup, Mark uses this coordinating conjunction (Mark 14:36). Other refs.: 1 Cor. 7:7, 21; 8:6, 7; 2 Cor. 4:16; 5:16; Col. 2:5; 2 Tim. 2:9. *

2 ***de*** [conj.: δέ <1161>] ► **Also, on the other hand, nevertheless** > But the Galatians knew that a man is not justified on the principle of works of law (Gal. 2:16). *

3 ***plēn*** [adv.: πλήν <4133>] ► **Moreover, nevertheless, yet** > But the Philippians took part in Paul's affliction (Phil. 4:14). *

BUT NOW – ***tanun*** [adv.: τανῦν <3569>] ► **At present** > Refs.: Acts 4:29; 5:38; 17:30; 20:32; 27:22. ¶ ‡

BUTCHER – Matt. 22:4 → KILL <2380>.

BUTTRESS – 1 Tim. 3:15 → FOUNDATION <1477>.

BUY – **1** ***agorazō*** [verb: ἀγοράζω <59>]; **lit.: to go to the marketplace (*agora*), hence: to buy** ► **The verb usually means to obtain an object by paying for it; also transl.: to redeem, to purchase** > In a particular way, the Christian who was before the slave of sin has been bought with a price (1 Cor. 6:20; 7:23; Rev. 5:9); the buying in this context suggests a change of master: previously a slave of Satan, the Christian now belongs to Christ. There are false teachers who deny the master who has bought them, bringing swift destruction on themselves (2 Pet. 2:1). The 144,000 will have been bought from the earth, bought from among men (Rev. 14:3, 4). Other refs.: Matt. 13:44, 46; 14:15; 21:12; 25:9, 10 {to make the purchase}; 27:7; Mark 6:36, 37 {to spend}; 11:15; 15:46; 16:1; Luke 9:13; 14:18, 19; 17:28; 19:45 in some mss.; 22:36; John 4:8; 6:5; 13:29; 1 Cor. 7:30; Rev. 3:18; 13:17; 18:11. ¶

2 ***ōneomai*** [verb: ὠνέομαι <5608>]; **from *ōnos*: price of a thing being bought ▶ To acquire an object by payment >** Abraham had bought {had purchased} a tomb from the sons of Emmor for a sum of money (Acts 7:16). ¶
– 3 Acts 1:18; 8:20 → PURCHASE (verb) <2932> 4 Acts 20:28 → PURCHASE (verb) <4046> 5 Acts 22:28 → OBTAIN <2932> 6 James 4:13 → to buy and sell → EXPLOIT <1710>.

BY – 1 ***para*** [prep.: παρά <3844>] ▶ **Beside, close to >** Jesus walked by the Sea of Galilee (Matt. 4:18; Mark 1:16). Some seed fell by the wayside (Matt. 13:4, 19; Mark 4:4, 15; Luke 8:5, 12). *
2 **but by: *ean mē*** [conj. and neg. particle: ἐὰν μή <3362>] ▶ **If not by, not otherwise >** The expr. "but by" is used in Gal. 2:16.
– 3 Acts 27:2 → ALONG <2596> 4 2 Cor. 10:15 → AMONG <1722>.

BY AND BY – 1 Matt. 13:21; Luke 21:9 → IMMEDIATELY <2112> <2117> 2 Mark 6:25 → ONCE (AT) <1824>.

BY NO MEANS – ***mēdamōs*** [adv.: μηδαμῶς <3365>]; **from *mēdamos*: not even one ▶ Not at all >** Refs.: Acts 10:14; 11:8. ¶ ‡

BY NO MEANS ALL – ***ouchi*** [adv.: οὐχί <3780>] ▶ **Not at all >** Refs.: John 13:10, 11; 1 Cor. 10:29. *

BY THIS PERSON, BY THIS THING – ***toutō*** [pron.: τούτῳ <5129>]. *

BYGONE – Acts 14:16 → PAST <3944>.

BYSTANDER – 1 Matt. 26:71 → lit.: those there (*tois ekei*) 2 Matt. 27:47 → lit.: those standing there → STAND (verb) <2476> 3 Mark 14:70; 15:35; Luke 19:24; Acts 23:4 → one who stands by → STAND (verb) <3936>.

 C

CABLE – ***boētheia*** [fem. noun: βοήθεια <996>]; **from *boētheō*: to help, which is from *boē*: cry, exclamation, and *theō*: to run ▶ Safety device** > Cables {Ropes, Helps, Supporting cables} were used to undergird Paul's ship (Acts 27:17). Other ref.: Heb. 4:16; see HELP (noun) <996>. ¶

CAESAR – ***Kaisar*** [Lat. masc. name: Καῖσαρ <2541>] ▶ **Title held by several Roman emperors belonging to the family of Gaius Julius Caesar** > This Caesar, the most famous, became the master of Rome after having conquered Gaul. He was assassinated in 44 B.C. The title of Caesar was given to the emperors Augustus (Luke 2:1), Tiberius (Matt. 22:17, 21a–c; Mark 12:14, 16, 17; Luke 3:1; 20:22, 24, 25a, b; 23:2; John 19:12a, b, 15), Caligula (Acts 17:7), Claudius (see Acts 18:2), Nero (Acts 25:8, 10–12a, b, 21; 26:32; 27:24; 28:19; Phil. 4:22), and Titus who besieged Jerusalem in A.D. 70. ¶

CAESAREA – ***Kaisareia*** [fem. name: Καισάρεια <2542>]; **from the name of Tiberius Augustus, the Roman emperor ▶ Seaport of Palestine, located northwest of Jerusalem** > Philip preached the gospel in all the cities, from Azotus until he came to Caesarea (Acts 8:40). The brothers brought Paul down at first to Caesarea, when the Hellenistic Jews of Jerusalem wanted to put him to death (9:30). Cornelius was of Caesarea (10:1, 24). Three men from Caesarea came to Peter (11:11); Peter stayed in this city (12:19). From Caesarea, Paul went up to Jerusalem to greet the church (18:22). He later returned to Caesarea, entering into the house of Philip the evangelist (21:8); disciples from this city came with him to Jerusalem (21:16). Paul was brought as a prisoner to Caesarea under military guard (23:23, 33); he appealed to Caesar and made his defense before King Agrippa (see 25:1, 4, 6, 13). ¶

CAESAREA PHILIPPI – ***Kaisareia tēs Philippou***; ***Kaisareia*** [fem. name: Καισάρεια <2542>], ***Philippos*** [masc. name: Φίλιππος <5376>]; **so named by Philip the tetrarch in honor of Tiberius Caesar and himself ▶ City located in Northern Palestine, at one of the sources of the Jordan River** > In this city, Jesus asked His disciples two questions: "Who do men say that I am?," "And you, who do you say that I am?" (Matt. 16:13, see v. 15; Mark 8:27, see v. 29). ¶

CAIAPHAS – ***Kaiaphas*** [masc. name: Καϊάφας <2533>] ▶ **High priest in Israel** > Caiaphas was high priest (Luke 3:2; John 11:49) at the same time as his father-in-law Annas (John 18:13). He was in Jerusalem when Peter spoke to the rulers and elders of the people of Israel (Acts 4:6). The chief priests gathered together and held counsel at his palace to put Jesus to death (Matt. 26:3, 57). When Jesus appeared before them (see Matt. 26:59–68), Caiaphas accused Him of blasphemy because He said that He was the "Messiah" and the "Son of God" (John 18:24, 28; see Matt. 26:63–65); then he tore his clothes (see Matt. 26:65) despite the law's prohibition (see Lev. 21:10) and delivered Jesus to Pilate. He was willing to let Jesus die for the people (John 18:14). He was dismissed from office in the year 36 by Vitellius, a representative of Rome. ¶

CAIN – ***Kain*** [masc. name: Κάϊν <2535>]: **acquisition, in Heb. ▶ First child of Adam and Eve (see Gen. 4:1)** > Because God took pleasure in the sacrifice of his brother Abel and not in his own, Cain killed Abel (1 John 3:12; see Gen. 4:1–16). The sacrifice of Cain evokes in figure the works performed by man in order to approach God. But God accepted, from the flock of Abel, the firstborn, a type of the excellence of the sacrifice of Jesus Christ, a more excellent sacrifice than that of Cain (Heb. 11:4). Cain lived in banishment in the land of Nod, east of Eden (see Gen. 4:16). Jude 11 speaks of those who have gone in the way of Cain, a way of distance from God, of irritation, and of opposition to that which is of God. ¶

CAINAN – ***Kainan*** [masc. name: Καϊνάν <2536>]: **possession, in Heb.; also spelled: *Kainam* ▶ Name of two men of the O.T.** > The name Cainan is mentioned in the genealogy of Jesus, one time before and the other time after the flood (Luke 3:36, 37). ¶

CALAMITY – 2 Cor. 6:4; 12:10 → DISTRESS <4730>.

CALCULATE – [1] ***sumpsēphizō*** [verb: συμψηφίζω <4860>]; **from *sun*: together, and *psēphizō*: to calculate, to vote ► To estimate, to evaluate; also transl.: to count, to reckon up** > The value of the books of magic which had been burned was calculated and it was found that the total came to fifty thousand pieces of silver (Acts 19:19). ¶
– [2] Luke 14:28; Rev. 13:18 → COUNT <5585>.

CALF – [1] ***moschos*** [masc. noun: μόσχος <3448>] ► **The young of a cow** > Following the return of his son, the father said to bring the fattened calf and kill it (Luke 15:23, 27, 30). It is not by the blood of goats and calves, but by His own blood, that Christ has entered in once for all into the Most Holy Place, having obtained an eternal redemption (Heb. 9:12). Moses took the blood of calves and goats, with water, scarlet wool, and hyssop; he sprinkled both the book of the law itself and all the people (Heb. 9:19). The second living creature which John saw was like a calf {an ox} (Rev. 4:7). ¶
[2] **to make a calf: *moschopoieō*** [verb: μοσχοποιέω <3447>]; **from *moschos*: see [1], and *poieō*: to make ► To fabricate the statue of a calf** > The Israelites made a calf and offered a sacrifice to the idol (Acts 7:41). ¶
– [3] Matt. 22:4 → fat calf → FATLING <4619>.

CALL (noun) – [1] Rom. 11:29; Eph. 4:4; Phil. 3:14; 2 Pet. 1:10 → CALLING <2821>
[2] 1 Cor. 7:18a, b → at the time of his call → when he was called → CALL (verb) <2564>
[3] Rev. 10:7 → to sound the trumpet call → to sound a trumpet → TRUMPET <4537>
[4] Rev. 13:10; 14:12 → "a call for" added in Engl.

CALL (verb) – [1] ***kaleō*** [verb: καλέω <2564>] ► **a. To name; to give a name, a surname** > The verb "to call" is used to designate Jesus (Matt. 1:21, 23, 25; 2:23; Luke 1:31, 32, 35; 2:21; 6:46; Rev. 19:13), John the Baptist (Luke 1:13, 59, 60), Simon the Zealot (Luke 6:15), Mary Magdalene (Luke 8:2), Mary of Bethany (Luke 10:39), Zaccheus (Luke 19:2), Simon Peter (John 1:42), Joseph Barsabas (Acts 1:23), Saul (Acts 7:58 {whose name was}), Simeon (Acts 13:1), Barnabas and Paul (Acts 14:12), and John (Acts 15:37 {whose surname was Mark}). This verb is also used to designate places (called): the potter's field (Matt. 27:8; Acts 1:19), Bethlehem (Luke 2:4), Nain (Luke 7:11), Bethsaida (Luke 9:10), the mount of Olives (Luke 19:29; 21:37; Acts 1:12), Calvary (Luke 23:33), the porch of Solomon (Acts 3:11), the street Straight (Acts 9:11), Fair Havens (Acts 27:8), Clauda (Acts 27:16), Malta (Acts 28:1), Patmos (Rev. 1:9), the great city (Rev. 11:8), and Armageddon (Rev. 16:16). **b. To ask to come, to invite** > In a parable, a king sent out his servants to call those who were invited to a wedding (Matt. 22:3) and other people (v. 9 {to bid, to invite}). Other refs.: Matt. 2:7, 15; 4:21; 5:9, 19; 9:13; 10:25; 20:8; 21:13; 22:43, 45; 23:7–10; 25:14; Mark 1:20; 2:17; 3:31; 11:17; Luke 1:36, 61, 62, 76; 2:23; 5:32; 15:19, 21; 19:13; 20:44; 22:25; John 10:3; Acts 4:18; 8:10; 10:1; 24:2; 27:14; Rom. 4:17; 8:30a, b; 9:7, 11, 24–26; 1 Cor. 1:9; 7:15, 17, 18a, b, 20, 21, 22a, b, 24; 15:9; Gal. 1:6, 15; 5:8, 13; Eph. 4:1, 4; Col. 3:15; 1 Thes. 2:12; 4:7; 5:24; 2 Thes. 2:14; 1 Tim. 6:12; 2 Tim. 1:9; Heb. 2:11; 3:13; 5:4; 9:15; 11:8, 18; Jas. 2:23; 1 Pet. 1:15; 2:9, 21; 3:6, 9; 5:10; 2 Pet. 1:3; 1 John 3:1; Rev. 12:9; 19:11 in some mss. ¶
[2] **to call in question: *enkaleō*** [verb: ἐγκαλέω <1458>]; **from *en*: in, and *kaleō*: see [1] ► To accuse; to prosecute at law** > The men of Ephesus were in danger of being called in question {being put in accusation, being accused, being charged} for the uproar against Paul (Acts 19:40). All other refs.: ACCUSATION <1458>, ACCUSE <1458>.
[3] ***epikaleō*** [verb: ἐπικαλέω <1941>]; **from *epi*: upon, and *kaleō*: see [1] ► a. To give a surname, to call upon** > Paul calls God

as a witness that if he had not yet gone to Corinth, it was to spare the Corinthians (2 Cor. 1:23). God is not ashamed to be called the God of those who have died in faith (Heb. 11:16). **b. To invoke by prayer >** The verb is used in relation to the name of the Lord (Acts 2:21; 9:14, 21; 22:16; Rom. 10:12–14; 1 Cor. 1:2; 2 Tim. 2:22; Jas. 2:7 {to belong}) and God the Father (1 Pet. 1:17 {to address, to invoke}). All other refs.: APPEAL <1941>, INVOKE <1941>, PRAY <1941>, SURNAME (verb) <1941>.

4 ***metakaleō*** [verb: μετακαλέω <3333>]**; from *meta*: denoting change, and *kaleō*: see 1 ▶ To convene, to convoke, to send for >** Joseph called {invited} his father Jacob and all his family to him (Acts 7:14). Cornelius was told to call for {invite, fetch} Simon (Acts 10:32). Paul called the elders of the church in Ephesus (Acts 20:17). Felix would call {summon} Paul when he would get an opportunity (Acts 24:25). ¶

5 to call for: *parakaleō* [verb: παρακαλέω <3870>]**; from *para*: beside, and *kaleō*: see 1; lit.: to call beside ▶ To ask to come >** Paul had called for {requested, asked} to see the leaders of the Jews in Rome (Acts 28:20). All other refs.: see entries in Lexicon at <3870>.

6 to call, to call unto, to call to: *proskaleō* [verb: προσκαλέω <4341>]**; from *pros*: to, and *kaleō*: see 1 ▶ To call to oneself; also transl.: to summon >** Jesus called to Himself His twelve disciples (Matt. 10:1; Mark 6:7; 12:43), the multitude (Matt. 15:10), His disciples (Matt. 15:32; Mark 8:1), a little child (Matt. 18:2), and the people (Mark 7:14; 8:34). Other refs.: Matt. 18:32 (some mss.: *parakaleō*); 20:25; Mark 3:13, 23; 10:42; 15:44; Luke 7:19; 15:26; 16:5; 18:16; Acts 2:39; 5:40; 6:2; 13:2, 7; 16:10; 20:1; 23:17, 18, 23; Jas. 5:14. ¶

7 to call together: *sunkaleō* [verb: συγκαλέω <4779>]**; from *sun*: together, and *kaleō*: see 1 ▶ To convene, to gather >** The soldiers called together the whole cohort against Jesus (Mark 15:16). Jesus called together His twelve disciples and gave them power over all devils and to heal diseases (Luke 9:1). The man who has found his lost sheep calls together the friends and the neighbors (Luke 15:6). Having found her drachma, the woman calls together the friends and neighbors to rejoice with her (Luke 15:9). Pilate called together {summoned} the chief priests, the rulers, and the people to talk to them about Jesus (Luke 23:13). The council was called together to bring the apostles before them (Acts 5:21). Cornelius had called together his relatives and close friends on the occasion of Peter's visit (Acts 10:24). In Rome, Paul called together the leaders of the Jews (Acts 28:17). ¶

8 ***legō*** [verb: λέγω <3004>] **▶ To speak of by name, to name >** This verb "to call" is used to designate Jesus (Matt. 1:16; 27:17, 22; Luke 20:37; John 4:25; 9:11), God (2 Thes. 2:4), Simon (Matt. 4:18; 10:2), the mother of Jesus (Matt. 13:55 {the name is}), Caiaphas (Matt. 26:3 {whose name was}), Judas Iscariot (Matt. 26:14; Luke 22:47), Thomas (John 11:16; 20:24; 21:2), and Justus (Col. 4:11). The verb also designates places: Nazareth (Matt. 2:23), Gethsemane (Matt. 26:36), Golgotha (Matt. 27:33; John 19:17), Ephraim (John 11:54), the Pavement (John 19:13 {known as}), and a gate of the temple (Acts 3:2). Other refs.: Mark 10:18; 12:37; 15:12; Luke 18:19; 22:1; John 10:36; 15:15a, b; Acts 6:9; 10:28; 24:14; 1 Cor. 8:5 {so-called}; Eph. 2:11a, b; Heb. 9:2, 3; 11:24 {known as}. Other refs.: Matt. 9:9; 27:16; Mark 15:7; John 4:5; Heb. 7:11; see NAME (verb) <3004>. Other refs.: SPEAK <3004>.

9 ***epilegō*** [verb: ἐπιλέγω <1951>]**; from *epi*: upon, and *legō*: see 8 ▶ To give a surname >** A pool in Jerusalem was called Bethesda (John 5:2). Other ref.: Acts 15:40; see CHOOSE <1951>. ¶

10 to call, to call over, to call upon: *onomazō* [verb: ὀνομάζω <3687>]**; from *onoma*: name ▶ a. To give a name >** Christians should not mix with a man called {named, so-called} brother who is sexually immoral or practices other serious sins (1 Cor. 5:11). **b. To invoke the name of someone in order to exorcise >** Some exorcists tried to call the name of the Lord Jesus over {to name over} those who had

wicked spirits (Acts 19:13). All other refs.: NAME (verb) <3687>.
11 ***phōneō*** [verb: φωνέω <5455>]; **from *phōnē*: sound, voice; lit.: to make a sound ▶ To speak, to address as** > The disciples of Jesus called Him the Teacher and the Lord (John 13:13). An angel called {cried} with a loud cry (Rev. 14:18). Other refs.: Matt. 20:32; 27:47; Mark 3:31; 9:35; 10:49; 15:35; Luke 14:12; 16:2; 19:15; John 1:48; 2:9; 4:16; 9:18, 24; 11:28; 12:17; 18:33; Acts 9:41; 10:7, 18. All other refs.: CROW <5455>, CRY (verb) <5455>.
12 ***prosphōneō*** [verb: προσφωνέω <4377>]; **from *pros*: to, and *phōneō*: see 11 ▶ To speak to, to summon** > Those of the generation of Jesus were like children calling to their companions (Matt. 11:16; Luke 7:32). Jesus called His disciples (Luke 6:13). He called a woman who had a spirit of infirmity eighteen years (Luke 13:12). Other refs.: Luke 23:20; Acts 21:40; 22:2; see ADDRESS (verb) <4377>. ¶
13 ***chrēmatizō*** [verb: χρηματίζω <5537>]; **from *chrēma*: matter, business; lit.: to behave like ▶ To be named** > A woman will be called an adulteress if she marries another man while her husband lives (Rom. 7:3). The disciples were first called Christians in Antioch (Acts 11:26). All other refs.: ORACLE <5537>, WARN <5537>.
– 14 Matt. 2:4; John 11:47 → to call together, to call a meeting → GATHER <4863> 15 Matt. 3:3; Mark 1:3; Luke 3:4; 18:7, 38; John 1:23 → CRY (verb) <994> 16 Matt. 9:27; Gal. 4:6; Rev. 6:10; 7:2; 10:3a, b; 14:15; 18:2; 19:17 → CRY (verb) <2896> 17 Matt. 19:17 → ASK <2065> 18 Matt. 20:16; 22:14; Rom. 1:1; et al. → CALLED <2822> 19 Matt. 21:16 → to call forth → PERFECT (verb) <2675> 20 Matt. 22:3a; Luke 14:13; Rev. 19:9 → INVITE <2564> 21 Mark 15:18 → to call out → GREET <782> 22 Luke 1:48; Jas. 5:11 → to call blessed → BLESSED <3106> 23 Luke 9:38 → CRY (verb) <310> 24 Luke 11:27 → RAISE <1869> 25 Luke 17:13 → called out in a loud voice → lit.: lifted up their voices → LIFT <142> 26 Luke 23:21 → to keep on calling out → SHOUT (verb) <2019> 27 John 11:43 → CRY (verb) <2905> 28 Acts 4:9 → to call to account, to call upon to answer → EXAMINE <350> 29 Acts 10:23 → to call in → to invite in → INVITE <1528> 30 Acts 16:29 → to call for → ASK <154> 31 Rom. 2:17 → NAME (verb) <2028> 32 1 Cor. 1:26; Eph. 1:18; 4:4; Phil. 3:14 → CALLING <2821> 33 Heb. 5:10 → DESIGNATE <4316> 34 Heb. 11:22 → to call to mind → to make mention → MENTION (noun) <3421> 35 Rev. 2:2 → SAY <5335> 36 Rev. 9:11 → to be called → lit.: to have the name → NAME (noun) <3686>.

CALLED – 1 ***klētos*** [verbal adj.: κλητός <2822>]; **from *kaleō*: to name, to give a name ▶ Invited, summoned (with emphasis on spiritual privilege); effectively summoned, chosen** > Many are called, but few are chosen (Matt. 20:16 in some mss.; 22:14). Paul says of himself: called to be an apostle (lit.: called an apostle; i.e., an apostle by God's calling) (Rom. 1:1; 1 Cor. 1:1). Christians in Rome were the called of Jesus Christ (Rom. 1:6); they, themselves, and the Christians in Corinth were called saints (i.e., saints by God's calling) (Rom. 1:7; 1 Cor. 1:2). All things work together for good to those who love God, to those who are called according to His purpose (Rom. 8:28). Christ is God's power and wisdom to those who are called (1 Cor. 1:24). Jude addressed himself to the called ones (v. 1). Those who are with the Lamb are called and chosen and faithful (Rev. 17:14). ¶
– 2 Luke 24:13 → NAME (noun) <3686>.

CALLING – 1 ***klēsis*** [fem. noun: κλῆσις <2821>]; **from *kaleō*: to call ▶ Vocation; the action of asking to come, invitation** > The gifts and calling {call} of God are irrevocable (Rom. 11:29). Paul tells the Corinthians to consider their calling (1 Cor. 1:26). Each Christian is to remain in the same calling {condition, situation} in which he has been called (1 Cor. 7:20). The Ephesians needed to know what was the hope of the calling of God (Eph. 1:18). Paul beseeches them to walk worthy of their calling (Eph. 4:1); they had been called in one hope of their calling (v. 4).

Paul himself was pursuing the goal for the prize of the calling on high {upward call} of God in Christ Jesus (Phil. 3:14). He was praying always that God might count the Thessalonians worthy of the calling (2 Thes. 1:11). God has called Christians with a holy calling {to a holy life} (2 Tim. 1:9); they are partakers of the heavenly calling (Heb. 3:1). Christians are exhorted by Peter to use diligence to make their calling and election sure (2 Pet. 1:10). ¶
– [2] Rev. 18:17 → to exercise one's calling → TRADE (verb) <2038>.

CALLING TO MIND – Heb. 10:3 → REMINDER <364>.

CALLOUS – Eph. 4:19 → to become callous → to cast off all feeling → FEELING <524>.

CALLOUSED – Matt. 13:15; Acts 28:27 → to become calloused → to become dull → DULL <3975>.

CALM (adj. and noun) – [1] ***galēnē*** [fem. noun: γαλήνη <1055>] ▶ **Stillness on a body of water, quietness** > Jesus rebuked the winds and the sea, and there was a great calm (Matt. 8:26; Mark 4:39; Luke 8:24). ¶
[2] **to be calm, to keep calm: *katastellō*** [verb: καταστέλλω <2687>]; **from *kata*: down, and *stellō*: to restrain ▶ a. Active voice: To quiet, to appease** > The town clerk quieted the crowd in Ephesus (Acts 19:35). **b. Pass. voice: To be quiet, to simmer down** > The town clerk told the inhabitants of Ephesus they should be calm {calmed down} (Acts 19:36). ¶

CALM (verb) – Acts 19:36 → to calm down → lit.: having been calmed → CALM (noun and adj.) <2687>.

CALUMNIATE – 1 Pet. 3:16 → to falsely accuse → ACCUSE <1908>.

CALVARY – See SKULL <2898>.

CAMEL – ***kamēlos*** [masc. and fem. noun: κάμηλος <2574>]; **other mss.: *kamilos*; in Heb. *gâmâl* ▶ Large domesticated ruminant, most useful to carry people and burdens on great distances** > John the Baptist was clothed with a garment of camel's hair (Matt. 3:4; Mark 1:6). It is easier for a camel to enter the eye of a needle, than for a rich man to enter the kingdom of God (Matt. 19:24; Mark 10:25; Luke 18:25); see NEEDLE <4476>. To "strain out a gnat and swallow a camel" (to filter a liquid in order to avoid swallowing a gnat) means to be preoccupied by insignificant details and not to pay attention to important matters, such as the moral prescriptions of the law (Matt. 23:24). ¶

CAMP – [1] ***parembolē*** [fem. noun: παρεμβολή <3925>]; **from *paremballō*: to set alongside, which is from *para*: near, beside, and *emballō*: to throw in, which is from *en*: in, and *ballō*: to throw ▶ a. Organized encampment of the people of Israel** > The bodies of the beasts were burned outside the camp (Heb. 13:11). **b. Figur., the Judaic religious system and, in general, any religious system established by men** > We must go forth to Jesus outside the camp (Heb. 13:13). **c. Defensive gathering** > At the end of the millennium, under the instigation of Satan, the nations will surround the camp of the saints and Jerusalem (Rev. 20:9). All other refs.: ARMY <3925>, FORTRESS <3925>.
– [2] Acts 1:20 → DWELLING PLACE <1886>.

CAN, CANNOT – Matt. 3:9; 5:14; et al. → ABLE (BE) <1410>.

CANA – ***Kana*** [fem. name: Κανά <2580>]: **place of reeds, in Heb. ▶ City of Galilee** > Jesus performed His first miracle in Cana during a wedding (John 2:1): He changed water into wine; He thus manifested His glory and His disciples believed in Him (v. 11). He later returned to Cana where He met a nobleman, from Capernaum whose son was dying; Jesus healed his son without traveling from Cana, performing this second miracle (John 4:46; see v. 54). Nathanael, one of the twelve disciples, was originally from Cana of Galilee (John 21:2). ¶

CANAAN – ***Chanaan*** [fem. name: Χανάαν <5477>]: **humiliated, in Heb. ▶ Region occupied by Ham, Noah's son (see Gen. 9:20–25); it corresponds to Palestine >** Luke recalls that a famine came upon Egypt and Canaan, which forced Jacob to seek food from Joseph in Egypt (Acts 7:11). The Israelites destroyed seven nations in Canaan when they entered the land to take possession of it (Acts 13:19). ¶

CANAANITE – [1] ***Chananaios*** [adj.: Χαναναῖος <5478>]; **from *Chanaan*: Canaan ▶ Person descended from the lineage of Canaan, the people occupying the land before the arrival of the Israelites >** The daughter of a Canaanite woman, tormented by a demon, was healed by Jesus (Matt. 15:22; see v. 28). ¶
– [2] Matt. 10:4; Mark 3:18 → CANANITE <2581>.

CANANAEAN – See CANANITE <2581>.

CANANITE – ***Kananaios*** [masc. name: Καναναῖος <2581>]: **zealous, in Aram.; also spelled: *Kananitēs* ▶ Member of a Jewish national party; also transl.: Canaanite, Cananaean >** Simon, one of the disciples of Jesus, was called "the Cananite" or "the Zealot" (in some mss.) (Matt. 10:4; Mark 3:18). ¶

CANCEL – [1] Matt. 18:27, 32 → FORGIVE <863> [2] Luke 7:42, 43 → FORGIVE <5483> [3] Col. 2:14 → to cancel out → to blot out → BLOT (verb) <1813>.

CANCER – 2 Tim. 2:17 → GANGRENE <1044>.

CANDACE – ***Kandakē*** [fem. name: Κανδάκη <2582>]; **possibly a general designation for Ethiopian queens ▶ Queen of Ethiopia >** An important official under Candace (Acts 8:27), who was reading the prophet Isaiah, was converted by the preaching of Philip and was baptized by him (see 8:26–40). ¶

CANDLE – Matt. 5:15; 6:22; Mark 4:21; Luke 8:16; 11:33, 34, 36; 12:35; 15:8; John 5:35; 2 Pet. 1:19; Rev. 18:23; 21:23; 22:5 → LAMP <3088>.

CANDLESTICK – Matt. 5:15; Mark 4:21; Luke 8:16; 11:33; Heb. 9:2; Rev. 1:12, 13, 20a, b; 2:1, 5; 11:4 → LAMPSTAND <3087>.

CANKER – [1] 2 Tim. 2:17 → GANGRENE <1044> [2] Jas. 5:3 → RUST <2447>.

CANKERED (BE) – Jas. 5:3 → RUSTED (BE) <2728>.

CAPERNAUM – ***Kapernaoum*** [fem. name: Καπερναούμ <2584>]: **comfortable village (or: village of consolation), in Heb.; also spelled: *Kapharnaoum* ▶ Village of Galilee, northwest of the Sea of Galilee >** After His miracle at Cana, Jesus went down to Capernaum and stayed there for a few days (John 2:12; also Matt. 4:13). He healed in Capernaum a centurion's servant who was paralyzed (Matt. 8:5; Luke 7:1; John 4:46). He taught in the synagogue of this city (John 6:59), and healed a man possessed by an unclean spirit (Mark 1:21; also vv. 23–26; Luke 4:31; also vv. 33–35). He preached the word of God there, and healed a paralytic carried by four people (Mark 2:1). He taught His disciples a lesson in humility at Capernaum (Mark 9:33). Jesus did many things at Capernaum (Luke 4:23), but He reproached this city for unbelief in spite of the miracles performed in its midst (Matt. 11:23; Luke 10:15). He performed another miracle there when He told Peter to take a fish in whose mouth there was a coin to pay a tax (Matt. 17:24; see v. 27). Jesus walked on the sea on His way to Capernaum (John 6:17); a crowd came there seeking Him (v. 24). ¶

CAPPADOCIA – ***Kappadokia*** [fem. name: Καππαδοκία <2587>] **▶ Roman province located in eastern Asia Minor >** Jews from

Cappadocia were present in Jerusalem at Pentecost (Acts 2:9). Peter addressed his first letter to the Christians of Cappadocia, among other Christians (1 Pet. 1:1). ¶

CAPSTONE – Matt. 21:42; Mark 12:10; Luke 20:17; Acts 4:11; 1 Pet. 2:7 → CHIEF CORNERSTONE <2776> <1137>.

CAPTAIN – [1] ***archēgos*** [masc. noun: ἀρχηγός <747>]; **from *archē*: beginning, rule, and *agō*: to lead ▶ First cause, one who occupies a preeminent position, chief** > Jesus is the captain {author, leader} of the salvation of Christians (Heb. 2:10). All other refs.: AUTHOR <747>, PRINCE <747>.

[2] ***stratēgos*** [masc. noun: στρατηγός <4755>]; **from *stratos*: army, and *agō*: to lead ▶ Chief of the guards, commanding officer; also transl.: officer** > The captains of the temple were guarding it (Luke 22:4, 52; Acts 4:1; 5:24, 26). They were Jews from the tribe of Levi. Other refs.: Acts 16:20, 22, 35, 36, 38; see MAGISTRATE <4755>. ¶

[3] **captain, chief captain, high captain, chiliarch, commander, military commander, high officer: *chiliarchos*** [masc. noun: χιλίαρχος <5506>]; **from *chilioi*: thousand, and *archō*: to command, which is from *archē*: beginning, authority ▶ Tribune, i.e., a commanding officer in the Roman army, in charge of one thousand soldiers; any military commander; also transl.: commander** > John the Baptist was beheaded at the time Herod was giving a feast for his captains and others (Mark 6:21). A band and its captain arrested Jesus (John 18:12). Lysias was a captain (Acts 24:7, 22). Captains {High ranking officers, High ranking military officers} were present when Paul appeared before Agrippa (Acts 25:23). The captains {generals} will hide themselves from the wrath of the Lamb (Rev. 6:15); the birds will eat the flesh of the captains {generals} (Rev. 19:18). Other refs.: Acts 21:31–33, 37; 22:24, 26–29; 23:10, 15, 17–19, 22. ¶

– [4] Acts 27:11 → SHIPOWNER <3490>.

CAPTAIN OF THE GUARD – Acts 28:16 → PRAETORIAN PREFECT <4759>.

CAPTIVATE – 2 Tim. 3:6 → to lead captive → CAPTIVE (adj.) <163>.

CAPTIVE (adj.) – [1] **to lead captive: *aichmalōteuō*** [verb: αἰχμαλωτεύω <162>]; **from *aichmalōtos*: captive, prisoner, which is from *aichmē*: end of a spear, and *alōtos*: which can be taken, or *haliskomai*: to be captured ▶ To make prisoner** > Christ has led captivity captive (Eph. 4:8). Other ref.: 2 Tim. 3:6; see [2]. ¶

[2] **to lead away captive, to lead captive, to make captive, to take captive, to bring into captivity: *aichmalōtizō*** [verb: αἰχμαλωτίζω <163>]; **from *aichmalōtos*: see [1] ▶ To make prisoner** > During the great tribulation, the Jews will be led captive {taken as prisoners} among all the nations (Luke 21:24). Some are leading captive {are captivating, gain control over} silly women laden with sins (2 Tim. 3:6); some mss. have *aichmalōteuō*; see [1]. Another law is bringing the man of Romans 7 into captivity {making him prisoner} to the law of sin (v. 23). Spiritual weapons lead captive every thought to the obedience of Christ (2 Cor. 10:5). ¶

– [3] Acts 8:23 → BOND[1] <4886> [4] Rom. 7:6 → to hold captive → lit.: to be held firmly → HOLD (verb) <2722> [5] 1 Cor. 9:27 → to lead captive → to bring into subjection → SUBJECTION <1396> [6] 2 Cor. 2:14 → to lead as captives → to lead in triumph → TRIUMPH (noun and verb) <2358> [7] Gal. 3:23 → to hold captive → GUARD (verb) <5432> [8] Col. 2:8 → to take captive → to lead away as a prey → PREY <4812> [9] 2 Tim. 2:26 → to take captive → CATCH (verb) <2221> [10] Rev. 13:10 → to take captive → lit.: to be for captivity, or in some mss.: to gather captivity → CAPTIVITY <161>.

CAPTIVE (noun) – [1] ***aichmalōtos*** [masc. noun: αἰχμάλωτος <164>]; **from *aichmē*: end of a spear, and *alōtos*: which can be taken, or *haliskomai*: to be captured ▶ Prisoner of war** > Jesus was sent to preach deliverance to captives {prisoners} (Luke 4:18). ¶

– [2] Eph. 4:8 → host of captives → CAPTIVITY <161>.

CAPTIVITY – [1] ***aichmalōsia*** [fem. noun: αἰχμαλωσία <161>]; **from *aichmalōtos*: a captive; which is from *aichmē*: end of a spear, and *alōtos*: which can be taken, or *haliskomai*: to be captured ▶ Deprivation of freedom, imprisonment** > Christ has led captivity captive (Eph. 4:8); other transl.: He has led captive a host of captives, He led captive in His train. In relation to the saints persecuted by the beast, he who leads into captivity will go into captivity (Rev. 13:10a, b). ¶

– [2] Matt. 1:17a, b → DEPORTATION <3350> [3] Rom. 7:23; 2 Cor. 10:5 → to bring into captivity → CAPTIVE (adj.) <163>.

CAPTURE (noun) – ***halōsis*** [fem. noun: ἅλωσις <259>]; **from *haliskō*: to capture ▶ What or who is caught, captured, taken** > Peter speaks of men who are like unreasoning animals, made to be caught and destroyed (lit.: for capture and destruction) (2 Pet. 2:12). ¶

CAPTURE (verb) – [1] Matt. 26:55; Mark 14:48 → TAKE <4815> [2] 2 Tim. 2:26 → CATCH (verb) <2221> [3] 2 Tim. 3:6 → to lead captive → CAPTIVE (adj.) <163> or <162> [4] 2 Pet. 2:12 → CAPTURE (noun) <259> [5] Rev. 19:20 → SEIZE <4084>.

CARAVAN – Luke 2:44 → COMPANY (noun) <4923>.

CARCASE – [1] Matt. 24:28 → CORPSE <4430> [2] Heb. 3:17 → CORPSE <2966>.

CARCASS – Matt. 24:28 → CORPSE <4430>.

CARE (noun) – [1] ***epimeleia*** [fem. noun: ἐπιμέλεια <1958>]; **from *epimeleomai*: see [2] ▶ Attention, hospitality** > Julius allowed Paul to go to his friends and receive care {and refresh himself, so they might provide for his needs, and to be cared for} (Acts 27:3). ¶

[2] **to take care of: *epimeleomai*** [verb: ἐπιμελέομαι <1959>]; **from *epi*: upon, and *melō*: to concern oneself ▶ To look after the well-being of a person** > The verb is used in the parable of the good Samaritan (Luke 10:34, 35). One must know how to manage his own household in order to take care of the church of God (1 Tim. 3:5). ¶

[3] ***merimna*** [fem. noun: μέριμνα <3308>]; **from *meris*: part ▶ Anxiety, concern, worry** > The cares of this life and the deceit of riches choke the word of God (Matt. 13:22 {anxious care}; Mark 4:19; Luke 8:14). Our hearts may be weighed down with cares of this life (Luke 21:34). There was the daily pressure on Paul of concern {burden} for all the churches (2 Cor. 11:28). The Christian may cast all his care on Jesus, for He cares for him (1 Pet. 5:7). ¶

[4] **to have care: *merimnaō*** [verb: μεριμνάω <3309>]; **from *merimna*: see [3] ▶ To be occupied with others and their interests >** The members of the body (Christians) are to have the same care {to have the same concern} for one another (1 Cor. 12:25). All other refs.: ANXIOUS (BE) <3309>, CARE <3309>, WORRY (verb) <3309>.

– [5] Matt. 10:29 → outside your Father's care → lit.: without your Father → WITHOUT <427> [6] Matt. 25:44 → to take care → SERVE <1247> [7] Luke 12:15 → to take care → BEWARE <3708> [8] John 21:16 → to take care of the sheep → to feed the sheep → SHEEP <4165> [9] Acts 5:35 → to take care → BEWARE <4337> [10] Acts 24:23 → to take care → MINISTER (verb) <5256> [11] 1 Cor. 3:10 → with care, to take care → to take heed → HEED (noun) <991> [12] 1 Cor. 7:32 → without care → free from concern → CONCERN (noun) <275> [13] 1 Cor. 9:9 → to take care → he is occupied about → OCCUPY <3199> [14] 2 Cor. 7:12; 8:16 → care, earnest care → ZEAL <4710> [15] 2 Cor. 11:28 → CONCERN (noun) <3308> [16] Phil. 2:25 → to take care → MINISTER (noun) <3011> [17] Phil. 4:10 → THINK <5426> [18] 1 Thes. 2:7 → to take care of → CHERISH <2282> [19] 1 Tim. 5:16 → "in her care" added in

Engl. 20 Heb. 2:6 → to take care → VISIT (verb) <1980> 21 2 Pet. 3:17 → to take care → to be on one's guard → GUARD (noun) <5442>.

CARE (verb) – 1 ***melō*** [verb: μέλω <3199>] ▶ **To be troubled, to be concerned** > It was said to Jesus that He did not care for {did not defer to, was not swayed by} anyone, for He did not regard the person of men (Matt. 22:16; Mark 12:14). The disciples said to Jesus: Do You not care that we are perishing? (Mark 4:38). Martha asked the Lord if He did not care that her sister had left her to serve alone (Luke 10:40). The hired hand does not care {is not concerned} about the sheep (John 10:13). Judas did not care about the poor (John 12:6). Gallio did not care {did not trouble himself, did not take notice, was not concerned, showed no concern} about the Jews beating Sosthenes (Acts 18:17). One who has been called being a bondman should not care {be concerned, worry, be troubled} about it (1 Cor. 7:21). Paul asks if God is concerned about {is occupied about, takes care of} the oxen? (1 Cor. 9:9). Christians are to cast all their care (or: anxiety) upon God, for He cares for them (1 Pet. 5:7). ¶

2 ***merimnaō*** [verb: μεριμνάω <3309>]; **from *merimna*: care, concern, worry ▶ a. To be occupied with others and their interests** > Timothy would care {would be concerned, would take an interest} genuinely for the welfare of the Philippians (Phil. 2:20). **b. To worry, to be uneasy; also transl.: to be concerned** > He who is unmarried cares for the things of the Lord (1 Cor. 7:32), but he who is married cares for the things of the world (v. 33); it is the same for the woman who is married and for the one who is unmarried (v. 34a, b). All other refs.: ANXIOUS (BE) <3309>, CARE (noun) <3309>, WORRY (verb) <3309>.

– 3 Luke 18:2, 4 → RESPECT (verb) <1788> 4 Acts 7:20 → cared for → nourished → NOURISH <397> 5 Acts 20:28 → SHEPHERD (verb) <4165> 6 Acts 27:3 → to be cared for → to enjoy care → CARE (noun) <1958>, ENJOY <5177> 7 2 Cor. 3:3 → MINISTER (verb) <1247> 8 Eph. 5:29; 1 Thes. 2:7 → to care for, to tenderly care → CHERISH <2282> 9 Phil. 4:10 → THINK <5426> 10 1 Thes. 2:8 → "we cared for you" added in Engl. 11 1 Thes. 5:12 → LEAD (verb) <4291> 12 1 Tim. 5:10, 16a, b → to care for → RELIEVE <1884> 13 Heb. 2:6 → VISIT (verb) <1980> 14 Heb. 8:9 → to not care for → DISREGARD <272> 15 Jude 12 → FEED <4165> 16 Rev. 12:6, 14 → to take care → NOURISH <5142>.

CAREFUL – 1 **to be careful: *phrontizō*** [verb: φροντίζω <5431>]; **from *phrontis*: care, concern, which is from *phrēn*: mind, faculty of thinking ▶ To take care, to be cautious** > Those who have believed in God should be careful to pay diligent attention to good works (Titus 3:8). ¶

– 2 Matt. 2:8; Eph. 5:15 → to make careful search, to be careful how you walk → lit.: to search carefully, to walk carefully → CAREFULLY <199> 3 Matt. 6:1; Luke 21:34; Acts 20:28 → to be careful, to pay careful attention → to take heed → HEED (noun) <4337> 4 Matt. 6:25, 28, 31; 10:19; Luke 10:41; 12:22, 25, 26 → to be careful → WORRY (verb) <3309> 5 Mark 13:11 → to be careful beforehand → to worry beforehand → WORRY (verb) <4305> 6 Rom. 12:17 → to be careful to do what is right → to provide things honest → PROVIDE <4306> 7 1 Cor. 3:10 → to be careful → to take heed → HEED (noun) <991> 8 Eph. 5:15; et al. → to be careful → to see, to see to it → SEE <991> 9 Phil. 4:6 → ANXIOUS (BE) <3309> 10 Phil. 4:10 → to be careful → THINK <5426> 11 2 Pet. 1:12 → to be careful → not to be negligent → NEGLIGENT <3195> 12 2 Pet. 1:15 → to be careful → to be diligent → DILIGENT <4704>.

CAREFUL (BE) – 1 Matt. 23:3 → OBSERVE <5083> 2 Luke 11:35 → WATCH (verb) <4648>.

CAREFULLY – 1 ***akribōs*** [adv.: ἀκριβῶς <199>]; **from *akribēs*: accurate, or *akron*: point ▶ a. Exactly, precisely** > Herod told the wise men to search carefully {search diligently, search accurately, make careful search} for the child Jesus (Matt. 2:8). Luke had followed carefully {had perfect understanding of, was accurately acquainted with} all things concerning Jesus (Luke 1:3). **b. Conscientiously, with attention** > The Christian is to see that he walks carefully {circumspectly} (Eph. 5:15). Other refs.: Acts 18:25; 1 Thes. 5:2; see ACCURATELY <199>, PERFECTLY <199>. ¶

2 ***epimelōs*** [adv.: ἐπιμελῶς <1960>]; **from *epimelēs*: careful, which is from: *epi*: upon, for, and *melō*: to care ▶ With care, diligently, painstakingly** > In a parable, the woman who has lost a coin searches carefully until she finds it (Luke 15:8). ¶

3 **fist: *pugmē*** [fem. noun: πυγμή <4435>]; **from *pux*: with the fist ▶ Meticulously, thoroughly** > The Jews wash their hands carefully {diligently, oft} (lit.: with the fist) before eating (Mark 7:3). ¶

– 4 Acts 2:14 → to listen carefully → to give heed → HEED (noun) <1801> 5 Acts 5:35 → to consider carefully → BEWARE <4337> 6 Acts 16:23 → SECURELY <806> 7 Acts 17:23 → to look carefully at → BEHOLD (verb) <333> 8 Phil. 2:28 → the more carefully → the more eagerly → EAGERLY <4708> 9 1 Tim. 4:6; 2 Tim. 3:10 → to follow carefully → FOLLOW <3877> 10 1 Pet. 1:10 → to search carefully → SEARCH (verb) <1830>.

CAREFULNESS – 1 Matt. 6:27 → lit.: by being careful → WORRY (verb) <3309> 2 1 Cor. 7:32 → without care → free from concern → CONCERN (noun) <275> 3 2 Cor. 7:11 → DILIGENCE <4710>.

CARELESS – Matt. 12:36 → IDLE <692>.

CARGO – 1 Acts 21:3 → BURDEN (noun) <1117> 2 Acts 27:10 → LADING <5414> 3 Acts 27:18 → to jettison the cargo → LIGHTEN <1546> 4 Rev. 18:11, 12 → MERCHANDISE <1117>.

CARNAL – 1 ***sarkikos*** [adj.: σαρκικός <4559>]; **from *sarx*: flesh ▶ Concerning the flesh; material, physical; also transl.: external, of flesh, fleshly, material, worldly** > A carnal Christian is one who has returned to an improper way of living which may have characterized him before his conversion (Rom. 7:14 {unspiritual}; 1 Cor. 3:1, 3a, b), e.g., to sexual immorality {carnal lusts, sinful desires} (1 Pet. 2:11). Carnal things (Rom. 15:27; 1 Cor. 9:11: see 2) are things of this material world. The carnal commandment (Heb. 7:16) and ordinances (9:10: for the body; lit.: of the flesh) are related to the law which concerned the flesh. The weapons of the Christian warfare are not carnal {of the world} (2 Cor. 10:4), but spiritual. By the grace of God, Paul did not conduct himself with carnal wisdom (2 Cor. 1:12). Other ref.: 1 Cor. 9:11; see 2. ¶

2 **carnal things: *ta sarkikai*; plur. of *sarkikos*** [adj. used as noun: σαρκικός <4559>]; **see 1 ▶ Matters which are temporal, material, of this world** > Paul was reaping the carnal things {material things, material harvest} of the Corinthians (1 Cor. 9:11).

CARNELIAN – Rev. 4:3 → SARDIUS <4555>.

CAROUSAL – 1 Pet. 4:3 → REVEL (noun) <2970>.

CAROUSE – 1 2 Pet. 2:13 → to carouse with → to feast with → FEAST (verb) <4910> 2 2 Pet. 2:13 → REVEL (verb) <1792> 3 2 Pet. 2:13 → INDULGENCE <5172>.

CAROUSING – 1 ***kraipalē*** [fem. noun: κραιπάλη <2897>]; ***crapula*, in Lat.: headache caused by excessive drinking, deep drunkenness ▶ Excessive drinking and its consequences** > The Lord says to be careful so that our hearts will not be weighted down with carousing {dissipation, surfeiting}, drunkenness, and the worries of life (Luke 21:34). ¶

– 2 Rom. 13:13; Gal. 5:21 → REVEL (noun) <2970> 3 1 Pet. 4:3 → DRINKING <4224>.

CARPENTER – ***tektōn*** [masc. noun: τέκτων <5045>]; **comp. *tiktō*: to pro-**

duce ► Craftsman who works in stone, wood, and metal; a builder > Some spoke of Jesus as the son of a carpenter (Matt. 13:55). He, Himself, was a carpenter (Mark 6:3). ¶

CARPUS – ***Karpos*** [masc. name: Κάρπος <2591>]: **fruit, profit ► Christian man of Troas** > Paul had left a cloak with Carpus; he asks Timothy to bring it to him (2 Tim. 4:13). ¶

CARRIAGE – 1 Acts 21:15 → to take one's carriages → PACK <643> 2 Rev. 18:13 → CHARIOT <4480>.

CARRY – 1 **to carry away: *apagō*** [verb: ἀπάγω <520>]; **from *apo*: from, and *agō*: to lead ► To take away, to drag along** > Before their conversion, the Corinthians were carried away {were led away, were led astray} to worship dumb idols (1 Cor. 12:2). All other refs.: BRING <520>, DEATH <520>, LEAD (verb) <520>, TAKE <520>.

2 **to carry away with, by: *sunapagō*** [verb: συναπάγω <4879>]; **from *sun*: together, and *apagō*: see 1 ► To take along with** > Barnabas was carried away {was led astray} by the hypocrisy of the Jews (Gal. 2:13). Peter speaks of being carried away {led away} with the error of the wicked (2 Pet. 3:17). Other ref.: Rom. 12:16; see ASSOCIATE (verb) <4879>. ¶

3 **to carry out: *ekteinō*** [verb: ἐκτείνω <1614>]; **from *ek*: from, and *teinō*: to stretch out ► To put far out, to remove at a distance** > The sailors pretended they were going to carry out {cast out, put out, lay out, lower} anchors from the prow (Acts 27:30). All other refs.: STRETCH <1614>.

4 ***pherō*** [verb: φέρω <5342>] **► To bring, to lead** > Another would carry the aged Peter where he did not desire to go (John 21:18), most likely to his execution. The verb is transl. "to lead" in Acts 12:10: an iron gate led to the city. All other refs.: see entries in Lexicon at <5342>.

5 **to carry up: *anapherō*** [verb: ἀναφέρω <399>]; **from *ana*: above, and *pherō*: see 4 ► To take higher** > Jesus was carried up {was taken up} into heaven (Luke 24:51 in some mss.). All other refs.: BEAR (verb) <399>, LEAD (verb) <399>, OFFER <399>.

6 **to carry, to carry away: *apopherō*** [verb: ἀποφέρω <667>]; **from *apo*: from, and *pherō*: see 4 ► To take away, to transport** > Jesus was carried away {led away} and delivered to Pilate (Mark 15:1). Lazarus was carried away by angels to Abraham's bosom (Luke 16:22). Handkerchiefs or aprons were carried from Paul's body to the sick, and the diseases left them and the evil spirits went out (Acts 19:12). Paul would send someone to carry the gift of the Corinthians to Jerusalem (1 Cor. 16:3 {to bear, to bring}). John was carried away in spirit to a desert (Rev. 17:3), then set on a great and high mountain (21:10). ¶

7 ***diapherō*** [verb: διαφέρω <1308>]; **from *dia*: through, and *pherō*: see 4 ► To transport somewhere** > Jesus would not permit anyone to carry merchandise through the temple (Mark 11:16). All other refs.: see entries in Lexicon at <1308>.

8 ***eispherō*** [verb: εἰσφέρω <1533>]; **from *eis*: in, and *pherō*: see 4 ► To introduce, to bring** > The blood of the bodies of beasts is carried, as sacrifices for sin, into the holy of holies (Heb. 13:11). All other refs.: BRING <1533>, LEAD (verb) <1533>.

9 **to carry out, to carry forth: *ekpherō*** [verb: ἐκφέρω <1627>]; **from *ek*: out, and *pherō*: see 4 ► To take out, to take away** > The young men carried out the bodies of Ananias and Sapphira (Acts 5:6, 9, 10). We brought nothing into this world, and we cannot carry out anything (1 Tim. 6:7). All other refs.: BRING <1627>.

10 **to carry, to carry about, away, along: *peripherō*** [verb: περιφέρω <4064>]; **from *peri*: around, and *pherō*: see 4 ► a. To bring here and there** > Those who were ill were being carried about in beds (Mark 6:55). Christians should no longer be carried about {be blown here and there} with every wind of teaching (Eph. 4:14). Jude speaks of evil men carried about {blown along} by the winds (Jude 12). **b. To lead to one opinion and then to another, to deceive** > One ought not to be carried away by various and

strange doctrines (Heb. 13:9). Other refs.: 2 Cor. 4:10; see BEAR (verb) <4064>. ¶

11 **to carry away: *bastazō*** [verb: βαστάζω <941>]: **from *basis*: base, foot, step ▶ To take away, to transport** > Mary asked the man she thought was the gardener if he had carried {borne} Jesus away (John 20:15). All other refs.: BEAR (verb) <941>.

12 **to carry out: *ekkomizō*** [verb: ἐκκομίζω <1580>]; **from *ek*: out, and *komizō*: to take away, to transport ▶ To take a dead body for burial** > The verb is used in regard to an only son who had died (Luke 7:12). ¶

13 **to carry to one's burial: *sunkomizō*** [verb: συγκομίζω <4792>]; **from *sun*: together, and *komizō*: to take away, to transport ▶ To bear together a dead body for its burial** > Pious men carried Stephen to his burial {buried him} (Acts 8:2). ¶

14 **to carry back, to carry over: *metatithēmi*** [verb: μετατίθημι <3346>]; **from *meta*: indicating change, and *tithēmi*: to put ▶ To transfer** > Jacob and the fathers of the Israelites, after their death, were carried over {were brought back, were removed} to Shechem (Acts 7:16). All other refs.: CHANGE (verb) <3346>, TAKE <3346>, TURN (verb) <3346>.

– 15 Matt. 1:11, 12, 17a, b → carrying away → DEPORTATION <3350> 16 Matt. 4:1 → LEAD (verb) <321> 17 Matt. 12:29a; Mark 3:27a → to carry off → PLUNDER (verb) <1283> 18 Matt. 27:32; Mark 2:3; 15:21 → BEAR (verb) <142> 19 John 3:21 → to carry out → PRACTICE (verb) <2038> 20 John 7:19 → to carry out → PRACTICE (verb) <4160> 21 Acts 7:43 → to carry away → TRANSPORT <3351> 22 Acts 8:39 → to carry away → to catch away → CATCH (verb) <726> 23 Acts 13:29 → to carry out → FULFILL <5055> 24 Acts 21:34; 1 Cor. 12:2 → to carry, to carry away → LEAD (verb) <71> 25 Acts 24:12 → to carry on a discussion → DISPUTE (verb) <1256> 26 Rom. 9:28 → to carry out with speed → to cut short → SHORT <4932> 27 Rom. 13:4 → who carries out → lit.: for (*eis*) 28 1 Cor. 16:10 → to carry on → MINISTER (verb) <2038> 29 Eph. 2:3 → to carry out → FULFILL <4160> 30 Eph. 3:11 → to carry out → ACCOMPLISH <4160> 31 Col. 1:25 → to fully carry out → FULFILL <4137> 32 Heb. 9:6 → to carry on → ACCOMPLISH <2005> 33 Jas. 1:14 → to carry away → to draw away → DRAW <1828> 34 1 Pet. 4:3 → to carry out → DO <2716> 35 2 Pet. 2:17 → DRIVE <1643> 36 Rev. 17:17 → to carry out → EXECUTE <4160>.

CARVE – 2 Cor. 3:7 → ENGRAVE <1795>.

CASE – 1 ***aitia*** [fem. noun: αἰτία <156>]; **from *aiteō*: to ask, or *aitios*: responsible ▶ Situation, condition** > The disciples were talking to Jesus about the case {relationship} of the man divorcing his wife (Matt. 19:10). All other refs.: ACCUSATION <156>, CAUSE (noun) <156>, FAULT <156>, REASON (noun) <156>.

2 ***ta*; fem. of *ho*** [art.: ὁ <3588>] **▶ Lit.: the (matters)** > Felix would make a decision on Paul's case (Acts 24:22).

– 3 Acts 19:38 → MATTER <3056> 4 Acts 24:1; 25:2, 15 → to lay a case, to lay out a case → to bring charges → CHARGE (noun)[1] <1718> 5 Acts 25:14 → CAUSE <3588> 6 Acts 25:18 → in his case → lit.: concerning whom 7 1 Cor. 6:1 → MATTER <4229> 8 1 Cor. 6:4 → JUDGMENT <2922>.

CAST (noun) – Luke 22:41 → THROW (noun) <1000>.

CAST (verb) – 1 ***ballō*** [verb: βάλλω <906>] **▶ To throw (in various applications, with a degree of violence or intensity)** > The soldiers divided up the clothes of Jesus by casting lots (Matt. 27:35; Mark 15:24; Luke 23:34). Simon and Andrew were casting a net into the sea (Mark 1:16; other mss.: *amphiballō*). The Jews were casting {throwing, tossing} dust in the air (Acts 22:23). There is no fear in love, but perfect love casts out fear (1 John 4:18). The serpent cast {spewed, poured} out of his mouth behind the woman water as a river (Rev. 12:15); the earth swallowed the river which the dragon cast {spewed, poured} out of his mouth (v. 16). Satan will be cast out {hurled down} into the earth as well as his angels (Rev. 12:9a–c). He will see that he has been cast out into the earth and he will persecute Israel (Rev. 12:13). All other refs.: see entries in Lexicon at <906>.

2 to cast away: *apoballō* [verb: ἀποβάλλω <577>]; **from *apo*: from, and *ballō*: see 1 ▶ To set aside, to throw away >** Christians are not to cast away their confidence, which has great recompense (Heb. 10:35). Other ref.: Mark 10:50 (to throw aside, away); see THROW (verb) <577>. ¶

3 to cast out: *ekballō* [verb: ἐκβάλλω <1544>]; **from *ek*: out, and *ballō*: see 1; lit.: to throw outside ▶ To send away, to expel, to drive away, to drive out >** If Satan casts out Satan, he is divided against himself (Matt. 12:26; Mark 3:23). The disciples could not cast out a demon from a boy (Matt. 17:19; Mark 9:18, 28; Luke 9:40). Jesus cast out all those who sold and bought in the temple (Matt. 21:12; Mark 11:15; Luke 19:45; John 2:15). The Jews cast out {thrust out} Jesus from Nazareth (Luke 4:29). Blessed are those whose name will be cast out {scorned, rejected} as wicked by their persecutors, for the Son of Man's sake (Luke 6:22). Jesus will not at all cast out {drive away} the one who comes to Him (John 6:37). The Pharisees cast out {put out, threw out} the blind man who had been healed by Jesus (John 9:34); Jesus heard that they had cast {had thrown} him out (v. 35). The Jews cast out {expelled} Paul and Barnabas from their coasts (Acts 13:50). Abraham had to cast out {get rid of} the servant and her son (Gal. 4:30). Diotrephes was casting out {putting out} of the church those who would receive the brothers (3 John 10). The expr. "to cast out demons (or: devils)" is often found in the synoptic Gospels (Matt. 7:22; 8:31; 9:33, 34; 10:1, 8; 12:24, 27a, b, 28; Mark 1:34, 39; 3:15, 22; 6:13; 7:26; 9:38; 16:9, 17; Luke 9:49; 11:14, 15, 18, 19a, b, 20; 13:32). John was told to cast out {to leave out, to exclude} the outer court of the temple (Rev. 11:2). The verb is also transl.: to bring out, to put forth, to put out, to put outside, to send out, to send off, to thrust out, to turn out (Matt. 9:25; Mark 5:40; Luke 8:54 [in some mss.]; John 10:4; Acts 9:40; 16:37; Jas. 2:25). All other refs.: see entries in Lexicon at <1544>.

4 to cast out: *exō* [adv.: ἔξω <1854>] ***ballō*** [verb: βάλλω <906>]; **lit.: to throw outside ▶ To exclude >** Perfect love casts out {drives out} fear (1 John 4:18). Other refs. (*ballō*): see 1.

5 to cast down, to cast out: *kataballō* [verb: καταβάλλω <2598>]; **from *kata*: down, and *ballō*: see 1; lit.: to throw on the ground ▶ To be overcome, to throw to a lower level >** During great trials, Paul and Timothy were cast down {struck down}, but not destroyed (2 Cor. 4:9). John heard a voice announcing that Satan had been cast down {thrown down, hurled down} (Rev. 12:10; *ballō* in other mss.). Other ref.: Heb. 6:1; see LAY <2598>. ¶

6 to cast away, to cast off: *apotithēmi* [verb: ἀποτίθημι <659>]; **from *apo*: away from, and *tithēmi*: to put ▶ To remove, to renounce; also transl.: to lay aside, to put aside, to rid, to throw off >** Christians are to cast away {to lay aside, to put aside} the works of darkness (Rom. 13:12), every weight and sin (Heb. 12:1), all filthiness and abounding of wickedness (Jas. 1:21), all malice, deceit, hypocrisy, envy, slander (1 Pet. 2:1). All other refs.: LAY <659>, PUT <659>.

7 *rhipteō* [verb: ῥιπτέω <4495>] **▶ To throw away, to throw off >** This verb is used in regard to clothes (Acts 22:23 {to tear, to throw}). ¶

8 to cast, to cast down, to cast up, to cast out: *rhiptō* [verb: ῥίπτω <4496>] **▶ To throw; also transl.: to lay, to lay down, to drop >** This verb is used in regard to people being laid down at the feet of Jesus (Matt. 15:30), pieces of silver in the temple (Matt. 27:5), a possessed man thrown down (Luke 4:35), casting into the sea (Luke 17:2), ship's tackle (Acts 27:19), and anchors (Acts 27:29). All other refs.: SCATTER <4496>.

9 *aporriptō* [verb: ἀπορρίπτω <641>]; **from *apo*: from, and *rhiptō*: see 8 ▶ To throw oneself off (into the water); to throw off >** The centurion commanded those who could swim to cast themselves first into the sea {to jump overboard} (Acts 27:43). Other ref.: 1 Pet. 5:7 in some mss. ¶

10 ***epiriptō*** [verb: ἐπιρίπτω <1977>]; **from *epi*: upon, and *riptō*: see 8; also spelled: *epirriptō*** ▶ **To throw upon, to confide to** > People threw their own garments on the colt (Luke 19:35). The Christian is to cast all his care upon God, for God cares for him (1 Pet. 5:7; *aporriptō* in some mss.). ¶

11 ***katapherō*** [verb: καταφέρω <2702>]; **from *kata*: down, against, and *pherō*: to carry** ▶ **To direct at; also transl.: to bring against** > Many serious charges were brought against Paul (Acts 25:7; some mss.: *pherontes kata*). Before his conversion, Paul was casting {giving} his vote against the saints, i.e., he was agreeing when they were put to death (Acts 26:10). Other refs.: Acts 20:9a, b; see FALL (verb) <2702>. ¶

– **12** Matt. 4:12 → to cast in prison → BETRAY <3860> **13** Mark 11:7; 1 Cor. 7:35 → to cast on → PUT <1911> **14** Mark 14:51 → to cast about → WEAR <4016> **15** Luke 1:29 → REASON (verb) <1260> **16** Luke 4:29 → to cast down → to throw down → THROW (verb) <2630> **17** Luke 9:25 → to be cast away → FORFEIT <2210> **18** Luke 19:43 → to cast about → to build around → BUILD <4016> **19** Acts 1:26 → DRAW <1325> **20** Acts 7:19, 21 → to cast out → EXPOSED <1570> **21** Acts 12:8 → to cast about → to wrap around → WRAP <4016> **22** Acts 27:29 → to be cast on → to run aground → RUN <1601> **23** Acts 27:30 → to cast out → to carry out → CARRY <1614> **24** Rom. 11:1, 2 → to cast away → REJECT <683> **25** 2 Cor. 10:5 → to cast down → DESTROY <2507> **26** Eph. 4:19 → to cast off all feeling → FEELING <524> **27** 1 Tim. 5:12 → to cast off → REJECT <114> **28** 1 Pet. 2:4, 7 → to cast away → REJECT <593> **29** 2 Pet. 2:4 → to cast down to the deepest pit of gloom, to cast down to hell → HELL <5020> **30** Jude 13 → to cast up like foam → to foam up → FOAM (verb) <1890>.

CAST AWAY (BEING) – Rom. 11:15 → REJECTION <580>.

CAST DOWN – ***tapeinos*** [adj.: ταπεινός <5011>]; **from which *tapeinoō*: to make lower, to humble** ▶ **One who is brought low, of a low estate** > God encourages those who are cast down {the downcast, the depressed, those who are low} (2 Cor. 7:6). All other refs.: HUMBLE (adj.) <5011>, LOWLY <5011>.

CASTAWAY – 1 Cor. 9:27 → WORTHLESS <96>.

CASTING AWAY – Rom. 11:15 → REJECTION <580>.

CASTLE – Acts 21:34, 37; 22:24; 23:10, 16, 32 → FORTRESS <3925>.

CASTOR AND POLLUX – See TWIN BROTHERS <1324>.

CATCH (noun) – ***agra*** [fem. noun: ἄγρα <61>]; **poss. from *agros*: countryside (where fishing and hunting are practiced)** ▶ **The act of catching fish; also transl.: draught, haul** > Jesus told Simon to let down his nets for a catch (Luke 5:4). Astonishment had taken hold of Peter and the other disciples because of the catch of fish they had taken (Luke 5:9). ¶

CATCH (verb) – **1** ***agreuō*** [verb: ἀγρεύω <64>]; **from *agreus*: hunter, fisherman, which is from *agra*: catch, capture** ▶ **To hunt, to fish; figur.: to ensnare, to trap** > Certain Pharisees and Herodians attempted to catch Jesus in His words (Mark 12:13). ¶

2 **to catch away, to catch up: *harpazō*** [verb: ἁρπάζω <726>] ▶ **To seize, to take by force** > The Spirit of the Lord caught away {snatched away, took away} Philip (Acts 8:39). John saw a woman whose child was caught up {snatched up} to God (Rev. 12:5). All other refs.: PULL <726>, SEIZE <726>, TAKE <726>.

3 ***sunarpazō*** [verb: συναρπάζω <4884>]; **from *sun*: together (intens.), and *harpazō*: see 2** ▶ **To seize with violence, to take by great force** > An unclean spirit had caught {had seized} a Gadarene man (Luke 8:29). Stephen was caught {seized, dragged away}

and brought to the council (Acts 6:12). The Ephesians rushed into the theater, having caught {having seized, dragging along} Gaius and Aristarchus (Acts 19:29). Paul's ship was caught in a hurricane (Acts 27:15). ¶
4 ***epilambanō*** [verb: ἐπιλαμβάνω <1949>]; **from *epi*: upon (intens.), and *lambanō*: to take ▶ To seize, to take hold, to trap** > Spies pretended to be righteous men in order to catch Jesus in some statement (Luke 20:20), but they could not (v. 26). All other refs.: SEIZE <1949>, TAKE <1949>.
5 ***katalambanō*** [verb: καταλαμβάνω <2638>]; **from *kata*: intens., and *lambanō*: to take ▶ a. To apprehend, to seize** > The scribes and the Pharisees brought to Jesus a woman caught {taken} in adultery (John 8:3, 4). **b. To overtake, to surprise** > The Thessalonians were not in darkness, that the day of the Lord should overtake them as a thief (1 Thes. 5:4). All other refs.: see entries in Lexicon at <2638>.
6 ***prolambanō*** [verb: προλαμβάνω <4301>]; **from *pro*: before, and *lambanō*: to take ▶ To surprise in the act, to discover** > Even if someone had been caught {had been overtaken, had been taken} in any fault, the Galatians were to restore such a one in a spirit of gentleness (Gal. 6:1). All other refs.: COME <4301>, TAKE <4301>.
7 ***zōgreō*** [verb: ζωγρέω <2221>]; **from *zōos*: living, and *agreuō*: to catch ▶ To take alive, to capture** > Simon would catch (lit.: would be catching alive) men henceforth (Luke 5:10). Some, caught {taken, taken captive, held captive} by the snare of the devil, might come to their senses and, by repentance, do the will of Jesus (2 Tim. 2:26). ¶
8 ***sunkleiō*** [verb: συγκλείω <4788>]; **from *sun*: together, and *kleiō*: to shut up, to close ▶ To take, to capture together** > The disciples caught {enclosed} a great number of fish (Luke 5:6). Other refs.: Rom. 11:32; Gal. 3:22, 23; see SHUT <4788>. ¶
9 ***thēreuō*** [verb: θηρεύω <2340>]; **from *thēra*: hunt, prey, trap ▶ To ensnare, to lay hold** > Luke uses this verb regarding those who attempted to catch something out of the mouth of Jesus, that they might accuse Him (Luke 11:54). ¶
– 10 Matt. 13:47 → GATHER <4863> 11 Matt. 21:39; Mark 12:3; Luke 5:5; 2 Cor. 12:16 → TAKE <2983> 12 Luke 8:29 → SEIZE <4884> 13 John 21:3, 10 → TAKE <4084> 14 Acts 26:21 → TAKE <4815> 15 1 Cor. 3:19 → TAKE <1405> 16 2 Cor. 12:3 → "was caught up into paradise" added in Engl. 17 2 Pet. 2:12 → CAPTURE (noun) <259>.

CATTLE – 1 ***thremma*** [neut. noun: θρέμμα <2353>]; **from *trephō*: to feed ▶ Domestic animals raised on a farm** > The cattle {flocks and herds, livestock} of Jacob had drunk at the well of Sychar (John 4:12). ¶
2 ***ktēnos*** [neut. noun: κτῆνος <2934>]; **from *ktaomai*: to acquire, to possess ▶ Wealth in the form of herd and flock** > After the fall of Babylon, no one will buy cattle {beasts} (Rev. 18:13). All other refs.: BEAST <2934>.
– 3 Matt. 22:4 → fatted cattle, fattened cattle → FATLING <4619> 4 John 2:14, 15 → OX <1016>.

CAUDA – See CLAUDA <2802>.

CAUSE (noun) – 1 ***aitia*** [fem. noun: αἰτία <156>]; **from *aiteō*: to ask, or *aitios*: responsible ▶ Charge, motive; also transl.: reason** > The Pharisees were asking if it was lawful for a man to divorce his wife for any cause (Matt. 19:3). Peter asked the men sent by Cornelius what was the cause for which they had come (Acts 10:21). Those who dwell in Jerusalem found no cause {ground} for death in Jesus, but asked Pilate that He might be put to death (Acts 13:28). There was no cause {no crime, no ground, nothing worthy} to put Paul to death (Acts 28:18). All other refs.: ACCUSATION <156>, CASE <156>, FAULT <156>, REASON (noun) <156>.
2 ***krima*** [neut. noun: κρίμα <2917>]; **from *krinō*: to decide, to judge ▶ Judgment** > In Rev. 18:20, God has avenged {pronounced judgment, has judged} (lit.: judged the cause of) His own, i.e., He made them justice. All other refs.: FAULT <2917>, JUDGMENT <2917>, LAWSUIT <2917>.

[3] ***logos*** [masc. noun: λόγος <3056>] ► **Reason, motive** > Whoever divorces his wife for any cause except sexual immorality causes her to commit adultery (Matt. 5:32). Other refs.: WORD <3056>.

[4] ***ta*: fem. plur. of *ho*** [art.: ὁ <3588>] ► **Lit.: the (matters)** > Festus laid Paul's cause {matter, case} before the king (Acts 25:14).

[5] **without a cause: *dōrean*** [adv.: δωρεάν <1432>]; **from *dōrea*: gift** ► **Freely, without reason** > Jesus was hated without a cause (John 15:25). All other refs.: FREELY <1432>.

[6] **without cause, without a cause: *eikē*** [adv.: εἰκῇ <1500>] ► **Without reason, vainly** > Whoever is angry with his brother without cause {lightly} is in danger of the judgment (Matt. 5:22 in some mss.). All other refs.: see "in vain" under VAIN <1500>.

– [7] Luke 2:10 → lit.: to be [8] Luke 23:22; Acts 19:40 → REASON (noun) <158> [9] 1 Cor. 16:10 → without cause to be afraid → without fear → FEAR (noun) <870> [10] 2 Cor. 5:12 → OCCASION <874> [11] Phil. 1:26 → to have ample cause → ABOUND <4052>.

CAUSE (verb) – [1] ***parechō*** [verb: παρέχω <3930>]; **from *para*: next to, and *echō*: to have** ► **To occasion, to provoke** > Fables and genealogies cause {bring, give rise, minister, promote} questionings (1 Tim. 1:4). Other ref.: Luke 11:7; see TROUBLE (noun) <2873>. All other refs.: see entries in Lexicon at <3930>.

[2] ***poieō*** [verb: ποιέω <4160>] ► **To bring, to procure, to produce** > Relating the conversion of the Gentiles, Paul and Barnabas caused great joy to all the brothers {made them glad} (Acts 15:3). Paul urges Christians to consider those who cause {create} divisions and occasions of falling, and to avoid them (Rom. 16:17). The body causes {makes, works} for itself the increase of the body according to the working of each part (Eph. 4:16). Other refs.: see entries in Lexicon at <4160>.

– [3] Matt. 17:27 → to cause offense → OFFEND <4624> [4] Acts 24:12 → to cause a riot → to raise up → RAISE <1999> <4160> [5] 2 Cor. 4:15 → to cause to abound → ABOUND <4052> [6] 2 Cor. 9:11 → PRODUCE <2716> [7] Phil. 1:16 → STIR (verb) <2018>.

CAUTERISE – 1 Tim. 4:2 → to sear with a hot iron → IRON <2743>.

CAUTION (noun) – Mark 8:15 → COMMAND (verb) <1291>.

CAUTION (verb) – Acts 23:22 → COMMAND (verb) <3853>.

CAVALRY – Acts 23:32 → lit.: horsemen → HORSEMAN <2460>.

CAVE – [1] ***spēlaion*** [neut. noun: σπήλαιον <4693>] ► **Cavern, usually large and underground** > Jesus came to the tomb of Lazarus, which was in a cave (John 11:38). All other refs.: DEN <4693>.

– [2] Heb. 11:38 → in dens and caves → in caves and holes → HOLES <3692>.

CAVERN – Heb. 11:38 → HOLES <3692>.

CEASE – [1] ***dialeipō*** [verb: διαλείπω <1257>]; **from *dia*: through (intens.), between, and *leipō*: to leave; lit.: to leave an interval** ► **To interrupt, to stop** > A woman had not ceased kissing the feet of Jesus (Luke 7:45). ¶

[2] ***katargeō*** [verb: καταργέω <2673>]; **from *kata*: intens., and *argeō*: to be inactive, which is from *argos*: idle, useless, which is from *a*: neg., and *ergon*: work** ► **To suppress, to abolish, to do away** > If Paul still preached circumcision, then the scandal of the cross had ceased (Gal. 5:11). All other refs.: see entries in Lexicon at <2673>.

[3] ***pauō*** [verb: παύω <3973>] ► **To bring to an end; also transl.: to finish, to stop** > When He had ceased {left} speaking to the crowds, Jesus spoke to Simon (Luke 5:4). The wind and the raging of the water ceased {subsided} after Jesus rebuked them (Luke 8:24). When Jesus ceased praying, one of His disciples asked Him to teach them how to pray (Luke 11:1). The apostles did not cease {never stopped, kept right on} teaching and

announcing the good news that Jesus was the Christ (Acts 5:42). False witnesses were saying that Stephen did not cease to speak {was incessantly speaking, never stopped speaking} blasphemous words against the holy place and the law (Acts 6:13). Paul wanted Elymas to cease perverting the straight paths of the Lord (Acts 13:10). After the tumult had ceased {ended}, Paul called the disciples to himself (Acts 20:1). He had not ceased admonishing the Ephesians with tears (Acts 20:31). The Jews ceased {left off} beating Paul (Acts 21:32). Whether there are tongues, they will cease {will be stilled} (1 Cor. 13:8). Paul did not cease giving thanks for the Ephesians (Eph. 1:16), and asking for the Colossians that they might be filled with the knowledge of the will of God (Col. 1:9). Sacrifices would have ceased to be offered if they could have made perfect the worshippers (Heb. 10:2). Christ, having suffered in the flesh, is our example to see suffering as a way to cease from {be done with} sin (1 Pet. 4:1). Other ref.: 1 Pet. 3:10; see REFRAIN <3973>. ¶

4 **who cannot cease, who cease not: *akatapaustos*** [adj.: ἀκατάπαυστος <180>]; **from *a*: neg., and *katapauō*: to stop, to make to cease, which is from *kata*: intens., and *pauō*: see 3 ► Who never stops, who does not abstain** > Peter speaks of those who cease not from sin (2 Pet. 2:14); other mss. have *akatapastos*: insatiable. ¶

– 5 Matt. 14:32; Mark 4:39; 6:51 → FALL (verb) <2869> 6 Luke 8:44 → STOP <2476> 7 Acts 21:14 → to be silent → SILENT <2270> 8 Heb. 4:10 → REST (verb) <2664> 9 Rev. 4:8 → to have rest → rest → REST (verb) <372>.

CEASING (WITHOUT) – 1 ***adialeiptos*** [adj.: ἀδιάλειπτος <88>]; **from *a*: neg., and *dialeipō*: to cease, which is from *dia*: across, between, and *leipō*: to leave ► Without intermission, continually** > Paul was thanking God that he remembered Timothy in his prayers without ceasing {constantly} (2 Tim. 1:3). Other ref.: Rom. 9:2; see UNINTERRUPTED <88>. ¶

2 ***adialeiptōs*** [adv.: ἀδιαλείπτως <89>]; **from *adialeiptos*: see 1 ► Relentlessly, continually; also transl.: constantly, unceasingly** > Paul was making mention without ceasing of the Christians in Rome in his prayers (Rom. 1:9). He was remembering without ceasing the work of faith, the labor of love, and the enduring constancy of hope of the Thessalonians (1 Thes. 1:3); he was giving thanks to God without ceasing that they had received and accepted God's word (2:13); he was telling them to pray without ceasing (5:17). Other ref.: 1 Thes. 1:2 in some mss. ¶

– 3 Acts 12:5 → without ceasing → UNCEASING <1618>.

CEDRON – See KIDRON <2748>.

CELEBRATE – 1 Matt. 14:6 → KEEP (verb) <1096> 2 Luke 15:23, 24, 29, 32 → to be merry → MERRY <2165> 3 1 Cor. 5:8 → to celebrate the feast → FEAST (noun) <1858>.

CELEBRATION – 1 Acts 7:41 → to hold a celebration → REJOICE <2165> 2 Col. 2:16 → the word "celebration" is added in Engl. in the expr. "new moon celebration."

CELESTIAL – 1 1 Cor. 15:40a, b → HEAVENLY <2032> 2 Jude 8 → celestial being → DIGNITARY <1391>.

CELL – 1 Acts 12:7 → PRISON <3612> 2 Acts 16:40 → PRISON <5438>.

CELLAR – Luke 11:33 → secret; secret place → PLACE (noun) <2926>.

CENCHREA – ***Kenchreai*** [fem. name: Κεγχρεαί <2747>]: **millet ► Port near Corinth on the Aegean Sea; also spelled: Cenchreae** > Paul shaved his head there after making a vow during his second missionary journey (Acts 18:18). He commended Phoebe, a servant of the church of Cenchrea, to the Christians of Rome (Rom. 16:1). ¶

CENCHREAE – Acts 18:18; Rom. 16:1 → CENCHREA <2747>.

CENSER – [1] ***thumiatērion*** [neut. noun: θυμιατήριον <2369>]; **from *thumiaō*: to burn incense ▶ Article used for burning incense** > There was a golden censer {some transl.: altar of incense} in the holy place of the Israelites' tabernacle (Heb. 9:4). ¶
[2] ***libanōtos*** [masc. noun: λιβανωτός <3031>]; **from *libanos*: incense, frankincense ▶ Container to burn incense or frankincense** > An angel stood at the altar having a golden censer; he filled it from the fire of the altar and cast it on the earth (Rev. 8:3, 5). ¶

CENSUS – [1] ***apographē*** [fem. noun: ἀπογραφή <582>]; **from *apographō*: see [2] ▶ Enrollment of individuals in a public register, enumeration of persons and property; also transl.: registration, taxing** > A census first took place when Quirinius had the government of Syria (Luke 2:2). A census is also mentioned in the account of Acts 5:37. ¶
[2] **to make a census, to take a census: *apographō*** [verb: ἀπογράφω <583>]; **from *apo*: from, and *graphō*: to write ▶ To make the enumeration of property and persons during a census; also transl.: to register, to tax** > Joseph and Mary were obliged to travel to Bethlehem in order to be registered since a decree had gone out from Caesar Augustus, that a census be made of all the inhabited earth (Luke 2:1); others went also to be registered (Luke 2:3, 5). There Mary gave birth to Jesus, as Micah had prophesied (see Mic. 5:2). Other ref.: Heb. 12:23; see REGISTER <583>. ¶

CENT – [1] Matt. 5:26; Mark 12:42 → QUADRANS <2835> [2] Matt. 10:29; Luke 12:6 → PENNY <787> [3] Luke 12:59 → MITE <3016>.

CENTER – John 8:3; 19:18 → in the center → in the midst → MIDST <3319>.

CENTURION – [1] ***hekatontarchēs*** [masc. noun: ἑκατοντάρχης <1543>] **and *hekatontarchos*** [masc. noun: ἑκατόνταρχος <1543>]; **from *hekaton*: one hundred, and *archō*: to begin, to command, which is from *archē*: beginning ▶ Commanding officer of a Roman century, i.e., a troop of 50 to 100 soldiers; a regiment (or band) was made of six centuries** > Jesus healed the servant of a centurion (Matt. 8:5, 8, 13; Luke 7:2, 6). After the death of Jesus, a centurion said that He was truly the Son of God and a righteous Man (Matt. 27:54; Luke 23:47). Peter preached the gospel to Cornelius, a centurion of the band called Italic (Acts 10:1, 22). Paul and other prisoners were delivered to a centurion named Julius (Acts 27:1, 6, 11, 31, 43). Other refs.: Acts 21:32; 22:25, 26; 23:17, 23; 24:23. ¶
[2] ***kenturiōn*** [masc. noun: κεντυρίων <2760>]; **from the Lat. *centurio*, which is from *centum*: one hundred ▶ See defin. of [1].** > When he saw that Jesus had expired, a centurion said that this man was truly the Son of God (Mark 15:39, 44, 45). ¶

CEPHAS – ***Kēphas*** [masc. name: Κηφᾶς <2786>]: **rock, in Aram. ▶ Surname of the apostle Peter** > Jesus gave this name to Simon, son of John (or: Jonas) (John 1:42). Peter (*Petros*) is the Greek equivalent of the Aram. Cephas. See PETER <4074>. Other refs.: 1 Cor. 1:12; 3:22; 9:5; 15:5; Gal. 1:18; 2:9, 11, 14. ¶

CEREMONIAL – [1] John 2:6; 3:25 → ceremonial washing → PURIFICATION <2512> [2] John 11:55 → for their ceremonial cleansing → lit.: to purify themselves → PURIFY <48> [3] Heb. 6:2; 9:10 → ceremonial washing → BAPTISM <909>.

CEREMONIALLY – [1] Mark 7:4a → to ceremonially wash → WASH <907> [2] Acts 24:18 → to be ceremonially clean → to be purified → PURIFY <48>.

CEREMONY – Heb. 9:21 → SERVICE <3009>.

CERTAIN – [1] **a certain, a certain man: *tis*** [pron. or adj.: τὶς <5100>] **▶ Indef. pron. or adj. designating a person, a place, a thing which is or is not specified; also transl.: one, some, someone** > A certain young man followed Jesus (Mark 14:51). A certain man, Simon, a Cyrenian, was compelled to carry the cross of Jesus (Mark 15:21; Luke 23:26). The term "certain" is used in apposition to a priest (Luke 1:5), a centurion (Luke 7:2), a man who wanted to follow Jesus (Luke 9:57), a city (Luke 18:2), Lazarus (John 11:1), Simon a tanner (Acts 9:43; 10:6), Bar-Jesus (Acts 13:6), disciples in Ephesus (Acts 19:1), Demetrius (Acts 19:24), Mnason (Acts 21:16), Ananias (Acts 22:12), Tertullus (Acts 24:1), Jews from Asia (Acts 24:18), Paul (Acts 25:14), Jesus (Acts 25:19), persons teaching other doctrines (1 Tim. 1:3), and men who had crept in among the faithful (Jude 4). Jesus was praying in a certain place (Luke 11:1). The Athenians were saying that Paul was bringing certain strange things to their ears (Acts 17:20). Human ordinances result in a certain honor to the satisfaction of the flesh (Col. 2:23). There remains a certain fearful expectation of judgment if one sins willfully after having received the knowledge of the truth (Heb. 10:27). *

– 2 Acts 2:36 → for certain → ASSUREDLY <806> 3 Acts 12:11 → for certain → SURELY <230> 4 Acts 22:30; 25:26 → for certain, certain → CERTAINTY <804> 5 Rom. 4:16; 2 Pet. 1:10 → SURE <949> 6 1 Cor. 4:11 → to have no certain dwelling place → to be homeless → HOMELESS <790> 7 1 Tim. 6:7 → EVIDENT <1212> 8 2 Pet. 1:19 → FIRM <949>.

CERTAINLY – 1 ***ontōs*** [adv.: ὄντως <3689>]; **from *on*: pres. ptcp. of "to be" ▶ Truly, definitely** > The centurion said of Jesus that certainly {in very deed, surely} He was righteous (Luke 23:47). All other refs.: INDEED <3689>, REALLY <3689>, TRULY <3689>.

– 2 Matt. 14:33; John 17:8 → with certainty → TRULY <230> 3 Matt. 17:12 → will certainly → lit.: is about to occur (*mellō*) 4 Matt. 26:73; Mark 14:70; Acts 12:11 → SURELY <230> 5 Acts 28:4 → no doubt → DOUBT (adv.) <3843>.

CERTAINTY – 1 ***asphaleia*** [fem. noun: ἀσφάλεια <803>]; **from *asphalēs*: see** 2 **▶ Firmness, truthfulness** > Luke wanted Theophilus to know the certainty {exact truth} of the things in which he had been instructed (Luke 1:4). Other refs.: Acts 5:23; 1 Thes. 5:3; see SAFETY <803>. ¶

2 ***asphalēs*** [adj. used as noun: ἀσφαλής <804>]; **from *a*: neg., and *sphallō*: to fail ▶ Something sure, precise reason** > The chief captain could not know the certainty {truth, facts} of the uproar concerning Paul (Acts 21:34). The commander was desirous to know the certainty {for certain, exactly} why Paul was accused by the Jews (Acts 22:30). The word is transl. "certain" {definite} in Acts 25:26: Festus had nothing certain to write to the emperor concerning Paul. All other refs.: SAFE <804>, SURE <804>.

– 3 Acts 24:8 → to know the certainty → to take knowledge → KNOWLEDGE <1921>.

CERTIFICATE – 1 ***biblion*** [neut. noun: βιβλίον <975>]; **dimin. of *biblos*: book ▶ Letter, written document** > Moses had commanded to write a certificate {writing, bill} of divorce (Matt. 19:7; Mark 10:4). All other refs.: BOOK <975>.

– 2 Col. 2:14 → HANDWRITING <5498>.

CERTIFY – 1 John 3:33 → SEAL (verb) <4972> 2 Gal. 1:11 → KNOW <1107>.

CHAFF – ***achuron*** [neut. noun: ἄχυρον <892>] **▶ Hay, stubble** > Chaff is the husk of cereal grain, e.g., from the wheat (Matt. 3:12; Luke 3:17), separated by threshing or winnowing. ¶

CHAIN (noun) – 1 ***halusis*** [fem. noun: ἅλυσις <254>]; **poss. from *a*: neg. and *luō*: to loose ▶ Succession of interlinked metal rings; chains were used to bind prisoners** > No one was able to bind with chains a man possessed by an unclean spirit; but every time he was bound, the chains had been pulled apart (Mark 5:3, 4a, b; Luke 8:29). Peter was sleeping in prison, bound with two chains; an angel woke him and the chains fell off from his hands (Acts 12:6, 7). The chiliarch commanded that Paul be bound with two

chains (Acts 21:33). Paul was bound with a chain on account of the hope of Israel (Acts 28:20). He said to the Ephesians that he was an ambassador in chains {in bonds} (Eph. 6:20). Onesiphorus had not been ashamed of Paul's chain (2 Tim. 1:16). John saw an angel with a great chain in his hand to bind the dragon (Rev. 20:1). ¶
[2] ***desmos*** [masc. noun: δεσμός <1199>]; **from *deō*: to bind ▶ That which restrains, tie; also transl.: band, bond, imprisonment** > The band {impediment, string} of a deaf man's tongue was loosed after Jesus healed him (Mark 7:35). A possessed man broke his chains {fetters} (Luke 8:29). Jesus loosed a woman with a spirit of infirmity from her bond {what bound her} on the Sabbath day (Luke 13:16). The chains of all the prisoners were loosened (Acts 16:26). Chains {Prison} and tribulations awaited Paul (Acts 20:23). Paul deserved neither death nor chains {imprisonment} (Acts 23:29; 26:31); nevertheless, he was put in chains (Acts 26:29). In Paul's chains, the Philippians had all been participants in his grace (Phil. 1:7). It became manifest that Paul's chains were in Christ (Phil. 1:13), and most of the brothers, trusting in the Lord through his chains, dared more abundantly to speak the word of God fearlessly (v. 14), but some thought they could add tribulation for his chains (v. 16 or v. 17). Paul asks the Colossians to remember his chains (Col. 4:18). He was suffering as an evil doer, even to chains {the point of being chained} (2 Tim. 2:9). He had begotten Onesimus while in his chains (Phm. 10); he would have been desirous that Onesimus minister to him in his chains for the gospel (v. 13). O.T. people of faith had trial of chains (Heb. 11:36). God has reserved in eternal chains the angels who abandoned their own dwelling (Jude 6). Other refs.: Acts 22:30 and Heb. 10:34 in some mss. ¶
[3] ***seira*** [fem. noun: σειρά <4577>]; **from *eirō*: to bind ▶ Bond, tie** > The angels who have sinned have been delivered to chains {pits: *siros* in some mss.} of darkness, to be kept for judgment (2 Pet. 2:4). ¶
– [4] Acts 22:5, 29; Col. 4:3 → in chains → BIND <1210>.

CHAIN (verb) – [1] ***deō*** [verb: δέω <1210>]; **lit.: to tie, to bind ▶ To detain, to keep in custody** > Barabbas was chained {was bound, was imprisoned, was in prison} with those who had made an insurrection with him (Mark 15:7). All other refs.: BIND <1210>.
– [2] 2 Tim. 2:9 → to the point of being chained → lit.: even unto chains → CHAIN (noun) <1199> [3] Heb. 13:3 → to bind with → BIND <4887>.

CHAINED – 2 Tim. 2:9 → BIND <1210>.

CHAIR – Matt. 23:2 → SEAT (noun) <2515>.

CHALCEDONY – ***chalkēdōn*** [masc. noun: χαλκηδών <5472>] ▶ **Precious stone found near an ancient city of the same name in Asia Minor, agate** > It is of a milky color, sometimes tinted blue or gray. The third foundation of the wall of the heavenly Jerusalem is adorned with chalcedony (Rev. 21:19). ¶

CHALDEAN – ***Chaldaios*** [masc. name: Χαλδαῖος <5466>] ▶ **Inhabitant of Chaldea or Babylonia, lands of Western Asia** > The land of the Chaldeans faces south toward the Persian Gulf. God had told Abraham to go out from the land of the Chaldeans; he stayed in Haran until the death of his father (Acts 7:4). The Chaldeans were known for their discoveries in astronomy and their astrological practices. ¶

CHALLENGE – [1] John 8:13; 18:26 → lit.: to say (*legō*) [2] Gal. 5:26 → PROVOKE <4292>.

CHAMBER – [1] Matt. 6:6; 24:26; Luke 12:3 → chamber, inner chamber, secret chamber → room, inner room → ROOM <5009> [2] Mark 14:14; Luke 22:11 → guest chamber → GUEST ROOM <2646> [3] Acts 1:13; 9:37, 39; 20:8 → upper chamber → upper room → ROOM <5253>.

CHAMBERING – Rom. 13:13 → LEWDNESS <766>.

CHAMBERLAIN – [1] ***oikonomos*** [masc. noun: οἰκονόμος <3623>]; **from *oikos*: house, and *nemō*: to distribute, to manage ▶ Administrator, manager** > Erastus was the chamberlain {treasurer, steward, director of public works} of a city (Rom. 16:23). All other refs.: STEWARD <3623>.

[2] ***ho epi tou koitōnos*; bedroom: *koitōn*** [masc. noun: κοιτών <2846>]; **from *koitē*: bed; lit.: one who is over the bedroom ▶ Person responsible for the room of the sovereign** > Blastus was the chamberlain {personal aide, personal servant} of King Herod Agrippa (Acts 12:20). ¶

CHANCE (noun) – [1] ***sunkuria*** [fem. noun: συγκυρία <4795>]; **from *sunkureō*: to happen together, which is from *sun*: together, and *kureō*: to meet ▶ Fortuitous, accidental meeting; by chance (*kata sunkurian*): fortuitously** > In a parable, a certain priest was coming down the road by chance {happened to go down that way} where a wounded man was lying (Luke 10:31); similar terms: *suntukia*, *tuchē* in some mss. ¶

– [2] Mark 6:31 → to have a chance → to have time → TIME <2119> [3] Acts 27:12 → on the chance → SOMEHOW <4458> [4] Heb. 12:17 → chance to repent → place for repentance → PLACE (noun) <5117>.

CHANCE (verb) – 1 Cor. 15:37 → to happen → PERHAPS <5177>.

CHANGE (noun) – [1] ***metathesis*** [fem. noun: μετάθεσις <3331>]; **from *metatithēmi*: to transfer, which is from *meta*: prep. indicating change, and *tithēmi*: to put ▶ Transfer, move** > When the priesthood is changed, there is a change of law also (Heb. 7:12). Other refs.: Heb. 11:5; 12:27; see TRANSLATION <3331>, REMOVING <3331>. ¶

– [2] John 2:15 → MONEY <2772> [3] Heb. 7:12 → CHANGE (verb) <3346> [4] Heb. 12:17 → change of mind → REPENTANCE <3341> [5] Jas. 1:17 → VARIATION <3883>.

CHANGE (verb) – [1] ***allassō*** [verb: ἀλλάσσω <236>]; **from *allos*: other ▶ To modify, to alter** > According to false witnesses, Stephen had said that Jesus would change the customs taught by Moses (Acts 6:14). Some men have changed {exchanged} the glory of the incorruptible God into the likeness of an image of corruptible man and beasts (Rom. 1:23). The Christians will all be changed at the coming of the Lord (1 Cor. 15:51), the living ones in particular (v. 52). Paul would have wished to change his tone with the Galatians (Gal. 4:20). The heavens will be changed (Heb. 1:12). ¶

[2] ***metallassō*** [verb: μεταλλάσσω <3337>]; **from *meta*: prep. indicating change, and *allassō*: see [1]; also transl.: to exchange ▶ To transform** > Some men have changed the truth of God into falsehood (Rom. 1:25); their women have changed the natural use {function, sexual relations} into that contrary to nature (v. 26). ¶

[3] ***metatithēmi*** [verb: μετατίθημι <3346>]; **from *meta*: prep. indicating a change, and *tithēmi*: to put ▶ To turn aside, to transform** > Paul wondered that the Galatians had changed so quickly to a different gospel (Gal. 1:6); also transl.: to be removed, to turn away, to desert, to desert and to turn. There is of necessity a change of law with the priesthood being changed {when there is a change of the priesthood} (Heb. 7:12). All other refs.: CARRY <3346>, TAKE <3346>, TURN (verb) <3346>.

– [4] Matt. 18:3 → CONVERT (verb) <4762> [5] Matt. 21:32 → to change one's mind → REPENT <3338> [6] Matt. 27:3 → to change one's mind → to be filled with remorse → REMORSE <3338> [7] Acts 2:20; Jas. 4:9 → TURN (verb) <3344> [8] Acts 28:13 → the wind having changed to south → lit.: the south wind having blown → BLOW (verb) <1920> [9] 2 Cor. 3:18 → TRANSFIGURE <3339> [10] Phil. 3:21 → TRANSFORM <3345> [11] Jas. 3:3, 4 → TURN (verb) <3329>.

CHANGER – [1] Matt. 21:12; Mark 11:15; John 2:15 → MONEY CHANGER <2855> [2] John 2:14 → MONEY CHANGER <2773>.

CHARACTER – 1 John 8:44 → out of his own character → lit.: out of his own 2 Acts 17:11 → of noble character → lit.: noble → NOBLE <2104> 3 Rom. 5:4a, b; 2 Cor. 9:13 → character, proven character → EXPERIENCE (noun) <1382> 4 1 Cor. 15:33 → HABIT <2239> 5 Phil. 2:22 → proven character → TEST (noun and verb) <1382> <1381> 6 Heb. 13:5 → CONDUCT (noun) <5158>.

CHARCOAL – John 18:18; 21:9 → charcoal fire → fire of coals → COAL <439>.

CHARGE (noun)[1] – 1 ***aitiōma*** [neut. noun: αἰτίωμα <159a>] **or *aitiama*** [neut. noun: αἰτίαμα <157>] ► **Grievance, accusation** > The Jews brought many and grievous charges {complaints} against Paul (Acts 25:7). ¶
2 ***enklēma*** [neut. noun: ἔγκλημα <1462>]**; from *enkaleō*: to accuse, which is from *en*: in, and *kaleō*: to call, to institute proceedings ► Indictment, accusation** > Paul had no charge laid {had no accusation, had nothing charged} against him deserving death or bonds (Acts 23:29). The custom of the Romans was to give the accused the opportunity of defense regarding the charge {crime} (Acts 25:16). Other ref.: Acts 23:25 in some mss. ¶
3 **to bring charges, to present charges: *emphanizō*** [verb: ἐμφανίζω <1718>]**; from *emphanēs*: manifest, known, which is from *en*: in, and *phainō*: to shine, to become evident, which is from *phōs*: light ► To make known, to declare** > Several people brought their charges {gave evidence, laid their information, informed} against Paul to the governor (Acts 24:1; 25:2, 15). All other refs.: APPEAR <1718>, MANIFEST (verb) <1718>, PLAINLY <1718>, REVEAL <1718>, SIGNIFY <1718>.
– 4 Matt. 12:10; Luke 23:14; Acts 24:2, 8, 13, 19; 25:5, 11; 28:19 → to bring, to make, to press charges → ACCUSE <2723> 5 Matt. 27:37; Mark 15:26; Acts 25:18, 27 → lit.: written charge, written accusation → ACCUSATION <156> 6 Mark 3:21 → to take charge → SEIZE <2902> 7 Luke 16:1 → to bring a charge → ACCUSE <1225> 8 Luke 23:4, 14 → basis for a charge → FAULT <158> 9 John 18:29; 1 Tim. 5:19; Titus 1:6 → ACCUSATION <2724> 10 John 18:38; 19:4, 6 → basis for a charge → FAULT <156> 11 Acts 7:60 → to lay to the charge → CHARGE (verb) <2476> 12 Acts 19:38 → to bring, to press charges against → ACCUSE <1458> 13 Acts 23:28 → REASON (noun) <156> 14 Acts 25:2 → to present charges → BESEECH <3870> 15 Acts 25:16 → CRIME <1462> 16 Rom. 3:9 → to make the charge already → to prove before → PROVE <4256> 17 Rom. 8:33 → to bring a charge, to lay anything to the charge → to bring an accusation → ACCUSATION <1458> 18 2 Thes. 3:8 → free of charge, without charge → FREELY <1432> 19 1 Tim. 3:10; Titus 1:6, 7 → without charge, free from all charge → BLAMELESS <410> 20 2 Tim. 4:16 → to lay to the charge → IMPUTE <3049> 21 Rev. 14:18 → AUTHORITY <1849>.

CHARGE (noun)[2] – 1 ***parangelia*** [fem. noun: παραγγελία <3852>]**; from *parangellō*: to command, which is from *para*: near, and *angellō*: to announce ► Commandment, prescription** > The council had strictly (lit.: by a charge) enjoined the apostles not to teach in the name of Jesus (Acts 5:28). The jailer had received a charge {command, order} to keep Paul and Silas safely (Acts 16:24). Love is the goal of the charge {what is enjoined, the commandment, the instruction} (1 Tim. 1:5). Paul committed a charge {command} to Timothy (1 Tim. 1:18). Other ref.: 1 Thes. 4:2; see COMMANDMENT <3852>. ¶
2 **to give charge: *entellomai*** [verb: ἐντέλλομαι <1781>]**; from *en*: in, and *tellō*: to accomplish ► To enjoin, to command** > God would give charge to His angels concerning Jesus (Matt. 4:6; Luke 4:10). Jesus, by the Holy Spirit, gave charge to {charged, gave commandment to, gave instructions to, gave orders to} His apostles (Acts 1:2). Joseph gave charge {gave commandment, gave instructions, gave orders} concerning his bones (Heb. 11:22). All other refs.: COMMAND (verb) <1781>.

– 3 Matt. 18:16; 2 Cor. 13:1 → WORD <4487> 4 Luke 19:17 → to take charge → to be in authority → AUTHORITY <1849> 5 John 8:6 → "some charge" added in Engl. 6 John 10:18 → COMMANDMENT <1785> 7 Acts 6:3 → to put in charge → APPOINT <2525> 8 Acts 24:9 → to join in the charge → JOIN <4934> 9 1 Cor. 7:10 → to give a charge → COMMAND (verb) <3853> 10 Col. 2:14 → HANDWRITING <5498> 11 1 Tim. 6:13 → to give charge → ENJOIN <3853> 12 2 Tim. 4:1 → to give charge → CHARGE (verb) <1263>.

CHARGE (noun)[3] – 1 John 12:6 → to have charge of → HAVE <2192> 2 Acts 21:24 → to be at charge → to pay the expenses → EXPENSE <1159> 3 1 Cor. 9:7 → EXPENSE <3800> 4 1 Cor. 9:18 → without charge, free of charge → COSTLESS <77> 5 2 Cor. 12:13, 14 → to be in laziness a charge → to be burdensome → BURDENSOME <2655> 6 1 Thes. 2:6 → BURDEN (noun) <922>.

CHARGE (verb) – 1 **to charge, to charge solemnly: *diamarturomai*** [verb: διαμαρτύρομαι <1263>]; **from *dia*: through (intens.), and *marturomai*: to attest, to witness, which is from *martus*: witness ▶ To adjure, to warn, to admonish; also transl.: to testify, to give charge** > Paul charged Timothy to keep his instructions without prejudice (1 Tim. 5:21). He charged him before God to preach the word (2 Tim. 4:1). He charged solemnly {testified earnestly, warned} before the Lord that there should not be disputes of words (2 Tim. 2:14). All other refs.: TESTIFY <1263>.

2 **to earnestly charge: *epitimaō*** [verb: ἐπιτιμάω <2008>]; **from *epi*: against, and *timaō*: to evaluate, which is from *timē*: honor, price ▶ To threaten, to reprimand** > Jesus earnestly charged {straitly charged, warned, strictly warned} His disciples, commanding them to say to no one He was the Christ of God (Luke 9:21). All other refs.: REBUKE (verb) <2008>, WARN <2008>.

3 ***histēmi*** [verb: ἵστημι <2476>] ▶ **To hold against** > Stephen cried out to the Lord not to charge those who stoned him with this sin (Acts 7:60 {to lay to the charge}). Other refs.: see entries in Lexicon at <2476>.

– 4 Matt. 10:5; Mark 6:8; Luke 5:14; 8:56; Acts 4:18; 5:28, 40; 16:23; 23:22 → COMMAND (verb) <3853> 5 Matt. 16:20; Mark 5:43; 7:36a, b; 8:15; 9:9 → COMMAND (verb) <1291> 6 Matt. 17:9; Mark 13:34 → to charge, to give charge → COMMAND (verb) <1781> 7 Matt. 24:45, 47; 25:21, 23; Luke 12:42, 44 → to put in charge → to make, to make ruler → MAKE <2525> 8 Mark 9:25 → COMMAND (verb) <2004> 9 Luke 11:50, 51 → REQUIRE <1567> 10 Acts 1:2 → to give charge → CHARGE (noun)[2] <1781> 11 Acts 19:40 → to call in question → CALL (verb) <1458> 12 Acts 23:29 → CHARGE (noun)[1] <1462> 13 Acts 25:18 → to bring an accusation → ACCUSATION <156> 14 Rom. 3:8 → to injuriously charge → to report slanderously → REPORT (verb) <987> 15 Rom. 3:9 → PROVE <4256> 16 1 Thes. 4:11; 1 Tim. 1:3; 6:17 → ENJOIN <3853> 17 1 Thes. 5:27 → ADJURE <3726> 18 1 Tim. 5:16 → to be charged → BURDEN (verb) <916> 19 2 Tim. 4:16 → IMPUTE <3049> 20 Phm. 18 → to charge the account → IMPUTE <1677>.

CHARGEABLE – 1 Thes. 2:9; 2 Thes. 3:8 → to be chargeable → to be a burden → BURDEN (noun) <1912>.

CHARGER – Matt. 14:8, 11; Mark 6:25, 28 → DISH <4094>.

CHARGES – Acts 25:15 → JUDGMENT <1349>.

CHARIOT – 1 ***harma*** [neut. noun: ἅρμα <716>]; **same radical as *ararisko*: to be adapted, to be equipped ▶ Two-wheeled cart drawn by a horse** > An Ethiopian, who was over all the treasure of Queen Candace, was sitting in his chariot and reading the prophet Isaiah (Acts 8:28); the Spirit said to Philip to approach and join this chariot

(v. 29); the Ethiopian commanded the chariot to stop so that Philip might baptize him (v. 38). The sound of the wings of the locusts was as the sound of chariots of many horses running to war (Rev. 9:9). ¶

[2] ***rhedē*** [fem. noun: ῥέδη <4480>]; **from the Lat. *rheda*: cart for travelling ▶ Carriage with four wheels used to travel** > Babylon was buying chariots {carriages} (Rev. 18:13). ¶

CHARITABLE – [1] Matt. 6:1 → charitable deeds → ALMS <1343> [2] Matt. 6:2–4; Acts 9:36 → charitable deeds → ALMS <1654>.

CHARITY – [1] See LOVE (noun) <26>. – [2] Luke 11:41; 12:33; Acts 9:36 → ALMS <1654> [3] Jude 12 → feasts of charity → LOVE FEASTS <26>.

CHARRAN – See HARRAN <5488>.

CHASM – ***chasma*** [neut. noun: χάσμα <5490>]; **from *chainō*: to open the mouth wide ▶ Abyss, gulf** > A great chasm is firmly established between believers and unbelievers after death (Luke 16:26). ¶

CHASTE – ***hagnos*** [adj.: ἁγνός <53>]; **same radical as *hagos*: respect of God, religious fear ▶ Pure, beyond reproach** > Paul tells the Corinthians that he had espoused them to one husband, that he may present them a chaste virgin to Christ (2 Cor. 11:2). Unbelieving husbands witness the chaste {pure} conduct of their wives (1 Pet. 3:2). Other refs.: 2 Cor. 7:11; Phil. 4:8; 1 Tim. 5:22; Titus 2:5; Jas. 3:17; 1 John 3:3; see PURE <53>. ¶

CHASTEN – [1] ***paideuō*** [verb: παιδεύω <3811>]; **from *pais*: child; lit.: to raise, to educate a child ▶ To correct, to chastise; also transl.: to discipline** > When the Christians are judged, they are chastened by the Lord (1 Cor. 11:32). Paul was as chastened {beaten, punished}, but not killed (2 Cor. 6:9). Whom the Lord loves, He chastens (Heb. 12:6). Fathers chasten their sons as seems good to them (Heb. 12:7, 10), but God does it for their profit so that they may partake of His holiness (see v. 10). The Lord rebukes and chastens as many as He loves (Rev. 3:19). The verb is transl. "to chastise" {to punish} in Luke 23:16, 22. All other refs.: CORRECT <3811>, EDUCATE <3811>, LEARN <3811>, TEACH <3811>.

– [2] Heb. 12:6 → SCOURGE (verb) <3146>.

CHASTENING – Heb. 12:5, 7, 8, 11 → TRAINING <3809>.

CHASTISE – [1] Luke 23:16, 22 → CHASTEN <3811> [2] Heb. 12:6 → SCOURGE (verb) <3146>.

CHATTER – 1 Tim. 6:20; 2 Tim. 2:16 → empty chatter, godless chatter → idle babbling → BABBLING <2757>.

CHATTERER – Acts 17:18 → BABBLER <4691>.

CHEAPER – John 2:10 → LESSER <1640>.

CHEAT – [1] ***pleonekteō*** [verb: πλεονεκτέω <4122>]; **from *pleion*: more, and *echō*: to have ▶ To become rich at the expense of another, to exploit** > Paul had cheated {defrauded, had taken advantage of, made gain of} no one (2 Cor. 7:2). The verb is transl. "to take advantage" {to make a gain} in 2 Cor. 12:17, 18. All other refs.: ADVANTAGE (noun) <4122>, WRONG (verb) <4122>.

– [2] Luke 19:8 → to accuse falsely → ACCUSE <4811> [3] 1 Cor. 6:7, 8 → DEFRAUD <650> [4] Col. 2:8 → to lead away as a prey → PREY <4812>.

CHECK – Jas. 3:2 → to keep in check → BRIDLE (verb) <5468>.

CHEEK – ***siagōn*** [fem. noun: σιαγών <4600>] ▶ **Side of the face between the temple and the chin** > If someone strikes us on one cheek, we must offer the other also (Matt. 5:39; Luke 6:29). ¶

CHEER – [1] Matt. 9:2, 22; 14:27; Mark 6:50; 10:49; Luke 8:48; John 16:33; Acts 23:11 → to be of good cheer → to take courage → COURAGE <2293> [2] Luke 16:19 → to make good cheer → to be merry → MERRY <2165> [3] Acts 27:22, 25 → to take heart → HEART <2114> [4] Acts 27:36 → lit.: to become courageous → ENCOURAGE <2115>.

CHEER UP – Mark 10:49 → to take courage → COURAGE <2293>.

CHEERED (BE) – Phil. 2:19 → to be encouraged → ENCOURAGE <2174>.

CHEERFUL – [1] ***hilaros*** [adj.: ἱλαρός <2431>]; **from *hilaskomai*: to appease, to propitiate, which is from *hilaos*: appeased, favorable ▶ Joyous, quick to act** > God loves a cheerful giver (2 Cor. 9:7). ¶
– [2] Jas. 5:13 → to be cheerful → to be happy → HAPPY <2114>.

CHEERFULLY – [1] **cheerfully, more cheerfully: *euthumōs*** [adv.: εὐθύμως <2115a>]; **from *eu*: well, and *thumos*: spirit, soul, feeling ▶ With gladness, with confidence** > Paul was cheerfully {gladly, readily} answering for himself (Acts 24:10; in other mss.: *euthumotheron*, compar. adj. used as an adv., more cheerfully), i.e., he was giving his apology with (more) confidence. Other ref.: Acts 27:36 (adj.: *euthumos*); see ENCOURAGE <2115>. ¶
– [2] Rom. 12:8 → lit.: with cheerfulness → CHEERFULNESS <2432>.

CHEERFULNESS – ***hilarotēs*** [fem. noun: ἱλαρότης <2432>]; **from *hilaros*: cheerful, which is from *hilaskomai*: to appease, to propitiate, which is from *hilaos*: appeased, favorable ▶ Enthusiasm, gaiety** > He who shows mercy is to do so with cheerfulness {cheerfully} (Rom. 12:8). ¶

CHERISH – [1] ***thalpō*** [verb: θάλπω <2282>] **▶ To surround with attention, to take care tenderly** > Every one cherishes {cares for} his own flesh, just as Christ does the church (Eph. 5:29). Paul had been gentle in the midst of the Thessalonians, as a nurse would cherish {take care of, tenderly care for} her own children (1 Thes. 2:7). ¶
– [2] Acts 24:15 → RECEIVE <4327>.

CHERUBIM – ***cheroubim*** [neut. noun plur.: χερουβίμ <5502>]; **transliteration of the Heb.; also written: *cheroubin, cheroubein, cheroubeim* ▶ Angels overseeing the administration of divine justice and judgment (e.g., Gen. 3:24; Ps. 80:1)** > The cherubim are mentioned only once in the N.T. (Heb. 9:5) in relation to the mercy seat: they were made of gold, were stretching out their wings above, covering the mercy seat with them, and their faces were turned toward the mercy seat (see Ex. 25:18–20). Comp.: SERAPHIM. ¶

CHEST – [1] Rev. 1:13 → BREAST <3149> [2] Rev. 15:6 → BREAST <4738>.

CHICK – [1] Matt. 23:37 → CHICKEN <3556> [2] Luke 13:34 → chicks → BROOD <3555>.

CHICKEN – ***nossion*** [neut. noun: νοσσίον <3556>]; **dimin. of *neossos*: young ▶ Bird, nestling** > Jesus would have gathered the children of Jerusalem as a hen gathers her chickens {brood} under her wings (Matt. 23:37). ¶

CHIDE – 1 Cor. 4:14 → SHAME (verb) <1788>.

CHIEF – [1] ***prōtos*** [adj.: πρῶτος <4413>]; **superl. of *pro*: before ▶ First in rank, leading; also transl.: chief man, leading man, leader** > The word is used in the following exprs.: the chief men of Galilee (Mark 6:21), the chief of the people (Luke 19:47), the chief men of the city (Acts 13:50), and the chief of the Jews (Acts 25:2; 28:17). All other refs.: BEST <4413>, FIRST <4413>, PROMINENT <4413>.
[2] **to be the chief: *hēgeomai*** [verb: ἡγέομαι <2233>] **▶ To take the lead** > Paul was called the "chief speaker" because he took the lead in Acts 14:12. All other refs.: see entries in Lexicon at <2233>.

– [3] Matt. 21:42; Mark 12:10; Luke 20:17; Acts 4:11; 1 Pet. 2:7 → chief corner stone → CORNER STONE <2776> <1137> [4] Luke 11:15 → PRINCE <758> [5] Luke 14:1 → RULER <758> [6] Luke 19:2 → chief among the publicans, chief tax collector → PUBLICAN <754> [7] Acts 18:8, 17 → chief ruler of the synagogue → SYNAGOGUE <752> [8] Acts 21:31–33, 37; 22:24, 26–29; 23:10, 15, 17–19, 22; 24:7, 22; 25:23; Rev. 6:15 → chief captain → CAPTAIN <5506> [9] Eph. 2:20; 1 Pet. 2:6 → corner stone, chief corner stone → CORNER STONE <3037> <204> [10] 1 Pet. 5:4 → chief shepherd → SHEPHERD (noun) <750>.

CHIEF CORNERSTONE – [1] ***akrogōniaios*** [adj.: ἀκρογωνιαῖος <204>]; **from *akros*: highest, and *gōnia*: angle ► The chief cornerstone formed the exterior angle at the meeting of two walls; it held them together and sustained them; also transl.: cornerstone** > The chief cornerstone is an image of Christ; He unites the Gentiles and the Jews (Eph. 2:20) for a dwelling of God in the Spirit (see v. 22). The chief cornerstone is also laid in Zion (1 Pet. 2:6; see Is. 28:16) in view of the future edification of the house of Israel. ¶

[2] **chief: *kephalē*** [fem. noun: κεφαλή <2776>]**; corner (stone): *gōnia*** [fem. noun: γωνία <1137>]**; lit.: head of the corner ► Every stone having this function, whether situated at the base or at the peak, was a cornerstone** > As in [1], the chief cornerstone {head of the corner, very corner stone, capstone} refers to the Lord Jesus who, although rejected, is the foundation upon which the church is built (Matt. 21:42; Mark 12:10; Luke 20:17; 1 Pet. 2:7). The Lord Jesus is the chief cornerstone {very corner stone, capstone}, i.e., the One through whom we must be saved (Acts 4:11). All other refs. (*kephalē*): see CORNER STONE <2776>, HEAD (noun) <2776>. All other refs. (*gōnia*): see CORNER <1137>, CORNER STONE <1137>.

CHIEFEST – 2 Cor. 11:5; 12:11 → the very chiefest → in surpassing degree → SURPASSING <5244a> <3029>.

CHIEFLY – [1] Rom. 3:2 → FIRST <4412> [2] Phil. 4:22; 2 Pet. 2:10 → ESPECIALLY <3122>.

CHILD – [1] ***nēpios*** [adj. and adj. used as noun: νήπιος <3516>]; **from *nē*: not, and *epos*: word; lit.: one who cannot talk ► Baby, infant, one at an early stage of life (male or female), a minor** > As long as the heir is a child, he does not differ from a servant (Gal. 4:1). When we were children, we were held in bondage under the principles of the world (v. 3). Paul and his companions had been like young children among the Thessalonians (1 Thes. 2:7 in some mss.). All other refs.: BABE <3516>.

[2] **to be children: *nēpiazō*** [verb: νηπιάζω <3515>]; **from *nēpios*: see [1] ► To react as a baby, an infant; also transl.: to be a babe, to be an infant** > In malice, Christians should be children (1 Cor. 14:20), i.e., incapable of thinking and speaking maliciously. ¶

[3] ***pais*** [masc. or fem. noun: παῖς <3816>] ► **Boy or girl** > Herod put to death all the male children who were in Bethlehem from two years old and under (Matt. 2:16). The children were crying in the temple (Matt. 21:15). The child Jesus remained behind in Jerusalem (Luke 2:43). Jesus healed a child possessed by an unclean spirit (Luke 9:42). All other refs.: BOY <3816>, DAUGHTER <3816>, SERVANT <3816>, SON <3816>.

[4] **child, little child, young child: *paidion*** [neut. noun: παιδίον <3813>]; **dimin. of *pais*: see [3] ► Young child, boy or girl** > The expr. "young child" and the word "child" are used concerning Jesus (Matt. 2:8, 9, 11, 13a, b, 14, 20a, b, 21; Luke 1:59, 76; 2:17, 27). Jesus called little children and let them come to Him (Matt. 18:2; 19:13, 14; Mark 9:36; 10:13, 14; Luke 9:47; 18:16). Unless people are converted and become as little children, they will not enter the kingdom of heaven (Matt. 18:3); whoever humbles himself as a little child is the greatest in that kingdom (v. 4). Whoever receives a little child in the name of Jesus receives Him (Matt. 18:5; Mark 9:37; Luke 9:48). One must receive the kingdom of God as a little child to enter it (Mark 10:15; Luke 18:17). Jesus compared His generation to children

sitting in the marketplace (Luke 7:32). John was writing to little children because they had known the Father (1 John 2:13; v. 14 in some mss.); he tells them it is the last hour (v. 18). Other refs.: Matt. 14:21; 15:38; Mark 5:39, 40a, b, 41; 7:28; 9:24; Luke 1:66, 80; 2:40; 11:7; John 4:49; 16:21; 21:5; Heb. 2:13, 14; 11:23. ¶

[5] ***paidarion*** [neut. noun: παιδάριον <3808>]; **dimin. of *pais*: see [3] ► Young child** > Jesus compared His generation to children sitting in the marketplaces (Matt. 11:16). Other ref.: John 6:9; see BOY <3808>. ¶

[6] ***teknon*** [neut. noun: τέκνον <5043>]; **from *tiktō*: to give birth, to beget ► One who is begotten by another person; the word puts the emphasis on the birth; also transl.: son** > Christians are children of God (John 1:12; 11:52; Rom. 8:16, 21; 9:8b; Phil. 2:15; 1 John 3:1, 2, 10a; 5:2) and children of the promise (Rom. 9:8c). Those who are the children of the flesh are not the children of God (Rom. 9:8a). Elders must have faithful children (Titus 1:6). John makes a contrast between the children of the devil (1 John 3:10b) and the children of God (v. 10b). Other refs.: Matt. 2:18; 3:9; 7:11; 9:2; 10:21a, b; 11:19; 15:26; 18:25; 19:29; 21:28a, b; 22:24; 23:37; 27:25; Mark 2:5; 7:27a, b; 10:24, 29, 30; 12:19; 13:12a, b; Luke 1:7, 17; 2:48; 3:8; 7:35; 11:13; 13:34; 14:26; 15:31; 16:25; 18:29; 19:44; 20:31; 23:28; John 8:39; Acts 2:39; 7:5; 13:33; 21:5, 21; Rom. 8:17; 9:7, 8a; 1 Cor. 4:14, 17; 7:14; 2 Cor. 6:13; 12:14a, b; Gal. 4:19 (some mss.: *teknion*), 25, 27, 28, 31; Eph. 2:3; 5:1, 8; 6:1, 4; Phil. 2:22; Col. 3:20, 21; 1 Thes. 2:7, 11; 1 Tim. 1:2, 18; 3:4, 12; 5:4; 2 Tim. 1:2; 2:1; Titus 1:4; Phm. 10; 1 Pet. 1:14; 3:6 {daughter}; 2 Pet. 2:14; 2 John 1, 4, 13; 3 John 4; Rev. 2:23; 12:4, 5. ¶

[7] **to bear, to have children: *teknogoneō*** [verb: τεκνογονέω <5041>]; **from *teknogonos*: child-bearing, which is from *teknon*: see [6], and *gennaō*: to beget, which is from *genna*: birth, race ► To procreate, to beget** > Paul desired that the younger widows marry and bear children (1 Tim. 5:14). ¶

[8] **loving one's children: *philoteknos*** [adj.: φιλότεκνος <5388>]; **from *phileō*: to love, and *teknon*: see [6] ► Having affection for one's own children** > Younger women must be admonished to love {be attached to} their children (lit.: to be loving one's children) (Titus 2:4). ¶

[9] **childless, without children: *ateknos*** [adj.: ἄτεκνος <815>]; **from *a*: neg., and *teknon*: see [6] ► Having no children** > Moses has written about one who dies without children (Luke 20:28–30). ¶

[10] **child, little child: *teknion*** [neut. noun: τεκνίον <5040>]; **dimin. of *teknon*: child ► Affectionate term for a child; see [6]; also transl.: dear child** > Jesus addressed His disciples as little children (John 13:33). John was writing to his little children so that they might not sin (1 John 2:1). Other refs.: Gal. 4:19 (some mss.: *teknon*); 1 John 2:12, 28; 3:7, 18; 4:4; 5:21. ¶

[11] **with child: *en gastri*; in: *en*** [prep.: ἐν <1722>]; **belly, womb: *gastēr*** [fem. noun: γαστήρ <1064>] **► In a state of pregnancy** > Mary was found to be with child by the Holy Spirit (Matt. 1:18), so was fulfilled what the prophet had predicted: that the virgin would be with child and bring forth a son (v. 23). When the abomination of desolation stands in the holy place, it will be a very difficult time for the women who are with child {pregnant} (Matt. 24:19; Mark 13:17; Luke 21:23). Sudden destruction will come upon those who say "Peace and safety!" as labor pains upon a woman who is with child {a pregnant woman} (1 Thes. 5:3). John saw a woman being with child, crying out in labor and in pain to give birth (Rev. 12:2). All other refs. (*gastēr*): see GLUTTON <1064>, WOMB <1064>.

[12] **with child: *enkuos*** [adj.: ἔγκυος <1471>]; **from *en*: in, and *kuō*: to conceive ► In a state of pregnancy** > Mary, the betrothed wife of Joseph, was with child (Luke 2:5). ¶

– [13] Matt. 5:9, 45; 17:25, 26; 23:15; Mark 3:28; Luke 6:35; 14:5 in some mss.; John 12:36; Rom. 8:14, 19; 9:26; Gal. 3:26; 4:7a, b; 1 Thes. 5:5a, b; Heb. 12:7a, b; Rev. 21:7 → child, children → lit.: son, sons → SON

<5207> [14] Mark 9:21 → of a child → from childhood → CHILDHOOD <3812> [15] Acts 7:19 → young child → BABE <1025> [16] 1 Tim. 2:15 → bearing of children → CHILDBEARING <5042> [17] 1 Tim. 5:10 → to bring up children → BRING <5044> [18] 2 Tim. 3:15 → CHILDHOOD <1025> [19] Rev. 12:17 → children → SEED <4690>.

CHILDBEARING – [1] ***teknogonia*** [fem. noun: τεκνογονία <5042>]; **from *teknogos*: bearing children, which is from *teknon*: child, and *ginomai*: to make ▶ Act of giving birth, maternity** > The woman will be preserved through childbearing {the bearing of children} (1 Tim. 2:15). ¶

– [2] Heb. 11:11 → past childbearing age → lit.: beyond time of age → TIME <2540>.

CHILDBIRTH – Gal. 4:19, 27; Rev. 12:2 → to be in the pains of childbirth, to have labor pains → to be in labor → LABOR (verb) <5605>.

CHILDHOOD – [1] **child: *brephos*** [neut. noun: βρέφος <1025>] ▶ **Baby, infant** > Timothy knew the Holy Scriptures from childhood {infancy} (lit.: from a child, i.e., from a very young age) (2 Tim. 3:15). All other refs.: see BABE <1025>.

[2] **from childhood: *paidiothen*** [adv.: παιδιόθεν <3812>]; **from *paidion*: young child, and suffix *then*: from a place or time ▶ Since being a young child** > The son of a man was seized by a spirit from childhood {of a child} (Mark 9:21). ¶

– [3] 1 Cor. 13:11 → of childhood → of a babe → BABE <3516>.

CHILDISH – 1 Cor. 13:11e → lit.: of a child → BABE <3516>.

CHILDLESS – [1] Luke 1:7 → to be childless → to have no child → CHILD <5043> [2] Luke 20:28 → childless, without children → CHILD <815> [3] Luke 23:29 → BARREN <4723>.

CHILDREN – [1] Matt. 22:24b, 25; Mark 12:19–22; Luke 20:28 → SEED <4690> [2] Acts 17:28, 29 → RACE[1] <1085>.

CHILIARCH – Mark 6:21; John 18:12; Acts 21:31–33, 37; 22:24, 26–29; 23:10, 15, 17–19, 22; 24:7, 22; 25:23; Rev. 6:15; 19:18 → CAPTAIN <5506>.

CHIOS – ***Chios*** [fem. name: Χίος <5508>] ▶ **Island in the Aegean Sea, at the entrance of the Gulf of Smyrna** > Paul's ship passed near the island of Chios during his third missionary journey (Acts 20:15). ¶

CHLOE – ***Chloē*** [fem. name: Χλόη <5514>]: **new verdure ▶ Christian woman of Corinth** > Those who were of the household of Chloe had told Paul that there were dissensions among the Corinthians (1 Cor. 1:11). ¶

CHOENIX – Rev. 6:6a, b → QUART <5518>.

CHOICE – [1] Acts 15:7 → to make choice → CHOOSE <1586> [2] Rom. 8:20 → by its own choice → WILLINGLY <1635> [3] Rom. 9:11; 11:5, 28; 1 Thes. 1:4 → ELECTION <1589> [4] Rom. 16:13; 1 Pet. 2:6 → ELECT <1588> [5] 1 Pet. 2:4 → CHOOSE <1588>.

CHOKE – [1] ***apopnigō*** [verb: ἀποπνίγω <638>]; **from *apo*: intens., and *pnigō*: to choke, which is from *pneō*: to breathe ▶ To strangle; to suffocate, whether by depriving of air, as in the case of plants, or with water, i.e., to drown** > In a parable, the thorns choked the seed that was sown (Matt. 13:7; other mss.: *pnigō*). The herd of swine were choked {drowned} in the sea (Luke 8:33). Other ref.: Luke 8:7 in some mss.; see [2]. ¶

[2] ***epipnigō*** [verb: ἐπιπνίγω <1970>]; **from *epi*: upon, and *pnigō*: see [1] ▶ To hinder the growth** > Luke uses this verb concerning the seed choked by the thorns (Luke 8:7). ¶

[3] ***sumpnigō*** [verb: συμπνίγω <4846>]; **from *sun*: together (intens.), and *pnigō*: see [1]; lit.: to choke together ▶ To hinder**

the growth > The cares of this life and the deceit of riches choke the word of God (Matt. 13:22; Mark 4:19; Luke 8:14). Mark uses this verb concerning the seed choked by the thorns (Mark 4:7). Other refs.: Luke 8:42; see THRONG (verb) <4846>; 12:1 in some mss. ¶

– 4 Matt. 18:28; Mark 5:13 → to take by the throat → THROAT <4155>.

CHOOSE – 1 ***haireō*** [verb: αἱρέω <138>]; **in the N.T., *haireomai* (a form of *haireō*): to take for oneself ▶ To decide, to select, to prefer** > Paul did not know if he should choose to live or to die (Phil. 1:22). God had chosen the Thessalonians from the beginning for salvation (2 Thes. 2:13). Moses chose to suffer affliction with the people of God (Heb. 11:25). ¶

2 ***hairetizō*** [verb: αἱρετίζω <140>]; **from *haireō*: to take ▶ To elect someone, to select** > God has chosen His servant Jesus, His beloved in whom His soul has found its delight (Matt. 12:18). ¶

3 ***eklegō*** [verb: ἐκλέγω <1586>]; **from *ek*: out, and *legō*: to choose ▶ To select, to elect; when God is choosing, it is His sovereign decision** > For the sake of the elect, whom He chose, God will shorten the days of the great tribulation (Mark 13:20). Jesus chose twelve disciples (Luke 6:13; John 6:70; 13:18; 15:16, 19; Acts 1:2). Mary of Bethany had chosen the good part in listening to Jesus (Luke 10:42). In a parable, those who were invited were choosing {picking} the first places (Luke 14:7). The apostles prayed the Lord to show them which one of two disciples He had chosen to replace Judas (Acts 1:24). The whole multitude of disciples chose seven men for the service (Acts 6:5). Paul reminds the Israelites that God chose their fathers (Acts 13:17). God had chosen {made choice of} Peter to present the gospel to the Gentiles (Acts 15:7). Men were chosen {selected} to accompany Paul and Barnabas to Antioch (Acts 15:22, 25). God has chosen the foolish things of this world that He may put to shame the wise, and the weak things to put to shame the strong things (1 Cor. 1:27a, b); He has also chosen the ignoble things of this world, the despised, and those which are not, to annul those which are (v. 28). Christians have been chosen in Christ before the foundation of the world, that they should be holy and blameless before Him in love (Eph. 1:4), but everyone is responsible to accept personally God's salvation. God has chosen the poor of this world to be rich in faith and heirs of the kingdom (Jas. 2:5). Other ref.: Luke 6:44 in some mss. rather that *sullegō*. ¶

4 **chosen: *eklektos*** [adj.: ἐκλεκτός <1588>]; **from *eklegō*: see 3 ▶ Selected, elected** > Christians come to the Lord as to a living stone, chosen {choice} by God and precious (1 Pet. 2:4). All other refs.: ELECT <1588>.

5 ***epilegō*** [verb: ἐπιλέγω <1951>]; **from *epi*: upon, and *legō*: to say ▶ To express the choice, to select** > Paul had chosen Silas to accompany him (Acts 15:40). Other ref.: John 5:2; see CALL (verb) <1951>. ¶

6 ***procheirizomai*** [verb: προχειρίζομαι <4400>]; **from *procheiros*: ready, at hand, which is from *pro*: before, and *cheir*: hand ▶ To select in advance** > God had chosen beforehand {appointed, chosen before hand} Paul to know His will, and to see the Just One, and to hear a voice out of His mouth (Acts 22:14). Other refs.: Acts 3:20; 26:16; see FOREORDAIN <4400>, MAKE <4400>. ¶

7 **to choose before, to choose beforehand: *procheirotoneō*** [verb: προχειροτονέω <4401>]; **from *pro*: before, in advance, and *cheirotoneō*: to chose, to designate, which is from *cheirotonos*: extending the hand, which is from *cheir*: hand, and *teinō*: to stretch out ▶ To select in advance** > The risen Christ appeared to witnesses who were chosen before of God (Acts 10:41). ¶

– 8 Matt. 20:14, 15; 1 Cor. 12:18 → WANT (verb) <2309> 9 Acts 6:3 → to look out → LOOK (verb) <1980> 10 Acts 14:23; 2 Cor. 8:19 → ORDAIN <5500> 11 Acts 15:14; Heb. 5:1 → to take out → TAKE <2983> 12 Rom. 11:5; 1 Thes. 1:4 → ELECTION <1589> 13 1 Cor. 15:38 → WILL (verb) <2309> 14 Eph. 1:11 → we were also chosen → lit.: we have obtained an inheritance → INHERITANCE <2820> 15 1 Pet. 1:20 → FOREKNOW <4267>.

CHOOSING – 2 Pet. 1:10 → ELECTION <1589>.

CHORAZIN – ***Chorazin*** [fem. name: Χοραζίν <5523>] ▶ **City of Galilee near Capernaum** > Jesus reproached Chorazin and Bethsaida for not having repented despite the miracles which He had performed there (Matt. 11:21; Luke 10:13). ¶

CHOSEN – **1** Matt. 20:16; 22:14; Luke 18:7; 23:35; Rom. 8:33; 16:13; Col. 3:12; 1 Tim. 5:21; 2 Tim. 2:10; Titus 1:1; 1 Pet. 1:1 (or 2); 2:6, 9; 2 John 1, 13; Rev. 17:14 → chosen, chosen one → ELECT <1588> **2** Acts 9:15; Rom. 11:7 → ELECTION <1589> **3** 1 Pet. 2:4 → CHOOSE <1588> **4** 1 Pet. 5:13 → chosen together with → elected together → ELECT <4899>.

CHOSEN ONE – John 1:34 → God's Chosen One → lit.: Son of God.

CHRIST – ***Christos*** [masc. name: Χριστός <5547>]: **anointed, consecrated; from *chriō*: to anoint ▶ Originally one of the titles of the Lord Jesus; see Ps. 2:2, 6; later one of His names** > The name "Christ" is the Greek equivalent of the Hebrew name "Messiah," He whom the Jews were to expect and who would reign over them (John 4:25; see v. 42). Simon Peter acknowledged Jesus as the Christ, the Son of the Living God (Matt. 16:16). Before His return, there shall arise false christs (see FALSE <5580>) who will seek to seduce men (Matt. 24:23, 24; Mark 13:22). *

CHRISTIAN – ***Christianos*** [masc. noun: Χριστιανός <5546>]; **from *Christos*: Christ, which is from *chriō*: to anoint ▶ Name given to people belonging to Christ and following Him** > The disciples of Jesus Christ were first called Christians in Antioch (Acts 11:26). Agrippa told Paul he almost persuaded him to become a Christian (Acts 26:28). Peter, speaking of anyone suffering as a Christian, says that he should not be ashamed but glorify God in this name (1 Pet. 4:16). ¶

CHRYSOLITE, CHRYSOLYTE – ***chrusolithos*** [masc. noun: χρυσόλιθος <5555>]; **from *chrusos*: gold, and *lithos*: stone ▶ Precious stone of a golden color** > The seventh foundation of the wall of the heavenly Jerusalem is adorned with chrysolite (Rev. 21:20). ¶

CHRYSOPRASE, CHRYSOPRASUS – ***chrusoprasos*** [masc. noun: χρυσόπρασος <5556>]; **from *chrusos*: gold, and *prason*: leek ▶ Precious stone, variety of chalcedony of a golden green and translucent** > The tenth foundation of the wall of the heavenly Jerusalem is adorned with chrysoprase {turquoise} (Rev. 21:20). ¶

CHURCH – **1** ***ekklēsia*** [fem. noun: ἐκκλησία <1577>]; **from *ekkaleō*: to call out, which is from *ek*: out, and *kaleō*: to call; lit.: an assembly by convocation ▶ a. The church (or assembly) of God is composed of all Christian believers redeemed by the blood of Christ, since the coming of the Holy Spirit at Pentecost until the return of the Lord** > Jesus is building His church (Matt. 16:18; see Eph. 2:20–22). In the meantime, the Christian church is made of all the true believers in the Lord Jesus, known by God, who live at a certain time on earth (see 2 Tim. 2:19–21). Christ has loved the church and has given Himself for her (Eph. 5:25). Other refs.: Acts 2:47; 5:11; 8:1, 3; 1 Cor. 12:28; 14:12; 15:9; Eph. 1:22; 3:10, 21; 5:23, 24, 27, 29, 32; Phil. 3:6; Col. 1:18, 24; 1 Tim. 3:5, 15; Heb. 2:12; 12:23. **b. The local church is made of all the true Christian believers living in a locality** > The term designates a gathering of Christians around the Lord in a given place (1 Cor. 11:16; 14:19, 34, 35). The local church is an expression of the universal church, the body of Christ (1 Cor. 1:2; 1 Thes. 1:1). Other refs.: Matt. 18:17a, b; Acts 9:31; 11:22, 26; 12:1, 5; 13:1; 14:23, 27; 15:3, 4, 22, 41; 16:5; 18:22; 20:17, 28; Rom. 16:1, 4, 5, 16, 23; 1 Cor. 4:17; 6:4; 7:17; 10:32; 11:18, 22; 14:4, 5, 23, 28, 33; 16:1, 19a, b; 2 Cor. 1:1; 8:1, 18, 19, 23, 24; 11:8, 28; 12:13; Gal. 1:2, 13, 22; Phil. 4:15; Col. 4:15, 16; 1 Thes. 2:14; 2 Thes. 1:1, 4;

1 Tim. 5:16; Phm. 2; Jas. 5:14; 3 John 6, 9, 10; Rev. 1:4, 11, 20a, b; 2:1, 7, 8, 11, 12, 17, 18, 23, 29; 3:1, 6, 7, 13, 14, 22; 22:16. **c. Group of people gathered together >** The Greek term is used for the assembly {congregation} of Israel in the desert (Acts 7:38). It designates also an assembly of citizens in Ephesus (Acts 19:32, 41) and a lawful assembly (v. 39). ¶
– 2 Acts 15:30 → MULTITUDE <4128>
3 Acts 19:37 → robber of churches → lit.: robber of temples → TEMPLE <2417>.

CHUZA – *Chouzas* [masc. name: Χουζᾶς <5529>] **▶ Herod's steward; also transl.: Cuza >** Chuza was the husband of Joanna; she was among the many women who were attending to Jesus out of their own means (Luke 8:3). ¶

CILICIA – *Kilikia* [fem. name: Κιλικία <2791>] **▶ Province located in southern Asia Minor and northeast of the Mediterranean Sea >** Paul was originally from Tarsus, the capital of Cilicia (Acts 21:39; 22:3; 23:34); in Acts 23:34, some mss. have *Kilix*: a Cilician. Men from Cilicia disputed with Stephen, but they could not resist the wisdom and the Spirit by which he spoke (Acts 6:9). Paul returned to Cilicia after his conversion (Gal. 1:21). Churches were found in Cilicia (Acts 15:23, 41). Other ref.: Acts 27:5. ¶

CINNAMON – *kinamōmon* [neut. noun: κινάμωμον <2792>]**; also spelled: *kinnamōmon* ▶ Yellowish-brown spice made from the inner bark of the tree of the same name >** The merchants of the earth will weep over the fall of Babylon who will no longer buy from them various products, including cinnamon (Rev. 18:13). ¶

CIRCLE ROUND – *perierchomai* [verb: περιέρχομαι <4022>]**; from *peri*: around, and *erchomai*: to go ▶ To sail along the coast >** Paul's boat circled round {sailed around, fetched a compass, went on a circuitous course} between Syracuse and Rhegium (Acts 28:13); some mss. have *periaireō*.: raise anchor. Other refs.: Acts 19:13 (to go here and there); 1 Tim. 5:13; Heb. 11:37; see ITINERANT <4022>, WANDER <4022>. ¶

CIRCUIT – 1 in a circuit: *kuklō* [adv.: κύκλῳ <2945>]**; from *kuklos*: circle ▶ All around, in a circular space >** Jesus went round the villages in a circuit, teaching (Mark 6:6). The expr. "*peri kuklō*" is transl. "around in a circuit" in Mark 3:34. All other refs.: AROUND <2945>, ROUND <2945>.
– 2 Acts 28:13 → to make a circuit → CIRCLE ROUND <4022>.

CIRCUITOUS – Acts 28:13 → to go on a circuitous course → CIRCLE ROUND <4022>.

CIRCULATE – Matt. 28:15 → to be widely circulated → to be widely spread → SPREAD <1310>.

CIRCUMCISE – 1 *peritemnō* [verb: περιτέμνω <4059>]**; from *peri*: around, and *temnō*: to cut ▶ To cut off the foreskin of a male, as a religious rite in Israel >** John the Baptist was circumcised (Luke 1:59), and Jesus as well (Luke 2:21). Other men were circumcised: Isaac (Acts 7:8), Timothy (Acts 16:3), and Paul (Phil. 3:5; lit.: as to circumcision: *peritomē*). Titus was not compelled to be circumcised (Gal. 2:3). If anyone was called while circumcised, he should not become uncircumcised (i.e., hide his circumcision); if anyone was called while uncircumcised, he should not become circumcised (1 Cor. 7:18a, b). Christians were circumcised with the circumcision not done with hands (Col. 2:11), i.e., spiritually by the setting aside of the flesh. Other refs.: John 7:22; Acts 15:1, 5, 24; 21:21; Gal. 5:2, 3; 6:12, 13a, b. ¶
– 2 Rom. 15:8; Phil. 3:5; Col. 3:11 → CIRCUMCISION <4061>.

CIRCUMCISING – Luke 2:21 → CIRCUMCISE <4059>.

CIRCUMCISION – 1 *peritomē* [fem. noun: περιτομή <4061>]**; from *peritemnō*:**

to circumcise, which is from *peri*: around, and *temnō*: to cut ▶ Cutting off the foreskin of a male, as a religious rite in Israel > Rite ordained by God to Abraham and his male descendants as a sign of a covenant, and performed on the eighth day after birth (Acts 7:8). Moses has given the circumcision to the Jews (John 7:22, 23). In the N.T., the Jews are those of the circumcision (Acts 10:45; 11:2; Gal. 2:12; Eph. 2:11; Col. 4:11; Titus 1:10); the Gentiles are uncircumcised men (see Acts 11:3). In the church, there is no difference between the Jews and the Gentiles, circumcision and uncircumcision {circumcised nor uncircumcised; lit.: circumcision nor uncircumcision} (Col. 3:11). In contrast with the circumcision of the flesh, the "circumcision" of the Christian is of the heart, in spirit (Rom. 2:25a, b, 26–29; Col. 2:11a, b), a spiritual sign of his belonging to the Lord. The Christians are now figur. the circumcision (Phil. 3:3). Other refs.: Rom. 3:1, 30; 4:9, 10a, b, 11, 12a, b; 15:8; 1 Cor. 7:19; Gal. 2:7–9; 5:6, 11; 6:15; Phil. 3:5 (lit.: as to circumcision). ¶
– [2] Luke 2:21 → CIRCUMCISE <4059> [3] 1 Cor. 7:18a → to seek to remove the marks of circumcision → lit.: to become uncircumcised [4] 1 Cor. 7:18b → to seek circumcision → lit.: to be circumcised [5] Gal. 6:13 → "circumcision" added in Engl. [6] Phil. 3:2 → false circumcision → CONCISION <2699>.

CIRCUMSPECTLY – Eph. 5:15 → CAREFULLY <199>.

CIRCUMSTANCE – [1] Eph. 6:16 → in all circumstances → lit.: above all [2] Col. 4:8 → AFFAIR <3588> [3] 2 Thes. 3:16 → MANNER <5158> [4] Jas. 1:9 → in humble circumstances → LOWLY <5011>.

CIS – See KISH <2797>.

CITIZEN – ***politēs*** [masc. noun: πολίτης <4177>]**; from *polis*: city ▶ One who is an inhabitant of a city, a state, a district, and who is entitled to full civil rights** > The prodigal son joined himself to one of the citizens of the country where he had gone (Luke 15:15). In a parable, the citizens {subjects} of a noble man hated him (Luke 19:14). Paul was a citizen of Tarsus (Acts 21:39). The word is used in Heb. 8:11 and is transl. "fellow citizen"; some mss. have *plēsion* (neighbor). ¶

CITIZENSHIP – [1] ***politeia*** [fem. noun: πολιτεία <4174>]**; from *politeuō*: to act as a citizen, which is from *politēs*: citizen, which is from *polis*: city ▶ Quality and right of a citizen** > The chiliarch told Paul he had bought his citizenship {freedom} for a great sum (Acts 22:28), but Paul had his citizenship by birth, referring to his Roman citizenship (see v. 25). The Gentiles were aliens from the citizenship {commonwealth} of Israel before the coming of Christ (Eph. 2:12). ¶
[2] ***politeuma*** [neut. noun: πολίτευμα <4175>]**; from *politeuō*: see [1] ▶ Participation in the matters of the state; the term means both "citizenship" and "state"** > The citizenship {commonwealth, conversation} of Christians is in heaven (Phil. 3:20). ¶

CITRON – ***thuinos*** [adj.: θύϊνος <2367>] **▶ Citron wood is an aromatic evergreen producing hard wood from which statues and expensive vessels were made** > Citron wood {Thyine wood} is mentioned in Rev. 18:12. ¶

CITY – [1] ***polis*** [fem. noun: πόλις <4172>] **▶ Significant agglomeration of dwellings, usually surrounded by a wall; also transl.: town** > Jesus was born in Bethlehem, the city of David (Luke 2:11). Abraham waited for the city, of which God is the builder and maker (Heb. 11:10). God has prepared a city for the believers who have died in the faith (Heb. 11:16). Christians have come to the city of the living God (Heb. 12:22); they do not have an abiding city here, but they seek the coming one (13:14). The name of the city of God will be written on him who overcomes (Rev. 3:12). Before the beginning of the millennium, the nations will tread underfoot the holy city,

Jerusalem, forty-two months (Rev. 11:2); at the end of the millennium, the nations will again surround Jerusalem, the beloved city (20:9). The holy city, the heavenly Jerusalem here, is mentioned in Rev. 21:2, 10, 14, 15, 16a, b, 18, 19, 21, 23; 22:14, 19. The term "city" designates Antioch (Acts 13:44, 50), Arimathea (Luke 23:51), Athens (Acts 17:16), Babylon the Great (Rev. 17:18; 18:10a, b, 16, 18, 19, 21), Bethlehem (Luke 2:4b), Bethsaida (Luke 9:10; John 1:44), Capernaum (Luke 4:31), Caesarea (Acts 10:9), Corinth (Acts 18:10; Rom. 16:23), Damascus (Acts 9:6; 2 Cor. 11:32), Ephesus (Acts 19:29, 35), Ephraim (John 11:54), Iconium (Acts 14:4), Jerusalem, the holy city (Matt. 4:5; 5:35; 21:10, 17, 18; 27:53; Mark 11:19; Luke 19:41; 24:49; John 19:20; Acts 4:27; 7:58; 21:29, 30; 22:3; 24:12; 25:23; Rev. 11:8, 13; 14:20; 16:19a), Joppa (Acts 11:5), Lasea (Acts 27:8), Lystra (Acts 14:13, 19), Nain (Luke 7:11, 12a, b), Nazareth (Matt. 2:23; Luke 1:26; 2:4a, 39; 4:29a, b), Philippi (Acts 16:12a, b, 20, 39), Sychar (John 4:5), Sodom and Gomorrah (2 Pet. 2:6) and the cities around them (Jude 7), Tarsus (Acts 21:39), Thessalonica (Acts 17:5), Thyatira (Acts 16:14), Tyr (Acts 21:5), the cities of Crete (Titus 1:5), a city in the country of the Gergesenes (Matt. 8:33, 34; Mark 5:14; Luke 8:27, 34, 39), agglomerations in Israel (Matt. 10:23b), a city of Judah (Luke 1:39), the cities of Lycaonia (Acts 14:6), cities of the nations (Rev. 16:19b), a city of Samaria (Acts 8:5, 8, 9), and the cities of the Samaritans (Matt. 10:5). Jesus traveled about all the cities and villages, teaching, preaching, and healing (Matt. 9:35; 11:1, 20; Mark 6:56; Luke 4:43; 5:12; 8:1; 13:22). Other refs.: Matt. 5:14; 9:1; 10:11, 14, 15, 23a; 12:25; 14:13; 22:7; 23:34a, b; 26:18; 28:11; Mark 1:33, 45; 6:11 (in some mss.), 33; 14:13, 16; Luke 2:3; 7:37; 8:4; 9:5; 10:1, 8, 10–12; 14:21; 18:2, 3; 19:17, 19; 22:10; 23:19; John 4:8, 28, 30, 39; Acts 5:16; 8:40; 12:10; 14:20, 21; 15:21, 36; 16:4; 20:23; 26:11; 2 Cor. 11:26; Jas. 4:13. ¶

– **2** Acts 17:6, 8 → city authority, city official → ruler of the city → RULER <4173>.

CITY CLERK – Acts 19:35 → TOWN CLERK <1122>.

CITY GATE – Acts 16:13; Heb. 13:12 → lit.: gate → GATE <4439>.

CLAIM (noun) – **1** John 14:30 → he has no claim on me → lit.: he has nothing in me **2** 1 Cor. 9:12 → rightful claim → RIGHT (noun)[2] <1849> **3** 2 Cor. 11:12a, b → to undermine the claim of those who would like to claim → to cut off the occasion of those wishing for an occasion → OCCASION <874> **4** 1 Tim. 2:10 → to make a claim → PROMISE (verb) <1861>.

CLAIM (verb) – **1** Acts 25:19; Rom. 1:22; Rev. 2:2 → to claim to be → SAY <5335> **2** Rom. 3:8 → AFFIRM <5346> **3** Rom. 6:17 → to claim the allegiance → lit.: into which you were instructed → INSTRUCT <3860> **4** 1 Cor. 5:11 → one who claims to be a brother or sister → one called brother → CALL (verb) <3687> **5** 1 Tim. 2:10 → to make a claim → to make profession → PROFESSION <1861> **6** Titus 1:16 → PROFESS <3670> **7** 1 John 4:20 → SPEAK <2036>.

CLAMOR – ***kraugē*** [fem. noun: κραυγή <2906>]; **from *krazō*: to shout ▶ Shouting, outcry** > All clamor {brawling} was to be removed from the Ephesians (Eph. 4:31). All other refs.: CRY (noun) <2906>.

CLAMOUR – Eph. 4:31 → CLAMOR <2906>.

CLANGING – **to clang: *alalazō*** [verb: ἀλαλάζω <214>]; **from *alalē*: war shout, noise ▶ To resound, to produce a noisy sound** > If Paul spoke in the tongues of men and of angels, but had no love, he would have become like a clanging {tinkling} (lit.: which clangs) cymbal (1 Cor. 13:1). Other ref.: Mark 5:38; see WAIL <214>. ¶

CLASP – Matt. 28:9 → SEIZE <2902>.

CLASS (noun) – Acts 13:50; 17:12 → of the upper class → PROMINENT <2158>.

CLASS (verb) – 2 Cor. 10:12 → CLASSIFY <1469>.

CLASSIFY – ***enkrinō*** [verb: ἐγκρίνω <1469>]; **from *en*: in, among, and *krinō*: to judge ▶ To place in the same rank, to make equal** > Paul did not dare to classify {to class, to make of the number} himself with some who commended themselves (2 Cor. 10:12). ¶

CLAUDA – ***Klauda*** [fem. name: Κλαύδα <2802>]; **also spelled: *Kauda*, *Kaudē* ▶ Small island of the Mediterranean Sea, southwest of Crete** > A violent storm drove Paul's ship, on the way to Rome, under the shelter of this island (Acts 27:16). ¶

CLAUDIA – ***Klaudia*** [fem. name: Κλαυδία <2803>]; **perhaps from the Lat. *clauda*: fem. of lame ▶ Christian woman of Rome** > Paul sent the greetings of Claudia to Timothy (2 Tim. 4:21). ¶

CLAUDIUS – ***Klaudios*** [masc. name: Κλαύδιος <2804>]; **perhaps from the Lat. *claudus*: lame ▶ Roman emperor** > At the beginning Claudius was in favor of the Jews, but then he banished them from Rome (Acts 18:2). A great famine took place under his reign (Acts 11:28). He died in A.D. 54. See LYSIAS for Claudius Lysias. ¶

CLAVE – Acts 17:34 → JOIN <2853>.

CLAY – [1] ***pēlos*** [masc. noun: πηλός <4081>] ▶ **a. Firm, fine-grained earth used to make pottery** > The potter has authority over the clay to make different vessels (Rom. 9:21). **b. Soil mixed with a liquid, mud** > Jesus spat on the ground and made clay {mud} with the saliva, which He used to heal the blind man (John 9:6a, b, 11, 14, 15). ¶
– [2] Luke 8:16 → clay jar → VESSEL[1] <4632> [3] 2 Cor. 4:7; 2 Tim. 2:20 → of clay → EARTHEN <3749>.

CLEAN (adj.) – [1] ***katharos*** [adj.: καθαρός <2513>] ▶ **Free from dirt or pollution, pure** > Jesus said to first make clean the inside of the cup, that the outside might also become clean (Matt. 23:26b). Joseph wrapped the body of Jesus in a clean linen cloth (Matt. 27:59). Jesus told the Pharisees to give alms, and then all things would be clean to them (Luke 11:41). The disciples of Jesus were clean, with the exception of Judas (John 13:10a, b, 11; 15:3). Paul was clean {clear} (Acts 18:6); he was clean {innocent} from the blood of all (20:26). All other refs.: PURE <2513>.
– [2] Matt. 8:2; 23:25, 26; Mark 1:40, 42; Luke 5:12; et al. → to make clean → CLEANSE <2511> [3] Acts 10:15; 11:9 → to make clean → PURIFY <2511> [4] Acts 24:18 → to be ceremonially clean → to be purified → PURIFY <48> [5] Heb. 9:13 → that they are outwardly clean → lit.: for the purity of the flesh → PURITY <2514>.

CLEAN (verb) – [1] Matt. 3:12; Luke 3:17 → to thoroughly clean out → PURGE <1245> [2] 1 Cor. 5:7 → to clean out → to purge out → PURGE <1571>.

CLEANSE – [1] ***katharizō*** [verb: καθαρίζω <2511>]; **from *katharos*: clean, pure ▶ To purify; also transl.: to make clean** > Jesus was able to cleanse a leper (Matt. 8:2; Mark 1:40; Luke 5:12); He said to him: Be cleansed (Matt. 8:3a; Mark 1:41; Luke 5:13). Immediately this leper was cleansed of his leprosy (Matt. 8:3b; Mark 1:42). Jesus told His disciples to cleanse lepers (Matt. 10:8). Jesus cleansed lepers (Matt. 11:5; Luke 7:22). The Pharisees made clean the outside of the cup and of the dish (Matt. 23:25; Luke 11:39); Jesus said to first make clean the inside (Matt. 23:26). Naaman was cleansed of his leprosy (Luke 4:27). Jesus cleansed ten leprous men (Luke 17:14, 17). James tells sinners to cleanse {wash} their hands (Jas. 4:8). All other refs.: PURIFY <2511>.
– [2] Mark 7:4a → to cleanse oneself → WASH <907> [3] 1 Cor. 5:7 → to cleanse out → to purge out → PURGE <1571> [4] 2 Tim. 2:21 → PURIFY <1571> [5] Heb. 10:2 → PURIFY <2508> [6] 2 Pet. 1:9 → that he was cleansed → lit.: the cleansing → PURIFICATION <2512>.

CLEANSING – [1] Mark 1:44; Luke 5:14 → PURIFICATION <2512> [2] John 11:55 → for their ceremonial cleansing → lit.: to purify themselves → PURIFY <48> [3] Heb. 9:13 → PURITY <2514>.

CLEANSING RITE – Heb. 6:2 → BAPTISM <909>.

CLEAR (adj.) – [1] ***phaneros*** [adj.: φανερός <5318>]; **from *phainō*: to shine, to become evident, which is from *phōs*: light ▶ Known, visible** > Each one's work will become clear {manifest, evident} {will be shown for what it is} (1 Cor. 3:13). All other refs.: see entries in Lexicon at <5318>.
– [2] Matt. 6:22; Luke 11:34 → SINGLE <573> [3] John 8:43 → to be clear → UNDERSTAND <1097> [4] Acts 18:6 → CLEAN (noun) <2513> [5] Acts 24:16 → without offense → OFFENSE <677> [6] 1 Cor. 4:4 → my conscience is clear → lit.: I know of nothing against myself → KNOW <4894> [7] 1 Cor. 14:8 → not clear → UNCERTAIN <82> [8] 1 Cor. 14:9 → INTELLIGIBLE <2154> [9] 1 Cor. 15:27; 1 Tim. 6:7 → EVIDENT <1212> [10] 2 Cor. 7:11 → PURE <53> [11] Phil. 1:28 → clear sign → PROOF <1732> [12] Col. 4:4 → to make clear → MANIFEST (verb) <5319> [13] 1 Thes. 3:11 → to make clear → DIRECT <2720> [14] 2 Tim. 3:9 → MANIFEST (adj.) <1552> [15] Heb. 5:11 → hard to make clear → HARD <1421> [16] Heb. 6:17 → very clear → more abundantly → ABUNDANTLY <4054> [17] Heb. 6:17 → to make very clear → SHOW (verb) <1925> [18] Heb. 7:14 → EVIDENT <4271> [19] Heb. 7:15 → EVIDENT <2612> [20] Heb. 11:14 → to make it clear → to declare plainly → PLAINLY <1718> [21] 1 Pet. 3:21 → clear conscience → good conscience → GOOD (adj. and noun) <18> [22] Rev. 21:11 → to be clear as crystal → CRYSTAL <2929> [23] Rev. 22:1 → BRIGHT <2986> [24] Rev. 21:18b → PURE <2513>.

CLEAR (verb) – [1] Matt. 3:12; Luke 3:17 → to clear, to thoroughly clear → PURGE <1245> [2] 2 Cor. 7:11 → eagerness to clear → EXCUSING <627> [3] Heb. 9:9 → to make perfect → PERFECT (verb) <5048> [4] 2 Pet. 1:14 → to make clear → SHOW (verb) <1213>.

CLEAR (BE) – Rom. 7:2, 6 → to be released → RELEASE (verb) <2673>.

CLEARING – 2 Cor. 7:11 → EXCUSING <627>.

CLEARLY – [1] ***tēlaugōs*** [adv.: τηλαυγῶς <5081>]; **from *tēlaugēs*: shining from a distance, which is from *tēle*: afar, and *augē*: radiance ▶ Distinctly, free from cloudiness** > The blind man healed by Jesus saw all things (other mss.: all men) clearly (Mark 8:25); other mss. have *dēlaugōs*: very clearly. ¶
[2] **clearly evident, quite evident: *prodēlos*** [adj.: πρόδηλος <4271>]; **from *pro*: before, and *dēlos*: visible, evident ▶ Known to all, openly manifest, obvious; also transl.: conspicuous** > Some men's sins are clearly evident {open beforehand, manifest beforehand} (1 Tim. 5:24); likewise, the good works of some are clearly evident {manifest beforehand} (v. 25). Other ref.: Heb. 7:14; see EVIDENT <4271>. ¶
[3] **to see clearly: *diablepō*** [verb: διαβλέπω <1227>]; **from *dia*: through (intens.), and *blepō*: to see ▶ To look distinctly** > By first removing the beam from one's own eye, one can see clearly to remove the mote out of the eye of one's brother (Matt. 7:5; Luke 6:42). The blind man healed by Jesus saw distinctly (Mark 8:25); other mss.: *anablepō*. ¶
– [4] John 3:21; 2 Cor. 3:3 → to be clearly seen, clearly → MANIFEST (verb) <5319> [5] John 16:29 → OPENLY <3954> [6] Acts 10:3 → PLAINLY <5320> [7] Gal. 3:1 → to portray clearly → PORTRAY <4270> [8] Gal. 3:11 → EVIDENT <1212> [9] 1 Tim. 4:1 → EXPRESSLY <4490> [10] Heb. 11:14 → to show clearly → to declare plainly → PLAINLY <1718>.

CLEAVE – [1] ***kollaō*** [verb: κολλάω <2853>]; **from *kolla*: glue ▶ To adhere, to cling** > Jesus told His disciples about the dust of a city cleaving on {sticking to} their

feet (Luke 10:11). All other refs.: CLING <2853>, COMPANY (noun) <2853>, JOIN <2853>, REACH <2853>.
– [2] Matt. 19:5; Mark 10:7 → JOIN <4347> [3] Luke 16:13 → HOLD (verb) <472> [4] Acts 11:23 → CONTINUE <4357>.

CLEMENCY – Acts 24:4 → COURTESY <1932>.

CLEMENT – ***Klēmēs*** [masc. name: Κλήμης <2815>]: **mild-tempered, merciful, indulgent; *clemens*, in Lat. ▶ Christian man of the city of Philippi** > Paul speaks of Clement as a fellow worker (Phil. 4:3). Perhaps this is Clement of Rome, one of the Fathers of the church. ¶

CLEOPAS – ***Kleopas*** [masc. name: Κλεοπᾶς <2810>]: **very renowned; or dimin. of *kleopatros*: illustrious father ▶ Disciple of Jesus** > Cleopas was one of the two disciples to whom Jesus manifested Himself on the evening of His resurrection on the road to Emmaus (Luke 24:18). These disciples did not recognize Jesus and constrained Him to stay with them. They recognized Him at table after Jesus had blessed and broken bread (see Luke 24:13–35). Some think this may be Clopas of John 19:25. ¶

CLERK – Acts 19:35 → city clerk, town clerk → TOWN CLERK <1122>.

CLEVERLY – 2 Pet. 1:16 → cleverly devised → DEVISED <4679>.

CLEVERNESS – [1] 1 Cor. 1:17 → WISDOM <4678> [2] 1 Cor. 1:19 → UNDERSTANDING <4907>.

CLIMB – Luke 19:4; John 10:1 → to climb up → GO UP <305>.

CLING – [1] ***kollaō*** [verb: κολλάω <2853>]; **from *kolla*: glue ▶ To attach firmly, to adhere** > Christians are to cling {to cleave} to that which is good (Rom. 12:9). All other refs.: CLEAVE <2853>, COMPANY (noun) <2853>, JOIN <2853>, REACH <2853>.
– [2] Acts 3:11 → HOLD (verb) <2902> [3] Titus 1:9 → to hold fast → FAST (HOLD) <472> [4] Heb. 12:1 → which clings so closely → which ensnares so easily → ENSNARE <2139>.

CLOAK – [1] ***himation*** [neut. noun: ἱμάτιον <2440>]; **comp. *hennumi*: to cover, to dress ▶ A large outer garment, a mantle** > Jesus said if anyone wants to go to law with a person and take away his body coat, to leave him one's cloak {coat, cloke} also (Matt. 5:40); Luke reverses the garments (Luke 6:29). All other refs.: CLOTHES <2440>, GARMENT <2440>.
[2] ***peribolaion*** [neut. noun: περιβόλαιον <4018>]; **from *periballō*: to cast around, which is from: *peri*: around, and *ballō*: to cast, to put ▶ Outer garment which one puts around oneself, coat** > The Lord will roll up the earth and the heavens like a cloak {covering, mantle, robe, vesture} (Heb. 1:12). Other ref.: 1 Cor. 11:15; see VEIL (noun) <4018>. ¶
[3] ***phailonēs*** [masc. noun: φαιλόνης <5341>]; **also spelled: *phelonēs* ▶ A travelling-coat, used for protection against stormy weather** > Paul asks Timothy to bring the cloak {cloke} which he had left behind in Troas (2 Tim. 4:13). ¶
– [4] Matt. 27:28, 31 → ROBE (noun) <5511> [5] Mark 15:17, 20 → in a purple cloak → lit.: in purple [6] John 15:22; 1 Thes. 2:5 → PRETEXT <4392> [7] 1 Pet. 2:16 → COVERING <1942>.

CLOKE – [1] Matt. 5:40; Luke 6:29 → CLOAK <2440> [2] 1 Thes. 2:5 → PRETEXT <4392> [3] 2 Tim. 4:13 → CLOAK <5341> [4] 1 Pet. 2:16 → COVERING <1942>.

CLOPAS – ***Klōpas*** [masc. name: Κλωπᾶς <2832>] ▶ **Man of the N.T.** > Clopas was the husband of the sister of Mary, the mother of Jesus (John 19:25). This is perhaps Cleopas in Luke 24:18. ¶

CLOSE (adj. and adv.) – [1] ***anankaios*** [adj.: ἀναγκαῖος <316>]; **from *anankē*:**

necessity ▶ Who is very close in terms of natural relations or friendship; lit.: indispensable person > Cornelius had gathered together his relatives and close {intimate, near} friends (Acts 10:24). All other refs.: NECESSARY <316>.
[2] ***paraplēsion*** [adv.: παραπλήσιον <3897>]; **neut. of *paraplēsios*: near, which is from *para*: close to, and *plēsios*: near ▶ Nearly; also transl.: almost, nigh, to the point** > Epaphroditus had been close to death (Phil. 2:27). ¶
– [3] Matt. 13:39, 40, 49; 24:3 → END (noun) <4930> [4] John 13:23 → close to → lit.: in the bosom of [5] John 19:42 → close at hand → NEAR (adv.) <1451> [6] John 21:20 → lit.: on His breast → BREAST <4738> [7] Phil. 2:30 → to come close → to draw near → NEAR (adv.) <1448>.

CLOSE (verb) – [1] ***kammuō*** [verb: καμμύω <2576>]; **from *kata*: down (intens.), and *muō*: to shut ▶ To block, to shut (the eyes)** > The Jews have closed their eyes, not seeing the things concerning the kingdom (Matt. 13:15; Acts 28:27). ¶
[2] **to close in: *sunechō*** [verb: συνέχω <4912>]; **from *sun*: together (intens.), and *echō*: to hold ▶ To press on all sides, to completely restrain** > The crowds were closing in {crowding, thronging} on Jesus and pressing against Him (Luke 8:45). The days were coming when the enemies of Jerusalem would cast a trench about her, surround her, and close her in {hem her in, keep her in} on every side (Luke 19:43). All other refs.: see entries in Lexicon at <4912>.
– [3] Matt. 6:6; 25:10; 1 John 3:17; Rev. 21:25 → SHUT <2808> [4] Luke 4:20 → to roll up → ROLL <4428> [5] Luke 13:25 → SHUT <608> [6] Luke 21:34 → COME <2186> [7] Rom. 3:19; 2 Cor. 11:10 → STOP <5420>.

CLOSELY – [1] Luke 1:3 → ACCURATELY <199> [2] Acts 23:20 → more closely → more accurately → ACCURATELY <197> [3] 1 Tim. 4:16 → to watch closely → to take heed → HEED (noun) <1907> [4] Heb. 12:1 → which clings so closely → which ensnares so easily → ENSNARE <2139>.

CLOSET – Matt. 6:6 → room, inner room → ROOM <5009>.

CLOTH – [1] ***rhakos*** [neut. noun: ῥάκος <4470>]; **from *rhēgnumi*: to tear ▶ A piece of fabric woven or knitted** > No one puts a patch of new (lit.: unmilled, unshrunk) cloth on an old garment (Matt. 9:16; Mark 2:21). ¶
[2] **cloth, burial cloth, face cloth: *soudarion*** [neut. noun: σουδάριον <4676>]; ***sudor*, in Lat.: perspiration, and *sudare*: to perspire ▶ Fabric used to wrap the head of a dead person; also transl.: handkerchief, napkin** > The face of Lazarus was wrapped with a cloth (John 11:44). The cloth which had been around the head of Jesus was folded up in a distinct place by itself (John 20:7). Other refs.: Luke 19:20; Acts 19:12; see HANDKERCHIEF <4676>. ¶
– [3] Matt. 27:59; Mark 14:51, 52 → LINEN, LINEN CLOTH <4616> [4] Luke 2:7, 12 → to wrap in cloths → WRAP <4683> [5] Luke 24:12; John 19:40; 20:5–7 → LINEN, LINEN CLOTH <3608>.

CLOTHE – [1] ***enduō*** [verb: ἐνδύω <1746>]; **from *en*: in, and *duō*: to put on ▶ To put on (as a garment), to clothe, to dress; also transl.: to put on, to wear** > Jesus said not to worry about what we shall put on (or: be clothed with) (Matt. 6:25; Luke 12:22). The king saw a man who was not clothed with wedding clothes (Matt. 22:11). The soldiers put Jesus's own clothes on Him after they had mocked Him (Matt. 27:31; Mark 15:20). John the Baptist was clothed in {wore clothing made of} camel's hair (Mark 1:6). The verb is used in regard to body tunics (Mark 6:9). In a parable, the father gave instructions to put on his son the best robe (Luke 15:22). A rich man was clothed in purple and fine linen (Luke 16:19). The disciples were to be clothed {to be endued} with power from on high (Luke 24:49). Herod was clothed in royal apparel (Acts 12:21 {to be arrayed, to wear}). The Christian is to put on the armor of light (Rom. 13:12), the Lord Jesus Christ (Rom. 13:14), the full armor of God (Eph. 6:11), and the breastplate of faith (1 Thes. 5:8).

The corruptible body of the Christian must put on incorruptibility and the mortal body must put on immortality (1 Cor. 15:53a, b, 54a, b). If Christians are clothed, they shall not be found naked (2 Cor. 5:3). The Galatians had put on Christ (Gal. 3:27). The Christian has put on the new man (Eph. 4:24; Col. 3:10) and the breastplate of righteousness (Eph. 6:14). Christians are to put on bowels of compassion, kindness, lowliness, meekness, longsuffering (Col. 3:12). The Son of Man was clothed in a robe reaching down to the feet (Rev. 1:13). The seven angels who had the seven plagues were clothed in pure bright linen (Rev. 15:6). The armies that followed the Lord were clothed in fine linen, white and clean (Rev. 19:14). Other ref.: Mark 6:9; see PUT <1746>. ¶

[2] ***endiduskō*** [verb: ἐνδιδύσκω <1737>]; **lengthened form of *enduō*; see [1] ▶ To dress, to put on a garment** > The soldiers clothed Jesus with purple (Mark 15:17); some mss. have [1]. A rich man was clothed in purple and fine linen (Luke 16:19). Other ref.: Luke 8:27; see WEAR <1737>. ¶

[3] **to put on: *ependuomai*** [verb: ἐπενδύομαι <1902>]; **from *epi*: upon, and *enduō*: see [1] ▶ Lit.: to put on over** > Christians ardently desire to be clothed {to have put on} their dwelling which is from heaven (2 Cor. 5:2), desiring to be clothed so that what is mortal may be swallowed up by life (v. 4). ¶

[4] ***amphiennumi*** [verb: ἀμφιέννυμι <294>]; **from *amphi*: around, and *ennumi*: to dress; lit.: to wrap clothes around oneself ▶ To dress, to put on clothes** > God clothes the grass of the field (Matt. 6:30; Luke 12:28: some mss. have *amphiazō*, others have *amphiezō*). John the Baptist was not clothed in fine clothes (Matt. 11:8; Luke 7:25). ¶

[5] ***himatizō*** [verb: ἱματίζω <2439>]; **from *himation*: garment ▶ To put on a garment, to dress** > The man who had been demon-possessed was found clothed (Mark 5:15; Luke 8:35).

[6] **to clothe with: *enkomboomai*** [verb: ἐγκομβόομαι <1463>]; **from *en*: in, and *komboō*: to tie; lit.: to fasten a garment ▶ To put on; from this verb comes *enkombōma*, a garment fastened with strings worn by slaves over their tunic** > All Christians are to clothe themselves with {to bind on} humility toward one another (1 Pet. 5:5). ¶

[7] ***periballō*** [verb: περιβάλλω <4016>]; **from *peri*: around, and *ballō*: to cast, to put ▶ To array, to dress; also transl.: to wear, to wear for clothing** > Solomon, in all his glory, was not clothed as one of the lilies of the field (Matt. 6:29; Luke 12:27). We are not to worry about what we shall be clothed with (Matt. 6:31). Jesus will say: I was naked, and you clothed me (Matt. 25:36), and the righteous will ask Him when (v. 38); He will say to others that they had not clothed Him (v. 43). In the tomb of Jesus, a young man was sitting, clothed in a white robe (Mark 16:5). Herod clothed {arrayed} Jesus with a splendid robe (Luke 23:11). The soldiers clothed Jesus in a purple robe (John 19:2). He who overcomes in Sardis will be clothed in white garments (Rev. 3:5). Laodicea needed to be clothed (Rev. 3:18). The twenty-four elders were clothed in white garments (Rev. 4:4). A great crowd was clothed in white robes (Rev. 7:9, 13). John saw a strong angel clothed with {robed in} a cloud (Rev. 10:1); he also saw a woman clothed with the sun (12:1). The two witnesses were clothed in sackcloth (Rev. 11:3). The woman (Babylon) was clothed in purple and scarlet (Rev. 17:4; 18:16). The wife of the Lamb is clothed in fine linen (Rev. 19:8). The Lord is clothed in a robe dyed in blood (Rev. 19:13). All other refs.: BUILD <4016>, WEAR <4016>, WRAP <4016>.

– [8] Luke 17:8 → GIRD <4024> [9] 1 Cor. 12:23 → BESTOW <4060> [10] Heb. 5:2 → to be clothed, to be subject → SUBJECT (verb) <4029>.

CLOTHED – [1] 1 Cor. 4:11 → to be poorly clothed → to be naked → NAKED <1130> [2] Rev. 16:15 → to remain clothed → to keep one's clothes → CLOTHES <2440>.

CLOTHES – [1] ***enduma*** [neut. noun: ἔνδυμα <1742>]; **from *enduō*: to clothe, to dress, which is from *en*: in, and *duō*: to put on ▶ Articles designed to cover**

the body; also transl.: clothing, garment, raiment > John the Baptist had clothes that were made of camel's hair (Matt. 3:4). The body is more than clothes (Matt. 6:25; Luke 12:23); we are not to worry about clothes (Matt. 6:28). The angel's clothes were white as snow (Matt. 28:3). Other refs.: Matt. 7:15; 22:11, 12; see CLOTHING <1742>, GARMENT <1742>. ¶

2 ***esthēs*** [fem. noun: ἐσθής <2066>]; **from *ennumi*: to clothe, to dress ▶ See defin. in 1; also transl.: apparel, clothing, garment, raiment, robe >** Herod put a gorgeous robe on Jesus (Luke 23:11). At the ascension of Jesus, two men in white clothing stood beside the disciples (Acts 1:10). A man stood before Cornelius in shining clothes (Acts 10:30). James speaks of the difference which might be made in the synagogue between a man in fine clothes and a poor man in dirty clothes (Jas. 2:2a, b, 3). Other ref.: Luke 24:4; see 3. Other ref.: Acts 12:21; see APPAREL <2066>. ¶

3 ***esthēsis*** [fem. noun: ἔσθησις <2067>]; **from *estheō*: to be dressed, which is from *esthēs*: see 2 ▶ Clothing, garment >** On the morning of the resurrection of the Lord, two men suddenly stood by the women, in shining clothes (Luke 24:4 {raiment}); other mss. have *esthēs* (see 2). ¶

4 ***himation*** [neut. noun: ἱμάτιον <2440>]; **comp. *hennumi*: to cover, to dress ▶ Garment in general, including outer and inner clothing; often a shirt over which a tunic could be worn; also transl.: apparel, cloak, clothing, coat, dress, garment, robe >** A woman who had a hemorrhage touched the edge of Jesus's clothes (Matt. 9:20, 21; Mark 5:27, 28, 30; Luke 8:44). John the Baptist was not dressed in fine clothes (Matt. 11:8; Luke 7:25a). Jesus was transfigured, and His clothes became white as the light (Matt. 17:2; Mark 9:3). The disciples put their coats on the donkey and the colt (Matt. 21:7; Mark 11:7; Luke 19:35), and a very large crowd spread their coats on the pathway of Jesus (Matt. 21:8; Mark 11:8; Luke 19:36). The scribes and the Pharisees lengthened the tassels of their garments (Matt. 23:5). During the tribulation, he who is in the field is not to go back to get his cloak (Matt. 24:18; Mark 13:16). The high priest tore his clothes (Matt. 26:65). The soldiers put His own clothes on Jesus (Matt. 27:31; Mark 15:20). Having crucified Him, the soldiers divided up His clothes (Matt. 27:35); Mark 15:24; Luke 23:34; John 19:23), so that the Scripture concerning His outer garments might be fulfilled (John 19:24). People begged Jesus to let the sick touch the edge of His garment (Mark 6:56). A blind man threw aside his cloak and came to Jesus (Mark 10:50). A demon-possessed man who wore no clothes met Jesus (Luke 8:27). Jesus told His disciples that whoever has no sword is to sell his coat (Luke 22:36). Jesus laid aside His outer clothing and wrapped a towel around His waist (John 13:4); He put on his clothes again after having washed the feet of His disciples (v. 12). A purple robe was put on Jesus (John 19:2); He came out wearing the crown of thorns and this robe (v. 5). The witnesses at the stoning of Stephen laid aside their clothes at the feet of Saul (Acts 7:58; 22:20). Dorcas had made tunics and garments while she was living (Acts 9:39). Peter was to wrap his cloak around himself and follow the angel (Acts 12:8). Barnabas and Paul tore their robes (Acts 14:14). The magistrates tore off the clothes of Paul and Silas (Acts 16:22). Paul shook out his clothes (Acts 18:6). The Jews were throwing off their cloaks (Acts 22:23). James speaks of the clothes of the rich which are eaten by moths (Jas. 5:2). The adornment of the wife must not be merely external, such as fine clothes, but the hidden disposition of the heart (1 Pet. 3:3). The term is also used in Rev. 3:4, 5, 18; 4:4; 16:15; 19:13, 16. All other refs.: CLOAK <2440>, GARMENT <2440>.

5 ***himatismos*** [masc. noun: ἱματισμός <2441>]; **from *himatizō*: to clothe, which is from *himation*: garment ▶ Clothing, apparel; also transl.: raiment, robe >** Those who are in splendid clothing and live luxuriously are in the courts of kings (Luke 7:25b). At the transfiguration, the clothes of Jesus became white and gleaming (Luke 9:29). All other refs.: CLOTHING <2441>.

6 *chitōn* [masc. noun: χιτών <5509>] ► **Inner garment, shirt worn next to the skin** > The high priest tore his clothes (Mark 14:63). Jude speaks of saving some people with fear, snatching them out of the fire, hating even the garment {clothing} polluted by the flesh (Jude 23). All other refs.: TUNIC <5509>.
– 7 Matt. 25:36, 38, 43, 44; Jas. 2:15 → needing clothes, without clothes → NAKED <1131> 8 Luke 2:7, 12 → to wrap in swaddling clothes → WRAP <4683> 9 John 11:44 → to take off the grave clothes → LOOSE <3089> 10 Acts 12:8 → to put on one's clothes → GIRD <4024>.

CLOTHING – 1 *enduma* [neut. noun: ἔνδυμα <1742>]; **from *enduō*: to clothe, which is from *en*: in, and *duō*: to put on** ► **Garment, clothes** > Jesus warns against false prophets who come in sheep's clothing (Matt. 7:15). All other refs.: CLOTHES <1742>, GARMENT <1742>.
2 *himatismos* [masc. noun: ἱματισμός <2441>]; **from *himatizō*: to clothe, which is from *himation*: garment** ► **Garment, also transl.: clothes** > The soldiers cast lots for the clothing {vesture} of Jesus (John 19:24). Paul had coveted the clothing {apparel} of no one (Acts 20:33). Christian women are not to adorn themselves with costly clothing {array, attire} (1 Tim. 2:9). All other refs.: CLOTHES <2441>.
3 *skepasma* [neut. noun: σκέπασμα <4629>]; **from *skepazō*: to cover** ► **Garment, clothes: also transl.: covering, raiment** > Having food and clothing, Christians will be content with these (1 Tim. 6:8). ¶
– 4 Matt. 11:8; Luke 7:25; 8:27; John 13:4 {outer clothing}; 1 Pet. 3:3; etc. → CLOTHES <2440> 5 Mark 1:6 → to wear clothing → CLOTHE <1746> 6 Mark 12:38 → in long clothing → in long robes → ROBE (noun) <4749> 7 Luke 10:30 → to take off the clothing → TAKE <1562> 8 Luke 23:11; Acts 1:10; 10:30; Jas. 2:2a, b, 3 → CLOTHES <2066> 9 Luke 24:4 → CLOTHES <2067> 10 1 Tim. 2:9 → proper clothing → modest apparel → APPAREL <2887> 11 Jas. 2:15 → without clothing → NAKED <1131> 12 Jude 23 → CLOTHES <5509>.

CLOUD – 1 *nephelē* [fem. noun: νεφέλη <3507>]; **dimin. of *nephos*: see defin. in 2** ► **Vapor mass of limited size and definite shape in the sky** > A bright cloud overshadowed Jesus and His disciples (Matt. 17:5a, b; Mark 9:7a, b; Luke 9:34a, b, 35). The Son of Man will come on the clouds of heaven (Matt. 24:30; 26:64; Mark 13:26; 14:62; Luke 21:27). If a cloud rises out of the west, a shower is coming (Luke 12:54). Jesus was taken up and a cloud received Him (Acts 1:9). The Israelites were under a cloud when they crossed the Red Sea (1 Cor. 10:1, 2). When Jesus returns, those who remain will be caught up together in the clouds with those who have fallen asleep (1 Thes. 4:17). Jude speaks of the wicked who are like clouds without water (Jude 12). The Son of Man comes with the clouds (Rev. 1:7). John saw an angel clothed with a cloud (Rev. 10:1) and another angel who sat on a cloud (14:15, 16). He saw a white cloud, and on the cloud one sitting like the Son of Man (Rev. 14:14a, b). The two witnesses went up to heaven in the cloud (Rev. 11:12). Other ref.: 2 Pet. 2:17: see MIST <3507>. ¶
2 *nephos* [neut. noun: νέφος <3509>] ► **Large, shapeless mass of cloud; lit.: what covers, in particular a cloud canopy; multitude** > A great cloud of witnesses are surrounding the Christians (Heb. 12:1). ¶

CLUB – Matt. 26:47, 55; Mark 14:43, 48; Luke 22:52 → STAVE <3586>.

CLUSTER – *botrus* [masc. noun: βότρυς <1009>] ► **Group of fruit, e.g., grapes, which grow together** > An angel called with a loud voice to another angel to harvest the clusters {bunches} of grapes from the vine of the earth (Rev. 14:18). ¶

CNIDUS – *Knidos* [fem. name: Κνίδος <2834>] ► **Greek city located in south-western Asia Minor** > Paul's ship passed near Cnidus (Acts 27:7). ¶

CO-HEIR – Rom. 8:17 → JOINT HEIR <4789>.

COAL – [1] ***anthrax*** [masc. noun: ἄνθραξ <440>] ▶ **Piece of charred wood used as a fuel** > The expr. "to heap coals of fire on the head of an enemy" (Rom. 12:20; see Prov. 25:22) means that by doing good in response to evil, one may reach the conscience and the heart of his enemy. An explanation is given in *Sondez les Écritures*: "In the Eastern countries, when the fire would die out, people felt the cold and were hungry (it was not possible anymore to cook the food). Then they would go to their neighbor to get fire by using a brazier (a metal bowl to hold burning coals) full of charcoal on fire carried on the head, according to the Eastern custom. The neighbor would literally heap coals of fire on the head of the requester. If it was normal to do this service to a friend, this verse (see also Prov. 25:21, 22) is an encouragement to do it to an enemy." If the enemy does not repent, the vengeance of the Lord (see Rom. 12:19) would be that much greater; the Christian, however, must overcome evil with good (see v. 21). ¶
[2] **fire of coals: *anthrakia*** [fem. noun: ἀνθρακιά <439>]; **from *anthrax*: see** [1] ▶ **Heap of burning coal lumps; also transl.: charcoal fire** > The servants and the officers had made a fire of coals (John 18:18). The disciples saw a fire of coals and fish laid on it (John 21:9). ¶

COARSE – Eph. 5:4 → coarse jesting, coarse joking → JESTING <2160>.

COAST (noun) – [1] ***horion*** [neut. noun: ὅριον <3725>]; **dimin. of *horos*: boundary** ▶ **Region, territory** > Jesus departed from the coasts {borders, region, vicinity} of Decapolis (Mark 7:31). All other refs.: BORDER <3725>, REGION <3725>.
[2] ***topos*** [masc. noun: τόπος <5117>] ▶ **Place, region, location** > The ship of Paul was to sail along the coasts of Asia (Acts 27:2). All other refs.: OPPORTUNITY <5117>, PLACE (noun) <5117>, ROCK <5117>.
– [3] Matt. 15:21; 16:13 → PART (noun) <3313> [4] Luke 6:17 → sea coast → SEA COAST, SEACOAST <3882> [5] Acts 19:1 → REGION <3313> [6] Acts 26:20 → coasts → COUNTRY <5561> [7] Acts 27:8 → to move along the coast → PASS <3881>.

COAST (verb) – [1] Acts 27:8 → PASS <3881> [2] Acts 27:13 → to sail close → SAIL (verb) <3881>.

COASTAL REGION – Luke 6:17 → SEA COAST <3882>.

COAT – [1] Matt. 5:40; Luke 6:29; → CLOAK <2440> [2] Matt. 10:10; Mark 6:9; Luke 3:11; 9:3; John 19:23a, b; Acts 9:39 → TUNIC <5509> [3] Matt. 21:7; Mark 11:7; Luke 19:35; 22:36; Acts 7:58; et al. → CLOTHES <2440> [4] John 21:7 → fisher's coat → OVERCOAT <1903>.

COCKCROW, COCKCROWING – Mark 13:35 → crowing of the rooster → ROOSTER <219>.

CODE – [1] Rom. 2:27, 29; 7:6 → written code → LETTER <1121> [2] Col. 2:14 → written code → HANDWRITING <5498>.

COFFIN – Luke 7:14 → coffin, open coffin → BIER <4673>.

COGNIZANCE – Acts 25:21 → DECISION <1233>.

COHORT – ***speira*** [fem. noun: σπεῖρα <4686>] ▶ **Body of infantry made of 500 to 600 men; ten cohorts made a legion; also transl.: band, band of soldiers, company, detachment, garrison, troop, regiment** > The whole cohort was gathered against Jesus (Matt. 27:27; Mark 15:16). Julius, to whom Paul was delivered, was a centurion of the Augustan cohort (Acts 27:1), most likely the imperial cohort. As a centurion, Cornelius was commanding the Italian cohort (Acts 10:1). Other refs.: John 18:3, 12; Acts 21:31. ¶

COIN – [1] **coin, silver coin:** ***drachmē*** [fem. noun: δραχμή <1406>]; **from** ***drassomai*:** **to seize, to take ► Greek piece of money worth approx. one Roman denarius; it was the average pay for an average work day; also transl.: drachma** > A woman had ten silver coins {pieces of silver} and she was carefully searching for one which was lost (Luke 15:8a, b, 9); this parable illustrates the Holy Spirit seeking a lost sinner in view of salvation. ¶

– [2] Matt. 18:28 → silver coins → lit.: denarii → DENARIUS <1220> [3] Matt. 22:19 → MONEY <3546> [4] Mark 12:42; Luke 21:2 → copper coin → MITE <3016> [5] John 2:15 → MONEY <2772>.

COLD – [1] ***psuchos*** [neut. noun: ψῦχος <5592>]; **from** ***psuchō*:** **to breathe, to blow ► Lack of heat** > The servants and the officers had made a fire because it was cold (John 18:18). The inhabitants of Malta had kindled a fire because of the cold (Acts 28:2). Paul had been in cold and nakedness (2 Cor. 11:27). ¶

[2] ***psuchros*** [adj.: ψυχρός <5593>]; **from** ***psuchō*:** **see** [1] **► Broader term than the preceding one; in the N.T. it speaks of something which refreshes, reinvigorates** > The church of Laodicea is neither cold nor hot (Rev. 3:15a, 16); the Lord would that it were cold or hot (v. 15b), not lukewarm. This term is transl. "cold water" in Matt. 10:42: Jesus is speaking of giving a cup of cold water to drink. ¶

[3] **to grow cold, to wax cold:** ***psuchō*** [verb: ψύχω <5594>] **► In a spiritual sense, to become cold by losing one's fervor** > During the tribulation, the love of many will grow cold (Matt. 24:12). ¶

COLLAPSE – [1] Matt. 15:32; Mark 8:3 → FAINT <1590> [2] Luke 6:49; Rev. 11:13; 16:19 → FALL (verb) <4098>.

COLLECT – [1] ***lambanō*** [verb: λαμβάνω <2983>] **► To receive, to levy** > Those who collected the didrachmas asked Peter if Jesus paid the didrachmas (Matt. 17:24). Other refs.: see entries in Lexicon at <2983>.

[2] ***prassō*** [verb: πράσσω <4238>]; **lit.: to practice, to perform ► To obtain money from a person as payment or tribute** > Jesus told the tax-gatherers to collect {to take, to exact} no more money than what was appointed them (Luke 3:13). The master would have collected {received, required} the money he had entrusted to his servant with interest if this money had been put in the bank (Luke 19:23); some mss. have *anaprassō*. Other refs.: CONTRARY <4238>, DO <4238>, KEEP (verb) <4238>, USE (verb) <4238>.

– [3] Matt. 13:48 → GATHER <4816> [4] Luke 19:21, 22 → TAKE <142> [5] Rom. 15:28 → what has been collected → lit.: this fruit → FRUIT <2590>.

COLLECTING – 1 Cor. 16:2 → COLLECTION <3048>.

COLLECTION – ***logeia*** [fem. noun: λογεία <3047a>] **or** ***logia*** [fem. noun: λογία <3048>]; **from** ***legō*:** **to choose, to set aside ► Gift made by Christians, as money given during a church service** > Scriptural practice for the Christian which consists in laying something aside on the first day of the week, according to how God has blessed him (1 Cor. 16:1, 2), for the saints who are poor and for the servants of the Lord (see 1 Cor. 9:11–14). God is well pleased with sacrifices of praise, but also with Christians doing good and sharing what they have (see 2 Cor. 9:6–14; Heb. 13:15, 16). ¶

COLLECTOR – [1] Matt. 17:24 → the collectors → lit.: those who collected → COLLECT <2983> [2] Luke 19:2 → chief tax collector, chief tax-gatherer → PUBLICAN <754>.

COLONNADE – John 5:2; 10:23; Acts 3:11; 5:12 → colonnade, covered colonnade, roofed colonnade → PORCH <4745>.

COLONY – ***kolōnia*** [fem. noun: κολωνία <2862>]; **similar to Lat.** ***colonia*:** **settlement ► District inhabited by Roman citizens (at first, veterans) and governed**

by Roman laws > Philippi in Macedonia was a Roman colony (Acts 16:12). ¶

COLOSSAE – ***Kolossai*** [fem. name: Κολοσσαί <2857>] **or** ***Kolassai*** [fem. name: Κολασσαί <2857>]**: giant, colossal statue ▶ City of Phrygia in Asia Minor, not far from Laodicea and Hierapolis; also transl.: Colosse** > Paul wrote a letter to the Christians of this city (Col. 1:2). He warns them against the deceptions of philosophy (see 2:8), against religious ordinances and the worship of angels (see 2:16–19). He reminds Christians that they are dead and risen with Christ, and that they are to live accordingly (see 2:20 to 3:4). In this same letter, the double supremacy of Christ, the firstborn of all creation and the firstborn from among the dead (see 1:13–20), and the effectiveness of His work on the cross (see 2:13, 14) have an important place. ¶

COLOSSE – See COLOSSAE <2857>.

COLOSSIAN – ***Kolassaeus*** [masc. name: Κολασσαεύς <2858>] **▶ Inhabitant of the city of Colossae, in Asia Minor** > The name is found only in the inscription to the Epistle to the Colossians. Paul addressed his letter to the brothers in Christ of the city of Colossae (see Col. 1:1, 2); see COLOSSAE <2857>. ¶

COLOUR – Acts 27:30 → PRETEXT <4392>.

COLT – ***pōlos*** [masc. noun: πῶλος <4454>] **▶ Young male donkey** > Jesus sat on a colt (Matt. 21:2, 5a, b, 7; Mark 11:2, 4, 5, 7; Luke 19:30, 33, 35; John 12:15). ¶

COMB – ***kērion*** [neut. noun: κηρίον <2781>]**; from *kērox*: wax ▶ The honeycomb is a cake of wax formed by bees whose cells are full of honey** > After His resurrection, Jesus ate some honeycomb (Luke 24:42 in some mss.). ¶

COMBAT (noun) – [1] 2 Cor. 7:5 → FIGHTING <3163> [2] Col. 2:1 → CONFLICT <73> [3] 1 Tim. 6:12; 2 Tim. 4:7 → FIGHT (noun) <75>.

COMBAT (verb) – [1] 1 Cor. 9:26 → FIGHT (verb) <4438> [2] Col. 1:29; 4:12; 2 Tim. 4:7 → to combat, to combat earnestly → FIGHT (verb) <75>.

COMBINE – [1] 1 Cor. 2:13 → COMPARE <4793> [2] 1 Cor. 12:24 → COMPOSE <4786> [3] Heb. 4:2 → to mix with → MIX <4786>.

COME – [1] **to come, to come to pass, to come upon, to come on, to come to be: *ginomai*** [verb: γίνομαι <1096>] **▶ a. To reach, to arrive** > The blessing of Abraham came to the nations in Christ Jesus (Gal. 3:14). **b. To become** > All those who obeyed Theudas were dispersed and came to nothing (Acts 5:36). **c. To become, to happen, to make, to seize** > The voice of Mary's salutation sounded in (lit.: came to) Elizabeth's ears (Luke 1:44). Fear came on the neighbors of Zacharias (Luke 1:65). Astonishment came upon all the people of Capernaum (Luke 4:36). The verb is used in regard to evening (Matt. 8:16), morning (Matt. 27:1), a voice (Mark 1:11; Luke 9:35), the Sabbath (Mark 6:2), a day (Mark 6:21), and salvation (Luke 19:9). The number of men who believed came to be (in the sense of: increased) to about five thousand (Acts 4:4). Other refs.: Matt. 24:6; Mark 9:21; Luke 1:8; 2:1, 15; 12:55; 21:9; 24:12; John 13:19a, b; 14:29a, b; Acts 5:5, 11, 36; 12:11; 21:17; 22:17; 26:22; 27:7; 28:6; 2 Cor. 1:8; 1 Thes. 3:4; 2 Tim. 3:11; Heb. 7:16. Other refs.: see entries in the Lexicon at <1096>.

[2] ***paraginomai*** [verb: παραγίνομαι <3854>]**; from *para*: near, and *ginomai*: see** [1] **▶ To appear, to arrive** > While Jesus was still speaking, Judas came up, and with him a great crowd with swords and clubs (Mark 14:43). A servant came up and brought back word of certain things to his master (Luke 14:21). The verb is used in regard to John the Baptist (Matt. 3:1), Jesus (Matt. 3:13; Luke 12:51). Other refs.: Matt. 2:1; Luke 11:6; 19:16; Acts 5:22, 25;

9:26, 39; 11:23; 13:14; 14:27; 15:4; 17:10; 18:27; 23:35; 25:7; 28:21. Other refs.: GO <3854>.

3 **to come together:** ***sumparaginomai*** [verb: συμπαραγίνομαι <4836>]**; from** ***sun*****: together, and** ***paraginomai*****: see** 2 ▶ **To assemble** > All the crowds who had come together {gathered} for the crucifixion of Jesus returned, beating their breasts (Luke 23:48). No man came together with {stood with, supported, came to the support of} Paul at his first defense (2 Tim. 4:16). ¶

4 ***erchomai*** [verb: ἔρχομαι <2064>] ▶ **a. To appear, to arrive, to go** > Jesus said He would come and heal the servant of the centurion (Matt. 8:7). The Son of Man has come to seek and to save that which was lost (Matt. 18:11; Luke 19:10). The Son of Man did not come to be served, but to serve and to give His life as a ransom for many (Matt. 20:28). Jesus came to a fig tree (Matt. 21:19; Mark 11:13a, b). The Lord Jesus is coming quickly (Rev. 22:7, 12, 20). The verb is employed many times, e.g., in regard to the Lord Jesus (Matt. 3:11, 14; 9:18b; 1 Cor. 4:5; 11:26; 2 Thes. 1:10; Heb. 10:37a; Rev. 1:4, 7, 8), the Father and the Son (John 14:23), the Holy Spirit (e.g., Matt. 3:16; John 15:26; 16:7), John the Baptist (Matt. 11:18; 21:32), wise men (Matt. 2:2), Elijah (e.g., Matt. 17:10–12), Peter (Matt. 14:29; Acts 5:15; 12:10), Paul (1 Cor. 14:6; 2 Cor. 12:1; 13:1, 2; Phil. 1:27; 1 Tim. 4:13), John (3 John 10; Rev. 6:1, 3, 5, 7), Nathanael (John 1:47), a Samaritan woman (John 4:7, 15, 16), Mary of Bethany (John 11:29), Mary of Magdala (e.g., John 20:18), Timothy (e.g., 1 Cor. 16:10, 11), Mark (Col. 4:10), Satan (Mark 4:15; Luke 8:12; John 14:30), Jairus (Mark 5:22; Luke 8:41), the Father's kingdom (Matt. 6:10; Luke 11:2), the wrath of God (Eph. 5:6; Col. 3:6; 1 Thes. 1:10), the day of the Lord (1 Thes. 5:2), false prophets (Matt. 7:15), the antichrist (John 5:43b; 1 John 2:18a; 4:3b), and false christs (Matt. 24:5; Mark 13:6; Luke 21:8). A famine came upon {struck} all the land of Egypt and Canaan (Acts 7:11). **b. To arrive, to reach** > Paul spoke of those who are always learning and never able to come to the knowledge of {to acknowledge} the truth (2 Tim. 3:7). Paul and Silas had come {come down} to Mysia (Acts 16:7). **c. To go meet, to return, to visit** > When he came home, the man who had lost his sheep invited his friends and neighbors to rejoice with him (Luke 15:6). The prodigal son came to himself {came to his senses} in the distant country (Luke 15:17). In the same parable, the older son came from the field (Luke 15:25). The judge feared that the woman would come continually to be avenged (Luke 18:5). The blind man came seeing from the pool of Siloam (John 9:7). Jesus will come again to take His own to Himself (John 14:3). Silas and Timothy had received a commandment to come to {to join} Paul (Acts 17:15). Paul did not want to come back {to make a visit} to the Corinthians in sorrow (2 Cor. 2:1). He speaks of coming again among the Corinthians (2 Cor. 12:21). Other refs.: Matt. 2:11, 23; 8:28; 9:18, 23, 28; 13:36; 14:12, 28, 29; 15:25; 18:7a, b; 21:1, 23; 27:33, 57; 28:11; Mark 1:29; 5:1; 6:31b; 10:46; 13:36; 14:16; Luke 2:16; 3:3; 7:7; 8:51; 10:1, 32; 14:20; 17:1a, b; 18:3; 22:7; John 1:39a, b; 6:17; 11:17, 30; 19:39a, b; 20:3, 4, 6, 8; 21:3b; Acts 8:36, 40; 20:6; 21:1, 22; 22:11; 27:8; 28:13, 14, 16; Rom. 1:10, 13; 3:8; 15:22, 23, 29a, b, 32; 1 Cor. 2:1a, b; 4:18, 19, 21; 11:34; 16:2, 12; 2 Cor. 1:15, 16, 23; 2:3, 12; 7:5; 12:14, 20; Gal. 1:21; Phil. 1:12 {to fall out, to turn out}; 1 Thes. 2:18; 3:6; 2 Thes. 2:3; 2 John 12; Rev. 9:12. Other refs.: FALL (verb) <2064>, GO <2064>, GROW <2064>.

5 ***dierchomai*** [verb: διέρχομαι <1330>]**; from** ***dia*****: through, and** ***erchomai*****: see** 4 ▶ **To go, to pass** > Peter was not to delay to come to Joppa (Acts 9:38). All other refs.: GO <1330>, PASS <1330>, PIERCE <1330>, SPREAD <1330>.

6 **to come, to come in:** ***eiserchomai*** [verb: εἰσέρχομαι <1525>]**; from** ***eis*****: in, and** ***erchomai*****: see** 4 ▶ **a. To enter, to go in** > Jairus pleaded with Jesus to come into his house (Luke 8:41b). **b. To return** > The Lord speaks of a servant who comes in from the field (Luke 17:7). Other refs.: Mark 15:43; Acts 11:20. All other refs.: ENTER <1525>.

7 **to come in: *pareiserchomai*** [verb: παρεισέρχομαι <3922>]; **from *para*: beside, *eis*: in, and *erchomai*: to enter ▶ To introduce, to appear on the scene** > The law came in {entered, was brought in} that the offense might abound (Rom. 5:20). Other ref.: Gal. 2:4 (to come in surreptitiously); see SURREPTITIOUSLY <3922>. ¶

8 **to come, to come forth, to come out: *exerchomai*** [verb: ἐξέρχομαι <1831>]; **from *ek*: out, and *erchomai*: see 4 ▶ To have one's origin; also transl.: to go out, to go forth, to originate, to proceed, to proceed forth** > The verb is used in regard to things that come out of the heart (Matt. 15:18, 19), Jesus (Mark 1:38; John 13:3; 16:30), a viper (Acts 18:3; *diexerchomai* in some mss.), and the brothers of Italy (Acts 28:15). This verb describes specifically the bond uniting people: Jesus came forth from God (John 8:42). The word of God did not come out from the Corinthians (1 Cor. 14:36). James warns against the mouth from which goes forth (sing. in Greek) both blessing and cursing (Jas. 3:10). All other refs.: DEPART <1831>, ESCAPE <1831>, GO <1831>, SPREAD <1831>, STEP (verb) <1831>.

9 **to come, to come on, to come upon: *eperchomai*** [verb: ἐπέρχομαι <1904>]; **from *epi*: upon, and *erchomai*: see 4 ▶ a. To arrive, to descend** > The Holy Spirit was to come upon Mary (Luke 1:35), the disciples (Acts 1:8). The verb is also used when the Lord speaks about things to come upon the inhabited earth (Luke 21:26) and to that day (v. 35; *epeiserchomai* in some mss.). Other refs.: Acts 8:24; Eph. 2:7; Jas. 5:1. **b. To happen, to come near** > What is spoken of in the prophets came upon those who were listening to Paul in Antioch (Acts 13:40). Other ref.: Acts 14:19. Other ref.: Luke 11:22; see ATTACK (verb) <1904>. ¶

10 **to come, to come down: *katerchomai*** [verb: κατέρχομαι <2718>]; **from *kata*: down, and *erchomai*: see 4 ▶ a. To descend, to go down** > The verb is used concerning Jesus (Luke 9:37), Peter (Acts 9:32 {to go}), prophets (Acts 11:27), men from Judea (Acts 15:1), Silas and Timothy (Acts 18:5), and Agabus (Acts 21:10). **b. To disembark** > Ref.: Acts 27:5 {to land}. All other refs.: DESCEND <2718>, GO <2718>, LAND (verb) <2718>.

11 ***parerchomai*** [verb: παρέρχομαι <3928>]; **from *para*: near, and *erchomai*: see 4 ▶ To come beside or in front** > At his return, the master will come {will come up, will come forth} and serve his servants (Luke 12:37). Lysias came up and with great force took Paul out of the hands of his enemies (Acts 24:7). Other ref.: Luke 17:7b. All other refs.: GO <3928>, PASS <3928>, SPEND <3928>, TRANSGRESS <3928>.

12 ***proserchomai*** [verb: προσέρχομαι <4334>]; **from *pros*: to, and *erchomai*: see 4 ▶ To draw near, to approach** > Various people, as well as angels, came to Jesus: the tempter (Matt. 4:3), angels (Matt. 4:11), His disciples (Matt. 5:1; 8:25; 13:10; 15:12, 23; 24:1), a leper (Matt. 8:2), a scribe (Matt. 8:19), a woman who had a flow of blood (Matt. 9:20; Luke 8:44), the Pharisees and the Sadducees (Matt. 16:1), the father of an epileptic (Matt. 17:14), Peter (Matt. 18:21), a rich young man (Matt. 19:16), Judas (Matt. 26:49; Mark 14:45), a multitude with swords and clubs (Matt. 26:50), godly women (Matt. 28:9), a scribe (Mark 12:28), the twelve apostles (Luke 9:12), a child possessed by an unclean spirit (Luke 9:42), some of the Sadducees (Luke 20:27), and soldiers (Luke 23:36). Jesus came to three of His disciples (Matt. 17:7); He came to the eleven disciples on a mountain in Galilee (Matt. 28:18); He came to the mother of Simon's wife (Mark 1:31); He came and touched the open coffin of a young man (Luke 7:14). The servants of the householder came to Him (Matt. 13:27). People came to Peter in the yard of the palace (Matt. 26:73). The verb is used in regard to disciples of John (Matt. 9:14), those of Jesus (Matt. 17:19), and scribes and Pharisees (Matt. 15:1). Paul came to Aquila and Priscilla (Acts 18:2). The chief captain came to Paul (Acts 22:27). Christians can come to God: Heb. 4:16 {to approach}; 7:25; 10:1, 22 {to draw near}; 11:6. Christians come to the Lord as to a living stone (1 Pet. 2:4). Other

refs.: CONSENT (verb) <4334>, DRAW <4334>, GO <4334>.

13 ***sunerchomai*** [verb: συνέρχομαι <4905>]; **from *sun*: together, and *erchomai*: see 4 ▶ a. To assemble, to meet together; also transl.: to resort, to meet, to gather** > The multitude came together near the house where Jesus was (Mark 3:20). The chief priests, the elders, and the scribes were assembled with Jesus (Mark 14:53). Great multitudes came together to hear Jesus and to be healed by Him (Luke 5:15). Paul used this verb in addressing the church of Corinth which gathered together to proclaim the Lord's death (1 Cor. 11:17, 18, 20, 33, 34) and for prophecy meetings (14:23, 26). **b. To proceed in the company of another** > The verb is used in John 11:33; Acts 10:45; 21:16; 25:17. **c. To return together, to be found together** > Paul speaks of spouses who come together again after having given themselves to prayer (1 Cor. 7:5). Other refs.: Matt. 1:18; Mark 6:33; John 18:20; Acts 1:6; 2:6; 5:16; 10:27; 16:13; 19:32; 21:22; 22:30; 28:17. All other refs.: ACCOMPANY <4905>, FOLLOW <4905>, GO <4905>.

14 ***eisporeuomai*** [verb: εἰσπορεύομαι <1531>]; **from *eis*: in, and *poreuomai*: to go ▶ To go in, to enter** > At the beginning of his conversion, Paul was with the apostles coming in and going out {moving about freely} in Jerusalem, and speaking boldly in the name of the Lord (Acts 9:28). Other ref.: Acts 28:30. All other refs.: ENTER <1531>.

15 ***epiporeuomai*** [verb: ἐπιπορεύομαι <1975>]; **from *epi*: to, and *poreuomai*: to go ▶ To go, to journey** > People were coming to Jesus out of every city (Luke 8:4). ¶

16 **to come to: *prosporeuomai*** [verb: προσπορεύομαι <4365>]; **from *pros*: to, and *poreuomai*: to go ▶ To go to, to go near** > James and John came to Jesus (Mark 10:35). ¶

17 ***anabainō*** [verb: ἀναβαίνω <305>]; **from *ana*: up, and *bainō*: to go ▶ To arise, to rise** > It came into the heart of Moses to visit his brothers, the sons of Israel (Acts 7:23). A report came up to the chiliarch that all Jerusalem was in a tumult (Acts 21:31). All other refs.: see GO <305>.

18 ***apobainō*** [verb: ἀποβαίνω <576>]; **from *apo*: away from, and *bainō*: to go ▶ To come out, to go down** > When the disciples had come to land {had gone out on the land, got out upon the land, landed}, they saw the meal prepared by Jesus (John 21:9). Other refs.: Luke 5:2; 21:13; Phil. 1:19; see GO <576>, TURN (verb) <576>. ¶

19 ***epibainō*** [verb: ἐπιβαίνω <1910>]; **from *epi*: upon, and *bainō*: to come ▶ To arrive** > The verb is used for Paul (Acts 20:18b {to set foot}) and Festus (Acts 25:1). All other refs.: BOARD (verb) <1910>, SIT <1910>.

20 **to come down: *katabainō*** [verb: καταβαίνω <2597>]; **from *kata*: down, and *bainō*: to go ▶ To go down; also transl.: to descend** > Jesus came down the mountain with Peter and James, and John his brother, after His transfiguration (Matt. 17:9; Mark 9:9). He was challenged to come down from the cross (Matt. 27:40; Mark 15:30, 32). The verb is used concerning Jesus (Matt. 8:1; Luke 6:17; John 4:47, 49) and the Father (Jas. 1:17). It is also used concerning Peter (Matt. 14:29), people during the tribulation (Matt. 24:17; Luke 17:31), scribes (Mark 3:22), a certain priest (Luke 10:31), Zaccheus (Luke 19:5, 6), the Lord (Acts 7:34), Peter and John (Acts 8:15), gods (Acts 14:11), Paul (Acts 16:8), Ananias (Acts 24:1), Lysias (Acts 24:22), Jews (Acts 25:7), and the devil (Rev. 12:12). The expr. "to come down from heaven" is found in Luke 9:54; John 3:13; 6:33, 38, 41, 42, 50, 51, 58; Rev. 3:12; 10:1; 13:13; 16:21; 18:1; 20:1, 9; 21:2. All other refs.: DESCEND <2597>, FALL (verb) <2597>, GO <2597>, STEP (verb) <2597>.

21 **to come up: *sunanabainō*** [verb: συναναβαίνω <4872>]; **from *sun*: together with, and *anabainō*: see 17 ▶ To go up** > Women came up with Jesus to Jerusalem (Mark 15:41). Jesus appeared to those, most likely the previous women, who had come up {had traveled} with Him from Galilee to Jerusalem (Acts 13:31). ¶

22 **to come into the neighborhood: *engizō*** [verb: ἐγγίζω <1448>]; **from *engus*:**

near ▶ To approach, to draw near; also transl.: to approach, to be near, to draw near, to near > Paul was coming near Damascus (Acts 9:3; 22:6). Other refs.: Luke 10:9, 11; 12:33; 18:35, 40; 19:29; Acts 21:33 {to come up}; 23:15 {to get}. All other refs.: DRAW <1448>, HAND (noun) <1448>, NEAR (adv.) <1448>, NEIGHBORHOOD <1448>.

23 **to come near, to come nigh, to get near, to get to: *prosengizō*** [verb: προσεγγίζω <4331>]**; from *pros*: to, and *engizō*: see** 22 **▶ To approach, to get closer >** The friends of the paralytic could not come near Jesus because of the crowd (Mark 2:4). Other refs. in some mss.: Acts 10:25; 27:27. ¶

24 ***enistēmi*** [verb: ἐνίστημι <1764>]**; from *en*: in, and *histēmi*: to stand ▶ To be near, to be imminent >** Paul warned Timothy that in the last days difficult times will come (2 Tim. 3:1). All other refs. (to be present): see PRESENT (BE) <1764>.

25 **to come on, there, up, upon: *ephistēmi*** [verb: ἐφίστημι <2186>]**; from *epi*: upon, and *histēmi*: to stand ▶ To occur suddenly, to surprise >** The day of the arrival of the kingdom of God might come {close} upon certain people unexpectedly (Luke 21:34). Claudius Lysias came up and delivered Paul (Acts 23:27). An angel of the Lord came and woke Peter up in the prison (Acts 12:7). Sudden destruction will come upon those saying: Peace and safety (1 Thes. 5:3). Other refs.: Luke 2:38; 10:40; 20:1; Acts 4:1. All other refs.: ASSAULT (verb) <2186>, FALL (verb) <2186>, HAND (noun) <2186>, READY <2186>, STAND (verb) <2186>.

26 ***pareimi*** [verb: πάρειμι <3918>]**; from *para*: beside, near, and *eimi*: to be ▶ To reach, to be present >** Jesus asked Judas for what purpose he had come (Matt. 26:50). The glad tidings had come to the Colossians (Col. 1:6). Other refs.: John 7:6; 11:28; Acts 10:21; 12:20; 17:6. All other refs. (to be present): PRESENT (BE) <3918>.

27 ***hupostrephō*** [verb: ὑποστρέφω <5290>]**; from *hupo*: under, and *strephō*: to turn ▶ To come back, to turn back; also transl.: to return >** The seventy returned with joy from their mission (Luke 10:17). One of the lepers who had been healed returned, glorifying God (Luke 17:15); he was the only one who returned (v. 18). In a parable, a nobleman went to receive for himself a kingdom and return (Luke 19:12). When they returned from the empty tomb of Jesus, the women told all the things they had seen to the eleven disciples and to all the others (Luke 24:9). Melchizedek blessed Abraham returning from the defeat of the kings (Heb. 7:1). All other refs.: RETURN (verb) <5290>.

28 ***phthanō*** [verb: φθάνω <5348>] **▶ To arrive at, to reach >** If Jesus cast out demons, then the kingdom of God had come upon Israel (Matt. 12:28; Luke 11:20). Israel has not attained to the law of righteousness (Rom. 9:31). Paul had come to the Corinthians with the gospel of Christ (2 Cor. 10:14). Christians are to live up to what they have already attained (or: come upon) (Phil. 3:16). Other refs.: 1 Thes. 2:16; 4:15. ¶

29 ***hēkō*** [verb: ἥκω <2240>] **▶ To arrive, to be present >** The Lord Jesus came to do His Father's will (Heb. 10:7, 9). The verb is used in regard to the Lord (John 8:42; Rom. 11:26; Heb. 10:37b; Rev. 2:25; 3:3a, b), many from the east and the west (Matt. 8:11; Luke 13:29), the end of times (Matt. 24:14; Luke 19:43), the master of a servant (Matt. 24:50; Luke 12:46), the day of the Lord (2 Pet. 3:10). *

30 **to come along with, to come with: *katakoloutheō*** [verb: κατακολουθέω <2628>]**; from *kata*: intens., and *akoloutheō*: to go with ▶ To follow closely, to accompany >** The women who had come along with Jesus from Galilee saw how His body was placed in the tomb (Luke 23:55). Other ref.: Acts 16:17; see FOLLOW <2628>. ¶

31 ***katantaō*** [verb: καταντάω <2658>]**; from *kata*: intens., and *antaō*: to come, to meet, which is from *anta*: face to face ▶ To arrive at, to reach >** The ends of the ages have come upon the Christians (1 Cor. 10:11). Other refs.: Acts 16:1; 18:19; 20:15; 21:7; 28:13. All other refs.: ARRIVE <2658>, ATTAIN <2658>.

32 **to come to nothing: *katargeō*** [verb: καταργέω <2673>]; **from *kata*: intens., and *argeō*: to be inactive, which is from *argos*: idle, useless, which is from *a*: neg., and *ergon*: work ▶ To disappear >** The rulers of this world are coming to nothing {are passing away, are coming to nought} (1 Cor. 2:6). All other refs.: see entries in Lexicon at <2673>.
33 ***mellō*** [verb: μέλλω <3195>] ▶ **To be about to occur >** The verb is used in regard to wrath (Matt. 3:7; Luke 3:7), future Christians (1 Tim. 1:16). Other refs.: see entries in the Lexicon at <3195>.
34 ***paristēmi*** [verb: παρίστημι <3936>]; **from *para*: near, and *histēmi*: to place ▶ To arrive >** The Lord speaks of the harvest that has come (Mark 4:29). Other refs.: see entries in Lexicon at <3936>.
35 **to come, to come fully: *plēthō*** [verb: πλήθω <4130>] ▶ **To be accomplished >** Elisabeth's full time came {time was fulfilled; lit.: time came fully} to have her baby (Luke 1:57). All other refs.: FILL (verb) <4130>.
36 **to come aforehand, to come beforehand, to have beforehand: *prolambanō*** [verb: προλαμβάνω <4301>]; **from *pro*: before, and *lambanō*: to take; lit.: to do something in advance ▶ To do something before its time, to anticipate the moment >** By pouring the ointment on Jesus's head, a woman had come beforehand to anoint His body for burial (Mark 14:8). All other refs.: CATCH (verb) <4301>, TAKE <4301>.
37 **to fully come, to come, to fill: *sumplēroō*** [verb: συμπληρόω <4845>]; **from *sun*: together (intens.), and *plēroō*: to fill ▶ To arrive, to be fulfilled >** The time had come {approached} (lit.: The days were fulfilled) for Jesus to be taken up to heaven (Luke 9:51). In Acts 2:1, when the day of Pentecost had come {was fully come, was accomplishing}, the disciples were all with one accord in one place. The verb also means "to fill" {to swamp; e.g., with water} and is used in Luke 8:23. ¶
38 **to come at: *suntunchanō*** [verb: συντυγχάνω <4940>]; **from *sun*: together, and *tunchanō*: to attain, to reach ▶ To reach, to get close, to draw near, to meet with >** The mother and the brothers of Jesus could not come at {approach, get at, get to, get near} Him because of the crowd (Luke 8:19). Other ref.: Acts 11:26 in some mss. ¶
39 **to come short: *hustereō*** [verb: ὑστερέω <5302>]; **from *husteros*: which comes after, last ▶ To stay behind, to not attain, to fall short >** All have sinned and come short of the glory of God (Rom. 3:23). Someone could seem to come short of entering {fail to enter} into the rest of God (Heb. 4:1). All other refs.: INFERIOR <5302>, LACK (verb) <5302>, PRIVATION <5302>, WANT (noun) <5302>, WORSE <5302>.
40 ***pherō*** [verb: φέρω <5342>] ▶ **Lit.: to carry, to bring >** A voice came {was uttered, was made} to Jesus by the excellent glory (2 Pet. 1:17, 18). All other refs.: see entries in Lexicon at <5342>.
41 ***chōreō*** [verb: χωρέω <5562>]; **from *chōra*: place ▶ To make place >** The Lord desires that all should come to repentance (2 Pet. 3:9). All other refs.: see entries in Lexicon at <5562>.
– 42 Matt. 9:7; Mark 7:30; Rom. 15:28 → GO <565> 43 Matt. 13:6; Mark 4:6 → to come up → RISE (verb) <393> 44 Matt. 13:26 → to come up → SPROUT <985> 45 Matt. 14:32 → to come into → to get into → GET <1684> 46 Matt. 18:20; 27:62; Mark 7:1; Luke 22:66; Acts 13:44; 15:6; 20:7 → to come together → GATHER <4863> 47 Matt. 21:18 → to come back → RETURN (verb) <1877> 48 Matt. 24:32; Mark 13:28 → its leaves come out → lit.: it produces leaves → PRODUCE <1631> 49 Mark 10:1 → to come, to come together → GATHER <4848> 50 Luke 1:68, 78; 7:16 → to come, to come to help → VISIT (verb) <1980> 51 Luke 4:22 → to come out → to go out → GO <1607> 52 Luke 7:16 → to come on → SEIZE <2983> 53 Luke 8:4 → to come together → to gather together → GATHER <4896> 54 Luke 10:35 → to come again, to come back → RETURN (verb) <1880> 55 Luke 12:36 → to come home → RETURN (verb) <360> 56 Luke 15:12 → property coming to someone → property falling to someone → FALL (verb) <1911> 57 Luke 16:26; Acts 16:9 → to come over → PASS <1224>

58 Luke 19:44 → God's coming to you → lit.: your visitation → VISITATION <1984> 59 John 7:8 → to be full come → FULFILL <4137> 60 John 7:29 → I come from Him → lit.: I am from Him 61 John 10:24 → to come round about → SURROUND <2944> 62 Acts 3:24 → those who came after him → lit.: those after (*tōn kathexēs*) 63 Acts 5:38 → to come to nothing, to come to nought → DESTROY <2647> 64 Acts 7:26 → to come upon → APPEAR <3700> 65 Acts 8:16; 10:10, 44; 11:15; 13:11 → to run aground → FALL (verb) <1968> 66 Acts 13:6 → to come upon → FIND <2147> 67 Acts 18:21 → to come back → RETURN (verb) <344> 68 Acts 20:19 → to come upon → HAPPEN <4819> 69 Acts 21:28 → to come to the aid → HELP (verb) <997> 70 Acts 25:5 → to come with → to go down with → GO <4782> 71 Acts 27:14 → to come down → ARISE <906> 72 Acts 27:16 → to come by → SECURING <4031> 73 Acts 28:12 → LAND (verb) <2609> 74 Acts 28:13 → to come up → BLOW (verb) <1920> 75 Rom. 16:19 → to come 76 Rom. 16:26 → the verb is added in Engl. abroad → to become known → KNOWN <864> 77 1 Cor. 16:22 → O Lord, Come! → MARANATHA <3134> 78 2 Cor. 11:28 → to come upon → PREOCCUPATION <1987a> 79 1 Tim. 6:19 → time to come → TIME <3195> 80 Heb. 1:12 → to come to an end → FAIL <1587> 81 Rev. 18:17 → to come to nothing → to change in desolation → DESOLATE <2049>.

COME NOW – ***age*** [interj.: ἄγε <33>]; **imper. of *agō*: to lead ▶ Go; also transl.: go to now, now** > James uses this word in his letter (Jas. 4:13; 5:1). ¶

COMELILY – 1 Cor. 14:40 → DECENTLY <2156>.

COMELINESS – Jas. 1:11 → GRACE <2143>.

COMELY – 1 **that which is comely: *euschēmōn*** [adj.: εὐσχήμων <2158>]; **from *eu*: well, and *schēma*: outward manner of being ▶ What is fitting, appropriate in behavior** > Paul was giving advice concerning marriage in view of that which is comely {what is proper, what is seemly, a right way} (1 Cor. 7:35). All other refs.: HONORABLE <2158>, PRESENTABLE <2158>, PROMINENT <2158>.

2 **to be comely: *prepō*** [verb: πρέπω <4241>] ▶ **To be appropriate, to be suitable** > Paul asks if it is comely {proper} that a woman should pray to God uncovered (1 Cor. 11:13), i.e., with her head uncovered. All other refs.: FITTING (BE) <4241>, PROPER <4241>.

COMFORT (noun) – 1 ***paramuthia*** [fem. noun: παραμυθία <3889>]; **from *paramutheomai*: to comfort, which is from *para*: near, and *muthos*: speech; lit.: to speak to, to console ▶ Consolation, encouragement** > He who prophesies speaks to persons in edification, encouragement, and comfort. (1 Cor. 14:3). ¶

2 ***parēgoria*** [fem. noun: παρηγορία <3931>]; **from *parēgoreō*: to console, which is from *para*: near, and *agoreuō*: to speak in public, to counsel ▶ Consolation, encouragement, solace** > Paul mentions three brothers in the Lord who had been a comfort to him (Col. 4:11). ¶

– 3 Matt. 9:22; Mark 10:49; Luke 8:48 → to be of good comfort → to take courage → COURAGE <2293> 4 Luke 6:24; Acts 9:31; Rom. 15:4, 5; 2 Cor. 1:3–5, 6a, b, 7; 7:4, 7, 13; Phil. 2:1; 2 Thes. 2:16; Phm. 7 → CONSOLATION <3874> 5 Rom. 1:12 → to have mutual comfort → to be encouraged together → ENCOURAGE <4837> 6 2 Cor. 13:11 → to be of good comfort → ENCOURAGE <3870> 7 Phil. 2:1 → comfort of love → consolation of love → CONSOLATION <3890> 8 Phil. 2:19 → to be of good comfort → to be encouraged → ENCOURAGE <2174>.

COMFORT (verb) – 1 ***paramutheomai*** [verb: παραμυθέομαι <3888>]; **from *para*: beside, to, and *mutheomai*: to speak, which is from *muthos*: speech; lit.: to speak to, to console ▶ To encourage, to console** > Many had come to comfort

Martha and Mary concerning their brother (John 11:19, 31). Paul had exhorted and comforted the Christians in Thessalonica (1 Thes. 2:11). He exhorted them to comfort the timid (1 Thes. 5:14). ¶
– [2] Matt. 2:18; 5:4; Luke 16:25; Acts 20:12; 2 Cor. 1:4a–c, 6; 2:7; 7:6a, b, 13; 13:11; Eph. 6:22; Col. 2:2; 4:8; 1 Thes. 3:2, 7; 4:18; 2 Thes. 2:17 → ENCOURAGE <3870> [3] Acts 16:40; 1 Cor. 14:31; 1 Thes. 5:11 → EXHORT <3870> [4] Rom. 1:12 → to comfort together → to be encouraged together → ENCOURAGE <4837>.

COMFORTER – John 14:16, 26; 15:26; 16:7 → ADVOCATE (noun) <3875>.

COMFORTLESS – John 14:18 → ORPHAN (noun) <3737>.

COMING – [1] ***eleusis*** [fem. noun: ἔλευσις <1660>]; **from *erchomai*: to come ► Arrival, advent >** The term is used in regard to the first coming of the Lord Jesus (Acts 7:52). ¶
[2] ***parousia*** [fem. noun: παρουσία <3952>]; **from *para*: beside, and *ousia*: pres. ptcp. of *eimi* (to be) ► Presence; arrival, advent >** The term is used in regard to the Lord Jesus (Matt. 24:3, 27, 37, 39; 1 Cor. 15:23; 1 Thes. 2:19; 3:13; 4:15; 5:23; 2 Thes. 2:1, 8; Jas. 5:7, 8; 2 Pet. 1:16; 3:4; 1 John 2:28), Stephanas and Fortunatus and Achaicus (1 Cor. 16:17), Titus (2 Cor. 7:6, 7), Paul (Phil. 1:26), the antichrist (2 Thes. 2:9), and the day of God (2 Pet. 3:12). Other refs.: 2 Cor. 10:10; Phil. 2:12; see PRESENCE <3952>. ¶
– [3] Acts 13:24; 1 Thes. 2:1 → ENTRY <1529> [4] 1 Cor. 1:7; 1 Pet. 1:13 → when Jesus Christ is revealed at His coming → lit.: at the revelation of Jesus Christ → REVELATION <602>.

COMMAND (noun) – [1] ***entolē*** [fem. noun: ἐντολή <1785>]; **from *entellō*: to command, which is from *en*: in, and *tellō*: to accomplish, to produce ► Order, commandment, instruction >** The chief priests and the Pharisees had given command to make known where Jesus was, that they might take Him (John 11:57). Paul had given a command that Silas and Timothy should come to him at Athens (Acts 17:15). The Colossians had received commands concerning Mark (Col. 4:10). All other refs.: COMMANDMENT <1785>.
– [2] Matt. 8:18; Acts 25:23 → to give a command, at the command → COMMAND (verb) <2753> [3] John 15:17 → lit.: this I command you → COMMAND (verb) <1781> [4] Acts 1:2 → to give commands → to give charge → CHARGE (noun)[2] <1781> [5] Acts 1:4; 1 Cor. 7:10; 2 Thes. 3:10 → to give the command → COMMAND (verb) <3853> [6] Acts 16:24; 1 Tim. 1:18 → CHARGE (noun)[2] <3852> [7] Rom. 5:14 → by breaking a command → lit.: in the likeness of the transgression → LIKENESS <3667> [8] Rom. 13:9b → WORD <3056> [9] 1 Thes. 4:16 → loud command → SHOUT (noun) <2752> [10] Heb. 11:23 → ORDINANCE <1297> [11] Heb. 12:20 → lit.: the having been commanded → COMMAND (verb) <1291>.

COMMAND (verb) – [1] ***diatassō*** [verb: διατάσσω <1299>]; **from *dia*: through, and *tassō*: to arrange, to order ► To give orders, to prescribe; also transl.: to give instructions, to instruct, to order, to tell >** Jesus finished commanding His twelve disciples (Matt. 11:1). He commanded that the little girl whom He had raised be given something to eat (Luke 8:55). The master does not have to be thankful to a servant because he did the things that were commanded to him (Luke 17:9); so likewise when we have done all those things that we were commanded to do, we will say that we are unworthy (rather: not indispensable) servants (v. 10). Claudius had commanded all the Jews to leave Rome (Acts 18:2). According to what was commanded them {Carrying out their orders}, the soldiers brought Paul to Antipatris (Acts 23:31). All other refs.: ORDAIN <1299>, ORDER (noun) <1299>.
[2] ***epitassō*** [verb: ἐπιτάσσω <2004>]; **from *epi*: upon, and *tassō*: to arrange, to order ► To enjoin, to give orders; also transl.: to charge, to order, to direct >** With

authority Jesus commanded the unclean spirits (Mark 1:27; Luke 4:36). Herod commanded to bring the head of John the Baptist (Mark 6:27). Jesus commanded to make the great multitude sit on the green grass (Mark 6:39). He commanded a dumb and deaf spirit to come out of a young child (Mark 9:25). He commanded even the winds and the water (Luke 8:25). The demons besought Jesus that He would not command them to go out into the bottomless pit (Luke 8:31). The slave had done as his master had commanded (Luke 14:22). Ananias commanded to smite Paul on the mouth (Acts 23:2). Paul had much boldness in Christ to command Philemon what was fitting (Phm. 8). ¶

3 ***prostassō*** [verb: προστάσσω <4367>]; **from *pros*: to, and *tassō*: to arrange, to order ▶ To prescribe, to give the order >** Peter commanded {ordered} that the Christians from the Gentiles be baptized (Acts 10:48). All other refs.: ORDAIN <4367>.

4 ***diastellō*** [verb: διαστέλλω <1291>]; **from *dia*: through, and *stellō*: to send ▶ To give a charge, to order; also transl.: to charge, to enjoin, to give order, to strictly charge, to warn >** Jesus commanded not to say certain things (Matt. 16:20; Mark 5:43; 9:9); He commanded to beware of the leaven of the Pharisees and of the leaven of Herod (Mark 8:15). He commanded people to tell to no one that He had healed the deaf; but the more He commanded them, the more widely they proclaimed it (Mark 7:36a, b). The Israelites could not endure what was commanded {the command} (Heb. 12:20). Other ref.: Acts 15:24; see COMMANDMENT <1291>. ¶

5 ***entellomai*** [verb: ἐντέλλομαι <1781>]; **from *en*: in, and *tellō*: to accomplish, to produce ▶ To give an order, to prescribe; also transl.: to enjoin >** God has commanded {in some mss.: has said (*legō*)} to honor one's father and one's mother (Matt. 15:4). Jesus commanded {charged, instructed} His disciples to tell the vision on the mountain to no one (Matt. 17:9). Moses had commanded to give a letter of divorce (Matt. 19:7); the Lord asks the Pharisees about this (Mark 10:3). The eleven were to teach the nations to observe all things that Jesus had commanded them (Matt. 28:20). The apostles spoke as Jesus had commanded {had told} them concerning the colt (Mark 11:6). A man who had gone out of the country commanded {told} the doorkeeper that he should watch (Mark 13:34). Moses commanded the Israelites to stone women caught in adultery (John 8:5); *diakeleuō* in some mss.: stronger than *entellomai*. Jesus was doing as the Father commanded Him {gave Him commandment} (John 14:31). Those who do whatever the Lord commands them are His friends (John 15:14). Jesus commands his disciples to love one another (John 15:17). The Lord had commanded Paul to accomplish what Scripture said about Christ: "I have set you as a light of the nations" (Acts 13:47). God had commanded a covenant to Israel (Heb. 9:20). All other refs.: CHARGE (noun)[2] <1781>.

6 ***epō*** [verb: ἔπω <2036>] **▶ To say, to tell >** In a parable, a nobleman commanded {ordered, desired} his servants to whom he had given money to be called to him (Luke 19:15).

7 ***keleuō*** [verb: κελεύω <2753>]; **similar to *kellō*: to drive on, to push ashore ▶ To give an order; also transl.: to give a command, to give commandment, to bid, to direct, to give orders, to order, to tell >** Jesus commanded his disciples to depart to the other side of the sea (Matt. 8:18). Herod commanded the head of John the Baptist to be given to the daughter of Herodias (Matt. 14:9). Jesus commanded {directed} the crowds to recline on the grass (Matt. 14:19). Peter said to the Lord to command him to come to Him on the water (Matt. 14:28). Jesus commanded the crowds to lie down on the ground (Matt. 15:35). The lord of a bondman commanded him to be sold (Matt. 18:25). Pilate commanded the body of Jesus to be given up to Joseph of Arimathea (Matt. 27:58). The chief priests and Pharisees asked Pilate to command that the tomb of Jesus be secured (Matt. 27:64). Jesus commanded that the blind beggar be led to Him (Luke 18:40). The chiliarch commanded his soldiers to take

Paul by force from the crowd (Acts 23:10). Other refs.: Acts 4:15; 5:34; 8:38; 12:19; 16:22; 21:33, 34; 22:24, 30; 23:3, 35; 24:8; 25:6, 17, 21, 23 {to give command, at the command, at the commandment; lit.: having commanded}; 27:43. ¶

[8] ***parangellō*** [verb: παραγγέλλω <3853>]; **from *para*: near, and *angellō*: to announce ▶ To announce, to give an order; also transl.: to charge, to direct, to enjoin, to give commandment, to give the command, to give instructions, to give order, to instruct, to order** > Jesus commanded the twelve apostles to go to the lost sheep of Israel (Matt. 10:5). Jesus commanded the twelve to take nothing for the way except a staff (Mark 6:8). He commanded {told} the crowd to sit down on the ground (Mark 8:6). He commanded the man whom He had healed from his leprosy to tell no one (Luke 5:14). He had commanded an unclean spirit to come out of a man (Luke 8:29). He commanded {strictly warned} to tell no man He was the Christ (Luke 9:21). He commanded His disciples not to depart from Jerusalem (Acts 1:4). He had commanded His disciples to preach to the people (Acts 10:42). Paul commanded {said to} the spirit of Python (or: divination), in the name of Jesus Christ, to come out of the woman (Acts 16:18). The praetors commanded the jailer to keep Paul and Silas safely (Acts 16:23). Claudius Lysias commanded Paul's accusers to say before Felix the things they had against him (Acts 23:30). Paul trusted in the Lord that the Thessalonians would do the things he had commanded them (2 Thes. 3:4). Other refs.: Luke 8:56; Acts 4:18; 5:28 {to give strict orders, to straitly command} (lit.: to command by order), 40; 15:5 {to require}; 23:22 {to caution}; 1 Cor. 7:10; 2 Thes. 3:6, 10 {to give the rule}, 12. Other ref.: 1 Thes. 4:11. All other refs.: ENJOIN <3853>, PRESCRIBE <3853>.

– [9] Matt. 20:21 → SPEAK <2036> [10] Matt. 27:10 → DIRECT <4929> [11] John 12:49; 14:15; 1 John 3:23b; 2 John 4 → COMMANDMENT <1785> [12] Acts 19:13 → ADJURE <3726> [13] 1 Cor. 7:6; 2 Cor. 8:8 → COMMANDMENT <2003>.

COMMANDER – Mark 6:21; John 18:12; Acts 21:31–33, 37; 22:24, 26–29; 23:10, 15, 17–19, 22; 24:7, 22; 25:23; Rev. 6:15; 19:18 → commander, military commander → CAPTAIN <5506>.

COMMANDMENT – [1] ***entalma*** [neut. noun: ἔνταλμα <1778>]; **from *entellō*: see [2] ▶ Ordinance, precept** > The commandments established by the Colossians were according to the commandments {injunctions} and teachings of men (Col. 2:22). Israel was teaching commandments {rules} of men (Matt. 15:9; Mark 7:7). ¶

[2] ***entolē*** [fem. noun: ἐντολή <1785>]; **from *entellō*: to command, which is from *en*: in, and *tellō*: to accomplish, to produce ▶ Ordinance, moral and religious precept; also transl.: command, law, order, precept, regulation** > References are often made in the N.T. to the commandments of God transmitted to Moses (Matt. 5:19; 15:3, 6; 19:17; 22:36, 38, 40; Mark 7:8, 9; 10:5, 19; 12:28–31; Luke 1:6; 18:20; 23:56; 1 Cor. 7:19; Eph. 2:15; 6:2; Heb. 7:5, 16, 18; 9:19; Rev. 12:17; 14:12). The Father gave Jesus a commandment, what He should say and what He should speak (John 12:49). Jesus has given a new commandment, that we love one another (John 13:34), as He has loved us (15:12). He speaks of keeping His commandments (John 14:15, 21; 15:10a), as He has kept His Father's commandment (John 15:10b). Peter refers to the commandment of the apostles of the Lord (2 Pet. 3:2); some mss. have: the commandment of the Lord by the apostles. In his epistles, John speaks of keeping the commandments of God (1 John 2:3, 4; 3:22, 23a, b, 24; 4:21; 5:2, 3a, b; 2 John 4, 5) and walking in them (2 John 6a, b). Other refs.: Luke 15:29; John 10:18; 12:50; Rom. 7:8–13; 13:9; 1 Cor. 14:37; 1 Tim. 6:14; Titus 1:14; 2 Pet. 2:21; 1 John 2:7a–c, 8; Rev. 22:14 in some mss. Other refs.: John 11:57; Acts 17:15; Col. 4:10; see COMMAND (noun) <1785>. ¶

[3] ***epitagē*** [fem. noun: ἐπιταγή <2003>]; **from *epitassō*: to command, which is from *epi*: upon, and *tassō*: to ordain, to set ▶ Order given with authority, prescription; also transl.: command** > Paul speaks of the commandment of the eternal God (Rom. 16:26). He was addressing himself to the Christian couple as a concession, not as commanding (lit.: not by commandment) (1 Cor. 7:6). He had no commandment from the Lord concerning virgins (1 Cor. 7:25). He spoke to the Corinthians concerning sharing their goods not as commanding it (lit.: not by commandment), but because of the zeal of others (2 Cor. 8:8). He was an apostle of Jesus Christ by the commandment of God (1 Tim. 1:1). Preaching had been entrusted to him according to the commandment of his Savior God (Titus 1:3). The word is transl. "authority" in Titus 2:15: Titus was to rebuke with all authority. ¶

[4] ***parangelia*** [fem. noun: παραγγελία <3852>]; **from *parangellō*: to transmit a message, to command, which is from *para*: intens., and *angellō*: to announce ▶ Order received from a superior and communicated to others nearby** > The Thessalonians knew what commandments {charges, instructions} Paul had given them through the Lord Jesus (1 Thes. 4:2). All other refs.: CHARGE (noun)[2] <3852>.

[5] **to give a commandment: *diastellō*** [verb: διαστέλλω <1291>]; **from *dia*: intens., and *stellō*: to send ▶ To order, to strongly recommend** > The apostles and the elders, with the whole church at Jerusalem, had given no commandment {had given no authorization, no instruction} concerning circumcision (Acts 15:24). All other refs.: COMMAND (verb) <1291>.

– [6] Matt. 8:18; Acts 25:23 → to give commandment, at the commandment (lit.: having commanded) → COMMAND (verb) <2753> [7] John 14:31 → to give commandment → COMMAND (verb) <1781> [8] Acts 1:2; Heb. 11:22 → to give commandment → to give charge → CHARGE (noun)[2] <1781> [9] Acts 23:30 → to give commandment → COMMAND (verb) <3853> [10] Rom. 10:5 → commandments → lit.: that [11] Heb. 11:23 → ORDINANCE <1297>.

COMMEND – [1] ***paristēmi*** [verb: παρίστημι <3936>]; **from *para*: beside, and *histēmi*: to place, to present ▶ To bring near, to recommend** > Meat, whether sacrificed to idols or not, does not commend a person to God (1 Cor. 8:8). Other refs.: see entries in Lexicon at <3936>.

[2] ***sunistēmi*** [verb: συνίστημι <4921>]; **from *sun*: together, and *histēmi*: to place, to set; lit.: to place together ▶ To present favorably to the attention of someone >** Our unrighteousness commends God's righteousness (Rom. 3:5). God commends His love to us, in that, while we were still sinners, Christ has died for us (Rom. 5:8). Paul commended Phoebe to the Christians in Rome (Rom. 16:1). He did not want to begin again to commend himself to the Corinthians (2 Cor. 3:1; 5:12); but he commended himself to every conscience of men by manifestation of the truth (4:2) and in everything as God's servant (6:4 {to approve}). Some commended themselves (2 Cor. 10:12), but it is not he who commends himself that is approved, but he whom the Lord commends (v. 18a, b). Paul ought to have been commended by the Corinthians (2 Cor. 12:11). All other refs.: MAKE <4921>, PROVE <4921>, STAND (verb) <4921>, SUBSIST <4921>.

– [3] Luke 16:8; 1 Cor. 11:2, 17, 22 → PRAISE (verb) <1867> [4] Luke 23:46; Acts 14:23; 20:32 → COMMIT <3908> [5] Acts 14:26; 15:40 → COMMIT <3860> [6] Rom. 13:3; 1 Pet. 2:14 → to receive, to give praise → PRAISE (noun) <1868> [7] Heb. 11:4b → WITNESS (verb) <3140>.

COMMENDABLE – [1] Phil. 4:8 → of good report → REPORT (noun) <2163> [2] 1 Pet. 2:19, 20 → ACCEPTABLE <5485>.

COMMENDABLY – ***kalōs*** [adv.: καλῶς <2573>]; **from *kalos*: good ▶ Rightly, in an honorable way** > Some were eagerly seeking the Galatians, but not commendably {for good, well} (Gal. 4:17). Other refs.:

PLACE (noun) <2573>, WELL (adv.) <2573>.

COMMENDATION – [1] 1 Cor. 4:5 → PRAISE (noun) <1868> [2] 2 Cor. 3:1a, b → EPISTLE OF COMMENDATION <4956> [3] Heb. 11:2 → to receive commendation → to obtain witness → WITNESS (verb) <3140>.

COMMENDATORY – 2 Cor. 3:1 → EPISTLE OF COMMENDATION <4956>.

COMMERCE – Matt. 22:5 → BUSINESS <1711>.

COMMISSION – [1] ***epitropē*** [fem. noun: ἐπιτροπή <2011>]; **from *epitrepō*: to permit, which is from *epi*: to, and *trepō*: to turn ▶ Permission, mandate** > Paul was journeying to Damascus with authority and commission {power} from the chief priests (Acts 26:12). ¶
– [2] Col. 1:25 → DISPENSATION <3622>.

COMMISSIONED – 2 Cor. 2:17 → as commissioned by God → lit.: as of (*ek*) God.

COMMIT – [1] ***ergazomai*** [verb: ἐργάζομαι <2038>]; **from *ergon*: work; lit.: to work ▶ To do, to accomplish** > By showing partiality, one commits sin {one sins} (Jas. 2:9). All other refs.: see entries in Lexicon at <2038>.

[2] ***katergazomai*** [verb: κατεργάζομαι <2716>]; **from *kata*: intens., and *ergazomai*: see [1] ▶ To do, to accomplish** > Men have committed {worked} what is shameful (Rom. 1:27). Paul had judged to deliver to Satan a man who had committed {done, wrought} a certain action (1 Cor. 5:3). All other refs.: see entries in Lexicon at <2716>.

[3] ***paradidōmi*** [verb: παραδίδωμι <3860>]; **from *para*: over to, and *didōmi*: to give ▶ To commend, to recommend** > Paul and Barnabas had been committed to the grace of God at Antioch (Acts 14:26). Paul and Silas were committed to the grace of God by the brothers of Antioch (Acts 15:40). All other refs.: see entries in Lexicon at <3860>.

[4] ***paratithēmi*** [verb: παρατίθημι <3908>]; **from *para*: near, in front, and *tithēmi*: to put ▶ a. To assign to the care of someone, to confide; also transl.: to entrust** > To whom much has been committed, more will be asked from him (Luke 12:48). Paul was committing a charge to Timothy (1 Tim. 1:18). Timothy was to commit the things heard from Paul to faithful men competent to teach others (2 Tim. 2:2). **b. To commend, to confide** > Jesus committed {commended} His spirit into the hands of His Father (Luke 23:46). The elders chosen in each church were committed to the Lord (Acts 14:23). Paul committed the elders of Ephesus to God and to the word of His grace (Acts 20:32). Those who suffer according to the will of God are to commit {to entrust} their souls in well-doing to a faithful Creator (1 Pet. 4:19). All other refs.: LAY <3908>, SET (verb) <3908>.

[5] ***pisteuō*** [verb: πιστεύω <4100>]; **from *pistis*: belief, assurance, which is from *peithō*: to persuade, to convince ▶ To give the responsibility; also transl.: to confide, to entrust, to commit to the trust, to put in trust, to trust with** > The true riches are committed to the trust of those who are faithful in the unrighteous mammon (Luke 16:11). The oracles of God were committed to the Jews (Rom. 3:2). A stewardship was committed to Paul (1 Cor. 9:17); the gospel of the uncircumcision had been committed to him (Gal. 2:7; 1 Thes. 2:4; 1 Tim. 1:11); preaching had been committed as well to him (Titus 1:3). All other refs.: BELIEVE <4100>, BELIEVER <4100>, ENTRUST <4100>.

[6] ***poieō*** [verb: ποιέω <4160>] **▶ To do, to make** > Barabbas and his fellow rebels had committed a murder (Mark 15:7). Paul asked if he had committed sin in humbling himself (2 Cor. 11:7). The verb is also transl. "to do," "to practice" in the expr. "every sin that a man commits" (1 Cor. 6:18). James speaks of forgiveness to the one who has committed sins {has sinned} (Jas. 5:15). Christ committed no sin (1 Pet. 2:22). Other refs.: see entries in Lexicon at <4160>.

7 **to commit previously, to commit beforehand:** ***proginomai*** [verb: προγίνομαι <4266>]; **from** ***pro*****: before, and** ***ginomai*****: to happen ▶ To happen (in the sense of: to commit) previously** > God showed forth His righteousness in respect of His forbearance of sins previously committed {that are past, that had taken place before} (Rom. 3:25). ¶

8 **what is committed, what is committed to the trust:** ***parathēkē*** [fem. noun: παραθήκη <3866>]; **from** ***paratithēmi*****: to deposit, which is from** ***para*****: beside, unto, and** ***tithēmi*****: to put ▶ Deposit, what is entrusted to someone** > Timothy was to guard what was committed to his trust {the entrusted deposit, what had been entrusted to him} (1 Tim. 6:20; 2 Tim. 1:14); other mss.: *parakatathēkē*. Paul was persuaded that He in whom he had believed was able to keep what he had committed {what he had entrusted, the entrusted deposit} to Him (2 Tim. 1:12). ¶

– 9 Matt. 5:27, 32a, b; 19:9, 18; John 8:4; et al. → to commit adultery → ADULTERY <3429> <3431> 10 John 5:22 → GIVE <1325> 11 John 8:34 → PRACTICE (verb) <4160> 12 Rom. 1:32; 2 Cor. 12:21 → DO <4238> 13 Rom. 2:22 → to commit sacrilege → SACRILEGE <2416> 14 Rom. 11:32 → to shut up → SHUT <4788> 15 2 Cor. 5:19 → LAY <5087> 16 1 Thes. 4:6 → "who commit such sins" added in Engl.

COMMITMENT – 1 Cor. 7:27 → to be free from such a commitment → lit.: to be loosed from a wife.

COMMITTED – 1 Tim. 6:20; 2 Tim. 1:14 → THING COMMITTED <3872>.

COMMODIOUS – Acts 27:12 → not commodious → not suitable → SUITABLE <428>.

COMMON – 1 ***koinos*** [adj.: κοινός <2839>] ▶ **a. Which belongs to many, shared by many** > At the beginning, all Christians had all things common {shared everything they had} (Acts 2:44; 4:32). Titus was Paul's own child according to the common faith (Titus 1:4). Jude wanted to write concerning the common salvation {the salvation they shared} (Jude 3). **b. Profane, shared by all, ordinary, not holy** > Peter had never eaten anything common or unclean (Acts 10:14). He was not to call any man common or unclean (Acts 10:28). Nothing common or unclean had ever entered into his mouth (Acts 11:8). He who has esteemed the blood of the covenant common {unclean, unholy} will be judged worthy of severe punishment (Heb. 10:29). Other refs.: Rev. 21:27 in some mss.; Mark 7:2; Rom. 14:14a–c; see UNCLEAN <2839>. ¶

2 **to call common, to make common:** ***koinoō*** [verb: κοινόω <2840>]; **from** ***koinos*****: see** 1 **▶ To consider as defiled** > Peter was not to call common {call impure, consider unholy} what God had purified (Acts 10:15). What God has cleansed must not be made common {be called impure, be considered unholy} (Acts 11:9). All other refs.: DEFILE <2840>.

3 **to be common:** ***tunchanō*** [verb: τυγχάνω <5177>] **▶ To encounter, to come upon** > The barbarians showed no common {unusual, no little, extraordinary} kindness (lit.: a kindness not being common, i.e., not encountered frequently) toward Paul and the passengers of the ship (Acts 28:2). All other refs.: ATTAIN <5177>, ENJOY <5177>, OBTAIN <5177>, ORDINARY <5177>, PERHAPS <5177>.

– 4 Acts 4:13 → UNINSTRUCTED <2399> 5 Acts 5:18 → PUBLIC <1219> 6 Rom. 9:21; 2 Tim. 2:20 → common use → DISHONOR (noun) <819> 7 1 Cor. 12:7 → the common good → lit.: the what is profitable → PROFIT (noun) <4851> 8 2 Cor. 6:14 → to have in common → PARTICIPATION <3352> 9 Phil. 2:1 → common sharing → FELLOWSHIP <2842>.

COMMONLY – 1 Cor. 5:1 → ACTUALLY <3654>.

COMMONWEALTH – [1] Eph. 2:12 → CITIZENSHIP <4174> [2] Phil. 3:20 → CITIZENSHIP <4175>.

COMMOTION – [1] Matt. 9:23 → to make a commotion → to make a noise → NOISE (noun) <2350> [2] Mark 5:38 → TUMULT <2351> [3] Mark 5:39 → to make a commotion → to make a tumult → TUMULT <2350> [4] Luke 21:9 → TUMULT <181> [5] Acts 12:18; 19:23 → DISTURBANCE <5017> [6] Acts 15:2 → DISSENSION <4714> [7] Acts 19:40 → CONCOURSE <4963>.

COMMUNE – [1] Luke 6:11 → DISCUSS <1255> [2] Luke 22:4 → to speak to → SPEAK <4814> [3] Luke 24:15; Acts 24:26 → TALK (verb) <3656>.

COMMUNICATE[1] – [1] ***koinōneō*** [verb: κοινωνέω <2841>]; **from *koinōnos*: associate, participant, which is from *koinos*: common ► To share, to associate (e.g., in giving)** > In the beginning of the gospel, no church communicated anything to Paul concerning giving and receiving, except the Philippians (Phil. 4:15). All other refs.: DISTRIBUTE <2841>, PARTICIPATE <2841>.
[2] **sharing of goods: *koinōnia*** [fem. noun: κοινωνία <2842>]; **from *koinōneō*: see [1] ► Fellowship, mutual help** > The Hebrews were not to forget to do good and to communicate {share} (lit.: the sharing of goods) (Heb. 13:16). All other refs.: CONTRIBUTION <2842>, DISPENSATION <2842>, FELLOWSHIP <2842>, SHARING <2842>.
– [3] Gal. 2:2 → to lay before → LAY <394> [4] Gal. 2:6 → ADD <4323> [5] Phil. 4:14 → to communicate with → to share in → SHARE (verb) <4790> [6] 1 Tim. 6:18: willing to communicate → willing to share → SHARE (verb) <2843>.

COMMUNICATE[2] – [1] Luke 2:26 → to be divinely communicated → to be divinely warned → WARN <5537> [2] 1 Cor. 2:13 → COMPARE <4793> [3] Rev. 1:1 → SIGNIFY <4591>.

COMMUNICATING – 2 Cor. 9:13 → SHARING <2842>.

COMMUNICATION – [1] ***homilia*** [fem. noun: ὁμιλία <3657>]; **from *homileō*: to talk, to converse, which is from *homilos*: crowd, which is from *homos*: similar ► Association of an individual with other individuals, company** > Christians must not be deceived: evil communications corrupt good manners (1 Cor. 15:33). ¶
– [2] Luke 24:17 → SAYING <3056> [3] Phm. 6 → FELLOWSHIP <2842>.

COMMUNION – [1] 1 Cor. 10:16a, b; 2 Cor. 6:14; 13:14 → FELLOWSHIP <2842> [2] 1 Cor. 10:18 → one who has communion, one who is in communion → PARTAKER <2844>.

COMMUNITY – Acts 25:24 → MULTITUDE <4128>.

COMPACT – Eph. 4:16 → to knit together → KNIT <4822>.

COMPANION – [1] ***hetairos*** [masc. noun: ἑταῖρος <2083>]; **from *ethos*: custom, or *etēs*: member of a clan ► Self-serving friend, opportunistic comrade** > Jesus likens His generation to children calling to their companions {their fellows, the other children} (Matt. 11:16); other mss. have *heteros*. Other refs.: Matt. 20:13; 22:12; 26:50; see FRIEND <2083>. ¶
[2] ***sunkoinōnos*** [masc. and fem. noun: συγκοινωνός <4791>]; **from *sun*: together, and *koinōnos*: companion, which is from *koinos*: common ► Co-participant, fellow partaker, one who shares with someone** > John was the brother and companion {partner} in tribulation of those from the seven churches (Rev. 1:9). Other refs.: Rom. 11:17; 1 Cor. 9:23; Phil. 1:7; see PARTAKER <4791>. ¶
– [3] Acts 17:1 → "Paul and his companions" added in Engl. [4] Acts 19:29 → travel companion, traveling companion → FELLOW TRAVELER <4898> [5] 2 Cor. 8:23 → PARTNER <2844> [6] Phil. 2:25 → FELLOW WORKER <4904> [7] Phil. 4:3

→ YOKEFELLOW <4805> 8 Heb. 1:9; 3:14 → PARTNER <3353> 9 Heb. 10:33 → PARTAKER <2844>.

COMPANY (noun) – 1 ***klisia*** [fem. noun: κλισία <2828>]; **from *klinō*: to incline, to recline ▶ Group of people reclining around a table for eating** > Jesus had a crowd of 5,000 men sit down in companies of 50 each before feeding them (Luke 9:14). ¶
2 ***homilos*** [masc. noun: ὅμιλος <3658>]; **from *homos*: similar ▶ Crowd, multitude** > The word is found in some mss. in Rev. 18:17. ¶
3 ***sunodia*** [fem. noun: συνοδία <4923>]; **from *sun*: together, and *hodos*: road ▶ Group of people who travel together** > The parents of Jesus believed that He was in the company {caravan} that journeyed together (Luke 2:44). ¶
4 **to keep company: *kollaō*** [verb: κολλάω <2853>]; **from *kolla*: to glue ▶ To join, to have relations, to associate** > It is unlawful for a Jew to keep company with a stranger (Acts 10:28). All other refs.: CLEAVE <2853>, CLING <2853>, JOIN <2853>, REACH <2853>.
5 **to keep company, to have company: *sunanamignumi*** [verb: συναναμίγνυμι <4874>]; **from *sun*: together, with, *ana*: particle of repetition, and *mignumi*: to mix; lit.: to mix together ▶ To associate; also transl.: to company, to mix** > Christians must not keep company with anyone called a brother who is a fornicator (1 Cor. 5:9, 11). The Thessalonians were not to keep company with those disobedient to the word of Paul (2 Thes. 3:14). ¶
– 6 Matt. 14:6 → before the company → lit.: in the midst → MIDST <3319> 7 Matt. 27:27; Mark 15:16; Acts 27:1 → COHORT <4686> 8 Mark 6:39 → GROUP <4849> 9 Luke 2:13; 23:1, 27 → MULTITUDE <4128> 10 Luke 5:29; Acts 1:15 → CROWD (noun) <3793> 11 John 18:2 → in company → lit.: gathered with → GATHER <4863> 12 Acts 17:5 → to gather a company → GATHER <3792> 13 1 Cor. 15:33 → COMMUNICATION <3657> 14 Heb. 12:22 → innumerable company → MYRIAD <3461> 15 Rev. 18:17 → company in ship → SAIL (verb) <4126>.

COMPANY (verb) – 1 Acts 1:21 → ACCOMPANY <4905> 2 1 Cor. 5:9 → to keep company, to have company → COMPANY (noun) <4874>.

COMPARE – 1 ***paraballō*** [verb: παραβάλλω <3846>]; **from *para*: alongside, and *ballō*: to throw, to put ▶ To present, to represent; also transl.: to describe, to picture** > Jesus asks with what comparison should He compare the kingdom of God (Mark 4:30). Other ref.: Acts 20:15; see ARRIVE <3846>. ¶
2 ***sunkrinō*** [verb: συγκρίνω <4793>]; **from *sun*: together, and *krinō*: to judge ▶ a. To communicate, to expound** > Paul was comparing {expressing, combining} spiritual things with spiritual words (1 Cor. 2:13); this can also be rendered by the fact that Paul was communicating spiritual things by spiritual means. **b. To examine in order to find similar and different aspects** > Paul and his companions did not compare themselves with some who commended themselves or were comparing themselves with themselves (2 Cor. 10:12a, b). ¶
– 3 Matt. 7:24; 11:16; Mark 4:30; Luke 7:31; 13:18, 20 → LIKEN <3666> 4 Matt. 13:24; 18:23; 22:2; 25:1 → to be like → LIKE (adj., adv., noun) <3666> 5 Rom. 5:16 → "can be compared" added in Engl.

COMPARISON – 1 Mark 4:30 → PARABLE <3850> 2 2 Cor. 4:17 → far beyond all comparison → beyond measure → MEASURE (noun) <5236>.

COMPASS (noun) – Acts 28:13 → to fetch a compass → CIRCLE ROUND <4022>.

COMPASS (verb) – 1 Matt. 23:15 → to go round → GO <4013> 2 Luke 19:43 → SURROUND <4033> 3 Luke 21:20; Heb. 11:30; Rev. 20:9 → SURROUND <2944> 4 Heb. 5:2 → to be subject → SUBJECT (verb) <4029> 5 Heb. 12:1 → SURROUND <4029>.

COMPASSION – [1] **to have compassion:** ***eleeō*** [verb: ἐλεέω <1653>]; **from** ***eleos*****: compassion, mercy ► To have mercy, to take pity** > Christians are to have compassion on {to be merciful to} those who are doubting (Jude 22); *eleaō* in some mss. All other refs.: MERCY <1653>.
[2] **to have compassion:** ***metriopatheō*** [verb: μετριοπαθέω <3356>]; **from** ***metriopathēs*****: moderate in expressing emotions, which is from** ***metriōs*****: moderate, and** ***pathos*****: emotion, sentiment ► To treat with indulgence, to sympathize** > The high priest is able to have compassion on {to deal gently with, to exercise forbearance toward} the ignorant and the erring (Heb. 5:2). ¶
[3] **to have compassion:** ***oikteirō*** [verb: οἰκτείρω <3627>]; **from** ***oiktos*****: compassion, pity; also spelled:** ***oiktirō*** **► To show mercy, to exercise grace** > God said to Moses He would have compassion on whom He would have compassion (Rom. 9:15a, b). ¶
[4] **to have, to feel, to be moved with compassion:** ***splanchnizomai*** [verb: σπλαγχνίζομαι <4697>]; **from** ***splanchna*****: bowels, or viscera in Classical Greek (mainly heart, liver, lungs) ► To be moved internally by the circumstances of others and to seek to share their sufferings; also transl.: to be moved with pity, to take pity** > The verb is used concerning the feelings of the Lord for people who were suffering (Matt. 20:34; Mark 1:41; Luke 7:13 {His heart went out to her}) and toward the crowds (Matt. 9:36; 14:14; 15:32; Mark 6:34; 8:2). In different parables, the master was moved with compassion for his servant (Matt. 18:27), a certain Samaritan for a wounded man (Luke 10:33), and the father for the prodigal son (Luke 15:20). A father asked Jesus to have compassion and heal his son who was possessed by a mute spirit (Mark 9:22). ¶
– [5] Matt. 9:13; 12:7 → MERCY <1656> [6] Luke 18:13 → to have compassion → to be merciful → MERCIFUL <2433> [7] Rom. 12:1; 2 Cor. 1:3; Phil. 2:1; Col. 3:12 → MERCY <3628> [8] Heb. 10:34 → to have compassion → SYMPATHIZE <4834> [9] Jas. 5:11 → full of compassion, full of tender compassion → very compassionate → COMPASSIONATE <4184> [10] 1 Pet. 3:8 → having compassion → SYMPATHETIC <4835>.

COMPASSIONATE – [1] **very compassionate:** ***polusplanchnos*** [adj.: πολύσπλαγχνος <4184>]; **from** ***polus*****: much, and** ***splanchnon*****: a bowel (but used in the plur.:** ***splanchna*****) ► Quality of one seeking to respond to the needs of others, to relieve their sufferings** > The Lord is very compassionate {full of compassion, full of tender compassion, very pitiful} (Jas. 5:11). ¶
– [2] Eph. 4:32; 1 Pet. 3:8 → TENDERHEARTED <2155> [3] Col. 3:12 → compassionate hearts → lit.: entrails of mercy → MERCY <3628>.

COMPEL – [1] ***angareuō*** [verb: ἀγγαρεύω <29>]; **from** ***angaros*****: mounted courier who had authority to press into service ► To constrain, to force** > Jesus says if someone compels us to go one mile, we should go with him two (Matt. 5:41). Simon of Cyrene was compelled {pressed} to carry the cross of Jesus (Matt. 27:32; Mark 15:21). ¶
[2] ***sunechō*** [verb: συνέχω <4912>]; **from** ***sun*****: together (intens.), and** ***echō*****: to have, to hold ► To press, to constrain; also transl.: to control** > Paul was compelled in respect of the word (other mss.: the Spirit) (Acts 18:5); other transl.: Paul devoted himself exclusively to teaching. The love of Christ compelled him (2 Cor. 5:14). All other refs.: see entries in Lexicon at <4912>.
– [3] Matt. 14:22; Mark 6:45; Luke 14:23; Acts 26:11; 28:19; 2 Cor. 12:11; Gal. 2:3, 14; 6:12 → CONSTRAIN <315> [4] Acts 20:22 → BIND <1210>.

COMPELLED (BE) – 1 Cor. 9:16; Jude 3 → NECESSITY <318>.

COMPETE – [1] 1 Cor. 9:25 → FIGHT (verb) <75> [2] 2 Tim. 2:5a, b → to compete, to compete in athletics → STRIVE <118>.

COMPETENCE, COMPETENCY – 2 Cor. 3:5 → SUFFICIENCY <2426>.

COMPETENT – 1 **to make competent:** ***hikanoō*** [verb: ἱκανόω <2427>]; **from *hikanos*: capable, sufficient ▶ To empower; also transl.: to make able, to make adequate, to make sufficient** > God has made Christians competent, as ministers of the new covenant (2 Cor. 3:6). Other ref.: Col. 1:12 (to make meet); see MEET (adj.) <2427>. ¶
– 2 Acts 18:24 → competent in the Scriptures → lit.: mighty in the Scriptures → MIGHTY (adj.) <1415> 3 Rom. 15:14 → to be competent → to be able → ABLE <1410> 4 1 Cor. 6:2 → not competent → UNWORTHY <370> 5 2 Cor. 3:5; 2 Tim. 2:2 → ABLE <2425> 6 2 Tim. 3:17 → COMPLETE (adj.) <739>.

COMPILE – Luke 1:1 → to draw up → DRAW <392>.

COMPLAIN – 1 ***stenazō*** [verb: στενάζω <4727>]; **from *stenō*: to moan, to lament, or *stenos*: narrow ▶ To groan, to murmur, to sigh** > Christians should not complain {grudge, grumble} one against another (Jas. 5:9). All other refs.: GROAN (verb) <4727>.
– 2 Matt. 20:11; Luke 5:30; John 6:41; 7:32 → MURMUR <1111> 3 Luke 15:2; 19:7 → MURMUR <1234> 4 Acts 6:1 → MURMURING <1112>.

COMPLAINER – ***mempsimoiros*** [adj. used as noun: μεμψίμοιρος <3202>]; **from *memphomai*: to find fault, and *moira*: allotment, destiny ▶ Dissatisfied, discontented person; one who finds fault with his situation** > Jude spoke of complainers {faultfinders} (Jude 16). ¶

COMPLAINING – John 7:12; Phil. 2:14 → MURMURING <1112>.

COMPLAINT – 1 ***momphē*** [fem. noun: μομφή <3437>]; **from *memphomai*: to find fault ▶ Blame, reprimand, censure** > We are to forgive one another if any should have a complaint {grievance, quarrel} against another (Col. 3:13); *mempsis* in some mss.: ground for complaint. ¶
– 2 Acts 6:1; 1 Pet. 4:9 → MURMURING <1112> 3 Acts 19:38 → MATTER <3056> 4 Acts 25:7 → CHARGE (noun)[1] <157>.

COMPLETE (adj.) – 1 ***artios*** [adj.: ἄρτιος <739>]; **from *arti*: exactly, precisely ▶ Sufficient, qualified** > Every Scripture is divinely inspired and profitable for teaching, for reproof, for correction, for instruction in righteousness; so that the man of God may be complete {adequate, perfect}, fully fitted to every good work (2 Tim. 3:17). ¶
2 **to be complete:** ***plērophoreō*** [verb: πληροφορέω <4135>]; **from *plērēs*: full, and *phoreō*: to fill, which is from *pherō*: to carry, to bear ▶ To give full measure, full guarantee; to make sure** > Epaphras was praying that the Thessalonians might stand perfect and complete {fully assured} (lit.: having been completed fully) in all the will of God (Col. 4:12); other mss. have *plēroō*. All other refs.: BELIEVE <4135>, PERSUADE <4135>, PREACH <4135>, PROOF <4135>.
– 3 Matt. 19:21; Col. 1:28 → PERFECT (adj.) <5046> 4 John 17:23; Jas. 2:22; 1 John 2:5; 4:12, 17 → to bring to complete unity, to make complete → PERFECT (verb) <5048> 5 1 Cor. 1:10 → to make complete → to perfectly unite → PERFECTLY <2675> 6 2 Cor. 13:9 → PERFECTING <2676> 7 2 Cor. 13:11 → to become complete, to be made complete → PERFECTED (BE) <2675> 8 Phil. 2:2; 1 John 1:4 → to make complete → FULFILL <4137> 9 Col. 2:2 → full assurance → ASSURANCE <4136> 10 1 Thes. 5:23; Jas. 1:4 → ENTIRE <3648> 11 Heb. 13:21 → to make complete → PERFECT (adj.) <2675> 12 Rev. 3:2 → lit.: completed → COMPLETE (verb) <4137> 13 Rev. 15:1, 8 → COMPLETE (verb) <5055>.

COMPLETE (verb) – 1 ***plēroō*** [verb: πληρόω <4137>]; **from *plērēs*: full ▶ To execute, to realize** > The works of the church in Sardis had not been found completed {complete, perfect} before God (Rev. 3:2). All other refs.: see entries in Lexicon at <4137>.

[2] ***teleō*** [verb: τελέω <5055>]; **from *telos*: end, goal ▶ To accomplish, to conclude, to finish >** When the seventh angel is about to sound the trumpet, the mystery of God also will be completed (Rev. 10:7). The fury of God is completed {complete, filled up, finished, fulfilled} in the last plagues (Rev. 15:1, 8). All other refs.: see entries in Lexicon at <5055>.

– [3] Luke 1:23; 2:6, 21, 22 → ACCOMPLISH <4130> [4] Luke 4:13; Acts 21:27 → END (verb) <4931> [5] Luke 14:28 → FINISH <535> [6] John 5:36; 17:4 → FINISH <5048> [7] Acts 21:7 → FINISH <1274> [8] Rom. 15:28; 2 Cor. 8:11; Phil. 1:6 → PERFORM <2005> [9] 2 Cor. 8:6 → FINISH <2005> [10] 2 Cor. 9:5 → to complete beforehand → to make up beforehand → MAKE <4294> [11] Phil. 2:30 → to fill up → SUPPLY (verb) <378> [12] 1 Thes. 3:10 → SUPPLY (verb) <2675> [13] Jas. 1:15 → FINISH <658>.

COMPLETED – Rev. 3:2 → COMPLETE (verb) <4137>.

COMPLETELY – [1] ***holos*** [adj.: ὅλος <3650>] ▶ **Entirely, fully >** The blind man who was healed was told that he was completely {altogether, wholly} born in sins (John 9:34). Other refs.: see WHOLE <3650>.

[2] ***holotelēs*** [adj.: ὁλοτελής <3651>]; **from *holos*: see [1], and *telos*: end, fulfillment ▶ Entirely, fully >** Paul prayed that the God of peace Himself might sanctify the Christians completely {wholly, through and through} (1 Thes. 5:23). ¶

[3] ***teleiōs*** [adv.: τελείως <5049>]; **from *teleios*: perfect, complete ▶ Perfectly, entirely >** Christians are to hope completely {fully, to the end, with perfect steadfastness} in the grace that will be brought to them at the revelation of Jesus Christ (1 Pet. 1:13). ¶

– [4] Mark 6:51 → exceedingly beyond measure → EXCEEDINGLY <3029> <1537> <4053> [5] Luke 18:5 → to completely harass → HARASS <5299> [6] Acts 3:16 → to completely heal → to give complete soundness → GIVE <1325>, SOUNDNESS <3647> [7] Heb. 12:5 → to completely forget → FORGET <1585>.

COMPLETENESS – 1 Cor. 13:10 → that which is perfect → PERFECT (adj.) <5046>.

COMPLETER – Heb. 12:2 → FINISHER <5051>.

COMPLETING – 2 Cor. 8:11 → performance → PERFORM <2005>.

COMPLETION – [1] Matt. 13:39, 40, 49; 24:3; 28:20 → END (noun) <4930> [2] Acts 21:26 → ACCOMPLISHMENT <1604> [3] 2 Cor. 7:1 → to bring to completion → PERFECT (verb) <2005> [4] 2 Cor. 8:6 → to bring to completion → FINISH <2005> [5] 2 Cor. 8:11; Phil. 1:6 → to carry on to completion → PERFORM <2005>.

COMPOSE – [1] ***sunkerannumi*** [verb: συγκεράννυμι <4786>]; **from *sun*: together, with, and *kerannumi*: to mix ▶ To organize, to harmonize >** God has composed {has combined, has tempered together} the body, having given more abundant honor to that part which lacks it (1 Cor. 12:24). Other ref.: Heb. 4:2; see MIX <4786>. ¶

– [2] Acts 1:1 → MAKE <4160>.

COMPOSURE – 2 Thes. 2:2 → from your composure → lit.: in mind → MIND (noun) <3563>.

COMPREHEND – [1] ***katalambanō*** [verb: καταλαμβάνω <2638>]; **from *kata*: intens., and *lambanō*: to take ▶ To perceive, to understand, to grasp; also transl.: to apprehend >** The darkness (i.e., the world) did not comprehend the light (i.e., Jesus Christ) (John 1:5). Paul was praying that the Ephesians would be fully able to comprehend {grasp} the dimensions of the love of Christ (Eph. 3:18). All other refs.: see entries in Lexicon at <2638>.

[2] ***suniēmi*** [verb: συνίημι <4920>]; **from *sun*: together, and *hiēmi*: to send ▶ To perceive mentally, to understand >**

Jesus opened the understanding of His disciples that they might comprehend the Scriptures (Luke 24:45). All other refs.: UNDERSTAND <4920>.
– [3] Rom. 13:9 → SUM UP <346> [4] 1 Cor. 2:11 → KNOW <1492>.

COMPULSION – [1] 1 Cor. 7:37; 9:16; 2 Cor. 9:7; Phm. 14 → NECESSITY <318> [2] 1 Cor. 9:16 → to be under compulsion → to be imposed → IMPOSE <1945> [3] 1 Pet. 5:2 → CONSTRAINT <317>.

COMRADE – Phil. 4:3 → YOKEFELLOW <4805>.

CONCEAL – [1] Matt. 10:26 → COVER <2572> [2] Luke 9:45 → HIDE <3871> [3] Luke 12:2 → COVER <4780> [4] 1 Tim. 5:25 → HIDE <2928>.

CONCEALED – Mark 4:22 → SECRET (adj.) <2927>.

CONCEIT – [1] 2 Cor. 12:20 → PUFFING UP <5450> [2] Phil. 2:3 → conceit, empty conceit, vain conceit → vain glory → VAIN <2754> [3] 1 Tim. 3:6; 6:4; 2 Tim. 3:4 → to become puffed up with conceit → to be puffed up → PUFF UP <5187>.

CONCEITED – [1] ***kenodoxos*** [adj.: κενόδοξος <2755>]; **from *kenos*: vain, empty, and *doxa*: glory ▶ Vain, boastful; also transl.: desirous of vain glory, vain-glorious** > Christians must not become conceited, provoking one another and envying one another (Gal. 5:26). ¶
[2] **to be conceited: *hupsēlophroneō*** [verb: ὑψηλοφρονέω <5309>]; **from *hupsēlos*: elevated, arrogant, and *phroneō*: to think, to feel, which is from *phrēn*: mind, understanding ▶ To be proud, to be arrogant** > Christians are not to be conceited {to be arrogant, to be haughty, to be high-minded} (Rom. 11:20; 1 Tim. 6:17). ¶
– [3] Rom. 11:25; 12:16 → WISE (adj.) <5429> [4] 2 Cor. 12:7 → to become conceited → to exalt above measure → EXALT <5229> [5] 1 Tim. 3:6; 6:4; 2 Tim. 3:4 → to become conceited → to be puffed up → PUFF UP <5187>.

CONCEIVE – [1] ***gennaō*** [verb: γεννάω <1080>]; **from *genna*: birth, race ▶ To procreate** > That which was conceived {begotten} in Mary was of the Holy Spirit (Matt. 1:20). All other refs.: see entries in Lexicon at <1080>.
[2] ***sullambanō*** [verb: συλλαμβάνω <4815>]; **from *sun*: together (intens.), and *lambanō*: to take ▶ To become pregnant** > Elizabeth conceived a son in her old age (Luke 1:24, 36). Jesus was given His name before He was conceived (Luke 1:31; 2:21). Lust having conceived gives birth to sin (figur. sense) (Jas. 1:15). All other refs.: HELP (verb) <4815>, SEIZE <4815>, TAKE <4815>.
[3] **conception: *katabolē*** [fem. noun: καταβολή <2602>]; **from *kataballō*: to cast down, which is from *kata*: down, and *ballō*: to cast ▶ Procreation; lit.: beginning** > Sarah received strength to conceive (lit.: for the conception of a posterity) (Heb. 11:11). All other refs.: FOUNDATION <2602>.
[4] In Rom. 9:10, the verb is lit.: to have (*echō*) the bed (*koitē*): Rebecca conceived by Isaac.
– [5] Matt. 1:23 → lit.: to be with child → CHILD <1064> [6] Luke 1:7, 36 → not able to conceive, unable to conceive → BARREN <4723> [7] Acts 5:4 → PURPOSE (verb) <5087>.

CONCEPTION – Heb. 11:11 → CONCEIVE <2602>.

CONCERN (noun) – [1] ***merimna*** [fem. noun: μέριμνα <3308>]; **from *meris*: part ▶ Burden, care, solicitude** > His concern for all the churches pressed daily upon Paul (2 Cor. 11:28). All other refs.: CARE (noun) <3308>.
[2] **free from concern: *amerimnos*** [adj.: ἀμέριμνος <275>]; **from *a*: neg., and *merimna*: see [1] ▶ Exempt from worries** > Paul would have the Corinthians to be free from concern {free from anxieties, without care, without carefulness} (1 Cor. 7:32).

Other ref.: Matt. 28:14 (out of trouble); see TROUBLE (noun) <275>. ¶
– 3 Matt. 16:23a, b; Mark 8:33a, b → lit.: the things 4 Acts 15:14 → to show concern → VISIT (verb) <1980> 5 Acts 18:17 → to show no concern → CARE <3199> 6 1 Cor. 12:25; Phil. 2:20 → to have concern, to show concern → to have care → CARE (noun) <3309> 7 2 Cor. 7:7 → ardent concern → fervent mind → MIND (noun) <2205> 8 2 Cor. 7:11; Col. 4:13 → ZEAL <2205> 9 2 Cor. 8:16 → ZEAL <4710> 10 2 Cor. 11:29 → without my intense concern → lit.: without me burning → BURN <4448> 11 Phil. 4:10 → THINK <5426> 12 Heb. 8:9 → to show no concern → DISREGARD <272>.

CONCERN (verb) – 1 Acts 15:14 → to concern oneself → VISIT (verb) <1980> 2 1 Cor. 9:9 → he is occupied about → OCCUPY <3199>.

CONCERNED (BE) – 1 John 10:13; 12:6; Acts 18:17; 1 Cor. 7:21 → CARE <3199> 2 1 Cor. 7:32, 33, 34a, b; Phil. 2:20 → CARE <3309> 3 Phil. 2:28 → to be less concerned → to be less sorrowful → SORROWFUL <253> 4 Phil. 4:10 → THINK <5426> 5 Heb. 2:6 → VISIT (verb) <1980>.

CONCERNING – 1 ***kata*** [prep.: κατά <2596>] ► **On the matter of, about, as far as** > Concerning {As regards, From the standpoint of} the gospel, the Jews are enemies for the sake of the Gentiles (Rom. 11:28a); but concerning {as touching, as regards, from the standpoint of} the election, they are beloved for the sake of the fathers (v. 28b). Paul speaks concerning {according, in accordance with, in reference to} the former conduct of the Ephesians (Eph. 4:22a, b). The prep. is transl. "according to" in Heb. 9:19. *

2 ***peri*** [prep.: περί <4012>] ► **About, regarding, touching** > The things concerning {referring to} Jesus were reaching their fulfillment (Luke 22:37). Paul was persuading his listeners concerning Jesus (Acts 28:23). The author of the Epistle to the Hebrews was persuaded of better things concerning them (Heb. 6:9). Moses spoke nothing concerning the priests (Heb. 7:14). John spoke concerning the word of life (1 John 1:1). The term is also used in regard to Jesus (Matt. 2:8; Luke 2:17; 24:19; Acts 25:19; Rom. 1:3), bread (Matt. 16:11), goodness (Matt. 19:17), a parable (Mark 7:17), words of Jesus (Luke 9:45; John 16:19), Galileans (Luke 13:1), purification (John 3:25), the disciples and the doctrine of Jesus (John 18:19a, b), Judas (Acts 1:16), David (Acts 2:29), the kingdom of God (Acts 8:12), questions of the law of the Jews (Acts 23:29), the Jewish system of worship (Acts 25:19), Mark (Col. 4:10), faith (1 Thes. 3:2), the seventh day (Heb. 4:4), the bones of Joseph (Heb. 11:22), those who lead astray (1 John 2:26), and the body of Moses (Jude 9). Other refs.: Matt. 4:6; 11:7; 16:11; Mark 5:16; 7:17; Luke 2:17; 7:24; 18:31; 24:19, 27, 44; John 7:12, 32; 9:18; 11:19; Acts 8:12; 19:8, 39; 21:24; 22:18; 23:15; 24:24; 25:16; 28:21–23; Rom. 1:3; 1 Cor. 7:1, 25; 8:4; 12:1; 16:1; 1 Thes. 3:2; 4:13; 1 Tim. 1:19; 6:21; 2 Tim. 2:18; 3:8; Heb. 7:14; 11:20, 22; 1 Pet. 4:12. *
– 3 Col. 2:16 → in respect of → RESPECT <1722>.

CONCESSION – ***sungnōmē*** [fem. noun: συγγνώμη <4774>]; **from *sun*: together, and *gnōmē*: opinion, which is from *ginōskō*: to know, to learn; lit.: shared opinion or understanding** ► **Permission, indulgence** > Paul said things to the Corinthians as a concession (1 Cor. 7:6). ¶

CONCILIATE – 1 Cor. 4:13 → to try to conciliate → PLEAD <3870>.

CONCISION – ***katatomē*** [fem. noun: κατατομή <2699>]; **from *katatemnō*: to cut off, which is from *kata*: intens., and *temnō*: to cut** ► **Cut, mutilation** > In contrast to circumcision, the apostle Paul uses the word "concision" {false circumcision, mutilators of the flesh} to designate a religious rite of circumcision of no value and against which he warns the Philippians (Phil. 3:2). ¶

CONCLUDE[1] – [1] ***logizomai*** [verb: λογίζομαι <3049>]; **from *logos*: word, account ► To determine, to deduce** > Paul was concluding {reckoning, maintaining} that a man is justified by faith without works of the law (Rom. 3:28). All other refs.: see entries in Lexicon at <3049>.
[2] ***sumbibazō*** [verb: συμβιβάζω <4822>]; **from *sun*: together, and *bibazō*: to cause to go ► To determine, to deduce** > Paul concluded {assuredly gathered} that the Lord had called him and his companions to preach the gospel in Macedonia (Acts 16:10). Other ref.: Acts 19:33; some mss. have *probibazō*: to draw out. All other refs.: INSTRUCT <4822>, KNIT <4822>, PROVE <4822>, UNITE <4822>.
– [3] John 7:26 → RECOGNIZE <1097> [4] Acts 21:25 → DECIDE <2919> [5] Rom. 11:32; Gal. 3:22 → to shut up → SHUT <4788>.

CONCLUDE[2] – ***plēroō*** [verb: πληρόω <4137>]; **from *plērēs*: full; lit.: to fill ► To accomplish, to terminate** > After having concluded {completed, ended, finished} all His words, Jesus entered Capernaum (Luke 7:1). All other refs.: see entries in Lexicon at <4137>.

CONCORD – ***sumphōnēsis*** [fem. noun: συμφώνησις <4857>]; **from *sumphōneō*: to agree, which is from *sun*: together, and *phonē*: sound, voice ► Agreement; also transl.: accord, consent, harmony** > There is no concord between Christ and Belial (2 Cor. 6:15). ¶

CONCOURSE – [1] ***sundromē*** [fem. noun: συνδρομή <4890>]; **from *suntrechō*: to run together, which is from *sun*: together, and *trechō*: to run; note: *dramein* and *dedroma* are forms of *trechō* ► Tumultuous gathering** > There was a concourse of the people {The people ran together, ran from all directions, rushed together} against Paul at Jerusalem (Acts 21:30). ¶
[2] ***sustrophē*** [fem. noun: συστροφή <4963>]; **from: *sustrephō*: to gather, which is from *sun*: together, and *strephō*: to turn, to gather ► Gathering, sedition** > The men of Ephesus could not give an account of their concourse {disorderly gathering, commotion} (Acts 19:40). Other ref.: Acts 23:12; see CONSPIRACY <4963>. ¶

CONCUPISCENCE – Rom. 7:8; Col. 3:5; 1 Thes. 4:5 → LUST (noun) <1939>.

CONCUR – Rom. 7:22 → to joyfully concur → DELIGHT (verb) <4913>.

CONDEMN – [1] ***kataginōskō*** [verb: καταγινώσκω <2607>]; **from *kata*: against, and *ginōskō*: to know ► To rebuke, to convict** > Paul withstood Peter to the face, because he was to be condemned {to be blamed, in the wrong} (Gal. 2:11), i.e., Peter had to be reprimanded. The heart can condemn a Christian (1 John 3:20, 21). Other ref.: Mark 7:2 in some mss. ¶
[2] **that cannot be condemned: *akatagnōstos*** [adj.: ἀκατάγνωστος <176>]; **from *a*: neg., and *kataginōskō*: see [1] ► That cannot be blamed, reprimanded** > Titus had to use sound speech that could not be condemned {that was beyond reproach} (Titus 2:8). ¶
[3] ***katadikazō*** [verb: καταδικάζω <2613>]; **from *kata*: against, and *dikazō*: to judge, which is from *dikē*: justice; lit.: to judge against, i.e., to find guilty ► To exercise justice, to pronounce a sentence** > The Lord told the Pharisees they would not have condemned the guiltless if they had known that God would have mercy and not sacrifice (Matt. 12:7). By their words, men will be condemned (Matt. 12:37). We will not be condemned if we do not condemn (Luke 6:37a, b). James tells the rich they have condemned and killed the just (Jas. 5:6). ¶
[4] ***katakrinō*** [verb: κατακρίνω <2632>]; **from *kata*: against, and *krinō*: to judge ► To pronounce a sentence, to judge** > At the time of judgment, men of Nineveh who have repented and the queen of the South will condemn the evil and adulterous generation during the life of the Lord on earth (Matt. 12:41, 42; Luke 11:31, 32). The chief priests and the scribes would condemn Jesus to death (Matt. 20:18; Mark 10:33). Seeing

that Jesus had been condemned, Judas returned the thirty pieces of silver (Matt. 27:3). All condemned Jesus to be guilty of death (Mark 14:64). Jesus says that he who disbelieves will be condemned {damned} (Mark 16:16). He did not condemn the woman caught in adultery (John 8:10, 11). The man who judges another condemns himself (Rom. 2:1). God condemned sin in the flesh by sending His own Son in the likeness of flesh of sin and for sin (Rom. 8:3). Christ is the answer to the one who condemns (Rom. 8:34). He who doubts, if he eats, is condemned {damned} (Rom. 14:23). When Christians are judged, they are disciplined by the Lord, that they may not be condemned with the world (1 Cor. 11:32). Noah condemned the world by his ark (Heb. 11:7). We should not complain against another brother so that we may not be condemned (Jas. 5:9). God has condemned to destruction the cities of Sodom and Gomorrah (2 Pet. 2:6). ¶

5 **self-condemned: *autokatakritos*** [adj.: αὐτοκατάκριτος <843>]; **from *autos*: oneself, and *katakrinō*: see 4 ▶ Judged by oneself** > A heretical man is self-condemned {condemned of himself} (Titus 3:11). ¶

– 6 Luke 19:22; John 3:17; 18a, b → JUDGE (verb) <2919> 7 Luke 24:20 → to be condemned → lit.: to the judgment → JUDGMENT <2917> 8 Acts 25:15 → that he be condemned → lit.: for a judgment → JUDGMENT <1349> 9 2 Cor. 7:3 → to condemn → lit.: for condemnation → CONDEMNATION <2633> 10 Col. 2:14 → "and condemned us" added in Engl. 11 Jas. 5:12 → to be condemned → lit.: to fall under judgment → FALL (verb) <4098> 12 Jude 9 → to bring a railing judgment → BRING <2018>.

CONDEMNATION – 1 ***katakrima*** [neut. noun: κατάκριμα <2631>]; **from *katakrinō*: to condemn, which is from *kata*: against, and *krinō*: to judge ▶ Sentence, judgment pronounced with a punishment in view** > Death is a condemnation extended to all men by one man's offense (Rom. 5:16, 18). But there is now no condemnation for those who are in Christ Jesus (Rom. 8:1). ¶

2 ***katakrisis*** [fem. noun: κατάκρισις <2633>]; **from *kata*: against, and *krisis*: judgment, which is from *krinō*: to judge; lit.: to judge against ▶ Judgment bringing condemnation against someone** > The expr. the "ministry of condemnation" (2 Cor. 3:9) relates to the ministry of the Mosaic law. Paul was not addressing himself to the Corinthians for condemnation {to condemn them} (2 Cor. 7:3). ¶

– 3 Mark 12:40; Luke 24:20 → JUDGMENT <2917> 4 John 3:19; 5:29; Jas. 5:12 → JUDGMENT <2920> 5 1 Tim. 3:6; 5:12 → FAULT <2917> 6 2 Pet. 2:3 → DESTRUCTION <684>.

CONDEMNED – 1 Cor. 4:9 → condemned to death → DEATH <1935>.

CONDEMNED (BE) – Gal. 1:8, 9 → lit.: to be a curse → ACCURSED <331>.

CONDESCEND – Rom. 12:16 → ASSOCIATE (verb) <4879>.

CONDITION – 1 Matt. 12:45; Luke 11:26 → last condition, final condition → last state → STATE <2078> 2 1 Cor. 7:20 → CALLING <2821>.

CONDUCT (noun) – 1 ***anastrophē*** [fem. noun: ἀναστροφή <391>]; **from *anastrephō*: to turn up, which is from *ana*: again (intens.), and *strephō*: to turn ▶ Way of life, behavior; also transl. in older versions: conversation** > Paul speaks of his former conduct {way of life, manner of life} in Judaism before his conversion (Gal. 1:13). He tells Timothy to be a model for the Christians in conduct {life} (1 Tim. 4:12). Considering the outcome of the conduct of their leaders, Christians should imitate their faith (Heb. 13:7). By a good conduct, they must show that their works are done in the meekness of wisdom (Jas. 3:13). They should be holy in all their conduct (1 Pet. 1:15), have an honest conduct (2:12), a conduct which is good (3:16), and a holy conduct (2 Pet. 3:11). They have been redeemed from their vain conduct {way of life} (1 Pet. 1:18) by the blood of Christ (see v. 19). Husbands can observe the chaste conduct of their wives (1 Pet. 3:2) and may be won without a word by their conduct (v. 1). Lot was oppressed by the filthy conduct of the godless people of Sodom and Gomorrah (2 Pet. 2:7). Other ref.: Eph. 4:22; see LIFE <391>. ¶

[2] ***tropos*** [masc. noun: τρόπος <5158>]; **from *trepō*: to turn ▶ Manner of life, behavior** > Our conduct {character, conversation, life} must be without love of money (Heb. 13:5). All other refs.: MANNER <5158>.

– [3] Acts 13:18 → to endure the conduct → ENDURE <5159> [4] Rom. 13:3 → good conduct → good work → WORK (noun) <2041> [5] Gal. 2:14 → their conduct was not in step → lit.: they did not walk straightforwardly → STRAIGHTFORWARD <3716> [6] Phil. 1:27 → to let the conduct be → LIVE <4176> [7] 1 Thes. 2:10 → was our conduct → we behaved → BEHAVE <1096> [8] 2 Tim. 3:10 → manner of life → LIFE <72> [9] 2 Pet. 2:2 → depraved conduct → dissolute way → DISSOLUTE <766>.

CONDUCT (verb)[1] – [1] ***anastrephō*** [verb: ἀναστρέφω <390>]; **from *ana*: again (intens.), and *strephō*: to turn ▶ To behave** > Paul conducted himself {had his conversation} in the world in simplicity and sincerity before God (2 Cor. 1:12). Before their conversion, Christians were conducting themselves {had their conversation, were living} in the lusts of their flesh (Eph. 2:3). Timothy had to know how to conduct himself in God's house (1 Tim. 3:15). The author of the Epistle to the Hebrews was desirous to conduct himself well {live honorably, conduct himself honorably, live honestly, walk rightly} in all things (Heb. 13:18). Christians should conduct themselves throughout {should pass, should live} the time of their stay on earth with fear (1 Pet. 1:17). All other refs.: LIVE <390>, RETURN (verb) <390>, TREAT <390>.

– [2] Acts 23:1 → LIVE <4176> [3] 2 Cor. 12:18; Col. 4:5 → WALK <4043> [4] 1 Thes. 2:10 → BEHAVE <1096> [5] 1 Tim. 3:4, 5, 12 → RULE (verb) <4291> [6] Heb. 12:7 → to conduct toward → to deal with → DEAL <4374>.

CONDUCT (verb)[2] – ***kathistēmi*** [verb: καθίστημι <2525>]; **from *kata*: down, and *histēmi*: to stand ▶ To be responsible for, to escort** > Those who conducted Paul brought him as far as Athens (Acts 17:15). All other refs.: APPOINT <2525>, MAKE <2525>, RENDER <2525>.

CONFER – [1] ***sullaleō*** [verb: συλλαλέω <4814>]; **from *sun*: together, and *laleō*: to speak ▶ To talk together, to deliberate** > Festus conferred with the council concerning Paul who had appealed to Caesar (Acts 25:12). All other refs.: SPEAK <4814>.

[2] ***sumballō*** [verb: συμβάλλω <4820>]; **from *sun*: together, and *ballō*: to throw ▶ To discuss, to deliberate** > The Jewish elders conferred with one another concerning Peter and John (Acts 4:15). All other refs.: HELP (verb) <4820>, MEET (verb) <4820>, PONDER <4820>.

[3] ***prosanatithēmi*** [verb: προσανατίθημι <4323>]; **from *pros*: before, and *anatithēmi*: to communicate, which is from *ana*: intens., and *tithēmi*: to put ▶ To place a subject before some people to obtain their advice; to consult** > Paul did not confer {took not counsel} with flesh and blood (i.e., other people) immediately before preaching the Son of God (Gal. 1:16). Other ref.: Gal. 2:6; see ADD <4323>. ¶

– [4] Luke 22:29a, b → APPOINT <1303>.

CONFESS – [1] ***homologeō*** [verb: ὁμολογέω <3670>]; **from *homologos*: assenting, of one mind, which is from *homos*: same, and *legō*: to speak ▶ To acknowledge, to openly declare the truth; to take sides with someone, to make confession** > If one confesses with his mouth the Lord Jesus and believes in his heart that God has raised Him from among the dead, he will be saved (Rom. 10:9). With the mouth, confession is made to salvation {one confesses and is saved} (Rom. 10:10). He who confesses {acknowledges} the Son has the Father also (1 John 2:23). Other verses concerning the confession of Jesus:

Matt. 10:32a, b; Luke 12:8a, b; John 9:22; 12:42; 1 John 4:2, 3, 15; 2 John 7. Timothy had confessed {professed, made} the good confession before many witnesses (1 Tim. 6:12). Offering sacrifice of praise is the fruit of the lips confessing {giving thanks to} the name of Jesus (Heb. 13:15). If we confess our sins, God is faithful and righteous to forgive us our sins (1 John 1:9). Other refs.: Matt. 7:23 {to declare}; 14:7 {to promise}; John 1:20a, b; Acts 23:8; 24:14 {to admit}; Titus 1:16 {to profess}; Heb. 11:13 {to admit}. ¶

[2] ***exomologeō*** [verb: ἐξομολογέω <1843>]; **from *ek*: out, and *homologeō*: see [1] ▶ a. To celebrate, to exalt; also transl.: to give praise, to praise** > David said he would confess to God among the nations (Rom. 15:9). In a future day, every tongue will confess that Jesus Christ is Lord to the glory of God the Father (Phil. 2:11); also, every tongue will confess to God (Rom. 14:11). **b. To admit, to acknowledge** > The N.T. speaks of the confession of sins (Matt. 3:6; Mark 1:5), deeds (Acts 19:18), and faults (Jas. 5:16). The Lord will confess {acknowledge} the name of the overcomer in Sardis before His Father and His angels (Rev. 3:5). All other refs.: PROMISE (verb) <1843>, THANK (verb) <1843>.

– [3] John 1:20 → to fail to confess → DENY <720> [4] Acts 19:18 → to openly confess → TELL <312> [5] 1 Tim. 3:16 → we confess → without controversy → CONTROVERSY <3672> [6] 2 Tim. 2:19 → NAME (verb) <3687> [7] Heb. 3:1 → whom we confess → lit.: of our confession → CONFESSION <3671>.

CONFESSEDLY – 1 Tim. 3:16 → without controversy → CONTROVERSY <3672>.

CONFESSION – [1] ***homologia*** [fem. noun: ὁμολογία <3671>]; **from *homologeō*: see [2] ▶ Declaration, profession, public acknowledgment** > The Corinthians made profession of submission in regard to the glad tidings of Christ (2 Cor. 9:13). Timothy confessed the good confession {professed a good profession} before many witnesses (1 Tim. 6:12). Jesus witnessed the good confession before Pontius Pilate (1 Tim. 6:13) by acknowledging He was the king of the Jews (see Matt. 27:11; Mark 15:2; Luke 23:3; John 18:33). He is the Apostle and High Priest of the Christians' confession {whom they confess} (Heb. 3:1); they must hold fast their confession {the faith they profess} (Heb. 4:14) and hold fast unwavering the confession of their hope (10:23). ¶

[2] **to make confession: *homologeō*** [verb: ὁμολογέω <3670>]; **from *homologos*: assenting, of one mind, which is from *homos*: same, and *legō*: to speak ▶ To acknowledge, to openly declare the truth; to take sides with someone** > With the mouth, confession is made to salvation {one confesses} (Rom. 10:10). All other refs.: CONFESS <3670>.

– [3] 1 Tim. 3:16 → by common confession → without controversy → CONTROVERSY <3672>.

CONFIDE – Gal. 2:7 → COMMIT <4100>.

CONFIDENCE – [1] ***parrēsia*** [fem. noun: παρρησία <3954>]; **from *pan*: all, and *rhēsis*: act of speaking; lit.: liberty of speech ▶ Full assurance, boldness** > Christians must hold fast the confidence {courage} and the rejoicing of the hope firm to the end (Heb. 3:6). They can come with confidence {with boldness, boldly} to the throne of grace (Heb. 4:16). They must not cast away their confidence, which has great reward (Heb. 10:35). By abiding in God, His children will have confidence {may be confident} at the coming of Jesus (1 John 2:28). They have confidence toward God if their heart does not condemn them (1 John 3:21). Love has been made perfect that they may have confidence in the day of judgment (1 John 4:17). Christians have confidence that the Son of God hears them when they ask anything according to His will (1 John 5:14). All other refs.: BOLDLY <3954>, BOLDNESS <3954>, OPENLY <3954>, PUBLIC <3954>.

[2] ***pepoithēsis*** [fem. noun: πεποίθησις <4006>]; **from *pepoitha*, perf. of *peithō*:**

to trust, to have confidence ▶ Assurance, boldness; also transl.: trust > In his confidence {Because he was confident} toward the Corinthians, Paul had purposed to come to them previously (2 Cor. 1:15); he had sent them a brother because of his great confidence in them (8:22). He had confidence through Christ toward God that the Corinthians were manifested to be Christ's epistle (2 Cor. 3:4). He thought of having to act with confidence {be bold} against some walking according to the flesh in Corinth (2 Cor. 10:2). Christians have boldness and access in confidence {confident access} to Christ Jesus, their Lord, through the faith they have in Him (Eph. 3:12). Paul also might have confidence in the flesh (Phil. 3:4). ¶

[3] ***hupostasis*** [fem. noun: ὑπόστασις <5287>]**; from *huphistēmi*: to place under, which is from *hupo*: under, and *histēmi*: to put; lit.: what we put underneath, foundation ▶ Firm conviction, trust** > Paul might have been ashamed in his confidence {of having been so confident} concerning the promised gift of the Corinthians (2 Cor. 9:4). We have become companions of the Christ if we hold the beginning of the confidence {assurance, conviction} firm to the end (Heb. 3:14). Other ref.: 2 Cor. 11:17. Other refs.: Heb. 1:3; 11:1; see SUBSTANCE <5287>. ¶

[4] **to have confidence, to put confidence, to be confident: *peithō*** [verb: πείθω <3982>] **▶ To trust, to have faith; also transl.: to be convinced, to have trust** > Paul had confidence in all the Corinthians (2 Cor. 2:3). He had confidence as to the Galatians in the Lord (Gal. 5:10). He had the confidence that he would remain with the Philippians (Phil. 1:25). He could have confidence in the flesh more than any other (Phil. 3:4), even though Christians should not have confidence in the flesh (v. 3). He had confidence in the Lord that the Thessalonians were doing and would do the things he had enjoined them (2 Thes. 3:4). He had confidence in the obedience of Philemon (Phm. 21). All other refs.: see entries in Lexicon at <3982>.

– [5] Acts 26:26 → to speak with confidence → to speak boldly → BOLDLY <3955> [6] 2 Cor. 1:12 → proud confidence → reason to boast → GLORIFY <2746> [7] 2 Cor. 7:16 → to have confidence → CONFIDENT <2292> [8] Phil. 1:26 → proud confidence → BOAST (noun) <2745>.

CONFIDENT – [1] **to be confident, to have confidence: *tharreō*** [verb: θαρρέω <2292>]**; form of *tharseō*, which is from *tharsos*: courage, boldness; also transl.: to be of good courage ▶ To show courage, to have assurance** > Paul was confident (2 Cor. 5:6, 8). He rejoiced that in everything he was confident as to the Corinthians (2 Cor. 7:16). All other refs.: BOLD <2292>, BOLDLY <2292>.

[2] **to be confident, to become confident: *peithō*** [verb: πείθω <3982>] **▶ To trust, to have faith, to be convinced; also transl.: to have confidence** > Paul addresses himself to those who were confident that they were guides to the blind (Rom. 2:19). He was confident that He who had begun a good work in the Philippians would complete it until the day of Jesus Christ (Phil. 1:6); most brothers in the Lord had become confident {waxed confident, were trusting, had been encouraged} in the Lord through Paul's bonds (v. 14); he was confident that he would remain with them (v. 25). The author of the Epistle to the Hebrews was confident {persuaded himself, was sure} that he had a good conscience (Heb. 13:18). All other refs.: see entries in Lexicon at <3982>.

– [3] 2 Cor. 1:15; Eph. 3:12 → in his confidence, confident access → CONFIDENCE <4006> [4] 2 Cor. 9:4 → having been so confident → lit.: in his confidence → CONFIDENCE <5287> [5] 1 John 2:28 → to be confident → to have confidence → CONFIDENCE <3954>.

CONFIDENTLY – [1] Acts 2:29 → with boldness → BOLDNESS <3954> [2] Heb. 13:6 → to have confidence → BOLDLY <2292>.

CONFINE – Gal. 3:22 → to shut up → SHUT <4788>.

CONFIRM – [1] ***bebaioō*** [verb: βεβαιόω <950>]; **from *bebaios*: solid, firm ► To assure, to establish** > The Lord was confirming the word preached by the apostles through the signs that accompanied it (Mark 16:20). Jesus Christ confirmed the promises made to the Jews (Rom. 15:8). The testimony of Christ had been confirmed in the Corinthians (1 Cor. 1:6). The Lord Jesus Christ will confirm {will keep strong} the Christians to the end (1 Cor. 1:8). The salvation of God had been confirmed {attested} by those who had heard it (Heb. 2:3). All other refs.: ESTABLISH <950>.

[2] ***kuroō*** [verb: κυρόω <2964>]; **from *kuros*: supreme authority, ratification ► To validate, to approve** > No one sets aside or adds other conditions to a covenant if it is confirmed {ratified, duly established} (Gal. 3:15). Other ref.: 2 Cor. 2:8; see REAFFIRM <2964>. ¶

[3] **to confirm before, to confirm beforehand: *prokuroō*** [verb: προκυρόω <4300>]; **from *pro*: before, and *kuroō*: see [2] ► To ratify, to confirm in advance** > The law does not annul the covenant that was confirmed {was established} beforehand by God (Gal. 3:17). ¶

– [4] Matt. 18:16 → ESTABLISH <2476> [5] Luke 22:32 → STRENGTHEN <4741> [6] Acts 14:22; 15:32, 41 → STRENGTHEN <1991> [7] Acts 15:27 → TELL <518> [8] Acts 16:5 → ESTABLISH <4732> [9] Rom. 9:1 → to bear witness → WITNESS (noun)[1] <4828> [10] Phil. 1:7; Heb. 6:16 → CONFIRMATION <951> [11] 1 Thes. 3:2, 13 → ESTABLISH <4741> [12] Heb. 6:17 → INTERVENE <3315> [13] 2 Pet. 1:10 → lit.: to make sure → SURE <949>, MAKE <4160>.

CONFIRMATION – ***bebaiōsis*** [fem. noun: βεβαίωσις <951>]; **from *bebaioō*: to confirm, to establish, which is from *bebaios*: solid, firm ► a. Strengthening, establishment** > In the confirmation of {In confirming} the gospel, the Philippians were all participants of grace with Paul (Phil. 1:7). **b. Corroboration, ratification** > An oath is for confirmation of that which has been agreed upon (Heb. 6:16). ¶

CONFIRMED – 2 Pet. 1:19 → lit.: more firm → FIRM <949>.

CONFISCATION – Heb. 10:34 → PLUNDERING <724>.

CONFLICT – [1] ***agōn*** [masc. noun: ἀγών <73>]; **from *agō*: to lead ► Battle, struggle** > Paul mentions to the Philippians the conflict they had seen in him (Phil. 1:30). He wanted the Colossians to know what a conflict {combat} he had for them and those in Laodicea (Col. 2:1). He had spoken the gospel of God in much conflict {earnest striving, contention, opposition} to the Thessalonians (1 Thes. 2:2). All other refs.: FIGHT (noun) <73>, RACE[2] <73>.

– [2] Luke 22:44 → AGONY <74> [3] 2 Cor. 7:5; Jas. 4:1 → FIGHTING <3163> [4] Gal. 5:17 → to be in conflict → to be opposed → OPPOSE <480> [5] Phil. 1:27 → to labor together in the same conflict → to strive together → STRIVE <4866> [6] Heb. 10:32 → FIGHT (noun) <119>.

CONFLICTING – Rom. 2:15 → "conflicting" added in Engl.

CONFORM – [1] ***suschēmatizō*** [verb: συσχηματίζω <4964>]; **from *sun*: together, and *schēmatizō*: to fashion, which is from *schēma*: form ► To become similar, to be in accord** > The Christian must not be conformed to this world (Rom. 12:2). He must not conform {fashion himself} to his former lusts in his ignorance (1 Pet. 1:14). ¶

[2] **to be conformed: *summorphoō*** [verb: συμμορφόω <4833>]; **from *summorphos*: conformed, which is from *sun*: together, and *morphē*: form ► To make similar** > Paul speaks of being conformed {being made conformable} to the death of Christ {becoming like Christ in His death} (Phil. 3:10); in other mss.: *summorphizō* [συμμορφίζω <4831a>]. ¶

– [3] Acts 26:5 → I (Paul) conformed to the strictest sect → lit.: according (*kata*) to the strictest sect.

CONFORMABLE – Phil. 3:10 → to be made conformable → to be conformed → CONFORM <4833>.

CONFORMED – 1 ***summorphos*** [adj.: σύμμορφος <4832>]; **from *sun*: together, and *morphē*: form ► Similar, in agreement** > Those whom God foreknew, He has also predestinated to be conformed to the image of His Son (Rom. 8:29). The Lord Jesus Christ will transform the Christian's lowly body that it may be conformed to {fashioned to, in conformity to, like} His glorious body (Phil. 3:21). ¶
– 2 Phil. 3:10 → to be conformed → CONFORM <4833>.

CONFORMITY – Phil. 3:21 → in conformity → lit.: that it may be conformed → CONFORMED <4832>.

CONFOUND – 1 ***suncheō*** [verb: συγχέω <4797>]; **from: *sun*: together, and *cheō*: to pour; lit.: to pour together ► To confuse (in the mind), to disconcert** > The multitude was confounded {bewildered, came together in bewilderment} because everyone heard the believers in the Lord speaking in his own language (Acts 2:6). Saul confounded {baffled} the Jews who dwelt in Damascus by proving that Jesus was the Christ (Acts 9:22). All other refs.: CONFUSED (BE) <4797>, STIR (verb) <4797>, UPROAR <4797>.
– 2 Luke 24:37 → TERRIFY <4422> 3 1 Cor. 1:27a, b → to put to shame → SHAME (noun) <2617> 4 1 Pet. 2:6 → to be confounded → ASHAMED (BE) <2617>.

CONFUSED (BE) – ***suncheō*** [verb: συγχέω <4797>]; **from *sun*: together, and *cheō*: to pour; lit.: to pour together ► To be troubled, to be agitated** > The assembly of Ephesians was confused {was tumultuous, was in confusion} (Acts 19:32). All other refs.: CONFOUND <4797>, STIR (verb) <4797>, UPROAR <4797>.

CONFUSION – 1 ***akatastasia*** [fem. noun: ἀκαταστασία <181>]; **from *akatastatos*: unstable, which is from *a*: neg., and *kathistēmi*: to establish firmly, which is from *kata*: down, and *histēmi*: to stand ► Disorder, perturbation** > God is not a God of confusion, but of peace (1 Cor. 14:33). Paul was fearing to find confusions {disturbances, tumults} among the Corinthians (2 Cor. 12:20). Where envy and self-seeking exist, there is confusion and every evil thing (Jas. 3:16). Other refs.: Luke 21:9; 2 Cor. 6:5; see TUMULT <181>, RIOT (noun) <181>. ¶
2 ***sunchusis*** [fem. noun: σύγχυσις <4799>]; **from *suncheō*: to pour together, which is from *sun*: together, and *cheō*: to pour ► Trouble, agitation** > The whole city of Ephesus was filled with confusion {was in an uproar} after it was said that the goddess Artemis might be despised (Acts 19:29). ¶
– 3 Acts 16:20 → to throw into confusion → to trouble exceedingly → TROUBLE (verb) <1613> 4 Acts 17:5 → to set in confusion → to set in an uproar → UPROAR <2350> 5 Acts 19:32 → to be in confusion → CONFUSED (BE) <4797> 6 Acts 21:31 → to be in confusion → to be in uproar → UPROAR <4797> 7 Gal. 1:7; 5:10 → to throw into confusion → TROUBLE (verb) <5015> 8 Gal. 5:12 → to throw into confusion → TROUBLE (verb) <387>.

CONGREGATION – 1 Acts 4:32; 6:2, 5; 15:30; 19:9 → MULTITUDE <4128> 2 Acts 7:38 → CHURCH (c.) <1577> 3 Acts 13:43 → SYNAGOGUE <4864>.

CONJUGAL – 1 Cor. 7:3 → to give conjugal rights → to give her due (lit.: what he owes); in some mss.: to give due good will → DUE <3784>, GOOD WILL <2133>.

CONNECTION – 1 Acts 11:19 → in connection with → on the occasion of → OCCASION <1909> 2 Col. 2:19 → to lose connection → lit.: to not hold fast → FAST (HOLD) <2902>.

CONQUER – 1 ***katagōnizomai*** [verb: καταγωνίζομαι <2610>]; **from *kata*: against, and *agōnizomai*: to contend for victory, which is from *agōn*: conflict,**

struggle ▶ To prevail against, to vanquish > By faith, believers of the O.T. conquered {overcame, subdued} kingdoms (Heb. 11:33). ¶
– [2] Rom. 8:37 → to more than conquer, to overwhelmingly conquer → to be more than conqueror → CONQUEROR <5245> [3] Rev. 2:7, 11, 17, 26; 3:5, 12, 21a, b; 5:5; 6:2a, b; 11:17; 13:7; 12:11; 17:14; 21:7 → OVERCOME <3528> [4] Rev. 15:2 → to gain the victory → VICTORY <3528>.

CONQUEROR – [1] **to be more than conqueror: *hupernikaō*** [verb: ὑπερνικάω <5245>]**; from *huper*: more, and *nikaō*: to overcome ▶ To be more than an overcomer, to vanquish overwhelmingly; also transl.: to more than conquer, to overwhelmingly conquer** > Christians are more than conquerors through Him who has loved them (Rom. 8:37). ¶
– [2] Rev. 6:2a → as a conqueror → lit.: conquering → OVERCOME <3528>.

CONQUEST – Rev. 6:2b → bent on conquest → lit.: to conquer → OVERCOME <3528>.

CONSCIENCE – [1] ***suneidēsis*** [fem. noun: συνείδησις <4893>]**; from *suneidō*: to be conscious, which is from *sun*: together, and *oida*: to know, to perceive ▶ Faculty to discern right and wrong, given by God to the human race since the fall of Adam and Eve; it is more or less blinded in the natural man** > The conscience of the Christian is purified (Heb. 9:14; 10:2 {consciousness, to feel guilty}), but the Christian must apply himself to have a good conscience (Acts 23:1; 1 Tim. 1:5, 19; Heb. 13:18; 1 Pet. 3:16, 21), a pure conscience (1 Tim. 3:9; 2 Tim. 1:3), and a conscience without offense toward God and men (Acts 24:16). Some will depart from faith, cauterized as to their own conscience (1 Tim. 4:2), i.e., having become insensitive to the word of God. Other refs.: John 8:9 in some mss.; Rom. 2:15; 9:1; 13:5; 1 Cor. 8:7 in some mss., 10, 12; 10:25, 27–29; 2 Cor. 1:12; 4:2; 5:11; Titus 1:15; Heb. 9:9; 1 Pet. 2:19. ¶
– [2] 1 Cor. 4:4 → my conscience is clear → lit.: I (Paul) am conscious of nothing → KNOW <4894>.

CONSCIOUS – [1] **to be conscious: *suneidō*** [verb: συνείδω <4894>]**; from *sun*: together, and *eidō*: to have the knowledge, to understand ▶ To be aware** > Paul was conscious {knew} of nothing against himself (1 Cor. 4:4). All other refs.: AWARE <4894>, CONSIDER <4894>, KNOW <4894>, PRIVY <4894>.
– [2] John 6:61; Acts 23:5 → to be conscious → KNOW <1492> [3] Rom. 3:20 → to become conscious → to be the knowledge → KNOWLEDGE <1922> [4] 1 Pet. 2:19 → because he is conscious → lit.: because of conscience → CONSCIENCE <4893>.

CONSCIOUSNESS – Heb. 10:2 → CONSCIENCE <4893>.

CONSECRATE – [1] ***enkainizō*** [verb: ἐγκαινίζω <1457>]**; from *en*: in, and *kainizō*: to make new, which is from *kainos*: new ▶ To inaugurate, to open** > Jesus has consecrated {dedicated} for Christians a new and living way, through the veil, that is, His flesh, to enter the Holiest by His blood (Heb. 10:20). Other ref.: Heb. 9:18; see INAUGURATE <1457>. ¶
– [2] John 10:36; 17:19; 1 Tim. 4:5 → SANCTIFY <37> [3] Heb. 7:28 → PERFECT (verb) <5048>.

CONSECRATED – [1] Luke 2:23 → HOLY <40> [2] Luke 21:5 → consecrated offering → OFFERING → <334>.

CONSENT (noun) – [1] ***sumphōnos*** [adj. used as noun: σύμφωνος <4859>]**; from *sun*: together, and *phōnē*: sound ▶ Mutual agreement** > A married couple must not deprive one another except by consent {agreement, mutual consent} for a time, that they may give themselves to fasting and prayer, and be together again (1 Cor. 7:5). ¶
– [2] 2 Cor. 6:15 → CONCORD <4857> [3] Phm. 14 → MIND (noun) <1106>.

CONSENT (verb) – 1 ***epineuō*** [verb: ἐπινεύω <1962>]; **from *epi*: upon, and *neuō*: to agree ▶ To express one's agreement** > Paul did not consent {did not accede, declined} to stay a longer time in Ephesus (Acts 18:20). ¶

2 ***proserchomai*** [verb: προσέρχομαι <4334>]; **from *pros*: to, and *erchomai*: to come ▶ To agree, to adhere** > If anyone does not consent {accede} to sound words, he is puffed up with pride (1 Tim. 6:3). Other refs.: COME <4334>, DRAW <4334>, GO <4334>.

3 ***sunkatatithemai*** [verb: συγκατατίθεμαι <4784>]; **from *sun*: together, and *katatithēmi*: to lay down, which is from *kata*: down, and *tithēmi*: to put ▶ To acquiesce, to accept** > Joseph of Arimathea had not consented {assented} to the counsel and deed of the Jews in regard to Jesus (Luke 23:51). ¶

4 ***sumphēmi*** [verb: σύμφημι <4852>]; **from *sun*: together, and *phēmi*: to say ▶ To approve, to agree** > If one does what he does not want, he consents to the law that it is good (Rom. 7:16). ¶

5 ***suneudokeō*** [verb: συνευδοκέω <4909>]; **from *sun*: together, and *eudokeō*: to think well, which is from *eu*: well, and *dokeō*: to think, to appear ▶ To approve fully, to assent** > Paul was consenting {was in hearty agreement, was approving, was giving approval} to Stephen being killed (Acts 8:1; 22:20). All other refs.: APPROVE <4909>, WILL (verb) <4909>.

– 6 Luke 22:6 → PROMISE (verb) <1843>.

CONSENTING – 1 Cor. 7:6 → CONCESSION <4774>.

CONSEQUENTLY – 1 ***toi*** [particle: τοι <5104>] ▶ Compound word: *kaitoi*; in some mss.: *kai toi* (Acts 14:17). *

2 ***toigaroun*** [particle: τοιγαροῦν <5105>] ▶ Refs.: 1 Thes. 4:8; Heb. 12:1. ¶

CONSIDER – 1 ***blepō*** [verb: βλέπω <991>] ▶ **To look, to see** > Paul was telling the Corinthians to consider {think of} their calling (1 Cor. 1:26). Other ref.: Matt. 7:3a {to observe}. Other refs.: BEHOLD (verb) <991>, SEE <991>.

2 ***bouleuō*** [verb: βουλεύω <1011>]; **from *boulē*: advice, will ▶ To take advice, to deliberate** > A king going to war considers {consults, takes counsel} first whether he is able to meet him who comes against him (Luke 14:31). All other refs.: CONSULT <1011>, PROPOSE <1011>, RESOLVE (verb) <1011>.

3 ***dokeō*** [verb: δοκέω <1380>] ▶ **To think, to believe** > The disciples were disputing as to which of them should be considered {should be accounted, should be held, was regarded} the greatest (Luke 22:24). All other refs.: REGARD (verb) <1380>, REPUTATION <1380>, SEEM <1380>, SUPPOSE <1380>, THINK <1380>.

4 ***theōreō*** [verb: θεωρέω <2334>]; **from *theoros*: spectator, which is from *theaomai*: to look, to see ▶ To look attentively, to discern** > The author of the Epistle to the Hebrews says to consider {observe, think} how great Melchizedek was (Heb. 7:4). Other refs.: SEE <2334>.

5 ***anatheōreō*** [verb: ἀναθεωρέω <333>]; **from *ana*: intens., and *theōreō*: see 4 ▶ To look very attentively, to contemplate** > Christians must consider the issue of the conduct of their leaders, who have spoken the word of God to them, and imitate their faith (Heb. 13:7). Other ref.: Acts 17:23; see BEHOLD (verb) <333>. ¶

6 ***hēgeomai*** [verb: ἡγέομαι <2233>]; **from *agō*: to lead ▶ To think, to believe; also transl.: to account, to regard, to suppose, to esteem** > Christ Jesus did not consider {esteem, regard, think} equality with God something to be grasped (Phil. 2:6). The things that were gain to himself, Paul considered as loss on account of Christ (Phil. 3:7); and he counted also all things to be loss (v. 8). Peter says to consider {bear in mind} that the longsuffering of the Lord is salvation (2 Pet. 3:15). Other refs.: Phil. 2:25; Heb. 10:29. All other refs.: see entries in Lexicon at <2233>.

7 ***katamanthanō*** [verb: καταμανθάνω <2648>]; **from *kata*: intens., and *manthanō*: to learn ▶ To study, to observe attentively** > Jesus said to consider {observe,

observe with attention, see} the lilies of the field, how they grow (Matt. 6:28). ¶

8 ***noeō*** [verb: νοέω <3539>]; **from *nous*: mind, understanding ▶ To understand, to think about >** Paul was telling Timothy to consider {reflect on, think of} what he was saying to him (2 Tim. 2:7). All other refs.: PERCEIVE <3539>, THINK <3539>, UNDERSTAND <3539>.

9 ***katanoeō*** [verb: κατανοέω <2657>]; **from *kata*: intens., and *noeō*: see 8 ▶ a. To distinguish, to perceive; also transl.: to behold, to look, to observe, to notice, to face the fact, to contemplate >** Jesus reproached the one judging another for not considering {paying attention to} the beam in his own eye (Matt. 7:3; Luke 6:41). Abraham did not consider his own body already become dead in relation to the promise of having a son (Rom. 4:19); other transl.: he considered his body as good as dead in relation to the promise. **b. To observe >** Jesus says to consider the ravens (Luke 12:24) and the lilies (v. 27). Moses went up to consider the burning bush, but he did not dare consider it after he had heard the voice of the Lord (Acts 7:31, 32). In a vision, Peter considered {looked into} an object like a great sheet and saw various animals (Acts 11:6). The author of the Epistle to the Hebrews invites his holy brothers to consider {fix the thoughts on} the Apostle and High Priest of their confession (Heb. 3:1). If anyone is a hearer of the word and not a doer, he is like a man observing {looking at, beholding} his natural face in a mirror; for he observes {looks at, beholdeth} himself, goes away, and immediately forgets what he was like (Jas. 1:23, 24). **c. To pay careful attention to, to look after >** Christians are to consider one another in order to stir each other up to love and good works (Heb. 10:24). All other refs.: DISCOVER <2657>, PERCEIVE <2657>.

10 ***logizomai*** [verb: λογίζομαι <3049>]; **from *logos*: word, account ▶ To think, to believe, to conclude; also transl.: to account, to reckon >** Paul considered that the sufferings of this present time are not worthy to be compared with the coming glory to be revealed to Christians (Rom. 8:18). Some believers were considered as sheep for slaughter (Rom. 8:36). To a man who considers {esteems, regards} anything to be unclean, to him it is unclean (Rom. 14:14). Paul considered {supposed, thought} that in nothing he was inferior to the most eminent apostles (2 Cor. 11:5). Abraham considered {counted, reasoned} that God was able to raise Isaac from among the dead (Heb. 11:19). Other refs.: 2 Cor. 10:11 {to realize}; 12:6 {to credit}. All other refs.: see entries in Lexicon at <3049>.

11 ***analogizomai*** [verb: ἀναλογίζομαι <357>]; **from *ana*: intens., and *logizomai*: see 10 ▶ To think attentively, to ponder again and again >** Christians must consider Jesus who endured so great contradiction from sinners against Himself, that they will not grow weary and discouraged in their souls (Heb. 12:3). ¶

12 ***dialogizomai*** [verb: διαλογίζομαι <1260>]; **from *dia*: intens., and *logizomai*: see 10 ▶ To think, to reason >** Caiaphas was telling the Jews they were not considering {realizing, taking into account} that it was profitable for them that one man should die for the people, and not that the whole nation perish (John 11:50). All other refs.: REASON (verb) <1260>.

13 ***skopeō*** [verb: σκοπέω <4648>]; **from *skopos*: observer, objective ▶ To direct one's attention, to take heed >** Paul beseeched the Christians at Rome to consider {mark, note, keep their eyes on, watch out for} those who create divisions and occasions of falling (Rom. 16:17). All other refs.: EYES <4648>, REGARD (verb) <4648>, WATCH (verb) <4648>.

14 ***suneidō*** [verb: συνείδω <4894>]; **from *sun*: completely, and *eidō*: to see, to know ▶ To perceive mentally, to be aware >** Having considered {become clearly conscious, realized} the place where he was, Peter went to the house of Mary, the mother of Mark (Acts 12:12). All other refs.: AWARE <4894>, CONSCIOUS <4894>, KNOW <4894>, PRIVY <4894>.

– **15** Matt. 1:20 → THINK <1760> **16** Mark 6:52 → UNDERSTAND <4920> **17** Mark 10:42 → REGARD (verb) <1380> **18** Mark 11:32 → COUNT

<2192> [19] Acts 4:29 → to look upon → LOOK (verb) <1896> [20] Rom. 11:22 → BEHOLD (verb) <1492> [21] Rom. 14:5a, b → ESTEEM (verb) <2919> [22] 1 Cor. 2:14 → considers them → lit.: they are to him [23] 2 Thes. 1:6 → "considers" added in Engl. [24] Rev. 2:5 → REMEMBER <3421>.

CONSIDERABLE – [1] Luke 7:12 → very considerable → LARGE <2425> [2] Acts 14:3; 27:9 → LONG (adj.) <2425>.

CONSIDERATE – [1] Titus 3:2; Jas. 3:17; 1 Pet. 2:18 → GENTLE <1933> [2] 1 Pet. 3:7 → being considerate → with knowledge → KNOWLEDGE <1108>.

CONSIDERATION – [1] Acts 27:3 → with consideration → KINDLY <5364> [2] Titus 3:2 → GENTLENESS <4236>.

CONSIGN – [1] Rom. 11:32 → to shut up → SHUT <4788> [2] Rev. 21:8 → they will be consigned → lit.: their part will be → PART (noun) <3313>.

CONSIST – [1] 1 Cor. 12:14 → does not consist → lit.: is not [2] Col. 1:17 → to subsist together → SUBSIST <4921>.

CONSISTENT – Mark 14:56, 59 → not to be consistent → to not agree → AGREE <2470> <3756> <1510>.

CONSOLATION – [1] ***paraklēsis*** [fem. noun: παράκλησις <3874>]; **from *parakaleō*: to comfort, to encourage, which is from *para*: near, and *kaleō*: to call ▶ Encouragement, exhortation; also transl.: comfort** > Simeon was waiting for the consolation of Israel (Luke 2:25). Barnabas means "son of consolation" (Acts 4:36). The churches increased through the consolation of the Holy Spirit (Acts 9:31). Those of the church in Antioch rejoiced over the consolation brought by the letter {the encouraging message} of the Christians in Jerusalem (Acts 15:31). We have hope through the patience and consolation of the Scriptures (Rom. 15:4). God is the God of consolation (Rom. 15:5), of all consolation (2 Cor. 1:3). Paul encouraged the afflicted by the consolation he had received from God (2 Cor. 1:4). The consolation of Paul was abounding through Christ (2 Cor. 1:5); he speaks of the consolation in Christ (Phil. 2:1). God has given Christians an eternal consolation and good hope (2 Thes. 2:16); by Him we have a strong consolation (Heb. 6:18). Other refs.: Luke 6:24; 2 Cor. 1:6a, b {endurance}, 7; 7:4, 7, 13; Phm. 7. All other refs.: ENTREATY <3874>, EXHORTATION <3874>.

[2] ***paramuthion*** [neut. noun: παραμύθιον <3890>]; **from *paramutheomai*: to comfort verbally, which is from *para*: to, and *mutheomai*: to speak, which is from *muthos*: speech, conversation ▶ Comfort, encouragement, solace** > Paul speaks to the Philippians of the consolation of love (Phil. 2:1). ¶

– [3] 1 Cor. 14:3 → COMFORT (noun) <3889> [4] Col. 4:11 → COMFORT (noun) <3931>.

CONSOLE – John 11:19, 31 → COMFORT (verb) <3888>.

CONSORT – Acts 17:4 → to consort with → to join oneself to → JOIN <4345>.

CONSPICUOUS – [1] Gal. 2:2, 6a, b, 9 → to be conspicuous → to be of reputation → REPUTATION <1380> [2] 1 Tim. 5:24, 25 → clearly evident → CLEARLY <4271>.

CONSPIRACY – [1] ***sunōmosia*** [fem. noun: συνωμοσία <4945>]; **from *sunomnumi*: to swear together, which is from *sun*: together, and *omnuō*: to swear ▶ A plot by individuals acting together secretly, especially for an evil purpose** > There were more than forty Jews who had formed a conspiracy {formed a plot, joined together in an oath} against Paul to kill him (Acts 23:13; see v. 12). ¶

[2] ***sustrophē*** [fem. noun: συστροφή <4963>]; **from *sustrephō*: to gather, which is from *sun*: together, and *strephō*: to turn ▶ Coalition in view of a conspiracy** > Jews formed a conspiracy {banded together} and bound themselves under an oath, saying

that they would neither eat nor drink until they had killed Paul (Acts 23:12). Other ref.: Acts 19:40; see CONCOURSE <4963>. ¶
– 3 Acts 9:23 → there was a conspiracy → lit.: they consulted together → CONSULT <4823>.

CONSPIRE – 1 Acts 5:9 → to agree together → AGREE <4856> 2 Acts 9:23 → CONSULT <4823>.

CONSTANT – 1 Acts 12:5 → UNCEASING <1618> 2 Rom. 12:12 → PERSEVERING <4342> 3 1 Tim. 6:5 → constant friction, constant quarrellings → useless wrangling → WRANGLING <1275a>.

CONSTANTLY – 1 Mark 5:5 → ALWAYS <1275> 2 Acts 27:33 → to constantly watch → TARRY <4328> 3 Rom. 1:9; 1 Thes. 1:2 in some mss., 3; 2:13; 5:17 → CEASING (WITHOUT) <89> 4 2 Cor. 4:11 → ALWAYS <104> 5 Phil. 1:4 → ALWAYS <3842> 6 2 Tim. 1:3 → CEASING (WITHOUT) <88>.

CONSTERNATION – 1 Pet. 3:6 → FEAR (noun) <4423>.

CONSTITUTE – 1 Acts 7:27; Heb. 8:3 → APPOINT <2525> 2 Rom. 5:19a, b; Heb. 7:28; Jas. 4:4 → to make, to make ruler → MAKE <2525> 3 Gal. 2:18 → MAKE <4921> 4 Heb. 3:2 → APPOINT <4160>.

CONSTRAIN – 1 ***anankazō*** [verb: ἀναγκάζω <315>]; **from *anankē*: necessity ▶ To oblige; also transl.: to force, to compel, to make** > Jesus constrained His disciples to get into a boat (Matt. 14:22; Mark 6:45). The servant of the parable had to constrain people to enter into the house of the master (Luke 14:23). Before his conversion, Paul constrained {tried to force} the saints to blaspheme (Acts 26:11). He was constrained to appeal to Caesar (Acts 28:19). The Corinthians had constrained {had driven} Paul to become a fool in boasting (2 Cor. 12:11). Titus was not constrained to be circumcised (Gal. 2:3). Peter was constraining the Gentiles to live as Jews (Gal. 2:14). Those desiring to have a good appearance in the flesh would constrain the Galatians to be circumcised (Gal. 6:12). ¶
2 ***parabiazomai*** [verb: παραβιάζομαι <3849>]; **from *para*: near (intens.), and *biazō*: to force ▶ To press, to make an earnest request** > The two disciples of Emmaus constrained {urged, urged strongly} Jesus to stay with them (Luke 24:29). Lydia constrained {persuaded, urged} Paul and others to come to her house and stay there (Acts 16:15). ¶
– 3 Acts 20:22 → BIND <1210> 4 2 Cor. 5:14 → COMPEL <4912>.

CONSTRAINT – 1 **by constraint: *anankastōs*** [adv.: ἀναγκαστῶς <317>]; **from *anankazō*: to constrain, to force, which is from *anankē*: necessity ▶ By necessity, by obligation** > The elders must shepherd the flock of God, not by constraint {by necessity, under compulsion, because they must}, but willingly (1 Pet. 5:2). ¶
– 2 Luke 12:50 → to be under constraint → to be distressed → DISTRESSED <4912> 3 1 Cor. 7:37 → NECESSITY <318>.

CONSTRUCT – Heb. 11:7 → PREPARE <2680>.

CONSTRUCTION – 1 Pet. 3:20 → during the construction of the ark → lit.: while the ark was being prepared → PREPARE <2680>.

CONSTRUCTIVE – 1 Cor. 10:23 → to be constructive → EDIFY <3618>.

CONSTRUCTOR – Heb. 11:10 → MAKER <1217>.

CONSULT – 1 ***bouleuō*** [verb: βουλεύω <1011>]; **from *boulē*: advice, will; lit.: to want ▶ To hold a council, to decide** > The chief priests consulted {took counsel, plotted, made plans} to put Lazarus to death (John 12:10). The Jews consulted {intended, took counsel, plotted, wanted} to kill the apostles (Acts 5:33). All other refs.:

CONSIDER <1011>, PROPOSE <1011>, RESOLVE (verb) <1011>.

[2] ***sumbouleuō*** [verb: συμβουλεύω <4823>]; **from *sun*: together (intens.), and *bouleuō*: see [1]; lit.: to hold a council ▶ To deliberate, to decide together; also transl.: to consult together, to give counsel, to take counsel, to plot, to plot together, to advise >** The Jews consulted to take Jesus by subtlety and kill Him (Matt. 26:4). Caiaphas gave counsel to the Jews that it was expedient that one man should die for the people (John 18:14). The Jews consulted together {conspired} to kill Paul (Acts 9:23). Other refs.: John 11:53; Rev. 3:18; see COUNSEL (noun) <4823>, COUNSEL (verb) <4823>. ¶

– [3] Matt. 28:12 → to hold a council → COUNSEL (noun) <4824> [4] Gal. 1:16 → CONFER <4323>.

CONSUME – [1] ***analiskō*** [verb: ἀναλίσκω <355>]; **from *ana*: away, and *aliskō*: to take ▶ To take away, to destroy >** James and John wanted to speak so that the fire would come down from heaven and consume a village of Samaritans (Luke 9:54). The Lord will consume {will slay, will overthrow} the lawless one with the breath of His mouth (2 Thes. 2:8; other mss.: *analoō*). If the Galatians were biting and devouring one another, they should see that they were not consumed by one another (Gal. 5:15). Other ref.: Mark 9:49 in some mss. ¶

– [2] John 2:17; Rev. 11:5; 20:9 → DEVOUR <2719> [3] Rom. 1:27 → BURN <1572> [4] 1 Cor. 3:15; Rev. 18:8 → BURN <2618> [5] 2 Cor. 4:16 → PERISH <1311> [6] Heb. 10:27 → DEVOUR <2068> [7] Jas. 4:3 → SPEND <1159>.

CONSUMING – **to consume: *katanaliskō*** [verb: καταναλίσκω <2654>]; **from *kata*: intens., and *analiskō*: to consume, to destroy, which is from *ana*: away, and *aliskomai*: to be taken ▶ To destroy completely, to devour >** God is a consuming fire (Heb. 12:29). ¶

CONSUMMATE – [1] Matt. 1:25 → to consummate marriage → KNOW <1097> [2] Heb. 8:8 → MAKE <4931>.

CONSUMMATION – Heb. 9:26 → END (noun) <4930>.

CONTAIN – [1] ***periechō*** [verb: περιέχω <4023>]; **from *peri*: about, and *echō*: to have ▶ To find, to include >** It is contained {is said} in Scripture: Behold I lay in Zion a chief cornerstone (1 Pet. 2:6). All other refs.: AFTER <4023>, SEIZE <4023>.

[2] ***chōreō*** [verb: χωρέω <5562>]; **from *chōra*: place ▶ To include, to hold >** The world could not contain {would not have room for} the books that would be written about the things Jesus did (John 21:25). All other refs.: see entries in Lexicon at <5562>.

– [3] 1 Cor. 10:26 → all it contains → FULLNESS <4138> [4] 3 John 8 → RECEIVE <618>.

CONTAINER – [1] Matt. 13:48 → VESSEL[1] <30> [2] Luke 8:16 → VESSEL[1] <4632>.

CONTAMINATE – 2 Cor. 7:1 → thing that contaminates → DEFILEMENT <3436>.

CONTAMINATED – Acts 15:20 → thing contaminated → thing polluted → POLLUTED <234>.

CONTEMPLATE – [1] John 1:14 → SEE <2300> [2] Rom. 4:19 → CONSIDER <2657> [3] 2 Cor. 3:18 → to behold as in a mirror → BEHOLD (verb) <2734> [4] 1 John 1:1 → to look upon → LOOK (verb) <2300>.

CONTEMPORARY – Gal. 1:14 → EQUAL <4915>.

CONTEMPT – [1] **to be treated with contempt: *exoudeneō*** [verb: ἐξουδενέω <1847>]; **from *ek*: intens., and *oudeneō*: to bring to nothing, which is from *ouden*: nothing; also spelled: *exoudenoō* ▶ To treat a person as though he or she were nothing >** The Son of Man had to suffer many things and be treated with contempt {be set at nought, be rejected} (Mark 9:12). ¶

[2] **to treat with contempt, to view with contempt: *exoutheneō*** [verb: ἐξουθενέω <1848>]; **from *ek*: intens., and *outheneō*: to bring to nothing, which is from *outhen*: nothing ▶ Verb equivalent to the preceding one >** Herod together with his troops treated Jesus with contempt {set Him at nought, ridiculed Him} (Luke 23:11). The verb is transl. "to despise," "to make nothing of," "to look down" in Luke 18:9. All other refs.: CONTEMPTIBLE <1848>, DESPISE <1848>, ESTEEM (verb) <1848>.

– [3] Rom. 2:4 → to show contempt → DESPISE <2706> [4] Heb. 6:6 → to hold up to contempt → to make a show → SHOW (noun) <3856>.

CONTEMPTIBLE – to treat with contempt: *exoutheneō* [verb: ἐξουθενέω <1848>]; **from *ek*: intens., and *outhenoō*: to bring to nothing, which is from *outhen*: nothing ▶ To treat a person or his words as though they were nothing or without value >** Some said Paul's speech was contemptible {was naught, was of no account, amounted to nothing} (lit.: was being treated with contempt) (2 Cor. 10:10). All other refs.: CONTEMPT <1848>, DESPISE <1848>, ESTEEM (verb) <1848>.

CONTEND – [1] *diakrinō* [verb: διακρίνω <1252>]; **from *dia*: denotes separation in two, and *krinō*: to judge ▶ To have a different opinion, to argue >** Those of the circumcision contended with {criticized, took issue with} Peter (Acts 11:2). Michael the archangel was contending {disputing} with the devil about the body of Moses (Jude 9). All other refs.: see entries in Lexicon at <1252>.

[2] **to contend, to contend earnestly: *epagōnizomai*** [verb: ἐπαγωνίζομαι <1864>]; **from *epi*: for, about, and *agōnizomai*: to fight ▶ To fight, to strive >** Jude was writing to exhort his readers to contend earnestly for the faith (Jude 3). ¶

– [3] John 6:52 → QUARREL (verb) <3164> [4] Acts 7:26 → FIGHT (verb) <3164> [5] Acts 23:9 → STRIVE <1264> [6] 1 Cor. 9:25 → FIGHT (verb) <75> [7] Phil. 1:27; 4:3 → to contend as one man, to contend → to strive together → STRIVE <4866> [8] Col. 1:29 → to strenuously contend → to labor, fighting → LABOR (verb) <2872>, FIGHT (verb) <75> [9] Col. 2:1 → how hard I am contending → how great a conflict I have → CONFLICT <73> [10] 2 Tim. 2:24 → STRIVE <3164>.

CONTENT (adj.) – [1] Luke 3:14; Heb. 13:5; 3 John 10 → to be content → to be satisfied → SATISFIED <714> [2] 2 Cor. 12:10 → to be well content → PLEASED (BE) <2106> [3] Phil. 4:11 → SATISFIED <842>.

CONTENT (verb) – [1] ***arkeō*** [verb: ἀρκέω <714>]; ***arcere*, in Lat.: to contain, to retain ▶ To satisfy, to suffice >** Paul says that having food and clothing, we will be content with that (1 Tim. 6:8). All other refs.: ENOUGH <714>, SATISFIED <714>, SUFFICIENT <714>.

[2] ***hikanos poiēsai*; *hikanos*** [adj.: ἱκανός <2425>], ***poieō*** [verb: ποιέω <4160>]; **lit.: to make sufficient ▶ To give satisfaction >** Pilate, desirous of satisfying {gratifying, contenting} the crowd, released Barabbas and delivered Jesus (Mark 15:15). Other refs. (*hikanos*): see entries in Lexicon at <2425>. Other refs. (*poieō*), see entries in Lexicon at <4160>.

CONTENTION – [1] *eritheia* [fem. noun: ἐριθεία <2052>]; **from *eritheuō*: to work for hire, in the sense of seeking only one's own interest ▶ Personal ambition with the intent of drawing others to one's cause; also transl.: dispute, selfish ambition, selfishness, strife >** Paul feared there might be contentions among the Corinthians (2 Cor. 12:20). Contentions are one of the works of the flesh (Gal. 5:20). Some people announced the Christ out of contention (Phil. 1:16 or 17). Nothing ought to be done in the spirit of strife (or: in contention}

(Phil. 2:3). All other refs.: SELF-SEEKING <2052>, STRIFE <2052>.
[2] ***eris*** [fem. noun: ἔρις <2054>] ▶ **Dispute; also transl.: discord, quarrel, strife >** There were contentions among the Corinthians (1 Cor. 1:11). Paul tells Titus to avoid contentions (Titus 3:9). Other refs.: Rom. 1:29; 13:13; 1 Cor. 3:3; 2 Cor. 12:20; Gal. 5:20; Phil. 1:15; 1 Tim. 6:4; see STRIFE <2054>. ¶
– [3] Acts 15:39 → sharp contention → sharp disagreement → DISAGREEMENT <3948> [4] 1 Thes. 2:2 → CONFLICT <73> [5] 1 Tim. 3:3 → not addicted to contention → not quarrelsome → QUARRELSOME <269> [6] Titus 3:9 → STRIVING <3163>.

CONTENTIOUS – [1] ***philoneikos*** [adj.: φιλόνεικος <5380>]; **from *phileō*: to love, and *neikos*: conflict ▶ Who likes to protest, fond of disputing; anti-authority >** Concerning the head covering, Paul says if anyone thinks to be contentious, there is no such custom (1 Cor. 11:16). ¶
– [2] Rom. 2:8 → SELF-SEEKING <2052> [3] Titus 3:2 → not contentious → not quarrelsome → QUARRELSOME <269>.

CONTENTMENT – ***autarkeia*** [fem. noun: αὐτάρκεια <841>]; **from *autarkēs*: self-sufficient, which is from *autos*: oneself, and *arkeō*: to be content, to be sufficient ▶ Satisfaction with what one has, condition of having one's needs met >** Paul speaks to the Corinthians as always having all contentment {sufficiency, all that they need} in everything (2 Cor. 9:8). Godliness with contentment is great gain (1 Tim. 6:6). ¶

CONTEST – Heb. 10:32 → FIGHT (noun) <119>.

CONTINUAL – [1] Luke 18:5 → PERPETUALLY <1519> <5056> [2] Rom. 9:2 → UNINTERRUPTED <88>.

CONTINUALLY – [1] ***diapantos*** [adv.: διαπαντός <1275>]; **from *dia*: across, and *pas*: all; lit.: through all ▶ Always, without ceasing >** After the ascension of Jesus, the disciples were continually in the temple praising and blessing God (Luke 24:53). Christians should offer the sacrifice of praise continually to God (Heb. 13:15). All other refs.: ALWAYS <1275>.
[2] ***eis to diēnekes*; *diēnekēs*** [adj.: διηνεκής <1336>]; **from *diēnenka*: a form of *diapherō*: to carry through ▶ Indefinitely, without interruption; also transl.: forever, for all time, in perpetuity, perpetually >** Melchizedek abides a priest continually (Heb. 7:3). The same sacrifices offered under the law continually {endlessly} yearly cannot make perfect those who approach (Heb. 10:1). Jesus Christ sat down in perpetuity at the right hand of God (Heb. 10:12); He had perfected in perpetuity the sanctified (v. 14). ¶
– [3] Matt. 18:10 → ALWAYS <1223> <3956> [4] Luke 18:5 → PERPETUALLY <1519> <5056> [5] Rom. 13:6 → to attend continually → ATTEND <4342> [6] Col. 1:3 → ALWAYS <3842> [7] Col. 1:9 → "continually" added in Engl. [8] 1 Thes. 1:2 (in some mss.), 3; 2:13; 5:17 → CEASING (WITHOUT) <89>.

CONTINUANCE – Rom. 2:7 → PATIENT CONTINUANCE <5281>.

CONTINUE – [1] ***menō*** [verb: μένω <3306>] ▶ **To remain, to persevere >** Jesus told the Jews who believed in Him that if they continued in {abode in, held to} His word, they were truly His disciples (John 8:31). In 1 Tim. 2:15, believing women are to continue in faith and love and holiness. All other refs.: AWAIT <3306>, LASTING <3306>, REMAIN <3306>, STAY (verb) <3306>, TARRY <3306>.
[2] ***emmenō*** [verb: ἐμμένω <1696>]; **from *en*: in, and *menō*: see [1]; lit.: to remain in the same place ▶ To persevere firmly >** Paul exhorted the disciples to continue {to abide, to remain true} in the faith (Acts 14:22). He who places himself under the law is cursed if he does not continue {abide} in all the things which are written in the book of the law to do them (Gal. 3:10). The Lord reproached Israel because they did not continue {remain faithful} in His covenant (Heb. 8:9). Paul

remained two whole years in his own rented house in Rome (Acts 28:30). ¶

[3] ***epimenō*** [verb: ἐπιμένω <1961>]; **from *epi*: upon (intens.), and *menō*: see [1] ► To persevere with determination, to refuse to give up; also transl.: to abide, to persist** > The scribes and the Pharisees continued {persisted in, kept on} asking Jesus (John 8:7). Peter continued {kept on} knocking at the door (Acts 12:16). Paul and Barnabas exhorted the Jews and the proselytes to continue in the grace of God (Acts 13:43; some mss. have *prosmenō*). In Romans 11, Paul says to abide (or: continue) in the goodness of God and not to abide (or: continue) in unbelief (vv. 22, 23). Timothy was to continue in various things (1 Tim. 4:16). Other refs.: Rom. 6:1 {to go on}; Col. 1:23. All other refs.: REMAIN <1961>, STAY (verb) <1961>, TARRY <1961>.

[4] ***paramenō*** [verb: παραμένω <3887>]; **from *para*: beside, and *menō*: see [1] ► To remain, to stay** > Death hindered the priests from continuing in their service (Heb. 7:23). He who continues in the law of liberty will be blessed (Jas. 1:25). Some mss. have Phil. 1:25; see [5]. Other ref.: 1 Cor. 16:6; see STAY (verb) <3887>. ¶

[5] **to continue with: *sumparamenō*** [verb: συμπαραμένω <4839>]; **from *sun*: with, and *paramenō*: see [4] ► To remain together** > Paul knew that he would continue with {abide with} the Philippians for their progress and joy in faith (Phil. 1:25); some mss. have *paramenō*. ¶

[6] ***prosmenō*** [verb: προσμένω <4357>]; **from *pros*: with, and *menō*: to stay ► To persevere, to remain; also transl.: to be with, to abide with** > The multitude had continued with Jesus for three days (Matt. 15:32; Mark 8:2). Barnabas encouraged all the Christians in Antioch to continue with {cleave unto, remain true to, remain faithful to} the Lord (Acts 11:23). She who is a widow indeed continues in supplications (1 Tim. 5:5). Other ref.: Acts 13:43 in some mss.; see [3]. Other refs.: Acts 18:18; 1 Tim. 1:3; see REMAIN <4357>. ¶

[7] ***ginomai*** [verb: γίνομαι <1096>] **► To be** > Paul taught in the school of Tyrannus, and this continued {took place, went on} (lit.: was) for two years (Acts 19:10).

[8] ***kathizō*** [verb: καθίζω <2523>]; **from *kata*: down, and *hizō*: to sit; lit.: to sit down ► To stay, to remain at the same place, to settle** > Paul continued a year and six months to teach the word of God among the Corinthians (Acts 18:11). All other refs.: JUDGE (verb) <2523>, SIT <2523>, TARRY <2523>.

[9] ***poieō*** [verb: ποιέω <4160>]; **lit.: to do ► To act, to behave** > The beast will be given power to continue forty-two months (Rev. 13:5). Other refs.: see entries in Lexicon at <4160>.

[10] ***proskartereō*** [verb: προσκαρτερέω <4342>]; **from *pros*: toward, and *kartereō*: to be strong, to endure, which is from *karteros*: strength ► a. To continue to do what one has proposed to do without stopping, to devote oneself to this matter, to persevere** > The apostles and others continued {joined constantly} with one accord in prayer in the upper chamber, after the ascension of the Lord (Acts 1:14). The early Christians continued in the teaching of the apostles (Acts 2:42) and continued in the temple with one accord (v. 46). The twelve apostles had resolved to give themselves continually {to devote themselves, to give their attention} to prayer and the ministry of the word (Acts 6:4). Paul exhorted the Colossians to continue in prayer (Col. 4:2). **b. To be at the disposition, to follow, to remain attached to someone** > Simon continued constantly with Philip (Acts 8:13). The verb is also used in regard to the servants and soldiers of Cornelius (Acts 10:7 {to wait on continually}). All other refs.: ATTEND <4342>, PERSEVERING <4342>, READY <4342>.

– [11] Luke 1:22; Gal. 2:5; Heb. 1:11; 2 Pet. 3:4 → REMAIN <1265> [12] Luke 22:28 → PERSEVERE <1265> [13] Luke 24:28 → to continue on as if → to act as if → ACT (verb) <4364> [14] John 11:54; Acts 15:35 → STAY (verb) <1304> [15] Acts 15:38 → to go with, to go along → GO <4905> [16] Acts 20:7 → PROLONG <3905> [17] Acts 20:9 → to continue speaking → lit.: to speak for longer (*epi pleion*) [18] Acts 21:7 → FINISH

<1274> 19 Acts 26:22 → STAND (verb) <2476> 20 1 Tim. 5:16 → "continue to" added In Engl. 21 Jas. 4:13 → PASS <4160> 22 1 Pet. 4:19 → to continue to do good → well doing → DOING <16>.

CONTINUING – 1 Rom. 12:12 → continuing instant, continuing steadfastly → PERSEVERING <4342> 2 Heb. 13:14 → LASTING <3306>.

CONTRADICT – 1 Luke 21:15 → RESIST <436> 2 Luke 21:15 → REPLY (verb) <471> 3 Acts 13:45a, b; Titus 1:9 → to speak against → SPEAK <483>.

CONTRADICTION – 1 ***antilogia*** [fem. noun: ἀντιλογία <485>]; **from *antilegō*: to contradict, which is from *anti*: against, and *legō*: to talk ▶ Opposition, revolt** > Beyond all contradiction {dispute, doubt, gainsaying}, the inferior (Abraham) is blessed by the better (Melchizedek) (Heb. 7:7). Jesus has endured contradiction {hostility} from sinners against Himself (Heb. 12:3). Jude refers to the contradiction {gainsaying, rebellion} of Korah (Jude 11). Other ref.: Heb. 6:16; see DISPUTE (noun) <485>. ¶
– 2 1 Tim. 6:20 → OPPOSITION <477>.

CONTRARIWISE – 2 Cor. 2:7; Gal. 2:7; 1 Pet. 3:9 → on the contrary → CONTRARY <5121>.

CONTRARY – 1 ***enantios*** [adj.: ἐναντίος <1727>]; **from *en*: in, and *antios*: set against ▶ In opposite direction, adverse, unfavorable** > The boat that Jesus compelled His disciples to board was tossed by the waves, for the wind was contrary {against it} (Matt. 14:24). On another occasion, the disciples were toiling in rowing, for the wind was contrary to them {against them} (Mark 6:48). The winds were contrary to Paul's ship (Acts 27:4). The word is transl. "in front," "opposite," "against" in Mark 15:39. Other refs.: Acts 26:9; 28:17. Other refs.: 1 Thes. 2:15; Titus 2:8; see OPPOSED <1727>. ¶
2 **on the contrary: *tounantion*** [adv.: τοὐναντίον <5121>]; **from *enantios*: see 1 ▶ Rather, instead, contrariwise** > On the contrary, i.e., instead of continuing the punishment, Christians should rather show grace toward and encourage the brother who had caused grief (2 Cor. 2:7). Those who seemed to be something added nothing to Paul, but, on the contrary, they had seen that the gospel for the uncircumcised had been committed to him (Gal. 2:7). The Christian must not render evil for evil, but on the contrary bless others (1 Pet. 3:9). ¶
3 ***hupenantios*** [adj. and adj. used as noun: ὑπεναντίος <5227>]; **from *hupo*: under, and *enantios*: see 1 ▶ Adverse, directly opposed** > God has effaced the handwriting in ordinances that was contrary to {hostile to, against} Christians (Col. 2:14). Other ref.: Heb. 10:27; see ADVERSARY <5227>. ¶
4 ***para*** [prep.: παρά <3844>] **▶ Against, in opposition to** > Paul was accused of persuading men to worship God contrary to the law (Acts 18:13).
5 **to break the law: *paranomeō*** [verb: παρανομέω <3891>]; **from *paranomos*: contrary to the law, which is from *para*: against, beyond, and *nomos*: law ▶ To transgress the law, to violate the law** > Contrary to the law {In violation of the law} (lit.: Breaking the law), the high priest Ananias had commanded Paul to be struck (Acts 23:3). ¶
6 **to do contrary, to act contrary: *prassō*** [verb: πράσσω <4238>] ***apenanti*** [adv.: ἀπέναντι <561>]; **from *apo*: from, and *enanti*: before ▶ To act against, to contravene** > Jason and certain brothers were accused of acting contrary to {defying} the decrees of Caesar, saying there was another king, Jesus (Acts 17:7). Other refs. (*prassō*): COLLECT <4238>, DO <4238>, KEEP (verb) <4238>, USE (verb) <4238>. Other refs. (*apenanti*): PRESENCE <561>.
– 7 Rom. 3:31 → on the contrary → RATHER <235> 8 Rom. 10:21 → to speak against → SPEAK <483> 9 Gal. 5:17; 1 Tim. 1:10 → to be contrary → OPPOSE <480>.

CONTRIBUTE – 1 Mark 12:43; Luke 21:4 → to throw into the treasury → THROW (verb) <906> 2 Mark 12:44 → to throw into the treasury → PUT <906> 3 Luke 8:3 →

to contribute to the support → MINISTER (verb) <1247> [4] Rom. 12:8 → GIVE <3330> [5] Rom. 12:13 → DISTRIBUTE <2841> [6] Gal. 2:6 → ADD <4323>.

CONTRIBUTION – [1] ***koinōnia*** [fem. noun: κοινωνία <2842>]; **from *koinōneō*: to share, which is from *koinōnos*: associate, participant, which is from *koinos*: common ▶ Practical expression of communion, solidarity** > Christians in Macedonia and Achaia were pleased to make a certain contribution for the poor among the saints in Jerusalem (Rom. 15:26). All other refs.: COMMUNICATE[1] <2842>, DISPENSATION <2842>, FELLOWSHIP <2842>, SHARING <2842>.
– [2] Rom. 15:28 → to make sure that they have received this contribution → lit.: to seal to them this fruit → FRUIT <2590> [3] Rom. 15:31 → the contribution I take to Jerusalem → lit.: my service to Jerusalem → SERVICE <1248>.

CONTRIVE – Acts 5:4 → PURPOSE (verb) <5087>.

CONTROL (noun) – [1] **to exercise self-control, to have control over oneself: *enkrateuomai*** [verb: ἐγκρατεύομαι <1467>]; **from *enkratēs*: self-control, continence, which is from *en*: in, and *kratos*: power, strength ▶ To exercise continence, to abstain** > Paul tells those who have no control over themselves {cannot exercise self-control, cannot contain} to marry (1 Cor. 7:9). Everyone who competes for the prize exercises self-control {is temperate} in all things {goes into strict training} (1 Cor. 9:25). ¶
– [2] Acts 5:4; 1 Cor. 7:37; Rev. 16:9 → AUTHORITY <1849> [3] Acts 27:16 → getting under control → SECURING <4031> [4] 1 Cor. 9:27 → to keep under control → to bring into subjection → SUBJECTION <1396> [5] Gal. 3:22 → "the control of" added in Engl. [6] Phil. 3:21 → to bring under control → SUBJECT (verb) <5293> [7] 1 Tim. 3:4 → SUBMISSION <5292> [8] 2 Tim. 3:6 → to gain control over → to make captive → CAPTIVE (adj.) <163> [9] Heb. 2:8 → He left nothing outside His control → lit.: He left nothing not subjected to Him → SUBJECT (verb) <506>.

CONTROL (verb) – [1] 1 Cor. 7:9 → to have control over oneself → CONTROL (noun) <1467> [2] 2 Cor. 5:14 → COMPEL <4912> [3] 1 Thes. 4:4 → POSSESS <2932>.

CONTROVERSIAL – [1] 1 Tim. 1:4 → controversial speculation → DISPUTE (noun) <2214> [2] 1 Tim. 6:4 → controversial question → QUESTION (noun) <2214>.

CONTROVERSY – [1] **without controversy: *homologoumenōs*** [adv.: ὁμολογουμένως <3672>]; **from *homologeō*: to confess, which is from *homos*: same, and *legō*: to speak ▶ Assuredly, unquestionably** > Without controversy {Confessedly, By common confession, Beyond all questions}, the mystery of piety is great (1 Tim. 3:16). ¶
– [2] Acts 26:3 → QUESTION (noun) <2213> [3] 1 Tim. 1:4 → DISPUTE (noun) <2214> [4] 1 Tim. 6:4; 2 Tim. 2:23; Titus 3:9 → QUESTION (noun) <2214>.

CONVENE – John 11:47 → GATHER <4863>.

CONVENIENT – [1] Mark 6:21 → OPPORTUNE <2121> [2] Acts 24:25 → convenient season, convenient time → SEASON (noun) <2540> [3] Rom. 1:28 → to be convenient → FITTING (BE) <2520> [4] 1 Cor. 16:12 → to have convenient time → to have opportunity → OPPORTUNITY <2119> [5] Eph. 5:4; Phm. 8 → to be convenient → FITTING (BE) <433>.

CONVENIENTLY – ***eukairōs*** [adv.: εὐκαίρως <2122>]; **from *eukairos*: convenient, which is from *eu*: well, and *kairos*: time, season ▶ At a favorable time, easily** > Judas sought how he might conveniently {opportunely, at an opportune time} {watched for an opportunity to} deliver Jesus (Mark 14:11). Other ref.: 2 Tim.

4:2 {in season}; see SEASON (noun) <2122>. ¶

CONVERSATION[1] – [1] Luke 1:65 → to be the subject of conversation → DISCUSS <1255> [2] Luke 24:17 → SAYING <3056> [3] 1 Tim. 1:6 → fruitless conversation → vain discourse → VAIN <3150>.

CONVERSATION[2] – [1] 2 Cor. 1:12; Eph. 2:3 → to have one's conversation → CONDUCT (verb)[1] <390> [2] Gal. 1:13; 1 Tim. 4:12; Heb. 13:7; Jas. 3:13; 1 Pet. 1:15, 18; 2:12; 3:1, 2, 16; 2 Pet. 2:7; 3:11 → CONDUCT (noun) <391> [3] Eph. 4:22 → manner of life → LIFE <391> [4] Phil. 3:20 → CITIZENSHIP <4175> [5] Heb. 13:5 → CONDUCT (noun) <5158>.

CONVERSE – [1] Luke 24:14, 15; Acts 20:11; 24:26 → TALK (verb) <3656> [2] Acts 17:18 → to converse with → MEET (verb) <4820>.

CONVERSION – ***epistrophē*** [fem. noun: ἐπιστροφή <1995>]; **from *epistrephō*: to turn about, which is from *epi*: again, anew, and *strephō*: to turn ► Stopping on the way to eternal loss, changing direction and turning to the Savior God** > Paul and Barnabas related the conversion of those among the Gentiles {how the Gentiles had been converted} (Acts 15:3). ¶

CONVERT (noun) – [1] Matt. 23:15; Acts 6:5; 13:43 → PROSELYTE <4339> [2] Rom. 16:5; 1 Cor. 16:15 → first convert → FIRSTFRUITS <536> [3] 1 Tim. 3:6 → new convert, recent convert → NOVICE <3504>.

CONVERT (verb) – [1] ***strephō*** [verb: στρέφω <4762>] **► To change direction on the way to eternal loss and return to the Savior God** > A person has to be converted and become as a little child to enter the kingdom of the heavens (Matt. 18:3). All other refs.: RETURN (verb) <4762>, TURN (verb) <4762>.

[2] ***epistrephō*** [verb: ἐπιστρέφω <1994>]; **from *epi*: anew, again, and *strephō*: to convert ► See [1]; also transl.: to return, to turn, to turn again** > The verb is used concerning Israel (Matt. 13:15; Mark 4:12; John 12:40; Acts 28:27). Peter said to the people of Israel to repent and be converted (Acts 3:19). Paul had declared to the Jews and to the Gentiles that they should repent and turn (or: to convert) to God, and do works worthy of repentance (Acts 26:20). The Thessalonians turned (or: converted) to God from idols (1 Thes. 1:9). All other refs.: BRING <1994>, RETURN (verb) <1994>, TURN (verb) <1994>.

– [3] Acts 15:3 → how the Gentiles had been converted → lit.: the conversion of the Gentiles → CONVERSION <1995>.

CONVEY – [1] John 5:13 → to convey oneself away → WITHDRAW <1593> [2] Col. 1:13 → TRANSFER <3179>.

CONVICT – [1] John 8:9, 46; 16:8; 1 Cor. 14:24; 1 Tim. 5:20; 2 Tim. 4:2; Jas. 2:9 → CONVINCE <1651> [2] Titus 1:9 → REFUTE <1651> [3] Jude 15 → CONVINCE <1827>.

CONVICTION – [1] 1 Thes. 1:5 → deep conviction, full conviction → much assurance → ASSURANCE <4136> [2] 2 Tim. 3:16 → REPROOF <1650> [3] Heb. 3:14 → CONFIDENCE <5287> [4] Heb. 11:1 → EVIDENCE <1650>.

CONVINCE – [1] ***elenchō*** [verb: ἐλέγχω <1651>] **► To prove, to reprove; also transl.: to convict, to bring demonstration, to rebuke** > Scribes and Pharisees were convicted in their conscience at the words of Jesus (John 8:9 in some mss.). Jesus asked the Jews who convinced {rebuke publicly} Him of sin (John 8:46). When the Holy Spirit had come, He would convince the world of sin (John 16:8). An unbeliever or simple person could be convinced by all if all prophesy (1 Cor. 14:24). Timothy had to convince before all {rebuke publicly} those who were sinning (1 Tim. 5:20); he was to convince with all longsuffering and doctrine

(2 Tim. 4:2). Those who show partiality commit sin and are convinced by the law as transgressors (Jas. 2:9). All other refs.: REFUTE <1651>, REPROVE <1651>.
[2] ***exelenchō*** [verb: ἐξελέγχω <1827>]; **from *ek*: intens., and *elenchō*: see [1] ▶ To convince completely, to convict** > The Lord will convince all who are ungodly of all their works of ungodliness (Jude 15). ¶
– [3] Luke 16:31; 20:6; Acts 19:26; 26:26; 28:23, 24; Rom. 8:38; 14:14; 15:14; 2 Tim. 1:12; Heb. 6:9 → PERSUADE <3982> [4] Acts 18:28 → REFUTE <1246> [5] 2 Cor. 10:7 → TRUST (verb) <3982> [6] Phil. 1:25 → to be convinced → to have confidence → CONFIDENCE <3982>.

CONVINCED (BE, BECOME) – [1] Acts 26:9 → THINK <1380> [2] Rom. 2:19; Phil. 1:25 → to be confident → CONFIDENT <3982> [3] Rom. 4:21; 14:5 → to be fully convinced → to be fully persuaded → PERSUADE <4135> [4] 2 Tim. 3:14 → to become convinced → ASSURED (BE) <4104>.

CONVINCING – Acts 1:3 → convincing proof → PROOF <5039>.

CONVINCINGLY – Heb. 6:17 → ABUNDANTLY <4054>.

CONVULSE – [1] ***sparassō*** [verb: σπαράσσω <4682>] ▶ **To shake violently, so as to injure; also transl.: to throw into convulsions, to tear, to rend** > The unclean spirit convulsed {shook violently} the possessed man, then cried out and came out of him (Mark 1:26). A dumb spirit came out of the son of a man, convulsing him greatly when rebuked by Jesus (Mark 9:26). Luke reports a similar incident of the son of a man convulsed by a spirit (Luke 9:39). ¶
[2] ***susparassō*** [verb: συσπαράσσω <4952>]; **from *sun*: together (intens.), and *sparassō*: see [1] ▶ To thoroughly shake or agitate with violence** > A dumb spirit convulsed the son of a man when he saw Jesus (Mark 9:20); some mss.: *sparassō*. A demon threw a child to the ground and convulsed him {tare him, threw him in convulsion}, but Jesus healed him (Luke 9:42); some mss.: *suntarassō*. ¶

CONVULSION – [1] Mark 1:26; 9:26; Luke 9:39 → to throw into convulsions → CONVULSE <4682> [2] Mark 9:20; Luke 9:42 → to throw in a convulsion → CONVULSE <4952>.

COOL – ***katapsuchō*** [verb: καταψύχω <2711>]; **from *kata*: down (intens.), and *psuchō*: to blow, to chill ▶ To refresh, to make fresh** > The wicked rich man wanted Lazarus to cool {to cool off} his tongue (Luke 16:24). ¶

COPE – Acts 6:10 → to cope with → RESIST <436>.

COPPER – [1] Matt. 10:9 → BRASS <5475> [2] Mark 6:8 → MONEY <5475> [3] Mark 7:4 → copper pot, copper vessel → BRAZEN VESSEL <5473>.

COPPER COIN – [1] Matt. 10:29; Luke 12:6 → PENNY <787> [2] Mark 12:42; Luke 21:2 → MITE <3016>.

COPPERSMITH – ***chalkeus*** [masc. noun: χαλκεύς <5471>]; **from *chalkos*: copper, brass ▶ Person whose work is to make articles in copper or other metals** > Alexander the coppersmith {metalworker, smith} did many evil things against Paul (2 Tim. 4:14). ¶

COPY – [1] ***antitupon*** [neut. noun: ἀντίτυπον <499>]; **from *anti*: in the place of, and *tupos*: figure, form ▶ What corresponds to a reality, representation** > The holy places of the tabernacle were copies {figures} of the heavenly places (Heb. 9:24). Other ref.: 1 Pet. 3:21; see FIGURE <499>. ¶
[2] ***hupodeigma*** [neut. noun: ὑπόδειγμα <5262>]; **from *hupodeiknumi*: to show, to illustrate, which is from *hupo*: under, and *deiknumi*: to show, from which *deigma*: example, specimen ▶ Example set forth as an imitation, pattern** > The priests under the law with their offerings

served at a sanctuary that is a copy {example, representation} and shadow of heavenly things (Heb. 8:5). The copies {figurative representations} of the things in the heavens must be purified (Heb. 9:23). All other refs.: EXAMPLE <5262>.

COR – Luke 16:7 → MEASURE (noun) <2884>.

CORBAN – ***korban*** [masc. noun: κορβᾶν <2878>] ▶ **Heb. or Aram. word meaning a gift** > In Mark 7:11, it is in particular an offering to God. Jesus reproached the Pharisees for telling children to declare corban what they could have used to assist their parents. ¶

CORD – ***schoinion*** [neut. noun: σχοινίον <4979>]; **dimin. of *schoinos*: rush, straw** ▶ **Thick string, rope** > Jesus made a scourge of cords, and cast out of the temple the vendors and the money changers (John 2:15). The soldiers cut away the cords of the skiff on board the boat where Paul was (Acts 27:32). ¶

CORE – Jude 11 → KORAH <2879>.

CORINTH – ***Korinthos*** [fem. name: Κόρινθος <2882>] ▶ **City of Greece located west of Athens; Corinth was the capital of Achaia** > Paul wrote two letters to the Christians of Corinth (1 Cor. 1:2; 2 Cor. 1:1). He stayed at Corinth for a year and a half, with Aquila and Priscilla (Acts 18:1); he discoursed in the synagogue and persuaded Jews and Greeks (see v. 4). Apollos also stayed at Corinth (Acts 19:1). Paul wrote a second letter to the Corinthians before returning to Corinth, in order to give a final warning to those who were dishonoring the Lord by their conduct (2 Cor. 1:23). He would say at the end of his life that Erastus remained at Corinth (2 Tim. 4:20). ¶

CORINTHIAN – ***Korinthios*** [masc. name.: Κορίνθιος <2881>] ▶ **Inhabitant of the city of Corinth, capital of the Roman province of Achaia in Greece** > Many Corinthians believed in the Lord Jesus and were baptized (Acts 18:8). Paul's heart was opened wide to them (2 Cor. 6:11). Two letters addressed by Paul to the Corinthians are included in the N.T. Other ref.: Acts 18:27 in some mss. ¶

CORN – [1] ***sitos*** [masc. noun: σῖτος <4621>] ▶ **Cereal used to make bread; it could be wheat** > Jacob heard that there was corn {grain} in Egypt (Acts 7:12); other mss. have *sition* (wheat) in the plur. which means food. All other refs.: GRAIN OF WHEAT <4621>, WHEAT <4621>.

[2] **corn, cornfield: *sporimos*** [adj. used as noun: σπόριμος <4702>]; **from *spora*: what is sown, which is from *speirō*: to sow** ▶ **Field sown with corn (or another cereal)** > Jesus went through the cornfields {grainfields} on the Sabbath (Matt. 12:1; Mark 2:23; Luke 6:1). ¶

– [3] Matt. 12:1; Mark 2:23; 4:28a, b; Luke 6:1 → ear of corn → head of grain → GRAIN <4719>.

CORN-MEASURE – Luke 11:33 → BUSHEL <3426>.

CORNELIUS – ***Kornēlios*** [masc. name: Κορνήλιος <2883>]; **Lat. name** ▶ **Roman centurion commanding a cohort stationed at Caesarea** > In a vision, an angel told Cornelius to send for Peter. The latter preached Jesus to Cornelius as well as to his relatives and close friends. While he was still speaking, the Holy Spirit fell upon all those who heard the word of God. They were then baptized in the name of the Lord. This event marked the introduction of the Gentiles into the church. Refs.: Acts 10:1, 3, 7, 17, 21 in some mss., 22, 24, 25, 30, 31. ¶

CORNER – [1] ***gōnia*** [fem. noun: γωνία <1137>] ▶ **Angle, junction, crossroads; the expr. "four corners" means the four extremities** > The hypocrites loved to pray standing in the synagogues and on the corners of the street (Matt. 6:5). John saw four angels standing on the four corners of the earth, holding the four winds of the earth (Rev. 7:1). After the millennium, Satan will go out to deceive the nations which are in the four corners {quarters} of the earth (Rev. 20:8). All other refs.: CHIEF CORNERSTONE <1137>, CORNER STONE <1137>.

[2] ***archē*** [fem. noun: ἀρχή <746>]; **lit.: beginning ▶ Extremity >** Peter saw an object like a great sheet bound at the four corners and it came to him (Acts 10:11; 11:5); in it were all kinds of quadrupeds, reptiles, and birds (see 10:12). All other refs.: BEGINNING <746>, MAGISTRATE <746>, POWER[2] <746>, PRINCIPALITY <746>, STATE <746>.

– [3] Matt. 21:42; Mark 12:10; Luke 20:17; Acts 4:11; 1 Pet. 2:7 → head of the corner → CHIEF CORNERSTONE <2776> <1137> [4] Matt. 22:9 → street corner → THOROUGHFARE <1327>.

CORNER STONE – [1] head: *kephalē* [fem. noun: κεφαλή <2776>]; **corner: *gōnia*** [fem. noun: γωνία <1137>]; **lit.: head of the corner; also transl.: chief corner stone, capstone ▶ Stone that plays a fundamental role in the stability of a construction; the word "head" emphasizes its importance >** Jesus Christ, as the stone rejected by the Jews, has become the corner-stone (Matt. 21:42; Mark 12:10; Luke 20:17; Acts 4:11; 1 Pet. 2:7), on which the church is built (see Matt. 16:18). All other refs. (*kephalē*): see CHIEF CORNERSTONE <2776>, HEAD (noun) <2776>. All other refs. (*gōnia*): see CHIEF CORNERSTONE <1137>, CORNER <1137>.

[2] **stone: *lithos*** [masc. noun: λίθος <3037>]; **corner: *akrogōniaios*** [adj. used as noun: ἀκρογωνιαῖος <204>]; **from *akron*: extreme, and *gonia*: corner; lit.: chief corner stone, or corner-foundation stone ▶ Stone that plays a fundamental role in the stability of a construction >** The corner stone (*lithos akrogōniaios*) has been laid in Zion (1 Pet. 2:6; see Is. 28:16). Jesus Christ Himself is the corner stone {*akrogōniaios*} of the church (Eph. 2:20). ¶

CORNERSTONE – See CHIEF CORNERSTONE.

CORPSE – [1] *kōlon* [neut. noun: κῶλον <2966>] **▶ Dead body of a person >** The corpses {bodies, carcases} of the Israelites who had sinned fell in the wilderness (Heb. 3:17). ¶

[2] ***ptōma*** [neut. noun: πτῶμα <4430>]; **from *piptō*: to fall; lit.: what is fallen ▶ Mortal remains, dead body >** The eagles will be gathered wherever the corpse {carcase, carcass} is (Matt. 24:28). The disciples of John took away his corpse {body} and laid it in a tomb (Mark 6:29). The bodies (i.e., the dead bodies) of the two prophets will lie in the street of the great city (Rev. 11:8, 9a, b). Other ref.: Matt. 14:12 (the body of John the Baptist); Mark 15:45 (the body of the Lord Jesus); in other mss.: *sōma*. ¶

– [3] Mark 15:45; Luke 17:37 → BODY <4983> [4] Rev. 16:3 → lit.: dead → DEAD <3498>.

CORRECT – [1] *paideuō* [verb: παιδεύω <3811>]; **from *pais*: child; lit.: to teach children ▶ To instruct, to teach >** A servant of the Lord must correct {set right} in humility those who oppose (2 Tim. 2:25). All other refs.: CHASTEN <3811>, EDUCATE <3811>, LEARN <3811>, TEACH <3811>.

[2] **who corrects: *paideutēs*** [masc. noun: παιδευτής <3810>]; **from *paideuō*: see [1] ▶ One who educates, who disciplines >** We have had our human fathers who corrected us and we respected them (Heb. 12:9). Other ref.: Rom. 2:20; see INSTRUCTOR <3810>. ¶

– [3] 2 Tim. 3:16 → for correcting → lit.: for correction → CORRECTION <1882>.

CORRECTION – ***epanorthōsis*** [fem. noun: ἐπανόρθωσις <1882>]; **from *epanorthoō*: to set right, which is from *epi*: upon, *ana*: again, and *orthoō*: to make straight ▶ Restoration to its original character >** Every Scripture is profitable for correction {correcting} (2 Tim. 3:16). ¶

CORRECTLY – [1] Luke 7:43; 20:21 → RIGHTLY <3723> [2] Luke 10:28 → PLAINLY <3723> [3] John 7:24 → to judge correctly → lit.: to judge righteous judgment

→ RIGHTEOUS <1342>, JUDGMENT <2920> 4 2 Tim. 2:15 → to handle correctly → to divide rightly → DIVIDE <3718>.

CORRECTOR – Rom. 2:20 → INSTRUCTOR <3810>.

CORRESPOND – 1 ***sustoicheō*** [verb: συστοιχέω <4960>]; **from *sun*: together, and *stoicheō*: to proceed in order, which is from *stoichos*: row ► To conform, to be similar** > Hagar corresponds {answers} to Jerusalem which is now (Gal. 4:25). ¶
– 2 2 Cor. 11:15 → their end will correspond to their deeds → lit.: whose end shall be according (*kata*) to their deeds 3 1 Pet. 3:21 → what corresponds → FIGURE <499>.

CORRODED (BE) – Jas. 5:3 → RUSTED (BE) <2728>.

CORROSION – Jas. 5:3 → RUST <2447>.

CORRUPT (adj.) – 1 ***sapros*** [adj.: σαπρός <4550>]; **from *sēpō*: to decompose ► Bad, dishonest** > No corrupt {unwholesome} word should go out of the mouth of a Christian (Eph. 4:29). Other refs.: Matt. 7:17a, 18b; 12:33a, b; 13:48; Luke 6:43a, b; see BAD <4550>. ¶
– 2 Luke 12:33 → DESTROY <1311> 3 Acts 2:40 → PERVERSE <4646> 4 Eph. 4:22 → to grow corrupt, to be corrupt → CORRUPT (verb) <5351> 5 1 Tim. 6:5 → CORRUPT (verb) <1311> 6 2 Tim. 3:8 → of corrupt mind; lit.: having the mind corrupted → CORRUPT (verb) <2704> 7 2 Pet. 2:10 → corrupt desire → lust of uncleanness → UNCLEANNESS <3394>.

CORRUPT (verb) – 1 ***phtheirō*** [verb: φθείρω <5351>]; **from *phthiō*: to consume, to waste ► To destroy, to perish; to pervert morally** > Evil communications corrupt good manners (1 Cor. 15:33). Paul had corrupted {ruined} no man (2 Cor. 7:2). He feared that the thoughts of the Corinthians might be corrupted {led astray} from the simplicity that is in the Christ (2 Cor. 11:3). The Christian has put off the old man which corrupts itself {grows corrupt, is corrupted} according to the deceitful lusts (Eph. 4:22). Jude speaks of those who corrupt themselves in what they understand by mere nature (Jude 10). God will judge the great prostitute which corrupted the earth with her sexual immorality (Rev. 19:2). Other ref.: 2 Pet. 2:12 (*kataphtheirō* in other mss.); see 3. Other refs.: 1 Cor. 3:17a, b; see DESTROY <5351>. ¶
2 ***diaphtheirō*** [verb: διαφθείρω <1311>]; **from *dia*: through (intens.), and *phtheirō*: see 1; lit.: to corrupt utterly ► To destroy completely; also transl.: to destroy** > Paul speaks of men corrupted in mind {of corrupt mind, of depraved mind} and destitute of the truth (1 Tim. 6:5). The wrath of God has come to destroy those who destroy the earth (Rev. 11:18a, b). All other refs.: DESTROY <1311>, PERISH <1311>.
3 ***kataphtheirō*** [verb: καταφθείρω <2704>]; **from *kata*: down (intens.), and *phtheirō*: see 1; lit.: to corrupt utterly ► To pervert, to render dishonest** > Paul speaks of men corrupted in mind {of depraved mind, of corrupt mind}, found worthless as regards the faith (2 Tim. 3:8). Other ref.: 2 Pet. 2:12; see PERISH <2704>. ¶
– 4 Matt. 6:19, 20 → DESTROY <853> 5 2 Cor. 2:17 → PEDDLE <2585> 6 Jas. 3:6 → DEFILE <4695>.

CORRUPTED – 1 Titus 1:15a, b → to be corrupted → to be defiled → DEFILE <3392> 2 Jas. 5:2 → to be corrupted → to become rotten → ROTTEN <4595>.

CORRUPTIBLE – 1 ***phthartos*** [adj.: φθαρτός <5349>]; **from *phtheirō*: to corrupt, which is from *phthiō*: to consume, to waste ► Which can be destroyed; also transl.: mortal, perishable** > Some men have changed the glory of the incorruptible God into the likeness of an image of corruptible man and animals (Rom. 1:23). Everyone who competes does it to receive a corruptible crown {a crown that will not last}, but Christians an incorruptible one (1 Cor. 9:25). The corruptible body of the Christians must put on incorruptibility (1 Cor. 15:53,

54). Christians have not been redeemed by corruptible things (1 Pet. 1:18), but by the precious blood of Christ (see v. 19). They have been born again, not of corruptible seed, but of incorruptible (1 Pet. 1:23). ¶

[2] 1 Pet. 3:4 → not corruptible → INCORRUPTIBLE <862>.

CORRUPTING – Eph. 4:29 → BAD <4550>.

CORRUPTION – [1] ***phthora*** [fem. noun: φθορά <5356>]; **from *phtheirō*: to corrupt, which is from *phthiō*: to consume, to waste ▶ Deterioration, destruction** > The creation will be set free from the bondage of corruption {decay} (Rom. 8:21). The body of the Christian is sown in corruption {perishable}, but it is raised in incorruptibility (1 Cor. 15:42). Corruption {The perishable} cannot inherit incorruption (1 Cor. 15:50). He who sows to his flesh will of the flesh reap corruption (Gal. 6:8). Christians have escaped the corruption that is in the world through lust (2 Pet. 1:4). Peter speaks of unbelievers who will perish in their own corruption (2 Pet. 2:12); they are slaves of corruption {depravity} (v. 19). Other ref.: Col. 2:22 {destruction}; see PERISH <5356>. ¶

[2] ***diaphthora*** [fem. noun: διαφθορά <1312>]; **from *diaphtheirō*: to corrupt completely, which is from *dia*: through (intens.), and *phtheirō*: see [1] ▶ Decomposition, destruction; also transl.: decay** > God did not allow His Holy One (the Lord Jesus) to see corruption (Acts 2:27, 31; 13:35). God has raised His Son from the dead, no more to return to corruption (Acts 13:34); David saw corruption (v. 36), but Jesus, whom God has raised up, saw no corruption (v. 37). ¶

– [3] 1 Pet. 4:4 → DISSIPATION <810> [4] 2 Pet. 2:20 → DEFILEMENT <3393>.

COS – ***Kōs*** [fem. name: Κῶς <2972>] ▶ **Island of the Mediterranean Sea located southwest of Asia Minor** > Paul's ship came to Cos during the apostle's third missionary journey (Acts 21:1). ¶

COSAM – ***Kōsam*** [masc. name: Κωσάμ <2973>]: **diviner, in Heb. ▶ Man of the O.T.** > Cosam is mentioned in the genealogy of Jesus (Luke 3:28). ¶

COSMIC – Eph. 6:12 → cosmic powers → RULER <2888>.

COST – [1] ***dapanē*** [fem. noun: δαπάνη <1160>]; **from *daptō*: to devour ▶ Expense, charge** > He who intends to build a tower first sits down and counts the cost (Luke 14:28). ¶

– [2] 2 Thes. 3:8; Rev. 22:17 → without cost → FREELY <1432>

COSTLESS – ***adapanos*** [adj.: ἀδάπανος <77>]; **from *a*: neg., and *dapanē*: expense ▶ Without cost, free of charge** > In announcing the glad tidings, Paul made the glad tidings costless {without charge, free of charge} to others (1 Cor. 9:18). ¶

COSTLINESS – Rev. 18:19 → WEALTH <5094>.

COSTLY – [1] ***polutelēs*** [adj.: πολυτελής <4185>]; **from *polus*: much, and *telos*: expense, cost ▶ Very expensive, magnificent, sumptuous** > Believing women are not to adorn themselves with costly {expensive} clothing (1 Tim. 2:9). Other refs.: Mark 14:3 and 1 Pet. 3:4 (of great price); see PRICE (noun) <4185>. ¶

– [2] Matt. 26:7 → very costly → very precious → PRECIOUS <927> [3] John 12:3 → very costly → of great price → PRICE (noun) <4186> [4] 1 Cor. 3:12; Rev. 21:11 → PRECIOUS <5093>.

COT – Acts 5:15 → little bed → BED <2824a>.

COUCH – ***krabattos*** [masc. noun: κράβαττος <2895>]; ***grabatus*, in Lat. ▶ Mattress, stretcher** > The sick were put on beds and couches {mats, pallets} so that Peter would heal them (Acts 5:15). All other refs.: see BED <2895>.

COUNCIL – [1] ***sumboulion*** [neut. noun: συμβούλιον <4824>]; **from *sumboulos*: counsel, which is from *sun*: together, and *boulē*: counsel, decision ▶ Assembly of counselors** > The Jews often held councils against Jesus to harm Him (Matt. 12:14; 22:15); the expr. in these verses is sometimes transl. "to take counsel": see COUNSEL (noun) <4824>. Festus conferred with the council (Acts 25:12). ¶
– [2] Matt. 5:22; 10:17; 26:59; et al. → SANHEDRIN <4892> [3] Mark 15:43; Luke 23:50 → council member → COUNSELLOR, COUNSELOR <1010> [4] Luke 22:66; Acts 22:5; 1 Tim. 4:14 → ELDER <4244>.

COUNCILLOR – Mark 15:43; Luke 23:50 → COUNSELLOR, COUNSELOR <1010>.

COUNSEL (noun) – [1] ***boulē*** [fem. noun: βουλή <1012>] ▶ **a. Plan, purpose of God; also transl.: decision, plan, purpose, will** > Divine and eternal principles determining irrevocable decisions; they are applied in time, according to God's plans (Luke 7:30; Acts 2:23; 4:28; 13:36; 20:27; Eph. 1:11; Heb. 6:17). **b. Goal, plan, intention; also transl.: decision, motive** > Joseph of Arimathea had not consented to the counsel and deed of the Jews to kill Jesus (Luke 23:51). The Lord will manifest the counsels of the hearts (1 Cor. 4:5). **c. Advice, opinion after reflection** > The counsel {plan} of the soldiers was to kill the prisoners after the shipwreck (Acts 27:42). Other refs.: Acts 5:38; 27:12 (in some mss.); see PLAN (noun) <1012>, ADVISE <1012>. ¶
[2] ***sumboulion*** [neut. noun: συμβούλιον <4824>]; **from *sumboulos*: counsel, which is from *sun*: together, and *boulē*: counsel, decision ▶ Common plan, counsel** > The Jews often took counsel against Jesus to harm Him (Matt. 12:14; 22:15; 27:1; 28:12; Mark 3:6; 15:1 {consultation}). Other transl.: to plot, to hold a consultation, to hold counsel, to take counsel, to counsel together, to consult, to lay plans, to devise a plan, to come to the decision. Other ref.: Matt. 27:7 {to take counsel, to consult, to decide}. ¶
[3] **to take counsel together: *sumbouleuō*** [verb: συμβουλεύω <4823>]; **from *sun*: together (intens.), and *bouleuō*: to consult, to determine, which is from *boulē*: counsel, decision; lit.: to consult together ▶ To advise, to decide** > The Jews took counsel {plotted; planned together} that they might kill Jesus (John 11:53). All other refs.: CONSULT <4823>, COUNSEL (verb) <4823>.
– [4] Matt. 12:14; 22:15 → COUNCIL <4824> [5] Luke 14:31 → to take counsel → CONSIDER <1011> [6] John 12:10; Acts 5:33 → to take counsel → CONSULT <1011> [7] Acts 5:38 → PLAN (noun) <1012>.

COUNSEL (verb) – [1] ***sumbouleuō*** [verb: συμβουλεύω <4823>]; **from *sun*: together (intens.), and *bouleuō*: to consult, to determine, which is from *boulē*: counsel, advice; lit.: to consult together ▶ To advise, to recommend** > The Lord counsels Laodicea to buy from Him gold purified by fire (Rev. 3:18). All other refs.: CONSULT <4823>, COUNSEL (noun) <4823>.
– [2] Matt. 12:14; 22:15; 27:7; 28:12 → to counsel together → COUNCIL <4824>, COUNSEL (noun) <4824> [3] Acts 27:9 → ADMONISH <3867> [4] Acts 27:12 → ADVISE <1014>.

COUNSELLOR, COUNSELOR – [1] ***bouleutēs*** [masc. noun: βουλευτής <1010>]; **from *bouleuō*: to consult, to determine, which is from *boulē*: advice, counsel ▶ Member of the Jewish Sanhedrin, an assembly of men giving advice** > Joseph of Arimathea was a counselor {council member, councilor} (Luke 23:50); Mark writes that he was an honorable counselor {a prominent council member} (Mark 15:43). ¶
[2] ***sumboulos*** [masc. noun: σύμβουλος <4825>]; **from *sun*: together, and *boulē*: advice, counsel ▶ Person who gives advice, counsel** > Paul asks who has been the counselor {counsellor} of the Lord (Rom. 11:34). ¶

– [3] John 14:16, 26; 15:26; 16:7 → ADVOCATE (noun) <3875>.

COUNT – [1] ***echō*** [verb: ἔχω <2192>]; **lit.: to have, to hold ▶ To consider** > All counted {held} John the Baptist to have been a prophet (Mark 11:32).
[2] ***hēgeomai*** [verb: ἡγέομαι <2233>]; **from *agō*: to lead ▶ To think, to believe; also transl.: to account, to consider, to regard** > Paul counted all things to be loss on account of the excellence of the knowledge of Christ Jesus His Lord; he considered all things rubbish that he might gain Christ (Phil. 3:8a, b). Christ Jesus had counted Paul faithful (1 Tim. 1:12). Some count {understand} there is delay concerning the promise of the return of the Lord (2 Pet. 3:9). Other refs.: 1 Tim. 6:1; Jas. 1:2; 2 Pet. 2:13. All other refs.: see entries in Lexicon at <2233>.
[3] ***logizomai*** [verb: λογίζομαι <3049>]; **from *logos*: account ▶ To consider, to impute; also transl.: to account, to credit, to number, to reckon, to regard** > Jesus was counted with the transgressors (Mark 15:28; Luke 22:37). Paul asks if the uncircumcision will be counted as circumcision by keeping the law (Rom. 2:26). Abraham believed God, and this was counted to him for righteousness (Rom. 4:3, 9, 22, 23; Gal. 3:6; Jas. 2:23). To him who works, the reward is not counted as grace but as debt (Rom. 4:4); but to him who does not work but believes on Him who justifies the ungodly, his faith is counted as righteousness (v. 5). God counts righteousness without works (Rom. 4:6). Blessed is the man to whom the Lord will not at all count {take into account} sin (Rom. 4:8). Faith was counted to Abraham before he was circumcised (Rom. 4:10). Because of Abraham, righteousness may be counted to those also who are uncircumcised (Rom. 4:11, 24). The children of the promise are counted as descendants of Abraham (Rom. 9:8). Christians should count themselves dead to sin and alive to God in Christ Jesus (Rom. 6:11). All other refs.: see entries in Lexicon at <3049>.
[4] ***psēphizō*** [verb: ψηφίζω <5585>]; **from *psēphos*: pebble, stone; lit.: to count with stones ▶ To determine the cost by counting, to calculate** > One who intends to build a tower sits down first and counts {estimates} the cost (Luke 14:28). Let him who has understanding count the number of the beast (Rev. 13:18). ¶
[5] **to count out: *histēmi*** [verb: ἵστημι <2476>]; **same as *stare*, in Lat.: to stand ▶ To weigh, to calculate** > The chief priest counted out to {covenanted with, appointed, weighed out to} Judas thirty pieces of silver to deliver Jesus to them (Matt. 26:15). Other refs.: SET (verb) <2476>, STAND (verb) <2476>.
– [6] Luke 20:35; 21:36; Acts 5:41; 2 Thes. 1:5 → to count worthy → WORTHY <2661> [7] John 6:63 → to count for → PROFIT (verb) <5623> [8] Acts 1:17 → NUMBER (verb) <2674> [9] Acts 19:19 → to reckon up → CALCULATE <4860> [10] Rom. 5:13 → to be counted → to be imputed → IMPUTE <1677> [11] 2 Thes. 1:11; 1 Tim. 5:17; Heb. 3:3 → to count worthy → WORTHY <515> [12] Heb. 7:6 → to count one's descent → to have genealogy → GENEALOGY <1075> [13] Jas. 5:11 → to count blessed → BLESSED <3106> [14] Rev. 7:9 → NUMBER (verb) <705>.

COUNTENANCE – [1] ***idea*** [fem. noun: ἰδέα <2397>]; **from *eidon*, form of *horaō*: to see; "idea" in Engl. is derived from the Greek word ▶ External aspect, shape** > At the tomb of Jesus, the countenance {look, appearance} of the angel was like lightning (Matt. 28:3; *eidea* in some mss.). The word is found also in Luke 9:29 in some mss. ¶
– [2] Matt. 6:16 → sad countenance, downcast in countenance → SAD <4659> [3] Luke 9:29; Acts 2:28; Rev. 10:1 → FACE (noun) <4383> [4] 2 Cor. 5:12 → APPEARANCE <4383> [5] Rev. 1:16 → FACE (noun) <3799>.

COUNTERFEIT – 2 Thes. 2:9; 1 John 2:27 → LIE (noun) <5579>.

COUNTLESS – [1] 2 Cor. 11:23 → to excess → EXCESS <5234> [2] Heb. 11:12 → INNUMERABLE <382>.

COUNTRY – [1] ***agros*** [masc. noun: ἀγρός <68>] ▶ **Field, rural area; also transl.: countryside** > Those who were feeding the swine reported in the city and in the country that the herd had run into the sea (Mark 5:14; Luke 8:34). The disciples wanted the people to be sent to the surrounding country and villages to buy bread (Mark 6:36; Luke 9:12). The sick in the country were laid in the streets so that they might touch Jesus and be healed (Mark 6:56). All other refs.: FIELD <68>, FIELD OF BLOOD <68>, LAND (noun) <68>.

[2] **to go to a far country, to go on a journey, etc.: *apodēmeō*** [verb: ἀποδημέω <589>]; **from *apodēmos*: traveler, which is from *apo*: away from, and *dēmos*: area of living, people ▶ To be absent from one's country, to travel** > In a parable, a landowner planted a vineyard and left the country (Matt. 21:33; Mark 12:1; Luke 20:9). Other refs.: Matt. 25:14, 15; Luke 15:13; 2 Cor. 5:6 in some mss. ¶

[3] ***patris*** [fem. noun: πατρίς <3968>]; **from *patēr*: father ▶ Native land, fatherland; also transl.: hometown** > The word is used in regard to Jesus (Matt. 13:54, 57; Mark 6:1, 4; Luke 4:23, 24; John 4:44). Those who confess that they are strangers and sojourners on the earth show clearly that they seek a heavenly country {homeland} (Heb. 11:14). Other ref.: Acts 18:27 in some mss. ¶

[4] ***chōra*** [fem. noun: χώρα <5561>]; **from *chōros*: field, place ▶ Land, region; also transl.: area, district, coasts, countryside** > With the coming of Jesus, light had sprung up to those sitting in the country and shadow of death (Matt. 4:16). There were shepherds in the same country where Jesus was born (Luke 2:8). The word is transl. "region" concerning Trachonitis of which Philip was the tetrarch (Luke 3:1). During the great tribulation, those who are in the country must not enter into Jerusalem (Luke 21:21). Jesus went to a country near the desert (John 11:54). Many went from the country up to Jerusalem before the Passover (John 11:55). The Christians of the church in Jerusalem were all scattered in the countries of Judea and Samaria (Acts 8:1). The word is also used in regard to the country of the wise men (Matt. 2:12), the country of the Gadarenes (Matt. 8:28; Mark 5:1; Luke 8:26), the country of Judea (Mark 1:5; Acts 26:20), the country of Legion (Mark 5:10), the country where the prodigal son dissipated his goods (Luke 15:13–15), the distant country where a high-born man went (Luke 19:12), the country of the Jews (Acts 10:39), the country of the Tyrians and the Sidonians (Acts 12:20), the whole country through which the word of the Lord was carried (Acts 13:49), and the Galatian country (Acts 16:6; 18:23). All other refs.: FIELD <5561>, LAND (noun) <5561>.

[5] **country around, surrounding country: *perichōros*** [adj.: περίχωρος <4066>]; **from *peri*: around, and *chōra*: see [4] ▶ Surrounding region; also transl.: region round about, surrounding area, surrounding district** > Men sent to the whole country around to bring to Jesus all who were ill (Matt. 14:35; Mark 6:55). The fame of Jesus went out into the whole surrounding country {countryside} (Luke 4:14), in every place of the country round about (v. 37). The report that God had visited His people went out in all Judea and in all the surrounding country (Luke 7:17). Other refs.: Matt. 3:5; Mark 1:28; Luke 3:3; 8:37; Acts 14:6 (region around); see REGION <4066>. ¶

– [6] Matt. 9:31; Acts 7:3, 4 → LAND (noun) <1093> [7] Mark 13:34 → gone out of the country → away on a journey → JOURNEY (noun) <590> [8] Luke 1:39, 65 → hill country → HILL <3714> [9] Luke 14:23 → country lane → HEDGE (noun) <5418> [10] Acts 4:36 → of the country of Cyprus → lit.: a Cyprian by birth → BIRTH <1085> [11] Acts 19:1 → REGION <3313> [12] 2 Cor. 11:26 → WILDERNESS <2047>.

COUNTRYMAN – [1] ***genos*** [neut. noun: γένος <1085>]; **from *ginomai*: to become ▶ Person of the same country, same race** > Paul had been in perils from his own countrymen {from his own race} (2 Cor. 11:26). All other refs.: see entries in Lexicon at <1085>.

2 ***sumphuletēs*** [masc. noun: συμφυλέτης <4853>]; **from *sun*: together, and *phuletēs*: one of the same tribe, which is from *phulē*: race, nation ► Person of the same nation** > The Thessalonians had suffered from their own countrymen the same things as the churches in Judea (1 Thes. 2:14). ¶
– 3 Rom. 9:3; 16:7, 11, 21 → RELATIVE <4773>.

COUNTRYSIDE – 1 Mark 5:14; 6:36, 56; Luke 8:34; 9:12 → COUNTRY <68> 2 Luke 4:14 → COUNTRY <4066> 3 John 3:22 → LAND (noun) <1093>.

COURAGE – 1 ***tharsos*** [neut. noun: θάρσος <2294>] **► Comfort, confidence, boldness** > When Paul saw the brothers, he thanked God and took courage {was encouraged} (Acts 28:15). ¶
2 **to take courage: *tharseō*** [verb: θαρσέω <2293>]; **from *tharsos*: see 1 ► To be courageous, to have comfort, to have confidence; also transl.: to be of good cheer, to cheer up, to be of good comfort, to be of good courage, to take heart** > Jesus told a paralytic to take courage, his sins were forgiven (Matt. 9:2). He told a woman who had a flow of blood to take courage, her faith had healed her (Matt. 9:22; Luke 8:48 in some mss.). A blind man was told to take courage, Jesus was calling him (Mark 10:49). In the middle of the sea tossed by the waves, Jesus told His disciples to take courage, not to be afraid (Matt. 14:27; Mark 6:50). Jesus says to take courage, He has overcome the world (John 16:33). The Lord stood by Paul and said to him to take courage (Acts 23:11). ¶
– 3 Mark 15:43 → to gather one's courage → to go boldly → BOLDLY <5111> 4 Luke 20:40 → to have courage → DARE <5111> 5 Acts 4:13; Phil. 1:20 → BOLDNESS <3954> 6 Acts 27:22, 25 → to be of good courage, to keep up the courage → to take heart → HEART <2114> 7 Acts 27:36 → to take courage → to become courageous → courageous → ENCOURAGE <2115> 8 2 Cor. 5:6, 8 → to be of good courage → to be confident → CONFIDENT <2292> 9 Phil. 1:14 → to have courage → to be bold → BOLD <5111> 10 Heb. 3:6 → CONFIDENCE <3954>.

COURAGEOUS – 1 1 Cor. 16:13 → to be courageous → to act like a man → MAN <407> 2 2 Cor. 10:2 → to be courageous → to be bold → BOLD <5111>.

COURSE – 1 ***aiōn*** [masc. noun: αἰών <165>]; **lit.: age ► Epoch, way of living** > The Ephesians had once walked in their sins, according to the course {age, ways} of this world, according to the ruler of the authority of the air (Eph. 2:2). Other refs.: AGE <165>, FOREVER <165>, TROUBLE (noun) <165>, WORLD <165>.
2 ***dromos*** [masc. noun: δρόμος <1408>]; **from *dremō*: to run ► Life activity; also transl.: race, work** > As John the Baptist was finishing his course, he asked people who they thought he was (Acts 13:25). Paul made no account of his life as dear to himself, so that he would finish his course and ministry (Acts 20:24). In 2 Tim. 4:7, he had finished the course, he had kept the faith. ¶
3 ***ephēmeria*** [fem. noun: ἐφημερία <2183>]; **from *ephēmeros*: daily, which is from *epi*: upon, and *hēmera*: day ► A group of Jewish priests serving daily in the temple; their term was seven days** > Zacharias, the father of John the Baptist, was a priest of the course {division} of Abia (Luke 1:5, 8). See 2 Chr. 13:10, 11 concerning the priests and their service. ¶
4 ***trochos*** [masc. noun: τροχός <5164>]; **from *trechō*: to run; lit.: wheel ► Cycle, unfolding** > The tongue sets fire to the course of nature (Jas. 3:6). ¶
– 5 Luke 13:32 → to finish one's course → to be perfected → PERFECT (verb) <5048> 6 Acts 16:11; 21:1 → to run a straight course → to sail straight → SAIL (verb) <2113> 7 Acts 21:7 → NAVIGATION <4144> 8 Acts 28:13 → to go on a circuitous course → CIRCLE ROUND <4022> 9 2 Cor. 8:20 → we take this course → lit.: avoiding this → AVOID <4724> 10 2 Cor. 12:18 → STEP (noun) <2487> 11 2 Thes. 3:1 → to have free course → RUN <5143>.

COURT – 1 ***agoraios*** [adj. used as noun: ἀγοραῖος <60>]; **from *agora*: marketplace ▶ Day on which justice is dispensed** > If Demetrius had a matter against Paul, the courts (lit.: court days) were being held {the law was open}, the proper setting for pressing charges (Acts 19:38). Other ref.: Acts 17:5 {from the marketplace}; see MARKETPLACE <60>. ¶

2 ***aulē*** [fem. noun: αὐλή <833>]; **poss. from *aēmi*: to blow (speaking of the wind), whence: open space ▶ Outer courtyard of the temple** > The angel ordered John not to measure the outer court (Rev. 11:2). All other refs.: COURTYARD <833>, FOLD (noun) <833>, PALACE <833>.

– 3 Matt. 5:22; 10:17; et al. → court, supreme court → SANHEDRIN <4892> 4 Matt. 21:12, 15 → temple courts → TEMPLE <2411> 5 Mark 11:11, 15; Luke 19:45; John 2:15; 8:20; 10:23; 11:56 → "courts" added in Engl. 6 Acts 13:1 → member of the court → lit. brought up with → BRING <4939> 7 Acts 18:12, 16, 17; 25:6, 10, 17 → JUDGMENT SEAT <968> 8 1 Cor. 6:2; Jas. 2:6 → law court, court → JUDGMENT SEAT <2922> 9 1 Cor. 6:6 → to take to court → to prosecute one's suit → SUIT (noun) <2919>.

COURTEOUS – ***philophrōn*** [adj.: φιλόφρων <5391>]; **from *philos*: friend, and *phrēn*: mind ▶ Friendly, favorably disposed** > Peter urges Christians to be courteous (1 Pet. 3:8); see HUMBLE (adj.) <5012a>. ¶

COURTEOUSLY – 1 ***philophronōs*** [adv.: φιλοφρόνως <5390>]; **from *philophrōn*: courteous, friendly, which is from *philos*: friend, and *phrēn*: mind ▶ With kindness, affably** > Publius received Paul and the other shipwrecked people courteously {in a very friendly way, hospitably} (Acts 28:7). ¶

– 2 Acts 27:3 → KINDLY <5364>.

COURTESY – ***epieikeia*** [fem. noun: ἐπιείκεια <1932>]; **from *epieikēs*: kindness, patience, which is from *epi*: upon (intens.), and *eikos*: equitable, fair ▶ Kindness; also transl.: indulgence, clemency** > Tertullus begged Felix to hear him briefly, by his courtesy, concerning his accusation against Paul (Acts 24:4). Other ref.: 2 Cor. 10:1; see GENTLENESS <1932>. ¶

COURTIER – John 4:46, 49 → NOBLEMAN <937>.

COURTYARD – ***aulē*** [fem. noun: αὐλή <833>]; **see** COURT <833> **▶ Open space, surrounded by the buildings of the palace** > Peter was sitting outside in the courtyard {palace, palace-court} (Matt. 26:69; Mark 14:66). The soldiers led Jesus away into the courtyard {court, hall, palace} called Praetorium (Mark 15:16). A fire was kindled in the midst of the courtyard {court, yard} (Luke 22:55). All other refs.: COURT <833>, FOLD (noun) <833>, PALACE <833>.

COUSIN – 1 ***anepsios*** [masc. noun: ἀνεψιός <431>]; **poss. from *nepous*: progeny, a relative; *nepos*, in Lat.: grandson, nephew ▶ Son of an uncle or an aunt; also transl.: nephew** > The Thessalonians had received instructions concerning Mark, the cousin of Barnabas (Col. 4:10). ¶

– 2 Luke 1:36, 58 → RELATIVE <4773>.

COVENANT (noun) – ***diathēkē*** [fem. noun: διαθήκη <1242>]; **from *diatithēmi*: to place in a particular order, which is from *dia*: intens., and *tithēmi*: to place ▶ Alliance; also transl.: testament** > A covenant, or an alliance, in the Bible is a disposition without prior conditions on the part of God; e.g., toward the earth with Noah (see Gen. 9:8–17) or toward His people with Abraham (Luke 1:72; Acts 3:25; Rom. 9:4; Eph. 2:12; Heb. 8:9a, b; 9:4, 15a, b, 20). The covenant with Israel was made at Mount Sinai with Moses. The signs of God's covenant are respectively the rainbow (see Gen. 9:16), the circumcision (Acts 7:8), and the Sabbath (Ex. 31:12–17). No one can set aside or add to a covenant that has been duly established (Gal. 3:15, 17). Gal. 4:24 speaks of two covenants, the old and the new. The old covenant (2 Cor. 3:14) had been concluded with Israel under the condition of their obedience. Israel was to be blessed if they would observe the law given by God to Moses. According to Heb. 8:8, a new covenant will be made by the Lord with the house of Israel and the house of Judah for their blessing without conditions; see also Rom. 11:27; 2 Cor. 3:6; Heb. 7:22; 8:6, 10; 10:16, 29; 12:24. This new covenant is based on the value of the blood of Christ, the blood of the new covenant (Matt. 26:28; Mark 14:24; Luke 22:20). The church already benefits from the blessing which will be introduced by this new order of things (Luke 22:20; 1 Cor. 11:25), because of this eternal covenant (Heb. 13:20). In Rev. 11:19, the ark of the covenant of God was seen within His temple. The term "covenant" is transl. "testament" {will} in Heb. 9:16, 17 by some translators with its ordinary meaning of a person's wishes concerning the disposal of his or her property after death. ¶

COVENANT (verb) – [1] Matt. 26:15 → to covenant with → to count out to → COUNT <2476> [2] Luke 22:5 → AGREE <4934> [3] Heb. 8:10 → MAKE <1303>.

COVENANT LAW – Acts 7:44; Rev. 15:5 → lit.: witness → WITNESS (noun)[1] <3142>.

COVENANTBREAKER – Rom. 1:31 → FAITHLESS <802>.

COVER – [1] ***kaluptō*** [verb: καλύπτω <2572>] ▶ **a. To submerge** > The waves were covering {swept over} the boat boarded by Jesus and His disciples (Matt. 8:24). **b. To hide** > There is nothing covered {concealed} that will not be revealed (Matt. 10:26). No one having lighted a lamp covers it with {hides it in} a vessel (Luke 8:16). During the great tribulation, people will say to the hills to cover them (Luke 23:30). He who brings back a sinner from the error of his way will cover a multitude of sins (Jas. 5:20). Love covers a multitude of sins (1 Pet. 4:8). Other ref.: Luke 24:32 in some mss. Other refs.: 2 Cor. 4:3a, b; see VEIL (verb) <2572>. ¶

[2] ***epikaluptō*** [verb: ἐπικαλύπτω <1943>]; **from *epi*: upon, and *kaluptō*: to cover, to hide; lit.: to cover over ▶ To place something on, to conceal** > Blessed are those whose sins have been covered (Rom. 4:7). ¶

[3] ***katakaluptō*** [verb: κατακαλύπτω <2619>]; **from *kata*: intens., and *kaluptō*: to cover ▶ To place something on, to veil** > Paul teaches that the woman should cover her head in the church (1 Cor. 11:6a, b), but not the man (v. 7). ¶

[4] ***perikaluptō*** [verb: περικαλύπτω <4028>]; **from *peri*: around, and *kaluptō*: to cover; lit.: to cover all around ▶ To cover completely (e.g., the eyes), also transl.: to blindfold** > Some began to spit on Jesus, to cover His face, and to urge Him to prophesy who had struck Him (Mark 14:65 {to cover his face}; Luke 22:64 {to cover}). The ark was covered {overlaid} in every part with gold (Heb. 9:4). ¶

[5] ***sunkaluptō*** [verb: συγκαλύπτω <4780>]; **from *sun*: together (intens.), and *kaluptō*: to cover ▶ To cover completely** > There is nothing covered {concealed} which will not be revealed (Luke 12:2). ¶

– [6] Matt. 13:44 → to cover up → HIDE <2928> [7] Matt. 17:5; Mark 9:7; Luke 9:34 → OVERSHADOW <1982> [8] Acts 7:57 → STOP <4912> [9] 2 Cor. 3:15 → LIE (verb)[1] <2749> [10] 1 Thes. 2:5 → nor did we put on a mask to cover up → lit.: nor with a pretext for → PRETEXT <4392>.

COVER-UP – 1 Pet. 2:16 → COVERING <1942>.

COVERED – [1] Luke 5:12 → FULL <4134> [2] Rev. 17:3 → to be covered → to be full → FULL <1073>.

COVERING – [1] ***epikalumma*** [neut. noun: ἐπικάλυμμα <1942>]; **from *epikaluptō*: to cover, to conceal, which is from *epi*: over, and *kaluptō*: to cover ▶ Cover, pretext** > Peter speaks of evil men who use freedom as a covering {cloak, cloke, cover-up} for evil (1 Pet. 2:16). ¶

– 2 1 Cor. 11:15; Heb. 1:12 → CLOAK <4018> 3 1 Tim. 6:8 → CLOTHING <4629>.

COVET – 1 ***epithumeō*** [verb: ἐπιθυμέω <1937>]; **from *epi*: upon, and *thumos*: great passion, emotion ▶ To greatly desire to possess something that one cannot or should not possess, to lust** > Paul had coveted the silver or gold or clothing of no one (Acts 20:33). The law says not to covet (Rom. 7:7; 13:9). All other refs.: see DESIRE (verb) <1937>, LUST (verb) <1937>.
2 ***zēloō*** [verb: ζηλόω <2206>]; **from *zēlos*: jealousy, passion ▶ To be jealous, to greatly desire** > James mentions those who covet {lust, desire to have} and have not (Jas. 4:2). All other refs.: DESIRE (verb) <2206>, ENVY (verb) <2206>, JEALOUS <2206>, ZEALOUS <2206>.
3 ***oregō*** [verb: ὀρέγω <3713>]; ***regere*, in Lat.: to direct, to rule ▶ To lust after, to strongly desire; also transl.: to be eager** > In their love of money, some have coveted {aspired, longed} after it and {some in their greediness} have wandered from the faith (1 Tim. 6:10). Other refs.: 1 Tim. 3:1; Heb. 11:16; see DESIRE (verb) <3713>. ¶

COVETING – 1 Mark 7:22 → deed of coveting → COVETOUSNESS <4124> 2 Rom. 7:7, 8 → LUST (noun) <1939>.

COVETOUS (adj.) – 1 ***philarguros*** [adj.: φιλάργυρος <5366>]; **from *philos*: friend, and *arguros*: money; lit.: friend of money, who loves money ▶ Avaricious, greedy; also transl.: lover of money** > The Pharisees were covetous (Luke 16:14). In the last days, men will be covetous (2 Tim. 3:2). ¶
– 2 2 Pet. 2:14 → covetous practices → COVETOUSNESS <4124>.

COVETOUS (noun) – ***pleonektēs*** [masc. noun: πλεονέκτης <4123>]; **from *pleonekteō*: to be covetous, to want more, which is from *pleion*: more, and *hektos*: verbal adj. from *echō*: to have, to hold; lit.: who wants to obtain more than others or more than he should have ▶ Avaricious, greedy** > Christians cannot avoid contact with the covetous of this world (1 Cor. 5:10), but they should not have company with anyone named a brother who is covetous (v. 11). The covetous will not inherit the kingdom of God (1 Cor. 6:10). No covetous person {person of unbridled lust}, who is an idolater, has any inheritance in the kingdom of the Christ and God (Eph. 5:5). ¶

COVETOUSNESS – 1 ***pleonexia*** [fem. noun: πλεονεξία <4124>]; **from *pleion*: more, and *hektos*: verbal adj. from *echō*: to have, to hold ▶ Avarice; also transl.: greed** > Covetousness {Deeds of coveting} and other evils proceed from within, out of the heart of men (Mark 7:22); they characterize the man who rejects God (Rom. 1:29). Jesus told his disciples to take heed and keep themselves from all covetousness (Luke 12:15). The gift of the Corinthians was not to be out of covetousness {a grudging obligation, grudgingly given, exaction} (2 Cor. 9:5). Covetousness {Unbridled lust} should not even be named among Christians (Eph. 5:3); it is idolatry (Col. 3:5; comp. Eph. 5:5). Paul had not been among the Thessalonians with a pretext for covetousness (1 Thes. 2:5). False prophets and false teachers will exploit by covetousness {covetous practices} (2 Pet. 2:3, 14). Other ref.: Eph. 4:19; see GREEDINESS <4124>. ¶
2 **without covetousness: *aphilarguros*** [adj.: ἀφιλάργυρος <866>]; **from *a*: neg., and *philarguros*: avaricious, greedy, which is from *philos*: friend, and *arguros*: money; lit.: who does not love money ▶ Without avarice, not greedy; also transl.: free from the love of money, without love of money** > The conduct of the Christian must be without covetousness (Heb. 13:5). Other ref.: 1 Tim. 3:3 (not greedy for money); see GREEDY <866>. ¶
– 3 Rom. 7:7, 8 → LUST (noun) <1939>.

COWARDICE – 2 Tim. 1:7 → FEAR (noun) <1167>.

COWARDLY – Rev. 21:8 → FEARFUL <1169>.

COWORKER – 1 Thes. 3:2 → FELLOW WORKER <4904>.

CRAFT[1] – 1 Acts 18:3 → TRADE (noun) <3673> 2 Acts 19:25 → BUSINESS <2039> 3 Acts 19:27 → PART (noun) <3313> 4 Rev. 18:22 → OCCUPATION <5078>.

CRAFT[2] – 1 Acts 13:10 → FRAUD <4468> 2 2 Cor. 11:3 → CRAFTINESS <3834>.

CRAFTINESS – ***panourgia*** [fem. noun: πανουργία <3834>]; **from *panourgeō*: to act deceitfully, which is from *panourgos*: crafty, shrewd, which is from *pan*: all, and *ergon*: deed, work ▶ Astuteness, unscrupulousness; also transl.: craft, cunning, deceit, deception, subtilty** > God takes the wise in their craftiness (1 Cor. 3:19). Paul did not walk in craftiness (2 Cor. 4:2). The serpent deceived Eve by his craftiness (2 Cor. 11:3). Other refs.: Luke 20:23; Eph. 4:14; see CUNNING <3834>, DECEIT <3834>. ¶

CRAFTSMAN – ***technitēs*** [masc. noun: τεχνίτης <5079>]; **from *technē*: art, handicraft ▶ Skilled worker in a trade, artisan** > Demetrius brought much business to his fellow craftsmen in Ephesus (Acts 19:24, 38). No craftsman {artificer, workman} of any craft will be found any more at all in Babylon (Rev. 18:22). Other ref.: Heb. 11:10; see BUILDER <5079>. ¶

CRAFTY – 1 ***panourgos*** [adj.: πανοῦργος <3835>]; **from *pan*: all, and *ergon*: deed, work ▶ Astute, clever** > Paul did not burden the Corinthians, but being crafty, he had taken them by guile (2 Cor. 12:16). ¶
– 2 Mark 14:1 → SUBTLETY <1388>.

CRASH – Matt. 7:27 → FALL <4431>.

CRAVE – 1 Matt. 12:39 → SEEK <1934> 2 Mark 15:43 → ASK <154> 3 1 Cor. 10:6a, b → LUST (verb) <1937> <1938> 4 1 Pet. 2:2 → to desire earnestly → DESIRE (verb) <1971>.

CRAVING – 1 1 Tim. 6:4 → to have an unhealthy craving → OBSESSED (BE) <3552> 2 1 Tim. 6:10 → through this craving → lit.: having coveted after → COVET <3713>.

CRAWLING – Acts 10:12; 11:6; Rom. 1:23 → crawling creature → REPTILE <2062>.

CREATE – 1 ***ktizō*** [verb: κτίζω <2936>] ▶ **Among the Greeks, this verb refers to the foundation of a city; in the N.T., it corresponds to the divine action of bringing to existence what did not exist before.** > God has created the creation (Mark 13:19). The Creator (lit.: He who creates) has made them (the man and the woman) from the beginning male and female (Matt. 19:4). He has created all things (Eph. 3:9; Col. 1:16a, b; Rev. 4:11a, b; 10:6); He has created foods (1 Tim. 4:3). Some people have honored and worshipped the creature rather than the One who has created {the Creator} (Rom. 1:25). Man was not created for the sake of the woman, but woman for the sake of the man (1 Cor. 11:9). The verb is used concerning the spiritual creation: Christians have been created in Christ Jesus for good works (Eph. 2:10); God has created {formed, made} in Christ Jesus the believing Gentiles and Jews into one new man (lit.: human being) (Eph. 2:15); the new man (lit.: human being) was created according to God in truthful righteousness and holiness (Eph. 4:24) and is renewed in full knowledge according to the image of Him who has created him {of its Creator} (Col. 3:10). ¶
– 2 Rom. 16:17 → CAUSE (verb) <4160> 3 1 Tim. 2:13 →FORM (verb) <4111> 4 1 Tim. 4:4; Jas. 1:18; Rev. 5:13 → created thing → CREATURE <2938> 5 Heb. 1:2 → MAKE <4160> 6 Heb. 11:3 → PREPARE <2675>.

CREATED THING – Rom. 1:25; 8:39; Heb. 4:13 → CREATURE <2937>.

CREATION – 1 ***ktisis*** [fem. noun: κτίσις <2937>]; **from *ktizō*: to create, to make ▶ Totality of beings and things which came**

into existence from the very beginning of time; also transl.: creature > From the beginning of creation, God made man male and female (Mark 10:6). In the future tribulation, there will be distress such as there has not been since the beginning of creation which God created (Mark 13:19). Jesus said to His disciples to preach the gospel to all the creation (Mark 16:15). From the creation of the world, the invisible qualities of God, His eternal power and His divinity, are discerned by the understanding (Rom. 1:20). The earnest expectation of the creation eagerly awaits the revelation of the sons of God (Rom. 8:19), for the creation has been made subject to vanity (v. 20); the creation itself will be set free from the bondage of corruption (v. 21); we know that the whole creation groans and labors until now (v. 22). Jesus Christ is the firstborn of all creation (Col. 1:15), referring to His supremacy over the first (physical) creation. The gospel was preached in the whole creation under heaven (Col. 1:23). Christ has come as high priest by means of the tabernacle not of this creation {building} (Heb. 9:11). Some say that all things continue as they were from the beginning of the creation (2 Pet. 3:4). Jesus is the beginning of the creation of God (Rev. 3:14). All other refs.: CREATURE <2937>, INSTITUTION <2937>, NEW CREATION <2937>.

– 2 Matt. 13:35; 25:34; John 17:24; Eph. 1:4; Heb. 4:3; 9:26; 1 Pet. 1:20; Rev. 13:8; 17:8 → FOUNDATION <2602> 3 Rom. 8:23 → "creation" added in Engl.

CREATOR – 1 ***ktistēs*** [masc. noun: κτίστης <2939>]; **from *ktizō*: to create, to make ► One who produces something from nothing** > This title is applied to God, a "faithful Creator" (1 Pet. 4:19); the word is found only in this verse. In Col. 1:16, we read that by Jesus Christ all things were created, including human beings (see Eccl. 12:1) and angels (see Job 1:6; 38:7). God is the Creator of (lit.: the One who has created; from the verb *ktizō*) the man and the woman (Matt. 19:4; in other mss.: *poieō*, to make). Creation (see John 1:1–3) has been defined as "the act of God calling into existence what did not exist before." ¶

– 2 Acts 24:5 → MOVE <2795> 3 Rom. 1:25; Col. 3:10 → the Creator → lit.: the one who has created → CREATE <2936>.

CREATURE – 1 ***ktisis*** [fem. noun: κτίσις <2937>]; **from *ktizō*: to create, to make ► Being who came into existence at a given moment in time; also transl.: created thing** > Paul speaks of those who have honored and served the creature more than the Creator (Rom. 1:25). He is persuaded that no creature will be able to separate Christians from the love of God which is in Christ Jesus (Rom. 8:39). There is no creature {nothing in all creation} hidden before God (Heb. 4:13). All other refs.: CREATION <2937>, INSTITUTION <2937>, NEW CREATION <2937>.

2 ***ktisma*** [neut. noun: κτίσμα <2938>]; **from *ktizō*: to create, to make ► Product of the creative act** > Every creature of {Everything created by} God is good (1 Tim. 4:4). Christians are a kind of first-fruits of His creatures {all He created} (Jas. 1:18). John heard all creatures {created things} praise Him who sits on the throne and the Lamb (Rev. 5:13). When the second angel sounded the trumpet, the third part of the creatures in the sea died (Rev. 8:9). ¶

– 3 Acts 10:12; 11:6; Rom. 1:23 → crawling creature → REPTILE <2062> 4 Acts 28:4, 5 → beast, wild beast → BEAST <2342> 5 Jas. 3:7 → creature in the sea, creature of the sea → SEA <1724> 6 2 Pet. 2:12 → born as creature of instinct → NATURAL <5446> 7 Rev. 4:6, 7a–d, 8, 9; 5:6, 8, 11, 14; 6:1, 3, 5–7; 7:11; 14:3; 15:7; 19:4 → living creatures → BEAST <2226>.

CREDIT (noun) – 1 ***charis*** [fem. noun: χάρις <5485>]; **from *chairō*: to rejoice ► Grace, gratitude; also transl.: thank** > It is no credit to us if we love those who love us (Luke 6:32), do good only to those who do good to us (v. 33), and lend only to those from whom we hope to receive (v. 34). Other refs.: see entries in Lexicon at <5485>.

– 2 Phil. 4:17 → ACCOUNT (noun) <3056> 3 1 Pet. 2:20 → GLORY (noun) <2811>.

CREDIT (verb) – 1 Rom. 4:3–6, 9, 10, 11, 22–24; Gal. 3:6; Jas. 2:23 → COUNT <3049> 2 2 Cor. 12:6 → CONSIDER <3049> 3 Phil. 4:17 → ABOUND <4121>.

CREDITOR – ***daneistēs*** [masc. noun: δανειστής <1157>]; **from *daneizō*: to lend with interest; also written: *danistēs* ▶ One who lends money >** Jesus told the parable of a creditor {moneylender} who had two debtors (Luke 7:41). ¶

CREEK – Acts 27:39 → BAY <2859>.

CREEP – **to creep into: *endunō*** [verb: ἐνδύνω <1744>]; **from *en*: in, and *dunō*: to penetrate ▶ To slip into, to insinuate one's way into >** Some people were creeping into {were entering into, were getting into, were worming into} houses and leading captive silly women loaded down with sins (2 Tim. 3:6). ¶

CREEPING – Acts 10:12; 11:6; Rom. 1:23; Jas. 3:7 → creeping thing → REPTILE <2062>.

CRESCENS – ***Krēskēs*** [masc. name: Κρήσκης <2913>]: **growing ▶ Christian man who had followed Paul >** Crescens had departed to Galatia (2 Tim. 4:10). ¶

CRETAN – ***Krēs*** [masc. name: Κρής <2912>] **▶ Person originally from the Island of Crete; also transl.: Cretian >** On the day of Pentecost, Cretans heard the gospel preached in their own language (Acts 2:11). A prophet among the Cretans had said that they were always liars (Titus 1:12). ¶

CRETE – ***Krētē*** [fem. name: Κρήτη <2914>] **▶ Large Greek Island in the Mediterranean Sea located southeast of Greece >** Paul's ship, heading toward Rome, sailed along the coast of the Island of Crete after having left Fair Havens in order to reach Phoenix (Acts 27:7, 12, 13, 21). Paul had left Titus in Crete so that he might, among other things, appoint elders (Titus 1:5). ¶

CRETIAN – See CRETAN <2912>.

CRIME – 1 ***enklēma*** [neut. noun: ἔγκλημα <1462>]; **from *enkaleō*: to accuse, which is from *en*: in, and *kaleō*: to call, to institute proceedings ▶ Accusation, indictment >** Roman custom gave an accused man the opportunity to defend himself before his accusers concerning the crime {charge} they were accusing him of (Acts 25:16). Other ref.: Acts 23:25, 29; see CHARGE (noun)[1] <1462>. ¶

2 ***rhadiourgēma*** [neut. noun: ῥᾳδιούργημα <4467>]; **from *rhadiourgeō*: to be ready to commit wickedness, which is from *rhadios*: easy, and *ergon*: action ▶ Misdeed, baseness, lack of scruples >** Gallio would have listened to the Jews if their accusations against Paul had been related to some vicious crime (Acts 18:14 {criminality, lewdness}). ¶

– 3 Acts 24:20 → WRONG (noun) <92> 4 Acts 25:27 → ACCUSATION <156> 5 Acts 28:18 → CAUSE (noun) <156> 6 Rev. 18:5 → INIQUITY <92>.

CRIMINAL – 1 ***kakourgos*** [masc. noun: κακοῦργος <2557>]; **from *kakos*: bad, evil, and *ergon*: action, work ▶ One who commits misdeeds, a wrong-doer >** Two criminals {malefactors} were crucified on either side of Jesus (Luke 23:32, 33, 39). Paul was bound in chains as a criminal {an evildoer, evil doer} (2 Tim. 2:9). ¶

– 2 Luke 23:4 → nothing criminal → lit.: no fault → FAULT <158> 3 John 18:30; 1 Pet. 4:15 → EVILDOER <2555>.

CRIMINALITY – Acts 18:14 → CRIME <4467>.

CRIPPLE – Acts 8:7; 14:8 → LAME <5560>.

CRIPPLED – 1 Matt. 15:30, 31; 18:8; Mark 9:43 → MAIMED <2948> 2 Matt.

18:8; Mark 9:45; Acts 3:2 → LAME <5560> 3 Luke 14:13, 21 → MAIMED <376> 4 Acts 4:9 → SICK (adj. and noun) <772>.

CRIPPLED (BE) – Luke 13:11 → lit.: to have a sickness → WEAKNESS <769>.

CRISIS – 1 Cor. 7:26 → NECESSITY <318>.

CRISPUS – ***Krispos*** [masc. name: Κρίσπος <2921>]**: curled ▶ Ruler of the synagogue who was converted** > Crispus believed in the Lord Jesus with all his household (Acts 18:8). Paul baptized him (1 Cor. 1:14). ¶

CRITICISM – 2 Cor. 8:20 → BLAME (verb) <3469>.

CRITICIZE – 1 Mark 14:5 → to rebuke harshly → REBUKE (verb) <1690> 2 Acts 11:2 → CONTEND <1252>.

CROOKED – 1 ***skolios*** [adj.: σκολιός <4646>]**; from *skellō*: to dry ▶ a. Tortuous, winding** > According to a passage in Isaiah, the crooked places will become straight (Luke 3:5). **b. Unjust, wicked** > Christians are to be blameless and pure, irreproachable children of God, in the midst of a crooked and perverse generation (Phil. 2:15). All other refs.: HARSH <4646>, PERVERSE <4646>.
– 2 Acts 13:10 → to make crooked → PERVERT (verb) <1294> 3 Phil. 2:15 → PERVERTED <1294>.

CROP – 1 Luke 12:16 → to produce a good crop → to bring forth plentifully → BRING <2164> 2 Luke 12:18 → GRAIN <1079a> 3 Acts 14:17 → crops in their seasons → lit.: fruitful seasons → FRUITFUL <2593> 4 1 Cor. 9:10 → "the crop" added in Engl. 5 Heb. 6:7 → VEGETATION <1008>.

CROSS (noun) – 1 ***stauros*** [masc. noun: σταυρός <4716>]**; from *histēmi*: to stand ▶ Vertical post, usually with a horizontal bar to which criminals were fastened to die** > This form of execution was originally used by the Phoenicians. The Romans nailed the hands of the sentenced person to the horizontal bar and his feet to the upright post. To accelerate the death of the crucified individuals, their legs were broken (John 19:31). Jesus went out of Jerusalem, bearing His cross (John 19:17); it was a custom that the sentenced person would bear his cross to the place of crucifixion. Simon of Cyrene was compelled to bear the cross of Jesus (Matt. 27:32; Mark 15:21; Luke 23:26). Pilate put a title on the cross: "Jesus of Nazareth, the King of the Jews" (John 19:19). Three women were standing by the cross of Jesus (John 19:25). Many were saying to Jesus to descend from the cross (Matt. 27:40; Mark 15:30, 32). The disciple of Jesus must take his cross and follow after Him (Matt. 10:38; 16:24; Mark 8:34; 10:21 in some mss.; Luke 9:23; 14:27). The apostle Paul often refers to the cross of Christ (1 Cor. 1:17, 18; Gal. 5:11; 6:12, 14; Eph. 2:16; Phil. 2:8; 3:18; Col. 1:20; 2:14; Heb. 12:2). ¶
– 2 Acts 2:23 → to nail to the cross → CRUCIFY <4362> 3 Acts 5:30; 10:39; 13:29; 1 Pet. 2:24 → TREE <3586>.

CROSS (verb) – 1 **to cross over: *diaperaō*** [verb: διαπεράω <1276>]**; from *dia*: denoting transition, and *peraō*: to pass, which is from *peran*: beyond; lit.: to traverse completely ▶ To pass over, to traverse** > Jesus crossed over a lake (Matt. 9:1). Jesus and His disciples passed over a lake (Matt. 14:34; Mark 6:53). He crossed over a lake in the ship again to the other side (Mark 5:21). Other refs.: Luke 16:26; Acts 21:2; see PASS <1276>. ¶
– 2 Matt. 8:18 → DEPART <565> 3 Mark 4:35; Luke 8:22; Acts 18:27 → to cross, to cross over → to go over → GO <1330> 4 John 5:24 → PASS <3327> 5 John 6:1, 17 → lit.: to go over → OVER <4008> 6 Acts 20:15 → to cross over → ARRIVE <3846> 7 Heb. 11:29 → to pass through → PASS <1224>.

CROSS-EXAMINE – Acts 12:19 → EXAMINE <350>.

CROSSWAY – Mark 11:4 → place where two ways meet → PLACE (noun) <296>.

CROW – ***phōneō*** [verb: φωνέω <5455>]; **from *phōnē*: sound, voice; lit.: to make sounds ▶ To make the shrill cry of a rooster** > Peter denied Jesus three times before the rooster had crowed (Matt. 26:34, 74, 75; Mark 14:30, 68, 72; Luke 22:34, 60, 61; John 13:38; 18:27). All other refs.: CALL (verb) <5455>, CRY (verb) <5455>.

CROWD (noun) – 1 ***ochlos*** [masc. noun: ὄχλος <3793>] ▶ **Large number of people, large company** > Great crowds gathered around Jesus (Matt. 4:25; 8:1; 12:15; 19:2). He was moved with compassion on seeing a great crowd (Matt. 14:14; Mark 6:34). The chief priests stirred up the crowd {people} to have Barabbas released (Mark 15:11). The crowd {gathering, group, number} of brothers who were together was about one hundred twenty when Peter addressed them (Acts 1:15). The town clerk had quieted the crowd {multitude, people} in Ephesus (Acts 19:35). This term is also found in Rev. 7:9; 17:15; 19:1, 6. Other ref.: Acts 24:18; see MULTITUDE <3793>.
– 2 Mark 3:7, 8; Luke 6:17; 19:37; Acts 2:6; 5:16; 21:36 → MULTITUDE <4128> 3 Luke 23:18 → whole crowd → lit.: they 4 Acts 17:5; 19:30 → PEOPLE <1218> 5 Acts 17:5 → to gather a crowd → GATHER <3792> 6 Acts 18:17 → the crowd → lit.: all; in some mss.: all of the Greeks.

CROWD (verb) – 1 Mark 3:9 → PRESS <2346> 2 Mark 5:24, 31 → PRESS <4918> 3 Luke 5:1 → to crowd around → to press around → PRESS <1945> 4 Luke 8:45 → PRESS <598> 5 Luke 8:45 → to close in → CLOSE (verb) <4912>.

CROWING – Mark 13:35 → crowing of the rooster → ROOSTER <219>.

CROWN (noun) – 1 ***diadēma*** [neut. noun: διάδημα <1238>]; **from *diadeō*: to bind around, which is from *dia*: around, and *deō*: to bind; lit.: diadem ▶ Band worn around the head representing the power and the dignity of a monarch; also transl.: diadem** > John saw a dragon having seven crowns on his heads (Rev. 12:3). The first beast had ten crowns on his horns (Rev. 13:1). He who sat on the white horse, i.e., the Lord Himself, had on His head many crowns (Rev. 19:12); the beast, the kings of the earth, and their armies, will be gathered together to make war against the Lord and His army (see vv. 19–21). ¶
2 ***stephanos*** [masc. noun: στέφανος <4735>]; **from *stephō*: to surround, to crown ▶ Ornament worn on the head which symbolizes kingship or victory (in a race, an arena, a military campaign)** > A crown of thorns was put on the head of Jesus in mockery (Matt. 27:29; Mark 15:17; John 19:2, 5), but God has given Him a golden crown (Rev. 14:14; see also Ps. 21:3). Those who compete in a race do so to obtain a corruptible crown {wreath}, but Christians for an incorruptible one (1 Cor. 9:25). The Philippians (Phil. 4:1) and the Thessalonians (1 Thes. 2:19) were crowns for the apostle Paul. The crown of righteousness is given to all who love the appearing of the Lord (2 Tim. 4:8); the unfading crown of glory is given to those who shepherd the flock of God (1 Pet. 5:4). The crown of life is promised to those who love the Lord (Jas. 1:12) and to the martyrs (Rev. 2:10). Philadelphia is told to hold fast what she has, that no one may take her crown (Rev. 3:11). The twenty-four elders had golden crowns on their heads (Rev. 4:4); they will cast their crowns before the throne of God (v. 10). A crown was given to Him who sat on the white horse (Rev. 6:2). There were as it were crowns like gold on the heads of the locusts (Rev. 9:7). The woman of Rev. 12:1 has on her head a crown {garland} of twelve stars. ¶
– 3 2 Tim. 2:5 → to receive the crown → lit.: to be crowned → CROWN (verb) <4737>.

CROWN (verb) – ***stephanoō*** [verb: στεφανόω <4737>]; **from *stephanos*: crown, which is from *stephō*: to surround, to crown ▶ To put a crown on the head of**

someone as a sign of victory in games or of honor > If anyone competes in the games, he is not crowned {does not win the prize, does not receive the crown} unless he competes according to the rules (2 Tim. 2:5). Jesus has been crowned with glory and honor (Heb. 2:7, 9; see Ps. 8:5). ¶

CRUCIFY – [1] ***stauroō*** [verb: σταυρόω <4717>]; **from *stauros*: cross ▶ To execute someone, usually a criminal, by fastening him to a cross** > Jesus would be delivered to the Gentiles to be crucified (Matt. 20:19; 26:2). The crowd was shouting that Jesus be crucified (Matt. 27:22, 23; Mark 15:13, 14; Luke 23:21a, b, 23; John 19:6a, b, 15a). Pilate delivered Jesus to be crucified (Matt. 27:26; Mark 15:15; John 19:6c, 16). Jesus was led away to be crucified (Matt. 27:31; Mark 15:20). Having crucified Jesus, the soldiers divided his garments (Matt. 27:35; Mark 15:24). Two robbers were crucified with Jesus (Matt. 27:38; Mark 15:27). Jesus was crucified at the third hour (i.e., nine o'clock in the morning) (Mark 15:25) at the place called Calvary (Golgotha, in Heb.) (Luke 23:33; John 19:18). The Son of Man had to be crucified (Luke 24:7). The first day of the week, there were women at the tomb seeking Jesus who had been crucified (Matt. 28:5; Mark 16:6). Other refs.: Matt. 23:34; Luke 24:20; John 19:10, 15b, 20, 23, 41; Acts 2:36; 4:10; 1 Cor. 1:13, 23; 2:2, 8; 2 Cor. 13:4; Gal. 3:1; 5:24; 6:14; Rev. 11:8. ¶

[2] **to crucify again: *anastauroō*** [verb: ἀνασταυρόω <388>]; **from *ana*: again (or: up), and *stauroō*: see [1] ▶ To crucify a person again** > It is impossible for those who have fallen away to renew them again to repentance, since they would crucify for themselves again the Son of God (Heb. 6:6). Note that these people had not really been converted; they were not born again, even though they appeared to be: they were once enlightened, had tasted of the heavenly gift, were made partakers of the Holy Spirit, etc., but there was no personal commitment and self-appropriation of these blessings (see Heb. 6:4, 5). ¶

[3] **to crucify with: *sustauroō*** [verb: συσταυρόω <4957>]; **from *sun*: together, and *stauroō*: see [1] ▶ To crucify one person with another one** > The robbers who were being crucified with Jesus reviled Him (Matt. 27:44; Mark 15:32). The soldiers broke the legs of the first and of the other who were crucified with Jesus (John 19:32). The old man (lit.: human being) of the Christian has been crucified with Christ (Rom. 6:6). Paul was crucified with Christ (Gal. 2:20). ¶

[4] ***prospēgnumi*** [verb: προσπήγνυμι <4362>]; **from *pros*: to, and *pēgnumi*: to fasten ▶ To put to death by nailing or binding to a cross** > Peter blamed the Jews for having crucified {nailed to the cross} and slain Jesus (Acts 2:23). ¶

CRUDE – Eph. 5:4 → crude joking → JESTING <2160>.

CRUELLY – Matt. 15:22 → SEVERELY <2560>.

CRUMB – ***psichion*** [neut. noun: ψιχίον <5589>]; **dimin. of *psix*: morsel, crumb, which is from *psaō*: to rub, to crumble ▶ Little bit or fragment** > A Syro-Phoenician woman said to Jesus that even the little dogs eat from the crumbs that fall from the table of their masters (Matt. 15:27; Mark 7:28). Lazarus desired to be fed with the crumbs that fell from the table of the rich man (Luke 16:21 in many mss.); *psix* in some mss. ¶

CRUSH – [1] Matt. 21:44; Luke 20:18 → to grind to powder → POWDER <3039> [2] Mark 3:9 → PRESS <2346> [3] Luke 4:18 → to oppress → OPPRESSED (BE) <2352> [4] Luke 8:42 → CHOKE <4846> [5] Luke 9:39; Rom. 16:20 → BRUISE <4937> [6] 2 Cor. 4:8 → RESTRAIN <4729>.

CRY (noun) – [1] ***boē*** [fem. noun: βοή <995>] ▶ **Shout, e.g., call for help** > The cries {outcry} of those who have reaped have entered in the ears of the Lord of Sabaoth (Jas. 5:4). ¶

[2] ***kraugē*** [fem. noun: κραυγή <2906>]; **from *krazō*: to shout ▶ Noise, clamor,**

strong voice > In the parable of the ten virgins, there was a cry {shout} at midnight (Matt. 25:6; some mss. have *phōnē*). There was a great cry {outcry, uproar} from those who had listened to Paul (Acts 23:9). In the days of His flesh, Christ offered up prayers and supplications, with strong cries {crying} and tears to God who was able to save Him from death (Heb. 5:7). In the new Jerusalem, there will be no more death, nor grief, nor cry {crying}, nor pain (Rev. 21:4). Some mss. have this word in Rev. 14:18; others have *phōnē*. Other refs.: Luke 1:42 in some mss.; Eph. 4:31; see CLAMOR <2906>. ¶
– 3 Mark 15:37; Luke 23:23; Rev. 14:18 → VOICE <5456> 4 Luke 1:42 → loud cry → VOICE <5456> (in some mss.) 5 1 Thes. 4:16 → cry of command → SHOUT (noun) <2752> 6 Rev. 8:13; 19:1, 6 → to cry, to cry out → SAY <3004> 7 Rev. 19:3 → to cry out → SAY <2046>.

CRY (verb) – 1 **to cry, to cry out: *boaō*** [verb: βοάω <994>]; **from *boē*: cry, shout ▶ To speak with a loud voice; also transl.: to shout** > John the Baptist was saying that he was the voice of one crying {calling} in the wilderness (Matt. 3:3; Mark 1:3; Luke 3:4; John 1:23). God's elect cry to Him day and night (Luke 18:7). A blind man who was begging cried out {called out, cried} to Jesus to have mercy on him (Luke 18:38). Jesus cried out with a loud voice: "My God, My God, why have You forsaken Me?" (Mark 15:34). Unclean spirits, crying with a loud voice {with shrieks}, were coming out of many who were possessed, because of Philip's miracles (Acts 8:7). The verb is also transl. "to cry," "to shout" in Acts 17:6; 21:34; Gal. 4:27. ¶
2 **to cry, to cry aloud, to cry out: *anaboaō*** [verb: ἀναβοάω <310>]; **from *ana*: intens., and *boaō*: see 1 ▶ To shout out** > The crowd crying out began to ask Pilate to release the prisoner of their choice (Mark 15:8 in some mss.). Jesus cried out with a loud voice: "My God, My God, why have You forsaken Me?" (Matt. 27:46). The verb "to cry" {to shout, to call out} is also used for a man whose son was possessed (Luke 9:38; some mss. have *boaō*). ¶
3 **to cry, to cry out: *epiboaō*** [verb: ἐπιβοάω <1916>]; **from *epi*: upon (intens.), and *boaō*: see 1 ▶ To shout, to scream** > The whole assembly of Jews had cried out {had loudly declared} that Paul was not to live any longer (Acts 25:24; some mss. have *boaō*). ¶
4 **to cry, to cry out: *krazō*** [verb: κράζω <2896>] ▶ **To utter an exclamation, to speak with a loud voice; also transl.: to shout, to scream** > John the Baptist cried out that Jesus, who was coming after him, was preferred before him (John 1:15). On many occasions, we read that demons or possessed people cried out (Matt. 8:29; Mark 1:26 {with a shriek; lit.: crying out}); 3:11; 5:5, 7; 9:26 {to shriek}; Luke 4:41; 9:39; Acts 16:17). We also read that afflicted people cried out to Jesus: two blind men on two different occasions (Matt. 9:27; 20:30, 31), a woman whose daughter was severely demon possessed (Matt. 15:23), the father of a child (Mark 9:24 {to exclaim}), and the blind man Bartimaeus (Mark 10:47, 48; Luke 18:39). The disciples cried out of fear when they saw Jesus walking on the sea (Matt. 14:26); Peter cried out when sinking (14:30). Jesus cried out as He taught in the temple (John 7:28). He cried out {said in a loud voice}, inviting anyone who thirsted to come to Him and drink (John 7:37; see also 12:44). The multitude was crying out "Hosanna" to Jesus (Matt. 21:9; Mark 11:9; John 12:13); the children were also crying out the same in the temple (Matt. 21:15). The Jews were crying out to Pilate concerning Jesus (John 19:12). The people at the cross were crying out (Matt. 27:23; Mark 15:13, 14). Jesus cried out with a loud voice and yielded up the spirit (Matt. 27:50; Mark 15:39 in some mss.). Crying out {Yelling} with a loud voice, those who were listening to Stephen stopped their ears and ran at him with one accord (Acts 7:57); Stephen cried out with a loud voice to the Lord to not charge them with this sin of stoning him (v. 60). By the Spirit of adoption, Christians cry out: "Abba Father!" (Rom. 8:15; Gal. 4:6). The souls of those who had been slain for the word of God were crying out to be avenged (Rev. 6:10). In Revelation, angels are crying out (7:2; 10:3a, b; 14:15; 18:2; 19:17). A great

multitude was crying out with a loud voice saying that salvation belonged to God and to the Lamb (Rev. 7:10). Other refs.: Luke 19:40; Acts 7:60; 14:14; 19:28, 32, 34; 21:28, 36; 23:6; 24:21; Rom. 9:27; Jas. 5:4; Rev. 12:2; 18:18 {to exclaim}, 19. ¶

5 **to cry out: *anakrazō*** [verb: ἀνακράζω <349>]; **from *ana*: intens., and *krazō*: see** 4 ▶ **To shout loudly** > The disciples cried out when they saw Jesus walking on the sea (Mark 6:49). The verb is also used concerning a man with an unclean spirit (Mark 1:23; Luke 4:33), a man who had demons (Luke 8:28), and the Jews (Luke 23:18). ¶

6 **to cry, to cry out: *kraugazō*** [verb: κραυγάζω <2905>]; **from *kraugē*: cry, noise ▶ To scream, to shout** > Isaiah had said concerning the Lord that He would not strive nor cry out (Matt. 12:19). This was effectively the case, except when Jesus cried {called} with a loud voice to Lazarus to come out of the tomb (John 11:43). A woman from Canaan cried out to Jesus (Matt. 15:22). The Jews cried out to Pilate to release Barabbas and to crucify Jesus (John 18:40; 19:6, 15). The Jews in Ephesus who were listening to Paul cried out and threw away their clothes when he said he was sent to the Gentiles (Acts 22:23). Other refs.: Luke 4:41; John 12:13; some mss.: *krazō* in both cases. ¶

7 **to cry, to cry out: *phōneō*** [verb: φωνέω <5455>]; **from *phōnē*: sound, shout ▶ To shout, to exclaim; also transl.: to call out** > Jesus was crying, " He who had ears to hear, let him hear" (Luke 8:8). He cried out and said to a little girl to arise (Luke 8:54). The rich man was crying to Abraham in Hades (Luke 16:24; other mss.: *ekphōneō*). Having cried out with a loud voice, Jesus committed His spirit into the hands of His Father (Luke 23:46). Paul cried out with a loud voice to the jailer to do no harm to himself (Acts 16:28). An angel cried with a loud cry to another to thrust his sharp sickle and gather the bunches of grapes from the vine of the earth (Rev. 14:18). All other refs.: CALL (verb) <5455>, CROW <5455>.

– 8 Mark 5:38; Luke 7:13, 32; John 20:11a, 13, 15; Acts 9:39 → WEEP <2799> 9 Mark 15:37 → to cry, to cry out → UTTER (verb) <863> 10 Luke 1:42 → to cry out → to speak out → SPEAK <400> 11 Luke 23:21; Acts 12:22; 22:24 → to cry out, to cry against → to shout against → SHOUT (verb) <2019>.

CRYING – Heb. 5:7; Rev. 21:4 → CRY (noun) <2906>.

CRYSTAL – 1 ***krustallos*** [masc. noun: κρύσταλλος <2930>]; **from *kruos*: cold; primary meaning: ice, i.e., frozen water ▶ White glass, very pure and transparent** > Before the throne of God, there was what looked like a glass sea, like crystal (Rev. 4:6). A river of water of life, bright as crystal, goes out of the throne of God and of the Lamb (Rev. 22:1). ¶

2 **to be clear as crystal: *krustallizō*** [verb: κρυσταλλίζω <2929>]; **from *krustallos*: see** 1 ▶ **To be transparent and shiny as crystal** > The shining of Jerusalem was like a most precious stone, like a jasper, clear as crystal (Rev. 21:11). ¶

CUBIT – ***pēchus*** [masc. noun: πῆχυς <4083>] ▶ **Measure of length of approx. 18 inches (45 centimeters); but some have transl. by "yard"** > The word is used in Matt. 6:27 and Luke 12:25 (stature of a person); John 21:8 (distance from the land); Rev. 21:17 (wall of Jerusalem). ¶

CULMINATION – 1 Rom. 10:4; 1 Cor. 10:11 → END (noun) <5056> 2 Heb. 9:26 → END (noun) <4930>.

CULPRIT – Luke 13:4 → SINNER <3781>.

CULTIVATE – ***geōrgeō*** [verb: γεωργέω <1090>]; **from *geōrgos*: farmer, which is from *gē*: soil, and *ergon*: work ▶ To prepare and work the earth for growing an agricultural product** > The ground produces useful crops for those by whom it is cultivated {tilled, dressed, farmed} (Heb. 6:7). ¶

CULTIVATED – Rom. 11:24 → cultivated olive tree → good olive tree → OLIVE TREE <2565>.

CUMBER – Luke 13:7 → to use up → USE (verb) <2673>.

CUMBERED (BE) – Luke 10:40 → DISTRACTED (BE) <4049>.

CUMBERSOME – Matt. 23:4 → HEAVY <926>.

CUMIN – ***kuminon*** [neut. noun: κύμινον <2951>] ► **Plant of which the aromatic seeds are used as seasoning; also transl.: cummin** > Cumin gives taste to bread and pastries. The scribes and the Pharisees were paying tithes of cumin, but had set aside the weightier matters of the law (Matt. 23:23). ¶

CUMMIN – Matt. 23:23 → CUMIN <2951>.

CUNNING – [1] ***panourgia*** [fem. noun: πανουργία <3834>]; **from *panourgeō*: to act deceitfully, which is from *panourgos*: deceitful, which is from *pan*: all, and *ergon*: action, work** ► **Craftiness, deceitfulness** > Men have the cunning to use circuitous ways in order to lead astray (Eph. 4:14 {sleight, trickery}). All other refs.: CRAFTINESS <3834>, DECEIT <3834>.
– [2] 2 Cor. 12:16 → DECEIT <1388> [3] Eph. 4:14 → TRICKERY <2940>.

CUNNINGLY – 2 Pet. 1:16 → cunningly devised → DEVISED <4679>.

CUP – ***potērion*** [neut. noun: ποτήριον <4221>]; **from *poō*, which became *pinō*: to drink, or dimin. of *potēr*: drinking cup** ► **Container for drinking** > Jesus speaks of giving a cup of cold water to drink (Matt. 10:42; Mark 9:41). He mentions that the Pharisees were cleaning the outside of the cup (Matt. 23:25, 26; Luke 11:39). The cup speaks often of the sufferings of the Lord (Matt. 20:22, 23; 26:39; Mark 10:38, 39; 14:36; Luke 22:42; John 18:11). The cup of the Lord's supper, more precisely its content, calls to mind the blood of the Lord Jesus that was to be shed and that was indeed shed at the cross (Matt. 26:27; Mark 14:23; Luke 22:20; 1 Cor. 11:25–28); it is also a cup of blessing (1 Cor. 10:16); it refers to the third cup of the Passover by which the Jews were praising and thanking God. The Corinthians could not drink the cup of the Lord and the cup of demons (1 Cor. 10:21a, b). John mentions in Revelation the cup of the wrath of God (14:10; 16:19) and the cup full of the abominations of Babylon the Great (17:4; 18:6). Other refs.: Mark 7:4, 8 in some mss.; Luke 22:17. ¶

CURE (noun) – ***iasis*** [fem. noun: ἴασις <2392>]; **from *iaomai*: to cure** ► **Healing, restoration to health** > The Lord accomplished cures (Luke 13:32). Other refs.: John 5:7 in some mss.; Acts 4:22, 30; see HEALING <2392>. ¶

CURE (verb) – [1] Mark 5:29; Luke 9:11; 17:15; Acts 28:8 → HEAL <2390> [2] Luke 8:36 → SAVE (verb) <4982> [3] Acts 19:12 → LEAVE (verb) <525>.

CURIOUS ARTS – Acts 19:19 → MAGIC <4021>.

CURRENT – Matt. 28:15 → to be current → to be widely spread → SPREAD <1310>.

CURRY – Col. 3:22 → to curry favor → lit.: as men-pleasers → MEN-PLEASER <441>.

CURSE (noun) – [1] ***katanathema*** [neut. noun: κατανάθεμα <2652>]; **from *kata*: against (intens.), and *anathema*: malediction, or from *anatithēmi*: to place, to lay up, which is from *ana*: intens., and *tithēmi*: to place** ► **Word invoking evil, execration, malediction** > In eternity there will be no more curse (Rev. 22:3; other mss.: *katathema*). ¶
[2] ***katara*** [fem. noun: κατάρα <2671>]; **from *kata*: against, and *ara*: cursing** ► **Word invoking evil on someone, imprecation, malediction** > The law is a curse

in that it condemns sinful man and likewise those who are under the principle of the works of the law; but Christ has redeemed us from the curse of the law, having become a curse for us at the cross (Gal. 3:10, 13a, b). The earth which bears thorns and briars is rejected and near to a curse {a cursing, being cursed} (Heb. 6:8). Blessing and curse {cursing} should not proceed out of the same mouth (Jas. 3:10). Peter calls unjust people children of curse {cursed children, accursed children} (2 Pet. 2:14). ¶

[3] **to invoke, to put, to bind oneself under a curse, an oath: *anathematizō*** [verb: ἀναθεματίζω <332>]; **see CURSE** (verb) <332> ▶ **To invoke a malediction on oneself should one not accomplish what one had vowed >** The Jews had put themselves under a curse to kill Paul (Acts 23:12, 14, 21). The Greek verb is transl. "to curse," "to call down curses" in Mark 14:71 when Peter denied the Lord. ¶

– [4] Matt. 26:74 → to call down curses → CURSE (verb) <2653> [5] John 7:49; Gal. 3:10 → CURSED <1944> [6] Rom. 3:14 → CURSING <685> [7] Rom. 9:3; 1 Cor. 12:3; 16:22; Gal. 1:8, 9 → ACCURSED <331>.

CURSE (verb) – [1] ***anathematizō*** [verb: ἀναθεματίζω <332>]; **from *anathēma*: curse, which is from *anatithēmi*: to put upon, which is from *ana*: intens., and *tithēmi*: to put; lit.: to anathematize** ▶ **To invoke a malediction on oneself should one not accomplish what one had vowed >** Peter began to curse {call down curses, put himself under a curse}, saying he did not know Jesus (Mark 14:71). Other refs.: Acts 23:12, 14, 21; see CURSE (noun) <332>. ¶

[2] ***katathematizō*** [verb: καταθεματίζω <2653>]; **from *kata*: intens., and *anathematizō*: see** [1] ▶ **Stronger verb than the previous one >** Peter cursed, saying he did not know Jesus (Matt. 26:74; other mss.: *katanathematizō*). ¶

[3] ***kakologeō*** [verb: κακολογέω <2551>]; **from *kakologos*: evil speaking, which is from *kakos*: evil, and *legō*: to speak** ▶ **To speak evil against someone >** Under the law, one who cursed {spoke evil to} his father or his mother was liable to be put to death (Matt. 15:4; Mark 7:10; see Ex. 21:17). Other refs.: Mark 9:39 and Acts 19:9 (to speak evil); see EVIL (adv.) <2551>. ¶

[4] ***kataraomai*** [verb: καταράομαι <2672>]; **from *kata*: against, and *araomai*: to wish something to happen, or from *katara*: imprecation, malediction, which is from *kata*: against, and *ara*: curse** ▶ **To verbally wish evil upon a person or thing >** The Lord tells us to bless those who curse us (Matt. 5:44 in some mss.; Luke 6:28). Paul says to bless and to curse not (Rom. 12:14). James warns us about the tongue with which we curse men (Jas. 3:9). The fig tree which the Lord cursed dried up (Mark 11:21). Other ref.: Matt. 25:41; see CURSED <2672>. ¶

– [5] 1 Cor. 4:12 → REVILE <3058> [6] Rev. 16:9, 11, 21 → BLASPHEME <987>.

CURSED – [1] ***epikataratos*** [adj.: ἐπικατάρατος <1944>]; **from *epi*: upon, and *kataratos*: cursed, which is from *kataraomai*: to curse; see CURSE** (verb) <2672> ▶ **Upon whom one invokes evil; who is under an imprecation, a malediction >** In the opinion of the Pharisees, the crowd who did not know the law was cursed {was accursed, had a curse on them} (John 7:49; *eparatos* in some mss.). He who does not continue to do all the things that are written in the book of the law is cursed {under a curse} (Gal. 3:10; see Deut. 27:26). Cursed is everyone hanged on a tree (Gal. 3:13; see Deut. 21:23). Other ref.: Luke 6:4 in some mss. ¶

[2] **to curse: *kataraomai*** [verb: καταράομαι <2672>]; **see CURSE** (verb) <2672> ▶ **To verbally wish evil upon a person or thing >** In judgment, the Lord will tell certain people whom He calls "cursed" {accursed ones} (lit.: those who are cursed) to go from Him into eternal fire (Matt. 25:41). All other refs.: CURSE (verb) <2672>.

– [3] Rom. 9:3; 1 Cor. 12:3; 16:22 → ACCURSED <331> [4] Heb. 6:8; 2 Pet. 2:14 → CURSE (noun) <2671>.

CURSING – [1] ***ara*** [fem. noun: ἀρά <685>] ▶ **Word invoking evil, imprecation, malediction >** The mouth is full of cursing and bitterness (Rom. 3:14). ¶

– [2] Heb. 6:8; Jas. 3:10 → CURSE (noun) <2671>.

CURTAIN – Matt. 27:51; Mark 15:38; Luke 23:45; Heb. 6:19; 9:3; 10:20 → VEIL (noun) <2665>.

CUSHION – ***proskephalaion*** [neut. noun: προσκεφάλαιον <4344>]; **from *pros*: for, and *kephalaios*: related to the head, which is from *kephalē*: head ▶ Headrest, pillow** > Jesus was in the stern of the ship sleeping on the cushion (Mark 4:38). ¶

CUSTODY – [1] Mark 3:21 → to take custody → SEIZE <2902> [2] Acts 4:3 → PRISON <5084> [3] Gal. 3:23 → to keep in custody, to hold in custody → GUARD (verb) <5432>.

CUSTOM[1] – [1] ***ethos*** [neut. noun: ἔθος <1485>]; **prob. from *ethō*: to be accustomed ▶ a. Prescription of the law, usage** > According to the custom of the priesthood, the lot fell on Zacharias to burn incense in the temple (Luke 1:9). The parents of Jesus went to Jerusalem according to the custom of the feast (Luke 2:42). Jesus went to the Mount of Olives, according to His custom {as He was accustomed, as He was wont, as usual} (Luke 22:39). Jesus was buried as was the custom {manner} of the Jews (John 19:40). False witnesses said that Jesus would change the customs taught by Moses (Acts 6:14). Certain people taught the Gentile Christians that if they had not been circumcised according to the custom {manner} of Moses, they could not be saved (Acts 15:1). Paul was accused of announcing customs that were not lawful for Romans to receive or practice (Acts 16:21), and teaching the Jews not to walk according to their customs (Acts 21:21). Agrippa was acquainted with all Jewish customs and questions (Acts 26:3). Paul had done nothing against the customs of his forefathers (Acts 28:17). **b. Usual manner of behavior** > It was not the custom {manner} of Romans to deliver the accused before he had an opportunity to defend himself (Acts 25:16). Some have the custom {habit, manner} of forsaking the assembling of themselves together (Heb. 10:25). ¶

[2] **to be customary: *ethizō*** [verb: ἐθίζω <1480>]; **from *ethos*: see [1] ▶ To be the habit, to be according to the tradition >** The parents of Jesus brought Him to the temple that they might do for Him according to the custom (lit.: what is customary) of the law (Luke 2:27). ¶

[3] ***sunētheia*** [fem. noun: συνήθεια <4914>]; **from *sunēthēs*: accustomed, common, which is from *sun*: together, and *ethos*: see [1] ▶ Habit, usage** > The Jews had a custom that someone would be released to them at the Passover (John 18:39). If anyone thought to be contentious about Paul's teachings on order in the church, he had no such custom {practice}, nor did the churches of God (1 Cor. 11:16). Other ref.: 1 Cor. 8:7 where the word is transl. "former association," "conscience," "to be accustomed" in relation to idols. ¶

[4] **to be the custom: *nomizō*** [verb: νομίζω <3543>]; **from *nomos*: law ▶ To follow a habit, a custom; the verb can also mean "to think"** > Paul went to the riverside, where it was the custom for prayer to be {where prayer was wont to be; where they expect, or suppose, there was a place for prayer; where prayer was customarily made} (Acts 16:13). All other refs.: SUPPOSE <3543>, THINK <3543>.

– [5] Matt. 27:15; Mark 10:1; Luke 4:16; Acts 17:2 → to be the custom, according to his custom → ACCUSTOMED (BE) <1486> [6] Gal. 2:14 → to follow Jewish customs → JUDAIZE <2450>.

CUSTOM[2] – [1] ***telos*** [neut. noun: τέλος <5056>]; **from *teleō*: to bring to completion, or: to discharge, to pay ▶ Levy, tax; also transl.: revenue** > The kings of the earth receive customs {duty} or taxes from strangers (Matt. 17:25). We are to render to all their dues: to whom custom, custom (Rom. 13:7a, b). All other refs.: END (noun) <5056>, FINALLY <5056>, PERPETUALLY <5056>.

– [2] Matt. 9:9; Mark 2:14; Luke 5:27 → receipt of custom → tax office → TAX (noun) <5058>.

CUT – 1 **to cut off:** ***aphaireō*** [verb: ἀφαιρέω <851>]; **from *apo*: away from, and *haireō*: to take, to remove ▶ To remove, to sever** > Simon Peter cut off {took off, smote off} the ear of the servant of the high priest with his sword (Matt. 26:51; Mark 14:47; Luke 22:50). All other refs.: TAKE <851>.

2 **to cut, to cut down:** ***koptō*** [verb: κόπτω <2875>] ▶ **To remove by giving a blow** > People were cutting down branches from the trees and strewing them on the way of Jesus (Matt. 21:8; Mark 11:8). All other refs.: LAMENT <2875>, MOURN <2875>.

3 **to cut off, to cut away, to cut oneself off:** ***apokoptō*** [verb: ἀποκόπτω <609>]; **from *apo*: away, and *koptō*: see** 2 ▶ **a. To remove, to sever** > If the right hand causes one to sin, it should be cut off (figur. speaking) (Mark 9:43), and the foot as well (v. 45). Simon Peter cut off the right ear of Malchus, a servant of the high priest (John 18:10, 26). The soldiers on Paul's boat cut away the ropes of the skiff (Acts 27:32). **b. To amputate, to separate oneself (from other Christians); also transl.: to emasculate oneself, to mutilate oneself** > Paul wished that those who were troubling the Galatians would cut themselves off (Gal. 5:12). ¶

4 **to cut, to cut down, to cut off, to cut out:** ***ekkoptō*** [verb: ἐκκόπτω <1581>]; **from *ek*: out, and *koptō*: see** 2 ▶ **To remove, to bring down, to separate** > Every tree that does not produce good fruit is cut {hewn} down and thrown into the fire (Matt. 3:10; 7:19; Luke 3:9). If the right hand or foot causes one to sin, it should be cut off (figur. speaking) and cast from oneself (Matt. 5:30; 18:8). In a parable, the keeper of the vineyard was told to cut down the fig tree that was not producing fruit (Luke 13:7); the keeper asked for another year before cutting it down (v. 9). The Christian can be cut off {cut away} from spiritual blessings (Rom. 11:22). The Christian has been cut out of the olive tree, which is wild by nature, i.e., separated from the Gentiles (Rom. 11:24). Paul wanted to cut off an opportunity from those who were boasting (2 Cor. 11:12). The verb is transl. "to hinder" in 1 Pet. 3:7 in relation to the prayers of the Christian couple. ¶

5 ***katakoptō*** [verb: κατακόπτω <2629>]; **from *kata*: down (intens.), and *koptō*: see** 2 ▶ **To bruise, to wound** > A man possessed by an unclean spirit was cutting {gashing} himself with stones (Mark 5:5). ¶

6 **to cut in two:** ***dichotomeō*** [verb: διχοτομέω <1371>]; **from *dicha*: separately, and *temnō*: to cut ▶ To punish severely, to destroy** > In a parable, the evil servant would be cut in two {cut asunder, cut in sunder, cut in pieces} and his portion appointed with the hypocrites (Matt. 24:51), with the unbelievers (Luke 12:46). ¶

– 7 Matt. 27:60; Mark 15:46 → to hew out → HEW <2998> 8 Acts 2:37 → PRICK <2660> 9 Acts 3:23 → to completely cut off → DESTROY <1842> 10 Acts 5:33; Acts 7:54 → to be cut to the heart, to be cut to the quick → to be furious → FURIOUS <1282> 11 Acts 18:18; 1 Cor. 11:6a, b → to cut the hair, to cut off the hair → lit.: to shear the head → SHEAR <2751> 12 Rom. 9:28 → to cut short → SHORT (CUT) <4932> 13 Gal. 5:7 → to cut in and keep from → HINDER (verb) <348> 14 2 Tim. 2:15 → to cut in a straight line → to divide rightly → DIVIDE <3718>.

CUZA – See CHUZA <5529>.

CYMBAL – ***kumbalon*** [neut. noun: κύμβαλον <2950>]; **from *kumbos*: hollow object ▶ Pieces of brass that produce a sound when clashed together** > The clanging cymbal in 1 Cor. 13:1 refers to a discordant and unpleasant sound. ¶

CYPRIAN – ***Kuprios*** [masc. name: Κύπριος <2953>]; **from *Kupros*: Cyprus ▶ Inhabitant of the island of Cyprus; also transl.: of Cyprus, man of Cyprus** > Barnabas was Cyprian by birth (Acts 4:36), as was Mnason (21:16). Men of Cyprus came to Antioch, preaching the Lord Jesus to the Greeks (Acts 11:20). ¶

CYPRUS – ***Kupros*** [fem. name: Κύπρος <2954>]: **fairness ▶ Large island in the northeast of the Mediterranean Sea** >

Christians preached the gospel to Jews at Cyprus (Acts 11:19). Paul and Barnabas came to Cyprus (Acts 13:4) and preached the word of God at Salamis (see v. 5). After he had separated from Paul, Barnabas took Mark and sailed away to Cyprus, where he was originally from, during a second missionary journey (Acts 15:39). Paul passed near Cyprus later during his third and fourth journeys (Acts 21:3; 27:4). ¶

CYPRUS (OF) – See CYPRIAN <2953>.

CYRENE – ***Kurēnē*** [fem. name: Κυρήνη <2957>] ▶ **City in northern Africa located southeast of the Island of Crete >** Libya is near Cyrene (Acts 2:10). For "of Cyrene" (Matt. 27:32; Mark 15:21; et al.), see CYRENIAN <2956>. ¶

CYRENIAN – ***Kurēnaios*** [masc. name: Κυρηναῖος <2956>] ▶ **Inhabitant of Cyrene, city of a Greek colony in North Africa (Tripoli); also transl.: of Cyrene >** A certain Simon, Cyrenian, was constrained to carry the cross of Jesus (Matt. 27:32; Mark 15:21; Luke 23:26). Cyrenians rose up against Stephen (Acts 6:9) and took part in stoning him (see 7:58). Cyrenians, who came to Antioch, announced the gospel of the Lord Jesus to the Greeks (Acts 11:20). Lucius was Cyrenian (Acts 13:1). ¶

CYRENIUS – See QUIRINIUS <2958>.

D

DAILY – [1] ***epiousios*** [adj.: ἐπιούσιος <1967>]; **from *epi*: upon, and *ousia*: substance, property ▶ Present, needed for subsistence** > Jesus told His disciples to ask the Father to give them each day their daily bread (Matt. 6:11; Luke 11:3). ¶
[2] ***ephēmeros*** [adj.: ἐφήμερος <2184>]; **from *epi*: upon, and *hēmera*: day ▶ That which is necessary for the day** > James speaks of a brother or a sister who is without clothing and daily food (Jas. 2:15). ¶
[3] ***kathēmerinos*** [adj.: καθημερινός <2522>]; **from *kata*: each, and *hēmera*: day ▶ Occurring each day** > Certain widows were being overlooked in the daily distribution of food among early Christians (Acts 6:1). ¶
– [4] Titus 3:14 → NECESSARY <316>.

DAINTY – Rev. 18:14 → RICH <3045>.

DALMANUTHA – ***Dalmanoutha*** [fem. name: Δαλμανουθά <1148>] **▶ Place in Palestine near the region of Magdala** > Jesus came to the region of Dalmanutha, and reproached the Pharisees for asking Him for a sign from heaven in order to test Him (Mark 8:10; see vv. 11–13). ¶

DALMATIA – ***Dalmatia*** [fem. name: Δαλματία <1149>] **▶ Region of Illyria in Europe on the eastern coast of the Adriatic Sea** > At the end of his life, Paul would say that Titus had departed to Dalmatia (2 Tim. 4:10). ¶

DAMAGE (noun) – [1] Acts 27:10 → DISASTER <5196> [2] Acts 27:10 → LOSS <2209> [3] Acts 27:21 → HARM (noun) <5196> [4] 2 Cor. 7:9 → to receive damage → to suffer loss → LOSS <2210>.

DAMAGE (verb) – Rev. 6:6 → INJURE <91>.

DAMARIS – ***Damaris*** [fem. name: Δάμαρις <1152>]; **perhaps: gentle ▶ Christian woman of Athens** > Damaris believed the preaching of Paul and joined him, as did others with her (Acts 17:34). ¶

DAMASCENE – ***Damaskēnos*** [adj. used as a name: Δαμασκηνός <1153>] **▶ Inhabitant of Damascus** > While the city of the Damascenes was kept under guard (2 Cor. 11:32), Paul was able to flee the city by being let down in a basket through an opening in the wall (see v. 33). ¶

DAMASCUS – ***Damaskos*** [fem. name: Δαμασκός <1154>] **▶ Major city in southern Syria, near Palestine** > It was on the road leading to Damascus that Paul saw the Lord in His glory and was converted; he preached the gospel first in this city, but he was obliged to flee, let down in a basket through an opening in the wall (Acts 9:2, 3, 8, 10, 19, 22, 27). He would later recall this milestone episode of his life (Acts 22:5, 6, 10, 11; 26:12, 20; 2 Cor. 11:32), and his return to Damascus later (Gal. 1:17). ¶

DAMN – Mark 16:16; Rom. 14:23 → CONDEMN <2632>.

DAMNABLE – 2 Pet. 2:1 → DESTRUCTION <684>.

DAMNATION – [1] Mark 12:40 → JUDGMENT <2917> [2] John 5:29 → JUDGMENT <2920> [3] 2 Pet. 2:3 → DESTRUCTION <684>.

DAMSEL – [1] Matt. 9:24, 25; 14:11; Mark 5:41, 42; 6:22, 28a, b → girl, little girl → DAUGHTER <2877> [2] Matt. 26:69; John 18:17; Acts 12:13; 16:16 → SERVANT GIRL <3814>.

DANCE – ***orcheomai*** [verb: ὀρχέομαι <3738>]; **prob. from *orchos*: line, row ▶ To perform rhythmic movements of the body to the sound of music** > Jesus spoke of children who did not dance when the flute was playing (Matt. 11:17; Luke 7:32). The daughter of Herodias danced at Herod's birthday celebration and pleased him (Matt. 14:6; Mark 6:22). ¶

DANCING – ***choros*** [masc. noun: χορός <5525>] **▶ Rhythmic movements of the body performed to the sound of music** > In the parable of the prodigal son, the older son heard music and dancing (Luke 15:25). The Greek word has also the meaning of a company of dancers and singers. ¶

DANGER – [1] ***kindunos*** [masc. noun: κίνδυνος <2794>]; **poss. from *kineō*: to move ▶ Something that may cause injury, peril** > No danger will separate Christians from the love of Christ (Rom. 8:35). Paul uses the word eight times in 2 Cor. 11:26 in relation to dangers he had faced. ¶
[2] **to be in danger, to be in great danger: *kinduneuō*** [verb: κινδυνεύω <2793>]; **from *kindunos*: see [1] ▶ a. To be in peril regarding one's life** > The disciples were in danger {were in jeopardy} in the ship (Luke 8:23). **b. To run the risk, to expose to the possibility of a loss** > The business of the craftsmen of Ephesus was in danger of falling into discredit as a result of Paul's preaching of the gospel (Acts 19:27); the Ephesians were in danger of being charged with sedition for a disorderly gathering (v. 40). Other ref.: 1 Cor. 15:30 (to stand in jeopardy); see JEOPARDY <2793>. ¶
– [3] Matt. 5:21, 22; Mark 3:29 → in danger of → SUBJECT (noun)[1] <1777>.

DANGEROUS – [1] ***episphalēs*** [adj.: ἐπισφαλής <2000>]; **from *epi*: upon, and *sphallō*: to fall ▶ Perilous, risky** > In Acts 27:9, sailing had become dangerous. ¶
– [2] Matt. 8:28 → DIFFICULT <5467>.

DANIEL – ***Daniēl*** [masc. name: Δανιήλ <1158>]: **God is judge, in Heb. ▶ Prophet of the O.T.** > Jesus mentions the name of Daniel in connection with the abomination of desolation (Matt. 24:15; Mark 13:14 in some mss.). ¶

DARE – ***tolmaō*** [verb: τολμάω <5111>]; **from *tolma*: boldness, courage, which is from *tlaō*: to endure, to suffer ▶ To have audacity, to allow oneself, to risk; also transl.: to venture, to presume, to be bold, to be daring, durst (past tense and past ptcp. of dare), to have courage** > Perhaps for a good man someone might dare to die (Rom. 5:7). The verb is also used in regard to those listening to Jesus (Matt. 22:46; Mark 12:34; Luke 20:40), His disciples (John 21:12), the Jews (Acts 5:13), Moses (Acts 7:32), Paul (Rom. 15:18 {to presume, to venture}; 2 Cor. 10:12; 11:21b), the Corinthians (1 Cor. 6:1; 2 Cor. 11:21a), and Michael the archangel (Jude 9). All other refs.: BOLD <5111>, BOLDLY <5111>.

DARING – [1] 2 Cor. 10:2 → BOLD <5111> [2] 2 Cor. 11:21a, b → to be daring → DARE <5111> [3] 2 Pet. 2:10 → PRESUMPTUOUS <5113>.

DARK – [1] Matt. 6:23; Luke 11:34, 36 → full of darkness → DARKNESS <4652> [2] Luke 12:3; John 6:17; 20:1; et al. → DARKNESS <4653> [3] 2 Pet. 1:19 → OBSCURE (adj.) <850> [4] Rev. 8:12 → to turn dark → DARKEN <4654>.

DARKEN – [1] ***skotizō*** [verb: σκοτίζω <4654>]; **from *skotos*: darkness ▶ To cover with darkness, to deprive of light physically or morally** > After the tribulation, the sun will be darkened (Matt. 24:29; Mark 13:24). When Jesus was on the cross, the sun was darkened {was obscured, stopped shining} between the sixth and the ninth hour (Luke 23:45); other mss.: *ekleipō*. The heart of men without understanding was darkened (Rom. 1:21). Concerning the wicked, David said: "Let their eyes be darkened to see not" (Rom. 11:10). The Gentiles are darkened in their understanding (Eph. 4:18). The third part of the stars was darkened {turned dark} (Rev. 8:12). The sun and the air were darkened with the smoke of the pit (Rev. 9:2). ¶
[2] ***skotoō*** [verb: σκοτόω <4656>]; **from *skotos*: darkness ▶ To obscure, to cover with darkness** > The kingdom of the beast became darkened {became full of darkness, was full of darkness, was plunged into darkness} (Rev. 16:10). Other mss. have Eph. 4:18; Rev. 9:2; see [1]. ¶

DARKLY – 1 Cor. 13:12 → OBSCURELY <1722> <135>.

DARKNESS – [1] ***zophos*** [masc. noun: ζόφος <2217>]; **related to *gnophos*: darkness, obscurity ▶ Blackness of the infernal regions** > The angels who had not kept their original state (see Gen. 6:2) are kept in eternal chains under darkness, in the deepest pit of gloom, until the day of their judgment (2 Pet. 2:4; Jude 6 {gloomy darkness}). In 2 Pet. 2:17 and Jude 13, the Greek expr. "*ho zophos tou skotous*" (lit.: the darkness of gloom) is transl.: the gloom of, the blackness, the black, the blackest darkness. Other mss. have this word in Heb. 12:18; see [2]. ¶

[2] ***skotia*** [fem. noun: σκοτία <4653>]; ***skotos*** [neut. noun: σκότος <4655>] ▶ **Obscurity, night** > Darkness is characterized by the absence of light (Matt. 10:27; 27:45; Mark 15:33; Luke 12:3; 23:44; Acts 2:20; 13:11; 2 Cor. 4:6; Heb. 12:18). The term is also used in the moral sense in the N.T. (Matt. 4:16; 6:23; Luke 1:79; 11:35; John 8:12; 12:35a, b, 46; Rom. 2:19; 13:12; 1 Cor. 4:5; 6:14; Eph. 5:11; 1 Pet. 2:9; 1 John 1:6; 2:8, 9, 11). Darkness symbolizes distance and separation from God who is light (John 1:5; 3:19; Acts 26:18; 1 John 1:5). It is the realm of man without God (Eph. 5:8; 1 Thes. 5:4, 5), subjected to the power of Satan, the ruler of darkness (Luke 22:53; Eph. 6:12; Col. 1:13). Outer darkness refers to the eternal dwelling place, removed from God, of wicked men, in company with Satan and demons (Matt. 8:12; 22:13; 25:30; 2 Pet. 2:17; Jude 13). Other refs.: John 6:17; 20:1. ¶

[3] **full of darkness: *skoteinos*** [adj.: σκοτεινός <4652>]; **from *skotos*: darkness** ▶ **Dark, full of blackness, in the lit. or moral sense** > If the eye is wicked, the whole body will be full of darkness (Matt. 6:23; Luke 11:34). If the body has no dark part, it will be wholly full of light (Luke 11:36). ¶

– [4] Heb. 12:18 → darkness and gloom → obscurity and darkness → OBSCURITY <1105> [5] Rev. 16:10 → to become full of darkness, to be full of darkness, to be plunged into darkness → DARKEN <4656>.

DARNEL – ***zizanion*** [neut. noun: ζιζάνιον <2215>] ▶ **Poisonous plant causing intoxication; it resembles wheat and grows in a similar fashion; also transl.: tares, weeds** > It is almost impossible to distinguish darnel from wheat when they are in the bud. When the ears appear, one can distinguish and separate them; this is done before threshing. The Lord explains that, in His parable, the tares are the sons of the evil one (Matt. 13:25–27, 29, 30, 36, 38, 40). ¶

DART – [1] ***belos*** [neut. noun: βέλος <956>]; **from *ballō*: to throw** ▶ **Wooden spear with an iron point at its extremity; javelin, arrow** > With the shield of faith, the Christians are able to quench all the burning darts {flaming missiles, flaming arrows} of Satan (Eph. 6:16), i.e., to fend off all his attacks. ¶

[2] ***bolis*** [fem. noun: βολίς <1002>]; **from *ballō*: to throw** ▶ **See [1].** > This word is added in some mss. at the end of Heb. 12:20. ¶

DASH – [1] Matt. 4:6; Luke 4:11 → STRIKE <4350> [2] Mark 9:18 → to dash (to the ground) → TEAR (verb) <4486> [3] Luke 19:44 → to dash to the ground → GROUND (noun)[1] <1474> [4] Acts 27:29 → to dash against → to run aground → RUN <1601> [5] Rev. 2:27 → to dash to pieces → BREAK <4937>.

DATE – [1] Acts 1:7; 1 Thes. 5:1 → SEASON (noun) <2540> [2] Gal. 4:2 → date set → time appointed → TIME <4287>.

DAUGHTER – [1] ***thugatēr*** [fem. noun: θυγάτηρ <2364>] ▶ **Person of the feminine gender, considered in relation to the father or the mother** > This word is found mainly in the Gospels (Matt. 9:18, 22; 10:35, 37; 14:6; 15:22, 28; 21:5; Mark 5:34, 35; 6:22; 7:26, 29, 30; Luke 1:5; 2:36; 8:42, 48, 49; 12:53a, b; 13:16; 23:28; John 12:15; Acts 2:17; 7:21; 21:9; 2 Cor. 6:18; Heb. 11:24). ¶

[2] **young daughter, little daughter: *thugatrion*** [neut. noun: θυγάτριον <2365>]; **dimin. of *thugatēr*: see [1]** ▶ **Little girl, young girl** > The little daughter of the ruler of the synagogue was at the point of death (Mark 5:23). The little daughter of a woman had an unclean spirit (Mark 7:25). ¶

[3] **girl, little girl: *korasion*** [neut. noun: κοράσιον <2877>]; **dimin. of *korē*: young girl** ▶ **Young female child; also transl.: damsel, maid** > Jesus said that the girl (the daughter of the ruler of the synagogue) was

not dead (Matt. 9:24); He took her hand, and the girl got up (v. 25). Other refs.: Matt. 14:11; Mark 5:41, 42; 6:22, 28a, b. ¶

4 ***pais*** [masc. or fem. noun: παῖς <3816>] ► **Child; also transl.: girl, little girl, maid, maiden** > Jesus resurrected a young girl (Luke 8:51, 54). All other refs.: BOY <3816>, CHILD <3816>, SERVANT <3816>, SON <3816>.

– 5 Heb. 2:10; 12:8 → "and daughters" added in Engl. 6 1 Pet. 3:6 → CHILD <5043>.

DAUGHTER-IN-LAW – Matt. 10:35; Luke 12:53a, b → BRIDE <3565>.

DAVID – ***Dauid*** [masc. name: Δαυίδ <1138>]**: beloved, in Heb.; also spelled: *Dabid*** ► **King in the O.T. from whom Jesus Christ, the Messiah, is descended** > He is a type of the Lord as the rejected king, and then as conqueror. He is mentioned in the genealogy of Jesus Christ (Matt. 1:1; Luke 3:31). God says of him: "I have found David … a man after my heart, who shall do all my will" (Acts 13:22a, b). Jesus is the root and the offspring of David (Rev. 22:16). Other refs.: Matt. 1:6a, b, 17a, b, 20; 9:27; 12:3, 23; 15:22; 20:30, 31; 21:9, 15; 22:42, 43, 45; Mark 2:25; 10:47, 48; 11:10; 12:35–37; Luke 1:27, 32, 69; 2:4, 11; 6:3; 18:38, 39; 20:41, 42, 44; John 7:42a, b; Acts 1:16; 2:25, 29, 34; 4:25; 7:45; 13:34, 36; 15:16; Rom. 1:3; 4:6; 11:9; 2 Tim. 2:8; Heb. 4:7; 11:32; Rev. 3:7; 5:5. ¶

DAWN (noun) – 1 Matt. 14:25; Mark 6:48 → shortly before dawn → lit.: about the fourth watch of the night → WATCH (noun) <5438> 2 Matt. 28:1 → at dawn → lit.: when it began to dawn → DAWN (verb) <2020> 3 Mark 13:35 → in the morning → MORNING <4404> 4 Luke 24:1; John 8:2 → at dawn → early in the morning → MORNING <3722> <901>.

DAWN (AT EARLY) – Mark 1:35 → MORNING (VERY EARLY IN THE) <1773>.

DAWN (verb) – 1 ***diaugazō*** [verb: διαυγάζω <1306>]**; from *dia*: through, and *augazō*: to shine, which is from *augē*: brilliance** ► **To appear (speaking of daybreak)** > We do well to take heed to the prophetic word until the day dawns and the morning star arises (2 Pet. 1:19). ¶

2 **to begin to dawn: *epiphōskō*** [verb: ἐπιφώσκω <2020>]**; from *epi*: upon, and *phōskō*: to shine, which is from *phōs*: light** ► **To start shining, i.e., at dawn, at daybreak** > Joseph of Arimathea laid the body of Jesus in a tomb, the day of Preparation, and the Sabbath drew near {drew on, was about to begin} (lit.: began to dawn) (Luke 23:54). Mary Magdalene and the other Mary came to see the tomb of Jesus as the first day of the week began to dawn (Matt. 28:1). ¶

– 3 Matt. 4:16 → RISE (verb) <393> 4 Acts 12:12 → this had dawned on him → lit.: having considered → CONSIDER <4894>.

DAY – 1 ***hēmera*** [fem. noun: ἡμέρα <2250>] ► **Interval of time between sunrise and sunset** > This term describes a future time (Matt. 24:50; Luke 1:20), a period of twenty-four hours (Mark 1:13), the period of natural light (Mark 4:35), a time of opportunity to serve (John 9:4; Rom. 13:13), an indefinite period of time (Rom. 2:5; 2 Cor. 6:2 a, b; Eph. 6:13), or an appointed time (Eph. 4:30). See DAY OF THE LORD. Other refs.: AGE <2250>, TIME <2250>, YEAR <2250>.

2 **next day, second day, day later: *deuteraios*** [adj. used as adv.: δευτεραῖος <1206>]**; from *deuteros*: second** ► **Second day, tomorrow** > The word is used in Acts 28:13. ¶

3 **next day, following day: *epaurion*** [adv.: ἐπαύριον <1887>]**; from *epi*: upon, and *aurion*: next day** ► **The day after today** > The word is used in Matt. 27:62; Mark 11:12 {the morrow}; John 1:29, 35, 43; 6:22; 12:12; Acts 10:9, 23, 24; 14:20; 20:7; 21:8; 22:30; 23:32; 25:6, 23. ¶

4 **next day, day following: *epiousa*** [fem. sing. ptcp. of verb: ἐπιοῦσα <1966>]**; from *epeimi*: to come after, which is from *epi*: on, and *eimi*: to be; lit.: the (day) that comes after** ► **The day after today** > The

word is used in Acts 16:11; 20:15. All other refs.: FOLLOWING <1966>.

5 **a night and day, a night and a day: *nuchthēmeron*** [neut. noun: νυχθήμερον <3574>]**; from *nux*: night, and *hēmera*: day ▶ A period of twenty-four hours** > Paul had passed a night and a day in the depths of the sea (2 Cor. 11:25). ¶

6 **this day, to day, today: *sēmeron*** [adv.: σήμερον <4594>]**; from *hēmera*: day ▶ On this very day** > This adv. is frequently used by Matthew (Matt. 6:11, 30; 11:23; 16:3; 21:28; 27:8, 19; 28:15) and Luke (Luke 2:11; 4:21; 5:26; 12:28; 13:32, 33; 19:5, 9; 22:34; 23:43; 24:21; Acts 4:9; 13:33; 19:40; 20:26; 22:3; 24:21; 26:2, 29; 27:33). Other refs.: Mark 14:30; Rom. 11:8; 2 Cor. 3:14, 15; Heb. 1:5; 3:7, 13, 15; 4:7a, b; 5:5; 13:8; Jas. 4:13. ¶

– 7 Mark 1:35 → a long while before day light {a great while before day} → lit.: quite in the night (*ennucha lian*) 8 Luke 12:55 → hot day → burning heat → HEAT <2742> 9 John 10:40 → in the early days → at first → FIRST <4412> 10 John 21:4 → MORNING <4405> 11 Acts 8:1 → TIME <2250> 12 Acts 20:11 → BREAK OF DAY <827> 13 Acts 20:15b → the next day → lit.: the next (*heteros*) 14 Rom. 15:4 → to write in former days → lit.: to write before → WRITE <4270>.

DAY OF ATONEMENT – Acts 27:9 → lit.: Fast → FAST <3521>.

DAY OF THE LORD – day: *hēmera* [fem. noun: ἡμέρα <2250>]**; Lord: *Kurios*** [masc. noun: Κύριος <2962>]**; from *kuros*: supremacy ▶ Future day of the Lord's dominion on earth** > This day will come as a thief in the night (1 Thes. 5:2; 2 Pet. 3:10), when the Lord returns. The Thessalonians thought that the day of the Lord had already come (2 Thes. 2:2). There are other exprs. which are equivalent to the day of the Lord (Acts 2:20) in the N.T.: the day of Christ (Phil. 1:10; 2:16), the day of Jesus Christ (Phil. 1:6), the day of the Lord Jesus (1 Cor. 5:5; 2 Cor. 1:14), the day of the Lord Jesus Christ (1 Cor. 1:8), the days of the Son of Man (Luke 17:22, 26), the day of God the Almighty (Rev. 16:14), and the day (2 Pet. 1:19). The day of the Lord (2 Pet. 3:10) will begin when He appears in glory, at His coming to judge the inhabited earth and to establish His kingdom. It will end with the dissolving of the present creation to give place to the day of God (2 Pet. 3:12), with new heavens and a new earth in which righteousness dwells (see v. 13).

DAYBREAK – 1 Luke 12:38 → toward daybreak → lit.: in the third watch → THIRD <5154>, WATCH (noun) <5438> 2 Acts 20:11 → BREAK OF DAY <827>.

DAYLIGHT – Acts 20:11 → BREAK OF DAY <827>.

DAYSPRING FROM ON HIGH – dayspring: *anatolē* [fem. noun: ἀνατολή <395>]**; from *anatellō*: to rise, which is from *ana*: high, and *tellō*: to accomplish, to rise; high: *hupsos*** [neut. noun: ὕψος <5311>]**; from *hupsi*: high ▶ Full light (rising sun) coming to enlighten a world of darkness** > Zacharias prophesied the coming of the Lord Jesus to the earth using this figure of speech: the dayspring {sunrise, rising sun} from on high has visited us (Luke 1:78). All other refs. (*anatolē*): see EAST <395>. All other refs. (*hupsos*): see EXALTATION <5311>, HEIGHT <5311>, HIGH (noun) <5311>.

DAYTIME – John 11:9 → DAY <2250>.

DAZZLING – 1 Mark 9:3 → EXCEEDINGLY <3029> 2 Mark 9:3 → to shine → SHINING <4744> 3 Luke 9:29 → GLISTENING <1823> 4 Luke 24:4 → SHINING <797>.

DEACON – Rom. 16:1; Phil. 1:1; 1 Tim. 3:8, 12 → SERVANT <1249>.

DEAD – 1 ***nekros*** [adj. and adj. used as noun: νεκρός <3498>]**; from *nekus*: corpse ▶ Without life (adj.); one who is without life (noun)** > Jesus said to let the dead bury their own dead (Matt. 8:22a, b). Other refs.: Matt. 10:8; 11:5; 14:2; 17:9; 22:31, 32;

23:27; 27:64; 28:4, 7; Mark 6:14, 16; 9:9, 10, 26a; 12:25–27; Luke 7:15, 22; 9:7, 60a, b; 15:24, 32; 16:30, 31; 20:35, 37, 38; 24:5, 46; John 2:22; 5:21, 25; 12:1b, 9, 17; 20:9; 21:14; Acts 3:15; 4:2, 10; 5:10; 10:41, 42; 13:30, 34; 17:3, 31, 32; 20:9; 23:6; 24:15 (in some mss.), 21; 26:8, 23; 28:6; Rom. 1:4; 4:17, 24; 6:4, 9, 11, 13; 7:4b, 8; 8:10, 11a, b; 10:7, 9; 11:15; 14:9; 1 Cor. 15:12a, b, 13, 15, 16, 20, 21, 29a, b, 32, 35, 42, 52; 2 Cor. 1:9; Gal. 1:1; Eph. 1:20; 2:1, 5; 5:14; Phil. 3:11; Col. 1:18; 2:12, 13; 1 Thes. 1:10; 4:16; 2 Tim. 2:8; 4:1; Heb. 6:1, 2; 9:14, 17; 11:19, 35; 13:20; Jas. 2:17, 20, 26a, b; 1 Pet. 1:3, 21; 4:5, 6; Rev. 1:5, 17, 18; 2:8; 3:1; 11:18; 14:13; 16:3; 20:5, 12a, b, 13. ¶

[2] **dead, as good as dead: *nenekrōmenos*** [perf. pass. ptcp.: νενεκρωμένος <3499>]; **from *nekroō*: to put to death, to make as dead, which is from *nekros*: see [1] ► Almost dead** > Abraham did not consider his own body already become dead (Rom. 4:19); other transl.: he considered his body as good as dead in relation to the promise of having a son. From Abraham, a man become dead {as good as dead}, was born a multitude of people (Heb. 11:12). Other ref.: Col. 3:5; see DEATH <3499>. ¶

[3] **half dead: *hēmithanēs*** [adj.: ἡμιθανής <2253>]; **from *hēmi*: half, and *thnēskō*: to die ► Semi-deceased, semi-dying** > Thieves left a man half dead (Luke 10:30). ¶

[4] **to be dead: *thnēskō*** [verb: θνήσκω <2348>] **► To be deceased, meaning that the soul and the spirit are separated from the body** > Those who sought the life of the young child Jesus were dead (Matt. 2:20). In Luke 7:12; John 11:39, 44 (he who had died, he who was dead); 12:1a means lit.: one having died. Other refs.: Mark 15:44a; Luke 8:49; John 11:21 and 41 in some mss., 44; 19:33; Acts 14:19; 25:19; 1 Tim. 5:6. ¶

[5] **to be dead, to die: *apothnēskō*** [verb: ἀποθνήσκω <599>]; **from *apo*: intens., and *thnēskō*: to be dead ► See defin. of [4].** > When we were still without strength, in due time Christ died for the ungodly (Rom. 5:6); He died for sinners (v. 8). The Lord raised a girl who was dead (Matt. 9:24; Mark 5:35, 39). Other refs.: Mark 9:26b; 15:44b; Luke 8:52, 53; John 6:49; 8:52a, 53a, b; 11:14, 21, 25, 32; 12:1 in some mss.; Acts 7:4; Rom. 5:15; 6:2, 7, 8, 10a, b; 7:6; 8:34; 14:9a, 15; 1 Cor. 8:11; 15:3; 2 Cor. 5:14a, b, 15a, b; Gal. 2:19, 21; Col. 2:20; 3:3; 1 Thes. 5:10; Heb. 11:4, 13; Jude 12. All other refs.: DIE <599>, DYING <599>.

[6] **to be dead, to die: *teleutaō*** [verb: τελευτάω <5053>]; **from *teleutē*: death, which is from *teleō*: to complete, which is from *telos*: end ► To finish life, to reach one's end** > The verb is used in regard to the death of the patriarch David (Acts 2:29) and Herod (Matt. 2:19). All other refs.: DIE <5053>.

– [7] Acts 2:27, 31 → realm of the dead → HADES <86> [8] Rom. 4:19 → DEADNESS <3500> [9] Rom. 7:4 → to become dead, to make dead → KILL <2289> [10] 1 Cor. 7:39 → to be dead → SLEEP (verb) <2837> [11] 2 Tim. 2:11 → to be dead with → to die with → DIE <4880> [12] Heb. 9:17 → a testament is in force after men are dead → lit.: a testament is firm over those dead (*nekros*) [13] 1 Pet. 2:24 → being dead → having died → DIE <581> [14] Rev. 11:8, 9a, b → dead body → CORPSE <4430>.

DEADEN – John 12:40 → HARDEN <4456>.

DEADENING – Rom. 4:19 → DEADNESS <3500>.

DEADLY – [1] ***thanasimos*** [adj.: θανάσιμος <2286>]; **from *thanatos*: death ► Causing death, poisonous** > Jesus spoke of those who will drink any deadly thing without being injured by it (Mark 16:18). ¶

[2] ***thanatēphoros*** [adj.: θανατηφόρος <2287>]; **from *thanatos*: death, and *pherō*: to carry ► Bringing death** > The tongue is an unruly evil, full of deadly {death-bringing} poison (Jas. 3:8). ¶

– [3] Rev. 13:3, 12 → deadly wound → lit.: wound of death (*thanatos*).

DEADNESS – ***nekrōsis*** [fem. noun: νέκρωσις <3500>]; **from *nekroō*: to put to death ► State of what is dead, sterility** > Abraham did not consider the deadness {barrenness, deadening} of Sarah's womb

(Rom. 4:19). Other refs.: Mark 3:5 in some mss.; 2 Cor. 4:10: see DYING <3500>. ¶

DEAF – ***kōphos*** [adj. and adj. used as noun: κωφός <2974>]; **from *koptō*: to cut down, to strike ▶ Incapable of hearing, hard of hearing** > Jesus healed the deaf (Matt. 11:5; Mark 7:32, 37; Luke 7:22). He commanded a dumb and deaf spirit to come out of a child and enter no more into him (Mark 9:25). All other refs.: DUMB <2974>.

DEAL – 1 **to deal treacherously: *katasophizomai*** [verb: κατασοφίζομαι <2686>]; **from *kata*: against, and *sophizō*: to deal with subtly; also transl.: to deal shrewdly, to deal subtilly ▶ To use deception, to act with artifice** > The king of Egypt dealt treacherously with {took shrewd advantage of} the Israelites and mistreated them (Acts 7:19). ¶

2 **to deal with: *prospherō*** [verb: προσφέρω <4374>]; **from *pros*: to, and *pherō*: to bring, to carry ▶ To behave toward, to treat (someone)** > God deals with {conducts himself toward} Christians as with sons (Heb. 12:7). All other refs.: BRING <4374>, OFFER <4374>.

– 3 Luke 16:8 → DO <4160> 4 Acts 1:1 → to deal with certain matters in a book → to make (*poieō*) an account of certain matters 5 Acts 25:24 → PETITION (verb) <1793> 6 Rom. 12:3 → DISTRIBUTE <3307> 7 1 Cor. 7:31 → to deal with → USE (verb) <5530> 8 Heb. 9:10 → "but deal" added in Engl. 9 Heb. 9:28 → not to deal with sin → lit.: without sin.

DEALER – Acts 16:14 → dealer in purple → PURPLE (noun) <4211>.

DEALING – 2 Cor. 13:4 → "in dealing," "in our dealing" added in Engl.

DEALINGS – 1 **to have dealings: *sunchraomai*** [verb: συγχράομαι <4798>]; **from *sun*: together, and *chraomai*: to behave toward, to conduct oneself ▶ To keep company, to have relations** > The Jews have no dealings {do not associate} with Samaritans (John 4:9). ¶

– 2 1 Cor. 7:31 → to have dealings → USE (verb) <2710>.

DEAR – 1 ***agapētos*** [adj.: ἀγαπητός <27>]; **from *agapaō*: to love ▶ Whom one loves, beloved** > The Thessalonians were dear to Paul {they had a fond affection for him} (1 Thes. 2:8). All other refs.: BELOVED <27>.

2 ***entimos*** [adj.: ἔντιμος <1784>]; **from *en*: in, and *timē*: price, honor, esteem ▶ Precious, who is appreciated** > A centurion had a servant who was dear to {highly regarded by, valued highly by} him (Luke 7:2). All other refs.: HONOR (noun) <1784>, HONORABLE <1784>, PRECIOUS <1784>.

– 3 Acts 20:24 → PRECIOUS <5093>.

DEARLY LOVED – Eph. 5:1 → BELOVED <27>.

DEARTH – Acts 7:11; 11:28 → FAMINE <3042>.

DEATH – 1 ***thanatos*** [masc. noun: θάνατος <2288>]; **from *thnēskō*: to die ▶ Death is the separation of the soul and spirit of a human being from the physical body** > At the coming of Jesus, light sprang up for those who sat in the shadow of death (Matt. 4:16; Luke 1:79). Death also designates the spiritual state of man at birth, as separated from God (John 5:24; Rom. 5:12a, b; see Eph. 2:1) and far from God (see Luke 15:24). Christians are seen as identified with Christ in His death and as joined to Him in resurrection (see Rom. 6:8; Col. 2:20; 3:1); they are to reckon themselves to be dead to sin, but alive to God (see Rom. 6:11). Death of the body is compared to sleep (see 1 Cor. 15:6, 17, 18; 1 Thes. 4:13, 15). After death and while awaiting judgment (see Heb. 9:27), unbelievers go to a place of torments (see Luke 16:23, 24); after judgment (see Rev. 20:11–15), they are cast into the lake of fire: this is the second death, eternal death. This expr., "the second death," is found in Rev. 2:11; 20:6, 14; 21:8. Death is the last enemy that will be destroyed (1 Cor. 15:26). Those who believe have passed from death into life (John 5:24). Other refs.: Matt. 10:21a; 15:4; 16:28; 20:18; 26:38, 66; Mark 7:10; 9:1; 10:33; 13:12a; 14:34, 64; Luke 2:26; 9:27; 22:33; 23:15, 22; 24:20; John 8:51, 52; 11:4, 13; 12:33; 18:32; 21:19; Acts 2:24; 13:28; 22:4; 23:29; 25:11, 25; 26:31; 28:18; Rom. 1:32; 5:10, 14, 17, 21; 6:3, 4, 5, 9, 16, 21, 23; 7:5, 10, 13a, b, 24; 8:2, 6, 38; 1 Cor. 3:22; 11:26; 15:21, 26, 54, 55a, 55b (lit.: Hades), 56; 2 Cor. 1:9, 10; 2:16a, b; 3:7; 4:11, 12; 7:10; 11:23; Phil. 1:20; 2:8a, b, 27, 30; 3:10; Col. 1:22; 2 Tim. 1:10; Heb. 2:9a, b, 14a, b, 15; 5:7; 7:23; 9:15, 16; 11:5; Jas. 1:15; 5:20; 1 John 3:14a, b; 5:16a–c, 17; Rev. 1:18; 2:10, 11, 23; 6:8a, b; 9:6a, b; 12:11; 13:3, 12 {mortally wounded, fatal wound} (lit.: wounded to death); 18:8 {pestilence}; 20:13, 14a, b; 21:4. ¶

[2] ***anairesis*** [fem. noun: ἀναίρεσις <336>]; **from *anaireō*: to take away, which is from *ana*: up (intens.), and *haireō*: to take ▶ Assassination, murder** > Saul was consenting to the death {execution} of Stephen {his being killed} (Acts 8:1; 22:20 in some mss.). ¶

[3] ***teleutē*** [fem. noun: τελευτή <5054>]; **from *teleō*: to accomplish, to complete, which is from *telos*: end ▶ End of life, decease** > The word is used in regard to the death of Herod (Matt. 2:15). ¶

[4] ***phonos*** [masc. noun: φόνος <5408>]; **from *phenō*: to kill ▶ Murder, slaughter** > O.T. people of faith died by the death of the sword {were slain with the sword, were put to death with the sword} (Heb. 11:37). Other refs.: MURDER (noun) <5408>, SLAY <5408>.

[5] **condemned to death, condemned to die: *epithanatios*** [adj.: ἐπιθανάτιος <1935>]; **from *epi*: to, on, and *thanatos*: see [1] ▶ Sentenced to death** > God had set up the apostles last of all, as condemned to death {appointed to death} (1 Cor. 4:9). ¶

[6] **to put to death: *anaireō*** [verb: ἀναιρέω <337>]; **from *ana*: up (intens.), and *haireō*: to take; lit.: to take away ▶ To kill, to execute** > Two criminals were led with Jesus to be put to death (Luke 23:32). Jesus was crucified and put to death by the hand of lawless men (Acts 2:23). Other refs.: Luke 22:2; Acts 9:29; 10:39; 12:2; 13:28; 26:10. All other refs.: KILL <337>, TAKE <337>.

[7] **to put to death: *apagō*** [verb: ἀπάγω <520>]; **from *apo*: from, and *agō*: to lead; lit.: to lead elsewhere ▶ To take away to punish, to execute** > Herod commanded that the guards should be put to death {executed, led away to execution} (Acts 12:19). All other refs.: BRING <520>, CARRY <520>, LEAD (verb) <520>, TAKE <520>.

[8] **to put to death, to deliver to death: *thanatoō*** [verb: θανατόω <2289>]; **from *thanatos*: see [1] ▶ To kill; also transl.: to cause to put to death** > The verb is used in regard to Jesus (Matt. 26:59; 27:1; Mark 14:55), relatives (Matt. 10:21; Mark 13:12), disciples (Luke 21:16), and Christians (Rom. 8:13 {to mortify}, 36 {to face death}). All other refs.: KILL <2289>.

[9] **to put to death: *nekroō*** [verb: νεκρόω <3499>]; **from *nekros*: dead ▶ To mortify** > The spiritual application of putting one's members to death {to consider them as dead} is to refrain from allowing them to behave in a way leading to sexual immorality, uncleanness, inordinate passion, evil desire, and other forms of sin (Col. 3:5). Other refs.: Rom. 4:19; Heb. 11:12; see DEAD <3499>. ¶

– [10] Matt. 14:5; Mark 6:19; 14:1; Luke 18:33; John 11:53; 12:10; 18:31; Acts 3:15; Eph. 2:16 → to put to death → KILL <615> [11] Matt. 15:4; Mark 7:10; Luke 7:2 → to be put to death, at the point of death → DIE <5053> [12] Matt. 21:41; 27:20 → to put to death → PERISH <622> [13] Mark 5:23 → at the point of death → at extremity → EXTREMITY <2079> [14] Luke 15:17 → to starve to death → lit.: to perish with hunger → HUNGER (noun) <3042> [15] John 4:47; 1 Cor. 15:31; Heb. 11:37 → at the point of death, to put to death, to face death → DIE <599> [16] Acts 5:30 → to put to death → MURDER (verb) <1315> [17] Acts 26:21 → to put to death → KILL <1315> [18] 2 Cor. 4:10 → DYING <3500> [19] 1 Thes. 4:13; Heb. 12:20 → "in death," "to death" added in Engl. [20] Heb. 9:17 → at death → after men are dead → DEAD

<3498> [21] Jas. 5:6 → to put to death → MURDER (verb) <5407>.

DEATH-BRINGING – Jas. 3:8 → DEADLY <2287>.

DEBASED – Rom. 1:28 → WORTHLESS <96>.

DEBATE (noun) – [1] Acts 15:2, 7 → DISPUTE (noun) <2214> [2] Rom. 1:29; 2 Cor. 12:20 → STRIFE <2054>.

DEBATE (verb) – [1] Mark 1:27 → QUESTION (verb) <4802> [2] Mark 12:28; Acts 9:29 → DISPUTE (verb) <4802> [3] Acts 17:18 → they began to debate with him → they met him → MEET (verb) <4820>.

DEBATER – 1 Cor. 1:20 → DISPUTER <4804>.

DEBAUCHERY – [1] Luke 15:13 → in debauchery → prodigally → PRODIGAL <811> [2] Rom. 13:13; 2 Cor. 12:21; Gal. 5:19; Eph. 4:19; 1 Pet. 4:3 → LEWDNESS <766> [3] Eph. 5:18; Titus 1:6; 1 Pet. 4:4 → DISSIPATION <810>.

DEBT – [1] ***daneion*** [neut. noun: δάνειον <1156>]; **from *danos*: gift, loan ► What one owes to another one lending money** > The master of a servant forgave him his debt {the loan} (Matt. 18:27). ¶

[2] ***opheilē*** [fem. noun: ὀφειλή <3782>]; **from *opheilō*: see [4] ► What one owes** > The master of a servant reminded him that he had forgiven him all his debt (Matt. 18:32). Other refs.: Rom. 13:7; 1 Cor. 7:3; see DUE <3782>. ¶

[3] ***opheilēma*** [neut. noun: ὀφείλημα <3783>]; **from *opheilō*: see [4] ► What one owes, offense** > Jesus taught His disciples to pray, asking God to forgive them their debts (Matt. 6:12). To him who works, the reward is not counted as a grace but as debt {an obligation, what is due} (Rom. 4:4). ¶

[4] **to owe: *opheilō*** [verb: ὀφείλω <3784>] ► **To have a financial obligation** > A servant threw a fellow servant into prison until he should pay his debt (lit.: what was owed) (Matt. 18:30). All other refs.: DEBTOR <3784>, DUE <3784>, INDEBTED (BE) <3784>, OUGHT <3784>, OWE <3784>.

– [5] Matt. 18:25 → to repay the debt → lit.: to make payment → PAYMENT <591> [6] Luke 7:42, 43 → to forgive the debt → FORGIVE <5483>.

DEBTOR – [1] ***opheiletēs*** [masc. noun: ὀφειλέτης <3781>]; **from *opheilō*: to owe ► One who owes something to someone else; also transl.: under obligation** > Jesus uses this word in giving His disciples instructions on prayer (Matt. 6:12). Paul was debtor {was obligated} to many, feeling the obligation to preach the gospel to them (Rom. 1:14). Christians are debtors {have an obligation}, not to the flesh, to live according to it, but they must put to death the deeds of the body (Rom. 8:12; see v. 13). Christians among the Gentiles were debtors of {indebted to, owed to} the believers in Jerusalem; it was their duty to minister to them in material things (Rom. 15:27). Paul testified that any man who accepts circumcision is debtor {obligated} to keep the whole law (Gal. 5:3). All other refs.: OWE <3781>, SINNER <3781>.

[2] ***chreōpheiletēs*** [masc. noun: χρεωφειλέτης <5533>]; **from *chraō*: to lend, or *chreos*: loan, and *opheiletēs*: debtor; also spelled: *chreopheiletēs* ► One who has a debt, debt-ower; stronger than [1]** > Jesus told two parables about debtors (Luke 7:41; 16:5). ¶

[3] **to be a debtor: *opheilō*** [verb: ὀφείλω <3784>] ► **To owe, to be under obligation; also transl.: to be obliged, to be obligated** > Whoever will swear by the gold of the temple is a debtor {is bound by his oath} (Matt. 23:16), as likewise whoever will swear by the gift that is on the altar (v. 18 {to be guilty}). Jesus told His apostles that they were unprofitable (or: unworthy) bondmen, in the sense that they had done what was their duty (or: what they were debtors) to do (Luke 17:10). All other refs.: DEBT <3784>, DUE <3784>, INDEBTED (BE) <3784>, OUGHT <3784>, OWE <3784>.

DECAPOLIS – ***Dekapolis*** [fem. name: Δεκάπολις <1179>]: **ten cities ► Roman**

region composed of a group of ten cities east of Samaria and southeast of Galilee > Great crowds from this region followed Jesus (Matt. 4:25). The demoniac possessed by Legion, after having been healed by Jesus, proclaimed in Decapolis all that Jesus had done for him (Mark 5:20). Jesus also healed a deaf man in this region (Mark 7:31). ¶

DECAY (noun) – [1] Acts 2:27, 31; 13:34–37 → CORRUPTION <1312> [2] Rom. 8:21 → CORRUPTION <5356>.

DECAY (verb) – [1] 2 Cor. 4:16 → PERISH <1311> [2] Heb. 8:13 → to grow old → OLD <3822>.

DECEASE (noun) – ***exodos*** [fem. noun: ἔξοδος <1841>]; **from *ek*: out, and *hodos*: way ▶ Departure from earthly life; a way out >** Moses and Elijah spoke of the decease {departure} Jesus was about to accomplish (Luke 9:31). Peter was careful to ensure that Christians should always have a reminder of his teachings after his decease {departure} (2 Pet. 1:15). Other ref.: Heb. 11:22; see DEPARTURE <1841>. ¶

DECEASE (verb) – Matt. 22:25 → DIE <5053>.

DECEIT – [1] ***apatē*** [fem. noun: ἀπάτη <539>] **▶ Delusion, seduction >** With regard to their former manner of living, the Ephesians were to have put off the old man which corrupts itself according to lusts of deceit {deceitful lusts} (Eph. 4:22). The Colossians were to beware so there would be no one leading them away as a prey through philosophy and vain deceit {deception} according to the teaching of men (Col. 2:8). All other refs.: DECEITFULNESS <539>.

[2] ***dolos*** [masc. noun: δόλος <1388>]; ***dolus*, in Lat.: trick, ruse, bad faith ▶ Cunning, trickery; also transl.: guile, lie >** Deceit comes forth from the heart of men (Mark 7:22). There was no deceit in Nathanael (John 1:47). Elymas was full of all deceit (Acts 13:10). Men living in iniquity are full of deceit (Rom. 1:29). Paul's opponents charged him of catching the Corinthians by trickery (2 Cor. 12:16), which he refutes in the verses that follow. Peter exhorts Christians to put aside all deceit (1 Pet. 2:1). There was no deceit found in the mouth of Jesus (1 Pet. 2:22). He who would love life and see good days is to keep his lips from speaking deceit (1 Pet. 3:10). The one hundred forty-four thousand of Revelation 14 are irreproachable, for in their mouths was found no deceit (v. 5). All other refs.: SUBTLETY <1388>.

[3] **to practice deceit, to use deceit: *dolioō*** [verb: δολιόω <1387>]; **from *dolos*: see [2] ▶ To deceive, to trick >** Men have used deceit with their tongues (Rom. 3:13). ¶

[4] ***panourgia*** [fem. noun: πανουργία <3834>]; **from *panourgeō*: to act deceitfully, which is from *panourgos*: crafty, which is from *pan*: all, and *ergon*: deed, work; lit.: capable of everything ▶ Disloyal, unscrupulous, sly conduct >** Jesus perceived the deceit {craftiness, trickery, duplicity} of the spies who sought to deliver Him up (Luke 20:23). All other refs.: CRAFTINESS <3834>, CUNNING <3834>.

– [5] 1 Thes. 2:3 → ERROR <4106>.

DECEITFUL – [1] ***dolios*** [adj.: δόλιος <1386>]; **from *dolioō*: to deceive, which is from *dolos*: deceit, trickery; *dolus*, in Lat.: trick, ruse, bad faith ▶ Who is a cheater, deceiver >** Paul speaks of men who are false apostles, deceitful workers, transforming themselves into apostles of Christ (2 Cor. 11:13). ¶

[2] **deceit: *planē*** [fem. noun: πλάνη <4106>] **▶ Wandering, delusion >** There are men who are capable of deceitful plotting {who lie in wait to deceive, have a view to systematized error} (lit.: of plotting of deceit) (Eph. 4:14). All other refs.: DECEPTION <4106>, DELUSION <4106>, ERROR <4106>.

– [3] Eph. 4:22 → lit.: of deceit → DECEIT <539> [4] 1 Tim. 4:1 → DECEIVER <4108> [5] Rev. 21:27 → LIE (noun) <5579>.

DECEITFULLY – 2 Cor. 4:2 → to handle deceitfully → FALSIFY <1389>.

DECEITFULNESS – ***apatē*** [fem. noun: ἀπάτη <539>] ▶ **Deceit, seduction, temptation; also transl.: deceiving, deception, pleasure** > The deceitfulness of riches may choke the word (Matt. 13:22; Mark 4:19). The coming of the antichrist will be in all deceitfulness {deceivableness} of unrighteousness for those who perish (2 Thes. 2:10). We ought to exhort one another so that none of us may be hardened by the deceitfulness of sin (Heb. 3:13). Peter speaks of those who revel in their own deceitfulness (2 Pet. 2:13). All other refs.: DECEIT <539>.

DECEIVABLENESS – 2 Thes. 2:10 → DECEITFULNESS <539>.

DECEIVE – [1] ***apataō*** [verb: ἀπατάω <538>]; **from *apatē*: deceitfulness** ▶ **To mislead into error, to seduce** > Christians should let no one deceive them with vain words (Eph. 5:6). Adam was not deceived (*apataō*); but the woman, having been deceived (*exapataō*), fell into transgression (1 Tim. 2:14). If anyone thinks himself to be religious and yet does not bridle his tongue, but deceives his own heart, this man's religion is vain (Jas. 1:26). ¶

[2] ***exapataō*** [verb: ἐξαπατάω <1818>]; **from *ek*: intens., and *apataō*: see [1]** ▶ **To completely mislead, to seduce entirely** > Paul speaks of sin which, having found an occasion by the commandment, deceived the man in Romans 7 and by it killed him (v. 11). Paul speaks of those who deceive the hearts of the unsuspecting (Rom. 16:18). The serpent deceived {beguiled} Eve (2 Cor. 11:3). The Thessalonians were to let no one deceive them in any way concerning the coming of the Lord Jesus Christ (2 Thes. 2:3). Other refs.: 1 Cor. 3:18; 1 Tim. 2:14b (see [1]). ¶

[3] ***phrenapataō*** [verb: φρεναπατάω <5422>]; **from *phrēn*: mind, and *apataō*: see [1]** ▶ **To mislead, to delude, to seduce the mind** > If anyone thinks he is something when he is nothing, he deceives himself (Gal. 6:3). ¶

[4] ***paralogizomai*** [verb: παραλογίζομαι <3884>]; **from *para*: aside, and *logizomai*: to reason, to judge** ▶ **To take in by false reasonings; also transl.: to beguile, to delude** > The Colossians were to let no one deceive them with persuasive words (Col. 2:4). James says to be a doer of the word, and not a hearer only, deceiving oneself (Jas. 1:22). ¶

[5] ***planaō*** [verb: πλανάω <4105>]; **from *planē*: seduction, wandering** ▶ **To lead into error, to seduce; also transl.: to delude, to lead astray, to mislead** > Jesus uses this verb in regard to events preceding His coming to establish His kingdom (Matt. 24:4, 5, 11, 24; Mark 13:5, 6; Luke 21:8). It was said that Jesus deceived the crowd (John 7:12, 47). Paul says not to be deceived, the unrighteous will not inherit the kingdom of God (1 Cor. 6:9), for bad company corrupts good morals (1 Cor. 15:33). He also says not to be deceived, for God is not mocked: whatever a man sows, that also he will reap (Gal. 6:7). Wicked men and imposters will go from bad to worse, deceiving and being deceived (2 Tim. 3:13a, b). If we say we are without sin, we deceive ourselves (1 John 1:8). It is Satan who deceives the whole habitable world (Rev. 12:9); he will be cast into the abyss so that he should not anymore deceive the nations during one thousand years (20:3). The false prophet will deceive those who dwell on the earth (Rev. 13:14); he will deceive those who receive the mark of the beast (19:20). All other refs.: ASTRAY <4105>, MISTAKEN (BE) <4105>, STRAY <4105>, WANDER <4105>.

[6] ***apoplanaō*** [verb: ἀποπλανάω <635>]; **from *apo*: from, and *planaō*: see [5]** ▶ **To mislead, to lead into error** > False christs and false prophets will show signs and wonders to deceive {to lead astray, to seduce}, if that were possible, even the elect (Mark 13:22). Other ref.: 1 Tim. 6:10; see STRAY <635>. ¶

– [7] Matt. 2:16 → MOCK <1702> [8] Rom. 3:13 → to keep deceiving → lit.: to practice deceit → DECEIT <1387> [9] Eph. 4:14 → DECEITFUL <4106> [10] 1 Thes. 2:3 → attempt to deceive → SUBTLETY <1388> [11] 2 Thes. 2:10 → evil that deceives → lit.: deceitfulness of evil → DECEITFULNESS <539>.

DECEIVER – [1] ***planos*** [adj. and adj. used as noun: πλάνος <4108>]; **from *planaō*: to deceive, to mislead ► Impostor, seducer** > Jesus was called a deceiver (Matt. 27:63). Paul had been regarded as a deceiver (2 Cor. 6:8). In the latter times some will apostatize from the faith, giving their mind to deceiving {deceitful, seducing} spirits and teachings of demons (1 Tim. 4:1). Those who do not confess Jesus Christ coming in the flesh are deceivers and antichrists (2 John 7a, b). ¶

[2] ***phrenapatēs*** [masc. noun: φρεναπάτης <5423>]; **from *phrenapataō*: to deceive the mind, which is from *phrēn*: mind, and *apataō*: to mislead, which is from *apatē*: deceitfulness, delusion ► One who misleads, seducer** > Paul warns Titus against numerous disorderly vain speakers and deceivers (lit.: deceivers of people's minds) (Titus 1:10). ¶

– [3] 2 Tim. 3:13 → IMPOSTOR <1114> [4] Rev. 12:9 → who deceives → DECEIVE <4105>.

DECEIVING – [1] 1 Tim. 4:1 → DECEIVER <4108> [2] 2 Pet. 2:13 → DECEITFULNESS <539>.

DECENCY – 1 Tim. 2:9 → MODESTY <127>.

DECENT – 1 Tim. 2:9 → decent deportment → modest apparel → APPAREL <2887>.

DECENTLY – ***euschēmonōs*** [adv.: εὐσχημόνως <2156>]; **from *euschēmōn*: honorable, which is from *eu*: well, and *schēma*: outward manner of being ► Honorably, appropriately** > In the church, all things must be done decently {properly, comelily, in a fitting way} and with order (1 Cor. 14:40). Other refs.: Rom. 13:13; 1 Thes. 4:12; see HONESTLY <2156>, PROPERLY <2156>.

DECEPTION – [1] ***planē*** [fem. noun: πλάνη <4106>] ► **a. Deceit, imposture** > When Jesus died, the chief priests and the Pharisees were fearful that His disciples would steal His body and say that He was risen, so the last deception {error} would be worse than the first (Matt. 27:64). **b. Moving away, deviation of conduct** > Having committed what is shameful, some men receive in themselves the penalty of their deception {error, perversion} (Rom. 1:27). The word is also transl. "error" in Jas. 5:20. All other refs.: DECEITFUL <4106>, DELUSION <4106>, ERROR <4106>.

– [2] 2 Cor. 4:2 → CRAFTINESS <3834> [3] Col. 2:8 → DECEIT <539> [4] 2 Thes. 2:10; 2 Pet. 2:13 → DECEITFULNESS <539> [5] Titus 1:10 → people full of deception → DECEIVER <5423>.

DECEPTIVE – [1] Col. 2:8 → hollow and deceptive philosophy → lit.: philosophy and vain deceit → DECEIT <539> [2] 2 Pet. 2:3 → FEIGNED <4112>.

DECIDE – [1] ***krinō*** [verb: κρίνω <2919>] ► **To conclude, to determine, to resolve** > Paul had decided {had thought it desirable, had determined} to sail past Ephesus (Acts 20:16). The brothers in Jerusalem had decided {concluded} that the Christians among the Gentiles did not have to observe the same things as the Jews (Acts 21:25). It was decided {determined} that Paul would sail to Italy (Acts 27:1). Festus had decided to send Paul to Augustus (Acts 25:25). Paul had decided to winter at Nicopolis (Titus 3:12). All other refs.: see entries in Lexicon at <2919>.

– [2] Matt. 27:7 → COUNSEL (noun) <4824> [3] Luke 1:3 → with this in mind, I decided → lit.: it has seemed good to me [4] Luke 16:4 → KNOW <1097> [5] Luke 23:24 → to give sentence → SENTENCE <1948> [6] John 9:22 → AGREE <4934> [7] Acts 4:28 → to decide beforehand → to determine before → DETERMINE <4309> [8] Acts 11:29 → DETERMINE <3724> [9] Acts 15:22 → THINK <1380> [10] Acts 19:21 → PURPOSE (verb) <5087> [11] Acts 24:22 → to make a decision → DECISION <1231> [12] Acts 27:12 → ADVISE <1014> [13] Acts 27:39 → RESOLVE (verb) <1011> [14] 1 Cor. 6:5 → JUDGE (verb) <1252> [15] 2 Cor. 9:7 → PURPOSE (verb) <4255>.

DECISION – [1] ***diagnōsis*** [fem. noun: διάγνωσις <1233>]; **from *diaginōskō*: see** [2] **▶ Hearing, examination** > Paul had appealed to be kept for the decision {cognizance} of Augustus (Nero at that time) (Acts 25:21). ¶

[2] **to make a decision: *diaginōskō*** [verb: διαγινώσκω <1231>]; **from *dia*: indicates separation (intens.), and *ginōskō*: to know ▶ To examine; also transl.: to decide** > Felix would make a decision {determine, know the uttermost} concerning the case of Paul (Acts 24:22). The verb is transl. "to determine" in Acts 23:15. ¶

– [3] Matt. 27:1; 28:12; Mark 15:1 → COUNSEL (noun) <4824> [4] Mark 14:64 → to be the decision → THINK <5316> [5] Luke 23:51 → COUNSEL (noun) <1012> [6] John 1:13 → human decision → lit.: the will of the flesh [7] Acts 16:4 → ORDINANCE <1378> [8] Acts 21:25 → our decision → lit.: having decided → DECIDE <2919>.

DECK – Rev. 17:4; 18:16 → to have ornaments → ORNAMENT <5558>.

DECLARATION – Luke 1:1 → ACCOUNT (noun) <1335>.

DECLARE – [1] ***anangellō*** [verb: ἀναγγέλλω <312>]; **from *ana*: upon (intens.), and *angellō*: to bring a message, to tell ▶ To announce, to communicate, to make known** > Jesus would declare {show} plainly to His disciples concerning the Father (John 16:25b). Paul had not shunned to declare {proclaim} all the counsel of God to the Ephesians (Acts 20:27). John declares that God is light (1 John 1:5). All other refs.: see entries in Lexicon at <312>.

[2] ***apangellō*** [verb: ἀπαγγέλλω <518>]; **from *apo*: from (intens.), and *angellō*: to bring a message, to tell ▶ To announce, to publish, to preach** > A woman declared to {told} Jesus the reason she had touched Him and how she was healed immediately (Luke 8:47). The Lord says that He will declare {proclaim} the name of God to His brothers (Heb. 2:12). All other refs.: RELATE <518>, REPORT (verb) <518>, SHOW (verb) <518>, TELL <518>.

[3] ***diangellō*** [verb: διαγγέλλω <1229>]; **from *dia*: through, and *angellō*: to bring a message, to tell ▶ To publicize fully, to announce everywhere** > The name of God is to be declared {proclaimed} in all the earth (Rom. 9:17). Other refs.: Luke 9:60; Acts 21:26; see PREACH <1229>, SIGNIFY <1229>. ¶

[4] ***dēloō*** [verb: δηλόω <1213>]; **from *dēlos*: certain, evident ▶ To manifest, to make known, to inform, to show** > The day will declare {bring to light} the work of each one (1 Cor. 3:13). Epaphras had declared {had told of} the love of the Colossians in the Spirit (Col. 1:8). It had been declared to Paul {Paul was informed} that there were strifes among the Corinthians (1 Cor. 1:11). All other refs.: INDICATE <1213>, SHOW (verb) <1213>.

[5] ***exēgeomai*** [verb: ἐξηγέομαι <1834>]; **from *ek*: out (intens.), and *hēgeomai*: to lead, to tell ▶ To reveal, to make known** > The only begotten Son, who is in the bosom of the Father, has declared {explained} Him (John 1:18). All other refs.: RELATE <1834>.

[6] ***legō*** [verb: λέγω <3004>] **▶ To tell, to say** > David declared {described, spoke of} the blessedness of the man to whom God reckons righteousness without works (Rom. 4:6). Other refs.: SAY <3004>, SPEAK <3004>.

[7] ***homologeō*** [verb: ὁμολογέω <3670>]; **from *homologos*: assenting, which is from *homos*: same, and *legō*: to say ▶ To maintain, to assert** > Jesus will declare {avow, profess, tell plainly} that He never knew some who have practiced lawlessness (Matt. 7:23). All other refs.: CONFESS <3670>.

– [8] Matt. 11:25; Acts 10:46 → ANSWER (verb) <611> [9] Matt. 13:36; 15:15 → EXPOUND <5419> [10] Matt. 15:5 → SPEAK <2036> [11] Luke 7:29 → to declare just → JUSTIFY <1344> [12] John 16:13 → SHOW (verb) <312> [13] John 17:26a, b; 1 Cor. 15:1; Col. 4:7 → to make known → KNOW <1107> [14] Acts 2:11; 11:14; 1 Cor. 2:7; Col. 4:3; 1 Thes. 2:2; Titus 2:15; Heb. 2:2, 3; 9:19 → SPEAK <2980>

15 Acts 8:33; 9:27; 12:17 → RELATE <1334> 16 Acts 13:41; 15:3 → RELATE <1555> 17 Acts 17:23; 1 Cor. 2:1 → PREACH <2605> 18 Acts 20:21 → TESTIFY <1263> 19 Acts 20:26; Gal. 5:3 → TESTIFY <3143> 20 Acts 25:14 → to lay before → LAY <394> 21 Acts 25:24 → to declare loudly → CRY (verb) <1916> 22 Rom. 3:25, 26 → DEMONSTRATE <1732> 23 2 Cor. 3:3 → to be manifestly declared → lit.: to be manifested → MANIFEST (verb) <5319> 24 Gal. 3:22 → to shut up → SHUT <4788> 25 Heb. 11:14 → to declare plainly → PLAINLY <1718> 26 1 Pet. 2:9 → to show forth → SHOW (verb) <1804> 27 1 Pet. 5:12 → TESTIFY <1957>.

DECLINE[1] – Luke 9:12; 24:29 → to wear away → WEAR <2827>.

DECLINE[2] – 1 Acts 18:20 → to not consent → CONSENT (verb) <1962> 2 1 Tim. 5:11 → REFUSE (verb) <3868> 3 Heb. 12:19 → BEG <3868>.

DECORATE – Matt. 23:29; Rev. 21:19 → ADORN <2885>.

DECOROUS – 1 Tim. 3:2 → RESPECTABLE <2887>.

DECREASE – ***elattoō*** [verb: ἐλαττόω <1642>]; **from *elattōn*: lesser, smaller ▶ To reduce, to diminish** > Jesus had to increase, but John the Baptist to decrease {become less} (John 3:30). Other refs.: Heb. 2:7, 9 (to make lower); see LOWER (adj.) <1642>. ¶

DECREE (noun) – 1 ***dogma*** [neut. noun: δόγμα <1378>]; **from *dokeō*: to think, to appear ▶ Official order proclaimed by an authority, decision, edict** > A decree went out by Caesar Augustus that a registered census should be made of all the habitable world (Luke 2:1). All other refs.: ORDINANCE <1378>.
– 2 Luke 1:6 → ORDINANCE <1345> 3 1 Cor. 2:7 → PREDESTINE <4309> 4 Col. 2:20 → to submit to decrees → to subject to ordinances → ORDINANCE <1379>.

DECREE (verb) – 1 Luke 22:22 → DETERMINE <3724> 2 1 Cor. 7:37 → DETERMINE <2919>.

DEDICATE – 1 Heb. 9:18 → INAUGURATE <1457> 2 Heb. 10:20 → CONSECRATE <1457>.

DEDICATION – John 10:22 → FEAST OF DEDICATION <1456>.

DEED – 1 ***ergon*** [neut. noun: ἔργον <2041>]; **from *ergō*: to work; lit.: work ▶ Action, work** > Moses was mighty in his words and deeds (Acts 7:22). The man who had done this deed, i.e., who had committed an act of sexual immorality, should have been removed from the church in Corinth (1 Cor. 5:2). Lot tormented his righteous soul with the lawless deeds he witnessed in Sodom and Gomorrah (2 Pet. 2:8). The children of God must love in deed and in truth (1 John 3:18). All other refs.: ACTION <2041>, WORK (noun) <2041>.
2 **good deed: *euergesia*** [fem. noun: εὐεργεσία <2108>]; **from *euergetēs*: benefactor, which is from *eu*: good, and *ergon*: see 1 Beneficial work** > Peter uses this word {benefit, act of kindness} in Acts 4:9. Other ref.: 1 Tim. 6:2; see SERVICE <2108>. ¶
3 ***praxis*** [fem. noun: πρᾶξις <4234>]; **from *prassō*: to do, to execute ▶ What one does; also transl.: practice, action** > Joseph of Arimathea had not assented to the counsel and deed of those who had Jesus crucified (Luke 23:51). Many of those who believed came confessing and declaring their deeds (Acts 19:18). The Christians have put off the old man with his deeds (Col. 3:9). The Christians live if they put to death the deeds {misdeeds} of the body by the Spirit (Rom. 8:13). All other refs.: FUNCTION (noun) <4234>, WORK (noun) <4234>.
– 4 Matt. 6:1 → charitable deeds → ALMS <1343> 5 Matt. 6:2–4; Acts 9:36 → charitable deeds → ALMS <1654> 6 Matt. 19:16; Phm. 14 → good deed → GOOD (adj. and noun) <18> 7 Mark 7:22

→ deed of coveting → COVETOUSNESS <4124> [8] Luke 1:51 → mighty deeds → STRENGTH <2904> [9] Luke 23:41 → of our deeds → lit.: of what we have done → DO <4238> [10] Luke 23:47 → in very deed → CERTAINLY <3689> [11] Acts 2:11 → mighty deed → wonderful work → WONDERFUL <3167> [12] Acts 5:4 → THING <4229> [13] Acts 24:2 → very worthy deeds → excellent measures → MEASURE (noun) <2735> [14] 2 Cor. 12:12 → mighty deed → MIRACLE <1411> [15] Jas. 1:25 → DOING <4162> [16] Rev. 19:8 → righteous deeds → righteousnesses → RIGHTEOUS <1345>.

DEEM – [1] John 5:31 → is not deemed true → lit.: is not true [2] Acts 27:27 → SUPPOSE <5282> [3] 1 Cor. 12:23 → THINK <1380>.

DEEP (adj.) – [1] ***bathus*** [adj.: βαθύς <901>] ► **a. Having a bottom which is distant** > The well of Sychar was deep (John 4:11). **b. Evoking profoundness, profundity** > Eutychus was sinking into a deep sleep (Acts 20:9). Other refs.: Luke 24:1; see MORNING <901>; Rev. 2:24 in some mss.: see DEPTH <899>. ¶
– [2] Rom. 8:26 → too deep for words → which cannot be uttered → UTTER (verb) <215> [3] 1 Cor. 2:10; 2 Cor. 8:2 → DEPTH <899>.

DEEP (noun) – [1] ***bathos*** [neut. noun: βάθος <899>]; **from *bathus*: deep ► Place far below the surface, deep water** > Jesus told Simon to draw out into the deep {deep water} and let down his nets for a catch (Luke 5:4). All other refs.: DEPTH <899>.
[2] ***buthos*** [masc. noun: βυθός <1037>] ► **Abyss, deep sea** > Paul had spent a night and day in the deep {open sea} (2 Cor. 11:25). ¶
– [3] Luke 6:48 → to dig deep → DIG <900> [4] Luke 8:31; Rom. 10:7 → BOTTOMLESS <12> [5] 2 Cor. 7:7 → deep sorrow → MOURNING <3602>.

DEEPEN – Phm. 6 → in deepening your understanding → through the knowledge → KNOWLEDGE <1922>.

DEEPLY – [1] Matt. 18:31 → GREATLY <4970> [2] Acts 8:2 → mourned deeply → lit.: made great lamentations → LAMENTATION <2870> [3] 1 Pet. 1:22 → FERVENTLY <1619> [4] 1 Pet. 4:8 → to love deeply → lit.: to have fervent love → FERVENT <1618>.

DEFAME – [1] ***blasphēmeō*** [verb: βλασφημέω <987>]; **from *blasphēmos*: blasphēmous, which is poss. from *blaptō*: to damage, and *phēmē*: reputation ► To lie by denouncing an imaginary or unproved evil; to slander, to libel** > Paul was defamed {slandered} (1 Cor. 4:13). Some mss. have *dusphēmeō* [verb: δυσφημέω <1425a>]. All other refs.: see entries in Lexicon at <987>.
– [2] 1 Pet. 3:16 → SPEAK AGAINST <2635>.

DEFEAT (noun) – [1] 1 Cor. 6:7 → FAULT <2275> [2] Heb. 7:1 → SLAUGHTER (noun) <2871>.

DEFEAT (verb) – Rev. 12:8 → to be strong enough → STRONG (adj.) <2480>.

DEFECT – 1 Pet. 1:19 → without defect → without spot → SPOT <784>.

DEFENCE – See DEFENSE.

DEFEND – [1] ***amunomai*: middle voice of *amunō*** [verb: ἀμύνω <292>] ► **To become involved in protecting, helping someone** > Moses defended and avenged an Israelite who was being oppressed (Acts 7:24). ¶
[2] **to defend oneself: *apologeomai*** [verb: ἀπολογέομαι <626>]; **from *apo*: from, and *logos*: word, speech ► To plead for oneself, to vindicate oneself** > The Corinthians had long been supposing that Paul was defending {was excusing} himself to them (2 Cor. 12:19). All other refs.: ANSWER (verb) <626>, DEFENSE <626>, EXCUSE (verb) <626>.
– [3] Phil. 1:7 → lit.: the defense → DEFENSE <627>.

DEFENSE – [1] ***apologia*** [fem. noun: ἀπολογία <627>]; **from *apologeomai*: see**

2; lit.: apology, justification ▶ Formal verbal, written reaction or vindication against an accusation, an attack** > Paul made his defense in Jerusalem to his Jewish brothers and fathers (Acts 22:1). He spoke of his defense {answer} as an apostle to people who were examining him (1 Cor. 9:3). In the defense and confirmation of {In defending and confirming} the gospel, the Philippians had all been partakers of grace with Paul (Phil. 1:7). He was set for the defense of the gospel (Phil. 1:16 or 17). At his first defense {answer}, no one stood with him (2 Tim. 4:16). All other refs.: ANSWER (noun) <627>, ANSWER (verb) <627>, EXCUSING <627>.

2 to make one's defense, to answer for one's defense: *apologeomai* [verb: ἀπολογέομαι <626>]; **from *apo*: from (intens.), and *logos*: word, speech; lit.: to plead for oneself ▶ To make an apology against an accusation, an attack** > Alexander was prevented from making his defense in Ephesus (Acts 19:33). In relation to Paul's apology before Felix (Acts 24:10) and Agrippa (26:1, 2), the verb is also transl.: to answer, to answer for oneself, to answer in one's defence. Paul answered for his defense {made his defense, said in his defense, spoke for himself} before Festus (Acts 26:24). All other refs.: ANSWER (verb) <626>, DEFEND <626>, EXCUSE (verb) <626>.
– 3 John 5:17 → "in his defense" added in Engl. 4 1 John 2:1 → one who speaks in the defense → ADVOCATE (noun) <3875>.

DEFER – 1 Matt. 22:16; Mark 12:14 → CARE <3199> 2 Acts 24:22 → ADJOURN <306>.

DEFIANT – Jude 15 → defiant words → hard things spoken → HARD <4642>.

DEFICIENT – 1 John 2:3 → to be deficient → LACK (verb) <5302> 2 Phil. 2:30 → what is deficient → what is lacking → LACK (noun) <5303>.

DEFILE – **1 *koinoō*** [verb: κοινόω <2840>]; **from *koinos*: common; lit.: to make common ▶ To make impure, to make unclean, to profane** > It is not what enters into the mouth which defiles a man; but what proceeds from the mouth, this defiles a man (Matt. 15:11a, b), for these things come out of the heart (v. 18); also Matt. 15:20a, b; Mark 7:15a, b, 18, 20, 23. Paul was accused of having defiled {profaned, polluted} the temple by bringing Greeks into it (Acts 21:28). The blood of animals was sprinkled on those who had been defiled (Heb. 9:13). Nothing that defiles {common} will enter into the new Jerusalem (Rev. 21:27; other mss.: *koinos*). Other refs.: Matt. 11:19; Acts 10:15; see COMMON <2840>. ¶

2 *miainō* [verb: μιαίνω <3392>] **▶ To contaminate, to infect** > The Jews did not enter into the Praetorium, so that they would not be defiled (John 18:28 {to avoid ceremonial uncleanness}). All things are pure to the pure; but to the defiled and unbelieving, nothing is pure, but both their mind and conscience are defiled (Titus 1:15a, b {to be corrupted}). A root of bitterness springing up may defile many (Heb. 12:15). Jude speaks of dreamers who defile the flesh (Jude 8 {to pollute}). ¶

3 *molunō* [verb: μολύνω <3435>] **▶ To contaminate, to soil, to stain** > Paul speaks of a weak conscience which is defiled by eating things sacrificed to idols (1 Cor. 8:7). A few people in Sardis had not defiled their garments (Rev. 3:4). There are those who have not been defiled with women; these are the ones who follow the Lamb wherever He goes (Rev. 14:4). Other ref.: Acts 5:38 in some mss. ¶

4 *spiloō* [verb: σπιλόω <4695>]; **from *spilos*: moral defect, spot, stain ▶ To soil, to stain** > The tongue defiles {corrupts} the whole body (Jas. 3:6). Those who are beloved in God are to snatch unbelievers out of the fire, hating even the garment defiled {polluted, spotted} by the flesh (Jude 23). ¶
– 5 1 Cor. 3:17a, b → DESTROY <5351> 6 1 Tim. 1:10 → one who defiles oneself with mankind → HOMOSEXUAL <733>.

DEFILED – 1 Mark 7:2 → UNCLEAN <2839> 2 Mark 7:5 → IMPURE <449>.

DEFILEMENT – [1] ***miasma*** [neut. noun: μίασμα <3393>]; **from *miainō*: to contaminate, to infect ▶ Corruption, what defiles morally** > Peter speaks of those who, after having escaped the defilements {pollutions} of the world through the knowledge of the Lord and Savior Jesus Christ, are again entangled in them (2 Pet. 2:20). ¶
[2] ***molusmos*** [neut. noun: μολυσμός <3436>]; **from *molunō*: to contaminate, to stain ▶ Corruption, impurity** > Paul exhorts to purify oneself from every defilement of {filthiness of, pollution of, thing that contaminates} flesh and spirit, perfecting holiness in the fear of God (2 Cor. 7:1). ¶

DEFILER – Jas. 3:6 → the defiler → lit.: it defiles → DEFILE <4695>.

DEFILING – 2 Pet. 2:10 → defiling passion → lust of uncleanness → UNCLEANNESS <3394>.

DEFINITE – [1] Acts 2:23 → DETERMINED <3724> [2] Acts 25:26 → CERTAINTY <804>.

DEFRAUD – [1] ***apostereō*** [verb: ἀποστερέω <650>]; **from *apo*: from, and *stereō*: to deprive, to rob ▶ To deprive someone of what legitimately belongs to that person, to do harm; also transl.: to cheat** > A commandment said not to defraud (Mark 10:19). Christians are to rather suffer wrong and let themselves be defrauded (1 Cor. 6:7), but the Corinthians did wrong and defrauded their brothers (v. 8). Other refs.: DEPRIVE <650>, KEEP (verb) <650>.
[2] **to defraud of the prize: *katabrabeuō*** [verb: καταβραβεύω <2603>]; **from *kata*: against, and *brabeuō*: to act as judge or referee at athletic games, which is from *brabeus*: judge, referee ▶ To disqualify, to cause to lose the reward; also transl.: to beguile of the reward, to cheat of the reward, to disqualify, to fraudulently deprive of the prize** > No one was to defraud the Colossians of their prize (Col. 2:18). ¶
– [3] Luke 19:8 → to accuse falsely → ACCUSE <4811> [4] 2 Cor. 7:2 → to make gain → CHEAT <4122> [5] 1 Thes. 4:6 → WRONG (verb) <4122>.

DEFY – Acts 17:7 → to do contrary → CONTRARY <4238> <561>.

DEGRADE – Rom. 1:24 → DISHONOR (verb) <818>.

DEGRADING – Rom. 1:26 → SHAMEFUL <819>.

DEGREE – [1] Luke 1:52; Jas. 1:9 → one of low degree → LOWLY <5011> [2] 2 Cor. 3:18 → from one degree of glory to another → lit.: from glory to glory [3] 1 Tim. 3:13 → STANDING <898>.

DEITY – [1] Acts 17:18 → GOD (other god) <1140> [2] Col. 2:9 → GODHEAD <2320>.

DELAY (noun) – [1] ***anabolē*** [fem. noun: ἀναβολή <311>]; **from *anaballō*: to defer, which is from *ana*: above, and *ballō*: to throw; lit.: what is thrown in the air ▶ Postponement, suspension** > Festus commanded that Paul be brought before him without any delay {without putting it off, without delaying} (Acts 25:17). ¶
[2] ***bradutēs*** [fem. noun: βραδύτης <1022>]; **from *bradus*: slow ▶ Slowness, tardiness** > Some calculate that there is delay concerning the coming of the Lord (2 Pet. 3:9). ¶
[3] ***chronos*** [masc. noun: χρόνος <5550>] ▶ **Time, determined duration of an event** > The angel swore that there should be no longer delay, but that the mystery of God would be completed with the heralding of the seventh angel (Rev. 10:6). Other refs.: TIME <5550>.
– [4] Luke 1:21 → at his delay → at his delaying → DELAY (verb) <5549> [5] Rom. 9:28 → to carry out without delay → to cut short → SHORT <4932>.

DELAY (verb) – [1] ***bradunō*** [verb: βραδύνω <1019>]; **from *bradus*: slow ▶ To be slow, to be held up; also transl.: to be slack, to**

tarry > Paul wrote to Timothy so that, if he was delayed, Timothy might know how to conduct himself in the house of God, the church of the living God (1 Tim. 3:15). The Lord does not delay His promise, but He is patient, not willing that any should perish, but that all should come to repentance (2 Pet. 3:9). ¶

[2] ***mellō*** [verb: μέλλω <3195>] ▶ **To be about to act, but to hesitate** > Saul was not to delay {to linger, to tarry, to wait}, but to rise and be baptized and have his sins washed away (Acts 22:16).

[3] ***okneō*** [verb: ὀκνέω <3635>]; **from *oknos*: hesitation, slowness** ▶ **To hesitate, to be slow to do something** > The disciples implored Peter not to delay coming to them (Acts 9:38). ¶

[4] ***chronizō*** [verb: χρονίζω <5549>]; **from *chronos*: time** ▶ **To be slow to do something, to take one's time** > The people wondered at the delaying of Zacharias in the temple (Luke 1:21 {to linger, to stay, to tarry}). A servant might say that his master delayed to come (Matt. 24:48; Luke 12:45). While the bridegroom was delaying, the virgins of the parable all slumbered and slept (Matt. 25:5). Yet a very little while, and He that comes will come and will not delay (Heb. 10:37). ¶

– [5] Luke 18:7 → to delay long → to have patience → PATIENCE <3114> [6] Acts 25:17 → DELAY (noun) <311>.

DELEGATION – ***presbeia*** [fem. noun: πρεσβεία <4242>]; **from *presbeuō*: to act as an ambassador, which is from *presbus*: older** ▶ **Deputation of people to communicate a message to someone important** > Jesus speaks of a king who sent a delegation {an embassy, an ambassage} to another king and asked for conditions of peace (Luke 14:32). The citizens of a nobleman sent a delegation {an embassy, a message} after him to say they would not have this man to reign over them (Luke 19:14). ¶

DELIBERATE (adj.) – Acts 2:23 → DETERMINED <3724>.

DELIBERATE (verb) – [1] Luke 14:31 → CONSIDER <1011> [2] John 16:19 → INQUIRE <2212>.

DELIBERATELY – Heb. 10:26 → VOLUNTARILY <1596>.

DELICACY – [1] Rev. 18:3 → LUXURY <4764> [2] Rev. 18:14 → delicacies → rich things → RICH <3045>.

DELICATE – ***malakos*** [adj.: μαλακός <3120>] ▶ **Fine to the touch, refined; also transl.: soft, fine** > The word is used in relation to garments (Matt. 11:8a, b; Luke 7:25). Other ref.: 1 Cor. 6:9; see HOMOSEXUAL <3120>. ¶

DELICATELY – Luke 7:25 → LUXURY <5172>.

DELICIOUSLY – Rev. 18:7, 9 → LUXURIOUSLY <4763>.

DELIGHT (noun) – [1] Matt. 3:17; 12:18; 17:5; Mark 1:11; Luke 3:22; 1 Thes. 2:8; 2 Pet. 1:17 → to find one's delight → to be well pleased → PLEASED (BE) <2106> [2] Mark 12:37 → with delight → GLADLY <2234> [3] Luke 1:14 → GLADNESS <20> [4] Rom. 1:32 → to have fellow delight → APPROVE <4909> [5] Rom. 10:1 → DESIRE <2107> [6] Rev. 12:12 → to be full of delight → REJOICE <2165>.

DELIGHT (verb) – [1] ***sunēdomai*** [verb: συνήδομαι <4913>]; **from *sun*: with, and *hēdomai*: to be pleased** ▶ **To rejoice (in oneself)** > The man of Romans 7 delights {joyfully concurs} in the law of God according to the inner man (v. 22). ¶

– [2] Matt. 12:18; 2 Cor. 12:10; 1 Thes. 2:8; 2 Thes. 2:12 → PLEASED (BE) <2106> [3] Col. 2:5 → REJOICE <5463>.

DELINEATION – 1 Tim. 1:16 → EXAMPLE <5296>.

DELIVER – [1] ***anadidōmi*** [verb: ἀναδίδωμι <325>]; **from *ana*: intens., and *didōmi*: to give; lit.: to give up** ▶ **To carry and hand**

over to someone, to present > A letter was delivered to the governor of Caesarea (Acts 23:33). ¶

2 ***epididōmi*** [verb: ἐπιδίδωμι <1929>]; **from *epi*: to (intens.), and *didōmi*: to give ▶ To give into the hands, to hand over >** Paul and other brothers delivered the letter of the apostles and elders to the brothers of Antioch (Acts 15:30). All other refs.: DRIVE <1929>, GIVE <1929>.

3 **to deliver, to deliver up: *paradidōmi*** [verb: παραδίδωμι <3860>]; **from *para*: over, and *didōmi*: to give ▶ a. To communicate, to teach; also transl.: to entrust, to hand down, to pass on >** The Jews invalidated the word of God by their tradition which they had delivered (Mark 7:13). Luke had undertaken to compose an account of things as they had been delivered by those who, from the beginning, had been eyewitnesses and servants of the Word (Luke 1:2). Moses had delivered {handed down} customs to the Jews (Acts 6:14). Paul and Timothy delivered the decrees decided upon by the apostles and elders (Acts 16:4). The Corinthians were keeping the directions just as Paul had delivered {had directed} them (1 Cor. 11:2). He had delivered to the Corinthians what he had received from the Lord (1 Cor. 11:23). He had delivered to them in the first place what also he had received concerning the death of Christ (1 Cor. 15:3), as well as His burial and resurrection (see v. 4). Some had turned from the holy commandment delivered to them (2 Pet. 2:21). **b. To give, to transmit; also transl.: to commit, to hand over >** All things have been delivered to Jesus by His Father (Matt. 11:27; Luke 10:22). In a parable, a man delivered his goods to his bondmen (Matt. 25:14 {to entrust}, 20, 22). The authority and the glory of the kingdoms of the earth have been delivered {given} to Satan (Luke 4:6). Judas had delivered Jesus to Pilate (John 19:11). Having bowed His head, Jesus delivered up His spirit (John 19:30). At the end, Christ will deliver the kingdom to God the Father (1 Cor. 15:24). Paul and other prisoners were delivered up to a centurion named Julius (Acts 27:1). The faith was once delivered to the saints (Jude 3). **c. To give up, to commit >** It is better for a person to be reconciled with an adversary than to be dragged to the judge, and the judge deliver him to the officer, and the officer cast him into prison (Luke 12:58). Saul dragged off Christians and delivered them up to {put them in} prison (Acts 8:3). All other refs.: see entries in Lexicon at <3860>.

4 **to deliver out, to deliver: *exaireō*** [verb: ἐξαιρέω <1807>]; **from *ek*: out, and *haireō*: to take, to choose ▶ To remove, to pull out; also transl.: to rescue, to take out >** God delivered Joseph out of all his tribulations (Acts 7:10). The Lord had come down to deliver {set free} His people from their ill treatment in Egypt (Acts 7:34). He had delivered Peter from the hand of Herod (Acts 12:11). Claudius Lysias had delivered Paul from the hands of the Jews (Acts 23:27). All other refs.: PLUCK <1807>, TAKE <1807>.

5 ***rhuomai*** [verb: ῥύομαι <4506>]; **from *rhuō*: to draw; *rhuma*: shelter, refuge; lit.: to pull out ▶ To save, to liberate; also transl.: to rescue >** Jesus taught his disciples to pray "Deliver from the evil one" (or: from evil) (Matt. 6:13). The robbers were defying God to deliver Jesus on the cross (Matt. 27:43). God had delivered the Jews from the hand of their enemies (Luke 1:74). The man of Romans 7 asks who will deliver him {set him free} from this body of death (v. 24). Paul was asking the Christians at Rome to pray that he might be delivered from those in Judea who did not believe (Rom. 15:31). God had delivered Paul from so great a death, and did deliver him; in Him he trusted that He would still deliver him (2 Cor. 1:10a–c). The Father has delivered Christians from the authority of darkness (Col. 1:13). Jesus delivers the Christians from the wrath to come (1 Thes. 1:10). Paul was asking to pray that he would be delivered from bad and evil men (2 Thes. 3:2). The Lord had delivered Paul out of all his persecutions (2 Tim. 3:11); Paul says that the Lord would deliver him from every wicked work (4:18). Paul was delivered out of the mouth of the lion (2 Tim. 4:17). God delivered righteous Lot (2 Pet. 2:7). The Lord knows how to deliver

the godly out of trial (2 Pet. 2:9). Other ref.: Rom. 11:26; see DELIVERER <4506>. ¶
[6] ***charizomai*** [verb: χαρίζομαι <5483>]; **from *charis*: grace, good will, which is from *chairō*: to rejoice; lit.: to surrender to the mercy ▶ To give up, to give over to, to hand over** > Paul uses this verb in relation to himself (Acts 25:11, 16). All other refs.: FORGIVE <5483>, GIVE <5483>, GRANT <5483>.
[7] **being delivered, delivered up: *ekdotos*** [adj.: ἔκδοτος <1560>]; **from *ek*: out, and *didōmi*: to give ▶ Remitted to the power or will of another** > Being delivered {Given up, Handed over} by the will of God, Jesus was put to death (Acts 2:23). ¶
– [8] Matt. 10:21; Mark 13:12 → to deliver to death → DEATH <2289> [9] Matt. 15:2; Mark 7:3, 5, 8, 9 → what has been delivered → lit.: the tradition → TRADITION <3862> [10] Matt. 27:58 → GIVE <591> [11] John 16:21 → to deliver the baby → to beget → BORN (BE) <1080> [12] Acts 7:25 → SALVATION <4991> [13] Rom. 7:25 → "who delivers me" added in Engl. [14] Rom. 8:21 → to make free, to set free → FREE (adj.) <1659> [15] Rom. 15:28 → to deliver to them what has been collected → lit.: to seal to them this fruit → SEAL (verb) <4972> [16] 2 Cor. 3:3 → letter delivered → epistle ministered → MINISTER (verb) <1247> [17] Heb. 2:15 → RELEASE (verb) <525> [18] Jude 5 → SAVE (verb) <4982>.

DELIVERANCE – [1] ***apolutrōsis*** [fem. noun: ἀπολύτρωσις <629>]; **from *apolutroō*: to let go after payment of a ransom, which is from *apo*: from, and *lutroō*: to redeem, which is from *lutron*: ransom paid to free someone ▶ Redemption, liberation after payment of a ransom** > O.T. people of faith were tortured, not having accepted deliverance {release, to be released} (Heb. 11:35). All other refs.: REDEMPTION <629>.
– [2] Luke 1:69, 71, 77; Acts 7:25 → SALVATION <4991> [3] Luke 4:18a → LIBERTY <859>.

DELIVERED – [1] Luke 4:18b → LIBERTY <859> [2] Acts 7:53 → delivered by angels → by the disposition of angels → DISPOSITION <1296>.

DELIVERED (BE) – [1] ***tiktō*** [verb: τίκτω <5088>] **▶ To give birth, to bring forth, to have a baby** > The verb is used for Elizabeth (Luke 1:57) and Mary (2:7). All other refs.: BIRTH <5088>.
– [2] Acts 2:23 → delivered → being delivered → DELIVER <1560>.

DELIVERER – [1] ***lutrōtēs*** [masc. noun: λυτρωτής <3086>]; **from *lutroō*: to redeem, which is from *lutron*: ransom, price paid to liberate captives ▶ Redeemer, liberator** > Moses was a ruler and a deliverer sent to Israel by God (Acts 7:35). ¶
[2] **to deliver: *rhuomai*** [verb: ῥύομαι <4506>]; **from *rhuō*: to draw; *rhuma*: shelter, refuge; lit.: to pull out ▶ To save, to liberate** > In Rom. 11:26, the Deliverer (lit.: the Delivering One) coming out of Zion is the Lord Jesus. All other refs.: DELIVER <4506>.
– [3] Acts 7:52 → deliverer up → BETRAYER <4273>.

DELUDE – [1] Col. 2:4; Jas. 1:22 → DECEIVE <3884> [2] Rev. 13:14 → DECEIVE <4105>.

DELUDING – 2 Thes. 2:11 → deluding influence → strong delusion → DELUSION <4106>.

DELUGE – ***katakluzō*** [verb: κατακλύζω <2626>]; **from *kata*: down (intens.), and *kluzō*: to flood, to wash; from which: cataclysm ▶ To cover completely with water; also transl.: to flood, to overflow** > During the flood, the world of Noah's time was destroyed, deluged by water (2 Pet. 3:6). ¶

DELUSION – **strong delusion: *energeia planēs*; *energeia*** [fem. noun: ἐνέργεια <1753>]; **from *energēs*: efficient, powerful, which is from *en*: in, and *ergon*: work; *planē*** [fem. noun: πλάνη <4106>]; **lit.: energy of error ▶ Powerful activity aimed at deceiving, misleading** > The expr. "strong delusion" {powerful delusion, working of error, deluding influence} describes the judgment of God on those who will have gone after the antichrist, that they should believe the lie (2 Thes. 2:11). All other refs. (*energeia*): WORKING (noun) <1753>. All other refs. (*planē*): DECEITFUL <4106>, DECEPTION <4106>, DELUSION <4106>, ERROR <4106>.

DEMAND (noun) – [1] Luke 23:24 → request → REQUEST (verb) <155> [2] Col. 2:14 → legal demands → ordinances against → ORDINANCE <1378> [3] 1 Thes. 2:6 → BURDEN (noun) <922>.

DEMAND (verb) – [1] **to demand, to demand back: *apaiteō*** [verb: ἀπαιτέω <523>]; **from *apo*: from, and *aiteō*: to ask ▶ To require from, to ask back** > Jesus told His disciples not to demand it back {to ask it back} from him who takes away what is theirs (Luke 6:30). The soul of the man who had accumulated many goods would be demanded from {required of him} that very night (Luke 12:20). Other ref.: 1 Pet. 3:15 in some mss.; other mss.: *aiteō*. ¶
– [2] Matt. 2:4 → INQUIRE <4441> [3] Matt. 16:13; John 16:19, 23a, 26, 30; 17:9a, b, 15; 18:19; et al. → ASK <2065> [4] Matt. 22:23, 35, 41; Mark 12:18; Luke 20:27; 23:3; John 18:21a in some mss.; et al. → ASK <1905> [5] Luke 12:48 → REQUIRE <2212> [6] Luke 12:48; 23:23 → ASK <154> [7] Luke 22:31 → ASK <1809> [8] Acts 21:33 → ASK <4441>.

DEMAS – ***Dēmas*** [masc. name: Δημᾶς <1214>]; **from Demeter, agrarian divinity ▶ Fellow worker of Paul** > Demas is one of those who sent greetings to Philemon (Phm. 24) and the church at Colossae (Col. 4:14). He later forsook the apostle, having loved the present age, i.e., the world (2 Tim. 4:10). ¶

DEMETRIUS – ***Dēmētrios*** [masc. name: Δημήτριος <1216>]; **from Demeter, agrarian divinity ▶ a. Ephesian who made silver shrines of the goddess Diana** > This Demetrius stirred up the other artisans against Paul, fearing that the temple of Diana (or: Artemis) would lose its prestige, which would have reduced their business (Acts 19:24, 38). **b. Believing man of the N.T.** > The apostle John wrote concerning a Demetrius who had a good report of all, and of the truth itself (3 John 12). ¶

DEMOLISH – [1] Rom. 11:3 → to dig down → DIG <2679> [2] 2 Cor. 10:4 → lit.: for the destruction → DESTRUCTION <2506> [3] 2 Cor. 10:5 → DESTROY <2507>.

DEMON – [1] ***daimonion*** [neut. of adj.: δαιμόνιον <1140>]; **from *daimonios*: that which is divine, which is from *daimōn*: demon, evil supernatural spirit ▶ For the pagans, they are inferior divinities, demigods; according to the word of God, they are fallen angels who have followed Satan in his fall; also transl.: devil** > Demons remain under the authority of Satan, their chief, awaiting the day when they will be thrown into the everlasting fire (see Matt. 25:41). Presently, demons are deceiving spirits inciting men to do evil (1 Tim. 4:1). We see men sacrificing to demons in the O.T. (e.g., Deut. 32:17). Jesus cast out demons on many occasions (Matt. 9:33; 17:18; Mark 1:34a, b, 39; 7:26, 29, 30; 16:9; Luke 9:42; 11:14a, b; 13:32). The twelve disciples also were casting out many demons (Mark 6:13; Luke 10:17), with the authority of the Lord (Matt. 10:8; Mark 3:15; Luke 9:1). Jesus was accused of casting out demons by the ruler of the demons (Matt. 9:34a, b; 12:24a, b, 27, 28; Mark 3:22a, b; Luke 4:33, 35; 8:2; 11:15a, b, 18–20), and of having a demon (John 7:20; 8:48, 49, 52; 10:20, 21). Demons believe that there is one God and they tremble (Jas. 2:19). Other refs.: Matt. 7:22; 11:18; Mark 9:38; 16:17; Luke 4:41; 7:33; 8:27, 30, 33, 35, 38; 9:49; 1 Cor. 10:20a, b, 21a, b; Rev. 9:20. Other ref.: Acts 17:18; see GOD (other god) <1140>. ¶
[2] ***daimōn*** [masc. or fem. noun: δαίμων <1142>] ▶ **See defin. of [1].** > Demons were beseeching Jesus to send them away into the herd of swine (Matt. 8:31; Mark 5:12 in some mss.). In a future day, spirits

of demons will incite the kings of the whole habitable world to make war against Christ (Rev. 16:14). Other refs.: Mark 5:12 in some mss.; Luke 8:29; Rev. 18:2. ¶

3 to be possessed by a demon, one who has a demon, demon-possessed: from *daimonizomai* [verb: δαιμονίζομαι <1139>]; **from *daimōn*: see 1 ► To be (a person) under the influence of a demon, which can lead that person astray mentally and physically; also transl.: demoniac** > The words of Jesus could not be those of one who is possessed by a demon (John 10:21). The daughter of a woman of Canaan was cruelly possessed by a demon {vexed with a devil, suffering from demon-possession} (Matt. 15:22). People who were possessed by demons were brought to the Lord (Matt. 4:24; 8:16; Mark 1:32; Luke 8:36). He healed men possessed by demons (Matt. 8:28, 33; Mark 5:15, 16, 18). He also healed a man, mute and possessed by a demon (Matt. 9:32), and another possessed by a demon, blind and mute (12:22). ¶

– 4 Acts 17:22 → given up to demon worship → RELIGIOUS <1174> 5 Rom. 8:38 → PRINCIPALITY <746>.

DEMON-OPPRESSED – Matt. 9:32; 12:22 → to be oppressed by a demon → to be possessed by a demon → DEMON <1139>.

DEMON-POSSESSED – Matt. 4:24; 8:16, 28, 33; 9:32; 12:22; Mark 1:32; 5:15, 16, 18; Luke 8:36 → to be possessed by a demon → DEMON <1139>.

DEMON-POSSESSION – Matt. 15:22 → to suffer from demon-possession → to be possessed by a demon → DEMON <1139>.

DEMONIAC – Matt. 4:24; 8:33 → to be possessed by a demon → DEMON <1139>.

DEMONIC – 1 ***daimoniōdēs*** [adj.: δαιμονιώδης <1141>]; **from *daimonion*: see** DEMON <1140> **► Which relates to demons, which takes its source in them** > The wisdom of bitter emulation and strife in the hearts does not come down from above, but is demonic {devilish, of the devil} (Jas. 3:15; see v. 14). ¶

– 2 Rev. 16:14 → of demons → DEMON <1142>.

DEMONSTRATE – 1 **demonstration: *endeixis*** [fem. noun: ἔνδειξις <1732>]; **from *endeiknumi*: to display, to demonstrate, which is from *en*: in, and *deiknumi*: to show ► To prove, to give evidence** > God set forth Jesus as a propitiation to demonstrate {show, declare} (lit.: in demonstration of) His righteousness (Rom. 3:25), to demonstrate {declare, show} (lit.: for the demonstration of) His righteousness at the present time (v. 26). Other refs.: 2 Cor. 8:24; Phil. 1:28; see PROOF <1732>. ¶

– 2 Acts 17:3 → to lay down → LAY <3908> 3 Acts 18:28 → SHOW (verb) <1925> 4 Acts 26:20 → demonstrate their repentance by their deeds → lit.: doing (*prassō*) works worthy of the repentance 5 Rom. 3:5; 5:8 → COMMEND <4921> 6 Rom. 9:17, 22; 1 Tim. 1:16 → SHOW (verb) <1731> 7 2 Cor. 7:11 → PROVE <4921> 8 2 Cor. 12:12 → I persevered in demonstrating the marks → lit.: the signs were worked out in all patience.

DEMONSTRATION – 1 ***apodeixis*** [fem. noun: ἀπόδειξις <585>]; **from *apodeiknumi*: to prove, which is from *apo*: from, and *deiknumi*: to show ► Manifestation, proof** > Paul's preaching had been in demonstration of the Spirit and of power (1 Cor. 2:4). ¶

– 2 John 16:8 → to bring demonstration → CONVINCE <1651> 3 Rom. 3:25, 26 → DEMONSTRATE <1732> 4 Phil. 1:28 → PROOF <1732>.

DEN – 1 ***spēlaion*** [neut. noun: σπήλαιον <4693>]; **from *speos*: cave ► Cavern, usually large and underground; also transl.: cave** > Those who were selling and buying in the temple had made it a den of robbers (Matt. 21:13; Mark 11:17; Luke 19:46). Jesus came to the tomb of Lazarus which was a cave (John 11:38). O.T. people of faith have wandered in dens and caverns of the earth (Heb. 11:38). Men will hide

themselves in the dens and in the rocks of the mountains during the great tribulation (Rev. 6:15). ¶
– 2 Matt. 8:20; Luke 9:58 → HOLE <5454>.

DENARII – Plur. of denarius → DENARIUS <1220>.

DENARIUS – ***dēnarion*** [neut. noun: δηνάριον <1220>] ▶ **Roman coin which was equivalent in value to the Greek drachma; a denarius (plur.: denarii) prob. represented the pay for a day's work of a laborer; also transl.: penny (plur.: pence), coin, silver coin** > The denarius shown to Jesus, which was used as tax money (Matt. 22:19; Mark 12:15; Luke 20:24), had the image and superscription of Caesar (see Matt. 22:20, 21; Mark 12:16). The Samaritan gave two denarii to the innkeeper to take care of the man who had fallen in the hands of robbers (Luke 10:35). A quart of wheat for a denarius and three quarts of barley for a denarius is an excessive price during a time of food shortage (Rev. 6:6a, b). Other refs.: Matt. 18:28; 20:2, 9, 10, 13; Mark 6:37; 14:5; Luke 7:41; John 6:7; 12:5. ¶

DENOTE – Heb. 12:27 → INDICATE <1213>.

DENOUNCE – 1 Matt. 11:20 → REPROACH (verb) <3679> 2 1 Cor. 10:30 → to speak evil → EVIL (adv.) <987>.

DENY – 1 ***arneomai*** [verb: ἀρνέομαι <720>] ▶ **To disclaim (sometimes under false pretense) knowing a person or something; to renounce, to reject; also transl.: to disown** > Whoever will deny Jesus before men, him will He also deny before His Father (Matt. 10:33a, b). Peter denied that he knew Jesus (Matt. 26:70, 72; Mark 14:68, 70; John 18:25, 27). All denied having touched Jesus (Luke 8:45). Luke writes that he who will have denied (*arneomai*) Jesus before men will be denied (*aparneomai*; see 2) before the angels of God (Luke 12:9). Peter denied Jesus (Luke 22:57); the Lord had told him that he would deny Him three times (John 13:38 {some mss.: *aparneomai*}). John the Baptist denied not {did not fail to confess}, and acknowledged, that he was not the Christ (John 1:20). The Jews denied Jesus in the presence of Pilate (Acts 3:13); they denied Jesus, the holy and righteous one (v. 14). If we deny Jesus, He also will deny us (2 Tim. 2:12a, b); He cannot deny Himself (v. 13). The Jews could not deny that an evident sign had been done through the means of Peter and John (Acts 4:16). Certain men who profess to know God deny Him by their deeds (Titus 1:16). Peter and Jude predicted that there would be false teachers who would deny the master who bought them (2 Pet. 2:1; Jude 4). Anyone who does not provide for his own has denied the faith (1 Tim. 5:8). Men having a form of piety have denied the power of it (2 Tim. 3:5). The grace of God teaches us to deny ungodliness and worldly lusts (Titus 2:12). The antichrist denies that Jesus is the Christ, and he denies the Father and the Son (1 John 2:22a, b). Whoever denies the Son does not have the Father either (1 John 2:23). The church of Pergamum did not deny the faith of the Lord (Rev. 2:13); the church of Philadelphia did not deny His name (3:8). Other refs.: Acts 7:35; Heb. 11:24; see REFUSE (verb) <720>. ¶

2 **to deny, to deny oneself: *aparneomai*** [verb: ἀπαρνέομαι <533>]; **from *apo*: intens., and *arneomai*: see 1** ▶ **a. To deny completely; also transl.: to disown** > This verb is related to the denial of Peter in the synoptic Gospels (Matt. 26:34, 75; Mark 14:30, 72; Luke 22:34, 61; John 13:38 in some mss.). It is also used when Peter told the Lord that he would surely not deny Him (Matt. 26:35; Mark 14:31). Luke uses it as the second verb in Luke 12:9b; see 1. **b. To completely renounce oneself** > Whoever desires to come after Jesus must deny himself (Matt. 16:24; Mark 8:34; Luke 9:23). ¶

3 ***antilegō*** [verb: ἀντιλέγω <483>]; **from *anti*: against, and *legō*: to speak** ▶ **To contradict, to oppose** > Some of the Sadducees denied that there is any {said there is no} resurrection (Luke 20:27). All

other refs.: ANSWER (verb) <483>, SPEAK <483>.
– 4 Acts 8:33 → justice was denied Him → judgment was taken away → TAKE <142> 5 Acts 19:36 → which cannot be denied → UNDENIABLE <368> 6 Jas. 3:14 → to lie against → LIE (verb)[2] <5574>.

DEPART – 1 ***anagō*** [verb: ἀνάγω <321>]; **from *ana*: above, again, and *agō*: to lead ► To go aboard a ship, to set sail >** When Paul departed {On his leaving, When he was setting sail, When he was ready to sail}, people of Malta provided him with what he needed (Acts 28:10). All other refs.: see entries in Lexicon at <321>.
2 ***analuō*** [verb: ἀναλύω <360>]; **from *ana*: indicates separation, and *luō*: to loose; lit.: to break, to untie ► To leave, to go >** The apostle Paul had a desire to depart {for departure} and to be with Christ (Phil. 1:23; see vv. 21–24). Other ref.: Luke 12:36; see RETURN (verb) <360>. ¶
3 **to depart, to let depart: *apoluō*** [verb: ἀπολύω <630>]; **from *apo*: from, and *luō*: to loose ► To let go freely, to send away, to dismiss >** Simeon asked the Lord to let him depart {go} in peace for his eyes had seen His salvation (Luke 2:29). The verb is transl. "to send away" {to send off, to let go} in Acts 13:3. At Rome, the Jews departed after Paul had spoken one final word to them (Acts 28:25). All other refs.: see entries in Lexicon at <630>.
4 ***anachōreō*** [verb: ἀναχωρέω <402>]; **from *ana*: particle indicating a reversal (intens.), and *chōreō*: to go ► To go away, to leave; also transl.: to return, to withdraw >** The wise men departed into their own country (Matt. 2:12, 13). Joseph and Mary departed into Egypt with Jesus (Matt. 2:14); later they departed {turned aside, withdrew} into the parts of Galilee (v. 22). Jesus departed into Galilee (Matt. 4:12), to a desert place (14:13), into the parts of Tyre and Sidon (15:21), to a mountain (John 6:15), from a place where the Pharisees wanted to kill Him (Matt. 12:15), and with His disciples to the sea (Mark 3:7). He told the crowd to withdraw {to give place, to make room} for the young girl was not dead (Matt. 9:24). Having cast down the pieces of silver in the temple, Judas departed from the place (Matt. 27:5). The chiliarch went apart {drew aside, stepped aside} (Acts 23:19). King Agrippa and others departed (Acts 26:31). ¶
5 ***apochōreō*** [verb: ἀποχωρέω <672>]; **from *apo*: from, and *chōreō*: to go ► To leave, to separate, to withdraw >** Jesus will tell workers of iniquity to depart from Him (Matt. 7:23). A spirit departed with difficulty from an only son after having crushed him (Luke 9:39). John (Mark) departed from Paul and his companions (Acts 13:13). Other ref.: Luke 20:20 in some mss. ¶
6 ***ekchōreō*** [verb: ἐκχωρέω <1633>]; **from *ek*: out of, and *chōreō*: to go ► To leave a place, to go away >** At the time of the great tribulation, those who will be in the midst of Jerusalem are to depart out of {get out of, leave} the city (Luke 21:21). ¶
7 ***aperchomai*** [verb: ἀπέρχομαι <565>]; **from *apo*: from, and *erchomai*: to come, to go ► To move away, to go away >** Jesus commanded the disciples to depart {to cross} to the other side (Matt. 8:18). The leprosy departed from a leper at the word of Jesus (Mark 1:42; Luke 5:13). The angel departed from Mary (Luke 1:38). Many disciples withdrew {turned back, went back} (or: departed) and walked no more with Jesus (John 6:66). The Jews went away (or: departed) after having listened to Paul (Acts 28:29). Other ref.: Luke 8:34 in some mss. All other refs.: see entries in Lexicon at <565>.
8 ***exerchomai*** [verb: ἐξέρχομαι <1831>]; **from *ek*: out, and *erchomai*: to go ► To go away, to leave >** Peter asked Jesus to depart from him because he was a sinful man (Luke 5:8). Certain Pharisees told Jesus to leave {to go away, to get out} and to go hence for Herod wanted to kill Him (Luke 13:31). When Paul departed from {came out of, left, set out from} Macedonia, only the Philippians communicated anything to him (Phil. 4:15). All other refs.: COME <1831>, ESCAPE <1831>, GO <1831>, SPREAD <1831>, STEP (verb) <1831>.
9 ***aphistēmi*** [verb: ἀφίστημι <868>]; **from *apo*: from, and *histēmi*: to stand ► a. To**

leave, to retire, to withdraw > Anna did not depart from the temple (Luke 2:37). The devil departed from Jesus after having tempted Him (Luke 4:13). Some fall away (or: depart) in time of temptation (Luke 8:13). The Lord will tell the workers of iniquity to depart from Him (Luke 13:27). The angel departed from Peter (Acts 12:10). Paul had pleaded with the Lord that the thorn in his flesh might depart from him (2 Cor. 12:8). Everyone who names the name of the Lord is to depart {to abstain, to turn away} from iniquity (2 Tim. 2:19). Paul departed from rebellious men (Acts 19:9). Those who were about to question Paul departed from him after he revealed his Roman citizenship (Acts 22:29). **b. To abandon, to desert** > Mark had departed from Paul in Pamphylia (Acts 15:38). A wicked heart of unbelief could depart {fall away, turn away} from the living God (Heb. 3:12). **c. To forsake the truth, to apostatize** > In the latter times, some will depart from {fall away from, apostatize from, abandon} the faith (1 Tim. 4:1). All other refs.: KEEP (verb) <868>, REVOLT <868>.

10 ***exeimi*** [verb: ἔξειμι <1826>]; **from *ek*: out, and *eimi*: to go ▶ To go away, to leave** > The verb is used in regard to Paul (Acts 17:15; 20:7). All other refs.: GET <1826>, GO <1826>.

11 ***metabainō*** [verb: μεταβαίνω <3327>]; **from *meta*: particle indicating change, and *bainō*: to go, to come ▶ To pass on to another place, to leave; also transl.: to go away, to go on, to remove** > The people of the city begged Jesus to depart out of their coasts (Matt. 8:34). The verb is also used in regard to Jesus elsewhere (Matt. 11:1; 12:9; 15:29; John 7:3) and to Paul (Acts 18:7). All other refs.: MOVE <3327>, PASS <3327>.

12 ***metairō*** [verb: μεταίρω <3332>]; **from *meta*: particle indicating change, and *airō*: to take up ▶ To move on, to withdraw** > Jesus departed after having finished His parables (Matt. 13:53). Other ref.: Matt. 19:1; see WITHDRAW <3332>. ¶

13 ***poreuomai*** [verb: πορεύομαι <4198>]; **from *poros*: passage ▶ To leave one place and go to another, to travel** > The apostles departed {left, went their way} from the presence of the council after having suffered shame (Acts 5:41). The verb is also used in regard to Jesus (Matt. 19:15 {to go on}), a king (Luke 14:31 {to go, to go one's way, to set out}), and Paul (Acts 20:1 {to go away, to leave, to set out}). All other refs.: FOLLOW <4198>, GO <4198>, TRAVEL <4198>, WALK <4198>.

14 ***ekporeuomai*** [verb: ἐκπορεύομαι <1607>]; **from *ek*: out, and *poreuomai*: see 13 ▶ To move away, to go out, to leave** > The verb is used in regard to the disciples (Mark 6:11) and to Festus (Acts 25:4). All other refs.: GO <1607>, PROCEED <1607>, SPREAD <1607>.

15 ***chōrizō*** [verb: χωρίζω <5563>]; **from *chōris*: separately ▶ To separate oneself** > If the unbelieving spouse departs {goes away, leaves}, let him or her depart (1 Cor. 7:15a, b). All other refs.: LEAVE (verb) <5563>, SEPARATE <5563>.

16 ***diachōrizō*** [verb: διαχωρίζω <1316>]; **from *dia*: through (intens.), and *chōrizō*: see 15; lit.: to withdraw completely ▶ To leave, to go away; also transl.: to part** > Moses and Elijah departed from Jesus on the mountain (Luke 9:33). ¶

– **17** Matt. 9:27 → to pass on → PASS <3855> **18** Mark 6:33; Jas. 2:16 → GO <5217> **19** Acts 13:4 → to go down → GO <2718> **20** Acts 13:14 → to pass through → PASS <1330> **21** Acts 15:39 → to depart asunder → SEPARATE <673> **22** Acts 19:12 → to depart from → LEAVE (verb) <525> **23** Acts 21:1 → GET <645> **24** 1 Tim. 1:6; 6:21; 2 Tim. 2:18 → STRAY <795> **25** Rev. 6:14 → RECEDE <673>.

DEPARTING – **1** Acts 20:29 → DEPARTURE <867> **2** Heb. 11:22 → DEPARTURE <1841>.

DEPARTURE – **1** ***analusis*** [fem. noun: ἀνάλυσις <359>]; **from *analuō*: to return, which is from *ana*: denotes separation, and *luō*: to loose ▶ Action of leaving the earthly life** > The time of Paul's departure {release} had come (2 Tim. 4:6). The word is used in Greek for the hoisting of a ship's anchor or for the dismantlement and departure of a military camp. ¶

[2] ***aphixis*** [fem. noun: ἄφιξις <867>]; **from *aphikneomai*, which is from *apo*: away from, and *hikneomai*: to come, to occur ► Action of leaving, going away >** After Paul's departure {departing}, grievous wolves would come in among the Christians of Ephesus (Acts 20:29).

[3] ***exodos*** [fem. noun: ἔξοδος <1841>]; **from *ek*: out of, and *hodos*: way ► Action of leaving a place for good, exodus >** By faith, Joseph when dying made mention of the departure of the sons of Israel (Heb. 11:22 {departing, going forth}). Other refs.: Luke 9:31; 2 Pet. 1:15; see DECEASE (noun) <1841>. ¶

– [4] Phil. 1:23 → DEPART <360>.

DEPEND – [1] Matt. 22:40 → HANG <2910> [2] Acts 12:20 → to depend for the food supply → to be nourished → NOURISH <5142> [3] Rom. 1:15 → as far as depends on me → for my part → PART (noun) <4289> [4] Rom. 4:14, 16 → the verb is added in Engl. [5] In Rom. 12:18, the expr. "as much as depends on you" is lit. "the (coming) from you."

DEPORTATION – ***metoikesia*** [fem. noun: μετοικεσία <3350>]; **from *metoikeō*: to move from one place to another, which is from *meta*: indicating displacement, and *oikia*: dwelling place ► Transportation of people out of their country, expatriation; also transl.: exile >** The term is used in regard to the deportation of the Jews to Babylon (Matt. 1:11, 12, 17a, b). ¶

DEPORTMENT – [1] 1 Tim. 2:9 → decent deportment → modest apparel → APPAREL <2689> [2] Titus 2:3 → BEHAVIOR <2688>.

DEPOSE – Acts 19:27 → DESTROY <2507>.

DEPOSIT (noun) – [1] Luke 19:23 → BANK[1] <5132> [2] 2 Cor. 1:22; 5:5; Eph. 1:14 → EARNEST (noun) <728> [3] 1 Tim. 6:20; 2 Tim. 1:12, 14 → entrusted deposit → what is committed → COMMIT <3866>.

DEPOSIT (verb) – [1] Matt. 25:27 → PUT <906> [2] Luke 19:21, 22 → LAY <5087>.

DEPRAVE – [1] 1 Tim. 6:5 → CORRUPT (verb) <1311> [2] 2 Tim. 3:8 → CORRUPT (verb) <2704>.

DEPRAVED – [1] Rom. 1:28 → WORTHLESS <96> [2] Phil. 2:15 → PERVERTED (BE) <1294> [3] 2 Pet. 2:2 → depraved conduct → dissolute way → DISSOLUTE <766> [4] 2 Pet. 2:7 → depraved conduct → conduct in lewdness → LEWDNESS <766>.

DEPRAVITY – [1] Rom. 1:29 → MALICE <2549> [2] 2 Pet. 2:19 → CORRUPTION <5356>.

DEPRECATE – Acts 25:11 → REFUSE (verb) <3868>.

DEPRESSED – [1] Matt. 26:37; Mark 14:33 → to be deeply depressed → to be full of heaviness → HEAVINESS <85> [2] 2 Cor. 7:6 → CAST DOWN <5011>.

DEPRIVE – [1] ***apostereō*** [verb: ἀποστερέω <650>]; **from *apo*: from, and *stereō*: to take away ► To frustrate out of something, to render someone destitute of something >** In the setting of the natural relations of a married couple, the man and the woman are not to deprive {defraud} one another (1 Cor. 7:5). In 1 Tim. 6:5, men are deprived {are destitute, are robbed} of the truth because of their corrupted minds. Other refs.: DEFRAUD <650>, KEEP (verb) <650>.

– [2] 1 Cor. 9:15 → to make void → VOID <2758> [3] Gal. 5:4 → to deprive of all profit → to make of no effect → EFFECT (noun) <2673> [4] Col. 2:18 → to deprive of the prize → to defraud of the prize → DEFRAUD <2603>.

DEPTH – [1] ***bathos*** [neut. noun: βάθος <899>]; **from *bathus*: deep ► Character of that which is deep; also transl.: deep >** No depth will be able to separate Christians from the love of God, which is in Christ Jesus (Rom. 8:39). Paul exclaimed: O depth of the riches both of the wisdom and knowledge of God! (Rom. 11:33). Paul wanted Christians to be fully able to understand the depth (he is not specifying of what), and to know the love of Christ (Eph. 3:18). Some of those who were in Thyatira had not known the depths {deep things, deep secrets} of Satan (Rev. 2:24; other mss.: *bathus*). The word is also used in regard to the soil (Matt. 13:5 and Mark 4:5 {deepness}), the depth of God (1 Cor. 2:10 {the deep things of God}), and the deep poverty of the churches of Macedonia (2 Cor. 8:2). All other refs.: DEEP (noun) <899>.

2 **to be sunk in the depth of the sea; to sink: *katapontizō*** [verb: καταποντίζω <2670>], **from *kata*: down, and *pontizō*: to sink; depth (lit.: open water): *pelagos*** [neut. noun: πέλαγος <3989>]; **sea: *thalassa*** [fem. noun: θάλασσα <2281>] ▶ **To plunge down into the broad open water (of the sea); i.e., far from land and any hope of rescue** > Jesus spoke of being drowned in the depths of the sea to emphasize the punishment of one who would cause little ones to sin (Matt. 18:6). Other ref.: Acts 27:5; see SEA <3989>. ¶

– 3 2 Cor. 2:4 → very abundantly → ABUNDANTLY <4056>.

DEPUTY – 1 Acts 13:7, 8, 12; 19:38 → PROCONSUL <446> 2 Acts 18:12 → to be the deputy → to be the proconsul → PROCONSUL <445>.

DERBE – 1 ***Derbē*** [fem. name: Δέρβη <1191>] ▶ **City of Asia Minor located in the plain of Lycaonia** > Paul and Barnabas preached the gospel in Derbe during their first missionary journey (Acts 14:6, 20). Paul, accompanied by Silas, returned there on his second missionary journey, and met Timothy (Acts 16:1). ¶

2 **of Derbe: *Derbaios*** [adj.: Δερβαῖος <1190>]; **from *Derbē*: see 1** ▶ **Native of Derbe** > Timothy was of Derbe (Acts 20:4; see 16:1). ¶

DERIDE – 1 Matt. 9:24; Mark 5:40; Luke 8:53 → to laugh at → LAUGH <2606> 2 Matt. 27:39; Mark 15:29 → REVILE <987> 3 Luke 16:14 → MOCK <1592> 4 Luke 23:35 → SNEER <1592>.

DERIVE – 1 Eph. 3:15 → to derive the name → NAME (verb) <3687> 2 Phm. 7 → HAVE <2192> 3 Heb. 7:6 → to derive one's genealogy → to have genealogy → GENEALOGY <1075>.

DESCEND – 1 ***katabainō*** [verb: καταβαίνω <2597>]; **from *kata*: down, and *bainō*: to go** ▶ **To go down; also transl.: to come down, to let down** > The Spirit of God descended upon Jesus at His baptism by John (Matt. 3:16; Mark 1:10; Luke 3:22; John 1:32, 33). A squall descended on the lake where was found the boat which Jesus and His disciples had boarded (Luke 8:23). The verb is also used concerning angels of God (John 1:51), a vessel (Acts 10:11; 11:5), Ananias (Acts 24:1), the abyss (Rom. 10:7), and Jesus (Eph. 4:9, 10). The expr. "to descend {to come down} from heaven" is found in Matt. 28:2; 1 Thes. 4:16; Rev. 21:10. All other refs.: COME <2597>, FALL (verb) <2597>, GO <2597>, STEP (verb) <2597>.

2 ***katabibazō*** [verb: καταβιβάζω <2601>]; **from *kata*: down, and *bibazō*: to cause to go** ▶ **To come down** > Capernaum will go down to the depths (Matt. 11:23; Luke 10:15); some mss. have *katabainō*. ¶

3 ***katerchomai*** [verb: κατέρχομαι <2718>]; **from *kata*: down, and *erchomai*: to go** ▶ **To come down** > James speaks of a wisdom which does not descend from above, which is characterized by bitter envy and strife in the hearts (Jas. 3:15). All other refs.: COME <2718>, GO <2718>, LAND (verb) <2718>.

– 4 Acts 23:6 → descended → lit.: son of 5 Rom. 1:3 → who was descended → lit.: the becoming (*ginomai*) of the seed (*sperma*) 6 2 Tim. 2:8 → descended from → lit.: descendant of → SEED <4690> 7 Heb. 7:14 → SPRING (verb) <393>.

DESCENDANT – 1 Luke 1:33 → one's descendants → one's house → HOUSE <3624> 2 Luke 1:55; John 7:42; Acts 13:23; Rom. 1:3; 4:13, 16, 18; 9:7a, b, 8, 29;

11:1; 2 Cor. 11:22; Gal. 3:29; 2 Tim. 2:8; Heb. 2:16; 11:18 → descendant, descendants → SEED <4690> [3] Rom. 1:3 → to be a descendant → to be born of the seed → BORN (BE) <1096> [4] 1 Tim. 5:4 → GRANDCHILD <1549> [5] Heb. 6:14 → and give you many descendants → lit.: and multiplying I will multiply you → MULTIPLY <4129> [6] Rev. 22:16 → OFFSPRING <1085>.

DESCENDANTS – John 8:33, 37; Acts 7:5, 6 → SEED <4690>.

DESCENT – [1] ***katabasis*** [fem. noun: κατάβασις <2600>]; **from *katabainō*: to descend, which is from *kata*: down, and *bainō*: to go ► Road, place which leads downward** > The multitude of disciples began to rejoice as Jesus drew near the descent of {where the road goes down} the Mount of Olives (Luke 19:37). ¶

– [2] John 1:13 → natural descent → BLOOD <129> [3] Acts 4:6 → RACE[1] <1085> [4] Rom. 9:8 → physical descent → FLESH <4561> [5] Heb. 7:3 → without descent → without genealogy → GENEALOGY <35> [6] Heb. 7:6 → to count a descent, to trace a descent → to trace a genealogy → GENEALOGY <1075> [7] Heb. 7:16 → concerning bodily descent → CARNAL <4559>.

DESCRIBE – [1] Mark 4:30 → COMPARE <3846> [2] Mark 5:16; Luke 8:39; Acts 8:33; 9:27; 12:17 → RELATE <1334> [3] Acts 13:41; 15:3 → RELATE <1555> [4] Acts 15:14 → RELATE <1834> [5] Rom. 4:6 → DECLARE <3004> [6] Rom. 10:5 → WRITE <1125>.

DESECRATE – Acts 24:6 → PROFANE <953>.

DESERT (adj.) – [1] See DESERTED <2048>.

– [2] Matt. 15:33; Mark 8:4 → desert place → WILDERNESS <2047>.

DESERT (noun) – [1] Matt. 24:26; Luke 1:80; 5:16; John 6:31; Rev. 12:14; et al. → WILDERNESS <2048> [2] 2 Cor. 11:26; Heb. 11:38 → WILDERNESS <2047>.

DESERT (verb) – [1] Matt. 26:56; Mark 14:50 → FORSAKE <863> [2] Acts 15:38 → DEPART <868> [3] Gal. 1:6 → to desert, to desert and to turn → CHANGE (verb) <3346> [4] 2 Tim. 1:15 → to turn away → TURN (verb) <654> [5] 2 Tim. 4:10, 16 → FORSAKE <1459> [6] Heb. 13:5 → LEAVE (verb) <447>.

DESERTED – ***erēmos*** [adj.: ἔρημος <2048>] ► **Abandoned, solitary; also transl.: desolate, desert, lonely, remote, unpopulated** > Jesus was often in deserted places (Matt. 14:13, 15; Mark 1:45; 6:31 {quiet}, 32, 35; Luke 4:42; 9:10 in some mss., 12). He prayed in a deserted place (Mark 1:35). Philip was to go down on the road from Jerusalem to Gaza which was deserted (Acts 8:26). The dwelling place of Judas was to be deserted (Acts 1:20). All other refs.: DESOLATE <2048>, WILDERNESS <2048>.

DESERTION – ***hupostolē*** [fem. noun: ὑποστολή <5289>]; **from *hupostellō*: to withdraw, which is from *hupo*: under, and *stellō*: to send, to draw ► Apostasy, withdrawal** > Christians are not those who draw back {those who shrink back} (lit.: who are of desertion) (Heb. 10:39). ¶

DESERVE – [1] Matt. 8:8; Luke 7:6; 1 Cor. 15:9 → WORTHY <2425> [2] Matt. 10:10, 13a, b; 22:8; Luke 7:4; 10:7; 23:15; Acts 25:11; 26:31; Rom. 1:32; 1 Tim. 1:15; 4:9; 5:18; Rev. 16:6 → WORTHY <514> [3] Luke 23:22 → no guilt deserving death → no reason for death → REASON (noun) <158> [4] Luke 23:41; Acts 23:29 → DESERVING <514> [5] Eph. 2:3 → "deserving" added in Engl. [6] Heb. 10:29 → to think worthy → WORTHY <515>.

DESERVING – [1] ***axios*** [adj.: ἄξιος <514>]; **from *agō*: to weigh ► Suitable, worthy** > He who knew not the will of his master, and did things deserving stripes, will be beaten with few stripes (Luke 12:48). The criminals on the cross received the things deserving of what they had done {the just recompense of what they had done, the due reward of their deeds, what they deserved for their deeds} (Luke 23:41). Paul had no charge laid against him deserving of {that deserved} death or chains (Acts 23:29). Other refs.: FITTING <514>, MEET (adj.) <514>, UNWORTHY <514>, WORTHY <514>.

[2] ***enochos*** [adj.: ἔνοχος <1777>]; **from *enechō*: to have to ▶ Liable, worthy** > Jesus was condemned as deserving {guilty of, liable of} death (Matt. 26:66; Mark 14:64). All other refs.: GUILTY <1777>, SUBJECT (noun)[1] <1777>.

– [3] Luke 7:4; 23:15; Acts 25:11, 25; 26:31; Rom. 1:32; 1 Tim. 1:15; 4:9 → WORTHY <514>.

DESIGN – [1] Acts 17:29 → ART <5078> [2] 2 Cor. 2:11 → DEVICE <3540>.

DESIGNATE – [1] ***prosagoreuō*** [verb: προσαγορεύω <4316>]; **from *pros*: to, and *agoreuō*: to speak, which is from *agora*: marketplace ▶ To name, to give a title publicly** > The Son of God was designated {addressed, called} by God as high priest according to the order of Melchizedek (Heb. 5:10). ¶

– [2] Matt. 28:16 → APPOINT <5021> [3] Heb. 4:7 → DETERMINE <3724> [4] Heb. 7:11 → NAME (verb) <3004> [5] Jude 4 → to mark out beforehand → MARK (verb) <4270>.

DESIGNER – Heb. 11:10 → BUILDER <5079>.

DESIRABLE – [1] ***arestos*** [adj.: ἀρεστός <701>]; **from *areskō*: to please, which is from *arō*: to fit, to adapt ▶ To be reasonable, to be suitable** > It was not desirable {right, reason} that the apostles should leave the word of God and serve tables (Acts 6:2). Other refs.: John 8:29; Acts 12:3; 1 John 3:22; see PLEASING <701>. ¶

– [2] Acts 20:16 → to think it desirable → DECIDE <2919>.

DESIRE (noun) – [1] ***epithumia*** [fem. noun: ἐπιθυμία <1939>]; **from *epithumeō*: to strongly desire, which is from *epi*: upon, and *thumos*: passion ▶ a. Ardent yearning, longing, but legitimate** > Jesus had desired with desire (*epithumia epethumēsa*) {earnestly desired, eagerly desired} to eat the Passover with His disciples before He suffered (Luke 22:15). Paul had the desire {desired} for departure and being with Christ (Phil. 1:23). He had used more abundant diligence to see the face of the Thessalonians with much desire (1 Thes. 2:17). **b. Covetousness, lust** > Those who desire to be rich fall into many unwise and harmful desires (1 Tim. 6:9). The ripe fruits that the soul of Babylon the great longed for {lusted after} (lit.: The ripe fruits of the desire of the soul of Babylon) have departed from her (Rev. 18:14). All other refs.: LUST (noun) <1939>.

[2] **ardent desire: *epipothēsis*** [fem. noun: ἐπιπόθησις <1972>]; **from *epipotheō*: to desire earnestly, which is from *epi*: upon, and *potheō*: to desire ▶ Very great desire; also transl.: longing, earnest desire, vehement desire** > Titus had told Paul of the ardent desire of the Corinthians (2 Cor. 7:7). Being grieved in a godly manner had produced an ardent desire among the Corinthians (2 Cor. 7:11). ¶

[3] **great desire: *epipothia*** [fem. noun: ἐπιποθία <1974>]; **from *epipotheō*: see [2] ▶ Strong desire, great yearning; also transl.: longing** > Paul had a great desire {had been longing} to come to the Christians in Rome (Rom. 15:23). ¶

[4] ***eudokia*** [fem. noun: εὐδοκία <2107>]; **from *eudokeō*: to please, which is from *eu*: well, and *dokeō*: to think, to appear ▶ Good wish, good pleasure, longing** > The desire {delight} of Paul's heart concerning the Jews, and the supplication which he addressed to God for them, was that they might be saved (Rom. 10:1). All other refs.: PLEASURE <2107>, WELL PLEASING <2107>, WILL (noun)[1] <2107>.

– [5] Acts 27:13 → PURPOSE (noun) <4286> [6] Rom. 1:27 → LUST (noun) <3715> [7] Rom. 7:18 → WILLING <2309> [8] 1 Cor. 7:37; Eph. 2:3 → WILL (noun)[1]

<2307> 9 2 Cor. 9:14; Phil. 2:26 → to be full of ardent desire, to have a longing desire → LONG (verb) <1971> 10 Gal. 5:17 → to set one's desire → LUST (verb) <1937> 11 1 Thes. 4:5 → PASSION <3806> 12 1 Tim. 5:11 → to feel sensual desire → to wax wanton → WANTON <2691> 13 Jas. 4:1, 3 → PLEASURE <2237> 14 Jude 7 → unnatural desire → lit.: other flesh → FLESH <4561>.

DESIRE (verb) – 1 ***axioō*** [verb: ἀξιόω <515>]; **from *axios*: worthy ▶ To think well, to think appropriate, to find good >** The leaders of the Jews in Jerusalem desired {wanted} to hear from Paul what he thought about Christianity (Acts 28:22). All other refs.: THINK <515>, WORTHY <515>.
2 ***epithumeō*** [verb: ἐπιθυμέω <1937>]; **from *epi*: upon, and *thumos*: passion ▶ To want greatly, to crave; also transl.: to long >** Many prophets and righteous men had desired to see the things done by Jesus (Matt. 13:17). The prodigal son desired to fill {would gladly have filled, would fain have filled} his belly with the husks which the swine were eating (Luke 15:16). Lazarus desired to be filled with the crumbs which fell from the table of the rich man (Luke 16:21). The disciples would desire to see one of the days of the Son of Man (Luke 17:22). Jesus had earnestly desired {eagerly desired} (*epithumia epethumēsa*; lit.: had desired with desire) to eat the Passover with His disciples before He suffered (Luke 22:15). If a man desires (*oregō*) {aspires} to exercise oversight, he desires (*epithumeō*) a good work (1 Tim. 3:1). The author of the Epistle to the Hebrews desired {desired earnestly} that each one of his readers show the same diligence to the full assurance of hope until the end (Heb. 6:11). Angels desire to look into the glories and the sufferings of Christ (1 Pet. 1:12). During the apocalyptic judgments, men will desire to die, and death will flee from them (Rev. 9:6). All other refs.: see: COVET <1937>, LUST (verb) <1937>.
3 **to desire; to desire earnestly, ardently, greatly, much: *epipotheō*** [verb: ἐπιποθέω <1971>]; **from *epi*: intens., and *potheō*: to long for, to yearn ▶ To feel a great tenderness, an ardent desire; also transl.: to long >** Christians desire ardently to have put on their habitation which is from heaven (2 Cor. 5:2). The Thessalonians much desired to see Paul (1 Thes. 3:6). Paul earnestly desired to see Timothy (2 Tim. 1:4). Christians should desire earnestly {should crave} the pure milk of the word (1 Pet. 2:2). All other refs.: LONG (verb) <1971>, YEARN <1971>.
4 **to desire; to desire earnestly, eagerly: *zēloō*** [verb: ζηλόω <2206>]; **from *zēlos*: zeal, passion ▶ To show zeal, to aspire; also transl.: to covet >** Paul says to desire earnestly the greater gifts (1 Cor. 12:31), to desire {be emulous of} spiritual gifts (14:1), and to desire to prophesy (14:39). All other refs.: COVET <2206>, ENVY (verb) <2206>, JEALOUS <2206>, ZEALOUS <2206>.
5 ***thelō*** [verb: θέλω <2309>] **▶ To have the intention; also transl.: to want, to wish, to be desirous >** The mother and the brothers of Jesus were desiring to see Him (Luke 8:20), as well as Herod (Luke 23:8). Many prophets and kings had desired to see the things done by Him (Luke 10:24). *
6 ***oregō*** [verb: ὀρέγω <3713>]; **lit.: to stretch toward, to aim ▶ To aspire, to seek, to strive >** If a man desires {sets his heart} (*oregō*) to exercise oversight, he desires (*epithumeō*) a good work (1 Tim. 3:1). Those who died in faith desire {long for} a better country, i.e., a heavenly one (Heb. 11:16). Other ref.: 1 Tim. 6:10; see COVET <3713>. ¶
– 7 Matt. 12:38; 14:5; 27:43; Mark 3:13; Heb. 12:17; 13:18 → WANT (verb) <2309> 8 Matt. 12:47; Luke 9:9 → SEEK <2212> 9 Matt. 16:1 → ASK <1905> 10 Matt. 20:20; Mark 10:35; 11:24; 15:6, 8; Luke 23:25; Acts 3:14; 7:46; 9:2; 12:20; 13:21, 28; 25:3; Eph. 3:13; 1 John 5:15b → ASK <154> 11 Mark 12:38; Luke 20:46 → LIKE (verb) <2309> 12 Luke 7:36; 14:32; John 12:21; Acts 16:39; 18:20; 23:20 → ASK <2065> 13 Luke 10:29; 14:28; 23:20; John 12:21; 1 Cor. 14:5 → WISH <2309> 14 Luke 19:15 → COMMAND (verb) <2036> 15 Luke 22:31 → to ask for → ASK <1809> 16 Acts 8:31; 9:38; 28:14; 1 Cor.

16:12; 2 Cor. 12:18 → BESEECH <3870> [17] Acts 13:7; Phil. 4:17 → SEEK <1934> [18] Acts 18:27 → PURPOSE (verb) <1014> [19] Acts 22:30; Jude 5 → WANT (verb) <1014> [20] Acts 25:15 → REQUIRE <154> [21] Rom. 9:22 → WILL (verb) <2309> [22] 1 Cor. 10:6 → LUST (verb) <1938> [23] 2 Cor. 8:6; Heb. 13:22 → EXHORT <3870> [24] Phil. 1:23 → lit.: to have the desire → DESIRE (noun) <1939>.

DESIROUS – [1] Luke 23:8 → to be desirous → DESIRE (verb) <2309> [2] Luke 23:20 → to be desirous → WISH <2309> [3] 1 Thes. 2:8 → to be affectionately desirous → AFFECTIONATELY <2442> [4] Heb. 13:18 → to be desirous → WANT (verb) <2309>.

DESOLATE – [1] *erēmos* [adj.: ἔρημος <2048>] ► **Deserted, abandoned, solitary** > The house of the Jews was left to them desolate (Matt. 23:38; Luke 13:35). The dwelling place of Judas was to be desolate (Acts 1:20). Isaiah wrote that the children of the desolate woman are more numerous than those of the one who has a husband (Gal. 4:27). All other refs.: DESERTED <2048>, WILDERNESS <2048>.

[2] **to make desolate, to bring to desolation, to bring to ruin, to change in desolation:** ***erēmoō*** [verb: ἐρημόω <2049>]; **from *erēmos*: desert, wilderness ► To make deserted, abandoned, solitary; to make a place uninhabited** > Every kingdom divided against itself is brought to desolation {laid waste, will be ruined} (Matt. 12:25; Luke 11:17). The ten horns of the beast will make the prostitute desolate and naked (Rev. 17:16). The great riches of Babylon will be made desolate {come to nothing, come to nought, be laid waste, brought to ruin} in one hour (Rev. 18:17); in one hour she will be made desolate (v. 19). ¶

[3] **to be desolate:** ***monoō*** [verb: μονόω <3443>]; **from *monos*: alone ► To be alone (having no one by whom to be helped)** > Paul mentions a real widow as one who is desolate {left alone, left all alone} (1 Tim. 5:5). ¶

– [4] Matt. 15:33; Mark 8:4 → desolate place → WILDERNESS <2047>.

DESOLATION – [1] *erēmōsis* [fem. noun: ἐρήμωσις <2050>]; **from *erēmoō*: to desolate, which is from *erēmos*: desert, wilderness ► Devastation, total destruction** > Jesus speaks of seeing the abomination of desolation (i.e., that causes desolation) standing in the holy place, where it should not be (Matt. 24:15; Mark 13:14). When Jerusalem is surrounded by armies, it will be known then that its desolation is near (Luke 21:20). ¶

– [2] Matt. 12:25; Luke 11:17; Rev. 18:17 → to bring to desolation → DESOLATE <2049>.

DESPAIR – to be in despair: ***exaporeomai*** [verb: ἐξαπορέομαι <1820>]; **from *ek*: intens., and *aporeō*: to be perplexed, which is from *aporos*: without resource ► To be entirely without resource, to be completely at an impasse** > In Asia, Paul had been in despair {had despaired, had been driven to despair} even of living (2 Cor. 1:8). He was perplexed, but not in despair {despairing, entirely shut up} (2 Cor. 4:8). ¶

DESPISE – [1] ***exoutheneō*** [verb: ἐξουθενέω <1848>]; **from *ek*: from, and *outheneō*: to reduce to nothing, which is from *outhen*: nothing ► To treat people as though they were nothing, to treat with contempt** > Jesus Christ was the stone despised {rejected, set at nought} by Israel (Acts 4:11). God has chosen the despised things to annul the things that are (1 Cor. 1:28). Paul wrote that no one was to despise {refuse to accept} Timothy (1 Cor. 16:11). He who eats certain things should not despise {make nothing of, regard with contempt, look down on} those who do not eat (Rom. 14:3). Christians should not despise {set at nought, regard with contempt, show contempt of, make little of, look down on} their brothers (Rom. 14:10). The Galatians did not despise Paul's temptation (or: infirmity) in his flesh (Gal. 4:14). Paul exhorts the Thessalonians not to despise {lightly esteem} prophecies (1 Thes. 5:20). All other refs.: CONTEMPT

<1848>, CONTEMPTIBLE <1848>, ESTEEM (verb) <1848>.

2 ***kataphroneō*** [verb: καταφρονέω <2706>]; **from *kata*: against, and *phroneō*: to think, which is from *phrēn*: mind, understanding ▶ To lower in one's esteem** > If a man follows two masters, he will despise one of them (Matt. 6:24; Luke 16:13). The Lord warns against despising {looking down on} a young believer in Him (Matt. 18:10). He who despises {thinks lightly of, shows contempt for} the riches of the goodness of God treasures up for himself wrath in the day of judgment (Rom. 2:4). Paul exhorts Timothy to let no one despise {look down} on his youth (1 Tim. 4:12). Servants must not despise {be disrespectful to, show less respect for} their believing masters because they are brothers in the Lord (1 Tim. 6:2). Paul asks the Corinthians if they were despising the church of God by their behavior (1 Cor. 11:22). Jesus endured the cross, having despised {scorned} the shame of the cross by enduring it (Heb. 12:2). Certain men despise authority by walking according to the flesh in the lust of uncleanness (2 Pet. 2:10). Other ref.: Titus 2:15; other mss.: see 5. ¶

3 **to count: *logizomai*** [verb: λογίζομαι <3049>]; **from *logos*: word, reputation ▶ To estimate, to consider** > There was fear that the temple of Diana might be despised {discredited, regarded as worthless} (lit.: counted for nothing) (Acts 19:27). All other refs.: see entries in Lexicon at <3049>.

4 ***oligōreō*** [verb: ὀλιγωρέω <3643>]; **from *oligos*: short, little, and *ōra*: care ▶ To neglect, to consider as of little importance** > One who is chastened by the Lord should not despise {regard lightly, make light of} His discipline (Heb. 12:5). ¶

5 ***periphroneō*** [verb: περιφρονέω <4065>]; **from *peri*: around, and *phroneō*: to think, which is from *phrēn*: mind, understanding; lit.: to think beyond ▶ To ignore, to deprecate in one's esteem** > Titus was to let no one despise {disregard} him (Titus 2:15). ¶

– 6 Luke 10:16a–d; 1 Thes. 4:8a, b; Heb. 10:28; Jude 8 → REJECT <114> 7 Jas. 2:6 → DISHONOR (verb) <818>.

DESPISED – 1 Mark 6:4 → without honor → HONOR (noun) <820> 2 1 Cor. 1:28 → DESPISE <1848> 3 1 Cor. 4:10 → DISHONORED <820>.

DESPISER – 1 ***kataphronētēs*** [masc. noun: καταφρονητής <2707>]; **from *kataphroneō*: to despise, which is from *kata*: against, and *phroneō*: to think, which is from *phrēn*: mind, understanding ▶ Person who criticizes, who is contemptuous, arrogant** > Despisers {Scoffers} will see a work which they will not believe (Acts 13:41). ¶

2 **despiser of good, of those who are good: *aphilagathos*** [adj.: ἀφιλάγαθος <865>]; **from *a*: neg., and *philagathos*: lover of good men or of what is good, which is from *philos*: friend, and *agathos*: benevolent ▶ Hostile to what is good, to good men** > In the last days, men will be despisers of what is good {not lovers of what is good, haters of what is good} (lit.: having no love for what is good) (2 Tim. 3:3). ¶

DESPITE – Heb. 10:29 → to do despite → INSULT (verb) <1796>.

DESPITEFUL – Rom. 1:30 → insolent man → INSOLENT <5197>.

DESPITEFULLY – Acts 14:5 → to use despitefully → MISTREAT <5195>.

DESTINE – 1 Luke 2:34 → LAY <2749> 2 1 Cor. 2:7 → PREDESTINE <4309> 3 1 Thes. 3:3 → APPOINT <2749> 4 1 Thes. 5:9; 1 Pet. 2:8 → APPOINT <5087> 5 Heb. 9:27 → APPOINT <606>.

DESTITUTE – 1 1 Tim. 6:5 → DEPRIVE <650> 2 Heb. 11:37 → to be destitute → to be in want → WANT (noun) <5302> 3 Jas. 2:15 → to be destitute → LACK (verb) <3007>.

DESTITUTION – Mark 12:44 → POVERTY <5304>.

DESTROY – 1 ***apollumi*** [verb: ἀπόλλυμι <622>]; **from *apo*: intens., and *ollumi*: to**

destroy ▶ To perish, to ruin completely > Jesus says to fear him who is able to destroy both soul and body in hell (Matt. 10:28). The unclean spirit asked Jesus if He had come to destroy them (Mark 1:24; Luke 4:34). The chief priests and the scribes sought how they might destroy {kill} the Lord Jesus (Mark 11:18; Luke 19:47). There is no profit for a man if he gains the whole world and is himself destroyed or lost {and loses himself or forfeits himself} (Luke 9:25). Contrary to the shepherd of the sheep, the thief comes to steal and kill and destroy (John 10:10). One must not destroy with his food the one for whom Christ has died (Rom. 14:15). God will destroy the wisdom of the wise (1 Cor. 1:19). There is one lawgiver and judge who is able to save and to destroy (Jas. 4:12). The Lord destroyed the Israelites who had come out of Egypt and had not believed (Jude 5). All other refs.: LOSE <622>, PERISH <622>.

[2] ***aphanizō*** [verb: ἀφανίζω <853>]; **from *aphanēs*: hidden, which is from *a*: neg., and *phainō*: to appear, which is from *phōs*: light; lit.: to make (something) disappear ▶ To corrupt, to consume; also transl.: to spoil >** Moth and rust spoil the treasures on earth (Matt. 6:19), but not in heaven (v. 20). All other refs.: DISFIGURE <853>, PERISH <853>, VANISH <853>.

[3] ***kathaireō*** [verb: καθαιρέω <2507>]; **from *kata*: down, and *haireō*: to take ▶ To bring down, to upset, to demolish >** God had destroyed {overthrown} seven nations in the land of Canaan (Acts 13:19). Demetrius in Ephesus feared that the greatness of the goddess Diana might be destroyed {dethroned, robbed} (Acts 19:27). The weapons of the Christian are mighty in God to destroy {cast down, overthrow} reasonings and every pretension (2 Cor. 10:5). All other refs.: PULL <2507>, PUT <2507>, TAKE <2507>.

[4] ***katargeō*** [verb: καταργέω <2673>]; **from *kata*: intens., and *argeō*: to be inactive, which is from *argos*: idle, useless, which is from *a*: neg. and *ergon*: work ▶ a. To annul, to make disappear; also transl.: to abolish, to put down >** In the end, Christ will destroy all rule, authority, and power (1 Cor. 15:24), and He will destroy {put an end to} death (v. 26). The Lord will destroy {bring to an end, overthrow} the lawless one by the appearing of His coming (2 Thes. 2:8). The Savior Jesus Christ has destroyed death (2 Tim. 1:10). **b. To render something useless, without profit >** God will destroy {bring to nothing, do away with} both food for the stomach and the stomach for food (1 Cor. 6:13). All other refs.: see entries in Lexicon at <2673>.

[5] ***exolethreuō*** [verb: ἐξολεθρεύω <1842>]; **from *ek*: intens., and *olothreuō*: to destroy, which is from *olethros*: destruction; other spelling: *exolothreuō* ▶ To exterminate (but not to the point of extinction), to punish greatly >** Whoever should not hear the prophet would be destroyed {utterly destroyed, completely cut off} (Acts 3:23). ¶

[6] **he who destroys: *olothreuōn*; pres. ptcp. of *olothreuō*** [verb: ὀλοθρεύω <3645>]; **see [5]; other spelling: *olethreuōn* ▶ The one who slays, who takes life away >** He who destroyed {The destroyer of} the firstborn in Egypt (Heb. 11:28) was the Lord (see Ex. 12:29). ¶

[7] ***phtheirō*** [verb: φθείρω <5351>]; **from *phthiō*: to consume, to waste ▶ To corrupt, to make worse >** If anyone destroys (lit.: corrupts, defiles) the temple of God, God will destroy him (1 Cor. 3:17a, b). All other refs.: CORRUPT (verb) <5351>.

[8] **destruction: *phthora*** [fem. noun: φθορά <5356>]; **from *phtheirō*: see [7] ▶ Perishing, loss, ruin >** Peter compares certain men to natural beasts, without reason, made to be caught and destroyed {be captured and killed} (lit.: for capture and destruction) (2 Pet. 2:12). All other refs.: CORRUPTION <5356>, PERISH <5356>.

[9] ***diaphtheirō*** [verb: διαφθείρω <1311>]; **from *dia*: through (intens.), and *phtheirō*: see [7] ▶ To corrupt completely, to perish >** Moths do not destroy {corrupt} a treasure that one provides for himself in heaven (Luke 12:33). When the second angel sounded the trumpet, the third part of the ships were destroyed (Rev. 8:9). The twenty-four elders said the time had come to destroy those who destroy the earth (Rev. 11:18a, b).

All other refs.: CORRUPT (verb) <1311>, PERISH <1311>.

10 ***luō*** [verb: λύω <3089>]; **lit.: to loose, to unbind ▶ To undo, to break** > Jesus said to destroy this temple (His body), and in three days He would raise it up (John 2:19). He has destroyed {broken down} the middle wall of separation (Eph. 2:14). The Son of God was manifested that He might destroy {undo} the works of the devil (1 John 3:8). All other refs.: ANNUL <3089>, BREAK <3089>, DISSOLVE <3089>, LOOSE <3089>, RELEASE (verb) <3089>.

11 ***kataluō*** [verb: καταλύω <2647>]; **from *kata*: down (intens.), and *luō*: see 10 ▶ To abolish, to abrogate; to demolish completely, to annihilate** > The Lord has not come to destroy {abolish, make void} the law or the prophets, but to fulfill them (Matt. 5:17a, b). According to false witnesses, Jesus had said He was able to destroy the temple of God and to build it in three days (Matt. 26:61; Mark 14:58), but Jesus was speaking of His body. When Jesus was on the cross, passers-by accused Him of saying that He would destroy the temple (Matt. 27:40; Mark 15:29). Concerning the preaching of the apostles, Gamaliel said that if this plan or work had its origin in men, it would be destroyed {be overthrown, come to nothing, come to nought, fail} (Acts 5:38); but if it was of God, it could not be destroyed {overthrown, put down, stopped} (v. 39). According to false witnesses, Stephen had said Jesus would destroy the place (i.e., the temple) (Acts 6:14). We must not destroy {tear down} the work of God for the sake of food (Rom. 14:20). If a Christian's earthly house (i.e., his body) is destroyed {torn down, dissolved}, he has a building from God (2 Cor. 5:1). Paul had destroyed the principle of justification by the works of the law (Gal. 2:18). All other refs.: LODGE <2647>, THROW (verb) <2647>.

12 ***portheō*** [verb: πορθέω <4199>]; **from *perthō*: to turn upside down; lit.: to devastate ▶ To handle roughly, to devastate** > It was said of Paul that he had destroyed {had raised havoc among} those who called on the name of Jesus in Jerusalem (Acts 9:21). Before his conversion, Paul was persecuting the church of God excessively and destroying {ravaging} it (Gal. 1:13); later, he was preaching the faith which formerly he destroyed {ravaged} (v. 23). ¶

– **13** Luke 9:39 → BRUISE <4937> **14** Luke 9:54; Gal. 5:15 → CONSUME <355> **15** Acts 8:3 → RAVAGE <3075> **16** Acts 26:21 → KILL <1315> **17** 1 Cor. 5:5 → lit.: for the destruction → DESTRUCTION <3639> **18** 2 Cor. 10:4, 8 → lit.: for the destruction → DESTRUCTION <2506> **19** Heb. 10:39 → and are destroyed → lit.: to destruction → DESTRUCTION <684> **20** 2 Pet. 2:12 → PERISH <2704>.

DESTROYER – **1** ***olothreutēs*** [masc. noun: ὀλοθρευτής <3644>]; **from *olothreuō*: to strip, to destroy ▶ The one who destroys, who takes life away** > Some Israelites complained and perished by the destroyer {destroying angel}, i.e., the Lord Himself (1 Cor. 10:10; see Num. 16:41). ¶

– **2** Heb. 11:28 → he who destroys → DESTROY <3645> **3** Rev. 9:11 → "that is, Destroyer" added in Engl. (i.e., probable translation of Apollyon) **4** Rev. 11:18 → destroyers → those who destroy → DESTROY <1311>.

DESTROYING – 1 Cor. 10:10 → destroying angel → DESTROYER <3644>.

DESTRUCTION – **1** ***apōleia*** [fem. noun: ἀπώλεια <684>]; **from *apollumi*: to destroy completely, which is from *apo*: intens., and *ollumi*: to destroy ▶ Loss, perdition, ruin** > Destruction is the opposite of eternal life (Matt. 7:13; Phil. 1:28; 3:19), in the sense that this latter is not communicated to those who remain in unbelief and ungodliness. God has endured with much longsuffering the vessels of wrath fitted for destruction (Rom. 9:22). False prophets will secretly introduce destructive heresies (lit.: heresies of destruction), bringing upon themselves swift destruction (2 Pet. 2:1a, b); the destruction {condemnation, damnation} of those following them does not slumber (v. 3). The heavens and the earth are kept for fire until the day of judgment and destruction {perdition} of ungodly men (2 Pet. 3:7). Some people were twisting the Scriptures to their own destruction (2 Pet. 3:16). The word is used in the expr. "the one doomed to destruction" {the son of perdition, the son of destruction} (solemn example of those who are eternally lost): John 17:12; 2 Thes. 2:3. Those who desire to be rich fall into hurtful lusts which plunge men into destruction and ruin (1 Tim. 6:9). Other refs.: Heb. 10:39 {those who are destroyed}; 2 Pet. 2:2 in some mss.; Rev. 17:8, 11. All other refs.: PERISH <684>, SON OF PERDITION <684>, WASTE (noun) <684>.

2 ***kathairesis*** [fem. noun: καθαίρεσις <2506>]; **from *kathaireō*: to destroy, to demolish, which is from *kata*: down, and *haireō*: to take ▶ Action of casting down, of demolishing** > The weapons of the Christian's warfare are mighty for the destruction of {for the pulling down of, for the overthrow of, to demolish} strongholds (2 Cor. 10:4). The Lord had given Paul authority for edification and not for destruction {destroying, overthrowing, pulling down, tearing down} (2 Cor. 10:8; 13:10). ¶

3 ***olethros*** [masc. noun: ὄλεθρος <3639>]; **from *ollumi*: to destroy ▶ Ruin, suppression, wiping out** > Paul had decided to deliver a certain man to Satan for the destruction of {to destroy} the flesh (1 Cor. 5:5). When men will say "Peace and safety," then sudden destruction will come upon them (1 Thes. 5:3). Those who do not obey the gospel will pay the penalty of everlasting destruction from the presence of the Lord (2 Thes. 1:9). Other ref.: 1 Tim. 6:9; see RUIN (noun) <3639>. ¶

4 ***suntrimma*** [neut. noun: σύντριμμα <4938>]; **from *suntribō*: to crush completely, which is from *sun*: together (intens.), and *tribō*: to break ▶ Crushing, ruin** > Destruction and misery are in the ways of evil men (Rom. 3:16). ¶

– 5 Luke 6:49 → RUIN (noun) <4485> 6 John 17:12; 2 Thes. 2:3 → one (man) doomed to destruction → lit.: son of perdition → SON OF PERDITION <5207> 7 Gal. 6:8; 2 Pet. 2:12 → CORRUPTION <5356> 8 Col. 2:22 → PERISH <5356> 9 2 Pet. 2:6 → RUIN (noun) <2692> 10 2 Pet. 3:12 → DISSOLVE <3089>.

DESTRUCTIVE – 1 2 Pet. 2:1a → destructive heresies → lit.: heresies of destruction → DESTRUCTION <684> 2 2 Pet. 2:2 → destructive ways → dissolute ways → DISSOLUTE <766>.

DETACHMENT – John 18:3, 12 → COHORT <4686>.

DETAIL – 1 ***meros*** [neut. noun: μέρος <3313>] ▶ **Element, part** > It was not the time to speak in detail {particularly}, for the author of the Epistle to the Hebrews, concerning the cherubim of glory overshadowing the mercy seat (Heb. 9:5). Other refs.: see entries in Lexicon at <3313>.
– 2 Acts 24:4 → TEDIOUS (BE) <1465> 3 Col. 2:18 → to go into great detail about → to intrude into → INTRUDE <1687>.

DETECT – Luke 20:23 → PERCEIVE <2657>.

DETER – Matt. 3:14 → PREVENT <1254>.

DETERMINATE – Acts 2:23 → DETERMINED <3724>.

DETERMINE – 1 ***akriboō*** [verb: ἀκριβόω <198>]; **from *akribēs*: accurate ▶ To find out exactly, to get precise information** > Herod had determined {diligently enquired of, accurately inquired of, ascertained, found out, learned} the time from the wise men concerning the birth of Christ (Matt. 2:7, 16). ¶

2 ***diaginōskō*** [verb: διαγινώσκω <1231>]; **from *dia*: intens., and *ginōskō*: to know ▶ To examine, to obtain information** > The chief priests and elders were to pretend they wanted to determine {to enquire, to make inquiries, to want information} more precisely concerning Paul (Acts 23:15). Other ref.: Acts 24:22 (to make a decision); see DECISION <1231>. ¶

3 ***epiluō*** [verb: ἐπιλύω <1956>]; **from *epi*: intens., and *luō*: to loose, to untie ▶ To**

decide, to resolve > In the city of Ephesus, inquiries made were to be determined {were to be settled} in the regular assembly (Acts 19:39). The verb is transl. "to explain" in Mark 4:34: Jesus explained all things to His disciples. ¶

4 ***krinō*** [verb: κρίνω <2919>] ► **To conclude, to establish; also transl.: to decide, to judge, to decree, to ordain** > Pilate had determined to let Jesus go (Acts 3:13). Paul and Timothy delivered the decrees determined {decisions reached} by the apostles and elders at Jerusalem (Acts 16:4). He who has determined {decreed, judged, decided} in his heart {made up his mind} that he will keep his virginity does well (1 Cor. 7:37). All other refs.: see entries in Lexicon at <2919>.

5 ***horizō*** [verb: ὁρίζω <3724>]; **from *horos*: limit** ► **a. To define, to decide** > The night before His death, Jesus said that the Son of Man was going as it had been determined {had been decreed} (Luke 22:22). The disciples in Antioch determined to send relief to the brothers in Judea (Acts 11:29). God has determined the preappointed times and the boundaries of the dwelling of men (Acts 17:26). He determines {designates, fixes, limiteth, sets} a certain day for people to hear His voice (Heb. 4:7). **b. To establish** > Jesus Christ is determined {declared, marked out} Son of God with power (Rom. 1:4). All other refs.: DETERMINED <3724>, ORDAIN <3724>.

6 **to determine before: *proorizō*** [verb: προορίζω <4309>]; **from *pro*: before, and *horizō*: see** 5 ► **To decide in advance; also transl.: to predestine** > God had determined before {had decided beforehand} what should come to pass concerning Jesus (Acts 4:28). All other refs.: PREDESTINE <4309>.

7 ***tassō*** [verb: τάσσω <5021>] ► **To decide; also transl.: to arrange, to appoint** > The disciples determined that Paul and Barnabas should go up to Jerusalem to settle a certain question (Acts 15:2). All other refs.: APPOINT <5021>.

– 8 Acts 15:37 → PROPOSE <1011> 9 Acts 17:26 in some mss. → ORDAIN <4367> 10 Acts 20:3 → PURPOSE (verb) <1106> 11 1 Cor. 12:11 → PLEASE <1014>.

DETERMINED – to determine: *horizō* [verb: ὁρίζω <3724>]; **from *horos*: limit, frontier** ► **To define, to decide** > Jesus was delivered by the determined {definite, deliberate, determinate, predetermined, set} counsel and foreknowledge of God (Acts 2:23). All other refs.: DETERMINE <3724>, ORDAIN <3724>.

DETERMINED (BE) – Luke 9:51 → to set steadfastly → STEADFASTLY <4741>.

DETESTABLE – 1 Luke 16:15; Rev. 21:27 → detestable, what is detestable → abomination, making an abomination → ABOMINATION <946> 2 Titus 1:16 → ABOMINABLE <947> 3 1 Pet. 4:3 → ABOMINABLE <111> 4 Rev. 18:2 → HATED (BE) <3404> 5 Rev. 21:8 → ABOMINABLE <948>.

DETHRONE – Acts 19:27 → DESTROY <2507>.

DEVELOP – Jas. 1:3 → PRODUCE <2716>.

DEVICE – 1 ***noēma*** [neut. noun: νόημα <3540>]; **from *noeō*: to perceive, to understand, which is from *nous*: mind, understanding** ► **Thought, intention; also transl.: design, scheme** > Christians are not ignorant of Satan's devices (2 Cor. 2:11). All other refs.: MIND (noun) <3540>, THOUGHT <3540>.

– 2 Acts 17:29 → IMAGINATION <1761>.

DEVIL – 1 ***diabolos*** [masc. noun: διάβολος <1228>]; **from *diaballō*: to accuse; which is from *dia*: through, *ballō*: to throw, to cast; lit.: one who throws between, divides, slanders** ► **One of the names characterizing Satan; the word means an "accuser," and more specifically a "slanderer"** > The devil is the great enemy of God and of man. He tempted Jesus at the beginning of His public ministry (Matt.

4:1, 5, 8, 11, Luke 4:2, 3, 5, 6, 13). In one parable, he sows the tares (Matt. 13:39); in another one, he removes the word of God from the hearts (Luke 8:12). Originally, the eternal fire was prepared for the devil and his angels (Matt. 25:41). Jesus told the Jews they were of their father the devil (John 8:44). The devil put into the heart of Judas to betray Jesus (John 13:2). He was defeated by Jesus at the cross (Heb. 2:14). The devil is the adversary of the Christian (1 Pet. 5:8); he is the serpent of old, also called Satan (Rev. 12:9), who oppresses men (Acts 10:38). Pride is the sin of the devil (1 Tim. 3:6, 7; see Ezek. 28:1–19). Christians must stand against the artifices of the devil (Eph. 6:11), resist him (Jas. 4:7), and not give place to him (Eph. 4:27). The devil will have great rage, knowing that he has a short time (Rev. 12:12). He will be bound for one thousand years (Rev. 20:2), after which he must be released for a little while (see v. 3). At the end of the thousand years, he will go out to deceive the nations, but he will be cast into the lake of fire and brimstone, and will be tormented eternally (20:10). The word is also used concerning Judas who betrayed Jesus (John 6:70). Other refs.: Acts 13:10; 2 Tim. 2:26; 1 John 3:8a–c, 10; Jude 9; Rev. 2:10. Other refs.: 1 Tim. 3:11; 2 Tim. 3:3; Titus 2:3; see false accuser under ACCUSER <1228>. ¶

– 2 The word "devil" used for "fallen angel" → DEMON 3 Jas. 3:15 → of the devil → DEMONIC <1141>.

DEVILISH – Jas. 3:15 → DEMONIC <1141>.

DEVISE – Acts 4:25 → MEDITATE <3191>.

DEVISED – to be cleverly devised, to be cunningly devised: *sophizō* [verb: σοφίζω <4679>]; **from *sophos*: wise ▶ To be conceived or imagined with wisdom, to be sophisticated, but also with the intention of deceiving** > Peter had not followed cleverly devised {cleverly imagined} fables (2 Pet. 1:16). Other ref.: 2 Tim. 3:15 (to make wise); see WISE (adj.) <4679>. ¶

DEVISING – Acts 17:29 → IMAGINATION <1761>.

DEVOTE – 1 **to devote oneself: *scholazō*** [verb: σχολάζω <4980>]; **from *scholē*: leisure ▶ To give oneself to something, to be occupied with something** > Spouses are not to deprive one another, except by mutual consent, for a time, so that they may devote themselves to prayer (1 Cor. 7:5). Other refs.: Matt. 12:44 (to be unoccupied); see UNOCCUPIED <4980>; Luke 11:25 in some mss. ¶

2 **to devote oneself: *tassō*** [verb: τάσσω <5021>] ▶ **To assign oneself, to dedicate oneself** > Those of the household of Stephanas had devoted {had addicted} themselves to the service of the saints (1 Cor. 16:15). All other refs.: APPOINT <5021>.

– 3 Acts 1:14; 2:42; 6:4; Col. 4:2 → to devote, to devote continually → CONTINUE <4342> 4 Acts 18:5 → COMPEL <4912> 5 Rom. 13:6 → ATTEND <4342> 6 1 Tim. 1:4; 4:1; Titus 1:14 → to give heed → HEED (noun) <4337> 7 1 Tim. 4:13 → to devote oneself → to give attendance → ATTENDANCE <4337> 8 1 Tim. 5:10 → to follow diligently → DILIGENTLY <1872> 9 Titus 3:14 → to devote themselves to do → MAINTAIN <4291>.

DEVOTED – 1 Matt. 6:24; Luke 16:13 → to be devoted → HOLD (verb) <472> 2 Rom. 12:10 → kindly affectionate → AFFECTIONATE <5387> 3 Rom. 12:12 → PERSEVERING <4342> 4 1 Cor. 7:34 → HOLY (adj.) <40>.

DEVOTED (BE) – 1 1 Tim. 6:2 → are devoted to the welfare of their slaves → lit.: those receiving of the good service in return → PROFIT (verb) <482> 2 Heb. 13:9 → those devoted to → lit.: those having walked in → WALK <4043>.

DEVOTION – 1 ***euparedros*** [adj. used as noun: εὐπάρεδρος <2137a>]; **from *eu*: well, *para*: beside, and *hedra*: seat ▶ Diligent application or effort, perseverance, faithfulness** > Paul spoke to the Corinthians for their profit and that they might have devotion for {attend upon, serve, wait on} the Lord without distraction (1 Cor. 7:35); some mss. have [2]. ¶

[2] ***euprosedros*** [adj. used as noun: εὐπρόσεδρος <2145>]; **from *eu*: well, *pros*: near, and *hedra*: seat, or *prosedros*: constant attendant ▶ See [1].** > Some mss. have this word in 1 Cor. 7:35; see [1]. ¶

– [3] Acts 17:23 → object of worship → WORSHIP (noun) <4574> [4] 1 Cor. 7:35 → in undivided devotion → without distraction → DISTRACTION <563>.

DEVOUR – [1] ***esthiō*** [verb: ἐσθίω <2068>] ▶ **To eat, to swallow** > The heat of fire is about to devour {consume} the adversaries (Heb. 10:27). All other refs.: EAT <2068>.

[2] ***katesthiō*** [verb: κατεσθίω <2719>]; **from *kata*: intens., and *esthiō*: see [1] ▶ To swallow, to engulf; also transl.: to consume, to eat, to eat up** > In a parable, the birds devoured the seed fallen along the wayside (Matt. 13:4; Mark 4:4; Luke 8:5). The scribes were devouring the houses of widows (Matt. 23:14 in some mss.; Mark 12:40; Luke 20:47). The zeal for the house of God had devoured {consumed} (i.e., occupied entirely) Jesus (John 2:17). The prodigal son had devoured {had squandered} the property of his father with prostitutes (Luke 15:30). The Corinthians were bearing one who devoured {exploited} them (2 Cor. 11:20). Biting and devouring one another can lead to being consumed by one another (Gal. 5:15). Fire goes out of the mouth of the two witnesses and devours their enemies (Rev. 11:5). At the end of the millennium, fire will come down from God out of heaven and will devour the nations gathered to battle (Rev. 20:9). John had to take and eat (lit.: devour) the little book given to him by the angel (Rev. 10:9, 10a). The dragon stood before the woman to devour her Child when He would be born (Rev. 12:4). ¶

[3] ***katapinō*** [verb: καταπίνω <2666>]; **from *kata*: down (intens.), and *pinō*: to drink ▶ To swallow, to engulf** > The devil seeks whom he may devour (1 Pet. 5:8). All other refs.: DROWN <2666>, SWALLOW <2666>.

– [4] Rev. 17:16 → EAT <5315>.

DEVOUT – [1] ***eulabēs*** [adj.: εὐλαβής <2126>]; **from *eu*: well, and *lambanō*: to take, to receive ▶ Characterized by reverence toward God, pious** > Simeon was just and devout (Luke 2:25). There were Jews dwelling at Jerusalem who were devout {God-fearing} men (Acts 2:5). Devout {Godly} men carried Stephen to his burial (Acts 8:2). Some mss. have Acts 22:12; see [2]. ¶

[2] ***eusebēs*** [adj.: εὐσεβής <2152>]; **from *eu*: well, and *sebomai*: to venerate, to worship ▶ Characterized by piety, pious** > Cornelius was devout (Acts 10:2); a devout soldier was constantly with him (v. 7). Ananias was a devout man according to the law (Acts 22:12); some mss. have [1]. The Lord knows how to deliver the godly (or: pious men) out of trial (2 Pet. 2:9). ¶

[3] ***hosios*** [adj.: ὅσιος <3741>] ▶ **Holy, pious, upright** > The overseer is to be devout (Titus 1:8). All other refs.: HOLY (adj.) <3741>, HOLY (noun) <3741>.

– [4] Acts 13:43, 50; 17:4, 17 → WORSHIP (verb) <4576>.

DEVOUTLY – ***hosiōs*** [adv.: ὁσίως <3743>]; **from *hosios*: holy, sacred ▶ With holiness, with piety** > The Thessalonians, and God also, were witnesses how devoutly {holily, holy, piously} Paul had behaved himself among those who believed (1 Thes. 2:10). ¶

DIADEM – Rev. 12:3; 13:1; 19:12 → CROWN (noun) <1238>.

DIALECT – [1] Acts 1:19; 2:6, 8 → LANGUAGE <1258> [2] Acts 21:40; 22:2; 26:14 → TONGUE <1258>.

DIANA – ***Artemis*** [fem. name: Ἄρτεμις <735>] ▶ **Goddess of hunting and fertility, mother goddess of Asia Minor, among the Romans; Artemis is her Greek name** > Diana was the goddess of the Ephesians (Acts 19:28, 34, 35), whose temple (Acts 19:27) was considered as one of the seven wonders of that time. Silversmiths, such as Demetrius, made great gain from the manufacture of miniature silver temples of Diana (Acts 19:24). ¶

DIDRACHMA – See TAX (noun) <1323>.

DIDYMUS – ***Didumos*** [masc. name: Δίδυμος <1324>]**: twin ▶ Surname of Thomas; also transl.: the Twin** > Thomas, one of the twelve apostles, was called Didymus (John 11:16; 20:24; 21:2). See THOMAS <2381>. ¶

DIE – [1] **to die, to be dead: *apothnēskō*** [verb: ἀποθνήσκω <599>]**; from *apo*: intens., and *thnēskō*: to be dead, to die ▶ To be deceased, meaning that the soul is separated from the body** > The verb is used in regard to the Lord Jesus (John 11:50, 51; 12:33; 18:14 (*apollumi* in some mss.), 32; 19:7; Rom. 6:9; 1 Thes. 4:14). It is also used in regard to a girl (Matt. 9:24; Mark 5:35, 39), a woman (Matt. 22:27; Mark 12:22; Luke 20:32), Peter (Matt. 26:35), a man (Mark 12:21; Luke 20:29), a poor man and a rich man (Luke 16:22a, b), those who will have part in the resurrection of the dead (Luke 20:36), the son of a nobleman (John 4:47 {at the point of death; lit.: about to die}, 49), the disciples (John 11:16), Lazarus (John 11:21; in some mss.: *thnēskō*), whoever believes in Jesus (John 11:26), a grain of wheat (John 12:24a, b), John (John 21:23a, b), Dorcas (Acts 9:37), and Paul (Acts 21:13; 25:11; Rom. 7:9; 1 Cor. 9:15; 15:31; Phil. 1:21). When we were still without strength, in due time Christ died for the ungodly (Rom. 5:6); He died for sinners (v. 8). Other refs.: Matt. 8:32 {to perish}; 22:24; Mark 9:26b; 12:19, 20; 15:44b; Luke 8:42 {to lie a dying}, 52, 53; 20:28a, b, 31; John 6:49, 50, 58; 8:21, 24a, b, 52a, 53a, b; 11:14, 25, 32, 37; Acts 7:4; Rom. 5:7a, b, 15; 6:2, 7, 10a, b; 7:2, 3, 6; 8:13, 34; 14:7, 8a–c, 9a, 15; 1 Cor. 8:11; 15:3, 22, 31, 36; 2 Cor. 5:14a, b, 15a, b; Gal. 2:19, 21; Col. 2:20; 3:3; 1 Thes. 5:10; Heb. 7:8 {mortal men, men who die}; 9:27; 10:28; 11:4, 13, 21, 37 {to be slain, to be put to death} (lit.: to die by murder of sword); Jude 12; Rev. 3:2; 8:9, 11; 9:6; 14:13; 16:3. All other refs.: DEAD <599>, DYING <599>.

[2] **to die with, to die together: *sunapothnēskō*** [verb: συναποθνήσκω <4880>]**; from *sun*: together, and *apothnēskō*: see [1] ▶ To lay down one's life with; to be deceased with** > The verb is used in regard to Peter (Mark 14:31) and the Corinthians (2 Cor. 7:3). If we have died together with {If we be dead with} Christ, we will also live with Him (2 Tim. 2:11). ¶

[3] ***teleutaō*** [verb: τελευτάω <5053>]**; from *teleutē*: death, which is from *teleō*: to complete, which is from *telos*: end ▶ To arrive at one's end, to expire; also transl.: to decease, to be dead, to be put to death, to die** > The verb is used in regard to the daughter of the chief of the synagogue (Matt. 9:18), a man (Matt. 22:25), the servant of a centurion (Luke 7:2), and Jacob and his sons (Acts 7:15 {to pass away}). By faith Joseph, when he was dying {when his end was near}, spoke of the departure of the sons of Israel and gave instructions concerning his bones (Heb. 11:22). Other refs.: Matt. 15:4 (lit.: to die of death); Mark 7:10 (lit.: to die of death); 9:44, 46, 48. All other refs.: DEAD <5053>.

[4] **having died: *apogenomenos*** [ptcp.: ἀπογενόμενος <581>]**; from *apo*: far from, and *ginomai*: to become ▶ To be separated from** > Christ bore our sins on the cross, in order that, having died {being dead, we might die} to sins, we may live for righteousness (1 Pet. 2:24). ¶

– [5] Matt. 14:32; Mark 4:39; 6:51 → to die down → FALL (verb) <2869> [6] Mark 15:39 → EXPIRE <1606> [7] Luke 7:12 → who had died → who was dead → DEAD <2348> [8] Luke 21:26 → to be ready to die → to have the heart failing → HEART <674> [9] Acts 5:5; 12:23 → EXPIRE <1634> [10] Rom. 1:32 → deserve to die → worthy of death → DEATH <2288> [11] Rom. 7:4; 2 Cor. 6:9 → to die, to make to die → KILL <2289> [12] 1 Cor. 4:9 → condemned to die → DEATH <1935> [13] 1 Cor. 7:39; 11:30 → SLEEP (verb) <2837> [14] 1 Cor. 10:8 → FALL (verb) <4098> [15] 1 Pet. 3:18 → SUFFER <3958>

16 Rev. 1:18 → to become dead → DEAD <3498>.

DIED – 1 John 11:44 → he who had died → DEAD <2348> 2 1 Pet. 2:24 → having died → DIE <581>.

DIFFER – 1 ***diapherō*** [verb: διαφέρω <1308>]; **from *dia*: through, and *pherō*: to carry ▶ To be dissimilar, to be distinct** > One star differs from another star in glory (1 Cor. 15:41). The heir, as long as he is a child, does not differ {is not different} from a slave (Gal. 4:1). All other refs.: see entries in Lexicon at <1308>.
– 2 Rom. 12:6 → DIFFERING <1313> 3 1 Cor. 4:7 → to make a distinction → DISTINCTION <1252>.

DIFFERENCE – 1 ***diastolē*** [fem. noun: διαστολή <1293>]; **from *diastellō*: to set apart, which is from *dia*: through, and *stellō*: to send ▶ Distinction, discrimination** > There is no difference (Rom. 3:22), for all have sinned and come short of the glory of God (see v. 23). Other refs.: Rom. 10:12; 1 Cor. 14:7; see DISTINCTION <1293>. ¶
2 **to make a difference: *diapherō*** [verb: διαφέρω <1308>]; **from *dia*: through, and *pherō*: to carry ▶ To be important, to matter** > Those who seemed to be something, whatever they were, it made no difference {made no matter} to Paul (Gal. 2:6). All other refs.: see entries in Lexicon at <1308>.
3 **there is a difference: *memeristai*, form of *merizō*** [verb: μερίζω <3307>]**: to divide, which is from *meris*: portion ▶ There is a distinction** > There is a difference between the wife and the virgin (1 Cor. 7:34), since the woman who is not married has more time to care for the things of the Lord. All other refs.: DISTRIBUTE <3307>, DIVIDE <3307>, GIVE <3307>.
– 4 Acts 15:9; Jude 22 → to make a difference, to put a difference → to make a distinction → DISTINCTION <1252> 5 Rom. 3:22 → difference between Jew and Gentile → "between Jew and Gentile" added in Engl. 6 1 Cor. 11:19 → SECT <139> 7 1 Cor. 12:5 → DIVERSITY <1243> 8 Jas. 2:4 → to make a difference → to show partiality → PARTIALITY <1252>.

DIFFERENT – 1 ***heteros*** [adj.: ἕτερος <2087>] **▶ Other, another** > Paul feared that the Corinthians would receive a different Spirit which they had not received, or a different gospel which they had not received (2 Cor. 11:4a, b). He wondered that the Galatians were quickly changing to a different gospel (Gal. 1:6). Other refs.: ANOTHER <2087>, OTHER <2087>.
– 2 Rom. 12:6 → DIFFERING <1313> 3 1 Cor. 4:7 → to make different, to see anything different → to make a distinction → DISTINCTION <1252> 4 1 Cor. 12:4–6 → different kinds → DIVERSITY <1243> 5 1 Cor. 14:10 → many different languages → many kinds of voices → KIND (noun) <1085> 6 Gal. 4:1 → to be different → DIFFER <1308> 7 Phil. 3:15 → to have a different attitude → to think otherwise → OTHERWISE <2088> 8 1 Tim. 1:3 → to teach any different doctrine → DOCTRINE <2085>.

DIFFERENTLY – 1 Phil. 3:15 → OTHERWISE <2088> 2 1 Tim. 6:3 → to teach differently → to teach other doctrine → DOCTRINE <2085>.

DIFFERING – ***diaphoros*** [adj.: διάφορος <1313>]; **from *diapherō*: to differ, which is from *dia*: prep. indicating different directions, and *pherō*: to carry ▶ Distinct, different** > Christians have gifts differing {gifts that differ} according to the grace given to them (Rom. 12:6). All other refs.: EXCELLENT <1313>, VARIOUS <1313>.

DIFFICULT – 1 ***chalepos*** [adj.: χαλεπός <5467>] **▶ Distressing, troublesome** > Paul warned Timothy that, in the last days, there would come difficult {perilous, terrible} times (2 Tim. 3:1), i.e., times difficult to traverse because of widespread evil (see vv. 2–5). Other ref.: Matt. 8:28; see VIOLENT (adj.) <5467>. ¶
– 2 Mark 10:23; Luke 18:24 → HARD <1423> 3 Mark 10:24 → HARD <1422>

4 John 6:60 → HARD <4642> 5 Acts 15:19 → to make it difficult → TROUBLE (verb) <3926>.

DIFFICULTY – 1 **with difficulty: *mogis*** [adv.: μόγις <3425>]; **from *mogos*: trouble, effort ▶ Hardly, scarcely, with pain** > An evil spirit departed from the son of a man with difficulty {with great difficulty, scarcely} after crushing him (Luke 9:39); some mss. have *molis*: see 2. ¶

2 **with difficulty: *molis*** [adv.: μόλις <3433>]; **from *molos*: trouble ▶ Hardly; also transl.: scarce, scarcely, very rarely, with much work** > Paul and Barnabas with difficulty kept the crowd from sacrificing to them (Acts 14:18). Paul's boat arrived with difficulty off Cnidus (Acts 27:7); it coasted Crete with difficulty (v. 8). With difficulty they were able to make themselves masters of the boat (Acts 27:16). With difficulty will one die for a just man (Rom. 5:7). The righteous one is with difficulty {scarcely} saved (1 Pet. 4:18); other transl.: It is hard for the righteous to be saved. Other ref.: Luke 9:39 in some mss.; see 1.¶

– 3 Matt. 19:23; Mark 10:23; Luke 18:24 → with difficulty → HARD <1423> 4 2 Cor. 12:10 → DISTRESS <4730> 5 2 Tim. 3:1 → times of difficulty → difficult times → DIFFICULT <5467>.

DIFFUSE – 2 Cor. 2:14 → MANIFEST (verb) <5319>.

DIG – 1 **to dig, to dig deep: *bathunō*** [verb: βαθύνω <900>]; **from *bathus*: deep ▶ To make a deep hole** > To build his house, a man dug (*skaptō*) and dug deep (*bathunō*), and laid the foundation on the rock (Luke 6:48). ¶

2 ***orussō*** [verb: ὀρύσσω <3736>] **▶ To make a hole by removing earth or something else; to excavate** > A landowner dug {digged} a winepress and built a tower (Matt. 21:33; Mark 12:1 {to dig a pit}). A slave dug {digged, dug a hole} in the ground and hid the money of his lord (Matt. 25:18). ¶

3 **to dig up, through, an opening: *exorussō*** [verb: ἐξορύσσω <1846>]; **from *ek*: out, and *orussō*: see 2 ▶ To make an opening (in the roof of a house)** > The friends of the paralytic dug up {broke up, broke through} the roof of a house to let down the couch on which he lay (Mark 2:4). Other ref.: Gal. 4:15; see PLUCK <1846>. ¶

4 **to dig, to dig around, to dig about: *skaptō*** [verb: σκάπτω <4626>] **▶ a. To turn the ground** > In the parable, the keeper of the vineyard requested to dig around the fig tree and fertilize it (Luke 13:8). In another one, the steward said he could not dig (Luke 16:3). **b. To make a hole by scooping out, to excavate** > To build a house, a man dug (*skaptō*) and dug deep (*bathunō*) (Luke 6:48). ¶

5 **to dig down: *kataskaptō*** [verb: κατασκάπτω <2679>]; **from *kata*: down, and *skaptō*: see 4; lit.: to undermine ▶ To raze, to demolish** > Israel had dug down {had torn down} God's altars (Rom. 11:3). Other ref.: Acts 15:16 (to ruin); see RUIN (noun) <2679>. ¶

– 6 Matt. 6:19, 20; 24:43; Luke 12:39 → to dig through → to break into → BREAK <1358>.

DIGNIFIED – 1 1 Tim. 2:2; Titus 2:7 → lit.: dignity → DIGNITY <4587> 2 1 Tim. 3:8, 11; Titus 2:2 → GRAVE <4586>.

DIGNITARY – ***doxa*** [fem. noun: δόξα <1391>]; **from *dokeō*: to think, to appear; lit.: glory ▶ Term describing most likely the angels in a position of authority and who must be respected; also transl.: dignity, angelic majesty** > There are dreamers speaking evil of dignitaries {celestial beings} (Jude 8). They are not afraid to speak injuriously of dignitaries {authority} (2 Pet. 2:10). Other refs.: GLORY (noun) <1391>.

DIGNITY – 1 ***semnotēs*** [fem. noun: σεμνότης <4587>]; **from *semnos*: honorable, venerable ▶ Seriousness, nobleness; also transl.: gravity, holiness, honesty, respect, reverence** > Christians pray that they may lead a peaceful and quiet life in all dignity (1 Tim. 2:2). The overseer must have his children in subjection in all dignity (1 Tim. 3:4). Titus was to show seriousness in teaching (Titus 2:7). ¶

– 2 1 Tim. 3:8 → man of dignity → GRAVE <4586> 3 Jude 8; 2 Pet. 2:10 → DIGNITARY <1391>.

DILIGENCE – 1 ***spoudē*** [fem. noun: σπουδή <4710>]; **from *speudō*: to hasten ► Zeal, perseverance to accomplish something; also transl.: earnestness** > He who leads is to lead with diligence {diligently} (Rom. 12:8). Having been sorrowed in a godly manner had produced diligence {carefulness} in the Corinthians (2 Cor. 7:11). The Corinthians abounded in all diligence {forwardness, zeal} (2 Cor. 8:7, 8). The author of the Epistle to the Hebrews desired that each one would show the same diligence to the full assurance of hope until the end (Heb. 6:11). Being partaker of the divine nature, the Christian must use all diligence {make every effort} to add to his faith virtue and other qualities (2 Pet. 1:5). Jude used all diligence {was very diligent, was making every effort, was very eager} to write his letter (Jude 3). All other refs.: HASTE <4710>, ZEAL <4710>, ZEALOUSNESS <4710>.

– 2 Luke 12:58 → to give diligence → to make every effort → EFFORT <2039> 3 Eph. 4:3; 1 Thes. 2:17 → to use diligence → ENDEAVOR (verb) <4704> 4 2 Tim. 4:9, 21; Titus 3:12 → to do one's diligence, to use diligence → to make every effort → EFFORT <4704> 5 Heb. 4:11 → to use diligence → LABOR (verb) <4704> 6 2 Pet. 1:10, 15 → to give diligence, to use diligence → to be diligent → DILIGENT <4704>.

DILIGENT – 1 **to be diligent: *spoudazō*** [verb: σπουδάζω <4704>]; **from *spoudē*: diligence, haste, zeal ► To make every effort, to hasten** > Paul was diligent {was forward, was eager} to remember the poor (Gal. 2:10). Timothy was to be diligent {do his best, strive diligently, study} to present himself approved to God (2 Tim. 2:15). Peter exhorts Christians to be even more diligent {give diligence, use diligence, be all the more eager} to make their calling and election sure (2 Pet. 1:10); he would be diligent {be careful, endeavour, use diligence} that they always have a reminder of these things after his death (v. 15). He also exhorts them to be diligent to be found by God in peace, without spot and blameless (2 Pet. 3:14). All other refs.: EFFORT <4704>, ENDEAVOR (verb) <4704>, LABOR (verb) <4704>.

– 2 Rom. 12:11 → diligent zealousness → ZEALOUSNESS <4710> 3 2 Cor. 8:17, 22 → more diligent → more zealous → ZEALOUS <4707> 4 2 Cor. 8:22 → diligent, of diligent zeal → ZEALOUS <4705> 5 1 Tim. 4:15 → to be diligent → to occupy oneself → OCCUPY <3191> 6 Jude 3 → to be very diligent → DILIGENCE <4710>.

DILIGENTLY – 1 **to follow diligently: *epakoloutheō*** [verb: ἐπακολουθέω <1872>]; **from *epi*: upon (intens.), and *akoloutheō*: to follow, to accompany ► To devote oneself to, to practice** > Paul speaks of the widow who has diligently followed every good work (1 Tim. 5:10). Other refs.: Mark 16:20; 1 Tim. 5:24; 1 Pet. 2:21; see FOLLOW <1872>. ¶

2 **very diligently: *spoudaioteron*** [compar. adj. used as adv.: σπουδαιότερον <4706>]; **from *spoudaios*: earnest, prompt, which is from *spoudē*: application, zeal ► More carefully, with greater zeal** > Onesiphorus had sought Paul out very diligently {eagerly, hard, very zealously} in Rome and had found him (2 Tim. 1:17); other mss. have *spoudaiōs*; see 3. ¶

3 ***spoudaiōs*** [adv.: σπουδαίως <4709>]; **from *spoudaios*: see 2 ► Diligently, promptly, with haste** > Paul told Titus to diligently set forth Zenas on his way (Titus 3:13). Other refs.: Luke 7:4; see EARNESTLY <4709>; 2 Tim. 1:17: see 2. ¶

– 4 Matt. 2:8 → CAREFULLY <199> 5 Matt. 2:16 → to enquire diligently → DETERMINE <198> 6 Mark 7:3 → CAREFULLY <4435> 7 Luke 15:8 → CAREFULLY <1960> 8 Acts 18:25 → ACCURATELY <199> 9 Rom. 12:8 → lit.: with diligence → DILIGENCE <4710> 10 Phil. 2:28 → the more diligently → the more eagerly → EAGERLY <4708> 11 1 Pet. 1:10 → to search diligently → to search carefully → SEARCH (verb) <1830>.

DILL – Matt. 23:23 → ANISE <432>.

DIMINISHING – Rom. 11:12 → FAILURE <2275>.

DIMLY – 1 Cor. 13:12 → OBSCURELY <1722> <135>.

DINE – [1] ***aristaō*** [verb: ἀριστάω <709>]; **from *ariston*: breakfast ► To take a meal, usually earlier in the day, but not necessarily** > A Pharisee asked Jesus to dine {have lunch, eat} with him (Luke 11:37). After His resurrection, Jesus invited His disciples on the shore of the Sea of Tiberias to come and dine {eat breakfast, have breakfast} (John 21:12), which they did (v. 15 {to eat}). ¶

– [2] Matt. 9:10; Mark 2:15; Luke 5:29; 1 Cor. 8:10; et al. → to be at the table → TABLE[1] <345>; etc. [3] Luke 14:1 → lit.: to eat bread → EAT <5315>, BREAD <740> [4] 1 Cor. 8:10 → to sit at table → SIT <2621> [5] Rev. 3:20 → SUP <1172>.

DINING – Mark 7:4 → dining couches → lit.: couches → BED <2825>.

DINNER – [1] ***ariston*** [neut. noun: ἄριστον <712>] ► **Meal usually taken earlier in the day, but not necessarily** > Jesus told whom to invite when making a dinner {luncheon} or a supper (Luke 14:12). A Pharisee wondered that Jesus had not first washed before dinner {the meal} (Luke 11:38). In a parable, a king had prepared his dinner (poss.: a banquet early in the day) for the wedding of his son (Matt. 22:4). Other ref.: Luke 14:15 in some mss. ¶

– [2] Matt. 9:10; Mark 2:15 → to have dinner → to be at the table → TABLE[1] <345> [3] Luke 14:12, 16, 17, 24; John 12:2 → SUPPER <1173>.

DIONYSIUS – ***Dionusios*** [masc. name: Διονύσιος <1354>]; **from Dionysius, Greek god of wine ► Member of the Areopagus, tribunal court of Athens** > Dionysius believed the preaching of Paul and joined him with others (Acts 17:34). ¶

DIOSCURI – See TWIN BROTHERS <1324>.

DIOTREPHES – ***Diotrephēs*** [masc. name: Διοτρέφης <1361>]: **nourished by Zeus ► Member of a gathering of Christians** > Diotrephes loved to have the first place in the church; he prevented receiving brothers from other localities; he even chased away those who wanted to receive them (3 John 9, see v. 10). ¶

DIP – [1] ***baptō*** [verb: βάπτω <911>] ► **a. To immerse, to plunge** > The wicked rich man wanted Lazarus to dip the tip of his finger in water so that he might cool off his tongue (Luke 16:24). It was the one to whom Jesus would give the piece of bread, after having dipped it, who would betray Him (John 13:26a). **b. To immerse, to stain** > He who was sitting on the white horse was clothed with a robe dipped in blood (Rev. 19:13); *rainō* in some mss.: to sprinkle. ¶

[2] ***embaptō*** [verb: ἐμβάπτω <1686>]; **from *en*: in, and *baptō*: see [1] ► To plunge, to put into** > The verb is used in regard to Judas who was about to betray Jesus and who dipped his hand in the dish with Jesus (Matt. 26:23; Mark 14:20; John 13:26b). ¶

DIRECT – [1] ***euthunō*** [verb: εὐθύνω <2116>]; **from *euthus*: straight ► To guide on a direct course, to steer** > Ships are directed wherever the pilot wants to go (Jas. 3:4). Other ref.: John 1:23 {to make straight}; see STRAIGHT <2116>. ¶

[2] ***kateuthunō*** [verb: κατευθύνω <2720>]; **from *kata*: down (intens.), and *euthunō*: see [1] ► To make straight, to guide, to incline** > Paul hoped that God the Father and the Lord Jesus would direct {would make clear} his way to the Thessalonians (1 Thes. 3:11); this verb is sing. in Greek, possibly a testimony to the unity of divine persons. Paul wished that the Lord would direct the hearts of the Thessalonians into the love of God and into the patience of Christ (2 Thes. 3:5). Other ref.: Luke 1:79; see GUIDE (verb) <2720>. ¶

[3] ***suntassō*** [verb: συντάσσω <4929>]; **from *sun*: together (intens.), and *tassō*: to designate, to establish ► To prescribe, to order** > The disciples did as Jesus had directed {appointed} them (Matt. 26:19). The chief priests gave the thirty pieces of silver for the field of the potter, according as the Lord directed {commanded, appointed} (Matt. 27:10). Other ref.: Matt. 21:6 in some mss. ¶

– [4] Matt. 14:19; 15:35 → COMMAND (verb) <2753> [5] Matt. 21:6 → ORDAIN <4367> [6] Matt. 28:15 → TEACH <1321> [7] Matt. 28:16 → APPOINT <5021> [8] Mark 6:39 → COMMAND (verb) <2004> [9] Mark 8:6; Acts 15:5 → COMMAND (verb) <3853> [10] Luke 8:55 → COMMAND (verb) <1299> [11] Acts 3:4 → to direct one's gaze → to fasten one's eyes → FASTEN <816> [12] Acts 7:44; 20:13; 1 Cor. 7:17; 9:14; 16:1; Titus 1:5 → ORDAIN <1299> [13] Acts 10:22 → to be divinely directed → to be divinely warned → WARN <5537> [14] 1 Cor. 11:2 → DELIVER <3860> [15] 1 Tim. 5:17 → to direct the affairs of the church → RULE (verb) <4291> [16] Jas. 3:4 → wherever the will of the pilot directs → lit.: wherever the inclination of the one steering wills → INCLINATION <3730>, WILL (verb) <1014>.

DIRECTION – [1] Mark 1:45 → from every direction → on every side → SIDE <3840> [2] Acts 7:53 → DISPOSITION <1296> [3] Acts 10:17 → to ask directions → to make inquiry → INQUIRY <1331> [4] 1 Cor. 11:2 → TRADITION <3862> [5] 1 Cor. 11:34 → to give further directions → to set in order → ORDER (noun) <1299> [6] Heb. 11:22 → to give directions → to give charge → CHARGE (noun)[2] <1781>.

DIRECTIVES – 1 Cor. 11:17 → in the following directives → lit.: in prescribing this → PRESCRIBE <3853>.

DIRECTLY – Mark 6:25 → ONCE (AT) <1824>.

DIRECTLY OVERHEAD – Rev. 8:13; 14:6; 19:17 → midst of heaven → HEAVEN <3321>.

DIRECTOR – Rom. 16:23 → director of public works → CHAMBERLAIN <3623>.

DIRGE – Matt. 11:17; Luke 7:32 → to sing a dirge → MOURN <2354>.

DIRT – 1 Pet. 3:21 → FILTH <4509>.

DIRTY – ***rhuparos*** [adj.: ῥυπαρός <4508>]; **from *rhupos*: filth ► Filthy, soiled** > James speaks of the welcome which is to be extended to a poor person in dirty {shabby, vile} clothes who enters a synagogue (Jas. 2:2). Other ref.: Rev. 22:11a; see FILTHY <4510>. ¶

DIS- – ***dus*** [particle: δυς <1418>] ► Inseparable particle implying difficulty, used as a prefix like the Engl. un-, in-, mis-, and dis-. Examples: *duskolos*, difficult; *dusphēmia*, defamation. * ‡

DISABILITY – Luke 13:12 → WEAKNESS <769>.

DISABLE – Heb. 12:13 → DISLOCATE <1624>.

DISABLED – John 5:3 → to be disabled → to be sick → SICK (adj. and noun) <770>.

DISABLING – Luke 13:11 → of weakness → WEAKNESS <769>.

DISAGREE – Acts 28:25 → one who does not agree → AGREE <800>.

DISAGREEMENT – [1] **sharp disagreement: *paroxusmos*** [masc. noun: παροξυσμός <3948>]; **from *paroxunō*: to agitate, to provoke, which is from *para*: beside (intens.), and *oxunō*: to irritate ► Serious dispute, sharp contention** > There was a sharp disagreement between Paul and Barnabas (Acts 15:39). Other ref.: Heb. 10:24 (provoking); see PROVOKE <3948>. ¶

– [2] Acts 25:19 → point of disagreement → QUESTION (noun) <2213>.

DISALLOW – 1 Pet. 2:4, 7 → REJECT <593>.

DISANNUL – [1] Gal. 3:15 → REJECT <114> [2] Gal. 3:17 → to make of no effect → EFFECT (noun) <208>.

DISANNULLING – Heb. 7:18 → putting away → PUTTING <115>.

DISAPPEAR – [1] **invisible:** ***aphantos*** [adj.: ἄφαντος <855>]; **from *a*: neg., and *phainō*: to appear, which is from *phōs*: light ▶ Hidden, which vanishes from view** > Jesus disappeared {vanished} (lit.: became invisible) from the disciples of Emmaus (Luke 24:31). ¶
– [2] Matt. 5:18a, b; Luke 16:17; 2 Pet. 3:10 → PASS <3928> [3] 1 Cor. 13:10 → to do away → AWAY <2673> [4] Heb. 8:13 → disappearance → VANISH <854> [5] Jas. 4:14 → to vanish away → VANISH <853>.

DISAPPEARING – Heb. 8:13 → disappearance → VANISH <854>.

DISAPPOINTED (BE) – Rom. 9:33; 10:11; 1 Pet. 2:6 → ASHAMED (BE) <2617>.

DISAPPROVED – 2 Tim. 3:8 → WORTHLESS <96>.

DISARM – ***apekduomai*** [verb: ἀπεκδύομαι <554>]; **from *apo*: from, and *ekduō*: to strip, which is from *ek*: out, and *duō*: to go ▶ To remove completely, to undress completely** > Christ has disarmed {spoiled} principalities and authorities (Col. 2:15). The verb is transl. "to put off" {to lay aside, to take off} in Col. 3:9: the Christian should have put off the old man with his deeds. ¶

DISASTER – ***hubris*** [fem. noun: ὕβρις <5196>] ▶ **Damage, harm** > Paul perceived that the voyage would be accompanied by disaster {hurt} and much loss (Acts 27:10). Other refs.: Acts 27:21; 2 Cor. 12:10; see HARM (noun) <5196>, INSULT (noun) <5196>. ¶

DISASTROUS – Acts 27:10 → to be disastrous → lit.: with disaster → DISASTER <5196>.

DISBELIEVE – [1] ***apeitheō*** [verb: ἀπειθέω <544>]; **from *apeithēs*: disobedient, which is from *a*: neg., and *peithō*: to persuade ▶ To refuse to believe, to be disobedient** > At Ephesus, some were hardened and disobedient to {became disobedient to, did not believe, refused to believe} the preaching of Paul (Acts 19:9). All other refs.: BELIEVE <544>, DISOBEDIENT <544>, OBEY <544>, UNBELIEVING <544>.
– [2] Luke 24:41 → to not believe → BELIEVE <569> [3] John 20:27 → to be unbelieving → UNBELIEVING <571>.

DISCERN – [1] ***anakrinō*** [verb: ἀνακρίνω <350>]; **from *ana*: intens., and *krinō*: to judge ▶ To distinguish; also transl.: to appraise, to judge** > The things of the Spirit of God are spiritually discerned (1 Cor. 2:14); he who is spiritual discerns {makes judgments about} all things, yet he himself is rightly discerned by {is subject to the judgment of} no one (v. 15a, b). All other refs.: ASK <350>, EXAMINE <350>, JUDGE (verb) <350>, SEARCH (verb) <350>.
[2] ***diakrinō*** [verb: διακρίνω <1252>]; **from *dia*: through, and *krinō*: to judge; lit.: to separate completely ▶ To distinguish accurately, to perceive distinctly** > The Pharisees and the Sadducees knew how to discern {interpret} the face of the sky, but not the signs of the times (Matt. 16:3). He who takes part in the Lord's supper in an unworthy manner, not discerning {distinguishing, judging, recognizing} the Lord's body, eats and drinks judgment to himself (1 Cor. 11:29). All other refs.: see entries in Lexicon at <1252>.
[3] ***dokimazō*** [verb: δοκιμάζω <1381>]; **from *dokimos*: tested, approved; comp. *dechomai*: to accept, to receive ▶ To examine, to test, to scrutinize, to discern by testing** > The multitudes could discern

{judge, analyze, interpret} the appearance of the sky and of the earth, but not the times they were going through (Luke 12:56a, b). The Jews discerned {approved, discerningly approved} the things that are excellent (Rom. 2:18). Being transformed by the renewing of his mind, the Christian can discern {prove, test and approve} what is the will of God (Rom. 12:2). Paul was praying that the Philippians would discern {approve} the things that are more excellent (Phil. 1:10). All other refs.: APPROVE <1381>, LIKE (verb) <1381>, TEST (noun and verb) <1381>.

– 4 Luke 1:29 → to try to discern → to reason in one's mind → REASON (verb) <1260> 5 Heb. 4:12 → discerning → DISCERNER <2924> 6 Heb. 5:14 → DISCERNING <1253>.

DISCERNER – ***kritikos*** [adj.: κριτικός <2924>]; **from *krinō*: to judge, or *kritēs*: judge ► Capable of judging, of perceiving distinctly** > The word of God is a discerner (lit.: discerning) of {is able to judge, judges} the thoughts and intents of the heart (Heb. 4:12). ¶

DISCERNING – 1 ***diakrisis*** [fem. noun: διάκρισις <1253>]; **from *diakrinō*: to separate completely, which is from *dia*: through, and *krinō*: to distinguish, to judge ► Capacity of good judgment, sound evaluation** > The discerning of {distinguishing of, ability to distinguish the} spirits (1 Cor. 12:10; other mss.: *diermēneia*) is a gift allowing to judge if what is said is from God or not. Those who are experienced in the word of God have their senses exercised for discerning {to discern, to distinguish, for distinguishing} (lit.: for the discerning of, for the distinction of) both good and evil (Heb. 5:14). Other refs.: Acts 4:32 in some mss.; Rom. 14:1; see DISPUTE (noun) <1253>. ¶

– 2 1 Cor. 1:19 → lit.: the understanding ones → UNDERSTANDING <4908> 3 1 Cor. 11:31 → to be more discerning → JUDGE (verb) <1252>.

DISCERNINGLY – Rom. 2:18 → to discerningly approve → DISCERN <1381>.

DISCERNMENT – 1 ***aisthēsis*** [fem. noun: αἴσθησις <144>]; **from *aisthanomai*: to perceive, to grasp with the senses or by thought ► Perception by the senses and by the intellect, discrimination; also transl.: depth of insight, intelligence, judgment** > Paul prayed that the love of the Philippians might abound in all discernment (Phil. 1:9). ¶

– 2 1 Cor. 1:19 → UNDERSTANDING <4907> 3 Heb. 5:14 → power of discernment → SENSE (noun) <145>.

DISCHARGE (noun) – 1 Matt. 9:20 → to suffer from a discharge of blood → to have a flow of blood → FLOW (noun) <131> 2 Mark 5:25; Luke 8:43, 44 → FLOW (noun) <4511>.

DISCHARGE (verb) – 1 Acts 21:3 → UNLOAD <670> 2 2 Tim. 4:5 → to discharge all the duties → to make full proof → PROOF <4135>.

DISCIPLE – 1 ***mathētēs*** [masc. noun: μαθητής <3101>]; **from *manthanō*: to learn, to understand ► One who follows a teacher, learns his teachings, and puts them into practice** > The disciple {student} is not above his teacher (Matt. 10:24). John the Baptist had his disciples (Matt. 9:14; John 1:35); the Pharisees also had their own (Matt. 22:16). The term is specifically applied to the apostles of the Lord (Matt. 10:1–4; Luke 6:13–16). A disciple is an individual who receives by faith the teachings of Jesus and of the apostles, and puts them into practice (e.g., Acts 1:15). The word appears more than 250 times in the four Gospels and in the Acts. *

2 ***mathētria*** [fem. noun: μαθήτρια <3102>]; **fem. of 1 ► A woman who follows the teachings of a teacher and puts them into practice** > Dorcas (or: Tabitha) was a disciple (Acts 9:36). ¶

3 **to become a disciple, to be a disciple, to make a disciple, to be discipled, to win disciples, to instruct, to teach: *mathēteuō***

[verb: μαθητεύω <3100>]; **from *mathētēs*: see [1] ▶ To become a disciple or to make someone else a disciple** > Jesus speaks of a scribe who has become a disciple concerning the kingdom of heaven (Matt. 13:52). Joseph of Arimathea had become a disciple of Jesus (Matt. 27:57). Jesus told His eleven disciples to make disciples of all the nations (Matt. 28:19). In a city, Paul and Barnabas preached the gospel and made many disciples (Acts 14:21). ¶

– [4] Mark 8:34; Luke 9:23 → wants to be my disciple → lit.: would come after me.

DISCIPLED – Matt. 13:52 → to be discipled → DISCIPLE <3100>.

DISCIPLINE (noun) – [1] 1 Cor. 4:21 → "of discipline" added in Engl. [2] Eph. 6:4; Heb. 12:5, 7, 8, 11 → TRAINING <3809> [3] Col. 2:5 → good discipline → ORDER (noun) <5010> [4] 1 Tim. 1:20 → to teach by discipline → LEARN <3811> [5] 1 Tim. 4:8 → EXERCISE (noun) <1129> [6] 2 Tim. 1:7 → sound mind → MIND (noun) <4995>.

DISCIPLINE (verb) – [1] ***hupōpiazō*** [verb: ὑπωπιάζω <5299>]; **from *hupōpion*: part of the face under the eyes, blow in the face, which is from *hupo*: under, and *ōps*: eye, sight; lit.: to hit below the eye ▶ To compel oneself to observe a severe training program** > Paul disciplined {beat, buffeted, kept under} his body (1 Cor. 9:27), perhaps through voluntary deprivation. Other ref.: Luke 18:5; see HARASS <5299>. ¶

– [2] 1 Cor. 11:32; Heb. 12:6, 7, 10; Rev. 3:19 → CHASTEN <3811> [3] Col. 2:5 → how disciplined you are → your order → ORDER (noun) <5010> [4] 1 Tim. 4:7 → EXERCISE (verb) <1128> [5] Heb. 12:9 → who corrects → CORRECT <3810>.

DISCLOSE – [1] Matt. 10:26; Luke 12:2 → REVEAL <601> [2] Mark 4:22; Rom. 16:26; 1 Cor. 4:5; Heb. 9:8 → MANIFEST (verb) <5319> [3] John 14:21, 22 → MANIFEST (verb) <1718> [4] Acts 19:18 → TELL <312> [5] Acts 23:30 → SHOW (verb) <3377> [6] 1 Cor. 3:13 → DECLARE <1213>.

DISCLOSED – [1] Mark 4:22; Luke 8:17 → to be disclosed → to light → LIGHT (noun) <1519> <5318> [2] Luke 8:17; 1 Cor. 14:25 → REVEALED <5318>.

DISCORD – [1] 2 Cor. 12:20 → CONTENTION <2054> [2] Gal. 5:20 → STRIFE <2054>.

DISCOURAGED – [1] **to become discouraged: *athumeō*** [verb: ἀθυμέω <120>]; **from *athumos*: discouragement, which is from *a*: neg., and *thumos*: passion ▶ To be overwhelmed, to be demoralized** > Fathers must not vex their children, to the end that they become discouraged {be discouraged, be disheartened, lose heart} (Col. 3:21). ¶

[2] **to be discouraged: *ekluō*** [verb: ἐκλύω <1590>]; **from *ek*: out (intens.), and *luō*: to unbind, to loose ▶ To lose courage, to be overwhelmed by circumstances** > By looking to Jesus, we do not become weary, discouraged {fainting, losing heart} in our minds (Heb. 12:3). Under the chastening of the Lord, we should not be discouraged {faint} (Heb. 12:5). All other refs.: FAINT <1590>, HEART <1590>, WEARY (adj.) <1590>.

– [3] Eph. 3:13 → to be discouraged → to lose heart → HEART <1573>.

DISCOURSE (noun) – [1] Luke 7:1 → SAYING <4487> [2] Acts 1:1 → ACCOUNT (noun) <3056> [3] Acts 20:7 → MESSAGE <3056> [4] 1 Tim. 1:6 → vain discourse → VAIN <3150>.

DISCOURSE (verb) – ***dialegomai*** [verb: διαλέγομαι <1256>]; **from *dia*: intens., and *legō*: to speak ▶ To explain, to reason** > While Paul discoursed {preached, spoke, talked} very much at length, Eutychus fell from the window (Acts 20:9). All other refs.: DISPUTE (verb) <1256>, REASON (verb) <1256>, SPEAK <1256>.

DISCOVER – [1] ***katanoeō*** [verb: κατανοέω <2657>]; **from: *kata*: intens., and *noeō*: to think, to understand, which is from *nous*: mind, understanding ▶ To see clearly, to distinguish** > A bay with a beach was

discovered {observed, perceived} from the boat on which Paul sailed (Acts 27:39). All other refs.: CONSIDER <2657>, PERCEIVE <2657>.
– [2] Acts 21:3 → SIGHT (verb) <398>.

DISCREDIT (noun) – [1] Acts 19:27 → DISREPUTE <557> [2] 2 Cor. 6:3; 8:20 → BLAME (verb) <3469>.

DISCREDIT (verb) – Acts 19:27 → DESPISE <3049>.

DISCREET – [1] ***sōphrōn*** [adj.: σώφρων <4998>]; **from *sōos*: sound, and *phrēn*: mind, understanding ▶ Temperate, self-controlled, of a sound mind; also transl.: prudent, self-controlled, sober, sober-minded** > The overseer is to be discreet (1 Tim. 3:2; Titus 1:8), as likewise the older men (Titus 2:2) and the younger women (2:5). ¶
– [2] Titus 2:6 → to be discreet → to be self-controlled → SELF-CONTROLLED <4993>.

DISCREETLY – [1] Mark 12:34 → INTELLIGENTLY <3562> [2] 1 Tim. 2:9 → lit.: with discretion → MODERATION <4997>.

DISCRETION – [1] 1 Tim. 2:9, 15 → MODERATION <4997> [2] 2 Tim. 1:7 → wise discretion → sound mind → MIND (noun) <4995>.

DISCRIMINATE – [1] Acts 15:9 → to make a distinction → DISTINCTION <1252> [2] Jas. 2:4 → to show partiality → PARTIALITY <1252>.

DISCUSS – [1] ***dialaleō*** [verb: διαλαλέω <1255>]; **from *dia*: through, and *laleō*: to talk ▶ To talk, to converse** > The sayings concerning Zacharias and his family were discussed {were the subject of conversations, were noised, were talked about} (Luke 1:65). The Jews were discussing {communing, speaking} together concerning what they might do to Jesus (Luke 6:11). ¶
– [2] Matt. 16:7, 8; Mark 8:16, 17; 9:33; 11:31 → REASON (verb) <1260> [3] Mark 9:10; Luke 22:23 → QUESTION (noun) <4802> [4] Mark 9:16; Acts 9:29 → to discuss with → to dispute with → DISPUTE (verb) <4802> [5] Mark 9:34 → DISPUTE (verb) <1256> [6] Luke 20:5 → REASON (verb) <4817> [7] Luke 22:4 → to speak to → SPEAK <4814> [8] Luke 24:15 → REASON (verb) <4802> [9] Luke 24:17 → EXCHANGE (verb) <474> [10] Acts 24:25 → REASON (verb) <1256> [11] Acts 25:14 → to lay before → LAY <394>.

DISCUSSION – [1] John 3:25; Acts 15:2, 7 → DISPUTE (noun) <2214> [2] Acts 19:9 → to have discussions → REASON (verb) <1256> [3] Acts 24:12 → to carry on a discussion → DISPUTE (verb) <1256> [4] Heb. 6:1 → the discussion of the elementary principles → lit.: the word of the beginning → WORD <3056>, BEGINNING <746>.

DISEASE – [1] ***malakia*** [fem. noun: μαλακία <3119>]; **from *malakos*: soft, delicate ▶ Physical weakness or infirmity** > Jesus healed all kinds of disease and every bodily weakness (Matt. 4:23; 9:35). He gave authority to His disciples to do the same (Matt. 10:1). ¶

[2] ***nosēma*** [neut. noun: νόσημα <3553>]; **from *noseō*: to be sick ▶ Health problem >** The first sick person, who went in the pool of Bethesda after an angel had stirred up the water, became well of whatever disease he had (John 5:4). ¶
– [3] Matt. 4:23, 24; 8:17; 9:35; 10:1; Mark 1:34; 3:15; Luke 4:40; 6:17; 7:21; 9:1; Acts 19:12 → SICKNESS <3554> [4] Mark 3:10; 5:29, 34 → AFFLICTION <3148> [5] Luke 8:2 → WEAKNESS <769> [6] Acts 28:9 → SICKNESS <769>.

DISEASED – [1] Matt. 7:17, 18 → BAD <4550> [2] Matt. 14:35; Mark 1:32 → SICK (adv.) <2560> [3] John 6:2 → to be diseased → to be sick, to fall sick → SICK (adj. and noun) <770>.

DISFIGURE – **to disfigure the face:** ***aphanizō*** [verb: ἀφανίζω <853>]; **from *aphanēs*: hidden, not apparent, which is from *a*: neg., and *phainō*: to appear, which is from *phōs*: light ▶ To become obscure, distorted** > The hypocrites disfigure their faces {put on a gloomy face} that they may appear to men to be fasting (Matt. 6:16). All other refs.: DESTROY <853>, PERISH <853>, VANISH <853>.

DISGRACE (noun) – [1] Matt. 1:19; Heb. 6:6 → to subject, to expose to public disgrace → to make a show → SHOW (noun) <3856> [2] Luke 1:25 → REPROACH (noun) <3681> [3] Acts 5:41 → to suffer disgrace → DISHONORED (BE) <818> [4] 1 Cor. 11:6 → SHAMEFUL <149> [5] 1 Cor. 11:14 → DISHONOR (noun) <819> [6] 1 Tim. 3:7; Heb. 11:26; 13:13 → REPROACH (noun) <3680>.

DISGRACE (verb) – [1] Matt. 1:19 → to make an example → EXAMPLE <1165> [2] 1 Cor. 11:4, 5 → DISHONOR (verb) <2617>.

DISGRACEFUL – [1] 1 Cor. 14:35; Eph. 5:12 → SHAMEFUL <149> [2] 2 Cor. 4:2 → SECRET (adj. and noun) <2927>.

DISGUISE – 2 Cor. 11:13–15 → TRANSFORM <3345>.

DISH – [1] ***paropsis*** [fem. noun: παροψίς <3953>]; **from *para*: with, and *opson*: food eaten with bread, cooked food ▶ Vessel used for side dishes, delicacies, dainties** > The scribes and the Pharisees made clean the outside of the cup and the dish {platter} (Matt. 23:25, 26). ¶

[2] ***pinax*** [masc. noun: πίναξ <4094>] ▶ **Plate, platter** > The head of John the Baptist was brought upon a dish {in a charger} (Matt. 14:8, 11; Mark 6:25, 28). The scribes and the Pharisees cleanse the outside of the cup and the dish (Luke 11:39). ¶

[3] ***trublion*** [neut. noun: τρύβλιον <5165>] ▶ **Shallow bowl, plate to bring food to the table or for eating** > He, who was about to dip his hand with Jesus in the dish {bowl}, would deliver Him up (Matt. 26:23; Mark 14:20). ¶

DISHEARTENED – [1] Mark 10:22 → SAD <4768> [2] Col. 3:21 → to be disheartened → to be discouraged → DISCOURAGED <120> [3] 1 Thes. 5:14 → FAINTHEARTED <3642>.

DISHONEST – [1] ***aischros*** [adj.: αἰσχρός <150>] ▶ **Inappropriate, unseemly, indecent** > Some were teaching things which ought not to be taught for the sake of dishonest {base, filthy, sordid} gain (Titus 1:11). For *aischron*, see SHAMEFUL <149>. ¶

– [2] Luke 16:8, 9 → UNRIGHTEOUSNESS <93> [3] Luke 16:10a, b → UNRIGHTEOUS (adj. and noun) <94> [4] 1 Tim. 3:8; Titus 1:7 → pursuing dishonest gain → greedy for money → GREEDY <146>.

DISHONESTY – 2 Cor. 4:2 → SHAME (noun) <152>.

DISHONOR (noun) – [1] ***atimia*** [fem. noun: ἀτιμία <819>]; **from *atimos*: without honor, which is from *a*: neg., and *timē*: esteem, honor ▶ Shame, ignominy, disgrace** > The potter can make one vessel for honor and another for dishonor {common use} (Rom. 9:21). If a man has long hair, it is a dishonor {disgrace} to him (1 Cor. 11:14). The body of the Christian is sown in dishonor, it is raised in glory (1 Cor. 15:43). Paul speaks about glory and dishonor concerning himself (2 Cor. 6:8). He was talking to the dishonor {reproach} of the Corinthians (2 Cor. 11:21). In a great house, there are some vessels for honor and some for dishonor {ignoble purposes} (2 Tim. 2:20). Other ref.: Rom. 1:26; see SHAMEFUL <819>. ¶

– [2] Acts 5:41 → to suffer dishonor → DISHONORED (BE) <818> [3] 1 Cor. 4:10 → in dishonor → DISHONORED <820>.

DISHONOR (verb) – [1] ***atimazō*** [verb: ἀτιμάζω <818>]; **from *atimos*: without honor, which is from *a*: neg., and *timē*: esteem, honor ▶ To treat shamefully,**

without honor > The Jews were dishonoring Jesus (John 8:49). Unbelievers dishonor {degrade} their bodies among themselves (Rom. 1:24). Paul asks the one who boasts in the law if he dishonors God by transgressing the law (Rom. 2:23). James reproaches his brothers for having dishonored {despised, insulted} the poor (Jas. 2:6). All other refs.: DISHONORED (BE) <818>, INSULT (noun) <818>, SHAMEFULLY <818>.

[2] ***kataischunō*** [verb: καταισχύνω <2617>]; **from *kata*: intens., and *aischunō*: to shame, which is from *aischos*: shame, disgrace ▶ To make shameful, to cover with shame >** Every man praying or prophesying, having his head covered, dishonors {disgraces, puts to shame} his head (1 Cor. 11:4); it is the same for every woman who prays or prophesies with her head uncovered (v. 5). All other refs.: ASHAMED <2617>, ASHAMED (BE) <2617>, SHAME (noun) <2617>.

– [3] 1 Cor. 13:5 → to dishonor others → to behave uncomely, unseemly → BEHAVE <807> [4] Titus 2:5 → BLASPHEME <987>.

DISHONORABLE – [1] Rom. 1:26 → SHAMEFUL <819> [2] Rom. 9:21; 2 Tim. 2:20 → for dishonorable use → lit.: to dishonor → DISHONOR (noun) <819> [3] 2 Tim. 2:21 → from what is dishonorable → lit.: from these.

DISHONORED – ***atimos*** [adj.: ἄτιμος <820>]; **from *a*: neg., and *timē*: esteem, honor ▶ Without honor, despised >** Paul told the Corinthians that they were distinguished, but that he himself was dishonored {in dishonor} (1 Cor. 4:10). All other refs.: HONOR (noun) <820>, HONORABLE <820>.

DISHONORED (BE) – ***atimazō*** [verb: ἀτιμάζω <818>]; **from *atimos*: without honor, which is from *a*: neg., and *timē*: esteem, honor ▶ To be disgraced, to be treated shamefully >** The apostles rejoiced that they were counted worthy to be dishonored {suffer shame, suffer disgrace} for the name of Jesus (Acts 5:41). All other refs.: DISHONOR (verb) <818>, INSULT (noun) <818>, SHAMEFULLY <818>.

DISHONOUR – See DISHONOR.

DISLOCATE – ***ektrepō*** [verb: ἐκτρέπω <1624>]; **from *ek*: from, and *trepō*: to turn ▶ To put out of joint; to turn away from the right path >** Paths must be made straight, so that what is lame may not be dislocated {disabled, turned out of the way, turned aside, put out of joint} (Heb. 12:13). All other refs.: AVOID <1624>, TURN (verb) <1624>.

DISMAY – Luke 21:25 → DISTRESS <4928>.

DISMISS – [1] ***apoluō*** [verb: ἀπολύω <630>]; **from *apo*: from, and *luō*: to unbind, to loose ▶ To let go, to send off >** When they were dismissed {sent away, let go} by the church in Jerusalem, Paul and Barnabas came to Antioch (Acts 15:30). The town clerk dismissed the assembly in Ephesus (Acts 19:41). All other refs.: see entries in Lexicon at <630>.

– [2] Matt. 13:36 → to send away → SEND <863> [3] Mark 6:46 → to send away → SEND <657> [4] Acts 13:43 → to break up → BREAK <3089>.

DISMISSAL – Matt. 5:31 → DIVORCE (noun) <647>.

DISOBEDIENCE – [1] ***apeitheia*** [fem. noun: ἀπείθεια <543>]; **from *apeithēs*: disobedient, which is from *a*: neg., and *peithō*: to persuade ▶ Refusal to be persuaded, to obey, to believe; also transl.: unbelief >** Gentiles have been objects of mercy through the disobedience of Israel (Rom. 11:30). God has shut up together Jews and Gentiles in disobedience, that He might show mercy to all (Rom. 11:32). Paul speaks of unbelievers as sons of disobedience {those who are disobedient} (Eph. 2:2), upon whom comes the wrath of God (Eph. 5:6; Col. 3:6). Some did not enter in the rest of God because of disobedience {not hearkening to the word} (Heb. 4:6, 11). ¶

2 ***parakoē*** [fem. noun: παρακοή <3876>]; **from *parakouō*: to disregard, to disobey, which is from *para*: aside, and *akouō*: to listen ▶ Refusal to obey following inattentive or careless hearing** > By the disobedience of one man, many were constituted sinners (Rom. 5:19). Paul was ready to avenge all disobedience (2 Cor. 10:6). Every transgression and disobedience to the things of God received a just retribution (Heb. 2:2). ¶

DISOBEDIENT – 1 ***apeithēs*** [adj.: ἀπειθής <545>]; **from *a*: neg., and *peithō*: to persuade, to believe ▶ Who refuses to be persuaded, to obey, to believe** > John the Baptist would turn the disobedient ones to the thoughts of just ones (Luke 1:17). Paul had not been disobedient to the heavenly vision (Acts 26:19). Some evil men are disobedient to {disobey their} parents (Rom. 1:30; 2 Tim. 3:2). Those who are defiled and unbelieving are disobedient (Titus 1:16). Christians were also once disobedient (Titus 3:3). ¶

2 **to disobey, to be disobedient: *apeitheō*** [verb: ἀπειθέω <544>]; **from *apeithēs*: see 1 ▶ To refuse to be persuaded, to disbelieve; also transl.: to believe not** > God had stretched out His hands to a disobedient (lit.: being disobedient) and opposing people (Rom. 10:21). Christians once had been disobedient to God (Rom. 11:30); Jews have also been disobedient (v. 31). To those who are disobedient {do not believe}, the Lord Jesus has become the chief cornerstone (1 Pet. 2:7); they stumble, being disobedient to {because they disobey} the word (v. 8). Peter speaks of those who formerly were disobedient in the days of Noah (1 Pet. 3:20). All other refs.: BELIEVE <544>, DISBELIEVE <544>, OBEY <544>, UNBELIEVING <544>.

– 3 Eph. 2:2; 5:6; Col. 3:6 → those who are disobedient → lit.: the sons of disobedience → DISOBEDIENCE <543> 4 1 Tim. 1:9; Titus 1:6 → INSUBORDINATE <506>.

DISOBEY – 1 See DISOBEDIENT <544>. – 2 Luke 15:29 → TRANSGRESS <3928>.

DISORDER – 1 Matt. 9:23 → the crowd in noisy disorder → lit.: the crowd making a noise → to make a noise → NOISE (noun) <2350> 2 1 Cor. 14:33; 2 Cor. 12:20; Jas. 3:16 → CONFUSION <181>.

DISORDERLY – 1 ***ataktōs*** [adv.: ἀτάκτως <814>]; **from *ataktos*: out of order, unruly, which is from *a*: neg., and *tassō*: to order ▶ In a confused, unruly manner** > The Thessalonians were to withdraw from every brother walking disorderly {leading an unruly life, being idle} (2 Thes. 3:6); some among them were walking disorderly {were walking in a disorderly manner, were leading an undisciplined life, were idle} (v. 11). ¶

2 **to be disorderly: *atakteō*** [verb: ἀτακτέω <812>]; **from *ataktos*: out of order, unruly, which is from *a*: neg., and *tassō*: to order ▶ To behave in a confused, unruly manner; without discipline** > Paul and his companions had not walked disorderly {acted in an undisciplined manner, been idle} among the Thessalonians (2 Thes. 3:7). ¶

– 3 1 Thes. 5:14 → UNRULY <813> 4 1 Tim. 3:3; Titus 1:7 → disorderly through wine → given to wine → GIVE <3943> 5 Titus 1:10 → INSUBORDINATE <506>.

DISOWN – 1 Matt. 10:33a, b; Luke 12:9a; Acts 3:13, 14; 2 Tim. 2:12a, b, 13 → DENY <720> 2 Matt. 26:34, 35, 75; Mark 14:30, 31, 72; Luke 12:9b 22:61 → DENY <533> 3 Acts 7:35 → REFUSE (verb) <720>.

DISPENSATION – 1 ***oikonomia*** [fem. noun: οἰκονομία <3622>]; **from *oikonomeō*: to manage a household, which is from *oikos*: house, and *nemō*: to distribute, to manage ▶ Conduct or supervision of a house or goods entrusted; administration, management, stewardship** > A dispensation {trust}, the preaching of the gospel, was entrusted {was committed} to Paul (1 Cor. 9:17). The dispensation of the grace of God was given to him concerning the church (Eph. 3:2) to make all see what is the dispensation {fellowship: see 2} of the mystery (v. 9). He was made a minister according to the dispensation {commission} of God to complete the word of God (Col. 1:25). The purpose of God was that, in the dispensation of the fullness of times {when the times will have reached their fulfillment}, He would gather together in one all things in Christ (Eph. 1:10). God's dispensation {edifying, edification, work} is in faith (1 Tim. 1:4). Other refs.: Luke 16:2–4; see STEWARDSHIP <3622>. ¶

[2] **fellowship:** ***koinōnia*** [fem. noun: κοινωνία <2842>]; **from *koinōneō*: to share, which is from *koinōnos*: associate, participant, which is from *koinos*: common ▶ Communion, sharing** > Some mss. have this word in Eph. 3:9 instead of *oikonomia*; see [1]. All other refs.: COMMUNICATE[1] <2842>, CONTRIBUTION <2842>, FELLOWSHIP <2842>, SHARING <2842>.

DISPERSE – [1] Acts 5:36 → SCATTER <1262> [2] Acts 5:37 → SCATTER <1287> [3] 2 Cor. 9:9 → to scatter abroad → SCATTER <4650>.

DISPERSED – John 7:35; Jas. 1:1 → DISPERSION <1290>.

DISPERSION – ***diaspora*** [fem. noun: διασπορά <1290>]; **from *diaspeirō*, which is from *dia*: through (denoting separation), and *speirō*: to sow, to scatter ▶ Dissemination, Diaspora** > The Jews were asking among themselves if Jesus was about to go to the dispersion {the dispersed, the people who live scattered} among the Greeks and teach them (John 7:35). James addresses himself to the twelve tribes who are in the dispersion {scattered abroad, scattered among the nations, dispersed} (Jas. 1:1). Peter addresses himself to the sojourners of the dispersion {who reside as aliens, scattered} in various regions (1 Pet. 1:1). ¶

DISPLAY (noun) – [1] Col. 2:15 → to make a display → to make a spectacle → SPECTACLE <1165> [2] 2 Thes. 2:9 → "displays of" added in Engl.

DISPLAY (verb) – [1] Matt. 14:2 → to display the force → WORK (verb) <1754> [2] Luke 1:58 → to display great mercy → MAGNIFY <3170> [3] John 9:3 → MANIFEST (verb) <5319> [4] Rom. 3:25 → to display publicly → to set forth → SET (verb) <4388> [5] Rom. 9:17 → SHOW (verb) <1731> [6] 2 Cor. 4:4, 6 → "that displays," "displayed" added in Engl. [7] 2 Thes. 2:4 → to show oneself → SHOW (verb) <584> [8] 1 Tim. 6:15 → SHOW (verb) <1166>.

DISPLEASE – 1 Thes. 2:15 → lit.: to not please → PLEASE <700>.

DISPLEASED – [1] Matt. 20:24; 21:15; Mark 10:14, 41 → to be greatly displeased → to be indignant → INDIGNANT <23> [2] Acts 12:20 → to be highly displeased → to be very angry → ANGRY <2371>.

DISPOSAL – [1] **to put at the disposal:** ***paristēmi*** [verb: παρίστημι <3936>]; **from *para*: nearby, and *histēmi*: to stand ▶ To put at (someone's) disposition** > The Father could have put at the disposal {have provided, have furnished} the Lord Jesus more than twelve legions of angels (Matt. 26:53). Other refs.: see entries in Lexicon at <3936>.
– [2] Acts 5:4 → AUTHORITY <1849>.

DISPOSE – [1] Acts 18:27 → PURPOSE (verb) <1014> [2] 1 Cor. 7:31 → USE (verb) <2710>.

DISPOSED (BE) – 1 Cor. 10:27 → WANT (verb) <2309>.

DISPOSITION – [1] ***diatagē*** [fem. noun: διαταγή <1296>]; **from *diatassō*: to arrange completely, which is from *dia*: through, and *tassō*; to appoint; lit.: ordinance ▶ Ministry, intermediary** > The Jews received the law by the disposition of {by the direction of, as ordained by, delivered by, that was put into effect by} the angels (Acts 7:53), i.e., the law was transmitted by angels. We read that the angels were present at Sinai (see Deut. 33:2; Ps. 68:17) when Moses received the law of God. Other ref.: Rom. 13:2; see ORDINANCE <1296>. ¶

– [2] Rom. 1:29 → evil dispositions → EVIL-MINDEDNESS <2550>.

DISPOSSESS – Acts 7:45 → lit.: when they entered into possession of the nations → POSSESSION <2697>.

DISPOSSESSION – Acts 7:45 → lit.: when they entered into possession of the nations → POSSESSION <2697>.

DISPUTABLE – Rom. 14:1 → disputable matter → REASONING <1261>.

DISPUTATION – [1] Acts 15:2 → DISPUTE (noun) <2214> or <4803> [2] Rom. 14:1 → DISPUTE (noun) <1253>.

DISPUTE (noun) – [1] ***antilogia*** [fem. noun: ἀντιλογία <485>]; **from *antilegō*: to contradict, to deny, which is from *anti*: against, and *legō*: to speak ► Contradiction, contestation** > For men, an oath is an end to all dispute {argument, strife}, as making matters sure (Heb. 6:16). All other refs.: CONTRADICTION <485>.
[2] ***diakrisis*** [fem. noun: διάκρισις <1253>]; **from *diakrinō*: to judge, to decide, which is from *dia*: through, and *krinō*: to distinguish, to judge ► Decision, judgment** > One who is weak in the faith should be received in the faith, not to disputes in reasoning {not to doubtful disputations, without passing judgment} on his opinions (Rom. 14:1). Other refs.: 1 Cor. 12:10; Heb. 5:14; see DISCERNING <1253>. ¶
[3] ***zētēsis*** [fem. noun: ζήτησις <2214>]; **from *zēteō*: to seek ► Argumentative questioning, debate** > There was a dispute {an argument, a reasoning, a question} between some of John's disciples and a Jew about purification (John 3:25). Paul and Barnabas had a dispute {disputation} with those who were forcing others to be circumcised (Acts 15:2). There had been much dispute {disputing} by the brothers concerning the observance of the law (Acts 15:7). The Jews had a great dispute {reasoning} among themselves when Paul declared that the salvation of God had been sent to the Gentiles (Acts 28:29). In the last three references, some mss. have *suzētēsis* [fem. noun: συζήτησις <4803>]. Fables and interminable genealogies cause disputes {controversial speculation, controversies, questionings, questions, mere speculation}; some mss. have *ekzētēsis* [fem. noun: ἐκζήτησις <1567a>] (1 Tim. 1:4). All other refs.: INQUIRY <2214>, QUESTION (noun) <2214>.
– [4] Luke 9:46 → REASONING <1261> [5] Luke 22:24 → STRIFE <5379> [6] Acts 15:2; 23:7 → DISSENSION <4714> [7] Acts 23:10 → TUMULT <4714> [8] Acts 25:19 → point of dispute → QUESTION (noun) <2213> [9] 1 Cor. 6:1 → MATTER <4229> [10] 1 Cor. 6:4 → JUDGMENT <2922> [11] 1 Cor. 6:5 → to settle a dispute → JUDGE (verb) <1252> [12] 2 Cor. 12:20; Gal. 5:20 → CONTENTION <2052> [13] Gal. 5:20 → DIVISION <1370> [14] 1 Tim. 6:4 → dispute of words → argument over words → ARGUMENT <3055> [15] 2 Tim. 2:14 → to have disputes of words → to strive about words → STRIVE <3054> [16] Titus 3:9 → STRIVING <3163>.

DISPUTE (verb) – [1] ***dialegomai*** [verb: διαλέγομαι <1256>]; **from *dia*: through, and *legō*: to say ► To discuss, to argue** > The disciples had disputed among themselves {had been reasoning} with one another who would be the greatest (Mark 9:34). Paul had not been found disputing with {discoursing to, carrying on a discussion with} anyone (Acts 24:12). Contending with the devil, Michael the archangel was disputing {reasoning} about the body of Moses (Jude 9). All other refs.: DISCOURSE (verb) <1256>, REASON (verb) <1256>, SPEAK <1256>.
[2] **to dispute, to dispute with, to dispute against: *suzēteō*** [verb: συζητέω <4802>]; **from *sun*: together, and *zēteō*: to seek ► To discuss with contentiously, to argue with; also transl.: to question with, to reason together** > The Pharisees began to dispute against Jesus (Mark 8:11). Scribes were disputing against Jesus's disciples (Mark 9:14); Jesus asked the scribes what they were disputing with the disciples (v. 16). A scribe

had heard the Sadducees and Jesus disputing {debating} (Mark 12:28). Some from the synagogue of the Freedmen were disputing with Stephen (Acts 6:9). Paul was disputing against {debating with} the Hellenists (Acts 9:29). All other refs.: QUESTION (verb) <4802>, REASON (verb) <4802>.
– 3 Mark 9:33 → REASON (verb) <1260> 4 John 6:52 → QUARREL (verb) <3164> 5 Jude 9 → CONTEND <1252>.

DISPUTER – ***suzētētēs*** [masc. noun: συζητητής <4804>]; **from *suzēteō*: to seek together, to dispute, which is from *sun*: together, and *zēteō*: to seek ▶ One who engages in an argument; sophist, i.e., one who reasons speciously** > Paul asks where is the disputer {debater, philosopher} of this world (1 Cor. 1:20). ¶

DISPUTING – 1 Acts 15:7 → DISPUTE (noun) <2214> <4803> 2 Phil. 2:14; 1 Tim. 2:8 → REASONING <1261> 3 1 Tim. 6:5 → perverse disputing → useless wrangling → WRANGLING <1275a>.

DISQUALIFIED – 1 Cor. 9:27; 2 Cor. 13:5–7; 2 Tim. 3:8; Titus 1:16 → WORTHLESS <96>.

DISQUALIFY – Col. 2:18 → to defraud of the prize → DEFRAUD <2603>.

DISREGARD – 1 ***ameleō*** [verb: ἀμελέω <272>]; **from *amelēs*: careless, which is from *a*: neg., and *melō*: to take care ▶ To neglect, to give up** > The Lord has disregarded {did not regard, did not care for, turned away from} the Israelites, because they did not continue in His covenant (Heb. 8:9). All other refs.: LIGHT (adj.) <272>, NEGLIGENT <272>.
– 2 Luke 11:42 → to pass over, to pass by → PASS <3928> 3 1 Thes. 4:8a, b; Heb. 10:28 → to set aside → REJECT <114> 4 Titus 2:15 → DESPISE <4065>.

DISREPUTE – 1 ***apelegmos*** [masc. noun: ἀπελεγμός <557>]; **from *apo*: intens., and *elenchō*: to refute ▶ Disfavor, rejection** > The trade of those making shrines of the goddess Diana was in danger of falling into disrepute {being set at nought, coming into discredit, losing its good name} (Acts 19:27). ¶
– 2 1 Cor. 4:10 → held in disrepute → DISHONORED <820> 3 2 Pet. 2:2 → to bring into disrepute → BLASPHEME <987>.

DISRESPECT – 1 Tim. 6:2 → to show disrespect → DESPISE <2706>.

DISRESPECTFUL – 1 Tim. 6:2 → to be disrespectful → DESPISE <2706>.

DISRUPT – Titus 1:11 → OVERTURN <396>.

DISRUPTIVE – 1 1 Thes. 5:14 → idle and disruptive → UNRULY <813> 2 2 Thes. 3:6, 11 → DISORDERLY <814>.

DISSEMBLE – Gal. 2:13 → to play the hypocrite → HYPOCRITE <4942>.

DISSENSION – 1 ***stasis*** [fem. noun: στάσις <4714>]; **from *histēmi*: to stand ▶ Quarrel, contention, conflict** > A dissension {commotion, dispute} having taken place, Paul and Barnabas had no small dispute with men who had come down from Judea (Acts 15:2). After Paul's declaration on the matter of resurrection, there was a dissension {dispute, tumult} between the Pharisees and the Sadducees (Acts 23:7). All other refs.: INSURRECTION <4714>, STANDING <4714>, TUMULT <4714>.
– 2 Rom. 13:13; 1 Tim. 6:4 → STRIFE <2054> 3 Rom. 16:17; Gal. 5:20 → DIVISION <1370> 4 1 Tim. 2:8 → REASONING <1261>.

DISSIMULATION – 1 Rom. 12:9 → without dissimulation → without hypocrisy → HYPOCRISY <505> 2 Gal. 2:13 → HYPOCRISY <5272>.

DISSIPATE – Luke 15:13 → WASTE (verb) <1287>.

DISSIPATION – [1] ***asōtia*** [fem. noun: ἀσωτία <810>]; **from *asōtos*: prodigal, which is from *a*: neg., and *sōzō*: to save completely ▶ Indulgence in immoral pleasure; also transl.: debauchery, corruption, excess, riot** > There is dissipation in being drunk with wine (Eph. 5:18). Overseers of Crete had to have children not accused of dissipation {being wild} (Titus 1:6). Unbelievers think it strange that Christians do not run with them in the same flood of dissipation (1 Pet. 4:4). ¶
– [2] Luke 21:34 → CAROUSING <2897>.

DISSOLUTE – **dissolute way: *aselgeia*** [fem. noun: ἀσέλγεια <766>]; **from *aselgēs*: licentious, violent ▶ Absence of restraint, debauchery** > Many will follow the dissolute ways {depraved conduct, shameful ways, sensuality} of false prophets and false teachers (2 Pet. 2:2); other mss.: destructive ways, pernicious ways (*apōleia*). All other refs.: LEWDNESS <766>.

DISSOLUTENESS – 2 Pet. 2:18; Jude 4 → LEWDNESS <766>.

DISSOLVE – [1] ***luō*** [verb: λύω <3089>]; **lit.: to loose ▶ To melt, to disaggregate** > In the day of the Lord, the elements will be dissolved {will be destroyed} with fervent heat (2 Pet. 3:10, 11); the heavens will be dissolved {their destruction will be brought about} (v. 12). All other refs.: ANNUL <3089>, BREAK <3089>, DESTROY <3089>, LOOSE <3089>, RELEASE (verb) <3089>.
– [2] 2 Cor. 5:1 → DESTROY <2647>.

DISSUADE – Acts 21:14 → lit.: to persuade → PERSUADE <3982>.

DISTANCE – [1] **at a distance: *apo*** [prep.: ἀπό <575>] ***makrothen*** [adv.: μακρόθεν <3113>]; **from *makros*: far ▶ Far, at a remote place; also transl.: far off, afar off** > At the cross, the acquaintances of Jesus and the women who had followed Him were standing at a distance (Luke 23:49). The kings of the earth will stand at a distance, for fear of the torment of Babylon the great (Rev. 18:10), as will also the merchants (v. 15) and all people who travel by ship and sailors also (v. 17). *
– [2] Luke 17:12 → at a distance → AFAR OFF <4207>.

DISTANT – [1] Luke 15:13; 19:12 → FAR <3117> [2] Luke 24:13 → to be distant → to be far → FAR <568>.

DISTINCT – [1] 1 Cor. 14:7 → distinct notes → distinction in sounds → DISTINCTION <1293> [2] 1 Cor. 14:9 → INTELLIGIBLE <2154>.

DISTINCTION – [1] ***diastolē*** [fem. noun: διαστολή <1293>]; **from *diastellō*: to separate, which is from *dia*: through, and *stellō*: to send ▶ Difference, discrimination** > There is no distinction between Jew and Greek, for the same Lord of all is rich toward all who call upon Him (Rom. 10:12). The flute and the harp must make a distinction in the sounds (1 Cor. 14:7). Other ref.: Rom. 3:22; see DIFFERENCE <1293>. ¶
[2] **to make a distinction, to make to differ: *diakrinō*** [verb: διακρίνω <1252>]; **from *dia*: through, and *krinō*: to distinguish, to judge ▶ To differentiate, to discriminate** > God made no distinction {made no difference, put no difference} between the Gentiles and the Israelites (Acts 15:9). Paul asks the Corinthians who makes a distinction of one {who makes one of them to differ, who makes one different, who regards one as superior} from the others (1 Cor. 4:7). Jude says to have compassion on some, making a distinction {making a difference, who are doubting} (Jude 22). All other refs.: see entries in Lexicon at <1252>.
– [3] Acts 25:23 → prominence → PROMINENT <1851> [4] 1 Cor. 12:4–6 → DIVERSITY <1243>.

DISTINCTLY – Acts 10:3 → PLAINLY <5320>.

DISTINGUISH – [1] 1 Cor. 11:29 → DISCERN <1252> [2] 1 Cor. 12:10 → ability to distinguish → DISCERNING <1253>.

DISTINGUISHED – [1] Luke 14:8 → more distinguished → more honorable → HONORABLE <1784> [2] 1 Cor. 4:10 → HONORED <1741>.

DISTINGUISHING – 1 Cor. 12:10; Heb. 5:14 → DISCERNING <1253>.

DISTORT – [1] ***strebloō*** [verb: στρεβλόω <4761>]; **from *streblos*: crooked, deformed, which is from *strephō*: to turn, to twist; a *streblē* was a winch, an instrument of torture ► To turn in the opposite direction, to pervert >** Untaught and unstable people distorted {twisted, wrested} the things which Paul had written, among which were things difficult to understand (2 Pet. 3:16). ¶
– [2] Acts 20:30 → to distort the truth → lit.: to speak perverted things → PERVERTED (BE) <1294> [3] 2 Cor. 4:2 → FALSIFY <1389> [4] Gal. 1:7 → PERVERT (verb) <3344>.

DISTRACTED (BE) – ***perispaō*** [verb: περισπάω <4049>]; **from *peri*: around, and *spaō*: to attract, to draw ► To be preoccupied, to have the mind diverted >** Martha was distracted {cumbered} with much serving (Luke 10:40). ¶

DISTRACTION – **without distraction: *aperispastōs*** [adv.: ἀπερισπάστως <563>]; **from *a*: neg., and *perispaō*: to be distracted, which is from *peri*: around, and *spaō*: to attract, to draw ► Without diversion, without disturbance >** One who is not married can serve the Lord without distraction {undistracted, in undivided devotion} (1 Cor. 7:35). ¶

DISTRESS – [1] ***anankē*** [fem. noun: ἀνάγκη <318>] **► Misery, trouble >** During the great tribulation, there will be great distress upon the land of Israel (Luke 21:23). All other refs.: MUST <318>, NECESSARY <318>, NECESSITY <318>.

[2] ***thlipsis*** [fem. noun: θλῖψις <2347>]; **from *thlibō*: to afflict ► Trouble, pressure >** It was not in order that there might be ease for others and that the Corinthians might be in distress {in affliction, burdened, hard pressed}, but on the principle of equality that the Corinthians were to share their goods (2 Cor. 8:13). All other refs.: AFFLICTION <2347>, ANGUISH <2347>, TRIBULATION <2347>, TROUBLE (noun) <2347>.

[3] ***stenochōria*** [fem. noun: στενοχωρία <4730>]; **from *stenos*: narrow, and *chōra*: space ► Anguish, anxiety >** Distress {Hardship} will not separate Christians from the love of Christ (Rom. 8:35). Paul was commending himself as a minister of God in distresses {straits} (2 Cor. 6:4). He was taking pleasure in distresses {difficulties, straits} for Christ's sake (2 Cor. 12:10). Other ref.: Rom. 2:9; see ANGUISH <4730>. ¶

[4] ***sunochē*** [fem. noun: συνοχή <4928>]; **from *sunechomai*: to be distressed, which is from *sun*: together, and *echō*: to hold; lit.: oppression, tightening ► Anguish, anxiety >** During the great tribulation, there will be on the earth distress of {dismay among} nations in perplexity (Luke 21:25). Other ref.: 2 Cor. 2:4; see ANGUISH <4928>. ¶
– [5] Luke 2:48 → in great distress → to be distressed → DISTRESSED <3600> [6] Luke 12:50 → great is my distress → to be distressed → DISTRESSED <4912> [7] 1 Tim. 5:10 → those in distress → lit.: to the distressed → AFFLICTED (BE) <2346> [8] Rev. 16:10, 11; Rev. 21:4 → PAIN (noun) <4192>.

DISTRESSED – [1] **to be distressed: *odunaō*** [verb: ὀδυνάω <3600>]; **from *odunē*: sorrow, anxiety ► To be anguished, to be very worried; also transl.: sorrowing, anxiously >** The parents of Jesus were distressed while they sought Him (Luke 2:48). All other refs.: GRIEVE <3600>, TORMENT (verb) <3600>.

[2] **to be distressed: *sunechomai*, middle voice of *sunechō*** [verb: συνέχω <4912>]; **from *sun*: together (intens.), and *echō*: to hold ► To be oppressed, to feel the pressure >** Jesus was distressed {under constraint, straitened} until His baptism of the cross was accomplished (Luke 12:50).

All other refs.: see entries in Lexicon at <4912>.
– 3 Matt. 9:36 → to be weary → WEARY (adj.) <1590> 4 Matt. 17:23; Rom. 14:15 → SORROW (noun) <3076> 5 Matt. 26:37; Phil. 2:26 → to be full of heaviness → HEAVINESS <85> 6 Mark 3:5 → to be distressed, to be deeply distressed → to be grieved → GRIEVE <4818> 7 Mark 6:26 → greatly distressed → very sorry → SORRY <4036> 8 Acts 4:2 → DISTURBED (BE) <1278> 9 Acts 16:18 → GRIEVE <1278> 10 Acts 17:16 → to be greatly distressed → to be painfully excited → EXCITE <3947> 11 2 Cor. 1:6; 1 Tim. 5:10 → AFFLICTED (BE) <2346> 12 2 Cor. 4:8 → RESTRAIN <4729> 13 2 Pet. 2:7 → VEXED (BE) <2669>.

DISTRIBUTE – 1 ***diadidōmi*** [verb: διαδίδωμι <1239>]; **from *dia*: through (denotes separation), and *didōmi*: to give ▶ To give to many people, to share among many people** > Jesus told a certain ruler to sell all that he had and to distribute {give} to the poor (Luke 18:22). He distributed the loaves to His disciples after having given thanks (John 6:11). At the beginning, the apostles distributed {made distribution of} the proceeds of the sale of Christians' possessions to each as anyone needed (Acts 4:35). All other refs.: DIVIDE <1239>, GIVE <1239>.

2 ***diaireō*** [verb: διαιρέω <1244>]; **from *dia*: through (denotes separation), and *haireō*: to take ▶ To divide, to give one's share** > The Spirit of God distributes {gives} to each one individually as He pleases (1 Cor. 12:11). Other ref.: Luke 15:12; see DIVIDE <1244>. ¶

3 ***koinōneō*** [verb: κοινωνέω <2841>]; **from *koinōnos*: associate, partner, which is from *koinos*: common ▶ To communicate, to contribute, to share** > Christians are to distribute to the needs of the saints (Rom. 12:13). All other refs.: COMMUNICATE[1] <2841>, PARTICIPATE <2841>.

4 ***merizō*** [verb: μερίζω <3307>]; **from *meris*: portion; lit.: to impart ▶ To attribute, to give, to assign** > God has distributed {allotted, dealt} to each one a measure of faith (Rom. 12:3). Each Christian must walk as the Lord has distributed {divided} to each one (1 Cor. 7:17). Paul boasted within the limits of the sphere which God had distributed to {apportioned to, appointed} him (2 Cor. 10:13). All other refs.: DIFFERENCE <3307>, DIVIDE <3307>, GIVE <3307>.
– 5 Mark 6:41; 8:6; Luke 9:16 → to set before → SET (verb) <3908> 6 Acts 2:3, 45 → DIVIDE <1266> 7 1 Cor. 12:4 → "distributes them" added in Engl. 8 2 Cor. 9:9 → to distribute freely → to scatter abroad → SCATTER <4650> 9 Eph. 4:28 → GIVE <3330>.

DISTRIBUTION – 1 Acts 4:35 → to make distribution → DISTRIBUTE <1239> 2 Acts 6:1 → distribution, distribution of food → SERVICE <1248> 3 2 Cor. 9:13 → liberal distribution → LIBERALITY <572>, SHARING <2842> 4 Heb. 2:4 → GIFT <3311>.

DISTRICT – 1 Matt. 2:16; Acts 13:50 → REGION <3725> 2 Matt. 2:22; 15:21; 16:13; Mark 8:10; Acts 2:10; 20:2 → PART (noun) <3313> 3 Matt. 3:5; 14:35; Mark 1:28; Luke 3:3; 4:14, 37; 7:17; 8:37 → district round, district around, surrounding district → regions around → REGION <4066> 4 Matt. 9:26, 31 → LAND (noun) <1093> 5 Mark 1:5 → COUNTRY <5561> 6 Acts 16:12 → PART (noun) <3310> 7 Acts 19:1 → REGION <3313>.

DISTRUST – Rom. 4:20 → UNBELIEF <570>.

DISTURB – 1 ***kineō*** [verb: κινέω <2795>]; **from *kiō*: to go ▶ To agitate, to move** > All the city of Ephesus was disturbed {aroused} after supposing Paul had brought Trophimus into the temple (Acts 21:30). All other refs.: MOVE <2795>, REMOVE <2795>, SHAKE <2795>.
– 2 Matt. 2:3; Acts 15:24; 17:8; Gal. 1:7; 5:10 → TROUBLE (verb) <5015> 3 Matt. 24:6, Mark 13:7; 2 Thes. 2:2 → to be disturbed → to be troubled → TROUBLE (verb) <2360> 4 Luke 11:7 → lit.: to cause

trouble → TROUBLE (noun) <2873> [5] Acts 16:20 → to trouble exceedingly → TROUBLE (verb) <1613> [6] 1 Thes. 3:3 → SHAKE <4525>.

DISTURBANCE – [1] ***tarachos*** [masc. noun: τάραχος <5017>]; **from *tarassō*: to disturb, to stir ► Agitation; also transl.: commotion, stir** > There was no small disturbance among the soldiers as to what had become of Peter, who had been imprisoned (Acts 12:18). There was no small disturbance about the Way at Ephesus (Acts 19:23). ¶
– [2] Luke 21:9 → TUMULT <181> [3] John 5:3 → MOVING <2796> [4] John 5:4 → TROUBLING <5016> [5] Acts 24:18 → TUMULT <2351> [6] 2 Cor. 12:20 → CONFUSION <181>.

DISTURBED (BE) – ***diaponeō*** [verb: διαπονέω <1278>]; **from *dia*: through (intens.), and *poneō*: to labor, which is from *ponos*: pain ► To be offended, to be dissatisfied** > Certain people were disturbed {were distressed, were grieved} on account of Peter and John teaching the people (Acts 4:2). Other refs.: Mark 14:4 in some mss.; Acts 16:18: see GRIEVE <1278>. ¶

DITCH – Matt. 15:14; Luke 6:39 → PIT <999>.

DIVERS – [1] Matt. 4:24; Mark 1:34; Luke 4:40; 2 Tim. 3:6; Titus 3:3; Heb. 2:4; 13:9; Jas. 1:2 → VARIOUS <4164> [2] Matt. 24:7; Mark 13:8; Luke 21:11 → VARIOUS <2596> [3] Heb. 1:1 → in divers manners → in various ways → WAY <4187> [4] Heb. 9:10 → VARIOUS <1313>.

DIVERSE – Heb. 13:9 → VARIOUS <4164>.

DIVERSITY – [1] ***diairesis*** [fem. noun: διαίρεσις <1243>]; **from *diaireō*: to divide, which is from *dia*: through (denotes separation), and *haireō*: to take ► Variety, plurality; also transl.: differences, distinction, different kinds** > There are diversities of gifts, but the same Spirit (1 Cor. 12:4); there are diversities of ministries, but the same Lord (v. 5); there are diversities of operations, but it is the same God who works all in all (v. 6). ¶
– [2] 1 Cor. 12:28 → KIND (noun) <1085>.

DIVIDE – [1] ***diadidōmi*** [verb: διαδίδωμι <1239>]; **from *dia*: throughout (denoting dispersion), and *didōmi*: to give ► To distribute, to apportion** > He, who overcomes the strong man, will divide {distribute} the spoil he has taken from him (Luke 11:22). All other refs.: DISTRIBUTE <1239>, GIVE <1239>.
[2] ***diaireō*** [verb: διαιρέω <1244>]; **from *dia*: through (denoting separation), and *haireō*: to take ► See [1].** > A father divided to his two sons his property (Luke 15:12). Other ref.: 1 Cor. 12:11; see DISTRIBUTE <1244>. ¶
[3] ***merizō*** [verb: μερίζω <3307>]; **from *meris*: part, portion ► To part, to separate, to distribute** > Every kingdom divided against itself is brought to desolation, and every city or house divided against itself will not subsist (Matt. 12:25a, b; Mark 3:24, 25). If Satan casts out Satan, he is divided against himself (Matt. 12:26; Mark 3:26). Jesus divided the two fish among all His disciples (Mark 6:41). A certain person wanted Jesus to tell his brother to divide the inheritance with him (Luke 12:13). Paul asks if Christ is divided (1 Cor. 1:13). All other refs.: DIFFERENCE <3307>, DISTRIBUTE <3307>, GIVE <3307>.
[4] ***diamerizō*** [verb: διαμερίζω <1266>]; **from *dia*: throughout (denoting separation), and *merizō*: see [3] ► To separate into parts, to distribute** > Every kingdom divided against itself is brought to desolation (Luke 11:17). If Satan is divided against himself, his kingdom cannot subsist (Luke 11:18). Because of Jesus, those in a house will be divided (Luke 12:52, 53). Jesus told His disciples to take a cup and to divide it among themselves (Luke 22:17). The soldiers divided {parted, parted out} the clothes of Jesus (Matt. 27:35; Mark 15:24; Luke 23:34; John 19:24). At Pentecost, there appeared divided {parted} tongues (Acts 2:3). Christians at the beginning were

selling their possessions and goods, and dividing {giving, parting} them among all as anyone had need (Acts 2:45). ¶

[5] ***ginomai*** [verb: γίνομαι <1096>] ► **To become** > The great city of Babylon was divided {was split} into (lit.: became) three parts (Rev. 16:19).

[6] **to divide rightly: *orthotomeō*** [verb: ὀρθοτομέω <3718>]; **from *orthos*: straight, and *temnō*: to cut ► To handle skillfully, to present with accuracy** > Timothy was to divide rightly {cut in a straight line, handle accurately, handle correctly} the word of truth (2 Tim. 2:15). ¶

[7] ***schizō*** [verb: σχίζω <4977>] ► **To split into factions, to break into parties** > The multitude of Iconium was divided, and some were with the Jews and some with the apostles (Acts 14:4). The multitude was divided between the Sadducees and the Pharisees (Acts 23:7). All other refs.: BREAK <4977>, SPLIT <4977>, TEAR (verb) <4977>.

– [8] Matt. 13:49; 25:32 → SEPARATE <873> [9] John 7:43 → lit.: there was a division → DIVISION <4978> [10] Jude 19 → to separate oneself → SEPARATE <592>.

DIVIDER – ***meristēs*** [masc. noun: μεριστής <3312>]; **from *merizō*: to divide, which is from *meris*: part, portion ► One who separates into parts, one who apportions** > Jesus asked a man, in the matter of dividing an inheritance with his brother, who had established Him as a judge or divider {arbiter, arbitrator} over them (Luke 12:14). ¶

DIVIDING – [1] Eph. 2:14 → SEPARATION <5418> [2] Heb. 4:12 → DIVISION <3311>.

DIVINATION – Acts 16:16 → PYTHON <4436>.

DIVINE – [1] ***theios*** [adj. and adj. used as noun: θεῖος <2304>]; **from *Theos*: God ► a. Which belongs to God** > Peter uses this term in relation to the power of God (2 Pet. 1:3) and His nature (v. 4). **b. Divine Nature: The Divinity, the only true God** > Paul told the Athenians they ought not to think that which is divine {the Divine Nature, the Godhead, the divine being} (*to theion*) is like gold or silver or stone (Acts 17:29). Other ref.: Titus 1:9 in some mss. ¶

– [2] Acts 19:27 → divine majesty → MAJESTY <3168> [3] Rom. 1:20 → divine nature → GODHEAD <2305> [4] Rom. 3:25 → lit.: of God [5] Rom. 11:4 → divine answer, divine response → ANSWER (noun) <5538> [6] 2 Cor. 11:2 → to feel a divine jealousy → lit. to be jealous with a jealousy of God [7] Gal. 4:23 → "divine" added in Engl. [8] Heb. 9:1 → divine service, divine worship → service, divine service → SERVICE <2999>.

DIVINELY – Matt. 2:12; Acts 10:22; Heb. 8:5; Heb. 11:7 → to be divinely warned, to be divinely instructed → WARN <5537>.

DIVINELY INSPIRED – ***theopneustos*** [adj.: θεόπνευστος <2315>]; **from *Theos*: God, and *pneō*: to breathe; lit.: God-breathed ► Breathed into by God; the term is used to describe the divine impulse under the impact of which the authors of the books of the Bible wrote them** > Every Scripture of the word of God is divinely inspired {breathed by God, inspired of God, given by inspiration of God} (2 Tim. 3:16). ¶

DIVINITIES – Acts 17:18 → GOD (other god) <1140>.

DIVINITY – Rom. 1:20 → GODHEAD <2305>.

DIVISION – [1] ***merismos*** [masc. noun: μερισμός <3311>]; **from *merizō*: to divide, which is from *meris*: portion, part ► Separation, partition** > The word of God penetrates even to the division {the dividing} of the soul and the spirit, and of joints and marrow (Heb. 4:12). Other ref.: Heb. 2:4; see GIFT <3311>. ¶

[2] ***diamerismos*** [masc. noun: διαμερισμός <1267>]; **from *dia*: through (denotes separation), and *merismos*: see [1] ► Dis-**

sension, discord > Jesus brought division on earth (Luke 12:51). ¶
[3] ***dichostasia*** [fem. noun: διχοστασία <1370>]; **from *dicha*: in two, and *stasis*: stance, dispute ► Dissension, taking away; also transl.: dispute, sedition** > Paul urges the Christians to note those who create divisions and occasions of falling (Rom. 16:17). Divisions are one of the works of the flesh (Gal. 5:20). Some mss. have the word in 1 Cor. 3:3. ¶
[4] ***schisma*** [neut. noun: σχίσμα <4978>]; **from *schizō*: to break, to divide ► Scission, dissension** > Because of Jesus, there was division in the crowd (John 7:43), among the Pharisees (9:16) and among the Jews (10:19). There were to be no divisions among the Corinthians (1 Cor. 1:10); Paul had heard that there existed divisions among them (11:18). God has composed the body that there should be no division {schism} in it (1 Cor. 12:25). Other refs.: Matt. 9:16; Mark 2:21; see TEAR (noun)[2] <4978>. ¶
– [5] Luke 1:5, 8 → COURSE <2183> [6] Gal. 5:20 → SECT <139> [7] Jude 19 → to cause divisions → to separate oneself → SEPARATE <592>.

DIVISIVE – Titus 3:10 → HERETICAL <141>.

DIVORCE (noun) – [1] ***apostasion*** [neut. noun: ἀποστάσιον <647>]; **from *aphistēmi*: to set aside, to separate, which is from *apo*: from, and *histēmi*: to stand; lit.: defection, desertion ► Official dissolution of marriage; the letter of divorce is the particular document authorizing it** > Moses had allowed a man to give his wife a letter of divorce {divorcement, dismissal} (Matt. 5:31; 19:7; Mark 10:4). But Jesus explains that Moses permitted to divorce because of the hardness of the hearts of the Israelites; He maintains the indissolubility of marriage before God, according to His thought from the beginning (see Matt. 19:6). ¶
– [2] 1 Cor. 7:27 → LOOSE <3080>.

DIVORCE (verb) – [1] ***apoluō*** [verb: ἀπολύω <630>]; **from *apo*: from, away from, and *luō*: to let go ► To send one's spouse away, breaking off the marriage; also transl.: to put away, to send away** > Joseph decided to divorce Mary secretly (Matt. 1:19). Jesus does not acknowledge divorce except for cause of adultery; whoever marries a woman who is divorced commits adultery, as likewise a woman who divorced her husband and marries another man; Moses allowed the Israelites to divorce their wives in view of their hardheartedness, but in the beginning it was not so (Matt. 5:31, 32; 19:3, 7–9; Mark 10:2, 4, 11, 12; Luke 16:18a, b). In the O.T. we find the solemn divine principle concerning divorce (or: putting away): "I hate divorce, says the Lord" (Mal. 2:16). Some mss. have the verb transl. "to let go" in Luke 22:68. All other refs.: see entries in Lexicon at <630>.
[2] ***aphiēmi*** [verb: ἀφίημι <863>]; **from *apo*: from, and *hiēmi*: to send ► See [1]; also transl.: to leave, to put away** > Paul speaks of the matter of leaving one's spouse in 1 Cor. 7:11–13. All other refs.: see entries in Lexicon at <863>.

DIVORCEMENT – Matt. 5:31; 19:7; Mark 10:4 → DIVORCE (noun) <647>.

DIVULGE – Acts 19:18 → TELL <312>.

DO – This verb used in the N.T. translates primarily the first three following Greek verbs.
[1] ***ginomai*** [verb: γίνομαι <1096>] ► **a. To occur, to take place** > Jesus did miracles (Mark 6:2 {to perform, to have wrought}; Luke 23:8 {to perform}). **b. To become, to happen** > Other refs.: Matt. 1:22; 18:31a, b; 21:4; 26:56; 27:54 {to happen}; Mark 5:14, 33; Luke 8:34, 35, 56; 23:47; Acts 5:7; 10:16; 11:10; 13:12; 28:9. *
[2] ***epiteleō*** [verb: ἐπιτελέω <2005>]; **from *epi*: upon (intens.), and *teleō*: to accomplish ► To accomplish, to perform** > The Lord was healing people (lit.: doing cures) (Luke 13:32). All other refs.: see entries in Lexicon at <2005>.
[3] ***ergazomai*** [verb: ἐργάζομαι <2038>]; **from *ergon*: work; lit.: to work ► To accomplish** > A woman had done a good

work toward Jesus (Matt. 26:10; Mark 14:6). Other refs.: John 9:4; Acts 13:41; Rom. 2:10; 13:10; Gal. 6:10; Eph. 4:28; Col. 3:23; 3 John 5b. All other refs.: see entries in Lexicon at <2038>.

4 ***katergazomai*** [verb: κατεργάζομαι <2716>]; **from *kata*: intens., and *ergazomai*: see 3 ▶ To accomplish, to produce; also transl.: to commit, to work** > There will be tribulation and anguish on every soul of man who does evil (Rom. 2:9). That which the man of Romans 7 does, he does not own (vv. 15a, 17); see also vv. 18, 20. Other refs.: Rom. 1:27; 5:3; 1 Cor. 5:3; 1 Pet. 4:3 {to carry out}. All other refs.: see entries in Lexicon at <2716>.

5 ***echō*** [verb: ἔχω <2192>] **▶ To keep, to be** > Paul wanted to return to see the brothers to find out how they were doing {getting on} (Acts 15:36). Other refs.: see entries in Lexicon at <2192>.

6 ***poieō*** [verb: ποιέω <4160>] **▶ To act, to behave** > Jesus was asked by what authority He did things such as miracles (Matt. 21:23; Mark 11:28; Luke 20:2). People asked John the Baptist what they should do in keeping with repentance (Luke 3:10, 12, 14), and they asked Jesus what they should do to inherit eternal life (10:25; 18:18). The unjust steward had done {dealt, acted} prudently (Luke 16:8). What Paul did before his conversion, he did ignorantly in unbelief (1 Tim. 1:13). Christians should speak and do as those who will be judged by the law of liberty (Jas. 2:12). Gaius was doing (*poieō*) faithfully whatever he did (*ergō*) for his brothers and for strangers (3 John 5). Other refs.: see entries in Lexicon at <4160>.

7 ***prassō*** [verb: πράσσω <4238>] **▶ To practice, to commit** > One of the two criminals at Calvary recognized that they were receiving the due reward of their deeds (lit.: of what they had done) (Luke 23:41). He who had done a certain deed should have been taken away out of the midst of the Corinthians (1 Cor. 5:2; some mss. have *poieō*). Others had not repented of the sins they had done {indulged in} (2 Cor. 12:21). Other refs.: Rom. 1:32a, b; 2:1–3; Gal. 5:21. Other refs.: COLLECT <4238>, CONTRARY <4238>, KEEP (verb) <4238>, USE (verb) <4238>.

– 8 Matt. 18:31 → to be done → to take place → PLACE (noun) <1096> 9 Luke 2:39 → PERFORM <5055> 10 Luke 3:14 → to do violence → OPPRESS <1286> 11 John 16:2 → OFFER <4374> 12 1 Cor. 6:13 → to do away → DESTROY <2673> 13 1 Cor. 13:11 → to do away → to put away → PUT <2673> 14 Gal. 3:17 → to do away → to make of no effect → EFFECT (noun) <2673> 15 Gal. 5:11 → to do away → CEASE <2673> 16 Eph. 2:10 → lit.: to walk in → WALK <4043> 17 2 Tim. 3:5 → to have nothing to do → to turn away → TURN (verb) <665> 18 2 Tim. 4:9, 21; Titus 3:12 → to do one's best → to make every effort → EFFORT <4704> 19 2 Tim. 4:14 → SHOW (verb) <1731> 20 Titus 3:8 → MAINTAIN <4291> 21 Titus 3:10 → to have done with, to have nothing to do with → AVOID <3868> 22 Heb. 4:13 → Him with whom we have to do → lit.: to whom the account (is given) by us, to whom we must give account → ACCOUNT (noun) <3056> 23 Jas. 1:25 → in what he does → lit.: in his doing → DOING <4162> 24 1 Pet. 4:1 → to have done with → to cease from → CEASE <3973> 25 Rev. 17:17a → EXECUTE <4160>.

DOCTOR[1] – Matt. 9:12; Mark 2:17; 5:26; Luke 5:31; 8:43; Col. 4:14 → PHYSICIAN <2395>.

DOCTOR[2] – 1 Luke 2:46 → TEACHER <1320> 2 Luke 5:17; Acts 5:34; 1 Tim. 1:7 → doctor of the law → TEACHER OF THE LAW <3547>.

DOCTRINE – 1 ***didaskalia*** [fem. noun: διδασκαλία <1319>]; **from *didaskō*: to teach, which is from *daō*: to learn ▶ What is taught, as well as the act of teaching; also transl.: teaching** > Isaiah speaks of those who teach as doctrines the commandments of men (Matt. 15:9; Mark 7:7). He who teaches must use his gift in doctrine (Rom. 12:7). Paul speaks of the danger of being carried about with every wind of doctrine (Eph. 4:14). He speaks of the Christian doctrine in his pastoral epistles (1 Tim. 1:10; 4:6; 6:1, 3; 2 Tim. 3:10; Titus 2:7). He speaks also of sound doctrine (2 Tim. 4:3; Titus 1:9; 2:1), as well as doctrines of men (Col. 2:22) and doctrines of {things taught by} demons (1 Tim. 4:1). Timothy was to give attention to doctrine (1 Tim. 4:13) and to take heed to it (v. 16). Elders who labor in the word of God and doctrine must be counted worthy of double honor (1 Tim. 5:17). Every Scripture is profitable for doctrine (2 Tim. 3:16). Titus was to show integrity in doctrine (Titus 2:7). By being obedient, bondservants adorn the doctrine of God the Savior (Titus 2:10). Other ref.: Rom. 15:4; see INSTRUCTION <1319>. ¶

[2] ***didachē*** [fem. noun: διδαχή <1322>]; **from *didaskō*: see [1] ► What is taught, instruction; also transl.: teaching** > Scripture speaks of the doctrine of Jesus in the Gospels (Matt. 7:28; 22:33; Mark 1:22, 27; 11:18; Luke 4:32; John 7:16, 17; 18:19), Christian doctrine (Acts 2:42; 5:28; 13:12; 17:19; Rom. 6:17; 16:17; 1 Cor. 14:6 {word of instruction}; 2 Tim. 4:2 {careful instruction}; Titus 1:9), and the doctrine of Christ (2 John 9, 10). But Scripture also speaks of other doctrines: the doctrine of the Pharisees and the Sadducees (Matt. 16:12), the doctrine of baptisms (or cleansing rites) and other matters (Heb. 6:2), strange doctrines (Heb. 13:9), the doctrine of Balaam (Rev. 2:14), of the Nicolaitans (2:15), and of Jezebel (2:24). Jesus gave His doctrine concerning the parable of the sower (Mark 4:2). He said in His doctrine {as He taught} to beware of the scribes (Mark 12:38). An overseer must be able to exhort by sound doctrine (Titus 1:9). When coming together, all brothers can have a doctrine {word of instruction} (1 Cor. 14:26). ¶

[3] **to teach other, strange, false doctrines: *heterodidaskaleō*** [verb: ἑτεροδιδασκαλέω <2085>]; **from *heteros*: other, strange, and *didaskō*: see [1] ► To give instruction diverging from that proper to the Christian faith and the Scriptures** > Timothy was to enjoin some not to teach other doctrines (1 Tim. 1:3). The verb is transl. "to teach differently" {to teach otherwise, to advocate a different doctrine} in 1 Tim. 6:3. ¶

– [4] Gal. 1:14 → TRADITION <3862> [5] Heb. 6:1 → elementary doctrine → word of the beginning → WORD <3056>.

DOER – [1] ***poiētēs*** [masc. noun: ποιητής <4163>]; **from *poieō*: to do, to put in practice ► One who accomplishes something, complies with a requirement** > The doers of {Those who obey} the law will be justified (Rom. 2:13). Christians should be doers of the word of God, and not hearers only, lest they deceive themselves (Jas. 1:22, 23). The doer of the work shall be blessed in his doing (Jas. 1:25). He who judges the law is not a doer of {keeping} the law (Jas. 4:11). Other ref.: Acts 17:28; see POET <4163>. ¶

– [2] 2 Tim. 2:9 → evil doer → CRIMINAL <2557>.

DOG – [1] ***kuōn*** [masc. and fem. noun: κύων <2965>] ► **Unclean and despised animal in Israel (see Deut. 23:18; 1 Sam. 17:43)** > The word is used with its usual meaning in Luke 16:21 and 2 Pet. 2:22. The term designates figur. people who cannot appreciate what is holy in the eyes of God (Matt. 7:6), who are unclean morally (Phil. 3:2), and who will be found as such in the judgment day (Rev. 22:15). ¶

[2] **dog, little dog: *kunarion*** [neut. noun: κυνάριον <2952>]; **dimin. of *kuōn*: see [1]; lit.: little dog ► See defin. of [1].** > The Jews were using the deprecatory term of "dog" about the Gentiles. Jesus Himself uses this word to show the grace of God toward the Gentiles (Matt. 15:26, 27; Mark 7:27, 28). ¶

DOING – [1] **well doing: *agathopoiia*** [fem. noun: ἀγαθοποιΐα <16>]; **from *agathopoieō*: to do good, which is from *agathos*: good, and *poieō*: to do, to make ► Course of action in performing good deeds** > Those who suffer according to the will of God must commit their souls to a faithful Creator in well doing {in doing good, in doing what is right, and continuing to do good} (1 Pet. 4:19). ¶

[2] ***poiēsis*** [fem. noun: ποίησις <4162>]; **from *poieō*: to do ▶ Achievement, activity, performance** > The doer of work shall be blessed in his doing {his deed, what he does} (Jas. 1:25). ¶
– [3] Matt. 16:27 → WORK (noun) <4234>.

DOMAIN – [1] Col. 1:13 → AUTHORITY <1849> [2] Jude 6 → own domain, proper domain → original state → STATE <746>.

DOMINEER – 1 Pet. 5:3 → to be lord → LORD (verb) <2634>.

DOMINION – [1] ***kuriotēs*** [fem. noun: κυριότης <2963>]; **from *kurios*: lord, master ▶ Authority, lordship** > God has seated Christ at His right hand in the heavenly places above every principality, authority, power, and dominion (Eph. 1:21). By the Lord Jesus were created all things, the things in the heavens and the things on the earth, the visible and the invisible, whether thrones, or dominions {powers}, or principalities, or authorities, all things have been created by Him and for Him (Col. 1:16). There are those who walk according to the flesh in the lust of uncleanness and despise authority (2 Pet. 2:10 {government}; Jude 8). ¶
[2] **to have dominion: *kurieuō*** [verb: κυριεύω <2961>]; **from *kurios*: see [1] ▶ To exercise authority, to rule, to reign; also transl.: to be master, to have authority, to exercise lordship** > The kings of the Gentiles have dominion over them (Luke 22:25). Death no longer has dominion {has mastery} over Christ (Rom. 6:9). Sin will not have dominion over the Christian (Rom. 6:14). The law has dominion {has jurisdiction, is binding} over a man as long as he lives (Rom. 7:1). Christ died and rose and lived again that He might have dominion over {rule over, be Lord of} both the dead and the living (Rom. 14:9). Paul did not have dominion {did not lord it} over the faith of the Corinthians (2 Cor. 1:24). God is the Lord of those who have dominion {of lords} (1 Tim. 6:15). ¶
– [3] Matt. 20:25 → to exercise dominion → to lord over → LORD (verb) <2634> [4] Acts 26:18; Col. 1:13 → AUTHORITY <1849> [5] 1 Cor. 15:24 → PRINCIPALITY <746> [6] 1 Tim. 6:16; 1 Pet. 4:11; 5:11; Jude 25; Rev. 1:6; 5:13 → MIGHT <2904> [7] Rev. 17:18 → KINGSHIP <932>.

DONATION – Luke 21:5 → consecrated offering → OFFERING <334>.

DONKEY – [1] ***onos*** [masc. noun: ὄνος <3688>] **▶ Domesticated beast of burden; also transl.: ass** > The Lord reminds the Jews that the owner of a donkey takes care of it even on the Sabbath day (Luke 13:15; 14:5 in some mss.). In accordance with a prophecy of the O.T. (see Zech. 9:9), Jesus entered into Jerusalem on a donkey that He had sent for (Matt. 21:2, 5a, 7; John 12:15); the Lord was thus manifesting both His humbleness and His kingship. ¶
[2] **young donkey: *onarion*** [neut. noun: ὀνάριον <3678>]; **dimin. of *onos*: see [1] ▶ See defin. of [1].** > Jesus sat upon a young donkey He had found (John 12:14). ¶
[3] **of a donkey: *onikos*** [adj.: ὀνικός <3684>]; **from *onos*: see [1] ▶ Which pertains to a donkey** > The word is found in Matt. 18:6; Mark 9:42; Luke 17:2. ¶
[4] ***hupozugion*** [neut. noun: ὑποζύγιον <5268>]; **from *hupo*: under, and *zugos*: yoke; lit.: animal under the yoke ▶ Animal used to carry burdens, beast of burden** > Zechariah had prophesized that the king of the daughter of Zion would come sitting upon a donkey (*onos*) and a colt, the foal of a donkey (*hupozugion*) (Matt. 21:5b). A mute donkey {ass, beast}, speaking with man's voice, reprimanded the madness of Balaam (2 Pet. 2:16). ¶
– [5] Luke 10:34 → BEAST <2934>.

DOOMED (BE) – 1 Cor. 2:6 → to be doomed to pass away → to come to nothing → COME <2673>.

DOOR – [1] ***thura*** [fem. noun: θύρα <2374>] **▶ That which permits entering in and going out; also transl.: doorway, entrance, gate** > The word, in addition to its lit. meaning (e.g., John 20:19; Acts 12:13), also designates Jesus Christ by whom one

enters to obtain salvation (John 10:9). It is He who knocks at the door of a person's heart, ready to enter, bringing salvation and fellowship with anyone who hears His voice and opens the door (Rev. 3:20a, b). God had opened a door of faith to the nations (Acts 14:27). Paul spoke of a great door and an effectual one that had been opened to him for the preaching of the glad tidings (1 Cor. 16:9; 2 Cor. 2:12); in his Epistle to the Colossians, he prayed that such a door might be opened to him (Col. 4:3). In Jas. 5:9, God is the Judge who stands before the door, ready to judge. The shut door, in the parable of the ten virgins (Matt. 25:10), speaks of the end of the period of grace at the second coming of Christ. Other refs.: Matt. 6:6; 24:33; 27:60; Mark 1:33; 2:2; 11:4; 13:29; 15:46; 16:3; Luke 11:7; 13:25a, b; John 10:1, 2, 7; 18:16; 20:26; Acts 3:2; 5:9, 19, 23; 12:6; 16:26, 27; 21:30; Rev. 3:8; 4:1. ¶
– [2] Matt. 23:13 → to shut the door of the kingdom of heaven → lit.: to shut the kingdom of heaven [3] Mark 13:34; John 10:3; 18:16, 17 → one at the door, one who keeps the door → DOORKEEPER <2377> [4] Luke 13:24 → GATE <4439>.

DOORKEEPER – ***thurōros*** [masc. and fem. noun: θυρωρός <2377>]**; from *thura*: door, and *ouros*: keeper ▶ Person, male or female, responsible for keeping watch at a door and permitting other people to enter** > In a parable, the man who had gone out of the country commanded the doorkeeper {porter, one at the door} to keep watch (Mark 13:34). The doorkeeper {porter, watchman} opens the door to the Shepherd of the sheep (John 10:3). The apostle John spoke to the doorkeeper {one who kept the door, one on duty, one at the door, porteress} of the palace of the high priest and brought Peter in (John 18:16, 17). ¶

DOORWAY – Mark 11:4 → DOOR <2374>.

DORCAS – ***Dorkas*** [fem. name: Δορκάς <1393>]**: gazelle; the word is associated with *derkomai*: to see clearly ▶ Christian woman of the city of Joppa** > Dorcas was a disciple full of good works and charitable deeds (Acts 9:36, 39). She died, but Peter prayed for her and she returned to life (see Acts 9:40). Her name was Tabitha in Hebrew and Dorcas in Greek. ¶

DOT – Matt. 5:18; Luke 16:17 → TITTLE <2762>.

DOTE – 1 Tim. 6:4 → OBSESSED (BE) <3552>.

DOUBLE (adj.) – [1] ***diplous*** [adj.: διπλοῦς <1362>]**; from *dis*: twice, and suffix *plous* denoting times ▶ Two times the quantity** > Elders who lead well must be esteemed worthy of double honor (1 Tim. 5:17). The angel said to repay Babylon the great double according to her works, and to mix double {twice} for her in the cup which she has mixed (Rev. 18:6a, b). Other ref.: Matt. 23:15 (twice as much); see TWICE <1362>. ¶
– [2] Luke 13:11 → to bend double → to bend over → BEND <4794>.

DOUBLE (verb) – Rev. 18:6 → REPAY <1363>.

DOUBLE-EDGED – Heb. 4:12; Rev. 1:16; 2:12 → TWO-EDGED <1366>.

DOUBLE-MINDED – ***dipsuchos*** [adj. and adj. used as noun: δίψυχος <1374>]**; from *dis*: twice, and *psuchē*: soul, mind ▶ Having divided feelings, wavering between adopting one of two paths (e.g., Christian or worldly)** > James speaks of a double-minded man, unstable in all his ways (Jas. 1:8). He exhorts the double-minded to purify their hearts (Jas. 4:8). ¶

DOUBLE-TONGUED – ***dilogos*** [adj.: δίλογος <1351>]**; from *dis*: twice, and *logos*: word; lit.: double in words ▶ Double in speech, i.e., saying one thing to one person and a different thing to another one** > Deacons must not be double-tongued {must be sincere} (1 Tim. 3:8). ¶

DOUBLY – Jude 12 → TWICE <1364>.

DOUBT (adv.) – 1 **no doubt:** ***pantōs*** [adv.: πάντως <3843>]**; from** ***pas*****: all ▶ Certainly, surely** > The natives first concluded that, no doubt {certainly, undoubtedly}, Paul was {that Paul must be} a murderer (Acts 28:4). Other refs.: ALTOGETHER <3843>, SURELY <3843>.
– 2 Luke 24:38 → THOUGHT <1261> 3 Acts 2:12 → to be in doubt → PERPLEXED (BE) <1280> 4 Acts 12:11 → without a doubt → SURELY <230> 5 Rom. 14:23 → to have doubt → DOUBT (verb) <1252> 6 Gal. 4:20 → to stand in doubt, to have doubts → PERPLEXED (BE) <639> 7 Heb. 7:7 → CONTRADICTION <485>.

DOUBT (verb) – 1 ***diakrinō*** [verb: διακρίνω <1252>]**; from** ***dia*****: through, in all directions, and** ***krinō*****: to separate, to judge ▶ To waver, to be of a divided mind, to deliberate; also transl.: to hesitate, to have misgivings** > Jesus spoke about having faith and not doubting (Matt. 21:21; Mark 11:23). Peter was to go with three men, doubting nothing (Acts 10:20; 11:12). He who doubts is condemned if he eats a particular food, because he is not acting on the principle of faith (Rom. 14:23). He who asks must do so in faith, with no doubting, for he who doubts is like a wave of the sea driven and tossed by the wind (Jas. 1:6a, b). All other refs.: see entries in Lexicon at <1252>.
2 ***distazō*** [verb: διστάζω <1365>]**; from** ***distos*****: doubtful, uncertain ▶ To vacillate, to be indecisive between two thoughts or actions** > Jesus asked Peter why he doubted (Matt. 14:31). Some doubted {were doubtful, i.e., they hesitated} when they saw Jesus risen (Matt. 28:17). ¶
– 3 John 13:22 → PERPLEXED (BE) <639> 4 Acts 5:24; 10:17 → PERPLEXED (BE) <1280> 5 Acts 25:20 → to doubt → to be uncertain → UNCERTAIN <639>.

DOUBTFUL – 1 Matt. 28:17 → to be doubtful → DOUBT (verb) <1365> 2 Luke 12:29 → to be of doubtful mind → to be in anxiety → ANXIETY <3349> 3 Rom. 14:1 → doubtful thing, doubtful disputation → REASONING <1261>.

DOUBTING – 1 John 20:27 → UNBELIEVING <571> 2 1 Tim. 2:8 → REASONING <1261>.

DOUBTLESS – Luke 4:23 → SURELY <3843>.

DOUGH – 1 Rom. 11:16 → first piece of dough → FIRSTFRUITS <536> 2 Rom. 11:16; 1 Cor. 5:6; Gal. 5:9 → lump of dough, batch of dough → LUMP <5445>.

DOVE – ***peristera*** [fem. noun: περιστερά <4058>] **▶ Female pigeon; this bird symbolizes purity, simplicity, and peace** > The disciples were to be guileless as doves (Matt. 10:16). The Spirit of God descended as a dove on Jesus at His baptism (Matt. 3:16; Mark 1:10; Luke 3:22; John 1:32). Doves were sold in the temple to be offered in sacrifice (Matt. 21:12; Mark 11:15; Luke 2:24 {pigeon}; John 2:14, 16). ¶

DOVE-SELLER – Mark 11:15 → lit.: one selling dove → SELL <4453>.

DOWN – 1 Matt. 11:23; Luke 10:15 → to go down → GO <2597> 2 Luke 5:4, 5 → to let down → LET <5465> 3 Luke 12:18 → to pull down → PULL <2507> 4 John 10:17, 18a, b; 13:37, 38; 15:13; 1 John 3:16a, b → to lay down → LAY <5087> 5 1 Cor. 15:24 → to put down → DESTROY <2673> 6 Eph. 4:26 → to go down → GO <1931>.

DOWNCAST – 1 Matt. 6:16; Luke 24:17 → downcast in countenance, downcast → sad countenance, sad → SAD <4659> 2 Matt. 9:36 → to be downcast → SCATTER <4496> 3 2 Cor. 7:6 → CAST DOWN <5011>.

DOWNWARDS – ***katō*** [adv.: κάτω <2736>]**; from** ***kata*****: down ▶** Refs.: Matt. 4:6; 27:51; Mark 14:66; 15:38; Luke 4:9; John 8:6, 8, 23; Acts 2:19; 20:9; Matt. 2:17: *katōterō*. ¶ ‡

DRACHMA – Luke 15:8a, b, 9 → silver coin → COIN <1406>.

DRAG – [1] ***helkuō*** [verb: ἑλκύω <1670>] **or *helkō*** [verb: ἕλκω <1670>] ▶ **To pull along, to take along (without necessarily using force)** > Paul and Silas were dragged into the market before the magistrates (Acts 16:19). People laid hold on Paul and dragged him out of the temple (Acts 21:30). All other refs.: DRAW <1670>.
[2] ***surō*** [verb: σύρω <4951>] ▶ **To draw, to pull forcefully (a person or an object)** > The disciples dragged {towed} the net of fish (John 21:8). Saul dragged off {haled} men and women, and put them in prison (Acts 8:3). Having stoned Paul, the Jews dragged him out of the city, supposing him to have died (Acts 14:19). Jason and other brothers were dragged before the city officials (Acts 17:6). Other ref.: Rev. 12:4; see DRAW <4951>. ¶
[3] ***katasurō*** [verb: κατασύρω <2694>]; **from *kata*: intens., and *surō*: see [2]** ▶ **To pull forcefully (e.g., to bring to a judge)** > The verb is used in regard to dragging someone before a judge (Luke 12:58 {to hale}). ¶
– [4] Matt. 10:18 → BRING <71> [5] Luke 9:42 → CONVULSE <4952> [6] Acts 6:12; 19:29 → to drag away, to drag along → CATCH (verb) <4884> [7] Acts 7:58 → to send out → SEND <1544> [8] Jas. 1:14 → to drag away → to draw away → DRAW <1828>.

DRAGNET – ***sagēnē*** [fem. noun: σαγήνη <4522>] ▶ **Large net for fishing** > Jesus compares the kingdom of heaven to a dragnet {net, seine} which has been cast into the sea and gathers together fish of every kind (Matt. 13:47). ¶

DRAGON – ***drakōn*** [masc. noun: δράκων <1404>]; **from a form of *derkomai*: to see clearly** ▶ **Monstrous animal in mythology; very big serpent** > In Revelation, Satan is represented as a great red dragon having seven heads and ten horns (12:3). The dragon stands before the woman (Israel) to devour her child (Christ) (v. 4); but the child is caught up to God (ascension of Christ) and the woman flees to the desert where she is fed (protection during the great tribulation under the antichrist; see vv. 5, 6). The archangel Michael and his angels will fight against the dragon, and the dragon with his angels will be cast to the earth (12:7a, b, 9). The dragon will then persecute Israel (12:13); the earth will help the woman (Israel) (12:16), which will enrage the dragon (12:17). The dragon will give his power, his throne, and great authority to the beast rising up out of the sea (13:2), i.e., the nations. People will worship the dragon who has given authority to the beast (13:4). The other beast will speak like a dragon (13:11). Later, unclean spirits will come out of the mouth of the dragon (16:13). Finally, the dragon, the serpent of old, who is the Devil and Satan, will be bound for one thousand years (20:2); after the thousand years, he will be cast into the lake of fire where the two other beasts will already be (see v. 10). ¶

DRAIN – Rev. 16:19 → to make her drain the cup → lit.: to give her the cup → GIVE <1325>.

DRAUGHT – [1] ***aphedrōn*** [masc. noun: ἀφεδρών <856>]; **from *apo*: from, and *hedra*: seat** ▶ **Place where human waste goes; pit** > The term is used in Matt. 15:17; Mark 7:19 (*ochetos* in some mss.: drain, sewer). The Greek expr. for "to go out into the draught," "to cast out into the draught" is also transl. "to be eliminated," "to go out of the body." ¶
– [2] Luke 5:4, 9 → CATCH (noun) <61>.

DRAVE – Acts 18:16 → DRIVE <556>.

DRAW – [1] **to draw, to draw up: *anabibazō*** [verb: ἀναβιβάζω <307>]; **from *ana*: up, and *bibazō*: to cause to go** ▶ **To drag, to pull to the shore** > In a parable, a net full of fish was drawn up on the shore (Matt. 13:48). ¶
[2] **to draw out: *probibazō*** [verb: προβιβάζω <4264>]; **from *pro*: before, and *bibazō*: to cause to go** ▶ **To cause to advance** > Alexander was drawn out of {was put forward from among} the crowd, the Jews

pushing him forward (Acts 19:33); other mss. have *sumbibazō*: to instruct. Other ref.: Matt. 14:8; see PROMPT <4264>. ¶

3 ***spaō*** [verb: σπάω <4685>] ▶ **To pull out, to unsheathe (in the case of a weapon)** > One of those who was with Jesus drew his sword and struck the servant of the high priest (Mark 14:47). The jailer drew his sword and was going to kill himself (Acts 16:27). ¶

4 **to draw, to draw away: *apospaō*** [verb: ἀποσπάω <645>]; **from *apo*: away from, and *spaō*: see** 3 ▶ **a. To pull out, to unsheathe (in the case of a weapon)** > One of those who was with Jesus, stretching out his hand, drew his sword and struck the servant of the high priest (Matt. 26:51). **b. To attract, to take along** > After Paul's departure, there would be men speaking perverse things to draw away the disciples after themselves (Acts 20:30). All other refs.: GET <645>, WITHDRAW <645>.

5 ***helkuō*** [verb: ἑλκύω <1670>] **or *helkō*** [verb: ἕλκω <1670>] ▶ **a. To pull, to attract (e.g., by an internal force or by divine power)** > No one can come to Jesus, unless the Father who sent Him draws him (John 6:44). If He was lifted up from the earth, Jesus would draw all to Himself (John 12:32). **b. To unsheathe (in the case of a weapon)** > Peter drew his sword and struck the servant of the high priest (John 18:10). **c. To drag (e.g., a net), to haul in, to pull back** > The apostles threw their net, and they could no longer draw it because of the large number of fish (John 21:6); Peter went up and drew the net ashore (v. 11). **d. To drag (e.g., into court)** > The rich drew their fellow citizens into court (Jas. 2:6). Other refs.: Acts 16:19; 21:30; see DRAG <1670>. ¶

6 **to draw near, to draw nigh: *engizō*** [verb: ἐγγίζω <1448>]; **from *engus*: near ▶ To come near; also transl.: to approach** > The publicans and sinners drew near to {gathered around} Jesus to hear Him (Luke 15:1). When the Son of Man will be seen coming in glory, then the redemption of Israel will draw near (Luke 21:28). The feast of unleavened bread drew near (Luke 22:1). Judas drew near to Jesus to kiss Him (Luke 22:47). The disciples of Emmaus drew near to the village where they were going (Luke 24:28); Jesus had drawn near {came up} to them before (v. 15). The time of the promise to Abraham drew near (Acts 7:17). James tells us to draw near to God, and He will draw near to us (Jas. 4:8a, b). By the introduction of a better hope, we draw near to God (Heb. 7:19). Other refs.: Matt. 15:8; 21:1, 34; Mark 11:1; Luke 7:12; 15:25; 19:29, 37; 24:15; Acts 10:9. All other refs.: COME <1448>, HAND (noun) <1448>, NEAR (adv.) <1448>, NEIGHBORHOOD <1448>.

7 **to draw up: *anatassomai*** [verb: ἀνατάσσομαι <392>]; **from *ana*: intens., and *tassō*: to arrange ▶ To compose, to write** > Many had undertaken to draw up an account {to set in order a narrative, to compile an account} of the things concerning the life of Jesus (Luke 1:1). ¶

8 **to draw away: *exelkō*** [verb: ἐξέλκω <1828>]; **from *ek*: from, and *helkō*: see** 5 ▶ **To attract, to carry away** > Every one is tempted when he is drawn away {dragged away} by his own lust (Jas. 1:14). ¶

9 **to draw near: *prosagō*** [verb: προσάγω <4317>]; **from *pros*: toward, and *agō*: to lead ▶ To come toward, to get closer** > The sailors deemed that they were drawing near to some land {they were approaching some land, some land neared them} (Acts 27:27; other mss.: *prosanechō*). Other refs.: Luke 9:41; Acts 16:20; 1 Pet. 3:18: see BRING <4317>; Acts 12:6 in some mss. ¶

10 **to draw near: *proserchomai*** [verb: προσέρχομαι <4334>]; **from *pros*: to, and *erchomai*: to go, to come ▶ To come close, to approach** > Moses drew near {went up, went over} to look at the burning bush (Acts 7:31). Christians are encouraged to draw near to {approach} God with a true heart, in full assurance of faith (Heb. 10:22). Other refs.: COME <4334>, CONSENT (verb) <4334>, GO <4334>.

11 **to draw near, to draw nigh: *ginomai*** [verb: γίνομαι <1096>] ***engus*** [adv.: ἐγγύς <1451>] ▶ **To become close** > The apostles saw Jesus drawing near {coming near, approaching} the boat (John 6:19).

12 ***surō*** [verb: σύρω <4951>] ▶ **To pull, to take forcefully (a person or an object)** >

The tail of the dragon drew {swept, swept away} a third of the stars of heaven (Rev. 12:4). All other refs.: DRAG <4951>.

13 ***antleō*** [verb: ἀντλέω <501>]; **from *antlos*: hold of a ship ▶ To take up a liquid by means of a container** > The water drawn by the servants at the wedding of Cana had been changed into wine (John 2:8, 9). The verb is also used in regard to drawing water when Jesus met the woman at the well of Sychar (John 4:7, 15). ¶

14 ***didōmi*** [verb: δίδωμι <1325>] **▶ To cast, to give** > The apostles drew lots on Barsabbas and Matthias (Acts 1:26). Other refs.: GIVE <1325>.

15 **vessel: *antlēma*** [neut. noun: ἄντλημα <502>]**; from *antleō*: see 13 ▶ Container for taking up a liquid** > The woman at the well had nothing to draw with (lit.: had no vessel) (John 4:11). ¶

– 16 Matt. 26:52 → TAKE <2983> 17 Luke 5:4 → to draw out → LAUNCH <1877> 18 Luke 9:51 → to draw near → to fully come → COME <4845> 19 Luke 23:54 → to draw near, to draw on → to begin to dawn → DAWN (verb) <2020> 20 Acts 5:37 → to draw away → to lead in revolt → REVOLT <868> 21 Acts 11:10 → to draw back, to draw up → to pull up → PULL <385> 22 Acts 23:19 → to draw aside → DEPART <402> 23 Gal. 2:12; Heb. 10:38 → to draw back → WITHDRAW <5288> 24 1 Tim. 5:11 → their passions draw them away → they wax wanton against → WANTON <2691> 25 Heb. 10:39 → to draw back → DESERTION <5289>.

DREADFUL – Heb. 10:31 → FEARFUL <5398>.

DREADFULLY – Matt. 8:6 → TERRIBLY <1171>.

DREAM (noun) – 1 ***enupnion*** [neut. noun: ἐνύπνιον <1798>]**; from *en*: in, and *hupnos*: sleep ▶ Something seen in sleep, vision while sleeping** > God says that in the last days old men will dream dreams (Acts 2:17). ¶

2 ***onar*** [neut. noun: ὄναρ <3677>] **▶ See 1.** > An angel of the Lord appeared to Joseph in a dream (Matt. 1:20; 2:13, 19, 22). The wise men were divinely instructed in a dream not to return to Herod (Matt. 2:12). The wife of Pilate had suffered many things in a dream because of Jesus (Matt. 27:19). ¶

– 3 Jude 8 → on the strength of their dreams → lit.: dreaming ones → DREAMER <1797>.

DREAM (verb) – ***enupniazō*** [verb: ἐνυπνιάζω <1797>]**; from *enupnion*: dream, which is from *en*: in, and *hupnos*: sleep ▶ To see in one's sleep** > God says that in the last days old men will dream dreams (Acts 2:17). Other ref.: Jude 8; see DREAMER <1797>. ¶

DREAMER – to dream: *enupniazō* [verb: ἐνυπνιάζω <1797>]**; from *enupnion*: dream, which is from *en*: in, and *hupnos*: sleep ▶ To have dreams, to imagine things (e.g., sensual ones)** > Jude speaks of dreamers (lit.: dreaming ones, i.e., those who are carried away by their reveries) who defile the flesh (Jude 8). Other ref.: Acts 2:17; see DREAM (verb) <1797>. ¶

DREGS – 1 Cor. 4:13 → REFUSE (noun) <4067>.

DRESS (noun) – 1 Pet. 3:3 → CLOTHES <2440>.

DRESS (verb) – 1 Matt. 6:29; Mark 16:5; Luke 12:27; 23:11; Rev. 3:5; 4:4; 7:13; 17:4; 18:16; 19:13 → CLOTHE <4016> 2 Matt. 11:8; Luke 7:25 → CLOTHE <294> 3 Matt. 22:11; Rev. 1:13; 15:6; 19:14 → CLOTHE <1746> 4 Mark 5:15; Luke 8:35 → CLOTHE <2439> 5 Mark 15:17; Luke 16:19 → CLOTHE <1737> 6 Luke 12:35; 17:8; Acts 12:8 → be dressed ready for service, stay dressed for action, to dress properly, to dress to serve → lit.: let your loins be girded about, to gird one's loins about → GIRD <4024> 7 John 21:18a, b → GIRD <2224> 8 Acts 1:10 → dressed in white → lit.: in white clothing → CLOTHES <2066> 9 1 Tim. 2:9 → to adorn oneself → ADORN <2885> 10 Heb. 6:7 → CULTIVATE <1090>.

DRESSED – [1] 1 Cor. 4:11 → to be poorly dressed → to be naked → NAKED <1130> [2] Rev. 21:2 → to be beautifully dressed → to be adorned → ADORN <2885>.

DRIED – [1] Mark 3:1, 3 → to be dried up → to wither → WITHERED <3583> [2] Rev. 14:15 → to be dried → RIPE (BE) <3583>.

DRIFT – [1] **to drift away: *pararreō*** [verb: παραρρέω <3901>]; **from *para*: past, beyond, and *rheō*: to flow; lit.: to slip far ▶ To move away, to stray** > We must give the more earnest heed to the things we have heard, lest we drift away {should slip away, should let them slip} (Heb. 2:1). ¶
– [2] Acts 27:32 → let it drift away → let it fall away → FALL (verb) <1601>.

DRINK (noun) – [1] ***poma*** [neut. noun: πόμα <4188>]; **from *pinō*: to drink ▶ Liquid which one takes and swallows** > The Israelites all drank the same spiritual drink (1 Cor. 10:4). Under the old covenant, the religious service was concerned with foods and drinks (Heb. 9:10). Other ref.: 1 Cor. 12:13 in some mss. ¶

[2] ***posis*** [fem. noun: πόσις <4213>]; **from *pinō*: to drink ▶ Act of taking and swallowing a liquid; practically equivalent to [1].** > Jesus says that His blood is truly drink (John 6:55). The kingdom of God is not food and drink (lit.: eating and drinking) (Rom. 14:17). No one should judge the Colossians in relation to their food or drink {what they eat or drink} (Col. 2:16). ¶

[3] **strong drink: *sikera*** [neut. noun: σίκερα <4608>]; **from the Heb. *shechar*: strong drink (see Num. 28:7) ▶ Beverage high in alcohol, which could intoxicate** > John the Baptist would not drink wine or strong drink {fermented drink, liquor} (Luke 1:15). ¶
– [4] Matt. 25:35, 37, 42; Rom. 12:20 → DRINK (verb) <4222> [5] John 4:7, 9, 10, 12–14; 1 Cor. 9:4 → DRINK (verb) <4095> [6] 1 Cor. 9:7 → EAT <2068> [7] Phil. 2:17 → to pour out as a drink offering → DRINK OFFERING <4689>.

DRINK (verb) – [1] ***pinō*** [verb: πίνω <4095>] **▶ To take and swallow a liquid; also used figur.** > Jesus says not to worry about what we will eat or drink (Matt. 6:25, 31; Luke 12:29). The Son of Man, in contrast to John the Baptist, came eating and drinking, i.e., partook of food and drank freely and sociably in contrast to John's austere lifestyle (Matt. 11:18, 19; Luke 7:33, 34). Jesus asked His disciples if they were able to drink the cup that He was about to drink (Matt. 20:22a, b, 23; Mark 10:38a, b, 39a, b). Jesus was criticized for eating and drinking with publicans and sinners (Mark 2:16 in some mss.; Luke 5:30), as well as His disciples (Luke 5:33). John the Baptist was not to drink {take} wine or strong drink (Luke 1:15). No one having drunk old wine immediately desires new (Luke 5:39). The verb "to drink" is used when Jesus met the Samaritan woman at the well of Sychar (John 4:7, 9, 10, 12–14; some transl. use the noun {a drink} in the first three verses). He who drinks the blood of the Son of Man, i.e., appropriates its value, has life in himself (John 6:53), has eternal life (v. 54), and abides in Jesus (v. 56). If anyone is thirsty, let this person come to Jesus and drink (John 7:37). The verb "to drink" is used in the accounts of the last supper of Jesus before His death (Matt. 26:27, 29a, b; Mark 14:23, 25a, b; Luke 22:18) and of His sufferings in Gethsemane (Matt. 26:42; John 18:11). On the cross, Jesus was given vinegar mingled with myrrh to drink, but He refused to drink (Matt. 27:34a, b); Mark speaks of wine mingled with myrrh (Mark 15:23) {to take}. As often as the Christians drink the cup, they do it in remembrance of the Lord Jesus (1 Cor. 11:25–29). Other refs.: Matt. 24:38, 49; Mark 16:18; Luke 10:7; 12:19, 45; 13:26; 17:8a, b, 27, 28; 22:30; Acts 9:9; 23:12, 21; Rom. 14:21; 1 Cor. 9:4; 10:4a, b, 7, 21, 31; 11:22; 15:32; Heb. 6:7; Rev. 14:10; 16:6; 18:3. ¶

[2] **to drink with: *sumpinō*** [verb: συμπίνω <4844>]; **from *sun*: together with, and *pinō*: see [1] ▶ To drink together** > Peter and others ate and drank with Jesus after His resurrection from among the dead (Acts 10:41). ¶

3 **to drink, to give to drink: *potizō*** [verb: ποτίζω <4222>]; **from *potos*: the action of drinking ▶ To take and swallow a liquid, to make someone or an animal swallow a liquid** > Jesus promises a reward to whoever gives a little one a cup of cold water to drink (Matt. 10:42), and to one belonging to Christ (Mark 9:41). Jesus spoke of those who gave Him drink (lit.: to drink) (Matt. 25:35, 37, 42). Jesus was given to drink from a sponge filled with vinegar on the cross (Matt. 27:48; Mark 15:36). The ox was loosed on the Sabbath to be led to drink {be given water} (Luke 13:15). One must give drink (lit.: to drink) to his enemy if he thirsts (Rom. 12:20). Paul had given the Corinthians milk to drink {had fed the Corinthians with milk} and not solid food (1 Cor. 3:2), i.e., he had communicated to them the basics of the word of God. All Christians have been made to drink into one Spirit (1 Cor. 12:13). Babylon makes all nations drink of the wine of the wrath of her sexual immorality (Rev. 14:8). Other refs.: 1 Cor. 3:6–8; see WATER (verb) <4222>. ¶
4 **to drink water only: *hudropoteō*** [verb: ὑδροποτέω <5202>]; **from *hudropotēs*: one who drinks water, which is from *hudōr*: water, and *pinō*: to drink ▶ To take and swallow water** > Paul advised Timothy to no longer drink only water (1 Tim. 5:23). ¶
5 **to drink well, to have too much to drink: *methuō*** [verb: μεθύω <3184>]; **from *methē*: drunkenness, intoxication, or *methu*: fermented drink, especially wine ▶ To drink an alcoholic beverage in full measure** > The inferior wine was served when the guests had well drunk (John 2:10). All other refs.: DRUNK (BE) <3184>.
– 6 Matt. 23:24; Rev. 12:16 → to drink down, to drink → SWALLOW <2666> 7 Rom. 14:17; Col. 2:16 → DRINK (noun) <4213>.

DRINK OFFERING – to be poured out as a drink offering, as a libation: *spendomai*: middle voice of *spendō* [verb: σπένδω <4689>] **▶ Verb used by Paul to speak of his death; it includes the sense of joy and consecration to God; other transl.: to be offered** > If Paul was being poured out as a drink offering on the sacrifice and service of the Philippians, he was glad and rejoiced with them (Phil. 2:17). He told Timothy that he was ready to be poured out as a drink offering, referring to his pending death and perhaps martyrdom (2 Tim. 4:6). In the O.T., a libation was an offering of wine (e.g., Ex. 29:40) or of water (e.g., 2 Sam. 23:16) to God. ¶

DRINKING – 1 ***potos*** [masc. noun: πότος <4224>]; **from *pinō*: to drink; lit.: a drink ▶ Occasion affording opportunity for excessive indulging in alcoholic beverages** > Before their conversion, Christians walked in drinkings {wine-drinkings, drinking parties, banqueting, carousing} (1 Pet. 4:3). ¶
– 2 Luke 21:34 → DRUNKENNESS <3178> 3 Rom. 14:17 → DRINK (noun) <4213>.

DRIVE – 1 ***elaunō*** [verb: ἐλαύνω <1643>] **▶ To impel, to push** > A man was driven by the demon into the deserts (Luke 8:29). The ships are driven by strong winds (Jas. 3:4). Peter spoke of those who are like mists driven {carried} by storm (2 Pet. 2:17). Other refs.: Mark 6:48; John 6:19; see ROW <1643>. ¶
2 ***apelaunō*** [verb: ἀπελαύνω <556>]; **from *apo*: from, and *elaunō*: see 1 ▶ To chase, to send away** > Gallio drove {ejected} the Jews from the court (Acts 18:16). ¶
3 **to drive out: *exōtheō*** [verb: ἐξωθέω <1856>]; **from *ek*: out, and *ōtheō*: to push ▶ To expel, to thrust out** > God drove out nations before Israel (Acts 7:45). Other ref.: Acts 27:39 (to run ashore); see RUN <1856>. ¶
4 **to let drive, to drive along: *epididōmi*** [verb: ἐπιδίδωμι <1929>]; **from *epi*: upon (intens.), and *didōmi*: to give ▶ To let go adrift** > Paul's ship was let go and driven (Acts 27:15). All other refs.: DELIVER <1929>, GIVE <1929>.
5 ***peritrepō*** [verb: περιτρέπω <4062>]; **from *peri*: about, around, and *trepō*: to turn ▶ To lead, to turn** > Festus said to Paul that his great learning was driving him to madness (Acts 26:24). ¶

6 ***pherō*** [verb: φέρω <5342>] ► **To carry away, to take away >** They let the ship which Paul had boarded be driven (Acts 27:15, 17). All other refs.: see entries in Lexicon at <5342>.
– 7 Matt. 12:26; 17:19; 21:12; Mark 3:23; 9:18, 28; 11:15; Luke 4:29; 9:40; 19:45; John 6:37; also in relation to demons: Matt. 7:22; 8:31; 9:33, 34; 10:8; 12:24, 27a, b, 28; Mark 1:34, 39; 3:15, 22; 6:13; 7:26; 9:38; 16:9, 17; Luke 9:49; 11:14, 15, 18:19a, b, 20; 13:32; John 2:15; Acts 13:50 → to drive out → to cast out → CAST (verb) <1544> 8 Mark 1:12; Acts 7:58 → to drive, to drive out → to send out → SEND <1544> 9 Mark 9:29 → to drive out → to go out → GO <1831> 10 Luke 11:49; 1 Thes. 2:15 → to drive out, to drive out by persecution → PERSECUTE <1559> 11 John 12:31 → to drive out → to throw out → THROW (verb) <1544> 12 Acts 19:13 → driving out evil spirits → EXORCIST <1845> 13 2 Cor. 12:11 → CONSTRAIN <315> 14 Jas. 1:6 → to drive by the wind → WIND (noun) <416> 15 1 John 4:18 → to drive out → to cast out → CAST (verb) <1854> <906>.

DRIVEN (BE) – to be driven about, across, up and down: *diapherō* [verb: διαφέρω <1308>]; **from *dia*: through, and *pherō*: to bear ► To be tossed about, to be carried here and there >** Paul and the other passengers were being driven about in the Adriatic sea (Acts 27:27). All other refs.: see entries in Lexicon at <1308>.

DROOP – Heb. 12:12 → to hang down → HANG <3935>.

DROP (noun) – ***thrombos*** [masc. noun: θρόμβος <2361>] ► **Large droplet, clot >** The sweat of the Lord became like drops {great drops} of blood at Gethsemane (Luke 22:44), so intense was His spiritual combat when He had before Him the terrible sufferings of the cross. ¶

DROP (verb) – 1 Luke 16:17 → to drop out → FALL (verb) <4098> 2 Acts 27:29 → CAST (verb) <4496>.

DROPSICAL – *hudrōpikos* [adj.: ὑδρωπικός <5203>]; **from *hudōr*: water, and *ōps*: appearance ► Afflicted with an illness consisting of the accumulation of body fluid, especially in the abdomen >** Jesus healed a dropsical man {a man who had dropsy, a man suffering from abnormal swelling of the body} (Luke 14:2). ¶

DROPSY – Luke 14:2 → having dropsy, suffering from dropsy → DROPSICAL <5203>.

DROWN – 1 ***katapinō*** [verb: καταπίνω <2666>]; **from *kata*: down (intens.), and *pinō*: to drink ► To be submerged, to be engulfed >** The Egyptians were drowned {swallowed up} when attempting to pass through the Red Sea (Heb. 11:29). All other refs.: DEVOUR <2666>, SWALLOW <2666>.
2 ***pnigō*** [verb: πνίγω <4155>]; **poss. from *pneō*: to breathe ► To strangle, to choke >** The herd of swine drowned {were choked} in the sea (Mark 5:13). Other refs.: Matt. 13:7 in some mss. (other mss.: *apopnigō*, see CHOKE <638>); Matt. 18:28 (to take by the throat): see THROAT <4155>. ¶
– 3 Matt. 8:32 → DIE <599> 4 Matt. 18:6 → SINK (verb) <2670> 5 Mark 4:38; Luke 8:24 → PERISH <622> 6 Luke 8:33 → CHOKE <638> 7 1 Tim. 6:9 → PLUNGE <1036>.

DROWSY – Matt. 25:5 → to get drowsy → SLUMBER (verb) <3573>.

DRUNK (BE) – 1 **to be drunk, to get drunk, to be made drunk: *methuō*** [verb: μεθύω <3184>]; **from *methē*: drunkenness, intoxication, or *methu*: fermented drink, especially wine ► To drink much, to be intoxicated with strong drink >** In a parable, a servant might be found drinking with drunkards (lit.: those who are drunk) (Matt. 24:49). The disciples in Acts 2 were not drunk {were not full of wine} (v. 15). At the Lord's supper among the Corinthians, one was hungry and another was drunk {drank to excess} (1 Cor. 11:21). The inhabitants of the earth were made drunk {were intoxicated} with the wine of the sexual immorality of the great prostitute (Rev. 17:2; some mss. have *methuskō*); she was drunk with the blood of the saints and the martyrs of Jesus (v. 6). See [2] for this Greek verb in 1 Thes. 5:7. Other ref.: John 2:10 (to have too much to drink; some mss. have *methuskō*); see DRINK (verb) <3184>. ¶

[2] **to be drunk, to get drunk: *methuskō*** [verb: μεθύσκω <3182>]**; form of *methuō*: see** [1] **► To become progressively intoxicated** > In a parable, a servant began to be drunk (Luke 12:45). Paul exhorts to not be drunk with wine (Eph. 5:18). Those who get drunk (*methuskō*), get drunk (*methuō*) at night (1 Thes. 5:7). Other mss.: John 2:10; Rev. 17:2; see [1]. ¶

DRUNKARD – [1] ***methusos*** [masc. noun: μέθυσος <3183>]**; from *methu*: fermented drink, especially wine ► Person who has the habit of drinking to excess, of getting drunk; heavy drinker** > Christians are not to associate or eat with one called a brother who is a drunkard (1 Cor. 5:11). Drunkards will not inherit the kingdom of God (1 Cor. 6:10). ¶

– [2] Matt. 11:19; Luke 7:34 → WINE-BIBBER <3630> [3] Matt. 24:49 → lit.: one who is drunk → to be drunk → DRUNK (BE) <3184> [4] 1 Tim. 3:3; Titus 1:7 → given to wine → GIVE <3943>.

DRUNKEN – 1 Cor. 15:34 → to wake up from one's drunken stupor → AWAKE (verb) <1594>.

DRUNKEN (BE) – Matt. 24:49 → to be drunk → DRUNK (BE) <3184>.

DRUNKENNESS – [1] ***methē*** [fem. noun: μέθη <3178>]**; from *methu*: fermented drink, especially wine ► Habit of drinking to the point of getting drunk; excessive drinking** > The word of God condemns drunkenness (Luke 21:34; Rom. 13:13; Gal. 5:21). ¶

[2] ***oinophlugia*** [fem. noun: οἰνοφλυγία <3632>]**; from *oinos*: wine, and *phluō*: to overflow ► Condition of one given to wine; alcoholism; stronger term than** [1] > Some Christians pursued a course of drunkenness {excess of wine, wine-drinking} before their conversion (1 Pet. 4:3). ¶

– [3] 1 Tim. 3:3; Titus 1:7 → given to drunkenness → given to wine → GIVE <3943>.

DRUSILLA – ***Drousilla*** [fem. name: Δρούσιλλα <1409>] **► Jewish woman** > She was the wife of the governor Felix (Acts 24:24). She died with her son during the eruption of Mount Vesuvius in A.D. 79. Other ref.: Acts 24:27 in some mss. ¶

DRY (noun) – [1] ***anudros*** [adj.: ἄνυδρος <504>]**; from *a*: neg., and *hudōr*: water ► Without water; also transl.: arid, waterless** > The term is used in regard to places through which an unclean spirit goes (Matt. 12:43; Luke 11:24). Other refs.: 2 Pet. 2:17 and Jude 12 (without water); see WATER (noun) <504>. ¶

[2] ***xēros*** [adj.: ξηρός <3584>] **► a. Not under water** > The Hebrews passed through the Red Sea as through dry land (Heb. 11:29). **b. Mature, ripe** > The term is used in Luke 23:31, where it is contrasted to a green tree. All other refs.: LAND (noun) <3584>, WITHERED <3584>.

DRY (verb) – [1] **to dry up: *xērainō*** [verb: ξηραίνω <3583>]**; from *xēros*: dry ► a. To become desiccated, to wither** > Certain plants withered because they had no root (Matt. 13:6; Mark 4:6); Luke adds that they had no moisture (Luke 8:6). The fig tree that Jesus had cursed dried up (Matt. 21:19; Mark 11:20). If someone does not abide in Jesus, that person is cast out as a branch and is dried up (John 15:6). The sun withered the grass (Jas. 1:11). The grass has withered and its flower has fallen (1 Pet. 1:24). **b. To cease to flow, to stop** > Jesus healed a woman who had a flow of blood for twelve years, and the flow of her blood was dried up (Mark 5:29). The sixth angel poured out his bowl on the great river Euphrates, and its water dried up (Rev. 16:12). All other refs.: RIGID <3583>, RIPE (BE) <3583>, WITHER <3583>, WITHERED <3583>.

– [2] John 13:5 → WIPE <1591>.

DUE – [1] ***opheilē*** [fem. noun: ὀφειλή <3782>]; **from *opheilō*: see [2] ▶ Something which must be paid, obligation** > The Christian must render to all their dues {what they owe them} (Rom. 13:7). Other refs.: Matt. 18:32: see DEBT <3782>; 1 Cor. 7:3: see [2]. ¶

[2] **to owe: *opheilō*** [verb: ὀφείλω <3784>]; **also transl.: duty, marital duty ▶ Obligation, what one must do** > The husband should render to his wife due benevolence (lit.: what he owes) (1 Cor. 7:3; other mss. have [1]). Other ref.: Phm. 18. All other refs.: DEBT <3784>, DEBTOR <3784>, INDEBTED (BE) <3784>, OUGHT <3784>, OWE <3784>.

– [3] Matt. 24:45; Luke 12:42; Rom. 5:6 → due season, due time → SEASON (noun) <2540> [4] Luke 23:41 → due reward → things deserving → DESERVING <514> [5] Rom. 1:27 → OUGHT <1163> [6] Rom. 4:4 → what is due → DEBT <3783> [7] Rev. 16:6 → it is their just due → they are worthy → WORTHY <514>.

DULL – [1] **to become dull, to grow dull: *pachunō*** [verb: παχύνω <3975>]; **from *pachus*: thick ▶ To become thick, hard, calloused** > The hearts of Israel have become dull {become fat, grown fat, waxed gross} (Matt. 13:15; Acts 28:27). ¶

– [2] Matt. 13:15; Acts 28:27 → HARD <917> [3] 2 Cor. 3:14 → to make dull → HARDEN <4456> [4] Heb. 5:11 → SLUGGISH <3576>.

DUMB – [1] ***alalos*** [adj.: ἄλαλος <216>]; **from *a*: neg., and *laleō*: to speak ▶ Without the faculty of speech, mute** > Jesus made the dumb {speechless} to speak (Mark 7:37). He healed a son who had been possessed by a dumb and deaf spirit at the father's request (Mark 9:17 {robbed of his speech}, 25). ¶

[2] ***aphōnos*** [adj.: ἄφωνος <880>]; **from *a*: neg., and *phōnē*: sound, voice; lit.: without a voice ▶ Mute, refraining from using the voice** > Jesus was like a lamb that is dumb {silent} before its shearer (Acts 8:32). Before their conversion, the Corinthians were led away to dumb idols (1 Cor. 12:2). Balaam was reproved by a dumb {without speech} donkey (2 Pet. 2:16). Other ref.: 1 Cor. 14:10 (without significance); see SIGNIFICANCE <880>. ¶

[3] ***kōphos*** [adj.: κωφός <2974>]; **from *kōphaō*: to silence, or *koptō*: to cut down ▶ Incapable of speaking, mute** > They brought a dumb man {a man who could not talk} possessed by a demon to Jesus (Matt. 9:32); the demon having been cast out, the dumb man spoke (v. 33). On another occasion, Jesus healed a man possessed by a demon, blind and dumb (Matt. 12:22a, b). He cast out a dumb demon; when the demon left, the dumb man spoke (Luke 11:14a, b). The crowds cast the dumb and other afflicted people at the feet of Jesus, and He healed them (Matt. 15:30); the crowds wondered, seeing the dumb speaking (v. 31). Zacharias remained dumb {unable to speak, speechless} (Luke 1:22). All other refs.: DEAF <2974>.

– [4] Luke 1:20 → to be dumb → to be silent → SILENT <4623>.

DUNG (noun) – [1] ***kopria*** [fem. noun: κοπρία <2874>]; **from *kopros*: refuse, dirt ▶ Manure or other refuse used as fertilizer** > The vineyard keeper wanted to put dung {fertilizer} around the fig tree so that it would produce fruit (Luke 13:8; *koprion* in other mss.). If the salt has lost its savor, it is not even good for dung (Luke 14:35). ¶

– [2] Phil. 3:8 → FILTH <4657>.

DUNG (verb) – Luke 13:8 → lit.: to put dung → PUT <906>, DUNG (noun) <2874>.

DUPLICITY – Luke 20:23 → DECEIT <3834>.

DURST – Matt. 22:46; Mark 12:34; Luke 20:40; John 21:12; Acts 5:13; 7:32; Rom. 15:18; Jude 9 → DARE <5111>.

DUST – [1] ***koniortos*** [masc. noun: κονιορτός <2868>]; **from *konia*: dust, and *ornu-***

***mi*: to raise ▶ Small organic or mineral particles raised or suspended in the air >** The disciples were to shake off the dust of their feet if they were not received (Matt. 10:14; Luke 9:5), which they did (Luke 10:11) as did also Paul and Barnabas (Acts 13:51). The Jews cast dust into the air as proof of their wrath and indignation (Acts 22:23). ¶

2 ***chous*** [masc. noun: χοῦς <5522>]**; from *cheō*: to pour; other spelling: *choos* ▶ Material reduced to powder, especially of earth >** The disciples were to shake the dust off their feet if they were not received (Mark 6:11). The sailors cast dust upon their heads, grieving over Babylon (Rev. 18:19). ¶

– 3 Matt. 21:44; Luke 20:18 → to scatter like dust → to grind to powder → POWDER <3039> 4 1 Cor. 15:47–49 → made of dust → EARTHY <5517>.

DUTY[1] – 1 Matt. 12:5 → on Sabbath duty → lit.: on the Sabbaths → SABBATH <4521> 2 Luke 17:10 → to do what is one's duty → to be a debtor → DEBTOR <3784> 3 John 18:16 → one on duty → DOORKEEPER <2377> 4 Acts 6:3 → BUSINESS <5532> 5 Acts 23:1 → to fulfill one's duty → LIVE <4176> 6 Rom. 15:27 → the duty of the nations is → lit.: the nations are indebted → INDEBTED (BE) <3784> 7 1 Cor. 7:3 in some mss. → DUE <3782> 8 2 Tim. 4:5 → to discharge all the duties → to make full proof → PROOF <4135> 9 Heb. 10:11 → to perform religious duties → MINISTER (verb) <3008>.

DUTY[2] – Matt. 17:25 → CUSTOM[2] <5056>.

DWELL – 1 ***oikeō*** [verb: οἰκέω <3611>]**; from *oikos*: dwelling place ▶ To live, to reside >** Paul speaks of the man in whom sin dwells (Rom. 7:17 {some mss. have 2}, 20), and not good (v. 18). The Spirit of God dwells in the Christian (Rom. 8:9, 11a; 1 Cor. 3:16). God dwells in unapproachable light (1 Tim. 6:16). Other refs.: 1 Cor. 7:12, 13. ¶

2 ***enoikeō*** [verb: ἐνοικέω <1774>]**; from *en*: in, and *oikeō*: see 1 ▶ To inhabit; used only in the spiritual sense >** God will quicken the mortal bodies of Christians on account of His Spirit which dwells in them (Rom. 8:11b). God dwells among His people (2 Cor. 6:16). The Holy Spirit dwells in the Christians {has been entrusted to them} (2 Tim. 1:14). Paul desired that the word of Christ might dwell in Christians richly (Col. 3:16). A sincere faith had dwelt in Timothy, as well as in his grandmother Lois and his mother Eunice (2 Tim. 1:5). Other ref.: Luke 13:4: some mss. have 3; Rom. 7:17: some mss. have 1. ¶

3 ***katoikeō*** [verb: κατοικέω <2730>]**; from *kata*: intens., and *oikeō*: see 1 ▶ To reside, to live; also transl.: to inhabit, dweller, inhabitant, inhabiter, resident, people, to live, to inhabit, to settle >** The suicide of Judas was known to all who dwelt in Jerusalem (Acts 1:19). It was evident to all who dwelt in Jerusalem that a noteworthy miracle had been done by Peter (Acts 4:16). God does not dwell in houses made with hands (Acts 7:48; 17:24). All the fullness of the Godhead dwells in Christ (Col. 1:19; 2:9). Abraham dwelt in tents with Isaac and Jacob (Heb. 11:9b). The Spirit who dwells in the Christians does not desire enviously (Jas. 4:5; other mss.: *katoikizō*). They wait for new heavens and a new earth in which righteousness dwells (2 Pet. 3:13). John saw an angel who had the everlasting gospel to announce to those who dwell on the earth (Rev. 14:6). Other refs.: Matt. 2:23; 4:13; 12:45; 23:21; Luke 11:26; 13:4 (some mss. have 2); Acts 1:20; 2:9, 14; 7:2, 4a, b; 9:22, 32, 35; 11:29; 13:27; 17:26; 19:10, 17; 22:12; Eph. 3:17; Rev. 2:13a, b; 3:10; 6:10; 8:13; 11:10a, b; 13:8, 12, 14a, b; 17:2, 8. Other ref.: Acts 2:5; see STAY (verb) <2730>. ¶

4 ***enkatoikeō*** [verb: ἐγκατοικέω <1460>]**; from *en*: in, and *katoikeō*: see 3 ▶ To settle down among >** Righteous Lot dwelt among wicked men (2 Pet. 2:8). ¶

5 ***paroikeō*** [verb: παροικέω <3939>]**; from *para*: near, and *oikeō*: see 1 ▶ To stay as a stranger, to remain >** Abraham dwelt {sojourned, made his home} in the land of promise (Heb. 11:9a). Other ref.: Luke 24:18; see VISIT (verb) <3939>. ¶

[6] **to dwell around:** ***perioikeō*** [verb: περιοικέω <4039>]; **from** ***peri*****: around, and** ***oikeō*****: see** [1] ▶ **To live nearby, to be a neighbor** > Fear came on all those dwelling around {the neighbors of} Elizabeth and Zacharias (Luke 1:65). ¶

[7] **to dwell with:** ***sunoikeō*** [verb: συνοικέω <4924>]; **from** ***sun*****: together, and** ***oikeō*****: see** [1] ▶ **To stay with, to remain with** > The husband must dwell with {live with} his wife with understanding (or: according to knowledge) (1 Pet. 3:7). ¶

[8] ***kathēmai*** [verb: κάθημαι <2521>]; **from** ***kata*****: down, and** ***hēmai*****: to sit** ▶ **To have a set dwelling** > Jesus speaks of a day which will come as a snare on all those who dwell on the face of the whole earth (Luke 21:35). All other refs.: SIT <2521>.

[9] ***skēnoō*** [verb: σκηνόω <4637>]; **from** ***skēnos*****: tabernacle, tent; lit.: to set up one's tent** ▶ **To abide, to reside** > The Word became flesh, and dwelt {made His dwelling} among us (John 1:14). In eternity, God will dwell with men (Rev. 21:3). Other refs.: Rev. 7:15 (see to spread one's tent under TENT <4637>); 12:12; 13:6 {to live}. ¶

[10] ***kataskēnoō*** [verb: κατασκηνόω <2681>]; **from** ***kata*****: intens., and** ***skēnoō*****: see** [9] ▶ **To remain, to repose** > David says that his flesh will dwell {rest, live} in hope (Acts 2:26). Other refs.: Matt. 13:32; Mark 4:32; Luke 13:19; see NEST (verb) <2681>. ¶

– [11] John 1:38, 39a; 5:38; 6:56; 14:10, 17; Acts 28:16, 30; 1 John 3:17, 24a; 4:12, 13, 15, 16a, b; 2 John 2, 9a, b → REMAIN <3306> [12] Rom. 7:23 → lit.: to be [13] 2 Cor. 12:9 → REST (verb) <1981> [14] Phil. 4:8 → to let the mind dwell → MEDITATE <3049>.

DWELLER – [1] ***paroikos*** [adj.: πάροικος <3941>]; **from** ***para*****: near, and** ***oikeō*****: to remain, to stay** ▶ **Temporary resident, sojourner** > Moses became a dweller {alien, foreigner, stranger} in the land of Midian (Acts 7:29). All other refs.: FOREIGNER <3941>.

– [2] Acts 1:19, 20; 2:9; Rev. 17:2, 8 → lit.: one who dwells → DWELL <2730>.

DWELLING – [1] ***katoikēsis*** [fem. noun: κατοίκησις <2731>]; **from** ***kata*****: down (intens.), and** ***oikos*****: house** ▶ **Act of inhabiting, residing** > A man with an unclean spirit had his dwelling {lived} in the tombs (Mark 5:3). ¶

– [2] Luke 16:9 → TABERNACLE <4633> [3] John 1:14 → to make one's dwelling → DWELL <4637> [4] Acts 7:46 → dwelling, dwelling place → TABERNACLE <4638> [5] Acts 17:26 → HABITATION <2733> [6] 2 Cor. 5:2; Jude 6 → HABITATION <3613> [7] 2 Cor. 6:16 → to make one's dwelling → DWELL <1774> [8] Eph. 2:22; Rev. 18:2 → DWELLING PLACE <2732> [9] 2 Pet. 1:13, 14 → earthly dwelling → TENT <4638>.

DWELLING PLACE – [1] ***epaulis*** [fem. noun: ἔπαυλις <1886>]; **from** ***epi*****: in, and** ***aulis*****: place to spend the night** ▶ **Habitation, abode (of the meaner sort)** > According to the Psalms, the dwelling place {homestead, place} of Judas was to be desolate (Acts 1:20). ¶

[2] ***katoikētērion*** [neut. noun: κατοικητήριον <2732>]; **from** ***kata*****: intens., and** ***oikētērion*****: habitation, which is from** ***oikeō*****: to dwell** ▶ **Place to settle down, habitation** > Christians are being built together for a dwelling place {dwelling} of God in the Spirit (Eph. 2:22). The angel shouted that Babylon was fallen and had become a dwelling place {home} of demons (Rev. 18:2). ¶

[3] ***skēnē*** [fem. noun: σκηνή <4633>] ▶ **Tent, habitation** > The beast blasphemed the name of God and of His dwelling place (Rev. 13:6). The dwelling place of God will be with men in the eternal state (Rev. 21:3). All other refs.: TABERNACLE <4633>, TENT <4633>.¶

– [4] John 14:2 → MANSION <3438> [5] Acts 17:26 → HABITATION <2733> [6] 1 Cor. 4:11 → to have no certain dwellingplace → to be homeless → HOMELESS <790>.

DYING – [1] ***nekrōsis*** [fem. noun: νέκρωσις <3500>]; **from** ***nekroō*****: to put to death,**

which is from *nekros*: dead ▶ The condition of death > Paul always carried about in the body the dying {death} of Jesus (2 Cor. 4:10). Other ref.: Rom. 4:19; see DEADNESS <3500>. ¶

2 **to die: *apothnēskō*** [verb: ἀποθνήσκω <599>]; **from *apo*: from (intens.), and *thnēskō*: to die ▶ To be deceased, which signifies that the immaterial part of man is separated from the body >** Paul was as one dying, and behold he lived (2 Cor. 6:9). When Jacob was dying, he blessed each of the sons of Joseph (Heb. 11:21). All other refs.: DEAD <599>, DIE <599>.

– 3 Mark 5:23 → at extremity → EXTREMITY <2079>.

DYSENTERY – ***dusenteria*** [fem. noun: δυσεντερία <1420>]; **from *enteron*: intestine, which is from *entos*: inside; other spelling: *dusenterion* ▶ Disease characterized by intestinal inflammation and severe diarrhea >** Paul prayed and laid his hands on the father of Publius who had dysentery, and cured him (Acts 28:8). ¶

E

EACH – ***hekastos*** [adj.: ἕκαστος <1538>]; **from *ekas*: separate ► Every one.** * ‡

EAGER – 1 Rom. 1:15 → I am so eager → lit.: the desire for me (for my part) → PART (noun) <4289> 2 1 Cor. 12:31 → to be eager → to eagerly desire → DESIRE (verb) <2206> 3 1 Cor. 14:12; Titus 2:14 → ZEALOUS <2207> 4 2 Cor. 8:11 → eager willingness → lit.: readiness to be willing → READINESS <4288> 5 Gal. 2:10; 2 Pet. 1:10 → to be eager, to be all the more eager → to be diligent → DILIGENT <4704> 6 Eph. 4:3; 1 Thes. 2:17 → ENDEAVOR (verb) <4704> 7 Phil. 1:20 → earnest expectation → EXPECTATION <603> 8 Phil. 2:28 → the more eager → the more eagerly → EAGERLY <4708> 9 1 Tim. 6:10 → eager for money → coveting after money → COVET <3713> 10 1 Pet. 3:13 → IMITATOR <3402> 11 Jude 3 → was very eager → used all diligence → DILIGENCE <4710>.

EAGERLY – 1 **the more eagerly: *spoudaioterōs*** [adv.: σπουδαιοτέρως <4708>]; **from *spoudaiōs*: eagerly, diligently ► With great diligence, in much haste >** Paul had sent Timothy the more eagerly {diligently, carefully} {was all the more eager to send Timothy} so that when the Philippians saw him they might rejoice again (Phil. 2:28). ¶
– 2 Luke 22:15 → to eagerly desire → lit.: to desire with desire → DESIRE (noun) <1939> 3 Rom. 8:19, 25; 1 Cor. 1:7; Gal. 5:5; Phil. 3:20; Heb. 9:28 → to wait eagerly → WAIT (verb) <553> 4 1 Cor. 12:31; 14:1 → to eagerly desire → DESIRE (verb) <2206> 5 Gal. 4:17, 18 → lit.: to be zealous → ZEALOUS <2206> 6 2 Tim. 1:17 → very diligently → DILIGENTLY <4706>.

EAGERNESS – 1 2 Cor. 7:11 → eagerness to clear oneself → EXCUSING <627> 2 2 Cor. 8:19 → eagerness to help → ready mind → MIND (noun) <4288> 3 2 Cor. 9:2 → eagerness to help, readiness of mind → READINESS <4288>.

EAGLE – ***aetos*** [masc. noun: ἀετός <105>] **► Large, strong bird of prey with sharp vision >** The eagle symbolizes the rapidity of God's judgment on corrupted humanity when the Son of Man will come to establish His reign (Matt. 24:28 {vulture}; Luke 17:37 {vulture}; Rev. 4:7; 8:13 {angel in some mss.}). In Rev. 12:14, two wings of a great eagle are given to the woman (Israel) that she might fly into the desert. ¶

EAR – 1 ***ous*** [neut. noun: οὖς <3775>] **► Organ of hearing >** What is heard in the ear is to be preached on the house tops (Matt. 10:27). Jesus said that he who has ears to hear, let him hear (Matt. 11:15; 13:9, 43; Mark 4:9, 23; 7:16; Luke 8:8; 14:35). He who has an ear is to hear what the Spirit says to the churches (Rev. 2:7, 11, 17, 29; 3:6, 13, 22). Other refs.: Matt. 13:15a, b, 16; Mark 7:33; 8:18; Luke 1:44; 4:21; 12:3; 22:50; Acts 7:51, 57; 11:22; 28:27a, b; Rom. 11:8; 1 Cor. 2:9; 12:16; Jas. 5:4; 1 Pet. 3:12; Rev. 13:9. ¶
2 ***ōtion*** [neut. noun: ὠτίον <5621>]; **dimin. of 1 ► Organ of hearing >** Peter struck the bondman of the high priest and cut off his ear (Matt. 26:51; Mark 14:47 {*ōtarion*, the outer ear, in some mss.}; Luke 22:50 {*ous* in some mss.}; John 18:10 {*ōtarion* in some mss.}, 26). Jesus touched the ear of Malchus and healed him (Luke 22:51). ¶
3 ***akoē*** [fem. noun: ἀκοή <189>]; **from *akouō*: to hear ► Organ of hearing >** The ears of the deaf man were opened (Mark 7:35). Paul speaks of a time when men will not bear sound teaching, having an itching ear (2 Tim. 4:3); they will turn away their ear from the truth (v. 4). All other refs.: FAME <189>, HEARING <189>, REPORT (noun) <189>, RUMOR <189>.
– 4 Matt. 12:1; Mark 2:23; 4:28a, b; Luke 6:1 → ear of corn → head of grain → GRAIN <4719> 5 Acts 2:14 → to give ear → to give heed → HEED (noun) <1801>.

EARLIER – 1 ***proteron*** [adv.: πρότερον <4386>]; **from *proteros*: first, previous, which is from *pro*: before ► Previous, former >** The Hebrews were to remember the earlier days, in which they had endured much conflict of sufferings (Heb. 10:32). All other refs.: BEFORE <4386>, FIRST <4386>, FORMER <4386>.
– 2 John 19:39 → at first → FIRST <4412>.

EARLY – 1 **early, very early:** ***orthrios*** [adj.: ὄρθριος <3721>]; **from** ***orthros*****: daybreak; lit.: up at daybreak; also spelled:** ***orthrinos*** ► **At dawn, first thing in the morning** > Certain women had arrived very early at the tomb of Jesus (Luke 24:22). ¶
2 ***prōimos*** [adj.: πρώϊμος <4406>]; **from** ***prōi*****: morning; also spelled:** ***proimos*** ► **This word describes the first rain which often falls in October** > The soil gets the early and latter rain {the autumn and spring rains} (Jas. 5:7). ¶
– 3 Matt. 21:18; 27:1; John 18:28; 21:4 → early, early in the morning → MORNING <4405> 4 Mark 16:9; John 20:1 → MORNING <4404> 5 Luke 24:1; John 8:2; Acts 5:21 → MORNING <3722> 6 John 10:40 → in the early days → at first → FIRST <4412> 7 Acts 15:7; 21:16 → OLD <744>.

EARN – 1 ***poieō*** [verb: ποιέω <4160>]; **lit.: to make, to do** ► **To produce, to yield** > A bondman's mina had earned {gained, made} five minas (Luke 19:18). Other refs.: see entries in Lexicon at <4160>.
– 2 Luke 19:16 → PRODUCE <4333> 3 Acts 16:16 → BRING <3930>.

EARNEST (adj.) – 1 Acts 12:5 → earnest prayer → unceasing prayer → UNCEASING <1618> 2 Rom. 8:19; Phil. 1:20 → earnest expectation → EXPECTATION <603> 3 2 Cor. 7:7 → earnest desire → ardent desire → DESIRE (noun) <1972> 4 2 Cor. 8:17, 22b → very earnest → more zealous → ZEALOUS <4707> 5 2 Cor. 8:22a → ZEALOUS <4705> 6 Heb. 2:1 → to give earnest heed → HEED (noun) <4337> 7 Rev. 3:19 → to be zealous → ZEALOUS <2206>.

EARNEST (noun) – ***arrabōn*** [masc. noun: ἀρραβών <728>]; **from a similar Heb. word: security pledge** ► **Amount given as a guarantee of the execution of a contract; in a general way, what is given or done as an assurance of something to come** > The Holy Spirit is given to the Christians as the earnest {guarantee, pledge} of their heavenly inheritance (2 Cor. 1:22; 5:5; Eph. 1:14). In modern Greek, *arrabōna* means an engagement ring. ¶

EARNESTLY – 1 **earnestness:** ***ekteneia*** [fem. noun: ἐκτένεια <1616>]; **from** ***ekteinō*****: to stretch out, which is from** ***ek*****: out, and** ***teinō*****: to stretch** ► **With ardor, with fervor** > The twelve tribes had served God earnestly {incessantly, instantly} (lit.: in earnestness) day and night (Acts 26:7). Other ref.: Acts 12:5 in some mss. ¶
2 **more earnestly:** ***ektenesteron*** [adv.: ἐκτενέστερον <1617>]; **compar. of** ***ektenēs*****: insistently, which is from** ***ekteinō*****: see** 1 ► **In a more pressing, urgent manner** > Being in agony, Jesus prayed more earnestly {very fervently, more intently} (Luke 22:44). ¶
3 ***polla*****; from** ***polus*** [adj.: πολύς <4183>] ► **Much, with insistence** > Jesus warned the unclean spirits strictly (or: much) (Mark 3:12). Legion implored Jesus earnestly {again and again} that He would not send them out of the country (Mark 5:10). Jairus implored Jesus earnestly {greatly} concerning his daughter (Mark 5:23). Other refs.: see MANY <4183>.
4 ***spoudaiōs*** [adv.: σπουδαίως <4709>]; **from** ***spoudaios*****: active, diligent** ► **Diligently, seriously** > The elders of the Jews implored Jesus earnestly {instantly} concerning a centurion's servant who was sick (Luke 7:4). Other ref.: Titus 3:13; see DILIGENTLY <4709>. ¶
5 **with prayer:** ***proseuchē*** [fem. noun: προσευχή <4335>]; **from** ***proseuchomai*****: to pray, which is from** ***pros*****: toward, and** ***euchē*****: prayer** ► **Demand, request to God** > Elijah prayed earnestly (lit.: prayed with prayer) that it would not rain (Jas. 5:17). All other refs.: PRAYER <4335>.
– 6 Matt. 9:38; Luke 10:2 → to pray earnestly → SUPPLICATE <1189> 7 Luke 9:21 → to earnestly charge → CHARGE (verb) <2008> 8 Luke 22:15 → lit.: with desire → DESIRE (noun) <1939> 9 Acts 12:5 → UNCEASING <1619> 10 Acts 23:1 → to behold earnestly, steadfastly → BEHOLD (verb) <816> 11 1 Cor. 12:31; 14:39 → to desire earnestly → DESIRE (verb) <2206> 12 2 Cor. 5:2; 2 Tim. 1:4 → to earnestly

desire → DESIRE (verb) <1971> **13** 2 Cor. 8:4 → with much entreaty → ENTREATY <3874> **14** Col. 4:12; 1 Tim. 6:12 → to combat earnestly, to strive earnestly, to labor earnestly → FIGHT (verb) <75> **15** 1 Thes. 3:10 → most earnestly → EXCEEDINGLY <5238a> **16** 2 Tim. 1:17 → DILIGENTLY <4706> **17** Heb. 13:19 → more earnestly → all the more → MORE <4056> **18** 1 Pet. 1:22 → FERVENTLY <1619> **19** 1 Pet. 4:8 → to love earnestly → lit.: to have fervent love → FERVENT <1618>.

EARNESTNESS – **1** 2 Cor. 7:11; 8:7, 8; Heb. 6:11 → DILIGENCE <4710> **2** 2 Cor. 7:12; 8:16 → ZEAL <4710>.

EARTH – **1** ***gē*** [fem. noun: γῆ <1093>] ► **a. Land, country** > At the indication of the angel, Joseph brought Mary and Jesus back to the land of Israel (Matt. 2:20, 21). The children of Israel had been enslaved for four hundred years in a foreign land (Acts 7:6). Other refs.: Matt. 2:6; 4:15a, b; Heb. 11:9; Rev. 20:9. **b. Soil, land where one is found** > The meek will inherit the earth (Matt. 5:5). Other refs.: Matt. 6:19; 9:6; 10:29; 12:40, 42; 15:35; 17:25; 18:18a, b, 19; 23:9, 35; 24:30; 27:51; Mark 4:1; 6:47; 8:6; 9:20; 14:35; Luke 5:3, 11; 6:49; 8:27; 11:31; 22:44; 24:5; John 6:21; 8:6, 8; 12:32; 17:4; 21:8, 9, 11; Acts 7:33; 9:4, 8; 10:11; 11:6; 26:14; 27:43, 44; 1 Cor. 15:47; Heb. 11:38; 12:25; Jas. 5:5; 2 Pet. 3:5; Rev. 12:16a, b. **c. Those who dwell on the earth considered as a whole** > Believers in the Lord Jesus are the salt of the earth (Matt. 5:13). Jesus asks if the Son of Man will find faith on earth when He comes (Luke 18:8). The whole earth wondered after the beast (Rev. 13:3). **d. Nation of Israel** > John saw another beast coming up out of the earth (Rev. 13:11), the antichrist, in contrast with the first beast which comes up out of the sea (see v. 1). **e. Earth considered as a whole (e.g., in contrast to heaven)** > God the Father is Lord of heaven and earth (Matt. 11:25; Luke 10:21; Acts 17:24). Heaven and earth will disappear, but everything which concerns the law will be fulfilled (Matt. 5:18) and the words of the Lord will never pass away (Matt. 24:35; Mark 13:31; Luke 21:33). The Christian is to set his mind on the things that are above, not on the things that are on the earth (Col. 3:2). Other refs.: Matt. 5:35; 6:10; 10:34; 16:19a, b; 28:18; Mark 2:10; 9:3; 13:27; Luke 2:14; 5:24; 12:49, 51, 56; 16:17; 21:25, 35; Acts 1:8; 2:19; 3:25; 4:24, 26; 7:49; 8:33; 10:12; 13:47; 14:15; 17:26; 22:22; Rom. 9:17, 28; 10:18; 1 Cor. 8:5; 10:26, 28 in some mss.; 15:47; Eph. 1:10; 3:15; 4:9; 6:3; Col. 1:16, 20; 3:5; Heb. 1:10; 8:4; 11:13; 12:26a, b; Jas. 5:12; 2 Pet. 3:7, 10; Rev. 1:5, 7; 3:10; 5:3a, b, 6, 10, 13a, b; 6:4, 8a, b, 10, 13, 15; 7:1a–c, 2, 3; 8:5, 7a, b, 13; 9:1, 3a, b; 10:2, 5, 6, 8; 11:4, 6; 12:4, 9, 12, 13; 13:8, 12, 13, 14a, b; 14:3, 6, 7, 16a, b, 18, 19a, b; 16:1, 2, 18; 17:2a, b, 5, 8, 18; 18:1, 3a, b, 9, 11, 23, 24; 19:2, 19; 20:8, 11; 21:1b, 24. **f. Arable land, soil that is cultivated** > The term is used in Matt. 13:5a, b, 8, 23; 25:18, 25; Mark 4:5a, b, 8, 20, 26, 28, 31a, b; Luke 8:8, 15; 13:7; 14:35; John 12:24; Heb. 6:7; Jas. 5:7, 17, 18; 1 John 5:8 in some mss.; Rev. 9:4; 11:18; 14:15; 16:14. **g. In contrast to that which is heavenly in character** > Jesus speaks of him who is of the earth and who speaks as of the earth (John 3:31a–c). Other refs.: Rev. 11:10a, b. **h. Future place** > Christians wait for new heavens and a new earth, in which righteousness dwells (2 Pet. 3:13). John saw a new heaven and a new earth, for the first heaven and the first earth had passed away (Rev. 21:1a). All other refs.: LAND (noun) <1093>.

2 **under the earth: *katachthonios*** [adj.: καταχθόνιος <2709>]**; from *kata*: down, and *chthōn*: ground, earth ► Which pertains to the lower regions of the earth** > At the name of Jesus every knee shall bow of heavenly, earthly, and infernal (lit. under-the-earth) beings (Phil. 2:10). The "under-the-earth beings" correspond to some fallen angels who already are suffering the punishment of eternal fire (see Jude 6), the devil and the other fallen angels (see Matt. 25:41) as well as unbelievers, whose names shall not be found written in the book of life (see Rev. 20:15). ¶

– **3** Matt. 24:14; Luke 2:1; 21:26; Acts 11:28; 17:31 → earth, habitable earth, inhabited earth → WORLD <3625> [4] Phil. 2:10 → in earth, on earth → EARTHLY <1919> [5] 2 Tim. 2:20 → of earth → EARTHEN <3749>.

EARTHEN – [1] ***ostrakinos*** [adj.: ὀστράκινος <3749>]; **from *ostrakon*: burnt clay ▶ Made of clay (which suggests fragility) >** Christians have the treasure of the knowledge of the glory of God in earthen vessels {jars of clay} (2 Cor. 4:7). In a large house, there are wooden and earthen vessels {vessels of clay, of earth, of earthenware} (2 Tim. 2:20). ¶
– [2] Rev. 2:27 → earthen pots → lit.: vessels of pottery → POTTERY <2764>.

EARTHENWARE – 2 Tim. 2:20 → of earthenware → EARTHEN <3749>.

EARTHLY – [1] ***epigeios*** [adj.: ἐπίγειος <1919>]; **from *epi*: upon, and *gē*: earth ▶ Which exists on earth, pertains to this world >** Jesus had spoken of earthly things (John 3:12). There are heavenly bodies and earthly bodies, but the glory of heavenly bodies differs from the glory of earthly bodies (1 Cor. 15:40a, b {terrestrial}). Christians know that if their earthly tent is destroyed, they have a building from God, a house which is not made with hands, eternal, in the heavens (2 Cor. 5:1). At the name of Jesus every knee will bow, of heavenly, earthly {in earth, on earth}, and infernal beings (Phil. 2:10). Paul speaks of those who mind earthly things (Phil. 3:19). Bitter envy and a spirit of strife correspond to the wisdom which is earthly, natural, demonic (Jas. 3:15). ¶
[2] ***kosmikos*** [adj.: κοσμικός <2886>]; **from *kosmos*: world, universe ▶ Made from materials of this world >** The first covenant had a sanctuary which was an earthly {worldly} one (Heb. 9:1). Other ref.: Titus 2:12; see WORLDLY <2886>. ¶
– [3] Rom. 1:3 → as to His earthly life → lit.: the becoming (*ginomai*) [4] 2 Cor. 1:12 → earthly wisdom → carnal wisdom → CARNAL <4559>.

EARTHQUAKE – ***seismos*** [masc. noun: σεισμός <4578>]; **from *seiō*: to agitate, to shake ▶ Shaking of the earth's crust, seism >** The centurion and others with him had seen the earthquake when Jesus yielded up His spirit (Matt. 27:54). There was a great earthquake when the women came to the tomb of Jesus (Matt. 28:2). There was a great earthquake, and the doors of the prison holding Paul and Silas were immediately opened (Acts 16:26). During the great tribulation, there will be earthquakes in various places (Matt. 24:7; Mark 13:8; Luke 21:11). The term is transl. by "storm" {tempest} in Matt. 8:24. Other refs.: Rev. 6:12; 8:5; 11:13a, b, 19; 16:18a, b. ¶

EARTHY – ***choikos*** [adj. used as noun: χοϊκός <5517>]; **from *chous* (or *choos*): dust ▶ Lit.: made of dust, i.e., dry particles from the earth >** The first man, taken out of the earth, is dust (1 Cor. 15:47). As he who is made of dust (Adam), so also are those who are made of dust (the human race) (1 Cor. 15:48a, b). As Christians have borne the image of the one made of dust, they will bear also the image of the heavenly One (Christ, the second man) (1 Cor. 15:49). ¶

EASE – [1] ***anesis*** [fem. noun: ἄνεσις <425>]; **from *aniēmi*: to let go ▶ Relief, rest >** For the Corinthians the willingness to give did not mean that there should be ease for others and burden for themselves {that others should be eased and them burdened, that others might be relieved and themselves hard pressed} (2 Cor. 8:13). All other refs.: LIBERTY <425>, REST (noun)[1] <425>.
– [2] Luke 12:19 → to take one's ease → REST (verb) <373> [3] 1 Cor. 16:10 → to put at ease → to see that someone may be without fear → SEE <991>, FEAR (noun) <870>.

EASED (BE) – 2 Cor. 8:13 → EASE <425>.

EASIER – ***eukopōteros*; compar. of *eukopos*** [adj.: εὔκοπος <2123>]; **from *eu*: well, and *kopos*: fatigue, labor ▶ Less difficult, simpler >** Jesus asked whether it was easier to tell a paralytic that his sins were forgiven or to tell him to get up and walk (Matt. 9:5;

Mark 2:9; Luke 5:23). It is easier for a camel to pass through the hole of a needle than for a rich man to enter into the kingdom of God (Matt. 19:24; Mark 10:25; Luke 18:25). It is easier that the heaven and earth should pass away than that one stroke of a letter of the law should fail (Luke 16:17). ¶

EASILY – [1] 2 Thes. 2:2 → QUICKLY <5030> [2] Heb. 12:1 → which ensnares so easily, which doth beset so easily → ENSNARE <2139>.

EAST – [1] ***anatolē*** [fem. noun: ἀνατολή <395>]; **from *anatellō*: to rise, which is from *ana*: up, and *tellō*: to rise ▶ The eastern side, the direction of the sunrise; one of the four cardinal points, opposite to the west** > The wise men came from the east to see the child Jesus (Matt. 2:1). They had seen His star in the east (Matt. 2:2), and it went before them (v. 9). Many will come from the east and lie down at table with Abraham, Isaac, and Jacob in the kingdom of heaven (Matt. 8:11 {rising sun}; Luke 13:29). The coming of the Son of Man will be as the lightning which goes forth from the east and shines to the west (Matt. 24:27). See DAYSPRING FROM ON HIGH (Luke 1:78). Other refs.: Rev. 7:2 {sunrising, rising of the sun}; 16:12 {rising of the sun}; 21:13. ¶

– [2] Rev. 7:2; 16:12 → lit.: rising of the sun → SUN <2246>.

EASY – [1] ***chrēstos*** [adj.: χρηστός <5543>]; **from *chraomai*: to use; lit.: which can be used ▶ Comfortable, gentle to bear** > The yoke of Jesus is easy and His burden is light (Matt. 11:30). All other refs.: BETTER <5543>, GOOD (adj.) <5543>, GOODNESS <5543>.

– [2] Matt. 7:13 → BROAD <2149> [3] Luke 12:19 → to take life easy → REST (verb) <373>.

EAT – [1] ***bibrōskō*** [verb: βιβρώσκω <977>]; **from which *brōma*: food ▶ To consume avidly, to devour** > This verb is used only in John 6:13 concerning those who had eaten the five barley loaves which had been multiplied by the Lord. ¶

[2] ***geuō*** [verb: γεύω <1089>] **▶ To taste, to take food** > The verb is used concerning Peter (Acts 10:10) and Paul (20:11). All other refs.: TASTE (verb) <1089>.

[3] ***esthiō*** [verb: ἐσθίω <2068>] **▶ To take food, to consume a meal** > The Pharisees asked why Jesus ate with publicans and sinners (Matt. 9:11). Other refs.: Matt. 11:18, 19; 12:1; 14:21; 15:2, 27, 38; 24:49; 26:21, 26a; Mark 1:6; 2:16a, b; 7:2–5, 28; 14:18, 22; Luke 5:30, 33; 6:1; 7:33, 34; 10:7, 8; 12:45; 15:16; 17:27, 28; 22:30; Acts 27:35; Rom. 14:2b, 3a–d, 6a–d, 20; 1 Cor. 8:7, 10; 9:7a, b, 13; 10:18, 25, 27, 28, 31; 11:22, 26–28, 29a, b, 34; 2 Thes. 3:10, 12. Other refs.: Heb. 10:27; see DEVOUR <2068>. ¶

[4] **to eat with: *sunesthiō*** [verb: συνεσθίω <4906>]; **from *sun*: together with, and *esthiō*: see [3] ▶ To take food together** > Jesus ate with sinners (Luke 15:2). Other refs.: Acts 10:41; 11:3; 1 Cor. 5:11; Gal. 2:12. ¶

[5] ***phagō*** [verb: φάγω <5315>]; **form of *esthiō*: see [3] ▶ To take food, to consume** > Christians should not worry about what they will eat (Matt. 6:25, 31). Other refs.: Matt. 12:4a, b; 14:16, 20; 15:20, 32, 37; 25:35, 42; 26:17, 26b; Mark 2:26a, b; 3:20; 5:43; 6:31, 36, 37a, b, 42, 44; 8:1, 2, 8, 9; 11:14; 14:12, 14, 22; Luke 4:2; 6:4a, b; 7:36; 8:55; 9:13, 17; 12:19, 22, 29; 13:26; 14:1, 15; 15:23; 17:8a, b; 22:8, 11, 15, 16; 24:43; John 4:31–33; 6:5, 23, 26, 31a, b, 49–53, 58a; 18:28; Acts 9:9; 10:13, 14; 11:7; 23:12, 21; Rom. 14:2a, 21, 23; 1 Cor. 8:8a, b, 13; 9:4; 10:3, 7; 11:20, 21, 33; 15:32; 2 Thes. 3:8; Heb. 13:10; Jas. 5:3; Rev. 2:7, 14, 20; 10:10b; 17:16; 19:18. ¶

[6] ***trōgō*** [verb: τρώγω <5176>] **▶ To take food (emphasizing a slow process); to chew** > Before the flood, people were eating and drinking (Matt. 24:38). He who eats the flesh and drinks the blood of the Lord Jesus (i.e., who feeds on Christ spiritually) has eternal life (John 6:54); he abides in Jesus and Jesus abides in him (v. 56). Always in the sense of spiritual appropriation, he who eats {feeds on} Jesus will live because of Him

(John 6:57); he who eats {feeds on} Jesus as the bread which came down from heaven will live forever (6:58b). In John 13:18 {to share}, the sense is to eat habitually with someone, as Judas did with Jesus. ¶
[7] Acts 27:38 → when they had eaten enough → lit.: having been filled (*korennumi*) [κορέννυμι <2880>] with food (*trophē*) [τροφή <5160>]. Other ref.: 1 Cor. 4:8; see FILL (verb) <2880>. ¶
– [8] Matt. 9:10; Mark 16:14; Luke 7:37; et al. → to be at the table → TABLE[1] <345>; etc. [9] Matt. 11:19, Luke 7:34 → a man who is eating → lit.: a man glutton → GLUTTON <5314> [10] Matt. 13:4; Mark 4:4; Luke 8:5; John 2:17; Rev. 10:9, 10a → to eat, to eat up → DEVOUR <2719> [11] Mark 7:27; Luke 16:21 → to be filled → FILL (verb) <5526> [12] Luke 9:12 → something to eat → FOOD <1979> [13] Luke 11:37; John 21:12, 15 → to eat, to eat breakfast, to have breakfast → DINE <709> [14] Luke 17:8; Rev. 3:20 → SUP <1172> [15] Luke 24:41 → something to eat → FOOD <1034> [16] John 6:11 → SET (verb) <345> [17] John 6:12 → to have enough to eat → to be filled → FILL (verb) <1705> [18] John 21:5 → something to eat → FOOD <4371> [19] Acts 1:4 → to eat with → ASSEMBLE <4871> [20] Acts 2:46 → to eat together → lit.: to receive the food → FOOD <5160> [21] Acts 27:33 → without eating → without taking food → FOOD <777> [22] Acts 27:33, 36 → to take food, to take → TAKE <4355> [23] Rom. 14:15a → what you eat → FOOD <1033> [24] 1 Cor. 8:4; Col. 2:16 → EATING <1035> [25] 1 Cor. 8:10 → to sit at table → SIT <2621> [26] 2 Tim. 2:17 → to eat as doth a canker → lit.: to have pasture as gangrene → PASTURE <3542> [27] Jas. 5:3 → to be eaten away → RUSTED (BE) <2728> [28] Jude 12 → to eat with → to feast with → FEAST (verb) <4910>.

EATING – [1] ***brōsis*** [fem. noun: βρῶσις <1035>]; **from *bibrōskō*: to eat ▶ Food, consumption of food; also transl. in older versions: meat** > The kingdom of God is not eating and drinking (Rom. 14:17). Paul speaks about the eating of things sacrificed to idols (1 Cor. 8:4). No one was to judge the Colossians in matters of food or drink (or: eating or drinking) (Col. 2:16). God supplies bread for eating (2 Cor. 9:10). All other refs.: FOOD <1035>, MEAL <1035>, RUST <1035>.
– [2] Rom. 14:15b → FOOD <1033>.

EATING CEREMONIAL – Heb. 13:9 → "eating ceremonial" added in Engl.

ECSTASY – ***ekstasis*** [fem. noun: ἔκστασις <1611>]; **from *existēmi*: to remove from its normal place, which is from *ek*: out, and *histēmi*: to stand; in the pass.: to be stupefied, to be amazed ▶ State of a person in a trance, as transported outside himself and unaware of the surroundings; also transl.: trance** > An ecstasy came upon Peter (Acts 10:10; 11:5), as likewise upon Paul (22:17). On this occasion, Peter saw a vision and heard a voice; as for Paul, he saw the Lord in his vision. All other refs.: AMAZEMENT <1611>.

EDGE – [1] ***stoma*** [neut. noun: στόμα <4750>] ▶ **Primary meaning: mouth; also: cutting side of an instrument** > Jesus speaks of those who will fall by the edge of the sword, and be led away captive into all the nations (Luke 21:24). O.T. people of faith escaped the edge of the sword (Heb. 11:34). All other refs.: MOUTH (noun) <4750>.
– [2] Matt. 4:5; Luke 4:9 → PINNACLE <4419> [3] Matt. 9:20; 14:36; Mark 6:56; Luke 8:44 → FRINGE <2899> [4] Luke 5:2 → water edge → LAKE <3041>.

EDICT – Heb. 11:23 → ORDINANCE <1297>.

EDIFICATION – [1] ***oikodomē*** [fem. noun: οἰκοδομή <3619>]; **from *oikos*: house, building, and *demō*: to build ▶ Result of activities contributing to the spiritual development of Christians; also transl.: edifying (to edify), building (to build) up, strengthening, upbuilding** > Christians must pursue the things which make for mutual edification (Rom. 14:19); they must please their neighbor with a view to what

is good, for edification (15:2). He who prophesies speaks for the edification of the church (1 Cor. 14:3, 5, 12); all things should be done for edification (v. 26). Paul had received his authority for edification from the Lord (2 Cor. 10:8; 13:10); he was doing all things for edification (12:19). The gifts have been given for the edifying of the body of Christ (Eph. 4:12, 16). Christians are to let what is good for necessary edification proceed out of their mouth (Eph. 4:29). All other refs.: BUILDING <3619>.
– 2 1 Tim. 1:4 → EDIFYING <3622>.

EDIFY – 1 ***oikodomeō*** [verb: οἰκοδομέω <3618>]; **from *oikodomos*: builder, building a house, which is from *oikos*: house, and *demō*: to build ► To build, to contribute to spiritual progress; also transl.: to strengthen** > The churches throughout Judea and Galilee and Samaria were edified (Acts 9:31). Paul did not want to build upon another's foundation (Rom. 15:20). Love edifies (1 Cor. 8:1). Not everything edifies {is constructive} (1 Cor. 10:23). He who speaks in tongues edifies himself, but he who prophesies edifies the church (1 Cor. 14:4a, b; also v. 17). The Thessalonians were to edify one another (1 Thes. 5:11). Christians are being built up as a spiritual house (1 Pet. 2:5). All other refs.: BUILD <3618>, EMBOLDENED (BE) <3618>.
– 2 Rom. 14:19; 1 Cor. 14:5 → lit.: for edification → EDIFICATION <3619>.

EDIFYING – 1 ***oikonomia*** [fem. noun: οἰκονομία <3622>]; **from *oikonomeō*: to manage a household, which is from *oikos*: house, and *nemō*: to distribute, to manage ► Administration, work** > Fables and endless genealogies cause disputes, rather than godly edifying {godly edification, God's work} (1 Tim. 1:4); some mss. have *oikodomia*: see 2. All other refs.: see DISPENSATION <3622>.
2 ***oikodomia*** [fem. noun: οἰκοδομία <3620>]; **from *oikodomeō*: to build, which is from *oikodomos*: builder, building a house, which is from *oikos*: house, building, and *demō*: to build ► Edification, spiritual progress** > This word is used in 1 Tim. 1:4 in some mss.; see 1. ¶
– 3 1 Cor. 14:5, 12, 26; 2 Cor. 12:19; Eph. 4:12, 16, 29 → EDIFICATION <3619>.

EDUCATE – ***paideuō*** [verb: παιδεύω <3811>]; **from *pais*: child ► To teach, to instruct with discipline** > Moses was educated {was instructed, was learned} in all the wisdom of the Egyptians (Acts 7:22). Paul had been educated {had studied} at the feet of Gamaliel (Acts 22:3). All other refs.: CHASTEN <3811>, CORRECT <3811>, LEARN <3811>, TEACH <3811>.

EFFACE – Col. 2:14 → to blot out → BLOT (verb) <1813>.

EFFECT (noun) – 1 **to make of no effect: *akuroō*** [verb: ἀκυρόω <208>]; **from *a*: neg., and *kuroō*: to confirm, which is from *kuros*: having authority, effective ► To annul, to make void; also transl.: to invalidate, to nullify** > The Jews had made the commandment of God, to honor father or mother, of no effect by their tradition (Matt. 15:6). They were making of no effect the word of God through their tradition (Mark 7:13). The law cannot make of no effect {set aside, disannul} a covenant confirmed before by God in Christ (Gal. 3:17), the one that God had concluded with Abraham on the principle of faith. ¶
2 **to take no effect: *ekpiptō*** [verb: ἐκπίπτω <1601>]; **from *ek*: out, from, and *piptō*: to fall ► To fail to give result** > It is not that the word of God has taken no effect {has failed} (Rom. 9:6). Other refs.: FAIL <1601>, FALL (verb) <1601>, RUN <1601>.
3 **to make of no effect, to make without effect, to become of no effect: *katargeō*** [verb: καταργέω <2673>]; **from *kata*: intens., and *argeō*: to be inactive, which is from *argos*: idle, useless, which is from *a*: neg. and *ergon*: work ► To abolish, to suppress; to render inoperative; also transl.: to nullify** > Unbelief does not make the faithfulness of God of no effect (Rom. 3:3). Faith does not make void {make of no effect} the law (Rom. 3:31). The promise

is made of no effect {is void, is worthless} if those who are of the law are heirs (Rom. 4:14). The body of sin is made of no effect {destroyed, done away, annulled} if the old man is crucified with Christ (Rom. 6:6). The law cannot annul the covenant confirmed before by God in Christ that it should make of no effect {do away with} the promise (Gal. 3:17). God has chosen base and despised things to make of no effect {bring to nought, bring to nothing, annul} things that are (1 Cor. 1:28). In justifying themselves by the law, the Galatians had made Christ to become of no effect unto them {they were deprived of all profit from Him, have been severed, alienated from Him, became estranged} (Gal. 5:4), in the sense that they were separated from Christ. All other refs.: see entries in Lexicon at <2673>.

– [4] Luke 18:1 → to the effect → to the purport (*pros*) [5] Acts 7:53 → that was put into effect → by the disposition → DISPOSITION <1296> [6] Acts 23:25 → to this effect → lit.: having this form → FORM (noun) <5179> [7] 1 Cor. 1:17 → to make of no effect → to make vain → VAIN <2758> [8] 1 Cor. 12:6 → OPERATION <1755> [9] 1 Cor. 15:10 → without effect → in vain → VAIN <2756> [10] Gal. 3:19 → to put into effect → ORDAIN <1299> [11] Heb. 9:17 → to take effect → PREVAIL <2480> [12] Heb. 9:18 → to put into effect → INAUGURATE <1457> [13] Jas. 1:4 → to have full effect → lit.: to have its perfect work → WORK (noun) <2041>.

EFFECT (verb) – [1] Rom. 7:13 → WORK (verb) <2716> [2] Heb. 8:8 → MAKE <4931>.

EFFECTING – 1 Cor. 12:10 → OPERATION <1755>.

EFFECTIVE – [1] ***energēs*** [adj.: ἐνεργής <1756>]; **from *en*: in, and *ergon*: work ▶ Apt to produce results (e.g., in the Christian service)** > A great and effective {effectual} door was opened to Paul in Ephesus (1 Cor. 16:9). Paul was praying that the participation in the faith of Philemon may become effective {active, effectual, operative} in the acknowledgment of every good thing which is in Christians toward Christ (Phm. 6). Other ref.: Heb. 4:12; see OPERATIVE <1756>. ¶

[2] **to act: *energeō*** [verb: ἐνεργέω <1754>]; **from *energēs*: active, see [1] ▶ To operate, to produce an effect** > The effective {effectual, fervent} supplication (lit.: supplication which acts) of the righteous man has much power (Jas. 5:16). All other refs.: WORK (verb) <1754>.

– [3] Eph. 4:16 → in its measure → MEASURE (noun) <3358>.

EFFECTIVELY – Gal. 2:8a, b; 1 Thes. 2:13 → to have wrought effectively, to work effectively → WORK (verb) <1754>.

EFFECTS – Acts 21:15 → to have the effects ready → PACK <643>.

EFFECTUAL – [1] 1 Cor. 16:9; Phm. 6 → EFFECTIVE <1756> [2] 2 Cor. 1:6 → to be effectual → WORK (verb) <1754> [3] Jas. 5:16 → EFFECTIVE <1754>.

EFFECTUALLY – Gal. 2:8a; 1 Thes. 2:13 → to have wrought effectually, to work effectually → WORK (verb) <1754>.

EFFEMINATE – 1 Cor. 6:9 → HOMOSEXUAL <3120>.

EFFORT – [1] **to make every effort, to make an effort: *didōmi*** [verb: δίδωμι <1325>], ***ergasia*** [fem. noun: ἐργασία <2039>]; **from *ergazomai*: to work ▶ To try, to endeavor** > Jesus says to make every effort {give diligence, strive, try hard} to settle with an adversary when going to a magistrate (Luke 12:58). Other refs. (*didōmi*): GIVE <1325>. All other refs. (*ergasia*): BUSINESS <2039>, GAIN (noun) <2039>, WORKING (noun) <2039>.

[2] **to make every effort: *spoudazō*** [verb: σπουδάζω <4704>]; **from *spoudē*: haste, diligence ▶ To hasten, to endeavor; also transl.: to use diligence, to be diligent, to do one's best, to do one's utmost** > Paul told Timothy to make every effort to come to see him soon (2 Tim. 4:9), and to

come before winter (v. 21). He also said to Titus to make every effort to come to him at Nicopolis (Titus 3:12). All other refs.: DILIGENT <4704>, ENDEAVOR (verb) <4704>, LABOR (verb) <4704>.

– [3] Luke 13:24 → to make every effort → STRIVE <75> [4] John 19:12 → to make efforts → SEEK <2212> [5] Acts 27:16 → to pass under → to run under → RUN <5295> [6] Rom. 14:19; Heb. 12:14 → to make every effort → PURSUE <1377> [7] Gal. 4:11 → to waste one's efforts → to labor in vain → LABOR (verb) <2872>, VAIN <1500> [8] 1 Thes. 3:5 → LABOR (noun) <2873> [9] 2 Pet. 1:5; Jude 3 → to make every effort → to use all diligence → DILIGENCE <4710> [10] 3 John 5 → all your efforts → whatever you do → DO <2038>.

EFFULGENCE – Heb. 1:3 → RADIANCE <541>.

EFFULGENT – Luke 9:29 → to become effulgent → to become glistening → GLISTENING <1823>.

EGG – ***ōon*** [neut. noun: ᾠόν <5609>] ▶ **Reproductive body produced by a female bird** > A father will not give a scorpion to a son who asks for an egg (Luke 11:12). ¶

EGYPT – ***Aiguptos*** [fem. name: Αἴγυπτος <125>] ▶ **Country of North Africa, located southwest of Palestine** > Jews from Egypt were present in Jerusalem at Pentecost (Acts 2:10). Egypt is mentioned in connection with the sojourn of the Israelites in this land at the time of Joseph (Acts 7:9, 10a, b, 11, 12, 15; 13:17) and of their exodus under the leadership of Moses (Acts 7:17, 18, 34a, b, 36, 39, 40; Heb. 3:16; 8:9; 11:26, 27; Jude 5). Joseph, the husband of Mary, was obliged to flee to Egypt with the child and Mary, for Herod sought to put Jesus to death (Matt. 2:13, 14, 15, 19). Jerusalem is called spiritually Sodom and Egypt in Rev. 11:8. ¶

EGYPTIAN – ***Aiguptios*** [adj. used as a noun: Αἰγύπτιος <124>] ▶ **Inhabitant of Egypt, a country of North Africa** > The Israelites were in captivity in this land. Moses, who led them out of Egypt, was himself instructed in all the wisdom of the Egyptians (Acts 7:22); he struck one of them to defend an Israelite (v. 24) and killed him (v. 28). Having attempted to pursue the Israelites, the Egyptians were drowned in the Red Sea (Heb. 11:29). The apostle Paul was mistaken for an Egyptian who had raised a rebellion (Acts 21:38). ¶

EH! – ***ea*** [interj.: ἔα <1436>]; **prob. from *eaō*: to allow ▶ Word expressing surprise, anger; some translate as "Let us alone!" >** A man possessed by an unclean spirit used this term in addressing Jesus (Mark 1:24; Luke 4:34). ¶

EIGHT – ***oktō*** [card. num.: ὀκτώ <3638>] ▶ This number is used in regard to years (Acts 9:33), days (Luke 2:21; 9:28; John 20:26; Acts 25:6), and people (1 Pet. 3:20). ¶

EIGHTEEN – ***oktō*** [card. num.: ὀκτώ <3638>] ***kai*** [conj.: καί <2532>] ***deka*** [card. num.: δέκα <1176>]; **lit.: eight and ten** ▶ This number is used in regard to people killed by the fall of a tower (Luke 13:4) and the years of infirmity of a woman (vv. 11, 16). ¶

EIGHTH – [1] ***ogdoos*** [ord. num.: ὄγδοος <3590>]; **from *oktō*: eight** ▶ This number is used in regard to a day (Luke 1:59; Acts 7:8), Noah (2 Pet. 2:5), the beast (Rev. 17:11), and a precious stone (Rev. 21:20). ¶

[2] **eighth day: *oktaēmeros*** [adj.: ὀκταήμερος <3637>]; **from *oktō*: eight, and *hēmera*: day** ▶ This word is used in Phil. 3:5 and has the meaning of "at the age of eight days." ¶

EIGHTY – ***ogdoēkonta*** [card. num.: ὀγδοήκοντα <3589>]; **from *oktō*: eight** ▶ This number is used in regard to measures of wheat (Luke 16:7). ¶

EIGHTY-FOUR – **eighty: *ogdoēkonta*** [card. num.: ὀγδοήκοντα <3589>], **four: *tessares*** [card. num.: τέσσαρες <5064>] ▶

This number is used in regard to the age of the prophetess Anna (Luke 2:37). ¶

EITHER – ***ētoi*** [conj.: ἤτοι <2273>]**; from *ē*: whether, or, and *toi*: truly (intens.) ▶ Whether truly, whether indeed** > Ref.: Rom. 6:16. ¶‡

EJECT – Acts 18:16 → DRIVE <556>.

ELABORATE HAIRSTYLE – [1] 1 Tim. 2:9 → BRAIDED HAIR <4117> [2] 1 Pet. 3:3 → BRAIDING <1708>, HAIR <2359>.

ELAMITE – ***Elamitēs*** [masc. name: Ἐλαμίτης <1639>] **▶ Inhabitant of Elam in Asia, a country north of the Persian Gulf; its capital was Susa** > On the day of Pentecost, the Elamites heard the gospel preached in their own language (Acts 2:9). ¶

ELAPSE – [1] ***diaginomai*** [verb: διαγίνομαι <1230>]**; from *dia*: through (intens.), and *ginomai*: to become ▶ To accomplish, to pass** > When some days had elapsed {After certain days, A few days later}, Agrippa and Bernice came to Caesarea (Acts 25:13). When much time had elapsed {had been spent, had been lost), Paul advised the men on the ship (Acts 27:9). Other ref.: Mark 16:1 (to be past); see PAST <1230>. ¶
– [2] Acts 9:23 → PAST <4137> [3] Acts 24:27 → when two years had elapsed → lit.: two years being fulfilled → FULFILL <4137>.

ELDER – [1] ***presbuteros*** [adj. and adj. used as noun: πρεσβύτερος <4245>]**; from *presbus*: old man, ambassador; lit.: more elderly; elder woman: *presbutera* ▶ a. Older person in general** > The elder {older} son was in the field when his prodigal brother came back home (Luke 15:25). Timothy was not to rebuke an elder {older man} sharply (1 Tim. 5:1); he was to rebuke the elder {older} women as mothers (v. 2). In some versions, the word is transl. "old man" in Acts 2:17. **b. Representative of the people** > Among the Jews, the elders were the representatives of the people (e.g., Matt. 21:23; Acts 4:8) and were members of the council in Jerusalem. Other refs.: Matt. 16:21; 26:3, 47, 57, 59; 27:1, 3, 12, 20, 41; 28:12; Mark 7:3, 5; 8:31; 11:27; 14:43, 53; 15:1; Luke 7:3; 9:22; 20:1; 22:52; John 8:9 {older one}; Acts 4:5, 23; 6:12; 23:14; 24:1; 25:15. **c. Much respected ancestor among the Israelites** > The tradition of the elders was not to be transgressed (Matt. 15:2). The elders {ancients, men of old} obtained a good testimony (Heb. 11:2). **d. Christian with spiritual maturity and experience that qualify him to oversee and respond to the spiritual needs of other Christians in a local church** > At the beginning, elders were to be established by the apostles or their delegates (Titus 1:5). As a fellow elder (*sumpresbuteros*: see [3]), Peter exhorts the elders to feed the flock of God (1 Pet. 5:1), and the younger people to submit themselves to the elders {those who are older} (v. 5). The function of elder is assimilated to the function of an overseer in Titus 1:5 (read vv. 6, 7) and to the one of ruling in 1 Tim. 5:17. Other refs.: Acts 11:30; 14:23; 15:2, 4, 6, 22, 23; 16:4; 20:17; 21:18; 1 Tim. 5:19; Jas. 5:14; 2 John 1; 3 John 1. **e. Priestly company of redeemed people glorified in heaven, and characterized by spiritual wisdom and intelligence** > We read about these elders in Revelation (4:4, 10; 5:5, 6, 8, 11, 14; 7:11, 13; 11:16; 14:3; 19:4). ¶
[2] **council of elders, elderhood: *presbuterion*** [neut. noun: πρεσβυτέριον <4244>]**; from *presbuteros*: see [1] ▶ Assembly of elders** > There were assemblies of elders among the Jews (Luke 22:66; Acts 22:5). In 1 Tim. 4:14, the word is also transl.: presbytery, eldership, elderhood, body of elders, estate of elders. This council is composed of the brothers having spiritual maturity and experience in a local church. ¶
[3] **elder with: *sumpresbuteros*** [masc. noun: συμπρεσβύτερος <4850>]**; from *sun*: together, and *presbuteros*: elder ▶ See d. in [1].** > Peter was himself an elder {a fellow-elder} (lit.: an elder with) (1 Pet. 5:1). ¶
– [4] Acts 5:21 → elders, full assembly of the elders → SENATE <1087> [5] 1 Tim. 5:20 → "elders" added in Engl.

ELDER MAN – Titus 2:2 → OLD MAN <4246>.

ELDER WOMAN – Titus 2:3 → AGED WOMAN <4247>.

ELDERHOOD – [1] Luke 22:66; Acts 22:5; 1 Tim. 4:14 → ELDER <4244> [2] Acts 5:21 → SENATE <1087>.

ELDERSHIP – 1 Tim. 4:14 → council of elders → ELDER <4244>.

ELDEST – ***presbuteros*** [adj.: πρεσβύτερος <4245>]; **from *presbus*: old man, ambassador ▶ Older in age** > The eldest {oldest ones, elder ones} went out first in the case of the adulterous woman (John 8:9). All other refs.: ELDER <4245>.

ELEAZAR – ***Eleazar*** [masc. name: Ἐλεάζαρ <1648>]: **God has helped, in Heb. ▶ Man of the O.T.; also transl.: Eliazar** > Eleazar is mentioned in the genealogy of Jesus Christ (Matt. 1:15a, b). ¶

ELECT – [1] ***eklektos*** [adj.: ἐκλεκτός <1588>]; **from *eklegō*: to choose, to select, which is from *ek*: from, and *legō*: to choose ▶ Selected, designated; election is the free and sovereign choice of God; also transl.: chosen, chosen one** > As the Christ, Jesus is the elect of God (Luke 23:35). He is also a chief cornerstone, elect {a choice stone} and precious (1 Pet. 2:6). Paul speaks of the elect angels (1 Tim. 5:21). Those who believe in Christ are called the "elect of God" (Luke 18:7; Rom. 8:33; Col. 3:12; Titus 1:1); also Rom. 16:13 {chosen, choice man}; 2 Tim. 2:10; 1 Pet. 1:1 (or v. 2); 2:9; 2 John 1, 13; Rev. 17:14). Many are called, but few elected (Matt. 20:16 in some mss.; 22:14). The days of the great tribulation will be cut short on account of the Lord's elect (Matt. 24:22, 24, 31; Mark 13:20, 22, 27). Other ref.: 1 Pet. 2:4 (chosen); see CHOOSE <1588>. ¶

[2] **elected together: *suneklektos*** [adj.: συνεκλεκτός <4899>]; **from *sun*: together, and *eklektos*: see** [1] **▶ Chosen with, selected with** > Peter speaks of a believing woman in Babylon who was elected with {chosen together with} the Christians of the dispersion and was greeting them (1 Pet. 5:13). ¶

– [3] Rom. 11:7 → ELECTION <1589>.

ELECTION – ***eklogē*** [fem. noun: ἐκλογή <1589>]; **from *eklegō*: to choose, to select, which is from *ek*: from, and *legō*: to choose ▶ Free and sovereign choice of God; also transl.: choice** > Paul was a chosen vessel {an elect vessel} (lit.: a vessel of election) of the Lord (Acts 9:15). The purpose of God according to the election abides in the choice of Jacob (Rom. 9:11). In the present time, there is a remnant among the Jews according to the election {chosen} of grace (Rom. 11:5). Israel has not obtained what it seeks, but the election {the elect, those who were chosen} has obtained it (Rom. 11:7); concerning the election, those of Israel are beloved on account of their fathers (v. 28). Paul knew the election by God of {that God had chosen} the Thessalonians (1 Thes. 1:4). Christians should use diligence to make their calling and election {choosing} sure (2 Pet. 1:10). ¶

ELEGANT – Luke 23:11 → BRIGHT <2986>.

ELEMENT – ***stoicheion*** [neut. noun: στοιχεῖον <4747>]; **dimin. of *stoichos*: row ▶ a. Principle, rudiment; also transl.: elemental thing, principle, spirit, basic principle, elementary principle** > When the Galatians were children, they were in bondage under the elements of the world (Gal. 4:3); Paul asked how they could turn again to these weak and beggarly elements (v. 9). Philosophy is according to the elements of the world (Col. 2:8); the Colossians had died with Christ to the elements of the world (v. 20). The Hebrews needed again someone to teach them what are the elements of the beginning of the oracles of God (Heb. 5:12). **b. Material substance of the world** > In the day of the Lord, the elements, burning with heat, will melt (2 Pet. 3:10, 12). ¶

ELEMENTAL – Gal. 4:3, 9; Col. 2:8, 20 → elemental things, elemental spirits → lit.: elements → ELEMENT <4747>.

ELEMENTARY – [1] Gal. 4:3, 9; Col. 2:8, 20 → elementary principles → lit.: elements → ELEMENT <4747> [2] Heb. 5:12 → the first {elementary} principles → lit.: the principles of the beginning (*tēs archēs*) [3] Heb. 6:1 → BEGINNING <746>.

ELEVATE – 2 Cor. 11:7 → EXALT <5312>.

ELEVATED – Acts 12:21 → elevated seat → THRONE <968>.

ELEVATION – Jas. 1:9 → EXALTATION <5311>.

ELEVEN – ***hendeka*** [card. num.: ἕνδεκα <1733>]; **from *eis*: one, and *deka*: ten** ▶ This number is used in regard to the remaining apostles after the death of Judas Iscariot and before the addition of Matthias (Matt. 28:16; Mark 16:14; Luke 24:9, 33; Acts 1:26; 2:14). ¶

ELEVENTH – ***hendekatos*** [ord. num.: ἑνδέκατος <1734>]; **from *hendeka*: eleven, which is from *eis*: (only) one, and *deka*: ten** ▶ This number is used in regard to an hour equivalent to 5 p.m. (Matt. 20:6, 9) and a precious stone (Rev. 21:20). ¶

ELI – [1] ***Ēli*** [masc. name: Ἠλί <2241>]: **my God, in Heb.** ▶ **Personal form of the name of God; also written: *Eloi*** > At the cross, Jesus cried "*Eli, Eli, lama sabachthani?* That is to say: My God, My God, why have You forsaken Me" (Matt. 27:46a, b). ¶
[2] ***Hēli*** [masc. name: Ἡλί <2242>]: **height, in Heb.** ▶ **Father of Joseph, himself the foster father of Jesus; also transl.: Heli** > Eli is mentioned in the genealogy of Jesus (Luke 3:23). ¶

ELIAKIM – ***Eliakim*** [masc. name: Ἐλιακίμ <1662>]: **God-appointed, in Heb.** ▶ **Name of two men in the O.T.; also spelled: Eliakeim** > Eliakim is mentioned in the genealogy of Jesus Christ: one of the men bearing this name is a descendant of David (Luke 3:30) and the other is a descendant of Zerubbabel (Matt. 1:13a, b). ¶

ELIAZAR – See ELEAZAR <1648>.

ELIEZER – ***Eliezer*** [masc. name: Ἐλιέζερ <1663>]: **God of help, in Heb.** ▶ **Man of the O.T.** > Eliezer is mentioned in the genealogy of Jesus (Luke 3:29). ¶

ELIHUD – Matt. 1:14, 15 → ELIUD <1664>.

ELIJAH – ***Ēlias*** [masc. name: Ἠλίας <2243>]: **my God is Jehovah, in Heb.** ▶ **Prophet in Israel** > Elijah is mentioned in connection with John the Baptist (Matt. 11:14; Luke 1:17; John 1:21, 25) and the Lord Jesus (Matt. 16:14; Mark 6:15; 8:28; Luke 9:8, 19). Elijah was a man having the same passions as we have, and God answered his prayer (James 5:17). In his time, he was sent to a widow in Zarephath, in a foreign land, although there were many widows in Israel (Luke 4:25, 26). Elijah thought he had been left alone, the only one faithful to the Lord, but the Lord had reserved to Himself 7,000 faithful men (Rom. 11:2). He appeared with Moses on the mountain at the transfiguration of the Lord (Matt. 17:3, 4, 10–12; Mark 9:4, 5, 11–13; Luke 9:30, 33). Some believed that on the cross Jesus was calling for Elijah (Matt. 27:47, 49; Mark 15:35, 36). James and John wanted to command fire to come down from heaven as Elijah had done (Luke 9:54; see 2 Kings 1). ¶

ELIMINATE – [1] ***ekballō*** [verb: ἐκβάλλω <1544>]; **from *ek*: out of, and *ballō*: to throw** ▶ **To throw out, to expel; also transl.: to go out, to cast forth, to cast out** > The Lord uses this verb in Matt. 15:17 (lit.: to cast out into the draught). All other refs.: see entries in Lexicon at <1544>.
– [2] Matt. 15:17; Mark 7:19 → to be eliminated → to go out, to cast out into the draught → DRAUGHT <856> [3] Mark 7:19 → to be eliminated → to go out → GO <1607>.

ELISHA – ***Elisaios*** [masc. name: Ἐλισαῖος <1666>] **my God is deliverance, in Heb.; also spelled: *Elissaios* ► Prophet in Israel >** Jesus mentions the name of Elisha in relation to a time when there were many lepers in Israel; only Naaman, a stranger, was cleansed (Luke 4:27). ¶

ELIUD – ***Elioud*** [masc. name: Ἐλιούδ <1664>]**: God of majesty, in Heb. ► Man of the O.T. >** Eliud is mentioned in the genealogy of Jesus Christ (Matt. 1:14, 15). ¶

ELIZABETH – ***Elisabet*** [fem. name: Ἐλισάβετ <1665>]**: God of the oath, in Heb. ► Wife of the priest Zacharias and mother of John the Baptist >** Elizabeth was from the daughters of Aaron (Luke 1:5). Previously barren, she conceived a son in her old age (Luke 1:7, 13, 24, 25, 36, 57). She was filled with the Holy Spirit and recognized Mary as the mother of the Lord (Luke 1:40, 41a, b). ¶

ELMADAM – ***Elmadam*** [masc. name: Ἐλμαδάμ <1678>]**; also spelled: *Elmōdam* ► Man of the O.T. >** Elmadam is mentioned in the genealogy of Jesus (Luke 3:28). ¶

ELMODAM – See ELMADAM <1678>.

ELOI – ***Elōi*** [masc. name: Ἐλωΐ <1682>]**: my God, in Aram.; also written: *Eli* ► Name of God >** At the cross, Jesus cried "*Eloi, eloi, lama sabachthani?* Which is, being interpreted: My God, My God, why have You forsaken Me?" (Mark 15:34a, b); comp. Ps. 22:1. ¶

ELOQUENCE – 1 1 Cor. 1:17 → wisdom and eloquence → lit.: wisdom of words, wisdom of speech → WORD <3056> 2 1 Cor. 2:1 → lit.: excellence of words → EXCELLENCE <5247>.

ELOQUENT – 1 ***logios*** [adj.: λόγιος <3052>]**; from *logos*: word, expression ► Graceful and persuasive in one's speech; erudite >** Apollos was an eloquent {a learned} man and mighty in the Scriptures (Acts 18:24). ¶ – 2 1 Cor. 1:17 → words of eloquent wisdom → lit.: wisdom of words, wisdom of speech → WORD <4678>.

ELSE – 1 ***ei de mē*** [cond. expr.: εἰ δὲ μή <1490>] **► Otherwise, if not; also transl.: if one does >** The Greek expr. for "else" is used in relation to reward (Matt. 6:1), wineskins (Matt. 9:17; Mark 2:22; Luke 5:37), a piece of cloth (Mark 2:21; Luke 5:37), and a king going to make war (Luke 14:32). It is transl. "if it were not so" in John 14:2. Other refs.: Luke 5:36; 10:6; 13:9; John 14:11; 2 Cor. 11:16; Rev. 2:5, 16. ¶
2 ***epei*** [conj.: ἐπεί <1893>] **► Otherwise, since >** The term is used in Rom. 11:6a, b, 22; 1 Cor. 14:16; 15:29; Heb. 10:2 {once}. *
3 ***epei*** [conj.: ἐπεί <1893>] ***ara*** [conj.: ἄρα <686>]**; intens. of 2 ► Then, otherwise >** This expr. is used in 1 Cor. 7:14.

ELSEWHERE – John 10:1 → some other way → WAY <237>.

ELUDE – 1 John 10:39 → ESCAPE <1831> 2 Rev. 9:6 → FLEE <5343>.

ELYMAS – ***Elumas*** [masc. name: Ἐλύμας <1681>]**: wise man; some mss.: *Etoimas* ► Other name of the magician or sorcerer Bar-Jesus >** Elymas tried to turn away the proconsul Sergius Paulus from the faith (Acts 13:8). ¶

EMASCULATE – Gal. 5:12 → to emasculate oneself → to cut oneself off → CUT <609>.

EMBALM – Mark 16:1 → ANOINT <218>.

EMBANKMENT – ***charax*** [masc. noun: χάραξ <5482>]**; from *charassō*: to sharpen, to engrave ► Stake of wood used in constructions for siege purposes; wall or mound employing such posts; also transl.: barricade, palisaded mound, trench >** The days were to come upon Jerusalem, when her enemies would make an embankment around her (Luke 19:43). ¶

EMBARK – [1] Mark 8:13 → ENTER <1684> [2] Acts 27:2 → BOARD (verb) <1910>.

EMBARRASSED (BE) – 2 Cor. 7:14 → ASHAMED (BE) <2617>.

EMBASSY – Luke 14:32; 19:14 → DELEGATION <4242>.

EMBITTER – [1] Acts 14:2 → POISON (verb) <2559> [2] Col. 3:21 → PROVOKE <2042>.

EMBITTERED (BE) – Col. 3:19 → to be bitter → BITTER <4087>.

EMBOLDEN – Mark 15:43 → to embolden oneself → to go boldly → BOLDLY <5111>.

EMBOLDENED (BE) – ***oikodomeō*** [verb: οἰκοδομέω <3618>]; **from *oikodomos*: builder, building a house, which is from *oikos*: house, and *demō*: to build ▶ To confirm, to establish (in a bad or ironic sense)** > By one being seen in a temple of idols, the conscience of another one who is weak could be emboldened {encouraged, strengthened} to eat the things sacrificed to idols (1 Cor. 8:10). All other refs.: BUILD <3618>, EDIFY <3618>.

EMBRACE – [1] ***aspazomai*** [verb: ἀσπάζομαι <782>] ▶ **To salute by surrounding with one's arms, to greet on arrival or before departure** > Paul embraced {took his leave from, said goodbye to} the disciples in Ephesus and departed to go to Macedonia (Acts 20:1). Paul and the disciples from Tyre embraced one another (Acts 21:6 {to take leave, to say goodbye, to say farewell}); some mss. have *apaspazomai* [verb: ἀπασπάζομαι <537a>]. When he had embraced {greeted, saluted} James and the elders, Paul related one by one the things which God had done among the Gentiles by his ministry (Acts 21:19). All other refs.: see GREET <782>.
[2] ***sumperilambanō*** [verb: συμπεριλαμβάνω <4843>]; **from *sun*: together, and *perilambanō*: to embrace, which is from *peri*: around, and *lambanō*: to take ▶ To take in one's arms** > Paul embraced {enfolded, put his arms around} Eutychus, and said that his life was in him (Acts 20:10). ¶
– [3] Luke 15:20; Acts 20:37 → to fall upon → lit.: to fall on the neck → FALL (verb) <1968>, NECK <5137> [4] Heb. 11:17 → RECEIVE <324>.

EMERALD – [1] ***smaragdos*** [masc. noun: σμάραγδος <4665>] ▶ **Bright-green transparent precious stone** > The fourth foundation of the wall of the heavenly Jerusalem is adorned with emerald (Rev. 21:19). ¶
[2] **of an emerald: *smaragdinos*** [adj.: σμαράγδινος <4664>]; **from *smaragdos*: emerald ▶ See [1].** > In John's vision, the rainbow around the throne was like the appearance of an emerald (Rev. 4:3). ¶

EMINENT – 2 Cor. 11:5; 12:11 → most eminent → in surpassing degree → SURPASSING <5244a>.

EMMANUEL – See IMMANUEL <1694>.

EMMAUS – ***Emmaous*** [fem. name: Ἐμμαοῦς <1695>]: **warm spring, in Heb. ▶ Village located about 7 miles (11 kilometers) northwest of Jerusalem** > On the evening of His resurrection, Jesus conversed with two disciples from Emmaus, and entered their home (Luke 24:13; read vv. 13–31). ¶

EMMOR – See HAMOR <1697>.

EMPATHIZE – Heb. 4:15 → SYMPATHIZE <4834>.

EMPEROR – [1] Acts 25:21 → for the decision of the emperor → lit.: for the decision of Augustus [2] 1 Pet. 2:13, 17 → KING <935>.

EMPLOY – [1] 1 Cor. 9:13 → to be employed in temple service → MINISTER (verb) <2038> [2] 1 Pet. 4:10 → to employ in serving → MINISTER (verb) <1247>.

EMPOWER – 1 Cor. 12:6, 11 → WORK (verb) <1754>.

EMPTINESS – 2 Pet. 2:18 → VANITY <3153>.

EMPTY (adj.) – [1] Matt. 6:7 → to heap up empty phrases → lit.: much speaking → SPEAKING <4180> [2] Matt. 12:36 → empty word → idle word → IDLE <692> [3] Matt. 12:44 → to be empty → to be unoccupied → UNOCCUPIED <4980> [4] Mark 12:3; Luke 1:53; 20:10, 11 → EMPTY-HANDED <2756> [5] 1 Cor. 9:15 → to make empty → to make void → VOID <2758> [6] 1 Cor. 15:14a, b; Eph. 5:6; Col. 2:8 → VAIN <2756> [7] 2 Cor. 9:3 → to be empty → to be in vain → VAIN <2758> [8] 2 Tim. 2:16 → empty chatter → idle babbling → BABBLING <2757> [9] Titus 1:10 → empty talker → idle talker → TALKER <3151> [10] 1 Pet. 1:18 → VAIN <3152> [11] 2 Pet. 2:18 → empty words → lit.: words of emptiness → VANITY <3153>.

EMPTY (verb) – Phil. 2:7 → to empty oneself → to make oneself of no reputation → REPUTATION <2758>.

EMPTY-HANDED – ***kenos*** [adj.: κενός <2756>] ► **Which has nothing, leaving nothing** > The vine-growers beat a servant and sent him away empty-handed (Mark 12:3; Luke 20:10), as well as another servant (Luke 20:11). God has sent away the rich empty-handed (Luke 1:53). All other refs.: VAIN <2756>.

EMULATION – [1] Rom. 11:14 → to provoke to emulation → to provoke to jealousy → JEALOUSY <3863> [2] Rom. 13:13; 1 Cor. 3:3 → ENVY (noun) <2205> [3] Gal. 5:20; Jas. 3:14 → JEALOUSY <2205>.

EMULOUS – [1] 1 Cor. 13:4 → to be emulous → ENVY (verb) <2206> [2] 1 Cor. 14:1 → to be emulous → to desire, to desire earnestly → DESIRE (verb) <2206>.

ENABLE – [1] John 6:65; Acts 14:3 → GIVE <1325> [2] Acts 2:4 → to utter → UTTERANCE <669>.

ENACT – Heb. 8:6 → ESTABLISH <3549>.

ENCIRCLE – [1] ***kukloō*** [verb: κυκλόω <2944>]; **from *kuklos*: circle ► To encompass, to go around** > By faith the walls of Jericho fell, after the people encircled {had marched around} them for seven days (Heb. 11:30). All other refs.: SURROUND <2944>.
– [2] Luke 19:43 → SURROUND <4033>.

ENCLOSE – Luke 5:6 → CATCH (verb) <4788>.

ENCLOSURE – Eph. 2:14 → SEPARATION <5418>.

ENCOMPASS – Luke 21:20 → SURROUND <2944>.

ENCOUNTER – [1] Luke 14:31 in some mss. → MEET (verb) <5221> [2] Acts 17:18 → MEET (verb) <4820> [3] Jas. 1:2 → to fall into → FALL (verb) <4045>.

ENCOURAGE – [1] ***parakaleō*** [verb: παρακαλέω <3870>]; **from *para*: beside, and *kaleō*: to call ► To inspire and stimulate with courage to face difficulties, to console, to exhort; also transl.: to comfort** > God encouraged Paul in all his tribulation, that he might be able to encourage those who were in any tribulation whatever, through the encouragement with which he himself was encouraged by God (2 Cor. 1:4a–c); if Paul was encouraged, it was for the encouragement of the Corinthians (v. 6). The Corinthians were to forgive and encourage the brother who had been under discipline (2 Cor. 2:7). Paul mentions occasions when he was encouraged (2 Cor. 7:6a, b, 13; 1 Thes. 3:7). He tells the Corinthians to be encouraged {be of good comfort, listen to his appeal} (2 Cor. 13:11). Tychicus was to encourage the hearts of the Christians in Ephesus

(Eph. 6:22) and in Colossae (Col. 4:8). Paul wanted the hearts of the Christians in Colossae, Laodicea, and elsewhere to be encouraged (Col. 2:2). He had sent Timothy to encourage the Thessalonians concerning their faith (1 Thes. 3:2). He had told them to encourage one another (1 Thes. 4:18). He prayed that the Lord Jesus and God the Father might encourage the hearts of the Christians in Thessalonica (2 Thes. 2:17). Other refs.: Matt. 2:18; 5:4; Luke 16:25; Acts 20:12. All other refs.: see entries in Lexicon at <3870>.

2 **to be encouraged together, mutually: *sumparakaleō*** [verb: συμπαρακαλέω <4837>]; **from *sun*: together, and *parakaleō*: see** 1 **► To encourage together by stimulating and inspiring one another to face difficulties, to console together >** Paul greatly desired to see the Christians in Rome so that they might be encouraged together {be comforted together, have mutual comfort} (Rom. 1:12). ¶

3 **encouraged: *euthumos*** [adj.: εὔθυμος <2115>]; **from *eu*: well, and *thumos*: spirit, passion ► Confident, of good spirit, cheerful >** The passengers on Paul's boat were all encouraged {were all of good cheer, took courage} (lit.: became cheerful) (Acts 27:36). Other ref.: Acts 24:10 (adv.: *euthumōs*); see CHEERFULLY <2115a>. ¶

4 **to be encouraged: *eupsucheō*** [verb: εὐψυχέω <2174>]; **from *eupsuchos*: courageous, which is from *eu*: well, and *psuchē*: soul ► To be comforted, to be more cheerful >** Paul would be encouraged {be refreshed, be of good comfort, be cheered} when he would know the state of the Philippians (Phil. 2:19). ¶

5 ***protrepō*** [verb: προτρέπω <4389>]; **from *pro*: toward, and *trepō*: to turn ► To urge morally, to inspire positively to do something >** Having encouraged Apollos, the brothers wrote to the disciples of Achaia to welcome him. (Acts 18:27; see EXHORT 3 for a less preferred transl.). ¶

– 6 Acts 9:31; 2 Cor. 7:4, 13; Heb. 6:18 → CONSOLATION <3874> 7 Acts 28:15 → to be encouraged → lit.: to take courage → COURAGE <2294>, TAKE <2983> 8 1 Cor. 8:10 → to be encouraged → EMBOLDENED (BE) <3618> 9 1 Thes. 2:11; 5:14 → COMFORT (verb) <3888> 10 Titus 2:4 → ADMONISH <4994>.

ENCOURAGEMENT – 1 Acts 4:36; 15:31; Rom. 15:4, 5; 2 Cor. 1:3–5, 6a; 7:4, 7, 13; 2 Thes. 2:16; Heb. 6:18; Phm. 7 → CONSOLATION <3874> 2 Acts 13:15; Rom. 12:8; 1 Cor. 14:3; Heb. 12:5 → EXHORTATION <3874> 3 Acts 20:2 → lit.: to encourage → EXHORT <3870> 4 Col. 4:11 → COMFORT (noun) <3931>.

ENCOURAGING – 1 Acts 15:31 → CONSOLATION <3874> 2 Rom. 12:8; 1 Cor. 14:3 → EXHORTATION <3874>.

ENCUMBRANCE – Heb. 12:1 → WEIGHT <3591>.

END (noun) – 1 ***akron*** [neut. noun: ἄκρον <206>]; **acc. of *akros*: highest ► Extremity, most distant part >** The Son of Man will send His angels to gather His elect from one end of heaven to the other end (Matt. 24:31a, b; Mark 13:27a and b {uttermost part, farthest part}). In Luke 16:24, it is transl. "tip" in relation to the tip of the finger of Lazarus. Jacob worshipped, leaning on the top (lit.: end) of his staff (Heb. 11:21). ¶

2 ***peras*** [neut. noun: πέρας <4009>]; **from *pera*: beyond ► Conclusion, term >** For men the oath is an end to all dispute, as making matters sure (Heb. 6:16). All other refs.: EXTREMITY <4009>, PART (noun) <4009>.

3 ***eschatos*** [adj. used as noun: ἔσχατος <2078>] **► Last, furthermost extremity or part >** Paul was to be light for salvation to the end of the earth (Acts 13:47). At the end of the days {In these last days} when God spoke to the fathers by (lit.: in) the prophets, God has spoken to us by His Son (lit.: in Son) (Heb. 1:2). Christ has appeared at the end of times {in the last times} (1 Pet. 1:20). At the end of the time {In the last time}, there shall be mockers (Jude 18). All other refs.: LAST (adv. and noun) <2078>, PART (noun) <2078>, STATE <2078>.

[4] ***telos*** [neut. noun: τέλος <5056>] ▶ **Termination, limit of a thing** > He who stands firm to the end shall be saved (Matt. 10:22; 24:13; Mark 13:13). The end will not come immediately after rumors of war (Matt. 24:6; Mark 13:7; Luke 21:9). The end will come after the preaching of the gospel of the kingdom (Matt. 24:14). The end will come after Jesus delivers up the kingdom to God the Father (1 Cor. 15:24). Peter followed Jesus at a distance to see the end (Matt. 26:58). If Satan is divided, his end has come (Mark 3:26). There will be no end of the kingdom of Jesus (Luke 1:33). It was necessary for the things concerning Jesus to have an end (i.e., to be fulfilled; Luke 22:37). Jesus loved His own to the end (John 13:1). Christ is the end {culmination} of the law for righteousness to everyone who believes (Rom. 10:4). Jesus will keep Christians strong to the end (1 Cor. 1:8). The Israelites could not look steadily at the end of what was passing away, i.e., the glory on Moses's face (2 Cor. 3:13). Christians receive the end of their faith, the salvation of their souls (1 Pet. 1:9). Jesus is the beginning and the end (Rev. 21:6; 22:13). Other refs.: Rom. 6:21, 22; 1 Cor. 10:11 {culmination}; 2 Cor. 1:13; 11:15; Phil. 3:19; 1 Tim. 1:5 {aim}; Heb. 6:8, 11; 7:3; Jas. 5:11; 1 Pet. 4:7, 17; Rev. 1:8 {ending} in some mss.; 2:26. All other refs.: CUSTOM[2] <5056>, FINALLY <5056>, PERPETUALLY <5056>.

[5] **until the end, unto the end: *achri telous*; *achri*** [adv.: ἄχρι <891>] ***telos*** [neut. noun: τέλος <5056>]; **from *achri*: until, and *telos*: see [4] ▶ Until the termination (e.g., of life on earth)** > The Hebrews were to show the same diligence to the full assurance of hope until the end {very end} (Heb. 6:11). Also transl. "as long as," "until," etc. elsewhere. *

[6] ***sunteleia*** [fem. noun: συντέλεια <4930>]; **from *sunteleō*: to complete fully, which is from *sun*: together, and *teleō*; to finish ▶ Full accomplishment of something** > Jesus uses the expr. "the end of the world {the completion of the age, the end of the age}" concerning the times of the end (Matt. 13:39, 40, 49; 24:3). He assures His own that He is with them until the end of the world {the completion of the age, the end of the age} (Matt. 28:20). He has appeared at the end {consummation, culmination} of the ages to put away sin by the sacrifice of Himself (Heb. 9:26). ¶

– [7] Matt. 11:1 → to make an end → FINISH <5055> [8] Matt. 21:41 → to bring to a wretched end → PERISH <622> [9] Luke 4:2 → END (verb) <4931> [10] Acts 2:24 → to put an end → LOOSE <3089> [11] Acts 21:5 → to come to the end → to fully accomplish → ACCOMPLISH <1822> [12] Rom. 9:28 → to bring to an end → FINISH <4931> [13] 1 Cor. 15:24 → to put an end → DESTROY <2673> [14] Phil. 1:14 → to be confident → CONFIDENT <3982> [15] Heb. 1:12 → to come to an end → FAIL <1587> [16] Heb. 11:22 → when his end was near → when dying → DIE <5053> [17] Heb. 13:7 → OUTCOME <1545> [18] 1 Pet. 1:13 → to the end → COMPLETELY <5049>.

END (verb) – [1] ***sunteleō*** [verb: συντελέω <4931>]; **from *sun*: together, and *teleō*: to finish; lit.: to complete fully ▶ To accomplish, to fulfill; to terminate** > When His forty days of temptation had ended {were finished} {At the end of them}, Jesus was hungry (Luke 4:2). After he had ended {Having completed, After he had finished} every temptation, the devil left Jesus (Luke 4:13). The seven days of Paul's purification were almost ended {nearly completed, almost over, nearly over} (Acts 21:27). All other refs.: FINISH <4931>, FULFILL <4931>, MAKE <4931>.

– [2] Matt. 7:28 in some mss.; Rev. 20:3, 5 → FINISH <5055> [3] Luke 1:23 → ACCOMPLISH <4130> [4] Luke 2:43 → FULFILL <5048> [5] Luke 7:1 → CONCLUDE[2] <4137> [6] Acts 19:21 → FULFILL <4137> [7] Acts 20:1 → CEASE <3973> [8] Acts 21:5 → ACCOMPLISH <1822> [9] Acts 21:26 → when it would end → lit.: the accomplishment → ACCOMPLISHMENT <1604> [10] 1 Cor. 13:8 → FAIL <1601> [11] 2 Cor. 3:7, 11, 13 → to be brought to an end → to pass away, to do away → AWAY <2673> [12] 2 Thes. 2:8 → to bring to an end → DESTROY <2673>

13 Heb. 1:12 → FAIL <1587> 14 Rev. 20:7 → EXPIRE <5055>.

ENDANGER – 1 Cor. 15:30 → to stand in jeopardy → JEOPARDY <2793>.

ENDEAVOR (noun) – Gal. 2:17 → in our endeavor to be justified → seeking to be justified → SEEK <2212>.

ENDEAVOR (verb) – 1 ***spoudazō*** [verb: σπουδάζω <4704>]; **from *spoudē*: haste, zeal ▶ To be diligent, to hasten, to make every effort >** The Christians should endeavor {use diligence} to keep the unity of the Spirit in the uniting bond of peace (Eph. 4:3). Paul had endeavored more eagerly {used more abundant diligence, was all the more eager} to see the Thessalonians personally (1 Thes. 2:17). All other refs.: DILIGENT <4704>, EFFORT <4704>, LABOR (verb) <4704>.
– 2 Acts 16:10 → SEEK <2212>.

ENDEAVOUR – See ENDEAVOR (verb).

ENDING – Rev. 1:8 → END (noun) <5056>.

ENDLESS – 1 ***aperantos*** [adj.: ἀπέραντος <562>]; **from *a*: neg., and *perainō*: to complete, which is from *peras*: end, limit ▶ Without end, interminable >** Timothy was to instruct certain people not to pay attention to fables and endless genealogies (1 Tim. 1:4). ¶
– 2 Heb. 7:16 → INDESTRUCTIBLE <179>.

ENDLESSLY – Heb. 10:1 → CONTINUALLY <1519> <1336>.

ENDUE – Luke 24:49 → CLOTHE <1746>.

ENDURANCE – 1 ***hupomonē*** [fem. noun: ὑπομονή <5281>]; **from *hupomenō*, which is from *hupo*: under (intens.), and *menō*: to remain ▶ Patience, perseverance (e.g., in trials) >** Salvation was effective in the Corinthians for the endurance of {for the patient endurance of, for enduring, in the patient enduring of} the same sufferings which Paul also suffered (2 Cor. 1:6). All other refs.: PATIENCE <5281>, PATIENT CONTINUANCE <5281>.
– 2 2 Cor. 1:6b → CONSOLATION <3874>.

ENDURE – 1 ***tinō*** [verb: τίνω <5099>] ▶ **To suffer, to be subjected, to undergo >** Paul speaks of those who will endure the punishment of {pay the penalty of, be punished with} everlasting destruction when the Lord comes to be glorified in His saints (2 Thes. 1:9). ¶
2 ***hupomenō*** [verb: ὑπομένω <5278>]; **from *hupo*: under (intens.), and *menō*: to remain; lit.: to stay in one place ▶ To bear, to suffer with patience; to persevere courageously, particularly in sufferings or trials >** He who endures {stands firm} to the end will be saved (Matt. 10:22; 24:13; Mark 13:13). Love endures all things (1 Cor. 13:7). Paul endured all things for the sake of the elect (2 Tim. 2:10). If we endure {suffer} with the Christ Jesus, we will also reign with Him (2 Tim. 2:12). The Hebrews had endured {had stood their ground in} much conflict of sufferings (Heb. 10:32). Jesus has endured the cross (Heb. 12:2); He has endured such contradiction from sinners against Himself (v. 3). The Hebrews were enduring chastening (Heb. 12:7). Blessed is the man who endures temptation {perseveres under trial} (Jas. 1:12); indeed, James counted them blessed who have endured (5:11). Peter makes a distinction between enduring {taking it patiently} for having done evil and having done good (1 Pet. 2:20a, b). All other refs.: LINGER <5278>, PATIENT <5278>, REMAIN <5278>, SUFFER <5278>.
3 ***pherō*** [verb: φέρω <5342>] ▶ **To bear, to suffer, to put up with >** God endured with much patience vessels of wrath fitted for destruction (Rom. 9:22). The Israelites could not endure that which was commanded (Heb. 12:20). All other refs.: see entries in Lexicon at <5342>.
4 ***hupopherō*** [verb: ὑποφέρω <5297>]; **from *hupo*: under (intens.), and *pherō*: see**

3 ▶ **To bear, to support patiently** > God is faithful, who will not allow Christians to be tempted (or: tested) above what they are able to bear, but will with the temptation (or: testing) also make a way of escape, so that they may be able to endure {to stand up under} it (1 Cor. 10:13). It is commendable, if a person, for conscience sake toward God, endures grief, suffering unjustly (1 Pet. 2:19 {to bear}). Paul endured persecutions and the Lord delivered him out of them all (2 Tim. 3:11). ¶

5 **to endure the conduct: *tropophoreō*** [verb: τροποφορέω <5159>]; **from *tropos*: manner, and *phoreō*: to bear, to endure, which is from *pherō*: to carry, to bear ▶ To put up with the behavior of someone** > God endured the conduct of {suffered the manners of, put up with, put up with the ways of} the Israelites in the desert (Acts 13:18); some mss. have: ***trophophoreō*** [verb: τροφοφορέω <5162a>], transl. by "to nourish," "to nurse." ¶

– 6 Mark 5:26 → SUFFER <3958> 7 John 6:27; 1 Cor. 3:14; 2 Cor. 9:9; 1 Pet. 1:25 → REMAIN <3306> 8 1 Cor. 4:12; 2 Thes. 1:4; 2 Tim. 4:3 → SUFFER <430> 9 1 Cor. 9:12 → BEAR (verb) <4722> 10 2 Cor. 1:6 → enduring, to patiently endure → patient endurance → ENDURANCE <5281> 11 2 Cor. 1:8 → ability to endure → STRENGTH <1411> 12 2 Tim. 2:24 → patiently enduring evil → FORBEARING <420> 13 2 Tim. 4:5 → to endure affliction → SUFFER <2553> 14 Heb. 11:27 → PERSEVERE <2594> 15 Heb. 13:13 → the reproach He endured → lit.: His reproach 16 Rev. 2:3 → to endure, to endure hardships → lit.: to have patience → BEAR (verb) <941>, PATIENCE <5281>.

ENDURING – 1 Rom. 12:12 → to be enduring → to be patient → PATIENT <5278> 2 2 Cor. 1:6 → enduring, patient enduring → ENDURANCE <5281> 3 1 Thes. 1:3 → enduring constancy → PATIENCE <5281> 4 Heb. 10:34; 13:14; 1 Pet. 1:23 → LASTING <3306>.

ENEMY – 1 ***echthros*** [adj. used as noun: ἐχθρός <2190>]; **from *echthos*: hatred, enmity ▶ Adversary, opponent** > The ancients said to hate one's enemy (Matt. 5:43); but Jesus said to love one's enemies (Matt. 5:44; Luke 6:27, 35). The enemies of the Lord will be put under His feet (Matt. 22:44; Mark 12:36; Luke 20:43; Acts 2:35 {foe}; Heb. 1:13; 10:13). In a parable, a nobleman said to slay his enemies before him (Luke 19:27). The enemies of Israel would build an embankment around Jerusalem (Luke 19:43). When they were enemies (i.e., before their conversion), Christians were reconciled to God through the death of His Son (Rom. 5:10; Col. 1:21 {hostile}). We must feed our enemy if he is hungry (Rom. 12:20). Christ will put all enemies under His feet (1 Cor. 15:25); the last enemy who will be destroyed is death (v. 26). A friend of the world is an enemy of God (Jas. 4:4). Other refs.: Matt. 10:36 {foe}; 13:25, 28, 39; Luke 1:71, 74; 10:19; Acts 13:10; Rom. 11:28; Gal. 4:16; Phil. 3:18; 2 Thes. 3:15; Rev. 11:5, 12. ¶

– 2 Luke 23:12; Jas. 4:4 → ENMITY <2189> 3 1 Tim. 5:14 → to be the adversary → ADVERSARY <480> 4 Heb. 10:27 → ADVERSARY <5227> 5 1 Pet. 5:8 → ADVERSARY <476>.

ENERGY – Col. 1:29 → WORKING (noun) <1753>.

ENFOLD – Acts 20:10 → EMBRACE <4843>.

ENFORCE – Heb. 11:33 → WROUGHT <2038>.

ENGAGE – 1 Acts 18:27 → EXHORT <4389> 2 Phil. 1:30 → to be engaged in the same conflict → to have the same conflict → HAVE <2192> 3 2 Tim. 2:4 → to engage in warfare → WARFARE <4758> 4 Titus 3:8, 14 → MAINTAIN <4291>.

ENGAGED (BE) – Luke 1:27; 2:5 → to be pledged to be married → MARRIED (BE) <3423>.

ENGAGEMENT – 1 Pet. 3:21 → ANSWER (noun) <1906>.

ENGRAVE – ***entupoō*** [verb: ἐντυπόω <1795>]; **from *en*: in, and *tupoō*: to mark with an imprint, which is from *tupos*: form, imprint ▶ To inscribe on hard material** > The ministry of death (i.e., the Mosaic law) had been engraved {carved} in letters on stone (the tables of the law) (2 Cor. 3:7). ¶

ENGROSS – 1 Cor. 7:31 → USE (verb) <2710>.

ENJOIN – [1] ***parangellō*** [παραγγέλλω <3853>]; **from *para*: intens., and *angellō*: to announce ▶ To declare, to command, to exhort; also transl.: to charge, to give charge, to urge** > God enjoins men to repent (Acts 17:30). Paul had enjoined the Thessalonians regarding certain things (1 Thes. 4:11). Timothy was to enjoin certain people not to teach other doctrines (1 Tim. 1:3). Paul uses this verb also in addressing Timothy (1 Tim. 4:11; 5:7; 6:13, 17). All other refs.: COMMAND (verb) <3853>, PRESCRIBE <3853>.

– [2] Matt. 1:24 → ORDAIN <4367> [3] Matt. 16:20; Mark 5:43; 7:36; 9:9; Heb. 12:20 → COMMAND (verb) <1291> [4] Matt. 28:20; Acts 13:47; Heb. 9:20 → COMMAND (verb) <1781> [5] 1 Tim. 1:5 → what is enjoined → CHARGE (noun)[2] <3852> [6] Phm. 8 → COMMAND (verb) <2004>.

ENJOY – [1] ***empiplēmi*** [verb: ἐμπίπλημι <1705>]; **from *en*: in, and *pimplēmi*: to fill ▶ To be filled, to be entirely satisfied (e.g., by someone's company)** > Paul wanted to first enjoy the company of the Christians in Rome (Rom. 15:24). All other refs.: FILL (verb) <1705>.

[2] ***tunchanō*** [verb: τυγχάνω <5177>] **▶ To obtain, to receive** > The Jews enjoyed {had attained} great peace through Felix (Acts 24:2). Julius allowed Paul to go to his friends and enjoy their care {receive care, refresh himself, be provided for his needs} (Acts 27:3). All other refs.: ATTAIN <5177>, COMMON <5177>, OBTAIN <5177>, ORDINARY <5177>, PERHAPS <5177>.

[3] **enjoyment: *apolausis*** [fem. noun: ἀπόλαυσις <619>]; **from *apolauō*: to seize, to enjoy something, which is from *apo*: from, and *lauō*: to enjoy ▶ Pleasure, satisfaction** > God gives us all things richly to enjoy (lit.: for our enjoyment) (1 Tim. 6:17). Moses chose to suffer affliction with the people of God, rather than to enjoy the temporary pleasures (lit.: to have the temporary enjoyment) of sin (Heb. 11:25). ¶

– [4] Mark 6:20; 12:37 → enjoyed listening → lit.: listened gladly → GLADLY <2234> [5] John 5:35 → REJOICE <21> [6] 3 John 2 → to enjoy good health → to prosper in health → PROSPER <2137>.

ENJOYMENT – 1 Tim. 6:17 → ENJOY <619>.

ENLARGE – [1] ***megalunō*** [verb: μεγαλύνω <3170>]; **from *megas*: great ▶ To increase more and more, to extend; to make great** > The scribes and the Pharisees enlarged {lengthened, made long} the borders of their garments (Matt. 23:5). Paul had hope, when the faith of the Corinthians was increased, he would be enlarged among them according to his rule {his area of activity would greatly expand} (2 Cor. 10:15). All other refs.: ESTEEM (verb) <3170>, MAGNIFY <3170>.

– [2] 2 Thes. 1:3 → to greatly enlarge → to grow exceedingly → GROW <5232>.

ENLIGHTEN – ***phōtizō*** [verb: φωτίζω <5461>]; **from *phōs*: light ▶ To make clear spiritually, to cause to understand** > Paul was praying that the eyes of the hearts of the Ephesians would be enlightened (Eph. 1:18). Some people were enlightened {were illuminated, received the light} once (Heb. 6:4; 10:32). All other refs.: ILLUMINATE <5461>, LIGHT (noun) <5461>.

ENMITY – ***echthra*** [fem. noun: ἔχθρα <2189>]; **from *echthros*: enemy ▶ Hostility, hatred, opposition** > Pilate and Herod had been at enmity {enemies} (Luke 23:12; *aēdia* in some mss.: disagreement). The mind of the flesh is enmity against {hostile toward} God (Rom. 8:7). Enmities are among the works of the flesh (Gal. 5:20). Christ has abolished in His flesh the enmity between Jews and Gentiles, enmity caused by the law, which separated Israel from other nations (Eph. 2:15, 16). The friendship of the world is enmity against {makes oneself enemy of} God (Jas. 4:4). ¶

ENOCH – ***Henōch*** [masc. name: Ἑνώχ <1802>]: **initiated, instructed, in Heb. ► Faithful man of the O.T.** > Enoch is mentioned in the genealogy of Jesus (Luke 3:37). He had the testimony of having pleased God, who took him up so that he should not see death (Heb. 11:5). Jude speaks of Enoch as having prophesied about the wicked who will be judged at the coming of the Lord (Jude 14). ¶

ENOS – See ENOSH <1800>.

ENOSH – ***Enōs*** [masc. name: Ἐνώς <1800>]: **man, in Heb. ► Man of the O.T.; also transl.: Enos** > Enosh is mentioned in the genealogy of Jesus (Luke 3:38). He was the grandson of Adam (see Gen. 4:26: Enosh). ¶

ENOUGH – 1 ***hikanos*** [adj.: ἱκανός <2425>]; **from *hikneomai*: to come, to occur ► Sufficient** > Jesus told His disciples who presented to Him two swords that it was enough (Luke 22:38), in the sense that they had not understood the words concerning Himself. In Acts 18:18, the expr. "a good while" {for some time} is lit. "enough days" (*hemeras hikanas*). The word is transl. "many" in 1 Cor. 11:30: in Corinth, many had fallen asleep (i.e., were dead) because of evil things in their lives that had not been judged. Other refs.: see entries in Lexicon at <2425>.

2 **it is enough: *apechei*** [verb: ἀπέχει <566>]; **from *apechō*: to have, to receive, which is from *apo*: from, and *echō*: to have ► It is adequate, it is sufficient** > Jesus said: It is enough, the hour had come for Him to be delivered up (Mark 14:41). ¶

3 **to be enough: *arkeō*** [verb: ἀρκέω <714>]; ***arcere*, in Lat.: to contain, to retain ► To be sufficient** > The virgins in the parable were afraid that there would not be enough {not suffice} oil for them and the others if they gave some to them (Matt. 25:9). All other refs.: CONTENT (verb) <714>, SATISFIED <714>, SUFFICIENT <714>.

– 4 Matt. 6:34; 10:25; 1 Pet. 4:3 → SUFFICIENT <713> 5 Luke 15:17 → to have enough and to spare → to have in abundance → ABUNDANCE <4052> 6 Eph. 6:3 → enjoy long life → lit.: living a long time → LIVE <3118> 7 Phil. 4:18 → to have more than enough → ABOUND <4052>.

ENQUIRE – 1 Matt. 2:16 → to diligently enquire → DETERMINE <198> 2 Matt. 10:11 → INQUIRE <1833> 3 Luke 22:23 → to question together → QUESTION (verb) <4802> 4 John 4:52; Acts 23:20 → INQUIRE <4441> 5 John 16:19 → INQUIRE <2212> 6 Acts 9:11 → to enquire for → SEEK <2212> 7 Acts 19:39 → SEEK <1934> 8 Acts 23:15 → DETERMINE <1231> 9 1 Pet. 1:10 → enquired and searched diligently → sought out and searched out → to seek out → SEEK <1567>.

ENQUIRY – Acts 10:17 → to make enquiry → to make inquiry → INQUIRY <1331>.

ENRAGED (BE) – 1 ***orgizō*** [verb: ὀργίζω <3710>]; **from *orgē*: wrath ► To be provoked to anger; also transl.: to be angry, to be furious, to be full of wrath, to be wroth** > A king was enraged at the treatment dealt out to his servants (Matt. 22:7). The nations were enraged (Rev. 11:18). The dragon was enraged against the woman (Rev. 12:17). All other refs.: ANGRY <3710>.

– 2 Matt. 2:16 → to be enraged → to be angry → ANGRY <2373> 3 Acts 5:33; 7:54 → to be furious → FURIOUS <1282> 4 Acts 19:28 → lit.: to be full of wrath → FULL <4134>, WRATH <2372> 5 Acts 26:11 → to be exceedingly enraged, to be furiously enraged → to be exceedingly furious → FURIOUS <1693>.

ENRICH – [1] ***ploutizō*** [verb: πλουτίζω <4148>]; **from *ploutos*: wealth ▶ To become rich, wealthy** > The Corinthians had been enriched in everything in Christ, in all word of doctrine (1 Cor. 1:5); they were enriched {were made rich} in every way for all liberality (2 Cor. 9:11). Paul was poor, but enriching many {making many rich} (2 Cor. 6:10). ¶
– [2] 1 Cor. 4:8; 2 Cor. 8:9; Rev. 18:3, 19 → to be enriched → to become rich → RICH <4147>.

ENROLL – [1] 1 Tim. 5:9 → to put on the list → LIST (noun) <2639> [2] 1 Tim. 5:11 → "to enroll" added in Engl.

ENROLLED (BE) – Heb. 12:23 → REGISTER <583>.

ENSAMPLE – Phil. 3:17; 1 Thes. 1:7; 2 Thes. 3:9; 1 Pet. 5:3 → PATTERN <5179>.

ENSIGN – Acts 28:11 → FIGUREHEAD <3902>.

ENSLAVE – [1] John 8:33; Gal. 4:8, 9 → to be enslaved → to be in bondage → BONDAGE <1398> [2] Acts 7:6; Rom. 6:22; Titus 2:3; 1 Cor. 7:15; Gal. 4:3 → to be enslaved → to bring into bondage → BONDAGE <1402> [3] Rom. 6:6; Titus 3:3 → to be enslaved to → SERVE <1398> [4] 1 Cor. 6:12 → to bring under the power → POWER[2] <1850> [5] 2 Cor. 11:20 → to be enslaved → to bring into bondage → BONDAGE <2615>.

ENSLAVER – 1 Tim. 1:10 → KIDNAPPER <405>.

ENSNARE – [1] **which ensnares so easily: *euperistatos*** [adj.: εὐπερίστατος <2139>]; **from *eu*: well, and *periistēmi*: to surround, which is from *peri*: around, and *histēmi*: to stand; *euperispastos* in some mss.: which distracts easily ▶ Which surrounds so easily, obsesses, assails** > The Christian must lay aside the sin which so easily ensnares {clings so closely, so easily besets, so easily entangles} him (Heb. 12:1). ¶
– [2] Matt. 22:15 → ENTANGLE <3802>.

ENSUE – 1 Pet. 3:11 → PURSUE <1377>.

ENSUING – Acts 13:42 → NEXT <3342>.

ENTANGLE – [1] **to entangle with, to entangle in: *emplekō*** [verb: ἐμπλέκω <1707>]; **from *en*: in, and *plekō*: to twist, to weave ▶ a. To worry about, to give importance to** > No one serving as a soldier entangles himself with {gets involved in} the affairs of life (2 Tim. 2:4). **b. To be caught, to be wrapped up** > Peter speaks of those who are again entangled in the pollutions of the world and subdued by them (2 Pet. 2:20). ¶
[2] ***pagideuō*** [verb: παγιδεύω <3802>]; **from *pagis*: snare, trap ▶ To catch in a snare** > The Pharisees held a council how they might entangle {ensnare, trap} Jesus in His words (Matt. 22:15). ¶
– [3] Heb. 12:1 → to entangle so easily → to ensnare so easily → ENSNARE <2139>.

ENTANGLED (BE) – ***enechō*** [verb: ἐνέχω <1758>]; **from *en*: in, and *echō*: to have, to hold ▶ To be subject to; other transl.: to be held in, to be burdened by** > The Galatians were not to be held again in a yoke of bondage (Gal. 5:1). Other refs.: Mark 6:19; Luke 11:53; see GRUDGE (noun) <1758>, PRESS <1758>. ¶

ENTER – [1] ***eiserchomai*** [verb: εἰσέρχομαι <1525>]; **from *eis*: in, and *erchomai*: to come ▶ To come in, to penetrate** > Jesus says to enter the kingdom of God by the narrow gate (Matt. 7:13; Luke 13:24). Jesus commanded the unclean spirit to come out of a child and to enter him no more (Mark 9:25). It is easier for a camel to go through the eye of a needle than for a rich man to enter the kingdom of God (Mark 10:25). Other refs. (the verb can be transl. "to enter," "to go into," "to come in," etc.): Matt. 5:20; 6:6; 7:21; 8:5, 8; 9:25; 10:5, 11, 12; 12:4, 29, 45; 15:11; 17:25; 18:3, 8, 9; 19:17, 23, 24; 21:10, 12; 22:11, 12; 23:13a–c; 24:38;

25:10, 21, 23; 26:41, 58; 27:53; Mark 1:21, 45; 2:1, 26; 3:1, 27; 5:12, 13, 39; 6:10, 22, 25; 7:17, 24; 8:26; 9:28, 43, 45, 47; 10:15, 23, 24, 25; 11:11, 15; 13:15; 14:14, 38; 15:43; 16:5; Luke 1:9, 28; 4:16, 38; 6:4, 6; 7:1, 6, 36, 44, 45; 8:30, 32, 33, 51; 9:4, 34, 46, 52; 10:5, 8, 10, 38; 11:26, 37, 52a, b; 14:23; 15:28; 17:7, 12, 27; 18:17, 24, 25; 19:1, 7; 21:21; 22:3, 10a, 40, 46; 24:3, 26, 29; John 3:4, 5; 4:38; 10:1, 2, 9a, b; 13:27; 18:1, 28, 33; 19:9; 20:5, 6, 8; Acts 1:13, 21; 3:8; 5:7, 10, 21; 9:6, 12, 17; 10:3, 24, 25, 27; 11:3, 8, 12, 20 (some mss.: *erchomai*); 13:14; 14:1, 20, 22; 16:15, 40; 17:2; 18:7 (some mss.: *erchomai*), 19; 19:8, 30; 20:29; 21:8; 23:16, 33; 25:23; 28:8; Rom. 5:12; 11:25; 1 Cor. 14:23, 24; Heb. 3:11, 18, 19; 4:1, 3, 5, 6a, b, 10, 11; 6:19, 20; 9:12, 24, 25; 10:5; Jas. 2:2a, b; 5:4; 2 John 7 (some mss.: *erchomai*); Rev. 3:20; 11:11; 15:8; 21:27; 22:14. ¶

[2] **to enter with: *suneiserchomai*** [verb: συνεισέρχομαι <4897>]**; from *sun*: together, and *eiserchomai*: see [1] ► To come in together, to go in together >** Jesus had not entered with {had not gone with} His disciples into the boat (John 6:22). John entered with {went with} Jesus into the courtyard of the high priest (John 18:15). Other ref.: Luke 8:51 in some mss. ¶

[3] ***eisporeuomai*** [verb: εἰσπορεύομαι <1531>]**; from *eis*: in, and *poreuomai*: to go ► To penetrate, to go into >** Jesus spoke about what enters man (Matt. 15:17; Mark 7:15, 18, 19). Other refs.: Mark 1:21; 4:19; 5:40; 6:56; 11:2; Luke 8:16; 11:33 {to come in}; 19:30; 22:10b; Acts 3:2; 8:3. All other refs.: COME <1531>.

[4] ***embainō*** [verb: ἐμβαίνω <1684>]**; from *en*: in, and *bainō*: to go, to come ► To go on board, to embark >** Jesus entered {embarked, got back, got into, went on board} the ship again (Mark 8:13). All other refs.: GET <1684>, STEP (verb) <1684>.

[5] **to enter before: *proagō*** [verb: προάγω <4254>]**; from *pro*: before, and *agō*: to go, to lead ► To go before, to precede >** Tax collectors and prostitutes were entering {going into, getting into} the kingdom of God before the chief priests and the elders (Matt. 21:31). All other refs.: see entries in Lexicon at <4254>.

– [6] Matt. 8:14; 12:9; 19:1 → to come into → COME <2064> [7] John 21:3; 1 Cor. 2:9 → GO UP <305> [8] Acts 21:26; Heb. 9:6 → to go in, to go into → GO <1524> [9] Acts 27:2 → to enter (into a ship) → BOARD (verb) <1910> [10] Rom. 5:20 → to come in → COME <3922> [11] Col. 2:18 → to enter into → to intrude into → INTRUDE <1687> [12] 2 Tim. 3:6 → to enter into → to creep into → CREEP <1744> [13] Heb. 10:19 → ENTRY <1529>.

ENTERING – 1 Thes. 1:9; 2:1; Heb. 10:19 → ENTRY <1529>.

ENTERTAIN – [1] Matt. 9:4 → THINK <1760> [2] Acts 28:7; Heb. 13:2 → LODGE <3579> [3] 1 Tim. 5:19 → RECEIVE <3858>.

ENTERTAINMENT – Luke 5:29 → FEAST (noun) <1403>.

ENTHRONED – Rev. 18:7 → "enthroned" added in Engl.

ENTHUSIASM – [1] 2 Cor. 8:17 → with much enthusiasm → more zealous → ZEALOUS <4707> [2] 2 Cor. 9:2 → ZEAL <2205>.

ENTICE – [1] ***deleazō*** [verb: δελεάζω <1185>]**; from *delear*: lure, bait ► To lure, to seduce >** Every man is tempted, drawn away, and enticed by his own lust (Jas. 1:14). There are those who entice {allure, beguile} unstable souls (2 Pet. 2:14) and entice {allure} new Christians with the lusts of the flesh (v. 18). ¶

– [2] Rev. 2:14 → lit.: to put a stumbling block before → STUMBLING BLOCK <4625>.

ENTICING – [1] 1 Cor. 2:4 → PERSUASIVE <3981> [2] Col. 2:4 → enticing words → persuasive words → WORD <4086>.

ENTIRE – [1] ***holoklēros*** [adj.: ὁλόκληρος <3648>]**; from *holos*: all, whole, and *klēros*:**

lot, share ▶ Perfect, accomplished; also transl.: complete, whole > Paul prays that the God of peace sanctify the Thessalonians wholly; and their whole spirit, soul, and body be preserved blameless at the coming of the Lord (1 Thes. 5:23). Patience must have its perfect work so that Christians may be perfect and entire (Jas. 1:4). ¶
– [2] Acts 2:2 → WHOLE <3650>.

ENTIRELY – [1] John 9:34 → COMPLETELY <3650> [2] 1 Thes. 5:23 → COMPLETELY <3651>.

ENTRAILS – ***splanchna*; plur. of *splanchnon*** [neut. noun: σπλάγχνον <4698>]; **comp. *splēn*: spleen; the word is always plur. in the N.T.; in Classical Greek, *splanchna* are the viscera (mainly heart, liver, lung) ▶ a. Inner organs of the body, bowels** > The entrails {intestines} of Judas gushed out when he fell headlong (Acts 1:18). **b. Affection, compassion; figur.: heart** > The word is transl. "tender" in the expr. "the tender mercy {the bowels of mercy} (lit.: the entrails of mercy) of our God" (Luke 1:78) and "affection" in the expr. "the affection {bowels} of Jesus Christ" (Phil. 1:8). Paul told the Corinthians they were straitened in their affections (or: entrails {bowels}) (2 Cor. 6:12). He exhorted the Colossians to put on tender mercies {bowels of mercies, bowels of compassion, a heart of compassion} (Col. 3:12). He used the Greek word (transl.: bowels, hearts) three times in his Epistle to Philemon (Phm. 7, 12, 20). In 1 John 3:17, "to shut up one's bowels (or: entrails {heart})" {to have no pity} most likely means to fail to show compassion to one's brother in need by sharing one's goods. Other refs.: 2 Cor. 7:15; Phil. 2:1; see AFFECTION <4698>, TENDERNESS <4698>. ¶

ENTRANCE – [1] Matt. 26:71; Acts 12:13, 14a, b → GATEWAY <4440> [2] Matt. 27:60; Mark 15:46; 16:3; Acts 12:6 → DOOR <2374> [3] John 8:37 → to have an entrance → to have a place → PLACE (noun) <5562> [4] Acts 14:13 → at the entrance → lit.: before (*pro*) [5] 1 Thes. 2:1; 2 Pet. 1:11 → ENTRY <1529>.

ENTREAT – [1] Matt. 8:31 → BESEECH <3870> [2] Matt. 22:6 → to entreat spitefully, to entreat shamefully → MISTREAT <5195> [3] Luke 15:28 → BESEECH <1831> [4] Luke 18:32 → to entreat spitefully → INSULT (verb) <5195> [5] Acts 7:6, 19 → to entreat evil → OPPRESS <2559> [6] Acts 27:3 → TREAT <5530> [7] 1 Cor. 4:13, 16; 2 Cor. 5:20; 10:1; Eph. 4:1; Phil. 4:2a, b → PLEAD <3870> [8] Gal. 4:12 → PRAY <1189>.

ENTREATY – [1] ***paraklēsis*** [fem. noun: παράκλησις <3874>]; **from *parakaleō*: to implore, to encourage, which is from *para*: near, and *kaleō*: to call ▶ Supplication, insistence** > The churches of Macedonia had begged with much entreaty {with much intreaty, urgency, urging; urgently} the grace and fellowship of a service to the saints (2 Cor. 8:4). All other refs.: CONSOLATION <3874>, EXHORTATION <3874>.
– [2] 1 Tim. 2:1; 5:5 → SUPPLICATION <1162> [3] Heb. 5:7 → SUPPLICATION <2428>.

ENTRUST – [1] ***pisteuō*** [verb: πιστεύω <4100>]; **from *pistis*: belief, assurance, faith, which is from *peithō*: to persuade, to convince ▶ To put in a capacity of trust by delivering (oneself)** > Jesus did not entrust {did not commit} Himself to those who believed in His name, because they saw His miracles (John 2:24). All other refs.: BELIEVE <4100>, BELIEVER <4100>, COMMIT <4100>.
[2] ***paradidōmi*** [verb: παραδίδωμι <3860>]; **from *para*: over to, and *didōmi*: to give ▶ To confide, to yield** > Jesus entrusted Himself to {committed Himself to, gave Himself over into the hands of} Him who judges righteously (1 Pet. 2:23). All other refs.: see entries in Lexicon at <3860>.
[3] **one who is entrusted to the charge (of another): *klēros*** [masc. noun: κλῆρος <2819>]; **from *klaō*: to break ▶ Allotted portion, share** > The elders are to shepherd the flock of God, not as lording over those entrusted to their charge {those allotted to their charge, their possessions, God's heri-

tage} (1 Pet. 5:3). All other refs.: INHERITANCE <2819>, LOT[2] <2819>, PART (noun) <2819>.
– 4 Luke 12:48; 1 Tim. 1:18; 2 Tim. 2:2; 1 Pet. 4:19 → COMMIT <3908> 5 John 5:22 → GIVE <1325> 6 1 Cor. 4:1; Titus 1:7 → one who is entrusted → STEWARD <3623> 7 2 Cor. 5:19 → LAY <5087> 8 Gal. 3:19 → entrusted to a mediator → lit.: by the hand of a mediator 9 1 Tim. 6:20 in some mss.; 2 Tim. 1:12 → entrusted, entrusted deposit → what is committed → COMMIT <3866> 10 2 Tim. 1:14 → DWELL <1774>.

ENTRUSTED – 1 Tim. 6:20; 2 Tim. 1:14 → entrusted deposit, entrusted treasure, what has been entrusted → THING COMMITTED <3872>.

ENTRY – 1 ***eisodos*** [fem. noun: εἴσοδος <1529>]; **from *eis*: in, and *hodos*: way ▶ Coming, entrance, arrival** > John had preached the baptism of repentance before the entry {coming} of Jesus (lit.: before the face of His entry) (Acts 13:24). Paul speaks of the entry {entering, entrance, coming, visit} he had to the Thessalonians (1 Thes. 1:9; 2:1). Christians have boldness for entering (lit.: of the entry) the Holiest by the blood of Jesus (Heb. 10:19). An entry {An entrance, A welcome} into the everlasting kingdom of the Lord and Savior Jesus Christ will be richly supplied to the Christians (2 Pet. 1:11). ¶
– 2 Acts 12:13, 14a, b → GATEWAY <4440>.

ENTRYWAY – Mark 14:68 → PORCH <4259>.

ENVELOP – Matt. 17:5; Mark 9:7; Luke 9:34 → OVERSHADOW <1982>.

ENVIOUS – 1 Acts 7:9 → to become envious → ENVY (verb) <2206> 2 Acts 17:5 → to become envious → to become jealous → JEALOUS <2206> 3 Rom. 11:11 → to make envious → to provoke to jealousy → JEALOUSY <3863>.

ENVIOUSLY – Jas. 4:5 → lit.: with envy → ENVY (noun) <5355>.

ENVY (noun) – 1 ***phthonos*** [masc. noun: φθόνος <5355>] ▶ **Discontent, irritation resulting from knowing that others possess something one does not possess; jealousy; also transl.: envying** > Jesus had been delivered because of envy (Matt. 27:18; Mark 15:10). Paul speaks of unbelievers full of envy (Rom. 1:29), and Christians living in envy before their conversion (Titus 3:3). Envy is one of the works of the flesh (Gal. 5:21). Christians must lay aside envy (Phil. 1:15; 1 Tim. 6:4; 1 Pet. 2:1). The Spirit in the Christians does not desire with envy {jealously, enviously} (Jas. 4:5), but He gives more grace (see v. 6). ¶
2 ***zēlos*** [masc. noun: ζῆλος <2205>]; **from *zeō*: to be fervent ▶ Jealousy** > Christians must not walk in strife and envy {envying, emulation} (Rom. 13:13; 1 Cor. 3:3). All other refs.: HEAT <2205>, JEALOUSY <2205>, MIND (noun) <2205>, ZEAL <2205>.
– 3 Acts 7:9 → to be moved with envy → ENVY (verb) <2206> 4 Acts 17:5 → to be moved with envy → to become jealous → JEALOUS <2206> 5 Rom. 11:14 → to arouse to envy → to provoke to jealousy → JEALOUSY <3863>.

ENVY (verb) – 1 ***zēloō*** [verb: ζηλόω <2206>]; **from *zēlos*: ardor, zeal ▶ To have a strong desire, to be jealous** > The brothers of Joseph, envying {being moved with envy of, becoming envious of, became jealous of, being jealous of} him, sold him (Acts 7:9). Love does not envy {is not emulous, is not jealous} (1 Cor. 13:4). All other refs.: COVET <2206>, DESIRE (verb) <2206>, JEALOUS <2206>, ZEALOUS <2206>.
2 ***phthoneō*** [verb: φθονέω <5354>]; **from *phthonos*: envy ▶ To be characterized by envy, jealousy** > Christians should not become conceited, provoking one another, envying one another (Gal. 5:26). ¶
– 3 Jas. 4:5 → YEARN <1971>.

ENVYING – 1 Rom. 13:13; 1 Cor. 3:3 → ENVY (noun) <2205> 2 2 Cor. 12:20; Jas.

3:14, 16 → JEALOUSY <2205> [3] Gal. 5:21; 1 Pet. 2:1 → ENVY (noun) <5355>.

EPAENETUS – ***Epainetos*** [masc. name: Ἐπαίνετος <1866>]: **praised ► Believing man of the church of Rome** > Paul sends greetings to his beloved Epaenetus, who is the first-fruits of Asia for Christ (Rom. 16:5). ¶

EPAPHRAS – ***Epaphras*** [masc. name: Ἐπαφρᾶς <1889>]; **from Epaphroditus: devoted to Aphrodite, a Greek goddess ► Fellow servant of the apostle Paul** > Paul speaks of Epaphras as a faithful servant of Christ for the Colossians (Col. 1:7), combating for them in prayer (4:12). Having become a fellow prisoner of Paul (Phm. 23), Epaphras sends greetings to Philemon in this letter (see v. 24). ¶

EPAPHRODITUS – ***Epaphroditos*** [masc. name: Ἐπαφρόδιτος <1891>]: **devoted to Aphrodite, a Greek goddess ► Fellow worker and fellow soldier of Paul** > Epaphroditus had been sent by the Philippians to bring a gift to Paul (Phil. 4:18). Paul thought it necessary to send him to the Philippians (Phil. 2:25), and he may have brought Paul's letter to the Philippians. He had been sick, very close to death (see Phil. 2:26, 27). ¶

EPARCHY – Acts 23:34; 25:1 → PROVINCE <1885>.

EPHESIAN – [1] ***Ephesios*** [adj.: Ἐφέσιος <2180>]; **maybe: desirable ► Inhabitant of the city of Ephesus, capital of the Roman province of Asia** > The Ephesians were devoted to the worship of the goddess Diana (Acts 19:28, 34, 35). Trophimus was Ephesian (Acts 21:29). ¶
[2] ***Ephesinos*** [adj.: Ἐφεσῖνος <2179>] ► **See [1].** > For this word in Rev. 2:1, see EPHESUS <2181>. ¶

EPHESUS – ***Ephesos*** [fem. name: Ἔφεσος <2181>] ► **City of Lydia on the west coast of Asia Minor** > Paul reasoned with the Jews in the synagogue of Ephesus during his second missionary journey (Acts 18:19, 21). Apollos came to Ephesus later (Acts 18:24). Paul returned to Ephesus and taught there for at least three years during his third missionary journey (Acts 19:1, 17, 26). Later, when he was at Miletus, he called the elders of the church of Ephesus to him to give them his recommendations (Acts 20:16, 17). He mentions his visits to Ephesus in his First Epistle to the Corinthians (1 Cor. 15:32; 16:8). He addressed a letter to the church of Ephesus (Eph. 1:1). Timothy had remained at Ephesus at the request of Paul (1 Tim. 1:3) who had sent Tychicus to him there (2 Tim. 4:12). Onesiphorus had rendered much service at Ephesus (2 Tim. 1:18). The church of Ephesus is one of the seven churches to which a letter is addressed in Revelation (1:11; 2:1 {Ephesian}); some mss. have *Ephesinos* <2179> in Rev. 2:1. ¶

EPHPHATHA – ***ephphatha*** [Aram. imper.: εφφαθα <2188>] ► **Aram. term meaning "Be opened"** > Jesus used this verb when He healed the person who was deaf and had an impediment of speech (Mark 7:34). ¶

EPHRAIM – ***Ephraim*** [masc. name: Ἐφραίμ <2187>]: **double fruitfulness, in Heb. ► City located approx. 15 miles (25 kilometers) from Jerusalem, near the desert** > Jesus stayed in Ephraim with His disciples (John 11:54). ¶

EPICUREAN – ***Epikoureios*** [masc. noun: Ἐπικούρειος <1946>] ► **Epicureans were philosophers seeking happiness in pleasure and avoidance of sufferings; for them, the soul died with the body and there was no future retribution** > Certain Epicurean and Stoic philosophers attacked Paul verbally in Athens (Acts 17:18). ¶

EPILEPTIC – **to be epileptic: *selēniazomai*** [verb: σεληνιάζομαι <4583>]; **from *selēnē*: moon; lit.: to be affected by the moon ► Someone afflicted by periodical seizures; prob. a person suffering from epilepsy which was believed to be influenced by the moon** > Jesus healed epileptics {lunatics, those having seizures} (lit.: those struck by the moon) (Matt. 4:24; 17:15). ¶

EPISTLE – [1] ***epistolē*** [fem. noun: ἐπιστολή <1992>]; **from *epistellō*: to send (a message), to write, which is from *epi*: to, and *stellō*: to send ▶** This word is most often transl. "letter"; see LETTER <1992>. It describes also, in the common language, the name given to the 21 books of the N.T. which are letters to local churches or to individuals. Titles such as "Epistle to the Philippians" should be lit. "To the Philippians." Paul wrote fourteen epistles (if we include Hebrews in which the author is not mentioned); James, one; Peter, two; John, three; Jude, one.

[2] See EPISTLE OF COMMENDATION.

– [3] Acts 15:30; 23:33; Rom. 16:22; 1 Cor. 5:9; 2 Cor. 3:2, 3; Col. 4:16; 1 Thes. 5:27; 2 Thes. 2:15; 3:14, 17; 2 Pet. 3:16 → LETTER <1992>.

EPISTLE OF COMMENDATION – letter: *epistolē* [fem. noun: ἐπιστολή <1992>]; **from *epistellō*: to send (a message), to write, which is from *epi*: to, and *stellō*: to send; of commendation: *sustatikos*** [adj.: συστατικός <4956>]; **from *sunistaō*: to approve, to recommend ▶ Letter facilitating the favorable introduction of a Christian to other Christians** > This letter, signed by several others of the local church to which he or she is associated, facilitates the reception of a Christian, including participation in the Lord's supper, at another local church to which he or she is traveling and receive help in whatever business he or she may have need (see Rom. 16:1, 2 where Phoebe is commended). In addressing the Corinthians, Paul mentions that such a letter {letter of recommendation} was not necessary for himself, since he was well known to them (2 Cor. 3:1a; b in some mss.). All other refs. (*epistolē*): see LETTER <1992>.

EPOCH – Acts 1:7; 1 Thes. 5:1 → SEASON (noun) <2540>.

EQUAL – [1] ***isos*** [adj.: ἴσος <2470>] ▶ **Same in quantity, quality, dignity** > The owner of the vineyard had made the laborers who had worked only one hour equal to those who had worked all day (Matt. 20:12). By saying that God was His own Father, Jesus was making Himself equal to God (John 5:18). Being in the form of God, Jesus did not consider it robbery to be equal to {on an equality with} God (Phil. 2:6). The length, the breadth, and the height of the heavenly Jerusalem are equal (Rev. 21:16). All other refs.: AGREE <2470>, LIKE (adj., adv., noun) <2470>, SAME <2470>.

[2] ***sunēlikiōtēs*** [masc. noun: συνηλικιώτης <4915>]; **from *sun*: together, and *hēlikiōtēs*: who is of the same age, which is from *hēlikia*: age ▶ Person of the same age** > Paul was progressing in Judaism beyond many his equals {contemporaries, of his own age} in his nation (Gal. 1:14). ¶

– [3] 1 Cor. 12:25 → SAME <846> [4] 2 Cor. 2:16 → SUFFICIENT <2425> [5] Col. 4:1 → what is equal → what is fair → FAIR <2471>.

EQUAL STANDING – 2 Pet. 1:1 → of equal standing → PRECIOUS <2472>.

EQUALITY – [1] ***isotēs*** [fem. noun: ἰσότης <2471>]; **from *isos*: equal ▶ Equivalence, similarity in quality and quantity** > By supplying the need of other Christians, the Corinthians were acting by equality, i.e., on the principle of equality; others, by their abundance, were also supplying the need of the Corinthians, that there might be equality (2 Cor. 8:13, 14). Masters must give to their servants what is just and what is fair {fairness} (lit.: equality) (Col. 4:1). ¶

– [2] Phil. 2:6 → on an equality → lit.: equal → EQUAL <2470>.

EQUIP – [1] Eph. 4:12 → PERFECTING <2677> [2] Eph. 4:16 → equipped → of supply → SUPPLY (noun) <2024> [3] Heb. 13:21 → to be perfect → PERFECT (adj.) <2675>.

EQUIPPED – 2 Tim. 3:17 → to be equipped, to be fully equipped → to be fully accomplished → ACCOMPLISH <1822>.

EQUIPPING – Eph. 4:12 → PERFECTING <2677>.

ER – ***Ēr*** [masc. name: Ἤρ <2262>]**: watchful, in Heb. ▶ Man of the O.T.** > Er is mentioned in the genealogy of Jesus (Luke 3:28). ¶

ERASE – Rev. 3:5 → to cancel out → to blot out → BLOT (verb) <1813>.

ERASTUS – ***Erastos*** [masc. name: Ἔραστος <2037>]**: beloved ▶ a. Administrator of the city of Corinth** > Erastus sent his greetings to the Christians at Rome (Rom. 16:23). **b. The same as the preceding or another Christian man** > Erastus ministered to Paul, who sent him to Macedonia (Acts 19:22). Later, Erastus remained at Corinth (2 Tim. 4:20). ¶

ERECT (adj.) – Luke 13:13 → to make erect → to make straight → STRAIGHT <461>.

ERECT (verb) – [1] ***pēgnumi*** [verb: πήγνυμι <4078>] ▶ **To set up, to assemble** > The Lord has erected {pitched} the true tabernacle (Heb. 8:2). ¶
– [2] Heb. 8:5a → MAKE <2005>.

ERR – [1] Matt. 22:29; Mark 12:24, 27 → MISTAKEN (BE) <4105> [2] 1 Cor. 6:9 → DECEIVE <4105> [3] 1 Tim. 6:10 → STRAY <635> [4] 1 Tim. 6:21; 2 Tim. 2:18 → STRAY <795> [5] Heb. 3:10; Jas. 1:16; 5:19 → STRAY <4105> [6] Heb. 5:2 → to go astray → ASTRAY <4105>.

ERROR – [1] ***planē*** [fem. noun: πλάνη <4106>] ▶ **Delusion, false judgment, belief of what is untrue, wandering** > Paul's exhortation was not of error, of impurity or by way of deceit (1 Thes. 2:3); older transl.: deceit, impurity, guile. He who turns a sinner from the error of his way will save a soul from death (Jas. 5:20). Peter speaks of those who walk in error (2 Pet. 2:18); he warns against being led away along with the error of the wicked (3:17). Those who are of God know the spirit of truth and the spirit of error {falsehood} (1 John 4:6). Jude speaks of those who have given themselves up to the error of Balaam for reward (Jude 11). All other refs.: DECEITFUL <4106>, DECEPTION <4106>, DELUSION <4106>.
– [2] Matt. 22:29; Mark 12:24 → to be in error → MISTAKEN (BE) <4105> [3] Titus 3:3 → to wander in error → STRAY <4105> [4] Heb. 9:7 → sin committed in ignorance → IGNORANCE <51>.

ESAIAS – See ISAIAH <2268>.

ESAU – ***Ēsau*** [masc. name: Ἠσαῦ <2269>]**: hairy, in Heb. ▶ Son of Isaac and Rebecca, and twin brother of Jacob** > Esau sold his birthright for a single meal (Heb. 12:16); he later sought to recover the inheritance of the paternal blessing, but he was rejected (see v. 17). Isaac blessed Jacob and Esau concerning things to come (Heb. 11:20). God loved Jacob and hated Esau (Rom. 9:13). One may assume that in the first case it is a matter of the sovereign grace of God who loves the sinner in spite of himself; in the second case, the attitude of God follows the contempt of Esau for the divine promises of blessing made to his fathers. ¶

ESCAPE – [1] ***pheugō*** [verb: φεύγω <5343>] ▶ **To flee, to avoid** > Jesus asked the Pharisees how they could escape the judgment of hell (Matt. 23:33). A young man escaped {fled} naked from those who had laid hold of him (Mark 14:52). O.T. people of faith escaped the edge of the sword (Heb. 11:34). All other refs.: FLEE <5343>.
[2] ***apopheugō*** [verb: ἀποφεύγω <668>]; **from *apo*: from, and *pheugō*: see [1] ▶ To flee far from, to completely avoid (by flight)** > Peter speaks of escaping the corruption which is in the world through lust (2 Pet. 1:4), of escaping from those who walk in error (2:18), and of escaping the pollutions of the world (2:20). ¶
[3] ***diapheugō*** [verb: διαφεύγω <1309>]; **from *dia*: through (intens.), and *pheugō*:**

see [1] ► **To flee, to get away (from pending danger)** > The soldiers were afraid that the prisoners would escape (Acts 27:42). ¶
[4] ***ekpheugō*** [verb: ἐκφεύγω <1628>]; **from *ek*: out, and *pheugō*: see** [1] ► **To flee (out of)** > Jesus says to pray to be counted worthy to escape the things that will come to pass (Luke 21:36). The man who judges cannot think that he will escape the judgment of God (Rom. 2:3). Paul escaped from {slipped through} the hands of king Aretas (2 Cor. 11:33). People who will say "Peace and safety!" in the day of the Lord will not escape at all (1 Thes. 5:3). People cannot escape if they neglect so great salvation first spoken of by the Lord (Heb. 2:3). Those who refused Him who spoke on earth did not escape (Heb. 12:25; some mss.: *pheugō*). All other refs.: FLEE <1628>.
[5] ***exerchomai*** [verb: ἐξέρχομαι <1831>]; **from *ek*: out, and *erchomai*: to go** ► **To go away out of** > Jesus escaped out of {went away from} the hands {eluded the grasp} of those who sought to seize Him (John 10:39). All other refs.: COME <1831>, DEPART <1831>, GO <1831>, SPREAD <1831>, STEP (verb) <1831>.
– [6] Mark 7:24; Luke 8:47; Acts 26:26; 2 Pet. 3:5, 8 → to escape notice, to escape attention → to be hidden → HIDDEN (BE) <2990> [7] Acts 25:11 → to seek to escape → REFUSE (verb) <3868> [8] Acts 28:1, 4 → SAVE (verb) <1295> [9] 1 Cor. 10:13 → way to escape → WAY <1545>.

ESCHEW – 1 Pet. 3:11 → TURN (verb) <1578>.

ESCORT – [1] Acts 17:15 → CONDUCT (verb)[2] <2525> [2] Acts 21:5 → to bring on the way → WAY <4311>.

ESLI – See HESLI <2069>.

ESPECIALLY – [1] ***malista*** [adv.: μάλιστα <3122>]; **superl. of *mala*: very, much** ► **a. Principally, above all; also transl.: chiefly, specially** > Festus had brought Paul especially before Agrippa (Acts 25:26). All the saints saluted the Philippians, and especially those of the household of Caesar (Phil. 4:22). Paul hoped in the living God who is the preserver (or: the savior, the protector) of all men, especially of those who believe (1 Tim. 4:10). If anyone does not provide for his relatives, and especially for his immediate family, he has denied the faith and is worse than an unbeliever (1 Tim. 5:8). The elders who take the lead well (among the saints) are to be esteemed worthy of double honor, especially those who labor in word and doctrine (1 Tim. 5:17). Timothy was to bring the books to Paul, especially the parchments (2 Tim. 4:13). Especially those of the circumcision were disorderly (Titus 1:10). Onesimus was a beloved brother, especially to Paul (Phm. 16). Especially those who walk after the flesh in the lust of uncleanness, and who despise lordship, will be punished in the day of judgment (2 Pet. 2:10). **b. Particularly, most of all** > The elders of Ephesus were grieved especially {most, most of all} over the word which Paul had spoken that they would not see his face again (Acts 20:38). Paul was happy to make his defense before Agrippa, especially because he was acquainted with all customs and questions among the Jews (Acts 26:3). Christians are to do good to all, especially to those who are of the household of faith (Gal. 6:10). ¶
[2] ***mallon*** [adv.: μᾶλλον <3123>]; **compar. of *mala*: very, much** ► **Much more, preferably; also transl.: even more, rather** > The Corinthians were to follow after love and earnestly desire spiritual gifts, but especially to prophesy (1 Cor. 14:1, 5). *
– [3] Matt. 8:33 → lit.: and (*kai*) [4] Acts 9:41 → "especially" added in Engl. [5] 1 Cor. 8:13; 10:14; 14:13 → WHEREFORE <1355> [6] 2 Cor. 2:4 → very abundantly → ABUNDANTLY <4056> [7] 2 Cor. 7:13 → EXCEEDINGLY <4056> [8] Heb. 13:19 → all the more → MORE <4056>.

ESPOUSE – 2 Cor. 11:2 → PROMISE (verb) <718>.

ESPOUSED (BE) – Matt. 1:18; Luke 1:27; 2:5 → to be pledged to be married → MARRIED (BE) <3423>.

ESROM – See HEZRON <2074>.

ESSAY – Acts 9:26 in some mss. → TRY[1] <3985>.

ESSENTIAL – 1 Acts 15:28 → NECESSARY <1876> 2 Rom. 2:18 → thing that is essential → more excellent thing → EXCELLENT <1308>.

ESTABLISH – 1 ***bebaioō*** [verb: βεβαιόω <950>]; **from *bebaios*: solid, firm ▶ To assure, to confirm; also transl.: to strengthen** > God firmly establishes {makes stand firm} Christians with one another in Christ (2 Cor. 1:21). The Christian is established {stablished} in the faith (Col. 2:7). It is good that the heart be established by grace (Heb. 13:9). All other refs.: to CONFIRM <950>.
2 ***histēmi*** [verb: ἵστημι <2476>] ▶ **a. To decide, to determine** > By two or three witnesses, every word is established (Matt. 18:16 {to confirm, to stand upon}; 2 Cor. 13:1). **b. To confirm** > Paul was establishing {upholding} the law through faith (Rom. 3:31). **c. To set up** > The Jews seek to establish their own righteousness (Rom. 10:3). Jesus takes away the first form of worship under the law that He may establish the second under grace (Heb. 10:9). Other refs.: SET (verb) <2476>, STAND (verb) <2476>.
3 ***nomotheteō*** [verb: νομοθετέω <3549>]; **from *nomothetēs*: legislator, which is from *nomos*: law, and *tithēmi*: to put, to place ▶ To constitute, i.e., to establish formally as by a law** > Christ is mediator of a better covenant, which is established {enacted, founded} on better promises (Heb. 8:6). Other ref.: Heb. 7:11 (to receive the law); see LAW <3549>. ¶
4 ***stereoō*** [verb: στερεόω <4732>]; **from *stereos*: solid, stable ▶ To solidify, to reinforce** > In the beginning, the churches were established {confirmed, strengthened} in the faith (Acts 16:5). Other refs.: Acts 3:7, 16 (to be made strong); see STRONG (adj.) <4732>. ¶
5 ***stērizō*** [verb: στηρίζω <4741>]; **comp. *stereos*: solid, stable ▶ To fortify, to strengthen; also transl.: to confirm, to stablish, to strengthen, to make strong** > Paul longed to see the Christians in Rome so that he might establish them by some spiritual gift (Rom. 1:11). God was able to establish them according to Paul's gospel and the preaching of Jesus Christ (Rom. 16:25). Paul had sent Timothy to establish the Christians in Thessalonica (1 Thes. 3:2); the Lord could establish their hearts blameless in holiness (1 Thes. 3:13) and in every good work and word (2 Thes. 2:17); the Lord would establish them (2 Thes. 3:3). James exhorts the Christians to establish their hearts {stand firm}, for the coming of the Lord is near (Jas. 5:8). The God of all grace will establish the Christians (1 Pet. 5:10). Christians to whom Peter wrote were established in the present truth (2 Pet. 1:12). All other refs.: FIX <4741>, STEADFASTLY <4741>, STRENGTHEN <4741>.
– 6 Mark 7:9 → KEEP (verb) <5083> 7 Luke 12:14; Acts 7:27 → to make, to make ruler → MAKE <2525> 8 Acts 6:3; Titus 1:5; Heb. 5:1 → APPOINT <2525> 9 Acts 14:22; 18:23 → STRENGTHEN <1991> 10 Rom. 13:1 → APPOINT <5021> 11 1 Cor. 7:37 → to be firmly established → lit.: to stand (*histēmi*) firm (*hedraios*) 12 Eph. 3:17; Col. 1:23 → to establish, to establish firmly → FOUND <2311> 13 Heb. 1:2 → APPOINT <5087> 14 Heb. 8:8 → MAKE <4931> 15 Heb. 8:10; 10:16 → MAKE <1303> 16 Heb. 9:16 → BRING <5342> 17 1 Pet. 5:10 → SETTLE <2311>.

ESTABLISHED (BE) – 1 Gal. 3:15 → to be duly established → CONFIRM <2964> 2 Gal. 3:17 → to confirm before → CONFIRM <4300>.

ESTATE – 1 Luke 1:48 → low estate → HUMILIATION <5014> 2 Luke 1:52 → one of humble estate → lowly one, one of low degree → LOWLY <5011> 3 Luke 15:12, 13 → GOOD (adj. and noun) <3776> 4 Acts 5:8 → FIELD <5564> 5 Acts 28:7 → LAND (noun) <5564> 6 Rom. 12:16 → men of low estate → HUMBLE (adj.)

<5011> 7 Col. 4:8 → AFFAIR <3588> 8 Jude 6 → first estate → original state → STATE <746>.

ESTEEM (noun) – 1 Acts 5:13 → to hold in high esteem → ESTEEM (verb) <3170> 2 Phil. 2:29 → in esteem → in honor → HONOR (noun) <1784>.

ESTEEM (verb) – 1 ***hēgeomai*** [verb: ἡγέομαι <2233>]; **from *agō*: to lead ▶ To consider, to think, to believe** > Christians should esteem {regard} others as more excellent than themselves (Phil. 2:3). They must esteem very highly {regard exceedingly, hold in the highest regard} in love those who labor among them, take the lead among them in the Lord, and admonish them (1 Thes. 5:13). Moses esteemed {regarded} the reproach of Christ greater riches than the treasures of Egypt (Heb. 11:26). All other refs.: see entries in Lexicon at <2233>.
2 **to esteem least: *exoutheneō*** [verb: ἐξουθενέω <1848>]; **from *ek*: intens., and *outheneō*: to bring to nothing, which is from *ouden*: nothing ▶ To despise, to consider of inferior value** > Paul said to appoint those who are least esteemed {are little esteemed, are of no account, are of little account} in the church to judge (1 Cor. 6:4). All other refs.: CONTEMPT <1848>, CONTEMPTIBLE <1848>, DESPISE <1848>.
3 ***krinō*** [verb: κρίνω <2919>] **▶ To judge, to consider; also transl.: to regard** > One person esteems one day above another; another esteems every day alike (Rom. 14:5a, b). All other refs.: see entries in Lexicon at <2919>.
4 **to esteem highly: *megalunō*** [verb: μεγαλύνω <3170>]; **from *megas*: great ▶ To magnify, to exalt** > The people esteemed highly {held in high esteem, magnified, highly regarded} the apostles (Acts 5:13). All other refs.: ENLARGE <3170>, MAGNIFY <3170>.
– 5 Mark 10:42 → REGARD (verb) <1380> 6 Rom. 14:14 → CONSIDER <3049> 7 1 Cor. 12:23 → THINK <1380> 8 Gal. 2:2, 9 → to be of reputation → REPUTATION <1380> 9 Gal. 2:6 → held in high esteem → lit.: seeming to be something.

ESTEEMED – highly esteemed: *hupsēlos* [adj.: ὑψηλός <5308>]; **from *hupsos*: elevation, exaltation ▶ What is high, superior** > What is highly esteemed {highly thought of, highly valued} among men is an abomination in the sight of God (Luke 16:15). All other refs.: HIGH (adj.) <5308>, UPLIFTED <5308>.

ESTIMATE – Luke 14:28 → COUNT <5585>.

ESTRANGED (BE) – 1 Gal. 5:4 → to become estranged → to make of no effect → EFFECT (noun) <2673> 2 Eph. 4:18 → ALIENATED (BE) <526>.

ETERNAL – 1 ***aidios*** [adj.: ἀΐδιος <126>]; **from *aei*: always ▶ a. Without beginning or end, self-existent** > The eternal power and divinity of God are apprehended by the mind through the things that are made (Rom. 1:20). **b. Perpetual, without end** > The angels who did not keep their original state (see Genesis 6) are being kept in eternal {everlasting} chains (Jude 6). ¶
2 ***aiōnios*** [adj.: αἰώνιος <166>]; **from *aiōn*: age, duration ▶ Without end, outside of time; also transl.: everlasting** > The first aspect of this word is a physical notion, that of a sphere where time does not exist: Paul speaks of the revelation of the mystery (the union of Christ with His church), as to which silence has been kept in the times of the ages {for long ages past}, i.e., the eternal times (Rom. 16:25; some have transl. "since the world began," but it should be: "since eternal times"). The second aspect of this word is a spiritual notion linked closely to the nature of God Himself (Rom. 16:26; 1 Tim. 6:16 {immortal}; Heb. 9:14: the eternal Spirit; 1 Pet. 5:10). Jesus Christ became the author of eternal salvation to all who obey Him (Heb. 5:9). He has obtained eternal redemption (Heb. 9:12), an eternal glory (2 Cor. 4:17; 2 Tim. 2:10), eternal things (2 Cor. 4:18), and an eternal inheritance (Heb. 9:15); He Himself

and God the Father, who has given eternal encouragement, strengthen the hearts of Christians (2 Thes. 2:16). Grace was given to us in Christ Jesus before the ages of time (lit.: before the eternal times) (2 Tim. 1:9). The believer in the Lord Jesus will be received into the eternal dwellings (Luke 16:9), into the eternal kingdom of the Lord and Savior Jesus Christ (2 Pet. 1:11); the future body of glory of the Christian is compared to a house not made with hands, eternal in the heavens (2 Cor. 5:1). The lot of the unbelievers is the eternal fire (Matt. 18:8; 25:41); their condemnation, or judgment, is eternal (Mark 3:29; Heb. 6:2), and their punishment and destruction are eternal (Matt. 25:46; 2 Thes. 1:9 {everlasting}). Sodom and Gomorrah suffered the judgment of eternal fire (Jude 7). John saw an angel who had the eternal gospel to preach to those settled on earth (Rev. 14:6). Other refs.: Titus 1:2; Heb. 13:20; Phm. 15 {forever}. *
3 See LIFE ETERNAL.

ETERNAL LIFE – See LIFE ETERNAL.

ETERNALLY – Rom. 9:5 → FOREVER <165>.

ETERNITY – 2 Cor. 9:9; 1 Pet. 1:25 → for eternity → for the age → FOREVER <165>.

ETHIOPIAN – ***Aithiops*** [masc. name: Αἰθίοψ <128>]: **burned by the sun ▶ Inhabitant of Ethiopia, a country of eastern Africa** > An Ethiopian of the royal court (Acts 8:27) was converted through the preaching of Philip, as he was returning after having worshiped at Jerusalem. Philip baptized him after his conversion (see Acts 8:26–40). ¶

ETHNARCH – 2 Cor. 11:32 → GOVERNOR <1481>.

EUBULUS – ***Euboulos*** [masc. name: Εὔβουλος <2103>]: **prudent, well-intentioned ▶ Christian man of Rome** > Paul sends the greetings of Eubulus to Timothy (2 Tim. 4:21). ¶

EUNICE – ***Eunikē*** [fem. name: Εὐνίκη <2131>]: **happily victorious; from *eu*: good, and *nikos*: victory ▶ Mother of Timothy** > Eunice was a believing Jewish woman who had married a Greek man (see Acts 16:1). The sincere faith in her son Timothy had first dwelt in Eunice (2 Tim. 1:5). ¶

EUNUCH – **eunuch: *eunouchos*** [masc. noun: εὐνοῦχος <2135>]; **to make eunuch: *eunouchizō*** [verb: εὐνουχίζω <2134>]; **from *eunē*: bed, and *echō*: to keep; lit.: keeper of the bed ▶ Man who cannot have a normal sexual life or procreate because of a forced or voluntary castration or birth defect; to become such** > Jesus speaks of three categories of eunuchs: those who were born as such, those who were made eunuchs by men (e.g., to serve in palaces), and those who have made themselves eunuchs (figur. speaking) for the kingdom of heaven (Matt. 19:12a–e). Philip preached Jesus to a man from Ethiopia and baptized him; this man was a eunuch of power under Candace, the queen of the Ethiopians (Acts 8:27, 34, 36, 38, 39). ¶

EUNUCH (MAKE) – Matt. 19:12c, e → EUNUCH <2134>.

EUODIA – ***Euodia*** [fem. name: Εὐοδία <2136>]: **pleasant journey or fragrant; from *eu*: good, and *odos*: journey ▶ Christian woman of Philippi; also transl.: Euodias** > Paul urged Euodia and Syntyche to have the same mind in the Lord (Phil. 4:2); they had shared Paul's struggle in the gospel (see v. 3). ¶

EUODIAS – See EUODIA <2136>.

EUPHRATES – ***Euphratēs*** [masc. name: Εὐφράτης <2166>]: **the abounding ▶ River in western Asia, approx. 1,740 miles (2,800 kilometers) in length, located east of Palestine; Babylon was built near the Euphrates River; it flows into the Persian Gulf** > Four angels bound at the great river Euphrates will be released so that they may kill the third part of men (Rev. 9:14). Its water will be dried up to prepare the way for the kings from the East (Rev. 16:12). ¶

EURAQUILO – See EUROCLYDON <2148>.

EUROCLYDON – ***Eurokludōn*** [masc. name: Εὐροκλύδων <2148>]; **from *euros*: east wind, and *kludōn*: wave; also written: *Eurakulōn, Eurukludōn* ► Very violent wind blowing from the east or from the northeast; also transl.: Euraquilo, Northeaster** > It endangered, near the island of Crete, the ship on which Paul was traveling to Italy (Acts 27:14); the ship ran aground on the island of Malta (see Acts 28:1). ¶

EUTYCHUS – ***Eutuchos*** [masc. name: Εὔτυχος <2161>]: **fortunate; from *eu*: good, and *tuchē*: fortune ► Young man of Troas** > Sitting on the edge of a window and overcome by deep sleep while Paul was preaching, Eutychus fell from the third floor and was taken up dead (Acts 20:9). But he came back to life thanks to the apostle Paul; people brought away the young man alive and were greatly comforted (see vv. 10, 12). ¶

EVANGELIST – ***euangelistēs*** [masc. noun: εὐαγγελιστής <2099>]; **from *euangelizō*: to evangelize, which is from *euangelos*: bringing good news, which is from *eu*: well, and *angellō*: to bring a message; lit.: one who announces good news ► This spiritual gift is for the preaching of the gospel concerning Jesus Christ, the Son of God** > The Lord has given evangelists (Eph. 4:11) for the edifying of the body of Christ (see v. 12). Philip is the only one to be called specifically "the evangelist" (Acts 21:8). Timothy was to do the work of an evangelist (2 Tim. 4:5). ¶

EVANGELIZE – Luke 7:22 → to preach the gospel → PREACH <2097>.

EVE – ***Eua*** [fem. name: Εὔα <2096>]: **life, in Heb. ► Name of the first woman** > God created Eve from Adam (see Gen. 2:22); the man called her by this name because she was the mother of all living (3:20). Eve was formed by God after Adam (1 Tim. 2:13). The serpent deceived Eve by his craftiness (2 Cor. 11:3). ¶

EVEN (adv.) – Matt. 10:42 → ONLY <3440>.

EVEN AS – Acts 15:11 → MANNER <5158>.

EVEN (noun) – 1 Matt. 8:16; 14:15, 23; 20:8; 26:20; 27:57; Mark 1:32; 4:35; 6:47; 15:42; John 6:16 → EVENING <3798> 2 Mark 11:19; 13:35 → EVENING <3796>.

EVENING – 1 ***hespera*** [fem. noun: ἑσπέρα <2073>] ► **End of the day** > The term is used in Luke 24:29; Acts 4:3 {eventide}; 28:23. Other ref.: Acts 20:15 in some mss. ¶
2 **evening, in the evening: *opse*** [adv.: ὀψέ <3796>] ► **Late in the day** > The term is used in Mark 11:19 {even}; 13:35 {even}. Other refs.: Matt. 28:1; see LATE <3796>; Mark 11:11 in some mss. ¶
3 ***opsios*** [adj.: ὄψιος <3798>]; **from *opse*: late in the day ► End of the day; also transl.: even** > The term is used in the Gospels (Matt. 8:16; 14:15, 23; 16:2; 20:8; 26:20; 27:57; Mark 1:32; 4:35; 6:47; 11:11 {eventide, late}; 14:17; 15:42; John 6:16; 20:19). ¶

EVENT – 1 Luke 21:11 → fearful event → FEARFUL <5400> 2 Acts 19:21; Heb. 11:7 → "events" added in Engl.

EVENTIDE – 1 Mark 11:11 → EVENING <3798> 2 Acts 4:3 → EVENING <2073>.

EVER – 1 Mark 15:8 → ALWAYS <104> 2 Luke 15:31; John 6:34; 18:20; 1 Thes. 4:17; 5:15; 2 Tim. 3:7; Heb. 7:25 → ALWAYS <3842>.

EVER AGAIN – ***mēketi eis ton aiōna*; ever: *mēketi*** [adv.: μηκέτι <3371>]; **age: *aiōn*** [masc. noun: αἰών <165>]; **lit.: no more for the ages (or: eternity) ► No more in the future** > Jesus told a fig tree that no one might eat its fruit ever again {hereafter, any more for ever, again} (Mark 11:14). *

EVERLASTING – 1 Matt. 18:8; 25:41, 46; Luke 16:9; Rom. 16:26; 2 Thes. 1:9; 2:16; 1 Tim. 6:16; 2 Pet. 1:11; Rev. 14:6 → ETERNAL <166> 2 John 4:14, 36; et al. → everlasting life → LIFE ETERNAL <2222> <166> 3 Jude 6 → ETERNAL <126>.

EVERMORE – 1 2 Cor. 11:31; Heb. 7:28 → evermore, for ever more → FOREVER <165> 2 1 Thes. 5:16 → ALWAYS <3842>.

EVERYDAY LIFE – Rom. 6:19 → I am using an example from everyday life → lit.: I speak humanly → HUMAN <442>.

EVERYTHING – 1 Acts 24:16 → in everything → ALWAYS <1275> 2 1 Cor. 10:26 → FULLNESS <4138>.

EVERYWHERE – 1 ***pantachou*** [adv.: πανταχοῦ <3837>]; **from *pas*: all, and suffix *chou* meaning a place ▶ In all places** > The disciples preached everywhere (Mark 16:20; Luke 9:6). God commands all men everywhere to repent (Acts 17:30). Paul was accused of preaching everywhere against the people and the law (Acts 21:28); *pantachē* in some mss. Other refs.: Mark 1:28 in some mss.; Acts 24:3 {every way, all places}; 28:22; 1 Cor. 4:17. ¶
– 2 1 Tim. 2:8 → PLACE (noun) <5117>.

EVIDENCE – 1 ***elenchos*** [masc. noun: ἔλεγχος <1650>]; **from *elenchō*: to convict; lit.: conviction ▶ Proof, demonstration** > Faith is the evidence {the conviction, being sure} of things not seen (Heb. 11:1). Other ref.: 2 Tim. 3:16; see REPROOF <1650>. ¶
2 **manifest evidence: *endeigma*** [neut. noun: ἔνδειγμα <1730>]; **from *endeiknumi*: to show, which is from *en*: in, and *deiknumi*: to show ▶ Proof, indication** > The persecutions and tribulations of the Thessalonians were manifest evidence {a manifest token, a plain indication} of the righteous judgment of God (2 Thes. 1:5). ¶
– 3 Matt. 18:16; 2 Cor. 13:1 → MOUTH (noun) <4750> 4 Mark 14:55 → WITNESS (noun)[1] <3141> 5 Acts 17:3 → to give evidence → to lay down → LAY <3908> 6 Acts 24:1; 25:2, 15 → to give evidence → to bring charges → CHARGE (noun)[1] <1718> 7 1 Tim. 5:19; Heb. 10:28 → "the evidence of" added in Engl. 8 Jas. 2:20 → to want evidence → lit.: to want to know → KNOW <1097> 9 Jas. 5:3 → WITNESS (noun)[1] <3142>.

EVIDENT – 1 ***gnōstos*** [adj.: γνωστός <1110>]; **from *ginoskō*: to know ▶ Known, remarkable** > An evident {notable, noteworthy, outstanding} miracle had been done through Peter and John (Acts 4:16) in healing the infirm man (see 3:1–11). All other refs.: ACQUAINTANCE <1110>, KNOWN <1110>.
2 ***dēlos*** [adj.: δῆλος <1212>] ▶ **Certain, understood** > It is evident {clear, manifest} that all things put under the feet of Jesus exclude God the Father (1 Cor. 15:27). It is evident that {Clearly} no one is justified by the law before God (Gal. 3:11). It is evident {clear} we can carry nothing out of this world (1 Tim. 6:7 in some mss.). Other ref.: Matt. 26:73; see MANIFEST (adj.) <1212>. ¶
3 ***katadēlos*** [adj.: κατάδηλος <2612>]; **from *kata*: intens., and *dēlos*: see 2 ▶ Notorious, more evident, clearer** > The word is used in Heb. 7:15 concerning the priesthood of the Lord which is in the likeness that of Melchizedek. ¶
4 ***prodēlos*** [adj.: πρόδηλος <4271>]; **from *pro*: intens., and *dēlos*: see 2 ▶ Openly evident, manifest before (all)** > It is evident {clear} that the Lord arose from Judah (Heb. 7:14). Other refs.: 1 Tim. 5:24, 25; see CLEARLY <4271>. ¶
5 ***phaneros*** [adj.: φανερός <5318>]; **from *phainō*: to shine, to become evident, which is from *phōs*: light ▶ Known, visible; also transl.: manifest** > The works of the flesh are evident {obvious} (Gal. 5:19). It became evident {clear, well known} that Paul's bonds were in Christ (Phil. 1:13). Timothy was to occupy himself with certain things that his progress might be evident to {appear to, be seen by} all (1 Tim. 4:15). All other refs.: see entries in Lexicon at <5318>.

– 6 Rom. 1:19; 2 Cor. 11:6 → to make evident → MANIFEST (verb) <5319> 7 Phil. 1:28 → evident token → PROOF <1732>.

EVIDENTLY – Gal. 3:1 → to evidently set forth → PORTRAY <4270>.

EVIL (adj.) – 1 ***kakos*** [adj.: κακός <2556>] ► **Bad, wicked** > The word is used in regard to a servant (Matt. 24:48), thoughts (Mark 7:21), things (Rom. 1:30; 9:11 in some mss.; 1 Cor. 10:6), works (Rom. 13:3), company (1 Cor. 15:33 {bad}), workers (Phil. 3:2), lust (Col. 3:5), Cretans (Titus 1:12), men (Rev. 2:2), a sore (Rev. 16:2 {foul, noisome, loathsome}). All other refs.: EVIL (noun) <2556>, HARM (noun) <2556>, WICKED (noun) <2556>.

2 ***ponēros*** [adj.: πονηρός <4190>]; **from *ponos*: pain ► Bad, grievous, of a wicked nature or condition; also transl.: lewd, lewdness, malicious, wicked** > Women who had been healed of evil spirits accompanied Jesus (Luke 8:2). Paul worked miracles, healing people possessed by evil spirits (Acts 19:12); certain Jews took it upon themselves to attempt to exorcise such spirits also (v. 13). A man, in whom an evil spirit was, wounded the seven sons of Sceva (Acts 19:15, 16). The Greek word is also used in regard to the eye (Matt. 6:23; 20:15; Mark 7:22), men (Matt. 7:11; 12:34, 35a; 22:10; Luke 6:45a; 11:13; Acts 17:5; 2 Thes. 3:2; 2 Tim. 3:13), fruit (Matt. 7:17b, 18a), treasure (Matt. 12:35b), things (Matt. 12:35c; Mark 7:23; Luke 3:19; 6:45b, c; Acts 25:18: adj. used as noun), a generation (Matt. 12:39, 45b; 16:4; Luke 11:29), thoughts (Matt. 15:19; Jas. 2:4), a servant (Matt. 18:32; 25:26; Luke 19:22), the name of believers in the Lord (Luke 6:22), spirits (Luke 7:21), the body (Luke 11:34), works (John 3:19; 7:7; Col. 1:21; 2 Tim. 4:18; 1 John 3:12; 2 John 11), crimes (Acts 18:14), the present age (Gal. 1:4), days (Eph. 5:16; 6:13), works (Col. 1:21), suspicions (1 Tim. 6:4), a heart (Heb. 3:12), conscience (Heb. 10:22), boasting (Jas. 4:16), and words (3 John 10). In Rev. 16:2, the Greek word is transl. "grievous" {loathsome}: An evil (*kakos*) and grievous (*ponēros*) sore came upon the men who had the mark of the beast and those who worshipped his image. All other refs.: EVIL (noun) <4190>, WICKED (noun) <4190>.

3 ***phaulos*** [adj.: φαῦλος <5337>] ► **That which is bad; also transl.: bad** > Whoever practices evil hates the light (John 3:20). Other refs.: John 5:29; Rom. 9:11; 2 Cor. 5:10 in some mss.; Titus 2:8; Jas. 3:16. ¶

– 4 Matt. 22:18 → evil intent → WICKEDNESS <4189> 5 Rom. 1:29 → evil dispositions → EVIL-MINDEDNESS <2550> 6 Eph. 4:31 → evil language → BLASPHEMY <988>.

EVIL (adv.) – 1 **to speak evil: *blasphēmeō*** [verb: βλασφημέω <987>]; **from *blasphēmos*: blasphemer; which is poss. from *blaptō*: to harm, and *phēmē*: reputation ► To blame, to say bad things** > The good of Christians in Rome was not to be spoken of as evil (Rom. 14:16). Paul ought not be evil spoken of {denounced, slandered} for that over which he gave thanks (1 Cor. 10:30). All other refs.: see entries in Lexicon at <987>.

2 **to speak evil: *kakologeō*** [verb: κακολογέω <2551>]; **from *kakologos*: evil speaking, which is from *kakos*: evil, and *legō*: to speak ► To say bad things about someone** > One who works a miracle in the name of Jesus cannot soon afterward speak evil {speak ill, say something bad} of Him (Mark 9:39). Some spoke evil of {maligned} the Way (Acts 19:9). Other refs.: Matt. 15:4; Mark 7:10; see CURSE (verb) <2551>. ¶

3 **to do evil: *kakopoieō*** [verb: κακοποιέω <2554>]; **from *kakopoios*: evildoer, which is from *kakos*: bad, and *poieō*: to do ► To do that which is bad, that which is harmful to others** > Jesus asked if it is lawful on the Sabbath to do good or to do evil {do harm} (Mark 3:4; Luke 6:9). It is better to suffer for doing good than for doing evil {doing what is wrong} (1 Pet. 3:17). He who does evil has not seen God (3 John 11b). ¶

– 4 Luke 11:26 → more evil → more wicked → WICKED (adj.) <4191> 5 John 18:23a; Acts 23:5 → SICK (adv.) <2560>.

EVIL (noun) – 1 ***kakon*; from *kakos*** [adj. used as noun: κακός <2556>] ▶ **That which is bad, wicked** > Pilate asked what evil Jesus had done (Matt. 27:23; Mark 15:14; Luke 23:22). Lazarus had received evil things {bad things} (lit.: the evils) during his lifetime (Luke 16:25). Jesus answered the officer that if He had spoken evil (*kakōs*), he should bear witness of the evil {the wrong} (*kakon*) (John 18:23b). The Greek word is also transl. "harm": Paul had done much harm to the saints at Jerusalem (Acts 9:13). He told the jailer to do himself no harm (Acts 16:28). The scribes of the Pharisee's party found no evil {nothing wrong} in Paul (Acts 23:9). Paul suffered no harm from the viper (Acts 28:5). Tribulation and distress are the portion of every soul of man who does evil (Rom. 2:9). Some slanderously claimed that Paul said to do evil that good might come (Rom. 3:8). The man of Romans 7 practices the evil which he would not do (v. 19); evil is present with him (v. 21). We should repay no one evil for evil (Rom. 12:17a, b; also 1 Thes. 5:15a, b; 1 Pet. 3:9a, b). We should not be overcome by evil, but overcome evil with good (Rom. 12:21a, b). We should fear the ruler if we do evil, for he executes the wrath of God on him who practices evil (Rom. 13:4a, b). The Greek word is transl. "harm" in Rom. 13:10 {ill, wrong}: Love does no harm to a neighbor. It is evil for the man who causes offense by what he eats (Rom. 14:20). We should be wise in what is good and simple concerning evil (Rom. 16:19). Love thinks no evil {wrong} (1 Cor. 13:5). At the judgment seat of Christ, we will receive according to what we have done, whether good or evil {bad} (2 Cor. 5:10). Paul prayed to God that the Corinthians should do no evil {wrong} (2 Cor. 13:7). The love of money is a root of all kinds of evil (1 Tim. 6:10). Those who are full grown men discern both good and evil (Heb. 5:14). God cannot be tempted by evil (Jas. 1:13). The tongue is an unruly evil (Jas. 3:8). He who would love life and see good days must refrain his tongue from evil (1 Pet. 3:10); he must turn away from evil (v. 11), for the face of the Lord is against those who do evil (v. 12). Gaius was not to imitate that which is evil (3 John 11a). All other refs.: EVIL (adj.) <2556>, HARM (noun) <2556>, WICKED (noun) <2556>.

2 ***ponēros*** [adj. used as noun: πονηρός <4190>]; **from *ponos*: pain** ▶ **A bad thing, wickedness; a wicked being** > The believer in the Lord Jesus is blessed when people say all kinds of evil {wicked thing} against him falsely for His sake (Matt. 5:11). Jesus tells us not to resist an evil (person) (Matt. 5:39). The scribes were thinking evil in their hearts (Matt. 9:4). At the end of the age, the angels will come forth and separate the evil from among the righteous (Matt. 13:49). No brother who came to the leaders of the Jews reported or spoke any evil {any harm, anything bad} concerning Paul (Acts 28:21). We should abhor what is evil (Rom. 12:9) and we should abstain from every form of evil (1 Thes. 5:22). The term may also designate Satan, the Evil one, in Matt. 5:37; 6:13; John 17:15. All other refs.: EVIL (adj.) <4190>, WICKED (noun) <4190>.

3 ***phaulos*** [adj. used as noun: φαῦλος <5337>] ▶ **That which is without value, wicked, base** > Those who have done evil will come forth from the tombs to the resurrection of judgment (John 5:29). All other refs.: EVIL (adj.) <5337>.

– 4 Matt. 6:34 → TROUBLE (noun) <2549> 5 Matt. 13:41 → INIQUITY <458> 6 Matt. 15:4; Mark 7:10 → to speak evil → CURSE (verb) <2551> 7 Luke 13:27; Rom. 2:8; Jas. 3:6 → INIQUITY <93> 8 John 18:30; 1 Pet. 2:14 → doing evil → EVILDOER <2555> 9 Acts 7:6, 19 → to entreat evil → OPPRESS <2559> 10 Acts 24:20 → WRONG (noun) <92> 11 1 Cor. 5:8; Eph. 6:12 → WICKEDNESS <4189> 12 1 Cor. 13:6 → UNRIGHTEOUSNESS <93> 13 1 Cor. 14:20; Jas. 1:21 → MALICE <2549> 14 2 Cor. 12:20; 1 Pet. 2:1 → evil speaking → BACKBITING <2636> 15 2 Tim. 2:24 → patiently enduring evil → FORBEARING <420> 16 2 Tim. 4:5 → to bear evils → to endure hardship → SUFFER <2553>, HARDSHIP <2553> 17 Titus 3:2; 1 Pet. 4:4; 2 Pet. 2:10, 12; Jude 8, 10 → to speak evil → REVILE <987> 18 1 Pet. 2:16 → WICKEDNESS <2549> 19 Rev. 22:11

→ to do evil → to do wrong → WRONG (noun) <91>.

EVIL-AFFECTED – Acts 14:2 → to make evil-affected → POISON (verb) <2559>.

EVIL DOER – See EVILDOER <2555>.

EVIL-MINDEDNESS – ***kakoētheia*** [fem. noun: κακοήθεια <2550>]; **from *kakoēthēs*: mischievous, vicious, which is from *kakos*: bad, and *ēthos*: custom, manner ▶ A disposition to wickedness; depravity; lit.: evil habits** > In Rom. 1:29, men are full of evil-mindedness {evil dispositions, malice, malignity}. ¶

EVIL SPEAKER – 2 Tim. 3:2 → BLASPHEMER <989>.

EVILDOER – 1 ***kakopoios*** [adj. used as noun: κακοποιός <2555>]; **from *kakos*: bad, and *poieō*: to do ▶ Wicked, harmful person, one who does that which is wrong** > Jesus was accused of being an evildoer {criminal, malefactor} before Pilate (John 18:30). Gentiles should not speak against us as evildoers {of doing wrong} (1 Pet. 2:12; also 3:16 in some mss.). We should submit to those sent by rulers to punish evildoers {those who do wrong} (1 Pet. 2:14). No one should suffer as an evildoer {a criminal} (1 Pet. 4:15). ¶
– 2 Matt. 7:23 → lit.: one who practices lawlessness → PRACTICE (verb) <2038>, INIQUITY <458> 3 Luke 13:27 → lit.: worker of iniquity → INIQUITY <93>, WORKMAN <2040> 4 Luke 18:11 → UNRIGHTEOUS (adj. and noun) <94> 5 Phil. 3:2 → evil workman → EVIL (adj.) <2556>, WORKMAN <2040> 6 2 Tim. 2:9 → CRIMINAL <2557> 7 2 Tim. 3:13 → lit.: evil men → EVIL (adj.) <4190>, MAN <444> 8 1 Pet. 3:17 → as evildoer → lit.: as doing evil → to do evil → EVIL (adv.) <2554> 9 Rev. 22:11 → him that is doing wrong → to do wrong → WRONG (noun) <91>.

EVILLY – Acts 23:5; Jas. 4:3 → SICK (adv.) <2560>.

EXACT (adj.) – 1 Luke 1:4 → exact truth → CERTAINTY <803> 2 Acts 17:26 → exact place → BOUNDARY <3734> 3 Acts 24:22 → more exact → more accurately → ACCURATELY <197> 4 Heb. 1:3 → exact representation → EXPRESSION <5481>.

EXACT (verb) – Luke 3:13 → COLLECT <4238>.

EXACTING – Luke 19:21, 22 → HARSH <840>.

EXACTION – 2 Cor. 9:5 → COVETOUSNESS <4124>.

EXACTLY – 1 Acts 18:25 → ACCURATELY <199> 2 Acts 18:26; 23:15 → more exactly → more accurately → ACCURATELY <197> 3 Acts 22:30 → CERTAINTY <804>.

EXACTLY LIKE – See WHOLLY AS <5618>.

EXACTNESS – Acts 22:3 → STRICTNESS <195>.

EXALT – 1 ***epairō*** [verb: ἐπαίρω <1869>]; **from *epi*: upon, and *airō*: to lift up ▶ To rise up, to oppose** > The spiritual weapons of God were casting down every high thing that exalted itself {lifted itself up, set itself up, raised up} against the knowledge of God (2 Cor. 10:5). The Corinthians put up with it if anyone exalted himself {pushed himself forward} (2 Cor. 11:20). All other refs.: LIFT <1869>, RAISE <1869>, TAKE <1869>.
2 **to exalt above measure, to exalt: *huperairō*** [verb: ὑπεραίρω <5229>]; **from *huper*: above (intens.), and *airō*: to lift up ▶ To rise up, to boast** > A thorn in the flesh was given to Paul that he might not be exalted above measure {become conceited} by the exceeding greatness of the revelations (2 Cor. 12:7a, b). The man of sin will oppose and exalt himself above all that is called God or is an object of veneration (2 Thes. 2:4). ¶
3 ***hupsoō*** [verb: ὑψόω <5312>]; **from *hupsos*: height ▶ To elevate, to glorify;**

also transl.: to lift up > Capernaum was exalted {raised up} to heaven (Matt. 11:23; Luke 10:15). Whoever exalts himself will be humbled, and he who humbles himself will be exalted (Matt. 23:12a, b; Luke 14:11a, b; 18:14a, b). The Lord has exalted the lowly (Luke 1:52). Jesus has been exalted by the right hand of God (Acts 2:33; 5:31). God has exalted {made great, made prosper} the people of Israel (Acts 13:17). Paul had humbled himself that the Corinthians might be exalted {be elevated} (2 Cor. 11:7). Those humbling themselves under the mighty hand of God will be exalted by Him in due time (1 Pet. 5:6). All other refs.: to lift up → LIFT <5312>.

[4] **to highly exalt: *huperupsoō*** [verb: ὑπερυψόω <5251>]**; from *huper*: above, and *hupsoō*: see [3] ▶ To lift up high, to raise supremely** > God has highly exalted Christ Jesus (Phil. 2:9). ¶

– [5] Luke 1:46; Acts 10:46; Phil. 1:20 → MAGNIFY <3170> [6] Heb. 5:5 → GLORIFY <1392> [7] Jas. 1:9 → EXALTATION <5311>.

EXALTATION – ***hupsos*** [neut. noun: ὕψος <5311>]**; from *hupsi*: high ▶ Elevation, action of raising in status or dignity** > The lowly brother ought to glory in his exaltation {high position, in that he is exalted} (Jas. 1:9). All other refs.: DAYSPRING FROM ON HIGH <5311>, HEIGHT <5311>, HIGH (noun) <5311>.

EXALTED – [1] Luke 16:15 → highly esteemed → ESTEEMED <5308> [2] Heb. 7:26 → higher → HIGH (adj.) <5308>.

EXAMINATION – Acts 25:26 → INVESTIGATION <351>.

EXAMINE – [1] ***anakrinō*** [verb: ἀνακρίνω <350>]**; from *ana*: intens., and *krinō*: to judge; lit.: to examine carefully ▶ To question, to discern** > Having examined Jesus, Pilate had found nothing criminal in Him (Luke 23:14). Peter and John were examined {were called to account, were called upon to answer, were judged, were being on trial} in regard to the healing of an infirm (Acts 4:9). Herod examined {cross-examined} the guards who had kept Peter (Acts 12:19). Felix might examine Paul (Acts 24:8). The Romans had examined Paul (Acts 28:18). Paul speaks of the defense he presented to those who were examining {were sitting in judgment on} him (1 Cor. 9:3). All other refs.: ASK <350>, DISCERN <350>, JUDGE (verb) <350>, SEARCH (verb) <350>.

[2] ***anetazō*** [verb: ἀνετάζω <426>]**; from *ana*: intens., and *etazō*: to examine, to test ▶ To interrogate in a judicial manner, even resorting to torture** > The chiliarch wanted Paul to be examined {questioned} by scourging (Acts 22:24), but those who were about to examine him did not do so when they learned that he was a Roman (v. 29). ¶

[3] ***peirazō*** [verb: πειράζω <3985>]**; from *peira*: experience, trial ▶ To scrutinize, to consider carefully** > Paul told the Corinthians to examine {test} themselves to see if they were in the faith (2 Cor. 13:5a). All other refs.: TEMPT <3985>, TEMPTER <3985>, TEST (noun and verb) <3985>, TRY[1] <3985>.

– [4] Luke 14:19; 1 Cor. 11:28; Gal. 6:4; 1 Thes. 2:4; 5:21 → TEST (noun and verb) <1382> <1381> [5] Acts 17:23 → BEHOLD (verb) <333> [6] Acts 25:26 → after we have examined → after the investigation has taken place → INVESTIGATION <351>.

EXAMPLE – [1] ***deigma*** [neut. noun: δεῖγμα <1164>]**; from *deiknuō*: to show; lit.: that which is shown ▶ Model to be imitated or to be used as a warning** > Sodom and Gomorrah, and the cities around them, which went after other flesh, serve as an example by undergoing the judgment of eternal fire (Jude 7). ¶

[2] ***hupodeigma*** [neut. noun: ὑπόδειγμα <5262>]**; from *hupodeiknumi*: to show, to forewarn, which is from *hupo*: under, and *deigma*: see [1] ▶ Model to be imitated or to be used as a warning** > Jesus had given an example to His disciples by washing their feet (John 13:15). Christians should use diligence to enter into the rest of God, that no one may fall after the same example of not listening to the word of God (Heb.

4:11). The prophets who have spoken in the name of the Lord are examples of suffering and having patience (Jas. 5:10). Sodom and Gomorrah are an example for those who would later live an ungodly life (2 Pet. 2:6). All other refs.: COPY <5262>.

[3] **to make an example: *deigmatizō*** [verb: δειγματίζω <1165>]**; from *deigma*: see [1] ▶ To defame, to exhibit** > Joseph did not wish to make an example of {disgrace, expose to public disgrace} Mary (Matt. 1:19); certain mss. have *paradeigmatizō*: to make a public example (see **4**). Other ref.: Col. 2:15 (to make a spectacle); see SPECTACLE <1165>. ¶

[4] **to make a public example: *paradeigmatizō*** [verb: παραδειγματίζω <3856>]**; from *para*: alongside, and *deigmatizō*: see [3] ▶ To expose publicly, to put to open shame** > Joseph did not wish to make a public example of Mary (Matt. 1:19); certain mss. have *deigmatizō*: to make an example (see [3]). Other ref.: Heb. 6:6 (to make a show); see SHOW (noun) <3856>. ¶

[5] ***hupogrammos*** [masc. noun: ὑπογραμμός <5261>]**; from *hupographō*: to write below, which is from *hupo*: under, and *graphō*: to write; lit.: handwriting model of the letters of the alphabet given to beginners to teach them to trace the letters ▶ Pattern, model to follow** > Christ has suffered for us, leaving us an example {a model}, so that we may follow His steps (1 Pet. 2:21). ¶

[6] ***hupotupōsis*** [fem. noun: ὑποτύπωσις <5296>]**; from *hupotupoō*: to make a sketch, which is from *hupo*: under, and *tupos*: model ▶ Model, pattern** > Paul was to be an example {a delineation} to those about to believe on Jesus Christ to eternal life (1 Tim. 1:16). Other ref.: 2 Tim. 1:13; see PATTERN <5296>. ¶

– [7] Rom. 6:19 → I am using an example from everyday life → lit.: I speak humanly → HUMAN <442> [8] 1 Cor. 10:6, 11 → TYPE <5179> [9] Eph. 5:1 → to follow the example → to become an imitator → IMITATOR <3402> [10] Phil. 3:17 → to follow the example → to be imitator together → imitator together → IMITATOR <4831> [11] 1 Thes. 1:7; 2 Thes. 3:9; 1 Tim. 4:12; Titus 2:7; 1 Pet. 5:3 → PATTERN <5179>.

EXASPERATE – [1] Eph. 6:4 → PROVOKE <3949> [2] Col. 3:21 → PROVOKE <2042>.

EXCEED – [1] ***perisseuō*** [verb: περισσεύω <4052>]**; from *perissos*: abundant ▶ To surpass the measure, to overflow, to abound** > The ministry of righteousness exceeds {far exceeds} in glory (2 Cor. 3:9). All other refs.: see entries in Lexicon at <4052>.

– [2] 1 Cor. 4:6 → THINK <5426> [3] 2 Cor. 8:5 → they exceeded our expectations → lit.: not as we hoped → HOPE (verb) <1679> [4] Rev. 2:19 → lit.: more than → MORE <4119>.

EXCEEDING – [1] **to exceed: *huperballō*** [verb: ὑπερβάλλω <5235>]**; from *huper*: above, and *ballō*: to throw ▶ To surpass, to excel** > Paul speaks to the Corinthians of the exceeding grace (lit.: the grace which exceeds) of God which was upon them (2 Cor. 9:14). All other refs.: EXCEL <5235>, SURPASS <5235>, SURPASSING <5235>.

– [2] Mark 6:26 → exceeding sorry → very sorry → SORRY <4036> [3] Mark 9:3 → EXCEEDINGLY <3029> [4] Acts 7:20 → exceeding fair → well pleasing to God → PLEASING <2316> [5] Rom. 7:13 → EXCEEDINGLY <2596> <5236> [6] 2 Cor. 4:17 → far more exceeding → beyond measure → MEASURE (noun) <5236> [7] 2 Cor. 7:4 → to be exceeding joyful → lit.: to overabound in joy → ABOUND <5248> [8] 2 Cor. 12:7 → exceeding greatness → GREATNESS <5236> [9] Jude 24 → exceeding joy → JOY (noun) <20>.

EXCEEDINGLY – [1] ***lian*** [adv.: λίαν <3029>] **▶ To a high degree, extremely** > During His transfiguration, the clothes of Jesus became exceedingly {dazzling, exceeding} white (Mark 9:3). The word is transl. "exceeding" in Matt. 8:28. All other refs.: VERY <3029>.

[2] ***perissōs*** [adv.: περισσῶς <4057>]**; from *perissos*: abundant, which is from *peri*:**

above, beyond ▶ Very much, extremely > The disciples were exceedingly {out of measure, greatly, even more} astonished at the words of Jesus, asking one another who could be saved (Mark 10:26). All other refs.: MORE <4057>, VEHEMENTLY <4057>.

[3] ***perissoterōs*** [adv.: περισσοτέρως <4056>]; **from *perissos*: abundant, which is from *peri*: above, beyond ▶ To a greater degree, in a great measure >** Paul rejoiced exceedingly {abundantly, even much} more for {was especially delighted to see} the joy of Titus (2 Cor. 7:13). Other refs.: ABUNDANT <4056>, ABUNDANTLY <4056>, MORE <4056>.

[4] ***huperekperissou*** [adv.: ὑπερεκπερισσοῦ <5238a>]; **from *huper*: above, *ek*: out of, and *perissos*: abundant, which is from *peri*: above, beyond ▶ With utmost fervor, most abundantly >** Paul prayed exceedingly {most earnestly} night and day that he might see the face of the Thessalonians to supply what was lacking in their faith (1 Thes. 3:10). Other ref.: 1 Thes. 5:13 in some mss.; also *huperekperissōs*. Other ref.: Eph. 3:20; see ABUNDANTLY <5238a>. ¶

[5] **exceedingly beyond measure: *lian ek perissou*; *lian*** [adv.: λίαν <3029>]***ek*** [prep.: ἐκ <1537>] ***perissos*** [adj. used as adv.: περισσός <4053>], **which is from *peri*: above, beyond ▶ Quite extraordinarily >** The disciples were exceedingly beyond measure {completely, greatly, greatly beyond measure, sore beyond measure} astonished and wondered that Jesus had calmed the storm (Mark 6:51; simply *lian* in some mss.). See [1].

[6] ***kath' huperbolēn*; from *kata*** [prep.: κατά <2596>]: **according to, and *huperbolē*** [fem. noun: ὑπερβολή <5236>]: **last degree, which is from *huperballō*: to throw beyond, which is from *huper*: above, and *ballō*: to throw ▶ Abundantly, in the extreme >** By the commandment, sin has become exceedingly {exceeding, utterly} sinful (Rom. 7:13). Paul had been exceedingly {excessively, out of measure, beyond measure} pressed in Asia (2 Cor. 1:8). All other refs. (*huperbolē*): EXCELLENCE <5236>, GREATNESS <5236>, MEASURE (noun) <5236>.

[7] ***sphodra*** [adv.: σφόδρα <4970>]; **from *sphodros*: violent, strong ▶ Extremely, greatly, very >** The wise men rejoiced with exceedingly great joy when they saw the star of the little child Jesus (Matt. 2:10). The disciples were exceedingly sorrowful that Jesus was going to die (Matt. 17:23). They were exceedingly amazed in regard to who could be saved (Matt. 19:25). They were exceedingly sorrowful that one among them would deliver up Jesus (Matt. 26:22). The centurion and those who were with him keeping guard over Jesus feared greatly (Matt. 27:54). The stone in front of the entrance of the tomb of Jesus was extremely large (Mark 16:4). The plague of hail was exceedingly terrible (Rev. 16:21). All other refs.: GREATLY <4970>.

– [8] Mark 6:26 → exceedingly sorry → very sorry → SORRY <4036> [9] 2 Cor. 7:4 → to be exceedingly joyful → lit.: to overabound in joy → ABOUND <5248> [10] 2 Thes. 1:3 → to grow exceedingly → GROW <5232> [11] Heb. 12:21 → exceedingly afraid → AFRAID <1630>.

EXCEL – [1] ***perisseuō*** [verb: περισσεύω <4052>]; **from *perissos*: abundant, which is from *peri*: above, beyond ▶ To surpass the measure, to abound >** The Corinthians were to seek to excel in spiritual gifts for the edification of the church (1 Cor. 14:12). All other refs.: see entries in Lexicon at <4052>.

[2] ***huperballō*** [verb: ὑπερβάλλω <5235>]; **from *huper*: above, and *ballō*: to throw ▶ To surpass, to be superior >** Paul speaks of the glory that excels {the surpassing glory} (2 Cor. 3:10). All other refs.: EXCEEDING <5235>, SURPASS <5235>, SURPASSING <5235>.

EXCELLENCE – [1] **excellence, surpassing excellence: *huperbolē*** [fem. noun: ὑπερβολή <5236>]; **from *huperballō*: to throw, which is from *huper*: above, beyond, and *ballō*: to throw ▶ That which excels, surpassing merit, superiority >** Paul showed a way of more surpassing excellence {a more excellent way} (lit.: a way according to excellence) (1 Cor. 12:31). The excellence {surpassing greatness,

excellency, surpassingness} of the power {all-surpassing power} in the Christian must be of God (2 Cor. 4:7). All other refs.: EXCEEDINGLY <5236>, GREATNESS <5236>, MEASURE (noun) <5236>.
[2] **from *huperechō*** [verb: ὑπερέχω <5242>]: **to surpass, which is from *huper*: over, above, and *echō*: to have ▶ Pre-eminence, supremacy** > Paul counted all things to be loss on account of the excellence {surpassing greatness, surpassing value} of the knowledge of Christ (Phil. 3:8). All other refs.: AUTHORITY <5242>, GOVERNING <5242>, IMPORTANT <5242>, SURPASS <5242>.
[3] ***huperochē*** [fem. noun: ὑπεροχή <5247>]; **from *huperechō*: see [2] ▶ Superiority, prestige** > Paul did not go to the Corinthians in excellence of word {with eloquence, with excellency of speech} (1 Cor. 2:1). Other ref.: 1 Tim. 2:2; see AUTHORITY <5247>. ¶
– [4] Phil. 4:8; 2 Pet. 1:3, 5a, b → excellence, moral excellence → VIRTUE <703>.

EXCELLENCY – [1] Acts 23:26 → his excellency → most excellent → EXCELLENT <2903> [2] 1 Cor. 2:1 → EXCELLENCE <5247> [3] 2 Cor. 4:7 → EXCELLENCE <5236> [4] 1 Pet. 2:9 → VIRTUE <703>.

EXCELLENT – [1] ***megaloprepēs*** [adj.: μεγαλοπρεπής <3169>]; **from *megas*: great, and *prepō*: to be suitable for ▶ Magnificent, glorious, splendid** > The voice of the Father spoke to the Lord Jesus from the excellent {majestic} glory (2 Pet. 1:17). ¶
[2] **the more excellent things: *ta diapheronta*; from *diapherō*** [verb: διαφέρω <1308>]: **to carry through, which is from *dia*: through, and *pherō*: to carry ▶ That which is important, that which is essential** > Paul speaks of a Jew who discerningly approves the things that are more excellent {the things that are essential, what is superior} (Rom. 2:18). Christians ought to discern and approve the things that are more excellent {what is best} (Phil. 1:10). All other refs.: see entries in Lexicon at <1308>.
[3] **more excellent: *diaphoros*** [adj.: διάφορος <1313>]; **from *diapherō*: see [2] ▶ Differing in a greater degree, distinct; also transl.: superior** > Jesus inherited a name more excellent than the angels (Heb. 1:4). Christ has obtained a more excellent ministry as the mediator of a new covenant (Heb. 8:6). All other refs.: DIFFERING <1313>, VARIOUS <1313>.
[4] **most excellent: *kratistos*** [adj.: κράτιστος <2903>]; **superl. of *kratos*: strong ▶ Very honorable; also transl.: noble** > Luke addresses Theophilus as most excellent (Luke 1:3). Paul addressed the most excellent governors Felix and Festus (Acts 23:26 {his excellency}; 24:3; 26:25). ¶
[5] **more excellent: *pleiōn*** [adj.: πλείων <4119>]; **compar. of *polus*: great, important ▶ Better** > By faith Abel offered to God a more excellent sacrifice than Cain (Heb. 11:4). *
– [6] Acts 24:2 → excellent measures → MEASURE (noun) <2735> [7] 1 Cor. 12:31 → surpassing excellence → EXCELLENCE <5236> [8] Phil. 2:3 → more excellent → more important → IMPORTANT <5242> [9] Phil. 4:8 → if anything is excellent → lit.: if any excellence → VIRTUE <703> [10] Jas. 2:7 → WORTHY <2570> [11] 1 Pet. 2:12 → HONEST <2570>.

EXCEPT – [1] ***ektos*** [adv.: ἐκτός <1622>]; **from *ek*: out ▶ With the exception of, other than** > All things are put into subjection to Jesus, except {excepted, this does not include} God who will put all things in subjection to Him (1 Cor. 15:27). *
[2] **except, except for: *parektos*** [adv.: παρεκτός <3924>]; **from *para*: intens., and *ektos*: see [1] ▶ With the exception, excluding** > Paul desired that those who heard him might become as he was, except for his chains (Acts 26:29). Other refs.: Matt. 5:32 {saving for}; 2 Cor. 11:28 {external, other, without}. Other ref.: Matt. 19:9 in some mss. ¶
[3] ***plēn*** [prep. and adv.: πλήν <4133>] ▶ **With the exclusion of, save** > During a persecution against the church, all were scattered except the apostles (Acts 8:1). *
[4] ***ei mē ti*** [cond. expr.: εἰ μή τι <1509>]; **from *ei*: if, and *mē*: not, and *ti*: some ▶ Also transl.: if not somewhat,**

unless perhaps > Refs.: Luke 9:13; 1 Cor. 7:5; 2 Cor. 13:5. ¶‡
– [5] Matt. 21:19; Mark 6:8 → ONLY <3440>.

EXCEPTED – 1 Cor. 15:27 → EXCEPT <1622>.

EXCESS – [1] ***anachusis*** [fem. noun: ἀνάχυσις <401>]; **from *anacheō*: to pour forth, which is from *ana*: intens., and *cheō*: to pour; lit.: outpouring ▶ Overflow, disorder** > Unbelievers think it strange that Christians do not run with them in the same excess {flood, sink} of corruption (1 Pet. 4:4). ¶
[2] **to excess: *huperballontōs*** [adv.: ὑπερβαλλόντως <5234>]; **from *huperballō*: to surpass, which is from *huper*: above, beyond, and *ballō*: to throw ▶ Much more, disproportionally** > Paul had been in stripes to excess {above measure, times without number, more severely, more} (2 Cor. 11:23). ¶
– [3] Matt. 23:25 → SELF-INDULGENCE <192> [4] 1 Cor. 11:21 → to drink to excess → to be drunk → DRUNK (BE) <3184> [5] 2 Cor. 8:15 → to have excess → to have something over → OVER <4121> [6] Eph. 5:18; Titus 1:6 → DISSIPATION <810> [7] 1 Tim. 3:3; Titus 1:7 → given to excesses from wine → given to wine → GIVE <3943>.

EXCESSIVE – ***perissoteros*** [adj.: περισσότερος <4055>]; **compar. of *perissos*: abundant; which is from *peri*: above, beyond ▶ Much greater** > The man disciplined by the church ought to be forgiven, lest he be swallowed up with excessive {overmuch, too much} sorrow (2 Cor. 2:7). *

EXCESSIVELY – [1] 2 Cor. 1:8 → EXCEEDINGLY <2596> <5236> [2] Gal. 1:13 → beyond measure → MEASURE (noun) <5236>.

EXCHANGE (noun) – [1] ***antimisthia*** [fem. noun: ἀντιμισθία <489>]; **from *anti*: in return, and *misthos*: reward, salary ▶ Retribution; also transl.: recompense, recompence** > The heart of Paul was open wide to the Corinthians; he tells them, in a like exchange, to also be open (2 Cor. 6:13). Other ref.: Rom. 1:27; see PENALTY <489>. ¶
[2] **in exchange: *antallagma*** [neut. noun: ἀντάλλαγμα <465>]; **from *antalassō*: to exchange, which is from *anti*: against, and *allassō*: to change ▶ Instead, in the place of** > Jesus asks what will a man give in exchange for his soul (Matt. 16:26; Mark 8:37). ¶

EXCHANGE (verb) – [1] ***antiballō*** [verb: ἀντιβάλλω <474>]; **from *anti*: reciprocally, and *ballō*: to throw ▶ To share words, to have a conversation** > Jesus asked the disciples of Emmaus what words they were exchanging with one another {were discussing together} (Luke 24:17). ¶
– [2] John 2:14 → one exchanging money → MONEYCHANGER <2773> [3] Rom. 1:23 → CHANGE (verb) <236> [4] Rom. 1:25, 26 → CHANGE (verb) <3337> [5] Rev. 11:10 → to exchange presents → lit.: to send one another gifts → SEND <3992>.

EXCHANGER – ***trapezitēs*** [masc. noun: τραπεζίτης <5133>]; **from *trapeza*: table (e.g., for money transactions), which is from *tetra*: four, and *peza*: foot ▶ Person exchanging money; also, person to whom money is entrusted to gain interest on the capital** > In the parable, the servant should have deposited the money of his master with the exchangers {with the money changers, with the bankers, in the bank} (Matt. 25:27). ¶

EXCITE – [1] **to be painfully excited: *paroxunō*** [verb: παροξύνω <3947>]; **from *para*: unto, and *oxunō*: to sharpen, which is from *oxus*: rapid, sharp ▶ To provoke, to irritate** > The spirit of Paul was painfully excited {was stirred, was provoked} {Paul was greatly distressed} seeing Athens given up to idolatry (Acts 17:16). Other ref.: 1 Cor. 13:5 (to be quickly provoked); see PROVOKE <3947>. ¶
[2] ***parotrunō*** [verb: παροτρύνω <3951>]; **from *para*: unto, and *otrunō*: to stimu-**

late ▶ **To agitate, to animate the emotions** > The Jews excited {aroused, incited, stirred up} the women of the upper classes and the leading men of Antioch of Pisidia against Paul (Acts 13:50). ¶

EXCLAIM – 1 Mark 9:24; Rev. 18:18 → CRY (verb) <2896> 2 Luke 1:42 → to speak out → SPEAK <400> 3 Acts 12:14; 1 Cor. 14:25 → REPORT (verb) <518>.

EXCLUDE – 1 ***aphorizō*** [verb: ἀφορίζω <873>]; **from *apo*: from, and *horizō*: to determine, to limit ▶ To excommunicate, to ostracize** > The disciples of Jesus would be blessed when men would exclude {separate} them from their midst (Luke 6:22). All other refs.: SEPARATE <873>.

2 ***ekkleiō*** [verb: ἐκκλείω <1576>]; **from *ek*: out of, and *kleiō*: to close ▶ To discard, to set aside, to remove** > Boasting has been excluded by the law of faith (Rom. 3:27). Some wanted to exclude {alienate, shut out} the Galatians from any communication with Paul (Gal. 4:17). ¶

– 3 Rev. 11:2 → CAST (verb) <1544>.

EXCLUDED (BE) – Eph. 2:12; 4:18 → ALIENATED (BE) <526>.

EXCOMMUNICATED – **excommunicated from the synagogue: *aposunagōgos*** [adj.: ἀποσυνάγωγος <656>]; **from *apo*: from, and *sunagogē*: synagogue, which is from *sunagō*: to lead together, to assemble ▶ Expelled from the synagogue; such a person might not go to the synagogue nor entertain relations with other Jews; also transl.: put out of the synagogue** > The Jews had agreed that if anyone confessed Jesus as the Christ, he should be excommunicated from the synagogue (John 9:22). Many rulers believed on Jesus, but did not confess Him, that they might not be excommunicated from the synagogue (John 12:42). Jesus warned His disciples that they would be excommunicated {be made outcasts} from the synagogues (John 16:2). ¶

EXCUSE (noun) – 1 Luke 14:18a → to make excuse → EXCUSE (verb) <3868> 2 John 15:22 → PRETEXT <4392> 3 Rom. 1:20; 2:1 → without excuse, no excuse → INEXCUSABLE <379>.

EXCUSE (verb) – 1 **to excuse oneself: *apologeomai*** [verb: ἀπολογέομαι <626>]; **from *apo*: from, and *logos*: word, speech ▶ To plead for oneself, to defend oneself** > The thoughts of those of the nations accuse or else excuse themselves between themselves {defend them} (Rom. 2:15). All other refs.: ANSWER (verb) <626>, DEFEND <626>, DEFENSE <626>.

2 ***paraiteomai*** [verb: παραιτέομαι <3868>]; **from *para*: near, and *aiteō*: to ask, to supplicate ▶ To express one's regrets, to ask forgiveness** > In a parable, various persons invited to a great supper excused themselves (Luke 14:18a {to make excuse}, b, 19). All other refs.: AVOID <3868>, BEG <3868>, REFUSE (verb) <3868>.

EXCUSING – ***apologia*** [fem. noun: ἀπολογία <627>]; **from *apologeomai*: to respond in defense of oneself, which is from *apo*: from, and *logos*: word, speech ▶ Reason given to be forgiven, defense against an accusation** > The Corinthians were excusing {clearing, vindicating, eager to clear} themselves because of godly sorrow (2 Cor. 7:11). All other refs.: ANSWER (noun) <627>, ANSWER (verb) <627>, DEFENSE <627>.

EXECUTE – 1 ***poieō*** [verb: ποιέω <4160>] ▶ **To perform, to realize; also transl.: to act, to accomplish, to do, to fulfill** > The Lord has come to execute judgment against all (Jude 15). God has given to the hearts of the ten horns to execute His mind and to act with one mind {to agree} in regard to great Babylon and the beast (Rev. 17:17a, b). Other refs.: see entries in Lexicon at <4160>.

– 2 Matt. 27:1 → to put to death → DEATH <2289> 3 Matt. 27:20 → PERISH <622> 4 Luke 23:32; Acts 13:28 → to put to death → DEATH <337> 5 John 5:27 → to execute judgment → lit.: to do judgment

→ DO <4160> 6 Acts 12:19 → to be put to death → DEATH <520> 7 Rom. 9:28 → FINISH <4931>.

EXECUTION – Acts 8:1 → DEATH <336>.

EXECUTIONER – Mark 6:27 → GUARD (noun) <4688>.

EXERCISE (noun) – ***gumnasia*** [fem. noun: γυμνασία <1129>]; **from *gumnazō*: to train athletically, which is from *gumnos*: naked ▶ Physical training, gymnastics >** Bodily exercise {discipline} is profitable for a little, but piety is profitable for everything (1 Tim. 4:8). ¶

EXERCISE (verb) – 1 ***askeō*** [verb: ἀσκέω <778>]; **lit.: to work at ▶ To endeavor, to make an effort >** Paul exercised himself {did his best, strived} to have in everything a conscience without offence toward God and men (Acts 24:16). ¶
2 ***gumnazō*** [verb: γυμνάζω <1128>]; **from *gumnos*: nude, wearing exercise clothes; original sense: to train in the nude (for athletic games) ▶ To train, to develop one's ability >** Timothy was to exercise himself to {discipline himself for the purpose of} piety (1 Tim. 4:7). Mature Christians have their senses exercised {trained} to discern both good and evil (Heb. 5:14). Chastening yields the peaceful fruit of righteousness to those who are exercised by it (Heb. 12:11). Peter speaks of those who have a heart exercised {practiced} {who are experts} in covetousness (2 Pet. 2:14). ¶
3 ***poieō*** [verb: ποιέω <4160>]; **lit.: to do, to perform ▶ To put into practice, to realize, to direct and manage >** There is not one that exercises {practices, does} goodness (Rom. 3:12). The second beast exercises all the authority of the first beast (Rev. 13:12). Other refs.: see entries in Lexicon at <4160>.
– 4 Matt. 20:25; Mark 10:42 → to exercise lordship, to exercise dominion → to lord over → LORD (verb) <2634> 5 Luke 22:25 → to exercise authority → AUTHORITY <1850> 6 1 Cor. 7:9 → to exercise self-control → CONTROL (noun) <1467> 7 1 Tim. 2:12 → to exercise authority → to usurp authority → AUTHORITY <831> 8 Rev. 13:5 → to exercise his authority → lit.: authority to continue → CONTINUE <4160> 9 Rev. 18:17 → to exercise one's calling → TRADE (verb) <2038>.

EXERTION – 1 Rom. 9:16 → human exertion → lit.: of the one running → RUN <5143> 2 Phil. 3:21 → WORKING (noun) <1753>.

EXHAUSTED – Luke 12:33 → that will not be exhausted → unfailing → FAIL <413>.

EXHIBIT – Jude 7 → to set forth → SET (verb) <4295>.

EXHORT – 1 ***paraineō*** [verb: παραινέω <3867>]; **from *para*: by the side, and *aineō*: to prescribe, to praise ▶ To warn, to advise >** Paul exhorted {urged} the sailors to be of good courage (Acts 27:22). Other refs.: Luke 3:18 in some mss.; Acts 27:9; see ADMONISH <3867>. ¶
2 ***parakaleō*** [verb: παρακαλέω <3870>]; **from *para*: beside, and *kaleō*: to call ▶ To encourage, to urge; also transl.: to appeal, to beg, to beseech, to comfort, to desire, to entreat, to implore, to intreat, to plead, to pray, to preach >** John the Baptist exhorted (Luke 3:18 {with many exhortations}) the people and preached the gospel. Peter exhorted {solemnly testified} in Acts (Acts 2:40) and in his first epistle (1 Pet. 2:11; 5:1, 12); Barnabas exhorted (Acts 11:23), as likewise Paul and Barnabas (Acts 14:22), Paul and Silas (Acts 16:40), Judas and Silas (Acts 15:32), Paul alone in Acts (Acts 20:2 {to give much exhortation}; 27:33, 34), and Jude (Jude 3). Paul uses the verb frequently in his epistles (e.g., Rom. 12:8; 1 Cor. 1:10; 2 Cor. 2:8; 8:6; 10:1; Eph. 4:1; 1 Thes. 2:11 (or v. 12); 4:1, 10; 5:14; 2 Thes. 3:12; 1 Tim. 2:1; 5:1; 6:2; Titus 2:6, 15). Other refs.: Rom. 12:1; 15:30; 16:17; 1 Cor. 14:31; 16:15; 2 Cor. 5:20 {to make an appeal}; 6:1; 1 Thes. 5:11; 2 Tim. 4:2; Titus 1:9; Heb. 3:13; 10:25; 13:22. All other refs.: see entries in Lexicon at <3870>.

3 ***protrepō*** [verb: προτρέπω <4389>]; **from *pro*: toward, and *trepō*: to turn ▶ To urge morally, to encourage** > The brothers of Ephesus exhorted {engaged} the disciples of Achaia to receive Apollos (Acts 18:27); more accurately: having encouraged Apollos, the brothers wrote to the disciples of Achaia to welcome him. See ENCOURAGE 5. ¶

EXHORTATION – 1 ***paraklēsis*** [fem. noun: παράκλησις <3874>]; **from *parakaleō*: see 2 ▶ Earnest advice or caution, encouragement, consolation; also transl.: appeal** > The rulers of the synagogue invited Paul and his companions to give some word of exhortation to the people (Acts 13:15). He who exhorts should occupy himself in exhortation {encouraging} (Rom. 12:8). He who prophesies speaks to men in exhortation (1 Cor. 14:3). Titus had received Paul's exhortation {entreaty} to go to the Corinthians (2 Cor. 8:17). Paul's exhortation was not of deceit, nor of uncleanness (1 Thes. 2:3). Timothy was to give himself to exhortation {preaching} until Paul came (1 Tim. 4:13). Other refs.: Heb. 12:5; 13:22. All other refs.: CONSOLATION <3874>, ENTREATY <3874>.
2 **to exhort: *parakaleō*** [verb: παρακαλέω <3870>]; **from *para*: beside, and *kaleō*: to call ▶ Admonition, encouragement** > With many other exhortations (lit.: Exhorting many other things), John the Baptist announced his glad tidings to the people (Luke 3:18). All other refs.: see entries in Lexicon at <3870>.

EXILE – 1 Matt. 1:11, 12, 17a, b → DEPORTATION <3350> 2 Acts 7:29 → became an exile → became a dweller → DWELLER <3941> 3 Acts 7:43 → to send into exile → TRANSPORT <3351> 4 Heb. 11:13; 1 Pet. 2:11 → SOJOURNER <3927> 5 1 Pet. 1:1 → STRANGER <3927> 6 1 Pet. 1:17 → STAY (noun) <3940>.

EXIST – 1 ***eimi*** [verb: εἰμί <1510>] **▶ To be** > The law of sin exists {is at work} in the members of one who has not been delivered (Rom. 7:23). There exists no authority except from God, and those that exist are set up of God (Rom. 13:1a, b).
2 ***huparchō*** [verb: ὑπάρχω <5225>]; **from *hupo*: under, and *archō*: to begin, which is from *archē*: beginning ▶ To put forward (as a pretext)** > No cause existed {There was no cause} whereby the Ephesians could give a reason for their disorderly gathering (Acts 19:40). Other refs.: see entries in Lexicon at <5225>.
– 3 John 17:5 → existed → lit.: was (*eimi*) 4 2 Pet. 3:7 → "that exist" added in Engl.

EXISTENCE – 1 Rom. 4:17 → calls into existence → lit.: calls as existing (or: being) 2 1 Cor. 8:4 → has no real existence → lit.: is nothing in the world.

EXODUS – Heb. 11:22 → DEPARTURE <1841>.

EXORCISE – Acts 19:13 → ADJURE <3726>.

EXORCIST – ***exorkistēs*** [masc. noun: ἐξορκιστής <1845>]; **from *exorkizō*: to require an oath, to adjure, which is from *ek*: intens., and *horkizō*: to adjure; lit.: someone who binds by an oath or a spell ▶ Individual who chases, or pretends to chase, demons from a possessed person** > Certain Jewish exorcists {driving out evil spirits} took in hand to call the name of the Lord Jesus upon those who had wicked spirits (Acts 19:13). ¶

EXPAND – 1 ***platunō*** [verb: πλατύνω <4115>]; **from *platus*: broad ▶ a. To make wider in a moral sense; also transl.: to enlarge, to open, to open wide** > Paul's heart was expanded for the Corinthians (2 Cor. 6:11); he tells them to expand their hearts also (v. 13). **b. To make wider** > The scribes and the Pharisees broaden {made broad, made wide} their phylacteries (Matt. 23:5). ¶
– 2 2 Cor. 10:15 → ENLARGE <3170>.

EXPECT – 1 ***prosdokaō*** [verb: προσδοκάω <4328>]; **from *pros*: to, and *dokaō*: to look for, from which *prosdokia*: expectation ▶**

To look for, to wait for > The lame man was expecting to receive something from Peter and John (Acts 3:5). All other refs.: EXPECTATION <4328>, LOOK (verb) <4328>, TARRY <4328>, WAIT (verb) <4328>.

2 ***huponoeō*** [verb: ὑπονοέω <5282>]; **from *hupo*: under, and *noeō*: to consider, to think, which is from *nous*: mind, understanding ▶ To conjecture, to suppose** > Paul's accusers brought no accusation against him of such things as Festus expected (Acts 25:18). Other refs.: Acts 13:25; 27:27; see SUPPOSE <5282>. ¶

– 3 Matt. 20:10 → SUPPOSE <3543> 4 Matt. 24:44; Luke 12:40 → THINK <1380> 5 Luke 6:35 → to expect in return, to expect to get something back → to hope in return → HOPE (verb) <560> 6 Acts 12:11 → what is expected → EXPECTATION <4329> 7 Acts 16:13 → to be the custom → CUSTOM <3543> 8 Rom. 8:19, 23, 25 → WAIT (verb) <553> 9 1 Cor. 16:11; Heb. 10:13 → WAIT (verb) <1551> 10 2 Cor. 10:2a → THINK <3049> 11 Phil. 1:20 → to expect eagerly → lit.: eager expectation → earnest expectation → EXPECTATION <603> 12 Jas. 1:7 → THINK <3633>.

EXPECTANTLY – Luke 3:15 → to wait expectantly → to be in expectation → EXPECTATION <4328>.

EXPECTATION – 1 **earnest expectation: *apokaradokia*** [fem. noun: ἀποκαραδοκία <603>]; **from *apokaradokeō*: to expect earnestly, which is from *apo*: intens., and *karadokeō*: to move the head to observe, to listen, which is from *kara*: head, and *dechomai*: to receive, or *dokeō*: to think, to appear ▶ Impatient, fervent, constant waiting** > The earnest expectation {anxious longing, anxious looking out} of the creation waits for the manifestation of the sons of God (Rom. 8:19). According to his earnest expectation and hope, Paul would be ashamed of nothing (Phil. 1:20); *karadokia* in some mss. ¶

2 ***prosdokia*** [fem. noun: προσδοκία <4329>]; **from *prosdokaō*: to wait, to expect, which is from *pros*: to, and *dokaō*: to expect, to look for ▶ Anticipation, what is waited for; also transl.: looking after, what is expected** > During the great tribulation, men will be ready to die through fear and expectation {to die apprehensive} of what is coming on the earth (Luke 21:26). The Lord had delivered Peter from all the expectation of the Jewish people {from everything they were anticipating} (Acts 12:11), i.e., from what they wanted to inflict on him. ¶

3 **to be in expectation: *prosdokaō*** [verb: προσδοκάω <4328>]; **see 2 ▶ To be waiting** > People were in expectation {were waiting expectantly} about John the Baptist whether he might be the Christ (Luke 3:15). All other refs.: EXPECT <4328>, LOOK (verb) <4328>, TARRY <4328>, WAIT (verb) <4328>.

4 ***ekdochē*** [fem. noun: ἐκδοχή <1561>]; **from *ekdechomai*: to expect, which is from *ek*: of, and *dechomai*: to receive ▶ Waiting, anticipation; also transl.: looking for** > If someone sins willfully after having received the knowledge of the truth, there remains a certain fearful expectation of judgment (Heb. 10:27). ¶

– 5 2 Cor. 8:5 → they exceeded our expectations → lit.: not as we hoped → HOPE (verb) <1679>.

EXPEDIENT – 1 John 11:50; 16:7; 18:14; 1 Cor. 6:12; 10:23; 2 Cor. 8:10 → to be expedient → to be profitable → PROFITABLE <4851> 2 2 Cor. 12:1 → of profit → PROFIT (noun) <4851>.

EXPEL – 1 Matt. 15:17 → ELIMINATE <1544> 2 Mark 7:19 → to be expelled → to go out → GO <1607> 3 Acts 13:50 → CAST (verb) <1544> 4 1 Cor. 5:13 → to take away → TAKE <1808>.

EXPEND – 1 Luke 10:35 → to expend more → to spend more → SPEND <4325> 2 2 Cor. 12:15b → SPEND <1550>.

EXPENSE – 1 ***opsōnion*** [neut. noun: ὀψώνιον <3800>]; **from *opson*: meat, food, and *ōneomai*: to buy ▶ Wage, cost** > Paul asks who there is that ever goes to war at his own expense {charges} (1 Cor. 9:7). Other refs.: Luke 3:14; Rom. 6:23; 2 Cor. 11:8; see WAGES <3800>. ¶

2 **to pay the expenses: *dapanaō*** [verb: δαπανάω <1159>]; **from *dapanē*: expense ▶ To pay the costs >** Paul was told to pay the expenses of {be at charges with} the men with whom he would purify himself (Acts 21:24). All other refs.: SPEND <1159>.

– 3 Luke 10:35 → for any extra expense → lit.: whatever would be spent more → to spend more → SPEND <4325> 4 Acts 28:30 → at his own expense → his own rented house → HOUSE <3410>.

EXPENSIVE – 1 Matt. 26:7 → very expensive → very precious → PRICE (noun) <927> 2 Mark 14:3 → very expensive → lit.: of great price → PRICE (noun) <4185> 3 Luke 7:25 → gorgeous → GORGEOUSLY <1741> 4 John 12:3 → of great price → PRICE (noun) <4186> 5 1 Tim. 2:9 → COSTLY <4185>.

EXPERIENCE (noun) – 1 ***dokimē*** [fem. noun: δοκιμή <1382>]; **from *dokimos*: approved; comp. *dechomai*: to receive ▶ Quality of being approved as a result of testing; also transl.: character, proven character >** Endurance produces experience, and experience produces hope (Rom. 5:4a, b). The saints glorified God through the experience (or: proof, experiment) of the ministry of other Christians in their regard (2 Cor. 9:13). All other refs.: PROOF <1382>, TEST (noun and verb) <1382>.

– 2 2 Cor. 1:15 → experience of grace → GRACE <5485>.

EXPERIENCE (verb) – 1 2 Cor. 1:6 → which you experience → lit.: being worked out → WORK (verb) <1754> 2 2 Cor. 1:8 → affliction we experienced → affliction which came to us → COME <1096> 3 Gal. 3:4 → SUFFER <3958> 4 Heb. 11:36 → to make trial → TRIAL <3984> 5 1 Pet. 5:9 → ACCOMPLISH <2005>.

EXPERIMENT – 2 Cor. 9:13 → EXPERIENCE (noun) <1382>.

EXPERT – 1 ***gnōstēs*** [masc. noun: γνώστης <1109>]; **from *ginoskō*: to know ▶ One who knows, authority, specialist >** Agrippa was an expert in {was well acquainted with} all Jewish customs and questions (Acts 26:3). ¶

– 2 Matt. 22:35; Luke 7:30; 10:25; 11:45, 46, 52; 14:3 → expert in the law → LAWYER <3544> 3 1 Cor. 3:10 → WISE (adj.) <4680> 4 2 Pet. 2:14 → those who are expert → lit.: those who have a heart trained (or: exercised) → EXERCISE (verb) <1128>.

EXPERT BUILDER – 1 Cor. 3:10 → MASTER BUILDER <753>.

EXPIRATION – Acts 21:26 → ACCOMPLISHMENT <1604>.

EXPIRE – 1 ***ekpneō*** [verb: ἐκπνέω <1606>]; **from *ek*: out, and *pneō*: to breathe, from which *pneuma*: breath, spirit ▶ To stop breathing, to die >** Jesus, having uttered a loud cry, expired {breathed His last, gave up the ghost} (Mark 15:37, 39; Luke 23:46). ¶

2 ***ekpsuchō*** [verb: ἐκψύχω <1634>]; **from *ek*: out, and *psuchō*: to breathe, from which *psuchē*: soul ▶ To stop breathing, to die; also transl.: to give up the ghost, to yield up the ghost, to breathe one's last, to die >** Ananias expired (Acts 5:5), as likewise Sapphira (v. 10). Herod expired (Acts 12:23). ¶

3 ***teleō*** [verb: τελέω <5055>]; **from *telos*: accomplishment, end ▶ To be accomplished, to be over >** When the thousand years have expired {have been completed, are over}, Satan will be released from his prison (Rev. 20:7). All other refs.: see entries in Lexicon at <5055>.

– 4 Acts 7:30 → PASS <4137>.

EXPLAIN – 1 ***dianoigō*** [verb: διανοίγω <1272>]; **from *dia*: through (intens.), and *anoigō*: to open ▶ To open completely, to cause to understand >** Paul explained {opened} and gave evidence that the Christ must have suffered and risen again (Acts 17:3). All other refs.: OPEN (verb) <1272>.

[2] ***diermēneuō*** [verb: διερμηνεύω <1329>]; **from *dia*: intens., and *hermēneuō*: to explain ▶ To interpret, to expound** > Jesus explained in all the Scriptures the things concerning Himself (Luke 24:27). Other refs.: Acts 9:36; 1 Cor. 12:30; 14:5, 13, 27; see INTERPRET <1329>. ¶

[3] ***ektithēmi*** [verb: ἐκτίθημι <1620>]; **from *ek*: out, and *tithēmi*: to put ▶ To expound, to set out, to set forth** > Peter began and explained the matter of his vision in order (Acts 11:4). Aquila and Priscilla explained {unfolded} to Apollos the way of God more exactly (Acts 18:26). Paul explained the truth, testifying of the kingdom of God (Acts 28:23). Other ref.: Acts 7:21; see EXPOSE <1620>. ¶

[4] ***epiluō*** [verb: ἐπιλύω <1956>]; **from *epi*: upon (intens.), and *luō*: to loosen ▶ To expose, to interpret** > Jesus explained {expounded} all things to His disciples (Mark 4:34). Other ref.: Acts 19:39; see SETTLE <1956>. ¶

– [5] Matt. 13:36; 15:15 → EXPOUND <5419> [6] John 1:18 → DECLARE <1834> [7] John 4:25 → TELL <312> [8] Acts 2:14 → let me explain → lit.: let it be known → KNOWN <1110> [9] Acts 10:8 → RELATE <1834> [10] 1 Cor. 2:13 → COMPARE <4793> [11] Heb. 5:11 → hard to explain → HARD <1421>.

EXPLICITLY – 1 Tim. 4:1 → EXPRESSLY <4490>.

EXPLOIT – [1] ***emporeuomai*** [verb: ἐμπορεύομαι <1710>]; **from *emporos*: merchant, one who trades, which is from *en*: in, and *poros*: passage, voyage; primary meaning: to do business ▶ To make use of someone for one's personal gain** > Peter speaks of those who by their greed will exploit {will make merchandise of} Christians with deceptive words (2 Pet. 2:3). The verb is also used in Jas. 4:13 and transl.: to buy and sell, to carry on business, to engage in business, to traffic. ¶

– [2] 2 Cor. 7:2; 12:17, 18 → CHEAT <4122> [3] 2 Cor. 11:20 → DEVOUR <2719> [4] Jas. 2:6 → OPPRESS <2616>.

EXPOSE – [1] ***ektithēmi*** [verb: ἐκτίθημι <1620>]; **from *ek*: out, and *tithēmi*: to put ▶ To set out, to set forth** > When Moses was exposed {placed outside, set out}, the daughter of Pharaoh took him up (Acts 7:21). All other refs.: see EXPLAIN <1620>.

– [2] Matt. 1:19 → to expose to public disgrace → to make a show → SHOW (noun) <3856> [3] John 3:20; Eph. 5:11, 13 → REPROVE <1651> [4] 1 Cor. 4:9 → to publicly expose → to make a public spectacle → SPECTACLE <2302> [5] Heb. 4:13 → OPEN (verb) <5136> [6] 2 Pet. 3:10 in some mss. → FIND <2147>.

EXPOSED – ***ekthetos*** [adj.: ἔκθετος <1570>]; **from *ektithēmi*: to expose, which is from *ek*: out of, and *tithēmi*: to put ▶ To put in danger, to put in peril; also transl.: to cast out** > An Egyptian king oppressed the Israelites, making them expose {forcing them to throw out} their newborn babies (lit.: making their babies exposed) (Acts 7:19). ¶

EXPOSITION OF THE LOAVES – **exposition: *prothesis*** [fem. noun: πρόθεσις <4286>]; **from *pro*: before, and *tithēmi*: to place; loaf: *artos*** [masc. noun: ἄρτος <740>] **▶ There were twelve loaves of bread in the holy place of the tabernacle which were arranged in two rows on the table of showbread** > The showbread {consecrated bread, sacred bread} (lit.: exposition of the loaves) represented the twelve tribes of Israel placed in perfection under the eyes of God, so that He might dwell in the midst of His people (see Ex. 25:23, 30; Lev. 24:5–9). The showbread was in the Holy Place of the tabernacle (Heb. 9:2). In a similar way, the redeemed of Christ form the present-day people of God represented as placed on the golden altar (figure of Christ who presents the people to God according to His own perfections). David ate the showbread reserved for the priests under the law (Matt. 12:4; Mark 2:26; Luke 6:4; see 1 Sam. 21:6); the priests ate the showbread on the Sabbath. Jesus availed Himself of this fact to show that He, the Son of God, who is greater than David, is the Lord of the Sabbath. All other refs. (*prothesis*): see PURPOSE (noun) <4286>. All other refs. (*artos*): see BREAD <740>, BREAK BREAD <740>.

EXPOSURE – 2 Cor. 11:27 → NAKEDNESS <1132>.

EXPOUND – 1 ***phrazō*** [verb: φράζω <5419>]; **has given the word *phrase* in Engl. ▶ To explain, to make known >** The disciples asked Jesus to expound {declare} His parables (Matt. 13:36; 15:15). ¶
– 2 Mark 4:34 → EXPLAIN <1956> 3 Luke 24:27 → EXPLAIN <1329> 4 Acts 11:4; 18:26; 28:23 → EXPLAIN <1620>.

EXPRESS (adj.) – Heb. 1:3 → express image → EXPRESSION <5481>.

EXPRESS (verb) – 1 1 Cor. 2:13 → COMPARE <4793> 2 Gal. 5:6 → WORKING (verb) <1754> 3 Eph. 2:15 → "expressed" added in Engl.

EXPRESSION – ***charaktēr*** [masc. noun: χαρακτήρ <5481>]; **from *charassō*: to sharpen, to engrave; lit.: imprint ▶ Exact representation and precise reproduction >** Jesus, the Son of God, is the expression {express image, exact representation} of the person (lit.: substance, essential being) of God (Heb. 1:3). ¶

EXPRESSLY – ***rhētōs*** [adv.: ῥητῶς <4490>]; **from *ereō*, which is derived from *legō*: to say ▶ Clearly, distinctly >** The Spirit speaks expressly {explicitly}, that in the latter times some will apostatize from the faith (1 Tim. 4:1). ¶

EXTEND – 1 Acts 4:30 → to stretch out → STRETCH <1614> 2 2 Cor. 4:15 → ABOUND <4121>.

EXTENT – 1 Cor. 11:18 → to some extent → in part → PART (noun) <3313>.

EXTERNAL – 1 2 Cor. 11:28 → except for → EXCEPT <3924> 2 Col. 3:22 → external service → EYESERVICE <3787> 3 Heb. 7:16 in some mss. → CARNAL <4559> 4 1 Pet. 3:3 → OUTWARD <1855>.

EXTINCTION – 2 Pet. 2:6 → RUIN (noun) <2692>.

EXTINGUISH – Eph. 6:16 → QUENCH <4570>.

EXTOL – 1 Acts 10:46; 19:17 → MAGNIFY <3170> 2 Rom. 15:11 → PRAISE (verb) <1867>.

EXTORT – Luke 3:14 → to extort money → OPPRESS <1286>.

EXTORTION – Matt. 23:25; Luke 11:39 → ROBBERY <724>.

EXTORTIONER – Luke 18:11; 1 Cor. 5:10, 11; 6:10 → RAPACIOUS <727>.

EXTRAORDINARY – 1 Luke 5:26 → STRANGE <3861> 2 Acts 19:11 → lit.: not the being ordinary → to be ordinary → ORDINARY <5177> 3 Acts 28:2 → lit.: not common → to be common → COMMON <5177>.

EXTREMELY – 1 Mark 16:4 → EXCEEDINGLY <4970> 2 Luke 18:23 → GREATLY <4970>.

EXTREMITY – 1 ***peras*** [neut. noun: πέρας <4009>]; **from *pera*: beyond ▶ End, remotest area >** The word is used in Rom. 10:18 in the expression "to the extremities of the habitable earth." All other refs.: END (noun) <4009>, PART (noun) <4009>.
2 **at extremity: *eschatōs*** [adv.: ἐσχάτως <2079>]; **from *eschatos*: last ▶ Near death >** The daughter of Jairus was at extremity {at the point of death, dying} (Mark 5:23). ¶
– 3 Matt. 24:31a, b; Mark 13:27a, b → END (noun) <206>.

EXULT – 1 ***agalliaō*** [verb: ἀγαλλιάω <21>]; **from *agan*: very much, and *hallomai*: to leap ▶ To be glad, to rejoice greatly; also transl.: to be exceeding glad,**

to be exceedingly glad > Jesus told His disciples to rejoice and exult (Matt. 5:12). Abraham exulted (John 8:56). David's tongue exulted (Acts 2:26). All other refs.: EXULTATION <21>, REJOICE <21>.
– 2 John 8:56 → REJOICE <5463>.

EXULTATION – 1 **to exult:** ***agalliaō*** [verb: ἀγαλλιάω <21>]**; from *agan*: very much, and *hallomai*: to leap ▶ To be glad, to be overjoyed** > To the extent that they are partakers of the sufferings of Christ, Christians are to rejoice, that in the revelation of His glory, they may rejoice with exultation {they may be glad with exceeding joy, they may be overjoyed} (lit.: they may rejoice in exulting) (1 Pet. 4:13). All other refs.: EXULT <21>, REJOICE <21>.
– 2 1 Thes. 2:19; et al. → reason to boast → GLORIFY <2746> 3 Jude 24 → exceeding joy → JOY (noun) <20>.

EYE – 1 ***ophthalmos*** [masc. noun: ὀφθαλμός <3788>]**; from *optomai*: to see; *oculus*, in Lat. ▶ Organ of vision** > Jesus spoke of the eye as a snare (Matt. 5:29; 18:9 a, c; Mark 9:47a, c), the question of eye for eye in the law (Matt. 5:38a, b), the eye as the lamp of the body (Matt. 6:22; Luke 11:34a, b), the wicked or evil eye (Matt. 6:23; 20:15; Mark 7:22), and the mote that is in the eye of one's brother and the beam that is in one's own eye (Matt. 7:3a, b, 4a, b, 5a, b; Luke 6:41a, b, 42a, b, c, d). In the twinkling of an eye, the dead in Christ will be raised incorruptible and the living will be changed (1 Cor. 15:52). A cloud received Jesus out of the sight (lit.: up from the eyes) of those who were watching (Acts 1:9). Other refs.: Matt. 9:29, 30; 13:15a, b, 16; 17:8; 20:33, 34a, b; 21:42; 26:43; Mark 8:18, 25; 12:11; 14:40; Luke 2:30; 4:20; 6:20; 10:23; 16:23; 18:13; 19:42; 24:16, 31; John 4:35; 6:5; 9:6, 10, 11, 14, 15, 17, 21, 26, 30, 32; 10:21; 11:37, 41; 12:40a, b; 17:1; Acts 9:8, 18, 40; 26:18; 28:27a, b; Rom. 3:18; 11:8, 10; 1 Cor. 2:9; 12:16, 17, 21; Gal. 3:1; 4:15; Eph. 1:18; Heb. 4:13; 1 Pet. 3:12; 2 Pet. 2:14; 1 John 1:1; 2:11, 16; Rev. 1:7, 14; 2:18; 3:18; 4:6, 8; 5:6; 7:17; 19:12; 21:4. ¶

2 ***omma*** [neut. noun: ὄμμα <3659>]**; from *optomai*: to see ▶ Word that is more poetical than the previous one** > It is used in some mss. in Matt. 20:34 and in Mark 8:23. ¶

3 **with one eye: *monophthalmos*** [adj.: μονόφθαλμος <3442>]**; from *monos*: only one, and *ophthalmos*: see 1; also transl.: one-eyed ▶ Having the use of only one eye** > It is better to enter into life with one eye than to have two eyes and to be cast into the hell of fire (Matt. 18:9b; Mark 9:47b). ¶
– 4 Matt. 19:24; Luke 18:25 → HOLE <5169>, <5168> 5 Acts 4:19 → in God's eyes → lit.: before God 6 Acts 7:55; 2 Cor. 3:13 → to fix one's eyes → to look steadfastly → LOOK (verb) <816> 7 Acts 23:1; 2 Cor. 3:7 → to fix the eyes → to behold earnestly → BEHOLD (verb) <816> 8 Rom. 16:17 → to keep one's eyes → CONSIDER <4648> 9 2 Cor. 10:7 → what is before your eyes → PRESENCE <4383> 10 Eph. 6:6; Col. 3:22 → when their eye is on you → lit.: not with eyeservice → EYESERVICE <3787> 11 Rev. 3:18 → eye salve → EYESALVE <2854>.

EYES – 1 **to fix the eyes: *skopeō*** [verb: σκοπέω <4648>]**; from *skopos*: goal ▶ To behold, to consider** > The Christian fixes his eyes {looks} not on the things that are seen but on the things that are not seen (2 Cor. 4:18). Paul exhorted the Philippians to fix their eyes on {to mark, to note, to observe, to take note of} those walking according to his model (Phil. 3:17). All other refs.: CONSIDER <4648>, REGARD (verb) <4648>, WATCH (verb) <4648>.
– 2 Luke 22:56 → to fix one's eyes upon → to look upon → LOOK (verb) <816> 3 Acts 1:9 → before their very eyes → lit.: while they were looking → LOOK (verb) <991>.

EYESALVE – ***kollourion*** [neut. noun: κολλούριον <2854>]; **from *kolla*: glue, or *kolloura*: coarse bread or cake; some mss. have *kollurion* ▶ Medicinal ointment applied to the eye for healing, collyrium** > The Lord tells the angel of the church of Laodicea to buy from Him eyesalve {eye salve, salve} and anoint his eyes that he may see (Rev. 3:18); this refers to the spiritual vision of the most responsible members of that church. ¶

EYESERVICE – ***ophthalmodouleia*** [fem. noun: ὀφθαλμοδουλεία <3787>]; **from *ophthalmos*: eye, and *douleia*: service; also spelled: *ophthalmodoulia*; from *doulos*: servant ▶ Service visible to the sight of men and accomplished to please men, in contrast to a service performed before God, in simplicity of heart and according to His will** > Servants are not to serve their masters with eye-service only {when their eye is on them} (Eph. 6:6; Col. 3:22). ¶

EYEWITNESS – 1 ***autoptēs*** [masc. noun: αὐτόπτης <845>]; **from *autos*: oneself, and *optomai*: to see ▶ One who sees with his own eyes** > In Luke 1:2, the eyewitnesses are those who have seen the Lord on earth with their own eyes. ¶

2 ***epoptēs*** [masc. noun: ἐπόπτης <2030>]; **from *epi*: on, and *optomai*: to see ▶ One who sees with his eyes** > In 2 Pet. 1:16, Peter writes that he was one of the eyewitnesses of the majesty of the Lord Jesus Christ at His transfiguration (see v. 17). ¶

EZECHIAS – See HEZEKIAH <1478>.

F

FABLE – ***muthos*** [masc. noun: μῦθος <3454>]; **close to *mutheō*: to say, to tell ▶ Invented story, imaginary event; also transl.: myth** > Fables seem to have been common among the Jews; Paul exhorts Timothy and Titus not to be attached to them (1 Tim. 1:4; Titus 1:14). Profane fables are to be rejected (1 Tim. 4:7). Paul also warns Timothy concerning those who will turn away from the truth and will turn aside to fables (2 Tim. 4:4). Peter had not made known the coming of the Lord by imagined fables (2 Pet. 1:16). ¶

FABRICATED – 2 Pet. 2:3 → FEIGNED <4112>.

FACE (noun) – 1 ***opsis*** [fem. noun: ὄψις <3799>]; **from *optanomai*: to see ▶ Front part of the head; appearance, visage** > The face of Lazarus was wrapped with a cloth (John 11:44). The face {countenance} of the Son of Man was like the sun (Rev. 1:16). Other ref.: John 7:24; see APPEARANCE <3799>. ¶

2 ***prosōpon*** [neut. noun: πρόσωπον <4383>]; **from *pros*: toward, and *ōps*: eye, face ▶ Visage, countenance, external appearance** > Jesus told the Pharisees and the Sadducees that they could discern the face {appearance} of the sky, but not the signs of the times (Matt. 16:3; Luke 12:56). John had preached the baptism of repentance before the coming of Jesus (lit.: before the face of His coming) (Acts 13:24). This term is also used in speaking of God or Christ (Matt. 11:10; 18:10; 26:39; Mark 1:2; Luke 1:76; 7:27; 9:51–53; 10:1; Acts 2:28; 3:19; 2 Cor. 4:6; Heb. 9:24; 1 Pet. 3:12; Rev. 6:16; 20:11; 22:4), Jesus (Matt. 17:2; 26:67; Mark 14:65; Luke 9:29), Moses (2 Cor. 3:7a, b, 13), those who fast (Matt. 6:16, 17), disciples (Matt. 17:6), people in the time of Jesus (Luke 5:12; 17:16), women at the tomb (Luke 24:5), Stephen (Acts 6:15a), angels (Acts 6:15b; Rev. 10:1), Paul (Acts 20:25, 38; Gal. 1:22 {sight, personally}; 2:11; Col. 2:1; 1 Thes. 2:17a {person, presence}, b; 3:10), Christians (1 Cor. 13:12a, b; 2 Cor. 3:18), an unbeliever or uninformed person (1 Cor. 14:25), the Corinthians (2 Cor. 11:20), angels (Rev. 7:11), and the twenty-four elders (Rev. 11:16). Other refs.: Luke 2:31; 21:35 (or: surface); 22:64 in some mss.; Acts 7:45; 17:26 (or: surface); 25:16; 2 Cor. 8:24 {before}; Jas. 1:23; Rev. 4:7; 9:7a, b; 12:14 {reach}. All other refs.: APPEARANCE <4383>, PERSON <4383>, PRESENCE <4383>.

– 3 Matt. 6:16 → to put on a gloomy face → to disfigure the face → DISFIGURE <853> 4 Mark 10:22 → his face fell → lit.: he was sad → to be sad → SAD <4768>.

FACE (verb) – 1 ***blepō*** [verb: βλέπω <991>] ▶ **To look** > Phoenix was facing southwest and northwest (Acts 27:12). Other refs.: SEE <991>.

– 2 Acts 27:15 → to head into → HEAD (verb) <503> 3 Rom. 4:19 → to face the fact → CONSIDER <2657> 4 1 Cor. 15:31 → to face death → DIE <599> 5 Heb. 11:36 → TRIAL <3984> 6 Jas. 1:2 → to fall into King Agrippa and others → FALL (verb) <4045>.

FACT – 1 **if in fact: *eiper*** [cond. expr.: εἴπερ <1512>] ▶ **If precisely, if it is thus** > God has not raised Christ if in fact {if indeed, if so be} those who are dead are not raised (1 Cor. 15:15). Other refs.: Rom. 8:9, 17; 1 Cor. 8:5; 2 Thes. 1:6; 1 Pet. 2:3. ¶

– 2 Matt. 16:8 → the fact that → lit.: because 3 Acts 21:34 → facts → CERTAINTY <804> 4 Acts 23:11; 2 Pet. 3:5 → "facts," "fact" added in Engl. 5 Rom. 4:19 → to face the fact → CONSIDER <2657> 6 2 Cor. 13:1 → WORD <4487>.

FACTION – 1 Cor. 11:19; Gal. 5:20 → SECT <139>.

FACTIOUS – Titus 3:10 → HERETICAL <141>.

FADE – 1 2 Cor. 3:7, 11, 13, 14 → to fade away → to do away → AWAY <2673> 2 Jas. 1:11b → to fade away → WITHER <3133> 3 1 Pet. 1:4 → that does not fade → UNFADING <263> 4 1 Pet. 5:4 → that does not fade away → UNFADING <262>.

FAIL – 1 ***ekleipō*** [verb: ἐκλείπω <1587>]; **from *ek*: out (intens.), and *leipō*: to fail ▶ To fall short of something; to cease,**

to stop > Jesus uses this verb in regard to unrighteous riches (Luke 16:9 {to be gone}). He had prayed for Peter, that his faith might not fail (Luke 22:32). The years of the Lord will not fail {will not come to an end, will never end} (Heb. 1:12). Other ref.: Luke 23:45; see DARKEN <4654>. ¶

[2] **unfailing, that does not fail:** ***anekleiptos*** [adj.: ἀνέκλειπτος <413>]; **from *a*: neg., and *ekleipō*: see [1] ▶ Which does not fall short of something; inexhaustible, that always remains** > Jesus told His disciples to make themselves a treasure in heaven that does not fail {that will not be exhausted} (Luke 12:33). ¶

[3] ***epileipō*** [verb: ἐπιλείπω <1952>]; **from *epi*: on (intens.), and *leipō*: to fail ▶ To lack, to be insufficient** > Time would have failed the author of the Epistle to the Hebrews {He did not have time} to tell of many people of faith in the O.T. (Heb. 11:32). ¶

[4] ***ekpiptō*** [verb: ἐκπίπτω <1601>]; **from *ek*: out of, and *piptō*: to fall ▶ To fall through, to lose one's place, to diminish** > Love never fails (1 Cor. 13:8). Other refs.: EFFECT (noun) <1601>, FALL (verb) <1601>, RUN <1601>.

– [5] Matt. 16:13 → fail to understand → lit.: do not understand [6] Luke 1:37 → to be impossible → IMPOSSIBLE <101> [7] Luke 16:17 → FALL (verb) <4098> [8] Luke 21:26 → HEART <674> [9] John 1:20 → to fail to confess → DENY <720> [10] Acts 5:38 → to be destroyed → DESTROY <2647> [11] Rom. 11:7 → failed to obtain → lit.: did not obtain [12] 2 Cor. 13:7 → to have failed → lit.: worthless → WORTHLESS <96> [13] Heb. 4:1 → to come short → COME <5302> [14] Heb. 12:15 → LACK (verb) <5302> [15] Jas. 5:4 → to fail to pay → to wrongfully keep back the pay → KEEP (verb) <650>.

FAILING – [1] Rom. 15:1 → WEAKNESS <771> [2] Heb. 12:12 → paralyzed → PARALYZED (BE) <3886>.

FAILURE – [1] ***hēttēma*** [neut. noun: ἥττημα <2275>]; **from *hēttaomai*: to be defeated, to be inferior ▶ What is missing, fault, diminution** > The failure {loss, diminishing} of Israel was riches for the Gentiles (Rom. 11:12). Other ref.: 1 Cor. 6:7; see FAULT <2275>. ¶

– [2] 1 Thes. 2:1 → a failure → lit.: in vain → VAIN <2756>.

FAIN – Luke 15:16 → would fain have → desired → DESIRE (verb) <1937>.

FAINT – [1] ***ekluō*** [verb: ἐκλύω <1590>]; **from *ek*: out (intens.), and *luō*: to loose ▶ To lose one's strength, to become weak** > If Jesus had the multitude sent away hungry to their own houses, they would have fainted {collapsed} on the way (Matt. 15:32; Mark 8:3). All other refs.: DISCOURAGED <1590>, HEART <1590>, WEARY (adj.) <1590>.

– [2] Luke 18:1, 2 Cor. 4:1, 16 → to lose heart → HEART <1457a> [3] Luke 21:26 → to have a failing heart → HEART <674> [4] Gal. 6:9 → to grow weary → WEARY (adj.) <1573>, under <1457a> [5] Eph. 3:13 → to lose heart → HEART <1573> [6] Rev. 2:3 → to grow weary → WEARY (adj.) <2872>.

FAINTHEARTED – [1] ***oligopsuchos*** [adj. used as noun: ὀλιγόψυχος <3642>]; **from *oligos*: small, and *psuchē*: soul ▶ Person who is discouraged, depressed** > Paul exhorts the church to encourage the fainthearted {feebleminded, disheartened, timid} (1 Thes. 5:14). ¶

– [2] Heb. 12:3 → DISCOURAGED <1590>.

FAIR – [1] **what is fair: *isotēs*** [fem. noun: ἰσότης <2471>]; **from *isos*: equal ▶ Likeness, equality, i.e., equal proportion** > Masters must give their bondservants what is just and fair {what is equal, fairness} (Col. 4:1). Other refs.: 2 Cor. 8:14a, b; see EQUALITY <2471>. ¶

– [2] Matt. 16:2 → fair weather → WEATHER <2105> [3] Acts 7:20 → exceeding fair, fair in the sight of God → well pleasing to God → PLEASING <791> <2316> [4] Rom. 16:18 → fair speeches →

SPEECH <2129> [5] Jas. 2:7 → WORTHY <2570> [6] Rev. 18:14 → RICH <3045>.

FAIR HAVENS – ***Kaloi Limenes*** [proper name: Καλοὶ Λιμένες <2568>]; **from *kalos*: beautiful, good, and *limēn*: port ▶ Seaport of southern Crete, near the city of Lasea** > The ship boarded by Paul came to Fair Havens on the way to Rome (Acts 27:8). ¶

FAIR-MINDED – Acts 17:11 → NOBLE <2104>.

FAIRLY – Col. 4:1 → to treat fairly → to give what is fair → FAIR <2471>.

FAIRNESS – 2 Cor. 8:13, 14; Col. 4:1 → EQUALITY <2471>.

FAITH – [1] ***pistis*** [fem. noun: πίστις <4102>]; **from *peithō*: to convince, to believe ▶ Trust, confidence; Heb. 11:1 says that faith is the assurance of things hoped for and the conviction of things not seen** > Faith comes by hearing, and hearing by the word of God (Rom. 10:17). It is a gift of God (Eph. 2:8). In the word of God, faith is not a mere opinion or belief, but a firm conviction based on God, Jesus Christ, invisible things, and spiritual things. Faith is presented in various aspects: a. the means by which one acquires salvation (e.g., Rom. 10:17; Eph. 2:8); b. the inner energy of the Christian fed by the word of God and directed by the Holy Spirit (e.g., 1 Tim. 4:12); c. the whole range of Christian truths and divine blessings received by faith (e.g., Eph. 4:5); d. a particular gift of grace of use in the church (e.g., 1 Cor. 12:9). Other refs.: FAITHFULNESS <4102>.

[2] **of little faith: *oligopistos*** [adj.: ὀλιγόπιστος <3640>]; **from *oligos*: little, and *pistis*: conviction, faith ▶ Not believing or trusting very much** > Jesus reproached His disciples, speaking to them as to people of little faith (Matt. 6:30; 8:26; 16:8; Luke 12:28); He addresses Peter as a man of little faith (Matt. 14:31). Jesus is the only one who uses this term. ¶

– [3] Matt. 13:58; 17:20; Mark 6:6; 16:14 → lack of faith, little faith, littleness of faith → UNBELIEF <570> [4] Matt. 21:22 → to have faith → BELIEVE <4100> [5] Rom. 4:22; 1 Cor. 7:22 → "faith" added in Engl. [6] Rom. 10:10 → to profess one's faith → lit: to make confession → CONFESSION <3670> [7] Gal. 3:9 → of faith → BELIEVING <4103> [8] Heb. 4:14 → the faith we profess → lit.: our profession → CONFESSION <3671> [9] Heb. 10:39 → BELIEVE <4102>.

FAITHFUL – [1] ***pistos*** [adj. and noun: πιστός <4103>]; **from *peithō*: to believe, to have confidence ▶ a. Which is reliable, sure; also transl.: trustworthy** > Paul uses the expr. "this is a faithful (or: true) saying" {the word is faithful} in his letters to Timothy and Titus (1 Tim. 1:15; 3:1; 4:9; 2 Tim. 2:11; Titus 3:8). John was told that the words spoken were faithful and true (Rev. 21:5; 22:6). **b. Worthy of confidence, person worthy of confidence; one who believes** > This term is often used to designate those who have faith, i.e., Christians (e.g., Col. 1:7). It designates a servant (Matt. 24:45; 25:21, 23), a manager (Luke 12:42), and men who are able to teach (2 Tim. 2:2). We find the exprs. "the faithful of the circumcision" (Acts 10:45) and the "saints and faithful in Christ Jesus" (Eph. 1:1). Those who are with the Lamb are called faithful (Rev. 17:14). Paul uses this Greek term several times in 1 Timothy (4:3, 10, 12; 5:16; 6:2). It is also used numerous times as an adj. to characterize God (e.g., 1 Cor. 1:9) and Jesus (e.g., Heb. 3:2). Other refs.: BELIEVING <4103>, SURE <4103>.

– [2] Matt. 1:19 → faithful to the law → RIGHTEOUS <1342> [3] Acts 11:23 → to remain faithful → CONTINUE <4357> [4] Rom. 12:12 → PERSEVERING <4342> [5] 1 Tim. 2:7 → faithful teacher → teacher in faith → FAITH <4102> [6] 1 Tim. 3:2, 12; Titus 1:6 → faithful to his wife → lit.: of one wife [7] Heb. 8:9 → to remain faithful → CONTINUE <1696> [8] 1 Pet. 4:10 → GOOD (adj.) <2570>.

FAITHFULLY – ***piston*** [adv.: πιστὸν <4102a>]; **from *pistos*: faithful, which is from *peithō*: to believe, to have confidence ▶ With faith, inspiring confidence** > John recognized that Gaius was acting faithfully in whatever he did toward the brothers (3 John 5).

FAITHFULNESS – ***pistis*** [fem. noun: πίστις <4102>]; **from *peithō*: to believe, to have confidence; lit.: faith, firm conviction ▶ Loyalty, trustworthiness; also transl.: faith, fidelity** > Faithfulness is one of the more important matters of the law (Matt. 23:23). The unbelief of some who did not have faith will not nullify the faithfulness of God (Rom. 3:3). Faithfulness is part of the fruit of the Spirit (Gal. 5:22). Titus was to teach servants to show faithfulness (Titus 2:10). Other refs.: FAITH <4102>.

FAITHLESS – 1 ***asunthetos*** [adj.: ἀσύνθετος <802>]; **from *a*: neg., and *suntithēmi*: to concur, which is from *sun*: together, and *tithēmi*: to put ▶ Oath breaker, disloyal** > Some men are faithless {covenantbreakers, untrustworthy} (Rom. 1:31). ¶

2 **to be faithless: *apisteō*** [verb: ἀπιστέω <569>]; **from *apistos*: unbelieving, untrustworthy, which is from *a*: neg., and *pistos*: believing, faithful ▶ To disbelieve, to be unfaithful** > If Christians are faithless (or: do not believe), Jesus Christ remains faithful (2 Tim. 2:13). All other refs. (to not believe): BELIEVE <569>.

– 3 Matt. 17:17; Mark 9:19; Luke 9:41; John 20:27; Rev. 21:8 → UNBELIEVING <571>.

FAITHLESSNESS – Rom. 3:3 → UNBELIEF <570>.

FALL (noun) – 1 ***paraptōma*** [neut. noun: παράπτωμα <3900>]; **from *parapiptō*: to fall beside, which is from *para*: beside, and *piptō*: to fall; figur.: to make a mistake, to miss ▶ Fault, sin; also transl.: transgression** > Through the fall of Israel, salvation has come to the Gentiles (Rom. 11:11); their fall is the wealth of the world (v. 12). All other refs.: TRANSGRESSION <3900>.

2 ***ptōsis*** [fem. noun: πτῶσις <4431>]; **from *piptō*: to fall ▶ Act of coming down** > The fall of the house built on the sand was great {it fell with a great crash} (Matt. 7:27). Jesus was set for the fall {falling} and rising up of many in Israel (Luke 2:34). ¶

FALL (verb) – 1 **to fall, to fall down: *piptō*** [verb: πίπτω <4098>] ▶ **a. To come down from a standing position, to collapse; also: to prostrate oneself** > The verb is used in regard to Jesus (Matt. 26:39; Mark 14:35), one house which withstood bad weather and another which collapsed (Matt. 7:25, 27; Luke 6:49: *sumpiptō* in other mss.), a sparrow (Matt. 10:29), seed (Matt. 13:4, 5, 7, 8; Mark 4:4, 5, 7, 8; Luke 8:5–8, 14; John 12:24), two blind men (Matt. 15:14: *sphallō* in other mss.; Luke 6:39), crumbs (Matt. 15:27; Luke 16:21), the disciples (Matt. 17:6), a boy who had seizures (Matt. 17:15), a servant (Matt. 18:26, 29), a stone (Matt. 21:44a, b; Luke 20:18a, b), stars (Matt. 24:29; Rev. 6:13; 8:10a, b; 9:1), Jairus (Mark 5:22; Luke 8:41), a child possessed by a spirit (Mark 9:20), a leper (Luke 5:12), Satan (Luke 10:18), a house set against itself (Luke 11:17), the tower in Siloam (Luke 13:4), one stroke of a letter of the law (Luke 16:17 {to drop out, to fail}), a Samaritan (Luke 17:16 {to throw}), Jews during the capture of Jerusalem (Luke 21:24), mountains during the great tribulation (Luke 23:30), Mary (John 11:32), those who wanted to seize Jesus (John 18:6), the lot that designated Matthias (Acts 1:26), Ananias and Sapphira (Acts 5:5, 10), Paul (Acts 9:4; 22:7), Cornelius (Acts 10:25), the tabernacle of David (Acts 15:16), Eutychus (Acts 20:9), Jews (Rom. 11:11, 22), a servant (Rom. 14:4), people who committed sexual immorality (1 Cor. 10:8 {to die}), he who thinks he is standing (1 Cor. 10:12), one whose secrets of the heart are manifested (1 Cor. 14:25), Israelites in the desert (Heb. 3:17), one who does not listen to the word of God (Heb. 4:11), the walls of Jericho (Heb. 11:30), the Christian brothers of James (Jas. 5:12), John (Rev. 1:17; 19:10;

22:8), twenty-four elders (Rev. 4:10; 5:8, 14; 11:16), the mountains and the rocks (Rev. 6:16), angels (Rev. 7:11), part of Jerusalem (Rev. 11:13), Babylon the Great (Rev. 14:8a, b; 18:2a, b), the cities of the nations (Rev. 16:19), five kings (Rev. 17:10), and fear (Rev. 11:11 {to strike}). **b. To bow down in order to worship** > The wise men fell down and worshipped Jesus at Bethlehem (Matt. 2:11). The devil wanted Jesus to fall down before him (Matt. 4:9). Twenty-four elders and four living creatures fell down and worshiped God (Rev. 19:4). All other refs.: PERISH <4098>, STRIKE <4098>.

2 to fall from: *apopiptō* [verb: ἀποπίπτω <634>]; **from *apo*: from, and *piptō*: see 1 ▶ To come down** > Something like scales fell from Paul's eyes (Acts 9:18). ¶

3 to fall; to fall away, down, off: *ekpiptō* [verb: ἐκπίπτω <1601>]; **from *ek*: out, and *piptō*: see 1 ▶ To drop down, to descend from its position** > By attempting to be justified by law, the Galatians had fallen from grace (Gal. 5:4). The error of the wicked may induce Christians to fall from their own steadfastness (2 Pet. 3:17). The church of Ephesus had to remember from where it had fallen (Rev. 2:5). The verb is also used in regard to the stars of heaven (Mark 13:25), chains (Acts 12:7), a ship and its passengers (Acts 27:17 {to run aground}), a ship's boat (Acts 27:32), and the flower (Jas. 1:11; 1 Pet. 1:24). Other refs.: EFFECT (noun) <1601>, FAIL <1601>, RUN <1601>.

4 to fall into: *empiptō* [verb: ἐμπίπτω <1706>]; **from *en*: in, and *piptō*: see 1 ▶ To be brought down** > The verb is used in regard to a sheep (Matt. 12:11), a man who fell into the hands of thieves (Luke 10:36), a donkey or an ox (Luke 14:5), a new convert (1 Tim. 3:6), an overseer (1 Tim. 3:7), and those who desire to become rich (1 Tim. 6:9). It is a fearful thing to fall into the hands of the living God (Heb. 10:31). ¶

5 *epipiptō* [verb: ἐπιπίπτω <1968>]; **from *epi*: upon, and *piptō*: see 1 ▶ a. To descend, to take possession** > The Holy Spirit had not yet fallen {come} upon any of those of Samaria (Acts 8:16). Peter fell into a trance (lit.: a trance fell on Peter) (Acts 10:10); some mss. have *ginomai*: to be, to become. The Holy Spirit fell upon all those who heard the message of Peter (Acts 10:44; 11:15). The verb is used in regard to a mist and darkness which fell upon Elymas (Acts 13:11). Reproaches fell upon Christ (Rom. 15:3). **b. To throw oneself, to rush** > Those who had afflictions fell upon {beset, pressed about, pressed upon, pressed around, pushed forward} Jesus that they might touch Him (Mark 3:10). The father fell upon his son's neck {embraced him, threw his arms around him} (Luke 15:20). Paul fell upon {threw himself on} Eutychus (Acts 20:10). The elders of Ephesus fell upon Paul's neck {embraced Paul} (Acts 20:37). Other refs.: Luke 1:12; Acts 19:17; see SEIZE <1968>. ¶

6 to fall down: *katapiptō* [verb: καταπίπτω <2667>]; **from *kata*: down, and *piptō*: see 1 ▶ To collapse** > Saul and those who accompanied him all fell to the ground (Acts 26:14). They expected Paul to suddenly fall down dead (Acts 28:6). Other ref.: Luke 8:6; some mss. have *piptō*. ¶

7 to fall away: *parapiptō* [verb: παραπίπτω <3895>]; **from *para*: beside, and *piptō*: see 1 ▶ To deviate from a path, to turn away** > Heb. 6:6 speaks of those having fallen away, crucifying for themselves the Son of God; they were not true Christians, having only tasted of the heavenly gift (see vv. 4, 5). ¶

8 to fall among, into, into the hands: *peripiptō* [verb: περιπίπτω <4045>]; **from *peri*: around, and *piptō*: see 1 ▶ a. To be surrounded by** > A man went down from Jerusalem to Jericho, and fell among robbers (Luke 10:30). **b. To be exposed, to go through** > James says to his brothers to count it all joy when they fall into {encounter, face} various trials (Jas. 1:2). Falling into {Striking} a place where two seas met, Paul's ship was run aground (Acts 27:41). ¶

9 to fall down before, to fall at the feet (or knees): *prospiptō* [verb: προσπίπτω <4363>]; **from *pros*: before, and *piptō*: see 1 ▶ To cast (oneself) before** > The unclean spirits fell down before Jesus (Mark 3:11). Women fell down at His feet (Mark 5:33; 7:25; Luke 8:47). Simon Peter fell at His knees (Luke 5:8). A possessed man fell down before Him (Luke 8:28). The jailer fell down before Paul and Silas (Acts 16:29). Other ref.: Matt. 7:25; see "to beat upon" under BEAT <4363>. ¶

10 **fallen down from heaven: *diopetēs*** [adj.: διοπετής <1356>]; **from *Dios*: Zeus, the chief god of the Greeks, and *piptō*: see** 1 ▶ **Come from heaven** > The town clerk maintained that the image of Diana had fallen down from heaven (Acts 19:35). ¶

11 **to fall, to fall down: *katabainō*** [verb: καταβαίνω <2597>]; **from *kata*: down, and *bainō*: to go ▶ To come down, to descend** > The verb is used in regard to rain (Matt. 7:25, 27). The sweat of the Lord became as great drops of blood falling down to the ground (Luke 22:44). All other refs.: COME <2597>, DESCEND <2597>, GO <2597>, STEP (verb) <2597>.

12 **to fall by transgression: *parabainō*** [verb: παραβαίνω <3845>]; **from *para*: away from, and *bainō*: to go ▶ To move away, to forsake; also transl.: to turn aside, to leave** > Judas by transgression fell {Judas transgressing fell} from his ministry and apostleship (Acts 1:25). Other refs.: Matt. 15:2, 3; 2 John 9 in some mss.; see TRANSGRESS <3845>. ¶

13 ***brechō*** [verb: βρέχω <1026>] ▶ **To rain** > During the great tribulation, the two prophets will have the power to shut up the sky, so that rain will not fall during the days of their prophesying (Rev. 11:6). All other refs.: RAIN (noun) <1026>, RAIN (verb) <1026>, WASH <1026>.

14 ***epiballō*** [verb: ἐπιβάλλω <1911>]; **from *epi*: upon, and *ballō*: to put ▶ To accrue, to be given by right of inheritance** > A son asked his father to give him the share of the property that fell to him (Luke 15:12). All other refs.: BEAT <1911>, LAY <1911>, PUT <1911>, THINK <1911>.

15 ***erchomai*** [verb: ἔρχομαι <2064>] ▶ **To come** > The verb is used in the expr. "to fall into disrepute" {to be set at nought, to come into discredit, to lose one's good name} (Acts 19:27). Other refs.: COME <2064>.

16 **to come upon, to come up to: *ephistēmi*** [verb: ἐφίστημι <2186>]; **from *epi*: upon, and *histēmi*: to stand ▶ To throw oneself on, to assail** > The people, the elders, and the scribes came upon Stephen and seized him (Acts 6:12). The verb is also transl. "to fall" and used in regard to rain (Acts 28:2). All other refs.: ASSAULT (verb) <2186>, COME <2186>, HAND (noun) <2186>, READY <2186>, STAND (verb) <2186>.

17 ***katapherō*** [verb: καταφέρω <2702>]; **from *kata*: down, and *pherō*: to carry ▶ To be oppressed, to be overwhelmed** > Eutychus, being fallen (*katapherō*) into {sinking into, overcome by, overpowered by} a deep sleep as Paul talked, fell down (*piptō*) from the third story (Acts 20:9a, b). Other refs.: Acts 25:7; 26:10; see CAST (verb) <2702>. ¶

18 ***kopazō*** [verb: κοπάζω <2869>]; **from *kopos*: work ▶ To cease; also transl.: to die down, to stop** > The verb is used in regard to the wind which died down at the Lord's command (Mark 4:39), likewise, when He went up into a ship (Matt. 14:32; Mark 6:51). ¶

– 19 Matt. 7:27 → FALL (noun) <4431> 20 Matt. 13:20, 22, 23 → SOW (verb) <4687> 21 Matt. 13:21; 17:27; 24:10; 26:31, 33; Mark 4:17; 14:27, 29; Luke 7:23; John 16:1; Rom. 14:21; 2 Cor. 11:29 → to fall, to fall away → OFFEND <4624> 22 Mark 5:6; Rev. 3:9 → to fall on one's knees, to fall down → WORSHIP (verb) <4352> 23 Luke 8:13; 1 Tim. 4:1; Heb. 3:12 → to fall away → DEPART <868> 24 Acts 5:15 → OVERSHADOW <1982> 25 Rom. 8:15 → to fall back into → lit.: again for 26 Rom. 9:33; 1 Pet. 2:8 → that makes them fall → of offense → OFFENSE <4625> 27 Rom. 14:13; 16:17 → cause to fall, occasion of falling, occasion to fall → STUMBLING BLOCK <4625> 28 Rom. 14:21 → STUMBLE <4350> 29 Heb. 12:15 → to fall short → LACK (verb) <5302> 30 Jas. 2:10; 2 Pet. 1:10 → STUMBLE <4417> 31 Jude 24 → without falling → without stumbling → STUMBLE <679>.

FALL-TRAP – 1 Rom. 11:9; 14:13 → STUMBLING BLOCK <4625> 2 1 Cor. 8:13a, b → to be a fall-trap → OFFEND <4624>.

FALLING – Luke 2:34 → FALL (noun) <4431>.

FALLING AWAY – 2 Thes. 2:3 → APOSTASY <646>.

FALSE – [1] ***pseudēs*** [adj.: ψευδής <5571>]; **from *pseudomai*: to lie, to deceive ► Lying, deceiving >** False witnesses were produced against Stephen (Acts 6:13). Other refs.: Rev. 2:2; 21:8; see LIAR (adj. and noun) <5571>. ¶
[2] **false brother: *pseudadelphos*** [masc. noun: ψευδάδελφος <5569>]; **from *pseudēs*: see [1], and *adelphos*: brother, which is from *a*: particle of union, and *delphus*: womb ► Person pretending to be a Christian, without being one in reality >** Paul had been in dangers among false brothers {false believers} (2 Cor. 11:26). False brothers had spied out the liberty which believers have in Christ Jesus (Gal. 2:4). ¶
[3] **false apostle: *pseudapostolos*** [masc. noun: ψευδαπόστολος <5570>]; **from *pseudēs*: see [1], and *apostolos*: one who is sent, apostle, which is from *apostellō*: to send, which is from *apo*: away, and *stellō*: to send ► Person who falsely pretends to be an apostle >** Paul speaks of false apostles of Christ (2 Cor. 11:13); they sought an occasion to lift themselves up against Paul and glorify themselves (see v. 12). ¶
[4] **false teacher: *pseudodidaskalos*** [masc. noun: ψευδοδιδάσκαλος <5572>]; **from *pseudēs*: see [1], and *didaskalos*: teacher, which is from *didaskō*: to teach ► One who falsely pretends to be a teacher; instructor of false principles, erroneous doctrine >** Peter warns against false teachers (2 Pet. 2:1). Paul also warns against teachers who do not bring sound doctrine (see 2 Tim. 4:3). ¶
[5] **false prophet: *pseudoprophētēs*** [masc. noun: ψευδοπροφήτης <5578>]; **from *pseudēs*: see [1], and *prophētēs*: prophet, which is from *prophēmi*: to announce beforehand, to predict ► One who falsely pretends to be a prophet, to communicate God's thoughts >** Jesus warns against false prophets (Matt. 7:15). When the abomination of desolation stands up, false prophets will arise (Matt. 24:11, 24; Mark 13:22). The fathers of the Jews had spoken well of false prophets (Luke 6:26). Bar-Jesus was a false prophet (Acts 13:6). There were false prophets in Israel (2 Pet. 2:1). Many false prophets have gone out into the world (1 John 4:1). The "false prophet" is another name for the antichrist (Rev. 16:13; 19:20; 20:10). ¶
[6] **false christ: *pseudochristos*** [masc. noun: ψευδόχριστος <5580>]; **from *pseudēs*: see [1], and *Christos*: Christ ► One who falsely pretends to be the Christ >** When the abomination of desolation stands up, false christs will arise (Matt. 24:24; Mark 13:22). ¶
– [7] John 7:18 → there is nothing false → lit.: there is no unrighteousness → UNRIGHTEOUSNESS <93> [8] Rom. 3:4 → LIAR (noun) <5583> [9] Phil. 3:2 → false circumcision → CONCISION <2699> [10] 2 Thes. 2:9, 11; Rev. 21:27 → LIE (noun) <5579> [11] 1 Tim. 1:3; 6:3 → to teach false doctrines → DOCTRINE <2085> [12] Titus 2:3 → false accuser → ACCUSER <1228> [13] 2 Pet. 2:3 → FEIGNED <4112>.

FALSE (BE) – Jas. 3:14 → to be false to → to lie against → LIE (verb)[2] <5574>.

FALSE-NAMED – 1 Tim. 6:20 → FALSELY NAMED <5581>.

FALSEHOOD – [1] John 7:18 → UNRIGHTEOUSNESS <93> [2] John 8:44; Rom. 1:25; Eph. 4:25; 2 Thes. 2:9; Rev. 22:15 → LIE (noun) <5579> [3] Rom. 3:7 → LIE (noun) <5582> [4] 1 John 4:6 → ERROR <4106>.

FALSELY – Matt. 5:11 → falsely, to say falsely → LIE (verb)[2] <5574>.

FALSELY CALLED – 1 Tim. 6:20 → FALSELY NAMED <5581>.

FALSELY NAMED – ***pseudōnumos*** [adj.: ψευδώνυμος <5581>]; **from *pseudēs*: false, and *onoma*: name ► Deceivingly so-called, self-styled, pretended >** Timothy was to avoid the oppositions of falsely named {falsely called, false-named} knowledge (1 Tim. 6:20). ¶

FALSIFY – ***doloō*** [verb: δολόω <1389>]; **from *dolos*: deceit; *dolus*, in Lat.: trick, ruse, bad faith; lit.: to cause to fall into a snare ▶ To corrupt with error, to alter; also transl.: to adulterate, to distort, to handle deceitfully** > Paul had not falsified the word of God (i.e., by mixing false teachings with its truths), but has commended himself by the manifestation of the truth (2 Cor. 4:2). ¶

FAME – [1] ***akoē*** [fem. noun: ἀκοή <189>]; **from *akouō*: to hear ▶ That which is reported regarding someone, reputation; also transl.: news, report** > The fame of Jesus went out into all Syria (Matt. 4:24) and into the whole region of Galilee (Mark 1:28). Herod heard of the fame of Jesus (Matt. 14:1). All other refs.: EAR <189>, HEARING <189>, REPORT (noun) <189>, RUMOR <189>.
[2] ***phēmē*** [fem. noun: φήμη <5345>]; **from *phēmi*: to say ▶ Rumor, that which is reported; also transl.: news, report** > After the resurrection of the young girl by Jesus, the fame of it went out into all that land (Matt. 9:26). Other ref.: Luke 4:14; see NEWS <5345>. ¶
– [3] Matt. 9:31 → to spread the fame → to spread the news → NEWS <1310> [4] Luke 4:37 → REPORT (noun) <2279> [5] Luke 5:15 → REPORT (noun) <3056> [6] 2 Cor. 8:18 → PRAISE (noun) <1868>.

FAMILIAR – [1] Acts 26:3 → to be familiar → to be an expert → EXPERT <1109> [2] Acts 26:26 → to be familiar with → KNOW <1987>.

FAMILY – [1] ***genos*** [neut. noun: γένος <1085>]; **from *ginomai*: to become ▶ Person closely related by blood, relatives; near relations** > The family {kindred} of Joseph became known to Pharaoh (Acts 7:13). All other refs.: see entries in Lexicon at <1085>.
[2] ***patria*** [fem. noun: πατριά <3965>]; **from *patēr*: father ▶ Lineage, descendants; also transl.: kindred, line** > Joseph, the husband of Mary, was of the family of David (Luke 2:4). All the families of the earth shall be blessed in the offspring of Abraham (Acts 3:25). From God the Father is named every family in the heavens and on earth (Eph. 3:15). It should be noted that Christians of the present period of grace have a spiritual relationship of adoption with God the Father (see Eph. 1:5), and thus constitute His family. ¶
– [3] Mark 3:21 → RELATIVE <846> [4] Luke 16:27 → father's house → FATHER <3962>, HOUSE <3624> [5] John 7:42 → SEED <4690> [6] Acts 7:14 → RELATIVES <4772> [7] Acts 7:20 → by his family → lit.: in his father's house [8] Acts 16:34 → with his whole family → with all the household → HOUSEHOLD <3832> [9] Rom. 16:10 → "family" added in Engl. [10] Gal. 6:10; 1 Tim. 5:8 → of the immediate family, who belongs to the family → of the household → HOUSEHOLD <3609> [11] 1 Thes. 4:10 → God's family → lit.: brothers [12] 1 Tim. 3:4, 5; 1 Pet. 4:17 → HOUSE <3624>.

FAMILY OF BELIEVERS – 1 Pet. 2:17; 5:9 → BROTHERHOOD <81>.

FAMINE – ***limos*** [masc. and fem. noun: λιμός <3042>] ▶ **Extreme lack of food, hunger affecting a wide area** > Before the end, there will be famines in various places (Matt. 24:7; Mark 13:8; Luke 21:11); famine will also come upon Babylon the great (Rev. 18:8). There was a great famine in the days of Elijah (Luke 4:25). A severe famine occurred in the land where the prodigal son had gone (Luke 15:14). In the days of Jacob, there was a famine {dearth} in all the land of Egypt (Acts 7:11). Agabus indicated by the Spirit that there was going to be a great famine {dearth} over all the inhabited earth (Acts 11:28). Paul asks rhetorically if famine shall separate Christians from the love of Christ (Rom. 8:35). Other refs.: Luke 15:17; 2 Cor. 11:27; Rev. 6:8; see HUNGER (noun) <3042>. ¶

FAMOUS – 2 Cor. 8:18 → who is famous for → whose praise is in → PRAISE (noun) <1868>.

FAN (noun) – Matt. 3:12; Luke 3:17 → WINNOWING FAN <4425>.

FAN (verb) – 2 Tim. 1:6 → to fan into flame → REKINDLE <329>.

FAR – [1] ***makros*** [adj.: μακρός <3117>] ▶ **At a great distance, remote; also transl.: distant** > The prodigal son journeyed to a far {long way off} country (Luke 15:13). A certain nobleman went into a far country (Luke 19:12). Other refs.: Matt. 23:14; Mark 12:40; Luke 20:47; see LONG (adj.) <3117>. ¶
[2] ***makran*** [adv. and adv. used as noun: μακράν <3112>]; **from *makros*: far, long, far off ▶ Long way, at a distance, opposed to one who is near** > Refs.: Matt. 8:30; Mark 12:34; Luke 7:6; 15:20; John 21:8; Acts 2:39; 17:27; 22:21; Eph. 2:13, 17. ¶ ‡
[3] ***porrō*** [adv.: πόρρω <4206>]; **from *pro*: in front, before ▶ Much distant, much remote** > God says that the heart of His people was far (lit.: was far far, was distant far) from Him (Matt. 15:8; Mark 7:6). The word is transl. "far off," "far away," "a great way off," "a long way off" in Luke 14:32. ¶
[4] **to be far: *porrō*** [adv: πόρρω <4206>]: **far, at a distance, a great way off; *apechō*** [verb: ἀπέχω <568>]; **from *apo*: from, and *echō*: to have, to hold ▶ To be at a great distance** > The heart of Israel was far (lit.: was far distant) from God (Matt. 15:8; Mark 7:6). Emmaus was (*apechō*; lit.: was distant) seven miles from Jerusalem (Luke 24:13). Other refs. (*apechō*): Luke 7:6; 15:20. All other refs.: HAVE <568>, POSSESS <568>.
– [5] Matt. 16:22 → far from you → lit.: be merciful to yourself → FAVORABLE <2436> [6] Matt. 25:14 → to travel to a far country → COUNTRY <589> [7] Mark 6:35 → far passed, far spent → PASS <4183> [8] Rom. 13:12 → to be far spent → SPEND <4298> [9] 2 Tim. 3:9 → to get far → lit.: to proceed further → PROCEED <4298> [10] 2 John 9 → to go too far → TRANSGRESS <4254>.

FAR OFF – Luke 23:49; Rev. 18:10, 15, 17 → at a distance → DISTANCE <575> <3113>.

FARE – Luke 16:19 → to fare → to be merry → MERRY <2165>.

FAREWELL – [1] **to bid farewell: *apotassō*** [verb: ἀποτάσσω <657>]; **from *apo*: from, and *tassō*: to place in order, to determine ▶ To say words, good wishes at parting** > A man asked Jesus to let him first go and bid farewell {bid adieu, say good-bye} to his own before following Him (Luke 9:61). Paul bade farewell to the Jews {took leave of them, left them} in the synagogue of Ephesus (Acts 18:21). Other ref.: Mark 6:46 {to leave}. All other refs.: FORSAKE <657>, LEAVE (noun) <657>, SEND <657>.
[2] **lit.: to farewell: *rhōnnumi*** [verb: ῥώννυμι <4517>] ▶ **To be strong; form of greetings similar to "good-bye"** > This verb is used in Acts 15:29 {Fare ye well}, and 23:30 in some mss. ¶
– [3] Acts 20:1; 21:5, 6 → to say farewell → EMBRACE <782>.

FARM (noun) – Matt. 22:5; et al. → FIELD <68>.

FARM (verb) – Heb. 6:7 → CULTIVATE <1090>.

FARMER – ***geōrgos*** [masc. noun: γεωργός <1092>]; **from *gē*: soil, and *ergon*: toil, labor ▶ One who prepares the soil for sowing and gathers the crop; also transl.: husbandman** > The hardworking farmer must work first before partaking of the crops (2 Tim. 2:6). The farmer {laborer} waits for the precious fruit of the earth (Jas. 5:7). All other refs.: VINEDRESSER <1092>.

FARTHER – [1] ***porrōteron*** [adv.: πορρώτερον <4208>]; **compar. of *porrō*: far off; also spelled: *porrōterō*** ▶ **At a greater distance** > With the disciples of Emmaus Jesus made as though He would go farther {further} (Luke 24:28). ¶
[2] **to go a little farther: *diistēmi*** [verb: διΐστημι <1339>]; **from *dia*: apart, and *histēmi*: to stand ▶ To move away, to pass** > The verb is used in Acts 27:28; also transl.: a little further, a short time later. In Luke 22:59, the verb is used in the expr.

"after about an hour had passed." Other ref.: Luke 24:51; see SEPARATE <1339>. ¶

FARTHEST – Mark 13:27a, b → farthest part → END (noun) <206>.

FARTHING – [1] Matt. 5:26; Mark 12:42 → QUADRANS <2835> [2] Matt. 10:29; Luke 12:6 → PENNY <787>.

FASHION (noun) – [1] ***eidos*** [neut. noun: εἶδος <1491>]; **from *eidō*: to see ► External appearance, what is seen >** The fashion of the countenance {appearance of the face} of Jesus became different on the mountain (Luke 9:29). All other refs.: FORM (noun) <1491>, SIGHT (noun) <1491>.
– [2] Acts 7:44 → PATTERN <5179> [3] 1 Cor. 7:31 → APPEARANCE <4976> [4] 2 Thes. 3:12 → in quiet fashion → lit.: in quietness → QUIETNESS <2271> [5] Jas. 1:11 → APPEARANCE <4383>.

FASHION (verb) – [1] 2 Cor. 5:5 → PREPARE <2716> [2] 1 Pet. 1:14 → CONFORM <4964>.

FASHIONED – Phil. 3:21 → CONFORMED <4832>.

FAST – [1] Matt. 19:5 → to hold fast → JOIN <4347> [2] Acts 16:24 → to make fast → FASTEN <805> [3] Acts 27:41 → to stick fast → STICK (verb) <2043> [4] 1 Cor. 16:13; Gal. 5:1; Phil. 1:27; 4:1; 1 Thes. 3:8; 2 Thes. 2:15 → to stand fast → to stand firm → FIRM <4739> [5] Rev. 12:17 → to hold fast → KEEP (verb) <5083>.

FAST (HOLD) – [1] ***antechō*** [verb: ἀντέχω <472>]; **from *anti*: to, against, and *echō*: to hold ► To firmly adhere, to stay attached >** The overseer must hold fast {cling to, hold firmly to} the faithful word according to the doctrine he has been taught (Titus 1:9). All other refs.: HOLD (verb) <472>, SUPPORT (verb) <472>.

[2] ***katechō*** [verb: κατέχω <2722>]; **from *kata*: intens., and *echō*: to hold ► To retain, to keep, to stay firmly attached >** Christians are to hold fast {to hold firmly, to keep in memory} the word which was announced to them as the gospel (1 Cor. 15:2). Christians are the house of Christ (or: of God, according to v. 4) if they hold fast {hold on to} the confidence and the rejoicing of hope to the end (Heb. 3:6). All other refs.: see entries in Lexicon at <2722>.

[3] ***krateō*** [verb: κρατέω <2902>]; **from *kratos*: strength, power ► To grasp firmly, to cling to >** Some did not hold fast {did not hold} the head (i.e., Christ) (Col. 2:19). Christians are to hold fast {to hold firmly} their confession (Heb. 4:14). Pergamum held fast the name of the Lord (Rev. 2:13). Those in Thyatira are to hold fast {to hold on to} what they have until the Lord's return (Rev. 2:25). Those in Philadelphia are to hold fast {to hold on to} what they have so that no one may take their crown (Rev. 3:11). All other refs.: see entries in Lexicon at <2902>.

FAST, FASTING, FAST – fast, fasting: *nēsteia* [fem. noun: νηστεία <3521>]; **to fast: *nēsteuō*** [verb: νηστεύω <3522>]; **from *nē*: neg. particle, and *esthiō*: to eat ► Voluntary deprivation of food; to voluntarily deprive oneself of food >** The Lord fasted forty days and forty nights at the beginning of His public ministry (Matt. 4:2). He gave instructions on how to conduct oneself while fasting (Matt. 6:16a, b, 17, 18). The disciples of John fasted often, but not the disciples of Jesus (Matt. 9:14a, b, 15; Mark 2:18a–c, 19a, b, 20; Luke 5:33–35). In a parable, a Pharisee fasted twice in a week (Luke 18:12). Fasting associated with prayer (Matt. 17:21; Mark 9:29; Luke 2:37; Acts 10:30; 13:2, 3; 14:23) symbolizes the refusal to act according to the flesh and the desire to wait on God. It may also refer to involuntary fasting as a result of difficult circumstances, as in the case of Paul (2 Cor. 6:5 and 11:27 {hunger}). The fast in Acts 27:9 is prob. related to the Day of Atonement (see Lev. 23:26–32), and is merely an indication of date. Other ref.: 1 Cor. 7:5 in some mss. ¶

FASTEN – [1] ***asphalizō*** [verb: ἀσφαλίζω <805>]; **from *asphalēs*: firm, safe, which is from *a*: neg., and *sphallō*: to throw down ▶ To tie up, to make secure in order to prevent any escape** > The jailer fastened {made fast, secured} the feet of Paul and Silas to the stocks (Acts 16:24). Other refs.: Matt. 27:64–66 (to make secure); see SECURE (adj.) <805>. ¶

[2] **to fasten, to fasten the eyes: *atenizō*** [verb: ἀτενίζω <816>]; **from *atenēs*: strained, earnest, which is from *a*: neg., and *teinō*: to stretch ▶ To fix with the eyes intently** > The eyes of all who were in the synagogue were fastened on {fixed upon} Jesus (Luke 4:20). Peter and John fastened their eyes on {fixed their eyes on, looked steadfastly at, looked straight at} the lame man (Acts 3:4). All other refs.: BEHOLD (verb) <816>, FIX <816>, LOOK (verb) <816>.

[3] ***kathaptō*** [verb: καθάπτω <2510>]; **from *kata*: down (intens.), and *haptō*: to bind ▶ To seize, to lay hold** > A viper fastened on {seized} Paul's hand (Acts 28:3). ¶

– [4] Matt. 18:6 → HANG <2910> [5] John 19:19 → SET (verb) <5087> [6] Eph. 6:14 → GIRD <4024>.

FASTER – ***tachion*** [adv.: τάχιον <5032>]; **neuter of *tachiōn*: quicker, more sudden, which is the compar. of *tachus*: rapid, prompt ▶ More rapidly, without delay** > John ran ahead faster than {outran} Peter, and came first to the tomb (John 20:4). All other refs.: QUICKLY <5032>, SHORTLY <5032>, SOONER <5032>.

FASTING – [1] Matt. 6:16a, b, 17, 18; et al. → FAST, FASTING, FAST <3521> [2] Matt. 15:32; Mark 8:3 → HUNGRY <3523>.

FAT – [1] Matt. 13:15; Acts 28:27 → to become fat, to grow fat → to grow dull → DULL <3975> [2] Matt. 22:4 → fat calf → FATLING <4619>.

FATHER – [1] ***patēr*** [masc. noun: πατήρ <3962>]; **from a root which means: feeder, protector, supporter ▶ a. He from whom one is issued** > Matt. 2:22; et al. **b. Ancestor, patriarch** > Matt. 3:9; 23:30; 1 Cor. 10:1; 2 Pet. 3:4; et al. **c. Christian who is mature in spiritual matters** > 1 John 2:13. **d. One who is at the origin of a family or a group of people animated by the same spirit as himself** > Abraham (Rom. 4:11, 12a, b, 16), Satan (John 8:38b, 41a, 44a–c). **e. One who looks after the spiritual well-being of those to whom he preaches the glad tidings and whom he instructs** > 1 Cor. 4:15 (which is distinct from the title that the Lord prohibits to use in Matt. 23:9). **f. Member of the Sanhedrin exercising religious authority over others** > Acts 7:2; 22:1. **g. God in relation to those who are born anew according to John 1:12, 13** > Christians have access to the Father who is over all (Eph. 2:18; 4:6); see 2 Cor. 6:18. They are imitators of their Father (Matt. 5:45, 48; 6:1, 4, 6, 8, 9; et al.). Christ never associated Himself with them by using the pronoun "our." He always used the sing. "My Father." His relationship was from eternity and essential in character, whereas the relationship of Christians with the Father is an effect of grace and regeneration (e.g., Matt. 11:27a–c; 25:34; John 20:17a–c; Rev. 2:27; 3:5, 21). The apostles spoke of God as the "Father" of the Lord Jesus Christ (e.g., Rom. 15:6; 2 Cor. 1:3a; 11:31; Eph. 1:3; Heb. 1:5; 1 Pet. 1:3; Rev. 1:6). **h. God in various aspects** > Father of lights (Jas. 1:17); Father of compassions (2 Cor. 1:3b), Father of glory (Eph. 1:17), Father of spirits (Heb. 12:9). (After W. E. Vine.) *

[2] **without father: *apatōr*** [masc. noun: ἀπάτωρ <540>]; **from *a*: neg, particle, and *patēr*: see [1] ▶ Not having a father** > Melchizedek was without father (Heb. 7:3). ¶

[3] **murderer of father: *patrolōas*** [masc. noun: πατρολῴας <3964>]; **from *patēr*: see [1], and *aloiaō*, same as *aloaō*: to smite; also spelled: *patralōas* ▶ One who kills his father; more generally, one who mistreats his father** > The law is for murderers {smiters} of fathers (1 Tim. 1:9). ¶

[4] **of one's fathers: *patrikos*** [adj.: πατρικός <3967>]; **from *patēr*; see [1] ▶ Coming from ancestors** > Paul was exceedingly zealous of the doctrines of his fathers (Gal. 1:14). ¶

[5] **of the fathers: *patrōos*** [adj.: πατρῷος <3971>]; **from *patēr*: see [1] ▶ Coming from ancestors** > Paul used this word in Acts 22:3; 24:14; 28:17. ¶

[6] **received by tradition from the fathers: *patroparadotos*** [adj.: πατροπαράδοτος <3970>]; **from *patēr*: see [1], and *paradidōmi*: to transmit, which is from *para*: beside, and *didōmi*: to give ▶ Transmitted by the fathers, inherited from the fathers** > Those to whom Peter speaks were redeemed from their vain conduct received by tradition from their fathers {handed down from their forefathers, inherited from the forefathers} (1 Pet. 1:18). ¶

– [7] Matt. 1:2–16; Acts 7:8, 29; 1 Cor. 4:15; Phm. 10 → be the father, to become the father → BEGET <1080>.

FATHER-IN-LAW – ***pentheros*** [masc. noun: πενθερός <3995>] ▶ **Father of the spouse** > Annas was the father-in-law of Caiaphas (John 18:13). ¶

FATHERLESS – Jas. 1:27 → ORPHAN (noun) <3737>.

FATHOM – ***orguia*** [fem. noun: ὀργυιά <3712>]; **from *oregō*: to stretch ▶ Measure of length or depth of about six feet (1.8 meters)** > The sailors on Paul's boat took soundings and found it to be twenty fathoms {one hundred and twenty feet}, and a little farther fifteen fathoms {ninety feet} (Acts 27:28a, b). ¶

FATLING – ***sitistos*** [adj. used as noun in the plur.: σιτιστός <4619>]; **from *sitizō*: to feed upon, to eat, which is from *sitos*: grain, wheat ▶ Animal fattened with grain for slaughter** > The king had his fatlings {fat calves, fatted beasts, fatted cattle, fattened livestock, fattened cattle} killed for the marriage of his son (Matt. 22:4). ¶

FATNESS – ***piotēs*** [fem. noun: πιότης <4096>]; **from *piōn*: fat ▶ Metaphor to describe oily sap; a figure of blessing** > The wild olive tree (the nations) was grafted in among the branches of the cultivated olive tree (Israel), and now shares in its root and fatness (Rom. 11:17). ¶

FATTED – [1] Matt. 22:4 → fatted cattle, fatted beasts → FATLING <4619> [2] Luke 15:23, 27, 30 → FATTENED <4618>.

FATTEN – Jas. 5:5 → NOURISH <5142>.

FATTENED – [1] ***siteutos*** [adj.: σιτευτός <4618>]; **from *siteuō*: to feed grain, which is from *sitos*: grain, wheat ▶ Which has been fattened on grain** > The father of the prodigal son had the fattened calf brought and killed (Luke 15:23, 27, 30). ¶

– [2] Matt. 22:4 → fattened livestock, fattened cattle → FATLING <4619>.

FAULT – [1] ***aitia*** [fem. noun: αἰτία <156>]; **from *aiteō*: to ask, or *aitios*: responsible ▶ Accusation, reason for condemnation; crime** > Pilate had found no fault {basis for a charge, guilt} in Jesus concerning the things He was accused of by the Jews (John 18:38; 19:4, 6). All other refs.: ACCUSATION <156>, CASE <156>, CAUSE (noun) <156>, REASON (noun) <156>.

[2] ***aition*** [adj. used as noun: αἴτιον <158>]; **neut. of *aitios*: responsible ▶ Cause, reason; also transl.: basis for a charge** > Pilate found no fault in Jesus (Luke 23:4 {no guilt}, 14 {no guilt, nothing criminal}). Other refs.: Luke 23:22; Acts 19:40; see REASON (noun) <158>. ¶

[3] ***hēttēma*** [neut. noun: ἥττημα <2275>]; **from *hēttaomai*: to be defeated, which is from *hētton*: lesser, inferior ▶ Failure, loss; also transl.: defeat, diminishing** > The loss of the Jews is riches for the Gentiles (Rom. 11:12). In 1 Cor. 6:7, this term signifies a spiritual loss: it was a fault for the Corinthians to have law suits with one another. ¶

[4] ***krima*** [neut. noun: κρίμα <2917>]; **from *krinō*: to distinguish, to judge ▶ Condemnation, guilt** > The fault {condemnation, judgment} of the devil was his pride (1 Tim. 3:6). Young widows may be at fault {bring judgment on themselves, incur condemnation, may be guilty} because they have cast off their first faith (1 Tim. 5:12). All

other refs.: CAUSE <2917>, JUDGMENT <2917>, LAWSUIT <2917>.

5 **to find fault: *memphomai*** [verb: μέμφομαι <3201>] ▶ **To blame, to be dissatisfied with** > One might have asked Paul why God yet finds fault (Rom. 9:19). While finding fault with Israel, the Lord speaks of making a new covenant with the house of Israel (Heb. 8:8; see Jer. 31:32 and Heb. 8:9). Some mss. have this verb also in Mark 7:2. ¶

6 **to sin: *hamartanō*** [verb: ἁμαρτάνω <264>]; **lit.: to miss the mark** ▶ **To commit a fault, to be disobedient to the will of God** > There is no glory when we are beaten for our faults {doing wrong} (lit.: if sinning) (1 Pet. 2:20). All other refs.: SIN (verb) <264>.

7 **improper: *atopos*** [adj.: ἄτοπος <824>]; **from *a*: neg., and *topos*: place; lit.: out of place** ▶ **Unsuitable, reprehensible** > Festus wanted to see if there was any fault {any wickedness, anything wrong} (lit.: if something was improper) in Paul (Acts 25:5). All other refs.: BAD <824>.

– 8 Matt. 18:15 → to tell the fault to someone, to show the fault to someone → REPROVE <1651> 9 2 Cor. 6:3 → to find fault → BLAME (verb) <3469> 10 Gal. 6:1; Jas. 5:16 → TRANSGRESSION <3900> 11 Phil. 2:15 → without fault → IRREPROACHABLE <298> 12 Jas. 1:5 → and without finding fault → lit.: and reproaches not → REPROACH (verb) <3679> 13 Jas. 3:2b → to be at fault → STUMBLE <4417> 14 Jude 16 → finding fault → lit.: faultfinder → COMPLAINER <3202> 15 Jude 24; Rev. 14:5 → without fault → BLAMELESS <299>.

FAULTFINDER – Jude 16 → COMPLAINER <3202>.

FAULTLESS – 1 Phil. 3:6; Heb. 8:7 → BLAMELESS <273> 2 Jas. 1:27 → UNDEFILED <283> 3 Jude 24 → BLAMELESS <299>.

FAVOR (noun) – 1 ***charis*** [fem. noun: χάρις <5485>]; **from *chairō*: to rejoice** ▶ **Grace, goodness, agreeable disposition** > The favor of God was on Jesus (Luke 2:40). Jesus increased in favor with God and men (Luke 2:52). Christians had favor with all the people (Acts 2:47). Festus was desirous of acquiring the favor {pleasure} of the Jews (Acts 24:27; 25:9). Christians stand in the favor of God, having been justified and having peace with God (Rom. 5:2; see v. 1). Other refs.: see entries in Lexicon at <5485>.

– 2 Luke 1:25 → to look with favor, to show one's favor → LOOK (verb) <1896> 3 Luke 2:14 → to men on whom His favor rests → lit.: good pleasure in men → PLEASURE <2107> 4 Luke 4:19 → lit.: favorable → ACCEPTABLE <1184> 5 Rom. 5:16b; 6:23 → act of favor → GIFT <5486> 6 2 Cor. 6:2a → in the time of His favor → lit.: in an accepted time → ACCEPTED <1184> 7 2 Cor. 6:2b → the time of God's favor → lit.: the acceptable time for God → ACCEPTABLE <2144> 8 Eph. 6:6; Col. 3:22 → to win the favor → lit.: as men-pleasers → MEN-PLEASER <441>.

FAVOR (verb) – ***charitoō*** [verb: χαριτόω <5487>]; **from *charis*: favor, grace, which is from *chairō*: to rejoice** ▶ **To bestow grace upon, to grant an advantage or privilege to someone** > God had favored {highly favored} Mary (Luke 1:28). Other ref.: Eph. 1:6 (to make accepted); see ACCEPTED <5487>. ¶

FAVORABLE – 1 ***hileōs*** [adj.: ἵλεως <2436>]; **from *hilaos*: appeased** ▶ **Merciful, gracious** > Peter uses the expr. "(Be it) favorable to you, Lord" {Far from you, Lord; God forbid it, Lord; Never, Lord} (lit.: Merciful to You, Lord) (Matt. 16:22). Other ref.: Heb. 8:12; see MERCIFUL <2436>. ¶

– 2 Luke 4:19; 2 Cor. 6:2a → ACCEPTABLE <1184> 3 2 Cor. 6:2b → ACCEPTABLE <2144>.

FAVORABLY – Rom. 15:31 → to be received favorably → lit.: to be acceptable → ACCEPTABLE <2144>.

FAVORED – 2 Cor. 12:13 → to be less favored → to be inferior → INFERIOR <2274>.

FAVORITISM – [1] Luke 20:21; Gal. 2:6; Jude 16 → PERSON <4383> [2] Acts 10:34 → to show favoritism → respecter of persons → RESPECT OF PERSONS <4381> [3] Rom. 2:11; Eph. 6:9; Col. 3:25; Jas. 2:1 → favoritism, personal favoritism → RESPECT OF PERSONS <4382> [4] 1 Tim. 5:21 → PARTIALITY <4346> [5] Jas. 2:9 → to show favoritism → to have respect of persons → RESPECT OF PERSONS <4380>.

FAVOUR (noun) – [1] See FAVOR (noun). – [2] 1 Tim. 5:21 → PARTIALITY <4346>.

FAVOUR (verb) – See FAVOR (verb).

FEAR (noun) – [1] ***ptoēsis*** [fem. noun: πτόησις <4423>]; **from *ptoeō*: to terrify ▶ Distressing emotion resulting from facing danger, evil, pain; dread, terror** > Imitating the conduct of Sarah, believing women become her children and are not frightened by any fear (1 Pet. 3:6 {amazement, consternation}). ¶

[2] ***phobos*** [masc. noun: φόβος <5401>]; **from *phebomai*: to fear, to be afraid ▶ Feeling of trouble and worry in the soul caused by danger, evil, pain; also transl.: awe, respect, reverence** > The guards at the tomb of Jesus trembled for fear (Matt. 28:4). The Gerasenes were gripped with great fear (Luke 8:37). The word is also used in regard to the disciples who saw Jesus walking on the sea (Matt. 14:26), shepherds (Mark 4:41; Luke 2:9; lit.: they feared [*phobeō*] with great fear [*phobos*]), and those who will be ready to die through fear of what is coming on the habitable earth (Luke 21:26 {terror}). Other refs.: Luke 1:65; Rom. 8:15 {to fear}; Rev. 11:11 {terror}. The word is transl. "terror" by some in Rom. 13:3 and means a respectful fear toward the authorities. Other refs.: Matt. 28:8 {afraid}; Luke 1:12; 5:26; 7:16; John 7:13; 19:38 {to fear}; 20:19; Acts 2:43 (in some mss.); 5:5, 11; 9:31; 19:17; Rom. 3:18; 13:7a, b; 1 Cor. 2:3; 2 Cor. 7:5, 11 {alarm}, 15; Eph. 5:21; 6:5; Phil. 2:12; 1 Tim. 5:20 {fearful, warning} (lit.: to have fear); Heb. 2:15; 1 Pet. 1:17; 2:18; 3:2 {respectful} (lit.: in respect, in fear), 14 {intimidation, terror, threat, what they fear}, 15; 1 John 4:18; Jude 23; Rev. 18:10, 15. ¶

[3] **without fear: *aphobōs*** [adv.: ἀφόβως <870>]; **from *aphobos*: fearless, which is from *a*: neg., and *phobos*: see [2] ▶ Without fright, without worry** > God had granted Israel to serve Him without fear (Luke 1:74). Timothy was to be without fear {be without cause to be afraid, have nothing to fear} among the Corinthians (1 Cor. 16:10). Brothers, trusting in the Lord, were much more bold to speak the word without fear {fearlessly} (Phil. 1:14). There were those feasting with the Christians without fear {without the slightest qualm} (Jude 12). ¶

[4] ***deilia*** [fem. noun: δειλία <1167>]; **from *deilos*: fearful, timid ▶ Fearfulness, reticence** > God has not given Christians a spirit of fear {cowardice, timidity} (2 Tim. 1:7). ¶

[5] **godly fear: *deos*** [neut. noun: δέος <1189a>] ▶ **Respectful attitude toward God** > Christians are invited to serve God acceptably with reverence (*eulabeia*) and godly fear (*deos*) {with respect (*aidōs*) and reverence (*eulabeia*), with reverence and awe} (Heb. 12:28); other mss. have *aidōs*: see MODESTY <127>. ¶

[6] **to be moved with fear: *eulabeomai*** [verb: εὐλαβέομαι <2125>]; **from *eulabēs*: one who receives well, which is from *eu*: well, and *lambanō*: to receive ▶ To act in a way which is respectful toward God** > Noah was moved with fear {moved with godly fear, in reverence, in holy fear} and prepared an ark for the saving of his household (Heb. 11:7). ¶

– [7] Matt. 17:7; Rom. 13:3 → have no fear, to have fear → don't be afraid, to be afraid → AFRAID <5399> [8] Mark 5:33 → trembling with fear → lit.: fearing and trembling → FEAR (verb) <5399> [9] Mark 9:6; Heb. 12:21 → AFRAID <1630> [10] Luke 24:5; Acts 10:4; 24:25; Rev. 11:13 → filled with fear, full of fear → AFRAID <1719> [11] John 14:27 → to fear → to be afraid → AFRAID <1168> [12] Acts 7:32 → to shake with fear → full of trembling → TREMBLING <1790> [13] Acts 22:9 → were filled with fear → lit.: were frightened → FRIGHTENED <1719> [14] Gal. 2:2;

1 Thes. 3:5 → for fear that → LEST <3381> [15] Eph. 6:5 → with respect and fear → lit.: with fear and trembling → TREMBLING <5156> [16] 1 Tim. 2:10 → fear of God → GODLINESS <2317> [17] Heb. 5:7 → godly fear → REVERENCE (noun) <2124>.

FEAR (verb) – [1] ***phobeō*** [verb: φοβέω <5399>]; **from *phobos*: fear; also transl.: to be afraid ► To feel anxious, to be agitated because of pain, danger, etc.; also, to show respect toward God or another person** > Jesus speaks of this fear of God (Matt. 10:28b; Luke 12:5a, b; 18:2, 4), as well as Mary (Luke 1:50) and one of the two criminals crucified with Jesus (Luke 23:40). Fearing and trembling {Frightened and trembling, Trembling with fear}, a woman healed by Jesus fell down before Him (Mark 5:33). This verb is used when Jesus spoke to His disciples (Matt. 14:27; 17:7; 28:10; Mark 4:41; 6:50; John 6:20), when the women were at His tomb (Matt. 28:5; Mark 16:8), and when the angel addressed the shepherds who feared (Luke 2:9, 10). The verb is used in regard to Peter (Matt. 14:30), the disciples at the transfiguration (Matt. 17:6; Luke 9:34) and when they saw Jesus walking on the sea (John 6:19), the centurion and those who were standing guard over Jesus (Matt. 27:54), the people who knew the man who had been possessed by the legion of demons (Mark 5:15; Luke 8:35), the praetors (Acts 16:38), and the chiliarch (Acts 22:29). Cornelius feared God {was God-fearing} with all his household (Acts 10:2, 22). Whoever fears God is accepted by Him (Acts 10:35). Bondservants are to obey their masters, fearing God {with reverence for the Lord} (Col. 3:22). Peter exhorts to fear God (1 Pet. 2:17). Other refs.: Acts 13:16 {to worship}, 26 {God-fearing}; 23:10 in some mss.; Rev. 11:18 {to reverence}; 14:7; 15:4; 19:5. All other refs.: AFRAID <5399>, RESPECT (verb) <5399>.
– [2] John 19:38; Rom. 8:15; 1 Pet. 3:14 → FEAR (noun) <5401> [3] 1 Cor. 16:10 → to have nothing to fear → without fear → FEAR (noun) <870> [4] 2 Cor. 12:21 → "I fear that" added in Engl. [5] Heb. 5:7 → in that He feared → lit.: because of His piety → PIETY <2124> [6] Heb. 12:21 → to fear exceedingly → exceedingly afraid → AFRAID <1630> [7] 2 Pet. 2:10 → TREMBLE <5141>.

FEARFUL – [1] ***deilos*** [adj.: δειλός <1169>]; **from *deidō*: to fear ► Who lacks assurance, timid; also transl.: afraid, cowardly** > Jesus asked His disciples in the great tempest why they were fearful (Matt. 8:26; Mark 4:40). In Rev. 21:8, the fearful, or cowardly, were unwilling to pronounce themselves in favor of Christ; their place for eternity will be in the lake which burns with fire. ¶
[2] ***phoberos*** [adj.: φοβερός <5398>]; **from *phobos*: fear, terror ► Which inspires horror, terror; also transl.: dreadful, terrible, terrifying** > The term is used in regard to a certain expectation of judgment (Heb. 10:27), of falling into the hands of the living God (10:31), and of what Moses saw (12:21). ¶
[3] **fearful event, fearful sight: *phobētron*** [neut. noun: φόβητρον <5400>]; **from *phobeō*: to frighten ► Dreadful sight, phenomenon that provokes terror** > There will be fearful sights {terrors} and great signs from heaven before the return of the Lord to establish His millennium of glory (Luke 21:11). ¶
– [4] Mark 10:32; Luke 8:25 → to be fearful → to be afraid → AFRAID <5399> [5] Luke 9:34 → to be fearful → FEAR (verb) <5399> [6] John 14:27 → to be fearful → to be afraid → AFRAID <1168> [7] 1 Tim. 5:20 → to be fearful → to have fear → FEAR (noun) <5401>.

FEARFULLY – Matt. 8:6 → TERRIBLY <1171>.

FEARLESSLY – [1] Acts 9:27 → to preach fearlessly → to preach boldly → BOLDLY <3955> [2] Eph. 6:19 → lit.: with boldness → BOLDNESS <3954> [3] Phil. 1:14 → without fear → FEAR (noun) <870>.

FEAST (noun) – [1] ***dochē*** [fem. noun: δοχή <1403>]; **from *dechomai*: to receive ► Banquet, reception** > Levi gave a great feast in his house (Luke 5:29 {entertainment}).

Jesus says to invite the poor, the crippled, the lame, the blind when one gives a feast (Luke 14:13). ¶

[2] ***heortē*** [fem. noun: ἑορτή <1859>] **▶ Celebration, commemoration; also transl.: festival** > This term designates the solemn Israelite celebrations: the Passover (Matt. 26:5; 27:15; Mark 14:2; 15:6; Luke 2:41, 42; 23:17; John 2:23; 6:4; 13:1, 29), the Feast of Unleavened Bread (Luke 22:1), the Feast of Tabernacles (John 7:2), and the Feast of the Dedication (John 10:22). Other refs.: John 4:45; 5:1; 7:8, 10, 11, 14, 37; 11:56; 12:12, 20; Acts 18:21. Paul reminded the Colossians (Col. 2:16) that the Israelite feasts {holidays, religious festivals} belonged to the past and that they prefigured the new things of the period of grace, e.g., the sacrifice of Christ in the Passover, the millennium in the Feast of Tabernacles, and the formation of the church on the day of Pentecost (see Acts 2). ¶

[3] **to celebrate the feast: *heortazō*** [verb: ἑορτάζω <1858>]**; from *heortē*: see [2] ▶ To keep a feast or a festival, a special occasion by a ceremony** > Christians celebrate the feast {keep the feast, keep the Festival} of unleavened bread, in a spiritual way, by behaving in the world with sincerity and truth (1 Cor. 5:8), in separation of evil (see v. 7). ¶

[4] **governor of the feast, master of the feast: *architriklinos*** [masc. noun: ἀρχιτρίκλινος <755>]**; from *archi*: denoting rank or degree, and *triklinos*: room with three couches, which is from *treis*: three, and *klinē*: couch ▶ Person responsible for arranging the table and couches, guiding guests, organizing the meal as well as tasting food and wine at a feast; also transl.: headwaiter, master of the banquet, ruler of the feast** > At the wedding of Cana, the servants brought some of the water that had been transformed into wine to the master of the feast (John 2:8, 9a, b). ¶

– [5] Matt. 22:2–4, 8–12; et al. → wedding feast → WEDDING <1062> [6] Matt. 23:6; Mark 6:21; 12:39; Luke 20:46 → SUPPER <1173> [7] John 7:2 → Feast of Booths → TABERNACLES (FEAST OF) <4634>.

FEAST OF DEDICATION – *enkainia* [neut. noun plur.: ἐγκαίνια <1456>]**; from *en*: in, and *kainos*: new ▶ Jewish feast lasting eight days and celebrated in the middle of the month of December** > The Feast of Dedication in Jerusalem (John 10:22) perpetuated the memory of the dedication of the temple purified and rebuilt after its profanation by Antiochus Epiphanes. The Dedication was instituted by Judas Maccabeus in 164 B.C. Jews today still celebrate the rededication of the temple during the Festival of Lights (Hanukkah). ¶

FEASTS OF CHARITY – Jude 12 → LOVE FEASTS <26>.

FEAST (verb) – [1] **to feast with, to feast together with: *suneuōcheō*** [verb: συνευωχέω <4910>]**; from *sun*: together, and *euōcheō*: to be well fed, which is from *eu*: well, and *echō*: to have ▶ To share good food, to make merry together** > Peter and Jude speak of wicked men who feast with Christians (2 Pet. 2:13 {to carouse with}; Jude 12 {to eat with}). ¶

– [2] Luke 16:19 → to be merry → MERRY <2165>.

FED (BE) – Mark 7:27; Luke 15:16 in some mss. → lit.: to be filled → FILL (verb) <5526>.

FEEBLE – [1] 1 Cor. 12:22 → WEAK <772> [2] Heb. 12:12 → to hang down → HANG <3935>.

FEEBLEMINDED – 1 Thes. 5:14 → FAINTHEARTED <3642>.

FEED – [1] ***boskō*** [verb: βόσκω <1006>] **▶ a. To give food (to animals); also transl.: to keep, to tend** > The prodigal son was sent into the fields to feed swine (Luke 15:15). Other refs.: Matt. 8:30, 33; Mark 5:11, 14; Luke 8:32, 34. **b. In a spiritual sense: to feed souls, to ensure they have good food** > Jesus told Peter to feed His lambs (John 21:15) and His sheep (John 21:17). ¶

[2] ***poimainō*** [verb: ποιμαίνω <4165>]**; from *poimēn*: shepherd ▶ To care for**

(oneself), to satisfy (oneself) > Jude speaks of ungodly men who feed {pasture, care for, serve} themselves only (Jude 12). All other refs.: SHEEP <4165>, SHEPHERD (verb) <4165>.

3 **to feed, to bestow to feed, to give to feed, to give: *psōmizō*** [verb: ψωμίζω <5595>]; **from *psōmion*: piece of food; lit.: to cut pieces, to put food in the mouth of someone ▶ To give food, to nourish** > If an enemy is hungry, we should feed him (Rom. 12:20). Without love, bestowing all our goods to feed the poor profits nothing (1 Cor. 13:3). ¶

– 4 Matt. 6:26; 25:37; Luke 12:24; Acts 12:20; Rev. 12:6 → NOURISH <5142> 5 Matt. 15:33; Mark 8:4; Luke 16:21; Phil. 4:12; Jas. 2:16 → FILL (verb) <5526> 6 Luke 6:25 → to be well fed, to be well-fed → to be filled → FILL (verb) <1705> 7 John 6:54, 56 → to feed on → EAT <5176> 8 1 Cor. 3:2 → DRINK (verb) <4222> 9 Eph. 5:29 → NOURISH <1625>.

FEEL – 1 **to feel after: *psēlaphaō*** [verb: ψηλαφάω <5584>]; **from *psaō*: to touch lightly ▶ To touch with the fingers, to sense physically** > Speaking to the Athenians, Paul uses the expr. "to feel after {to grope for, to reach after} and to find" concerning God (Acts 17:27). Other refs.: Luke 24:39; Heb. 12:18; 1 John 1:1; see TOUCH <5584>. ¶

– 2 Mark 5:29 → KNOW <1097> 3 Acts 28:5 → SUFFER <3958> 4 1 Cor. 13:11; Phil. 1:7 → THINK <5426> 5 2 Cor. 2:3 → to feel sure → to have confidence → CONFIDENCE <3982> 6 2 Cor. 11:2 → to feel a divine jealousy → lit.: to be jealous with a godly jealousy → JEALOUS <2206> 7 Gal. 4:15 → "felt" added in Engl. 8 1 Thes. 3:9 → the joy we feel → lit.: the joy with which we rejoice → REJOICE <5463>.

FEELING – 1 **to cast off all feeling: *apalgeō*** [verb: ἀπαλγέω <524>]; **from *apo*: from, and *algeō*: to feel pain ▶ To become insensitive to the impact of one's behavior** > Paul speaks of the rest of the Gentiles who cast off all feeling {are past feeling, have become callous, have lost all sensitivity} (Eph. 4:19). ¶

– 2 Acts 15:39 → very warm feeling → sharp disagreement → DISAGREEMENT <3948>.

FEET – Acts 27:28a, b → FATHOM <3712>.

FEIGN – Luke 20:20 → PRETEND <5271>.

FEIGNED – ***plastos*** [adj.: πλαστός <4112>]; **from *plassō*: to shape ▶ Deceitful, false** > Peter warns against false teachers who will exploit (lit.: make merchandise of) Christians with feigned {deceptive} words {with stories they have made up} (2 Pet. 2:3). ¶

FELIX – ***Phēlix*** [masc. name: Φῆλιξ <5344>]: **happy, in Lat. ▶ Governor of Judea** > Paul was brought to Felix (Acts 23:24, 26). Felix married Drusilla, the daughter of Herod Agrippa I. Tertullus accused Paul before him (Acts 24:3). Felix was terrified at the preaching of Paul; but he expected to be bribed by Paul for his release (Acts 24:22, 24, 25; see v. 26). He was succeeded by Porcius Festus and left Paul prisoner in order to gain the favor of the Jews (Acts 24:27a, b; 25:14). ¶

FELLOW – 1 Matt. 11:16 → COMPANION <2083> 2 Acts 2:22; 3:12; 13:16, 26; 19:35; 21:28; et al. → fellow, fellow Israelites, etc. → lit.: men, brothers 3 Rom. 16:7, 11, 21 → my fellow Jew → lit.: my relative → RELATIVE (noun) <4773> 4 1 Cor. 3:9 → fellow worker → LABORER TOGETHER <4904> 5 2 Cor. 1:24; 1 Thes. 3:2; Phm. 1, 24 → fellow worker, fellow laborer → FELLOW WORKER <4904> 6 2 Cor. 11:26 → fellow Jews → COUNTRYMAN <1085> 7 Eph. 3:6 → fellow-heir, fellow heir → JOINT HEIR <4789> 8 Heb. 1:9 → PARTNER <3353> 9 Heb. 13:3 → fellow prisoner → lit.: bound with prisoners → to bind with → BIND <4887>.

FELLOW BELIEVER – [1] 2 Thes. 3:15; 1 Tim. 6:2a; Jas. 3:1 → lit.: brother → BROTHER <80> [2] 1 Tim. 6:2b → lit.: are believing and beloved → BELIEVING <4103>.

FELLOW BOND-SERVANT – Col. 1:7; 4:7 → FELLOW SERVANT <4889>.

FELLOW BONDMAN – Matt. 18:28, 29, 31, 33; 24:49; Col. 1:7; 4:7; Rev. 6:11; 19:10; 22:9 → FELLOW SERVANT <4889>.

FELLOW CAPTIVE – Rom. 16:7; Col. 4:10; Phm. 23 → FELLOW PRISONER <4869>.

FELLOW CITIZEN – [1] ***sumpolitēs*** [masc. noun: συμπολίτης <4847>]; **from *sun*: together, and *politēs*: citizen ▶ Inhabitant of a city, a state, a district, who is entitled to the same full civil rights as those enjoyed by his compatriots >** Christians are fellow citizens with the saints and members of the household of God (Eph. 2:19). ¶

– [2] Heb. 8:11 in some mss. → CITIZEN <4177>.

FELLOW DISCIPLE – ***summathētēs*** [masc. noun: συμμαθητής <4827>]; **from *sun*: together, and *mathētēs*: disciple, which is from *manthanō*: to learn ▶ Learning companion who follows a teacher >** Thomas addressed himself to his fellow disciples, i.e., the rest of the disciples of Jesus (John 11:16). ¶

FELLOW-ELDER – 1 Pet. 5:1 → elder with → ELDER <4850>.

FELLOW HEIR – Rom. 8:17; Eph. 3:6; Heb. 11:9; 1 Pet. 3:7 → JOINT HEIR <4789>.

FELLOW HELPER – Rom. 16:3, 9, 21; 2 Cor. 1:24; 8:23; Phil. 2:25; 4:3; Col. 4:11; 1 Thes. 3:2; Phm. 1, 24; 3 John 8 → FELLOW WORKER <4904>.

FELLOW ISRAELITE – Heb. 7:5 → their fellow Israelites → lit.: their brothers → BROTHER <80>.

FELLOW LABORER – Rom. 16:3, 9, 21; 2 Cor. 1:24; 8:23; Phil. 2:25; 4:3; Col. 4:11; 1 Thes. 3:2; Phm. 1, 24; 3 John 8 → FELLOW WORKER <4904>.

FELLOW MAN – Phm. 16 → as a fellow man → in the flesh → FLESH <4561>.

FELLOW MEMBER – Eph. 3:6 → fellow member of the body → same body → BODY <4954>.

FELLOW PARTAKER – [1] Rom. 11:17; 1 Cor. 9:23 → PARTAKER <4791> [2] Eph. 3:6 → PARTAKER <4830>.

FELLOW-PARTAKER – Eph. 5:7 → PARTAKER <4830>.

FELLOW PRISONER – ***sunaichmalōtos*** [masc. noun: συναιχμάλωτος <4869>]; **from *sun*: together, and *aichmalōtos*: captive; also transl.: fellow captive ▶ One who is held captive together with another >** Andronicus and Junias were fellow prisoners of {had been in prison with} Paul (Rom. 16:7), as well as Aristarchus (Col. 4:10) and Epaphras (Phm. 23); most likely they were imprisoned at the same time as Paul. ¶

FELLOW REBEL – ***sustasiastēs*** [masc. noun: συστασιαστής <4955>]; **from *sun*: together, and *stasis*: insurrection, revolt ▶ Accomplice with others during an insurrection, a rebellion >** Barabbas was bound with his fellow rebels {insurrectionists, those who had made an insurrection with him} (Mark 15:7); other mss.: *stasiastēs*: rebel. ¶

FELLOW SERVANT – ***sundoulos*** [masc. noun: σύνδουλος <4889>]; **from *sun*: together, and *doulos*: slave, servant; lit.: companion of slavery ▶ a. Collaborator, associate in the work of the Lord >** Paul uses this term (also transl.: fellow bondman, fellow bond-servant) concerning Epaphras (Col. 1:7) and Tychicus (4:7). **b. Slave with someone else** > The term is used of men (Matt. 18:28, 29, 31, 33; 24:49; Rev. 6:11) and of angels (Rev. 19:10; 22:9). ¶

FELLOW SLAVE – Matt. 18:28, 29, 31, 33; 24:49; Rev. 6:11 → FELLOW SERVANT <4889>.

FELLOW SOLDIER – ***sustratiōtēs*** [masc. noun: συστρατιώτης <4961>]; **from *sun*: together with, and *stratiōtēs*: soldier; lit.: person who goes to war with another one ▶ Collaborator in the service for Christ** > Epaphroditus was a fellow soldier with Paul (Phil. 2:25), as well as Archippus (Phm. 2). ¶

FELLOW TRAVELER – ***sunekdēmos*** [masc. noun: συνέκδημος <4898>]; **from *sun*: together, and *ekdēmos*: traveler, which is from *ek*: from, and *demos*: people ▶ Person who journeys with another one; also spelled: fellow traveller** > Paul uses this word {travel companion, traveling companion, companion in travel} concerning the Macedonians Gaius and Aristarchus (Acts 19:29), and a brother who was recognized for preaching the gospel and who was chosen by the churches to travel with {accompany} him (lit.: fellow traveler of him) (2 Cor. 8:19; see v. 18). ¶

FELLOW WORKER – ***sunergos*** [adj. and masc. noun: συνεργός <4904>]; **from *sun*: together, and *ergon*: work ▶ One who exercises an activity with someone else to achieve something, collaborator; also transl.: companion, helper, fellow helper, fellow laborer, workfellow** > Paul and others were fellow workers for the joy of the Christians in Corinth {workers with them} (2 Cor. 1:24). He also uses this term concerning: Prisca and Aquila (Rom. 16:3), Urbanus (Rom. 16:9), Timothy (Rom. 16:21; 1 Thes. 3:2), Titus (2 Cor. 8:23), Epaphroditus (Phil. 2:25), Clement and others (Phil. 4:3), Aristarchus, Mark and Jesus called Justus (Col. 4:11), as well as Philemon, Demas, and Luke (Phm. 1, 24). We should receive those who have gone forth for the name of Jesus that we may become fellow workers for the truth (3 John 8). Other ref.: 1 Cor. 3:9; see LABORER TOGETHER <4904>. ¶

FELLOW-WORKER – 1 Cor. 16:16 → to work with, to work together → WORK (verb) <4903>.

FELLOW-WORKMAN – [1] 1 Cor. 3:9 → LABORER TOGETHER <4904> [2] 2 Cor. 6:1 → to work together → WORK (verb) <4903>.

FELLOWSHIP – [1] ***koinōnia*** [fem. noun: κοινωνία <2842>]; **from *koinōneō*: to share, which is from *koinōnos*: associate, participant, which is from *koinos*: common ▶ Common interest and portion, association; also transl.: communion** > The first Christians continued steadfastly in the doctrine and fellowship of the apostles (Acts 2:42). By participating in the Lord's supper, Christians have fellowship of {a sharing of, a participation in} the blood and the body of Christ (1 Cor. 10:16a, b). The faithful Christian, as light, has no fellowship with darkness (2 Cor. 6:14). Paul speaks to the Philippians of their fellowship {participation, partnership} in the gospel (Phil. 1:5). Christians have fellowship with divine persons: the Father and the Son (1 Cor. 1:9; 1 John 1:3a, b, 6), and the Holy Spirit (2 Cor. 13:14; Phil. 2:1); they also have fellowship one with another (1 John 1:7). Other refs.: 2 Cor. 8:4 {participation, sharing}; Phil. 3:10 {fellowship of sharing}; Phm. 6 {communication, sharing, participation}. All other refs.: COMMUNICATE[1] <2842>, CONTRIBUTION <2842>, DISPENSATION <2842>, SHARING <2842>.

[2] **to have fellowship with: *sunkoinōneō*** [verb: συγκοινωνέω <4790>]; **from *sun*: together, and *koinōneō*: see [1] ▶ To have something in common with, to associate with** > Christians should not have fellowship with {not participate in, have nothing to do with} the unfruitful works of darkness

(Eph. 5:11). All other refs.: PARTICIPATE <4790>, SHARE (verb) <4790>.

[3] **to give the right hand of fellowship; right: *dexios*** [adj.: δεξιός <1188>]; **to give: *didōmi*** [verb: δίδωμι <1325>]; **fellowship: *koinōnia*** [fem. noun: κοινωνία <2842>]; **from *koinōnos*: see [1] ▶ To give the hand (lit.: the right) as a token of support, communion; the right hand is a sign of a loyal engagement >** James, Cephas, and John gave the right hands {the right hand} of fellowship to Paul and Barnabas in their service for the Lord (Gal. 2:9). Other refs. (*didōmi*): GIVE <1325>. All other refs. (*dexios*): see RIGHT[1] <1188>. All other refs. (*koinōnia*): see COMMUNICATE[1] <2842>, CONTRIBUTION <2842>, DISPENSATION <2842>, SHARING <2842>.
– [4] 1 Cor. 10:20 → to have fellowship with → lit.: to become partaker of → PARTAKER <2844> [5] 2 Cor. 6:14 → PARTICIPATION <3352>.

FEMALE – [1] ***gunaikeios*** [adj.: γυναικεῖος <1134>]; **from *gunē*: woman ▶ Characteristic of a woman, feminine >** Husbands are to dwell with their wives according to knowledge, as with a weaker, i.e., the female, vessel {as with someone weaker, since she is a woman} (1 Pet. 3:7). ¶

[2] ***thēlus*** [adj.: θῆλυς <2338>] **▶ Woman, who belongs to the feminine gender >** From the beginning of the creation, God made man male and female (Matt. 19:4; Mark 10:6). In Christ Jesus, there is neither male nor female (Gal. 3:28). The word is used as a noun in Rom. 1:26, 27. ¶
– [3] Luke 12:45; Acts 16:16 → female servant, female slave → SERVANT GIRL <3814> [4] Acts 2:18 → female servant → BONDWOMAN <1399>.

FENCE – Matt. 21:33; Mark 12:1; Luke 14:23 → HEDGE (noun) <5418>.

FERMENTED – Luke 1:15 → fermented drink → strong drink → DRINK (noun) <4608>.

FEROCIOUS – Matt. 7:15 → RAPACIOUS <727>.

FERTILIZE – Luke 13:8 → lit.: to put fertilizer → PUT <906>, DUNG (noun) <2874>.

FERTILIZER – Luke 13:8 → DUNG (noun) <2874>.

FERVENT – [1] ***ektenēs*** [adj.: ἐκτενής <1618>]; **from *ekteinō*: to stretch, to reach out, which is from *ek*: out, and *teinō*: to stretch ▶ With warm and earnest feeling toward others; intense, ardent >** Peter exhorts Christians to have fervent love among themselves (1 Pet. 4:8 {to love deeply, to love earnestly}). Other ref.: Acts 12:5; see UNCEASING <1618>. ¶

[2] **to be fervent: *zeō*** [verb: ζέω <2204>]; **lit.: to bubble, to boil ▶ To demonstrate zeal, to show enthusiasm >** Apollos was fervent in his spirit (Acts 18:25). Christians are encouraged to be fervent in spirit (Rom. 12:11). ¶
– [3] Heb. 5:7 → STRONG <2478> [4] Jas. 5:16 → EFFECTIVE <1754> [5] 2 Pet. 3:10, 12 → HEAT <2741>.

FERVENTLY – [1] ***ektenōs*** [adv.: ἐκτενῶς <1619>]; **from *ektenēs*: fervent, intense, which is from *ekteinō*: to stretch, to extend ▶ With intensity, ardor of spirit >** Prayers were made fervently {earnestly} for Peter (Acts 12:5). Peter tells Christians to love one another fervently {deeply} with a pure heart (1 Pet. 1:22). ¶
– [2] Luke 22:44 → very fervently → more earnestly → EARNESTLY <1617> [3] Col. 4:12 → to labor {labour} fervently → FIGHT (verb) <75> [4] Jas. 5:17 → EARNESTLY <4335>.

FERVOR – Acts 18:25; Rom. 12:11 → with great fervor, keeping the spiritual fervor → lit.: being fervent, fervent in spirit → FERVENT <2204>.

FESTAL GATHERING – Heb. 12:23 → ASSEMBLY <3831>.

FESTERING – Rev. 16:2 → EVIL (adj.) <4190>.

FESTIVAL – [1] Matt. 26:5; 27:15; Mark 14:2; 15:6; Luke 2:41, 42; 22:1; John 2:23; 4:45; 5:1; 6:4; 7:2, 8a, b, 10, 11, 14, 37; 11:56; 12:12, 20; 13:1, 29; Col. 2:16 → FEAST (noun) <1859> [2] Matt. 26:17; Mark 14:1, 12; Acts 12:3; 20:6 → Festival of Unleavened Bread → lit.: unleavened bread, the unleavened, of the unleavened, days of Unleavened Bread [3] Luke 2:43 → after the festival was over → lit.: fulfilling the days → DAY <2250> [4] John 7:2 → Festival of Tabernacles → TABERNACLES (FEAST OF) <4634> [5] John 10:22 → the Festival of Dedication → lit.: the Dedication [6] 1 Cor. 5:8 → to keep the Festival → to celebrate the feast → FEAST (noun) <1858>.

FESTUS – ***Phēstos*** [masc. name: Φῆστος <5347>]**: festive ► Procurator of Judea** > Porcius Festus succeeded Felix (Acts 24:27). The apostle Paul had to defend himself before him against the accusations of the Jews; he appealed to Caesar (see Acts 25:11). Festus summoned Paul before Agrippa and Bernice; Paul then spoke in his own defense (see Acts 26). Other refs.: Acts 25:1, 4, 9, 12–14, 22–24; 26:24, 25, 32. ¶

FETCH – [1] Acts 10:32 → CALL (verb) <3333> [2] Acts 16:37 → to fetch out → to lead out → LEAD (verb) <1806> [3] Acts 28:13 → to fetch a compass → CIRCLE ROUND <4022>.

FETTER – [1] Mark 5:4a, b; Luke 8:29 → SHACKLE <3976> [2] Luke 8:29 → CHAIN (noun) <1199>.

FEVER – [1] ***puretos*** [masc. noun: πυρετός <4446>]**; from *pur*: fire ► Abnormal increase in body temperature that accompanies illness** > Jesus touched Peter's mother-in-law, and the fever left her (Matt. 8:15; Mark 1:31; Luke 4:38, 39); Luke specifies it was a high fever. Jesus also healed the son of a royal official, who was sick and stricken with fever (John 4:52). Paul healed the father of Publius who was much afflicted with fever (Acts 28:8). ¶

[2] **to be in a fever, with a fever; to be sick in a fever, with a fever: *puressō*** [verb: πυρέσσω <4445>]**; from *puretos*: see [1] ► To suffer an abnormal increase in body temperature accompanying illness** > Peter's mother-in-law lay in a fever (Matt. 8:14; Mark 1:30). ¶

FEW – [1] ***oligos*** [adj.: ὀλίγος <3641>]**; adv.: *oligon* ► Not many, some** > Few find the way that leads to life (Matt. 7:14). Jesus laid His hands on a few infirm people in His own country (Mark 6:5). Someone asked if those who are to be saved are few in number (Luke 13:23). A few, that is, eight souls, were saved through water, meaning: through the course of the flood in the time of Noah (1 Pet. 3:20). Other refs.: see entries in Lexicon at <3641>.

[2] **not a few: *ouk*** [neg. particle: οὐκ <3756>] ***oligos*** [adj., adv.: ὀλίγος <3641>] **► A good number, many** > Of the leading women, not a few believed in Thessalonica (Acts 17:4). Among the honorable women and men in Berea, not a few {a number} believed (Acts 17:12). Other refs. (*oligos*): see entries in Lexicon at <3641>.

[3] Acts 24:4 → a few words → WORD <4935>.

FICKLE – 2 Cor. 1:17 → to be fickle → lit.: to use lightness → LIGHTNESS <1644>.

FIDELITY – [1] Rom. 1:31 → to have no fidelity → to be faithless → FAITHLESS <802> [2] Rom. 16:10 → whose fidelity has stood the test → lit.: approved → APPROVE <1384> [3] Gal. 5:22; Titus 2:10 → FAITHFULNESS <4102>.

FIELD – [1] ***agros*** [masc. noun: ἀγρός <68>] **► Parcel of land in the country; also transl.: country, farm, land** > Jesus says to consider the lilies of the field (Matt. 6:28). God clothes the grass of the field (Matt. 6:30; Luke 12:28). The kingdom of heaven is like a man who sows good seed in his field (Matt. 13:24, 27) and a grain of mustard which a man sowed in his field (v. 31). To His disciples who were asking Him to explain to them the parable of the tares of the field (Matt. 13:36), Jesus said that the field represents the world (v. 38). The kingdom of heaven is like a treasure hidden in a field;

a man buys that field (Matt. 13:44a, b). Some would leave their fields for the sake of the Lord (Matt. 19:29; Mark 10:29); they would receive a hundred fold later (Mark 10:30). In a parable, a guest made light of an invitation to a wedding and went to his field (Matt. 22:5; Luke 14:18 {piece of ground}). During the great tribulation, he who is in the field must not return back to take his clothes or his goods (Matt. 24:18; Mark 13:16; Luke 17:31). At the coming of the Son of Man, two men will be in the field; one will be taken and the other one left (Matt. 24:40; Luke 17:36 in some mss.). The potter's field was bought with the price of Judas's treason (Matt. 27:7, 10); this field was called the Field of Blood (Matt. 27:8a, b). Simon, who was coming from the field, was compelled to bear the cross of Jesus (Mark 15:21; Luke 23:26). Jesus appeared to two disciples who were going to the field (Mark 16:12). The grass which is today in the field is thrown into the oven tomorrow (Luke 12:28). The prodigal son was sent into the fields to feed swine (Luke 15:15); when he came back to his father, the older son was in the field (v. 25). Jesus spoke of a servant coming in from the field (Luke 17:7). All other refs.: COUNTRY <68>, FIELD OF BLOOD <68>, LAND (noun) <68>.

[2] **to abide in the field, to stay out in the fields: *agrauleō*** [verb: ἀγραυλέω <63>]; **from *agros*: see [1], and *aulizomai*: to stay outside ▶ To live in the fields, outside** > The shepherds were abiding in the field {living out in the field, abiding without} when the angel announced to them the birth of Jesus (Luke 2:8). ¶

[3] ***geōrgion*** [neut. noun: γεώργιον <1091>]; **from *georgos*: farmer, which is from *gē*: soil, ground, and *ergon*: work ▶ Plowing the earth in preparation for sowing, cultivation of the soil** > In the figur. sense, the Corinthians were God's field {husbandry} (1 Cor. 3:9). ¶

[4] ***chōra*** [fem. noun: χώρα <5561>] ▶ **Land, region, countryside; a larger tract than [1]** > In a parable, the field {ground, land} of a rich man had yielded plentifully (Luke 12:16). Jesus invited His disciples to look at the fields (John 4:35). James speaks of laborers who have reaped the fields of rich men (Jas. 5:4). All other refs.: COUNTRY <5561>, LAND (noun) <5561>.

[5] ***chōrion*** [neut. noun: χωρίον <5564>]; **dimin. of *chōra*: see [4] ▶ Domain, parcel of land** > Judas had bought a field with the reward of iniquity (Acts 1:18); this field was called the Field of Blood (Acts 1:19a, b). In the beginning, Christians were selling their fields {lands} (Acts 4:34), and the money was distributed according to need (see v. 35). Peter asked the wife of Ananias if they had sold their field {land, estate} for a certain amount (Acts 5:8). All other refs.: GROUND (noun)[1] <5564>, LAND (noun) <5564>, PLACE (noun) <5564>.

– [6] Mark 2:23; Luke 6:1 → corn field → CORN <4702> [7] 2 Cor. 10:13, 15 → RULE (noun) <2583>.

FIELD OF BLOOD – ***Agros Aimatos* or *Chōrion Haimatos*; *agros*** [masc. noun: ἀγρός <68>], ***chōrion*** [neut. noun: χωρίον <5564>], ***haima*** [neut. noun: αἷμα <129>] ▶ For this place name in Matt. 27:8 and Acts 1:19, see ACELDAMA <184>. Other refs. (*agros*): COUNTRY <68>, FIELD <68>, LAND (noun) <68>. Other refs. (*chōrion*): FIELD <5564>, GROUND (noun)[1] <5564>, LAND (noun) <5564>, PLACE (noun) <5564>. Other refs. (αἷμα): BLOOD <129>. ¶

FIERCE – [1] Matt. 8:28 → DIFFICULT <5467> [2] Luke 23:5 → to be the more fierce → to be insistent → INSIST <2001> [3] Acts 20:29 → SAVAGE <926> [4] 2 Tim. 3:3 → BRUTAL <434> [5] Jas. 3:4 → VIOLENT (adj.) <4642> [6] Rev. 16:19 → fierce wrath → lit.: fierceness of the wrath → FURY <2372>.

FIERCELY – Luke 11:53 → VEHEMENTLY <1171>.

FIERCENESS – Rev. 16:19; 19:15 → FURY <2372>.

FIERY – [1] **fiery trial, fiery ordeal: *purōsis*** [fem. noun: πύρωσις <4451>]; **from *pur*: fire ▶ Intense suffering, persecution** >

Christians were not to be surprised at the fiery trial {painful trial, fire} which had come upon them for their testing (1 Pet. 4:12). Other refs.: Rev. 18:9, 18; see BURNING <4451>. ¶

[2] **to inflame: *puroō*** [verb: πυρόω <4448>]; **from *pur*: fire ▶ To set on fire, to set ablaze >** The shield of faith makes one able to quench all the fiery {burning, flaming} (lit.: inflamed) darts of the wicked one (Eph. 6:16). All other refs.: BURN <4448>, FIRE <4448>, PURIFY <4448>, REFINE <4448>.

– [3] Rev. 9:17a → fiery red → FIRE <4447>.

FIFTEEN – *dekapente* [card. num.: δεκαπέντε <1178>]; **from *deka*: ten, and *pente*: five ▶** This number is used in regard to stadia (John 11:18), fathoms (Acts 27:28), and days (Gal. 1:18). Other ref.: Acts 27:5 in some mss. ¶

FIFTEENTH – *pentekaidekatos* [ord. num.: πεντεκαιδέκατος <4003>]; **from *pente*: five, *kai*: and, *dekatos*: tenth ▶** Pontius Pilate was governor of Judaea in the fifteenth year of the government of Tiberius Caesar (Luke 3:1). ¶

FIFTH – *pemptos* [ord. num.: πέμπτος <3991>]; **from *pente*: five ▶** This number is used in regard to a seal (Rev. 6:9), an angel (9:1; 16:10), and a foundation of the holy city (21:20). In Acts 20:6, some mss. have: on the fifth day (*pemptaios*). ¶

FIFTY – *pentēkonta* [card. num.: πεντήκοντα <4004>]; **from *pente*: five ▶** This number is used in regard to people (Mark 6:40; Luke 9:14), denarii (Luke 7:41), measures of oil (Luke 16:6), and years (John 8:57). Other refs.: John 21:11 (one hundred and fifty-three large fish); Acts 13:20 (four hundred and fifty years). ¶

FIFTY THOUSAND – *pente muriadas*; *pente* [card. num.: πέντε <4002>], ***murias*** [fem. noun: μυριάς <3461>]; **lit.: five myriads, or five times ten thousand ▶** The value of occult books burned in Ephesus totaled fifty thousand pieces of silver (Acts 19:19). All other refs. (*murias*): see INNUMERABLE <3461>, MYRIAD <3461>.

FIG – [1] *sukon* [neut. noun: σῦκον <4810>] **▶ Edible fruit of the fig tree; the fleshy receptacle has seeds on the inside >** One does not gather figs from thistles (Matt. 7:16) or from thornbushes (Luke 6:44). Jesus found nothing but leaves on a fig tree, for it was not yet the season for figs (Mark 11:13). A grapevine cannot produce figs (Jas. 3:12). ¶

[2] **unseasonable fig: *olunthos*** [masc. noun: ὄλυνθος <3653>] **▶ Fig which is not ripe >** John saw the stars fall, as a fig tree shaken by a strong wind drops its unseasonable figs (Rev. 6:13). ¶

FIG TREE – *sukē* [fem. noun: συκῆ <4808>]; **from *sukon*: fig ▶ Fruit tree which is the most common in Israel and which can live up to 200 years >** The fig tree produces its leaves at the end of spring (Matt. 24:32; Mark 13:28; Luke 21:29). Its flowers are invisible to the human eye, but one can obtain several harvests of figs each year. The Lord's curse upon a fig tree which bore no fruit, only leaves (Matt. 21:19a, b, 20, 21; Mark 11:13, 20, 21), is an illustration of Israel which bore no fruit for God. The fig tree mentioned in Luke 13 (vv. 6, 7) may represent more specifically the Jews who, during the public ministry of Jesus, for the most part did not produce fruit for God. Jesus had seen Nathanael under the fig tree (John 1:48, 50). Other refs.: Jas. 3:12; Rev. 6:13. ¶

FIGHT (noun) **– [1] *agōn*** [masc. noun: ἀγών <73>]; **from *agō*: to lead ▶ Battle, struggle >** Paul exhorted Timothy to fight the good fight {conflict, combat} of faith (1 Tim. 6:12). He himself had fought the good fight (2 Tim. 4:7). All other refs.: CONFLICT <73>, RACE[2] <73>.

[2] ***athlēsis*** [fem. noun: ἄθλησις <119>]; **from *athleō*: to fight ▶ Battle, struggle >** The Hebrew Christians had endured a great fight {conflict, contest} of sufferings (Heb. 10:32). ¶

3 ***polemos*** [masc. noun: πόλεμος <4171>] ▶ **War, battle** > O.T. people of faith became valiant in fight (Heb. 11:34). All other refs.: BATTLE (noun) <4171>, WAR (noun) <4171>.
– 4 1 Tim. 1:18 → WARFARE <4752>
5 Jas. 4:1 → FIGHTING <3163>.

FIGHT (verb) – 1 ***agōnizomai*** [verb: ἀγωνίζομαι <75>]; **from *agōn*: battle, conflict, which is from *agō*: to lead ▶ To struggle, to wrestle** > Jesus says that if His kingdom were of this world, His servants would have fought so that He would have not been delivered to the Jews (John 18:36). Everyone who fights {strives, competes, contends} for the mastery is temperate in all things (1 Cor. 9:25). Paul was fighting {was combating, was striving, was struggling} according to the working of Christ (Col. 1:29). Epaphras was fighting {combating earnestly, laboring fervently, laboring earnestly, wrestling} for the Colossians in prayers (Col. 4:12). Paul exhorts Timothy to fight {strive earnestly in} the good fight of faith (1 Tim. 6:12). He himself had fought the good fight {combated the good combat} (2 Tim. 4:7). Other refs.: Luke 13:24; see STRIVE <75>; 1 Tim. 4:10; see REPROACH (noun) <3679>. ¶
2 ***machomai*** [verb: μάχομαι <3164>] ▶ **To take part in a physical struggle** > Moses tried to reconcile two Israelites as they were fighting {were contending, strove} (Acts 7:26). Other refs.: John 6:52; 2 Tim. 2:24; Jas. 4:2; see QUARREL (verb) <3164>, STRIVE <3164>. ¶
3 **to fight against God: *theomacheō*** [verb: θεομαχέω <2313>]; **from *theomachos*: fighter against God, which is from *Theos*: God, and *machomai*: see 2 ▶ To struggle against, to oppose God Himself** > This verb is used in Acts 23:9 in some mss. (but this portion of text is questionable). ¶
4 ***polemeō*** [verb: πολεμέω <4170>]; **from *polemos*: war, battle ▶ To combat; also transl.: to wage war, to make war, to go to war** > The Lord will fight against those who are unrepentant in Pergamum (Rev. 2:16). Michael and his angels were fighting with the dragon, and the dragon and his angels fought {fought back} (Rev. 12:7a, b). The world will say: Who is able to fight against the beast? (Rev. 13:4). Ten kings will fight against the Lamb (Rev. 17:14). He who sat on the white horse judges and makes war (Rev. 19:11). Other ref.: Jas. 4:2; see WAR (verb) <4170>. ¶
5 ***pukteuō*** [verb: πυκτεύω <4438>]; **from *puktēs*: athlete fighting with his fists, which is from *pux*: with the fist ▶ To strike with the fists; to engage in boxing, which was an Olympic discipline** > Paul was fighting {combating, boxing}, not as one beating the air (1 Cor. 9:26). ¶
– 6 Acts 5:39 → to fight against God → lit.: fighter against God → FIGHTER <2314>
7 1 Tim. 1:18 → WAR (verb) <4754>.

FIGHTER – fighter against God: *theomachos* [adj. used as noun: θεομάχος <2314>]; **from *Theos*: God, and *machomai*: to fight ▶ One who combats against God** > Gamaliel warned the Jews against opposing the Christian doctrine or else they would be found fighters against God (Acts 5:39). ¶

FIGHTING – *machē* [fem. noun: μάχη <3163>]; **from *machomai*: to fight, to make war ▶ Dispute; also transl.: fight, combat, conflict** > Paul was troubled: outside were fightings, within were fears (2 Cor. 7:5). James links the wars and fightings among Christians to the lusts that war in their members (Jas. 4:1). All other refs.: STRIFE <3163>, STRIVING <3163>.

FIGURATIVE – 1 John 16:25a, b, 29 → figurative language, figurative speech → ALLEGORY <3942> 2 Heb. 11:19 → in a figurative sense → lit.: in a figure → FIGURE <3850>.

FIGURATIVELY – 1 John 16:25a, b → lit.: figurative language → ALLEGORY <3942> 2 Gal. 4:24 → to take figuratively → to be an allegory → ALLEGORY <238>
3 Heb. 11:19 → lit.: in a figure → FIGURE <3850>.

FIGURE – **1** ***antitupon*** [neut. noun of an adj.: ἀντίτυπον <499>]; **from *anti*: in place of, instead of, and *tupos*: type; lit.: which corresponds to the type ▶ That which is foreshadowed, represented by a type >** Baptism is the figure of {is the antitype of, is what corresponds to, symbolizes} Noah's ark going through the water of the flood (1 Pet. 3:21), i.e., Christian baptism is represented by Noah's ark. Other ref.: Heb. 9:24; see COPY <499>. ¶
2 ***parabolē*** [fem. noun: παραβολή <3850>]; **from *paraballō*: to compare, which is from *para*: along, near, and *ballō*: to throw ▶ Symbolic narrative or comparison of everyday life to illustrate more clearly a moral or spiritual lesson >** The tabernacle is a figure {illustration, image, symbol} for the present time (Heb. 9:9). Abraham received Isaac in a figure {in a type, figuratively} as risen from among the dead (Heb. 11:19). All other refs.: PARABLE <3850>.
– **3** John 10:6; 16:25a, b, 29 → figure of speech → ALLEGORY <3942> **4** Acts 7:43; Rom. 5:14 → TYPE <5179> **5** Phil. 2:8 → APPEARANCE <4976>.

FIGUREHEAD – ***parasēmos*** [adj.: παράσημος <3902>]; **from *para*: near, and *sēma*: sign ▶ Carved figure on the front part of a ship >** Paul sailed on a ship whose figurehead {ensign, sign} was the Twin Brothers, i.e., the Dioscuri Castor and Pollux (Acts 28:11). ¶

FILL (noun) – John 6:12 → they had eaten their fill → lit.: when they were filled.

FILL (verb) – **1** **to fill, to fill up: *gemizō*** [verb: γεμίζω <1072>]; **from *gemō*: to be full ▶ To be full, to make full >** The waves were beating on the boat Jesus and His apostles were in, so that it was already filled {was now full, was filling up, was nearly swamped} (Mark 4:37). A sponge filled with vinegar was fixed at the end of a reed and presented to the Lord on the cross (Mark 15:36). The prodigal son longed to fill his stomach with the husks which the swine were eating (Luke 15:16). At the wedding in Cana, Jesus said to fill the water-vessels with water, and they were filled up to the brim (John 2:7a, b). The verb is also used in regard to a house (Luke 14:23), baskets (John 6:13), a censer (Rev. 8:5), and the temple (Rev. 15:8). ¶
2 **to fill up: *plēroō*** [verb: πληρόω <4137>]; **from *plērēs*: full ▶ To complete, to make full >** The scribes and the Pharisees were filling up the measure of their fathers (Matt. 23:32). As a child, Jesus grew, being filled {increasing} with wisdom (Luke 2:40). With the coming of Jesus, every valley would be filled up (Luke 3:5). As head of the church, Christ fills all in all (Eph. 1:23); He fills with all the fullness of God (3:19); He fills all things (4:10). Paul was filled up {was full, was amply supplied}, having received the gift of the Philippians (Phil. 4:18). The verb is used in the expr. "filled with the Spirit" (Eph. 5:18). We find the following exprs.: "filled with joy" (Acts 2:28; 2 Tim. 1:4), "filled with joy and the Holy Spirit" (Acts 13:52), "filled (*plērēs* <4134>) with rage" (Acts 19:28), "filled with all unrighteousness, etc." (Rom. 1:29), "to fill with all joy and peace" (Rom. 15:13), "filled with knowledge" (Rom. 15:14 {to be complete}; Col. 1:9), "filled with encouragement" (2 Cor. 7:4 {to be greatly encouraged}), and "filled {complete} as regards the fruit of righteousness" (Phil. 1:11). Other exprs. are also found: "filled with the fragrance of the perfume" (John 12:3), "to fill the heart" (John 16:6; Acts 5:3), "to fill with a doctrine" (Acts 5:28), and "to fill all the house" (Acts 2:2). All other refs.: see entries in Lexicon at <4137>.
3 **to fill, to fill up: *anaplēroō*** [verb: ἀναπληρόω <378>]; **from *ana*: up (intens.), and *plēroō*: see 2 ▶ a. To occupy the whole, to complete >** He who fills {occupies} the place of a simple Christian must understand what is said in order to say "Amen" at the giving of thanks (1 Cor. 14:16). **b. To accomplish completely >** Those who were forbidding Paul to speak to the Gentiles were always filling up their sins (1 Thes. 2:16 {heap up}). All other refs.: FULFILL <378>, SUPPLY (verb) <378>.
4 **to fill up: *antanaplēroō*** [verb: ἀνταναπληρόω <466>]; **from *anti*: in the place of, in return, and *anaplēroō*: see**

3 ▶ **To accomplish completely** > Paul was filling up in his flesh what was lacking in the afflictions of Christ for the church (Col. 1:24). ¶

5 ***sumplēroō*** [verb: συμπληρόω <4845>]; **from *sun*: together (intens.), and *plēroō*: see** 2 ▶ **To fill completely** > The boat Jesus and His disciples were in was filled {was filling, was swamped} with water (Luke 8:23). Other refs.: Luke 9:51; Acts 2:1; see COME <4845>. ¶

6 ***korennumi*** [verb: κορέννυμι <2880>]; **from *koros*: satiety ▶ To have enough, to gratify to satiation** > Paul told the Corinthians that they were filled {were full, had all they wanted} already (1 Cor. 4:8). Other ref.: Acts 27:38; see EAT <2880>. ¶

7 ***pimplēmi*** [verb: πίμπλημι <4130>] ▶ **a. To impregnate** > At the cross, a soldier filled a sponge with vinegar and gave Jesus to drink (Matt. 27:48). **b. To make full** > In Matt. 22:10, the wedding hall was filled {furnished} with guests. Both boats of the disciples were filled with fish (Luke 5:7}). The verb is also used in the expr. "filled with the Holy Spirit" in regard to John the Baptist (Luke 1:15), Elizabeth (Luke 1:41), Zacharias (Luke 1:67), believers in the Lord on the day of Pentecost (Acts 2:4), Christians a little later (Acts 4:31), Peter (Acts 4:8), and Paul (Acts 9:17; 13:9). In regard to feelings, we find the following exprs.: "filled with rage" (Luke 4:28 {to be furious}), "filled with fear" (Luke 5:26), "filled with wonder and amazement" (Acts 3:10), "filled with jealousy" (Acts 5:17; 13:45), and "filled with confusion" (Acts 19:29). Other refs.: Matt. 27:48; Luke 1:23, 57; 2:6, 21, 22; 6:11; John 19:29 (*plēthō*; see 9). ¶

8 ***empiplēmi*** [verb: ἐμπίπλημι <1705>]; **from *en*: in, and *pimplēmi*: see** 7 ▶ **a. To satisfy** > God has filled the hungry with good things (Luke 1:53). **b. To be satisfied, to be full** > Woe awaits those who are filled {are full, are well fed, are well-fed}, for they will hunger (Luke 6:25). The verb is used in John 6:12 in regard to the people whom Jesus had fed and who had been filled {had enough to eat}. God fills hearts with food and gladness (Acts 14:17). All other refs.: ENJOY <1705>.

9 ***plēthō*** [verb: πλήθω <4130>] ▶ **To make full** > They (soldiers, most likely) filled {soaked} a sponge with {They put a sponge full of} vinegar and gave it to Jesus (John 19:29). All other refs. (*pimplēmi*): see 7.

10 ***chortazō*** [verb: χορτάζω <5526>]; **from *chortos*: grass, hay ▶ To satisfy hunger with food; also transl.: to eat, to feed, to satisfy** > The crowds whom Jesus fed were filled (Matt. 14:20; 15:33, 37; Mark 6:42; 8:4, 8; Luke 9:17; John 6:26). Those who hunger and thirst after righteousness will be filled (Matt. 5:6; Luke 6:21). Jesus told a Greek woman to let the children, i.e., Israel, be first filled (Mark 7:27). The prodigal son longed to fill his stomach (lit.: to fill) with the pods that the swine were eating (Luke 15:16 in some mss.). Lazarus desired to be filled with the crumbs that fell from the table of the rich man (Luke 16:21). Paul had been instructed to be full (or: to be filled) as well as to be hungry (Phil. 4:12). There is no profit to tell people to fill themselves without giving them the needful things for the body (Jas. 2:16). In Rev. 19:21, all the birds were filled {gorged themselves} with the flesh of the armies gathered together to make war against the Lord. ¶

– 11 Matt. 12:34; Luke 6:45 → that which fills → ABUNDANCE <4051> 12 Matt. 27:54; Mark 4:41 → to be filled with awe, to be filled with great fear → lit.: to fear a great fear → FEAR (verb) <5399> 13 Luke 1:65 → to come on → COME <1096> 14 Luke 7:16 → SEIZE <2983> 15 2 Cor. 9:12 → to fill up the measure → SUPPLY (verb) <4322> 16 Rev. 13:3 → to fill with wonder → WONDER (verb) <2296> 17 Rev. 15:1 → COMPLETE (verb) <5055> 18 Rev. 18:6a, b → to pour out → POUR <2767>.

FILLED – 1 Luke 4:1 → FULL <4134> 2 Acts 2:13 → filled with new wine → full of new wine → FULL <3325>.

FILLED (BE) – 1 ***plēroō*** [verb: πληρόω <4137>]; **from *plērēs*: full ▶ To be replete, to be complete; also transl.: to be full** > The verb is used in regard to a seine cast into the sea (Matt. 13:48), and unrighteousness

and various wicked things (Rom. 1:29). All other refs.: see entries in Lexicon at <4137>.
– [2] Matt. 23:27; Rev. 15:7; 17:4; 21:9 → to be filled → to be full → FULL <1073>.

FILTH – [1] ***perikatharma*** [neut. noun: περικάθαρμα <4027>]; **from *perikathairō*: to purify completely, which is from *peri*: around, and *kathairō*: to purify, to clean, which is from *kathairos*: pure, clean ▶ Dirt, refuse; unclean person or thing, an outcast** > Paul and Apollos had been made similar to the filth {offscouring, scum} of the world (1 Cor. 4:13); *katharma* in some mss. ¶
[2] ***rhupos*** [masc. noun: ῥύπος <4509>] ▶ **That which is unclean, dirt** > Peter speaks of the putting away of the filth {dirt} of the flesh (1 Pet. 3:21). ¶
[3] ***skubalon*** [neut. noun: σκύβαλον <4657>]; **akin to *kusibalon*: something thrown to the dogs, which is from *kuon*: dog, and *ballō*: to throw ▶ Waste, trash** > Paul counted all things to be filth {dung, loss, rubbish} on account of the excellency of the knowledge of Christ Jesus (Phil. 3:8). ¶
– [4] Jas. 1:21 → moral filth → FILTHINESS <4507>.

FILTHINESS – [1] ***aischrotēs*** [fem. noun: αἰσχρότης <151>]; **from *aischros*: improper, shameful ▶ Coarse talk, improper conduct; also transl.: obscenity** > One ought not to hear of any filthiness on the part of Christians (Eph. 5:4). ¶
[2] ***rhuparia*** [fem. noun: ῥυπαρία <4507>]; **from *rhuparos*: dirty, filthy ▶ Defilement, contamination** > The Christian is to lay aside all filthiness {moral filth} and overflow of wickedness (Jas. 1:21). ¶
– [3] 2 Cor. 7:1 → DEFILEMENT <3436> [4] Rev. 17:4 → unclean thing → UNCLEAN <168>.

FILTHY – [1] **filthy language, filthy communication: *aischrologia*** [fem. noun: αἰσχρολογία <148>]; **from *aischrologeō*: to make shameful remarks, which is from *aischros*: improper, shameful, and *legō*: to say ▶ Coarse talk, inappropriate language** > The Colossians were to put off filthy language {abusive speech, vile language} coming out of their mouth (Col. 3:8). ¶
[2] **to be filthy, to make oneself filthy: *rhupoō*** [verb: ῥυπόω <4510>]; **from *rhupos*: dirt ▶ To soil, to defile oneself morally** > The angel said to John: Let him who is unjust, be unjust still; and let him who is filthy (*rhuparos*), make himself filthy {be vile} (*rhupoō*) still (Rev. 22:11); some mss. have *rhupainō* [verb: ῥυπαίνω <4506a>]. ¶
– [3] 1 Tim. 3:3 → greedy of filthy lucre → GREEDY <866> [4] Titus 1:11 → DISHONEST <150> [5] Jas. 2:2 → DIRTY <4508> [6] 2 Pet. 2:7 → filthy lives → conduct in lewdness → LEWDNESS <766>.

FINAL – [1] Matt. 12:45; Luke 11:26 → LAST (adv. and noun) <2078> [2] Heb. 6:16 → END (noun) <4009>.

FINALLY – [1] ***loipon*** [adv.: λοιπόν <3063>]; **from *loipos*: remaining ▶ From now on** > Finally {Now, Henceforth, In the future}, the crown of righteousness was laid up for Paul (2 Tim. 4:8). The word is transl. "from that time" in Heb. 10:13: From that time {Henceforth, Since that time}, Christ waits until His enemies are made His footstool. Other ref.: Acts 27:20 {in the end, finally, from then on}. All other refs.: NOW <3063>, REST (noun)[2] <3063>.
[2] ***to de telos*; *de*** [particle: δέ <1161>]; ***telos*** [neut. noun: τέλος <5056>] ▶ **In conclusion, to sum up** > Peter uses this Greek expr. in 1 Pet. 3:8. All other refs. (*telos*): CUSTOM[2] <5056>, END (noun) <5056>, PERPETUALLY <5056>.
– [3] Matt. 21:37 → at last → LAST (adv. and noun) <5305> [4] 1 Cor. 11:32 → "finally" added in Engl.

FIND – [1] ***heuriskō*** [verb: εὑρίσκω <2147>] ▶ **a. To become, to discover** > Mary was found to be with child by the Holy Spirit (Matt. 1:18). Other refs.: Mark 7:30; Luke 9:36; 17:18; Acts 5:10, 39; Rom. 7:10, 18, 21; 2 Cor. 5:3; 11:12; Gal. 2:17; Phil. 2:8; Rev. 5:4. **b. To perceive, to encounter** > Jesus speaks of an unclean spirit who found the house from which he had come unoccupied (Matt. 12:44). He speaks of a hidden treasure that a man found (Matt. 13:44). Peter would find a stater {coin} in the mouth of a fish (Matt. 17:27). Jesus found nothing but leaves on a fig tree (Matt. 21:19; Mark 11:13a, b). The master of the house might find his servants sleeping (Mark 13:36). Jesus found His disciples sleeping (Matt. 26:40, 43; Mark 14:37, 40; Luke 22:45). He asks when He, the Son of Man, comes, shall He find faith on the earth (Luke 18:8). Other refs.: Matt. 18:28; 20:6; 21:2; 22:9, 10; 24:46; 27:32; Mark 11:2, 4; 14:16; Luke 2:12; 7:9, 10; 8:35; 12:37, 38, 43; 13:6, 7; 19:30, 32; 22:13; 23:2; 24:2, 3, 23, 24, 33; John 1:41a, b, 43, 45a, b; 2:14; 5:14; 9:35; 11:17; 12:14; Acts 5:22, 23a, b; 8:40; 9:2, 33; 10:27; 13:6, 22; 17:23; 18:2; 19:1; 21:2 (or in the sense of: to discover after searching); 28:14; Rom. 10:20; 1 Cor. 4:2; 2 Cor. 9:4; 12:20a, b; Phil. 3:9; 1 Pet. 1:7; 2:22; 2 Pet. 3:14; 2 John 4; Rev. 12:8; 18:22, 24. **c. To discover after searching >** When the wise men had found the child Jesus, they were to report to Herod (Matt. 2:8). Jesus says to seek and we shall find (Matt. 7:7, 8). There are few who find the gate which leads to life (Matt. 7:14). Jesus had not found, not even in Israel, so great faith as that of the centurion (Matt. 8:10). He mentions the unclean spirit that seeks rest but does not find it (Matt. 12:43; Luke 11:24). He also mentions a merchant who seeks beautiful pearls and finds one pearl of great value (Matt. 13:46). He speaks of a man who finds his lost sheep (Matt. 18:13; Luke 15:4–6) and a woman who finds her lost drachma (Luke 15:8, 9a, b). No false witnesses (Matt. 26:60), false testimonies (Mark 14:55), or proper ground were found against Jesus for a death sentence (Acts 13:28). Pilate found no fault in Jesus (Luke 23:4, 14, 22; John 18:38; 19:4, 6). Other refs.: Mark 1:37; Luke 2:45, 46; 4:17; 5:19; 6:7; 11:9, 10, 25; 19:48; John 6:25; 7:34–36; Acts 4:21; 7:11; 11:26; 12:19; 17:6, 27; 19:19; 23:9, 29; 24:5, 12, 18, 20; 27:6, 28a, b; 1 Cor. 15:15; 2 Cor. 2:13; 2 Tim. 1:17; Heb. 11:5; Rev. 2:2; 3:2; 9:6; 14:5; 16:20; 18:14, 21; 20:11, 15. **d. To acquire, to obtain >** He who finds his life shall lose it; and he who loses his life, for the sake of Jesus, shall find it (Matt. 10:39a, b; 16:25). Jesus says to take His yoke upon us, and to learn from Him, for He is meek and lowly in heart; and we will find rest for our souls (Matt. 11:29). Mary found grace with God (Luke 1:30). David found grace before God (Acts 7:46a). Other refs.: Luke 9:12; John 10:9; 21:6; Acts 7:46b; Rom. 4:1; 2 Tim. 1:18; Heb. 4:16; 12:17. **e. To obtain, to recover >** As far as his father was concerned, the son who had been lost was now found (Luke 15:24, 32). Other refs.: Matt. 2:11 and 2 Pet. 3:10 {to lay bare} in some mss.; Heb. 9:12: see OBTAIN <2147>. ¶

[2] to find, to find out: *aneuriskō* [verb: ἀνευρίσκω <429>]**; from *ana*: intens., and *heuriskō*: see [1] ► To discover after diligent searching >** The shepherds came with haste, and they found both Mary and Joseph, and the little child Jesus lying in the manger (Luke 2:16). Paul found out {looked up} the disciples at Tyre (Acts 21:4). ¶

[3] *katalambanō* [verb: καταλαμβάνω <2638>]**; from *kata*: intens., and *lambanō*: to take ► To seize, to obtain, to understand >** Festus had found that Paul had done nothing worthy of death (Acts 25:25). All other refs.: see entries in Lexicon at <2638>.

[4] *metalambanō* [verb: μεταλαμβάνω <3335>]**; from *meta*: with, and *lambanō*: to take ► To get, to obtain >** Felix would have Paul called when he found a more convenient time (Acts 24:25). All other refs.: PARTAKE <3335>, PARTICIPATE <3335>, RECEIVE <3335>, TAKE <3335>.

– [5] Matt. 2:7 → to find out → DETERMINE <198> [6] Matt. 10:11 → to find out → INQUIRE <1833> [7] Mark 6:38; 15:45; Luke 19:15; John 11:57; 12:9; Acts 17:13; 22:30; 2 Cor. 13:6 → to find out → KNOW <1097> [8] Luke 9:12 → to find lodging → LODGE <2647> [9] John 8:37 → to find room → to have a place → PLACE (noun) <5562> [10] Acts 9:30; 19:34; 22:24, 29; 28:1 → to find out → KNOW <1921> [11] Acts 10:17 → to find out → to make inquiry → INQUIRY <1331> [12] Acts 14:6 → to find out → to be aware → AWARE <4894> [13] Acts 24:8 → to find out → to take knowledge → KNOWLEDGE <1921> [14] 2 Cor. 1:20 → "find" added in Engl. [15] 2 Cor. 6:3 → to find fault → BLAME (verb) <3469> [16] Gal. 3:2 → to find out → LEARN <3129> [17] Eph. 5:10 → to find out → TEST (noun and verb) <1381> [18] 1 Pet. 1:11 in some mss. → to try to find out → SEEK <2037a>.

FINDING – Rom. 11:33 → beyond finding out → UNTRACEABLE <421>.

FINE – [1] Matt. 11:8a, b; Luke 7:25 → DELICATE <3120> [2] Matt. 13:45 → BEAUTIFUL <2570> [3] Jas. 2:2, 3 → BRIGHT <2986>.

FINE LINEN – **fine linen: *bussos*** [fem. noun: βύσσος <1040>]; **from a Heb. verb: to be white; with fine linen, in fine linen: *bussinos*** [adj.: βύσσινος <1039>] ▶ **Fabric made from high quality linen** > In the parable of Lazarus and the rich man, the latter was clothed in fine linen (Luke 16:19). The Lamb's bride was clothed in fine linen corresponding to the righteous acts of the saints (Rev. 19:8a, b); here fine linen represents the holiness and moral purity of the one who wears it (see v. 14). Babylon is also clothed with fine linen (Rev. 18:12, 16). The armies that follow the Lord in Rev. 19:14 are clothed with fine linen. ¶

FINGER – ***daktulos*** [masc. noun: δάκτυλος <1147>] ▶ **One of the five jointed parts extending from the human hand** > The scribes and the Pharisees did not want to move with one of their fingers the heavy burdens they laid on men's shoulders (Matt. 23:4; Luke 11:46). Jesus put His fingers in the ears of the deaf man (Mark 7:33). He was casting out demons by the finger of God (Luke 11:20). The rich man was asking that Lazarus dip the tip of his finger in water and cool his tongue (Luke 16:24). Jesus wrote with His finger on the ground (John 8:6). Thomas wanted to put his finger into the mark of the nails in the hands of Jesus (John 20:25); eight days later, Jesus told him to reach out his finger and to look at His hands (v. 27). ¶

FINISH – [1] ***teleō*** [verb: τελέω <5055>]; **from *telos*: end, accomplishment** ▶ **To accomplish, to execute** > The verb "to finish" is used about the things Jesus was saying (Matt. 7:28 {to end; some mss.: *sunteleō*}; 19:1; 26:1), His instructions (11:1 {to make an end}), and His parables (13:53). The Son of Man will come before the disciples have finished {finished going through, gone through, completed, gone over} the cities of Israel (Matt. 10:23). At the cross, Jesus said: "It is finished (*Tetelestai*)" (John 19:30). Paul had finished the race (2 Tim. 4:7). When the two witnesses will have finished {completed} their testimony, the beast will kill them (Rev. 11:7). Satan will be kept in the abyss until the thousand years are finished {fulfilled, completed, ended} (Rev. 20:3). The rest of the dead will not come to life until the thousand years have been finished {have been completed, are ended} (Rev. 20:5). All other refs.: see entries in Lexicon at <5055>.

[2] ***apoteleō*** [verb: ἀποτελέω <658>]; **from *apo*: intens., and *teleō*: see [1]** ▶ **To arrive at its end** > Sin, when it is finished {completed, fully completed, full-grown, accomplished}, brings forth death (Jas. 1:15). Other ref.: Luke 13:32 in some mss. ¶

[3] ***ekteleō*** [verb: ἐκτελέω <1615>]; **from *ek*: out (intens.), and *teleō*: see [1]** ▶ **To carry to completion** > The verb is used in regard to a tower, whose builder will be mocked if he is unable to finish it because of the cost involved (Luke 14:29, 30). ¶

[4] ***epiteleō*** [verb: ἐπιτελέω <2005>]; **from *epi*: until (intens.), and *teleō*: see [1]** ▶ **To accomplish, to carry to completion** > Titus would finish {complete, bring to completion} the act of grace among the Corinthians by encouraging them to make a gift (2 Cor. 8:6). All other refs.: see entries in Lexicon at <2005>.

[5] ***sunteleō*** [verb: συντελέω <4931>]; **from *sun*: together (intens.), and *teleō*: see [1]** ▶ **To complete, to end** > Isaiah speaks of God finishing {bringing to an end, carrying out, executing} the work of saving the remnant (Rom. 9:28). All other refs.: END (verb) <4931>, FULFILL <4931>, MAKE <4931>.

[6] ***teleioō*** [verb: τελειόω <5048>]; **from *teleios*: complete, perfect, which is from *telos*: end, accomplishment ▶ To achieve, to end successfully; also transl.: to accomplish, to complete** > The food of Jesus was to finish the work of His Father (John 4:34); the works to be finished by Jesus bore witness that the Father had sent Him (5:36). Jesus told His Father He had finished {completed} the work He gave Him to do (John 17:4). Paul wanted to finish his race and the ministry he had received from the Lord with joy (Acts 20:24). All other refs.: FULFILL <5048>, PERFECT (adj.) <5048>, PERFECT (verb) <5048>.

[7] ***dianuō*** [verb: διανύω <1274>]; **from *dia*: through (intens.), and *anuō*: to accomplish, to perform ▶ To terminate, to complete; to resume** > When Paul and his companions had finished {continued} their voyage from Tyre, they came to Ptolemais (Acts 21:7). ¶

[8] **completion: *apartismos*** [masc. noun: ἀπαρτισμός <535>]; **from *apartizō*: to perfect, which is from *apo*: particle of completion, and *artizō*: to render functional ▶ Action of completing something, to go to the end** > One who wants to build a tower estimates the cost to see if he has enough to finish it {complete it} (lit.: if he has enough for completion) (Luke 14:28). ¶

– [9] Luke 5:4; 11:1 → CEASE <3973> [10] Luke 7:1 → CONCLUDE[2] <4137> [11] John 19:24; Acts 13:25 → FULFILL <4137> [12] Acts 15:13 → to be silent → SILENT <4601> [13] Acts 20:36 → when Paul finished speaking → lit.: having said these things [14] 2 Cor. 9:5 → MAKE <4294> [15] Jas. 1:4a → must finish its work → lit.: must have its perfect work → PERFECT (adj.) <5046>.

FINISHER – ***teleiōtēs*** [masc. noun: τελειωτής <5051>]; **from *teleioō*: to finish, to accomplish, which is from *teleios*: complete, of highest quality ▶ One who makes perfect and brings a thing to its final state** > Jesus is the author and finisher {completer, perfecter} of our faith (Heb. 12:2). ¶

FIRE – [1] ***pur*** [neut. noun: πῦρ <4442>] ▶ **Release of heat, light, and flames by the combustion of certain materials** > This term is used in its habitual sense; e.g., in Luke 22:55, a fire was lit in the middle of the courtyard of the high priest. It is also used in regard to the sanctification of believers in the Lord and to divine judgment of those who reject Christ (Matt. 3:11, 12; Luke 3:16), the eternal fire of hell (Matt. 5:22; 18:8, 9; 25:41; Mark 9:43–48; Jude 7, 23; Rev. 14:10; 19:20; 20:10, 14a, b, 15; 21:8), the judgment of people (Mark 9:49), hostility between men (Luke 12:49), repaying an enemy with kindness (Rom. 12:20), the testing of the works of Christians (1 Cor. 3:13, 15), the vengeance of God (2 Thes. 1:8), angels (Heb. 1:7), the holiness of God (Heb. 10:27; 12:29; Rev. 1:14; 2:18; 4:5; 19:12), and the tongue (Jas. 3:6). Other refs.: Matt. 3:10; 7:19; 13:40, 42, 50; 17:15; Mark 9:22; Luke 3:9, 17; 9:54; 17:29; John 15:6; Acts 2:3, 19; 7:30; 28:5; Heb. 11:34; 12:18; Jas. 3:5; 5:3; 1 Pet. 1:7; 2 Pet. 3:7; Rev. 3:18; 8:5, 7, 8; 9:17b, 18; 10:1; 11:5; 13:13; 14:18; 15:2; 16:8; 17:16; 18:8; 20:9. ¶

[2] ***pura*** [fem. noun: πυρά <4443>]; **from *pur*: see [1] ▶ Pile of combustible materials** > The islanders of Malta kindled a fire (Acts 28:2); Paul put branches on the fire (v. 3). ¶

[3] **to be on fire: *puroō*** [verb: πυρόω <4448>]; **from *pur*: see [1] ▶ To consume by flames, to burn** > At the coming of the day of God, the heavens being on fire will be dissolved (2 Pet. 3:12). All other refs.: BURN <4448>, FIERY <4448>, PURIFY <4448>, REFINE <4448>.

[4] **of fire, the color of fire, fiery red: *purinos*** [adj.: πύρινος <4447>]; **from *pur*: see [1] ▶ Of the color of flames, glittering** > Those sitting on the horses had breastplates of fire (Rev. 9:17a). ¶

[5] ***phōs*** [neut. noun: φῶς <5457>]; **from *phaō*: to shine ▶ Light, flame** > Peter warmed himself at the fire (Mark 14:54). All other refs.: LIGHT (noun) <5457>, SON OF LIGHT <5457>.

[6] **to set fire, to set on fire: *phlogizō*** [verb: φλογίζω <5394>]; **from *phlox*: flame ▶ To**

light, to set ablaze > The tongue sets fire to the course of nature, and it is set on fire by hell (Jas. 3:6a, b). ¶
– [7] Matt. 6:30; Luke 12:28 → OVEN <2823> [8] Matt. 22:7 → to set on fire → BURN <1714> [9] John 18:18; 21:9 → charcoal fire → fire of coals → COAL <439> [10] Jas. 3:5 → to set on fire → KINDLE <381> [11] 1 Pet. 4:12 → fiery trial → FIERY <4451>.

FIRELIGHT – Luke 22:56 → LIGHT (noun) <5457>.

FIRKIN – John 2:6 → MEASURE (noun) <3355>.

FIRM – [1] ***bebaios*** [adj.: βέβαιος <949>]; **from *bainō*: to go, to walk ▶ Assured, reliable; also transl.: binding, firmly, firmly grounded, steadfast, sure, unalterable** > Paul's hope regarding the Corinthians was firm (2 Cor. 1:7). The word that was spoken by angels was firm (Heb. 2:2). We have become the companions of Christ if we hold the beginning of our assurance firm to the end (Heb. 3:14). The hope set before Christians is like an anchor of the soul, secure and firm (Heb. 6:19). We have the prophetic word made more sure {more certain, confirmed} (2 Pet. 1:19). All other refs.: SURE <949>, VALID <949>.
[2] ***hedraios*** [adj.: ἑδραῖος <1476>]; **from *hedra*: seat ▶ Determined, resolved** > He who has decided not to marry and who stands firm {steadfast} in his heart does well (1 Cor. 7:37). Paul exhorts his beloved brothers to be firm (1 Cor. 15:58). Christians will be presented before God holy, blameless, and irreproachable if they remain in the faith, grounded and firm (Col. 1:23; see v. 22). ¶
[3] ***stereos*** [adj.: στερεός <4731>] **▶ Solid, unmoved** > We are to resist the devil, being firm {steadfast} in the faith (1 Pet. 5:9). Other refs.: 2 Tim. 2:19; Heb. 5:12, 14; see SOLID <4731>. ¶
[4] **to stand firm: *stēkō*** [verb: στήκω <4739>]; **from *estēka*, a form of *histēmi*: to stand ▶ To persevere, to remain steadfast; also transl.: to stand fast** > Christians are to stand firm in the faith (1 Cor. 16:13) and in freedom (Gal. 5:1). The Philippians were to stand firm in the Lord (Phil. 1:27; 4:1). Paul lived if the Thessalonians stood firm in the Lord (1 Thes. 3:8). All other refs.: STAND (verb) <4739>.
– [5] Matt. 10:22; 24:13; Mark 13:13 → to stand firm → ENDURE <5278> [6] Luke 21:19 → standing firm → PATIENCE <5281> [7] 1 Cor. 1:8 → to keep firm → CONFIRM <950> [8] 1 Cor. 7:37 → to stand firm → DETERMINE <2919> [9] 2 Cor. 1:21 → to make stand firm → ESTABLISH <950> [10] Col. 2:5 → how firm your faith is → lit.: the steadfastness of your faith → STEADFASTNESS <4733> [11] Titus 1:9 → to hold firm → FAST (HOLD) <472> [12] Heb. 6:19 → SURE <804> [13] Jas. 5:8 → to stand firm → lit.: to establish the hearts → ESTABLISH <4741>.

FIRMLY – [1] 1 Cor. 15:2; Heb. 3:6 → to hold firmly → FAST (HOLD) <2722> [2] 2 Cor. 1:7 → firmly, firmly grounded → FIRM <949> [3] Phil. 2:16 → to hold firmly → HOLD (verb) <1907> [4] 2 Tim. 3:14 → to believe firmly → ASSURED (BE) <4104> [5] Titus 1:9 → to hold firmly → FAST (HOLD) <472> [6] Heb. 4:14 → to hold firmly → FAST (HOLD) <2902>.

FIRMNESS – Col. 2:5 → STEADFASTNESS <4733>.

FIRST – [1] **first, at first, at the first, first of all, the first time: *proteron*** [adj. used as adv.: πρότερον <4386>]; **from *proteros*: first ▶ Previously, before (anything else)** > Paul had announced the gospel to the Galatians at first in weakness of flesh (Gal. 4:13). Those who first {formerly} received the gospel had been disobedient (Heb. 4:6). The high priests first offer up sacrifices for their own sins and then for those of the people (Heb. 7:27). All other refs.: BEFORE <4386>, EARLIER <4386>, FORMER <4386>.
[2] **first, at first: *prōton*** [adj. used as adv.: πρῶτον <4412>]; **from *prōtos*: first ▶ Primarily, before** > One must first be reconciled to his brother, and then offer his gift (Matt. 5:24). The gospel must first be

preached to all the nations before the events of the end (Mark 13:10). Jesus began to say to His disciples first of all to beware of the leaven of the Pharisees, i.e., hypocrisy (Luke 12:1). The Son of Man had to suffer many things first (Luke 17:25). Jesus went to the place where John was baptizing at first {in the early days} (John 10:40). The disciples did not understand at first the things Jesus was telling them (John 12:16). Nicodemus at first {earlier} came to Jesus by night (John 19:39). First {Chiefly, First of all} to the Jews were entrusted the oracles of God (Rom. 3:2). Paul wanted first to enjoy the company of Christians in Rome (Rom. 15:24). He did not praise the Corinthians, for first {in the first place}, when they came together as a church there existed divisions among them (1 Cor. 11:18). God has first appointed apostles in the church (1 Cor. 12:28). The apostasy will come first before the day of the Lord (2 Thes. 2:3). Paul exhorts Timothy first of all to pray for all men (1 Tim. 2:1). He recalled the unfeigned faith that had dwelt first in the grandmother and the mother of Timothy (2 Tim. 1:5). We should know this first {above all}, that no prophecy of Scripture is a matter of any private interpretation (2 Pet. 1:20). We should know first {first of all} that mockers will come in the last days (2 Pet. 3:3). Other refs.: Matt. 6:33; 7:5; 8:21; 12:29; 13:30; 17:10, 11 (in some mss.); 23:26; Mark 3:27; 4:28; 7:27; 9:11, 12; 16:9; Luke 6:42; 9:59, 61; 10:5; 11:38; 14:28, 31; 21:9; John 2:10 {at the beginning}; 15:18; 18:13; Acts 3:26; 7:12 {first time, first visit}; 11:26; 13:46; 15:14; 26:20; Rom. 1:8, 16; 2:9, 10; 1 Cor. 15:46; 2 Cor. 8:5; Eph. 4:9 in some mss.; 1 Thes. 4:16; 1 Tim. 3:10; 5:4; Heb. 7:2; Jas. 3:17; 1 Pet. 4:17. ¶

3 ***prōtos*** [adj.: πρῶτος <4413>]**; superl. of *pro*: before, forward ► Before, primarily; also transl.: chief >** Jesus said that if anyone wants to be first, he shall be last of all and servant of all (Mark 9:35). We love because God has first loved us (1 John 4:19). Other refs.: Matt. 10:2; 12:45; 17:27; 19:30a, b; 20:8, 10, 16a, b, 27; 21:28, 31, 36; 22:25, 38; 26:17; 27:64; Mark 6:21; 10:31a, b, 44; 12:20, 28–30; 14:12; 16:9; Luke 2:2; 11:26; 13:30a, b; 14:18; 15:22; 16:5; 19:16, 47; 20:29; John 1:15, 30; 41; 5:4; 8:7; 19:32; 20:4, 8; Acts 1:1; 12:10; 13:50; 16:12; 17:4; 20:18; 25:2; 26:23; 27:43; 28:7, 17; Rom. 10:19; 1 Cor. 14:30; 15:3, 45, 47; Eph. 6:2; Phil. 1:5; 1 Tim. 1:15, 16; 2:13; 5:12; 2 Tim. 2:6; 4:16; Heb. 8:7, 13; 9:1, 2, 6, 8, 15, 18; 10:9; 2 Pet. 2:20; Rev. 1:11, 17; 2:4, 5, 8, 19; 4:1, 7; 8:7; 13:12a, b; 16:2; 20:5, 6; 21:1a, b, 4, 19; 22:13. ¶

4 second-first, second after the first: *deuteroprōtos* [adj.: δευτερόπρωτος <1207>]**; from *deuteros*: second, and *prōtos*: see 3 ► The second-first Sabbath was the Sabbath after the second day of unleavened bread connected with the Passover >** Jesus went through cornfields on the second-first Sabbath (Luke 6:1 in some mss.). ¶

5 ***mia*** [card. num.: μία <3391>] **► Fem. of *heis*: one >** In Mark 16:2, "the first day of the week" renders the lit. expr. "first of the week"; likewise in John 20:1, 19; Acts 20:7; 1 Cor. 16:2; other refs.: Matt. 28:1 {the next day after the Sabbath}; Luke 24:1 {the morrow of the Sabbath}. The word is used concerning admonition (Titus 3:10) and woes (Rev. 9:12). *

6 from the very first: *anōthen* [adv.: ἄνωθεν <509>]**; from *anō*: above, and suffix *then*: from ► From the beginning >** Luke had perfect understanding from the very first {from the beginning, the first, the origin} of things received among the Christians (Luke 1:3). All other refs.: ABOVE <509>, AGAIN <509>, BEGINNING <509>, TOP <509>.

7 to be there first: *prokeimai* [verb: πρόκειμαι <4295>]**; from *pro*: before, and *keimai*: to be found ► To be present >** If the readiness to give is there first, it is accepted according to what one may have (2 Cor. 8:12). All other refs.: SET (verb) <4295>.

– **8** Eph. 1:12 → to first trust → TRUST (verb) <4276> **9** Heb. 5:12 → the first {elementary} principles → lit.: the principles of the beginning (*tēs archēs*).

FIRSTBEGOTTEN – Heb. 1:6; Rev. 1:5 → FIRSTBORN <4416>.

FIRSTBORN – ***prōtotokos*** [masc. noun: πρωτότοκος <4416>]; **from *protos*: first, and *tiktō*: to give birth ▶ First in order of birth; preeminent; also transl.: first-begotten** > This word designates the order of birth of Jesus Christ (Matt. 1:25; Luke 2:7) and the firstborn of the Israelites in Egypt (Heb. 11:28). It is also used to draw attention to the preeminence of the Lord Jesus (Heb. 1:6) over creation (Col. 1:15), as the Creator (see v. 16), among many brothers (Rom. 8:29), and in resurrection (Col. 1:18; Rev. 1:5). The church is called the church of the firstborn (Heb. 12:23), because it occupies the first place in the counsels of God. ¶

FIRSTFRUITS – [1] ***aparchē*** [fem. noun: ἀπαρχή <536>]; **from *aparchomai*: to offer the firstfruits, which is from *apo*: from, and *archē*: beginning ▶ First ripe fruits of the harvest; also transl.: first convert** > This was the occasion of a feast instituted by the Lord (or: Jehovah) (see Lev. 23:9–14). The Holy Spirit who dwells in the Christian is the firstfruits of the fruits of redemption (Rom. 8:23). The first Christians in a region constitute its firstfruits (Rom. 16:5; 1 Cor. 16:15). Jesus Christ, raised from among the dead, is the firstfruits of those who have fallen asleep in Him (1 Cor. 15:20, 23). The 144,000 of Revelation 14 are the firstfruits to God and the Lamb (v. 4). See also Rom. 11:16 {first piece of dough} in relation to Israel. Christians are a kind of firstfruits of God's creatures (Jas. 1:18). Other ref.: 2 Thes. 2:13 in some mss. ¶
– [2] 2 Thes. 2:13 → as firstfruits → lit.: from beginning → BEGINNING <746>.

FISH (noun)– [1] ***ichthus*** [masc. noun: ἰχθύς <2486>] **▶ Animal that lives in water and breathes through gills** > A father will not give his son a serpent if he asks him for a fish (Matt. 7:10; Luke 11:11a, b). The disciples had only five loaves and two fish (Matt. 14:17, 19; Mark 6:38; Luke 9:13), but Jesus multiplied them (Mark 6:41a, b; Luke 9:16), and they gathered the remnants (Mark 6:43). On another occasion, Jesus multiplied seven loaves and a fish (Matt. 15:36). Peter was to take the first fish that came up (Matt. 17:27). The disciples enclosed a great multitude of fish in their net (Luke 5:6, 9; John 21:6, 8). The disciples gave Jesus a piece of a broiled fish (Luke 24:42). Peter drew the net to land full of 153 large fish (John 21:11). The flesh of fish differs from other flesh (1 Cor. 15:39). ¶
[2] **small fish, little fish: *ichthudion*** [neut. noun: ἰχθύδιον <2485>]; **dimin. of *ichthus*: see [1] ▶ Little fish** > The disciples had seven loaves and a few small fish (Matt. 15:34; Mark 8:7). ¶
[3] **fish, small fish: *opsarion*** [neut. noun: ὀψάριον <3795>]; **dimin. of *opson*: cooked food or food eaten with bread ▶ Cooked fish** > A little boy had five barley loaves and two small fish (John 6:9); Jesus multiplied them (v. 11). The disciples saw a fire of coals and fish laid on it (John 21:9); Jesus told them to bring of the fish which they had just taken (v. 10). He gave the fish to His disciples (John 21:13). ¶
– [4] Matt. 12:40 → great fish, huge fish → WHALE <2785> [5] John 21:5 → FOOD <4371>.

FISH (verb) – [1] ***halieuō*** [verb: ἁλιεύω <232>]; **from *halieus*: fisher, which is from *hals*: sea ▶ To catch fish** > Simon Peter told his companions that he was going to fish (John 21:3). ¶
– [2] Matt. 4:19; Mark 1:17 → to send out to fish, to send to fish for people → lit.: to become fishers of men → FISHER <231> [3] Luke 5:10 → CATCH (verb) <2221>.

FISHER – ***halieus*** [masc. noun: ἁλιεύς <231>]; **from *hals*: sea ▶ One who catches fish; also transl.: fisherman** > Simon Peter and his brother Andrew were fishers (Matt. 4:18; Mark 1:16). Jesus told them He would make them fishers of men (Matt. 4:19; Mark 1:17). He saw two fishermen who were washing their nets (Luke 5:2). ¶

FISHERMAN – Matt. 4:18; Mark 1:16; Luke 5:2 → FISHER <231>.

FIT (adj.) – [1] ***euthetos*** [adj.: εὔθετος <2111>]; **from *eu*: well, and *tithēmi*: to**

place ▶ Appropriate, useful, suitable > The word is used in regard to the kingdom of God (Luke 9:62) and to salt (Luke 14:35 {proper}). Other ref.: Heb. 6:7; see USEFUL <2111>. ¶
– 2 Matt. 3:11; 8:8; Mark 1:7; Luke 3:16; 1 Cor. 15:9 → WORTHY <2425> 3 Rom. 1:28 → to see fit → LIKE (verb) <1381> 4 Col. 1:12 → to make fit → to make meet → MEET (adj.) <2427>.

FIT (noun) – 2 Cor. 12:20; Gal. 5:20 → fit of rage, fit of rages → wrath, outbursts of wrath → WRATH <2372>.

FIT (verb) – 1 **to fit together: *sunarmologeō*** [verb: συναρμολογέω <4883>]**; from *sun*: together, and *harmologeō*: to join together, which is from *harmos*: joint, articulation ▶ To be well adjusted together >** The church is a building fitted together {fitly framed together, joined together} in Christ Jesus (Eph. 2:21); see also Eph. 4:16 {to join together, to fitly join together}. ¶
– 2 Eph. 4:16 → to fit together → to knit together → KNIT <4822>.

FIT (BE) – 1 Acts 22:22 → FITTING (BE) <2520> 2 Acts 25:24 → he was not fit to live → lit.: he ought not to live → OUGHT <1163> 3 Col. 3:18 → FITTING (BE) <433>.

FITTED – 1 Rom. 9:22 → PREPARED <2675> 2 Eph. 6:15 → SHOD <5265> 3 2 Tim. 3:17 → to be fitted → to be fully accomplished → ACCOMPLISH <1822>.

FITTING – 1 ***axios*** [adj.: ἄξιος <514>]**; from *agō*: to weigh ▶ Proper, right >** It was fitting for Paul to thank God always for the Thessalonians (2 Thes. 1:3). Other refs.: DESERVING <514>, MEET (adj.) <514>, UNWORTHY <514>, WORTHY <514>.
– 2 Rom. 8:26 → OUGHT <1163> 3 1 Cor. 14:40 → in a fitting way → DECENTLY <2156> 4 Eph. 5:4 → FITTING (BE) <433>.

FITTING (BE) – 1 ***anēkō*** [verb: ἀνήκω <433>]**; from *ana*: above, and *hēkō*: to happen ▶ To be appropriate, suitable >** Filthiness, foolish talking, and jesting are not fitting {are not convenient, are out of place} among the Christians (Eph. 5:4). Wives are exhorted to submit themselves to their own husbands as is fitting {it is fit} in the Lord (Col. 3:18). Paul was very bold in Christ to command Philemon what was fitting {was convenient, was proper, he ought to do} (Phm. 8). ¶
2 ***kathēkō*** [verb: καθήκω <2520>]**; from *kata*: with, and *hēkō*: to happen ▶ To be suitable, to be appropriate; also transl.: to be fit >** Those who were listening to Paul said it was not fit for him {he was not fit, he should not be allowed} to live (Acts 22:22). God has given evil men over to a reprobate mind to do things which are not fitting {are not convenient, are unseemly, are not proper, ought not to be done} (Rom. 1:28). ¶
3 ***prepō*** [verb: πρέπω <4241>] **▶ To be appropriate, to be convenient; also transl.: to become >** It was fitting for {was proper for} Jesus to fulfill all righteousness (Matt. 3:15). Sexual immorality, all uncleanness, or covetousness should not even be named as is fitting for {as is proper for} saints (Eph. 5:3); other transl.: these things are improper for God's people. Paul told Titus to speak things which are fitting for {are proper to, in accord with} sound teaching (Titus 2:1). It was fitting for God to make the author of our salvation perfect through sufferings (Heb. 2:10). Jesus is a high priest who was fitting for Christians {meets their need} (Heb. 7:26). All other refs.: COMELY <4241>, PROPER <4241>.
– 4 Luke 15:32 → OUGHT <1163>.

FIVE – 1 ***pente*** [card. num.: πέντε <4002>] **▶** This number is used in regard to loaves of bread (Matt. 14:17, 19; 16:9; Mark 6:38, 41; 8:19; Luke 9:13, 16; John 6:9, 13), wise and foolish virgins (Matt. 25:2a, b), talents (Matt. 25:15, 16a, b, 20a–d), months (Luke 1:24; Rev. 9:5, 10), sparrows (Luke 12:6), people in a house (Luke 12:52), yoke of oxen (Luke 14:19), brothers (Luke 16:28), minas (Luke 19:18), cities (Luke 19:19), husbands (John 4:18), porches (John 5:2), days (Acts 20:6; 24:1),

words (1 Cor. 14:19), and kings (Rev. 17:10). ¶
– [2] Matt. 20:6, 9 → five in the afternoon → lit.: the eleventh hour → ELEVENTH <1734>.

FIVE HUNDRED – ***pentakosioi*** [card. num.: πεντακόσιοι <4001>]; **from *pente*: five, and *hekaton*: hundred** ▶ This number is used in regard to denarii (Luke 7:41) and brothers to whom the Lord appeared after His resurrection (1 Cor. 15:6). ¶

FIVE THOUSAND – [1] ***pentakischilioi*** [adj. num.: πεντακισχίλιοι <4000>]; **from *pentakis*: five times, and *chilioi*: thousands** ▶ Jesus miraculously fed about five thousand men on one occasion (Matt. 14:21; 16:9; Mark 6:44; 8:19; Luke 9:14; John 6:10). ¶
[2] **five: *pente*** [card. num.: πέντε <4002>] **thousand: *chilias*** [fem. noun: χιλιάς <5505>] ▶ The number of men who heard and believed the word preached by Peter and John was about five thousand (Acts 4:4). ¶

FIX – [1] **to fix the eyes, to fix one's gaze: *atenizō*** [verb: ἀτενίζω <816>]; **from *atenēs*: strained, earnest, which is from *a*: intens., and *teinō*: to stretch ▶ To look fixedly, to scrutinize; also transl.: to behold stedfastly, to look earnestly, to look intently, to look directly, to look straight, to observe, to observe intently, to set the eyes, to stare** > Peter asked the Israelites why they had fixed their eyes {were gazing} on himself and John (Acts 3:12). Cornelius fixed his eyes on the angel (Acts 10:4). Having fixed his eyes on a certain vessel like a great sheet, Peter considered the vision (Acts 11:6). Paul fixed his eyes on Elymas (Acts 13:9). He also fixed his eyes on the man who had no strength in his feet (Acts 14:9). All other refs.: BEHOLD (verb) <816>, FASTEN <816>, LOOK (verb) <816>.
[2] **to fix the eyes: *aphoraō*** [verb: ἀφοράω <872>]; **from *apo*: intens., and *horaō*: to see ▶ To turn one's eyes, to concentrate one's attention; also transl.: to look, to look steadfastly (stedfastly)** > The Christian is to run with perseverance the race that is set before him, fixing the eyes on Jesus, the author and the perfecter of faith (Heb. 12:2). Other ref.: Phil. 2:23; see SEE <872>. ¶
[3] ***stērizō*** [verb: στηρίζω <4741>]; **comp. *stereos*: solid, stable ▶ To set, to firmly establish** > A great chasm is fixed in the hereafter between those who suffer and those who are in paradise (Luke 16:26). All other refs.: ESTABLISH <4741>, STEADFASTLY <4741>, STRENGTHEN <4741>.
[4] ***tithēmi*** [verb: τίθημι <5087>] ▶ **To place, to put, to set** > God the Father has fixed the times and the seasons by His own authority for the restoration of Israel (Acts 1:7). All other refs.: see entries in Lexicon at <5087>.
– [5] Matt. 27:48; Mark 15:36 → to fix on → to put on → PUT <4060> [6] Acts 3:5 → fixed his attention → gave his attention → ATTENTION <1907> [7] 1 Tim. 6:17 → to fix one's hope → TRUST (verb) <1679> [8] Heb. 3:1 → to fix the thoughts → CONSIDER <2657> [9] Heb. 4:7 → DETERMINE <3724>.

FIXED – [1] Luke 16:26 → FIX <4741> [2] Gal. 4:2 → period fixed → time appointed → TIME <4287>.

FIXEDLY – Acts 6:15 → to look fixedly → to look steadfastly → LOOK (verb) <816>.

FLAME – [1] ***phlox*** [fem. noun: φλόξ <5395>]; **from *phlegō*: to burn, to illuminate ▶ Light produced by the combustion of a substance** > The rich man, in Hades, was tormented in the flame (Luke 16:24). An angel appeared to Moses in the flame of a burning bush (Acts 7:30). The angels of God's power, in flaming {blazing} (lit.: flames of) fire, take vengeance on those who do not know God (2 Thes. 1:7 or 8). God makes His servants a flame of fire (Heb. 1:7). The Son of God has eyes like a flame of fire {blazing fire} (Rev. 1:14; 2:18; 19:12). ¶
– [2] 1 Cor. 13:3 → BURN <2545> [3] 2 Tim. 1:6 → to fan into flame → REKINDLE <329>.

FLAMING – [1] Eph. 6:16 → FIERY <4448> [2] 2 Thes. 1:8 → FLAME <5395>.

FLASH (noun) – 1 Cor. 15:52 → MOMENT <823>.

FLASH (verb) – [1] Matt. 24:27 → APPEAR <5316> [2] Luke 17:24 → SHINE <797> [3] Acts 9:3; 22:6 → to flash around → to shine around → SHINE <4015>.

FLASK – [1] Matt. 25:4 → VESSEL[1] <30> [2] Matt. 26:7; Mark 14:3a, b → alabaster flask → alabaster box → ALABASTER <211>.

FLATTER – Jude 16 → to have in admiration → ADMIRATION <2296>.

FLATTERING – [1] **flattery:** ***kolakeia*** [fem. noun: κολακεία <2850>]; **from** ***kolakeuō*****: to flatter, to adulate ► Act of seeking to please, but with an ulterior motive** > The apostle Paul had never used flattering speech (lit.: speech of flattery) in regard to the Thessalonians (1 Thes. 2:5). ¶
– [2] Rom. 16:18 → flattering speech → fair speeches → SPEECH <2129>.

FLATTERY – [1] Rom. 16:18 → fair speeches → SPEECH <2129> [2] 1 Thes. 2:5 → FLATTERING <2850>.

FLAVOR – [1] Matt. 5:13; Luke 14:34 → to lose its flavor → LOSE <3471> [2] Mark 9:50 → to lose the flavor → to become unsalty → UNSALTY <358>.

FLAX – ***linon*** [neut. noun: λίνον <3043>] **► Fiber of a plant from which linen is obtained; also transl.: wick** > Lamp wicks were made from braided flax. The Lord will not quench smoking flax (Matt. 12:20; see Is. 42:3). Other refs.: Mark 1:18 in some mss.; Rev. 15:6; see LINEN, LINEN CLOTH <3043>. ¶

FLEE – [1] ***pheugō*** [verb: φεύγω <5343>]; ***fugere*****, in Lat.: to run, to flee ► To run away in order to escape; also transl.: to run away, to run off** > Joseph was to flee into Egypt (Matt. 2:13). John the Baptist asked who had forewarned the crowds to flee from the coming wrath (Matt. 3:7; Luke 3:7). Those who fed the herd of swine fled (Matt. 8:33; Mark 5:14; Luke 8:34). When they will see the abomination of desolation, Jesus told those who will be persecuted in one city to flee into another (Matt. 10:23). Those who are in Judea will have to flee to the mountains (Matt. 24:16; Mark 13:14; Luke 21:21). All the disciples left Jesus and fled (Matt. 26:56; Mark 14:50). The women fled from the tomb of Jesus (Mark 16:8). The sheep of Jesus flee from a stranger (John 10:5). He who is not the shepherd flees when he sees the wolf coming (John 10:12, 13). Moses fled to the land of Midian (Acts 7:29); *phugadeuō* in some mss.: to live in exile. The sailors on board Paul's ship were seeking to flee {escape} (Acts 27:30). Christians are to flee sexual immorality (1 Cor. 6:18) and to flee from idolatry (10:14). Timothy was to flee various things (1 Tim. 6:11), including the love of money (see vv. 10, 11). He was also to flee youthful lusts (2 Tim. 2:22). If Christians resist the devil, he will flee from them (Jas. 4:7). The earth and the heaven fled away from the face of the One who was sitting on the great white throne (Rev. 20:11). Other refs.: Rev. 9:6 {to elude}; 12:6; 16:20. All other refs.: ESCAPE <5343>.

[2] ***ekpheugō*** [verb: ἐκφεύγω <1628>]; **from** ***ek*****: from, and** ***pheugō*****: see [1] ► To escape** > The jailer thought the prisoners had fled {had escaped} (Acts 16:27). The exorcists fled out {ran out} of the house of the man in whom the evil spirit was (Acts 19:16). All other refs.: ESCAPE <1628>.

[3] **to flee, to flee for refuge:** ***katapheugō*** [verb: καταφεύγω <2703>]; **from** ***kata*****: intens., and** ***pheugō*****: see [1] ► To escape in order to find refuge** > Paul and Barnabas fled to Lystra and Derbe (Acts 14:6). Believers in the Lord have fled for refuge to lay hold of the hope set before them (Heb. 6:18). ¶

FLEETING – Heb. 11:25 → for a time → TIME <4340>.

FLESH – [1] ***sarx*** [fem. noun: σάρξ <4561>] ► In the N.T., this word has different meanings: **a. the substance of the body, whether of animals or men** (1 Cor. 15:39); **b. the human body** (2 Cor. 10:3; Gal. 2:20; Phil. 1:22); **c. the human nature, which includes the spirit, the soul, and the body of people** (Matt. 24:22; John 1:13; Rom. 3:20); **d. the holy humanity of the Lord Jesus, which includes His spirit, His soul, and His body** (John 1:14; 1 Tim. 3:16; 1 John 4:2, 3; 2 John 7); in Heb. 5:7, the expr. "the days of his flesh" refers to the life of the Lord spent on the earth in contrast to His present life in resurrection; **e. the complete person** (2 Cor. 7:5; Jas. 5:3); **f. the weakest element of the human nature** (Matt. 26:41; Rom. 6:19; 8:3a); **g. the non-regenerated state of men** (Rom. 7:5; 8:8, 9); **h. the seat of sin in the inward man** (2 Pet. 2:18; 1 John 2:16); **i. the inferior and temporal element in the Christian** (Gal. 3:3; 6:8) **and in the ordinances of the flesh** (Heb. 9:10); **j. the human person with its natural abilities** (1 Cor. 1:26; 2 Cor. 10:2, 3b); **k. circumstances** (1 Cor. 7:28); concerning what is external to Christians (2 Cor. 7:1; Eph. 6:5; Heb. 9:13); **l. what is external and visible in contrast with the spirit, which is internal and true** (John 6:63); **m. natural relationships** (1 Cor. 10:18; Gal. 4:23) **or marital ones** (Matt. 19:5, 6; Mark 10:8; 1 Cor. 6:16; Eph. 5:31). (After Walter Scott.) Other refs.: Matt. 16:17; Mark 13:20; 14:38; Luke 3:6; 24:39; John 3:6a, b; 6:51–56; 8:15; 17:2; Acts 2:17, 26, 30 (in some mss.), 31; Rom. 1:3; 2:28; 4:1; 7:18, 25; 8:1 (in some mss.), 3a–c, 4, 5a, b, 6, 7, 12a, b, 13; 9:3, 5, 8; 11:14; 13:14; 1 Cor. 1:29; 5:5; 15:39a–d, 50; 2 Cor. 1:17; 4:11; 5:16a, b; 10:3a, b; 11:18; 12:7; Gal. 1:16; 2:16; 4:13, 14, 29; 5:13, 16, 17a, b, 19, 24; 6:8a, b, 12, 13; Eph. 2:3a, b, 11a, b, 15; 5:29, 30; 6:12; Phil. 1:24; 3:3, 4a, b; Col. 1:22, 24; 2:1, 5, 11, 13, 18, 23; 3:22; Phm. 16; Heb. 2:14; 9:10; 10:20; 12:9; 1 Pet. 1:24; 3:18, 21; 4:1a, b, 2, 6; 2 Pet. 2:10; Jude 7, 8, 23; Rev. 17:16; 19:18, 21. ¶

[2] ***kreas*** [neut. noun: κρέας <2907>] ► **Meat** > It is good neither to eat flesh nor to drink wine, or to do other things that could scandalize our brother (Rom. 14:21). Paul would never again eat flesh if it made his brother stumble (1 Cor. 8:13). ¶

– [3] Rom. 7:14; 1 Cor. 3:1, 3a, b; 2 Cor. 10:4; 1 Pet. 2:11 → of flesh, of the flesh → CARNAL <4559> [4] 2 Cor. 3:3 → of flesh → FLESHLY <4560> [5] Phil. 3:2 → mutilator of the flesh → CONCISION <2699>.

FLESHLY – [1] ***sarkinos*** [adj.: σάρκινος <4560>]; **from *sarx*: flesh** ► **Made of the substance corresponding to the physical body** > The Corinthians were the epistle of Christ written by the Spirit in the heart of Paul, not on tablets of stone, but on fleshly tablets {fleshy tablets, tablets of flesh, tablets of human hearts} (2 Cor. 3:3). Other refs.: in some mss.: Rom. 7:14; 1 Cor. 3:1; Heb. 7:14. ¶

– [2] Rom. 15:27; 1 Cor. 3:3a, b; 9:11; 2 Cor. 1:12; 10:4; 1 Pet. 2:11 → CARNAL <4559> [3] Col. 1:22; 2:18, 23; Heb. 9:10; 2 Pet. 2:18 → FLESH <4561>.

FLESHY – 2 Cor. 3:3 → FLESHLY <4560>.

FLIGHT – [1] ***phugē*** [fem. noun: φυγή <5437>]; **from *pheugō*: to flee** ► **Hasty departure to avoid danger** > The Jews were to pray that their flight might not be in winter time (Matt. 24:20; Mark 13:18 in some mss.). ¶

[2] **to put to flight, to turn to flight: *klinō*** [verb: κλίνω <2827>] ► **To induce to bow, to make to give way** > O.T. people of faith put to flight {routed} the armies of strangers (Heb. 11:34). All other refs.: BOW (verb) <2827>, LAY <2827>, WEAR <2827>.

– [3] Rev. 4:7 → in flight → flying → FLY <4072>.

FLOCK – [1] ***poimnē*** [fem. noun: ποίμνη <4167>]; **from *poimēn*: shepherd** ► **a. Animals, particularly sheep, raised together** > Shepherds kept watch over their flocks at night (Luke 2:8). One who tends a flock drinks of the milk of the flock (1 Cor. 9:7a, b). **b. The term is used to designate**

those who follow the Lord Jesus > Jesus said that the sheep of the flock would be scattered (Matt. 26:31). He says that there shall be one flock and one shepherd (John 10:16). ¶

[2] ***poimnion*** [neut. noun: ποίμνιον <4168>]; **from *poimēn*: shepherd ▶ The term is used in the N.T. only in regard to the disciples of the Lord Jesus** > Jesus says: Fear not, little flock, for your Father has been pleased to give you the kingdom (Luke 12:32). Paul told the elders of Ephesus to keep watch over themselves and all the flock, among which the Holy Spirit had set them as overseers to shepherd the church of God, which He had purchased with the blood of His own Son (Acts 20:28); he knew that after his departure there would enter among them savage wolves, not sparing the flock (v. 29). Peter exhorts the elders to shepherd the flock of God which is with them, not by constraint, but willingly, and not for dishonest gain, but with eagerness (1 Pet. 5:2), not as lords over those entrusted to them, but as models for the flock (v. 3). ¶

– [3] John 4:12 → flocks and herds → CATTLE <2353> [4] John 10:26 → part of my flock → lit.: of my sheep → SHEEP <4263>.

FLOG – [1] Matt. 10:17; 20:19; 23:34; Mark 10:34; Luke 18:33; John 19:1 → SCOURGE (verb) <3146> [2] Matt. 27:26; Mark 15:15 → SCOURGE (verb) <5417> [3] Mark 13:9; Luke 12:48; Acts 5:40 → BEAT <1194> [4] Acts 16:23 → lit.: to strike with many blows → STRIKE <2007>, STRIPE <4127> [5] Acts 22:24 → to flog and interrogate → lit.: to examine by scourging → SCOURGING <3148> [6] 2 Cor. 11:23 → STRIPE <4127>.

FLOGGING – [1] Luke 12:48 → STRIPE <4127> [2] Acts 22:24; Heb. 11:36 → SCOURGING <3148>.

FLOOD (noun) – [1] ***kataklusmos*** [masc. noun: κατακλυσμός <2627>]; **from *katakluzō*: to overflow, which is from *kata*: intens., and *kluzō*: to dash, to flood ▶ Overflowing of water which becomes a cataclysm** > The flood happened during the days of Noah. We read that "all the fountains of the great deep were broken up, and the windows of heaven were opened" (Gen. 7:11), to such an extent that "the high hills under the whole heaven were covered" (v. 19). The flood was a judgment of God upon the world of the ungodly (2 Pet. 2:5). Only Noah, the righteous, and his household were saved (Matt. 24:38, 39; Luke 17:27; see also 1 Pet. 3:20). ¶

[2] ***plēmmura*** [fem. noun: πλήμμυρα <4132>]; **similar to *plēmmē* or *plēsmē*: rising of a river, which is from *pimplēmi*: to fill ▶ Rise in the water level, overflow of a river** > In a parable, when a flood {great rain} came, the stream beat with violence against the house (Luke 6:48). ¶

– [3] Matt. 7:25, 27; Rev. 12:15a, 16 → RIVER <4215> [4] 1 Pet. 4:4 → EXCESS <401> [5] Rev. 12:15b → carried away by a flood, swept away with the flood → carried away by a river → RIVER <4216>.

FLOOD (verb) – 2 Pet. 3:6 → DELUGE <2626>.

FLOOR – [1] Matt. 3:12; Luke 3:17 → THRESHING FLOOR <257> [2] Acts 20:9 → third floor → third story → STORY <5152>.

FLOUR – [1] ***aleuron*** [neut. noun: ἄλευρον <224>]; **from *aleō*: to grind ▶ Powder obtained by grinding cereal grain such as wheat** > In a parable, a woman hid leaven in three measures of flour (Matt. 13:33; Luke 13:21). ¶

[2] **fine flour: *semidalis*** [fem. noun: σεμίδαλις <4585>] **▶ Fine wheat flour, i.e., very white and very fine flour** > After the fall of Babylon, no one will buy fine flour anymore (Rev. 18:13). ¶

FLOURISH – [1] Acts 12:24 → MULTIPLY <4129> [2] Phil. 4:10 → REVIVE <330>.

FLOW (noun) – [1] ***pēgē*** [fem. noun: πηγή <4077>]; **lit.: fountain, source ▶ Issue, as of blood** > A woman touched the clothes of Jesus and immediately the flow of her blood {the fountain of her blood, her bleeding} dried up (Mark 5:29). All other refs.: FOUNTAIN <4077>.

[2] ***rhusis*** [fem. noun: ῥύσις <4511>]; **from *rheō*: to flow ► Flowing, as of blood; i.e., bleeding** > Jesus healed a woman who had had a flow {a flux, an issue} of blood {who had had a hemorrhage, who had been subject to bleeding} for twelve years (Mark 5:25; Luke 8:43, 44). ¶

[3] **to have a flow of blood: *haimorroeō*** [verb: αἱμορροέω <131>]; **from *haima*: blood, and *rheō*: to flow ► To suffer a hemorrhage** > Jesus healed a woman who had had a flow of blood {had a bloody flux, was diseased with an issue of blood, had been suffering from a hemorrhage, had been subject to bleeding} for twelve years (Matt. 9:20). ¶

FLOW (verb) – [1] ***rheō*** [verb: ῥέω <4482>] ► **To spurt out, to stream** > Rivers of living water will flow out of the belly of one who believes in Jesus (John 7:38). ¶

– [2] 2 Cor. 1:5a → to flow over → ABOUND <4052> [3] 2 Cor. 9:13 → "flowing" added in Engl.

FLOWER – [1] ***anthos*** [neut. noun: ἄνθος <438>] ► **Part of certain plants that has color other than the usual green of the stems and leaves, and which is sometimes fragrant** > The rich will pass away like the flower of the grass {flowering grass} (Jas. 1:10). Under the burning heat of the sun, the flower has fallen and the beauty of its appearance has perished (Jas. 1:11). Human glory is like the flower of the grass: the grass has withered and its flower has fallen, but the word of the Lord endures eternally (1 Pet. 1:24a, b). ¶

– [2] Matt. 6:28; Luke 12:27 → flower, wild flower → LILY <2918> [3] 1 Cor. 7:36 → who has passed the flower of youth → who has passed the flower of age → AGE <5230>.

FLOWERING – Jas. 1:10 → flowering grass → lit.: the flower of the grass → FLOWER <438>.

FLUTE – [1] ***aulos*** [masc. noun: αὐλός <836>] ► **Musical wind instrument** > The flute {pipe} is an inanimate thing that gives a sound (1 Cor. 14:7). ¶

[2] **to play the flute: *auleō*** [verb: αὐλέω <832>]; **from *aulos*: see [1] ► To play this instrument** > Little children had played the flute (Matt. 11:17; Luke 7:32). One recognizes what is played on the flute by the distinct sound of the instrument (1 Cor. 14:7). ¶

– [3] Matt. 9:23; Rev. 18:22 → FLUTE PLAYER <834>.

FLUTE PLAYER – ***aulētēs*** [masc. noun: αὐλητής <834>]; **from *auleō*: to play the flute ► Flutist; also transl.: piper, person who plays the pipe, minstrel** > Jesus saw the flute players (Matt. 9:23). The sound of flute players will be heard no more in Babylon (Rev. 18:22). ¶

FLUTE-PLAYER – Matt. 9:23; Rev. 18:22 → FLUTE PLAYER <834>.

FLUTIST – Rev. 18:22 → FLUTE PLAYER <834>.

FLUX – Mark 5:25; Luke 8:43, 44 → FLOW (noun) <4511>.

FLY – ***petomai*** [verb: πέτομαι <4072>] ► **To propel oneself through the atmosphere by means of wings** > John saw a fourth animal like a flying eagle (Rev. 4:7); he saw and heard an eagle flying in mid-heaven (8:13); he saw a woman who was given the two wings of a great eagle that she might fly into the desert (Rev. 12:14); he saw an angel flying in the mid-heaven (14:6) and another angel crying in a loud voice to all the birds which fly in mid-heaven (19:17). ¶

FOAL – ***huios*** [masc. noun: υἱός <5207>]; **lit.: son ► Offspring of an animal** > As king, Jesus came mounted on a donkey, and even on a colt, the foal of a donkey (Matt. 21:5). Other refs.: SON <5207>.

FOAM (noun) – Jude 13 → to cast up like foam → to foam up → FOAM (verb) <1890>.

FOAM (verb) – [1] ***aphrizō*** [verb: ἀφρίζω <875>]; **from *aphros*: see [3] ► To produce froth formed from saliva in the mouth** > Jesus healed a possessed child who was foaming and gnashing his teeth (Mark 9:18, 20). ¶

[2] **to foam up: *epaphrizō*** [verb: ἐπαφρίζω <1890>]; **from *epi*: upon (intens.), and *aphrizō*: see [1] ► To pour out like foam on the surface of agitated waters** > Jude speaks of those who are like raging waves of the sea, foaming up {foaming out, casting up like foam} their own shames (Jude 13). ¶

[3] **foam: *aphros*** [masc. noun: ἀφρός <876>] **► Whitish substance that comes on the lips during a crisis** > An unclean spirit was throwing a child into convulsion so that he foamed at the mouth (lit.: with foam) (Luke 9:39). ¶

FOAMING – Luke 9:39 → foam → FOAM (verb) <876>.

FOE – Matt. 10:36; Acts 2:35; Rev. 11:5 → ENEMY <2190>.

FOLD (noun) – ***aulē*** [fem. noun: αὐλή <833>]; **see** COURT <833> **► Enclosed space open to the wind in front of a house where sheep are kept; also transl.: pen** > He who does not enter the fold of the sheep by the door is a thief and a robber (John 10:1). Jesus has other sheep which are not of the fold of Israel (John 10:16), i.e., Christian believers. All other refs.: COURT <833>, COURTYARD <833>, PALACE <833>.

FOLD (verb) – [1] **to fold up, to fold together: *entulissō*** [verb: ἐντυλίσσω <1794>]; **from *en*: in, and *tulissō*: to twist, to roll up ► To wrap around** > The burial cloth, which was on the head of Jesus, was folded up in a distinct place by itself (John 20:7); the Greek verb means it was lying in the way it had been rolled around His head, evidence that neither enemy or follower had disturbed the wrappings. Other refs.: Matt. 27:59; Luke 23:53; see WRAP <1794>. ¶
– [2] Heb. 1:12 → ROLL <1667>.

FOLLOW – [1] ***akoloutheō*** [verb: ἀκολουθέω <190>]; **from *a*: particle of union, and *keleuthos*: way ► To accompany, to go with** > Various men said to Jesus that they would follow Him (Matt. 8:19; Luke 9:57, 61). Jesus said: "Follow me" to a man, but he wanted to bury his father first (Matt. 8:22; Luke 9:59); He said the same to Matthew who followed Him (Matt. 9:9a, b; Mark 2:14a, b; Luke 5:27, 28), a rich young man (Matt. 19:21; Mark 10:21; Luke 18:22), Philip (John 1:43), and Peter (John 21:19, 22). Jesus, with His disciples, followed a certain ruler to his house (Matt. 9:19). The verb is used in regard to one who does not take up his cross (Matt. 10:38). If anyone desires to come after Jesus, he must deny himself, take up his cross, and follow Him (Matt. 16:24; Mark 8:34; Luke 9:23). John saw someone casting out demons in the name of Jesus, who did not follow with the Lord's disciples (Mark 9:38a, b; Luke 9:49). The disciples were to follow a man carrying a pitcher of water (Mark 14:13; Luke 22:10). Jesus is the light of the world; he who follows Him will not walk in darkness, but will have the light of life (John 8:12). The good shepherd's sheep follow Him (John 10:4, 27); they will not follow a stranger (v. 5). The Jews followed Mary (John 11:31). If anyone serves Jesus, he must follow Him (John 12:26). Peter could not follow Jesus in His death, but he would follow Him later (John 13:36a, b, 37). Peter saw the disciple whom Jesus loved following (John 21:20). Crowds followed Jesus (Matt. 4:25; 8:1; 12:15; 14:13; 19:2; 20:29; 21:9; Mark 2:15; 3:7; 5:24; 11:9; Luke 7:9; 9:11; 23:27; John 6:2), as well as one or several disciples (Matt. 4:20, 22; 8:10, 23; 19:27, 28; 26:58; Mark 1:18; 6:1; 10:28, 32; 14:54; Luke 5:11; 18:28; 22:39, 54; John 1:37, 38, 40; 18:15; 20:6), women (Matt. 27:55; Mark 15:41), the blind (Matt. 9:27; 20:34; Mark 10:52; Luke 18:43), and a certain young man (Mark 14:51; some mss.: *sunakoloutheō*). The angel told Peter to follow him (Acts

12:8), and he followed him (v. 9). Many Jews and proselytes who served God followed Paul and Barnabas (Acts 13:43). A multitude of people followed, crying: "Away with Paul" (Acts 21:36). The spiritual rock which followed the Israelites was Christ (1 Cor. 10:4). Their works will follow those who die in the Lord (Rev. 14:13). Hades followed with Death (Rev. 6:8). There are some who will follow the Lamb wherever He goes (Rev. 14:4). The verb is also used in regard to angels (Rev. 14:8, 9). The armies that are in heaven followed the Lord on white horses (Rev. 19:14). Other refs.: Matt. 10:38; Rev. 18:5. ¶

[2] ***exakoloutheō*** [verb: ἐξακολουθέω <1811>]; **from *ek*: out (intens.), and *akoloutheō*: see [1] ► To walk in the same path, to imitate** > Peter uses this verb regarding invented stories (2 Pet. 1:16), shameful ways (2:2), and the way of Balaam (2:15). ¶

[3] **to follow; to follow after, in, later: *epakoloutheō*** [verb: ἐπακολουθέω <1872>]; **from *epi*: upon (intens.), and *akoloutheō*: see [1] ► a. To follow upon, to accompany** > The Lord worked with the disciples and confirmed the word by the following signs (Mark 16:20). **b. To come next** > The sins of some men follow after {trail behind them} (1 Tim. 5:24). **c. To walk in the same path, to imitate** > Christ has suffered for us, leaving Christians a model, so that they should follow in His steps (1 Pet. 2:21). Other ref.: 1 Tim. 5:10 (to follow diligently); see DILIGENTLY <1872>. ¶

[4] ***katakoloutheō*** [verb: κατακολουθέω <2628>]; **from *kata*: intens., and *akoloutheō*: see [1] ► To accompany closely** > A possessed woman followed Paul (Acts 16:17). Other ref.: Luke 23:55 (to come along with); see COME <2628>. ¶

[5] **to follow, to follow carefully, to follow closely: *parakoloutheō*** [verb: παρακολουθέω <3877>]; **from *para*: near, and *akoloutheō*: see [1] ► a. To accompany closely** > The Lord speaks of signs that will follow {accompany} those who have believed (Mark 16:17). **b. To comprehend, to understand fully** > Timothy had fully followed {attained} the good teaching (1 Tim. 4:6); he had carefully followed {fully known} Paul's teaching (2 Tim. 3:10). Other ref.: Luke 1:3; see INVESTIGATE <3877>. ¶

[6] ***sunakoloutheō*** [verb: συνακολουθέω <4870>]; **from *sun*: together, and *akoloutheō*: see [1] ► To come along with others, to accompany** > Jesus allowed only three disciples to follow Him to the house of the ruler of the synagogue (Mark 5:37). There were women who followed Jesus from Galilee when He gave His life (Luke 23:49). Other refs.: Mark 14:51; John 10:36a, b in some mss. ¶

[7] ***diōkō*** [verb: διώκω <1377>]; **from *diō*: to pursue ► To run after** > The verb is used in Luke 17:23 in relation to the coming of the kingdom of God. All other refs.: GIVE <1377>, PERSECUTE <1377>, PRESS <1377>, PURSUE <1377>.

[8] **to follow after: *katadiōkō*** [verb: καταδιώκω <2614>]; **from *kata*: intens., and *diōkō*: see [7] ► To follow earnestly, to pursue** > Simon and those who were with him followed after {searched for, went after, went to look for} Jesus (Mark 1:36). ¶

[9] ***sunerchomai*** [verb: συνέρχομαι <4905>]; **from *sun*: together, and *erchomai*: to come ► To come together, to meet together** > Women who had accompanied Jesus from Galilee, having followed those who were about to bury Him, saw the tomb and how His body was placed (Luke 23:55). All other refs.: ACCOMPANY <4905>, COME <4905>, GO <4905>.

[10] ***poreuomai*** [verb: πορεύομαι <4198>]; **from *poros*: passage ► To go, to conduct; also transl.: to indulge, to walk** > The unjust will be punished, and especially those who follow after the flesh in the lust of uncleanness and who despise authority (2 Pet. 2:10). All other refs.: DEPART <4198>, GO <4198>, TRAVEL <4198>, WALK <4198>.

– [11] Luke 22:49 → BE <2071> [12] John 6:66 → WALK <4043> [13] Acts 5:36, 37; Rom. 2:8 → OBEY <3982> [14] Acts 8:11; 1 Tim. 4:1 → to give heed → HEED (noun) <4337> [15] Acts 8:13 → to continue with → CONTINUE <4342> [16] Acts 27:21 → to follow the advice → LISTEN

<3980> **17** Rom. 4:12 → WALK <4748> **18** Eph. 5:1 → to follow the example → to become an imitator → IMITATOR <3402> **19** 2 Thes. 3:7, 9; Heb. 13:7; 3 John 11 → to follow, to follow the example → IMITATE <3401> **20** 2 Tim. 1:13 → to follow the pattern → to have (*echō*) an outline → FORM (noun) <5296>.

FOLLOWER – **1** Acts 5:37 → lit.: one who obeys → OBEY <3982> **2** Acts 17:34 → to become follower → JOIN <2853> **3** 1 Cor. 4:6 → "being a follower" added in Engl. **4** 1 Cor. 4:16; 11:1; Eph. 5:1; 1 Thes. 1:6; 2:14; Heb. 6:12; 1 Pet. 3:13 → IMITATOR <3402> **5** Phil. 3:17 → follower together → imitator together → IMITATOR <4831>.

FOLLOWING – **1** ***epiousa*** [ptcp.: ἐπιοῦσα <1966>]**; from *epi*: on, and *eimi*: to go ▶ Next, which comes after** > The Greek word is found in exprs. such as "following day," "following night," and "next day." See Acts 7:26; 16:11; 20:15; 21:18; 23:11. ¶
– **2** Mark 11:12 → following day → DAY <1887>.

FOLLOWS (AS) – Acts 23:25 → lit.: containing → AFTER <4023>.

FOLLY – **1** Mark 7:22; 2 Cor. 11:1, 17, 21 → FOOLISHNESS <877> **2** Rom. 1:21 → to fall into folly → to become vain → VAIN <3154> **3** 1 Cor. 1:18, 21, 23; 2:14; 3:19 → FOOLISHNESS <3472> **4** 2 Tim. 3:9 → MADNESS <454> **5** 2 Pet. 2:16 → MADNESS <3913> **6** 2 Pet. 2:18 → VANITY <3153>.

FOND – **1** 1 Thes. 2:8 → to have a fond affection → to be affectionately desirous → AFFECTIONATELY <2442> **2** 1 Tim. 3:8; Titus 1:7 → fond of sordid gain → GREEDY <146>.

FOOD – **1** **food, solid food: *brōma*** [neut. noun: βρῶμα <1033>]**; from *bibroskō*: to eat ▶ Nourishment, sustenance; also transl. in older versions: meat** > The disciples wanted the crowd to go and buy food {victuals} for themselves (Matt. 14:15). Jesus told the crowd that he who has food is to give to him that has none (Luke 3:11). The food of Jesus, figur. speaking, was to do the will of Him who had sent Him, and to accomplish His word (John 4:34). If, because of our food, our brother is hurt, we are no longer walking according to love; we are not to destroy through our food him for whom Christ died (Rom. 14:15a, b). Paul says not to destroy the work of God for the sake of food (Rom. 14:20). He had given the Corinthians milk to drink, not solid food (1 Cor. 3:2). Food is for the stomach, and the stomach for food (1 Cor. 6:13a, b). Food does not commend us to God (1 Cor. 8:8). If food (*brōma*) caused his brother to stumble, Paul would not eat meat (*kreas*) again (1 Cor. 8:13). All the Israelites ate the same spiritual food in the desert (1 Cor. 10:3). Paul speaks of those who prescribed abstaining from foods which God had prepared to be received with thanks (1 Tim. 4:3). In the O.T., worship related only to foods, drinks, and various washings (Heb. 9:10). It is good that the heart be strengthened by grace, not by foods (Heb. 13:9). Other refs.: Mark 7:19; Luke 9:13. ¶
2 ***brōsis*** [fem. noun: βρῶσις <1035>]**; from *bibroskō*: to eat ▶ What one eats** > Jesus had food to eat that His disciples did not know (John 4:32). He says to work, not for the food which perishes, but for the food which endures to eternal life (John 6:27a, b). He says that His flesh is truly food {meat} indeed (John 6:55). All other refs.: EATING <1035>, MEAL <1035>, RUST <1035>.
3 ***brōsimos*** [adj.: βρώσιμος <1034>]**; from *brōsis*: see 2; lit.: eatable ▶ Something edible** > Jesus asked His disciples if they had any food {meat, something to eat} (Luke 24:41). ¶
4 ***episitismos*** [masc. noun: ἐπισιτισμός <1979>]**; from *episitizō*: to give food, which is from *epi*: upon, and *sitizō*: to feed ▶ Provisions, victuals** > The disciples wanted Jesus to send the crowd away so that they may get food {something to eat} in the surrounding area (Luke 9:12). ¶
5 ***prosphagion*** [neut. noun: προσφάγιον <4371>]**; from *pros*: in addition, and *phagō*: to eat ▶ Food eaten with bread**

(e.g., fish) > Jesus asked His disciples if they had food {fish, something to eat} (John 21:5). ¶

6 ***trophē*** [fem. noun: τροφή <5160>]; **from *trephō*: to nourish ▶ Nourishment, that which one eats; also transl. in older versions: meat** > The food {nourishment} of John the Baptist was locusts and wild honey (Matt. 3:4). Life is more than food (Matt. 6:25; Luke 12:23). The workman is worthy of his food {keep, nourishment, support} (Matt. 10:10). A faithful bondman had been established to give food to the household servants (Matt. 24:45). The disciples of Jesus had gone away into the city to buy food (John 4:8). The Christians received their food {ate together, were taking their meals} with gladness and simplicity of heart (Acts 2:46). Having received food, Paul got strength (Acts 9:19). God fills our hearts with food and gladness (Acts 14:17). Paul exhorted the passengers to take food (Acts 27:33, 34 {nourishment}), which they did (v. 36). The Hebrews had need of milk, and not of solid food (Heb. 5:12); solid food belongs to full-grown men (v. 14). James speaks of a brother or a sister in the Lord who is in need of daily food (Jas. 2:15). Other refs.: Acts 27:38; see EAT <5160>. ¶

7 ***diatrophē*** [fem. noun: διατροφή <1305>]; **from *diatrephō*: to maintain, which is from *dia*: through, and *trophē*: see 6 ▶ Nurture, nourishment** > Having food {sustenance} and covering, we will be content (1 Tim. 6:8). ¶

8 **without taking food: *asitos*** [adj.: ἄσιτος <777>]; **from *a*: neg. particle, and *sitos*: food ▶ Without eating** > It was the fourteenth day that the passengers on Paul's ship had passed without taking food {having taken nothing, without eating} (Acts 27:33). ¶

– 9 Matt. 25:35, 42 → EAT <5315> 10 Luke 11:6 → I have no food to offer him → lit.: I do not have what I may set before him 11 Acts 6:1 → distribution of food, serving of food → SERVICE <1248> 12 Acts 7:11 → SUSTENANCE <5527> 13 Acts 12:20 → to supply with food, to depend for the food supply → to be nourished → NOURISH <5142> 14 Acts 16:34 → to set food → lit.: set the table → SET (verb) <3908> 15 Acts 23:14 → to taste no food → lit.: to taste nothing 16 Acts 27:21 → without food → ABSTINENCE <776> 17 1 Cor. 8:10; 10:19 → food offered to idols → IDOL <1494> 18 2 Thes. 3:12 → BREAD <740>.

FOOD ALLOWANCE – Luke 12:42 → MEASURE OF CORN <4620>.

FOOL – 1 ***aphrōn*** [adj. and adj. used as noun: ἄφρων <878>]; **from *a*: neg., and *phrēn*: mind, understanding; lit.: without comprehension, without understanding ▶ Unintelligent, unthinking; also transl.: foolish** > Jesus called the Pharisees fools {foolish ones, foolish people} (Luke 11:40). God called a rich man a fool (Luke 12:20). Paul uses this term in 1 Cor. 15:36 when he talks about sowing. He uses it in regard to himself in 2 Cor. 11:16a, b: no one should consider him to be a fool. The Corinthians gladly put up with fools (2 Cor. 11:19). All other refs.: FOOLISH <878>.

2 ***mōros*** [adj.: μωρός <3474>] **▶ Thoughtless, senseless; also transl.: foolish** > Whoever says to his brother, "Fool," shall be subject to the penalty of the hell of fire (Matt. 5:22). Jesus called the scribes and Pharisees fools and blind (Matt. 23:17, 19 in some mss.). In a parable, five virgins were foolish (Matt. 25:2, 3, 8). God has chosen the foolish things of the world to put to shame the wise (1 Cor. 1:27). If a Christian thinks himself to be wise in this world, let him become foolish, so that he may become wise (1 Cor. 3:18). Paul was a fool for the love of Christ (1 Cor. 4:10). Timothy was to avoid foolish questions (2 Tim. 2:23), as likewise was Titus (Titus 3:9). All other refs.: FOOLISH <3474>, FOOLISHNESS <3474>.

3 **to become a fool: *mōrainō*** [verb: μωραίνω <3471>]; **from *mōros*: see 2 ▶ To become senseless, foolish** > Claiming to be wise, men became fools (Rom. 1:22). All other refs.: FOOLISH <3471>, LOSE <3471>.

– 4 Luke 24:25 → FOOLISH <453> 5 2 Cor. 11:17, 21 → as a fool → lit.: as in foolishness → FOOLISHNESS <877> [6] 2 Cor. 11:23 → to be a fool → to be out of one's mind → MIND (noun) <3912> [7] Eph. 5:15 → WISE (noun) <781>.

FOOLISH – [1] ***anoētos*** [adj.: ἀνόητος <453>]; **from *a*: neg., and *noeō*: to perceive, to understand; lit.: lacking sense ► Without comprehension, understanding; also transl.: fool, senseless, unintelligent, unwise, without intelligence >** Jesus addressed the disciples of Emmaus, calling them "foolish" (Luke 24:25). Paul was a debtor to the foolish (Rom. 1:14). He addresses the Galatians as foolish on two occasions (Gal. 3:1, 3). Those who desire to become rich fall into many foolish lusts (1 Tim. 6:9); *anonētos* in some mss.: worthless. Before their conversion, Christians were foolish (Titus 3:3). ¶

[2] ***aphrōn*** [adj. and adj. used as noun: ἄφρων <878>]; **from *a*: neg., and *phrēn*: mind, understanding; lit.: without understanding ► Unintelligent, unthinking; also transl.: fool, senseless >** Certain Jews might think themselves to be instructors of the foolish (Rom. 2:20). If he had wanted to boast, Paul would not have been foolish (2 Cor. 12:6); he had been compelled to become foolish (v. 11). He says not to be foolish {unwise}, but understand what is the will of the Lord (Eph. 5:17). The will of God is that, by well-doing, we put to silence the ignorance of foolish men (1 Pet. 2:15). All other refs.: FOOL <878>.

[3] ***mōros*** [adj.: μωρός <3474>] **► Thoughtless, senseless; morally worthless >** A foolish man built his house on the sand (Matt. 7:26). All other refs.: FOOL <3474>, FOOLISHNESS <3474>.

[4] **foolish talk, foolish talking: *mōrologia*** [fem. noun: μωρολογία <3473>]; **from *mōros*: see [3], and *logos*: word ► Thoughtless, senseless comments >** Foolish talking {Silly talk} is not fitting for saints (Eph. 5:4). ¶

[5] **to make foolish: *mōrainō*** [verb: μωραίνω <3471>]; **from *moros*: foolish ► To make (something) unreasonable, senseless >** God has made foolish the wisdom of the world (1 Cor. 1:20). All other refs.: FOOL <3471>, LOSE <3471>.

– [6] Rom. 1:21, 31; 10:19 → without understanding → UNDERSTANDING <801> [7] Jas. 2:20 → VAIN <2756>.

FOOLISHLY – 2 Cor. 11:17, 21 → lit.: in foolishness → FOOLISHNESS <877>.

FOOLISHNESS – [1] ***aphrosunē*** [fem. noun: ἀφροσύνη <877>]; **from *aphrōn*: foolish, unintelligent, which is from *a*: neg., and *phrēn*: spirit, judgment ► Folly; lack of wisdom, of common sense >** Folly proceeds out of the heart of men (Mark 7:22). Paul hoped that the Corinthians would put up with a little of his foolishness (2 Cor. 11:1). What Paul said was said as in foolishness {as in folly, as a fool, foolishly} (2 Cor. 11:17). He spoke in foolishness {as in folly, as a fool, foolishly} (2 Cor. 11:21). ¶

[2] ***mōria*** [fem. noun: μωρία <3472>]; **from *moros*: foolish ► Absurdity, that which displays a lack of sense >** The word of the cross is foolishness to those who perish (1 Cor. 1:18). By the foolishness of preaching, God saves those who believe (1 Cor. 1:21). Christ crucified was foolishness to the Gentiles (1 Cor. 1:23). The things of the Spirit of God are foolishness to the natural man (1 Cor. 2:14). The wisdom of the world is foolishness before God (1 Cor. 3:19). ¶

[3] ***mōros*** [adj. used as noun: μωρός <3474>] **► That which is deemed unreasonable, absurd >** The foolishness of God is wiser than men (1 Cor. 1:25). All other refs.: FOOL <3474>, FOOLISH <3474>.

FOOT[1] – [1] ***pous*** [masc. noun: πούς <4228>] **► Lower extremity of the leg, enabling standing and walking >** The word is used in regard to Jesus (Matt. 4:6; 15:30; 18:8a, b; 22:44; 28:9; Mark 5:22; 7:25; Luke 4:11; 7:38a, b, 44a, b, 45, 46; 8:35, 41; 10:39; 17:16; 20:43; 24:39, 40; John 11:2, 32; 12:3a, b; 20:12; Acts 2:35; 7:49; 13:25; 1 Cor. 15:25, 27; Eph. 1:22; Heb. 1:13; 2:8; 10:13; Rev. 1:15, 17; 2:18; 3:9), God (Matt. 5:35), the disciples (Matt. 10:14; Mark 6:11; Luke 9:5; John 13:5, 6, 8–10, 12, 14a, b), the prodigal son (Luke

15:22), Lazarus (John 11:44), the apostles (Acts 4:35, 37; 5:2), those who had buried Ananias (Acts 5:9), Peter (Acts 5:10; 10:25), Abraham (Acts 7:5), Moses (Acts 7:33), Paul (Acts 7:58; 26:16), Paul and Barnabas (Acts 13:51; 16:24), a man impotent in his feet (Acts 14:8, 10), Agabus (Acts 21:11), Gamaliel (Acts 22:3), wicked men (Rom. 3:15), those who announce peace (Rom. 10:15), Christians (Rom. 16:20; Eph. 6:15; 1 Tim. 5:10), an angel (Rev. 10:1, 2; 19:10; 22:8), two prophets (Rev. 11:11), a woman clothed with the sun (Rev. 12:1), and the beast that John saw (Rev. 13:2). Other refs.: Matt. 7:6; 22:13; Mark 9:45a, b; 12:36; Luke 1:79; 1 Cor. 12:15, 21; Heb. 12:13. ¶

2 ***basis*** [fem. noun: βάσις <939>]; **from *bainō*: to walk; lit.: base ▶ Sole of the foot or, more generally, foot of a person, i.e., the base on which one stands or goes** > A lame man was healed by Peter, and his feet and his ankle bones were made strong (Acts 3:7). ¶

3 **reaching to the feet, down to the feet: *podērēs*** [adj.: ποδήρης <4158>]; **from *pous*: see 1, and *arō*: to adapt, to adjust ▶ Descending to the ground** > John saw someone like the Son of Man, clothed with a garment reaching to the feet (Rev. 1:13). ¶

4 **on foot: *pezē*** [adv.: πεζῇ <3979>] **▶ By land (rather than by sea)** > The crowds followed Jesus on foot {afoot} (Matt. 14:13 {other mss.: *pezos*}; Mark 6:33). ¶

5 **to go on foot: *pezeuō*** [verb: πεζεύω <3978>]; **from *pous*: foot ▶ To walk** > Paul intended to go on foot {go by land} to Assos (Acts 20:13). ¶

– 6 Matt. 5:13 → to be trampled under people's feet → lit.: to be trampled under → TREAD <2662> 7 Acts 20:18b → to set foot → COME <1910> 8 Jas. 2:3 → by my feet → lit.: under my footstool → FOOTSTOOL <5286>.

FOOT[2] – Acts 27:28a, b → FATHOM <3712>.

FOOTHOLD – Eph. 4:27 → OPPORTUNITY <5117>.

FOOTMAN – Acts 23:23 → light-armed footman → SPEARMAN <1187>.

FOOTSTEP – Rom. 4:12; 2 Cor. 12:18 → STEP (noun) <2487>.

FOOTSTOOL – ***hupopodion*** [neut. noun: ὑποπόδιον <5286>]; **from *hupopodios*: underfoot, which is from *hupo*: under, and *pous*: foot ▶ A low foot-rest** > The earth is God's footstool (Matt. 5:35; 22:44 in some mss.; Acts 7:49). The enemies of the Lord will be made His footstool (Mark 12:36 in some mss.; Luke 20:43; Acts 2:35; Heb. 1:13; 10:13). One might tell a poor man to sit under his footstool {by his feet} (Jas. 2:3). ¶

FORASMUCH – 1 ***epeidēper*** [conj.: ἐπειδήπερ <1895>]; **from *epeidē*: since, and *per*: truly, a particle of abundance ▶ Inasmuch, since** > Luke uses this word at the beginning of his Gospel (Luke 1:1). ¶ ‡

2 ***kathoti*** [adv.: καθότι <2530>]; **from *kata*: according to, and *hoti*: that ▶** Refs.: Luke 1:7; 19:9; Acts 2:24. All other refs.: ACCORDING AS <2530>. ‡

FORBEAR – 1 ***pheidomai*** [verb: φείδομαι <5339>] **▶ To avoid, to refrain** > Paul was forbearing from boasting (2 Cor. 12:6) of the abundance of the revelations made to him (see v. 7). All other refs.: SPARE <5339>.

– 2 Eph. 4:2; Col. 3:13 → SUFFER <430> 3 Eph. 6:9 → to give up → GIVE <447>.

FORBEARANCE – 1 ***anochē*** [fem. noun: ἀνοχή <463>]; **from *anechō*: to bear, to suffer, which is from *ana*: up, and *echō*: to have, to hold; lit.: (self) restraint ▶ Tolerance, longsuffering, indulgence** > Paul speaks of the forbearance of God (Rom. 2:4; 3:25). ¶

– 2 Gal. 5:22 → LONGSUFFERING <3115> 3 Heb. 5:2 → to exercise forbearance → to have compassion → COMPASSION <3356>.

FORBEARING – 1 ***anexikakos*** [adj.: ἀνεξίκακος <420>]; **from *anechō*: to bear, to suffer, which is from *ana*: in, and *echō*:**

to have, and *kakos*: bad ▶ Which bears wickedness and faults; also transl.: not resentful, patient, patient when wronged, patiently enduring evil > The servant of the Lord must not contend, but be gentle toward all, able to teach, forbearing (2 Tim. 2:24). ¶
– 2 Phil. 4:5 → GENTLENESS <1933>.

FORBID – 1 ***ginomai*** [verb: γίνομαι <1096>] **▶ To be, to occur, to happen** > In Luke 20:16, "God forbid!" is lit.: "May this not become" (*ginomai*). In Gal. 6:14, the expr. "God forbid" is lit. "May it not happen" {May I never, Far be it}. Other refs.: see entries in Lexicon at <1096>.
2 ***kōluō*** [verb: κωλύω <2967>]**; from *kolos*: truncated ▶ To prevent, to prohibit; also transl.: to hinder, to withstand, to stand in one's way** > Jesus said to not forbid little children to come to Him (Matt. 19:14; Mark 10:14; Luke 18:16). John and other disciples had forbidden {told to stop, tried to stop} someone to cast out demons in the name of Jesus (Mark 9:38; Luke 9:49), but Jesus said not to forbid him (Mark 9:39; Luke 9:50). He said to not forbid {withhold} our garment from him who takes away our coat (Luke 6:29 {to stop, to withhold}). Jesus was accused of forbidding {opposing} to pay taxes to Caesar (Luke 23:2). Peter could not forbid God to give the gift of the Holy Spirit to the nations (Acts 11:17). Paul was forbidden {had been kept} by the Holy Spirit to preach the word in Asia (Acts 16:6). The Corinthians were not to forbid speaking in tongues (1 Cor. 14:39). The Spirit expressly says that in latter times some will forbid to marry (1 Tim. 4:3). Other refs.: Acts 10:47 {to refuse, to keep from}; 24:23 {to permit; lit.: to not forbid}; 27:43 {to keep from}; 1 Thes. 2:16 {to keep from}; Heb. 7:23 {to not suffer}; 3 John 10 {to stop}. All other refs.: HELP (verb) <2967>, REFUSE (verb) <2967>, RESTRAIN <2967>.
3 **no one forbidding: *akōlutōs*** [adv.: ἀκωλύτως <209>]**; from *a*: neg., and *koluō*: see** 2 **▶ Without obstacle, without hindrance** > In Rome, Paul preached the kingdom of God and taught the things concerning the Lord Jesus Christ with all freedom, no one forbidding him {unhindered, unhinderedly, without hindrance} (Acts 28:31). ¶
– 4 Matt. 3:14 → PREVENT <1254> 5 Matt. 16:22 → God forbid it → lit.: Be merciful to Yourself, Lord → FAVORABLE <2436> 6 John 5:10 → the law forbids → it is not lawful → LAWFUL <1832>.

FORCE (noun) – 1 Matt. 11:12 → to take by force → SEIZE <726> 2 Matt. 14:2 → to display the force → WORK (verb) <1754> 3 Luke 3:14 → to take money by force → OPPRESS <1286> 4 Acts 5:26; 24:7; 27:41 → VIOLENCE <970> 5 Acts 23:10 → to take by force → TAKE <726> 6 Gal. 4:9; Col. 2:8, 20 → ELEMENT <4747> 7 Gal. 5:6 → to have force → to have value → VALUE (noun) <2480> 8 Eph. 6:12 → world force → RULER <2888> 9 Heb. 9:17 → in force, of force → VALID <949> 10 Heb. 9:17 → to be in force, to be of force → PREVAIL <2480>.

FORCE (verb) – 1 Matt. 5:41; 27:32; Mark 15:21 → COMPEL <29> 2 Luke 16:16 → to force one's way → to strive violently to go in → VIOLENCE <971> 3 Acts 7:19 → OPPRESS <2559> 4 Acts 26:11; 28:19; 2 Cor. 12:11; Gal. 2:3, 14; 6:12 → to try to force, to force → CONSTRAIN <315>.

FORCED – 1 Phm. 14 → lit.: by necessity → NECESSITY <318> 2 Phm. 14 → not forced → VOLUNTARY <1595>.

FORCEFUL – 1 Matt. 11:12 → forceful men → lit.: the violent → VIOLENT (noun) <973> 2 2 Cor. 10:10 → STRONG (adj.) <2478>.

FORCEFULLY – Matt. 11:12 → to forcefully advance → to take by violence → VIOLENCE <971>.

FORCES – Matt. 22:7 → TROOPS <4753>.

FOREBODING – Luke 21:26 → foreboding of what is coming → expectation of what is coming → EXPECTATION <4329>.

FOREFATHER – 1 ***progonos*** [adj. used in the plur.: πρόγονος <4269>]; **from *proginomai*: to become, which is from *pro*: before, and *ginomai*: to be born ▶ Ancestor, parent** > Paul was serving God, as his forefathers did, with a pure conscience (2 Tim. 1:3). Other ref.: 1 Tim. 5:4; see PARENT <4269>. ¶
2 In Rom. 4:1, some mss. have *propatōr*; the word means an ancestor. ¶
– 3 Acts 7:12; Rom. 9:10; 11:28 → FATHER <3962> 4 1 Pet. 1:18 → handed down from the forefathers, inherited from the forefathers → received by tradition from the fathers → FATHER <3970>.

FOREHEAD – ***metōpon*** [neut. noun: μέτωπον <3359>]; **from *meta*: with, and *ōps*: eye, face ▶ Upper portion of the face, from the eyebrows to the hairline** > The servants of God are sealed on their foreheads (Rev. 7:3). Other men do not have the seal of God on their foreheads (Rev. 9:4). The beast will give to all a mark on their right hand or on their forehead (Rev. 13:16; 14:9). There will be people who will not receive the mark on their forehead and hand (Rev. 20:4). One hundred forty-four thousand had the name of the Lamb and the name of His Father written on their foreheads (Rev. 14:1). The name written on the forehead of the great prostitute was a mystery (Rev. 17:5). The name of the Lamb will be on the foreheads of His servants (Rev. 22:4). Other ref.: Luke 23:48 in some mss. ¶

FOREIGN – 1 ***allotrios*** [adj.: ἀλλότριος <245>]; **from *allos*: other ▶ Pertaining to another, unknown** > The descendants of Abraham would dwell in a foreign {strange} land (Acts 7:6). Abraham dwelt in the land of promise as in a foreign {strange} country (lit.: a foreign) (Heb. 11:9). All other refs.: ANOTHER <245>, STRANGER <245>.
2 ***exō*** [adv.: ἔξω <1854>]; **from *ek*: out ▶ Outside, abroad** > Paul was persecuting Christians even to foreign {strange} cities (lit.: to cities out) (Acts 26:11). *
3 ***xenos*** [adj.: ξένος <3581>] ▶ **Which comes from somewhere else; also transl.: strange** > Paul seemed to be a proclaimer of foreign gods (Acts 17:18). Other ref.: Heb. 13:9. All other refs.: HOST[2] <3581>, STRANGE <3581>, STRANGER <3581>.

FOREIGNER – 1 ***allogenēs*** [adj. used as noun: ἀλλογενής <241>]; **from *allos*: other, and *genos*: race ▶ Person who belongs to another nation** > Only a foreigner {stranger} among the ten lepers who had been healed, a Samaritan, returned and gave glory to God (Luke 17:18). ¶
2 ***paroikos*** [adj. used as noun: πάροικος <3941>]; **from *para*: near, and *oikos*: house ▶ Person who sojourns, who remains in a place for a certain time; also transl.: alien, stranger** > On the one hand, the Christian is no longer a stranger or a foreigner, because he is part of the household of God (Eph. 2:19). On the other hand, on an earthly level, he is a foreigner and a stranger {an alien and a stranger, a sojourner and a pilgrim} in relation to this world (1 Pet. 2:11). Other ref.: Acts 7:6 in some mss. Other ref.: Acts 7:29; see DWELLER <3941>. ¶
– 3 Matt. 27:7; Acts 17:21; Eph. 2:12, 19; Heb. 11:13 → STRANGER <3581> 4 Acts 10:28 → one of another nation → NATION <246> 5 1 Cor. 14:11 → BARBARIAN <915> 6 1 Pet. 1:17 → your time as foreigners → lit.: the time of your stay → STAY (noun) <3940>.

FOREKNOW – ***proginōskō*** [verb: προγινώσκω <4267>]; **from *pro*: before, and *ginōskō*: to know ▶ To know in advance** > God has predestined the Christians whom He has foreknown to be conformed to the image of His Son (Rom. 8:29). God foreknew His people Israel (Rom. 11:2). Christ was foreknown {was chosen, was foreordained} before the foundation of the world as a lamb without blemish and without spot (1 Pet. 1:20). Other refs.: Acts 26:5; 2 Pet. 3:17 (to know already); see KNOW <4267>. ¶

FOREKNOWLEDGE – ***prognōsis*** [fem. noun: πρόγνωσις <4268>]; **from *proginoskō*: to know in advance, which is from *pro*: before, and *ginoskō*: to know ▶ Knowledge of something before it happens; prior cognition, prescience** > Jesus was delivered by the predetermined plan and foreknowledge of God (Acts 2:23). Christians have been elected according to the foreknowledge of God the Father (1 Pet. 1:2). ¶

FOREMAN – Matt. 20:8 → STEWARD <2012>.

FOREORDAIN – 1 ***procheirizomai*** [verb: προχειρίζομαι <4400>]; **from *procheiros*: ready, which is from *pro*: before, and *cheir*: hand ▶ To be designated in advance, to be predetermined** > God had sent Jesus Christ, who was foreordained {appointed, preached before} (Acts 3:20). Other refs.: Acts 22:14; 26:16; see CHOOSE <4400>, MAKE <4400>. ¶
– 2 1 Pet. 1:20 → FOREKNOW <4267>.

FOREPART – Acts 27:41 → PROW <4408>.

FORERUNNER – ***prodromos*** [adj. used as a masc. noun: πρόδρομος <4274>]; **from *protrechō*: to run before, which is from *pro*: ahead, before, and *trechō*: to run; note: *dramein* (close to *dromos*) is a form of the verb *trechō* ▶ One who goes ahead in order to prepare the way** > Jesus has entered as a forerunner for Christians within the veil (Heb. 6:20). ¶

FORESAIL – Acts 27:40 → MAINSAIL <736>.

FORESEE – 1 ***problepō*** [verb: προβλέπω <4265>]; **from *pro*: before, and *blepō*: to see; lit.: to see beforehand ▶ To anticipate, to plan; also transl.: to provide** > O.T. people of faith did not receive what had been promised, God having foreseen something better for Christians, that they should not be made perfect without believers of the N.T. (Heb. 11:40). ¶
2 ***proeidon*** [verb: προεῖδον <4275>]; **from *pro*: before, and *eidon*; form of *horaō*: to see; lit.: to see beforehand ▶ To view in advance** > David foresaw the resurrection of Christ (Acts 2:31); also transl.: to see before, to look ahead, to see what was ahead. The Scripture foresaw that God would justify the nations on the principle of faith (Gal. 3:8). ¶
3 ***prooraō*** [verb: προοράω <4308>]; **from *pro*: before, and *horaō*: to see; lit.: to see beforehand ▶ To see in front of self** > David foresaw {saw, was beholding} the Lord always before him (Acts 2:25). Other ref.: Acts 21:29 (to see before); see SEE <4308>. ¶

FORESHIP – Acts 27:30 → PROW <4408>.

FORESIGHT – Acts 24:2 → FORETHOUGHT <4307>.

FOREST – ***hulē*** [fem. noun: ὕλη <5208>] ▶ **Area of land covered with trees** > The tongue is like a little fire which sets on fire a large forest {matter} (Jas. 3:5). ¶

FORETELL – 1 ***prokatangellō*** [verb: προκαταγγέλλω <4293>]; **from *pro*: before, and *katangellō*: to declare, to preach, which is from *kata*: intens., and *angellō*: to preach ▶ To declare in advance; to predict, to prophesy** > The prophets had foretold {announced} the times of refreshing, of restoration of all things (Acts 3:24; see vv. 18–23); other mss. have *katangellō*. All other refs.: ANNOUNCE <4293>.
– 2 Mark 13:23; 2 Cor. 13:2 → to tell before → TELL <4302> 3 Acts 1:16; 1 Thes. 4:6 → to say before → SAY <4277> 4 Acts 11:28 → SHOW (verb) <4591>.

FORETHOUGHT – ***pronoia*** [fem. noun: πρόνοια <4307>]; **from *pronoeō*: to look ahead, which is from *pro*: in advance, and *noeō*: to think ▶ Provision beforehand; precaution, prudence** > Tertullus spoke of the forethought {foresight, providence} of Felix regarding the measures executed for Israel (Acts 24:2). Other ref.: Rom. 13:14; see PROVISION <4307>. ¶

FOREVER – [1] **unto the age: *eis ton aiōna*; age: *aiōn*** [masc. noun: αἰών <165>]; **from *aei*: always ▶ For eternity, eternally >** Jesus is the living bread which has come down from heaven; if anyone eats of this bread, he will live forever (John 6:51, 58). The Christ abides forever (John 12:34); Jesus continues forever {ever} (Heb. 7:24). The Holy Spirit abides with the Christians forever (John 14:16). The righteousness of God remains forever (2 Cor. 9:9). The word of the Lord abides forever (1 Pet. 1:25). He who does the will of God abides forever (1 John 2:17). Other refs.: AGE <165>, COURSE <165>, TROUBLE (noun) <165>, WORLD <165>.

[2] **for the ages: *eis tous aiōnas*; age: see [1] ▶ Eternally >** The Creator is blessed forever (Rom. 1:25). Christ is overall God blessed forever (Rom. 9:5). The glory is to God forever (Rom. 11:36; 16:27). The Lord Jesus Christ is blessed forever {for evermore} (2 Cor. 11:31). Jesus Christ is the same yesterday and today and forever {to the ages to come} (Heb. 13:8).

[3] ***aiōn*** [masc. noun: αἰών <165>] **▶ Era, period of time of undetermined duration >** Christ is a priest and a high priest forever (Heb. 5:6; 6:20; 7:17, 21, 28 {evermore}), i.e., eternally. To Him be the glory both now and forever {to the day of eternity} (2 Pet. 3:18). Other refs.: see [1].

– [4] Rom. 11:10 → ALWAYS <1275> [5] Gal. 5:21a, b → to tell beforehand → TELL <4302> [6] 1 Thes. 4:17 → ALWAYS <3842> [7] 1 Tim. 5:25 → "forever" added in Engl. [8] Heb. 7:3; 10:12, 14 → CONTINUALLY <1519> <1336> [9] Heb. 7:25 → to the uttermost → UTTERMOST <3838>.

FOREVERMORE – Rom. 16:27 → lit.: for the ages → FOREVER <165>.

FOREWARN – [1] Matt. 3:7; Luke 3:7 → WARN <5263> [2] Luke 12:5 → SHOW (verb) <5263> [3] Gal. 5:21 → to tell before → TELL <4302> [4] 2 Pet. 3:17 → to know beforehand → KNOW <4267>.

FOREWARNED (BE) – 2 Pet. 3:17 → FOREKNOW <4267>.

FORFEIT – ***zēmioō*** [verb: ζημιόω <2210>]; **from *zēmia*: privation, divestiture ▶ To be under the penalty of loss, to be despoiled >** It will profit a man nothing if he gains the whole world, and loses (*apollumi*) or forfeits (*zēmioō*) himself (Luke 9:25). Other refs.: Matt. 16:26; Mark 8:36; 1 Cor. 3:15; 2 Cor. 7:9; Phil. 3:8 (to suffer the loss); see LOSS <2210>. ¶

FORGET – [1] ***eklanthanomai*** [verb: ἐκλανθάνομαι <1585>]; **from *ek*: intens., and *lanthanō*: to be hidden, to forget ▶ To completely cease remembering or noticing, to be entirely oblivious of >** Hebrew Christians had forgotten the exhortation that spoke to them as to sons (Heb. 12:5). ¶

[2] ***epilanthanō*** [verb: ἐπιλανθάνω <1950>]; **from *epi*: intens., and *lanthanō*: see [1] ▶ To fail to be mindful of, to neglect >** The disciples had forgotten to take bread (Matt. 16:5; Mark 8:14). Not one sparrow is forgotten before God (Luke 12:6). Paul voluntarily forgot the things that were behind him (Phil. 3:13). God is not unrighteous to forget the work of love shown to his name (Heb. 6:10). Christians should not forget {be forgetful of, neglect} hospitality (Heb. 13:2), or sharing what they have (v. 16). James speaks of a man who has forgotten what he was like (Jas. 1:24). ¶

[3] **forgetfulness: *lēthē*** [fem. noun: λήθη <3024>]; **from *lanthanō*: see [1] ▶ Loss of recollection, oblivion >** Peter speaks of him who has forgotten (lit.: taking on forgetfulness of) the purging of his former sins (2 Pet. 1:9). ¶

– [4] Jas. 1:25 → not forgetting what he has heard → lit.: not a hearer of forgetfulness → forgetfulness → FORGETFUL <1953> [5] 2 Pet. 3:5, 8 → HIDDEN (BE) <2990>.

FORGETFUL – [1] **forgetfulness: *epilēsmonē*** [fem. noun: ἐπιλησμονή <1953>]; **from *epi*: in, and *lanthanō*: to forget, to be ignorant of ▶ Loss of recollection; negligence, heedlessness >** He who is

not a forgetful hearer (lit.: hearer of forgetfulness) will be blessed (Jas. 1:25). ¶
– [2] Heb. 13:2, 16 → to be forgetful → FORGET <1950>.

FORGIVE – [1] ***apoluō*** [verb: ἀπολύω <630>]; **from *apo*: from, and *luō*: to untie, to loose ▶ To free up, to release somebody of the obligation of paying a debt, to absolve; also transl.: to pardon, to remit** > Jesus tells us to forgive, and we will be forgiven (Luke 6:37a, b). All other refs.: see entries in Lexicon at <630>.

[2] ***aphiēmi*** [verb: ἀφίημι <863>]; **from *apo*: from, and *hiēmi*: to send away ▶ To remit someone's fault and, consequently, to exempt him from punishment; to release from an obligation. Divine forgiveness also includes removal of the offence or sin.** > Jesus taught us to pray to God to forgive us our debts as we forgive our debtors (Matt. 6:12a, b; Luke 11:4a, b). Our heavenly Father forgives us our offences in the measure that we forgive others their offences (Matt. 6:14, 15a, b; Mark 11:25a, b, 26a, b). Jesus forgave the sins of a paralytic and healed him (Matt. 9:2, 5, 6; Mark 2:5, 7, 9, 10; Luke 5:20, 21, 23, 24); He also forgave the sins of a sinful woman (Luke 7:47a, b, 48, 49). Every sin and blasphemy will be forgiven to man, including a word spoken against the Son of Man, but speaking blasphemy of the Holy Spirit will not be forgiven (Matt. 12:31a, b, 32a, b; Mark 3:28; Luke 12:10a, b). The lord of a bondman forgave him his debt (Matt. 18:27, 32). Those whose iniquities have been forgiven are blessed (Rom. 4:7). Jesus said to forgive until seventy times seven (Matt. 18:21; see v. 22), i.e., continually. He illustrates by a parable what awaits one who does not forgive his brother (Matt. 18:35; see vv. 23–35; Mark 11:26a, b). In Mark 4:12, the expr. "lest it may be, they should be converted and they should be forgiven" shows that for a while God abandons the nation of Israel which rejected His Son; comp. Is. 6:10–13. Jesus said to forgive one's brother if he repents (Luke 17:3, 4). On the cross, Jesus said: "Father, forgive them, for they know not what they do" (Luke 23:34). Jesus told the apostles that whosesoever sins they forgave, they would be forgiven (John 20:23a). Peter commanded Simon the magician to repent so that the thought of his heart might be forgiven him (Acts 8:22). If we confess our sins, God is faithful and righteous to forgive us our sins (1 John 1:9); our sins are forgiven for the sake of the name of Jesus (2:12). Jas. 5:15 mentions a sick person who is forgiven. All other refs.: see entries in Lexicon at <863>.

[3] ***charizomai*** [verb: χαρίζομαι <5483>]; **from *charis*: grace ▶ To use grace toward a person, not holding a personal offense against him or her; to cancel the debt of someone** > A creditor forgave two men who could not pay what they owed him (Luke 7:42, 43). God, in Christ, forgave us; therefore we ought to forgive one another (Eph. 4:32a, b; Col. 3:13a, b). God has forgiven Christians all their offences (Col. 2:13). Paul urged the Corinthians to forgive the man who had been disciplined by the church, and to assure him of their love (2 Cor. 2:7 {to show grace}; 2 Cor. 2:10a–c). Other ref.: 2 Cor. 12:13. All other refs.: DELIVER <5483>, GIVE <5483>, GRANT <5483>.

– [4] Mark 3:29 → will never be forgiven → lit.: has no forgiveness → FORGIVENESS <859> [5] John 20:23b → to not forgive → lit.: to retain → HOLD (verb) <2902> [6] Acts 5:31 → lit.: to give forgiveness, to give remission → GIVE <1325>, REMISSION <859>.

FORGIVENESS – [1] ***aphesis*** [fem. noun: ἄφεσις <859>]; **from *aphiēmi*: to send away, to release, which is from *apo*: far, and *hiēmi*: to send ▶ Granting pardon to someone; remission of an offence, i.e., to reckon it as not imputed** > He who will blaspheme against the Holy Spirit has no forgiveness {will never be forgiven} (Mark 3:29). All other refs.: LIBERTY <859>, REMISSION <859>.

– [2] John 20:23 → to withhold forgiveness → lit.: to hold; i.e., to hold or retain sins → HOLD (verb) <2902>.

FORM (noun) – [1] ***eidos*** [neut. noun: εἶδος <1491>]; **from *eidō*: to see, to examine; lit.: that which is seen ▶ Outward appearance, aspect** > The Holy Spirit descended on Jesus in a bodily form {shape}, like a dove (Luke 3:22). The Jews had never seen the form {shape} of the Father (John 5:37). The Christians of Thessalonica were to abstain from every form {appearance, kind} of evil (1 Thes. 5:22). All other refs.: FASHION (noun) <1491>, SIGHT (noun) <1491>.

[2] ***morphē*** [fem. noun: μορφή <3444>] ▶ **Intrinsic nature of a person or an object, essence of a being** > Jesus appeared in another form to two disciples (Mark 16:12). Existing in the form {nature} of God, Jesus took the form of a servant (Phil. 2:6, 7). ¶

[3] ***morphōsis*** [fem. noun: μόρφωσις <3446>]; **from *morphoō*: to form ▶ External appearance, outward resemblance** > Men have the form {embodiment} of knowledge and of the truth in the law (Rom. 2:20). There are men who have a form of godliness, but deny the power of it (2 Tim. 3:5). ¶

[4] ***tupos*** [masc. noun: τύπος <5179>]; **from *tuptō*: to strike (as to produce an imprint) ▶ Representation, model** > Claudius Lysias wrote a letter in a certain form {manner} (Acts 23:25). The Christians of Rome had obeyed from the heart the form {pattern} of teaching into which they had been instructed (Rom. 6:17). All other refs.: MARK (noun) <5179>, PATTERN <5179>, TYPE <5179>.

[5] **graven form: *charagma*** [neut. noun: χάραγμα <5480>]; **from *charassō*: to engrave ▶ Sculpture, i.e., a work fashioned out of a hard material** > The Athenians ought not to think that which is divine (i.e., the Divine Nature) was like a graven form of {an image formed by, an image made by, something shaped by} man's art (Acts 17:29). Other refs.: Rev. 13:16, 17; 14:9, 11; 15:2 in some mss.; 16:2; 19:20; 20:4; see MARK (noun) <5480>. ¶

– [6] Acts 14:11 → in form of → lit.: having become like → LIKE (adj., adv., noun) <3666> [7] Rom. 1:23 → LIKENESS <3667> [8] 1 Cor. 7:31; Phil. 2:8 → APPEARANCE <4976> [9] 2 Tim. 1:13 → PATTERN <5296> [10] Heb. 10:1 → IMAGE <1504> [11] 1 Pet. 4:10 → in its many forms → MANIFOLD <4164>.

FORM (verb) – [1] ***morphoō*** [verb: μορφόω <3445>]; **from *morphē*: form ▶ To fashion inwardly, to bring to maturity** > Paul was again in labor until Christ should be formed in the Christians of Galatia (Gal. 4:19). ¶

[2] ***plassō*** [verb: πλάσσω <4111>] ▶ **To shape, to mold** > Shall the thing formed (*plasma*) say to him who has formed (*plassō*) it {to the molder}: Why did you make me like this? (Rom. 9:20). Adam was formed {was created} first (1 Tim. 2:13). ¶

– [3] Acts 17:5 → to form a mob → to gather a mob → GATHER <3792> [4] 1 Cor. 12:13 → so as to form → lit.: into (*eis*) [5] Eph. 2:15 → CREATE <2936> [6] Heb. 11:3 → PREPARE <2675> [7] 2 Pet. 3:5 → to subsist together → SUBSIST <4921>.

FORMED – Rom. 9:20 → thing formed, what is formed → thing molded → MOLDED <4110>.

FORMER – [1] ***proteron*** [neut. adj. used as an adv. of time: πρότερον <4386>]; **from *proteros*: see [2] ▶ Beforehand, previously** > Christians must not conform themselves to the former lusts {the lusts they had in their ignorance} (1 Pet. 1:14). All other refs.: BEFORE <4386>, EARLIER <4386>, FIRST <4386>.

[2] ***proteros*** [adj.: πρότερος <4387>]; **from *pro*: before ▶ Previous, prior** > Paul spoke to the Ephesians of their "former manner of life" (Eph. 4:22). ¶

[3] **to go before: *proagō*** [verb: προάγω <4254>]; **from *pro*: before, and *agō*: to lead ▶ To precede, e.g., in time** > The former commandment (lit.: The commandment going before) (i.e., under the law) is set aside for its weakness and uselessness (Heb. 7:18). All other refs.: see entries in Lexicon at <4254>.

– [4] Rom. 3:25 → former sins → lit.: sins committed previously → COMMIT <4266> [5] Gal. 1:13 → in time(s) past →

PAST <4218> 6 1 Tim. 5:12 → FIRST <4413> 7 2 Pet. 1:9 → OLD (adj.) <3819>.

FORMERLY – 1 ***pote*** [adv.: ποτέ <4218>] ► **In the past, previously** > After his conversion, Paul, who had formerly {once} persecuted Christians, now announced the faith which he had formerly {once} tried to destroy (Gal. 1:23a, b). Peter describes the way in which holy women adorned themselves inwardly formerly {of the past, heretofore, in former times, in the old time} (1 Pet. 3:5). Other refs.: AFORETIME <4218>, PAST <4218>.
– 2 John 9:8; 1 Tim. 1:13 → BEFORE <4386> 3 Heb. 1:1 → in time past → PAST <3819> 4 Heb. 4:6 → at first → FIRST <4386>.

FORNICATION – 1 **fornication: *porneia*** [fem. noun: πορνεία <4202>]; **to commit fornication: *porneuō*** [verb: πορνεύω <4203>]; **from *pornos*: male prostitute, which is from *pernaō*: to sell** ► **Sexual relations outside the bonds of marriage; also transl.: sexual immorality** > Whoever puts away his wife, except for cause of fornication, makes her commit adultery (Matt. 5:32). Whoever shall put away his wife, not for fornication, and shall marry another, commits adultery (Matt. 19:9). The Jews said they were not born of fornication (John 8:41). This sin existed among the Corinthians (1 Cor. 5:1a, b). On account of fornications, each man was to have his own wife, and each woman was to have her own husband (1 Cor. 7:2). Fornication is expressly forbidden by God (Acts 15:20, 29; 21:25; 1 Cor. 6:18a, b; 10:8; Eph. 5:3; 1 Thes. 4:3). This term (*porneia*) also describes figur. worldly unbelievers (Rev. 14:8; 17:2b, 4; 18:3a, b, 9; 19:2). Other refs.: Matt. 15:19; Mark 7:21; Rom. 1:29 in some mss.; 1 Cor. 6:13; 2 Cor. 12:21; Gal. 5:19; Col. 3:5; Rev. 2:14, 20, 21; 9:21; 17:2a. ¶

2 **to give oneself over to fornication: *ekporneuō*** [verb: ἐκπορνεύω <1608>]; **from *ek*: intens., and *porneuō*: to commit prostitution, to prostitute oneself** ► **To practice unlawful sexual intercourse, including adultery** > Sodom and Gomorrah, and the surrounding towns, gave themselves over to fornication {committed greedily fornication, indulged in gross immorality, gave themselves up to sexual immorality} (Jude 7). ¶
– 3 1 Cor. 6:9 → one who commits fornication → FORNICATOR <4205>.

FORNICATOR – ***pornos*** [masc. noun: πόρνος <4205>]; **from *pernēmi*: to sell** ► **One who has sexual relations outside the bonds of marriage; also transl.: immoral people, sexually immoral people** > This term is found in 1 Cor. 5:9–11; 6:9; Eph. 5:5; 1 Tim. 1:10; Heb. 12:16; 13:4; Rev. 21:8; 22:15. ¶

FORSAKE – 1 ***apotassō*** [verb: ἀποτάσσω <657>]; **from *apo*: from, and *tassō*: to arrange** ► **To abandon, to give up** > Whoever does not forsake all that is his own cannot be the Lord's disciple (Luke 14:33). All other refs.: FAREWELL <657>, LEAVE (noun) <657>, SEND <657>.

2 ***aphiēmi*** [verb: ἀφίημι <863>]; **from *apo*: from, and *hiēmi*: to send** ► **To leave behind, to abandon** > All the disciples forsook {deserted, left} Jesus and fled (Matt. 26:56; Mark 14:50). All other refs.: see entries in Lexicon at <863>.

3 ***enkataleipō*** [verb: ἐγκαταλείπω <1459>]; **from *en*: in, and *kataleipō*: to leave behind, which is from *kata*: intens., and *leipō*: to leave behind, to forsake** ► **To withdraw from, to abandon; also transl.: to desert** > On the cross, Jesus asked God why He had forsaken Him (Matt. 27:46; Mark 15:34). Paul and Timothy were persecuted, but not forsaken {abandoned} (2 Cor. 4:9). Demas had forsaken Paul (2 Tim. 4:10); at his first defense, all forsook Paul (v. 16). Christians must not forsake {give up} the assembling of themselves together (i.e., neglect, abandon their meetings) (Heb. 10:25). God will never forsake the Christian believers (Heb. 13:5). All other refs.: LEAVE (verb) <1459>.
– 4 Acts 21:21 → lit.: apostasy → APOSTASY <646> 5 Heb. 11:27; 2 Pet. 2:15 → LEAVE (verb) <2641>.

FORSAKEN – Luke 13:35 → DESOLATE <2048>.

FORSWEAR – ***epiorkeō*** [verb: ἐπιορκέω <1964>]; **from *epiorkos*: perjurer, which is from *epi*: against, and *horkos*: oath ▶ To swear falsely, to violate one's oath; also transl.: to make false vows, to break one's oath** > Jesus reminded His listeners that it had been said not to forswear oneself, but to render to the Lord what one has sworn (Matt. 5:33). ¶

FORTH – [1] Matt. 1:21, 23, 25; Jas. 1:15; Rev. 12:2, 4a, b, 5, 13 → to bring forth → to give birth → BIRTH <5088> [2] Matt. 21:16 → to call forth → PERFECT (verb) <2675>.

FORTHWITH – Matt. 13:5; 26:49; et al. → IMMEDIATELY <2112> <2117>.

FORTRESS – [1] ***parembolē*** [fem. noun: παρεμβολή <3925>]; **from *paremballō*: to surround, which is from *para*: beside, and *emballō*: to interpose, which is from *en*: in, and *ballō*: to throw ▶ Lit.: soldier's quarters, barracks; hence, fortified castle, stronghold; also transl.: castle** > Paul was brought into a fortress (Acts 21:34, 37; 22:24; 23:10, 16, 32). All other refs.: ARMY <3925>, CAMP <3925>.

[2] ***ochurōma*** [neut. noun: ὀχύρωμα <3794>]; **from *ochuroō*: to fortify ▶ Fortified place, stronghold** > Reasonings against the knowledge of God are compared to fortresses; but the Christian, by spiritual weapons, is able to destroy such fortresses (2 Cor. 10:4). ¶

FORTUNATE – Acts 26:2 → HAPPY <3107>.

FORTUNATUS – ***Phortounatos*** [masc. name: Φορτουνάτος <5415>]: **happy, fortunate, in Lat. ▶ Christian man of Corinth** > The coming of Fortunatus had gladdened the apostle Paul at Ephesus (1 Cor. 16:17). He was to return with Paul's letter to the Corinthians (see v. 18). ¶

FORTUNE-TELLING – Acts 16:16 → PROPHESY <3132>.

FORTY – [1] ***tessarakonta*** [card. num.: τεσσαράκοντα <5062>]; **from *tessares*: four ▶** This number is used in regard to days (Matt. 4:2; Mark 1:13; Luke 4:2; Acts 1:3), nights (Matt. 4:2), years (Acts 4:22; 7:30, 36, 42; 13:21; Heb. 3:9, 17), conspirators (Acts 23:13, 21), and stripes (2 Cor. 11:24; the word "stripes" is added in Engl.). ¶
– [2] Acts 7:23; 13:18 → forty years old, of forty years → YEAR <5063>.

FORTY-SIX – **forty: *tessarakonta*** [card. num.: τεσσαράκοντα <5062>]**; and: *kai*** [conj.: καί <2532>]**; six: *hex*** [card. num.: ἕξ <1803>] ▶ This number is used in regard to the years spent in building the temple (John 2:20). ¶

FORTY-TWO – **forty: *tessarakonta*** [card. num.: τεσσαράκοντα <5062>]**; two: *duo*** [card. num: δύο <1417>] ▶ This number is used in regard to months the holy city will be treaded under foot (Rev. 11:2) and the beast will exercise its authority (13:5). ¶

FORUM OF APPIUS – See MARKET OF APPIUS <675> <5410>.

FORWARD – [1] Matt. 25:20, 22, 24 → to come forward → to come up, to come near → COME <4334> [2] Acts 1:23 → to put forward → APPOINT <2476> [3] 2 Cor. 8:17 → more forward → more zealous → ZEALOUS <4707>.

FORWARD (BE) – Gal. 2:10 → to be diligent → DILIGENT <4704>.

FORWARDNESS – 2 Cor. 8:8 → DILIGENCE <4710>.

FOSTER-BROTHER – Acts 13:1 → brought up with → BRING <4939>.

FOUL – [1] Matt. 16:3 → foul weather → STORM <5494> [2] Rev. 16:2 → EVIL (adj.) <2556>.

FOUND – [1] ***themelioō*** [verb: θεμελιόω <2311>]; **from *themelios*: foundation, which is from *tithēmi*: to establish, to set ▶ To establish a base, a foundation >** A house had been founded on the rock (Matt. 7:25; Luke 6:48). Christians are to be rooted and founded {established, grounded} in love (Eph. 3:17); they are to continue in the faith, founded {established, grounded, firmly established} and firm (Col. 1:23). The Lord has founded {has laid the foundation of} the earth (Heb. 1:10). Other ref.: 1 Pet. 5:10; see SETTLE <2311>. ¶

– [2] Heb. 8:6 → ESTABLISH <3549>.

FOUNDATION – [1] ***hedraiōma*** [neut. noun: ἑδραίωμα <1477>]; **from *hedraioō*: to make firm ▶ Basis, ground, support >** The church of the living God is the pillar and foundation {base, buttress} of the truth (1 Tim. 3:15). ¶

[2] ***katabolē*** [fem. noun: καταβολή <2602>]; **from *kataballō*: to throw down, which is from *kata*: down, and *ballō*: to throw ▶ Creation, beginning; also transl.: founding >** Jesus uttered things hidden from the world's foundation (Matt. 13:35). The kingdom is prepared for the blessed from the foundation of the world (Matt. 25:34). The blood of the prophets has been poured out from the foundation of the world (Luke 11:50). The Father loved the Son before the foundation of the world (John 17:24). God the Father has chosen Christians before the foundation of the world (Eph. 1:4). The works of God have been finished from the foundation of the world (Heb. 4:3). In keeping with the example of the high priest, Christ would have had to suffer many times from the foundation of the world, but now He has been manifested one time for the putting away of sin (Heb. 9:26). As a lamb without blemish and without spot, Christ was foreknown before the foundation of the world (1 Pet. 1:20). All who dwell on the earth, whose names have not been written from the foundation of the world in the book of life of the Lamb who was slain, will worship the beast (Rev. 13:8). Previously, they were astonished on seeing the beast (Rev. 17:8). Other ref.: Heb. 11:11 (conception); see CONCEIVE <2602>. ¶

[3] ***themelios*** [adj. used as noun: θεμέλιος <2310>]; **from *tithēmi*: to establish, to set ▶ Base, footing of a building; principle >** A man had laid the foundation of his house on the rock (Luke 6:48); another man built his house on the earth, without a foundation (v. 49). A person might lay the foundation of a tower without being able to finish it (Luke 14:29). The foundations of the prison where Paul was were shaken (Acts 16:26; *to themelion*). Paul did not want to build on another's foundation (Rom. 15:20). As a wise architect, he had laid the foundation (1 Cor. 3:10). Jesus Christ is the foundation which has been laid (1 Cor. 3:11); it is on this foundation that one builds (v. 12). Christians have been built on the foundation of the apostles and prophets (Eph. 2:20). Being rich in good works, those who are rich lay up for themselves a good foundation (1 Tim. 6:19; *keimēlion* in a mss.: treasure). The solid foundation of God remains: He knows those who are His and they are to withdraw from iniquity (2 Tim. 2:19). The Christian is not to lay again the foundation of repentance and faith in God (Heb. 6:1). Abraham waited for the city which has foundations (Heb. 11:10). In Revelation 21, we read about the foundation of the walls of the new Jerusalem (vv. 14, 19a, b). ¶

– [4] Matt. 7:25; Heb. 1:10 → to have the foundation, to lay the foundation → to be founded, to found → FOUND <2311>.

FOUNDER – [1] Heb. 2:10 → CAPTAIN <747> [2] Heb. 12:2 → AUTHOR <747>.

FOUNDING – Rev. 13:8; 17:8 → FOUNDATION <2602>.

FOUNTAIN – ***pēgē*** [fem. noun: πηγή <4077>] **▶ Well fed by a source; also transl.: spring, well >** In Sychar there was a fountain of Jacob's; Jesus sat thus as He was at the fountain (John 4:6a, b). The water which Jesus gives is a fountain of water springing up to eternal life in Christians (John 4:14). James asks if a fountain can pour forth both sweet and bitter out of the same opening (Jas. 3:11, 12 in some mss.). Peter speaks of people who are springs without water (2 Pet. 2:17). The Lamb shall lead those who come out of the great tribulation to fountains of waters of life (Rev. 7:17). A great star fell upon the fountains of waters (Rev. 8:10). God has made the fountains of waters (Rev. 14:7). An angel poured out his bowl on the fountains of waters (Rev. 16:4). To him who thirsts, Jesus will give of the fountain of the water of life freely (Rev. 21:6). Other ref.: Mark 5:29; see FLOW (noun) <4077>. ¶

FOUR – [1] ***tessares*** [card. num.: τέσσαρες <5064>] ► This number is used in regard to winds (Matt. 24:31; Mark 13:27; Rev. 7:1), people (Mark 2:3), days (John 11:17), parts (John 19:23), corners (Acts 10:11; 11:5; Rev. 7:1; 20:8), squads of soldiers (Acts 12:4), the daughters of Philip (Acts 21:9), men (Acts 21:23), anchors (Acts 27:29), living creatures (Rev. 4:6, 8; 5:6, 8, 14; 6:1, 6; 7:11; 14:3; 15:7; 19:4), angels (Rev. 7:2; 9:14, 15), and horns (Rev. 9:13). ¶
[2] **four days: *tetartaios*** [adj.: τεταρταῖος <5066>]; **from *tessares*: four** ► Lazarus had been dead four days (John 11:39). ¶
[3] **fourth: *tetartos*** [ord. num.: τέταρτος <5067>]; **from *tessares*: four** ► Four days ago (lit.: From the fourth day) Cornelius had been fasting (Acts 10:30). All other refs.: FOURTH <5067>. ¶
– [4] Luke 19:8 → four times as much, four times the amount → FOURFOLD <5073>
[5] John 4:35 → four months → MONTH <5072>.

FOUR-FOOTED ANIMAL – Acts 10:12; 11:6; Rom. 1:23 → QUADRUPED <5074>.

FOUR HUNDRED – ***tetrakosioi*** [card. num.: τετρακόσιοι <5071>]; **from *tessares*: four, and *ekaton*: hundred** ► This number is used in regard to men (Acts 5:36), years (Acts 7:6). ¶

FOUR HUNDRED AND FIFTY – **four hundred: *tetrakosioi*** [card. num.: τετρακόσιοι <5071>], **and: *kai*** [conj.: καί <2532>], **fifty: *pentēkonta*** [card. num.: πεντήκοντα <4004>] ► This number is used in regard to years (Acts 13:20). ¶

FOUR HUNDRED AND THIRTY – **four hundred: *tetrakosioi*** [card. num.: τετρακόσιοι <5071>], **thirty: *triakonta*** [card. num.: τριάκοντα <5144>] ► This number is used in regard to years (Gal. 3:17). ¶

FOUR THOUSAND – ***tetrakischilioi*** [card. num.: τετρακισχίλιοι <5070>]; **from *tessares*: four, and *chilioi*: thousand** ► This number is used in regard to men whom Jesus fed (Matt. 15:38; 16:10; Mark 8:9, 20) and to assassins (Acts 21:38). ¶

FOURFOLD – ***tetraplous*** [adj.: τετραπλοῦς <5073>]; **from *tessares*: four, and *haploos*: simple, onefold ► Quantity that is four times that of another quantity** > Zachaeus returned fourfold {four times as much, four times the amount} to any man if he had taken anything from him by false accusation (Luke 19:8). ¶

FOURSQUARE – ***tetragōnos*** [adj.: τετράγωνος <5068>]; **from *tessares*: four, and *gōnia*: angle, corner ► Quadrangular, i.e., which has four angles** > The new Jerusalem is laid out foursquare {as a square, like a square} (Rev. 21:16). ¶

FOURTEEN – ***dekatessares*** [card. num.: δεκατέσσαρες <1180>]; **from *deka*: ten, and *tessares*: four** ► This number is used in regard to generations (Matt. 1:17a–c) and years (2 Cor. 12:2; Gal. 2:1). ¶

FOURTEENTH – ***tessareskaidekatos*** [ord. num.: τεσσαρεσκαιδέκατος <5065>]; **from *tessares*: four, *kai*: and, *dekatos*: tenth** ► This number is used in regard to night (Acts 27:27) and day (v. 33). ¶

FOURTH – ***tetartos*** [ord. num.: τέταρτος <5067>]; **from *tessares*: four ► One of four portions of a whole** > Authority was given to Death over the fourth of the earth (Rev. 6:8). This number is also used in regard to a watch (Matt. 14:25; Mark 6:48), a living creature (Rev. 4:7; 6:7b), a seal (Rev. 6:7a), an angel (Rev. 8:12; 16:8), and the new Jerusalem (Rev. 21:19). Other ref.: Acts 10:30; see FOUR <5067>. ¶

FOWL – See BIRD.

FOX – ***alōpēx*** [fem. noun: ἀλώπηξ <258>] ► **Carnivorous mammal of the same family as the dog, which customarily makes a den for itself** > Jesus mentioned the foxes: they have a dwelling place, whereas He did not have a place where He might lay His head (Matt. 8:20; Luke 9:58). Jesus compared Herod Antipas to a fox (Luke 13:32), because he was a crafty, malicious person. ¶

FRAGMENT – ***klasma*** [neut. noun: κλάσμα <2801>]; **from** ***klaō*****: to break** ► **Piece of food, leftover food; also transl.: broken piece, piece** > The disciples took up twelve baskets full of the fragments that remained from the multiplication of loaves (Matt. 14:20; Mark 6:43; 8:19; Luke 9:17; John 6:12, 13). On another occasion, they took up seven baskets full of fragments {broken meat} (Matt. 15:37; Mark 8:8, 20). ¶

FRAGRANCE – 1 John 12:3; 2 Cor. 2:14, 16b → ODOR <3744> 2 2 Cor. 2:15 → sweet odor → ODOR <2175>.

FRAGRANT – 1 Eph. 5:2 → fragrant offering → OFFERING <4376> 2 Eph. 5:2; Phil. 4:18 → fragrant aroma, sweet odor → ODOR <2175>.

FRAGRANT OIL – Matt. 26:7, 9, 12; Mark 14:3–5; Luke 7:37, 38, 46; 23:56; John 11:2; 12:3a, b, 5 → OINTMENT <3464>.

FRAME – Heb. 11:3 → PREPARE <2675>.

FRAMED TOGETHER (FITLY) – Eph. 2:21 → to fit together → FIT (verb) <4883>.

FRANKINCENSE – ***libanos*** [masc. noun: λίβανος <3030>]; **from a Heb. word: white** ► **White and fragrant gum which is obtained by making an incision in the tree which produces it** > The wise men who had come to worship Jesus presented to Him gifts of gold, frankincense {incense}, and myrrh (Matt. 2:11). Frankincense is also mentioned in Rev. 18:13 in the list of precious merchandise bought by Babylon. ¶

FRANKNESS – 2 Cor. 7:4 → BOLDNESS <3954>.

FRAP – Acts 27:17 → UNDERGIRD <5269>.

FRAUD – 1 ***rhadiourgia*** [fem. noun: ῥᾳδιουργία <4468>]; **from** ***rhadiourgeō*****: to act without loyalty, which is from** ***rhadios*****: easy, reckless, and** ***ergon*****: work** ► **Deceitful conduct, facility for doing evil** > Elymas was full of all fraud {craft, mischief, trickery} (Acts 13:10). ¶
– 2 Matt. 27:64 → DECEPTION <4106> 3 Jas. 5:4 → to keep back by fraud → KEEP (verb) <650>.

FREE (adj.) – 1 ***eleutheros*** [adj.: ἐλεύθερος <1658>] ► **Liberated, not bound by an obligation; unconstrained, independent** > Jesus told the Jews they would become free (John 8:33). Those set free by the Son are free indeed (John 8:36b). The sons of the kings of the earth are free {exempt} from paying custom or tribute (Matt. 17:26). Paul often uses this Greek word in his letters (Rom. 6:20; 7:3 {released}; 1 Cor. 7:21, 22, 39 {at liberty}; 9:1, 19; 12:13; Gal. 3:28; 4:26, 31; Eph. 6:8; Col. 3:11 {freeman}). Peter uses it in 1 Pet. 2:16 {free man}, and John in Rev. 13:16; 19:18. The word is transl. "free woman" (*eleuthera*) in Gal. 4:22, 23, 30, and "free man" (*eleutheros*) in Rev. 6:15. ¶
2 **to set free, to make free, to free:** ***eleutheroō*** [verb: ἐλευθερόω <1659>]; **from** ***eleutheros*****: see** 1 ► **To liberate, to deliver from slavery or bondage** > The Son of God and the truth set free (John 8:32, 36a). Being set free {Having got his freedom, Having been freed} from sin, the Christian has become

the servant of righteousness and of God (Rom. 6:18, 22). The law of the Spirit of life in Christ Jesus has set Christians free from the law of sin and of death (Rom. 8:2). The creature {creation} itself will be set free {delivered, liberated} from the bondage of corruption (Rom. 8:21). Christians must stand fast in the liberty by which Christ has set them free (Gal. 5:1). ¶

[3] **to set free: *apoluō*** [verb: ἀπολύω <630>]; **from *apo*: from, and *luō*: to loose ▶ To release, to liberate (e.g., from imprisonment)** > Timothy had been set free {set at liberty} (Heb. 13:23). All other refs.: see entries in Lexicon at <630>.

– [4] Luke 1:64 → set free → added in Engl. [5] Luke 4:18 → to set free → SEND <649> [6] Luke 4:18b → LIBERTY <859> [7] Luke 13:16; 1 Cor. 7:27b → to set free → LOOSE <3089> [8] Acts 7:34 → to set free → DELIVER <1807> [9] Acts 13:39; Rom. 6:7 → JUSTIFY <1344> [10] Rom. 5:15, 16 → free gift → GIFT <5486> [11] Rom. 7:24 → to set free → DELIVER <4506> [12] 1 Cor. 7:32 → free from concern, free from anxieties → CONCERN (noun) <275> [13] Gal. 5:13a → to be free → lit.: to liberty → LIBERTY <1657> [14] 2 Thes. 3:1 → to have free course → RUN <5143> [15] 1 Tim. 3:3; Heb. 13:5 → free from the love of money → not greedy for money → GREEDY <866> [16] 1 Tim. 5:22 → free from sin → PURE <53> [17] 1 Tim. 6:14 → free from reproach → REPROACH (noun) <423> [18] Heb. 2:15 → to set free → RELEASE (verb) <525> [19] Rev. 20:3 → RELEASE (verb) <3089>.

FREE (verb) – [1] Acts 2:24 → LOOSE <3089> [2] Acts 13:39; Rom. 6:7 → to obtain justification → to be justified → JUSTIFY <1344> [3] Heb. 2:15 → RELEASE (verb) <525> [4] Rev. 1:5 → WASH <3068>.

FREED – 1 Cor. 7:22 → freed person → FREEDMAN <558>.

FREEDMAN – [1] ***apeleutheros*** [masc. noun: ἀπελεύθερος <558>]; **from *apo*: from, and *eleutheros*: free ▶ Man released from slavery or bondage** > The servant called in the Lord is the Lord's freedman {freeman} (1 Cor. 7:22). ¶

[2] ***Libertinos*** [masc. name: Λιβερτῖνος <3032>]: **person who has been liberated; *libertinus*, in Lat. ▶ Person made prisoner and freed later; also transl.: Libertine** > Some men from the Synagogue of the Freedmen argued with Stephen (Acts 6:9). ¶

FREEDOM – [1] Luke 4:18a → LIBERTY <859> [2] Acts 2:29; 28:31; Eph. 3:12 → BOLDNESS <3954> [3] Acts 22:28 → CITIZENSHIP <4174> [4] Acts 24:23 → LIBERTY <425> [5] Acts 26:26 → to speak with all freedom → to speak boldly → BOLDLY <3955> [6] Rom. 6:18, 22 → to get the freedom → to be set free → FREE (adj.) <1659> [7] Rom. 8:21; 1 Cor. 10:29; Gal. 2:4; 5:1; 5:13a, b; Jas. 1:25; 2:12; 1 Pet. 2:16; 2 Pet. 2:19 → LIBERTY <1657> [8] 1 Cor. 7:21 → you can gain your freedom → lit.: you can become free → FREE (adj.) <1658> [9] 1 Cor. 8:9 → exercise of the freedom → LIBERTY <1849>.

FREELY – [1] ***dōrean*** [adv.: δωρεάν <1432>]; **from *dōrea*: gift, present ▶ Without charge, gratuitously; also transl.: free of charge, without cost** > The disciples of Jesus had received freely and they were to give freely (Matt. 10:8a, b). We are justified freely {as a gift} by the grace of God through the redemption which is in Christ Jesus (Rom. 3:24). Paul had freely preached the gospel of God to the Corinthians (2 Cor. 11:7). Paul had not eaten anyone's bread free of charge (or: freely) (2 Thes. 3:8). Jesus will give of the fountain of the water of life freely to the one who thirsts (Rev. 21:6). Whoever wills may take the water of life freely (Rev. 22:17). This term is transl. "for nothing," "in vain," "needlessly" in Gal. 2:21. Other ref.: John 15:25 (without a cause); see CAUSE <1432>. ¶

– [2] Acts 2:29 → lit.: with freedom → with boldness → BOLDNESS <3954> [3] Acts 9:28 → to move about freely → lit.: to come in and go out → COME <1531> [4] Acts 26:26 → to speak freely → to speak boldly → BOLDLY <3955> [5] 2 Cor. 9:9

→ to scatter freely → to scatter abroad → SCATTER <4650> 6 Gal. 3:18 → to freely give → GIVE <5483> 7 Eph. 1:6 → to bestow one's grace freely → to make accepted → ACCEPTED <5487> 8 Jas. 1:5 → LIBERALLY <574>.

FREEMAN – 1 1 Cor. 7:22 → FREEDMAN <558> 2 Col. 3:11 → FREE (adj.) <1658>.

FREEWOMAN – Gal. 4:22, 23, 30 → FREE (adj.) <1658>.

FREQUENT – 1 ***puknos*** [adj.: πυκνός <4437>]; **from *pux*: fist ▶ Which occurs often** > Timothy was to use a little wine because of his frequent illnesses (1 Tim. 5:23). Other refs.: Mark 7:3 in some mss.; Luke 5:33; Acts 24:26; see OFTEN <4437>. ¶
– 2 2 Cor. 11:23b → more frequent → more abundant → ABUNDANT <4056>.

FREQUENTLY – 2 Cor. 11:23b → more frequently → more abundant → ABUNDANT <4056>.

FRESH – ***glukus*** [adj.: γλυκύς <1099>] ▶ **Having a taste which is neither salty nor bitter; also transl.: sweet** > James asks if a fountain sends forth fresh and bitter water out of the same opening (Jas. 3:11); no fountain can produce both salt and fresh water (v. 12). Other refs.: Rev. 10:9, 10; see SWEET <1099>. ¶

FRICTION – 1 Tim. 6:5 → constant friction → useless wrangling → WRANGLING <1275a> <3859>.

FRIEND – 1 ***hetairos*** [masc. noun: ἑταῖρος <2083>]; **comp. *etēs* which is a man of the same social group or related by marriage ▶ Opportunistic companion** > Jesus uses the word "friend" in the parable of the workmen sent in a vineyard (Matt. 20:13) and in the one of the king who made a marriage for his son (22:12). Before being betrayed, Jesus addressed Himself to Judas with the name "friend" (Matt. 26:50). Other ref.: Matt. 11:16; see COMPANION <2083>. ¶

2 ***philos*** [adj. and masc. noun: φίλος <5384>] ▶ **Dear person, for whom one has affection; one who seeks the good of another** > Jesus was accused of being a friend of tax-gatherers and sinners (Matt. 11:19; Luke 7:34). A centurion sent friends to Jesus (Luke 7:6). Jesus speaks of friends in His parables (Luke 11:5a, b, 6, 8; 14:10; 15:6, 29) and of the friend of the bridegroom (John 3:29). He calls His disciples friends (Luke 12:4; John 15:15), and He speaks of Lazarus as "our friend" (John 11:11). When one makes a meal, he should not call his friends lest they also invite him back (Luke 14:12). The woman who has found the piece of silver in the parable calls her friends to rejoice with her (Luke 15:9). Jesus said to make ourselves friends of the wealth of unrighteousness (Luke 16:9). The disciples of Jesus would be betrayed by friends (Luke 21:16). Pilate and Herod became friends the day before the crucifixion of Jesus (Luke 23:12). There is no greater love than laying down one's life for His friends (John 15:13); those doing whatever Jesus commands them are His friends (v. 14). The Jews cried out to Pilate that he would not be Caesar's friend if he let Jesus go (John 19:12). Cornelius called his close friends to listen to Peter (Acts 10:24). Paul had some of the Asiarchs as his friends (Acts 19:31). Julius gave Paul liberty to go to his friends (Acts 27:3). Abraham was called the friend of God (Jas. 2:23). Whoever wants to be a friend of the world makes himself an enemy of God (Jas. 4:4). The friends of John greeted Gaius, and John asked to greet the friends by name (3 John 14a, b). ¶
– 3 Matt. 5:25 → to make friends → AGREE <2132> 4 Mark 3:21 → RELATIVE <846> 5 Luke 2:44 → ACQUAINTANCE <1110> 6 Acts 4:23 → their friends → lit.: their own 7 Acts 12:20 → to make a friend → to win over → WIN <3982> 8 Acts 13:38; 14:15; 19:25 → friends → lit.: men brothers, men 9 Rom. 12:19; 16:8 → friend, dear friend → BELOVED <27>.

FRIENDLY – Acts 28:7 → in a very friendly way → COURTEOUSLY <5390>.

FRIENDSHIP – 1 ***philia*** [fem. noun: φιλία <5373>]; **from *philos*: dear, friend ▶ Feeling of affection, attachment between two people** > The friendship with the world is enmity with God (Jas. 4:4). ¶
– 2 Luke 11:8 → because of friendship → because he is his friend → FRIEND <5384>.

FRIGHT – Luke 24:5 → in fright → AFRAID <1719>.

FRIGHTEN – 1 Matt. 24:6; Mark 13:7 → to be frightened → to be troubled → TROUBLE (verb) <2360> 2 Luke 21:9; 24:37 → TERRIFY <4422> 3 2 Cor. 10:9 → TERRIFY <1629> 4 Phil. 1:28 → TERRIFY <4426> 5 1 Pet. 3:14 → TROUBLE (verb) <5015>.

FRIGHTENED – 1 ***emphobos*** [adj.: ἔμφοβος <1719>]; **from *en*: in, and *phobos*: fear ▶ Fearful, scared, terrified** > The disciples were confounded and frightened {affrighted} when Jesus appeared in the midst of them (Luke 24:37). Those who were with Paul saw the light and were afraid {were filled with fear} (lit.: became frightened) (Acts 22:9 in some mss.). All other refs.: AFRAID <1719>.
– 2 Matt. 14:30; 27:54; Mark 5:15; Luke 8:35; John 6:19 → to be frightened, to become frightened → FEAR (verb) <5399> 3 Mark 5:33; 1 Pet. 3:6 → to be frightened → to be afraid → AFRAID <5399> 4 Mark 9:6 → lit.: to be greatly afraid → AFRAID <1630>.

FRIGHTENING – 1 Pet. 3:6 → anything that is frightening → lit.: (not any) fear → FEAR (noun) <4423>.

FRINGE – ***kraspedon*** [neut. noun: κράσπεδον <2899>]; **from *kras*: head, summit, and *pedon*: ground, earth ▶ Strip of cloth used to border a garment; also transl.: border, edge, hem, tassel** > Jesus reproached the Pharisees for enlarging the tassels of their garments to attract the attention of men (Matt. 23:5). This border prob. refers to the thread of blue which Israelites were to wear at the corners of their garments (see Num. 15:38), to recall the commandments of the Lord and to remember to practice them. The term is also used in Matt. 9:20; 14:36; Mark 6:56; Luke 8:44. ¶

FROG – ***batrachos*** [masc. noun: βάτραχος <944>] ▶ **Amphibian known for its croaking; symbol of impurity due to the fact it lives nears swamps and in the mud** > The unclean spirits that come out of the mouths of the dragon, the beast, and the false prophet are like frogs (Rev. 16:13); they are the spirits of demons performing miraculous signs to gather together the kings of the earth for the battle of Armageddon (see vv. 14–16). ¶

FROM – ***ek*** [prep.: ἐκ <1537>] ▶ **Inside, among** > This prep. is also transl.: from among, of, out from, out of, with. For example: Luke 11:27; 12:13; Acts 26:17; 27:29; 1 Cor. 5:13; 1 John 2:19; Rev. 18:4. *

FROM EVERYWHERE – ***pantachothen*** [adv.: πανταχόθεν <3836>]; **from *pas*: all, and suffix *then*: from a place ▶ Also transl.: from every side, from every quarter, from every direction** > Ref.: Mark 1:45. ¶

FROM WHERE – ***pothen*** [adv.: πόθεν <4159>] ▶ Ref.: Matt. 15:33; Mark 8:4; John 4:11; 6:5. *

FRONT – 1 Matt. 6:1 → in front of → in the presence of → PRESENCE <1715> 2 Matt. 21:2 → in front of → lit.: in the presence of → PRESENCE <561> 3 Luke 18:39 → to be in front → to go before → GO <4254>.

FROWARD – 1 Pet. 2:18 → HARSH <4646>.

FRUIT – 1 ***karpos*** [masc. noun: καρπός <2590>]; ***carpere*, in Lat.: to pick, to harvest ▶ Primarily, the fleshy, edible, seed-bearing product of trees, plants or the**

ground > This term is used in various places (Matt. 3:10; 7:17a, b, 18a, b, 19; 12:33a–c; 13:8, 26; 21:19, 34a, b, 41; Mark 4:7, 8, 29; 11:14; 12:2; Luke 3:9; 6:43a, b, 44; 8:8; 12:17; 13:6, 7, 9; 20:10; John 15:4; 1 Cor. 9:7; 2 Tim. 2:6; Jas. 5:7, 18; Rev. 22:2a, b). It designates someone's descendants (Luke 1:42; Acts 2:30). It is also used to describe the visible works or actions produced by a person (Matt. 3:8; 7:16, 20; 21:43; Luke 3:8; John 4:36; 12:24; 15:2a–c, 5, 8, 16a, b; Rom. 1:13; 6:21, 22; 15:28; Gal. 5:22; Eph. 5:9; Phil. 1:11, 22 (lit.: this is to me the fruit of labor); 4:17; Heb. 12:11; 13:15; Jas. 3:17, 18). ¶

2 **without fruit:** ***akarpos*** [adj.: ἄκαρπος <175>]; **from** ***a*****: neg., and** ***karpos*****: see** 1 ► **Without results, ineffective; also transl.: unfruitful >** Christians must not participate in the unfruitful deeds of darkness (Eph. 5:11). Other refs.: Matt. 13:22; Mark 4:19; 1 Cor. 14:14; Titus 3:14; 2 Pet. 1:8 {unproductive}; Jude 12. ¶

3 **to bear fruit, to bring forth fruit:** ***karpophoreō*** [verb: καρποφορέω <2592>]; **from** ***karpophoros*****: fruitful, which is from** ***karpos*****: see** 1**, and** ***phoreō*****: to bear, which is from** ***pherō*****: to carry, to bear ► To yield results, to produce an effect; also transl.: to be fruitful, to produce a crop, to produce grain >** The verb is used in Matt. 13:23; Mark 4:20, 28; Luke 8:15; Rom. 7:4, 5; Col. 1:6, 10. ¶

4 ***genēma*** [neut. noun: γένημα <1079a>]; **from** ***gennaō*****: to give birth, which is from** ***genna*****: race ► Produce of the ground (e.g., grapes of the vine) >** This term is used when Jesus instituted the Last Supper (Matt. 26:29; Mark 14:25; Luke 22:18). The word is also transl. "harvest" in 2 Cor. 9:10. Other ref.: Luke 12:18; see GRAIN <1079a>. ¶

5 ***opōra*** [fem. noun: ὀπώρα <3703>] ► **Ripe fruit (late summer or early fall) >** This term is used in Rev. 18:14 in relation to Babylon the great. ¶

6 **to bring fruit to maturity, to bring fruit to perfection:** ***telesphoreō*** [verb: τελεσφορέω <5052>]; **from** ***telos*****: end, and and** ***phoreō*****: to bear, which is from** ***pherō*****: to carry, to bear ► To produce fruit which is ready to be picked >** The seed that fell among the thorns did not bring fruit to maturity in Luke 8:14. ¶

FRUITFUL – 1 ***karpophoros*** [adj.: καρποφόρος <2593>]; **from** ***karpos*****: fruit, and** ***pherō*****: to bring ► Fruit bearing, productive >** God gives rain from heaven and fruitful seasons (Acts 14:17). Other ref.: John 15:2 in some mss. ¶

– 2 Phil. 1:22 → fruitful labor → lit.: fruit of labor → FRUIT <2590> 3 Col. 1:10 → to be fruitful → to bear fruit → FRUIT <2592>.

FRUITION – 2 Thes. 1:11 → bring to fruition → FULFILL <4137>.

FRUITLESS – 1 Eph. 5:11 → UNFRUITFUL <175> 2 1 Tim. 1:6 → fruitless conversation → vain discourse → VAIN <3150> 3 Jude 12 → lit.: without fruit → FRUIT <175>.

FRUSTRATE – 1 Cor. 1:19; Gal. 2:21 → REJECT <114>.

FRUSTRATION – Rom. 8:20 → VANITY <3153>.

FULFILL – 1 ***teleō*** [verb: τελέω <5055>]; **from** ***telos*****: end, completion ► To execute, to accomplish, to satisfy; also transl.: to carry out, to keep >** The people of Jerusalem and their rulers had fulfilled (carried out) all things written concerning Jesus (Acts 13:29). Paul speaks about the physically uncircumcised fulfilling {who obeys} the law (Rom. 2:27). He tells the Galatians to walk in the Spirit and they will not fulfill {gratify} the lust of the flesh (Gal. 5:16). Those who fulfill {keep} the royal law to love their neighbor as themselves are doing well (Jas. 2:8). The nations will give their kingdom to the beast until the words of God will be fulfilled (Rev. 17:17). All other refs.: see entries in Lexicon at <5055>.

2 ***sunteleō*** [verb: συντελέω <4931>]; **from** ***sun*****: together (intens.), and** ***teleō*****: see** 1 ► **To accomplish, to happen >** Four disciples asked Jesus what the sign will be that all the things of the end will be fulfilled (Mark

13:4). All other refs.: END (verb) <4931>, FINISH <4931>, MAKE <4931>.

3 ***teleioō*** [verb: τελειόω <5048>]; **from *teleios*: complete ▶ To accomplish, to complete** > When they had fulfilled the {finished the, spent the full number of} days of the Feast {After the Feast was over}, the boy Jesus remained behind in Jerusalem (Luke 2:43). Jesus said that He was thirsty so that the Scriptures might be fulfilled (John 19:28). All other refs.: FINISH <5048>, PERFECT (adj.) <5048>, PERFECT (verb) <5048>.

4 ***ginomai*** [verb: γίνομαι <1096>] **▶ To happen, to be accomplished** > Everything written in the law will be fulfilled {come to pass} (Matt. 5:18). Other ref.: Luke 21:32 {to come to pass, to take place}. Other refs.: see entries in Lexicon at <1096>.

5 ***plēroō*** [verb: πληρόω <4137>]; **from *plērēs*: full ▶ To make full, to accomplish, to realize; also transl.: to complete, to be complete, to make complete, to end, to finish, to be full, to make full, to come full, to come fully, to pass** > The verb "fulfill" confirms the accomplishment of what God had predicted in His word (e.g., Matt. 1:22). It underlies the accomplishment of something, e.g., the righteousness that was proper for Jesus to fulfill (Matt. 3:15), as well as the law or the prophets (5:17). It also means the fulfillment of a period of time, e.g., the time that has elapsed before the establishment of the kingdom (Mark 1:15). When he was forty years old {When he was approaching the age of forty} (lit.: When a period of forty years was fulfilled to him), it came into the heart of Moses to visit his brothers (Acts 7:23). Paul speaks of John fulfilling his course (Acts 13:25). The righteous requirement of the law is fulfilled in those walking according to the Spirit (Rom. 8:4). Paul speaks of the obedience of the Corinthians being fulfilled (2 Cor. 10:6). He had received the ministry of fulfilling the word of God (Col. 1:25). The Christians are fulfilled in Christ (Col. 2:10). Other refs.: Matt. 2:15, 17, 23; 4:14; 8:17; 12:17; 13:35; 21:4; 26:54, 56; 27:9, 35 in some mss.; Mark 14:49; 15:28; Luke 1:20; 4:21; 9:31; 21:22, 24; 22:16; 24:44; John 3:29; 7:8; 12:38; 13:18; 15:11, 25; 16:24; 17:12, 13; 18:9, 32; 19:24, 36; Acts 1:16; 3:18; 12:25; 13:27; 14:26; 19:21; 24:27; Rom. 13:8; Gal. 5:14; Phil. 2:2; Col. 4:17; 2 Thes. 1:11; Jas. 2:23; 1 John 1:4; 2 John 12; Rev. 6:11. All other refs.: see entries in Lexicon at <4137>.

6 ***anaplēroō*** [verb: ἀναπληρόω <378>]; **from *ana*: intens., and *plēroō*: see 5 ▶ To accomplish, to realize thoroughly** > A prophecy of Isaiah was fulfilled {filled} in the fact that the people did not understand the parables of Jesus (Matt. 13:14). In bearing one another' burdens, we fulfill the law of Christ (Gal. 6:2). All other refs.: FILL (verb) <378>, SUPPLY (verb) <378>.

7 ***ekplēroō*** [verb: ἐκπληρόω <1603>]; **from *ek*: intens., and *plēroō*: see 5 ▶ To accomplish completely** > God has fulfilled His promise to the fathers of Israel for us, their children, by raising up Jesus (Acts 13:33). ¶

8 ***poieō*** [verb: ποιέω <4160>]; **lit.: to make ▶ To accomplish, to do** > Before their conversion, Christians were fulfilling {gratifying, indulging in) the desires of the flesh and of the mind (Eph. 2:3). Other refs.: see entries in Lexicon at <4160>.

– **9** Matt. 5:33 → RENDER <591> **10** Luke 1:1 → to believe most surely → BELIEVE <4135> **11** Luke 1:45 → lit.: to be a performance → PERFORMANCE <5050> **12** Luke 1:57 → to come fully → COME <4130> **13** Luke 9:51 → to fully come → COME <4845> **14** Acts 23:1 → to fulfill one's duty → LIVE <4176> **15** Phil. 2:13 → in order to fulfill → according to (*huper*) **16** 2 Tim. 4:5 → to make full proof → PROOF <4135> **17** 2 Pet. 3:9 → "to fulfill" added in Engl. **18** Rev. 17:17a, b → EXECUTE <4160>.

FULFILLED – **1** Acts 9:23 → to be past → to be fulfilled → PAST <4137> **2** Acts 26:7 → to see fulfilled → ARRIVE <2658>.

FULFILLING – Rom. 13:10 → FULFILLMENT <4138>.

FULFILLMENT – **1** ***plērōma*** [neut. noun: πλήρωμα <4138>]; **from *plēroō*: to fill**

up ► **Accomplishment, fullness** > Love is the fulfillment of the law (Rom. 13:10 {fulfilling, whole}). All other refs.: FULL <4138>, FULLNESS <4138>, PATCH <4138>, PIECE <4138>.

– 2 Luke 1:45 → PERFORMANCE <5050>.

FULL – 1 ***plērēs*** [adj.: πλήρης <4134>]; **comp. *pimplēmi*: to fill, *pleos*: full ► Replete, complete** > The word is used in regard to baskets and fragments of bread (Matt. 14:20; 15:37; Mark 6:43; 8:19), the ear and the corn (Mark 4:28 {mature}), Jesus and the Holy Spirit (Luke 4:1 {filled}), a man and his leprosy (Luke 5:12 {covered}), the Son full of grace and truth (John 1:14), Stephen and the Holy Spirit (Acts 6:3, 5; 7:55), Stephen and grace and power (Acts 6:8), Dorcas and good works and alms-deeds (Acts 9:36 {abounding}), Barnabas and the Holy Spirit and faith (Acts 11:24), Elymas and deceit and craft (Acts 13:10), and John writing to the chosen lady concerning their reward (2 John 8). The word is also used in the expr. "filled with rage" (Acts 19:28). ¶

2 **filling: *plērōma*** [neut. noun: πλήρωμα <4138>]; **from *plēroō*: to fill, which is from *plērēs*: complete, full ► State of that which is complete, abundance** > This word is used when Jesus spoke about baskets full (lit.: the filling of many baskets) of fragments of bread (Mark 8:20). All other refs.: FULFILLMENT <4138>, FULLNESS <4138>, PATCH <4138>, PIECE <4138>.

3 ***mestos*** [adj.: μεστός <3324>] ► **Filled, replete** > The word is used in regard to scribes and Pharisees and their hypocrisy and lawlessness (Matt. 23:28), a vessel and vinegar (John 19:29), a net with 153 large fish (John 21:11), unrighteous men and wicked things (Rom. 1:29), brothers and goodness (Rom. 15:14), uncontrolled tongue and deadly poison (Jas. 3:8), the wisdom from above with mercy and good fruits (Jas. 3:17), and unrighteous men and adultery (2 Pet. 2:14). ¶

4 **to be full: *mestoō*** [verb: μεστόω <3325>]; **from *mestos*: see 3 ► To have too much** > The verb is used in regard to disciples in Jerusalem accused mockingly of being full of new wine (Acts 2:13). ¶

5 **to be full: *gemō*** [verb: γέμω <1073>] ► **To be replete, to be stuffed; also transl.: to be covered, to be filled** > The verb is used in regard to the inside of a cup and dish with robbery and intemperance (Matt. 23:25), whitewashed tombs with bones and uncleanness (Matt. 23:27), Pharisees and wickedness (Luke 11:39), the mouth of unrighteous men and their cursing and bitterness (Rom. 3:14), four beasts and their eyes (Rev. 4:6, 8), golden bowls and incenses (Rev. 5:8), golden bowls and the fury of God (Rev. 15:7), a scarlet beast and names of blasphemy (Rev. 17:3), a golden cup with abominations and unclean things (Rev. 17:4), and the seven bowls and seven last plagues (Rev. 21:9). ¶

– 6 Matt. 6:22; Luke 11:34, 36 → full of light → LIGHT (noun) <5460> 7 Matt. 12:34; Luke 6:45 → what the heart is full of → of the abundance of the heart → ABUNDANCE <4051> 8 Matt. 13:48 → to be full → FILLED (BE) <4137> 9 Mark 4:37; Luke 14:23 → to be full → FILL (verb) <1072> 10 Luke 6:25 → to be full → to be filled → FILL (verb) <1705> 11 Luke 6:34 → in full → the like → LIKE (adj., adv., noun) <2470> 12 John 3:29; 7:8; 15:11; 16:24; 17:13; 1 John 1:4; 2 John 12 → to be full come, to make full, to be full → FULFILL <4137> 13 John 6:63 → the words are full of the Spirit and life → lit.: the words are Spirit and are life 14 John 10:10 → to the full → ABUNDANTLY <4053> 15 John 19:29 → they put a sponge full of → lit.: they filled a sponge with → FILL (verb) <4130> 16 Acts 2:28; Phil. 4:18 → to make full, to be full → to fill up → FILL (verb) <4137> 17 1 Cor. 4:8 → to be full → to be filled → FILL (verb) <2880> 18 Phil. 2:2 → being in full accord → joined in soul → SOUL <4861> 19 Phil. 4:12 → to be full → to be filled → FILL (verb) <5526> 20 Col. 2:2 → full assurance → ASSURANCE <4136> 21 Jas. 1:4 → to have full effect → lit.: to have its perfect work → PERFECT (adj.) <5046> 22 Rev. 1:16 → "full" added in Engl. 23 Rev. 6:11 → until the full number → until the number should be fulfilled → FULFILL <4137> **24** Rev. 6:12 in some mss. → WHOLE <3650> **25** Rev. 14:10 → full strength → STRENGTH <194>.

FULL-GROWN – 1 Cor. 14:20; Eph. 4:13; Heb. 5:14 → full grown man → mature man → MATURE <5046>.

FULL-GROWN (BE) – Jas. 1:15 → FINISH <658>.

FULL WELL – 1 Thes. 5:2 → PERFECTLY <199>.

FULLER – Mark 9:3 → LAUNDERER <1102>.

FULLNESS – ***plērōma*** [neut. noun: πλήρωμα <4138>]; **from *plēroō*: to fill, which is from *plērēs*: complete, full ▶ a. Content** > The earth is the Lord's, and its fullness {all it contains, everything in it} (1 Cor. 10:26). **b. Abundance, completeness, plenitude** > When the fullness of the time had come {When the time had fully come}, God sent forth His Son (Gal. 4:4). All the fullness of the Godhead was pleased to dwell in Christ (Col. 1:19; 2:9). The church is the fullness of Christ, as being His body (Eph. 1:23). Of the fullness of Jesus Christ, all Christians have received, and grace upon grace (John 1:16). Paul spoke of the fullness {full measure} of the blessing of Christ (Rom. 15:29) and of the stature of the fullness of Christ (Eph. 4:13); he prayed that the Ephesians might be filled to all the fullness of God (Eph. 3:19). In Rom. 11:12, the fullness {fulfillment} of Israel refers to the day when this people will turn toward their Messiah and to the blessing that will thereby result for all nations; in Rom. 11:25, the fullness {full number} of the nations corresponds to all the various nations. In Eph. 1:10, the fullness {fulfillment} of times refers to the millennial day. Other ref.: 1 Cor. 10:28 in some mss. All other refs.: FULL <4138>, FULFILLMENT <4138>, PATCH <4138>, PIECE <4138>.

FULLY – **1** John 7:8 → to come fully → FULFILL <4137> **2** Acts 23:20 → more fully → more accurately → ACCURATELY <197> **3** Rom. 9:28 → to carry out fully → FINISH <4931> **4** Rom. 15:19 → to preach fully → PREACH <4137> **5** 1 Cor. 15:58 → to give oneself fully → ABOUND <4052> **6** 2 Cor. 1:13 → to the end → END (noun) <5056> **7** Gal. 4:4 → FULLNESS <4138> **8** Col. 4:12 in some mss. → fully assured → to be complete → COMPLETE (adj.) <4135> **9** 1 Thes. 5:2 → PERFECTLY <199> **10** 2 Tim. 3:10 → to fully know → to follow carefully → FOLLOW <3877> **11** 2 Tim. 4:17 → to preach fully → PREACH <4135> **12** 1 Pet. 1:13 → COMPLETELY <5049> **13** Jude 5 → to fully know → KNOW <1492> **14** Rev. 14:15 → to be fully ripe → RIPE (BE) <3583>.

FULLY HUMAN – Heb. 2:17 → like them, fully human → lit.: like to the brothers → BROTHER <80>.

FULNESS – See FULLNESS <4138>.

FUN – Acts 2:13 → to make fun → MOCK <5512>.

FUNCTION (noun) – **1** ***praxis*** [fem. noun: πρᾶξις <4234>]; **from *prassō*: to practice, to accomplish; lit.: action ▶ Role, activity** > In one body, all members do not have the same function {office} (Rom. 12:4). All other refs.: DEED <4234>, WORK (noun) <4234>.

– **2** Rom. 1:26, 27 → USE (noun) <5540>.

FUNCTION (verb) – Heb. 9:8 → to be functioning → lit.: to have its standing → STANDING <4714>.

FURIOUS – **1 to be furious: *diapriō*** [verb: διαπρίω <1282>]; **from *dia*: through, and *priō*: to saw; lit.: to saw through or asunder ▶ To be vexed, to be exasperated, to be enraged; also transl.: to be cut to the heart, to be cut to the quick** > Those who had heard the words of Peter were furious

(Acts 5:33). Those who heard the words of Stephen were furious (Acts 7:54). ¶

2 **to be exceedingly furious: *emmainomai*** [verb: ἐμμαίνομαι <1693>]; **from *en*: in, and *mainomai*: to act like a madman ▶ To be carried away with rage, to be consumed with anger; also transl.: to be exceedingly mad, to be exceedingly enraged, to be furiously enraged, to be obsessed with persecution** > Before his conversion, Paul was exceedingly furious against Christians (Acts 26:11). ¶

– 3 Matt. 2:16 → to be furious → to be angry → ANGRY <2373> 4 Matt. 22:7; Rev. 12:17 → to be furious, to become furious → ENRAGED (BE) <3710> 5 Luke 4:28; 6:11; Acts 19:28 → to be furious → lit.: to be filled with wrath, madness → FILL (verb) <4130>, WRATH <2372>, MADNESS <454>.

FURLONG – See STADION.

FURNACE – 1 ***kaminos*** [fem. noun: κάμινος <2575>]; **comp. *kamara*: arch, curved object ▶ Large oven where a blazing fire burns** > Those who commit iniquity will be cast into the furnace of fire (Matt. 13:42), as will likewise the wicked (v. 50). The feet of the Son of Man were like fine brass, as burning in a furnace (Rev. 1:15). Smoke went up out of the bottomless pit, as the smoke of a great furnace (Rev. 9:2). ¶

– 2 Matt. 6:30; Luke 12:28 → OVEN <2823>.

FURNISH – 1 ***strōnnumi*** [verb: στρώννυμι <4766>] ▶ **To be supplied with the necessary furniture** > The disciples were to find a large room furnished where they were to make preparations for the Passover (Mark 14:15; Luke 22:12). ¶

– 2 Matt. 22:10 → FILL (verb) <4130> 3 Matt. 26:53 → to put at the disposal → DISPOSAL <3936> 4 Acts 17:31 → GIVE <3930> 5 Acts 28:10 → SUPPLY (verb) <2007> 6 2 Pet. 1:11 → to richly furnish → SUPPLY (verb) <2023>.

FURNISHED (BE THOROUGHLY) – 2 Tim. 3:17 → to be fully accomplished → ACCOMPLISH <1822>.

FURNITURE – Acts 27:19 → TACKLING <4631>.

FURTHER (adv.) – 1 ***peraiterō*** [adv.: περαιτέρω <4007a>]; **from *pera*: beyond ▶ More distant than; also transl.: beyond** > Ref.: Acts 19:39. ¶

– 2 Luke 24:28 → FARTHER <4208> 3 Acts 4:17 → MORE <4119> 4 Acts 23:15 → more accurately → ACCURATELY <197> 5 Acts 27:28 → FARTHER <1339> 6 1 Cor. 4:2; Phil. 3:1 → for the rest → REST (noun)[2] <3063>.

FURTHER (verb) – Titus 1:1 → to further the faith → lit.: according to (*kata*) *the* faith.

FURTHERANCE – ***prokopē*** [fem. noun: προκοπή <4297>]; **from *prokoptō*: to progress, which is from *pro*: forward, and *koptō*: to strike, to impel ▶ Progress, advancement; also transl.: greater progress** > Paul wanted the Philippians to know that his circumstances had turned out for the furtherance of {to advance} the gospel (Phil. 1:12). He knew that he would remain and abide with them all for their furtherance and joy in faith (Phil. 1:25). Other ref.: 1 Tim. 4:15; see PROGRESS <4297>. ¶

FURY – 1 ***thumos*** [masc. noun: θυμός <2372>]; **from *thuō*: to move impetuously ▶ Primary meaning: perfume, smoke, whence: strong anger, passion** > The devil will be precipitated to the earth and shall be in a great fury {rage, wrath} (Rev. 12:12). Babylon has made all the nations drink of the wine of the fury {passion, wrath} of her sexual immorality (Rev. 14:8; 18:3). Anyone who receives a mark on his forehead or on his hand will drink of the wine of the fury {wrath} of God (Rev. 14:10). God will give Babylon the cup of the wine of the fury {fierceness} of His wrath (Rev. 16:19). The Lord will tread the wine press of the fury {fierceness} of the wrath of God the

Almighty (Rev. 19:15). All other refs.: INDIGNATION <2372>, WRATH <2372>.
– 2 Luke 6:11 → MADNESS <454> 3 Acts 26:11 → in raging fury → to be exceedingly furious → FURIOUS <1693> 4 Rom. 2:8 → WRATH <3709> 5 Heb. 10:27 → HEAT <2205> 6 Heb. 11:34 → STRENGTH <1411>.

FUTILE – 1 Acts 4:25 → VAIN <2756> 2 Rom. 1:21 → to become futile → to become vain → VAIN <3154> 3 1 Cor. 3:20; 1 Pet. 1:18 → VAIN <3152>.

FUTILITY – Rom. 8:20; Eph. 4:17 → VANITY <3153>.

FUTURE – 1 Matt. 26:64 → in the future → HEREAFTER <534> 2 1 Cor. 3:23 → the future → lit.: things coming (*mellō*) 3 1 Tim. 6:19 → time to come → TIME <3195> 4 2 Tim. 4:8 → in the future → FINALLY <3063>.

 G 

GABBATHA – ***Gabbatha*** [fem. name: Γαββαθᾶ <1042>]**: elevated place, in Aram. ▶ Place where there was a tribunal (or: platform) and judgments were delivered** > Pilate sat at Gabbatha; he presented Jesus to the Jews and delivered Him up to them; in Greek, the term is transl. by "Pavement" (John 19:13); see PAVEMENT <3038>. ¶

GABRIEL – ***Gabriēl*** [masc. name: Γαβριήλ <1043>]**: man of God, in Heb. ▶ Angel of God** > Gabriel was sent to Zechariah to announce to him that his wife would conceive a son (Luke 1:19). He was also sent to Mary to announce to her the conception of Jesus, the Son of God (Luke 1:26; see v. 31). In the O.T., he was sent to Daniel to explain a vision (see Dan. 8:16; 9:21. ¶

GAD – ***Gad*** [masc. name: Γάδ <1045>]**: good fortune, in Heb.; see Gen. 30:11, 12 ▶ One of the twelve sons of Jacob and the tribe which is descended from him** > Twelve thousand out of the tribe of Gad will be sealed (Rev. 7:5). ¶

GADARENE – ***Gadarēnos*** [masc. name: Γαδαρηνός <1046>] ▶ See GERASENE <1086>.

GAILY – Luke 16:19 → to live gaily → to be merry → MERRY <2165>.

GAIN (noun) – 1 ***ergasia*** [fem. noun: ἐργασία <2039>]**; from *ergazomai*: to work, which is from: *ergon*: work ▶ Result of working or other activity, whence money, profit** > A servant girl, having a spirit of divination, brought much gain to her masters by prophesying (Acts 16:16); after Paul had commanded the spirit to come out of her, her masters saw that the hope of their gains was gone (v. 19). The fabrication of temples of Diana brought no small gain {profit, business} to the craftsmen of Ephesus (Acts 19:24). All other refs.: BUSINESS <2039>, EFFORT <2039>, WORKING (noun) <2039>.

2 ***kerdos*** [neut. noun: κέρδος <2771>] **▶ Advantage, benefit** > Paul says that for him, to live is Christ and to die is gain (Phil. 1:21). He had counted as loss the things that were a gain to him, on account of Christ (Phil. 3:7). Some were teaching things which ought not to be taught for the sake of dishonest gain {lucre} (Titus 1:11). ¶

3 **for base, dishonest, sordid gain: *aischrokerdōs*** [adv.: αἰσχροκερδῶς <147>]**; from *aischrokerdēs*: greedy for shameful profit, which is from *aischros*: dirty, shameful, and *kerdos*: see 2 ▶ Basely, with greed** > The elders are to shepherd the flock of God, not for dishonest gain {filthy lucre}, but with eagerness (1 Pet. 5:2). ¶

4 **gain, means of gain, means to financial gain: *porismos*** [masc. noun: πορισμός <4200>]**; from *porizō*: to acquire, to procure, which is from *poros*: means ▶ Source of profit, that which contributes to prosperity** > Men who are corrupted in mind and destitute of the truth think that godliness is a means of gain (1 Tim. 6:5). Godliness with contentment is a great gain (1 Tim. 6:6). ¶

– 5 2 Cor. 7:2; 12:17, 18 → to make a gain → CHEAT <4122> 6 1 Tim. 3:8; Titus 1:7 → seeking gain by base mean, fond of sordid gain, pursuing dishonest gain → greedy for money → GREEDY <146> 7 Jas. 4:13 → to make gain → GAIN (verb) <2770> 8 2 Pet. 2:15 → WAGES <3408> 9 Jude 11 → REWARD (noun) <3408>.

GAIN (verb) – 1 **to gain, to gain by trading: *diapragmateuomai*** [verb: διαπραγματεύομαι <1281>]**; from *dia*: through (intens.), and *pragmateuomai*: to do business, which is from *pragma*: matter, business ▶ To make a profit by doing business, to obtain return from investments** > In a parable, a nobleman wanted to know how much each of his servants had gained by trading {what business they had done} (Luke 19:15). ¶

2 ***kerdainō*** [verb: κερδαίνω <2770>]**; from *kerdos*: advantage, profit ▶ a. To make a profit, to acquire; also transl.: to get gain, to make gain, to make a profit, to win** > Jesus asks what will it profit a man if he should gain the whole world and forfeit his soul (Matt. 16:26; Mark 8:36) or if he loses or forfeits himself (Luke 9:25). In the parable of the talents, he who had received two gained two more besides them (Matt.

25:17, 22: *epikerdainō* in some mss.); he who had received five gained five more besides them (v. 20: *epikerdainō* in some mss.). James addresses those who say they will engage in business and make gain {get gain, make a profit, make money} for a year without knowing what will happen the next day (Jas. 4:13). **b. To bring closer to oneself, to obtain a favorable disposition >** A believer in the Lord may gain his brother who had sinned against him (Matt. 18:15). Husbands who are disobedient to the word may be won by the behavior of their wives (1 Pet. 3:1). **c. To obtain adherence to what one believes (e.g., believing in the gospel of salvation) >** Paul had made himself servant to all to win as many people as possible (1 Cor. 9:19). He had become as a Jew to win the Jews who were under the law (1 Cor. 9:20a, b), as though he were without law in order to win those who were without law (v. 21) and as weak that he might win the weak (v. 22). **d. To appropriate for oneself >** Paul had suffered the loss of all things that he might gain Christ (Phil. 3:8). Other refs.: Matt. 25:16; Acts 27:21. MAKE <2770>, INCUR <2770>. ¶

[3] ***krateō*** [verb: κρατέω <2902>]; **from *kratos*: strength ▶ To obtain, to realize >** This verb is used in Acts 27:13: to gain one's object. All other refs.: FAST (HOLD) <2902>, HOLD (verb) <2902>, KEEP (verb) <2902>, SEIZE <2902>, TAKE <2902>.

– [4] Matt. 15:5; Mark 7:11; 1 Cor. 13:3 → PROFIT (verb) <5623> [5] Matt. 27:24; John 12:19 → PREVAIL <5623> [6] Luke 18:12; 21:19 → POSSESS <2932> [7] Luke 19:16 → PRODUCE <4333> [8] Luke 19:18 → EARN <4160> [9] Acts 12:20 → to win over → WIN <3982> [10] Rom. 4:1 → FIND <2147> [11] 1 Cor. 15:32 → lit.: to be the profit → PROFIT (noun) <3786> [12] 2 Cor. 12:1 → to be gained → of profit → PROFIT (noun) <4851> [13] 2 Thes. 2:14 → that they may gain → lit.: for the obtaining → OBTAINING <4047> [14] 1 Tim. 3:13 → PURCHASE (verb) <4046> [15] Heb. 11:33 → OBTAIN <2013> [16] Heb. 11:35 → OBTAIN <5177> [17] Rev. 18:15 → to gain one's wealth → to become rich → RICH <4147>.

GAINSAY – [1] Luke 21:15 → REPLY (verb) <471> [2] Titus 2:9 → ANSWER (verb) <483>.

GAINSAYER – Titus 1:9 → to speak against → SPEAK <483>.

GAINSAYING – [1] Acts 10:29 → without gainsaying → without objection → OBJECTION <369> [2] Rom. 10:21 → to speak against → SPEAK <483> [3] Titus 2:9 → to be gainsaying → to answer back → ANSWER (verb) <483> [4] Heb. 7:7; Jude 11 → CONTRADICTION <485>.

GAIUS – ***Gaios*** [masc. name: Γάϊος <1050>] ▶ **a. Macedonian Christian man >** Gaius was a travel companion of Paul (Acts 19:29). **b. Christian man of Derbe >** This Gaius accompanied Paul to Asia (Acts 20:4). **c. Christian man of Corinth >** This Gaius was hospitable; Paul dictated his letter to the Romans while staying in his house (Rom. 16:23). Paul had baptized him (1 Cor. 1:14). **d. Christian man well known of John >** The apostle John addresses his third letter to this other Gaius (3 John 1). ¶

GALATIA – [1] ***Galatia*** [fem. name: Γαλατία <1053>] ▶ **Central province of Asia Minor >** Paul speaks of the churches of Galatia without giving their exact location (1 Cor. 16:1; Gal. 1:2). At the end of his life, Paul would say that Crescens had departed to Galatia (2 Tim. 4:10); other mss.: *Gallia* (Gaul, an ancient region of Western Europe). Peter addresses his first letter to the Christians of Galatia among other Christians (1 Pet. 1:1). ¶

[2] **of Galatia: *Galatikos*** [adj.: Γαλατικός <1054>] ▶ **Which concerns the province of Galatia in Asia Minor; also transl.: Galatian >** Paul, during his second missionary journey, accompanied by Timothy, passed through the land of Galatia, but without preaching the gospel there (Acts 16:6). He returned there during his third jour-

ney, strengthening all the disciples (Acts 18:23). ¶

GALATIAN – [1] ***Galatēs*** [masc. name: Γαλάτης <1052>] ▶ **Inhabitant of Galatia, a province of central Asia Minor** > Paul had written a letter to the Galatians; he called them foolish because they were abandoning the gospel of grace and returning to a religion based on works (Gal. 3:1). ¶
– [2] Acts 18:23 → of Galatia → GALATIA <1054>.

GALE – [1] Mark 4:37; Luke 8:23 → STORM <2978> [2] Rev. 6:13 → lit.: great wind → GREAT <3173>, WIND (noun) <417>.

GALILEAN – ***Galilaios*** [adj.: Γαλιλαῖος <1057>] ▶ **Inhabitant of Galilee, most northern province of Palestine** > Peter denied having been with Jesus the Galilean (Matt. 26:69; Mark 14:70: see v. 71; Luke 22:59: see v. 60). Pilate mixed the blood of certain Galileans with their sacrifices (Luke 13:1, 2). Pilate sent Jesus back to Herod, having learned that He was a Galilean (Luke 23:6; see v. 7). Having seen the things that Jesus had done at Jerusalem, the Galileans received Him (John 4:45). The apostles, "men of Galilee" (lit.: "Galilean" men), were present at the ascension of Jesus to heaven (Acts 1:11). They spoke in other tongues at Pentecost (Acts 2:7). See also Judas the Galilean under the name JUDAS d. <2455>. ¶

GALILEE – ***Galilaia*** [fem. name: Γαλιλαία <1056>]**: circle, circuit** ▶ **Most northern province of Palestine** > Jesus spent His childhood in Nazareth of Galilee (Matt. 2:22) and served the greater part of His ministry in Galilee (e.g., Matt. 4:23). Galilee was inhabited primarily by people of the nations (Matt. 4:15). There were later churches in Galilee (Acts 9:31), where the good news had begun to be announced (Acts 10:37). *

GALL – ***cholē*** [fem. noun: χολή <5521>]**; comp. *chloē*: green, *cheō*: to pour** ▶ **Bile of animals or birds; this liquid is secreted by the liver to facilitate absorption and digestion** > Gall was mingled with the wine offered to Jesus to drink before His crucifixion (Matt. 27:34), but He did not want to drink it after tasting it. Mark says that He was offered wine mixed with myrrh, but He did not take it (see Mark 15:23). These mixtures may have dulled the senses and alleviated the pain of the crucified victim. In Acts 8:23, the gall of bitterness evokes the wickedness of Simon the magician, and his bitterness at not being able to give the Holy Spirit by the imposition of hands. ¶

GALLIO – ***Galliōn*** [masc. name: Γαλλίων <1058>] ▶ **Proconsul (i.e., governor or military commander) of Achaia** > The Jews brought Paul before the tribunal of Gallio (Acts 18:12, 14). He was not concerned that they were beating Sosthenes, the ruler of the synagogue, in front of him (Acts 18:17). ¶

GALLON – [1] Luke 16:6 → nine hundred gallons → lit.: one hundred measures → MEASURE (noun) <943> [2] John 2:6 → MEASURE (noun) <3355>.

GAMALIEL – ***Gamaliēl*** [masc. name: Γαμαλιήλ <1059>]**: reward of God, in Heb.** ▶ **Pharisee, doctor of the law and a man held in honor by all the Jewish people** > Gamaliel advised to let the apostles alone, for if their work was of God, the Jews would not be able to destroy it (Acts 5:34; see v. 39). Paul was instructed at the feet of this doctor of the Jewish law (Acts 22:3). ¶

GAME – Luke 23:36 → to make game → MOCK <1702>.

GANGRENE – ***gangraina*** [fem. noun: γάγγραινα <1044>]**; from *graō* or *grainō*: to consume** ▶ **Destruction of body tissues resulting from cessation of blood circulation; in the spiritual dimension, errors which spread and cause damage** > The talk of those who engage in profane and vain babblings will spread as gangrene {cancer, canker} (lit.: will have pasture like gangrene) (2 Tim. 2:17); see PASTURE <3542>. ¶

GARBAGE – [1] 1 Cor. 4:13 → REFUSE (noun) <4067> [2] Phil. 3:8 → FILTH <4657>.

GARDEN – ***kēpos*** [masc. noun: κῆπος <2779>] ▶ **Ground where one can cultivate various things** > A man threw a grain of mustard seed into his garden (Luke 13:19). Jesus entered into a garden beyond the brook of Kidron (John 18:1). A servant had seen Peter in the garden with Jesus (John 18:26). There was a garden in the place where Jesus was crucified, and in the garden a new tomb (John 19:41a, b). ¶

GARDENER – [1] ***kēpouros*** [masc. noun: κηπουρός <2780>]; **from *kēpos*: garden, and *ouros*: guardian** ▶ **He who takes care of a garden** > Mary, seeing Jesus after His resurrection, thought that He was the gardener (John 20:15). ¶
– [2] John 15:1 → VINEDRESSER <1092>.

GARLAND – [1] ***stemma*** [neut. noun: στέμμα <4725>]; **from *stephō*: to encircle the head, to crown** ▶ **Crown or something else worn on the head** > The priest of Zeus brought oxen and garlands {wreaths} in honor of Paul and Barnabas (Acts 14:13). ¶
– [2] Rev. 12:1 → CROWN (noun) <4735>.

GARMENT – [1] ***enduma*** [neut. noun: ἔνδυμα <1742>]; **from *enduō*: to clothe, to dress, which is from *en*: in, and *duō*: to put on** ▶ **Outer clothes** > In a parable, the king saw a man who was not clothed with a wedding garment {wedding clothes} (Matt. 22:11, 12). All other refs.: CLOTHES <1742>, CLOTHING <1742>.
[2] ***himation*** [neut. noun: ἱμάτιον <2440>]; **comp. *hennumi*: to cover, to dress** ▶ **Clothing, clothes** > No one puts a patch of new cloth on an old garment (Matt. 9:16a; Mark 2:21), for the patch pulls away part of the garment (Matt. 9:16b). Those who were ill begged Jesus that they might only touch the hem of His garment (Matt. 14:36). No one puts a piece of a new garment on an old garment (Luke 5:36a, b). The heavens and the earth will grow old like a garment (Heb. 1:11). All other refs.: CLOAK <2440>, CLOTHES <2440>.
[3] **to clothe with a garment: *enduō*** [verb: ἐνδύω <1746>]; **from *en*: in, and *duō*: to put on** ▶ **To dress, to clothe** > John saw someone like the Son of Man, clothed with a garment {clothed in a robe, dressed in a robe} reaching to the feet (Rev. 1:13). All other refs.: CLOTHE <1746>.
– [4] Mark 14:51, 52 → linen garment → LINEN <4616> [5] Mark 14:63; John 19:23 → TUNIC <5509> [6] Luke 24:4 → CLOTHES <2067> [7] John 19:24; 1 Tim. 2:9 → CLOTHING <2441> [8] John 21:7 → outer garment → OVERCOAT <1903> [9] Acts 10:30 → CLOTHES <2066> [10] Jude 23 → CLOTHES <5509>.

GARNER – Matt. 3:12; Luke 3:17 → BARN <596>.

GARNISH – Matt. 12:44; 23:29; Luke 11:25; Rev. 21:19 → ADORN <2885>.

GARRISON – Matt. 27:27; Mark 15:16; Acts 21:31 → COHORT <4686>.

GASH – Mark 5:5 → CUT <2629>.

GATE – [1] ***pulē*** [fem. noun: πύλη <4439>] ▶ **Door of a city, of a rampart** > Jesus said to enter by the narrow gate, for wide is the gate that leads to destruction (Matt. 7:13a, b, 14). He even says to strive in earnestness to enter in through the narrow gate {door} (Luke 13:24). Hades' gates will not prevail against the church (Matt. 16:18). Jesus suffered without the gate {city gate} (Heb. 13:12). Other refs.: Luke 7:12; Acts 3:10; 9:24; 12:10; 16:13 in some mss. ¶
[2] ***pulōn*** [masc. noun: πυλών <4440>]; **from *pulē*: see [1]** ▶ **Porch; door of a walled city** > Lazarus was laid at the gate {gateway} of the rich man (Luke 16:20). John saw the new Jerusalem with twelve gates (Rev. 21:12a, b, 13a–d, 15, 21a, b, 25); blessed are those who go in by the gates into the city (22:14). Other refs.: Acts 10:17; 14:13. All other refs.: GATEWAY <4440>.

– [3] Matt. 24:33; Mark 13:29; John 10:1, 2, 7; Acts 3:2; 5:19; 21:30 → DOOR <2374> [4] John 5:2 → Sheep Gate → SHEEP <4262>.

GATEKEEPER – John 10:3 → DOORKEEPER <2377>.

GATEWAY – [1] ***pulōn*** [masc. noun: πυλών <4440>]**; from *pulē*: door, gate ▶ Door or gate at the entrance of a house** > A servant girl saw Peter in the gateway {entrance, porch} of the palace of the high priest (Matt. 26:71). On another occasion, Peter knocked at the door of the entrance {entry, gate} of the house of Mary, and Rhoda came to listen, but she did not open the gate; she ran to report that Peter was standing before the gate {door} (Acts 12:13, 14a, b). All other refs.: GATE <4440>.
– [2] Mark 14:68 → PORCH <4259>.

GATHER – [1] **to gather, to gather together, etc.: *sunagō*** [verb: συνάγω <4863>]**; from *sun*: together, and *agō*: to lead ▶ To bring together, to come together; also transl.: to assemble, to assemble together (people or things), to meet, to meet together, to meet with** > In a parable, the lord gathered from where he had not scattered (Matt. 25:24, 26). In another one, the younger son, having gathered all together, went away into a country a long way off (Luke 15:13). The verb is also used in regard to crowds (Matt. 13:2; Mark 4:1; 5:21), fish (lit.: of every kind) (Matt. 13:47 {to catch}), the apostles (Mark 6:30), and the children of God (John 11:52). The rulers were gathered together against the Lord and against His Christ (Acts 4:26). Barnabas and Saul were gathered together for one year in the church of Antioch (Acts 11:26). Later, both of them gathered together {brought together} this church to relate all that God had done with them (Acts 14:27). The term applies to Christians gathered together in the name of the Lord (Matt. 18:20; Acts 20:7). It designates meetings of Jews in various circumstances (e.g., Matt. 2:4 {to call together}; 22:41; 26:57; 27:17; 28:12). All nations will be gathered before the Son of Man when He will come in His glory (Matt. 25:32). After having fed the crowd, Jesus told the disciples to gather up the fragments that remained (John 6:12); therefore they gathered them up (v. 13). Men gathered {picked up} branches and burned them (John 15:6). The verb is used concerning the gathering of the harvest, e.g., of wheat (Matt. 13:30; Luke 3:17). Other refs.: Matt. 3:12; 6:26 {to store away}; 12:30; 22:10, 34 {to get together}; 24:28; 26:3; 27:27, 62 {to go to}; Mark 2:2; 7:1; Luke 11:23; 12:17 and 18 {to bestow, to store, to lay up}; 17:37; 22:66; John 4:36 {to harvest}; 11:47 {to convene, to call a meeting}; 18:2 {to resort, in company}; 20:19 in some mss.; Acts 4:6 (or v. 5), 27, 31; 13:44; 15:6, 30; 20:8; 1 Cor. 5:4; Rev. 13:10 in some mss.; 16:14, 16; 19:17, 19; 20:8. All other refs.: INVITE <4863>, LEAD (verb) <4863>.
[2] **to gather, to gather together: *episunagō*** [verb: ἐπισυνάγω <1996>]**; from *epi*: upon, moreover, and *sunagō*: see [1] ▶ To assemble, to bring together** > Jesus said that often He would have gathered the children of Jerusalem (Matt. 23:37a, b; Luke 13:34). The angels will gather together God's elect (Matt. 24:31; Mark 13:27). An entire city was gathered together at the door on account of Jesus (Mark 1:33). Jesus spoke to a crowd of many thousands who had gathered (Luke 12:1); *sumperiechō* in some mss.: to stand around together. The eagles will gather together where the body is (Luke 17:37); some mss. have *sunagō*. ¶
[3] **to gather together: *epathroizō*** [verb: ἐπαθροίζω <1865>]**; from *epi*: upon, and *athroizō*: to assemble a great number ▶ To come together in a great number** > The crowds were gathering thick together {were thickly gathered, were thronging together, were increasing} to hear Jesus (Luke 11:29). ¶
[4] **to gather together: *sunathroizō*** [verb: συναθροίζω <4867>]**; from *sun*: together, and *athroizō*: to assemble a great number ▶ To assemble together, to meet together** > The two disciples returned to Jerusalem from Emmaus and found the eleven apostles gathered together (Luke 24:33; some mss.: *athroizō*). Peter came

to the house of Mary, the mother of John (Mark) where many were gathered together and praying (Acts 12:12). Demetrius gathered together {called together, brought together} other silversmiths with workmen of like occupation (Acts 19:25). ¶

[5] **to gather a mob, a company, a crowd: *ochlopoieō*** [verb: ὀχλοποιέω <3792>]; **from *ochlos*: crowd, and *poieō*: to make, to do ▶ To assemble, to bring together a crowd** > The Jews gathered a crowd {formed a mob} in Thessalonica against Paul and his companions (Acts 17:5). ¶

[6] **to gather, to gather together: *suneimi*** [verb: σύνειμι <4896>]; **from *sun*: together, and *eimi*: to go ▶ To come together, to assemble** > Many people were gathering {were coming together} and were coming to Jesus out of every city (Luke 8:4). ¶

[7] ***sullegō*** [verb: συλλέγω <4816>]; **from *sun*: together, and *legō*: to gather ▶ To pick, to reap, to collect** > Jesus spoke about gathering grapes and figs (Matt. 7:16), wheat and tares (13:28–30), darnel (13:40), things that offend (13:41 {to weed out}), the good fish (13:48 {to collect}), and figs (Luke 6:44). ¶

[8] ***trugaō*** [verb: τρυγάω <5166>]; **from *trugē*: harvest, vintage ▶ To harvest the grapes of the vine** > Jesus says that men do not gather {vintage, pick} grapes from a bramble bush (Luke 6:44b). An angel put his sickle to the earth, gathered the clusters from the vine of the earth, and threw the clusters of grapes into the great winepress of the wrath of God (Rev. 14:18, 19). ¶

[9] **to gather together, to gather together in one: *anakephalaioō*** [verb: ἀνακεφαλαιόω <346>]; **from *ana*: again (intens.), and *kephalaioō*: to sum up, which is from *kephalē*: head; lit.: to recapitulate ▶ To regroup under, to sum up** > God purposed in Himself to gather together in one {to bring together, to head up} all things in the Christ (Eph. 1:10). Other ref.: Rom. 13:9; see SUM UP <346>. ¶

[10] ***sumporeuomai*** [verb: συμπορεύομαι <4848>]; **from *sun*: with, together, and *poreuomai*: to come ▶ To congregate, to assemble** > Crowds gathered around {came to, came together to, resorted unto} Jesus (Mark 10:1). All other refs.: GO <4848>.

[11] ***sustrephō*** [verb: συστρέφω <4962>]; **from *sun*: with, together, and *strephō*: to turn ▶ To amass, to collect** > Paul had gathered a quantity of sticks (Acts 28:3). Other ref.: Matt. 17:22; see STAY (verb) <4962>. ¶

– [12] Matt. 16:9, 10 → to pick up → PICK <2983> [13] Mark 9:25 → to gather rapidly → to run together → RUN <1998> [14] Mark 14:53; Luke 5:15; Acts 28:17; 1 Cor. 11:33 → COME <4905> [15] Luke 15:1 → to gather around → to draw near → DRAW <1448> [16] Luke 23:48 → to come together → COME <4836> [17] John 10:24; Acts 14:20 → to gather around → SURROUND <2944> [18] Acts 1:4 → to be gathered together → to be assembled together → ASSEMBLE <4871> [19] Acts 1:6 → to gather around → to assemble together → ASSEMBLE <4905> [20] Acts 16:10 → to assuredly gather → CONCLUDE <4822> [21] 2 Tim. 4:3 → to gather around → HEAP <2002>.

GATHERED – John 18:38; 19:4 → "gathered there" added in Engl.

GATHERING – [1] Acts 1:15 → CROWD (noun) <3793> [2] Acts 6:5 → MULTITUDE <4128> [3] Acts 19:40 → disorderly gathering → CONCOURSE <4963> [4] Acts 24:12 → to make a tumultuous gathering → to raise up → RAISE <1999> <4160> [5] 2 Thes. 2:1 → gathering together → ASSEMBLING <1997>.

GAY – Jas. 2:3 → BRIGHT <2986>.

GAZA – ***Gaza*** [fem. name: Γάζα <1048>]: **strong, in Heb. ▶ City near the Mediterranean Sea and southwest of Jerusalem** > Philip was sent by the Holy Spirit to an Ethiopian on the road leading from Jerusalem to Gaza, and he presented the gospel to him (Acts 8:26). ¶

GAZE (noun) – [1] Acts 3:4 → direct his gaze → fastened his eyes → FASTEN <816>

2 Acts 6:15 → to fix one's gaze → to look steadfastly → LOOK (verb) <816>.

GAZE (verb) – 1 Acts 1:10; 6:15; 7:55; 2 Cor. 3:13 → to gaze, to gaze intently → to look intently, to look steadfastly → LOOK (verb) <816> 2 Acts 1:11 in some mss. → LOOK (verb) <991> 3 Acts 3:12; 10:4 → to fix the eyes → FIX <816> 4 2 Cor. 3:7, 13 → to gaze at → to behold steadfastly → BEHOLD (verb) <816>.

GAZINGSTOCK – 1 Cor. 4:9 → to make a gazingstock → to make a public spectacle → SPECTACLE <2302>.

GEAR – Acts 27:17 → SAIL (noun) <4632>.

GEHENNA – See HELL <1067>.

GENDER – 1 Gal. 4:24 → BEAR (verb) <1080> 2 2 Tim. 2:23 → GENERATE <1080>.

GENEALOGY – 1 ***genealogia*** [fem. noun: γενεαλογία <1076>]; **from *genealogeō*: see 2 ► Ordered sequence of ancestors of a person, of a family; especially genealogical tales** > Paul urged Timothy to command some men not to devote themselves to interminable genealogies (1 Tim. 1:4) and Titus to avoid genealogies (Titus 3:9). ¶
2 **to have genealogy: *genealogeō*** [verb: γενεαλογέω <1075>]; **from *genea*: generation, descent, and *logos*: calculation, reasoning ► To recognize one's descent from certain people, to retrace one's genealogy** > Melchizedek had no genealogy {His genealogy was not derived, was not traced; His descent was not counted, not traced} from the sons of Levi (Heb. 7:6). ¶
3 ***genesis*** [fem. noun: γένεσις <1078>]; **from *ginomai*: to become ► Ancestry, lineage of a person** > Matthew gives the genealogy {generation} of Jesus Christ, Son of David, Son of Abraham (Matt. 1:1; Luke 1:14 in some mss.). Other refs.: Jas. 1:23; 3:6; see NATURE <1078>. ¶
4 **without genealogy: *agenealogētos*** [adj.: ἀγενεαλόγητος <35>]; **from *a*: neg., and *genealogeō*: see 2 ► Without recorded ancestry; also transl.: without descent** > This term in Heb. 7:3 applies to Melchizedek; it leads us to consider him as a type of the yet more remarkable Lord Jesus. ¶

GENERAL – Rev. 6:15; 19:18 → CAPTAIN <5506>.

GENERATE – ***gennaō*** [verb: γεννάω <1080>]; **from *genna*: birth, race ► To give birth; also transl.: to beget, to breed, to gender, to produce** > Foolish and senseless questionings generate contentions (2 Tim. 2:23). All other refs.: see entries in Lexicon at <1080>.

GENERATION – 1 ***genea*** [fem. noun: γενεά <1074>]; **from *ginomai*: to become ► a. Descendants of a man, counted by lifespan** > All the generations, from Abraham to David are 14 generations; from David until the captivity in Babylon, 14; from the captivity in Babylon to the Christ, 14 (Matt. 1:17a–d). **b. Group of people living in a given period of time: 30 to 35 years on the average** > See e.g., Acts 14:16; 15:21. A generation may be marked by specific moral characteristics: a wicked generation (Matt. 12:45; Luke 11:29), perverse (Acts 2:40), unbelieving and perverted (Matt. 17:17; Mark 9:19; Luke 9:41), wicked and adulterous (Matt. 12:39; 16:4), adulterous and sinful (Mark 8:38), and crooked and perverted (Phil. 2:15). Other refs.: Matt. 11:16; 12:41, 42; 23:36; 24:34; Mark 8:12a, b; 13:30; Luke 1:48, 50a, b; 7:31; 11:30–32, 50, 51; 16:8; 17:25; 21:32; Acts 8:33; 13:36; Eph. 3:5, 21; Col. 1:26; Heb. 3:10. ¶
– 2 Matt. 1:1 → GENEALOGY <1078> 3 Matt. 3:7; 12:34; 23:33; Luke 3:7 → BROOD <1081> 4 Acts 15:21 → throughout many generations → OLD <744> 5 1 Pet. 2:9 → RACE[1] <1085>.

GENEROSITY – 1 Matt. 20:15 → one's generosity → lit.: to be good → GOOD (adj.) <18> 2 Rom. 12:8 → SIMPLICITY <572> 3 2 Cor. 8:2; 9:11, 13 → LIBERALITY <572>.

GENEROUS – 1 *eumetadotos* [adj.: εὐμετάδοτος <2130>]; **from *eu*: well, and *metadidomi*: to impart, which is from *meta*: with, and *didōmi*: to give ▶ Quality of one who is ready to share or to give, who is liberal in doing so** > Those who are rich are to be generous {liberal in distributing, ready to distribute, ready to give} (1 Tim. 6:18). ¶
– 2 Matt. 20:15 → GOOD (adj.) <18> 3 2 Cor. 8:20 → generous gift → ABUNDANCE <100> 4 2 Cor. 9:5 → generous gift → GIFT <2129>.

GENEROUS (BE) – 1 Luke 11:41 → to be generous to the poor → lit.: to give alms → GIVE <1325>, ALMS <1654> 2 Acts 2:46 → generous hearts → simplicity of heart → SIMPLICITY <858> 3 Acts 28:7 → generous hospitality → lit.: hospitality → LODGE <3579>.

GENEROUSLY – 1 Rom. 12:8 → lit.: with generosity → SIMPLICITY <572> 2 2 Cor. 9:6a, b → BOUNTIFULLY <2129> 3 Titus 3:6 → RICHLY <4146> 4 Jas. 1:5 → LIBERALLY <574>.

GENNESARET – *Gennēsaret* [fem. name: Γεννησαρέτ <1082>] **▶ Very fertile plain near the Sea of Galilee (or Lake of Gennesaret)** > Jesus came to this land and healed many who were sick (Matt. 14:34; Mark 6:53). He taught the crowds from a boat on the Lake of Gennesaret (Luke 5:1; see vv. 2, 3). ¶

GENTILE, GENTILES – 1 See NATION.
– 2 Acts 15:10 → Gentiles → lit.: disciples 3 1 Cor. 12:13; Gal. 3:28; Col. 3:11 → GREEK <1672>.

GENTLE – 1 *epieikēs* [adj.: ἐπιεικής <1933>]; **from *epi*: upon (intens.), and *eikos*: equitable, fair ▶ Patient, reasonable, forbearing; also transl.: considerate, mild** > If a man desires the position of an overseer, he must be gentle (1 Tim. 3:3). Christians should be gentle {mild} (Titus 3:2). The wisdom from above is gentle (Jas. 3:17). Servants must be subject not only to good and gentle masters, but also to the ill-tempered (1 Pet. 2:18). Other ref.: Phil. 4:5; see GENTLENESS <1933>. ¶
2 *ēpios* [adj.: ἤπιος <2261>] **▶ Affable, mild** > Paul had been gentle in the midst of the Thessalonians (1 Thes. 2:7). A servant of the Lord must be gentle {kind} to everyone (2 Tim. 2:24). ¶
3 *praos* [adj.: πρᾶος <4235>] **▶ Mild, kind, forgiving** > Jesus says He is gentle {meek} and humble in heart (Matt. 11:29). ¶
4 *praus* [adj.: πραΰς <4239>] **▶ Humble of heart and mind** > The adorning of Christian wives is the ornament of a gentle {meek} and quiet spirit, which is of great price in the eyes of God (1 Pet. 3:4). For Matt. 11:29, some mss. have *praos*: see 3. Other refs.: Matt. 5:5; 21:5; see MEEK <4239>. ¶
– 5 1 Cor. 4:21; Eph. 4:2 → GENTLENESS <4236>.

GENTLENESS – 1 *epieikeia* [fem. noun: ἐπιείκεια <1932>]; **from *epieikēs*: see 2 ▶ Kindness, mildness** > Paul was appealing to the Corinthians by the meekness and gentleness of Christ (2 Cor. 10:1). Other ref.: Acts 24:4; see COURTESY <1932>. ¶
2 *epieikēs* [adj. used as noun: ἐπιεικής <1933>]; **from *epi*: upon (intens.), and *eikos*: equitable, fair ▶ Mildness, patience; it is the character of one who does not insist on his rights** > Christians must let their gentleness {moderation, forbearing spirit} be known to all men (Phil. 4:5). All other refs.: GENTLE <1933>.
3 *praotēs* [fem. noun: πραότης <4236>]; **from *praos*: meek, gentle ▶ Humble attitude of the heart and spirit, first before God and then before men; also transl.: meekness** > Paul wanted to come to the Corinthians with a spirit of gentleness {a gentle spirit} (1 Cor. 4:21). He was entreating them by the gentleness and kindness of Christ (2 Cor. 10:1). Part of the fruit of the Spirit is gentleness (Gal. 5:23). One who has been taken in some fault must be restored in a spirit of gentleness {gently} (Gal. 6:1). The Christian must walk with all gentleness (Eph. 4:2) and put on gentleness (Col. 3:12). Timothy was to

pursue gentleness (1 Tim. 6:11; some mss.: *praupathia*). A servant of the Lord must correct in gentleness {in humility, gently} those who oppose (2 Tim. 2:25). Titus was to remind Christians to show all gentleness {humility, consideration} to all men (Titus 3:2). ¶
4 ***chrēstotēs*** [fem. noun: χρηστότης <5544>]; **from *chrēstos*: useful, agreeable, which is from *chraomai*: to use ► Kindness, helpfulness, attitude of being obliging** > Part of the fruit of the Spirit is gentleness {kindness} (Gal. 5:22). Other refs.: GOODNESS <5544>, KINDNESS <5544>.
– 5 Jas. 3:13; 1 Pet. 3:15 → MEEKNESS <4240>.

GENTLY – 1 Gal. 6:1; 2 Tim. 2:25 → GENTLENESS <4236> 2 Heb. 5:2 → to deal gently → to have compassion → COMPASSION <3356>.

GENUINE – 1 Rom. 12:9; 2 Cor. 6:6; 2 Tim. 1:5 → without hypocrisy → HYPOCRISY <505> 2 1 Cor. 11:19 → approved → APPROVE <1384> 3 2 Cor. 6:8 → TRUE <227> 4 2 Cor. 8:8 → SINCERITY <1103> 5 Phil. 2:20 → with genuine feeling, genuine interest → SINCERELY <1104> 6 2 Tim. 1:5 → SINCERE <505>.

GENUINELY – Phil. 2:20 → SINCERELY <1104>.

GENUINENESS – 1 2 Cor. 8:8 → SINCERITY <1103> 2 2 Thes. 3:17 → sign of genuineness → SIGN <4592> 3 1 Pet. 1:7 → TESTING <1383>.

GERASENE – ***Gerasēnos*** [masc. name: Γερασηνός <1086>] **► Inhabitant of a region east of Lake Tiberias; also written: Gaderane (*Gadarēnos*), Gergesene (*Gergesēnos*)** > Two demon-possessed men of this region came to meet the Lord. He cast their demons into a herd of swine; the herd rushed into the sea, and the swine died (Matt. 8:28; see v. 32). In the Gospels of Mark and of Luke, mention is made of only one man possessed by an unclean spirit (Mark 5:1; see vv. 1–13; Luke 8:26; see vv. 26–33). The people of the surrounding area, terrified, begged Jesus to leave them (Luke 8:37). The liberated man published what Jesus had done for him (see Mark 5:20; Luke 8:37–39). ¶

GERGESENE – See GERASENE <1086>.

GESTURE – John 13:24 → to make a sign → SIGN <3506>.

GET – 1 **to get, to get away: *apospaō*** [verb: ἀποσπάω <645>]; **from *apo*: from, and *spaō*: to draw ► To depart with difficulty; pass.: to tear oneself from someone** > Paul and his companions got away {departed, parted, tore themselves away} from the Christians in Miletus and Ephesus (Acts 21:1). All other refs.: DRAW <645>, WITHDRAW <645>.
2 **to get into: *embainō*** [verb: ἐμβαίνω <1684>]; **from *en*: in, and *bainō*: to go ► To enter, to embark; also transl.: to enter into, to go into, to come into, to take (shipping)** > This verb is found in regard to a boat in Matt. 8:23; 9:1; 13:2; 14:22, 32; 15:39; Mark 4:1; 5:18; 6:45; 8:10; Luke 5:3; 8:22, 37; John 6:17, 22, 24. All other refs.: ENTER <1684>, STEP (verb) <1684>.
3 ***exeimi*** [verb: ἔξειμι <1826>]; **from *ek*: out, and *eimi*: to go ► To head toward, to reach** > The centurion ordered those who could swim to jump overboard and get to land (Acts 27:43). Other refs.: Acts 13:42; 17:15 and 20:7 {to depart, to leave}. All other refs.: DEPART <1826>, GO <1826>.
4 **to get in unnoticed: *pareisduō*** [verb: παρεισδύω <3921>]; **from *para*: beside, and *eisduō*: to enter in, which is from *eis*: in, and *duō*: to sink ► To infiltrate, to enter surreptitiously** > Certain ungodly men had gotten in among the Christians unnoticed (Jude 4). ¶
– 5 Matt. 8:26; 9:19; et al. → ARISE <1453> 6 Matt. 10:9 → PROVIDE <2932> 7 Matt. 16:23; Mark 8:33 → GO <5217> 8 Matt. 21:34 → RECEIVE <2983> 9 Matt. 22:34; Luke 15:13 → to get together → to gather together → GATHER

<4863> 10 Matt. 24:17, 18; Mark 13:15, 16; 15:24; Luke 17:31 → TAKE <142> 11 Matt. 25:27 → RECEIVE <2865> 12 Matt. 27:24; John 12:19 → PREVAIL <5623> 13 Matt. 27:48, 59; John 18:3; 2 Cor. 11:20; 12:16 → TAKE <2983> 14 Mark 2:4 → to get near → to come near → COME <4331> 15 Luke 6:34 → to get back → RECEIVE <618> 16 Luke 8:19 → to get at, to, near → to come at → COME <4940> 17 Luke 8:27 → to get out → to step out → STEP (verb) <1831> 18 Luke 13:31 → to get out → DEPART <1831> 19 Luke 17:8 → to get oneself ready → GIRD <4024> 20 Luke 18:12 → POSSESS <2932> 21 Luke 21:21 → to get out → DEPART <1633> 22 John 21:3 → to get into → to go up → GO <305> 23 John 21:9 → to get out → COME <576> 24 Acts 5:8 → GIVE <591> 25 Acts 10:20 → to get down → to go down → GO <2597> 26 Acts 10:26 → to make get up → RAISE <1453> 27 Acts 16:37 → to get out → to lead out → LEAD (verb) <1806> 28 Acts 23:15 → to come near → COME <1448> 29 1 Cor. 9:7 → getting some of the milk → lit.: eats of the milk → EAT <2068> 30 1 Cor. 9:24 → to get the prize → lit.: to get → OBTAIN <2638> 31 2 Tim. 3:6 → to get into → to creep into → CREEP <1744> 32 2 Tim. 4:11 → TAKE <353> 33 Heb. 6:15 → OBTAIN <2013> 34 Heb. 8:6; 11:35 → OBTAIN <5177> 35 3 John 2 → to get along well → PROSPER <2137>.

GETHSEMANE – ***Gethsēmani*** [fem. name: Γεθσημανί <1068>]**: oil press, in Aram.; also spelled: *Gethsēmanē* ► Garden located near Jerusalem, at the foot of the Mount of Olives** > Jesus went to Gethsemane with His disciples for the last time on the night during which He was betrayed by Judas (Matt. 26:36; Mark 14:32). ¶

GHOST – 1 ***phantasma*** [neut. noun: φάντασμα <5326>]**; from *phantazō*: to cause to appear, which is from *phainō*: to appear, which is from *phōs*: light ► Apparition of a dead or absent person believed to be seen** > Seeing Jesus walking on the sea, His disciples believed it was a ghost {apparition, spirit} (Matt. 14:26; Mark 6:49). ¶
2 See SPIRIT <4151>.
– 3 Mark 15:37, 39; Luke 23:46 → to give up the ghost → EXPIRE <1606> 4 Acts 5:5, 10; 12:23 → to give up the ghost → EXPIRE <1634>.

GIDEON – ***Gedeōn*** [masc. name: Γεδεών <1066>]**: a hewer, in Heb. ► Judge of Israel** > Gideon delivered and judged Israel (see Judges 6–8); he is mentioned among the O.T. people of faith (Heb. 11:32). ¶

GIFT – 1 ***doma*** [neut. noun: δόμα <1390>]**; from *didōmi*: to give ► Good thing offered voluntarily and freely** > God has given gifts to men (Eph. 4:8). Paul was not seeking a gift from the Philippians, but fruit abounding to their account (Phil. 4:17). Other refs.: Matt. 7:11; Luke 11:13. ¶
2 ***dōrea*** [fem. noun: δωρεά <1431>]**; from *didōmi*: to give ► Free present from God; also transl.: free gift** > Jesus spoke to the Samaritan woman about the gift of God (John 4:10). The Holy Spirit is presented as a gift of God (Acts 2:38; 8:20; 10:45; 11:17). Paul speaks of the gift in grace by Jesus Christ (Rom. 5:15) and the gift of righteousness (v. 17). He gives thanks to God for His unspeakable gift (2 Cor. 9:15). He had become a minister of the gospel according to the gift of the grace of God (Eph. 3:7). Grace was given to each Christian according to the measure of the gift of Christ (Eph. 4:7). Some have tasted of the heavenly gift (Heb. 6:4). ¶
3 ***dōrēma*** [neut. noun: δώρημα <1434>]**; from *dōreō*: to make a gift ► Thing given, present, offering** > Every good gift (*dosis*; see GIVING <1394>) and every perfect gift (*dōrēma*) comes down from the Father of lights (Jas. 1:17b). In Rom. 5:16a, the gift (*dōrēma*) refers to Jesus Christ; this free gift (*charisma*) brings justification (see 5:16b). ¶
4 ***dōron*** [neut. noun: δῶρον <1435>]**; from *didōmi*: to give ► Present, sacrifice; also transl.: offering** > The wise men offered gifts to Jesus (Matt. 2:11). Jesus says to

be reconciled with one's brother before presenting one's gift at the altar (Matt. 5:23, 24a, b). The leper who was healed had to offer the gift that Moses ordained (Matt. 8:4). Some evil children were saying to their parents that whatever profit they might have received from them was a gift {had been given} to God (and thus were not taking care of the needs of their parents) (Matt. 15:5; Mark 7:11). Jesus saw the rich casting their gifts into the treasury (Luke 21:1); He spoke of those who out of their abundance cast into the gifts of God (v. 4). Salvation by grace, through faith, is the gift of God (Eph. 2:8). Those who dwell on the earth will send gifts one to another after the death of the two witnesses (Rev. 11:10). Other refs.: Matt. 23:18, 19a, b; Heb. 5:1; 8:3, 4; 9:9; 11:4. ¶

5 **generous gift: *eulogia*** [fem. noun: εὐλογία <2129>]; **from *eulogeō*: to bless, to praise, which is from *eu*: well, and *logos*: word ► Blessing; monetary gift** > The generous gift {The bounty, The bountiful gift} of the Corinthians (2 Cor. 9:5), i.e., their gift to help other Christians, signifies lit. a "blessing." All other refs.: BLESSING <2129>, BOUNTIFULLY <2129>, SPEECH <2129>.

6 ***merismos*** [masc. noun: μερισμός <3311>]; **from *merizō*: to divide into parts, which is from *meris*: part ► What is being shared, distributed; the act of sharing** > The great salvation has been confirmed by the gifts {distributions} of the Holy Spirit (Heb. 2:4). Other ref.: Heb. 4:12; see DIVISION <3311>. ¶

7 ***charis*** [fem. noun: χάρις <5485>]; **from *chairō*: to rejoice; lit.: grace ► Generous present** > Paul would send those approved by the Corinthians with letters to carry their gift {liberality, bounty} to Jerusalem (1 Cor. 16:3). Other refs.: see entries in Lexicon at <5485>.

8 **gift, free gift, spiritual gift: *charisma*** [neut. noun: χάρισμα <5486>]; **from *charizomai*: to freely give, which is from *charis*: gift, grace, which is from *chairō*: to rejoice ► Free present from God; spiritual capacity** > This free gift {act of favor} is related to spiritual instruction (Rom. 1:11), the salvation of repenting sinners (Rom. 5:15, 16b; 6:23), the calling of God concerning Israel (Rom. 11:29), self-control (1 Cor. 7:7), and the answer to prayers (2 Cor. 1:11 {favor}). God grants different gifts, by the operation of the Holy Spirit, for the building of the church (Rom. 12:6, 1 Cor. 1:7; 12:4, 9, 28, 30, 31). Timothy was not to neglect the gift that was in him (1 Tim. 4:14); Paul reminds him to rekindle the gift of God in him (2 Tim. 1:6). Christians must use their gift to minister to one another (1 Pet. 4:10). ¶

9 ***pneumatikos*** [adj.: πνευματικός <4152>]; **from *pneuma*: spirit ►** 1 Cor. 12:1 → spiritual gift → lit.: spiritual (spiritual matters implied). All other refs.: see SPIRITUAL <4152>.

– 10 Luke 21:5 → gift, votive gift → consecrated offering → OFFERING <334> 11 Rom. 3:24 → as a gift → FREELY <1432> 12 Rom. 11:35 → to give a gift → to give first → GIVE <4272> 13 2 Cor. 8:20 → lavish gift, generous gift, liberal gift → ABUNDANCE <100> 14 Jas. 1:17 → GIVING <1394>.

GIN – Rom. 11:9 → TRAP (noun) <2339>.

GIRD – 1 ***zōnnumi*** [verb: ζώννυμι <2224>]; **has given *zōnē*: belt ► To encircle or fasten with a belt; to bind** > When he was younger, Peter girded {dressed} himself; when he would be old, another would gird {dress} him (John 21:18a, b). Other ref.: Acts 12:8 in some mss.; see **4**. ¶

2 **to gird up: *anazōnnumi*** [verb: ἀναζώννυμι <328>]; **from *ana*: particle of repetition, and *zōnnumi*: see 1; lit.: to gird again ► To encircle a part of the body** > Peter exhorts the Christians to gird up the loins of {prepare for action} their mind (1 Pet. 1:13), i.e., to be morally fitted for serving the Lord. ¶

3 ***diazōnnumi*** [verb: διαζώννυμι <1241>]; **from *dia*: intens., and *zōnnumi*: see 1 ► To encircle a part of the body** > Jesus girded Himself with {wrapped around Him, wrapped around His waist} a towel, washed the feet of His disciples, and wiped them with the towel (John 13:4, 5). Simon Peter

girded on him {put on him, wrapped around him} his outer garment (John 21:7). ¶
[4] **to gird, to gird about: *perizōnnumi*** [verb: περιζώννυμι <4024>]; **from *peri*: around, and *zōnnumi*: see [1]; lit.: to gird all around ► To encircle a part of the body >** A belt could be used to gird oneself in order to accomplish a service more efficiently or to move more quickly. The loins of the servants must be girded about {The servants must be dressed in readiness, dressed ready for service}, and their lamps burning (Luke 12:35). When He returns, the Lord will gird Himself {will dress Himself to serve}, make His servants who are found watching to sit down to eat, and serve them (Luke 12:37). A master asked his servant to prepare his meal, to gird himself {clothe himself, get himself ready}, and to serve him (Luke 17:8). An angel told Peter to gird himself {put on his clothes} and bind on his sandals (Acts 12:8). Christians must have their loins girded about with truth {the belt of truth buckled around their waist} (Eph. 6:14). John saw the Son of Man girded about the chest with a golden band (Rev. 1:13). The seven angels with the seven plagues had their chests girded with golden bands (Rev. 15:6 {to wear}). ¶

GIRDLE – Matt. 3:4; Mark 1:6; 6:8; Acts 21:11a, b; Rev. 1:13; 15:6 → BELT <2223>.

GIRL – [1] Luke 8:51, 54 → girl, little girl → DAUGHTER <3816> [2] John 18:16 → servant girl who kept watch, servant girl on duty → DOORKEEPER <2377> [3] John 18:17; Acts 12:13 → SERVANT GIRL <3814>.

GIVE – [1] ***didōmi*** [verb: δίδωμι <1325>] ► **a. To let, to allow, to yield >** No one can come to Jesus unless it is given {granted} to him by the Father (John 6:65). Christians should not avenge themselves, but give place {leave room} to wrath (Rom. 12:19), i.e., the wrath of God. **b. To grant, to bestow; to put >** God has given His only begotten Son (John 3:16). The Father has given all things to be in the hand of the Son (John 3:35 {to place}), into His hands (13:3 {to put under the power}). He has given {committed, entrusted} all judgment to the Son (John 5:22). He has given to {has granted} the Son to have life in Himself (John 5:26). He has given Him glory {has glorified Him} (1 Pet. 1:21). Jesus has completed the work which the Father had given Him to do (John 17:4). The Lord Jesus has given Himself for our sins (Gal. 1:4). **c. To pay, to give voluntarily >** Jesus was asked if it was lawful to give tribute (or: pay taxes) to Caesar (Matt. 22:17; Mark 12:14, 15a, b; Luke 20:22). **d. To present, to utter, to speak >** The Corinthians were to give a distinct speech in speaking with their tongue (1 Cor. 14:9). Other refs.: Mark 10:37 {to let}; Luke 19:23; Acts 14:3 {to enable}; 1 Cor. 9:12 {to hinder, to put hindrance, to cause hindrance} (lit.: to give an obstacle); 2 Cor. 8:16; Heb. 8:10; 10:16; 1 John 3:1 {to lavish}; Rev. 3:8 {to place, to set}; 17:17. Other refs.: see entries in Lexicon at <1325>.
[2] ***apodidōmi*** [verb: ἀποδίδωμι <591>]; **from *apo*: from, and *didōmi*: see [1] ► To remit, to return >** Pilate commanded the body of Jesus be given up {be delivered} to Joseph of Arimathea (Matt. 27:58). Zaccheus gave half of his goods to the poor (Luke 19:8). The Lord will give {award} to Paul the crown of righteousness on the day of His appearing (2 Tim. 4:8). Other refs.: Luke 10:35 {to sell}; Luke 20:25 {to give back}; Acts 5:8 {to sell, to get}; Rev. 18:6a, b {to render, to reward, to recompense, to pay}. Other refs.: see entries in Lexicon at <591>.
[3] ***diadidōmi*** [verb: διαδίδωμι <1239>]; **from *dia*: through, and *didōmi*: see [1] ► To deliver, to hand over >** The ten kings will give their power and authority to the beast (Rev. 17:13). All other refs.: DISTRIBUTE <1239>, DIVIDE <1239>.
[4] ***epididōmi*** [verb: ἐπιδίδωμι <1929>]; **from *epi*: to (intens.), and *didōmi*: see [1] ► To share personally, to deliver into another's hands >** A father would not give his son a stone if he asked him for bread, or a serpent if he asked for a fish (Matt. 7:9, 10; Luke 11:11a, b in some mss.); he would not give {offer} him a scorpion if he asked him for an egg (Luke 11:12). In the synagogue of Nazareth, Jesus was given {delivered,

handed} the book of the prophet Isaiah (Luke 4:17). He blessed and broke bread, and gave it to the disciples of Emmaus (Luke 24:30); *prosdidōmi* in some mss. The disciples gave to Jesus a piece of broiled fish (Luke 24:42). Jesus gave the piece of bread to Judas (John 13:26a, b). All other refs.: DELIVER <1929>, DRIVE <1929>.

5 ***metadidōmi*** [verb: μεταδίδωμι <3330>]; **from *meta*: with, and *didōmi*: see 1 ► To distribute, to share; also transl.: to impart >** He who has two tunics has to give to him who has none (Luke 3:11). Paul wanted to give some spiritual gift (Rom. 1:11). He who gives must do so with liberality (Rom. 12:8). The one who stole before his conversion must work to be able to give to him who has need (Eph. 4:28). Other ref.: 1 Thes. 2:8; see IMPART <3330>. ¶

6 **to give over: *paradidōmi*** [verb: παραδίδωμι <3860>]; **from *para*: beside, over to, and *didōmi*: see 1 ► To yield, to surrender oneself >** Paul speaks of those who have given themselves over to debauchery (Eph. 4:19). All other refs.: see entries in Lexicon at <3860>.

7 **to give first: *prodidōmi*** [verb: προδίδωμι <4272>]; **from *pro*: before, and *didōmi*: see 1 ► To grant beforehand >** Paul asks who has first given to the Lord (Rom. 11:35). ¶

8 **to give up: *aniēmi*** [verb: ἀνίημι <447>]; **from *ana*: back, and *hiēmi*: to send; lit.: to desist ► To abstain from, to cease from >** Masters are to give up {to forbear} threatening their bondmen (Eph. 6:9). All other refs.: LEAVE (verb) <447>, LOOSE <447>.

9 ***aponemō*** [verb: ἀπονέμω <632>]; **from *apo*: from, and *nemō*: to distribute ► To bestow, to grant >** Husbands are to give {to show} honor to {to treat with respect} their wives (1 Pet. 3:7). ¶

10 ***diōkō*** [verb: διώκω <1377>]; **from *diō*: to pursue ► To apply oneself to do something; to do it with attentiveness, with zeal >** Paul exhorts his readers to be given to {practice} hospitality (Rom. 12:13). All other refs.: FOLLOW <1377>, PERSECUTE <1377>, PRESS <1377>, PURSUE <1377>.

11 ***dōreomai*** [verb: δωρέομαι <1433>]; **from *dōrea*: gift, offering ► To give freely; also transl.: to grant >** Pilate gave the body of Jesus to Joseph of Arimathea (Mark 15:45). God has given us all things which relate to life and godliness, and the greatest and precious promises (2 Pet. 1:3, 4). ¶

12 **to give oneself up: *ekcheō*** [verb: ἐκχέω <1632>]; **from *ek*: out, and *cheō*: to pour; lit.: to pour out ► To abandon oneself to something, to yield entirely >** Jude speaks of those who have given themselves up to {run greedily in, rushed headlong into, rushed for profit into} the error of Balaam (Jude 11). All other refs.: POUR <1632>.

13 ***epitithēmi*** [verb: ἐπιτίθημι <2007>]; **from *epi*: on, and *tithēmi*: to put ► To put on, to place on >** Jesus gave the name (lit.: put the name on) Peter to Simon, and Boanerges to James and John (Mark 3:16, 17). All other refs.: see entries in Lexicon at <2007>.

14 ***merizō*** [verb: μερίζω <3307>]; **from *meris*: portion ► To share, to divide >** Abraham gave {apportioned} the tenth portion of all to Melchizedek (Heb. 7:2). All other refs.: DIFFERENCE <3307>, DISTRIBUTE <3307>, DIVIDE <3307>.

15 ***pareispherō*** [verb: παρεισφέρω <3923>]; **from *para*: near, and *eispherō*: to bring in ► To bring in addition, to add >** Christians must give {use, apply} all diligence {must make every effort} to add virtue to their faith (2 Pet. 1:5). ¶

16 ***parechō*** [verb: παρέχω <3930>]; **from *para*: near, and *echō*: to have, to hold ► To provide, to grant >** God has given {furnished} the proof of the judgment to come by raising Christ from the dead (Acts 17:31). Masters must give their bondservants what is just and fair (Col. 4:1). God gives {affords, supplies} us all things richly to enjoy (1 Tim. 6:17). The verb is transl. "to trouble," "to bother" (lit.: to give trouble) in Matt. 26:10; Mark 14:6. All other refs.: see entries in Lexicon at <3930>.

17 **to be given to: *prosechō*** [verb: προσέχω <4337>]; **from *pros*: to, and *echō*: to have, to hold ► To yield oneself to, to indulge >** Deacons must not be given {addicted} to much wine (1 Tim. 3:8). All other refs.:

ATTENDANCE <4337>, BEWARE <4337>, HEED (noun) <4337>.

18 **to freely give, to graciously give, to give: *charizomai*** [verb: χαρίζομαι <5483>]; **from *charis*: favor, gift, grace, which is from *chairō*: to rejoice ► To bestow as a favor; also transl.: to grant** > Jesus gave sight to many blind people (Luke 7:21). God had graciously given Paul all those who were sailing with him (Acts 27:24). God, who has not spared His Son, freely gives us also all things (Rom. 8:32). Christians have things freely given to them by God (1 Cor. 2:12). God gave to Abraham the inheritance of the law by promise (Gal. 3:18). It has been given to the Christian to suffer for the sake of Christ (Phil. 1:29). God has given {bestowed on} Jesus the name which is above every name (Phil. 2:9). Paul trusted that, by the prayers of the Christians, he would be given {restored} to them (Phm. 22). All other refs.: DELIVER <5483>, FORGIVE <5483>, GRANT <5483>.

19 **given to wine: *paroinos*** [adj.: πάροινος <3943>]; **from *para*: near, and *oinos*: wine ► Drinking excessively** > An overseer must not be given to wine (1 Tim. 3:3; Titus 1:7); the word is also transl.: addicted to wine, given to excesses from wine, disorderly through wine, given to drunkenness. ¶

– **20** Matt. 5:12 → to be glad, to be exceedingly (exceeding) glad → EXULT <21> **21** Matt. 6:33; Luke 12:31 → to give as well → ADD <4369> **22** Matt. 15:5; Mark 7:11 → GIFT <1435> **23** Matt. 20:8 → PAY (verb) <591> **24** Matt. 21:41 → RENDER <591> **25** Matt. 24:24; Mark 13:22; Acts 2:19 → SHOW (verb) <1325> **26** Matt. 26:73 → to give away → to make manifest → MANIFEST (adj.) <1212> **27** Mark 11:6 → to give permission → LET <863> **28** Mark 15:37, 39; Luke 23:46 → to give up the ghost → EXPIRE <1606> **29** Luke 1:54 → to give help → HELP (verb) <482> **30** Luke 2:38 → to give praise → THANKS (GIVE) <437> **31** Luke 12:58 → to give diligence → to make every effort → EFFORT <1325> <2039> **32** Luke 14:33 → to give up → FORSAKE <657> **33** Luke 17:5 → INCREASE (verb) <4369> **34** Luke 18:1 in some mss. → to give up → to lose heart → HEART <1457a> **35** Luke 18:12 → to give tithe → TITHE (noun and verb) <586> **36** John 1:16 → "already given" added in Engl. **37** John 2:3 → to give out → LACK (verb) <5302> **38** John 7:51; Acts 13:16; 15:12; 22:22 → to give a hearing, to give audience → HEAR <191> **39** John 10:11 → LAY <5087> **40** Acts 1:14; 6:4 → to give oneself continually; to give oneself up continually → CONTINUE <4342> **41** Acts 1:26 → DRAW <1325> **42** Acts 2:4 → to give utterance → to utter → UTTERANCE <669> **43** Acts 2:23 → being given up → being delivered → DELIVER <1560> **44** Acts 2:27 → LET <1325> **45** Acts 2:45 → DIVIDE <1266> **46** Acts 2:46 → with glad hearts → lit.: with gladness of hearts → JOY (noun) <20> **47** Acts 5:5, 10; 12:23 → to give up the ghost → EXPIRE <1634> **48** Acts 12:22 → to give a shout → SHOUT (verb) <2019> **49** Acts 21:14 → to give up → to be silent → SILENT <2270> **50** Acts 23:21 → to give in → YIELD <3982> **51** Acts 23:33 → to give up → DELIVER <325> **52** Acts 26:10 → CAST (verb) <2702> **53** Acts 27:20 → to give up → to take away → TAKE <4014> **54** Acts 27:34 → to give strength → lit.: to be for survival → SURVIVAL <4991> **55** Rom. 1:27 → to give up → LEAVE (verb) <863> **56** Rom. 8:2, 10 → the verb is added in Engl. **57** Rom. 12:17 → to give thought to do what is honorable → to provide things honest → PROVIDE <4306> **58** Rom. 13:6 → to give one's full time → to attend continually → ATTEND <4342> **59** Rom. 14:11; 15:9 → to give praise → CONFESS <1843> **60** 1 Cor. 7:5 → to give oneself → to devote oneself → DEVOTE <4980> **61** 1 Cor. 12:11 → DISTRIBUTE <1244> **62** 1 Cor. 13:3 → to give, to give to feed → FEED <5595> **63** 1 Cor. 13:11 → to give up → to put away → PUT <2673> **64** 1 Cor. 15:58 → to give oneself fully → ABOUND <4052> **65** 2 Cor. 8:24 → to give proof → to show the proof → SHOW (verb) <1731> **66** Gal. 3:5 → SUPPLY (verb) <2023> **67** Gal. 3:15 → to give a human example → lit.: I speak according to man **68** Gal. 3:19a → "was given at all" added in Engl. **69** Gal. 3:19b →

ORDAIN <1299> 70 Gal. 4:24 → to give birth → BEAR (verb) <1080> 71 Gal. 6:9 → to give up → to lose heart → HEART <1590> 72 Eph. 1:21 → NAME (verb) <3687> 73 Eph. 4:29 → MINISTER (verb) <1325> 74 Phil. 2:28; Rev. 19:7 → to be glad → REJOICE <5463> 75 1 Thes. 5:12 → to give instructions → ADMONISH <3560> 76 1 Tim. 6:13 → to give life → to preserve in life → LIFE <2227> 77 Titus 2:3 → to be given → to bring into bondage → BONDAGE <1402> 78 Heb. 10:25 → to give up → FORSAKE <1459> 79 1 Pet. 1:13 → BRING <5342> 80 1 Pet. 4:11 → SUPPLY (verb) <5524> 81 Jude 7 → to give oneself over to fornication → FORNICATION <1608> 82 Rev. 18:6 → to give back → REPAY <1363> 83 Rev. 18:20 → God had given judgment for you against her → lit.: God has judged your judgment on her → JUDGE (verb) <2919>.

GIVEN – Acts 7:53 → given through angels → by the disposition of angels → DISPOSITION <1296>.

GIVER – ***dotēs*** [masc. noun: δότης <1395>]; **from *didōmi*: to give ▶ Donator, one who gives** > God loves a cheerful giver (2 Cor. 9:7). ¶

GIVING – 1 ***dosis*** [fem. noun: δόσις <1394>]; **from *didōmi*: to give ▶ The act of bestowing, what is given** > At the beginning, no church shared with Paul concerning giving and receiving but the Philippians only (Phil. 4:15). Every good gift {thing} (*dosis*; lit.: giving) and every perfect gift (*dōrēma*) comes down from the Father of lights (Jas. 1:17a). ¶
2 **giving of the law: *nomothesia*** [fem. noun: νομοθεσία <3548>]; **from *nomotheteō*: to legislate, which is from *nomos*: law, and *tithēmi*: to put ▶ Privilege of having received the law** > The giving of the law {law-giving, receiving of the law} pertained to the Israelites (Rom. 9:4). ¶
– 3 Matt. 6:4 → ALMS <1654>.

GLAD – 1 John 11:15; Rom. 16:19; 1 Cor. 16:17; 2 Cor. 7:16; et al. → to be glad → REJOICE <5463> 2 Acts 2:26; 2 Cor. 2:2; Gal. 4:27 → to be glad, to make glad → REJOICE <2165> 3 Acts 15:3 → to make glad → to cause great joy → CAUSE (verb) <4160> 4 Rev. 19:7 → to be glad → REJOICE <21>.

GLAD (BE) – 1 John 6:21 → were glad → lit.: were willing → WILLINGLY <2309> 2 Phm. 13 → I would have been glad → WANT (verb) <1014>.

GLAD TIDINGS – See GOSPEL <2098>.

GLADDEN – 2 Cor. 2:2 → REJOICE <2165>.

GLADLY – 1 ***asmenōs*** [adv.: ἀσμένως <780>]; **from *hēsmenos*: perf. pass. ptcp. of *hēdomai*: to delight ▶ Joyfully, with pleasure** > Those who received the word of God gladly were baptized (Acts 2:41 in some mss.). The brothers of Jerusalem received Paul gladly {warmly} (Acts 21:17). ¶
2 ***hēdeōs*** [adv.: ἡδέως <2234>]; **from *hēdus*: soft, gentle, sweet ▶ With pleasure, willingly** > Herod listened to John the Baptist gladly (Mark 6:20). The mass of the people heard Jesus gladly {with delight} (Mark 12:37). The Corinthians gladly tolerated fools (2 Cor. 11:19). ¶
3 **all the more gladly, most gladly, very gladly: *hēdista*** [adv.: ἥδιστα <2236>]; **superl. of *hēdus*: see 2 ▶ With great pleasure** > Paul would most gladly boast in his weaknesses (2 Cor. 12:9). He would most gladly spend and be utterly spent for the souls of the Corinthians (2 Cor. 12:15). ¶
– 4 Luke 12:32 → to choose gladly → PLEASED (BE) <2106> 5 Luke 15:16 → to gladly have → DESIRE (verb) <1937> 6 Luke 19:6 → REJOICE <5463> 7 Acts 24:10 → CHEERFULLY <2115a>.

GLADNESS – 1 ***agalliasis*** [fem. noun: ἀγαλλίασις <20>]; **from *agalliaō*: to rejoice much, which is from *agan*: very much, and *hallomai*: to leap ▶ Extreme joy, exultation, jubilation** > John the Baptist would be a subject of joy and gladness {delight} for his father Zacharias (Luke

1:14). Other refs.: Luke 1:44; Acts 2:46; Heb. 1:9; Jude 24; see JOY (noun) <20>. ¶
– [2] Acts 2:28; 14:17 → JOY (noun) <2167>.

GLASS – [1] ***hualos*** [masc. noun: ὕαλος <5194>] ► **Transparent stone, crystal** > The new Jerusalem, in the vision of John at Patmos, was like pure glass (Rev. 21:18), and her street like transparent glass (v. 21). He also saw a sea of glass (*hualinos*) (Rev. 4:6; 15:2a, b; see SEA <5193>). ¶
– [2] 1 Cor. 13:12; Jas. 1:23 → MIRROR <2072> [3] 2 Cor. 3:18 → to behold as in a glass → to behold as in a mirror → BEHOLD (verb) <2734> [4] Rev. 4:6; 15:2a, b → sea of glass → SEA <5193>.

GLEAM – Luke 24:4 → to gleam like lightning → to shine → SHINING <797>.

GLEAMING – Luke 9:29 → to become gleaming → to become glistening → GLISTENING <1823>.

GLISTENING – **to become glistening: *exastraptō*** [verb: ἐξαστράπτω <1823>]; **from *ek*: out, and *astraptō*: to illuminate like lightning, which is from *astrapē*: lightning ► To become brilliant, to flash out as lightning** > On the mountain, the clothes of Jesus became white and glistening {dazzling white, white and effulgent, white and gleaming, as bright as a flash of lightning} (Luke 9:29). ¶

GLITTER – Rev. 17:4; 18:16 → to have ornaments → ORNAMENT <5558>.

GLOAT – Rev. 11:10 → REJOICE <2165>.

GLOOM – [1] ***katēpheia*** [fem. noun: κατήφεια <2726>]; **from *katēphēs*: downcast because of shame or sadness ► Heaviness, shame, sorrow** > James tells sinners to change their laughter to mourning and their joy to gloom (Jas. 4:9). ¶
– [2] 2 Pet. 2:4 → to cast down to the deepest pit of gloom → to cast down to hell → HELL <5020> [3] 2 Pet. 2:17; Jude 13 → BLACKNESS <2217>.

GLOOMY – [1] Matt. 6:16 → to put on a gloomy face → to disfigure the face → DISFIGURE <853> [2] Jude 6 → gloomy darkness → DARKNESS <2217>.

GLORIFY – [1] ***doxazō*** [verb: δοξάζω <1392>]; **from *doxa*: glory, honor ► To magnify, to praise** > This verb is used in regard to the Lord Jesus (Luke 4:15; John 7:39; 8:54a, b; 11:4; 12:16, 23; 13:31a, 32b, c; 16:14; 17:1a, 5, 10; Acts 3:13; Heb. 5:5; Rev. 15:4), the Father (Matt. 5:16; John 12:28a–c; 14:13; 15:8; 17:1b, 4; Rom. 15:6), God (Matt. 9:8; 15:31; Mark 2:12; Luke 2:20; 5:25, 26; 7:16; 13:13; 17:15; 18:43; 23:47; John 13:31b, 32a; 21:19; Acts 4:21; 11:18; 21:20; Rom. 1:21; 15:9; 1 Cor. 6:20; 2 Cor. 9:13; Gal. 1:24; 1 Pet. 2:12; 4:11, 16), the word of the Lord (Acts 13:48; 2 Thes. 3:1), those who have been justified (Rom. 8:30), and Babylon the great (Rev. 18:7). Other refs.: Matt. 6:2; Rom. 11:13; 1 Cor. 12:26; 2 Cor. 3:10a, b; 1 Pet. 1:8 {glorious}; 4:14 in some mss. ¶

[2] ***endoxazō*** [verb: ἐνδοξάζω <1740>]; **from *endoxos*: glorious, which is from *en*: in, and *doxazō*: see [1] ► To magnify, to praise** > Jesus will come to be glorified in His saints (2 Thes. 1:10). His name is glorified in them (2 Thes. 1:12). ¶

[3] **to be glorified with: *sundoxazō*** [verb: συνδοξάζω <4888>]; **from *sun*: with, and *doxazō*: see [1] ► To partake in the glory of another** > If we suffer with Christ, we shall also be glorified with Him (Rom. 8:17). ¶

[4] ***kauchaomai*** [verb: καυχάομαι <2744>]; **from *kauchē*: acccomplishment, exploit ► To show off, to take pride; also transl.: to do boasting, to make a boast, to glory** > He who boasts, let him boast in the Lord (1 Cor. 1:31a, b). Speaking to the Corinthians, Paul says to receive him as a fool that he may boast of himself a little (2 Cor. 11:16). We are not saved on the principle of works, that no one may boast (Eph. 2:9). Other refs.: Rom. 2:17, 23; 5:2, 3, 11; 1 Cor. 1:29; 3:21; 4:7; 13:3 in some mss.; 2 Cor. 5:12b; 7:14a; 9:2; 10:8, 13, 15, 16, 17a, b; 11:12, 18a, b, 30a, b; 12:1, 5a, b, 6, 9, 11 in some mss.; Gal. 6:13, 14; Phil.

3:3; 2 Thes. 1:4 (other mss.: *enkauchaomai*); Jas. 1:9; 4:16. ¶

5 ***katakauchaomai*** [verb: κατακαυχάομαι <2620>]; **from *kata*: against (intens.), and *kauchaomai*: see 4 ▶ To show off, to take great pride** > This verb is used in Rom. 11:18a, b {to be arrogant, to consider oneself superior} where it is a matter of Gentiles boasting over the Jews. James says not to boast {be arrogant, glory} and lie against the truth (3:14). The verb is transl. "to triumph" {to glory, to rejoice} in Jas. 2:13: mercy triumphs over judgment. ¶

6 **something to boast: *kauchēma*** [neut. noun: καύχημα <2745>]; **from *kauchaomai*: see 4 ▶ A reason for taking pride, for bragging; also transl.: boast, reason to glory** > If Abraham had been justified on the principle of works, he had something of which to boast (Rom. 4:2). It would have been good for Paul rather to die, than that anyone should make vain his boast (1 Cor. 9:15). Though Paul preached the gospel, he had nothing to boast of (1 Cor. 9:16). The Philippians held forth the word of life so as to be a boast for Paul in the day of Christ (Phil. 2:16). The Christian is to hold fast the boldness and the boast of hope firm to the end (Heb. 3:6). Other refs.: 2 Cor. 5:12a; 9:3; Gal. 6:4. All other refs.: BOAST (noun) <2745>, BOASTING <2745>.

7 **reason to glorify: *kauchēsis*** [fem. noun: καύχησις <2746>]; **from *kauchaomai*: see 4 ▶ Reason for boasting, to take pride; also transl.: boast, boasting, confidence, proud, reason to boast, rejoicing** > Paul had whereof to boast in Christ Jesus (Rom. 15:17). His boasting was to have conducted himself in simplicity and sincerity (2 Cor. 1:12). His boasting of being a burden to no one was not to be stopped in the regions of Achaia (2 Cor. 11:10). Other refs.: 2 Cor. 7:4, 14b; 8:24; 1 Thes. 2:19. All other refs.: BOASTING <2746>.

– 8 Luke 1:46 → MAGNIFY <3170>
9 1 Pet. 1:21 → lit.: to give glory → GIVE <1325>.

GLORIOUS – 1 ***endoxos*** [adj.: ἔνδοξος <1741>]; **from *en*: in, and *doxa*: glory, honor ▶ Marvelous, worthy of praise** > The crowd rejoiced at all the glorious things that were being done by Jesus (Luke 13:17). Christ will present the church to Himself, glorious {in all her glory, radiant} (Eph. 5:27). Other refs.: Luke 7:25; 1 Cor. 4:10; see GORGEOUSLY <1741>, HONORED <1741>. ¶

2 **to glorify: *doxazō*** [verb: δοξάζω <1392>]; **from *doxa*: glory, honor ▶ To magnify, to praise; also transl.: filled with glory, full of glory** > Those who believe in Jesus Christ rejoice with inexpressible and glorious (lit.: glorified) joy (1 Pet. 1:8). All other refs.: GLORIFY <1392>.

– 3 Acts 2:20 → AWESOME <2016>
4 1 Cor. 4:10 → HONORED <1741>
5 2 Pet. 2:10; Jude 8 → glorious ones → also transl.: celestial beings → DIGNITARY <1391>.

GLORIOUSLY – Acts 2:20 → gloriously appearing → AWESOME <2016>.

GLORY (noun) – 1 ***doxa*** [fem. noun: δόξα <1391>]; **from *dokeō*: to think ▶ Honor resulting from a good opinion, distinctive praise; the glory of God relates to what God is essentially in His magnificence** > This term concerns: a. The nature and the acts of God in self-manifestation, i.e., what He essentially is and does. He reveals Himself particularly in the Person of Christ, in whom essentially His glory has ever shone forth and ever will do (John 17:5, 24; Heb. 1:3). The glory of God was manifested in the character and acts of Christ in the days of His flesh (John 1:14a, b; 2:11); at Cana both His grace and His power were manifested, and these constituted His glory; so also in the resurrection of Lazarus (John 11:4, 40); the glory of the Father was exhibited in the resurrection of Christ (Rom. 6:4) and in His ascension and exaltation (1 Pet. 1:21), as well as at the transfiguration (2 Pet. 1:17). In Rom. 1:20, His "eternal power and His divinity" are spoken of as His glory (v. 23), i.e., His attributes and power as revealed through creation. In Rom. 3:23, the word denotes the manifested perfection of His character, especially His righteousness. In

Col. 1:11, the "might of His glory" signifies the "might which is characteristic of His glory." In Eph. 1:6, 12, 14, the "praise of the glory of His grace" and the "praise of His glory" signify the due acknowledgment of the exhibition of His attributes and ways. In Eph. 1:17, the "Father of glory" describes Him as the source from whom all divine splendor and perfection proceed. b. The character and ways of God as exhibited through Christ to and through Christians (2 Cor. 3:18; 4:6). c. The state of blessedness into which Christians are to enter hereafter through being brought into the likeness of Christ (e.g., Rom. 8:18, 21; Phil. 3:21; 1 Pet. 5:1, 10; Rev. 21:11). d. The supernatural brightness or splendor emanating from God (Luke 2:9; Acts 22:11; Rom. 9:4; Jas. 2:1; Titus 2:13 refer to the return of Christ to reign) or belonging to heavenly bodies (1 Cor. 15:40, 41). e. Honor, praise, and good reputation (Luke 14:10; John 5:41; 7:18a, b; 8:50; 12:43a, b; 2 Cor. 6:8; Phil. 3:19; Heb. 3:3); see also 1 Cor. 11:7 and 1 Thes. 2:6. f. Praise to God (e.g., Luke 2:14; 17:18; John 9:24; Acts 12:23; Rom. 11:36; 16:27; Gal. 1:5; Rev. 1:6). (After W. E. Vine.) *

2 ***kleos*** [neut. noun: κλέος <2811>]; **from *kleō*: to tell ▶ Value, credit** > Peter asks what glory is it to endure being beaten for doing wrong (1 Pet. 2:20). ¶

– 3 Matt. 5:16; 6:2; Heb. 5:5; Rev. 15:4 → to bring, give, have, take the glory → GLORIFY <1392> 4 Eph. 5:27 → in all her glory → lit.: glorious → GLORIOUS <1741> 5 1 Pet. 1:8 → filled with glory, full of glory → lit.: glorified → to glorify → GLORIOUS <1392>.

GLORY (verb) – 1 Rom. 4:2; 1 Cor. 9:16; Phil. 1:26; 2:16; Heb. 3:6; et al. → reason to glory → something to boast → GLORIFY <2745> 2 Rom. 15:17 → reason to glory → reason to boast → GLORIFY <2746> 3 1 Cor. 1:31a, b; Jas. 1:9; et al. → GLORIFY <2744> 4 1 Cor. 15:31 → lit.: glory → BOASTING <2746> 5 Phil. 1:26 → ample cause to glory → your boasting may abound → BOAST (noun) <2745> 6 Jas. 2:13; 3:14 → GLORIFY <2620>.

GLORYING – 1 1 Cor. 5:6 → BOASTING <2745> 2 1 Cor. 9:15 → something to boast → GLORIFY <2745> 3 Jas. 4:16 → BOASTING <2746>.

GLOW – 1 Rev. 1:15 → to glow, to cause to glow → REFINE <4448> 2 Rev. 15:2 → glowing with fire → mingled with fire → MINGLE <3396>.

GLUTTON – 1 ***gastēr*** [fem. noun: γαστήρ <1064>] ▶ **Lit.: belly, stomach** > The Cretans were lazy gluttons {slow bellies} (Titus 1:12), i.e., they wanted to eat well without working. All other refs.: CHILD <1064>, WOMB <1064>.

2 ***phagos*** [masc. noun: φάγος <5314>]; **from *phagō*: to eat ▶ Greedy, voracious person** > It was said that the Son of Man was a glutton {a man who is eating, gluttonous} and a wine-drinker (Matt. 11:19; Luke 7:34). ¶

GLUTTONOUS – Matt. 11:19, Luke 7:34 → GLUTTON <5314>.

GNASH – 1 ***trizō*** [verb: τρίζω <5149>]; **describes primarily the sound of an animal ▶ To make a strident noise by grinding the teeth** > The son of a man was possessed by a mute spirit and he gnashed {ground} his teeth (Mark 9:18). ¶

2 ***bruchō*** [verb: βρύχω <1031>] ▶ **To make an unpleasant sound by abrasion of the teeth** > The Jews gnashed their teeth against Stephen (Acts 7:54). ¶

GNASHING – ***brugmos*** [masc. noun: βρυγμός <1030>]; **from *bruchō*: to bite, to grind the teeth ▶ Unpleasant sound produced by abrasion of teeth** > There will be weeping and gnashing of teeth in the outer darkness (Matt. 8:12; 22:13; 25:30; Luke 13:28), in the furnace of fire (Matt. 13:42, 50), and with the hypocrites (Matt. 24:51). ¶

GNAT – ***kōnōps*** [masc. noun: κώνωψ <2971>] ▶ **Small fly, mosquito, wine-gnat** > The word is found in Matt. 23:24; see CAMEL <2574>. ¶

GNAW – ***masaomai*** [verb: μασάομαι <3145>]; **from *massō*: to clench; also spelled: *massaomai* ▶ To bite (particularly the tongue because of pain)** > When the fifth bowl was poured out, men gnawed their tongues with distress (Rev. 16:10). ¶

GO – 1 ***agō*** [verb: ἄγω <71>] **▶ To depart, to leave, to proceed** > Jesus said to His disciples: Let us go into Judaea again (John 11:7). Thomas said to the other disciples: Let us go to Lazarus with Jesus, expecting to die (John 11:15, 16). Jesus said to His disciples: Let us go (John 14:31). Other refs.: Matt. 26:46; Mark 1:38; 11:2; 14:42. Other refs.: BRING <71>, LEAD (verb) <71>.

2 **to go before, ahead of: *proagō*** [verb: προάγω <4254>]; **from *pro*: in front, and *agō*: see 1 ▶ To precede, to go ahead** > The star went before the wise men (Matt. 2:9). Jesus made the disciples go before Him to Bethsaida (Mark 6:45). Other refs.: Matt. 14:22; 21:9; 26:32; 28:7; Mark 10:32; 11:9; 14:28; 16:7; Luke 18:39; 1 Tim. 5:24 {to precede}. Other ref.: 2 John 9 in some mss. All other refs.: see entries in Lexicon at <4254>.

3 **to go, to go about, to go around, etc.: *periagō*** [verb: περιάγω <4013>]; **from *peri*: around, and *agō*: see 1 ▶ a. To go from one place to another** > Jesus went round the whole of Galilee, teaching in the synagogues, preaching the glad tidings, and healing those who were ill (Matt. 4:23). **b. To cover, to travel in a circuit** > Jesus went about all the cities and villages, teaching in the synagogues (Matt. 9:35). He went around the villages (Mark 6:6). The scribes and the Pharisees went round {compassed} the sea and the dry land to make a proselyte (Matt. 23:15). Being blinded, Elymas went about, seeking someone to lead him by the hand (Acts 13:11). Other ref.: 1 Cor. 9:5 (to take along); see TAKE <4013>. ¶

4 **to go, to go away: *hupagō*** [verb: ὑπάγω <5217>]; **from *hupo*: under, and *agō*: see 1 ▶ To depart, to withdraw** > Jesus told Satan to go away from Him (Matt. 4:10). Other refs.: Matt. 5:24, 41b; 8:4, 13, 32a; 9:6; 13:44; 16:23 {to get}; 18:15; 19:21; 20:4a, 7, 14; 21:28; 26:18, 24; 27:65; 28:10b; Mark 1:44; 2:11; 5:19, 34; 6:31, 33, 38; 7:29; 8:33 {to get}; 10:21, 52; 11:2; 14:13, 21; 16:7a; Luke 4:8 in some mss.; 8:42; 10:3; 12:58; 17:14b; 19:30; John 3:8; 4:16; 6:21, 67; 7:3, 33; 8:14a, b, 21a, b, 22; 9:7a, 11a; 11:8, 31b, 44; 12:11, 35; 13:3, 33, 36a, b; 14:4, 5, 28a; 15:16; 16:5a, b, 10, 17; 18:8; 21:3a; Jas. 2:16; 1 John 2:11; Rev. 10:8; 13:10; 14:4; 16:1; 17:8, 11. ¶

5 ***diateleō*** [verb: διατελέω <1300>]; **from *dia*: through (intens.), and *teleō*: to finish ▶ To finish completely** > The verb is used in the expr. "to go without eating" (Acts 27:33). ¶

6 ***erchomai*** [verb: ἔρχομαι <2064>] **▶ To walk, to come** > The verb is used in Matt. 13:36; Luke 2:44 {to travel}; 14:1. Other refs.: COME <2064>.

7 **to go up: *anerchomai*** [verb: ἀνέρχομαι <424>]; **from *ana*: up, and *erchomai*: see 6 ▶ To move to a higher place, to ascend** > Jesus went up on the mountain (John 6:3). Paul did not go up to Jerusalem immediately (Gal. 1:17), he only went up to Jerusalem later (v. 18). ¶

8 **to go away, to go back: *aperchomai*** [verb: ἀπέρχομαι <565>]; **from *apo*: from, and *erchomai*: see 6 ▶ To leave one place and proceed to another** > A scribe told Jesus he would follow Him wherever He went (Matt. 8:19; Luke 9:57b). The disciples went away again to their own homes on the morning of the resurrection (John 20:10). They commanded Peter and John to go out of the Sanhedrin (Acts 4:15). Other refs.: Matt. 2:22; 8:21, 31 (*apostellō* in some mss.), 32b, 33; 9:7; 10:5; 13:25, 28, 46; 14:15, 16, 25 {to pass}; 16:4, 21; 18:30; 19:22; 20:4b; 21:29, 30; 22:5, 22; 25:10, 18, 25, 46; 26:36, 42, 44; 27:5, 60; 28:10b; Mark 1:20, 35b; 5:17, 20, 24; 6:27, 32, 36, 46; 7:24, 30 {to pass}; 8:13; 9:43; 10:22; 11:4; 12:12; 14:10, 39; 16:13; Luke 1:23; 2:15a; 5:14, 25; 7:24; 8:31, 37a, 39; 9:12, 59, 60; 10:30; 17:23; 19:32; 22:4, 13; 23:33; 24:12, 24; John 4:3, 8, 28, 47; 5:15; 6:1, 22, 68; 9:7b, 11b; 10:40; 11:28, 46, 54; 12:19, 36; 16:7a, b; Acts 5:26; 9:17; 10:7; 23:32 (some mss.: *poreuomai*); Rom. 15:28; Gal. 1:17b; Jas. 1:24; Jude 7; Rev. 10:9; 12:17; 16:2; 18:14a; 21:1 (some mss.:

parerchomai) {to pass away}. All other refs.: see entries in Lexicon at <565>.

9 to go; to go around, over, etc.: *dierchomai* [verb: διέρχομαι <1330>]**; from *dia*: through, and *erchomai*: see 6 ▶ To go to different places, to traverse; also transl.: to come, to pass, to pass over, to pass through, to cross over** > When an unclean spirit goes out (*exerchomai*) of a man, it goes through (*dierchomai*) {he walketh through} arid places seeking rest (Matt. 12:43; Luke 11:24). Jesus said to go over to the other side (Mark 4:35; Luke 8:22). He passed through the midst of the crowd (Luke 4:30). He was going to pass a certain way (Luke 19:4). He went about doing good (Acts 10:38). Christians who had been scattered preached the word of God wherever they went (Acts 8:4). By sin, death passed upon {spread to} all men (Rom. 5:12). Other refs.: Matt. 19:24; Luke 2:15b; John 8:59; Acts 8:40; 11:19 {to travel, to make one's way}, 22; 12:10; 17:23 {to walk around}; 18:27 {to cross}; 19:21; 20:25; 1 Cor. 10:1; 2 Cor. 1:16 {to visit}. All other refs.: COME <1330>, PASS <1330>, PIERCE <1330>, SPREAD <1330>.

10 to go out into: *eiserchomai* [verb: εἰσέρχομαι <1525>]**; from *eis*: in, and *erchomai*: see 6 ▶ To enter, to come** > Many deceivers have gone out into the world (2 John 7). All other refs.: ENTER <1525>.

11 to go; to go away, to go out, to go forth, to go forward, to leave, etc.: *exerchomai* [verb: ἐξέρχομαι <1831>]**; from *ek*: out, and *erchomai*: see 6 ▶ To come out, to leave, to set out, to proceed** > Out of Bethlehem was to go forth a leader for Israel (Matt. 2:6). Jesus went out to a mountain to pray (Luke 6:12). He went forth toward those who had come to seize Him (John 18:4). The verb is used in regard to Jesus (Matt. 15:21; Mark 7:31; John 4:43), and also in regard to the disciples (Matt. 10:11, 14; Mark 6:10, 12; 16:20; Luke 9:4, 6 {to set out}), blind men (Matt. 9:31), and Paul (Acts 15:40; 16:10, 40a {to come out}, b; 20:11; 21:5 {to set out}, 8; 2 Cor. 2:13 {to come away}). The whole city went out to meet Jesus (Matt. 8:34). Rising in the morning long before day, Jesus went out into a desert place, and there He prayed (Mark 1:35). The apostles believed that Jesus came out from God (John 16:27); He had come out from the Father; again, He left the world (v. 28). Having sung a hymn, Jesus and His apostles went out to the Mount of Olives (Mark 14:26). Jesus went out, bearing His cross (John 19:17). One of the soldiers pierced the side of Jesus with a spear, and immediately there came out blood and water (John 19:34). As the lightning goes forth from the east and shines to the west, so will be the coming of the Son of Man (Matt. 24:27). In the completion of the age, the angels will go forth and sever the wicked from the midst of the just (Matt. 13:49). In a parable, ten virgins went forth to meet the bridegroom (Matt. 25:1, 6). Christians are to come out from the midst of those who are in darkness (2 Cor. 6:17). Christians are called to go forth to Jesus, bearing His reproach (Heb. 13:13). Other refs.: Matt. 5:26; 8:28, 32; 9:32; 11:7–9; 12:14, 43, 44; 13:1, 3; 14:14; 15:22; 17:18; 18:28; 20:1, 3, 5, 6; 21:17; 22:10; 24:1, 26; 26:30, 55, 71, 75; 27:32, 53; 28:8; Mark 1:25, 26, 29, 45; 2:12, 13; 3:6, 21; 4:3; 5:2, 8, 13, 14, 30; 6:1, 24, 34, 54; 7:29, 30; 8:11, 27; 9:25, 26, 29, 30; 11:11, 12; 14:16, 48, 68; 16:8; Luke 1:22; 2:1; 4:35, 36, 41, 42; 5:27; 6:19; 7:24–26; 8:2, 5, 29, 33, 35a, b, 38, 46; 9:5; 10:10; 11:14, 24a, b; 12:59; 14:18, 21, 23; 15:28; 17:29; 21:37; 22:39, 52, 62; John 1:43; 4:30; 8:9, 59; 10:9; 11:31, 44; 12:13; 13:30, 31; 17:8; 18:1, 16, 29, 38; 19:4, 5; 20:3; 21:3; Acts 1:21; 7:3, 4, 7; 8:7; 10:23; 11:25; 12:9, 10, 17b; 14:20; 15:24; 16:3, 13, 18a, b, 19, 36, 39, 40; 17:33; 18:23; 19:12; 20:1; 22:18; 28:3; Rom. 10:18; 1 Cor. 5:10; 2 Cor. 8:17; Heb. 3:16; 7:5; 11:8a, b; 15 (*ekbainō* in some mss.); 1 John 2:19; 4:1; 3 John 7; Rev. 3:12; 6:2, 4; 9:3; 14:15, 17, 18, 20; 15:6; 16:17; 18:4; 19:5; 20:8. All other refs.: COME <1831>, DEPART <1831>, ESCAPE <1831>, SPREAD <1831>, STEP (verb) <1831>.

12 to go, to go down, to depart: *katerchomai* [verb: κατέρχομαι <2718>]**; from *kata*: down, and *erchomai*: see 6 ▶ To descend, to come down** > The verb is used concerning Jesus (Luke 4:31), Philip (Acts

8:5), Paul and Barnabas (Acts 13:4), and Herod (Acts 12:19). All other refs.: COME <2718>, DESCEND <2718>, LAND (verb) <2718>.

13 ***parerchomai*** [verb: παρέρχομαι <3928>]; **from *para*: near, and *erchomai*: see 6 ► To come** > Ref.: Luke 17:7 {to come}. All other refs.: COME <3928>, PASS <3928>, SPEND <3928>, TRANSGRESS <3928>.

14 **to go farther, ahead, before, forward, on, through: *proerchomai*** [verb: προέρχομαι <4281>]; **from *pro*: before, in front, and *erchomai*: see 6 ► To precede, to go in front** > At Gethsemane, Jesus went a little farther and prayed to His Father (Matt. 26:39; Mark 14:35). John the Baptist was to go before the Lord in the spirit and power of Elijah (Luke 1:17). There were brothers who had gone ahead and were waiting for Paul at Troas (Acts 20:5). Other refs.: Mark 6:33 {to outgo}; Luke 22:47 {to precede}; Acts 12:10 {to pass on, to go down}; 20:13; 2 Cor. 9:5 {to go ahead of time, to visit in advance}. ¶

15 **to go to, to go unto, to go near: *proserchomai*** [verb: προσέρχομαι <4334>]; **from *pros*: to, and *erchomai*: see 6 ► To come to, to approach** > Joseph of Arimathea went to Pilate and asked for the body of Jesus (Matt. 27:58). The Spirit said to Philip to approach the chariot of the Ethiopian (Acts 8:29). Other refs.: Luke 10:34; Acts 9:1; 10:28 {to visit}. Other refs.: COME <4334>, CONSENT (verb) <4334>, DRAW <4334>.

16 **to go with, to go along: *sunerchomai*** [verb: συνέρχομαι <4905>]; **from *sun*: together, and *erchomai*: see 6 ► To go together** > Peter went with the men to Joppa (Acts 9:39). John, whose surname was Mark, did not go {did not continue} with Paul and Barnabas to the work (Acts 15:38). All other refs.: ACCOMPANY <4905>, COME <4905>, FOLLOW <4905>.

17 **to go up: *anabainō*** [verb: ἀναβαίνω <305>]; **from *ana*: up, and *bainō*: to go ► To move to a higher place, to ascend, to climb, to rise, to spring up, to enter; also transl.: to arise, to bring up, to climb up, to come up, to get into, to grow up, to rise up, etc.** > Jesus was baptized and immediately came up from the water (Matt. 3:16; Mark 1:10). He went up on a mountain (Matt. 5:1; 15:29; Mark 3:13; Luke 9:28). Thorns came up (Matt. 13:7; Mark 4:7). Jesus went up on a mountain to pray (Matt. 14:23). Peter was to take the fish that came up first (Matt. 17:27). Jesus went up to Jerusalem (Matt. 20:17, 18; Mark 10:32, 33; Luke 18:31; 19:28; John 2:13; 5:1). A crop sprang up (Mark 4:8). A mustard plant grew up (Mark 4:32). Jesus went up into the boat (Mark 6:51). Joseph went up from Galilee (Luke 2:4). Jesus went up to Jerusalem with His parents (Luke 2:42). Men went up on the housetop to let down a paralyzed man through the tiling before Jesus (Luke 5:19). Two men went up to the temple to pray (Luke 18:10). Zaccheus climbed up into a sycamore tree (Luke 19:4). Jesus asked His disciples why certain doubts had arisen in their hearts (Luke 24:38). The disciples would see angels ascending and descending on Jesus (John 1:51). No one has ascended to heaven but He who has come down from heaven (John 3:13). Jesus said the disciples would see Him ascend where He was before (John 6:62). His brothers were to go up to the feast, but not Jesus (John 7:8a, b); when His brothers went up, then Jesus also went up, but as it were in secret (v. 10a, b). He went up to the temple (John 7:14). The thief climbs up into the sheepfold by a way other than the door (John 10:1). Many went up to Jerusalem (John 11:55); certain Greeks came up (John 12:20). Jesus would ascend to His Father (John 20:17a, b). The disciples got (lit.: went up) into the boat (John 21:3). Simon Peter went up and dragged the net to land (John 21:11). The disciples went up into the upper room (Acts 1:13). David did not ascend into the heavens (Acts 2:34). Peter and John went up to the temple (Acts 3:1). The Ethiopian invited Philip to come up and sit with him in his chariot (Acts 8:31). Following the baptism of the eunuch, he and Philip came up (or: went up) out of the water (Acts 8:39). The prayers and alms of Cornelius had come up for a memorial before God (Acts 10:4). Peter went up on the housetop to pray (Acts 10:9). Peter came up to Jerusalem (Acts 11:2). Paul and

certain others should go up to Jerusalem (Acts 15:2); he went up to Jerusalem (Acts 21:15; 24:11). Paul went up into the upper room (Acts 20:11). Paul was told not to go up to Jerusalem (Acts 21:4, 12). When Paul landed at Caesarea, he went up and greeted the church (Acts 18:22). Festus went up to Jerusalem (Acts 25:1), and went down to Caesarea where he asked Paul if he were willing to go up to Jerusalem (v. 9). Paul asks who will ascend into heaven to bring Christ down from above (Rom. 10:6: *anabainō*) and who will descend into the abyss to bring up (*anagō*) Christ from the dead (v. 7). Paul went up again to Jerusalem (Gal. 2:1, 2). The things that God has prepared for those who love Him have not entered into the heart of man (1 Cor. 2:9). Jesus ascended on high (Eph. 4:8–10). A voice told John to come up here (Rev. 4:1). John saw another angel ascending from the east (Rev. 7:2). The smoke of the incense ascended with the prayers of the saints (Rev. 8:4). Smoke arose out of the pit (Rev. 9:2). A beast ascended out of the bottomless pit (Rev. 11:7; 13:11; 17:8); another beast rose up out of the sea (Rev. 13:1). A loud voice from heaven told the two witnesses to come up here (i.e., into heaven), and they did indeed ascend to heaven (Rev. 11:12a, b). The smoke of the torment of those who accept the beast ascends forever and ever (Rev. 14:11), likewise, the smoke of Babylon rises up for ever and ever (Rev. 19:3). The nations went up on the breadth of the earth (Rev. 20:9). Other refs.: Acts 7:23; 21:31; see COME <305>. ¶

18 ***apobainō*** [verb: ἀποβαίνω <576>]; **from *apo*: from, and *bainō*: to go ▶ To come out** > The fishermen had gone from {had left} their boats (Luke 5:2). Other refs.: Luke 21:13; John 21:9; Phil. 1:19 see COME <576>, TURN (verb) <576>. ¶

19 **to go down: *katabainō*** [verb: καταβαίνω <2597>]; **from *kata*: down, and *bainō*: to go ▶ To descend; to abase, to bring down** > Capernaum will go down to the depths (Matt. 11:23; Luke 10:15); some mss. have *katabibazō*. The verb is used concerning Jews during the great tribulation (Matt. 24:17; Mark 13:15), Jesus (Luke 2:51; John 2:12), a man wounded by thieves (Luke 10:30), a tax collector (Luke 18:14), a nobleman (John 4:51), an angel (John 5:4), the disciples (John 6:16), Jacob (Acts 7:15), a road to Gaza (Acts 8:26), Philip and the eunuch (Acts 8:38), Peter (Acts 10:20 {to get down}, 21), Paul (Acts 14:25; 18:22; 20:10), soldiers (Acts 23:10), and Festus (Acts 25:6). All other refs.: COME <2597>, DESCEND <2597>, FALL (verb) <2597>, STEP (verb) <2597>.

20 **to go on: *probainō*** [verb: προβαίνω <4260>]; **from *pro*: ahead, and *bainō*: to go ▶ To pass further on** > The verb is used of Jesus (Matt. 4:21; Mark 1:19). All other refs.: ADVANCE <4260>.

21 **to go up: *prosanabainō*** [verb: προσαναβαίνω <4320>]; **from *pros*: to, and *anabainō*: see 17 ▶ To move to a higher level (to a place of honor)** > He who had invited someone might tell him to go up {move up} higher if he had sat down in the lowest place (Luke 14:10). ¶

22 **to go down with: *sunkatabainō*** [verb: συγκαταβαίνω <4782>]; **from *sun*: together, and *katabainō*: see 19 ▶ To descend with** > Festus wanted certain men of authority to go down with him to Caesarea and accuse Paul there (Acts 25:5). ¶

23 ***poreuomai*** [verb: πορεύομαι <4198>]; **from *poros*: passage ▶ To proceed on one's way, to travel; also transl.: to depart, to journey** > Herod told the wise men to go and search diligently for the young child (Matt. 2:8). As Jesus went, many spread their clothes on the road (Luke 19:36). Other refs.: Matt. 2:9a, 20; 8:9a, b; 9:13; 10:6, 7; 11:4, 7; 12:1, 45; 17:27; 18:12; 21:2, 5, 6; 22:9; 24:1; 25:9, 16, 41; 26:14; 27:66; 28:7a, 9, 11, 16, 19; Mark 16:10, 15; Luke 1:39; 2:3, 41; 4:30, 42; 5:24; 7:6, 8a, b, 11a, 22, 50; 8:14 {to go forth, to go out}, 48; 9:13, 51, 53, 56, 57; 10:37, 38; 11:5, 26; 13:31, 32; 14:10; 15:4, 15, 18; 16:30; 17:11, 14a, 19; 19:12, 28; 21:8; 22:8, 22, 39; 24:13, 28a, b; John 4:50a, b; 7:35a, b, 53; 8:1, 11; 10:4; 11:11; 14:2, 3, 12, 28b; 16:7, 28; 20:17; Acts 1:10, 11, 25; 5:20; 8:26a, 27, 36, 39; 9:3; 11, 15; 10:20b; 12:17; 16:7, 16, 36; 17:14; 18:6; 19:21; 20:1, 22; 21:5 {to go one's way}; 22:5, 6,

10, 21; 23:23, 32; 24:25; 25:12, 20; 26:12, 13; 27:3; 28:26; Rom. 15:24, 25; 1 Cor. 10:27; 16:4a, b, 6; 1 Tim. 1:3; 2 Tim. 4:10; Jas. 4:13b; 1 Pet. 3:19, 22. All other refs.: DEPART <4198>, FOLLOW <4198>, TRAVEL <4198>, WALK <4198>.

24 to go through, to go by: *diaporeuomai* [verb: διαπορεύομαι <1279>]**; from *dia*: through, and *poreuomai*: see 23 ▶ To traverse a place, to pass through** > The verb is used in regard to Jesus (Luke 6:1; 13:22), the crowd (Luke 18:36 {to pass, to pass by}), and Paul and Barnabas (Acts 16:4). Other refs.: Mark 2:23 in some mss.; Rom. 15:24; see PASS <1279>. ¶

25 to go out, to go forth: *ekporeuomai* [verb: ἐκπορεύομαι <1607>]**; from *ek*: out, and *poreuomai*: see 23 ▶ a. To go out, to come forth** > Many people went out to Jesus (Matt. 3:5). Spirits of demons will go out {go forth} to the kings of the whole world to gather them for the battle of the great day of God Almighty (Rev. 16:14). Other refs.: Matt. 17:21; 20:29; Mark 1:5; 10:17, 46; 11:19; 13:1; Luke 3:7; John 5:29; Acts 9:28. **b. To come from, to proceed** > All bore witness to Jesus and wondered at the words of grace that were coming out of His mouth (Luke 4:22). Man will live by every word that goes out of the mouth of God (Matt. 4:4). The things that go forth out of the mouth come from the heart, and these things defile a man (Matt. 15:11, 18; Mark 7:15, 20, 21, 23). No corrupt word is to go out of our mouth (Eph. 4:29). John saw a river of water of life, bright as crystal, going out of the throne of God and of the Lamb (Rev. 22:1). **c. To come out** > What enters a man goes out {is eliminated} from his body (Mark 7:19). Other refs.: Rev. 1:16; 4:5; 9:17, 18; 11:5; 19:15, 21. All other refs.: DEPART <1607>, PROCEED <1607>, SPREAD <1607>.

26 to go before: *proporeuomai* [verb: προπορεύομαι <4313>]**; from *pro*: before, in front, and *poreuomai*: see 23 ▶ To precede, to walk before** > John the Baptist would go before the face of the Lord to prepare His ways (Luke 1:76). The Israelites asked Aaron to make them gods who would go before them (Acts 7:40). ¶

27 to go along with: *sumporeuomai* [verb: συμπορεύομαι <4848>]**; from *sun*: together, and *poreuomai*: see 23 ▶ To go together, to travel with** > Great multitudes went with Jesus (Luke 7:11b; 14:25). Other refs.: Mark 10:1 {to gather}; Luke 24:15 {to walk along}. ¶

28 to go to, into: *apeimi* [verb: ἄπειμι <549>]**; from *apo*: from, and *eimi*: to go ▶ To enter** > Paul and Silas went into the synagogue of Berea (Acts 17:10). ¶

29 to go in, to go into: *eiseimi* [verb: εἴσειμι <1524>]**; from *eis*: into, and *eimi*: to go ▶ To enter, to penetrate** > The priests always went into {entered} the first part of the tabernacle to accomplish the services (Heb. 9:6). Other refs.: Acts 3:3; 21:18, 26. ¶

30 to go out: *exeimi* [verb: ἔξειμι <1826>]**; from *ek*: out, and *eimi*: to be ▶ To depart, to leave** > The verb is used in Acts 13:42 concerning Paul and Barnabas going out of the synagogue. All other refs.: DEPART <1826>, GET <1826>.

31 to go through, throughout, around: *diodeuō* [verb: διοδεύω <1353>]**; from *dia*: through, and *hodeuō*: to travel, which is from *hodos*: way ▶ To traverse, to travel about** > Jesus went through every city and every village (Luke 8:1). Other ref.: Acts 17:1 (to pass through); see PASS <1353>. ¶

32 to go down: *epiduō* [verb: ἐπιδύω <1931>]**; from *epi*: upon, and *dunō*: to set ▶ To disappear behind the horizon** > We should not let the sun go down {set upon} on our wrath (Eph. 4:26). ¶

33 *paraginomai* [verb: παραγίνομαι <3854>]**; from *para*: near, and *ginomai*: to become ▶ To come to join** > The nephew of Paul went and entered into the fortress and told him about an ambush against him (Acts 23:16). Other refs.: COME <3854>.

34 to go on: *pherō* [verb: φέρω <5342>]**; lit.: to carry ▶ To progress** > Christians should go on to full growth (Heb. 6:1). All other refs.: see entries in Lexicon at <5342>.

35 to go into: *chōreō* [verb: χωρέω <5562>]**; from *chōros*: space, region ▶ To pass into** > Whatever goes into {enters} the mouth goes into the stomach (Matt.

15:17). All other refs.: see entries in Lexicon at <5562>.
– 36 Matt. 2:12, 13, 22; 9:24; 14:13; 15:21; 27:5; Acts 23:19; 26:31 → to go apart, aside, away → DEPART <402> 37 Matt. 2:12; Acts 5:22; et al. → to go back → RETURN (verb) <344> <390> <5290> 38 Matt. 8:25 → to go down → PERISH <622> 39 Matt. 8:31 in some mss.; Acts 15:33 in some mss. → to go away, to let go → SEND <649> 40 Matt. 8:34; 12:9; 15:29 → to go away, to go on → DEPART <3327> 41 Matt. 9:9, 27; 20:30; John 9:1 → to go on, to go by, to go along → to pass on → PASS <3855> 42 Matt. 10:23 → to go through, to go over, to finish going through → FINISH <5055> 43 Matt. 13:2; 14:22; Luke 8:37 → to go into → to get into → GET INTO <1684> 44 Matt. 13:53 → to go away → DEPART <3332> 45 Matt. 15:17 → to go out → ELIMINATE <1544> 46 Matt. 25:8 → to go out → QUENCH <4570> 47 Matt. 27:62 → to go to → GATHER <4863> 48 Matt. 28:16 → to tell to go → APPOINT <5021> 49 Mark 1:16; 12:38; Luke 20:46; John 7:1; 21:18; Rev. 16:15 → to go; to go about, around, along → WALK <4043> 50 Mark 1:36 → to go after, to go to look for → to follow after → FOLLOW <2614> 51 Mark 2:23; 9:30 → to go through → to pass through → PASS <3899> 52 Luke 2:29; Acts 13:3 → to go, to let go → DEPART <630> 53 Luke 10:7 → PASS <3327> 54 Luke 16:9 → FAIL <1587> 55 Luke 16:26 → PASS <1224> 56 Luke 19:11 → to go on → ADD <4369> 57 John 5:4 → to go in → to step in → STEP (verb) <1684> 58 John 6:22; 18:15 → to go with → to enter with → ENTER <4897> 59 John 7:19, 20; Acts 21:31; 27:30; Rom. 10:3 → to go about → SEEK <2212> 60 Acts 9:23 → to go by → PAST <4137> 61 Acts 9:29 → to go about → SEEK <2021> 62 Acts 15:30 → to let go → DISMISS <630> 63 Acts 19:10 → to go on → CONTINUE <1096> 64 Acts 19:13 → to go here and there, about, around, from place to place → ITINERANT <4022> 65 Acts 20:13 → to go by land → to go on foot → FOOT[1] <3978> 66 Acts 21:2 → to go aboard → BOARD (verb) <1910> 67 Acts 26:21 → to go about → TRY[1] <3987> 68 Acts 27:32 → let it go → let it fall away → FALL (verb) <1601> 69 Rom. 3:12 → to go out of the way → to turn aside → TURN (verb) <1578> 70 Rom. 6:1 → to go on → CONTINUE <1961> 71 Rom. 12:16 → to go along → ASSOCIATE (verb) <4879> 72 1 Cor. 4:6 → to go beyond → lit.: to think above → THINK <5426> 73 1 Cor. 7:15a, b → to go away → DEPART <5563> 74 1 Tim. 5:13; Heb. 11:37 → to go about, to go around → WANDER <4022> 75 Heb. 5:2; 1 Pet. 2:25 → to go astray → ASTRAY <4105> 76 Heb. 6:20 → who went before → lit.: as a forerunner → FORERUNNER <4274> 77 2 Pet. 3:4 → to go on → REMAIN <1265>.

GO (LET) – Mark 7:8 → to lay aside → LAY <863>.

GO TO NOW – Jas. 4:13; 5:1 → COME NOW <33>.

GOAD – Acts 26:14 → STING (noun) <2759>.

GOAL – 1 Luke 13:32; Phil. 3:12 → to reach one's goal, to arrive at the goal → to be perfected → PERFECT (verb) <5048> 2 Rom. 9:31 → have not attained their goal → lit.: have not attained a law of righteousness 3 2 Cor. 5:9 → to make one's goal → LABOR (verb) <5389> 4 2 Cor. 8:14 → the goal is equality → lit.: so as there may be equality 5 Gal. 3:3 → to try to attain one's goal → to make perfect → PERFECT (adj.) <2005> 6 Phil. 3:14 → MARK (noun) <4649> 7 Col. 2:2 → "my goal is" added in Engl.

GOAT – 1 ***eriphos*** [masc. noun: ἔριφος <2056>] ► **Domesticated bovid ruminant, a caprine animal, particularly an adult male; also: a kid** > As a shepherd separates the sheep from the goats, the Son of Man will separate the just from the unjust when He comes in His glory (Matt. 25:32). The brother of the prodigal son told his father he had never been given a young goat {a kid} to make merry with his friends (Luke 15:29); some mss. have *aix*, others have 2. ¶

2 ***eriphion*** [neut. noun: ἐρίφιον <2055>]; **dimin. of 1 ▶ Small goat** > The Son of Man in His glory will set the sheep on His right hand, and the goats on His left (Matt. 25:33). The goats designate those who will have refused to receive the messengers of the Lord during His reign (see vv. 41–43). ¶

3 ***tragos*** [masc. noun: τράγος <5131>]; **poss. from *trōgō*: to graze ▶ Male domesticated bovid ruminant** > Christ did not enter in the most holy place with the blood of goats and calves (Heb. 9:12); this blood sanctified for the purifying of the flesh (v. 13). Moses took the blood of calves and goats, and sprinkled the book of the law and the people (Heb. 9:19). It is not possible that the blood of bulls and goats take away sins (Heb. 10:4). ¶

4 **of a goat: *aigeios*** [adj.: αἴγειος <122>]; **from *aix*: goat ▶ Which belongs to a goat** > O.T. people of faith wandered about in sheepskins and goatskins (lit.: skins of goats) (Heb. 11:37). ¶

– 5 Rev. 6:12 → made of goat hair → lit.: made of hair → HAIR <5155>.

GOATSKIN – Heb. 11:37 → lit.: skin of goat → GOAT <122>, SKIN <1192>.

GOD – ***Theos*** [masc. noun used as name: Θεός <2316>] **▶ The supreme, eternal Being** > God is known by His works in His eternal power and His divinity (Rom. 1:19, 20; Ps. 19:1). He is the Lord God, the Almighty (Rev. 4:8). He is God in three Persons: Father, Son, and Holy Spirit. He has revealed Himself in the Person of the Lord Jesus Christ, who is God manifested in flesh, the Word of God become flesh (John 1:13, 14; 1 Tim. 3:16). "God is love" (1 John 4:8, 16; see John 3:16); "God is light" (1 John 1:5). He reveals Himself to all the Christians by the gracious name of Father (John 20:17). The principal characteristics and attributes of God mentioned in the Scriptures are: His eternal being (Is. 57:15; 1 Tim. 1:17), immortality (1 Tim. 6:16; Ps. 90:2), omnipotence (Job 11:7; Rom. 1:20), sovereignty (1 Tim. 6:15), invisibility (1 Tim. 1:17; 6:16), omnipresence (Ps. 139:7–10; Jer. 23:23, 24), omniscience (1 Chr. 28:9; Jer. 1:5; Rom. 8:29, 30; Heb. 4:13), incorruptibility (Rom. 1:23; James 1:13), immutability (Mal. 3:6; James 1:17), wisdom (Ps. 104:24; Rom. 11:33–36), holiness (Amos 4:2; Luke 1:49), righteousness (Rom. 2:5–7; 2 Tim. 4:8), grace and mercy (Luke 1:50; Rom. 3:24; Eph. 2:4), patience (Rom. 2:4; 15:5), and faithfulness (Ps. 92:2; 1 Cor. 1:9). How blessed to be able to say with the Psalmist: "This is our God for ever and ever" (Ps. 48:14). (After Walter Scott.) *

GOD (other god) – 1 ***daimonion*** [neut. noun: δαιμόνιον <1140>]; **dimin. of *daimōn*: demon ▶ Pagan divinity** > Philosophers from Athens were saying that Paul seemed to be a proclaimer of foreign gods {demons, deities} (Acts 17:18). All other refs.: DEMON <1140>.

2 ***theos*** [masc. noun: θεός <2316>] **▶ Superior spiritual being or its representation** > God calls gods those to whom the word of God came (John 10:34, 35; citing Ps. 82:6). The Israelites asked Moses to make them gods to go before them (Acts 7:40); they took up the star of their god Remphan (v. 43). The people kept shouting that the voice of Herod was the voice of a god and not of a man (Acts 12:22). People in Lystra said about Paul and Barnabas that the gods had come down to them (Acts 14:11). Paul saw in Athens an altar to the unknown god (Acts 17:23). He was saying that the gods of the Ephesians were not gods (Acts 19:26). The natives of Malta said that Paul was a god (Acts 28:6). Paul speaks of those who are called gods in heaven or on earth (1 Cor. 8:5a, b). The god of this age (Satan) has veiled the thoughts of the unbelievers (2 Cor. 4:4). Before their conversion, the Galatians were serving those that by nature are not gods (Gal. 4:8). The god of some was their belly; they had set their mind on earthly things (Phil. 3:19). See GOD <2316>.

GOD-BREATHED – 2 Tim. 3:16 → DIVINELY INSPIRED <2315>.

GOD-FEARING – [1] ***theosebēs*** [adj.: θεοσεβής <2318>]; **from *Theos*: God, and *sebomai*: to venerate, to worship ▶ Demonstrating respect and reverence toward God; see GODLINESS** > A blind man who had been healed by Jesus said that God hears anyone who is God-fearing {a worshipper of God, a godly man} (John 9:31). ¶
– [2] Acts 2:5 → DEVOUT <2126> [3] Acts 10:2, 22; 13:26 → FEAR (verb) <5399> [4] Acts 13:43, 50; 17:4 → WORSHIP (verb) <4576>.

GOD (WITHOUT) – ***atheos*** [adj.: ἄθεος <112>]; **from *a*: neg., and *theos*: god ▶ Not believing in a supreme being, atheist; also, being given up by God, thus not having fellowship with Him** > The Gentiles had no hope and were without God in the world (Eph. 2:12). ¶

GODDESS – [1] ***thea*** [fem. noun: θεά <2299>]; **fem. of *theos*: god ▶ Female god** > Diana (or: Artemis) was a Greek goddess, particularly revered in Ephesus (Acts 19:27, 35 in some mss., 37). ¶
– [2] Acts 28:4 → goddess Justice → JUSTICE <1349>.

GODHEAD – [1] ***theiotēs*** [fem. noun: θειότης <2305>]; **from *Theos*: God ▶ Term which characterizes the nature of God and His infinite power** > The eternal power and Godhead {divinity, divine nature} of God are understood by the things that are made (Rom. 1:20). ¶
[2] ***theotēs*** [fem. noun: θεότης <2320>]; **from *Theos*: God ▶ God, in all the plenitude of His being, without restriction** > In Christ dwells all the fullness of the Godhead {Deity} bodily (Col. 2:9). ¶
– [3] Acts 17:29 → Divine Nature → DIVINE <2304>.

GODLESS – [1] Acts 2:23 → LAWLESS (adj.) <459> [2] 1 Tim. 4:7; 6:20; 2 Tim. 2:16; Heb. 12:16 → PROFANE (adj. and noun) <952> [3] 1 Pet. 4:18 → UNGODLY <765> [4] 2 Pet. 2:7 → LAWLESS MAN <113>.

GODLESSNESS – Rom. 1:18; 11:26; 2 Tim. 2:16 → UNGODLINESS <763>.

GODLINESS – [1] ***eusebeia*** [fem. noun: εὐσέβεια <2150>]; **from *eusebēs*: devout, godly, which is from *eu*: well, and *sebomai*: to experience a sense of religious fear, to adore ▶ Living relationship of the Christian with God characterized by fear, respect, and confidence; also transl.: piety** > Peter did not make the lame man walk by his own godliness {holiness} (Acts 3:12). The Christian is to pray that he may lead a quiet life in all godliness (1 Tim. 2:2). The mystery of godliness is related to all that concerns the person of Christ (1 Tim. 3:16). Timothy was to exercise himself unto godliness {to be godly} (1 Tim. 4:7), for godliness is profitable for everything (v. 8). The teaching of Jesus Christ is according to godliness (1 Tim. 6:3). Corrupted men esteem godliness to be a source of gain (1 Tim. 6:5); but for the Christian piety is a great gain (v. 6) and is to be pursued (v. 11). In the last days, men will have nothing more than the form of godliness (2 Tim. 3:5). Knowledge of the truth is also according to godliness (Titus 1:1). Peter speaks of godliness that characterizes Christian conduct (2 Pet. 1:3, 6, 7; 3:11). ¶
[2] ***theosebeia*** [fem. noun: θεοσέβεια <2317>]; **from *theosebēs*: God-fearing, devout, which is from *Theos*: God, and *sebomai*: see [1] ▶ Fear of God, piety, reverence toward God** > Good works are proper for women professing godliness (1 Tim. 2:10). ¶
– [3] 1 Tim. 5:4 → PIETY <2151>.

GODLY – [1] ***eusebōs*** [adv.: εὐσεβῶς <2153>]; **from *eusebēs*: devout, godly, which is from *eu*: well, and *sebomai*: to venerate, to adore ▶ With reverence toward God, piously** > All who desire to live godly (i.e., a godly life) in Christ will be persecuted (2 Tim. 3:12). Christians are called to live godly (i.e., godly lives) (Titus 2:12). ¶
– [2] John 9:31 → a godly man → lit.: God-fearing → GOD-FEARING <2318> [3] Acts 8:2 → DEVOUT <2126> [4] 1 Tim. 2:2;

4:7; 6:3; 2 Pet. 1:3 → godly in every way, to be godly, godly life → lit.: in all godliness, unto godliness, life and godliness → GODLINESS <2150> [5] Heb. 5:7 → godly fear → PIETY <2124> [6] Heb. 11:7 → to be moved with godly fear → to be moved with fear → FEAR (noun) <2125> [7] Heb. 12:28 in some mss. → godly fear → FEAR (noun) <1189a> [8] 2 Pet. 2:9 → DEVOUT <2152>.

GOD'S HOLY PEOPLE – Rev. 13:7; 17:6; 18:24; 19:8 → lit.: saints → SAINT <40>.

GOD'S PEOPLE – [1] 1 Thes. 5:26 → lit.: brothers → BROTHER <80> [2] 2 Tim. 2:14 → "God's people" added in Engl. [3] Rev. 5:8; 8:3, 4; 13:10 → lit.: saints → SAINT <40>.

GOG – ***Gōg*** [masc. name: Γώγ <1136>]; **from Gog, the chief prince of Meshech and Tubal in Ezek. 38:2; 39:1 ▶ Gog and Magog are the symbolical names of nations that are enemies of God** > Gog and Magog will be gathered together by Satan at the end of the millennium for the great battle (Rev. 20:8). The fire of God will come down from heaven and devour them (see Rev. 20:9). ¶

GOING – Jas. 1:11 → PURSUIT <4197>.

GOING FORTH – Heb. 11:22 → DEPARTURE <1841>.

GOLD (adj.) – [1] 2 Tim. 2:20; Rev. 21:15; et al. → gold, in gold, of gold → GOLDEN <5552> [2] Jas. 2:2 → with a gold ring → RING (noun) <5554>.

GOLD (noun) – [1] ***chrusos*** [masc. noun: χρυσός <5557>] **▶ Precious metal of a brilliant yellow color, very ductile and malleable; in virtue of its brilliance and costliness, it symbolizes divine righteousness** > The wise men offered gold, frankincense, and myrrh (Matt. 2:11). The disciples were not to provide themselves with gold or silver for the way (Matt. 10:9). Some swore by the gold of the temple (Matt. 23:16, 17a, b). The Greeks ought not to think that which is divine to be like gold (Acts 17:29). The outward dress of believing women does not consist in being adorned with gold (1 Tim. 2:9). James told the rich that their gold and silver was eaten away (Jas. 5:3). The great prostitute was adorned with gold (Rev. 17:4; 18:16). Babylon will not buy merchandise of gold any more (Rev. 18:12). Other refs.: 1 Cor. 3:12; Rev. 9:7. ¶

[2] ***chrusion*** [neut. noun: χρυσίον <5553>]; **dimin. of [1] ▶ Object or money made of gold** > Peter had neither silver nor gold (Acts 3:6). Paul had not coveted anyone's silver or gold (Acts 20:33). The ark of the covenant was completely covered in gold (Heb. 9:4). The proving of the faith of a Christian is much more precious than that of gold (1 Pet. 1:7). Christians have not been redeemed from their vain manner of life by gold (1 Pet. 1:18). The adorning of a believing woman is to be an inward adorning rather than an outward adorning consisting of wearing gold (1 Pet. 3:3). The heavenly Jerusalem was of pure gold (Rev. 21:18), as likewise its street (v. 21). Other ref.: Rev. 3:18. ¶

– [3] Matt. 18:24; 25:15, 16, 20a, b, 22a, b, 24, 25, 28 → gold, bag of gold → lit.: talent → TALENT <5007> [4] Matt. 25:17 → two bags of gold → lit.: two.

GOLDEN – [1] ***chruseos*** [adj.: χρυσέος <5552>]; **from *chrusos*: gold; also spelled: *chrusous* ▶ Made of gold; also transl.: of gold, in gold, gold** > Paul speaks of gold vessels in a great house, i.e., Christians who honor God in the church (2 Tim. 2:20). The tabernacle had a golden censer (Heb. 9:4a), and in the ark of the covenant was the golden pot (v. 4b). The word is found many times in Revelation (1:12, 13, 20; 2:1; 4:4; 5:8; 8:3a, b; 9:13, 20; 14:14; 15:6, 7; 17:4; 21:15). ¶

– [2] Jas. 2:2 → with a golden ring → RING (noun) <5554>.

GOLGOTHA – ***Golgotha*** [proper name: Γολγοθᾶ <1115>]**: skull, in Aram. ▶ Place of the crucifixion of Jesus** > See SKULL <2898>.

GOMORRAH – ***Gomorra*** [fem. name: Γόμορρα <1116>]**: submersion, in Heb. ▶ City of the plain of the Jordan which was destroyed at the same time as Sodom; its inhabitants were destroyed because their sin was grievous (see Gen. 18:20, 21; 19:24, 25)** > Jesus recalls the fate of Sodom and Gomorrah (Matt. 10:15; Mark 6:11; see Matt. 11:23, 24 and Luke 10:12), as likewise do Paul (Rom. 9:29), Peter (2 Pet. 2:6), and Jude (v. 7). ¶

GONE – Acts 14:16 → PAST <3944>.

GONG – 1 Cor. 13:1 → BRASS <5475>.

GOOD (adj.) – 1 ***agathos*** [adj.: ἀγαθός <18>] **▶ This word defines what produces a beneficial effect, being agreeable in its character and nature** > He who would love life and see good days must keep his tongue from evil (1 Pet. 3:10). It qualifies physical objects, e.g., a tree (Matt. 7:17), the ground (Luke 8:8); morally, it is applied frequently to persons and things. God is essentially, absolutely, and perfectly good (Matt. 19:17a, b; Mark 10:18a, b; Luke 18:19a, b); His will is also good (Rom. 12:2). The word is used in relation to Jesus (John 7:12) and certain persons (Matt. 20:15 {generous}; 25:21, 23; Luke 19:17; 23:50; Acts 11:24; Titus 2:5 {kind}); in a general sense: Matt. 5:45; 12:35a, b; Luke 6:45a–c; Rom. 5:7; 1 Pet. 2:18. Christians must do what is good {useful} (Eph. 4:28), pursue what is good {kind} (1 Thes. 5:15), and become imitators of what is good (1 Pet. 3:13). Other refs.: see GOOD (adj. and noun) <18>.

2 ***kalos*** [adj.: καλός <2570>] **▶ Agreeable, beautiful, honorable** > This word is applied to various things, e.g., fruit (Matt. 3:10), a tree (Matt. 12:33a, b), the ground (Matt. 13:8, 23), fish (Matt. 13:48), the law (Rom. 7:16; 1 Tim. 1:8), every creature of God (1 Tim. 4:4), and a servant of God and the doctrine he teaches (1 Tim. 4:6a, b). It relates also to what is morally good, just, right, noble, and honorable (1 Tim. 5:10a, 25; 6:18; Titus 2:7; 3:14). Christians must do what is good {honorable, honest} (2 Cor. 13:7), hold fast what is good (1 Thes. 5:21), be zealous for good works (Titus 2:14), maintain good works (Titus 3:8a, b), provoke one another to good works (Heb. 10:24), and give a good testimony by their good works to those around them (1 Pet. 2:12). *Kalos* and *agathos* are found together in Luke 8:15: a heart which is honest {noble} (*kalos*), i.e., with the right attitude before God, and good (*agathos*), i.e., acting with goodness toward others. Timothy had confessed the good confession (of faith) in the presence of many witnesses (1 Tim. 6:12). Jesus had made a good confession before Pilate (1 Tim. 6:13). *

3 ***chrēstos*** [adj.: χρηστός <5543>]**; from *chraomai*: to use; lit.: which can be used ▶ Which is pleasant, beneficial** > Evil company corrupts good habits (1 Cor. 15:33). The word is transl. "kind" in Eph. 4:32: Christians must be kind to one another. It is transl. "gracious" in 1 Pet. 2:3: the Lord is gracious. Other ref.: Luke 6:35 {kind}. All other refs.: BETTER <5543>, EASY <5543>, GOODNESS <5543>.

– 4 Matt. 9:2, 22; 14:27; Mark 6:50; 10:49; Luke 8:48; John 16:33; Acts 23:11 → to be of good cheer, to be of good comfort → to take courage → COURAGE <2293> 5 Rom. 12:17; 1 Pet. 2:12 → HONEST <2570> 6 2 Tim. 3:3 → despiser of, hater of what is good → DESPISER <865> 7 Titus 1:8 → lover of what is good → LOVER <5358> 8 Titus 2:3 → teacher of good things → TEACHER <2567>.

GOOD (adj. and noun) – 1 **good, good thing: *agathos*** [adj. and noun: ἀγαθός <18>] **▶ Agreeable, beneficial; what is such** > God has filled the hungry with good things (Luke 1:53). Other refs.: Luke 12:18, 19; 16:25; John 5:29; Rom. 2:10; 3:8; 7:18a, 19; 8:28; 9:11; 12:9, 21; 13:3, 4; 15:2; 16:19; 2 Cor. 5:10; Gal. 6:6, 10; Eph. 6:8; Phm. 6, 14 {benefit, good deed}; Heb. 9:11; 10:1; 1 Pet. 3:11; 3 John 11b. *

2 ***eupoiia*** [fem. noun: εὐποιΐα <2140>]**; from *eu*: well, and *poieō*: to do, to make ▶ Charitable deeds** > We must not forget to do good and to share, for God is pleased with such sacrifices (Heb. 13:16). ¶

3 ***kalon***; **neut. of *kalos*** [adj. used as noun: καλός <2570>] ► **What is right, honest, valuable** > The man in Romans 7 wants to do good {practice what is right} (v. 21). Other refs.: Rom. 7:18b; Gal. 4:18b {good thing}; 6:9 {well}; Jas. 4:17.

4 **goods: *ousia*** [fem. noun: οὐσία <3776>]; **from *ousa*: being ► What one owns, possesses** > In a parable, the younger son asked his father to give him the portion of goods {the estate} that fell to him (Luke 15:12). He wasted his goods {estate, substance, possessions, wealth} in living prodigally (v. 13). ¶

5 ***skeuos*** [neut. noun: σκεῦος <4632>] ► **Object, possession** > Before anyone can plunder the goods {property} of a strong man, he must first bind the strong man (Matt. 12:29; Mark 3:27). During the tribulation, he who has his goods {stuff} in the house should not come down from the housetop to take them away (Luke 17:31). All other refs.: ARTICLE <4632>, SAIL (noun) <4632>, VESSEL[1] <4632>.

6 ***huparxis*** [fem. noun: ὕπαρξις <5223>]; **from *huparchō*: to begin, which is from *hupo*: under, and *archō* to begin, which is from *archē*: beginning; lit.: existence ► Means of existing, possession, resource; also transl.: substance** > The first Christians sold their possessions and goods {property and possessions} (Acts 2:45). Christians have in heaven a better and enduring possession {or: good} (Heb. 10:34). ¶

7 **goods: *huparchonta*** [pres. ptcp. neut. plur. of a verb: ὑπάρχοντα <5224>]; **from *huparchō*: see 6 ► Means of existing, resource; also transl.: possession, substance** > The master will establish the faithful servant over all his goods (Matt. 24:47; Luke 12:44 {all that he has}). A man delivered his goods to his servants (Matt. 25:14). Other refs.: Matt. 19:21; Luke 11:21; 12:15 {things one possesses}, 33 {what one has}; 14:33; 16:1; 19:8; 1 Cor. 13:3; Heb. 10:34 {property}. All other refs.: POSSESSIONS <5224>, SUBSTANCE <5224>.

8 **to do good: *agathoergeō*** [verb: ἀγαθοεργέω <14>]; **from *agathoergos*: doing good to benefit others, which is from *agathos*: good, and *ergon*: action, work ► To do useful and profitable things to others** > Paul told Timothy to command those who are rich in this present age to do good (1 Tim. 6:18). Other ref.: Acts 14:17 in some mss.; see 9. ¶

9 **to do good: *agathopoieō*** [verb: ἀγαθοποιέω <15>]; **from *agathopoios*: doing what is good, helpful to others, which is from *agathos*: good, and *poieō*: to do, to make ► To do useful and profitable things to others** > Jesus asked if it was lawful to do good on the Sabbath (Mark 3:4; Luke 6:9). Other refs.: Luke 6:33a, b, 35; Acts 14:17 {to show kindness}; 1 Pet. 2:15 and 20 {to do well}; 3:6 {to do what is right}, 17 {to do well}; 3 John 11. ¶

10 **to do good: *euergeteō*** [verb: εὐεργετέω <2109>]; **from *eu*: well, and *ergon*: action ► To do useful and profitable things to others** > Jesus went about doing good (Acts 10:38). ¶

11 **to be good: *ischuō*** [verb: ἰσχύω <2480>]; **from *ischus*: capacity, strength ► To be fit, to have strength** > If the salt has become insipid, it is no longer good for anything (Matt. 5:13). All other refs.: see entries in Lexicon at <2480>.

– 12 Matt. 6:22; Luke 11:34 → SINGLE <573> 13 Matt. 15:26; Mark 7:27 → MEET (adj.) <2570> 14 Matt. 16:26; Mark 8:36; Luke 9:25; 1 Cor. 14:6 → to be good → PROFIT (verb) <5623> 15 Matt. 19:10; John 16:7; 18:14 → to be for the good, to be good → PROFITABLE <4851> 16 Matt. 24:46; Luke 12:37, 38, 43; → it will be good → BLESSED <3107> 17 In Luke 6:30, Jesus said to not ask for our goods (lit.: what is our own) again from one who takes them away. 18 Luke 23:51 → good deed → DEED <4234> 19 Acts 18:18 → a good while → lit.: a considerable number of days (*hēmeras hikanas*) 20 Acts 24:13 → to make good → PROVE <3936> 21 Acts 27:22, 25 → to be of good cheer → to take heart → HEART <2114> 22 Acts 28:6 → a good while → lit.: after much (*epi polu*) 23 Rom. 1:28 → to think good → LIKE (verb) <1381> 24 Rom. 3:12 → GOODNESS <5544> 25 Rom. 16:18 → good word → smooth word → SMOOTH <5542> 26 1 Cor. 7:35 in some mss.; 10:33

→ PROFIT (noun) <4852a> [27] Gal. 4:17 → for good → COMMENDABLY <2573> [28] Gal. 6:12 → to make a good showing → SHOWING <2146> [29] Eph. 5:9 → all that is good → all goodness → GOODNESS <19> [30] 2 Thes. 3:13 → to do good → WELL (adv.) <2569> [31] 2 Tim. 2:14 → which does no good → profitable for nothing → PROFITABLE <5539> [32] 2 Tim. 3:3 → despiser of good, despiser of those that are good, hater of what is good → DESPISER <865> [33] Titus 1:8 → lover of what is good → LOVER <5358> [34] Heb. 12:10 → PROFIT (noun) <4851> [35] Jas. 2:14, 16 → PROFIT (noun) <3786> [36] 1 Pet. 2:14 → who does good → who does well → WELL <17> [37] 1 Pet. 4:19 → doing good → well doing → DOING <16> [38] 1 John 3:17 → LIVING (noun) <979>.

GOOD (adv.) – [1] **to do good: *eu*** [adv.: εὖ <2095>] ***poieō*** [ποιέω <4160>]**; from *eu*: well, and *poieō*: to do, to make ▶ To do to someone what is beneficial, helpful for that person** > Jesus told some people that they may always do good to {help} the poor (Mark 14:7).
– [2] Matt. 12:12; Luke 6:26, 27 → WELL (adv.) <2573>.

GOOD-FOR-NOTHING – Matt. 5:22 → RACA <4469>.

GOOD NEWS – [1] Mark 1:1; Acts 20:24 → GOSPEL <2098> [2] 1 Pet. 1:12, 25 → to preach the good news, good news that was preached → PREACH <2097>.

GOOD WILL – [1] ***eunoia*** [fem. noun: εὔνοια <2133>]**; from *eunoeō*: to be benevolent, which is from *eu*: well, and *nous*: mind, understanding ▶ Favorable disposition, free will; also transl.: affection, benevolence** > The husband must render to his wife the affection due her {due benevolence} (1 Cor. 7:3 in some mss.). Servants are to serve with good will {wholeheartedly} as to the Lord (Eph. 6:7). ¶
– [2] 2 Cor. 8:19 → READINESS <4288>.

GOODBYE – [1] Luke 9:61 → to say goodbye → to bid farewell → FAREWELL <657> [2] Acts 20:1; 21:6 → to say goodbye → EMBRACE <782> [3] 2 Cor. 2:13 → to say goodbye → to take leave → LEAVE (noun) <657>.

GOODLY – Jas. 2:2; Rev. 18:14 → BRIGHT <2986>.

GOODMAN – Matt. 20:11; 24:43; Mark 14:14; Luke 12:39; 22:11 → master of the house → MASTER (noun) <3617>.

GOODNESS – [1] ***agathōsunē*** [fem. noun: ἀγαθωσύνη <19>]**; from *agathos*: good ▶ Benevolence, kindness** > Paul was confident that the Romans were full of goodness (Rom. 15:14). Part of the fruit of the Spirit is goodness (Gal. 5:22). The fruit of the Spirit is in all goodness (Eph. 5:9). Paul was praying that God would fulfill all the good pleasure of His goodness {every good purpose} in the Thessalonians (2 Thes. 1:11). ¶
[2] ***chrēston*** [adj. used as noun: χρηστόν <5543>]**; neut. of *chrēstos*: good, profitable, which is from *chraomai*: to use ▶ Good quality, charity** > The goodness {kindness} of God leads to repentance (Rom. 2:4b). All other refs.: BETTER <5543>, EASY <5543>, GOOD (adj.) <5543>.
[3] ***chrēstotēs*** [fem. noun: χρηστότης <5544>]**; from *chrēstos*: see [2] ▶ Kindness, virtue** > Paul asks the man who judges if he despises the riches of the goodness of God (Rom. 2:4a). There is none who practices goodness {who does good} (Rom. 3:12). Christians should consider the goodness of God and continue in His goodness (Rom. 11:22a–c). Other refs.: GENTLENESS <5544>, KINDNESS <5544>.
– [4] Titus 1:8 → lover of goodness → LOVER <5358> [5] 2 Pet. 1:3, 5a, b → VIRTUE <703>.

GOODS – [1] Matt. 24:47; 25:14; Luke 12:44; etc. → GOODS (adj. and noun) <5224> [2] Luke 15:12, 13 → GOODS (adj. and noun) <3776> [3] Acts 16:13 → a seller of purple goods → lit.: a seller of purple

4 1 Cor. 7:30 → to have goods → POSSESS <2722>.

GORGE (noun) – Luke 3:5 → VALLEY <5327>.

GORGE (verb) – Rev. 19:21 → to be filled → FILL (verb) <5526>.

GORGEOUS – Luke 23:11 → BRIGHT <2986>.

GORGEOUSLY – gorgeous: *endoxos* [adj.: ἔνδοξος <1741>]**; from *en*: in, and *doxa*: glory ▶ Splendid, glorious >** Those who are gorgeously appareled {are splendidly clothed, wear expensive clothes} (lit.: those in gorgeous clothing) are in the courts of kings (Luke 7:25). All other refs.: GLORIOUS <1741>, HONORED <1741>.

GOSPEL – 1 *euangelion* [neut. noun: εὐαγγέλιον <2098>]**; from *euangelos*: who brings a good news, which is from *eu*: well, and *angelos*: who brings news, messenger ▶ Good news, good message; also transl.: glad tidings >** This is the gospel of the grace of God (Acts 20:24), bringing salvation (Eph. 1:13) and peace (6:15) to sinners. Its message calls for faith in the person and work of Jesus Christ (see 1 Cor. 15:1–4). The gospel of the kingdom was preached by Jesus (Matt. 4:23; 9:35; Mark 1:14), and it will be preached before the return of Christ to inaugurate the millennium (Matt. 24:14; Mark 13:10; 16:15). The everlasting gospel (Rev. 14:6) is the gospel of the kingdom; its subject is the Creator God, worthy of homage (see v. 7). We also find the exprs. "gospel of God" (Rom. 1:1; 15:16; 2 Cor. 11:7; 1 Thes. 2:2, 8, 9; 1 Pet. 4:17) and "the glorious gospel" of the blessed God (1 Tim. 1:11). In relation to the Son of God, we find the exprs. "the gospel of His Son" (Rom. 1:9), "the gospel of Jesus Christ, the Son of God" (Mark 1:1), "the gospel of our Lord Jesus Christ" (2 Thes. 1:8), "the gospel of Christ" (Rom. 15:19; 1 Cor. 9:12; 2 Cor. 2:12; 9:13; 10:14; Gal. 1:7; Phil. 1:27; 1 Thes. 3:2), and "the gospel of the glory of Christ" (2 Cor. 4:4). Paul spoke about his gospel, i.e., the gospel he was preaching (Rom. 2:16; 16:25; 2 Cor. 4:3; Gal. 1:11; 2:2; 1 Thes. 1:5; 2 Thes. 2:14; 2 Tim. 2:8). The gospel to the uncircumcised had been committed to Paul, and the gospel to the circumcised to Peter (Gal. 2:7). Other refs.: Matt. 26:13; Mark 1:15; 8:35; 10:29; 14:9; Acts 15:7; Rom. 1:16; 10:16; 11:28; 1 Cor. 4:15; 9:14, 18, 23; 2 Cor. 8:18; 11:4; Gal. 1:6; 2:5, 14; Eph. 3:6; 6:19; Phil. 1:5, 7, 12, 17; 2:22; 4:3, 15; Col. 1:5, 23; 2 Tim. 1:8, 10; Phm. 13. ¶

2 Name later given to each of the four accounts of the life of Jesus Christ narrated in the N.T. > Each Gospel presents a particular aspect of the person of Christ: Matthew presents the King of Israel; Mark, the humble and perfect Servant; Luke, the Son of Man; John, the Son of God.

3 For the expr. "to preach the gospel," see PREACH <2097> <4283>.

– 4 Phil. 1:14 → to proclaim the gospel → lit.: to speak the word → WORD <3056>.

GOSSIP (noun) – 1 Rom. 1:29 → WHISPERER <5588> 2 2 Cor. 12:20 → WHISPERING <5587> 3 1 Tim. 3:11; 2 Tim. 3:3; Titus 2:3 → malicious gossip → false accuser → ACCUSER <1228> 4 1 Tim. 5:13 → TATTLER <5397>.

GOSSIP (verb) – 3 John 10 → to gossip maliciously → PRATE <5396>.

GOSSIPER – 1 Tim. 5:13 → TATTLER <5397>.

GOUGE – 1 Matt. 5:29; 18:9 → to gouge out → to pluck out → PLUCK <1807> 2 Gal. 4:15 → PLUCK <1846>.

GOVERN – 1 Luke 2:2 → to be the governor → GOVERNOR <2230> 2 Luke 22:26 → he who governs → LEADER <2233> 3 Rom. 8:6a, b, 7 → "governed" added in Engl.

GOVERNING – from *huperechō* [verb: ὑπερέχω <5242>]**: to surpass, which is from *huper*: over, above, and *echō*: to have ▶ Which is above >** Every soul should be subject to the governing authorities {higher powers} for they are established by God (Rom. 13:1). All other refs.: AUTHORITY <5242>, EXCELLENCE <5242>, IMPORTANT <5242>, SURPASS <5242>.

GOVERNMENT – [1] Luke 2:2 → to have the government → to be the governor → GOVERNOR <2230> [2] Luke 3:1 → REIGN <2231> [3] 1 Cor. 12:28 → ADMINISTRATION <2941> [4] 2 Pet. 2:10 → DOMINION <2963>.

GOVERNOR – [1] ***ethnarchēs*** [masc. noun: ἐθνάρχης <1481>]; **from *ethnos*: people, nation, and *archō*: to begin, to reign, which is from *archē*: beginning, domination; lit.: ethnarch ▶ Ruler of people, chief** > The governor {ethnarch} of the king was guarding Damascus in order to arrest Paul (2 Cor. 11:32). ¶

[2] ***hēgemōn*** [masc. noun: ἡγεμών <2232>]; **from *hēgeomai*: to lead, to administer ▶ He to whom one has entrusted an administration** > This term is used in a general manner in Matt. 2:6; 10:18; Mark 13:9; Luke 20:20; 21:12; 1 Pet. 2:14. Roman governors bore the title of procurators and exercised civil and military authority: Pontius Pilate (Matt. 27:2, 11a, b, 14, 15, 21, 23, 27; 28:14), Felix (Acts 23:24, 26, 33; 24:1, 10), and Porcius Festus (Acts 26:30). ¶

[3] **to be the governor: *hēgemoneuō*** [verb: ἡγεμονεύω <2230>]; **from *hēgemōn*: governor, ruler ▶ To guide, to direct; also transl.: to govern, to have the government** > Cyrenius had the government of Syria when a census took place (Luke 2:2). Pontius Pilate was governor of Judea (Luke 3:1; *epitropeuō* in some mss.: to be the administrator). ¶

[4] **to govern: *hēgeomai*** [verb: ἡγέομαι <2233>]; **from *agō*: to lead ▶ To rule, to administer** > Pharaoh established Joseph governor (lit.: governing) over Egypt and all his house (Acts 7:10). All other refs.: see entries in Lexicon at <2233>.

– [5] Matt. 2:6 → RULER <2232> [6] Gal. 4:2 → STEWARD <3623>.

GOVERNOR OF THE FEAST – John 2:8, 9a, b → FEAST (noun) <755>.

GOVERNOR'S HEADQUARTERS – Matt. 27:27a; Mark 15:16; John 18:28a, b → PRAETORIUM <4232>.

GRAB – Matt. 18:28 → SEIZE <2902>.

GRACE – [1] ***charis*** [fem. noun: χάρις <5485>]; **from *chairō*: to rejoice; the word *chara* (joy) is also derived from *chairō* ▶ Unmerited favor which God, in His love, extends to the sinner who repents** > Grace is a "favor done without expectation of return; the absolutely free expression of the loving kindness of God to men finding its only motive in the bounty and benevolence of the Giver; unearned and unmerited favor. *Charis* stands in direct antithesis to *erga*, works, the two being mutually exclusive. God's grace affects man's sinfulness and not only forgives the repentant sinner, but brings joy and thankfulness to him. It changes the individual to a new creature without destroying his individuality (2 Cor. 5:17; Eph. 2:8, 9)." (S. Zodhiates). The grace of God brings salvation to the sinner (Eph. 2:5, 8; Titus 2:11), justifying him freely (Rom. 3:24; Titus 3:7). Grace and truth came (sing. in Greek) by Jesus Christ (John 1:17); these divine traits are closely linked to the person of Jesus. Grace also accompanies Christians during their life on earth (e.g., 1 Cor. 15:10a–c; 2 Cor. 12:9) and they can be strong in grace (2 Tim. 2:1). To find grace means to find favor, e.g., as in the case of David before God (Acts 7:46). To give thanks (*eucharisteō*) to God means to thank Him, a verb frequently found in the epistles of Paul (e.g., 1 Thes. 1:1). God also grants a gift of grace to each Christian for His service, for the benefit of other Christians, and for the formation and edification of the church. The term is also used in the expr. of greetings, e.g., "Grace be with you all" (Col. 4:18; Heb. 13:25; et al.). Other refs.: see entries in Lexicon at <5485>.

[2] ***euprepeia*** [fem. noun: εὐπρέπεια <2143>]; **from *euprepēs*: beautiful, decent, which is from *eu*: well, and *prepō*: to be**

suitable ▶ Beauty, noble appearance > The grace {comeliness} (*euprepeia*) of the appearance (*prosōpon*) of the flower has perished with the burning heat of the sun (Jas. 1:11). ¶
– 3 2 Cor. 2:7 → to show grace → FORGIVE <5483> 4 Eph. 1:6 → to bestow, to give one's grace freely → to make accepted → ACCEPTED <5487>.

GRACIOUS – 1 Matt. 11:26; Luke 10:21 → to be the gracious will → to be well-pleasing → WELL PLEASING <2107> 2 Acts 2:27; 13:35 → gracious one → HOLY (noun) <3741> 3 Col. 4:6 → with grace → GRACE <5485> 4 1 Pet. 2:3 → GOOD (adj.) <5543> 5 1 Pet. 2:19, 20 → gracious thing → ACCEPTABLE <5485>.

GRAFT – ***enkentrizō*** [verb: ἐγκεντρίζω <1461>]; **from *en*: in, and *kentrizō*: to goad, to graft, which is from *kentron*: goad, sting; lit.: to sting in ▶ To insert a shoot of a cultivated tree into the stem of a wild tree; the branch continues to grow there and becomes a permanent part of it >** Paul speaks of the Christians among the Gentiles as branches of a wild olive tree having been grafted into a cultivated olive tree, an image of Israel (Rom. 11:17, 19, 23a, b, 24a, b), which is contrary to the normal process. ¶

GRAFTED – Jas. 1:21 → IMPLANTED <1721>.

GRAIN – 1 ***genēma*** [neut. noun: γένημα <1079a>]; **from *gennaō*: to give birth, which is from *genna*: birth, race ▶ That which the earth produces, the fruit of agriculture >** A man was going to lay up all his grain {produce, fruits, crops} and his goods in greater barns (Luke 12:18 in some mss.; other mss. have *sitos*). All other refs.: FRUIT <1079a>.
2 **head of grain, head: *stachus*** [masc. noun: στάχυς <4719>]**▶ Tip of the stalk of certain cereal plants; also transl.: ear of corn >** The disciples plucked heads of grain and ate them (Matt. 12:1; Mark 2:23; Luke 6:1). The earth produces the blade, then the head of grain, after the full grain in the head of grain (Mark 4:28a, b). ¶
– 3 Matt. 13:8; Mark 4:8 → FRUIT <2590> 4 Matt. 13:26 → BLADE <5528> 5 Mark 4:28; Acts 27:38 → WHEAT <4621> 6 Luke 12:19 → lit.: goods → GOOD (adj. and noun) <18> 7 Acts 7:12 → CORN <4621> 8 Heb. 11:12 → "grains of" added in Engl.

GRAIN OF MUSTARD – ***kokkos sinapeōs***; ***kokkos*** [masc. noun: κόκκος <2848>]; ***sinapi*** [neut. noun: σίναπι <4615>] **▶ Kernel of seed of a plant, black or white mustard, which abounds in Israel; its size is approx. three millimeters (0.1 inch), which makes it the smallest grain of seed among those that were sown in N.T. times >** Since the plant can attain a height of more than ten feet (three meters) and attract birds, Jesus uses it in the parable of the sower, in order to illustrate the rapid development of the kingdom of the heavens (Matt. 13:31; Mark 4:31; Luke 13:19). Those who have faith as a grain of mustard seed (Matt. 17:20; Luke 17:6) may have very little faith, but they realize great things for God because they rely on Him. All other refs. (*kokkos*): see GRAIN OF WHEAT <2848> <4621>.

GRAIN OF WHEAT – ***kokkos tou sitou***; ***kokkos*** [masc. noun: κόκκος <2848>]; ***sitos*** [masc. noun: σῖτος <4621>] **▶ Cereal originating from the Middle East; wheat is used for making bread >** Man sows a bare grain of wheat (1 Cor. 15:37), but God gives it a body (see v. 38). Jesus compares Himself to a grain of wheat that, after it has fallen into the ground, dies; but if it dies, it bears much fruit (John 12:24). Satan can seek to sift a believer in the Lord like wheat, to make his faith falter (Luke 22:31). All other refs. (*kokkos*): see GRAIN OF MUSTARD <2848>. All other refs. (*sitos*): see CORN <4621>, WHEAT <4621>.

GRAINFIELD – Matt. 12:1; Mark 2:23; Luke 6:1 → CORN <4702>.

GRANARY – Matt. 6:26; 13:30; Luke 12:18, 24 → BARN <596>.

GRANDCHILD – ***ekgonos*** [adj. used as noun: ἔκγονος <1549>]; **from *ekginomai*: to be born of, which is from *ek*: out, and *ginomai*: to become, to be born ▶ Child of one's son or daughter; also transl.: descendant, nephew** > Children and grandchildren must learn to repay their parents, especially if the parent is a widow (1 Tim. 5:4). ¶

GRANDEE – Mark 6:21 → LORD (noun) <3175>.

GRANDMOTHER – ***mammē*** [fem. noun: μάμμη <3125>]; **an infant's word for *mamma*: mom, mother, and later: grandmother ▶ Mother of a mother or a father** > Genuine faith dwelt in Lois, the grandmother of Timothy (2 Tim. 1:5). ¶

GRANDPARENT – 1 Tim. 5:4 → parents and grandparents → lit.: parents → PARENT <4269>.

GRANT – [1] ***didōmi*** [verb: δίδωμι <1325>] ▶ **To give, to allow** > James and John asked Jesus to grant them to {let them} sit at His right hand and His left hand in His glory (Mark 10:37). The Lord granted {enabled} that signs and wonders be done by Paul and Barnabas (Acts 14:3). Other refs.: GIVE <1325>.

[2] ***charizomai*** [verb: χαρίζομαι <5483>]; **from *charis*: grace, favor, which is from *chairō*: to rejoice ▶ To give (what is requested) as a favor** > The Jews asked for a murderer to be granted {be released} to them (Acts 3:14). All other refs.: DELIVER <5483>, FORGIVE <5483>, GIVE <5483>.

– [3] Matt. 20:21 → SPEAK <2036> [4] Mark 15:45; 2 Pet. 1:3, 4 → GIVE <1433> [5] Luke 22:29a, b → APPOINT <1303> [6] John 5:26 → GIVE <1325> [7] Acts 2:19 → SHOW (verb) <1325> [8] Acts 7:17 → PROMISE (verb) <3660> [9] Acts 24:27 → ACQUIRE <2698> [10] Col. 4:1 → GIVE <3930> [11] 2 Thes. 1:7 → "to grant" added in Engl.

GRAPE – ***staphulē*** [fem. noun: σταφυλή <4718>] ▶ **Fruit of the vine from which one obtains wine** > One does not gather a bunch of grapes from thorns (Matt. 7:16) or from a bramble (Luke 6:44); accordingly, a good or wicked man is recognized by the good or wicked fruit which he brings forth. An angel gathered the bunches of the vine of the earth and cast the bunches of grapes into the great wine-press of the fury of God (Rev. 14:18), which refers to a future divine judgment on unbelieving people. ¶

GRAPE HARVEST – Rev. 14:19 → VINE <288>.

GRASP – [1] Luke 9:45 → PERCEIVE <143> [2] Luke 18:34 → KNOW <1097> [3] Eph. 3:18 → COMPREHEND <2638> [4] Phil. 2:6 → thing to be grasped → ROBBERY <725>.

GRASS – ***chortos*** [masc. noun: χόρτος <5528>] ▶ **a. Thin green plant growing in the fields** > God clothes the grass of the fields (Matt. 6:30; Luke 12:28). Jesus commanded the crowd to sit down on the grass (Matt. 14:19; John 6:10), on the green grass (Mark 6:39). In 1 Cor. 3:12, grass {hay} represents work without value which will be burned up. Hail and fire mixed with blood burned up all the green grass (Rev. 8:7). The locusts were not to harm the grass of the earth (Rev. 9:4). Other refs.: Jas. 1:10, 11; 1 Pet. 1:24a–c. **b. Blade of corn** > The earth produce first the blade {stalk}, then the head, then the mature grain in the head (Mark 4:28). Other ref.: Matt. 13:26; see BLADE <5528>. ¶

GRATEFUL – Heb. 12:28 → let us be grateful → lit.: let us have grace → GRACE <5485>.

GRATIFY – [1] Mark 15:15 → CONTENT (verb) <2425> <4160> [2] Gal. 5:16 → FULFILL <5055> [3] Eph. 2:3 → FULFILL <4160>.

GRATITUDE – Acts 24:3 → THANKFULNESS <2169>.

GRATUITOUSLY – Matt. 10:8a, b; 2 Cor. 11:7 → FREELY <1432>.

GRAVE (adj.) – ***semnos*** [adj.: σεμνός <4586>]; **from *sebomai*: to honor, to venerate ▶ Serious, worthy of respect; also transl.: dignified, man of dignity, reverent** > The deacons must be grave (1 Tim. 3:8), as likewise their wives (1 Tim. 3:11) and older men (Titus 2:2). Other ref.: Phil. 4:8; see NOBLE <4586>. ¶

GRAVE (noun) – 1 Matt. 27:52, 53; 28:8; Luke 11:44; John 5:28; 11:17, 31, 38; 12:17 → TOMB <3419> 2 Matt. 27:61, 64, 66; 28:1; Rom. 3:13 → TOMB <5028> 3 Rev. 11:9 → TOMB <3418>.

GRAVE (verb) – 2 Cor. 3:7 → ENGRAVE <1795>.

GRAVECLOTHES – ***keiria*** [fem. noun: κειρία <2750>] ▶ **Bands of cloth binding the limbs of a dead body** > Lazarus came forth, his feet and hands bound with graveclothes {strips of linen, wrappings} (John 11:44). ¶

GRAVEN – Acts 17:29 → graven form → FORM (noun) <5480>.

GRAVITY – ***semnotēs*** [fem. noun: σεμνότης <4587>]; **from *semnos*: honorable, venerable ▶ Seriousness, dignity; also transl.: dignified, dignity, holiness, honesty, respect, reverence** > Christians pray that they may lead tranquil and quiet lives in all godliness and gravity (1 Tim. 2:2). One who aspires to exercise oversight must have his children in subjection with all gravity (1 Tim. 3:4). Paul exhorts Titus to show gravity in teaching (Titus 2:7). ¶

GREAT – 1 ***megas*** [adj.: μέγας <3173>] ▶ **This Greek term is most often used to describe importance or size** ▶ Simon Peter's mother-in-law was suffering from a great {high} fever (Luke 4:38). Simon Peter's net was full of one hundred fifty-three great {large} fish (John 21:11). There was a great hailstorm when the temple of God in heaven was opened (Rev. 11:19). Other refs.: Matt. 2:10; 4:16; 5:19, 35; 7:27; 8:24, 26; 15:28; 20:26; 22:36, 38; 24:21, 24, 31; 27:60; 28:2, 8; Mark 4:32, 37, 39, 41; 5:11, 42; 10:43; 13:2; 14:15; 15:37; 16:4; Luke 1:15, 32; 2:9, 10; 4:25; 5:29; 6:49; 7:16; 8:37; 9:48; 13:19; 14:16; 16:26; 21:11, 23; 22:12; 23:23; 24:52; John 6:18; 7:37; 19:31; Acts 2:20; 4:33; 5:5, 11; 6:8; 7:11; 8:1, 2, 8, 9, 10a, b, 13; 10:11; 11:5, 28; 15:3; 16:26; 19:27, 28, 34, 35; 23:9; 26:24; Rom. 9:2; 1 Cor. 16:9; 1 Cor. 9:11; 2 Cor. 11:15; Eph. 5:32; 1 Tim. 3:16; 6:6; 2 Tim. 2:20; Titus 2:13; Heb. 4:14; 8:11; 10:21, 35; 11:24; 13:20; Jude 6; Rev. 1:10; 2:22; 6:4, 12, 13, 17; 7:14; 8:8, 10; 9:2, 14; 11:8, 11–13, 15, 17; 12:1, 3, 9, 10, 12, 14; 13:2, 5, 13; 14:2, 8, 18, 19; 15:1, 3; 16:1, 9, 12, 14, 17, 18a, b, 19a, b, 21a, b; 17:1, 5, 6, 18; 18:1, 2, 10, 16, 18, 19, 21a, b; 19:1, 2, 17; 20:1, 11; 21:3, 10, 12. See also entries in Lexicon at <3173>.

2 **greater, greatest: *meizōn*** [adj.: μείζων <3187>]; **compar. of *megas*: see** 1 ▶ **More important; better, larger, more, more valuable, older, superior** > Matt. 11:11a, b; 12:6; 13:32; 18:1, 4; 23:11, 17, 19; Mark 4:32; 9:34; 12:31; Luke 7:28a, b; 9:46; 12:18; 22:24, 26, 27; John 1:50; 4:12; 5:20, 36; 8:53; 10:29; 13:16a, b; 14:12, 28; 15:13, 20; Rom. 9:12; 1 Cor. 12:31; 13:13; 14:5; Heb. 6:13, 16; 9:11; 11:26; Jas. 4:6; 2 Pet. 2:11; 1 John 3:20; 4:4; 5:9. All other refs.: GREAT (adj. expressing the majesty of God) <3187>, STRICT <3187>.

3 **greater: *meizoteros*** [adj.: μειζότερος <3186>]; **double compar. of *megas*: great ▶ More important, more excellent** > Ref.: 3 John 4. ¶

4 **greatest: *megistos*** [adj.: μέγιστος <3176>]; **superl. of *megas*: great ▶ Very important, very excellent** > Ref.: 2 Pet. 1:4. ¶

5 ***hikanos*** [adj.: ἱκανός <2425>]; **from *hikneomai*: to come, to occur ▶ Considerable, important** > Mark 10:46; Luke 8:32; Acts 11:24, 26; 19:26; 22:6. Other refs.: see entries in Lexicon at <2425>.

6 ***ischuros*** [adj.: ἰσχυρός <2478>]; **from *ischuō*: to be capable ▶ Mighty** > Luke 15:14 {violent}; Heb. 5:7. All other refs.:

MAN <2478>, MIGHTY (adj.) <2478>, STRONG (adj.) <2478>.

[7] **greater: *perissoteros*** [adj.: περισσότερος <4055>]; **compar. of *perissos*: abundant, which is from *peri*: above, beyond ▶ More important** > 1 Cor. 12:23, 24.

[8] **how great: *pēlikos*** [adj.: πηλίκος <4080>] ▶ **How important** > Refs.: Gal. 6:11 {what large}; Heb. 7:4. ¶

[9] **greater: *pleiōn*** [adj.: πλείων <4119>]; **compar. of *polus*: see** [11] ▶ **Even more important** > Ref.: Heb. 3:3. Other refs.: EXCELLENT <4119>, MORE <4119>.

[10] ***pleistos*** [adj.: πλεῖστος <4118>]; **superl. of *polus*: much ▶ Immense, numerous** > All refs.: Matt. 11:20; Mark 4:1 in some mss.; 1 Cor. 14:27; see MOST <4118>.

[11] ***polus*** [adj.: πολύς <4183>] ▶ **Numerous, important** > Matt. 2:18; 4:25; 5:12; 8:1, 18, 30; 9:37; 12:15; 13:2; 14:14; 15:30; 19:2, 22; 20:29; 24:30; 26:47; Mark 3:7, 8; 5:21, 24, 38; 6:34; 8:31; 9:14; 10:22; 12:27, 37; 13:26; 14:43; Luke 5:6, 15, 29; 6:17, 23, 35; 7:11; 8:4; 9:37; 10:2; 14:25; 16:10; 21:27; 23:27; John 6:2, 5; 7:12; 12:9, 12; Acts 6:7; 11:21; 14:1; 15:7; 16:16; 17:4; 18:10; 21:40; 22:28; 23:10; 24:2, 7; 25:23; 28:10, 23, 29; Rom. 3:2; 9:22; 1 Cor. 2:3; 2 Cor. 2:4; 3:12; 6:4; 7:4; 8:2, 4, 22; Eph. 2:4; Col. 4:13; 1 Thes. 1:5, 6; 2:17; 1 Tim. 3:13; Phm. 7, 8; Heb. 10:32; 1 Pet. 1:3; Rev. 1:15; 7:9; 19:6.

[12] **so great: *tēlikoutos*** [pron.: τηλικοῦτος <5082>]; **from *hēlikos*: so great ▶ So important, such** > 2 Cor. 1:10; Heb. 2:3; Jas. 3:4; Rev. 16:18. ¶

[13] **so great: *tosoutos*** [pron.: τοσοῦτος <5118>] ▶ **Such, such a large** > Matt. 8:10; 15:33; Luke 7:9; Heb. 12:1. *

– [14] Matt. 12:40 → great fish → WHALE <2785> [15] Mark 9:42 → great millstone → lit.: millstone of a donkey (in some Greek mss.) → DONKEY <3684> [16] Mark 12:40; Luke 20:47 → greater → severer → SEVERE <4055> [17] Luke 1:58 → to show {shew} great → MAGNIFY <3170> [18] Acts 13:17 → to make great → EXALT <5312> [19] Eph. 1:19 → great power → lit.: greatness of the power → GREATNESS <3174> [20] Heb. 7:4 → how great → what large → LARGE <4080> [21] Jas. 3:1 → greater → stricter → STRICT <3187>.

GREAT (adj. expressing the majesty of Jesus and God) – [1] ***megas*** [adj.: μέγας <3173>] ▶ **Adj. which expresses the importance and excellence of a person** > Jesus was to be great (Luke 1:32). Christians look for the appearing of the glory of their great God and Savior Jesus Christ (Titus 2:13). The God of peace brought again from among the dead the great shepherd of the sheep (Heb. 13:20). All other refs.: GREAT <3173>.

[2] **greater: *meizōn*** [adj.: μείζων <3187>]; **compar. of *megas*: great ▶ See** [1]. > The woman at the well of Sychar asked Jesus if He was greater than Jacob (John 4:12). The Jews asked if He was greater than Abraham (John 8:53). Jesus said that His Father is greater than all (John 10:29) and greater than Him (14:28). God is greater than our heart (1 John 3:20). He who is in the Christian is greater than he who is in the world (1 John 4:4). All other refs.: GREAT <3187>, STRICT <3187>.

GREAT (noun) – ***megas*** [adj. used as noun: μέγας <3173>] ▶ **Person who is more important, physically or otherwise, than another** > This term is used in association with the noun "small" in Acts 8:10a; 26:22; Rev. 11:18; 13:16; 19:5, 18; 20:12. Other refs.: Matt. 20:25; Mark 10:42; Acts 8:10b. All other refs.: GREAT <3173>.

GREAT TRIBULATION – ***thlipsis megalē*; tribulation: *thlipsis*** [fem. noun: θλῖψις <2347>]; **from *thlibō*: to afflict; great: *megas*** [adj.: μέγας <3173>] ▶ **Great distress, severe trouble** > Jesus speaks of a great tribulation that will come upon the earth, such as has not been from the beginning of the world (Matt. 24:21: great tribulation; Mark 13:19: tribulation). The Jews will be mainly affected by this time of persecution and of Jacob's trouble (see Jer. 30:7). The great tribulation will take place before the Lord's return to establish His kingdom on earth. The Jews in particular, but also the nations, will suffer greatly at the hand of the antichrist (see 2 Thes. 2) invested with the power of the dragon (Satan) (see Rev. 12:13–17; 13:1–18). The gospel of the kingdom will be preached to all nations and then the great tribulation will occur (see Matt. 24:14). An innumerable crowd, come out of the great tribulation (Rev. 7:14), will give glory to God and to the Lamb (see v. 17). Great tribulation shall come upon Jezebel and those who commit adultery with her (Rev. 2:22). All other refs. (*thlipsis*): see AFFLICTION <2347>, ANGUISH <2347>, DISTRESS <2347>, TRIBULATION <2347>, TROUBLE (noun) <2347>. Other refs. (*megas*): see GREAT <3173>.

GREAT WHITE THRONE – throne: *thronos* [masc. noun: θρόνος <2362>]**; from *thraō*: to sit; great: *megas*** [adj.: μέγας <3173>]**; white: *leukos*** [adj.: λευκός <3022>] **► Seat of judgment, set up immediately after the millennium** > John saw a great white throne and Him who was sitting on it (Rev. 20:11). Before the throne will stand all those who have died in their sins (see v. 12). They are judged by the Lord according to their works and are cast into the lake of fire, for they do not have eternal life. Comp.: JUDGMENT SEAT. All other refs. (*thronos*): see THRONE <2362>. All other refs. (*megas*): see GREAT <3173>. Other refs. (*leukos*): see WHITE (adj.) <3022>.

GREATER – [1] John 3:30 → to become greater → INCREASE (verb) <837> [2] 2 Cor. 7:15; 11:23 → more greater, far greater → more abundant → ABUNDANT <4056> [3] Heb. 7:7 → BETTER <2909>.

GREATLY – [1] ***megalōs*** [adv.: μεγάλως <3171>]**; from *megas*: great ► Much, a lot** > Paul had rejoiced greatly in the Lord in regard to the Philippians (Phil. 4:10). ¶

[2] ***sphodra*** [adv.: σφόδρα <4970>]**; from *sphodros*: eager, violent ► Profoundly, exceedingly** > The disciples were greatly terrified when they heard the voice out of the cloud at the occasion of the transfiguration of Jesus (Matt. 17:23). In a parable, the bondmen were greatly {very, deeply} grieved by the behavior of one of their fellow-bondmen (Matt. 18:31). One of the rulers of the people, who was greatly {very, extremely} rich {of great wealth}, became very sorrowful when Jesus told him to sell everything and follow Him (Luke 18:23). Other ref.: Acts 6:7. All other refs.: EXCEEDINGLY <4970>.

– [3] Matt. 2:16; Luke 23:8; 2 Tim. 4:15; 2 John 4 → VERY <3029> [4] Matt. 17:15 → SEVERELY <2560> [5] Mark 5:23 → EARNESTLY <4183> [6] Mark 9:6 → greatly afraid → AFRAID <1630> [7] Mark 10:26 → EXCEEDINGLY <4057> [8] Mark 14:33 → to be greatly distressed → to be alarmed → ALARM (verb) <1568> [9] Acts 3:11 → greatly amazed, greatly wondering → AMAZED <1569> [10] Acts 16:18 → to greatly annoy → GRIEVE <1278> [11] Acts 20:12 → not moderately → MODERATELY <3357> [12] 1 Thes. 3:6; 2 Tim. 1:4 → to greatly desire → DESIRE (verb) <1971> [13] 2 Pet. 2:7 → to be greatly distressed → VEXED (BE) <2669>.

GREATNESS – [1] ***megaleiotēs*** [fem. noun: μεγαλειότης <3168>]**; from *megaleios*: glorious, magnificent, which is from *megas*: great ► Magnificence, great power; also transl.: majesty** > When Jesus rebuked the unclean spirit, all were astonished at the greatness of God (Luke 9:43). Other refs.: Acts 19:27; 2 Pet. 1:16; see MAJESTY <3168>. ¶

[2] ***megethos*** [neut. noun: μέγεθος <3174>]**; from *megas*: strong, great ► Power, importance** > Paul speaks of the exceeding greatness of the power of God toward those who believe (Eph. 1:19). ¶

[3] **exceeding greatness, surpassing greatness, surpassingly great: *huperbolē*** [fem. noun: ὑπερβολή <5236>]**; from *huperballō*: to surpass, which is from *huper*: above, and *ballō*: to throw ► Exceptional character, excellence** > On account of the exceeding greatness {abundance} of the revelations granted him, Paul had been given a thorn in the flesh (2 Cor. 12:7). All other refs.: EXCEEDINGLY

<5236>, EXCELLENCE <5236>, MEASURE (noun) <5236>.
– [4] Phil. 3:8 → surpassing greatness → EXCELLENCE <5242> [5] Heb. 1:3; 8:1 → MAJESTY <3172>.

GREECE – ***Hellas*** [fem. name: Ἑλλάς <1671>] ► **Region of Southern Europe; see ACHAIA** <882> > Paul sojourned three months in Greece (Acts 20:2; see v. 3). ¶

GREED – [1] Matt. 23:25; Luke 11:39 → ROBBERY <724> [2] Mark 7:22; Luke 12:15; Rom. 1:29; Eph. 5:3; Col. 3:5; 1 Thes. 2:5; 2 Pet. 2:3, 14 → COVETOUSNESS <4124> [3] 1 Cor. 5:11 → one who is guilty of greed → COVETOUS (noun) <4123> [4] Eph. 4:19 → full of greed → with greediness → GREEDINESS <4124>.

GREEDILY – Jude 11 → to run greedily → to give oneself up → GIVE <1632>.

GREEDINESS – [1] ***pleonexia*** [fem. noun: πλεονεξία <4124>]; **from *pleion*: more, and *hektos*: verbal adj. from *echō*: to have, to hold ► Greed, cupidity; unrestrained manner** > Paul speaks of Gentiles who have given themselves up to lewdness to work all uncleanness with greediness {with greedy unsatisfied lust, with a continual lust for more} (Eph. 4:19). All other refs.: COVETOUSNESS <4124>.
– [2] 1 Tim. 6:10 → COVET <3713>.

GREEDY – [1] **greedy for money, greedy of filthy lucre, given to filthy lucre: *aischrokerdēs*** [adj.: αἰσχροκερδής <146>]; **from *aischros*: improper, shameful, and *kerdos*: gain, profit ► Who seeks gain by dishonest means** > Deacons must not be greedy of filthy lucre {seeking gain by base mean, fond of sordid gain, pursuing dishonest gain} (1 Tim. 3:8). The same applies to the overseer (Titus 1:7). ¶
[2] **not greedy for money, not greedy of filthy lucre: *aphilarguros*** [adj.: ἀφιλάργυρος <866>]; **from *a*: neg., and *philarguros*: loving money, which is from *philos*: friend, and *arguros*: silver, money ► Not loving money, without avarice, not covetous of wealth; also transl.: free from the love of money, not a lover of money** > A man desiring the position of an overseer must not be greedy for money (1 Tim. 3:3). Other ref.: Heb. 13:5 (without covetousness); see COVETOUSNESS <866>. ¶
– [3] 1 Cor. 5:10, 11; 6:10; Eph. 5:5 → COVETOUS (noun) <4123> [4] Eph. 4:19 → greedy unsatisfied lust → GREEDINESS <4124>.

GREEK – [1] ***Hellēn*** [masc. name: Ἕλλην <1672>], ***Hellēnis*** [fem. name: Ἑλληνίς <1674>] ► **Person inhabiting Greece (*Hellas*) or of the Greek race** > The Greeks sought wisdom (1 Cor. 1:22); they symbolized the civilized pagan world of that time. Jesus cast a demon out of the daughter of a Greek woman, of the Syrophoenican race (Mark 7:26). The Jews thought that Jesus would go teach the Greeks (John 7:35a, b). Some Greeks told Philip that they wanted to see Jesus (John 12:20; see v. 21). Cyprians and Cyrenians announced the Lord Jesus to Greeks (Acts 11:20). Paul was obliged to announce the gospel to the Greeks (Rom. 1:14, 16; 1 Cor. 1:22, 24). At Iconium, a great number of Jews and Greeks believed after Paul and Barnabas preached to them (Acts 14:1). At Thessalonica, a great number of Greeks who worshiped God joined Paul and Silas (Acts 17:4). At Berea, Greek women of the upper classes were among the number of those who believed (Acts 17:12). At Athens, Paul persuaded Jews and Greeks (Acts 18:4). In Asia, particularly at Ephesus, Jews and Greeks heard the word of the Lord (Acts 19:10, 17; 20:21). Timothy was the son of a Greek father (Acts 16:1, 3), and Titus was a Greek (Gal. 2:3). The Jews accused Paul of having profaned the temple by bringing Greeks into it (Acts 21:28). Christian liberty was not to be a stumbling block for Jews or Greeks or the church of God at Corinth (1 Cor. 10:32). God does not show partiality (Rom. 2:9, 10), for all are under sin (Rom. 3:9), but He is rich in grace to save individuals from among all nations (Rom. 10:12). The church of God is one body formed of the redeemed from every origin (1 Cor. 12:13; Gal. 3:28; Col. 3:11). ¶

[2] ***Hellēnikos*** [adj.: Ἑλληνικός <1673>]; **from *Hellas*: Greece ▶ Which pertains to Greece; Greek language** > The inscription written above Jesus on the cross was in Greek, Latin, and Hebrew letters (Luke 23:38). The name of the angel of the abyss is Apollyon in Greek (Rev. 9:11). ¶

[3] ***Hellēnisti*** [adv.: Ἑλληνιστί <1676>]; **from *Hellas*: Greece ▶ Greek language** > The title above Jesus on the cross was written in Hebrew, Greek, and Latin (John 19:20). The commander was surprised that Paul knew Greek (Acts 21:37). ¶

GREEN – [1] ***hugros*** [adj.: ὑγρός <5200>]; **poss. from *huō*: to rain ▶ Moist, full of sap** > Jesus compares Himself to a green tree in regard to the things which were inflicted on Him (Luke 23:31). ¶

[2] ***chlōros*** [adj.: χλωρός <5515>]; **from *chloē*: green herb or grass ▶ a. Of the color of verdant vegetation; also transl.: pale** > Jesus commanded the crowd to sit down by companies on the green grass (Mark 6:39). In Rev. 8:7, all green grass was burned up. The scorpions of the earth were commanded not to hurt any green thing {any plant} (Rev. 9:4). **b. Pale or yellowish color like the grass when dried up** > John saw a pale {ashen} horse, and he who sat on it had the name Death (Rev. 6:8). ¶

GREET – [1] ***aspazomai*** [verb: ἀσπάζομαι <782>] **▶ To salute, to welcome; also transl.: to acclaim, to call out, to give greetings, to send greetings** > This verb is used in regard to Jesus (Mark 9:15; 15:18) as well as to the brothers (Matt. 5:47), a house (Matt. 10:12), Elizabeth (Luke 1:40), those whom the disciples met (Luke 10:4), the church of Caesarea (Acts 18:22), Paul and the brothers in Tyre (Acts 21:7), and Festus (Acts 25:13 {to pay respects}). Paul uses this verb several times: in his letters to the Romans (Rom. 16:3, 5–7, 9, 10a, b, 11a, b, 12a, b, 13–15, 16a, b, 21, 22, 23a, b), the Corinthians (1 Cor. 16:19a, b, 20a, b; 2 Cor. 13:12, 13), the Philippians (Phil. 4:21a, b, 22), the Colossians (Col. 4:10, 12, 14, 15), the Thessalonians (1 Thes. 5:26), Timothy (2 Tim. 4:19, 21), Titus (Titus 3:15a, b), Philemon (Phm. 23), and the Hebrews (Heb. 13:24a, b; assuming Paul is the author of this epistle). Peter uses this verb (1 Pet. 5:13, 14) and John also (2 John 13; 3 John 14a, b). Those who died in faith have seen the promises from afar off and embraced {welcomed} (or: greeted, saluted) them (Heb. 11:13). All other refs.: see EMBRACE <782>.

– [2] Matt. 23:7; Mark 12:38; Luke 20:46 → to be greeted → lit.: greetings → GREETINGS <783> [3] Matt. 28:9; Acts 15:23; 23:26; Jas. 1:1; 2 John 10, 11 → HAIL (verb) <5463>.

GREETINGS – [1] **greetings, respectful greetings: *aspasmos*** [masc. noun: ἀσπασμός <783>]; **from *aspazomai*: to greet, to salute ▶ Oral or written salutation** > Jesus spoke of scribes and Pharisees who loved greetings {to be greeted} in public places (Matt. 23:7; Mark 12:38; Luke 11:43; 20:46). Mary reasoned concerning the salutation of the angel (Luke 1:29). Elizabeth heard Mary's salutation (Luke 1:41, 44). Paul wrote the salutation at the end of three letters with his own hand (1 Cor. 16:21; Col. 4:18; 2 Thes. 3:17). ¶

– [2] Matt. 10:12; Rom. 16:21, 23; 1 Cor. 16:19a; 20a; 2 Tim. 4:21; et al. → to give greetings, to send greetings → GREET <782> [3] Matt. 26:49; 28:9; Luke 1:28; Acts 15:23; 23:26; Jas. 1:1; 2 John 10, 11 → greetings, to give greetings, to send greetings → HAIL (verb) <5463> [4] Acts 15:33 → with greetings → lit.: in peace → PEACE <1515>.

GRIEF – [1] Mark 14:34 → full of grief → exceedingly sorrowful → SORROWFUL <4036> [2] Luke 22:45; John 16:6, 20, 21, 22; Rom. 9:2; 2 Cor. 2:1, 3, 7; 7:10a, b; Heb. 12:11; 1 Pet. 2:19 → SORROW (noun) <3077> [3] John 16:20a; 2 Cor. 2:5; 7:9, 11; et al. → to cause grief → to cause sorrow → SORROW (noun) <3076> [4] Rom. 9:2; 1 Tim. 6:10 → SORROW (noun) <3601> [5] 1 Cor. 5:2 → to be filled with grief → MOURN <3996> [6] Heb.

13:17 → with grief → lit.: groaning → GROAN (verb) <4727> 7 Rev. 18:7a, b, 8; 21:4 → MOURNING <3997>.

GRIEVANCE – 1 Acts 19:38 → MATTER <3056> 2 1 Cor. 6:1 → MATTER <4229> 3 Col. 3:13 → COMPLAINT <3437>.

GRIEVE – 1 ***diaponeō*** [verb: διαπονέω <1278>]; **from *dia*: through (intens.), and *poneō*: to labor, which is from *ponos*: sorrow, tiredness; lit.: to trouble, to endure with difficulty ► To sadden, to irritate >** Paul was grieved {was annoyed, was annoyed greatly, was distressed, became troubled} to hear a slave girl possessed with a spirit of divination (Acts 16:18). Other ref.: Acts 4:2; see DISTURBED (BE) <1278>. ¶
2 ***odunaō*** [verb: ὀδυνάω <3600>]; **from *odunē*: grief, distress ► To be deeply saddened >** The elders of the church of Ephesus were especially grieved {pained, sorrowing} by the word which Paul had said, that they would no more see his face (Acts 20:38). All other refs.: DISTRESSED <3600>, TORMENT (verb) <3600>.
3 **to be grieved: *sullupeō*** [verb: συλλυπέω <4818>]; **from *sun*: together (intens.), and *lupeō*: to afflict, to grieve; *sun* could suggest the mingling of grief and anger ► To sadden, to afflict >** Jesus was grieved {distressed, deeply distressed} at the hardness of the hearts of those in the synagogue (Mark 3:5). ¶
– 4 Matt. 17:23; 18:31; 26:37; John 21:17; 2 Cor. 7:8; Eph. 4:30; 1 Thes. 4:13; 1 Pet. 1:6; et al. → SORROW (verb) <3076> 5 Mark 16:10; Rev. 18:11, 15 → MOURN <3996> 6 John 16:20 (to cause sorrow) → SORROW (noun) <3076> 7 2 Cor. 12:21 → BEWAIL <3996> 8 Jas. 4:9 → LAMENT <5003>.

GRIEVED – 1 Matt. 19:22; Mark 10:22 → to be grieved → to be sad → SAD <3076> 2 Matt. 26:38; Mark 14:34 → deeply grieved → exceedingly sorrowful → SORROWFUL <4036> 3 Acts 4:2 → DISTURBED (BE) <1278> 4 Heb. 3:10, 17 → to be grieved → to be angry → ANGRY <4360>.

GRIEVING – Matt. 19:22; Mark 10:22 → to be grieving → to be sad → SAD <3076>.

GRIEVINGLY – **grief: *lupē*** [fem. noun: λύπη <3077>] **► Sorrow, heartache >** We are to share our goods, not grievingly {grudgingly, reluctantly} (lit.: not of grief), but freely and joyfully (2 Cor. 9:7). All other refs.: SORROW (noun) <3077>.

GRIEVOUS – 1 Matt. 23:4; Luke 11:46 → grievous to be borne → hard to bear → HARD <1419> 2 Acts 20:29 → SAVAGE <926> 3 Acts 25:7 → SERIOUS <926> 4 Phil. 3:1 → TEDIOUS <3636> 5 Heb. 12:11 → lit.: of grief → SORROW (noun) <3077> 6 1 John 5:3 → BURDENSOME <926> 7 Rev. 16:2 → EVIL (adj.) <4190>.

GRIEVOUSLY – 1 Matt. 8:6 → TERRIBLY <1171> 2 Matt. 15:22 → SEVERELY <2560>.

GRIND – 1 ***alēthō*** [verb: ἀλήθω <229>]; **later form of *aleō*, from which *aleuron*: flour ► To crush cereal grains using a mill >** At the Lord's return to reign on earth, two women will be grinding at the mill; one will be taken and the other will be left (Matt. 24:41; Luke 17:35). ¶
– 2 Matt. 21:44; Luke 20:18 → to grind to powder → POWDER <3039> 3 Mark 9:18 → GNASH <5149> 4 Acts 7:54 → GNASH <1031>.

GRIP – 1 ***echō*** [verb: ἔχω <2192>] **► To seize, to take hold of >** Trembling and astonishment had gripped the women at the tomb of Jesus (Mark 16:8).
– 2 Luke 1:12 → SEIZE <1968> 3 Luke 7:16 → SEIZE <2983>.

GROAN (noun) – Acts 7:34; Rom. 8:26 → GROANING <4726>.

GROAN (verb) – 1 ***stenazō*** [verb: στενάζω <4727>]; **from *stenos*: narrow, pressed (by circumstances), or *stenō*: to moan, to lament ► To sigh under affliction or oppression >** Jesus groaned {sighed} and said to the deaf man: Be opened, and immediately his ears were opened (Mark 7:34). Christians, who have the first fruits of the Spirit, groan in themselves, waiting for the adoption, i.e., the redemption of their body (Rom. 8:23). While in their tent (i.e., their earthly body), Christians groan, desiring to be clothed with their heavenly dwelling (2 Cor. 5:2, 4). Christians are to obey their leaders, so they may watch over their souls with joy, and not groaning {with grief, a burden} (Heb. 13:17). Other ref.: Jas. 5:9; see COMPLAIN <4727>. ¶

[2] ***anastenazō*** [verb: ἀναστενάζω <389>]; **from *ana*: intens., and *stenazō*: see [1]; lit.: to groan deeply ▶ To sigh deeply >** Jesus groaned (lit.: groaned deeply) in His spirit in regard to those seeking a sign (Mark 8:12). ¶

[3] **to groan together: *sustenazō*** [verb: συστενάζω <4959>]; **from *sun*: together, and *stenazō*: see [1] ▶ To sigh together >** The whole creation groans together and suffers the pains of childbirth together (Rom. 8:22). ¶

– [4] John 11:33, 38 → to be deeply moved → MOVED (BE) <1690>.

GROANING – ***stenagmos*** [masc. noun: στεναγμός <4726>]; **from *stenazō*: to groan, to sigh, which is from *stenos*: narrow, pressed (by circumstances) ▶ Sighing under affliction or oppression; also transl.: groan >** The Lord had heard the groaning of His people in Egypt (Acts 7:34). The Spirit Himself intercedes for Christians with groanings which cannot be expressed by words (Rom. 8:26). ¶

GROPE – Acts 17:27 → to grope for → to feel after → FEEL <5584>.

GROSS – Matt. 13:15; Acts 28:27 → to wax gross → to become dull → DULL <3975>.

GROUND (noun)[1] – [1] ***bēma*** [neut. noun: βῆμα <968>]; **from *bainō*: to go; lit.: step ▶ Space covered by the foot, place >** God did not give Abraham a foot of ground (lit.: the ground of foot) even what his foot could stand on {not even to set his foot on, not even what his foot could stand on} (Acts 7:5). All other refs.: JUDGMENT SEAT <968>, THRONE <968>.

[2] ***edaphos*** [neut. noun: ἔδαφος <1475>] **▶ Earth >** Saul fell to the ground (Acts 22:7). ¶

[3] **to lay even with the ground, to level to the ground, to dash to the ground: *edaphizō*** [verb: ἐδαφίζω <1474>]; **from *edaphos*: see [2] ▶ To destroy, to raze >** Jesus warned Jerusalem that her enemies would lay her even with the ground (Luke 19:44). ¶

[4] **on the ground, to the ground: *chamai*** [adv.: χαμαί <5476>] **▶ On the earth, on the soil >** Jesus spat on the ground and made clay with His saliva, and put it, as an ointment, on the eyes of the blind man (John 9:6). People fell to the ground when Jesus told them He was the one they were seeking (John 18:6). ¶

[5] **parcel of ground, plot of ground: *chōrion*** [neut. noun: χωρίον <5564>]; **dimin. of *choros*: field, space ▶ Field, parcel of land >** Jesus came to Sychar, near the parcel of ground {land} which Jacob gave to Joseph (John 4:5). All other refs.: FIELD <5564>, LAND (noun) <5564>, PLACE (noun) <5564>.

– [6] Matt. 10:29; 13:8, 23; Mark 4:8, 20; 8:6; Acts 7:33; 26:14; Heb. 6:7; et al. → EARTH <1093> [7] Matt. 13:20 → rocky ground → rocky places → ROCK <4075> [8] Luke 8:6, 13 → rocky ground → ROCK <4073> [9] Luke 9:42 → to slam to the ground, to throw down to the ground → TEAR (verb) <4486> [10] Luke 12:16 → FIELD <5561> [11] Luke 14:18 → piece of ground → FIELD <68> [12] John 8:59 → from the temple grounds → lit.: from the temple [13] 1 Cor. 9:15 → to deprive me of my ground → to make void → VOID <2758> [14] 1 Cor. 10:25, 27 → on the ground of → because (*dia*) [15] Eph. 6:13 → to stand one's ground → RESIST <436> [16] 1 Tim. 3:15 → FOUNDATION <1477> [17] Heb. 10:32 → to stand one's ground → ENDURE <5278>.

GROUND (noun)[2] – [1] Luke 23:22 → REASON (noun) <158> [2] Acts 13:28; 28:18 → CAUSE (noun) <156>.

GROUND (verb) – [1] Eph. 3:17; Col. 1:23 → FOUND <2311> [2] 1 Pet. 5:10 → SETTLE <2311>.

GROUP – [1] **rank: *prasia*** [fem. noun: πρασιά <4237>]; **from *prason*: leek; lit.: plot of leeks; from which: group ▶ Number of persons arranged in a square >** Jesus made a great crowd sit down in groups (*prasiai prasiai*; lit.: ranks in ranks) of 100 and of 50 before feeding them (Mark 6:40a, b). ¶
[2] ***sumposion*** [neut. noun: συμπόσιον <4849>]; **from *sunpinō*: to drink together, which is from *sun*: together, and *pinō*: to drink ▶ Cluster, company >** Jesus commanded to make all the people sit down in groups (lit.: groups by groups) on the green grass (Mark 6:39a, b). ¶
– [3] Mark 6:40 → COMPANY (noun) <4237> [4] Luke 2:44 → COMPANY (noun) <4923> [5] Luke 9:14 → COMPANY (noun) <2828> [6] Acts 1:15 → CROWD (noun) <3793> [7] Acts 5:36 → NUMBER (noun) <706> [8] Acts 6:5 → MULTITUDE <4128> [9] Acts 23:6 → PART (noun) <3313>.

GROW – [1] ***auxanō*** **or** ***auxō*** [verb: αὐξάνω or αὔξω <837>] ▶ **To increase, to augment, to progress >** Jesus says to consider the lilies of the field, how they grow (Matt. 6:28; Luke 12:27). In a parable, the grain of mustard, when it is grown, is greater than the herbs and becomes a tree (Matt. 13:32; Luke 13:19). The verb is used concerning John the Baptist and Jesus: the child grew (Luke 1:80; 2:40). The people of Israel grew and multiplied {greatly increased} in Egypt (Acts 7:17). In Acts 12:24, the word of God grew and spread itself; see also Acts 6:7 and 19:20 {to spread}. The household of God grows into {rises to become} a holy temple in the Lord (Eph. 2:21). By holding the truth in love, Christians grow up in all things into Christ (Eph. 4:15). The gospel was growing among the Colossians (Col. 1:6 in some mss.). The church grows with the increase of God (Col. 2:19). Peter speaks of growing by desiring the pure milk of the word (1 Pet. 2:2) and of growing in the grace and knowledge of the Lord and Savior Jesus Christ (2 Pet. 3:18). All other refs.: INCREASE (noun) <837>, INCREASE (verb) <837>.
[2] **to grow together: *sunauxanō*** [verb: συναυξάνω <4885>]; **from *sun*: together, and *auxanō*: see [1] ▶ To increase together >** In a parable, the servants were instructed to let the tares and the wheat grow together (Matt. 13:30). ¶
[3] **to grow exceedingly, to grow more and more: *huperauxanō*** [verb: ὑπεραυξάνω <5232>]; **from *huper*: intens., and *auxanō*: see [1] ▶ To increase much, to progress a lot >** The faith of the Thessalonians was growing exceedingly {increasing exceedingly, greatly enlarged} (2 Thes. 1:3). ¶
[4] ***erchomai*** [verb: ἔρχομαι <2064>] ▶ **To become >** A woman who had suffered many things was growing {was getting} worse (Mark 5:26). Other refs.: COME <2064>.
[5] ***mēkunō*** [verb: μηκύνω <3373>]; **from *mēkos*: length ▶ To increase, to spread >** In a parable, the seed sprouts and grows without the sower knowing how (Mark 4:27). ¶
[6] ***prokoptō*** [verb: προκόπτω <4298>]; **from *pro*: before, in front, and *koptō*: to hit repeatedly ▶ To advance, to progress >** Evil men and seducers will grow {will wax, will advance, will proceed} worse and worse {will go from bad to worse} (2 Tim. 3:13). All other refs.: INCREASE (verb) <4298>, PROCEED <4298>, SPEND <4298>.
– [7] Matt. 13:15; Acts 28:27 → to grow fat, to grow dull → DULL <3975> [8] Mark 4:8, 32 → to grow up → to go up → GO <305> [9] Luke 8:6, 8; Heb. 12:15 → to grow up → to spring up → SPRING (verb) <5453> [10] Luke 8:7 → to grow up with → to spring up with → SPRING (verb) <4855> [11] John 6:18 → to grow rough → ARISE <1326> [12] Acts 9:31 → to grow in number → MULTIPLY <4129> [13] Acts 13:46 → to grow bold → BOLD <3955> [14] Acts 16:5 → INCREASE (verb) <4052> [15] 1 Cor. 7:29 → to grow very short → to be straitened → SHORT <4958> [16] Eph. 4:16; Col. 2:19 → INCREASE (noun) <838> [17] Eph. 4:22 → to grow corrupt → CORRUPT (verb) <5351> [18] 2 Thes. 1:3

→ to grow greater → ABOUND <4121> [19] 1 Tim. 5:11 → to grow wanton → to wax wanton → WANTON <2691> [20] Jas. 1:15 → when it is fully grown → FINISH <658> [21] Rev. 2:3 → to grow weary → WEARY (adj.) <2872> [22] Rev. 18:19 → to grow rich → RICH <4147>.

GROWING – Luke 13:6 → planted → PLANT (verb) <5452>.

GROWTH – [1] Matt. 6:27 → STATURE <2244> [2] 1 Cor. 3:6, 7 → to give the growth → to give the increase → INCREASE (noun) <837> [3] Eph. 4:16; Col. 2:19 → INCREASE (noun) <838> [4] Heb. 6:1 → full growth → PERFECTION <5047>.

GRUDGE (noun) – **to hold a grudge, to nurse a grudge: *enechō*** [verb: ἐνέχω <1758>]; **from *en*: in, upon, and *echō*: to have ▶ To have resentment, to hold something against someone** > Herodias held a grudge against John the Baptist, because he said it was not lawful for Herod to have her, since she was already the wife of Herod's brother (Mark 6:19). Other refs.: Gal. 5:1; Luke 11:53; see ENTANGLED (BE) <1758>, PRESS <1758>. ¶

GRUDGE (verb) – Jas. 5:9 → COMPLAIN <4727>.

GRUDGING – [1] 2 Cor. 9:5 → grudging obligation → COVETOUSNESS <4124> [2] 1 Pet. 4:9 → MURMURING <1112>.

GRUDGINGLY – 2 Cor. 9:5 → as grudgingly given → as of covetousness → COVETOUSNESS <4124>.

GRUMBLE – [1] Matt. 20:11; Luke 5:30; John 6:41, 43, 61; 1 Cor. 10:10a, b → MURMUR <1111> [2] Luke 15:2; 19:7 → MURMUR <1234> [3] Jas. 5:9 → COMPLAIN <4727>.

GRUMBLER – Jude 16 → MURMURER <1113>.

GRUMBLING – John 7:12; Phil. 2:14; 1 Pet. 4:9 → MURMURING <1112>.

GUARANTEE (noun) – [1] 2 Cor. 1:22; Eph. 1:14 → EARNEST <728> [2] Heb. 7:22 → GUARANTOR <1450>.

GUARANTEE (verb) – Heb. 6:17 → to guarantee with an oath → to intervene by an oath → INTERVENE <3315>.

GUARANTEED – Rom. 4:16 → SURE <949>.

GUARANTOR – ***enguos*** [masc. noun: ἔγγυος <1450>]; **from *enguē*: pledge, promise ▶ Person who is legally responsible** > Jesus has become the guarantor {guarantee, surety} of a better covenant (Heb. 7:22). ¶

GUARD (noun) – [1] ***koustōdia*** [fem. noun: κουστωδία <2892>]; **from the Lat. *custodia*: military surveillance, post ▶ Soldiers responsible for keeping watch; also transl.: watch** > Pilate told the Jews that they had a guard and that they were to secure the tomb of Jesus as well as they knew how (Matt. 27:65); they posted the guard there (v. 66). Men of the guard reported to the chief priest the things that had happened concerning the resurrection of Jesus (Matt. 28:11). ¶
[2] ***spekoulatōr*** [masc. noun: σπεκουλάτωρ <4688>]; ***speculator*, in Lat.: spy, scout ▶ Soldier responsible for certain missions, executioner** > King Herod sent one of his guards, and commanded him to bring the head of John the Baptist (Mark 6:27). ¶
[3] ***phulax*** [masc. noun: φύλαξ <5441>]; **from *phulassō*: to guard ▶ Keeper, sentinel; also transl.: sentry** > The guards stood outside before the doors of the prison where the apostles had been placed (Acts 5:23). Guards kept the prison in which Peter was (Acts 12:6). Herod examined the guards about Peter (Acts 12:19). Other ref.: Matt. 27:65 in some mss. ¶
[4] ***phulakē*** [fem. noun: φυλακή <5438>]; **from *phulassō*: to guard ▶ People responsible for surveillance; guard post** > The

angel and Peter passed through a first and second guard (Acts 12:10). All other refs.: HOLD (noun) <5438>, PRISON <5438>, WATCH (noun) <5438>.

[5] **to guard: *tēreō*** [verb: τηρέω <5083>]; **from *tēros*: warden, guard ► To watch over (to prevent from escaping) >** The guards {keepers} of (lit.: those guarding) the tomb of Jesus trembled and became as dead men at the appearance of the angel of the Lord (Matt. 28:4). All other refs.: see entries in Lexicon at <5083>.

[6] **to be on one's guard: *phulassō*** [verb: φυλάσσω <5442>] **► To watch, to pay attention >** Peter says to Christians to be on their guard so that they may not fall from their own steadfastness (2 Pet. 3:17). All other refs.: GUARD (verb) <5442>, KEEP (verb) <5442>, PRESERVE <5442>.

– [7] Matt. 5:25; 26:58; Mark 14:54, 65; John 7:32, 45, 46; 18:3, 12, 18, 22; 19:6 → guard, temple guard → OFFICER <5257> [8] Matt. 10:17; 16:6, 11; Luke 12:1; 17:3; 21:34 → to be on guard → BEWARE <4337> [9] Mark 14:44 → under guard → SECURELY <806> [10] Acts 20:31; 1 Cor. 16:13 → to be on one's guard → WATCH (verb) <1127>.

GUARD (verb) – [1] ***phulassō*** [verb: φυλάσσω <5442>] **► To abstain, to refrain; also transl.: to beware, to be on guard, to keep, to watch >** Jesus says to keep oneself from all covetousness (Luke 12:15). The nations are to keep themselves from what is sacrificed to idols, from blood, from what is strangled, and from sexual immorality (Acts 21:25). Timothy was to be on his guard against Alexander (2 Tim. 4:15). John tells the little children to guard themselves from idols (1 John 5:21). All other refs.: GUARD (noun) <5442>, KEEP (verb) <5442>, PRESERVE <5442>.

[2] ***diaphulassō*** [verb: διαφυλάσσω <1314>]; **from *dia*: intens., and *phulassō*: see [1] ► To watch closely and carefully, to protect, i.e., to look after carefully >** The angels were to guard {to keep, to guard carefully} the Son of God (Luke 4:10). ¶

[3] ***phroureō*** [verb: φρουρέω <5432>]; **from *phrouros*: sentinel, guardian ► a. To watch over with a military guard >** The ethnarch of the king kept the city of Damascus, in order to arrest Paul (2 Cor. 11:32). **b. To protect, to preserve; also transl.: to shield >** Before faith came, we were guarded under the law (Gal. 3:23). The peace of God keeps the hearts and minds of those who make their requests known to Him by Christ Jesus (Phil. 4:7). Christians are guarded by the power of God through faith (1 Pet. 1:5). ¶

– [4] Matt. 16:12; Acts 20:28 → to be on guard → BEWARE <4337> [5] Matt. 27:54 → WATCH (verb) <5083> [6] Acts 12:6 → stood guard, were guarding → KEEP (verb) <5083>.

GUARDIAN – [1] ***epitropos*** [masc. noun: ἐπίτροπος <2012>]; **from *epitrepō*: to permit, which is from *epi*: upon, and *trepō*: to turn ► Person who has responsibility for a minor child, whether the father is living or not >** Paul speaks of the heir, as long as he is a child, who is under guardians {tutors} and trustees until the time set by the father (Gal. 4:2). Other refs.: Matt. 20:8; Luke 8:3; see STEWARD <2012>. ¶

[2] **temple guardian: *neōkoros*** [masc. noun: νεωκόρος <3511>]; **from *naos*: temple, and *koreō*: to sweep ► One who takes care, who protects a place of worship; also, honorary title of certain cities in which special worship of some deity had been established >** Ephesus was temple guardian {temple keeper, guardian of the temple, worshipper} of the great goddess Diana (Acts 19:35). ¶

– [3] 1 Cor. 4:15 → INSTRUCTOR <3807> [4] Gal. 3:24, 25 → TUTOR <3807> [5] 1 Pet. 2:25 → OVERSEER <1985>.

GUEST – [1] Matt. 14:6 → for the guests → lit.: in the midst → MIDST <3319> [2] Matt. 22:10, 11 → to be at the table → TABLE[1] <345> [3] Mark 14:14; Luke 2:7; 22:11 → guest chamber, guest room → INN <2646> [4] Luke 2:7 → guest room: same as room → PLACE (noun) <5117> [5] Luke 14:7 → lit.: one invited to eat → INVITE <2564> [6] Luke 19:7 → to be a guest → LODGE

<2647> 7 Acts 10:23, 32 → to be a guest → LODGE <3579>.

GUEST CHAMBER – Mark 14:14; Luke 22:11 → GUEST ROOM <2646>.

GUEST ROOM – 1 ***kataluma*** [neut. noun: κατάλυμα <2646>]; **from *kataluō*: to unloose, to lodge, which is from *kata*: down (intens.), and *luō*: to loose, suggesting the idea of unpacking one's baggage ► Chamber for visitors, reception room; lodging place, inn** > The Lord spoke of the guest room {chamber, guest chamber} where He would eat the Passover (Mark 14:14; Luke 22:11). Other ref.: Luke 2:7; see INN <2646>. ¶

2 ***xenia*** [fem. noun: ξενία <3578>]; **from *xenos*: stranger, foreigner ► Housing, accommodation, also transl.: lodging** > Paul had a guest room {place where he was staying} in Rome where many came to him (Acts 28:23). He asked Philemon to prepare a guest room for him (Phm. 22). ¶

GUIDANCE – 1 Cor. 12:28 → ADMINISTRATION <2941>.

GUIDE (noun) – 1 ***hodēgos*** [masc. noun: ὁδηγός <3595>]; **from *hodos*: road, way, and *hēgeomai*: to lead, to show the direction ► One who shows the way, conductor** > Jesus spoke of blind guides {leaders} of the blind (Matt. 15:14). He addressed the scribes and Pharisees as blind guides (Matt. 23:16, 24). Judas became a guide to those who took Jesus (Acts 1:16). A Jew might think he was a guide {leader} to the blind (Rom. 2:19). ¶

– 2 1 Cor. 4:15 → INSTRUCTOR <3807>.

GUIDE (verb) – 1 ***kateuthunō*** [verb: κατευθύνω <2720>]; **from *kata*: intens., and *euthunō*: to make straight, which is from *euthus*: straight ► To lead, to direct** > The dayspring from on high had visited Israel to guide their feet into the way of peace (Luke 1:79). All other refs.: DIRECT <2720>.

– 2 Matt. 15:14; John 16:13; Acts 8:31; Rev. 7:17 → LEAD (verb) <3594> 3 Jas. 3:3, 4 → TURN (verb) <3329>.

GUILE – 1 John 1:47; 2 Cor. 12:16; 1 Pet. 2:1, 22; 3:10; Rev. 14:5 → DECEIT <1388> 2 1 Thes. 2:3 → SUBTLETY <1388>.

GUILELESS – Matt. 10:16 → INNOCENT <185>.

GUILT – 1 Mark 3:29 → to lie under the guilt → to be subject → SUBJECT (noun)[1] <1777> 2 Luke 23:4, 14 → FAULT <158> 3 Luke 23:22 → REASON (noun) <158> 4 John 18:38; 19:4, 6 → FAULT <156> 5 Acts 13:28 → guilt worthy of death → cause for death → CAUSE (noun) <156> 6 Jas. 2:10 → under the guilt → GUILTY <1777>.

GUILTLESS – 1 ***anaitios*** [adj.: ἀναίτιος <338>]; **from *a*: neg., and *aitia*: accusation ► Innocent, blameless** > If the Pharisees had known the meaning of mercy, they would not have condemned the guiltless (Matt. 12:7). Other ref.: Matt. 12:5; see BLAMELESS <338>. ¶

– 2 Matt. 27:4, 24 → INNOCENT <121> 3 1 Cor. 1:8 → BLAMELESS <410>.

GUILTY – 1 ***enochos*** [adj.: ἔνοχος <1777>]; **from *enechō*: to contain, which is from *en*: in, and *echō*: to have, to hold ► Culpable, responsible** > Whoever participates to the Lord's supper unworthily will be guilty in respect of the body and of the blood of the Lord (1 Cor. 11:27). Whoever will keep the whole law and will offend in one point, this person is guilty {under the guilt} of all (Jas. 2:10). All other refs.: DESERVING <1777>, SUBJECT (noun)[1] <1777>.

2 ***hupodikos*** [adj.: ὑπόδικος <5267>]; **from *hupo*: under, and *dikē*: judgment, justice ► Liable to or under a judgment for punishment, blamable** > The law says that all the world is guilty {under judgment, accountable} before God (Rom. 3:19). ¶

– 3 Matt. 23:18 → to be guilty → to be a debtor → DEBTOR <3784> 4 Luke 13:4 → SINNER <3781> 5 Luke 23:14 → Pilate did not find Jesus guilty → Pilate found no fault in Jesus → FAULT <158> **6** Acts 22:25 → not found guilty → UNCONDEMNED <178> **7** 1 Cor. 5:11 → is guilty of sexual immorality or greed → lit.: is a fornicator <4205> or covetous <4123> **8** Heb. 10:2 → to feel guilty CONSCIENCE <4893>.

GULF – Luke 16:26 → CHASM <5490>.

GULLIBLE WOMAN – 2 Tim. 3:6 → SILLY WOMAN <1133>.

GUSH – to gush out: *ekchunō* [verb: ἐκχύνω <1632a>]**; from *ek*: out, and *cheō*: to pour ► To come out, to spill out >** The body of Judas burst open and all his intestines gushed out (Acts 1:18). All other refs.: POUR <1632a>.

GUST – Mark 4:37 → STORM <2978>.

H

HA! – ***oua*** [interj.: οὐά <3758>] ▶ **Interj. of mockery** > Those who passed by hurled insults at Jesus, saying: Ha! {Ah!, Aha!, So!} You who destroy the temple… come down from the cross! (Mark 15:29; see v. 30). ¶

HABIT – [1] ***hexis*** [fem. noun: ἕξις <1838>]; **from *echō*: to have, to hold ▶ Practice, experience; also transl.: use** > On account of habit, full-grown men (i.e., spiritually mature Christians) have their senses exercised for distinguishing both good and evil (Heb. 5:14). ¶
[2] ***ēthos*** [neut. noun: ἦθος <2239>]; **from *ethos*: custom, manner ▶ Custom, moral conduct** > Evil company corrupts good habits {character, manners, morals} (1 Cor. 15:33). ¶
– [3] Heb. 10:25 → CUSTOM[1] <1485>.

HABITATION – [1] ***katoikia*** [fem. noun: κατοικία <2733>]; **from *katoikeō*: to dwell, which is from *kata*: intens., and *oikeō*: to dwell ▶ Dwelling place, residence** > God had determined the boundaries of the habitation of men (Acts 17:26 {dwelling, land}). ¶
[2] ***oikētērion*** [neut. noun: οἰκητήριον <3613>]; **from *oikētēr*: inhabitant, which is from *oikeō*: to dwell ▶ Dwelling, abode** > Christians desire to be clothed with their habitation {house} which is from heaven (2 Cor. 5:2). Certain angels have abandoned their own habitation {home} (Jude 6), by taking wives for themselves among the daughters of men (see Gen. 6:2). ¶
– [3] Luke 16:9 → TABERNACLE <4633> [4] Acts 1:20 → DWELLING PLACE <1886> [5] Eph. 2:22; Rev. 18:2 → DWELLING PLACE <2732>.

HADES – ***hadēs*** [masc. noun: ᾅδης <86>]; **from *a*: neg., and *eidon*: conjugated form of "to see" ▶ Invisible place where the souls of men go after death; KJV translates: hell, but see the meaning of that word** > Capernaum will be brought down to Hades (Matt. 11:23; Luke 10:15). The gates of Hades shall not prevail against the church (Matt. 16:18). In Hades, the rich man saw Lazarus in Abraham's bosom (Luke 16:23). Christ Jesus was not left in Hades (Acts 2:31); His soul was not left in Hades (v. 27). The Son of Man has the keys of Death and of Hades (Rev. 1:18). Hades accompanies Death (Rev. 6:8; 20:13): they will both be cast into the lake of fire, after the judgment of the great white throne (20:14). Other ref.: 1 Cor. 15:55 (in some mss.). ¶

HAGAR – ***Hagar*** [fem. name: Ἁγάρ <28>] ▶ **Egyptian bondservant, handmaid of Sarah, by whom Abraham begat Ishmael; also spelled: Agar** > Hagar illustrates the bondage of the law to which the Galatians were returning (Gal. 4:24, 25). In contrast with the "Jerusalem which is now," still under this yoke of bondage, in spite of the preaching of the apostles, the "Jerusalem that is above," represented by Sarah, speaks of the grace which the freed Christian enjoys. ¶

HAIL (noun) – ***chalaza*** [fem. noun: χάλαζα <5464>]; **from *chalaō*: to let fall, to strike ▶ Frozen raindrops** > Hail will constitute a judgment of God (Rev. 8:7; 11:19; 16:21a) because of which men will blaspheme Him (16:21b); one may believe that the hailstones will be of significant size. ¶

HAIL (verb) – ***chairō*** [verb: χαίρω <5463>]; **lit.: to rejoice ▶ To greet, to salute; also transl.: to bid God speed, to give a greeting, to give greetings, to rejoice, to welcome** > Judas said "Hail" to Jesus (Matt. 26:49). Jesus was saluted by "Hail, King of the Jews" (Matt. 27:29; Mark 15:18; John 19:3). He said "Hail" to certain women (Matt. 28:9). An angel said "Hail" to Mary (Luke 1:28). If someone comes to us and does not bring the doctrine of Christ, John says not to receive him into our house or to greet him (2 John 10) for he who greets him partakes of his wicked works (v. 11). Other refs.: Acts 15:23; 23:26; Jas. 1:1. All other refs.: REJOICE <5463>.

HAIR – [1] ***thrix*** [fem. noun: θρίξ <2359>] ▶ **a. Fine outgrowth from the skin on the head** > One cannot make one hair white or black (Matt. 5:36). Jesus told His disciples that even the very hairs of their head were all numbered (Matt. 10:30; Luke

12:7). A woman who was a sinner washed the feet of Jesus with her tears and wiped them with the hair of her head (Luke 7:38, 44). Mary of Bethany anointed the feet of Jesus with fragrant oil and wiped His feet with her hair (John 11:2; 12:3). Jesus said that not a hair of the head of His persecuted disciples will perish (Luke 21:18); Paul uses a similar expr. to encourage the passengers of the boat in peril (Acts 27:34). The adornment of Christian women must not be that outward one of the hair and the wearing of gold, or of putting on fine clothes (1 Pet. 3:3). In John's vision, the head and hair of the Son of Man were white like white wool (Rev. 1:14); the locusts had hair like women's hair (9:8a, b). **b. Pelt of an animal >** The garment of John the Baptist was made of camel's hair (Matt. 3:4; Mark 1:6). ¶

[2] **made of hair: *trichinos*** [adj.: τρίχινος <5155>]**; from *thrix*: see [1] ▶ Made of the hair of an animal >** John saw the sun become black as a sackcloth made of hair {made of goat hair} (Rev. 6:12). ¶

[3] ***komē*** [fem. noun: κόμη <2864>]**; poss. from *komeō*: to take care; akin to *coma*, in Lat. ▶ Growth covering the human head >** Her hair {Long hair} is given to the woman for a covering (1 Cor. 11:15). ¶

[4] **to have long hair, to wear long hair: *komaō*** [verb: κομάω <2863>]**; from *komē*: see [3] ▶ To grow long hair >** If a man has long hair, it is a dishonor to him; but it is a glory to the woman (1 Cor. 11:14, 15). ¶

HAKELDAMA – See ACELDAMA <184>.

HALE – [1] Luke 12:58 → DRAG <2694> [2] Acts 8:3 → DRAG <4951>.

HALF – [1] ***hēmisu*** [adj. used as noun: ἥμισυ <2255>] **▶ One of two equal parts into which a thing may be divided >** Herod was ready to give up half of his kingdom (Mark 6:23). Zaccheus gave half of his goods to the poor (Luke 19:8). The dead bodies of the two prophets will be seen for three and a half days (Rev. 11:9, 11). The woman (Israel) will be nourished in the wilderness for a time and times and half a time (Rev. 12:14), i.e., three and a half years. ¶

– [2] Luke 10:30 → half dead → DEAD <2253>.

HALF YEAR – Luke 4:25; Acts 18:11; Jas. 5:17 → lit.: six months → SIX <1803>.

HALFWAY – John 7:14 → to be halfway → to be the middle → MIDDLE <3322>.

HALL – [1] Matt. 27:27; John 18:28, 33; 19:9; Acts 23:35 → common hall, judgment hall → PRAETORIUM <4232> [2] Mark 15:16 → COURTYARD <833> [3] Acts 25:23 → hall of audience → place of hearing → HEARING <201>.

HALLELUJAH – See ALLELUIA <239>.

HALLOW – Matt. 6:9; Luke 11:2 → SANCTIFY <37>.

HALT – [1] Matt. 18:8; Mark 9:45; Luke 14:21; John 5:3 → LAME <5560> [2] Luke 7:14 → to come to a halt → STAND (verb) <2476>.

HAMOR – ***Hemmor*** [masc. name: Ἑμμώρ <1697>]**: donkey, in Heb. ▶ Prince of Shechem; also transl.: Emmor >** Abraham had bought a tomb from the sons of Hamor (Acts 7:16). Shechem {Sychem} was one of the sons of Hamor (see Gen. 33:19). ¶

HAND (noun) – [1] ***cheir*** [fem. noun: χείρ <5495>] **▶ Part of the human body enabling touching and grasping, among other functions >** The left hand (lit.: the left) should not know what the right hand (lit.: the right) is doing when one is doing a charitable deed, in the sense that one should not be keeping count (Matt. 6:3). For ceremonial religious reasons, the Pharisees scrupulously washed their hands before meals (Matt. 15:2; Mark 7:2–5). The act of washing one's hands expresses a profession of innocence (Matt. 27:24). The right hand symbolizes power and authority (Matt. 27:29, lit.: the right; Rev. 1:16). To lay hands on someone is to take hold of him (e.g., Luke 20:19 {to arrest}; Acts 4:3 {to seize}; 5:18 {to arrest}). To commit into the hands of someone is to confide something to his care: Jesus committed His spirit into His Father's hands (Luke 23:46). The act of lifting up hands accompanies the act of blessing (Luke 24:50). The hands of the Lord Jesus were pierced (John 20:20, 25, 27). The hand of God with someone suggests His help (Acts 11:21). The hand of God upon someone suggests His control over that person (Acts 13:11). The heavens are the works of God's hands (Heb. 1:10); He has set Jesus over the works of His hands (2:7 in some mss.). To strengthen the hands {arms} that hang down is to take courage in Christian service (Heb. 12:12). We should humble ourselves under the mighty hand of God (1 Pet. 5:6). See IMPOSITION OF HANDS. *

2 **made with, made by, built by hands: *cheiropoiētos*** [adj.: χειροποίητος <5499>]; **from *cheir*: see 1, and *poieō*: to make ▶ Man made** > The temple was made with hands (Mark 14:58). The Lord of heaven and earth does not dwell in temples made with hands (Acts 7:48; also 17:24). Circumcision is made {done, performed} in the flesh by hands (Eph. 2:11). Christ came with the tabernacle not made with hands (Heb. 9:11). He has not entered the holy places made with hands (Heb. 9:24). ¶

3 **made without hands, not made with hands: *acheiropoiētos*** [adj.: ἀχειροποίητος <886>]; **from *a*: neg., and *cheiropoiētos*: see 2 ▶ Not man made** > False witnesses claimed that Jesus had said He would build another temple made without hands (Mark 14:58). Christians have a house not made with hands, eternal in the heavens (2 Cor. 5:1). They have been circumcised with a circumcision made without hands (Col. 2:11). ¶

4 **to take in hand: *epicheireō*** [verb: ἐπιχειρέω <2021>]; **from *epi*: to, and *cheir*: see 1 ▶ To undertake, to assume the responsibility** > Many had taken in hand to set in order a narrative of those things concerning the life of Jesus (Luke 1:1). Some Jewish exorcists took in hand {attempted, tried} to call the name of the Lord over those who had evil spirits (Acts 19:13). Other ref.: Acts 9:29; see SEEK <2021>. ¶

5 **to be at hand: *engizō*** [verb: ἐγγίζω <1448>]; **from *engus*: near; lit.: to draw near ▶ To approach, to get closer** > The day of salvation is at hand (Rom. 13:12; Heb. 10:25). The end of all things is at hand (1 Pet. 4:7). Other refs.: Matt. 3:2; 4:17; 10:7; 26:45, 46; Mark 1:15; 14:42. All other refs.: COME <1448>, DRAW <1448>, NEAR (adv.) <1448>, NEIGHBORHOOD <1448>.

6 **to be at hand: *ephistēmi*** [verb: ἐφίστημι <2186>]; **from *epi*: upon, and *histēmi*: to stand ▶ To be there, to be about to occur** > The time of Paul's departure was at hand {had come} (2 Tim. 4:6). All other refs.: ASSAULT (verb) <2186>, COME <2186>, FALL (verb) <2186>, READY <2186>, STAND (verb) <2186>.

– 7 Matt. 18:28; 21:46; Mark 12:12 → to lay hands → SEIZE <2902> 8 Matt. 19:13, 15; et al. → to lay, to place, to put, to impose hands → see LAYING ON OF HANDS <1936>, <2007>, <5495> 9 Matt. 26:18; Luke 21:31; John 2:13; 6:4; 7:2; 11:55; 19:42; Phil. 4:5; Rev. 1:3; 22:10 → at hand, nigh at hand → NEAR (adv.) <1451> 10 Mark 10:13; Luke 18:15 → to place one's hand → TOUCH <680> 11 Luke 12:58 → to hand over → DELIVER <3860> 12 Luke 21:8 → to be at hand → to be near → NEAR (adv.) <1448> 13 John 8:20 → to lay hands on → TAKE <4084> 14 Acts 9:8; 22:11 → to lead by the hand → LEAD (verb) <5496> 15 Acts 13:11 → someone to lead by the hand → LEAD (verb) <5497> 16 Acts 27:19 → with their own hands → OWN HANDS <849> 17 2 Cor. 11:24 → "at the hands" added in Engl. 18 Gal. 2:9 → to give the right hand of fellowship → FELLOWSHIP <1188> <1325> <2842> 19 2 Thes. 2:2 → to be at hand → to be present → PRESENT (BE) <1764> 20 1 Pet. 2:23 → to give oneself over into the hands → ENTRUST <3860>.

HAND (verb) – 1 Matt. 5:25; 10:17; 27:18; Mark 15:10 → to hand over → BETRAY <3860> 2 Matt. 5:40 → to hand over → to let have → LET <863> 3 Matt. 11:27; Mark 7:13; Luke 1:2; 4:6; 10:22; John 19:11; Acts 6:14; 27:1; 1 Cor. 15:24 → to hand over, to hand down → DELIVER <3860> 4 Luke 4:17 → GIVE <1929> 5 Acts 2:23 → to hand over → DELIVER <1560> 6 Acts 23:33 → to hand over → PRESENT (verb) <3936> 7 Acts 25:11, 16 → to hand over → DELIVER <5483> 8 1 Pet. 1:18 → handed down from the fathers, the forefathers → received by tradition from the fathers → FATHER <3970> 9 Rev. 17:13 → to hand over → GIVE <1239> 10 Rev. 17:17 → to hand over → GIVE <1325>.

HAND-BASKET – Matt. 14:20; 16:9; Mark 6:43; 8:19; Luke 9:17; John 6:13 → BASKET <2894>.

HANDIWORK – Eph. 2:10 → WORKMANSHIP <4161>.

HANDKERCHIEF – 1 ***soudarion*** [neut. noun: σουδάριον <4676>]; **from *sudor*, in Lat.: perspiration, and *sudare*: to perspire ▶ Cloth to wipe away perspiration and for other uses** > A man had kept his master's mina (a unit of money) in a handkerchief {piece of cloth, towel, napkin} (Luke 19:20). Handkerchiefs {Napkins} and aprons were brought from the body of Paul upon the sick (Acts 19:12). Other refs.: John 11:44; 20:7; see CLOTH <4676>. ¶
– 2 John 11:44; 20:7 → CLOTH <4676>.

HANDLE – 1 Mark 12:4 in some mss. → to handle shamefully → to insult → INSULT (noun) <818> 2 Luke 24:39; 1 John 1:1 → TOUCH <5584> 3 2 Cor. 4:2 → to handle deceitfully → FALSIFY <1389> 4 Col. 2:21 → TOUCH <2345> 5 2 Tim. 2:15 → to handle accurately, correctly → to divide rightly → DIVIDE <3718>.

HANDMAID – ***doulē*** [fem. noun: δούλη <1399>]; **fem. of *doulos*: servant, slave ▶ Female servant or slave; also transl.: bondslave, maidservant, bondmaid, bondwoman, servant** > The word is used concerning Mary, the mother of Jesus (Luke 1:38, 48). Other ref.: Acts 2:18; see BONDWOMAN <1399>. ¶

HANDWRITING – ***cheirographon*** [neut. noun: χειρόγραφον <5498>]; **from *cheir*: hand, and *graphō*: to write ▶ Written order, necessity, obligation** > Christ has effaced the handwriting {certificate of debt, written code} in ordinances which stood out against us, i.e., the necessity of submitting to ordinances of the law (Col. 2:14; see Eph. 2:15), for the Christian is not under law, but under grace (see Rom. 6:14). ¶

HANG – 1 ***apanchō*** [verb: ἀπάγχω <519>]; **from *apo*: intens., and *anchō*: to strangle ▶ To suffocate, to commit suicide by hanging oneself** > Having cast down the pieces of silver in the temple, Judas went away and hanged himself (Matt. 27:5). ¶
2 ***kremannumi*** [verb: κρεμάννυμι <2910>] **▶ To attach, to suspend, to depend** > Whoever will offend one of the little ones who believes in Jesus, it would be better for him to hang a great millstone upon his neck and he be sunk in the depths of the sea (Matt. 18:6). On two commandments (to love God and to love our neighbor) hang all the law and the prophets (Matt. 22:40). One of the malefactors who had been hanged (or: crucified) insulted Jesus (Luke 23:39). Jesus was hanged on a cross (Acts 5:30; 10:39). The native people saw the viper hanging from Paul's hand (Acts 28:4). It is written: Cursed is everyone hanged on a tree (Gal. 3:13). ¶
3 **to hang on: *ekkremannumi*** [verb: ἐκκρεμάννυμι <1582>]; **from *ek*: from, and *kremannumi*: see 2 ▶ To listen very closely** > People were hanging on {were very attentive} to every word the Lord said (Luke 19:48). ¶
4 **to hang down: *pariēmi*** [verb: παρίημι <3935>]; **from *para*: near, and *hiēmi*: to release, to let fall ▶ To be faltering, to slack off** > Christians were to strengthen the hands that hang down {drooping hands, weak hands, feeble hands} and the feeble knees (an indication of tiredness and lack of prayers) (Heb. 12:12). Other ref.: Luke 11:42 (to leave aside, to neglect) in some mss. ¶
5 **to hang about, to hang around: *perikeimai*** [verb: περίκειμαι <4029>]; **from**

***peri*: around, and *keimai*: to lay ► To put around, to surround >** The verb is used in Mark 9:42 and Luke 17:2, where Jesus warned that it would be better if a millstone were hung about (lit.: be hung around about) {tied around} a man's neck than that he should be an offence to others. All other refs.: BIND <4029>, SUBJECT (verb) <4029>, SURROUND <4029>.
– [6] 2 Pet. 2:3 → to hang over → to not be idle → IDLE (BE) <691>.

HAPLY – Mark 11:13 → PERHAPS <686>.

HAPPEN – [1] ***ginomai*** [verb: γίνομαι <1096>] **► To take place, to occur >** The verb is used in Matt. 26:54; 27:54; Mark 5:16; 9:21; Luke 24:12; Acts 11:28; 22:17; Rom. 11:25; 1 Thes. 3:4; 2 Tim. 3:11. Other refs.: see entries in Lexicon at <1096>.
[2] ***sumbainō*** [verb: συμβαίνω <4819>]**; from *sun*: together, and *bainō*: to go, to walk ► To take place, to occur together >** On His way to Jerusalem, Jesus began to tell His apostles what was going to happen to Him (Mark 10:32). On the day of Jesus's resurrection, the disciples of Emmaus talked together of all the things that had happened (Luke 24:14). Other refs.: Acts 3:10; 20:19 {to befall, to come upon}; 21:35 {to be, to have to be}; 1 Cor. 10:11; 1 Pet. 4:12; 2 Pet. 2:22. ¶
– [3] Matt. 8:33 → what had happened to the possessed → lit.: the (things) of the possessed [4] Matt. 13:21 → ARISE <1096> [5] Matt. 18:31 → to take place → PLACE (noun) <1096> [6] Mark 13:4 → FULFILL <4931> [7] Luke 10:31 → by chance → CHANCE (noun) <4795> [8] Luke 22:49 → BE <2071> [9] Acts 12:11 → everything they were hoping would happen → lit.: all their expectation → EXPECTATION <4329> [10] Acts 13:40 → COME <1904> [11] Acts 17:17 → those who happen to be there → those he met with → MEET (verb) <3909> [12] Acts 20:22 → BEFALL <4876>.

HAPPY – [1] ***makarios*** [adj.: μακάριος <3107>]**; from *makar*: blessed one ► Blessed, possessing the favor of God >** It is more blessed to give than to receive (Acts 20:35). Paul counted himself happy {fortunate} to make his apology before Agrippa (Acts 26:2). The woman whose husband has died is happier if she does not remarry (1 Cor. 7:40). All other refs.: BLESSED <3107>.
[2] **to be happy: *euthumeō*** [verb: εὐθυμέω <2114>]**; from *euthumos*: who is cheerful, full of courage, which is from *eu*: well, and *thumos*: feeling, passion ► To be cheerful, to be glad >** He who is happy {is merry} is to sing psalms (Jas. 5:13). Other refs.: Acts 27:22, 25 (to take heart); see HEART <2114>. ¶
– [3] Matt. 18:13; 2 Cor. 7:9; et al. → to be happy → REJOICE <5463> [4] Jas. 5:11 → to call happy → BLESSED <3106>.

HAR-MAGEDON – See ARMAGEDDON <707>.

HARAN – Acts 7:2, 4 → HARRAN <5488>.

HARASS – [1] **to completely harass: *hupōpiazō*** [verb: ὑπωπιάζω <5299>]**; from *hupōpion*: part of the face under the eyes, blow in the face, which is from *hupo*: under, and *ōps*: eye; lit.: to strike below the eye ► To exasperate, to importune, to weary; also transl.: to wear out >** The unjust judge in a parable feared that a widow would completely harass him (Luke 18:5). Other ref.: 1 Cor. 9:27; see DISCIPLINE (verb) <5299>. ¶
– [2] Acts 12:1 → OPPRESS <2559> [3] 2 Cor. 12:7 → BEAT <2852>.

HARASSED (BE) – [1] Matt. 9:36 → to be weary → WEARY (adj.) <1590> [2] 2 Cor. 7:5 → AFFLICTED (BE) <2346>.

HARBOR – ***limēn*** [masc. noun: λιμήν <3040>]**; akin to *limnē*: inlet, standing water in general ► Maritime shelter for receiving ships; also transl.: haven >** Sailing to Rome, Paul's ship landed at a place called Fair Havens (Acts 27:8), but the harbor was not adapted to winter in (Acts 27:12a); it was decided to set sail in order to reach Phoenicia, a harbor {port} of Crete, to winter (v. 12b). ¶

HARD – [1] ***bareōs*** [adv.: βαρέως <917>]; **from *barus*: heavy ► With difficulty, hardly** > The ears of the Jews were hard {dull} of hearing {They had heard heavily with their ears} (Matt. 13:15; Acts 28:27). ¶
[2] ***duskolos*** [adj.: δύσκολος <1422>]; **from *dus*: with difficulty, and *kolon*: food; lit.: difficult to satisfy with food ► Arduous, difficult** > It is hard {difficult} for those who trust in riches to enter into the kingdom of God (Mark 10:24). ¶
[3] ***duskolōs*** [adv.: δυσκόλως <1423>]; **from *duskolos*: see [2] ► With difficulty, painfully** > It is hard for those who have riches to enter {A rich man enters with difficulty in; hardly} the kingdom of God (Matt. 19:23; Mark 10:23; Luke 18:24). ¶
[4] **hard to bear: *dusbastaktos*** [adj.: δυσβάστακτος <1419>]; **from *dus*: with difficulty, and *bastazō*: to bear ► Difficult to carry, burdensome** > The scribes and the Pharisees were binding heavy burdens on men that were hard to bear {grievous to be borne} (Matt. 23:4 in some mss.; Luke 11:46 {heavy to bear, they can hardly carry}). ¶
[5] **hard to explain: *dusermēneutos*** [adj.: δυσερμήνευτος <1421>]; **from *dus*: with difficulty, and *hermēneuō*: to interpret ► Difficult to expose, to interpret** > The author of the Epistle to the Hebrews had much to say about a matter, but hard to explain {hard to be interpreted, hard to be uttered} (Heb. 5:11). ¶
[6] ***sklēros*** [adj.: σκληρός <4642>]; **from *skellō*: to harden, to dry up ► a. Harsh, tough** > A servant in a parable knew that his master was a hard man (Matt. 25:24). **b. Offensive, intolerable** > The word of Jesus concerning eating His flesh and drinking His blood was hard {difficult} for many of His disciples (John 6:60). It was hard for Paul to kick against goads (Acts 26:14). Ungodly men have spoken hard {harsh} things against the Lord (Jude 15). Other ref.: Acts 9:5 in some mss. Other ref.: Jas. 3:4; see VIOLENT (adj.) <4642>. ¶
– [7] Matt. 7:14 → to be hard → AFFLICTED (BE) <2346> [8] Matt. 19:8; Mark 10:5 → your hearts were hard → lit.: the hardness of your heart → hardness of heart → HARDNESS <4641> [9] Luke 11:53 → to press hard → to oppose vehemently → VEHEMENTLY <1171> [10] Luke 12:58 → to try hard → to make every effort → EFFORT <1325> <2039> [11] Luke 19:21, 22 → HARSH <840> [12] Rom. 2:5 → your hard heart → lit.: your hardness → HARDNESS <4643> [13] 2 Tim. 1:17 → very diligently → DILIGENTLY <4706> [14] Heb. 10:32 → GREAT <4183> [15] 1 Pet. 4:18 → it is hard → DIFFICULTLY <3433>.

HARD-PRESSED – Phil. 1:23 → PRESS <4912>.

HARD PRESSED (BE) – 2 Cor. 8:13 → in distress → DISTRESS <2347>.

HARDEN – [1] ***pōroō*** [verb: πωρόω <4456>]; **from *pōros*: porous stone ► To make rigid, to petrify** > The heart of the disciples was hardened (Mark 6:52; 8:17: *pēroō* in some mss.). Paul speaks of those who were hardened {were blinded} (Rom. 11:7). The minds of the Jews were hardened {were blinded, were made dull} (2 Cor. 3:14); God has blinded their eyes and hardened {deadened} their heart (John 12:40; *pēroō* in some mss.). ¶
[2] ***sklērunō*** [verb: σκληρύνω <4645>]; **from *sklēros*: hard, which is from *skellō*: to dry up ► To become hard, sclerosed; to become dry** > Some were hardened {became obstinate} and did not believe Paul (Acts 19:9). God hardens whom He wills (Rom. 9:18). Christians must exhort one another that none of them be hardened through the deceitfulness of sin (Heb. 3:13). The author of the Epistle to the Hebrews warns them not to harden their hearts (Heb. 3:8, 15; 4:7). ¶

HARDENING – Mark 3:5; Rom. 11:25; Eph. 4:18 → HARDNESS <4457>.

HARDHEARTEDNESS – Matt. 19:8; Mark 10:5 → hardness of heart → HARDNESS <4641>.

HARDLY – [1] Matt. 13:15; Acts 28:27 → HARD <917> [2] Matt. 19:23; Mark 10:23; Luke 18:24 → HARD <1423> [3] Luke 9:39 → with difficulty → DIFFICULTY <3425> [4] Luke 11:46 → they can hardly carry → hardly to bear → HARD <1419> [5] Acts 27:8, 16; Rom. 5:7 → with difficulty → DIFFICULTY <3433>.

HARDNESS – [1] ***pōrōsis*** [fem. noun: πώρωσις <4457>]; **from *pōroō*: to harden, which is from *pōros*: porous stone ▶ State of being hard, rigid; resistance; also transl.: hardening, blindness** > Jesus was grieved by the hardness of the heart {stubborn hearts} of the Jews (Mark 3:5; *pērosis* in some mss.). Hardness in part has happened to Israel (Rom. 11:25). Unbelievers among the Gentiles walk in the vanity of their mind because of the hardness of their heart (Eph. 4:18). ¶

[2] **hardness of heart, hardheartedness: *sklērokardia*** [fem. noun: σκληροκαρδία <4641>]; **from *sklēros*: harsh, tough, which is from *skellō*: to harden, to dry up, and *kardia*: heart ▶ Absence of understanding and of affection** > Jesus uses this term in relation to the Pharisees (Matt. 19:8; Mark 10:5) and to His disciples after His resurrection (Mark 16:14 {stubborn refusal}). ¶

[3] ***sklērotēs*** [fem. noun: σκληρότης <4643>]; **from *sklēros*: see [2] ▶ Insensitivity, stubbornness** > Paul speaks of the hardness of some who despise the grace of God (Rom. 2:5). ¶

– [4] 2 Tim. 2:3 → to endure hardness → to endure hardship → HARDSHIP <2553>.

HARDSHIP – [1] **to endure hardship, to suffer hardship: *kakopatheō*** [verb: κακοπαθέω <2553>]; **from *kakos*: evil, and *pathos*: affliction ▶ To endure difficulties, to be afflicted; also transl.: to bear evils, to endure afflictions, to endure hardness, to suffer, to suffer trouble, to take one's share in suffering** > Timothy was to endure hardship as a good soldier of Jesus Christ (2 Tim. 2:3; also 4:5). Paul suffered hardship in his gospel (2 Tim. 2:9). He who is suffering hardship {is afflicted, is in trouble} should pray (Jas. 5:13). ¶

– [2] Acts 14:22; Acts 20:23 → TRIBULATION <2347> [3] Rom. 8:35 → DISTRESS <4730> [4] 1 Cor. 13:3 → "to hardship" added in Engl. [5] 2 Cor. 1:8 → TROUBLE (noun) <2347> [6] 2 Cor. 6:4; 12:10 → NECESSITY <318>.

HARLOT – Matt. 21:31, 32; 1 Cor. 6:15, 16; Heb. 11:31; Jas. 2:25; Rev. 17:1, 5, 15, 16; 19:2 → PROSTITUTE <4204>.

HARM (noun) – [1] ***kakon*** [adj. used as noun: κακόν <2556>] ▶ **Evil; something morally wrong, injurious** > Alexander did much harm {evil things} to Paul (2 Tim. 4:14). All other refs.: EVIL (adj.) <2556>, EVIL (noun) <2556>, WICKED (noun) <2556>.

[2] ***hubris*** [fem. noun: ὕβρις <5196>]; **lit.: excess ▶ Damage, injury** > Paul uses this word {disaster} concerning the ship on which he was sailing (Acts 27:21). Other refs.: Acts 27:10; 2 Cor. 12:10; see DISASTER <5196>; INSULT (noun) <5196>. ¶

– [3] Mark 3:4; Luke 6:9 → to do harm → to do evil → EVIL (adv.) <2554> [4] Luke 4:35 → to do harm → HURT (verb) <984> [5] Acts 18:10; 1 Pet. 3:13 → HURT (verb) <2559> [6] Acts 28:6 → no harm → lit.: nothing unusual → UNUSUAL <824> [7] Acts 28:21 → EVIL (noun) <4190> [8] Heb. 6:6 → to their own harm → lit.: for themselves [9] 2 Pet. 2:13 → INIQUITY <93>.

HARM (verb) – [1] Luke 10:19; Rev. 6:6; 7:2, 3; 9:4, 19; 11:5a, b → INJURE <91> [2] Acts 18:10 → HURT (verb) <2559> [3] 1 John 5:18 → TOUCH <680>.

HARMED (BE) – 2 Cor. 7:9 → to suffer loss → LOSS <2210>.

HARMFUL – [1] ***blaberos*** [adj.: βλαβερός <983>]; **from *blaptō*: to harm ▶ Injurious, noxious** > Those who desire to be rich fall into many unwise and harmful {hurtful} lusts (1 Tim. 6:9). ¶

– [2] Rev. 16:2 → EVIL (adj.) <2556>.

HARMLESS – [1] Matt. 10:16 → INNOCENT <185> [2] Phil. 2:15 → PURE <185> [3] Heb. 7:26 → SIMPLE <172>.

HARMONIOUS – 1 Pet. 3:8 → of one mind → MIND (noun) <3675>.

HARMONY – [1] Rom. 12:16; Phil. 4:2 → to live in harmony → lit.: to be of the same mind → MIND (noun) <5426> [2] Rom. 15:5 → to live in harmony → to be like-minded → THINK <5426> [3] 2 Cor. 6:15 → CONCORD <4857> [4] Col. 3:14 → perfect harmony → PERFECTION <5047> [5] 1 Pet. 3:8 → in harmony → of one mind → MIND (noun) <3675>.

HARP (noun) – [1] ***kithara*** [fem. noun: κιθάρα <2788>]; **from which: *cithara*, in Lat.; *guitar*, in English ▶ Stringed musical instrument; lyre** > The harp gives a distinct sound (1 Cor. 14:7). The four living creatures and the twenty-four elders each had a harp (Rev. 5:8). John heard a voice as of harpists, harping with their harps (or: playing on their harps) (Rev. 14:2b). Those who had gained the victory over the beast had harps of God (Rev. 15:2). ¶

[2] **to play the harp, to play on the harp: *kitharizō*** [verb: κιθαρίζω <2789>]; **from *kitaris*, same as *kithara*: see [1] ▶ To play this stringed musical instrument; also transl.: to harp, to play** > The harp must give a distinct sound so that one may recognize what is played on it (1 Cor. 14:7). The voice which John heard was like the sound of harpists playing on their harps (Rev. 14:2a). ¶

HARP (verb) – 1 Cor. 14:7; Rev. 14:2 → to play on the harp → HARP (noun) <2789>.

HARP-SINGER – Rev. 14:2; 18:22 → HARPIST <2790>.

HARPER – Rev. 14:2; 18:22 → HARPIST <2790>.

HARPIST – ***kitharōdos*** [masc. noun: κιθαρῳδός <2790>]; **from *kithara*: harp ▶ Person who sings and accompanies himself with the harp; also transl.: harper, harp-singer** > John heard a voice as of harpists (Rev. 14:2). The voice of harpists shall be heard no more in Babylon (Rev. 18:22). ¶

HARRAN – ***Charran*** [fem. name: Χαρράν <5488>]: **parched, in Heb. ▶ City of Mesopotamia located northeast of Canaan; also transl.: Charran** > Abraham lived in Harran after having left from the land of the Chaldeans, before going into Canaan (Acts 7:2, 4). ¶

HARSH – [1] ***austēros*** [adj.: αὐστηρός <840>]; ***austerus*, in Lat.: serious, severe ▶ Earnest, severe** > A servant esteemed his master as a harsh {austere, exacting, hard} man (Luke 19:21, 22). ¶

[2] ***skolios*** [adj.: σκολιός <4646>]; **from *skellō*: to parch; lit.: bent, crooked ▶ Dishonest, unscrupulous** > Believing servants are to submit themselves even to harsh {forward, ill-tempered, unreasonable} masters (1 Pet. 2:18). All other refs.: CROOKED <4646>, PERVERSE <4646>.

– [3] 2 Cor. 13:10 → to have to be harsh → lit.: to deal severely → SEVERITY <664> [4] Col. 2:23 → harsh treatment → NEGLECT (noun) <857> [5] Col. 3:19 → to be harsh → to be bitter → BITTER <4087> [6] Jude 15 → HARD <4642>.

HARVEST (noun) – [1] ***therismos*** [masc. noun: θερισμός <2326>]; **from *therizō*: to reap, which is from *theros*: hot season, summer ▶ The season for gathering in crops** > The word is used in the lit. sense to designate harvest time (Mark 4:29; John 4:35a, b). The harvest began in April and lasted approx. seven weeks. The feast of the First Fruits was celebrated at the beginning of the harvest, and fifty days later the feast of Pentecost (see Lev. 23:10, 11, 15–17). Jesus also used this word to designate those to whom the gospel was addressed (Matt. 9:37, 38a, b; Luke 10:2a–c). Elsewhere, the harvest corresponds to the time of judgment at the end (Matt. 13:30a, b, 39; Rev. 14:15). ¶

– [2] Luke 12:16 → to yield an abundant harvest → to bring forth abundantly → BRING <2164> [3] 2 Cor. 9:10 → FRUIT <1079a>.

HARVEST (verb) – [1] Matt. 25:24, 26; Jas. 5:4b; Rev. 14:16 → REAP <2325> [2] John 4:36 → GATHER <4863> [3] Jas. 5:4a → MOW <270>.

HARVESTER – [1] Matt. 13:30, 39 → REAPER <2327> [2] Jas. 5:4 → lit.: who has harvested → who has reaped → REAP <2325>.

HARVESTMAN – Matt. 13:30, 39 → REAPER <2327>.

HAS NOT? – ***mē ou*** [interrogative expr.: μὴ οὐ <3378>]**; from *mē*: not even, and *ou*: not** ▶ Refs.: Rom. 10:18, 19; 1 Cor. 9:4, 5; 11:22. ¶ ‡

HASTE (noun) – [1] ***spoudē*** [fem. noun: σπουδή <4710>]**; from *speudō*: see [2]** ▶ **Promptness, rapidity** > The daughter of Herodias came in with haste {hurried in} to the king and asked for the head of John the Baptist (Mark 6:25). Mary went into the hill country with haste {in a hurry} (Luke 1:39). All other refs.: DILIGENCE <4710>, ZEAL <4710>, ZEALOUSNESS <4710>.
[2] **to come with haste, to make haste: *speudō*** [verb: σπεύδω <4692>] ▶ **To hurry, to rush** > The shepherds came with haste {came in a hurry, hurried off} and found Mary and Joseph, and the little child (Luke 2:16). Zaccheus made haste {hurried} and came down from the tree (Luke 19:5, 6). All other refs.: HASTEN <4692>.
– [3] Titus 3:13 → with haste → DILIGENTLY <4709>.

HASTE (verb) – Acts 20:16 → HASTEN <4692>.

HASTEN – ***speudō*** [verb: σπεύδω <4692>] ▶ **a. To hurry, to rush** > Paul hastened {hasted, hurried, was in a hurry} to be in Jerusalem on the day of Pentecost (Acts 20:16). Jesus told Paul to make haste (or: to hasten) and get out of Jerusalem quickly (Acts 22:18). **b. To accelerate, to speed; other sense: to be zealous, to take seriously** > Peter speaks of waiting for and hastening the coming of the day of God (2 Pet. 3:12). All other refs.: HASTE (noun) <4692>.

HASTILY – ***tacheōs*** [adv.: ταχέως <5030>]**; from *tachus*: prompt, rapid** ▶ **Rapidly, thoughtlessly** > Timothy was to lay hands hastily {hasty, quickly, suddenly} on no man (1 Tim. 5:22). All other refs.: QUICKLY <5030>, SHORTLY <5030>.

HASTY – 1 Tim. 5:22 → HASTILY <5030>.

HATE – [1] ***miseō*** [verb: μισέω <3404>]**; from *misos*: hatred, aversion** ▶ **To experience a sentiment of hostility, to detest** > Jesus says to do good to those who hate us (Matt. 5:44; Luke 6:27). He speaks of being hated because of His name (Matt. 10:22; 24:9; Mark 13:13; Luke 21:17). Everyone who does evil hates the light (John 3:20). The man of Romans 7 does what he hates (v. 15). God loved Jacob and hated Esau (Rom. 9:13). The Son of God has loved righteousness and hated iniquity (Heb. 1:9). Those of Ephesus and the Lord hate the deeds of the Nicolaitans (Rev. 2:6a, b). Other refs.: Matt. 5:43; 6:24; 24:10; Luke 1:71; 6:22; 14:26 (hate here in the sense of: to not prefer, to not love; comp. Matt. 10:37); Luke 16:13; 19:14; John 7:7a, b; 12:25; 15:18a, b, 19, 23a, b, 24, 25; 17:14; Eph. 5:29; Titus 3:3; 1 John 2:9, 11; 3:13, 15; 4:20; Jude 23; Rev. 2:15; 17:16; 18:2 {hated, hateful}. ¶
– [2] Rom. 12:9 → ABHOR <655>.

HATED – Titus 3:3 → being hated → HATEFUL <4767>.

HATED (BE) – ***miseō*** [verb: μισέω <3404>]**; from *misos*: hatred, aversion** ▶ **To be detested, to be odious** > Great Babylon has become the habitation of every unclean and hated {hateful, detestable} (lit.:

being hated) bird (Rev. 18:2). All other refs.: HATE <3404>.

HATEFUL – [1] ***stugētos*** [adj.: στυγητός <4767>]**; from *stugeō*: to hate ► Odious, detestable** > Before their conversion, Christians were hateful {being hated, hated by others} and hating one another (Titus 3:3). ¶
– [2] Rom. 1:30 → hateful to God → hater of God → HATER <2319> [3] Rev. 18:2 → HATED (BE) <3404>.

HATER – [1] **hater of God: *theostugēs*** [adj.: θεοστυγής <2319>]**; from *Theos*: God, and *stugeō*: to hate ► In Classical Greek, hated by God; in the N.T., one who turns against God** > Men who reject God are haters of God {hateful to God}, practicing various abominations (Rom. 1:30). ¶
– [2] 2 Tim. 3:3 → hater of what is good → despiser of good → DESPISER <865>.

HATRED – Gal. 5:20 → ENMITY <2189>.

HAUGHTINESS – Mark 7:22 → PRIDE <5243>.

HAUGHTY (adj.) – [1] Rom. 1:30 → PROUD (adj.) <5244> [2] Rom. 11:20; 1 Tim. 6:17 → CONCEITED <5309> [3] Rom. 12:16 → HIGH (adj.) <5308> [4] 2 Tim. 3:4 → PUFF UP <5187> [5] Rev. 13:5 → haughty words → lit.: great things → GREAT <3173>.

HAUGHTY (noun) – Luke 1:51 → PROUD (noun) <5244>.

HAUL (noun) – Luke 5:4, 9 → CATCH (noun) <61>.

HAUL (verb) – John 21:6, 11 → DRAW <1670>.

HAUNT – Rev. 18:2a, b → HOLD (noun) <5438>.

HAVE – [1] ***echō*** [verb: ἔχω <2192>] **► To hold in possession, to come, to occur** > This verb is the most frequent Greek verb transl. by "to have" in Engl.; more than 700 times in the Greek N.T. Men lacked the moral sense to have God in their knowledge (Rom. 1:28). The Christians of Thessalonica always had good remembrance of Paul (1 Thes. 3:6). Timothy was to have faith and a good conscience (1 Tim. 1:19). Deacons are to hold (or: have) the mystery of the faith in a pure conscience (1 Tim. 3:9). Christians are to have grace (i.e., to be thankful) by which they may serve God in a way that is pleasing to Him (Heb. 12:28). *
[2] ***apechō*** [verb: ἀπέχω <568>]**; from *apo*: from, and *echō*: see [1]; lit.: to obtain from someone, to receive ► To receive (e.g., payment) in full** > Matt. 6:2, 5, 16; Luke 6:24. All other refs.: FAR <568>, POSSESS <568>.
[3] ***katechō*** [verb: κατέχω <2722>]**; from *kata*: intens., and *echō*: to hold ► To be afflicted, to suffer** > This verb is found in John 5:4 and Rom. 7:6. All other refs.: see entries in Lexicon at <2722>.
[4] ***huparchō*** [verb: ὑπάρχω <5225>]**; from *hupo*: under, and *archō*: to start ► To possess** > Acts 3:6; 4:37; et al. Other refs.: see entries in Lexicon at <5225>.
– [5] Luke 11:5 → to let have → LEND <5531> [6] Rom. 1:13 → OBTAIN <2192> [7] Eph. 6:17 → TAKE <1209> [8] Rev. 18:2a, b → HOLD (noun) <5438>.

HAVEN – Acts 27:12a → HARBOR <3040>.

HAVOC – [1] Acts 8:3 → to make havoc → RAVAGE <3075> [2] Acts 9:21 → to raise havoc → DESTROY <4199>.

HAY – ***chortos*** [masc. noun: χόρτος <5528>] **► Grass for feeding livestock** > In 1 Cor. 3:12, hay {grass} represents work without value that will be burned up. All other refs.: BLADE <5528>, HAY <5528>.

HAZARD – Acts 15:26 → RISK <3860>.

HE WHO IS, AND WAS, AND IS COMING – ***ho ōn kai ho ēn kai ho***

erchomenos [ὁ ὢν καὶ ὁ ἦν καὶ ὁ ἐρχόμενος <3801>] ▶ Refs.: Rev. 1:4, 8; 4:8; 11:17. ¶

HEAD (noun) – [1] ***kephalē*** [fem. noun: κεφαλή <2776>] ▶ **a. Upper or forward portion of a creature's body** > Jesus says not to swear by one's head (Matt. 5:36), nor to anoint one's head when one is fasting (Matt. 6:17). The hairs of our head are all numbered (Matt. 10:30; Luke 12:7). As in the body, so in the church: the head cannot say to the feet that it has no need of them (1 Cor. 12:21). The term is also used in regard to Jesus (Matt. 8:20; 26:7; 27:29, 30, 37; Mark 14:3; 15:19; Luke 7:46; 9:58; John 19:2, 30; 20:7, 12; Rev. 1:14; 14:14; 19:12), John the Baptist (Matt. 14:8, 11; Mark 6:24, 25, 27, 28), those who passed by and saw Jesus on the cross (Matt. 27:39; Mark 15:29), a woman who anointed the feet of Jesus with perfume (Luke 7:38), the disciples of Jesus (Luke 21:18, 28), Peter (John 13:9), certain Jews (Acts 18:6), Paul (Acts 18:18), Paul's companions (Acts 21:24), passengers aboard ship with Paul (Acts 27:34), one's enemy (Rom. 12:20), a man who prays or prophesies (1 Cor. 11:4a, b), a woman who prays or prophesies (1 Cor. 11:5a, b), a man in the church (1 Cor. 11:7), a woman in the church (1 Cor. 11:10), twenty-four elders (Rev. 4:4), locusts (Rev. 9:7), horses (Rev. 9:17a, b), serpents (Rev. 9:19), an angel (Rev. 10:1), a woman clothed with the sun (Rev. 12:1), the dragon (Rev. 12:3a, b), the beast (Rev. 13:1a, b, 3), a woman sitting on a scarlet beast (Rev. 17:3, 7, 9), and those who see the ruin of Babylon (Rev. 18:19). **b. One who is above** > The word is used as a symbol of authority and is applied to God (1 Cor. 11:3c), Christ (1 Cor. 11:3a; Eph. 1:22; 4:15; 5:23b; Col. 1:18; 2:10, 19), man (1 Cor. 11:3b), and the husband (Eph. 5:23a). All other refs.: see CHIEF CORNERSTONE <2776>, CORNER STONE <2776>.

[2] **to strike on the head, to wound in the head: *kephalaioō*** [verb: κεφαλαιόω <2775>]; **from *kephalaios*: dimin. of *kephalē*: see [1] ▶ To hit, to wound the head** > In a parable, vine-growers struck a servant on the head and treated him shamefully (Mark 12:4). ¶

– [3] Matt. 10:25; 13:52; 24:43; Luke 12:39; 13:25; 14:21 → head of the house, head of the household → master of the house → MASTER (noun) <3617> [4] Matt. 12:1; Mark 2:23; 4:28a, b; Luke 6:1 → head of grain → GRAIN <4719> [5] Acts 27:15 → to bring one's head to → to head into → HEAD (verb) <503> [6] 2 Tim. 4:5 → to keep one's head → to be sober → SOBER <3525> [7] Heb. 11:21 → END (noun) <206>.

HEAD (verb) – [1] **to head into: *antophthalmeō*** [verb: ἀντοφθαλμέω <503>]; **from *anti*: against, and *ophthalmos*: eye; lit.: to look a person in the face ▶ To face, to resist** > The ship Paul had boarded was not able to head into {to bear up into, to bring her head to, to face} the wind (Acts 27:15). ¶

– [2] John 6:21 → GO <5217> [3] Acts 27:40 → to head for the beach → to make for the shore → SHORE <2722> [4] Eph. 1:10 → to head up → to gather together → GATHER <346>.

HEADLONG – [1] ***prēnēs*** [adj.: πρηνής <4248>] ▶ **Head first** > The term is used in regard to the death of Judas (Acts 1:18). ¶

– [2] Acts 19:36 → RASH <4312> [3] 2 Tim. 3:4 → HEADSTRONG <4312> [4] Jude 11 → to rush headlong into → to give oneself up → GIVE <1632>.

HEADQUARTERS – Matt. 27:27; Mark 15:16; John 18:28a, b, 33; 19:9 → governor's headquarters; his, i.e., Pilate's, headquarters → PRAETORIUM <4232>.

HEADSTRONG – [1] ***propetēs*** [adj.: προπετής <4312>]; **from *propiptō*: to fall forward, which is from *pro*: forward, and *piptō*: to fall ▶ Who acts precipitously, in a foolhardy manner** > In the last days, men will be headstrong (2 Tim. 3:4 {headlong, heady, rash, reckless}). Other ref.: Acts 19:36; see RASH <4312>. ¶

– [2] Titus 1:7 → SELF-WILLED <829>.

HEADWAITER – John 2:8, 9a, b → master of the feast → FEAST (noun) <755>.

HEADWAY – 1 Mark 6:48 → to make headway painfully → to be tormented at rowing → TORMENT (verb) <928>, ROWING <1643> 2 Acts 27:7a → to make slow headway → to sail along → SAIL (verb) <1020>.

HEADY – 2 Tim. 3:4 → HEADSTRONG <4312>.

HEAL – 1 ***therapeuō*** [verb: θεραπεύω <2323>]; **from *therapōn*: attendant, servant ► To restore someone's health, to relieve from an illness** > Jesus healed many sick and infirm people of their diseases (Matt. 4:23, 24; 8:7, 16; 9:35; 12:15, 22; 14:14; 15:30; 17:18; 19:2; 21:14; Mark 1:34; 3:10; 6:5, 13; Luke 4:40; 5:15; 6:18; 7:21; 8:2, 43; 9:6; John 5:10; Acts 5:16). He gave authority to heal (Matt. 10:1, 8; 17:16; Luke 9:1; 10:9). Some raised the question of healing or being healed on the Sabbath (Matt. 12:10; Mark 3:2; Luke 6:7; 13:14a, b; 14:3). This verb is transl. "to serve," "to worship" in Acts 17:25. Other refs.: Luke 4:23; Acts 4:14; 8:7; 28:9; Rev. 13:3, 12. ¶

2 ***iaomai*** [verb: ἰάομαι <2390>]; **akin to *iainō*: to cheer, to relieve the pain ► See 1; also transl.: to cure** > This verb is used in the physical sense (Matt. 8:8, 13; 15:28; Mark 5:29; Luke 5:17; 6:17, 19; 7:7; 8:47; 9:2, 11, 42; 14:4; 17:15; 22:51; John 4:47; 5:13; Acts 9:34; 10:38; 28:8; Jas. 5:16) and in the moral sense (Matt. 13:15; John 12:40; Acts 28:27; Heb. 12:13; 1 Pet. 2:24). ¶

3 ***sōzō*** [verb: σῴζω <4982>]; **from *sōs*: safe and sound ► See 1.** > This verb is used in Matt. 9:21, 22a, b; Mark 5:28, 34; 6:56; 10:52; Luke 8:48; 17:19; 18:42; John 11:12; Acts 4:9; 14:9. All other refs.: PRESERVE <4982>, SAVE (verb) <4982>.

4 ***diasōzō*** [verb: διασῴζω <1295>]; **from *dia*: through (intens.), and *sōzō*: see 3; lit.: to completely heal ► To save entirely from illness, infirmity** > This verb is used in Matt. 14:36. All other refs.: SAFELY <1295>, SAVE (verb) <1295>.

– 5 Luke 13:32 → lit.: to perform cures → PERFORM <2005>, CURE (noun) <2392> 6 John 5:11, 15 → SOUND (adj.) <5199> 7 John 6:2 → "by healing" added in Engl. 8 Acts 3:16 → to completely heal → to give complete soundness → GIVE <1325>, SOUNDNESS <3647> 9 Acts 4:22, 30 → who was miraculously healed, to heal → lit.: on whom this miracle of healing had been performed, for healing → HEALING <2392>.

HEALED – 1 John 5:6, 9 → SOUND (adj.) <5199> 2 Acts 4:10 → in good health → HEALTH <5199>.

HEALING – 1 ***therapeia*** [fem. noun: θεραπεία <2322>]; **from *therapeuō*: to serve, to heal ► Curing, restoring of health** > Jesus healed those who had need of healing (Luke 9:11). The leaves of the tree of life are for the healing of the nations (Rev. 22:2). Other refs.: Matt. 24:45; Luke 12:42; see HOUSEHOLD <2322>. ¶

2 ***iama*** [neut. noun: ἴαμα <2386>]; **from *iaomai*: to heal ► Result or means of curing** > The gifts of grace of physical healing were given in the church at its beginning Paul speaks of these gifts in 1 Cor. 12:9, 28, 30. They are among the "sign gifts," which differ from the gifts of teacher, pastor, and evangelist. ¶

3 ***iasis*** [fem. noun: ἴασις <2392>]; **from *iaomai*: to heal ► Process or act of restoring to health** > A miraculous healing had been performed on a man who was over forty years old (Acts 4:22). Acts 4:30 speaks of the Lord stretching out His hand to heal (lit.: for healing). Other ref.: Luke 13:32; see CURE (noun) <2392>. ¶

– 4 Luke 9:2 → to perform healing → lit.: to heal the sick → SICK (adj. and noun) <770> 5 Acts 3:16 → complete healing → complete soundness → SOUNDNESS <3647>.

HEALTH – 1 **in good health: *hugiēs*** [adj.: ὑγιής <5199>] **► Whose organism enjoys a sound physiological condition** > A sick man had been healed by the name of Jesus Christ and was in good health {healed, sound in body, whole} (Acts 4:10). All other refs.: SOUND (adj.) <5199>.

[2] **to be in health, in good health, in sound health: *hugiainō*** [verb: ὑγιαίνω <5198>]; **from *hugiēs*: see [1] ▶ To be healthy, to be well physically, to be healed** > Those who are in sound health {are well, are whole} do not need a physician (Luke 5:31). The bondman was found in good health {whole, well} (Luke 7:10). John desired that Gaius might be in good health {that all may go well for him} (3 John 2). All other refs.: SAFELY <5198>, SOUND (adj.) <5198>.

– [3] Acts 3:16 → perfect health → complete soundness → SOUNDNESS <3647> [4] Acts 27:34 → SURVIVAL <4991>.

HEALTHY – [1] **to be healthy: *ischuō*** [verb: ἰσχύω <2480>]; **from *ischus*: strength ▶ To have physical and moral strength** > Those who are healthy {are strong, are well, are whole} do not need a physician (Matt. 9:12; Mark 2:17). All other refs.: see entries in Lexicon at <2480>.

– [2] Matt. 6:22; Luke 11:34 → SINGLE <573> [3] Matt. 7:17, 18 → GOOD (adj. and noun) <18> [4] Matt. 12:13; 15:31 → SOUND (adj.) <5199> [5] Luke 5:31 → lit.: those who are in good health → HEALTH <5198>.

HEAP – [1] ***sōreuō*** [verb: σωρεύω <4987>]; **from *sōros*: heap ▶ To pile up, to accumulate** > By feeding and giving a drink to one's enemy, one heaps coals of fire upon his head (Rom. 12:20); for the explanation of this, see COAL <440>. Other ref.: 2 Tim. 3:6 (to load down); see LOAD (verb) <4987>. ¶

[2] ***episōreuō*** [verb: ἐπισωρεύω <2002>]; **from *epi*: upon, and *sōreuō*: see [1] ▶ To gather more, to surround oneself** > Paul warns Timothy that men will heap for {accumulate for, gather around} themselves teachers according to their own lusts (2 Tim. 4:3). ¶

[3] **to heap up treasure together: *thēsaurizō*** [verb: θησαυρίζω <2343>]; **from *thēsauros*: treasure ▶ To gather, to put in a reserve** > The rich men have heaped up treasure together {stored up their treasure, hoarded wealth} in the last days (Jas. 5:3). All other refs.: LAY <2343>, RESERVE <2343>, STORE (verb) <2343>, TREASURE (verb) <2343>.

– [4] Matt. 6:7 → to heap up empty phrases → lit.: much speaking → SPEAKING <4180> [5] Acts 13:45 → to heap abuse → BLASPHEME <987> [6] 1 Thes. 2:16 → to heap up → to fill up → FILL (verb) <378> [7] 2 Pet. 2:10; Jude 8 → to heap abuse → REVILE <987> [8] 2 Pet. 2:11 → to heap abuse when bringing judgment → lit.: to bring a reviling judgment → BRING <5342>, REVILING <989>, JUDGMENT <2920> [9] Rev. 18:5 → to heap up → REACH <2853>.

HEAR – [1] ***akouō*** [verb: ἀκούω <191>] ▶ **To listen to, to understand, to learn** > The mother and the brothers of Jesus are those who hear the word of God and do it (Luke 8:21); they are blessed (11:28). Mary of Bethany was sitting at Jesus's feet and hearing His word (Luke 10:39). The sheep of Jesus hear His voice (John 10:3, 16, 27). The people had heard that Jesus had done a miracle (John 12:18). The people had heard from the law that Christ abides forever (John 12:34). Everyone who is of the truth hears the voice of Jesus (John 18:37). The apostles heard that Samaria had received the word of God (Acts 8:14). The apostles and the brothers in Judea heard that the Gentiles had also received the word of God (Acts 11:1). Paul wanted to hear that the Philippians were standing fast in one spirit (Phil. 1:27); they were to do what they had heard from Paul (4:9). Paul had heard of the love and faith of Philemon (Phm. 5). Every man must be swift to hear, slow to speak, slow to anger (Jas. 1:19). If we ask anything according to the will of God, He hears us; and if we know that He hears us, whatever we ask, we know that we have what we have asked for (1 John 5:14, 15). This verb is also used in regard to Herod (Matt. 2:3; 14:1; Mark 6:14; Luke 9:7), the wise men (Matt. 2:9), a voice in Rama (Matt. 2:18), Joseph (Matt. 2:22), Jesus (Matt. 4:12; John 8:26, 40; 15:15 {to learn}), the Jews (Matt. 5:21, 27, 33, 38, 43; 13:15a, b; 26:65; Mark 2:1

{to noise, to report}; Mark 14:64; Luke 2:18; 4:23; John 8:43; 9:32; 12:12; Acts 11:18; 28:27a, b), John the Baptist (Matt. 11:2), two blind men (Matt. 20:30), the Pharisees (Matt. 22:34), a woman who had a flux of blood (Mark 5:27), a mother whose daughter was possessed (Mark 7:25), a scribe (Mark 12:28), the master of a bondman (Luke 7:3), Andrew (John 1:40), a father whose son was about to die (John 4:47), the disciples (John 6:60), Martha (John 11:20), Christians (Acts 1:4; 2:37; 4:4), lying men (Acts 6:11), Jacob (Acts 7:12), Ananias (Acts 9:13), Peter (Acts 11:7), the nations (Acts 15:7), the apostles and the elders at Jerusalem (Acts 15:24), the Athenians and the strangers sojourning at Athens (Acts 17:21 {to listen}, 32), the Corinthians (Acts 18:8), the disciples at Ephesus (Acts 19:2, 5), those who inhabited Asia (Acts 19:10), the brothers at Jerusalem (Acts 21:20), Paul's nephew (Acts 23:16), the Galatians (Gal. 1:13), Paul (Eph. 1:15; Col. 1:4, 9), the Colossians (Col. 1:23), the twelve tribes in the dispersion (Jas. 5:11), the beloved who are addressed by John (1 John 4:3), John (Rev. 1:10; 4:1; 5:11; 6:6; 9:13; 10:4, 8; 11:12; 12:10; 14:2, 13; 16:1; 18:4; 19:1, 6; 21:3), the voice of musicians (Rev. 18:22a), the sound of millstone (Rev. 18:22b), and the voice of the bridegroom and the bride (Rev. 18:23). Other refs.: Matt. 7:24, 26; 10:14; 11:15; 13:18; 14:13a, b; 15:10; 17:5; 18:15, 16; 21:33; Mark 4:3; 6:11, 16, 20, 29; 7:14; 9:7; 12:29; 16:11; Luke 1:58; 2:46; 6:27, 47; 9:35; 10:16a, b; 16:29, 31; 18:6; 20:45; John 9:27a, b, 31a, b, 35; 10:8, 20; Acts 2:22; 3:22, 23; 4:19; 5:5, 24; 6:14; 7:2, 37; 9:38; 10:46; 13:16; 14:14; 15:12, 13; 16:14, 38; 19:26; 22:1, 14, 22; 24:4; 26:3; 28:15, 28; Rom. 11:8; 1 Cor. 2:9; 5:1 {to report}; 11:18; 2 Cor. 12:4, 6; Gal. 1:23; 4:21; Eph. 1:13; Phil. 1:30; 2:26; 2 Thes. 3:11; 1 Tim. 4:16; 2 Tim. 2:14; Jas. 2:5; 1 John 4:5, 6a, b; Rev. 1:3; 2:7, 11, 17, 29; 3:3, 6, 13, 20, 22; 13:9. *

2 **to hear fully: *diakouō*** [verb: διακούω <1251>]**; from *dia*: through (intens.), and *akouō*: see 1 ► To listen thoroughly, e.g., in the case of a legal hearing >** Felix would hear Paul fully {give him a hearing} when his accusers had come (Acts 23:35). ¶

3 ***eisakouō*** [verb: εἰσακούω <1522>]**; from *eis*: to, and *akouō*: see 1 ► a. To listen with the idea of obeying >** The Lord said He would speak to His people by people of other tongues, but they would not hear Him (1 Cor. 14:21). **b. To answer prayers favorably (used in regard to God's answer to prayers) >** Some think they will be heard through their much speaking (Matt. 6:7). The supplications of Zacharias had been heard (Luke 1:13); the prayer of Cornelius had been heard (Acts 10:31); the Lord Jesus was heard because of His piety (Heb. 5:7). ¶

4 ***parakouō*** [verb: παρακούω <3878>]**; from *para*: aside, and *akouō*: see 1 ► To listen without paying attention >** Jesus speaks of a brother who refuses to hear {listen to} his brothers or the church (Matt. 18:17a, b). Other ref.: Mark 5:36; other mss. have *akouō*. ¶

5 **to hear already, before, previously: *proakouō*** [verb: προακούω <4257>]**; from *pro*: before, and *akouō*: see 1 ► To hear (to apprehend by the ear) previously >** The Colossians had heard before about the hope laid up for them in heaven (Col. 1:5). ¶

– 6 John 10:9 → who heard these words → lit.: because of these words 7 John 12:38; Rom. 10:16 → REPORT (noun) <189> 8 Acts 2:6 → to be heard → OCCUR <1096> 9 Acts 16:25 → LISTEN <1874> 10 Rom. 2:13; Jas. 1:25 → one who hears → HEARER <202> 11 Rom. 10:17b; Gal. 3:2, 5; 2 Pet. 2:8 → HEARING <189> 12 2 Cor. 6:2 → LISTEN <1873> 13 1 Thes. 2:13 → which you heard from us → lit.: of the report from us → REPORT (noun) <189>.

HEARD – 1 Acts 1:19 → KNOWN <1110> 2 Rom. 16:19 → to become known → KNOWN <864>.

HEARER – 1 ***akroatēs*** [masc. noun: ἀκροατής <202>]**; from *akroaomai*: to listen ► One who listens >** It is not the hearers of {those who hear} the law who are just before God (Rom. 2:13). James exhorts his audience to be not only hearers of {those who listen to} the word, but doers also (Jas. 1:22, 23). The one who is not a forgetful hearer of the law of liberty will be blessed in what he does (Jas. 1:25). ¶

[2] **to hear:** ***akouō*** [verb: ἀκούω <191>] ▶ **To listen, to understand** > Striving about words can only lead to the subversion of the hearers (lit.: those who hear) (2 Tim. 2:14). Other refs.: HEAR <191>.

– [3] Heb. 12:19 → those who heard → HEAR <191>.

HEARING – [1] ***akoē*** [fem. noun: ἀκοή <189>]**; from *akouō*: to hear, to understand ▶ a. Sense enabling the perception of sounds** > Just as in the human body the ear has been set among the other members for its own function of hearing, so in the body of Christ one Christian has been set among other Christians for a particular function (1 Cor. 12:17a {sense of hearing}, b {ear}). The Holy Spirit is received on the principle of the hearing {report, what is heard} of faith (Gal. 3:2, 5), i.e., the doctrine of faith. **b. What is heard, what is understood** > Faith comes by hearing, and hearing by the word of God (Rom. 10:17a, b). The Hebrews had become dull in hearing {to learn} (Heb. 5:11). Lot tormented his righteous soul by seeing and hearing {by what he saw and heard,} the lawless works of the men around him (2 Pet. 2:8). All other refs.: EAR <189>, FAME <189>, REPORT (noun) <189>, RUMOR <189>.

[2] **place of hearing:** ***akroatērion*** [neut. noun: ἀκροατήριον <201>]**; from *akroaomai*: to listen ▶ Place where someone is admitted and allowed to speak** > Paul was brought forth in the place of hearing {auditorium, hall of audience, audience room} (Acts 25:23). ¶

– [3] Luke 4:21 → in your hearing → lit.: in your ear (*ous*) → EAR <3775> [4] Luke 7:1 → in the hearing of the people → lit.: at the ears (*akoē*; see [1]) of the people [5] John 7:51 → to give a hearing → HEAR <191> [6] Acts 23:35 → to give a hearing → to hear fully → HEAR <1251> [7] Acts 25:21 → DECISION <1233>.

HEARKEN – [1] Mark 4:3; 7:14; Acts 4:19; 7:2; 15:13; Jas. 2:5 → HEAR <191> [2] Acts 2:14 → to give heed → HEED (noun) <1801> [3] Acts 12:13 → ANSWER (verb) <5219> [4] Acts 27:21 → LISTEN <3980>.

HEARKENING – Heb. 4:6, 11 → not hearkening to the word → DISOBEDIENCE <543>.

HEART – [1] ***kardia*** [fem. noun: καρδία <2588>] ▶ "The heart occupies the most important place in the human system. By an easy transition the word came to stand for man's entire mental and moral activity, both the rational and the emotional elements. In other words, the heart is used figuratively for the hidden springs of the personal life. As to its usage in the N.T., it denotes **a. the seat of physical life** (Acts 14:17; Jas. 5:5), **b. the seat of moral nature and spiritual life, i.e., the seat of grief** (John 14:1; Rom. 9:2; 2 Cor. 2:4), **c. joy** (John 16:22; Eph. 5:19), **d. the desires** (Matt. 5:28; 2 Pet. 2:14), **e. the affections** (Luke 24:32; Acts 21:13), **f. the perceptions** (John 12:40; Eph. 4:18), **g. the thoughts** (Matt. 9:4; Heb. 4:12), **h. the understanding** (Matt. 13:15; Rom. 1:21), **i. the reasoning powers** (Mark 2:6; Luke 24:38), **j. the imagination** (Luke 1:51), **k. conscience** (Acts 2:37; 1 John 3:20), **l. the intentions** (Heb. 4:12; see 1 Pet. 4:1), **m. purpose** (Acts 11:23; 2 Cor. 9:7), **n. the will** (Rom. 6:17; Col. 3:15), **o. faith** (Mark 11:23; Rom. 10:10; Heb. 3:12)." (a. to o.: after W. E. Vine.) **p. Middle, depth** > The Lord was three days and three nights in the heart of the earth (Matt. 12:40). In Eph. 1:18, some mss. have *kardia* and others have *dianoia* (understanding).

[2] **who knows the hearts:** ***kardiognōstēs*** [masc. noun: καρδιογνώστης <2589>]**; from *kardia*: heart, and *ginōskō*: to know ▶ Who understands the human heart, who perceives what are the most intimate feelings of human beings** > The Lord knows the hearts of all (Acts 1:24), and likewise God knows the hearts (15:8). ¶

[3] **to have one's heart fail:** ***apopsuchō*** [verb: ἀποψύχω <674>]**; from *apo*: far from, and *psuchō*: to breathe ▶ To faint, to die** >

During the great tribulation, men's hearts will be failing them {men will be ready to die, men will faint} from fear (Luke 21:26). ¶

[4] **to lose heart: *enkakeō*** [verb: ἐγκακέω <1457a>]; **from *en*: in, and *kakos*: bad ▶ To lack courage, to grow weary; also transl.: to faint** > Jesus told a parable to show that one ought always to pray and not lose heart {give up} (Luke 18:1). Paul did not lose heart (2 Cor. 4:1, 16); some mss. have *ekkakeō*. Other refs.: Eph. 3:13; see [5]; Gal. 6:9; 2 Thes. 3:13 in other mss. ¶

[5] **to lose heart: *ekkakeō*** [verb: ἐκκακέω <1573>] **or *enkakeō*** [verb: ἐγκακέω <1457a>]; **from *ek*: out (intens.), or *en*: in, and *kakos*: bad, evil ▶ To be discouraged, to be overwhelmed; also transl.: to faint** > Paul asked the Ephesians to not lose heart {faint, be discouraged} at his tribulations (Eph. 3:13). All other refs. (*ekkakeō*): see WEARY (adj.) <1573>, under <1457a>. Other refs. (*enkakeō*): 2 Cor. 4:1, 16; see [4]. ¶

[6] **to lose heart: *ekluō*** [verb: ἐκλύω <1590>]; **from *ek*: out (intens.), and *luō*: to loose ▶ To loose one's strength, to become weak, to slacken** > Christians will reap in due season if they do not lose heart {faint, give up} (Gal. 6:9). All other refs.: DISCOURAGED <1590>, FAINT <1590>, WEARY (adj.) <1590>.

[7] **to take heart: *euthumeō*** [verb: εὐθυμέω <2114>]; **from *euthumos*: who is cheerful, full of courage, which is from *eu*: well, and *thumos*: spirit, soul, feeling ▶ To have good courage, to have confidence, to be in good spirit** > Paul urged the men on the boat to take heart {be of good courage, keep up their courage, be of good cheer} (Acts 27:22, 25). Other ref.: Jas. 5:13 (to be happy); see HAPPY <2114>. ¶

[8] In Eph. 6:6 and Col. 3:23, "heart" translates the Greek word *psuchē*. See SOUL <5590> for the meaning of this word.

– [9] Matt. 9:2, 22; Mark 6:50; 10:49; 14:27; John 16:33 → to take heart → to take courage → COURAGE <2293> [10] Luke 7:13 → to have one's heart going to someone → to have compassion → COMPASSION <4697> [11] Luke 12:29 → to set one's heart on → SEEK <2212> [12] John 5:42 → in your hearts → lit.: in you [13] John 7:38 → WOMB <2836> [14] Acts 5:33; 7:54 → to be cut to the heart → to be furious → FURIOUS <1282> [15] Rom. 15:6 → with one heart → with one accord → ACCORD <3661> [16] 1 Cor. 10:6 → to set one's heart → LOVE (verb) <1937> [17] 2 Cor. 9:14 → to have the heart going out to → to long for → LONG (verb) <1971> [18] Gal. 6:9; 2 Thes. 3:13 → to lose heart → to become weary → WEARY (adj.) <1573>, under <1457a> [19] Col. 3:12; Phm. 7, 12, 20; 1 John 3:17 → ENTRAILS <4698> [20] Col. 3:21 → to lose heart → to become discouraged → DISCOURAGED <120> [21] 1 Tim. 3:1 → to set one's heart → DESIRE (verb) <3713> [22] 1 Pet. 3:8 → having a tender heart → TENDER-HEARTED <2155>.

HEARTILY – *polla*; from *polus* [plur. neut. of adj.: πολύς <4183>]; **lit.: much ▶ Much (with the idea of affection)** > Aquila and Priscilla greeted the Corinthians heartily {warmly} (1 Cor. 16:19). Other refs.: see entries in Lexicon at <4183>.

HEARTLESS – Rom. 1:31; 2 Tim. 3:3 → without natural affection → AFFECTION <794>.

HEARTY – [1] Acts 8:1 → to be in hearty agreement → CONSENT (verb) <4909> [2] 1 Cor. 16:19 → to send hearty greetings → lit.: to greet much → GREET <782>.

HEAT – [1] ***zēlos*** [masc. noun: ζῆλος <2205>]; **from *zeō*: to be hot, to be fervent; lit.: zeal ▶ Strength, vigor** > If we sin willfully after having received the knowledge of the truth, there remains a fearful expectation of judgment and heat of {fury of, raging} fire {and fiery indignation} which will devour the adversaries (Heb. 10:27). All other refs.: ENVY (noun) <2205>, JEALOUSY <2205>, MIND (noun) <2205>, ZEAL <2205>.

[2] ***thermē*** [fem. noun: θέρμη <2329>]; **from *thermos*: warm, which is from *therō*: to heat ▶ Increase in temperature caused by fire** > A viper came out because of the

heat of the fire and seized Paul's hand (Acts 28:3). ¶

3 ***kauma*** [neut. noun: καῦμα <2738>]; **from *kaiō*: to burn ► Scorching, burning heat; the result of burning, the heat produced by burning** > No heat {burning heat} will affect the saints coming out of the great tribulation (Rev. 7:16). When the fourth bowl was poured out on the sun, men were scorched with great heat (Rev. 16:9). ¶

4 **burning heat, scorching heat, heat: *kausōn*** [masc. noun: καύσων <2742>]; **from *kaiō*: to burn ► Scorching, burning hotness** > In a parable, some laborers in the vineyard had borne the burden of the day and the heat (Matt. 20:12). The Jews said there would be heat {hot day, hot weather} when they saw the south wind blow (Luke 12:55). The sun has risen with its burning heat (Jas. 1:11). ¶

5 **to burn with fervent heat, to be destroyed with intense heat, to be destroyed by fire: *kausoō*** [verb: καυσόω <2741>]; **from *kausis*: act of burning ► To consume by an intense conflagration** > In the day of the Lord, the elements will melt with fervent heat (lit.: will melt burning with fervent heat) (2 Pet. 3:10, 12). ¶

HEATEDLY – Acts 23:9 → to argue heatedly → STRIVE <1264>.

HEATHEN – See NATION <1484> <1482>.

HEAVEN – 1 ***ouranos*** [masc. noun: οὐρανός <3772>] ► **a. Atmosphere above the earth, firmament; also transl.: air, sky** > The word is used, for instance, in Matt. 6:26; 16:3 (see Gen. 1:8, 26). **b. Interstellar space of the creation** > The word is used in Acts 4:24 (see Gen. 1:1). Christians look for new heavens and a new earth (2 Pet. 3:13) to replace the present creation which will be destroyed by fire (v. 10). **c. Abode of God and the angels** > See, for instance, Matt. 5:16; 21:25; 24:36; John 3:13a–c, 31. When He returns, the Lord Himself will descend from heaven (1 Thes. 4:16); believers who have risen or been changed will go to meet Him (see v. 17). **d. Abode of the Christians** > The habitation of Christians is from heaven (2 Cor. 5:2). **e. Term designating the divine origin of something** > It is used concerning the kingdom of heaven (Matt. 19:14), John's baptism (Matt. 21:25; Luke 20:4, 5), a gift received from above (John 3:27). *

2 **from heaven: *ouranothen*** [adv.: οὐρανόθεν <3771>]; **from *ouranos*: heaven, and suffix *then*: from a place ►** This adv. is used in Acts 14:17; 26:13. ¶

3 **midst of heaven: *mesouranēma*** [neut. noun: μεσουράνημα <3321>]; **from *mesos*: midst, and *ouranos*: heaven ► Mid-sky; also transl.: midair, midheaven** > This Greek word is used in Rev. 8:13; 14:6; 19:17. ¶

– 4 Matt. 5:48 in some mss.; Acts 26:19 → in heaven, from heaven → HEAVENLY <3770> 5 Matt. 21:9; Mark 11:10; Luke 2:14 → "heaven" added in Engl. 6 1 Cor. 15:48a, b, 49; Phil. 2:10 → in heaven, from heaven → HEAVENLY <2032>.

HEAVENLIES – Eph. 1:3, 20; 2:6; 3:10; 6:12 → HEAVENLY <2032>.

HEAVENLY – 1 ***ouranios*** [adj.: οὐράνιος <3770>]; **from *ouranos*: heaven ► Which relates to heaven, celestial** > The word is applied to God the Father by Matthew (Matt. 5:48 {in heaven; some mss.: *ouranos*}; 6:14, 26, 32; 15:13) and to the host of angels praising God (Luke 2:13). Paul was not disobedient to the heavenly vision {vision from heaven} (Acts 26:19). ¶

2 ***epouranios*** [adj.: ἐπουράνιος <2032>]; **from *epi*: upon, in, and *ouranos*: heaven ► Who, which is in heaven** > The word is applied to God the Father (Matt. 18:35). The Jews would have not believed Jesus if He had told them heavenly things (John 3:12). The glory of the heavenly {celestial} bodies is different than that of terrestrial bodies (1 Cor. 15:40a, b). As is the heavenly (the Lord Jesus), so also are those who are heavenly {from heaven} (the Christians) (1 Cor. 15:48a, b); they will bear the image of the heavenly one {of the man from heaven} (v. 49). God the Father has blessed the Christians with all spiritual blessing in

the heavenly places {heavenly realms} (lit.: the heavenlies) (Eph. 1:3). He has seated Christ at His right hand in the heavenly places {heavenly realms} (lit.: the heavenlies) (Eph. 1:20), and the Christians as well (2:6). The manifold wisdom of God is made known to the principalities and powers in the heavenly places {heavenly realms} (lit.: the heavenlies) (Eph. 3:10). Christians wrestle against spiritual wickedness in the heavenly places {high places, the heavenly realms} (lit.: in the heavenlies) (Eph. 6:12). Knees in heaven (lit.: Heavenly knees) will bow at the name of Jesus (Phil. 2:10). God would preserve Paul for His heavenly kingdom (2 Tim. 4:18). The Hebrews were holy brothers, partakers of the heavenly calling (Heb. 3:1). The word is also used in the Epistle to the Hebrews concerning the heavenly gift (Heb. 6:4), the heavenly things (8:5; 9:23), a heavenly country (11:16), and the heavenly Jerusalem (12:22). ¶

HEAVENLY BODY – 2 Pet. 3:10, 12 → heavenly bodies → ELEMENT <4747>.

HEAVENWARD – Phil. 3:14 → HIGH (adv.) <507>.

HEAVILY – Matt. 13:15; Acts 28:27 → HARD <917>.

HEAVINESS – 1 **to be full of heaviness: *adēmoneō*** [verb: ἀδημονέω <85>]; **from a derivative of *adeō*: to be disgusted, to be overwhelmed ▶ To be depressed, preoccupied, tormented** > Epaphroditus was full of heaviness {distressed} because the Philippians had heard that he was sick (Phil. 2:26). Other refs.: Matt. 26:37; Mark 14:33 (to be very heavy); see HEAVY <85>. ¶
– 2 Rom. 9:2; 2 Cor. 2:1 → SORROW (noun) <3077> 3 Jas. 4:9 → GLOOM <2726> 4 1 Pet. 1:6 → to be in heaviness → SORROW (verb) <3076>.

HEAVY – 1 ***barus*** [adj.: βαρύς <926>] ▶ **Burdensome, oppressive** > The scribes and the Pharisees bound heavy {cumbersome} burdens on the shoulders of men (Matt. 23:4). All other refs.: BURDENSOME <926>, SAVAGE <926>, SERIOUS <926>, WEIGHTIER <926>.
2 **to be heavy: *bareō*** [verb: βαρέω <916>]; **from *barus*: see** 1 ▶ **To be oppressed, to be overcome** > The eyes of the disciples were heavy in Gethsemane (Matt. 26:43). On the mountain, Peter and those with him were heavy {were oppressed, were overcome} with sleep {were very sleepy} (Luke 9:32). All other refs.: BURDEN <916>.
3 **to be heavy: *katabareō*** [verb: καταβαρέω <2599>]; **from *kata*: down, and *bareō*: see** 2 ▶ **To be much oppressed, to be overcome** > The eyes of the disciples were heavy {very heavy} in Gethsemane (Mark 14:40); some mss. have *bareō, katabarunō.* Other ref.: 2 Cor. 12:16 in some mss. ¶
4 **to be very heavy: *adēmoneō*** [verb: ἀδημονέω <85>]; **from *adēmōn*: worried, tormented, which is from *adeō*: to be worried, to be tormented ▶ To feel a great weight, to be deeply depressed; also transl.: to be distressed, to be troubled** > In Gethsemane, Jesus began to be sorrowful and very heavy (Matt. 26:37; Mark 14:33: *akēdemoneō* in some mss.). Other ref.: Phil. 2:26 (to be full of heaviness); see HEAVINESS <85>. ¶
– 5 Matt. 11:28 → to be heavy laden → LOAD (verb) <5412> 6 Matt. 25:5 → to grow heavy → SLUMBER (verb) <3573> 7 Matt. 26:37; Mark 14:33 → to be very heavy → to be full of heaviness → HEAVINESS <85> 8 Luke 11:46 → heavy to bear → HARD <1419> 9 Rev. 11:19 → GREAT <3173>.

HEBER – ***Eber*** [masc. name: Ἔβερ <1443>]: **beyond, in Heb. ▶ Hebrew patriarch** > Heber is mentioned in the genealogy of Jesus (Luke 3:35; see Gen. 10:24: Eber). ¶

HEBREW – 1 ***Hebraios*** [masc. name: Ἑβραῖος <1445>]: **from Eber; see Gen. 10:21 ▶ The Hebrews are the ancestors of the Israelites who came from the east bank of the Euphrates River; the Jews called themselves by this name because they spoke Hebrew, or rather Aramaic, a related language** > The Hellenists murmured against the Hebrews because their widows were neglected in the daily service (Acts 6:1). Paul was a Hebrew (2 Cor. 11:22; Phil. 3:5a, b). ¶

2 ***Hebraikos*** [adj.: Ἑβραϊκός <1444>] ▶ **Hebraic** > The inscription over Jesus on the cross was written in Hebrew letters, as well as Greek and Latin (Luke 23:38). ¶

3 ***Hebrais*** [fem. noun: Ἑβραΐς <1446>] ▶ **Term describing the language of the Hebrews** > Paul spoke to the people in the Hebrew language (Acts 21:40; 22:2). The voice which spoke to Saul on the road to Damascus was in the Hebrew language (Acts 26:14). ¶

4 **in Hebrew: *Hebraisti*** [adv.: Ἑβραϊστί <1447>] ▶ **In the Hebraic language** > A pool of water in Jerusalem was called in Hebrew Bethesda (John 5:2). The place of the tribunal court was called in Hebrew Gabbatha (John 19:13) and the Place of the Skull, Golgotha (v. 17). The inscription above Jesus on the cross was written in Hebrew, Greek, and Latin (John 19:20). "Rabboni" is the term in Hebrew for "Teacher" (John 20:16 in some mss.). The name of the angel of the abyss in Hebrew is "Abaddon" (Rev. 9:11). Armageddon is the name in Hebrew of the place where the armies of the earth will be gathered together to fight the Lord (Rev. 16:16). ¶

HEDGE (noun) – ***phragmos*** [masc. noun: φραγμός <5418>]; **from *phrassō*: to enclose, to stop ▶ Fence or any sort of surrounding barrier to enclose a property, to prevent access to it; poss. also: narrow pathway between country plots** > In a parable, a landowner planted a vineyard and made a hedge {fence, wall} around it (Matt. 21:33 {hedged it round about}; Mark 12:1). The servant was to go into the highways and along the hedges {country lanes}, and constrain people to come in to the great supper (Luke 14:23). Other ref.: Eph. 2:14; see SEPARATION <5418>. ¶

HEDGE (verb) – Matt. 21:33 → to hedge round about → lit.: to make a hedge around → HEDGE (noun) <5418>.

HEED (noun) – 1 **to take heed: *blepō*** [verb: βλέπω <991>] ▶ **To look, to consider** > Every Christian must take heed {must see, must be careful} how he builds on Paul's foundation (1 Cor. 3:10). Other refs.: SEE <991>.

2 **to take heed, to give heed: *epechō*** [verb: ἐπέχω <1907>]; **from *epi*: upon, and *echō*: to have, to hold ▶ To be careful, to be attentive** > Paul tells Timothy to take heed {pay close attention, watch closely} to himself and to the teaching (1 Tim. 4:16). All other refs.: ATTENTION <1907>, HOLD (verb) <1907>, REMARK <1907>, STAY (verb) <1907>.

3 **to give heed, to give earnest heed, to heed, to take heed: *prosechō*** [verb: προσέχω <4337>]; **from *pros*: to, and *echō*: to have, to hold ▶ To hold, to give attention, to pay close attention, to attach oneself; also transl.: to pay attention, to follow** > Jesus says to take heed to oneself in order to not offend one's brother (Luke 17:3). He says to take heed to oneself in regard to carousing, drunkenness, and the anxieties of this life (Luke 21:34). The people gave heed to the things spoken by Philip (Acts 8:6). All had given heed to Simon the magician (Acts 8:10, 11 {to have regard}). Lydia gave heed to {attended, responded to} the things spoken by Paul (Acts 16:14). Paul told the elders of Ephesus to take heed to themselves and to all the flock (Acts 20:28). Paul urged Timothy to charge some not to give heed {turn their mind, devote themselves} to fables and endless genealogies (1 Tim. 1:4). Likewise, he charged Titus to rebuke certain people severely, that they might not give heed {turn their minds, pay attention} to Jewish fables and commandments of men (Titus 1:14). In the latter times, some will give heed to seducing spirits and doctrines of demons (1 Tim. 4:1). We must give the more earnest heed to the things we have heard, lest we drift away (Heb. 2:1). Christians do well to take heed to the prophetic word (2 Pet. 1:19). All other refs.: ATTENDANCE <4337>, BEWARE <4337>, GIVE <4337>.

4 **to give heed: *enōtizomai*** [verb: ἐνωτίζομαι <1801>]; **from *en*: in, and *ous*: ear ▶ To open the ear, to listen** > Peter

told the men of Judea and inhabitants of Jerusalem to give heed {hearken, heed, listen carefully} to his words (Acts 2:14). ¶

– [5] Matt. 18:10 → to take heed → SEE <3708> [6] Luke 11:35 → to take heed → WATCH (verb) <4648>.

HEED (verb) – [1] Acts 2:14 → to give heed → HEED (noun) <1801> [2] Acts 8:6, 11; 2 Pet. 1:19 → HEED (noun) <4337> [3] Rom. 10:16 → OBEY <5219>.

HEEL – ***pterna*** [fem. noun: πτέρνα <4418>] ▶ **Back part of the foot; "to lift up the heel against someone" is to harm him, with the idea of contempt, insolence, or betrayal** > Judas, who ate bread with Jesus, had lifted up his heel against Him (John 13:18). ¶

HEIFER – ***damalis*** [fem. noun: δάμαλις <1151>]; **from *damazō*: to tame ▶ Young cow, female of domestic cattle** > In the O.T. the ashes of a heifer were used for the cleansing of the flesh (i.e., of defiled persons) (Heb. 9:13). ¶

HEIGHT – [1] ***hupsos*** [neut. noun: ὕψος <5311>]; **from *hupsi*: high ▶ Elevation** > Paul wanted Christians to be fully able to understand the height (he is not specifying of what), and to know the love of Christ (Eph. 3:18). The length and the width and the height of the heavenly Jerusalem were equal (Rev. 21:16). All other refs.: DAYSPRING FROM ON HIGH <5311>, EXALTATION <5311>, HIGH (noun) <5311>.

[2] ***hupsōma*** [neut. noun: ὕψωμα <5313>]; **from *hupsi*: high ▶ Something elevated, high thing** > Neither height, nor other things, will be able to separate Christians from the love of God (Rom. 8:39). The weapons of Paul's warfare could overthrow every high thing {lofty thing, pretension} which exalts itself against the knowledge of God (2 Cor. 10:5). ¶

– [3] Matt. 6:27; Luke 12:25 → STATURE <2244>.

HEIR – [1] ***klēronomos*** [masc. noun: κληρονόμος <2818>]; **from *klēros*: portion, and *nemō*: to distribute ▶ He who receives goods by means of succession** > In a parable, the vine-growers wanted to kill the heir (Matt. 21:38; Mark 12:7; Luke 20:14). The promise that he would be the heir of the world was made to Abraham (Rom. 4:13, 14). Christians are heirs of God (Rom. 8:17a, b), heirs through God (Gal. 4:7), and heirs according to the promise to Abraham (Gal. 3:29; Heb. 6:17). The heir, as long as he is underage, does not differ at all from a servant, although he is master of all (Gal. 4:1). Christians have become heirs according to the hope of eternal life (Titus 3:7). God has established His Son heir of all things; the latter has inherited a name more excellent than the angels (Heb. 1:2, see v. 4). Noah became heir of righteousness (Heb. 11:7). James speaks of the poor of the world who are heirs of the kingdom (Jas. 2:5). ¶

[2] **heir together: *sunklēronomos*** [masc. noun: συγκληρονόμος <4789>]; **from *sun*: together, and *klēronomos*: see [1] ▶ One who receives with another goods by means of succession or inheritance** > The Christian husband and wife are heirs together of the grace of life (1 Pet. 3:7). Other refs.: Rom. 8:17; Eph. 3:6; Heb. 11:9; see JOINT HEIR <4789>. ¶

– [3] Gal. 4:2 → "heir" added in Engl.

HELD – [1] 1 Cor. 4:10 → held in disrepute → DISHONORED <820> [2] Heb. 2:15 → subject → SUBJECT (noun)[1] <1777> [3] Also past tense of HOLD (verb).

HELI – See ELI <2242>.

HELL – [1] ***geenna*** [fem. noun: γέεννα <1067>]; **from the Heb.: valley of Hinnom ▶ This term represents the lake of fire, the place of eternal torment** > The Israelites sacrificed their children by fire to the gods of the nations in the valley of Hinnom (see 2 Kgs. 23:10). Later, the detritus of Jerusalem, as well as the dead bodies of animals and brigands, were burned there; fire was kept continually burning there. The body and soul of unbelievers are the objects of eternal destruction in hell (Matt. 5:29, 30; 10:28). God has the power to cast into hell (Luke 12:5). Jesus speaks of the "judgment of hell" (Matt. 23:33) and of the "hell of fire," "hell, the fire unquenchable" (Matt. 5:22; 18:9; Mark 9:43, 45, 47). The tongue is set on fire by hell (Jas. 3:6), in the sense that it is capable of evil things. Other ref.: Matt. 23:15; see SON OF HELL <5207> <1067>. ¶

[2] **to cast to hell, to cast down to hell: *tartaroō*** [verb: ταρταρόω <5020>]**; from *tartaros*: the Tartar; lit.: to precipitate into the Tartarus, or bottom of gloom ▶ In the Greek mythology, Tartarus was a part of Hades where evil persons were kept and tormented >** God cast down to hell {cast down to the deepest pit of gloom} the angels who sinned (2 Pet. 2:4). ¶

[3] See HADES <86> for this word used in the KJV.

HELLENIST – See HELLENISTIC JEW <1675>.

HELLENISTIC JEW – *Hellēnistēs* [masc. name: Ἑλληνιστής <1675>]**; from *Hellas*: Greece ▶ Israelite who spoke the Greek language and who had adopted Greek customs; also transl.: Hellenist >** The Hellenistic Jews murmured against the Hebrews because their widows were neglected in the daily service (Acts 6:1). Saul disputed against the Hellenistic Jews at Jerusalem; they attempted to put him to death (Acts 9:29). Other ref.: Acts 11:20. ¶

HELMET – *perikephalaia* [fem. noun: περικεφαλαία <4030>]**; from *peri*: around, and *kephalē*: head; lit.: what surrounds the head ▶ Covering to protect the head >** Paul exhorts the Christian to take the helmet of salvation (Eph. 6:17), to put on the hope of salvation as a helmet (1 Thes. 5:8). ¶

HELMSMAN – Acts 27:11; Rev. 18:17 → PILOT <2942>.

HELP (noun) – [1] ***antilēmpsis*** [fem. noun: ἀντίλημψις <484>]**; from *antilambanō*: to come to the rescue, which is from *anti*: against, and *lambanō*: to take; lit.: laying hold; also spelled: *antilēpsis* ▶ Aid, assistance to anyone >** A service mentioned in 1 Cor. 12:28 which consists of aiding other Christians by responding to their various needs. ¶

[2] ***boētheia*** [fem. noun: βοήθεια <996>]**; from *boētheō*: to help, which is from *boē*: cry, and *theō*: to run ▶ Aid, assistance in response to the cry of a person in distress >** We must approach the throne of grace with boldness, that we may receive mercy and find grace for seasonable help (Heb. 4:16; some translate: to help, but it should be the noun). Other ref.: Acts 27:17; see CABLE <996>. ¶

[3] ***epikouria*** [fem. noun: ἐπικουρία <1947>]**; from *epikouros*: one who helps, especially during war ▶ Divine assistance, succor >** Paul had obtained that help which is from God (Acts 26:22). ¶

[4] ***epichorēgia*** [fem. noun: ἐπιχορηγία <2024>]**; from *epichorēgeō*: to supply, which is from *epi*: moreover, and *chorēgeō*: see SUPPLY** (verb) <5524> **▶ Aid, assistance; also transl.: provision, supply >** The supplication of the Philippians and the help given by the Spirit of Jesus Christ would turn out for Paul's deliverance (Phil. 1:19). Other ref.: Eph. 4:16; see SUPPLY (noun) <2024>. ¶

– [5] Matt. 15:5; Mark 7:11; John 6:63 → to receive help, to be help → PROFIT (verb) <5623> [6] Luke 1:54 → to give help → HELP (verb) <482> [7] Acts 11:29 → SERVICE <1248> [8] Acts 18:27 → to be a great help → HELP (verb) <4820> [9] Acts 27:17 → CABLE <996> [10] Rom. 8:26 → to join help → HELP (verb) <4878> [11] Rom. 16:2 → a great help → HELPER <4368> [12] Phil. 2:30 → SERVICE <3009> [13] Phil. 2:30 → LACK (noun) <5303> [14] Phil. 4:16 → "help" added in Engl. [15] Heb. 2:16a, b → to give help → to take hold → TAKE <1949> [16] Rev. 12:16 → to come to the help of → HELP (verb) <997>.

HELP (verb) – [1] ***boētheō*** [verb: βοηθέω <997>]**; from *boē*: cry, and *theō*: to run ▶ To assist, to support; also transl.: to aid,**

to come to the aid, to succour > A woman from Canaan asked the Lord to help her (Matt. 15:25). The father of a possessed child asked the Lord to help him (Mark 9:22), to help his unbelief (v. 24). A man prayed for Paul, in a vision, to come over to Macedonia and help them (Acts 16:9). Jews from Asia shouted to the men of Israel to help them {come to their aid} in arresting Paul (Acts 21:28). The Lord has said: "I have listened to you in an accepted time, and I have helped you in a day of salvation. Behold, now is the well-accepted time; behold, now is the day of salvation." (2 Cor. 6:2). In that He Himself has suffered, being tempted, Jesus is able to help those who are tempted (Heb. 2:18). The earth helped the woman who gave birth to the male Child (Rev. 12:16). ¶

[2] ***antilambanō*** [verb: ἀντιλαμβάνω <482>]; **from *anti*: particle of substitution, and *lambanō*: to take ▶ To take the cause of someone, to intervene on behalf of someone** > The Lord has helped {has given help, has holpen} Israel His servant (Luke 1:54). We must help the weak (Acts 20:35). Other ref.: 1 Tim. 6:2; see PROFIT (verb) <482>. ¶

[3] ***sullambanō*** [verb: συλλαμβάνω <4815>]; **from *sun*: together (intens.), and *lambanō*: to take ▶ To assist, to give a hand** > The fishermen signaled to their partners in the other boat to help them with the great multitude of fish in their net (Luke 5:7). Paul urges a companion to help {assist} those women who had labored with him in the gospel (Phil. 4:3). All other refs.: CONCEIVE <4815>, SEIZE <4815>, TAKE <4815>.

[4] ***sunantilambanō*** [verb: συναντιλαμβάνω <4878>]; **from *sun*: together, and *antilambanō*: see [2]; lit.: to join help ▶ To assist, to aid** > Martha asked the Lord to tell her sister to help her (Luke 10:40). The Spirit helps {joins its help to} the weaknesses of the Christians (Rom. 8:26). ¶

[5] ***eparkeō*** [verb: ἐπαρκέω <1884>]; **from *epi*: unto (intens.), and *arkeō*: to be strong ▶ To come in aid of, to assist with one's resources; also transl.: to assist, to impart relief, to relieve** > Paul speaks of a widow who had helped those in trouble (1 Tim. 5:10). Christians should assist their dependent widows, so that the church can assist those widows who are really in need, having no one to help them (1 Tim. 5:16a, b). ¶

[6] ***sumballō*** [verb: συμβάλλω <4820>]; **from *sun*: together, and *ballō*: to throw ▶ To be useful, to contribute to the progress** > Apollos greatly helped {contributed much to, was a great help to} those who had believed in Achaia (Acts 18:27). All other refs.: CONFER <4820>, MEET (verb) <4820>, PONDER <4820>.

[7] **to help, to help together: *sunupourgeō*** [verb: συνυπουργέω <4943>]; **from *sun*: together, and *hupourgos*: rendering service, which is from *hupo*: under, and *ergon*: work ▶ To work together, to cooperate** > The Christians in Corinth were helping together {were joining in helping} in prayer for Paul's deliverance (2 Cor. 1:11). ¶

– [8] Matt. 15:5; Mark 7:11; John 6:63 → PROFIT (verb) <5623> [9] Matt. 25:44; 2 Tim. 1:18; Heb. 6:10a, b → SERVE <1247> [10] Mark 14:7 → lit.: to do good → GOOD (adv.) <2095> [11] John 12:6 → to help oneself → more likely: to carry → BEAR (verb) <941> [12] John 14:16 → advocate to help → COMFORTER <3875> [13] Acts 26:22 → God has helped me → lit.: having obtained help from God → HELP (noun) <1947> [14] Rom. 16:2 → ASSIST <3936> [15] 1 Cor. 12:28 → those able to help others → lit.: helps → HELP (noun) <484> [16] 1 Cor. 16:11 → to help on the way → to set forward → SET (verb) <4311> [17] 1 Cor. 16:16 → to work with → WORK (verb) <4903> [18] 2 Cor. 8:19 → eagerness to help → ready mind → MIND (noun) <4288> [19] 1 Thes. 5:14 → SUPPORT (verb) <472> [20] 1 Tim. 5:10, 16a, b → RELIEVE <1884> [21] Heb. 2:16a, b → to take hold → TAKE <1949> [22] Heb. 4:16 → lit.: for help → HELP (noun) <996>.

HELPED (BE) – ***ōpheleō*** [verb: ὠφελέω <5623>]; **from *ophelos*: gain, interest ▶ To benefit, to become better** > A woman who had had a hemorrhage for twelve years had not been helped {had found no advantage, was nothing bettered} from medical consultations (Mark 5:26). All other refs.: PREVAIL <5623>, PROFIT (verb) <5623>, VALUE (noun) <5623>.

HELPER – [1] ***boēthos*** [masc. noun: βοηθός <998>]; **from *boētheō*: to help, which is from *boē*: cry, and *theō*: to run ▶ One who assists, one who responds to a shout of distress** > The Christian can boldly say that the Lord is his helper and he will not be afraid (Heb. 13:6). ¶

[2] ***prostatis*** [fem. noun: προστάτις <4368>]; **from *proistēmi*: to place oneself in front, which is from *pro*: before, and *histēmi*: to stand ▶ Woman who assists other people; patroness** > Phoebe had been a helper of {benefactor of, great help to, succourer of} many, and of Paul also (Rom. 16:2); *parastatis* in other mss. ¶

[3] See COMFORTER <3875>.

– [4] John 14:16, 26; 15:26; 16:7 → ADVOCATE (noun) <3875> [5] Acts 13:5 → SERVANT <5257> [6] Rom. 16:3, 9; 2 Cor. 1:24 → FELLOW WORKER <4904>.

HELPFUL – [1] Acts 20:20; 1 Cor. 6:12; 10:23 → to be helpful → PROFITABLE <4851> [2] 2 Tim. 4:11 → USEFUL <2173>.

HELPLESS – [1] Matt. 9:36 → scattered → SCATTER <4496> [2] Acts 4:9 → SICK <772> [3] Rom. 5:6 → POWERLESS <772>.

HEM (noun) – Matt. 9:20; 14:36; Mark 6:56; Luke 8:44 → FRINGE <2899>.

HEM (verb) – Luke 19:43 → to hem in → to close in → CLOSE (verb) <4912>.

HEMORRHAGE – [1] Matt. 9:20 → to suffer from a hemorrhage → to have a flow of blood → FLOW (noun) <131> [2] Mark 5:25; Luke 8:43, 44 → lit.: a flow of blood → BLOOD <129>, FLOW (noun) <4511>.

HEN – ***ornis*** [fem. noun: ὄρνις <3733>] **▶ Domestic farmyard bird known for watching over her little ones** > Jesus would have gathered the children of Jerusalem as a hen gathers her chickens under her wings (Matt. 23:37; Luke 13:34). ¶

HENCEFORTH – [1] ***loipou*** [adj.: λοιποῦ <3064>]; **from *loipos*: remaining; used as an adv.: *tou loipou*, referring to time ▶ From now on, for the rest** > Ref.: Gal. 6:17. ¶ ‡

– [2] Matt. 26:64; Rev. 14:13 → HEREAFTER <534> [3] Luke 1:48; 5:10; Acts 18:6; 2 Cor. 5:16 → NOW <3568> [4] Acts 4:17 → from now on → NOW <3371> [5] 2 Tim. 4:8; Heb. 10:13 → FINALLY <3063>.

HERALD – ***kērux*** [masc. noun: κῆρυξ <2783>]; **from *kērussō*: to proclaim, to preach ▶ Preacher, public messenger** > A herald presents a message on behalf of God. Paul was a herald of the glad tidings (1 Tim. 2:7; 2 Tim. 1:11). Noah was a preacher (or: herald) of righteousness (2 Pet. 2:5); he announced the righteousness of God in judgment upon the world of the ungodly. It has been noted that "herald" emphasizes the person who delivers the message; "evangelist," the message itself of the good news; "apostle," the relationship between God, who sends, and the messenger. ¶

HERB – [1] Matt. 13:32; Mark 4:32; Luke 11:42 → herb, garden herb → garden plant → PLANT (noun) <3001> [2] Heb. 6:7 → VEGETATION <1008>.

HERBAGE – Matt. 6:30 → GRASS <5528>.

HERD (noun) – [1] ***agelē*** [fem. noun: ἀγέλη <34>]; **from *agō*: to lead ▶ Number of animals gathered together** > The Greek term is used in the N.T. only in regard to swine (Matt. 8:30–32; Mark 5:11, 13; Luke 8:32, 33). ¶

– [2] John 4:12 → flocks and herds → CATTLE <2353>.

HERD (verb) – 1 Cor. 9:7 → SHEPHERD (verb) <4165>.

HERDSMAN – Matt. 8:33; Mark 5:14; Luke 8:34 → lit.: one who feeds → FEED <1006>.

HERE – [1] ***autou*** [adv.: αὐτοῦ <847>] ▶ **In this place, in that place; also transl.: there** > Refs.: Matt. 26:36; Acts 15:34; 18:19; 21:4. ¶

[2] ***deute*** [adv.: δεῦτε <1205>]; **plur. of *deuro*: here, hither, up to this time ▶ Come, come hither** > With the prep. *eis*, into or to: come to (Matt. 22:4; Mark 6:31). With the prep. *pros*, toward: come to (Matt. 11:28). With *opisō*, behind or after: come after, follow me (Matt. 4:19; Mark 1:17). With an impersonal (Matt. 21:38; Mark 12:7; Luke 20:14). Come see (Matt. 28:6; John 4:29). See also Matt. 25:34; John 21:12; Rev. 19:17. ¶ ‡

[3] ***enthade*** [adv.: ἐνθάδε <1759>]; **from *entha*: here, there ▶ To this place** > Refs.: Luke 24:41; John 4:15, 16; Acts 10:18; 16:28; 17:6; 25:17, 24. ¶ ‡

HEREAFTER – [1] ***aparti*** [adv.: ἀπάρτι <534>]; **from *apo*: from, and *arti*: now ▶ In the future, from now on** > Jesus says that hereafter (*ap' aparti*) {henceforth} the Son of Man would be seen sitting at the right hand of Power (Matt. 26:64). In Rev. 14:13, the word is transl. "from now on" {henceforth}. The word is found in John 1:51 in some mss. ¶

– [2] Mark 11:14 → EVER AGAIN <3371> [3] Luke 22:69 → NOW <3568>.

HERESY – Acts 24:14; 1 Cor. 11:19; Gal. 5:20; 2 Pet. 2:1 → SECT <139>.

HERETICAL – ***hairetikos*** [adj.: αἱρετικός <141>]; **from *haireō*: to choose, to take ▶ Who causes divisions, who introduces or promotes sects** > A heretical {divisive, factious} person {An heretick} must be rejected (Titus 3:10), for he divides by means of subversive teaching (see Acts 16:17; 20:30). ¶

HERETICK – Titus 3:10 → lit.: heretical person → HERETICAL <141>.

HERETOFORE – 1 Pet. 3:5 → FORMERLY <4218>.

HERITAGE – [1] 1 Pet. 5:3 → God's heritage → one who is entrusted to the charge → ENTRUST <2819> [2] Rev. 21:7 → will have this heritage → lit.: will inherit these things → INHERIT <2816>.

HERMAS – ***Hermas*** [masc. name: Ἑρμᾶς <2057>]; **perhaps from Hermes, a Greek god ▶ Christian man of Rome** > Paul sends greetings to Hermas in his letter to the church at Rome (Rom. 16:14). ¶

HERMES – ***Hermēs*** [masc. name: Ἑρμῆς <2060>]; **name of a Greek god ▶ Messenger and interpreter of the messages of the gods in Greek mythology (known as Mercurius among the Romans, or Mercury in Engl.); also a Christian man** > Witnesses of the healing of a man who had never walked, the people of Lystra called Paul "Hermes" because he took the lead in speaking (Acts 14:12). Paul sends greetings to Hermes in his letter to the church at Rome (Rom. 16:14). ¶

HERMOGENES – ***Hermogenēs*** [masc. name: Ἑρμογένης <2061>]: **born of Hermes, a Greek god ▶ Christian man of Asia** > Hermogenes turned away from Paul (2 Tim. 1:15). ¶

HEROD – ***Hērōdēs*** [masc. name: Ἡρῴδης <2264>] ▶ **a. Herod the Great, king of Judea** > Jesus was born during the reign of Herod (Matt. 2:1; Luke 1:5). This Herod sent soldiers to kill all the male children of Bethlehem from two years old and under (Matt. 2:3, 7, 12, 13, 15, 16, 19, 22); he died shortly after this massacre (see v. 19). **b. Herod Antipas, son of Herod the Great; tetrarch of Galilee** > This Herod had John the Baptist beheaded (Matt. 14:1, 3, 6; Mark 6:14, 16, 18, 20–22; Luke 3:1, 19; 9:7, 9). He wanted to kill Jesus (Luke 13:31), who called him "that fox" (see v. 32). He questioned Jesus at length, but Jesus answered him nothing; Herod clothed Him in a splendid robe in mockery; then he sent Him back to Pilate, and the two became friends that day, for previously they had been enemies (Luke 23:7, 8, 11, 12, 15).

Herod and Pontius Pilate are responsible for being gathered together with the nations and the people of Israel against Jesus (Acts 4:27). He died in A.D. 39. Johanna, the wife of Herod's steward Chuza, followed Jesus with others who ministered to Him out of their personal possessions (Luke 8:3). Manaen, of the church of Antioch, had been brought up with him (Acts 13:1). **c. Herod Agrippa I, grandson of Herod the Great, nephew of Herod Antipas** > This Herod was king of Judea (Acts 12:1). He laid his hands on certain Christians and had James, the son of Zebedee, put to death (see v. 2). He also had Peter taken and imprisoned; but the Lord delivered Peter out of the hand of Herod (Acts 12:6, 11, 19, 21). He died, eaten by worms, because he had not given glory to God (see v. 23). Paul was kept under guard in Herod's courtroom (Acts 23:35). **d. Herod Agrippa II, son of Herod Antipas** > See AGRIPPA <67> for the reference to this Herod in Acts 25:13. ¶

HERODIANS – ***Hērōdianoi*** [masc. noun plur.: Ἡρῳδιανοί <2265>] ▶ **Sectarian followers of King Herod who attempted to lead the people into the practices and leisure entertainment of the people of the nations** > They are mentioned in Matt. 22:16; Mark 3:6; 12:13. Herod urged the people to submit to the Romans and to pay tribute. ¶

HERODIAS – ***Hērōdias*** [fem. name: Ἡρῳδιάς <2266>] ▶ **Wife of Philip, the brother of Herod Antipas** > Herodias married Herod while her husband was still living, for which John the Baptist reproved her (Matt. 14:3 {see v. 4}; Mark 6:17 {v. 22 in some mss.}; Luke 3:19). Herodias resented John the Baptist and wanted to have him put to death (Mark 6:19). Her daughter danced and pleased Herod (Matt. 14:6; Mark 6:22). She incited her daughter to ask for the head of John. Herod sent to behead John in the prison (see Matt. 14:9–11). ¶

HERODION – ***Hērōdiōn*** [masc. name: Ἡρῳδίων <2267>] ▶ **Christian man of Rome** > Paul calls Herodion his relative and sends greetings to him in his letter to the church in Rome (Rom. 16:11). ¶

HESITATE – [1] Acts 10:20 → DOUBT (verb) <1252> [2] Acts 20:20 → to keep back → KEEP (verb) <5288> [3] Acts 20:27 → SHRINK <5288> [4] Rom. 4:20 → WAVER <1252>.

HESITATION – Acts 10:20; 11:12 → DOUBT (verb) <1252>.

HESLI – ***Hesli*** [masc. name: Ἑσλί <2069>]**: reserved by Jehovah, in Heb.; also spelled and transl.: Esli** ▶ **Man of the O.T.** > Hesli is mentioned in the genealogy of Jesus (Luke 3:25). ¶

HEW – [1] **to hew, to hew out: *latomeō*** [verb: λατομέω <2998>]**; from *las*: stone, and *temnō*: to cut** ▶ **To cut stones, to excavate; also transl.: to cut out** > Joseph of Arimathea laid the body of Jesus in his new tomb which he had hewn out in the rock (Matt. 27:60; Mark 15:46). Other ref.: Luke 23:53 in some mss. ¶

– [2] Matt. 3:10; 7:19; Luke 3:9 → to cut down → CUT <1581>.

HEZEKIAH – ***Ezekias*** [masc. name: Ἐζεκίας <1478>]**: strength from Jehovah, in Heb.** ▶ **King of Judah; also transl.: Ezechias** > Hezekiah is mentioned in the genealogy of Jesus Christ (Matt. 1:9, 10). He did what was right in the eyes of the Lord and put his trust in the God of Israel (see 2 Kgs. 18:1–8). ¶

HEZRON – ***Hesrōm*** [masc. name: Ἑσρώμ <2074>]**: walled in, in Heb.** ▶ **Man of the O.T.; also transl.: Esrom** > Hezron is mentioned in the genealogy of Jesus Christ (Matt. 1:3a, b; Luke 3:33). ¶

HID – Matt. 10:26; Luke 8:17; 12:2 → SECRET (adj. and noun) <2927>.

HIDDEN – [1] Matt. 10:26; Mark 4:22; Luke 8:17; 12:2; 1 Cor. 4:5; 2 Cor. 4:2; 1 Pet. 3:4 → SECRET (adj. and noun) <2927> [2] Luke 1:24 → to keep oneself hidden → to hide oneself → HIDE <4032> [3] Rom. 16:25 → to keep hidden → to keep silence → SILENCE (noun) <4601> [4] Heb. 4:13 → not manifest → MANIFEST (adj.) <852>.

HIDDEN (BE) – ***lanthanō*** [verb: λανθάνω <2990>] ► **To be concealed, to be unknown; other transl.: to escape the attention, to escape the notice, to forget, to be ignorant** > Jesus could not be hidden {keep His presence secret} (Mark 7:24). A woman saw that she was not hidden (Luke 8:47). Paul was persuaded that, of the things which he said, nothing was hidden from King Agrippa (Acts 26:26). This is hidden from men through their own willfulness: that heavens were of old, and an earth having its subsistence out of water and in water, by the word of God (2 Pet. 3:5). This is not to be hidden from us: that one day with the Lord is as a thousand years, and a thousand years as one day (2 Pet. 3:8). Other ref.: Heb. 13:2; see KNOW <2990>.

HIDE – [1] ***kruptō*** [verb: κρύπτω <2928>] ► **To keep from being seen, to conceal** > A city set on a hill cannot be hidden (Matt. 5:14). Jesus was going to utter things which had been hidden {kept secret} from the world's foundation (Matt. 13:35). He compares the kingdom of God to a treasure hidden in a field, which a man found and hid (Matt. 13:44a, b). A servant hid the talent of his master in the ground (Matt. 25:25). The saying of Jesus was hidden from the disciples (Luke 18:34). The things that belong to the peace of Jerusalem were hidden from her eyes (Luke 19:42). Jesus hid Himself from those who wanted to stone Him (John 8:59); He also hid Himself on another occasion (12:36). The life of the Christians is hidden with the Christ in God (Col. 3:3). Works that are not good cannot be hidden (1 Tim. 5:25). Moses was hidden three months by his parents (Heb. 11:23). To him who overcomes in Pergamum, the Lord will give to eat of the hidden manna (Rev. 2:17). Men will hide themselves in the caves and in the rocks of the mountains (Rev. 6:15); they will tell the mountains and the rocks to hide them from the face of God and from the wrath of the Lamb (v. 16). ¶

[2] ***apokruptō*** [verb: ἀποκρύπτω <613>]; **from *apo*: from, and *kruptō*: see [1] ► To keep secret, to keep concealed** > The Father has hidden things from the wise and prudent (Matt. 11:25; Luke 10:21). A servant hid his master's money (Matt. 25:18). Paul speaks of the hidden wisdom of God (1 Cor. 2:7). He was to make all Gentiles see what is the fellowship of the mystery hidden in God (Eph. 3:9; Col. 1:26). ¶

[3] ***enkruptō*** [verb: ἐγκρύπτω <1470>]; **from *en*: in, and *kruptō*: see [1] ► To dissimulate, to bury** > In a parable, a woman hid {mixed} leaven in three measures of meal (Matt. 13:33; Luke 13:21). ¶

[4] ***perikruptō*** [verb: περικρύπτω <4032>]; **from *peri*: around, and *kruptō*: see [1] ► To keep secret, to conceal** > Elizabeth conceived and hid herself {kept herself in seclusion, remained in seclusion for} five months (Luke 1:24). ¶

[5] ***parakaluptō*** [verb: παρακαλύπτω <3871>]; **from *para*: along, and *kaluptō*: to cover, to hide ► To veil, to conceal from someone's understanding** > The saying of Jesus was hidden {was concealed} from His disciples (Luke 9:45). ¶

[6] **hid, hidden: *apokruphos*** [adj.: ἀπόκρυφος <614>]; **from *apokruptō*: see [2] ► Concealed from the eyes, kept secret** > There is nothing hidden which will not become manifest (Mark 4:22; Luke 8:17). All the treasures of wisdom and knowledge are hidden in Christ (Col. 2:3). ¶

[7] **hidden: *kruptos*** [adj.: κρυπτός <2927>]; **from *kruptō*: see [1] ► Secret, concealed** > The Lord will bring to light the hidden things of darkness (1 Cor. 4:5). Peter mentions the hidden person {inner self} of the heart (1 Pet. 3:4). All other refs.: SECRET (adj. and noun) <2927>.

– [8] Luke 8:16; Jas. 5:20 → COVER <2572> [9] Luke 11:33 → a place to hide → a secret place → PLACE (noun) <2926> [10] Acts 1:9 → RECEIVE <5274> [11] 2 Cor. 4:3a, b → VEIL (verb) <2572> [12] Heb. 4:13 → hidden → not manifest → MANIFEST (adj.) <852>.

HIERAPOLIS – ***Hierapolis*** [fem. name: Ἱεράπολις <2404>]**: holy city; from *hieros*: holy, sacred, and *polis*: city ▶ City near Colossae and Laodicea in Asia Minor** > Epaphras had a particular concern for the Christians of this city (Col. 4:13). ¶

HIGH (adj.) – [1] ***hupsēlos*** [adj.: ὑψηλός <5308>]**; from *hupsos*: height ▶ a. Elevated** > The devil took Jesus to a very high mountain (Matt. 4:8); Luke says "into a high mountain" (Luke 4:5). Jesus took three of His disciples up on a high mountain (Matt. 17:1; Mark 9:2). **b. Elevated, glorious** > Christians must not set their mind on high things {be haughty in mind, be proud} (Rom. 12:16). Jesus has become higher than {exalted above} the heavens (Heb. 7:26). Other refs.: Heb. 1:3; Rev. 21:10, 12. All other refs.: ESTEEMED <5308>, UPLIFTED <5308>.
[2] **highest, most high: *hupsistos*** [adj. and adj. used as noun: ὕψιστος <5310>]**; superl. from the base of *hupsos*: height ▶ a. Very elevated** > The heavenly host said: Glory to God in the highest (Luke 2:14). The crowds who went before Jesus cried, saying: Hosanna in highest! (Matt. 21:9; Mark 11:10; Luke 19:38). A possessed girl said that Paul and others were the servants of the Most High God (Acts 16:17). Melchizedek was the priest of the Most High God (Heb. 7:1). **b. Very elevated in speaking of God** > For this title of God, see MOST HIGH <5310>. All other refs.: HIGHEST <5310>.
– [3] Mark 6:21 → high captain, high officer → CAPTAIN <5506> [4] Luke 4:38 → GREAT <3173> [5] Acts 17:12 → of high standing → PROMINENT <2158> [6] Eph. 1:3, 20; 2:6; 3:10; 6:12 → high places → HEAVENLY <2032> [7] Eph. 3:18 → how high → lit.: the height → HEIGHT <5311> [8] Jas. 1:9 → high position → EXALTATION <5311>.

HIGH (adv.) – ***anō*** [adv.: ἄνω <507>] **▶ From above, heavenly** > Paul was pressing toward the goal for the prize of the high calling {upward call, upward calling, calling on high} of God {the prize for which he had been called heavenward by God} in Christ Jesus (Phil. 3:14). All other refs.: HIGH (ON) <507>.

HIGH (ON) – ***anō*** [adv.: ἄνω <507>] **▶ Upward, above, in a higher place** > The water-vessels were filled up to the brim (or: on high) (John 2:7). Jesus was from on high (John 8:23). He lifted up His eyes on high, and addressed His Father (John 11:41). Christians are to seek the things which are above (or: on high) (Col. 3:1) and have their minds on these things (v. 2). Other refs.: Acts 2:19; Gal. 4:26; Heb. 12:15. Other ref.: Phil. 3:14; see HIGH (adv.) <507>. ¶

HIGH (noun) – ***hupsos*** [neut. noun: ὕψος <5311>]; **from *hupsi*: high ▶ Elevated place** > The disciples were to be clothed with power from on high (Luke 24:49). Having ascended up on high, Jesus has led captivity captive (Eph. 4:8). All other refs.: DAYSPRING FROM ON HIGH <5311>, EXALTATION <5311>, HEIGHT <5311>.

HIGH-BORN – Luke 19:12; 1 Cor. 1:26 → NOBLE <2104>.

HIGH-MINDED – Rom. 11:20; 1 Tim. 6:17 → to be high-minded → to be conceited → CONCEITED <5309>.

HIGH OFFICIAL – Mark 6:21 → LORD (noun) <3175>.

HIGH PRIEST – [1] ***archiereus*** [masc. noun: ἀρχιερεύς <749>]**; from *archē*: denoting dignity, rank, and *hiereus*: priest ▶ Chief priest who was to exercise the priesthood until his death (see Num. 35:25)** > Under the law, he was the only one who might enter the Most Holy Place of the tabernacle once a year, with blood and incense (Heb. 9:7, 25; 13:11; see Leviticus 16). The Gospels and Acts make reference to the high priest of those times (e.g., Matt. 26:3; Acts 4:6). The Epistle to the Hebrews reveals Christ as the High Priest in heaven (2:17; see 10:21). He sustains Christians until salvation is finalized (Heb. 7:26). He presents them to God and He presents their offerings to God, sanctifying them (see Heb.

13:15); He intercedes for them (see Rom. 8:34). At His entrance into heaven after His resurrection, He received the honor of High Priest for eternity according to the order of Melchizedek (see Heb. 5:6; 7:3, 23, 24). He will exercise this priestly office, in the order of this priesthood, for the blessing of the future kingdom (Heb. 9:11). *
– [2] Acts 4:6 → lit.: high priestly → HIGH-PRIESTLY <748>.

HIGH-PRIESTLY – ***archieratikos*** [adj.: ἀρχιερατικός <748>]; **from *archiereus*: chief priest, which is from *archē*: denoting dignity, rank, and *hiereus*: priest, which is from *hieros*: holy, sacred ▶ Which belongs to the high priest** > Peter and John appeared before all who were of the high-priestly family (Acts 4:6). ¶

HIGH RANKING – Acts 25:23 → high ranking military officer → CAPTAIN <5506>.

HIGHER – [1] ***anōteron*** [adv.: ἀνώτερον <511>]; **compar. of *anō*: on high ▶ Term describing a more important place** > One might tell a person who had sat down in the last place to go up higher (Luke 14:10). Other ref.: Heb. 10:8 {above, previously}. ¶
– [2] Rom. 13:1 → GOVERNING <5242> [3] 1 Cor. 12:31 → BETTER <2909> [4] 1 Cor. 12:31 in some mss. → greater → GREAT <3187>.

HIGHEST – ***hupsistos*** [adj.: ὕψιστος <5310>]; **superl. of *hupsos*: height ▶ Most elevated region, i.e., the dwelling place of God** > The term is used in Matt. 21:9; Mark 11:10; Luke 2:14; 19:38. All other refs.: HIGH (adj.) <5310>.

HIGHEST POINT – Matt. 4:5; Luke 4:9 → PINNACLE <4419>.

HIGHFLOWN – 2 Pet. 2:18 → highflown words → boastful words → WORD <5246>.

HIGHLY – [1] Luke 16:15 → highly esteemed → ESTEEMED <5308> [2] Acts 5:13 → to esteem highly → ESTEEM (verb) <3170>.

HIGHLY (VERY) – ***huperekperissou*; from *huper*: above, *ek*: from, and *perissos*: abundant ▶ Very intensely, exceedingly** > Christians are to esteem very highly in love those who admonish them (1 Thes. 5:13). All other refs. (*perissos*): see ABUNDANTLY <4053>, ADVANTAGE <4053>, SUPERFLUOUS <4053>.

HIGHMINDED – [1] Rom. 11:20 → to be highminded → to be haughty → HAUGHTY (adj.) <5309> [2] 2 Tim. 3:4 → PUFF UP <5187>.

HIGHWAY – Matt. 22:9, 10; Mark 10:46; Luke 14:23 → WAY <3598>.

HILL – [1] ***bounos*** [masc. noun: βουνός <1015>] ▶ **Elevated ground, small mountain** > John was preaching that every mountain and hill would be brought low at the coming of the Lord (Luke 3:5). There would be days when people of Jerusalem would say to the hills to cover them (Luke 23:30). ¶
[2] **hill country: *oreinos*** [adj.: ὀρεινός <3714>]; **from *oros*: mountain ▶ Mountainous region** > Mary went into the hill country (Luke 1:39). People discussed what had happened to Zacharias throughout all the hill country of Judea (Luke 1:65). ¶
– [3] Matt. 5:14; Luke 4:29; 9:37 → MOUNTAIN <3735>.

HIMSELF – ***autou*** [pron.: αὐτοῦ <848>] ▶ Refs.: Matt. 1:21; 3:12; Luke 5:25; 9:14; 2 Tim. 2:19; Rev. 16:17.

HINDER (adj.) – Mark 4:38; Acts 27:41 → hinder part → STERN <4403>.

HINDER (verb) – [1] ***anakoptō*** [verb: ἀνακόπτω <348>]; **from *ana*: backward, and *koptō*: to hit repeatedly, to stop abruptly ▶ To stop, to restrain** > Paul asks the Galatians who did hinder them {cut in on them and kept them} that they should not obey the truth (Gal. 5:7); some mss. have *enkoptō*: see [2]. ¶

[2] ***enkoptō*** [verb: ἐγκόπτω <1465>]; **from *en*: in, and *koptō*: to cut ► a. To hamper, to impede** > Paul had been often hindered from coming to the Christians in Rome (Rom. 15:22). Satan had hindered him {stopped him, thwarted him, blocked his way} from coming to the Thessalonians (1 Thes. 2:18). **b. To interrupt, to obstruct** > Husbands are to honor their wives so their prayers may not be hindered (1 Pet. 3:7). For this verb in Gal. 5:7; see [1]. Other ref.: Acts 24:4; see TEDIOUS (BE) <1465>. ¶

[3] ***kōluō*** [verb: κωλύω <2967>]; **from *kolos*: truncated ► To prevent, to stop** > The lawyers had hindered those who were entering (Luke 11:52). The eunuch asked what was hindering him from being baptized {why shouldn't he be baptized} (Acts 8:36). Paul had been hindered {had been let} to go to Rome (Rom. 1:13). All other refs.: FORBID <2967>, REFUSE (verb) <2967>, RESTRAIN <2967>.

– [4] 1 Cor. 9:12 → lit.: to give a hindrance → GIVE <1325>, HINDRANCE <1464> [5] Heb. 12:1 → something that hinders → WEIGHT <3591>.

HINDRANCE – [1] ***enkopē*** [fem. noun: ἐγκοπή <1464>]; **from *enkoptō*: to cut in, to impede, which is from *en*: in, and *koptō*: to cut down, to strike ► Impediment, obstacle** > Paul bore all things, that he might put no hindrance {not hinder, cause no hindrance} in the way of the gospel of Christ (1 Cor. 9:12); *ekkopē* in some mss. ¶

– [2] Matt. 16:23; Rom. 14:13; 16:17 → STUMBLING BLOCK <4625> [3] Acts 28:31 → without hindrance → no one forbidding → FORBID <209>.

HINT – Eph. 5:3 → to be a hint → NAME (verb) <3687>.

HIRE (noun) – [1] Matt. 20:8; Luke 10:7; 1 Tim. 5:18; Jas. 5:4 → WAGES <3408> [2] 2 Cor. 11:8 → WAGES <3800>.

HIRE (verb) – [1] ***misthoō*** [verb: μισθόω <3409>]; **from *misthos*: salary, reward ► To engage, to employ for pay** > A landowner went out to hire workmen for his vineyard (Matt. 20:1, 7). ¶

– [2] Luke 15:15 → to hire oneself out → to join oneself → JOIN <2853>.

HIRED – [1] Mark 1:20; John 10:12, 13a, b → hired man, hired servant, hired hand → he who serves for wages → WAGES <3411> [2] Luke 15:17, 19 → hired man, hired servant → SERVANT <3407> [3] Acts 28:30 → hired house, hired lodging → rented house → HOUSE <3410>.

HIRELING – John 10:12, 13a, b → he who serves for wages → WAGES <3411>.

HISTORY – Acts 17:26 → "in history" added in Engl.

HIT – [1] Matt. 26:68; Luke 22:64 → STRIKE <3817> [2] Luke 6:29 → STRIKE <5180> [3] 2 Cor. 11:20 → BEAT <1194>.

HITHER – ***hōde*** [adv.: ὧδε <5602>] ► Refs.: Matt. 8:29; 14:18; 17:17. *

HITHERTO – [1] ***arti*** [adv.: ἄρτι <737>] ► **Until this moment, until now** > The disciples had asked nothing in the name of Jesus hitherto (John 16:24). Most of the five hundred brothers who had seen the risen Lord were living until now {unto this present, to the present, still} (or: hitherto; i.e., until the moment when Paul wrote his letter) (1 Cor. 15:6). *

– [2] Rom. 1:13 → present time → PRESENT TIME <1204>.

HOARD – Jas. 5:3 → to hoard wealth → to heap up treasure together → HEAP <2343>.

HOIST – [1] Acts 27:17 → to take on board → BOARD (noun) <142> [2] Acts 27:40 → LIFT <1869>.

HOLD (noun) – [1] ***phulakē*** [fem. noun: φυλακή <5438>]; **from *phulassō*: to keep, to watch ► Refuge of dangerous and evil creatures; also transl.: haunt, prison** > Great Babylon will become a hold of every unclean spirit and a hold of every unclean and hated bird (Rev. 18:2a, b). All other refs.: GUARD (noun) <5438>, PRISON <5438>, WATCH (noun) <5438>.

[2] **to lay hold, to take hold: *katalambanō*** [verb: καταλαμβάνω <2638>]; **from *kata*: intens., and *lambanō*: to take ▶ To take over, to take possession; also transl.: to apprehend** > Paul sought to take hold {get possession} of Christ, seeing that also he had been taken hold {had been taken possession} by Christ (Phil. 3:12a, b); he did not count to have taken hold {got possession} himself (v. 13). All other refs.: see entries in Lexicon at <2638>.

– [3] Matt. 11:12 → to lay hold → SEIZE <726> [4] Matt. 12:11; Mark 5:41; 9:27 → to lay hold, to take hold → TAKE <2902> [5] Matt. 21:46; 22:6; 26:57; 28:9; Mark 3:21; 12:12; 14:51; Heb. 6:18; Rev. 20:2 → to lay hold, to take hold of → SEIZE <2902> [6] Luke 5:9 → to lay hold on → SEIZE <4023> [7] Luke 20:20, 26 → to take hold → CATCH (verb) <1949> [8] Luke 22:54 → to lay hold → SEIZE <4815> [9] Acts 2:24 → to keep one's hold → HOLD (verb) <2902> [10] Acts 4:3 → PRISON <5084> [11] Acts 18:17; 21:30, 33; 1 Tim. 6:12, 19 → to lay hold, to take hold → SEIZE <1949>.

HOLD (verb) – [1] ***krateō*** [verb: κρατέω <2902>]; **from *kratos*: power, strength ▶ To keep, to hold firm, to observe, to retain, to restrain** > The Jews washed their hands diligently, thus holding {observing} the tradition of the elders (Mark 7:3). They have received many things traditionally to hold {observe} (Mark 7:4). They held the tradition of men (Mark 7:8). The eyes of the disciples of Emmaus were restrained {were kept, were prevented} from recognizing the Lord (Luke 24:16). If the disciples retained (or: held) the sins of anyone, they were retained (John 20:23b {to not forgive}). It was not possible that Jesus should be held by death (Acts 2:24). A lame man held {was clinging to} Peter and John (Acts 3:11). Paul exhorted the Thessalonians to hold fast the instructions taught by his word or by his letter (2 Thes. 2:15). One holding the seven stars in His right hand sent a message to the church in Ephesus (Rev. 2:1). Some held the doctrine of Balaam (Rev. 2:14, 15). John saw four angels holding fast {holding back} the four winds of the earth (Rev. 7:1). All other refs.: FAST (HOLD) <2902>, GAIN (verb) <2902>, KEEP (verb) <2902>, SEIZE <2902>, TAKE <2902>.

[2] ***antechō*** [verb: ἀντέχω <472>]; **from *anti*: in face, and *echō*: to hold ▶ To hold firmly, to honor** > A man who wants to serve two masters will hold {will be loyal, will be devoted} to one and despise the other (Matt. 6:24; Luke 16:13 {to cleave}). All other refs.: FAST (HOLD) <472>, SUPPORT (verb) <472>.

[3] **to hold forth, fast, out: *epechō*** [verb: ἐπέχω <1907>]; **from *epi*: upon, over, and *echō*: to hold; lit.: to hold above ▶ To carry, to have, to hold firm** > The Philippians were to hold forth the word of life, for the glory of Paul in Christ's day (Phil. 2:16). All other refs.: ATTENTION <1907>, HEED (noun) <1907>, REMARK <1907>, STAY (verb) <1907>.

[4] **to hold, to hold firmly: *katechō*** [verb: κατέχω <2722>]; **from *kata*: intens., and *echō*: to hold ▶ To keep, to retain** > The Christians of Corinth were holding firmly to the teachings of Paul (1 Cor. 11:2). Other ref.: Rom. 7:6. All other refs.: see entries in Lexicon at <2722>.

[5] **to hold, to hold in custody: *sunechō*** [verb: συνέχω <4912>]; **from *sun*: together, and *echō*: to have ▶ To guard, to keep under close watch** > The men who held Jesus mocked him, beating Him (Luke 22:63). All other refs.: see entries in Lexicon at <4912>.

[6] ***chōreō*** [verb: χωρέω <5562>]; **from *chōra*: place; lit.: to make a place ▶ To contain, to include within its volume** > At the wedding of Cana, the water jars held from twenty to thirty gallons (John 2:6). All other refs.: see entries in Lexicon at <5562>.

– [7] Matt. 19:5; Mark 10:7; Eph. 5:31 → to hold fast → to be joined → JOIN <4347> [8] Mark 6:19 → to hold against → to hold a grudge → GRUDGE (noun) <1758> [9] Mark 11:32 → COUNT <2192> [10] Luke 22:24 → to be held → CONSIDER <1380> [11] Luke 24:17 →

to hold conversation → lit.: to exchange words → EXCHANGE (verb) <474> 12 John 4:37 → here the saying holds true → lit.: in this the word is true 13 John 8:31 → CONTINUE <3306> 14 John 8:44; Rom. 14:4b → STAND (verb) <2476> 15 John 19:29 → they held a sponge to His mouth → OFFER <4374> 16 Acts 7:60 → to hold against → CHARGE (verb) <2476> 17 Acts 25:21; 2 Pet. 2:9 → to hold, to hold over → RESERVE <5083> 18 Rom. 3:28 → CONCLUDE[1] <3049> 19 Rom. 10:21 → to hold out → to stretch out → STRETCH <1600> 20 Rom. 12:9 → to hold fast → CLING <2853> 21 Gal. 2:6 → to be held in high esteem → to be of reputation → REPUTATION <1380> 22 Gal. 5:1 → to be held in → ENTANGLED (BE) <1758> 23 Eph. 4:16 → to hold together → to knit together → KNIT <4822> 24 Phil. 3:16 → to hold true → to walk by the same; to walk by the same rule (in some mss.) → WALK <4748> 25 Col. 1:17 → to hold together → to subsist together → SUBSIST <4921> 26 Col. 2:19 → to hold together → to unite together → UNITE <4822> 27 1 Tim. 6:5 → SUPPOSE <3543> 28 2 Tim. 4:16 → to hold against → IMPUTE <3049>.

HOLE – 1 ***opē*** [fem. noun: ὀπή <3692>] ► **Cavern, opening in the earth** > O.T. people of faith wandered in deserts and mountains, and in caves and holes in the ground {in dens and caves of the earth} (Heb. 11:38). Other ref.: Jas. 3:11; see OPENING <3692>. ¶

2 ***trumalia*** [fem. noun: τρυμαλιά <5168>]; **from *truō*: to wear out, to consume ► Perforation at the end of a sewing needle allowing one to insert thread; eye (of a needle)** > It is easier for a camel to go through the eye of a needle, than for a rich man to enter the kingdom of God (Mark 10:25; Luke 18:25: other mss. have *trēma*). See NEEDLE <4476>. ¶

3 ***trupēma*** [neut. noun: τρύπημα <5169>]; **from *trupaō*: to perforate ► See 2.** > It is easier for a camel to go through the eye of a needle, than for a rich man to enter the kingdom of God (Matt. 19:24; other mss.: *trēma, trumalia*). See NEEDLE <4476>. ¶

4 ***phōleos*** [masc. noun: φωλεός <5454>] ► **Place where an animal lurks, in which he makes his den** > Foxes have holes {dens}, but the Son of Man had nowhere to lay His head (Matt. 8:20; Luke 9:58). ¶

– 5 Matt. 25:18 → to dig a hole → DIG <3736>.

HOLIDAY – 1 Mark 6:21 → lit.: opportune day → OPPORTUNE <2121> 2 Col. 2:16 → FEAST (noun) <1859>.

HOLIEST – Heb. 9:8; 10:19 → holiest, holiest of all → SANCTUARY <39>.

HOLILY – 1 Thes. 2:10 → DEVOUTLY <3743>.

HOLINESS – 1 ***hagiasmos*** [masc. noun: ἁγιασμός <38>]; **from *hagiazō*: to sanctify, which is from *hagios*: holy, which is from *hagos*: religious respect, reverence toward God ► Sanctification, moral purity** > Christians are to yield their members in bondage to righteousness unto holiness (Rom. 6:19); they have their fruit to holiness (v. 22). Christ Jesus has been made to Christians holiness from God (1 Cor. 1:30). The will of God, their holiness, is that Christians should abstain from sexual immorality (1 Thes. 4:3) and that each one of them should possess his own vessel in sanctification {a way that is holy} (v. 4); God has not called Christians to uncleanness, but in sanctification {to live a holy life} (v. 7). They have been chosen in sanctification {sanctifying work} of the Spirit (2 Thes. 2:13) and elected by sanctification {sanctifying work} of the Spirit (1 Pet. 1:2). The Christian woman is enjoined to continue in holiness {sanctity} (1 Tim. 2:15). We are exhorted to pursue holiness, without which no one will see the Lord (Heb. 12:14). ¶

2 ***hagiotēs*** [fem. noun: ἁγιότης <41>]; **from *hagios*: holy ► Separation from evil according to the character and the nature of God** > God disciplines Christians for their good that they may share in His holiness (Heb. 12:10). ¶

3 ***hagiōsunē*** [fem. noun: ἁγιωσύνη <42>]; **from *hagios*: holy ► Setting apart,**

separation in moral purity > The Holy Spirit is called the Spirit of holiness (Rom. 1:4). Paul desires that the Lord Jesus might establish the hearts of the Thessalonians in holiness before God the Father (1 Thes. 3:13). He invites the Corinthians to perfect holiness in the fear of God (2 Cor. 7:1). ¶

4 ***hosiotēs*** [fem. noun: ὁσιότης <3742>]; **from *hosios*: holy, sacred ▶ Godliness, obedience to God** > God had granted Israel to serve Him in holiness {piety} and righteousness (Luke 1:75). The Christian is called to put on the new man, which according to God is created in true righteousness and holiness (Eph. 4:24). ¶

– 5 Acts 3:12 → GODLINESS <2150> 6 2 Cor. 1:12 → SIMPLICITY <572> 7 1 Tim. 2:2 → GRAVITY <4587> 8 Titus 2:3 → as becometh holiness → REVERENT <2412> 9 2 Pet. 3:11 → lives of holiness → lit.: holy conduct (plural in Greek) → HOLY <40>, CONDUCT (noun) <391>.

HOLLOW – 1 2 Cor. 9:3 → to prove hollow → to be in vain → VAIN <2758> 2 Col. 2:8 → VAIN <2756>.

HOLY (adj.) – 1 ***hagios*** [adj.: ἅγιος <40>]; **from *hagos*: religious respect, reverence toward God; same root as *hagnos*: pure ▶ Quality of one who or of that which is consecrated to God, set apart for Him; holiness is also an attribute of God Himself who is separate from evil; other transl.: sacred** > The term qualifies God the Father (John 17:11), Jesus, the Servant of God (Acts 4:27), and God (1 Pet. 1:15a, 16b; Rev. 4:8a–c; 6:10); the name of God is holy (Luke 1:49), as well as His temple (1 Cor. 3:17), His law (Rom. 7:12a), His commandment (Rom. 7:12b; 2 Pet. 2:21), His covenant (Luke 1:72), and His calling (2 Tim. 1:9). It designates the angels who have not sinned (Mark 8:38; Luke 9:26; Acts 10:22; Rev. 14:10), the prophets (Luke 1:70; Acts 3:21; 2 Pet. 3:2), men of God (2 Pet. 1:21), the apostles (Eph. 3:5), John the Baptist (Mark 6:20), Christians (Eph. 1:4; Col. 1:22; 3:12; 1 Thes. 5:27; Heb. 3:1; 1 Pet. 1:15b, 16a; Rev. 20:6), and children of married parents of whom only one is a Christian (1 Cor. 7:14). Christians greet one another with a holy kiss (Rom. 16:16; 1 Cor. 16:20; 2 Cor. 13:12; 1 Thes. 5:26). They are exhorted to present their bodies a living sacrifice, holy to God (Rom. 12:1). They are built up a holy priesthood (1 Pet. 2:5); they are a holy nation (v. 9) and a holy temple (Eph. 2:21); as the bride of Christ, the church is holy and blameless (Eph. 5:27). In relation to Israel, the olive tree: the firstfruit, the lump, the root, and the branches are holy (Rom. 11:16). The first sanctuary of the tabernacle is called Holy (Heb. 9:2), the second is called the Holy of Holies (v. 3); see SANCTUARY <39>. The new Jerusalem is the holy city (Rev. 11:2; 21:2, 10; 22:19: *hagion*). Enoch spoke of the Lord who has come amidst His holy myriads (Jude 14). Moses stood on holy ground (Acts 7:33). The prophets of God had promised the gospel of God in the Holy Scriptures (Rom. 1:2). The unmarried woman is occupied with the things of the Lord, that she may be holy both in body and in spirit (1 Cor. 7:34). Christians are to be characterized by holy conduct while waiting for the day of the Lord (2 Pet. 3:11). They build themselves up on their most holy faith (Jude 20). According to the law, every male who opened the womb was called holy to the Lord (Luke 2:23). Other refs.: see SAINT <40>.

2 **that which is holy, what is holy, what is sacred: *hagion*; neut. of *hagios*** [adj. used as noun: ἅγιος <40>] **▶ The sacred** > Jesus says not to give that which is holy (which has value in the eyes of God) to dogs (those who are unable to appreciate such things) (Matt. 7:6). Other refs. for *hagios*: see 1.

3 ***hieros*** [adj.: ἱερός <2413>] **▶ Sacred** > Timothy knew the Holy Scriptures (i.e., the writings of the O.T.) from childhood (2 Tim. 3:15 {sacred letters, the sacred writings}). Other ref.: 1 Cor. 9:13; see SACRED <2413>. ¶

4 ***hosios*** [adj.: ὅσιος <3741>] **▶ Godly, righteous** > One translator's footnote to the related Heb. word in the O.T. suggests it is a matter of goodness in God, as well as piety in man toward God or one's fellows. Paul desired that men pray lifting up holy

hands (1 Tim. 2:8). The Son of God, as high priest, is holy (Heb. 7:26). The Lord God only is holy (Rev. 15:4; 16:5). Other ref.: Acts 13:34 (the holy and sure blessings of David). All other refs.: DEVOUT <3741>, HOLY (noun) <3741>.

– [5] 1 Cor. 7:14a, b; Eph. 5:26; 1 Tim. 4:5; 2 Tim. 2:21; Heb. 2:11a, b; 10:10, 14; 13:12; 1 Pet. 3:15; Rev. 22:11 → to make holy, to be holy → SANCTIFY <37> [6] 1 Thes. 2:10 → DEVOUTLY <3743> [7] 1 Thes. 3:13 → to be holy → lit.: in holiness → HOLINESS <42> [8] 1 Thes. 4:4, 7 → way that is holy, to live a holy life → HOLINESS <38> [9] Heb. 11:7 → in holy fear → to be moved with fear → FEAR (noun) <2125>.

HOLY (noun) – [1] ***hosios*** [adj. used as noun: ὅσιος <3741>] ▶ **One who is gracious, pious, righteous** > The term is used in Acts 2:27; 13:35. All other refs.: DEVOUT <3741>, HOLY (adj.) <3741>.

– [2] Matt. 7:6 → HOLY (adj.) <40> [3] Mark 1:24; Luke 4:34; Acts 3:14; 1 John 2:20; et al. → holy one → SAINT <40> [4] Heb. 9:2, 3; 10:19 → Holy, Holy of Holies, Holy Place, Holiest of all, Most Holy Place → SANCTUARY <39>.

HOLY, HOLY ONE – For this title of the Lord Jesus, see HOLY (adj.) <3741> and HOLY ONE, HOLY THING <40>.

HOLY ONE, HOLY THING – holy: *hagios* [adj.: ἅγιος <40>]**; from *hagos*: religious respect, reverence toward God ▶ Venerable; separated from sin and set apart for God** > This word is used by the angel Gabriel to characterize Jesus before His birth: the holy thing {that Holy One, the holy offspring} who was to be born would be called the Son of God (Luke 1:35). Other refs.: HOLY (adj.) <40>.

HOLY PEOPLE – Rom. 1:7 → SAINT <40>.

HOLY PLACE – Heb. 9:2, 24, 25; et al. → holy place, most holy place → SANCTUARY <39>.

HOLY PLACES – Heb. 9:8, 12; 10:19; 13:11 → SANCTUARY <39>.

HOLY SPIRIT – ***Hagion Pneuma*; holy: *hagios*** [adj.: ἅγιος <40>]**; from *hagos*: religious respect, reverence toward God; spirit: *pneuma*** [neut. name: πνεῦμα <4151>]**; from *pneō*: to breath ▶ Third person of the Trinity** > The Holy Spirit is named with the Father and the Son in Matt. 28:19. He was sent by God the Father and by the Lord Jesus (John 14:26; 15:26). Many passages attest to His personality and divine authority. Ananias lied to the Holy Spirit (Acts 5:3); Paul and Timothy were forbidden by the Holy Spirit to preach in Asia and He did not permit them to go into Bithynia (Acts 16:6, 7). The saints are built together to be a habitation of God by the Spirit (Eph. 2:22; 1 Cor. 3:16). It is the Holy Spirit who gives life to those who are saved (John 6:63) and seals them (Eph. 1:13); He dwells in them and baptizes them into one body in Christ (1 Cor. 12:13). He is their Comforter (*paraklētos*) or Advocate on the earth, as Jesus Christ is in heaven (John 14:16, 26). Although the influence of the Holy Spirit acted in the saints of the O.T., He did not come to earth as a Person before the ascension of Christ (see John 16:7). In addition to His work in the saints and by them, His presence on earth after the crucifixion of the Lord brings demonstration to the world of sin, of righteousness, and of judgment (see John 16:8–11). (After Walter Scott.) *

HOMAGE – Matt. 2:2, 8, 11; 4:9; 8:2; 9:18; 14:33; 15:25; 18:26; 20:20; 28:9, 17; Mark 5:6; 15:19; Luke 4:7; 24:52; John 9:38; Acts 7:43; 10:25; 1 Cor. 14:25; Rev. 3:9; 4:10; 5:14; 13:4a, b, 8, 12, 15; 14:7, 9, 11; 15:4; 19:4, 10a, b; 20:4; 22:8, 9 → to do homage, to pay homage → WORSHIP (verb) <4352>.

HOME – [1] **busy at home, worker at home, diligent in home work, keeper at home, homemaker: *oikourgos*** [adj. or adj. used as noun: οἰκουργός <3626>]**; from *oikos*: house, and *ouros*: keeper ▶ One**

looking after domestic matters with care > Older sisters are to teach younger women to be diligent in home work (Titus 2:5); *oikouros* in other mss. ¶
– [2] Matt. 9:6, 7 → HOUSE <3624> [3] Matt. 13:57; Mark 6:4; 13:34; 2 Cor. 5:1 → HOUSE <3614> [4] Luke 12:36 → to come home → RETURN (verb) <360> [5] Luke 16:9 → TABERNACLE <4633> [6] Luke 23:48 → to return home → lit.: to return → RETURN (verb) <5290> [7] John 14:23 → MANSION <3438> [8] 1 Cor. 4:11 → to be without a home → to be homeless → HOMELESS <790> [9] 2 Cor. 5:6, 8, 9 → to be at home → lit.: to be present → PRESENT (BE) <1736> [10] Heb. 11:9a → to make one's home → DWELL <3939> [11] Jude 6 → HABITATION <3613> [12] Rev. 18:2 → DWELLING PLACE <2732>.

HOMELAND – Heb. 11:14 → COUNTRY <3968>.

HOMELESS – to be homeless: *astateō* [verb: ἀστατέω <790>]; **from *astatos*: unstable, which is from *a*: neg., and *histēmi*: to stand ► To wander, to be without a home >** Paul was homeless {had no certain dwelling place, was without a home} (1 Cor. 4:11). ¶

HOMEMAKER – Titus 2:5 → diligent in home work → DILIGENT <3626>.

HOMESTEAD – Acts 1:20 → DWELLING PLACE <1886>.

HOMETOWN – Matt. 13:54, 57; Mark 6:1, 4; Luke 4:23, 24; John 4:44 → COUNTRY <3968>.

HOMOSEXUAL – [1] ***arsenokoitēs*** [masc. noun: ἀρσενοκοίτης <733>]; **from *arsēn*: man, and *koitē*: bed ► Person sexually active with a member of one's own sex >** Homosexuals {Abusers of themselves with men, Sodomites} will not inherit the kingdom of God (1 Cor. 6:9; see v. 10). The law is made for the homosexual {one who defiles himself with men, perverts, sodomites} (1 Tim. 1:10; see v. 9). ¶
[2] ***malakos*** [adj. and adj. used as noun: μαλακός <3120>]; **lit.: soft ► Man without virility, submissive in same-sex relationship >** Homosexuals {Male prostitutes, Effeminate} will not inherit the kingdom of God (1 Cor. 6:9). Other refs.: Matt. 11:8a, b; Luke 7:25; see DELICATE <3120>. ¶

HOMOSEXUALITY – 1 Cor. 6:9; 1 Tim. 1:10 → who practice homosexuality → HOMOSEXUAL <733>.

HONEST – [1] ***kalos*** [adj.: καλός <2570>] **► Morally upright, just; worthy of the esteem of others; also transl.: excellent, good, honorable, noble, right >** Those who keep the word in an honest heart bring forth fruit (Luke 8:15). The Christian is exhorted to provide things honest before all men (Rom. 12:17). Paul was careful to provide for things honest before the Lord and before men (2 Cor. 8:21). Peter exhorts his readers to have their conduct honest among the Gentiles (1 Pet. 2:12). Other refs.: see entries in Lexicon at <2570>.
– [2] Phil. 4:8 → NOBLE <4586>.

HONESTLY – [1] ***euschēmonōs*** [adv.: εὐσχημόνως <2156>]; **from *euschēmōn*: becoming, honorable, which is from *eu*: well, and *schēma*: appearance ► Decently, honorably; also transl.: becomingly, properly >** Christians are exhorted to conduct themselves honestly (Rom. 13:13). Other refs.: 1 Cor. 14:40; 1 Thes. 4:12; see DECENTLY <2156>, PROPERLY <2156>. ¶
– [2] 1 Tim. 2:2 → DIGNITY <4587> [3] Heb. 13:18 → to live honestly → lit.: to conduct oneself well → CONDUCT (verb)[1] <390>, WELL <2573>.

HONESTY – 1 Tim. 2:2 → GRAVITY <4587>.

HONEY – ***meli*** [neut. noun: μέλι <3192>] **► Sweet, syrupy substance produced by bees from the nectar of flowers; bee: *melissa* in Greek >** John the

Baptist ate locusts and wild honey (Matt. 3:4; Mark 1:6). In his vision, the apostle John ate a little book which was as sweet as honey in his mouth (Rev. 10:9, 10). ¶

HONEYCOMB – comb (see COMB) of honey: *melissios* [adj.: μελίσσιος <3193>]; **from *melissa*: bee, which is from *meli*: honey ▶ Made with honey** > After His resurrection, Jesus ate some honeycomb (lit.: comb of honey) (Luke 24:42 in some mss.). ¶

HONOR (noun) – [1] ***euschēmosunē*** [fem. noun: εὐσχημοσύνη <2157>]; **from *euschēmōn*: comely, honorable, which is from *eu*: good, well, and *schēma*: form, aspect ▶ Respect, regard** > Our members which are less presentable obtain a greater honor (1 Cor. 12:23). ¶

[2] ***timē*** [fem. noun: τιμή <5092>]; **from *tiō*: to esteem, to respect ▶ Respect, esteem; also transl.: honorable use, special purposes** > A prophet has no honor in his own country (John 4:44). Paul was honored with many honors {in many ways, with many marks of respect} (Acts 28:10). Some seek honor by persevering in good works (Rom. 2:7). There will be glory and honor to every man who does good (Rom. 2:10). The potter has power to make a vessel to honor (Rom. 9:21). Christians are to render honor to others (Rom. 12:10; 13:7a, b). We clothe the less honorable members of the body with more abundant honor (1 Cor. 12:23); God has given more abundant honor to the part that lacked (v. 24). Ordinances give the body a certain honor (Col. 2:23); other transl.: these ordinances are of no value against the satisfaction of the flesh. Everyone should know how to possess his own vessel in honor (1 Thes. 4:4). To God alone belongs honor and glory (1 Tim. 1:17), as well as honor and eternal might (6:16). Elders who take the lead among the saints well are to be esteemed worthy of double honor (1 Tim. 5:17). Servants are to consider their own masters worthy of all honor {of full respect} (1 Tim. 6:1). In a great house, there are such vessels (2 Tim. 2:20). If someone purifies himself from vessels of dishonor, he will be a vessel to honor (2 Tim. 2:21). God has crowned His Son with glory and honor (Heb. 2:7, 9). He who builds the house has more honor than the house (Heb. 3:3). No one could take the honor of being high priest to himself, only if he was called by God (Heb. 5:4). The proving of the faith of Christians will be found to honor at the revelation of Jesus Christ (1 Pet. 1:7). The husband is to give honor to {treat with respect} his wife (1 Pet. 3:7). Jesus received from God the Father honor and glory (2 Pet. 1:17). He who sits on the throne and the Lamb receive honor (Rev. 4:9, 11; 5:12, 13; 7:12; 21:26). Salvation, glory, honor, and power belong to God (Rev. 19:1 in some mss.). The kings of the earth will bring their glory and their honor into the new Jerusalem (Rev. 21:24). All other refs.: PRICE (noun) <5092>.

[3] **in honor: *timios*** [adj.: τίμιος <5093>]; **from *timē*; honor, respect ▶ Respected, precious** > Marriage is to be held in honor {to be honourable, to be honored} in every way (Heb. 13:4). All other refs.: HONORED <5093>, PRECIOUS <5093>.

[4] **without honor: *atimos*** [adj.: ἄτιμος <820>]; **from *a*: neg., and *timē*: see [1] ▶ Without respect, without esteem, despised** > A prophet is not without honor, except in his own country and in his own house (Matt. 13:57; Mark 6:4). All other refs.: DISHONORED <820>, HONORABLE <820>.

[5] **in honor: *entimos*** [adj.: ἔντιμος <1784>]; **from *en*: in, and *timē*: see [1] ▶ In respect, in esteem; also transl.: in reputation, in high regard** > Paul told the Philippians to have in honor {to honor} men like Epaphroditus (Phil. 2:29). All other refs.: DEAR <1784>, HONORABLE <1784>, PRECIOUS <1784>.

– [6] Acts 19:17 → to hold in high honor → MAGNIFY <3170> [7] Rom. 14:6a–c → added in Engl. [8] 1 Cor. 4:10 → without honor → DISHONORED <820> [9] 1 Pet. 2:7 → PRICE (noun) <5092> [10] 1 Pet. 2:17a → to show honor → HONOR (verb) <5091>.

HONOR (verb) – 1 *timaō* [verb: τιμάω <5091>]; **from *timē*: esteem, honor ▶ To respect, to esteem >** God commanded all to honor their father and mother (Matt. 15:4; 19:19; Mark 7:10; 10:19; Luke 18:20; Eph. 6:2), which some did not do (Matt. 15:6). Israel honored God with their lips (Matt. 15:8; Mark 7:6). All are to honor the Son, as they honor the Father; he who does not honor the Son does not honor the Father who has sent Him (John 5:23a–d). Jesus honored His Father (John 8:49). If anyone serves Jesus, the Father will honor him (John 12:26). The inhabitants of Malta honored Paul and his travel companions with great honors (Acts 28:10). Timothy was to honor {to give proper recognition to} widows who were really widows (1 Tim. 5:3). We are to honor all people and the king (1 Pet. 2:17a, b). Other refs.: Matt. 27:9a, b; see PRICE (verb) <5091>. ¶
– 2 Luke 4:15; John 8:54a, b → GLORIFY <1392> 3 Rom. 1:25 → WORSHIP (verb) <4573> 4 Rom. 12:10 → honor one another above yourselves → lit.: take the lead to pay honor to the other → HONOR (noun) <5092> 5 Phil. 1:20 → MAGNIFY <3170> 6 Phil. 2:29 → lit.: to have in honor → HONOR (noun) <1784> 7 1 Pet. 3:15 → to honor as holy → SANCTIFY <37> 8 3 John 6 → in a manner that honors God → in a manner worthy of God → WORTHY <516>.

HONORABLE – 1 *euschēmōn* [adj.: εὐσχήμων <2158>]; **from *eu*: well, and *schēma*: appearance ▶ Distinguished, eminent >** Joseph of Arimathea was an honorable {a prominent, a respected} member of the council (Mark 15:43). All other refs.: COMELY <2158>, PRESENTABLE <2158>, PROMINENT <2158>.
2 **one more honorable: *entimoteros*; compar. of *entimos*** [adj.: ἔντιμος <1784>]; **from *en*: in, and *timē*: esteem, honor ▶ More important, more distinguished >** A guest at a wedding might be obliged to yield his place to a more honorable person (Luke 14:8). All other refs. (*entimos*): DEAR <1784>, HONOR (noun) <1784>, PRECIOUS <1784>.
3 **less honorable: *atimos*** [adj.: ἄτιμος <820>]; **from *a*: neg., and *timē*: honor ▶ Without honor, unworthy of respect >** We clothe the less honorable members of the body with more abundant honor (1 Cor. 12:23). All other refs.: DISHONORED <820>, HONOR (noun) <820>.
– 4 Rom. 9:21; 2 Tim. 2:20, 21 → for honorable use → lit.: to honor, for honor → HONOR (noun) <5092> 5 Rom. 12:17; 2 Cor. 8:21; 1 Pet. 2:12 → HONEST <2570> 6 1 Cor. 4:10 → HONORED <1741> 7 2 Cor. 13:7 → GOOD (adj.) <2570> 8 Phil. 4:8 → NOBLE <4586> 9 Heb. 13:4 → in honor → HONOR (noun) <5093> 10 Jas. 2:7 → WORTHY <2570>.

HONORABLY – 1 1 Cor. 7:36 → to not act honorably → to behave unseemly → BEHAVE <807> 2 Heb. 13:18 → to live honorably → to conduct oneself well → CONDUCT (verb)[1] <390>, WELL (adv.) <2573>.

HONORED – 1 *endoxos* [adj.: ἔνδοξος <1741>]; **from *en*: in, and *doxa*: glory ▶ Distinguished, esteemed >** The Corinthians were honored {distinguished, glorious, honourable}, but Paul and his companions were despised (1 Cor. 4:10). All other refs.: GLORIOUS <1741>, GORGEOUSLY <1741>.
2 *timios* [adj.: τίμιος <5093>]; **from *timē*: honor, respect ▶ Esteemed, respected >** Gamaliel was honored {respected, held in honor, held in respect} by all the people (Acts 5:34). All other refs.: HONOR (noun) <5093>, PRECIOUS <5093>.

HONOUR (noun) – See HONOR (noun).

HONOUR (verb) – See HONOR (verb).

HONOURABLE – See HONORABLE.

HOOK – *ankistron* [neut. noun: ἄγκιστρον <44>]; **from *ankos*: bend, curve ▶ Bent device for catching fish >** Jesus told Peter to throw a hook {line} and take the first fish that would come up (Matt. 17:27). ¶

HOPE (noun) – 1 ***elpis*** [fem. noun: ἐλπίς <1680>]; **comp. *elpō*: to give hope, to believe ▶ Contrary to human hope which includes uncertainty, the Christian hope has been described as a happy and confident expectation** > Hope is related to what is invisible and future (Rom. 8:24a–c; see v. 25). The hope of the Christian is in God (Acts 24:15; 1 Pet. 1:21); He is the God of hope (Rom. 15:13a, b). Jesus Christ is the hope of the Christian (Col. 1:27; 1 Tim. 1:1; 1 John 3:3). The hope of Israel is mentioned in Acts 23:6; 26:6, 7; 28:20 and the hope of Abraham in Rom. 4:18a, b. Formerly having no hope (Eph. 2:12; 1 Thes. 4:13), the Christian now possesses the hope of glory (Rom. 5:2; 2 Cor. 3:12), righteousness (Gal. 5:5), the calling of God (Eph. 1:18; 4:4), the gospel (Col. 1:23), salvation (1 Thes. 5:8), and eternal life (Titus 1:2; 3:7). This hope is good (2 Thes. 2:16) and living (1 Pet. 1:3). The blessed hope in Titus 2:13 is the coming of the Lord for His saints (see 1 Thes. 4:15–18). Other refs.: Acts 2:26; 16:19; 27:20; Rom. 5:4, 5; 8:20; 12:12; 15:4; 1 Cor. 9:10a, b; 13:13; 2 Cor. 1:7; 10:15; Phil. 1:20; Col. 1:5; 1 Thes. 2:19; Heb. 3:6; 6:11, 18; 7:19; 10:23; 1 Pet. 1:21; 3:15. ¶

2 **to have hope: *elpizō*** [verb: ἐλπίζω <1679>]; **from *elpis*: hope, trust ▶ To have confidence, to trust** > If in this life only Christians have hope {have hoped} in Christ, they are the most pitiable of all men (1 Cor. 15:19). All other refs.: HOPE (verb) <1679>.

– 3 Acts 8:22 → in the hope → lit.: if perhaps 4 1 Cor. 15:32 → no more than human hopes → lit.: after the manner of man 5 Eph. 1:12 → to be the first to put hope in → to first trust → TRUST (verb) <4276> 6 1 Tim. 6:17 → to set one's hopes → TRUST (verb) <1679> 7 2 Tim. 2:25 → in the hope → PERHAPS <3379>.

HOPE (verb) – 1 ***elpizō*** [verb: ἐλπίζω <1679>]; **from *elpō*: to wait upon, or *elpis*: hope, trust ▶ To place one's trust, one's hope in someone, something; also transl.: to trust, to have hope, to set hope** > The Gentiles hope in the Lord (Matt. 12:21; Rom. 15:12). The Jews trust in Moses (John 5:45). Love hopes all things (1 Cor. 13:7). Paul was hoping to send Timothy to the Philippians (Phil. 2:19, 23). He was hoping to come to Timothy shortly (1 Tim. 3:14). Faith is the substance of things hoped for (Heb. 11:1). John was hoping to come to the elect lady and her children (2 John 12); he was hoping to see Gaius shortly (3 John 14). Other refs.: Luke 6:34; 23:8; 24:21; John 5:45; Acts 24:26; 26:7; Rom. 8:24, 25; 15:24; 1 Cor. 15:19; 16:7; 2 Cor. 1:10, 13; 5:11; 8:5; 13:6; 1 Tim. 4:10; 5:5; Phm. 22; 1 Pet. 1:13; 3:5. Other ref.: 1 Tim. 6:17; see TRUST (verb) <1679>. ¶

2 **to hope in return: *apelpizō*** [verb: ἀπελπίζω <560>]; **from *apo*: from, and *elpizō*: see 1 ▶ To expect in return, to wish for in return** > Jesus says to lend, hoping for nothing in return {hoping for nothing again, without expecting to get anything back} (Luke 6:35). ¶

– 3 Acts 12:11 → everything they were hoping would happen → lit.: all their expectation → EXPECTATION <4329> 4 Eph. 1:12 → to be the first to hope → to first trust → TRUST (verb) <4276> 5 1 John 3:3 → to have hope → HOPE (noun) <1680>.

HORN – ***keras*** [neut. noun: κέρας <2768>]; **akin to *kara*: head ▶ Bony projection on the head of an animal, or object with the same shape; symbol of strength, power** > In Luke 1:69, it represents the power of deliverance wrought by God, who has visited His people Israel in the person of His Son. The word also has this meaning of great strength in relation to the Lamb (Rev. 5:6), the dragon (12:3), and the two beasts (13:1a, b, 11; 17:3, 7, 12, 16). The horns of the golden altar in Rev. 9:13 are prob. part of the altar and resemble the horns of animals; in the O.T., the sacrifices were bound with cords to the horns of the altar (Ps. 118:27) and the blood was put on the horns of the altar of fragrant incense (Lev. 4:7). ¶

HORSE – 1 ***hippos*** [masc. noun: ἵππος <2462>] **▶ Domesticated mammal used for transport or carrying loads** > Bits are

put in the mouths of the horses, that they may obey (Jas. 3:3). In his vision, John saw a white horse (Rev. 6:2), a red horse (v. 4), a black horse (v. 5), and a pale horse (v. 8); these horses are related to the judgment of God upon the inhabitants of the earth. John also saw the Lord sitting on a white horse, judging in righteousness and making war (Rev. 19:11, 19, 21). Other refs.: Rev. 9:7, 9, 17a, b, 19 in some mss.; 14:20; 18:13; 19:14, 18. ¶
– 2 Acts 23:24 → BEAST <2934>.

HORSEMAN – 1 ***hippeus*** [masc. noun: ἱππεύς <2460>]; **from *hippos*: horse ▶ Person riding on horseback >** Seventy horsemen accompanied Paul to Caesarea (Acts 23:23, 32 {cavalry}). ¶
2 ***hippikon*** [adj. used as noun: ἱππικόν <2461>]; **from *hippos*: horse; as an adj.: equestrian ▶ The Greek word is used in the N.T. with the collective meaning: troops for battle mounted on horses, cavalry >** In the vision of John, the number of the army of the horsemen {the number of the mounted troops} was two hundred million (Rev. 9:16). ¶

HOSANNA – ***Hōsanna*** [interj.: Ὡσαννά <5614>] **▶ Hebrew term composed of two words meaning: "Save, we pray!" (see Ps. 118:25); it became an expr. of praise, a wish for prosperity >** Jesus was greeted with this cry of joy and rejoicing at His entrance into Jerusalem (Matt. 21:9a, b, 15; Mark 11:9, 10; John 12:13). ¶

HOSEA – ***Hōsēe*** [masc. name: Ὡσηέ <5617>]: **liberator, in Heb. ▶ Prophet of the O.T. >** Paul quotes Hosea in his letter to the Christians of Rome (Rom. 9:25). ¶

HOSPITABLE – ***philoxenos*** [adj.: φιλόξενος <5382>]; **from *philos*: friend, and *xenos*: guest, stranger ▶ Given to hospitality; welcoming people in one's home >** We are exhorted to be hospitable {to offer hospitality} to one another (1 Pet. 4:9). The overseer, in particular, is to be hospitable (1 Tim. 3:2 {given to hospitality}; Titus 1:8 {lover of hospitality}). ¶

HOSPITABLY – Acts 28:7 → COURTEOUSLY <5390>.

HOSPITALITY – 1 ***philoxenia*** [fem. noun: φιλοξενία <5381>]; **from *philoxenos*: hospitable, which is from *philos*: friend, and *xenos*: guest, stranger ▶ Readiness to welcome to one's home people who are passing on their way >** Christians are to practice hospitality (Rom. 12:13). They are exhorted not to forget to show hospitality {to entertain strangers} (Heb. 13:2). ¶
– 2 Acts 28:7; Heb. 13:2b → to give hospitality, to show hospitality → LODGE <3579> 3 Rom. 16:23 → whose hospitality I enjoy → lit.: my host → HOST[2] <3581> 4 1 Tim. 3:2; Titus 1:8; 1 Pet. 4:9 → given to hospitality, lover of hospitality; to offer hospitality → lit.: hospitable; to be hospitable → HOSPITABLE <5382> 5 1 Tim. 5:10 → to exercise hospitality, to show hospitality to strangers → to lodge strangers → STRANGER <3580> 6 3 John 8 → to show hospitality → RECEIVE <618>.

HOST[1] – 1 ***stratia*** [fem. noun: στρατιά <4756>]; **from *stratos*: army ▶ Military troop. a. This word designates a great gathering of angels >** When Jesus was born, a multitude of the heavenly host praised God (Luke 2:13). **b. This word also designates celestial bodies (sun, moon, stars) >** God gave up the Israelites to worship the host of heaven {heavenly bodies} after they had offered a sacrifice to the golden calf (Acts 7:42; see Deut. 4:19; 17:3). Other ref.: 2 Cor. 10:4 in some mss. ¶
– 2 Rom. 9:29; Jas. 5:4 → hosts of Sabaoth → SABAOTH <4519> 3 Eph. 4:8 → host of captives → CAPTIVITY <161> 4 Rev. 9:16 → ARMY <4753>.

HOST[2] – 1 ***xenos*** [adj. used as noun: ξένος <3581>] **▶ Person who receives another in his home >** Gaius was the host of Tertius and of the whole church (Rom. 16:23). All other refs.: FOREIGN <3581>, STRANGE <3581>, STRANGER <3581>.
– 2 Luke 10:35 → INNKEEPER <3830>.

HOSTILE – 1 Luke 11:53 → to be very hostile → PRESS <1758> 2 Luke 11:53 → to be very hostile → lit.: to oppose vehemently → VEHEMENTLY <1171> 3 Rom. 8:7 → ENMITY <2189> 4 Col. 1:21 → ENEMY <2190> 5 Col. 2:14 → CONTRARY <5227> 6 1 Thes. 2:15 → he who is hostile → he who is opposed → OPPOSED <1727>.

HOSTILITY – 1 Acts 12:20 → to be in bitter hostility → to be very angry → ANGRY <2371> 2 2 Cor. 12:20 → CONTENTION <2052> 3 Eph. 2:16 → ENMITY <2189> 4 Heb. 12:3 → CONTRADICTION <485>.

HOT – 1 ***zestos*** [adj.: ζεστός <2200>]; **from *zeō*: to boil ▶ Very warm; figur.: fervent** > The angel of the church of Laodicea was neither cold nor hot, but should have been cold or hot (Rev. 3:15a, b, 16). ¶
– 2 Luke 12:55 → hot, hot weather, hot day → burning heat → HEAT <2742> 3 1 Tim. 4:2 → to sear with a hot iron → IRON <2743>.

HOUR – 1 ***hōra*** [fem. noun: ὥρα <5610>]; ***hora*, in Lat. ▶ a. Unit of measurement of time corresponding to one twelfth of the day or night** > It is important to notice that the authors of the synoptic Gospels (Matthew, Mark, and Luke) count hours in the manner of the Jews, for whom the day began at six o'clock in the morning; e.g., the ninth hour corresponds to three o'clock in the afternoon. Jesus was crucified at the third hour (Mark 15:25). Pilate presented Jesus as king to the Jews about the sixth hour (John 19:14). While He was on the cross, from the sixth hour, there was darkness over the whole land until the ninth hour (Matt. 27:45a, b; Mark 15:33a, b; Luke 23:44a, b). At the ninth hour, Jesus cried out: "My God, My God, why have You forsaken Me?" (Matt. 27:46; Mark 15:34). Other refs.: Matt. 14:15; 20:3, 5, 6, 9, 12; Mark 6:35a; Luke 22:59; John 1:39; 4:6, 52a, b; 11:9; Acts 2:15; 3:1; 5:7; 10:3, 9, 30; 19:34; 23:23. **b. Period of time of indefinite, but short duration** > Jesus reproached His disciples of not being able to watch one hour with Him (Matt. 26:40; Mark 14:37). Jesus will keep the Christians of Philadelphia out of the hour of trial (Rev. 3:10). Ten kings will receive authority as kings for one hour with the beast (Rev. 17:12). Other refs.: Rev. 18:10, 17, 19. **c. Precise moment in time** > At the hour when Jesus spoke to the centurion, his servant was healed (Matt. 8:13). When the hour was come, Jesus sat down at table with the twelve apostles (Luke 22:14). The hour is coming when true worshippers will worship the Father in spirit and truth (John 4:23). The hour had come for the Father to glorify His Son (John 17:1). Jesus asked His Father to save Him from this hour (i.e., the hour of the sufferings of the cross), but it was on account of this that He had come to this hour (John 12:27a, b; also Mark 14:35). Other refs.: Matt. 9:22; 10:19; 15:28; 17:18; 18:1; 24:36, 42, 44, 50; 25:13; 26:45, 55; Mark 11:11; 13:11, 32; 14:41; Luke 1:10; 2:38; 7:21; 10:21; 12:12, 39, 40, 46; 14:17; 20:19; 22:53; 24:33; John 2:4; 4:21, 53; 5:25, 28; 7:30; 8:20; 12:23; 13:1; 16:2, 4, 21, 25, 32; 19:27; Acts 16:18, 33; 22:13; Rom. 13:11; 1 Cor. 4:11; 15:30; Gal. 2:5; 1 John 2:18a, b; Rev. 3:3; 9:15; 11:13; 14:7, 15. All other refs.: TIME <5610>.
2 **half an hour: *hēmiōrion*** [neut. noun: ἡμιώριον <2256>]; **from *hēmi*: half, and *hōra*: hour ▶ Thirty minutes** > When the seventh seal was opened, there was a silence in heaven about half an hour (Rev. 8:1). ¶

HOUSE – 1 ***oikia*** [fem. noun: οἰκία <3614>]; **from *oikos*: see 2 ▶ Building, residence** > The term is used most of the time in the general sense of a dwelling. For example, the house of a certain man named Justus was next door to the synagogue (Acts 18:7); other examples: Matt. 2:11; 5:15; 7:24–27; 2 Tim. 2:20; 2 John 10. The word is not used to designate the tabernacle or the temple. It is used in John 14:2 by Jesus: "My Father's house," which will be the eternal dwelling place of the children of God. The term also describes the Christian's present body and future body in 2 Cor. 5:1a, b. In other passages, it describes a person's possessions (e.g., Mark 12:40) and the inhabitants of a house (e.g., Matt. 12:25 {household}; see also John 4:53 and 1 Cor. 16:15). *

[2] ***oikos*** [masc. noun: οἶκος <3624>] ► **Place of residence; also transl.: family, home, household, palace, temple (the house of God)** > The term is used in the general sense of a dwelling (e.g., Matt. 9:6, 7; 11:8). It also corresponds to the tabernacle, the house of God (Matt. 12:4), and to the temple (e.g., Matt. 21:13; Luke 11:51 {sanctuary}; John 2:16, 17), which the Lord calls "your house" (Matt. 23:38; Luke 13:35). It describes Israel as the house of God (Heb. 3:2, 5) as well as Christians (Heb. 3:6; 10:21; 1 Pet. 2:5; 4:17). It may also refer to the body (Matt. 12:44; Luke 11:24). Additionally, this term may be applied to the members of a house or family (Luke 10:5; Acts 7:10; 11:14; 1 Tim. 3:4, 5, 12, 15; 2 Tim. 1:16; 4:19; Titus 1:11), to the church of God (1 Tim. 3:15), and to the descendants of Jacob and of David: the house of Israel (Matt. 10:6; Luke 1:27, 33; Acts 2:36; 7:42). *

[3] **rented house: *misthōma*** [neut. noun: μίσθωμα <3410>]; **from *misthoō*: to hire ► Housing leased for a price** > Paul dwelt two whole years in Rome in his own rented house {hired house, hired lodging, rented quarters} (Acts 28:30). ¶

– [4] Matt. 10:25; 13:27, 52; 20:1; 21:33; 24:43; Luke 12:39; 13:25; 14:21 → head of the house, head of the household → master of the house → MASTER (noun) <3617> [5] Matt. 10:27; 24:17; Mark 13:15; Luke 17:31; Acts 10:9 → house, roof of the house → HOUSETOP <1430> [6] Luke 11:21 → PALACE <833> [7] John 18:28; Acts 21:16; 2 Tim. 2:21 → added in Engl. [8] Acts 16:34 → with all his house → will all the household → HOUSEHOLD <3832> [9] 2 Cor. 5:2 → HABITATION <3613> [10] 1 Tim. 5:8 → of the house → of the household → HOUSEHOLD <3609> [11] 1 Tim. 5:14 → to guide, to keep, to manage, to rule the house → to manage the home → MANAGE <3616>.

HOUSEHOLD – [1] ***therapeia*** [fem. noun: θεραπεία <2322>]; **from *therapeuō*: to serve, to heal, which is from *therapōn*: servant ► Group of servants working in a house** > Jesus spoke of a steward who is made ruler over the household {servants} of his master (Luke 12:42); some mss.: Matt. 24:45. Other refs.: Luke 9:11; Rev. 22:2; see HEALING <2322>. ¶

[2] **one of the household: *oikiakos*** [masc. noun: οἰκιακός <3615>]; **from *oikia*: house, dwelling, which is from *oikos*: house ► Those who belong to the house** > The Greek word is used in Matt. 10:25, 36. ¶

[3] **of the household: *oikeios*** [adj.: οἰκεῖος <3609>]; **from *oikos*: house ► Who belongs to a family; also transl.: of the immediate family, of one's own house, who belong to the family** > Christians are exhorted to do good toward all, and especially toward those of the household of faith (Gal. 6:10). They are members of the household of God (Eph. 2:19), i.e., they are His spiritual family. The Christian must especially provide for those of his household (1 Tim. 5:8). ¶

[4] ***oiketeia*** [fem. noun: οἰκετεία <3609a>]; **from *oiketēs*: domestic servant ► Group of servants working in a house** > Jesus spoke of a servant who was made ruler over the household of his master (Matt. 24:45; some mss.: *therapeia* <2322>). ¶

[5] **with all the household: *panoikei*** [adv.: πανοικεί <3832>]; **from *pas*: all, and *oikos*: house; also spelled *panoiki* ► With all the members of the family** > The jailer brought Paul and Barnabas into his house (*oikos*) and rejoiced with all those of his household {with all his house, with his whole family} (*panoikei*) (Acts 16:34). ¶

– [6] Matt. 12:25; John 4:53; 1 Cor. 16:15 → HOUSE <3614> [7] Matt. 13:52; Luke 14:21 → head of the household → master of the house → MASTER (noun) <3617> [8] Luke 11:17; Acts 11:14; 1 Tim. 3:5, 12, 15; 5:4; 2 Tim. 1:16; 4:19; Titus 1:11 → HOUSE <3624> [9] Acts 10:7 → household servant → SERVANT <3610> [10] 1 Tim. 5:14 → to manage the household → MANAGE <3616> [11] Titus 1:7 → since (he) manages

God's household → lit.: as God's steward → STEWARD <3623>.

HOUSEHOLDER – Matt. 13:27, 52; 20:1; 21:33 → master of the house → MASTER (noun) <3617>.

HOUSETOP – ***dōma*** [neut. noun: δῶμα <1430>]; **from *demō*: to build ▶ Summit of the house, often used as a terrace in the East; also transl.: house, roof, roof of the house** > What Jesus says in the darkness is to be preached on the housetops (Matt. 10:27). During the great tribulation, he who is on the housetop is not to go down to take away anything out of his house (Matt. 24:17; Mark 13:15; Luke 17:31). Four men went up on the housetop and let down a paralyzed man lying on his bed through the tiling before Jesus (Luke 5:19). That which is spoken in the ear in inner rooms will be proclaimed on the housetops (Luke 12:3). Peter went up on the housetop to pray (Acts 10:9). ¶

HOW – [1] ***pōs*** [particle: πώς <4458>] ▶ **In what manner, in what way; also transl.: what manner, by any means, somehow** > The word is found in Rom. 1:10; 2 Cor. 11:3; Gal. 2:2; Phil. 3:11. *

[2] ***pōs*** [particle: πῶς <4459>] ▶ **In what manner, in what way; also transl.: what manner, by any means, somehow** > The word is found in Luke 22:4; Acts 20:18; 1 Thes. 4:1. *

HOW GREAT – ***hēlikos*** [particle: ἡλίκος <2245>]; **from *hēlis*: adult** ▶ Refs.: Col. 2:1; Jas. 3:5. Other ref.: Gal. 6:11 in some mss. ¶ ‡

HOW GREAT?, HOW MUCH MORE? – ***posos*** [pron.: πόσος <4214>]; **from *polus*: many** ▶ Ref.: Matt. 6:23; 7:11; Rom. 11:12, 24. *

HOW LONG? – ***pote*** [pron.: πότε <4219>] ▶ Ref.: Matt. 24:3; 25:37–39; Rev. 6:10. *

HOW MUCH MORE – ***mētige*** [interrog. adv.: μήτιγε <3386>]; **from *mē*: denoting a question, and *tis*: anyone** ▶ Ref.: 1 Cor. 6:3. ¶ ‡

HOWEVER – John 4:2 → ALTHOUGH <2544>.

HOWL – ***ololuzō*** [verb: ὀλολύζω <3649>] ▶ **To shout, to scream, to lament** > James tells the rich to weep and howl {wail} for their miseries that are coming upon them (Jas. 5:1). ¶

HUMAN – [1] **human, in human terms: *anthrōpinos*** [adj.: ἀνθρώπινος <442>]; **from *anthrōpos*: human being ▶ a. Which pertains to mankind** > Paul spoke of the things given by God, not in words taught by human wisdom {by man's wisdom}, but in those taught by the Spirit (1 Cor. 2:13). It was a very small matter for Paul to be judged by a human court (1 Cor. 4:3). No testing overtakes a Christian except what is human {such as is common to man, is common to mankind} (1 Cor. 10:13). Every species of animal is tamed by the human race {by mankind} (Jas. 3:7). We are to submit ourselves to every human institution {ordinance of man} for the Lord's sake (1 Pet. 2:13). **b. In a way that people can understand (given their limitations) >** Paul speaks in human terms {humanly, in the manner of men} when speaking of bondage to righteousness (Rom. 6:19). Paul's message and preaching were not in persuasive words of human wisdom, but in demonstration of the Spirit and of power (1 Cor. 2:4 in some mss.). ¶

– [2] Matt. 15:9; 16:23; 21:25, 26; Mark 7:7, 8; et al. → lit.: of man, of men → MAN <444> [3] Matt. 24:22 → human being → FLESH <4561> [4] Mark 14:58; Heb. 9:11, 24 → made with human hands → lit.: made with hands [5] Luke 20:4, 6; John 12:43 → of human origin, human → lit.: from men [6] Acts 17:24; 1 Cor. 2:1 → "human" added in Engl. [7] Acts 19:26 → by human hands → lit.: by hands [8] Rom. 6:19 → human limitations → lit.: weakness of the flesh → WEAKNESS <769>, FLESH <4561>

[9] Rom. 9:16 → human will → lit.: of the one willing [10] 2 Cor. 3:3 → FLESHLY <4560> [11] Col. 3:23 → human masters → lit.: men.

HUMAN BEING – [1] John 5:41; et al. → lit.: man [2] Rom. 3:20; 1 Cor. 1:29 → FLESH <4561> [3] Gal. 1:16 → flesh and blood → FLESH <4561>, BLOOD <129> [4] Rev. 18:13 → human beings sold as slaves → lit.: bodies and souls of men.

HUMAN LEADER – 1 Cor. 3:21 → human leaders → lit.: men → MAN <444>.

HUMAN STANDARDS – 1 Pet. 4:6 → according to human standards → lit.: according to men in flesh → MAN <444>, FLESH <4561>.

HUMANITY – Eph. 2:15 → MAN <444>.

HUMANLY – [1] Rom. 6:19 → in human terms → HUMAN <442> [2] 1 Cor. 15:32 → humanly speaking → lit.: after the manner of man.

HUMBLE (adj.) – [1] ***tapeinos*** [adj.: ταπεινός <5011>] ▶ **Which voluntarily lowers himself, self-effacing; also transl.: lowly** > Jesus said of Himself that He was meek and humble in heart (Matt. 11:29). Paul exhorts Christians to associate with the humble {men of low estate, people of low position} (Rom. 12:16). God gives grace to the humble (Jas. 4:6; 1 Pet. 5:5). All other refs.: CAST DOWN <5011>, LOWLY <5011>.

[2] **humble state, lowly state: *tapeinōsis*** [fem. noun: ταπείνωσις <5014>]; **from *tapeinoō*: to lower, which is from *tapeinos*: see [1]** ▶ **Low condition** > God had regarded the humble state {low estate} of Mary, who would become the mother of Jesus (Luke 1:48). All other refs.: HUMILIATION <5014>.

[3] **humble, humble minded, humble in spirit: *tapeinophrōn*** [adj.: ταπεινόφρων <5012a>]; **from *tapeinos*: see [1], and *phrēn*: mind** ▶ **Modest in willingly lowering oneself, which shows humility of mind** > Peter urges Christians to be humble minded {courteous} (1 Pet. 3:8). Other mss. have *philophrōn*; see COURTEOUS <5391>. ¶

– [4] Matt. 21:5 → GENTLE <4239> [5] Acts 14:15 → of like passions → PASSION <3663> [6] 2 Cor. 3:3 → FLESHLY <4560> [7] Eph. 4:2 → be completely humble → lit.: in all humility → HUMILITY <5012>.

HUMBLE (verb) – ***tapeinoō*** [verb: ταπεινόω <5013>]; **from *tapeinos*: humble** ▶ **To bring down, to make unpretentious; also transl.: to abase** > Whoever humbles himself like a little child is the greatest in the kingdom of heaven (Matt. 18:4). Whoever exalts himself will be humbled, and whoever humbles himself will be exalted (Matt. 23:12a, b; Luke 14:11a, b; 18:14a, b). Paul feared that God would humble {humiliate} him in regard to the Corinthians (2 Cor. 12:21). Christ Jesus humbled Himself and became obedient to the death of the cross (Phil. 2:8). James says to humble yourself before the Lord and He will exalt you (Jas. 4:10). Peter also says to Christians to humble themselves under the mighty hand of God so that He may exalt them in due time (1 Pet. 5:6). All other refs.: ABASE <5013>, LOW <5013>.

HUMBLY – [1] Gal. 5:13 → to serve humbly → to serve as slaves → SERVE <1398> [2] Jas. 1:21 → with meekness → MEEKNESS <4240>.

HUMILIATE – [1] Luke 13:17; 1 Cor. 11:22 → to put to shame → SHAME (noun) <2617> [2] 1 Cor. 11:22 → DESPISE <2706> [3] 2 Cor. 12:21 → HUMBLE (verb) <5013>.

HUMILIATED (BE) – 2 Cor. 9:4 → ASHAMED (BE) <2617>.

HUMILIATION – ***tapeinōsis*** [fem. noun: ταπείνωσις <5014>]; **from *tapeinoō*: to make lower, to humble, which is from *tapeinos*: humble** ▶ **Low condition, low state** > God has regarded the humiliation {lowly state, low estate, humble state} of

Mary, His maidservant (Luke 1:48). In the humiliation of Jesus, His judgment was taken away (Acts 8:33). The Lord will change the body of humiliation {the lowly body, the body of the humble state, the vile body} of the Christians into conformity to His glorious body (Phil. 3:21). The brother who is rich should glory in his humiliation {in his low position, in that he is made low} (Jas. 1:10), because whoever exalts himself will be humbled; and whoever humbles himself will be exalted (see Matt. 23:12). ¶

HUMILITY – 1 **humility, humility of mind:** ***tapeinophrosunē*** [fem. noun: ταπεινοφροσύνη <5012>]**; from *tapeinos*: humble, and *phrēn*: mind ▶ Characteristic of a person who lowers himself before others, which manifests this disposition of spirit; also transl.: lowliness** > Paul had served the Lord in all humility (Acts 20:19). Humility is to characterize the life of the Christian (Eph. 4:2; Phil. 2:3; Col. 3:12; 1 Pet. 5:5). But there is another kind of humility {self-abasement} that is inappropriate: that which stems from self-will (Col. 2:18) and has an appearance of wisdom (v. 23). ¶
– 2 2 Cor. 10:1; 2 Tim. 2:25; Titus 3:2 → GENTLENESS <4236> 3 Jas. 1:21; 3:13 → with meekness, in meekness → MEEKNESS <4240>.

HUNDRED – 1 ***hekaton*** [card. num.: ἑκατόν <1540>] ▶ This number is used in regard to fruit (hundredfold, hundred times: Matt. 13:8, 23; Mark 4:8, 20), sheep (Matt. 18:12; Luke 15:4), denarii (Matt. 18:28), people (Mark 6:40), measures of oil (Luke 16:6), measures of wheat (Luke 16:7), and pounds (John 19:39). ¶
– 2 Matt. 19:29; Mark 10:30; Luke 8:8 → hundred times → HUNDREDFOLD <1542> 3 Rom. 4:19 → hundred years old → YEAR <1541>.

HUNDRED AND FIFTY-THREE – **hundred:** ***hekaton*** [card. num.: ἑκατόν <1540>] **fifty:** ***pentēkonta*** [card. num.: πεντήκοντα <4004>] **three:** ***treis*** [card. num.: τρεῖς <5140>] ▶ Peter dragged the net to the land, full of one hundred and fifty-three large fish (John 21:11). ¶

HUNDRED AND FORTY-FOUR – **hundred:** ***hekaton*** [card. num.: ἑκατόν <1540>] **forty:** ***tessarakonta*** [card. num.: τεσσαράκοντα <5062>] **four:** ***tessares*** [card. num.: τέσσαρες <5064>] ▶ This number is used in regard to cubits, the measure of the new Jerusalem (Rev. 21:17). ¶

HUNDRED AND FORTY-FOUR THOUSAND – **hundred:** ***hekaton*** [card. num.: ἑκατόν <1540>] **forty:** ***tessarakonta*** [card. num.: τεσσαράκοντα <5062>] **four:** ***tessares*** [card. num.: τέσσαρες <5064>] **thousand:** ***chilias*** [fem. noun: χιλιάς <5505>] ▶ This number is used in regard to those who are sealed from every tribe of the sons of Israel (Rev. 7:4) and those standing with the Lamb (Rev. 14:1, 3). ¶

HUNDRED AND TWENTY – **hundred:** ***hekaton*** [card. num.: ἑκατόν <1540>] **twenty:** ***eikosi*** [card. num.: εἴκοσι <1501>] ▶ Peter addressed himself to about a hundred and twenty disciples at the beginning (Acts 1:15). ¶

HUNDREDFOLD – 1 ***hekatontaplasiōn*** [adj.: ἑκατονταπλασίων <1542>]**; from *hekaton*: one hundred, and *plasiōn*: suffix indicating a numeral termination ▶ Hundred times as much** > The word is used in Matt. 19:29; Mark 10:30; Luke 8:8. Other ref.: Luke 18:30 in some mss. ¶
– 2 Matt. 13:8, 23 → HUNDRED <1540> 3 Matt. 19:29; Mark 10:30 → hundred times as much → TIME <1542>.

HUNGER (noun) – 1 ***limos*** [masc. noun: λιμός <3042>] ▶ **Famine, need of food** > The prodigal son was perishing with hunger {starving to death} (Luke 15:17). Paul had been in hunger and thirst (2 Cor. 11:27). Authority was given to death to kill with famine (Rev. 6:8). All other refs.: FAMINE <3042>.
– 2 2 Cor. 6:5; 11:27 → FAST, FASTING, FAST <3521> <3522> 3 Phil. 4:12 → to

face hunger → to be hungry → HUNGRY <3983>.

HUNGER (verb) – Matt. 4:2; 12:1, 3; 21:18; Mark 2:25; 11:12; Luke 4:2; 6:3; 1 Cor. 4:11; Rev. 7:16; et al. → to be hungry → HUNGRY <3983>.

HUNGRY – [1] ***nēstis*** [adj.: νῆστις <3523>]; **from *nē*: neg., and *esthiō*: to eat ► Not having eaten >** Jesus did not want to send the crowd away hungry {fasting} (Matt. 15:32; Mark 8:3). ¶

[2] ***prospeinos*** [adj.: πρόσπεινος <4361>]; **from *pros*: intens., and *peina*: hunger ► Needing food >** Peter became hungry and wanted to eat (Acts 10:10). ¶

[3] **to be hungry, to become hungry: *peinaō*** [verb: πεινάω <3983>]; **from *peina*: hunger ► To have the need and the desire to eat, lit. or metaphorically; also transl.: to hunger >** This verb is used in speaking of Jesus (Matt. 4:2; 21:18; 25:35, 37, 42, 44; Mark 11:12; Luke 4:2), His disciples (Matt. 12:1), David (Matt. 12:3; Mark 2:25; Luke 6:3), and Paul (1 Cor. 4:11; Phil. 4:12). Other refs.: Matt. 5:6; Luke 1:53; 6:21, 25; John 6:35; Rom. 12:20; 1 Cor. 11:21, 34; Rev. 7:16. ¶

HUNT – Acts 26:11 → "hunted down" added in Engl.

HURL – [1] 1 Pet. 2:23a → to hurl insults → REVILE <3058> [2] Rev. 8:5 → THROW (verb) <906> [3] Rev. 12:9a–c, 13 → to hurl down → to cast out → CAST (verb) <906> [4] Rev. 12:10 → to hurl down → to cast down → CAST (verb) <2598>.

HURRICANE – Acts 27:14 → lit.: tempestuous wind → TEMPESTUOUS <5189>, WIND (noun) <417>.

HURRY (noun) – [1] Luke 1:39 → HASTE (noun) <4710> [2] Luke 2:16 → to come in a hurry → to come with haste → HASTE (noun) <4692> [3] Acts 20:16 → to be in a hurry → HASTEN <4692>.

HURRY (verb) – [1] Matt. 28:8 → to hurry away → lit.: to leave quickly → QUICKLY <5035> [2] Mark 6:25; Luke 1:39 → lit.: to go in a hurry → HASTE (noun) <4710> [3] Luke 2:16; 19:6 → to hurry, to hurry off → to come with haste → HASTE (noun) <4692> [4] Acts 20:16 → HASTEN <4692>.

HURT (noun) – [1] Acts 12:1 → to do hurt → OPPRESS <2559> [2] Acts 27:10 → DISASTER <5196>.

HURT (verb) – [1] ***adikeō*** [verb: ἀδικέω <91>]; **from *adikos*: unjust, which is from *a*: neg., and *dikē*: justice ► To injure, to damage >** He who overcomes in Smyrna will not be hurt by the second death (Rev. 2:11). All other refs.: INJURE <91>, WRONG (noun) <91>.

[2] ***blaptō*** [verb: βλάπτω <984>] **► To injure, to wound >** A demon came out of a man without hurting {injuring, doing injury to, doing harm to} him (Luke 4:35). Other ref.: Mark 16:18; see INJURE <984>. ¶

[3] ***kakoō*** [verb: κακόω <2559>]; **from *kakos*: bad, evil ► To do that which is bad, that which is harmful to others >** No one would hurt {injure, harm} Paul because Jesus was with him (Acts 18:10). Peter asks who will hurt {injure, harm} Christians if they become followers of what is good (1 Pet. 3:13). All other refs.: OPPRESS <2559>, POISON (verb) <2559>.

HURTFUL – 1 Tim. 6:9 → HARMFUL <983>.

HUSBAND – [1] ***anēr*** [masc. noun: ἀνήρ <435>] **► Spouse of a woman >** The word is used in regard to Joseph (Matt. 1:16, 19), the husband of Anna (Luke 2:36), the husbands of the woman at Sychar's well (John 4:16, 17a, b, 18a, b), Ananias (Acts 5:9, 10), Christ (2 Cor. 11:2; Rev. 21:2), an overseer (1 Tim. 3:2), deacons (1 Tim. 3:12), and an elder (Titus 1:6). Other refs.: Mark 10:12; Luke 16:18; Rom. 7:2b–d, 3a, b; 1 Cor. 7:2, 3a, b, 4a, b, 10, 11a, b, 13a, b {him}, 14a, b, 16a, b {man}, 34, 39a, b; 14:35; Gal. 4:27; Eph. 5:22–25, 28, 33;

Col. 3:18, 19; 1 Tim. 5:9 {man}; Titus 2:5; 1 Pet. 3:1, 5, 7. *

2 who has a husband: *hupandros* [adj.: ὕπανδρος <5220>]; **from *hupo*: under, and *anēr*: see 1 ▶ Under the legal authority of a husband** > Paul speaks of a woman who has a husband {is married} (Rom. 7:2). ¶

3 loving one's husband: *philandros* [adj.: φίλανδρος <5362>]; **from *philos*: friend or loving as a friend, and *anēr*: see 1 ▶ Affectionate toward or fond of one's husband** > The older women should teach the young women to love their husbands {be attached to their husbands} (lit.: to be loving their husbands) (Titus 2:4). ¶

– 4 John 1:13 → a husband's will → lit.: the will of man 5 1 Cor. 11:3 → MAN <435>.

HUSBANDMAN – 1 Matt. 21:33–35, 38, 40, 41; Mark 12:1, 2, 7, 9; Luke 20:9, 10a, b, 14, 16; John 15:1 → VINEDRESSER <1092> 2 2 Tim. 2:6; Jas. 5:7 → FARMER <1092>.

HUSBANDRY – 1 Cor. 3:9 → FIELD <1091>.

HUSH – 1 Mark 4:39 → to make hush → QUIET (BE) <5392> 2 Acts 21:40 → SILENCE (noun) <4602>.

HUSK – ***keration*** [neut. noun: κεράτιον <2769>]; **dimin. of *keras*: horn; lit.: little horn ▶ Food eaten by pigs; also transl.: pod** > This is the horn-shaped seed pod of the carob tree, which can attain a height of 40 feet (12 meters). The prodigal son longed to eat them, during the famine which occurred in the country where he was (Luke 15:16). ¶

HYMENAEUS – ***Humenaios*** [masc. name: Ὑμέναιος <5211>]; **from *Humēn*, the god of marriage ▶ Man of the N.T.** > Paul had delivered Hymenaeus and Alexander to Satan, so that they might learn not to blaspheme (1 Tim. 1:20). Hymenaeus and Philetus had gone astray from the truth (2 Tim. 2:17), saying that the resurrection had already taken place; they overthrew the faith of some (see v. 18). ¶

HYMN – 1 ***humnos*** [masc. noun: ὕμνος <5215>] **▶ Song of praise addressed to God** > Christians are to speak to one another with psalms, hymns, and spiritual songs (Eph. 5:19; Col. 3:16). ¶

– 2 Matt. 26:30; Mark 14:26; Acts 16:25 → to sing a hymn → SING <5214> 3 1 Cor. 14:26 → PSALM <5568>.

HYPOCRISY – 1 ***hupokrisis*** [fem. noun: ὑπόκρισις <5272>]; **from *hupokrinomai*: to pretend, which is from *hupo*: under, and *krinō*: to judge ▶ Dissimulation, pretention of being what one is not** > The scribes and the Pharisees were full of hypocrisy inside (Matt. 23:28). Jesus knew the hypocrisy of the Pharisees and the Herodians (Mark 12:15). The leaven of the Pharisees is hypocrisy (Luke 12:1). Barnabas was carried away by the hypocrisy {dissimulation} of the Jews (Gal. 2:13). In the latter times, some will speak lies in hypocrisy (1 Tim. 4:2). We are to reject hypocrisy (1 Pet. 2:1). ¶

2 without hypocrisy: *anupokritos* [adj.: ἀνυπόκριτος <505>]; **from *a*: neg., and *hupokrinomai*: see 1 ▶ Without disguise, sincere; also transl.: genuine, unfeigned, without dissimulation** > Love is to be without hypocrisy (Rom. 12:9; 2 Cor. 6:6), as likewise brotherly love (1 Pet. 1:22). The wisdom from above is without hypocrisy (Jas. 3:17). Paul speaks of sincere faith (1 Tim. 1:5; 2 Tim. 1:5). ¶

– 3 Gal. 2:13 → to join in hypocrisy → to play the hypocrite → HYPOCRITE <4942>.

HYPOCRITE – 1 ***hupokritēs*** [masc. noun: ὑποκριτής <5273>]; **from *hupokrinomai*: to pretend, to feign, which is from *hupo*: under, and *krinō*: to judge ▶ Person who acts with hypocrisy, i.e., dissimulating his true feeling or pretending to be what he is not** > Originally, on-stage actor; later, individual who disguises his real feelings, who presents a facade which does not correspond to what he truly is. The Lord often addresses Pharisees as hypocrites (Matt. 15:7; 22:18; 23:13, 15, 23, 25, 27, 29; Mark 7:6) and others manifesting the same fault (Matt. 6:2, 5, 16; 7:5; 24:51; Luke 6:42; 12:56; 13:15). Other refs. in some mss.: Matt. 16:3; Luke 11:44. ¶

2 **to play the hypocrite with: *sunupokrinomai*** [verb: συνυποκρίνομαι <4942>]; **from *sun*: together, and *hupokrinomai*: see 1 ► To pretend, to feign with** > Some Jews played the hypocrite {joined in hypocrisy, dissembled, played the dissembled part} with Cephas (Gal. 2:13), in the sense that they were hiding their real motive. ¶

HYPOCRITICAL – 1 Tim. 4:2 → hypocritical liars → lit.: lies in hypocrisy → HYPOCRISY <5272>.

HYPOCRITICALLY – Gal. 2:13 → to act hypocritically → to play the hypocrite → HYPOCRITE <4942>.

HYSSOP – ***hussōpos*** [masc. noun: ὕσσωπος <5301>] ► **Small aromatic plant** > A sponge full of vinegar was put on a branch of hyssop and presented to Jesus on the cross (John 19:29). Hyssop was used to sprinkle the blood of sacrifices (Heb. 9:19). ¶

I

I ALSO – ***kagō*** [contraction of two words.: κἀγώ <2504>]; **from *kai*: and, and *egō*: I ▶** Refs.: Matt. 2:8; 10:32; 11:28; Luke 2:48; John 1:34; 2 Cor. 11:28; 1 Thes. 3:5. * ‡

ICONIUM – ***Ikonion*** [neut. name: Ἰκόνιον <2430>]: **like an image ▶ Major city of Lycaonia in Asia Minor** > Paul and Barnabas, during the first missionary journey, came to Iconium and preached the gospel in such a way that a great multitude of Jews and Greeks believed; they had to leave, being driven away by persecution; the Jews of Iconium even pursued Paul to Lystra, stoned him, and dragged him out of the city; but Paul rose up and returned to Lystra to strengthen the disciples (Acts 13:51; 14:1, 19, 21; 2 Tim. 3:11). Timothy had a good testimony of the brothers of Iconium (Acts 16:2). ¶

IDEA – 1 John 5:13; 8:14b; Acts 12:9 → to have an idea → KNOW <1492> 2 Acts 17:21 → NEW <2537> 3 1 Tim. 6:20 → opposing idea → OPPOSITION <477> 4 2 Pet. 2:13 → their idea of pleasure → they count pleasure → COUNT <2233>.

IDENTIFIED – ***sumphutos*** [adj. used as noun: σύμφυτος <4854>]; lit.: same plant; **from *sumphuō*: to grow together, which is from *sun*: together, and *phuō*: to generate, to grow, from which *phullon*: leaf ▶ Organically unified with, intimately associated with** > Christians have become identified {have been planted together, have been united together, have become united, have been united} (lit.: have become the same plant) with Christ in the likeness of His death (Rom. 6:5; see vv. 4, 8). ¶

IDLE – 1 ***argos*** [adj.: ἀργός <692>]; **from *a*: neg., and *ergon*: work ▶ a. Vain, useless, unprofitable** > In the day of judgment, men will render an account of every idle {careless} word they have spoken (Matt. 12:36). **b. Inactive, unemployed, without an occupation** > A landowner saw workmen standing idle {doing nothing} in the marketplace (Matt. 20:3, 6a, b). Young widows may learn to be idle (1 Tim. 5:13a, b {idler}). Faith, virtue, knowledge, and other qualities subsisting in Christians make them to be neither idle {barren, ineffective, useless} nor unfruitful as regards the knowledge of their Lord (2 Pet. 1:8). Other ref.: Titus 1:12; see LAZY <692>. ¶
– 2 Luke 24:11 → idle tale → TALE <3026> 3 1 Thes. 5:14 → UNRULY <813> 4 2 Thes. 3:6, 11 → who is idle → walking disorderly → DISORDERLY <814> 5 1 Tim. 1:6 → idle talk → vain discourse → VAIN <3150> 6 1 Tim. 6:20; 2 Tim. 2:16 → idle babbling → BABBLING <2757> 7 Titus 1:10 → idle talker → TALKER <3151>.

IDLE (BE) – 1 ***argeō*** [verb: ἀργέω <691>]; **from *argos*: idle, which is from *a*: neg., and *ergon*: work ▶ To be unemployed, to remain inactive** > The judgment of false prophets and false teachers is not idle {lingereth not, has been hanging over them} (2 Pet. 2:3). ¶
– 2 2 Thes. 3:7 → to be disorderly → DISORDERLY <812>.

IDLENESS – 2 Thes. 3:6, 11 → in idleness → DISORDERLY <814>.

IDLER – 1 Tim. 5:13b → IDLE <692>.

IDOL – 1 ***eidōlon*** [neut. noun: εἴδωλον <1497>]; **from *eidos*: appearance, what one sees ▶ Material representation of a false god for the purpose of religious worship; the false god itself** > Sacrifices were offered to idols (Acts 7:41; 1 Cor. 8:4, 7; 10:19). James was minded to write to the Christians of the nations to abstain from things polluted by idols (Acts 15:20). Paul asks the person who abhors idols if he commits sacrilege (Rom. 2:22). Before their conversion, the Corinthians were led away to mute idols (1 Cor. 12:2). There is no agreement between the temple of God and idols (2 Cor. 6:16). The Thessalonians had turned to God from idols (1 Thes. 1:9). Men will not repent of worshiping idols (Rev. 9:20). Greed for material wealth, or other things which take the place of God in the life of the Christian, are considered as idols (see Eph. 5:5; Col. 3:5). The injunction to keep oneself from idols (i.e., anything that would display worship due to God) always remains valid for the Christian today (1 John 5:21). ¶

2 **idol's temple:** ***eidōleion*** [neut. noun: εἰδωλεῖον <1493>]; **from *eidōlon*: see 1 ▶ Place of pagan religious worship** > If a Christian is eating in an idol's temple and is seen by a weak person, the conscience of this person could be emboldened to eat things sacrificed to idols (1 Cor. 8:10). ¶

3 **thing sacrificed to the idol, thing offered to idols, etc.:** ***eidōlothuton*** [neut. noun: εἰδωλόθυτον <1494>]; **from *eidōlon*: see 1, and *thuō*: to sacrifice ▶ Remains of victims sacrificed to idols (i.e., false gods)** > Paul addresses the subject of things sacrificed to idols (1 Cor. 8:1, 4, 7, 10). Balaam wanted the sons of Israel to eat of things sacrificed to idols (Rev. 2:14). Jezebel misleads servants of the Lord to eat things sacrificed to idols (Rev. 2:20). Other refs.: Acts 15:29; 21:25; 1 Cor. 10:19, 28 in some mss. ¶

4 **full of idols:** ***kateidōlos*** [adj.: κατείδωλος <2712>]; **from *kata*: intens., and *eidōlon*: see 1 ▶ Filled with idols (i.e., false gods), given up to idolatry** > Athens was full of idols (Acts 17:16). ¶

– 5 Acts 7:43 → TYPE <5179>.

IDOLATER – ***eidōlolatrēs*** [masc. noun: εἰδωλολάτρης <1496>]; **from *eidōlon*: idol, and *latris*: worshiper, servant ▶ One who worships idols (i.e., false gods)** > It is not always possible for the Christian to avoid associating with the idolaters of this world (1 Cor. 5:10), but he is not to associate with anyone called brother who is an idolater (v. 11). Idolaters will not inherit the kingdom of God (1 Cor. 6:9; Eph. 5:5). The Christian must not be an idolater (1 Cor. 10:7). The part of idolaters will be in the lake of fire (Rev. 21:8); they will be outside the heavenly Jerusalem (22:15). ¶

IDOLATRY – 1 ***eidōlolatreia*** [fem. noun: εἰδωλολατρεία <1495>]; **from *eidōlon*: idol, and *latreia*: divine service, which is from *latreuō*: to worship; also spelled: *eidōlolatria* ▶ Religious worship of idols** > The word of God condemns idolatry (Gal. 5:20; Col. 3:5; 1 Pet. 4:3). The Christian is to flee idolatry (1 Cor. 10:14). ¶

– 2 Acts 17:16 → given up to idolatry, given over to idols, wholly given to idolatry → full of idols → IDOL <2712>.

IDUMEA – ***Idoumaia*** [fem. name: Ἰδουμαία <2401>]: **belonging to Edom, in Heb. ▶ Region occupied by the descendants of Edom (or Esau, the twin brother of Jacob), located southwest of the Dead Sea** > People from Idumea followed Jesus (Mark 3:8). ¶

IF – 1 ***ean*** [conj.: ἐάν <1437>]; **formed by combining *ei*, a cond. particle meaning if, and *an*, a particle denoting supposition, wish, possibility, or uncertainty ▶ Also transl.: What, where, whither, whosoever.** * ‡

2 ***ei*** [conj.: εἰ <1487>] ▶ This cond. expresses a condition which is merely hypothetical and separate from all experience in indicating a mere subjective possibility. * ‡

3 ***per*** [emphatic particle: περ <4007>]; **from *peri*: concerning, about, with respect ▶ Very, wholly, ever** > In the N.T., it is always joined with a pron. or a particle for greater emphasis and strength; e.g., *eanper* (Heb. 3:6, 14; 6:3) and *eiper*, if perhaps; *epeiper*, since indeed; *epeidēper*, since indeed, because of; *ēper*, than indeed; *kathaper*, exactly as, even as, as well; *kaiper*, and yet, although; *hosper*, whomsoever (Mark 15:6); *hōsper*, exactly like, even. * ‡ ¶

IF ALSO, EVEN IF, IF THAT, THOUGH – ***ei kai*** [cond. expr.: εἰ καί <1499>]; **from *ei*: if, and *kai*: and ▶** Generally, the expr. means: if also (1 Cor. 7:21; 2 Cor. 11:15; Phil. 3:12; 1 Pet. 3:14). It can also mean: if even, though, although, implying the reality and natural existence of that which is assumed. Other refs.: Mark 14:29; Luke 11:8; 18:4; 2 Cor. 4:16; 7:8, 12; 8:5; 12:11, 15; 13:4; Phil. 2:17; Col. 2:5; Heb. 6:9; 1 Pet. 3:1. ¶ ‡

IF (AND, ALSO) – ***kan*** [contraction of two words: κἄν <2579>]; **from *kai*: and, and**

***ean*: if** ▶ Refs.: Matt. 21:21; 26:35; Mark 5:28; 6:56; 16:18; Luke 13:9; John 8:14; 10:38; 11:25; Acts 5:15; 2 Cor. 11:16; Heb. 12:20; Jas. 5:15. * ‡

IF ANY, IF SOMEONE – ***ei tis*** [cond. expr.: εἴ τις <1536>]; **from *ei*: if, and *tis*: any ▶ This expr. is most often used to set items in contrast or opposition to one another; also transl.: and if.** > Refs.: Mark 9:35; Luke 14:26; 1 Cor. 3:14, 15; 2 Cor. 5:17; Gal. 1:9; 1 Tim. 5:16; 6:3. * ‡

IF INDEED, IF SO BE, IF AT LEAST – ***eige*** [particle: εἴγε <1489>]; **from *ei*: if, and *ge*: indeed** ▶ A particle of emphasis or qualification meaning if at least, if indeed, if so be, followed by the indic. and spoken of what is taken for granted (Eph. 3:2; 4:21; Col. 1:23). Other refs.: 2 Cor. 5:3; Gal. 3:4. ¶ ‡

IF ONLY – Acts 20:24 → SO THAT <5613>.

IF POSSIBLY – ***ei pōs*** [cond. expr.: εἴ πως <1513>]; **from *ei*: if, and *pōs*: how ▶ Also transl.: if by any means** > Refs.: Acts 27:12; Rom. 1:10; 11:14; Phil. 3:11. ¶ ‡

IGNOBLE – [1] 1 Cor. 1:28 → BASE (adj.) <36> [2] 2 Tim. 2:20 → ignoble purpose → DISHONOR (noun) <819>.

IGNORANCE – [1] **sin committed in ignorance: *agnoēma*** [neut. noun: ἀγνόημα <51>]; **from *agnoeō*: to ignore, which is from *a*: neg., and *noeō*: to understand, to perceive, which is from *nous*: mind, understanding ▶ Thing which one ignores, fault; also transl.: error** > The high priest offered blood for the sins committed in ignorance by the people (Heb. 9:7). ¶
[2] ***agnoia*** [fem. noun: ἄγνοια <52>]; **from *agnoeō*: to be ignorant, which is from *a*: neg., and *noeō*: see [1] ▶ Lack of knowledge or perception** > The Jews put Jesus to death through ignorance (Acts 3:17). Having overlooked the times of ignorance, God commands all men to repent (Acts 17:30). The Gentiles are strangers to the life of God because of the ignorance that is in them (Eph. 4:18). Before their conversion, Christians were in ignorance (1 Pet. 1:14). Other ref.: 2 Pet. 2:13 in some mss. ¶
[3] ***agnōsia*** [fem. noun: ἀγνωσία <56>]; **from *a*: neg., and *gnōsis*: knowledge ▶ Lack of understanding, lack of knowledge** > Some of the Corinthians were ignorant {did not have the knowledge} (lit.: had the ignorance) of God (1 Cor. 15:34). By doing good, Christians put to silence the ignorance {ignorant talk} of senseless people (1 Pet. 2:15). ¶
– [4] Acts 17:23 → in ignorance → to know not → KNOW <50> [5] 1 Tim. 1:13 → to act in ignorance → to be ignorant → IGNORANT <50>.

IGNORANT – [1] **to be ignorant: *agnoeō*** [verb: ἀγνοέω <50>]; **from *a*: neg., and *noeō*: to conceive, to think, which is from *nous*: mind, understanding ▶ To be unacquainted with, to not know; also transl.: to be unaware, to be uninformed, to act in ignorance, to act ignorantly** > Paul did not want the Corinthians to be ignorant regarding spiritual gifts (1 Cor. 12:1). If anyone is ignorant about the things which Paul wrote, let him be ignorant (1 Cor. 14:38a, b {to ignore, to not recognize}). He did not wish the Thessalonians to be ignorant concerning those who had fallen asleep (1 Thes. 4:13). Before his conversion, Paul had acted in ignorance, in unbelief (1 Tim. 1:13). The high priest is able to use forbearance toward the ignorant (lit.: the being ignorant) and the misguided (Heb. 5:2). Paul uses this verb in relation to baptism (Rom. 6:3), the law (Rom. 7:1), God's righteousness (Rom. 10:3), and the devices of Satan (2 Cor. 2:11). He uses the expr. "I do not wish you to be ignorant, brothers" in Rom. 1:13; 11:25; 1 Cor. 10:1; 2 Cor. 1:8. Men blaspheme in things they are ignorant of {do not understand, have no knowledge} (2 Pet. 2:12). All other refs.: KNOW <50>, UNDERSTAND <50>, UNKNOWN <50>.
– [2] Acts 4:13 → UNINSTRUCTED <2399> [3] 1 Cor. 15:34; 1 Pet. 2:15 → IGNORANCE <56> [4] 2 Tim. 2:23 →

SENSELESS <521> 5 2 Pet. 3:5, 8 → to be ignorant → HIDDEN (BE) <2990> 6 2 Pet. 3:16 → UNTAUGHT <261>.

IGNORANTLY – 1 Acts 17:23 → to know not → KNOW <50> 2 1 Tim. 1:13 → to act ignorantly, to do something ignorantly → to be ignorant → IGNORANT <50>.

IGNORE – 1 1 Cor. 14:38a, b → to be ignorant → IGNORANT <50> 2 Heb. 2:3 → to be negligent → NEGLIGENT <272>.

ILL – 1 Matt. 4:24; 8:16; 14:35; Mark 6:55 → SICK (adv.) <2560> 2 Matt. 12:15 → all who were ill → lit.: them all → ALL <3956> 3 Matt. 17:15 → very ill → SEVERELY <2560> 4 Matt. 17:15 → to be ill → SUFFER <3958> 5 Matt. 22:6; Acts 14:5 → to treat ill, to use ill → MISTREAT <5195> 6 Matt. 25:36 → to be ill → to be sick → SICK (adj. and noun) <770> 7 Matt. 25:39, 43, 44 → SICK (adj. and noun) <772> 8 Mark 1:30 → ill with a fever → FEVER <4445> 9 Mark 1:32; Luke 7:2 → to be ill → to be sick → SICK (adv.) <2192> <2560> 10 Mark 9:39 → to speak ill → to speak evil → EVIL (adv.) <2551> 11 Luke 7:10; John 4:46; 11:1, 2, 3, 6; Acts 9:37; Phil. 2:26, 27; 2 Tim. 4:20 → to be ill → to be sick → SICK (adv.) <770> 12 John 5:5 → who had been ill → lit.: who had an infirmity → INFIRMITY <769> 13 Acts 7:34 → ill treatment → OPPRESSION <2561> 14 Acts 27:12 → ill adapted → not suitable → SUITABLE <428> 15 Rom. 13:10 → EVIL (noun) <2556> 16 1 Cor. 11:30 → SICK (adj. and noun) <732>.

ILL (BE) – Luke 4:38 → to be ill with → to suffer from → SUFFER <4912>.

ILL-ESTABLISHED – 2 Pet. 3:16 → UNSTABLE <793>.

ILL-TEMPERED – 1 Pet. 2:18 → HARSH <4646>.

ILL-TREATMENT – Heb. 11:25 → to endure ill-treatment with → to suffer affliction with → AFFLICTION <4778>.

ILLEGITIMATE – 1 ***nothos*** [adj.: νόθος <3541>] ► **Born of parents not married to each other** > God chastens His children as sons; if He acted otherwise, they would be illegitimate {illegitimate children, bastards} and not sons (Heb. 12:8). ¶
– 2 John 8:41 → to be illegitimate → lit.: to be born of fornication → FORNICATION <4202>, <4203>.

ILLNESS – 1 ***astheneia*** [fem. noun: ἀσθένεια <769>]; **from *asthenēs*: weak, which is from *a*: neg., and *sthenos*: strength** ► **Weakness, lack of strength** > Timothy was to use a little wine because of his stomach and his frequent illnesses {ailments, infirmities} (1 Tim. 5:23). All other refs.: INFIRMITY <769>, SICKNESS <769>, WEAKNESS <769>.
– 2 Acts 19:12 → SICKNESS <3554> 3 Gal. 4:14 → TEMPTATION <3986>.

ILLUMINATE – 1 ***phōtizō*** [verb: φωτίζω <5461>]; **from *phōs*: light** ► **To enlighten, to give light; also transl.: to lighten, to illumine, to make bright** > The earth was illuminated {was lightened, was illumined} by the glory of the angel descending out of the heaven (Rev. 18:1). The glory of God will illuminate {enlighten} the new Jerusalem (Rev. 21:23). All other refs.: ENLIGHTEN <5461>, LIGHT (noun) <5461>.
– 2 Eph. 5:13 → LOVE (verb) <5319>.

ILLUMINE – 1 Luke 11:36; Rev. 22:5 → to give light, to bring to light → LIGHT (noun) <5461> 2 Rev. 18:1; 21:23 → ILLUMINATE <5461>.

ILLUSTRATION – 1 John 10:6 → ALLEGORY <3942> 2 Heb. 9:9 → PARABLE <3850>.

ILLYRICUM – ***Illurikon*** [neut. name: Ἰλλυρικόν <2437>] ► **Region located northeast of the Adriatic Sea** > Paul had fully preached the gospel of Christ from Jerusalem as far as Illyricum (Rom. 15:19). ¶

IMAGE – 1 ***eikōn*** [fem. noun: εἰκών <1504>]; **from *eikō*: to resemble** ►

a. Representation of a person or an object > Men have changed the glory of the incorruptible God into the likeness of an image of corruptible man (Rom. 1:23). God has predestined Christians to be conformed to the image of His Son (Rom. 8:29). Man is the image and glory of God (1 Cor. 11:7). As Christians have borne the image of the one made of dust (Adam), they shall bear also the image of the heavenly one (Christ) (1 Cor. 15:49a, b). Contemplating the glory of the Lord, Christians are transformed into the same image (2 Cor. 3:18). Christ is the image of God (2 Cor. 4:4), of the invisible God (Col. 1:15). The new man is according to the image of Him who has created him (Col. 3:10). The law does not have the image itself {the very form, the realities} of things to come (Heb. 10:1). The term is used in regard to the beast (Rev. 13:14, 15a–c; 14:9, 11; 15:2; 16:2; 19:20; 20:4). **b. Effigy, likeness** > Jesus asked whose image was on the denarius (Matt. 22:20; Mark 12:16; Luke 20:24). ¶

– [2] Acts 7:43 → TYPE <5179> [3] Acts 17:29 → image formed, image made → graven form → FORM (noun) <5480> [4] Heb. 1:3 → express image → EXPRESSION <5481> [5] Heb. 9:9 → PARABLE <3850>.

IMAGINATION – [1] ***enthumēsis*** [fem. noun: ἐνθύμησις <1761>]; **from *enthumeomai*: to think, which is from *en*: in, and *thumos*: strong feeling, passion ► Thought, device; also transl.: devising, skill** > The Divine Nature is not like a graven form of man's art and imagination (Acts 17:29). Other refs.: Matt. 9:4; 12:25; Heb. 4:12; see THOUGHT <1761>. ¶

– [2] Luke 1:51 → UNDERSTANDING <1271> [3] Rom. 1:21 → REASONING <1261> [4] 2 Cor. 10:5 → REASONING <3053>.

IMAGINE – [1] Acts 4:25 → MEDITATE <3191> [2] 1 Cor. 2:9 → nor the heart of man imagined → and have not gone up into the heart of man → GO UP <305> [3] 1 Cor. 8:2 → THINK <1380> [4] Eph. 3:20 → THINK <3539> [5] 1 Tim. 6:5 → SUPPOSE <3543>.

IMAGINED – 2 Pet. 1:16 → cleverly imagined → cleverly devised → DEVISED <4679>.

IMITATE – [1] ***mimeomai*** [verb: μιμέομαι <3401>]; **from *mimos*: imitator ► To reproduce the behavior of another; to follow a model; also transl.: to follow, to follow the example** > The Thessalonians were to imitate Paul (2 Thes. 3:7, 9). Christians are to imitate the faith of their leaders (Heb. 13:7). Gaius was not to imitate what is evil, but what is good (3 John 11). ¶

– [2] 1 Cor. 4:16; Heb. 6:12 → lit.: to be imitators → IMITATOR <3402> [3] Phil. 3:17 → to join in imitating → to become imitators together → IMITATOR <4831>.

IMITATOR – [1] ***mimētēs*** [masc. noun: μιμητής <3402>]; **from *mimeomai*: to imitate, to follow ► Person who reproduces the behavior of another, who follows a model; also transl.: example, follower** > Paul told the Corinthians to be his imitators (1 Cor. 4:16; 11:1), and similarly told the Ephesians to be imitators of God (Eph. 5:1). The Thessalonians had become imitators of Paul and his companions as well as of the Lord (1 Thes. 1:6); they had become also imitators of the churches of God (2:14). The Hebrews were to become imitators of those who inherit what has been promised (Heb. 6:12). Peter speaks of becoming imitators of that which is good {zealous for what is good, eager to do good} (1 Pet. 3:13); other mss. have *zēlōtēs* <2207>: zealous. ¶

[2] **imitator together: *summimētēs*** [masc. noun: συμμιμητής <4831>]; **from *sun*: together, and *mimētēs*: see [1] ► Imitator with another person** > Paul told the Philippians to be his imitators together {to be followers together of him, to follow his example} (Phil. 3:17). ¶

IMMANUEL – ***Emmanouēl*** [masc. name: Ἐμμανουήλ <1694>]: **God with us, in Heb. ► Name of the Lord Jesus; also transl.: Emmanuel** > Isaiah had said that the virgin would be with child and that they would call the name of her son Immanuel (Matt. 1:23; see Isaiah 7:14; 8:8, 10). ¶

IMMATURE – Rom. 2:20 → BABE <3516>.

IMMEASURABLE – 1 Eph. 1:19 → surpassing → SURPASS <5235> 2 Eph. 2:7 → SURPASSING <5235>.

IMMEASURABLY – Eph. 3:20 → immeasurably more → far more abundantly → ABUNDANTLY <5238a>.

IMMEDIATE – Gal. 1:16 → my immediate response was not to consult → I did not consult immediately → IMMEDIATELY <2112>.

IMMEDIATELY – 1 ***euthеōs*** [adv.: εὐθέως <2112>] ¶, ***euthus*** [adv.: εὐθύς <2117>]; **from *euthus*: straight, direct ▶ Without delay, at once** > Jesus asks if the master will tell his servant to come immediately {at once, now} and sit down to eat (Luke 17:7). If God is glorified in the Son of Man, God will also glorify Him in Himself, and will glorify Him immediately {straightway} (John 13:32). Immediately John was in the Spirit, and behold, a throne was set in heaven, and One was sitting on the throne (Rev. 4:2). These Greek words are transl. by "immediately," "straightway," and "forthwith" in the Gospels (occurring particularly frequently in the Gospel of Mark) and in Acts; also Gal. 1:16; Jas. 1:24. Other refs.: Matt. 3:16; 4:20, 22; 8:3; 13:5; 14:22, 27, 31; 20:34; 21:2, 3; 24:29; 25:15; 26:49, 74; 27:48; Mark 1:10, 12, 18, 20, 21, 28–31, 42, 43; 2:2, 8, 12; 3:6; 4:5, 15–17, 29; 5:2, 13, 29, 30, 36 {as soon}, 42; 6:25, 27, 45, 50, 54; 7:35; 8:10; 9:15, 20, 24; 10:52; 11:2 {as soon}, 3; 14:43, 45; 15:1; Luke 5:13, 39; 6:49; 12:36, 54; 14:5; 21:9; John 5:9; 6:21; 13:30, 32; 18:27; 19:34; 21:3; Acts 9:18, 20, 34; 12:10; 16:10; 17:10, 14; 21:30; 22:29; 3 John 14 {shortly}. All other refs. (*euthus*): see STRAIGHT <2117>.
2 ***exautēs*** [adv.: ἐξαυτῆς <1824>]; **from *ek*: from, and *autos*: it, this ▶ Instantly, suddenly, at once** > Paul hoped to send Timothy to the Philippians immediately {presently} (Phil. 2:23). The word is also found in Acts 11:11; 21:32; 23:30 {straightway, at that moment, at once, right then}. Other refs.: Mark 6:25; Acts 10:33. ¶
3 ***parachrēma*** [adv.: παραχρῆμα <3916>]; **from *para*: at, and *chrēma*: matter ▶ At once, instantly, right away** > At the word of Jesus, the fig tree dried up immediately (Matt. 21:19, 20). The young girl who had been dead got up immediately {straightway} (Luke 8:55). People thought that the kingdom of God was going to appear immediately (Luke 19:11). The jailer took Paul and Silas during the night and washed their wounds; and immediately {straightway} he was baptized, he and all his household (Acts 16:33). The term is also used in regard to Zacharias (Luke 1:64), the mother-in-law of Simon (Luke 4:39), a paralyzed man (Luke 5:25), a woman who had a hemorrhage (Luke 8:44, 47), a woman who had a spirit of infirmity (Luke 13:13), a blind man (Luke 18:43), Peter (Luke 22:60), a lame man (Acts 3:7), Sapphira (Acts 5:10), Herod (Acts 12:23), Elymas (Acts 13:11), and the doors of the prison where Paul and Silas were kept (Acts 16:26). ¶
– 4 Acts 22:18 → QUICKLY <5034>.

IMMENSE – 1 Tim. 1:16 → immense patience → lit.: all (*pas*) patience.

IMMERSE – 1 Tim. 4:15 → to immerse oneself in → lit.: to be in.

IMMINENT – ***tachinos*** [adj.: ταχινός <5031>]; **from *tachus*: prompt, swift ▶ Quick, close; also transl.: shortly, speedily** > Peter knew that the moment of putting off his tabernacle was imminent as the Lord had shown him (2 Pet. 1:14). Other ref.: 2 Pet. 2:1; see SWIFT <5031>. ¶

IMMORAL – 1 Cor. 5:9–11; 6:9; Eph. 5:5; 1 Tim. 1:10; Heb. 12:16; 13:4; Rev. 21:8; 22:15 → immoral people, sexually immoral people → FORNICATOR <4205>.

IMMORALITY – 1 Matt. 5:32; 19:9; John 8:41; 1 Cor. 5:1a, b; 7:2; Rev. 2:14;

et al. → immorality, sexual immorality → FORNICATION <4202>, <4203> 2 Rom. 13:13 → sexual immorality → LEWDNESS <2845> 3 1 Cor. 5:11 → one who is guilty of sexual immorality → FORNICATOR <4205> 4 Jude 4 → license for immorality → LEWDNESS <766> 5 Jude 7 → to give oneself up to sexual immorality, to indulge in gross immorality → to give oneself over to fornication → FORNICATION <1608>.

IMMORTAL – 1 Rom. 1:23; 1 Tim. 1:17 → INCORRUPTIBLE <862> 2 1 Tim. 6:16 → who alone is immortal → lit.: who alone has immortality → IMMORTALITY <110> 3 1 Tim. 6:16 → ETERNAL <166>.

IMMORTALITY – 1 ***athanasia*** [fem. noun: ἀθανασία <110>]; **from *athanatos*: immortal, which is from *a*: neg., and *thanatos*: death ▶ Quality of that which cannot die** > At the resurrection of Christians, their mortal body will put on immortality (1 Cor. 15:53, 54). Immortality characterizes the nature of God (1 Tim. 6:16). ¶
– 2 Rom. 2:7; 2 Tim. 1:10 → INCORRUPTIBILITY <861>.

IMMOVABLE – 1 ***ametakinētos*** [adj.: ἀμετακίνητος <277>]; **from *a*: neg., and *metakinētos*: disturbed, displaced, which is from *metakineō*: to move away, which is from *meta*: indicates change and *kineō*: to displace ▶ Which one cannot displace, not being subject to negative influences; not turned aside by others** > Paul enjoins the Corinthians to be immovable {unmoveable} (1 Cor. 15:58). ¶

2 ***asaleutos*** [adj.: ἀσάλευτος <761>]; **from *a*: neg., and *saleuō*: to agitate, to stir ▶ Which one cannot move, fixed** > The prow of the ship remained immovable {unmoveable, unmoved} (Acts 27:41). Other ref.: Heb. 12:28 (which cannot be shaken); see SHAKEN <761>. ¶

IMMUTABILITY – Heb. 6:17 → UNCHANGEABLE <276>.

IMMUTABLE – Heb. 6:18 → UNCHANGEABLE <276>.

IMPART – 1 ***metadidōmi*** [verb: μεταδίδωμι <3330>]; **from *meta*: with, and *didōmi*: to give ▶ To share, to communicate** > Paul and his companions were well pleased to impart to the Thessalonians not only the gospel of God, but also their own lives (1 Thes. 2:8). Other refs.: Luke 3:11; Rom. 1:11; 12:8; Eph. 4:28; see GIVE <3330>. ¶
– 2 1 Cor. 2:6, 7, 13 → SPEAK <2980> 3 Eph. 4:29 → MINISTER (verb) <1325>.

IMPARTIAL – Jas. 3:17 → UNQUESTIONING <87>.

IMPARTIALLY – 1 Pet. 1:17 → without respect of persons → RESPECT OF PERSONS <678>.

IMPEDIMENT – 1 Mark 7:32 → who has an impediment in his speech → who cannot speak right → SPEAK <3424> 2 Mark 7:35 → CHAIN (noun) <1199>.

IMPEL – Mark 1:12 → to impel to go → to send out → SEND <1544>.

IMPENITENT – Rom. 2:5 → UNREPENTANT <279>.

IMPERFECT – 1 Cor. 13:10 → the imperfect → that which is in part → PART (noun) <3313>.

IMPERIAL – 1 Matt. 22:17; Mark 12:14 → imperial tax → TRIBUTE <2778> 2 Phil. 1:13 → imperial guard → PRAETORIUM <4232>.

IMPERISHABLE – 1 1 Cor. 9:25; 15:52; 1 Pet. 1:4, 23; 3:4 → INCORRUPTIBLE <862> 2 1 Cor. 15:42, 50, 53, 54 → INCORRUPTIBILITY <861>.

IMPETUOUS – Acts 2:2 → RUSHING <5342>.

IMPIETY – Rom. 1:18; 11:26; Titus 2:12; Jude 15, 18 → UNGODLINESS <763>.

IMPIOUS – 1 Tim. 1:9; 1 Pet. 4:18 → UNGODLY <765>.

IMPLACABLE – 1 ***aspondos*** [adj.: ἄσπονδος <786>]; **from *a*: neg., and *spondē*: libation which usually accompanied a treaty ▶ Which cannot be persuaded to reach an agreement, irreconcilable; also transl.: unforgiving, trucebreakers** > In the last days, men will be implacable (2 Tim. 3:3); one translator's note suggests: "who do not keep their commitments." Paul speaks of unbelievers who are implacable (Rom. 1:31 in some mss.). ¶
– 2 2 Tim. 3:3 → BRUTAL <434>.

IMPLANTED – ***emphutos*** [adj.: ἔμφυτος <1721>]; **from *emphuō*: to implant, which is from *en*: in, and *phuō*: to produce, to grow ▶ Which is grafted and develops** > James exhorts to accept with humility the implanted {grafted, planted} word (Jas. 1:21). ¶

IMPLEAD – Acts 19:38 → ACCUSE <1458>.

IMPLORE – 1 ***deomai*** [verb: δέομαι <1189>]; **from *deō*: to bind ▶ To ask urgently, to make a request demanding immediate attention** > The churches of Macedonia had implored {begged, pleaded, prayed} Paul that he would receive the gift and the fellowship of ministering to the saints (2 Cor. 8:4). All other refs.: PRAY <1189>, REQUEST (noun) <1189>, SUPPLICATE <1189>.
– 2 Matt. 8:5; Mark 1:40; 5:23; Luke 8:41; 2 Cor. 12:8; Phil. 4:2a, b → PLEAD <3870> 3 Matt. 8:34; 14:36; Mark 5:10, 12, 17, 18; 6:56; 7:32; 8:22; Luke 7:4; Acts 9:38 → BESEECH <3870> 4 Matt. 15:23; John 4:47 → ASK <2065> 5 Matt. 18:26 → lit.: to say (*legō*) 6 Mark 5:7 → ADJURE <3726> 7 Acts 2:40; 27:33 → EXHORT <3870>.

IMPLY – 1 1 Cor. 10:19 → SAY <5346> 2 1 Cor. 10:20 → "I imply" added in Engl. 3 Gal. 3:20 → an intermediary implies more than one → lit.: the mediator is not of one.

IMPORTANT – 1 **more important: from the verb: *huperechō*** [verb: ὑπερέχω <5242>]; **from *huper*: above, and *echō*: to have, to hold; lit.: to stand above ▶ Better, more excellent, superior** > In humility, one is to esteem the other more important than himself (Phil. 2:3). All other refs.: AUTHORITY <5242>, EXCELLENCE <5242>, GOVERNING <5242>, SURPASS <5242>.
– 2 Matt. 23:23 → more important → WEIGHTIER <926> 3 Luke 14:9 → least important → LAST (adv. and noun) <2078> 4 Gal. 2:6a, b → to seem to be important → to be of reputation → REPUTATION <1380> 5 Rev. 18:23 → important person → LORD (noun) <3175>.

IMPORTUNITY – Luke 11:8 → PERSISTENCE <335>.

IMPOSE – 1 ***ballō*** [verb: βάλλω <906>]; **lit.: to throw ▶ To put, to place; also transl.: to cast** > The Son of God does not impose any other burden on those of Thyatira (Rev. 2:24). All other refs.: see entries in Lexicon at <906>.
2 ***epikeimai*** [verb: ἐπίκειμαι <1945>]; **from *epi*: upon, and *keimai*: to put ▶ To direct, to dictate; also transl.: to lay upon** > To preach the gospel was a necessity for Paul which had been imposed upon him (1 Cor. 9:16); other transl.: he was under compulsion, he was compelled to preach the gospel. The carnal ordinances of the O.T. had been imposed {applying} until the time of setting things right (Heb. 9:10). All other refs.: BEAT <1945>, INSISTENT <1945>, LAY <1945>, PRESS <1945>.
– 3 Rev. 18:20 → God has judged her with the judgment she imposed on you → lit.: God has judged your judgment by her.

IMPOSSIBLE – 1 ***adunatos*** [adj.: ἀδύνατος <102>]; **from *a*: neg., and *dunatos*: capable, possible, which is from *dunamai*: to be capable, to have power ▶ Unrealizable, incapable of being done** > Without the intervention of God in grace, it is impossible for men to be saved (Matt. 19:26; Mark 10:27). The things that are impossible with men are possible with God (Luke 18:27). The law could not {was powerless to} (or: It was impossible for the law to) set us free from sin and death (Rom. 8:3). It is impossible for those who have once been enlightened, and have fallen away, to be renewed again to repentance (Heb. 6:4 or v. 6). It was impossible that God should lie (Heb. 6:18). It is impossible {not possible} for the blood of bulls and goats to take away sins (Heb. 10:4). Without faith it is impossible to please God (Heb. 11:6). Other refs.: Acts 14:8 (without strength); Rom. 15:1; see STRENGTH <102>; WEAK <102>. ¶

[2] **to be impossible: *adunateō*** [verb: ἀδυνατέω <101>]; **from *adunatos*: see [1] ▶ To be unrealizable, incapable of being done** > With faith, nothing shall be impossible (Matt. 17:20). Nothing shall be impossible with God (Luke 1:37). ¶

[3] ***anendektos*** [adj.: ἀνένδεκτος <418>]; **from *a*: neg., and *endechomai*: to allow, to be possible, which is from *en*: in, and *dechomai*: to receive ▶ Inevitable, unavoidable** > Jesus told His disciples that it was impossible but that offenses will come (or: it was inevitable that offenses come) (Luke 17:1). ¶

– [4] Acts 2:24 → lit.: not possible → POSSIBLE <1415>.

IMPOSTER – Matt. 27:63 → DECEIVER <4108>.

IMPOSTOR – [1] ***goēs*** [masc. noun: γόης <1114>]; **from *goaō*: to wail, no doubt an allusion to the weird incantations of charlatans; lit.: sorcerer, magician ▶ Person who deceives by false appearances, who cheats** > Evil men and imposters {deceivers} will go from bad to worse in the times of the end, deceiving and being deceived (2 Tim. 3:13). ¶

– [2] 2 Cor. 6:8 → DECEIVER <4108>.

IMPOTENT – [1] John 5:3 → to be impotent → to be sick → SICK (adj. and noun) <770> [2] John 5:7 → to be impotent → to be sick → SICK (adv.) <770> [3] Acts 4:9 → SICK (adj. and noun) <772> [4] Acts 14:8 → without strength → STRENGTH <102>.

IMPRESS – Gal. 6:12 → to impress people → to make a good showing → SHOWING <2146>.

IMPRESSION – Gal. 6:12 → to make a good impression → to make a good showing → SHOWING <2146>.

IMPRINT – [1] John 20:25a → MARK (noun) <5179> [2] Heb. 1:3 → exact imprint → EXPRESSION <5481>.

IMPRISON – [1] ***phulakizō*** [verb: φυλακίζω <5439>]; **from *phulakē*: prison ▶ To put in prison, to incarcerate** > Paul imprisoned those who believed in the Lord (Acts 22:19). ¶

– [2] Mark 15:7 → CHAIN (verb) <1210> [3] Acts 21:13; 24:27 → BIND <1210> [4] Gal. 3:22, 23 → to shut up → SHUT <4788>.

IMPRISONED – [1] Matt. 11:2 → while imprisoned → lit.: in the prison → PRISON <1201> [2] 1 Pet. 3:19 → imprisoned spirits → spirits in prison → PRISON <5438>.

IMPRISONMENT – [1] Acts 20:23; 23:29; 26:31; Phil. 1:7, 13, 14, 16 (or 17); Col. 4:18; 2 Tim. 2:9; Phm. 10, 13; Heb. 11:36 → CHAIN (noun) <1199> [2] 2 Cor. 6:5; 11:23; Heb. 11:36 → PRISON <5438>.

IMPROPER – [1] 1 Cor. 14:35 → SHAMEFUL <149> [2] Eph. 5:3 → to be improper → to not be fitting → FITTING (BE) <4241>.

IMPROPERLY – 1 Cor. 7:36 → to behave improperly → to behave uncomely → BEHAVE <807>.

IMPUDENCE – Luke 11:8 → PERSISTENCE <335>.

IMPULSE – [1] Acts 7:57 → with one impulse → with one accord → ACCORD

<3661> 2 2 Tim. 3:6 → LUST (noun) <1939>.

IMPURE – 1 ***aniptos*** [adj.: ἄνιπτος <449>]; **from *a*: neg. part, and *niptō*: to wash ▶ Unclean, unwashed** > Jesus was asked why His disciples ate bread with impure {defiled, unwashen} hands (Mark 7:5). Other refs.: Matt. 15:20; Mark 7:2; see UNWASHED <449>. ¶
– 2 Matt. 10:1; 12:43; Mark 1:23, 26, 27; Eph. 5:5; Rev. 16:13; et al. → UNCLEAN <169> 3 Mark 7:2 → UNCLEAN <2839> 4 Acts 10:14 → COMMON <2839> 5 Acts 10:15; 11:9 → to call impure → to call common → COMMON <2840> 6 1 Thes. 2:3; 4:7 → impure motives, to be impure → UNCLEANNESS <167> 7 Rev. 21:27 → to be impure → DEFILE <2840>.

IMPURITY – 1 Rom. 1:24; 6:19; 2 Cor. 12:21; Gal. 5:19; Eph. 4:19; 5:3; Col. 3:5; 1 Thes. 2:3; 4:7 → UNCLEANNESS <167> 2 Rev. 17:4 → unclean things → UNCLEAN <168>.

IMPUTE – 1 ***logizomai*** [verb: λογίζομαι <3049>]; **from *logos*: word, account ▶ To keep account, to take into consideration** > Love does not impute {think} evil (1 Cor. 13:5); other transl.: does not take into account a wrong suffered, keeps no record of wrongs. God has not imputed {counted, reckoned} their offences to the sinners of the world (2 Cor. 5:19). All had abandoned Paul at his first defense, but he did not want that to be imputed to them (2 Tim. 4:16 {to count against, to lay to the charge, to charge, to hold against}). All other refs.: see entries in Lexicon at <3049>.
2 ***ellogeō*** [verb: ἐλλογέω <1677>]; **from *en*: in, and *logos*: word, account ▶ To attribute, to ascribe** > Sin is not imputed {put to account, taken into account} when there is no law (Rom. 5:13). If Onesimus had wronged or owed anything to Philemon, the later was to impute that to {put that on the account of, charge the account of} Paul (Phm. 18). ¶

IN- – See DIS- <1418>.

IN EVERY WAY, IN ALL THINGS – ***pantē*** [adv.: πάντῃ <3839>]; **from *pas*: all, every ▶** Ref.: Acts 24:3. ¶ ‡

INASMUCH – Luke 1:1 → NOW (SINCE) <1894>.

INAUGURATE – ***enkainizō*** [verb: ἐγκαινίζω <1457>]; **from *en*: in, and *kainizō*: to make new, which is from *kainos*: new ▶ To do something for the first time, to begin** > The first covenant was not inaugurated {dedicated, put into effect} without blood (Heb. 9:18). Jesus has inaugurated {has consecrated, has dedicated, has opened} a new and living way through the veil into the holy of holies by His blood (Heb. 10:20). ¶

INCAPABLE – Heb. 10:4 → IMPOSSIBLE <102>.

INCENSE – 1 ***thumiama*** [neut. noun: θυμίαμα <2368>]; **from *thumiaō*: see 2 ▶ Substance which releases a pleasing odor when burned** > The multitude prayed at the hour of incense (Luke 1:10). An angel appeared to Zacharias, standing on the right of the altar of incense (Luke 1:11). The golden bowls of the living creatures and elders are full of incenses {incense, odours}, which are the prayers of the saints (Rev. 5:8). Much incense was given to an angel, that he might give efficacy to the prayers of the saints (Rev. 8:3); the smoke of the incense went up with the prayers of the saints (v. 4). Merchants will grieve over the fall of Babylon because no one buys their various products, including incense {odours}, any more (Rev. 18:13). ¶
2 **to burn incense: *thumiaō*** [verb: θυμιάω <2370>]; **from *thuō*: to offer in sacrifice ▶ To set alight a particular substance which releases a pleasing odor** > It fell to Zacharias by lot to enter into the temple to burn incense (Luke 1:9). ¶
– 3 Matt. 2:11 → FRANKINCENSE <3030> 4 Heb. 9:4 → altar of incense → CENSER <2369>.

INCESSANTLY – 1 Acts 6:13 → to speak incessantly → lit.: to not cease to speak → CEASE <3973> [2] Acts 26:7 → EARNESTLY <1616>.

INCITE – [1] Luke 23:14 → to incite to rebellion → to turn away → TURN (verb) <654> [2] Acts 13:50 → EXCITE <3951>.

INCLINATION – ***hormē*** [fem. noun: ὁρμή <3730>]; **from *ornumi*: to excite, to stir up ▶ Desire, impulsion** > Ships are directed wherever the inclination {pleasure} of the pilot desires (Jas. 3:4). Other ref.: Acts 14:5; see ATTEMPT (noun) <3730>. ¶

INCLUDE – 1 Cor. 15:27 → this does not include → EXCEPT <1622>.

INCLUSION – Rom. 11:12 → full inclusion → FULLNESS <4138>.

INCOME – Acts 19:25 → good income → WEALTH <2142>.

INCOMPARABLE – [1] Eph. 1:19 → surpassing → SURPASS <5235> [2] Eph. 2:7 → SURPASSING <5235>.

INCOMPETENT – 1 Cor. 6:2 → UNWORTHY <370>.

INCONTINENCY – [1] 1 Cor. 7:5 → lack of self-control → SELF-CONTROL (noun) <192> [2] 2 Tim. 3:3 → without self-control → SELF-CONTROL (adj.) <193>.

INCONTINENT – 2 Tim. 3:3 → without self-control → SELF-CONTROL (adj.) <193>.

INCORRUPTIBILITY – [1] ***aphtharsia*** [fem. noun: ἀφθαρσία <861>]; **from *aphtartos*: incorruptible, which is from *a*: neg., and *phtartos*: corruptible, which is from *phtheirō*: to corrupt, to waste ▶ a. Purity, sincerity** > Paul desired that grace might be with all who love the Lord in incorruptibility {incorruption} (Eph. 6:24). Titus was to show incorruptibility {integrity, uncorruptedness, uncorruptness} and dignity in his teaching (Titus 2:7); other mss. have *adiaphtoria* (see [2]), *aphthonia*, *aphthoria*. **b. Quality of that which cannot be corrupted, i.e., decomposed; also transl.: immortality, imperishable, incorruption** > God will render to every person according to his works, in particular to those who by perseverance in good works seek for incorruptibility (Rom. 2:7). At the resurrection, the bodies of believers in the Lord who have died will be resurrected in incorruptibility (1 Cor. 15:42, 50, 53, 54). Jesus Christ has brought to light life and incorruptibility by the gospel (2 Tim. 1:10). ¶

[2] ***adiaphthoria*** [fem. noun: ἀδιαφθορία <90>]; **from *adiaphthoros*: incorrupt, which is from *a*: neg., and *diaphtheirō*: to corrupt ▶ Purity, sincerity** > This word is found in Titus 2:7 in certain mss.; see [1]. ¶

INCORRUPTIBLE – [1] ***aphthartos*** [adj.: ἄφθαρτος <862>]; **from *a*: neg., and *phtartos*: corruptible, which is from *phtheirō*: to corrupt, to waste ▶ Unalterable, which cannot be corrupted; also transl.: immortal, imperishable, not corruptible, that can never perish, unfading, which lasts forever** > God is incorruptible (Rom. 1:23; 1 Tim. 1:17; *athanatos* in some mss.: immortal), and His word is an incorruptible seed (1 Pet. 1:23). The rewards of the saints are represented by incorruptible crowns (1 Cor. 9:25); their inheritance is also incorruptible (1 Pet. 1:4). At the resurrection, believers in the Lord who have died will be resurrected incorruptible (1 Cor. 15:52). Peter speaks of the incorruptible quality of a meek and quiet spirit (1 Pet. 3:4). ¶

– [2] Eph. 6:24 → love incorruptible → lit.: love in incorruptibility → INCORRUPTIBILITY <861>.

INCORRUPTION – 1 Cor. 15:42, 50, 53, 54; Eph. 6:24 → INCORRUPTIBILITY <861>.

INCREASE (noun) – [1] ***auxēsis*** [fem. noun: αὔξησις <838>]; **from *auxō*: see [2] ▶ Growth, progression** > Christ works the increase {causes the growth of} the body, the church, for the edifying of itself in love

(Eph. 4:16). This body increases with the increase {grows with a growth} which is from God (Col. 2:19). ¶
[2] **to give the increase: *auxanō* or *auxō*** [verb: αὐξάνω or αὔξω <837>] ▶ **To make grow, to make progress, to augment** > Paul planted the seed, Apollos watered it, but God had given the increase {had given the growth} (1 Cor. 3:6, 7). All other refs.: GROW <837>, INCREASE (verb) <837>.

INCREASE (verb) – [1] ***auxanō* or *auxō*** [verb: αὐξάνω or αὔξω <837>] ▶ **To progress; also transl.: to grow** > Jesus had to increase {become greater}, and John the Baptist to decrease (John 3:30). In a parable, seed increased and produced (Mark 4:8). God will increase the fruits of the righteousness of Christians (2 Cor. 9:10). Paul was hoping that the faith of the Corinthians would increase {continue to grow} (2 Cor. 10:15). The gospel was increasing among the Colossians (Col. 1:6 in some mss.); Paul was praying they would increase in the knowledge of God (v. 10). The church increases with the increase that is from God (Col. 2:19). All other refs.: GROW <837>, INCREASE (noun) <837>.
[2] ***perisseuō*** [verb: περισσεύω <4052>]; **from *perissos*: abundant, which is from *peri*: above, beyond** ▶ **To grow, to augment** > At the beginning, the churches increased in number every day (Acts 16:5). All other refs.: see entries in Lexicon at <4052>.
[3] ***prokoptō*** [verb: προκόπτω <4298>]; **from *pro*: before, in front, and *koptō*: to hit, to cut** ▶ **Primarily: to beat forward (as a smith elongating metal) or to cut forward (as blazing a trail); from which: to advance, to progress** > Jesus increased {grew} in wisdom and stature, and in favor with God and men (Luke 2:52). Paul increased {advanced, profited} in Judaism beyond many of his contemporaries (Gal. 1:14). Those who indulge in profane and vain babblings will increase to more ungodliness {will become more and more ungodly} (2 Tim. 2:16 {to lead}). All other refs.: GROW <4298>, PROCEED <4298>, SPEND <4298>.
[4] ***prostithēmi*** [verb: προστίθημι <4369>]; **from *pros*: moreover, and *tithēmi*: to put, to place** ▶ **To add, to augment** > The apostles said to the Lord to increase their {give them more} faith (Luke 17:5). All other refs.: ADD <4369>.
– [5] Matt. 24:12 → ABOUND <4129> [6] Luke 2:40 → FILL (verb) <4137> [7] Luke 11:29 → to gather tick together → GATHER <1865> [8] Acts 6:1, 7; 7:17; 9:31; 2 Cor. 9:10 → MULTIPLY <4129> [9] Rom. 5:20; 6:1; Phil. 4:17; 2 Thes. 1:3; 2 Pet. 1:8 → ABOUND <4121> [10] Rom. 5:20 → to increase all the more → to abound much more → ABOUND <5248> [11] 2 Thes. 1:3 → to increase exceedingly → to grow exceedingly → GROW <5232>.

INCREDIBLE – ***apistos*** [adj.: ἄπιστος <571>]; **from *a*: neg., and *pistos*: believing, faithful** ▶ **Which one cannot believe, improbable, which one cannot accept as true** > Some considered it incredible that God should raise the dead (Acts 26:8). All other refs.: UNBELIEVING <571>.

INCUR – [1] ***kerdainō*** [verb: κερδαίνω <2770>]; **from *kerdos*: gain; lit.: to make a gain** ▶ **To happen, to occur** > If the men navigating the ship had listened to Paul, they would not have incurred {would have not gained, would have been spared} the disaster and loss of the ship (Acts 27:21). All other refs.: GAIN (verb) <2770>, MAKE <2770>.
– [2] Rom. 13:2 → BRING <2983>.

INDEBTED – Rom. 15:27 → DEBTOR <3781>.

INDEBTED (BE) – ***opheilō*** [verb: ὀφείλω <3784>] ▶ **To owe something, to have the obligation to repay** > The Christians of the nations were indebted {the nations ought, owed it; their duty was} to help the poor of the saints who were in Jerusalem (Rom. 15:27). All other refs.: DEBT <3784>, DEBTOR <3784>, DUE <3784>, OUGHT <3784>, OWE <3784>.

INDEBTEDNESS – Col. 2:14 → legal indebtedness → ordinances against → ORDINANCE <1378>.

INDECENT – Rom. 1:27 → indecent acts → shameful acts → SHAMEFUL <808>.

INDEED – [1] ***kai ge*** [conj.: καί γε <2534>]; **from *kai*: and, and *ge*: intens. ▶ In fact, in reality** > Refs.: Luke 19:42; Acts 2:18. ¶ ‡
[2] ***ontōs*** [adv.: ὄντως <3689>]; **from *ōn*: being, pres. ptcp. of *eimi* ▶ Really, in truth** > If the law had been able to quicken, then indeed {certainly, truly, verily} righteousness would have been on the principle of the law (Gal. 3:21). All other refs.: CERTAINLY <3689>, REALLY <3689>, TRULY <3689>.
– [3] John 1:47; 4:42; 6:55a, b; 7:26; 8:31 → TRULY <230> [4] Acts 16:37 → VERILY <1063> [5] Rom. 10:18 → yes indeed → VERILY <3304> [6] 1 Cor. 15:15 → if indeed → if in fact → FACT <1512> [7] 2 Cor. 12:12 → TRULY <3303> [8] Heb. 2:16 → VERILY <1222>.

INDESCRIBABLE – ***anekdiēgētos*** [adj.: ἀνεκδιήγητος <411>]; **from *a*: neg., and *ekdiēgeomai*: to tell, to narrate in full, which is from *ek*: out, *dia*: intens., and *diēgeomai*: to declare, to relate ▶ Which one cannot express adequately with words** > Paul says: Thanks be to God for His indescribable {unspeakable} gift (2 Cor. 9:15). ¶

INDESTRUCTIBLE – ***akatalutos*** [adj.: ἀκατάλυτος <179>]; **from *a*: neg., and *kataluō*: to dissolve, which is from *kata*: intens., and *luō*: to loosen ▶ Indissoluble, imperishable** > As high priest, Jesus has been established according to the power of an indestructible {endless, indissoluble} life (Heb. 7:16). ¶

INDICATE – [1] ***dēloō*** [verb: δηλόω <1213>]; **from *dēlos*: evident ▶ To make manifest, to declare; also transl.: to denote, to point out, to show, to signify** > The Holy Spirit indicates that the way of the Most Holy Place was not yet made manifest under the law (Heb. 9:8). The "yet once" of Hag. 2:6 indicated the removal of what can be shaken (Heb. 12:27). The Holy Spirit indicated to the prophets what might be the time of the manifestation of grace toward Christians (1 Pet. 1:11). All other refs.: DECLARE <1213>, SHOW (verb) <1213>.
– [2] John 12:33; 21:19; Acts 25:27 → SIGNIFY <4591> [3] Acts 11:28 → SHOW (verb) <4591>.

INDICATION – 2 Thes. 1:5 → plain indication → manifest evidence → EVIDENCE <1730>.

INDIGNANT – [1] **to be, to become, to feel indignant: *aganakteō*** [verb: ἀγανακτέω <23>]; **from *agan*: excessively, and *achtos*: grief, pain ▶ To be appalled, to be angry; also transl.: to be moved with indignation, to be greatly displeased** > The ten other apostles were indignant against James and John (Matt. 20:24; Mark 10:41). This verb is also used in regard to the chief priests and the scribes (Matt. 21:15), the disciples (Matt. 26:8; Mark 14:4), Jesus (Mark 10:14), and a synagogue official (Luke 13:14). ¶
– [2] Mark 1:41 → to be indignant → lit.: to be moved with compassion → COMPASSION <4697> [3] 2 Cor. 11:29 → to be indignant → BURN <4448>.

INDIGNANTLY – Mark 14:4 → some were indignantly saying → lit.: there were some being indignant in themselves saying → to be indignant → INDIGNANT <23>.

INDIGNATION – [1] ***aganaktēsis*** [fem. noun: ἀγανάκτησις <24>]; **from *aganakteō*: to be angry, to be indignant, which is from *agan*: much, and *achthos*: pain, sorrow ▶ Irritation, vexation** > The fact of having been grieved according to God had produced in the Corinthians indignation against those among them who had stumbled or against the fact that they had carelessly allowed sin in their midst (2 Cor. 7:11). ¶
[2] ***thumos*** [masc. noun: θυμός <2372>]; **from *thuō*: to move impetuously ▶ Sud-**

den anger, fury > Wrath (*orgē*) and indignation (*thumos*) are the portion of those who obey unrighteousness (Rom. 2:8). All other refs.: FURY <2372>, WRATH <2372>.
– 3 Matt. 20:24; 26:8; Mark 14:4; Luke 13:14 → to be moved with, to have indignation → to be indignant → INDIGNANT <23> 4 Acts 5:17 → JEALOUSY <2205> 5 Heb. 10:27 → HEAT <2205>.

INDISPENSABLE – 1 Cor. 12:22 → NECESSARY <316>.

INDISSOLUBLE – Heb. 7:16 → INDESTRUCTIBLE <179>.

INDISTINCT – 1 Cor. 14:8 → UNCERTAIN <82>.

INDIVIDUAL – Jude 4 → MAN <444>.

INDIVIDUALLY – 1 1 Cor. 12:11 → PRIVATELY <2398> 2 1 Cor. 12:27 → in particular → PARTICULAR <3313>.

INDUCE – Acts 6:11 → to secretly induce → SUBORN <5260>.

INDULGE – 1 Luke 7:25 → LIVE <5225> 2 1 Cor. 10:8 → to indulge in sexual immorality → to commit fornication → FORNICATION <4203> 3 2 Cor. 12:21 → to indulge in → DO <4238> 4 Gal. 5:13 → lit.: into an occasion → OCCASION <874> 5 Eph. 2:3 → FULFILL <4160> 6 Eph. 4:19 → as to indulge in → lit.: in view of the working of → WORKING (noun) <2039> 7 1 Tim. 3:8 → GIVE <4337> 8 Jas. 5:5 → to indulge oneself → to live in self-indulgence → SELF-INDULGENCE <4684> 9 2 Pet. 2:10 → FOLLOW <4198> 10 Jude 7 → to indulge in gross immorality → to give oneself over to fornication → FORNICATION <1608>.

INDULGENCE – 1 ***plēsmonē*** [fem. noun: πλησμονή <4140>]; **from *plethō*: to fill; lit.: fulfillment, satiety ▶ Contentment, gratification** > The ordinances of men are for the indulgence {satisfaction, satisfying} of the flesh (Col. 2:23). ¶

2 ***truphē*** [fem. noun: τρυφή <5172>]; **from *thruptō*: to become soft, to enfeeble (by sensuality, debauchery) ▶ Luxury, sensual life** > Some count the indulgence of a day as pleasure (2 Pet. 2:13); also freely transl. as a verb: to riot, to revel, to carouse. Other ref.: Luke 7:25; see LUXURY <5172>. ¶

INEFFECTIVE – 2 Pet. 1:8 → IDLE <692>.

INEVITABLE – Matt. 18:7 → it is inevitable → lit.: it is a necessity → necessity → NECESSARY <318>.

INEXCUSABLE – ***anapologētos*** [adj.: ἀναπολόγητος <379>]; **from *a*: neg., and *apologeomai*: to excuse, to plead for, which is from *apo*: from, and *logos*: word, speech ▶ Without excuse, having merely a pretext which one cannot defend** > The creation renders men inexcusable for not believing in God (Rom. 1:20). He who judges is inexcusable {has no excuse} (Rom. 2:1). ¶

INEXPRESSIBLE – 1 ***aneklalētos*** [adj.: ἀνεκλάλητος <412>]; **from *a*: neg., and *eklaleō*: to disclose, to say, which is from *ek*: out, and *laleō*: to speak ▶ Unutterable, which one cannot express in words** > The joy of Christians is inexpressible {unspeakable} (1 Pet. 1:8). ¶
2 ***arrētos*** [adj.: ἄρρητος <731>]; **from *a*: neg., and *rētos*: said, spoken, which is from *eirō*: to speak, to say ▶ Unutterable, which one cannot express in words** > Caught up into paradise, Paul heard inexpressible {unspeakable} things (2 Cor. 12:4). ¶
– 3 2 Cor. 9:15 → INDESCRIBABLE <411>.

INFALLIBLE – Acts 1:3 → infallible proof → PROOF <5039>.

INFANCY – 2 Tim. 3:15 → CHILDHOOD <1025>.

INFANT – 1 Matt. 21:16; Rom. 2:20; 1 Cor. 3:1; Eph. 4:14; Heb. 5:13 → BABE <3516> 2 Matt. 24:19; Mark 13:17; Luke

21:23 → to nurse infants → NURSE (verb) <2337> 3 Luke 18:15; Acts 7:19; 1 Pet. 2:2 → BABE <1025> 4 1 Cor. 14:20 → to be infants → to be children → CHILD <3515> 5 Heb. 5:13 → being still an infant → UNSKILLED <552>.

INFERIOR – 1 **to be inferior: *hēttaomai*** [verb: ἡττάομαι <2274>]; **from *hētton*: lower, lesser ▶ To be less, to be of lower rank** > Paul asks in what the Corinthians had been inferior to other churches (2 Cor. 12:13). Other refs.: 2 Pet. 2:19, 20; see OVERCOME <2274>. ¶

2 **to be inferior: *hustereō*** [verb: ὑστερέω <5302>]; **from *husteros*: coming after, last ▶ To fall short, to be deficient** > Paul considered that he was inferior in nothing to {was not a whit behind} the most eminent apostles (2 Cor. 11:5; 12:11). All other refs.: COME <5302>, LACK (verb) <5302>, PRIVATION <5302>, WANT (noun) <5302>, WORSE <5302>.

– 3 John 2:10; Heb. 7:7 → LESSER <1640> 4 Heb. 2:7, 9 → to make inferior → to make lower → LOWER (adj.) <1642>.

INFERNAL – Phil. 2:10 → under the earth → EARTH <2709>.

INFIDEL – 2 Cor. 6:15; 1 Tim. 5:8 → UNBELIEVING <571>.

INFILTRATE – 1 Gal. 2:4 → to infiltrate the ranks → had been secretly brought in → SECRETLY <3920> 2 Gal. 2:4 → to infiltrate the ranks → to come in surreptitiously → SURREPTITIOUSLY <3922>.

INFIRM – 1 Matt. 10:8; Mark 6:56 → to be infirm → to be sick → SICK (adj. and noun) <770> 2 Matt. 14:14; Mark 6:5, 13; 16:18 → SICK (adj. and noun) <732> 3 John 5:7 → to be infirm → to be sick → SICK (adv.) <770> 4 Acts 4:9; 1 Cor. 11:30 → SICK (adj. and noun) <772>.

INFIRMITY – 1 ***astheneia*** [fem. noun: ἀσθένεια <769>]; **from *asthenēs*: weak, sick ▶ Weakness, sickness** > Jesus Himself took our infirmities and bore our diseases (Matt. 8:17). At the pool of Bethesda, Jesus healed a man who had an infirmity {had been ill, had been invalid} (John 5:5). All other refs.: ILLNESS <769>, SICKNESS <769>, WEAKNESS <769>.

– 2 Luke 7:21 → SICKNESS <3554> 3 Rom. 15:1 → WEAKNESS <771>.

INFLAME – Rom. 1:27 → BURN <1572>.

INFLATE – 1 Col. 2:18 → PUFF UP <5448> 2 1 Tim. 3:6 → PUFF UP <5187>.

INFLICT – 1 ***epipherō*** [verb: ἐπιφέρω <2018>]; **from *epi*: upon, and *pherō*: to carry, to bring ▶ To unleash, to release** > Paul asks if God is unrighteous for inflicting wrath {in bringing His wrath, who takes vengeance} (Rom. 3:5). All other refs.: BRING <2018>, STIR (verb) <2018>.

– 2 Luke 10:30 → to inflict wounds → to cover with wounds → WOUND (verb) <2007> <4127> 3 Acts 16:23 → to inflict many blows → to strike with many blows → STRIKE <2007> 4 2 Thes. 1:8 → to inflict vengeance → to take vengeance → TAKE <1325> 5 Rev. 9:19 → to inflict injury → INJURE <91>.

INFLUENCE – 1 2 Cor. 10:13, 15, 16 → area of influence → one's rule, measure of rule → RULE (noun) <2583> 2 2 Thes. 2:11 → deluding influence → strong delusion → DELUSION <4106>.

INFLUENTIAL – 1 Acts 25:5 → of authority → AUTHORITY <1415> 2 1 Cor. 1:26 → POWERFUL <1415> 3 Gal. 2:2, 6b → to seem to be influential → to be of reputation → REPUTATION <1380> 4 Gal. 2:6a → seemed to be influential → lit.: seeming to be something.

INFORM – 1 ***gnōrizō*** [verb: γνωρίζω <1107>]; **from *ginōskō*: to be acquainted, to know ▶ To make known, to communicate** > Tychicus and Onesimus were to inform {to tell} the Colossians about everything happening in the place where Paul was (Col. 4:9). All other refs.: KNOW <1107>.

2 **to be informed:** ***katēcheō*** [verb: κατηχέω <2727>]; **from *kata*: intens., and *ēcheō*: to sound, which is from: *ēchos*: sound ▶ To be advised orally, to learn, to be told >** The verb is used in regard to the Jews and those things they had been informed of concerning Paul (Acts 21:21, 24). All other refs.: TEACH <2727>.
– 3 Acts 23:22 → REVEAL <1718> 4 Acts 23:30; 1 Cor. 10:28 → SHOW (verb) <3377> 5 Acts 24:1; 25:2, 15 → to lay information → to bring charges → CHARGE (noun)[1] <1718> 6 Acts 26:26 → to be informed → KNOW <1987> 7 1 Cor. 1:11; Col. 1:8 → DECLARE <1213>.

INFORMATION – 1 Acts 23:15 → to want more accurate information → lit.: to determine more precisely → DETERMINE <1231> 2 Acts 23:30 → to receive information → SHOW (verb) <3377> 3 Acts 24:1; 25:2, 15 → to lay information → to bring charges → CHARGE (noun)[1] <1718> 4 Col. 4:7 → to bring information → KNOW <1107>.

INFURIATED (BE) – Matt. 2:16 → to be angry → ANGRY <2373>.

INHABIT – Acts 1:19; 2:9; 4:16; 9:32, 35; 17:26 → DWELL <2730>.

INHABITANT – Acts 2:14; 4:16; Rev. 3:10; 6:10; 8:13; 11:10a, b; 13:8, 12, 14; 17:2 → DWELL <2730>.

INHABITER – Rev. 8:13 → DWELL <2730>.

INHERIT – ***klēronomeō*** [verb: κληρονομέω <2816>]; **from *klēronomos*: heir, which is from *klēros*: portion, and *nemō*: to distribute ▶ To receive goods by means of succession, to obtain something reserved >** The meek will inherit the earth (Matt. 5:5). He who has left everything for the sake of Jesus's name will inherit eternal life (Matt. 19:29). A person asked Jesus what one must do to inherit eternal life (Mark 10:17; Luke 10:25; 18:18). Those who are blessed of His Father will inherit the kingdom (Matt. 25:34). Unrighteous people will not inherit the kingdom of God (1 Cor. 6:9), nor other people who practice evil things (1 Cor. 6:10; Gal. 5:21). Flesh and blood cannot inherit God's kingdom, nor does corruption inherit incorruptibility (1 Cor. 15:50a, b). The son of the maidservant (Ishmael) shall not inherit with the son of the free woman (Isaac) (Gal. 4:30). Jesus has inherited a name more excellent than the angels (Heb. 1:4). The angels are sent out for service on account of those who will inherit salvation (Heb. 1:14). We are to imitate those who through faith and patience inherit the promises (Heb. 6:12). Afterwards, Esau wanted to inherit the blessing (Heb. 12:17). Christians are to bless others because they have been called to inherit blessing (1 Pet. 3:9). He who overcomes will inherit the new things which God will make (Rev. 21:7). ¶

INHERITANCE – 1 ***klēronomia*** [fem. noun: κληρονομία <2817>]; **from *klēronomos*: heir, which is from *klēros*: see 2, and *nemō*: to distribute ▶ Goods transmitted by means of succession at a person's death, something reserved to be passed on >** In a parable, the vinegrowers killed the heir in order to take his inheritance (Matt. 21:38; Mark 12:7; Luke 20:14). Someone said to Jesus to tell his brother to share the inheritance with him (Luke 12:13). God did not give Abraham an inheritance in the land to which he had come, and He promised to give it to him for a possession and to his descendants after him (Acts 7:5). The word of God's grace is able to build Christians up and give them an inheritance among all those who are sanctified (Acts 20:32). If the inheritance is on the principle of law, it is no longer on the principle of promise (Gal. 3:18). The Holy Spirit is the guarantee of the inheritance of the Christians (Eph. 1:14). Paul prayed that the Ephesians might know what are the riches of the glory of God's inheritance in the saints (Eph. 1:18). No fornicator, or unclean person, or person of unbridled lust, has an inheritance in the kingdom of Christ and of God (Eph. 5:5). Christians will receive of the Lord the reward of the inheritance (Col. 3:24). Abraham went out into a place which he was to receive as an inheritance (Heb. 11:8). Those who are called receive the promise of the eternal inheritance (Heb. 9:15). God the Father has regenerated the Christians to an incorruptible inheritance (1 Pet. 1:4). ¶

2 ***klēros*** [masc. noun: κλῆρος <2819>]; **from *klaō*: to break ▶ Allotted portion, share** > The Father has made the Christian fit to share in the inheritance of the saints in light (Col. 1:12). All other refs.: ENTRUST <2819>, LOT (noun) <2819>, PART (noun) <2819>.

3 **to give as an inheritance: *kataklērodoteō*** [verb: κατακληροδοτέω <2624>]; **from *kata*: according, and *klērodoteō*: to distribute by lot, which is from *klēros*: see 2, and *didōmi*: to give ▶ To distribute a heritage, to give something reserved** > God gave the land of Canaan to the Israelites as an inheritance (Acts 13:19); other mss. have *kataklēronomeō* (see 4). ¶

4 **to give as an inheritance: *kataklēronomeō*** [verb: κατακληρονομέω <2624a>]; **from *kata*: according, and *klēronomeō*: to distribute by lot, which is from *klēros*: see 2, and *nemō*: to distribute ▶ To distribute a heritage** > See 3. ¶

5 **to obtain an inheritance: *klēroō*** [verb: κληρόω <2820>]; **from *klēros*: see 2 ▶ To receive goods by means of succession** > Christians have obtained an inheritance in Christ (Eph. 1:11). ¶

INHERITANCE RIGHTS – Heb. 12:16 → BIRTHRIGHT <4415>.

INHERITED – 1 Pet. 1:18 → inherited from the forefathers → received by tradition from the fathers → FATHER <3970>.

INIQUITY – 1 ***adikēma*** [neut. noun: ἀδίκημα <92>]; **from *adikeō*: to act unjustly, which is from *adikos*: unjust, which is from *a*: neg., and *dikē*: justice ▶ Wrongdoing, injustice** > God will remember the iniquities {crimes, unrighteousnesses} of Babylon the great (Rev. 18:5). Other refs.: Acts 18:14; 24:20; see WRONG (noun) <92>. ¶

2 ***adikia*** [fem. noun: ἀδικία <93>]; **from *adikos*: see 1 ▶ Injustice; it is the opposite of what is right, for those who know what is right before God; also transl.: doing wrong, evil, harm, sin, unrighteousness, wickedness, wrongdoing** > Jesus speaks of workers of iniquity {evildoers} who must depart from Him (Luke 13:27). The wrath of God is revealed against all ungodliness and unrighteousness {wickedness} of men who live in unrighteousness (Rom. 1:18a, b). The tongue is a world of iniquity (Jas. 3:6). All unrighteousness is sin (1 John 5:17). Everyone who pronounces the name of the Lord is to depart from iniquity (2 Tim. 2:19). If we confess our sins, God is faithful and just to purify us from all unrighteousness (1 John 1:9). Other refs.: Acts 1:18; 8:23; Rom. 2:8; 6:13; 2 Pet. 2:13, 15. All other refs.: UNJUST (adj.) <93>, UNRIGHTEOUSNESS <93>, WRONG (noun) <93>.

3 ***anomia*** [fem. noun: ἀνομία <458>]; **from *anomos*: without law, which is from *a*: neg., and *nomos*: law ▶ Conduct, without restraint, characterized by wickedness; also transl.: evil, iniquity, lawless acts, lawless deeds, transgression of the law, unrighteousness, wickedness** > Jesus Christ gave Himself for us, that He might redeem us from all lawlessness {lawless deed} (Titus 2:14). To practice sin is to practice lawlessness, and sin is lawlessness (1 John 3:4a, b). Lawlessness will prevail on earth before the establishment of the kingdom of God (Matt. 24:12); but it is already at work (2 Thes. 2:7). Other refs.: Matt. 7:23; 13:41; 23:28; 24:12; Rom. 4:7; 6:19a, b; 2 Cor. 6:14; 2 Thes. 2:3 in some mss. (see LAWLESSNESS <458>), 7; Titus 2:14; Heb. 1:9; 10:17. ¶

4 ***paranomia*** [fem. noun: παρανομία <3892>]; **from *paranomeō*: to transgress the law, which is from *para*: against, and *nomos*: law ▶ Transgression, disobedience** > Balaam was rebuked for his own iniquity {wickedness, wrongdoing} when a donkey spoke to him to restrain his madness (2 Pet. 2:16). ¶

– 5 Acts 3:26 → WICKEDNESS <4189>.

INITIATE – Phil. 4:12 → LEARN <3453>.

INITIATIVE – John 8:28 → on my own initiative → lit.: on my own.

INJUNCTION – 1 Col. 2:22 → COMMANDMENT <1778> 2 Heb. 11:23 → ORDINANCE <1297>.

INJURE – 1 ***adikeō*** [verb: ἀδικέω <91>]; **from *adikos*: unjust, wicked, which is from *a*: neg., and *dikē*: justice ▶ To inflict damage, to wound; also transl.: to hurt, to harm** > Nothing would injure those to whom Jesus gave authority (Luke 10:19). He who sat on the black horse was not to injure {damage} the oil and the wine (Rev. 6:6). It had been given to four angels to injure the earth and the sea (Rev. 7:2); they were told not to hurt them, until the bondmen of God were sealed upon their foreheads (v. 3). The power of the scorpions was in their tails to injure {torment} men five months (Rev. 9:10); they were told not to injure the grass of the earth, nor any green thing, nor any tree, but only the men who have not the seal of God on their foreheads (v. 4). In the vision of John, the horses injure {inflict injury} with their tails (Rev. 9:19). No one can injure the two witnesses (Rev. 11:5a, b). All other refs.: HURT (verb) <91>, WRONG (noun) <91>.

2 ***blaptō*** [verb: βλάπτω <984>] ▶ **To hurt, to wound** > Jesus said if those who believed should drink any deadly thing it would not injure {hurt} them (Mark 16:18). Other ref.: Luke 4:35; see HURT (verb) <984>.

3 ***blasphēmeō*** [verb: βλασφημέω <987>]; **from *blasphēmos*: blasphemer; which is poss. from *blaptō*: to harm, and *phēmē*: reputation ▶ To insult, to blaspheme** > The men who held Jesus said many injurious {blasphemous, blaspheming, insulting} things to Him (Luke 22:65). All other refs.: see entries in Lexicon at <987>.

– 4 Acts 18:10; 1 Pet. 3:13 → HURT (verb) <2559>.

INJURED (BE) – 2 Cor. 7:9 → to suffer loss → LOSS <2210>.

INJURIOUS – 1 **injurious speech, injurious word: *blasphēmia*** [fem. noun: βλασφημία <988>]; **prob. from *blaptō*: to injure, and *phēmē*: reputation ▶ Calumny, insult, abuse** > Injurious speeches shall be forgiven men (Mark 3:28 {blasphemy, slander}). Injurious words arise out of disputes over words (1 Tim. 6:4 {railing, reviling, abusive language, malicious talk}). All other refs.: BLASPHEMY <988>, RAILING <988>.

– 2 Luke 22:65 → INJURE <987> 3 1 Tim. 1:13 → insolent man → INSOLENT <5197> 4 2 Pet. 2:11 → REVILING <989>.

INJURIOUSLY – 1 Pet. 4:4; 2 Pet. 2:10, 12 → to speak injuriously → REVILE <987>.

INJURY – 1 Luke 4:35 → to do injury → HURT (verb) <984> 2 Acts 27:10 → DISASTER <5196> 3 Acts 27:21 → HARM (noun) <5196> 4 2 Cor. 12:13 → WRONG (noun) <93> 5 Rev. 9:19 → to inflict injury → INJURE <91>.

INJUSTICE – Rom. 9:14 → UNRIGHTEOUSNESS <93>.

INK – ***melan*** [neut. noun: μέλαν <3188>]; **from *melas*: black ▶ Black liquid used to write** > The Corinthians were an epistle of Christ, written not with ink, but by the Spirit of the living God (2 Cor. 3:3). Having many things to write, John did not wish to do so with paper and ink to the elect lady and her children (2 John 12), nor did he wish to write with pen and ink to Gaius (3 John 13). ¶

INLAND – Acts 19:1 → inland country → lit.: upper regions → UPPER <510>.

INN – 1 ***kataluma*** [neut. noun: κατάλυμα <2646>]; **from *kataluō*: to untie, which is from *kata*: intens., and *luō*: to untie; lit.: place where one unpacks his luggage and unties his sandals ▶ a. Lodging place, common room** > There was no place for

Joseph, Mary, and her firstborn son in the inn (Luke 2:7). **b. Common room** > The disciples were to ask where was the guest room {guest chamber} where Jesus may eat the Passover with His disciples (Mark 14:14; Luke 22:11). ¶

2 ***pandocheion*** [neut. noun: πανδοχεῖον <3829>]; **from *pandocheus*: innkeeper, which is from *pas*: all, and *dechomai*: to receive ▶ Public lodging place, house for receiving strangers** > In a parable, a Samaritan brought a wounded man to the inn and took care of him (Luke 10:34). ¶

INNER – 1 ***esōteros*** [adj.: ἐσώτερος <2082>]; **compar. of *esō*: inside ▶ Situated within** > The jailer put Paul and Barnabas into the inner prison (Acts 16:24). The hope of the Christian enters within {behind, the inner place behind, the inner sanctuary behind} the veil (Heb. 6:19). ¶

– 2 Matt. 24:26; Luke 12:3 → inner room → ROOM <5009> 3 1 Pet. 3:4 → hidden → HIDE <2927>.

INNERMOST BEING – John 7:38 → WOMB <2836>.

INNKEEPER – ***pandocheus*** [masc. noun: πανδοχεύς <3830>]; **from *pas*: all, and *dechomai*: to receive ▶ Keeper of a public lodging place** > In a parable, a Samaritan gave an innkeeper {a host} two denarii (a denarius was the equivalent of a day's wages) to take care of a wounded man (Luke 10:35). ¶

INNOCENT – 1 ***athōos*** [adj.: ἀθῷος <121>]; **from *a*: neg., and *thōē*: punishment, penalty; lit.: unpunished ▶ Not guilty, i.e., not having committed an offence; also transl.: guiltless** > Judas had sinned in having betrayed the innocent blood (Matt. 27:4). Pilate said he was innocent of the blood of this righteous man, Jesus (Matt. 27:24). ¶

2 ***akakos*** [adj.: ἄκακος <172>]; **from *a*: neg., and *kakos*: bad ▶ Without evil, blameless** > Jesus is an innocent {blameless, harmless} high priest (Heb. 7:26). Other ref.: Rom. 16:18; see SIMPLE <172>. ¶

3 ***akeraios*** [adj.: ἀκέραιος <185>]; **from *a*: neg., and *kerannumi*: to mix ▶ Pure; without compromise with evil; also transl.: guileless, harmless, simple** > Jesus tells us to be innocent like doves (Matt. 10:16). Paul wished the Christians at Rome to be wise as to that which is good and innocent {simple} as to evil (Rom. 16:19). Other ref.: Phil. 2:15; see PURE <185>. ¶

– 4 Matt. 12:5, 7 → GUILTLESS <338> 5 Matt. 23:35 → RIGHTEOUS <1342> 6 Acts 18:6; 20:26 → CLEAN (noun) <2513> 7 1 Cor. 4:4 → to make innocent → JUSTIFY <1344> 8 2 Cor. 7:11 → PURE <53> 9 Phil. 2:15 → PURE <185>.

INNUMERABLE – 1 ***anarithmētos*** [adj.: ἀναρίθμητος <382>]; **from *a*: neg., and *arithmeō*: to count ▶ Which cannot be counted, in very great quantity** > From Abraham were born people as innumerable {countless, numerous} as the sand which is by the seashore (Heb. 11:12). ¶

2 ***murias*** [fem. noun: μυριάς <3461>]; **from *murioi*: too many to be counted; lit.: myriads ▶ This word describes a very large number; also transl.: thousand** > An innumerable multitude of people {A crowd of many thousands} had gathered together to listen to Jesus (Luke 12:1). Many thousands of Jews had believed (Acts 21:20). All other refs.: FIFTY THOUSAND <3461>, MYRIAD <3461>.

INORDINATE – Col. 3:5 → inordinate affection → AFFECTION <3806>.

INQUIRE – 1 ***exetazō*** [verb: ἐξετάζω <1833>]; **from *ek*: intens., and *etazō*: to examine ▶ To ask, to search** > On entering into a city or village, the disciples were to inquire {to enquire} who in it was worthy and stay there until their departure (Matt. 10:11). All other refs.: ASK <1833>, SEARCH (verb) <1833>.

2 ***zēteō*** [verb: ζητέω <2212>] **▶ To seek, to try to find out** > The disciples were inquiring {were enquiring, were deliberating} among themselves {were asking one another} about what Jesus had said (John 16:19).

All other refs.: REQUIRE <2212>, SEEK <2212>.

[3] ***punthanomai*** [verb: πυνθάνομαι <4441>] ► **To ask, to find out; also transl.: to enquire** > Herod inquired {demanded} where the Christ was to be born (Matt. 2:4). The nobleman inquired the hour when his son got better (John 4:52). The verb is also used concerning a commander (Acts 23:20). See also ASK <4441>.

– [4] Matt. 2:7, 16 → to accurately inquire → DETERMINE <198> [5] Luke 1:62 → inquiring what → lit.: as to what [6] Acts 19:39 → SEEK <1934> [7] 1 Pet. 1:10 → inquired and searched carefully → sought out and searched out → to seek out → SEEK <1567> [8] 1 Pet. 1:11 → SEEK <2037a>.

INQUIRER – 1 Cor. 14:16, 23, 24 → the simple → SIMPLE <2399>.

INQUIRY – [1] ***zētēsis*** [fem. noun: ζήτησις <2214>]; **from *zēteō*: to seek** ► **Questioning, investigation** > Festus was at loss as to an inquiry {as to how to investigate, of such questions} concerning the case of Paul (Acts 25:20). All other refs.: DISPUTE (noun) <2214>, QUESTION (noun) <2214>.

[2] **to make inquiry: *dierōtaō*** [verb: διερωτάω <1331>]; **from *dia*: intens., and *erōtaō*: to ask** ► **To ask with insistence, to try to find out with diligence** > The men sent by Cornelius had made inquiry {had made enquiry, had sought out, had asked directions} for Simon's house (Acts 10:17). ¶

– [3] Acts 19:39 → to have an inquiry → SEEK <1934> [4] Acts 23:15 → to make inquiries → DETERMINE <1231> [5] 1 Cor. 10:25, 27 → to make inquiry → to ask questions → ASK <350> [6] 1 Pet. 1:10 → to make inquiry → to search carefully → SEARCH (verb) <1830>.

INSANE – [1] John 10:20 → to be insane → to be mad → MAD <3105> [2] Acts 26:24b → to drive insane → to drive to insanity → MADNESS <3130> [3] Acts 26:25 → to be insane → to be out of one's mind → MIND (noun) <3105> [4] 2 Cor. 11:23 → to be insane → to be out of one's mind → MIND (noun) <3912>.

INSATIABLE – 2 Pet. 2:14 → who cannot cease → CEASE <180>.

INSCRIBE – [1] ***epigraphō*** [verb: ἐπιγράφω <1924>]; **from *epi*: upon, and *graphō*: to write** ► **To mark a surface with words, to write on it** > Paul had found at Athens an altar on which was inscribed {with this inscription}: To the unknown God (Acts 17:23). Other refs.: Mark 15:26; Heb. 8:10; 10:16; Rev. 21:12; see WRITE <1924>. ¶

– [2] Luke 2:3 → REGISTER <583>.

INSCRIPTION – [1] ***epigraphē*** [fem. noun: ἐπιγραφή <1923>]; **from *epigraphō*: to write upon, to inscribe, which is from *epi*: upon, and *graphō*: to write** ► **Words marked on a surface, what is written on it** > Jesus asked whose was the image and inscription {superscription} on the denarius (Matt. 22:20; Mark 12:16; Luke 20:24). At the cross, the inscription {superscription, written notice} of the accusation of Jesus was written above Him (Mark 15:26; Luke 23:38). ¶

– [2] John 19:19, 20 → TITLE <5102> [3] Acts 17:23 → with this inscription → lit.: on which was inscribed → INSCRIBE <1924>.

INSCRUTABLE – Rom. 11:33 → UNTRACEABLE <421>.

INSIDE – Matt. 26:58 → INTO <2080>.

INSIGHT – [1] Mark 6:52 → to gain insight → UNDERSTAND <4920> [2] Eph. 1:8 → INTELLIGENCE <5428> [3] Eph. 3:4; 2 Tim. 2:7 → UNDERSTANDING <4907> [4] Phil. 1:9 → depth of insight → DISCERNMENT <144>.

INSIGNIFICANT – ***asēmos*** [adj.: ἄσημος <767>]; **from *a*: neg., and *sēma*: distinctive sign** ► **Without reputation, without renown** > Tarsus was no insignificant {mean, ordinary} city (Acts 21:39). ¶

INSINCERITY – 1 Tim. 4:2 → HYPOCRISY <5272>.

INSIPID – Matt. 5:13 → to become insipid → to lose its flavor → LOSE <3471>.

INSIST – 1 ***epischuō*** [verb: ἐπισχύω <2001>]; **from *epi*: upon, and *ischuō*: to be strong, which is from *ischus*: strength ▶ To declare forcefully, to assert with emphasis, to be more violent** > The Jews insisted {were the more fierce}, saying that Jesus was stirring up the people (Luke 23:5). ¶
– 2 Luke 22:59; Acts 12:15 → to insist, to keep insisting → to confidently affirm → AFFIRM <1340> 3 Acts 15:38 → to think not wise → THINK <515> 4 1 Cor. 13:5 → to insist on one's own way → to seek its own → SEEK <2212> 5 Eph. 4:17 → TESTIFY <3143> 6 Col. 2:18 → insisting on asceticism → willing to do so in (false) humility → WILL (verb) <2309> 7 1 Tim. 6:2 → EXHORT <3870> 8 Titus 3:8 → to insist strenuously → AFFIRM <1226>.

INSISTENT – to be insistent: *epikeimai* [verb: ἐπίκειμαι <1945>]; **from *epi*: upon, and *keimai*: to be placed ▶ To declare in a pressing manner, to assert with emphasis >** The Jews were insistent {were instant, were urgent} with loud voices, requiring that Jesus be crucified (Luke 23:23). All other refs.: BEAT <1945>, IMPOSE <1945>, LAY <1945>, PRESS <1945>.

INSISTENTLY – 1 Mark 14:31 → more vehemently → VEHEMENTLY <1537> 2 Luke 23:23 → they insistently demanded → they were insistent → INSISTENT <1945>.

INSOLENT – insolent man: *hubristēs* [masc. noun: ὑβριστής <5197>]; **from *hubrizō*: to treat shamefully, which is from *hubris*: insult, injury ▶ Easily provoked, impetuous, violent person >** Paul was an insolent man {an insolent overbearing man, injurious, a violent aggressor, a violent man} before his conversion (1 Tim. 1:13). Rom. 1:30 speaks of insolent {despiteful, violent} men. ¶

INSPIRATION – 2 Tim. 3:16 → given by inspiration of God → DIVINELY INSPIRED <2315>.

INSPIRE – Rev. 22:6 in some mss. → God who inspires the prophets → lit.: God of the spirits of the prophets → SPIRIT <4151>.

INSPIRED – 2 Tim. 3:16 → divinely inspired, inspired of God → DIVINELY INSPIRED <2315>.

INSPIRED OF GOD – 2 Tim. 3:16 → DIVINELY INSPIRED <2315>.

INSTANT – 1 Luke 2:38 → HOUR <5610> 2 Luke 4:5 → lit.: moment of time → MOMENT <4743> 3 Luke 23:23 → to be instant → to be insistent → INSISTENT <1945> 4 1 Cor. 15:52 → MOMENT <823> 5 2 Tim. 4:2 → to be instant → to be ready → READY <2186>.

INSTANTLY – 1 Matt. 9:22; 15:28; 17:18 → lit.: from that hour → HOUR <5610> 2 Luke 7:4 → EARNESTLY <4709> 3 Acts 26:7 → EARNESTLY <1616>.

INSTEAD – 1 ***anti*** [prep.: ἀντί <473>] **▶ Rather than, in place of >** Archelaus reigned instead of {in the room of} Herod his father (Matt. 2:22). The term is used also in Jas. 4:15.
– 2 2 Cor. 2:7; 1 Pet. 3:9 → on the contrary → CONTRARY <5121>.

INSTIGATE – 1 Acts 6:11 → SUBORN <5260> 2 Acts 13:50 → to raise, to raise up → RAISE <1892>.

INSTINCT – 1 2 Pet. 2:12 → born as creature of instinct → NATURAL <5446> 2 Jude 10 → NATURE <5447> 3 Jude 19 → who follow mere natural instincts → lit.: who are natural → NATURAL <5591>.

INSTINCTIVELY – [1] Rom. 2:14 → by nature → NATURE <5449> [2] Jude 10 → by mere nature → NATURE <5447>.

INSTITUTE – [1] Rom. 13:1 → APPOINT <5021> [2] Rom. 13:2 → what God has instituted → lit.: the ordinance of God → ORDINANCE <1296>.

INSTITUTION – ***ktisis*** [fem. noun: κτίσις <2937>]; **from *ktizō*: to create, to found ▶ Ordinance, authority** > Christians are to be in subjection to every human institution {ordinance} for the Lord's sake (1 Pet. 2:13). All other refs.: CREATION <2937>, CREATURE <2937>, NEW CREATION <2937>.

INSTRUCT – [1] ***paradidōmi*** [verb: παραδίδωμι <3860>]; **from *para*: beside, and *didōmi*: to give; lit.: to deliver ▶ To expound, to communicate** > The Romans had obeyed the form of doctrine in which they had been instructed {which was delivered to them, to which they were committed, that had claimed their allegiance} (Rom. 6:17). All other refs.: see entries in Lexicon at <3860>.

[2] ***sumbibazō*** [verb: συμβιβάζω <4822>]; **from *sun*: together, and *bibazō*: to cause to go ▶ To teach, to persuade by reasoning** > Paul asks: Who has known the mind of the Lord that he may instruct Him? (1 Cor. 2:16). All other refs.: CONCLUDE[1] <4822>, KNIT <4822>, PROVE <4822>, UNITE <4822>.

– [3] Matt. 2:12, 22; Acts 10:22 → to be divinely instructed → WARN <5537> [4] Matt. 10:5; Mark 6:8; Luke 8:56; 9:21; Acts 23:22, 30 → COMMAND (verb) <3853> [5] Matt. 11:1 → COMMAND (verb) <1299> [6] Matt. 13:52 → to be instructed → to become a disciple → DISCIPLE <3100> [7] Matt. 14:8 → to instruct before → PROMPT <4264> [8] Matt. 17:9 → COMMAND (verb) <1781> [9] Matt. 21:6 → ORDAIN <4367> [10] Luke 1:4; Acts 18:25; Rom. 2:18; 1 Cor. 14:19 → TEACH <2727> [11] Acts 7:22 → EDUCATE <3811> [12] Rom. 15:14 → ADMONISH <3560> [13] Eph. 4:21; 2 Tim. 2:2 → TEACH <1321> [14] Phil. 4:12 → LEARN <3453> [15] 1 Thes. 4:11 → ENJOIN <3853> [16] 1 Tim. 4:6 → to point out → POINT (verb) <5294> [17] 2 Tim. 2:25 → CORRECT <3811> [18] Titus 2:12 → TEACH <3811>.

INSTRUCTION – [1] ***didaskalia*** [fem. noun: διδασκαλία <1319>]; **from *didaskō*: to teach, which is from *daō*: to teach, to learn ▶ Teaching, learning** > All the things that had been written before (i.e., those of the O.T.) were written for our instruction {to teach us} (Rom. 15:4). All other refs.: DOCTRINE <1319>.

– [2] Matt. 10:5; Mark 6:8; 1 Cor. 7:10 → with instructions, to give instructions → COMMAND (verb) <3853> [3] Matt. 11:1; Acts 23:31 → to give instructions → COMMAND (verb) <1299> [4] Acts 1:2; Heb. 11:22 → to give instructions → to give charge → CHARGE (noun)[2] <1781> [5] Acts 15:24 → COMMANDMENT <1291> [6] Acts 17:15; Col. 4:10 → COMMAND (noun) <1785> [7] Acts 19:33 → to shout instructions → to draw out → DRAW <4264> [8] 1 Cor. 10:11; Eph. 6:4 → ADMONITION <3559> [9] 1 Cor. 11:17 → in giving instructions → lit.: in prescribing this → PRESCRIBE <3853> [10] 1 Cor. 14:6, 26; 2 Tim. 4:2; Heb. 6:2 → DOCTRINE <1322> [11] Gal. 6:6a → to receive instruction → to be taught → TEACH <2727> [12] 1 Thes. 4:2 → COMMANDMENT <3852> [13] 1 Thes. 5:12 → to give instructions → ADMONISH <3560> [14] 2 Thes. 2:15; 3:6 → TRADITION <3862> [15] 1 Tim. 1:5 → CHARGE (noun)[2] <3852> [16] 1 Tim. 2:11 → to receive instruction → LEARN <3129> [17] 2 Tim. 3:16 → TRAINING <3809>.

INSTRUCTOR – [1] ***paidagōgos*** [masc. noun: παιδαγωγός <3807>]; **from *pais*: boy, and *agōgos*: leader, which is from *agō*: to lead ▶ Pedagogue, teacher** > Even though the Corinthians might have ten thousand instructors {tutors, guardians} in Christ, yet they did not have many fathers (1 Cor. 4:15). Other refs.: Gal. 3:24, 25; see TUTOR <3807>. ¶

[2] ***paideutēs*** [masc. noun: παιδευτής <3810>]; **from *paideuō*: to teach children, which is from *pais*: child ▶ Educator, teacher** > Paul speaks of a Jew under the law who might consider himself to be an instructor {a corrector} of the foolish (Rom. 2:20). Other ref.: Heb. 12:9 (he who corrects); see CORRECT <3810>. ¶
– [3] Matt. 23:8, 10 → TEACHER <2519> [4] Gal. 6:6b → lit.: him who teaches → TEACH <2727>.

INSTRUMENT – [1] ***hoplon*** [neut. noun: ὅπλον <3696>] ▶ **Tool, weapon** > Christians are not to yield their members as instruments of unrighteousness to sin, but to yield them as instruments of righteousness to God (Rom. 6:13a, b). Other refs.: John 18:3; Rom. 13:12; 2 Cor. 6:7; 10:4; see WEAPON <3696>. ¶
– [2] Acts 9:15; 2 Tim. 2:21 → VESSEL[1] <4632> [3] 1 Cor. 14:7 → lifeless instruments → LIFELESS <895>.

INSUBORDINATE – ***anupotaktos*** [adj. and adj. used as noun: ἀνυπότακτος <506>]; **from *a*: neg., and *hupotassō*: to submit oneself, which is from *hupo*: under, and *tassō*: to put in order ▶ Who refuses to accept an order of subjection, not submitting to authority; also transl.: disobedient, disorderly, rebel, rebellious, unruly** > The law is for the insubordinate (1 Tim. 1:9). Elders are not to have insubordinate children (Titus 1:6 {insubordination, rebellion}). Paul remarks that there are many insubordinate vain talkers and deceivers (1:10). Other ref.: Heb. 2:8c (not subject); see SUBJECT (verb) <506>. ¶

INSUBORDINATION – Titus 1:6 → INSUBORDINATE <506>.

INSULT (noun) – [1] ***hubris*** [fem. noun: ὕβρις <5196>] ▶ **Reproach, injurious treatment** > Paul took pleasure in insults (2 Cor. 12:10), for they gave him an occasion to glory in Christ. Other refs.: Acts 27:10, 21; see DISASTER <5196>, HARM (noun) <5196>. ¶
[2] **to insult: *atimazō*** [verb: ἀτιμάζω <818>]; **from *atimos*: without honor, which is from *a*: neg. and *timē*: honor ▶ To dishonor, to treat without dignity** > In a parable, the husbandmen sent away a bondman with insult (lit.: insulting him) (Mark 12:4 {to shamefully handle, to shamefully treat}); some mss. have *atimaō*, and others *atimoō* (see [3]). All other refs.: DISHONOR (verb) <818>, DISHONORED (BE) <818>, SHAMEFULLY <818>.
[3] **to insult: *atimoō*** [verb: ἀτιμόω <821>]; **from *atimos*: see [2]** ▶ Mark 12:4; see [2]. ¶
– [4] Matt. 27:39; Mark 15:29; Luke 23:39 → to hurl insults → REVILE <987> [5] Matt. 27:44; Mark 15:32 → to heap insults → INSULT (verb) <3679> [6] John 9:28; 1 Pet. 2:23a → to hurl insults → REVILE <3058> [7] Rom. 15:3; Heb. 10:33 → REPROACH <3680> [8] 1 Pet. 3:9a, b → REVILING <3059>.

INSULT (verb) – [1] ***hubrizō*** [verb: ὑβρίζω <5195>]; **from *hubris*: insolence, insult ▶ To revile, to abuse** > Jesus insulted {reproached} the doctors of the law, according to their estimation (Luke 11:45). People would insult {mistreat, spitefully entreat} the Son of Man (Luke 18:32). Other refs.: Matt. 22:6; Acts 14:5; 1 Thes. 2:2; see MISTREAT <5195>. ¶
[2] ***enubrizō*** [verb: ἐνυβρίζω <1796>]; **from *en*: against, and *hubrizō*: see [1] ▶ To offend, to treat shamefully** > He who has insulted {has done despite unto} the Spirit of grace will be judged worthy of a severe punishment (Heb. 10:29). ¶
[3] ***oneidizō*** [verb: ὀνειδίζω <3679>]; **from *oneidos*: reproach, shame ▶ To reproach, to revile, to abuse; also transl.: to cast reproaches, to heap insults** > The thieves crucified with Jesus were insulting Him (Matt. 27:44; Mark 15:32). Christians are blessed when they are insulted for the Son of Man's sake (Luke 6:22). They are blessed when they are insulted for the name of Christ (1 Pet. 4:14). All other refs.: REPROACH <3679>, REPROACH (verb) <3679>, REVILE <3679>.
– [4] Matt. 5:22 → to say "Raca" → RACA <4469> [5] Matt. 5:44 → to use despitefully

→ USE (verb) <1908> 6 Acts 23:4 → REVILE <3058> 7 Jas. 2:6 → DISHONOR (verb) <818>.

INSULTING – Luke 22:65 → injurious → INJURE <987>.

INSURRECTION – 1 ***stasis*** [fem. noun: στάσις <4714>]; **from *histēmi*: to stand ▶ Rising in revolt, sedition; also transl.: dissension, rebellion, riot, rioting, tumult, uprising, uproar** > Barabbas and others had committed a murder during an insurrection (Mark 15:7; Luke 23:19, 25). The Ephesians were in danger of being accused of sedition (Acts 19:40). Tertullus accused Paul of moving sedition among all the Jews (Acts 24:5). All other refs.: DISSENSION <4714>, STANDING <4714>, TUMULT <4714>.

– 2 Acts 18:12 → to make insurrection against → to rise up against → RISE (verb) <2721>.

INSURRECTIONIST – Mark 15:7 → FELLOW REBEL <4955>.

INTEGRITY – 1 Matt. 22:16; Mark 12:14 → a man of integrity → TRUE <227> 2 2 Cor. 1:12 → SIMPLICITY <572> 3 Titus 2:7 → INCORRUPTIBILITY <861>.

INTELLECTUAL – ***logikos*** [adj.: λογικός <3050>]; **from *logos*: word, reasoning, intelligence ▶ Rational, mental; also transl.: spiritual, of the word** > Peter uses the expr. "the pure intellectual milk" (1 Pet. 2:2) to describe the effect of the word of God on the regenerated spirit: reading it contributes to the spiritual growth of the Christian. Other ref.: Rom. 12:1; see INTELLIGENT <3050>. ¶

INTELLIGENCE – 1 ***phronēsis*** [fem. noun: φρόνησις <5428>]; **from *phroneō*: to think, which is from *phrēn*: mind, understanding ▶ Practical wisdom, prudence; also transl.: insight, understanding** > God has caused His grace to abound toward us in all wisdom and intelligence (Eph. 1:8). Other ref.: Luke 1:17; see THOUGHT <5428>. ¶

– 2 Matt. 15:16 → without intelligence → without understanding → UNDERSTANDING <801> 3 Mark 12:33; 1 Cor. 1:19; Eph. 3:4 → UNDERSTANDING <4907> 4 Phil. 1:9 → depth of insight → DISCERNMENT <144> 5 Titus 3:3 → without intelligence → FOOLISH <453>.

INTELLIGENT – 1 ***logikos*** [adj.: λογικός <3050>]; **from *logos*: word, reasoning, intelligence ▶ Reasonable, characterized by spiritual discernment** > The intelligent {reasonable, spiritual, true and proper} service of Christians is to present their bodies as a living sacrifice (Rom. 12:1). Other ref.: 1 Pet. 2:2; see INTELLECTUAL <3050>. ¶

2 ***phronimos*** [adj.: φρόνιμος <5429>]; **from *phroneō*: to think, which is from *phrēn*: mind, understanding ▶ Wise, prudent** > Paul spoke as to intelligent {sensible} people (1 Cor. 10:15). All other refs.: PRUDENT <5429>, WISE (adj.) <5429>.

– 3 Matt. 11:25; Luke 10:21; Acts 13:7 → UNDERSTANDING <4908> 4 2 Cor. 10:12 → to be intelligent → UNDERSTAND <4920>.

INTELLIGENTLY – ***nounechōs*** [adv.: νουνεχῶς <3562>]; **from *nounechēs*: reasonable, wise, which is from *nous*: comprehension, mind, and *echō*: to have ▶ Judiciously** > Jesus saw that a scribe had answered Him intelligently {discreetly, wisely} (Mark 12:34). ¶

INTELLIGIBLE – 1 ***eusēmos*** [adj.: εὔσημος <2154>]; **from *eu*: well, and *sēma*: mark, sign ▶ Distinct, clear; also transl.: easy to understand** > A listener cannot know what is said if one does not speak intelligible words (1 Cor. 14:9). ¶

– 2 1 Cor. 14:19 → five intelligible words → lit.: five words with my understanding → UNDERSTANDING <3563>.

INTEMPERANCE – Matt. 23:25 → SELF-INDULGENCE <192>.

INTEND – [1] ***mellō*** [verb: μέλλω <3195>] ► **To have in mind, to plan** > The ship's company intended to take Paul on board at Assos; Paul intended {minded} himself to go {was going} on foot to Assos (Acts 20:13a, b). Peter intended to always remind Christians of certain things (2 Pet. 1:12 in some mss.). Other refs.: see entries in Lexicon at <3195>.
– [2] Acts 5:33 → CONSULT <1011> [3] Rom. 1:13 → PURPOSE (verb) <4388> [4] Rom. 2:4 → is intended to lead you → lit.: leads you [5] 1 Cor. 16:5 → I intend to pass → lit.: I am passing through [6] 2 Cor. 1:17 → PROPOSE <1011> [7] 2 Cor. 10:2a → THINK <3049>.

INTENSE – 2 Cor. 11:29 → without my intense concern → lit.: without me burning → BURN <4448>.

INTENSELY – [1] Mark 9:3 → EXCEEDINGLY <3029> [2] Gal. 1:13 → beyond measure → MEASURE (noun) <5236>.

INTENT – [1] ***ennoia*** [fem. noun: ἔννοια <1771>]; **from *en*: in, and *nous*: mind** ► **What the mind proposes, idea** > The word of God discerns the thoughts and intents {attitudes, intentions} of the heart (Heb. 4:12). Other ref.: 1 Pet. 4:1; see MIND (noun) <1771>. ¶
– [2] Matt. 5:28 → with lustful intent → to lust after → LUST (verb) <1937> [3] Matt. 22:18 → evil intent → WICKEDNESS <4189> [4] Acts 8:22 → THOUGHT <1963> [5] Acts 10:29 → REASON (noun) <3056>.

INTENTION – [1] Acts 8:22 → THOUGHT <1963> [2] Acts 27:43 → PURPOSE (noun) <1013> [3] Eph. 1:5, 9 → PLEASURE <2107> [4] Heb. 4:12 → INTENT <1771>.

INTENTLY – [1] Luke 22:44 → more intently → more earnestly → EARNESTLY <1617> [2] Acts 6:15; 2 Cor. 3:13 → to look intently → to look steadfastly → LOOK (verb) <816> [3] Acts 14:9 → to look intently → to fix one's eyes → FIX <816> [4] Acts 23:1; 2 Cor. 3:7 → to look intently → to behold earnestly → BEHOLD (verb) <816> [5] Jas. 1:23 → to look intently → CONSIDER <2657>.

INTERCEDE – [1] ***entunchanō*** [verb: ἐντυγχάνω <1793>]; **from *en*: in, and *tunchanō*: to arrive, to intervene** ► **To plead the cause of someone, to intervene in their favor; also transl.: to make intercession** > The Holy Spirit intercedes for the saints, according to God (Rom. 8:27); Christ also intercedes for Christians (Rom. 8:34; Heb. 7:25). All other refs.: PETITION (verb) <1793>, PLEAD <1793>.

[2] ***huperentunchanō*** [verb: ὑπερεντυγχάνω <5241>]; **from *huper*: in favor of, and *entunchanō*: see [1]** ► **To present a request in favor of someone; also transl.: to make intercession** > The Holy Spirit Himself intercedes for the saints with groanings that cannot be uttered (Rom. 8:26). ¶

INTERCESSION – [1] ***enteuxis*** [fem. noun: ἔντευξις <1783>]; **from *entunchanō*: to intercede, which is from *en*: in, and *tunchanō*: to arrive, to intervene** ► **Prayer, request in favor of someone** > The Christian is exhorted to make intercessions {petitions} for all men (1 Tim. 2:1). Every creature is sanctified by God's word and prayer {and freely addressing Him} (1 Tim. 4:5). ¶
– [2] Rom. 8:26 → to make intercession → INTERCEDE <5241> [3] Rom. 8:27, 34; Heb. 7:25 → to make intercession → INTERCEDE <1793> [4] Rom. 11:2 → to make intercession → PLEAD <1793> [5] 2 Cor. 1:11 → through the intercession → lit.: through (*ek*).

INTEREST[1] – ***tokos*** [masc. noun: τόκος <5110>]; **from *tiktō*: to produce** ► **Amount charged for borrowing money; KJV: usury** > This Greek term has the sense of interest on a bank loan in Matt. 25:27 and Luke 19:23. ¶

INTEREST[2] – [1] Phil. 2:20 → to take an interest → CARE <3309> [2] 1 Tim. 6:4 →

to have a morbid, an unhealthy interest → OBSESSED (BE) <3552>.

INTERIOR – Acts 19:1 → lit.: upper regions → REGION <3313>, UPPER <510>.

INTERMEDIARY – Gal. 3:19, 20 → MEDIATOR <3316>.

INTERMINABLE – 1 Tim. 1:4 → ENDLESS <562>.

INTERPOSE – Heb. 6:17 → INTERVENE <3315>.

INTERPRET – [1] ***diermēneuō*** [verb: διερμηνεύω <1329>]; **from *dia*: intens., and *hermēneuō*: to interpret ▶ To explain, to translate** > Interpreted {Translated, By interpretation}, Tabitha signifies Dorcas (Acts 9:36). Paul uses this verb in relation to the interpretation of tongues (1 Cor. 12:30; 14:5, 13, 27). Other ref.: Luke 24:27; see EXPLAIN <1329>. ¶
– [2] Matt. 1:23; Mark 5:41; 15:22, 34; John 1:41; Acts 4:36 → TRANSLATE <3177> [3] Matt. 16:3 → DISCERN <1252> [4] Luke 12:56a, b → DISCERN <1381> [5] John 1:38, 42; 9:7; Heb. 7:2 → TRANSLATE <2059> [6] 1 Cor. 2:13 → COMPARE <4793> [7] 1 Cor. 14:28 → one to interpret → INTERPRETER <1328> [8] Gal. 4:24 → to be interpreted allegorically → to be an allegory → ALLEGORY <238>.

INTERPRETATION – [1] ***epilusis*** [fem. noun: ἐπίλυσις <1955>]; **from *epiluō*: to resolve, to explain, which is from *epi*: upon (intens.), and *luō*: to loosen ▶ Explanation, exposition** > No prophecy of Scripture is a matter of its own particular interpretation (2 Pet. 1:20). ¶
[2] ***hermēneia*** [fem. noun: ἑρμηνεία <2058>]; **from *hermēneuō*: to explain, to interpret ▶ Explanation of what is said more or less clearly by others** > A Christian might have received the gift of interpretation of tongues (1 Cor. 12:10; *diermēneia* in some mss.), or might have an interpretation (14:26). ¶
– [3] John 1:42; 9:7; Heb. 7:2 → to be by interpretation → lit.: to be translated → TRANSLATE <2059> [4] Acts 9:36 → by interpretation → lit.: interpreted → INTERPRET <1329> [5] Acts 13:8 → to be by interpretation → TRANSLATE <3177>.

INTERPRETED (BE) – Heb. 5:11 → hard to be interpreted → hard to explain → HARD <1421>.

INTERPRETER – ***diermēneutēs*** [masc. noun: διερμηνευτής <1328>]; **from *diermēneuō*: to interpret fully, to explain, which is from *dia*: intens., and *hermēneuō*: to explain, to interpret ▶ He who gives a thorough explanation of what is said more or less clearly by others** > If there is no interpreter, one may not speak in tongues in the church (1 Cor. 14:28; other mss.: *hermēneutēs*). ¶

INTERROGATE – Acts 22:24, 29 → EXAMINE <426>.

INTERVAL – [1] ***diastēma*** [neut. noun: διάστημα <1292>]; **from *diistēmi*: to separate ▶ Space of time** > This word is used in Acts 5:7. ¶
– [2] Luke 22:59 → after an interval of about an hour → lit.: having passed about an hour → SEPARATE <1339>.

INTERVENE – [1] ***mesiteuō*** [verb: μεσιτεύω <3315>]; **from *mesitēs*: mediator, which is from *mesos*: middle, in the midst ▶ To commit oneself, to be involved** > In relation to the unchangeableness of His purpose, God intervened by {confirmed it by, interposed with} an oath (Heb. 6:17). ¶
– [2] Acts 15:14 → VISIT (verb) <1980>.

INTESTINES – Acts 1:18 → ENTRAILS <4698>.

INTIMATE – Acts 10:24 → CLOSE (adj. and adv.) <316>.

INTIMIDATE – Luke 3:14 → OPPRESS <1286>.

INTIMIDATION – 1 Pet. 3:14 → FEAR (noun) <5401>.

INTO – ***esō*** [adv.: ἔσω <2080>]; **from *eis*: in ▶ In the direction of what is located inside, within** > Peter followed Jesus until He had gone into the courtyard of the high priest (Mark 14:54). *

INTOXICATED – Rev. 17:2 → to be intoxicated → to get drunk → DRUNK (BE) <3184>.

INTREAT – 1 Luke 15:28 → BESEECH <3870> 2 Phil. 4:3 → ASK <2065> 3 1 Tim. 5:1 → EXHORT <3870> 4 Heb. 12:19 → BEG <3868>.

INTREATED (BE) – Jas. 3:17 → easy to be intreated → YIELDING <2138>.

INTREATY – 2 Cor. 8:4 → ENTREATY <3874>.

INTRODUCE – Gal. 3:17 → ARISE <1096>.

INTRODUCTION – 1 ***epeisagōgē*** [fem. noun: ἐπεισαγωγή <1898>]; **from *epi*: furthermore, and *eisagō*: to introduce, which is from *eis*: in and *agō*: to lead ▶ Act of bringing in something additional, possibly in replacement** > There is the introduction of a better hope by which we draw near to God (Heb. 7:19). ¶
– 2 Rom. 5:2 → ACCESS <4318>.

INTRUDE – 1 **to intrude into: *embateuō*** [verb: ἐμβατεύω <1687>]; **from *en*: in, and *bateuō*: to step ▶ To inquire, to scrutinize minutely** > The Colossians were not to intrude into {to enter into, to go into great detail about, to take a stand on} things which they had not seen (Col. 2:18). Among the Greeks, this verb signified frequenting a place consecrated to the gods. ¶
– 2 Acts 24:4 → to intrude on the time → TEDIOUS (BE) <1465>.

INVALID – 1 John 5:3, 7 → to be sick → SICK <770> 2 John 5:5 → who had been invalid → lit.: who had an infirmity → INFIRMITY <769>.

INVALIDATE – Matt. 15:6; Mark 7:13; Gal. 3:17 → to make of no effect → EFFECT (noun) <208>.

INVENT – Rom. 1:30 → they invent → lit.: inventors of → INVENTOR <2182>.

INVENTOR – ***epheuretēs*** [masc. noun: ἐφευρετής <2182>]; **from *epheuriskō*: to discover, to invent, which is from *epi*: upon, and *heuriskō*: to find ▶ One who imagines, who contrives** > Paul speaks of inventors of evil things (Rom. 1:30). ¶

INVEST – Matt. 25:27 → to put on deposit → PUT <906>.

INVESTIGATE – 1 ***parakoloutheō*** [verb: παρακολουθέω <3877>]; **from *para*: near, and *akoloutheō*: to follow, which is from *akolouthos*: follower, which is from *a*: particle of union, and *keleuthos*: way ▶ To follow faithfully, to examine, to inquire** > Luke had carefully investigated all things concerning Jesus from the beginning (Luke 1:3 {to be acquainted with, to have understanding}). Other refs.: Mark 16:17; 1 Tim. 4:6; 2 Tim. 3:10; see FOLLOW <3877>. ¶
– 2 Acts 25:20 → INQUIRY <2214>.

INVESTIGATION – ***anakrisis*** [fem. noun: ἀνάκρισις <351>]; **from *anakrinō*: to examine, which is from *ana*: up, again (intens.) and *krinō*: to judge ▶ Examination, search for information before judging** > Festus was desirous that Agrippa would proceed with an investigation {examination} of Paul (Acts 25:26). ¶

INVISIBLE – ***aoratos*** [adj.: ἀόρατος <517>]; **from *a*: neg., and *horaō*: to see ▶ Which one cannot see, not perceptible by the eye** > The invisible attributes of God are understood through what has been made (Rom. 1:20). The Son is the image of the invisible God (Col. 1:15). By Him were created all things visible and invisible (Col.

1:16). God is invisible (1 Tim. 1:17). Moses persevered, as seeing Him who is invisible {unseen} (Heb. 11:27). ¶

INVITE – [1] ***kaleō*** [verb: καλέω <2564>] ▶ **To ask to come; also transl.: to call, to bid** > A king sent his slaves to call {to tell to come} (or: to invite) those who were invited {were bidden} to the wedding (Matt. 22:3a, b, 4), but they were not worthy (v. 8); so others were invited (v. 9). A Pharisee had invited Jesus to eat with him (Luke 7:39). Jesus told a parable to those who were invited to eat {to the guests} and were choosing the best places (Luke 14:7); the parable concerned a man who sent his bondman to say to those who were invited that all things were ready (v. 17). Jesus gave instructions on how to behave when invited to a wedding feast (Luke 14:8a, b, 9, 10a, b, 12a, 13, 16). He then gave a parable about a man who invited many to a great supper (Luke 14:16, 24). Jesus and His disciples were invited to a wedding in Cana of Galilee (John 2:2). Paul talks about an unbeliever who invites a Christian to a dinner (1 Cor. 10:27). Blessed are those who are invited to the marriage supper of the Lamb (Rev. 19:9). All other refs.: CALL (verb) <2564>.

[2] **to invite back, to invite in return: *antikaleō*** [verb: ἀντικαλέω <479>]; **from *anti*: in return, and *kaleō*: see [1] ▶ To ask to come in return** > Jesus says to not ask people close to us for a meal, otherwise they may also invite us in return {bid us again} and we should be repaid (Luke 14:12). ¶

[3] **to invite in: *eiskaleō*** [verb: εἰσκαλέω <1528>]; **from *eis*: in, and *kaleō*: see [1] ▶ To make someone enter** > Peter invited in {called in} the men sent by Cornelius (Acts 10:23). ¶

[4] ***sunagō*** [verb: συνάγω <4863>]; **from *sun*: together, and *agō*: to bring ▶ To offer hospitality, to welcome; also transl.: to take in** > The Son of Man will praise those who will have invited Him, and will reproach some who will not have invited Him (Matt. 25:35, 38, 43). All other refs.: GATHER <4863>, LEAD (verb) <4863>.

– [5] Luke 7:36; 11:37 → ASK <2065> [6] Acts 7:14; 10:32 → CALL (verb) <3333> [7] Acts 8:31; 16:15; 19:31; 28:14 → BESEECH <3870> [8] Acts 13:42 → BEG <3870> [9] Acts 18:26 → to take aside → TAKE <4355>.

INVITED – Matt. 22:14 → CALLED <2822>.

INVOKE – [1] ***epikaleō*** [verb: ἐπικαλέω <1941>]; **from *epi*: upon, and *kaleō*: to call ▶ To call upon, to call to be one's own** > James speaks of the nations on whom the name of the Lord is invoked (Acts 15:17); other transl.: upon whom the name of the Lord is called, who are called by His name, who bear His name. All other refs.: APPEAL <1941>, CALL (verb) <1941>, PRAY <1941>, SURNAME (verb) <1941>.

– [2] Matt. 26:74; Mark 14:71 → to invoke a curse → CURSE (verb) <2653> [3] Mark 14:71 → to invoke a curse → CURSE (noun) <332> [4] Acts 19:13 → to call over → CALL (verb) <3687> [5] Eph. 1:21 → NAME (verb) <3687> [6] Heb. 11:20 → to invoke blessings on → BLESS <2127>.

INVOLVE – [1] John 2:4 → why do you involve me → lit.: what does this have to do with me [2] 2 Tim. 2:4 → to get involved → ENTANGLE <1707> [3] Heb. 9:16 → "is involved" added in Engl.

INWARD – 2 Cor. 7:15 → inward affection → AFFECTION <4698>.

INWARDLY – [1] Acts 10:17 → lit.: in himself [2] Rom. 2:29 → SECRET (adj. and noun) <2927> [3] 2 Cor. 4:16 → lit.: inner man → MAN <2080>, <444> [4] 2 Cor. 11:29 → to burn inwardly → BURN <4448>.

IOTA – ***iōta*** [neut. noun: ἰῶτα <2503>] ▶ **Ninth letter of the Greek alphabet which is written simply "ι"** > Jesus says that not one iota {smallest letter} or one tittle will pass away from the law, until all is accomplished (Matt. 5:18). ¶

IRKSOME – Phil. 3:1 → TEDIOUS <3636>.

IRON – [1] ***sidēros*** [masc. noun: σίδηρος <4604>] ▶ **Gray metal used in the manufacture of objects** > This term is used in Rev. 18:12. ¶
[2] **iron, of iron: *sidēreos* or *sidērous*** [adj.: σιδήρεος or σιδηροῦς <4603>]; **from *sidēros*: see** [1] ▶ **Made of iron** > This term is used to describe a gate (Acts 12:10), a rod (Rev. 2:27; 12:5; 19:15), and breastplates (Rev. 9:9). ¶
[3] **to sear with a hot (or: branding) iron: *kautēriazō*** [verb: καυτηριάζω <2743>]; **from *kautērion*: hot iron to cauterize, which is from *kaiō*: to light a fire, to burn; also spelled: *kaustēriazō*** ▶ **To cauterize, i.e., to burn the tissues with an instrument such as a hot iron; to mark as with a brand** > In latter times, those departing from the faith will have their conscience seared with a hot iron (1 Tim. 4:2); they will have become morally insensitive, having given heed to deceiving spirits and doctrines of demons (see v. 1). ¶
– [4] Mark 5:4b → SHACKLE <3976>.

IRRATIONAL – 2 Pet. 2:12; Jude 10 → without reason → REASON (noun) <249>.

IRRELIGIOUS – 1 Tim. 1:9 → PROFANE (adj. and noun) <952>.

IRREPROACHABLE – [1] ***amōmētos*** [adj.: ἀμώμητος <298>]; **from *a*: neg., and *mōmaomai*: to blame** ▶ **Concerning whom one cannot make any reproach, blameless** > Christians are seen in the eyes of God as irreproachable {above reproach, without fault, without rebuke} (Phil. 2:15). However, they must be diligent to be found blameless before Him practically (2 Pet. 3:14). ¶
– [2] Phil. 2:15 → BLAMELESS <273> [3] Col. 1:22 → above reproach → REPROACH <410> [4] 1 Tim. 3:2; 5:7; 6:14 → above reproach → REPROACH <423>.

IRREVERENT – 1 Tim. 4:7; 6:20; 2 Tim. 2:16 → PROFANE (adj. and noun) <952>.

IRREVOCABLE – ***ametamelētos*** [adj.: ἀμεταμέλητος <278>]; **from *a*: neg., and *metamelomai*: to regret, to change opinion, which is from *meta*: denoting change, and *melō*: to care** ▶ **That concerning which one has no regret, does not wish to change one's mind** > The gifts of grace and the calling of God are irrevocable {not subject to repentance, without repentance} (Rom. 11:29). Other ref.: 2 Cor. 7:10 (never to be regretted); see REGRET <278>. ¶

IRRITABLE (BE) – 1 Cor. 13:5 → to be quickly provoked → PROVOKE <3947>.

ISAAC – ***Isaak*** [masc. name: Ἰσαάκ <2464>]: **one who laughs, in Heb.** ▶ **Patriarch of the O.T.** > Isaac was the son of Abraham and the father of Jacob (Matt. 1:2a, b) and Esau (see Gen. 25:25, 26). Paul teaches the Galatians that they are children of promise like Isaac (Gal. 4:28). Isaac is mentioned among O.T. people of faith (Heb. 11:9, 17, 18, 20). God tested Abraham, telling him to offer up his son Isaac on the altar (James 2:21; Heb. 11:17). Other refs.: Matt. 8:11; 22:32; Mark 12:26; Luke 3:34; 13:28; 20:37; Acts 3:13; 7:8, 32; Rom. 9:7, 10. ¶

ISAIAH – ***Ēsaias*** [masc. name: Ἠσαΐας <2268>]: **Jehovah's salvation, in Heb.** ▶ **Prophet of the O.T.; also transl.: Esaias** > John the Baptist quotes the prophet Isaiah (Matt. 3:3; John 1:23) as does also Jesus (Matt. 13:14; 15:7; Mark 7:6). An Ethiopian of the court of Candace was reading the prophet Isaiah and Philip asked him if he understood what he was reading (Acts 8:28, 30). Paul quotes Isaiah in his letter to the Christians of Rome (Rom. 9:27, 29; 10:16, 20; 15:12). Other refs.: Matt. 4:14; 8:17; 12:17; Mark 1:2; Luke 3:4; 4:17; John 12:38, 39, 41; Acts 28:25. ¶

ISCARIOT – ***Iskariōthēs*** [masc. name: Ἰσκαριώθης <2469>]; **prob.: man of Kerioth, locality in the south of Judah** ▶ **Surname of Judas who betrayed Jesus** > See JUDAS c. <2455>.

ISLAND – [1] ***nēsos*** [fem. noun: νῆσος <3520>]; ***insula*, in Lat. ▶ Area of land (smaller than a continent) surrounded by water** > This term is used in regard to Cyprus (Acts 13:6), Malta (Acts 28:1, 7, 9, 11), and Patmos (Rev. 1:9). Other refs.: Acts 27:26; Rev. 6:14; 16:20. ¶
[2] **small island, certain island: *nēsion*** [neut. noun: νησίον <3519>]; **dimin. of [1] ▶ Islet, a very little island** > The term is used in regard to Clauda (Acts 27:16). ¶

ISLANDER – Acts 28:2, 4 → BARBARIAN <915>.

ISLE – See ISLAND.

ISRAEL – ***Israēl*** [masc. name: Ἰσραήλ <2474>]: **wrestler, or prince of God, in Heb. ▶ Name of the earthly people of God, descended from Jacob, who himself received this name after having struggled with God (see Gen. 32:28); the people of Israel are formed of twelve tribes, essentially corresponding to the twelve sons of Jacob** > Jesus was acclaimed as the king of Israel (John 1:49; 12:13). He commanded His disciples to go to the lost sheep of the house of Israel (Matt. 10:6), to whom He Himself had been sent (Matt. 15:24; Acts 13:23). During the period of grace, Israel is partially hardened to the message of the gospel, but later all true Israel shall be saved (Rom. 11:25, 26). *

ISRAELITE – ***Israēlitēs*** [masc. name: Ἰσραηλίτης <2475>]: **from Israel, in Heb. ▶ Descendant of Israel, i.e., of Jacob, grandson of Abraham (see Gen. 32:28)** > Christ comes from this people who had received various favors and promises from God (Rom. 9:4; see v. 5). Jesus calls Nathanael a true Israelite (John 1:47). The expr. "men of Israel" is used as an interpolation in the Acts by Peter (2:22; 3:12), Gamaliel (5:35), Paul (13:16), and the Jews from Asia (21:28). Paul was an Israelite (Rom. 11:1; 2 Cor. 11:22). ¶

ISSACHAR – ***Isachar*** [masc. name: Ἰσαχάρ <2466>]: **he will bring a reward, in Heb.; see Gen. 30:18 ▶ Son of Jacob and name of one of the twelve tribes descended from him** > Twelve thousand out of the tribe of Issachar shall be sealed (Rev. 7:7). ¶

ISSUE (noun)[1] – [1] Matt. 22:25 → SEED <4690> [2] Acts 11:2 → to take issue → CONTEND <1252> [3] Acts 15:2 → QUESTION (noun) <2213>.

ISSUE (noun)[2] – Mark 5:25; Luke 8:43, 44 → FLOW (noun) <4511>.

ISSUE (noun)[3] – [1] 2 Cor. 4:8 → to see no apparent issue → PERPLEXED (BE) <639> [2] Heb. 13:7 → OUTCOME <1545>.

ISSUE (verb) – 1 Tim. 1:5 → "that issues" added in Engl.

ITALIAN – ***Italikos*** [adj.: Ἰταλικός <2483>]: **which belongs to Italy ▶ Name of a cohort; also transl.: Italic** > Cornelius was a centurion to a cohort called Italian (Acts 10:1). ¶

ITALIC – See ITALIAN <2483>.

ITALY – ***Italia*** [fem. name: Ἰταλία <2482>] **▶ Country of Europe whose capital is Rome** > Aquila and Priscilla had come from Italy to Athens where Paul met them (Acts 18:2). Paul was brought to Italy as a prisoner, having appealed to Caesar (Acts 27:1, 6). The author of the Epistle to the Hebrews sends them greetings from those of Italy (Heb. 13:24). ¶

ITCHING – **to itch: *knēthō*** [verb: κνήθω <2833>]; **from *knaō*: to scrape, to scratch ▶ To tickle, to irritate** > Paul speaks of the time when men will not endure sound doctrine, but according to their own desires, because they have itching ears (lit.: ears that itch), they will heap up for themselves teachers (2 Tim. 4:3). ¶

ITINERANT – **to go here and there, about, around, from place to place: *perierchomai*** [verb: περιέρχομαι <4022>]; **from *peri*: around, and *erchomai*: to go ▶**

To go to various localities, to travel from place to place > Some of the itinerant (lit.: the going here and there, i.e., the ambulant) Jewish exorcists took it upon themselves to call the name of the Lord Jesus over those who had evil spirits (Acts 19:13). Other refs.: Acts 28:13 (to go here and there); 1 Tim. 5:13; Heb. 11:37; see CIRCLE AROUND <4022>, WANDER <4022>. ¶

ITSELF – of itself: *automatos* [adj.: αὐτόματος <844>]; **from *autos*: itself ▶ Which happens from its own impulse, spontaneous** > The earth bears fruit of itself (Mark 4:28). An iron gate opened by itself to an angel and Peter (Acts 12:10). ¶

ITURAEA – *Itouraia* [fem. name: Ἰτουραία <2484>]; **prob.: encircled ▶ Province northeast of Galilee** > Philip was tetrarch of Ituraea (Luke 3:1). ¶

IVORY – of ivory: *elephantinos* [adj.: ἐλεφάντινος <1661>]; **from *elephas*: elephant, ivory ▶ Made of the hard white substance of the elephant tusks** > After the fall of Babylon, merchants will weep because no one will buy their merchandise, including articles of ivory (Rev. 18:12). ¶

 J

JACINTH – [1] ***huakinthos*** [masc. noun: ὑάκινθος <5192>] ► **Precious stone whose color resembles the hyacinth flower** > The eleventh foundation of the wall of the heavenly Jerusalem was adorned with jacinth (Rev. 21:20). ¶
[2] **of jacinth: *huakinthinos*** [adj.: ὑακίνθινος <5191>] ► **Which resembles the precious stone; see [1]** > The breastplates in Rev. 9:17 are of jacinth, i.e., they look like this stone. ¶

JACOB – ***Iakōb*** [masc.: Ἰακώβ <2384>]**: supplanter, in Heb.** ► **a. Son of Isaac** > Jacob is mentioned in the genealogy of Jesus Christ (Matt. 1:2a, b; Luke 3:34). Following a famine, his sons went down to Egypt to buy wheat; later his son Joseph sent for him (Acts 7:12, 14, 15). Jacob, when he was dying, worshiped, leaning on the top of his staff (Heb. 11:21). Other refs.: Matt. 8:11; 22:32; Mark 12:26; Luke 1:33; 13:28; 20:37; John 4:5, 6, 12; Acts 3:13; 7:8, 32, 46; Rom. 9:13; 11:26; Heb. 11:9, 20. **b. Other man of the O.T.** > This Jacob is mentioned in the genealogy of Jesus Christ and is the father of Joseph, the husband of Mary (Matt. 1:15, 16). ¶

JAIL – [1] Acts 4:3; 5:18 → PRISON <5084> [2] Acts 5:19, 22, 25 → PRISON <5438> [3] Acts 5:23 → PRISON <1201>.

JAILER – ***desmophulax*** [masc. noun: δεσμοφύλαξ <1200>]**; from *desmos*: bond, and *phulax*: guardian** ► **Prison keeper, person responsible for a jail; also spelled: jailor** > The jailer in Philippi who was guarding Paul and Silas was about to kill himself, supposing that the prisoners had fled. But on that same night, he was converted and baptized (Acts 16:23, 27, 36). ¶

JAILOR – See JAILER <1200>.

JAIRUS – ***Iairos*** [masc. name: Ἰάϊρος <2383>]**: whom Jehovah enlightens; also spelled: *Iaeiros*** ► **Chief of a synagogue** > Jairus came to Jesus (Mark 5:22; Luke 8:41), and Jesus resurrected his daughter (see Mark 5:41, 42; Luke 8:54, 55). ¶

JAMBRES – ***Iambrēs*** [masc. name: Ἰαμβρῆς <2387>] ► **Egyptian magician** > Jambres and Jannes opposed Moses by imitating the miracles which he performed before Pharaoh (2 Tim. 3:8; see Ex. 7:11, 22; 8:7, 18). ¶

JAMES – ***Iakōbos*** [masc. name: Ἰάκωβος <2385>]**; Greek name of Jacob** ► **a. Father of Judas** > This James is the father of Judas (Luke 6:16; Acts 1:13c), not Judas Iscariot (see John 14:22), but the Judas otherwise known as the Thaddaeus of Matt. 10:3; Mark 3:18. Nothing more is known about him. **b. James the brother of John and one of the twelve apostles (Matt. 10:2; Mark 3:17; Luke 6:14; Acts 1:13a)** > James and John, sons of Zebedee, were repairing their nets when Jesus called them to follow Him (Matt. 4:21, 22; Mark 1:19, 20; Luke 5:10). James was with Jesus when He was transfigured on the mountain (Matt. 17:1; Mark 9:2; Luke 9:28). Jesus also took James along with Him at Gethsemane (Mark 14:33). James and John asked the Lord to sit one at His right hand and the other at His left hand in glory (Mark 10:35, 41). King Herod had James put to death with the sword (Acts 12:2). Other refs.: Mark 1:29; 5:37a, b; 13:3; Luke 8:51; 9:54. **c. Son of Alphaeus** > This other James was also one of the twelve apostles, and is mentioned in Matt. 10:3; Mark 3:18; Luke 6:15; Acts 1:13b. He is called James the Less, i.e., the smaller (Matt. 27:56; Mark 15:40; 16:1; Luke 24:10). **d. James the Lord's brother** > The name of this James is mentioned in Matt. 13:55; Mark 6:3. James, Cephas, and John gave the right hand of fellowship to Paul and Barnabas to preach to the nations (Gal. 2:9). The Epistle of James was most likely written by this brother of the Lord (James 1:1). Other refs.: Acts 12:17; 15:13; 21:18; 1 Cor. 15:7; Gal. 1:19; 2:12; Jude 1. ¶

JANGLING – 1 Tim. 1:6 → vain jangling → VAIN <3150>.

JANNA – See JANNAI <2388>.

JANNAI – ***Ianna*** [masc. name: Ἰαννά <2388>]**: whom Jehovah bestows** ► **Man of the O.T.; also spelled: Janna** > Jannai is mentioned in the genealogy of Jesus (Luke 3:24). ¶

JANNES – ***Iannēs*** [masc. name: Ἰάννης <2389>] ▶ **Egyptian magician** > See JAMBRES <2387>.

JAR – [1] Matt. 25:4 → VESSEL[1] <30> [2] Matt. 26:7; Mark 14:3a, b; Luke 7:37 → alabaster jar → alabaster box → ALABASTER <211> [3] Mark 14:13; Luke 22:10 → PITCHER <2765> [4] Luke 8:16; John 19:29; 2 Cor. 4:7 → VESSEL[1] <4632> [5] John 2:6, 7; 4:28 → jar, water jar → WATER POT <5201> [6] Heb. 9:4 → POT <4713>.

JARED – ***Iared*** [masc. name: Ἰάρεδ <2391>]**: descent, in Heb.** ▶ **Man of the O.T., father of Enoch: see Gen. 5:18; also spelled: *Iaret*** > Jared is mentioned in the genealogy of Jesus (Luke 3:37). ¶

JASON – ***Iasōn*** [masc. name: Ἰάσων <2394>]**: who heals** ▶ **a. Christian man of Thessalonica** > Jason had received Paul and Silas; the Jews attacked his house and dragged him before the rulers of the city, but he was released after they had received a pledge from Jason and others (Acts 17:5–7, 9). **b. Relative of the apostle Paul** > Jason greets the Christians of Rome in the letter from Paul (Rom. 16:21). ¶

JASPER – ***iaspis*** [fem. noun: ἴασπις <2393>] ▶ **Precious stone colored by spots or bands** > He who was sitting on the throne was like a stone of jasper (Rev. 4:3). The shining of the heavenly Jerusalem was like a jasper stone, crystal clear (Rev. 21:11). The wall of the heavenly Jerusalem is built of jasper (Rev. 21:18), and the first foundation of this wall is adorned with jasper (21:19). ¶

JEALOUS – [1] **to be jealous, to become jealous, to be stirred up to jealousy: *zēloō*** [verb: ζηλόω <2206>]**; from *zēlos*: zeal, which is from *zeō*: to be hot, to be fervent** ▶ **To envy the advantages of others or to be upset regarding those advantages; in a positive sense, to desire good things for others** > Becoming jealous {Becoming envious, Having been stirred up to jealousy, Moved with envy}, the Jews sought Paul and Silas (Acts 17:5). Paul was jealous for the Corinthians with a godly jealousy (2 Cor. 11:2). All other refs.: COVET <2206>, DESIRE (verb) <2206>, ENVY (verb) <2206>, ZEALOUS <2206>.

– [2] Acts 7:9; 1 Cor. 13:4 → to be jealous, to become jealous → ENVY (verb) <2206> [3] Rom. 11:11, 14 → to make jealous → to provoke to jealousy → JEALOUSY <3863>.

JEALOUSLY – Jas. 4:5 → with envy → ENVY (noun) <5355>.

JEALOUSY – [1] ***zēlos*** [masc. noun: ζῆλος <2205>]; **from *zeō*: to be hot, to be fervent** ▶ **Attitude of a person who envies the advantages of another or who is upset in regard to those advantages; also transl.: emulation, envy, envying, indignation, wrath** > The high priest and the Sadducees were filled with jealousy against the apostles (Acts 5:17). The Jews were filled with jealousy against Paul and Barnabas (Acts 13:45). Paul was jealous as to the Corinthians with a godly jealousy (2 Cor. 11:2); but he feared there might be jealousies in their midst (2 Cor. 12:20). Jealousies are among the works of the flesh (Gal. 5:20). Jealousy and self-ambition engender disorder and evil deeds (Jas. 3:14, 16). All other refs.: ENVY (noun) <2205>, HEAT <2205>, MIND (noun) <2205>, ZEAL <2205>.

[2] **to arouse the jealousy of, to move to jealousy, to provoke to jealousy: *parazēloō*** [verb: παραζηλόω <3863>]; **from *para*: to the point of, and *zēloō*: to be filed with zeal, which is from *zēlos*: see** [1] ▶ **To excite to rivalry, emulation; also transl.: to arouse to envy, to make jealous, to make envious, to provoke to emulation** > The Lord told Israel that He would provoke them to jealousy by another nation (Rom. 10:19). Salvation came to the nations to provoke Israel to jealousy (Rom. 11:11); Paul speaks of provoking them which are his own flesh to jealousy in order to save some of Israel (v. 14). To partake of the table of the Lord and of the table of demons would be to provoke the Lord to jealousy (1 Cor. 10:22). ¶

JECHONIAH – Matt. 1:11, 12 → JECONIAH <2423>.

JECHONIAS – See JECONIAH <2423>.

JECONIAH – ***Iechonias*** [masc. name: Ἰεχονίας <2423>]: **Jehovah will establish, in Heb. ▶ Name of a King of Judah (Jehoiachin or Coniah; see 2 Kgs. 24:8; Jer. 22:24–30); also spelled: Jechoniah, Jechonias** > Jeconiah is mentioned in the genealogy of Jesus Christ (Matt. 1:11, 12). ¶

JEHOSHAPHAT – ***Iōsaphat*** [masc. name: Ἰωσαφάτ <2498>]: **Jehovah is judge, in Heb. ▶ King of Judah; also transl.: Josaphat** > Jehoshaphat is mentioned in the genealogy of Jesus Christ (Matt. 1:8a, b). ¶

JEOPARDY – **to stand in jeopardy:** ***kinduneuō*** [verb: κινδυνεύω <2793>]; **from *kindunos*: danger ▶ To be in peril, to expose oneself to danger** > Paul asks why did he stand in jeopardy {did he endanger himself, was he in danger} every hour (1 Cor. 15:30), if the dead do not rise (see v. 29). Other refs.: Luke 8:23; Acts 19:27, 40 (to be in danger); see DANGER <2793>. ¶

JEPHTHAH – ***Iephthae*** [masc. name: Ἰεφθάε <2422>]: **he delivered, in Heb. ▶ Judge of Israel** > Illegitimate child, Jephthah was driven from his father's house by his brothers; he delivered Israel from the Ammonites (see Judg. 11:1 to 12:7). He is mentioned among believers of the O.T. who have distinguished themselves by their faith (Heb. 11:32). ¶

JEREMIAH – ***Ieremias*** [masc. name: Ἰερεμίας <2408>]: **appointed of Jehovah, in Heb. ▶ Prophet of the O.T.** > Some said that Jesus was Jeremiah (Matt. 16:14). The Gospel of Matthew reports two prophecies of Jeremiah which were fulfilled in the time of the Lord: the massacre of the little children at the order of Herod (2:17) and the price of the betrayal by Judas (27:9). ¶

JERICHO – ***Ierichō*** [fem. name: Ἰεριχώ <2410>]: **fragrance, in Heb. ▶ Major city of Palestine, located approx. 17 miles (27 kilometers) northeast of Jerusalem and 787 feet (240 meters) below the level of the Mediterranean Sea** > Jericho, which was in Canaan, was the first city taken by the Israelites during the conquest of the land; the walls of Jericho fell after the Israelites had encircled them for seven days (Heb. 11:30). Jesus healed two blind men as He was going out of Jericho (Matt. 20:29); one of them was Bartimaeus (Mark 10:46a, b; Luke 18:35). The parable of the "Good Samaritan" takes place between Jerusalem and Jericho (Luke 10:30). Zaccheus received Jesus in his house at Jericho (Luke 19:1). ¶

JERUSALEM – **[1]** ***Hierosoluma*** [plur. neut. name: Ἱεροσόλυμα <2414>]; ***Ierousalēm*** [fem. name: Ἰερουσαλήμ <2419>]: **habitation of peace, in Heb. ▶ Capital of Palestine, located in Judea at 2,460–2,620 feet (750–800 meters) above sea level** > The foundation of Jerusalem dates back to at least 1500 B.C., perhaps to the time of Melchizedek, called "king of Salem" (see Gen. 14:18). David made it his capital, and Solomon built the temple there. The Babylonians destroyed it in 587 B.C., but it was rebuilt in the time of Ezra and Nehemiah after the return from captivity. Titus destroyed it in A.D. 70. The city and its holy places were subsequently restored. Jesus went there several times. He reproached Jerusalem for being the city that kills the prophets and stones those who are sent to her (Matt. 23:37a, b; Luke 13:34a, b). Jesus was crucified there. *

[2] people of Jerusalem: ***Hierosolumitēs*** [masc. name: Ἱεροσολυμίτης <2415>]; **from *Hierosoluma*: see [1] ▶ Inhabitant of this city** > This name is used in Mark 1:5; John 7:25. ¶

JESSE – ***Iessai*** [masc. name: Ἰεσσαί <2421>]: **strong, in Heb. ▶ Man of the O.T.; see 1 Sam. 17:17** > Jesse is the father of David (Acts 13:22). He is mentioned in the genealogy of Jesus Christ (Matt. 1:5, 6; Luke 3:32). Jesus arose from the root of Jesse to reign over the nations (Rom. 15:12). ¶

JESTING – ***eutrapelia*** [fem. noun: εὐτραπελία <2160>]; **from *eu*: easily, and *trepō*: to turn ▶ Coarse pleasantry; remarks intended to make people laugh, but of a light and even vulgar character; also transl.: coarse jesting, coarse joking, crude joking** > Jesting and any other thing which is not becoming is not to be even named among Christians (Eph. 5:4). ¶

JESUS – ***Iēsous*** [masc. name: Ἰησοῦς <2424>]: **Jehovah saves, in Heb. ▶ a. Name of the Son of God manifested in flesh** > Jesus is the personal name of the Lord as man (Matt. 1:21). Conceived by the Holy Spirit (Matt. 1:20), He was born of the virgin Mary (v. 20). We read concerning His childhood that He grew and became strong, being full of wisdom, and the grace of God was upon Him (Luke 2:40). When He was twelve years old, his parents found Him sitting in the temple in the midst of the doctors, listening to them and asking them questions; the latter were astonished at His intelligence and His answers (vv. 41–48); He thus was occupied in His Father's business (v. 49). At Nazareth, where He grew up, He was subject to His parents. He advanced in wisdom and in stature, and in favor with God and man (v. 52). When He was about thirty years of age, He came to John the Baptist to be baptized by him; at this baptism, the Holy Spirit descended upon Him, and the Father declared that He was His beloved Son in whom He had found His pleasure (Matt. 3:13–17). He was then tempted by the devil, and overcame him by the word of God (Matt. 4:1–11; Luke 4:1–13). After having been presented as the Lamb of God who takes away the sin of the world (John 1:29), Jesus began His public ministry. He preached the gospel of the kingdom, healed the sick, cast out demons, and raised the dead. He fulfilled the prophecies of the O.T. which had predicted what the Messiah would do. Jesus was also on earth for another purpose, that of saving souls; to all those who received Him, He gave to them the right to be children of God (John 1:12). He revealed God to them as Father and gave them eternal life. Christ was the second Man, the last Adam, the Head, so to speak, of a new race. Those who are sanctified in Him are delivered from sin and their former condition in Adam; they are justified and are given a new position in Christ. By the baptism of the Holy Spirit at Pentecost, they have become one body, united to the Lord in glory: He is the Head of the church. From the beginning, the leaders in Israel rejected the Lord Jesus: "His own did not receive Him" (John 1:11). But some believers were gathered around Him; He chose among them twelve apostles. After a ministry of about three and a half years, the time came for Jesus to offer Himself as a sacrifice for sin, according to the counsel of God. In the garden of Gethsemane, He was filled with dread at the prospect of bearing sin. He asked His Father: "My Father, if it is possible, let this cup pass from me"; but that was not possible, and He bowed before the will of His Father. He was arrested and crucified; His blood was shed, and by His blood redemption was accomplished. On the third day, He rose from among the dead; He breathed into the apostles the Holy Spirit as the power of life (John 20:19–23). After having appeared on several occasions to many witnesses, He ascended to heaven. The Scriptures clearly demonstrate by direct affirmations and by the works of the Lord Jesus that He was at the same time God and man; He had indeed accomplished what no mere man could do, e.g., read the thoughts of men, forgive sins, cast out demons, raise the dead and raise Himself from among the dead (John 10:18). The Lord Jesus is truly God and man. This mystery which surrounds His person is beyond human comprehension. We read that no one knows the Father except the Son, and no one knows the Son except the Father, and he to whom the Son may be pleased to reveal Him (Matt. 11:27; Luke 10:22). This is not to be a stumbling block, but calls forth reverence, praise, and adoration. (After Walter Scott.) *
b. Disciple at Rome, also called Justus > Paul commends Jesus called Justus to the Colossians; he had been a consolation to Paul (Col. 4:11); this Jesus greets the Colossians (see v. 10). **c. Name or surname**

of Barabbas in some mss. > Ref.: Matt. 27:16, 17.

JETTISON – Acts 27:18 → to jettison the cargo, to throw cargo overboard → LIGHTEN <1546>.

JEW – [1] ***Ioudaios*** [adj. used as noun: Ἰουδαῖος <2453>]: **man of Judea ▶ At the beginning, member of the tribe of Judah; later, person of this race** > The name "Jew" (or: Judean) was not used until after the division of Israel into two kingdoms of ten tribes and two tribes (see 2 Kgs. 16:6). It is thought to be derived from "Judah," the kingdom formed of the tribes of Judah and of Benjamin. Those who returned from the captivity belonged to these two tribes. After the captivity, all the descendants of the twelve tribes were called Jews; the Lord is called "King of the Jews" (Matt. 27:37); He told the Samaritan woman that salvation is of the Jews (John 4:22). In the Gospel of John, the "Jews" designate the inhabitants of Judea, in contrast with the people from elsewhere who gathered for the feast. The expr. "those who say they are Jews" is used with respect to religious groups claiming to represent Judaism or Christianity, and seeking to give a Judaic form to Christianity; they are under the influence of Satan ("the synagogue of Satan") and oppose the faithful represented by two churches: Smyrna and Philadelphia (Rev. 2:9; 3:9), to whom no reproach is made. (After Walter Scott.) *
[2] **like the Jews:** ***Ioudaikōs*** [adv.: Ἰουδαϊκῶς <2452>] **▶ According to the customs of the Jewish people** > Paul told Peter that he lived like the Gentiles and not like the Jews (Gal. 2:14). ¶
– [3] Gal. 1:13, 14 → Jews' religion → JUDAISM <2454> [4] Gal. 2:14 → to live like Jews → JUDAIZE <2450>.

JEWEL – Rev. 17:4; 18:12, 16; 21:19 → jewels → lit.: precious stones → PRECIOUS <5093>, STONE (noun) <3037>.

JEWISH – [1] ***Ioudaikos*** [adj.: Ἰουδαϊκός <2451>]; **from *Iouda*: Judah ▶ Pertaining to Judaism** > Paul asks Titus to rebuke the Cretans so that they may not pay attention to Jewish myths (Titus 1:14). ¶
– [2] John 1:19, 5:10; et al. → Jewish leader → lit.: Jew [3] John 10:31 → His Jewish opponents → lit.: the Jews [4] John 18:28 → "Jewish leaders" added in Engl. [5] Gal. 2:14 → to follow Jewish customs → JUDAIZE <2450>.

JEWISH FESTIVAL – John 5:1 → lit.: feast of the Jews.

JEZEBEL – ***Iezabel*** [fem. name: Ἰεζάβελ <2403>]: **chaste, in Heb. ▶ Daughter of a king of the Sidonians and wife of Ahab (see 1 Kgs. 16:29–31)** > This wicked queen exterminated the prophets of the Lord (see 1 Kgs. 18:4) and had Naboth murdered so that Ahab might take possession of his vineyard (ch. 21). In Rev. 2:20, Jezebel is a woman who incites the Christians of Thyatira to commit sexual immorality and to eat things sacrificed to idols. Symbolically, she represents those who, in Christendom, join idolatrous practices to true Christianity. ¶

JOANAN – ***Iōannas*** [masc. name: Ἰωαννᾶς <2490>]; **also spelled: *Iōanan* ▶ Man of the O.T.; also transl.: Joanna, Joannas, Joannes** > Joanan is mentioned in the genealogy of Jesus (Luke 3:27). ¶

JOANNA – ***Iōanna*** [fem. name: Ἰωάννα <2489>] **▶ Wife of Chuza, Herod's steward** > Joanna ministered to Jesus out of her own means (Luke 8:3). She was one of the women who announced the Lord's resurrection to the apostles (Luke 24:10). ¶

JOANNA, JOANNAS, JOANNES – See JOANAN <2490>.

JOATHAM – See JOTHAM <2488>.

JOB (name) – ***Iōb*** [masc. name: Ἰώβ <2492>]: **persecuted, poorly treated, in Heb. ▶ Patriarch of the O.T., which contains a book bearing his name** > James speaks of the patience of Job and how the Lord showed Himself to be full of compassion and tender mercy toward him (James 5:11). ¶

JOB (noun) – Luke 16:3, 4 → STEWARDSHIP <3622>.

JODA – See JUDAH <2455>.

JOEL – ***Iōēl*** [masc. name: Ἰωήλ <2493>]: **Jehovah is God, in Heb. ► Prophet of the O.T., which contains a book bearing his name >** A prophecy of Joel was fulfilled at Pentecost when the Holy Spirit descended from heaven and the disciples prophesied (Acts 2:16; see 17–21). ¶

JOHN – ***Iōannēs*** [masc. name: Ἰωάννης <2491>]: **Jehovah has been gracious, in Heb. ► a. John the Baptist or John the Baptizer, cousin of Jesus >** The father of John, Zacharias, and his mother, Elizabeth, were both righteous before God (see Luke 1:5, 6); they were both well advanced in years when John was born (see v. 7). John had been sent from God as the forerunner of Christ, to bear witness concerning Him (John 1:6; see v. 7). He preached repentance and the coming of the kingdom of the heavens; he baptized with water for repentance. Jesus Himself came to be baptized by John: although righteous and having nothing to confess, He associated Himself with the repentant remnant of Israel (Matt. 3:13; see v. 15). After a short ministry, John was beheaded in prison by order of Herod the tetrarch (Matt. 14:10). Although John the Baptist had performed no miracle (John 10:41), Jesus speaks of him as the greatest of the prophets (Luke 7:28). * **b. Son of Zebedee, brother of James and disciple of the Lord >** In the Gospel which bears his name, the apostle John describes himself as the "disciple whom Jesus loved" (see John 13:23; 19:26; 20:2; 21:7, 20). Jesus surnamed John and his brother James "Boanerges," i.e., "Sons of Thunder" (see Mark 3:17), perhaps because of their impetuous character (Matt. 20:20–24; Mark 10:35–41; see Luke 9:49, 54). When on the cross, Jesus entrusted His mother to John (see John 19:25–27). The Gospel of John presents the Lord Jesus as the Son of God. John is the author of three epistles which bear his name and of Revelation, which he wrote in exile on the island of Patmos (Rev. 1:1, 4, 9; 22:8). Other refs.: Mark 9:38; Luke 9:49; 22:8; Acts 3:1, 4, 11; 4:13, 19; 8:14; Gal. 2:9. * **c. John, called Mark >** See MARK (name) <3138>. **d. Important Jewish man, of the high priestly family >** Peter and John, and others with them, appeared before him (Acts 4:6). **e. Father of Peter >** The name is found in John 1:42; 21:15–17 in some mss.; see JONAH <2495>. ¶

JOIN – **1 to join, to join oneself: *kollaō*** [verb: κολλάω <2853>]; **from *kolla*: glue; lit.: to glue together ► To bind together, to firmly unite; also transl.: to associate >** The prodigal son joined himself {hired himself out} to a citizen of the distant country where he had gone (Luke 15:15). Among the people, some did not dare to join the apostles (Acts 5:13). The Spirit told Philip to join {to overtake, to stay near} the chariot of the Ethiopian (Acts 8:29). Paul tried to join himself to the disciples (Acts 9:26). Some Athenians joined themselves to {clave unto, became followers of} Paul and believed (Acts 17:34). He who joins {unites} himself with a prostitute is one body with her (1 Cor. 6:16), but he who unites himself with the Lord is one with Him in spirit (v. 17). All other refs.: CLEAVE <2853>, CLING <2853>, COMPANY (noun) <2853>, REACH <2853>.

2 *proskollaō* [verb: προσκολλάω <4347>]; **from *pros*: to, and *kollaō*: see 1 ► a. To adhere >** About four hundred men were joined {rallied} to Theudas (Acts 5:36); *prosklinō* in some mss. **b. To closely join together; also transl.: to cleave, to unite >** A man shall leave his father and mother, and shall be united to his wife; the two shall be one flesh (Matt. 19:5; Mark 10:7). A man shall be joined {shall be united} to his wife (Eph. 5:31). ¶

3 to join oneself to: *prosklēroō* [verb: προσκληρόω <4345>]; **from *pros*: to, and *klēroō*: to designate by drawing lots, which is from *klēros*: lot, portion randomly selected ► To be added to, to share the**

lot of > Some of the Thessalonians joined themselves to {consorted with} Paul and Silas (Acts 17:4). ¶

4 **to join together: *suzeugnumi*** [verb: συζεύγνυμι <4801>]; **from *sun*: together, and *zeugos*: yoke, pair ► To unite, forming a pair; to unite by marriage** > Speaking of marriage, Jesus says that man is not to separate what God has joined together (Matt. 19:6; Mark 10:9). ¶

5 **to join in pressing a matter, an attack, an accusation: *suntithēmi*** [verb: συντίθημι <4934>]; **from *sun*: together, and *tithēmi*: to put ► To get together, to support** > The Jews joined Tertullus in pressing a matter against Paul (Acts 24:9 {to assent}); other mss.: *sunepitithēmi*. Other refs.: Luke 22:5; John 9:22; Acts 23:20; see AGREE <4934>. ¶

– 6 John 6:17; Acts 17:15 → COME <2064> 7 Acts 1:14 → to join constantly → CONTINUE <4342> 8 Acts 10:28 → to keep company → COMPANY (noun) <2853> 9 Acts 18:7 → to join hard → ADJOINED (BE) <4927> 10 1 Cor. 1:10 → to perfectly join → PERFECTLY <2675> 11 1 Cor. 16:16 → to join in the work → to work together → WORK (verb) <4903> 12 Gal. 2:13 → to join in hypocrisy → to play the hypocrite → HYPOCRITE <4942> 13 Eph. 2:21; 4:16 → to join together, to fitly join together → to fit together → FIT (verb) <4883> 14 2 Tim. 2:3 in some mss. → to join in suffering → SUFFERING <4777> 15 1 Pet. 4:4 → to run together → RUN <4936>.

JOINT – 1 ***harmos*** [masc. noun: ἁρμός <719>]; **comp. *arariskō*: to fit together ► Juncture, articulation in the case of bones** > In Heb. 4:12, "the joints and marrow" refers to the inner man, to his moral and spiritual characteristics. ¶

2 ***haphē*** [fem. noun: ἁφή <860>]; **from *haptō*: to join, to connect ► Articulation, contact; also transl.: ligament** > In the figur. sense, the church is a body fitted together and connected by every supporting ligament (Eph. 4:16; Col. 2:19). ¶

– 3 Heb. 12:13 → to put out of joint → DISLOCATE <1624>.

JOINT HEIR – ***sunklēronomos*** [masc. noun: συγκληρονόμος <4789>]; **from *sun*: together, and *klēronomos*: heir, which is from *klēros*: portion, and *nemō*: to distribute ► One who receives reserved goods together with another person, e.g., by means of succession; also transl.: co-heir, fellow heir, fellow-heir, heir together, heir with** > Christians are heirs of God and joint heirs with Christ (Rom. 8:17). The Gentiles would be joint heirs of the same body (Eph. 3:6). Isaac and Jacob were the joint heirs with their father Abraham of the promise (Heb. 11:9). Husbands and their wives are joint heirs of the promise of life (1 Pet. 3:7). ¶

JOINT PARTAKER – Eph. 3:6 → PARTAKER <4830>.

JOKING – Eph. 5:4 → coarse joking → JESTING <2160>.

JONA – See JONAH <2495>.

JONAH – ***Iōnas*** [masc. name: Ἰωνᾶς <2495>]: **dove, in Heb. ► a. Prophet of the O.T., which contains a book bearing his name; also transl.: Jonas** > Jesus speaks of the sign of Jonah: as Jonah was three days and three nights in the belly of the great fish, so He would remain in death for three days (Matt. 12:39–41; 16:4; Luke 11:29, 30, 32). **b. Father of Simon Peter; also transl.: Jona, Jonas** > This Jonah is mentioned in John 1:42; 21:15–17; other mss.: John. ¶

JONAM – ***Iōnam*** [masc. name: Ἰωνάμ <2494>]: **Jehovah is gracious, in Heb. ► Man of the O.T.; also spelled: Jonan** > Jonam is mentioned in the genealogy of Jesus (Luke 3:30). ¶

JONAN – See JONAM <2494>.

JONAS – See JONAH <2495>.

JOPPA – ***Ioppē*** [fem. name: Ἰόππη <2445>]: **beauty, in Heb. ► Seaport city of Palestine facing the Mediterranean Sea, located northwest of Jerusalem; its**

present name is Jaffa > A woman named Dorcas, who was a disciple, was resurrected by Peter at Joppa (Acts 9:36, 38, 42). While he was staying in Joppa, Peter had a vision preparing him to go to Cornelius, a Gentile (Acts 9:43; 10:5, 8, 23, 32; 11:5, 13). ¶

JORAM – ***Iōram*** [masc. name: Ἰωράμ <2496>]: **Jehovah is exalted, in Heb. ▶ Name of a king of Judah, son of Jehoshaphat (see 2 Kgs. 8:16, 17)** > Joram is mentioned in the genealogy of Jesus Christ (Matt. 1:8a, b). ¶

JORDAN – ***Iordanēs*** [masc. name: Ἰορδάνης <2446>]: **the descender, in Heb. ▶ River which the Israelites crossed when they entered the promised land (see Josh. 3:1–17); it is the main river of Palestine** > John baptized in the Jordan; he baptized Jesus there (Matt. 3:5, 6, 13; Mark 1:5, 9; Luke 3:3; 4:1; John 1:28). Several times we find the exprs. "across the Jordan," "beyond the Jordan" (or similar exprs.) (Matt. 4:15, 25; 19:1; Mark 3:8; 10:1; John 1:28; 3:26; 10:40). ¶

JOREIM – ***Iōreim*** [masc. name: Ἰωρείμ <2497>]**; also spelled and transl.: Jorim ▶ Man of the O.T.** > Joreim is mentioned in the genealogy of Jesus (Luke 3:29). ¶

JORIM – See JOREIM <2497>.

JOSAPHAT – See JEHOSHAPHAT <2498>.

JOSE – See JOSHUA <2424>.

JOSEK – Luke 3:26 → JOSEPH <2501>.

JOSEPH – ***Iōsēph*** [masc. name: Ἰωσήφ <2501>]: **He will add, in Heb.; see Gen. 30:24 ▶ a. Son of Jacob and name of one of the twelve tribes descended from him** > Joseph had received from Jacob a plot of ground which was near the city of Sychar (John 4:5). Joseph's brothers were full of envy against him; they sold him for twenty pieces of silver, and he was led away to Egypt. In that land, he prospered, for God was with him; he saved his father, his brothers and their families from famine (Acts 7:9, 13, 14, 18). At the end of his life, Jacob blessed the sons of Joseph (Heb. 11:21); before dying, Joseph made mention of the departure of the sons of Israel out of Egypt and gave orders to carry away his bones (v. 22). In the land of Canaan, the descendants of Joseph became two tribes, Ephraim and Manasseh (see Josh. 14:4). Twelve thousand out of the tribe of Joseph will be sealed (Rev. 7:8). **b. Husband of Mary, the mother of Jesus** > This Joseph is mentioned in the genealogy of Jesus Christ (Matt. 1:16; Luke 1:27). An angel appeared to him in a dream and told him not to fear to take Mary as his wife, for the child she was expecting had been conceived by the Holy Spirit (Matt. 1:18–20, 24; see also v. 25; Luke 2:33 and, in some mss., v. 43). Joseph went up to Bethlehem with Mary, who was pregnant, on the occasion of a census (Luke 2:4). Shepherds found Mary and Joseph, and the baby lying in a manger (Luke 2:16). An angel appeared to him on a second occasion to tell him to flee to Egypt, for Herod was going to search for the little child to kill him (Matt. 2:13). Once again, an angel appeared to him so that he would return to Israel after the death of Herod (Matt. 2:19; see v. 20); he lived in Nazareth (see 2:19–23). People regarded Jesus as the son of Joseph (Luke 3:23; 4:22; John 6:42); Jesus was known as the son of Joseph, who is from Nazareth (John 1:45). **c. Man of the N.T. originally from Arimathea** > Joseph of Arimathea was a rich man; he was a disciple of Jesus (Matt. 27:57). Mark says that he was an honorable counselor, waiting for the kingdom of God (Mark 15:43), while Luke mentions that he was a counselor, a good and righteous man (Luke 23:50). He asked for the body of Jesus, wrapped it in a clean linen cloth, and put it in a tomb which belonged to him (Matt. 27:57, 59; Mark 15:45, 46). Joseph of Arimathea and Nicodemus wrapped the body of Jesus in linen with aromatic spices, and embalmed it with a mixture of myrrh and aloes weighing about 100 pounds (45 kilograms) (John 19:38; see 38–42). **d. Name of three men of the O.T.** > Their names are mentioned in the genealogy of Jesus (Luke 3:24, 26 {other mss.: *Iōsēch*}, 30). **e. Christian man at the beginning of Acts >** Joseph was a disciple called Barsabbas and surnamed Justus (Acts 1:23), proposed to replace Judas; but the lot fell on Matthias (see v. 26). **f. Levite from Cyprus, surnamed Barnabas >** This Joseph is mentioned in Acts 4:36; see BARNABAS <921>. **g.** Matt. 13:55; 27:56 → JOSES <2500>. ¶

JOSES – [1] ***Iōsēs*** [masc. name: Ἰωσῆς <2500>]**: adding, in Heb. ► a. One of the brothers of the Lord; also transl.: Joseph >** Joses is mentioned in Matt. 13:55; Mark 6:3. **b. Other name of Jude, son of Mary and brother of James; also transl.: Joseph >** This Joses is mentioned in Matt. 27:56; Mark 15:40, 47. **c. Other name of Joseph, surnamed Barnabas >** See BARNABAS <921>.

– [2] See JOSHUA <2499>.

JOSHUA – [1] ***Iēsous*** [masc. name: Ἰησοῦς <2424>]**: Jehovah saves, in Heb.; same spelling in Greek of the name of Jesus ► Leader of Israel who succeeded Moses >** Joshua brought the Israelites into Canaan, the promised land (Acts 7:45). Heb. 4:8 underlines the fact that Joshua did not bring this people into rest; in v. 9 it is a matter of the rest to come for the people of God.

[2] ***Iōsē*** [masc. name: Ἰωσή <2499>]**: adding, in Heb. ► Man of the O.T.; also transl.: Jose, Joses >** Joshua is mentioned in the genealogy of Jesus (Luke 3:29). ¶

JOSIAH – ***Iōsias*** [masc. name: Ἰωσίας <2502>]**: Jehovah heals, in Heb. ► King of Judah (see 2 Kgs. 22:1) >** Josiah is mentioned in the genealogy of Jesus Christ (Matt. 1:10, 11). ¶

JOSIAS – See JOSIAH <2502>.

JOTHAM – ***Iōatham*** [masc. name: Ἰωάθαμ <2488>]**: Jehovah is perfect, in Heb. ► Name of a king of Judah (Jotham, son of Uzziah, or Azariah: 2 Kgs. 15:32, 33); also transl.: Joatham >** Jotham is mentioned in the genealogy of Jesus Christ (Matt. 1:9a, b). ¶

JOURNEY (noun) – [1] ***hodos*** [fem. noun: ὁδός <3598>] **► Travel, voyage >** The friend of a man had come to him on his journey (Luke 11:6). All other refs.: WAY <3598>.

[2] ***hodoiporia*** [fem. noun: ὁδοιπορία <3597>]**; from *hodoiporeō*: see [3] ► Same as [1]. >** Being wearied from His journey {the way he had come}, Jesus sat by the well of Sychar (John 4:6). Paul had been on frequent journeys (2 Cor. 11:26). ¶

[3] **to go on one's journey: *hodoiporeō*** [verb: ὁδοιπορέω <3596>]**; from *hodoiporos*: traveler, which is from *hodos*: road, way, and *poros*: passage ► To travel; to be a traveler, especially on foot >** The verb is used in Acts 10:9 {to journey, to be on one's way, to be on one's journey}. ¶

[4] **to have a prosperous journey: *euodoō*** [verb: εὐοδόω <2137>]**; from *euodos*: easy to travel, which is from *eu*: well, and *hodos*: journey; lit.: to allow a good journey ► To be granted a successful opportunity further to a travel >** Paul was praying that he might have a prosperous journey {he might find a way, prosper, succeed; the way might be opened} to come to the Christians in Rome (Rom. 1:10). Other refs.: 1 Cor. 16:2; 3 John 2a, b; see PROSPER <2137>. ¶

[5] **to bring on one's journey: *propempō*** [verb: προπέμπω <4311>]**; from *pro*: before, and *pempō*: to send ► To help (in view of a voyage), to provide (for the needs of someone) >** Titus was to diligently bring on their journey {send, set forward on their way, help on their way} Zenas the lawyer and Apollos (Titus 3:13). All other refs.: ACCOMPANY <4311>, SET (verb) <4311>, WAY <4311>.

[6] **away on a journey, taking a far journey: *apodēmos*** [adj.: ἀπόδημος <590>]**; from *apo*: away from, and *dēmos*: people, country ► Going on a voyage >** In a parable, a man taking a far journey {gone out of the country, gone away} gave authority to his servants and to each his work (Mark 13:34). ¶

– [7] Matt. 10:10; Mark 6:8; 10:17; Luke 2:44; 9:3; Acts 1:12 → WAY <3598> [8] Matt. 21:33; 25:14, 15; Mark 12:1; Luke 15:13; 20:9 → to go on a journey, etc. → COUNTRY <589> [9] Luke 10:33 → to be on a journey → JOURNEY (verb) <3593> [10] Acts 22:6; 26:12 → GO <4198> [11] Rom. 15:24 → on (in) my journey → lit.: in passing → PASS <1279>.

JOURNEY (verb) – [1] ***hodeuō*** [verb: ὁδεύω <3593>]; **from *hodos*: way, journey ▶ To go one's way, to travel** > In a parable, a certain Samaritan was journeying {was on a journey} (Luke 10:33). ¶

[2] **way: *poreia*** [fem. noun: πορεία <4197>]; **from *poreuomai*: to go ▶ Voyage, journey** > Jesus was journeying {proceeding on His way} (lit.: making His way) toward Jerusalem (Luke 13:22). Other ref.: Jas. 1:11; see PURSUIT <4197>. ¶

[3] ***poieō*** [verb: ποιέω <4160>] ▶ **To make (one's way), to proceed (on one's way)** > Jesus journeyed to Jerusalem (Luke 13:22). Other refs.: see entries in Lexicon at <4160>.

– [4] Luke 13:33 → WALK <4198> [5] Acts 9:3; 22:5, 6; 26:13 → GO <4198> [6] Acts 9:7 → to journey with → to travel with → TRAVEL <4922> [7] Acts 10:9 → to go on one's journey → JOURNEY (noun) <3596> [8] Acts 17:1 → to journey through → to pass through → PASS <1353>.

JOURNEYING – John 4:6; 2 Cor. 11:26 → JOURNEY (noun) <3597>.

JOY (noun) – [1] ***agalliasis*** [fem. noun: ἀγαλλίασις <20>]; **from *agalliaō*: to rejoice greatly, which is from *agan*, and *hallomai*: to leap ▶ Exuberant joy, exultation; also transl.: elation, exultation, great joy, gladness** > John the Baptist leaped with joy in the womb of his mother (Luke 1:44). The disciples received their food with gladness (Acts 2:46). God anointed Jesus with the oil of joy above His companions (Heb. 1:9). God is able to present the Christians before His glorious presence faultless with exceeding joy {exultation} (Jude 24). Other ref.: Luke 1:14; see GLADNESS <20>. ¶

[2] ***euphrosunē*** [fem. noun: εὐφροσύνη <2167>]; **from *euphrōn*: cheerful, which is from *eu*: well, and *phrēn*: mind ▶ Joyfulness, gladness** > David said that God would fill him with joy (Acts 2:28). God filled the hearts of men with food and joy (Acts 14:17). ¶

[3] ***chara*** [fem. noun: χαρά <5479>]; **from *chairō*: to rejoice; the word *charis* (grace) is also derived from *chairō* ▶ Gladness, delight** > This term is used in regard to the wise men (Matt. 2:10), he who hears the word of God (Matt. 13:20; Luke 8:13), a man who finds a treasure hidden in a field (Matt. 13:44), a good and faithful servant (Matt. 25:21, 23), women at the tomb of Jesus (Matt. 28:8), people who have heard the word (Mark 4:16), John the Baptist (Luke 1:14; John 3:29), the shepherds (Luke 2:10), the seventy disciples of Jesus (Luke 10:17), a repenting sinner (Luke 15:7, 10), the disciples of Jesus (Luke 24:41, 52; John 15:11b; 16:20, 22, 24; Acts 13:52), the joy of Jesus (John 15:11a; 17:13), a woman who has given birth (John 16:21), a city of Samaria (Acts 8:8), Rhoda (Acts 12:14), brothers (Acts 15:3), the kingdom of God (Rom. 14:17), the God of hope (Rom. 15:13), and Paul and the Romans (Rom. 15:32). This term is found frequently in the epistles of Paul: to the Corinthians (2 Cor. 1:24; 2:3; 7:4, 13; 8:2), to the Galatians (Gal. 5:22), to the Philippians (Phil. 1:4, 25; 2:2, 29; 4:1), to the Colossians (Col. 1:11), to the Thessalonians (1 Thes. 1:6; 2:19, 20; 3:9), to Timothy (2 Tim. 1:4), and to the Hebrews (Heb. 10:34; 12:2, 11; 13:17, assuming Paul wrote this epistle). James also uses this term (Jas. 1:2; 4:9), as well as Peter (1 Pet. 1:8) and John (1 John 1:4; 2 John 12; 3 John 4). ¶

[4] ***charis*** [fem. noun: χάρις <5485>]; **from *chairō*: to rejoice ▶ Gladness, thankfulness** > Paul had great joy {thankfulness} in the love of Philemon (Phm. 7). Other refs.: see entries in Lexicon at <5485>.

[5] **to leap for joy: *skirtaō*** [verb: σκιρτάω <4640>]; **comp. *skairō*: to leap ▶ To jump for joy** > The disciples of Jesus were to leap for joy when they suffered at the hands of

men (Luke 6:23). Other refs.: Luke 1:41, 44; see LEAP <4640>. ¶

– 6 Luke 1:58; Phil. 2:17, 18 → to share one's joy → REJOICE <4796> 7 Luke 10:21; Acts 16:34 → to be full of joy, to be filled with joy → REJOICE <21> 8 Rom. 16:19; 2 Cor. 2:3; 7:7; et al. → to be full of joy, to have joy, etc. → REJOICE <5463> 9 Gal. 4:15 → all the joy → BLESSEDNESS <3108> 10 Gal. 4:27 → to shout for joy → to break forth → BREAK <4486> 11 Phil. 1:26 → BOAST (noun) <2745> 12 Phm. 20 → to have joy → BENEFIT <3685> 13 1 Pet. 4:13 → with exceeding joy → lit.: in exulting → EXULTATION <21>.

JOY (verb) – 2 Cor. 7:13; Col. 2:5; et al. → REJOICE <5463>.

JOYFUL – Col. 1:12 → "joyful" added in Engl.

JOYFULLY – 1 Luke 15:5; 19:6 → REJOICE <5463> 2 Rom. 7:22 → to joyfully concur → DELIGHT (verb) <4913>.

JUDA – See JUDAH.

JUDAH – 1 ***Iouda*** [masc. name: Ἰούδα <2448>]: **praise, in Heb. ▶ Region of southern Palestine; also transl.: Juda, Judea** > Mary went to a city of Judah (Luke 1:39). ¶

2 ***Ioudas*** [masc. name: Ἰούδας <2455>]: **praise, in Heb.; see Gen. 29:35; 49:8 ▶ a. Son of Jacob and name of one of the twelve tribes descended from him** > Judah is mentioned in the genealogy of Jesus Christ (Matt. 1:2, 3; Luke 3:33). The city of Bethlehem was situated in the territory of Judah (Matt. 2:6). The Lord descended from the tribe of Judah (Heb. 7:14). Twelve thousand out of the tribe of Judah will be sealed (Rev. 7:5). **b. Name of two other men of the O.T.** > They are mentioned in the genealogy of Jesus (Luke 3:26; 3:30). See JUDAS <2455>.

JUDAISM – ***Ioudaismos*** [masc. noun: Ἰουδαϊσμός <2454>]; **from *Iouda*: Judah ▶ Religious system based on the law of Moses, to which the Jews had added traditional practices** > Paul speaks of his behavior in Judaism before his conversion as well as of his progress in Judaism {the Jews' religion} (Gal. 1:13, 14). ¶

JUDAIZE – ***ioudaizō*** [verb: ἰουδαΐζω <2450>]; **from *Ioudaios*: Jewish ▶ To impose Jewish customs and ways; also transl.: to live like Jews, to follow Jewish customs** > Paul had reproved Peter who compelled the nations to Judaize (Gal. 2:14), i.e., to adopt Jewish religious practices tainted with traditions (see Mark 7:3–9). ¶

JUDAS – ***Ioudas*** [masc. name: Ἰούδας <2455>]: **form of Judah, in Heb. ▶ a. One of the brothers of Jesus** > Judas is mentioned in Matt. 13:55; Mark 6:3. This Judas was probably the author of the book that bears his name (Jude 1). **b. The brother of James and prob. the same as Lebbaeus surnamed Thaddaeus (Matt. 10:3; Mark 3:18)** > This Judas was one of the twelve apostles (Luke 6:16a; John 14:22; Acts 1:13). **c. Disciple of Jesus** > Judas Iscariot was one of the twelve disciples of Jesus (Matt. 26:14, 47; Mark 14:10, 43; Luke 22:47; John 12:4). He was the disciple who had the money bag (John 13:29), but he was a thief (see John 12:6). We read that the devil had put it into his heart to betray Jesus (John 13:2), and that Satan entered into him (Luke 22:3). He betrayed Jesus (Matt. 10:4; 26:25; Mark 3:19; Luke 6:16; 22:48; John 6:71; 13:26; 18:2, 3, 5; Acts 1:16) for thirty pieces of silver (see Matt. 26:15). Filled with remorse, Judas brought back the thirty pieces of silver and confessed that he had sinned by betraying innocent blood; he went away and hanged himself (Matt. 27:3–5). Matthias replaced Judas as an apostle (Acts 1:25; see v. 26). **d. Believing man of Jerusalem** > This Judas is mentioned in Acts 15:22, 27, 32; see BARSABBAS <923>. **e. Inhabitant of Damascus** > Saul of Tarsus stayed with this Judas (Acts 9:11). **f. Man of Galilee** > Judas of Galilee led many people after him in revolt; he perished in the revolt (Acts 5:37). ¶

JUDE – See JUDAS b. <2455>.

JUDEA – [1] ***Ioudaia*** [fem. name: Ἰουδαία <2449>] ▶ **Region of southern Palestine, west of the Dead Sea and the Jordan River; Judea corresponds to the territory assigned to the tribe of Judah** > Bethlehem (Matt. 2:1) and Jerusalem (3:5) are located in Judea. Large crowds from Judea followed Jesus (Matt. 4:25; Mark 3:7). There were several churches in Judea (Acts 9:31; 10:37; Gal. 1:22; 1 Thes. 2:14). Paul solicited the prayers of the saints that he might be delivered from the unbelievers in Judea (Rom. 15:31). *
– [2] See JUDAH <2448>.

JUDGE (noun) – [1] ***dikastēs*** [masc. noun: δικαστής <1348>]**; from *dikazō*: to render a judgment, which is from *dikē*: justice ▶ He who administers justice** > Jesus said He had not come to be a judge in matters of this world (Luke 12:14); other mss. have [2]. An Israelite asked Moses who had established him ruler and judge over them (Acts 7:27, 35). ¶
[2] ***kritēs*** [masc. noun: κριτής <2923>]**; from *krinō*: to decide, to judge ▶ He who pronounces a judgment on something, on an individual; he dispenses justice and applies laws** > Jesus is established by God as judge of the living and the dead (Acts 10:42). This term is also used in regard to Him elsewhere (Matt. 5:25a, b; Luke 12:58a, b; 18:2, 6; 2 Tim. 4:8; Jas. 4:12 in some mss.; 5:9), the sons of the Jews (Matt. 12:27; Luke 11:19), the judges under the law (Acts 13:20), Gallio (Acts 18:15), Felix (Acts 24:10), God (Heb. 12:23), those who discriminate between men coming into their synagogue (Jas. 2:4), and he who judges the law (Jas. 4:11). ¶
– [3] 1 Cor. 6:4 → to appoint as judge → JUDGE (verb) <2523>.

JUDGE (verb) – [1] ***krinō*** [verb: κρίνω <2919>] ▶ **To deliver a judgment, to render a verdict, to decide; also transl.: to condemn** > This verb is used in relation to Jesus (Matt. 7:1a, b, 2a, b; 19:28; Luke 6:37a, b; 7:43; 12:57; 22:30; John 3:17, 18a, b; 5:22, 30; 7:24a, b, 51; 8:15a, b, 16, 26, 50; 12:47a, b, 48a, b; 16:11), God (Acts 7:7), the master of a servant (Luke 19:22), Pilate (John 18:31), Peter and John (Acts 4:19), Paul and Barnabas (Acts 13:46), Lydia (Acts 16:15), Paul (Acts 13:27; 17:31; 23:3; 25:10; 26:8; Rom. 2:1a–c, 3, 12, 16, 27; 3:4, 6, 7; 14:3, 4, 10, 13a, b, 22; 1 Cor. 2:2; 4:5; 5:3, 12a, b, 13; 6:2a, b, 3; 10:15, 29 {to judge}; 11:13, 31b, 32; 2 Cor. 2:1; 5:14; Col. 2:16; 2 Thes. 2:12; 2 Tim. 4:1; Heb. 10:30; 13:4), Tertullus (Acts 24:6), Festus (Acts 25:9, 20), James (Jas. 2:12; 4:11a–c, 12), Peter (1 Pet. 1:17; 2:23; 4:5, 6), the souls of martyrs (Rev. 6:10), the twenty-four elders (Rev. 11:18), the angel of the waters (Rev. 16:5), a voice out of the heaven (Rev. 18:8, 20), a loud voice of a great multitude (Rev. 19:2), and John (Rev. 19:11; 20:12, 13). All other refs.: see entries in Lexicon at <2919>.
[2] ***anakrinō*** [verb: ἀνακρίνω <350>]**; from *ana*: going back (to the evidence) (intens.), and *krinō*: see [1] ▶ To investigate, to scrutinize; also transl.: to examine** > Paul uses this verb in 1 Cor. 4:3a, b, 4; 14:24. All other refs.: ASK <350>, DISCERN <350>, EXAMINE <350>, SEARCH (verb) <350>.
[3] ***diakrinō*** [verb: διακρίνω <1252>]**; from *dia*: indicates separation, and *krinō*; see [1] ▶ To examine; also transl.: to come under judgment, to pass judgment, to weigh carefully, to judge rightly, to judge truly** > Paul said to the shame of the Corinthians that there was not a wise man among them who would be able to judge {decide} between his brothers (1 Cor. 6:5). He also uses this verb in 1 Cor. 11:31a; 14:29. All other refs.: see entries in Lexicon at <1252>.
[4] ***hēgeomai*** [verb: ἡγέομαι <2233>]**; from *agō*: to lead ▶ To think, to believe** > Sarah judged {counted, considered} God faithful who had promised (Heb. 11:11). All other refs.: see entries in Lexicon at <2233>.
[5] **to appoint to judge: *kathizō*** [verb: καθίζω <2523>]**; from *kata*: down (intens.), and *hizō*: to sit ▶ To put**

in place, to designate > Paul tells the Christians of Corinth to appoint to judge {set to judge, appoint as judges} those who are less esteemed by the church (1 Cor. 6:4). All other refs.: CONTINUE <2523>, SIT <2523>, TARRY <2523>.

6 ***katakrinō*** [verb: κατακρίνω <2632>]; **from *kata*: against (intens.), and *krinō*: see 1 ▶ To pass a judgment, to condemn** > Christians should not complain one against the other, so that they may not be judged (Jas. 5:9). All other refs.: CONDEMN <2632>.

– 7 Luke 12:56a → DISCERN <1381> 8 Luke 17:9 → THINK <1380> 9 John 5:24 → to be judged → lit.: to come into judgment → COME <2064>, JUDGMENT <2920> 10 John. 5:27 → lit.: to do judgment → DO <4160> JUDGMENT <2920> 11 1 Cor. 6:2 → JUDGMENT SEAT <2922> 12 2 Cor. 10:7 → to judge by appearances → to look at what concerns appearance → LOOK (verb) <991> 13 Heb. 4:12 → able to judge, to judge → DISCERNER <2924> 14 Jas. 5:9 → CONDEMN <2632> 15 Rev. 18:20 → lit.: to judge the cause → CAUSE <2917>.

JUDGE'S SEAT – Matt. 27:19; John 19:13 → JUDGMENT SEAT <968>.

JUDGMENT – 1 ***gnōmē*** [fem. noun: γνώμη <1106>]; **from *ginōskō*: to know, to understand, to discern ▶ Thought, decision; also transl.: opinion** > Paul was pleading with the Corinthians to be joined together in the same judgment (1 Cor. 1:10). According to Paul's judgment, the believing widow is happier if she remains as she is (1 Cor. 7:40). All other refs.: ADVICE <1106>, MIND (noun) <1106>, OPINION <1106>, PURPOSE (verb) <1106>.

2 **righteous judgment: *dikaiokrisia*** [fem. noun: δικαιοκρισία <1341>]; **from *dikaios*: just, and *krisis*: judgment ▶ Judgment that results in justice** > Paul speaks of the day of wrath and the revelation of the righteous judgment of God (Rom. 2:5). ¶

3 ***dikē*** [fem. noun: δίκη <1349>]; **lit.: justice ▶ Condemnation, punishment** > The chief priests and elders had asked for a judgment {sentence of condemnation, charges} against Paul (Acts 25:15; other mss.: *katadikē*). Sodom, Gomorrah, and the cities around them are set forth as examples, undergoing the judgment {vengeance} of eternal fire (Jude 7). Other refs.: 2 Thes. 1:9; see PUNISHMENT <1349>; Acts 28:4: see JUSTICE <1349>. ¶

4 ***krima*** [neut. noun: κρίμα <2917>]; ***krisis*** [fem. noun: κρίσις <2920>]; **from *krinō*: to decide, to judge ▶ a. Both words relate to a tribunal, when men appear before the judge** > Judgment is reserved after death (Heb. 9:27). The Scriptures do not speak of a general judgment at which all humanity will be judged. The Scriptures declare that the Christian will not come into judgment, but that he has passed out of death to life (John 5:24). He must appear before the judgment seat of Christ (see Rom. 14:10; 2 Cor. 5:10); he will not be judged for his sins, because Christ was judged for them, but each one must give account for himself and be manifested before Christ. Other ref.: Luke 11:31. **b. Sentence, decision taken by a judge; also transl.: condemnation, damnation, punishment** > Those who devour the houses of widows will receive a more severe judgment (Mark 12:40; Luke 20:47). The chief priests and the rulers delivered Jesus to the judgment {sentence, condemnation} of death {to be condemned, to be sentenced to death} (Luke 24:20). An angel would show John the judgment of the great prostitute (Rev. 17:1). **c. Action of executing judgments** > This may be of a temporal character as in the case of the judgments in Revelation. It may also be a matter of the final and eternal lot of Satan and the wicked (Heb. 6:2; see Rev. 20:10, 15). (After Walter Scott.) Other refs.: Matt. 5:21, 22; 7:2; 10:15; 11:22, 24; 12:18, 20, 36, 41, 42; 23:14 in some mss., 23, 33; Mark 3:29; 6:11; Luke 5:27; 10:14; 11:32, 42; 23:40; John 3:19; 5:22, 27, 29, 30; 7:24; 8:16; 9:39; 12:31; 16:8, 11; Acts 8:33; 24:25; Rom. 2:2, 3; 3:8; 5:16; 11:33; 13:2; 1 Cor. 6:7; 11:29, 34; Gal. 5:10; 2 Thes. 1:5; 1 Tim. 3:6; 5:12, 24; Heb. 10:27; Jas. 2:13a, b; 3:1; 5:12; 1 Pet. 4:17; 2 Pet. 2:3, 4, 9, 11; 3:7; 1 John 4:17; Jude 4, 6, 9, 15; Rev.

14:7; 16:7; 18:10, 20; 19:2; 20:4. All other refs.: CAUSE <2917>, FAULT <2917>, LAWSUIT <2917>.

5 ***kritērion*** [neut. noun: κριτήριον <2922>]; **from *kritēs*: he who decides, judge, which is from *krinō*: to judge ▶ Subject of controversy, lawsuit, case** > Paul spoke of those who have judgments {disputes, law courts} as to things of this life (1 Cor. 6:4). Other refs.: 1 Cor. 6:2; Jas. 2:6; see JUDGMENT SEAT <2922>. ¶

6 **to be judged: *krinō*** [verb: κρίνω <2919>] **▶ To stand for trial, to be brought into judgment** > This verb is used in Acts 23:6; 24:21; 26:6. All other refs.: see entries in Lexicon at <2919>.

7 **to have sound judgment, to have sober judgment: *sōphroneō*** [verb: σωφρονέω <4993>]; **from *sōphron*: sober-minded, which is from *sōos*: sound, and *phrēn*: mind, understanding ▶ To behave wisely, reasonably** > Paul says to think so as to have sound judgment {so as to be wise, soberly, with sober judgment} (Rom. 12:3). All other refs.: MIND (noun) <4993>, SELF-CONTROLLED <4993>, THINK <4993>.

– 8 Matt. 26:66 → what is your judgment? → what do you think? → THINK <1380> 9 Acts 18:12 → place of judgment → JUDGMENT SEAT <968> 10 Rom. 3:19 → under judgment → GUILTY <5267> 11 Rom. 14:1 → passing judgment → DISPUTE (noun) <1253> 12 1 Cor. 2:15a → to make judgments, to be subject to judgment → DISCERN <350> 13 1 Cor. 4:3a, b, 4; 4:14 → to come under judgment, to pass judgment, to be brought under judgment → JUDGE (verb) <350> 14 1 Cor. 9:3 → to sit on judgment → EXAMINE <350> 15 Phil. 1:9 → depth of insight → DISCERNMENT <144> 16 Jude 9 → railing judgment → BLASPHEMY <988>.

JUDGMENT SEAT – 1 ***bēma*** [neut. noun: βῆμα <968>]; **from *bainō*: to go; lit.: step ▶ Place where justice is dispensed, tribunal; also transl.: court, judge's seat** > Jesus appeared before the judgment seat of Pilate (Matt. 27:19; John 19:13). Paul was brought before the judgment seat of Gallio (Acts 18:12, 16) and that of Festus (25:6, 10, 17). Sosthenes was beaten before the judgment seat of Gallio (Acts 18:17). All men will stand before the judgment seat of God {of Christ, in some mss.} (Rom. 14:10); Christians will not be judged, because Jesus Christ has suffered the judgment of God in their place at the cross. Nevertheless, the works of Christians will be judged when they will be manifested before the judgment seat of Christ, so that they may receive the reward for their faithfulness; they will suffer a loss in respect to anything that has not been done for the Lord and His glory during their life (2 Cor. 5:10; see 1 Cor. 3:15). All other refs.: GROUND (noun)[1] <968>, THRONE <968>.

2 ***kritērion*** [neut. noun: κριτήριον <2922>]; **from *kritēs*: he who decides, judge, which is from *krinō*: to judge ▶ See defin. in 1; also transl.: court, law court, tribunal** > Paul asks if the saints are not competent to constitute the smallest law courts {unworthy to judge the smallest matters, unworthy of the smallest judgments, not competent to judge trivial cases} (1 Cor. 6:2). The rich drag those whom they oppress before the judgment seats (Jas. 2:6). Other ref.: 1 Cor. 6:4; see JUDGMENT <2922>. ¶

JULIA – ***Ioulia*** [fem. name: Ἰουλία <2456>]; **fem. of Julius ▶ Christian woman of Rome** > Paul sends his greetings to Julia (Rom. 16:15). Other ref.: Rom. 16:7 in some mss. rather than Junia (or Junias, a masc. name). ¶

JULIUS – ***Ioulios*** [masc. name: Ἰούλιος <2457>] **▶ Centurion of the cohort of Augustus** > Paul and other prisoners were delivered up to Julius (Acts 27:1). He treated Paul with consideration and allowed him to go to his friends (v. 3). ¶

JUMP – 1 **to jump up: *anapēdaō*** [verb: ἀναπηδάω <375a>]; **from *ana*: up (intens.), and *pēdaō*: to dash forward, to jump ▶ To rise up with a bound** > Bartimaeus jumped up {jumped to his feet, rose, started up} and came to Jesus (Mark 10:50). ¶

– [2] Acts 3:8 → to jump to one's feet → STAND (verb) <2476> [3] Acts 3:8a → to leap up → LEAP <1814> [4] Acts 3:8b; 14:10 → LEAP <242> [5] Acts 19:16 → LEAP <2177> [6] Acts 27:43 → CAST (verb) <641>.

JUNIAS – ***Iounias*** [masc. name: Ἰουνιᾶς <2458>] **► Christian man of Rome; also transl.: Junia, a fem. name** > In his letter to the Christians of Rome, Paul greets Andronicus and Junias, his kinsmen and former fellow prisoners (Rom. 16:7); some mss. have Julia, a fem. name, rather than Junias. ¶

JUPITER – See ZEUS <2203>.

JURISDICTION – [1] ***exousia*** [fem. noun: ἐξουσία <1849>]; **from *exesti*: it is permissible, which is from *ek*: out, and *eimi*: to be ► Right to exercise justice; authority of an individual over the inhabitants of a region** > Jesus was Galilean, of the jurisdiction of Herod (Luke 23:7). All other refs.: AUTHORITY <1849>.

– [2] Rom. 7:1 → to have jurisdiction → to have dominion → DOMINION <2961>.

JUST (adj.) – [1] ***endikos*** [adj.: ἔνδικος <1738>]; **from *en*: in, and *dikē*: justice, righteousness ► In accordance with what is right, according to justice** > Every transgression and disobedience to the word of angels received just retribution (Heb. 2:2). The condemnation of some evil men is just (Heb. 3:8). ¶

– [2] Matt. 5:45; 13:49; 23:29; Luke 1:17; 14:14; Rom. 2:13; 1 Tim. 1:9 et al. → RIGHTEOUS <1342> [3] Matt. 8:8; 14:36; Mark 5:36; Luke 8:50; John 13:9; Gal. 3:2; 4:18 → ONLY <3440> [4] Luke 7:29 → to declare just → JUSTIFY <1344> [5] Luke 23:41 → DESERVING <514> [6] Acts 18:2 → RECENTLY <4373> [7] Rom. 2:26 → just requirement → REQUIREMENT <1345> [8] 2 Tim. 3:8 → just as → in like manner as → MANNER <5158> [9] Rev. 16:6 → it is their just due → they are worthy → WORTHY <514>.

JUST (adv.) – ***oligōs*** [adv.: ὀλίγως <3643a>]; **from *oligos*: few, little ► Almost not; also transl.: barely** > Peter mentions those who just escape from the ones who live in error (2 Pet. 2:18). ¶

JUST AS – See WHOLLY AS <5618>.

JUSTICE (name) – ***Dikē*** [fem. name: Δίκη <1349>]: **Justice ► Personification of divine justice among the Greeks; also transl.: vengeance, Nemesis, the goddess Justice** > The barbarians of the island of Malta believed that Paul, after having been saved from a shipwreck, was a murderer whom Justice punished by means of a viper (Acts 28:4); but Paul shook the creature off into the fire and suffered no harm (see Acts 28:1–6). All other refs.: see JUDGMENT <1349>, PUNISHMENT <1349>.

JUSTICE (noun) – [1] ***ekdikēsis*** [fem. noun: ἐκδίκησις <1557>]; **from *ekdikeō*: see [2] ► Retribution, act of obtaining justice after a wrong committed** > God will bring about justice for {will avenge} His elect (Luke 18:7, 8). All other refs.: PUNISHMENT <1557>, VENGEANCE <1557>.

[2] **to give justice, to see that one gets justice: *ekdikeō*** [verb: ἐκδικέω <1556>]; **from *ekdikos*: avenger, which is from *ek*: out, and *dikē*: justice ► To render justice, to avenge** > A judge was going to give justice {to avenge, to give legal protection} to a widow (Luke 18:5). All other refs.: AVENGE <1556>.

– [3] Luke 18:3 → to get justice from, to grant justice against → AVENGE <1556> [4] Heb. 1:8 → RIGHTEOUSNESS <2118>.

JUSTIFICATION – [1] ***dikaiōma*** [neut. noun: δικαίωμα <1345>]; **from *dikaioō*: to justify, which is from *dikaios*: just, righteous, which is from *dikē*: justice ► Result of being justified, acquittal** > The free gift of God's grace was in justification (Rom. 5:16). All other refs.: ORDINANCE <1345>, REQUIREMENT <1345>, RIGHTEOUS <1345>.

[2] ***dikaiōsis*** [fem. noun: δικαίωσις <1347>]; **from *dikaioō*: see [1] ► Acquittal of an**

individual from all charges that could weigh on him > He is then considered as being without fault. In His death, Jesus Christ has accomplished all that was necessary for our justification (Rom. 5:18). God has made this manifest by raising the Lord from among the dead for the justification of those who would believe (Rom. 4:25). ¶
– 3 Acts 13:39 → to obtain justification → to be justified → JUSTIFY <1344>.

JUSTIFIER – Rom. 3:26 → lit.: one who justifies → JUSTIFY <1344>.

JUSTIFY – 1 ***dikaioō*** [verb: δικαιόω <1344>]; **from *dikaios*: just, righteous, which is from *dikē*: justice ▶ To render just, righteous by acquitting an individual from all charges that could weigh on him or her; also transl.: to free, to consider righteous, to declare righteous, to practice righteousness, to vindicate** > Before God, man is justified freely by divine grace (Rom. 3:24), by faith without works of law (v. 28); it is God who justifies (Rom. 8:33). Fulfilling the law of Moses or works of the law cannot justify a man before God (Acts 13:39 {to obtain justification}; Rom. 2:13; 3:20; 4:2; Gal. 2:16; 3:11; 5:4). The man who has died is justified from sin (Rom. 6:7) by the grace of God, by faith in Jesus Christ (Acts 13:39; Rom. 3:24, 26, 28; 5:1, 9; 1 Cor. 6:11; Gal. 2:16, 17; 3:24; Titus 3:7). It is God who justifies (Rom. 3:30; 4:5; 8:30a, b; Gal. 3:8). In James 2, Abraham (vv. 21, 24) and Rahab (v. 25) were justified by their works which proved their faith (see v. 18). Other refs.: Matt. 11:19 {to prove}; 12:37; Luke 7:29 {to acknowledge}, 35; 10:29; 16:15; 18:14; Rom. 3:4 {to prove right}; 1 Cor. 4:4 {to acquit, to make innocent}; 1 Tim. 3:16; Rev. 22:11. ¶
– 2 Acts 19:40 → lit.: to give an account, a reason → REASON (noun) <3056>.

JUSTLY – 1 ***dikaiōs*** [adv.: δικαίως <1346>]; **from *dikaios*: just, righteous, which is from *dikē*: justice ▶ In a manner corresponding to that which is upright, just; also transl.: righteously, uprightly** > One of the malefactors at the cross acknowledged that he was justly under judgment (Luke 23:41). Paul exhorts the Corinthians to awake to righteousness {to become sober-minded, to come back to their senses} (lit.: to awake up righteously; 1 Cor. 15:34). He had conducted himself justly among the Thessalonians (1 Thes. 2:10). We are taught to live righteously in this present age (Titus 2:12). Christ committed Himself to Him who judges righteously (1 Pet. 2:23). ¶
– 2 Col. 4:1 → to treat justly → to give what is righteous → RIGHTEOUS <1342>.

JUSTUS – ***Ioustos*** [masc. name: Ἰοῦστος <2459>]: **just ▶ a. Surname of Joseph, called Barsabbas** > Joseph, surnamed Justus, was proposed to replace Judas (Acts 1:23). **b. Man who served God and whose house was next to the synagogue** > Paul lodged at the home of this Justus (Acts 18:7); other mss.: Titius Justus. **c. Surname of a man called Jesus** > Ref.: Col. 4:11. ¶

K

KANDAKE – Acts 8:27 → CANDACE <2582>.

KEEP (noun) – Matt. 10:10 → FOOD <5160>.

KEEP (verb) – [1] **to wrongfully keep back, to keep back by fraud: *apostereō*** [verb: ἀποστερέω <650>]**; from *apo*: from, and *stereō*: to take away, to rob ▶ To deprive, to withhold fraudulently** > The wages of the laborers were wrongfully kept back by the rich (Jas. 5:4; other mss.: *aphustereō*). Other refs.: DEFRAUD <650>, DEPRIVE <650>.

[2] ***tērēō*** [verb: τηρέω <5083>]**; from *tēros*: warden, guard ▶ a. To watch over (in order to prevent from escaping)** > Guards kept the prison where Peter was (Acts 12:6). Paul and Silas were to be kept safely (Acts 16:23). **b. To look after carefully, to take care of, to preserve** > On earth, Jesus kept His own in the Father's name (John 17:12a). He asked His Father to keep those whom He has given to Him (John 17:11), to keep them from the evil (v. 15). Timothy was to keep himself pure (1 Tim. 5:22). Certain angels had not kept their original state (Jude 6a). **c. To conserve, to store** > The master of the feast thought that the good wine had been kept until the end of the wedding (John 2:10). Mary had kept the perfume for the day of Jesus's burial (John 12:7). He who has decided to keep his own virginity does well (1 Cor. 7:37). Christians are to keep the unity of the Spirit (Eph. 4:3). Paul had kept the faith (2 Tim. 4:7). Because the angel of Philadelphia had kept the word of the patience of the Lord, He would keep (i.e., shelter) him out of the hour of trial (Rev. 3:10a, b). The angel of Sardis is to remember how he received and heard, and keep it (i.e., to keep watch over himself), and repent (Rev. 3:3). **d. To practice, to observe** > Some of the Pharisees said that Jesus did not keep the Sabbath (John 9:16). **e. To detain, to watch; to reserve; also transl.: to keep, to keep in custody, to keep under guard** > Peter was kept in the prison (Acts 12:5). Felix ordered the centurion that Paul should be kept in custody (Acts 24:23). Festus answered that Paul should be kept at Caesarea (Acts 25:4, 21a, b). The angels who sinned are kept in chains of darkness for judgment (2 Pet. 2:4). The present heavens and the earth are kept for the day of judgment and destruction of ungodly men (2 Pet. 3:7). This verb is also used with "commandment," "thing commanded" (Matt. 19:17; 28:20; John 14:15, 21; 15:10a, b; 1 Tim. 6:14; 1 John 2:3; 3:22, 24; 5:2, 3; Rev. 12:17; 14:12), "law" (Acts 15:5, 24; Jas. 2:10), "work" (Rev. 2:26), "word" (John 8:51, 52, 55; 14:23, 24; 15:20a, b; 17:6; 1 John 2:5; Rev. 3:8; 22:7, 9), "things written" (Rev. 1:3), "tradition" (Mark 7:9), and "garments" (Rev. 16:15). All other refs.: see entries in Lexicon at <5083>.

[3] ***diatēreō*** [verb: διατηρέω <1301>]**; from *dia*: intens., and *tēreō*: see [2] ▶ To keep, to retain** > The mother of Jesus kept {treasured} all the things concerning Him in her heart (Luke 2:51). Other ref.: Acts 15:29; see BEWARE <1301>. ¶

[4] ***suntēreō*** [verb: συντηρέω <4933>]**; from *sun*: intens., and *tēreō*: see [2] ▶ a. To protect** > Herod kept John the Baptist safe (Mark 6:20). **b. To retain, to keep carefully** > Mary kept all the things that the shepherds had told her in her mind and pondered them in her heart (Luke 2:19). Other refs.: Matt. 9:17; Luke 5:38; see PRESERVE <4933>. ¶

[5] ***ginomai*** [verb: γίνομαι <1096>] **▶ To become, to happen, to arrive** > When Herod's birthday was kept {was celebrated, came} (lit.: had arrived), the daughter of Herodias danced (Matt. 14:6). Other ref.: Mark 4:22 {to be, to take place}. Other refs.: see entries in Lexicon at <1096>.

[6] **to keep, to keep back: *katechō*** [verb: κατέχω <2722>]**; from *kata*: down, and *echō*: to have ▶ To not let go, to prevent from leaving; also transl.: to hold, to hold fast, to hold on, to restrain, to retain** > The crowds would have kept Jesus back {would have stayed Him} to prevent Him from leaving (Luke 4:42). In a parable, some who heard the word kept it in an honest and good heart (Luke 8:15). Paul says to keep that which is good (1 Thes. 5:21). He would have liked to keep Onesimus with himself (Phm. 13). The author of Hebrews speaks of holding fast the boldness and the rejoicing of hope (Heb. 3:6), the beginning

of assurance (3:14), and the confession of hope (10:23). In 2 Thes. 2:6, that which restrains (or: "that which keeps back") (*to katechon*) corresponds to the church, i.e., to the presence of the redeemed Christians on earth; in v. 7, He who restrains (or: "He who keeps back") (*ho katechōn*) corresponds to the Holy Spirit. All other refs.: see entries in Lexicon at <2722>.

7 ***poieō*** [verb: ποιέω <4160>]; **lit.: to make ▶ To accomplish, to obey** > Every man who becomes circumcised is a debtor to keep {to do, to obey} the whole law (Gal. 5:3). Other refs.: see entries in Lexicon at <4160>.

8 ***prassō*** [verb: πράσσω <4238>] **▶ To accomplish, to observe** > Circumcision is profitable for the one who keeps {observes, practices} the law (Rom. 2:25). Other refs.: COLLECT <4238>, CONTRARY <4238>, DO <4238>, USE (verb) <4238>.

9 ***phulassō*** [verb: φυλάσσω <5442>] **▶ a. To observe, to practice** > A young man had kept the commandments (Matt. 19:20; Mark 10:20); Luke speaks of a certain ruler (Luke 18:21). Jesus kept those whom the Father had given Him (John 17:12). Timothy was to keep certain things without partiality (1 Tim. 5:21), which had been committed to his trust (1 Tim. 6:20), and, by the Holy Spirit, the good deposit entrusted (2 Tim. 1:14). This verb is also used with the nouns "law" (Acts 7:53; 21:24; Rom. 2:26; Gal. 6:13), "decree" (Acts 16:4), and "word" (Luke 11:28; John 12:47 in some mss.). **b. To look after, to oversee** > Shepherds were keeping watch over their flock when Jesus was born (Luke 2:8). The strong man, image of Satan, keeps his house (Luke 11:21). Peter was delivered to four squads of four soldiers each to keep him (Acts 12:4). Saul kept the clothes of those who killed Stephen (Acts 22:20). **c. To protect, to preserve** > He who hates his life in this world will keep it for eternal life (John 12:25). A soldier kept Paul in Rome (Acts 28:16). The Lord will keep Christians from evil (2 Thes. 3:3). God the Savior is able to keep Christians from stumbling (Jude 24). **d. To hold, to preserve, to save** > Jesus was able to keep the deposit that Paul had entrusted to Him (2 Tim. 1:12). **e. To watch, to pay attention** > A possessed man had been kept in chains (Luke 8:29). Felix commanded that Paul should be kept in Herod's Praetorium (Acts 23:35). All other refs.: GUARD (noun) <5442>, GUARD (verb) <5442>, PRESERVE <5442>.

10 **to keep away: *aphistēmi*** [verb: ἀφίστημι <868>]; **from *apo*: from, and *histēmi*: to stand, to hold oneself ▶ To refrain from occupying oneself (with some person or matter), to distance oneself** > Gamaliel said to keep away {refrain from, withdraw from, stay away from, leave alone} the apostles (Acts 5:38). All other refs.: DEPART <868>, REVOLT <868>.

11 ***krateō*** [verb: κρατέω <2902>]; **from *kratos*: power, strength ▶ To retain, to remember** > The disciples kept {seized upon} the word spoken by the Lord Jesus concerning the resurrection (Mark 9:10). All other refs.: FAST (HOLD) <2902>, GAIN (verb) <2902>, HOLD (verb) <2902>, SEIZE <2902>, TAKE <2902>.

12 **to keep back, to keep for oneself: *nosphizō*** [verb: νοσφίζω <3557>]; **from *nosphi*: aside, secretly ▶ To retain, to misappropriate for one's own profit** > Ananias and Sapphira kept back {put aside} part of the proceeds of the possession they had sold (Acts 5:2), and Peter reproached them (v. 3). The verb is transl. "to pilfer" {to rob, to steal} in Titus 2:10. ¶

13 **to keep back: *hupostellō*** [verb: ὑποστέλλω <5288>]; **from *hupo*: under, and *stellō*: to send ▶ To hide, to conceal** > Paul kept back nothing {held back nothing, did not shrink from anything, did not hesitate} to announce what was profitable to the elders in Ephesus (Acts 20:20). Other refs.: Acts 20:27; Gal. 2:12; Heb. 10:38; see SHRINK <5288>, WITHDRAW <5288>. ¶

– 14 Matt. 5:19; John 7:19 → PRACTICE (verb) <4160> 15 Matt. 8:33 → FEED <1006> 16 Mark 3:9 → to keep ready → READY <4342> 17 Mark 13:33 → to keep awake → WATCH (verb) <69> 18 Luke 1:66 → LAY <5087> 19 Luke 4:10 → GUARD (verb) <1314> 20 Luke 9:36 → to keep close, to keep quiet, to keep to oneself, to keep silence → to be silent → SILENT <4601> [21] Luke 17:7 → to keep sheep → SHEPHERD (verb) <4165> [22] Luke 17:33 → PURCHASE (verb) <4046> [23] Luke 19:20 → to keep put away, to keep laid → PUT <606> [24] Luke 19:43 → to keep in → to close in → CLOSE (verb) <4912> [25] Luke 20:20; Acts 9:24 → to keep a close watch → OBSERVE <3906> [26] John 8:7; Acts 12:16 → to keep on → CONTINUE <1961> [27] John 16:1 → to keep you from falling away → lit.: so that you would not be offended [28] Acts 5:42 → to keep right on → to not cease → CEASE <3973> [29] Acts 7:19 → to be kept alive → LIVE <2225> [30] Acts 9:33 → to keep one's bed → to be lying → BEDRIDDEN (BE) <2621> [31] Acts 10:28 → to keep company → COMPANY (noun) <2853> [32] Acts 10:47; 16:6; 27:43; 1 Thes. 2:16 → to keep from → FORBID <2967> [33] Acts 14:18 → RESTRAIN <2664> [34] Acts 20:7 → to keep on → PROLONG <3905> [35] Rom. 2:27; Gal. 5:16; Jas. 2:8 → FULFILL <5055> [36] Rom. 11:4 → RESERVE <2641> [37] Rom. 15:31 → to be kept safe → to be delivered → DELIVER <4506> [38] Rom. 16:17 → to keep one's eyes → CONSIDER <4648> [39] Rom. 16:17 → to keep away → AVOID <1578> [40] 1 Cor. 5:8 → to keep the feast → to celebrate the feast → FEAST (noun) <1858> [41] 1 Cor. 9:27 → to keep under control → to bring into subjection → SUBJECTION <1396> [42] 2 Cor. 4:4 → to keep them from seeing the light of the gospel → lest the light of the gospel should shine on them → SHINE <826> [43] 2 Cor. 11:32; Gal. 3:23; Phil. 4:7 → GUARD (verb) <5432> [44] Gal. 3:23 → to shut up → SHUT <4788> [45] Gal. 5:7 → to cut in and keep from → HINDER (verb) <348> [46] Gal. 5:14 → "keeping" added in Engl. [47] Phil. 3:17 → to keep one's eyes on → to fix one's eyes on → EYES <4648> [48] Jas. 4:11 → keeping → DOER <4163> [49] 1 Pet. 3:10 → REFRAIN <3973> [50] 2 Pet. 1:8 → to keep from → RENDER <2525> [51] 2 Pet. 3:7 → RESERVE <2343>.

KEEPER – [1] Matt. 28:4 → GUARD (noun) <5083> [2] Acts 5:23; 12:6, 19 → GUARD (noun) <5441> [3] Acts 19:35 → temple keeper → temple guardian → GUARDIAN <3511>.

KEEPING – [1] ***tērēsis*** [fem. noun: τήρησις <5084>]; **from *tēreō*: to keep watch, to observe a commandment ▶ Compliance with a requirement; observance >** In 1 Cor. 7:19, the keeping of God's commandments has the meaning of strict compliance with them. Other refs.: Acts 4:3; 5:18; see PRISON <5084>. ¶

– [2] Matt. 3:8; Luke 3:8 → in keeping with → WORTHY <514> [3] Acts 26:20 → in keeping → MEET (adj.) <514> [4] Rom. 16:25 → in keeping with → lit.: according (*kata*) to.

KERNEL – 1 Cor. 15:37 → GRAIN OF WHEAT <2848>.

KETTLE – Mark 7:4 → BRAZEN VESSEL <5473>.

KEY – ***kleis*** [fem. noun: κλείς <2807>]; **akin to *kleiō*: to shut ▶ Instrument to operate a lock, thus to open or close >** The term is used metaphorically in the N.T. Jesus would give Peter the keys of the kingdom of heaven (Matt. 16:19). He reproaches the lawyers of having taken away the keys of knowledge (Luke 11:52). The Lord Jesus has the keys of Hades and of Death (Rev. 1:18); He has the key of David (3:7). The key of the bottomless pit was given to the fifth angel (Rev. 9:1); he had the key to the bottomless pit and a great chain in his hand (20:1). ¶

KICK – ***laktizō*** [verb: λακτίζω <2979>]; **from *lax*: with the foot; lit.: to deliver a blow with the foot ▶ To rebel, to resist >** The Lord told Paul that it was hard for him to kick against the goads (Acts 26:14). Other ref.: Acts 9:5 in some mss. ¶

KID – Luke 15:29 → GOAT <2056>.

KIDNAPPER – ***andrapodistēs*** [masc. noun: ἀνδραποδιστής <405>]; **from *andrapodizō*: to enslave, which is from *andra-***

***podon*: slave, which is from *anēr*: man, and *pous*: foot ► One who steals men, most likely to make them slaves** > The law is for kidnappers {menstealers, slave traders} (1 Tim. 1:10). ¶

KIDRON – ***Kedrōn*** [masc. name: Κεδρών <2748>]: **dark, confused, in Heb. ► Ravine where a brook flowed east of Jerusalem, separating the city from the Mount of Olives** > The garden where Jesus went, on the night He was betrayed, was beyond the brook Kidron (John 18:1); other mss. have: of the cedar tree(s) (*kedros*). ¶

KILL – 1 ***anaireō*** [verb: ἀναιρέω <337>]; **from *ana*: intens., and *haireō*: to take ► To take life away; also transl.: to put to death, to slay** > Herod gave orders to kill all the children who were in Bethlehem and its vicinity, from two years of age and under (Matt. 2:16). An Israelite asked Moses if he wanted to kill him as he had killed the Egyptian (Acts 7:28a, b). Certain Jews wanted to kill Paul (Acts 9:23 {to do away}, 24; 23:15, 27; 25:3). The jailer was going to kill himself (Acts 16:27). Paul kept the clothes of those who killed Stephen (Acts 22:20). The verb is used regarding the Lord Jesus (Luke 22:2 {to get rid of}; Acts 10:39; 13:28 {to execute}), Stephen (Acts 5:33), Paul (Acts 9:29), James (Acts 12:2), and Christians (Acts 26:10). Other refs.: Acts 5:36; 23:21. All other refs.: DEATH <337>, TAKE <337>.

2 ***apokteinō*** [verb: ἀποκτείνω <615>]; **from *apo*: off (intens.), and *kteinō*: to put to death; lit.: to kill off ► To slay, to cause to perish; also transl.: to put to death** > Jesus says not to fear those who kill the body and cannot kill the soul (Matt. 10:28a, b; Luke 12:4). Jesus showed His disciples that He must be killed (Matt. 16:21; Mark 8:31; 9:31a, b; Luke 9:22; 18:33 {or v. 32}). He says that Jerusalem is the city which kills the prophets and stones those who are sent to her (Matt. 23:37; Luke 13:34). He asked if it were lawful to save life or to kill on the Sabbath day (Mark 3:4). God has the power to kill and to cast into hell (Luke 12:5). Herod wanted to kill Jesus (Luke 13:31). Some Jews sought to kill Paul (Acts 21:31; 23:12, 14). The soldiers wanted to kill the prisoners (Acts 27:42). The letter kills, but the Spirit gives life (2 Cor. 3:6). By the cross God has put to death the enmity between the nations and those of Israel (Eph. 2:16). He who was seated on the pale horse had received authority to kill with the sword (Rev. 6:8). The verb is also used elsewhere in regard to Jesus (Matt. 17:23; 26:4; Mark 9:31a, b; 10:34; 14:1; John 5:16 (in some mss.), 18; 7:1, 19, 20, 25; 8:37, 40; 11:53; 18:31), John the Baptist (Matt. 14:5; Mark 6:19), the disciples (Matt. 24:9), Lazarus (John 12:10), and the children of Jezebel (Rev. 2:23). Other refs.: Matt. 21:35, 38, 39; 22:6; 23:34; Mark 12:5a, b, 7, 8; Luke 11:47, 48; 13:4; 20:14, 15; John 8:22; 16:2; Acts 3:15; 7:52; Rom. 7:11; 11:3; 1 Thes. 2:15; Rev. 2:13; 6:11; 9:5, 15, 18, 20; 11:5, 7, 13; 13:10a, b, 15; 19:21. ¶

3 ***diacheirizō*** [verb: διαχειρίζω <1315>]; **from *dia*: by means of (intens.), and *cheirizō*: to manipulate, which is from *cheir*: hand ► To mistreat, to put to death with one's own hands** > The Jews sought to kill Paul (Acts 26:21 {to destroy, to put to death}). Other ref.: Acts 5:30; see MURDER (verb) <1315>. ¶

4 ***sphazō*** [verb: σφάζω <4969>] **► To put to death, to slaughter** > It was granted to the one who sat on the fiery red horse that people should kill {slay} one another (Rev. 6:4). All other refs.: MURDER (verb) <4969>, SLAY <4969>.

5 ***katasphazō*** [verb: κατασφάζω <2695>]; **from *kata*: intens., and *sphazō*: see 4 ► To slaughter, to slay** > A master said to bring his enemies who did not want him to reign over them, and to slay them before him (Luke 19:27). ¶

6 ***thanatoō*** [verb: θανατόω <2289>]; **from *thanatos*: death ► To slay; also transl.: to put to death, to face death, to become dead, to make dead** > For Jesus's sake, there were those who were killed all day long (Rom. 8:36). Other refs.: Rom. 7:4 {to die}; 2 Cor. 6:9 {to make to die}; 1 Pet. 3:18. All other refs.: to put to death, to deliver to death under DEATH <2289>.

[7] ***thuō*** [verb: θύω <2380>] ▶ **To slaughter, to sacrifice an animal** > The thief of the sheep comes only to steal and kill and destroy (John 10:10). A voice told Peter to kill and eat (Acts 10:13; 11:7). The father had killed the fattened calf for his son returned safe and sound (Luke 15:23, 27, 30). Other ref.: Matt. 22:4 {to butcher}. All other refs.: SACRIFICE (verb) <2380>.
[8] ***phoneuō*** [verb: φονεύω <5407>]; **from *phonos*: murder, or *phoneus*: murderer ▶ To assassinate, to put to death; also transl. more precisely: to commit murder, to murder** > The commandment said not to murder (Matt. 5:21a, b; 19:18; Mark 10:19; Luke 18:20; Rom. 13:9; Jas. 2:11a, b). The Jews were the sons of those who had killed the prophets (Matt. 23:31), including Zechariah (v. 35). James speaks of those who kill and who are envious (Jas. 4:2). Other ref.: Jas. 5:6; see MURDER (verb) <5407>. ¶
– [9] Matt. 2:13; 12:14; Mark 3:6; 9:22; 12:9; Luke 11:51; 20:16; Acts 5:37; 1 Cor. 10:9, 10 → PERISH <622> [10] Mark 11:18; Luke 19:47 → DESTROY <622> [11] Acts 8:1 → to his being killed → lit.: to his death → DEATH <336> [12] Acts 11:19 → when Stephen was killed → lit.: over Stephen [13] 2 Thes. 2:8 → CONSUME <355> [14] 1 Tim. 1:9 → one who kills his father, one who kills his mother → murderer of father, murderer of mother → MURDERER <3964> <3389> [15] Heb. 11:31 → PERISH <4881> [16] Heb. 11:37 → to be killed by the sword → lit.: to die by murder of sword → DIE <599> [17] 2 Pet. 2:12 → destruction → DESTROY <5356>.

KILLING – Acts 8:1 → DEATH <336>.

KIN – Mark 6:4 → own kin → RELATIVE <4773>.

KIND (adj.) – [1] **to be kind: *chrēsteuomai*** [verb: χρηστεύομαι <5541>]; **from *chrēstos*: good, useful ▶ To be helpful, to be pleasant** > Love is kind (1 Cor. 13:4). ¶
– [2] Luke 6:35; Eph. 4:32 → GOOD (adj.) <5543> [3] Acts 24:4 → to be kind enough → by his courtesy → COURTESY <1932> [4] Phil. 4:14 → it was kind of you → you have done well → WELL (adv.) <2573> [5] 1 Thes. 5:15; Titus 2:5 → GOOD (adj.) <18> [6] 2 Tim. 2:24 → GENTLE <2261>.

KIND (noun) – [1] ***genos*** [neut. noun: γένος <1085>]; **from *ginomai*: to become ▶ Sort, type** > A certain kind of demon does not go out except by prayer and fasting (Matt. 17:21; Mark 9:29). Various kinds of tongues are given to Christians (1 Cor. 12:10, 28 {diversity, variety}). There are a great many kinds of voices in the world (1 Cor. 14:10). Other ref.: Matt. 13:47. All other refs.: see entries in Lexicon at <1085>.
[2] ***phusis*** [fem. noun: φύσις <5449>]; **from *phuō*: to produce ▶ Race, nature** > Every kind {species} of animals has been tamed by mankind {the human species, the human race, man} (lit.: the human kind) (Jas. 3:7a, b). All other refs.: NATURE <5449>.
– [3] Matt. 5:11 → all kinds of evil → lit.: all evil [4] Rom. 1:29 → with every kind → lit.: with all [5] 1 Cor. 7:7 → one of one kind and one of another → lit.: one thus, the other thus [6] 1 Cor. 12:4–6 → different kinds → DIVERSITY <1243> [7] 1 Thes. 5:22 → FORM (noun) <1491> [8] 2 Tim. 3:6; Titus 3:3; Heb. 13:9; Jas. 1:2; 1 Pet. 1:6 → of all kinds, of many kinds → VARIOUS <4164> [9] 2 Pet. 1:1 → of the same kind → lit.: as precious → PRECIOUS <2472>.

KINDHEARTED – 1 Pet. 3:8 → TENDER-HEARTED <2155>.

KINDLE – [1] ***anaptō*** [verb: ἀνάπτω <381>]; **from *ana*: intens., and *haptō*: to light ▶ To light, to set on fire** > Jesus speaks of a fire already kindled on the earth (Luke 12:49). The natives of Malta kindled a fire for Paul and the other shipwrecked people (Acts 28:2). The tongue is a little fire, but kindles {sets aflame, sets ablaze} a great forest (Jas. 3:5). ¶
[2] ***periaptō*** [verb: περιάπτω <4014a>]; **from *peri*: around, and *haptō*: to light ▶ See [1].** > A fire was kindled {was lit} in the midst of the courtyard of the high priest's house (Luke 22:55); some mss. have *aptō*: see LIGHT (verb) <681>. ¶

– [3] 2 Cor. 8:7 → "have kindled" added in Engl. [4] 2 Tim. 1:6 → to kindle afresh → REKINDLE <329>.

KINDLY – ***philanthrōpōs*** [adv.: φιλανθρώπως <5364>]; **see KINDNESS** <5363> ► **With grace, with consideration; also transl.: courteously, in kindness** > Julius treated Paul kindly (Acts 27:3). ¶

KINDNESS – [1] ***philanthrōpia*** [fem. noun: φιλανθρωπία <5363>]; **from *philos*: loving, and *anthrōpos*: human being, which is from *anēr*: man, and *ōps*: appearance** ► **Benevolence toward mankind, philanthropy** > The natives showed no common kindness to Paul and his companions (Acts 28:2). Other ref.: Titus 3:4; see LOVE (noun) <5363>. ¶
[2] ***chrēstotēs*** [fem. noun: χρηστότης <5544>]; **from *chrēstos*: of good quality, useful, which is from *chraomai*: to use** ► **Goodness, virtue** > God has shown His kindness toward us in Christ Jesus (Eph. 2:7). Paul commended himself as a minister of God by his kindness (2 Cor. 6:6). Christians must put on kindness (Col. 3:12). The kindness and the love of the Savior God toward man has appeared (Titus 3:4). Other refs.: GENTLENESS <5544>, GOODNESS <5544>.
– [3] Acts 4:9 → act of kindness → good deed → DEED <2108> [4] Acts 14:17 → to show kindness → to do good → GOOD (adj. and noun) <15> [5] Acts 24:4 → COURTESY <1932> [6] Acts 27:3 → in kindness → KINDLY <5364> [7] Rom. 2:4b → GOODNESS <5543> [8] 2 Pet. 1:7 → brotherly kindness → brotherly love → LOVE (noun) <5360>.

KINDRED – [1] Luke 1:61; Acts 7:3, 14 → RELATIVES <4772> [2] Acts 3:25 → FAMILY <3965> [3] Acts 4:6; 7:19 → RACE[1] <1085> [4] Acts 7:13 → FAMILY <1085> [5] Phil. 2:20 → of kindred spirit → LIKEMINDED <2473> [6] Rev. 1:7; 5:9; 7:9; 11:9; 13:7; 14:6 → TRIBE <5443>.

KING – [1] ***basileus*** [masc. noun: βασιλεύς <935>] ► **Sovereign, head of state** > The term is used in regard to Jesus (Matt. 5:35; 18:23; 21:5; 22:2, 7, 11, 13; 25:34, 40; 27:42; Mark 15:32; Luke 19:38; 23:2; John 1:49; 12:13, 15; 18:37a, b; 19:14, 15; Acts 17:7; 1 Tim. 1:17; 6:15; Rev. 15:3; 17:14a; 19:16a), and in particular as king of the Jews (Matt. 2:2; 27:11, 29, 37; Mark 15:2, 9, 12, 18, 26; Luke 23:3, 37, 38; John 6:15; 18:33, 39; 19:3, 12, 19, 21). Christians have been made kings and priests (Rev. 1:6 and 5:10 {kingdom}). The term also designates David (Matt. 1:6a, b; Acts 13:22), Herod the Great (Matt. 2:1, 3, 9; Luke 1:5), kings in general (Matt. 10:18; 11:8; 17:25; Mark 13:9; Luke 10:24; 14:31a, b; 21:12; 22:25; Acts 4:26; 9:15; 13:21; 1 Tim. 2:2; 1 Pet. 2:13, 17; Rev. 1:5; 6:15; 9:11; 10:11; 16:12, 14; 17:2, 10, 12, 14b, 18; 18:3, 9; 19:16b, 18, 19; 21:24), Herod Antipas (Matt. 14:9; Mark 6:14, 22 or 23, 25–27), Caesar (John 19:15b), the pharaoh of Egypt (Acts 7:10, 18; Heb. 11:23, 27), Herod Agrippa I (Acts 12:1, 20), Herod Agrippa II (Acts 25:13, 14, 24, 26; 26:2, 7, 13, 19, 26, 27, 30), Aretas (2 Cor. 11:32), Melchizedek (Heb. 7:1, 2a–c), and Satan (Rev. 9:11). ¶
[2] **court of kings: *basileion*** [adj. used as plur. noun: βασίλειον <933>]; **from *basileios*: royal** ► **Court, habitation of the king** > Those who are dressed in splendid clothing and who live luxuriously are in the courts of kings {palaces, royal palaces} (Luke 7:25). ¶
[3] **king's: *basilikos*** [adj.: βασιλικός <937>]; **from *basileus*: see** [1] ► **Which belongs to the king** > The country of the Tyrians and of the Sidonians was nourished by the king's country (Acts 12:20). All other refs.: NOBLEMAN <937>, ROYAL <937>.
– [4] 1 Cor. 4:8 → to become kings → REIGN (verb) <936> <4821>.

KINGDOM – [1] ***basileia*** [fem. noun: βασιλεία <932>]; **from *basileus*: king** ► **Sphere of the exercise of a sovereign's power** > Jesus taught his disciples to pray to the Father, in relation to His kingdom (Matt. 6:10; Luke 11:2). The scepter of the kingdom of the Son is a scepter of uprightness (Heb. 1:8). Paul charged Timothy to preach the word prior to the judgment of the living and the dead and by the appearing and kingdom of Christ (2 Tim. 4:1). See KINGDOM OF GOD and KINGDOM OF HEAVEN. * – [2] Rev. 1:6; 5:10 → KING <935>.

KINGDOM OF GOD – kingdom: *basileia* [fem. noun: βασιλεία <932>]**; from *basileus*: king; God: *Theos*** [masc. noun: Θεός <2316>] **▶ Sphere in which God reigns and exercises His authority (moral authority currently) >** The expr. "kingdom of God" is found frequently in the N.T., particularly in the Gospel of Luke and in the Acts (approx. forty times). In order to enter into the kingdom of God, it is necessary to be born anew, to be born of water and of the Spirit (John 3:3, 5); see BORN AGAIN (BE). The kingdom of God is righteousness, peace, and joy in the Holy Spirit (Rom. 14:17), i.e., it procures these blessings for one who submits himself to divine authority. Jesus Himself preached the kingdom of God (e.g., Mark 1:14) as likewise did His disciples (Luke 9:2). Other servants will preach this gospel before the reign of Christ is established (see Matt. 24:14). The kingdom of God was in the midst of men when Jesus Christ (the king) was on earth (Luke 17:21). Presently Jesus is represented as a nobleman who has gone to a far country to receive for Himself a kingdom and return (see Luke 19:12). During the age of the new covenant, the kingdom of God also morally bears the character of the kingdom of heaven.

KINGDOM OF HEAVEN – kingdom: *basileia* [fem. noun: βασιλεία <932>]**; from *basileus*: king; heaven: *ouranos*** [masc. noun: οὐρανός <3772>] **▶ The kingdom of heaven (lit.: of the heavens) emphasizes the present session of the king, the Lord Jesus, in heaven >** Matthew alone uses the expr. "kingdom of heaven" in his Gospel to designate the kingdom of God. The ten parables of the kingdom of heaven (see Matt. 13:24–50; 18:23–35; 20:1–16; 22:1–14; 25:1–13) illustrate the fact that there are presently in this kingdom those who serve the king who is in heaven, and there are those who deny Him by their conduct. At the coming of Jesus, the kingdom of heaven had drawn near (3:2; 4:17; 10:7). Jesus gives the characteristics of those who will and of those who will not enter into the kingdom of heaven (5:3, 10, 19, 20; 7:21; 8:11; 11:11; 18:1, 3, 4; 19:12, 14, 23). He says that the violent seize on the kingdom of heaven (11:12), for John the Baptist had preached the repentance necessary for entering into it. The scribes and the Pharisees shut up the kingdom of heaven against men (23:13). To the disciples of Jesus, it was given to know the mysteries of the kingdom of heaven (13:11).

KINGLY – 1 Pet. 2:9 → ROYAL <934>.

KINGSHIP – *basileia* [fem. noun: βασιλεία <932>]**; from *basileus*: king ▶ Royal authority, royal power >** The ten horns that John saw are ten kings who have not received royal power {kingship} (Rev. 17:12). The ten horns will hand over their kingship {royal authority} to the beast (Rev. 17:17). Babylon the great has kingship over the kings of the earth (Rev. 17:18). Other refs.: KINGDOM <932>.

KINSFOLK – [1] Luke 1:58; 2:44; 14:12; 21:16 → RELATIVE <4773> [2] Luke 1:61 → RELATIVES <4772>.

KINSMAN – Mark 6:4; Luke 1:36, 58; John 18:26; Acts 10:24; Rom. 9:3; 16:7, 11, 21 → RELATIVE <4773>.

KINSWOMAN – Luke 1:36 → RELATIVE <4773>.

KIS – See KISH <2797>.

KISH – *Kis* [masc. name: Κίς <2797>]**: bow, in Heb. ▶ Man of the O.T.; also transl.: Cis, Kis >** Kish was the father of King Saul (Acts 13:21). ¶

KISS (noun) – ***philēma*** [neut. noun: φίλημα <5370>]**; from *phileō*: to love, which is from *philos*: loved one, friend ▶ A touch with the lips >** Jesus reproached Simon for not having given Him a kiss (Luke

7:45). Judas betrayed the Son of Man with a kiss (Luke 22:48). Paul exhorts Christians to greet one another with a holy kiss (Rom. 16:16; 1 Cor. 16:20; 2 Cor. 13:12; 1 Thes. 5:26). Peter exhorts them to greet one another with a kiss of love (1 Pet. 5:14). ¶

KISS (verb) – [1] ***phileō*** [verb: φιλέω <5368>]; **from *philos*: loved one, friend ▶ To touch with the lips >** The crowd was to seize Him whom Judas would kiss (Matt. 26:48; Mark 14:44); Judas drew near to Jesus to kiss Him (Luke 22:47). All other refs.: LOVE (verb) <5368>.
[2] ***kataphileō*** [verb: καταφιλέω <2705>]; **from *kata*: intens., and *phileō*: see [1] ▶ To cover tenderly with kisses >** Judas kissed Jesus (Matt. 26:49; Mark 14:45). A woman kissed the feet of Jesus (Luke 7:38, 45). The father in the parable kissed his son upon his return home (Luke 15:20). The elders in Ephesus kissed Paul before his departure (Acts 20:37). ¶

KNEE – [1] ***gonu*** [neut. noun: γόνυ <1119>] **▶ Part of the body formed by the articulation of the thigh and the lower leg; to kneel down is lit.: to place the knees >** The soldiers bent the knee in mockery before Jesus (Mark 15:19). Simon Peter fell at Jesus's knees (Luke 5:8). Jesus knelt down and prayed at Gethsemane (Luke 22:41). Stephen knelt down and cried with a loud voice to the Lord (Acts 7:60). Peter knelt down and prayed for Dorcas (Acts 9:40). Paul knelt down and prayed with the elders of Ephesus (Acts 20:36). Paul and his companions knelt down on the shore outside the city of Tyre and prayed (Acts 21:5). Seven thousand men had not bowed the knee to Baal (Rom. 11:4). Every knee shall bow to the Lord (Rom. 14:11). Paul bowed his knees to the Father (Eph. 3:14). At the name of Jesus every knee shall bow, of heavenly and earthly and infernal beings (Phil. 2:10). We are to lift up the hands that hang down and the failing knees (Heb. 12:12). ¶
[2] **to kneel down, to fall on the knees, to bow the knee: *gonupeteō*** [verb: γονυπετέω <1120>]; **from *gonu*: see [1], and *piptō*: to fall ▶ To bend the knees >** Various men fell to their knees before Jesus (Matt. 17:14; Mark 1:40; 10:17). The soldiers bowed the knee before Jesus to mock Him (Matt. 27:29). ¶
– [3] Matt. 18:26; Mark 5:6 → to fall on one's knees → WORSHIP (verb) <4352>.

KNEEL – [1] Matt. 8:2; 9:18; 15:25; 20:20 → to kneel down → WORSHIP (verb) <4352> [2] Matt. 17:14; 27:29; Mark 1:40; 10:17 → to fall on the knees → KNEE <1120> [3] Luke 22:41; Acts 7:60; 9:40; 20:36; 21:5 → to kneel down; lit.: to place the knee → KNEE <1119>, LAY <5087> [4] Eph. 3:14 → lit.: to bow the knees → BOW (verb) <2578>.

KNIT – [1] **to knit together: *sumbibazō*** [verb: συμβιβάζω <4822>]; **from *sun*: together, and *bibazō*: to cause to go ▶ To fit together, to fuse together; also transl.: to compact, to hold together >** The body of Christ (His church) is joined and knit together (Eph. 4:16). All other refs.: CONCLUDE[1] <4822>, INSTRUCT <4822>, PROVE <4822>, UNITE <4822>.
– [2] Acts 10:11 → BIND <1210> [3] Eph. 4:16 → to join together → to fit together → FIT (verb) <4883>.

KNOCK – ***krouō*** [verb: κρούω <2925>] **▶ To tap at a door >** This verb is used lit. in regard to a master returning from a wedding (Luke 12:36) and to Peter (Acts 12:13, 16). It is also used in the figur. sense to encourage laying one's request before God (Matt. 7:7, 8; Luke 11:9, 10), and in regard to unbelievers for whom it will be too late to knock at the door (Luke 13:25). The Lord stands at the door of Laodicea and is knocking (Rev. 3:20). ¶

KNOW – [1] ***ginōskō*** [verb: γινώσκω <1097>] **▶ To perceive, to comprehend; the term often suggests a progression in knowledge; also transl.: to be aware, to be sure, to find out, to have knowledge, to keep in mind, to learn, to mark, to realize, to recognize, to resolve, to see, to speak, to take notice, to understand >** The world did not know {recognize} the Word (John 1:10). The world did not know God through wisdom (1 Cor. 1:21). God has made Christ, who knew no sin, to be sin for us (2 Cor. 5:21). The Lord knows those who are His (2 Tim. 2:19). Joseph did not know (Hebrew expr. to designate the sexual relation between a man and a woman) {had no union with} Mary before she gave birth to Jesus (Matt. 1:25; Luke 1:34). The disciples did not know the things that were spoken by Jesus (Luke 18:34). The apostles did not know for what reason Jesus had said to Judas: "What you do, do quickly" (John 13:28). Pilate knew from {learned from} the centurion that Jesus was dead (Mark 15:45). The chief captain could not know the certainty of {ascertain, get at the truth because of} the tumult concerning Paul (Acts 21:34). The Hebrews knew that they had for themselves a better and enduring possession (Heb. 10:34). Other refs.: Matt. 6:3; 7:23; 9:30; 10:26; 12:7, 12, 15, 33; 13:11; 16:3, 8; 21:45; 22:18; 24:32, 33, 39, 43a, b, 50; 25:24; 26:10; Mark 4:11, 13b; 5:29 {to feel}, 43; 6:38; 7:24; 8:17; 9:30; 12:12; 13:28, 29; 15:10; Luke 1:18; 2:43; 6:44; 7:39; 8:10, 17, 46; 9:11; 10:11, 22; 12:2, 39a, b, 46–48; 16:4, 15; 19:15, 42, 44; 20:19; 21:20, 30, 31; 24:18, 35; John 1:48; 2:24, 25; 3:10; 4:1, 53; 5:6, 42; 6:15, 69; 7:17, 26, 27b, 49, 51; 8:27, 28, 32, 43, 52, 55a; 10:6, 14a, b, 15a, b, 27, 38; 11:57; 12:9, 16; 13:7b, 12, 35; 14:7a–c, 9, 17a, b, 20, 31; 15:18; 16:3, 19; 17:3, 7, 8, 23, 25a–c; 19:4; 21:17b; Acts 1:7; 2:36; 8:30; 9:24; 17:13, 19, 20; 19:15a, 35; 20:34; 21:24, 37; 22:14, 30; 23:6, 28; 24:11 {to ascertain}; Rom. 1:21; 2:18; 3:17; 6:6; 7:1b, 7a, 15; 10:19; 11:34; 1 Cor. 2:8a, b, 14, 16; 3:20; 4:19; 8:2a, b, 3; 13:9, 12a; 14:7, 9; 2 Cor. 2:4, 9; 3:2; 5:16b, c; 8:9; 13:6; Gal. 2:9; 3:7; 4:9a, b; Eph. 3:19; 5:5; 6:22; Phil. 1:12; 2:19, 22; 3:10; 4:5; Col. 4:8; 1 Thes. 3:5; 2 Tim. 1:18; 3:1; Heb. 3:10; 8:11a; 13:23; Jas. 1:3; 2:20; 5:20; 2 Pet. 1:20; 3:3; 1 John 2:3a, b, 4, 5, 18, 29b, 13a, b, 14; 3:1, 6, 16, 19, 20, 24; 4:2, 6a, b, 7, 8, 13, 16; 5:2, 20; 2 John 1; Rev. 2:17, 23, 24; 3:3, 9. ¶

[2] **to know well: *anaginōskō*** [verb: ἀναγινώσκω <314>]; **from *ana*: intens., and *ginōskō*: see [1] ▶ To be thoroughly acquainted with, to know by reading >** Paul did not write other things to the Corinthians but what they well knew {they read} and understood (2 Cor. 1:13). All other refs.: READ <314>.

[3] ***epiginōskō*** [verb: ἐπιγινώσκω <1921>]; **from *epi*: upon, and *ginōskō*: see [1]; lit.: to know fully ▶ To recognize, to discover, to discern >** No one knows the Son except the Father; nor does anyone know the Father except the Son (Matt. 11:27a, b). Luke had written his orderly account so that Theophilus might know the certainty of those things in which he had been instructed (Luke 1:4). Pilate knew {learned} that Jesus belonged to Herod's jurisdiction (Luke 23:7). The chief captain wanted to know {find out} why the Jews were shouting against Paul (Acts 22:24). The chief captain knew that Paul was a Roman (Acts 22:29). The shipwrecked people knew {found out} that the island was called Malta (Acts 28:1). Christians will know {will know fully} just as they are also known (1 Cor. 13:12b, c). Paul speaks of himself as unknown, and yet well known (2 Cor. 6:9). The Colossians heard and knew {understood} the grace of God in truth (Col. 1:6). Other refs.: Mark 2:8 {to perceive}; 5:30 {to realize}; Luke 5:22 {to perceive}; 7:37; Acts 9:30; 19:34 {to find out}; 25:10; Rom. 1:32; 1 Tim. 4:3; 2 Pet. 2:21a, b. All other refs.: KNOWLEDGE <1921>, RECOGNIZE <1921>.

[4] **to know; to know already, before, beforehand, etc.: *proginōskō*** [verb: προγινώσκω <4267>]; **from *pro*: in advance, and *ginōskō*: see [1] ▶ To know in advance, to find out in advance >** The Jews knew Paul from the outset (Acts 26:5). Peter speaks about knowing beforehand things concerning the day of the Lord (2 Pet. 3:17). Other refs.: Rom. 8:29; 11:2; 1 Pet. 1:20; see FOREKNOW <4267>. ¶

[5] **to know, to make known: *gnōrizō*** [verb: γνωρίζω <1107>]; **comp. *gnōrimos*: well-known, familiar ▶ To explain, to declare, to reveal; also transl.: to bring information, to certify, to remind, to tell, to understand, to wit >** The shepherds made widely known {made known abroad,

made known about the country, spread} the saying concerning the child Jesus (Luke 2:17; some mss. have *diagnōrizō*). Jesus has made known to His disciples all things that He heard from His Father (John 15:15). He had made known to them His name and would make it known (John 17:26a, b). The Lord had made known to David the way of life (Acts 2:28). God has made known the riches of His glory toward the vessels of mercy which He had prepared beforehand for glory (Rom. 9:23). The manifold wisdom of God is made known by the church to the angels (Eph. 3:10). We ought to let our requests be made known {present our requests} to God by prayer and supplication with thanksgiving (Phil. 4:6). Other refs.: Luke 2:15; Rom. 9:22; 16:26; 1 Cor. 12:3; 15:1; 2 Cor. 8:1 {to wit}; Gal. 1:11; Eph. 1:9; 3:3, 5; 6:19, 21b; Phil. 1:22; Col. 1:27; 4:7, 9 {to inform}; 2 Pet. 1:16. ¶

6 to make known, to make widely known: *diagnōrizō* [verb: διαγνωρίζω <1232>]**; from *dia*: indicating separation, and *gnōrizō*: see 5 ▶ To know by distinguishing, to spread** > Some mss. have this verb for Luke 2:17; see 5. ¶

7 *eidō* [verb: εἴδω <1492>] **▶ To be acquainted with, to comprehend; the verb suggests thorough knowledge; also transl.: to be aware, to be conscious, to be sure, to have an idea, to realize, to remember, to seem to tell, to suppose, to understand, to wit (archaic)** > The Father knows what His children have need of (Matt. 6:8, 32; Luke 12:30). No one knows the day and the hour of the great tribulation (Matt. 24:36; Mark 13:32). Peter said he did not know Jesus (Matt. 26:72, 74; Mark 14:71; Luke 22:57). Jesus knew God for He was from Him (John 7:29); He knew Him and kept His word (8:55b–d). Jesus, knowing that His hour had come that He should depart out of this world to the Father, having loved His own who were in the world, loved them to the end (John 13:1). He knew whom He had chosen (John 13:18). Christians have received the Spirit that they may know {understand} the things given freely by God (1 Cor. 2:12). Timothy knew the Holy Scriptures from childhood which were able to make him wise for salvation (2 Tim. 3:15). We know that we have eternal life if we believe in the name of the Son of God (1 John 5:13). The Lord knows the works of the various churches (Rev. 2:2, 9, 19; 3:1, 8, 15); in the case of Smyrna, He also knows its tribulation and poverty (see 2:9). Other refs.: Matt. 7:11; 9:6; 12:25; 15:12; 20:22, 25; 21:27; 22:16, 19; 24:42, 43b; 25:12, 13, 26; 26:2, 70; 27:18; 28:5; Mark 1:24, 34; 2:10; 4:13a, 27; 5:33; 6:20; 9:6 10:19, 38, 42; 11:33; 12:14, 15, 24; 13:25, 33, 35; 14:40, 68; Luke 2:49; 4:34, 41; 5:24; 6:8; 8:53; 9:33, 55 in some mss; 11:13, 17, 44; 12:39a, b, 46, 56; 13:25, 27; 18:20; 19:22; 20:7, 21; 22:34, 60; 23:34; John 1:26, 31, 33; 2:9a, b; 3:2, 8, 11; 4:10, 22a, b, 25, 32, 42; 5:13, 32; 6:6, 42, 61, 64; 7:15, 27a, 28a, b; 8:14a, b, 19a–c, 37; 9:12, 20, 21a, b, 24, 25a, b, 29a, b, 30, 31; 10:4, 5; 11:22, 24, 42, 49; 12:35, 50; 13:3, 7a, 11, 17; 14:4a, b, 5a, b; 15:15, 21; 16:18, 30a, b; 18:2, 4, 21; 19:10, 28, 35; 20:2, 9, 13, 14; 21:4, 12, 15–17a, 24; Acts 2:22, 30; 3:16, 17; 5:7; 7:18, 40; 10:37; 12:9, 11; 16:3; 19:32; 20:22, 25, 29; 23:5; 26:27; Rom. 2:2; 3:19; 5:3; 6:9, 16; 7:7b, 14, 18; 8:22, 26–28; 11:2; 13:11; 14:14; 15:29; 1 Cor. 1:16; 2:2, 11a, b; 3:16; 5:6; 6:2, 3, 9, 15, 16, 19; 7:16a, b; 8:1, 2a, 4; 9:13, 24; 11:3; 12:2; 13:2; 14:11, 16; 15:58; 16:15; 2 Cor. 1:7; 4:14; 5:1, 6, 11, 16a; 9:2; 11:11, 31; 12:2a–d. 3; Gal. 2:16; 4:8, 13; Eph. 1:18; 6:8, 9, 21a; Phil. 1:17, 19, 25; 4:12a, b, 15; Col. 2:1; 3:24; 4:1, 6; 1 Thes. 1:4, 5; 2:1, 2, 5, 11; 3:3, 4; 4:2, 5; 5:2, 12 {to recognize}; 2 Thes. 1:8; 2:6; 3:7; 1 Tim. 1:8, 9; 3:15; 2 Tim. 1:12, 15; 2:23; 3:14; Titus 1:16; 3:11; Phm. 21; Heb. 8:11b; 10:30; Jas. 3:1; 4:4; 1 Pet. 1:18; 5:9; 2 Pet. 1:12, 14; 2:9; 1 John 2:11, 20, 21a, b, 29a; 3:2, 5, 14, 15; 5:15a, b, 18–20; 3 John 12; Jude 5, 10 (some mss.: *epistamai*); Rev. 2:13; 3:17; 7:14; 12:12; 19:12. *

8 *oida* [verb: οἶδα <1492>]**; form of *eidō*: see 7 ▶ To have the knowledge, to understand** > The Jews were to secure the tomb of Jesus as well as they knew how {as they could} (Matt. 27:65). All the Jews knew the manner of Paul's life (Acts 26:4). Jude speaks of those who corrupt themselves in whatever they know naturally, like brute beasts (v. 10). *

9 ***suneidō*** [verb: συνείδω <4894>]; **from *sun*: together, and *eidō*: see 7 ▶ To be aware, to have knowledge** > Paul knew {was conscious} of nothing against himself {His conscience was clear} (1 Cor. 4:4). All other refs.: AWARE <4894>, CONSCIOUS <4894>, CONSIDER <4894>, PRIVY <4894>.

10 **to know not: *agnoeō*** [verb: ἀγνοέω <50>]; **from *a*: neg., and *noeō*: to perceive, to understand, which is from *nous*: mind, understanding ▶ To not have the knowledge, to ignore** > The people in Jerusalem and their rulers did not know {did not recognize} Jesus (Acts 13:27). Paul proclaimed to the Athenians the god they worshipped without knowing {ignorantly, in ignorance, as something unknown} (Acts 17:23). The person who judges others does not know {does not realize} that the goodness of God leads him to repentance (Rom. 2:4). All other refs.: IGNORANT <50>, UNDERSTAND <50>, UNKNOWN <50>.

11 **to not know: *lanthanō*** [verb: λανθάνω <2990>] ▶ **To not realize, to be unconscious** > Some have lodged angels without knowing it {unawares, unwittingly} (Heb. 13:2). All other refs.: HIDDEN (BE) <2990.

12 ***isēmi*** [verb: ἴσημι <2467>]; **from *eisō*, the future of *eidō*: see 7 ▶ To be acquainted, to understand** > This verb is used in Acts 26:4 and Heb. 12:17. ¶

13 ***epistamai*** [verb: ἐπίσταμαι <1987>]; **from *epi*: upon, and *histēmi*: to stand ▶ To understand well, to grasp** > Apollos knew only the baptism of John (Acts 18:25). Agrippa knew {was informed about, was familiar with} the things of which Paul was speaking (Acts 26:26). Abraham went out, not knowing where he was going (Heb. 11:8). Other refs.: Mark 14:68 {to understand}; Acts 10:28 {to be aware}; 15:7; 19:15, 25; 20:18, 22:19; 24:10; 1 Tim. 6:4; Jas. 4:14; Jude 10. ¶

– 14 Matt. 7:16, 20; 17:12; Mark 6:33, 54; Luke 24:16, 31; Acts 3:10; 12:14; 27:39; 2 Cor. 13:5 → RECOGNIZE <1921> 15 John 7:26 → RECOGNIZE <1097> 16 John 8:43; 10:6; 12:16; Acts 8:30 → UNDERSTAND <1097> 17 John 11:57 → to make known, to let known → REPORT (verb) <3377> 18 John 19:13; Heb. 11:24 → known as → called → CALL (verb) <3004> 19 Acts 1:24; 15:8 → who knows the hearts → HEART <2589> 20 Acts 4:10; 13:38; 28:22, 28 → KNOWN <1110> 21 Acts 10:18 → SURNAME (verb) <1941> 22 Acts 24:22 → to know the uttermost → to make a decision → DECISION <1231> 23 Rom. 14:16; 1 John 3:20; Rev. 2:3 → the verb is added in Engl. 24 Rom. 15:20 → NAME (verb) <3687> 25 2 Cor. 5:11a, b; 7:12 → to be well known, to make known → to be manifested → MANIFEST (verb) <5319> 26 Eph. 1:17; 2 Tim. 2:25 → to know better; that they may know → in the knowledge of; to the knowledge → KNOWLEDGE <1922> 27 Eph. 4:20 → LEARN <3129> 28 1 Tim. 1:7 → UNDERSTAND <3539> 29 2 Tim. 3:10 → to know, to fully know → to follow carefully → FOLLOW <3877> 30 2 Tim. 4:17 → to know fully → to preach fully → PREACH <4135>.

KNOWLEDGE – 1 ***gnōsis*** [fem. noun: γνῶσις <1108>]; **from *ginōskō*: to know ▶ What one knows, understands** > Jesus told the lawyers they had taken away the key of knowledge (Luke 11:52). A Jew may have the form of knowledge (Rom. 2:20). Paul marvels at the knowledge of God (Rom. 11:33). He was confident that the Christians in Rome were filled with all knowledge (Rom. 15:14). Husbands must dwell with their wives with knowledge {with understanding, being considerate} (1 Pet. 3:7). Peter exhorts to grow in the grace and knowledge of the Lord and Savior Jesus Christ (2 Pet. 3:18). Other refs.: Luke 1:77; 1 Cor. 1:5; 8:1a, b, 7, 10, 11; 12:8; 13:2, 8; 14:6; 2 Cor. 2:14; 4:6; 6:6; 8:7; 10:5; 11:6; Eph. 3:19; Phil. 3:8; Col. 2:3; 1 Tim. 6:20 {science}; 2 Pet. 1:5, 6. ¶

2 ***epignōsis*** [fem. noun: ἐπίγνωσις <1922>]; **from *epiginōskō*: to know fully, which is from *epi*: upon (intens.), and *ginōskō*: to know; lit.: full knowledge ▶ a. More**

advanced knowledge, more accurate understanding > Men did not like to retain God in their knowledge {to acknowledge Him} (Rom. 1:28). By the law is the knowledge {we become conscious} of sin (Rom. 3:20). Jews have a zeal for God, but not according to knowledge (Rom. 10:2). Paul was praying that God would give the Ephesians the spirit of wisdom and revelation in the knowledge of Him {to know Him better} (Eph. 1:17); he speaks of coming to the unity of faith and of the knowledge of the Son of God (4:13). He was praying that the love of the Philippians might abound in knowledge (Phil. 1:9); he was praying also that the Colossians might be filled with the knowledge of the will of God (Col. 1:9), that they might increase in the knowledge of God (v. 10). Christians are knit together to the knowledge {understanding} of the mystery of God (Col. 2:2). If we sin willfully after having received the knowledge of the truth, there no longer remains a sacrifice for sins (Heb. 10:26). Other refs.: Col. 3:10; 1 Tim. 2:4; 2 Tim. 3:7; Titus 1:1 {acknowledging, acknowledgment}; 2 Pet. 1:2, 3, 8; 2:20. **b. Perception, discernment; also transl.: acknowledging, acknowledgment, understanding** > God may give repentance to acknowledgment of the truth (2 Tim. 2:25). Philemon's participation in the faith became operative in acknowledgment of every good thing which was in Paul toward Christ (Phm. 6). ¶

[3] **to take knowledge: *epiginōskō*** [verb: ἐπιγινώσκω <1921>]; **see** [2] ▶ **To know with certainty** > Felix could take knowledge of {ascertain, know the certainty of, learn the truth about} all the things Paul was accused of (Acts 24:8). All other refs.: KNOW <1921>, RECOGNIZE <1921>.

[4] **to have knowledge: *eidō*** [verb: εἴδω <1492>] ▶ **To know, to understand** > Felix had more accurate knowledge {knew accurately} (Acts 24:22).

– [5] Acts 17:13 → to have knowledge → KNOW <1097> [6] Acts 18:24 → with a thorough knowledge → lit.: he was mighty → MIGHTY (adj.) <1415> [7] 1 Cor. 15:34 → not to have the knowledge → lit.: to have the ignorance → IGNORANCE <56> [8] Eph. 3:4 → UNDERSTANDING <4907> [9] Jas. 3:13 → endued with knowledge → UNDERSTANDING <1990> [10] 2 Pet. 2:12 → to have no knowledge → to be ignorant → IGNORANT <50> [11] 1 John 2:20 → to have knowledge → KNOW <1492>.

KNOWN – [1] ***gnōstos*** [adj.: γνωστός <1110>]; **from *ginōskō*: to know** ▶ **Learned, found out; familiar** > The apostle John was known to the high priest (John 18:15, 16). What happened to Judas became known to {was heard by} all those dwelling in Jerusalem (Acts 1:19). The resurrection of Dorcas became known throughout all Joppa (Acts 9:42). What the man with an evil spirit had done became known to the inhabitants of Ephesus (Acts 19:17). Other refs.: Acts 2:14; 4:10; 13:38; 15:18; 28:22, 28; Rom. 1:19. All other refs.: ACQUAINTANCE <1110>, EVIDENT <1110>.

[2] ***phaneros*** [adj.: φανερός <5318>]; **from *phainō*: to seem, to shine, which is from *phōs*: light** ▶ **Visible, brought to the attention** > Jesus warned the unclean spirits that they should not make Him known {make Him manifest, tell who He was} (Mark 3:12). Joseph's family became known to the Pharaoh {He learned about this family} (Acts 7:13b). All other refs.: see entries in Lexicon at <5318>.

[3] **to make known: *anagnōrizō*** [verb: ἀναγνωρίζω <319>]; **from *ana*: again, and *gnōrizō*: to know, to reveal** ▶ **To reveal, to disclose oneself** > Joseph was made known to his brothers {told his brothers who he was} (Acts 7:13). ¶

[4] **to become known: *aphikneomai*** [verb: ἀφικνέομαι <864>]; **from *apo*: from, and *hikneomai*: to come, to occur** ▶ **To be brought to the attention, to be heard** > The obedience of the Christians in Rome had become known to {had come abroad to, had reached} all (Rom. 16:19). ¶

– [5] John 1:18 → to make known → DECLARE <1834> [6] John 11:16; 20:24; 21:2 → to be known CALLED (BE) <3004> [7] John 16:13, 14 → to make known → SHOW (verb) <312> [8] Col. 1:8

→ to make known → DECLARE <1213> **9** Col. 1:25 → to make fully known → FULFILL <4137> **10** Col. 4:9 → to make known → INFORM <1107> **11** 1 Thes. 1:8 → to become known → SPREAD <1831> **12** Rev. 1:1 → to make known → SIGNIFY <4591>.

KORAH – ***Kore*** [masc. name: Κόρε <2879>]; **from *korah*: bald, in Heb. ▶ Man of the tribe of Levi** > Jude 11 speaks of the rebellion of Korah who incited the Israelites to revolt against the authority of Moses (see Num. 16:1–19). The earth opened and swallowed Korah, all those who supported him and their possessions; the earth closed over them and they perished in the midst of Israel (see Num. 16:20–35). Num. 26:11 specifies that the sons of Korah, however, did not die. ¶

KOS – Acts 21:1 → COS <2972>.

KYRIA – 2 John 1, 5 → LADY <2959>.

L

LABOR (noun) – [1] ***kopos*** [masc. noun: κόπος <2873>]; **from *koptō*: to cut, to strike ▶ Intense work, toil; also transl.: efforts, hard work, weariness, work** > The disciples had entered into the labors of other people (John 4:38). Each shall receive his own reward according to his own labor (1 Cor. 3:8). The labor of Christians is not in vain in the Lord (1 Cor. 15:58). Paul commended himself as God's servant in labors (2 Cor. 6:5). He did not boast in things beyond his measure, in the labors of others (2 Cor. 10:15). As a servant of Christ he had been in labors more abundantly (2 Cor. 11:23). He had been in labor and toil (2 Cor. 11:27; 1 Thes. 2:9; 2 Thes. 3:8). He remembered the labor of love of the Thessalonians (1 Thes. 1:3). He feared that his labor among the Thessalonians might come to nothing (1 Thes. 3:5). The Lord knows the works, the labor, and the endurance of the church of Ephesus (Rev. 2:2). The dead who die in the Lord will rest from their labors (Rev. 14:13). Other ref.: Heb. 6:10 in some mss. All other refs.: TROUBLE (noun) <2873>, TROUBLE (verb) <2873>.

[2] **to be in labor, to have labor pains: *ōdinō*** [verb: ὠδίνω <5605>]; **from *ōdin*: pain of childbirth ▶ To go through the pain of giving birth** > The barren woman is not in labor {travails not, has no labor pains} (Gal. 4:27). John saw a woman crying out in labor {in pain, being in travail, travailing in birth} (lit.: being in labor) (Rev. 12:2). Other ref.: Gal. 4:19; see LABOR (verb) <5605>. ¶

– [3] John 16:21; Gal. 4:27 → to be in labor → to give birth → BIRTH <5088> [4] 1 Thes. 5:3 → labor pain → PAIN (noun) <5604>.

LABOR (verb) – [1] ***kopiaō*** [verb: κοπιάω <2872>]; **from *kopos*: work, effort ▶ To exert a major effort in order to accomplish something, to work; also transl.: to labour, to toil, to work hard** > The lilies of the field do not labor or spin (Matt. 6:28; Luke 12:27). Peter and the other disciples had labored through the whole night (Luke 5:5). Jesus speaks to His disciples of not having labored, but others having labored (John 4:38a, b). In everything he did, Paul had shown the Christians of Ephesus that, just as he labored for his own needs and the needs of his companions, they too must help the weak (Acts 20:35). Paul said to greet a certain Mary who had labored much for the Christians at Rome (Rom. 16:6), as well as Tryphaena, Tryphosa, and Persis (v. 12a, b). He labored, working with his own hands (1 Cor. 4:12). He had labored more abundantly than all the other apostles, nevertheless, not he, but the grace of God which was with him (1 Cor. 15:10). The Christians of Corinth were to submit themselves to everyone who joined in the work and labored with Paul (1 Cor. 16:16). Paul feared for the Galatians, lest perhaps he had labored over them in vain (Gal. 4:11). He who steals must steal no longer, but he must labor, working with his hands what is good (Eph. 4:28). Paul had not run in vain nor labored in vain (Phil. 2:16). He labored that he might present every man perfect in Christ (Col. 1:29). He requested his brothers in Thessalonica to know those who labored among them (1 Thes. 5:12). He labored and suffered reproach because he trusted in the living God (1 Tim. 4:10). The elders who take the lead well are to be esteemed worthy of double honor, especially those who labor in the word and doctrine (1 Tim. 5:17). The hardworking farmer must first labor before partaking of the fruits (2 Tim. 2:6); other transl.: the farmer who works hard must be the first to receive his share of the crops. Other refs.: Matt. 11:28; John 4:6; Rev. 2:3; see WEARY (adj.) <2872>. ¶

[2] ***ōdinō*** [verb: ὠδίνω <5605>]; **from *ōdin*: pain of childbirth ▶ To go through the pain of giving birth** > Paul uses this verb {to travail in birth, to be in the pains of childbirth} to describe his efforts to free the Galatians from the influence of Judaism until Christ would be formed in them (Gal. 4:19); he was working at this "again" since he had worked at their liberation from idolatry (see vv. 8–11). Other refs.: Gal. 4:27; Rev. 12:2; see LABOR (noun) <5605>. ¶

[3] ***spoudazō*** [verb: σπουδάζω <4704>]; **from *spoudē*: haste, zeal ▶ To hasten; also transl.: to be diligent, to use diligence, to make every effort** > The Christians should labor to enter into the rest of God (Heb. 4:11). All other refs.: DILIGENT <4704>,

EFFORT <4704>, ENDEAVOR (verb) <4704>.

[4] ***philotimeomai*** [verb: φιλοτιμέομαι <5389>]; **from *philotimos*: fond of honor, ambitious, which is from *philos*: friend, and *timē*: honor ▶ To be zealous, to make it a point of honor** > Paul was laboring {had as his ambition, made it his goal, made it his aim} to be accepted of the Lord (2 Cor. 5:9). All other refs.: STRIVE <5389>, STUDY <5389>.

– [5] Matt. 11:28 → WEARY (BE) <2872> [6] Mark 6:48 → TORMENT (verb) <928> [7] John 6:27; 1 Thes. 2:9; 2 Thes. 3:8 → WORK (verb) <2038> [8] 1 Cor. 9:13 → MINISTER (verb) <2038> [9] 2 Cor. 11:27; 2 Thes. 3:8 → lit.: in labor → LABOR (noun) <2873> [10] Phil. 4:3 → to strive together → STRIVE <4866> [11] Col. 4:12 → to labor fervently, to labor earnestly → FIGHT (verb) <75> [12] Col. 4:13 → he labors much → lit.: he has a great work → ZEAL <2205>.

LABORER – [1] Matt. 9:37, 38; 10:10; 20:1, 2, 8; Luke 10:2a, b, 7; 1 Tim. 5:18; James 5:4 → WORKMAN <2040> [2] 1 Cor. 16:16 → every laborer → everyone who labors → LABOR (verb) <2872> [3] 1 Thes. 3:2; Phm. 1, 24 → fellow laborer → FELLOW WORKER <4904> [4] Jas. 5:7 → FARMER <1092>.

LABORER TOGETHER – ***sunergos*** [adj. used as noun: συνεργός <4904>]; **from *sun*: together, and *ergon*: work; lit.: who works together ▶ Person working with another one, co-worker** > Christians are laborers together of God {God's fellow workers, fellow-workmen} (1 Cor. 3:9). All other refs.: FELLOW WORKER <4904>.

LABOUR (noun) – See LABOR (noun).

LABOUR (verb) – [1] See LABOR (verb).
– [2] Col. 3:23 → DO <2038>.

LABOURER – See LABORER, LABORER TOGETHER.

LACK (noun) – [1] **what is lacking: *husterēma*** [neut. noun: ὑστέρημα <5303>]; **from *hustereō*: to lack, which is from *husteros*: last ▶ Need, requirement; also transl.: want** > Fortunatus and Achaicus had supplied what was lacking on the part {absence} of the Corinthians (1 Cor. 16:17). Epaphroditus completed what was lacking {completed what was deficient, completed their lack, made up for the help they could not give} in the service of the Philippians toward Paul (Phil. 2:30). Paul filled up in his flesh that which was lacking {that which was behind} in regard to the afflictions of Christ for His body (Col. 1:24). He prayed that he might supply that which was lacking in the faith of the Thessalonians (1 Thes. 3:10). The brothers from Macedonia had supplied what was lacking to Paul (2 Cor. 11:9). Other refs.: Luke 21:4 {need}; 2 Cor. 8:14a, b; 9:12. ¶

[2] **to have lack: *elattoneō*** [verb: ἐλαττονέω <1641>]; **from *elattōn*: less ▶ To have less (of something)** > He who gathered little manna had no lack {was nothing short, did not have too little} (2 Cor. 8:15). ¶
– [3] 1 Thes. 4:12 → NEED <5532>.

LACK (verb) – [1] ***hustereō*** [verb: ὑστερέω <5302>]; **from *husteros*: last ▶ To be without, to be in want of something** > The rich young man asked Jesus what he still lacked (Matt. 19:20); Jesus told him he lacked one thing (Mark 10:21). The disciples lacked nothing when Jesus had sent them without moneybag, knapsack, or shoes (Luke 22:35). The verb is transl. "to run out of" {to want, to be deficient, to give out, to be gone} in John 2:3: they ran out of wine at the wedding in Cana. The Corinthians were not lacking {coming behind, coming short} in any gift of grace (1 Cor. 1:7). God has given greater honor to our members which lack it (1 Cor. 12:24). We must look carefully lest anyone lacks {comes short, falls short, fails} of {misses} the grace of God (Heb. 12:15). All other refs.: COME <5302>, INFERIOR <5302>, PRIVATION <5302>, WANT (noun) <5302>, WORSE <5302>.

[2] ***leipō*** [verb: λείπω <3007>] **▶ To fail, to be absent** > The rich young man lacked one

thing (Luke 18:22; lit.: one thing was lacking to him). Titus was to see that nothing was lacking {wanting} to Zenas and Apollos {that they had everything needed} (Titus 3:13). Other refs.: Titus 1:5 {to remain}; Jas. 1:4 {to be wanting}, 5; 2:15 {to be destitute, to be in need, to be without}. ¶

– 3 Acts 4:34 → any that lacked, anyone who lacked → person in want → WANT (noun) <1729> 4 1 Cor. 9:6 → to not have 5 1 Cor. 16:17; 2 Cor. 8:14a, b; 9:12; 11:9; Phil. 2:30; 1 Thes. 3:10 → what is lacking → LACK (noun) <5303> 6 Phil. 4:10 → to lack opportunity → OPPORTUNITY <170> 7 2 Pet. 1:9 → lit.: to not be present → to be present → PRESENT <3918>.

LACKING – 1 Rom. 12:11 → SLOTHFUL <3636> 2 1 Cor. 16:17; 2 Cor. 8:14a, b; 9:12; Phil. 2:30; Col. 1:24; 1 Thes. 3:10 → what is lacking → LACK (noun) <5303>.

LAD – John 6:9 → BOY <3808>.

LADE – 1 Luke 11:46 → LOAD (verb) <5412> 2 Luke 21:34 → to be laden → OVERCHARGED (BE) <925> 3 Acts 28:10 → to make presents → SUPPLY (verb) <2007>.

LADEN – 1 Matt. 11:28 → to be heavy laden → LOAD (verb) <5412> 2 2 Tim. 3:6 → to load down → LOAD (verb) <4987>.

LADING – ***phortos*** [masc. noun: φόρτος <5414>]; **from *pherō*: to carry ▶ Freight of a ship; also transl.: cargo** > Paul warned that there would be much damage to the lading of the ship (Acts 27:10). ¶

LADY – ***kuria*** [fem. noun: κυρία <2959>]; **fem. of *kurios*: master, mister ▶ Title given to a woman** > Person to whom John addresses himself in his second epistle (2 John 1, 5). It has been suggested that this person could be Kyria, a proper name of a woman. ¶

LAGGING – Rom. 12:11 → SLOTHFUL <3636>.

LAID OUT (BE) – ***keimai*** [verb: κεῖμαι <2749>] **▶ To lie, to be built** > The holy city is laid out as a square {lies four-square} (Rev. 21:16). Other refs.: APPOINT <2749>, LAY <2749>, LIE (verb)[1] <2749>, SITUATE <2749>, STAND (verb) <2749>.

LAKE – 1 ***limnē*** [fem. noun: λίμνη <3041>]; **comp. *limēn*: harbor ▶ a. An expanse of water surrounded by land** > Luke uses this term for the lake of Gennesaret. Jesus stood by that lake (Luke 5:1); He saw two boats standing by the lake {at the water's edge} (v. 2). He said to His disciples: Let us cross over to the other side of the lake (8:22); a storm of wind came down on the lake (v. 23). A herd of swine ran violently down a steep place into the lake (8:33). **b. The lake of fire is a place of eternal suffering and damnation reserved for unbelievers as well as fallen angels** > The beast and the false prophet will be cast alive into the lake of fire burning with brimstone at the beginning of the millennium (Rev. 19:20), and the devil as well at the end of the millennium (Rev. 20:10). Death and Hades will be cast into the lake of fire (Rev. 20:14); anyone not found written in the book of life will be cast into the lake of fire (v. 15). The lake burns with fire and brimstone, which is the second death (Rev. 21:8). ¶

– 2 Matt. 4:13 → by the lake → by the sea → SEA <3864> 3 John 6:22, 25; et al. → SEA <2281>.

LAMA – ***lama*** [adv.: λαμά <2982>] **▶ Heb. word meaning "Why?"** > It is found in Matt. 27:46 and Mark 15:34: see SABACHTHANI. Some mss. have the Aram. form "*lema.*" ¶

LAMB (name) – ***Arnion*** [neut. noun used as masc. name: Ἀρνίον <721>]; **dimin. of *arēn*: young sheep; lit.: small lamb ▶ Name of the Lord Jesus, the Son of God, who offered Himself as the sin-offering to redeem us** > This name appears 28 times in Revelation as a name of the Lord: Rev. 5:6, 8, 12, 13; 6:1, 16; 7:9, 10, 14, 17; 12:11; 13:8; 14:1, 4a, b, 10; 15:3; 17:14a, b; 19:7,

9; 21:9, 14, 22, 23, 27; 22:1, 3. Other refs.: John 21:15; Rev. 13:11. ¶

LAMB (noun) – [1] ***amnos*** [masc. noun: ἀμνός <286>]**; *agnus*, in Lat. ▶ Young sheep** > John the Baptist said that Jesus was the Lamb of God who takes away the sin of the world (describing His work of redemption; John 1:29) and the Lamb of God (describing His person; v. 36). Isaiah had spoken of Jesus as a lamb that is silent before his shearer (Acts 8:32). Peter speaks of the precious blood of Christ, as of a lamb without blemish and without spot (1 Pet. 1:19). ¶

[2] ***arēn*** [masc. noun: ἀρήν <704>] **▶ Young sheep** > The Lord sent out His disciples as lambs among wolves (Luke 10:3). ¶

[3] ***arnion*** [neut. noun: ἀρνίον <721>]**; dimin. of *arēn*: see [2]; lit.: small lamb ▶ Young sheep** > Jesus told Peter to feed His lambs (John 21:15). John saw a Lamb as it had been slain, standing in the midst of the elders (Rev. 5:6). The second beast had two horns like a lamb (Rev. 13:11). All other refs.: LAMB (name) <721>.

LAME – [1] ***chōlos*** [adj. and adj. used as noun: χωλός <5560>]**; *claudus*, in Lat. ▶ Crippled person having an injured leg or foot, disabled; also transl.: crippled, halt** > Jesus healed the lame so they could walk (Matt. 11:5; 15:30, 31; Luke 7:22). It is better to enter into life lame than to have two feet and be cast into the everlasting fire (Matt. 18:8; Mark 9:45). Jesus healed the lame who came to Him in the temple (Matt. 21:14). He told a host to invite the lame (Luke 14:13, 21). Lame people were waiting to be healed at the pool of Bethesda (John 5:3). Peter healed a certain lame man at the gate of the temple (Acts 3:2). Philip healed lame people {cripples} (Acts 8:7). At Lystra Paul healed a man who had been lame {a cripple} from his mother's womb (Acts 14:8). In their walk, Christians are to make straight paths for their feet, so that what is lame may not be disabled, i.e., become worse during the walk, but rather be healed (Heb. 12:13). ¶

– [2] Acts 4:9 → SICK (adj. and noun) <772>.

LAMECH – ***Lamech*** [masc. name: Λάμεχ <2984>]**: strong, in Heb. ▶ Father of Noah (see Lamech: Gen. 5:28, 29)** > Lamech is mentioned in the genealogy of Jesus (Luke 3:36). ¶

LAMENT – [1] ***koptō*** [verb: κόπτω <2875>]**; lit.: to beat ▶ To beat oneself on the breast as an expr. of grief; hence, to bewail; also transl.: to wail, to mourn** > All wept and lamented for the young girl who had died (Luke 8:52). The generation of the Lord was like children saying that they had mourned and their companions did not lament (Matt. 11:17). All the tribes of the earth will lament when they see the Son of Man coming in the clouds of heaven (Matt. 24:30); see also Rev. 1:7. The kings of the earth will lament for Babylon (Rev. 18:9). All other refs.: CUT <2875>, MOURN <2875>.

[2] ***thrēneō*** [verb: θρηνέω <2354>]**; from *thrēnos*: dirge, lamentation, funeral moaning; an outward demonstration of an inner grief ▶ To bewail, to mourn** > A great multitude of the people and of women mourned and lamented {wailed for} Jesus, following Him (Luke 23:27). After the departure of Jesus, the disciples would weep and lament, but the world would rejoice (John 16:20). Other refs.: Matt. 11:17; Luke 7:32; see MOURN <2354>. ¶

[3] ***talaipōreō*** [verb: ταλαιπωρέω <5003>]**; from *talaiporos*: afflicted, miserable, which is from *talas*: suffering, and an uncertain Greek word ▶ To feel one's own distress; to be miserable** > James exhorts sinners to lament {be afflicted, grieve, be wretched} and mourn (Jas. 4:9). ¶

LAMENTATION – [1] ***kopetos*** [masc. noun: κοπετός <2870>]**; from *koptō*: to beat one's breast, to lament, to mourn ▶ Mourning, expression of bereavement** > Devout men made great lamentations {mourned deeply} over Stephen's death (Acts 8:2). ¶

[2] ***thrēnos*** [masc. noun: θρῆνος <2355>]**; comp. *threomai*: to cry aloud, to lament >**

This word is found in Matt. 2:18 in some mss. ¶
– [3] Matt. 2:18; 2 Cor. 7:7 → MOURNING <3602>.

LAMP – [1] ***lampas*** [fem. noun: λαμπάς <2985>]; **from *lampō*: to shine ▶ Torch; a lamp that is fed with oil** > In the parable, ten virgins took their lamps and went out to meet the bridegroom (Matt. 25:1, 3, 4, 7, 8). There were many lamps {lights} in the upper chamber where Paul continued his speech (Acts 20:8); *hupolampas* in some mss. John saw seven lamps of fire burning before the throne (Rev. 4:5). Other refs.: John 18:3; Rev. 8:10; see TORCH <2985>. ¶
[2] ***luchnos*** [masc. noun: λύχνος <3088>]; **comp. *leukos*: white ▶ A portable lamp or other means of illumination; this is not a candle as we understand it, which feeds of its own substance, but rather a lamp fed by oil, figure of the Holy Spirit; also transl.: candle, light** > Men do not light a lamp and put it under a bushel (Matt. 5:15; Mark 4:21; Luke 8:16; 11:33), but on a lampstand. The lamp of the body is the eye (Matt. 6:22; Luke 11:34). The body may be full of light, as when the bright shining of a lamp gives light (Luke 11:36). Our loins should be girded and our lamps burning (Luke 12:35). The woman who has lost a piece of silver lights a lamp and sweeps the house (Luke 15:8). John the Baptist was a burning and shining lamp (John 5:35). The word of prophecy is like a lamp that shines in a dark place (2 Pet. 1:19). The light of a lamp will shine no more at all in Babylon (Rev. 18:23). The Lamb is the lamp of the new Jerusalem (Rev. 21:23); there will be no more need of a lamp (Rev. 22:5). ¶
– [3] Rev. 1:12, 13, 20a, b; 2:1, 5; 11:4 → LAMPSTAND <3087>.

LAMPSTAND – ***luchnia*** [fem. noun: λυχνία <3087>]; **from *luchnos*; see** LAMP <3088> **▶ Support for a lamp; also transl.: candlestick, lamp, stand** > There was a lampstand in the holy place of the tabernacle (Heb. 9:2); it was made of pure gold and its seven lamps were constantly lighted (see Ex. 25:31–40). The word is also used in Matt. 5:15; Mark 4:21; Luke 8:16; 11:33. John saw seven golden lampstands (Rev. 1:12, 13, 20a, b; 2:1). The lampstand of the church of Ephesus was in danger of being removed from its place (Rev. 2:5). The two witnesses during the great tribulation are like two lampstands (Rev. 11:4). ¶

LAND (noun) – [1] ***agros*** [masc. noun: ἀγρός <68>] **▶ Field, piece of ground** > Owning land, Barnabas sold it and brought the money to the apostles (Acts 4:37). All other refs.: COUNTRY <68>, FIELD <68>, FIELD OF BLOOD <68>.
[2] ***gē*** [fem. noun: γῆ <1093>] **▶ Region, country; earth as a whole** > Jesus and His disciples came to the land of {landed at} Gennesaret (Matt. 14:34; Mark 6:53). The word is used for those places where darkness appeared when Jesus was on the cross (Matt. 27:45; Mark 15:33; Luke 23:44), as well for the land where Jesus had resurrected a young girl (Matt. 9:26), the land where He had healed two blind men (Matt. 9:31), the land of Sodom and Gomorrah (Matt. 10:15; 11:24), the land where a great famine took place in the days of Elijah (Luke 4:25), the land upon which there will be great tribulation (Luke 21:23), the land {countryside} of Judea (John 3:22), the land which Abraham left and the land which he entered (Acts 7:3a, b, 4a, b), the land of Egypt (Acts 7:11, 36, 40; 13:17; Heb. 8:9; Jude 5), the land of Midian (Acts 7:29), the land of Canaan (Acts 13:19a, b), and an unfamiliar land (Acts 27:39). All other refs.: EARTH <1093>.
[3] ***chōra*** [fem. noun: χώρα <5561>]; **from *chōros*: field ▶ Country, region** > The term is used in Acts 27:27. All other refs.: COUNTRY <5561>, FIELD <5561>.
[4] ***chōrion*** [neut. noun: χωρίον <5564>]; **from *chōra*: region, or dimin. of *chōros*: field, place ▶ Region, grounds** > Publius had lands {possessions, an estate} on the island of Malta (Acts 28:7). All other refs.: FIELD <5564>, GROUND (noun)[1] <5564>, PLACE (noun) <5564>.
[5] **dry land, dry: *xēros*** [adj. used as noun: ξηρός <3584>] **▶ This term designates earth as opposed to water** > The scribes

and the Pharisees traveled over the sea and the land (lit.: the dry) to win a single convert (Matt. 23:15). All other refs.: DRY (noun) <3584>, WITHERED <3584>.
– 6 Matt. 2:6, 20, 21; Mark 4:1; 6:47; Luke 8:27; 14:35; Eph. 6:3; Heb. 11:9; Rev. 1:7; et al. → EARTH <1093> 7 Matt. 4:16 → COUNTRY <5561> 8 Acts 17:26 → HABITATION <2733> 9 Acts 20:13 → to go by land → to go on foot → FOOT[1] <3978> 10 Acts 21:3 → to make the land → LAND (verb) <2718> 11 2 Cor. 10:16 → in lands beyond you → lit.: to the things beyond you 12 Heb. 11:15 → "land" added in Engl.

LAND (verb) – 1 ***katagō*** [verb: κατάγω <2609>]; **from *kata*: down (intens.), and *agō*: to lead ▶ To go ashore, to reach land** > After having landed at {come to, put in} Syracuse, Paul remained there for three days (Acts 28:12). All other refs.: BRING <2609>, TOUCH <2609>.
2 ***katerchomai*** [verb: κατέρχομαι <2718>]; **from *kata*: down, and *erchomai*: to go ▶ To descend, to dock** > Paul landed at Caesarea (Acts 18:22). Paul and his companions landed {made the land} at Tyre (Acts 21:3); other mss.: *katagō* (see 1). All other refs.: COME <2718>, DESCEND <2718>, GO <2718>.
– 3 Matt. 14:34; Mark 6:53 → lit.: to come to the land (noun) → LAND <1093> 4 Mark 3:20 → to come together → COME <4905> 5 John 21:9 → COME <576>.

LANDOWNER – Matt. 13:27; 20:1, 11; 21:33 → master of the house → MASTER (noun) <3617>.

LANE – 1 ***rhumē*** [fem. noun: ῥύμη <4505>] ▶ **Alley, small street** > The master of the house sent his servant out into the streets and lanes of the city to bring in the poor, the crippled, the blind, and the lame to his great supper (Luke 14:21). Other refs.: Matt. 6:2; Acts 9:11; 12:10; see STREET <4505>. ¶
– 2 Luke 14:23 → country lane → HEDGE (noun) <5418>.

LANGUAGE – 1 ***dialektos*** [fem. noun: διάλεκτος <1258>]; **from *dialegomai*: to deliberate, which is from *dia*: denoting separation, and *legō*: to speak ▶ The entire body of words in use in a given community; also transl.: dialect, tongue** > The field purchased by Judas was called Aceldama in the language of those dwelling in Jerusalem (Acts 1:19). Everyone heard the early Christians speaking in his or her own language (Acts 2:6, 8). Other refs.: Acts 21:40; 22:2; 26:14; see TONGUE <1258>. ¶
– 2 John 8:43 → SPEECH <2981> 3 John 8:44 → his native language → lit.: his own things → his own nature → NATURE <2398> 4 John 16:25a, b → figurative language → ALLEGORY <3942> 5 Rev. 5:9; 7:9; 10:11; 11:9; 13:7; 14:6; 17:15 → TONGUE <1100>.

LANTERN – ***phanos*** [masc. noun: φανός <5322>]; **from *phainō*: to shine, to show, which is from *phōs*: light ▶ A torch consisting of strips of resinous wood tied together, usually held in the hand** > Judas and those who accompanied him came with lanterns and torches {some translate: torches and lanterns} and weapons to take hold of Jesus (John 18:3). ¶

LAODICEA – ***Laodikeia*** [fem. name: Λαοδίκεια <2993>]; **from *laos*: people, and *dikē*: justice ▶ City in western Asia Minor, in Phrygia** > Paul mentions the Christians at Laodicea (Col. 2:1; 4:13), greets the brothers there (4:15), and encourages the Colossians to read the letter from them (4:16). The church of Laodicea is the last of seven churches to which a letter is addressed; its lukewarm condition is emphasized (Rev. 1:11; 3:14). ¶

LAODICEAN – ***Laodikeus*** [masc. name: Λαοδικεύς <2994; **from *Laodikeia*: Laodicea, which is from *laos*: people, and *dikē*: justice ▶ Inhabitant of Laodicea, in Asia Minor, near Colossae and Hierapolis** > Paul asked the Colossians and Laodiceans to read the respective letters from each other (Col. 4:16). Other ref.: Rev. 3:14 in some mss. ¶

LAP – Luke 6:38 → BOSOM <2859>.

LARGE – [1] ***hikanos*** [adj.: ἱκανός <2425>]; **from *hikneomai*: to come, to occur ▶ Great, considerable** > A large {very considerable, sizeable} crowd was {Much people were} with the widow whose son was being carried out (Luke 7:12). Other refs.: see entries in Lexicon at <2425>.
[2] **what large: *pēlikos*** [adj.: πηλίκος <4080>] ▶ **How great** > Paul told the Galatians to see what large letters (i.e., characters) he had written with his own hand (Gal. 6:11). The term is transl. "how great" in Heb. 7:4 concerning Melchizedek. ¶
– [3] Matt. 12:15 → numerous → GREAT <4183> [4] Matt. 21:8 → very large → very great → MOST <4118> [5] Matt. 26:9 → large sum → lit.: much (*polus*) [6] Mark 8:1 → VERY GREAT <3827> [7] John 21:11 → GREAT <3173>.

LARGER – Matt. 21:36 → MORE <4119>.

LASCIVIOUSNESS – Mark 7:22; 2 Cor. 12:21; Gal. 5:19; Eph. 4:19; 1 Pet. 4:3; Jude 4 → LEWDNESS <766>.

LASEA – ***Lasaia*** [fem. name: Λασαία <2996> ▶ **City in southern Crete near Fair Havens** > Paul's ship approached Lasea when he was traveling to Rome (Acts 27:8). ¶

LAST (adv. and noun) – [1] ***eschatos*** [adj. used as noun: ἔσχατος <2078>] ▶ **Which comes at the end, least important** > Jesus said that many who are first will be last, and the last first (Matt. 19:30a, b; 20:16a, b; Mark 10:31a, b; Luke 13:30a, b). If anyone desires to be first, he will be last of all and servant of all (Mark 9:35). Jesus will raise all the Father has given Him at the last day (John 6:39, 40, 44, 54). The last Adam became a life-giving spirit (1 Cor. 15:45). The Christians will be changed at the last trumpet (1 Cor. 15:52). Jesus is the first and the last (Rev. 1:17; 2:8; 22:13). He knows the last works of Thyatira which are more than the first (Rev. 2:19). Other refs.: Matt. 5:26 {uttermost}; 12:45 {final}; 20:8, 12, 14; 27:64; Mark 12:6, 22; Luke 11:26 {final}; 12:59; 14:9 {least important, lowest}, 10 {lowest}; John 7:37; 8:9; 11:24; 12:48; Acts 2:17; 1 Cor. 4:9 {at the end of the procession}; 15:8, 26; 2 Tim. 3:1; Jas. 5:3; 1 Pet. 1:5; 2 Pet. 3:3; 1 John 2:18a, b; Rev. 15:1; 21:9. All other refs.: END (noun) <2078>, PART (noun) <2078>, STATE <2078>.
[2] **at the last: *husteron*** [adv.: ὕστερον <5305>]; **from *husteros*: which comes after ▶ Finally, later** > At the last {At last, Later on}, two false witnesses testified against Jesus (Matt. 26:60).
[3] **last of all, at last: *husteron*** [adv.: ὕστερον <5305>] ***de*** [conj.: δέ <1161>] ▶ **Later, finally** > At last {Afterward} the landowner sent his son to the vinedressers (Matt. 21:37). Other refs.: Matt. 4:2; 21:29, 32; 22:27; 25:11; 26:60 (see [2]); Mark 16:14; Luke 4:2; 20:32; John 13:36; Heb. 12:11. ¶
[4] **at last: *ēdē*** [adv.: ἤδη <2235>] ▶ **Finally** > Paul rejoiced that now at last {at the last, at length} the care of the Philippians for him had flourished again (Phil. 4:10). *
– [5] Mark 15:37, 39; Luke 23:46 → to breathe one's last → EXPIRE <1606> [6] Acts 5:5, 10 → to breathe one's last → EXPIRE <1634>.

LAST (verb) – [1] Matt. 13:21 → lit.: to be [2] 1 Cor. 9:25 → to last forever → INCORRUPTIBLE <862> [3] 1 Cor. 9:25 → that will not last → CORRUPTIBLE <5349>.

LASTING – **to last: *menō*** [verb: μένω <3306>] ▶ **To remain, to stay forever** > The Hebrew Christians knew that they had a better possession, and a lasting {abiding, enduring} one, in comparison to the goods that had been taken from them (Heb. 10:34). Christians do not have a lasting {abiding, continuing, enduring} city here on earth (Heb. 13:14). They are born again by the living and abiding {enduring} word of God (1 Pet. 1:23). All other refs.: AWAIT <3306>, CONTINUE <3306>, REMAIN

<3306>, STAY (verb) <3306>, TARRY <3306>.

LATCHET – Mark 1:7; Luke 3:16; John 1:27 → STRAP <2438>.

LATE – [1] **late on:** ***opse*** [adv.: ὀψέ <3796>] ▶ **At the end of; also transl.: after** > Women came to the tomb of Jesus late on the Sabbath, as it was the dusk of the first day of the week (Matt. 28:1). Other refs.: Mark 11:19; 13:35; see EVENING <3796>. ¶
– [2] Matt. 14:15 → it is already late → lit.: the hour is already passed → PASS <3928> [3] Mark 6:35a, b → far passed → PASS <4183> [4] Mark 11:11 → EVENING <3798>.

LATELY – Acts 18:2 → RECENTLY <4373>.

LATER – [1] Matt. 14:23 → later that night → when evening came → EVENING <3798> [2] Mark 16:14; John 13:36; Heb. 12:11 → AFTERWARD <5305> [3] Acts 27:28 → a short time later → lit.: having gone a little farther → FARTHER <1339> [4] 1 Tim. 4:1 → LATTER <5306> [5] Jude 5 → SECOND <1208>.

LATIN – **in Latin:** ***Rhōmaisti*** [adv.: Ῥωμαϊστί <4515>]; **from *Rhōmē*: Rome** ▶ **In the language spoken by the Romans** > The title above Jesus on the cross was written in Hebrew, Greek, and Latin (John 19:20). ¶

LATTER – [1] ***husteros*** [adj.: ὕστερος <5306>] ▶ **Which comes at the end** > The Spirit expressly says that in the latter {later} times, some will apostatize from the faith, giving their mind to deceiving spirits and doctrines of demons (1 Tim. 4:1). ¶
– [2] Jas. 5:7 → late rain, latter rain → RAIN (noun) <3797> [3] 2 Pet. 2:20 → latter end → last state → STATE <2078> [4] Rev. 2:19 → LAST (adv. and noun) <2078>.

LAUD – Rom. 15:11 → PRAISE (verb) <134>.

LAUGH – [1] ***gelaō*** [verb: γελάω <1070>] ▶ **To express one's joy, one's satisfaction out loud** > Blessed are those who weep now, for they will laugh (Luke 6:21); woe to those who laugh now, for they will mourn and weep (v. 25). ¶
[2] **to laugh at, to laugh to scorn: *katagelaō*** [verb: καταγελάω <2606>]; **from *kata*: against (intens.), and *gelaō*: see [1]** ▶ **To mock at; also transl.: to deride, to ridicule** > People laughed at Jesus for saying that the young girl was not dead (Matt. 9:24; Mark 5:40; Luke 8:53). ¶

LAUGHTER – ***gelōs*** [masc. noun: γέλως <1071>]; **from *gelaō*: to laugh** ▶ **Audible expression of joy, of satisfaction** > The laughter of sinners will be changed to mourning (Jas. 4:9). ¶

LAUNCH – [1] **to launch forth: *anagō*** [verb: ἀνάγω <321>]; **from *ana*: up, again, and *agō*: to lead, to drive** ▶ **To sail away** > Jesus launched forth {launched out, set out, set off from shore} with His disciples in a boat (Luke 8:22). All other refs.: see entries in Lexicon at <321>.
[2] **to launch out: *epanagō*** [verb: ἐπανάγω <1877>]; **from *epi*: toward, and *anagō*: see [1]** ▶ **To advance (nautical term)** > Jesus told Simon to launch out {draw out, put out} into the deep (Luke 5:4). Other refs.: Matt. 21:18; Luke 5:3; see RETURN (verb) <1877>, PUT <1877>. ¶

LAUNDERER – ***gnapheus*** [masc. noun: γναφεύς <1102>]; **from *gnaphos*: teasel-cloth** ▶ **Worker who cleans soiled garments or bleaches new material** > At the transfiguration of Jesus, His clothes became exceedingly white, such as no launderer {fuller} on earth can whiten them (Mark 9:3). ¶

LAVISH (adj.) – 2 Cor. 8:20 → lavish gift → ABUNDANCE <100>.

LAVISH (verb) – [1] Eph. 1:8 → ABOUND <4052> [2] 1 John 3:1 → BESTOW <1325>.

LAW – [1] ***nomos*** [masc. noun: νόμος <3551>]; **from *nemō*: to distribute ► Rules that allow, restrict, or prohibit individual and institutional behavior >** The term describes a law in general (Rom. 4:15; 5:13). Most frequently, it describes the divine law given through Moses, whether it be moral, ceremonial, or judicial (Matt. 5:17, 18; 7:12; 23:23; Luke 2:22; John 7:51; 8:5). Sometimes it means the books of Moses or the Pentateuch containing the law (Luke 24:44; 1 Cor. 14:21). The gospel method of justification is called the "law of faith," the opposite of the "law of works" (Rom. 3:27). The "law of the Spirit of life" is the opposite of the law of sin and death (Rom. 8:2). In James we find the "royal law" (2:8). The "perfect law of liberty" (Jas. 1:25; 2:12) frees Christians from the yoke of ceremonial observances and from the slavery of sin; it is opposed to the Mosaic law which made nothing perfect (Heb. 7:19; 10:1). The term also describes a force or principle of action which is equivalent to a law (Rom. 7:21, 23, 25; 8:2). (After S. Zodhiates.) *

[2] **to receive the law, to have the law given: *nomotheteō*** [verb: νομοθετέω <3549>]; **from *nomothetēs*: legislator, which is from *nomos*: see [1], and *tithēmi*: to put ► To make the object of a piece of legislation >** In Heb. 7:11, the thought is that the Levitical priesthood was at the base of the legislation given to the people. Other ref.: Heb. 8:6; see ESTABLISH <3549>. ¶

[3] **he who is without law, he who does not have the law: *anomos*** [adj. used as a noun: ἄνομος <459>]; **from *a*: neg., and *nomos*: law (see [1]) ► Person who does not observe the law >** Paul uses this word in 1 Cor. 9:21a–d. All other refs.: LAWLESS (adj.) <459>, LAWLESS (noun) <459>.

[4] **without the law, apart from the law: *anomōs*** [adv.: ἀνόμως <460>]; **from *anomos*: see [3] ► Outside the law >** All who have sinned without the law will also perish without the law, and all who have sinned under the law will be judged by the law (Rom. 2:12a, b). ¶

[5] **about the law: *nomikos*** [adj.: νομικός <3544>]; **from *nomos*: see [1] ► Concerning the law >** Titus was to avoid disputes about the law (Titus 3:9). All other refs.: LAWYER <3544>.

– [6] Matt. 1:19 → faithful to the law → RIGHTEOUS <1342> [7] Matt. 5:40 → to go to law, to sue at law → SUE <2919> [8] Matt. 8:14; 10:35; Mark 1:30; Luke 4:38; 12:53 → mother-in-law → MOTHER <3994> [9] Matt. 12:38; 26:57; Luke 20:1; et al. → teacher of the law → SCRIBE <1122> [10] Matt. 27:6; John 5:10 → to be against the law, the law forbids → to not be lawful, it is not lawful → LAWFUL <1832> [11] Mark 10:5; Heb. 7:5 → COMMANDMENT <1785> [12] Luke 5:17; Acts 5:34; 1 Tim. 1:7 → TEACHER OF THE LAW <3547> [13] Acts 7:44 → covenant law → lit.: witness → WITNESS (noun)[1] <3142> [14] Acts 10:28 → against the law → UNLAWFUL <111> [15] Acts 15:21 → the law of Moses has been preached → lit.: Moses has been preached [16] Acts 19:38 → COURT <60> [17] Acts 23:3 → contrary to the law → to break the law, to violate the law → CONTRARY <3891> [18] Rom. 9:4 → giving of the law, receiving of the law → GIVING <3548> [19] 1 Cor. 6:1, 6 → to go to law → to prosecute one's suit → SUIT (noun) <2919> [20] 1 Cor. 6:7 → to go to law → lit.: to have lawsuit → LAWSUIT <2917> [21] 1 Cor. 9:21: under the law, under law → LAWFUL <1772>.

LAW-BREAKER – Matt. 13:41 → lit.: the ones practicing iniquity → INIQUITY <458>.

LAW COURT – 1 Cor. 6:4 → JUDGMENT <2922>.

LAW-GIVING – Rom. 9:4 → giving of the law → GIVING <3548>.

LAWBREAKER – [1] Gal. 2:18; Jas. 2:9, 11 → TRANSGRESSOR <3848> [2] 1 Tim. 1:9 → LAWLESS (noun) <459>.

LAWFUL – [1] ***ennomos*** [adj.: ἔννομος <1772>]; **from *en*: in, and *nomos*: law, which is from *nemō*: to distribute ► Within the law, legal >** The lawful {regular} assembly of Acts 19:39 refers to a gathering which is legitimate. The word is transl. "under {the) law" {legitimately subject} in 1 Cor. 9:21. ¶

[2] **to be lawful: *exesti*** [verb: ἔξεστι <1832>]; **from *ek*: out of, and *eimi*: to be ▶ To be legal, to be exempt from penalization, to be allowed, to be permitted, to be permissible** > The verb is used in regard to the disciples (Matt. 12:2; Mark 2:24; Luke 6:2), David (Matt. 12:4; Mark 2:26; Luke 6:4), Herod (Matt. 14:4; Mark 6:18), a master of a house (Matt. 20:15 {to have the right}), paying tribute to Caesar {to be right} (Matt. 22:17; Mark 12:14; Luke 20:22), and the pieces of silver of Judas (Matt. 27:6 {to be against the law; lit.: to not be lawful}). It is also used concerning Jesus (Luke 6:9; 14:3), Peter (Acts 2:29), and Paul and in regard to himself (Acts 21:37 {to be allowed}; 22:25 {to be legal}; 2 Cor. 12:4). Other refs.: Matt. 12:10, 12; 19:3; Mark 3:4; 10:2; John 5:10; 18:31; Acts 8:37 (in some mss.); 16:21; 1 Cor. 6:12a, b; 10:23a, b. ¶

LAWFULLY – ***nomimōs*** [adv.: νομίμως <3545>]; **from *nomimos*: lawful, which is from *nomos*: law, which is from *nemō*: to distribute ▶ In an equitable manner, according to the law** > The law is good if one uses it lawfully {properly} (1 Tim. 1:8); it is not made for a righteous person but for the lawless and insubordinate (see v. 9). If a man competes in the games, he is not crowned, unless he competes lawfully {according to the rules} (2 Tim. 2:5). ¶

LAWGIVER – ***nomothetēs*** [masc. noun: νομοθέτης <3550>]; **from *nomos*: law, which is from *nemō*: to distribute, and *tithēmi*: to establish, to lay down ▶ He who promulgates the laws, legislator** > God only is the Lawgiver and Judge (Jas. 4:12). ¶

LAWLESS (adj.) – [1] ***anomos*** [adj.: ἄνομος <459>]; **from *a*: neg., and *nomos*: law, which is from *nemō*: to distribute ▶ Which observes neither moral rule nor the law** > Peter reproaches the Jews for having put Jesus to death by the hand of lawless {godless, wicked} men (lit.: by lawless hands) (Acts 2:23). Lot tormented his soul with the lawless {unlawful} deeds of the evil men of Sodom and Gomorrah (2 Pet. 2:8). All other refs.: LAW <459>, LAWLESS (noun) <459>.

– [2] Rom. 4:7; Heb. 10:17 → lawless deeds, lawless acts → INIQUITY <458> [3] 1 Pet. 4:3 → ABOMINABLE <111> [4] 2 Pet. 2:7; 3:17 → LAWLESS MAN <113>.

LAWLESS (noun) – ***anomos*** [adj. used as noun: ἄνομος <459>]; **from *a*: neg., and *nomos*: law, which is from *nemō*: to distribute ▶ Which does not observe any moral rule; without faith or law** > The Lord was counted among the lawless (Mark 15:28; Luke 22:37). In 2 Thes. 2:8, the lawless one {the wicked} refers to the antichrist. The law is for the lawless {lawbreakers} and insubordinate (1 Tim. 1:9). All other refs.: LAW <459>, LAWLESS (adj.) <459>.

LAWLESS MAN – ***athesmos*** [adj. used as noun: ἄθεσμος <113>]; **from *a*: neg., and *thesmos*: law, ordinance, which is from *tithēmi*: to set, to enact ▶ One without restriction, disobedient to rules; also transl.: godless, unprincipled man, wicked** > Lot was distressed with the filthy conduct of the lawless men of Sodom and Gomorrah (2 Pet. 2:7). Peter spoke of the error of lawless men (2 Pet. 3:17). ¶

LAWLESSNESS – ***anomia*** [fem. noun: ἀνομία <458>]; **from *a*: neg., and *nomos*: law, which is from *nemō*: to distribute ▶ Conduct without law, unrestrained, characterized by wickedness** > The man of lawlessness {in some mss.: of sin (*hamartia*)} will be revealed before the return of the Lord to reign on the earth (2 Thes. 2:3, 7). All other refs.: INIQUITY <458>.

LAWSUIT – ***krima*** [neut. noun: κρίμα <2917>] ▶ **Disagreement brought before a court** > It is a fault for Christians to have lawsuits {suits} between themselves (1 Cor. 6:7). All other refs.: CAUSE <2917>, FAULT <2917>, JUDGMENT <2917>.

LAWYER – [1] ***nomikos*** [adj. used as noun: νομικός <3544>]; **from *nomos*: law, which is from *nemō*: to distribute ▶ Interpreter and teacher of the law of Moses; also transl.: expert in the law** > There were many lawyers in Israel (Matt. 22:35; Luke 7:30; 10:25; 11:45, 46, 52; 14:3). Zenas was a lawyer (Titus 3:13). Other ref.: Titus 3:9 (about the law); see LAW <3544>. ¶
– [2] Acts 24:1 → ORATOR <4489>.

LAY – [1] ***tithēmi*** [verb: τίθημι <5087>]; **from *theō*: to place, to put ▶ a. To place, to put, to deposit, to set aside; also transl.: to make** > Jesus laid His hands on little children (Mark 10:16). A man might lay the foundation of a tower and not be able to finish it (Luke 14:29). The good Shepherd lays down His life for the sheep (John 10:11 {to give}, 15). Jesus was laid in a new tomb where no one had yet been laid (John 19:41, 42). Paul had laid the foundation (1 Cor. 3:10). No man can lay (*tithēmi*) a foundation other than that which is laid (lit.: beside the One being laid: *ton keimenon*), which is Christ Jesus (1 Cor. 3:11). Jesus is waiting until His enemies are made His footstool (Heb. 10:13). God says He has laid a corner stone (1 Pet. 2:6). Other refs.: Matt. 5:15; 12:18; 22:44; 27:60; Mark 4:21a, b {to set}; 6:29; 12:36; 15:19 {to bow the knee}, 46, 47; 16:6; Luke 1:66 {to keep}; 5:18; 6:48; 8:16; 11:33; 19:21 and 22 {to deposit}; 20:43; 21:14 {to settle}; 22:41 {to kneel} (lit. to place the knees); 23:53; John 11:34; 20:2, 13, 15; Acts 2:35; 3:2; 4:35, 37; 5:2, 15, 25; 7:16, 60 {to kneel}; 9:37, 40 {to kneel}; 12:4; 13:29; 20:36 {to kneel}; 21:5 {to kneel}; Rom. 9:33; 14:13; 1 Cor. 15:25; 16:2; 2 Cor. 3:13; 5:19 {to commit}; Heb. 1:13; Rev. 1:17 in some mss.; 10:2 {to set}. **b. to lay aside: To put down** > Jesus laid aside {took off} His garments before washing His disciples' feet (John 13:4). **c. to lay, to lay down: To put, to leave** > There were women observing how the body of Jesus was laid in the tomb (Luke 23:55). The Father loves the Son, because He lays down His life (John 10:17). He lays it down of Himself and He has the power to lay it down (John 10:18a, b). Peter said he was ready to lay down his life for the Lord (John 13:37, 38). No one has a greater love than to lay down his life for his friends (John 15:13). Jesus has laid down His life for us, and Christians also ought to lay down their lives for the brothers (1 John 3:16a, b). All other refs.: see entries in Lexicon at <5087>.

[2] **to lay before: *anatithēmi*** [verb: ἀνατίθημι <394>]; **from *ana*: intens., and *tithēmi*: see [1] ▶ To present, to explain** > Festus laid before {declared unto, discussed with} the king the matters relating to Paul (Acts 25:14). Paul went up to Jerusalem and laid before {communicated to, set before, submitted to} the leading brothers the glad tidings which he preached (Gal. 2:2). ¶

[3] **to lay aside, to lay down: *apotithēmi*** [verb: ἀποτίθημι <659>]; **from *apo*: from, aside, and *tithēmi*: see [1] ▶ To put on the ground** > Before Stephen was stoned, witnesses laid aside their clothes at the feet of Saul (Acts 7:58). All other refs.: CAST (verb) <659>, PUT <659>.

[4] **to lay on: *epitithēmi*** [verb: ἐπιτίθημι <2007>]; **from *epi*: upon, and *tithēmi*: see [1] ▶ To put on, to impose** > A ruler of the synagogue asked Jesus to lay His hand on his daughter who had just died so that she might live (Matt. 9:18). Jesus laid His hands on a blind man (Mark 8:23) and on an infirm woman (Luke 13:13). The cross of Jesus was laid on Simon the Cyrenian, that he might bear it after Him (Luke 23:26; other mss.: *epilambanō*). Paul laid sticks on the fire (Acts 28:3). In Acts 18:10, the verb is transl. "to attack" {to set on, to set upon}: The Lord told Paul that no one would attack him. The Lord laid {placed} His right hand on John (Rev. 1:17); other mss.: *tithēmi*. Other refs.: Matt. 21:7; 23:4; 27:29; Luke 15:5; John 9:15 {to apply}; 19:2; Acts 15:10, 28 {to burden; lit.: to lay a burden}. See LAYING ON OF HANDS <1936> <2007> <5495>. All other refs.: see entries in Lexicon at <2007>.

[5] ***katatithēmi*** [verb: κατατίθημι <2698>]; **from *kata*: down (intens.), and *tithēmi*: see [1] ▶ To lay down, to place (e.g., in a tomb)** > Joseph laid {placed} the body of Jesus in a tomb (Mark 15:46). Other refs.: Acts 24:27 and 25:9 {to acquire, to do}. ¶

[6] **to lay down:** ***paratithēmi*** [verb: παρατίθημι <3908>]; **from** ***para*****: near, and** ***tithēmi*****: see** [1] ▶ **To establish, to explain** > Paul laid down {demonstrated, alleged, gave evidence, proved} that Christ must have suffered and risen up (Acts 17:3). All other refs.: COMMIT <3908>, SET (verb) <3908>.

[7] ***keimai*** [verb: κεῖμαι <2749>]; **lit.: to be lying, hence: to be deposited** ▶ **a. To be stored** > A man was saying to himself that he had much goods laid up for many years (Luke 12:19). **b. To be placed, to find oneself, to be** > The axe is laid to {is applied to, is at} the root of the trees (Matt. 3:10; Luke 3:9). In Luke 2:34, the verb is transl. "to be destined" {to be set, to be appointed}: Christ was destined for the fall and rising of many in Israel. **c. To be established** > See [1] for this verb in 1 Cor. 3:11b. Other refs.: APPOINT <2749>, LAID OUT (BE) <2749>, LIE (verb)[1] <2749>, SITUATE <2749>, STAND (verb) <2749>.

[8] **to lay up:** ***apokeimai*** [verb: ἀπόκειμαι <606>]; **from** ***apo*****: from, and** ***keimai*****: to lie** ▶ **To set aside, to preserve** > The hope of Christians is laid up {is stored up} for them in the heavens (Col. 1:5). The crown of righteousness was laid up {was in store} for Paul (2 Tim. 4:8). All other refs.: APPOINT <606>, PUT <606>.

[9] **to lay, to lay on:** ***epikeimai*** [verb: ἐπίκειμαι <1945>]; **from** ***epi*****: on, and** ***keimai*****: to lie** ▶ **To place upon** > A stone lay {was lying} against the tomb of Lazarus (John 11:38). The disciples saw the fish laid upon the coals (John 21:9). All other refs.: BEAT <1945>, IMPOSE <1945>, INSISTENT <1945>, PRESS <1945>.

[10] ***katakeimai*** [verb: κατάκειμαι <2621>]; **from** ***kata*****: down, and** ***keimai*****: to lie** ▶ **To lie in bed because of sickness** > Jesus saw Peter's wife's mother laying {was lying} sick with a fever (Mark 1:30). A great multitude of sick people lay {used to lie} by the pool of Bethesda (John 5:3). The father of Publius lay ill {was lying in bed, was sick in bed} of fever and dysentery (Acts 28:8). All other refs.: BEDRIDDEN (BE) <2621>, LIE (verb)[1] <2621>, SIT <2621>, TABLE[1] <2621>.

[11] ***klinō*** [verb: κλίνω <2827>] ▶ **To recline, to lie down** > The Son of Man had nowhere to lay His head (Matt. 8:20; Luke 9:58). All other refs.: BOW (verb) <2827>, FLIGHT <2827>, WEAR <2827>.

[12] ***anaklinō*** [verb: ἀνακλίνω <347>]; **from** ***ana*****: backward (intens.), and** ***klinō*****: see** [11] ▶ **To put down** > Mary laid Jesus in a manger (Luke 2:7). All other refs.: SIT <347>, TABLE[1] <347>.

[13] **to lay aside:** ***aphiēmi*** [verb: ἀφίημι <863>]; **from** ***apo*****: from, and** ***hiēmi*****: to send** ▶ **To forsake, to leave aside** > The Pharisees and scribes were laying aside {were neglecting, had let go} the commandment of God (Mark 7:8). All other refs.: see entries in Lexicon at <863>.

[14] **to lay up:** ***thēsaurizō*** [verb: θησαυρίζω <2343>]; **from** ***thēsauros*****: treasure, which is from** ***tithēmi*****: to put, to set** ▶ **To gather, to put in a reserve** > Jesus says to not lay up {store up} for ourselves treasures upon earth (Matt. 6:19), but to lay up for ourselves treasures in heaven (v. 20). The parents should lay up {save up} for their children (2 Cor. 12:14). He who lays up treasure {stores up things} for himself is not rich toward God (Luke 12:21). All other refs.: HEAP <2343>, RESERVE <2343>, STORE (verb) <2343>, TREASURE (verb) <2343>.

[15] **to lay by, to lay up in store:** ***apothēsaurizō*** [verb: ἀποθησαυρίζω <597>]; **from** ***apo*****: from, away, and** ***thēsaurizō*****: see** [14] ▶ **To keep in reserve** > By giving what they have, those who are rich are laying by {are storing up, are laying up treasure} for themselves a good foundation for the future (1 Tim. 6:19). ¶

[16] ***epiballō*** [verb: ἐπιβάλλω <1911>]; **from** ***epi*****: upon, and** ***ballō*****: to throw** ▶ **To seize, to take hold forcibly** > Men laid hands on Jesus (Matt. 26:50; Mark 14:46). Other refs.: Luke 9:62 {to put}; 20:19; 21:12; John 7:30, 44; Acts 4:3; 5:18; 12:1 {to stretch forth, to stretch out}; 21:27. All other refs.: BEAT <1911>, FAIL <1911>, PUT <1911>, THINK <1911>.

[17] ***kataballō*** [verb: καταβάλλω <2598>]; **from** ***kata*****: down, and** ***ballō*****: to throw** ▶ **To establish, to build** > Christians are not

to lay again a foundation of repentance from dead works and faith in God (Heb. 6:1). Other refs.: 2 Cor. 4:9; Rev. 12:10; see CAST (verb) <2598>. ¶

18 **to lay low: *katastrōnnumi*** [verb: κατα-στρώννυμι <2693>]; **from *kata*: down, and *strōnnumi*: to spread out ▶ To be brought down, to be killed** > The Israelites were laid low {were overthrown, were scattered, were strewed} in the desert (1 Cor. 10:5). ¶

– **19** Matt. 8:14; 9:2; Mark 7:30; Luke 16:20 → LIE (verb)[1] <906> **20** Matt. 12:25; Luke 11:17; Rev. 18:17, 19 → to lay waste → to make desolate → DESOLATE <2049> **21** Matt. 15:30 → to lay, to lay down → to cast, to cast down → CAST (verb) <4496> **22** Mark 15:46 → ACQUIRE <2698> **23** Luke 11:46 → LOAD (verb) <5412> **24** Luke 12:17, 18 → to lay up → GATHER <4863> **25** Luke 19:44 → to lay even with the ground → GROUND (noun)[1] <1474> **26** Luke 22:53 → to stretch out → STRETCH <1614> **27** Acts 13:36 → ADD <4369> **28** Acts 20:3; 23:30 → to lay wait, to lay in wait → PLOT (noun) <1917> **29** Acts 24:14 → "laid down" added in Engl. **30** Acts 25:7 → BRING <5342> **31** Acts 27:30 → to lay out → to carry out → CARRY <1614> **32** Rom. 16:4 → to lay down → RISK <5294> **33** 1 Cor. 6:4 → to lay before → to set to judge → JUDGE (verb) <2523> **34** Eph. 4:22, 25 → to lay aside → to put off, to put away → PUT <659> **35** Col. 3:9 → to lay aside → DISARM <554> **36** 1 Tim. 4:6 → to lay before → to point out → POINT (verb) <5294> **37** Rev. 2:24 → IMPOSE <906> **38** Rev. 11:9 → PUT <5087>.

LAYING ASIDE – 2 Pet. 1:14 → REMOVAL <595>.

LAYING AWAIT – Acts 9:24 → PLOT (noun) <1917>.

LAYING ON OF HANDS – **laying on: *epithesis*** [fem. noun: ἐπίθεσις <1936>] ¶; **to lay on, to lay upon: *epitithēmi*** [verb: ἐπιτίθημι <2007>]; **from *epi*: upon, and *tithēmi*: to put; hand: *cheir*** [fem. noun: χείρ <5495>] ▶ **a. Practice consisting of laying hands on the sick and the infirm to heal them, invoking upon them the power of God** > Jesus laid on hands on various occasions (Mark 5:23; 6:5; 7:32; 8:25; Luke 4:40). He speaks of laying hands on the infirm (Mark 16:18). Saul saw in a vision Ananias lay his hands on him (Acts 9:12); after Ananias laid his hands on him, Saul regained his sight (v. 17). Paul laid his hands on the father of Publius and healed him (Acts 28:8). **b. Practice for publicly recognizing Christians having received a gift of grace for a service** > This was the case of seven men chosen to serve tables (Acts 6:6), Barnabas and Saul (13:3), Timothy (1 Tim. 4:14; 2 Tim. 1:6) and those on whom he was to lay hands (1 Tim. 5:22). **c. Practice through which a person receives the Holy Spirit** > The Christians of Samaria received the Holy Spirit thus by Peter and John (Acts 8:17); Simon offered money to receive this power (v. 19; see v. 18). Paul having laid his hands on the Christians of Ephesus, the Holy Spirit came upon them, and they spoke with tongues and prophesied (Acts 19:6). **d. Practice of O.T. times** > The Christian is not to lay again a foundation of this practice (Heb. 6:2). **e. Practice of the times of Jesus** > Jesus laid His hands on little children (Matt. 19:13, 15).

LAZARUS – ***Lazaros*** [masc. name: Λάζαρος <2976>]: **God is my help, in Heb. ▶ a. Poor man in a parable** > Lazarus was laid at the gate of a rich man (Luke 16:20); after his death, he was comforted in the bosom of Abraham (vv. 23–25). **b. Brother of Martha and Mary** > Jesus resurrected Lazarus who had died of an illness (John 11:1, 2, 5, 11, 14, 43). Afterwards, Lazarus was one of those who were at table with Jesus during a supper at Bethany (John 12:1, 2). The chief priests wanted to kill him, because on his account many of the Jews believed in Jesus (John 12:9, 10, 17). ¶

LAZILY – 2 Cor. 11:9 → to lazily burden → to be burdensome → BURDENSOME <2655>.

LAZINESS – 2 Cor. 12:13, 14 → to be in laziness a charge → to be burdensome → BURDENSOME <2655>.

LAZY – [1] ***argos*** [adj.: ἀργός <692>]; **from *a*: neg., and *ergon*: work ► Inactive, without fruit** > A Cretan prophet said the Cretans were lazy gluttons {slow bellies} (Titus 1:12). All other refs.: IDLE <692>.
– [2] Matt. 25:26 → SLOTHFUL <3636> [3] Heb. 6:12 → SLUGGISH <3576>.

LEAD (noun) – [1] Acts 14:12 → to take the lead → to be the chief → CHIEF <2233> [2] Rom. 12:10 → to take the lead → to give preference → PREFERENCE <4285> [3] 1 Thes. 5:12 → to take the lead → LEAD (verb) <4291>.

LEAD (verb) – [1] **to lead, to lead away, to lead about: *agō*** [verb: ἄγω <71>] ► **To bring, to take, to conduct** > The disciples would be led away {arrested} and delivered up (Mark 13:11). Jesus was led by the Spirit in the wilderness (Luke 4:1). The devil led Him to Jerusalem and had Him stand on the pinnacle of the temple (Luke 4:9). Jesus was led to the brow of the mountain (Luke 4:29). He was led and brought into the house of the high priest (Luke 22:54). Two criminals were led with Jesus to be put to death (Luke 23:32). Jesus was led away to Annas first (John 18:13); they led Him after to the Praetorium (v. 28). Jesus was led as a sheep to slaughter (Acts 8:32). The commander gave the order for Paul to be led {carried} into the fortress (Acts 21:34). The goodness of God leads to repentance (Rom. 2:4). Those led by the Spirit of God are sons of God (Rom. 8:14). Before their conversion the Corinthians were led away (*agō*) {carried away} to dumb idols, however they were led (*apagō*) (1 Cor. 12:2a). If we are led by the Spirit, we are not under the law (Gal. 5:18). Paul speaks of those who are led away {are swayed} by various lusts (2 Tim. 3:6). Other refs.: BRING <71>, GO <71>.
[2] **to lead, to lead up: *anagō*** [verb: ἀνάγω <321>]; **from *ana*: upwards, and *agō*: see [1] ► To bring, to take** > Jesus was led up {carried up} by the Spirit into the wilderness (Matt. 4:1). He was led into the council of the elders, the chief priests, and the scribes (Luke 22:66). All other refs.: see entries in Lexicon at <321>.
[3] **to lead, to lead away: *apagō*** [verb: ἀπάγω <520>]; **from *apo*: from, away, and *agō*: see [1] ► To take along, to take (somebody somewhere)** > The way that leads to destruction is broad (Matt. 7:13); the way that leads to life is narrow (v. 14). Those who had laid hold on Jesus led Him away to Caiaphas (Matt. 26:57; Mark 14:53). Jesus was led away and delivered to Pilate (Matt. 27:2). He was led away to be crucified (Matt. 27:31; Luke 23:26; John 19:16). Jesus was to be seized and led away (Mark 14:44); He was led away {taken away} into the Praetorium (15:16). Each one leads his ox or his donkey away to give it water on a Sabbath day (Luke 13:15). Other ref.: 1 Cor. 12:2b (see [1]). All other refs.: BRING <520>, CARRY <520>, DEATH <520>, TAKE <520>.
[4] ***diagō*** [verb: διάγω <1236>]; **from *dia*: through, and *agō*: see [1] ► To live with the sense of quietness and tranquility** > We ought to pray that we may lead {live} a quiet and peaceable life (1 Tim. 2:2). Other ref.: Titus 3:3; see LIVE <1236>. ¶
[5] ***eisagō*** [verb: εἰσάγω <1521>]; **from *eis*: in, toward, and *agō*: see [1] ► To take, to bring** > Paul being blind was led by the hand and brought into Damascus (Acts 9:8). All other refs.: BRING <1521>.
[6] **to lead out: *exagō*** [verb: ἐξάγω <1806>]; **from *ek*: out, and *agō*: see [1] ► To conduct out, to take out** > Jesus led {brought} the blind man out of town (Mark 8:23). Jesus was led out to be crucified (Mark 15:20). Jesus led His disciples out as far as Bethany (Luke 24:50). The shepherd leads his sheep out (John 10:3). In Acts 16:37, the Greek verb is transl. "to get out" {to bring out, to fetch out}: Paul said the magistrates ought to come to get himself and Silas out of the prison (Acts 16:37), which, in fact, they proceeded to do (v. 39). An Egyptian had led out assassins into the wilderness (Acts 21:38). God took the Israelites by the hand to lead them out of the land of Egypt (Heb. 8:9). All other refs.: BRING <1806>.

7 ***sunagō*** [verb: συνάγω <4863>]; **from *sun*: together, and *agō*: see 1 ► To bring along, to convey** > He who leads into captivity will go into captivity (Rev. 13:10). All other refs.: GATHER <4863>, INVITE <4863>.

8 ***hodēgeō*** [verb: ὁδηγέω <3594>]; **from *hodēgos*: guide, which is from *hodos*: way, and *hēgeomai*: to lead, to command ► To show the way; also transl.: to guide** > Jesus asked if the blind could lead the blind (Luke 6:39). He said that if the blind leads the blind, both will fall into a ditch (Matt. 15:14). The Spirit of truth would lead into all truth (John 16:13). The Ethiopian needed to be led to understand what he was reading (Acts 8:31). The Lamb will lead those who come out of the great tribulation to living fountains of waters (Rev. 7:17). ¶

9 ***pherō*** [verb: φέρω <5342>] **► To take, to bring** > An iron gate leading into the city opened by itself to let Peter and the angel go through (Acts 12:10). All other refs.: see entries in Lexicon at <5342>.

10 **to lead up: *anapherō*** [verb: ἀναφέρω <399>]; **from *ana*: up, and *pherō*: see 9 ► To take up** > Jesus led up {brought up} three disciples on a high mountain by themselves (Matt. 17:1; Mark 9:2). All other refs.: BEAR (verb) <399>, CARRY <399>, OFFER <399>.

11 **to lead away: *apopherō*** [verb: ἀποφέρω <667>]; **from *apo*: from, and *pherō*: see 9 ► To take away** > Jesus was led away {carried away} and delivered to Pilate (Mark 15:1). All other refs.: CARRY <667>.

12 ***eispherō*** [verb: εἰσφέρω <1533>]; **from *eis*: toward, in, and *pherō*: see 9 ► To bring, to expose** > Jesus taught to pray to the Father not to lead us into temptation (Matt. 6:13; Luke 11:4). All other refs.: BRING <1533>, CARRY <1533>.

13 ***proistēmi*** [verb: προΐστημι <4291>]; **from *pro*: before, and *histēmi*: to stand ► To direct, to give direction, to preside** > He who leads {rules} in a local church is to do so diligently (Rom. 12:8). Christians are to respect (sense of: to have consideration for) those who labor among them, taking the lead among them in the Lord and giving them instruction (1 Thes. 5:12 {to take the lead, to be over, to have charge over}). All other refs.: MAINTAIN <4291>, RULE (verb) <4291>.

14 **to lead by the hand: *cheiragōgeō*** [verb: χειραγωγέω <5496>]; **from *cheiragōgos*: see 15 ► To take, to show the way by the hand** > Led by the hand, Saul who was blind was brought to Damascus (Acts 9:8; 22:11). ¶

15 **someone who leads by the hand: *cheiragōgos*** [adj. used as noun: χειραγωγός <5497>]; **from *cheir*: hand, and *agō*: see 1 ► Someone who shows the way to another person by taking his hand** > Having become blind, Elymas went around seeking someone to lead him by the hand (Acts 13:11). ¶

– 16 Matt. 12:20 → to bring forth → BRING <1544> 17 Matt. 24:4, 5, 11, 24; Mark 13:5, 6; Luke 21:8; John 7:12 or 13, 47; 2 Tim. 3:13a, b; Rev. 12:9 → to lead astray → DECEIVE <4105> 18 Mark 9:2 → TAKE <3880> 19 Mark 13:22 → to lead astray → DECEIVE <635> 20 Luke 21:13 → to turn out → TURN (verb) <576> 21 Luke 22:47 → PRECEDE <4281> 22 John 11:4 → does not lead to death → lit.: is not to death 23 Acts 5:24 → to lead to → BECOME <1096> 24 Acts 5:31 → PRINCE <747> 25 Acts 5:37 → to lead in revolt → REVOLT <868> 26 Acts 15:22 → lit.: leading man → LEADING <2233> 27 Acts 16:30 → to lead out → to bring out → BRING <4254> 28 Acts 19:26 → to lead astray → to turn away → TURN (verb) <3179> 29 Rom. 5:18a, b, 21; 9:31; Jude 21 → the verb is added in Engl. 30 1 Cor. 7:17; 2 Thes. 3:6, 11 → WALK <4043> 31 1 Cor. 9:5 → to lead about → to take along → TAKE <4013> 32 2 Cor. 11:3 → to lead astray → CORRUPT (verb) <5351> 33 Gal. 2:13; 2 Pet. 3:17 → to lead astray, to lead away → to carry away → CARRY <4879> 34 Gal. 3:24 → in charge to lead → TUTOR <3807> 35 1 Thes. 4:11 → to lead a quiet life → QUIET (adj.) <2270> 36 2 Tim. 2:16 → INCREASE (verb) <4298> 37 Heb. 3:12 → "leading you to" added in Engl. 38 Heb. 13:9 → to lead away → to carry away → CARRY <4064>.

LEADER – [1] ***hēgoumenos*; from *hēgeomai*** [verb: ἡγέομαι <2233>]**: to lead ▶ One who gives direction, who commands** > Among believers in the Lord, the leader {he who governs, he who is chief, the one who rules} should be as the one who serves (Luke 22:26). All other refs.: see entries in Lexicon at <2233>.

– [2] Matt. 2:6 → RULER <2232> [3] Matt. 9:18, 23; Luke 8:41; 14:1; John 12:42; Acts 3:17; 14:5 → RULER <758> [4] Matt. 15:14 → GUIDE (noun) <3595> [5] Matt. 23:10 → TEACHER <2519> [6] Mark 5:22, 35, 38; Luke 8:49; 13:14; Acts 13:15; 18:8, 17 → leader of the synagogue → ruler of the synagogue → SYNAGOGUE <752> [7] John 1:19, 5:10; et al. → Jewish leader, leader → lit.: Jew [8] John 18:28 → "Jewish leaders" added in Engl. [9] Acts 24:5 → RINGLEADER <4414> [10] Acts 25:2; 28:17 → CHIEF <4413> [11] Gal. 2:2 → to seem to be leader → to be of reputation → REPUTATION <1380> [12] Heb. 2:10 → CAPTAIN <747> [13] Heb. 12:2 → AUTHOR <747>.

LEADERSHIP – [1] Acts 1:20 → place of leadership → OFFICE <1984> [2] Rom. 12:8 → if it is leadership → lit.: he who leads → LEAD (verb) <4291>.

LEADING – [1] **to lead: *hēgeomai*** [verb: ἡγέομαι <2233>] **▶ To have authority, to be considered** > Judas, called Barsabbas, and Silas were leading men {chief men, leaders} among the brothers (Acts 15:22). All other refs.: see entries in Lexicon at <2233>.

– [2] Mark 6:21; Acts 25:2; 28:17 → CHIEF <4413> [3] Acts 17:4 → PROMINENT <4413> [4] Acts 25:23 → lit.: prominence → PROMINENT <1851>.

LEAF – [1] ***phullon*** [neut. noun: φύλλον <5444>]**; from *phuō*: to produce, to grow ▶ Part of a plant which is attached to a stem or branch, and is usually green** > Jesus found nothing but leaves on the fig tree (Matt. 21:19; Mark 11:13a, b). One knows that summer is near when the fig tree produces leaves (Matt. 24:32; Mark 13:28). The leaves of the tree of life are for the healing of the nations (Rev. 22:2). ¶

– [2] Luke 21:30 → to come out in leaf, to put forth leaves, to sprout leaves → SPROUT <4261>.

LEAN – **to lean, to lean back: *anapiptō*** [verb: ἀναπίπτω <377>]**; from *ana*: backwards {intens.}, and *piptō*: to fall ▶ To bend the body so as to rest on someone** > John was leaning {was lying, was leaning back} against Jesus (John 13:25; 21:20); in John 13:25, some mss. have *epipiptō*. All other refs.: SIT <377>, TABLE[1] <377>.

LEAP – [1] ***hallomai*** [verb: ἅλλομαι <242>] **▶ To bound, to jump** > Healed by Peter and John, a lame man leaped up (*exallomai*), stood and walked, leaping (*hallomai*) and praising God (Acts 3:8b). Healed by Paul, a man crippled in his feet leaped {leaped up, sprang up} and walked (Acts 14:10). Other ref.: John 4:14 (to spring up); see SPRING (verb) <242>. ¶

[2] **to leap up: *exallomai*** [verb: ἐξάλλομαι <1814>]**; from *ek*: out, and *hallomai*: see [1] ▶ To jump up, to rise with a bound** > The verb is used in Acts 3:8a; see [1]. ¶

[3] ***ephallomai*** [verb: ἐφάλλομαι <2177>]**; from *epi*: upon, and *hallomai*: see [1] ▶ To jump, to assault** > The man, in whom the evil spirit was, leaped on the exorcists (Acts 19:16); *enallomai* in other mss. ¶

[4] ***skirtaō*** [verb: σκιρτάω <4640>]**; related to *skairō*: to jump ▶ To jump for joy, to exult** > Elizabeth's child leaped in her womb (Luke 1:41, 44). The disciples of Jesus are to leap for joy (lit.: are to leap) when they suffer at the hands of men (Luke 6:23). ¶

LEARN – [1] ***manthanō*** [verb: μανθάνω <3129>] **▶ To acquire knowledge, to study** > Jesus says to learn what it means to have mercy (Matt. 9:13). He says to learn from Him, for He is meek and lowly (Matt. 11:29). Everyone who has learned from the Father comes to Jesus (John 6:45). Jesus knew letters without having learned {studied} them (John 7:15). The Christians in Rome were to be careful concerning matters that were not according to the doctrine which they had learned (Rom. 16:17). The Ephesians had learned {had known} Christ according to the truth which is in Jesus (Eph. 4:20; see v. 21). Paul had learned to be content in all his circumstances (Phil. 4:11). The Colossians had learned from Epaphras concerning the grace of God (Col. 1:7). Some are always learning and never able to come to the knowledge of the truth (2 Tim. 3:7). Christians must learn to maintain good works for necessary uses (Titus 3:14). Though He was Son, Jesus learned obedience by the things which He suffered (Heb. 5:8). Other refs.: Matt. 24:32; Mark 13:28; Acts 23:27; 1 Cor. 4:6; 14:31, 35; Gal. 3:2 {to find out}; Phil. 4:9; 1 Tim. 2:11 {to receive instruction}; 5:4, 13; 2 Tim. 3:14; Rev. 14:3. ¶

[2] ***mueō*** [verb: μυέω <3453>]; **from *muō*: to shut the mouth; lit.: to initiate into mysteries ► To instruct, to teach** > Paul had learned {was initiated} both to be full and to be hungry (Phil. 4:12). ¶

[3] ***paideuō*** [verb: παιδεύω <3811>]; **from *pais*: child ► To educate; pass.: to be instructed** > Hymenaeus and Alexander had to learn {be taught, be taught by discipline} not to blaspheme (1 Tim. 1:20). All other refs.: CHASTEN <3811>, CORRECT <3811>, EDUCATE <3811>, TEACH <3811>.

– [4] Matt. 2:16 → DETERMINE <198> [5] Mark 15:45; Luke 9:11; John 4:1; 5:6; 7:51; 12:9; Acts 17:13; 21:34; 1 Thes. 3:5; Rev. 3:9 → KNOW <1097> [6] Luke 7:37; 23:7; Acts 9:30; 28:1 → KNOW <1921> [7] John 15:15 → HEAR <191> [8] Acts 7:13b → KNOWN <5318> [9] Acts 14:6 → to become aware → AWARE <4894> [10] Acts 23:34 → UNDERSTAND <4441> [11] Eph. 5:10 → to try to learn → TEST (noun and verb) <1381> [12] Heb. 5:11 → lit.: in hearing → HEARING <189>.

LEARNED – [1] Matt. 11:25; Luke 10:21 → UNDERSTANDING <4908> [2] Acts 18:24 → ELOQUENT <3052>.

LEARNING – [1] ***gramma*** [neut. noun: γράμμα <1121>]; **from *graphō*: to write; lit.: writing ► Knowledge in its written form, study** > According to Festus, Paul's great learning (lit.: numerous studies) was driving him insane (Acts 26:24). All other refs.: BILL <1121>, LETTER <1121>, WRITING <1121>.

– [2] Rom. 15:4 → INSTRUCTION <1319>.

LEASE – ***ekdidōmi*** [verb: ἐκδίδωμι <1554>]; **from *ek*: out, and *didōmi*: to give; lit.: to remit ► To give temporary possession and use in return for payment** > A landlord leased {let out, rented, rented out} his vineyard to vine-growers (Matt. 21:33, 41; Mark 12:1; Luke 20:9 {to let forth}). ¶

LEASH – ***brochos*** [masc. noun: βρόχος <1029>] **► Slipknot, snare** > Paul did not want to put a leash on {cast a snare on, put a restraint on, restrict} the Corinthians (1 Cor. 7:35). ¶

LEAST – [1] ***elachistos*** [adj.: ἐλάχιστος <1646>]; **superl. of *mikros*: small, little (the compar. of *mikros* is *elassōn*: smaller) ► Smallest in importance, most insignificant** > Paul wrote that he was the least of the apostles (1 Cor. 15:9). The word is used in regard to Bethlehem (Matt. 2:6), a commandment of God (Matt. 5:19a), a place in the kingdom of heaven (Matt. 5:19b), a disciple of the Lord (Matt. 25:40, 45), judgments (1 Cor. 6:2 {smallest, trivial}), and a rudder (Jas. 3:4 {very small}). Other refs. (very little): Luke 12:26; 16:10a, b; 19:17. Other ref.: 1 Cor. 4:3; see VERY SMALL <1646>. ¶

[2] **the very least, less than the least: *elachistoteros*** [adj.: ἐλαχιστότερος <1647>]; **compar. of *elachistos*: see [1] ► More insignificant than the most insignificant, lower than the lowest** > Paul said he was the least of all saints (Eph. 3:8). ¶

[3] ***mikroteros*** [adj.: μικρότερος <3398a>]; **compar. of *mikros*: small ► Smaller in importance or rank** > He who is least in the kingdom of heaven (or: of God) is greater than John the Baptist (Matt. 11:11; Luke 7:28). ¶

[4] See also LESS.

– 5 1 Cor. 6:4 → to esteem least → ESTEEM (verb) <1848>.

LEATHER – ***dermatinos*** [adj.: δερμάτινος <1193>]; **from *derma*: skin ▶ Made with the skin of an animal** > John the Baptist had a leather belt {a leathern girdle; a girdle of a skin} around his waist (Matt. 3:4; Mark 1:6: *derris* in some mss.). ¶

LEATHERN – Matt. 3:4 → LEATHER <1193>.

LEAVE (noun) – 1 **to take leave: *apotassō*** [verb: ἀποτάσσω <657>]; **from *apo*: from, and *tassō*: to place in order, to determine ▶ To say words, good wishes at parting; also transl.: to leave** > Paul took leave of the brothers and sailed for Syria (Acts 18:18); he took leave of the Jews {he bade farewell to them} in the synagogue of Ephesus (v. 21). He took his leave of {bade adieu to, said good-by to} the Christians in Troas (2 Cor. 2:13). All other refs.: FAREWELL <657>, FORSAKE <657>, SEND <657>.
– 2 Mark 5:13; John 19:38; Acts 27:3 → to give leave → PERMIT <2010> 3 Acts 20:1; 21:6 → to take leave → EMBRACE <782>.

LEAVE (verb) – 1 ***aniēmi*** [verb: ἀνίημι <447>]; **from *ana*: again, and *hiēmi*: to send ▶ To abandon, to give up** > God has promised that He will never leave {desert} Christians nor forsake them (Heb. 13:5). All other refs.: GIVE <447>, LOOSE <447>.
2 ***aphiēmi*** [verb: ἀφίημι <863>]; **from *apo*: from, and *hiēmi*: to send ▶ a. To go away from, to depart from** > The devil left Jesus (Matt. 4:11). Jesus left His disciples in Gethsemane to pray (Matt. 26:44). The Father has not left Jesus alone (John 8:29), i.e., the Father has not forsaken His Son. Jesus was leaving the world and going to the Father (John 16:28). Other refs.: Matt. 22:22, 25; Mark 1:20; 8:13; 13:34; Luke 10:30; John 10:12; 14:18; 16:32; Acts 14:17. **b. To not take away, to allow to remain** > One must leave his gift before the altar and first be reconciled with his brother (Matt. 5:24). A man will leave his sheep to seek the one that is straying (Matt. 18:12; Luke 15:4: *kataleipō*). The house of the Jews was left to them desolate (Matt. 23:38). Not one stone of the temple would be left that would not be thrown down (Matt. 24:2; Mark 13:2; Luke 19:44; 21:6). One person will be taken and the other left when wicked people will be removed from the earth before the millennium (Matt. 24:40, 41; Luke 17:34–36). Jesus was leaving peace with His disciples (John 14:27). Other refs.: Matt. 4:20; John 4:28. **c. To have descendants who remain behind** > A man might leave no children after his death (Mark 12:19b, 20–22). **d. To forget, to overlook** > The scribes and the Pharisees had left {omitted, neglected} justice, mercy, and faith; they should have done these without leaving other less important matters of the law undone (Matt. 23:23a, b; Luke 11:42). God has left nothing that is not put under Christ (Heb. 2:8). Other refs.: Rom. 1:27; Heb. 6:1. **e. To abandon; also transl.: to forsake** > James and John left the boat and their father, and followed Jesus (Matt. 4:22). Jesus touched the hand of Peter's mother-in-law, and the fever left her (Matt. 8:15; Mark 1:31; Luke 4:39). The disciples had left all things to follow Jesus (Matt. 19:27; Mark 10:28; Luke 18:28). Jesus speaks of leaving various people and things for His name's sake (Matt. 19:29; Mark 10:29; Luke 18:29). Simon and Andrew left their trawl-nets and followed Jesus (Mark 1:18); Luke says they left all (Luke 5:11). Jesus left Judea and went away to Galilee (John 4:3). The fever had left the son of a royal official after the healing effected by Jesus (John 4:52). The church of Ephesus had left {abandoned} her first love (Rev. 2:4). All other refs.: see entries in Lexicon at <863>.
3 ***apallassō*** [verb: ἀπαλλάσσω <525>]; **from *apo*: from, and *allassō*: to change, to go away ▶ The verb is used in regard to the healing of diseases** > God wrought extraordinary miracles by the hands of Paul, so that the diseases left the sick {departed from the sick, were cured} (Acts 19:12). Other refs.: Luke 12:58; Heb. 2:15; see RELEASE (verb) <525>, SETTLE <525>. ¶
4 ***aperchomai*** [verb: ἀπέρχομαι <565>]; **from *apo*: from, and *erchomai*: to go ▶ To**

go away, away into, to, into > The verb is used in regard to Jesus (John 4:43). All other refs.: see entries in Lexicon at <565>.

5 ***apoleipō*** [verb: ἀπολείπω <620>]; **from: *apo*: from, and *leipō*: to leave ▶ To forget; to depart from >** Paul had left his cloak with Carpus (2 Tim. 4:13). He had left Trophimus sick in Miletus (2 Tim. 4:20). Angels who did not keep their first state left {abandoned} their own abode (Jude 6; see Gen. 6:1, 2). Other refs.: Titus 1:5 in some mss.; Heb. 4:6, 9; 10:26: see REMAIN <620>. ¶

6 ***kataleipō*** [verb: καταλείπω <2641>]; **from *kata*: intens., and *leipō*: to leave ▶ To abandon; to depart from, to forsake >** Leaving Nazareth, Jesus went and dwelt in Capernaum (Matt. 4:13). A man will leave his father and mother and be joined to his wife (Matt. 19:5; Mark 10:7; Eph. 5:31). Levi left all, rose up and followed Jesus (Luke 5:28). A young man following Jesus left the linen cloth thrown around his body and fled from those who were trying to seize him (Mark 14:52). The soul of Christ was not left in Hades (Acts 2:31). By faith Moses left {forsook} Egypt (Heb. 11:27). Other refs.: Matt. 16:4; 21:17; Mark 12:19a; Luke 10:40; 15:4; 20:31; John 8:9; Acts 6:2 {to neglect}; 18:19; 21:3 {to pass on}; 24:27; 25:14; 1 Thes. 3:1; Titus 1:5 (some mss. have 5); Heb. 4:1 {to remain}; 2 Pet. 2:15. Other ref.: Rom. 11:4; see RESERVE <2641>. ¶

7 ***enkataleipō*** [verb: ἐγκαταλείπω <1459>]; **from *en*: in, and *kataleipō*: to leave behind ▶ To abandon, to forsake >** God would not leave the soul of David in Hades (Acts 2:27). Other ref.: Rom. 9:29. All other refs.: FORSAKE <1459>.

8 ***hupoleipō*** [verb: ὑπολείπω <5275>]; **from *hupo*: under, and *leipō*: to leave ▶ To stay, to remain >** Elijah thought that he alone was left faithful to the Lord (Rom. 11:3; see 1 Kgs. 19:10). ¶

9 ***hupolimpanō*** [verb: ὑπολιμπάνω <5277>]; **form of *hupoleipō*: see 8 ▶ To bequeath, to give something for use after one's departure >** Christ has suffered for us, leaving us a model (1 Pet. 2:21). ¶

10 ***chōrizō*** [verb: χωρίζω <5563>]; **from *chora*: region, country, or *chōris*: without ▶ To depart, to go away from >** Jesus commanded His disciples not to leave Jerusalem, but to await the promise of the Father (Acts 1:4). Paul left Athens (Acts 18:1). Claudius had ordered all the Jews to leave Rome (Acts 18:2). All other refs.: DEPART <5563>, SEPARATE <5563>.

– 11 Matt. 2:12–14, 22; 9:24; 27:5; Acts 26:31 → DEPART <402> 12 Matt. 8:34; John 7:3; Acts 18:7 → DEPART <3327> 13 Matt. 10:11, 14; 15:21; Mark 6:10; 7:31; Luke 9:4; John 4:43; Acts 15:40; 16:10, 40; 20:11; 21:5, 8 → GO <1831> 14 Matt. 19:1 → WITHDRAW <3332> 15 Mark 6:46; Acts 18:21 → to bid farewell → FAREWELL <657> 16 Luke 2:37; Luke 4:13; Acts 12:10; 19:9; 22:29; 2 Cor. 12:8 → DEPART <868> 17 Luke 4:1 → RETURN (verb) <5290> 18 Luke 5:2 → GO <576> 19 Luke 5:4; Acts 21:32 → CEASE <3973> 20 Luke 9:33 → DEPART <1316> 21 Luke 9:39; Acts 13:13 → DEPART <672> 22 Luke 12:36 → RETURN (verb) <360> 23 Luke 21:21 → DEPART <1633> 24 John 6:67 → to go away → GO <5217> 25 John 13:1 → PASS <3327> 26 John 14:31 → GO <71> 27 Acts 1:25 → to fall by transgression → FALL (verb) <3845> 28 Acts 5:38 → to leave alone → to keep away → KEEP (verb) <868> 29 Acts 5:41; 20:1 → DEPART <4198> 30 Acts 14:16; 23:32 → ALLOW <1439> 31 Acts 17:15; 20:7 → DEPART <1826> 32 Acts 18:18, 21 → to take leave → LEAVE (noun) <657> 33 Acts 20:29 → after I leave → lit.: after my departure → DEPARTURE <867> 34 Acts 25:4 → DEPART <1607> 35 Acts 28:25 → DEPART <630> 36 Rom. 11:4 → RESERVE <2641> 37 Phil. 4:15 → DEPART <1831> 38 1 Tim. 5:5 → to be left alone, to be left all alone → to be desolate → DESOLATE <3443> 39 Titus 1:5 → things left unfinished → things that remained → REMAIN <3007> 40 Rev. 11:2 → to leave out → CAST (verb) <1544>.

LEAVEN (noun) – ***zumē*** [fem. noun: ζύμη <2219>]; **from *zeō*: to heat ▶ Fermenting substance used in baking to cause bread**

to rise; also transl.: yeast > The term is used in the lit. sense in Matt. 16:12: the leaven of bread. Elsewhere in the word of God, leaven always represents evil; the Christian must recognize it and remove it from his personal life. Scripture mentions the leaven of error mixed with truth (Matt. 13:33; Luke 13:21), the religious hypocrisy of the Pharisees and the rationalism of the Sadducees (Matt. 16:6, 11; Mark 8:15a; Luke 12:1), the materialism of Herod (Mark 8:15b), pride and boasting (1 Cor. 5:6), false doctrines (Gal. 5:9), as well as malice and wickedness intrinsic to the old nature (1 Cor. 5:7, 8a, b). See UNLEAVENED BREAD. ¶

LEAVEN (verb) – ***zumoō*** [verb: ζυμόω <2220>]**; from *zumē*: leaven ▶ To make rise by the action of leaven; also transl.: to work through >** The verb is used in relation to three measures of meal (Matt. 13:33; Luke 13:21) and a lump (1 Cor. 5:6; Gal. 5:9). ¶

LEAVENED – 1 Cor. 5:8 → old bread leavened with malice → lit.: old leaven, leaven of malice → LEAVEN (noun) <2219>.

LEAVING – Acts 28:10 → DEPART <321>.

LEBBAEUS – ***Lebbaios*** [masc. name: Λεββαῖος <3002>] **▶ One of the twelve apostles of Jesus; this name appears in some mss. >** Lebbaeus was surnamed Thaddaeus and was the brother of James (Matt. 10:3).¶

LECTURE HALL – Acts 19:9 → SCHOOL <4981>.

LEE – Acts 27:4, 7b → to pass under the lee, to sail under the lee → to sail under → SAIL (verb) <5284>.

LEFT – 1 **left, left hand, the left: *aristeros*** [adj.: ἀριστερός <710>] **▶ On the side of the heart >** One who gives to the poor is not to let his left hand know what his right hand does (Matt. 6:3). James and John wanted to sit, one on the right and the other on the left of Jesus in His glory (Mark 10:37; some mss. have 2). A criminal was crucified on the left of Jesus (Luke 23:33). Paul had the weapons of righteousness on the right hand and on the left hand (2 Cor. 6:7). ¶

2 **left, the left, on the left hand: *euōnumos*** [adj.: εὐώνυμος <2176>]**; from *eu*: well, and *onoma*: name; lit.: of a good name; euphemism for *aristeros* (see 1), since the bad omens came from the left ▶ On the side of the heart >** The mother of the sons of Zebedee wanted her two sons to sit, one on the right and the other on the left of Jesus in His kingdom (Matt. 20:21), but that would be given to those for whom it was prepared by the Father (Matt. 20:23; Mark 10:40). The Son of Man will put the goats on His left (Matt. 25:33) and will tell them to depart from Him into the eternal fire (v. 41). A thief was crucified on the left of Jesus (Matt. 27:38; Mark 15:27). The ship Paul had boarded passed Cyprus on the left (Acts 21:3). An angel set his left foot on the earth (Rev. 10:2). ¶

LEFT (BE) – 1 Matt. 14:20; 15:37; Luke 9:17; John 6:12, 13 → to be left over → REMAIN <4052> 2 Mark 8:8 → to be left over → that remained → REST (noun)[2] <4051> 3 1 Thes. 4:15, 17 → REMAIN <4035> 4 Heb. 10:26 → REMAIN <620>.

LEFT OVER – 2 Cor. 8:15 → to have left over → OVER <4121>.

LEFTOVER – John 6:12 → that remained → REMAIN <4052>.

LEG – ***skelos*** [neut. noun: σκέλος <4628>] **▶ Member of the body between the hip and the foot >** The soldiers broke the legs of the two criminals but not those of Jesus (John 19:31–33). ¶

LEGAL – 1 Acts 19:39 → LAWFUL <1772> 2 Acts 22:25 → to be legal → to be lawful → LAWFUL <1832> 3 Heb. 7:16 → legal requirement → LAW <3551>.

LEGION – ***legiōn*** [masc. noun: λεγιών <3003>]; **from Lat.: *legio*; also spelled: *legeōn* ▶ a. The most important unit of the Roman army, consisting of 5,000 to 6,000 men and divided into 10 cohorts of 500 to 600 men each** > The expr. "twelve legions of angels" is syn. with a significantly high number in Matt. 26:53. **b. Evil spirits** > Legion was the name of evil spirits who had taken possession of a man who was healed by Jesus (Mark 5:9, 15; Luke 8:30); the name Legion comes from the fact that there were many demons in him. Later, the evil spirits entered into a herd of swine which rushed into the sea (see Mark 5:13). ¶

LEGITIMATE – Heb. 12:8 → not legitimate → ILLEGITIMATE <3541>.

LEGITIMATELY – 1 Cor. 9:21 → legitimately subject → LAWFUL <1772>.

LEISURE – Mark 6:31 → to have leisure → to have time → TIME <2119>.

LEMA – Matt. 27:46; Mark 15:34 → LAMA <2982>.

LEND – [1] ***daneizō*** [verb: δανείζω <1155>]; **from *daneion*: loan, debt, which is from *danos*: gift, interest loan ▶ To put something (such as money) at the disposition of someone for a time** > We should lend to those from whom we do not hope to receive back (Luke 6:34a, b, 35). Other ref.: Matt. 5:42; see BORROW <1155>. ¶

[2] ***chraō*** [verb: χράω <5531>] ▶ **See [1].** > A man asked his friend to lend him {to let him have} three loaves of bread (Luke 11:5; other mss.: *kichrēmi*). ¶

LENGTH – [1] ***mēkos*** [neut. noun: μῆκος <3372>] ▶ **Dimension of a thing, in the sense opposed to its breadth** > Paul wanted Christians to be fully able to understand the length (he is not specifying of what), and to know the love of Christ (Eph. 3:18). The length, the breadth, and the height of the new Jerusalem are equal (Rev. 21:16a, b). ¶

– [2] Acts 7:5 → not even a foot's length → not even the ground of foot → GROUND (noun)[1] <968> [3] Phil. 4:10 → at length → at last → LAST (adv. and noun) <2235>.

LENGTHEN – Matt. 23:5 → ENLARGE <3170>.

LENGTHY – Mark 12:40; Luke 20:47 → LONG (adj.) <3117>.

LEOPARD – ***pardalis*** [fem. noun: πάρδαλις <3917>]; **comp. *pardos*: leopard or panther ▶ Rapid African panther with brusque movements** > The beast John saw resembled a leopard {leopardess} (Rev. 13:2). ¶

LEOPARDESS – Rev. 13:2 → LEOPARD <3917>.

LEPER – ***lepros*** [adj. used as noun: λεπρός <3015>]; **from *lepō*: to peel, or *lepos*: scale; lit.: scaly ▶ Person afflicted with leprosy; also transl.: man with leprosy, one with leprosy** > Jesus healed many lepers in Israel (Matt. 8:2; 11:5; Mark 1:40; Luke 7:22; 17:12). He sent out the twelve disciples to cleanse the lepers (Matt. 10:8). He went to the house of a man named Simon the leper (Matt. 26:6; Mark 14:3). There were many lepers {with leprosy} in Israel in the time of Elisha, but only Naaman the Syrian was cleansed (Luke 4:27). ¶

LEPROSY – [1] ***lepra*** [fem. noun: λέπρα <3014>]; **from *lepis*: scale, which is from *lepō*: to peel ▶ Contagious illness, which was incurable** > Leprosy symbolizes sin especially since the leper gradually loses feeling in the afflicted members. Jesus healed various individuals of their leprosy (Matt. 8:3; Mark 1:42; Luke 5:12, 13). According to the law, one who was completely covered with leprosy was declared clean (see Lev. 13:12, 13); today this symbolizes the fact that one who realizes he is completely sinful may be saved by faith in the Son of God. ¶

– [2] Matt. 8:2; 10:8; 11:5; Mark 1:40; Luke 4:27; 17:12 → man with leprosy, one with leprosy → LEPER <3015>.

LESS – [1] ***mikros*** [adj.: μικρός <3398>]; **lit.: small ▶ Young, not adult** > A certain James, the son of Alphaeus and Mary, was surnamed the "Less" {Younger} (Mark 15:40). Other refs.: see LITTLE <3398>.
– [2] John 3:30 → to become less → DECREASE <1642> [3] Rom. 9:12 → YOUNGER <1640>.

LESSER – ***elassōn*** [adj. used as noun: ἐλάσσων <1640>]; **compar. of *micros*: small ▶ Inferior in quality** > Men usually set out lesser {inferior, worse, poorer, cheaper} wine after the guests have well drunk (John 2:10). The word is transl. "under" {less than} in 1 Tim. 5:9; lit.: of not less than sixty years. The lesser {inferior} is blessed by the greater (Heb. 7:7). Other ref.: Rom. 9:12; see YOUNGER <1640>. ¶

LESSON – 1 Cor. 14:26 → DOCTRINE <1322>.

LEST – [1] ***mēpote*** [conj.: μήποτε <3379>]; **from *mē*: not, and *pote*: at any time ▶ For fear that; also transl.: otherwise, so that** > The word is used by the devil (Matt. 4:6; Luke 4:11), by the Lord (Matt. 5:25; 7:6; 13:15, 29; 15:32; Mark 4:12; Luke 12:58; 14:8, 12, 29; 21:34), by the prudent virgins (Matt. 25:9), concerning the body of Jesus (Matt. 27:64), by Gamaliel (Acts 5:39), and by Paul (Acts 28:27; Heb. 2:1). *
[2] ***mēpōs*** [conj.: μήπως <3381>]; **from *mē*: not, and *pōs*: by any means ▶ For fear that, so that, otherwise** > Paul was afraid, lest {perhaps, somehow} he had labored in vain (Gal. 4:11).The Greek word is also used by Paul in 1 Cor. 9:27; 2 Cor. 2:7; 9:4; Gal. 2:2; 1 Thes. 3:5. *
[3] ***hina mē*** [expr.: ἵνα μή <3363>]>]; **from *hina*: in order that, and *mē*: not ▶** Refs.: Matt. 26:5; Mark 4:12; Acts 5:26. * ‡

LET – [1] ***aphiēmi*** [verb: ἀφίημι <863>]; **from *apo*: from, and *hiēmi*: to send ▶ To allow, to permit; also transl.: to suffer, to leave, to give permission** > The verb is used by Jesus and in regard to Himself (Matt. 7:4; 23:13; Mark 1:34; 5:19, 37; 7:12: *enaphiēmi* in some mss.; 11:16; Luke 6:42; 8:51; John 12:7). It is also used when Jesus spoke with John the Baptist (Matt. 3:15a, b). If anyone wants to take our tunic, we should let him have our cloak also (Matt. 5:40). Jesus told a man to let the dead bury their own dead (Matt. 8:22; Luke 9:60). Jesus said to let the little children come to Him (Matt. 19:14; Mark 10:14; Luke 18:16). Other refs.: Matt. 13:30; 15:14; 27:49; Mark 7:27; 11:6; 14:6; 15:36; Luke 12:39; 13:8; John 11:44, 48; 18:8; Rev. 11:9. All other refs.: see entries in Lexicon at <863>.
[2] **to let down: *kathiēmi*** [verb: καθίημι <2524>]; **from *kata*: down, and *hiēmi*: to send ▶ To send below, to lower** > A man who was paralyzed was let down {lowered} with his bed through the tiling (Luke 5:19). The disciples let Paul down through the wall (Acts 9:25). Peter saw an object like a great sheet descending to him and let down {lowered} to the earth (Acts 10:11; 11:5). ¶
[3] ***didōmi*** [verb: δίδωμι <1325>] **▶ To allow, to give (one's accord), to suffer** > God would not let His Holy One (i.e., the Lord Jesus) see corruption (Acts 2:27; 13:35). Other refs.: GIVE <1325>.
[4] ***tithēmi*** [verb: τίθημι <5087>]; **from *theō*: to place ▶ To make, to put** > Jesus told His disciples to let His words sink into their ears (Luke 9:44). All other refs.: see entries in Lexicon at <5087>.
[5] **to let down: *chalaō*** [verb: χαλάω <5465>] **▶ To lower** > The bed on which the paralytic was lying was let down (Mark 2:4). Jesus told Simon to let down his nets for a catch (Luke 5:4), which Simon did (v. 5). The disciples let down Paul in a large basket (Acts 9:25; 2 Cor. 11:33). The ship's gear and the skiff were let down (Acts 27:17, 30) on Paul's ship. ¶
– [6] Matt. 8:21; Luke 9:59, 61; Acts 21:39 → PERMIT <2010> [7] Matt. 18:27; Acts 3:13; 4:21, 23; 5:40; 16:35, 36; 17:9; 26:32; 28:18 → to let go → RELEASE (verb) <630> [8] Matt. 21:33, 41; Mark 12:1; Luke 20:9 → to let out, to let forth → LEASE <1554> [9] Matt. 24:43; Acts 5:38; 14:16; 19:30; 23:32; 27:32; 1 Cor. 10:13 → ALLOW <1439> [10] Mark 10:37 → GRANT <1325> [11] Acts 15:30 → to let go → DISMISS <630> [12] Acts 24:1

→ to let down → DESCEND <2597> 13 Acts 27:29 → to let down anchors → to cast anchors → CAST (verb) <4496> 14 Rom. 1:13 → HINDER (verb) <2967>.

LET BE – ***ētō*** [verb: ἤτω <2277>]; **pres. imperfect of *eimi* (I am) ▶ let him or it be** > Refs.: 1 Cor. 16:22; Jas. 5:12. ¶ ‡

LETTER – 1 ***gramma*** [neut. noun: γράμμα <1121>]; **from *graphō*: to write; lit.: writing ▶ a. Character, symbol of an alphabet** > The inscription over Jesus crucified was written in letters of Greek, Latin, and Hebrew (in some mss.: Luke 23:38). The ministry of death (i.e., the law given to Moses), in letters engraved on stones, came with glory (2 Cor. 3:7). **b. The Scriptures of the O.T.** > The Jews wondered that Jesus knew letters {got such learning} (John 7:15). Timothy knew the sacred letters {Holy Scriptures, sacred writings} from childhood (2 Tim. 3:15). **c. Message, writing transmitted to someone** > The brothers in Rome had not received letters from Judea concerning Paul (Acts 28:21). Paul had written a large letter (lit.: large letters) to the Galatians (Gal. 6:11); some believe it could mean he had written a long letter, but most likely he used big characters in his letter since he may have had an eye infirmity (see 4:13–15). **d. Written commandment from God; also transl.: written code** > The word is used with this sense in Rom. 2:27, 29; 7:6; 2 Cor. 3:6a, b. All other refs.: BILL <1121>, LEARNING <1121>, WRITING <1121>.

2 ***epistolē*** [fem. noun: ἐπιστολή <1992>]; **from *epistellō*: to send, which is from *epi*: to, and *stellō*: to send ▶ Message, writing transmitted to someone; often transl.: epistle** > Saul asked the high priest for letters to the synagogues (Acts 9:2; 22:5). Barnabas and Paul delivered the letter to the multitude at Antioch (Acts 15:30). Claudius Lysias wrote a letter (Acts 23:25), which was delivered to the governor (v. 33). Tertius had written Paul's epistle (Rom. 16:22), i.e., under Paul's dictation. Paul had written in his epistle not to keep company with sexually immoral people (1 Cor. 5:9). He would send Corinthians with letters to Jerusalem (1 Cor. 16:3). The Corinthians were Paul's epistle written in his heart (2 Cor. 3:2); they were manifested as being the epistle of Christ by the ministry of Paul (v. 3). Paul had made the Corinthians sorry with his letter (2 Cor. 7:8a, b). He did not want to terrify them by his letters (2 Cor. 10:9); it was said that his letters were weighty and powerful (v. 10); what he was in word by his letters when absent, Paul was also when present (v. 11). The Epistle to the Colossians was to be read also in the church of the Laodiceans (Col. 4:16). The Epistle to the Thessalonians was also to be read to all the holy brothers (1 Thes. 5:27). They were not to be troubled by word or by letter as though the day of Christ (some mss.: of the Lord) had come (2 Thes. 2:2). They were to hold the traditions (i.e., the teachings) which were taught by word or Paul's letter (2 Thes. 2:15). Paul's word in his letter was to be obeyed (2 Thes. 3:14); he wrote the salutation with his own hand in every letter (v. 17). Peter had written a second letter to stir up the pure mind of his readers (2 Pet. 3:1). Paul was writing in all his epistles according to the wisdom given to him (2 Pet. 3:16; see v. 15). Other ref.: 2 Cor. 3:1; see EPISTLE OF COMMENDATION <1992> <4956>. ¶

– 3 Matt. 5:18 → smallest letter → IOTA <2503> 4 Matt. 19:7 → CERTIFICATE <975> 5 Acts 21:25 → to send a letter → WRITE <1989>.

LETTER OF RECOMMENDATION – 2 Cor. 3:1 → EPISTLE OF COMMENDATION <1992> <4956>.

LEVEL (adj.) – 1 ***pedinos*** [adj.: πεδινός <3977>]; **from *pedion*: field, plain ▶ Flat, of an equal plane** > Jesus stood on a level place {on a plain} (Luke 6:17). ¶

– 2 Luke 3:5 → level ways → smooth ways → SMOOTH <3006> 3 Heb. 12:13 → STRAIGHT <3717>.

LEVEL (verb) – Luke 19:44 → to level to the ground → GROUND <1474>.

LEVI (man of the N.T.) – ***Leuis*** [masc. name: Λευΐς <3018>]**: joining, in Heb.; see Gen. 29:34 ▶ One of the twelve apostles of Jesus >** Levi was a tax collector (Mark 2:14; Luke 5:27). He is also called Matthew (Matt. 9:9; 10:3; Mark 3:18; Luke 6:15; Acts 1:13). He left everything to follow Jesus, and made Him a great feast in his house (Luke 5:29). ¶

LEVI (men of the O.T.) – ***Leui*** [masc. name: Λευί <3017>]**: joining, in Heb.; see Gen. 29:34 ▶ a. Son of Jacob and name of one of the twelve tribes descended from him >** A family of the sons of Levi had received the service of the priesthood in Israel (Heb. 7:5, 9). Twelve thousand out of the tribe of Levi will be sealed (Rev. 7:7). **b. Name of two men of the O.T. >** These men named Levi are mentioned in the genealogy of Jesus (Luke 3:24, 29).

LEVITE – ***Leuitēs*** [masc. noun: Λευίτης <3019>]**; from *Leui*: Levi ▶ Member of the tribe of Levi >** In the parable of the Good Samaritan, a Levite seeing the man who was stripped and wounded passed by on the other side (Luke 10:32). The Jews sent priests and Levites to ask John the Baptist who he was (John 1:19). Barnabas was a Levite (Acts 4:36). ¶

LEVITICAL – ***Leuitikos*** [adj.: Λευιτικός <3020>]**; from *Leui*: Levi ▶ Pertaining to the tribe of Levi >** The Levitical priesthood was so named because it was entrusted to the tribe of Levi (Heb. 7:11). ¶

LEWD – Acts 17:5 → EVIL (adj.) <4190>.

LEWDNESS – 1 ***aselgeia*** [fem. noun: ἀσέλγεια <766>]**; from *aselgēs*: licentious, brutal ▶ Dissoluteness, absence of control in enjoying sensual pleasures, shamelessness; also transl.: debauchery, lasciviousness, licentiousness, sensuality, wantonness >** Lewdness proceeds out of the heart of man (Mark 7:22). Christians must walk properly, not in lewdness {chambering, lust} (Rom. 13:13). Many at Corinth had not repented of the lewdness which they had practiced (2 Cor. 12:21). Lewdness is a work of the flesh (Gal. 5:19). Paul speaks of those who have given themselves over to lewdness (Eph. 4:19). Some were walking in lewdness before their conversion (1 Pet. 4:3). Lot was oppressed by the lewdness {abandoned, depraved, filthy, sensual conduct, filthy lives} of the wicked of his time (2 Pet. 2:7). Peter speaks of those who influence new converts by their lewdness (2 Pet. 2:18). In Jude 4, certain men turn the grace of God into lewdness {license for immorality}. Other ref.: 2 Pet. 2:2 (dissolute way); see DISSOLUTE <766>. ¶
2 ***koitē*** [fem. noun: κοίτη <2845>]**; from *keimai*: to lie; lit.: bed for sleeping ▶ Sexual relations outside of marriage >** Christians are not to conduct themselves in lewdness {sexual promiscuity, sexual immorality, chambering} (Rom. 13:13). All other refs.: BED <2845>.
– 3 Acts 18:14 → CRIME <4467>.

LIABLE – 1 Matt. 5:21, 22 → SUBJECT (noun)[1] <1777> 2 Matt. 26:66 → DESERVING <1777>.

LIAR (adj. and noun) – 1 ***pseudēs*** [adj. used as noun: ψευδής <5571>]**; from *pseudomai*: to lie ▶ Character of one who deceives with lies, through falsehood; person who lies >** The church at Ephesus tested those who falsely said they were apostles and found them liars {false} (Rev. 2:2). The part of liars will be in the lake of fire and brimstone (Rev. 21:8). Other ref.: Acts 6:13; see FALSE <5571>. ¶
– 2 Rev. 3:9 → to be a liar → LIE (verb)[2] <5574>.

LIAR (noun) – 1 ***pseustēs*** [masc. noun: ψεύστης <5583>]**; from *pseudomai*: to lie ▶ Person who deceives with lies, through falsehood >** The devil is a liar (John 8:44). Jesus would be a liar if He were to say that He does not know the Father (John 8:55). Paul exclaims in Rom. 3:4: Let God be true but every man a liar {false}. The law is made for liars (1 Tim. 1:10). One of the Cretans' own prophets said: "Cretans are always liars" (Titus 1:12).

Those who say they have never sinned make God a liar (1 John 1:10). The one who says he knows Jesus Christ and does not keep His commandments is a liar (2:4), likewise the one who denies that Jesus is the Christ (2:22), he who hates his brother (4:20), and he who does not believe God (5:10). ¶
– [2] 1 Tim. 4:2 → hypocrisy of liars → lie, liar → LIE (noun) <5573>.

LIBATION – Phil. 2:17; 2 Tim. 4:6 → to be poured out as a libation → DRINK OFFERING <4689>.

LIBERAL – [1] 2 Cor. 8:20 → liberal gift → ABUNDANCE <100> [2] 2 Cor. 9:13 → liberal, liberal sharing distribution → LIBERALITY <572> [3] 1 Tim. 6:18 → liberal in distributing → GENEROUS <2130>.

LIBERALITY – [1] ***haplotēs*** [fem. noun: ἁπλότης <572>]; **from *haplous*: simple, singular ► Generous gift offered in simplicity; also transl.: free-hearted liberality, generosity** > The churches of Macedonia had abounded in the riches of their liberality (2 Cor. 8:2). The Corinthians would be enriched in every way unto all liberality {bountifulness} (2 Cor. 9:11); Paul speaks of their liberality in communicating {liberal distribution, liberal sharing} what they had to others (v. 13). Other refs.: Rom. 12:8; 2 Cor. 1:12; 11:3; Eph. 6:5; Col. 3:22; see SIMPLICITY <572>. ¶
– [2] Rom. 12:8 → SIMPLICITY <572> [3] 1 Cor. 16:3 → GIFT <5485>.

LIBERALLY – ***haplōs*** [adv.: ἁπλῶς <574>]; **from *haplous*: simple, loyal; lit.: without folds ► Freely, generously and without condition** > God gives to all liberally (Jas. 1:5). ¶

LIBERATE – Rom. 8:21 → to set free → FREE (adj.) <1659>.

LIBERTINE – See FREEDMAN <3032>.

LIBERTY – [1] ***anesis*** [fem. noun: ἄνεσις <425>]; **from *aniēmi*: to loose ► Slackening, loosening (in relation to conditions of captivity)** > Felix commanded that Paul be granted a measure of liberty {freedom} (Acts 24:23). All other refs.: EASE <425>, REST (noun)[1] <425>.
[2] ***aphesis*** [fem. noun: ἄφεσις <859>]; **from *aphiēmi*: to send away, which is from *apo*: from, and *hiēmi*: to send ► Deliverance, release** > Jesus was sent to preach liberty {deliverance, freedom, release} to the captives, to set at liberty {deliver, free} those who are oppressed {to release the oppressed} (Luke 4:18a, b). All other refs.: FORGIVENESS <859>, REMISSION <859>.
[3] ***eleutheria*** [fem. noun: ἐλευθερία <1657>]; **from *eleutheros*: free person ► Emancipation, freedom, liberation** > Creation will enjoy the liberty of the glory of the children of God (Rom. 8:21). Paul asks why his liberty is judged by another's conscience (1 Cor. 10:29). Where the Spirit of the Lord is, there is liberty (2 Cor. 3:17). False brothers were spying out the liberty of believers in Christ Jesus (Gal. 2:4). Christians are to stand fast in the liberty by which Christ has made them free (Gal. 5:1). The Galatians were called to liberty {to be free}, however were not to use that liberty as an opportunity for the flesh, but by love serve one another (Gal. 5:13a, b). James speaks of the perfect law, that of liberty (Jas. 1:25). Christians are to act as those who will be judged by the law of liberty (Jas. 2:12). Liberty should not be used as a cloak of malice (1 Pet. 2:16). Wicked men, themselves slaves of corruption, promise liberty (2 Pet. 2:19). ¶
[4] ***exousia*** [fem. noun: ἐξουσία <1849>]; **from *exesti*: it is permissible, which is from *ek*: out, and *eimi*: to be ► Authority, permission, right** > The liberty {exercise of the freedom} of the Corinthians might potentially become a stumbling block to the weak (1 Cor. 8:9). All other refs.: AUTHORITY <1849>.
– [5] Luke 4:18 → to set at liberty → SEND <649> [6] Acts 26:32; 28:18 → to set at liberty → RELEASE (verb) <630> [7] Acts 27:3 → to give liberty → PERMIT <2010> [8] 1 Cor. 7:39 → at liberty → FREE (adj.)

<1658> [9] Heb. 13:23 → to set at liberty → to set free → FREE (adj.) <630>.

LIBYA – ***Libuē*** [fem. name: Λιβύη <3033>] ▶ **Region of northeast Africa, bordering Egypt and near Cyrene** > Jews of Libya were present in Jerusalem at Pentecost (Acts 2:10). ¶

LICENCE – [1] Acts 21:40 → to give licence→ PERMIT <2010> [2] Acts 25:16 → OPPORTUNITY <5117>.

LICENSE – Jude 4 → license for immorality → LEWDNESS <766>.

LICENTIOUSNESS – Mark 7:22; 2 Cor. 12:21; Gal. 5:19; Jude 4 → LEWDNESS <766>.

LICK – [1] ***epileichō*** [verb: ἐπιλείχω <1952a>]; **from *epi*: upon, and *leichō*: to lap with the tongue; lit.: to lick over** ▶ **To pass the tongue over** > The dogs came and licked the sores of Lazarus (Luke 16:21); some mss. have *apoleichō*: see [2]. ¶
[2] ***apoleichō*** [verb: ἀπολείχω <621>]; **from *apo*: from, and *leichō*: see [1]** ▶ **To pass the tongue over** > See [1]. ¶

LICTOR – Acts 16:35, 38 → OFFICER <4465>.

LIE (noun) – [1] ***pseudos*** [neut. noun: ψεῦδος <5579>]; **from *pseudomai*: to lie, to speak deceitfully** ▶ **Affirmation contrary to the truth with the intent to deceive; also transl.: lying, falsehood** > When the devil speaks a lie {lies}, he speaks of what is his own, for he is a liar and its father (John 8:44). Certain persons exchanged the truth of God for a lie (Rom. 1:25). Christians ought to put off lying and each one of them ought to speak truth with their neighbor (Eph. 4:25). The coming of the antichrist will be characterized by lying wonders {wonders of falsehood, false wonders, counterfeit miracles} (lit.: wonders of a lie) (2 Thes. 2:9); God will send a strong delusion, such that men should believe the lie {what is false} (v. 11). No lie is of the truth (1 John 2:21, 27 {counterfeit}). No lie {Not what is deceitful} will enter into the heavenly Jerusalem (Rev. 21:27); whoever loves and practices a lie will be outside (22:15). Other ref.: Rev. 14:5 in some mss.; see DECEIT <1388>. ¶
[2] **one speaking lies, liar: *pseudologos*** [adj. used as noun: ψευδολόγος <5573>]; **from *pseudēs*: false, and *legō*: to speak** ▶ **False language, deception** > Certain apostates speak lies in hypocrisy {hypocrisy of liars} (1 Tim. 4:2). ¶
[3] ***pseusma*** [neut. noun: ψεῦσμα <5582>]; **from *pseudomai*: see [1]** ▶ **Falsehood** > In Rom. 3:7, the lie which Paul attributes to himself refers to the generalized attitude of falsehood of man before God. ¶
– [4] John 13:25 → LEAN <377> [5] Acts 27:20 → BEAT <1945> [6] Gal. 1:20 → what I am writing is no lie → lit.: I do not lie → LIE (verb)[2] <5574>.

LIE (verb)[1] – [1] ***keimai*** [verb: κεῖμαι <2749>] ▶ **a. To be in a horizontal position, to rest** > The shepherds would find a baby lying in a manger (Luke 2:12); they went and they found him lying there (v. 16). **b. To remain, to stay** > When Moses is read, a veil lies on {covers, is upon} the heart of the Jews (2 Cor. 3:15). **c. To rest (in regard to one who has died)** > After the resurrection, an angel invited the women to see the place where the Lord was lying {lay} (Matt. 28:6). No one had ever lain {been laid} before in the tomb of Jesus (Luke 23:53). Mary saw two angels where the body of Jesus had lain {had been} (John 20:12). **d. To be under the control** > The whole world lies in the wicked one (1 John 5:19), i.e., in his power. Other refs.: see entries in Lexicon at <2749>.
[2] ***anakeimai*** [verb: ἀνάκειμαι <345>]; **from *ana*: intens., and *keimai*: see [1]** ▶ **To rest in a horizontal position** > Jesus entered where the child was lying {was} (Mark 5:40). All other refs.: SET (verb) <345>, TABLE[1] <345>.
[3] ***katakeimai*** [verb: κατάκειμαι <2621>]; **from *kata*: down (intens.), and *keimai*: see [1]** ▶ **To lay because of sickness** > The men let down the bed on which the paralytic was lying {laying} (Mark 2:4). The paralytic

who was healed by Jesus took up what he had been lying {laying} on, and departed to his own house, glorifying God (Luke 5:25). A man of thirty-eight years was lying by the pool of Bethesda, waiting to be healed (John 5:6). All other refs.: BEDRIDDEN (BE) <2621>, LAY <2621>, SIT <2621>, TABLE[1] <2621>.

[4] ***ballō*** [verb: βάλλω <906>]; **lit.: to put down ▶ To be in a horizontal position >** The servant of the centurion was lying at home paralyzed (Matt. 8:6). Jesus saw the mother of Peter's wife lying sick {laid, laid down, sick} with a fever (Matt. 8:14). A paralytic lying {laid} on a bed was brought to Jesus (Matt. 9:2). The mother found her daughter lying on {laid upon} the bed and the demon gone out (Mark 7:30). Lazarus was lying {was laid at} the gate of a rich man (Luke 16:20). All other refs.: see entries in Lexicon at <906>.

– [5] Matt. 15:35 → to lie down → to sit down → SIT <377> [6] Luke 8:42 → to lie a dying → DIE <599> [7] John 11:38 → LAY <1945> [8] Acts 23:21 → to lie in wait → WAIT (verb) <4327> [9] Rom. 7:21 → to lie close at hand → to be present → PRESENT (BE) <3873>.

LIE (verb)[2] – [1] ***pseudomai*** [verb: ψεύδομαι <5574>] **▶ To assert something untrue, to make an affirmation contrary to the truth in order to deceive >** Believers in the Lord are blessed when others say evil against them lying {falsely, falsely saying} for the sake of the Lord Jesus (Matt. 5:11). Ananias and Sapphira lied to the Holy Spirit and to God (Acts 5:3, 4). On several occasions Paul takes God as his witness that he is not lying (Rom. 9:1; 2 Cor. 11:31; Gal. 1:20; 1 Tim. 2:7). Christians should not lie to one another (Col. 3:9) nor should they lie against {deny} the truth (Jas. 3:14). In His promise to Abraham, it was impossible for God to lie (Heb. 6:18). If we say that we have fellowship with God, and we walk in darkness, we lie (1 John 1:6). Those of the synagogue of Satan lie {are liars} (Rev. 3:9). ¶

[2] **who cannot lie, that cannot lie: *apseudēs*** [adj.: ἀψευδής <893>]; **from *a*: neg., and *pseudēs*: false, a liar ▶ Who cannot be untruthful (lit.: never-lying) >** God who cannot lie {does not lie} promised eternal life before time began (Titus 1:2). ¶

– [3] John 8:44 → lit.: to speak a lie → LIE (noun) <5579>.

LIE IN WAIT – Luke 11:54; Acts 23:21 → to wait in ambush → AMBUSH <1748>.

LIFE – [1] **manner, way of life: *agōgē*** [fem. noun: ἀγωγή <72>]; **from *agō*: to lead ▶ Conduct, behavior >** Timothy had carefully followed Paul's manner of life (2 Tim. 3:10). ¶

[2] **manner of life, way of life: *anastrophē*** [fem. noun: ἀναστροφή <391>]; **from *anastrephō*: to return, which is from *ana*: again, and *strephō*: to turn ▶ Conduct, behavior >** With regard to his former manner of life {conduct, conversation}, the Christian is to have put off the old man which corrupts itself according to the deceitful lusts (Eph. 4:22). All other refs.: CONDUCT (noun) <391>.

[3] ***bios*** [masc. noun: βίος <979>] **▶ The present state of existence >** This term is used in regard to the duration of life (Luke 8:14; 2 Tim. 2:4), as well as to our life in this world (1 Tim. 2:2; 1 John 2:16). Other ref.: 1 Pet. 4:3 in some mss. All other refs.: LIVELIHOOD <979>, LIVING (noun) <979>.

[4] **manner of life: *biōsis*** [fem. noun: βίωσις <981>]; **from *bioō*: to live, which is from *bios*: see [3] ▶ Way of living, behavior, conduct >** Paul speaks of his manner of life {the way he lived} from his youth (Acts 26:4). ¶

[5] **things that pertain to this life, things of this life, matters of this life: *biōtika*; fem. plur. of *biōtikos*** [adj.: βιωτικός <982>]; **from *bioō*: to live, which is from *bios*: see [3] ▶ That which relates to present existence on earth >** Jesus says to be careful so that our hearts will not be weighed down with the worries of this life (Luke 21:34). Christians should judge themselves the matters of this life (1 Cor. 6:3); if they have judgments concerning things pertaining to this life {such matters}, they should appoint

those who are least esteemed by the church to judge (v. 4). ¶

6 ***zōē*** [fem. noun: ζωή <2222>]; **from *zaō*: to live ► The state of one who is living >** This term is used in regard to life as a principle, life in the absolute sense, life as God has it, that which the Father has in Himself and which He gave to the Incarnate Son to have in Himself (John 5:26a, b) and which the Son manifested in the world (1 John 1:2a, b). In consequence of the fall, man has become alienated from this life of God (Eph. 4:18); but he is able to become a partaker of it through faith in the Lord Jesus Christ (John 3:15) who becomes the Prince (or: Originator) to all who believe in Him (Acts 3:15). Christ is therefore the Christian's life (Col. 3:4) and He sustains this life (John 6:35, 63). The Christians possess eternal life presently in virtue of their relationship with God (John 5:24; 1 John 3:14). The resurrection of Christ assures them that this life will become that of their bodies one day (2 Cor. 5:4; 2 Tim. 1:10). God gives to all life and breath (Acts 17:25). He will give life to a brother who has sinned a sin which does not lead to death, if request is made for him (1 John 5:16). The term describes the duration of the present sojourn of man on the earth (Luke 16:25; 1 Cor. 15:19; 1 Tim. 4:8a; 1 Pet. 3:10). The expr. "this life" corresponds to "the gospel," "the faith," and "Christianity" (Acts 5:20). Sin has introduced death (see Rom. 5:12), and sin is to rebel against God. "The soul of the flesh is in the blood" (Lev. 17:11); consequently, the communication of life to the sinner must be by the death caused by the shedding of blood. "It is the blood that makes atonement for the soul" (Lev. 17:11). Only a sacrifice in which the victim and the offerer became identified could figuratively remove this separation from God. This was made possible by the voluntary offering of Christ, which the offerings in Israel had previously typified. The shedding of blood, in the language of Scripture, involves the taking or giving of the "life." Since Christ was without sin, and therefore had no sins of His own to die for, His death was a voluntary one for us (John 10:15: *psuchē*; comp. Is. 53:5, 10, 12; 2 Cor. 5:21). In His sacrifice, He endured the divine judgment due to the sin of man. By this means, the Christian becomes identified with Him in newness of life, through His resurrection, and he enjoys conscious and eternal fellowship with God. (After W. E. Vine.) In Heb. 2:15, the term translates the verb *zaō* (lit.: the activities of life). See LIFE ETERNAL for the verses containing this expr. *

7 ***psuchē*** [fem. noun: ψυχή <5590>]; **from *psuchō*: to breathe ► Breath, breath of life >** This term designates the natural life (e.g., Matt. 2:20; 6:25a, b; Mark 10:45; Luke 12:22; John 10:15; Acts 20:10; Rev. 8:9; 12:11). It also designates the seat of personality (Luke 9:24a, b). All other refs.: SOUL <5590>.

8 **to come to life: *zaō*** [verb: ζάω <2198>]; **contracted form: *zō* ► To live, to be alive >** He who died and came to life addresses the church of Smyrna (Rev. 2:8). The beast who was wounded by the sword will come to life (Rev. 13:14). All other refs.: LIVE <2198>, LIVING (adj.) <2198>, LIVING (noun) <2198>.

9 **to come to life, to come to life again: *anazaō*** [verb: ἀναζάω <326>]; **from *ana*: again, and *zaō*: see 8 ► To be alive once again, to return to life >** For his father, the prodigal son had come to life again (Luke 15:24); also v. 32 in some mss. All other refs.: LIVE <326>, REVIVE <326>.

10 **to come to life, to give life: *zōopoieō*** [verb: ζωοποιέω <2227>]; **from *zōos*: alive, and *poieō*: to make ► To communicate life, especially eternal life, to vivify; also transl.: to make alive, to quicken >** The Father and the Son give life (John 5:21a, b), as well as the Holy Spirit (John 6:63; 2 Cor. 3:6; 1 Pet. 3:18; v. 19 in some mss.). God gives life to the dead (Rom. 4:17). This working is also attributed to God by His Spirit (Rom. 8:11). The principle of giving life is the following: that which is sown must die before being given life (1 Cor. 15:36). The last Adam, Jesus Christ, is a life-giving spirit (1 Cor. 15:45); He will give life to the mortal bodies of Christians, whether living or fallen asleep, at His coming. The law is not able to give life (Gal. 3:21). God

preserves in life {quickens} all things (1 Tim. 6:13). Other ref.: 1 Cor. 15:22; see ALIVE <2227>. ¶

11 living long, long-lived: *makrochronios* [adj.: μακροχρόνιος <3118>]; **from *makros*: long, and *chronos*: time ▶ Enjoying an extended lifetime >** Paul says to honor one's father and mother in order to prosper and live long (lit.: to be of living life) on the earth (Eph. 6:3). ¶

– **12** Matt. 13:22; Mark 4:19 → AGE <165> **13** John 10:15; Acts 20:10; et al. → SOUL <5590> **14** Rom. 1:3 → as to His earthly life → lit.: the becoming (*ginomai*) **15** Rom. 16:4 → NECK <5137> **16** 1 Cor. 6:4 → those whose way of life is scorned → those who are least esteemed → ESTEEM (verb) <1848> **17** 1 Cor. 7:17; Col. 2:6 → to lead the life, to live your lives → WALK <4043> **18** 1 Cor. 14:7 → without life → LIFELESS <895> **19** 2 Cor. 1:23 → SOUL <5590> **20** Gal. 1:13; 1 Tim. 4:12; Jas. 3:13; 1 Pet. 1:15, 18; 3:2, 16; 2 Pet. 2:7; 3:11 → way of life, good life, life → CONDUCT (noun) <391> **21** Eph. 4:20 → the way of life → lit.: the Christ **22** Eph. 6:3 → enjoy long life → lit.: living a long time → LIVE <3118> **23** Phil. 1:27 → to let one's manner of life be worthy → to live in a worthy manner → LIVE <4176> **24** 1 Thes. 4:11 → to lead a quiet life → QUIET (adj.) <2270> **25** 2 Thes. 3:6, 11 → unruly life, undisciplined life → DISORDERLY <814> **26** 2 Tim. 1:9 → to call to a holy life → lit.: to call with a holy calling → CALLING <2821> **27** Titus 3:3 → to spend one's life → LIVE <1236> **28** Heb. 11:22 → at the end of his life → dying → DIE <5053> **29** Heb. 13:5 → CONDUCT (noun) <5158> **30** Jas. 3:6 → NATURE <1078> **31** Rev. 13:15 → BREATH <4151>.

LIFE ETERNAL – life: *zōē* [fem. noun: ζωή <2222>]; **from *zaō*: to live; eternal: *aiōnios*** [adj.: αἰώνιος <166>]; **from *aiōn*: age ▶ Life eternal is communicated at new birth. It is new life, divine life transmitted by God. >** God communicates life eternal to whoever believes in the Son of God (John 3:15, 16, 36; 6:40, 47, 54; 1 Tim. 1:16; 1 John 1:2). Jesus gives life eternal (John 10:28; 17:2). He who hears the word of the Lord and believes Him who sent Him has life eternal (John 5:24). God has given eternal life to the Christian, and this life is in His Son (1 John 5:11); Jesus Christ is the true God and eternal life (v. 20); the Christian already possesses eternal life while here on earth and enjoys it presently (v. 13). The perfect and definitive enjoyment of blessings related to this life is seen as yet future (Matt. 19:29; Rom. 2:7; 6:22; Gal. 6:8; 1 Tim. 6:12). Other refs.: Matt. 19:16; 25:46; Mark 10:17, 30; Luke 10:25; 18:18, 30; John 4:14, 36; 5:39; 6:27, 68; 12:25, 50; 17:3; Acts 13:46, 48; Rom. 5:21; 6:23; 1 Tim. 6:19 in some mss.; Titus 1:2; 3:7; 1 John 2:25; Jude 21. Other refs. (*zōē*): see LIFE <2222>. All other refs. (*aiōnios*): see ETERNAL <166>.

LIFEBOAT – Acts 27:16, 30, 32 → BOAT <4627>.

LIFELESS – *apsuchos* [adj.: ἄψυχος <895>]; **from *a*: neg., and *psuchē*: life ▶ Without life, inanimate >** Paul speaks of lifeless things {things without life} that give distinct sounds (1 Cor. 14:7). ¶

LIFETIME – Luke 16:25 → LIFE <2222>.

LIFT – 1 to lift, to lift up: *airō* [verb: αἴρω <142>] **▶ a. To lift up (the eyes), i.e., to look at a person or an object; also transl.: to raise >** Jesus lifted up His eyes {looked up} and addressed His Father (John 11:41). **b. To raise >** Ten lepers lifted up their voices {called out in a loud voice}, saying to Jesus to have compassion on them (Luke 17:13). The apostles lifted up the voice with one accord to God (Acts 4:24). An angel lifted up his right hand to heaven (Rev. 10:5). All other refs.: see entries in Lexicon at <142>.

2 *epairō* [verb: ἐπαίρω <1869>]; **from *epi*: upon, and *airō*: to lift, to raise ▶ To lift up (the eyes), i.e., to look at a person or an object; also transl.: to look up >** The verb is used concerning three disciples (Matt. 17:8), Jesus (Luke 6:20 {to turn one's gaze}; John 6:5; 17:1), the rich man in Hades (Luke 16:23), a tax collector (Luke 18:13 {to raise}), and the disciples (John 4:35). The verb is also used for lifting the head (Luke 21:28), the hands (Luke 24:50; 1 Tim. 2:8), the heel (John 13:18), and the foresail (Acts 27:40 {to hoist}). All other refs.: EXALT <1869>, RAISE <1869>, TAKE <1869>.

3 **to lift up: *anakuptō*** [verb: ἀνακύπτω <352>]; **from *ana*: upwards, back again, and *kuptō*: to bend ▶ To regain an upright position** > A woman was bent over for eighteen years and unable to lift herself up {raise herself up, straighten up} (Luke 13:11). All other refs.: LOOK (verb) <352>, STRAIGHTEN <352>.

4 **to lift up: *egeirō*** [verb: ἐγείρω <1453>] **▶ To make stand upright, to raise** > Jesus took hold of the hand of the man who appeared to be dead, lifted him up, and the man arose (Mark 9:27). All other refs.: ARISE <1453>, RAISE <1453>, RISE (verb) <1453>, WAKE <1453>.

5 **to lift up: *hupsoō*** [verb: ὑψόω <5312>]; **from *hupsos*: height ▶ To elevate, to rise** > As Moses lifted up the serpent in the wilderness, even so the Son of Man had to be lifted up (John 3:14a, b; 12:34). When they would have lifted up the Son of Man, the Jews would know who He was, i.e., the one He claimed to be (John 8:28). If He was lifted up from the earth, Jesus would draw all people to Himself (John 12:32). Those humbling themselves in the sight of the Lord will be lifted up {exalted} by Him (Jas. 4:10). All other refs.: to EXALT <5312>.

– 6 Luke 11:46 → to lift one finger to help → lit.: to touch the burden with one of the fingers → TOUCH <4379> 7 John 19:29 → OFFER <4374> 8 Acts 7:43 → to lift up → to take up → TAKE <353> 9 Acts 9:41 → to lift up → ARISE <450> 10 1 Tim. 3:6 → to be lifted up with pride → PUFF UP <5187> 11 Heb. 12:12 → to lift up → STRENGTHEN <461>.

LIGAMENT – 1 Eph. 4:16; Col. 2:19 → supporting ligaments, ligaments and sinews → lit.: joint of supply, joints and bands → JOINT <860> 2 Col. 2:19 → BOND[1] <4886>.

LIGHT (adj.) – 1 ***elaphros*** [adj.: ἐλαφρός <1645>] **▶ Which has little weight** > The burden of Jesus is light (Matt. 11:30). The momentary and light affliction of Christians works for them an eternal weight of glory (2 Cor. 4:17). ¶

2 **to make light: *ameleō*** [verb: ἀμελέω <272>]; **from *amelēs*: careless, which is from *a*: neg., and *melei*: to care ▶ To remain indifferent, to neglect** > Those invited to the wedding of the king's son made light of {paid no attention to} the invitation (Matt. 22:5). All other refs.: DISREGARD <272>, NEGLIGENT <272>.

– 3 Luke 12:48 → to receive a light beating → lit.: to be beaten with few (stripes) → FEW <3641> 4 Heb. 12:5 → to make light → DESPISE <3643>.

LIGHT (noun) – 1 ***phōs*** [neut. noun: φῶς <5457>]; **from *phaō*: to shine, to make manifest ▶ Brightness produced by a luminous source** > The term is used in regard to Jesus (Matt. 4:16a, b; John 1:4, 5, 7, 8a, b, 9; 3:19a, b; 8:12a, b; 9:5; 12:35a, b, 36a, b, 46; Acts 26:18), God (1 John 1:5), John the Baptist (John 5:35), believers in the Lord (Matt. 5:14, 16; Luke 11:35; 16:8; Eph. 5:8a, b, 9 {some mss.: Spirit}), a lamp (Luke 8:16), Paul (Acts 13:47), and Satan (2 Cor. 11:14). When Jesus was transfigured, His clothes became as white as the light (Matt. 17:2). The Father of lights gives us every good gift and every perfect gift (Jas. 1:17). Other refs.: Matt. 6:23; 10:27; Luke 2:32; 12:3; 22:56 {fire, firelight}; John 3:20a, b, 21; 11:9, 10; Acts 9:3; 12:7; 16:29; 22:6, 9, 11; 26:13, 23; Rom. 2:19; 13:12; 2 Cor. 4:6; 6:14; Eph. 5:13a, b; Col. 1:12; 1 Tim. 6:16; 1 Pet. 2:9; 1 John 1:7a, b; 2:8–10; Rev. 18:23; 21:24; 22:5a. All other refs.: FIRE <5457>, SON OF LIGHT <5457>.

2 ***phōstēr*** [masc. noun: φωστήρ <5458>]; **from *phōs*: see 1 ▶ Source of brightness** > Christians are called to shine like lights {stars} in the world (Phil. 2:15). The light {shining, brilliance} of Jerusalem in the future will be like a most precious stone (Rev. 21:11). ¶

3 **light, full of light: *phōteinos*** [adj.: φωτεινός <5460>]; **from *phōs*: see 1 ▶**

Well illuminated, luminous > The Greek word is used in regard to the body being full of light (Matt. 6:22; Luke 11:34, 36a, b). Other ref.: Matt. 17:5; see BRIGHT <5460>. ¶

4 ***phōtismos*** [masc. noun: φωτισμός <5462>]; **from *phōtizō*: to enlighten, which is from *phōs*: see 1 ► Brilliant radiance, brightness, illumination** > Paul spoke of the light {radiancy} of the gospel of the glory of Christ (2 Cor. 4:4); this light has shone in the hearts of Christians to give the light of (lit.: for the light of) the knowledge of the glory of God in the face of Jesus Christ (v. 6). ¶

5 ***phengos*** [neut. noun: φέγγος <5338>] ► **a. Brilliance of the moon** > After the tribulation the moon will not give its light (Matt. 24:29; Mark 13:24). **b. Illumination of a lamp** > A lamp is set on a lamp-stand in order that people may see the light (Luke 11:33). ¶

6 **to give light: *epiphainō*** [verb: ἐπιφαίνω <2014>]; **from *epi*: over, upon, and *phainō*: to give illumination, which is from *phōs*: see 1 ► To shine upon, to make clearly known** > The Dayspring from on high gives light to {shines on} those who sit in darkness and the shadow of death (Luke 1:79). Other refs.: Acts 27:20; Titus 2:11; 3:4; see APPEAR <2014>. ¶

7 **to give light: *epiphauskō*** [verb: ἐπιφαύσκω <2017>]; **a form of *epiphainō*: see 6 ► To shine on (upon), to radiate** > Christ will give light to one who awakes and rises from among the dead (Eph. 5:14). ¶

8 **to give light, to bring to light: *phōtizō*** [verb: φωτίζω <5461>]; **from *phōs*: see 1 ► To shine, to shed light on; to enlighten spiritually, to cause to understand** > A lamp gives light {lights, illumines} (Luke 11:36). Jesus, the true light, gives light to {lights, lightens, enlightens} every man coming into the world (John 1:9). The Lord will bring to light the hidden things of darkness (1 Cor. 4:5). It was given to Paul to bring to light {to make to see, to make plain, to enlighten} what is the fellowship of the hidden mystery of the church (Eph. 3:9). Jesus Christ brought life and incorruptibility to light (2 Tim. 1:10). The Lord God will give light to {shine upon, illumine} His servants (Rev. 22:5c). All other refs.: ENLIGHTEN <5461>, ILLUMINATE <5461>.

9 **to light: *eis phaneron*; *eis*** [prep.: εἰς <1519>]; ***phaneros*** [adj. used as noun: φανερός <5318>]; **from *phainō*: to shine, which is from *phōs*: see 1 ► Open, in evidence** > Anything kept secret will come to light {will come abroad, is meant to be disclosed} (Mark 4:22; Luke 8:17). All other refs. (*phaneros*): see entries in Lexicon at <5318>.

– 10 Matt. 5:15 → to give light → SHINE <2989> 11 Matt. 6:22; Luke 11:34; 12:35; 15:8; John 5:35; 2 Pet. 1:19; Rev. 18:23; 21:23; 22:5 → LAMP <3088> 12 Luke 11:36 → SHINING <796> 13 Luke 23:45 → the sun's light → lit.: the sun → SUN <2246> 14 John 5:35 → to give light → to shine → SHINING <5316> 15 Acts 20:8 → LAMP <2985> 16 1 Cor. 3:13 → to bring to light → DECLARE <1213>.

LIGHT (verb) – 1 ***haptō*** [verb: ἅπτω <681>] ► **To set burning, to kindle** > No man, when he had lighted a lamp, covers it with a vessel (Luke 8:16) or puts it in a secret place (11:33). The woman who has lost one piece of silver lights a lamp and seeks it diligently (Luke 15:8). Other ref.: Luke 22:55; see KINDLE <4014a>. ¶

2 ***kaiō*** [verb: καίω <2545>] ► **To set something on fire so that it can shine, to burn** > Men light a lamp and put it on a lampstand (Matt. 5:15). All other refs.: BURN <2545>.

– 3 Luke 2:32 → lit.: for revelation → REVELATION <602> 4 Luke 11:36; John 1:9 → to give light → LIGHT (noun) <5461> 5 Luke 17:24 → SHINE <2989> 6 John 1:9 → to give light → LIGHT (noun) <5461> 7 Rev. 7:16 → to light down → STRIKE <4098> 8 Rev. 18:1 → ILLUMINATE <5461>.

LIGHTEN – 1 ***kouphizō*** [verb: κουφίζω <2893>]; **from *kouphos*: light ► To unload, to make lighter** > The ship on which Paul was aboard was lightened by throwing out the wheat into the sea. (Acts 27:38). ¶

[2] **to lighten the ship:** ***poieō ekbolēn; poieō*** [verb: ποιέω <4160>]; ***ekbolē*** [fem. noun: ἐκβολή <1546>]; **from** ***poieō*****: to make,** ***ek*****: outside, and** ***ballō*****: to throw; lit.: to make casting out ▶ To throw merchandise overboard; also transl.: to jettison the cargo, to throw cargo overboard** > The ship on which Paul was aboard was lightened (Acts 27:18). ¶

LIGHTLY – [1] ***tachu*** [adj. used as adv.: ταχύ <5035>]; **from** ***tachus*****: quick ▶ Quickly; by implication: without being careful** > No man doing a miracle in Jesus's name can lightly {soon afterward, soon after, in the next moment} speak evil of Him (Mark 9:39). All other refs.: QUICKLY <5035>.
– [2] Matt. 5:22 → without cause, without a cause → CAUSE <1500> [3] Rom. 2:4 → to think lightly → DESPISE <2706> [4] 2 Cor. 1:17 → do so lightly; lit.: use lightness → LIGHTNESS <1644> [5] 1 Thes. 5:20 → to lightly esteem → DESPISE <1848> [6] Heb. 12:5 → to regard lightly → DESPISE <3643>.

LIGHTNESS – ***elaphria*** [fem. noun: ἐλαφρία <1644>]; **from** ***elaphros*****: light ▶ Fickleness, levity, the character of that which lacks gravity or serious consideration** > Paul did not use lightness {did not do so lightly, was not vacillating} when he purposed to go to the Corinthians (2 Cor. 1:17). ¶

LIGHTNING – [1] ***astrapē*** [fem. noun: ἀστραπή <796>] **▶ Dazzling light in the sky during a storm** > The coming of the Son of Man will be as the lightning (Matt. 24:27; Luke 17:24). The countenance of the angel at the tomb of Jesus was like lightning (Matt. 28:3). Jesus said He saw Satan fall like lightning from heaven (Luke 10:18). In John's vision, lightnings {flashes of lightning} proceeded from the throne (Rev. 4:5); lightnings {flashes of lightning} are also mentioned in Rev. 8:5; 11:19; 16:18. Other ref.: Luke 11:36; see SHINING <796>. ¶
– [2] Luke 9:29 → as bright as a flash of lightning → lit.: white and glistening → GLISTENING <1823> [3] Luke 24:4 → to gleam like lightning → to shine → SHINING <797>.

LIKE (adj., adv., noun) – [1] **the like:** ***isos*** [adj. and adj. used as noun: ἴσος <2470>] **▶ The same thing, the equivalent, the equal** > Sinners lend to sinners that they may receive the like (Luke 6:34); also transl.: as much again, as much back, the same amount, in full. All other refs.: AGREE <2470>, EQUAL <2470>, SAME <2470>.
[2] ***homoios*** [adj.: ὅμοιος <3664>]; **from** ***homos*****: one and the same ▶ Of the same kind, similar** > Jesus uses this tem in regard to His generation (Matt. 11:16). He also uses it in regard to the kingdom of heaven and the kingdom of God (Matt. 13:31, 33, 44, 45, 47, 52; 20:1; Luke 13:18, 19, 21). Christians know that when the Lord Jesus will be manifested, they will be like Him (1 John 3:2). Other refs.: Matt. 22:39; Mark 12:31; Luke 6:47–49; 7:31, 32; 12:36; John 8:55; 9:9; Acts 17:29; Gal. 5:21; Jude 7 {same, similar}; Rev. 1:13, 15; 2:18; 4:3a, b, 6, 7a–c; 9:7; 10, 19; 11:1; 13:2, 4, 11; 14:14; 16:13; 18:18; 21:11, 18. ¶
[3] **to be like, to become like, to make like:** ***homoioō*** [verb: ὁμοιόω <3666>]; **from** ***homoios*****: see** [2] **▶ a. To compare, to be similar; also transl.: to liken, to resemble** > Jesus uses this verb in regard to the kingdom of heaven (Matt. 13:24; 18:23; 22:2; 25:1). He had to be made like His brothers in all things, that He might be a merciful and faithful high priest in things relating to God (Heb. 2:17). **b. To be made such as (another), to present identical traits** > Jesus says to not be like those who use vain repetitions when they pray (Matt. 6:8). Other refs.: Acts 14:11; Rom. 9:29. All other refs.: LIKEN <3666>.
[4] **to make like:** ***aphomoioō*** [verb: ἀφομοιόω <871>]; **from** ***apo*****: intens., and** ***homoioō*****: see** [3] **▶ To consider similar, to assimilate** > Melchizedek, priest of the most high God, is made like the Son of God (Heb. 7:3). ¶
[5] ***paromoios*** [adj.: παρόμοιος <3946>]; **from** ***para*****: beside, near, and** ***homoios*****: see** [2] **▶ Resembling, similar** > This word is found in Mark 7:8, 13. ¶

[6] **to be like: *paromoiazō*** [verb: παρομοιάζω <3945>]**; from *para*: beside, and *homoiazō*: to be like, which is from *homoios*: see [2] ▶ To be as, to be similar to** > Jesus says the scribes and the Pharisees are like whitewashed tombs (Matt. 23:27). ¶
[7] **like, the like: *toioutos*** [adj. and pron.: τοιοῦτος <5108>]**; from *toi*: certainly, and *outos*: this ▶ Of the same kind, of the same sort; also transl.: related, similar, such** > Jesus speaks of a tribulation such as there has not been the like {such as has not occurred} since the beginning of creation (Mark 13:19). Other refs.: Acts 19:25; 21:25; Eph. 5:27. *
[8] ***hōs*** [adv.: ὡς <5613>] ▶ **As, in the same manner** > Power was given to the locusts like the power of scorpions (Rev. 9:3). *
[9] **to be like: *eikō*** [verb: εἴκω <1503>] ▶ **To be as, to resemble** > He who doubts is like a wave of the sea (Jas. 1:6). James also uses this term regarding a man who is not a doer of the word (Jas. 1:23). ¶
– [10] Matt. 7:24, 26; Mark 4:30; Luke 13:18 → to be like → LIKEN <3666> [11] Mark 4:16; Luke 16:25 → in the same way, in a similar way → in like manner → MANNER <3668> [12] Acts 14:15; Jas. 5:17 → subject to like passions, a nature like, just like → of like passions → PASSION <3663> [13] Rom. 1:23 → made like, made to look like → LIKENESS <3667> [14] Phil. 2:20 → like him → LIKEMINDED <2473>.

LIKE (verb) – [1] ***dokimazō*** [verb: δοκιμάζω <1381>]**; from *dokimos*: tested, approved; comp. *dechomai*: to accept, to receive ▶ To think fit, to discern as being worthy** > Men did not like {think good, think worthwhile, see fit} to retain God in their knowledge (Rom. 1:28). All other refs.: APPROVE <1381>, DISCERN <1381>, TEST (noun and verb) <1381>.
[2] ***thelō*** [verb: θέλω <2309>] ▶ **To want, to take pleasure** > The scribes liked {loved, desired} to walk about in long robes (Mark 12:38; Luke 20:46). Other refs.: see entries in Lexicon at <2309>.
– [3] Mark 6:20 → to like to listen → lit.: to listen gladly → GLADLY <2234> [4] John 12:21; 1 Cor. 14:5 → WISH <2309> [5] 3 John 9 → to like to put oneself first → to love to have the preeminence → PREEMINENCE <5383>.

LIKE-MINDED – [1] Rom. 15:5; 2 Cor. 13:11; Gal. 5:10 → to be like-minded → THINK <5426> [2] 1 Pet. 3:8 → of one mind → MIND (noun) <3675>.

LIKEMINDED – [1] ***isopsuchos*** [adj.: ἰσόψυχος <2473>]**; from *isos*: equal, and *psuchē*: breath, life, soul ▶ Animated by the same feeling; lit.: equal of soul** > Paul had no one likeminded {of kindred spirit, like-minded, like him} other than Timothy, who would naturally care for the state of the Philippians (Phil. 2:20). ¶
– [2] Phil. 2:2 → to be likeminded → MIND (verb) <5426>.

LIKEN – ***homoioō*** [verb: ὁμοιόω <3666>]**; from *homoios*: similar ▶ To compare, to establish a similitude, to be like** > The Lord likened whoever puts His words into practice to a prudent man building his house on the rock (Matt. 7:24), and whoever does not to a foolish man building his house on the sand (v. 26). He asked to what He should liken His generation (Matt. 11:16; Luke 7:31). He asked the same question concerning the kingdom of God (Mark 4:30; Luke 13:18 {to resemble}, 20). All other refs.: LIKE (adj., adv., noun) <3666>.

LIKENESS – [1] ***homoiōma*** [neut. noun: ὁμοίωμα <3667>]**; from *homoioō*: to make like, which is from *homoios*: like, similar ▶ That which is made like, similitude** > Foolish men have changed the glory of God into the likeness of an image of {an image made like, an image in the form of, an image made to look like} corruptible men and animals (Rom. 1:23). Death reigned even on those who had not sinned in the likeness of Adam's transgression (Rom. 5:14). By baptism, the Christian is identified with Christ, in the likeness of His death (Rom. 6:5). The Son of God was sent in the likeness of flesh of sin (Rom. 8:3); He took His place in the likeness of men (Phil. 2:7). In the vision of John, the likenesses

{appearance, shapes} of the locusts were like horses prepared for war (Rev. 9:7). ¶
[2] ***homoiōsis*** [fem. noun: ὁμοίωσις <3669>]; **from *homoioō*: see [1] ► Image, similitude** > Men are made in the likeness of God (Jas. 3:9). ¶
[3] ***homoiotēs*** [fem. noun: ὁμοιότης <3665>]; **from *homoios*: like, similar ► Which resembles, similitude** > Christ was tempted in all things as we are {in like manner to us} (lit.: according to likeness), sin apart (Heb. 4:15). Jesus is the different priest who appears according to the likeness of Melchizedek (Heb. 7:15). ¶
– [4] Matt. 22:20; Mark 12:16; Luke 20:24 → IMAGE <1504> [5] Acts 14:11 → in the likeness of → lit.: having become like → LIKE (adj., adv., noun) <3666>.

LIKEWISE – [1] ***homoiōs*** [adv.: ὁμοίως <3668>]; **from *homoios*: alike, similar ► In like manner, similarly; also transl.: in the same manner, in the same way, too** > Luke 13:3; Heb. 9:21 {moreover}; Jude 8. Other refs. (in like manner): Matt. 27:41; Mark 4:16; 15:31; Luke 10:32; 16:25; 17:31; John 5:19; Rom. 1:27; 1 Cor. 7:3, 4; Jas. 2:25; 1 Pet. 3:1, 7; 5:5; see MANNER <3668>.
[2] **in like manner: *paraplēsiōs*** [adv.: παραπλησίως <3898>]; **from *paraplēsion*: similarly, which is from *para*: beside, and *plēsios*: near ► In like manner, in the same way** > Since the children have partaken of flesh and blood, Jesus also, in like manner, took part in the same, that through death He might annul him who has the power of death (Heb. 2:14). ¶
[3] ***hōsautōs*** [adv.: ὡσαύτως <5615>]; **from *hōs*: as, and *autōs*: likewise, the same ► In the same or like manner** > Refs.: Matt. 20:5; 21:30, 36; 25:17; Mark 12:21; 14:31; Luke 13:3; 20:31; 22:20; Rom. 8:26; 1 Cor. 11:25; 1 Tim. 2:9; 3:8, 11; 5:25; Titus 2:3, 6. ‡

LILY – ***krinon*** [neut. noun: κρίνον <2918>] **► Prob. anemones which cover the hills of Israel at the end of winter; these flowers may be purple, blue, or pink in color** > Jesus said to consider the lilies of the field, how they grow: they neither toil nor spin; Solomon in all his glory was not clothed like one of these (Matt. 6:28; Luke 12:27). ¶

LIMIT (noun) – John 3:34 → MEASURE (noun) <3358>.

LIMIT (verb) – [1] 1 Cor. 7:5 → "limited" added in Engl. [2] Heb. 4:7 → DETERMINE <3724>.

LIMITATION – Rom. 6:19 → human limitations → lit.: weakness of the flesh → WEAKNESS <769>, FLESH <4561>.

LINE – [1] Matt. 17:27 → HOOK <44> [2] Luke 2:4 → FAMILY <3965> [3] 2 Cor. 10:16 → line of things → RULE (noun) <2583> [4] Gal. 2:14 → to act in line with → to be straightforward → STRAIGHTFORWARD <3716> [5] 2 Tim. 2:15 → to cut in a straight line → to divide rightly → DIVIDE <3718>.

LINEAGE – Luke 2:4 → FAMILY <3965>.

LINEN, LINEN CLOTH – [1] ***linon*** [neut. noun: λίνον <3043>]; ***linum*, in Lat. ► Plant (flax) from which fabric is made for clothing** > A linen garment may represent the holiness and moral purity of the person wearing it. In Rev. 15:6, seven angels are clothed in pure bright linen. Other ref.: Matt. 12:20; see FLAX <3043>. ¶
[2] ***othonion*** [neut. noun: ὀθόνιον <3608>]; **dimin. of *othonē*: linen, sheet ► Linen bandage used to wrap a body; also transl. (plur.): linen clothes, linen wrappings, strips of linen** > The body of Jesus was bound in linen with the spices (John 19:40). Peter saw the linen cloths lying in the tomb of Jesus (Luke 24:12; John 20:6), as also did John (John 20:5). The handkerchief that had been upon His head was not lying with the linen cloths (John 20:7). ¶
[3] ***sindōn*** [fem. noun: σινδών <4616>] ► **a. Clothing made of linen** > After Judas betrayed Jesus, the young man who followed Him was covered with a linen cloth, which he left behind when he fled (Mark 14:51,

52). **b. Piece of linen used for wrapping the dead; also transl.: fine linen** > Joseph wrapped the body of Jesus in a clean linen cloth and laid it in his tomb (Matt. 27:59; Mark 15:46a, b; Luke 23:53). ¶
– 4 John 11:44 → strips of linen → GRAVECLOTHES <2750> 5 John 13:4, 5 → linen towel → TOWEL <3012>.

LINGER – 1 **to linger behind:** ***hupomenō*** [verb: ὑπομένω <5278>]; **from** ***hupo*****: under, and** ***menō*****: to stay ▶ To stay behind, to remain behind** > The boy Jesus lingered behind {tarried behind} in Jerusalem (Luke 2:43); *apomenō* in other mss.: to remain behind. All other refs.: ENDURE <5278>, PATIENT <5278>, REMAIN <5278>, SUFFER <5278>.
– 2 Luke 1:21 → DELAY (verb) <5549> 3 Acts 22:16 → DELAY (verb) <3195> 4 2 Pet. 2:3 → IDLE (BE) <691>.

LINUS – ***Linos*** [masc. name: Λίνος <3044>]; **perhaps from** ***linon*****: flax, linen ▶ Christian man of Rome** > Paul sends greetings from Linus to Timothy (2 Tim. 4:21). According to history, he was the first bishop (overseer) of the church at Rome. ¶

LION – ***leōn*** [masc. noun: λέων <3023>] **▶ Well known carnivorous feline mammal** > Paul was delivered from the mouth of the lion (2 Tim. 4:17): the expr. may be understood in the lit. sense (a lion in the Roman arena) or in the figur. sense in reference to a tyrant (e.g., Satan, Nero). Through faith, O.T. men of faith stopped the mouths of lions (Heb. 11:33), prob. an allusion to the occasion when Daniel the prophet was in the den of lions (see Dan. 6:22). The devil is compared to a roaring lion (1 Pet. 5:8), i.e., a cruel adversary. Christ is called the Lion of the tribe of Judah (Rev. 5:5), i.e., He who has conquered. The term is used lit. elsewhere in comparisons (Rev. 4:7; 9:8, 17; 10:3; 13:2). ¶

LIP – ***cheilos*** [neut. noun: χεῖλος <5491>] **▶ One of two parts which form the contour of the mouth; figur.: means of expression; the word is used in the plur.:** ***cheilē*** > Israel honored God with their lips (Matt. 15:8; Mark 7:6). The poison of asps is under the lips of the wicked (Rom. 3:13). God spoke to Israel with other lips (1 Cor. 14:21). The fruit of the lips that confess the name of Jesus is a sacrifice of praise to God (Heb. 13:15). He who would love life and see good days must keep his lips from speaking evil (1 Pet. 3:10). Other ref.: Heb. 11:12; see SHORE <5491>. ¶

LIQUOR – Luke 1:15 → strong drink → DRINK (noun) <4608>.

LIST (noun) – **to put on the list:** ***katalegō*** [verb: καταλέγω <2639>]; **from** ***kata*****: with (intens.), and** ***legō*****: to say ▶ To register** > A widow was not to be put upon the list {to be taken into the number} unless she was at least sixty years old (1 Tim. 5:9), in order to receive assistance from the local church. ¶

LIST (verb) – John 3:8 → archaic verb; syn.: to wish, to want (*thelō*).

LISTEN – 1 ***epakouō*** [verb: ἐπακούω <1873>]; **from** ***epi*****: upon, and** ***akouō*****: to hear ▶ To answer prayers favorably (used in regard to God's answer to prayers)** > God listened to {heard} Israel in an accepted time (2 Cor. 6:2, quoting Is. 49:8). ¶
2 ***epakroaomai*** [verb: ἐπακροάομαι <1874>]; **from** ***epi*****: upon (intens.), and** ***akroaomai*****: to hear, to listen ▶ To hear with thoughtful attention** > The prisoners listened to {heard} Paul and Silas singing hymns to God (Acts 16:25). ¶
3 ***peitharcheō*** [verb: πειθαρχέω <3980>]; **from** ***peithō*****: to persuade, and** ***archō*****: to begin, to dominate, which is from** ***archē*****: beginning ▶ To obey someone in a position of authority** > Paul told the sailors they should have listened to him {hearkened to him, followed his advice, taken his advice} and not have left Crete (Acts 27:21). All other refs.: OBEDIENT <3980>, OBEY <3980>.
– 4 Matt. 2:9; Mark 4:3; Luke 2:46; 6:27; 10:39; John 8:43; 10:3, 16, 20, 27; 18:37; Acts 4:19; 7:2; 13:16; 15:12, 13; 17:21; 22:22; Heb. 4:2; Jas. 1:19; 2:5; et al. →

HEAR <191> 5 Matt. 18:17a, b → HEAR <3878> 6 Luke 7:1 → to the people who were listening → in the hearing of the people → HEARING <189> 7 Acts 2:14 → to listen carefully → to give heed → HEED (noun) <1801> 8 Acts 5:40 → AGREE <3982> 9 Acts 12:13 → ANSWER (verb) <5219> 10 Acts 18:14 → SUFFER <430> 11 Acts 23:21 → YIELD <3982> 12 1 Cor. 14:21 → HEAR <1522> 13 2 Cor. 13:11 → listen to my appeal → lit.: be encouraged → ENCOURAGE <3870> 14 2 Tim. 4:4 → to turn away from listening to → lit.: to turn the ear away from → EAR <189> 15 Jas. 1:22, 23 → one who listens → HEARER <202>.

LITERAL – John 11:13 → literal sleep → lit.: rest of sleep → REST (noun)[1] <2838>.

LITTLE – 1 ***mikros*** [adj. and adj. used as noun: μικρός <3398>]; **compar. degree: *mikroteros*: smaller, less ▶ Small or smaller in size; person who is of small or smaller stature, who exercises a small or smaller degree of influence; also transl.: less, least, low, short, smallest >** The word is used in regard to a disciple of the Lord (Matt. 10:42; 18:6, 10, 14; Mark 9:42; Luke 17:2), a grain of mustard seed (Matt. 13:32; Mark 4:31), a person who occupies a humble place (Luke 9:48 {*mikroteros*}), the Lord's flock (Luke 12:32), the stature of Zaccheus (Luke 19:3), the people of a city of Samaria (Acts 8:10), those to whom Paul witnessed (Acts 26:22), those who will know the Lord (Heb. 8:11), a member of the body (Jas. 3:5a), those who fear the name of the Lord (Rev. 11:18), those who receive the mark of the beast (Rev. 13:16), those who fear God (Rev. 19:5), those whom the Lord will fight (Rev. 19:18), and those who will be judged according to their works (Rev. 20:12). Other refs.: John 7:33; 12:35; 1 Cor. 5:6; 2 Cor. 11:1, 16. *

2 ***oligos*** [adj.: ὀλίγος <3641>] **▶ Unimportant, not very intense >** A little {small} fire kindles a large forest (Jas. 3:5b). Other refs.: see entries in Lexicon at <3641>.

– 3 Matt. 15:26, 27; Mark 7:27, 28 → little dog → DOG <2952> 4 Luke 12:26; 16:10a, b → very little → LEAST <1646> 5 Acts 20:12 → a little → MODERATELY <3357> 6 Acts 26:28 → in a little → ALMOST <3641> 7 Acts 28:2 → no little → no common → to be common → COMMON <5177> 8 2 Cor. 8:15 → to have too little → to have lack → LACK (noun) <1641> 9 Heb. 2:7, 9 → to make a little lower → to make lower → LOWER (adj.) <1642>.

LITTLE (A) – ***mikron*; neut. of *mikros* (small)** [adv.: μικρόν <3397>]; **neut. of *mikros*: small ▶ A small space of time or degree >** Refs.: Matt. 26:39, 73; Mark 14:35, 70; John 13:33; 14:19; 16:16–19. ‡

LITTLE FAITH (OF) – Matt. 6:30; 8:26; 14:31; 16:8; Luke 12:28 → FAITH <3640>.

LIVE – 1 ***zaō*** [verb: ζάω <2198>]; **contracted form: *zō* ▶ To be alive, to breathe >** Man shall not live by bread alone, but by every word that proceeds out of the mouth of God (Matt. 4:4; Luke 4:4). Anna had lived with her husband seven years (Luke 2:36). In a parable, the younger son dissipated his wealth in living in debauchery (Luke 15:13). All live for God (Luke 20:38). Jesus told a man that his son lived (John 4:50, 51, 53). Jesus is the living bread which came down out of heaven; if anyone eats of this bread, he will live eternally (John 6:51, 57b, 58). Jesus lives on account of the Father (John 6:57). He who believes in Jesus, though he have died, yet shall he live (John 11:25). Whoever lives and believes in Jesus shall never die (John 11:26). Because Jesus lives, His disciples would also live (John 14:19a, b). Some said that Paul ought not to live any longer (Acts 22:22; 25:24). According to the strictest sect of his religion, Paul had lived a Pharisee (Acts 26:5). The just shall live by faith (Rom. 1:17; Gal. 3:11; Heb. 10:38; see Hab. 2:4). In that Christ lives, He lives to God (Rom. 6:10a, b). If Christians live according to the flesh, they will die; but if by the Spirit they put to death the actions of the body, they will live (Rom.

8:13a, b). Whether Christians live, they live to the Lord, or whether they die, they die to the Lord; whether they live therefore, or die, they are the Lord's (Rom. 14:8a–c). The Lord directed those who preach the gospel should receive their living from the gospel (1 Cor. 9:14). Paul had despaired even of living (2 Cor. 1:8). Christ died for all, that those who live should no longer live for themselves, but for Him who died for them and was raised again (2 Cor. 5:15a, b). Christ lives by the power of God, and Christians shall live with Him by the power of God toward them (2 Cor. 13:4a, b). At Antioch, Peter lived as the Gentiles, but compelled them to Judaize (Gal. 2:14). Through the law, Paul died to the law, that he might live to God (Gal. 2:19). He was crucified with Christ; and it was no longer he who lived, but Christ lived in him; the life which he then lived in the flesh, he lived now by faith in the Son of God (Gal. 2:20a–d). If we live by the Spirit, we are to also walk by the Spirit (Gal. 5:25). For Paul to live was Christ and to die was gain (Phil. 1:21); but if it were his lot to live in the flesh, this was for him worth the while (v. 22). Whether they are awake or they sleep, Christians will live together with Jesus (1 Thes. 5:10). The widow who lives in pleasure is dead even while she lives (1 Tim. 5:6b). All who desire to live godly in Christ Jesus will be persecuted (2 Tim. 3:12). Christians are called to live sober, righteous, and godly lives in the present age (Titus 2:12). Being dead to sins, they are to live to righteousness (1 Pet. 2:24). God sent His one and only Son into the world, that we might live through Him (1 John 4:9). The angel of the church at Sardis has a name that he lives, but is dead (Rev. 3:1). The living creatures will give glory to the Lord who lives to the age of ages (Rev. 4:9), as will also the elders (v. 10); the angel will swear by Him who lives to the ages of ages (10:6). God lives to the age of ages (Rev. 15:7). Those who had not done homage to the beast or his image and had not received his mark lived and reigned with Christ for one thousand years (Rev. 20:4). Other refs.: Matt. 9:18; 27:63; Mark 5:23; Luke 10:28; John 5:25; Acts 17:28; 28:4; Rom. 6:2; 7:1, 2, 9; 8:12, 13a, b; 10:5; 14:7; 1 Cor. 7:39; 2 Cor. 4:11; 6:9; Gal. 3:12; Col. 2:20; 3:7; 1 Thes. 3:8; Heb. 7:8; 9:17; 12:9; Jas. 4:15; 1 Pet. 4:6; Rev. 16:3. All other refs.: LIFE <2198>, LIVING (adj.) <2198>, LIVING (noun) <2198>.

2 to live again: *anazaō* [verb: ἀναζάω <326>]**; from *ana*: again, and *zaō*: see 1 ► To revive, to come back to life >** The rest of the dead did not live again {did not come to life} until the thousand years were ended (Rev. 20:5). All other refs.: LIFE <326>, REVIVE <326>.

3 to live together, to live with: *suzaō* [verb: συζάω <4800>]**; from *sun*: together, and *zaō*: see 1 ► To be alive with others >** If we have died with Christ, we believe that we shall also live with Him (Rom. 6:8; 2 Tim. 2:11). The Corinthians were in Paul's heart, to live together and to die together (2 Cor. 7:3). ¶

4 *anastrephō* [verb: ἀναστρέφω <390>]**; from *ana*: again, and *strephō*: to turn ► To behave, to conduct oneself >** Peter speaks of those who have just escaped from those who live {walk} in error (2 Pet. 2:18). All other refs.: CONDUCT (verb)[1] <390>, RETURN (verb) <390>, TREAT <390>.

5 *bioō* [verb: βιόω <980>]**; from *bios*: life ► To spend one's existence >** The Christian should not live the rest of his life in the flesh for the lusts of men, but for the will of God (1 Pet. 4:2). ¶

6 *ginomai* [verb: γίνομαι <1096>] **► To be, to behave >** The elders in Ephesus knew in what manner Paul always lived among them (Acts 20:18). Other refs.: see entries in Lexicon at <1096>.

7 *diagō* [verb: διάγω <1236>]**; from *dia*: through, and *agō*: to lead ► To spend one's life >** Paul speaks of those who, before their conversion, lived in malice and envy (Titus 3:3). Other refs.: Luke 7:25 in some mss.; 1 Tim. 2:2: see LEAD (verb) <1236>. ¶

8 *zōogoneō* [verb: ζῳογονέω <2225>]**; from *zōogonos*: life-giving, which is from *zoos*: living, and *gonos*: procreation, birth ► To remain living, to survive >** An Egyptian king did not want the children of the Israelites to live (Acts 7:19). Other refs.:

Luke 17:33 {to preserve life}; 1 Tim. 6:13 in some mss. {to give life}. ¶

9 ***peripateō*** [verb: περιπατέω <4043>]; **from *peri*: around, and *pateō*: to walk ▶ To comply, to confirm** > Some accused Paul of telling the Jews among the nations not to live according to ancestral customs (Acts 21:21). All other refs.: WALK <4043>.

10 ***politeuō*** [verb: πολιτεύω <4176>]; **from *politēs*: citizen ▶ To behave, to conduct oneself as a good citizen** > Paul had lived {walked, fulfilled his duty, conducted himself} in all good conscience before God (Acts 23:1). He tells the Philippians to let their conduct be worthy (lit.: to conduct themselves, or: to live, worthily) of the gospel of Christ (Phil. 1:27). ¶

11 ***huparchō*** [verb: ὑπάρχω <5225>]; **from *hupo*: under, and *archō*: to begin, which is from *archē*: beginning ▶ To be found, to be** > Those who live {indulge} in luxury are in kings' palaces (Luke 7:25). Other refs.: see entries in Lexicon at <5225>.

12 **living a long time: *makrochronios*** [adj.: μακροχρόνιος <3118>]; **from *makros*: long, and *chronos*: time, duration ▶ Having an extended life span, whose days are prolonged** > A child must obey his parents so that he may live long {be longlived, enjoy long life} (lit.: so that he may be living a long time) on the earth (Eph. 6:3). ¶

– 13 Matt. 2:23; 4:13; 12:45; Luke 11:26; 13:4; Acts 1:19, 20; 2:14; 4:16; 7:2, 4a, b, 48; 9:22, 32, 35; 11:29; 17:24; 19:10, 17; 22:12; Col. 2:9; Heb. 11:9b; Jas. 4:5; Rev. 2:13a, b; 14:6 → DWELL <2730> 14 Mark 5:3 → lit.: to have one's dwelling → DWELLING <2731> 15 Mark 7:5; Rom. 6:4; 8:4; 2 Cor. 5:7; 10:2, 3; Gal. 5:16; Eph. 2:2; 4:1, 17a; 5:2, 8, 15; Phil. 3:17; Col. 1:10; 2:6; 1 Thes. 2:12; 4:1; 2 Thes. 3:6 → WALK <4043> 16 Mark 12:44; Luke 21:4 → what one has to live on → LIVELIHOOD <979> 17 Luke 2:8 → to live out in the field → FIELD <63> 18 Luke 8:27; Acts 28:30 → REMAIN <3306> 19 Luke 16:19 → to live gaily → to be merry → MERRY <2165> 20 Luke 21:35 → DWELL <2521> 21 John 3:21 → to live by → PRACTICE (verb) <4160> 22 Acts 1:20 → was living → lit.: came in and went out 23 Acts 2:5 → STAY (verb) <2730> 24 Acts 2:26 → DWELL <2681> 25 Acts 9:31 → WALK <4198> 26 Acts 17:21 → STAY (verb) <1927> 27 Acts 21:24; Gal. 6:16; Phil. 3:16 → WALK <4748> 28 Acts 26:4 → the way I have lived → my manner of life → LIFE <981> 29 Rom. 7:5 → we were living in the flesh → lit.: we were in the flesh 30 Rom. 7:17, 20; 8:9, 11a; 1 Cor. 7:12, 13; 1 Tim. 6:16 → DWELL <3611> 31 Rom. 8:11b; 2 Cor. 6:16; 2 Tim. 1:5, 14 → DWELL <1774> 32 Rom. 8:15; Heb. 11:38; 1 Pet. 2:16 → "to live in," "living" added in Engl. 33 Rom. 12:16 → to live in harmony → lit.: to be of the same mind → MIND (noun) <5426> 34 Rom. 12:18; 2 Cor. 13:11; 1 Thes. 5:13 → to live in peace, to live at peace, to live peaceably → PEACE <1514> 35 1 Cor. 3:1; Gal. 6:1 → who live by the Spirit → spiritual ones → SPIRITUAL <4152> 36 2 Cor. 5:1 → the earthly tent we live in → lit.: our earthly tent house → HOUSE <3614> 37 Gal. 1:6 → "to live" added in Engl. 38 Phil. 4:12a → to live in prosperity → ABOUND <4052> 39 1 Tim. 2:2 → LEAD (verb) <1236> 40 Titus 2:3 → the way one lives → BEHAVIOR <2688> 41 Heb. 5:13 → to live on → USE (verb) <3348> 42 Heb. 11:9 → to go to live → DWELL <3939> 43 Jas. 5:5 → to live in pleasure, in luxury, luxuriously → PLEASURE <5171> 44 1 Pet. 3:7 → to live with → to dwell with → DWELL <4924> 45 2 Pet. 2:8 → DWELL <1460> 46 Rev. 13:6 → DWELL <4637> 47 Rev. 18:7, 9 → to live sensuously, to live deliciously → to live luxuriously → LUXURIOUSLY <4763>.

LIVELIHOOD – ***bios*** [masc. noun: βίος <979>]; **lit.: life ▶ What one has to subsist on** > A poor widow had cast the whole of her livelihood {living} into the treasury of the temple (Mark 12:44). A woman cast in the offering all her livelihood {all her living, all she had to live on} (Luke 21:4). All other refs.: LIFE <979>, LIVING (noun) <979>.

LIVESTOCK – [1] Matt. 22:4 → fattened livestock → FATLING <4619> [2] John 4:12 → CATTLE <2353>.

LIVING (adj.) – [1] **to live:** ***zaō*** [verb: ζάω <2198>]>]; **contracted form:** ***zō*** ► **Which is alive, as opposed to being dead or not existing; which has vital power** > Jesus is the Christ, the Son of the living God (Matt. 16:16). The high priest adjured Jesus by the living God to tell if He was the Christ, the Son of God (Matt. 26:63). The term is used in regard to Jesus risen (Mark 16:11; Luke 24:5, 23; Acts 1:3). Jesus gives living water (John 4:10, 11). He is the living bread which has come down out of heaven (John 6:51). He was sent by the Father who is living (John 6:57). He who believes in Him, out of his belly will flow rivers of living water (John 7:38). Moses received the living oracles (Acts 7:38). Peter presented Dorcas living to the saints and widows (Acts 9:41). The men of Lystra were exhorted to turn to the living God (Acts 14:15). Eutychus was taken home alive (Acts 20:12). Paul affirmed that Jesus was living (Acts 25:19). We are to consider ourselves dead to sin, but alive to God in Christ Jesus (Rom. 6:11, 13). While her husband is living, if the married woman is joined to another man, she will be called an adulteress (Rom. 7:3). Those of Israel will be called sons of the living God, and are prompted to offer their bodies a living sacrifice, acceptable to God (Rom. 9:26; 12:1). As I live (or: I am living), says the Lord, every knee will bow to me, and every tongue confess to God (Rom. 14:11). The first man Adam became a living soul (1 Cor. 15:45). The Corinthians were manifested as being the letter of Christ, the result of the ministry of the apostle Paul, written not with ink, but by the Spirit of the living God (2 Cor. 3:3). Christians are the temple of the living God (2 Cor. 6:16). The Thessalonians had turned to God from idols, to serve the living and true God (1 Thes. 1:9). Timothy was to know how one ought to conduct oneself in God's house, which is the church of the living God (1 Tim. 3:15). Paul hoped in the living God, who is the preserver of all men (1 Tim. 4:10). The brothers are told to see to it that there not be in anyone of them an evil heart of unbelief in abandoning the living God (Heb. 3:12). The word of God is living and operative, and more penetrating than any two-edged sword (Heb. 4:12). Christ is always living to intercede for those who come to God by Him (Heb. 7:25). The blood of Christ purifies our conscience from dead works, to serve the living God (Heb. 9:14). Christians have full liberty to enter into the Most Holy Place by the blood of Jesus, by the new and living way which He has inaugurated for them through the veil, i.e., His flesh (Heb. 10:20). It is a terrible thing to fall into the hands of the living God (Heb. 10:31). Christians have come to the city of the living God (Heb. 12:22). God the Father has given them new birth into a living hope (1 Pet. 1:3). They are born again by the living and enduring word of God (1 Pet. 1:23). They come to the Lord as to a living stone, rejected by men (1 Pet. 2:4); they also are living stones (v. 5). Jesus is living (Rev. 1:18b). John saw another angel ascending from the rising of the sun, having the seal of the living God (Rev. 7:2). The beast and the false prophet were both thrown alive into the lake of fire burning with brimstone (Rev. 19:20). Other ref.: 1 Tim. 6:17 in some mss. All other refs.: LIFE <2198>, LIVE <2198>, LIVING (noun) <2198>.

– [2] living creatures → Rev. 4:6, 7a–d, 8, 9; 5:6, 8, 11, 14; 6:1, 3, 5–7; 7:11; 14:3; 15:7; 19:4 → BEAST <2226>.

LIVING (noun) – [1] ***bios*** [masc. noun: βίος <979>]; **lit.: life** ► **What is required to live, resources; also transl.: livelihood, substance** > A woman had spent all her living to be healed (Luke 8:43 in some mss.). In a parable, the father divided to his sons his living {what he was possessed of, his wealth, his property} (Luke 15:12); the older son told his father that the younger brother had devoured his living with prostitutes (v. 30). John speaks of one having the world's goods (lit.: living) and shutting up his heart from his brother (1 John 3:17). All other refs.: LIFE <979>, LIVELIHOOD <979>.

[2] **to live:** ***zaō*** [verb and verb used as a noun: ζάω <2198>]; **contracted form:** ***zō*** ► **Per-**

son who has life, who is alive > God is not God of the dead, but of the living (Matt. 22:32; Mark 12:27; Luke 20:38). Jesus is established by God as judge of the living and the dead (Acts 10:42). Christ has died and lived again, that He might rule over both the dead and the living (Rom. 14:9). The living, who remain to the coming of the Lord, will by no means precede those who have fallen asleep (1 Thes. 4:15); we, the living who remain, shall be caught up together with them in the clouds to meet the Lord (v. 17). Christ Jesus shall judge the living and the dead (2 Tim. 4:1). Evil men will give account to Him who is ready to judge the living and the dead (1 Pet. 4:5). Jesus reveals Himself to John as the Living One (Rev. 1:18a). All other refs.: LIFE <2198>, LIVE <2198>, LIVING (adj.) <2198>.
– [3] 2 Thes. 3:12 → BREAD <740> [4] Rev. 18:17 → to make, to earn one's living → TRADE (verb) <2038>.

LO AND BEHOLD! – ***idou*** [particle: ἰδού <2400>] ▶ **Demonstrative particle serving to call attention to something external or exterior to oneself** > Refs.: Matt. 23:34; Luke 13:16; Acts 2:7. * ‡

LOAD (noun) – Matt. 23:4; Gal. 6:5 → BURDEN (noun) <5413>.

LOAD (verb) – [1] **to be heavy laden, to load: *phortizō*** [verb: φορτίζω <5412>]; **from *pherō*: to carry, or *phortos*: burden, freight of a ship ▶ To carry or impose a burden, to have a burden put upon oneself** > Jesus invites those who are weary and heavy laden {burdened} to come to Him (Matt. 11:28). The lawyers loaded {lay, lade, loaded down, weighed down} men with burdens hard to bear (Luke 11:46). ¶
[2] **to load down: *sōreuō*** [verb: σωρεύω <4987>]; **from *sōros*: heap ▶ To pile up, to accumulate** > Paul speaks of gullible women loaded down {laden, weighed down} with sins (2 Tim. 3:6). Other ref.: Rom. 12:20; see HEAP <4987>. ¶

LOAF – Matt. 14:17, 19a, b; Acts 27:35; 1 Cor. 10:17a, b; et al. → BREAD <740>.

LOAN – Matt. 18:27 → DEBT <1156>.

LOATHE – Gal. 4:14 → REJECT <1609>.

LOATHSOME – Rev. 16:2 → EVIL (adj.) <2556> <4190>.

LOCAL – [1] Acts 21:12 → local resident → he who is from that place → PLACE (noun) <1786> [2] Acts 28:17 → "local" added in Engl.

LOCK – [1] Luke 3:20; Acts 26:10 → to lock, to lock up → to shut up → SHUT <2623> [2] Luke 11:7; John 20:19, 26; Acts 5:23; Rev. 20:3 → SHUT <2808> [3] Gal. 3:22, 23 → SHUT <4788>.

LOCUST – ***akris*** [fem. noun: ἀκρίς <200>] ▶ **Type of insect (large grasshopper) invading Eastern countries and destroying vegetation; the Mosaic law permitted eating the locusts (Lev. 11:21, 22)** > John the Baptist fed himself on locusts (Matt. 3:4; Mark 1:6). Locusts will receive power to injure those men who do not have the seal of God on their foreheads (Rev. 9:3, 7); the angel of the abyss is their king (see ABADDON <3>). ¶

LODGE – [1] ***kataluō*** [verb: καταλύω <2647>]; **from *kata*: down (intens.), and *luō*: to loose; suggests the idea of unpacking one's baggage ▶ To dwell (usually, in a temporary manner)** > The disciples wanted Jesus to send the multitude away so that they might lodge {find lodging} in the surrounding villages (Luke 9:12). People said that Jesus had gone to lodge with {to be the guest of} a sinful man (Luke 19:7). All other refs.: DESTROY <2647>, THROW (verb) <2647>.
[2] ***xenizō*** [verb: ξενίζω <3579>]; **from *xenos*: stranger; lit.: to receive as a guest ▶ To receive hospitality, to give hospitality; also transl.: to stay, to be a guest** > Peter lodged with a certain Simon, a tanner (Acts 10:6, 18, 32); the men who had been sent from Cornelius lodged {were given lodging} there also (v. 23). Paul was to lodge with Mnason (Acts 21:16). Publius lodged

{gave hospitality to, entertained} Paul with courtesy (Acts 28:7). Some have lodged {entertained} angels without knowing it (Heb. 13:2). All other refs. for "to think strange": STRANGE <3579>.
– 3 Matt. 13:32; Mark 4:32; Luke 13:19 → NEST (verb) <2681> 4 Matt. 21:17 → to spend the night → NIGHT <835> 5 Luke 21:37 → to stay at night → STAY (verb) <835> 6 1 Tim. 5:10 → to lodge strangers → STRANGER <3580>.

LODGING – 1 Luke 9:12 → to find lodging → LODGE <2647> 2 Acts 10:23 → to give lodging → LODGE <3579> 3 Acts 28:23; Phm. 22 → GUEST ROOM <3578> 4 Acts 28:30 → hired lodging → rented house → HOUSE <3410> 5 Jas. 2:25 → to give lodging → RECEIVE <5264>.

LOFTY – 1 Cor. 2:1 → lofty speech → lit.: excellence of speech → EXCELLENCE <5247>.

LOG – Matt. 7:3–5; Luke 6:41, 42a, b → BEAM <1385>.

LOINS – ***osphus*** [fem. noun: ὀσφύς <3751>] ▶ **Lower region of the back, hips** > The word is used twice with this meaning (Matt. 3:4; Mark 1:6; see Ex. 12:11). It is also used in the sense of the organ of reproduction (Acts 2:30; Heb. 7:5, 10) and of spiritual energy (Luke 12:35; Eph. 6:14; 1 Pet. 1:13; see Is. 11:5). ¶

LOIS – ***Lōis*** [fem. name: Λωΐς <3090>] ▶ **Grandmother of Timothy** > The sincere faith in Timothy had first dwelt in his grandmother Lois (2 Tim. 1:5). ¶

LONELY – Matt. 14:15; Mark 1:35, 45; 6:31, 32; Luke 4:42 → DESERTED <2048>.

LONG (adj.) – 1 ***hikanos*** [adj.: ἱκανός <2425>]; **from *hikneomai*: to come, to occur** ▶ **Sufficient, enough** > Paul and Barnabas abode a long time {a good while, considerable time} in Iconium (Acts 14:3). The word is transl. "much" {considerable} in Acts 27:9: much time had been spent since the departure of Paul to go to Rome. All other refs.: see entries in Lexicon at <2425>.
2 ***makros*** [adj.: μακρός <3117>] ▶ **Lengthy, lasting for a considerable time** > The scribes made long prayers for a pretense (Mark 12:40; Luke 20:47). Other ref.: Matt. 23:14 in some mss. All other refs.: FAR <3117>.
3 **not: *ouk*** [particle οὐκ <3756>] **short: *oligos*** [adj.: ὀλίγος <3641>] ▶ **Considerable, extended** > Paul and Barnabas stayed a long time (lit.: not a short time) with the disciples in Antioch (Acts 14:28). Other refs.: see entries in Lexicon at <3641>.
4 **long ago: *palai*** [adv.: πάλαι <3819>] ▶ **a. In time past** > The term is used regarding Tyre and Sidon (Matt. 11:21; Luke 10:13 {a great while ago}, the Lord Jesus in death (Mark 15:44 in some mss. {for some time, any while, already}), and the Corinthians (2 Cor. 12:19 in some mss. {again, all this time, all along}). **b. Formerly** > Ungodly men of old were marked out long ago {of old} for judgment because they turned grace into dissolution and denied the Lord (Jude 4). All other refs.: OLD <3819>, PAST <3819>.
5 **long ago: *ekpalai*** [adv.: ἔκπαλαι <1597>]; **from *ek*: from, and *palai*: see 4; lit.: of old** ▶ **In the distant past, formerly** > By the word of God, the heavens existed long ago {of old} (2 Pet. 3:5). Other ref.: 2 Pet. 2:3 (for a long time); see TIME <1597>. ¶
6 **as long as: *eph' hoson chronon*; *epi*** [prep.: ἐπί <1909>]; ***hosos*** [pron.: ὅσος <3745>]; ***chronos*** [masc. noun: χρόνος <5550>] ▶ **During all the time** > The expr. is employed in regard to the authority of the law over man (Rom. 7:1) and to the heir who is yet a minor (Gal. 4:1).
– 7 Matt. 23:5 → to make long → ENLARGE <3170> 8 Mark 2:19 → as long (as) → lit.: what time (*hoson chronon*) <3745> <5550> 9 Luke 8:27 → long time → *chronos hikanos* <5550> <2425> 10 Luke 23:8 → long season → long time → TIME <2425> <5550> 11 John 14:9 → so long a time {so long} → *tosoutos chronos* <5118> <5550> 12 Acts 14:28 → long time → lit.:

a time not little (*chronon ouk oligon*) 13 Acts 18:20 → longer time → lit.: over a longer time (*epi pleiona chronon*) 14 Acts 20:9 → to preach long → lit.: to preach for longer (*epi pleion*) 15 Acts 20:11 → a long while → lit.: over enough (time) (*eph' hikanon*) 16 Acts 27:21 → lit.: much (*polu*) 17 Rom. 2:4 → long suffering → SUFFERING <3115> 18 1 Tim. 3:14 → before long → SHORTLY <5032> 19 Heb. 4:7 → after such a long time, after so long a time → lit.: after all this time (*meta tosouton chronon*) <3326> <5118> <5550> 20 2 Pet. 2:3 → from long, as long → for a long time → TIME <1597>.

LONG (verb) – 1 ***epipotheō*** [verb: ἐπιποθέω <1971>]; **from *epi*: intens., and *potheō*: to desire something far away, to yearn ► To feel a great tenderness, an ardent desire >** Paul longed {greatly desired} to see the Christians in Rome (Rom. 1:11). Some Christians were longing after {were full of ardent desire for, were yearning for; their hearts would go out to} the Corinthians (2 Cor. 9:14), having been helped by them. Paul was longing after the Philippians (Phil. 1:8) and Epaphroditus was likewise longing after them {he had a longing desire} (2:26). All other refs.: DESIRE (verb) <1971>, YEARN <1971>.
– 2 Matt. 13:17; Luke 15:16; 16:21; 17:22; 1 Pet. 1:12; Rev. 9:6 → DESIRE (verb) <1937> 3 Rom. 15:23 → lit.: to have a great desire → great desire → DESIRE (noun) <1974> 4 Phil. 4:1 → LONGED-FOR <1973> 5 1 Thes. 2:8 → to affectionately long → to be affectionately desirous → AFFECTIONATELY <2442> 6 1 Tim. 6:10 → COVET <3713> 7 Heb. 11:16 → to long for → DESIRE (verb) <3713> 8 Rev. 18:14 → to long for → DESIRE (noun) <1939>.

LONGED – longed for: *epipothētos* [adj.: ἐπιπόθητος <1973>]; **from *epi*: upon (intens.), and *potheō*: to desire ► Which is the object of a strong desire >** The Philippians were Paul's beloved and longed for {whom he longed for, i.e., whom he longed to see} brothers (Phil. 4:1). ¶

LONGING – 1 Luke 22:15; 1 Thes. 2:17 → DESIRE (noun) <1939> 2 Rom. 8:19 → anxious longing → earnest expectation → EXPECTATION <603> 3 Rom. 15:23 → great desire → DESIRE (noun) <1974> 4 2 Cor. 7:7, 11 → ardent desire → DESIRE (noun) <1972>.

LONGLIVED – Eph. 6:3 → living a long time → LIVE <3118>.

LONGSUFFERING – 1 ***makrothumia*** [fem. noun: μακροθυμία <3115>]; **from *makrothumeō*: to suffer long, which is from *makros*: long, and *thumos*: soul, emotion, passion ► Disposition of a spirit characterized by great patience, perseverance in difficult circumstances; also transl.: patience >** Paul asks whether a man despises the riches of the longsuffering of God (Rom. 2:4). Longsuffering characterized Paul (2 Cor. 6:6). Longsuffering is part of the fruit of the Spirit (Gal. 5:22). Christians are to walk with longsuffering {being patient} (Eph. 4:2) and put on longsuffering (Col. 3:12). Paul spoke of being strengthened for all patience (or: great endurance) and longsuffering (Col. 1:11). Timothy was thoroughly acquainted with Paul's longsuffering {patience} (2 Tim. 3:10). Timothy was to exhort with all longsuffering (2 Tim. 4:2). All other refs.: PATIENCE <3115>.
– 2 2 Pet. 3:9 → to be longsuffering → to be patient → PATIENT <3114>.

LOOK (noun) – 1 Matt. 28:3 → COUNTENANCE <2397> 2 Acts 7:31 → to get a closer look → CONSIDER <2657> 3 Jas. 1:11 → APPEARANCE <4383>.

LOOK (verb) – 1 **to look intently, steadfastly, steadily, up, upon: *atenizō*** [verb: ἀτενίζω <816>]; **from *atenēs*: strained, earnest, which is from *a*: intens., and *teinō*: to stretch, to strain ► To fix with the eyes, to examine with attention, to scrutinize >** A maid looked upon {fixed her eyes upon} Peter (Luke 22:56). The disciples were looking steadfastly toward {gazing into} heaven at the ascension of Jesus (Acts 1:10). All those sitting in the council were looking steadfastly at {fixing their gaze on, were looking fixedly at} Stephen (Acts 6:15). Stephen was looking up steadfastly into {gazed into, gazed intently into, was fixing his eyes on} heaven (Acts 7:55). The sons of Israel could not look steadfastly {fix their eyes on, gaze} the face of Moses (2 Cor. 3:13). All other refs.: BEHOLD (verb) <816>, FASTEN <816>, FIX <816>.

2 ***blepō*** [verb: βλέπω <991>] ► **To see with the eyes, to direct the eyes toward** > Jesus spoke of looking at {beholding} the speck in the eye of one's brother (Matt. 7:3; Luke 6:41). He who looks upon (or: regards) a woman to lust for her has already committed adultery with her in his heart (Matt. 5:28). No one who has laid his hand on the plough and who looks back is fit for the kingdom of God (Luke 9:62). The disciples looked {stared} at one another, not knowing who would betray Jesus (John 13:22). Jesus was taken up from the earth as His disciples were looking {were beholding} (Acts 1:9); two men in white clothing asked them why they stood looking {gazing} into heaven (v. 11; some mss. have *emblepō*: to fix one's gaze on). Peter told the lame man to look at him (Acts 3:4). Paul asks the Corinthians if they were looking at things according to the outward appearance (2 Cor. 10:7). No one was able to look {to regard} the book in the right hand of Him who sat upon the throne (Rev. 5:3); no one had been found worthy to look at {regard} it (v. 4). Other refs.: SEE <991>.

3 **to look up: *anablepō*** [verb: ἀναβλέπω <308>]; **from *ana*: up, again, and *blepō*: see 2 ► To direct the eyes upward, to look above** > Jesus looked up to heaven and blessed the loaves before breaking them and giving them to the crowds (Matt. 14:19; Mark 6:41; Luke 9:16). He looked up to heaven before healing the mute man (Mark 7:34). The verb is used in regard to a blind man whom Jesus healed (Mark 8:24, 25). When the women looked up, they saw that the stone of the tomb had been rolled away (Mark 16:4). Jesus looked up and saw Zaccheus (Luke 19:5). He looked up and saw the rich casting their gifts into the treasury (Luke 21:1). Saul looked up at {saw} Ananias (Acts 22:13). All other refs.: SEE <308>.

4 ***apoblepō*** [verb: ἀποβλέπω <578>]; **from *apo*: intens., and *blepō*: see 2; lit.: to look away from every other thing ► To concentrate one's attention on one particular object** > Moses looked to the reward {had respect to the recompense} (Heb. 11:26). ¶

5 **to look at, into, on, upon, closely: *emblepō*** [verb: ἐμβλέπω <1689>]; **from *en*: on, and *blepō*: see 2 ► To fix one's gaze on; also transl.: to behold** > Jesus said to look at the birds of the heaven to learn from them (Matt. 6:26). He looked on His disciples before telling them that with God all things were possible (Matt. 19:26; Mark 10:27). Looking at a man who had kept the commandments, He loved him (Mark 10:21). The maid looked at Peter (Mark 14:67). Jesus looked at the people and told them about the cornerstone (Luke 20:17). The Lord looked at Peter (Luke 22:61; John 1:42). John the Baptist, looking at {seeing} Jesus as He walked, said that He was the Lamb of God (John 1:36). Men of Galilee were looking {were gazing} into the sky (Acts 1:11). All other refs.: see SEE <1689>.

6 **to look upon: *epiblepō*** [verb: ἐπιβλέπω <1914>]; **from *epi*: upon, and *blepō*: see 2 ► To rest one's gaze on, to examine** > God had looked upon {had regarded, had had regard for, had been mindful of} the low estate of Mary (Luke 1:48). A man implored Jesus to look upon his son (Luke 9:38). James condemned looking upon {having respect to, paying attention to, paying special attention to, showing special attention to} him who wears splendid clothing and making a distinction between the poor and the rich (Jas. 2:3). ¶

7 **to look around, round upon, etc.: *periblepō*** [verb: περιβλέπω <4017>]; **from *peri*: around, and *blepō*: see 2 ► To cast one's eyes all around** > Jesus looked around with anger upon those who were in the synagogue (Mark 3:5; Luke 6:10). He looked around at those who were seated around Him (Mark 3:34). He looked around about to see her who had touched His clothes (Mark 5:32). After He had told

the rich man to follow Him, Jesus looked around and addressed His disciples (Mark 10:23). He entered into the temple, and having looked around at all things, He went out to Bethany (Mark 11:11). After the transfiguration, having looked around, the disciples no longer saw anyone, but Jesus only (Mark 9:8). ¶

8 **to look out: *episkeptomai*** [verb: ἐπισκέπτομαι <1980>]; **from *epi*: upon, and *skopeō*: to view ► To see, in the sense of seeking out, choosing** > The apostles said to look out {to choose, to seek, to select} seven men to settle a matter (Acts 6:3). All other refs.: VISIT (verb) <1980>. ¶

9 ***horaō*** [verb: ὁράω <3708>] **► To behold, to consider** > Jesus said to look {to see} how many loaves of bread the disciples had (Mark 6:38 in some mss.). In regard to the temple, a disciple said to Jesus: "Look {See, Behold} what stones and what buildings!" (Mark 13:1 in some mss.). Zechariah had said they would look on Him whom they pierced (John 19:37 in some mss.). All those who knew Jesus and the women who had followed Him beheld {saw, watched} the things concerning the crucifixion of Jesus (Luke 23:49 in some mss.). Jesus told Thomas to look at {to see} His hands (John 20:27 in some mss.). Other refs.: APPEAR <3708>, BEWARE <3708>, SEE <3708>.

10 **to look at: *eidō*** [verb: εἴδω <1492>]; **form of *horaō*: see 9 ► To see, to consider** > Jesus, looking at His disciples, rebuked Peter (Mark 8:33).

11 **to look upon, on, with favor; to show one's favor: *epeidon*** [verb: ἐπεῖδον <1896>]; **from *epi*: upon, and *eidō*: see 10 ► To consider favorably or unfavorably** > Elizabeth spoke of the days in which the Lord had looked upon her (Luke 1:25). Peter and John asked the Lord to look upon {to behold, to take note of, to consider} the threatenings of the Jews (Acts 4:29). ¶

12 **to look for: *prosdechomai*** [verb: προσδέχομαι <4327>]; **from *pros*: toward, and *dechomai*: to receive, to welcome ► To expect, to remain in anticipation of, to wait for** > Anna spoke to many who were looking for {were looking forward to the} redemption in Jerusalem (Luke 2:38). Christians are looking for {awaiting} the blessed hope and the appearing of the glory of the Lord (Titus 2:13), and for His mercy (Jude 21 {to wait anxiously for}). All other refs.: ACCEPT <4327>, RECEIVE <4327>, TAKE <4327>, WAIT (verb) <4327>.

13 **to look for, to look when, to look forward: *prosdokaō*** [verb: προσδοκάω <4328>]; **from *pros*: for, and *dokaō*: to expect, to look, from which *prosdokia*: expectation ► To hope for, to expect, to wait** > John the Baptist was asking if people should look for another than Jesus (Matt. 11:3; Luke 7:19, 20). The master of a servant would come in a day when he did not look for him (Matt. 24:50; Luke 12:46). The people in Malta looked for Paul to die after the viper hung on his hand, but, after having looked for a long time, they saw that no harm came to him (Acts 28:6a, b). Christians must look for the coming of the day of God (2 Pet. 3:12); they look for new heavens and a new earth in which righteousness dwells (v. 13); while they look for these things, they should be diligent to be found by Him in peace, without spot and blameless (v. 14). All other refs.: EXPECT <4328>, EXPECTATION <4328>, TARRY <4328>, WAIT (verb) <4328>.

14 **to look upon, to look at: *theaomai*** [verb: θεάομαι <2300>]; **from *thaomai*: to wonder ► To examine, to contemplate, to behold** > Jesus said to look at {behold} the fields which were already white to harvest (John 4:35). John speaks about what he has looked upon concerning the Word of life (1 John 1:1). Other refs.: SEE <2300>.

15 **to look up: *anakuptō*** [verb: ἀνακύπτω <352>]; **from *ana*: up, and *kuptō*: to bend, to lean ► To straighten oneself up, to lift up** > When the things that will take place during the great tribulation begin to come to pass, Jesus said to look up {to stand up, to straighten up} (Luke 21:28). All other refs.: LIFT <352>, STRAIGHTEN <352>.

16 **to look into: *parakuptō*** [verb: παρακύπτω <3879>]; **from *para*: beside, and *kuptō*: to bend, to lean ► To examine attentively** > He who looks into {fixes his view on, looks intently into} the law of liberty will be blessed (Jas. 1:25). The angels

desire to look into the things concerning Christ (1 Pet. 1:12). Other refs.: Luke 24:12; John 20:5, 11; (to stoop down); see STOOP <3879>. ¶
– [17] Matt. 5:28 → to look lustfully → LUST (verb) <1937> [18] Matt. 16:4; Heb. 11:14; 13:14 → to look for → SEEK <1934> [19] Matt. 17:8; Luke 6:20; 16:23; 18:13; John 4:35; 6:5; 17:1 → lit.: to lift up (the eyes) → LIFT <1869> [20] Matt. 18:10; 1 Tim. 4:12 → to look down → DESPISE <2706> [21] Matt. 25:36, 43; Acts 7:23; Jas. 1:27 → to look after, to look upon → VISIT (verb) <1980> [22] Matt. 27:55; 28:1; Mark 15:40, 47; Luke 21:6; 23:35; John 6:40; Rev. 11:11 → SEE <2334> [23] Matt. 28:5; Mark 1:37; 3:32; 16:6; Luke 2:48, 49; 4:42; 13:6, 7; Acts 10:19, 21; 1 Cor. 1:22; Heb. 8:7; et al. → to look for → SEEK <2212> [24] Mark 1:36 → to go to look for → to follow after → FOLLOW <2614> [25] Luke 2:44, 45; Acts 11:25 → to look for → SEEK <327> [26] Luke 10:35 → to look after → to take care of → CARE (noun) <1959> [27] Luke 17:7 → to look after → SHEPHERD (verb) <4165> [28] Luke 18:9 → to look down → to treat with contempt → CONTEMPT <1848> [29] John 11:41 → to look up → lit.: to lift up the eyes → LIFT <142> [30] Acts 2:31 → to look ahead → FORESEE <4275> [31] Acts 7:31, 32; 11:6; Jas. 1:23, 24 → CONSIDER <2657> [32] Acts 13:25 → "you are looking for" added in Engl. [33] Acts 17:23 → to look carefully at → BEHOLD (verb) <333> [34] Acts 18:15 → to look after it, to look to it → to see to it → SEE <3700> [35] Acts 21:4 → FIND <429> [36] Rom. 14:3, 10 → to look down on → DESPISE <1848> [37] 1 Cor. 16:11; Heb. 11:10 → to look for, to look forward → WAIT (verb) <1551> [38] 2 Cor. 3:18 → to look on → to behold as in a mirror → BEHOLD (verb) <2734> [39] 2 Cor. 4:18 → to fix the eyes → EYES <4648> [40] Gal. 6:1 → WATCH (verb) <4648> [41] Phil. 3:20; Heb. 9:28 → to look for → WAIT (verb) <553> [42] Heb. 12:2 → to look, to look steadfastly → to fix the eyes → FIX <872> [43] Heb. 12:15 → to look carefully, to look diligently → WATCH (verb) <1983> [44] Rev. 9:7 → the locusts looked like → lit.: the likenesses of the locust were like → LIKENESS <3667>.

LOOKING – [1] Luke 21:26; Acts 12:11 → looking after → EXPECTATION <4329> [2] Heb. 10:27 → looking for → EXPECTATION <1561>.

LOOSE – [1] ***aniēmi*** [verb: ἀνίημι <447>]; **from *ana*: back, upward, and *hiēmi*: to send, to throw ► To untie, to free >** The chains of Paul, Silas, and the other prisoners were loosed {unfastened} (Acts 16:26). The verb is used for loosing the rudder ropes of a ship (Acts 27:40). All other refs.: GIVE <447>, LEAVE (verb) <447>.
[2] ***luō*** [verb: λύω <3089>] **► To unbind, to free; also transl.: to unfasten, to unloose, to untie >** Jesus told Peter that whatever he loosed on earth would be loosed in heaven (Matt. 16:19a, b); He says the same thing to believers in Him (18:18a, b). John the Baptist said he was not worthy to loose the sandal strap of Jesus (Mark 1:7; Luke 3:16; John 1:27; Acts 13:25). The impediment of the tongue of the one who was deaf was loosed {was removed, was loosened} when Jesus healed him (Mark 7:35). Jesus had to loose {release, set free} a woman from her bond (i.e., her spirit of infirmity) on the Sabbath day (Luke 13:16; see vv. 11, 12). Jesus said to loose {take off the grave clothes of} Lazarus and let him go (John 11:44). God has raised up Jesus, having loosed {putting an end to, freeing Him from} the pains of death (Acts 2:24). The Lord told Moses to loose the sandals of {take his sandals off, put off his shoes from} his feet (Acts 7:33). Paul tells one who is loosed {free, released} from a wife {unmarried} not to seek a wife (1 Cor. 7:27b). The verb is used also concerning animals (Matt. 21:2; Mark 11:2, 4, 5; Luke 13:15; 19:30, 31, 33a, b). All other refs.: ANNUL <3089>, BREAK <3089>, DESTROY <3089>, DISSOLVE <3089>, RELEASE (verb) <3089>.
[3] ***apoluō*** [verb: ἀπολύω <630>]; **from *apo*: from, and *luō*: see [2] ► To liberate, to deliver, to free >** Jesus loosed {set free} a woman from her infirmity (Luke 13:12). All other refs.: see entries in Lexicon at <630>.

[4] ***periaireō*** [verb: περιαιρέω <4014>]; **from *peri*: around, and *haireō*: to take, to lift ▶ To remove, to cut** > On Paul's boat, they let go the anchors and left them in the sea, meanwhile loosing the ropes of the rudders (Acts 27:40). All other refs.: TAKE <4014>.
[5] **loosening: *lusis*** [fem. noun: λύσις <3080>]; **akin to *luō*: to loose ▶ Divorce, separation** > If one is bound to a wife, he should not seek to be loosed {to be released} (lit.: a loosening) (1 Cor. 7:27). ¶
– [6] Luke 9:25b → FORFEIT <2210> [7] Acts 13:13; 16:11 → SAIL (verb) <321> [8] Acts 24:26: the verb *luō* is added in some mss. [9] Acts 27:13 → loosing → WEIGH <142> [10] Acts 27:21 → SAIL (noun) <321> [11] Rom. 7:2 → RELEASE (verb) <2673> [12] Eph. 3:13 → to loose heart → HEART <1573>.

LOOSEN – Mark 7:35 → LOOSE <3089>.

LORD (noun) – [1] ***Kurios, kurios*** [masc. noun: Κύριος, κύριος <2962>]; **from *kuros*: might, supremacy ▶ a. Title of God and of the Lord Jesus as those who have authority** > This title is used in regard to God (e.g., Matt. 1:20, 22, 24; Rev. 21:22). Jesus uses "the Lord your God" when responding to Satan, (Matt. 4:7, 10). Jesus is Lord of all (Acts 10:36). In anticipation of His return, Christians say: Amen; come, Lord Jesus! (Rev. 22:20). **b. Person who has authority over another, master, sir** > The servant is not above his lord (Matt. 10:24; John 13:16); it is sufficient for the servant to be as his lord (Matt. 10:25). The term is used in parables (Matt. 18:25–27, 31, 32, 34; 21:30; 25:11a, b; Luke 19:25). The word designates Pilate (Matt. 27:63). It is used when the jailer addressed Paul and Silas (Acts 16:30). Sarah called Abraham her lord (1 Pet. 3:6). The term designates an elder in Rev. 7:14. The Lamb is Lord of lords (Rev. 17:14a, b; 19:16a, b). Other refs.: 1 Cor. 8:5; Gal. 4:1 {owner}. **c. Sovereign, emperor** > Festus had nothing certain to write to his lord {majesty} concerning Paul (Acts 25:26). *
[2] ***Despotēs*** [masc. noun: Δεσπότης <1203>] **▶ Sovereign master, one possessing supreme authority** > The term is used in addressing God (Luke 2:29 {Sovereign Lord}). Christians address God by this title in Acts 4:24, as well as those who were slain for the word of God and for their testimony in Rev. 6:10. All other refs.: MASTER (noun) <1203>.
[3] **Lord's: *kuriakos*** [adj.: κυριακός <2960>]; **from *kurios*: see [1] ▶ Which belongs particularly to the Lord** > This word is used only in relation to the Lord's supper (1 Cor. 11:20) and the Lord's day, most likely the first day of the week (Rev. 1:10). ¶
[4] **lords: *megistanes*** [plur. masc. noun: μεγιστάνες <3175>]; **plur. of *megistos*, superl. of *megas* ▶ People who are very important, e.g., politically** > Herod on his birthday gave a banquet for his lords {grandees, high officials, nobles}, the military commanders, and the leading men of Galilee (Mark 6:21). The word is transl. "great," "great men," "great ones," "important people," or "princes" in Rev. 6:15; 18:23. ¶
– [5] Matt. 15:27; 20:8; 21:40; 24:45, 46, 48, 50; 25:18–22, 23a, b, 24, 26; Mark 12:9; Luke 12:36, 37, 42, 43, 45–47; 13:8; 14:21–23; 16:3, 5, 8; 19:16, 18, 20, 34; 20:13, 15; John 15:15, 20 → MASTER (noun) <2962> [6] Mark 10:51 → RABBONI <4462> [7] Rom. 14:9; 1 Tim. 6:15 → to be lord → to have dominion → DOMINION <2961> [8] Eph. 6:12 → universal lord → RULER <2888> [9] 1 Pet. 5:3 → to be lord → LORD (verb) <2634>.

LORD (verb) – [1] **to lord over, to be lord of: *katakurieuō*** [verb: κατακυριεύω <2634>]; **from *kata*: intens., and *kurieuō*: to dominate, to rule, which is from *kurios*: lord, master ▶ To dominate, to rule** > The rulers of the Gentiles lord it {exercise dominion, exercise lordship} over them (Matt. 20:25; Mark 10:42). Elders must shepherd the flock of God, not lording it over {as being lord of} those entrusted to them (1 Pet. 5:3). Other ref.: Acts 19:16; see OVERPOWER <2634>. ¶
– [2] Luke 22:25; 2 Cor. 1:24 → to have dominion → DOMINION <2961>.

LORD'S PEOPLE – Rom. 12:13; 15:25, 26; et al. → lit.: the saints → SAINT <40>.

LORDSHIP – 1 Mark 10:42 → to exercise lordship → to lord over → LORD (verb) <2634> 2 Luke 22:25; Rom. 6:9, 14; 14:9; 2 Cor. 1:24; 1 Tim. 6:15 → to exercise lordship → to have dominion → DOMINION <2961> 3 Col. 1:16; 2 Pet. 2:10; Jude 8 → DOMINION <2963>.

LOSE – 1 ***apollumi*** [verb: ἀπόλλυμι <622>]; **from *apo*: intens., and *ollumi*: to destroy, or *olethros*: loss ▶ To destroy, to ruin; also: to doom to eternal punishment** > The verb is used in regard to wine skins {to mar, to perish} (Matt. 9:17; Mark 2:22; Luke 5:37), the lost sheep of the house of Israel (Matt. 10:6; 15:24), life (Matt. 10:39a, b; 16:25a, b; Mark 8:35a, b; Luke 6:9; 9:24a, b; 17:33a, b; John 12:25), a reward (Matt. 10:42; Mark 9:41), those whom the Son of Man came to save (Matt. 18:11; Luke 19:10), a sheep (Luke 15:4a, b, 6), a drachma (Luke 15:8, 9), the prodigal son (Luke 15:24, 32), the fragments of the loaves which were over and above (John 6:12 {to waste}), all that the Father had given to the Son (John 6:39), the disciples of Jesus (John 17:12 {to perish}; 18:9), and that which John had wrought (2 John 8). All other refs.: DESTROY <622>, PERISH <622>.

2 **to lose its flavor: *mōrainō*** [verb: μωραίνω <3471>]; **from *moros*: foolish, thoughtless; lit.: to act foolishly ▶ To become insipid** > Believers in the Lord are the salt of the earth, but if the salt loses its flavor {loses its savor, becomes insipid, becomes savorless, becomes tasteless, loses its saltiness}, how will it be seasoned? (Matt. 5:13; Luke 14:34). All other refs.: FOOL <3471>, FOOLISH <3471>.

– 3 Matt. 16:26; Mark 8:36; Phil. 3:8 → to suffer the loss → LOSS <2210> 4 Luke 16:4 → to be removed → REMOVE <3179> 5 Luke 18:1; 2 Cor. 4:1, 16 → to lose heart → HEART <1457a> 6 Acts 19:27 → FALL (verb) <2064> 7 Acts 19:27 → to lose one's good name → lit.: to come into disrepute → DISREPUTE <557> 8 Acts 27:9 → to be lost → ELAPSE <1230> 9 Acts 27:34 → PERISH <4098> 10 Gal. 6:9; 2 Thes. 3:13 → to lose heart → to grow weary → WEARY <1573> 11 Col. 3:21 → to lose heart → to become discouraged → DISCOURAGED <120> 12 Heb. 12:3 → to lose heart → to be discouraged → DISCOURAGED <1590> 13 2 Pet. 3:17 → to lose one's own stability → to fall from one's own steadfastness → FALL (verb) <1601>.

LOSS – 1 ***apobolē*** [fem. noun: ἀποβολή <580>]; **from *apoballō*: to cast off, which is from *apo*: away, and *ballō*: to throw ▶ Deprivation of something** > There would be no loss of life of anyone on board Paul's ship (Acts 27:22). Other ref.: Rom. 11:15; see REJECTION <580>. ¶

2 ***zēmia*** [fem. noun: ζημία <2209>] ▶ **a. Damage, prejudice** > Paul said that the voyage would end with disaster and much loss (Acts 27:10, 21). **b. Deprivation, damage** > The things which were a gain for Paul, he counted as loss on account of Christ (Phil. 3:7); he counted also all things to be loss on account of the excellency of the knowledge of Christ Jesus (v. 8a). ¶

3 **to suffer the loss, to suffer loss: *zēmioō*** [verb: ζημιόω <2210>]; **from *zēmia*: see 2 ▶ a. To receive detriment, to be divested, to lose** > It will profit a man nothing to gain the whole world and suffer the loss of {forfeit, lose} his soul (Matt. 16:26; Mark 8:36). If the work of anyone is consumed, he will suffer loss (1 Cor. 3:15). Paul had suffered the loss of all things on account of Christ Jesus (Phil. 3:8b). **b. To suffer a wrong, to be injured** > The Corinthians did not suffer loss {were not injured, did not receive damage, were not harmed} from Paul following his first corrective letter (2 Cor. 7:9). Other ref.: Luke 9:25 (to be under the penalty of loss); see FORFEIT <2210>. ¶

– 4 John 13:22 → to be at a loss → PERPLEXED (BE) <639> 5 Acts 5:24 → to be at a loss → PERPLEXED (BE) <1280> 6 Acts 25:20 → to be at a loss → to be uncertain → UNCERTAIN <639> 7 Rom. 11:12 → FAILURE <2275> 8 Phil. 3:8 → FILTH <4657>.

LOST – [1] Matt. 18:14; 1 Cor. 15:18; 2 Cor. 4:3 → to be lost → PERISH <622> [2] Acts 27:22 → not one will be lost → lit.: there will be no loss of life → LOSS <580> [3] Rev. 18:14 → to be lost → PERISH <565>.

LOT (name) – ***Lōt*** [masc. name: Λώτ <3091>]**: veil, in Heb. ► Nephew of Abraham** > God preserved Lot at the destruction of Sodom (Luke 17:28, 29). His wife, who looked back, became a pillar of salt (Luke 17:32; see Gen. 19:26). God delivered Lot who was oppressed by the dissolute behavior of his fellow citizens; Lot is recognized a "righteous" man (2 Pet. 2:7). ¶

LOT (noun) – [1] ***klēros*** [masc. noun: κλῆρος <2819>]**; from *klaō*: to break ► Portion, share** > To draw someone's name by lot, i.e., to cast lot, is to choose his name by random selection. The soldiers divided up the clothes of Jesus by casting lots (Matt. 27:35; Mark 15:24; Luke 23:34; John 19:24b). The apostles cast lots to determine who would replace Judas, and the lot fell on Matthias (Acts 1:26a, b). All other refs.: ENTRUST <2819>, INHERITANCE <2819>, PART (noun) <2819>.
[2] **to fall by lot, to cast lots, to choose by lot, to decide by lot: *lanchanō*** [verb: λαγχάνω <2975>] **► To assign randomly, to obtain by a draw of chance** > It fell to Zacharias by lot to burn incense in the temple (Luke 1:9). The soldiers cast lots for the outer garments of Jesus (John 19:24a). Other refs.: Acts 1:17; 2 Pet. 1:1; see RECEIVE <2975>. ¶
– [3] Acts 19:24 → a lot of business → lit.: not little trade → LITTLE <3641> [4] Acts 22:28 → a lot of money → a great sum → GREAT <4183>.

LOUD – [1] ***megas*** [adj.: μέγας <3173>] **► Great in intensity, highly audible** > Jesus cried with a loud voice: "My God, My God, why have You forsaken Me?" (Matt. 27:46; Mark 15:34; Luke 23:46). He cried again with a loud voice and yielded up His spirit (Matt. 27:50). A possessed man shouted with a loud voice (Mark 5:7). Other refs.: Mark 1:26; Luke 1:42; 4:33; 8:28; 17:15; 19:37; John 11:43; Acts 7:57, 60; 8:7; 14:10; 16:28; 26:24; Rev. 5:2, 12; 6:10; 7:2, 10; 8:13; 10:3; 14:7, 9, 15; 19:17. All other refs.: GREAT <3173>.
– [2] 1 Thes. 4:16 → loud command → SHOUT (noun) <2752> [3] Heb. 5:7; Rev. 18:2 → STRONG <2478>.

LOUD-MOUTHED – Jude 16 → loud-mouthed boasters → lit.: their mouth speaks boastful words → MOUTH (noun) <4750>.

LOUDER – [1] Matt. 27:23 → all the louder → more than ever → MORE <4057> [2] Mark 15:14 → all the louder → the more → MORE <4056>.

LOUDLY – Acts 25:24 → to declare loudly → CRY (verb) <1916>.

LOVE (noun) – [1] ***agapē*** [fem. noun: ἀγάπη <26>]**; from *agapaō*: to love ► Deep feeling of affection, of attachment toward another person** > In the N.T., the term is used only concerning divine persons (e.g., John 15:9; Rom. 15:30; 1 John 2:15) and Christians (e.g., Phil. 1:9; 2 Thes. 1:3). Love has its source in God, and is expressed only by God and by those who are born of God (e.g., John 15:13; 1 John 4:8, 16, 18). The word is sometimes transl. "charity" (e.g., 1 Thes. 3:6). Other refs.: Matt. 24:12; Luke 11:42; John 5:42; 13:35; 15:10a, b; 17:26; Rom. 5:5, 8; 8:35, 39; 12:9; 13:10a, b; 14:15; 1 Cor. 4:21; 8:1; 13:1–3, 4a–c, 8, 13a, b; 14:1; 16:14, 24; 2 Cor. 2:4, 8; 5:14; 6:6; 8:7, 8, 24; 13:11, 13 (or v. 14); Gal. 5:6, 13, 22; Eph. 1:4, 15; 2:4; 3:18 (or v. 17), 19; 4:2, 15, 16; 5:2; 6:23; Phil. 1:16 (or v. 17); 2:1, 2; Col. 1:4, 8, 13; 2:2; 3:14; 1 Thes. 1:3; 3:6, 12; 5:8, 13; 2 Thes. 2:10; 3:5; 1 Tim. 1:5, 14; 2:15; 4:12; 6:11; 2 Tim. 1:7, 13; 2:22; 3:10; Titus 2:2; Phm. 5, 7, 9; Heb. 6:10; 10:24; 1 Pet. 4:8a, b; 5:14; 2 Pet. 1:7; 1 John 2:5; 3:1, 16, 17; 4:7, 9, 10, 12, 16a–c, 17, 18a–c; 5:3; 2 John 3, 6; 3 John 6; Jude 2, 12, 21; Rev. 2:4, 19. See LOVE FEASTS <26>. ¶
[2] **love of the brothers, love of the brethren, brotherly love: *philadelphia*** [fem.

noun: φιλαδελφία <5360>]; **from *philadelphos*: one who loves his brother, which is from *philos*: friend, and *adelphos*: brother ▶ Affection, friendship between the brothers and sisters in faith** > We must be kindly affectionate to one another with brotherly love (Rom. 12:10). Concerning brotherly love, the Thessalonians had not need that Paul should write to them (1 Thes. 4:9). Brotherly love must continue (Heb. 13:1). Peter speaks of unfeigned brotherly love {brotherly kindness} (1 Pet. 1:22; 2 Pet. 1:7a, b). ¶

[3] **love, love toward man, love to man: *philanthrōpia*** [fem. noun: φιλανθρωπία <5363>]; **from *philanthrōpos*: one who loves mankind, which is from *philos*: friend, and *anthrōpos*: human being ▶ Benevolence, feeling of goodness toward the human race** > When the kindness and the love toward man {love for mankind} of God the Savior appeared, He saved us (Titus 3:4). Other ref.: Acts 28:2; see KINDNESS <5363>. ¶

[4] **love of money: *philarguria*** [fem. noun: φιλαργυρία <5365>]; **from *philarguros*: one who loves money, which is from *philos*: friend, and *arguros*: money ▶ Avarice, inordinate greed for money** > Paul reminds Timothy that the love of money is a root of every evil (1 Tim. 6:10). ¶

– [5] Luke 7:47; 2 Tim. 4:10 → as her great love has shown, in love with → lit.: for she loved much, loving → LOVE (verb) <25> [6] Rom. 1:31; 2 Tim. 3:3 → natural affection → AFFECTION <794> [7] 1 Cor. 13:7 → "love" added in Engl. [8] Heb. 13:5 → free from the love of money → not greedy for money → GREEDY <866> [9] Jude 12 → LOVE FEASTS <26>.

LOVE (verb) – [1] ***agapaō*** [verb: ἀγαπάω <25>] **▶ To take a deep and caring interest in someone or something. It denotes a deliberate choice, originating in the will and disposition of the agent and it is expressed by action.** > The Father loves the Son (John 3:35), the human race in general (John 3:16), and those who love the Lord Jesus (John 14:21). The new command of Jesus for believers in Him is to love one another, as He has loved us; by this all men will know that they are His disciples (John 13:34a–c). Other refs.: Matt. 5:43, 44, 46a, b; 6:24; 19:19; 22:37, 39; Mark 10:21; 12:30, 31, 33a, b; Luke 6:27, 32a–d, 35; 7:5, 42, 47a, b; 10:27; 11:43; 16:13; John 3:19; 8:42; 10:17; 11:5; 12:43; 13:1a, b, 23; 14:15, 21a–d, 23a, b, 24, 28, 31; 15:9a, b, 12a, b, 17; 17:23a, b, 24, 26; 19:26; 21:7, 15a, 16a, 20; Rom. 8:28, 37; 9:13; 13:8a, b, 9; 1 Cor. 2:9; 8:3; 2 Cor. 9:7; 11:11; 12:15a, b; Gal. 2:20; 5:14; Eph. 2:4; 5:2, 25a, b, 28a–c, 33; 6:24; Col. 3:19; 1 Thes. 1:4; 4:9; 2 Thes. 2:13, 16; 2 Tim. 4:8, 10; Heb. 1:9; 12:6; Jas. 1:12; 2:5, 8; 1 Pet. 1:8, 22; 2:17; 3:10; 2 Pet. 2:15; 1 John 2:10, 15a, b; 3:10, 11, 14a, b, 18, 23; 4:7a, b, 8, 10a, b, 11a, b, 12, 19a, b, 20a–c, 21a, b; 5:1a, b, 2a, b; 2 John 1, 5; 3 John 1; Rev. 1:5; 3:9; 12:11. For the following refs.: Rom. 9:25a, b; Eph. 1:6; Jude 1; Rev. 20:9, see BELOVED <25>. ¶

[2] ***phileō*** [verb: φιλέω <5368>]; **from *philos*: friend ▶ To have tenderness, affection; to love as a friend** > This verb expresses the love of the Father for the Son (John 5:20) and for the believer in Jesus (John 16:27). Jesus loved Lazarus (John 11:36). The man who loves his life will lose it (John 12:25). Other refs.: Matt. 6:5; 10:37a, b; 23:6; Luke 20:46; John 11:3; 15:19; 16:27b; 20:2; 21:15b, 16b, 17a, b; 1 Cor. 16:22; Titus 3:15; Rev. 3:19; 22:15. Other refs.: Matt. 26:48; Mark 14:44; Luke 22:47, see KISS (verb) <5368>. ¶

– [3] Matt. 3:17; 12:18; 17:5; Mark 1:11; 9:7; 12:6; Luke 3:22; 9:35; 20:13; Rom. 1:7; 2 Pet. 1:17 → BELOVED <27> [4] Mark 12:38 → LIKE (verb) <2309> [5] 1 Thes. 2:8 → to be affectionately desirous → AFFECTIONATELY <2442> [6] 1 Tim. 3:3; Heb. 13:5 → free from the love of money → not greedy for money → GREEDY <866> [7] 2 Tim. 3:3 → not loving good → despiser of good → DESPISER <865> [8] Titus 1:8 → one who loves what is good → lover of what is good → LOVER <5358> [9] Titus 2:4 → loving one's husband → HUSBAND <5362> [10] Titus 2:4 → loving one's children → CHILDREN <5388> [11] Heb. 13:1 → to love as brothers → love of the brothers → LOVE (noun) <5360> 12 1 Pet. 3:8 → to love as brothers, to love one another → BROTHERLY <5361> 13 3 John 9 → to love to be first, to love to have the first place → to love to have the preeminence → PREEMINENCE <5383>.

LOVE FEASTS – *agapai*; plur. of *agapē* [fem. noun: ἀγάπη <26>]; **affection, love ▶ Meal expressing and nurturing mutual affection eaten together by early Christians >** Jude speaks of certain persons who were spots in the love feasts {feasts of charity} of Christians (Jude 12). At the beginning of the church, the Lord's supper was celebrated during those feasts. All other refs. (*agapē*): see LOVE (noun) <26>.

LOVELY – 1 *prosphilēs* [adj.: προσφιλής <4375>]; **from *pros*: to, and *phileō*: to feel tenderness, affection ▶ Agreeable, worthy of being loved >** Whatsoever things are lovely {amiable} should occupy the thoughts of Christians (Phil. 4:8). ¶

– 2 Acts 7:20 → exceedingly lovely, lovely in the sight of God → well pleasing to God → PLEASING <791> <2316>.

LOVER – 1 lover of what is good, lover of goodness, loving what is good, lover of good men: *philagathos* [adj.: φιλάγαθος <5358>]; **from *philos*: friend, loving, and *agathos*: good ▶ Having affection for what is good, for good people >** The overseer must be a lover of what is good {one who loves what is good} (Titus 1:8). ¶

2 **lover of self: *philautos*** [adj.: φίλαυτος <5367>]; **from *philos*: friend, loving, and *autos*: himself ▶ Occupied only with self, egoist >** In the last days, men will be lovers of self {lovers of themselves} (2 Tim. 3:2). ¶

3 **lover of pleasure: *philēdonos*** [adj.: φιλήδονος <5369>]; **from *philos*: friend, loving, and *hēdonē*: pleasure ▶ Liking pleasures, especially sensual pleasures >** In the last days, men will be lovers of pleasure {pleasures} rather than lovers of God (2 Tim. 3:4). ¶

4 **lover of God: *philotheos*** [adj.: φιλόθεος <5377>]; **from *philos*: friend, loving, and *Theos*: God ▶ Having affection for God >** In the last days, men will be lovers of pleasure rather than lovers of God (2 Tim. 3:4). ¶

– 5 Luke 16:14; 2 Tim. 3:2 → lover of money → COVETOUS (adj.) <5366> 6 1 Tim. 3:3 → not a lover of money → not greedy for money → GREEDY <866> 7 2 Tim. 3:3 → not lover of what is good → DESPISER <865>.

LOW – 1 to bring low, to make low: *tapeinoō* [verb: ταπεινόω <5013>]; **from *tapeinos*: humble ▶ To reduce the height, to make humble >** At the Lord's return, every mountain and hill will be brought low (Luke 3:5). All other refs.: ABASE <5013>, HUMBLE (verb) <5013>.

– 2 Luke 1:48; Jas. 1:10 → low estate, low position, to be made low → HUMILIATION <5014> 3 Acts 8:10 → LITTLE <3398> 4 1 Cor. 1:28 → BASE (adj.) <36> 5 2 Cor. 7:6 → CAST DOWN <5011> 6 Jas. 1:9 → of low degree → LOWLY <5011>.

LOWER (adj.) – **1 *katōteros*** [adj.: κατώτερος <2737>]; **compar. of *katō*: below ▶ Which is located below >** Jesus descended into the lower parts of the earth (Eph. 4:9). The adv. *katōterō* is used in Matt. 2:16 and transl. "lower." ¶

2 **to make lower: *elattoō*** [verb: ἐλαττόω <1642>]; **from *elattōn*: less, lesser ▶ To set at an inferior level, to decrease >** Jesus was made a little lower {was made inferior} than the angels (Heb. 2:7, 9). Other ref.: John 3:30; see DECREASE <1642>. ¶

LOWER (verb) – 1 Mark 2:4; Acts 9:25; 27:17, 30; 2 Cor. 11:33 → to let down → LET <5465> 2 Luke 5:19; Acts 9:25; 10:11; 11:5 → to let down → LET <2524> 3 Acts 27:30 → to carry out → CARRY <1614> 4 2 Cor. 11:7 → ABASE <5013>.

LOWERING – Matt. 16:3 → to be lowering → to be overcast → OVERCAST <4768>.

LOWEST – Luke 14:9, 10 → LAST (adv. and noun) <2078>.

LOWLINESS – Acts 20:19; Eph. 4:2; Phil. 2:3; Col. 3:12 → lowliness of mind → HUMILITY <5012>.

LOWLY – [1] ***tapeinos*** [adj. and adj. used as noun: ταπεινός <5011>] ► **Humble, meek, of humble condition, voluntarily lowering oneself** > God has exalted the lowly {one of low degree} (Luke 1:52). Paul said that in presence he was lowly {base, mean, timid} among the Corinthians (2 Cor. 10:1). The brother who is lowly {of low degree, in humble circumstances} can glory in his exaltation (Jas. 1:9). All other refs.: CAST DOWN <5011>, HUMBLE (adj.) <5011>.
– [2] Matt. 18:4 → to take the lowly position → HUMBLE (verb) <5013> [3] Matt. 21:5 → MEEK <4239> [4] Luke 1:48; Phil. 3:21 → lowly state, lowly → HUMILIATION <5014> [5] 1 Cor. 1:28 → BASE[2] <36>.

LOYAL – [1] Matt. 6:24; Luke 16:13 → to be loyal → HOLD (verb) <472> [2] Phil. 4:3 → TRUE <1103>.

LUCIUS – ***Loukios*** [masc. name: Λούκιος <3066>]; ***lux*, in Lat.: light** ► **a. Christian man of Antioch** > Lucius of Cyrene taught in the church of Antioch (Acts 13:1). **b. Relative of Paul** > This Lucius sent his greetings to the Christians of Rome (Rom. 16:21). ¶

LUCRE – [1] 1 Tim. 3:3 → not greedy of filthy lucre → GREEDY <866> [2] Titus 1:11 → GAIN (noun) <2771> [3] 1 Pet. 5:2 → for filthy lucre → for dishonest gain → GAIN (noun) <147>.

LUKE – ***Loukas*** [masc. name: Λουκᾶς <3065>]; ***lux*: light, in Lat.** ► **Author of the Gospel that bears his name** > Luke presents the Lord Jesus as the "Son of Man." He also wrote the Acts of the Apostles. Paul speaks of him as the beloved physician (Col. 4:14) and also a fellow worker (Phm. 24). He was still with Paul when the latter wrote the Second Epistle to Timothy (2 Tim. 4:11). ¶

LUKEWARM – ***chliaros*** [adj.: χλιαρός <5513>]; **from *chliainō*: to warm** ► **Tepid; indifferent, showing little fervor** > Because the angel of the church in Laodicea is lukewarm and is neither cold nor hot, the Lord will spit him out of His mouth (Rev. 3:16); this angel is the symbolic administrative representative of the church in Laodicea. ¶

LUMP – ***phurama*** [neut. noun: φύραμα <5445>]; **from *phuraō*: to dissolve, to knead** ► **a. Mixture with a base of flour and water that is kneaded; also transl.: lump of dough, batch of dough, batch** > A little leaven leavens the whole lump (1 Cor. 5:6; Gal. 5:9). The Corinthians were to purge out the old leaven so that they might be a new lump (1 Cor. 5:7). **b. Substance which one mixes, a mass** > The potter has power over the clay to make different vessels from the same lump (Rom. 9:21). Other ref.: Rom. 11:16 {dough}. ¶

LUNCH – Luke 11:37 → to have lunch → DINE <709>.

LUNCHEON – Luke 14:12 → DINNER <712>.

LURE – Jas. 1:14 → to draw away → DRAW <1828>.

LUST (noun) – [1] ***epithumia*** [fem. noun: ἐπιθυμία <1939>]; **from *epithumeō*: to greatly desire, to lust, which is from *epi*: upon, and *thumos*: great passion, emotion** ► **a. Great desire, but in a negative sense, to possess something that one cannot or should not possess; also transl.: concupiscence, coveting, covetousness, desire** > The lusts of various things choke the word of God (Mark 4:19). Paul speaks of the lusts (*epithumia*) of the hearts (Rom. 1:24), and of men who were inflamed in their lust (*orexis*) one toward another (v. 27; see [2]). Christians should not obey the lusts of their bodies (Rom. 6:12). The N.T. mentions in particular the lust of the flesh (Gal. 5:16, 24; 1 Pet. 2:11; 2 Pet. 2:18; 1 John 2:16a, b). The world is passing, and the lust of it (1 John 2:17). When lust has conceived, it gives birth to sin (Jas. 1:15). Other refs.: John 8:44; Rom. 7:7, 8; 13:14; Eph. 2:3; 4:22; Col. 3:5; 1 Thes. 4:5 {lustful; lit.: of lust}; 2 Tim. 2:22; 3:6 {impulse}; 4:3; Titus 2:12; 3:3; Jas. 1:14; 1 Pet. 1:14; 4:2, 3; 2 Pet. 1:4; 2:10; 3:3; Jude 16, 18. **b. Great legitimate and positive desire >** In Luke 22:15, the Lord had desired with desire {earnestly} to eat the Passover with His disciples before He suffered. In Phil. 1:23, Paul had a desire to depart and be with Christ. In 1 Thes. 2:17, Paul had endeavored to see the face of the Thessalonians with much desire. All other refs.: DESIRE (noun) <1939>.

2 ***orexis*** [fem. noun: ὄρεξις <3715>]**; from *oregō*: to try to reach, to desire, to covet ▶ Excitement of the mind, covetousness >** Some men were inflamed in their lust {desire} for one another, men with men committing what is shameful (Rom. 1:27). ¶

– 3 Rom. 1:26; 1 Thes. 4:5 → PASSION <3806> 4 Rom. 13:13 → LEWDNESS <766> 5 Eph. 4:19; 5:3 → greedy unsatisfied lust, unbridled lust, continual lust for more → COVETOUSNESS <4124> 6 Eph. 5:5 → of unbridled lust → COVETOUS (noun) <4123> 7 Col. 3:5 → inordinate affection → AFFECTION <3806> 8 Jas. 4:1, 3 → PLEASURE <2237>.

LUST (verb) – 1 ***epithumeō*** [verb: ἐπιθυμέω <1937>]**; from *epi*: in, upon, and *thumos*: great passion, emotion ▶ a. To greatly desire to possess something that one cannot or should not possess, to covet >** Whoever looks at a woman to lust after her {lustfully} has already committed adultery with her in his heart (Matt. 5:28). Things that happened to the Israelites in the desert have happened as examples to the intent that we should not lust after {should not be lusters after, should not crave after, set our hearts on} (lit.: are not those who lust; see 2) evil things as they also lusted {craved} (1 Cor. 10:6b). James tells his readers that they lust {covet} and have not (Jas. 4:2). **b. To oppose >** The flesh lusts {sets its desire, desires} against the Spirit, and the Spirit against the flesh (Gal. 5:17). All other refs.: see: COVET <1937>, DESIRE (verb) <1937>.

2 **one who lusts: *epithumētēs*** [masc. noun: ἐπιθυμητής <1938>]**; from *epithumeō*: see 1 ▶ One who greatly desires to possess something that one cannot or should not possess; one who covets; also transl.: to crave >** The expr. "we should not lust" is lit.: "we should not be those who lust" in 1 Cor. 10:6. ¶

– 3 Jas. 4:2 → COVET <2206> 4 Jas. 4:5 → YEARN <1971> 5 Rev. 18:14 → to lust after → DESIRE (noun) <1939>.

LUSTER – 1 Cor. 10:6 → LUST (verb) <1937>.

LUSTFUL – 1 Matt. 5:28 → with lustful intent → to lust after → LUST (verb) <1937> 2 1 Thes. 4:5 → lit.: of lust → LUST <1939> 3 2 Pet. 2:18 → LEWDNESS <766>.

LUSTFULLY – Matt. 5:28 → to look lustfully → LUST (verb) <1937>.

LUXURIOUS – 1 Rev. 18:3 → luxurious living → LUXURY <4764> 2 Rev. 18:14 → RICH <3045>.

LUXURIOUSLY – 1 **to live luxuriously: *strēniaō*** [verb: στρηνιάω <4763>]**; from *strēnos*: luxury, voluptuousness ▶ To live in luxury, in extravagance >** Babylon lived luxuriously {lived sensuously, lived deliciously, gave herself luxury} and the kings of the earth lived luxuriously with her (Rev. 18:7, 9). ¶

– 2 Luke 7:25 → lit.: in luxury → LUXURY <5172> 3 Jas. 5:5 → to live luxuriously → to live in pleasure → PLEASURE <5171>.

LUXURY – 1 ***strēnos*** [neut. noun: στρῆνος <4764>]**; comp. *stereos*: strong ▶ Manner of life characterized by excessive expense in order to possess superfluous goods >** Babylon the great is characterized by the wealth of her luxury {delicacies, sensuality} (Rev. 18:3). ¶

2 ***truphē*** [fem. noun: τρυφή <5172>]**; from *thruptō*: to soften ▶ Sensual life, enjoy-**

ment of the best things > Those who live in luxury {delicately, luxuriously} are in kings' courts (Luke 7:25). Other ref.: 2 Pet. 2:13; see PLEASURE <5172>. ¶
– 3 Luke 16:19 → in luxury → SUMPTUOUSLY <2988> 4 Jas. 5:5 → to live in luxury → to live in pleasure → PLEASURE <5171> 5 Rev. 18:7, 9 → to live luxuriously → LUXURIOUSLY <4763> 6 Rev. 18:14 → rich things → RICH <3045>.

LYCAONIA – ***Lukaonia*** [fem. name: Λυκαονία <3071>] ▶ **Region located in the center of Asia Minor** > On their first missionary journey, Paul and Barnabas preached the gospel to the cities of Lycaonia (Acts 14:6). ¶

LYCAONIAN – in the Lycaonian language: ***Lukaonisti*** [adv.: Λυκαονιστί <3072>] ▶ **In the language of the people of Lycaonia** > The crowds of Lystra said in the Lycaonian language that the gods had become like men, coming down in the form of Paul and Barnabas (Acts 14:11). ¶

LYCIA – ***Lukia*** [fem. name: Λυκία <3073>] ▶ **Province of Asia Minor** > On his way to Italy, Paul visited Myra in Lycia (Acts 27:5). ¶

LYDDA – ***Ludda*** [fem. name: Λύδδα <3069>]; **from Lod, in Heb.: a town situated near Joppa on the road to Jerusalem** ▶ **City of Judea northwest of Jerusalem** > Peter went down to the saints who lived in Lydda (Acts 9:32). There he healed Aeneas, a paralyzed man; the inhabitants of Lydda and of Sharon saw Aeneas and they turned to the Lord (Acts 9:35). Lydda is near Joppa (Acts 9:38). ¶

LYDIA – ***Ludia*** [fem. name: Λυδία <3070>]; **prob. "from Lydia," a coastal region of Asia Minor** ▶ **Christian woman of Thyatira in Lydia** > Lydia was a seller of purple fabrics who served God; the Lord opened her heart to be attentive to the things Paul was saying (Acts 16:14). After she had been baptized, she urged Paul to enter her house and stay there (see Acts 16:15). After Paul and Silas went out of the prison, they returned to her house (Acts 16:40). Lydia thus became the first Christian woman of Macedonia and of Europe. ¶

LYING – Eph. 4:25; 2 Thes. 2:9; Rev. 21:27; 22:15 → LIE (noun) <5579>.

LYING IN WAIT – 1 Acts 20:19 → PLOT (noun) <1917> 2 Acts 23:16 → AMBUSH <1749>.

LYSANIAS – ***Lusanias*** [masc. name: Λυσανίας <3078>]**: who drives away sorrow** ▶ **Tetrarch of the region of Abilene** > The word of God came to John the Baptist during the rule of Lysanias (Luke 3:1). ¶

LYSIAS – ***Lusias*** [masc. name: Λυσίας <3079>] ▶ **Chiliarch commanding the garrison of Jerusalem** > Claudius Lysias delivered Paul from Jews who wanted to kill him, and sent him under escort to the governor Felix residing in Caesarea (Acts 23:26; 24:7, 22). ¶

LYSTRA – ***Lustra*** [fem. name: Λύστρα <3082>] ▶ **City of Lycaonia in Asia Minor, near Derbe** > Paul and Barnabas preached the gospel in Lystra during their first missionary journey (Acts 14:6). There Paul was considered as a god after he healed a man who had never walked (Acts 14:8; see v. 12). After he had been stoned (see Acts 14:19), Paul returned to Lystra to strengthen the disciples (Acts 14:21). He returned again to Derbe and Lystra; there he met Timothy (Acts 16:1, 2). At the end of his life, Paul spoke of persecutions he had endured at Lystra (2 Tim. 3:11). ¶

MAATH – ***Maath*** [masc. name: Μάαθ <3092>]: **small, in Heb. ▶ Man of the O.T. >** Maath is mentioned in the genealogy of Jesus (Luke 3:26). ¶

MACEDONIA – ***Makedonia*** [fem. name: Μακεδονία <3109>]: **extended land ▶ Region of northern Greece >** After having seen a vision (Acts 16:9, 10), Paul went to Macedonia and preached the gospel there, particularly in the cities of Philippi (Acts 16:12) and Thessalonica (see Acts 17:1–15) during his second missionary journey. Later, Paul sent Timothy and Erastus into Macedonia (Acts 19:21, 22), and returned there himself on his third missionary journey (Acts 20:1, 3). The Christians of Macedonia had made a contribution to support the poor among the saints at Jerusalem (Rom. 15:26; 2 Cor. 8:1). The Christians of Philippi had made a gift to Paul to supply his need (Phil. 4:15; 2 Cor. 11:9). Other refs.: Acts 18:5; 1 Cor. 16:5a, b; 2 Cor. 1:16a, b; 2:13; 7:5; 1 Thes. 1:7, 8; 4:10; 1 Tim. 1:3. ¶

MACEDONIAN – **Macedonian, Macedonian man, man of Macedonia: *Makedōn*** [masc. name: Μακεδών <3110>]: **see MACEDONIA** <3109> **▶ Inhabitant of Macedonia in northern Greece >** Paul saw in a vision a Macedonian man begging him to come over to Macedonia (Acts 16:9; see v. 10). Gaius and Aristarchus, who were Macedonians, were traveling companions of Paul (Acts 19:29; 27:2). Paul boasted to the Macedonians of the zeal of the Corinthians for service to the saints (2 Cor. 9:2, 4).

MAD – [1] **to be mad: *mainomai*** [verb: μαίνομαι <3105>] **▶ To be out of one's senses, to be demented; also transl.: to be out of one's mind >** This verb is used by the Jews about Jesus (John 10:20 {to be insane, to be raving mad}), of Rhoda (Acts 12:15 {to be beside oneself, to be out of one's mind}), of the Corinthians if they were all to speak in tongues (1 Cor. 14:23). Other refs.: Acts 26:24a, 25 (to be out of one's mind); see MIND (noun) <3105>. ¶
– [2] Acts 26:11 → to be exceedingly mad → to be exceedingly furious → FURIOUS <1693> [3] Acts 26:24b → to drive mad → to drive to madness → MADNESS <3130>.

MADE (BE) – 1 Cor. 11:8, 12 → verb added in Engl.

MADIAM, MADIAN – See MIDIAN <3099>.

MADMAN – 2 Cor. 11:23 → to be like a madman → to be out of one's mind → MIND (noun) <3912>.

MADNESS – [1] ***anoia*** [fem. noun: ἄνοια <454>]; **from *a*: neg., and *nous*: spirit ▶ Lack of common sense; also transl.: folly >** The scribes and the Pharisees were filled with madness {rage} when Jesus healed a man's withered hand on the Sabbath (Luke 6:11). The folly of wicked men will be manifest to all in the last days (2 Tim. 3:9). ¶
[2] ***mania*** [fem. noun: μανία <3130>]; **from *mainomai*: to be mad, to rave ▶ Insanity, state of being out of one's mind >** Festus said to Paul that his great learning was driving him to madness (Acts 26:24). ¶
[3] ***paraphronia*** [fem. noun: παραφρονία <3913>]; **from *paraphroneō*: to be beside oneself (in the sense of: to be out of one's senses), which is from *para*: beside, and *phroneō*: to think, which is from *phrēn*: mind, understanding ▶ Folly, irrationality >** A beast of burden restrained the madness of Balaam (2 Pet. 2:16); *paraphrosunē* in other mss. ¶

MAGADAN – ***Magadan*** [fem. name: Μαγαδάν <3092a>] **▶ Locality situated west of the Sea of Galilee, perhaps including Magdala >** Jesus came to Magadan (Matt. 15:39), and reproached the Pharisees and the Sadducees for not discerning the signs of the times (see Matt. 16:3). See MAGDALA <3093>. ¶

MAGDALA – [1] ***Magdala*** [fem. name: Μαγδαλά <3093>]: **tower, in Heb. ▶ City situated on the western shore of the Sea of Galilee >** In Matt. 15:39, some mss. have this name instead of "Magadan"; see MAGADAN <3092a>. ¶
[2] **of Magdala: *Magdalēnē*** [fem. name: Μαγδαληνή <3094>]: **see** [1] **▶ Who lives at Magdala; also transl.: Magdalene >** This

name is the surname of a Mary mentioned in the gospels; see MARY (b).

MAGDALENE – See MAGDALA <3094>.

MAGI – Matt. 2:1, 7, 16 → wise men → WISE MAN <3097>.

MAGIC – [1] ***periergos*** [adj. used as noun: περίεργος <4021>]; **from *peri*: around (intens.), and *ergō*: to work ▶ Marginal, strange activity; certainly linked to the occult; also transl.: curious arts, sorcery** > In Acts 19:19, it was a matter of magical practices; many had books which taught such practices. Other ref.: 1 Tim. 5:13; see BUSYBODY <4021>. ¶
– [2] Acts 8:9 → to practice magic, to use magic arts → to practice sorcery → SORCERY <3096> [3] Acts 8:11 → magic, magic arts → SORCERY <3095> [4] Rev. 9:21; 18:23 → magic arts, magic spell → SORCERY <5331> [5] Rev. 21:8 in some mss.; 22:15 → one who practices magic arts → SORCERER <5333>.

MAGICIAN – Acts 13:6, 8 → SORCERER <3097>.

MAGISTRATE – [1] ***archē*** [fem. noun: ἀρχή <746>] ▶ **Lit.: beginning; by metonymy: person in a position of authority, ruler** > Believers in the Lord should not worry about what they should say before magistrates (Luke 12:11). All other refs.: BEGINNING <746>, CORNER <746>, POWER[2] <746>, PRINCIPALITY <746>, STATE <746>.
[2] ***archōn*** [masc. noun: ἄρχων <758>]; **ptcp. of *archō*: to rule, which is from *archē*: beginning ▶ Person in a position of authority; also transl.: authority, ruler** > Jesus speaks of going with one's adversary to the magistrate (Luke 12:58). Paul and Silas were dragged before the magistrates (Acts 16:19). Magistrates are not a terror to good works (Rom. 13:3); the ruler (lit.: he) is God's minister (v. 4). All other refs.: PRINCE <758>, RULER <758>.
[3] ***stratēgos*** [masc. noun: στρατηγός <4755>]; **from *stratos*: army, and *agō*: to lead, to conduct ▶ Primary sense: military commander; also: principal magistrate of a Roman province** > The magistrates {praetors} dispensed justice at Rome or in governed Roman colonies (Acts 16:20, 22, 35, 36, 38). The magistrate was escorted by two officers (lictors). Other refs.: Luke 22:4, 52; Acts 4:1; 5:24, 26; see CAPTAIN <4755>. ¶

MAGNIFICENCE – Acts 19:27 → MAJESTY <3168>.

MAGNIFICENT – Acts 2:20 → AWESOME <2016>.

MAGNIFY – ***megalunō*** [verb: μεγαλύνω <3170>]; **from *megas*: great, strong ▶ a. To celebrate the greatness of God, to give Him high praise; also transl.: to exalt, to extol, to glorify, to praise** > The soul of Mary magnified the Lord, i.e., Jehovah Elohim of the O.T. (Luke 1:46). Peter heard the Gentiles magnifying God (Acts 10:46). The name of the Lord Jesus was magnified {was held in high honor} at Ephesus (Acts 19:17). Paul spoke of Christ being magnified in his body, whether by life or by death (Phil. 1:20). **b. To demonstrate** > The Lord had magnified His {had shown great, had displayed His great} mercy with Elizabeth (Luke 1:58). All other refs.: ENLARGE <3170>, ESTEEM (verb) <3170>.

MAGOG – ***Magōg*** [masc. name: Μαγώγ <3098>] ▶ **Northern country whose people are descended from Japheth, one of the sons of Noah (see Gen. 10:2)** > Gog and Magog will be gathered together by Satan at the end of the millennium for the great battle (Rev. 20:8). Fire will come down from God out of the heaven and devour them (see Rev. 20:9). ¶

MAHALALEEL – ***Maleleēl*** [masc. name: Μαλελεήλ <3121>]: **praise of God, in Heb. ▶ Man of the O.T.; also transl.: Mahalalel, Maleleel** > Mahalaleel is mentioned in the genealogy of Jesus (Luke 3:37; see Gen. 5:12, 15: Mahalalel). ¶

MAHALALEL – See MAHALALEEL <3121>.

MAID – [1] Matt. 9:24, 25 → girl, little girl → DAUGHTER <2877> [2] Matt. 26:69; Mark 14:66, 69; Luke 12:45; 22:56; John 18:17; Acts 12:13 → SERVANT GIRL <3814> [3] Luke 8:54 → DAUGHTER <3816>.

MAID SERVANT – [1] Luke 12:45; Gal. 4:22, 23, 30a, b, 31 → SERVANT GIRL <3814> [2] Acts 2:18 → HANDMAID <1399>.

MAIDEN – Luke 8:51 → DAUGHTER <3816>.

MAIDSERVANT – Luke 1:38, 48; Acts 2:18 → HANDMAID <1399>.

MAIMED – [1] ***anapēros*** [adj.: used as noun: ἀνάπηρος <376>]; **from *ana*: intens., and *pēros*: disabled, mutilated; also spelled: *anapeiros* ▶ One who has lost a member or the use of a member; also transl.: crippled** > Jesus said to invite the maimed when giving a feast (Luke 14:13). In a parable, the master of the house told a slave to bring the maimed in to his great supper (Luke 14:21). ¶
[2] ***kullos*** [adj. used as noun: κυλλός <2948>] ▶ **Disabled; also transl.: crippled** > Jesus healed many maimed people (Matt. 15:30, 31). To obtain salvation it is better to be lame or maimed, in the figur. sense, if necessary, i.e., to give up some advantage (Matt. 18:8; Mark 9:43). ¶

MAINSAIL – ***artemōn*** [masc. noun: ἀρτέμων <736>]; **from *artaō*: to hoist, to suspend ▶ Sail poss. at the fore of a ship; also transl.: foresail** > The mainsail was hoisted up to the wind (Acts 27:40). ¶

MAINTAIN – [1] ***proistēmi*** [verb: προΐστημι <4291>]; **from *pro*: before, and *histēmi*: to stand ▶ To take the lead, to give the example** > Those who have believed God are to be careful to maintain {to pay diligent attention to, to engage in, to do, to apply themselves to, to devote themselves to do} good works (Titus 3:8, 14). All other refs.: LEAD (verb) <4291>, RULE (verb) <4291>.
– [2] Luke 22:59; Acts 12:15 → to stoutly maintain, to maintain → to confidently affirm → AFFIRM <1340> [3] Acts 24:9 → SAY <5335> [4] Rom. 3:28 → CONCLUDE[1] <3049> [5] 1 Cor. 11:2 → to hold firmly → HOLD (verb) <2722> [6] Eph. 4:3 → KEEP (verb) <5083>.

MAJESTIC – 2 Pet. 1:17 → EXCELLENT <3169>.

MAJESTY – [1] ***megaleiotēs*** [fem. noun: μεγαλειότης <3168>]; **from *megaleios*: glorious, which is from *megas*: great ▶ Magnificence, glory** > Peter speaks of having been witness of the majesty of the Lord when He was transfigured (2 Pet. 1:16). The Greek word is transl. "divine majesty" {magnificence, greatness} in Acts 19:27, where it is used to describe Diana, the goddess of the Ephesians. Other ref.: Luke 9:43; see GREATNESS <3168>. ¶
[2] ***megalōsunē*** [fem. noun: μεγαλωσύνη <3172>]; **from *megas*: great ▶ Greatness, dignity** > Term which characterizes God the Father in His greatness, His glory, and His dignity (Heb. 1:3; 8:1). It is also used in ascribing praise to God (Jude 25). ¶
– [3] Acts 25:26 → LORD (noun) <2962> [4] 2 Pet. 2:10; Jude 8 → angelic majesty → DIGNITARY <1391>.

MAJORITY – 2 Cor. 2:6 → the majority → the many → MORE <4119>.

MAKE – [1] ***diatithemai*** [verb: διατίθεμαι <1303>]; **from *dia*: intens., and *tithēmi*: to put, to place ▶ To establish, to conclude** > God made {appointed} a covenant with the fathers of the Jews (Acts 3:25). In the future, God will make {will covenant} a covenant with the house of Israel (Heb. 8:10; 10:16). All other refs.: APPOINT <1303>, TESTATOR <1303>.
[2] ***ginomai*** [verb: γίνομαι <1096>] ▶ **To take place, to happen** > Refs.: Luke 23:19;

John 5:14. Other refs.: see entries in Lexicon at <1096>.

3 ***kataskeuazō*** [verb: κατασκευάζω <2680>]; **from *kata*: intens., and *skeuazō*: to make ready, to prepare, which is from *skeuē*: equipment, which is from *skeuos*: vessel, instrument ▶ To build, to prepare** > A tabernacle was made {prepared, set up} (Heb. 9:2). The divine longsuffering waited while the ark was being made {was a preparing, was being prepared, was being built} (1 Pet. 3:20). All other refs.: BUILD <2680>, PREPARE <2680>.

4 ***katergazomai*** [verb: κατεργάζομαι <2716>]; **from *kata*: intens., and *ergazomai*: to work ▶ To cause, to produce** > Sin made {became} death by that which is good (i.e., the law) (Rom. 7:13). All other refs.: see entries in Lexicon at <2716>.

5 ***kerdainō*** [verb: κερδαίνω <2770>]; **from *kerdos*: gain, profit ▶ To acquire, to gain** > In a parable, the man who had received five talents made five more (Matt. 25:16). All other refs.: GAIN (verb) <2770>, INCUR <2770>.

6 ***poieō*** [verb: ποιέω <4160>] ▶ **a.** To do > The servants and the officers made (i.e., lighted up) a fire of coals, and Peter was warming himself with them (John 18:18). Luke had made {composed, wrote} the former account (his Gospel) of all that Jesus began both to do and teach (Acts 1:1). Christians should not make provision for {take forethought for, think about how to gratify} for the flesh (Rom. 13:14). The fruit of righteousness in peace is sown for them who make peace (Jas. 3:18). **b. To treat, to deal (with someone)** > The prodigal son asked his father to make him like one of his hired servants (Luke 15:19). **c. To produce, to accomplish** > Demetrius made articles of silver (Acts 19:24). Other refs.: see entries in Lexicon at <4160>.

7 ***epiteleō*** [verb: ἐπιτελέω <2005>]; **from *epi*: intens., and *teleō*: to finish, which is from *telos*: end, goal ▶ To build, to execute** > When he was about to make {erect, build} (*epiteleō*) the tabernacle, Moses was divinely instructed to make (*poieō*) all things according to the pattern (Heb. 8:5a). All other refs.: see entries in Lexicon at <2005>.

8 ***sunteleō*** [verb: συντελέω <4931>]; **from *sun*: together, and *teleō*: see 7 ▶ To conclude, to complete** > The Lord will make {effect, consummate} a new covenant with the house of Israel and with the house of Judah (Heb. 8:8). All other refs.: END (verb) <4931>, FINISH <4931>, FULFILL <4931>.

9 **to make, to make ruler, to make oneself: *kathistēmi*** [verb: καθίστημι <2525>]; **from *kata*: down (intens.), and *histēmi*: to stand ▶ To constitute, to designate, to establish; also transl.: to appoint, to be, to set, to put in charge** > The master made the faithful and wise servant ruler over his household (Matt. 24:45, 47; Luke 12:42, 44). Good and faithful servants had gained more talents and were made rulers over many things (Matt. 25:21, 23). Joseph was made governor over Egypt (Acts 7:10). For as by one man's (Adam) disobedience many were made sinners, so also by one man's (Christ) obedience many will be made righteous (Rom. 5:19a, b). Whoever wants to be a friend of the world makes himself {becomes} an enemy of God (Jas. 4:4). Other refs.: Luke 12:14; Acts 7:27, 35; Heb. 7:28; Jas. 3:6. All other refs.: APPOINT <2525>, CONDUCT (verb)[2] <2525>, RENDER <2525>.

10 ***sunistēmi*** [verb: συνίστημι <4921>]; **from *sun*: together, and *histēmi*: to set, to stand ▶ To constitute, to establish** > If Paul was building again those things which he destroyed, he was making {constituting} himself {he proved that he was} a transgressor (Gal. 2:18). All other refs.: COMMEND <4921>, PROVE <4921>, STAND (verb) <4921>, SUBSIST <4921>.

11 **to make up beforehand: *prokatartizō*** [verb: προκαταρτίζω <4294>]; **from *pro*: before, in advance, and *katartizō*: to establish, which is from *kata*: intens., and *artizō*: to adjust, which is from *artios*: fit, perfect ▶ To prepare, to fulfill in advance** > Brothers were to make up {arrange, complete, finish, prepare} beforehand the bounty of the Corinthians (2 Cor. 9:5). ¶

12 ***procheirizō*** [verb: προχειρίζω <4400>]; **from *procheiros*: ready, at hand, which is from *pro*: before, and *cheir*: hand; lit.: to designate by the hand ▶ To designate, to establish officially, to name** > Jesus had appeared to Paul to make {appoint} him a minister and a witness (Acts 26:16). Other refs.: Acts 3:20 in some mss.; 22:14; see CHOOSE <4400>, FOREORDAIN <4400>. ¶

– **13** Matt. 9:16; 23:15; Mark 1:17; 2:21; John 2:9; 1 Cor. 4:13; 7:21 → BECOME <1096> **14** Matt. 14:22; Mark 6:45; Luke 14:23; Acts 26:11 → CONSTRAIN <315> **15** Matt. 21:33; Mark 12:1 → to make round → to set around → SET (verb) <4060> **16** Matt. 22:5 → to make light → LIGHT (adj.) <272> **17** Matt. 22:44; Mark 12:36; Luke 20:43; Acts 2:35; Heb. 1:13; 10:13 → LAY <5087> **18** Matt. 23:5 → to make broad, to make wide → EXPAND <4115> **19** Matt. 23:5 → to make long → ENLARGE <3170> **20** Matt. 27:24 → RISE (verb) <1096> **21** Mark 15:7 → COMMIT <4160> **22** Luke 2:17 → to make widely known, to make known abroad → KNOW <1107> <1232> **23** Luke 8:36 → to make well → SAVE (verb) <4982> **24** Luke 12:58 → to make every effort → EFFORT <2039> **25** Luke 13:22 → JOURNEY (verb) <4160> **26** Luke 18:9 → to make nothing → to treat with contempt → CONTEMPT <1848> **27** Luke 19:16 → PRODUCE <4333> **28** Luke 19:18; Eph. 4:16 → EARN <4160> **29** Luke 19:43 → to make about → to build around → BUILD <4016> **30** Luke 23:14; Acts 24:19 → to make charges, to make accusations → ACCUSE <2723> **31** Luke 24:28 → to make as if → to act as if → ACT (verb) <4364> **32** John 12:10 → to make plans → CONSULT <1011> **33** Acts 10:17 → to make inquiry, to make enquiry → INQUIRY <1331> **34** Acts 11:12 → making no distinction → doubting nothing → DOUBT (verb) <1252> **35** Acts 13:47; 20:28; Rom. 4:17 → SET (verb) <5087> **36** Acts 16:13 → to make customarily, to wont to be made → to be the custom → CUSTOM <3543> **37** Acts 18:12 → to make insurrection against → to rise up against → RISE (verb) <2721> **38** Acts 20:28; Rom. 4:17; 2 Pet. 2:6 → APPOINT <5087> **39** Acts 21:26 → OFFER <4374> **40** Acts 21:38 → to make an uproar → to raise a sedition → SEDITION <387> **41** Acts 26:24 → DRIVE <4062> **42** Rom. 1:3 → to be made → BORN (BE) <1096> **43** Rom. 1:11; 1 Pet. 5:10 → to make strong → ESTABLISH <4741> **44** Rom. 1:20 → the things that are made → WORKMANSHIP <4161> **45** Rom. 6:12 → to make to obey → lit.: to obey **46** Rom. 7:23 → to make prisoner → to lead captive → CAPTIVE (adj.) <163> **47** Rom. 14:19 → what makes for peace → lit.: the things of peace **48** 1 Cor. 4:7; Jude 22 → to make a distinction, to make to differ → DISTINCTION <1252> **49** 1 Cor. 9:18 → OFFER <5087> **50** 1 Cor. 12:15, 16 → would not make → lit.: is not **51** 1 Cor. 16:17; Phil. 2:30 → to make up for → SUPPLY (verb) <378> **52** 2 Cor. 6:10 → to make rich → ENRICH <4148> **53** 2 Cor. 7:2; 12:17, 18 → to make gain, to make a gain → CHEAT <4122> **54** Gal. 3:17 → to make of no effect → EFFECT (noun) <2673> **55** Gal. 4:17a, b, 18 → to make much → lit.: to be zealous → ZEALOUS <2206> **56** Gal. 6:12 → to make a good showing → SHOWING <2146> **57** Eph. 5:16; Col. 4:5 → to make the most → REDEEM <1805> **58** 1 Tim. 1:18 → to make previously, to make once → PREVIOUSLY <4254> **59** 1 Tim. 1:19 → to make shipwreck → SHIPWRECK <3489> **60** Heb. 2:7, 9 → to make lower → LOWER (adj.) <1642> **61** Heb. 7:3 → to make like → LIKE (adj., adv. noun) <871> **62** Heb. 7:16 → COME <1096> **63** Heb. 11:14 → to make it clear → to declare plainly → PLAINLY <1718> **64** Heb. 12:5 → to make light → DESPISE <3643> **65** 2 Pet. 1:5 → to make every effort → lit.: to give all effort (or: diligence) → GIVE <3923> **66** 2 Pet. 1:17, 18 → COME <5342> **67** 2 Pet. 2:3 → to make up → FEIGNED <4112> **68** 2 Pet. 2:12 → to be made → BORN (BE) <1080> **69** Jude 3 → to make every effort → to use all diligence → DILIGENCE <4710>

[70] 1 John 2:25 → PROMISE (verb) <1861> [71] Rev. 16:19 → to make her drain the cup → lit.: to give her the cup → GIVE <1325> [72] Rev. 18:15 → to make rich → RICH <4147> [73] Rev. 21:18 → the wall was made → lit.: the building of the wall → BUILDING <1739>.

MAKER – ***dēmiourgos*** [adj. used as noun: δημιουργός <1217>]; **from *dēmos*: people, and *ergon*: work ▶ Creator, craftsman, public builder >** God is the architect and maker {builder, constructor} of the city which Abraham was waiting for (Heb. 11:10). ¶

MALCHUS – ***Malchos*** [masc. name: Μάλχος <3124>]: **counselor, in Aram. ▶ Servant of the high priest >** Peter struck Malchus and cut off his right ear (John 18:10). Jesus healed him (see Luke 22:51). ¶

MALCONTENT – Jude 16 → COMPLAINER <3202>.

MALE (adj.) – [1] Luke 12:45 → male slave → SERVANT <3816> [2] Acts 2:18 → male servant → SERVANT <1401>.

MALE (noun) – [1] ***arsēn*** [adj. used as noun: ἄρσην <730>]; **also spelled *arrēn* ▶ Person of the masculine sex, a man >** God made man and woman from the beginning, male and female (Matt. 19:4; Mark 10:6). Under the law of the O.T., every first born male was to be called holy to the Lord (Luke 2:23). Under grace, God makes no distinction between male and female (Gal. 3:28); all may obtain salvation and enjoy divine blessings. Men (lit.: The males) have committed what is shameful, males with males (Rom. 1:27a–c). The male son of Rev. 12:5, 13 is Jesus Christ borne by Israel, according to the context of the chapter. ¶

– [2] 1 Cor. 6:9 → male prostitute → HOMOSEXUAL <3120>.

MALEFACTOR – [1] Luke 23:32, 33, 39 → CRIMINAL <2557> [2] John 18:30 → EVILDOER <2555>.

MALELEEL – See MAHALALEEL <3121>.

MALICE – [1] ***kakia*** [fem. noun: κακία <2549>]; **from *kakos*: bad ▶ Characteristic of a person who seeks to do evil, who is wicked >** Malice {Maliciousness, Depravity} is evident in the unregenerated man (Rom. 1:29), likewise in the Christians before their conversion (Titus 3:3). Christians are to keep the feast, not with the leaven of malice (1 Cor. 5:8). Paul exhorts the Corinthians to be babes in respect to malice {evil} (1 Cor. 14:20), i.e., to be without malice. All malice was to be put away from the Ephesians (removed from their midst) (Eph. 4:31). The Colossians were to put off (i.e., to renounce) malice (Col. 3:8). They are to lay aside (i.e., reject) all malice (Jas. 1:21 {evil, naughtiness, wickedness}; 1 Pet. 2:1). All other refs.: TROUBLE (noun) <2549>, WICKEDNESS <2549>.

– [2] Matt. 22:18; Mark 7:22 → WICKEDNESS <4189> [3] Rom. 1:29 → EVIL-MINDEDNESS <2550>.

MALICIOUS – [1] 1 Tim. 3:11; Titus 2:3 → malicious gossip, malicious talker → false accuser → ACCUSER <1228> [2] 1 Tim. 6:4 → malicious talk → injurious word → INJURIOUS <988> [3] 3 John 10 → EVIL (adj.) <4190>.

MALICIOUSLY – [1] 1 Pet. 3:16 → to speak maliciously against → to falsely accuse → ACCUSE <1908> [2] 1 Pet. 3:16 → to speak maliciously → SPEAK <2635> [3] 3 John 10 → to gossip maliciously → PRATE <5396>.

MALICIOUSNESS – [1] Rom. 1:29 → MALICE <2549> [2] 1 Pet. 2:16 → WICKEDNESS <2549>.

MALIGN – [1] Acts 19:9 → to speak evil → EVIL (adv.) <2551> [2] Titus 2:5 → BLASPHEME <987> [3] Titus 3:2; 1 Pet. 4:4 → REVILE <987>.

MALIGNITY – Rom. 1:29 → EVIL-MINDEDNESS <2550>.

MALTA – ***Melitē*** [fem. name: Μελίτη <3194>] ► **Mediterranean island located south of Sicily; also transl.: Melita** > Traveling to Rome, Paul's ship ran aground on this island. Its inhabitants showed kindness to those who had been shipwrecked. Paul stayed there for three months (Acts 28:1; see also v. 11). ¶

MAMMON – ***mamōnas*** [masc. noun: μαμωνᾶς <3126>] ► **Aram. word; this term personifies material possessions or riches which enslave; also transl.: money, wealth** > One cannot serve God and mammon (Matt. 6:24; Luke 16:13). Jesus says to make to yourself friends with the mammon of unrighteousness (Luke 16:9), i.e., the riches of this world that rejects Christ. Who will entrust the true riches to those who have not been faithful in the unrighteous mammon? (Luke 16:11). ¶

MAN – [1] ***anēr*** [masc. noun: ἀνήρ <435>] ► **Person of the masculine gender** > Jesus speaks of a wise man who built his house on the rock and of a foolish man who built his house on the sand (Matt. 7:24, 26). Other refs.: see HUSBAND <435>.

[2] ***anthrōpos*** [masc. noun or fem.: ἄνθρωπος <444>] ► **Human being, man or woman** > The first mention of this term in the N.T. is in Matt. 4:4: Man shall not live by bread alone, but by every word that proceeds from the mouth of God. This term appears more than 550 times in the Greek. *

[3] **to act like a man: *andrizō*** [verb: ἀνδρίζω <407>]; **from *anēr*: man, husband** ► **To behave as a mature man, to conduct oneself in a manly fashion; also transl.: to be brave, to be courageous, to quit oneself like a man** > Paul told the Corinthians to act like men, to be strong (1 Cor. 16:13). ¶

[4] **a certain man: *deina*** [indef. pron.: δεῖνα <1170>] ► **Someone, such a one** > Ref.: Matt. 26:18. ¶

[5] **inner man, inward man; inner: *esō*** [adv.: ἔσω <2080>]; **man: *anthrōpos*** [masc. noun: ἄνθρωπος <444>]: **see [2]** ► **Expr. used to designate the spirit of the Christian; also transl.: inner being** > The inward man delights in the law of God (Rom. 7:22). Paul said his inward man was renewed day by day (2 Cor. 4:16; *exō* in some mss.: outward). He prayed that the Ephesians might be strengthened with might in the inner man (Eph. 3:16).

[6] **strong man: *ischuros*** [adj. used as noun: ἰσχυρός <2478>]; **from *ischuō*: to be able, which is from *ischus*: ability, power** ► **Powerful, robust man** > One must first bind the strong man before plundering his house (Matt. 12:29a, b; Mark 3:27a, b; Luke 11:21). All other refs.: GREAT <2478>, MIGHTY (adj.) <2478>, STRONG (adj.) <2478>.

– [7] Matt. 2:1, 7, 16 → WISE MAN <3097> [8] Matt. 16:17; Gal. 1:16 → lit.: flesh and blood → BLOOD <129> [9] Matt. 19:20, 22; Mark 14:51; 16:5; Luke 7:14; Acts 2:17; 1 John 2:13, 14; see young man under YOUNG <3495> [10] Acts 2:17 → old man → ELDER <4245> [11] Rom. 1:27a–c → MALE (noun) <730> [12] 1 Cor. 2:13; 10:13; 1 Pet. 2:13 → by man, such as is common to man, of man → HUMAN <442> [13] 1 Cor. 7:16b, 1 Tim. 5:9 → HUSBAND <435> [14] Rev. 6:15 → free man → FREE (adj.) <1658>.

MAN-MADE – [1] Mark 14:58; Heb. 9:11, 24 → lit.: made with hands → HAND (noun) <5499> [2] Gal. 3:15 → lit.: of man.

MAN OF GOD – ***anthrōpos Theou*; man: *anthrōpos*** [masc. noun: ἄνθρωπος <444>]; **God: *Theos*** [masc. noun: Θεός <2316>] ► **Person serving the interests of God** > Paul addresses Timothy as a man of God who is to pursue righteousness, godliness, faith, love, patience, and gentleness (1 Tim. 6:11). By using the word of God for teaching, correction, and instruction in righteousness, the man of God is complete and thoroughly equipped for every good work (2 Tim. 3:17). Holy men of God (i.e., prophets) spoke, under the power of the Holy Spirit (2 Pet. 1:21). ¶

MANAEN – ***Manaēn*** [masc. name: Μαναήν <3127>]: **comforter, consoler, in Heb.** ► **Teacher in the church of Antioch** >

Manaen had been brought up with Herod the tetrarch (Acts 13:1). ¶

MANAGE – [1] ***oikodespoteō*** [verb: οἰκοδεσποτέω <3616>]; **from *oikos*: house, and *despotēs*: master ▶ To assume responsibility for the domestic affairs of a home** > Paul would have the young widows manage their home (1 Tim. 5:14). ¶

– [2] Acts 27:16 → to be able → ABLE <2480> [3] 1 Tim. 3:4, 5, 12 → RULE (verb) <4291> [4] Titus 1:7 → since (he) manages God's household → lit.: as God's steward → STEWARD <3623>.

MANAGEMENT – Luke 16:2–4 → STEWARDSHIP <3622>.

MANAGER – [1] Luke 8:3 → manager of a household → STEWARD <2012> [2] Luke 12:42; 16:1, 3, 8; Gal. 4:2 → STEWARD <3623> [3] Luke 16:2 → to be a manager → to be a steward → STEWARD <3621> [4] 1 Tim. 3:12 → good manager of → lit.: managing well → RULE (verb) <4291>.

MANASSEH – ***Manassēs*** [masc. name: Μανασσῆς <3128>]: **causing to forget, in Heb. ▶ a. Older son of Joseph and the tribe descended from him (see Gen. 41:50–52; 48:8–20); also transl.: Manasses** > Twelve thousand out of the tribe of Manasseh will be sealed (Rev. 7:6). **b. King of Judah** > Manasseh is mentioned in the genealogy of Jesus Christ (Matt. 1:10a, b). He did that which is evil in the eyes of the Lord according to the abominations of the nations which the Lord had dispossessed before the sons of Israel (see 2 Kgs. 21:2). ¶

MANASSES – See MANASSEH <3128>.

MANGER – ***phatnē*** [fem. noun: φάτνη <5336>] **▶ Trough containing food for cattle to eat** > When Jesus was a new born infant, Mary laid Him in a manger (Luke 2:7, 12), and that is where the shepherds found Him (v. 16). Jesus spoke of loosing one's ox or donkey from the manger {stall} on the Sabbath (Luke 13:15). ¶

MANHOOD – Eph. 4:13 → mature manhood → MAN <435>, MATURE <5046>.

MANIFEST (adj.) – [1] ***dēlos*** [adj.: δῆλος <1212>] **▶ Making recognizable** > Peter's speech made him manifest {betrayed him, bewrayed him, gave him away} (Matt. 26:73). Other refs.: 1 Cor. 15:27; Gal. 3:11; 1 Tim. 6:7; see EVIDENT <1212>. ¶

[2] ***phaneros*** [adj.: φανερός <5318>]; **from *phainō*: to shine, to become evident, which is from *phōs*: light ▶ a. Evident, clear** > It was manifest {apparent, known} that Peter and John had done a notable miracle (Acts 4:16). **b. Known, visible** > What may be known of God is manifest {evident, plain} from the world's creation (Rom. 1:19). In this the children of God are manifest {obvious}: by the practice of righteousness and by brotherly love (1 John 3:10). All other refs.: see entries in Lexicon at <5318>.

[3] ***emphanēs*** [adj.: ἐμφανής <1717>]; **from *emphainō*: to appear, which is from *en*: in, and *phainō*: see [2] ▶ Made apparent, known, visible** > God raised up Jesus and showed Him openly {granted that He should become visible, caused Him to be seen} (lit.: has given Him to become manifest) to witnesses (Acts 10:40). God was made manifest to those who did not ask for Him (Rom. 10:20). ¶

[4] **manifest, completely manifest: *ekdēlos*** [adj.: ἔκδηλος <1552>]; **from *ek*: intens., and *dēlos*: visible, evident ▶ Evident, publicly known** > The folly of certain men will be completely manifest {clear, obvious} to all (2 Tim. 3:9). ¶

[5] **not manifest: *aphanēs*** [adj.: ἀφανής <852>]; **from *a*: neg., and *phainō*: see [2] ▶ Hidden, invisible** > There is no creature that is not manifest {hidden, unapparent} in the sight of God (Heb. 4:13). ¶

– [6] Mark 4:22; John 1:31; Rom. 1:19; 16:26; 1 Cor. 4:5; 2 Cor. 2:14; 5:11a, b; 11:6; Eph. 5:13a, b; Col. 1:26; 4:4; 2 Tim. 1:10; Heb. 9:8; 1 John 1:2a, b; 2:19, 28; 4:9; Rev. 15:4 → to make manifest, to be manifested → MANIFEST (verb) <5319> [7] 1 Cor. 15:27 → EVIDENT <1212> [8] 2 Thes. 1:5 → manifest evidence, manifest token → EVIDENCE <1730>

[9] 1 Tim. 5:24, 25 → manifest beforehand → clearly evident → CLEARLY <4271>.

MANIFEST (verb) – [1] ***anaphainō*** [verb: ἀναφαίνω <398>]; **from *ana*: up, and *phainō*: to appear, which is from *phōs*: light ▶ To be or to come into sight, to become visible >** The disciples thought that the kingdom of God was about to be immediately manifested (Luke 19:11). Other ref.: Acts 21:3; see SIGHT (verb) <398>. ¶

[2] ***phaneroō*** [verb: φανερόω <5319>]; **from *phaneros*: visible, apparent, which is from *phainō*: see [1] ▶ To render apparent, to make known; also transl.: to be made manifest, to be manifested, to make evident, to make clear, to make known, to appear, to become visible, to disclose, to display, to reveal, to shew, to show >** There is nothing hidden which will not be manifested (Mark 4:22). The verb is used in regard to the Lord Jesus (John 1:31; 2:11 {to manifest forth}), the deeds of him who practices the truth (John 3:21 {to be clearly seen, to see plainly}, and the works of God (John 9:3). Jesus manifested the name of the Father to the men the Father had given Him out of the world (John 17:6). He manifested Himself again to His disciples after His resurrection (John 21:1a, b, 14). Paul often uses this Greek verb in his epistles (Rom. 1:19; 3:21; 16:26; 1 Cor. 4:5; 2 Cor. 2:14 {to diffuse}; 3:3 {to be manifestly declared}; 4:10, 11; 5:10, 11a, b {to be well known}; 7:12; 11:6; Eph. 5:13a, b; Col. 1:26; 3:4a, b; 4:4; 1 Tim. 3:16; 2 Tim. 1:10; Titus 1:3; Heb. 9:8, 26). Jesus was manifested in these last times for us (1 Pet. 1:20). One day the Chief Shepherd will be manifested (1 Pet. 5:4). John also uses this verb (1 John 1:2a, b; 2:19, 28; 3:2a, b, 5, 8; 4:9; Rev. 3:18; 15:4). Other refs.: Mark 16:12, 14; John 7:4; see APPEAR <5319>, SHOW (verb) <5319>. ¶

[3] ***emphanizō*** [verb: ἐμφανίζω <1718>]; **from *emphanēs*: manifest, known, which is from *en*: in, and *phainō*: see [1] ▶ To make known >** Jesus will manifest {disclose, show} Himself to the one who loves Him and keep His commandments (John 14:21, 22). All other refs.: APPEAR <1718>, CHARGE (noun)[1] <1718>, PLAINLY <1718>, REVEAL <1718>, SIGNIFY <1718>.

– [4] Col. 1:8 → DECLARE <1213> [5] 1 Tim. 6:15 → SHOW (verb) <1166> [6] 2 Pet. 1:14 → SHOW (verb) <1213>.

MANIFESTATION – [1] ***anadeixis*** [fem. noun: ἀνάδειξις <323>]; **from *anadeiknumi*: to show plainly, openly, which is from *ana*: intens., and *deiknumi*: to show ▶ Public presentation >** John the Baptist was in the deserts until the day of his manifestation {public appearance, shewing} {until he appeared publicly} to Israel (Luke 1:80). ¶

[2] ***phanerōsis*** [fem. noun: φανέρωσις <5321>]; **from *phaneroō*: to make manifest, which is from *phaneros*: manifest, visible ▶ The act of making visible, of rendering visible >** The manifestation of the Spirit is given to each Christian for the common good (1 Cor. 12:7), in particular by the exercise of gifts. By manifestation of {setting forth plainly} the truth, Paul was commending himself to every conscience of men before God (2 Cor. 4:2). ¶

– [3] Rom. 8:19 → REVELATION <602> [4] 1 Cor. 14:12 → of manifestations of the Spirit → lit.: of the Spirit → HOLY SPIRIT <40> <4151>.

MANIFESTED – 1 Cor. 14:25 → REVEALED <5318>.

MANIFESTLY – 2 Cor. 3:3 → to be manifestly declared; lit.: to be manifested → MANIFEST (verb) <5319>.

MANIFOLD – [1] ***poikilos*** [adj.: ποικίλος <4164>] **▶ Diverse, various >** According as each Christian has received some gift of grace, they are to employ it in serving one another as good stewards of the manifold grace {the grace in its many forms} of God (1 Pet. 4:10). All other refs.: VARIOUS <4164>.

[2] ***polupoikilos*** [adj.: πολυποίκιλος <4182>]; **from *polus*: much, and *poikilos*: see [1] ▶ Much diversified, having many forms >** The manifold {all-various} wisdom of God is now made known by the church to

the principalities and powers in the heavenly places (Eph. 3:10). ¶

MANKIND – 1 John 1:4; 2:25; Acts 4:12; 1 Thes. 2:15; 1 Tim. 2:5; Heb. 2:6; Rev. 14:4; 16:18 → lit.: men → MAN <444> 2 Acts 17:25; Eph. 2:3; 1 Thes. 4:13 → added in Engl. 3 1 Cor. 6:9; 1 Tim. 1:10 → abuser of oneself with mankind, one who defiles oneself with mankind → HOMOSEXUAL <733> 4 1 Cor. 10:13; Jas. 3:7 → human race → HUMAN <442> 5 Titus 3:4 → love for mankind → love toward man → LOVE (noun) <5363> 6 Jas. 3:7b → KIND {noun) <5449>.

MANNA – ***manna*** [neut. noun: μάννα <3131>]; **from the Heb.: *man*, which means: What is it? or: gift ▶ Food which God provided for the Israelites during their forty year journey in the wilderness after their departure out of Egypt** > The manna is called the "bread from heaven" (John 6:31). During the sojourn in the promised land, a golden pot contained the manna; the pot itself was in the ark of the covenant (Heb. 9:4; see Ex. 16:34) as a testimony to the generations of Israelites which were to follow. As food, the manna did not prevent death, but Jesus is the bread which came down from heaven and which gives eternal life (John 6:49; v. 58 in some transl.). In Rev. 2:17, the hidden manna corresponds to an appreciation of Christ in His perfect humanity. ¶

MANNER – 1 **in like manner: *homoiōs*** [adv.: ὁμοίως <3668>]; **from *homoios*: same, similar ▶ Likewise, similarly, in the same way** > The word is used in Matt. 27:41; Mark 4:16; 15:31; Luke 5:33; 10:32; 13:5; 16:25; 17:31; John 5:19; Rom. 1:27; 1 Cor. 7:3, 4; Jas. 2:25; 1 Pet. 3:1, 7; 5:5; Rev. 2:15 in some mss. Other refs.: Luke 13:3 in some mss.; Heb. 9:21; Jude 8; see LIKEWISE <3668>.

2 ***tropos*** [masc. noun: τρόπος <5158>]; **from *trepō*: to turn ▶ Way, character; also transl.: as, means** > Jesus will come in like manner {in the same way} as His disciples saw Him go into heaven (Acts 1:11). Other refs.: Acts 15:11 {even as}; Rom. 3:2 {respect}; Phil. 1:18; 2 Thes. 2:3; 3:16 {circumstance}; 2 Tim. 3:8 {just as, in like manner}; Jude 7. Other refs.: Matt. 23:37; Luke 13:34; Acts 7:28; 27:25. Other ref.: Heb. 13:5; see CONDUCT (noun) <5158>. ¶

– 3 Matt. 5:11 → all manner of evil → lit.: all evil 4 Luke 13:3 in some mss.; Heb. 9:21; Jude 8 → in the same manner, in like manner → LIKEWISE <3668> 5 John 19:40; Acts 15:1; 25:16; Heb. 10:25 → CUSTOM <1485> 6 Acts 13:18 → to suffer the manners → to endure the conduct → ENDURE <5159> 7 Acts 20:18 → what manner → HOW <4459> 8 Acts 22:3 → perfect manner → STRICTNESS <195> 9 Acts 23:25 → FORM (noun) <5179> 10 Rom. 1:29 → with all manner → lit.: with all 11 Rom. 6:19 → in the manner of men → HUMAN <442> 12 1 Cor. 7:7a, b → one in this matter and another in that (*ho men houtōs, ho de houtōs*) → lit.: one this way, the other this way 13 1 Cor. 15:33 → HABIT <2239> 14 Gal. 1:13 → manner of life → CONDUCT (noun) <391> 15 2 Thes. 3:7 → to act in an undisciplined manner → to be disorderly → DISORDERLY <812> 16 1 Tim. 3:4 → in a manner worthy of full respect → with all gravity → DIGNITY <4587> 17 2 Tim. 3:10 → manner of life → LIFE <72> 18 Heb. 1:1 → in divers manners → in various ways → WAY <4187> 19 Heb. 2:14 → in like manner → LIKEWISE <3898> 20 Heb. 4:15 → in like manner to us → lit.: according to likeness → LIKENESS <3665> 21 Heb. 11:19 → in a manner of speaking → lit.: in a parable → PARABLE <3850>.

MANSERVANT – Luke 12:45 → SERVANT <3816>.

MANSION – ***monē*** [fem. noun: μονή <3438>]; **from *menō*: to stay ▶ Habitation, residence; also transl.: abode, dwelling place, home** > In the Father's house, there are many mansions {rooms} (John 14:2). Jesus and His Father will make their home with anyone who keeps the word of Jesus (John 14:23). ¶

MANSLAYER – 1 Tim. 1:9 → MURDERER <409>.

MANTLE – Heb. 1:12 → CLOAK <4018>.

MANURE – Luke 13:8 → DUNG (noun) <2874>.

MANY – 1 **many, good many: *hikanos*** [adj.: ἱκανός <2425>]; **from *hikneomai*: to come, to occur ▶ Several, a number** > A good many Christians at Corinth had fallen asleep (1 Cor. 11:30b). Other refs.: see entries in Lexicon at <2425>.
2 ***polus*** [adj.: πολύς <4183>] ▶ **A great number, numerous** > Many enter in through the gate that leads to destruction (Matt. 7:13). Many tax collectors and sinners followed Jesus (Mark 2:15). A woman had suffered much under many physicians (Mark 5:26). A woman's many sins were forgiven (Luke 7:47). Many stripes were laid on Paul and Silas (Acts 16:23). The Jews brought against Paul many and grievous charges which they were not able to prove (Acts 25:7). Paul was seeking the profit of the many, that they might be saved (1 Cor. 10:33). John heard something like a loud voice of a great multitude (lit.: a crowd of many people) in the heaven (Rev. 19:1, 6). Other ref.: Gal. 4:27 {more, more numerous}. Other refs.: see entries in Lexicon at <4183>.

MANY TIMES MORE – ***pollaplasiōn*** [adj.: πολλαπλασίων <4179>]; **from *polus*: many** ▶ Refs.: Matt. 19:29 in some mss.; Luke 18:30 (*eptaplasiōn* in some mss.: seven times more). ¶

MAR – Mark 2:22 → LOSE <622>.

MARANATHA – ***marana tha*** [μαράνα θά <3134>] ▶ **Aram. expr. meaning "the Lord comes"** > Paul uses this expr. at the end of his First Epistle to the Corinthians (1 Cor. 16:22). ¶

MARBLE – ***marmaros*** [masc. noun: μάρμαρος <3139>]; **from *marmairō*: to glisten ▶ Calcareous rock, often veined with various colors, which may be polished** > It is one of the things which Babylon buys (Rev. 18:12). ¶

MARCH – Heb. 11:30 → to march around → SURROUND <2944>.

MARK (name) – ***Markos*** [masc. name: Μᾶρκος <3138>]; ***Marcus*, in Lat. ▶ Surname of a Christian named John** > Mark was the son of a certain Mary (Acts 12:12) and the nephew (or cousin) of Barnabas (Col. 4:10). Barnabas and Saul took along with them John, surnamed Mark, for service (Acts 12:25; see 13:5). John abandoned them during their first journey (see Acts 13:13). Later, Barnabas proposed to take John, called Mark, along with them (Acts 15:37), but Paul refused (see v. 38), which caused a sharp disagreement between Paul and Barnabas. The latter took Mark with him and sailed away to Cyprus (Acts 15:39). Toward the end of his life, Paul asked Timothy to bring Mark to him, for he was useful to him for service (2 Tim. 4:11). He mentions him as a fellow worker (Phm. 24). Peter speaks of Mark as his son, in the spiritual sense no doubt (1 Pet. 5:13). Mark is the author of the Gospel which bears his name; he presents the Lord Jesus as the perfect Servant. ¶

MARK (noun) – 1 ***skopos*** [masc. noun: σκοπός <4649>]; **from *skeptomai*: to look carefully, to examine; *scopus*, in Lat. ▶ Objective, goal** > Paul was pressing on toward the mark for the prize of the calling on high of God in Christ Jesus (Phil. 3:14). ¶
2 ***stigma*** [neut. noun: στίγμα <4742>]; **from *stizō*: to imprint a sign ▶ Imprint made by a pointed or branding instrument in the body** > Paul uses this word to describe what were prob. the scars left by wounds which had been inflicted on him for preaching the gospel: he bore in his body the marks {brands, brand-marks} of the Lord Jesus (Gal. 6:17). ¶
3 ***tupos*** [masc. noun: τύπος <5179>]; **from *tuptō*: to strike ▶ Imprint, print, trace** > Thomas wanted to see the mark of the nails in the hands of Jesus and to put his finger

in them (John 20:25a, b {place}). All other refs.: FORM (noun) <5179>, PATTERN <5179>, TYPE <5179>.

4 ***charagma*** [neut. noun: χάραγμα <5480>]; **from *charassō*: to sharpen to a point, to cut, to incise ▶ Engraving, impression, stamp** > The mark of the beast will be given upon the forehead or the right hand of those who accept his authority (Rev. 13:16, 17; 14:9, 11; 15:2 in some mss.; 16:2; 19:20; 20:4). Other ref.: Acts 17:29 (graven form); see FORM (noun) <5480>. ¶

– 5 2 Thes. 3:17 → SIGN <4592>.

MARK (verb) – 1 ***sēmeioō*** [verb: σημειόω <4593>]; **from *sēmeion*: sign, mark ▶ To take note, to take into account** > If anyone did not obey Paul's letter, the Thessalonians were to mark {note, take special note of} that man (2 Thes. 3:14). ¶

2 **to mark out beforehand: *prographō*** [verb: προγράφω <4270>]; **from *pro*: before, and *graphō*: to write ▶ To write, to register in advance; also transl.: to designate** > Certain ungodly men had crept in unnoticed among the faithful, who were marked out beforehand for condemnation {who were before of old ordained, whose condemnation was written about long ago} (Jude 4). Other refs.: Rom. 15:4a; Eph. 3:3; Gal. 3:1; see WRITE <4270>, PORTRAY <4270>. ¶

– 3 Luke 14:7 → REMARK <1907> 4 Acts 17:26; Rom. 1:4 → to mark out → DETERMINE <3724> 5 Rom. 16:17 → CONSIDER <4648> 6 Eph. 1:5, 11 → to mark out beforehand → PREDESTINE <4309> 7 Phil. 3:17 → to fix the eyes → EYES <4648> 8 2 Tim. 3:1 → KNOW <1097> 9 Heb. 12:1 → to mark out → to set before → SET (verb) <4295> 10 Rev. 13:16 → lit.: to receive a mark → MARK (noun) <5480>.

MARKET – 1 Matt. 11:16; 23:7; Mark 7:4; 12:38; Luke 7:32; 11:43; 20:46; Acts 16:19; 17:17 → MARKETPLACE <58> 2 John 2:16 → lit.: place of business → BUSINESS <1712> 3 John 5:2 → sheep market → Sheep Gate → SHEEP <4262> 4 1 Cor. 10:25 → meat market → SHAMBLES <3111>.

MARKET OF APPIUS – ***Appiou Phoron*** [masc. name: Ἀππίου Φόρον <675>, <5410>] ▶ **The Appian Way was built by Appius Claudius and was a main road connecting Rome to Greece and Asia; the Market of Appius was a station 37 miles (sixty kilometers) southeast of Rome; also transl.: Appii Forum, Forum of Appius** > Brothers from the Market of Appius came to meet Paul; seeing them, he gave thanks to God and took courage (Acts 28:15). ¶

MARKETPLACE – 1 ***agora*** [fem. noun: ἀγορά <58>]; **from *ageirō*: to gather together ▶ Public place, town-square; place where assemblies are held** > Jesus spoke of little children sitting in the marketplaces (Matt. 11:16 {markets}; Luke 7:32). A landowner saw laborers in the marketplace (Matt. 20:3). In the cities where Jesus entered, they laid the sick in the marketplaces {streets} so that He might heal them (Mark 6:56). When they come from the marketplace, the Jews do not eat unless they carefully wash their hands (Mark 7:4). Jesus spoke of those who love salutations in marketplaces (Matt. 23:7; Mark 12:38; Luke 11:43; 20:46). Paul and Silas were dragged into the marketplace (Acts 16:19). Paul reasoned in the marketplace (Acts 17:17). ¶

2 **from the marketplace: *agoraios*** [adj.: ἀγοραῖος <60>]; **from *agora*: see 1; lit.: one who frequents the public place ▶ Individual of the common people, base loafer** > The Jews took certain wicked men from the marketplace {of the lowest rabble, of the baser sort} to set the city of Thessalonica in confusion and seek to bring out Paul and Silas (Acts 17:5). Other ref.: Acts 19:38; see COURT <60>. ¶

MARRIAGE – 1 ***gamos*** [masc. noun: γάμος <1062>] ▶ **a. Married state of a man and a woman; also transl.: wedding** > Marriage, i.e., the conjugal state, is to be held in honor among all, or in every respect (Heb. 13:4). **b. Ceremonial and social celebration of entering into the married**

state > Jesus was invited to a wedding in Cana of Galilee (John 2:1, 2). The marriage of the Lamb, which illustrates the union of Christ with the church, is described in Rev. 19:7, 9. Other refs.: Matt. 22:2–4, 8–12; 25:10; Luke 12:36; 14:8. See WEDDING <1062>. ¶

2 **to give in marriage: *gamiskō*** [verb: γαμίσκω <1061>]; **from *gamos*: see 1 ► To marry one's children** > In contrast to the practice of marriage on earth, one does not give (one's children) in marriage after the present life (Mark 12:25). ¶

3 **to give in marriage: *ekgamiskō*** [verb: ἐκγαμίσκω <1548>]; **from *ek*: out, and *gamiskō*: see 2 ► To marry one's children** > One is not given in marriage after the present life (Luke 20:34, 35); other mss. have 2. ¶

4 **to give in marriage: *ekgamizō*** [verb: ἐκγαμίζω <1547>]; **from *ek*: out, from, and *gamos*: see 1 ► To marry one's children** > In the days before the flood, people were marrying and given in marriage (Matt. 24:38; Luke 17:27). One is not given in marriage after the present life (Matt. 22:30). For 1 Cor. 7:38a, b, see MARRY <1547>. ¶

– 5 Matt. 1:25 → to consummate marriage → KNOW <1097> 6 Luke 2:36 → VIRGINITY <3932> 7 Luke 3:19 → "marriage" added in Engl. 8 Heb. 13:4 → marriage bed → BED <2845>.

MARRIED – 1 Rom. 7:2 → who has a husband → HUSBAND <5220> 2 1 Cor. 7:27a → to be married → lit.: to be bound to a wife → to be bound → BIND <1210>.

MARRIED (BE) – to be pledged to be married: *mnēsteuō* [verb: μνηστεύω <3423>]; **from *mnaomai*: to remember, since one was to remember the engagement; comp. *mimnēskō*: to recall to one's mind ► To be promised in marriage; also transl.: to be engaged, to be espoused** > Mary was pledged in marriage to Joseph (Matt. 1:16 in some mss., 18; Luke 1:27; 2:5). ¶

MARROW – *muelos* [masc. noun: μυελός <3452>] **► Fatty substance within the bones** > In a spiritual sense, the word of God pierces even to the division of joints and marrow (Heb. 4:12), or, in other words, to the deepest core of our being. ¶

MARRY – 1 *gameō* [verb: γαμέω <1060>]; **from *gamos*: marriage; for some refs., some mss. have *gamizō* ► To join as spouses, to take as life partner** > People do not marry after the present life (Matt. 22:30; Mark 12:25; Luke 20:34, 35). In the days before the flood, people were marrying and given in marriage (Matt. 24:38; Luke 17:27). Herod had married the wife of his brother Philip (Mark 6:17). In a parable, a man had married a wife and said he could not come to the great supper (Luke 14:20). Paul speaks much on marriage in 1 Cor. 7 (vv. 9a, b; 10, 28a, b, 33, 34, 36, 39). He wanted the younger widows to marry (1 Tim. 5:14). Several verses speaking about marrying a man or a woman who is divorced: Matt. 5:32; 19:9a, b; Mark 10:11, 12; Luke 16:18a, b. Other refs.: Matt. 19:10; 22:25; 1 Tim. 4:3; 5:11. ¶

2 ***ekgamizō*** [verb: ἐκγαμίζω <1547>]; **from *ek*: out, and *gamos*: marriage ► To give in marriage, as a life partner** > He who marries himself does well; and he who does not marry does better (1 Cor. 7:38a, b). Other transl. of this verse: He who gives his own virgin daughter in marriage does well, and he who does not give her in marriage does better. For Matt. 22:30; 24:38; Luke 17:27, "to give in marriage," see MARRIAGE <1547>. ¶

3 ***epigambreuō*** [verb: ἐπιγαμβρεύω <1918>]; **from *epi*: to, and *gambreuō*: to marry, which is from *gambros*: relative by marriage ► To take a woman as spouse** > According to the law, if a man died not having children, his brother had to marry his wife (Matt. 22:24). ¶

– 4 Mark 12:19–21; Luke 20:28, 29, 31 → TAKE <2983>.

MARTHA – *Martha* [fem. name: Μάρθα <3136>]: **lady, lady of the household, in Aram. ► Sister of Lazarus and Mary of Bethany** > Martha received Jesus into her house; she was distracted with much serving

(Luke 10:38, 40, 41a, b). She was witness to the resurrection of Lazarus (John 11:1, 5, 19–21, 24, 30, 39; see vv. 42–44). In John 12:2, Martha is found again serving at a supper they made for Jesus. ¶

MARVEL (noun) – 2 Cor. 11:14 → WONDER (adj. and noun) <2298>.

MARVEL (verb) – [1] ***thaumazō*** [verb: θαυμάζω <2296>]; **from *thauma*: object of amazement; lit.: to be surprised ▶ To respect, to estimate highly; to be astonished, to be filled with wonder; also transl.: to wonder, to be amazed, to be surprised** > Jesus marveled at the response of the centurion (Matt. 8:10). He marveled because of the unbelief of the people (Mark 6:6). The disciples marveled when Jesus calmed the winds and the sea (Matt. 8:27). The people marveled at the miracles of Jesus (Matt. 9:33; 15:31; Mark 5:20; 6:51; Luke 11:14). The Jews marveled at Jesus (Mark 12:17; other mss.: *ekthaumazō*). Jesus marveled at a centurion (Luke 7:9). The disciples marveled when Jesus rebuked the wind and the raging of the water (Luke 8:25). The Father would show greater works that the Jews might marvel (John 5:20). Other refs.: Matt. 21:20; 22:22; 27:14; Mark 15:5, 44; Luke 1:21, 63; 2:18, 33; 4:22; 9:43; 11:38; 20:26; 24:12, 41; John 3:7; 4:27; 5:28; 7:15, 21; Acts 2:7; 3:12; 4:13; 7:31; 13:41; Gal. 1:6; 1 John 3:13; Rev. 17:7, 8. All other refs.: ADMIRATION <2296>, ADMIRE <2296>, WONDER (verb) <2296>.

– [2] Matt. 9:8 → to be afraid, to fear → AFRAID <5399>.

MARVELLOUS – See MARVELOUS.

MARVELOUS – ***thaumastos*** [adj.: θαυμαστός <2298>]; **from *thaumazō*: to admire, to wonder, which is from *thauma*: admiration, astonishment ▶ Remarkable, worthy of admiration, surprising; also transl.: wonderful** > The chief cornerstone is marvelous in our eyes (Matt. 21:42; Mark 12:11). The blind man healed by Jesus found it marvelous {amazing, remarkable} that the Pharisees did not know where Jesus was from (John 9:30). Christians have been called out of darkness into the marvelous light of God (1 Pet. 2:9). In Rev. 15:1, a great and marvelous sign appeared in heaven; in v. 3, those who have the victory over the beast sing of the great and marvelous works of the Lord. Other ref.: 2 Cor. 11:14; see WONDER (adj. and noun) <2298>. ¶

MARY – ***Maria*** [fem. name: Μαρία <3137>] **or *Mariam*** [fem. name: Μαρίαμ <3137>] ▶ **a. Mother of Jesus** > Mary conceived Jesus miraculously (Matt. 1:16, 18, 20). She had four other sons and at least two daughters (Matt. 13:55; see also v. 56; Mark 6:3). Mary had found favor with God to become the mother of Jesus (Luke 1:30; see v. 31). On the cross, Jesus entrusted His mother to the disciple John who took her into his own home (see John 19:26, 27). After the ascension of the Lord, Mary was one of those who persevered in prayer in the upper room (Acts 1:14). Other refs.: Matt. 2:11; Luke 1:27, 34, 38, 39, 41, 46, 56; 2:5, 16, 19, 34. **b. Mary Magdalene (Mary of Magdala)** > Seven demons had been cast out of Mary Magdalene (Mark 16:9; Luke 8:2). She had followed Jesus from Galilee, ministering to Him (Matt. 27:56; see v. 55; Mark 15:40; see v. 41). She stood by the cross and saw where the body of the Lord was laid (Matt. 27:61; Mark 15:47; John 19:25). An angel appeared to her at the tomb on the first day of the week following the death of the Lord and told her about His resurrection; Jesus appeared to her when she went to announce this news (Matt. 28:1; Mark 16:1; Luke 24:10; John 20:1, 11, 16, 18). **c. Mary of Bethany** > This Mary sat at the feet of Jesus and listened to His word (Luke 10:39, 42). She was a sister of Lazarus and was witness to his resurrection by Jesus (John 11:1, 19, 20, 28, 31, 32, 45). She anointed Jesus with an ointment and wiped His feet with her hair (John 11:2; 12:3). **d. Mary, the wife of Clopas** > This Mary (her name in Greek is *Maria*) is the sister of Mary (*Mariam*, in Greek), the mother of Jesus (John 19:25). This could be the same person as Mary, the mother of James and

Joseph (or Joses) (Matt. 27:56; Mark 15:40, 47; 16:1; Luke 24:10), and "the other Mary" (Matt. 27:61; 28:1). She was near the cross and the tomb; Jesus may have appeared to her also after His resurrection, since the name of her husband may also be Cleopas (Luke 24: 13–35). **e. Mary, mother of John surnamed Mark** > Many Christians were gathered together at the house of this Mary, and were praying for Peter in prison (see Acts 12:5). After his miraculous deliverance, Peter went to her house (Acts 12:12). **f. Christian woman of Rome** > Paul greets this Mary in his letter to the church of Rome (Rom. 16:6). ¶

MASK – 1 Thes. 2:5 → nor did we put on a mask to cover up → lit.: nor with a pretext for → PRETEXT <4392>.

MASQUERADE – 2 Cor. 11:13–15 → TRANSFORM <3345>.

MASTER (noun) – [1] ***despotēs*** [masc. noun: δεσπότης <1203>] ► **One who has the power to exercise absolute authority over another** > If any Christian has purified himself, he will be a vessel useful to the Master, prepared for every good work (2 Tim. 2:21). Peter speaks of false teachers who deny the Master {Lord, sovereign Lord} who bought them (2 Pet. 2:1). Certain men deny the only Master {Sovereign} (*Despotēs*) and Lord (*Kurios*) Jesus Christ (Jude 4); other mss.: Lord God and the Lord Jesus Christ. Other refs.: 1 Tim. 6:1, 2; Titus 2:9; 1 Pet. 2:18. All other refs.: LORD (noun) <1203>.
[2] ***epistatēs*** [masc. noun: ἐπιστάτης <1988>]**; from *ephistēmi*: to stand over, which is from *epi*: over, and *histēmi*: to be established** ► **Person in charge, overseer** > The disciples, in addressing the Lord, recognized His authority of Master (Luke 5:5; 8:24a, b, 45; 9:33, 49), as did the ten lepers addressing Jesus (Luke 17:13). ¶
[3] ***kurios*** [masc. noun: κύριος <2962>]**; from *kuros*: power, supremacy** ► **One who exercises power; also transl.: lord** > The term is used in regard to the Lord Jesus (Eph. 6:9b; Col. 4:1b) and to a person whom one serves (Matt. 6:24). The Greek word is also transl. "owner" and is used for the owner of a vineyard: Matt. 20:8; 21:40; Mark 12:9; Luke 13:8 {sir}; 19:34; 20:13, 15. The term is used for a master who makes a servant ruler over his household: Matt. 24:45, 46, 48, 50; Luke 12:42, 43, 45–47. A master delivered his goods to his servants (Matt. 25:18–22, 23a, b, 24, 26; Luke 19:16, 18, 20). The term is used for the master of a house who is coming (Mark 13:35), a master returning from a wedding (Luke 12:36, 37), a master who gave a great supper (Luke 14:21a, 22, 23), a master of an unjust steward (Luke 16:3, 5, 8), and a master of servants (John 15:15, 20; Rom. 14:4; Eph. 6:5, 9a; Col. 3:22; 4:1a). Other refs.: Matt. 13:27; 15:27; Luke 16:13; Acts 16:16, 19. *
[4] **master of the house: *oikodespotēs*** [masc. noun: οἰκοδεσπότης <3617>]**; from *oikos*: house, and *despotēs*: master, lord; also transl.: goodman of the house, head of the house, head of the household, householder, landowner, owner, owner of the house** ► **One who has authority over the house** > The Greek word is used in Matt. 10:25b; 13:27, 52; 20:1, 11; 21:33; 24:43; Mark 14:14; Luke 12:39; 13:25; 14:21b; 22:11. ¶
– [5] Matt. 8:19; 9:11; 10:24, 25a; 12:38; 17:24; 19:16; 22:16, 24, 36; 26:18; Mark 4:38; 5:35; 9:17, 38; 10:17, 20, 35; 12:14, 19, 32; 13:1; 14:14; Luke 3:12; 6:40a, b; 7:40; 8:49; 9:38; 10:25; 11:45; 12:13; 18:18; 19:39; 20:21, 28, 39; 21:7; 22:11; John 1:38; 3:10; 8:4; 11:28; 13:13, 14; 20:16; Jas. 3:1 → TEACHER <1320> [6] Matt. 10:24, 25; 18:25–27, 31, 32, 34; Luke 19:25; John 13:16; Gal. 4:1; 1 Pet. 3:6 → LORD (noun) <2962> [7] Matt. 23:8, 10 → TEACHER <2519> [8] Matt. 26:25, 49; Mark 9:5; 11:21; 14:45 a, b; John 4:31; 9:2; 11:8 → RABBI <4461> [9] Acts 27:11 → PILOT <2942> [10] Acts 27:16 → making oneself master → SECURING <4031> [11] Rom. 6:9, 14 → to be master → to have dominion → DOMINION <2961>.

MASTER (verb) – [1] Acts 19:16 → OVERPOWER <2634> [2] 1 Cor. 6:12

→ to master → to bring under the power → POWER[2] <1850> [3] 2 Pet. 2:19 → OVERCOME <2274>.

MASTER BUILDER – ***architektōn*** [masc. noun: ἀρχιτέκτων <753>]**; from *archō*: to begin, to command, which is from *arkē*: *beginning*, and *tektōn*: craftsman ▶ Architect, building contractor, person responsible for public works** > As a wise master builder {masterbuilder, expert builder}, Paul had laid the foundation (which is Jesus Christ) of God's building (i.e., the church) (1 Cor. 3:10). ¶

MASTER OF THE BANQUET – John 2:8, 9a, b → FEAST (noun) <755>.

MASTER OF THE FEAST – John 2:8, 9a, b → FEAST (noun) <755>.

MASTERY – [1] Rom. 6:9 → to have mastery → to have dominion → DOMINION <2961> [2] 2 Tim. 2:5a → to strive for masteries → STRIVE <118>.

MAT – [1] Matt. 9:2, 6; Luke 5:18 → BED <2825> [2] Mark 2:4, 9, 11, 12; 6:55; John 5:8–12 → BED <2895> [3] Luke 5:19, 24 → little bed → BED <2826> [4] Acts 5:15 → BED <2824a> [5] Acts 5:15 → COUCH <2895> [6] Acts 9:34 → roll up your mat → make your bed → BED <4766>.

MATCH – Luke 5:36 → AGREE <4856>.

MATERIAL – [1] Rom. 15:27; 1 Cor. 9:11 → CARNAL <4559> [2] Rev. 21:18 → BUILDING <1739>.

MATHUSALA – See METHUSELAH <3103>.

MATTATHA – ***Mattatha*** [masc. name: Ματταθά <3160>]**: gift of Jehovah, in Heb. ▶ Man of the O.T.; also transl.: Mattathah** > Mattatha is mentioned in the genealogy of Jesus (Luke 3:31). ¶

MATTATHAH – See MATTATHA <3160>.

MATTATHIAH – See MATTATHIAS <3161>.

MATTATHIAS – ***Mattathias*** [masc. name: Ματταθίας <3161>]**: gift of Jehovah, in Heb. ▶ Name of two men of the O.T.; also transl.: Mattathiah** > These two men are mentioned in the genealogy of Jesus (Luke 3:25, 26). ¶

MATTER – [1] ***pragma*** [neut. noun: πρᾶγμα <4229>]**; from *prassō*: to do, to make ▶ Case, affair; also transl.: thing** > If a Christian has a matter {dispute, grievance} against another, he should not go to law before the unrighteous (1 Cor. 6:1). The Corinthians proved themselves in every way to be pure in the matter of a brother who had to be disciplined (2 Cor. 7:11). No one should transgress and defraud his brother in a matter of sexual immorality (1 Thes. 4:6). Other refs.: Matt. 18:19; Luke 1:1; Heb. 6:18; 10:1; 11:1. All other refs.: BUSINESS <4229>, THING <4229>, WORK (noun) <4229>.

[2] ***logos*** [masc. noun: λόγος <3056>]**; from *legō*: to say ▶ Word, subject, news** > The leper proclaimed the matter of his healing (Mark 1:45). Simon the magician had no part or portion in the matter {ministry} of the reception of the Holy Spirit (Acts 8:21). The apostles and elders came together to consider the matter {question} of the circumcision of Gentiles (Acts 15:6). Demetrius and the craftsmen had a matter {case, complaint, grievance} against Paul and his companions (Acts 19:38). Other refs.: WORD <3056>.

– [3] Matt. 5:25 → to settle matters → AGREE <2132> [4] Mark 8:32 → SAYING <3056> [5] Luke 12:26 → other matters → REST (noun)[2] <3062> [6] Acts 25:14 → CAUSE <3588> [7] Rom. 2:27 → "a matter" added in Engl. [8] Rom. 9:28 → WORK (noun) <3056> [9] Rom. 13:5 → as a matter of → lit.: because (*dia*) [10] 1 Cor. 6:3, 4 → matters of this life, such matters → LIFE <982> [11] 1 Cor. 7:37 → to settle the matter → lit.: to stand (*histēmi*) firm (*hedraios*) [12] 1 Cor. 11:22 → in this matter → lit.: in this (*en toutō*) [13] 2 Cor. 8:13, 22 → added in Engl. [14] 2 Cor. 13:1 → WORD <4487> [15] Gal. 2:6 → to make matter → to make a difference → DIFFERENCE <1308> [16] Col. 2:16 → in matter → in regard → REGARD (noun) <1722> <3313> [17] 1 Thes. 4:1; 2 Thes. 3:1 → for other matters → for the rest → REST (noun)[2] <3063> [18] Jas. 3:5 → FOREST <5208> [19] 1 Pet. 4:15 → busybody in other people's matters → BUSYBODY <244>.

MATTHAN – ***Matthan*** [masc. name: Ματθάν <3157>]**: gift, in Heb. ▶ Man of the O.T.** > Matthan is mentioned in the genealogy of Jesus Christ (Matt. 1:15a, b). ¶

MATTHAT – ***Matthat*** [masc. name: Ματθάτ <3158>]**: gift of God, in Heb. ▶ Name of two men of the O.T.** > These men named Matthat are mentioned in the genealogy of Jesus Christ (Luke 3:24, 29). ¶

MATTHEW – ***Matthaios*** [masc. name: Ματθαῖος <3156>]**: gift of God, in Heb. ▶ One of the twelve apostles of Jesus** > See LEVI (man of the N.T.) <3018>. The Gospel of Matthew presents the Lord Jesus as the King of Israel.

MATTHIAS – ***Matthias*** [masc. name: Ματθίας <3159>]**: gift of Jehovah, in Heb. ▶ Disciple who replaced Judas Iscariot** > Matthias was added to the eleven apostles (Acts 1:23, 26). ¶

MATURE – [1] **mature, mature man: *teleios*** [adj. used as noun: τέλειος <5046>]**; from *telos*: end; lit.: having reached its end ▶ Adult evidencing spiritual maturity; also transl.: full-grown man, one of full age, perfect** > In their minds, the Corinthians were to be grown men (1 Cor. 14:20). Paul speaks to the Ephesians of reaching the state of the mature man {full-grown man, perfect man} (Eph. 4:13). Solid food is for full-grown men (Heb. 5:14). All other refs.: PERFECT (adj.) <5046>.
– [2] Mark 4:28 → FULL <4134> [3] Luke 8:14 → lit.: to bring fruit to maturity → FRUIT <5052> [4] Eph. 4:15 → "the mature body of" added in Engl.

MATURITY – Heb. 6:1 → PERFECTION <5047>.

MAUL – Luke 9:39 → BRUISE <4937>.

MAY, MIGHT – ***ō*** [verb: ὦ <5600>]**; subjunctive of *eimi*: to be ▶** Refs.: Matt. 6:4, 22, 23; 2 John 12. *

ME – [1] ***egō*** [pron.: ἐγώ <1473>] ▶ Personal pron.; also transl.: I. *
[2] ***me*** [pron.: μέ <3165>] ▶ Personal pron.; also transl.: I, my. * ‡
[3] ***moi*** [pron.: μοι <3427>] ▶ Personal pron.; also transl.: mine, my. * ‡

MEAK – 2 Cor. 10:1 → LOWLY <5011>.

MEAL – [1] ***brōsis*** [fem. noun: βρῶσις <1035>]**; from *bibroskō*: to eat ▶ Dish, food** > Esau sold his birthright for one meal {morsel} (Heb. 12:16). All other refs.: EATING <1035>, FOOD <1035>, RUST <1035>.
– [2] Matt. 13:33; Luke 13:21 → FLOUR <224> [3] Luke 11:38 → DINNER <712> [4] John 13:2, 4; 1 Cor. 11:21 → evening meal, meal → SUPPER <1173> [5] Acts 2:46 → FOOD <5160>.

MEAN (adj.) – [1] Acts 21:39 → INSIGNIFICANT <767> [2] 2 Cor. 10:1 → LOWLY <5011>.

MEAN (verb) – [1] Matt. 1:23; Mark 5:41; 15:22, 34; John 1:38 in some mss., 41; Acts 4:36; 13:8 → TRANSLATE <3177> [2] Matt. 26:22, 25 → you don't mean me → lit.: is (*eimi*) it me? [3] Matt. 26:70 → what you mean → lit.: what you are saying (*legō*) [4] John 1:42; 9:7; Heb. 7:2 → TRANSLATE <2059> [5] Acts 7:18 → to whom Joseph meant nothing → lit.: who had not known Joseph [6] Rom. 2:4; 11:15a, b → the verb is added in Engl. [7] Rom. 4:14 → to mean nothing → to be made vain → VAIN <2758> [8] Gal. 4:1 → SAY <3004> [9] Gal. 5:6 → to mean something → to have value → VALUE (noun) <2480>.

MEANING – [1] ***dunamis*** [fem. noun: δύναμις <1411>]; **from *dunamai*: to be able ► Capacity, value** > One must know the meaning {power} of the voice in order to communicate effectively (1 Cor. 14:11). All other refs.: ABILITY <1411>, MIRACLE <1411>, POWER[1] <1411>, POWER[3] <1411>, STRENGTH <1411>.
– [2] Acts 13:8 → to be the meaning → to be translated → TRANSLATE <3177> [3] 1 Cor. 14:10 → without meaning → without significance → SIGNIFICANCE <880>.

MEANINGLESS – [1] Matt. 6:7 → to use meaningless repetitions → REPETITION <945> [2] 1 Tim. 1:6 → meaningless talk → vain discourse → VAIN <3150> [3] Titus 1:10 → people full of meaningless talk → idle talkers → TALKER <3151>.

MEANS – [1] **to have means: *euporeomai*** [verb: εὐπορέομαι <2141>]; **from *euporos*: prosperous, which is from *eu*: well, and *poros*: means, financial means ► To have resources** > The disciples determined to send a contribution for the relief of the brothers living in Judea, each according as he had means {according to his ability} (Acts 11:29). ¶
[2] **by no means: *ou mē*** [neg. expr.: οὐ μή <3364>]; **ellipsis for: there is nothing to fear, there is no danger ► Certainly not** > At the coming of the Lord, the living Christians will by no means {in no way, not} precede those who are asleep (1 Thes. 4:15). *
[3] **through means of, by the means of: *ek*** [prep.: ἐκ <1537>] ► **Through the intervention of, through the intercession of** > The word is used in 2 Cor. 1:11.
– [4] Matt. 2:6 → by no means → WISE (IN NO) <3760> [5] Luke 8:3 → own means, private means → SUBSTANCE <5224> [6] Rom. 3:4, 6, 31; 7:7; 9:14; 11:11 → by no means → lit.: not at all [7] Rom. 11:14 → by any means → SOMEHOW <4458> [8] 2 Cor. 8:3a, b → ABILITY <1411> [9] 2 Cor. 11:3; Phil. 3:11 → by any means → HOW <4458> [10] 2 Thes. 2:3; 3:16 → like manner → MANNER <5158>.

MEANS (IF BY ANY) – See IF POSSIBLY <1513>.

MEANTIME – [1] **in the meantime:** ἐν οἷς; ***en*** [prep.: ἐν <1722>]; ***hos*** [pron.: ὅσ <3739>] ► **Lit.: in those (moments)** > Ref.: Luke 12:1.
– [2] John 4:31 → MEANWHILE <3342>.

MEANWHILE – ***metaxu*** [adv.: μεταξύ <3342>]; **from *meta*: after, and *mesos*: middle ► In the meantime** > The term is used in John 4:31. All other refs.: Matt. 18:15; 23:35; Luke 11:51; 16:26; Acts 12:6; 13:42; 15:9; Rom. 2:15. ¶

MEASURE (noun) – [1] ***batos*** [masc. noun: βάτος <943>] ► **Bath, a liquid standard equaling from 6 to 10 gallons (approx. 35 liters)** > A debtor owed to his master one hundred measures of oil (Luke 16:6); in some mss.: *kabos, kados*. ¶
[2] ***koros*** [masc. noun: κόρος <2884>] ► **Largest standard for dry things in Israel, of about 275 dry quarts (300 liters)** > A man owed one hundred measures {one hundred cors, one thousand bushels} of wheat (Luke 16:7). ¶
[3] ***metrētēs*** [masc. noun: μετρητής <3355>]; **from *metreō*: to measure ► Standard of capacity for liquids of approx. 40 liters or 10 U.S. gallons** > In John 2:6, the vessels for purification could each hold two or three measures {two or three firkins; twenty or thirty gallons}. ¶
[4] ***metron*** [neut. noun: μέτρον <3358>] ► **Determination of the value of an object; portion** > With the measure {standard of measure} a person uses, it will be measured back to this person (Matt. 7:2; Mark 4:24; Luke 6:38). In Matt. 23:32, "to fill up the measure" has the meaning of "to behave according to the measure of." God does not give the Spirit by {or: in) measure {He gives the Spirit without limit} (John 3:34), i.e., not in a limited manner. It is becoming to have sober thoughts according to the measure of faith that God has dealt to each one (Rom. 12:3). The word has the meaning of "proportion" in 2 Cor. 10:13a, b: the measure of the rule which the God

of measure has apportioned to us. Grace has been given according to the measure of the gift of Christ {as Christ apportioned it} (Eph. 4:7). The word also has the meaning of "standard" in Eph. 4:13: the measure of the stature of the fullness of Christ. The working in its measure of each one part {effective working, proper working} of every member in the body (i.e., each member of the body of Christ, the church) causes growth (Eph. 4:16). The wall of the heavenly Jerusalem is measured according to the measure {measurement} of a man (Rev. 21:17). ¶

5 ***saton*** [neut. noun: σάτον <4568>]; **from the Heb. *seah*** ▶ **Standard of volume corresponding to between 8 to 11 liters** > In a parable, a woman hid leaven in three measures {three pecks, a large amount} of flour (Matt. 13:33; Luke 13:21). ¶

6 **excellent measures: *katorthōma*** [neut. noun: κατόρθωμα <2735>]; **from *katorthoō*: to make straight, which is from *kata*: intens.; and *orthoō*: to set straight, which is from *orthos*: straight** ▶ **Beneficial and valuable action; lit.: excellent attainments** > Felix had brought excellent measures {very worthy deeds, prosperity, reforms} for the Jewish nation (Acts 24:2); other mss. have *diorthōma*: improvement, correction. ¶

7 **beyond measure, in surpassing measure: *huperbolē*** [fem. noun: ὑπερβολή <5236>]; **from *huperballō*: to throw beyond, which is from *huper*: beyond, and *ballō*: to throw** ▶ **Used as an adv., the Greek word has the meaning of "excessively"** > The Greek expr. *kat' huperbolēn* is transl. "beyond measure" {intensely}: Paul persecuted the church of God beyond measure (Gal. 1:13). The Greek expr. *huperbolē eis huperbolēn* is also transl. "far more exceeding," "far beyond all comparison" in 2 Cor. 4:17. All other refs.: EXCEEDINGLY <5236>, EXCELLENCE <5236>, GREATNESS <5236>.

8 **above measure, beyond measure: *huperperissōs*** [adv.: ὑπερπερισσῶς <5249>]; **from *huper*: above, and *perissōs*: abundantly** ▶ **Excessively, utterly** > The Jews were astonished above measure {were overwhelmed with amazement} by the things Jesus did (Mark 7:37). ¶

9 **beyond, out of, without measure: *ametros*** [adj.: ἄμετρος <280>]; **from *a*: neg., and *metron*: see 4** ▶ **Beyond what is reasonable** > Paul would not boast out of measure (*eis ta ametra*) (2 Cor. 10:13, 15). ¶

– 10 Mark 6:51 → sore, greatly beyond measure → exceedingly beyond measure → EXCEEDINGLY <3029> <1537> <4053> 11 Mark 10:26 → out of measure → EXCEEDINGLY <4057> 12 Rom. 15:29 → full measure → FULLNESS <4138> 13 2 Cor. 2:5 → in some measure → in part (*meros*) 14 2 Cor. 11:23 → above measure → to excess → EXCESS <5234> 15 2 Cor. 12:7a, b → to exalt above measure → EXALT <5229> 16 2 Tim. 4:5 → to fill up the full measure → to make full proof → PROOF <4135> 17 1 Pet. 1:2 → to be in fullest measure → MULTIPLY <4129> 18 Rev. 6:6 → QUART <5518>.

MEASURE (verb) – 1 ***metreō*** [verb: μετρέω <3354>]; **from *metron*: measure** ▶ **To determine the value, to estimate** > With the same measure a person measures {metes, uses}, it will be measured back to him (Matt. 7:2a, b; Mark 4:24a, b; Luke 6:38a). The verb means to esteem oneself in 2 Cor. 10:12. In Revelation 11, John is told to measure the temple of God (v. 1), but not the court which is outside the temple (v. 2). In Revelation 21, a gold reed is used to measure the heavenly Jerusalem (vv. 15, 16) and its wall (v. 17). ¶

2 **to measure; to measure again, back, in return: *antimetreō*** [verb: ἀντιμετρέω <488>]; **from *anti*: in return, and *metreō*: see 1** ▶ **To render the same, to repay** > With the same measure with which a person measures, it will be measured to him again (Matt. 7:2b in some mss.; Luke 6:38b). ¶

MEASURE OF CORN – ***sitometrion*** [neut. noun: σιτομέτριον <4620>]; **from *sitos*: grain, corn, and *metron*: measure** ▶ **Specified measure of grain, ration of food; also transl.: food allowance, portion of food, portion of meat, ration** > The Lord spoke of a steward giving domestic servants their measure of corn (Luke 12:42). ¶

MEASUREMENT – Rev. 21:17 → MEASURE <3358>.

MEAT – [1] Matt. 3:4; 6:25; 10:10; 24:45; Luke 12:23; John 4:8; Acts 2:46; 27:33, 34, 36; Heb. 5:12, 14 → FOOD <5160> [2] Matt. 25:35, 42 → EAT <5315> [3] Luke 3:11; 9:13; Rom. 14:15a, b, 20; 1 Cor. 3:2; et al. → FOOD <1033> [4] Luke 24:41 → FOOD <1034> [5] John 4:32; 6:27a, b, 55 → FOOD <1035> [6] Acts 9:19 → having received meat → lit.: having taken (*lambanō*) nourishment (*trophē*) [7] Rom. 14:21; 1 Cor. 8:13 → FLESH <2907> [8] 1 Cor. 8:10 → to sit at meat → to sit at table → SIT <2621> [9] 1 Cor. 10:25 → meat market → SHAMBLES <3111> [10] Col. 2:16; Rom. 14:17 → EATING <1035>.

MEDDLER – 1 Tim. 5:13 → being a busybody → BUSYBODY <4021>.

MEDE – ***Mēdos*** [masc. name: Μῆδος <3370>] ▶ **Inhabitant of Media, region situated south of the Caspian Sea and east of Palestine** > Medes, i.e., Jews of Media, were present in Jerusalem at Pentecost (Acts 2:9). ¶

MEDIATE – Heb. 8:6 → to be a mediator → MEDIATOR <3316>.

MEDIATOR – ***mesitēs*** [masc. noun: μεσίτης <3316>]; **from *mesos*: middle, and *eimi*: to go** ▶ **Intermediary, conciliator** > Christ is the mediator between God and men (1 Tim. 2:5). Moses was the mediator between God and Israel, having transmitted the divine commandments to this people and having represented this people before God (Gal. 3:19, 20; see Ex. 34:27). In the Epistle to the Hebrews, Jesus is the mediator, i.e., the intermediary guaranteeing a better covenant, for that covenant is one founded upon the glories of His Person and upon the perfection of His work (8:6; 9:15; 12:24). ¶

MEDICATE – Mark 15:23 → to medicate with myrrh → to mingle with myrrh → MINGLE <4669>.

MEDITATE – [1] ***logizomai*** [verb: λογίζομαι <3049>]; **from *logos*: word, reasoning** ▶ **To reckon, to consider** > Paul speaks of things which are true, noble, etc., which we should meditate {think, let the mind dwell} on (Phil. 4:8). All other refs.: see entries in Lexicon at <3049>.

[2] ***meletaō*** [verb: μελετάω <3191>]; **from *meletē*: care, meditation, which is from *melō*: to take care** ▶ **To intend, to plan; also transl.: to devise, to imagine, to plot** > David said that the people had meditated vain things (Acts 4:25). Other refs.: Mark 13:11; 1 Tim. 4:15; see PREMEDITATE <3191>, OCCUPY <3191>. ¶

[3] **to meditate beforehand: *promeletaō*** [verb: προμελετάω <4304>]; **from *pro*: before, and *meletaō*: see [2]** ▶ **To worry in advance, to be distressed in advance** > Jesus told His disciples not to meditate {to prepare, to worry} beforehand {before} their defense (Luke 21:14). ¶

MEEK – [1] ***praus*** [adj.: πραΰς <4239>] ▶ **Who shows gentleness, kindness, forgiveness; also transl.: gentle** > Blessed are the meek, for they will inherit the earth (Matt. 5:5). The Messiah, the King of Israel, came to His people meek {lowly} (Matt. 21:5). Other ref.: 1 Pet. 3:4; see GENTLE <4239>. ¶

– [2] Matt. 11:29 → GENTLE <4235>.

MEEKNESS – [1] ***prautēs*** [fem. noun: πραΰτης <4240>]; **from *praus*: kind, forgiving** ▶ **Humble attitude of the heart and the mind, first before God and then before men; also transl.: gentleness, humility** > We must receive with meekness {humbly} the implanted word which is able to save our souls (Jas. 1:21). Works done in meekness of wisdom are shown by good conduct (Jas. 3:13). Christians must always be ready to respond with meekness and fear to everyone who asks them a reason for the hope that is in them (1 Pet. 3:15). ¶

– [2] 1 Cor. 4:21; 2 Cor. 10:1; Gal. 5:23; 6:1; Eph. 4:2; Col. 3:12; 1 Tim. 6:11; 2 Tim. 2:25; Titus 3:2 → GENTLENESS <4236>.

MEET (adj.) – 1 ***axios*** [adj.: ἄξιος <514>]; **from *agō*: to weigh ▶ Suitable, appropriate, worthy** > Paul had declared to the Gentiles that they should repent and do works meet for {befitting} repentance (Acts 26:20). If it was meet {advisable, fitting} for Paul to go to Jerusalem, he would go (1 Cor. 16:4). Other refs.: DESERVING <514>, FITTING <514>, UNWORTHY <514>, WORTHY <514>.
2 **to make meet: *hikanoō*** [verb: ἱκανόω <2427>]; **from *hikanos*: able, sufficient ▶ To able, to make capable** > The Father has made Christians meet {has made them fit, has qualified them} to be partakers of the inheritance of the saints in light (Col. 1:12). Other ref.: 2 Cor. 3:6 (to make competent); COMPETENT <2427>. ¶
3 **it is meet: *esti*** [verb: εστι <2076>] ***kalos*** [καλός <2570>] **▶ To be suitable, lit.: to be good** > Jesus told a woman it was not meet {good, right, well} to take the children's bread and throw it to the little dogs (Matt. 15:26; Mark 7:27).
– 4 1 Cor. 15:9 → WORTHY <2425> 5 2 Tim. 2:21 → USEFUL <2173> 6 Heb. 6:7 → USEFUL <2111>.

MEET (verb) – 1 ***apantaō*** [verb: ἀπαντάω <528>]; **from *apo*: from, and *antaō*: to encounter, meet ▶ To encounter from opposite directions, to come face to face** > Jesus met the women who went to announce His resurrection (Matt. 28:9). A man would meet the disciples to show them the place where they might eat the Passover (Mark 14:13). Ten leprous men met Jesus (Luke 17:12). The servants of the nobleman met him and told him that his son was living (John 4:51). A slave girl, having a spirit of divination, met Paul (Acts 16:16). Other refs. in some mss.: Mark 5:2; Luke 14:31; other mss. have *hupantaō*; see 3. ¶
2 ***sunantaō*** [verb: συναντάω <4876>]; **from *sun*: together, and *antaō*: see 1 ▶ To come together, to come face to face with someone** > For the same occasion as of Mark 14:13 (see 1), Luke uses this verb (Luke 22:10). A great crowd met the Lord (Luke 9:37). Melchizedek met Abraham (Heb. 7:1, 10). Cornelius met Peter (Acts 10:25). Other ref.: Acts 20:22; see BEFALL <4876>. ¶
3 ***hupantaō*** [verb: ὑπαντάω <5221>]; **from *hupo*: under, and *antaō*: see 1 ▶ a. To encounter with hostility, to resist** > A king who goes to war against another king deliberates whether he is able to meet {to encounter, to oppose} the one coming against him (Luke 14:31). **b. To come toward (with the nuance: furtively or secretly)** > Two demoniacs met Jesus (Matt. 8:28), as well as a man possessed by an unclean spirit (Mark 5:2) and a demoniac (Luke 8:27). Martha went and met Jesus (John 11:20). Jesus was in the place where Martha came to meet Him (John 11:30). Many people met Jesus after the resurrection of Lazarus (John 12:18). ¶
4 **to meet, to meet with: *sumballō*** [συμβάλλω <4820>]; **from *sun*: together, and *ballō*: to cast ▶ To encounter** > Paul met with Luke and others at Assos (Acts 20:14). Other refs.: Luke 14:31; Acts 17:18 {to encounter, to converse with}. All other refs.: CONFER <4820>, HELP (verb) <4820>, PONDER <4820>.
5 **meeting: *apantēsis*** [fem. noun: ἀπάντησις <529>]; **from *apantaō*: to encounter, which is from *apo*: from, and *antaō*: to meet ▶ Encounter of people** > The virgins of the parable went forth to meet (lit.: a meeting of) the bridegroom (Matt. 25:1, 6). The brothers came to meet (lit.: to the meeting of) Paul and others (Acts 28:15). Christians will be caught up together to meet (lit.: a meeting of) the Lord in the air when He returns (1 Thes. 4:17). ¶
6 ***paratunchanō*** [verb: παρατυγχάνω <3909>]; **from *para*: near, and *tunchanō*: to happen ▶ To be found (perhaps fortuitously) in a place** > Paul reasoned in the marketplace of Athens with those he met {who happened to be there} (Acts 17:17). ¶
7 **meeting: *sunantēsis*** [fem. noun: συνάντησις <4877>]; **from *sunantaō*: to meet, which is from *sun*: together, and *antaō*: to meet ▶ Encounter of people** > This word is found in Matt. 8:34; see 8. ¶
8 **meeting: *hupantēsis*** [fem. noun: ὑπάντησις <5222>]; **from *hupantaō*: to come opposite, which is from *hupo*: under, and**

***antaō*: to meet ▶ See 7. >** The whole city came out to meet (lit.: to the meeting of) Jesus (Matt. 8:34); other mss. have *sunantēsis*. The people went out to meet {to the meeting of} Jesus (John 12:13). Other ref.: Matt. 25:1 in some mss.; see 5. ¶
– 9 Matt. 28:12; Luke 22:66; John 18:2; Acts 4:6 (or v. 5), 27, 31; 11:26; 15:6; 20:8 → to meet, to meet with, to meet together → GATHER <4863> 10 Mark 11:4 → place where two ways met → PLACE (noun) <296> 11 Mark 14:53; Acts 16:13; 21:22; 1 Cor. 11:20, 34 → to come together → COME <4905> 12 Acts 27:41 → where two seas meet → SEA <1337> 13 2 Cor. 13:5 → to fail to meet the test → lit.: to be worthless → WORTHLESS <96> 14 2 Cor. 13:7 → appear to have met the test → appear approved → APPROVE <1384> 15 Gal. 2:2 → "meeting" added in Engl. 16 Phil. 4:19 → SUPPLY (verb) <4137> 17 Heb. 10:25 → to meet together → ASSEMBLING <1997> 18 Jas. 1:2 → to fall into → FALL (verb) <4045>.

MEETING – 1 John 11:47 → to call a meeting → GATHER <4863> 2 1 Cor. 11:17 → your meetings → lit.: you come together → COME <4905> 3 Heb. 10:25 → ASSEMBLING <1997>.

MELCHI – ***Melchi*** [masc. name: Μελχί <3197>]**: my king, in Heb. ▶ Name of two men of the O.T.; also transl.: Melki >** These men named Melchi are mentioned in the genealogy of Jesus (Luke 3:24, 28). ¶

MELCHISEDEC – See MELCHIZEDEK <3198>.

MELCHIZEDEK – 1 ***Melchisedek*** [masc. name: Μελχισέδεκ <3198>]**: king of righteousness, in Heb. ▶ King and priest of the O.T.; also transl.: Melchisedec >** Melchizedek blessed Abraham and the Most High God after the victory of Abraham over the kings (Heb. 7:1, 10; see Gen. 14:13–20). The Son of God is a priest forever according to the order of Melchizedek (Heb. 5:6, 10; 6:20; 7:11, 15, 17, 21). The priesthood of Christ during the millennium will be a priesthood of blessing, according to the order of Melchizedek (see Ps. 110:4). ¶
– 2 Heb. 7:2 → the name Melchizedek means → lit.: being translated.

MELEA – ***Meleas*** [masc. name: Μελεᾶς <3190>] **▶ Man of the O.T.; also transl.: Meleas >** Melea is mentioned in the genealogy of Jesus (Luke 3:31). ¶

MELEAS – See MELEA <3190>.

MELITA – See MALTA <3194>.

MELKI – See MELCHI <3197>.

MELODY – Eph. 5:19 → to make melody → SING <5567>.

MELT – 1 ***tēkō*** [verb: τήκω <5080>] **▶ To liquefy under the effect of heat >** At the end of the millennium, the heavens, being on fire, will be dissolved and the elements will melt with burning heat (2 Pet. 3:12). ¶
– 2 2 Pet. 3:10 → DISSOLVE <3089>.

MEMBER – 1 ***melos*** [neut. noun: μέλος <3196>] **▶ Part of the human body attached to the trunk, or any part of the body >** The word is used in the lit. sense in Matt. 5:29, 30; Rom. 6:13, 19; 7:5, 23a, b; Col. 3:5; Jas. 3:5, 6; 4:1. In the spiritual sense, the bodies of Christians are members of Christ (1 Cor. 6:15a–c); they are members one of another (Rom. 12:4a, b, 5; Eph. 4:25). Christians are members of the mystical body of Christ (1 Cor. 12:27; Eph. 5:30), and as such they have different functions (1 Cor. 12:12a, b, 14, 18–20, 22, 25, 26a–d, 27). ¶
– 2 Mark 15:43; Luke 23:50 → council member → COUNSELLOR, COUNSELOR <1010> 3 Acts 7:54 → "members of the Sanhedrin" added in Engl. 4 Acts 13:1 → member of the court → lit. brought up with → BRING <4939> 5 Acts 22:30 → all the members of the Sanhedrin → lit.: all the Sanhedrin 6 Rom. 11:1; 1 Tim. 5:8 → added in Engl. 7 Eph. 3:6 → fellow member of the body → same body → BODY <4954>.

MEMORIAL – ***mnēmosunon*** [neut. noun: μνημόσυνον <3422>]; **from *mnēmoneuō*: to remember, which is from *mnēmōn*: who remembers ▶ Commemoration of a person or an object** > The word is used in regard to the woman who poured perfume on the head of Jesus (Matt. 26:13 and Mark 14:9 {memory}). The prayers and alms of Cornelius had gone up as a memorial {a memorial offering} before God (Acts 10:4). ¶

MEMORY – [1] Matt. 26:13; Mark 14:9 → MEMORIAL <3422> [2] 1 Cor. 15:2 → to keep in memory → FAST (HOLD) <2722> [3] 2 Pet. 1:13 → by refreshing their memory → lit.: by memory → REMEMBRANCE <5280>.

MEN-PLEASER – ***anthrōpareskos*** [adj. used as noun: ἀνθρωπάρεσκος <441>]; **from *anthrōpos*: human being, and *areskō*: to please ▶ Seeking human approval, favor (rather than of God)** > Paul exhorted to serve not as men-pleasers (Eph. 6:6). Bondmen are to obey their masters not as men-pleasers (Col. 3:22). ¶

MENAN – See MENNA <3104>.

MEND – ***katartizō*** [verb: καταρτίζω <2675>]; **from *kata*: with, and *artizō*: to adjust, which is from *artios*: fit, complete ▶ To repair, to put in order** > James and John were mending {were preparing} their nets when Jesus called them (Matt. 4:21; Mark 1:19). All other refs.: see entries in Lexicon at <2675>.

MENNA – ***Mainan*** [masc. name: Μαϊνάν <3104>] **▶ Man of the O.T.; also transl.: Menan** > His name is mentioned in the genealogy of Jesus (Luke 3:31). ¶

MENSTEALER – 1 Tim. 1:10 → KIDNAPPER <405>.

MENTAL – 1 Pet. 2:2 → INTELLECTUAL <3050>.

MENTION (noun) – [1] ***mneia*** [fem. noun: μνεία <3417>]; **from *mnaomai*: to remember, to recall ▶ In the N.T., to make mention is to name, to remember in prayer** > Paul made mention unceasingly of {remembered constantly} the believers of Rome in his prayers (Rom. 1:9). He also made mention of the Ephesians (Eph. 1:16 {to remember}), the Thessalonians (1 Thes. 1:2 {to mention}), and Philemon (Phm. 4 {to remember}). All other refs.: REMEMBRANCE <3417>.

[2] **to make mention: *mnēmoneuō*** [verb: μνημονεύω <3421>]; **from *mnaomai*: see [1] ▶ To evoke, to speak of** > Joseph made mention of {called to mind, spoke about} the departure of the children of Israel out of Egypt (Heb. 11:22). All other refs.: REMEMBER <3421>.

MENTION (verb) – 1 Thes. 1:2 → lit.: to make mention → MENTION (noun) <3417>.

MERCHANDISE – [1] ***gomos*** [masc. noun: γόμος <1117>]; **from *gemō*: to be full ▶ Cargo (of a ship), load; wares, every product which is sold** > After the fall of Babylon, no one will buy anymore the merchandise of the merchants who did business with her (Rev. 18:11, 12). Other ref.: Acts 21:3; see BURDEN (noun) <1117>. ¶
– [2] Matt. 22:5 → BUSINESS <1711> [3] Mark 11:16 → VESSEL[1] <4632> [4] John 2:16 → BUSINESS <1712> [5] 2 Pet. 2:3 → to make merchandise → EXPLOIT <1710>.

MERCHANT – ***emporos*** [masc. noun: ἔμπορος <1713>]; **from *en*: in, and *poros*: passage, voyage; originally: a passenger on board a boat, a commercial traveler ▶ A person who buys for resale in order to make a profit** > Jesus compares the kingdom of God to a merchant who is seeking beautiful pearls (Matt. 13:45). Merchants will do business with Babylon the great (Rev. 18:3, 11, 15, 23). ¶

MERCIFUL – [1] ***eleēmōn*** [adj.: ἐλεήμων <1655>]; **from *eleos*: compassion, mercy**

▶ Manifesting compassion for the misery of others > The merciful will find mercy (Matt. 5:7). Jesus Christ is a merciful and faithful High Priest (Heb. 2:17). ¶

[2] ***hileōs*** [adj.: ἵλεως <2436>]; **from *hilaos*: appeased, favorable ▶ Compassionate, clement >** The Lord says He will be merciful to the unrighteousness of the house of Israel (Heb. 8:12). Other ref.: Matt. 16:22; see FAVORABLE <2436>. ¶

[3] **to be merciful: *hilaskomai*** [verb: ἱλάσκομαι <2433>]; **from *hilaos*: see [2] ▶ To be favorable toward someone, to have compassion, to have mercy >** The publican asked God to be merciful to him a sinner (Luke 18:13). Other ref.: Heb. 2:17 (to make propitiation); see PROPITIATION <2433>. ¶

[4] ***oiktirmōn*** [adj.: οἰκτίρμων <3629>]; **from *oikteirō*: to have compassion, which is from *oiktos*: pity ▶ Showing sympathy for the misery of others >** Christians should be merciful just as their Father also is merciful (Luke 6:36a, b). The Lord is merciful {full of mercy, of tender mercy, pitiful} (Jas. 5:11). ¶

– [5] Luke 1:54; Jas. 2:13b → MERCY <1656> [6] Jude 22 → to be merciful → to have compassion → COMPASSION <1653>.

MERCILESS – Jas. 2:13 → without mercy → MERCY <448>.

MERCURIUS – See HERMES <2060>.

MERCURY – See HERMES <2060>.

MERCY – [1] ***eleos*** [neut. noun: ἔλεος <1656>] **▶ Compassion for the misery of others, forbearing disposition exercised toward others >** It supposes a need for help on the part of the one who is its object, and a movement of the heart on the part of the one responding to the need: God is rich in mercy (Eph. 2:4); He saves according to His own mercy (Titus 3:5). Mary, the mother of Jesus, exalted the mercy of God, her Savior (Luke 1:50, 54 {merciful}, 58); likewise, Zacharias exalted the mercy of the Lord God of Israel (Luke 1:72, 78). God expects man to exercise mercy (Matt. 9:13 and 12:7 {compassion}; 23:23; Luke 10:37; Jas. 2:13b {merciful}, c). Christians look for the mercy of the Lord Jesus Christ unto eternal life (Jude 21). Other refs.: Rom. 9:23; 11:31a; 15:9; Gal. 6:16; 1 Tim. 1:2; 2 Tim. 1:2, 16, 18; Heb. 4:16; Jas. 3:17; 1 Pet. 1:3; 2 John 3; Jude 2. ¶

[2] **to be object of, to enjoy, to find, to have, to obtain, to receive, to show mercy: *eleeō*** [verb: ἐλεέω <1653>]; **from *eleos*: see [1] ▶ To show or be given compassion for the misery of others; also transl.: to have compassion >** The merciful will find mercy (Matt. 5:7). Jesus had mercy on a demoniac and healed him (Mark 5:19). God shows mercy on whom He will show mercy (Rom. 9:15a, b, 16: *eleaō* in some mss., 18). The Christians in Rome had been objects of mercy (Rom. 11:30, 31b, 32). He who shows mercy should do so with cheerfulness (Rom. 12:8). Mercy was shown to Paul (1 Tim. 1:13, 16). Other refs.: Matt. 9:27; 15:22; 17:15; 18:33; 20:30, 31; Mark 10:47, 48; Luke 16:24; 17:13; 18:38, 39; 1 Cor. 7:25; 2 Cor. 4:1; Phil. 2:27; 1 Pet. 2:10a, b. Other ref.: Jude 22; see COMPASSION <1653>. ¶

[3] ***oiktirmos*** [masc. noun: οἰκτιρμός <3628>]; **from *oikterō*: to have compassion, which is from *oiktos*: compassion, pity ▶ Compassion; attitude of one seeking to respond to the needs of others, to relieve their sufferings >** God is the Father of mercies (2 Cor. 1:3). Paul besought the Christians in Rome by the mercies of God to present their bodies a living sacrifice (Rom. 12:1); he uses the same word concerning the mercies in Christ (Phil. 2:1). The Christian is to put on tender mercies {compassionate hearts} (Col. 3:12). In Heb. 10:28, it is written that anyone who has disregarded Moses' law dies without mercy. ¶

[4] **without mercy: *aneleos*** [adj.: ἀνέλεος <448>]; **from *a*: neg., and *eleos*: see [1] ▶ Without compassion or forbearance for the misery of others >** Judgment will be without mercy {merciless} to one who has shown no mercy (Jas. 2:13a). ¶

– [5] Luke 18:13 → to have mercy → to be merciful → MERCIFUL <2433> [6] Rom. 1:31 → to have no mercy → to be implacable → IMPLACABLE <786> [7] Jas. 5:11 → full of mercy, of tender mercy → MERCIFUL <3629>.

MERCY SEAT – ***hilastērion*** [neut. noun: ἱλαστήριον <2435>]; **from *hilaskomai*: to be propitious, to be gracious, which is from *hilaōs*: favorable, propitious; also spelled: mercy-seat, mercyseat ▶ a. Cover of the ark surmounted by cherubim** > The cherubim of glory overshadowed the mercy-seat (Heb. 9:5). Once a year, on the day of atonement, the high priest entered the most holy place and sprinkled the blood of the sacrifice for sin, before and upon the mercy seat {atonement cover} (see Lev. 16). **b. He who is invested with propitiatory power** > The root of the Heb. word signifies "to cover" (see Ps. 32:1), whence the application to Christ: God sets Him forth as the mercy seat {propitiation, sacrifice of atonement} for the benefit of those who believe in the efficacy of the blood shed on the cross to cover their sins (Rom. 3:25). ¶

MERE – [1] 1 Cor. 15:37 → BARE <1131> [2] Titus 1:10 → mere talker → idle talker → TALKER <3151> [3] Heb. 8:2 → mere human being → lit.: man.

MERELY – [1] Rom. 4:12 → only (*monon*) [2] Col. 2:22 → "merely" added in Engl. [3] 1 Tim. 5:13; Jas. 1:22 → ONLY <3440>.

MERRY – [1] **to be merry, to make merry: *euphrainō*** [verb: εὐφραίνω <2165>]; **from *euphrōn*: cheerful, which is from *eu*: well, and *phrēn*: mind ▶ To rejoice, to feast; also transl.: to celebrate** > In a parable, a man who had many goods laid up wanted to be merry (Luke 12:19). People made merry when the prodigal son came back (Luke 15:23, 24, 32), which the older son did not appreciate (v. 29). In another parable, a certain rich man made merry {fared, lived gaily, made good cheer} in splendor {fared sumptuously} every day (Luke 16:19). All other refs.: REJOICE <2165>.

– [2] Jas. 5:13 → to be merry → to be happy → HAPPY <2114>.

MESOPOTAMIA – ***Mesopotamia*** [fem. name: Μεσοποταμία <3318>]: **region between rivers ▶ Region situated between the rivers Euphrates and Tigris northeast of Palestine** > Abraham was in Mesopotamia when God appeared to him (Acts 7:2). Jews of Mesopotamia were present in Jerusalem at Pentecost (Acts 2:9). ¶

MESSAGE – [1] ***angelia*** [fem. noun: ἀγγελία <31>]; **from *angellos*: messenger ▶ Communication transmitted to a person, announcement** > John heard a message regarding the fact that God is light (1 John 1:5); other mss.: *epangelia* <1860>. His readers heard the message that they should love one another (3:11). ¶

[2] ***logos*** [masc. noun: λόγος <3056>]; **from *legō*: to say, to speak ▶ Speech, discourse** > Paul continued his message {kept on talking} until midnight (Acts 20:7). Other refs.: WORD <3056>.

– [3] Mark 1:7 → this was his message → lit.: he preached, saying → PREACH <2784> [4] Luke 19:14 → DELEGATION <4242> [5] John 12:38; Rom. 10:16 → REPORT (noun) <189> [6] Acts 26:23 → to bring the message → PREACH <2605> [7] Rom. 10:8 → WORD <4487> [8] Rom. 16:25 → "message" added in Engl.

MESSENGER – [1] ***angelos*** [masc. noun: ἄγγελος <32>] ▶ **Person sent by another and charged with a mission; frequently of transmitting a message** > John the Baptist was a messenger of God, charged to prepare the way before Jesus Christ (Matt. 11:10; Mark 1:2; Luke 7:27). John himself sent messengers to Jesus to know if He was the Christ (Luke 7:24). Jesus sent messengers ahead of Himself to Jerusalem (Luke 9:52). In O.T. times, Rahab received the messengers {spies} (Jas. 2:25), i.e., the spies sent by Israel into Canaan (see Joshua 2). A messenger of Satan buffeted Paul (2 Cor. 12:7). All other refs.: ANGEL <32>.

– [2] John 13:16a; 2 Cor. 8:23; Phil. 2:25 → he who is sent → SENT <652>.

MESSIAH – ***Messias*** [masc. name: Μεσσίας <3323>]: **who is anointed, consecrated, in**

Heb. ▶ **One of the titles of the Lord Jesus; see CHRIST** <5547> > Andrew told Peter that he and another had found the Messiah (John 1:41). The woman at the well of Sychar knew that the Messiah, who is called Christ, was coming (John 4:25). ¶

METALWORKER – 2 Tim. 4:14 → COPPERSMITH <5471>.

METE – Matt. 7:2a; Mark 4:24a; Luke 6:38a → MEASURE (verb) <3354>.

METHOD – Luke 1:3 → with method → in order → ORDER (noun) <2517>.

METHUSALA – See METHUSELAH <3103>.

METHUSELAH – ***Mathousala*** [masc. name: Μαθουσάλα <3103>]**: man of the dart, in Heb.; see Gen. 5:25 ▶ Man of the O.T.; also transl.: Mathusala, Methusala** > Methuselah is mentioned in the genealogy of Jesus (Luke 3:37). This son of Enoch had the longest human life span recorded in the Bible: 969 years (see Gen. 5:27). ¶

METROPOLIS – ***mētropolis*** [fem. noun.: μητρόπολις <3390>]**; from *mētēr*: mother, and *polis*: city ▶ Mother city or principal city** > The word is found only in the spurious subscription following 1 Tim. 6:21. ¶ ‡

MICHAEL – ***Michaēl*** [masc. name: Μιχαήλ <3413>]**: who is like God?, in Heb. ▶ Archangel of God** > He is seen disputing with the devil concerning the body of Moses (Jude 9). Michael is also mentioned by Daniel (see Dan. 10:13, 21; 12:1) in regard to the assistance provided to the people of Israel in their battles. Michael and his angels will wage war against Satan and his angels; the latter will be thrown down to the earth and will persecute Israel (Rev. 12:7; see vv. 8, 9). ¶

MID-DAY – Acts 22:6 → NOON <3314>.

MIDAIR – Rev. 8:13; 14:6; 19:17 → midst of heaven → HEAVEN <3321>.

MIDDAY – Acts 26:13 → at midday → lit.: about the middle (*mesos*) of the day (*hēmera*). All other refs. (*mesos*): MIDST <3319>.

MIDDLE – [1] **to be the middle: *mesoō*** [verb: μεσόω <3322>]**; from *mesos*: middle ▶ To be midway in point of time** > When it was the middle {halfway, midst} of the feast, Jesus went up into the temple (John 7:14); *mesazō* in other mss.: to be at mid-point. ¶
– [2] Matt. 14:24; Mark 6:47; Acts 1:18; Rev. 22:2 → in the middle → in the midst → MIDST <3319> [3] Luke 12:38 → in the middle of the night → lit.: in the second watch → SECOND <1208>, WATCH (noun) <5438>.

MIDHEAVEN – Rev. 8:13; 14:6; 19:17 → midst of heaven → HEAVEN <3321>.

MIDIAN – ***Madiam*** [masc. name: Μαδιάμ <3099>]**: strife, in Heb. ▶ Country northeast of the Red Sea; also transl.: Madiam, Madian** > Moses fled to the land of Midian, where he became the father of two sons (Acts 7:29). ¶

MIDNIGHT – [1] ***mesonuktion*** [neut. noun: μεσονύκτιον <3317>]**; from *mesos*: middle, and *nux*: night ▶ Middle of the night** > The master of the house might come at midnight (Mark 13:35). A man might go to his friend at midnight and ask him to lend him three loaves of bread (Luke 11:5). At midnight, Paul and Silas were praying and praising God with singing (Acts 16:25). Paul prolonged his message until midnight (Acts 20:7). ¶
– [2] Matt. 25:6; Acts 27:27 → at midnight, about midnight → in the midst → MIDST <3319>.

MIDST – [1] **in the midst, into the midst: *mesos*** [adj.: μέσος <3319>] **▶ Used with a prep. such as *en* or *eis* to give the sense of "in the midst," this term means: among, in the center** > The Lord Jesus is in the midst of two or three gathered to His name (Matt. 18:20). The word is also transl. "among," "in the middle," etc. Other refs.: Matt. 10:16; 13:25, 49; 14:6, 24; 18:2; 25:6; Mark 3:3; 6:47; 7:31; 9:36; 14:60; Luke 2:46; 4:30, 35; 5:19; 6:8; 8:7; 10:3; 17:11; 21:21; 22:27, 55a, b; 23:45; 24:36; John 1:26; 8:3, 9, 59; 19:18; 20:19, 26; Acts 1:15, 18; 2:22; 4:7; 17:22, 33; 23:10; 26:13; 27:21, 27; 1 Cor. 5:2; 6:5; 2 Cor. 6:17; Phil. 2:15; Col. 2:14; 1 Thes. 2:7; 2 Thes. 2:7; Heb. 2:12; Rev. 1:13; 2:1, 7; 4:6; 5:6a, b; 6:6; 7:17; 22:2. ¶

– [2] John 7:14 → to be the midst → to be the middle → MIDDLE <3322> [3] Rev. 8:13; 14:6; 19:17 → midst of heaven → HEAVEN <3321>.

MIGHT – [1] ***kratos*** [neut. noun: κράτος <2904>] ▶ **Strength, sovereign power; also transl.: dominion, power** > The word of the Lord increased with might {grew mightily, spread widely} (Acts 19:20). The glory and the might {dominion, power} are attributed to Jesus Christ (1 Pet. 4:11) and to God (5:11). The power (*dunamis*) of God is exercised toward Christians according to the working of the might (*kratos*) of His strength (Eph. 1:19). The Christian is to be strong in the Lord and in the might of His strength (Eph. 6:10). To God be honor and eternal might {dominion, power} (1 Tim. 6:16), and might and authority (Jude 25). To Jesus be the glory and the might (Rev. 1:6). To Him who sits on the throne and to the Lamb is the might (Rev. 5:13). Paul was praying that the Colossians would be strengthened with all power according to the might of God's glory (Col. 1:11). Other refs.: Luke 1:51; Heb. 2:14; see STRENGTH <2904>, POWER[3] <2904>. ¶

– [2] Acts 18:28 → with great force → VIGOROUSLY <2159> [3] 2 Cor. 1:8 → STRENGTH <1411> [4] Eph. 1:21 → POWER[3] <1411> [5] 2 Thes. 1:9; 2 Pet. 2:11; Rev. 5:12; 7:12 → STRENGTH <2479>.

MIGHT BE – ***eiēn*** [verb: εἴην <1498>] ▶ Pres. optative form of *eimi*: to be. Refs.: Luke 1:29; 3:15; 8:9; 9:46; 15:26; 18:36; 22:23; John 13:24; Acts 8:20; 10:17; 21:33; Rev. 3:15. ¶ ‡

MIGHTILY – [1] Acts 18:28 → VIGOROUSLY <2159> [2] Acts 19:20 → lit.: with might → MIGHT <2904>.

MIGHTY (adj.) – [1] ***dunatos*** [adj.: δυνατός <1415>]; **from *dunamai*: to be able, to be powerful** ▶ **Strong, capable; also transl.: able, powerful** > This word is used in regard to the Lord Jesus (Luke 24:19; Rom. 14:4), Moses (Acts 7:22), Apollos (Acts 18:24 {competent}), God (Rom. 4:21; 11:23; 2 Cor. 9:8), the spiritual arms of Christians (2 Cor. 10:4), and the Corinthians (2 Cor. 13:9). All other refs.: see entries in Lexicon at <1415>.

[2] ***ischuros*** [adj.: ἰσχυρός <2478>]; **from *ischuō*: to be able, which is from *ischus*: might, strength** ▶ **Powerful, strong, valiant** > John the Baptist described Jesus, who was about to begin His public ministry, as mightier than himself (Matt. 3:11; Mark 1:7; Luke 3:16). The Greek word also describes the Lord God (Rev. 18:8) and angels (5:2; 10:1; 18:21). In Revelation, the birds gather together to eat the flesh of mighty men (lit.: the mighty) (Rev. 19:18). All other refs.: GREAT <2478>, MAN <2478>, STRONG (adj.) <2478>.

[3] ***krataios*** [adj.: κραταιός <2900>]; **from *kratos*: strength, power** ▶ **Strong, powerful** > Word which qualifies the hand of God (1 Pet. 5:6). ¶

– [4] Matt. 7:22; 11:20, 21, 23; 13:54, 58; 14:2; Mark 6:2, 5, 14; 9:39; Luke 10:13; 19:37; Acts 2:22; 2 Cor. 12:12 → mighty work, might deed → MIRACLE <1411> [5] Luke 1:49; 1 Cor. 1:26 → POWERFUL <1415> [6] Luke 1:51 → mighty deeds → STRENGTH <2904> [7] Acts 2:2 → VIOLENT <972> [8] Acts 13:17 → mighty power → lit.: uplifted arm → UPLIFTED <5308> [9] 2 Cor. 13:3 → to be mighty → to be powerful → POWERFUL <1414> [10] Gal. 2:8b → to be mighty → WORK (verb) <1754> [11] Eph. 1:19; 6:10 → His mighty strength → lit.: the strength of His might → MIGHT <2904>.

MIGHTY (noun) – [1] Luke 1:52 → the mighty → rulers → RULER <1413> [2] Rev. 6:15 → STRONG (noun) <1415>.

MILD – 1 Tim. 3:3; Titus 3:2 → GENTLE <1933>.

MILE – 1 ***milion*** [neut. noun: μίλιον <3400>]; ***mille*, in Lat.: thousand, a measure of distance equivalent to 1,000 *passus* or paces ► Roman measure of distance of approx. 1,480 meters (1,611 yards)** > Jesus says if someone compels us to go one mile, we should go with him two (Matt. 5:41). ¶
– 2 See STADION.

MILETUS – ***Milētos*** [fem. name: Μίλητος <3399>] ► **City located in the southwest of Asia Minor, south of Ephesus** > Paul came to Miletus and called the elders of Ephesus to a meeting, and prayed with them during his third missionary journey (Acts 20:15, 17; see v. 36). He left Trophimus sick there. (2 Tim. 4:20). ¶

MILITARY – 1 Mark 6:21 → military commander → CAPTAIN <5506> 2 Acts 23:27 → TROOP <4753>.

MILK – ***gala*** [neut. noun: γάλα <1051>]; ***lac*, in Lat. ► White liquid secreted by the mammary glands** > He who tends a flock eats of the milk of the flock (1 Cor. 9:7). Figur., milk also symbolizes the word of God (1 Pet. 2:2), and in particular the first principles of the word of God (1 Cor. 3:2; Heb. 5:12, 13). ¶

MILL – 1 ***mulōn*** [masc. noun: μύλων <3459>] ► **Very heavy stone cylinder used to grind; some believe it is a hand mill; poss. a mill-house** > At the Lord's return before establishing His kingdom (see vv. 36–40), two women will be grinding at the mill; one will be taken and one will be left (Matt. 24:41); other mss. have *mulos*: millstone. ¶
– 2 Mark 9:42 → stone of a mill → MILLSTONE <3457> 3 Rev. 18:22 → MILLSTONE <3458>.

MILLION – Rev. 9:16 → two hundred million → twice ten thousand times ten thousand → MYRIAD <3461>.

MILLSTONE – 1 ***mulos*** [masc. noun: μύλος <3458>]; **from *mulē*: mill ► Very heavy stone cylinder used to grind** > Speaking of one who causes a young believer in the Lord to sin, Jesus says it would be better for him that a great millstone be hung around his neck and he be drowned in the depths of the sea (Matt. 18:6; Luke 17:2). Certain mss. have "stone of a mill" (*lithos mulikos*) in Luke 17:2. Babylon will be thrown into the sea like a great millstone (Rev. 18:21; some mss. have *mulinos*: made of millstone); the sound of a millstone {mill} will no longer be heard in this city (v. 22). ¶
2 **of a mill: *mulikos*** [adj.: μυλικός <3457>]; **from *mulē*: mill ► Belonging to a mill** > Jesus said in regard to whoever causes one of the little ones who believes in Him to stumble, that it would be better for him if a millstone (lit.: stone of a mill) were hung around his neck and he were thrown into the sea (Mark 9:42; some mss.: *mulos*). ¶

MINA – ***mna*** [fem. noun: μνᾶ <3414>] ► **Measure of weight and of money amounting to approx. 100 Greek drachmas or 100 Roman denarii; one mina weighed slightly less than 500 grams** > Jesus told a parable of a nobleman who gave a mina {pound} to each of his ten servants so that they might gain more by trading (Luke 19:13, 16a, b, 18a, b, 20, 24a, b, 25). ¶

MIND (noun) – 1 ***gnōmē*** [fem. noun: γνώμη <1106>]; **from *ginoskō*: to know, to understand ► a. Thought, advice** > Paul would do nothing without the mind {consent} of Philemon (Phm. 14). **b. Intention, plan** > The ten kings have one mind {purpose} (Rev. 17:13); God has given to their hearts to do His mind {will, purpose}, and to act with one mind {to agree, to have a common purpose} (v. 17a, b). All other refs.: ADVICE <1106>, JUDGMENT <1106>, OPINION <1106>, PURPOSE (verb) <1106>.
2 ***dianoia*** [fem. noun: διάνοια <1271>]; **from *dia*: denotes separation, and *noos*: intelligence, thought ► Intelligence, understanding, ability to think** > Unbelievers

have their mind darkened (Eph. 4:18) and are enemies of God in their mind (Col. 1:21). God will put His laws in the mind of the people of Israel (Heb. 8:10), and will write them in their minds (10:16). While waiting for the revelation of Jesus Christ, Christians must gird up the loins of their mind (1 Pet. 1:13). Peter stirred up the pure mind {thinking} of the beloved ones to whom he wrote (2 Pet. 3:1). The Son of God has given an understanding to Christians so they may know Him who is true (1 John 5:20). All other refs.: UNDERSTANDING <1271>.

3 ***ennoia*** [fem. noun: ἔννοια <1771>]; **from *en*: in, and *nous*: spirit ▶ Consideration, conviction** > The Christian is to arm himself with the same mind {attitude, purpose} as Christ, for he who has suffered in the flesh has done with sin (1 Pet. 4:1). Other ref.: Heb. 4:12; see INTENT <1771>. ¶

4 ***noēma*** [neut. noun: νόημα <3540>]; **from *noeō*: to understand, to perceive, which is from *nous*: mind, understanding ▶ Thought, plan** > The minds of the sons of Israel were blinded (2 Cor. 3:14). All other refs.: DEVICE <3540>, THOUGHT <3540>.

5 ***nous*** [masc. noun: νοῦς <3563>] ▶ **Understanding, as well as perception and judgment** > God gave over evil men to a reprobate mind as they did not think it good to have God in their knowledge (Rom. 1:28). The law of sin may war against the law of the mind (Rom. 7:23), but with the mind one may serve the law of God (v. 25). Paul asked who has known the mind of the Lord (Rom. 11:34; 1 Cor. 2:16a). Christians are transformed by the renewing of their mind (Rom. 12:2); they are renewed in the spirit of their mind (Eph. 4:23). Paul speaks of being persuaded in one's own mind concerning matters of faith (Rom. 14:5). He exhorted the Corinthians to be perfectly united in the same mind and in the same judgment (1 Cor. 1:10). He himself had the mind of Christ (1 Cor. 2:16b). The Ephesians were no longer to walk as the rest of the nations walk in the vanity of their mind {thinking} (Eph. 4:17). The word of God mentions men corrupted in mind (1 Tim. 6:5; 2 Tim. 3:8); their mind and conscience are defiled (Titus 1:15). Other refs.: Col. 2:18 {notion}; 2 Thes. 2:2 {composure}; Rev. 17:9. All other refs.: UNDERSTANDING <3563>.

6 **fervent mind: *zēlos*** [masc. noun: ζῆλος <2205>]; **from *zeō*: to be hot, to be fervent ▶ Zeal, enthusiasm** > Titus had told Paul about the fervent mind {ardent concern, zeal} of the Corinthians for him (2 Cor. 7:7). All other refs.: ENVY (noun) <2205>, HEAT <2205>, JEALOUSY <2205>, ZEAL <2205>.

7 **ready mind: *prothumia*** [fem. noun: προθυμία <4288>]; **from *prothumos*: ready, which is from *pro*: before, and *thumos*: spirit, ardor ▶ Willingness, zealousness** > A brother had been chosen to travel with Paul with the gift of the Corinthians showing the ready mind {readiness, eagerness to help} of the two (some mss.: the ready mind of the Corinthians) (2 Cor. 8:19). Other refs.: Acts 17:11; 2 Cor. 8:11, 12; 9:2; see READINESS <4288>. ¶

8 **sound mind: *sōphronismos*** [masc. noun: σωφρονισμός <4995>]; **from *sōphronizō*; to admonish by encouraging sound judgment, which is from *sōphrōn*: sober, temperate ▶ Sober, moderated, rational mind** > God has given to Christians a spirit of a sound mind {discipline, self-discipline, wise discretion} (2 Tim. 1:7). ¶

9 ***phronēma*** [neut. noun: φρόνημα <5427>]; **from *phroneō*: see 10 ▶ What one has in thought, in one's spirit** > The mind of the flesh is death; but the mind of the Spirit is life and peace (Rom. 8:6a, b). The mind of the flesh is enmity against God (Rom. 8:7). He who searches the hearts knows what the mind of the Spirit is (Rom. 8:27). ¶

10 **to be of the mind, to set the mind, to have the mind: *phroneō*** [verb: φρονέω <5426>]; **from *phrēn*: mind, understanding ▶ To think, to concentrate, to behave** > Christians should be of the same mind {have the same respect, live in harmony} and not to set the mind on high things (Rom. 12:16a, b). The Philippians were to be of one mind {to think of one thing, to be intent on one purpose, to be one in purpose} (Phil. 2:2). The Christian

is to set his mind {affection} on the things that are above, not on the things that are on the earth (Col. 3:2). All other refs.: MIND (verb) <5426>, THINK <5426>.

[11] **to be out of one's mind: *paraphroneō*** [verb: παραφρονέω <3912>]**; from *para*: beside, beyond, and *phroneō*: see [10] ▶ To be a fool, to be insane; also transl.: to be beside oneself** > Paul spoke as if he were a man out of his mind regarding his service (2 Cor. 11:23). ¶

[12] **to be of sound mind, to be in one's right mind: *sōphroneō*** [verb: σωφρονέω <4993>]**; from *sōphron*: sober-minded, which is from *sōzō*: to save, and *phrēn*: mind, understanding ▶ To be sound-minded, to possess the faculty of thinking soundly** > Healed by Jesus, the man who had been possessed by demons was now in his right mind {was sensible} (Mark 5:15; Luke 8:35). If Paul was of sound mind {was sober}, it was for the Corinthians (2 Cor. 5:13). All other refs.: JUDGMENT <4993>, SELF-CONTROLLED <4993>, THINK <4993>.

[13] **to be out of one's mind: *existēmi*** [verb: ἐξίστημι <1839>]**; from *ek*: out, and *histēmi*: to put, to place ▶ To have lost one's reason, to be beside oneself** > The relatives of Jesus said that He was out of His mind (Mark 3:21). Paul says that if he was beside himself, it was for God (2 Cor. 5:13). All other refs.: AMAZED (BE) <1839>, ASTONISHED (BE) <1839>.

[14] **of one mind: *homophrōn*** [adj.: ὁμόφρων <3675>]**; from *homos*: same, and *phrēn*: mind, understanding ▶ Of one accord, of the same understanding** > Peter exhorts his readers to be all of one mind {harmonious, in harmony} (1 Pet. 3:8). ¶

[15] **to be out of one's mind: *mainomai*** [verb: μαίνομαι <3105>] **▶ To be mad, to rave; also transl.: to be beside oneself, to be insane** > Festus said to Paul that he was out of his mind (Acts 26:24a), his great learning was driving him to madness; but Paul answered him that he was not out of his mind (v. 25). Other refs.: John 10:20; Acts 12:15; 1 Cor. 14:23 (to be mad); see MAD <3105>. ¶

[16] **to change one's mind: *metamelomai*** [verb: μεταμέλομαι <3338>]**; from *meta*: denoting change, and *melō*: to care ▶ To regret, to reconsider one's decision** > The Lord has sworn, and will not change his mind {repent, relent}, that Jesus Christ is priest for ever according to the order of Melchizedek (Heb. 7:21). All other refs.: REGRET <3338>, REMORSE <3338>, REPENT <3338>.

[17] **to change one's mind: *metaballō*** [verb: μεταβάλλω <3328>]**; from *meta*: particle indicating change, and *ballō*: to throw, to put ▶ To change one's opinion, to reconsider** > The people of Malta changed their minds in regard to Paul (Acts 28:6). ¶

– [18] Matt. 27:63 → to call to mind → REMEMBER <3415> [19] Mark 14:72 → to call to mind → REMEMBER <363> [20] Luke 1:3 → with this in mind → lit.: it has seemed good to me [21] Luke 12:29 → to be of doubtful mind, to have an anxious mind → to be in anxiety → ANXIETY <3349> [22] John 6:6 → to have in mind → KNOW <1492> [23] John 14:26; 2 Pet. 1:12; 3 John 10 → to put in mind, to call to mind → REMIND <5279> [24] John 15:18 → to keep in mind → KNOW <1097> [25] Acts 1:14; 2:46; 15:25; Rom. 15:6 → with one mind → with one accord → ACCORD <3661> [26] Rom. 15:15 → to put in mind → REMIND <1878> [27] 1 Cor. 4:17; 2 Cor. 7:15; 2 Tim. 1:6; Heb. 10:32 → to put in mind, to call to mind → REMIND <363> [28] 1 Cor. 14:20a, b → UNDERSTANDING <5424> [29] 2 Cor. 4:4; 11:3; Phil. 4:7 → THOUGHT <3540> [30] 2 Cor. 8:12; 9:2 → willing mind, forwardness of mind → READINESS <4288> [31] Phil. 3:4 → to have a mind → THINK <1380> [32] Phil. 4:8 → to let the mind dwell → MEDITATE <3049> [33] 1 Thes. 1:3; Heb. 11:15 → to bear in mind, to call to mind → REMEMBER <3421> [34] 1 Tim. 1:4; Titus 1:14 → to turn one's mind → to give heed → HEED (noun) <4337> [35] Heb. 11:22 → to call to mind → to make mention → MENTION (noun) <3421> [36] Heb. 12:17 → change of mind → REPENTANCE <3341> [37] 1 Pet. 4:7 → to be of sober mind → WATCH (verb)

<3525> [38] 1 Pet. 5:8 → to be of sober mind → WATCH (verb) <1127> [39] 2 Pet. 3:15 → to bear in mind → CONSIDER <2233> [40] Rev. 2:23 → REINS <3510>.

MIND (verb) – [1] ***phroneō*** [verb: φρονέω <5426>]; **from *phrēn*: spirit, reason, manner of thinking, understanding ▶ To exercise the mental faculties of understanding, to think; also transl.: to have the mind on something, to let a certain mind be in oneself, to be of a certain mind >** Peter's mind was not on the things that are of God (lit.: Peter did not mind the things of God) (Matt. 16:23 and Mark 8:33 {to have in mind, to be mindful, to set one's mind, to savour}). Those who are according to the flesh mind {set their minds on} the things of the flesh; and those who are according to the Spirit mind the things of the Spirit (Rom. 8:5). The Philippians were to think the same thing {to be like-minded, to be of the same mind} (Phil. 2:2); they were to let the mind of Jesus Christ be in them also (v. 5 {to have the attitude, to let the attitude be}). Some mind {set their mind on} earthly things (Phil. 3:19). Paul exhorted Euodia and Syntyche to be of the same mind {to live in harmony, to agree with each other} (lit.: to mind the same thing) in the Lord (Phil. 4:2). Other ref.: Phil. 3:16 in some mss. All other refs.: MIND (noun) <5426>, THINK <5426>.

– [2] Matt. 1:19 → PURPOSE (verb) <1014> [3] Acts 20:13 → to mind oneself → INTEND <3195>.

MIND (CALL TO) – [1] **mind: *mnēmē*** [fem. noun: μνήμη <3420>]; **from *mnaomai*: to recall, comp. *mimnēskō*: to recall to one's mind; to call (lit.: to make): *poieō*** [verb: ποιέω <4160>] **▶ To remember, to retain in the memory >** Peter used diligence, that after his departure his readers might at any time call to mind {to have in remembrance, to have a reminder, to remember} the things which he had written to them (2 Pet. 1:15). ¶

[2] **mind: *hupomnēsis*** [fem. noun: ὑπόμνησις <5280>]; **from *hupo*: under, and *mimnēskō*: to recall, to remember; to call (lit.: to take): *lambanō*** [verb: λαμβάνω <2983>] **▶ To recollect, to remember >** Paul called to mind {called to remembrance, was mindful of, was reminded of} the unfeigned faith in Timothy, and in his grandmother and mother (2 Tim. 1:5). Other refs.: 2 Pet. 1:13; 3:1; see REMEMBRANCE <5280>. ¶

MINDED (BE) – [1] Acts 27:39 → RESOLVE (verb) <1011> [2] Rom. 8:6a, b → to be carnally minded → lit.: the mind of the flesh → MIND (noun) <5427> [3] Gal. 5:10; Phil. 3:15 → THINK <5426>.

MINDFUL – [1] Matt. 16:23; Mark 8:33 → to be mindful → MIND (verb) <5426> [2] Luke 1:48 → to be mindful → to look upon → LOOK (verb) <1914> [3] 1 Cor. 11:2; 2 Tim. 1:4; 2 Pet. 3:2 → to be mindful → REMEMBER <3415> [4] 2 Tim. 1:5 → to be mindful → to call to mind → MIND (CALL TO) <5280> <2983> [5] Heb. 2:6 → to be mindful → REMEMBER (T0) <3403> [6] 1 Pet. 2:19 → mindful of → for the sake of conscience toward → CONSCIENCE <4893>.

MINDSET – Phil. 2:5 → to have the same mindset → to mind the same thing → MIND (verb) <5426>.

MINE – [1] ***emoi*** [pron.: ἐμοί <1698>] **▶ The emphatic form of *moi*: I, me, my.** * ‡

[2] ***emos*** [pron.: ἐμός <1699>] **▶ Possessive pron. of the first person sing. Also transl.: I, my own.** * ‡

[3] ***emou*** [pron.: ἐμοῦ <1700>] **▶ The emphatic form of *mou*: of me, my.** * ‡

[4] ***mou*** [pron.: μου <3450>] **▶ Personal pron.; also transl.: of me.** * ‡

MINGLE – [1] ***mignumi*** [verb: μίγνυμι <3396>] **▶ To mix, to blend substances which differ and usually remain distinct >** The soldiers gave Jesus sour wine mingled with gall (Matt. 27:34). Pilate had mingled the blood of the Galileans with their sacrifices (Luke 13:1). In judgment, there will be hail and fire mingled with blood (Rev. 8:7). John saw a sea of glass mingled with fire (Rev. 15:2). ¶

2 **to mingle with myrrh:** ***smurnizō*** [verb: σμυρνίζω <4669>]; **from** ***smurna*****: myrrh** ▶ **To make a mixture of substances which includes myrrh** > They gave Jesus wine mingled with myrrh {mixed, medicated with myrrh} to drink, but He did not take it (Mark 15:23). ¶

MINISTER (noun) – **1** ***diakonos*** [masc. noun: διάκονος <1249>] ▶ **Servant, deacon** > This word is used regarding Christians who are ministers of the new covenant (2 Cor. 3:6) and the ministers of Christ (2 Cor. 11:23). The fallen angels are called ministers of Satan (2 Cor. 11:15). Christ can in no way be a minister of sin {promote sin} (Gal. 2:17). All other refs.: SERVANT <1249>.

2 ***leitourgos*** [masc. noun: λειτουργός <3011>]; **from** ***leitos*****: of the people, and** ***ergon*****: work** ▶ **He who exercises a public service; official administrator** > The word is used in regard to rulers {officers, servants}, i.e., public magistrates (Rom. 13:6), Paul as minister of Christ Jesus (Rom. 15:16), Epaphroditus as minister to the need of Paul (Phil. 2:25 {the one who ministers, he that ministers, to take care}), angels as ministers, servants of God (Heb. 1:7), and Christ as minister of, who serves in the sanctuary (Heb. 8:2). ¶

3 ***hupēretēs*** [masc. noun: ὑπηρέτης <5257>]; **from** ***hupo*****: under, and** ***eretēs*****: rower** ▶ **Servant who has received a special service** > The word is used in the expr. "ministers of the word" {attendants on the word, servants of the word} in Luke 1:2. All other refs.: ATTENDANT <5257>, OFFICER <5257>, SERVANT <5257>.

MINISTER (verb) – **1** ***diakoneō*** [verb: διακονέω <1247>]; **from** ***dia*****: intens., and** ***enkoneō*****: to hurry, or from** ***diakonos*****: servant, deacon** ▶ **a. To assist, to aid; to assume a service, to serve** > Many women were ministering to {were providing for, were supporting, were contributing to the support of} Jesus from their substance (Luke 8:3). Paul went to Jerusalem, ministering to the saints (Rom. 15:25). The O.T. prophets did not minister to themselves, but to those who have heard the gospel (1 Pet. 1:12). Each gift is to be ministered to {employed in serving} one another (1 Pet. 4:10). **b. To set up by the service** > The Corinthians were an epistle of Christ ministered by {cared for by, the result of the ministry of} Paul (2 Cor. 3:3). All other refs.: ADMINISTER <1247>, SERVE <1247>.

2 ***didōmi*** [verb: δίδωμι <1325>] ▶ **To give, to communicate** > The word of the Christian should minister {impart} grace to {should benefit} the hearers (Eph. 4:29). Other refs.: GIVE <1325>.

3 ***ergazomai*** [verb: ἐργάζομαι <2038>]; **from** ***ergon*****: work, toil** ▶ **To work, to ensure the service** > Those who minister {labour at, perform} the sacred things eat of the offerings of the temple (1 Cor. 9:13). Timothy was ministering {was carrying on, was doing} the work of the Lord as also did Paul (1 Cor. 16:10). All other refs.: see entries in Lexicon at <2038>.

4 ***leitourgeō*** [verb: λειτουργέω <3008>]; **from** ***leitourgos*****: public servant, which is from** ***leitos*****: of the people, and** ***ergon*****: work** ▶ **a. To help others by sharing one's resources, to worship** > The Christians at Antioch ministered to the Lord and fasted (Acts 13:2). The nations had the duty to minister to {to share with) Christians at Jerusalem in material things (Rom. 15:27). **b. To attend to the occupations of the tabernacle and the temple, to perform religious duties** > The priests of the O.T. stood daily ministering and offering often the same sacrifices which can never take away sins (Heb. 10:11). ¶

5 ***hupēreteō*** [verb: ὑπηρετέω <5256>]; **from** ***hupēretēs*****: servant, which is from** ***hupo*****: under, and** ***eressō*****: to row** ▶ **To act as a servant** > David had ministered to {had served} the purpose of God (Acts 13:36). Paul's friends were permitted to minister to {to provide for, to take care of} him (Acts 24:23). Other ref.: Acts 20:34; see PROVIDE <5256>. ¶

– **6** Acts 11:29 → SERVICE <1248> **7** Acts 20:34 → PROVIDE <5256> **8** Rom. 15:16 → to minister, to minister as a priest → to carry on as a sacrificial service → SACRIFICIAL <2418> **9** 2 Cor.

9:10b → SUPPLY (verb) <5524> **10** Gal. 3:5; 2 Pet. 1:11 → SUPPLY (verb) <2023> **11** Phil. 2:25 → one who ministers to, he that ministers → MINISTER (noun) <3011> **12** Col. 2:19 → having nourishment ministered → nourished → NOURISH <2023> **13** 1 Tim. 1:4 → CAUSE (verb) <3930> **14** Heb. 13:10 → SERVE <3000>.

MINISTERING – **1** ***leitourgikos*** [adj.: λειτουργικός <3010>]; **from *leitourgos*: minister, which is from *leitos*: of the people, and *ergon*: work ▶ Pertaining or related to a service (especially religious) >** Angels are ministering spirits sent out for service on account of those who will inherit salvation (Heb. 1:14). ¶

– **2** Rom. 12:7; 2 Cor. 8:4; 9:1 → SERVICE <1248> **3** 1 Cor. 3:5 → ministering servant → SERVANT <1249>.

MINISTRATION – **1** Luke 1:23 → MINISTRY <3009> **2** Acts 6:1; 2 Cor. 9:1, 13 → SERVICE <1248> **3** 2 Cor. 3:7, 8, 9 → MINISTRY <1248> **4** 2 Cor. 9:12 → ADMINISTRATION <1248> **5** Phil. 2:17, 30 → SERVICE <3009>.

MINISTRY – **1** ***diakonia*** [fem. noun: διακονία <1248>]; **from *diakonos*: servant, deacon ▶ Charge, function which a servant must fulfill; also transl.: ministration, service, office >** Paul speaks of his ministry to the Gentiles (Rom. 11:13; 2 Cor. 4:1). He contrasts the ministry of the law (2 Cor. 3:7) and that of the Holy Spirit (v. 8), and the ministry of condemnation and the ministry of righteousness (v. 9a, b). All other refs.: ADMINISTRATION <1248>, SERVE <1248>, SERVICE <1248>.

2 ***leitourgia*** [fem. noun: λειτουργία <3009>]; **from *leitourgos*: minister, which is from *leitos*: of the people, and *ergon*: work ▶ Official public service in regard to God >** Zacharias departed to his house when the days of his service {ministration, i.e., ministry} were completed (Luke 1:23). Christ has obtained a more excellent ministry because He is the Mediator of a better covenant (Heb. 8:6). Other refs.: 2 Cor. 9:12; Phil. 2:17, 30; Heb. 9:21; see SERVICE <3009>. ¶

– **3** Acts 7:53 → DISPOSITION <1296> **4** Acts 8:21 → MATTER <3056> **5** Rom. 15:19 → to fulfill the ministry → to preach fully → PREACH <4137> **6** 2 Cor. 3:3 → the result of the ministry → ministered → MINISTER (verb) <1247> **7** Gal. 2:8 → APOSTLESHIP <651>.

MINSTREL – Matt. 9:23 → FLUTE PLAYER <834>.

MINT – ***hēduosmon*** [neut. noun: ἡδύοσμον <2238>]; **from *hēdus*: sweet, pleasant, and *osmē*: odor ▶ Very aromatic herb that grows near water currents or in other humid places >** Jesus contrasts the payment of traditional and unimportant tithes of mint, anise, and cummin to the practical justice, mercy, and faith which ought to have characterized the scribes and the Pharisees (Matt. 23:23; Luke 11:42). ¶

MIRACLE – **1** ***dunamis*** [fem. noun: δύναμις <1411>]; **from *dunamai*: to be capable; lit.: power ▶ Work or deed whose cause is of a supernatural character; also transl.: power, work of power, act of power, wonder, wonderful work, mighty work, mighty deed >** Miracles confirmed the words of Jesus and manifested God's approval of Him (Acts 2:22). God worked unusual miracles by the hands of Paul (Acts 19:11). Men who perform miracles will not necessarily enter into the kingdom of heaven (Matt. 7:22). The antichrist will perform miracles (2 Thes. 2:9). Other refs.: Matt. 11:20, 21, 23; 13:54, 58; 14:2; Mark 6:2, 5, 14; 9:39; Luke 10:13; 19:37; Acts 8:13; 1 Cor. 12:10, 28, 29; 2 Cor. 12:12; Gal. 3:5; Heb. 2:4; 6:5. All other refs.: ABILITY <1411>, MEANING <1411>, POWER[1] <1411>, POWER[3] <1411>, STRENGTH <1411>.

2 ***sēmeion*** [neut. noun: σημεῖον <4592>]; **from *sēma*: mark ▶ Work or deed whose cause is of a supernatural character; also transl.: sign, miraculous sign >** The miracle of healing in Acts 4:22 refers to the divine power exercised by Peter and John in healing

the man who had been lame from his birth. Other refs.: Luke 23:8; John 2:11, 23; 3:2; 4:54; 6:2, 14, 26; 7:31; 9:16; 10:41; 11:47; 12:18, 37; Acts 4:16; 6:8; 8:6, 13; 15:12; Rev. 13:14; 16:14; 19:20. All other refs.: SIGN <4592>.
– [3] Matt. 24:24; Mark 13:22; Rom. 15:19 → WONDER (adj. and noun) <5059> [4] John 7:21 → WORK (noun) <2041>.

MIRACULOUS SIGN – John 2:11; 11:47; et al. → SIGN <4592>.

MIRE – ***borboros*** [masc. noun: βόρβορος <1004>] ▶ **Mud, filth** > A sow that was washed returns to her wallowing in the mire {mud} (2 Pet. 2:22). ¶

MIRROR – [1] ***esoptron*** [neut. noun: ἔσοπτρον <2072>]; **from *eisopsomai*: to look into, which is from *eis*: into, and *optomai*: to look ▶ Surface reflecting the images of objects, looking glass; also transl.: glass, window** > The mirrors of antiquity were usually made of polished metal (see Ex. 38:8; Job 37:18). Christians see now in a mirror {window} obscurely, but in the hereafter they will see face to face (1 Cor. 13:12). In Jas. 1:23, the word of God is compared to a mirror revealing to a man that which he is morally. ¶
– [2] 2 Cor. 3:18 → to behold as in a mirror → BEHOLD (verb) <2734>.

MIS- – See DIS- <1418>.

MISCHIEF – Acts 13:10 → FRAUD <4468>.

MISDEED – [1] Acts 24:20 → WRONG (noun) <92> [2] Rom. 8:13 → DEED <4234>.

MISDEMEANOR – Acts 18:14 → WRONG (noun) <92>.

MISERABLE – [1] ***eleeinos*** [adj.: ἐλεεινός <1652>]; **from *eleos*: compassion, mercy ▶ Prompting pity on account of an unfavorable condition** > If Christians have hope in Christ in this life only, they are of all men the most miserable {pitiable, to be pitied} (1 Cor. 15:19). The Lord said that the angel of the church of the Laodiceans was miserable {pitiful} (Rev. 3:17). ¶
– [2] Matt. 21:41 → to put to a miserable death → to destroy miserably → MISERABLY <2560> [3] Gal. 4:9 → BEGGARLY <4434> [4] Jas. 4:9 → to be miserable → LAMENT <5003>.

MISERABLY – ***kakōs*** [adv.: κακῶς <2560>]; **from *kakos*: bad, miserable ▶ Pitifully, wickedly** > In one parable, the word is used in the expr. "to destroy miserably" {to bring to a wretched end, to put to a miserable death} those men who killed the son of the landowner (Matt. 21:41). All other refs.: SEVERELY <2560>, SICK (adv.) <2560>.

MISERY – ***talaipōria*** [fem. noun: ταλαιπωρία <5004>]; **from *talaipōreō*: to be afflicted, to be distressed, which is from *talaiporos*: afflicted, miserable, which is from *talas*: suffering, and an uncertain Greek word ▶ Calamity, distress** > Ruin and misery characterize the ways of men living under the dominion of the flesh (Rom. 3:16). James exhorts those who are rich to weep on account of the miseries which are coming upon them (Jas. 5:1). ¶

MISFORTUNE – Acts 28:6 → no misfortune → nothing bad → BAD <824>.

MISGIVING – Acts 10:20; 11:12 → without misgivings → lit.: doubting nothing → DOUBT (verb) <1252>.

MISGUIDED – Heb. 5:2 → to be misguided → to go astray → ASTRAY <4105>.

MISLEAD – [1] Matt. 24:4, 5, 11, 24; Mark 13:5, 6; Luke 21:8; 1 Cor. 15:33 → DECEIVE <4105> [2] Luke 23:2 → PERVERT (verb) <1294> [3] Luke 23:14 → to turn away → TURN (verb) <654>.

MISREPRESENTING – 1 Cor. 15:15 → to be misrepresenting → to be false witnesses → WITNESS (noun)[2] <5575>.

MISS – [1] 1 Tim. 1:6; 6:21; 2 Tim. 2:18 → to miss, to miss the mark → STRAY <795> [2] Heb. 12:15 → LACK (verb) <5302>.

MISSILE – Eph. 6:16 → DART <956>.

MISSION – [1] Acts 12:25 → SERVICE <1248> [2] 2 Cor. 11:12 → in their boasted mission → lit.: in that which they boast.

MIST – [1] ***achlus*** [fem. noun: ἀχλύς <887>] ▶ **Obscurity, dimness; especially of the eye in medical writings** > A mist and darkness fell on the magician Elymas (Acts 13:11); this mist was deprivation of vision. ¶

[2] ***nephelē*** [fem. noun: νεφέλη <3507>]; **dimin. of *nephos*: cloud** ▶ **Mass of water particles suspended in the air possessing a specific form, small cloud** > Peter speaks of wicked men who are like mists {clouds} driven by the storm (2 Pet. 2:17); other mss. have *homichlē*. All other refs.: CLOUD <3507>.

[3] ***homichlē*** [fem. noun: ὁμίχλη <3658a>] ▶ Ref.: 2 Pet. 2:17; see [2].

– [4] Jas. 4:14 → VAPOR <822>.

MISTAKEN (BE) – ***planaō*** [verb: πλανάω <4105>]; **from *planē*: error, wandering** ▶ **To go astray, to be in error** > Jesus answered the Sadducees that they were mistaken {did err} (Matt. 22:29; Mark 12:24, 27 {to be mistaken badly}). All other refs.: ASTRAY <4105>, DECEIVE <4105>, STRAY <4105>, WANDER <4105>.

MISTREAT – [1] ***hubrizō*** [verb: ὑβρίζω <5195>]; **from *hubris*: insult, injury** ▶ **To treat shamefully** > In a parable, bondmen were mistreated {were entreated spitefully, were treated spitefully, were treated ill} and slain (Matt. 22:6). Many rose up to mistreat {abuse, use despitefully, use ill} and stone Paul and Barnabas (Acts 14:5). Paul was mistreated {was insulted, was shamefully entreated, was spitefully treated} at Philippi (1 Thes. 2:2). Other refs.: Luke 11:45; 18:32; see INSULT (verb) <5195>. ¶

– [2] Luke 6:28 → to use despitefully → USE (verb) <1908> [3] Acts 7:6, 19; 12:1 → OPPRESS <2559> [4] Acts 7:24 → to suffer wrong → WRONG (noun) <91> [5] Acts 7:27 → to do wrong → WRONG (verb) <91>.

MISTREATED (BE) – [1] Acts 7:24 → OPPRESSED (BE) <2669> [2] Heb. 11:25 → to be mistreated along with → to suffer affliction with → AFFLICTION <4778> [3] Heb. 11:37; 13:3 → TORMENTED (BE) <2558>.

MISUSE – 1 Cor. 7:31 → USE (verb) <2710>.

MITE – ***lepton*** [neut. noun: λεπτόν <3016>]; **from *leptos*: thin** ▶ **The smallest bronze coin, worth one eighth of a Roman penny; also transl.: small copper coin, cent, penny** > Jesus noticed the poor widow who cast two mites into the temple treasury (Mark 12:42; Luke 21:2). He spoke of paying to the very last mite (Luke 12:59). See PENNY. ¶

MITYLENE – ***Mitulēnē*** [fem. name: Μιτυλήνη <3412>]: **poss.: hornless** ▶ **City of the island of Lesbos in the Aegean Sea to the west of Pergamum** > Paul came to Mitylene on his third missionary journey (Acts 20:14). ¶

MIX – [1] ***kerannumi*** [verb: κεράννυμι <2767>] ▶ **To mingle substances in order to obtain a drink** > John heard a voice saying to mix double to Babylon in the cup which she has mixed (Rev. 18:6a, b {to fill}). Other ref.: Rev. 14:10 (to pour out); see POUR <2767>. ¶

[2] **to mix with: *sunkerannumi*** [verb: συγκεράννυμι <4786>]; **from *sun*: together, and *kerannumi*: see** [1] ▶ **To mix together, to temper together** > The word which certain ones heard was not mixed {combined, united} with faith (Heb. 4:2). Other ref.: 1 Cor. 12:24; see COMPOSE <4786>. ¶

– 3 Matt. 13:33; Luke 13:21 → HIDE <1470> 4 Matt. 27:34; Luke 13:1; Rev. 8:7; 15:2 → MINGLE <3396> 5 Mark 15:23 → to mix with myrrh → to mingle with myrrh → MINGLE <4669> 6 1 Cor. 5:9, 11 → to keep company → COMPANY (noun) <4874>.

MIXTURE – 1 ***migma*** [neut. noun: μίγμα <3395>]; **from *mignumi*: to mingle, to mix ▶ Mingling, combination of distinct substances** > Nicodemus brought a mixture (other mss.: *eligma, smēgma, smigma*) of myrrh and aloes to embalm the body of Jesus (John 19:39). ¶
– 2 Rev. 14:10 → without mixture → full strength → STRENGTH <194>.

MNASON – ***Mnasōn*** [masc. name: Μνάσων <3416>]: **remembering ▶ Man from Cyprus and an early disciple** > Mnason accompanied Paul from Caesarea to Jerusalem; Paul was to lodge with him (Acts 21:16). ¶

MOB – 1 Acts 17:5 → to form a mob → to gather a mob → GATHER <3792> 2 Acts 21:36 → MULTITUDE <4128> 3 Acts 24:18 → MULTITUDE <3793>.

MOCK – 1 ***empaizō*** [verb: ἐμπαίζω <1702>]; **from *en*: at, and *paizō*: to play ▶ a. To outwit, to fool; also transl.: to trick, to deceive** > The wise men had mocked Herod (Matt. 2:16). **b. To scorn, to treat with contempt** > The verb is used in regard to Christ, the object of the mockery of the Gentiles (Matt. 20:19; Mark 10:34; Luke 18:32; also Luke 23:11 about the mockery of Herod and his soldiers), soldiers (Matt. 27:29, 31; Mark 10:34; 15:20; Luke 22:63; 23:36 {to make game}), as well as chief priests, scribes, and elders (Matt. 27:41; Mark 15:31). The verb is also used in Luke 14:29 {to ridicule} in regard to one who is unable to finish the tower he began to build. ¶
2 ***muktērizō*** [verb: μυκτηρίζω <3456>]; **from *mukaomai*: to vociferate; lit.: to turn up the nose (*muktēr*) as a sign of derision, i.e., to mock, to sneer ▶ To despise, to treat with contempt** > God is not mocked (Gal. 6:7). ¶
3 ***ekmuktērizō*** [verb: ἐκμυκτηρίζω <1592>]; **from *ek*: intens., and *muktērizō*: see 2 ▶ To despise harshly, to treat with great contempt** > The Pharisees, who were covetous, mocked {derided, were scoffing at, were sneering at} Jesus (Luke 16:14). Other ref.: Luke 23:35; see SNEER <1592>. ¶
4 ***chleuazō*** [verb: χλευάζω <5512>]; **from *chleuē*: derision, joke ▶ To despise, to scoff at** > On the Day of Pentecost, some mocked {made fun of} those who announced the wonderful works of God (Acts 2:13); *diachleuazō* in some mss.: more intens. than *chleuazō*. Some mocked {sneered} when they heard of the resurrection of the dead (Acts 17:32). ¶

MOCKER – ***empaiktēs*** [masc. noun: ἐμπαίκτης <1703>]; **from *empaizō*: to deride, to mock, which is from *en*: at, *paizō*: to play ▶ A person who derides another person, who treats others with contempt** > There will be mockers {scoffers} in the last days (2 Pet. 3:3; Jude 18). ¶

MOCKING – 1 ***empaigmos*** [masc. noun: ἐμπαιγμός <1701>]; **from *empaizō*: to mock, which is from *en*: at, and *paizō*: to play ▶ The action of deriding someone** > People of faith of the O.T. endured trials by mockings (Heb. 11:36). ¶
2 ***empaigmonē*** [fem. noun: ἐμπαιγμονή <1700a>]; **from *empaizō*: see 1 ▶ Contempt, derision** > Mockers will come with their mockings {scoffing} in the last days, walking according to their own lusts (2 Pet. 3:3 in some mss.). ¶

MODEL – 1 Acts 7:44; Phil. 3:17; 1 Thes. 1:7; 2 Thes. 3:9; 1 Tim. 4:12; Titus 2:7; 1 Pet. 5:3 → PATTERN <5179> 2 1 Pet. 2:21 → EXAMPLE <5261>.

MODERATELY – ***metriōs*** [adv.: μετρίως <3357>]; **from *metrios*: moderate, which is from *metron*: measure ▶ With measure, a little** > The disciples were not moderately {no little, greatly} comforted, when they saw that Eutychus was alive (Acts 20:12). ¶

MODERATION – [1] ***sōphrosunē*** [fem. noun: σωφροσύνη <4997>]; **from *sōphron*: of a sound mind, temperate, which is from *sōs*: healthy, and *phrēn*: spirit, reason ▶ Good sense, sobriety; also transl.: propriety** > Believing women are enjoined to clothe themselves with moderation {with discretion, discreetly} (1 Tim. 2:9); they are also enjoined to persevere in faith, love, and holiness with moderation {discretion, self-control, self-restraint} (v. 15). Other ref.: Acts 26:25; see SOBERNESS <4997>. ¶
– [2] Phil. 4:5 → GENTLENESS <1933>.

MODEST – 1 Tim. 2:9 → modest apparel → APPAREL <2689> <2887>.

MODESTLY – 1 Tim. 2:9 → lit.: with modesty → MODESTY <127>.

MODESTY – ***aidōs*** [fem. noun: αἰδώς <127>]; **from which *aideomai*: to show respect ▶ Decency, seemliness, discretion** > Believing women are to adorn themselves with modesty {decency, propriety, shamefacedness} (1 Tim. 2:9). Some mss. also have this word at Heb. 12:28 {godly fear}. ¶

MOISTURE – ***ikmas*** [fem. noun: ἰκμάς <2429>] ▶ **Characteristic of that which contains water, humidity** > Some seed dried up because it had no moisture (Luke 8:6). ¶

MOLDED – **thing molded: *plasma*** [neut. noun: πλάσμα <4110>]; **from *plassō*: to form, to shape ▶ That which is formed or fashioned** > Shall the thing molded say to the molder: Why did you make me like this? (Rom. 9:20). ¶

MOLDER – Rom. 9:20 → lit.: one who molds → FORM (verb) <4111>.

MOLECH – Acts 7:43 → MOLOCH <3434>.

MOLEK – Acts 7:43 → MOLOCH <3434>.

MOLOCH – ***Moloch*** [masc. name: Μολόχ <3434>]: **king, in Heb. ▶ Idol-god worshipped by the Ammonites, to whom human sacrifices were offered; also spelled: Molech, Molek** > Stephen reproaches the Jews of having taken along the tabernacle of Moloch and of having worshiped him (Acts 7:43). ¶

MOMENT – [1] ***atomos*** [adj. used as a noun: ἄτομος <823>]; **from *a*: neg., and *tomē*: incision, which is from *temnō*: to cut ▶ Instant, indivisible unit of time** > At the return of Christ, Christians will all be changed in an instant {a flash}, in the twinkling of an eye, at the last trumpet (1 Cor. 15:52). ¶
[2] ***stigmē*** [fem. noun: στιγμή <4743>]; **from *stigma*: mark, which is from *stizō*: to sting, to make a mark ▶ Instant, very brief point in time** > The devil showed Jesus all the kingdoms of the habitable world in a moment of time {in an instant} (Luke 4:5). ¶
[3] **for a moment: *parautika*** [adv.: παραυτίκα <3910>]; **from *para*: at, and *autika*: immediately, which is from *autos*: this (referring to time), and *hikō*: to come ▶ For the present instant, momentarily** > The light affliction of Christians, which is but for a moment, is working for them a far more exceeding and eternal weight of glory (2 Cor. 4:17). ¶
– [4] Matt. 15:28; Luke 2:38; Gal. 2:5 → HOUR <5610> [5] Mark 9:39 → in the next moment → LIGHTLY <5035> [6] 1 Thes. 2:17 → TIME <2540> [7] Heb. 12:11 → for the moment → lit.: for the being present → PRESENT <3918>.

MOMENTARY – 2 Cor. 4:17 → for a moment → MOMENT <3910>.

MONEY – [1] ***kerma*** [neut. noun: κέρμα <2772>]; **from *keirō*: to cut; lit.: slice, because coins were often sliced off larger pieces of metal to do a transaction ▶ A small coin; also transl.: change, coin** > Jesus poured out the money of the money-changers (John 2:15). ¶
[2] ***nomisma*** [neut. noun: νόμισμα <3546>]; **from *nomizō*: to assume, to hold as**

customary, which is from *nomos*: law; *numisma*, in Lat. ▶ Currency, cash used as legal tender > Jesus asked to be shown the money {coin} of the tribute (Matt. 22:19). ¶
[3] ***chalkos*** [masc. noun: χαλκός <5475>]; **lit.: copper ▶ Copper coin >** Jesus saw how the crowd was casting money in the treasury (Mark 12:41). He commanded His disciples to take no money {copper} for the journey (Mark 6:8). Other refs.: Matt. 10:9; 1 Cor. 13:1; Rev. 18:12; see BRASS <5475>. ¶
[4] ***chrēma*** [neut. noun: χρῆμα <5536>]; **from *chraomai*: to use, to need; lit.: something being used ▶ Pieces of metal used to buy, monetary value >** Barnabas sold a tract of land; he brought the money and laid it at the feet of the apostles (Acts 4:37). The word is also used in Acts 8:18, 20b; 24:26 {bribe}. Other refs.: Mark 10:23, 24; Luke 18:24; see RICHES <5536>. ¶
– [5] Matt. 6:24; Luke 16:13 → MAMMON <3126> [6] Matt. 10:9; Mark 6:8 → money belt → BELT <2223> [7] Matt. 25:18, 27; 28:12, 15; Mark 14:11; Luke 9:3; 19:15, 23; 22:5; Acts 7:16; 8:20a → SILVER <694> [8] Matt. 27:6; Acts 4:34; 5:2, 3 → PRICE (noun) <5092> [9] Luke 3:14 → to extort money, to take money by force → OPPRESS <1286> [10] Luke 7:41 → two men owed money to → lit.: two debtors were to → DEBTOR <5533> [11] Luke 10:4; 12:33; 22:35, 36 → money bag → PURSE <905> [12] Luke 16:14; 2 Tim. 3:2 → lover of money, who loves money → COVETOUS (adj.) <5366> [13] Luke 19:13 → to put money to work → to do business → BUSINESS <4231> [14] John 2:14 → one exchanging money → MONEYCHANGER <2773> [15] John 12:6; 13:29 → money box, money bag → BAG <1101> [16] Acts 3:3 → ALMS <1654> [17] Acts 16:16, 19 → GAIN (noun) <2039> [18] Acts 17:9 → money as security → lit.: security → SECURITY <2425> [19] 1 Tim. 3:3; Heb. 13:5 → without love of money, not fond of money, not greedy for money, free from the love of money, not a lover of money → without covetousness → COVETOUSNESS <866> or GREEDY <866> [20] 1 Tim. 3:8; Titus 1:7 → greedy for money → GREEDY <146> [21] 1 Tim. 6:10 → love of money → LOVE (noun) <5365> [22] Jas. 4:13 → to make money → GAIN (verb) <2770>.

MONEYCHANGER – [1] **changer, money changer, money-changer: *kollubistēs*** [masc. noun: κολλυβιστής <2855>]; **from *kollubos*: small coin ▶ Person sitting at a table in the temple and exchanging currency >** Jesus overthrew the tables of the moneychangers (Matt. 21:12; Mark 11:15; John 2:15) because they were profaning the temple. Other ref.: Luke 19:45 in some mss. ¶
[2] ***kermatistēs*** [masc. noun: κερματιστής <2773>]; **from *kermatizō*: to divide into coins, which is from *kerma*: small coin of money ▶ See defin. of [1]. >** John uses this Greek word (John 2:14 {one exchanging money}). ¶
– [3] Matt. 25:27 → EXCHANGER <5133>.

MONEYLENDER – Luke 7:41 → CREDITOR <1157>.

MONSTER – Matt. 12:40 → sea monster → WHALE <2785>.

MONTH – [1] ***mēn*** [masc. noun: μήν <3376>] **▶ Period of time lasting thirty days >** This word is used particularly by Luke (Luke 1:24, 26, 36, 56; 4:25; Acts 7:20; 18:11; 19:8; 20:3; 28:11). Elsewhere, it is found in Gal. 4:10; Jas. 5:17; Rev. 9:5, 10, 15; 11:2; 13:5; 22:2. ¶
[2] **four months: neut. of *tetramēnos*** [adj.: τετράμηνος <5072>]; **from *tetra* or *tessares*: four, and *mēn*: see [1] ▶ A duration of four months >** The word is found in John 4:35 in relation to the harvest. ¶
[3] **three months: *trimēnos*** [neut. noun: τρίμηνος <5150>]; **from *treis*: three, and *mēn*: see [1] ▶ A duration of three months >** Moses was hidden for three months by his parents (Heb. 11:23). ¶

MONUMENT – Acts 2:29 → TOMB <3418>.

MOON – [1] ***selēnē*** [fem. noun: σελήνη <4582>]; **from *selas*: brilliance ▶ Heavenly body that reflects the light of the**

sun > When Jesus returns, the moon will not give its light (Matt. 24:29; Mark 13:24). There will be signs in the sun, in the moon and in the stars (Luke 21:25); the sun will be turned into darkness and the moon into blood (Acts 2:20; Rev. 6:12). The moon has its own particular glory (1 Cor. 15:41). Other refs.: Rev. 8:12; 12:1; 21:23. ¶

2 **new moon:** ***neomēnia*** [fem. noun: νεομηνία <3500a>] **or** ***noumēnia*** [fem. noun: νουμηνία <3561>]; **from** ***neos*****: new, and** ***mēn*****: month ▶ Term used to describe a Jewish feast** > No one should judge a Christian regarding a new moon {New Moon celebration} (Col. 2:16). ¶

– 3 Acts 7:42 → the sun, moon and stars → lit.: the host of heaven → HOST[1] <4756>, HEAVEN <3772>.

MOOR – Mark 6:53 → to moor to the shore → SHORE <4358>.

MORAL – 1 Cor. 15:33 → HABIT <2239>.

MORBID – 1 Tim. 6:4 → to have a morbid interest → OBSESSED (BE) <3552>.

MORE – 1 ***eti*** [adv.: ἔτι <2089>] ▶ **Additionally, further** > The author of the Epistle to the Hebrews, after having spoken about men and women of faith, asks what more he should say (Heb. 11:32). *

2 **more, the more, more so, more than ever, more and more, even more:** ***mallon*** [adv.: μᾶλλον <3123>]; **compar. of** ***mala*****: much ▶ a. Increasingly, in increased measure** > Bartimaeus cried out all the more (Mark 10:48; Luke 18:39). When Pilate heard that Jesus had made himself the Son of God, he was the more afraid (John 19:8). Paul could have confidence in the flesh more so than anyone else (Phil. 3:4). **b. In greater number** > Christians were more than ever {increasingly} added to the Lord (Acts 5:14).

3 **the more:** ***meizon*** [adv.: μεῖζον <3185>]; **compar. of** ***megas*****: great ▶ To a greater extent, surpassingly** > Two blind men shouted the more to attract the attention of Jesus (Matt. 20:31). ¶

4 **the more, all the more:** ***perissoterōs*** [adv.: περισσοτέρως <4056>]; **from** ***perissoteros*****: see** 8 ▶ **a. More excessively, in greater measure** > The crowd cried out all the more {all the louder} to crucify Jesus (Mark 15:14). **b. More abundantly, more ardently** > The author of the Epistle to the Hebrews urged his readers to pray all the more {especially, particularly, the rather} for him (Heb. 13:19). Other refs.: ABUNDANT <4056>, ABUNDANTLY <4056>, EXCEEDINGLY <4056>.

5 **more than ever:** ***perissōs*** [adv.: περισσῶς <4057>]; **from** ***perissos*****: abundant, exceeding a measure, which is from** ***peri*****: above, beyond ▶ In greater measure, exceedingly** > The crowd cried out more than ever {the more, out the more, all the more, all the louder} that Jesus should be crucified (Matt. 27:23). Other ref.: Acts 26:11. All other refs.: EXCEEDINGLY <4057>, VEHEMENTLY <4057>.

6 ***pleion*** [adj.: πλεῖον <4119>]; **neut. of** ***pleiōn*****: greater number ▶ Greater in quantity, larger group** > A husbandman sent other servants, more than the first time, to receive his fruit (Matt. 21:36). Other ref.: 2 Cor. 2:6 {many, the majority}.

7 ***pleiōn*** [adv.: πλείων <4119>]; **compar. of** ***polus*****: much ▶ Additionally, further** > In a parable, the laborers of the first hour supposed that they would receive more for their work (Matt. 20:10). The one who has been forgiven more {most, has the biggest debt cancelled} will love more {most} his creditor (Luke 7:42, 43 {bigger}). The expr. "*epi pleion*" is transl. "further" in Acts 4:17 and 24:4.

8 ***perissoteros*** [adj.: περισσότερος <4055>]; **compar. of** ***perissos*****: see** 5 ▶ **In a greater measure** > To him whom much has been committed, of him more will be asked (Luke 12:48).

– 9 Phil. 2:28 → the more eagerly, the more carefully → EAGERLY <4708>.

MOREOVER – Heb. 9:21 → LIKEWISE <3668>.

MORN – See MORNING.

MORNING – 1 **morning, early in the morning:** ***orthros*** [masc. noun: ὄρθρος

<3722>] ► **Dawn, daybreak** > Women came to the tomb of Jesus very early in the morning {at early dawn} (Luke 24:1); lit.: in dawn deep (*orthrou batheōs*). Jesus came to the temple early in the morning (John 8:2). The apostles entered early in the morning {very early} into the temple and taught (Acts 5:21). ¶
2 **to come early in the morning: *orthrizō*** [verb: ὀρθρίζω <3719>]; **from *orthros*: see** 1 ► **To come at dawn** > All the people came early in the morning to Jesus in the temple to hear Him (Luke 21:38). ¶
3 **very early in the morning: *ennuchon*** [adj.: ἔννυχον <1773>]; **from *en*: in, and *nux*: night ► While it was still dark, at early dawn** > Ref.: Mark 1:35. ¶ ‡
4 **early in the morning, in the morning, early, from morning: *prōi*** [adv.: πρωΐ <4404>]; **from *pro*: before ► Day-break, first thing at the beginning of the day** > In the morning, people say there will be a storm if the sky is red and threatening (Matt. 16:3). A householder went out early in the morning to hire workmen (Matt. 20:1). In the morning, having risen a long while before daylight, Jesus departed to a desert place and prayed (Mark 1:35). In the morning the disciples saw the fig tree dried up from the roots (Mark 11:20). The master of the house might come in the morning {at dawn} (Mark 13:35). In the morning Jesus was delivered to Pilate (Mark 15:1). Very early in the morning women came to the tomb (Mark 16:2 in some mss.). In Mark 16:9 the Greek word is transl. "early": Jesus rose early on the first day of the week. In John 20:1 the Greek word is again transl. "early": Mary Magdalene went to the tomb early. Paul taught from morning to evening (Acts 28:23). ¶
5 ***prōia*** [fem. noun: πρωΐα <4405>]; **from *prōi*: see** 4 ► **Beginning of the day, day-dawn; also transl.: early in the morning** > In the morning Jesus was hungry and returned to the city (Matt. 21:18). When morning came, the chief priests and the elders plotted against Jesus to put Him to death (Matt. 27:1). They led Him to the governor's headquarters in the early morning {early} (John 18:28). When morning {the day} had come, Jesus stood on the shore (John 21:4). ¶
6 See MORNING STAR.
– 7 Matt. 20:3; Mark 15:25 → nine in the morning → lit.: the third hour → HOUR <5610>.

MORNING STAR – 1 ***astēr*** [masc. noun: ἀστήρ <792>] ***orthrinos*** [adj.: ὀρθρινός <3720>]; **from *orthros*: morning, dawn ► One of the titles of the Lord Jesus** > In Rev. 22:16, the expr. is used in relation to the second coming of Christ; He is the "bright Morning Star." He will come later as the Sun of Righteousness for Israel and the world (see Mal. 4:2) and establish His kingdom of one thousand years. Actually, the morning star (which is the planet Venus) appears in the east before the sunrise. Certain mss. have 2 in Rev. 22:16. All other refs. (*astēr*): STAR <792>. ¶
2 ***astēr*** [masc. noun: ἀστήρ <792>] ***prōinos*** [adj.: πρωϊνός <4407>]; **from *prōi*: early in the morning ► See defin. of** 1. > The morning star is promised to the faithful of the church of Thyatira (Rev. 2:28). Other ref.: Rev. 22:16; see 1. All other refs. (*astēr*): STAR <792>. ¶
3 ***phōsphoros*** [adj.: φωσφόρος <5459>]; **from *phōs*: light, and *pherō*: to bring; lit.: light carrier ► Term designating the morning star which appears before the sunrise** > Christians do well to take heed to the prophetic word until the day dawns and the morning star arises in their hearts (2 Pet. 1:19). ¶

MORROW – 1 Matt. 6:30; Luke 10:35; et al. → morrow, to morrow → TOMORROW <839> 2 Mark 11:12 → next day → DAY <1887>.

MORSEL – 1 John 13:26a, b, 27, 30 → piece of bread → PIECE <5596> 2 Heb. 12:16 → MEAL <1035>.

MORTAL (adj.) – 1 ***thnētos*** [adj.: θνητός <2349>]; **from *thnēskō*: to die ► Liable to die** > We should not let sin reign in our mortal bodies (Rom. 6:12). God will give life to the mortal bodies of the Christians (Rom.

8:11). Other refs.: 1 Cor. 15:53, 54; 2 Cor. 4:11; 5:4 {mortality; lit.: the mortal}. ¶
– 2 Rom. 1:23 → CORRUPTIBLE <5349> 3 Heb. 7:8 → mortal men → DIE <599> 4 Rev. 13:3a, 12 → mortal wound → DEATH <2288>.

MORTAL (noun) – Heb. 13:6 → mere mortal → lit.: man → MAN <444>.

MORTALITY – 2 Cor. 5:4 → MORTAL <2349>.

MORTALLY – Rev. 13:3 → mortally wounded; lit.: wounded to death → DEATH <2288>.

MORTIFY – 1 Rom. 8:13 → to put to death → DEATH <2289> 2 Col. 3:5 → to put to death → DEATH <3499>.

MOSES – ***Mōseus*** [masc. name: Μωσεύς <3475>]**: drawn out (from the water), in Heb.; other Greek spellings: *Mōsēs*, *Mōuseus*, *Mōusēs* ▶ Author of the Pentateuch, the first five books of the O.T.** > Under his leadership, God delivered the Israelites from the Egyptian yoke of bondage and led them through the Red Sea. Moses received the law of God and His commandments. He walked with Israel in the wilderness for forty years. See Acts 7:21–43; Heb. 11:23–29. In the N.T., the giving of the law is associated with his name, whereas grace and truth came into being through Jesus (John 1:17; 7:19; Rom. 10:5). *

MOST – 1 ***pleistos*** [adj.: πλεῖστος <4118>]**; superl. of *polus*: many ▶ The largest number, the majority** > Jesus reproached the cities in which most of His works of power had taken place (Matt. 11:20). Other refs.: Matt. 21:8 {very great, very large}; 1 Cor. 14:27 {the most}. ¶
– 2 Luke 7:42, 43 → MORE <4119> 3 Eph. 5:16; Col. 4:5 → to make the most → REDEEM <1805>.

MOST HIGH – ***Hupsistos*** [adj. and adj. used as noun: Ὕψιστος <5310>]**; superl. of *hupsos*: height ▶ Title of God, indicating His great elevation** > Jesus would be called Son of the Highest (Luke 1:32) and prophet of the Highest (v. 76). The power of the Highest was to overshadow Mary (Luke 1:35). A possessed man addressed Jesus as the Son of the Most High God (Mark 5:7; Luke 8:28). Jesus tells how to be sons of the Highest (Luke 6:35). The Most High dwells not in houses made with hands (Acts 7:48). All other refs.: see HIGH (adj.) <5310>, HIGHEST <5310>.

MOTE – Matt. 7:3–5; Luke 6:41, 42a, b → SPECK <2595>.

MOTH – ***sēs*** [masc. noun: σής <4597>] ▶ **Mite, clothes moth (insect whose larvae attack clothing)** > Moth and rust destroy treasures on earth, but not in heaven (Matt. 6:19, 20). In heaven, no moth destroys (Luke 12:33). ¶

MOTH-EATEN – ***sētobrōtos*** [adj.: σητόβρωτος <4598>]**; from *sēs*: moth, and *bibriskō*: to eat ▶ Devoured by moths, which are stout-bodied winged insects** > The garments of the rich are moth-eaten (Jas. 5:2). ¶

MOTHER – 1 ***mētēr*** [fem. noun: μήτηρ <3384>] ▶ **Woman who has given birth to one or more children** > The word is used in regard to Mary, the mother of Jesus (Matt. 1:18; 2:11, 13, 14, 20, 21; 12:46, 47; 13:55; Mark 3:31, 32; Luke 1:43; 2:33, 34, 48, 51; 8:19, 20; John 2:1, 3, 5, 12; 19:25a, 26a, b, 27; Acts 1:14); Herodias (Matt. 14:8, 11; Mark 6:24, 28; John 6:42); the mother of the sons of Zebedee (Matt. 20:20; 27:56b); the mother of James and Joses (Matt. 27:56a; Mark 15:40); Elizabeth (Luke 1:15, 60); Mary, the wife of Clopas (John 19:25b); the mother of John Mark (Acts 12:12); the mother of Rufus (Rom. 16:13); the mother of Paul (Gal. 1:15); and Eunice (2 Tim. 1:5). The word is also used figur. in regard to the heavenly Jerusalem (Gal. 4:26) and Babylon the Great (Rev. 17:5). Other refs.: Matt. 10:35, 37; 12:48–50; 15:4a, b, 5, 6; 19:5, 12, 19, 29; Mark 3:33–35; 5:40; 7:10a, b,

11, 12; 10:7, 19, 29, 30; Luke 7:12, 15; 8:21, 51; 12:53a, b; 14:26; 18:20; John 3:4; Acts 3:2; 13:18 (in some mss.); 14:8; Eph. 5:31; 6:2; 1 Tim. 5:2. ¶

[2] **murderer of mother, smiter of mother, who kills his mother: *mētralōas*** [masc. noun: μητραλῴας <3389>]; **from *mētēr*: see [1], and *aloiaō*: to beat ▶ Matricide; one who mistreats or kills his mother** > The law is made for murderers of mothers (1 Tim. 1:9). ¶

[3] **without mother: *amētōr*** [adj.: ἀμήτωρ <282>]; **from *a*: neg., and *mētēr*: see [1] ▶ Not having a mother (or whose mother is not known or named)** > Melchizedek was without mother (Heb. 7:3). ¶

[4] **wife's mother, mother in law, mother-in-law: *penthera*** [fem. noun: πενθερά <3994>]; **fem. of *pentheros*: father-in-law ▶ Mother of the spouse** > Jesus saw Peter's wife's mother lying sick with a fever (Matt. 8:14; Mark 1:30; Luke 4:38). He has come to set a daughter-in-law against her mother-in-law (Matt. 10:35a, b; Luke 12:53). ¶

– [5] Matt. 1:16 → Mary was the mother of Jesus → lit.: Mary, of whom Jesus was born → BORN (BE) <1080> [6] 1 Thes. 2:7 → NURSE (noun) <5162>.

MOTHER-IN-LAW – Matt. 8:14; 10:35; Mark 1:30; Luke 4:38; 12:53 → MOTHER <3994>.

MOTION (noun) – Rom. 7:5 → PASSION <3804>.

MOTION (verb) – [1] John 13:24; Acts 24:10 → to make a sign → SIGN <3506> [2] Acts 12:17; 13:16; 19:33; 21:40 → to make a sign → SIGN <2678> [3] Acts 26:1 → to motion with → to stretch out → STRETCH <1614>.

MOTIVE – [1] 1 Cor. 4:5 → COUNSEL (noun) <1012> [2] Phil. 1:17 → from pure motives → PURELY <55> [3] Phil. 1:18 → false motives → PRETEXT <4392> [4] Jas. 2:4 → THOUGHT <1261> [5] Jas. 4:3 → with wrong motives → SICK (adv. and noun) <2560>.

MOUND – Luke 19:43 → palisaded mound → EMBANKMENT <5482>.

MOUNT (noun)[1] – ***ktēnos*** [neut. noun: κτῆνος <2934>]; **from *ktaomai*: to possess, to buy; lit.: property ▶ Animal used to transport a person** > The commander ordered two centurions to provide mounts {beasts} to put Paul on and bring him to Felix the governor (Acts 23:24). All other refs.: BEAST <2934>.

MOUNT (noun)[2] – ***oros*** [neut. noun: ὄρος <3735>] ▶ **Mountain, hill** > Paul spoke of the covenant from Mount Sinai (Gal. 4:24); Hagar is Mount Sinai (v. 25). All other refs.: MOUNTAIN <3735>.

MOUNT (verb) – Matt. 21:5 → SIT <1910>.

MOUNT OF OLIVES – [1] ***Oros tōn Elaiōn*; mount: *oros*** [neut. noun: ὄρος <3735>], **olive: *elaia*** [fem. noun: ἐλαία <1636>] ▶ **Mountain east of Jerusalem** > Jesus sat on the Mount of Olives to teach His disciples about events to come (Matt. 24:3; Mark 13:3). After having instituted the Supper, He went out to the Mount of Olives (Matt. 26:30; Mark 14:26; Luke 22:39). It was His custom to go to this place (Luke 21:37; John 8:1). He went there before being acclaimed at His triumphal entry into Jerusalem the week before His death (Matt. 21:1; Mark 11:1; Luke 19:29, 37). All other refs. for *elaia*: OLIVE <1636>, OLIVE TREE <1636>.

[2] ***Oros tou Elaiōnos*; mount: *oros*** [neut. noun: ὄρος <3735>], **olive tree: *elaiōn*** [masc. noun: ἐλαιών <1638>] ▶ **See [1].** > After the ascension of Jesus, the disciples returned to Jerusalem, from the mount called Olivet (or: of Olives) (Acts 1:12). ¶

MOUNTAIN – ***oros*** [neut. noun: ὄρος <3735>] ▶ **Significant elevation of terrain; also transl.: hill, mount, mountainside** > The word is used in a general sense (Matt. 4:8; 5:1, 14; 8:1; 14:23; 15:29; 17:1, 9, 20; 18:12; 21:21; 24:16; 28:16; Mark 3:13; 5:5, 11; 6:46; 9:2, 9; 11:23;

13:14; Luke 3:5; 4:5, 29; 6:12; 8:32; 9:28, 37; 21:21; 23:30; John 4:20, 21; 6:3, 15; 1 Cor. 13:2; Heb. 8:5; 11:38; 12:18, 20; 2 Pet. 1:18; Rev. 6:14–16; 8:8; 16:20; 17:9; 21:10). When used more specifically, the Greek word is generally transl. "mount"; i.e., it is used in regard to the Mount of Olives (Matt. 21:1; 24:3; 26:30; Mark 11:1; 13:3; 14:26; Luke 19:29, 37; 21:37; 22:39; John 8:1; Acts 1:12), Mount Sinai (Acts 7:30, 38; Gal. 4:24, 25), and Mount Zion (Heb. 12:22; Rev. 14:1). ¶

MOUNTAINSIDE – Matt. 5:1; 8:1; John 6:3; et al. → MOUNTAIN <3735>.

MOURN – 1 ***thrēneō*** [verb: θρηνέω <2354>]; **from *thrēnos*: lamentation ▶ To sing laments, songs of sorrow and grief** > Jesus compared His generation to children mourning {singing a dirge} and reproaching their companions that they had not lamented (Matt. 11:17) or wept (Luke 7:32). Other refs.: Luke 23:27; John 16:20; see LAMENT <2354>. ¶

2 ***koptō*** [verb: κόπτω <2875>] ▶ **To strike oneself on the chest as a sign of mourning; to mourn** > A great multitude of people, and of women who wailed {bewailed} and lamented Jesus, followed Him (Luke 23:27). All other refs.: CUT <2875>, LAMENT <2875>.

3 ***pentheō*** [verb: πενθέω <3996>]; **from *penthos*: pain, affliction ▶ To be afflicted, to grieve for the death of someone; also transl.: to grieve, to wail** > Blessed are those who mourn, for they will be comforted (Matt. 5:4). The friends of the bridegroom could not mourn as long as the bridegroom was with them (Matt. 9:15). Mary Magdalene announced the resurrection of Jesus to those who had been with Him, as they mourned and wept (Mark 16:10). Some who laugh now will mourn and weep (Luke 6:25). The Corinthians should have mourned {have been filled with grief} and taken away an evil man from their midst (1 Cor. 5:2). James exhorts his audience to be miserable and mourn and weep (Jas. 4:9). Babylon will be mourned when she falls (Rev. 18:11, 15, 19). Other ref.: 2 Cor. 12:21; see BEWAIL <3996>. ¶

– 4 John 11:31; Rom. 12:15a, b; 1 Cor. 7:30a, b → WEEP <2799> 5 Acts 8:2 → mourned deeply → lit.: made great lamentations → LAMENTATION <2870> 6 Rev. 18:7 → I will never mourn → lit.: I will not see mourning → MOURNING <3997>.

MOURNING – 1 ***odurmos*** [masc. noun: ὀδυρμός <3602>]; **from *oduromai*: to complain ▶ Complaint, lamentation, sorrow** > Great mourning was heard in Rama (Matt. 2:18). Titus had reported to Paul the mourning {deep sorrow} of the Corinthians (2 Cor. 7:7). ¶

2 ***penthos*** [neut. noun: πένθος <3997>]; **related to *pathos*: suffering ▶ Pain, affliction, bereavement; also transl.: grief, sorrow** > The laughter of sinners is to be turned to mourning (Jas. 4:9). Babylon the great will receive torment and mourning, because she said she would not see mourning, (Rev. 18:7a, b); her mourning will come in one day (v. 8). In the new Jerusalem, there will be no more death, mourning, crying, pain (Rev. 21:4). ¶

– 3 1 Cor. 5:2 → to go into mourning → MOURN <3996>.

MOUTH (noun) – 1 ***stoma*** [neut. noun: στόμα <4750>] ▶ **Opening in the lower portion of the face through which we can eat, drink, talk** > Man will live by every word that proceeds from the mouth of God (Matt. 4:4). Jesus frequently opened His mouth to teach (Matt. 5:2; 13:35; Luke 4:22); some were seeking to catch something out of His mouth that they might accuse Him (Luke 11:54 {something He might say}; 22:71). On the cross, a sponge filled with sour wine was put to His mouth (John 19:29). Jesus did not open His mouth when He was accused (Acts 8:32); guile was not found in His mouth (1 Pet. 2:22). Paul had been chosen by God to hear a voice out of His mouth (Acts 22:14). The Lord will consume the lawless one with the breath of His mouth (2 Thes. 2:8); there was a sharp two-edged sword going out of His mouth

(Rev. 1:16; 2:16; 19:15, 21); He will spew Laodicea out of His mouth (Rev. 3:16). The word is also used in relation to a fish (Matt. 17:27), witnesses (Matt. 18:16; 2 Cor. 13:1), children (Matt. 21:16), Zacharias (Luke 1:64), prophets (Luke 1:70; Acts 3:18, 21), David (Acts 1:16; 4:25), Philip (Acts 8:35), Peter (Acts 10:34; 11:8; 15:7), Paul (Acts 18:14; 23:2; 2 Cor. 6:11; Eph. 6:19), unbelievers (Rom. 3:14; 10:8, 9; Jude 16), Christians (Rom. 10:10; 15:6; Eph. 4:29; Col. 3:8), lions {2 Tim. 4:17; Heb. 11:33), horses (Jas. 3:3; Rev. 9:17, 18), the apostle John (2 John 12a, b; 3 John 14a, b; Rev. 10:9, 10), the two prophets (Rev. 11:5), the serpent (Rev. 12:15), the earth (Rev. 12:16a), the dragon (Rev. 12:16b; 16:13a), the beast (Rev. 13:2, 5, 6; 16:13b), and the false prophet (Rev. 16:13c). Other refs.: Matt. 12:34; 15:11a, b, 17, 18; Luke 6:45; 19:22; 21:15; Rom. 3:19; Jas. 3:10; Rev. 14:5. Other refs.: Luke 21:24; Heb. 11:34; see EDGE <4750>. ¶

[2] **to stop the mouth: *epistomizō*** [verb: ἐπιστομίζω <1993>]; **from *epi*: upon, and *stoma*: see [1] ▶ To shut up** > The mouths of many insubordinate people had to be stopped {They had to be silenced} (Titus 1:11). ¶

[3] **word: *logos*** [masc. noun: λόγος <3056>] **▶ To communicate by mouth, or word of mouth, is to communicate verbally** > Judas and Silas were to tell by word of mouth (lit.: by word) the same things as Barnabas and Paul (Acts 15:27). Other refs.: WORD <3056>.

– [4] 1 Cor. 9:9 → to muzzle the mouth → MUZZLE <5392> [5] 2 Thes. 2:2 → "of mouth" added in Engl.

MOUTH (verb) – [1] 2 Pet. 2:18 → SPEAK <5350> [2] Jude 16 → lit.: the mouth speaks → SPEAK <2980>.

MOVE – [1] ***kineō*** [verb: κινέω <2795>]; **from *kiō*: to go, to put in motion ▶ a. To stir, to displace** > In God we live and move and exist (Acts 17:28). The scribes and the Pharisees did not want to move with their finger the heavy burdens that they laid on the shoulders of others (Matt. 23:4). **b. To instigate** > Paul was accused of moving {being a creator of, a mover of, stirring up} sedition among all the Jews (Acts 24:5). All other refs.: DISTURB <2795>, REMOVE <2795>, SHAKE <2795>.

[2] **to move, to move away: *metakineō*** [verb: μετακινέω <3334>]; **from *meta*: indicating a change of position, and *kineō*: see [1] ▶ To displace, to shift from one position to another; to be diverted** > The Colossians were not to be moved away from the hope of the gospel which they had heard (Col. 1:23). ¶

[3] ***metabainō*** [verb: μεταβαίνω <3327>]; **from *meta*: indicating change, and *bainō*: to walk ▶ To transport from one place to another** > Jesus speaks of the faith that is able to move {to remove, to transport} a mountain (Matt. 17:20a, b). All other refs.: DEPART <3327>, PASS <3327>.

[4] ***metoikizō*** [verb: μετοικίζω <3351>]; **from *meta*: particle of change, and *oikos*: habitation ▶ To change one's habitation, to emigrate** > God moved {removed, sent} Abraham into the land where the Jews now dwell (Acts 7:4). Other ref.: Acts 7:43; see TRANSPORT <3351>. ¶

[5] **to be moved: *seiō*** [verb: σείω <4579>]; **lit.: to tremble, to stir ▶ To be touched, to be filled with a great emotion** > When Jesus had come into Jerusalem, the whole city was moved {was stirred} (Matt. 21:10). All other refs.: SHAKE <4579>.

[6] ***pherō*** [verb: φέρω <5342>] **▶ To lead, to conduct; to carry (primary meaning)** > Holy men of God spoke being moved by {being carried by, under the power of} the Holy Spirit (2 Pet. 1:21). All other refs.: see entries in Lexicon at <5342>.

– [7] Matt. 11:7; Acts 2:25 → to move about, to move → SHAKE <4531> [8] Matt. 13:53 → to move on → DEPART <3332> [9] Matt. 18:34 → to be moved with anger → to be angry → ANGRY <3710> [10] Matt. 21:33 → to move to another place → to go to another country → COUNTRY <589> [11] Mark 15:11 → to stir, to stir up → STIR (verb) <383> [12] Luke 14:10 → to move up → to go up → GO <4320> [13] John 11:54 → to move about → WALK <4043> [14] Acts 7:9 → to be moved with envy →

ENVY (verb) <2206> [15] Acts 9:28 → to move about freely → lit.: to come in and go out → COME <1531> [16] Acts 20:24 → the expr. "none of these things move me" is lit.: "I make (*poieō*) account (*logos*) of nothing" [17] Acts 27:8 → to move along, to move along the coast → PASS <3881> [18] Acts 27:41 → would not move → lit.: remained immovable → IMMOVABLE <761> [19] Rom. 10:19 → to move to anger → ANGER (verb) <3949> [20] 1 Cor. 13:2 → REMOVE <3179> [21] 1 Cor. 15:58 → let nothing move you → lit.: be immovable → IMMOVABLE <277> [22] 1 Thes. 3:3 → SHAKE <4525> [23] Heb. 6:1 → to move beyond → LEAVE (verb) <863> [24] Heb. 11:7 → to be moved by fear, to be moved by godly fear → to be moved with fear → FEAR (noun) <2125> [25] Heb. 12:28 → which cannot be moved → which cannot be shaken → SHAKEN <761>.

MOVED (BE) – to be deeply moved: *embrimaomai* [verb: ἐμβριμάομαι <1690>]; **from *en*: in, and *brimaomai*: to express anger ▶ To be violently affected by circumstances** > Jesus was deeply moved in His spirit (John 11:33: *brimaomai* in some mss., 38). Other refs.: REBUKE (verb) <1690>, WARN <1690>.

MOVER – Acts 24:5 → MOVE <2795>.

MOVING – *kinēsis* [fem. noun: κίνησις <2796>]; **from *kineō*: to move, to stir ▶ Agitation, motion** > A multitude of sick people waited for the moving {disturbance} of the water at the pool of Bethesda (John 5:3 in some mss.). ¶

MOW – *amaō* [verb: ἀμάω <270>]; **from *hama*: together ▶ To gather, to collect a crop; to cut down** > James speaks of laborers who had mowed {harvested, reaped down} the fields of the rich (Jas. 5:4). ¶

MUCH – [1] ***polus*** [adj. used as adv.: πολύς <4183>] ▶ **A great deal, greatly** > Jesus charged much {gave strict orders} that no one should know that He had raised the young girl (Mark 5:43). Paul had made every effort to see the Thessalonians with much desire (1 Thes. 2:17). John wept much because no one had been found worthy to open the book (Rev. 5:4). *

[2] **so much: *tosoutos*** [pron.: τοσοῦτος <5118>] ▶ **Enough, sufficient** > The disciples were asking if they would have so much {enough, so many} bread in the wilderness to feed the great multitude (Matt. 15:33). *

– [3] Mark 5:10, 23 → EARNESTLY <4183> [4] Luke 7:12 → LARGE <2425> [5] Acts 27:9 → LONG (adj.) <2425>.

MUD – [1] John 9:6, 11, 14, 15 → CLAY <4081> [2] 2 Pet. 2:22 → MIRE <1004>.

MULBERRY TREE – Luke 17:6 → SYCAMINE TREE <4807>.

MULTIPLY – *plēthunō* [verb: πληθύνω <4129>]; **from *plēthos*: company, multitude; lit.: to make full ▶ To augment, to increase; to be in abundance** > The verb is used in regard to the number of disciples (Acts 6:1, 7), the Israelite people in Egypt (Acts 7:17), the churches in the beginning (Acts 9:31 {to grow in number}), and the word of God, which grew and multiplied {spread} (Acts 12:24). God would multiply {make abundant} the sowing of the Corinthians (2 Cor. 9:10). God would multiply Abraham (Heb. 6:14a, b); other transl.: God would give him many descendants. Peter wished grace and peace to be multiplied (1 Pet. 1:2 {to be in fullest measure}; 2 Pet. 1:2). Jude also uses this form of greeting (Jude 2). Other ref.: Matt. 24:12; see ABOUND <4129>. ¶

MULTITUDE – [1] ***ochlos*** [masc. noun: ὄχλος <3793>] ▶ **Crowd, gathering** > Paul was found in the temple without a multitude {mob} (Acts 24:18). Other ref.: see CROWD (noun) <3793>.

[2] ***plēthos*** [neut. noun: πλῆθος <4128>]; **from *plēthō*: to fill ▶ A very large number; a large company; also transl.: all, assembly, church, company, community, congregation, crowd, group, number, people** > The word is used in regard to the men and women of Israel or elsewhere

(Mark 3:7, 8; Luke 1:10; 6:17; 8:37; 23:1, 27; Acts 2:6; 5:16; 14:4; 15:12; 19:9; 21:36; 23:7; 25:24; Heb. 11:12 {numerous}), angels (Luke 2:13), the disciples of Jesus (Luke 19:37; Acts 6:2), sick people (John 5:3), fish (John 21:6), Christians (Acts 4:32; 5:14 {more and more}; 6:5; 14:1; 15:30; 17:4; 21:22 in some mss.), and sins (Jas. 5:20; 1 Pet. 4:8). Other refs.: Luke 5:6; Acts 28:3; see QUANTITY <4128>. ¶

MURDER (noun) – 1 ***phonos*** [masc. noun: φόνος <5408>]; **from *phenō*: to kill ▶ Action of willfully killing a person** > Barabbas had been imprisoned for murder (Mark 15:7; Luke 23:19, 25). Saul was still breathing threat and murder {threat and slaughter, murderous threats} against the Christians when Jesus met him on the road to Damascus (Acts 9:1). Murders are works of the flesh (Gal. 5:21 in some mss.; see also: Rom. 1:29). They proceed out of the heart (Matt. 15:19; Mark 7:21). In Rev. 9:21, men did not repent of their murders. Other ref.: Heb. 11:37; see DEATH <5408>. ¶
– 2 Matt. 5:21a, b; 19:18; Jas. 2:11a, b; 4:2 → to commit murder, to do murder → KILL <5407>.

MURDER (verb) – 1 ***diacheirizō*** [verb: διαχειρίζω <1315>]; **from *dia*: by means of (intens.), and *cheirizō*: to manipulate, which is from *cheir*: hand ▶ To kill, to cause to perish by violently laying on hands** > The verb is used in regard to Jesus (Acts 5:30 {to slay, to put to death}). Other ref.: Acts 26:21; see KILL <1315>. ¶
2 ***phoneuō*** [verb: φονεύω <5407>]; **from *phoneus*: murderer, or *phonos*: murder ▶ To kill willfully, to assassinate** > The Jews murdered {killed, put to death} the just (Jas. 5:6). All other refs.: KILL <5407>.
3 ***sphazō*** [verb: σφάζω <4969>] **▶ To kill, to slay** > Cain was of the wicked one and slew his brother (1 John 3:12a, b). All other refs.: KILL <4969>, SLAY <4969>.
– 4 Acts 7:52 → lit.: to become the murderers → MURDERER <5406>.

MURDERER – 1 ***androphonos*** [masc. noun: ἀνδροφόνος <409>]; **from *anēr*: man, and *phonos*: murder ▶ Person who kills another person** > The law is, among other applications, for murderers {manslayers} (1 Tim. 1:9). ¶
2 ***anthrōpoktonos*** [adj. used as noun: ἀνθρωποκτόνος <443>]; **from *anthrōpos*: man, and *kteinō*: to kill ▶ One who willfully kills another person; one who commits homicide** > The devil was a murderer from the beginning (John 8:44). In the eyes of God, everyone who hates his brother is a murderer, and no murderer has eternal life in him (1 John 3:15a, b). ¶
3 ***sikarios*** [masc. noun: σικάριος <4607>]; **from the Lat. *sicarius*: assassin, which is from *sica*: dagger ▶ Killer, assassin** > An Egyptian had led out into the wilderness four thousand men who were murderers {terrorists} (Acts 21:38). ¶
4 ***phoneus*** [masc. noun: φονεύς <5406>]; **from *phoneuō*: to kill ▶ Person who commits murder** > In a parable, the king destroyed the murderers of his servants (Matt. 22:7). The Jews asked Pilate to release Barabbas, a murderer, rather than Jesus (Acts 3:14). They had become the murderers of {They had murdered} the Just (Acts 7:52). The natives of Malta believed that Paul was a murderer (Acts 28:4). No Christian should suffer as a murderer (1 Pet. 4:15). The part of murderers is in the lake of fire (Rev. 21:8); they will be outside (22:15). ¶
– 5 1 Tim. 1:9 → murderer of mother, murderer of father → MOTHER <3389>, FATHER <3964>.

MURDEROUS – Acts 9:1 → murderous threats → lit.: threat and murder → MURDER (noun) <5408>.

MURMUR – 1 ***gonguzō*** [verb: γογγύζω <1111>] **▶ To speak in a low voice, to grumble; often: to complain, to express one's discontent** > In a parable, workmen murmured against the master of the house (Matt. 20:11). The scribes and the Pharisees murmured at the disciples of Jesus (Luke 5:30). The Jews murmured about Jesus (John 6:41, 43). The disciples murmured concerning a word of the Lord (John 6:61). The crowd murmured {muttered, whispered things}, thinking that Jesus must be the Christ (John 7:32). Christians should not murmur as some Jews did (1 Cor. 10:10a, b). ¶

[2] ***diagonguzō*** [verb: διαγογγύζω <1234>]; **from *dia*: through (intens.), and *gonguzō*: see [1]; lit.: to complain throughout a whole crowd ▶ To murmur, but always pejoratively; also transl.: to complain, to grumble, to mutter >** The Pharisees and the scribes murmured against Jesus (Luke 15:2). All murmured when Jesus turned in to lodge with Zaccheus (Luke 19:7). ¶

– [3] Mark 14:5 → to murmur against → to rebuke harshly → REBUKE (verb) <1690>.

MURMURER – ***gongustēs*** [masc. noun: γογγυστής <1113>]; **from *gonguzō*: to grumble, to murmur ▶ Person who complains, who expresses his discontent >** Jude speaks of murmurers {grumblers} complaining about their lot and walking after their lusts (v. 16). ¶

MURMURING – ***gongusmos*** [masc. noun: γογγυσμός <1112>]; **from *gonguzō*: to murmur, to grumble ▶ Whispering, word (often of discontent) spoken in a low voice; also transl.: complaining, complaint, grudging, grumbling, muttering >** There was much murmuring concerning Jesus among the crowds (John 7:12). There arose a murmuring {Some complained} of the Hellenists against the Hebrews (Acts 6:1). Paul exhorts Christians to do all things without murmurings and reasonings (Phil. 2:14). Peter exhorts them to be hospitable without murmuring (1 Pet. 4:9). ¶

MUSE – Luke 3:15 → REASON (verb) <1260>.

MUSIC – [1] ***sumphōnia*** [fem. noun: συμφωνία <4858>]; **from *sumphonos*: harmonious, which is from *sun*: together, and *phōnē*: sound ▶ Melodious sounds produced by instruments >** The elder son heard music {KJV: musick} and dancing (Luke 15:25). ¶

– [2] Eph. 5:19 → to make music → SING <5567>.

MUSICIAN – ***mousikos*** [adj. used as noun: μουσικός <3451>]; **from *mousa*: muse (one of the nine goddesses presiding over arts, literature, and science); lit.: one who is devoted to the muses ▶ Person who plays a musical instrument >** The sound of musicians will not be heard any more in Babylon (Rev. 18:22). ¶

MUSICK – Luke 15:25 → MUSIC <4858>.

MUST – [1] ***dei*** [impersonal verb: δεῖ <1163>] ▶ **It is logically necessary >** Jesus said that one must be born again to see the kingdom of God (John 3:7), that the Son of Man must be lifted up (3:14; 12:34), that those who worship the Father must worship Him in spirit and in truth (4:24), and that He must work the works of Him who had sent Him (9:4). This Greek verb is used in particular regarding the fact that the Christ had to suffer (Luke 24:26, 46; Acts 17:3). Other ref.: see entries in Lexicon at <1163>.

[2] **need: *ananke*** [fem. noun: ἀνάγκη <318>] ▶ **Requirement, obligation >** A man excused himself, saying that he must (lit.: had need to) go out to see his land (Luke 14:18). All other refs.: DISTRESS <318>, NECESSARY <318>, NECESSITY <318>.

MUSTARD – Matt. 13:31; 17:20; Mark 4:31; Luke 13:19; 17:6 → mustard seed, grain of mustard seed → GRAIN OF MUSTARD <2848>.

MUTE – [1] Matt. 9:32, 33; 12:22a, b; 15:30, 31; Luke 1:22; 11:14a, b → DUMB <2974> [2] Mark 4:39; Luke 1:20 → to be mute → to be silent → SILENT <4623> [3] Mark 7:37; 9:17, 25 → DUMB <216> [4] 1 Cor. 12:2 → DUMB <880>.

MUTILATE – [1] Gal. 5:12 → to mutilate oneself → to cut oneself off → CUT <609> [2] Phil. 3:2 → those who mutilate the flesh → CONCISION <2699>.

MUTILATOR – Phil. 3:2 → mutilator of the flesh → CONCISION <2699>.

MUTTER – [1] Luke 15:2; 19:7 → MURMUR <1234> [2] John 7:32 → MURMUR <1111>.

MUTTERING – John 7:12 → MURMURING <1112>.

MUTUAL – [1] Rom. 1:12 → to have mutual comfort → to be encouraged together → ENCOURAGE <4837> [2] Rom. 14:19 → ONE ANOTHER <240>.

MUTUAL AFFECTION – 2 Pet. 1:7a, b → brotherly love → LOVE (noun) <5360>.

MUTUALLY – Rom. 1:12 → to be encouraged mutually → ENCOURAGE <4837>.

MUZZLE – ***phimoō*** [verb: φιμόω <5392>]; **from *phimos*: muzzle, a device used to prevent an animal from opening its mouth ▶ To prevent from opening one's mouth** > The law says that an ox should not be muzzled while it treads out the grain (1 Cor. 9:9 {to muzzle the mouth}: other mss. have *kēmoō*; 1 Tim. 5:18). All other refs.: QUIET (adj.) <5392>, SILENCE (noun) <5392>, SPEECHLESS <5392>.

MY OWN – ***hēmeteros*** [pron.: ἡμέτερος <2251>] ▶ Refs.: Acts 2:11; 24:6; 26:5; Rom. 15:4; 1 Cor. 15:31; 2 Tim. 4:15; Titus 3:14; 1 John 1:3; 2:2. ¶ ‡

MYRA – ***Mura*** [neut. name: Μύρα <3460>] ▶ **City of Lycia in Asia Minor** > On his way to Italy, Paul landed at Myra in Lycia (Acts 27:5). ¶

MYRIAD – ***murias*** [fem. noun: μυριάς <3461>]; **from *murios*: ten thousand ▶ Ten thousand, or a very large number; also transl.: thousands upon thousands** > The word is used to describe armies of angels (Heb. 12:22 {innumerable company}; Jude 14), angels, living creatures and elders (Rev. 5:11a, b), and horses (Rev. 9:16a, b {two hundred million; lit.: two myriads of myriads}; other mss.: *dismuriades muriadōn*). All other refs.: FIFTY THOUSAND <3461>, INNUMERABLE <3461>.

MYRRH – [1] ***smurna*** [fem. noun: σμύρνα <4666>] ▶ **Resinous gum extracted from a shrub native to Arabia and Ethiopia** > It may flow spontaneously (liquid or pure myrrh; see Ex. 30:23), or be extracted by an incision in the bark; it was used as perfume and medicinally. Very fragrant and of a bitter taste, myrrh is a figure representing the sweet odor of Christ, the Man of Sorrows suffering in His life and in His death on the cross. The wise men, who had come from the east to do homage to the child Jesus, offered Him myrrh and gold and frankincense (Matt. 2:11). Nicodemus came to embalm the body of Jesus with a mixture of myrrh and aloes (John 19:39). Christians of the church of Smyrna (Smyrna means "myrrh") were warned of the things they were about to suffer (Rev. 2:8; see v. 10). ¶
– [2] Mark 15:23 → to mingle with myrrh, to mix with myrrh → MINGLE <4669> [3] Luke 7:37, 38, 46; Rev. 18:13 → OINTMENT <3464>.

MYSELF – [1] ***emautou*** [pron.: ἐμαυτοῦ <1683>] ▶ **Also transl.: of myself, to myself** > Refs.: Matt. 8:9; Luke 7:7, 8; John 5:30, 31; 7:17; 8:14, 18, 54; 12:32, 49; 14:10; 1 Cor. 4:3; 2 Cor. 2:1; Phm. 13. * ‡
[2] ***eme*** [pron.: ἐμέ <1691>] ▶ **The emphatic form of *me*: me, my.** * ‡

MYSIA – ***Musia*** [fem. name: Μυσία <3465>]: **beach, region ▶ Region in north-western Asia Minor** > After they had come to Mysia during their second missionary journey, Paul and Silas attempted to go to Bithynia, but the Spirit did not allow them (Acts 16:7, 8). ¶

MYSTERY – ***mustērion*** [neut. noun: μυστήριον <3466>]; **from *mustēs*: person initiated to mysteries; lit.: that which is known by the initiated ▶ In the N.T., a mystery is a truth which was hidden, but is now revealed; also transl.: secret, secret**

thing > Col. 1:26 illustrates this definition: "the mystery which had been hidden ... but has now been made manifest," relative to the church (see also Eph. 3:3, 4, 9; 5:32). The following are examples of mysteries: the kingdom of God (Matt. 13:11; Mark 4:11; Luke 8:10), the blindness (or hardening) of Israel (Rom. 11:25), the resurrection of the saints (1 Cor. 15:51), the gospel (Eph. 6:19), Christ the hope of glory (Col. 1:27), lawlessness (2 Thes. 2:7 {secret power}: see MYSTERY OF LAWLESSNESS), and godliness (1 Tim. 3:16). Other refs.: Rom. 16:25; 1 Cor. 2:7; 4:1; 13:2; 14:2; Eph. 1:9; Col. 2:2; 4:3; 1 Tim. 3:9 {deep truths}; Rev. 1:20; 10:7; 17:5, 7. ¶

MYSTERY OF LAWLESSNESS – The mystery {secret power} of lawlessness in 2 Thes. 2:7 (see MYSTERY <3466> and LAWLESSNESS <458>) corresponds to the wickedness of man, which is unrestrained and will reach a level of full development in the person of the antichrist.

MYTH – **1** 1 Tim. 1:4; 4:7; 2 Tim. 4:4; Titus 1:14 → FABLE <3454> **2** 2 Pet. 1:16 → FABLE <3454>.

N

NAAMAN – ***Naiman*** [masc. name: Ναιμάν <3497>]**: pleasantness, in Heb.; other Greek spelling: *Neeman* ▶ Captain of the army of Syria** > Naaman, who was a leper, was healed by Elisha (Luke 4:27; see 2 Kgs. 5). ¶

NAASSON – See NAHSHON <3476>.

NACHOR – See NAHOR <3493>.

NAGGAI – ***Nangai*** [masc. name: Ναγγαί <3477>]**: shining, in Heb. ▶ Man of the O.T.; also transl.: Nagge** > Naggai is mentioned in the genealogy of Jesus (Luke 3:25). ¶

NAGGE – See NAGGAI <3477>.

NAHOR – ***Nachōr*** [masc. name: Ναχώρ <3493>]**: who snorts, in Heb. ▶ Man of the O.T.; also transl.: Nachor** > Grandfather of Abraham (see Gen. 11:22–26), Nahor is mentioned in the genealogy of Jesus (Luke 3:34). ¶

NAHSHON – ***Naassōn*** [masc. name: Ναασσών <3476>]**: diviner, in Heb. ▶ Man of the O.T.; also transl.: Naasson** > Nahshon is mentioned in the genealogy of Jesus Christ (Matt. 1:4a, b; Luke 3:32); he was the grandfather of Boaz (see Ruth 4:20). ¶

NAHUM – ***Naoum*** [masc. name: Ναούμ <3486>]**: comfort, in Heb. ▶ Man of the O.T.; also transl.: Naoum, Naum** > Nahum is mentioned in the genealogy of Jesus (Luke 3:25). ¶

NAIL (noun) – ***hēlos*** [masc. noun: ἧλος <2247>] **▶ Piece of metal pointed at one end and flat at the other to fasten something in place** > Thomas would not believe that Jesus was risen, unless he saw in His hands the print of the nails and put his finger into the print of the nails (John 20:25a, b). ¶

NAIL (verb) – 1 ***prosēloō*** [verb: προσηλόω <4338>]**; from *pros*: to, and *hēloō*: to sharpen, to nail, which is from *hēlos*: nail ▶ To fasten with nails or to hang an object** > Jesus has effaced the handwriting of ordinances that was against us, having nailed it to the cross (Col. 2:14). ¶
– 2 Acts 2:23 → to nail to the cross → CRUCIFY <4362>.

NAIN – ***Nain*** [fem. name: Ναΐν <3484>]**: beauty, in Heb. ▶ City of Galilee southeast of Nazareth** > Jesus resurrected the only son of a widow in Nain (Luke 7:11). ¶

NAIVE – Rom. 16:18 → SIMPLE <172>.

NAKED – 1 ***gumnos*** [adj.: γυμνός <1131>] **▶ Undressed, without clothing; wearing only an under garment** > The word is used in regard to the Lord Jesus {needing clothes} (Matt. 25:36, 38, 43, 44), a certain young man (Mark 14:51 {wearing nothing}, 52), Peter (John 21:7 {stripped, taken off}), the sons of Sceva (Acts 19:16), Christians (2 Cor. 5:3), all things to the eyes of God (Heb. 4:13 {bare, uncovered}), a brother or a sister {without clothes} (Jas. 2:15), Laodicea (Rev. 3:17), he who watches (Rev. 16:15), and the great prostitute (Rev. 17:16). Other ref.: 1 Cor. 15:37; see BARE <1131>. ¶
2 **to be naked: *gumnēteuō*** [verb: γυμνητεύω <1130>]**; from *gumnos*: see 1 ▶ To be lightly or poorly clothed** > Paul said that he was naked {was in nakedness, was poorly clothed, was poorly dressed, was in rags} (1 Cor. 4:11); some mss. have *gumniteuō*. ¶

NAKEDNESS – 1 ***gumnotēs*** [fem. noun: γυμνότης <1132>]**; from *gumnos*: naked ▶ State of a (fully or partially) naked person; deprivation of the necessities of life, destitution** > Nakedness cannot separate Christians from the love of Christ (Rom. 8:35). Paul had been in cold and nakedness {exposure} (2 Cor. 11:27). The shame of the nakedness of Laodicea ought not to be made manifest (Rev. 3:18). ¶
– 2 1 Cor. 4:11 → to be in nakedness → to be naked → NAKED <1130>.

NAME (noun) – 1 ***onoma*** [neut. noun: ὄνομα <3686>] **▶ Word or group of words used to designate a person** > The term is used in regard to the Lord Jesus (Matt. 1:21, 23, 25; 7:22a–c; 10:22; 12:21;

18:5, 20; 19:29; 24:5, 9; Mark 6:14; 9:37–39, 41; 13:6, 13; 16:17; Luke 1:31; 2:21a; 9:48, 49; 10:17; 21:8, 12, 17; 24:47; John 1:12; 2:23; 3:18; 14:13, 14, 26; 15:16, 21; 16:23, 24, 26; 20:31; Acts 2:21, 38; 3:6, 16a, b; 4:7, 10, 12, 17, 18, 30; 5:28, 40, 41; 8:12, 16; 9:14–16, 21, 27, 29; 10:43, 48; 19:5, 13, 17; 21:13; 22:16; 26:9; Rom. 1:5; 10:13; 1 Cor. 1:2, 10; 5:4; 6:11; Eph. 5:20; Phil. 2:9a, 10; Col. 3:17; 2 Thes. 1:12; 3:6; 2 Tim. 2:19; Heb. 1:4; 2:12; 13:15; Jas. 2:7; 5:10, 14; 1 Pet. 4:14, 16 in some mss.; 1 John 2:12; 3:23; 5:13; 3 John 7; Rev. 2:3, 13; 3:8, 12c; 14:1a; 15:4; 19:12, 13, 16; 22:4), God (Matt. 21:9; 23:39; Mark 11:9; Luke 1:49; 13:35; 19:38; John 12:13; Acts 15:14, 17, 26; 16:18; Rom. 2:24; 9:17; 15:9; 1 Tim. 6:1; Heb. 6:10; Rev. 3:12a; 11:18; 13:6; 16:9), the Father (Matt. 6:9; Luke 11:2; John 5:43a; 10:25; 12:28; 17:6, 11, 12, 26; Rev. 14:1b), and the three persons of the Trinity (Matt. 28:19). The term is also used in regard to the apostles (Matt. 10:2; Rev. 21:14), Simon, a man of Cyrene (Matt. 27:32), Jairus (Mark 5:22; Luke 8:41), a demon called Legion (Mark 5:9a, b; Luke 8:30), Gethsemane (Mark 14:32), Elizabeth (Luke 1:5), Zacharias (Luke 1:5, 59), John the Baptist (Luke 1:13, 61, 63; John 1:6), Nazareth (Luke 1:26), Joseph and Mary (Luke 1:27a, b), Simeon (Luke 2:25), Levi (Luke 5:27), disciples (Luke 6:22; 10:20), Martha (Luke 10:38), Lazarus (Luke 16:20), Zaccheus (Luke 19:2), Joseph of Arimathea (Luke 23:50), Emmaus (Luke 24:13 {called}; lit.: to which name), Cleopas (Luke 24:18), Nicodemus (John 3:1), the antichrist (John 5:43b; Rev. 13:17a, b; 14:11; 15:2), the sheep of the Good Shepherd (John 10:3), Malchus (John 18:10), Ananias (Acts 5:1), Gamaliel (Acts 5:34), Simon the magician (Acts 8:9), another Ananias (Acts 9:10, 12), Saul of Tarsus (Acts 9:11), Aeneas (Acts 9:33), Dorcas (Acts 9:36), Cornelius (Acts 10:1), Agabus (Acts 11:28; 21:10), Rhoda (Acts 12:13), Bar-Jesus (Acts 13:6), Elymas (Acts 13:8), Timothy (Acts 16:1), Lydia (Acts 16:14), Damaris (Acts 17:34), Aquila (Acts 18:2), Justus (Acts 18:7), names according to Jewish law (Acts 18:15), Apollos (Acts 18:24), Demetrius (Acts 19:24), Eutychus (Acts 20:9), Julius (Acts 27:1), Publius (Acts 28:7), Paul (1 Cor. 1:13, 15), everyone (Eph. 1:21; Phil. 2:9b), Christians (Phil. 4:3; Rev. 3:4, 5a, b), the friends of John (3 John 14), a name written on a white stone (Rev. 2:17), Sardis (Rev. 3:1), the city of God (Rev. 3:12b), Death (Rev. 6:8), the star Wormwood (Rev. 8:11), the angel of the abyss (Rev. 9:11a, b), seven thousand men (Rev. 11:13), the first beast and its names of blasphemy (Rev. 13:1), those who do homage to the antichrist (Rev. 13:8; 17:8), great Babylon (Rev. 17:3, 5), and the twelve tribes of Israel (Rev. 21:12). Other refs.: Matt. 10:41a, b, 42, see [2]. ¶

[2] **in:** ***eis*** [prep.: εἰς <1519>] **the name of:** ***onoma*** [neut. noun: ὄνομα <3686>] ▶ **In the capacity of, as; also transl.: because >** Jesus spoke of receiving a prophet in the name of a prophet and a righteous man in the name of a righteous man, and of receiving the reward of a prophet and of a righteous man (Matt. 10:41a, b); whoever will give to drink a cup of cold water to a little one, in the name of a disciple, will in no wise lose his reward (v. 42). All other refs. (*onoma*): see [1].

– [3] Matt. 9:31 → to spread the name → to spread the news → NEWS <1310> [4] Matt. 13:55; 26:3, 14 → the name is, whose name is → called → CALL (verb) <3004> [5] Matt. 27:16 → whose name was → named → NAME (verb) <3004> [6] Luke 2:21b → which was the name given → lit.: that was called [7] Luke 6:14; Eph. 3:15 → to give the name, to derive the name → NAME (verb) <3687> [8] Rom. 2:17 → to bear the name → NAME (verb) <2028> [9] 1 Cor. 5:11 → one who bears the name of brother → one called brother → CALL (verb) <3687>.

NAME (verb) – [1] ***legō*** [verb: λέγω <3004>] ▶ **To give a specific name; also transl.: to call >** The verb is used in regard to Matthew (Matt. 9:9), Barabbas (Matt. 27:16; Mark 15:7), and the city of Sychar (John 4:5). As a priest, Jesus is not named {designated} after the order of Aaron (Heb. 7:11). Other refs.: SPEAK <3004>.

[2] ***onomazō*** [verb: ὀνομάζω <3687>]; **from *onoma*: name ▶ a. To give a name, to call; to mention** > Jesus chose twelve disciples, whom He also named apostles (Luke 6:13), including Simon whom He named Peter (v. 14). God seated Christ at His right hand in the heavenly places, above every name named {every title given} (Eph. 1:21). Every family in the heavens and on earth is named {derives its name} of God the Father (Eph. 3:15). Neither sexual immorality, nor uncleanness nor lust should be named among the saints of God (Eph. 5:3 {to be a hint}). **b. To identify by name, to profess, to mention** > Paul announced the glad tidings, not where Christ had been named {had been known} (Rom. 15:20). Everyone who names {confesses} the name of the Lord is to withdraw from iniquity (2 Tim. 2:19). All other refs.: CALL (verb) <3687>.

[3] ***eponomazō*** [verb: ἐπονομάζω <2028>]; **from *epi*: upon, and *onomazō*: see [2] ▶ To be called** > Paul spoke of one who is named a {is called a, bears the name} Jew, and rests entirely on the law (Rom. 2:17). ¶

[4] The partic. "named" is often lit. "of the name." See NAME (noun) <3686>.

– [5] Luke 1:59; 2:21; 19:2; Heb. 11:18 et al. → CALL (verb) <2564> [6] Acts 4:36; 10:5 → SURNAME (verb) <1941> [7] Acts 13:47; 20:28; Rom. 4:17 → APPOINT <5087> [8] Acts 19:14 → "named" added in Engl.

NAMED – [1] **the name: *tounoma*** [neut. noun: τοὔνομα <5122>]; **from *to*: the, and *onoma*: name ▶ By name, called** > A rich man from Arimathea, named (lit.: the name) Joseph, had become a disciple of Jesus (Matt. 27:57). ¶

– [2] Acts 11:28; 21:10; et al. → lit.: of the name of → NAME (noun) <3686> [3] Acts 19:14 → "named" added in Engl.

NAMELY – Rom. 1:20 → "namely" added in Engl.

NAOUM – See NAHUM <3486>.

NAPHTALI – ***Nephthalim*** [masc. name: Νεφθαλίμ <3508>]: **my wrestling, in Heb.; see Gen. 30:8; also spelled: *Nephthaleim* ▶ One of the twelve sons of Jacob and the tribe descended from him; also transl.: Nephtalim, Nepthalim** > Capernaum is in the borders of Zebulun and Naphtali (Matt. 4:13, 15). Twelve thousand out of the tribe of Naphtali will be sealed (Rev. 7:6). ¶

NAPKIN – [1] Luke 19:20; Acts 19:12 → HANDKERCHIEF <4676> [2] John 11:44; 20:7 → CLOTH <4676>.

NARCISSUS – ***Narkissos*** [masc. name: Νάρκισσος <3488>]: **from the same name as the flower ▶ Christian man of Rome** > Paul greets the Christians of the household of Narcissus (Rom. 16:11). ¶

NARD – ***nardos*** [fem. noun: νάρδος <3487>] ▶ **Perfume of a pleasant odor extracted from a herbaceous plant; it was very costly; also transl.: spikenard** > Mary of Bethany poured pure nard on the head and feet of Jesus (Mark 14:3; John 12:3). The Lord received it in anticipation of the day of His burial. Thus, for the Christian, this perfume of great price also evokes the death of the Lord. ¶

NARRATIVE – Luke 1:1 → ACCOUNT (noun) <1335>.

NARROW – ***stenos*** [adj.: στενός <4728>] ▶ **Small in width, tight** > Jesus said to enter by the narrow {strait} gate which leads to life (Matt. 7:13, 14), to strive to enter through this gate (Luke 13:24). ¶

NATHAN – ***Nathan*** [masc. name: Ναθάν <3481>]: **(God) has given, in Heb. ▶ Man of the O.T.** > Nathan, one of the sons of David, is mentioned in the genealogy of Jesus (Luke 3:31). ¶

NATHANAEL – ***Nathanaēl*** [masc. name: Ναθαναήλ <3482>]: **gift of God, in Heb. ▶ Disciple of Jesus** > Nathanael was an Israelite of Cana in Galilee (John 21:2).

Philip led him to Jesus; he recognized that Jesus was the Son of God, the King of Israel (John 1:46–50). After Jesus had risen, He manifested Himself to him at the Sea of Tiberias (John 21:2). See BARTHOLOMEW. ¶

NATION – 1 ***genos*** [neut. noun: γένος <1085>]; **from *ginomai*: to become ▶ Race, kinship** > Paul advanced in Judaism beyond many of his contemporaries in his nation {many among his countrymen, many Jews of his own age} (Gal. 1:14). All other refs.: see entries in Lexicon at <1085>.

2 ***ethnos*** [neut. noun: ἔθνος <1484>]; **comp. *ethos*: custom ▶ Multitude, people, ethnic group** > In the sing., the word refers to the nation of Israel (e.g., Luke 7:5; 23:2; John 11:51). In the plur., the word designates the nations, the peoples, the Gentiles; it relates to Christians from among nations other than Israel (e.g., Rom. 16:4; Eph. 2:11; 3:6), or to the unconverted (the heathen, in certain versions) in contrast to believers of the church. God has made of one blood every nation of men to dwell upon the whole face of the earth (Acts 17:26). *

3 **one who is of the nations, one of the nations: *ethnikos*** [adj.: ἐθνικός <1482>]; **from *ethnos*: see 2; also transl.: heathen, Gentile, pagan ▶ Person who belongs to a nation other than Israel** > The Greek word is found in Matt. 6:7 and 18:17. ¶

4 **as the nations: *ethnikōs*** [adv.: ἐθνικῶς <1483>]; **from *ethnos*: see 2 ▶ After the manner of those who do not belong to Israel** > Paul told Peter he was living as the nations {in, after the manner of Gentiles, like the Gentiles, like a Gentile}, and not as the Jews (Gal. 2:14). ¶

5 **one of another nation: *allophulos*** [adj.: ἀλλόφυλος <246>]; **from *allos*: other, and *phulē*: tribe ▶ Stranger, foreigner** > It was unlawful for a Jewish man to keep company with one of another nation {one of a strange race, a foreigner, a Gentile} (Acts 10:28). Other ref.: Acts 13:19 in some mss. ¶

– 6 Matt. 24:30 → TRIBE <5443> 7 Acts 8:9 → PEOPLE <1484>.

NATIVE – 1 Acts 4:36 → a native of Cyprus → lit.: Cyprian by birth 2 Acts 18:2, 24 → RACE[1] <1085> 3 Acts 28:2, 4 → BARBARIAN <915>.

NATURAL – 1 ***phusikos*** [adj.: φυσικός <5446>]; **from *phusis*: nature, which is from *phuō*: to engender, to grow ▶ a. According to the order of nature** > Females changed natural relations into that contrary to nature (Rom. 1:26), and in like manner the males also (v. 27). **b. Governed by instincts of nature** > Peter writes about those who walk according to the flesh, acting as natural animals {as animals born as creatures of instinct} (2 Pet. 2:12). ¶

2 **natural, natural man: *psuchikos*** [adj.: ψυχικός <5591>]; **from *psuchē*: breath, life, soul ▶ Animated only by the created soul, the principle of natural life** > The natural man {man without the Spirit} does not receive the things of the Spirit of God (1 Cor. 2:14). The body of the Christian is sown a natural body; if there is a natural body, there is also a spiritual one (1 Cor. 15:44a, b). What is natural comes before what is spiritual (1 Cor. 15:46). Jude speaks of mockers, who are natural {sensual, worldly-minded} men {who follow mere natural instincts}, not having the Spirit (Jude 19). Other ref.: Jas. 3:15; see SENSUAL <5591>. ¶

3 **nature: *genesis*** [fem. noun: γένεσις <1078>]; **from *genos*: race, or *ginomai*: to become ▶ Birth** > James speaks of a man who considers his natural face (lit.: face of nature) in a mirror (Jas. 1:23). Other refs.: Matt. 1:1; Luke 1:14; Jas. 3:6; see GENEALOGY <1078>, NATURE <1078>. ¶

– 4 John 11:13 → natural sleep → lit.: rest of sleep → REST (noun)[1] <2838> 5 Rom. 11:21, 24c → according to nature, natural → NATURE <5449>.

NATURALLY – 1 Phil. 2:20 → SINCERELY <1104> 2 Jude 10 → by mere nature → NATURE <5447>.

NATURE – 1 ***phusis*** [fem. noun: φύσις <5449>]; **from *phuō*: to engender, to**

grow ▶ The whole combination of traits characterizing a being > Females changed natural relations to that contrary to nature {unnatural ones} (Rom. 1:26). The Gentiles practice by nature {instinctively} the things of the law (Rom. 2:14). Paul speaks of uncircumcision by nature {the physically uncircumcised} (Rom. 2:27). God had not spared the natural (lit.: according to nature; *kata phusin*) branches (Rom. 11:21); in Rom. 11:24a–c: nature. Nature teaches that long hair is a dishonor to a man (1 Cor. 11:14). Paul and Peter were Jews by nature {birth} (Gal. 2:15). Before their conversion, the Galatians were in bondage to those who by nature are not gods (Gal. 4:8). Before their conversion, Christians were children, by nature, of wrath (Eph. 2:3). They are partakers of the divine nature (2 Pet. 1:4). Other refs.: Jas. 3:7a, b; see KIND (noun) <5449>. ¶

[2] **by mere nature: *phusikōs*** [adv.: φυσικῶς <5447>]; **from *phusikos*: natural, which is from *phusis*: see [1] ▶ Naturally, under the guidance of physical senses** > Jude speaks of those who corrupt themselves in the things they understand by mere nature {by instinct, naturally}, as the irrational animals (Jude 10). ¶

[3] ***genesis*** [fem. noun: γένεσις <1078>]; **from *genos*: race, or *ginomai*: to become ▶ Existence, birth** > James speaks of a man who considers his natural face (lit.: face of nature) in a mirror (Jas. 1:23). The tongue sets fire to the course of nature {life} (Jas. 3:6). Other refs.: Matt. 1:1; Luke 1:14; see GENEALOGY <1078>. ¶

[4] **his own nature: *idios*** [adj.: ἴδιος <2398>] **▶ Which belongs exclusively to an individual** > The devil speaks from his own nature (lit.: of his own things), i.e., according to what his true nature is, a murderer and a liar (John 8:44). Other refs.: see entries in Lexicon at <2398>.

– [5] Acts 14:15 → of the same nature, with the same nature → of like passions → PASSION <3663> [6] Acts 17:29 → Divine Nature → DIVINE <2304> [7] Rom. 1:20 → divine nature → GODHEAD <2305> [8] Phil. 2:6, 7 → FORM (noun) <3444> [9] Heb. 1:3 → SUBSTANCE <5287>.

NAUGHT – 2 Cor. 10:10 → to be naught → to treat with contempt → CONTEMPTIBLE <1848>.

NAUGHTINESS – Jas. 1:21 → MALICE <2549>.

NAUM – See NAHUM <3486>.

NAVIGATE – Acts 27:2 → SAIL (verb) <4126>.

NAVIGATION – ***ploos*** [masc. noun: πλόος <4144>]; **from *pleō*: to navigate ▶ Voyage by sea; also transl.: course, sailing, voyage** > The word is used concerning Paul's journeys in Acts 21:7; 27:9, 10. ¶

NAY – Rom. 8:37 → RATHER <235>.

NAZARENE – **Nazarene, of Nazareth: *Nazarēnos*** [masc. name: Ναζαρηνός <3479>], ***Nazōraios*** [masc. name: Ναζωραῖος <3480>]; **from the Heb. *netser*: branch; see Is. 11:1 ▶ Inhabitant of Nazareth. This name also makes reference to a person who is consecrated to God (see Num. 6:1–21) with respect to the law of the Nazirite; see also Gen. 49:26 and Deut. 33:16.** On many occasions, Jesus is called a Nazarene in the Gospels (Matt. 2:23; 26:71; Mark 1:24; 10:47; 14:67; 16:6; Luke 4:34; 18:37; 24:19; John 18:5, 7; 19:19) and in Acts (2:22; 3:6; 4:10; 6:14; 22:8; 26:9). This name was a derogatory term for Christians; Paul was accused of being a leader of the sect of the Nazarenes (Acts 24:5). ¶

NAZARETH – [1] ***Nazaret*** [masc. name: Ναζαρέτ <3478>]; **also spelled: *Nazareth* ▶ City of Galilee** > Jesus lived in Nazareth (Matt. 2:23; 4:13; 21:11; Mark 1:9; Luke 2:51; 4:16; Acts 10:38). Joseph and Mary were from Nazareth (Luke 1:26, see v. 27; 2:4, 39). This city was despised by the Jews (John 1:45, 46). ¶

– [2] of Nazareth → NAZARENE <3479>, <3480>.

NEAPOLIS – ***Neapolis*** [fem. name: Νεάπολις <3496>]**: new city ▶ Port of Macedonia, north of the Aegean Sea** > Paul entered Europe by way of this port of the city of Philippi (Acts 16:11). ¶

NEAR (adv.) – [1] ***engus*** [adv.: ἐγγύς <1451>] **▶ Close in time or in space; also transl.: at hand, nigh at hand, nearby, almost time** > The word is used in regard to summer (Matt. 24:32; Mark 13:28; Luke 21:30), things of which the Lord spoke (Matt. 24:33; Mark 13:29), the Lord's time (Matt. 26:18), the kingdom of God (Luke 21:31), the Passover of the Jews (John 2:13; 6:4; 11:55), the feast of tabernacles (John 7:2), the tomb (John 19:42), and the time of the words of the prophecy (Rev. 1:3; 22:10). The Lord is near (Phil. 4:5), i.e., that He stands beside those who are His own or He will soon be coming for His own. *

[2] **to be near, to be nigh, to draw near, to draw nigh: *engizō*** [verb: ἐγγίζω <1448>]**; from *engus*: see** [1] **▶ To come close, to approach** > When Jesus drew near Jerusalem, He wept over it (Luke 19:41). Many will come in the name of Jesus and say the time is near (Luke 21:8). The desolation of Jerusalem will be near when it is encompassed with armies (Luke 21:20). For the sake of the work, Epaphroditus had drawn near {had come close} to death (Phil. 2:30). The coming of the Lord is near {is at hand} (Jas. 5:8). All other refs.: COME <1448>, DRAW <1448>, HAND (noun) <1448>, NEIGHBORHOOD <1448>.

– [3] Acts 10:24 → CLOSE <316> [4] Phil. 2:27 → CLOSE <3897> [5] 2 Tim. 4:6 → to be at hand → HAND <2186>.

NEAR (adv. and verb) – [1] Acts 9:3 → to come near → COME <1448> [2] Acts 27:27 → to draw near → DRAW <4317>.

NEARBY – John 19:42 → NEAR (adv.) <1451>.

NEARER – [1] ***enguteron*** [adv.: ἐγγύτερον <1452>]**; compar. of *engus*: near ▶ Closer in time** > The salvation of the Christians (i.e., the return of the Lord) is nearer than when they had believed (Rom. 13:11). ¶

– [2] Acts 27:13 → to raise nearer → WEIGH <142> <788>.

NEARLY – [1] Acts 13:44; Heb. 9:22 → ALMOST <4975> [2] Phil. 2:30 → to nearly die → lit.: to draw near as far as death → NEAR (adv.) <1448>.

NEARSIGHTED (BE) – 2 Pet. 1:9 → SHORTSIGHTED (BE) <3467>.

NECESSARILY – [1] 1 Cor. 5:10 → ALTOGETHER <3843> [2] Heb. 7:12 → of necessity → NECESSITY <318>.

NECESSARY – [1] ***anankaios*** [adj.: ἀναγκαῖος <316>]**; from *anankē*: see** [3] **▶ Needful, indispensable** > It was necessary that the word of God should first be spoken to the Jews (Acts 13:46). The members of the body that seem to be weaker are necessary (1 Cor. 12:22). Paul thought it necessary to encourage the brothers to go beforehand to the Corinthians (2 Cor. 9:5). It was more necessary for Paul to remain in the flesh (Phil. 1:24). He thought it necessary to send Epaphroditus to the Philippians (Phil. 2:25). Christians should learn to apply themselves to good works for necessary {pressing, urgent, daily} needs (Titus 3:14). It was necessary {of necessity} that Jesus, as high priest, should have something to offer (Heb. 8:3). Other ref.: Acts 10:24; see CLOSE (adj. and adv.) <316>. ¶

[2] ***epanankes*** [adv. and adv. used as noun: ἐπάναγκες <1876>]**; from *epi*: upon (intens.), and *anankē*: see** [3] **▶ Indispensable, absolutely required** > Paul speaks to Christians of certain necessary things {essentials, requirements} (Acts 15:28; see v. 29). ¶

[3] **necessity: *anankē*** [fem. noun: ἀνάγκη <318>] **▶ Need, obligation** > Jesus said it must needs be {it is inevitable, such things must come} (lit.: it is a necessity) that offences come (Matt. 18:7). It is necessary {You must, You must needs} (lit.: It is a necessity} to be subject to authority (Rom. 13:5). The death of the testator must needs

(lit.: of necessity) come in {is necessary} for a testament to be valid (Heb. 9:16). It was necessary (lit.: a necessity) that the copies of the things in the heavens should be purified (Heb. 9:23). Other ref.: Luke 23:17 in some mss. All other refs.: DISTRESS <318>, MUST <318>, NECESSITY <318>.
– [4] Luke 10:42; Acts 28:10 → NEED (noun) <5532> [5] Acts 17:3 → it was necessary → MUST <1163> [6] Acts 19:36 → it is necessary → it ought → OUGHT <1163> <2076> [7] Acts 27:34 → this had to do with → this is for (*huparchō*) [8] Jas. 2:16 → NEEDFUL <2006> [9] 1 Pet. 1:6 → it is needed → NEEDED <1163>.

NECESSITY – [1] ***anankē*** [fem. noun: ἀνάγκη <318>] ► **a. Need, obligation; also transl.: compulsion, constraint** > On account of the present necessity {crisis, distress}, it is good for a man to remain as he is (i.e., unmarried) (1 Cor. 7:26). He who has no necessity does well not to marry (1 Cor. 7:37). Announcing the good news was a necessity laid upon Paul {he was compelled} (1 Cor. 9:16). The Christian must not give of necessity, for God loves a cheerful giver (2 Cor. 9:7). The good deed that Paul wished Philemon to do was not to be as by way of necessity {forced} (Phm. 14). The priesthood being changed, there takes place of necessity also {there must also be} a change of law (Heb. 7:12). The high priests had day by day need {They needed} to offer up sacrifices (Heb. 7:27). Jude felt the necessity {was compelled, was obliged, found it necessary, felt he had; it was needful for him} to exhort Christians to contend for the faith (Jude 3). **b. Calamity, difficulty; also transl.: need, distress, hardship** > Paul commended himself as a servant of God in necessities (2 Cor. 6:4). He took pleasure in necessities (2 Cor. 12:10). He had been comforted in all his necessity by the faith of the Thessalonians (1 Thes. 3:7). All other refs.: DISTRESS <318>, MUST <318>, NECESSARY <318>.
[2] ***chreia*** [fem. noun: χρεία <5532>]; **from *chreos*: debt ► Need, what is required** > Christians ought to distribute to the necessities {needs} of the saints (Rom. 12:13). All other refs.: BUSINESS <5532>, NEED (noun) <5532>.
– [3] Heb. 8:3 → of necessity → NECESSARY <316> [4] 1 Pet. 5:2 → by necessity → by constraint → CONSTRAINT <317>.

NECK – ***trachēlos*** [masc. noun: τράχηλος <5137>] ► **Part of a human joining the head to the body** > The word is used in the expr. "to hang a millstone around the neck" (Matt. 18:6; Mark 9:42; Luke 17:2) and "to fall on the neck" {to embrace, to throw the arms around} (Luke 15:20; Acts 20:37). Peter says that it is putting a yoke on the neck of the disciples to add something other than grace (Acts 15:10). Prisca and Aquila had risked their own necks (in Greek, "neck" is sing.) {risked their lives} for Paul's life (Rom. 16:4). ¶

NEED (noun) – [1] ***chreia*** [fem. noun: χρεία <5532>]; **from *chreos*: debt ► Necessity, what is required; also transl.: to need** > John had need to be baptized by Jesus (Matt. 3:14). God the Father knows what things we have need of (Matt. 6:8). Jesus told the disciples the crowds had no need to go, but to give them something to eat (Matt. 14:16). The Lord had need of a donkey and a colt (Matt. 21:3; Mark 11:3; Luke 19:31, 34). Jesus cured those who had need of healing (Luke 9:11). He had no need that anyone should testify of man (John 2:25). The hands of Paul had ministered to his needs {wants} and to those who were with him (Acts 20:34). When Paul left, he was presented with what should minister to his needs {his wants, such things as were necessary} (Acts 28:10). Epaphroditus ministered to the need {the wants} of Paul (Phil. 2:25). The Philippians had sent something for Paul's need (Phil. 4:16); Paul told them that God would supply all their need (4:19). The Hebrews had need to be taught again, and had become such as had need of milk (Heb. 5:12a, b); they had need of endurance (10:36). The angel of the church in Laodicea says that he has need of nothing (Rev. 3:17). The holy city has no need of the sun to shine in it

(Rev. 21:23); there will be no need of a lamp or the light of the sun (22:5). Other refs.: Matt. 9:12; 26:65; Mark 2:17, 25; 14:63; Luke 5:31; 10:42 {necessary, needful}; 15:7; 22:71; John 13:10, 29; 16:30; Acts 2:45; 4:35; 1 Cor. 12:21a, b, 24; Eph. 4:28, 29 {use; needful, lit.: of the need}; 1 Thes. 1:8; 4:9, 12 {lack, to lack}; 5:1; Titus 3:14; Heb. 7:11; 1 John 2:27; 3:17. All other refs.: BUSINESS <5532>, NECESSITY <5532>.

2 **to have need, to need: *chrēzō*** [verb: χρῄζω <5535>]; **from *chreia*: see** 1 ► **To feel the necessity of something** > Our heavenly Father knows that we have need of various things for this life (Matt. 6:32; Luke 12:30). Other refs.: Luke 11:8 {to want}; Rom. 16:2; 2 Cor. 3:1. ¶

3 ***husterēma*** [neut. noun: ὑστέρημα <5303>]; **from *hustereō*: to lack, which is from *husteros*: lack ► Poverty, indigence, penury** > A poor widow out of her need had cast into the treasury of the temple all the living which she had (Luke 21:4). All other refs.: LACK (noun) <5303>.

– 4 Matt. 27:55 → to care for the needs → SERVE <1247> 5 Luke 15:14; 2 Cor. 11:9 → to be in need → to be in want → WANT (noun) <5302> 6 Acts 27:3 → to be provided for one's needs → lit.: to receive care → CARE (noun) <1958> 7 1 Cor. 7:37; 2 Cor. 6:4; 12:10; Heb. 7:27 → NECESSITY <318> 8 2 Cor. 9:1 → there was no need → lit.: it was superfluous → SUPERFLUOUS <4053> 9 2 Cor. 9:12; 11:9 → what is lacking → LACK (noun) <5303> 10 Phil. 4:11 → PRIVATION <5304> 11 Phil. 4:12 → to suffer need → to suffer privation → PRIVATION <5302> 12 Phil. 4:12 → to be in need → to be abased → ABASE <5013> 13 Heb. 4:16 → in time of need → SEASONABLE <2121> 14 Heb. 7:26 → to meet the need → FITTING (BE) <4241> 15 Jas. 2:15 → to be in need → LACK (verb) <3007>.

NEED (verb) – 1 ***prosdeomai*** [verb: προσδέομαι <4326>]; **from *pros*: besides, and *deomai*: to require, which is the middle voice of *deō*: to lack, to need something ► To require, to want (anything)** > God is not worshipped with men's hands as needing something (Acts 17:25). ¶

– 2 Matt. 3:14; 6:8; 9:12; 14:16; 21:3; Mark 2:17; 11:3; Luke 5:31; 9:11; 10:42; 15:7; 19:31, 34; 22:71; John 2:25; 13:10, 29; 16:30; Acts 28:10; Eph. 4:28; 1 Thes. 1:8; 4:9; Heb. 5:12a, b; 10:36; 1 John 2:27; Rev. 3:17; 21:23; 22:5 → lit.: to have need, to have no need; to be a need → NEED (noun) <5532> 3 Matt. 18:7; Rom. 13:5; Heb. 9:16 → NECESSARY <318> 4 Luke 11:8; 12:30; 2 Cor. 3:1 → NEED (noun) <5535> 5 2 Cor. 9:8 → having all that you need → having all contentment → CONTENTMENT <841> 6 2 Cor. 11:9 → to be in want → WANT (noun) <5302> 7 Titus 3:13 → LACK (verb) <3007> 8 Heb. 7:27 → NECESSITY <318> 9 1 Pet. 1:6 → it is needed → NEEDED <1163>.

NEEDED – 1 **it is needed: *dei*** [impersonal verb: δεῖ <1163>] ► **It is necessary** > Jesus needed {had} to go through Samaria (John 4:4). A Christian may be put to grief by various trials, if needed {need be, necessary} (1 Pet. 1:6).

– 2 Matt. 6:11; Luke 11:3 → DAILY <1967> 3 Jas. 2:16 → which is needed → NEEDFUL <2006>.

NEEDFUL – 1 ***epitēdeios*** [adj.: ἐπιτήδειος <2006>]; **from *epitēdēs*: beneficial, useful ► Indispensable, obligatory** > One must give the needful things {things which are needed, what is necessary} for the body to a brother or sister without clothing and destitute of daily food (Jas. 2:16). ¶

– 2 Luke 10:42; Eph. 4:29 → NEED (noun) <5532> 3 Phil. 1:24; Heb. 8:3 → NECESSARY <316> 4 Jude 3 → NECESSITY <318>.

NEEDLE – ***rhaphis*** [fem. noun: ῥαφίς <4476>]; **from *rhaptō*: to sew ► Small and slender piece of metal or other material, sharpened at one end and pierced at the other, allowing a thread to pass through; used for sewing** > It is easier for a camel to go through the eye of a needle, than for a rich man to enter into the kingdom of God (Matt. 19:24; Mark 10:25; Luke 18:25); some mss. have *belonē* in Luke 18:25. ¶

NEEDLESSLY – Gal. 2:21 → FREELY <1432>.

NEEDY – [1] Matt. 6:2, 3; Luke 12:33 → to give to the needy → lit.: to give alms → GIVE <1325>, ALMS <1654> [2] Acts 4:34 → needy person → person in want → WANT (noun) <1729>.

NEEMAN – See NAAMAN <3497>.

NEGLECT (noun) – ***apheidia*** [fem. noun: ἀφειδία <857>]; **from *a*: neg., and *pheidomai*: to spare; lit.: the fact of not sparing ▶ Severity, austerity; asceticism >** The commandments and the doctrines of men have an appearance of wisdom in self-imposed religion, humility, and neglect {neglecting, harsh treatment, severe treatment} of the body (Col. 2:23). ¶

NEGLECT (verb) – [1] Matt. 23:23 → LEAVE (verb) <863> [2] Mark 7:8 → to lay aside → LAY <863> [3] Luke 11:42 → to pass over → PASS <3928> [4] Luke 15:29 → TRANSGRESS <3928> [5] Acts 6:1 → OVERLOOK <3865> [6] Acts 6:2 → LEAVE (verb) <2641> [7] 1 Tim. 4:14; Heb. 2:3 → to be negligent → NEGLIGENT <272> [8] Heb. 10:25 → FORSAKE <1459> [9] Heb. 13:2, 16 → FORGET <1950>.

NEGLECTING – Col. 2:23 → NEGLECT (noun) <857>.

NEGLIGENT – [1] **to be negligent: *ameleō*** [verb: ἀμελέω <272>]; **from *amelēs*: careless, which is from *a*: neg., and *melō*: to take care of ▶ To remain indifferent to something; also transl.: to neglect, to ignore >** Timothy was not to be negligent of the gift that was in him (1 Tim. 4:14). How will men escape judgment if they are negligent of so great a salvation? (Heb. 2:3). Some mss. have this verb in 2 Pet. 1:12. All other refs.: DISREGARD <272>, LIGHT (adj.) <272>.

[2] **to not be negligent: *mellō*** [verb: μέλλω <3195>] ▶ **To be careful, to use diligence >** Peter would not be negligent {would be ready} to remind his readers of various exhortations (2 Pet. 1:12); other mss. have *ouk ameleō*; see [1].

NEIGHBOR – [1] ***geitōn*** [masc. and fem. noun: γείτων <1069>] ▶ **One who lives in the same region or the same country >** The term is used in the plur. (*geitones*) and in relation to one inviting for a meal (Luke 14:12), a man who found his lost sheep (15:6), a woman who finds her lost coin (15:9), and a beggar (John 9:8). ¶

[2] ***perioikos*** [adj. used as noun: περίοικος <4040>]; **from *peri*: around, and *oikos*: house ▶ One who lives nearby >** The neighbors and relatives of Elizabeth heard that the Lord had magnified His mercy toward her (Luke 1:58). ¶

[3] ***plēsion*** [adv. used as masc. noun: πλησίον <4139>]; **from *pelas*: near ▶ Person who lives near another one >** The Lord related that it had been said to love one's neighbor and hate one's enemy (Matt. 5:43); He commanded to love one's enemies (see v. 44). He commanded anew (see Lev. 19:18) to love one's neighbor as oneself (Matt. 19:19; 22:39; Mark 12:31, 33; Luke 10:27; Rom. 13:9; Gal. 5:14; Jas. 2:8). In Luke 10, Jesus uses a Samaritan to demonstrate what neighbors do for one another (vv. 29, 36); He showed mercy in "coming up to" him, so that He might bring him grace and life. He who was mistreating his neighbor pushed Moses away (Acts 7:27). Love works no ill to its neighbor, but seeks to please his neighbor (Rom. 13:10; 15:2). Everyone is to speak truth with his neighbor (Eph. 4:25) and not to judge him (Jas. 4:12). Those from Israel will not teach every man his neighbor, for all will know the Lord (Heb. 8:11); some mss.: *politēs* (citizen). ¶

– [4] Luke 1:65 → lit.: those dwelling around → DWELL <4039> [5] 1 Cor. 10:24; Gal. 6:4 → ANOTHER <2087>.

NEIGHBORHOOD – **to come into the neighborhood: *engizō*** [verb: ἐγγίζω

<1448>]; **from *engus*: near ▶ To approach, to come near** > When Jesus came into the neighborhood of Jericho, a blind man was sitting by the roadside begging (Luke 18:35). All other refs.: COME <1448>, DRAW <1448>, HAND (noun) <1448>, NEAR (adv.) <1448>.

NEIGHBOUR – See NEIGHBOR.

NEIGHBOURHOOD – See NEIGHBORHOOD.

NEITHER – [1] ***mēde*** [neg. conj.: μηδέ <3366>]; **from *mē*: not, and *de*: but, and** ▶ Nor, not even. * ‡
[2] ***oute*** [conj.: οὔτε <3777>]; **from *ou*: not, and *te*: particle of connection or addition** ▶ Also transl.: nor, not even, and not, also not. Refs.: Matt. 6:20; 1 Thes. 2:3, 5, 6. *

NEMESIS – See JUSTICE (name) <1349>.

NEPHEW – [1] Col. 4:10 → COUSIN <431> [2] 1 Tim. 5:4 → GRANDCHILD <1549>.

NEPHTALIM, NEPTHALIM – See NAPHTALI <3508>.

NEREUS – ***Nēreus*** [masc. name: Νηρεύς <3517>]: **Lat. name of a god of the sea ▶ Christian man of Rome** > Paul sends his greetings to Nereus and his sister (Rom. 16:15). ¶

NERI – ***Nēri*** [masc. name: Νηρί <3518>]: **lamp of Jehovah, in Heb. ▶ Man of the O.T.** > Neri is mentioned in the genealogy of Jesus (Luke 3:27). ¶

NERO – ***Nerōn*** [masc. name: Νέρων <3505>] ▶ **Roman emperor from A.D. 54 to 68** > Certain mss. have this name in a subscription, of no inspired authority, at the end of 2 Tim. 4. Paul appealed to Nero in Acts 25:10, 11. ¶

NEST (noun) – [1] ***kataskēnōsis*** [fem. noun: κατασκήνωσις <2682>]; **from *kataskēnoō*: to lodge, to rest, which is from *kata*: down (intens.), and *skēnoō*: to dwell, which is from *skēnos*: tent ▶ Place for birds to shelter themselves** > Foxes have holes and birds of the air have nests {roosting-places}, but the Son of God had nowhere to lay His head (Matt. 8:20; Luke 9:58). ¶
– [2] Matt. 13:32; Mark 4:32; Luke 13:19 → to make nests → NEST (verb) <2681>.

NEST (verb) – ***kataskēnoō*** [verb: κατασκηνόω <2681>]; **from *kata*: down (intens.), and *skēnoō*: to dwell, which is from *skēnos*: tent ▶ To live in a nest** > In a parable, birds nested {lodged, roosted, perched} in the branches of a mustard seed which had become a tree (Matt. 13:32; Mark 4:32; Luke 13:19). Other ref.: Acts 2:26; see DWELL <2681>. ¶

NET – [1] ***amphiblēstron*** [neut. noun: ἀμφίβληστρον <293>]; **from *amphiballō*: to throw around, which is from *amphi*: around, and *ballō*: to throw ▶ Mesh webbing to catch fish; this fishing net was cast from over the shoulder and sank down because of weights attached to it** > Jesus saw Simon and Andrew casting a net into the sea (Matt. 4:18; Mark 1:16). ¶
[2] ***diktuon*** [neut. noun: δίκτυον <1350>]; **poss. from *dikō*: to cast ▶ General term for a fish net in the N.T.; also transl.: trawl-net** > Simon and Andrew left their nets and followed Jesus (Matt. 4:20; Mark 1:18). James and John were mending their nets (Matt. 4:21; Mark 1:19). Fishermen were washing their nets (Luke 5:2). Jesus told Simon to let down his nets for a catch (Luke 5:4); Simon would let down the net at the Lord's word (v. 5); having done this, they caught a large number of fish, and their net broke (v. 6). After His resurrection, Jesus told His disciples to cast the net on the right side of the ship (John 21:6); they dragged the net full of fish (v. 8); Simon Peter dragged the net to land, and the net was not broken (v. 11a, b). ¶
– [3] Matt. 13:47 → DRAGNET <4522>.

NEVER – 1 ***ou mē*** [neg. expr.: οὐ μή <3364>]; **from *ou*: not, and *mē*: at all ▶ Certainly not, surely not** > Tribulation will come such as never was or shall be (Mark 13:19). Other refs.: Heb. 8:12; 10:17; 2 Pet. 1:10; Rev. 3:12; 18:14.

2 ***mēdepote*** [adv.: μηδέποτε <3368>]; **from *mēde*: not even, and *pote*: ever ▶ Term similar to the following one, but not quite as strong** > Some people are always learning, but never able to come to the knowledge of the truth (2 Tim. 3:7). ¶

3 **never more, (no one) any more: *mēketi*** [adv.: μηκέτι <3371>] ▶ **No longer, not henceforth** > There was to be never more fruit on a certain fig tree forever (Matt. 21:19); no one was to eat of it any more forever (Mark 11:14).

4 ***oudepote*** [adv.: οὐδέποτε <3763>]; **from *oude*: not even, and *pote*: ever ▶ In no case, under no circumstances** > Never did any man speak as Jesus spoke (John 7:46). Love never fails (1 Cor. 13:8). Other refs.: Matt. 7:23; 9:33; 21:16, 42; 26:33; Mark 2:12, 25; Luke 15:29a, b; Acts 10:14; 11:8; 14:8; Heb. 10:1, 11. ¶

5 ***oudepō*** [adv.: οὐδέπω <3764>]; **from *oude*: not even, and *pō*: yet ▶ Not yet, not up to now** > No one had ever been laid in the tomb of Joseph of Arimathea where the body of Jesus was laid (Luke 23:53; John 19:41). Other refs.: John 7:39; 20:9; 1 Cor. 8:2. ¶

– 6 Matt. 16:22 → Never, Lord → lit.: Be merciful to Yourself, Lord → FAVORABLE <2436> 7 Gal. 6:14 → FORBID <1096>.

NEVERTHELESS – 1 ***ara*** [adv.: ἆρα <687>] ▶ As an interrog., *ara* at the beginning of a clause, serves merely to denote a question and it cannot be expressed in Engl. It requires the answer to be neg. as in Luke 18:8, "Nevertheless [*ara*], when the Son of Man comes, will He find faith on the earth?" The answer must be "no." The same in Gal. 2:17. When strengthened by *ge*, a particle of emphasis as *ara ge*, it means whether indeed (Acts 8:30). ¶ ‡

2 ***kaitoi*** [particle: καίτοι <2543>] ▶ **But, however** > Nevertheless God did not leave Himself without witness (Acts 14:17 in some mss.). Other ref.: Heb. 4:3. ¶

3 ***homōs*** [adv.: ὅμως <3676>]; **from *homos*: like, similar ▶ Notwithstanding, yet** > Refs.: John 12:42; 1 Cor. 14:7; Gal. 3:15. ¶ ‡

4 ***plēn*** [prep. and adv.: πλήν <4133>] ▶ **Yet, however** > Jesus asked His Father, if it were possible, that the cup might pass from Him; nevertheless, not as He would, but as His Father would (Matt. 26:39; Luke 22:42). Other refs.: Luke 10:20; 1 Cor. 11:11; Eph. 5:33; Phil. 1:18; 3:16. *

– 5 1 Cor. 7:28; Heb. 12:11 → YET <1161>.

NEW – 1 ***agnaphos*** [adj.: ἄγναφος <46>]; **from *a*: neg., and *knaptō*: to mill or to full a cloth ▶ Never before worn, unused, unshrunk** > No one puts a patch of new {unshrunk} cloth on an old garment (Matt. 9:16; Mark 2:21a). ¶

2 ***kainos*** [adj.: καινός <2537>] ▶ **New in nature, never before used** > Men put new (*neos*) wine into new (*kainos*) skins (Matt. 9:17c; Mark 2:22c; Luke 5:38b). Joseph laid the body of Jesus in a new tomb (Matt. 27:60; John 19:41). A new piece sewn on an old garment might pull away part of the old garment (Mark 2:21b; Luke 5:36a–c). The word is also used in regard to things (Matt. 13:52; Rev. 21:5), a covenant (Matt. 26:28; Mark 14:24; Luke 22:20; 1 Cor. 11:25; 2 Cor. 3:6; Heb. 8:8, 13; 9:15), wine (Matt. 26:29; Mark 14:25), doctrine (Mark 1:27; Acts 17:19), tongues (Mark 16:17), a commandment (John 13:34; 1 John 2:7, 8; 2 John 5), a creation (2 Cor. 5:17a; Gal. 6:15), all things (2 Cor. 5:17b), a man (Eph. 2:15; 4:24), the heavens and the earth (2 Pet. 3:13a, b; Rev. 21:1a, b), a name (Rev. 2:17; 3:12b), the new Jerusalem (Rev. 3:12a; 21:2), and a song (Rev. 5:9; 14:3). The word is used as a noun by some in Acts 17:21: the news {ideas}; lit.: newer thing {something new}. ¶

3 ***neos*** [adj.: νέος <3501>] ▶ **Young, recent** > The word is used in regard to wine (Matt. 9:17a, b; Mark 2:22a, b; Luke 5:37a, b, 38, 39), a lump (1 Cor. 5:7), and a covenant (Heb. 12:24). The lit. expr. "the

new" in Col. 3:10 is transl. by some "the new man," "the new self." All other refs.: YOUNG <3501>.

[4] ***prosphatos*** [adj.: πρόσφατος <4372>]; **from *pro*: before, and *sphazō*: to slaughter, to sacrifice, or *phenō*: to kill ▶ Recently, newly made and retaining its freshness** > Christians have boldness to enter the holy of holies by the new (in the sense of: inaugurated by a sacrifice) and living way which Jesus has dedicated for them through the veil (Heb. 10:20). ¶

– [5] Matt. 19:28 → new world → REGENERATION <3824> [6] Acts 7:18 → a new king → lit.: another king [7] Rom. 6:4; 7:6 → NEWNESS <2538> [8] Eph. 4:23 → to be made new → RENEW <365> [9] 1 Tim. 3:6 → new convert → NOVICE <3504>.

NEW BIRTH – See BORN AGAIN (BE).

NEW CREATION – ***kainos*** [adj.: καινός <2537>] ***ktisis*** [fem. noun: κτίσις <2937>]; **from *ktizō*: to create ▶ Creation that will succeed the present creation and will be eternal** > This new creation {creature} includes Christians who have eternal life: the Christian is in Christ (2 Cor. 5:17), being born anew and God's child through faith in the Lord Jesus. Neither is circumcision anything, nor uncircumcision for a Christian, because he is a new creation {creature} (Gal. 6:15). All other refs. (*ktisis*): see CREATION <2937>, CREATURE <2937>, INSTITUTION <2937>. All other refs. (*kainos*): see NEW <2537>.

NEW CREATURE – 2 Cor. 5:17; Gal. 6:15 → NEW CREATION <2537> <2937>.

NEWBORN – ***artigennētos*** [adj.: ἀρτιγέννητος <738>]; **from *arti*: newly, and *gennētos*: born ▶ Newly come into the world, newly engendered** > Christians, as newborn babies, should earnestly desire the pure mental milk of the word (1 Pet. 2:2). ¶

NEWNESS – ***kainotēs*** [fem. noun: καινότης <2538>]; **from *kainos*: new in nature, completely new ▶ Character of that which appears for the first time** > The Christian is called to walk in newness of life {to live a new life}, in accordance with his new situation (Rom. 6:4) and in contrast with his previous life in sin (see v. 2). Christian service is in newness of spirit {the new way of the Spirit} (Rom. 7:6), because the Holy Spirit dwells in the Christian (see 8:11). ¶

NEWS – [1] ***phēmē*** [fem. noun: φήμη <5345>]; **from *phēmi*: to affirm, to say ▶ Reputation, what is said concerning someone; also transl.: fame, rumour** > News about Jesus went out into all Galilee (Luke 4:14). Other ref.: Matt. 9:26; see FAME <5345>. ¶

[2] **to spread the news: *diaphēmizō*** [verb: διαφημίζω <1310>]; **from *dia*: denoting dispersion, and *phēmē*: see [1]; also transl.: to spread the fame, to spread the name ▶ To speak about someone, to report on that person** > Two blind men spread the news of Jesus abroad (Matt. 9:31). Other refs.: Matt. 28:15; Mark 1:45; see SPREAD <1310>. ¶

– [3] Matt. 4:24; 14:1; Mark 1:28 → FAME <189> [4] Mark 1:1 → good news → GOSPEL <2098> [5] Mark 1:45 → MATTER <3056> [6] Luke 2:10 → to bring good news → PREACH <2097> [7] Luke 4:37 → REPORT (noun) <2279> [8] Luke 5:15 → REPORT (noun) <3056> [9] Luke 7:17 → RUMOR <3056> [10] John 20:18 → with the news → lit.: reporting → REPORT (verb) <518> [11] Acts 11:22 → TIDINGS <3056> [12] Acts 17:21 → NEW <2537> [13] Acts 21:31 → TIDINGS <5334> [14] Rom. 15:21 → to have news → SPEAK <312>.

NEXT – [1] ***metaxu*** [adv.: μεταξύ <3342>]; **from *meta*: after, and *mesos*: middle ▶ Which comes immediately after, ensuing** > The term is used in relation to the Sabbath (Acts 13:42). All other refs.: Matt. 18:15; 23:35; Luke 11:51; 16:26; John 4:31; Acts 12:6; 15:9; Rom. 2:15. ¶

[2] See THEREUPON <1899>.

– [3] John 13:23 → next to → lit.: on the bosom of → BOSOM <2859> [4] Acts

18:7 → to be next, to be next door → ADJOINED (BE) <4927> [5] Acts 18:23 → went from one place to the next → lit.: passing through in order [6] Acts 28:13 → next day → DAY <1206>.

NICANOR – ***Nikanōr*** [masc. name: Νικάνωρ <3527>]: **conqueror, victorious ▶ Christian man of the N.T.** > Nicanor was one of seven men who were chosen to attend to service in the church of Jerusalem (Acts 6:5). ¶

NICODEMUS – ***Nikodēmos*** [masc. name: Νικόδημος <3530>]: **victorious in the midst of the people ▶ A Pharisee, member of the Sanhedrin and doctor of the law** > Nicodemus came by night to Jesus, who taught him that it is necessary to be born anew in order to enter into the kingdom of God (John 3:1, 4, 9). Later, he took a public stand in favor of Jesus, when some wanted to seize Him (John 7:50, see v. 51). With Joseph of Arimathea, he embalmed the body of Jesus before laying it in the tomb (John 19:39, see v. 40). ¶

NICOLAITAN – ***Nikolaitēs*** [masc. name: Νικολαΐτης <3531>]**; from Nicolas: victorious over the people ▶ Follower of the doctrine of Nicolas** > The Christians of the church of Ephesus hated the works of the Nicolaitans (Rev. 2:6). Those of the church of Pergamum who held the doctrine of the Nicolaitans are ordered to repent (v. 15, see v. 16). According to the doctrine of Balaam, the Nicolaitans taught Christians that they were free to eat things sacrificed to idols and to commit sexual immorality (see Rev. 2:14). ¶

NICOLAS – ***Nikolaos*** [masc. name: Νικόλαος <3532>]: **victorious over the people ▶ Proselyte of Antioch** > Nicolas was chosen with six other Christians to be occupied with service in the church of Jerusalem (Acts 6:5; see vv. 1–6). ¶

NICOLAUS – Acts 6:5 → NICOLAS <3532>.

NICOPOLIS – ***Nikopolis*** [fem. name: Νικόπολις <3533>]: **city of victory ▶ Prob. the city founded by Augustus in the region of Epirus in Greece** > Paul had decided to spend winter in Nicopolis and Titus was to rejoin him there (Titus 3:12). ¶

NIGER – ***Niger*** [masc. name: Νίγερ <3526>]: **black, dark, in Lat. ▶ Christian man of Antioch** > Niger was the surname of Simeon, a prophet teaching in the church of Antioch (Acts 13:1). ¶

NIGH – [1] See NEAR (adv.) <1448>, <1451>.
– [2] Eph. 2:13 → to make nigh, to become nigh → to bring near → BRING <1096> <1451> [3] Phil. 2:27 → CLOSE (adj. and adv.) <3897>.

NIGHT – [1] ***nux*** [fem. noun: νύξ <3571>] ▶ This word is used lit. to describe **a. The period between the setting and the rising of the sun** (e.g., Matt. 4:2; 12:40a, b; 2 Tim. 1:3; Rev. 4:8), **b. The period of the absence of light, the time in which something takes place** (e.g., Matt. 2:14; Luke 2:8; John 3:2; Acts 5:19; 9:25), **c. A point of time** (e.g., Luke 12:20; Acts 27:23), **d. A duration of time** (e.g., Luke 2:37; 5:5; Acts 20:31; 26:7). It also describes, in the figur. sense, the time of sinful man's alienation from God (Rom. 13:12; 1 Thes. 5:5) and death (John 9:4). (After W. E. Vine.) *

[2] **to pass the night, to spend the night: *aulizomai*** [verb: αὐλίζομαι <835>]**; from *aulē*: courtyard of a building, sheepfold ▶ To stay at a place, to lodge** > Jesus passed the night at Bethany (Matt. 21:17). Other ref.: Luke 21:37 (to stay at night); see STAY (verb) <835>. ¶

[3] **to spend the night, to continue all night: *dianuktereuō*** [verb: διανυκτερεύω <1273>]; **from *dia*: through, and *nuktereuō*: to pass the night, which is from *nux*: night ▶ To continue throughout the night** > Jesus spent the night in prayer to God (Luke 6:12). ¶
– [4] Matt. 14:23 → later that night → when evening came → EVENING <3798>

[5] 2 Cor. 6:5; 11:27 → sleepless nights → SLEEPLESSNESS <70>.

NINE – [1] ***ennea*** [card. num.: ἐννέα <1767>] ▶ This number is used in regard to leprous men whom Jesus healed (Luke 17:17). ¶
– [2] Matt. 20:3; Mark 15:25 → nine in the morning → lit.: the third hour → THIRD <5154>.

NINE HUNDRED – Luke 16:6 → nine hundred gallons → lit.: one hundred measures → MEASURE (noun) <943>.

NINETY AND NINE – ***ennenēkontaennea*** [card. num.: ἐννενηκονταεννέα <1768>]; **from *ennenēkonta*: ninety, and *ennea*: nine** ▶ This number is used in regard to sheep (Matt. 18:12, 13; Luke 15:4) and to righteous people who have no need of repentance (Luke 15:7). ¶

NINEVEH – [1] ***Nineuē*** [fem. name: Νινευή <3535>]: **dwelling of Nin ▶ Capital of the Assyrian Empire northeast of Palestine** > Some transl. have this name in Luke 11:32. See NINEVITE <3536>. ¶
– [2] Luke 11:30 → the people of Nineveh → NINEVITE <3536>.

NINEVITE – ***Nineuitēs*** [masc. name: Νινευΐτης <3536>] ▶ **Inhabitant of Nineveh: see NINEVEH** <3535>. > Jonah was a sign, i.e., a testimony, to the Ninevites, calling them to repent (Luke 11:30, 32). The men of Nineveh will stand up at the judgment and condemn the generation of the time of the Lord (Matt. 12:41). ¶

NINTH – ***ennatos*** [ord. num.: ἔννατος <1766>]; **from *ennea*: nine; *enatos* in some mss.** ▶ This number is used in regard to an hour (Matt. 20:5; 27:45, 46; Mark 15:33, 34; Luke 23:44; Acts 3:1; 10:3, 30) and a precious stone (Rev. 21:20). ¶

NO MORE – ***ouketi*** [adv.: οὐκέτι <3765>]; **from *ouk*: not, and *eti*: yet, still** ▶ Refs.: Matt. 19:6; Mark 10:8; Luke 15:19. *

NO ONE – [1] ***oudeis*** [adj.: οὐδείς <3762>]; **from *oude*: not even, and *eis*: one ▶ Nobody, nothing, none** > No one can come to Jesus except the Father draws him (John 6:44, 65). No one comes to the Father unless by Jesus (John 14:6). No one is good but one, that is God (Mark 10:18; Luke 18:19). No one can serve two masters (Matt. 6:24; Luke 16:13). No one can plunder the goods of the strong man unless he first binds the strong man (Mark 3:27). No one having laid his hand on the plough and looking back is fit for the kingdom of God (Luke 9:62). No one among the Jews practiced the law (John 7:19). No one, speaking in the power of the Spirit of God, says: "Curse on Jesus"; and no one can say: "Lord Jesus," unless in the power of the Holy Spirit (1 Cor. 12:3a, b). No one going as a soldier entangles himself with the affairs of life (2 Tim. 2:4). No one will see the Lord without pursuing peace with all (Heb. 12:14). Other refs.: John 4:27; 7:4; 8:10, 11; Acts 5:13; Rom. 14:7a, b; Rev. 2:17; 3:7a, b; 5:4. *
[2] ***mēdeis*** [adj.: μηδείς <3367>]; **from *mē*: not, and *eis*: one ▶ Nobody, no man** > No one among the Thessalonians was to be moved by afflictions (1 Thes. 3:3). Let no one, being tempted, say, I am tempted by God (Jas. 1:13). *

NOAH – ***Nōe*** [masc. name: Νῶε <3575>]: **consolation, rest, in Heb.; see Gen. 5:28, 29 ▶ Patriarch living at the time of the flood** > Noah is mentioned in the genealogy of Jesus (Luke 3:36). The time of the coming of the Lord to establish His kingdom will be as it was in the days of Noah when everyone went about their business before the flood (Matt. 24:37, 38; Luke 17:26, 27). Noah is mentioned among the men of faith: he built an ark for the saving of his household, and by that ark, he condemned the world of that time (Heb. 11:7). God waited with patience during the days of the ark's construction (1 Pet. 3:20). Noah is called a preacher of righteousness (2 Pet. 2:5). ¶

NOBLE – [1] ***eugenēs*** [adj.: εὐγενής <2104>]; **from *eu*: well, and *ginomai*:**

to be born, or *genos*: race, family; also transl.: high-born ▶ Of high rank, honorable > Jesus told a parable about a noble man {nobleman, man of noble birth} who went to a distant country and gave ten minas to his bondmen for trading (Luke 19:12). Among the Corinthians, there were not many noble {of noble birth} (1 Cor. 1:26), i.e., not many persons of high rank by birth. The Berean Jews were more noble {fair-minded, noble-minded, of more noble character} than those of Thessalonica (Acts 17:11), as was demonstrated by their conduct in receiving Paul and Silas, and the word of God with all readiness of mind, searching daily the Scriptures. ¶

[2] ***semnos*** [adj.: σεμνός <4586>]; **from *sebomai*: to venerate, to worship ▶ Venerable, honorable** > All things that are noble {honest, honorable} are to occupy our thoughts (Phil. 4:8). Other refs.: 1 Tim. 3:8, 11; Titus 2:2; see GRAVE <4586>. ¶

– [3] Mark 6:21 → LORD (noun) <3175> [4] Luke 8:15 → GOOD (adj.) <2570> [5] Luke 21:5 → BEAUTIFUL <2570> [6] Acts 24:3; 26:25 → EXCELLENT <2903> [7] Jas. 2:7 → WORTHY <2570>.

NOBLE-MINDED – Acts 17:11 → NOBLE <2104>.

NOBLEMAN – [1] ***basilikos*** [adj. used as noun: βασιλικός <937>]; **from *basileus*: king ▶ Officer of the king, important person at the court** > A nobleman {courtier, official, royal official} asked Jesus to heal his son who was at the point of death (John 4:46, 49); *basiliskos* in some mss. All other refs.: KING <937>, ROYAL <937>.

– [2] Luke 19:12 → lit.: noble man → NOBLE <2104>.

NOD – Acts 24:10 → to make a sign → SIGN <3506>.

NOISE (noun) – [1] **with a rushing noise: *rhoizēdon*** [adv.: ῥοιζηδόν <4500>]; **from *rhoizos*: intense noise, roar ▶ With a crash, with a roar** > In the day of the Lord, the heavens will pass away with a rushing noise {with a great noise, with a roar} (2 Pet. 3:10). ¶

[2] **to make a noise: *thorubeō*** [verb: θορυβέω <2350>]; **from *thorubos*: great noise, tumult ▶ To make a commotion, to agitate oneself** > The people were making a noise {tumult} {The noisy crowd was wailing, The crowd was in noisy disorder} at the ruler's house (Matt. 9:23). All other refs.: TUMULT <2350>, UPROAR <2350>.

– [3] Acts 2:2 → SOUND (noun) <2279> [4] Rev. 9:9a, b → SOUND (noun) <5456>.

NOISE (verb) – [1] Luke 1:65 → DISCUSS <1255> [2] Acts 2:6 → this was noised abroad → lit.: the sound occurred → SOUND (noun) <5456> [3] Acts 2:6 → to be noised → OCCUR <1096>.

NOISOME – Rev. 16:2 → EVIL (adj.) <2556>.

NOISY – [1] Matt. 9:23 → the noisy crowd was wailing, the crowd was in noisy disorder → lit.: the crowd was making a noise → to make a noise → NOISE (noun) <2350> [2] 1 Cor. 13:1 → sounding → SOUND (verb) <2278>.

NOMINATE – Acts 1:23 → APPOINT <2476>.

NON-GREEK – Rom. 1:14 → BARBARIAN <915>.

NONSENSE – [1] Luke 24:11 → idle tale → TALE <3026> [2] 1 Tim. 5:13 → who talk nonsense → TATTLER <5397> [3] 3 John 10 → to spread malicious nonsense about → to prate against with malicious words → WORD <3056>.

NOON – [1] ***mesēmbria*** [fem. noun: μεσημβρία <3314>]; **from *mesos*: middle, and *hēmera*: day ▶ Hour corresponding to the middle of the day** > Around noon {noontime, mid-day} a great light shone around Paul (Acts 22:6). Other ref.: Acts 8:26; see SOUTH <3314>. ¶

– [2] Matt. 20:5; 27:45; Mark 15:33; Luke 23:44; John 4:6; 19:14 → lit.: the sixth hour → SIXTH <1623>, HOUR <5610>.

NOONTIME – Acts 22:6 → NOON <3314>.

NORMAL – Matt. 12:13 → to normal → SOUND (adj.) <5199>.

NORTH – ***borras*** [masc. noun: βορρᾶς <1005>]; **contracted from *boreas*: north ► One of the four cardinal points, opposite of south >** Believers in the Lord will come from everywhere, including the north, and sit down in the kingdom of God (Luke 13:29). The new Jerusalem has three gates on the north (Rev. 21:13). ¶

NORTHEASTER – See EUROCLYDON <2148>.

NORTHWEST – ***chōros*** [masc. noun: χῶρος <5566>]; ***corus*, in Lat.: name of the wind coming from the northwest ► Direction situated between the north and the west >** Phoenix was facing southwest and northwest (Acts 27:12). ¶

NOT – [1] ***mē*** [neg. particle: μή <3361>] ► This word implies a dependent and cond. neg., i.e., depending on the idea, concept or thought of some subject, and, thus, subjective. * ‡
[2] ***oude*** [conj.: οὐδέ <3761>]; **from *ou*: not, and *de*: but ►** Refs.: Matt. 5:15; 6:20; Gal. 1:1. *
– [3] The word also translates the neg. particles *ou* and *ouk* <3756>.

NOT AT ALL – ***mēti*** [neg. particle: μήτι <3385>]; **from *mē*: not, and *ti*: anything ►** Refs.: Matt. 7:16; 12:23; 26:22, 25; Mark 4:21; 14:19; Luke 6:39; John 4:29; 7:31; 8:22; 18:35; Acts 10:47; 2 Cor. 1:17; Jas. 3:11. ¶

NOT EVEN, AND NOT, ALSO NOT, NEITHER – ***mēte*** [conj.: μήτε <3383>]; **from *mē*: not, and *te*: and ►** Refs.: Matt. 5:34–36; 11:18; Mark 3:20; Luke 7:33; 9:3; Acts 23:8, 12, 21; 27:20; Eph. 4:27; 2 Thes. 2:2; 1 Tim. 1:7; Heb. 7:3; Jas. 5:12; Rev. 7:1, 3. ¶ ‡

NOT YET – [1] ***mēdepō*** [adv.: μηδέπω <3369>]; **from *mēde*: not even, and *pō*: yet ►** Ref.: Heb. 11:7. ¶ ‡
[2] ***mēpō*** [adv.: μήπω <3380>]; **from *mē*: not, and *pō*: yet ►** Refs.: Rom. 9:11; Heb. 9:8. ¶ ‡

NOT YET, NOT EVEN YET – ***oupō*** [adv.: οὔπω <3768>]; **from *ou*: not, and *pō*: yet ►** Also transl.: accordingly, thereupon, now, certainly. Refs.: Matt. 24:6; John 2:4; 3:24; 7:39; 8:57. *

NOTABLE – [1] Matt. 27:16 → NOTORIOUS <1978> [2] Acts 2:20 → AWESOME <2016> [3] Acts 4:16 → EVIDENT <1110>.

NOTE (noun) – [1] **of note: *episēmos*** [adj.: ἐπίσημος <1978>]; **from *epi*: upon, and *sēma*: mark, sign ► Eminent, remarkable >** Paul mentions Andronicus and Junias who were of note {outstanding} among the apostles (Rom. 16:7). Other ref.: Matt. 27:16; see NOTORIOUS <1978>. ¶
– [2] Acts 3:10; 4:13 → to take note → RECOGNIZE <1921> [3] Acts 4:29 → to take note → to look upon → LOOK (verb) <1896> [4] 1 Cor. 14:7 → SOUND <5353> [5] Phil. 3:17 → to take note → to fix the eyes → EYES <4648>.

NOTE (verb) – [1] Luke 14:7 → REMARK <1907> [2] Rom. 11:22 → to consider, to behold (*eidō*) [3] Rom. 16:17 → CONSIDER <4648> [4] Phil. 3:17 → to fix the eyes → EYES <4648> [5] 2 Thes. 3:14 → to note, to take special note → MARK (verb) <4593>.

NOTEWORTHY – Acts 4:16 → EVIDENT <1110>.

NOTHING – [1] Luke 1:37 → lit.: no word → WORD <4487> [2] Rom. 13:4; Gal. 3:4a, b → for nothing → in vain → VAIN <1500> [3] 1 Cor. 1:19 → to bring to nothing → REJECT <114> [4] 1 Cor. 1:28 → to bring to nothing → EFFECT (noun) <2673> [5] 1 Cor. 2:6 → to come to nothing → COME <2673> [6] Gal. 2:21 → for nothing → FREELY <1432> [7] Phil. 2:7 → to make oneself nothing → to make oneself of no reputation → REPUTATION <2758> [8] Phil. 2:16a, b → for nothing → in vain → VAIN <1519> <2756>.

NOTICE (noun) – [1] Mark 7:24; Luke 8:47 → to escape notice → to be hidden → HIDDEN (BE) <2990> [2] Mark 15:26; Luke 23:38 → written notice → INSCRIPTION <1923> [3] John 19:19 → TITLE <5102> [4] Acts 18:17 → to take notice → CARE <3199> [5] Acts 21:26 → to give notice → SIGNIFY <1229> [6] Acts 23:15 → to give notice → SIGNIFY <1718> [7] Acts 26:26; 2 Pet. 3:5 → to escape the attention, to escape the notice → HIDDEN (BE) <2990> [8] Heb. 13:23 → to take notice → KNOW <1097>.

NOTICE (verb) – [1] **to notice before: *prokatangellō*** [verb: προκαταγγέλλω <4293>]; **from *pro*: before, and *katangellō*: to declare, to preach, which is from *kata*: intens., and *angellō*: to preach ▶ To announce in advance** > The Corinthians had noticed before {had foreannounced, had promised, had previously promised} a generous gift (2 Cor. 9:5). Some mss. have *proepangellō* <4279>: to previously promise. All other refs.: ANNOUNCE <4293>.

– [2] Matt. 7:3; Luke 6:41 → CONSIDER <2657> [3] Matt. 22:11 → SEE <1492> [4] Luke 14:7 → REMARK <1907> [5] Acts 27:39 → DISCOVER <2657>.

NOTIFY – [1] Acts 23:15 → SIGNIFY <1718> [2] Acts 23:22 → REVEAL <1718>.

NOTION – [1] Col. 2:18 → MIND (noun) <3563> [2] Col. 2:18 → with idle notions → in vain → VAIN <1500>.

NOTORIOUS – ***episēmos*** [adj.: ἐπίσημος <1978>]; **from *epi*: upon, and *sēma*: mark ▶ Unfavorably known, outstanding** > Barabbas was a notorious {notable} prisoner (Matt. 27:16), known for his participation in an insurrection and who was a murderer (see Mark 15:7; Luke 23:18; Acts 3:14). Other ref.: Rom. 16:7 (of note); see NOTE (noun) <1978>. ¶

NOUGHT – [1] Mark 9:12 → to be set at nought → to be treated with contempt → CONTEMPT <1847> [2] Luke 23:11 → to set at nought → to treat with contempt → CONTEMPT <1848> [3] Acts 4:11; Rom. 14:10 → to set at nought → DESPISE <1848> [4] Acts 19:27 → to be set at nought → to fall in disrepute → DISREPUTE <557> [5] 1 Cor. 1:28 → to bring to nought → to make of no effect → EFFECT (noun) <2673> [6] 1 Cor. 2:6 → to come to nought → COME <2673>.

NOURISH – [1] ***epichorēgeō*** [verb: ἐπιχορηγέω <2023>]; **from *epi*: upon, and *chorēgeō*: see SUPPLY** (verb) <5524> ▶ **To supply abundantly** > The church is compared to a body nourished {ministered, ministered to, having nourishment, supplied} and united together (Col. 2:19). All other refs.: ADD <2023>, SUPPLY (verb) <2023>.

[2] ***trephō*** [verb: τρέφω <5142>] ▶ **To give nourishment, to feed, to feast** > God the heavenly Father nourishes the birds of the heaven (Matt. 6:26), including the ravens (Luke 12:24). The righteous will say to the Lord: When did we nourish You? (Matt. 25:37). The country of the Tyrians and Sidonians was nourished {supplied with food} by {depended for their food supply on} King Herod's country (Acts 12:20). James reproached the rich for having nourished {having fattened} their hearts as in a day of slaughter (5:5). God will prepare a place in the wilderness, that the woman (Israel) should be nourished {taken care of} there one thousand two hundred sixty days (Rev. 12:6); she is nourished {taken care of} there three and one half years, from the face of the serpent (Satan) (v. 14). Other ref.: Luke 4:16 (to bring up); see BRING <5142>. ¶

3 ***anatrephō*** [verb: ἀνατρέφω <397>]; **from *ana*: intens., and *trephō*: see 2 ▶ To feed (a small child), to nurse; also transl.: to bring up, to nurture >** Moses was brought up nourished by Pharaoh's daughter (Acts 7:20, 21). Paul had been brought up in Jerusalem (Acts 22:3). Other ref.: Luke 4:16 in some mss. ¶

4 ***ektrephō*** [verb: ἐκτρέφω <1625>]; **from *ek*: out (intens.), and *trephō*: see 2 ▶ To look after, to maintain >** No one has ever hated his own flesh, but nourishes {feeds} and cherishes it, as also the Christ the church (Eph. 5:29). Other ref.: Eph. 6:4 {to bring up}; see BRING <1625>. ¶

5 ***entrephō*** [verb: ἐντρέφω <1789>]; **from *en*: in, and *trephō*: see 2 ▶ To feed (in the figur. sense), to instruct >** Timothy was to be nourished with {to be brought up in} the words of the faith and of the good teaching (1 Tim. 4:6). ¶

– 6 Acts 7:21 → to bring up → BRING <397>.

NOURISHMENT – 1 Matt. 3:4; 10:10; Acts 27:34 → FOOD <5160> 2 Col. 2:19 → having nourishment ministered → NOURISH <2023>.

NOVICE – ***neophutos*** [adj.: νεόφυτος <3504>]; **from *neos*: new, and *phuō*: to produce; lit.: new plant ▶ Person recently converted, i.e., who has turned to God >** The overseer must not be a novice {new convert, recent convert}, that he may not be inflated with pride (1 Tim. 3:6). ¶

NOW – 1 ***gar*** [particle: γάρ <1063>] ▶ **Indeed, therefore; also transl.: why, well >** The word is used in John 9:30.

2 ***nun*** [adv.: νῦν <3568>] ▶ **At the present time >** The word is used in contrast with the past, e.g., the husband whom a woman now had (at the moment when the Lord spoke with her) was not her husband, because she had previously had five husbands (John 4:18). It is also used in contrast to the future: now the soul of the Lord Jesus was troubled (at the moment when He was speaking) on account of what He was about to suffer (John 12:27). Peter now knew that the Lord had certainly sent His angel to deliver him (Acts 12:11). The term occurs more than 130 times in the N.T. It is also transl. "henceforth" (Luke 1:48; Acts 18:6; 2 Cor. 5:16), "from now on" (Luke 12:52; Acts 18:6; 2 Cor. 5:16), and "hereafter" (Luke 22:69). Other refs.: Acts 24:13; Heb. 9:5. *

3 ***nuni*** [adv.: νυνί <3570>] ▶ **Stronger term than the previous one >** Paul was now going to Jerusalem to minister to the saints (Rom. 15:25). It is employed in regard to the present time (e.g., Eph. 2:13; Col. 1:21, 26) and also to indicate a logical reason (e.g., Rom. 7:17; 1 Cor. 12:18; 13:13). *

4 **now, from now on, hereafter: *arti*** [adv.: ἄρτι <737>] ▶ **At the present moment, henceforth >** Refs.: Matt. 11:12; 23:39; 26:29; John 1:51; Gal. 1:9, 10; et al.

5 ***loipon*** [adj. used as noun: λοιπόν <3063>]; **from *leipō*: to remain; lit.: for the rest ▶ In the future, henceforth >** In Gethsemane, Jesus said to His disciples to sleep on now (Matt. 26:45; Mark 14:41). All other refs.: FINALLY <3063>, REST (noun)[2] <3063>.

6 from now on: ***mēketi*** [adv.: μηκέτι <3371>]; **from *mē*: neg., and *eti*: more ▶ Not any more, in the future, henceforth >** Ref.: Acts 4:17.

– 7 Mark 6:25 → right now → at once → ONCE <1824> 8 Luke 17:7 → IMMEDIATELY <2112> 9 John 16:24; 1 Cor. 15:6 → until now → HITHERTO <737> 10 Acts 24:25; 27:22 in some mss. → for the present → PRESENT TIME <3568> 11 Rom. 1:13 → present time → PRESENT <1204> 12 Phil. 4:10 → now at last, now at the last → at last → LAST (adv. and noun) <2235> 13 Rev. 14:13 → from now on → HEREAFTER <534>.

NULL – 1 Luke 7:30 → to render null → REJECT <114> 2 Rom. 4:14 → to be null → to be made vain → VAIN <2758>.

NULLIFY – 1 Matt. 15:6; Mark 7:13 → to make of no effect → EFFECT (noun) <208> 2 Rom. 3:3, 31; 4:14; 1 Cor. 1:28; Gal. 3:17

→ to make of no effect → EFFECT (noun) <2673> [3] Gal. 2:21 → REJECT <114>.

NUMBER (noun) – [1] ***arithmos*** [masc. noun: ἀριθμός <706>] ► **Numeric value; group** > Judas was of the number of {numbered among} the twelve (Luke 22:3). The men sat down, in number about five thousand (John 6:10). The number of men who believed had become about five thousand (Acts 4:4). A number of men, about four hundred, were joined to Theudas (Acts 5:36). The number of disciples in Jerusalem was very greatly multiplied (Acts 6:7). A great number believed and turned to the Lord (Acts 11:21). The churches increased in number every day (Acts 16:5). Should the number of the children of Israel be as the sand of the sea, the remnant only will be saved (Rom. 9:27). The word is used ten times in Rev. (5:11 {numbering}; 7:4; 9:16a, b; 13:17, 18a–c; 15:2; 20:8). ¶

– [2] Luke 5:6 → great number, large number → great quantity → QUANTITY <4128> [3] John 5:3; 21:6; Acts 4:32; 6:2; 14:1; 17:4; Heb. 11:12 → number; great, large, full number → MULTITUDE <4128> [4] Acts 1:15 → CROWD (noun) <3793> [5] Acts 1:17 → to be one of the number → to be numbered → NUMBER (verb) <2674> [6] Acts 17:12 → not a few → FEW <3756> <3641> [7] Acts 27:7; 1 Cor. 11:30b → MANY <2425> [8] Rom. 11:25 → full number → FULLNESS <4138> [9] 2 Cor. 10:12 → to make of the number → CLASS <1469> [10] 2 Cor. 11:23 → times without number → to excess → EXCESS <5234> [11] 1 Tim. 5:9 → to be taken into the number → to put on the list → LIST (noun) <2639>.

NUMBER (verb) – [1] ***arithmeō*** [verb: ἀριθμέω <705>]; **from *arithmos*: number** ► **To count, to enumerate** > The very hairs of our head are all numbered (Matt. 10:30; Luke 12:7). John saw a great crowd which no one could number {count} (Rev. 7:9). ¶

[2] ***katarithmeō*** [verb: καταριθμέω <2674>]; **from *kata*: among, with, and *arithmeō*: see [1]** ► **To be counted among** > Judas was numbered among {was one of the number of} the apostles (Acts 1:17). ¶

[3] ***sunkatapsēphizō*** [verb: συγκαταψηφίζω <4785>]; **from *sun*: together, *kata*: according to (intens.), and *psēphizō*: to decide, to vote, which is from *psēphos*: pebble (used to vote)** ► **To choose, to elect; to adjoin** > Matthias was numbered with {was added to} the eleven apostles (Acts 1:26); *katapsēphizomai* in some mss. ¶

– [4] Mark 15:28; Luke 22:37 → COUNT <3049> [5] Luke 22:3; Rev. 5:11 → numbered among, numbering → lit.: of the number of, their number was → NUMBER (noun) <706>.

NUMBERING – Mark 5:13 → lit.: about (*ōs*).

NUMEROUS – [1] Heb. 11:12a → as numerous as the stars → lit.: as the stars in multitude → MULTITUDE <4128> [2] Heb. 11:12b → INNUMERABLE <382>.

NURSE (noun) – ***trophos*** [fem. noun: τροφός <5162>]; **from *trephō*: to nourish** ► **Mother who nurses her child** > In regard to the Thessalonians, Paul had been like a nurse {mother, nursing mother} who cherishes her own children (1 Thes. 2:7). ¶

NURSE (verb) – [1] **to nurse, to nurse babies: *thēlazō*** [verb: θηλάζω <2337>]; **from *thēlē*: breast** ► **To breast feed a child; also transl.: to give suck** > Out of the mouth of infants and nursing babies {babes and nursing infants, babes and sucklings, children and infants}, God has perfected praise (Matt. 21:16). During the establishment of the abomination of desolation in Jerusalem, the escape of pregnant women and those who are nursing babies {and nursing mothers} will be more difficult (Matt. 24:19; Mark 13:17; Luke 21:23). A woman told Jesus that blessed was

the womb that bore Him and the breasts which nursed Him (Luke 11:27). Days are coming in which it will be said: Blessed are the breasts that have not nursed (Luke 23:29). ¶
– [2] Acts 13:18 → ENDURE <5159>.

NURSING – [1] Matt. 21:16; 24:19; Mark 13:17; Luke 21:23 → NURSE (verb) <2337> [2] 1 Thes. 2:7 → nursing mother → NURSE (noun) <5162>.

NURTURE (noun) – Eph. 6:4 → TRAINING <3809>.

NURTURE (verb) – [1] Acts 7:20 → NOURISH <397> [2] Acts 7:21 → to bring up → BRING <397>.

NYMPHA – See NYMPHAS <3564>.

NYMPHAS – ***Numphas*** [masc. name: Νυμφᾶς <3564>]**: bridegroom ► Christian man of Laodicea or Colossae; also transl.: Nympha (Christian woman)** > The church met in the house of Nymphas; Paul sent his greetings to this Christian (Col. 4:15). ¶

O

O!, OH! – ***ō*** [ὦ <5599>] ▶ Refs.: Matt. 15:28; 17:17; Mark 9:19; Luke 9:41; 24:25; Acts 1:1; 13:10; 18:14; 27:21; Rom. 2:1, 3; 9:20; 11:33; Gal. 3:1; Jas. 3:20; 1 Tim. 6:20. ¶

OAR – Mark 6:48 → at the oars → lit.: rowing → ROW <1643>.

OATH – 1 ***horkos*** [masc. noun: ὅρκος <3727>] ▶ **Solemn commitment, promise** > Those of old were told to perform their oaths {vows} to the Lord (Matt. 5:33). Herod promised with an oath to give the daughter of Herodias whatever she might ask (Matt. 14:7, 9; Mark 6:26). Peter denied with an oath that he knew Jesus (Matt. 26:72). God remembered the oath that He had sworn to Abraham (Luke 1:73). God had sworn to David, with an oath, that He would raise up someone from the fruit of his loins to sit on his throne (Acts 2:30). An oath is for men the term of all dispute (Heb. 6:16); God intervened by an oath (v. 17). James says not to swear, either by heaven or by earth or by any other oath (Jas. 5:12). ¶
2 ***horkōmosia*** [fem. noun: ὁρκωμοσία <3728>]; **from *horkos*: see 1, and *omnuō*: to swear ▶ Swearing of an oath, sworn affirmation** > The term is used in regard to the establishment of the priesthood of Christ (Heb. 7:20, 21a, b, 28). ¶
– 3 Matt. 5:33 → to break one's oath → FORSWEAR <1964> 4 Matt. 5:34, 36 → to make, take, swear, to promise with an oath → SWEAR <3660> 5 Matt. 26:63 → to put, to charge under oath → ADJURE <1844> 6 Acts 23:12, 14, 21 → to bind oneself under an oath, to take a solemn oath, to take an oath → CURSE (noun) <332> 7 Acts 23:13 → to join together in an oath → lit.: to make a conspiracy → CONSPIRACY <4945> 8 Acts 23:14 → ACCURSED <331> 9 1 Thes. 5:27 → to put under oath → ADJURE <3726>.

OBED – ***Ōbēd*** [masc. name: Ὠβήδ <5601>]**: who serves (God), in Heb. ▶ Man of the O.T.** > Obed is mentioned in the genealogy of Jesus Christ (Matt. 1:5a, b; Luke 3:32). He is the son of Boaz and Ruth (see Ruth 4:13–22). ¶

OBEDIENCE – 1 ***hupakoē*** [fem. noun: ὑπακοή <5218>]; **from *hupakouō*: to listen, to obey, which is from *hupo*: under, and *akouō*: to hear, to understand ▶ Voluntary submission, deference** > Paul had received grace and apostleship for obedience of faith among all the nations (Rom. 1:5). By the obedience of Jesus, many will be constituted righteous (Rom. 5:19). We are bondmen for obedience to him whom we obey, whether of sin unto death, or of obedience unto righteousness (Rom. 6:16a, b). All that Paul had accomplished for the obedience of the Gentiles {to make the Gentiles obedient, obey} was through Christ (Rom. 15:18). The obedience of the Romans had come to the knowledge of all (Rom. 16:19). The mystery had been made known for obedience of faith to all the nations (Rom. 16:26 {to obey}). Titus remembered the obedience of all the Corinthians {that they were obedient} (2 Cor. 7:15). The arms of Paul's warfare lead captive every thought into the obedience of the {to make it obedient to} Christ (2 Cor. 10:5). The obedience of the Corinthians was to be fulfilled (2 Cor. 10:6). Paul was confident in the obedience of Philemon (Phm. 21). Though He was a Son, Christ learned obedience from the things that He suffered (Heb. 5:8). Christians have been chosen for the obedience and sprinkling of {that they may obey and be sprinkled with} the blood of Jesus Christ (1 Pet. 1:2). Christians are to behave as children of obedience {obedient children} (1 Pet. 1:14). Christians have purified their souls by obedience to {in obeying} the truth (1 Pet. 1:22). ¶
– 2 1 Cor. 14:34 → to be under obedience → SUBJECT (verb) <5293> 3 2 Cor. 9:13 → SUBMISSION <5292>.

OBEDIENT – 1 ***hupēkoos*** [adj.: ὑπήκοος <5255>]; **from *hupakouō*: to listen, to obey, which is from *hupo*: under, and *akouō*: to hear, to understand ▶ Docile, submitted** > The fathers of the Jews would not be obedient {subject} to Moses (Acts 7:39). Paul wanted to know if the Corinthians were obedient in everything (2 Cor.

2:9). Christ Jesus became obedient even to death (Phil. 2:8). ¶

[2] **to be obedient: *peitharcheō*** [verb: πειθαρχέω <3980>]; **from *peithō*: to persuade, and *archō*: to begin, to dominate, which is from *archē*: beginning ▶ To submit to those in a position of authority >** Titus was to remind those of Crete to be obedient (Titus 3:1). All other refs.: LISTEN <3980>, OBEY <3980>.

– [3] Luke 2:51; Titus 2:9 → to be obedient → to be subject → SUBJECT <5293> [4] Acts 6:7; Rom. 6:17; Eph. 6:5; Col. 3:20 → to be, to become obedient → OBEY <5219> [5] Rom. 6:16; 15:18; 2 Cor. 7:15; 10:5; 1 Pet. 1:2, 14, 22 → OBEDIENCE <5218>.

OBEY – [1] ***hupakouō*** [verb: ὑπακούω <5219>]; **from *hupo*: under, and *akouō*: to hear, to understand ▶ To submit oneself to someone, to execute his will; also transl.: to be obedient, to become obedient >** The winds and the sea obeyed Jesus (Matt. 8:27; Mark 4:41; Luke 8:25). The unclean spirits obeyed Him (Mark 1:27). The mulberry tree would have obeyed one having faith (Luke 17:6). A great crowd of priests obeyed the faith (Acts 6:7). Sin ought not to reign in our body to obey its lusts (Rom. 6:12). We are bondmen to him whom we obey (Rom. 6:16b); Rom. 6:16a, in some transl., should be "for obedience" (*hupakoē*). The Christians in Rome had obeyed from the heart the form of teaching by which they had been instructed (Rom. 6:17). All have not obeyed {did not heed, have not accepted} the gospel (Rom. 10:16). Children are to obey their parents in the Lord (Eph. 6:1) and in all things (Col. 3:20). Servants are to obey their masters (Eph. 6:5; Col. 3:22). The Philippians had always obeyed Paul (Phil. 2:12). The angels will take vengeance on those who do not know God and on those who do not obey the gospel of the Lord Jesus Christ (2 Thes. 1:8). If anyone obeyed not Paul's word by the letter, the Thessalonians were to note that person (2 Thes. 3:14). To all them who obey Him, Christ became author of eternal salvation (Heb. 5:9). Abraham obeyed to go out into the place which he was to receive for an inheritance (Heb. 11:8). Sarah obeyed Abraham, calling him lord (1 Pet. 3:6). Other ref.: Acts 12:13; see ANSWER (verb) <5219>. ¶

[2] ***peithō*** [verb: πείθω <3982>] **▶ To trust, to submit; also transl.: to follow >** Those who obeyed {rallied to} Theudas were dispersed (Acts 5:36); those who obeyed Judas the Galilean {his followers} were also scattered abroad (v. 37). Paul spoke of those who obey unrighteousness (Rom. 2:8). The Galatians did not obey the truth (Gal. 5:7). Christians ought to obey their leaders (Heb. 13:17). We put bits in the mouths of horses that they may obey us (Jas. 3:3). Other refs.: Gal. 3:1 in some mss. All other refs.: see entries in Lexicon at <3982>.

[3] ***peitharcheō*** [verb: πειθαρχέω <3980>]; **from *peitharchos*: submission to authority, which is from *peithō*: see [2], and *archō*: to begin, to rule, which is from *archē*: beginning ▶ To be subject to a sovereign, to a superior >** God must be obeyed rather than men (Acts 5:29). God has given the Holy Spirit to those who obey Him (Acts 5:32). Titus was to remind the saints to obey {to be obedient to, to be subject to} rulers and authorities (Titus 3:1). Other ref.: Acts 27:21; see LISTEN <3980>. ¶

[4] **to obey not: *apeitheō*** [verb: ἀπειθέω <544>]; **from *apeithēs*: disobedient, which is from *a*: neg., and *peithō*: see [2] ▶ To refuse subjection, to disobey >** Even if any husbands do not obey {are disobedient to, do not believe in} the word, they may be gained by the manner of life of their wives (1 Pet. 3:1). Peter asks what will be the end of those who do not obey {are disobedient to} the gospel of God (1 Pet. 4:17). All other refs.: BELIEVE <544>, DISBELIEVE <544>, DISOBEDIENT <544>, UNBELIEVING <544>.

– [5] Matt. 23:3 → OBSERVE <5083> [6] Luke 2:51 → to be subject → SUBJECT <5293> [7] John 8:51, 52, 55; 1 John 5:2 → KEEP (verb) <5083> [8] Acts 7:39 → lit.: to be obedient → OBEDIENT <5255> [9] Rom. 2:13 → one who obey → DOER <4163> [10] Rom. 2:25 → to obey the law → to keep the law → KEEP (verb) <4238> [11] Rom. 2:27 → FULFILL <5055>

12 Rom. 15:18; 16:26; 2 Cor. 10:5; 1 Pet. 1:22 → OBEDIENCE <5218> 13 Gal. 5:3 → KEEP (verb) <4160> 14 1 Tim. 3:4 → to see that his children obey → lit.: to have his children in submission → SUBMISSION <5292> 15 Heb. 4:2 → HEAR <191>.

OBJECT (noun) – 1 Acts 10:11, 16; 11:5; Rom. 9:22, 23 → VESSEL[1] <4632> 2 Acts 27:13 → PURPOSE (noun) <4286>.

OBJECT (verb) – 1 Acts 24:19 → ACCUSE <2723> 2 Acts 25:11 → REFUSE (verb) <3868> 3 Acts 28:19 → to speak against → SPEAK <483>.

OBJECTION – 1 **without objection, without raising any objection: *anantirrētōs*** [adv.: ἀναντιρρήτως <369>]; **from *anantirrētos*: indisputable, which is from *a*: neg., *anti*: against, and *rētos*: agreed, spoken ▶ Without difficulty, without hesitation** > Peter had come without objection {without saying, without gainsaying} when he was sent for by Cornelius (Acts 10:29). ¶
– 2 Acts 11:18 → to have no further objections → lit.: to be silent → SILENT <2270>.

OBLIGATED (BE) – 1 Matt. 23:16, 18 → to be a debtor → DEBTOR <3784> 2 Rom. 1:14; Gal. 5:3 → DEBTOR <3781> 3 2 Cor. 12:14 → OUGHT <3784>.

OBLIGATION – 1 Rom. 1:14; 8:12 → under obligation, to have an obligation → lit.: to be debtor → DEBTOR <3781> 2 Rom. 4:4 → DEBT <3783> 3 Rom. 15:1 → to have an obligation → OUGHT <3784> 4 2 Cor. 9:5 → grudging obligation → COVETOUSNESS <4124>.

OBLIGED (BE) – 1 Matt. 23:16, 18 → to be a debtor → DEBTOR <3784> 2 Jude 3 → NECESSITY <318>.

OBSCENE – Col. 3:8 → obscene talk → filthy language → FILTHY <148>.

OBSCENITY – Eph. 5:4 → FILTHINESS <151>.

OBSCURE (adj.) – 1 ***auchmēros*** [adj.: αὐχμηρός <850>]; **from *auchmos*: dryness, dirt ▶ Somber** > The prophetic word is like a lamp shining in an obscure {dark} place (2 Pet. 1:19). ¶
– 2 Acts 21:39 → INSIGNIFICANT <767>.

OBSCURE (verb) – Luke 23:45 → DARKEN <4654>.

OBSCURELY – ***en ainigmati***; **en** [prep.: ἐν <1722>] ***ainigma*** [neut. noun: αἴνιγμα <135>]; **from *ainissomai*: to hint obscurely, which is from *ainos*: discourse; lit.: in enigma ▶ Indistinctly, enigmatically** > The Christians do not see all things distinctly at the present time; they see as through a mirror, obscurely {dimly, darkly, but a poor reflection} (1 Cor. 13:12). ¶

OBSCURITY – ***gnophos*** [masc. noun: γνόφος <1105>]; **comp. *nephos*: cloud ▶ Thick cloud** > Christians have not come to obscurity {blackness} and darkness {to darkness and gloom} (Heb. 12:18). ¶

OBSERVANCE – Acts 16:4; 21:24 → KEEP (verb) <5442>.

OBSERVATION – **with observation, with careful observation: *meta paratērēseōs*; *paratērēsis*** [fem. noun: παρατήρησις <3907>], **from *paratēreō*: to observe, which is from *para*: near, and *tēreō*: to observe; lit.: in a way to attract attention ▶ As an observable matter, in a spectacular way** > The kingdom of God does not come with observation {with signs to be observed} (Luke 17:20). ¶

OBSERVE – 1 ***tēreō*** [verb: τηρέω <5083>]; **from *tēros*: warden, guard ▶ To take care of, to maintain, to preserve; also transl.: to keep, to obey** > Jesus told the crowds and His disciples to do and observe (some mss. inverse the verbs: to observe and do) all things told to them by the scribes and Pharisees (Matt. 23:3). Those of the nations were not required to observe the requirements of the law, as the Jews did

(Acts 21:25 in some mss.). All other refs.: see entries in Lexicon at <5083>.

[2] ***paratēreō*** [verb: παρατηρέω <3906>]; **from *para*: near, and *tēreō*: see [1] ▶ To respect religiously >** The Galatians observed days and months and times and years (Gal. 4:10). The verb is also transl. "to watch," "to keep a close watch" (Mark 3:2; Luke 6:7; 14:1; 20:20; Acts 9:24). ¶

– [3] Matt. 6:28 → to observe, to observe with attention → CONSIDER <2648> [4] Matt. 7:3a → CONSIDER <991> [5] Matt. 7:3b; Luke 6:41; Acts 7:31, 32; 11:6 → CONSIDER <2657> [6] Mark 7:3, 4 → HOLD (verb) <2902> [7] Mark 12:41; 15:47 → SEE <2334> [8] Luke 1:6 → to walk in → WALK <4198> [9] Luke 17:20 → with signs to be observed → with observation → OBSERVATION <3326> <3907> [10] Luke 23:55 → SEE <2300> [11] Acts 10:4; 11:6 → to observe, to observe intently, to fix the eyes → FIX <816> [12] Acts 16:21 → PRACTICE (verb) <4160> [13] Acts 17:23 → BEHOLD (verb) <333> [14] Acts 27:39 → DISCOVER <2657> [15] Rom. 2:25 → KEEP (verb) <4238> [16] Rom. 14:6 → THINK <5426> [17] 1 Cor. 10:18 → BEHOLD (verb) <991> [18] Phil. 3:17 → to fix the eyes → EYES <4648> [19] Heb. 7:4 → CONSIDER <2334> [20] 1 Pet. 2:12; 3:2 → WITNESS (verb) <2029>.

OBSESSED (BE) – [1] ***noseō*** [verb: νοσέω <3552>]; **from *nosos*: sickness, disease ▶ To be sick >** In 1 Tim. 6:4, "to be obsessed {to dote, to have a morbid interest, to have an unhealthy craving, to have an unhealthy interest} with disputes and arguments over words" is lit.: to be sick concerning such things; it is a matter of those who question in an exaggerated fashion and with bad intentions. ¶

– [2] Acts 26:11 → to be exceedingly furious → FURIOUS <1693>.

OBSOLETE – Heb. 8:13 → to be, to become, to make obsolete → to grow old → OLD <3822>.

OBSTACLE – [1] Rom. 14:13; 16:17 → STUMBLING BLOCK <4625> [2] 1 Cor. 9:12 → HINDRANCE <1464> [3] 2 Cor. 6:3 → obstacle in anyone's way → STUMBLING BLOCK <4349>.

OBSTINATE – [1] Acts 19:9 → to become obstinate → HARDEN <4645> [2] Rom. 10:21 → to speak against → SPEAK <483>.

OBTAIN – [1] ***heuriskō*** [verb: εὑρίσκω <2147>] **▶ To discover, to acquire, to procure >** Christ had obtained {found} an eternal redemption (Heb. 9:12). All other refs.: FIND <2147>.

[2] ***echō*** [verb: ἔχω <2192>] **▶ To have, to possess >** Paul had proposed to visit the Christians in Rome in order that he might obtain some fruit among them (Rom. 1:13). All other refs.: see entries in Lexicon at <2192>.

[3] ***katalambanō*** [verb: καταλαμβάνω <2638>]; **from *kata*: intens., and *lambanō*: to take ▶ To gain, to attain >** The Christian is to run so as to obtain {to get, to win} the prize (1 Cor. 9:24). All other refs.: see entries in Lexicon at <2638>.

[4] ***ktaomai*** [verb: κτάομαι <2932>] **▶ To acquire, to buy, to pay >** A chief captain had obtained his citizenship with a great sum of money (Acts 22:28). All other refs.: POSSESS <2932>, PROVIDE <2932>, PURCHASE (verb) <2932>.

[5] ***tunchanō*** [verb: τυγχάνω <5177>] **▶ To attain, to receive >** Paul had obtained help from God (Acts 26:22). He endured all things for the sake of the elect, that they also might obtain the salvation which is in Christ Jesus (2 Tim. 2:10). Christ has obtained {has got, has received} a more excellent ministry (Heb. 8:6). O.T. people of faith were tortured, not having accepted deliverance, that they might obtain {gain, get} a better resurrection (Heb. 11:35). All other refs.: ATTAIN <5177>, COMMON <5177>, ENJOY <5177>, ORDINARY <5177>, PERHAPS <5177>.

[6] ***epitunchanō*** [verb: ἐπιτυγχάνω <2013>]; **from *epi*: intens., and *tunchanō*: see [5] ▶ Stronger than [5]; to succeed in attaining, to secure >** Israel has not obtained what he seeks for, but the election has obtained it (Rom. 11:7a, b). Abraham obtained {got,

received} the promise (Heb. 6:15). O.T. people of faith obtained {gained} promises (Heb. 11:33). James speaks of those who cannot obtain {have what they want} although they are full of envy (Jas. 4:2). Other ref.: Acts 13:29 in some mss. ¶

– [7] Matt. 26:59; Mark 14:55 → to keep trying to obtain → SEEK <2212> [8] Acts 1:17; 2 Pet. 1:1 → RECEIVE <2975> [9] Acts 8:20 → PURCHASE (verb) <2932> [10] Acts 13:39 → a justification you were not able to obtain → lit.: from which you could not be justified [11] Acts 20:28; 1 Tim. 3:13 → PURCHASE (verb) <4046> [12] Rom. 8:21 → to obtain → lit.: for (*eis*) [13] 2 Thes. 2:14 → that you may obtain → lit.: for the obtaining → OBTAINING <4047> [14] Heb. 12:15 → to fail to obtain → LACK (verb) <5302> [15] 1 Pet. 1:9 → RECEIVE <2865> [16] 1 Pet. 3:9 → INHERIT <2816>.

OBTAINING – ***peripoiēsis*** [fem. noun: περιποίησις <4047>]; **from *peripoieō*: to acquire for oneself, which is from *peri*: around (denoting acquisition), and *poieō*: to make, to gain ▶ Possession, acquisition** > Christians have been called for the obtaining of {that they may gain, share in} the glory of the Lord Jesus Christ (2 Thes. 2:14). All other refs.: POSSESSION <4047>, RECEIVE <4047>, SAVING <4047>.

OBVIOUS – [1] Gal. 5:19 → EVIDENT <5318> [2] 1 Tim. 5:24, 25 → clearly evident → CLEARLY <4271> [3] 2 Tim. 3:9 → MANIFEST (adj.) <1552> [4] 1 John 3:10 → MANIFEST (adj.) <5318>.

OCCASION – [1] ***aphormē*** [fem. noun: ἀφορμή <874>]; **from *apo*: from, and *hormē*: impulse, violent attempt ▶ Point of departure, beginning; also transl.: opportunity** > Sin found an occasion {a point of attack} by the commandment (Rom. 7:8, 11). Paul gave the Corinthians an occasion to boast on his behalf (2 Cor. 5:12). The younger widows ought to give no occasion to the adversary (1 Tim. 5:14). Christians ought not to turn liberty into an occasion for {to indulge} the flesh (Gal. 5:13). Other refs.: Luke 11:53 in some mss.; 2 Cor. 11:12a, b. ¶

[2] ***kairos*** [masc. noun: καιρός <2540>] ▶ **Defined time, opportunity** > As they have occasion, Christians should do good toward all, and especially toward those of the household of faith (Gal. 6:10). They are to seize the occasion {to make most of the time, to make the most of the opportunity, to redeem the time}, i.e., to seize every good and favorable opportunity (Eph. 5:16; Col. 4:5). All other refs.: SEASON (noun) <2540>, TIME <2540>.

[3] **on the occasion of: *epi*** [prep.: ἐπί <1909>] ▶ **Over, about** > Christians had been scattered abroad through the tribulation that took place on the occasion of {in connection with} Stephen (Acts 11:19). *

– [4] Eph. 4:29 → as fits the occasion → lit.: of the need → NEED (noun) <5532>.

OCCUPATION – [1] ***technē*** [fem. noun: τέχνη <5078>]; **prob. from *tektōn*: craftsman ▶ Trade practiced by a person in order to earn his living** > The occupation of Aquila and Priscilla was to make tents (Acts 18:3). After the fall of Babylon, no craftsman of any occupation {craft, art, trade} will be found in her anymore (Rev. 18:22). Other ref.: Acts 17:29; see ART <5078>. ¶

[2] Acts 19:25 → of like (similar) occupations → lit.: concerning such things: *peri ta toiauta*.

OCCUPIED (BE) – Heb. 13:9 → WALK <4043>.

OCCUPY – [1] ***meletaō*** [verb: μελετάω <3191>]; **from *meletē*: care, which is from *melō*: see [2] ▶ To apply oneself, to practice** > Timothy was to occupy himself with {meditate on, take pain with, be diligent in} diverse things as a good servant of Christ Jesus (1 Tim. 4:15). Other refs.: Mark 13:11; Acts 4:25; see MEDITATE <3191>, PREMEDITATE <3191>. ¶

[2] **he is occupied about: *melei*; impersonal form of *melō*** [verb: μέλω <3199>]; **third person sing. of *mellō*: to occupy oneself ▶ He is interested in** > Paul asks if God is

occupied about {is concerned about, takes care of} the oxen (1 Cor. 9:9). *
– [3] Luke 14:9 → TAKE <2722> [4] Acts 18:5 → occupied with the word → compelled in respect of the word → COMPEL <4912> [5] 1 Cor. 14:16 → FILL (verb) <378>.

OCCUR – [1] ***ginomai*** [verb: γίνομαι <1096>]; **lit.: to become ▶ To happen, to circulate** > When the sound of people speaking in other tongues occurred {was heard, was noised, spread}, people came together (Acts 2:6). Other refs.: see entries in Lexicon at <1096>.
– [2] Mark 13:19 → to be like → LIKE (adj., adv., noun) <5108> [3] Luke 6:48; 15:14 → ARISE <1096> [4] Luke 19:13 → to do business → BUSINESS <4231> [5] Acts 13:12 → what had occurred → what had been done → DO <1096> [6] 1 Cor. 7:2 → "is occurring" added in Engl.

ODOR – [1] ***osmē*** [fem. noun: ὀσμή <3744>]; **from *ozō*: to emit a scent ▶ Scent; used primarily of agreeable, attractive perfume in the N.T.; also transl.: aroma, sweet aroma, fragrance, savor** > The house was full of the odor of Mary's ointment (John 12:3). God makes manifest the odor of His knowledge through Christians (2 Cor. 2:14). For those who perish, Christians are an odor {smell} from death unto death, but to the saved an odor from life unto life (2 Cor. 2:16a, b). Other refs.: Eph. 5:2; Phil. 4:18; see AROMA <3744>. ¶
[2] **sweet odor: *euōdia*** [fem. noun: εὐωδία <2175>]; **from *euōdēs*: sweet-smelling, which is from *eu*: good, and *ozō*: to emit a scent ▶ Perfume, a good and pleasing smell** > Christians are a sweet odor {sweet savor, fragrance, aroma} of Christ to God (2 Cor. 2:15). Christ delivered Himself up for us, an offering and a sacrifice to God for a sweet-smelling fragrance (lit.: fragrance of sweet odor; also transl.: sweet-smelling aroma, sweet-smelling savour, fragrant aroma, fragrant offering) (Eph. 5:2). That which the Philippians had sent to Paul was like a fragrance of sweet odor {sweet savor, sweet smell, fragrant aroma, fragrant offering}, agreeable to God (Phil. 4:18). ¶
– [3] John 11:39 → to be a bad odor → to be a stench → STENCH <3605>.

ODOUR – [1] See ODOR.
– [2] Phil. 4:18 → AROMA <3744> [3] Rev. 5:8; 18:13 → INCENSE <2368>.

OF ITS – ***tou*** [art. τοῦ <5120>]. *

OF THEE, THY, THINE – ***sou*** [sing. pron.: σοῦ <4675>]; **from *su*: thou, you ▶ Archaic form of "your, of you"** > Refs.: Matt. 7:3; 15:28; 25:25. *

OF THESE PERSONS, OF THESE THINGS – ***toutōn*** [pron.: τούτων <5130>]. *

OF THIS KIND, SUCH – ***toiosde*** [pron.: τοιόσδε <5107>] > Ref.: 2 Pet. 1:17. ¶

OF THIS PERSON, OF THIS THING – ***toutou*** [pron.: τούτου <5127>]. *

OF THYSELF – ***seautou*** [pron.: σεαυτοῦ <4572>]; **from *se*, and *autos*: self** > Refs.: John 1:22; Acts 9:34; 26:1. *

OF WHAT KIND – ***hoios*** [pron.: οἷος <3634>] ▶ **Of what kind or sort, what manner of, such as** > Refs.: Matt. 24:21; Mark 9:3; 13:19; Luke 9:55; Rom. 9:6; 1 Cor. 15:48; 2 Cor. 10:11; 12:20; Phil. 1:30; 1 Thes. 1:5; 2 Tim. 3:11; Rev. 16:18. ¶ ‡

OF WHAT KIND, OF WHAT SORT – ***hopoios*** [pron.: ὁποῖος <3697>]; **from *homos*: like, similar ▶** Refs.: Acts 26:29; 1 Cor. 3:13; Gal. 2:6; 1 Thes. 1:9; Jas. 1:24. ¶ ‡

OFF – Acts 20:15 → OPPOSITE <481>.

OFFENCE – [1] See OFFENSE.
– [2] Matt. 13:41; 16:23; 18:7a–c; Luke 17:1; 1 Cor. 1:23; Gal. 5:11 → STUMBLING BLOCK <4625> [3] Matt. 17:27, Luke 7:23 → to be an offence → OFFEND <4624> [4] 2 Cor. 6:3 → STUMBLING BLOCK <4349> [5] 2 Cor. 11:7 → SIN (noun) <266>.

OFFEND – [1] ***skandalizō*** [verb: σκανδαλίζω <4624>]; **from *skandalon*: occasion of stumbling, scandal; lit.: to cause to stumble and fall ▶ To affront, to scandalize, to wound morally; also transl.: to cause offense, to fall away, to go astray, to stumble, to take offense, to turn away** > This verb is used when the Lord describes the effect He had on men in general (Matt. 11:6; Luke 7:23), the Jews (Matt. 13:57; 17:27; Mark 6:3), the Pharisees (Matt. 15:12), and His disciples (Matt. 26:31; Mark 14:27; John 6:61). Some are offended when tribulation or persecution arises on account of the word (Matt. 13:21; Mark 4:17). During the tribulation, many will be offended (Matt. 24:10). Peter had assured the Lord that he would never be offended because of Him (Matt. 26:33; Mark 14:29). The Lord warned His disciples of tribulations yet future so that they would not be offended (John 16:1). It is good for the Christian to abstain from certain legitimate things so as not to offend his brother (Rom. 14:21); he is to avoid offending {being a snare to} one of the little ones (Luke 17:2). Paul suffered for those who were offended (2 Cor. 11:29 {to be led into sin}). Other refs.: Matt. 5:29, 30; 18:6, 8, 9; Mark 9:42, 43, 45, 47; 1 Cor. 8:13a, b. ¶

– [2] Matt. 13:41 → thing that offends → STUMBLING BLOCK <4625> [3] Acts 25:8 → SIN (verb) <264> [4] Jas. 2:10; 3:2a, b → STUMBLE <4417>.

OFFENDER – [1] Luke 13:4 → SINNER <3781> [2] Acts 25:11; 2 Cor. 7:12a → to be an offender → lit.: to do wrong → WRONG (verb) <91>.

OFFENSE – [1] ***proskomma*** [neut. noun: πρόσκομμα <4348>]; **from *proskoptō*: to stumble, which is from *pros*: against, and *koptō*: to cut, to strike ▶ Obstacle against which one stumbles, a matter that can scandalize someone** > It is evil for the man who eats with offense {while stumbling, and gives offense, that causes someone else to stumble} (Rom. 14:20). Other refs.: Rom. 9:32, 33; 14:13; 1 Cor. 8:9; 1 Pet. 2:8; see STUMBLING BLOCK <4348>. ¶

[2] **without offense: *aproskopos*** [adj.: ἀπρόσκοπος <677>]; **from *a*: neg., and *proskoptō*: see [1] ▶ Blameless, irreproachable** > Paul exercised himself to always have a conscience without offense {void to offence, blameless, clear} toward God and men (Acts 24:16). He was praying that the Philippians would be without offense (Phil. 1:10). Other ref.: 1 Cor. 10:32 (not giving occasion to stumble); see STUMBLE <677>. ¶

[3] ***skandalon*** [neut. noun: σκάνδαλον <4625>]; **lit.: snare set in the way ▶ Obstacle that is a cause for stumbling** > Jesus was a rock of offense {that makes them fall} in Zion (Rom. 9:33; 1 Pet. 2:8). All other refs.: STUMBLING BLOCK <4625>.

– [4] Matt. 6:14, 15a, b; Mark 11:25, 26; Rom. 4:25; 5:15–18, 20; 2 Cor. 5:19; Gal. 6:1; Eph. 2:1, 5; Col. 2:13a, b; Jas. 5:16 → TRANSGRESSION <3900> [5] Matt. 11:6; 13:57; 17:27; Mark 6:3; John 6:61 → to take offense → OFFEND <4624> [6] Matt. 16:23; 18:7a–c; Luke 17:1; Rom. 16:17; Gal. 5:11 → STUMBLING BLOCK <4625> [7] Acts 25:8 → to commit offense → SIN (verb) <264> [8] Rom. 5:14 → TRANSGRESSION <3847> [9] 2 Cor. 6:3 → STUMBLING BLOCK <4349> [10] 2 Cor. 11:7 → SIN (noun) <266>.

OFFER – [1] ***anagō*** [verb: ἀνάγω <321>]; **from *ana*: up, and *agō*: to lead ▶ To bring, to present** > The Israelites offered a sacrifice to their idol, the golden calf (Acts 7:41). All other refs.: see entries in Lexicon at <321>.

[2] **to offer, to offer up: *anapherō*** [verb: ἀναφέρω <399>]; **from *ana*: up, and *pherō*: to carry ▶ To bring up (on the altar)** > The high priests offered up sacrifices for their own sins and for those of the people (Heb. 7:27). Christians are to offer the sacrifice of praise continually to God (Heb. 13:15). Abraham offered his son Isaac upon the altar (Jas. 2:21). Christians offer spiritual sacrifices acceptable to God by Jesus Christ (1 Pet. 2:5). All other refs.: BEAR (verb) <399>, CARRY <399>, LEAD (verb) <399>.

[3] ***parechō*** [verb: παρέχω <3930>]; **from *para*: next to, and *echō*: to hold ▶ To**

present, to show > Jesus taught to offer {to turn} the other cheek to him that smites on a cheek (Luke 6:29). All other refs.: see entries in Lexicon at <3930>.

4 **to offer, to offer up: *prospherō*** [verb: προσφέρω <4374>]; **from *pros*: near, to, and *pherō*: to carry ▶ To bring, to bear, to present** > The wise men offered {presented} gifts to Jesus (Matt. 2:11). Jesus told the Israelites to offer their gifts (Matt. 5:23, 24; 8:4; Mark 1:44; Luke 5:14 {to make an offering}). The soldiers offered Jesus vinegar (Luke 23:36; John 19:29 {to put up, to lift}). Jesus told His disciples that the time was coming that whoever would kill them would think that he offers {renders, does} God service (John 16:2). Simon the magician offered money to the apostles that the Holy Spirit might be given by the laying on of his hands (Acts 8:18). An offering was to be offered {be made} on the occasion when Paul and other men had been purified before entering into the temple (Acts 21:26). The house of Israel had offered {had brought} God victims and sacrifices in the wilderness (Acts 7:42; also Heb. 10:2, 8 {to make}). The high priest offered gifts and sacrifices for sins (Heb. 5:1, 3; 8:3a {for the offering}, b, 4; 9:7, 9; 10:11). In the days of his flesh, Jesus offered up both prayers and supplications to Him who was able to save him out of death (Heb. 5:7). Christ offered Himself spotless to God (Heb. 9:14). Jesus did not offer Himself often (Heb. 9:25), but rather once to bear the sins of many (9:28 {to sacrifice}; 10:12). The same sacrifices were offered {were repeated} continually year by year (Heb. 10:1). Abel offered to God a more excellent sacrifice than Cain (Heb. 11:4). Abraham offered up his only begotten son (Heb. 11:17). All other refs.: BRING <4374>, DEAL <4374>.

5 ***didōmi*** [verb: δίδωμι <1325>] ▶ **To give, to present** > The parents of Jesus brought Him to Jerusalem to offer a sacrifice (Luke 2:24). Other refs.: GIVE <1325>.

6 ***tithēmi*** [verb: τίθημι <5087>] ▶ **To make, to present** > Paul was offering the gospel without charge (1 Cor. 9:18). All other refs.: see entries in Lexicon at <5087>.

– 7 Luke 10:8; 11:6 → to set before → SET (verb) <3908> 8 Luke 11:12 → GIVE <1929> 9 Acts 15:29; 21:25; 1 Cor. 8:1, 4, 7, 10; 10:19 → offered to idols → sacrificed to idols → SACRIFICE (verb) <1494> 10 Rom. 6:13a, b, 16; 12:1; 19a, b → PRESENT (verb) <3936> 11 1 Cor. 10:20 → SACRIFICE (verb) <2380> 12 1 Cor. 10:28 → offered to holy purposes, offered to idols → offered in sacrifice → SACRIFICE (noun) <1494> 13 Phil. 2:17; 2 Tim. 4:6 → to be offered → DRINK OFFERING <4689> 14 Titus 2:11 → that offers salvation → that brings salvation → SALVATION <4992> 15 Heb. 6:18 → to set before → SET (verb) <4295>.

OFFERING – 1 **consecrated offering: *anathēma*** [neut. noun: ἀνάθημα <334>]; **from *anatithēmi*: to lay up, which is from *ana*: above, and *tithēmi*: to put ▶ Offering in the temple, ex-voto** > The temple was adorned with beautiful stones and consecrated offerings {donations, gifts, votive gifts} (Luke 21:5). ¶

2 ***prosphora*** [fem. noun: προσφορά <4376>]; **from *prospherō*: to offer, which is from *pros*: to, and *pherō*: to bring ▶ Gift presented to God; also transl.: sacrifice** > An offering was to be presented by Paul and the men who were with him following their vow (Acts 21:26); later Paul came to Jerusalem with offerings (24:17). The offering up of the Gentiles (Rom. 15:16) refers to the presentation to God of Christians who are not Jews. Christ delivered Himself up for us, an offering {a fragrant offering} and sacrifice to God (Eph. 5:2). God did not want sacrifice and offering like those offered under the law, therefore Christ came (Heb. 10:5, 8). Christians have been sanctified by the offering of the body of Jesus Christ once for all (Heb. 10:10); they have been perfected in perpetuity by this one offering (v. 14) and, consequently, there is no longer an offering for sin (v. 18). ¶

– 3 Matt. 5:23, 24a, b; 8:4; 23:18, 19a, b; Luke 21:4; Heb. 11:4 → GIFT <1435> 4 Mark 12:41, 43; Luke 21:1 → offering box → temple treasury → TREASURE (noun) <1049> 5 Luke 5:14; Heb. 8:3a →

to make an offering → OFFER <4374> [6] Phil. 2:17; 2 Tim. 4:6 → DRINK OFFERING <4689> [7] Phil. 2:17b → sacrificial offering → sacrifice and service → SERVICE <3009> [8] Phil. 4:18 → fragrant offering → sweet odor → ODOR <2175> [9] Heb. 10:6, 8 → offering for, offerings for sin → lit.: for sin (*peri hamartias*). Such sacrifices were offered in the O.T. to make atonement of sins committed (see Lev. 4). [10] Heb. 11:4 → SACRIFICE (noun) <2378>.

OFFICE – [1] ***episkopē*** [fem. noun: ἐπισκοπή <1984>]; **from *episkopeō*: to look after, which is from *epi*: upon, and *skopeō*: to watch, to give attention, which is from *skopos*: goal, mark ▶ Duties, responsibilities of an overseer; see OVERSEER** <1985> > It was necessary that another should take the office {bishoprick, overseership, place of leadership} of Judas (Acts 1:20). All other refs.: VISITATION <1984>.
– [2] Rom. 11:13 → MINISTRY <1248> [3] Rom. 12:4 → FUNCTION (noun) <4234>.

OFFICER – [1] ***praktōr*** [masc. noun: πράκτωρ <4233>]; **from *prassō*: to do; lit.: agent, doer ▶ Justice officer, guard** > A judge could turn a person over to an officer, and the officer could throw this person in prison (Luke 12:58a, b). ¶
[2] ***rhabdouchos*** [masc. noun: ῥαβδοῦχος <4465>]; **from *rhabdos*: scepter, baton, and *echō*: to have, to hold ▶ Roman officer responsible to carry out the orders of the emperor and of the chief magistrates** > The magistrates sent officers {serjeants, lictors, policemen} to release Paul and Silas (Acts 16:35, 38). ¶
[3] ***hupēretēs*** [masc. noun: ὑπηρέτης <5257>]; **from *hupo*: under, and *eretēs*: rower ▶ a. Servant, especially responsible for implementing decisions of the Sanhedrin or the synagogue; also transl.: guard, guard of the temple, official** > Peter sat with the officers (Matt. 26:58; Mark 14:54; John 18:18). Some struck Jesus with their hands (Mark 14:65; John 18:22). Officers had been sent to arrest Jesus (John 7:32, 45, 46). Officers had accompanied Judas to arrest Jesus (John 18:3, 12). They cried out to crucify Jesus (John 19:6). The officers did not find the apostles in the prison (Acts 5:22); they found them in the temple and brought them before the Sanhedrin (Acts 5:26). **b. Subordinate officer, constable** > Matthew uses this Greek word in Matt. 5:25 rather than *praktōr* (see [1]). All other refs.: ATTENDANT <5257>, MINISTER (noun) <5257>, SERVANT <5257>.
– [4] Mark 6:21; Acts 25:23 → high officer, high ranking officer, high-ranking military officer → CAPTAIN <5506> [5] Luke 22:4, 52 → CAPTAIN <4755> [6] Rom. 13:6 → MINISTER (noun) <3011>.

OFFICIAL – [1] **court official, important official: *dunastēs*** [masc. noun: δυνάστης <1413>]; **from *dunamai*: to be capable ▶ Person in a position of authority; also transl.: man of great authority, man in power** > An Ethiopian eunuch was a court official who was over all the treasures of the queen of the Ethiopians (Acts 8:27). Other refs.: Luke 1:52; 1 Tim. 6:15; see RULER <1413>. ¶
– [2] Mark 6:21 → high official → LORD (noun) <3175> [3] John 4:46, 49 → official, royal official → NOBLEMAN <937> [4] John 18:3, 12; 19:6 → guard, temple guard → OFFICER <5257> [5] Acts 17:6, 8 → city official → ruler of the city → RULER <4173> [6] Acts 19:31 → official of Asia, official of the province → see ASIA <775>.

OFFICIATE – Heb. 7:13 → to give attendance → ATTENDANCE <4337>.

OFFSCOURING – [1] 1 Cor. 4:13 → FILTH <4027> [2] 1 Cor. 4:13 → REFUSE (noun) <4067>.

OFFSPRING – [1] ***genos*** [neut. noun: γένος <1085>]; **from *ginomai*: to be born ▶ Descendant, progeny** > Jesus is the root and offspring of David (Rev. 22:16). All other refs.: see entries in Lexicon at <1085>.

– [2] Matt. 3:7; 12:34; 23:33; Luke 3:7 → BROOD <1081> [3] Luke 1:35 → the holy offspring → the holy one → HOLY ONE, HOLY THING <40> [4] Luke 1:55; John 7:42; Acts 3:25; Rom. 4:13, 16, 18; 9:7b, 8, 29; Heb. 11:18; Rev. 12:17; et al. → SEED <4690>.

OFT – Mark 7:3 → CAREFULLY <4435>.

OFTEN – [1] **as often as: *hosakis*** [adv.: ὁσάκις <3740>]**; from *hosos*: how ▶ Every time that, whenever** > This term is used in 1 Cor. 11:25, 26; Rev. 11:6. ¶

[2] ***pollakis*** [adv.: πολλάκις <4178>]**; from *polus*: many ▶ Frequently** > A boy who was a lunatic often fell into the fire and often into the water (Matt. 17:15a, b {*eniote* in some mss.: sometimes}; Mark 9:22). Jesus had often met with His disciples in a garden beyond the brook Kidron (John 18:2). Paul had often proposed to visit the Christians in Rome (Rom. 1:13), but he had been often (*ta polla*) hindered from doing so (15:22). Onesiphorus had often refreshed Paul (2 Tim. 1:16). Every priest stands daily ministering and offering often the same sacrifices, which can never take away sins (Heb. 10:11). Other refs.: Mark 5:4; Acts 26:11; 2 Cor. 8:22; 11:23, 26, 27a, b; Phil. 3:18; Heb. 6:7; 9:25, 26. ¶

[3] **how often: *posakis*** [adv.: ποσάκις <4212>]**; from *posos*: how ▶ How many times** > This term is used in Matt. 18:21; 23:37; Luke 13:34. ¶

[4] ***puknos*** [adj.: πυκνός <4437>]**; used in the plur. as an adv.: *pukna* ▶ More frequently** > The Pharisees asked Jesus why the disciples of John fasted often (Luke 5:33). Felix sent for Paul often and talked with him (Acts 24:26). Other ref.: 1 Tim. 5:23; see FREQUENT <4437>. ¶

– [5] Luke 8:29 → often, often times → lit.: many times (*pollois chronois*).

OH THAT!, WOULD THAT! – *ophelon* (ὄφελον)**; from *opheilō*** [verb.: ὀφείλω <3785>] ▶ Refs.: 1 Cor. 4:8; 2 Cor. 11:1; Gal. 5:12; Rev. 3:15. ¶ ‡

OIL – [1] ***elaion*** [neut. noun: ἔλαιον <1637>]**; from *elaia*: olive, olive oil ▶ This term refers to olive oil** > In the parable of the ten virgins, some took oil with them, but others did not (Matt. 25:3, 4, 8); oil represents the Holy Spirit. The apostles had anointed with oil many sick people and had healed them (Mark 6:13). Jesus reproached His host Simon of not having anointed His head with oil (Luke 7:46). In the parable of the Good Samaritan, oil and wine were used as medications (Luke 10:34). In a parable, an unjust steward owed one hundred baths (a bath is about eight or nine gallons) of oil to his master (Luke 16:6). God has anointed His Son with the oil of gladness above His companions, thus showing His preeminence and His royalty (Heb. 1:9). James recommends anointing the sick with oil in the name of the Lord (5:14). In Revelation we find references to oil sold in the market (Rev. 6:6; 18:13). ¶

– [2] Matt. 6:17; Luke 7:46a → to put oil → ANOINT <218>.

OINTMENT – [1] ***muron*** [neut. noun: μύρον <3464>] ▶ **Aromatic liquid substance; myrrh; also transl.: fragrant oil, perfume** > A woman poured out a very precious ointment on the head of Jesus (Matt. 26:7, 9 in some mss., 12; Mark 14:3–5). A woman anointed the feet of Jesus with ointment (Luke 7:37, 38, 46; John 11:2; 12:3a, b, 5). Women prepared aromatic spices and ointments for the body of Jesus (Luke 23:56). Merchants will weep over the fall of Babylon who will not longer buy from them various products, including ointment {myrrh, perfume, unguent} (Rev. 18:13). ¶

– [2] John 9:6 → to put as ointment → ANOINT <2025>.

OLD – [1] ***archaios*** [adj.: ἀρχαῖος <744>]**; from *archē*: beginning ▶ Of the past, since a long time, long ago, some time ago** > Some said that Jesus was one of the old prophets risen again (Luke 9:8, 19). God had chosen Peter among the apostles a good while ago {since the earliest days, in the early days} (lit.: since the older days) (Acts 15:7). Of old time {Throughout many generations,

From generations of old, From ancient generations} (lit.: Since old generations), Moses is preached in the synagogues (Acts 15:21). Mnason was an old {early} disciple {a disciple of long standing} (Acts 21:16). If anyone is in Christ, he is a new creation, the old things have passed away; behold, all things have become new (2 Cor. 5:17). God did not spare the old {ancient} world (2 Pet. 2:5). Satan is the old {ancient} serpent (Rev. 12:9; 20:2). Other ref.: Matt. 5:27 in some mss. Other refs.: Matt. 5:21, 33; see ANCIENT <744>. ¶

2 ***gerōn*** [masc. noun: γέρων <1088>] ► **Elderly man, aged man** > Nicodemus asked Jesus how a man could be born being old (John 3:4). ¶

3 ***palai*** [adv.: πάλαι <3819>] ► **Formerly, from long ago, in the past** > Peter speaks of one who has forgotten that he was cleansed from his old {former, past} sins (lit.: his sins from long ago) (2 Pet. 1:9). All other refs.: LONG (adj.) <3819>, PAST <3819>.

4 ***palaios*** [adj.: παλαιός <3820>]; **from *palai*: see 3 ► Ancient, former, worn out** > The Christian's old man has been crucified with Christ (Rom. 6:6). The veil (i.e., the blinding of the minds) remains unlifted from the children of Israel in the reading of the old covenant (2 Cor. 3:14). The Christian is to have put off the old man, which corrupts itself according to deceitful lusts (Eph. 4:22), with its deeds (Col. 3:9). The term is also used in regard to an old garment (Matt. 9:16; Mark 2:21a, b; Luke 5:36a, b), wineskins (Matt. 9:17; Mark 2:22; Luke 5:37), things brought out of a treasure (Matt. 13:52), wine (Luke 5:39a, b), and leaven (1 Cor. 5:7, 8). John was writing an old commandment which the saints had heard from the beginning (1 John 2:7a, b). ¶

5 **to grow old, to make old: *palaioō*** [verb: παλαιόω <3822>]; **from *palaios*: see 4 ► To become obsolete, to wear out** > Jesus says to make ourselves money bags that do not grow old (Luke 12:33). The heavens and the earth will all grow old like a garment (Heb. 1:11). God has made old {has made obsolete} the first covenant, and what grows old {becomes obsolete, decays} and aged is ready to vanish away (Heb. 8:13a, b). ¶

6 **old wives': *graōdēs*** [adj.: γραώδης <1126>]; **from *graus*: old woman ► Absurd (stories) told by elderly women** > Timothy was to reject profane and old wives' fables {fables fit only for women} (1 Tim. 4:7). ¶

7 **to be old, to grow old: *gēraskō*** [verb: γηράσκω <1095>]; **from *gēras*: old age ► To become old** > When he would grow old, Peter would stretch out his hands and someone else would gird him, and bring him where he did not wish to go (John 21:18). What is becoming obsolete and growing old {aged, aging} is near disappearing (Heb. 8:13). ¶

– 8 Matt. 2:16 → from two years old and under → lit.: from two years and under 9 Luke 1:7 → to be very old → to be well advanced in years → ADVANCE <4260> 10 Luke 2:36 → very old → lit.: advanced in many days → AGE <2250> 11 Acts 2:17; Heb. 11:2 → old man, man of old → ELDER <4245> 12 Acts 15:18 → from of old → lit.: from eternity → FOREVER <165> 13 Rom. 4:19 → one hundred years old → YEAR <1541> 14 Jas. 2:2 → filthy old → DIRTY <4508> 15 2 Pet. 2:3 → of old → for a long time → TIME <1597> 16 2 Pet. 3:5 → of old → long ago → LONG (adj.) <1597>.

OLD AGE – 1 ***gēras*** [neut. noun: γῆρας <1094>] ► **Advanced age** > Elizabeth had conceived a son in her old age (Luke 1:36). ¶

2 ***palaiotēs*** [fem. noun: παλαιότης <3821>]; **from *palaios*: old ► Which belongs to the past and should not influence the present** > The Christian serves God in newness of spirit, not in oldness of the letter (Rom. 7:6). ¶

OLD MAN – 1 ***presbuteros*** [adj.: πρεσβύτερος <4245>]; **compar. of *presbus*: old man ► Elderly man** > In the last days, old men {elders} will dream dreams (Acts 2:17). All other refs.: ELDER <4245>.

2 ***presbutēs*** [masc. noun: πρεσβύτης <4246>]; **from *presbus*: old man ► Elderly man** > Zacharias was an old man (Luke 1:18). The older men {elder men} are to be sober, dignified, sensible, sound in faith, in

love, in perseverance (Titus 2:2). Paul had become an old man (Phm. 9 {the aged}). ¶

OLDER – [1] Luke 15:25; John 8:9; 1 Tim. 5:1, 2; 1 Pet. 5:5 → older, one who is older → ELDER <4245> [2] Titus 2:3 → older woman → AGED WOMAN <4247>.

OLDEST – John 8:9 → ELDEST <4245>.

OLIVE – ***elaia*** [fem. noun: ἐλαία <1636>] ► **Fruit of the olive tree, of a greenish color and then blackish at maturity, smooth skinned; oil is extracted from the olive** > A fig tree cannot produce olives {olive berries} (Jas. 3:12); similarly the Christian should not produce fruit according to his old nature, but rather fruit in conformity to his new nature. All other refs.: MOUNT OF OLIVES <1636>, OLIVE TREE <1636>.

OLIVE TREE – [1] ***elaia*** [fem. noun: ἐλαία <1636>] ► **Tree very widespread in Israel; the oil extracted from its fruit is used for food, lighting, fabrication of ointment or soap; the olive tree may live to 1,000 years, producing fruit throughout its entire life span** > Paul uses an illustration to recall the grace of God that has grafted the branches of the wild olive tree (the nations; see [2]) into the good olive tree (Israel; see [3]), i.e., a procedure which is contrary to the usual one wherein one grafts a branch of the good olive tree into the wild olive tree (Rom. 11:17 {wild olive shoot}, 24). The two olive trees and the two lamps of Rev. 11:4 are two witnesses operating in the power of the Holy Spirit (represented by the oil, according to Zech. 4:2, 6) to perform miracles, like Moses and Elijah formerly (see Ex. 7:20; 2 Kgs. 1:10). All other refs.: OLIVE <1636>, MOUNT OF OLIVES <1636>.

[2] **wild olive tree: *agrielaios*** [masc. noun: ἀγριέλαιος <65>]; **from *agrios*: growing in the fields, and *elaia*: see** [1] ► **Olive tree that grows naturally (i.e., an olive tree that is not cultivated by man)** > The Greek word is used in Rom. 11:17, 24. ¶

[3] **good olive tree: *kallielaios*** [adj. used as noun: καλλιέλαιος <2565>]; **from *kallos*: beauty, and *elaia*: see** [1] ► **Cultivated olive tree** > The Greek word is used in Rom. 11:24. ¶

OLIVET – Acts 1:12 → mount of Olivet → see MOUNT OF OLIVES <3735>, <1638>.

OLYMPAS – ***Olumpas*** [masc. name: Ὀλυμπᾶς <3652>]; **prob. from Olympus which was the celestial dwelling place of pagan gods in Greece** ► **Christian man living in Rome** > Paul sends his greetings to Olympas (Rom. 16:15). ¶

OMEGA – ***Ō*** [Ω <5598>] ► **Last letter of the Greek alphabet written "ω"** > The letter "omega" is used with the letter "alpha," the first letter of the same alphabet. The expr. "the Alpha and the Omega" is a name of God and of Christ found only in Revelation (1:8, 11 in some mss.; 21:6; 22:13). It underlines their eternal existence. ¶

OMIT – Matt. 23:23 → LEAVE (verb) <863>.

OMNIPOTENT – Rev. 19:6 → ALMIGHTY <3841>.

ONCE – [1] ***hapax*** [adv.: ἅπαξ <530>] ► **On one occasion** > This term is used in 2 Cor. 11:25; Phil. 4:16; 1 Thes. 2:18; Heb. 6:4; 9:7, 26–28; 10:2; 12:26, 27; 1 Pet. 3:18, 20; Jude 3, 5. ¶

[2] **once for all, at once: *ephapax*** [adv.: ἐφάπαξ <2178>]; **from *epi*: upon (intens.), and *hapax*: see** [1] ► **A single time, with the sense that there will not be other times; on the same occasion** > This term is used in Rom. 6:10; 1 Cor. 15:6; Heb. 7:27; 9:12; 10:10. ¶

[3] **at once: *exautēs*** [adv.: ἐξαυτῆς <1824>]; **from *ek*: from, and *autēs*: the same** ► **Instantly** > The daughter of Herodias wanted the king to give her at once {by and by, directly, right now} the head of John the Baptist (Mark 6:25). All other refs.: IMMEDIATELY <1824>.

– [4] Matt. 21:3; 27:48; Luke 17:7; Rev. 4:2; et al. → at once → IMMEDIATELY <2112>

[5] Matt. 21:19, 20; Luke 1:64; 8:55; Acts 16:26; et al. → IMMEDIATELY <3916> [6] Luke 14:21 → at once → QUICKLY <5030> [7] John 13:32 → IMMEDIATELY <2117> [8] Rom. 7:9; Eph. 2:2, 3, 11, 13; 5:8; Col. 1:21; 3:7; Titus 3:3; Phm. 11; 1 Pet. 2:10 → in time(s) past → PAST <4218> [9] Rom. 15:24 → FIRST <4412> [10] 1 Tim. 1:13 → BEFORE <4386> [11] Heb. 10:2 → ELSE <1893>.

ONE – ***heis*** [card. num.: εἷς <1520>] ▶ **Unique, single** > This number is used in regard to the beloved son of a man who rented out his vineyard to vine-growers (Mark 12:6). *

ONE ANOTHER – ***allēlōn*** [pron.: ἀλλήλων <240>]; **from *allos*: other** ▶ **Reciprocal, mutual** > Christians ought to pursue the things whereby one builds up another {for mutual edification} (Rom. 14:19). Other refs.: Matt. 24:10; 25:32; Mark 4:41; 8:16; John 4:43; 5:44; Eph. 4:2, 25, 32; et al. *

ONE BY ONE – ***heis kath' heis*** [adverbial expr.: εἷς καθ' εἷς <1527>]; **from *heis*: one, and *kata*: according to** ▶ Refs.: Mark 14:19; John 8:9. ¶ ‡

ONE-EYED – Mark 9:47b → with one eye → EYE <3442>.

ONESIMUS – ***Onēsimos*** [masc. name: Ὀνήσιμος <3682>]: **useful; from *oninēmi*: to be useful, to be beneficial** ▶ **Servant of Philemon** > Onesimus had formerly been useless to Philemon (Phm. 10, see v. 11) and had fled from his master. He had met Paul in Rome and had been converted. He had been useful to Paul, who now sent him back to his former master, that he might receive him as a brother in Christ. When bringing the letter to Philemon, Onesimus and Tychicus also brought the letter to the Colossians, in which Paul speaks of Onesimus as the faithful and beloved brother who is one of them (Col. 4:9). ¶

ONESIPHORUS – ***Onēsiphoros*** [masc. name: Ὀνησίφορος <3683>]: **who brings a profit; from *onēsis*: benefit, profit, and *pherō*: to bring** ▶ **Christian man who most likely lived at Ephesus** > Onesiphorus had visited and consoled the apostle Paul in prison at Rome; he had rendered many services at Ephesus (2 Tim. 1:16; see vv. 17, 18). Paul greets his household (2 Tim. 4:19). ¶

ONLY – [1] ***monon*** [adv.: μόνον <3440>]; **from *monos*: see** [2] ▶ **Uniquely; also transl.: alone, even, except, just, merely, simply** > The term is used in Matt. 5:47; 8:8; 9:21; 10:42; 14:36; 21:19, 21; Mark 5:36; 6:8; Luke 8:50; John 5:18; 11:52; 12:9; 13:9; 17:20; Acts 8:16; 11:19; 18:25; 19:26, 27; 21:13; 26:29; 27:10; Rom. 1:32; 3:29; 4:12, 16, 23; 5:3, 11; 8:23; 9:10, 24; 13:5; 1 Cor. 7:39; 15:19; 2 Cor. 7:7; 8:10, 19, 21; 9:12; Gal. 1:23; 2:10; 3:2; 4:18; 5:13; 6:12; Eph. 1:21; Phil. 1:27, 29; 2:12, 27; 1 Thes. 1:5, 8; 2:8; 2 Thes. 2:7; 1 Tim. 5:13; 2 Tim. 2:20; 4:8; Heb. 9:10; 12:26; Jas. 1:22; 2:24; 1 Pet. 2:18; 1 John 2:2; 5:6. ¶

[2] ***monos*** [adj.: μόνος <3441>] ▶ **Unique, solitary; also transl.: alone** > Eternal life is to know God as the only true God and Him whom He has sent, Jesus Christ (John 17:3). God only is wise (Rom. 16:27). To God only is honor and glory rendered to the age of ages (1 Tim. 1:17). He only has immortality (1 Tim. 6:16). Jesus Christ is the only Master and Lord (Jude 4). Other refs.: Matt. 4:4, 10; 12:4; 14:23; 17:8; 18:15; 24:36; Mark 6:47; 9:2, 8; Luke 4:4, 8; 5:21; 6:4; 9:36; 10:40; 24:12, 18; John 5:44; 6:15, 22; 8:9, 16, 29; 12:24; 16:32; Rom. 11:3; 16:4; 1 Cor. 9:6; 14:36; Gal. 6:4; Phil. 4:15; Col. 4:11; 1 Thes. 3:1; 1 Tim. 6:15; 2 Tim. 4:11; Heb. 9:7; 2 John 1; Jude 25; Rev. 9:4; 15:4. ¶

[3] ***plēn*** [prep. and adv.: πλήν <4133>] ▶ **Except, apart from** > The term is used in Acts 20:23; 27:22; Rev. 2:25. *

– [4] Luke 7:12; 8:42; 9:38; John 1:14, 18; 3:16, 18; Heb. 11:17; 1 John 4:9 → one and only, only → ONLY BEGOTTEN <3439> [5] Acts 5:2 → only a part → lit.: a certain part.

ONLY BEGOTTEN – ***monogenēs*** [adj.: μονογενής <3439>]; **from *monos*: only, and *genos*: offspring, family; also spelled: only-begotten ▶ One and only son or daughter** > The term is used five times by John in regard to Jesus, the only begotten {one and only} Son of God the Father (John 1:14, 18; 3:16, 18; 1 John 4:9). It is also used in regard to Isaac (Heb. 11:17). The Greek word is also transl. "only" and is used for a widow's son who had died and whom Jesus raised (Luke 7:12), the daughter of Jairus who died and whom Jesus likewise raised (Luke 8:42), and a man's son whom a spirit seized (Luke 9:38). ¶

ONYX – Rev. 21:20 → SARDONYX <4557>.

OPEN (adj.) – [1] Luke 7:14 → open coffin → BIER <4673> [2] Acts 1:18 → to burst open → BURST <2997> [3] 2 Cor. 3:18 → UNVEIL <343> [4] 2 Cor. 4:2 → open statement → MANIFESTATION <5321> [5] 2 Cor. 6:11, 13 → to be wide open, to be open → EXPAND <4115> [6] Col. 2:15 → to put to an open shame → to make a display in public → PUBLIC <3954> [7] 1 Tim. 5:24 → open beforehand → clearly evident → CLEARLY <4271>.

OPEN (verb) – [1] ***anaptussō*** [verb: ἀναπτύσσω <380>]; **from *ana*: back again, and *ptussō*: to roll up ▶ To unroll, to spread out (a scroll)** > Jesus opened the book of the prophet Isaiah (Luke 4:17). ¶
[2] ***anoigō*** [verb: ἀνοίγω <455>]; **from *ana*: again, and *oigō*: to open ▶ To render something that was shut or closed no longer so** > The wise men opened their treasures (Matt. 2:11). The heavens were opened to Jesus (Matt. 3:16; Luke 3:21). Having opened His mouth, Jesus taught (Matt. 5:2). He said to knock, and it will be opened (Matt. 7:7, 8; Luke 11:9, 10). He opened His mouth in parables (Matt. 13:35). The verb is used in regard to the eyes of the blind (Matt. 9:30; 20:33; John 9:10, 14, 17, 21, 26, 30, 32; 11:37). Peter was to open the mouth of a fish (Matt. 17:27). The virgins asked the Lord to open the door to them (Matt. 25:11). At the death of Jesus, many tombs were opened (Matt. 27:52). The mouth of Zacharias was opened (Luke 1:64). Jesus told Nathanael that he and others would see the heaven opened (John 1:51). The officers opened the doors of the prison, but the apostles were no longer there (Acts 5:23), for an angel of the Lord had already opened the doors (v. 19). Stephen saw the heavens opened (Acts 7:56). Jesus was like a lamb, silent in the presence of His shearers, not opening His mouth (Acts 8:32). Saul's eyes were opened, but he saw no one (Acts 9:8). Peter saw the heaven opened (Acts 10:11). God had opened a door of faith to the nations (Acts 14:27). The throat of wicked men is like an open tomb (Rom. 3:13). A great and effectual door was opened to Paul (1 Cor. 16:9). A door was opened to him at Troas (2 Cor. 2:12). Paul's mouth was opened to the Corinthians (2 Cor. 6:11). Jesus had set before the church of Philadelphia an opened door which no one could shut (Rev. 3:7a, b, 8). John saw a door opened in heaven (Rev. 4:1); He saw the heaven opened (19:11). The temple of God in the heaven was opened (Rev. 11:19) as well as the temple of the tabernacle of witness (15:5). The books were opened and another book, which is that of life (Rev. 20:12a, b). Other refs.: Luke 12:36; 13:25; John 10:3, 21; Acts 8:35; 9:40; 10:34; 12:10, 14, 16 (*exanoigō* in some mss.); 16:26, 27; 18:14; 26:18; Col. 4:3; Rev. 3:20; 5:2–4, 5 (some mss. have *luō*), 9; 6:1, 3, 5, 7, 9, 12; 8:1; 9:2; 10:2, 8; 12:16; 13:6. ¶
[3] ***dianoigō*** [verb: διανοίγω <1272>]; **from *dia*: intens., and *anoigō*: see [2] ▶ To open completely** > The eyes of the disciples of Emmaus were opened and they recognized Jesus (Luke 24:31); their heart burned as He opened the Scriptures to them (v. 32). He opened the understanding of His disciples (Luke 24:45). Jesus used this verb with a deaf man (Mark 7:34, 35). Every male who opens the womb was called holy to the Lord (Luke 2:23). The Lord opened Lydia's heart (Acts 16:14). Other ref.: Acts 17:3; see EXPLAIN <1272>. ¶
[4] ***trachēlizō*** [verb: τραχηλίζω <5136>]; **from *trachēlos*: throat ▶ To lay bare, to**

expose > All things are naked and opened {open} to the eyes of Him to whom we must give account (Heb. 4:13). ¶
– 5 Mark 1:10 → SPLIT <4977> 6 Luke 10:38 → to open one's home → lit.: to receive into one's home → RECEIVE <5264> 7 Rom. 1:10 → that the way may be opened → that he may have a prosperous journey → JOURNEY (noun) <2137> 8 2 Cor. 7:2 → to open the heart → RECEIVE <5562> 9 Eph. 6:19 → that I may open → lit.: in the opening → OPENING <457> 10 Heb. 9:8 → MANIFEST (verb) <5319> 11 Heb. 10:20 → CONSECRATE <1457>.

OPEN TO REASON – Jas. 3:17 → YIELDING <2138>.

OPENING – 1 ***anoixis*** [fem. noun: ἄνοιξις <457>]; **from *anoigō*: to open ▶ The act of moving from closed position** > Paul asked the Ephesians to pray that utterance might be given to him in the opening of his mouth to make known with boldness the mystery of the glad tidings (Eph. 6:19). ¶
2 ***opē*** [fem. noun: ὀπή <3692>] ▶ **Hole, orifice** > A fountain does not pour forth sweet and bitter out of the same opening {place, spring} (Jas. 3:11). Other ref.: Heb. 11:38; see HOLE <3692>. ¶
– 3 Mark 2:4 → to make an opening → UNCOVER <648>.

OPENLY – 1 ***parrēsia*** [fem. noun used as adv.: παρρησία <3954>]; **from *pas*: all, and *rhēsis*: act of speaking ▶ Freedom or frankness to speak unreservedly, cheerful confidence; also transl.: plainly, publicly** > Jesus spoke openly of His sufferings (Mark 8:32). The brothers of Jesus told Him that no one does anything in secret if he seeks to be known openly (John 7:4). No one spoke openly concerning Jesus (John 7:13). Jesus said plainly that Lazarus had died (John 11:14). He walked no longer openly among the Jews (John 11:54). He would speak openly concerning the Father (John 16:25). His disciples told Him that He was speaking openly {clearly} (John 16:29). He had spoken openly in the world (John 18:20). All other refs.: BOLDLY <3954>, BOLDNESS <3954>, CONFIDENCE <3954>, PUBLIC <3954>.
2 **open: *phaneros*** [adj.: φανερός <5318>]; **from *phainō*: to shine, which is from *phōs*: light ▶ Public, visible** > The expr. "to reward openly" (Matt. 6:4, 6, 18 in some mss.) is lit.: to reward in the open. All other refs.: see entries in Lexicon at <5318>.
3 ***phanerōs*** [adv.: φανερῶς <5320>]; **from *phaneros*: see 2 ▶ Publicly, visibly** > Jesus could no longer enter openly into the city (Mark 1:45). He went up to the feast, not openly, but as in secret (John 7:10). Other ref.: Acts 10:3; see PLAINLY <5320>. ¶
– 4 John 12:42 → to openly acknowledge → CONFESS <3670> 5 Acts 10:40 → MANIFEST (adj.) <1717> 6 Acts 16:37 → PUBLIC <1219>.

OPENNESS – Acts 28:31 → BOLDNESS <3954>.

OPERATE – 1 Cor. 12:6, 11 → WORK (verb) <1754>.

OPERATION – 1 ***energēma*** [neut. noun: ἐνέργημα <1755>]; **from *energeō*: to effect, to work, which is from *en*: in, and *ergon*: work ▶ Effect produced** > There are distinctions of operations {activities, effects, working} among Christians (1 Cor. 12:6); some have received operations {effecting, working} of miracles {miraculous powers} (v. 10). ¶
– 2 Col. 2:12 → WORKING (noun) <1753>.

OPERATIVE – ***energēs*** [adj.: ἐνεργής <1756>]; **from *en*: in, and *ergon*: work ▶ Active, effectual** > The word of God is living and operative {powerful} (Heb. 4:12); *enargēs* in other mss.: clear. Other refs.: 1 Cor. 16:9; Phm. 6; see EFFECTIVE <1756>. ¶

OPINION – 1 ***gnōmē*** [fem. noun: γνώμη <1106>]; **from *ginōskō*: to know, to understand ▶ View, judgment** > Paul gives his opinion concerning virgins (1 Cor. 7:25). All other refs.: ADVICE <1106>, JUDG-

MENT <1106>, MIND (noun) <1106>, PURPOSE (verb) <1106>.
– 2 Matt. 22:16 → anyone's opinion → lit.: anyone 3 Matt. 22:17 → to be the opinion → THINK <1380> 4 Acts 28:6 → to change one's opinion → to change one's mind → MIND (noun) <3328> 5 Rom. 14:1 → REASONING <1261> 6 2 Cor. 10:5 → lofty opinion → high thing → HEIGHT <5313> 7 Gal. 5:20 → school of opinion → SECT <139>.

OPPONENT – 1 Matt. 5:25a, b; Luke 12:58; 18:3 → ADVERSARY <476> 2 Luke 13:17; 21:15; 1 Cor. 16:9; Phil. 1:28 → to be the opponent → to be the adversary → ADVERSARY <480> 3 John 10:31; Acts 18:28; 20:19 → His Jewish opponents → lit.: the Jews 4 1 Tim. 1:13 → insolent opponent → INSOLENT <5197> 5 2 Tim. 2:25 → those who oppose → OPPOSE <475> 6 Titus 2:8 → he who is an opponent → he who is opposed → OPPOSED <1727>.

OPPORTUNE – 1 ***eukairos*** [adj.: εὔκαιρος <2121>]; **from *eu*: well, and *kairos*: favorable time, convenient occasion ▶ Appropriate, timely** > When an opportune {convenient, strategic} day had come, on his birthday, Herod gave a great banquet (Mark 6:21). Other ref.: Heb. 4:16; see SEASONABLE <2121>. ¶
– 2 Mark 14:11 → at an opportune time → CONVENIENTLY <2122> 3 John 7:6 → READY <2092>.

OPPORTUNELY – Mark 14:11 → CONVENIENTLY <2122>.

OPPORTUNITY – 1 ***eukairia*** [fem. noun: εὐκαιρία <2120>]; **from *eukairos*: convenient, which is from *eu*: good, and *kairos*: time, occasion ▶ Suitable moment, favorable occasion** > Judas sought an opportunity {a good opportunity} to deliver up Jesus (Matt. 26:16; Luke 22:6). ¶
2 **to lack opportunity: *akaireomai*** [verb: ἀκαιρέομαι <170>]; **from *a*: neg., and *kairos*: time, occasion ▶ To be without a suitable occasion, to have no suitable circumstance** > The Philippians lacked opportunity to revive their thinking of Paul (Phil. 4:10). ¶
3 **to have opportunity: *eukaireō*** [verb: εὐκαιρέω <2119>]; **from *eukairos*: appropriate, timely ▶ To find a convenient moment, to find a favorable time** > Apollos would go to the Corinthians when he would have opportunity {have convenient time, have good opportunity} (1 Cor. 16:12). Other refs.: Mark 6:31 {to have time}; Acts 17:21 {to spend time}; see TIME <2119>, SPEND <2119>. ¶
4 ***topos*** [masc. noun: τόπος <5117>] ▶ **Place, occasion** > Among the Romans, the accused had the opportunity {licence} to defend himself against the charge of which he was accused (Acts 25:16). We ought not to give an opportunity {foothold, room, way} to the devil (Eph. 4:27). All other refs.: COAST (noun) <5117>, PLACE (noun) <5117>, ROCK <5117>.
– 5 Mark 6:21 → opportune day → OPPORTUNE <2121> 6 Mark 14:11 → for an opportunity → CONVENIENTLY <2122> 7 Acts 24:25 → SEASON (noun) <2540> 8 Acts 27:13 → they saw their opportunity → lit.: supposing that they had obtained their purpose → PURPOSE (noun) <4286> 9 Rom. 7:8, 11; 2 Cor. 5:12; 11:12a, b; Gal. 5:13; 1 Tim. 5:14 → OCCASION <874> 10 1 Cor. 7:21 → to avail oneself of the opportunity → USE (verb) <5530> 11 Gal. 6:10; Eph. 5:16; Col. 4:5 → OCCASION <2540> 12 Heb. 11:15 → TIME <2540>.

OPPOSE – 1 ***antidiatithēmi*** [verb: ἀντιδιατίθημι <475>]; **from *anti*: against, and *diatithemai*: to separate, which is from *dia*: through (intens.), and *tithēmi*: to place ▶ To give a contrary opinion; to position oneself as an adversary** > The bondman of the Lord ought to teach in meekness those who oppose {those who are in opposition} (lit.: the opposing) (2 Tim. 2:25). ¶
2 ***antikeimai*** [verb: ἀντίκειμαι <480>]; **from *anti*: against, and *keimai*: to stand, to position oneself ▶ To rise up against, to lift oneself up against** > The Spirit and

the flesh are opposed one to another {are contrary to one another, are in opposition to one another, are in conflict with each other} (Gal. 5:17). The antichrist opposes himself against all called God (2 Thes. 2:4). The law has its application to anything opposed {contrary} to sound teaching (1 Tim. 1:10). All other refs. (to be the adversary): ADVERSARY <480>.

3 ***antitassō*** [verb: ἀντιτάσσω <498>]; **from *anti*: against, and *tassō*: to arrange ▶ To resist, to rebel against** > The Jews opposed Paul's testimony that Jesus was the Christ (Acts 18:6). All other refs.: RESIST <498>.

– 4 Mark 3:26 → to rise up → RISE (verb) <450> 5 Luke 2:34; John 19:12; Acts 13:45a; Titus 1:9 → to speak against → SPEAK <483> 6 Luke 11:53 → PRESS <1758> 7 Luke 13:17; 1 Cor. 16:9; Phil. 1:28 → those who oppose → to be the adversary → ADVERSARY <480> 8 Luke 14:31 in some mss. → MEET (verb) <5221> 9 Luke 23:2 → FORBID <2967> 10 Acts 5:39 → opposing God → fighter against God → FIGHTER <2314> 11 Acts 13:8; Rom. 13:2a, b; Gal. 2:11; 2 Tim. 3:8a, b → RESIST <436> 12 Rom. 13:2a; Jas. 4:6; 5:6; 1 Pet. 5:5 → RESIST <498> 13 2 Tim. 4:15 → WITHSTAND <436> 14 Titus 2:8 → those who opposed → lit.: those who are opposed → OPPOSED <1727>.

OPPOSED – 1 **he who is opposed: *enantios*** [adj.: ἐναντίος <1727>]; **from *en*: toward, and *antios*: set against ▶ Enemy, adversary** > Paul speaks of those who are opposed to {those who are against, those who are contrary to, those who are hostile to} all men (1 Thes. 2:15). He who is opposed {He who is an opponent, He that is of the contrary part} to sound doctrine would be ashamed in the presence of good deportment and sound teaching (Titus 2:8). All other refs.: CONTRARY <1727>.

– 2 Col. 2:14 → that stood opposed → ADVERSARY <5227>.

OPPOSER – Luke 21:15; Phil. 1:28 → to be the adversary → ADVERSARY <480>.

OPPOSING – 1 Acts 26:9 → lit.: against (*pros*) 2 Rom. 10:21 → to speak against → SPEAK <483> 3 1 Tim. 6:20 → opposing idea → OPPOSITION <477>.

OPPOSITE – 1 ***antikrus*** [adv.: ἄντικρυς <481>]; **from *anti*: against; also spelled: *antikru* ▶ Facing, directly in front of** > Paul's ship arrived opposite {against, off} Chios (Acts 20:15). ¶

2 ***antiperan*** [adv.: ἀντιπέραν <495>]; **from *anti*: against, and *peran*: beyond; some mss. have *antipera* ▶ On the other side, on the opposite shore** > The country of the Gadarene is opposite {across, over against} Galilee (Luke 8:26). ¶

3 ***katenanti*** [adv.: κατέναντι <2713>]; **from *kata*: against, and *enanti*: opposite, before ▶** Lit. it means down over against, at the point over against, opposite (Mark 11:2; 12:41; 13:3). With the definite art. used as an adj. meaning opposite (Luke 19:30). In the sense of "before" or "in the sight of" (Rom. 4:17). ¶ ‡

OPPOSITION – 1 ***antithesis*** [fem. noun: ἀντίθεσις <477>]; **from *antithēmi*: to oppose, which is from *anti*: against, and *tithēmi*: to place ▶ Subject of dispute, objection** > Paul enjoins Timothy to flee the oppositions {arguments, contradictions, opposing ideas} of false-named knowledge (1 Tim. 6:20). ¶

– 2 Acts 4:14 → to say in opposition → to say in reply → REPLY (verb) <471> 3 Gal. 5:17 → to be in opposition to one another → OPPOSE <480> 4 1 Thes. 2:2 → CONFLICT <73> 5 2 Tim. 2:25 → those who are in opposition → OPPOSE <475> 6 Heb. 12:3 → CONTRADICTION <485>.

OPPRESS – 1 ***diaseiō*** [verb: διασείω <1286>]; **from *dia*: intens., and *seiō*: to shake; lit.: to shake thoroughly ▶ To do violence to someone, to exert pressure on a person in order to obtain some benefit** > The Lord told people engaged in military service to oppress {intimidate, do violence to, extort money from, take money by force from} no one (Luke 3:14). ¶

[2] ***kakoō*** [verb: κακόω <2559>]; **from *kakos*: bad, evil ▶ To do harm to another, to treat harshly** > Israel was oppressed {afflicted, evil entreated, mistreated} for four hundred years (Acts 7:6, 19). Herod stretched out his hand to oppress {hurt, harass, mistreat, persecute, vex} some from the church (Acts 12:1). All other refs.: HURT (verb) <2559>, POISON (verb) <2559>.

[3] ***katadunasteuō*** [verb: καταδυναστεύω <2616>]; **from *kata*: against, and *dunasteuō*: to rule, which is from *dunastēs*: of great authority ▶ To exercise power against someone; to dominate over him, to exploit** > Jesus healed all those who were oppressed by {were under the power of} the devil (Acts 10:38). James speaks of the rich who oppress (Jas. 2:6). ¶

– [4] Matt. 4:24; 8:16; 15:22; John 10:21 → oppressed by demons → lit.: having been demon-possessed → DEMON <1139>.

OPPRESSED – Mark 1:32 → oppressed by demons → lit.: having been demon-possessed → DEMON <1139>.

OPPRESSED (BE) – [1] ***kataponeō*** [verb: καταπονέω <2669>]; **from *kata*: intens., and *poneō*: to labor, which is from *ponos*: pain, tiredness ▶ To afflict, to overwhelm with hard labor or suffering** > Moses avenged the Israelite who was being oppressed {being mistreated} (Acts 7:24). Other ref.: 2 Pet. 2:7; see VEXED (BE) <2669>. ¶

[2] ***thrauō*** [verb: θραύω <2352>] ▶ **To bruise, to crush** > Jesus has come to set free those who were oppressed (Luke 4:18); *thraumatizō* in some mss. Other ref.: Mark 14:3 in some mss. ¶

– [3] Luke 9:32 → to be heavy → HEAVY <916>.

OPPRESSION – ***kakōsis*** [fem. noun: κάκωσις <2561>]; **from *kakoō*: to hurt ▶ Bad treatment, misery** > God had seen the oppression {affliction, ill treatment} of His people who were in Egypt (Acts 7:34; see Ex. 3:7, 17). ¶

OR – ***ē*** [particle: ἤ <2228>] ▶ Disjunctive, interrog. or compar. particle. Refs.: Matt. 5:17, 36; Mark 4:30; Luke 9:25; John 6:19; Acts 3:12; Heb. 2:6. * ‡

ORACLE – [1] ***logion*** [neut. noun: λόγιον <3051>]; **dimin. of *logos*: word, declaration, or from *logios*: orator ▶ Divine answer or affirmation; in a general sense: word of God transmitted by His servants** > The oracles of God refer to the Mosaic law (Acts 7:38) and the other inspired writings of the O.T. committed to the Jews (Rom. 3:2), and leading to the Christian doctrine (Heb. 5:12). The Christian who teaches, having received this ministry from God, must also speak as one having received the oracles {utterances} of God (1 Pet. 4:11). ¶

[2] **to utter the oracles: *chrēmatizō*** [verb: χρηματίζω <5537>]; **from *chrēma*: matter, business ▶ To transmit a message, a warning from God** > Before the Lord's coming, prophets uttered the oracles {spoke, warned}, transmitting the thoughts of God (Heb. 12:25). All other refs.: CALL (verb) <5537>, WARN <5537>.

ORACULARLY – Heb. 8:5; 11:7 → to be told, to be warn oracularly → to be divinely warned → WARN <5537>.

ORATION – **to make a public oration, to make an oration, to give an oration: *dēmēgoreō*** [verb: δημηγορέω <1215>]; **from *dēmos*: people, and *agoreuō*: to speak at a public assembly, which is from *agora*: public place ▶ To deliver a speech before people, to speak before a crowd** > Herod made a public oration {delivered an address, delivered a public address} (Acts 12:21). ¶

ORATOR – ***rhētōr*** [masc. noun: ῥήτωρ <4489>]; **from *rhēma*: word, or *rheō*: to speak ▶ Person who pronounces a discourse, speaker** > A certain orator {attorney, lawyer} called Tertullus accused Paul before the governor Felix (Acts 24:1). ¶

ORDAIN – [1] ***diatassō*** [verb: διατάσσω <1299>]; **from *dia*: through (intens.),**

and *tassō*: to designate, to establish ▶ To prescribe, to decide; also transl.: to appoint, to arrange, to authorize, to command, to direct, to give orders, to order, to require > The tax collectors were to take no more money than what was ordained to them (Luke 3:13). The Israelites had the tent of the testimony in the wilderness, as God ordained (Acts 7:44). Paul had ordained {had made the arrangement} that they take him on board ship at Assos (Acts 20:13). Felix ordained the centurion to keep Paul under guard (Acts 24:23). Paul ordained certain things in all the churches (1 Cor. 7:17 {laid down the rule concerning}; 16:1 {told to do}). The Lord has ordained to those who announce the glad tidings to live of the glad tidings (1 Cor. 9:14). The law was ordained by {put into effect through} angels (Gal. 3:19). Titus was to establish elders, as Paul had ordained him (Titus 1:5). All other refs.: COMMAND (verb) <1299>, ORDER (noun) <1299>.

[2] ***prostassō*** [verb: προστάσσω <4367>]; **from *pros*: to, and *tassō*: see [1] ▶ To command, to prescribe; also transl.: to bid, to direct, to enjoin, to order** > Joseph did as the angel of the Lord had ordained him (Matt. 1:24). The cleansed leper was to offer the gift that Moses had ordained (Matt. 8:4; Mark 1:44; Luke 5:14). The disciples did as Jesus had ordained {instructed} them (Matt. 21:6); other mss.: *suntassō*. Cornelius and his kinsmen and friends were all present to hear all things that were commanded {ordained} Peter by God (Acts 10:33). God ordained {determined, appointed, preappointed, before appointed} times (lit.: the times having been ordained) (Acts 17:26); some mss. have *protassō*; see [3]. Other refs.: Acts 10:48; see COMMAND (verb) <4367>. ¶

[3] ***protassō*** [verb: προτάσσω <4384>]; **from *pro*: before, and *tassō*: see [1] ▶ To command, to prescribe; also transl.: to bid, to direct, to enjoin, to order** > Some mss. have this verb in Acts 17:26; see [2]. ¶

[4] ***horizō*** [verb: ὁρίζω <3724>]; **from *horos*: limit ▶ To determine, to designate; also transl.: to appoint** > God has ordained {appointed, determinately appointed} Jesus to be the judge of the living and the dead (Acts 10:42). God will judge the world in righteousness by the Man whom He has ordained (Acts 17:31), the Lord Jesus. All other refs.: DETERMINE <3724>, DETERMINED <3724>.

[5] ***cheirotoneō*** [verb: χειροτονέω <5500>]; **from *cheirotonos*: stretching out the hands, which is from *cheir*: hand, and *teinō*: to raise; lit.: to raise the hand to vote ▶ To choose, to designate, to appoint** > Paul and Barnabas ordained elders in each church (Acts 14:23). Titus was chosen by the churches to travel with Paul (2 Cor. 8:19). ¶

– [6] Matt. 21:16 → PERFECT (verb) <2675> [7] Mark 3:14 → APPOINT <4160> [8] John 15:16; 1 Tim. 2:7 → APPOINT <5087> [9] Acts 13:48; Rom. 13:1 → APPOINT <5021> [10] Acts 16:4 → DETERMINE <2919> [11] 1 Cor. 2:7 → PREDESTINE <4309> [12] Eph. 2:10 → to ordain before → to prepare before → PREPARE <4282> [13] Titus 1:5; Heb. 5:1; 8:3 → APPOINT <2525> [14] Heb. 9:6 → PREPARE <2680> [15] Jude 4 → to ordain before of old → to mark out beforehand → MARK (verb) <4270>.

ORDAINED – Acts 7:53 → DISPOSITION <1296>.

ORDEAL – [1] 2 Cor. 8:2 → TEST (noun and verb) <1382> <1381> [2] 1 Pet. 4:12 → fiery ordeal → FIERY <4451>.

ORDER (noun) – [1] ***taxis*** [fem. noun: τάξις <5010>]; **from *tassō*: to arrange in order, to establish ▶ Rank, position** > Zacharias fulfilled his priestly service in the order of his division (Luke 1:8). All things are to be done fittingly and with order {in an orderly manner, way} with respect to prophecy and speaking in tongues (1 Cor. 14:40). Paul saw the order {good discipline} of the Colossians {how orderly they were} (Col. 2:5). Jesus is a priest forever according to the order of Melchizedek (Heb. 5:6, 10; 6:20; 7:11a, 17; 7:21 in some mss.), and not after the order of Aaron (7:11b). ¶

[2] **in order, in consecutive order: *kathexēs*** [adv.: καθεξῆς <2517>]; **from *kata*: ac-**

cording to (intens.), and *hexēs*: consecutively ► Successively, logically sequenced > It seemed good to Luke, accurately acquainted from the origin with all things, to write in order {with method, an orderly account} the matters concerning the Lord (Luke 1:3). Peter began to set forth the matter in order {in orderly sequence} (concerning his vision) (Acts 11:4). Other refs.: Luke 8:1; Acts 3:24; 18:23. ¶

[3] **to set in order: *diatassō*** [verb: διατάσσω <1299>]; **from *dia*: through, and *tassō*: to arrange ► To make precise arrangements so as to resolve matters** > Paul would set in order {arrange, give further directions for} other matters whenever he would go to the Corinthians (1 Cor. 11:34). All other refs.: COMMAND (verb) <1299>, ORDAIN <1299>.

– [4] Matt. 6:1 → in order to → lit.: before (*pros*) [5] Matt. 8:18; 27:64; Acts 5:34; 8:38; 23:35; 24:8 → to give orders → COMMAND (verb) <2753> [6] Matt. 12:16; Mark 3:12 → WARN <2008> [7] Matt. 12:44; Luke 11:25 → to put in order → ADORN <2885> [8] Matt. 26:59; Acts 20:16 → in order that → SO THAT <3704> [9] Mark 1:27; 6:27; Luke 4:36 → to give orders → COMMAND (verb) <2004> [10] Mark 5:43; 7:36; 8:15; 9:9; Heb. 12:20 → to give orders, to give strict orders → COMMAND (verb) <1291> [11] Luke 1:1 → to set in order → to draw up → DRAW <392> [12] Luke 8:55; Acts 23:31 → to give order, to carry orders → COMMAND (verb) <1299> [13] Luke 15:29 → COMMANDMENT <1785> [14] John 11:57; Col. 4:10 → COMMAND (noun) <1785> [15] Acts 1:2; Heb. 11:22 → to give orders → to give charge → CHARGE (noun)[2] <1781> [16] Acts 5:28; 2 Thes. 3:10 → to give strict orders, to give order → lit.: to command by order → COMMAND (verb) <3853> [17] Acts 16:24 → CHARGE (noun)[2] <3852> [18] Acts 18:23 → in order → SUCCESSIVELY <2517> [19] Acts 20:13; 24:23; 1 Cor. 16:1 → to give orders → ORDAIN <1299> [20] 1 Cor. 7:35 → to promote good order → for what is comely → COMELY <2158> [21] 1 Cor. 15:23 → RANK (noun) <5001> [22] Heb. 9:10 → new order → REFORMATION <1357>.

ORDER (verb) – [1] Matt. 14:19; 18:25; 27:58; Luke 18:40; Acts 4:15; 5:34; 8:38; 12:19; 16:22; 21:33, 34; 22:24, 30; 23:3, 10, 35; 24:8; 25:6, 17, 21; 27:43 → COMMAND (verb) <2753> [2] Matt. 21:6 → ORDAIN <4367> or <4384> [3] Mark 3:12 → WARN <2008> [4] Mark 6:27, 39; Luke 8:31; 14:22; Acts 23:2; Phm. 8 → COMMAND (verb) <2004> [5] Mark 7:36b → COMMAND (verb) <1291> [6] Luke 3:13; Acts 24:23; Titus 1:5 → ORDAIN <1299> [7] Luke 5:14; 8:56; Acts 1:4; 5:40; 10:42; 15:5; 16:23; 23:30 → COMMAND (verb) <3853> [8] Luke 17:9, 10; Acts 18:2; 23:31 → COMMAND (verb) <1299> [9] Luke 19:15 → COMMAND (verb) <2036> [10] Acts 10:48 → COMMAND (verb) <4367> [11] Heb. 9:6 → PREPARE <2680>.

ORDERLY – [1] Luke 1:3; Acts 11:4 → orderly account, in orderly sequence → in order → ORDER (noun) <2517> [2] Acts 21:24 → WALK <4748> [3] 1 Cor. 14:40; Col. 2:5 → in an orderly manner, in an orderly way, how orderly → lit.: with order → ORDER (noun) <5010>.

ORDERS – Acts 16:22 → to give orders → COMMAND (verb) <2753>.

ORDINANCE – [1] ***diatagē*** [fem. noun: διαταγή <1296>]; **from *diatassō*: to prescribe, to appoint, from *dia*: through, and *tassō*: to arrange, to order ► Order, prescription** > He who sets himself up in opposition to the authority resists the ordinance of God {what God has instituted} (Rom. 13:2). Other ref.: Acts 7:53; see DISPOSITION <1296>. ¶

[2] ***diatagma*** [neut. noun: διάταγμα <1297>]; **from *diatassō*: to prescribe, to command ► Order, commandment** > The parents of Moses did not fear the ordinance {command, edict, injunction} of the king (Heb. 11:23). ¶

[3] ***dikaiōma*** [neut. noun: δικαίωμα <1345>]; **from *dikaioō*: to demonstrate**

one's righteousness, to justify ▶ That which has been commanded by someone; also transl.: regulation, requirement > Zacharias and Elizabeth walked blameless in all the commandments and ordinances of the Lord (Luke 1:6). The first covenant had ordinances of service (Heb. 9:1), ordinances of flesh (v. 10). All other refs.: JUSTIFICATION <1345>, REQUIREMENT <1345>, RIGHTEOUS <1345>.

4 ***dogma*** [neut. noun: δόγμα <1378>]; **from *dokeō*: to think ▶ a. Decree, edict of an authority; also transl.: regulation** > The Jews claimed that Paul and his companions contravened the ordinances of Caesar (Acts 17:7). The law of commandments consisted in ordinances (Eph. 2:15). The handwriting, or obligation, against us consisted in ordinances {legal demands, requirements} (Col. 2:14). **b. Ordinance relative to a virtuous life** > The apostles and elders at Jerusalem had determined the ordinances {reached decisions} (Acts 16:4). Other ref.: Luke 2:1; see DECREE (noun) <1378>. ¶

5 **to subject to ordinances, to submit to rules: *dogmatizō*** [verb: δογματίζω <1379>]; **from *dogma*: see 4 ▶ To be subject to precepts, doctrines** > Paul asks why subject ourselves to ordinances {decrees, regulations} if we have died with Christ to the elements of the world (Col. 2:20). ¶

– 6 1 Cor. 11:2 → TRADITION <3862> 7 1 Pet. 2:13 → INSTITUTION <2937>.

ORDINARY – 1 **to be ordinary: *tunchanō*** [verb used as an adj.: τυγχάνω <5177>] ▶ **To be common, to be usual** > God worked no ordinary {extraordinary, special, unusual} miracles (lit.: the miracles not the being ordinary) by the hands of Paul (Acts 19:11). All other refs.: ATTAIN <5177>, COMMON <5177>, ENJOY <5177>, OBTAIN <5177>, PERHAPS <5177>.

– 2 Acts 7:20; Heb. 11:23 → no ordinary → BEAUTIFUL <791> 3 Acts 21:39 → INSIGNIFICANT <767>.

ORGY – Rom. 13:13; Gal. 5:21; 1 Pet. 4:3 → REVEL (noun) <2970>.

ORIGIN – 1 Matt. 21:25, 26 → of human origin → of man → MAN <444> 2 Luke 1:3 → from the origin → from the very first → FIRST <509> 3 Luke 20:4, 6; Gal. 1:11 → of human origin → lit.: from men.

ORIGINAL – 1 Heb. 3:14 → our original conviction → lit.: the beginning of the assurance → BEGINNING <746> 2 Jude 6 → original state → STATE <746>.

ORIGINATE – 1 Cor. 14:36 → to come forth → COME <1831>.

ORIGINATOR – Acts 3:15 → PRINCE <747>.

ORNAMENT – 1 ***perithesis*** [fem. noun: περίθεσις <4025>]; **from *peritithēmi*: to set about, which is from *peri*: around, and *tithēmi*: to put ▶ Piece of jewelry** > The outward adorning of some women consists of putting ornaments of {wearing, wearing of} gold all around (1 Pet. 3:3). ¶

2 **to have ornaments: *chrusoō*** [verb: χρυσόω <5558>]; **from *chrusos*: gold ▶ To overlay or adorn with gold** > Great Babylon had ornaments of {was decked, was glittering with} gold (Rev. 17:4; 18:16). ¶

ORPHAN (noun) – ***orphanos*** [adj.: ὀρφανός <3737>]; ***orbus*, in Lat. ▶ Used of a child who has lost one or both parents** > The Lord will not leave His disciples orphans {comfortless} (John 14:18). To visit orphans {fatherless} and widows is part of pure and undefiled religion before God and the Father (Jas. 1:27). Other ref. in some mss.: Mark 12:40. ¶

ORPHAN (verb) – 1 Thes. 2:17 → SEPARATE <642>.

OSTRACIZE – Luke 6:22 → EXCLUDE <873>.

OTHER – 1 ***allos*** [adj.: ἄλλος <243>] ▶ **Another numerically** > Paul did not seek glory from the Thessalonians or from others (1 Thes. 2:6). Other refs.: Matt. 2:12; 4:21; Heb. 4:8. *

2 ***heteros*** [adj.: ἕτερος <2087>] ▶ **Other but different, another** > God would speak to His people with men of other lips {of strange lips, by the lips of strangers} (1 Cor. 14:21). Other refs.: ANOTHER <2087>, DIFFERENT <2087>.

– 3 Matt. 17:25, 26 → STRANGER <245> 4 2 Cor. 10:15; 1 Tim. 5:22 → other man's → ANOTHER <245>.

OTHERWISE – 1 ***allōs*** [adv.: ἄλλως <247>]; **from *allos*: other** ▶ **In another manner** > The good works of some are manifest beforehand; and they that are otherwise cannot be hidden (1 Tim. 5:25). ¶

2 ***heterōs*** [adv.: ἑτέρως <2088>]; **from *heteros*: other, different** ▶ **In a different way, divergently** > If in anything the Philippians were thinking otherwise {had a different attitude, were thinking differently}, God would reveal that to them (Phil. 3:15). ¶

– 3 Matt. 6:1; 9:17; Mark 2:21, 22; Luke 5:37; 2 Cor. 11:16 → ELSE <1490> 4 Matt. 13:15; 27:64; Mark 4:12; Luke 14:12, 29; Acts 28:27 → LEST <3379> 5 Rom. 11:6a, b, 22; 1 Cor. 7:14 → ELSE <1893> <686> 6 2 Cor. 9:4 → LEST <3381> 7 1 Tim. 6:3 → to teach otherwise → to teach other doctrine → DOCTRINE <2085>.

OUGHT – 1 ***dei*** [impersonal verb: δεῖ <1163>] ▶ **It is necessary, it must; it is appropriate, it is suitable** > The Scriptures had said that Jesus ought to {must, had to} rise again from the dead (John 20:9). We do not know what we should pray for as we ought {as is fitting, as we should} (Rom. 8:26). We should not think of ourselves more highly than we ought to {should} think (Rom. 12:3). Younger widows could say things that they ought not {not becoming, not proper} (1 Tim. 5:13). Some were teaching things that they ought not {they should not} (Titus 1:11). Other refs.: Matt. 18:33 {should}; 25:27; Mark 13:14; Luke 18:1; Acts 9:6 {must}, 16 {must}; 24:19; 25:10, 24 {to be fit}; 27:21 {should}; Rom. 1:27 {to be due}; 2 Cor. 2:3; Eph. 6:20; Col. 4:4, 6; Heb. 2:1 {must}; 2 Pet. 3:11; Rev. 1:1 {must}; 4:1 {must}; 22:6 {must}. *

2 **it ought: *deon estin*; *dei*** [verb: δεῖ <1163>]; ***esti*** [verb: εστι <2076>] ▶ **It is appropriate** > People from Ephesus ought (lit.: They ought, It was necessary for them) to be quiet and do nothing rashly (Acts 19:36). *

3 **ought: *opheilō*** [verb: ὀφείλω <3784>] ▶ **To have an obligation (to do something), to be compelled to** > Christians must wash one another's feet (John 13:14). The Jews said that, according to their law, Jesus ought to die (John 19:7). The children of God ought not to think that the Divine Nature is like gold or silver or stone (Acts 17:29). Christians who are strong ought to bear the weaknesses of the weak (Rom. 15:1). Husbands ought to love their own wives as their own bodies (Eph. 5:28). Other refs.: 1 Cor. 5:10 {should, would}; 7:36; 9:10; 11:7, 10; 2 Cor. 12:11, 14; 2 Thes. 1:3; 2:13; Heb. 2:17; 5:3, 12; 1 John 2:6; 3:16; 4:11; 3 John 8. All other refs.: DEBT <3784>, DEBTOR <3784>, DUE <3784>, INDEBTED (BE) <3784>, OWE <3784>.

4 ***chrē*** [impersonal verb: χρή <5534>] ▶ **It must, it is suitable** > It ought not to be so that from the mouth proceed blessing and cursing (Jas. 3:10). ¶

OUR – ***hēmas*** [pron.: ἡμᾶς <2248>] ▶ Also transl.: us, we. * ‡

OUT – 1 Acts 5:6, 9, 10; 1 Tim. 6:7 → to carry out → CARRY <1627> 2 Acts 27:29; 1 John 2:19; Rev. 18:4 → out from, out of → FROM <1537>.

OUTBURST – 2 Cor. 12:20; Gal. 5:20 → outburst of wrath, outburst of anger → WRATH <2372>.

OUTCAST – John 16:2 → made outcast from the synagogue → excommunicated from the synagogue → EXCOMMUNICATED → <656>.

OUTCOME – 1 ***ekbasis*** [fem. noun: ἔκβασις <1545>]; **from *ekbainō*: to go outside, which is from *ek*: out, outside,**

and ***bainō*****: to go ▶ Issue, end; also transl.: result** > Christians are to consider the outcome of the conduct of their leaders and imitate their faith (Heb. 13:7). Other ref.: 1 Cor. 10:13 (way to escape}; see WAY <1545>. ¶
– 2 2 Cor. 3:13 → END (noun) <5056>.

OUTCRY – 1 Acts 23:9 → CRY (noun) <2906> 2 Jas. 5:4 → CRY (noun) <995>.

OUTDATED – Heb. 8:13 → to grow old → OLD <1095>.

OUTDO – Rom. 12:10 → to outdo one another → to give preference → PREFERENCE <4285>.

OUTER – 1 ***exōteros*** [adj.: ἐξώτερος <1857>]**; from** ***exō*****: out ▶ Exterior** > Matt. 8:12; 22:13 refer to a place for unbelievers, while Matt. 25:30 may refer to a place of less reward for servants who did not use their God-given talents. ¶ ‡
– 2 John 13:12 → outer garments → lit.: garments 3 2 Cor. 4:16 → OUTWARD <1854> 4 Rev. 11:2 → OUTWARD <1855>.

OUTGO – Mark 6:33 → to go farther → GO <4281>.

OUTLINE – 2 Tim. 1:13 → PATTERN <5296>.

OUTRAGE – Heb. 10:29 → INSULT (verb) <1796>.

OUTRAGED (BE) – Matt. 18:31 → to sorrow greatly → SORROW (verb) <3076>.

OUTRAGEOUSLY – 1 Thes. 2:2 → to treat outrageously → MISTREAT <5195>.

OUTRUN – John 20:4 → to run ahead, to run before → lit.: to run ahead faster → RUN <4390>, FASTER <5032>.

OUTSET – Acts 26:5 → from the outset → lit.: from the beginning → BEGINNING <509>.

OUTSIDE – Mark 7:15; Rev. 11:2 → OUTWARD <1855>.

OUTSIDER – 1 Cor. 14:16, 23, 24 → the simple → SIMPLE <2399>.

OUTSTANDING – 1 Acts 4:16 → EVIDENT <1110> 2 Rom. 16:7 → of note → NOTE (adj.) <1978>.

OUTWARD – 1 ***exō*** [adv.: ἔξω <1854>]**; from** ***ek*****: out ▶ From outside, i.e., that which one sees** > If the outward {outer} man of {If outwardly} the Christian is consumed, yet the inward is renewed day by day (2 Cor. 4:16). *
2 ***exōthen*** [adv.: ἔξωθεν <1855>]**; from** ***exō*****: see** 1**, and suffix** ***then*****: from or at a place ▶ Exterior, outside** > Peter speaks of the adorning of the woman which is not to be an outward {external} one (1 Pet. 3:3). Other refs.: Matt. 23:27 {outside, outwardly}; Mark 7:15 {outside}; Rev. 11:2 {without, outer, outside}. *
3 ***phaneros*** [adj.: φανερός <5318>]**; from** ***phainō*****: to shine, to become evident, which is from** ***phōs*****: light ▶ Visible** > Circumcision is outward in the flesh (Rom. 2:28). All other refs.: see entries in Lexicon at <5318>.
– 4 2 Cor. 5:12 → outward appearance → APPEARANCE <4383> 5 2 Cor. 10:7 → outward appearance → PRESENCE <4383>.

OUTWARDLY – 1 Matt. 23:27 → OUTWARD <1855> 2 2 Cor. 4:16 → OUTWARD <1854> 3 2 Cor. 10:7 → outward appearance → PRESENCE <4383>.

OUTWEIGH – 2 Cor. 4:17 → an eternal glory that far outweighs them all → lit.: an eternal weight of glory → WEIGHT <922>.

OUTWIT – 1 Matt. 2:16 → MOCK <1702> 2 2 Cor. 2:11 → to take advantage → ADVANTAGE (noun) <4122>.

OVEN – ***klibanos*** [masc. noun: κλίβανος <2823>] **▶ Device dug into the ground with clay walls where bread and cakes**

were baked; also transl.: fire, furnace > The grass of the field is used to fuel the fire which heats the oven (Matt. 6:30; Luke 12:28). ¶

OVER – 1 ***peran*** [adv.: πέραν <4008>]; **from *pera*: across, beyond ▶ On the other side, beyond** > Jesus went over {crossed} the sea of Galilee (John 6:1); the disciples went over {crossed} the sea toward Capernaum (v. 17). The word is transl. "on the other side" {opposite shore} in John 6:22, 25. *
2 **to have something over: *pleonazō*** [verb: πλεονάζω <4121>]; **from *pleon*: more ▶ To abound, to have in excess** > Concerning the manna, he who gathered much had nothing over {had no excess, had nothing left over, did not have too much} (2 Cor. 8:15). All other refs.: ABOUND <4121>.
– 3 Matt. 10:23 → to go over → FINISH <5055> 4 Mark 16:1 → to be over → to be past → PAST <1230> 5 Luke 19:17, 19; John 3:31 → ABOVE <1883> 6 Acts 20:28 → AMONG <1722> 7 Rom. 13:12 → to be nearly over → to be far spent → SPEND <4298> 8 1 Thes. 5:12 → to be over, to have charge over → LEAD (verb) <4291>.

OVER AGAINST – Luke 8:26 → OPPOSITE <495>.

OVERABOUND – 1 Rom. 5:20; 2 Cor. 7:4 → to abound much more → ABOUND <5248> 2 1 Tim. 1:14 → to surpassingly over-abound → to be more than abundant → ABUNDANT <5250>.

OVERBEARING – Titus 1:7 → SELF-WILLED <829>.

OVERCAST – **to be overcast: *stugnazō*** [verb: στυγνάζω <4768>]; **from *stugnos*: hateful, gloomy ▶ To be covered with clouds, to become somber** > We know there will be a storm when the sky is red and overcast (Matt. 16:3 {to be lowering, to be threatening}). Other ref.: Mark 10:22 (to be sad); see SAD <4768>. ¶

OVERCHARGE – ***epibareō*** [verb: ἐπιβαρέω <1912>]; **from *epi*: upon (intens.), and *bareō*: to burden ▶ To impose a burden on someone** > If anyone had caused grief at Corinth, it was not Paul whom he had grieved, but, in some degree, that Paul might not overcharge all of them {be too severe, put it too severely, say to much} (2 Cor. 2:5). Other refs.: 1 Thes. 2:9 and 2 Thes. 3:8 (to be a burden); see BURDEN (noun) <1912>. ¶

OVERCHARGED (BE) – ***barunō*** [verb: βαρύνω <925>]; **from *barus*: heavy ▶ To be made heavier, to be burdened** > Jesus says to take heed to ourselves lest our hearts be overcharged {be laden, be weighed down} with surfeiting, drunkenness, and the cares of life (Luke 21:34). Other refs. in some mss.: Acts 3:14; 28:27; 2 Cor. 5:4. ¶

OVERCOAT – ***ependutēs*** [masc. noun: ἐπενδύτης <1903>]; **from *ependuō*: to clothe, which is from *epi*: upon, and *enduō*: to clothe, which is from *en*: in, and *duō*: to put on ▶ Outer garment, tunic** > Peter girded his overcoat {fisher's coat, outer garment} on him and threw himself into the sea (John 21:7). ¶

OVERCOME – 1 ***nikaō*** [verb: νικάω <3528>]; **from *nikē*: victory ▶ To win the victory, to conquer, to triumph; also transl.: to overpower, to prevail** > The strong man (Satan) has been overcome by someone stronger (Christ) (Luke 11:22). Jesus has overcome the world (John 16:33). Paul speaks of God overcoming {prevailing} when one is judged (Rom. 3:4). Paul says not to be overcome by evil, but to overcome evil with good (Rom. 12:21a, b). John writes to the young men because they have overcome the wicked one (1 John 2:13, 14). Whatever is born of God overcomes the world, and faith is the victory that has overcome the world (1 John 5:4a, b {to get the victory over}). He who believes that Jesus is the Son of God gets the victory over the world (1 John 5:5). Christians have overcome the spirits which are not of God (1 John 4:4). The Spirit addresses him who overcomes in the churches (Rev. 2:7, 11, 17), as does likewise the Son of God (2:26; 3:5, 12, 21a). The Lord Himself has also overcome

(Rev. 3:21b; 5:5). He who sat on the white horse went forth conquering (Rev. 6:2a, b). The beast will overcome the two witnesses (Rev. 11:7). The brothers overcame Satan because of the blood of the Lamb (Rev. 12:11). It was given to the beast to make war with the saints and to overcome them (Rev. 13:7). The Lamb will overcome those who make war against Him (Rev. 17:14). He who was seated on the throne told John that he who overcomes will inherit the new Jerusalem, and He will be his God, and he who overcomes shall be His son (Rev. 21:7). Other ref.: Rev. 15:2 (to gain the victory); see VICTORY <3528>. ¶

2 ***hēttaomai*** [verb: ἡττάομαι <2274>]; **from *hētton*: less, inferior ▶ To conquer, to defeat; also transl.: to master, to subdue >** In relation to corruption, Peter says that he who overcomes another enslaves that one (2 Pet. 2:19). He also speaks of those who are overcome by the defilements of the world (2 Pet. 2:20). Other ref.: 2 Cor. 12:13 (to be inferior); see INFERIOR <2274>. ¶

– 3 Matt. 16:18 → to prevail against → PREVAIL <2729> 4 Mark 5:42 → ASTONISHED (BE) <1839> 5 Luke 8:37 → SEIZE <4912> 6 John 1:5 → darkness has not overcome it → darkness did not comprehend it → COMPREHEND <2638> 7 Acts 19:16 → OVERPOWER <2634> 8 Heb. 11:33 → CONQUER <2610> 9 2 Pet. 3:6 → DELUGE <2626>.

OVERCOME (BE) – 1 Luke 9:32 → to be heavy → HEAVY <916> 2 Acts 20:9 → FALL (verb) <2702>.

OVEREXTEND – ***huperekteinō*** [verb: ὑπερεκτείνω <5239>]; **from *huper*: above, and *ekteinō*: to extend, which is from *ek*: out, and *teinō*: to stretch ▶ To stretch out excessively, to surpass the limit >** Paul was not overextending himself {overstretching himself, stretching himself beyond measure, going too far} (2 Cor. 10:14). ¶

OVERFLOW (noun) – 1 ***perisseia*** [fem. noun: περισσεία <4050>]; **from *perissos*: over and above, which is from *peri*: above, beyond ▶ Excess, surplus >** James exhorts to lay aside all filthiness and overflow {abounding, superfluity, the evil that is so prevalent, all that remains} of wickedness (Jas. 1:21). All other refs.: ABUNDANCE <4050>.

– 2 Matt. 12:34; Luke 6:45 → ABUNDANCE <4051> 3 2 Cor. 7:4 → to abound much more → ABOUND <5248>.

OVERFLOW (verb) – 1 Rom. 5:15; 15:13; 2 Cor. 4:15; 8:2; 9:12; Phil. 1:26; Col. 2:7; 1 Thes. 3:12 → ABOUND <4052> 2 1 Thes. 3:12 → ABOUND <4121> 3 1 Tim. 1:14 → to be more than abundant → ABUNDANT <5250>.

OVERFLOWING – 2 Cor. 8:2 → ABUNDANCE <4050>.

OVERJOYED (BE) – 1 Pet. 4:13 → they may be overjoyed → lit.: they may rejoice in exulting → EXULTATION <21>.

OVERLAY – Heb. 9:4 → COVER <4028>.

OVERLOOK – 1 ***paratheōreō*** [verb: παραθεωρέω <3865>]; **from *para*: beyond, and *theōreō*: to look ▶ To fail to notice; also transl.: to neglect >** The widows of the Hellenists were overlooked in the daily service (Acts 6:1). ¶

2 ***huperōraō*** [verb: ὑπεροράω <5237>]; **from *huper*: over, and *hōraō*: to see, to perceive ▶ To see beyond, to not take into account >** Having overlooked {Having winked at} the times of ignorance, God now enjoins all men to repent (Acts 17:30); *paroraō* in some mss. ¶

– 3 Heb. 6:10 → FORGET <1950> 4 2 Pet. 3:5, 8 → HIDDEN (BE) <2990>.

OVERPOWER – 1 ***ischuō*** [verb: ἰσχύω <2480>]; **from *ischus*: strength ▶ To prevail against someone by using force >** A man who had an evil spirit overpowered {gave a beating to, prevailed against} exorcists (Acts 19:16). All other refs.: see entries in Lexicon at <2480>.

2 ***katakurieuō*** [verb: κατακυριεύω <2634>]; **from *kata*: intens., and *kurieuō*: to have dominion over, which is from**

***kurios*: master ► To master, to dominate; lit.: to overmaster >** A possessed man overpowered {overcame} exorcists (Acts 19:16). Other refs.: Matt. 20:25; Mark 10:42; 1 Pet. 5:3; see LORD (verb) <2634>. ¶
– [3] Matt. 16:18 → to prevail against → PREVAIL <2729> [4] Luke 11:22; Rev. 11:7 → OVERCOME <3528> [5] Acts 20:9a, b → FALL (verb) <2702>.

OVERSEER – [1] ***episkopos*** [masc. noun: ἐπίσκοπος <1985>]; **from *epi*: upon, and *skopos*: watchman ► Christian who watches over souls with authority and care. At the beginning overseers were chosen by the apostles or their delegates by virtue of their moral qualities. Also transl.: bishop.** > An elder exercised this office in a local church (Acts 20:28; Phil. 1:1: *sunepiskopos* in some mss., i.e., fellow-overseer). The overseer must be above reproach (1 Tim. 3:2) and free from legal charges (Titus 1:7). Christ is the Overseer {Guardian} of the Christians' souls (1 Pet. 2:25). ¶
– [2] 1 Tim. 3:1 → the office of an overseer, be an overseer → OVERSIGHT <1984> [3] 1 Pet. 4:15 → overseer of other people's matters → busybody of other people's matters → BUSYBODY <244> [4] 1 Pet. 5:2 → to exercise oversight → OVERSIGHT <1983>.

OVERSEERSHIP – Acts 1:20 → OFFICE <1984>.

OVERSHADOW – [1] ***episkiazō*** [verb: ἐπισκιάζω <1982>]; **from *epi*: over, and *skiazō*: to cast a shadow, which is from *skia*: shadow ► To cover with shade, to cast a shadow over** > A bright cloud overshadowed {enveloped} Jesus and those who were with Him on the high mountain (Matt. 17:5; Mark 9:7; Luke 9:34). The power of the Highest was to overshadow Mary (Luke 1:35). They brought out the sick that the shadow of Peter might overshadow {fall on} some of them (Acts 5:15). ¶
– [2] Heb. 9:5 → SHADOW (verb) <2683>.

OVERSIGHT – [1] ***episkopē*** [fem. noun: ἐπισκοπή <1984>]; **from *episkopeō*: see [2] ► Responsibilities and duties of the overseer** > If anyone aspires to oversight {the office of a bishop, the position of a bishop, the office of an overseer, to be an overseer} he desires a good work (1 Tim. 3:1). See OVERSEER <1985>. All other refs.: VISITATION <1984>.
[2] **to exercise oversight, to take the oversight: *episkopeō*** [verb: ἐπισκοπέω <1983>]; **from *epi*: upon, and *skopeō*: to watch ► To watch over and see to the welfare of other Christians, to serve as overseer** > The elders are to shepherd the flock of God, exercising oversight, not by constraint, but willingly; not for base gain but with eagerness (1 Pet. 5:2). Other ref.: Heb. 12:15; see WATCH (verb) <1983>. ¶

OVERSTEP – 1 Thes. 4:6 → to overstep the rights → to take advantage → ADVANTAGE (noun) <5233>.

OVERSTRETCH – 2 Cor. 10:14 → OVEREXTEND <5239>.

OVERTAKE – [1] ***lambanō*** [verb: λαμβάνω <2983>] **► To get hold of, to seize, to take** > No temptation had overtaken {taken} the Corinthians (1 Cor. 10:13). Other refs.: TAKE <2983>.
[2] ***katalambanō*** [verb: καταλαμβάνω <2638>]; **from *kata*: down (intens.), and *lambanō*: to take ► To seize, to surprise >** Darkness was not to overtake the disciples of Jesus (John 12:35). All other refs.: see entries in Lexicon at <2638>.
– [3] Acts 8:29 → JOIN <2853> [4] Gal. 6:1 → CATCH (verb) <4301>.

OVERTHROW (noun) – 2 Cor. 10:4 → DESTRUCTION <2506>.

OVERTHROW (verb) – [1] Matt. 21:12; Mark 11:15 → OVERTURN <2690> [2] John 2:15 in some mss.; 2 Tim. 2:18 → OVERTURN <396> [3] Acts 5:38, 39 → DESTROY <2647> [4] Acts 13:19; 2 Cor. 10:5 → DESTROY <2507> [5] Rom. 3:31 → to make of no effect → EFFECT (noun)

<2673> 6 1 Cor. 10:5 → to lay low → LAY <2693> 7 2 Thes. 2:8 → CONSUME <355> 8 2 Thes. 2:8 → DESTROY <2673> 9 2 Pet. 2:6 → RUIN (noun) <2692>.

OVERTHROWING – 2 Cor. 10:8; 13:10 → DESTRUCTION <2506>.

OVERTURN – 1 ***anatrepō*** [verb: ἀνατρέπω <396>]; **from *ana*: again (intens.), and *trepō*: to turn ▶ a. To upturn** > Jesus scattered the change of the money-changers and overturned {overthrew} the tables (John 2:15); some mss. have *anastrephō*. **b. To upset, to corrupt, to ruin** > Paul speaks of those who overthrow (or: overturn) the faith of some (2 Tim. 2:18) and of those who subvert (or: overturn) whole houses, teaching things which ought not to be taught (Titus 1:11). ¶
2 ***katastrephō*** [verb: καταστρέφω <2690>]; **from *kata*: down, and *strephō*: to turn ▶ To throw down to the ground, to overthrow** > Jesus overturned the tables of the money-changers (Matt. 21:12; Mark 11:15). Other refs. in some mss.: John 2:15; Acts 15:16. ¶

OVERWHELM – 2 Cor. 2:7 → SWALLOW <2666>.

OVERWHELMED (BE) – Mark 9:15 → to be overwhelmed with wonder → AMAZED (BE) <1568>.

OWE – 1 ***opheilō*** [verb: ὀφείλω <3784>] ▶ **To have an obligation (e.g., financial)** > In a parable (Matt. 18:23–34), a slave owed another slave one hundred denarii (Matt. 18:28); the latter owed a much smaller sum to his lord who forgave him his debt. Due to his unforgiving spirit, he was eventually required to pay all that he owed (v. 34). In another parable, a moneylender forgave two debtors their debts (Luke 7:41). In Luke 16:1–10, the verb is used concerning an unrighteous manager (vv. 5, 7). Christians must owe no one anything (Rom. 13:8) All other refs.: DEBT <3784>, DEBTOR <3784>, DUE <3784>, INDEBTED (BE) <3784>, OUGHT <3784>.

2 ***prosopheilō*** [verb: προσοφείλω <4359>]; **from *pros*: in addition, and *opheilō*: see 1 ▶ To have an additional debt, to have the obligation (to pay something more)** > Philemon owed his own self also to Paul (Phm. 19). ¶
3 **one who owes: *opheiletēs*** [masc. noun: ὀφειλέτης <3781>]; **from *opheilō*: see 1 ▶ Debtor, one who has an obligation (to pay something)** > A servant who owed his king ten thousand talents was brought to him (Matt. 18:24). All other refs.: DEBTOR <3781>, SINNER <3781>.
– 4 Rom. 13:7a → what one owes → DUE <3782> 5 Rom. 13:7b–e → "owed" added in Engl. 6 Rom. 15:27 → INDEBTED (BE) <3784>.

OWN (adj. and pron.) – 1 ***autos*** [pron.: αὐτός <846>] ▶ **Himself, herself** > The word is used in regard to Mary's soul (Luke 2:35), ways (Acts 14:16), profit (1 Cor. 7:35), corruption (2 Pet. 2:12), mercy (Titus 3:5), and deceits (2 Pet. 2:13). *
2 ***heautou*** [pron.: ἑαυτοῦ <1438>] ▶ **Himself, herself** > The word is used in regard to life (Luke 14:26; 1 Thes. 2:8), a generation (Luke 16:8), shoulders (Luke 15:5), bondmen (Luke 19:13), the body (Rom. 4:19; Eph. 5:28), the Son (Rom. 8:3), the neck (Rom. 16:4), the belly (Rom. 16:18), a wife (1 Cor. 7:2; Eph. 5:25, 28, 33), virginity (1 Cor. 7:37), advantage (1 Cor. 10:24; 13:5; Phil. 2:21), work (Gal. 6:4), the flesh (Gal. 6:8; Eph. 5:29), salvation (Phil. 2:12), children (1 Thes. 2:7, 11), God's kingdom and glory (1 Thes. 2:12), a vessel (1 Thes. 4:4), time (2 Thes. 2:6), bread (2 Thes. 3:12), lusts (Jude 18), and voices (Rev. 10:3). *
3 ***idios*** [adj.: ἴδιος <2398>] ▶ **Belonging to oneself, particular** > The word is used in regard to a city (Matt. 9:1; Luke 2:3), bondmen (Matt. 25:14), ability (Matt. 25:15), clothes (Mark 15:20), eye (Luke 6:41), fruit (Luke 6:44), beast (Luke 10:34), brother (John 1:41), country (John 4:44), the Father (John 5:18), name (John 5:43), glory (John 7:18), the devil (John 8:44), sheep (John 10:3, 4, 12), authority (Acts 1:7), dialect (Acts 1:19), place (Acts 1:25),

hands (Acts 2:6, 8; 1 Cor. 4:12; 1 Thes. 4:11a), power (Acts 3:12), generation (Acts 13:36), the Son (Acts 20:28; Rom. 8:32), righteousness (Rom. 10:3), olive tree (Rom. 11:24), master (Rom. 14:4; 1 Tim. 6:1; Titus 2:9), mind (Rom. 14:5), labor (1 Cor. 3:8), reward (1 Cor. 3:8), body (1 Cor. 6:18; 7:4a, b; 15:38), gift of grace (1 Cor. 7:7), will (1 Cor. 7:37), charges (1 Cor. 9:7), supper (1 Cor. 11:21), husbands (1 Cor. 14:35; Eph. 5:22; Titus 2:5; 1 Pet. 3:1, 5), rank (1 Cor. 15:23), burden (Gal. 6:5), time (Gal. 6:9; 1 Tim. 2:6; 6:15; Titus 1:3), countrymen (1 Thes. 2:14), affairs (1 Thes. 4:11), house (1 Tim. 3:4, 5, 12; 5:4), conscience (1 Tim. 4:2), purpose and grace (2 Tim. 1:9), lusts (2 Tim. 4:3; Jas. 1:14), a prophet (Titus 1:12), work (Heb. 4:10), sin (Heb. 7:27), blood (Heb. 9:12; 13:12), wickedness (2 Pet. 2:16), destruction (2 Pet. 3:16), steadfastness (2 Pet. 3:17), and dwelling (Jude 6). Other refs.: see entries in Lexicon at <2398>.

OWN (verb) – [1] Acts 4:34 → those who owned → lit.: the owners → OWNER <2935> [2] Rom. 7:15 → RECOGNIZE <1097> [3] 1 Cor. 16:18 → RECOGNIZE <1921> [4] Gal. 4:1 → he owns → lit.: he is the owner → LORD (noun) <2962>.

OWN HANDS – with their own hands: *autocheir* [adv.: αὐτόχειρ <849>]; **from *autos*: self, and *cheir*: hand ▶ Done personally** > People on board Paul's ship threw the ship's tackle overboard with their own hands (Acts 27:19). ¶

OWNER – [1] ***ktētōr*** [masc. noun: κτήτωρ <2935>]; **from *ktaomai*: to obtain, to acquire ▶ Proprietor, possessor** > Owners of {Those who owned} lands and houses were selling them at the beginning of the church (Acts 4:34). ¶
– [2] Matt. 13:27; Mark 14:14; Luke 22:11 → owner, owner of the house → master of the house → MASTER (noun) <3617> [3] Matt. 20:8; 21:40; Mark 12:9; Luke 20:13, 15; et al. → MASTER (noun) <2962> [4] Acts 27:11 → owner of the ship → SHIPOWNER <3490> [5] Gal. 4:1 → LORD (noun) <2962>.

OX – [1] ***bous*** [masc. and fem. noun: βοῦς <1016>] ▶ **Bovid ruminant, used for domestic work; also transl.: cattle** > The ox was loosed on the Sabbath to be led to drink (Luke 13:15); an ox would also have been pulled out from a pit on the Sabbath day (14:5). A man had bought five yoke of oxen (Luke 14:19). The law says to not muzzle an ox while it treads out the grain (1 Cor. 9:9a; 1 Tim. 5:18). Paul asks rhetorically if God takes care of oxen (1 Cor. 9:9b). Jesus drove out of the temple those who sold oxen (John 2:14) and their oxen (v. 15). ¶
– [2] Rev. 4:7 → CALF <3448>.

OXEN – Matt. 22:4; Acts 14:13 → BULL <5022>.

P

PACATIANA – ***Pakatianē*** [fem. name: Πακατιανή <3818>] ▶ **Province of Western part of Phrygia; Laodicea was its capital** > Some mss. have this name at the end of 1 Tim. 6:21. ¶

PACK – [1] ***aposkeuazō*** [verb: ἀποσκευάζω <643>]; **from *apo*: from, and *skeuazō*: to prepare, which is from *skeuē*: equipment, which is from *skeuos*: goods, belongings** ▶ **To gather one's personal belongings in view of a journey** > Paul and his companions packed {took their carriages, had their effects ready, got ready} and went up to Jerusalem (Acts 21:15); some mss. have *episkeuazomai*; see [2]. ¶
[2] ***episkeuazomai*** [verb: ἐπισκευάζομαι <1980a>]; **from *epi*: upon, and *skeuazō*: see [1]** ▶ **To prepare for a journey** > Some mss. have this verb in Acts 21:15; see [1]. ¶

PACKAGE – Mark 11:16 → VESSEL[1] <4632>.

PAGAN – [1] Matt. 6:7; 18:17 → one of the nations → NATION <1482> [2] 1 Thes. 4:5 → like the pagans → as the nations → NATION <1484>.

PAIN (noun) – [1] ***ponos*** [masc. noun: πόνος <4192>]; **from *penomai*: to take the trouble, to work hard** ▶ **Suffering, distress** > People of the kingdom of the beast gnawed their tongues because of the pain {in agony} (Rev. 16:10); they blasphemed the God of heaven because of their pains and their sores (v. 11). When all things are made new, neither grief, nor crying, nor pain will exist anymore (Rev. 21:4). ¶
[2] **pain, labor pain: *ōdin*** [fem. noun: ὠδίν <5604>]; **lit.: pain of childbirth** ▶ **Physical suffering; also transl.: birth pain, birth pang** > Jesus spoke of the end of the age, which will be the beginning of pains {sorrows, throes} (Matt. 24:8; Mark 13:8). God has loosed the pains {agony} of death concerning Jesus (Acts 2:24). A sudden destruction will come upon men, as labor pains {travail} upon a pregnant woman (1 Thes. 5:3). ¶
[3] **to be in pain: *basanizō*** [verb: βασανίζω <928>]; **from *basanos*: suffering, torture** ▶ **To be put to the test, to be tortured; also transl.: to be pained** > The woman of Revelation 12 was pregnant and cried out being in labor and in pain to give birth (v. 2). All other refs.: TORMENT (verb) <928>.
[4] **to suffer the pains of childbirth, to travail in pain, to labor with birth pangs: *sunōdinō*** [verb: συνωδίνω <4944>]; **from *sun*: together, and *ōdinō*: to have labor pains** ▶ **To be in pain (as a woman in labor) together** > The whole creation groans and suffers the pains of childbirth until now (Rom. 8:22). ¶
– [5] Matt. 4:24 → pain, severe pain → TORMENT (noun) <931> [6] John 16:21; 2 Cor. 2:3; 1 Pet. 2:19 → SORROW (noun) <3077> [7] Acts 24:16 → to take pains → to exercise oneself → EXERCISE (verb) <778> [8] Rom. 9:2 → SORROW (noun) <3601> [9] 2 Cor. 2:2 → to cause pain → SORROW (verb) <3076> [10] 2 Cor. 8:21 → to take pains to do → PROVIDE <4306> [11] Gal. 4:19, 27; Rev. 12:2 → to be in the pains of childbirth, to have labor pains → to be in labor → LABOR (verb) <5605> [12] 1 Tim. 4:15 → to take pains → OCCUPY <3191>.

PAIN (verb) – [1] 2 Cor. 2:2, 4, 5 → SORROW (verb) <3076> [2] Rev. 12:2 → to be in pain → PAIN (noun) <928>.

PAINED (BE) – Acts 20:38 → GRIEVE <3600>.

PAINFUL – 2 Cor. 2:1; Heb. 12:11 → to make a painful visit, painful → lit.: to come in sorrow, of sorrow → SORROW (noun) <3077>.

PAINFULLY – Mark 6:48 → to make headway painfully → to be tormented at rowing → TORMENT (verb) <928>.

PAINFULNESS – 2 Cor. 11:27 → TOIL (noun) <3449>.

PAIR – [1] ***zeugos*** [neut. noun: ζεῦγος <2201>]; **from *zeugnumi*: to join** ▶ **Couple, two of the same sort** > It was prescribed in the law of the Lord to offer a pair of turtle doves or two young pigeons for a first born son, which the parents of Jesus

did (Luke 2:24). Other ref.: Luke 14:19; see YOKE <2201>. ¶
– [2] Rev. 6:5 → pair of balances, pair of scales → BALANCE <2218>.

PALACE – [1] ***aulē*** [fem. noun: αὐλή <833>]; **see COURT** <833> ▶ **Sumptuous building; also transl.: court, courtyard, house** > The Greek word is used in regard to the dwelling of the high priest (Matt. 26:3, 58; Mark 14:54; John 18:15) and that of the strong man (Luke 11:21). All other refs.: COURT <833>, COURTYARD <833>, FOLD (noun) <833>.
– [2] Matt. 11:8; Acts 7:10 → HOUSE <3624> [3] Luke 7:25 → palace, royal palace → court of kings → KING <933> [4] John 18:28, 33; 19:9; Acts 23:35; Phil. 1:13 → PRAETORIUM <4232>.

PALACE-COURT – Matt. 26:69; Mark 14:66 → COURTYARD <833>.

PALE – ***chlōros*** [adj.: χλωρός <5515>]; **from *chloē*: green or yellowish** ▶ **Light green, livid** > Death was seated on a pale {an ashen} horse (Rev. 6:8). Other refs.: Mark 6:39; Rev. 8:7; 9:4; see GREEN <5515>. ¶

PALESTINE – In the time of Jesus, Palestine was the name given by the Greeks and the Romans to the whole region inhabited by the Israelites. The name is derived from the name Philistia, the land of the Philistines, who are mentioned in the O.T. This region of the Middle East extends from the Mediterranean Sea at the west, to the Syrian Desert at the east, and to Lebanon at the north, and to a desert that separates it from Egypt at the south. The Jordan River runs through Palestine from north to south. In the Gospels, Palestine is divided into three territories: Galilee in the north, Samaria in the center, and Judea in the south. The ancient Hebrews called the territory situated west of the Jordan River "Canaan": the land of promise for them (Heb. 11:9) and the holy land (Zech. 2:12). The main events of the O.T. took place in Palestine, and it is there that Jesus spent His life. Many prophetic events to come will take place in Palestine. This name does not appear in the N.T.

PALISADED – Luke 19:43 → palisaded mound → EMBANKMENT <5482>.

PALLET – [1] Mark 2:4, 9, 11, 12; John 5:8–12 → BED <2895> [2] Acts 5:15 → COUCH <2895>.

PALM, PALM TREE – ***phoinix*** [masc. noun: φοῖνιξ <5404>] ▶ **Tree growing abundantly in parts of Israel, able to reach 65 feet (20 meters) in height** > The palm tree is an image of the righteous (see Ps. 92:12). A great crowd went out to meet Jesus, the Righteous Man above all others, with branches of palms, to welcome Him as the King of Israel (John 12:13). In Rev. 7:9, a great crowd stood before the throne of the Lamb with palm branches in their hands and worshipped Him. Jericho was called the city of palm trees (see Deut. 34:3; 2 Chr. 28:15). ¶

PALSY – See PARALYTIC <3885>, PARALYZED <3886>.

PAMPHYLIA – ***Pamphulia*** [fem. name: Παμφυλία <3828>]: **of every tribe, i.e., heterogeneous; from *pas*: all, and *phulē*: union of citizens, tribe** ▶ **Region in the south of Asia Minor** > Jews of Pamphylia were present in Jerusalem at Pentecost (Acts 2:10). Paul went there during his first missionary journey (Acts 13:13; 14:24). Mark had abandoned him in Pamphylia (Acts 15:38). Paul passed near the coast of Pamphylia during his fourth missionary journey (Acts 27:5). ¶

PANG – [1] Matt. 24:8; Mark 13:8; Acts 2:24 → birth pang, pang → pain, labor pain → PAIN (noun) <5604> [2] Rom. 8:22 → to labor with birth pangs → PAIN (noun) <4944> [3] 1 Tim. 6:10 → SORROW (noun) <3601>.

PANOPLY – Luke 11:22; Eph. 6:11, 13 → ARMOR <3833>.

PAP – Luke 11:27; 23:29 → BREAST <3149>.

PAPER – ***chartēs*** [masc. noun: χάρτης <5489>]; **from *charassō*: to engrave, to inscribe ▶ Sheet made of fibers coming from the inside of the stem of the papyrus, a plant that grows in Egypt** > The apostle John wrote his second letter on paper (2 John 12). See BOOK. ¶

PAPHOS – ***Paphos*** [fem. name: Πάφος <3974>]**: boiling, hot ▶ City situated in the west of Cyprus** > Paul met the proconsul Sergius Paulus and the magician Barjesus in Paphos during his first missionary journey (Acts 13:6, 13). ¶

PARABLE – 1 ***parabolē*** [fem. noun: παραβολή <3850>]; **from *paraballō*: to compare, which is from *para*: beside, and *ballō*: to put, to throw ▶ Symbolic narrative drawn from contemporary life to illustrate more clearly a moral or spiritual lesson** > The word is used only in the synoptic Gospels (Matthew, Mark, and Luke); it is transl. by "image" {figure, symbol, illustration} in Heb. 9:9; and by "in a figure" {in a figurative sense, figuratively, as a type} in Heb. 11:19. The majority of the Lord's parables, e.g., those in Matt. 13, are related to truths concerning the kingdom of God. A prophecy of the O.T. was fulfilled by the fact that the Lord spoke in parables (Matt. 13:34a, b, 35; comp. Ps. 78:2). Jesus spoke the word with many parables (Mark 4:33). Other refs.: Matt. 13:3, 10, 13, 18, 24, 31, 33, 36, 53; 15:15; 21:33, 45; 22:1; 24:32; Mark 3:23; 4:2, 10, 11, 13a, b, 30 (with what comparison should we compare it?; lit: with what parable should we compare [*paraballō*] it?), 34; 7:17; 12:1, 12; 13:28; Luke 4:23; 5:36; 6:39; 8:4, 9–11; 12:16, 41; 13:6; 14:7; 15:3; 18:1, 9; 19:11; 20:9, 19; 21:29. ¶
– 2 John 10:6 → ALLEGORY <3942>.

PARACLETE – See COMFORTER <3875>.

PARADE – 1 Cor. 13:4 → BOAST (verb) <4068>.

PARADISE – 1 ***paradeisos*** [masc. noun: παράδεισος <3857>] **▶ Word of Asian origin designating the parks of kings and nobles of Persia; in the N.T., it designates a place of delights and heavenly happiness, where the redeemed rejoice in the presence of the Lord Jesus after their death** > Jesus promised the thief on the cross that he would be there with Him that same day (Luke 23:43). Paul was caught up into paradise where he heard unspeakable things said (2 Cor. 12:4). The tree of life is found in the paradise of God (Rev. 2:7). ¶
– 2 2 Cor. 12:3 → "was caught up into paradise" added in Engl.

PARALYTIC – ***paralutikos*** [adj. and adj. used as noun: παραλυτικός <3885>]; **from *paraluō*: to be paralyzed, which is from *para*: beside, and *luō*: to loosen, to weaken ▶ Invalid who has lost the capacity for movement in a region of the body, particularly in the lower limbs** > Paralysis calls to mind the inability of man to approach God and to serve Him. The Lord Jesus healed paralytics (Matt. 4:24; 9:2, 6); in Mark 2, seeing the faith of those who carried a paralytic, Jesus forgave the sins of the latter and healed him (vv. 3–5, 9, 10). The servant of the centurion at Capernaum was paralytic (Matt. 8:6). ¶

PARALYZED – Matt. 9:2, 6; Mark 2:3, 5, 9 → paralyzed man → PARALYTIC <3885>.

PARALYZED (BE) – ***paraluō*** [verb: παραλύω <3886>]; **from *para*: beside, and *luō*: to loosen, to weaken ▶ To suffer an incapacity for movement in a region of the body, particularly in the lower limbs** > A man who was paralyzed was brought up to the housetop and let down into the midst of a room where Jesus was (Luke 5:18). Jesus said to the paralyzed man (lit.: one being paralyzed) to rise up, to take up his little bed and to go to his house (Luke 5:24). Philip and Peter healed many who were paralyzed (Acts 8:7; 9:33). The Hebrews were told to lift up the hands that hang down and the paralyzed {failing, feeble, weak} knees (Heb. 12:12). ¶

PARCHMENT – ***membrana*** [fem. noun: μεμβράνα <3200>]; **Lat. word for: skin, tablets, parchment to write or to wrap a volume ▶ Animal skin used for writing manuscripts** > The Engl. word "parchment" is derived from the city of "Pergamum," where this material was used for writing. Paul asked Timothy to bring his parchments (2 Tim. 4:13). See BOOK. ¶

PARDON – Luke 6:37a, b → FORGIVE <630>.

PARENT – 1 ***goneus*** [masc. noun: γονεύς <1118>]; **from *ginomai*: to become, to generate ▶ Father or mother of a child** > The word is used in regard to parents against whom children will rise up (Matt. 10:21; Mark 13:12) and be disobedient (Rom. 1:30; 2 Tim. 3:2), Joseph and Mary (Luke 2:27, 41, 43), the parents of a young girl brought back to life (Luke 8:56), and the parents of a blind man (John 9:2, 3, 18, 20, 22, 23). Children ought to obey their parents in the Lord (Eph. 6:1) and in all things (Col. 3:20). Other refs.: Luke 18:29; 21:16; 2 Cor. 12:14a, b. ¶

2 ***progonos*** [adj. used as noun: πρόγονος <4269>]; **from *proginomai*: to be done before, which is from *pro*: before, and *ginomai*: to become ▶ Living mother or father, or grandparent** > Christians must repay their parents {parents and grandparents} for what they have received from them (1 Tim. 5:4). Other ref.: 2 Tim. 1:3; see FOREFATHER <4269>. ¶

3 ***patēr*** [masc. noun: πατήρ <3962>]; **lit.: father ▶ In the plur., designates both the father and the mother** > Moses was hidden three months by his parents (Heb. 11:23). Other refs.: FATHER <3962>.

PARMENAS – ***Parmenas*** [masc. name: Παρμενᾶς <3937>]: **steadfast ▶ Christian man of the N.T.** > Parmenas was one of seven Christians chosen to be occupied with service (as deacons) in the church of Jerusalem (Acts 6:5). ¶

PART (noun) – 1 ***klēros*** [masc. noun: κλῆρος <2819>]; **from *klaō*: to break ▶ Allotment, portion** > Judas had received a part {had received his share, had shared} in the apostolic service (Acts 1:17); another was to receive the part {lot} of this service and apostleship (v. 25). Simon had neither part nor portion in the matter of the laying on of the hands to receive the Holy Spirit (Acts 8:21). All other refs.: ENTRUST <2819>, INHERITANCE <2819>, LOT (noun) <2819>.

2 ***meris*** [fem. noun: μερίς <3310>]; **from *meros*: see 3 ▶ a. Portion (e.g., of an inheritance) assigned to an individual** > Mary had chosen the good part {what is better}, which would not be taken away from her (Luke 10:42). **b. Region, district, country** > The word is used in regard to Macedonia (Acts 16:12). Other refs.: Acts 8:21; 2 Cor. 6:15. All other refs.: PARTAKER <3310>, SHARE (verb) <3310>.

3 ***meros*** [neut. noun: μέρος <3313>] ▶ **a. Division, partition, region; also transl.: area, coast, district** > Joseph went away into the parts of Galilee (Matt. 2:22). Jesus went forth into the parts of Tyre and Sidon (Matt. 15:21), Caesarea Philippi (16:13), and Dalmanutha (Mark 8:10). We read in Acts about the parts of Libya (2:10) and of Macedonia (20:2). **b. Portion, constituent element** > If the whole body is full of light, there is no dark part (Luke 11:36). Ananias kept back for himself some of the price of the sale of a possession and brought a certain part to the feet of the apostles (Acts 5:2); in v. 3, we read lit. "put aside for yourself ('a part' added in Engl. by some translators) of the price of the estate." Demetrius feared that the business {craft, trade} (lit.: part) of the Ephesians (i.e., their industry in the service of the worship of Diana) would come into discredit (Acts 19:27). Paul knew that one part {group} of the Sanhedrin were of the Sadducees and the other of the Pharisees (Acts 23:6). He heard there were divisions among the Corinthians and in part {partly, to

some extent) gave credit to it (1 Cor. 11:18). Hardening in part {A partial hardening} has happened to Israel (Rom. 11:25). On earth, Christians know in part and prophesy in part (1 Cor. 13:9a, b); that which is in part {the partial, the imperfect} will be done away when that which is perfect has come (v. 10). Now Paul knew in part {partially} (1 Cor. 13:12). The Corinthians had recognized Paul in part {partially} (2 Cor. 1:14). Jesus descended into the lower parts {regions} of the earth (Eph. 4:9). The working of each part of the body allows the body to function effectively (Eph. 4:16). Babylon was divided into three parts (Rev. 16:19). Other refs.: see entries in Lexicon at <3313>.

[4] **uttermost part, remotest part: *eschatos*** [adj. used as noun: ἔσχατος <2078>] ▶ **Extremity, furthest limit** > The disciples gathered at Pentecost would be the witnesses of Jesus unto the uttermost part {the end} of the earth (Acts 1:8). All other refs.: END (noun) <2078>, LAST (adv. and noun) <2078>, STATE <2078>.

[5] **uttermost part: *peras*** [neut. noun: πέρας <4009>]; **from *pera*: beyond ▶ See** [4]. > The queen of the South came from the uttermost parts {ends} of the earth to hear Solomon (Matt. 12:42; Luke 11:31). All other refs.: END (noun) <4009>, EXTREMITY <4009>.

[6] **desire: *prothumos*** [adj. used as noun: πρόθυμος <4289>]; **from *pro*: before, and *thumos*: passion ▶ Strong desire, will** > In Rom. 1:15, the expr. "for my part" {as far as depends on me, I am so eager} is lit. "my desire." Other refs.: Matt. 26:41; Mark 14:38; see WILLING <4289>. ¶

– [7] Matt. 5:29, 30; Rom. 6:13, 19; Jas. 3:5; et al. → part, part of the body → MEMBER <3196> [8] Matt. 23:30 → to take part → lit.: to be partaker → PARTAKER <2844> [9] Matt. 24:43 → part of the night → WATCH (noun) <5438> [10] Mark 13:27a, b → uttermost part, farthest part → END (noun) <206> [11] Luke 20:35 → to have part, to take part → ATTAIN <5177> [12] Rom. 9:14 → on God's part → lit.: with God [13] Rom. 15:23 → REGION <2824> [14] 1 Cor. 10:21, 30; Heb. 2:14 → to have a part, to take part → PARTAKE <3348> [15] 2 Cor. 8:4 → taking part → FELLOWSHIP <2842> [16] Eph. 5:11 → to take part → to have fellowship with → FELLOWSHIP <4790> [17] Phil. 4:14 → to take part → SHARE (verb) <4790> [18] 1 Tim. 5:22; 2 John 11 → to take part → PARTICIPATE <2841> [19] Titus 2:8 → he that is of the contrary part → he who is opposed → OPPOSED <1727> [20] Heb. 1:1 → in many parts → TIMES (AT MANY) <4181> [21] Rev. 11:13 → the tenth part → lit.: the tenth [22] Rev. 18:4 → to take part → PARTICIPATE <4790>.

PART (verb) – [1] Matt. 27:35; Mark 15:24; Luke 23:34; John 19:24; Acts 2:3, 45 → to part, to part out → DIVIDE <1266> [2] Mark 1:10 → to part, to part asunder → SPLIT <4977> [3] Luke 9:33 → DEPART <1316> [4] Luke 24:51 → to set apart → SEPARATE <1339> [5] Acts 15:39 → to part from one another, to part company → to depart from one another → SEPARATE <673> [6] Acts 21:1 → to get away → GET <645> [7] Phm. 15 → SEPARATE <5563>.

PARTAKE – [1] ***metalambanō*** [verb: μεταλαμβάνω <3335>]; **from *meta*: with, and *lambanō*: to take ▶ To obtain, to receive one's share** > The hard-working farmer must first labor before he partakes of the fruits (2 Tim. 2:6). All other refs.: FIND <3335>, PARTICIPATE <3335>, RECEIVE <3335>, TAKE <3335>.

[2] ***metechō*** [verb: μετέχω <3348>]; **from *meta*: with, and *echō*: to have ▶ To have a part, to take part, to have communion; also transl.: to be partaker, to share** > Christians partake of one loaf (1 Cor. 10:17). They cannot partake of the Lord's table and of the table of demons (1 Cor. 10:21). Paul speaks of partaking with thanksgiving (1 Cor. 10:30). Christ partook of blood and flesh (Heb. 2:14). Other refs.: 1 Cor. 9:10, 12. All other refs.: PERTAIN <3348>, USE (verb) <3348>.

[3] ***summerizō*** [verb: συμμερίζω <4829>]; **from *sun*: with, and *merizō*: to divide ▶ To share with another; also transl.: to be partaker, to have one's share, to share >**

Those who attend at the altar partake from the altar (1 Cor. 9:13). ¶
– 4 Acts 27:33 → TAKE <4355> 5 Rom. 11:17 → PARTAKER <4791> 6 1 Tim. 6:2 → PROFIT (verb) <482> 7 2 John 11; Heb. 2:14; 1 Pet. 4:13 → PARTICIPATE <2841>.

PARTAKER – 1 ***koinōnos*** [adj. and adj. used as noun: κοινωνός <2844>]; **from *koinos*: common ▶ Partner, companion, associate; one who shares, has communion; also transl.: participant, sharer** > The Israelites who were eating the sacrifices were partakers of {participated in} the altar (1 Cor. 10:18). Paul did not want the Corinthians to have fellowship with (lit.: to become partakers of) demons (1 Cor. 10:20). As the Corinthians were partakers of the sufferings, so also of the encouragement (2 Cor. 1:7). The Hebrews had become partakers {companions} of {stood side by side with} those who were ill-treated (Heb. 10:33). Peter was also a partaker of the glory about to be revealed (1 Pet. 5:1). Christians are partakers of {participate in} the divine nature (2 Pet. 1:4). Other ref.: Matt. 23:30. All other refs.: PARTNER <2844>.
2 ***sunkoinōnos*** [masc. and fem. noun: συγκοινωνός <4791>]; **from *sun*: with, together, and *koinōnos*: see 1 ▶ Coparticipant, one who shares with someone; also transl.: fellow-partaker** > The wild olive tree (i.e., the Gentiles) was grafted in among the branches of the olive tree (i.e., Israel), and became a partaker of {shared in, partook of} the root and fatness of the latter (Rom. 11:17). Paul was partaker {was sharing} with the Corinthians in relation to the gospel (1 Cor. 9:23). The Philippians had been partakers {participators} in the grace of God in Paul (Phil. 1:7). Other ref.: Rev. 1:9; see COMPANION <4791>. ¶
3 ***metochos*** [adj. used as noun: μέτοχος <3353>]; **from *metechō*: to be a participant, to use, which is from *meta*: with, and *echō*: to have ▶ Person who shares a part with another, participant** > Christians are partakers of the heavenly calling (Heb. 3:1) and partakers of the Holy Spirit (6:4). All Christians have been made partakers of the discipline of God (Heb. 12:8). Other refs.: Luke 5:7; Heb. 1:9; 3:14; see PARTNER <3353>. ¶
4 ***summetochos*** [adj. used as noun: συμμέτοχος <4830>]; **from *sun*: with, together, and *metochos*: see 3 ▶ a. Associate** > The Gentiles would become partakers {joint partakers, fellow partakers, sharers together} of the promise of God in Christ Jesus by the gospel (Eph. 3:6). **b. Person in complicity with another** > Christians are not to be partakers {fellow-partakers, partners} with the sons of disobedience (Eph. 5:7). ¶
5 **share: *meris*** [fem. noun: μερίς <3310>] **▶ Part, portion** > God has made the Christians fit to be partakers of the inheritance of the saints (lit.: fit for the share (*meris*) of the inheritance of the saints) (Col. 1:12). All other refs.: PART (noun) <3310>, SHARE (verb) <3310>.
– 6 Rom. 15:27; 1 Tim. 5:22; Heb. 2:14; 1 Pet. 4:13; 2 John 11 → to be partaker → PARTICIPATE <2841> 7 1 Cor. 9:10, 12; 10:17, 21, 30 → to be partaker → PARTAKE <3348> 8 1 Cor. 9:13 → to be partaker → PARTAKE <4829> 9 1 Tim. 6:2 → to be partaker → PROFIT (verb) <482> 10 Heb. 12:10 → to be partaker → PARTICIPATE <3335> 11 Rev. 18:4 → to be partaker → PARTICIPATE <4790>.

PARTAKING – Heb. 12:10 → PARTICIPATE <3335>.

PARTHIAN – ***Parthos*** [masc. name: Πάρθος <3934>] **▶ Inhabitant of Parthia in Asia, a country southeast of the Caspian Sea** > The Parthians conquered the Romans in 53 B.C, but were conquered by them in 39–38 B.C., which led to their decline. On the day of Pentecost, Parthians heard the gospel in their own language (Acts 2:9; see v. 8). ¶

PARTIAL – 1 Matt. 22:16; Mark 12:14 → to be partial → REGARD (verb) <991> 2 Luke 20:21 → PERSON <4383> 3 Rom. 11:25; 1 Cor. 13:10 → a partial, the partial → in part, that which is in part → PART (noun) <3313> 4 Jas. 2:4 → to be partial → to show partiality → PARTIALITY <1252>.

PARTIALITY – [1] ***prosklisis*** [fem. noun: πρόσκλισις <4346>]; **from *prosklinō*: to incline toward, which is from *pros*: toward, and *klinō*: to incline, to lean ► The fact of taking sides for someone or something, without concern for truth or righteousness; favoritism** > Paul exhorted Timothy to do nothing by partiality {favour} (1 Tim. 5:21; other mss.: *prosklēsis*). ¶

[2] **to show partiality: *diakrinō*** [verb: διακρίνω <1252>]; **from *dia*: through, and *krinō*: to judge; lit.: to separate completely ► To discriminate, to make a difference, to make distinctions** > Christians of Jewish origin were showing partiality {being partial} between the rich and the poor (Jas. 2:4). All other refs.: see entries in Lexicon at <1252>.

– [3] Acts 10:34 → to show partiality → respecter of persons → RESPECT OF PERSONS <4381> [4] Rom. 2:11; Eph. 6:9; Col. 3:25; Jas. 2:1 → RESPECT OF PERSONS <4382> [5] Gal. 2:6 → PERSON <4383> [6] 1 Tim. 5:21 → PREJUDICE <4299> [7] Jas. 2:9 → to show partiality → to have respect of persons → RESPECT OF PERSONS <4380> [8] Jas. 3:17 → without partiality → UNQUESTIONING <87> [9] 1 Pet. 1:17 → without partiality → without respect of persons → RESPECT OF PERSONS <678>.

PARTIALLY – 1 Cor. 13:12; 2 Cor. 1:14 → in part → PART <3313>.

PARTICIPANT – 1 Cor. 10:18, 20 → PARTAKER <2844>.

PARTICIPATE – [1] ***koinōneō*** [verb: κοινωνέω <2841>]; **from *koinōnos*: associate, partaker, which is from *koinos*: common ► To have part, to share; also transl.: to partake, to be partaker** > The nations have participated in the spiritual things of Israel (Rom. 15:27). He who is taught in the word is to share with {to communicate to} (or: to participate with) him who teaches in all good things (Gal. 6:6). Timothy was not to participate in the sins of others (1 Tim. 5:22). The children participate in blood and flesh (Heb. 2:14). Christians should rejoice that they participate {have share} in the sufferings of Christ (1 Pet. 4:13). He who greets one who does not bring the doctrine of Christ participates in his wicked works (2 John 11). All other refs.: see COMMUNICATE[1] <2841>, DISTRIBUTE <2841>.

[2] ***sunkoinōneō*** [verb: συγκοινωνέω <4790>]; **from *sun*: with, together, and *koinōneō*: see [1] ► To be associated with someone** > The people of God are not to participate in {to have fellowship in, to be partakers of, to share in} the sins of Babylon (Rev. 18:4). All other refs.: FELLOWSHIP <4790>, SHARE (verb) <4790>.

[3] ***metalambanō*** [verb: μεταλαμβάνω <3335>]; **from *meta*: with, and *lambanō*: to take, to receive ► To obtain, to receive part; also transl.: to be partaker, to share** > God chastens Christians for their profit, in order to participate in {to the partaking of} His holiness (Heb. 12:10). All other refs.: FIND <3335>, PARTAKE <3335>, RECEIVE <3335>, TAKE <3335>.

– [4] 1 Cor. 10:18; 2 Pet. 1:4 → lit.: to be partaker → PARTAKER <2844> [5] Heb. 12:8 → to be partakers → PARTAKER <3353>.

PARTICIPATION – [1] ***metochē*** [fem. noun: μετοχή <3352>]; **from *metechō*: to partake, which is from *meta*: with, and *echō*: to have ► Affinity, communion** > Paul asks what participation {fellowship, partnership} is there between righteousness and lawlessness (2 Cor. 6:14). ¶

– [2] 1 Cor. 10:16a, b; 2 Cor. 8:4; Phil. 1:5; 2:1; 3:10; Phm. 6 → FELLOWSHIP <2842>.

PARTICIPATOR – Phil. 1:7 → PARTAKER <4791>.

PARTICULAR – [1] **in particular: *ek merous*; *meros*** [neut. noun: μέρος <3313>]; **lit.: for his part ► Individually, separately and distinctively** > Christians are Christ's body, and members in particular (1 Cor.

12:27). Other refs.: see entries in Lexicon at <3313>.
– [2] 1 Cor. 12:11 → in particular → PRIVATELY <2398>.

PARTICULARLY – [1] Heb. 9:5 → in detail → DETAIL <3313> [2] Heb. 13:19 → all the more → MORE <4056>.

PARTITION – Eph. 2:14 → SEPARATION <5418>.

PARTLY – 1 Cor. 11:18 → PART (noun) <3313>.

PARTNER – [1] ***koinōnos*** [adj. used as noun: κοινωνός <2844>]; **from *koinos*: common ► Associate, companion >** James and John were partners with Simon (Luke 5:10). Titus was the partner and fellow worker of Paul concerning the Corinthians (2 Cor. 8:23). Philemon was to count Paul as a partner (Phm. 17). All other refs.: PARTAKER <2844>.
[2] ***metochos*** [adj. and masc. noun: μέτοχος <3353>]; **from *metechō*: to share with, which is from *meta*: with, and *echō*: to have ► Associate, person engaged in the same activity; also transl.: companion, fellow >** God has set His Son above His companions (Heb. 1:9). Christians have become companions of {have become partakers of, have come to share in} Christ (Heb. 3:14). The word is used to designate other fishermen in Luke 5:7. Other refs.: Heb. 3:1; 6:4; 12:8; see PARTAKER <3353>. ¶
– [3] 1 Cor. 7:15 → "partner" added in Engl. [4] Eph. 5:7 → PARTAKER <4830> [5] Heb. 10:33 → PARTAKER <2844> [6] 1 Pet. 3:7 → VESSEL[1] <4632> [7] Rev. 1:9 → COMPANION <4791>.

PARTNERSHIP – [1] Phil. 1:5; Phm. 6 → FELLOWSHIP <2842> [2] 2 Cor. 6:14 → PARTICIPATION <3352> [3] Phil. 4:15 → to enter into partnership → COMMUNICATE[1] <2841>.

PARTY – [1] ***meros*** [neut. noun: μέρος <3313>] **► Group, movement >** The scribes of the Pharisees' party {part} contended against Paul (Acts 23:9). Other refs.: see entries in Lexicon at <3313>.
– [2] Acts 5:17; 15:5 → SECT <139> [3] Acts 11:2 → the circumcision party → lit.: they of the circumcision [4] Acts 26:5 → SECT <139> [5] Titus 1:10 → "party" added in Engl. [6] 1 Pet. 4:3 → drinking party → DRINKING <4224>.

PASS – [1] **to pass, to pass away: *aperchomai*** [verb: ἀπέρχομαι <565>]; **from *apo*: from, and *erchomai*: to come, to go ► To go away >** This verb is used in Rev. 9:12; 11:14; 21:4 concerning woes and former things. All other refs.: see entries in Lexicon at <565>.
[2] **to pass through: *dierchomai*** [verb: διέρχομαι <1330>]; **from *dia*: through, and *erchomai*: to go, to come ► To traverse, to go from one place to another; also transl.: to depart, to go on, to go through, to travel, to travel through >** The twelve disciples passed through the villages announcing the glad tidings and healing everywhere (Luke 9:6). Jesus passed through the midst of Samaria and Galilee as He was going up to Jerusalem (Luke 17:11). He entered and passed through Jericho (Luke 19:1). He had to pass through Samaria (John 4:4). Peter passed through all quarters (Acts 9:32). Paul passed through the whole island of Cyprus as far as Paphos (Acts 13:6). Paul and his companions passed through Perga (Acts 13:14). Paul passed through Syria and Cilicia, strengthening the churches (Acts 15:41). We have a great high priest who has passed through the heavens, Jesus the Son of God (Heb. 4:14). The verb is also used in regard to other journeys of Paul: Acts 13:14; 14:24; 15:3; 16:6; 18:23; 19:1 {to take the road through}; 20:2; 1 Cor. 16:5a, b. All other refs.: COME <1330>, GO <1330>, PIERCE <1330>, SPREAD <1330>.
[3] **to pass; to pass over, by: *parerchomai*** [verb: παρέρχομαι <3928>]; **from *para*: beside, near, and *erchomai*: to come, to go ► a. To move away, to disappear; to elapse >** Jesus used this verb in regard to the fulfilling of the law (Matt. 5:18a, b; Luke 16:17), His words (Matt. 24:35a, b; Mark 13:31a, b; Luke 21:33a, b), the cup He was

about to drink (Matt. 26:39 and 42 {to take}), and the hour of His sufferings (Mark 14:35). Jesus passed by (Luke 18:37). The verb is also used in regard to the generation of the Lord's time (Matt. 24:34; Mark 13:30; Luke 21:32). The rich will pass away as the grass's flower (Jas. 1:10). When the Day of the Lord comes, the heavens will pass away {will disappear} with a roar (2 Pet. 3:10). Other refs.: Matt. 8:28; 14:15 {to go by}; Mark 6:48; Acts 16:8; 27:9 {to spend}; 2 Cor. 5:17 {to go}. **b. To go past, to go by >** Jesus walked on the sea and would have passed by His disciples (Mark 6:48). **c. To neglect, to omit >** The Pharisees passed by {disregarded} the judgment and the love of God (Luke 11:42). All other refs.: COME <3928>, GO <3928>, SPEND <3928>, TRANSGRESS <3928>.

4 **to pass, to pass through:** ***diabainō*** [verb: διαβαίνω <1224>]**; from *dia*: through, and *bainō*: to go ▶ To cross, to come over, to traverse >** By faith, the Israelites passed through the Red Sea (Heb. 11:29). The verb is also used in Luke 16:26 {to go}; Acts 16:9. ¶

5 ***metabainō*** [verb: μεταβαίνω <3327>]**; from *meta*: particle of change, and *bainō*: to go, to walk ▶ To go from one place to another >** The disciples were not to move {go, remove} (or: to pass) from house to house (Luke 10:7). He who hears the word of Jesus and Him who sent Jesus is passed out of {has crossed over from} death into life (John 5:24). Jesus was about to depart {to leave} (or: to pass) out of this world to the Father (John 13:1). Christians know they have passed from death to life (1 John 3:14). All other refs.: DEPART <3327>, MOVE <3327>.

6 **to pass, to pass over:** ***diaperaō*** [verb: διαπεράω <1276>]**; from *dia*: through, and *peraō*: to pass, which is from *peran*: beyond ▶ To cross over >** A great chasm was fixed between Lazarus and the wicked rich man, so that those in the flame could not pass over to Abraham and the faithful (Luke 16:26). A ship passing over {crossing over, sailing over} to Phoenicia was found (Acts 21:2). All other refs.: CROSS (verb) <1276>.

7 **to pass through:** ***diodeuō*** [verb: διοδεύω <1353>]**; from *dia*: through, and *odeuō*: to travel, which is from *hodos*: way ▶ To go through, to travel through >** Having passed through Amphipolis and Apollonia, Paul and his companions came to Thessalonica (Acts 17:1 {to journey through}). Other ref.: Luke 8:1 (to go through); see GO <1353>. ¶

8 **to pass; to pass away, by, forth, on:** ***paragō*** [verb: παράγω <3855>]**; from *para*: by, and *agō*: to lead ▶ a. To go ahead, to go on; also transl.: to depart, to go by >** The verb is used in regard to Jesus (Matt. 9:9, 27; 20:30; Mark 2:14 {to walk along}; John 9:1), and to Simon, a Cyrenian (Mark 15:21 {passer-by; lit.: one passing by}). The fashion of this world passes away (1 Cor. 7:31). **b. To go away, to disappear >** The darkness is passing {is past} and the true light already shines (1 John 2:8); the world and its lusts are passing {pass away}, but he who does the will of God abides forever (v. 17). Other ref.: John 8:59 in some mss. ¶

9 ***paralegō*** [verb: παραλέγω <3881>]**; from *para*: near, and *legō*: to lie ▶ To sail near the coastline >** Paul's ship passed {coasted, sailed past, moved along the coast of} Crete with difficulty (Acts 27:8). Other ref.: Acts 27:13 (to sail close); see SAIL (verb) <3881>. ¶

10 ***diaporeuomai*** [verb: διαπορεύομαι <1279>]**; from *dia*: through, and *poreuomai*: to go ▶ To go through, to travel through >** Paul hoped to see the Romans in passing {on his journey} (Rom. 15:24). All other refs.: GO <1279>.

11 **to pass through, to pass by:** ***paraporeuomai*** [verb: παραπορεύομαι <3899>]**; from *para*: near, and *poreuomai*: to go, to pass ▶ To go near a place, to go through, to cross >** Jesus passed through {went through} (or: passed by) the cornfields on the Sabbath (Mark 2:23). Jesus and His disciples passed through Galilee (Mark 9:30). Those who passed by the cross reviled Jesus (Matt. 27:39 {the passers-by}; Mark 15:29). Other ref.: Mark 11:20. ¶

12 ***plēroō*** [verb: πληρόω <4137>]**; from *plērēs*: full ▶ To accomplish, to spend >** Forty years had passed {expired, were fulfilled} between the time Moses had fled to

Midian and the appearance of the angel of the Lord (Acts 7:30). All other refs.: see entries in Lexicon at <4137>.
13 ***poieō*** [verb: ποιέω <4160>] ▶ **To do** > Paul passed {spent, had been} (lit.: did) a night and a day in the depths of the sea (2 Cor. 11:25). Other ref.: the expr. "to spend {to continue} a year" in Jas. 4:13. Other refs.: see entries in Lexicon at <4160>.
14 **far passed, far spent: *polus*** [adj.: πολύς <4183>] ▶ **Late, long** > Since the day was far spent, the hour was late, the disciples wanted Jesus to send the people away (Mark 6:35a, b). Other refs.: see entries in Lexicon at <4183>.
– 15 Mark 1:16; John 1:36 → to pass, to pass by → WALK <4043> 16 Luke 10:31, 32 → to pass by on the other side → SIDE <492> 17 Luke 21:7; Acts 11:28 → to come to pass: transl. of *ginomai*: to take place 18 Luke 21:32 → to come to pass → FULFILL <1096> 19 Acts 7:15 → to pass away → DIE <5053> 20 Acts 12:10 → to pass on → to go farther → GO <4281> 21 Acts 21:3 → to pass on → LEAVE (verb) <2641> 22 Acts 25:13; 27:9 → ELAPSE <1230> 23 Acts 26:22 → to come to pass → COME <1096> 24 Acts 27:17 → to pass under → UNDERGIRD <5269> 25 Rom. 3:25 → passing by, passing over → PASSING <3929> 26 Rom. 14:3, 4, 10, 13, 22 → to pass judgment → JUDGE (verb) <2919> 27 1 Cor. 2:6 → to pass away → to come to nothing → COME <2673> 28 1 Cor. 7:36 → who has passed the flower of age, of youth → AGE <5230> 29 1 Cor. 11:2, 23; 15:3; 2 Pet. 2:21 → to pass on → DELIVER <3860> 30 1 Cor. 13:10; 2 Cor. 3:7, 11, 13, 14 → to pass away → to do away → AWAY <2673> 31 Phil. 4:7 → SURPASS <5242> 32 Heb. 10:33 → to pass through → TREAT <390> 33 1 Pet. 1:17 → CONDUCT (verb)[1] <390>.

PASSAGE – 1 ***periochē*** [fem. noun: περιοχή <4042>]; **from *periechō*: to contain, which is from *peri*: around, and *echō*: to have** ▶ **Portion, content of a text** > An Ethiopian read a passage {place} of Scripture corresponding to the verses of Isaiah 53 (Acts 8:32). ¶
– 2 Mark 12:10; John 13:18 → this passage of Scripture → lit.: this Scripture 3 Heb. 4:7b → as in the passage already quoted → lit.: as He has previously said → SAY <4280>.

PASSENGER – Rev. 18:17 in some mss. → lit.: one sailing to a place → SAIL (verb) <4126>.

PASSER-BY – 1 Matt. 27:39 → lit.: those passing by → to pass by → PASS <3899> 2 Mark 15:21 → to pass on → PASS <3855>.

PASSING – 1 **passing by, passing over: *paresis*** [fem. noun: πάρεσις <3929>]; **from *pariēmi*: to let go, which is from *para*: beside, and *hiēmi*: to send** ▶ **Act of not taking into account, setting aside** > God had presented Christ as propitiation, through faith in His blood, to demonstrate His righteousness, in respect of the passing by {remission} of sins that had taken place before in the forbearance of God (Rom. 3:25). ¶
2 **in passing: *en parodō*; *en*** [prep.: ἐν <1722>]; ***parodos*** [fem. noun: πάροδος <3938>]; **from *para*: beside, and *hodos*: way** ▶ **On the way** > Paul did not wish to see the Corinthians now in passing {by the way, on the way, and make only a passing visit} (1 Cor. 16:7). ¶
– 3 Heb. 11:25 → for a time → TIME <4340>.

PASSION – 1 ***pathos*** [neut. noun: πάθος <3806>]; **from *paschō*: to suffer** ▶ **In the N.T., the word is used in relation to evil passions, affection lacking restraint** > The Christian must abstain from inordinate passion {affection, vile passions} (Col. 3:5). God gave corrupted men up to vile passions {lusts} (Rom. 1:26). Paul uses the expr. "passion of lust" (*pathos epithumias*) {passionate desire, lust of concupiscence, lustful passion, passionate lust} in 1 Thes. 4:5. ¶
2 ***pathēma*** [neut. noun: πάθημα <3804>]; **from *paschō*: to suffer** ▶ **Emotional or intellectual condition dominating a**

person > The word has a negative connotation: the passions {motions} of sin (Rom. 7:5) and the flesh with the passions {affections} and lusts (Gal. 5:24). All other refs.: SUFFERING <3804>. ¶

[3] **of like passions: *homoiopathēs*** [adj.: ὁμοιοπαθής <3663>]; **from *homoios*: similar, and *pathos*: passion ▶ Having the same tendencies, the same feelings, i.e., an emotional or intellectual condition influencing people in the same way; also transl.: subject to like passions, of the same nature, with the same nature, a nature like, just like, human** > Paul and Barnabas were men of like passions with the men of Lystra (Acts 14:15). Elias was a man of like passions to us (Jas. 5:17). ¶

– [4] Acts 1:3 → after His suffering → after He had suffered → SUFFER <3958> [5] Rom. 1:27 → LUST (noun) <3715> [6] Rom. 6:12; Eph. 2:3; 2 Tim. 2:22; 3:6; 4:3; 1 Pet. 1:14; 2:11; 4:2, 3; 2 Pet. 2:10, 18; Jude 18 → LUST (noun) <1939> [7] 1 Cor. 7:36 → if the passions are too strong → who has passed the flower of age → AGE <5230> [8] 1 Tim. 5:11 → their passions draw them away → they wax wanton against → WANTON <2691> [9] 2 Tim. 3:3 → of unsubdued passion → without self-control → SELF-CONTROL <193> [10] Jas. 4:1, 3 → PLEASURE <2237> [11] Rev. 14:8; 18:3 → FURY <2372>.

PASSIONATE – [1] 1 Thes. 4:5 → passionate desire, passionate lust → lit.: passion of lust → PASSION <3806> [2] Titus 1:7 → soon angry → ANGRY <3711>.

PASSOVER – ***Pascha*** [neut. noun: Πάσχα <3957>]; **from the Heb. word *pesach*: to pass over, to spare ▶ The first of seven feasts of the Lord, celebrated in Israel on the fourteenth day of the first month of the Jewish calendar (see Lev. 23:4, 5; Deut. 16:1–8)** > The first Passover was celebrated by Moses (Heb. 11:28; see Exodus 12); it marks the beginning of the history of Israel as a redeemed people. The firstborn of Israel were spared by virtue of the blood of the lamb, sprinkled on the door frames. This feast was celebrated during the Lord's time on earth (Matt. 26:2; Mark 14:1; Luke 2:41; 22:1; John 2:13, 23; 6:4; 11:55; 12:1; 13:1; 18:39; 19:14) and thereafter (Acts 12:4). The "Passover" also refers to the paschal lamb that was sacrificed and eaten on the occasion of this feast (Mark 14:12a, b; Luke 22:7; John 18:28). Jesus, in particular, ate the Passover with His disciples (Matt. 26:17–19; Mark 14:12, 14, 16; Luke 22:8, 11–13); He had greatly desired to eat this Passover with them before He suffered (Luke 22:15). In 1 Cor. 5:7, we read: "... our Passover, Christ, has been sacrificed," for the paschal lamb represented Christ who would come to offer Himself as the atoning sacrifice and to carry out the work of redemption through shedding His blood (see 1 Pet. 1:18, 19). ¶

PAST – [1] **to be past: *diaginomai*** [verb: διαγίνομαι <1230>]; **from *dia*: through, and *ginomai*: to be, to become ▶ To end, to be over** > The verb is used in regard to the Sabbath (Mark 16:1). Other refs.: Acts 25:13; 27:9; see ELAPSE <1230>. ¶

[2] **to be past: *plēroō*** [verb: πληρόω <4137>]; **from *plērēs*: full ▶ To accomplish, to spend** > After many days were past {had elapsed, were fulfilled, had gone by}, the Jews plotted to kill Paul (Acts 9:23). All other refs.: see entries in Lexicon at <4137>.

[3] **to pass: *paroichomai*** [verb: παροίχομαι <3944>]; **from *para*: by, and *oichomai*: to go, to leave ▶ To finish, to be past** > The verb is used as an adj. in the expr. "the past {bygone, gone} generations" (Acts 14:16). ¶

[4] **in time past, in the past: *palai*** [adv.: πάλαι <3819>] **▶ Formerly, a long time ago** > God spoke in time past to the fathers in Israel by the prophets (Heb. 1:1). All other refs.: LONG (adj.) <3819>, OLD <3819>.

[5] **in time(s) past: *pote*** [adv.: ποτέ <4218>] **▶ Formerly, long ago; also transl.: sometimes, once, at one time** > The word is used in relation to the conduct and the state of Christians before their conversion (Rom. 11:30; Eph. 2:2, 3, 11, 13; 5:8; Col. 1:21; 3:7; 1 Pet. 2:10), Paul before his conversion (Rom. 7:9; Gal. 1:13 {former}, 23; Titus

3:3), and Onesimus (Phm. 11). The spirits in prison in Noah's time were sometimes (lit.: in time past) disobedient (1 Pet. 3:20). Other refs.: AFORETIME <4218>, FORMERLY <4218>.
– 5 Luke 1:3 → for some time past → lit.: from the beginning 6 Rom. 3:25 → that is past → that is committed previously → COMMIT <4266> 7 Eph. 4:19 → to be past feeling → to cast off all feeling → FEELING <524> 8 2 Tim. 2:18 → to be past → transl. of *ginomai* <1096>: to take place 9 1 John 2:8 → to be past → PASS <3855>.

PASTOR – Eph. 4:11 → SHEPHERD (noun) <4166>.

PASTURE – 1 ***nomē*** [fem. noun: νομή <3542>]; **from *nemō*: to distribute, to apportion ► a. Food for animals** > In the figur. sense, anyone who enters in by Jesus will go in and will go out and will find pasture (John 10:9), i.e., anyone who believes in Jesus will find food for his soul. **b. Place where one provides grazing for livestock, action of feeding livestock** > The talk of those who engage in profane and vain babblings will spread as gangrene (lit.: will have pasture like gangrene) (2 Tim. 2:17). ¶
– 2 Jude 12 → FEED <4165>.

PATARA – ***Patara*** [neut. name: Πάταρα <3959>] ► **Seaport in Lycia** > Paul went to Patara on his third missionary journey (Acts 21:1). ¶

PATCH – 1 ***plērōma*** [neut. noun: πλήρωμα <4138>]; **from *plēroō*: to make full, to complete ► Added part, that which completes** > No one puts a patch {piece} of new cloth on an old garment (Matt. 9:16; Mark 2:21). All other refs.: FULL <4138>, FULFILLMENT <4138>, FULLNESS <4138>, PIECE <4138>.
– 2 Matt. 9:16; Mark 2:21; Luke 5:36a, b → PIECE <1915>.

PATH – 1 ***tribos*** [fem. noun: τρίβος <5147>]; **from *tribō*: to rub, to wear away ► Trail, worn road** > John the Baptist exhorted his listeners to prepare the way of the Lord and make His paths straight (Matt. 3:3; Mark 1:3; Luke 3:4). ¶
2 ***trochia*** [fem. noun: τροχιά <5163>]; **from *trochos*: wheel; lit.: wheel track; or from *trechō*: to run, hence a track made by the feet of runners ► Track, way** > Christians are to make straight paths for their feet, so that which is lame may not be disabled, but rather be healed (Heb. 12:13). ¶
– 3 Acts 13:10; Rom. 3:16; et al. → WAY <3598>.

PATIENCE – 1 ***makrothumia*** [fem. noun: μακροθυμία <3115>]; **from *makrothumeō*: see 2 ► Forbearance through contrary events, perseverance in difficult circumstances; also transl.: longsuffering** > God endured with much patience vessels of wrath (Rom. 9:22). Jesus Christ displayed His patience in Paul (1 Tim. 1:16). By faith and patience, Christians inherit the promises (Heb. 6:12). The prophets who spoke in the name of the Lord are an example of suffering and patience (Jas. 5:10). The patience of God waited in the days of Noah (1 Pet. 3:20). The patience of the Lord is salvation (2 Pet. 3:15). All other refs.: LONGSUFFERING <3115>.
2 **to have patience: *makrothumeō*** [verb: μακροθυμέω <3114>]; **from *makrothumos*: who is longsuffering, which is from *makros*: long, and *thumos*: disposition of soul, feeling ► To endure contrary circumstances, to persevere in difficult circumstances; also transl.: to be patient** > A bondman asked his lord to have patience with him (Matt. 18:26); another bondman asked his fellow-bondman the same thing (v. 29). God has patience {bears long, delays long, keeps putting off} before intervening for His elect (Luke 18:7). The Thessalonians were to be patient (or: have patience) with everyone (1 Thes. 5:14). Abraham had long patience (Heb. 6:15); other transl.: he had patiently endured, waited. James exhorted his brothers to have patience until the coming of the Lord (Jas. 5:7a); the laborer has patience waiting for the fruit of the earth (v. 7b); we are to have patience also (v. 8).

All other refs.: PATIENT <3114>, SUFFER <3114>.

[3] ***hupomonē*** [fem. noun: ὑπομονή <5281>]; **from *hupomenō*: to persevere, which is from *hupo*: under, and *menō*: to remain; lit.: to remain under (a burden) ▶ Perseverance, endurance; the quality of not surrendering in difficult circumstances >** The word is used in the expr. "bring forth fruit with patience {by persevering}" (Luke 8:15). Jesus told His listeners to gain (or: possess) their souls by their patience {patient endurance, standing firm} (Luke 21:19). Tribulation works patience (Rom. 5:3), and endurance works experience (v. 4). Christians expect in patience {patiently} what they see not, i.e., the redemption of their body (Rom. 8:25). We have hope through patience and encouragement of the Scriptures (Rom. 15:4). God is the God of patience and encouragement (Rom. 15:5). Paul commended himself as God's minister, in much patience (2 Cor. 6:4). He remembered the patience {enduring constancy, steadfastness} of hope in the Lord Jesus Christ, evidenced among the Thessalonians (1 Thes. 1:3); he boasted about their patience (2 Thes. 1:4); he prayed that the Lord would direct their hearts into the patience {patient waiting, steadfastness} of the Christ (2 Thes. 3:5). Timothy was to pursue patience (1 Tim. 6:11). Christians are to run with patience the race that lies before them (Heb. 12:1). The proving of faith produces patience (Jas. 1:3); patience is to have its perfect work (v. 4). We have heard of the endurance of Job (Jas. 5:11). Philadelphia kept the word of the patience {patient endurance} of the Lord (Rev. 3:10 {to persevere, to endure patiently}). Other refs.: 2 Cor. 12:12; Col. 1:11; 2 Tim. 3:10; Titus 2:2; Heb. 10:36; 2 Pet. 1:6a, b; Rev. 1:9; 2:2, 3 {to endure, to bear, to persevere; lit.: to have patience}, 19; 13:10; 14:12. Also: Rom. 2:7; 2 Cor. 1:6; see PATIENT CONTINUANCE <5281>, ENDURANCE <5281>. ¶

– [4] Rev. 2:3 → to have patience → BEAR <941>.

PATIENT – [1] to be patient: *makrothumeō* [verb: μακροθυμέω <3114>]; **from *makrothumos*: who is long-suffering, which is from *makros*: long, and *thumos*: disposition of the soul, feeling ▶ To endure contrary circumstances, to persevere in difficult situations >** The Lord is patient {is long-suffering}, not willing that any should perish (2 Pet. 3:9). All other refs.: PATIENCE <3114>, SUFFER <3114>.

[2] **to be patient: *hupomenō*** [verb: ὑπομένω <5278>]; **from *hupo*: under, and *menō*: to remain; lit.: to remain under (a weight) ▶ To bear, to persevere >** Paul encourages Christians to be patient {enduring, persevering} in tribulation (Rom. 12:12). All other refs.: ENDURE <5278>, LINGER <5278>, REMAIN <5278>, SUFFER <5278>.

– [3] Luke 21:19; 2 Thes. 3:5; Rev. 2:2, 19; 3:10 → patient endurance, patient waiting → PATIENCE <5281> [4] 2 Cor. 1:6 → patient enduring, patient endurance → ENDURANCE <5281> [5] Eph. 4:2 → being patient → with longsuffering → LONGSUFFERING <3115> [6] 1 Tim. 3:3 → GENTLE <1933> [7] 2 Tim. 2:24 → patient, patient when wronged → FORBEARING <420>.

PATIENT CONTINUANCE – *hupomonē* [fem. noun: ὑπομονή <5281>]; **from *hupomenō*: to be patient, which is from *hupo*: under, and *menō*: to remain, to continue ▶ Patience, endurance >** To those who in patient continuance {perseverance, persistence} of good works seek for glory and honor and incorruptibility, God will render eternal life (Rom. 2:7). All other refs.: ENDURANCE <5281>, PATIENCE <5281>.

PATIENTLY – [1] *makrothumōs* [adv.: μακροθύμως <3116>]; **from *makrothumos*: who is longsuffering, which is from *makros*: long, and *thumos*: disposition of the soul, feeling ▶ With endurance, with perseverance in relation to people >** Paul asked Agrippa to hear him patiently (Acts 26:3). ¶

– [2] Rom. 8:25; Rev. 2:3; 3:10 → PATIENCE <5281> [3] 2 Cor. 1:6 → to patiently endure → patient endurance → ENDURANCE <5281> [4] 2 Tim. 2:24 → patiently enduring evil → FORBEARING <420> [5] Heb. 6:15; Jas. 5:7b → he had patiently endured, waited → lit.: he had long patience → PATIENCE <3114> [6] 1 Pet. 2:20a, b → to take it patiently → ENDURE <5278> [7] 1 Pet. 3:20 → God waited patiently → lit.: the patience of God waited → PATIENCE <3115>.

PATMOS – ***Patmos*** [fem. name: Πάτμος <3963>] ▶ **Small rocky island in the south of the Aegean Sea, west of Miletus** > The apostle John was exiled on the island called Patmos, where he wrote the book of Revelation after having seen a vision (Rev. 1:9). ¶

PATRIARCH – ***patriarchēs*** [masc. noun: πατριάρχης <3966>]; **from *patria*: family, race, and *archē*: beginning** ▶ **For a Jew, significant ancestor who was the founder of a family or a tribe** > Mention is made of the patriarch David (Acts 2:29), the twelve patriarchs, the sons of Jacob (Acts 7:8, 9), and the patriarch Abraham (Heb. 7:4). ¶

PATROBAS – ***Patrobas*** [masc. name: Πατροβᾶς <3969>]: **who proceeds from the father, paternal** ▶ **Christian man of Rome** > Paul sends greetings to Patrobas in his letter to the Christians of Rome (Rom. 16:14). ¶

PATRON – [1] Rom. 16:2 → HELPER <4368> [2] 1 John 2:1 → ADVOCATE (noun) <3875>.

PATTERN – [1] ***tupos*** [masc. noun: τύπος <5179>]; **from *tuptō*: to strike, as when using a stamp** ▶ **Example to follow, model; also transl.: ensample, example** > The word is used in regard to the tabernacle built by Moses (Acts 7:44 {fashion}; Heb. 8:5). It is also used in regard to people: Paul (Phil. 3:17; 2 Thes. 3:9), the Christians of Thessalonica (1 Thes. 1:7), Timothy (1 Tim. 4:12), Titus (Titus 2:7), and the elders among the company of believers (1 Pet. 5:3). All other refs.: FORM (noun) <5179>, MARK (noun) <5179>, TYPE <5179>.
[2] ***hupotupōsis*** [fem. noun: ὑποτύπωσις <5296>]; **from *hupotupoō*: to draw a sketch, which is from *hupo*: under, and *tupos*: see [1]** ▶ **Model, example** > Timothy was to have a pattern {form, outline, standard} of sound words that he had heard from Paul (2 Tim. 1:13). Other ref.: 1 Tim. 1:16; see EXAMPLE <5296>. ¶
– [3] Heb. 9:23 → COPY <5262>.

PAUL – ***Paulos*** [masc. name: Παῦλος <3972>]; ***paulus*, in Lat.: small, in small quantity** ▶ **Principal apostle of the Gentiles and author of several epistles of the N.T.** > Paul was of the tribe of Benjamin, a citizen of Rome and native of Tarsus, a city of Cilicia. He was a Pharisee, and was taught by Gamaliel (Acts 22:3; see 5:34). His original name, Saul, is mentioned for the first time when witnesses of the stoning of Stephen laid their clothes at the feet of this young man (see Acts 7:58). He violently persecuted the church, thinking to render service to God. At his conversion (about A.D. 36), he received the Holy Spirit when Ananias, a disciple living in Damascus, laid hands on him. After his conversion, he began to preach that Jesus was the Son of God (see Acts 9:20). His new Roman name, Paul, appears for the first time in Acts 13:9, after meeting the proconsul of Cyprus. He received his gospel and his mission directly from heaven, so that he did not need to be commissioned by the brothers of Jerusalem; but he did not act independently of the church, which had already been formed. Through the preaching of the apostle Paul, the church received a new teaching concerning its heavenly character. The truth of the church, the body of Christ, was revealed to Paul; he taught that, in Christ Jesus, there is neither Jew nor Gentile, the middle wall of enclosure, having been destroyed. Although the question of ordinances of the law (which had become obsolete for Gentile Christians) had been settled at Jerusalem, Paul nevertheless endured much persecution from Jews and Judaizing teachers, who could not accept that the Gentiles were placed at the same level as themselves. Paul was truly the apostle of the nations, which led him to make several journeys to Asia and then pass on to Europe. A reading of 2 Cor. 11:24–27 makes evident the fact that the book of Acts does not give us a complete account of the labors of Paul. He was arrested at Jerusalem, and then sent to Caesarea for his safety, because plots had been made to kill him. He appealed to Caesar (Nero) and was sent to Rome. After two years of imprisonment (Acts 28:30, 31), he was no doubt liberated, as is implied by these final verses of Acts. We do not know all his movements, but he visited Palestine, Cyprus, Asia Minor, Macedonia, Achaia, and Crete; he was taken to Rome as a prisoner. He had desired to visit Spain (Rom. 15:24, 28). When he wrote the Second Epistle to Timothy, he was again a prisoner at Rome, expecting his imminent death. According to history, he was beheaded by the sword, a form of execution usually reserved for a Roman citizen. (After Walter Scott.) *

PAVEMENT – ***lithostrōtos*** [adj. used as a noun: λιθόστρωτος <3038>]; **from *lithos*: stone, and *strōnnumi*: to overlay ► Place located in front of the courtroom (judgment seat) at Jerusalem; it was overlaid with mosaic paving and was used as a public tribunal** > Jesus appeared before the people at a place called Pavement, Gabbatha in Heb. (John 19:13). ¶

PAY (noun) – 1 Matt. 10:8 → without pay → FREELY <1432> 2 Luke 3:14 → WAGES <3800> 3 Jude 11 → REWARD (noun) <3408>.

PAY (verb) – 1 ***apodidōmi*** [verb: ἀποδίδωμι <591>]; **from *apo*: from, and *didōmi*: to give ► To discharge, to settle a debt; also transl.: to repay, to pay back** > This verb is used in the parable about a lord to whom a bondman owed a large sum and another bondman who was in debt to the first bondman (Matt. 18:25, 26, 28–30, 34). The lord of a vineyard told his steward to pay the workmen their wages (Matt. 20:8). Other refs.: Matt. 5:26; Luke 7:42; 12:59. Other refs.: see entries in Lexicon at <591>.

2 ***teleō*** [verb: τελέω <5055>]; **from *telos*: end, goal ► To give money in order to obtain something or by obligation** > Peter was asked if Jesus paid the drachmas (Matt. 17:24). Other ref.: Rom. 13:6. All other refs.: see entries in Lexicon at <5055>.

3 ***tinō*** [verb: τίνω <5099>] **► To suffer, to endure (a penalty)** > Those who know not God and those who do not obey the gospel of the Lord Jesus Christ will pay the penalty of {will be punished with} everlasting destruction from the presence of the Lord and from the glory of His might (2 Thes. 1:9). ¶

– 4 Matt. 7:3; Luke 6:41 → to pay attention → CONSIDER <2657> 5 Matt. 21:41 → RENDER <591> 6 Matt. 22:5 → to pay no attention → to make light → LIGHT (adj.) <272> 7 Matt. 22:17; Mark 12:14, 15a, b; Luke 20:22 → GIVE <1325> 8 Matt. 23:23; Luke 11:42 → to pay tithes → TITHE (noun and verb) <586> 9 Matt. 26:15 → to count out → COUNT <2476> 10 Mark 4:24 → to pay attention → SEE <991> 11 Luke 17:3; Acts 8:6, 10, 11; 20:28; 1 Tim. 1:4; 4:1; Titus 1:14; Heb. 2:1; 2 Pet. 1:19 → to give attention, to pay attention, to pay close attention → to give heed → HEED (noun) <4337> 12 Acts 22:28 → OBTAIN <2932> 13 Acts 27:11 → to pay attention → PERSUADED (BE) <3982> 14 Rom. 11:35; 2 Thes. 1:6 → to pay back → RENDER <467> 15 Gal. 5:10 → to pay the penalty → to bear the judgment → BEAR <941> 16 Col. 3:25; 2 Pet. 2:13 → to be paid back → RECEIVE <2865> 17 1 Tim. 4:16 → to pay close attention → to take heed → HEED (noun) <1907> 18 Phm. 19 → to pay back → REPAY <661> 19 Jas. 5:4 → WAGES <3408> 20 Rev. 18:6a, b → GIVE <591>.

PAYING – Matt. 10:8 → without paying → FREELY <1432>.

PAYMENT – 1 **to make payment: *apodidōmi*** [verb: ἀποδίδωμι <591>]; **from *apo*: from, and *didōmi*: to give ► To discharge, to settle a debt** > A king com-

manded a bondman and his family to be sold so that payment {repayment} of his debt might be made {to repay the debt} (Matt. 18:25). Other refs.: PAY (verb) <591>.
– 2 Acts 1:18 → payment he received → WAGES <3408> 3 Rev. 21:6 → without payment → FREELY <1432>.

PEACE – 1 ***eirēnē*** [fem. noun: εἰρήνη <1515>] ▶ **Cordial relations among individuals, mutual harmony; absence of violence, tranquility** > God is called the "God of peace" (Rom. 15:33; 16:20; 1 Cor. 14:33; 2 Cor. 13:11; Phil. 4:9; 1 Thes. 5:23; Heb. 13:20). Jesus is called the "Lord of peace" (2 Thes. 3:16). The word is often used in various salutations of peace (e.g., Luke 24:36; Rom. 1:7; 1 Cor. 1:3; 2 Cor. 1:2). Christians have peace with God (Rom. 5:1); Christ is their peace (Eph. 2:14). Peace is an integral part of the fruit of the Spirit (Gal. 5:22; also: Rom. 8:6; 14:17; Eph. 4:3). God has called us to peace (1 Cor. 7:15). Though the Christian has tribulation in the world, he has peace in Jesus (John 16:33). Christians are exhorted to pursue peace with all (Heb. 12:14). They are to seek peace and pursue it (2 Tim. 2:22; 1 Pet. 3:11), and they are to pursue the things that tend to peace (Rom. 14:19). When the Lord left His own, He left them His peace (John 14:27a, b). The expr. "to go in peace" means "to go without care or worry" (Mark 5:34; Luke 2:29; 7:50; 8:48; Acts 16:36; Jas. 2:16). The peace of God guards their hearts and their thoughts in Christ Jesus (Phil. 4:7). Other refs.: Matt. 10:13a, b, 34; Luke 1:79; 2:14; 10:5, 6; 11:21; 12:51; 14:32; 19:38, 42; John 20:19, 21, 26; Acts 7:26; 9:31 {rest}; 10:36; 12:20; 15:33 {greetings}; 24:2 {quietness}; Rom. 2:10; 3:17; 10:15; 15:13; 1 Cor. 16:11; Gal. 1:3; 6:16; Eph. 1:2; 2:15, 17a, b; 6:15, 23; Phil. 1:2; Col. 1:2; 3:15; 1 Thes. 1:1; 5:3; 2 Thes. 1:2; 1 Tim. 1:2; 2 Tim. 1:2; Titus 1:4; Phm. 3; Heb. 7:2; 11:31; Jas. 3:18a, b; 1 Pet. 1:2; 5:14; 2 Pet. 1:2; 3:14; 2 John 3; 3 John 14; Jude 2; Rev. 1:4; 6:4. ¶
2 **to be in, to be at, to have, to live at, to live in peace: *eirēneuō*** [verb: εἰρηνεύω <1514>]; **from *eirēnē*: see** 1 ▶ **To enjoy cordial relations, mutual harmony among people** > Jesus said to be at peace with one another (Mark 9:50). If possible, as far as depends on them, Christians are to live in peace {to live peaceably} with all men (Rom. 12:18). Paul also exhorts the Corinthians to be at peace (2 Cor. 13:11), and the Thessalonians to be at peace among themselves (1 Thes. 5:13). ¶
3 **to make peace: *eirēnopoieō*** [verb: εἰρηνοποιέω <1517>]; **from *eirēnē*: see** 1, **and *poieō*: to make** ▶ **To procure reconciliation, to bring about harmony** > Christ has made peace by the blood of His cross (Col. 1:20). ¶
– 4 Matt. 20:31; 26:63; Mark 3:4; 9:34; 10:48; 14:61; Luke 19:40; Acts 18:9 → to hold one's peace → to be silent → SILENT <4623> 5 Mark 1:25; 4:39; Luke 4:35 → to hold one's peace → to be quiet → QUIET (adj.) <5392> 6 Luke 14:4; Acts 11:18 → to hold one's peace → to be silent → SILENT <2270> 7 Luke 20:26; Acts 12:17; 15:13; 1 Cor. 14:30 → to hold one's peace → to be silent → SILENT <4601> 8 2 Cor. 2:13 → peace of mind → lit.: rest for the spirit → REST (noun)[1] <425> 9 Heb. 12:11 → harvest of peace: lit.: peaceful fruit → PEACEFUL <1516>.

PEACE-LOVING – Jas. 3:17 → PEACEFUL <1516>.

PEACEABLE – 1 1 Tim. 2:2 → QUIET (adj.) <2272> 2 1 Tim. 3:3; Titus 3:2 → lit.: not quarrelsome → QUARRELSOME <269> 3 Heb. 12:11; Jas. 3:17 → PEACEFUL <1516>.

PEACEABLY – Rom. 12:18 → to live peaceably → lit.: to live in peace → PEACE <1514>.

PEACEFUL – 1 ***eirēnikos*** [adj.: εἰρηνικός <1516>]; **from *eirēnē*: peace** ▶ **Relative to peace, promoting peace; without violence, quarrel** > Chastening afterwards yields the peaceful {peaceable} fruit of righteousness (Heb. 12:11). The wisdom from above is peaceful {peaceable, peace-loving} (Jas. 3:17). ¶
– 2 1 Tim. 2:2 → QUIET (adj.) <2263>.

PEACEMAKER – [1] ***eirēnopoios*** [masc. noun: εἰρηνοποιός <1518>]; **from *eirēnopoieō*: to make peace, which is from *eirēnē*: peace, and *poieō*: to make ▶ One who makes peace, e.g., by promoting reconciliation** > Blessed are the peacemakers (Matt. 5:9). ¶
– [2] Jas. 3:18 → lit.: one who makes peace → MAKE <4160>, PEACE <1515>.

PEARL – ***margaritēs*** [masc. noun: μαργαρίτης <3135>]; ***margarita*, in Lat. ▶ Solid body formed in a mollusk by the secretion of nacre around a foreign body (e.g., a grain of sand) which has been introduced in the shell** > Pearls are used as ornaments (1 Tim. 2:9; Rev. 17:4; 18:12, 16). In the teaching of Matt. 7:6, the injunction "not to throw pearls before swine" means not to share with anyone indiscriminately the precious truths of the word of God. In a mystery, the church is compared to a pearl of great price (Matt. 13:45, 46). The twelve gates of the heavenly Jerusalem are represented by twelve pearls, each of the gates made of a single pearl (Rev. 21:21a, b). ¶

PECK – Matt. 13:33; Luke 13:21 → MEASURE (noun) <4568>.

PECK-MEASURE – Matt. 5:15; Mark 4:21; Luke 11:33 → BUSHEL <3426>.

PECULIAR – ***periousios*** [adj.: περιούσιος <4041>]; **from *peri*: over and above, and *eimi*: to be ▶ Chosen, acquired** > Jesus Christ has purified for Himself a peculiar people {His own special people, a people for His own possession, a people that are His very own} (Titus 2:14). ¶

PEDDLE – ***kapēleuō*** [verb: καπηλεύω <2585>]; **from *kapēlos*: dealer in secondhand goods ▶ To falsify, to corrupt for personal gain** > Paul was not as some who peddled {corrupted, were peddlers of, made a trade of} the word of God for profit (2 Cor. 2:17). ¶

PEDDLER – 2 Cor. 2:17 → many, peddlers of God's word → many, peddling God's word → PEDDLE <2585>.

PELEG – Luke 3:35 → PHALEK <5317>.

PELT – 2 Cor. 11:25 → to pelt with stones → STONE (verb) <3034>.

PEN[1] – ***kalamos*** [masc. noun: κάλαμος <2563>] ▶ **Instrument for writing, prob. a piece of reed** > The apostle John preferred to see Gaius rather than to write to him with ink and pen (3 John 13). All other refs.: REED <2563>.

PEN[2] – John 10:1, 16 → FOLD (noun) <833>.

PENALTY – [1] ***antimisthia*** [fem. noun: ἀντιμισθία <489>]; **from *anti*: in return, and *misthos*: reward, salary ▶ Retribution; also transl.: recompense, recompence** > Wicked men will receive the due penalty of their perversion (Rom. 1:27). The word is used in a good sense in 2 Cor. 6:13; see EXCHANGE (noun) <489>. ¶
– [2] 2 Thes. 1:9 → to pay the penalty → to endure the punishment → ENDURE <5099>, PUNISHMENT <1349> [3] Heb. 2:2 → RETRIBUTION <3405>.

PENCE – See DENARIUS <1220>.

PENETRATE – Heb. 4:12 → PIERCE <1338>.

PENNY – [1] ***assarion*** [neut. noun: ἀσσάριον <787>]; **from the Lat. *assarius* (worth one *as*) ▶ Roman copper coin worth about 1/16 of a Roman denarius; the denarius was equivalent to the salary of a laborer for a day; also transl.: *assaria* (plur. of *assarion*), cent, coin, copper, farthing** > Two sparrows were sold for a penny (Matt. 10:29) and five sparrows for two pennies (Luke 12:6). ¶
[2] See DENARIUS <1220>.
– [3] Matt. 5:26; Mark 12:42 → penny, fraction of a penny → QUADRANS <2835> [4] Luke 12:59 → MITE <3016>.

PENTECOST – ***Pentēkostē*** [adj. used as fem. noun: Πεντηκοστή <4005>]; **from *pentēkostos*: fiftieth, which is from *pente*: five ▶ Annual Jewish feast celebrated fifty days after the Feast of the Harvest of the firstfruits** > On this occasion, the Israelites were to bring two wave-loaves baked with leaven as an offering to the Lord (see UNLEAVENED BREAD). Details of this feast are provided in Lev. 23:15–21 and Deut. 16:9–12. The church began to be formed on the day of Pentecost by the Holy Spirit descended from heaven (Acts 2:1). Paul had thought it desirable to be at Jerusalem the day of Pentecost (Acts 20:16). In 1 Cor. 16:8, he said he had remained at Ephesus until Pentecost. ¶

PENUEL – Luke 2:36 → PHANUEL <5323>.

PENURY – Luke 21:4 → NEED (noun) <5303>.

PEOPLE – [1] ***dēmos*** [masc. noun: δῆμος <1218>]; **from *deō*: to bind ▶ Crowd gathered in a public place, members of the public** > The word is used in Acts 12:22; 17:5; 19:30, 33. ¶

[2] ***ethnos*** [neut. noun: ἔθνος <1484>] ▶ **Those living together in a region** > Simon the magician was astonishing people from {the nation of} Samaria (Acts 8:9). Other refs.: see NATION <1484>.

[3] ***laos*** [masc. noun: λαός <2992>] ▶ **Population, nation sharing the same language** > The word is used in regard to a group of individuals in a general manner (e.g., Luke 2:10, 31, 32), a group assembled in a particular manner (e.g., Matt. 27:25; Luke 1:21; 3:15; Acts 4:27), a nation of the same race and language (e.g., Rev. 5:9; in the plur.: Luke 2:31; Rom. 15:11; Rev. 7:9; 11:9; Israel in particular: Matt. 2:6; 4:23; Acts 4:8; Heb. 2:17; as distinct from the chief priests and leaders: Matt. 26:5; Luke 20:19; Heb. 5:3; as distinct from the Gentiles: Acts 26:17, 23; Rom. 15:10), and Christians as the people of God (e.g., Acts 15:14; Titus 2:14; Heb. 4:9; 1 Pet. 2:9). *

– [4] Matt. 5:47 → BROTHER <80> [5] Matt. 12:46; Mark 15:11; John 6:22, 24; Acts 19:35 → CROWD (noun) <3793> [6] Matt. 13:38a, b → SON <5207> [7] Matt. 24:30; Rev. 1:7 → TRIBE <5443> [8] Mark 3:8; Luke 8:37; Acts 5:16; 14:4; 25:24 → MULTITUDE <4128> [9] Mark 3:21 → RELATIVE <846> [10] Acts 7:3 → RELATIVES <4772> [11] Acts 7:19; 1 Pet. 2:9 → RACE[1] <1085> [12] Acts 9:32; 26:10; et al. → Lord's people → lit.: saints [13] Acts 13:27 → the people of Jerusalem → lit.: those who dwell in Jerusalem → DWELL <2730> [14] Acts 21:12 → people there → he who is from that place → PLACE (noun) <1786> [15] 1 Pet. 4:15 → busybody in other people's matters → BUSYBODY <244> [16] Jude 16 → PERSON <4383>.

PEOPLE OF GOD – Rev. 14:12 → lit.: saints → SAINT <40>.

PEOPLE-PLEASER – Eph. 6:6; Col. 3:22 → MEN-PLEASER <441>.

PERADVENTURE – [1] Rom. 5:7 → PERHAPS <5029> [2] 2 Tim. 2:25 → PERHAPS <3379>.

PERCEIVE – [1] ***aisthanomai*** [verb: αἰσθάνομαι <143>]; **from *aiō*: to hear, to listen ▶ To grasp, to understand** > The disciples did not perceive the saying of Jesus (Luke 9:45). ¶

[2] ***katalambanō*** [verb: καταλαμβάνω <2638>]; **from *kata*: intens., and *lambanō*: to take ▶ To understand, to grasp by the intelligence; also transl.: to realize** > Rulers, elders, and scribes perceived that Peter and John were unlettered and uninstructed men (Acts 4:13). Peter perceived that God showed no partiality (Acts 10:34). All other refs.: see entries in Lexicon at <2638>.

[3] ***noeō*** [verb: νοέω <3539>]; **from *nous*: mind, understanding ▶ To understand, to grasp by the intelligence** > The disciples did not perceive {see} (*noeō*) nor understand (*suniēmi*) what Jesus had said about the leaven (Mark 8:17). Other ref.: Mark 7:18 {to see}. All other refs.: CONSIDER

<3539>, THINK <3539>, UNDERSTAND <3539>.
[4] ***katanoeō*** [verb: κατανοέω <2657>]; **from: *kata*: intens., and *noeō*: see [3] ▶ To discern, to detect >** Jesus perceived {saw through} the deceit of those who wanted to test Him (Luke 20:23). All other refs.: CONSIDER <2657>, DISCOVER <2657>.
– [5] Matt. 13:14; Mark 4:12; Acts 28:26 → SEE <1492> [6] Matt. 16:8; 21:45; 22:18; Mark 12:12; 15:10; Luke 8:46; 20:19; John 6:15; Acts 23:6; 1 John 3:16 → KNOW <1097> [7] Mark 2:8; Luke 5:22 → KNOW <1921> [8] Luke 1:22 → RECOGNIZE <1921> [9] Rom. 1:20 → to see clearly → SEE <2529> [10] Gal. 2:9 → RECOGNIZE <1097>.

PERCH – Matt. 13:32; Mark 4:32; Luke 13:19 → NEST (verb) <2681>.

PERDITION – John 17:12; Phil. 1:28; 2 Thes. 2:3; Heb. 10:39; 2 Pet. 3:7; Rev. 17:8, 11 → DESTRUCTION <684>.

PERFECT (adj.) – [1] ***teleios*** [adj.: τέλειος <5046>]; **from *telos*: end, accomplishment, perfection; lit.: having reached completion ▶ Accomplished, excellent; also transl.: mature, complete >** The children of God are to be perfect as their heavenly Father is perfect (Matt. 5:48a, b). To be perfect, a certain man was to sell all that he had and give to the poor (Matt. 19:21). The will of God is perfect (Rom. 12:2). Paul spoke wisdom among the perfect (1 Cor. 2:6). When that which is perfect {When perfection} has come, that which is in part will be done away (1 Cor. 13:10). Paul speaks of Christians who are perfect (i.e., spiritually mature) (Phil. 3:15; Col. 1:28; 4:12). Christ has come by the better and more perfect tabernacle not made by hand (Heb. 9:11). Endurance is to have its perfect work, that we may be perfect (Jas. 1:4a, b). Every perfect gift comes down from above, from the Father of lights (Jas. 1:17). The perfect law is the law of liberty (Jas. 1:25). Anyone who does not offend in word is a perfect man (Jas. 3:2). Perfect love casts out fear (1 John 4:18). All other refs.: MATURE <5046>.
[2] **to make perfect: *epiteleō*** [verb: ἐπιτελέω <2005>]; **from *epi*: until (intens.), and *teleō*: to finish ▶ To accomplish, to terminate, to achieve >** Paul asks the Galatians if having begun in the Spirit, they were being made perfect {were finishing, were being perfected, were trying to attain their goal} now by the flesh (Gal. 3:3). All other refs.: see entries in Lexicon at <2005>.
[3] **to be perfect, to make perfect: *katartizō*** [verb: καταρτίζω <2675>]; **from *kata*: intens., and *artizō*: to develop, to perfect, which is from *artios*: complete ▶ a. To fully accomplish >** Everyone who is perfect {is perfectly trained, is fully trained, is perfected} will be like his teacher (Luke 6:40). The God of peace can make perfect {make complete, make perfect, equip} Christians in every good work to do His will (Heb. 13:21). **b. To restore, to reestablish >** The God of all grace will make perfect {will perfect} those who have suffered a while (1 Pet. 5:10). All other refs.: see entries in Lexicon at <2675>.
[4] **to make perfect: *teleioō*** [verb: τελειόω <5048>]; **from *teleios*: complete, mature ▶ a. To be accomplished, to be realized >** The strength of Christ is made perfect {is perfected} in weakness (2 Cor. 12:9). **b. To bring to perfection, to complete >** The law made nothing perfect {perfected nothing} (Heb. 7:19). All other refs.: FINISH <5048>, FULFILL <5048>, PERFECT (verb) <5048>.
– [5] Luke 1:3 → CAREFULLY <199> [6] Acts 3:16 → perfect health, perfect soundness → SOUNDNESS <3647> [7] Acts 22:3 → perfect manner → STRICTNESS <195> [8] Acts 24:22 → more perfect → more accurately → ACCURATELY <197> [9] 2 Cor. 7:16 → to have perfect confidence → lit.: to have confidence in everything (*en panti*) [10] Rev. 3:2 → lit.: completed → COMPLETE (verb) <4137>.

PERFECT (verb) – [1] ***epiteleō*** [verb: ἐπιτελέω <2005>]; **from *epi*: intens., and *teleō*: to finish ▶ To accomplish, to terminate, to achieve >** Christians should perfect

{bring to completion} holiness in God's fear (2 Cor. 7:1). All other refs.: see entries in Lexicon at <2005>.
2 *katartizō* [verb: καταρτίζω <2675>]; **from *kata*: intens., and *artizō*: to adjust, to develop, which is from *artios*: well adjusted, complete ▶ To prepare, to establish** > God has perfected {ordained} His praise out of the mouth of babes and nursing infants (Matt. 21:16). All other refs.: see entries in Lexicon at <2675>.
3 **to perfect, to make perfect, to be perfected: *teleioō*** [verb: τελειόω <5048>]; **from *teleios*: complete, mature ▶ To reach a state of completion, to attain the final goal; also transl.: to make perfect** > The third day, Jesus would be perfected {reach His goal} (Luke 13:32). He wanted His own to be perfected in one {be brought to complete unity} (John 17:23). Paul applied the expr. "to be already perfected" {to be already perfect, to arrive at the goal} to himself (in the negative sense) in Phil. 3:12; this was a reference to his spiritual aspirations, in which he was always short of perfection. God has perfected Jesus through sufferings (Heb. 2:10); having been perfected, Jesus became the author of eternal salvation to all who obey Him (5:9); He has been perfected {consecrated} forever (7:28). The law perfected nothing (Heb. 7:19). The men and women of faith in Hebrews 11 did not receive the promise, that they would not be made perfect without the Christians of the new covenant era (v. 40). The gifts and sacrifices under the law were unable to perfect as to conscience {to clear the conscience of} him who worshipped (Heb. 9:9). The law can never perfect those who approach (Heb. 10:1). By one offering Christ has perfected in perpetuity the sanctified (Heb. 10:14). Christians have come to the spirits of just men perfected (Heb. 12:23). The faith of Abraham was perfected {was made complete} by his works (Jas. 2:22). The love of God is perfected {is made complete} in the Christians (1 John 2:5; 4:12) and among believers (4:17). He who fears has not been perfected in love (1 John 4:18). All other refs.: FINISH <5048>, FULFILL <5048>>, PERFECT (adj.) <5048>.
– 4 2 Tim. 3:17 → COMPLETE (adj.) <739>.

PERFECTED (BE) – ***katartizō*** [verb: καταρτίζω <2675>]; **from *kata*: intens., and *artizō*: to adjust, to develop, which is from *artios*: well adjusted, complete ▶ To pursue and attain a moral state suitable to the glory of God** > Paul exhorted the Corinthians to be perfected {to be perfect, to become complete, to be made complete, to aim for perfection} (2 Cor. 13:11). The verb is transl. "to make perfect" {to restore} in 1 Pet. 5:10. All other refs.: see entries in Lexicon at <2675>.

PERFECTER – Heb. 12:2 → FINISHER <5051>.

PERFECTING – 1 ***katartisis*** [fem. noun: κατάρτισις <2676>]; **from *katartizō*: to put in order, to perfectly achieve, which is from *kata*: with (intens.), and *artizō*: to adjust, to develop, which is from *artios*: well adjusted, complete ▶ Pursuit and attainment of a suitable moral condition** > Paul prayed for the perfecting {perfection} of the Corinthians {that they may be made complete} (2 Cor. 13:9), i.e., a state of moral progress honoring God. ¶
2 ***katartismos*** [masc. noun: καταρτισμός <2677>]; **from *katartizō*: see 1 ▶ Pursuit and attainment of a suitable moral state, with the additional thought of excellence** > The gifts are for the perfecting {equipping} of {to prepare} the saints (Eph. 4:12). ¶

PERFECTION – 1 ***teleiotēs*** [fem. noun: τελειότης <5047>]; **from *teleios*: complete, perfect ▶ a. State of plenitude, achievement** > Love is the bond of perfection {perfectness, unity} (Col. 3:14) in that it unites and completes other moral qualities such as compassion, kindness (see vv. 12, 13). **b. Maturity, adulthood, in a spiritual sense** > Christians must go on to perfection {full growth} (Heb. 6:1). ¶
2 ***teleiōsis*** [fem. noun: τελείωσις <5050>]; **from *teleios*: complete, perfect ▶ Completion, fulfillment** > Perfection could

not be attained by the Levitical priesthood (Heb. 7:11). Other ref.: Luke 1:45; see PERFORMANCE <5050>. ¶

– [3] 1 Cor. 13:10 → lit.: that which is perfect → PERFECT (adj.) <5046> [4] 2 Cor. 13:9 → PERFECTING <2676> [5] 2 Cor. 13:11 → to aim for perfection → PERFECTED (BE) <2675>.

PERFECTLY – [1] ***akribōs*** [adv.: ἀκριβῶς <199>]; **from *akribēs*: exact, accurate ► Precisely, exactly; also transl.: full well, perfectly well, very well** > The Thessalonians themselves knew perfectly that the day of the Lord comes as a thief in the night (1 Thes. 5:2). Other refs.: Matt. 2:8; Luke 1:3; Acts 18:25; Eph. 5:15; see ACCURATELY <199>, CAREFULLY <199>. ¶

[2] **to perfectly unite, to perfectly join: *katartizō*** [verb: καταρτίζω <2675>]; **from *kata*: with, and *artizō*: to adjust, to develop, which is from *artios*: well adjusted, complete ► To completely unite, to fully join** > The Corinthians were to be perfectly united {to be made complete} in the same mind and in the same opinion (1 Cor. 1:10). All other refs.: see entries in Lexicon at <2675>.

– [3] John 17:23 → to become perfectly → to be perfected → PERFECT (verb) <5048> [4] Acts 18:26; 23:15, 20 → more perfectly → more accurately → ACCURATELY <197>.

PERFECTNESS – Col. 3:14 → PERFECTION <5047>.

PERFORM – [1] ***ginomai*** [verb: γίνομαι <1096>] **► To become, to happen** > Ref.: Luke 1:20 {to take place}. Other refs.: see entries in Lexicon at <1096>.

[2] ***teleō*** [verb: τελέω <5055>]; **from *telos*: completion, goal ► To accomplish, to execute** > Joseph and Mary had performed {completed, had done} all things according to the law of the Lord (Luke 2:39). All other refs.: see entries in Lexicon at <5055>.

[3] ***epiteleō*** [verb: ἐπιτελέω <2005>]; **from *epi*: until, and *teleō*: to finish ► To accomplish, to carry to completion; also transl.: to complete, to finish** > The Lord was performing cures {was doing cures, was healing people} (Luke 13:32). Paul would be performing {completing} the task of the saints of Macedonia by ensuring their gift would be received by the poor among the saints in Jerusalem (Rom. 15:28). He also addresses himself directly to the Corinthians prompting them to perform the preparation of their gift (i.e., to finalize their gift); this way, they would complete {there would be a completion, a performance} out of that which they had (2 Cor. 8:11a, b). He who had begun a good work in the Philippians would perform it {would perfect it, carry it on to completion} until the day of Jesus Christ (Phil. 1:6). All other refs.: see entries in Lexicon at <2005>.

[4] ***poieō*** [verb: ποιέω <4160>]; **lit.: to make ► To accomplish, to do** > Abraham was fully convinced that God was able to perform {to do} what He had promised (Rom. 4:21). Other refs.: see entries in Lexicon at <4160>.

– [5] Matt. 5:33 → RENDER <591> [6] Matt. 24:24; Mark 13:22 → SHOW (verb) <1325> [7] Mark 6:2; Luke 23:8 → DO <1096> [8] Luke 1:51 → SHOW (verb) <4160> [9] John 6:26 → "I performed" added in Engl. [10] John 6:30 → WORK (verb) <2038> [11] 1 Cor. 9:13 → MINISTER (verb) <2038> [12] 2 Cor. 9:12 → the service they performed → lit.: the administration of their service → ADMINISTRATION <1248> [13] 2 Cor. 12:12 → WORK (verb) <2716> [14] Eph. 2:11 → performed with hands → made with hands → HAND (noun) <5499> [15] Col. 2:11 → not performed by human hands → not made with hands → HAND (noun) <886> [16] Heb. 9:9 → to perform the service → WORSHIP (verb) <3000> [17] Heb. 11:33 → to perform acts → WROUGHT (HAVE) <2038>.

PERFORMANCE – [1] ***teleiōsis*** [fem. noun: τελείωσις <5050>]; **from *teleioō*: to accomplish, to complete ► Fulfillment, the action of carrying to completion, which is from *teleios*: complete, mature** > There would be a performance of those things spoken to Mary from the Lord {those

things would be accomplished} (Luke 1:45). Other ref.: Heb. 7:11; see PERFECTION <5050>. ¶
– [2] 2 Cor. 8:11 → PERFORM <2005>.

PERFUME – Matt. 26:7, 9, 12; Mark 14:3–5; Luke 7:37, 38, 46; 23:56; John 11:2; 12:3a, b, 5; Rev. 18:13 → OINTMENT <3464>.

PERGA – ***Pergē*** [fem. name: Πέργη <4011>]: **tower ▶ City of Pamphylia >** Paul announced the word of God in Perga during his first missionary journey (Acts 13:13, 14; 14:25). ¶

PERGAMOS – See PERGAMUM <4010>.

PERGAMUM – ***Pergamos*** [fem. name: Πέργαμος <4010>]: **citadel ▶ City of Mysia, in the northwest of Asia Minor; also written: Pergamos >** A letter is addressed to the church of Pergamum, as well as to six other churches; the Christians of Pergamum had not denied the faith (Rev. 1:11; 2:12; see v. 13). ¶

PERHAPS – [1] ***an*** [adv.: ἄν <302>] ▶ This particle is sometimes properly rendered by "perhaps"; more commonly not expressed in Engl. by any corresponding particle, but only giving to a proposition or sentence a stamp of uncertainty and mere possibility, and indicating a dependence on circumstances. Refs.: Matt. 2:13; 5:18, 19, 21, 22, 26, 31; etc. * ‡
[2] ***ara*** [inferential particle: ἄρα <686>] ▶ **By chance >** Jesus drew near a fig tree to see if perhaps {haply} He might find something on it (Mark 11:13). *
[3] ***isōs*** [adv.: ἴσως <2481>]; **from *isos*: equal ▶ Probably, possibly >** The lord of the vineyard hoped that perhaps the husbandmen would respect his son (Luke 20:13). ¶
[4] ***mēpote*** [conj.: μήποτε <3379>]; **from *mē*: not, and *pote*: at any time ▶ If, in some way, in the hope >** God perhaps {peradventure} might sometimes give repentance to those who oppose (2 Tim. 2:25).
[5] ***tacha*** [adv.: τάχα <5029>]; **from *tachus*: rapid; lit.: rapidly ▶ Maybe >** Perhaps for a good man someone might dare to die (Rom. 5:7). Paul used this word in addressing Philemon (Phm. 15). ¶
[6] **it may be that: *tunchanō*** [verb: τυγχάνω <5177>] ▶ **To happen by chance, fortuitously >** Paul thought perhaps he might stay with the Corinthians (1 Cor. 16:6). ¶
[7] **it may be: *ei tuchoi*; to happen: *tunchanō*** [verb: τυγχάνω <5177>]; **lit.: if it happens ▶ To occur, to be found >** Paul speaks of a bare grain, perhaps (lit.: it may be) of wheat or something else (1 Cor. 15:37). Other ref.: 1 Cor. 14:10 {undoubtedly}. All other refs.: ATTAIN <5177>, COMMON <5177>, ENJOY <5177>, OBTAIN <5177>, ORDINARY <5177>.
– [8] Gal. 4:11 → LEST <3381>.

PERIL – Rom. 8:35; 2 Cor. 11:26 → DANGER <2794>.

PERILOUS – 2 Tim. 3:1 → DIFFICULT <5467>.

PERIOD – [1] Acts 17:26 → TIME <2540> [2] Acts 18:20 → for a longer period → lit.: for more time [3] Gal. 4:2 → period fixed → time appointed → TIME <4287>.

PERISH – [1] ***apollumi*** [verb: ἀπόλλυμι <622>]; **from *apo*: intens., and *ollumi*: to destroy, or *olethros*: loss ▶ To destroy, to kill; also transl.: to put to death, to die, to execute, to ruin >** Everyone who believes in Jesus will not perish, but have eternal life (John 3:15, 16). The Good Shepherd's sheep will never perish (John 10:28). The word of the cross is foolishness to those who are perishing (1 Cor. 1:18). The Lord is not willing that any should perish, but that all should come to repentance (2 Pet. 3:9). The verb is also used in regard to Jesus (Matt. 2:13; 12:14; 27:20; Mark 3:6), a member of the body (Matt. 5:29 and 30 {to lose}), the disciples {to go down, to drown} (Matt. 8:25; Mark 4:38; Luke 8:24), one of the little ones in the kingdom of heaven (Matt. 18:14 {to be lost}), evil vinedressers (Matt. 21:41 {to bring to a wretched end}; Mark 12:9; Luke 20:16), murderers (Matt. 22:7), all who take the sword (Matt. 26:52), a possessed child (Mark 9:22), Zechariah (Luke 11:51), those who have not repented (Luke 13:3, 5), a prophet (Luke 13:33), the prodigal son (Luke 15:17 {to starve}), people before the flood (Luke 17:27), the people of Sodom and Gomorrah (Luke 17:29), a hair of the head (Luke 21:18 {to lose}), food (John 6:27 {to spoil}), the Jewish nation or the Jews (John 11:50; 1 Cor. 10:9, 10), Judas the Galilean (Acts 5:37), those who have sinned without the law (Rom. 2:12), a brother in Christ (1 Cor. 8:11), those who have fallen asleep in Christ {to be lost} (1 Cor. 15:18), unbelievers (2 Cor. 2:15; 4:3 {to be lost}; 2 Thes. 2:10; Heb. 1:11; Jude 11), Paul (2 Cor. 4:9), the grass's flower (Jas. 1:11), gold (1 Pet. 1:7 {to be perishable}), and the world in Noah's days (2 Pet. 3:6). Other ref.: John 18:14 in some mss. All other refs.: DESTROY <622>, LOSE <622>.

2 **to perish with: *sunapollumi*** [verb: συναπόλλυμι <4881>]; **from *sun*: with, together, and *apollumi*: see 1 ▶ To die with** > Rahab did not perish along with {was not killed with} the unbelieving (Heb. 11:31). ¶

3 ***aperchomai*** [verb: ἀπέρχομαι <565>]; **from *apo*: from, and *erchomai*: to come, to go ▶ To leave, to depart** > All the fair and splendid things have perished {are departed, have gone, have passed away, have vanished} from Babylon (Rev. 18:14). All other refs.: see entries in Lexicon at <565>.

4 ***aphanizō*** [verb: ἀφανίζω <853>]; **from *aphanēs*: hidden, which is from *a*: neg., and *phainō*: to shine, which is from *phōs*: light ▶ To disappear, to be annihilated** > The prophets had said to the scoffers that they would perish (Acts 13:41). All other refs.: DESTROY <853>, DISFIGURE <853>, VANISH <853>.

5 ***diaphtheirō*** [verb: διαφθείρω <1311>]; **from *dia*: through (intens.), and *phtheirō*: to corrupt, to destroy ▶ To corrupt, to destroy** > Even though the Christian's outward man is perishing {is consumed, is decaying, is wasting away}, yet the inward man is being renewed day by day (2 Cor. 4:16). All other refs.: CORRUPT (verb) <1311>, DESTROY <1311>.

6 ***kataphtheirō*** [verb: καταφθείρω <2704>]; **from *kata*: intens., and *phtheirō*: to corrupt, to destroy ▶ To become corrupt, to destroy oneself** > Peter spoke of those who will perish in their own corruption (2 Pet. 2:12). Other ref.: 2 Tim. 3:8; see CORRUPT (verb) <2704>. ¶

7 ***piptō*** [verb: πίπτω <4098>] **▶ To fall, to lose** > Paul used this verb in regard to a hair (Acts 27:34). All other refs.: FALL (verb) <4098>, STRIKE <4098>.

8 **destruction: *apōleia*** [fem. noun: ἀπώλεια <684>]; **from *apollumi*: see 1 ▶ Perdition, loss** > Peter said to Simon the magician: May your money perish (lit.: be for your destruction) (Acts 8:20). All other refs.: DESTRUCTION <684>, SON OF PERDITION <684>, WASTE (noun) <684>.

9 **destruction: *phthora*** [fem. noun: φθορά <5356>]; **from *phtheirō*: to corrupt, to destroy ▶ Corruption, decay** > Paul spoke of things that are all destined to perish (lit.: for destruction) with use (Col. 2:22). All other refs.: CORRUPTION <5356>, DESTROY <5356>.

– **10** Matt. 8:32 → DIE <599> **11** 1 Pet. 1:4 → that can never perish → INCORRUPTIBLE <862>.

PERISHABLE – **1** 1 Cor. 9:25; 15:53, 54; 1 Pet. 1:18, 23 → CORRUPTIBLE <5349> **2** 1 Cor. 15:42, 50 → CORRUPTION <5356> **3** 1 Pet. 1:7 → to be perishable → PERISH <622>.

PERJURED – 1 Tim. 1:10 → perjured person → PERJURER <1965>.

PERJURER – ***epiorkos*** [adj. used as noun: ἐπίορκος <1965>]; **from *epi*: against, and *horkos*: oath ▶ Person who swears falsely or who violates his oath** > The law has its application to perjurers {perjured persons} (1 Tim. 1:10). ¶

PERMANENT – **1** 2 Cor. 3:11 → what is permanent → what remains → REMAIN

<3306> [2] Heb. 7:24 → UNCHANGEABLE <531>.

PERMANENTLY – Heb. 7:24 → UNCHANGEABLE <531>.

PERMISSIBLE – John 5:10; 1 Cor. 6:12; 10:23 → to be permissible → to be lawful → LAWFUL <1832>.

PERMISSION – [1] Mark 5:13; Luke 8:32b; John 19:38; Acts 21:40; 26:1 → to give, to grant permission → PERMIT <2010> [2] Mark 11:6 → to give permission → LET <863>.

PERMIT – [1] ***epitrepō*** [verb: ἐπιτρέπω <2010>]; **from *epi*: to, and *trepō*: to turn ▶ To give permission; also transl.: to allow, to give license, to let, to suffer >** The verb is used in regard to a disciple of the Lord (Matt. 8:21), demons (Matt. 8:31), the Lord Jesus (Matt. 19:8; Mark 5:13 {to give leave}; Luke 8:32a, b), Moses (Mark 10:4), men who wanted to follow Jesus (Luke 9:59, 61), Pilate (John 19:38), Paul (Acts 21:39 (*sunchōreō* in some mss.: to grant), 40; 26:1; 28:16; 1 Tim. 2:12), Julius (Acts 27:3 {to give liberty}), and God (Heb. 6:3). Other refs.: 1 Cor. 14:34; 16:7. ¶
– [2] Matt. 3:15; Mark 5:19, 37; 7:12; 11:16; Luke 8:51; Rev. 11:9 → LET <863> [3] Mark 4:29 → PRODUCE <3860> [4] Luke 22:51; Acts 16:7; 28:4; Rev. 2:20 → ALLOW <1439> [5] Acts 24:23 → lit.: to not forbid → FORBID <2967> [6] Acts 27:7 → to permit to proceed, to permit to go → PROCEED <4330> [7] Rev. 6:4 → GIVE <1325>.

PERMITTED – [1] John 5:10; 18:31; 2 Cor. 12:4 → to be permitted → to be lawful → LAWFUL <1832> [2] Acts 26:1 → PERMIT <2010>.

PERNICIOUS – 2 Pet. 2:2 → pernicious ways → dissolute ways → DISSOLUTE <766>.

PERPETUALLY – [1] ***eis*** [prep.: εἰς <1519>] ***telos*** [neut. noun: τέλος <5056>]; **lit.: until the end ▶ Without ceasing >** In a parable, an unjust judge was afraid that a widow would completely harass him by perpetually {her continual, continually} coming (Luke 18:5). All other refs. (*telos*): CUSTOM[2] <5056>, END (noun) <5056>, FINALLY <5056>.
– [2] Heb. 7:3 → CONTINUALLY <1519> <1336>.

PERPETUITY – Heb. 10:12, 14 → in perpetuity → CONTINUALLY <1519> <1336>.

PERPLEXED (BE) – [1] ***aporeō*** [verb: ἀπορέω <639>]; **from *aporos*: without means, without resources, which is from *a*: neg., and *poros*: resources ▶ To be in confusion, to be in a quandary >** The disciples of Jesus were perplexed about {doubted, were at a loss} who would deliver up their Master (John 13:22). Paul was perplexed {saw no apparent issue}, but he was not in despair (2 Cor. 4:8). He was perplexed {stood in doubt, had doubts} as to the Galatians (Gal. 4:20) who were desirous of being under law. Other refs. in some mss.: Mark 6:20; Luke 24:4. Other ref.: Acts 25:20 (to be uncertain); see UNCERTAIN <639>. ¶
[2] ***diaporeō*** [verb: διαπορέω <1280>]; **from *dia*: through (intens.), and *aporeō*: see [1] ▶ To be in great doubt, almost driven to despair; also transl.: to be in perplexity, to be greatly perplexed, to be much perplexed, to be puzzled, to wonder >** Herod the tetrarch was perplexed, because it was said by some that John the Baptist was risen from among the dead (Luke 9:7). The women who had entered the tomb of Jesus were in perplexity because they had not found His body (Luke 24:4). At Pentecost, the multitude was in perplexity, hearing the Galileans speaking the great things of God in their own tongues (Acts 2:12). The priest and others were in perplexity as to what would happen since the apostles had gone out of the prison without the knowledge of the guards (Acts 5:24). Peter was perplexed {doubted} in himself in regard to a vision (Acts 10:17). ¶
– [3] Luke 1:29 → to be troubled → TROUBLE (verb) <1298>.

PERPLEXITY – [1] ***aporia*** [fem. noun: ἀπορία <640>]; **from *aporeō*: to be perplexed, which is from *aporos*: without resource ▶ Confusion, quandary** > Before the Lord's return, there will be upon the earth distress of nations in perplexity at the roar of the sea and rolling waves (Luke 21:25). ¶
– [2] Luke 9:7; 24:4; Acts 2:12; 5:24 → to be in perplexity → PERPLEXED (BE) <1280>.

PERSECUTE – [1] ***diōkō*** [verb: διώκω <1377>]; **from *diō*: to pursue ▶ To pursue with the intention of inflicting harm; also transl.: to suffer persecution** > The Lord warned His own about persecutions to come (Matt. 5:10, 11; 10:23; 23:34 {to pursue}). The prophets had been persecuted (Matt. 5:12; Acts 7:52). The world would persecute the disciples of Jesus (Luke 21:12; John 15:20b). Jesus was persecuted by the Jews (John 5:16; 15:20a) and by Paul (Acts 9:4, 5; 22:7, 8; 26:14, 15). Paul persecuted the church of God (Acts 22:4; 26:11 {to pursue}; 1 Cor. 15:9; Gal. 1:13, 23; Phil. 3:6 {a persecutor of}). Christians are to bless those who persecute them (Rom. 12:14) and pray for their persecutors (Matt. 5:44). Paul himself was persecuted (1 Cor. 4:12; 2 Cor. 4:9; Gal. 5:11). All who desire to live piously in Christ will be persecuted (2 Tim. 3:12). The dragon (Satan) persecuted {pursued} the woman (Israel) that bore the male child (Jesus Christ) (Rev. 12:13). Other refs.: Gal. 4:29; 6:12. All other refs.: FOLLOW <1377>, GIVE <1377>, PRESS <1377>, PURSUE <1377>.

[2] ***ekdiōkō*** (verb: ἐκδιώκω <1559>); **from *ek*: out, and *diōkō*: see [1] ▶ To pursue with the intention of inflicting harm, to drive out by persecution** > The prophets and the apostles would be persecuted (Luke 11:49). Paul had been driven out by persecution (1 Thes. 2:15). ¶
– [3] Matt. 24:9 → AFFLICTION <2347> [4] Acts 12:1 → OPPRESS <2559>.

PERSECUTED (BE) – 1 Thes. 3:4; Heb. 11:37 → AFFLICTED (BE) <2346>.

PERSECUTION – [1] ***diōgmos*** [masc. noun: διωγμός <1375>]; **from *diōkō*: to follow, to persecute, which is from *diō*: to pursue ▶ Pursuit with the intent of inflicting harm** > The Lord spoke of persecutions (Matt. 13:21; Mark 4:17; 10:30). There arose a great persecution against the church at the beginning (Acts 8:1). Persecution rose up against Paul on various occasions (Acts 13:50; Rom. 8:35; 2 Cor. 12:10; 2 Tim. 3:11a, b); he boasted about the faith of the Thessalonians in all their persecutions (2 Thes. 1:4). ¶
– [2] Luke 11:49 → to drive out by persecution → PERSECUTE <1559> [3] Acts 11:19; 1 Thes. 3:7; Rev. 2:10 → TRIBULATION <2347> [4] Acts 26:11 → to be obsessed with persecution → to be exceedingly furious → FURIOUS <1693> [5] Gal. 5:11; 6:12; 2 Tim. 3:12 → to suffer persecution → to be persecuted → PERSECUTE <1377> [6] Heb. 10:33 → AFFLICTION <2347>.

PERSECUTOR – [1] ***diōktēs*** [masc. noun: διώκτης <1376>]; **from *diōkō*: to follow, to persecute ▶ One who pursues with the intention of inflicting harm** > Paul was a persecutor before his conversion (1 Tim. 1:13). ¶
– [2] Phil. 3:6 → a persecutor of the church → lit.: persecuting the church → PERSECUTE <1377>.

PERSEVERANCE – [1] ***proskarterēsis*** [fem. noun: προσκαρτέρησις <4343>]; **from *proskartereō*: to continue steadfastly, which is from *pros*: toward, and *kartereō*: to be strong, to endure, which is from *karteros*: strength or *kratos*: might, strength ▶ Action of continuing to do that which one has proposed to do, to consecrate oneself to it** > Paul exhorted the Ephesians to watch with all prayer and supplication, and with this in mind to keep alert with all perseverance and supplication for all the saints (Eph. 6:18). ¶
– [2] Luke 8:15; Rom. 5:3, 4; 8:25; 15:4, 5; 2 Cor. 12:12; 2 Thes. 1:4; 3:5; 1 Tim. 6:11; 2 Tim. 3:10; Titus 2:2; Heb. 10:36; 12:1; Jas. 1:3, 4; 5:11; 2 Pet. 1:6a, b; Rev. 1:9; 2:2, 19; 3:10; 13:10; 14:12 → PATIENCE

<5281> 3 Rom. 2:7 → PATIENT CONTINUANCE <5281>.

PERSEVERE – 1 ***diamenō*** [verb: διαμένω <1265>]; **from *dia*: through (intens.), and *menō*: to remain, to continue ► To continue without interruption, to persist** > The apostles persevered with {continued with, stood by} the Lord in His trials (Luke 22:28). All other refs.: REMAIN <1265>.

2 ***kartereō*** [verb: καρτερέω <2594>]; **from *karteros*: strength or *kratos*: might, strength ► To remain firm, to be patient** > Moses persevered {endured}, as seeing Him who is invisible (Heb. 11:27). ¶

– 3 Acts 2:42; Col. 4:2 → CONTINUE <4342> 4 1 Cor. 13:7; Jas. 1:12; 5:11 → ENDURE <5278> 5 2 Cor. 12:12 → I persevered in demonstrating the marks → lit.: the signs were worked out in all patience 6 1 Tim. 4:16 → CONTINUE <1961> 7 Jas. 1:25 → CONTINUE <3887> 8 Rev. 2:3; 3:10 → to persevere, my command to persevere → lit.: to have patience, the word of my patience → PATIENCE <5281>.

PERSEVERING – 1 **to persevere: *proskartereō*** [verb: προσκαρτερέω <4342>]; **from *pros*: toward, and *kartereō*: to be strong, to endure, which is from *karteros*: strength ► Demonstrating perseverance, continuing steadfastly** > Paul urged the Christians at Rome to be persevering in {constant in, continuing instant in, continuing steadfastly in, devoted to, faithful in} prayer (Rom. 12:12). All other refs.: ATTEND <4342>, CONTINUE <4342>, READY <4342>.

– 2 Luke 8:15 → by persevering → lit.: with perseverance → PATIENCE <5281> 3 Rom. 12:12 → to be persevering → to be patient → PATIENT <5278>.

PERSIS – ***Persis*** [fem. name: Περσίς <4069>]: **woman of Persia ► Christian woman of Rome** > Paul sends greetings to Persis in his letter to the Christians of Rome (Rom. 16:12). ¶

PERSIST – 1 John 8:7; Rom. 11:23; 1 Tim. 4:16 → CONTINUE <1961> 2 1 Tim. 5:20 → "persist in" added in Engl.

PERSISTENCE – 1 ***anaideia*** [fem. noun: ἀναίδεια <335>]; **from *anaidēs*: impudent, insolent, which is from *a*: neg., and *aidōs*: shame, modesty ► Audacity, impudence** > Because of the persistence {importunity, shameless audacity, shamelessness} of his friend, a man will get up and give him bread (Luke 11:8). ¶

– 2 Rom. 2:7 → PATIENT CONTINUANCE <5281>.

PERSON – 1 ***prosōpon*** [neut. noun: πρόσωπον <4383>]; **from *pros*: toward, and *ōps*: face ► a. Lit.: face, individual** > The word is used in 2 Cor. 1:11; 2:10 {presence, sight}; Jude 16 {people}. **b. Appearance** > Jesus was told that He did not regard the person of men (Matt. 22:16; Mark 12:14). God accepts no man's person (Luke 20:21; Gal. 2:6); also transl.: God shows personal favoritism to no man; God is not partial to any; God shows no partiality. All other refs.: APPEARANCE <4383>, FACE (noun) <4383>, PRESENCE <4383>.

– 2 Acts 4:34 → needy person → person in want → WANT (noun) <1729> 3 Acts 27:37; 1 Pet. 3:20 → SOUL <5590> 4 2 Cor. 10:10 → lit.: presence in the body → BODY <4983>, PRESENCE <3952> 5 Heb. 1:3 → SUBSTANCE <5287>.

PERSONAL – 1 Luke 20:21; Gal. 2:6 → personal favoritism → PERSON <4383> 2 John 7:18 → personal glory → own glory → OWN (adj. and pron.) <2398> 3 Acts 12:20 → personal aide, personal servant → CHAMBERLAIN <2846> 4 2 Cor. 10:10 → personal presence → lit.: presence in the body → BODY <4983> 5 Jas. 2:1 → personal favoritism → RESPECT OF PERSONS <4382>.

PERSONALLY – Gal. 1:22; Col. 2:1 → FACE (noun) <4383>.

PERSUADE – 1 ***peithō*** [verb: πείθω <3982>] ► **a. To convince, to assure, to**

believe; also transl.: to try to persuade > Paul and Barnabas persuaded {urged} Christians at Antioch to continue in the grace of God (Acts 13:43). Paul was persuaded that nothing will be able to separate the Christian from the love of God that is in Christ Jesus (Rom. 8:38). The verb is also used in regard to the chief priests and the elders (Matt. 27:20; 28:14 {to appease, to win over, to satisfy}), the Jews (Luke 16:31; 20:6), the Thessalonians (Acts 17:4), Paul (Acts 18:4; 19:8, 26; 21:14; 26:26; 28:23; Rom. 14:14; 15:14 {to be confident}; 2 Cor. 5:11; 2 Tim. 1:5 {to be sure}, 12; Heb. 6:9), Agrippa (Acts 26:28), Paul's hearers (Acts 28:24), and O.T. people of faith (Heb. 11:13 in some mss.). **b. To seek to please >** Paul asks if he was now persuading {seeking to satisfy, striving to please, trying to win the approval of} God or men (Gal. 1:10). All other refs.: see entries in Lexicon at <3982>.
[2] ***anapeithō*** [verb: ἀναπείθω <374>]; **from *ana*: intens., and *peithō*: see [1] ▶ To agitate by persuasion, to incite >** The Jews said that Paul was persuading men to worship God contrary to the law (Acts 18:13). ¶
[3] **to be fully persuaded: *plērophoreō*** [verb: πληροφορέω <4135>]; **from *plērēs*: full, and *phoreō*: to fill, which is from *pherō*: to carry, to bear ▶ To be fully convinced, to be entirely assured >** Abraham was fully persuaded that what God had promised, He was able also to do (Rom. 4:21). Each one is to be fully persuaded in his own mind concerning the observance of certain days (Rom. 14:5). All other refs.: BELIEVE <4135>, COMPLETE (adj.) <4135>, PREACH <4135>, PROOF <4135>.
– [4] Acts 6:11 → to secretly persuade → SUBORN <5260> [5] Acts 16:15 → CONSTRAIN <3849> [6] 2 Tim. 3:14 → to be fully persuaded → ASSURED (BE) <4104>.

PERSUADED (BE) – [1] ***peithō*** [verb: πείθω <3982>] **▶ To believe, to trust >** The centurion was more persuaded by the pilot and owner of the ship than by Paul (Acts 27:11). All other refs.: see entries in Lexicon at <3982>.
– [2] 2 Tim. 3:14 → to be fully persuaded → ASSURED (BE) <4104>.

PERSUASIBLENESS – Gal. 5:8 → PERSUASION <3988>.

PERSUASION – ***peismonē*** [fem. noun: πεισμονή <3988>]; **from *peithō*: to persuade, to convince ▶ Influence, conviction which can be negative >** The persuasion {persuasibleness} of the Galatians was not of Him who had called them (Gal. 5:8). ¶

PERSUASIVE – [1] ***peithos*** [adj.: πειθός <3981>]; **from *peithō*: to persuade, to convince ▶ Convincing, prompting to believe >** Paul's preaching had not been in persuasive {enticing} words of wisdom (1 Cor. 2:4); *peithō* (fem. noun) in some mss.: in persuasiveness (*en peithoi*). ¶
– [2] Col. 2:4 → persuasive word, speech, argument → persuasive word → WORD <4086>.

PERSUASIVELY – Acts 19:8 → lit.: and persuading → PERSUADE <3982>.

PERTAIN – [1] ***metechō*** [verb: μετέχω <3348>]; **from *meta*: with, and *echō*: to have, to hold; lit.: to have a part with ▶ To belong, to be a member >** The Lord pertains to a different tribe than the one that was responsible for the priesthood (Heb. 7:13). All other refs.: PARTAKE <3348>, USE (verb) <3348>.
[2] ***pros*** [prep.: πρός <4314>] **▶ About, concerning >** The prep. is used in the expr. "things which pertain {pertaining, relating} to God" (Rom. 15:17; Heb. 2:17; 5:1). *

PERTAINING – 1 Cor. 6:3 → "pertaining" added in Engl.

PERVERSE – [1] ***skolios*** [adj.: σκολιός <4646>]; **from *skellō*: to dry ▶ Twisted, crooked >** Peter exhorted the inhabitants of Jerusalem to save themselves from a perverse {corrupt, untoward} generation (Acts 2:40). All other refs.: CROOKED <4646>, HARSH <4646>.

– [2] Matt. 17:17; Luke 9:41; Phil. 2:15 → PERVERTED (BE) <1294> [3] 2 Thes. 3:2 → BAD <824> [4] 1 Tim. 6:5 → perverse disputing → useless wrangling → WRANGLING <1275a> <3859>.

PERVERSION – Rom. 1:27 → DECEPTION <4106>.

PERVERT (noun) – 1 Tim. 1:10 → HOMOSEXUAL <733>.

PERVERT (verb) – [1] ***diastrephō*** [verb: διαστρέφω <1294>]; **from *dia*: through, and *strephō*: to turn, to change ▶ To corrupt; to lead astray** > The Jews accused Jesus of perverting {misleading, subverting} their nation (Luke 23:2). Paul accused Elymas of perverting {making crooked} the right paths of the Lord (Acts 13:10). All other refs.: PERVERTED (BE) <1294>, TURN (verb) <1294>.

[2] ***metastrephō*** [verb: μεταστρέφω <3344>]; **from *meta*: particle indicating change, and *strephō*: to turn ▶ To change into something else** > There were some who desired to pervert {to distort} the glad tidings of the Christ (Gal. 1:7). Other refs.: Acts 2:20; Jas. 4:9; see TURN (verb) <3344>. ¶

– [3] Luke 23:14 → to turn away → TURN (verb) <654> [4] Jude 4 → TURN (verb) <3346>.

PERVERTED (BE) – [1] ***diastrephō*** [verb used as adj.: διαστρέφω <1294>]; **from *dia*: through, and *strephō*: to turn ▶ To be vicious, to be corrupted; also transl.: to be depraved, to be perverse** > Jesus accused His generation of being unbelieving and perverted (Matt. 17:17; Luke 9:41). Paul warned the elders of Ephesus that there would arise from among them men speaking perverted things (Acts 20:30). Christians appear as lights in the midst of a perverted {crooked} generation (Phil. 2:15). All other refs.: PERVERT (verb) <1294>, TURN (verb) <1294>.

[2] ***ekstrephō*** [verb: ἐκστρέφω <1612>]; **from *ek*: out, and *strephō*: to turn, to change ▶ To change for the worse, to be subverted** > A sectarian man is perverted {is warped} and is sinning (Titus 3:11). ¶

PEST – ***loimos*** [masc. noun: λοιμός <3061>] ▶ **Person who causes annoyance** > Tertullus accused Paul of being a pest {pestilent fellow, real pest, plague, troublemaker} (Acts 24:5). Other refs.: Matt. 24:7; Luke 21:11; see PESTILENCE <3061>. ¶

PESTILENCE – [1] ***loimos*** [masc. noun: λοιμός <3061>] ▶ **Infectious and epidemic disease** > Before the return of Christ, there will be pestilences {plagues} (Matt. 24:7 in some mss.; Luke 21:11). Other ref.: Acts 24:5; see PEST <3061>. ¶

– [2] Rev. 18:8 → DEATH <2288>.

PETER – ***Petros*** [masc. name: Πέτρος <4074>]: **a stone; in contrast with the rock: *petra* (Matt. 16:18; see 1 Cor. 3:11; 1 Pet. 2:3–8) ▶ One of the twelve apostles** > The original name of Peter was Simon, son of John; Jesus gave him the name of Cephas (Peter) thereafter (Luke 5:8; 6:14; John 1:40–42). He was a fisherman and worked with James, John, and Andrew. At the call of Jesus, they left everything and followed Him (Mark 1:16–19). Peter had a prominent place among them. When Jesus chose a few disciples in particular circumstances, Peter is always among them and is named first; but we do not read that he exercised any formalized authority over the other apostles. The Gospels relate many incidents in connection with Peter. He was energetic and impulsive. When he refused to admit that the Christ should suffer, Jesus rebuffed him as speaking on behalf of Satan (Matt. 16:23). His self-confidence led him to deny his Lord, but he sincerely repented. After the resurrection, the Lord asked him if he loved Him more than the other disciples did; He then entrusted to him the shepherding and feeding of the lambs and sheep of Christ (John 21:15–17). Peter was entrusted with the keys of the kingdom (Matt. 16:19), and we see him preaching to large crowds after the Holy Spirit had come at Pentecost (see Acts 2:14–36). Three thousand souls were then saved and added to the church (these were primarily Jews of various nations). He was also the means by which Cornelius, a Gentile, was converted (Acts 10). Thus Peter opened the kingdom to both Jews and Gentiles. Peter was the apostle of the circumcision (and Paul was the apostle to the nations) (Gal. 2:7); it seems he did not get completely clear of his Jewish prejudices. Paul was obliged to withstand him to the face at Antioch because he was guilty of separating himself from Christians of the nations who did not follow Jewish customs (Gal. 2:11, 12–16). Peter remarks that Paul speaks in his epistles of some things that are hard to be understood (2 Pet. 3:15, 16); those who were not established in the teaching of the apostles took this opportunity to twist those things to their own destruction. Peter wrote the two epistles that bear his name. According to history, he was crucified at Rome and was nailed, at his own request, upside down. Tradition says that his wife also suffered with him. (After Walter Scott.) *

PETITION (noun) – 1 ***aitēma*** [neut. noun: αἴτημα <155>]**; from *aiteō*: to ask, to request ▶ Request, demand** > Christians know that they have the petitions that they have asked of God (1 John 5:15). Other refs.: Phil. 4:6; Luke 23:24; see REQUEST (noun) <155>, REQUEST (verb) <155>. ¶

– 2 Luke 1:13; Eph. 6:18a, b; Phil. 4:6b → SUPPLICATION <1162> 3 1 Tim. 2:1 → INTERCESSION <1783>.

PETITION (verb) – 1 ***entunchanō*** [verb: ἐντυγχάνω <1793>]**; from *en*: in, and *tunchanō*: to obtain ▶ To appeal, to intercede** > The Jews had petitioned Festus regarding Paul, crying out that he ought not to live any longer (Acts 25:24 {to appeal, to apply, to deal}). All other refs.: INTERCEDE <1793>, PLEAD <1793>.

– 2 Acts 23:15 → SIGNIFY <1718> 3 Acts 25:2 → BESEECH <3870>.

PHALEC – Luke 3:35 → PHALEK <5317>.

PHALEK – ***Phalek*** [masc. name: Φάλεκ <5317>]**: division, in Heb.; see Peleg, son of Eber: Gen. 11:16 ▶ Man of the O.T.; also transl.: Phalec, Peleg** > Phalek is mentioned in the genealogy of Jesus (Luke 3:35). ¶

PHANUEL – ***Phanouēl*** [masc. name: Φανουήλ <5323>]**: face of God, in Heb. ▶ Israelite man of the tribe of Asher** > Phanuel was the father of Anna, a prophetess (Luke 2:36). ¶

PHARAOH – ***Pharaō*** [masc. name: Φαραώ <5328>]**: great house ▶ Title of the kings of Egypt** > Joseph and his family found favor in the sight of the Pharaoh of that time (Acts 7:10, 13). Moses was brought up by the daughter of another Pharaoh (Acts 7:21), but he refused to be called her son (Heb. 11:24). God showed His power by delivering the Israelites from the hand of Pharaoh (Rom. 9:17). ¶

PHARES – ***Phares*** [masc. name: Φαρές <5329>]**: breach, in Heb.; see Gen. 38:29 ▶ Son of Judah and Tamar; also transl.: Perez** > Phares is mentioned in the genealogy of Jesus Christ (Matt. 1:3a, b; Luke 3:33). ¶

PHARISEE – ***Pharisaios*** [masc. noun: Φαρισαῖος <5330>]**; from an Aram. word signifying: to separate ▶ Member of a Jewish sect separated from the mass of the people on the principle of a life of superior holiness, devotion to God (e.g., fasting and long prayers) and knowledge of the law** > The Pharisees became attached to a form of godliness rather that to spiritual reality. They are mentioned repeatedly in the four Gospels and in Acts. Jesus reproached them particularly for annulling the commandment of God by their tradition (Matt. 15:1–9) and their hypocrisy (Matt. 23:23; Luke 18:9–14). They tried to tempt Jesus (e.g., Matt. 19:3) and to kill Him (e.g., Matt. 12:14). The Pharisees originated from the Jewish sect known as the Hasidim (lit.: those who are godly), founded in the second century B.C. Paul was a Pharisee as to the law (Phil. 3:5). *

PHEBE – Rom. 16:1 → PHOEBE <5402>.

PHENICE – [1] Acts 11:9; 15:3 → PHOENICIA <5403> [2] Acts 27:12 → PHOENIX <5405>.

PHENICIA – Acts 21:2 → PHOENICIA <5403>.

PHILADELPHIA – ***Philadelpheia*** [fem. name: Φιλαδέλφεια <5359>]: **brotherly love ► City of Lydia in Asia Minor; it was built by the king of Pergamum, and several times more or less destroyed by earthquakes.** > One of the seven letters to the churches of Asia was addressed to Philadelphia (Rev. 1:11; 3:7); the Christians of Philadelphia had shown remarkable faithfulness; they had kept the word of God (see Rev. 3:8, 10). ¶

PHILEMON – ***Philēmōn*** [masc. name: Φιλήμων <5371>]: **affectionate; from *phileō*: to love, which is from *philos*: dear, friend ► Christian man of the city of Colossae** > The church of Colossae met in the house of Philemon (Phm. 1; see v. 2). In the letter that he addresses to Philemon, Paul asks him to receive Onesimus, the slave who had fled from his home (see v. 17). His wife was probably Apphia and his son Archippus (see v. 2). Onesimus probably had been converted by means of Paul at Rome (see v. 10). ¶

PHILETUS – ***Philētos*** [masc. name: Φίλητος <5372>]: **beloved; from *phileō*: to love, which is from *philos*: dear, friend ► Man of the N.T.** > Philetus and Hymenaeus had erred from the truth (2 Tim. 2:17), saying that the resurrection had already taken place; they thus overturned the faith of some (see v. 18). ¶

PHILIP – ***Philippos*** [masc. name: Φίλιππος <5376>]: **lover of horses; from *philos*: friend, and *hippos*: horse ► a. One of the twelve apostles** > Philip is mentioned in Matt. 10:3; Mark 3:18; Luke 6:14; Acts 1:13. Jesus found Philip, who was from Bethsaida, and told him to follow Him (John 1:44, 45). Philip in turn spoke of Jesus to Nathanael (John 1:46, see vv. 47, 49). Jesus tested Philip, asking him to find bread to feed a large crowd (John 6:5, 7). Greeks came to Philip and expressed their desire to see Jesus; Philip spoke of this to Andrew (John 12:21, 22). Philip asked the Lord to show him the Father (John 14:8, 9). **b. Tetrarch of Ituraea and Trachonitis** > The word of God came to John the Baptist when Philip ruled (Luke 3:1). He was the first husband of Herodias; his brother Herod also had Herodias as his wife (Matt. 14:3, see v. 4; Mark 6:17). **c. Christian man of Jerusalem** > Philip the Evangelist was one of seven chosen to be occupied with service in the church of Jerusalem (Acts 6:5). He preached Christ in a city of Samaria and did miracles there (Acts 8:5, 6). A certain man named Simon, a magician, believed the preaching of Philip, was baptized by him, and continued constantly with him (Acts 8:12, 13, see v. 9), but he was a hypocrite. Philip announced Jesus to the Ethiopian eunuch who was returning from Jerusalem and then baptized him before being caught away by the Spirit of the Lord; passing through the land of Azotus, he preached the gospel in all the cities until he came to Caesarea (Acts 8:26, 29–31, 34, 35, 38–40). Philip lived in Caesarea (Acts 21:8) with his four daughters, who prophesied (see v. 9). ¶

PHILIPPI – ***Philippoi*** [masc. plur. name: Φίλιπποι <5375>]: **belonging to Philip ► City of Macedonia bearing the name of Philip, the father of Alexander the Great; Caesar Augustus established a Roman colony there** > Paul stayed in Philippi several days during his second missionary journey (Acts 16:12), and passed through the city on his third journey (20:6). During his visit, Paul had suffered and been insulted at Philippi (1 Thes. 2:2); he had been publicly beaten and thrown into prison (see Acts 16:22–37). The apostle Paul wrote a letter to the church of Philippi (Phil. 1:1). ¶

PHILIPPIAN – ***Philippēsios*** [masc. adj.: Φιλιππήσιος <5374>] ► **Inhabitant of the city of Philippi, in Macedonia** > Paul wrote a letter to them (see Phil. 1:1). The church of the Philippians had sent a gift to Paul to supply his needs (Phil. 4:15). ¶

PHILOLOGUS – ***Philologos*** [masc. name: Φιλόλογος <5378>]: **lover of words, who loves to talk** ► **Christian man of Rome** > Paul sends greetings to Philogus in his letter to the Christians of Rome (Rom. 16:15). ¶

PHILOSOPHER – 1 ***philosophos*** [masc. noun: φιλόσοφος <5386>]; **from *philos*: friend, and *sophia*: wisdom** ► **One who devotes himself to philosophy, the study of wisdom** > Some of the Epicurean and Stoic philosophers conversed with Paul at Athens (Acts 17:18). ¶

– 2 1 Cor. 1:20 → DISPUTER <4804>.

PHILOSOPHY – ***philosophia*** [fem. noun: φιλοσοφία <5385>]; **from *philos*: friend, and *sophia*: wisdom** ► **Search for wisdom and truth by intellectual efforts; in the N.T., the word has certainly a negative connotation** > Paul warns against philosophy (Col. 2:8), because most of the time it rejects or ignores divine revelation. ¶

PHLEGON – ***Phlegōn*** [masc. name: Φλέγων <5393>]: **burning, zealous; from *phlegō*: to set fire, to light** ► **Christian man of Rome** > Paul sends greetings to Phlegon in his letter to the Christians of Rome (Rom. 16:14). ¶

PHOEBE – ***Phoibē*** [fem. name: Φοίβη <5402>]: **radiant; from *phoibos*: clear, brilliant** ► **Christian woman of Cenchrea; also transl.: Phebe** > Paul commends Phoebe to the Christians of Rome, that they might assist her in her needs; she herself had been a helper of many people and of Paul (Rom. 16:1, see v. 2). ¶

PHOENICE – Acts 27:12 → PHOENIX <5405>.

PHOENICIA – ***Phoinikē*** [fem. name: Φοινίκη <5403>]: **land of palm trees; from *phoinix*: palm tree** ► **Region of Palestine along the Mediterranean Sea, northeast of Sidon; also transl.: Phenice, Phenicia** > Some Christians who had been scattered on the occasion of the stoning of Stephen traveled to Phoenicia (Acts 11:19). Paul and Barnabas passed through Phoenicia, telling about the conversion of the nations (Acts 15:3). Paul returned to this region during his third missionary journey (Acts 21:2). ¶

PHOENIX – ***Phoinix*** [fem. name: Φοίνιξ or Φοῖνιξ <5405>]: **palm tree** ► **A harbor of the island of Crete; also transl.: Phenice, Phoenice** > The men traveling with Paul had attempted to reach this Mediterranean port during his fourth journey, but without success (Acts 27:12). ¶

PHRASE – 1 Matt. 6:7 → to heap up empty phrases → lit.: much speaking → SPEAKING <4180> 2 Heb. 12:27 → "phrase" added in Engl.

PHRYGIA – ***Phrugia*** [fem. name: Φρυγία <5435>] ► **Region of central Asia Minor** > Jews of Phrygia were present in Jerusalem at Pentecost (Acts 2:10). Paul passed through Phrygia during his second missionary journey (Acts 16:6), and strengthened all the disciples there during his third journey (Acts 18:23). ¶

PHYGELLUS – 2 Tim. 1:15 → PHYGELUS <5436>.

PHYGELUS – ***Phugelos*** [masc. name: Φύγελος <5436>]: **fugitive; akin to *phugē*: escape; also spelled: Phugellos** ► **Christian man of Asia; also transl.: Phygellus** > Phygelus had turned away from Paul (2 Tim. 1:15). ¶

PHYLACTERY – ***phulaktērion*** [neut. noun: φυλακτήριον <5440>]; **from *phulassō*: to watch over, to keep** ► **Portion of the law, i.e., Scripture verses, written on a small strip of parchment** > It was worn on the forehead or the arm to remind its owner of his duty to keep the words of the Lord (see Ex. 13:9, 16; Deut. 6:8; 11:18). Jesus reproached the Pharisees for broadening their phylacteries (Matt. 23:5) to attract attention and flaunt their piety. ¶

PHYSICAL – [1] 1 Tim. 4:8 → BODILY (adj.) <4984> [2] Heb. 7:16 → CARNAL <4559>.

PHYSICALLY – Rom. 2:27 → physically uncircumcised → lit.: uncircumcision by nature → NATURE <5449>.

PHYSICIAN – ***iatros*** [masc. noun: ἰατρός <2395>]; **from *iaomai*: to heal ► Person who treats the sick; also transl.: doctor** > Those who are well have no need of a physician (Matt. 9:12; Mark 2:17; Luke 5:31). A woman had suffered many things under many physicians (Mark 5:26; Luke 8:43). Jesus calls Himself a physician (Luke 4:23). Paul calls Luke the beloved physician (Col. 4:14). ¶

PICK – [1] **to pick up: *airō*** [verb: αἴρω <142>] ► **a. To transport, to carry away; also transl.: to take up** > The verb is used concerning the fragments of bread that were over and above at the time of the miracles of the multiplication of bread (Matt. 14:20; 15:37; Mark 6:43; 8:8; Luke 9:17). Jesus asked His disciples to recall how many baskets and hand-baskets of the bread they picked up that was left over after having fed the crowds (Mark 8:19, 20). **b. To raise up, to set upright** > Eutychus was picked up {was taken up} dead after having fallen from the third story (Acts 20:9). All other refs.: see entries in Lexicon at <142>.
[2] **to pick up: *lambanō*** [verb: λαμβάνω <2983>] ► **To take up, to gather** > Jesus asked His disciples how many large baskets and hand baskets they had taken up of the bread that remained after having fed the crowds (Matt. 16:9, 10). Other refs.: see entries in Lexicon at <2983>.
– [3] Matt. 7:16; Luke 6:44 → GATHER <4816> [4] Matt. 12:1; Mark 2:23; Luke 6:1 → PLUCK <5089> [5] Matt. 27:6 → to pick up → TAKE <2983> [6] Luke 6:44b → GATHER <5166> [7] Luke 14:7 → CHOOSE <1586> [8] John 10:31 → to pick up → to take up → TAKE <941> [9] John 15:6 → to pick up → GATHER <4863> [10] Acts 6:3 → to look out → LOOK (verb) <1980> [11] 2 Tim. 4:11 → to pick up → TAKE <353>.

PICTURE – Mark 4:30 → COMPARE <3846>.

PIECE – [1] ***epiblēma*** [neut. noun: ἐπίβλημα <1915>]; **from *epiballō*: to put on, which is from *epi*: on, and *ballō*: to throw ► Patch, addition** > No one puts a piece of unshrunk cloth on an old garment (Matt. 9:16; Mark 2:21a; Luke 5:36a, b). ¶
[2] ***meros*** [neut. noun: μέρος <3313>] ► **Part, portion** > They gave Jesus a piece of a broiled fish (Luke 24:42). Other refs.: see entries in Lexicon at <3313>.
[3] ***plērōma*** [neut. noun: πλήρωμα <4138>]; **from *plēroō*: to fill ► Patch of cloth** > No one puts a patch of unshrunk cloth on an old garment, for the new piece will tear away part of the garment (Matt. 9:16; Mark 2:21). All other refs.: FULL <4138>, FULFILLMENT <4138>, FULLNESS <4138>, PATCH <4138>.
[4] **piece of bread, bread: *psōmion*** [neut. noun: ψωμίον <5596>]; **dimin. of *psōmos*: morsel, a mouthful ► Fragment, bit** > Jesus gave the piece of bread {morsel, sop} to Judas (John 13:26a, b, 27, 30). ¶
[5] **to tear to pieces, to pull to pieces: *diaspaō*** [verb: διασπάω <1288>]; **from *dia*: through, and *spaō*: to draw (the sword) ► To cut up into bits, to destroy** > The chiliarch feared lest Paul would have been torn to pieces (Acts 23:10). Other ref.: Mark 5:4 (to tear apart); see TEAR (verb) <1288>. ¶
[6] **to break in pieces: *suntribō*** [verb: συντρίβω <4937>]; **from *sun*: together (intens.), and *tribō*: to rub ► To smash, to shatter** > When he was bound with chains, a possessed man broke the shackles in pieces (Mark 5:4). All other refs.: BREAK <4937>, BRUISE <4937>.
– [7] Matt. 14:20; 15:37; Mark 6:43; 8:8, 19; Luke 9:17 → piece, broken piece →

FRAGMENT <2801> [8] Matt. 24:51; Luke 12:46 → to cut in two → CUT <1371> [9] Luke 14:18 → piece of ground → FIELD <68> [10] Luke 15:8a, b, 9 → piece of silver → COIN <1406> [11] Luke 19:20 → piece of cloth → HANDKERCHIEF <4676>.

PIERCE – [1] ***dierchomai*** [verb: διέρχομαι <1330>]; **from *dia*: through, and *erchomai*: to come, to go ► To go through, to penetrate** > A sword would pierce the soul of Mary, the mother of Jesus (Luke 2:35). All other refs.: COME <1330>, GO <1330>, PASS <1330>, SPREAD <1330>.
[2] ***diikneomai*** [verb: διϊκνέομαι <1338>]; **from *dia*: through, and *hikneomai*: to come, to occur ► To penetrate, to go through, to reach** > The word of God pierces to the division of soul and spirit (Heb. 4:12). ¶
[3] ***ekkenteō*** [verb: ἐκκεντέω <1574>]; **from *ek*: out (intens.), and *kenteō*: to sting, to puncture ► To penetrate, to stab through** > Those of Israel will look on Him whom they have pierced (John 19:37). Every eye will see Him, and those who have pierced Him (Rev. 1:7). ¶
[4] ***nussō*** [verb: νύσσω <3572>] **► To stab, to penetrate** > A soldier pierced the side of Jesus with a spear (John 19:34). Other ref.: Acts 12:7 in some mss. ¶
[5] ***peripeirō*** [verb: περιπείρω <4044>]; **from *peri*: around, and *peirō*: to pierce ► To torture, to afflict one's soul** > Because of the love of money, some have strayed from the faith and have pierced themselves through with many griefs (1 Tim. 6:10). ¶
– [6] Acts 2:37 → PRICK <2660>.

PIETY – [1] ***eulabeia*** [fem. noun: εὐλάβεια <2124>]; **from *eulabēs*: devout, which is from *eu*: well, and *lambanō*: to take, to receive ► Respectful fear in regard to God; also transl.: reverence** > Jesus Christ was heard because of His piety {godly fear, reverent submission, reverence} {in that He feared} (Heb. 5:7). It is by grace that Christians serve God acceptably, with reverence and godly fear (Heb. 12:28). ¶
[2] **to be pious, to show piety, to practice piety, to put religion in practice: *eusebeō*** [verb: εὐσεβέω <2151>]; **from *eusebēs*: devout, godly, which is from *eu*: well, and *sebomai*: to experience a sense of religious fear, to adore ► To practice a reverent, respectful fear in regard to God** > Piety should be shown first at home (1 Tim. 5:4). Other ref.: Acts 17:23; see WORSHIP (verb) <2151>. ¶
– [3] Luke 1:75 → HOLINESS <3742> [4] Acts 3:12; 1 Tim. 2:2; 3:16; 4:7, 8; 6:5, 6; 2 Tim. 3:5; Titus 1:1 → GODLINESS <2150>.

PIG – Matt. 7:6; 8:30, 31, 32a, b; Mark 5:11–13, 16; Luke 8:32, 33; 15:15, 16 → SWINE <5519>.

PIGEON – Matt. 21:12; Mark 11:15; Luke 2:24; John 2:14, 16 → DOVE <4058>.

PILATE – See PONTIUS PILATE <4194> <4091>.

PILE (noun) – Acts 28:3 → QUANTITY <4128>.

PILE (verb) – Rev. 18:5 → to pile up → REACH (verb) <2853>.

PILFER – [1] ***nosphizō*** [verb: νοσφίζω <3557>]; **from *nosphi*: apart ► To set aside, to withhold for oneself something that belongs to another** > Believing bondservants were not to pilfer {purloin, rob, steal}, but to show all good fidelity (Titus 2:10). The verb is transl. "to keep back" {to put aside} in Acts 5:2, 3. ¶
– [2] John 12:6 → more likely: to carry → BEAR <941>.

PILGRIM – [1] Heb. 11:13; 1 Pet. 2:11 → SOJOURNER <3927> [2] 1 Pet. 1:1 → STRANGER <3927>.

PILLAR – ***stulos*** [masc. noun: στῦλος <4769>]; **poss. from *istēmi*: to stand ► Vertical structure supporting the weight of a building, column; the word is used to indicate strength, stability, and authority** > James, Cephas, and John were pillars in the church of Jerusalem (Gal.

2:9), having a moral authority. The church on earth is the pillar and foundation of the truth (1 Tim. 3:15). Figur., a pillar indicates the firm, stable, and permanent position of the Christian in the temple of God (Rev. 3:12). In Rev. 10:1, the feet of the angel as pillars of fire suggest divine holiness and righteousness (see Rev. 1:15). ¶

PILLOW – Mark 4:38 → CUSHION <4344>.

PILOT – ***kubernētēs*** [masc. noun: κυβερνήτης <2942>]; **from *kubernaō*: to direct, to govern ► Person who steers a ship; also transl.: helmsman, master, shipmaster, steersman >** The centurion believed the helmsman of the ship rather than what Paul said (Acts 27:11). Other ref.: Rev. 18:17. ¶

PINE – Mark 9:18 → to pine away → to become rigid → RIGID <3583>.

PINNACLE – ***pterugion*** [neut. noun: πτερύγιον <4419>]; **dimin. of *pterux*: wing ► Highest part of the temple, its spire >** Satan set Jesus on the pinnacle {highest point} of the temple (Matt. 4:5; Luke 4:9). ¶

PINT – John 12:3 → POUND <3046>.

PIONEER – 1 Heb. 2:10 → CAPTAIN <747> 2 Heb. 12:2 → AUTHOR <747>.

PIOUS – 1 Luke 2:25; Acts 2:5; 8:2 → DEVOUT <2126> 2 Acts 10:2, 7; 22:12 → DEVOUT <2152> 3 1 Tim. 5:4 → to be pious → PIETY <2151> 4 Titus 1:8 → DEVOUT <3741>.

PIOUSLY – 1 1 Thes. 2:10 → DEVOUTLY <3743> 2 2 Tim. 3:12; Titus 2:12 → GODLY <2153>.

PIPE (noun) – 1 Matt. 9:23 → people playing pipe → FLUTE-PLAYER <834> 2 Matt. 11:17; Luke 7:32 → to play the pipe → to play the flute → FLUTE <832> 3 1 Cor. 14:7 → FLUTE <836>.

PIPE (verb) – Matt. 11:17; Luke 7:32; 1 Cor. 14:7b → to play the flute → FLUTE <832>.

PIPER – Rev. 18:22 → FLUTE PLAYER <834>.

PISIDIA – ***Pisidia*** [fem. name: Πισιδία <4099>] **► Region south of Phrygia, in Asia Minor >** Paul came to Antioch of Pisidia {Pisidian (*Pisidios*) Antioch} on his first missionary journey, and spoke in the synagogue (Acts 13:14). He passed through the region again during this same journey (Acts 14:24). ¶

PISIDIAN – See PISIDIA <4099>.

PIT – 1 ***bothunos*** [masc. noun: βόθυνος <999>] **► Ditch, hole in the ground >** A man will take hold of a sheep and lift it out of a pit even if it is the Sabbath (Matt. 12:11). Two blind men could fall into a pit (Matt. 15:14: *bothros* in some mss.; Luke 6:39). ¶

– 2 Mark 12:1 → to dig a pit → DIG <3736>, WINEVAT <5276> 3 Luke 14:5; Rev. 9:1, 2a–c → WELL (noun) <5421> 4 2 Pet. 2:4 → to cast down to the deepest pit of gloom → to cast down to hell → HELL <5020> 5 2 Pet. 2:4 → CHAIN (noun) <4577>.

PITCH – Heb. 8:2 → ERECT (verb) <4078>.

PITCHER – 1 ***keramion*** [neut. noun: κεράμιον <2765>]; **from *keramon*: clay ► Earthen vessel used to contain water >** A man would meet the disciples carrying a pitcher {jar} of water (Mark 14:13; Luke 22:10). ¶

– 2 Mark 7:4, 8 → VESSEL[1] <3582>.

PITIABLE – 1 Cor. 15:19; Rev. 3:17 → MISERABLE <1652>.

PITIED (BE) – 1 Cor. 15:19 → MISERABLE <1652>.

PITIFUL – [1] Jas. 5:11 → very pitiful → very compassionate → COMPASSIONATE <4184> [2] Jas. 5:11 → MERCIFUL <3629> [3] 1 Pet. 3:8 → TENDER-HEARTED <2155> [4] Rev. 3:17 → MISERABLE <1652>.

PITY – [1] Matt. 18:27; 20:34; Mark 1:41; 9:22; Luke 10:33 → to be moved with pity, to take pity → to have compassion → COMPASSION <4697> [2] 1 John 3:17 → ENTRAILS <4698> [3] 1 John 3:17 → to have not pity → lit.: to shut up one's heart → SHUT <2808>.

PLACE (noun) – [1] ***topos*** [masc. noun: τόπος <5117>] ▶ **a. Room, space** > There was no room (or: place) for Jesus and His parents in the inn (Luke 2:7). One might tell a guest to give place to another, such that he must take the last place (Luke 14:9a, b {seat}); one is rather to go and put oneself down in the last place (v. 10). The bondman told the master of the house that there was still room (or: place) at the great supper (Luke 14:22). Jesus was going to prepare a place (John 14:2), and then return (v. 3). Christians must give place unto {leave room for} wrath and not avenge themselves (Rom. 12:19). Paul spoke of him who fills the place of the simple (1 Cor. 14:16). Every mountain and island was removed out of their places (Rev. 6:14). The place of the dragon and his angels was not found any more in the heaven (Rev. 12:8). **b. Spot, location** > This term is used in the expr. "dry (arid) places" (Matt. 12:43; Luke 11:24), "deserted place" or "desert place" (Matt. 14:13, 15; Mark 1:45; 6:31, 32, 35; Luke 4:42; 9:10, 12), "solitary place" (Mark 1:35), the "holy place" of the temple (Matt. 24:15; Acts 6:13, 14; 21:28b), "level place" {plain} (Luke 6:17), and "place of torment" (Luke 16:28). The term is used in reference to Golgotha (Matt. 27:33; Mark 15:22; Luke 23:33; John 19:17, 20, 41; 20:7), Jerusalem (John 4:20), the Pavement (John 19:13), and Armageddon (Rev. 16:16). Other refs.: Matt. 14:35; 24:7; 26:52; 28:6; Mark 13:8; 16:6; Luke 4:37; 10:1, 32; 11:1; 19:5; 21:11; 22:40; John 5:13; 6:10, 23; 10:40; 11:6, 30, 48; 18:2; Acts 1:25; 4:31; 7:7, 33, 49; 12:17; 16:3 {region, quarters}; 21:28a; 27:2 {coasts}, 8, 29, 41; 28:7 {region, quarters}; Rom. 9:26; 1 Cor. 1:2; 2 Cor. 2:14; 1 Thes. 1:8; 1 Tim. 2:8 {everywhere}; Heb. 8:7; 11:8; 12:17; 2 Pet. 1:19; Rev. 2:5; 12:6, 14; 18:17 (lit.: all sailing to a place); 20:11. **c. Location (in a book)** > Jesus found a certain place in the book of the prophet Isaiah (Luke 4:17). **d. Opportunity, occasion** > The term is used in Rom. 15:23. All other refs.: COAST (noun) <5117>, OPPORTUNITY <5117>, ROCK <5117>.

[2] **chief place, place of honor, best place, first place: *prōtoklisia*** [fem. noun: πρωτοκλισία <4411>]; **from *prōtos*: first, and *klisia*: place to rest, to recline ▶ Principal seat at a table** > Jesus spoke of those who love the chief place at suppers (Matt. 23:6; Mark 12:39 {most important seat, chief seat}; Luke 14:7, 8; 20:46). ¶

[3] ***chōrion*** [neut. noun: χωρίον <5564>]; **dimin. of *chora*: country, region ▶ Region, domain** > The Greek term is used in ref. to Gethsemane (Matt. 26:36; Mark 14:32). All other refs.: FIELD <5564>, GROUND (noun)[1] <5564>, LAND (noun) <5564>.

[4] **to have a place: *chōreō*** [verb: χωρέω <5562>]; **from *chora*: country, region ▶ To enter, to penetrate** > The word of Jesus had no place {had no entrance, had no room} in the Jews (John 8:37). All other refs.: see entries in Lexicon at <5562>.

[5] **place where two ways meet: *amphodon*** [neut. noun: ἄμφοδον <296>]; **from *amphi*: around, or *amphō*: both, and *hodos*: way ▶ Crossroads, street** > The disciples found the colt in a place where two ways met {on the street, in the street, at the crossway} (Mark 11:4). Other ref.: Acts 19:28 in some mss. ¶

[6] **in a good place: *kalōs*** [adv.: καλῶς <2573>]; **from *kalos*: good, nice; lit.: well ▶ At ease, comfortably** > Telling someone rich to sit in a good place {in a good seat, well} in the church and someone poor to stand would be treating the two differently (Jas. 2:3). Other refs.: COMMENDABLY <2573>, WELL (adv.) <2573>.

7 **steep place: *krēmnos*** [masc. noun: κρημνός <2911>]**; from *kremannumi*: to hang ► Escarpment, precipice >** The whole herd of swine ran violently down the steep place {steep slope, steep bank} into the sea (Matt. 8:32; Mark 5:13; Luke 8:33). ¶

8 **secret place: *kruptē*** [fem. noun: κρύπτη <2926>]**; from *kruptos*: hidden, secret, which is from *kruptō*: to hide ► Hiding room >** A lighted candle is not put in a secret place {in secret, in a cellar, in a place where it will be hidden} (Luke 11:33). ¶

9 **to take place: *ginomai*** [verb: γίνομαι <1096>] **► To become, to happen >** Bondmen recounted all that had taken place (Matt. 18:31). Death took place for the redemption of transgressions (Heb. 9:15). The Greek verb is transl. variably "to be" (Matt. 24:20; Mark 13:18; Luke 23:19); "to be made" (Acts 15:7);"it had thundered" {it thundered; lit.: thunder to have occurred} (John 12:29); "to be done," "to take place" (Acts 10:16; 11:10); "to come to pass" (Acts 11:28b); and "to be past" (2 Tim. 2:18). Other refs.: Luke 1:20; 21:7, 32. Other refs.: see entries in Lexicon at <1096>.

10 **to give place: *eikō*** [verb: εἴκω <1502>]**; lit.: to back up ► To not resist, to submit >** Paul had not given place {yielded} by subjection {given in} to false brothers (Gal. 2:5). ¶

11 **to have the first place: *prōteuō*** [verb: πρωτεύω <4409>]**; from *prōtos*: first, foremost ► To occupy the position of honor; also transl.: to have the preeminence, to have the supremacy >** Christ must have the first place in all things (Col. 1:18). ¶

12 **he who is from that place: *entopios*** [adj.: ἐντόπιος <1786>]**; from *en*: in, and *topos*: place ► One who inhabits an area, one who is a native of an area, local resident >** Those of the place, i.e., from Caesarea, begged Paul not to go to Jerusalem (Acts 21:12 {people there}). ¶

– 13 Matt. 8:11; Luke 13:29 → to take a place → to sit down → SIT <347> 14 Matt. 9:24 → to give place → DEPART <402> 15 Matt. 15:33; Mark 8:4 → desert, desolate, remote place → WILDERNESS <2047> 16 Matt. 21:33 → to move to another place → to go to another country → COUNTRY <589> 17 Mark 12:39 → place of honor → first seat → SEAT (noun) <4410> 18 Mark 13:29; Acts 19:10 → to take place → CONTINUE <1096> 19 Luke 16:26 → to set in place → FIX <4741> 20 Luke 24:14 → to take place → HAPPEN <4819> 21 John 20:25b → MARK (noun) <5179> 22 John 21:9 → in place → lit.: lying 23 Acts 8:26 → this is a desert place → lit.: this is desert 24 Acts 8:32 → PASSAGE <4042> 25 Acts 18:23 → from place to place → SUCCESSIVELY <2517> 26 Acts 24:3 → all places → EVERYWHERE <3837> 27 Acts 28:23 → place where one stays → GUEST ROOM <3578> 28 Rom. 3:25 → to take place before → to commit previously → COMMIT <4266> 29 1 Cor. 7:17 → to retain the place → WALK <4043> 30 Gal. 3:17 → to take place → ARISE <1096> 31 Eph. 2:22; Rev. 18:2 → DWELLING PLACE <2732> 32 Eph. 4:27 → OPPORTUNITY <5117> 33 Eph. 5:4 → are out of place → are not fitting → FITTING (BE) <433> 34 Eph. 6:14 → with the breastplate of righteousness → lit.: having put it on → CLOTHE <1746> 35 Heb. 9:2, 24, 25; et al. → holy place, most holy place → SANCTUARY <39> 36 Jas. 3:11 → OPENING <3692>.

PLACE (verb) – 1 ***tassō*** [verb: τάσσω <5021>] **► To set, to post >** The centurion was a man placed under authority (Luke 7:8). All other refs.: APPOINT <5021>.

2 ***epitithēmi*** [verb: ἐπιτίθημι <2007>]**; from *epi*: on, and *tithēmi*: to put ► To put, to set >** The Lord placed {laid} His right hand on John (Rev. 1:17); other mss. have *tithēmi*. All other refs.: see entries in Lexicon at <2007>.

– 3 Matt. 18:2; 25:33; Mark 9:36; John 8:3; Acts 4:7 → SET (verb) <2476> 4 Mark 6:56; Acts 13:47; 1 Cor. 12:18 → SET (verb) <5087> 5 Mark 10:13; Luke 18:15 → to place one's hand → TOUCH <680> 6 Mark 10:16; Acts 5:15 → LAY <5087> 7 Mark 15:46 → LAY <2698> 8 Luke 10:8; 1 Cor. 10:27 → SET (verb) <3908> 9 John 3:35; Rev. 3:8 → GIVE <1325> 10 John 20:27 → PUT <906> 11 John 21:9 → to place upon → to lay on → LAY <1945> 12 Acts 1:7 → FIX <5087> 13 Acts 13:47 → APPOINT <5087> 14 Eph. 6:12 → heavenly place → HEAVENLY <2032> 15 Rev. 2:24 → IMPOSE <906> 16 Rev. 11:9 → PUT <5087>.

PLACE OF HOLINESS – Heb. 9:1 → SANCTUARY <39>.

PLAGUE – 1 ***plēgē*** [fem. noun: πληγή <4127>]; **from *plēssō*: to strike ► Blow; also transl.: stripe, wound** > The word is frequently used in Rev. with the sense of "calamity" (9:18, 20; 11:6; 15:1, 6, 8; 16:9, 21a, b; 18:4, 8; 21:9; 22:18). The first beast of Rev. 13 had been healed of his deadly wound (vv. 3, 12); this plague is called the "wound of the sword" (v. 14). The jailer washed the wounds of Paul and Silas (Acts 16:33). All other refs.: STRIPE <4127>, WOUND (verb) <4127>.

– 2 Mark 3:10; 5:29, 34; Luke 7:21 → AFFLICTION <3148> 3 Luke 21:11 → PESTILENCE <3061> 4 Acts 24:5 → PEST <3061>.

PLAIN (adj.) – 1 Mark 7:35 → PLAINLY <3723> 2 Rom. 1:19 → MANIFEST (adj.) <5318> 3 1 Cor. 15:27 → EVIDENT <1212> 4 2 Cor. 11:6; 1 John 2:19 → to make plain, to become plain → MANIFEST (verb) <5319> 5 Eph. 3:9 → to make plain → to bring to light → LIGHT <5461> 6 2 Tim. 3:9 → MANIFEST (adj.) <1552>.

PLAIN (noun) – 1 Luke 6:17 → lit.: level place → LEVEL (adj.) <3977>, PLACE (noun) <5117> 2 Rev. 20:9 → broad plain → BREATH <4114>.

PLAINLY – 1 ***orthōs*** [adv.: ὀρθῶς <3723>]; **from *orthos*: right; lit.: rightly ► Distinctly, correctly; also transl.: right** > The deaf man with the impediment of his tongue could speak plainly {plain} once Jesus healed him (Mark 7:35). The word is transl. "rightly" {correctly} in Luke 10:28. Other refs.: Luke 7:43; 20:21; see RIGHTLY <3723>. ¶

2 ***phanerōs*** [adv.: φανερῶς <5320>]; **from *phainō*: to shine, which is from *phōs*: light ► Distinctly, clearly** > Cornelius saw plainly {clearly, evidently} in a vision an angel of God addressing himself to him (Acts 10:3). Other refs.: Mark 1:45; John 7:10; see OPENLY <5320>. ¶

3 **to declare plainly: *emphanizō*** [verb: ἐμφανίζω <1718>]; **from *emphanēs*: manifest, known, which is from *en*: in, and *phainō*: see 2 ► To demonstrate, to prove** > Those who confess they are strangers and pilgrims on the earth declare plainly {show, show clearly, make it clear} that they seek a homeland (Heb. 11:14). All other refs.: APPEAR <1718>, CHARGE[1] <1718>, MANIFEST (verb) <1718>, REVEAL <1718>, SIGNIFY <1718>.

– 4 Matt. 7:23 → to tell plainly → DECLARE <3670> 5 Mark 8:32; John 11:14; 16:25, 29 → OPENLY <3954> 6 John 9:3 → to see plainly → MANIFEST (verb) <5319> 7 John 10:24 → lit.: with boldness → BOLDNESS <3954> 8 2 Cor. 4:2 → by setting forth plainly → lit.: by manifestation of → MANIFESTATION <5321>.

PLAINNESS – 2 Cor. 3:12 → BOLDNESS <3954>.

PLAIT – Mark 15:17; John 19:2 → to twist together → TWIST <4120>.

PLAITED HAIR – 1 Tim. 2:9 → BRAIDED HAIR <4117>.

PLAITING – 1 Pet. 3:3 → BRAIDING <1708>.

PLAN (noun) – 1 ***boulē*** [fem. noun: βουλή <1012>]; **from *boulomai*: to want ► Will, purpose, scheme** > In relation to the preaching of the apostles, Gamaliel said that if this plan {counsel} or this work had its origin from men, it would be destroyed (Acts 5:38). All other refs.: COUNSEL (noun) <1012>.

– 2 Matt. 1:19 → to have in mind → PURPOSE (verb) <1014> 3 Matt. 22:15; 27:1; Mark 15:1 → COUNCIL <4824>,

COUNSEL (noun) <4824> [4] John 11:53 → to make plans → to take counsel together → COUNSEL (noun) <4823> [5] John 12:10 → to make plans → CONSULT <1011> [6] Acts 9:24 → PLOT (noun) <1917> [7] Acts 25:3 → to plan an ambush → lit.: to make (*poieō*) an ambush → MAKE <4160>, AMBUSH <1747> [8] Acts 27:43 → PURPOSE (noun) <1013> [9] Eph. 1:10; 3:9 → DISPENSATION <3622> [10] Eph. 1:11 → PURPOSE (noun) <4286>.

PLAN (verb) – [1] Matt. 1:19 → PURPOSE (verb) <1014> [2] John 11:53 → to plan together → to take counsel together → COUNSEL (noun) <4823> [3] Acts 27:39 → RESOLVE (verb) <1011> [4] Acts 27:42 → lit.: plan → COUNSEL (noun) <1012> [5] Rom. 1:13 → PURPOSE (verb) <4388> [6] 2 Cor. 1:17 → PROPOSE <1011> [7] Heb. 11:40 → FORESEE <4265>.

PLANK – [1] Matt. 7:3–5; Luke 6:41, 42a, b → BEAM <1385> [2] Acts 27:44 → BOARD (noun) <4548>.

PLANT (noun) – [1] ***phuteia*** [fem. noun: φυτεία <5451>]; **from *phuteuō*: to plant, which is from *phuō*: to grow ▶ Vegetation emerging from the soil** > Every plant that the Father has not planted will be rooted up (Matt. 15:13). ¶
[2] **garden plant: *lachanon*** [neut. noun: λάχανον <3001>]; **from *lachainō*: to dig ▶ Garden herb, vegetable; also transl.: herb** > The grain of mustard seed becomes larger than all the garden plants (Matt. 13:32; Mark 4:32). The Pharisees paid tithes of every kind of garden herbs (Luke 11:42). One Christian believes he may eat all things, a weak Christian eats vegetables only (Rom. 14:2). ¶
– [3] Matt. 13:26 → BLADE <5528> [4] Rev. 9:4 → lit.: green thing → GREEN <5515>.

PLANT (verb) – [1] ***phuteuō*** [verb: φυτεύω <5452>]; **from *phuton*: plant, which is from *phuō*: to generate, to grow ▶ To put a plant into the earth so it may grow; also used figur.** > Every plant that the Father has not planted will be rooted up (Matt. 15:13). A landowner planted a vineyard (Matt. 21:33); Mark and Luke speak of a man who planted a vineyard (Mark 12:1; Luke 20:9). A certain man had a fig tree planted in his vineyard (Luke 13:6). With faith, one can tell a mulberry tree to be rooted up and be planted in the sea (Luke 17:6); *metaphuteuō* in some mss.: to transplant. In the days of Lot people planted (Luke 17:28). Paul had planted and Apollos had watered (1 Cor. 3:6); neither is he who plants anything, nor he who waters (v. 7); he who plants and he who waters are one (v. 8). He who plants a vineyard eats of its fruit (1 Cor. 9:7). ¶
– [2] Matt. 13:31; Mark 4:31, 32; 1 Cor. 15:37b → SOW (verb) <4687>.

PLANTED – [1] Rom. 6:5 → planted together → lit.: same plant → IDENTIFIED <4854> [2] Jas. 1:21 → IMPLANTED <1721>.

PLANTER – 1 Cor. 3:7, 8 → lit.: he who plants → PLANT (verb) <5452>.

PLAT – Matt. 27:29; Mark 15:17; John 19:2 → to twist together → TWIST <4120>.

PLATE – Matt. 23:25, 26 → DISH <3953>.

PLATTER – [1] Matt. 14:8, 11; Mark 6:25, 28; Luke 11:39 → DISH <4094> [2] Matt. 23:25, 26 → DISH <3953>.

PLAUSIBLE – [1] 1 Cor. 2:4 → PERSUASIVE <3981> [2] Col. 2:4 → plausible arguments → persuasive words → WORD <4086>.

PLAY – [1] ***paizō*** [verb: παίζω <3815>]; **from *pais*: child ▶ To entertain oneself, to revel** > The Israelites rose up to play {to indulge in revelry} (1 Cor. 10:7). ¶
– [2] Matt. 9:23 → people playing pipes → FLUTE PLAYER <834> [3] 1 Cor. 14:7 → to play on the harp → HARP (noun) <2789> [4] Gal. 2:13 → to play the hypocrite → HYPOCRITE <4942>.

PLAYMATE – Matt. 11:16 → COMPANION <2083>.

PLEAD – [1] ***entunchanō*** [verb: ἐντυγχάνω <1793>]; **from *en*: in, and *tunchanō*: to meet ▶ To solicit, to intercede; also transl.: to appeal, to make intercession >** Elijah pleaded with God against Israel (Rom. 11:2). All other refs.: INTERCEDE <1793>, PETITION (verb) <1793>.

[2] **to plead with: *parakaleō*** [verb: παρακαλέω <3870>]; **from *para*: beside, and *kaleō*: to call ▶ To address, to pray, to implore; also transl.: to ask, to beg, to beseech, to entreat, to exhort, to urge >** A centurion pleaded with Jesus regarding his paralyzed servant (Matt. 8:5). The Greek verb is also used in regard to a servant (Matt. 18:29), a leper (Mark 1:40), Jairus (Mark 5:23; Luke 8:41), friends of Paul (Acts 21:12), and Paul (1 Cor. 4:13 {to intreat, to answer kindly, to try to conciliate}, 16; 2 Cor. 12:8; Phil. 4:2a, b). All other refs.: see entries in Lexicon at <3870>.

– [3] Luke 7:3; 2 John 5 → ASK <2065> [4] 2 Cor. 8:4 → IMPLORE <1189>.

PLEASE – [1] ***areskō*** [verb: ἀρέσκω <700>]; **from *arō*: to fit, to adapt ▶ To be agreeable, to be a source of pleasure >** The daughter of Herodias pleased Herod (Matt. 14:6; Mark 6:22). The saying of the twelve pleased {found approval with} the multitude (Acts 6:5). Those who are in the flesh cannot please God (Rom. 8:8). Those who are strong ought not to please themselves (Rom. 15:1). Each Christian is to please his neighbor (Rom. 15:2). Christ did not please Himself (Rom. 15:3). Paul speaks of pleasing the Lord (1 Cor. 7:32), one's wife (v. 33), and one's husband (v. 34). On the one hand, Paul was pleasing all men in all things, seeking the profit of many, that they might be saved (1 Cor. 10:33), and, on the other hand, he knew that if he still was trying to please men, he would not be a bond-servant of Christ (Gal. 1:10a, b). He did not speak as pleasing men, but God (1 Thes. 2:4). He mentions those who do not please {displease} God (1 Thes. 2:15). The Thessalonians were to please God (1 Thes. 4:1). One going as a soldier is to please him who has enlisted him (2 Tim. 2:4). ¶

[2] **all pleasing, all well-pleasing: *areskeia*** [fem. noun: ἀρεσκεία <699>]; **from *areskō*: to please ▶ Desire, endeavor to be agreeable, to please >** Paul prayed that the Colossians might walk worthily of the Lord unto all well-pleasing {to please Him in every way, to please Him in all respects, to fully please Him} (Col. 1:10). ¶

[3] ***euaresteō*** [verb: εὐαρεστέω <2100>]; **from *euarestos*: well-pleasing, which is from *eu*: well, and *areskō*: to be agreeable, which is from *arō*: to fit, to adapt ▶ To be agreeable, to occasion pleasure >** Enoch had the testimony that he had pleased God (Heb. 11:5). Without faith it is impossible to please God (Heb. 11:6). Other ref.: Heb. 13:16; see PLEASED (BE) <2100>. ¶

[4] ***boulomai*** [verb: βούλομαι <1014>] **▶ To will (with a determined purpose), to determine >** The Spirit divides to each one in particular according as He pleases (1 Cor. 12:11). Other refs.: ADVISE <1014>, PURPOSE (verb) <1014>, WANT (verb) <1014>, WILL (verb) <1014>.

– [5] Matt. 17:12; Mark 9:13 → WANT (verb) <2309> [6] Luke 2:14 → men with whom He is pleased → lit.: good pleasure in men → PLEASURE <2107> [7] Luke 14:18 → ASK <2065> [8] John 8:29; Acts 12:3; 1 John 3:22 → PLEASING <701> [9] Acts 8:34 → please tell me → lit.: I ask you → PRAY <1189> [10] Acts 15:22 → THINK <1380> [11] 2 Cor. 5:9; Eph. 5:10 → ACCEPTABLE <2101> [12] Gal. 1:10 → to strive to please → PERSUADE <3982> [13] Col. 3:20; Titus 2:9 → to please, to please well, to try to please → lit.: to be well pleasing → PLEASING <2101> [14] Col. 3:22 → one who merely pleases men → MEN-PLEASER <441> [15] 1 Tim. 2:3; 5:4 → lit.: pleasing → ACCEPTABLE <587>.

PLEASED (BE) – [1] ***euaresteō*** [verb: εὐαρεστέω <2100>]; **from *euarestos*: well pleasing, which is from *eu*: well, and *areskō*: to be agreeable, which is from *arō*: to fit, to adapt ▶ To find agreeable, to give approval; also transl.: to be well pleased >** God is pleased with the sacrifice of doing good and sharing (Heb. 13:16). Other refs.: Heb. 11:5, 6; see PLEASE <2100>. ¶

[2] ***eudokeō*** [verb: εὐδοκέω <2106>]; **from *eu*: well, and *dokeō*: to think, to appear ▶ a. To take delight in, to approve; also transl.: to find one's delight, to delight** > God the Father was well pleased in His beloved Son (Matt. 3:17; 17:5; Mark 1:11; Luke 3:22; 2 Pet. 1:17) and His servant, whom He had chosen, His beloved (Matt. 12:18). The Christians in Macedonia and Achaia had been well pleased to minister to the needs of the poor among the saints in Jerusalem (Rom. 15:26, 27). God was not pleased {was not well pleased} with most of the Israelites before their entry into the promised land (1 Cor. 10:5). Paul was well pleased to be absent from the body and present with the Lord (2 Cor. 5:8). The verb is transl. "to take pleasure" in 2 Cor. 12:10: Paul took pleasure {was well content} in weaknesses. He was well pleased {was willing, found his delight, was delighted} to impart to the Thessalonians not only the gospel of God, but also his own life (1 Thes. 2:8). Those who have found pleasure in unrighteousness will be judged (2 Thes. 2:12). God was not pleased {took no pleasure} in burnt offerings and sacrifices for sin (Heb. 10:6, 8). If someone shrinks back, the soul of God does not take pleasure in him (Heb. 10:38). **b. To seem good, to find good; also transl.: to choose gladly, to be the good pleasure** > It has pleased {been the pleasure of} the Father to give the kingdom to the little flock (Luke 12:32). God has been pleased {was well-pleased} by the foolishness of the preaching to save those who believe (1 Cor. 1:21). God was pleased to reveal His Son in Paul (Gal. 1:15). All the fullness of the Godhead was pleased to dwell in the Son (Col. 1:19). Other refs.: Rom. 15:26; 1 Thes. 3:1; see THINK <2106>. ¶

– [3] Matt. 11:26 → to be well-pleasing → WELL PLEASING <2107>.

PLEASING – [1] ***arestos*** [adj.: ἀρεστός <701>]; **from *areskō*: to please, to be agreeable, which is from *arō*: to fit, to adapt ▶ Acceptable, agreeable, worthy of being approved** > Jesus always did the things that were pleasing to {that pleased} the Father who had sent Him (John 8:29). Herod saw it pleased (lit.: was pleasing) to the Jews to do harm to those of the church (Acts 12:3). John writes concerning doing those things that are pleasing in the sight of {that please} (lit.: those pleasing things to) God (1 John 3:22). Other ref.: Acts 6:2; see DESIRABLE <701>. ¶

[2] **well pleasing to God: *asteios tō Theō*; *asteios*** [adj.: ἀστεῖος <791>], ***Theos*** [masc. noun: Θεός <2316>] **▶ Agreeable to God** > Moses was well pleasing to {lovely in the sight of, fair in the sight of} God {was exceedingly fair, was exceedingly lovely} (Acts 7:20). Other ref. (*asteios*): Heb. 11:23; see BEAUTIFUL <791>. ¶

[3] **well-pleasing: *euarestos*** [adj.: εὐάρεστος <2101>]; **from *eu*: well, and *arestos*: see [1] ▶ Acceptable, agreeable** > It is well pleasing unto {It pleases} the Lord for children to obey their parents (Col. 3:20). Servants are exhorted to be well pleasing to {try to please} their own masters in all things (Titus 2:9). All other refs.: ACCEPTABLE <2101>.

– [4] 2 Cor. 2:15 → pleasing aroma → sweet odor → ODOR <2175> [5] 1 Tim. 2:3 → ACCEPTABLE <587>.

PLEASURE – [1] ***apolausis*** [fem. noun: ἀπόλαυσις <619>]; **from *apolauō*: to enjoy, which is from *apo*: from, and *lauō*: to enjoy ▶ Delight, enjoyment** > God gives us all things richly to enjoy (lit.: for our pleasure) (1 Tim. 6:17). Moses chose rather to suffer affliction with the people of God than to enjoy the temporary pleasures (but sing. in Greek) of sin (Heb. 11:25). ¶

[2] **good pleasure: *eudokia*** [fem. noun: εὐδοκία <2107>]; **from *eudokeō*: to please, which is from *eu*: well, and *dokeō*: to think, to appear ▶ Benevolence, kindness, goodwill, satisfaction; also transl.: intention, purpose** > A multitude of the heavenly host said: Good pleasure in {Good will toward} men (Luke 2:14). God has marked out Christians beforehand for adoption through Jesus Christ to Himself, according to the good pleasure of His will (Eph. 1:5). He has made known to them the mystery of His will, according to His good pleasure (Eph. 1:9). God works in Christians

both the willing and the working according to His good pleasure (Phil. 2:13). Paul prayed that God might fulfill all the good pleasure {desire, purpose} of His goodness in the Thessalonians (2 Thes. 1:11). All other refs.: DESIRE (noun) <2107>, WELL PLEASING <2107>, WILL (noun)[1] <2107>.

3 ***hēdonē*** [fem. noun: ἡδονή <2237>]; **from *handanō*: to please, or *hēdos*: delight, which is from *hēdomai*: to have sensual pleasure, sensual delight; also transl.: desire, lust ▶ Enjoyment, gratification, voluptuousness** > The pleasures of life can choke the word of God (Luke 8:14). Christians once were enslaved to various lusts and pleasures (Titus 3:3). Pleasures battle in the members of the body (Jas. 4:1). Some asked so that they might spend it on their pleasures (Jas. 4:3). Peter spoke of those who count it pleasure to revel in the daytime (2 Pet. 2:13). ¶

4 **to live in pleasure: *truphaō*** [verb: τρυφάω <5171>]; **from *truphē*: luxury, sensual life ▶ To live luxuriously, to live a sensual life** > James reproaches the rich for having lived in pleasure {lived in luxury} (Jas. 5:5). ¶

5 **to live in pleasure: *spatalaō*** [verb: σπαταλάω <4684>]; **from *spatalē*: luxury ▶ To lead a luxurious life of voluptuousness and entertainment** > The believing widow who lives in pleasure {who lives for pleasure, who gives herself to wanton pleasure, who lives in habits of self-indulgence} is dead while living (1 Tim. 5:6). Other ref.: Jas. 5:5 (to live in self-indulgence); see SELF-INDULGENCE <4684>. ¶

– 6 Luke 12:32; 2 Cor. 12:10; Col. 1:19; 2 Thes. 2:12; Heb. 10:6, 8, 38 → to be the good pleasure; to find, to have, to take pleasure → PLEASED (BE) <2106> 7 Acts 24:27; 25:9 → FAVOR (noun) <5485> 8 Rom. 1:32 → to have pleasure → APPROVE <4909> 9 2 Tim. 3:4 → lover of pleasure → LOVER <5369> 10 Heb. 12:10 → after their own pleasure → as they thought best → to think best → THINK <1380> 11 Jas. 3:4 → INCLINATION <3730> 12 2 Pet. 2:13b → DECEITFULNESS <539>.

PLEDGE (noun) – 1 Acts 17:9 → SECURITY <2425> 2 2 Cor. 1:22; Eph. 1:14 → EARNEST (noun) <728> 3 1 Pet. 3:21 → ANSWER (noun) <1906>.

PLEDGE (verb) – 1 Cor. 7:27 → pledged to a woman → bound to a wife → BIND <1210>.

PLENTIFUL – John 3:23 → water was plentiful → lit.: there were many waters.

PLENTIFULLY – Luke 12:16 → to bring forth plentifully, to yield plentifully → to bring forth plentifully → BRING <2164>.

PLENTY – 1 2 Cor. 8:14a, b → ABUNDANCE <4051> 2 Phil. 4:12a, b → to have plenty, to live in plenty → ABOUND <4052>.

PLOT (noun) – 1 ***epiboulē*** [fem. noun: ἐπιβουλή <1917>]; **from *epi*: against, and *boulē*: plan, purpose ▶ Secret project to try to kill someone; conspiracy, trap; also transl.: lying in wait, plotting** > Paul learned of the plot {plan, laying await} of the Jews to kill him (Acts 9:24). The Jews set a treacherous plot {plotted} against Paul (Acts 20:3, 19). The word is also used in Acts 23:30 {to lay wait, to lay in wait}. ¶

– 2 Luke 11:54; Acts 23:21 → to plot against → to wait in ambush → AMBUSH <1748> 3 Acts 14:5 → ATTEMPT (noun) <3730> 4 Acts 23:12 → to make a plot → lit.: to form a conspiracy → CONSPIRACY <4963> 5 Acts 23:13 → CONSPIRACY <4945> 6 Acts 23:16 → AMBUSH <1749>.

PLOT (verb) – 1 Matt. 12:14; 22:15; 27:1; Mark 3:6 → COUNCIL <4824>, COUNSEL (noun) <4824> 2 Matt. 26:4; Acts 9:23 → CONSULT <4823> 3 John 11:53 → to take counsel together → COUNSEL (noun) <4823> 4 John 12:10; Acts 5:33 → CONSULT <1011> 5 Acts 4:25 → MEDITATE <3191> 6 Acts 20:3 → PLOT (noun) <1917>.

PLOTTING – 1 ***methodeia*** [fem. noun: μεθοδεία <3180>]; **from *meta*: particle of**

change, and *hodos*: way, road, or *methodeuō*: to work with method ▶ Method to do evil, wile > There are men who are capable of deceitful plotting {are capable of deceitful scheming, lie in wait to deceive} (Eph. 4:14). Other ref.: Eph. 6:11; see WILE <3180>. ¶
– [2] Acts 20:19 → PLOT <1917>.

PLOUGH – See PLOW <723>.

PLOUGHMAN – See PLOWMAN <723>.

PLOW (noun) – ***arotron*** [neut. noun: ἄροτρον <723>]; **from *aroō*: to plow ▶ Instrument used to work the soil** > No one, having put his hand to the plow, and looking back, is fit for the kingdom of God (Luke 9:62). ¶

PLOW (verb) – ***arotriaō*** [verb: ἀροτριάω <722>]; **from *arotron*: plow ▶ To till the earth in preparation for sowing, to cultivate** > Jesus speaks of a servant plowing (Luke 17:7). He who plows {The plowman} (in the figur. sense: one who serves the Lord) should plow (i.e., should serve) in hope (1 Cor. 9:10a, b). ¶

PLOWMAN – 1 Cor. 9:10a → lit.: he who plows → PLOW (verb) <722>.

PLUCK – [1] **to pluck out: *ekballō*** [verb: ἐκβάλλω <1544>]; **from *ek*: out, and *ballō*: to throw ▶ To draw out with force** > Jesus speaks figur. of plucking out one's eye if it is causing one to sin (Mark 9:47). All other refs.: see entries in Lexicon at <1544>.
[2] **to pluck out: *exaireō*** [verb: ἐξαιρέω <1807>]; **from *ek*: out, and *haireō*: to take ▶ To remove, to extirpate** > Jesus speaks figur. of plucking out {gouging out} one's eye and casting it from oneself if it is causing one to sin (Matt. 5:29 {tearing out}; 18:9). All other refs.: DELIVER <1807>, TAKE <1807>.
[3] **to pluck out: *exorussō*** [verb: ἐξορύσσω <1846>]; **from *ek*: out, and *orussō*: to dig; lit.: to dig out ▶ To remove, to extirpate** > If it had been possible, the Christians in Galatia would have plucked out {have torn out} their own eyes and given them to Paul (Gal. 4:15). Other ref.: Mark 2:4; see DIG <1846>. ¶
[4] ***tillō*** [verb: τίλλω <5089>] **▶ To pull, to remove** > The disciples of Jesus began to pluck {pick} the ears of corn, and to eat, on a Sabbath day (Matt. 12:1; Mark 2:23; Luke 6:1). ¶
– [5] Mark 5:4 → to pluck asunder → to tear apart → TEAR (verb) <1288> [6] Luke 17:6; Jude 12 → to pluck up by the roots → UPROOT <1610> [7] John 10:28, 29 → SEIZE <726>.

PLUNDER (noun) – [1] Luke 11:22 → SPOILS <4661> [2] Luke 11:39 → ROBBERY <724> [3] Heb. 7:4 → SPOILS <205> [4] Heb. 10:34 → PLUNDERING <724>.

PLUNDER (verb) – ***diarpazō*** [verb: διαρπάζω <1283>]; **from *dia*: intens., and *harpazō*: to seize ▶ To spoil, to take by force; also transl.: to carry off, to rob** > The strong man must first be bound before one can enter into his house and plunder {spoil} his goods (Matt. 12:29a, b; Mark 3:27a, b). ¶

PLUNDERING – ***harpagē*** [fem. noun: ἁρπαγή <724>]; **from *harpazō*: to seize with force ▶ Robbery, taking away** > Hebrew Christians had accepted joyfully the plundering {confiscation, plunder, seizure, spoiling} of their goods, knowing that they had a better and enduring possession in heaven (Heb. 10:34). Other refs.: Matt. 23:25; Luke 11:39; see ROBBERY <724>. ¶

PLUNGE – [1] ***buthizō*** [verb: βυθίζω <1036>]; **from *buthos*: the depth ▶ To drown, to send to the bottom** > Those who desire to be rich fall into unwise and hurtful lusts, which plunge men into destruction and ruin (1 Tim. 6:9). Other ref.: Luke 5:7; see SINK (verb) <1036>. ¶
– [2] 1 Pet. 4:4 → to run together → RUN <4936>.

POD – Luke 15:16 → HUSK <2769>.

POET – ***poiētēs*** [masc. noun: ποιητής <4163>]; **from *poieō*: to make, to create ► Author of a poem or song** > Paul quoted to the Athenians the words of their poets (Acts 17:28). Other refs.: Rom. 2:13; Jas. 1:22, 23, 25; 4:11; see DOER <4163>. ¶

POINT (noun) – [1] Mark 5:23 → at the point of death → at extremity → EXTREMITY <2079> [2] Luke 7:2 → at the point of death → about (to be about: *mellō*) to die [3] Acts 25:19 → point of disagreement, point of dispute → QUESTION (noun) <2213> [4] 2 Cor. 9:6 → "the point is" added in Engl. [5] Phil. 2:27 → to the point → CLOSE (adj. and adv.) <3897> [6] Heb. 8:1 → point, main point → SUM <2774>.

POINT (verb) – [1] **to point out: *hupotithēmi*** [verb: ὑποτίθημι <5294>]; **from *hupo*: under, and *tithēmi*: to put ► To expose, to suggest** > Timothy was to point out certain things to the brothers (1 Tim. 4:6 {to instruct, to lay before, to put in remembrance}). Other ref.: Rom. 16:4; see RISK <5294>. ¶

– [2] Matt. 12:49 → to stretch out → STRETCH <1614> [3] Matt. 18:15 → to point out the fault to → REPROVE <1651> [4] Matt. 24:1 → to point out → SHOW (verb) <1925> [5] 1 Cor. 10:28 → to point out → SHOW (verb) <3377> [6] 1 Pet. 1:11 → to point out → INDICATE <1213>.

POISON (noun) – ***ios*** [masc. noun: ἰός <2447>]; ***virus*, in Lat. ► Specifically, an animal's poison; venom, the poison in the mouth of a serpent** > Paul quotes a Psalm that speaks of wicked men who have the poison of asps under their lips (Rom. 3:13). The tongue is a restless evil, full of deadly poison (Jas. 3:8). Other ref.: Jas. 5:3; see RUST <2447>. ¶

POISON (verb) – [1] ***kakoō*** [verb: κακόω <2559>]; **from *kakos*: bad ► To embitter, to put in a bad disposition** > The unbelieving Jews poisoned {made evil-affected} the minds of those of the nations against the brothers (Acts 14:2). All other refs.: HURT (verb) <2559>, OPPRESS <2559>.

– [2] Acts 8:23 → to be poisoned by bitterness → lit.: to be in the gall of bitterness → GALL <5521>.

POLE – Gal. 3:13 → hung on a pole → hanged on a tree → TREE <3586>.

POLICE – Acts 16:35, 38 → OFFICER <4465>.

POLICEMAN – Acts 16:35, 38 → OFFICER <4465>.

POLITARCH – Acts 17:6, 8 → ruler of the city → RULER <4173>.

POLL-TAX – Matt. 17:25; 22:17, 19; Mark 12:14 → TRIBUTE <2778>.

POLLUTE – [1] Acts 21:28 → DEFILE <2840> [2] Jude 8 → DEFILE <3392> [3] Jude 23 → DEFILE <4695>.

POLLUTED – [1] **food polluted, thing polluted: *alisgēma*** [neut. noun: ἀλίσγημα <234>]; **from *alisgeō*: to defile, to pollute ► Something contaminated, defiled object** > Christians are to abstain from things polluted {pollutions, things contaminated} by idols (Acts 15:20). ¶

– [2] Jas. 1:27 → from being polluted → UNSPOTTED <784>.

POLLUTION – [1] Acts 15:20 → thing polluted → POLLUTED <234> [2] 2 Cor. 7:1 → DEFILEMENT <3436> [3] 2 Pet. 2:20 → DEFILEMENT <3393>.

POMP – ***phantasia*** [fem. noun: φαντασία <5325>]; **from *phantazō*: to make visible, to show, which is from *phainō*: to appear, which is from *phōs*: light ► Pageantry, deployment of magnificence** > Agrippa and Bernice came with great pomp to hear Paul (Acts 25:23). ¶

POND – Jas. 3:12 → FOUNTAIN <4077>.

PONDER – [1] ***sumballō*** [verb: συμβάλλω <4820>]; **from *sun*: together, and *ballō*: to throw ▶ To consider, to reflect >** Mary pondered in her heart the things that the angel had said (Luke 2:19). All other refs.: CONFER <4820>, HELP (verb) <4820>, MEET (verb) <4820>.
– [2] Matt. 1:20; Acts 10:19 → THINK <1760> [3] Luke 1:29 → REASON (verb) <1260>.

PONTIUS PILATE – ***Pontios*** [masc. name: Πόντιος <4194>] ***Pilatos*** [masc. name: Πιλᾶτος <4091>] **▶ Governor of Judea >** Pilate ruled from A.D. 26 to 36 (Luke 3:1). Jesus was delivered to him by the chief priests and elders of the people to be put to death (Matt. 27:2; Mark 15:1; Luke 23:1, 3; Acts 3:13; 13:28). These Jews accused Jesus of perverting the Jewish nation, forbidding them to give tribute to Caesar, and proclaiming Himself to be the Christ, the king of the Jews; but Jesus did not defend Himself before Pilate. Paul reminds Timothy of the good confession that Jesus made before Pontius Pilate, in connection with maintaining the truth (1 Tim. 6:13). Pilate proposed to the crowd to release Jesus rather than Barabbas. After the crowd chose Barabbas, Pilate declared himself to be innocent of the blood of Jesus, whom he called righteous. Pilate released Barabbas, had Jesus scourged, and delivered Him up to be crucified (see Matt. 27:11–26; Mark 15:2–15; Luke 23:2–25; John 18:28 to 19:16; Acts 4:27). He placed a title on the cross with the words: "Jesus the Nazarene, the king of the Jews" (see John 19:17–22). Pilate commanded that the dead body of Jesus be given to Joseph of Arimathea; he gave the Jews permission to secure the tomb with a watch (see Matt. 27:57–66; Mark 15:42–45; Luke 23:50–53; John 19:38). Tradition relates that Pilate was obliged to go to Rome, was banished to Gaul, and committed suicide. *

PONTUS – [1] ***Pontos*** [masc. name: Πόντος <4195>]; **sea, from the name of the Black Sea, which borders this county ▶ Region in the northeast of Asia Minor >** Jews of Pontus were present in Jerusalem at Pentecost (Acts 2:9). Peter addresses his first letter to the Christians of Pontus, among others (1 Pet. 1:1). ¶
[2] **of Pontus, in Pontus: *Pontikos*** [adj.: Ποντικός <4193>] **▶ Who inhabits this region >** Aquila and Priscilla were natives of {born in} Pontus (Acts 18:2). ¶

POOL – ***kolumbēthra*** [fem. noun: κολυμβήθρα <2861>]; **from *kolumbaō*: to swim ▶ Reservoir, a small body of water >** There were two pools at Jerusalem (John 5:2, 3 (or 4) in some mss., 7; John 9:7, 11 in some mss.). See BETHESDA and SILOAM. ¶

POOR (adj.) – [1] ***penichros*** [adj.: πενιχρός <3998>]; **from *penomai*: to toil for one's daily subsistence ▶ Needy, indigent >** A poor widow put two mites in the treasury of the temple (Luke 21:2). ¶
[2] ***ptōchos*** [adj.: πτωχός <4434>]; **from *ptōssō*: to hide, to crouch (like a beggar) ▶ Deprived of wealth, needy; possibly reduced to begging >** A poor widow cast two mites into the treasury of the temple (Mark 12:42, 43; Luke 21:3). Paul was poor, but enriching many (2 Cor. 6:10). Laodicea is poor (Rev. 3:17). All other refs.: BEGGARLY <4434>, POOR (noun) <4434>.
[3] **to become poor: *ptōcheuō*** [verb: πτωχεύω <4433>]; **from *ptōchos*: see [2] ▶ To live in poverty, to become indigent >** The Lord became poor for us (2 Cor. 8:9). ¶
– [4] Luke 16:20, 22; Rom. 15:26; Jas. 2:2, 3, 5, 6 → poor man, poor → POOR (noun) <4434> [5] John 2:10 → LESSER <1640>.

POOR (noun) – [1] ***penēs*** [adj. used as noun: πένης <3993>]; **from *penomai*: to toil for one's daily subsistence ▶ Needy, indigent person >** God has given to the poor (2 Cor. 9:9). ¶
[2] ***ptōchos*** [adj. used as noun: πτωχός <4434>]; **from *ptōssō*: to hide, to crouch (like a beggar) ▶ Person who is deprived of wealth, needy; possibly reduced to begging >** Jesus said that the poor in spirit are blessed (Matt. 5:3). He preached the glad tidings to the poor (Matt. 11:5; Luke 4:18;

7:22). He spoke of giving to the poor (Matt. 19:21; Mark 10:21; Luke 18:22). We will always have the poor with us (Matt. 26:11; Mark 14:7; John 12:8). The poor are blessed for the kingdom of God is theirs (Luke 6:20). Lazarus, in a parable, was a poor man {beggar} (Luke 16:20, 22). Zaccheus gave half of his goods to the poor (Luke 19:8). The believers of Macedonia and Achaia made a certain contribution for the poor of the saints who were in Jerusalem (Rom. 15:26). Other refs.: Matt. 26:9; Mark 14:5; Luke 14:13, 21; John 12:5, 6; 13:29; Gal. 2:10; Jas. 2:2, 3, 5, 6; Rev. 13:16. All other refs.: BEGGARLY <4434>, POOR (adj.) <4434>.

– 3 Luke 11:41; 12:33; Acts 9:36; 10:4, 31; 24:17 → to give to the poor, to help the poor, gifts to the poor → lit.: to give alms, to do alms-deeds, alms → ALMS <1654> 4 1 Cor. 13:3 → "the poor" is added in Engl.

POORER – John 2:10 → LESSER <1640>.

POORLY – 1 Cor. 4:11 → to be poorly clothed, to be poorly dressed → to be naked → NAKED <1130>.

POORLY CLOTHED – Jas. 2:15 → NAKED <1131>.

PORCH – 1 ***proaulion*** [neut. noun: προαύλιον <4259>]; **from *pro*: before, in front, and *aulē*: court, yard ▶ Exterior court between the door and the street; also transl.: entryway, vestibule** > Peter went out onto the porch of the palace of the high priest (Mark 14:68). ¶

2 ***stoa*** [fem. noun: στοά <4745>]; **poss. from *histēmi*: to stand up ▶ Covered gallery supported by columns; also transl.: portico, colonnade, covered colonnade** > The pool called Bethesda had five porches (John 5:2). Solomon's porch corresponded to the porch of the temple at Jerusalem; it sheltered merchants, money changers, and the multitude (Acts 3:11; 5:12); Jesus walked in it (John 10:23). ¶

– 3 Matt. 26:71 → GATEWAY <4440>.

PORCIUS – ***Porkios*** [masc. name: Πόρκιος <4201>] **▶ Procurator of Judea** > See FESTUS <5347>. ¶

PORT – Acts 27:12b → HARBOR <3040>.

PORTER, PORTERESS – Mark 13:34; John 10:3; 18:16, 17 → DOORKEEPER <2377>.

PORTICO – John 5:2; 10:23; Acts 3:11; 5:12 → PORCH <4745>.

PORTION – 1 Luke 10:42; 2 Cor. 6:15 → PART (noun) <3310> 2 Col. 1:12 → part → PARTAKER <3310> 3 Heb. 1:1 → in many portions → TIMES (AT MANY) <4181> 4 Heb. 9:27 → to be the portion → APPOINT <606> 5 Rev. 21:8 → PART (noun) <3313>.

PORTION OF FOOD – Luke 12:42 → MEASURE OF CORN <4620>.

PORTION OF MEAT – Luke 12:42 → MEASURE OF CORN <4620>.

PORTRAY – to portray, to portray clearly, to portray publicly: *prographō* [verb: προγράφω <4270>]; **from *pro*: before, and *graphō*: to write, to describe ▶ To proclaim, to expose** > Jesus Christ was clearly portrayed {evidently set forth} before the eyes of the Galatians as crucified (Gal. 3:1). Other refs.: Rom. 15:4a; Eph. 3:3; Jude 4; see WRITE <4270>, MARK (verb) <4270>. ¶

POSITION – 1 Matt. 18:4 → to take the lowly position → HUMBLE (verb) <5013> 2 Rom. 12:16 → people of low position → HUMBLE (adj.) <5011> 3 1 Cor. 14:16 → PLACE (noun) <5117> 4 1 Tim. 2:2 → high position → AUTHORITY <5247> 5 Jas. 1:9 → high position → EXALTATION <5311> 6 Jas. 1:10 → low position → HUMILIATION <5014> 7 2 Pet. 3:17 → secure position → STEADFASTNESS <4740> 8 Jude 6 → position of authority → lit.: position → original state → STATE <746>.

POSSESS – 1 ***echō*** [verb: ἔχω <2192>] ▶ **To have** > God only possesses immortality (1 Tim. 6:16). Other refs.: see entries in Lexicon at <2192>.

2 ***apechō*** [verb: ἀπέχω <568>]**; from** ***apo*****: from, and** ***echō*****: see 1** ▶ **To receive, to retain** > Philemon was to possess Onesimus fully {have him back} forever (Phm. 15). Paul had received everything in full (Phil. 4:18). All other refs.: FAR <568>, HAVE <568>.

3 ***katechō*** [verb: κατέχω <2722>]**; from** ***kata*****: down, and** ***echō*****: see 1** ▶ **To take ownership; also transl.: to hold, to take, to seize** > The husbandmen wanted to kill the son and possess his inheritance (Matt. 21:38). Certain men possess {suppress} the truth while living in unrighteousness (Rom. 1:18). Those who buy are to be as not possessing (1 Cor. 7:30). Paul was as having nothing, and possessing all things (2 Cor. 6:10). All other refs.: see entries in Lexicon at <2722>.

4 ***ktaomai*** [verb: κτάομαι <2932>] ▶ **To acquire, to gain** > A Pharisee tithed everything he possessed {got} (Luke 18:12). Jesus said to gain our souls by patient endurance (Luke 21:19). Every Christian is to possess {to control} his own vessel (i.e., his body) in sanctification and honor (1 Thes. 4:4). All other refs.: OBTAIN <2932>, PROVIDE <2932>, PURCHASE (verb) <2932>.

– **5** Matt. 4:24; 8:16, 28, 33; 9:32; 12:22; Mark 1:32; 5:15, 16, 18; Luke 8:36 → possessed with, of devils → DEMON <1139> **6** Matt. 19:21; Luke 12:15; Acts 4:32 → things one possesses → GOOD (adj. and noun) <5224> **7** Mark 16:8 → GRIP <2192> **8** Luke 4:32 → His word possessed authority → lit.: His word was with authority **9** Luke 8:37 → SEIZE <4912> **10** Luke 15:12 → what he was possessed of → lit.: his living → LIVING (noun) <979> **11** Acts 4:32 → what one possesses → POSSESSIONS <5224> **12** Acts 7:5, 45 → lit.: to give to him for possession, when they entered into possession of the nations → POSSESSION <2697> **13** 1 Cor. 8:7 → "possesses" added in Engl. **14** 1 Cor. 12:30 → HAVE <2192>.

POSSESSION – 1 ***kataschesis*** [fem. noun: κατάσχεσις <2697>]**; from** ***katechō*****: to retain, to own, which is from** ***kata*****: down, and** ***echō*****: to have** ▶ **Property belonging to someone** > God promised Abraham to give him the land for a possession (Acts 7:5). Israel entered into possession of the lands of the nations, whom God drove out from before them (Acts 7:45). Other refs. in some mss.: Acts 13:33; 20:15. ¶

2 ***ktēma*** [neut. noun: κτῆμα <2933>]**; from** ***ktaomai*****: to acquire, to possess** ▶ **What is owned, property** > A young man went away grieved from Jesus, for he had great possessions {much property, great wealth} (Matt. 19:22; Mark 10:22). The Christians sold their possessions and goods {one transl.: property and possessions} (Acts 2:45). Ananias sold a possession {piece of property} (Acts 5:1). ¶

3 acquired possession, own possession: ***peripoiēsis*** [fem. noun: περιποίησις <4047>]**; from** ***peripoieō*****: to obtain, which is from** ***peri*****: around (denoting acquisition), and** ***poieō*****: to make, to gain** ▶ **Acquisition, what is obtained; conservation** > Christians were sealed with the Holy Spirit of promise until the redemption of the acquired possession (Eph. 1:14). They are a people for God's own possession {a people peculiar, own special, belonging to God} (1 Pet. 2:9). All other refs.: OBTAINING <4047>, RECEIVE <4047>, SAVING <4047>.

– **4** Matt. 12:29; Mark 3:27; Luke 17:31 → GOOD (adj. and noun) <4632> **5** Matt. 19:21; 24:47; 25:14; Luke 11:21; 12:15, 33, 44; 14:33; 16:1; 19:8; 1 Cor. 13:3 → goods → GOOD (adj. and noun) <5224> **6** Luke 15:13 → GOOD (adj. and noun) <3776> **7** Acts 2:45; Heb. 10:34 → GOOD (adj. and noun) <5223> **8** Acts 28:7 → LAND (noun) <5564> **9** Phil. 3:12a, b, 13 → to get possession, to take possession → to lay hold, to take hold → HOLD (noun) <2638> **10** Titus 2:14 → for one's own possession → PECULIAR <4041> **11** 1 Pet. 5:3 → one who is entrusted to the charge → ENTRUST <2819> **12** 1 John 2:16 → pride in possessions → pride of life → LIFE <979>.

POSSESSIONS – ***huparchonta*** [pres. active ptcp. used as plur. noun: ὑπάρχοντα <5224>]; **from *hupo*: under, and *archō*: to exist, to be at the disposition ▶ What one owns, property** > Not one of the Christians said that any of his possessions {anything of what he possessed, anything belonging to him} was his own (Acts 4:32). All other refs.: GOOD (adj. and noun) <5224>, SUBSTANCE <5224>.

POSSESSOR – Acts 4:34 → OWN <2935>.

POSSIBLE – [1] ***dunatos*** [adj.: δυνατός <1415>]; **from *dunamai*: to be able ▶ Achievable, realizable** > All things are possible with God (Matt. 19:26; Mark 10:27; Luke 18:27). False christs and false prophets will seek to mislead, if possible, even the elect (Matt. 24:24; Mark 13:22). Jesus prayed that, if it were possible, the cup might pass from Him (Matt. 26:39; Mark 14:36) and that the hour of expiatory sufferings might pass away from Him (Mark 14:35). All things are possible to him who believes (Mark 9:23). It was not possible {impossible} that Jesus should be held by the power of death (Acts 2:24). Paul hastened, if it was possible for him, to be in Jerusalem on the day of Pentecost (Acts 20:16). Christians are to live in peace with all men, if possible, as far as depends on them (Rom. 12:18). If possible {If they could have done so}, the Galatians would have plucked out their own eyes so they might give them to Paul (Gal. 4:15). All other refs.: see entries in Lexicon at <1415>.

[2] **to be possible: *dunamai*** [verb: δύναμαι <1410>] **▶ To be achieved, to be realized** > Jesus prayed His Father that, if it was not possible that the cup could pass from Him unless He drank it, His will be done (Matt. 26:42). The Greek verb is transl. "they might" {they could} in Acts 27:12: They counseled to set sail from Fair Havens if perhaps they might reach Phoenicia. All other refs.: ABLE <1410>.

– [3] Heb. 10:4 → not possible → IMPOSSIBLE <102>.

POSTERITY – Matt. 22:24, 25; Mark 12:19–22; Luke 20:28 → SEED <4690>.

POT – [1] ***stamnos*** [masc. noun: στάμνος <4713>]; **from *histēmi*: to stand ▶ Urn, vase** > The golden pot {jar} in the ark of the covenant had the manna in it (Heb. 9:4). ¶

– [2] Mark 7:4 → copper pot → BRAZEN VESSEL <5473> [3] Mark 7:4, 8 → VESSEL[1] <3582> [4] Rev. 2:27 → VESSEL[1] <4632>.

POTENTATE – 1 Tim. 6:15 → RULER <1413>.

POTTER – [1] ***kerameus*** [masc. noun: κεραμεύς <2763>]; **from *keramos*: potter's clay ▶ One who makes vessels of clay** > The field of the potter was bought for a burial place for foreigners with the thirty pieces of silver returned by Judas (Matt. 27:7, 10). The potter is able to make out of clay one vessel to honor and another to dishonor (Rom. 9:21). ¶

– [2] Rev. 2:27 → of the potter → lit.: of pottery → POTTERY <2764>.

POTTERY – [1] **of pottery: *keramikos*** [adj.: κεραμικός <2764>]; **from *keramos*: potter's clay, or *kerameus*: potter ▶ Made of clay** > The vessels of pottery {of the potter} in Rev. 2:27 are lit. vessels of clay made by potters. ¶

– [2] Rom. 9:21 → VESSEL[1] <4632>.

POUND – [1] ***litra*** [fem. noun: λίτρα <3046>]; **Lat.: *libra* ▶ Measure of weight: about 12 ounces, or approx. 327 grams** > Mary anointed the feet of Jesus with a pound {pint} of ointment of pure nard of great price (John 12:3). Nicodemus brought a mixture of myrrh and aloes, about one hundred {some: seventy-five} pounds weight for the burial of Jesus (John 19:39). ¶

– [2] Matt. 13:33; Luke 13:21 → sixty pounds → lit.: three measures → MEASURE (noun) <4568> [3] Luke 19:13; 16a, b, 20, 24a, b, 25 → MINA <3414> [4] Rev. 6:6a, b → two pounds, six pounds → a quart, three quarts → QUART <5518> [5] Rev. 16:21 → one hundred pounds each → the weight of a talent → TALENT <5006>.

POUNDING – Acts 27:41 → VIOLENCE <970>.

POUR – [1] ***ballō*** [verb: βάλλω <906>]; **primary meaning: to throw ▶ To make a liquid flow, to cause to flow freely** > Jesus used this verb in regard to the woman who had poured the ointment on His body (Matt. 26:12). He poured water into a basin and began to wash the feet of the disciples (John 13:5). All other refs.: see entries in Lexicon at <906>.

[2] **to pour out: *ekcheō*** [verb: ἐκχέω <1632>] **and *ekchunō*** [verb: ἐκχύνω <1632a>]; **from *ek*: out, and *cheō*: to pour ▶ a. To spill, to run out, to shed** > The verb is used in regard to the blood of: Jesus (Matt. 26:28; Mark 14:24; Luke 22:20), O.T. people of faith (Matt. 23:35), prophets (Luke 11:50), and saints and prophets (Rev. 16:6). It is also used in regard to the seven bowls of the wrath of God (Rev. 16:1–4, 8, 10, 12, 17). The love of God has been poured out in the Christians' hearts by the Holy Spirit who has been given to them (Rom. 5:5). Paul spoke of those whose feet are swift to shed blood (Rom. 3:15). The wine is poured out (on the ground) when old wineskins burst (Matt. 9:17; Mark 2:22; Luke 5:37: *ekchunō*). **b. To give profusely** > Joel prophesied that God would pour out {pour forth} His Spirit upon all flesh in the last days (Acts 2:17, 18). Shortly after Pentecost, the gift of the Holy Spirit was poured out upon the nations (Acts 10:45). Jesus has poured out {poured forth, shed forth} that which His disciples saw and heard at Pentecost (Acts 2:33). Paul was present when the blood of Stephen was shed (or: poured out) (Acts 22:20). God has richly poured out His own mercy on Christians through Jesus Christ (Titus 3:6). **c. To scatter by throwing on the ground** > Jesus poured out {scattered} the change of the money-changers in the temple (John 2:15). Other ref.: Jude 11; see GIVE <1632>. ¶

[3] ***epicheō*** [verb: ἐπιχέω <2022>]; **from *epi*: upon, and *cheō*: to pour ▶ To cause to flow in a stream onto something** > The good Samaritan poured oil and wine on the wounds of the man who had fallen into the hands of robbers (Luke 10:34). ¶

[4] ***katacheō*** [verb: καταχέω <2708>]; **from *kata*: down, and *cheō*: to pour ▶ To cause to flow freely down on** > A woman poured out a very precious ointment on the head of Jesus (Matt. 26:7; Mark 14:3). ¶

[5] **to pour out: *kerannumi*** [verb: κεράννυμι <2767>] ▶ **To mingle, e.g., wine mixed with something else** > He who worships the beast and his image shall drink of the wine of the fury of God, which is poured out without mixture into the cup of His wrath (Rev. 14:10 {to mix, to prepare}). Other refs.: Rev. 18:6a, b; see MIX <2767>. ¶

– [6] Mark 2:22; Luke 5:38 → which must be poured → which must be put → PUT <992> [7] Mark 14:8 → to pour perfume → ANOINT <3462> [8] Luke 7:38; 46b; John 11:2; 12:3 → ANOINT <218> [9] Phil. 2:17; 2 Tim. 4:6 → to be poured out as a drink offering → DRINK OFFERING <4689> [10] 1 Tim. 1:14 → to pour out abundantly → to be more than abundant → ABUNDANT <5250> [11] Jas. 3:11 → to pour forth → to send forth → SEND <1032> [12] Rev. 11:5 → to go out → GO <1607>.

POVERTY – [1] ***ptōcheia*** [fem. noun: πτωχεία <4432>]; **from *ptōchos*: poor and helpless, which is from *ptōssō*: to hide, to crouch ▶ Condition of a person destitute of wealth** > The deep poverty of the saints of Macedonia had abounded to the riches of their liberality (2 Cor. 8:2). We have been enriched by the poverty of the Lord Jesus Christ (2 Cor. 8:9). The Lord knew the poverty of Smyrna (Rev. 2:9). ¶

[2] ***husterēsis*** [fem. noun: ὑστέρησις <5304>]; **from *hustereō*: to lack, which is from *husteros*: last ▶ Deficiency in necessary possessions, indigence** > The widow who had cast two mites into the treasury had put in, out of her poverty {destitution, want}, all that she had (Mark 12:44). Other ref.: Phil. 4:11; see PRIVATION <5304>. ¶

– [3] Luke 21:4 → NEED <5303>.

POWDER – to grind to powder: *likmaō* [verb: λικμάω <3039>]**; from *likmos*: winnowing basket ▶ To winnow, to crush >** On whomever the rejected stone (Jesus Christ) falls, it will grind him to powder {it will scatter him like dust} (Matt. 21:44 in some mss.; Luke 20:18). ¶

POWER[1] – [1] ***dunamis*** [fem. noun: δύναμις <1411>]**; from *dunamai*: to be able ▶ Might, capability, strength >** The word is used in regard to God (Matt. 22:29; Mark 12:24; Luke 24:49; Acts 8:10; Rom. 1:20; 9:17; 1 Cor. 2:4, 5; 6:14; 2 Cor. 4:7; 6:7; 13:4a, b; Eph. 1:19; 3:7, 16, 20; 2 Tim. 1:8; 1 Pet. 1:5; Rev. 11:17), the Lord during His life on earth (Mark 5:30; Luke 4:14, 36; 5:17; 6:19; 8:46; 9:1), the Lord in glory (Matt. 26:64; Luke 22:69; Rom. 1:4; 1 Cor. 1:24; 5:4; 2 Cor. 12:9a, b; Phil. 3:10; Col. 1:29; 2 Thes. 1:7; Heb. 1:3; 2 Pet. 1:3, 16; Rev. 15:8), the Lord at His coming to establish His future kingdom and reign (Matt. 24:30; Mark 9:1; 13:26; 14:62; Luke 21:27; Rev. 12:10), the Holy Spirit (Luke 1:35; Acts 1:8; 10:38; Rom. 15:13, 19), Satan (Luke 10:19b; Acts 10:38b; Rev. 13:2), Elijah (Luke 1:17), Stephen (Acts 6:8), the apostles (Acts 3:12; 4:7, 33), angels (2 Pet. 2:11), and Babylon (Rev. 18:3). The word is also used in regard to the glad tidings (Rom. 1:16; 1 Cor. 1:18; 1 Thes. 1:5), the kingdom of God (1 Cor. 4:20), sin (1 Cor. 15:56), piety (2 Tim. 3:5), and signs and wonders (Rom. 15:19a). Power is attributed in praise to God (Rev. 4:11; 7:12; 19:1) and to the Lamb (Rev. 5:12). Other refs.: 1 Cor. 4:19; 15:24, 43; 2 Thes. 1:11; 2 Tim. 1:7; Heb. 7:16; Rev. 17:13. All other refs.: ABILITY <1411>, MEANING <1411>, MIRACLE <1411>, POWER[3] <1411>, STRENGTH <1411>.

[2] ***dunatos*** [adj. used as noun: δυνατός <1415>]**; from *dunamai*: to be able ▶ See [1].** > God could make His power known (Rom. 9:22). All other refs.: see entries in Lexicon at <1415>.

– [3] Matt. 9:6, 8; Mark 2:10; Luke 5:24; John 10:18a, b; Rom. 9:21; 13:1; Jude 25; Rev. 6:8; et al. → AUTHORITY <1849> [4] Luke 9:43 → mighty power → GREATNESS <3168> [5] Acts 7:18 → to come to power → lit.: to arise [6] Acts 7:22; Rom. 4:21; 2 Cor. 10:4 → to have the power, to be a man of power, to have divine power → lit.: to be mighty, to be mighty according to God → MIGHTY (adj.) <1415> [7] Acts 19:20; Heb. 9:17 → to grow in power, to have power → PREVAIL <2480> [8] Rom. 3:9 → under the power of sin → lit.: under sin [9] Rom. 16:25; Phil. 3:21 → to have the power → to be able → ABLE <1410> [10] 1 Cor. 1:17 → to be empty of power → to make vain → VAIN <2758> [11] 1 Cor. 13:2 → prophetic powers → lit.: prophecy → PROPHECY <4394> [12] 1 Cor. 14:13 → for the power to interpret → lit.: that he may interpret [13] Eph. 1:19; 6:10; 2 Thes. 1:9; 2 Pet. 2:11 → STRENGTH <2479> [14] Col. 1:11; 1 Tim. 6:16; 1 Pet. 4:11; 5:11; Rev. 1:6; 5:13 → MIGHT <2904> [15] Col. 1:16 → DOMINION <2963> [16] 2 Thes. 2:11 → powerful delusion → strong delusion → DELUSION <4106> [17] Heb. 4:12 → OPERATIVE <1756> [18] Heb. 5:14 → power of discernment → SENSE (noun) <145> [19] Heb. 11:11 → STRENGTH <2983> [20] 2 Pet. 1:21 → under the power → lit.: being carried → MOVE <5342> [21] Rev. 19:6 → to take to oneself kingly power → REIGN (verb) <936>.

POWER[2] – [1] ***archē*** [fem. noun: ἀρχή <746>] **▶ Rule, authority, dominion >** Spies were sent to seize on the Lord's words in order to deliver Him to the power and authority of the governor (Luke 20:20). All other refs.: BEGINNING <746>, CORNER <746>, MAGISTRATE <746>, PRINCIPALITY <746>, STATE <746>.

[2] **man in power: *dunastēs*** [masc. noun: δυνάστης <1413>]**; from *dunamai*: to be able, to be powerful ▶ Man of high rank, top level functionary, officer >** Philip met an Ethiopian, a man in power {of great authority, court official, important official} at the court of Queen Candace, who had come to worship at Jerusalem (Acts 8:27). Other refs.: Luke 1:52; 1 Tim. 6:15; see RULER <1413>. ¶

3 to bring under the power: *exousiazō* [verb: ἐξουσιάζω <1850>]; **from *exousia*: authority, which is from *exesti*: it is allowed, which is from *ek*: out, and *eimi*: to be ▶ To dominate, to have the authority; pass.: to be submitted to an authority** > Paul would not be brought under the power of {be mastered by} anything (1 Cor. 6:12). Other refs.: Luke 22:25; 1 Cor. 7:4a, b; see AUTHORITY <1850>. ¶

– 4 Matt. 28:18; Acts 1:7; 1 Cor. 7:37; 11:10; et al. → AUTHORITY <1849> 5 John 1:12; 1 Cor. 9:4, 5, 6, 12a, b, 18; 2 Thes. 3:9 → RIGHT (noun)[2] <1849> 6 John 13:3 → to put under the power → lit.: to give into the hands → GIVE <1325> 7 Acts 7:22; 2 Cor. 10:4; 13:9 → MIGHTY (adj.) <1415> 8 Acts 10:38 → to be under the power → to be oppressed → OPPRESS <2616> 9 Acts 13:17 → ARM (noun)[1] <1023> 10 Acts 26:12 → COMMISSION <2011> 11 1 Cor. 12:10 → miraculous powers → lit.: powers (or: operations) of miracles → OPERATION <1755> 12 Eph. 1:19; Col. 1:29; 2:12 → WORKING (noun) <1753> 13 Eph. 3:18 → to have power → to be able → ABLE <1840> 14 2 Thes. 2:7 → secret power → MYSTERY OF LAWLESSNESS <3466> 15 Heb. 2:14 → to break the power → to render powerless → POWERLESS <2673>.

POWER[3] – **1 *dunamis*** [fem. noun: δύναμις <1411>]; **from *dunamai*: to be able ▶ Spiritual being, prob. of superior rank, characterized by might** > God set Jesus down above every power {might} (Eph. 1:21). After the great tribulation, the powers of the heavens {heavenly bodies} will be shaken (Matt. 24:29; Mark 13:25; Luke 21:26). Powers will not be able to separate Christians from the love of God (Rom. 8:38). Angels, authorities, and powers are subjected to Jesus Christ (1 Pet. 3:22). All other refs.: ABILITY <1411>, MEANING <1411>, MIRACLE <1411>, POWER[1] <1411>, STRENGTH <1411>.

2 *kratos* [adj.: κράτος <2904>] ▶ **Might, domination** > Jesus has rendered Satan powerless, him who has the power of death (Heb. 2:14). All other refs.: MIGHT <2904>, STRENGTH <2904>.

– 3 Col. 2:10, 15 → PRINCIPALITY <746>.

POWERFUL – **1 *dunatos*** [adj. and adj. used as a noun: δυνατός <1415>]; **from *dunamai*: to be powerful ▶ High ranking person mighty in wealth or influence** > There were not many powerful {mighty, influential} among the Christians of Corinth (1 Cor. 1:26). The Greek word is a title of God in Luke 1:49: the Mighty (or: Powerful) One. All other refs.: ABLE <1415>, see entries in Lexicon at <1415>.

2 to be powerful: *dunateō* [verb: δυνατέω <1414>]; **from *dunatos*: see 1 ▶ To have power, to be mighty** > Christ was powerful among the Corinthians (2 Cor. 13:3). Other refs. in some mss.: Rom. 14:4; 2 Cor. 9:8. ¶

– 3 2 Cor. 10:10; Heb. 11:34 → STRONG (adj.) <2478> 4 Rev. 6:15 in some mss. → STRONG (noun) <1415>.

POWERFULLY – 1 Acts 4:33 → God's grace was so powerfully at work in them all → lit.: great grace was upon them all 2 Acts 18:28 → VIGOROUSLY <2159>.

POWERLESS – **1 *asthenēs*** [adj.: ἀσθενής <772>]; **from *a*: neg., and *sthenos*: physical strength, vigor ▶ Weak, without strength; also transl.: helpless** > When we were still without strength, Christ died for the ungodly (Rom. 5:6). All other refs.: SICK (adj. and noun) <772>, WEAK <772>, WEAKNESS <772>.

2 to render powerless: *katargeō* [verb: καταργέω <2673>]; **from *kata*: intens., and *argeō*: to be inactive, which is from *argos*: idle, useless, which is from *a*: neg., and *ergon*: work ▶ To cause to have no further efficacy, to deprive of strength; also transl.: to annul, to break the power, to destroy** > Jesus has rendered the devil powerless through His death (Heb. 2:14). All other refs.: see entries in Lexicon at <2673>.

– 3 Rom. 8:3 → IMPOSSIBLE <102>.

PRACTICALLY – Acts 19:26 → ALMOST <4975>.

PRACTICE (noun) – 1 **to put in practice:** ***poieō*** [verb: ποιέω <4160>] ► **To implement; also transl.: to act on, to do** > Jesus spoke of hearing and putting in practice His words, and not hearing or putting into practice the same (Matt. 7:24, 26; Luke 6:47, 49). He also spoke of hearing the word of God and putting it in practice (Luke 8:21). Other refs.: see entries in Lexicon at <4160>.
– 2 Acts 19:18; Col. 3:9 → DEED <4234> 3 1 Cor. 11:16 → CUSTOM[1] <4914> 4 Eph. 4:19 → WORKING (noun) <2039> 5 Heb. 5:14 → HABIT <1838> 6 2 Pet. 2:14 → covetous practices → COVETOUSNESS <4124>.

PRACTICE (verb) – 1 ***ergazomai*** [verb: ἐργάζομαι <2038>]; **from *ergon*: work** ► **To commit, to do, to exercise** > Jesus spoke of those who practice {evildoers of, workers of, those who work} lawlessness (Matt. 7:23). He also spoke about one who practices {lives by} (*poieō*) the truth, that his works may be manifested that they have been wrought {carried out} (*ergazomai*) in God (John 3:21). He who practices righteousness is acceptable to God (Acts 10:35). All other refs.: see entries in Lexicon at <2038>.
2 ***poieō*** [verb: ποιέω <4160>] ► **To implement, to put into practice; also transl.: to commit, to do, to keep, to live by, to observe** > Jesus spoke of practicing one of the least commandments (Matt. 5:19), the truth (John 3:21), and good (John 5:29). He said that everyone who practices sin is the bondman of sin (John 8:34). The Jews did not practice {carry out, keep} the law (John 7:19). It was not lawful for the Romans to practice certain Jewish customs (Acts 16:21). Wicked men were given up to a reprobate mind to practice unseemly things (Rom. 1:28). Men practice things worthy of death (Rom. 1:32; 2:3). The man of Romans 7 practices what he does not will and does not practice the good that he wills (vv. 15, 16, 19–21). The man who has practiced the things of the law will live by them (Rom. 10:5). The Spirit and the flesh are opposed to each other so that Christians should not practice the things that they desire (Gal. 5:17). John speaks of practicing or not practicing the truth (1 John 1:6), righteousness (2:29; 3:7, 10), sin (3:4a, 8, 9), lawlessness (3:4b), and the things that are pleasing in God's sight (3:22). He who is righteous is to practice righteousness (Rev. 22:11); some mss. have *dikaioō* <1344>. Other refs.: see entries in Lexicon at <4160>.
– 3 Acts 19:19 → USE (verb) <4238> 4 Rom. 1:32a, b; 2:1–3; 2 Cor. 12:21; Gal. 5:21 → DO <4238> 5 Rom. 2:25 → KEEP (verb) <4238> 6 Rom. 3:12 → EXERCISE (verb) <4160> 7 Rom. 12:13 → GIVE <1377> 8 1 Cor. 6:18 → COMMIT <4160> 9 2 Cor. 4:2 → to refuse to practice → lit.: not walking in → WALK <4043> 10 1 Tim. 4:15 → to occupy oneself with → OCCUPY <3191> 11 2 Pet. 2:14 → EXERCISE (verb) <1128> 12 Rev. 2:14, 20 → to practice sexual immorality → to practice fornication → FORNICATION <4203>.

PRAETOR – Acts 16:20, 22, 35, 36, 38 → MAGISTRATE <4755>.

PRAETORIAN PREFECT – ***stratopedarchēs*** [masc. noun: στρατοπεδάρχης <4759>]; **from *stratopedon*: encampment of troops, which is from *stratos*: army, *pedon*: ground, and *archō*: to begin, to rule, which is from *archē*: beginning** ► **Commanding officer, captain of the guard** > Certain mss. have this word in Acts 28:16. This is prob. a reference to the commander of praetorian cohorts. ¶

PRAETORIUM – ***praitōrion*** [neut. noun: πραιτώριον <4232>]; **from the Lat. *praetorium*** ► **Place where the praetor of the governor dispensed justice; also transl.: common hall, judgment hall, palace** > Jesus was taken to the Praetorium (Matt. 27:27; Mark 15:16; John 18:28a, b, 33; 19:9). Paul was kept in Herod's Praetorium at Caesarea (Acts 23:35), and in the Praetorium at Rome (Phil. 1:13). ¶

PRAISE (noun) – 1 ***ainesis*** [fem. noun: αἴνεσις <133>] ▶ **Celebration, glorification of a person** > The sacrifice of praise to God is the fruit of lips that confess His name (Heb. 13:15). ¶
2 ***ainos*** [masc. noun: αἶνος <136>]; **from *aineō*: to praise** ▶ **Term similar to 1** > God has ordained praise from the lips of children and infants (Matt. 21:16). All the people gave praise to {praised} God (Luke 18:43). ¶
3 ***epainos*** [masc. noun: ἔπαινος <1868>]; **from *epi*: over, upon, and *ainos*: see 2** ▶ **This term is stronger than the preceding ones with the idea of approval** > One receives praise from {is being commended by} the authority for a good work (Rom. 13:3). Each one's praise will come from God (1 Cor. 4:5). Paul speaks of the praise of the glory of the grace of God (Eph. 1:6) and of the praise of His glory (vv. 12, 14). The rulers are sent for the praise of {to commend} those who do well (1 Pet. 2:14). Other refs.: Rom. 2:29; 2 Cor. 8:18 {fame}; Phil. 1:11; 4:8 {praiseworthy}; 1 Pet. 1:7. ¶
4 **to sing praises: *humneō*** [verb: ὑμνέω <5214>]; **from *humnos*: hymn** ▶ **To sing hymns** > Paul and Silas sang praises to God {praised God with singing} in prison (Acts 16:25). The Lord Jesus sings the praise of God in the midst of the church (Heb. 2:12). Other refs.: Matt. 26:30; Mark 14:26 (to sing a hymn); see SING <5214>. ¶
– 5 Luke 1:64 → in praise → lit.: to praise → PRAISE (verb) <2127> 6 Luke 1:68; Rom. 1:25; 9:5; 2 Cor. 1:3; 11:31; Eph. 1:3a; 1 Pet. 1:3 → BLESSED ONE <2128> 7 Luke 2:38 → to give praise → THANKS (GIVE) <437> 8 Rom. 14:11; 15:9 → to give praise → CONFESS <1843> 9 Rom. 15:9; 1 Cor. 14:15 → to sing the praises → SING <5567> 10 1 Cor. 11:17 → to have praise → PRAISE (verb) <1867> 11 2 Cor. 6:8 → good report → REPORT (noun) <2162> 12 Jas. 3:10; Rev. 5:12, 13; 7:12 → BLESSING <2129> 13 1 Pet. 2:9 → VIRTUE <703> 14 Rev. 19:5 → to give praise → PRAISE (verb) <134>.

PRAISE (verb) – 1 ***aineō*** [verb: αἰνέω <134>] ▶ **To celebrate, to glorify a person** > The verb is used only in relation to God. The psalmist tells all the nations to praise {laud} the Lord (Rom. 15:11a citing Ps. 117:1). Other refs.: Luke 2:13, 20; 19:37; 24:53; Acts 2:47; 3:8, 9; Rev. 19:5 {to give praise}. ¶
2 ***epaineō*** [verb: ἐπαινέω <1867>]; **from *epi*: over, upon, and *aineō*: see 1** ▶ **This verb is stronger than the preceding one and adds the idea of approval** > The master in the parable praised {commended} the unjust steward (Luke 16:8). Paul praised the Corinthians because they remembered him and kept the directions just as he had delivered them (1 Cor. 11:2). All the nations are invited to praise {extol} the Lord (Rom. 15:11b). Other refs.: 1 Cor. 11:17 {to have praise}, 22. ¶
3 ***eulogeō*** [verb: εὐλογέω <2127>]; **from *eu*: good, well, and *logos*: word** ▶ **To bless, i.e., to say good things about, to give thanks** > Zacharias praised God (Luke 1:64). All other refs.: BLESS <2127>.
– 4 Matt. 6:2; Luke 4:15; Acts 4:21; et al. → GLORIFY <1392> 5 Matt. 11:25; Luke 10:21 → THANK (verb) <1843> 6 Luke 18:43 → lit.: to give praise → PRAISE (noun) <136> 7 Acts 10:46 → MAGNIFY <3170> 8 Acts 16:25 → to praise God with singing → to sing praises → PRAISE (noun) <5214> 9 Rom. 15:9 → CONFESS <1843> 10 2 Cor. 8:18 → PRAISE (noun) <1868>.

PRAISEWORTHY – Phil. 4:8 → lit.: if any praise → PRAISE (noun) <1868>.

PRATE – ***phluareō*** [verb: φλυαρέω <5396>]; **from *phluaros*: talkative, which is from *phluō*: to bubble; lit.: to overflow with talk** ▶ **To tell lies, to accuse falsely** > Diotrephes was prating against {was babbling against, was unjustly accusing} John with malicious words {was gossiping maliciously about him} (3 John 10). ¶

PRAY – 1 ***deomai*** [verb: δέομαι <1189>]; **middle voice of *deō*: to lack, to need something** ▶ **To supplicate, to express one's need; also transl.: to ask, to beseech** > Jesus said to pray at every season (Luke 21:36). He had prayed for Peter that his faith might not fail (Luke 22:32). The verb is used in regard to Christians in Acts 4:31. The eunuch used this verb in speaking to Philip (Acts 8:34). Cornelius prayed to God continually (Acts 10:2). Paul used this verb in Acts 21:39; 26:3; Gal. 4:12; 1 Thes. 3:10. All other refs.: IMPLORE <1189>, REQUEST (noun) <1189>, SUPPLICATE <1189>.

2 ***epikaleō*** [verb: ἐπικαλέω <1941>]; **from *epi*: upon, and *kaleō*: to call ▶ To call upon, to invoke** > Stephen prayed {called on, called upon God} when they stoned him (Acts 7:59). All other refs.: APPEAL <1941>, CALL (verb) <1941>, INVOKE <1941>, SURNAME (verb) <1941>.

3 ***euchomai*** [verb: εὔχομαι <2172>] ▶ **To communicate spiritually with God to ask, thank, praise, worship** > Paul used this verb (lit.: I pray God, I would to God) with Agrippa in Acts 26:29. He prayed to God that the Corinthians might do nothing evil (2 Cor. 13:7). He was praying {wishing} {His prayer was} for the perfecting of the Corinthians (2 Cor. 13:9). Christians are to pray one for another (Jas. 5:16). Other refs.: Acts 27:29; Rom. 9:3; 3 John 2; see WISH <2172>. ¶

4 ***proseuchomai*** [verb: προσεύχομαι <4336>]; **from *pros*: for, to, and *euchomai*: to pray ▶ See 3.** > Jesus often spoke of praying (Matt. 5:44; 6:5a, b, 6a, b, 7, 9; 24:20; 26:41; Mark 11:24; 13:18, 33; 14:38; Luke 6:28; 11:2; 18:1, 10, 11; 22:40, 46). Jesus Himself prayed (Matt. 14:23; 26:36, 39, 42, 44; Mark 1:35; 6:46; 14:32, 35, 39; Luke 3:21; 5:16; 6:12a; 9:18, 28, 29; 22:41, 44). Little children were brought to Jesus that He may lay hands on them and pray (Matt. 19:13). We do not know what we should pray for as is fitting (Rom. 8:26). The verb is also used in regard to the multitude of the people (Luke 1:10), a disciple (Luke 11:1), the apostles (Acts 1:24; 6:6; 8:15), Paul (Acts 9:11; 20:36; 22:17; 28:8; Col. 1:3, 9; 2 Thes. 1:11), Peter (Acts 9:40; 10:9), Cornelius (Acts 10:30), Christians assembled in the house of the mother of Mark (Acts 12:12), the Christians of Antioch (Acts 13:3), Paul and Barnabas (Acts 14:23), Paul and Silas (Acts 16:25), Paul and the disciples of Tyre (Acts 21:5), believers (1 Cor. 11:4, 5, 13; 14:13, 14a, b; 15a, b; Eph. 6:18; 1 Thes. 5:17; Jas. 5:13, 14), the Colossians (Col. 4:3), the Thessalonians (1 Thes. 5:25; 2 Thes. 3:1), men (1 Tim. 2:8), the readers of the letter to the Hebrews (Heb. 13:18), and Elijah (Jas. 5:17, 18). Jude spoke of praying in the Holy Spirit (Jude 20). Other refs.: Mark 11:25; 12:40; Luke 11:1; 20:47; Acts 11:5; Phil. 1:9 (to make a prayer); see PRAYER <4336>. ¶

– 5 Matt. 26:53; Mark 5:17, 18; Acts 16:9; 24:4 → BESEECH <3870> 6 Luke 5:3; 14:18, 19; 16:27; John 4:31; 14:16; 16:26; 17:9a, b, 15, 20; Acts 10:48; 23:18; 1 John 5:16 → ASK <2065> 7 Luke 5:33 → lit.: to make prayer → PRAYER <1162> 8 John 4:31 → ASK <2065> 9 Acts 27:34 → EXHORT <3870> 10 2 Cor. 9:14 → while they pray for you → in their supplication for you → SUPPLICATION <1162> 11 Col. 1:9 → ASK <154>.

PRAYER – 1 ***deēsis*** [fem. noun: δέησις <1162>]; **from *deomai*: to ask, to make known a need, which is the middle voice of *deō*: to lack, to need something ▶ Supplication addressed to God prompted by a need** > Anna served God night and day with fasting and prayers (Luke 2:37). The disciples of John made prayers (Luke 5:33). When on earth, the Lord offered up both prayers and supplications to Him who was able to save Him out of death (Heb. 5:7). All other refs.: SUPPLICATION <1162>.

2 ***enteuxis*** [fem. noun: ἔντευξις <1783>]; **from *entunchanō*: to intercede, which is from *en*: in, and *tunchanō*: to obtain ▶ Request, intercession** > The Christian is exhorted to make intercessions {petitions} for all men (1 Tim. 2:1). Every creature is sanctified by God's word and prayer {and freely addressing Him} (1 Tim. 4:5). ¶

3 ***euchē*** [fem. noun: εὐχή <2171>]; **from *euchomai*: to wish for, to pray ▶ Address to God** > James spoke of the prayer of faith that can heal the sick (Jas. 5:15). Other refs.: Acts 18:18; 21:23; see VOW (noun) <2171>. ¶

4 ***proseuchē*** [fem. noun: προσευχή <4335>]; **from *proseuchomai*: to pray, which is from**

***pros*: to, toward, and *euchomai*: see 3 ▶ Spiritual communication of the Christian with God to ask, thank, praise, worship Him** > The Lord spoke of prayer (Matt. 17:21; 21:13, 22; Mark 9:29; 11:17; Luke 19:46); He Himself prayed (Luke 6:12; 22:45). Believers in the Lord Jesus are often seen in prayer in Acts (Acts 1:14; 2:42; 3:1; 6:4; 10:4, 31; 12:5; 16:13, 16). Paul was a man of prayer (Rom. 1:9 or 10; Eph. 1:16; 1 Thes. 1:2; Phm. 4), and he encouraged others to persevere in prayer (Rom. 12:12; 15:30; 1 Cor. 7:5; Eph. 6:18; Phil. 4:6; Col. 4:2; 1 Tim. 2:1; 5:5; Phm. 22). The prayers of a believing couple are not to be interrupted (1 Pet. 3:7). Other refs.: Col. 4:12; 1 Pet. 4:7; Rev. 5:8; 8:3, 4. Other ref.: Jas. 5:17; see EARNESTLY <4335>. ¶

5 **to make a prayer, to offer a prayer, to be praying, to pray: *proseuchomai*** [verb: προσεύχομαι <4336>]; **from *pros*: toward, and *euchomai*: to pray ▶ See 4.** > Jesus gave instructions to those praying (Mark 11:25). He spoke of scribes who made long prayers (Mark 12:40; Luke 20:47). Jesus was praying (Luke 11:1). Peter was praying (Acts 11:5). Paul prayed that the love of the Philippians might abound (Phil. 1:9). All other refs.: PRAY <4336>.

– 6 2 Cor. 13:9 → PRAY <2172> 7 1 Tim. 4:5 → INTERCESSION <1783> 8 Heb. 5:7 → SUPPLICATION <2428>.

PRE-TRUST – Eph. 1:12 → to first trust → TRUST (verb) <4276>.

PREACH – 1 ***diangellō*** [verb: διαγγέλλω <1229>]; **from *dia*: through, and *angellō*: to bring news, a message ▶ To declare, to announce** > Jesus told a man to go and preach {proclaim} the kingdom of God (Luke 9:60). Other refs.: Mark 5:19 in some mss.; Acts 21:26; Rom. 9:17: see SIGNIFY <1229>, DECLARE <1229>. ¶

2 ***katangellō*** [verb: καταγγέλλω <2605>]; **from *kata*: intens., and *angellō*: to bring news, a message ▶ To announce, to declare, to proclaim** > This verb is used concerning the resurrection from the dead (Acts 4:2), the word of God (Acts 13:5; 15:36; 17:13), the forgiveness of sins (Acts 13:38), the way of salvation (Acts 16:17 {to tell}, 21 {to advocate, to teach}), Christ (Acts 17:3, 23; Phil. 1:17, 18; Col. 1:28), the light by Christ (Acts 26:23 {to show}), the testimony of God (1 Cor. 2:1), the gospel (1 Cor. 9:14), and the death of the Lord (1 Cor. 11:26 {to show}). Other ref.: Rom. 1:8; see PROCLAIM <2605>. ¶

3 **to preach, to preach the gospel, to preach the glad tidings, to preach the good news: *euangelizō*** [verb: εὐαγγελίζω <2097>]; **from *euangelos*: bringing good news, which is from *eu*: well, and *angellō*: to bring news, a message ▶ To announce, to communicate good news; most often it is concerning Jesus Christ, the Son of God** > This verb is used concerning the preaching of Jesus or the gospel (Matt. 11:5; Luke 2:10 {to bring good news, to bring good tidings, to announce good tidings}; 4:18; 7:22; 20:1 in some mss.; Acts 5:42; 8:4, 35; 10:36; 11:20; 13:32 {to declare glad tidings}; 14:15; 15:35; 17:18; Rom. 1:15; 10:15a, b; 1 Cor. 15:1, 2; 2 Cor. 11:7; Gal. 1:11, 16, 23; Eph. 2:17; 3:8; 1 Pet. 1:12, 25), the birth of John the Baptist (Luke 1:19 {to show, to bring the glad tidings, to bring the good news}), the kingdom (Luke 4:43; 8:1; 16:16; Acts 8:12), the mystery of God (Rev. 10:7 {to declare, to make known}), and the everlasting gospel (Rev. 14:6). John the Baptist preached to the people (Luke 3:18). The twelve apostles preached the gospel (Luke 9:6). Peter and John preached the word of the Lord (Acts 8:25); as did Philip (v. 40); Paul, Barnabas, and others (14:7, 21; 16:10). Paul often said he was called to preach the gospel (Rom. 15:20; 1 Cor. 1:17; 9:16a, b, 18; 2 Cor. 10:16; Gal. 1:8b; 4:13). Other refs.: Gal. 1:8a, 9; Heb. 4:2, 6; 1 Pet. 4:6. Other ref.: 1 Thes. 3:6 (to bring good news); see BRING <1994>. ¶

4 **to preach the gospel before: *proeuangelizomai*** [verb: προευαγγελίζομαι <4283>]; **from *pro*: before, and *euangelizō*: see 3 ▶ To announce in advance the good news** > The Scripture preached the gospel before {announced beforehand the glad tidings, preached the gospel beforehand} to Abraham (Gal. 3:8). ¶

[5] ***kērussō*** [verb: κηρύσσω <2784>]; **from *kērux*: herald, preacher ▶ To proclaim, to announce, to publish** > John the Baptist preached the baptism of repentance (Matt. 3:1; Mark 1:4, 7; Luke 3:3; Acts 10:37). Jesus preached the glad tidings of the kingdom of the heavens (Matt. 4:17, 23; 9:35; 11:1) and the glad tidings of the kingdom of God (Mark 1:14, 38, 39; Luke 4:44; 8:1). The apostles were sent to preach (Matt. 10:7, 27; Mark 3:14; 6:12; 13:10; 16:15, 20; Luke 9:2; 24:47; Acts 10:42). Others also went forth to preach the glad tidings of the kingdom (Matt. 24:14; 26:13; Mark 14:9). Philip preached the Christ (Acts 8:5). Paul preached the glad tidings, i.e., that which concerns Jesus Christ (Acts 9:20; 19:13; 20:25; 28:31; Rom. 10:8; 1 Cor. 1:23; 9:27; 15:11, 12; 2 Cor. 1:19; 4:5; 11:4a, b; Gal. 2:2; 1 Thes. 2:9). He exhorted Timothy to preach the word (2 Tim. 4:2). Some preached Christ out of envy and strife (Phil. 1:15). The preaching of Christ to the spirits in prison (1 Pet. 3:19) makes reference to His preaching by the Holy Spirit, employing Noah, before the flood; Noah's contemporaries refused this preaching, perished at the time of the flood, and are now in prison awaiting the final judgment. Other refs.: Acts 15:21 (those who preach Moses); Rom. 2:21 (to preach not to steal); Rom. 10:14, 15 and Col. 1:23 (to preach the glad tidings); Gal. 5:11 (to preach circumcision); 1 Tim. 3:16 (God preached among the nations). All other refs.: PROCLAIM <2784>, PUBLISH <2784>.

[6] ***laleō*** [verb: λαλέω <2980>] **▶ To speak, to announce, to tell** > Jesus was preaching the word (Mark 2:2). We read about the preaching of the word of God in Acts (8:25; 11:19, 20; 13:42; 14:25; 16:6). Other refs.: see entries in Lexicon at <2980>.

[7] **to preach fully: *plērophoreō*** [verb: πληροφορέω <4135>]; **from *plērēs*: full, and *phoreō*: to fill, which is from *pherō*: to carry, to bear ▶ To accomplish, to give full measure** > The Lord stood at Paul's side and gave him strength, so that through him the message might be preached fully {fully proclaimed, fully accomplished, known, made} (2 Tim. 4:17). All other refs.: BELIEVE <4135>, COMPLETE (adj.) <4135>, PERSUADE <4135>, PROOF <4135>.

[8] **to preach fully: *plēroō*** [verb: πληρόω <4137>]; **from *plērēs*: full; lit.: to accomplish fully ▶ To announce fully** > Paul had fully preached {had fully proclaimed} the gospel of Christ (Rom. 15:19). All other refs.: see entries in Lexicon at <4137>.

– [9] Acts 3:20 in some mss. → to preach before → FOREORDAIN <4400> [10] Acts 6:2 → to give up preaching → lit.: to leave → LEAVE (verb) <2641> [11] Acts 9:27–29 → to preach boldly, to preach fearlessly → BOLDLY <3955> [12] Acts 13:24 → to preach first, to preach before → to proclaim before → PROCLAIM <4296> [13] Acts 20:7 → SPEAK <1256> [14] Acts 20:9 → DISCOURSE (verb) <1256> [15] Acts 20:20 → ANNOUNCE <312> [16] Acts 26:20 → SHOW (verb) <518> [17] 1 Cor. 1:21; 2 Tim. 4:17 → the message preached, what was preached → lit.: the preaching → PREACHING <2782> [18] 1 Tim. 2:7; 2 Tim. 1:11; 2 Pet. 2:5 → HERALD <2783> [19] 2 Tim. 2:8 → as preached in my gospel → lit.: according to (*kata*) my gospel.

PREACHER – [1] Acts 17:18 → PROCLAIMER <2604> [2] 1 Cor. 9:18 → rights as a preacher of the gospel → lit.: right in the gospel.

PREACHING – [1] ***kērugma*** [neut. noun: κήρυγμα <2782>]; **from *kērussō*: to announce publicly ▶ Public proclamation, announcement of a message** > The inhabitants of Nineveh repented at the preaching of Jonah (Matt. 12:41; Luke 11:32). God has been pleased by the foolishness of the preaching {the message preached, what was preached} to save those who believe (1 Cor. 1:21). The preaching {proclamation} of Paul concerned Jesus Christ (Rom. 16:25; 1 Cor. 2:4; 15:14; 2 Tim. 4:17; Titus 1:3). ¶

– [2] 2 Cor. 8:18 → "preaching of" added in Engl. [3] 1 Tim. 4:13 → EXHORTATION <3874>.

PREAPPOINTED – Acts 17:26 → ORDAIN <4367> <4384>.

PRECAUTION – 2 Cor. 8:20 → to take precaution → AVOID <4724>.

PRECEDE – [1] ***proerchomai*** [verb: προέρχομαι <4281>]; **from *pro*: ahead, and *erchomai*: to go ▶ To outpace, to walk ahead** > Judas preceded {went before, led} the crowd (Luke 22:47). All other refs.: GO <4281>.
[2] ***phthanō*** [verb: φθάνω <5348>] ▶ **To go before** > Those who are alive and remain until the coming of the Lord are in no way to precede {anticipate, prevent} those who are asleep (1 Thes. 4:15). All other refs.: COME <5348>.
– [3] 1 Tim. 1:18 → to make previously → PREVIOUSLY <4254> [4] 1 Tim. 5:24 → GO <4254>.

PRECEPT – [1] Matt. 15:9; Mark 7:7; Col. 2:22 → COMMANDMENT <1778> [2] Mark 10:5; Heb. 9:19 → COMMANDMENT <1785> [3] Rom. 2:26 → REQUIREMENT <1345>.

PRECIOUS – [1] **very precious: *barutimos*** [adj.: βαρύτιμος <927>]; **from *barus*: heavy, and *timē*: value of a thing, price ▶ Very valuable, of great price** > A woman poured out an alabaster vase of very precious {very costly, very expensive} ointment on the head of Jesus (Matt. 26:7). ¶
[2] ***entimos*** [adj.: ἔντιμος <1784>]; **from *en*: in, and *timē*: honor, value ▶ Of great value, having a high price** > Christians come to the Lord, the precious Living Stone (1 Pet. 2:4, 6). All other refs.: DEAR <1784>, HONOR (noun) <1784>, HONORABLE <1784>.
[3] **like precious, as precious: *isotimos*** [adj.: ἰσότιμος <2472>]; **from *isos*: equal, and *timē*: honor, value ▶ Equally valuable; also transl.: of equal standing** > Peter addressed those who had received like precious faith with him (2 Pet. 1:1). ¶
[4] ***timios*** [adj.: τίμιος <5093>]; **from *timē*: honor, value ▶ Of great price, worthy of respect, dear** > Paul made no account of his life as precious to himself (Acts 20:24). He spoke of building with precious {costly} stones (1 Cor. 3:12). The laborer waits for the precious {valuable} fruit of the earth (Jas. 5:7). The proving of the Christian's faith is much more precious {of greater worth} than of gold, which perishes (1 Pet. 1:7). Christians have been redeemed by the precious blood of Christ (1 Pet. 1:19); they have received the greatest and precious promises (2 Pet. 1:4). Other refs.: Rev. 17:4; 18:12a, b, 16; 21:11 {costly} (most precious: *timiōtatos*), 19. All other refs.: HONOR (noun) <5093>, HONORED <5093>.
– [5] Mark 14:3; 1 Pet. 3:4 → precious, very precious → lit.: of great price → PRICE (noun) <4185> [6] 1 Pet. 2:7 → precious value → PRICE (noun) <5092>.

PRECIOUSNESS – 1 Pet. 2:7 → PRICE (noun) <5092>.

PRECISE – Acts 23:20 → more precise → more accurately → ACCURATELY <197>.

PREDESTINATE – See PREDESTINE <4309>.

PREDESTINE – ***proorizō*** [verb: προορίζω <4309>]; **from *pro*: before, and *horizō*: to determine, to limit ▶ To designate, to determine in advance; also transl.: to predestinate** > Predestination accompanies election, and defines that for which Christians are set apart in the plans of God. The redeemed forming the church are predestined to be conformed to the image of the Son of God (Rom. 8:29, 30). God has predestined them {marked them out beforehand} for adoption (see ADOPTION <5206>) through Jesus Christ to Himself (Eph. 1:5). They have been marked out beforehand (or: predestinated) so that they should be to the praise of His glory (Eph. 1:11; see v. 12). God has predestined {has predetermined, has destined, has ordained} His wisdom before the ages to the glory of Christians (1 Cor. 2:7). Other ref.: Acts 4:28 (to determine before); see DETERMINE <4309>. ¶

PREDETERMINE – 1 Cor. 2:7 → PREDESTINE <4309>.

PREDETERMINED – Acts 2:23 → to determine → DETERMINED <3724>.

PREDICT – [1] Acts 11:28 → SHOW (verb) <4591> [2] Rom. 9:29 → to say before, to say previously → SAY <4280> [3] 1 Pet. 1:11 → to testify beforehand → TESTIFY <4303>.

PREDICTION – 2 Pet. 3:2; Jude 17 → predictions → lit.: words having been said previously → SAY <4280>, WORD <4487>.

PREEMINENCE – [1] **to love to have the preeminence: *philoprōteuō*** [verb: φιλοπρωτεύω <5383>]**; from *philos*: one who loves, friend, and *prōteuō*: to be first, to be preeminent, which is from *prōtos*: first ▶ To love the first place, to be fond of occupying the chief position** > Diotrephes loved to have the preeminence {loved to be first, loved to have the first place} among the Christians (3 John 9). ¶

– [2] Col. 1:18 → to have the preeminence → to have the first place → PLACE (noun) <4409>.

PREEMINENT – Col. 1:18 → to be preeminent → to have the first place → PLACE (noun) <4409>.

PREFER – [1] Rom. 12:10 → to give preference → PREFERENCE <4285> [2] 1 Tim. 5:21 → preferring one before another → PREJUDICE <4299> [3] Phm. 9 → I prefer to appeal → I rather (*mallon*) appeal [4] Phm. 14 → I preferred to do nothing → I wanted to do nothing → WANT (verb) <2309>.

PREFERENCE – **to give preference: *proēgeomai*** [verb: προηγέομαι <4285>]**; from *pro*: before, and *hēgeomai*: to lead ▶ To take the lead, to give the example, to outdo** > Christians should give preference to {should prefer} one another in honor (Rom. 12:10). ¶

PREFERRED (BE) – John 1:15, 30 → is preferred before me → lit.: has been before me.

PREGNANCY – Luke 1:26 → "Elizabeth's pregnancy" added in Engl.

PREGNANT – [1] Matt. 1:18; 24:19; Mark 13:17; Luke 21:23; 1 Thes. 5:3 → with child → CHILD <1064> [2] Luke 1:24 → to become pregnant → CONCEIVE <4815>.

PREJUDGING – 1 Tim. 5:21 → PREJUDICE <4299>.

PREJUDICE – ***prokrima*** [neut. noun: πρόκριμα <4299>]**; from *prokrinō*: to prefer, which is from *pro*: before, and *krinō*: to judge ▶ Preconceived judgment, partiality** > Timothy was to keep the instructions of Paul without prejudice {bias, partiality, preferring one before another}, doing nothing out of favoritism (1 Tim. 5:21). ¶

PREMEDITATE – ***meletaō*** [verb: μελετάω <3191>]**; from *meletē*: care, which is from *melō*: to be of interest ▶ To be occupied with** > The disciples were not to premeditate what they would say when they would be delivered up (Mark 13:11 in some mss.). Other refs.: Acts 4:25; 1 Tim. 4:15; see MEDITATE <3191>, OCCUPY <3191>. ¶

PREOCCUPATION – [1] ***epistasis*** [fem. noun: ἐπίστασις <1987a>]**; from *epi*: upon, and *histēmi*: to stand ▶ What presses on the mind, what is upon the heart** > The preoccupation of {What came upon, The crowd (of cares) pressing on, The pressure on, The pressure of the concern of} Paul daily was the burden of all the churches (2 Cor. 11:28); in some mss.: *episustasis*; see [2]. ¶

[2] ***episustasis***: [fem. noun: ἐπισύστασις <1999>]**; from *episunistēmi*: to unite against, which is from *epi*: against, and *sunistemi*: to gather, which is from *sun*: together, and *histēmi*, to stand ▶ Disturbance, opposition** > Ref.: 2 Cor. 11:28;

see [1]. Other ref.: Acts 24:12; see RAISE <1999>. ¶

PREPARATION – [1] ***hetoimasia*** [fem. noun: ἑτοιμασία <2091>]; **from *hetoimos*: ready ▶ Readiness, promptitude** > Paul exhorts Christians to have shod their feet with the preparation of the glad tidings of peace (Eph. 6:15). The Greek word also has the sense of "foundation, base"; it is transl. thus in the Septuagint for Ps. 89:14: Righteousness and justice are the foundation of Your throne. In this sense, the gospel is the foundation of the Christian walk in Eph. 6:15. ¶
– [2] Matt. 26:17; Mark 14:12; Luke 9:52 → to make preparations → PREPARE <2090> [3] Mark 14:15; Luke 22:8, 12 → to make preparation → to make ready → READY <2090> [4] Luke 10:40 → preparations → SERVICE <1248> [5] Acts 10:10 → to make preparations → to make ready → READY <3903> [6] Heb. 9:6 → these preparations having been made → lit.: these things having been prepared → PREPARE <2680>.

PREPARATION DAY – Preparation, Preparation Day: ***Paraskeuē*** [fem. noun: Παρασκευή <3904>]; **from *paraskeuazō*: to prepare, which is from *para*: for, and *skeuazō*: to prepare, which is from *skeuē*: equipment, which is from *skeuos*: vessel, instrument ▶ Day preceding a Sabbath, i.e., a Friday** > The next day, after the Preparation, Pilate was asked to secure the tomb of Jesus (Matt. 27:62). Jesus was put to death on the Preparation Day (Mark 15:42; Luke 23:54; John 19:14, 31, 42). ¶

PREPARE – [1] ***hetoimazō*** [verb: ἑτοιμάζω <2090>]; **from *hetoimos*: ready ▶ To make ready, to get ready, to organize for a purpose** > Isaiah had said to prepare the way of the Lord (Matt. 3:3; Mark 1:3; Luke 3:4). The Father had prepared the privilege of sitting on the right hand or the left hand of Jesus for certain ones (Matt. 20:23; Mark 10:40). In a parable, the king had prepared his dinner (Matt. 22:4). The kingdom of God is prepared from the world's foundation (Matt. 25:34). Eternal fire is prepared for the devil and his angels (Matt. 25:41). The disciples of Jesus wanted to prepare {to make preparations} for Him to eat the Passover (Matt. 26:17; Mark 14:12). John the Baptist prepared the ways of the Lord (Luke 1:76). He was to prepare (*hetoimazō* <2090>) a people prepared (*kataskeuazō* <2680>) for the Lord (Luke 1:17). God had prepared His salvation before the face of all peoples (Luke 2:31). Messengers prepared {made ready, made arrangements, got ready} for Jesus (Luke 9:52). A rich man had prepared {provided} things, but his soul was to be required of him (Luke 12:20). A bondman knew his own lord's will, but had not prepared himself (Luke 12:47). Women prepared aromatic spices and ointments for Jesus (Luke 23:56; 24:1). Jesus was going to prepare a place for His redeemed in the house of His Father (John 14:2, 3). The chiliarch said to prepare men of war to conduct Paul to Caesarea (Acts 23:23). Paul speaks of the things that God has prepared for those who love Him (1 Cor. 2:9). The Christian is to be a vessel prepared for every good work (2 Tim. 2:21). Paul asked Philemon to prepare him a lodging (Phm. 22). God has prepared a city (Heb. 11:16). The verb is used in Revelation in regard to angels (Rev. 8:6; 9:15 {to keep ready}), horses, (9:7), a place (12:6), the way of the kings from the rising of the sun (16:12), the wife of the Lamb (19:7), and the new Jerusalem (21:2). Other refs.: READY <2090>.

[2] **to prepare afore, before, beforehand, in advance: *proetoimazō*** [verb: προετοιμάζω <4282>]; **from *pro*: before, and *hetoimazō*: see [1] ▶ To make ready in advance** > God has before prepared vessels of mercy for glory (Rom. 9:23). He has before prepared {before ordained} good works that we should walk in them (Eph. 2:10). ¶

[3] ***katartizō*** [verb: καταρτίζω <2675>]; **from *kata*: with (intens.), and *artizō*: to adjust, which is from *artios*: complete, perfect ▶ To form, to make** > God had prepared a body for the Lord Jesus (Heb. 10:5). The worlds were prepared {framed} by the word of God (Heb. 11:3). All other refs.: see entries in Lexicon at <2675>.

[4] ***kataskeuazō*** [verb: κατασκευάζω <2680>]; **from *kata*: intens., and *skeuazō*: to prepare, which is from *skeuē*: equipment, which is from *skeuos*: vessel, instrument ▶ a. To build, to construct >** A tabernacle was prepared {made, set up} (Heb. 9:2). The divine longsuffering waited while the ark was being prepared {was a preparing, was being made} {during the construction of the ark} (1 Pet. 3:20). Noah prepared an ark for the saving of his household (Heb. 11:7). **b. To be willing, to make ready >** John the Baptist prepared the way before Jesus (Matt. 11:10; Mark 1:2; Luke 7:27). He would prepare (*hetoimazō* <2090>) a people prepared (*kataskeuazō* <2680>) for the Lord (Luke 1:17). **c. To install >** The things in the tabernacle had been prepared {arranged, ordained, ordered} in a certain way (Heb. 9:6). All other refs.: BUILD <2680>, MAKE <2680>.

[5] ***paraskeuazō*** [verb: παρασκευάζω <3903>]; **from *para*: next to, and *skeuazō*: see [4] ▶ To get ready, to be ready >** The trumpet must not give an uncertain sound when it is a matter of preparing oneself for war (1 Cor. 14:8). Paul uses this verb in regard to Achaia (2 Cor. 9:2) and the Corinthians (v. 3). Other ref.: Acts 10:10 (to make ready); see READY <3903>. ¶

[6] ***katergazomai*** [verb: κατεργάζομαι <2716>]; **from *kata*: intens., and *ergazomai*: to work ▶ To accomplish, to work out >** God has prepared {has fashioned} Christians so that what is mortal may be swallowed up by life (2 Cor. 5:5). All other refs.: see entries in Lexicon at <2716>.

– [7] Luke 21:14 → to prepare beforehand → to meditate beforehand → MEDITATE <4304> [8] John 19:40 → to prepare for burial → BURY <1779> [9] 2 Cor. 9:5 → to prepare beforehand → to make beforehand → MAKE <4294> [10] Eph. 4:12 → lit.: for the perfecting → PERFECTING <2677> [11] 1 Pet. 1:13 → to prepare for action → to gird up → GIRD <328> [12] Rev. 14:10 → to pour out → POUR <2767>.

PREPARED – [1] **to prepare: *katartizō*** [verb: καταρτίζω <2675>]; **from *kata*: down, and *artizō*: to adjust, which is from *artios*: suitable ▶ To make ready, to form >** God endured with much patience vessels of wrath prepared {fitted} for destruction (Rom. 9:22; the middle voice in Greek here indicates that they have prepared themselves, emphasizing the fact that the responsibility for this is all of their own doing). All other refs.: see entries in Lexicon at <2675>.

– [2] Mark 14:15; 1 Pet. 3:15 → READY <2092> [3] 2 Tim. 4:2 → to be prepared → to be ready → READY <2186>.

PREPARING – 1 Pet. 3:20 → PREPARE <2680>.

PRESBYTERY – 1 Tim. 4:14 → ELDER <4244>.

PRESCRIBE – ***parangellō*** [verb: παραγγέλλω <3853>]; **from *para*: before, and *angellō*: to tell, to declare, which is from *angelos*: messenger ▶ To command, to ordain >** In prescribing {declaring} certain things to the Corinthians, Paul did not praise them (1 Cor. 11:17). All other refs.: COMMAND (verb) <3853>, ENJOIN <3853>.

PRESENCE – [1] ***parousia*** [fem. noun: παρουσία <3952>]; **from *para*: beside, and *ousia*: pres. ptcp. of *eimi* (to be) ▶ The fact of a person being in a place, his manifestation >** It was said that the personal presence of Paul was weak (2 Cor. 10:10). The Philippians had always obeyed in the presence and in the absence of Paul (Phil. 2:12). All other refs.: COMING <3952>.

[2] ***prosōpon*** [neut. noun: πρόσωπον <4383>]; **from *pros*: toward, and *ōps*: eye ▶ Person, appearance, face; also transl.: outward appearance >** In presence, Paul was lowly among the Corinthians (2 Cor. 10:1). He asked them if they looked on things after the outward appearance {on things outwardly, on the surface of things} (v. 7). Those who do not obey the glad tidings of the Lord Jesus Christ will pay the penalty of everlasting destruction from before the presence of the Lord (2 Thes. 1:9). Other refs.: Acts 3:13; 5:41. All other refs.:

APPEARANCE <4383>, FACE (noun) <4383>, PERSON <4383>.

3 **in the presence of: *apenanti*** [adv.: ἀπέναντι <561>]; **from *apo*: from, and *enanti*: before ► In front of, over against** > Faith in the name of Jesus had made a man strong in the presence of all (Acts 3:16). Other refs.: Matt. 21:2 {against, ahead, opposite}; 27:24 {before, in front of}, 61 {against, opposite}; Rom. 3:18 {before}. Other ref.: Acts 17:7; see CONTRARY <561>. ¶

4 **in the presence of: *emprosthen*** [adv.: ἔμπροσθεν <1715>]; **from *en*: in, and *prosthen*: in front ► Before, in front of** > The healed paralytic went out in the presence of {before, in the sight of, in full view of} all (Mark 2:12). Certain mss. have *enantion*. *

5 **in the presence: *enōpion*** [adv.: ἐνώπιον <1799>]; **from *en*: in, and *ōps*: eye ► Before, in front of** > Some will say that they have eaten and drunk in the presence of the Lord (Luke 13:26), but He will tell them He does not know them (see v. 27). *

– 6 Matt. 12:4; Mark 2:26; Luke 6:4; Heb. 9:2 → bread of the Presence → EXPOSITION OF THE LOAVES <4286> <740> 7 Mark 7:24 → to keep one's presence secret → to be hidden → HIDDEN (BE) <2990> 8 Acts 10:33 → we are in the presence → lit.: we are present → PRESENT <3918> 9 Phil. 1:26 → COMING <3952> 10 Rev. 7:15 → to shelter with one's presence → lit.: to spread one's tent → TENT <4637>.

PRESENCE OF (IN THE VERY) – ***katenōpion*** [adv.: κατενώπιον <2714>]; **from *kata*: against, and *enōpion*: before, which is from *en*: in, and *ōps*: eye ► Before, right in front of** > Refs.: 2 Cor. 2:17; 12:19; Eph. 1:4; Col. 1:22; Jude 24. ¶ ‡

PRESENT (adj.) – Eph. 6:12 → this present darkness → darkness of this age → AGE <165>.

PRESENT (noun) – 1 Acts 28:10 → to make presents → SUPPLY (verb) <2007> 2 Rev. 11:10 → GIFT <1435>.

PRESENT (verb) – 1 ***paristēmi*** [verb: παρίστημι <3936>]; **from *para*: beside, and *histēmi*: to stand ► a. This verb is used in regard to an ordinance of Jewish law, according to which every firstborn was to be set apart for Jehovah (or: the Lord) (see Ex. 13:2; 22:29, 30) and redeemed (see Num. 18:15, 16)** > Jesus was presented in the temple (Luke 2:22). Different offerings were specified in the law; the parents of Jesus offered that of the poor: two turtle doves (see Luke 2:24 and Lev. 12:8). **b. To manifest oneself, to appear; also transl.: to show** > Jesus presented Himself living after He had suffered (Acts 1:3). Peter presented Dorcas living (Acts 9:41). Paul had espoused the Corinthians to one man, to present them as a chaste virgin to Christ (2 Cor. 11:2). Timothy was to strive diligently to present himself approved to God (2 Tim. 2:15). **c. To bring before, to make (someone) appear** > Paul was presented {handed} to the governor (Acts 23:33). He who has raised the Lord Jesus will raise Paul also with Jesus and will present him with the Corinthians (2 Cor. 4:14). Christ will present the church to Himself (Eph. 5:27). He presents Christians holy before Himself (Col. 1:22). Paul wanted to present every man perfect in Christ (Col. 1:28). **d. To yield, to offer** > We must not present our members to sin, but rather present ourselves to God (Rom. 6:13a, b); we are slaves to whom we present ourselves, whether of sin or of obedience (v. 16); as we have presented our members to uncleanness and lawlessness, so we ought now to present our members as slaves of righteousness (v. 19a, b). Paul exhorts Christians to present their bodies a living sacrifice (Rom. 12:1). Other refs.: see entries in Lexicon at <3936>.

– 2 Matt. 2:11; 5:23, 24; 8:4; Acts 21:26 → to offer, to offer up → OFFER <4374> 3 Matt. 13:24, 31 → to set before → SET (verb) <3908> 4 Mark 4:30 → COMPARE <3846> 5 Acts 6:6; Jude 24 → SET (verb) <2476> 6 Acts 25:2 → to present charges → BESEECH <3870> 7 Rom. 3:25 → to set forth → SET (verb) <4388> 8 1 Cor. 9:18 → OFFER <5087> 9 Gal. 2:2 → to lay before → LAY <394> [10] Phil. 4:6 → to make known → KNOW <1107>.

PRESENT (BE) – [1] ***endēmeō*** [verb: ἐνδημέω <1736>]; **from *endēmos*: one who is at home, which is from *en*: in, and *dēmos*: people; lit.: at one's place ▶ To remain, to dwell; also transl.: to be at home** > We know that while present in the body, we are absent from the Lord (2 Cor. 5:6); we would rather be absent from the body and present with the Lord (v. 8); whether present or absent, we are zealous to be agreeable to Him (v. 9). ¶

[2] ***enistēmi*** [verb: ἐνίστημι <1764>]; **from *en*: in, and *histēmi*: to stand ▶ To be near, to be at hand** > Things present (lit.: Things which are present) cannot separate Christians from the love of God (Rom. 8:38). Things present belonged to the Corinthians (1 Cor. 3:22). Paul speaks of the present necessity (1 Cor. 7:26). Jesus gave Himself for sins, so that He would deliver Christians out of the present evil world (Gal. 1:4). Other refs.: 2 Thes. 2:2 {to come, to be at hand}; Heb. 9:9. Other ref.: 2 Tim. 3:1; see COME <1764>. ¶

[3] ***pareimi*** [verb: πάρειμι <3918>]; **from *para*: near, and *eimi*: to be ▶ To be there** > Paul was present in spirit in the midst of the Corinthians (1 Cor. 5:3a, b). He had been present with the Corinthians and in need, but he had been a burden to no one (2 Cor. 11:9). No chastening for the present {at the time, for the moment} (lit.: for the being present) seems to be a matter of joy (Heb. 12:11). Other refs.: Luke 13:1; Acts 10:33; 24:19; 2 Cor. 10:2, 11; 13:2, 10; Gal. 4:18, 20; Heb. 13:5; 2 Pet. 1:9, 12; Rev. 17:8 in some mss. All other refs.: COME <3918>.

[4] ***sumpareimi*** [verb: συμπάρειμι <4840>]; **from *sun*: with, together, and *pareimi*: see [3] ▶ To be found together** > The verb is used in Acts 25:24. ¶

[5] ***parakeimai*** [verb: παράκειμαι <3873>]; **from *para*: near, and *keimai*: to lie ▶ To be near, to be there** > The will to perform what is good is present with the man of Romans 7 (v. 18), but evil is also present with him (v. 21). ¶

– [6] John 14:25 → to be present → REMAIN <3306> [7] 1 Cor. 5:3 → to not be present physically → ABSENT (BE) <548>.

PRESENT TIME – [1] ***deuro*** [adv. and adv. used as noun: δεῦρο <1204>] **▶ Now, currently** > Paul had been hindered until the present time {hitherto, now, so far} from going to the Christians at Rome (Rom. 1:13). All other refs.: Matt. 19:21; Mark 10:21; Luke 18:22; John 11:43; Acts 7:3, 34; Rev. 17:1; 21:9. ¶

[2] ***nun*** [adv.: νῦν <3568>] **▶ Now, currently** > Felix told Paul to go for the present (Acts 24:25). God shows forth His righteousness in the present time Rom. 3:26). The sufferings of this present time are not worthy to be compared with the coming glory (Rom. 8:18). At the present time, there is a remnant of Israel according to the election of grace (Rom. 11:5). Other refs.: Acts 27:22; 2 Cor. 8:14; 1 Tim. 4:8; 6:17; 2 Tim. 4:10; Titus 2:12. Other refs.: see NOW <3568>.

PRESENT (TO THE, UNTO THIS) – John 16:24; 1 Cor. 15:6 → HITHERTO <737>.

PRESENTABLE – ***euschēmōn*** [adj.: εὐσχήμων <2158>]; **from *eu*: well, and *schēma*: shape, aspect ▶ Decent, not immodest** > Our presentable {comely, seemly} parts have no need of greater modesty (1 Cor. 12:24; see v. 23). All other refs.: COMELY <2158>, HONORABLE <2158>, PROMINENT <2158>.

PRESENTLY – Phil. 2:23 → IMMEDIATELY <1824>.

PRESERVATION – Acts 27:34 → SURVIVAL <4991>.

PRESERVE – [1] ***zōogoneō*** [verb: ζῳογονέω <2225>]; **from *zoos*: living, and *gonos*: procreation ▶ To maintain living, to retain life** > Whoever loses his life for the Lord will preserve it (Luke 17:33). Other refs.: Acts 7:19 {to live, to survive}; 1 Tim. 6:13 {to give life} in some mss. ¶

2 ***tēreō*** [verb: τηρέω <5083>]; **from *tēros*: warden, guard ▶ To keep, to guard** > The spirit, the soul, and the body of the Christian [ed: some believe soul and spirit are one and the same] must be preserved blameless at the coming of the Lord Jesus Christ (1 Thes. 5:23). The service of the Christian is to preserve himself unspotted from the world (Jas. 1:27). Christians have an inheritance preserved {reserved} in heaven for them (1 Pet. 1:4). Whoever is born of God preserves himself (1 John 5:18). Jude writes his epistle to those who are preserved in Jesus Christ (Jude 1); he exhorts them to preserve themselves in the love of God (v. 21). All other refs.: see entries in Lexicon at <5083>.

3 ***suntēreō*** [verb: συντηρέω <4933>]; **from *sun*: together, and *tēreō*: see 2 ▶ To keep, to save** > By putting new wine into new skins, both are preserved (Matt. 9:17; Luke 5:38 in some mss.). Other refs.: Mark 6:20; Luke 2:19; see KEEP (verb) <4933>. ¶

4 ***sōzō*** [verb: σῴζω <4982>]; **from *sōs*: safe, delivered ▶ To save, to guard** > Paul was saying that the Lord would preserve him for {would bring him safely to} His heavenly kingdom (2 Tim. 4:18). All other refs.: HEAL <4982>, SAVE (verb) <4982>.

5 ***phulassō*** [verb: φυλάσσω <5442>] **▶ To protect, to save** > God did not spare the old world, but preserved Noah (2 Pet. 2:5). All other refs.: GUARD (noun) <5442>, GUARD (verb) <5442>, KEEP (verb) <5442>.

– 6 Luke 17:33 → PURCHASE (verb) <4046> 7 Gal. 2:5 → to be preserved → REMAIN <1265> 8 1 Tim. 6:13 → to preserve in life → LIFE <2227> 9 Heb. 10:39 → those who have faith and preserve their souls → those who believe to the saving of the soul → SAVING <4047>.

PRESERVING – Heb. 10:39 → SAVING <4047>.

PRESIDE – Col. 3:15 → RULE (verb) <1018>.

PRESS – 1 ***diōkō*** [verb: διώκω <1377>]; **from *diō*: to pursue ▶ To run straight toward, to rush forward** > Paul was pressing {pursuing} toward the goal for the prize of the upward call of God in Christ Jesus (Phil. 3:14). All other refs.: FOLLOW <1377>, GIVE <1377>, PERSECUTE <1377>, PURSUE <1377>.

2 ***enechō*** [verb: ἐνέχω <1758>]; **from *en*: in, and *echō*: to hold ▶ To strive furiously against, to seek to trap** > The scribes and the Pharisees began to press Jesus vehemently (Luke 11:53); the verb is also transl.: to assail, to be very hostile, to oppose, to urge. Other refs.: Mark 6:19; Gal. 5:11; see GRUDGE (noun) <1758>, ENTANGLED (BE) <1758>. ¶

3 ***sunechō*** [verb: συνέχω <4912>]; **from *sun*: with, together, and *echō*: to hold ▶ To pull, to tear, to feel pressure; also transl.: to be in a strait, to be hard-pressed** > Paul was pressed by both, whether to die in order to be with Christ, or whether to live in order to serve Him (Phil. 1:23). All other refs.: see entries in Lexicon at <4912>.

4 ***thlibō*** [verb: θλίβω <2346>] **▶ To exercise pressure, to crush; also transl.: to crowd, to throng** > Jesus did not want the crowd to press upon Him (Mark 3:9). All other refs.: AFFLICTED (BE) <2346>.

5 ***apothlibō*** [verb: ἀποθλίβω <598>]; **from *apo*: from (intens.)., and *thlibō*: see 4 ▶ To exercise pressure from all sides** > The crowds closed Jesus in and pressed upon Him (Luke 8:45); also transl.: to crowd, to throng. ¶

6 ***sunthlibō*** [verb: συνθλίβω <4918>]; **from *sun*: with (intens.), and *thlibō*: see 4 ▶ To exercise pressure on all sides** > A large crowd pressed on {crowded, thronged} Jesus (Mark 5:24, 31). ¶

7 **to press around, on, etc.: *epikeimai*** [verb: ἐπίκειμαι <1945>]; **from *epi*: upon, and *keimai*: to put ▶ To push, to squash against** > The crowd pressed around {crowded around} Jesus to hear the word of God (Luke 5:1). All other refs.: BEAT <1945>, IMPOSE <1945>, INSISTENT <1945>, LAY <1945>.

8 **to press down: *piezō*** [verb: πιέζω <4085>] **▶ To compress, to pack down; comp. *piazō*: to press, to squeeze** > To him who gives, good measure, pressed down and

shaken together will be given into his bosom (Luke 6:38). ¶

– [9] Matt. 27:32; Mark 15:21 → COMPEL <29> [10] Mark 3:10 → to press, about, around, upon → to fall upon → FALL (verb) <1968> [11] Luke 8:42 → to press against → THRONG (verb) <4846> [12] Luke 13:33 → to press on → WALK <4198> [13] Luke 16:16 → to press into → to strive violently to go in → VIOLENCE <971> [14] 2 Cor. 11:28 in some mss. → crowd pressing on → PREOCCUPATION <1987a>.

PRESSED (BE) – [1] 2 Cor. 1:8 → to be pressed out, to be pressed beyond → BURDEN (verb) <916> [2] 2 Cor. 4:8; 1 Thes. 3:4 → to be hard pressed → AFFLICTED (BE) <2346>.

PRESSING – Titus 3:14 → NECESSARY <316>.

PRESSURE – [1] 2 Cor. 1:8 → to be under great pressure → to be burdened → BURDEN (verb) <916> [2] 2 Cor. 11:28 in some mss. → pressure, pressure of the concern → PREOCCUPATION <1987a>.

PRESUME – [1] Matt. 3:9 → THINK <1380> [2] Luke 7:7 → to count worthy → WORTHY <515> [3] Rom. 2:4 → to presume on → DESPISE <2706> [4] Rom. 15:18; Jude 9 → DARE <5111>.

PRESUMPTUOUS – ***tolmētēs*** [masc. noun: τολμητής <5113>]; **from *tolmaō*: to dare, to have audacity ▶ Self-assured, audacious** > Peter speaks of presumptuous {bold, daring} and self-willed people who are not afraid to speak injuriously of dignities (2 Pet. 2:10). ¶

PRETENCE – Mark 12:40; Phil. 1:18 → PRETEXT <4392>.

PRETEND – [1] ***hupokrinomai*** [verb: ὑποκρίνομαι <5271>]; **from *hupo*: under, and *krinō*: to judge ▶ To feign, to dissimulate** > Spies pretending to be righteous were sent to Jesus, so that they might catch Him in some statement (Luke 20:20). ¶

– [2] Acts 27:30 → pretending → PRETEXT <4392>.

PRETENSE – Mark 12:40; Luke 20:47; Acts 27:30; Phil. 1:18 → PRETEXT <4392>.

PRETENSION – [1] 2 Cor. 10:5 → high thing → HEIGHT <5313> [2] 2 Tim. 3:4 → of vain pretensions → PUFF UP <5187>.

PRETEXT – ***prophasis*** [fem. noun: πρόφασις <4392>]; **from *prophainō*: to appear before, which is from *pro*: before, and *phainō*: to appear, to shine, which is from *phōs*: light ▶ Appearance, reason invoked to dissimulate a real motive; also transl.: appearance, excuse, pretence, pretense, show** > The scribes made long prayers as a pretext (Matt. 23:14; Mark 12:40; Luke 20:47). When the Lord came, men had no pretext {cloak} for their sin (John 15:22). The sailors of Paul's ship had let down the boat into the sea under pretext {colour} of being about to carry out anchors from the prow (Acts 27:30). Even if Christ was announced in pretext, Paul rejoiced (Phil. 1:18 {false motives}). Paul had never used a pretext {cloak, cloke} for covetousness in his preaching of the glad tidings (1 Thes. 2:5). ¶

PREVAIL – [1] ***ischuō*** [verb: ἰσχύω <2480>]; **from *ischus*: power, strength ▶ To have vigor, to be effective; also transl.: to be in force, to be of force, to be of strength, to have power, to take effect** > The word of the Lord increased and prevailed {grew in power} (Acts 19:20). A testament is not in force while the testator is alive (Heb. 9:17). All other refs.: see entries in Lexicon at <2480>.

[2] **to prevail, to prevail against: *katischuō*** [verb: κατισχύω <2729>]; **from *kata*: against, and *ischuō*: to dominate; see also [1] ▶ To gain the upper hand, to be stronger** > The gates of Hades will not prevail against {overpower, overcome} the church (Matt. 16:18). The voices of the

people prevailed asking that Jesus be crucified (Luke 23:23). ¶
[3] ***ōpheleō*** [verb: ὠφελέω <5623>]; **from *ophelos*: advantage, profit ► To obtain an advantage, to profit; also transl.: to accomplish, to avail, to get, to profit** > Pilate saw that he could prevail nothing, addressing the crowd about Jesus (Matt. 27:24). The Pharisees said among themselves that they would not prevail for the world had gone after Jesus (John 12:19). All other refs.: HELPED (BE) <5623>, PROFIT (verb) <5623>, VALUE (noun) <5623>.
– [4] Matt. 24:12 → ABOUND <4129> [5] Rom. 3:4; Rev. 5:5 → OVERCOME <3528>.

PREVALENT – Jas. 1:21 → that is so prevalent → OVERFLOW (noun) <4050>.

PREVENT – [1] ***diakōluō*** [verb: διακωλύω <1254>]; **from *dia*: intens., and *koluō*: to forbid, to withhold ► To oppose vigorously, to prevent** > John was preventing {deterring, forbidding} Jesus from being baptized by him (Matt. 3:14). ¶
– [2] Matt. 17:25 → ANTICIPATE <4399> [3] Luke 24:16 → HOLD (verb) <2902> [4] Acts 8:36; Rom. 1:13 → HINDER (verb) <2967> [5] Acts 24:23; Heb. 7:23; 3 John 10 → FORBID <2967> [6] 2 Cor. 3:13 → to prevent the Israelites from seeing → lit.: for the sons of Israel not to gaze at [7] 1 Thes. 4:15 → PRECEDE <5348>.

PREVIOUSLY – [1] **to make previously: *proagō*** [verb: προάγω <4254>]; **from *pro*: before, and *agō*: to go, to lead; lit.: to precede ► To pronounce formerly, to utter beforehand** > Prophecies had been made previously {had preceded, had been made once} concerning Timothy (1 Tim. 1:18). All other refs.: see entries in Lexicon at <4254>.
– [2] Luke 23:12 → to be before → BEFORE <4391> [3] John 9:8; 2 Cor. 1:15 → BEFORE <4386> [4] Acts 21:29 → to see previously → SEE <4308> [5] 2 Cor. 8:6 → to make a beginning previously → BEGIN <4278> [6] Col. 1:5 → to hear previously → HEAR <4257> [7] Heb. 10:8 → HIGHER <511>.

PREY – [1] **to lead away as a prey: *sulagōgeō*** [verb: συλαγωγέω <4812>]; **from *sulon*: spoil, plunder, which is from *sulaō*: to strip, to rob, and *agō*: to lead away ► To ensnare; also transl.: to cheat, to spoil, to take captive** > The Colossians were to see that no one lead them away as prey through philosophy and vain deceit (Col. 2:8). ¶
– [2] Acts 11:6 → beasts of prey → wild beasts → BEAST <2342>.

PRICE (noun) – [1] ***timē*** [fem. noun: τιμή <5092>]; **from *tiō*: to revere, to pay honor ► Value of a thing, what one pays in order to obtain it; also transl.: money, proceeds, value** > The pieces of silver of Judas were the price of blood (Matt. 27:6), the price (*timē*) of Him on whom a price was set (*timaō*) on (v. 9). The early Christians sold their lands and houses, and brought the price of what was sold to the apostles to distribute according to need (Acts 4:34). Ananias set aside part of the price from the sale of a possession (Acts 5:2, 3). Abraham bought a tomb for a sum of money (lit.: for a price of silver) (Acts 7:16). The price of the books of magic that were burned was found to be fifty thousand pieces of silver (Acts 19:19). Christians have been bought with a price (1 Cor. 6:20; 7:23). Christ, as the head of the corner, has preciousness {is precious, has precious value} (or: price) for Christians (1 Pet. 2:7). All other refs.: HONOR (noun) <5092>.
[2] **very precious: *barutimos*** [adj.: βαρύτιμος <927>]; **from *barus*: heavy, and *timē*: see [1] ► Very valuable** > A woman poured out an alabaster vase of very precious {very costly, very expensive} ointment on the head of Jesus (Matt. 26:7). ¶
[3] **of great price: *polutelēs*** [adj.: πολυτελής <4185>]; **from *polus*: much, and *telos*: cost, payment ► Very precious, valuable** > A woman poured out an alabaster flask of ointment of great price {very costly, very expensive, very precious} (or: ointment of great price) on the head of Jesus (Mark 14:3). The hidden person of the heart is of great price {precious, very precious, of great worth} before God (1 Pet. 3:4). Other ref.: 1 Tim. 2:9; see COSTLY <4185>. ¶

[4] **of great price: *polutimos*** [adj.: πολύτιμος <4186>]; **from *polus*: much, and *timē*: see** [1] ► **Of very great worth** > A man sold all that he had in order to buy a pearl of great price {of great value} (Matt. 13:46). Mary anointed the feet of Jesus with an ointment of great price {expensive, very costly} (John 12:3). Other refs. in some mss.: Matt. 26:7; 1 Pet. 1:7. ¶
– [5] Matt. 27:9a, b → to set a price → PRICE (verb) <5091> [6] Acts 22:28 → SUM <2774> [7] Rev. 22:17 → without price → FREELY <1432>.

PRICE (verb) – ***timaō*** [verb: τιμάω <5091>]; **from *timē*: honor, price ► To estimate, to fix the value, to set a price** > Jesus was priced {valued} at thirty pieces of silver by the children of Israel (Matt. 27:9a, b). All other refs.: HONOR (verb) <5091>.

PRICK – [1] ***katanussō*** [verb: κατανύσσω <2660>]; **from *kata*: through (intens.), and *nussō*: to pierce; lit.: to pierce completely ► To experience a feeling of sadness and indignity as a sinner before God** > Those who heard Peter were pricked in {cut to, pierced to} their heart after listening to his preaching (Acts 2:37). ¶
– [2] Acts 26:14 → STING (noun) <2759>.

PRIDE – [1] ***alazoneia*** [fem. noun: ἀλαζονεία <212>]; **from *alazōn*: boaster, which is from *alē*: error ► Ostentation, arrogance** > The pride {boastful pride, boasting} of life is not of the Father (1 John 2:16). Other ref.: Jas. 4:16; see ARROGANCE <212>. ¶
[2] ***huperēphania*** [fem. noun: ὑπερηφανία <5243>]; **from *huperēphanos*: proud, which is from *huper*: above, and *phainō*: to appear, which is from *phōs*: light ► Exaggerated sense of one's importance, arrogance** > Pride {Haughtiness} comes out of the heart of men (Mark 7:22). ¶
– [3] Rom. 11:13 → to take pride → GLORIFY <1392> [4] 1 Cor. 4:6 → to take pride → to be puffed up → PUFF UP <5448> [5] 1 Cor. 15:31 → BOASTING <2746> [6] 1 Tim. 3:6 → to be lifted up with pride → PUFF UP <5187>.

PRIEST – [1] ***hiereus*** [masc. noun: ἱερεύς <2409>]; **from *hieros*: holy, sacred ► Person who exercised priesthood (see PRIESTHOOD** <2405>**) in Israel; the term applies also to Christ and to Christians** > There were priests in the time of the Lord (e.g., Matt. 8:4; Mark 1:44; Acts 4:1), and previously (Heb. 7:14, 15, 21, 23; 9:6). Jesus Christ is the great priest established over the house of God (Heb. 10:21). He is a priest forever according to the order of Melchizedek (Heb. 5:6; 7:17). He has made Christians of the present dispensation priests for His God and Father (Rev. 1:6), as likewise the redeemed of all dispensations (5:10). Other refs.: Matt. 12:4, 5; Mark 2:26; Luke 1:5; 5:14; 6:4; 10:31; 17:14; John 1:19; Acts 4:1; 6:7; 14:13 (priest of Zeus); Heb. 7:1, 3, 11; 8:4; 10:11; Rev. 20:6. ¶
[2] **chief priest: *archiereus*** [masc. noun: ἀρχιερεύς <749>]; **from *archē*: chief, and *hiereus*: see** [1] ► **Principal person among those who exercised the priesthood in Israel** > Chief priests were recognized among the larger group of priests (e.g., Matt. 2:4; Acts 4:23); they are responsible for having delivered Jesus to be condemned to death and for having crucified Him (Luke 24:20). Other refs.: HIGH PRIEST <749>, PRIESTHOOD <749>.
[3] **to execute the priest's office, to fulfill priestly service, to serve as priest, to perform priestly service: *hierateuō*** [verb: ἱερατεύω <2407>]; **from *hiereus*: priest ► To accomplish the functions of a priest in Israel; see** [1] > Zacharias fulfilled his priestly service before God (Luke 1:8). ¶
– [4] Luke 1:9; Heb. 7:5 → priest's office → PRIESTHOOD <2405> [5] Acts 4:6 → of the high priest → high-priestly → PRIESTLY <748>.

PRIESTHOOD – [1] ***hierateia*** [fem. noun: ἱερατεία <2405>]; **from *hierateuō*: to officiate as a priest, which is from *hiereus*: priest, which is from *hieros*: holy, sacred ► Priestly functions consisting essentially in offering the sacrifices prescribed by God under the law, interceding for the people**

and carrying out the divine service of the tabernacle, then later of the temple; also transl.: priest's office, priestly office > According to the custom of the priesthood, it fell to Zacharias by lot to enter into the temple to burn incense (Luke 1:9). Those from among the sons of Levi who receive the priesthood {the office of the priesthood} have a commandment to take tithes from the people according to the law (Heb. 7:5). ¶

[2] ***hierateuma*** [neut. noun: ἱεράτευμα <2406>]; **from *hierateuō*: to officiate as a priest, which is from *hiereus*: see [1] ▶ Body or order of priests exercising priestly functions; see [1].** > Christians of the present dispensation of grace constitute a holy priesthood (1 Pet. 2:5); they currently offer spiritual sacrifices to God; they also form a royal priesthood, in testimony before the world (v. 9). ¶

[3] ***hierōsunē*** [fem. noun: ἱερωσύνη <2420>]; **from *hieros*: holy, sacred ▶ See [1].** > In Israel, the exercise of the priesthood was reserved for the descendants of Aaron, the sons of Levi (Heb. 7:11). With the coming of Jesus, the priesthood is changed (Heb. 7:12); He has a priesthood that is not transmitted (v. 24). Other ref.: Heb. 7:14 in some mss. ¶

[4] **high priest: *archiereus*** [masc. noun: ἀρχιερεύς <749>]; **from *archē*: chief, and *hiereus*: see [1] ▶ Principal person among those who exercised the priesthood in Israel** > Under the high priesthood (lit.: the high priest) of Annas and Caiaphas, the word of God came to John, son of Zacharias (Luke 3:2). Other refs.: HIGH PRIEST <749>, PRIEST <749>.

– [5] Heb. 7:11b → established that priesthood → lit.: under it.

PRIESTLY – [1] Luke 1:8 → to fulfill priestly service, to perform priestly service → PRIESTHOOD <2407> [2] Luke 1:9; Heb. 7:5 → priestly office → PRIESTHOOD <2405> [3] Acts 4:6 → HIGH-PRIESTLY <748> [4] Rom. 15:16 → with the priestly duty → to carry on as a sacrificial service → SACRIFICIAL <2418>.

PRINCE – [1] ***archēgos*** [masc. noun: ἀρχηγός <747>]; **from *archē*: first, and *agō*: to lead ▶ Initiator, leader** > The word is reserved in the N.T. for the Lord Jesus Christ: the Prince {author, originator} of life (Acts 3:15), and the Prince {leader} and Savior exalted by God (Acts 5:31). All other refs.: AUTHOR <747>, CAPTAIN <747>.

[2] ***archōn*** [masc. noun: ἄρχων <758>]; **ptcp. of *archō*: to begin, to command, which is from *archē*: beginning ▶ Angel or man in a position of authority, chief, ruler** > This word is used concerning the demons (Matt. 9:34; 12:24; Mark 3:22; Luke 11:15); Satan, the prince of this world (John 12:31; 14:30; 16:11); and the power of the air (Eph. 2:2). It is also used of the Gentiles (Matt. 20:25) and of the authorities of this world (1 Cor. 2:6, 8). All other refs.: MAGISTRATE <758>, RULER <758>.

– [3] Rev. 6:15 → LORD (noun) <3175>.

PRINCIPAL – [1] Luke 19:47; Acts 25:2 → principal man → CHIEF <4413> [2] Acts 25:23 → lit.: prominence → PROMINENT <1851>.

PRINCIPALITY – ***archē*** [fem. noun: ἀρχή <746 **▶ Dignitary exercising a certain authority; also transl.: dominion, power, rule, ruler** > This word especially concerns spiritual powers, good or evil, of an invisible world. They have been created by the Lord and He is the head of them (Col. 1:16; 2:10). Principalities are found among the elect angels and upon earth (1 Cor. 15:24; Eph. 1:21; 3:10; Titus 3:1), as well as among the fallen angels (Rom. 8:38 {demons}; Eph. 6:12; Col. 2:15). Christ has created the faithful principalities for Himself, and He is their head (Eph. 1:21; Col. 2:10). At the end of the millennium, Christ will have annulled all rule (or: principality) and all authority and power (1 Cor. 15:24). Today, we are to submit ourselves to every principality established on earth (Titus 3:1). All other refs.: BEGINNING <746>, CORNER <746>, MAGISTRATE <746>, POWER[2] <746>, STATE <746>.

PRINCIPLE – [1] Gal. 4:3, 9; Col. 2:8, 20; Heb. 5:12 → principle, basic principle → ELEMENT <4747> [2] Heb. 6:1 → BEGINNING <746>.

PRISCA, PRISCILLA – ***Priska*** [fem. name: Πρίσκα <4251>], ***Priskilla*** [fem. name, dimin. of *Priska*: Πρίσκιλλα <4252>]: **ancient, virtuous (*priscus*, in Lat.) ► Christian woman of Jewish origin** > Priscilla is the wife of Aquila. She is referred to as Prisca (dimin. of Priscilla) in 2 Tim. 4:19 and as Priscilla in Acts 18:2, 18, 26; Rom. 16:3; 1 Cor. 16:19. See AQUILA <207>. ¶

PRISON – [1] ***desmōtērion*** [neut. noun: δεσμωτήριον <1201>]; **from *desmoō*: to bind; comp. *desmōma*: bonds, fetters ► Place where prisoners are kept in bonds** > The word is used in regard to John the Baptist (Matt. 11:2), the apostles (Acts 5:21, 23 {jail}), and Paul and Barnabas (Acts 16:26). ¶

[2] ***oikēma*** [neut. noun: οἴκημα <3612>]; **from *oikeō*: to dwell, to reside, which is from *oikos*: dwelling ► Place where one dwells; a euphemism for a jail cell** > The word is used to designate the cell where Peter was imprisoned (Acts 12:7). ¶

[3] ***tērēsis*** [fem. noun: τήρησις <5084>]; **from *tēreō*: to keep watch, to guard, which is from *tēros*: guard ► Place where prisoners are kept under guard** > The word is used in regard to Peter and John (Acts 4:3 {custody, hold, jail ward}), and the apostles (Acts 5:18 {jail}). Other ref.: 1 Cor. 7:19; see KEEPING <5084>. ¶

[4] ***phulakē*** [fem. noun: φυλακή <5438>]; **from *phulassō*: to keep, to preserve ► Place where prisoners are kept under guard; also transl.: imprisonment** > The word is used in regard to John the Baptist (Matt. 14:3, 10; Mark 6:17, 27; Luke 3:20; John 3:24), Jesus (Matt. 25:36, 39, 43, 44), disciples (Luke 21:12), Peter (Luke 22:33; Acts 12:4–6, 17), Barabbas (Luke 23:19, 25), the apostles (Acts 5:19, 22, 25), believers of the church (Acts 8:3; 22:4; 26:10), Paul and Barnabas (Acts 16:23, 24 {cell}, 27, 37, 40), Paul (2 Cor. 6:5; 11:23), O.T. people of faith (Heb. 11:36), spirits (1 Pet. 3:19), some of those of Smyrna (Rev. 2:10), and Satan (Rev. 20:7). Other refs.: Matt. 5:25; 18:30; Luke 12:58. All other refs.: GUARD (noun) <5438>, HOLD (noun) <5438>, WATCH (noun) <5438>.

– [5] Matt. 4:12; Mark 1:14 → to cast, to put in prison → BETRAY <3860> [6] Mark 15:7 → to be in prison → to be chained → CHAIN (verb) <1210> [7] Acts 20:23 → CHAIN (noun) <1199> [8] Acts 24:27; Col. 4:3 → in prison, to be in prison → lit.: imprisoned, to be bound → BIND <1210> [9] Rom. 16:7 → had been in prison with → FELLOW PRISONER <4869> [10] Heb. 10:34; 13:3 → one in prison → lit.: a prisoner → PRISONER <1198> [11] Heb. 13:3 → in prison → lit.: bound → to bind with → BIND <4887>.

PRISONER – [1] ***desmios*** [masc. noun: δέσμιος <1198>]; **from *desmeō*: to bind, which is from *desmos*: bond, chain ► Person who is deprived of liberty by being shut up in a prison while awaiting judgment** > Pilate released to the crowd one prisoner whom they wished (Matt. 27:15; Mark 15:6). Barabbas was a notorious prisoner at that time (Matt. 27:16), whom the crowd preferred to Jesus. In prison, Paul and Silas, in praying, were praising God with singing, and the other prisoners listened to them (Acts 16:25); the doors of the prison were miraculously opened, and the jailer thought that the prisoners had fled (v. 27). Paul was later once again made prisoner (Acts 23:18; 25:14, 27; 28:16, 17). He presents himself as a prisoner of Christ Jesus (Eph. 3:1; 4:1; 2 Tim. 1:8; Phm. 1, 9). The Hebrew Christians had sympathized with prisoners (Heb. 10:34); they were urged to remember prisoners (13:3). ¶

[2] ***desmōtēs*** [masc. noun: δεσμώτης <1202>]; **from *desmoō*: to bind ► See [1].** > Paul was sent to Rome with other prisoners (Acts 27:1, 42). ¶

– [3] Luke 4:18 → CAPTIVE (noun) <164> [4] Luke 21:24; Rom. 7:23 → to take as prisoners, to make prisoner → to make captive → CAPTIVE (adj.) <163> [5] Acts 9:2, 21; 22:5 → to take, to bring as prisoners

→ BIND <1210> [6] Rom. 16:7; Col. 4:10; Phm. 23 → FELLOW PRISONER <4869>.

PRIVATE – [1] Matt. 17:19 → in private → PRIVATELY <2596> [2] Mark 4:34; Gal. 2:2 → in private → PRIVATELY <2398> [3] Luke 9:18 → in private → ALONE <2651> [4] Luke 12:3 → private room → inner room → ROOM <5009> [5] John 7:10 → in private → in secret → SECRET (adj. and noun) <2927> [6] John 11:28 → in private → SECRETLY <2977> [7] 1 Cor. 11:21 → own private → own (*idios* <2398>).

PRIVATELY – [1] ***idios*** [adj. used as adv.: ἴδιος <2398>]; **lit.: one's own, personal ► Not publicly, apart; also transl.: in private, in particular, alone** > The disciples came to Jesus privately (Matt. 24:3). They questioned Him privately (Mark 9:28; 13:3). Jesus explained all things to His disciples privately (Luke 10:23; Mark 4:34). The Spirit divides the gifts to each privately {severally, individually} as He pleases (1 Cor. 12:11). Paul privately laid the gospel before those who were of reputation (Gal. 2:2). Other refs.: see entries in Lexicon at <2398>.

[2] ***kat'idian; kata*** [prep.: κατά <2596>]**: at, in, and *idios*** [adj.: ἴδιος <2398>]**: alone, private ► Apart, alone; also transl.: by himself, by themselves** > Having heard that John the Baptist was dead, Jesus departed to a desert place privately (Matt. 14:13); at this occasion, He took the apostles and went aside privately (Luke 9:10). He went up on a mountain to pray privately (Matt. 14:23). He led three of His disciples up on a high mountain by themselves (Matt. 17:1; Mark 9:2). The disciples came to Jesus privately (Matt. 17:19 {in private}). Jesus told His disciples to come aside privately (Mark 6:31, 32). He took a deaf man privately {aside from the crowd} (Mark 7:33). Other refs. (*idios*): see entries in Lexicon at <2398>.

PRIVATION – [1] ***husterēsis*** [fem. noun: ὑστέρησις <5304>]**; from *hustereō*: see [2] ► Lack of something, destitution** > Paul did not speak as regard to privation {need, want} (Phil. 4:11). Other ref.: Mark 12:44; see POVERTY <5304>. ¶

[2] **to suffer privation: *hustereō*** [verb: ὑστερέω <5302>]**; from *husteros*: last ► To lack something, to be in want** > Paul had learned both to abound and to suffer privation {to suffer need, to live in want} (Phil. 4:12). All other refs.: COME <5302>, INFERIOR <5302>, LACK (verb) <5302>, WANT (noun) <5302>, WORSE <5302>.

PRIVILY – [1] Matt. 1:19; 2:7; Acts 16:37 → SECRETLY <2977> [2] Gal. 2:4 → to come in privily → to come in surreptitiously → SURREPTITIOUSLY <3922>.

PRIVY – **to be privy: *suneidō*** [verb: συνείδω <4894>]**; from *sun*: together, and *eidō*: to know ► To be aware of something with someone else; to be his accomplice** > The wife of Ananias was privy to {was aware of, had full knowledge of} the fact that he was hiding a part of the sum for a possession that had been sold (Acts 5:2). The verb is transl. "I know {am conscious} of nothing," "my conscience is clear" (*oiden sunoida*) in 1 Cor. 4:4; lit.: "I have conscience of nothing." All other refs.: AWARE <4894>, CONSCIOUS <4894>, CONSIDER <4894>, KNOW <4894>.

PRIZE – [1] ***brabeion*** [neut. noun: βραβεῖον <1017>]**; from *brabeuō*: to assign a prize, to rule as an arbitrator ► Award to be won at stadium games held by the Greeks** > It is used in 1 Cor. 9:24 in regard to the Christian race. Paul ran straight to the goal for the prize of the calling on high (Phil. 3:14) that he might gain Christ (see v. 8), i.e., to be with Him and to be made like Him. ¶

– [2] 2 Tim. 2:5 → to win the prize → CROWN (verb) <4737>.

PROBABLY – Luke 20:13 → PERHAPS <2481>.

PROCEED – [1] ***ekporeuomai*** [verb: ἐκπορεύομαι <1607>]**; from *ek*: from, out, and *poreuomai*: to go ► To come from, to issue from** > The Spirit of truth proceeds {goes forth, goes out} from the Father (John

15:26). All other refs.: DEPART <1607>, GO <1607>, SPREAD <1607>.

2 **to proceed further: *prokoptō*** [verb: προκόπτω <4298>]; **from *pro*: before, in front, and *koptō*: to hit repeatedly ▶ To advance, to progress** > Evil men opposed to truth will proceed {make progress} no further {will not get far}, their folly will be clear to everyone (2 Tim. 3:9). All other refs.: GROW <4298>, INCREASE (verb) <4298>, SPEND <4298>.

3 **to permit to proceed, to permit to go: *proseaō*** [verb: προσεάω <4330>]; **from *pros*: in front, and *eaō*: to let, to permit ▶ To let come near** > The wind did not permit Paul's boat to proceed {did not suffer Paul's boat, did not allow to hold their course} (Acts 27:7). ¶

4 **to proceed, to proceed further: *prostithēmi*** [verb: προστίθημι <4369>]; **from *pros*: in front, and *tithēmi*: to put ▶ To continue, to add** > Herod had stretched out his hand to harass some of the church, and he proceeded further {went on} to seize Peter also (Acts 12:3). All other refs.: ADD <4369>.

– 5 Luke 13:22 → JOURNEY (verb) <4160> 6 John 8:42; Jas. 3:10 → to proceed forth → to come forth → COME <1831> 7 Rom. 14:23 → the verb is added in Engl.

PROCEEDS – 1 Acts 2:45 → "the proceeds" added in Engl. 2 Acts 4:34; 5:2, 3 → PRICE (noun) <5092>.

PROCESSION – 1 Cor. 4:9 → at the end of the procession → lit.: as the last ones → LAST (adv. and noun) <2078>.

PROCHORUS – ***Prochoros*** [masc. name: Πρόχορος <4402>]: **who leads the chorus or praise; from *pro*: before, and *choros*: dancing ▶ Christian man of the N.T.; also transl.: Procorus** > Prochorus was one of seven men chosen to be occupied with service in the church at Jerusalem (Acts 6:5). ¶

PROCLAIM – 1 ***katangellō*** [verb: καταγγέλλω <2605>]; **from *kata*: intens., and *angellō*: to bring a message, to tell ▶ To know, to report** > The faith of the Christians at Rome was proclaimed {spoken of} in the whole world (Rom. 1:8). All other refs.: PREACH <2605>.

2 ***kērussō*** [verb: κηρύσσω <2784>]; **from *kērux*: herald, preacher ▶ To announce, to declare; also transl.: to preach, to publish, to talk, to tell** > The leper who had been healed began to proclaim what had happened to him (Mark 1:45), as likewise the demoniac who had been healed (Mark 5:20; Luke 8:39) and those who had witnessed the healing of a deaf man (Mark 7:36). Jesus had been sent to preach deliverance to captives and to preach the acceptable year of the Lord (Luke 4:18, 19). A strong angel proclaimed with a loud voice: Who is worthy to open the book? (Rev. 5:2). Other ref.: Luke 12:3. All other refs.: PREACH <2784>, PUBLISH <2784>.

3 **to proclaim before: *prokērussō*** [verb: προκηρύσσω <4296>]; **from *pro*: before, and *kērussō*: see 2 ▶ To announce beforehand** > John had proclaimed before {had preached first, had preached before} the baptism of repentance (Acts 13:24). Other ref.: Acts 3:20 in some mss. ¶

– 4 Matt. 11:5; Luke 3:18; 4:43; 7:22; 9:6; 20:1; Acts 8:12; Heb. 4:2, 6 → PREACH <2097> 5 Matt. 12:18; 1 John 1:2, 3 → SHOW (verb) <518> 6 Luke 9:60 → PREACH <1229> 7 John 7:28 → to cry out → CRY (verb) <2896> 8 Acts 3:24 → ANNOUNCE <4293> 9 Acts 9:15 → to proclaim the Lord's name → to bear the Lord's name → BEAR <941> 10 Acts 20:20 → ANNOUNCE <312> 11 Acts 20:27; 1 John 1:5 → DECLARE <312> 12 Rom. 9:17 → DECLARE <1229> 13 Rom. 15:19 → to proclaim fully → to preach fully → PREACH <4137> 14 Rom. 16:25 → the message I proclaim → lit.: the preaching → PREACHING <2782> 15 Eph. 6:19 → to make known → KNOW <1107> 16 Phil. 1:14; Col. 4:3; Heb. 9:19 → SPEAK <2980> 17 2 Thes. 2:4 → to show oneself → SHOW (verb) <584> 18 2 Tim. 4:17 → to proclaim fully → to preach fully → PREACH <4135> 19 Heb. 2:12 → DECLARE <518> 20 1 Pet. 2:9 → to show forth → SHOW (verb) <1804>.

PROCLAIMER – ***katangeleus*** [masc. noun: καταγγελεύς <2604>]; **from *katangellō*: to declare, to preach, which is from *kata*: intens., and *angellō*: to bring a message ▶ One who announces, who declares in a formal manner** > Some philosophers said that Paul seemed to be a proclaimer of {an announcer of, a setter forth of, advocating} foreign gods (Acts 17:18). ¶

PROCLAMATION – Rom. 16:25; 2 Tim. 4:17; Titus 1:3 → PREACHING <2782>.

PROCONSUL – 1 ***anthupatos*** [masc. noun: ἀνθύπατος <446>]; **from *anti*: in place of, and *hupatos*: consul, which is from *huper*: over, above ▶ Originally, one invested with full military power, who acted in place of the consul to govern a Roman province; in N.T. times, one who governed a settled senatorial Roman province** > Sergius Paulus was the proconsul {deputy} of Cyprus (Acts 13:7, 8, 12). There were proconsuls {deputies} at Ephesus (Acts 19:38). ¶

2 **to be proconsul: *anthupateuō*** [verb: ἀνθυπατεύω <445>]; **from *anthupatos*: see 1 ▶ To act in place of the consul** > Gallio was proconsul {was the deputy} of Achaia (Acts 18:12). ¶

– 3 Acts 18:17 → in front of the proconsul → lit.: in front of the judgment seat.

PROCORUS – Acts 6:5 → see PROCHORUS <4402>.

PROCURE – John 18:3 → TAKE <2983>.

PRODIGAL – **prodigally: *asōtōs*** [adv.: ἀσώτως <811>]; **from *asōtos*: prodigal, extremely wasteful ▶ In an exceedingly wasteful, dissolute, immoral manner of life** > The younger son wasted his possessions with prodigal living {with riotous living, with loose living, in wild living, living in debauchery} (lit.: living prodigally) (Luke 15:13). ¶

PRODUCE – 1 ***blastanō*** [verb: βλαστάνω <985>]; **from *blastos*: bud, germ ▶ To grow, to cause to sprout** > Elijah prayed and the earth produced its fruit (Jas. 5:18 {to bring forth, to spring forth}). All other refs.: BUD <985>, SPROUT <985>.

2 ***didōmi*** [verb: δίδωμι <1325>] ▶ **To give, to yield** > In a parable, grain produced {brought forth} fruit (Matt. 13:8). Other refs.: GIVE <1325>.

3 ***ekphuō*** [verb: ἐκφύω <1631>]; **from *ek*: out, and *phuō*: to push, to spring up ▶** To put forth, to grow > Jesus spoke of the fig tree that produces leaves (Matt. 24:32; Mark 13:28). ¶

4 ***katergazomai*** [verb: κατεργάζομαι <2716>]; **from *kata*: intens., and *ergazomai*: to work, which is from *ergon*: work ▶ To generate, to accomplish, to give rise; also transl.: to bring about, to work** > Law produces {works, brings, brings about} wrath (Rom. 4:15). Tribulation produces endurance (Rom. 5:3). Sin works every lust (Rom. 7:8). The fact of having godly sorrow had produced much diligence in the Corinthians (2 Cor. 7:11). Their liberality worked through Paul thanksgiving to God (2 Cor. 9:11 {to cause, to result}). The proving of faith works {develops} endurance (Jas. 1:3). All other refs.: see entries in Lexicon at <2716>.

5 ***paradidōmi*** [verb: παραδίδωμι <3860>]; **from *para*: next to, and *didōmi*: to give ▶ To deliver, to bring forth; i.e., when its ripeness allows** > When the fruit is produced {is brought forth, is ripe, ripens}, the sickle is immediately put to it (Mark 4:29). All other refs.: see entries in Lexicon at <3860>.

6 ***prosergazomai*** [verb: προσεργάζομαι <4333>]; **from *pros*: to the advantage of, and *ergazomai*: to work, to trade ▶ To yield as a result of work or trade** > A bondman's mina produced {earned, gained, made} ten minas (Luke 19:16). ¶

7 ***poieō*** [verb: ποιέω <4160>]; **lit.: to make ▶ To bear (fruit), to bring forth, to yield** > The kingdom of God was to be given to a nation producing {bringing forth} the fruits of it (Matt. 21:43). The verb is used in regard to the subject of fruit by John the Baptist (Matt. 3:8, 10; Luke 3:8, 9), by Jesus (Matt. 7:17a, b, 18a, b, 19; 13:23b, 26; Luke 6:43a, b; 8:8). A fig tree cannot

produce olives (Jas. 3:12). Other refs.: see entries in Lexicon at <4160>.
[8] ***tiktō*** [verb: τίκτω <5088>] ▶ **To bear, to bring forth** > The ground produces useful herbs (Heb. 6:7). All other refs.: BIRTH <5088>.
– [9] Matt. 13:23; Mark 4:20, 28; Luke 8:15 → to produce a crop, to produce grain → to bear fruit → FRUIT <2592> [10] Mark 4:8; John 12:24 → BRING <5342> [11] Luke 6:45a, b → to bring forth → BRING <4393> [12] Luke 12:16 → to produce a good crop → to bring forth plentifully → BRING <2164> [13] Acts 22:30 → SET (verb) <2476> [14] Rom. 5:4a, b → "produces" added in Engl. [15] 1 Tim. 6:4 → which produce → lit.: out of which comes (*ginomai*) [16] 2 Tim. 2:23 → GENERATE <1080> [17] 2 Pet. 1:21 → produced by the will of man → came (*pherō*) by the will of man.

PRODUCTIVE – Luke 12:16 → to be very productive → to bring forth plentifully → BRING <2164>.

PROFANE (adj. and noun) – [1] ***bebēlos*** [adj. and adj. used as noun: βέβηλος <952>]; **from *bainō*: to walk, and *bēlos*: threshold; denotes one who was or should have been forbidden to enter the temple ▶ Foreign to God, impious, in contrast to that which is holy; also transl.: godless, worldly** > The law is for the unholy and profane {irreligious} (1 Tim. 1:9). Timothy was to reject profane fables (1 Tim. 4:7) as well as to avoid and shun profane, vain babblings (1 Tim. 6:20; 2 Tim. 2:16). Esau is qualified as profane on account of having sold his birthright for one meal (Heb. 12:16). ¶
– [2] 2 Tim. 3:2 → UNHOLY <462>.

PROFANE (verb) – [1] ***bebēloō*** [verb: βεβηλόω <953>]; **from *bebēlos*: see PROFANE** (adj. and noun) <952> ▶ **To desecrate, to defile** > Jesus reminded the Pharisees that the priests in the temple profaned {broke} the Sabbath and were blameless (Matt. 12:5). The orator Tertullus accused Paul of having attempted to profane the temple (Acts 24:6). ¶
– [2] Acts 21:28 → DEFILE <2840> [3] Heb. 10:29 → to consider common → COMMON <2839>, CONSIDER <2233>.

PROFESS – [1] ***homologeō*** [verb: ὁμολογέω <3670>]; **from *homologos*: assenting, which is from *homos*: same, and *logos*: word ▶ To declare, to publicly acknowledge** > The expr. "to profess {claim} to know" in Titus 1:16 is applied to unbelievers who falsely confess to know God, but who in works deny Him. All other refs.: CONFESS <3670>.
– [2] Rom. 1:22 → SAY <5335> [3] 1 Tim. 2:10; 6:21 → to make profession → PROFESSION <1861> [4] Heb. 4:14; 10:23 → lit.: to make confession → CONFESSION <3671>.

PROFESSED – 2 Cor. 9:13 → professed subjection → lit.: subjection by profession → CONFESSION <3671>.

PROFESSION – [1] **to make profession: *epangellō*** [verb: ἐπαγγέλλω <1861>]; **from *epi*: intens., and *angellō*: to tell, to declare, which is from *angelos*: messenger ▶ To declare, to acknowledge** > Good works are proper for women making profession of {making a claim of, professing} the fear of God (1 Tim. 2:10). Some have made profession of what is falsely called knowledge and have missed the faith (1 Tim. 6:21). All other refs.: PROMISE (noun) <1861>, PROMISE (verb) <1861>.
– [2] 2 Cor. 9:13; 1 Tim. 6:12; Heb. 3:1; 4:14; 10:23 → CONFESSION <3671>.

PROFIT (noun) – [1] ***ophelos*** [neut. noun: ὄφελος <3786>]; **from *ophellō*: to augment ▶ Gain, advantage** > There was no profit to Paul if the dead do not rise (1 Cor. 15:32). There is no profit if any one says he has faith, but does not have works (Jas. 2:14) and does not provide for physical needs (v. 16). ¶
[2] ***ōpheleia*** [fem. noun: ὠφέλεια <5622>]; **from *opheleō*: to profit, which is from *ophelos*: see [1] ▶ Benefit, advantage** > Paul asked what is the profit of circumcision (Rom. 3:1). Jude spoke of those who

admire men for the sake of their own profit {advantage} (v. 16). ¶

[3] **profit, of profit: *sumpheron*; neut. ptcp. of *sumpherō*** [verb: συμφέρω <4851>]; **see** [4] ▶ **Benefit, advantage** > It was not of profit {expedient, profitable} to {There was nothing to be gained for} Paul to boast (2 Cor. 12:1). God disciplines Christians for their profit {good} (Heb. 12:10). See [4]. All other refs.: BRING <4851>, PROFITABLE <4851>.

[4] **to be profitable: *sumpherō*** [verb: συμφέρω <4851>]; **from *sun*: together, and *pherō*: to bring; lit.: to bring together for the benefit of someone** ▶ **Advantage, benefit** > To each Christian is given the manifestation of the Spirit for mutual profit {the common good} (lit.: of the what is profitable) (1 Cor. 12:7). See [3].

[5] ***sumphoron*** [neut. noun: σύμφορον <4852a>]; **from *sumpherō*: see** [4] ▶ **Advantage, interest; also transl.: good** > Paul was speaking to the Corinthians for their own profit {benefit} (1 Cor. 7:35); he was not seeking his own profit, but that of the many that they may be saved (10:33). Some mss. have *sumpheron* <4851>. ¶

– [6] Matt. 15:5; 16:26; Mark 7:11; 8:36; Luke 9:25 → to receive profit, to be profit → PROFIT (verb) <5623> [7] Acts 16:16, 19; 19:24 → GAIN (noun) <2039> [8] Gal. 5:4 → to deprive of all profit → to make of no effect → EFFECT (noun) <2673> [9] 1 Tim. 4:8a → to be of profit → lit.: to be profitable → PROFITABLE <5624> [10] 2 Tim. 2:14 → to no profit → profitable for nothing → PROFITABLE <5539> [11] Phm. 20 → to have profit → BENEFIT <3685> [12] Jas. 4:13 → to make a profit → GAIN (verb) <2770> [13] Jude 11 → REWARD (noun) <3408> [14] Jude 11 → to rush for profit into → to give oneself up → GIVE <1632>.

PROFIT (verb) – [1] ***antilambanō*** [verb: ἀντιλαμβάνω <482>]; **from *anti*: in turn, mutually, and *lambanō*: to take** ▶ **To receive, to benefit** > Believing masters profit {partake, are partakers} from the good and ready service rendered by their servants (1 Tim. 6:2). Other refs.: Luke 1:54; Acts 20:35; see HELP (verb) <482>. ¶

[2] ***ōpheleō*** [verb: ὠφελέω <5623>]; **from *ophelos*: gain, advantage** ▶ **To be of value, to help, to benefit** > Jesus reproached the scribes and Pharisees for teaching people to declare their goods as corban (i.e., a gift) rather than permitting their parents to profit from {to be helped with} those goods (Matt. 15:5; Mark 7:11). A man does not profit if he should gain the whole world and suffer the loss of his soul (Matt. 16:26 {to be profited, to be good for}; Mark 8:36 {to be good for; Luke 9:25 {to be profited, to be good for, to be advantaged}). The flesh profits nothing {counts for nothing, is no help at all} (John 6:63). If a Christian does not have love, he profits {gains} nothing (1 Cor. 13:3). If Paul had come speaking only with tongues, without edifying his listeners, he would not have profited {have been good to} the Corinthians (1 Cor. 14:6). Christ will profit nothing {be of no benefit, be of no value} to those who are circumcised (Gal. 5:2). The word did not profit certain people, not being mixed with faith in those who heard it (Heb. 4:2). Meats have not profited {have not been of value to} those who have made them a question of observance (Heb. 13:9). All other refs.: HELPED (BE) <5623>, PREVAIL <5623>, VALUE (noun) <5623>.

– [3] 1 Cor. 6:12 → to be profitable → PROFITABLE <4851> [4] 1 Cor. 15:32; Jas. 2:14, 16 → lit.: to be the profit → PROFIT (noun) <3786> [5] Gal. 1:14 → INCREASE (verb) <4298> [6] 1 Tim. 4:8a → lit.: to be profitable → PROFITABLE <5624>.

PROFITABLE – [1] ***ōphelimos*** [adj.: ὠφέλιμος <5624>]; **from *ōpheleō*: to be useful, to be beneficial, which is from *ophelos*: profit, advantage** ▶ **Advantageous, beneficial; also transl.: of profit, of value, useful** > Bodily exercise is profitable for a little, but godliness is profitable for all things (1 Tim. 4:8a, b). Every Scripture is inspired by God, and profitable for teaching, for conviction, for correction, for instruction in righteousness (2 Tim. 3:16). Paul speaks of things that are good and profitable for people (Titus 3:8). ¶

[2] **to be profitable: *sumpherō*** [verb: συμφέρω <4851>]; **from *sun*: with, together,**

and *pherō*: to carry; lit.: to bring together for the benefit of someone ▶ To be to the advantage, to be in the interest; also transl.: to be better, to be good, to be expedient > It is profitable that one member perish, and not that the whole body be cast into hell (Matt. 5:29, 30). The disciples told Jesus it was not profitable to marry if one could not divorce his wife (Matt. 19:10). It was profitable for {It was for the good of} the disciples that Jesus went away (John 16:7). Paul says that all things are lawful, but not all things are profitable {are helpful, are beneficial, do profit} (1 Cor. 6:12; 10:23). In 2 Cor. 8:10, Paul gives his opinion, which is profitable {is expedient, is to the advantage, is best} for the Corinthians. Other refs.: Matt. 18:6; John 11:50; 18:14. See 3. All other refs.: BRING <4851>, PROFIT (noun) <4851>.

3 **what is profitable: *sumpheron*; neut. ptcp. of *sumpherō*** [verb: συμφέρω <4851>]; **see 2 ▶ Beneficial, advantageous thing >** Paul had held back nothing from the Ephesians of what is profitable {helpful} (Acts 20:20). See 2 for other refs. with *sumpherō*.

4 ***chrēsimos*** [adj.: χρήσιμος <5539>]; **from *chraomai*: to use, to meet a need ▶ Useful, beneficial >** Disputes of word are profitable for nothing {useless, of no value, to no profit} (2 Tim. 2:14). ¶

– 5 Luke 17:2 → lit.: to be more profitable → to be better → BETTER <3081> 6 Rom. 2:25 → to be profitable → to have value → VALUE (noun) <5623> 7 2 Tim. 4:11; Phm. 11 → USEFUL <2173>.

PROFITING – 1 Tim. 4:15 → PROGRESS <4297>.

PROGRESS – 1 ***prokopē*** [fem. noun: προκοπή <4297>]; **from *prokoptō*: to advance, to progress, which is from *pro*: before, forward, and *koptō*: to cut, to impel ▶ Advancement, growth (e.g., spiritual) >** The spiritual progress {profiting} of Timothy was to be evident to all (1 Tim. 4:15). Other refs.: Phil. 1:12, 25; see FURTHERANCE <4297>. ¶

– 2 John 13:2 → to be in progress → lit.: being (*ginomai*) 3 2 Tim. 3:9 → to make progress → PROCEED <4298>.

PROLONG – ***parateinō*** [verb: παρατείνω <3905>]; **from *para*: along, and *teinō*: to stretch ▶ To draw out, to continue, to carry on >** Paul prolonged {continued, kept on} his discourse until midnight on the first day of the week (Acts 20:7). ¶

PROMINENCE – Acts 13:50 → of prominence → PROMINENT <2158>.

PROMINENT – 1 ***euschēmōn*** [adj.: εὐσχήμων <2158>]; **from *eu*: well, and *schēma*: appearance ▶ Honorable, distinguished; also transl.: honourable, of the upper classes, of prominence, of high standing >** There were prominent women at Antioch who worshipped God (Acts 13:50). At Thessalonica, not a few Grecian women who were prominent believed the preaching of the word (Acts 17:12). All other refs.: COMELY <2158>, HONORABLE <2158>, PRESENTABLE <2158>.

2 ***prōtos*** [adj.: πρῶτος <4413>]; **superl. of *pro*: before, ahead ▶ Eminent, superior; also transl.: chief, leading >** Prominent women believed the preaching of Paul and Silas (Acts 17:4); they were most likely upper class women. All other refs.: BEST <4413>, CHIEF <4413>, FIRST <4413>.

3 **prominence: *exochē*** [fem. noun: ἐξοχή <1851>]; **from *exechō*: to be prominent, which is from *ek*: out of, and *echō*: to have, to be ▶ Excellence, distinction >** Paul was brought before the prominent {leading, principal} men (lit.: the men of prominence) of the city (Acts 25:23). ¶

– 4 Luke 14:1 → of a prominent Pharisee → lit.: of one of the rulers of the Pharisees → RULER <758>.

PROMISCUITY – Rom. 13:13 → sexual promiscuity → LEWDNESS <2845>.

PROMISE (noun) – 1 ***epangelia*** [fem. noun: ἐπαγγελία <1860>]; **from *epangellō*: to announce, which is from *epi*: upon (intens.), and *angellō*: to proclaim, to**

announce ▶ Commitment, assurance of a person to give or do something that which is promised > We have received of the Father the promise of the Holy Spirit (Acts 2:33). The nations have received the promise of the Spirit through faith (Gal. 3:14). We are to be imitators of those who through faith and patience have been inheritors of the promises (Heb. 6:12). Abraham got the promise (Heb. 6:15). The word is used in regard to the Father (Luke 24:49; Acts 1:4), the Holy Spirit (Acts 2:39; Gal. 3:14; Eph. 1:13), God (Acts 7:17; 13:23, 32; 26:6; Rom. 4:13, 14, 16, 20; 9:4, 8, 9; 15:8; 2 Cor. 1:20; 7:1; Gal. 3:16, 17, 18a, b, 21, 22, 29; 4:23, 28; Eph. 2:12; 3:6; 1 Tim. 4:8; 2 Tim. 1:1; Heb. 4:1; 6:17; 7:6; 8:6; 11:9a, b, 17; 1 John 2:25), a chiliarch (Acts 23:21), and a commandment (Eph. 6:2). Some say: Where is the promise of His coming? (2 Pet. 3:4), but the Lord does not delay His promise (v. 9). Other refs.: Heb. 9:15; 10:36; 11:13, 33, 39; 1 John 1:5. ¶

[2] ***epangelma*** [neut. noun: ἐπάγγελμα <1862>]; **from *epangellō*: see [1] ▶ Declaration, commitment which a person has made to do something** > Divine power has given to Christians the great and precious promises (2 Pet. 1:4). According to the promise of God, we wait for new heavens and a new earth, in which righteousness dwells (2 Pet. 3:13). ¶

[3] **to make a promise: *epangellō*** [verb: ἐπαγγέλλω <1861>]; **see [1] ▶ To commit, to engage oneself to doing something** > The promise was made to the Seed that should come (Gal. 3:19). God made a promise {promised} to Abraham (Heb. 6:13). All other refs.: PROFESSION <1861>, PROMISE (verb) <1861>.

PROMISE (verb) – [1] ***harmozō*** [verb: ἁρμόζω <718>]; **from *harmos*: bond; lit.: to join ▶ To engage, to give in marriage; also transl.: to betroth, to espouse** > Paul had promised the Corinthians to one husband, to present them to Christ as a pure virgin (2 Cor. 11:2). ¶

[2] ***epangellō*** [verb: ἐπαγγέλλω <1861>]; **from *epi*: upon (intens.), and *angellō*: to proclaim, to announce ▶ To commit, engage oneself to doing something** > The chief priests promised Judas to give him money for delivering Jesus up (Mark 14:11). God promised Abraham to give him an inheritance in the promised land (Acts 7:5). God is able to do what He has promised (Rom. 4:21). God promised eternal life before the ages of time (Titus 1:2). He who promised is faithful (Heb. 10:23). Sarah counted Him faithful who had promised {had made the promise} (Heb. 11:11). God promised that He will shake not only the earth, but also the heaven (Heb. 12:26). The Lord has promised the crown of life to those who love Him (Jas. 1:12). God has promised the kingdom to those who love Him (Jas. 2:5). Some who are slaves of corruption promise liberty to others (2 Pet. 2:19). The promise which God has promised {has made to} is life eternal (1 John 2:25). Other refs.: Gal. 3:19 {to make the promise}; 1 Tim. 2:10 {to make profession, to profess, to make a claim}; 6:21 {to make profession, to profess}; Heb. 6:13. ¶

[3] **to promise beforehand, before, afore: *proepangellō*** [verb: προεπαγγέλλω <4279>]; **from *pro*: before, and *epangellō*; see [2] ▶ To announce in advance, to commit oneself to doing something** > God had promised beforehand the glad tidings by His prophets in the Holy Scriptures (Rom. 1:2). Other ref. in some mss.: 2 Cor. 9:5. ¶

[4] ***omnuō*** [verb: ὀμνύω <3660>] **▶ To swear, to promise with an oath, to assure** > The time of promise drew near which God had promised to Abraham (Acts 7:17). All other refs.: SWEAR <3660>.

[5] ***homologeō*** [verb: ὁμολογέω <3670>]; **from *homologos*: assenting, of one mind, which is from *homos*: same, and *logos*: word ▶ To consent, to declare** > Herod promised with an oath to give the daughter of Herodias whatever she should ask (Matt. 14:7). All other refs.: CONFESS <3670>.

[6] ***exomologeō*** [verb: ἐξομολογέω <1843>]; **from *ek*: out (intens.), and *homologeō*: see [5] ▶ To accept, to commit oneself** > Judas promised {came to an agreement, consented} and sought an opportunity to betray Jesus (Luke 22:6). All other refs.: CONFESS <1843>, THANK (verb) <1843>.

– 7 Luke 1:45, 55 → SPEAK <2980> 8 Luke 10:6 → someone who promotes peace → lit.: son of peace 9 Luke 24:49; Acts 1:4; 2:33; Eph. 1:13; Heb. 6:12; 9:15; 10:36; 11:13, 33; et al. → what one promises → lit.: promise → PROMISE (noun) <1860> 10 Rom. 7:10 → "promised" added in Engl. 11 2 Cor. 9:5 → to promise, to previously promise → NOTICE (verb) <4293>.

PROMISED – Gal. 3:14 → the promised Spirit → the promise of the Spirit → PROMISE (noun) <1860>.

PROMOTE – 1 Gal. 2:17 → promotes sin → lit.: is a minister of sin → MINISTER (noun) <1249> 2 Col. 2:23 → in promoting → lit.: in (*en*) 3 1 Tim. 1:4 → CAUSE (verb) <3930>.

PROMPT – 1 ***probibazō*** [verb: προβιβάζω <4264>]; **from *pro*: forward, and *bibazō*: to cause to go ▶ To incite, to persuade; also transl.: to be set on, to instruct before** > Having been prompted by her mother, the daughter of Herodias asked for the head of John the Baptist (Matt. 14:8). Other ref.: Acts 19:33 (to draw out); see DRAW <4264>. ¶
– 2 John 13:2 → PUT <906>.

PRONOUNCE – 1 Matt. 7:2; 1 Cor. 4:5; 5:3 → to pronounce judgment → JUDGE (verb) <2919> 2 2 Pet. 2:11 → BRING <5342> 3 Jude 9 → BRING <2018>.

PROOF – 1 ***dokimē*** [fem. noun: δοκιμή <1382>]; **from *dokimos*: approved; comp. *dechomai*: to accept, to receive ▶ Sign of the reality of something** > The Corinthians sought a proof of Christ speaking in Paul (2 Cor. 13:3). All other refs.: EXPERIENCE (noun) <1382>, TEST (noun and verb) <1382>.
2 ***endeixis*** [neut. noun: ἔνδειξις <1732>]; **from *endeiknumi*: to display, to demonstrate, which is from *en*: in, and *deiknumi*: to show ▶ Manifestation, evidence** > The Corinthians were to show the proof of their love (2 Cor. 8:24). The efforts of the adversaries of the Philippians to terrify them was a proof {a clear sign, an evident token, a sign} of perdition for them (Phil. 1:28). Other refs.: Rom. 3:25, 26 (demonstration); see DEMONSTRATE <1732>. ¶
3 **infallible proof, convincing proof: *tekmērion*** [neut. noun: τεκμήριον <5039>]; **from *tekmar*: proof, sign ▶ Irrefutable substantiation, indubitable evidence** > Jesus presented Himself alive after His suffering by many infallible proofs (Acts 1:3). ¶
4 **to make full proof: *plērophoreō*** [verb: πληροφορέω <4135>]; **from *plērēs*: full, and *phoreō*: to fill, which is from *pherō*: to carry, to bear ▶ To accomplish, to give full measure** > Paul told Timothy to make full proof of {fill up the full measure, fulfill, discharge all the duties of} his ministry (2 Tim. 4:5). All other refs.: BELIEVE <4135>, COMPLETE (adj.) <4135>, PERSUADE <4135>, PREACH <4135>.
– 5 Matt. 8:4; Mark 1:44; Luke 5:14 → WITNESS (noun)[1] <3142> 6 Acts 17:31 → ASSURANCE <4102> 7 1 Pet. 1:7 → TESTING <1383>.

PROPER – 1 **to be proper: *prepō*** [verb: πρέπω <4241>] **▶ To be suitable, to be seemly; also transl.: to be appropriate, to become** > Believing women are to adorn themselves with good works, which is proper for women who make profession of serving God (1 Tim. 2:10). All other refs.: COMELY <4241>, FITTING (BE) <4241>.
– 2 Luke 14:35 → FIT <2111> 3 Rom. 1:28 → to be proper → FITTING (BE) <2520> 4 1 Cor. 7:35 → what is proper → that which is comely → COMELY <2158> 5 1 Cor. 11:13 → to be proper → to be comely → COMELY (BE) <4241> 6 Eph. 4:16 → in its measure → MEASURE (noun) <3358> 7 1 Tim. 2:9 → proper clothing → modest apparel → APPAREL <2887> 8 1 Tim. 5:13 → OUGHT <1163> 9 Phm. 8 → to be proper → FITTING (BE) <433> 10 Heb. 11:23 → BEAUTIFUL <791>.

PROPERLY – 1 ***euschēmonōs*** [adv.: εὐσχημόνως <2156>]; **from *euschēmōn*: honorable, which is from *eu*: well, and**

***schēma*: external form, attitude ▶ In a distinguished manner, honestly** > The Thessalonians were to behave properly {reputably} toward {win the respect of} those outside (1 Thes. 4:12). Other refs.: 1 Cor. 14:40; Rom. 13:13; see DECENTLY <2156>, HONESTLY <2156>. ¶
– [2] 1 Cor. 7:36 → to not behave properly → to behave unseemly → BEHAVE <807> [3] Eph. 4:16 → working properly → working in measure → MEASURE (noun) <3358> [4] 1 Tim. 1:8 → LAWFULLY <3545> [5] 1 Tim. 2:9 → lit.: with modest apparel → APPAREL <2887>.

PROPERTY – [1] Matt. 12:29; Mark 3:27 → GOOD (adj. and noun) <4632> [2] Matt. 19:22; Mark 10:22; Acts 5:1 → property, piece of property → POSSESSION <2933> [3] Luke 15:12, 30 → LIVING (noun) <979> [4] Luke 16:12 → someone's else property → ANOTHER <245> [5] Heb. 10:34 → GOOD (adj. and noun) <5224>.

PROPHECY – [1] ***prophēteia*** [fem. noun: προφητεία <4394>]**; from *prophēteuō*: to prophesy, which is from *prophētēs*: see PROPHET** <4396> **▶ a. Prediction of future events** > Many of the O.T. prophecies have been fulfilled, e.g., that of Isaiah about the condition of the Jewish people at the coming of Jesus (Matt. 13:14). Peter affirmed that no prophecy of Scripture is explained by its own particular meaning (2 Pet. 1:20): it is understood in relation to the whole of the entire prophetic revelation; prophets, holy men of God, spoke under the power of the Holy Spirit (v. 21): He is truly the author of all prophecy. Revelation is the book of the N.T. that unfolds the most concerning future events that are to take place after the return of Christ (chaps. 4–22), and that gives a prophetic outline of the history of the church up to that moment (chap. 2 and 3). The expr. "the words of the prophecy" occurs five times in the book of Revelation (1:3; 22:7, 10, 18, 19); the spirit of prophecy is the testimony of Jesus (19:10); during the days of the prophecy of the two prophets, no rain will fall (11:6). **b. Presentation of the mind of God** > Prophecy is a gift of grace (Rom. 12:6) given by the Spirit (1 Cor. 12:10; see vv. 8, 9). The exercise of prophecy is done in love (1 Cor. 13:2); prophecies will be done away (v. 8). The purpose of prophecy is to edify Christians (1 Cor. 14:6); it is a sign for them from God (v. 22). Paul exhorted the Thessalonians not to lightly esteem prophecies (1 Thes. 5:20). Preceding prophecies had been made in regard to Timothy (1 Tim. 1:18); he had received a gift of grace through prophecy (4:14). ¶
– [2] 2 Pet. 1:19 → of prophecy → PROPHETIC <4397>.

PROPHESY – [1] ***manteuomai*** [verb: μαντεύομαι <3132>]**; from *mantis*: diviner, soothsayer; related to *mania*: frenzy, madness ▶ To exercise divination, to make predictions** > By prophesying {soothsaying, fortune-telling}, a slave girl brought much profit to her masters (Acts 16:16). See PYTHON. ¶
[2] ***prophēteuō*** [verb: προφητεύω <4395>]**; from *prophētēs*: see PROPHET** <4396> **▶ To express that which God has communicated by His Spirit** > Some will say that they have prophesied in the name of Jesus (Matt. 7:22). Jesus spoke of the O.T. prophets who prophesied (Matt. 11:13; 15:7; Mark 7:6), as did Peter likewise (1 Pet. 1:10) and Jude (Jude 14). Some asked Jesus to prophesy by naming the person who had struck Him (Matt. 26:68; Mark 14:65; Luke 22:64). Zechariah prophesied (Luke 1:67). Caiaphas prophesied that Jesus was going to die for the nation (John 11:51). God said that, in the last days, sons and daughters will prophesy (Acts 2:17), as likewise His bondmen and bondwomen (v. 18). The disciples of Ephesus prophesied (Acts 19:6). Philip the evangelist had four virgin daughters who prophesied (Acts 21:9). Paul used this verb frequently in addressing the Corinthians (1 Cor. 11:4, 5; 13:9; 14:1, 3, 4, 5a, b, 24, 31, 39). The verb is also used in Rev. 10:11; 11:3. ¶

PROPHET – [1] ***prophētēs*** [masc. noun: προφήτης <4396>]**; from *prophēmi*: to tell beforehand, which is from *pro*: before,**

forth, and *phēmi*: to affirm, to say ▶ One who expresses the thought which God communicates to him by His Spirit > Prophets are found in the N.T. (e.g., Luke 11:49) and in the O.T. (e.g., Acts 3:18). The Lord Himself was the prophet who had been promised (Acts 3:22, 23). At the beginning of Christianity, some, like Agabus, foretold future events (Acts 11:27, see v. 28; 21:10, see v. 11). Christian believers are built on the foundation of the apostles and prophets, to whom the mystery of the Christ has been revealed (Eph. 2:20; 3:5). A prophet is also one who speaks in the name of the Lord to believers of the church for edification, encouragement, and comfort (Acts 13:1; 15:32; 1 Cor. 12:28, 29; 14:29, 32, 37; Eph. 4:11; see 1 Cor. 14:3, 4). Prophecy is a gift from God for the church; it is a sign for those who believe (see 1 Cor. 14:22). The word is used in regard to Isaiah (Matt. 1:22; 3:3; 4:14; 8:17; 12:17; Mark 1:2; Luke 3:4; 4:17; John 1:23, 25; 6:45; 12:38; Acts 7:48; 8:28, 30, 34; 28:25), Micah (Matt. 2:5; see v. 6; Mic. 5:2), Hosea (Matt. 2:15; see Hos. 11:1), Jeremiah (Matt. 2:17; 27:9), John the Baptist (Matt. 11:9a, b; 14:5; 21:26; Mark 11:32; Luke 1:76; 7:26a, b, 28; 20:6), Jonah (Matt. 12:39), Jesus (Matt. 13:57; 21:11, 46; Mark 6:4; Luke 4:24; 7:16, 39; 13:33; 24:19; John 4:19, 44; 6:14; 7:40; 9:17), Zechariah (Matt. 21:4; see Zech. 9:9), Daniel (Matt. 24:15), Elisha (Luke 4:27), Joel (Acts 2:16), David (Acts 2:30), Samuel (Acts 13:20), Habakkuk (Acts 13:40; see Hab. 1:5), a Cretan (Titus 1:12), Balaam (2 Pet. 2:16), and two witnesses (Rev. 11:10). Other refs.: Matt. 2:23; 5:12, 17; 7:12; 10:41a–c; 11:13; 13:17; 16:14; 22:40; 23:29–31, 34, 37; 26:56; Mark 6:15a, b; 8:28; Luke 1:70; 6:23; 9:8, 19; 10:24; 11:47, 50; 13:28, 34; 16:16, 29, 31; 18:31; 24:25, 27, 44; John 1:21, 45; 7:52; 8:52, 53; Acts 3:21, 24, 25; 7:37, 42, 52; 10:43; 13:15, 27; 15:15; 24:14; 26:22, 27; 28:23; Rom. 1:2; 3:21; 11:3; 1 Thes. 2:15; Heb. 1:1; 11:32; Jas. 5:10; 1 Pet. 1:10; 2 Pet. 3:2; Rev. 10:7; 11:18; 16:6; 18:20, 24; 22:6, 9. ¶
– [2] Luke 2:36; Rev. 2:20 → lit.: prophetess → PROPHETESS <4398> [3] 2 Pet. 1:19 → of the prophets → PROPHETIC <4397> [4] 2 Pet. 1:21 → prophets → lit.: holy men of God.

PROPHETESS – ***prophētis*** [fem. noun: προφῆτις <4398>]; **from *prophēmi*: see PROPHET** <4396> **▶ Woman who expresses the thought that God has communicated to her by His Spirit >** Anna, a prophetess, served God in the temple (Luke 2:36; see v. 37). Jezebel calls herself a prophetess (Rev. 2:20). ¶

PROPHETIC – [1] ***prophētikos*** [adj.: προφητικός <4397>]; **from *prophētēs*: see PROPHET** <4396> **▶ Concerning prophecy, whether the revelation of hidden things or future events >** Prophetic writings, such as those of Paul, have made known the mystery, as to which silence had been kept during eternal times (Rom. 16:26); this mystery concerns the nations that would be part of the church. The prophetic word {word of the prophets, word of prophecy} has been made more certain (2 Pet. 1:19) because of the transfiguration of the Lord Jesus; this event confirmed the reality of His next return to reign on earth and the prophetic testimony as a whole. ¶
– [2] 1 Cor. 13:2 → prophetic powers → lit.: prophecy → PROPHECY <4394>.

PROPITIATION – [1] ***hilasmos*** [masc. noun: ἱλασμός <2434>]; **from *hilaskomai*: to be propitious, to be gracious, which is from *hilaos*: favorable, propitious ▶ Among the ancient pagans, to make propitiation meant to propitiate the gods, to appease them. In the word of God we find that He is propitiated, not by what man on his own initiative can bring to Him, but by the expiatory sacrifice of Christ at Calvary. >** By giving His life as the sacrifice for sin, Jesus Christ accomplished a work that allows God to receive the sinner in grace; the sinner believes and obtains salvation by appropriating the virtues of this sacrifice. Christ is the propitiation {atoning sacrifice} for ours sins (1 John 2:2; 4:10). ¶
[2] **to make propitiation: *hilaskomai*** [verb: ἱλάσκομαι <2433>]; **see** [1] **▶ See defin. in** [1]. > As high priest, Jesus made propitiation

{made atonement, made reconciliation} for the sins of the people (Heb. 2:17). Other refs.: Luke 18:13 (to be merciful); see MERCIFUL <2433>. ¶
– [3] Rom. 3:25 → MERCY SEAT <2435>.

PROPORTION – ***analogia*** [fem. noun: ἀναλογία <356>]; **from *ana*: indicates distribution, and *logos*: account ▶ Measure** > He who has received the gift of prophecy is to exercise it according to the proportion of faith (Rom. 12:6). ¶

PROPOSE – [1] ***bouleuō*** [verb: βουλεύω <1011>]; **from *boulē*: decision, will ▶ To consider, to will** > Barnabas proposed {determined, wanted} to take John, called Mark, with himself and Paul (Acts 15:37). Other refs.: 2 Cor. 1:17a–c {to plan, to intend, to purpose}. All other refs.: CONSIDER <1011>, CONSULT <1011>, RESOLVE (verb) <1011>.
– [2] Acts 1:23 → APPOINT <2476> [3] 2 Cor. 10:2a → THINK <3049>.

PROPRIETY – [1] 1 Tim. 2:9 → MODESTY <127> [2] 1 Tim. 2:9, 15 → MODERATION <4997>.

PROSECUTE – Acts 25:5 → ACCUSE <2723>.

PROSELYTE – ***prosēlutos*** [masc. noun: προσήλυτος <4339>]; **from *proserchomai*: to approach, to come near, which is from: *pros*: to, and *erchomai*: to go, to come ▶ Stranger from among the Gentiles who adhered to Judaism; also transl.: convert** > Jesus denounced the hypocrisy of the scribes and Pharisees who manifested great zeal to make a proselyte adhering to their sect, but who closed the way of salvation to him (Matt. 23:15). Proselytes were present on the day of Pentecost (Acts 2:10). Nicholas was a proselyte of Antioch (Acts 6:5). Many of the Jews and proselytes who worshipped God followed Paul and Barnabas (Acts 13:43). ¶

PROSPER – [1] ***euodoō*** [verb: εὐοδόω <2137>]; **from *euodos*: easy to travel through, which is from *eu*: well, and *hodos*: way, road ▶ a. To succeed in the acquisition of material possessions** > On the first day of the week the Christians are to set aside for the collection according as they may have prospered {have saved} (1 Cor. 16:2). **b. To succeed in the acquisition of material and spiritual benefits or possessions** > The apostle John desired that Gaius might prosper {get along well} in health as his soul prospered (3 John 2a, b). Other ref.: Rom. 1:10 (to have a prosperous journey); see JOURNEY (noun) <2137>. ¶
– [2] Acts 13:17 → to make prosper → EXALT <5312> [3] Rev. 3:17 → to become wealthy → WEALTHY <4147>.

PROSPERITY – [1] Acts 19:25 → WEALTH <2142> [2] Acts 24:2 → excellent measures → MEASURE (noun) <2735> [3] Phil. 4:12a → to live in prosperity → ABOUND <4052>.

PROSPEROUS – Rom. 1:10 → to have a prosperous journey → JOURNEY (noun) <2137>.

PROSTITUTE – [1] ***pornē*** [fem. noun: πόρνη <4204>]; **from *pernēmi*: to sell ▶ One who engages in sexual relations for money; also transl.: harlot** > The word is found in Matt. 21:31, 32; Luke 15:30; 1 Cor. 6:15, 16. Rahab was a prostitute (Heb. 11:31; Jas. 2:25). The word is found in the figur. sense in regard to Babylon the great (Rev. 17:1, 5, 15, 16; 19:2). See FORNICATION <4202>. ¶
– [2] 1 Cor. 6:9 → male prostitute → HOMOSEXUAL <3120>.

PROSTRATE – Matt. 18:26 → to prostrate oneself → WORSHIP (verb) <4352>.

PROTECT – [1] 1 Cor. 13:7 → BEAR <4722> [2] 1 Pet. 1:5 → GUARD (verb) <5432> [3] 2 Pet. 2:5 → PRESERVE <5442> [4] 1 John 5:18 → he who was born of God protects himself → he who was born of God preserves himself → PRESERVE <5083>.

PROTECTION – [1] Luke 18:3 → to give legal protection from → AVENGE <1556> [2] Luke 18:5 → to give legal protection → to give justice → JUSTICE <1556>.

PROTEST – [1] Acts 23:9 → STRIVE <1264> [2] 1 Cor. 15:31 → I protest by my pride in you → lit.: by (*nē*) your boasting.

PROUD (adj.) – [1] ***huperēphanos*** [adj.: ὑπερήφανος <5244>]; **from *huper*: above, and *phainō*: to appear, to shine, which is from *phōs*: light ▶ Arrogant, conceited** > Men who reject God are proud (Rom. 1:30); in the last days, men will be proud (2 Tim. 3:2). Other refs.: Luke 1:51; Jas. 4:6; 1 Pet. 5:5; see PROUD (noun) <5244>. ¶

– [2] Rom. 11:20 → to become proud → to be conceited → CONCEITED <5309> [3] Rom. 12:16 → higher → HIGH (adj.) <5308> [4] Rom. 15:17 → to be proud → GLORIFY <2746> [5] 1 Cor. 5:2; 13:4 → to be proud → to be puffed up → PUFF UP <5448> [6] 2 Cor. 1:14; Phil. 1:26 → reason to be proud, proud confidence → BOAST (noun) <2745> [7] Phil. 2:16 → to be proud → GLORIFY <2745> [8] 1 Tim. 6:4 → to be proud → to be puffed up → PUFF UP <5187>.

PROUD (noun) – ***huperēphanos*** [adj. used as noun: ὑπερήφανος <5244>]; **from *huper*: above, and *phainō*: to appear, to shine, which is from *phōs*: light ▶ Arrogant, haughty** > God has scattered the proud {haughty} (Luke 1:51). God sets Himself against the proud, but gives grace to the lowly (Jas. 4:6; 1 Pet. 5:5). Other refs.: Rom. 1:30; 2 Tim. 3:2; see PROUD (adj.) <5244>. ¶

PROVE – [1] ***apodeiknumi*** [verb: ἀποδείκνυμι <584>]; **from *apo*: from (intens.), and *deiknumi*: to show ▶ To demonstrate the veracity, to justify** > The Jews brought many and grievous charges against Paul that they could not prove (Acts 25:7). All other refs.: APPROVE <584>, SET (verb) <584>, SHOW (verb) <584>.

[2] ***paristēmi*** [verb: παρίστημι <3936>]; **from *para*: near, and *histēmi*: to stand ▶ To substantiate, to demonstrate the truth** > The Jews could not prove {make good} the things of which they accused Paul (Acts 24:13). Other refs.: see entries in Lexicon at <3936>.

[3] **to prove before: *proaitiaomai*** [verb: προαιτιάομαι <4256>]; **from *pro*: before, and *aitiaomai*: to accuse, which is from *aitia*: reason, accusation ▶ To accuse previously, to establish before** > Paul had before proved {charged before, made the charge already} that both Jews and Greeks were all under sin (Rom. 3:9). ¶

[4] ***sumbibazō*** [verb: συμβιβάζω <4822>]; **from *sun*: together, and *bibazō*: to cause to go ▶ To show, to demonstrate** > Saul was proving that Jesus is the Christ (Acts 9:22). All other refs.: CONCLUDE[1] <4822>, INSTRUCT <4822>, KNIT <4822>, UNITE <4822>.

[5] ***sunistēmi*** [verb: συνίστημι <4921>]; **from *sun*: together, and *histēmi*: to place ▶ To give evidence, to establish** > The Corinthians had proved {approved, demonstrated} themselves clear in the matter of judging evil among themselves (2 Cor. 7:11). All other refs.: COMMEND <4921>, MAKE <4921>, STAND (verb) <4921>, SUBSIST <4921>.

– [6] Matt. 11:19 → JUSTIFY <1344> [7] Matt. 13:22 → it proves unfruitful → lit.: it becomes unfruitful → BECOME <1096> [8] Mark 4:19 → lit.: to become (*ginomai*) [9] Luke 14:19; 2 Cor. 8:8, 22; 13:5; Gal. 6:4; Eph. 5:10; 1 Thes. 2:4; 5:21; 1 Tim. 3:10; 1 John 4:1 → TEST (noun and verb) <1382> <1381> [10] John 6:6 → TEST (noun and verb) <3985> [11] John 8:46; John 16:8 → CONVINCE <1651> [12] Acts 17:3 → to lay down → LAY <3908> [13] Acts 18:28 → SHOW (verb) <1925> [14] Rom. 12:2 → DISCERN <1381> [15] 2 Cor. 9:3 → to prove hollow → to be in vain → VAIN <2758>.

PROVEN – [1] Phil. 2:22 → proven character → TEST (noun and verb) <1382> <1381> [2] 1 Pet. 1:7 → proven genuineness → TESTING <1383>.

PROVERB – 1 ***paroimia*** [fem. noun: παροιμία <3942>]; **from *para*: alongside, and *oimos*, also written *oimē*: way; story, poem ▶ Saying expressing a popular truth or experience** > Peter quoted a proverb to illustrate what had happened to those who had once again become slaves of corruption: The dog has turned back to his own vomit and the washed sow to her rolling in the mud (2 Pet. 2:22). Other refs.: John 10:6; 16:25a, b, 29; see ALLEGORY <3942>. ¶
– 2 John 16:25a, b, 29 → ALLEGORY <3942>.

PROVIDE – 1 **to provide oneself with: *ktaomai*** [verb: κτάομαι <2932>] ▶ **To obtain, to possess; also transl.: to acquire, to get, to take along** > When Jesus sent His disciples out to preach, He charged them not to provide themselves with gold, silver, or copper for their belts (Matt. 10:9). All other refs.: OBTAIN <2932>, POSSESS <2932>, PURCHASE (verb) <2932>.
2 ***paristēmi*** [verb: παρίστημι <3936>]; **from *para*: next to, and *histēmi*: to stand ▶ To supply, to place at the disposition** > Mounts were to be provided in order to carry Paul to the governor (Acts 23:24). Other refs.: see entries in Lexicon at <3936>.
3 ***pronoeō*** [verb: προνοέω <4306>]; **from *pro*: before, previously, and *noeō*: to understand, to consider, which is from *nous*: mind, understanding ▶ To think in advance, to anticipate** > Christians are to provide {to have regard for} things honest {to respect what is right, to be careful to do what is right} in the sight of all men (Rom. 12:17). Paul provided for {had regard for, took pains to do} what is honorable not only before the Lord, but also before men (2 Cor. 8:21). If any one does not provide for his own and especially those of his own household, he has denied the faith and is worse than an unbeliever (1 Tim. 5:8). ¶
4 ***hupēreteō*** [verb: ὑπηρετέω <5256>]; **from *hupēretēs*: assistant, which is from *hupo*: under, and *eretēs*: rower; lit.: to serve as a rower on a boat ▶ To serve, to be used** > Paul's hands had provided {had supplied, had ministered} for his necessities and for those who were with him (Acts 20:34). Other refs.: Acts 13:36; 24:23; see MINISTER (verb) <5256>. ¶
– 5 Luke 8:3 → MINISTER (verb) <1247> 6 Luke 10:7 → what they provide → lit.: the things with them 7 Luke 12:20 → PREPARE <2090> 8 Acts 27:3 → ENJOY <5177> 9 Acts 28:10 → to make presents → SUPPLY (verb) <2007> 10 Rom. 15:4 → the verb is added in Engl. 11 Gal. 3:5; 2 Pet. 1:11 → SUPPLY (verb) <2023> 12 Col. 4:1; 1 Tim. 6:17 → GIVE <3930> 13 Heb. 11:40 → FORESEE <4265> 14 1 Pet. 4:11 → SUPPLY (verb) <5524>.

PROVIDED – Rom. 8:17 → if in fact → FACT <1512>.

PROVIDENCE – Acts 24:2 → FORETHOUGHT <4307>.

PROVINCE – 1 ***eparcheia*** [fem. noun: ἐπαρχεία <1885>]; **from *eparchos*: governor of a province, which is from *epi*: over, and *archō*: to begin, to reign, which is from *archē*: beginning; also spelled: *eparchia* ▶ Administrative region of the Roman Empire** > Paul was of the province {eparchy} of Cilicia (Acts 23:34). The word is also used in Acts 25:1 (some mss. have the adj. *eparcheios*). ¶
– 2 Acts 10:37; 1 Pet. 1:1 → "province," "the provinces of" added in Engl.

PROVING – Jas. 1:3; 1 Pet. 1:7 → TESTING <1383>.

PROVISION – 1 ***pronoia*** [fem. noun: πρόνοια <4307>]; **from *pronoeō*: to think ahead, which is from *pro*: before, and *noeō*: to think, which is from *nous*: mind, understanding ▶ Concern, preoccupation** > The Christian is not to make provision for {take forethought for, think about} the flesh in regard to its lusts (Rom. 13:14). Other ref.: Acts 24:2; see FORETHOUGHT <4307>. ¶
– 2 Rom. 5:17 → abundant provision → ABUNDANCE <4050> 3 1 Cor. 9:15 → to secure provision → lit.: that it should be

so done in my case [4] Phil. 1:19 → SUPPLY (noun) <2024>.

PROVISIONS – [1] Luke 9:12 → FOOD <1979> [2] John 4:8 → FOOD <5160>.

PROVOCATION – ***parapikrasmos*** [masc. noun: παραπικρασμός <3894>]; **from *parapikrainō*: to make bitter, to exasperate, which is from *para*: intens., and *pikrainō*: to render bitter, which is from *pikros*: bitter ▶ Irritation, exasperation causing bitterness; also transl.: rebellion** > The Hebrews were not to harden their hearts as in the provocation, in the day of temptation in the wilderness (Heb. 3:8, 15). ¶

PROVOKE – [1] ***erethizō*** [verb: ἐρεθίζω <2042>]; **from *erethō*: to provoke, to trouble ▶ To irritate; also transl.: to embitter, to exasperate, to vex** > Fathers are not to provoke their children (Col. 3:21). Other ref.: 2 Cor. 9:2; see STIMULATE <2042>. ¶

[2] ***parapikrainō*** [verb: παραπικραίνω <3893>]; **from *para*: unto, and *pikrainō*: to embitter, which is from: *pikros*: bitter ▶ To irritate, to aggravate** > Those who came out of Egypt provoked {rebelled against} God (Heb. 3:16). ¶

[3] **to be quickly (easily) provoked: *paroxunō*** [verb: παροξύνω <3947>]; **from *para*: intens., and *oxunō*: to sharpen, which is from *oxus*: rapid, sharp ▶ To be vexed, to be frustrated, to become angry quickly** > Love is not quickly provoked {is not easily angered, does not take into account a wrong suffered, keeps no record of wrongs} (1 Cor. 13:5). Other ref.: Acts 17:16 (to be provoked; to be painfully excited); see EXCITE <3947>. ¶

[4] **provoking: *paroxusmos*** [masc. noun: παροξυσμός <3948>]; **from *paroxunō*: see [3] ▶ Incitement, stimulation** > Christians are to consider one another for provoking {for stirring up, to stimulate, how they may spur} to love and good works (Heb. 10:24). Other ref.: Acts 15:39 (sharp disagreement); see DISAGREEMENT <3948>. ¶

[5] ***parorgizō*** [verb: παροργίζω <3949>]; **from *para*: toward, and *orgizō*: to make angry, which is from *orgē*: anger ▶ To incite to anger, to irritate** > Fathers are told not to provoke to anger {to provoke to wrath, to exasperate} (lit.: to anger) their children, but bring them up in the discipline and instruction of the Lord (Eph. 6:4). Other ref.: Rom. 10:19; see ANGER <3949>. ¶

[6] **to provoke one another: *prokaleō*** [verb: προκαλέω <4292>]; **from *pro*: before, forward, and *kaleō*: to call ▶ To become angry, to quarrel** > Christians are not to provoke {to challenge} one another, envying one another (Gal. 5:26). ¶

– [7] Luke 11:53 → to provoke to speak → SPEAK <653> [8] Heb. 3:8, 15 → as when they provoked me → as in the provocation → PROVOCATION <3894> [9] Heb. 3:10, 17 → to be provoked → to be angry → ANGRY <4360>.

PROW – ***prōra*** [fem. noun: πρῷρα <4408>]; **from *pro*: before, forward ▶ Forward part of a ship; also transl.: bow, forepart, foreship** > The sailors of Paul's ship wanted to carry out anchors from the prow (Acts 27:30); the prow of the wrecked ship remained unmovable, but the stern was broken by the force of the waves (v. 41). ¶

PROWL – 1 Pet. 5:8 → to prowl around → to walk about → WALK <4043>.

PRUDENCE – Eph. 1:8 → INTELLIGENCE <5428>.

PRUDENT – [1] ***phronimos*** [adj.: φρόνιμος <5429>]; **from *phroneō*: to think, which is from *phrēn*: mind, understanding ▶ Wise, sagacious; also transl.: sensible, shrewd** > In a parable, the prudent man built his house upon the rock (Matt. 7:24). Jesus told His disciples to be as prudent as serpents (Matt. 10:16). He spoke of a faithful and prudent bondman awaiting his lord's return (Matt. 24:45); a faithful and prudent steward is mentioned in Luke 12:42. Five of ten virgins in a parable were prudent (Matt. 25:2, 4, 8, 9). The sons of this world, i.e., unbelievers, are more prudent {more shrewd, wiser} (*phronimōteros*) than the sons of light (Luke 16:8). All other refs.: INTELLIGENT <5429>, WISE (adj.) <5429>.

– [2] Matt. 11:25; Luke 10:21; Acts 13:7 → UNDERSTANDING <4908> [3] 1 Tim. 3:2 → DISCREET <4998>.

PRUDENTLY – *phronimōs* [adv.: φρονίμως <5430>]; **from *phronimos*: prudent, sensible, which is from *phroneō*: to think, which is from *phrēn*: mind, understanding ▶ With practical wisdom, in a wise manner** > In a parable, the lord praised the unrighteous steward because he had acted prudently {shrewdly, wisely} {for his shrewdness} (Luke 16:8). ¶

PRUNE – *kathairō* [verb: καθαίρω <2508>]; **from *katharos*: clean, pure ▶ To remove impurities; in the case of a tree, to remove extraneous parts (dead or living) to increase the production of fruit** > The Father prunes {purges} every branch bearing fruit that it may bring forth more fruit (John 15:2). Other ref.: Heb. 10:2; see PURIFY <2508>. ¶

PSALM – [1] *psalmos* [masc. noun: ψαλμός <5568>]; **from *psallō*: to sing ▶ In the O.T., a psalm corresponded firstly to the act of playing a stringed instrument; the word also signifies a sacred song accompanied by a musical instrument.** > The N.T. makes reference to the Psalms in the O.T. (Luke 20:42; 24:44; Acts 1:20), and to the second Psalm in particular (Acts 13:33). When the Corinthians came together, they had psalms {hymns} (1 Cor. 14:26); these were songs of praise. Christians are invited to speak to themselves and exhort one another in psalms, hymns, and spiritual songs (Eph. 5:19; Col. 3:16). ¶

– [2] Jas. 5:13 → to sing psalms → SING <5567>.

PTOLEMAIS – *Ptolemais* [fem. name: Πτολεμαΐς <4424>] **▶ City in northern Palestine on the Mediterranean Sea** > During his third missionary journey, Paul greeted the brothers in Ptolemais and stayed with them for a day (Acts 21:7). ¶

PUBLIC – [1] public, in public: *dēmosios* [adj. and adj. used as adv.: δημόσιος <1219>]; **from *dēmos*: people; lit.: belonging to the people ▶ a. Common** > The apostles were thrown into the public prison (Acts 5:18). **b. In view of all, publicly, openly** > Paul had been beaten publicly (Acts 16:37). With great force Apollos convinced the Jews publicly (Acts 18:28). Other ref.: Acts 20:20; see PUBLICLY <1219>. ¶

[2] ***parrēsia*** [fem. noun used as adv.: παρρησία <3954>]; **from *pas*: all, and *rhēsis*: act of speaking ▶ "In public" translates the Greek expr. *en parrēsia*** > God made a public display (lit.: made a display in public) of the principalities and powers (Col. 2:15). All other refs.: BOLDLY <3954>, BOLDNESS <3954>, CONFIDENCE <3954>, OPENLY <3954>.

[3] ***phaneros*** [adj.: φανερός <5318>]; **from *phainō*: to appear, to shine, which is from *phōs*: light ▶ Well known, eminent** > The name of Jesus had become public {was spread abroad} (Mark 6:14). In Matt. 12:16, it is lit.: that they should not make Him public. All other refs.: see entries in Lexicon at <5318>.

– [4] Luke 1:80 → public appearance → MANIFESTATION <323> [5] 1 Tim. 4:13 → public reading → READING <320>.

PUBLIC SQUARE – Rev. 11:8 → STREET <4113>.

PUBLICAN – [1] chief among the publicans: *architelōnēs* [masc. noun: ἀρχιτελώνης <754>]; **from *archō*: to begin, to command, which is from *archē*: beginning, and *telōnēs*: tax collector ▶ Person in charge of those responsible to collect taxes** > Zaccheus was the chief among the publicans {a chief tax collector, chief tax-gatherer} (Luke 19:2). ¶

– [2] Matt. 5:46, 47; 9:10, 11; 11:19; etc. → TAX COLLECTOR <5057>.

PUBLICLY – [1] *dēmosia* [adj. used as adv.: δημοσία <1219>]; **from *dēmosios*: public,**

which is from *dēmos*: people ► In a public place, in the sight of all > Paul had preached and taught publicly (Acts 20:20). Other refs.: Acts 5:18; 16:37; 18:28; see PUBLIC <1219>. ¶
– [2] Mark 1:45; John 7:10 → OPENLY <5320> [3] Luke 1:80 → until he appeared publicly → lit.: until the day of his manifestation → MANIFESTATION <323> [4] Luke 12:8 → to publicly acknowledge → CONFESS <3670> [5] John 7:13; 11:54 → OPENLY <3954> [6] John 7:26 → BOLDLY <3954> [7] Acts 19:9 → lit.: before the multitude → MULTITUDE <4128> [8] Gal. 3:1 → to portray publicly → PORTRAY <4270>.

PUBLISH – [1] ***kērussō*** [verb: κηρύσσω <2784>]; **from *kērux*: herald, preacher ► To announce, to preach** > The word of God was published {proclaimed} by John throughout all Judea (Acts 10:37). All other refs.: PREACH <2784>, PROCLAIM <2784>.
– [2] Acts 13:49 → to publish throughout → SPREAD <1308>.

PUBLIUS – ***Poplios*** [masc. name: Πόπλιος <4196>]; **Roman name: Publius ► Chief man of the island of Malta** > Publius lodged Paul and the others who had been shipwrecked with him and gave them hospitality in a very friendly way. Paul prayed for his father who was ill, laid his hands on him, and healed him (Acts 28:7, 8). ¶

PUDENS – ***Poudēs*** [masc. name: Πούδης <4227>]; ***pudens*, in Lat.: honest, modest ► Christian man of Rome** > Paul sends greetings to Pudens in his letter to Timothy (2 Tim. 4:21). ¶

PUFF UP – [1] ***phusioō*** [verb: φυσιόω <5448>]; **from *phusa*: breath of air, or *phusaō*: to breathe, to inflate ► To display vanity, arrogance; also transl.: to be arrogant, become arrogant, make arrogant, be proud** > Some at Corinth were puffed up (1 Cor. 4:18; 5:2). The Corinthians were not to be puffed up {take pride} on behalf of one against the other (1 Cor. 4:6); Paul would know the power of those who were puffed up (v. 19). Knowledge puffs up, but love edifies (1 Cor. 8:1); love is not puffed up (13:4); the mind of the flesh can vainly puff up {inflate without cause} (Col. 2:18). ¶
[2] ***tuphoō*** [verb: τυφόω <5187>]; **from *tuphos*: smoke ► To have exaggerated self-esteem; also transl.: to be conceited, to become conceited** > A newly converted overseer might be puffed up {be inflated, be lifted up with pride} (1 Tim. 3:6). One who teaches and does not accede to sound words is puffed up {is proud} (1 Tim. 6:4). In the last days men will be puffed up {of vain pretensions, haughty, highminded} (2 Tim. 3:4). ¶

PUFFING UP – ***phusiōsis*** [fem. noun: φυσίωσις <5450>]; **from *phusioō*: to puff up, to display vanity ► Vanity, arrogance** > Paul feared that perhaps he might find puffings up {swellings, conceits} among the Corinthians (2 Cor. 12:20). ¶

PUGNACIOUS – 1 Tim. 3:3; Titus 1:7 → STRIKER <4131>.

PULL – [1] **to pull away: *airō*** [verb: αἴρω <142>] **► To tear, to pull out** > An unshrunk patch on an old garment pulls away {takes, takes away} from the garment (Matt. 9:16; Mark 2:21). All other refs.: see entries in Lexicon at <142>.
[2] **to pull out, to pull up: *anaspaō*** [verb: ἀνασπάω <385>]; **from *ana*: again, up, and *spaō*: to draw ► To bring out, to draw back, to draw up** > One who has an animal that has fallen into a well immediately pulls him up even on a Sabbath day (Luke 14:5). The vessel, which was like a great sheet, was lowered down to Peter, then pulled up into heaven (Acts 11:10). ¶
[3] **to pull out: *harpazō*** [verb: ἁρπάζω <726>]; **from *harpax*: rapacious, pillaging ► To remove forcefully** > Certain Christians must be saved with fear, pulled out {snatched out} of the fire (Jude 23). All other refs.: CATCH (verb) <726>, SEIZE <726>, TAKE <726>.

[4] **to pull down: *kathaireō*** [verb: καθαιρέω <2507>]; **from *kata*: down, and *haireō*: to take, to seize ► To take away, to tear down, to demolish** > The rich man in the parable wanted to pull down his barns and build greater ones (Luke 12:18). All other refs.: DESTROY <2507>, PUT <2507>, TAKE <2507>.
– [5] Matt. 7:4, 5a, b; Luke 6:42a–c → to pull out → REMOVE <1544> [6] Matt. 13:29; 15:13 Luke 17:6; Jude 12 → to pull up, to pull by the roots → UPROOT <1610> [7] Matt. 13:48 → to pull up → to draw up → DRAW <307> [8] Mark 5:4 → to pull apart → to tear apart → TEAR (verb) <1288> [9] Luke 5:11 → BRING <2609> [10] 2 Cor. 10:8 → pulling down → DESTRUCTION <2506>.

PUNISH – [1] ***ekdikeō*** [verb: ἐκδικέω <1556>]; **from *ekdikos*: avenger, which is from *ek*: from, out, and *dikē*: justice ► To avenge, to execute justice** > Paul was ready to avenge {to revenge} all disobedience (2 Cor. 10:6). All other refs.: AVENGE <1556>.
[2] ***kolazō*** [verb: κολάζω <2849>]; **from *kolos*: abridged, cut short or *klaō*: to strike, to break ► To chastise, to correct** > The Jewish rulers and others found no way how they might punish Peter and John, on account of the people (Acts 4:21). The Lord knows how to keep the unjust to be punished {under punishment} (2 Pet. 2:9). Other ref.: 1 Pet. 2:20 in some mss. ¶
[3] ***timōreō*** [verb: τιμωρέω <5097>]; **from *timoros*: watching one's honor, which is from *timē*: honor, and *horaō*: to see ► To avenge, to do justice** > Before his conversion, Paul brought brothers, bound, to Jerusalem to be punished (Acts 22:5); punishing them in synagogues, he compelled them to blaspheme (Acts 26:11). ¶
– [4] Mark 12:40; Luke 20:47 → will be punished more severely → lit.: will receive a severer judgment → JUDGMENT <2917> [5] Luke 23:16, 22; 2 Cor. 6:9 → CHASTEN <3811> [6] 1 Thes. 4:6 → lit.: to be the avenger → AVENGER <1558> [7] 2 Thes. 1:8 → lit.: to take vengeance → VENGEANCE <1557> [8] 2 Thes. 1:9 → lit.: to endure the punishment → ENDURE <5099>, PUNISHMENT <1349> [9] Heb. 10:29 → to be punished → lit.: punishment → PUNISHMENT <5098> [10] Heb. 12:6 → SCOURGE (verb) <3146> [11] 1 Pet. 2:14 → to punish → lit.: for the punishment of → PUNISHMENT <1557>.

PUNISHED (BE) – 2 Thes. 1:9 → lit.: to pay the penalty → PAY (verb) <5099>.

PUNISHMENT – [1] ***dikē*** [fem. noun: δίκη <1349>]; **justice, judgment ► Penalty imposed as a sentence** > Those who do not obey the gospel of the Lord Jesus Christ will endure the punishment {will be punished, will pay the penalty} with everlasting destruction from the presence of the Lord and the glory of His power (2 Thes. 1:9; see v. 8). All other refs.: JUDGMENT <1349>; also JUSTICE <1349>.
[2] ***ekdikēsis*** [fem. noun: ἐκδίκησις <1557>]; **from *ekdikeō*: to execute justice, which is from *ek*: of, out of, and *dikē*: see [1] ► Revenge, vengeance, retributive justice** > Rulers are sent for the punishment of {for vengeance on, to punish} evildoers (1 Pet. 2:14). All other refs.: JUSTICE <1557>, VENGEANCE <1557>.
[3] ***epitimia*** [fem. noun: ἐπιτιμία <2009>]; **from *epi*: upon, and *timē*: honor ► Censure, reproof** > The discipline of the church of Corinth toward one of their own was sufficient for him as punishment {rebuke} (2 Cor. 2:6). ¶
[4] ***timōria*** [fem. noun: τιμωρία <5098>]; **from *timōreō*: to punish ► Vengeance, act of meting out justice** > He who despises the Son of God and the blood of the covenant will be judged worthy of a worse punishment than he who despised the law of Moses (Heb. 10:29). ¶
– [5] Matt. 25:46; 1 John 4:18 → TORMENT (noun) <2851> [6] Rom. 13:5 → WRATH <3709> [7] Heb. 2:2 → RETRIBUTION <3405> [8] 2 Pet. 2:9 → under punishment → lit.: to be punished → PUNISH <2849> [9] Rev. 17:1 → JUDGMENT <2917>.

PURCHASE (noun) – Matt. 25:10 → to make the purchase → BUY <59>.

PURCHASE (verb) – 1 ***ktaomai*** [verb: κτάομαι <2932>] ► **To acquire, to obtain, to buy** > Judas purchased {got} a field with the reward he got for his iniquity (Acts 1:18). Simon had thought he could purchase the gift of God for money (Acts 8:20). All other refs.: OBTAIN <2932>, POSSESS <2932>, PROVIDE <2932>.

2 ***peripoieō*** [verb: περιποιέω <4046>]; **from *peri*: denoting acquisition and *poieō*: to do; lit.: to do for oneself** ► **a. To acquire, to obtain for oneself** > God has purchased the church by the blood of His own Son (Acts 20:28). Those who have served well purchase {gain, obtain} for themselves a good standing (1 Tim. 3:13). **b. To keep, to secure for oneself** > Whoever seeks to preserve {save, keep} his life will lose it (Luke 17:33 in some mss.). ¶

– 3 Acts 7:16 → BUY <5608> 4 Rev. 5:9; 14:3, 4 → BUY <59>.

PURE – 1 ***hagnos*** [adj.: ἁγνός <53>]; **same radical as *hagos*: respect of God, religious fear** ► **Innocent, irreproachable, chaste** > The Corinthians had proved themselves to be pure {clear, innocent} in a certain matter (2 Cor. 7:11). Things that are pure are to occupy the thoughts of Christians (Phil. 4:8). Paul exhorted Timothy to keep himself pure {free from sin} (1 Tim. 5:22). The young women are to be taught to be pure (Titus 2:5). The wisdom from above is first pure (Jas. 3:17). Everyone who has this hope in God, i.e., to be like Him, purifies himself even as He is pure (1 John 3:3). Other refs.: 2 Cor. 11:2; 1 Pet. 3:2; see CHASTE <53>. ¶

2 ***adolos*** [adj.: ἄδολος <97>]; **from *a*: neg., and *dolos*: guile, deception** ► **Without deceit, sincere** > Christians are to desire the pure spiritual milk of the word (1 Pet. 2:2). ¶

3 ***akeraios*** [adj.: ἀκέραιος <185>]; **from *a*: neg., and *kerannumi*: to mix** ► **Without mixture, sincere, blameless** > Paul exhorted the Philippians to be blameless and pure {harmless, innocent, simple} (Phil. 2:15). Other refs.: Matt. 10:16; Rom. 16:19; see INNOCENT <185>. ¶

4 ***eilikrinēs*** [adj.: εἰλικρινής <1506>]; **poss. from *eilē*: heat of the sun, and *krinō*: to judge; lit.: judged by the light of the sun** ► **Without mixture, without spot, sincere** > Paul prayed that the Philippians might approve the things that are more excellent, in order that they might be pure (Phil. 1:10). In his letters, Peter stirred up the pure {sincere, wholesome} mind of his readers (2 Pet. 3:1). ¶

5 ***katharos*** [adj.: καθαρός <2513>] ► **Clear, clean, unsoiled** > Jesus blessed those who are pure in heart (Matt. 5:8). Paul recalled that all things (i.e., foods) are pure (Rom. 14:20). Love proceeds out of a pure heart (1 Tim. 1:5). Ministering servants are to hold the mystery of faith in a pure conscience (1 Tim. 3:9). Paul served God with a pure conscience (2 Tim. 1:3). Timothy was to pursue righteousness, faith, love, and peace with those who call on the Lord out of a pure heart (2 Tim. 2:22). All things are pure to the pure; but to the defiled and unbelieving, nothing is pure (Titus 1:15a–c). Christians are invited to approach God, having the body washed with pure water (Heb. 10:22). Pure (*katharos*) religious service is to visit orphans and widows in their affliction, and to keep oneself unspotted (*aspilos*) from the world (Jas. 1:27). Christians are to love one another out of a pure heart fervently (1 Pet. 1:22). The seven angels who had the seven plagues were clothed in pure bright linen (Rev. 15:6). The fine linen of the wife of the Lamb is bright and pure (Rev. 19:8); the armies that followed the Lord are clothed in white, pure, fine linen (v. 14). In John's vision, the heavenly Jerusalem was pure gold, like pure glass (Rev. 21:18a, b); the street of the city was pure gold (v. 21). Some mss. have this word in Rev. 22:1. All other refs.: CLEAN (adj.) <2513>.

6 ***pistikos*** [adj.: πιστικός <4101>]; **from *pistis*: faith, fidelity** ► **Authentic, natural, reliable** > A woman poured out a pure and very costly ointment on the head of Jesus (Mark 14:3). Mary of Bethany anointed His feet with an ointment of pure nard of great price (John 12:3). ¶

– [7] Phil. 1:17 → from pure motives → PURELY <55> [8] Heb. 7:26; 13:4 → UNDEFILED <283> [9] Jas. 1:2 → ALL <3956>.

PURELY – ***hagnōs*** [adv.: ἁγνῶς <55>]; **from *hagnos*: pure ▶ With sincerity, with true motives** > Some announced Christ out of contention, not purely {from pure motives, sincerely} (Phil. 1:17; some mss. have v. 16). ¶

PURENESS – 2 Cor. 6:6 → PURITY <54>.

PURGE – [1] **to thoroughly purge: *diakatharizō*** [verb: διακαθαρίζω <1245>]; **from *dia*: intens., and *katharizō*: to cleanse, which is from *katharos*: pure, clean ▶ To cleanse completely, to thoroughly purify** > Jesus Christ will thoroughly purge {clear, thoroughly clean out, thoroughly clear} His threshing floor (Matt. 3:12; Luke 3:17). ¶
[2] **to purge out: *ekkathairō*** [verb: ἐκκαθαίρω <1571>]; **from *ek*: out, and *kathairō*: to clean, to cleanse, which is from *katharos*: pure, clean ▶ To completely cleanse, to purify** > The Corinthians were to purge out {clean out, cleanse out, get rid of} the old leaven that they might be a new lump (1 Cor. 5:7). Other ref.: 2 Tim. 2:21; see PURIFY <1571>. ¶
– [3] Mark 7:19; Heb. 9:14, 22 → PURIFY <2511> [4] John 15:2 → PRUNE <2508> [5] 1 Cor. 5:13 → to take away → TAKE <1808> [6] Heb. 1:3; 2 Pet. 1:9 → He had purged; that he was purged → lit.: He made the purification; the purging → PURIFICATION <2512> [7] Heb. 10:2 → PURIFY <2508>.

PURGING – 2 Pet. 1:9 → PURIFICATION <2512>.

PURIFICATION – [1] ***hagnismos*** [masc. noun: ἁγνισμός <49>]; **from *hagnizō*: to consecrate, to purify, which is from *hagnos*: pure, clean ▶ Religious ritual to make pure** > An offering was presented at the end of the days of purification (Acts 21:26). ¶
[2] ***katharismos*** [masc. noun: καθαρισμός <2512>]; **from *katharizō*: to make clean, which is from *katharos*: pure, clean ▶ a. Religious ritual under the law following which a person is declared pure, undefiled; also transl.: cleansing, purifying, ceremonial washing** > Moses had commanded certain things for the purification of lepers (Mark 1:44; Luke 5:14) and at a birth (Luke 2:22). Water was used for the purification of the Jews (John 2:6). The disciples of John the Baptist reasoned with a Jew about purification (John 3:25). **b. Expiation** > Jesus made the purification {purging} of sins (Heb. 1:3; 2 Pet. 1:9). ¶
– [3] Acts 21:24 → join in the purification rites → lit.: be purified with them → PURIFY <48> [4] Heb. 9:13 → PURITY <2514>.

PURIFY – [1] ***hagnizō*** [verb: ἁγνίζω <48>]; **from *hagnos*: pure, clean ▶ To cleanse from all defilement** > It was customary among Jews to ceremonially purify themselves before the Passover (John 11:55). Paul was himself purified before entering the temple (Acts 21:24, 26; 24:18 {to be ceremonially clean}). The verb also has a moral meaning relative to a person considered in his entirety (1 John 3:3), the heart (Jas. 4:8), or the soul (1 Pet. 1:22). ¶
[2] ***kathairō*** [verb: καθαίρω <2508>]; **from *katharos*: pure, clean ▶ To remove impurities, to remove guilt** > Blood purified {cleansed, purged} those who worshipped (Heb. 10:2); some mss. have [4]. Other ref.: John 15:2; see PRUNE <2508>. ¶
[3] ***ekkathairō*** [verb: ἐκκαθαίρω <1571>]; **from *ek* (intens.): out, and *kathairō*: see [2] ▶ To thoroughly cleanse, to separate oneself** > The Christian is to purify {to cleanse, to purge} himself from vessels of dishonor (2 Tim. 2:21). Other ref.: 1 Cor. 5:7 (to purge out); see PURGE <1571>. ¶
[4] ***katharizō*** [verb: καθαρίζω <2511>]; **from *katharos*: pure, clean ▶ To cleanse from every impurity** > The organs of the body purify all foods (Mark 7:19). Peter was not to make common what God had

purified {had made clean} (Acts 10:15; 11:9). God has purified the hearts of Christians by faith (Acts 15:9). Christians are to purify themselves from all filthiness of flesh and spirit (2 Cor. 7:1). Christ purifies the church by the word (Eph. 5:26); He has purified for Himself a people for His own possession (Titus 2:14). The blood of Christ purifies {purges} the Christian's conscience from dead works (Heb. 9:14); under the law, almost all things were purified with blood (v. 22); the heavenly things are purified by the blood of Christ (v. 23). The blood of Jesus purifies us from all sin (1 John 1:7). He purifies from all unrighteousness one who confesses his sins (1 John 1:9). All other refs.: CLEANSE <2511>.

[5] ***puroō*** [verb: πυρόω <4448>]; **from *pur*: fire ▶ To burn, to refine** > Laodicea was counseled to buy from the Lord gold purified by {tried in the} fire (Rev. 3:18). All other refs.: BURN <4448>, FIERY <4448>, FIRE <4448>, REFINE <4448>.

PURIFYING – [1] Luke 2:22; John 2:6; 3:25 → PURIFICATION <2512> [2] Heb. 9:13 → PURITY <2514>.

PURITY – [1] ***hagneia*** [fem. noun: ἁγνεία <47>]; **from *hagnos*: pure, chaste; same radical as *hagos*: respect of God, religious fear ▶ Chastity; purity in manner of thinking and acting** > Timothy was to be a model in purity (1 Tim. 4:12); he was to exhort younger women as sisters, with all purity (5:2). ¶

[2] ***hagnotēs*** [fem. noun: ἁγνότης <54>]; **from *hagnos*: see [1] ▶ Sincerity, the opposite of duplicity** > Purity {Pureness} characterized Paul (2 Cor. 6:6). ¶

[3] ***katharotēs*** [fem. noun: καθαρότης <2514>]; **from *katharos*: pure, clean ▶ Cleanness; bodily cleanliness following a religious ritual** > Under the law, the blood of goats and bulls, and a heifer's ashes, sanctified for the purity {cleansing, purifying} of the flesh (Heb. 9:13). ¶

– [4] Titus 2:7 → INCORRUPTIBILITY <861> [5] 1 Pet. 3:2 → lit.: pure → CHASTE <53>.

PURLOIN – Titus 2:10 → PILFER <3557>.

PURPLE (adj.) – ***porphurous*** [adj.: πορφυροῦς <4210>]; **from *porphura*: purple dye or garment ▶ Dyed purple** > The soldiers put a purple robe on Jesus, in mockery, before they crucified Him (John 19:2, 5). Babylon was clothed with purple (Rev. 18:16). Other ref.: Rev. 17:4 in some mss. ¶

PURPLE (noun) – [1] ***porphura*** [fem. noun: πορφύρα <4209>] ▶ **The color purple was the imperial color; the bright red-blue dye was obtained from mollusks, and used to dye fabrics** > The soldiers clothed Jesus with purple (i.e., with a garment of this color), in mockery, before His crucifixion (Mark 15:17), and they took the purple off Him after they had mocked Him (v. 20). The rich man, in the parable, was clothed in purple (Luke 16:19). The great prostitute was clothed in purple (Rev. 17:4); other mss. have the adj. *porphurous*. The word is also used in Rev. 18:12. ¶

[2] **seller of purple, dealer in purple: *porphuropōlis*** [fem. noun: πορφυρόπωλις <4211>]; **from *porphura*: see [1], and *pōleō*: to sell ▶ One who sells objects dyed purple** > Lydia, a Christian living in the time of the apostle Paul, was a seller of purple (Acts 16:14). ¶

PURPOSE (noun) – [1] ***boulēma*** [neut. noun: βούλημα <1013>]; **from *boulomai*: to want ▶ Will, plan, scheme** > The centurion kept the soldiers from executing their purpose {intention} to kill Paul and the other prisoners (Acts 27:43). Other refs.: 1 Pet. 4:3 in some mss.; Rom. 9:19: see WILL <1013>. ¶

[2] ***prothesis*** [fem. noun: πρόθεσις <4286>]; **from *protithēmi*: to plan, which is from *pro*: before, and *tithēmi*: to put ▶ Intention, design, plan** > Barnabas exhorted the Christians with purpose of heart to abide with the Lord (Acts 11:23). Supposing that they had gained their purpose {desire, object, what they wanted}, the sailors put out to sea (Acts 27:13). All things work

together for good to those who are called according to the purpose of God (Rom. 8:28). The purpose of God according to election stood before the birth of Jacob (Rom. 9:11). Christians have been marked out beforehand according to the purpose of Him who works all things according to the counsel of His own will (Eph. 1:11). The eternal purpose concerning the church was accomplished in Christ Jesus (Eph. 3:11). God has called us according to His own purpose and grace (2 Tim. 1:9). Timothy had carefully followed the purpose {aim in life} of Paul (2 Tim. 3:10). All other refs.: EXPOSITION OF THE LOAVES <4286>.

– 3 Luke 7:30; Acts 2:23; 4:28; 13:36; 20:27; 1 Cor. 4:5; Eph. 1:11; Heb. 6:17 → COUNSEL (noun) <1012> 4 John 1:31; 18:37a, b → for this purpose → lit.: for this 5 Acts 5:38 → PLAN (noun) <1012> 6 Rom. 4:11 → the purpose was → lit.: that 7 Gal. 2:21 → for no purpose → FREELY <1432> 8 Gal. 4:17 → for no good purpose → not commendably → COMMENDABLY <2573> 9 Eph. 1:5, 9; Phil. 2:13; 2 Thes. 1:11 → PLEASURE <2107> 10 Phil. 2:2 → to be intent on one purpose, to be one in purpose → to have the same mind → MIND (noun) <5426> 11 2 Thes. 1:11 → every good purpose → lit.: all the good pleasure of goodness → GOODNESS <19> 12 Jas. 4:5 → to no purpose → in vain → VAIN <2761> 13 Jas. 5:11 → END (noun) <5056> 14 1 Pet. 4:1 → MIND (noun) <1771> 15 Rev. 17:13, 17a, b → MIND (noun) <1106>.

PURPOSE (verb) – 1 ***boulomai*** [verb: βούλομαι <1014>] **▶ To intend, to determine** > Joseph purposed {minded, planned, had in mind} to send Mary away secretly (Matt. 1:19). Paul purposed {desired, was disposed, wanted} to go to Achaia (Acts 18:27). Other refs.: ADVISE <1014>, PLEASE <1014>, WANT (verb) <1014>, WILL (verb) <1014>.

2 ***proaireō*** [verb: προαιρέω <4255>]; **from *pro*: before, and *aireō*: to choose ▶ To determine, to resolve** > Regarding service to the saints, each is to give according to what he has purposed {has decided} in his heart (2 Cor. 9:7). ¶

3 ***tithēmi*** [verb: τίθημι <5087>]; **lit.: to place, to put ▶ To imagine, to determine** > Peter asked Ananias why it was that he had purposed {had conceived, had thought} in his heart to lie (Acts 5:4). Paul purposed {decided} in his spirit to pass through Macedonia and Achaia (Acts 19:21). All other refs.: see entries in Lexicon at <5087>.

4 ***protithēmi*** [verb: προτίθημι <4388>]; **from *pro*: before, and *tithēmi*: see 2 ▶ To intend, to determine** > Paul had often purposed (planned, proposed} to go to the brothers at Rome (Rom. 1:13). God has made known the mystery of His will that He purposed in Himself (Eph. 1:9). Other ref.: Rom. 3:25 (to set forth); see SET (verb) <4388>. ¶

5 **opinion: *gnōmē*** [fem. noun: γνώμη <1106>]; **from *ginōskō*: to learn, to understand ▶ Thought, decision** > The opinion {resolution} was for Paul and his companions {It was decided, determined, purposed} to return to Macedonia (Acts 20:3). All other refs.: ADVICE <1106>, JUDGMENT <1106>, MIND (noun) <1106>, OPINION <1106>.

– 6 2 Cor. 1:17 → PROPOSE <1011> 7 Eph. 3:11 → ACCOMPLISH <4160>.

PURSE – 1 ***ballantion*** [neut. noun: βαλλάντιον <905>]; **also spelled: *balantion* ▶ Bag to put money in; also transl.: money bag** > Jesus told His disciples to not carry a purse (Luke 10:4; 22:35), to provide themselves bags that do not grow old (12:33), to each take his purse (22:36). ¶

– 2 Matt. 10:9; Mark 6:8 → BELT <2223>.

PURSUE – 1 ***diōkō*** [verb: διώκω <1377>]; **from *diō*: to pursue (in a good sense) ▶ To search, to follow after** > The nations did not pursue righteousness (Rom. 9:30), but Israel pursued a law of righteousness (v. 31). Christians are to pursue the things that tend to peace and the things that tend to mutual edification (Rom. 14:19 {to make every

effort}). The Corinthians were to pursue love (1 Cor. 14:1). Paul pursued {pressed on}, that he might apprehend Christ (Phil. 3:12). We are to always pursue what is good (1 Thes. 5:15 {to seek, to try}). Timothy was to pursue righteousness, piety, faith, love, endurance, meekness of spirit (1 Tim. 6:11). He was to pursue righteousness, faith, love, peace, with those who called upon the Lord out of a pure heart (2 Tim. 2:22). We are to pursue peace {to make every effort to live} with all and holiness (Heb. 12:14). He who will love life and see good days is to seek peace and pursue {ensue} it (1 Pet. 3:11). All other refs.: FOLLOW <1377>, GIVE <1377>, PERSECUTE <1377>, PRESS <1377>.
– [2] 1 Pet. 4:3 → WALK <4198> [3] 1 Pet. 5:2 → pursuing dishonest gain → GAIN (noun) <147> [4] Jude 7 → to go away → GO <565>.

PURSUIT – [1] ***poreia*** [fem. noun: πορεία <4197>]; **from *poreuomai*: to go ► Walk, journey; hence, a manner of life** > The rich man will wither in his pursuits {business, goings, ways} (Jas. 1:11). Other ref.: Luke 13:22 (way); see JOURNEY (verb). ¶
– [2] 2 Tim. 2:4 → AFFAIR <4230>.

PUSH – [1] **to push forward: *proballō*** [verb: προβάλλω <4261>]; **from *pro*: forward, and *ballō*: to throw ► To put forward** > The Jews pushed Alexander forward (Acts 19:33). Other ref.: Luke 21:30; see SPROUT <4261>. ¶
– [2] Mark 3:10 → to push forward → to fall upon → FALL (verb) <1968> [3] Acts 7:27 → to push aside, to push away → REJECT <683> [4] 2 Cor. 11:20 → to push forward → EXALT <1869>.

PUT – [1] ***tithēmi*** [verb: τίθημι <5087>] ► **To bring, to place** > God will put the enemies of the Lord Jesus under His feet (Matt. 22:44). Peter and John were put in jail (Acts 4:3). The apostles were put in the public jail (Acts 5:18). People will not permit the bodies of the two witnesses to be put {be laid} in a tomb {Rev. 11:9). All other refs.: see entries in Lexicon at <5087>.

[2] **to put, to put off, to put away: *apotithēmi*** [verb: ἀποτίθημι <659>]; **from *apo*: away, and *tithēmi*: see [1] ► a. To lay aside, to get rid of** > The Christian must put off the old man (Eph. 4:22) and put away lying (v. 25). **b. To throw** > Herod had put John in prison (Matt. 14:3; *tithēmi* in other mss.). The Colossians were to discard {were to rid themselves of} various evil things (Col. 3:8). All other refs.: CAST <659>, LAY <659>.
[3] ***epitithēmi*** [verb: ἐπιτίθημι <2007>]; **from *epi*: on, and *tithēmi*: see [1] ► To place, to set on** > A lamp should be put on a lamp stand (Mark 4:21). All other refs.: see entries in Lexicon at <2007>.
[4] **to put on: *peritithēmi*** [verb: περιτίθημι <4060>]; **from *peri*: around, and *tithēmi*: see [1] ► a. To fix around, at the end** > A sponge full of sour wine was put on {was fixed on} a reed and offered to Jesus (Matt. 27:48; Mark 15:36). **b. To put, to put on, to put upon: lit.: to put around, to surround** > The soldiers put a scarlet robe on Jesus (Matt. 27:28). The soldiers put {bound, set} a crown of thorns on His head (Mark 15:17). A sponge full of sour wine was put on a hyssop branch and offered to Him on the cross (John 19:29). All other refs.: BESTOW <4060>, SET (verb) <4060>.
[5] **to keep put away: *apokeimai*** [verb: ἀπόκειμαι <606>]; **from *apo*: aside, and *keimai*: to put ► To keep aside, to lay down** > One of the servants in a parable had kept put away {kept laid away} the mina of his master (Luke 19:20). All other refs.: APPOINT <606>, LAY <606>.
[6] ***ballō*** [verb: βάλλω <906>] ► **a. To throw, to pour, to introduce; also transl.: to cast** > New wine must be put {poured} into new wineskins (Luke 5:38). The devil put it into the heart of {prompted} Judas to betray Jesus (John 13:2). Thomas wanted to put his finger into the print of the nails in the hands of Jesus and put {thrust} his hand into His side (John 20:25a, b); Jesus told him to put {thrust} his hand in His side (v. 27). Other refs.: Matt. 9:17a, b; 10:34a, b {to bring, to send}; 27:6; Mark 2:22; 7:33; 12:43, 44a, b; Luke 5:37; 13:8 {to fertilize, to dung} (lit.: to put dung, to throw

manure); John 12:6; 15:6a, b; Jas. 3:3; Rev. 14:16 {to swing, to thrust}, 19 {to swing, to thrust}; 20:3. **b. To place, to deposit** > The bondman should have put his lord's money with the bankers (Matt. 25:27). Jesus told Peter to put his sword into the sheath (John 18:11). All other refs.: see entries in Lexicon at <906>.

[7] ***epiballō*** [verb: ἐπιβάλλω <1911>]; **from *epi*: on, and *ballō*: see [6] ▶ To throw, to apply, to cast on** > People put their own clothes on a colt, and they set Jesus on it (Mark 11:7). Paul did not want to put a leash {cast a snare, set a snare, put a restraint} on {restrict} the Corinthians (1 Cor. 7:35). Other refs.: Matt. 9:16 and Luke 5:36 {to sew}. All other refs.: BEAT <1911>, FALL (verb) <1911>, LAY <1911>, THINK <1911>.

[8] **which must be put: *blēteos*** [adj.: βλητέος <992>]; **from *ballō*: see [6] ▶ Which must be poured** > New wine must be put in new wineskins (Mark 2:22; Luke 5:38). ¶

[9] **to put down: *kathaireō*** [verb: καθαιρέω <2507>]; **from *kata*: down, and *haireō*: to take ▶ To make go down, to make descend** > God has put down (brought down) rulers from their thrones (Luke 1:52). All other refs.: DESTROY <2507>, PULL <2507>, TAKE <2507>.

[10] **to put away, to put behind: *katargeō*** [verb: καταργέω <2673>]; **from *kata*: intens., and *argeō*: to do nothing, to be inactive, which is from *argos*: useless, harmful, which is from *a*: neg., and *ergon*: work ▶ To abolish, to make to cease** > Paul had put away childish things (1 Cor. 13:11 {to do away}). All other refs.: see entries in Lexicon at <2673>.

[11] **to put in: *apostellō*** [verb: ἀποστέλλω <649>]; **from *apo*: from, and *stellō*: to set, to place ▶ To send** > When the grain is produced, immediately one puts in the sickle (Mark 4:29). All other refs.: SEND <649>.

[12] **to put on: *enduō*** [verb: ἐνδύω <1746>]; **from *en*: in, and *duō*: to sink into, as: to sink into clothing ▶ To wear, to don** > The verb is used in regard to body tunics (Mark 6:9). All other refs.: CLOTHE <1746>.

[13] **to put out: *epanagō*** [verb: ἐπανάγω <1877>]; **from *epi*: upon, *ana*: above, and *agō*: to lead ▶ To head for the more open sea** > Jesus asked Simon to put out {draw out, thrust out} a little from the land (Luke 5:3). All other refs.: LAUNCH <1877>, RETURN (verb) <1877>.

[14] **to put on board: *embibazō*** [verb: ἐμβιβάζω <1688>]; **from *en*: in, and *bibazō*: to cause to go ▶ To place (on a vessel)** > The centurion put Paul on board {made him go on board} a ship sailing to Italy (Acts 27:6). ¶

– [15] Matt. 1:19; 5:31, 32; 19:3, 7–9; et al. → to put away → DIVORCE (verb) <630> [16] Matt. 4:12; Mark 1:14 → to put in prison → BETRAY <3860> [17] Matt. 6:16 → to put on a gloomy face → to disfigure the face → DISFIGURE <853> [18] Matt. 6:31; Luke 23:11; John 19:2 → to put on → CLOTHE <4016> [19] Matt. 8:3; Mark 1:41; Luke 5:13 → to put out, to put forth → to stretch out → STRETCH <1614> [20] Matt. 9:25; Mark 5:40; Luke 8:54; John 10:4; Acts 9:40; 16:37; 3 John 10 → to put outside, to put out, to put forth → CAST <1544> [21] Matt. 12:20; 1 Thes. 5:19 → to put out → QUENCH <4570> [22] Matt. 12:44; Luke 11:25 → to put in order → ADORN <2885> [23] Matt. 13:24, 31; 1 Cor. 10:27 → to put forth → to set before → SET (verb) <3908> [24] Matt. 15:30 → CAST <4496> [25] Matt. 17:17; Mark 9:19; Luke 9:41; Acts 18:14; 2 Cor. 11:1a, 4, 19, 20; 2 Tim. 4:3 → to put up with → SUFFER <430> [26] Matt. 18:2; 25:33; Mark 9:36; Acts 22:30 → SET (verb) <2476> [27] Matt. 21:41 → to put to death → to cause to perish → PERISH <622> [28] Matt. 22:18 → to put to the test → TEMPT <3985> [29] Matt. 24:32; Mark 13:28 → to put forth → PRODUCE <1631> [30] Matt. 24:45, 47; 25:21, 23; Luke 12:42, 44 → to put in charge → to make, to make ruler → MAKE <2525> [31] Matt. 26:52 → to put, to put again, to put back → RETURN (verb) <654> [32] Matt. 26:59; 27:1; Mark 14:55; Luke 21:16; Rom. 8:13 → to put to death → DEATH <2289> [33] Mark 15:17 → to put on → CLOTHE <1737> [34] Luke 8:27 →

to put on → WEAR <1737> **35** Luke 10:34; 19:35; Acts 23:24 → SET (verb) <1913> **36** Luke 16:4 → to put out → REMOVE <3179> **37** Luke 18:7 → to keep putting off → to have patience → PATIENCE <3114> **38** Luke 19:23; 2 Cor. 8:16; Heb. 8:10; 10:16; Rev. 3:8; 17:17 → GIVE <1325> **39** Luke 21:12 → to hand over … and put → BETRAY <3860> **40** John 9:6, 11 → ANOINT <2025> **41** John 9:22; 12:42; 16:2 → put out of the synagogue → excommunicated from the synagogue → EXCOMMUNICATED <656> **42** John 13:3 → to put under the power → lit.: to give in the hands → GIVE <1325> **43** John 13:12 → to put on → to take again → TAKE <2983> **44** John 19:29 → to put up → OFFER <4374> **45** John 21:7 → to put on → GIRD <1241> **46** Acts 2:24; 7:33 → to put an end, to put off → LOOSE <3089> **47** Acts 5:2, 3 → to put aside → PILFER <3557> **48** Acts 5:39 → to put down → DESTROY <2647> **49** Acts 6:3 → to put in charge → APPOINT <2525> **50** Acts 8:3 → DELIVER <3860> **51** Acts 12:8 → to put on → to wrap around → WRAP <4016> **52** Acts 12:8 → to put on one's clothes → GIRD <4024> **53** Acts 12:8; Eph. 6:15 → to put on → SHOD <5265> **54** Acts 12:19 → to put to death → DEATH <520> **55** Acts 13:18 → to put up, to put up with the ways → to endure the conduct → ENDURE <5159> **56** Acts 13:46; 1 Tim. 1:19 → to put, to put away → REJECT <683> **57** Acts 19:33 → to put forward → to push forward → PUSH <4261> **58** Acts 19:33 → to put forward → to draw out → DRAW <4264> **59** Acts 20:15 → to put in → ARRIVE <3846> **60** Acts 24:22 → to put off → ADJOURN <306> **61** Acts 25:17 → to put off → DELAY <311> **62** Acts 26:10 → to shut up → SHUT <2623> **63** Acts 27:3 → to put in → TOUCH <2609> **64** Acts 27:13 → to put out to sea → WEIGH <142> **65** Acts 27:30 → to put out → to carry out → CARRY <1614> **66** Acts 28:12 → to put in → LAND (verb) <2609> **67** Rom. 3:25 → to put forward → to set forth → SET (verb) <4388> **68** 1 Cor. 5:13 → to put away, to put out → to take away → TAKE <1808> **69** 1 Cor. 10:9 → to put to the test → TEMPT <1598> **70** 1 Cor. 11:4, 5 → to put to shame → DISHONOR (verb) <2617> **71** 1 Cor. 12:24 → to put together → COMPOSE <4786> **72** 1 Cor. 14:16 → to be put in the position → to fill the place → FILL (verb) <378> **73** 1 Cor. 15:27; Eph. 1:22; Heb. 2:8 → to put under → SUBJECT (verb) <5293> **74** 1 Cor. 16:10 → to put at ease → to see that someone may be without fear → SEE <991>, FEAR <870> **75** 2 Cor. 5:2 → to put on → CLOTHE <1902> **76** 2 Cor. 10:8; Phil. 1:20 → to put to shame → ASHAMED (BE) <153> **77** 2 Cor. 11:20 → to put on airs → to exalt oneself → EXALT <1869> **78** Eph. 4:31 → to put away → to take away → TAKE <142> **79** Eph. 6:13 → to put on → TAKE <353> **80** Phil. 1:16 or 17 → APPOINT <2749> **81** Col. 2:11 → to put off → putting off → PUTTING <555> **82** Col. 3:9 → to put off → DISARM <554> **83** 1 Tim. 4:6 → to put before → to point out → POINT (verb) <5294> **84** Titus 1:5 → to put in order → to set in order → SET (verb) <1930> **85** Phm. 18 → to put on the account → IMPUTE <1677> **86** Heb. 2:8c → not put under → SUBJECT (verb) <506> **87** Heb. 3:9 → to put to the test → TEST (noun and verb) <1382> <1381> **88** Heb. 9:26 → to put away → putting away → PUTTING <115> **89** Heb. 12:13 → to put out of joint → DISLOCATE <1624> **90** 1 Pet. 3:21; 2 Pet. 1:14 → to put aside, away, off → REMOVAL <595> **91** 3 John 9 → to like to put oneself first → to love to have the preeminence → PREEMINENCE <5383> **92** Rev. 3:18 → to put on → ANOINT <1472> **93** Rev. 14:15, 18 → to put in → THRUST <3992>.

PUTEOLI – ***Potioloi*** [masc. plur. name: Ποτίολοι <4223>]: **sulfurous wells or springs; *Puteoli*, in Lat. ▶ Port of Italy near Naples >** Paul stayed in Puteoli with brothers for seven days, while he was on his way to Rome (Acts 28:13). ¶

PUTTING – **1** **putting away: *athetēsis*** [fem. noun: ἀθέτησις <115>]; **from *a*: neg., and *tithēmi*: to set, to place; lit.:**

setting aside ▶ Nullification, abrogation, rejection > With Christ's priesthood, there is a putting away {annulling, disannulling, setting aside} of the commandment concerning the previous priesthood (Heb. 7:18). Christ has been manifested to put away {to do away with} sin (lit.: for the putting away of sin) by the sacrifice of Himself (Heb. 9:26). ¶

2 **putting off: *apekdusis*** [fem. noun: ἀπέκδυσις <555>]; **from *apekduomai*: to put off from oneself, which is from *apo*: from, and *ekduō*: to strip, to put off, which is from *ek*: out of, and *duō*: to go, to sink, specifically, into or out of clothing ▶ Removal, setting aside** > Spiritual circumcision of Christians is by the putting off of the sinful nature (Col. 2:11). ¶

3 **putting on: *endusis*** [fem. noun: ἔνδυσις <1745>]; **from *enduō*: to clothe, which is from *en*: in, and *duō*: see 2 ▶ Wearing of clothes** > The adornment of the woman is not to consist of putting on fine clothes (1 Pet. 3:3), but her adornment is the disposition of her heart. ¶

PUZZLED (BE) – Acts 5:24 → were puzzled, wondering → were perplexed → PERPLEXED (BE) <1280>.

PYRRHUS – ***Purros*** [masc. name: Πύρρος <4450a>]: **red like fire; from *pur*: fire ▶ Father of Sopater** > Sopater of Berea was the son of Pyrrhus (Acts 20:4, but not in some mss.). ¶

PYTHON – ***Puthōn*** [masc. name: Πύθων <4436>]; **from *Puthō*: region where Delphi, an ancient Greek city, was situated ▶ In Greek mythology, it was a serpent or dragon that guarded the oracle of Delphi and was killed by Apollo; also transl.: divination** > In Acts 16:16, the slave girl who had a spirit of Python (i.e., a demon spirit of divination) brought much profit to her masters by prophesying; the apostle Paul delivered her in the name of Jesus Christ. ¶

Q

QUADRANS – ***kodrantēs*** [masc. noun: κοδράντης <2835>]; **from Lat. *quadrans*: quarter of an *assarion*** ► **Small coin worth two mites or 1/64 of a denarius; also transl.: cent, farthing, penny** > Jesus spoke of a man who was obliged to remain in prison until he had paid the last quadrans (Matt. 5:26); in some mss.: Luke 12:59. A poor widow put two mites (or: small copper coins), which make a quadrans {fraction of a penny}, in the treasury of the temple (Mark 12:42). ¶

QUADRUPED – ***tetrapous*** [adj. used as noun: τετράπους <5074>]; **from *tessares*: four, and *pous*: foot** ► **Animal with four feet; also transl.: four-footed animal** > Peter saw a great sheet in which were all the quadrupeds and reptiles of the earth, and the birds of heaven (Acts 10:12; 11:6). Men have changed the glory of the incorruptible God into an image of corruptible man, birds, quadrupeds, and reptiles (Rom. 1:23). ¶

QUAKE – Matt. 27:51 → SHAKE <4579>.

QUALIFIED – 2 Tim. 2:2 → ABLE <2425>.

QUALIFY – Col. 1:12 → to make meet → MEET (adj.) <2427>.

QUALITY – 2 Pet. 1:10, 12 → "qualities" added in Engl.

QUALM – Jude 12 → without the slightest qualm → without fear → FEAR (noun) <870>.

QUANTITY – [1] ***plēthos*** [neut. noun: πλῆθος <4128>]; **from *plēthō*: to fill** ► **Great number, multitude; also transl.: great quantity** > At the commandment of Jesus, the disciples let down their net and enclosed a great quantity {great number, large number, great multitude} of fish (Luke 5:6). Paul gathered a quantity {bundle, pile} of branches together to fuel the fire in order to warm himself and others (Acts 28:3). All other refs.: MULTITUDE <4128>.
– [2] John 21:6 → MULTITUDE <4128>.

QUARREL (noun) – [1] 1 Cor. 1:11; Titus 3:9 → CONTENTION <2054> [2] Col. 3:13 → COMPLAINT <3437> [3] 1 Tim. 6:4 → quarrel of words → argument over words → ARGUMENT <3055> [4] 2 Tim. 2:23 → STRIFE <3163> [5] Titus 3:9 → STRIVING <3163>.

QUARREL (verb) – [1] ***machomai*** [verb: μάχομαι <3164>] ► **To dispute, to fight over a subject, to discuss sharply** > The Jews quarreled {argued, argued sharply, strove, contended} among themselves regarding the saying that Jesus was giving them His flesh to eat (John 6:52). Other refs.: Acts 7:26; 2 Tim. 2:24; Jas. 4:2; see STRIVE <3164>, FIGHT (verb) <3164>. ¶
– [2] Matt. 12:19 → STRIVE <2051> [3] Rom.14:1 → DISPUTE (noun) <1253> [4] 2 Tim. 2:14 → to quarrel about words → to strive about words → STRIVE <3054>.

QUARRELING, QUARRELLING – [1] Acts 12:20 → to be quarreling → to be very angry → ANGRY <2371> [2] Rom. 13:13 → STRIFE <2054> [3] Rom. 14:1 → DISPUTE (noun) <1253> [4] 1 Cor. 1:11 → CONTENTION <2054> [5] 1 Cor. 3:3; 2 Cor. 12:20 → STRIFE <2054> [6] 1 Tim. 2:8 → REASONING <1261> [7] 1 Tim. 6:5 → constant quarrelling → useless wrangling → WRANGLING <1275a> <3859>.

QUARRELSOME – [1] **not quarrelsome: *amachos*** [adj.: ἄμαχος <269>]; **from *a*: neg., and *machē*: dispute, quarrel** ► **Not disposed to fight; also transl.: not a brawler, not addicted to contention, not contentious, peaceable** > The overseer must not be quarrelsome (1 Tim. 3:3). Titus was to remind the Cretans not to be quarrelsome (Titus 3:2). ¶
– [2] 2 Tim. 2:24 → to be quarrelsome → STRIVE <3164>.

QUART – ***choinix*** [fem. noun: χοῖνιξ <5518>] ► **Daily ration of food for a man** > In Rev. 6:6a, b, a quart {choenix, measure, pound} designates a Greek measure for dry things poss. almost equivalent to one quart or a liter; it is used concerning wheat and barley. ¶

QUARTER – [1] Mark 1:45 in some mss. → from every quarter → on every side →

SIDE <3840> [2] Acts 16:3; 28:7 → PLACE (noun) <5117> [3] Rev. 20:8 → CORNER <1137>.

QUARTERS – Acts 28:30 → rented quarters → rented house → HOUSE <3410>.

QUARTUS – ***Kouartos*** [masc. name: Κούαρτος <2890>]: **fourth, in Lat. ► Christian man living at Corinth** > The brother Quartus sent his greetings to the Christians of Rome (Rom. 16:23). ¶

QUATERNION – ***tetradion*** [neut. noun: τετράδιον <5069>]; **from *tessares*: four ► Group of four soldiers** > Herod delivered Peter to four quaternions {squads} of soldiers to keep him (Acts 12:4). ¶

QUEEN – ***basilissa*** [fem. noun: βασίλισσα <938>]; **fem. of *basileus*: king ► Woman who exercises sovereign power** > The queen of the south (Matt. 12:42; Luke 11:31) corresponds to the queen of Sheba who came to Solomon (see 1 Kgs. 10:1–13; 2 Chr. 9:1–12). Candace was queen of the Ethiopians (Acts 8:27). Great Babylon says in her heart: "I sit a queen" (Rev. 18:7). ¶

QUENCH – [1] ***sbennumi*** [verb: σβέννυμι <4570>] ► **To stop from burning, to extinguish; also transl.: to put out, to go out, to snuff out** > In speaking about Jesus who would come, Isaiah said that He would not quench smoking flax (i.e., Israel) (Matt. 12:20). In a parable, the lamps of the foolish virgins were being quenched (Matt. 25:8). The fire is not quenched in hell (Mark 9:44 in some mss., 46 in some mss., 48). With the shield of faith one is able to quench {extinguish} all the inflamed darts of the wicked one (Eph. 6:16). Christians must not quench the Spirit (1 Thes. 5:19). By faith, O.T. people of faith quenched the power of fire (Heb. 11:34). ¶
– [2] Matt. 3:12; Mark 9:43, 45; Luke 3:17 → that cannot be quenched → UNQUENCHABLE <762>.

QUESTION (noun) – [1] ***zētēma*** [neut. noun: ζήτημα <2213>]; **from *zēteō*: to seek, to inquire ► Syn. of [2], controversy** > The question {issue} of the circumcision was to be settled by the apostles and elders (Acts 15:2). The Roman proconsul Gallio did not want to judge questions about words (Acts 18:15). Paul was accused of questions of the law of the Jews (Acts 23:29) and their religion (25:19 {points of disagreement, points of dispute}). Agrippa was acquainted with all the customs and questions {controversies} among the Jews (Acts 26:3). ¶
[2] ***zētēsis*** [fem. noun: ζήτησις <2214>]; **from *zēteō*: to seek, to inquire ► Topic which is the subject of discussion; also transl.: arguments, controversial questions, controversies, disputes, questionings, speculations** > Paul speaks of one who is sick about questions (1 Tim. 6:4). Timothy and Titus were to avoid foolish and ignorant questions (2 Tim. 2:23; Titus 3:9). All other refs.: DISPUTE (noun) <2214>, INQUIRY <2214>.
– [3] Matt. 22:35; Mark 12:18; Luke 5:22; et al. → ASK <1905> [4] Luke 5:22 → REASONING <1261> [5] Acts 15:6 → MATTER <3056> [6] Acts 19:40 → to call in question → CALL (verb) <1458> [7] 1 Cor. 10:25, 27 → to ask questions, to raise questions → ASK <350> [8] Col. 2:16 → "questions of" added in Engl. [9] 1 Tim. 3:16 → beyond all questions → without controversy → CONTROVERSY <3672>.

QUESTION (verb) – [1] **to question together: *suzēteō*** [verb: συζητέω <4802>]; **from *sun*: together, and *zēteō*: to seek ► To seek to find an answer together; also transl.: to debate, to discuss, to enquire** > The Jews questioned together among themselves {asked each other} concerning the doctrine of Jesus (Mark 1:27). The disciples questioned among themselves what rising from among the dead meant (Mark 9:10). They began to question together among themselves which of them would betray Jesus (Luke 22:23). All other refs.: DISPUTE (verb) <4802>, REASON (verb) <4802>.
– [2] Matt. 12:10; 22:23, 46; 27:11; Mark 12:18, 34; Luke 23:9; et al. → ASK <1905> [3] Mark 2:6, 8a, b; Luke 3:15; 5:21 →

REASON (verb) <1260> 4 Luke 11:53 → to make to speak → SPEAK <653> 5 John 1:25; 8:7; 9:19; 16:19, 30 → ASK <2065> 6 John 21:12 → ASK <1833> 7 Acts 22:24, 29 → EXAMINE <426>.

QUESTIONING – 1 Phil. 2:14 → REASONING <1261> 2 2 Tim. 2:23 → STRIFE <3163>.

QUICK – 1 Acts 5:33; 7:54 → to be cut to the quick → to be furious → FURIOUS <1282> 2 Acts 12:7 → QUICKLY <1722> <5034> 3 Acts 22:18 → HASTEN <4692> 4 Jas. 1:19 → SWIFT <5036>.

QUICK-TEMPERED – Titus 1:7 → soon angry → ANGRY <3711>.

QUICKEN – 1 John 5:21a, b; 6:63; Rom. 4:17; 8:11; 1 Cor. 15:36; 2 Cor. 3:6; Gal. 3:21; 1 Tim. 6:13; 1 Pet. 3:18 → to give life, to preserve in life → LIFE <2227> 2 Eph. 2:5; Col. 2:13 → to quicken with → to make alive with → ALIVE <4806>.

QUICKENING – 1 Cor. 15:45 → life-giving → to give life → LIFE <2227>.

QUICKLY – 1 ***tacheōs*** [adv.: ταχέως <5030>]**; from *tachus*: prompt ▶ Rapidly, without delay >** A master of a house told his bondman to go out quickly {at once} to bring other people to his supper (Luke 14:21). The steward told a debtor to quickly write a false number of baths of oil (Luke 16:6). Mary rose up quickly {hastily} and went out (John 11:31). The Galatians had quickly {soon} changed to a different gospel (Gal. 1:6). The Thessalonians were not to be quickly {soon, easily} shaken in mind (2 Thes. 2:2). All other refs.: HASTILY <5030>, SHORTLY <5030>.

2 ***tachion*** [adv.: τάχιον <5032>]**; neuter of *tachiōn*, which is the compar. of *tachus*: rapid, prompt ▶ More rapidly, without delay >** Jesus said to Judas: "What you do, do quickly" (John 13:27). All other refs.: FASTER <5032>, SHORTLY <5032>, SOONER <5032>.

3 **as quickly as possible: *tachista*** [adv.: τάχιστα <5033>]**; superl. of *tachus*: rapid, prompt ▶ Very rapidly, as rapidly as possible >** Silas and Timothy had received a command to join Paul as quickly as possible {as soon as possible, with all speed} (Acts 17:15). ¶

4 ***en tachei*; *en*** [prep.: ἐν <1722>]**; *tachos*** [neut. noun: τάχος <5034>]**; from *en*: in, and *tachos*: speed ▶ Rapidly, swiftly >** An angel told Peter to rise up quickly (Acts 12:7). Paul was to go quickly {immediately} out of Jerusalem (Acts 22:18). Other refs. (*tachos*): SHORTLY <5034>, SPEEDILY <5034>.

5 ***tachu*** [adv.: ταχύ <5035>]**; from *tachus*: prompt, rapid ▶ Rapidly, without delay >** Jesus spoke of making friends quickly with one's adverse party while in the way with him (Matt. 5:25). The women were to go quickly and say to the disciples that Jesus was risen from the dead (Matt. 28:7); they went out quickly {hurried away} from the tomb with fear and great joy (v. 8). Mary rose up quickly and came to Jesus (John 11:29). The Lord was going to come quickly {soon} to Pergamos (Rev. 2:16). In a future day, the third woe will come quickly [soon} (Rev. 11:14). Jesus says three times that He is coming quickly {soon} in the last book of the N.T. (Rev. 3:11; 22:7, 20). Other refs.: Mark 16:8 and Rev. 2:5 in some mss. All other refs.: LIGHTLY <5035>.

QUICKSANDS – See SYRTIS <4950>.

QUIET (adj.) – 1 ***ēremos*** [adj.: ἤρεμος <2263>]**; from *ērema*: softly, peacefully ▶ State of calm that comes from the outside >** Christians pray that they may lead a quiet and tranquil life (1 Tim. 2:2); some versions translate: tranquil and quiet life, peaceful and quiet lives. ¶

2 ***hēsuchios*** [adj.: ἡσύχιος <2272>] **▶ Calm resulting from inner peace, occasioning no disturbance to others >** We are to pray for kings and all who are in authority, that we may lead a tranquil and quiet {peaceful and quiet, quiet and peaceable, quiet and tranquil} life, in all godliness and dignity

(1 Tim. 2:2). A gentle and quiet spirit is precious in the sight of God (1 Pet. 3:4). ¶
3 **to be quiet, to lead a quiet life: *hēsuchazō*** [verb: ἡσυχάζω <2270>]; **from *hēsuchos*: quiet, still ► To lead a tranquil life >** The Thessalonians were to seek earnestly to lead a quiet life (1 Thes. 4:11). All other refs.: REST (verb) <2270>, SILENT <2270>.
4 **to be quiet: *phimoō*** [verb: φιμόω <5392>]; **from *phimos*: muzzle ► To close one's mouth, to keep silence >** Jesus commanded a demon to be quiet (Mark 1:25; Luke 4:35). He told the sea to be quiet (Mark 4:39). All other refs.: see MUZZLE <5392>, SILENCE (noun) <5392>, SPEECHLESS <5392>.
– 5 Matt. 20:31; Mark 9:34; 10:48; Luke 19:40 → to be quiet, to keep quiet → to be silent → SILENT <4623> 6 Mark 6:31 → DESERTED <2048> 7 Acts 12:17; 1 Cor. 14:28 → to be quiet → to be silent → SILENT <4601> 8 Acts 19:36 → to be quiet → to be calm → CALM (noun and adj.) <2687> 9 Acts 22:2; 1 Tim. 2:12 → SILENCE (noun) <2271> 10 2 Thes. 3:12 → in quiet fashion → lit.: with quietness → QUIETNESS <2271>.

QUIET (verb) – 1 Acts 11:18 → to quiet down → to be silent → SILENT <2270> 2 Acts 19:35 → APPEASE <2687>.

QUIETLY – 1 Matt. 1:19; Acts 16:37 → SECRETLY <2977> 2 1 Thes. 4:11 → to live quietly → to lead a quiet life → QUIET (adj.) <2270> 3 2 Thes. 3:12 → lit.: with quietness → QUIETNESS <2271> 4 1 Tim. 2:11, 12 → SILENCE (noun) <2271>.

QUIETNESS – 1 ***hēsuchia*** [fem. noun: ἡσυχία <2271>]; **from *hēsuchos*: quiet, still ► Tranquility, as describing the life of one who minds his own affairs rather than interfering in the affairs of others >** Paul enjoined certain brothers among the Thessalonians to work in quietness {quietly, in quiet fashion} (2 Thes. 3:12). Other refs.: Acts 22:2; 1 Tim. 2:11, 12; see SILENCE (noun) <2271>. ¶
– 2 Acts 24:2 → PEACE <1515>.

QUIRINIUS – ***Kurēnios*** [masc. name: Κυρήνιος <2958>]; ***Quirinus* (not *Quirinius*) was the name given to Romulus, the founder of Rome, after his death ► Governor of Syria >** The census under Caesar Augustus took place when Quirinius (also spelled: *Cyrenius*, in some older transl.) was governing Syria (Luke 2:2). ¶

QUOTE – Heb. 4:7 in some mss. → as in the passage already quoted → lit.: as He has previously said → SAY <4280>.

R

RABBI – [1] ***Rhabbi*** [masc. noun: Ῥαββί <4461>]; **from the Heb. *rab*: elder, master ▶ Aram. word designating a master who teaches; a doctor of the law among the Jews** > The scribes and Pharisees loved to be called Rabbi, Rabbi (Matt. 23:7a, b); but Jesus told the crowds and His disciples not to be called Rabbi (v. 8). The disciples of Jesus gave Him this title (Matt. 26:25, 49; Mark 9:5; 11:21; 14:45; John 1:38, 49; 4:31; 6:25; 9:2; 11:8), as also did Nicodemus (John 3:2). John the Baptist was also called Rabbi (John 3:26). ¶
– [2] Mark 10:51 → RABBONI <4462>.

RABBLE – Acts 17:5 → from the lowest rabble → from the market place → MARKET PLACE <60>.

RABBONI – ***Rhabboni*** [masc. noun: Ῥαββονί <4462>]; **intens. form of *Rhabbi*: master; also spelled *Rhabbouni* ▶ Aram. word signifying "my great master" and indicating respect** > Blind Bartimaeus used the title Rabboni {Rabbi, Lord} in addressing Jesus (Mark 10:51), as did also Mary Magdalene when she recognized Jesus after He had risen from the dead (John 20:16). ¶

RACA – ***rhaka*** [adj.: ῥακά <4469>] ▶ **Aram. word of contempt meaning: stupid, worthless** > Jesus said that whoever will say to his brother, Raca {good-for-nothing}, will be subject to the judgment of the Sanhedrin (Matt. 5:22). ¶

RACE[1] – [1] ***genos*** [neut. noun: γένος <1085>]; **from *ginomai*: to become, to be born ▶ Descent, lineage; also transl.: birth, children, descent, family, generation, kindred, nation, offspring, people, stock, tribe** > Aquila was of Pontus by race {born in Pontus, a native of Pontus} (Acts 18:2). Apollos was an Alexandrian by race {born at Alexandria, native of Alexandria, an Alexandrian by birth} (Acts 18:24). The word is also used in regard to a Syro-Phoenician woman (Mark 7:26), men of the high priestly family (Acts 4:6), Israel (Acts 7:19; Phil. 3:5), Abraham (Acts 13:26), God (Acts 17:28, 29), and the chosen race that Christians constitute (1 Pet. 2:9). All other refs.: see entries in Lexicon at <1085>.
– [2] Acts 10:28 → one of a strange race → one of another nation → NATION <246> [3] Rom. 9:3 → those of my own race → lit.: my relatives according to the flesh → RELATIVE <4773> [4] Rom. 9:5 → from their race → lit.: of whom [5] Jas. 3:7b → KIND (noun) <5449>.

RACE[2] – [1] ***agōn*** [masc. noun: ἀγών <73>]; **from *agō*: to lead; lit.: gathering place, specifically athletic games ▶ Contest, run** > Christians should run the race that is set before them with endurance (Heb. 12:1). All other refs.: CONFLICT <73>, FIGHT (noun) <73>.
[2] ***stadion*** [neut. noun: στάδιον <4712>]; **from *histēmi*: to stand ▶ Race track, stadium** > Of those who run in a race {racecourse}, only one receives the prize (1 Cor. 9:24). All other refs.: STADION <4712>.
– [3] Acts 20:24; 2 Tim. 4:7 → COURSE <1408>.

RACE-COURSE – 1 Cor. 9:24 → RACE[2] <4712>.

RACHAB – Matt. 1:5 → RAHAB <4477>.

RACHEL – ***Rhachēl*** [fem. name: Ῥαχήλ <4478>]: **ewe or sheep, in Heb. ▶ Wife of Jacob (see Gen. 29:9–20, 28)** > The mention of Rachel weeping for her children during the massacre of the children of Bethlehem by Herod (Matt. 2:18) is related to a prophecy of Jeremiah (see Jer. 31:15). This latter passage alludes to the persecutions that Israel had endured over the course of centuries, until the tribes, which have been scattered throughout the world, return to the land of Israel. ¶

RADIANCE – [1] ***apaugasma*** [neut. noun: ἀπαύγασμα <541>]; **from *apaugazō*: to emit light, which is from *apo*: from, and *augazō*: to shine, which is from *augē*: dawn ▶ Brightness, effulgence, splendor** > The Son of God is the radiance of the glory of God (Heb. 1:3). ¶
– [2] Rev. 21:11 → LIGHT (noun) <5458>.

RADIANCY – 2 Cor. 4:4 → LIGHT (noun) <5462>.

RADIANT – [1] Mark 9:3 → SHINING <4744> [2] Eph. 5:27 → GLORIOUS <1741>.

RAG – 1 Cor. 4:11 → to be in rags → to be naked → NAKED <1130>.

RAGAU – See REU <4466>.

RAGE (noun) – [1] Luke 4:28; Acts 19:28; 2 Cor. 12:20; Gal. 5:20; Col. 3:8 → WRATH <2372> [2] Luke 6:11 → MADNESS <454> [3] Rev. 12:12 → FURY <2372>.

RAGE (verb) – [1] ***phruassō*** [verb: φρυάσσω <5433>]**; lit.: to snort; used of the spirited behavior of horses and the arrogance of men; comp. *bruō*: to overflow ▶ To agitate, to unleash** > David asked why did the nations rage against the Lord and His Christ (Acts 4:25). ¶
– [2] Acts 27:20 → to continue raging → BEAT <1945> [3] Rev. 11:18 → ENRAGED (BE) <3710>.

RAGING – [1] ***agrios*** [adj.: ἄγριος <66>]**; from *agros*: field, alluding to the wild, untamed nature of life forms in the country ▶ Impetuous, tumultuous** > Jude compares ungodly men to raging {wild} waves of the sea (Jude 13). Other refs.: Matt. 3:4; Mark 1:6; see WILD <66>. ¶
– [2] Luke 8:24 → WAVE <2830> [3] Acts 26:11 → in raging fury → to be exceedingly furious → FURIOUS <1693> [4] Heb. 10:27 → raging fire → lit.: heat of fire → HEAT <2205>.

RAHAB – [1] ***Rhaab*** [fem. name: Ῥαάβ <4460>]**: proud, in Heb. ▶ Prostitute of Jericho who received the Israelite spies and hid them** > By faith, Rahab received the spies sent by Joshua; she and her relatives were spared during the destruction of the city of Jericho (Heb. 11:31; see Joshua 6). James tells us that she was justified by her works (Jas. 2:25). ¶
[2] ***Rhachab*** [fem. name: Ῥαχάβ <4477>] ▶ **Same as [1]** > Rachab is one of four women, in addition to Mary, mentioned in the genealogy of Jesus Christ (Matt. 1:5). She was the mother of Boaz and the great-grandmother of David. ¶

RAID – Matt. 11:12 → to seize by force → SEIZE <726>.

RAIL – [1] Mark 15:29; Luke 23:39 → REVILE <987> [2] John 9:28; Acts 23:4; 1 Cor. 4:12 → to rail at, to rail against → REVILE <3058>.

RAILING – [1] ***blasphēmia*** [fem. noun: βλασφημία <988>]; **prob. from *blaptō*: to hurt, and *phēmē*: reputation ▶ Insult, blasphemy** > In Rev. 2:9, the Lord knows the railing {slander} of those who say they are Jews but are not. All other refs.: BLASPHEMY <988>, INJURIOUS <988>.
– [2] 1 Pet. 3:9a, b → REVILING <3059> [3] 2 Pet. 2:11 → REVILING <989>.

RAILINGLY – Jude 8, 10 → to speak railingly → REVILE <987>.

RAIMENT – [1] Matt. 3:4; 6:25, 28; 28:3; Luke 12:23 → CLOTHES <1742> [2] Matt. 11:8; 17:2; Mark 9:3; et al. → CLOTHES <2440> [3] Luke 9:29 → CLOTHES <2441> [4] Luke 24:4 → CLOTHES <2067> [5] 1 Tim. 6:8 → CLOTHING <4629> [6] Jas. 2:2a, b → CLOTHES <2066>.

RAIN (noun) – [1] ***brochē*** [fem. noun: βροχή <1028>]**; *from brechō*: see [2] ▶ Water that falls in drops from the clouds, sometimes abundantly** > Jesus spoke of the rain that came and of one house that withstood the inclement weather (Matt. 7:25) while another house fell (v. 27). ¶
[2] **to send rain: *brechō*** [verb: βρέχω <1026>] ▶ **To make it rain** > The Father sends rain on the just and the unjust (Matt. 5:45). All other refs.: FALL (verb) <1026>, RAIN (verb) <1026>, WASH <1026>.
[3] ***huetos*** [masc. noun: ὑετός <5205>]**; *from huō*: to rain ▶ See defin. in [1].** > God gives from heaven rain and fertile seasons (Acts 14:17). Because of the rain that was falling and because of the cold, the natives of the island of Malta took in Paul and his companions (Acts 28:2). The ground drinks

the rain that comes often upon it (Heb. 6:7). The laborer waits to receive the early and the latter rain (Jas. 5:7 in some mss.). Elias prayed and the heaven gave rain (Jas. 5:18). The two witnesses will have power to shut the heaven that no rain may fall (Rev. 11:6). ¶

4 **late rain, latter rain: *opsimos*** [adj.: ὄψιμος <3797>]; **from *opse*: late ▶ Rain falling in Palestine in March and April** > The rain of the latter season falls in early spring, immediately before the beginning of the harvest; the early rain falls in October. The laborer waits for the precious fruit of the earth, having patience for it until it receives the early and the late rains {the autumn and spring rains} (lit.: the early and the latter) (Jas. 5:7). ¶

– 5 Luke 6:48 → great rain → FLOOD (noun) <4132> 6 Jude 12 → without rain → without water → WATER (noun) <504>.

RAIN (verb) – 1 ***brechō*** [verb: βρέχω <1026>] ▶ **a. To fall like rain** > When Lot went out from Sodom, it rained fire and sulfur from heaven (Luke 17:29). **b. To fall, speaking of rain** > Elias prayed that it would not rain, and it did not rain upon the earth three years and six months. (Jas. 5:17a, b). All other refs.: FALL (verb) <1026>, RAIN (noun) <1026>, WASH <1026>.

– 2 Luke 12:54 → it's going to rain → lit.: rain (or: shower) comes → SHOWER <3655> 3 Acts 28:2 → because it was raining → lit.: because of the rain that was falling → RAIN (noun) <5205>.

RAINBOW – ***iris*** [fem. noun: ἶρις <2463>] ▶ **Luminous phenomenon shaped in a half circle, containing the colors of the spectrum, and appearing in the sky** > In the Greek mythology, the robe of Iris was of bright colors; she was a messenger of the gods and was assimilated to the rainbow. John saw a rainbow around the throne (Rev. 4:3) and a rainbow upon the head of a mighty angel (10:1). ¶

RAISE – 1 **to raise up, to rise, to arise: *egeirō*** [verb: ἐγείρω <1453>] ▶ **a. To take out, to bring out** > The man whose sheep falls into a pit on the Sabbath will raise it up {will lift it out} (Matt. 12:11). **b. To make a deceased person return to life** > The Lord would raise up {raise again} the temple of His body in three days (John 2:19, 20 {to rear}). The resurrection of Jesus from among the dead constitutes a fundamental doctrine of Christianity (1 Corinthians 15): if Christ has not been raised the Christians' faith is vain (vv. 12–17); but now Christ has been raised from among the dead (v. 20). Christ has been raised for the Christians' justification (Rom. 4:25). Many passages mention His resurrection that would be accomplished (Matt. 16:21; 17:23; 26:32; 27:63; Mark 14:28; Luke 9:22), and His actual resurrection (Matt. 27:64; 28:6, 7; Mark 16:6, 14; Luke 24:6, 34; John 2:22; 12:1, 9, 17; 21:14; Rom. 6:4, 9; 7:4; 8:34; 1 Cor. 15:4; 2 Cor. 5:15; 2 Tim. 2:8). Many passages state that God the Father has raised Jesus, His Son, from among the dead (Acts 3:15; 4:10; 5:30; 10:40; 13:30, 37; Rom. 4:24; 8:11; 10:9; 1 Cor. 6:14a; 2 Cor. 4:14a; Gal. 1:1; Eph. 1:20; Col. 2:12b; 1 Thes. 1:10; Heb. 11:19; 1 Pet. 1:21). Herod believed that John the Baptist was risen from the dead (Matt. 14:2; Mark 6:14, 16; Luke 9:7). At the return of Christ, God will raise Christians who have died (1 Cor. 15:52; 2 Cor. 4:14b). It is God who raises the dead (Acts 26:8; 2 Cor. 1:9). Other refs.: Matt. 10:8 in some mss.; 11:5; 27:52; Mark 12:26; Luke 7:22; 20:37; 1 Cor. 15:29, 32, 35, 42–44. **c. To set upright again** > Cornelius had fallen down at the feet of Peter who raised him up {lifted him up, made him rise, made him get up, took him up} (Acts 10:26). Other ref.: Mark 10:49. **d. To arise, to cause to appear, to rise** > The verb is used in regard to the children of Abraham (Matt. 3:9; Luke 3:8), David (Acts 13:22), John the Baptist (Matt. 11:11), Jesus (Luke 1:69; 7:16), and a prophet (John 7:52 {to come out}). Other ref.: Acts 13:23. **e. To restore health** > In Jas. 5:15, it is the Lord who raises up the sick. All other refs.: ARISE <1453>, LIFT <1453>, RISE (verb) <1453>, WAKE <1453>.

2 **to raise, to raise up: *exegeirō*** [verb: ἐξεγείρω <1825>]; **from *ek*: out, and *egeirō*:**

see 1 ▶ **a. To cause to appear** > The Scripture says to Pharaoh that God had raised him up that He might display His power in him (Rom. 9:17). **b. To make a deceased person return to life, to resurrect** > God both raised (*egeirō*) the Lord and will also raise up (*exegeirō*) the Christians by His power (1 Cor. 6:14b). ¶

3 **to raise, to raise up: *epegeirō*** [verb: ἐπεγείρω <1892>]; **from *epi*: upon, and *egeirō*: see** 1 ▶ **To provoke; also transl.: to instigate, to stir** > The Jews raised up a persecution against Paul and Barnabas (Acts 13:50). The unbelieving Jews stirred up the minds of the Gentiles and embittered them against the brethren (Acts 14:2). ¶

4 **to raise up together, to raise with: *sunegeirō*** [verb: συνεγείρω <4891>]; **from *sun*: together, and *egeirō*: see** 1 ▶ **To come alive again together** > Having believed through faith in the person and work of the Lord Jesus, Christians are viewed as risen with Christ (Eph. 2:6; Col. 2:12a and 3:1 {to rise with}). ¶

5 **to raise up: *anistēmi*** [verb: ἀνίστημι <450>]; **from *ana*: upward, and *histēmi*: to set, to present** ▶ **To give, to produce** > The verb is used in regard to the posterity that is to be ensured to a brother who had died (Matt. 22:24), a prophet (Acts 3:22), and Jesus (Acts 3:26; 7:37; 13:33). Other refs.: ARISE <450>, RISE (verb) <450>.

6 **to raise up: *exanistēmi*** [verb: ἐξανίστημι <1817>]; **from *ek*: out, and *anistēmi*: see** 5 ▶ **To produce** > The verb is used in regard to the posterity that is to be ensured to a brother who has died (Mark 12:19; Luke 20:28). Other ref.: Acts 15:5 {to rise up}; see RISE (verb) <1817>. ¶

7 ***epairō*** [verb: ἐπαίρω <1869>]; **from *epi*: upon, and *airō*: to lift up** ▶ **To elevate, to lift; also transl.: to lift up** > A woman from the crowd raised her voice {called out} and spoke to Jesus (Luke 11:27). Peter raised his voice (Acts 2:14). The people raised their voices {shouted} (Acts 14:11). The Jews raised their voices (Acts 22:22). All other refs.: EXALT <1869>, LIFT <1869>, TAKE <1869>.

8 **to raise up; lit.: to make an uprising: *episustasin poieō*; uprising: *episustasis*:** [fem. noun: ἐπισύστασις <1999>]; **from *episunistēmi*: to unite against, which is from *epi*: against, and *sunistemi*: to gather, which is from *sun*: together, and *histēmi*: to stand; to make: *poieō*** [verb: ποιέω <4160>] ▶ **To instigate a riot** > Paul had not been found raising up {making a tumultuous gathering of} the people {causing a riot, stirring up a crowd} (Acts 24:12). Other ref. (*episustasis*): 2 Cor. 11:8; see PREOCCUPATION <1999>. ¶

– 9 Matt. 11:23; Luke 10:15 → to raise up → EXALT <5312> 10 Luke 13:11 → to raise up → to lift up → LIFT <352> 11 Luke 17:13; John 11:41; Acts 4:24; Rev. 10:5 → LIFT <142> 12 John 8:7, 10 → to raise oneself up → to straighten oneself up → STRAIGHTEN <352> 13 Acts 10:29 → without raising any objection → OBJECTION <369> 14 Acts 21:38 → to raise a sedition → SEDITION <387> 15 1 Cor. 10:25, 27 → to raise questions → to ask questions → ASK <350>.

RALLY – Acts 5:36 → to be joined → JOIN <4347>.

RAM – See ARAM <689>.

RAMA – See RAMAH <4471>.

RAMAH – ***Rhama*** [fem. name: Ῥαμά <4471>]: **elevated place, in Heb.** ▶ **Locality north of Jerusalem; also transl.: Rama** > The mention of Ramah in Matt. 2:18, concerning the massacre of the children of Bethlehem under Herod, refers to a prophecy of the O.T. (see Jer. 31:15). ¶

RAMPANT – Jas. 1:21 → rampant wickedness → lit.: overflow of wickedness → OVERFLOW (noun) <4050>.

RANK (noun) – 1 ***tagma*** [neut. noun: τάγμα <5001>]; **from *tassō*: to order** ▶ **Order of importance** > All who are made alive are made alive each in his own rank {order, turn} (1 Cor. 15:23). ¶

– 2 Mark 6:40a, b → GROUP <4237> 3 John 1:15, 30 → has a higher rank than I → lit.: has been before me.

RANK (verb) – John 1:15, 30 → ranks before me → lit.: has been before me.

RANSOM (noun) – [1] ***lutron*** [neut. noun: λύτρον <3083>]; **from *luō*: to unbind ▶ Price paid to liberate a captive person** > Jesus Christ gave Himself a ransom for us, for our sins (Matt. 20:28; Mark 10:45). ¶
[2] ***antilutron*** [neut. noun: ἀντίλυτρον <487>]; **from *anti*: instead of, in return, and *lutron*: see [1] ▶ Same meaning as [1], with the idea of exchange** > Christ Jesus gave Himself a ransom for all (1 Tim. 2:6). ¶
– [3] Heb. 9:15 → REDEMPTION <629>.

RANSOM (verb) – [1] 1 Pet. 1:18 → REDEEM <3084> [2] Rev. 5:9 → BUY <59>.

RAPACIOUS – ***harpax*** [adj. and masc. or fem. noun: ἅρπαξ <727>]; **from *harpazō*: to seize ▶ Person who ravishes, snatches away by force; excessively greedy of gain; also transl.: extortioner, ferocious, ravening, ravenous, robber, swindler** > Jesus spoke of false prophets who within are rapacious wolves (Matt. 7:15). The Pharisee who prayed treated the rest of men as rapacious (Luke 18:11). Paul distinguished, on the one hand, between mixing, if necessary, with the rapacious of the world and, on the other hand, not mixing or eating with someone called brother if he is rapacious (1 Cor. 5:10, 11). The rapacious will not inherit the kingdom of God (1 Cor. 6:10). ¶

RAPINE – [1] Matt. 23:25; Luke 11:39; Heb. 10:34; see PLUNDERING <724> [2] Phil. 2:6 → object of rapine → ROBBERY <725>.

RAPTURE – See TRANSLATION <3331>.

RARE – Rev. 21:11 → PRECIOUS <5093>.

RARELY – Rom. 5:7 → very rarely → with difficulty → DIFFICULTY <3433>.

RASH – [1] ***propetēs*** [adj.: προπετής <4312>]; **from *propiptō*: to fall forward, which is from *pro*: forward, and *piptō*: to fall ▶ Characterized by hastiness, thoughtlessness** > The town clerk urged the Ephesians to do nothing rash {headlong, rashly} against Paul (Acts 19:36). Other ref.: 2 Tim. 3:4; see HEADSTRONG <4312>. ¶
– [2] 1 Cor. 13:4 → to be insolent and rash → BOAST (verb) <4068>.

RASHLY – Acts 19:36 → RASH <4312>.

RATE – Luke 18:5 → at any rate → YET <1065>.

RATHER – [1] ***alla*** [particle: ἀλλά <235>]; **from *allos*: other ▶ To the contrary, but** > The master would not serve his servant, but would rather tell the servant to serve him (Luke 17:8). Paul was not making the law void through faith, but he was rather {yea, on the contrary} establishing the law (Rom. 3:31). Paul was not overwhelmed by adverse circumstances, rather {nay, no, yet} he was more than conqueror (Rom. 8:37). *
[2] **rather than: *mallon*** [adv.: μᾶλλον <3123>] ▶ **More, in a greater degree, instead of** > Men loved darkness rather than the light that has come into the world (John 3:19). *
– [3] 1 Cor. 14:1, 5 → ESPECIALLY <3123> [4] Heb. 13:19 → the rather → all the more → MORE <4056>.

RATIFY – [1] Gal. 3:15 → CONFIRM <2964> [2] Gal. 3:17 → CONFIRM <4300>.

RATION – Luke 12:42 → MEASURE OF CORN <4620>.

RATIONAL – Acts 26:25 → rational words → words of soberness → SOBERNESS <4997>.

RAVAGE – [1] ***lumainomai*** [verb: λυμαίνομαι <3075>]; **from *lumē*: destruction ▶ To violently mistreat, to cause damage** > Saul ravaged {destroyed, made havoc of} the church before his conversion (Acts 8:3). ¶
– [2] Gal. 1:13, 23 → DESTROY <4199>.

RAVE – John 10:20 → to rave, to rave mad → to be mad → MAD <3105>.

RAVEN – ***korax*** [masc. noun: κόραξ <2876>]; ***corvus*, in Lat. ▶ Omnivorous bird, which feeds habitually on dead animals; it is frequently seen in Palestine** > If God feeds the ravens, how much more valuable are we than the birds (Luke 12:24). ¶

RAVENING – [1] Matt. 7:15 → RAPACIOUS <727> [2] Luke 11:39 → ROBBERY <724>.

RAVENOUS – Matt. 7:15 → RAPACIOUS <727>.

RAVINE – [1] Luke 3:5 → VALLEY <5327> [2] John 18:1 → TORRENT <5493>.

RAY – Luke 11:36 → SHINING <796>.

REACH (noun) – Rev. 12:14 → FACE (noun) <4383>.

REACH (verb) – [1] ***epekteinō*** [verb: ἐπεκτείνω <1901>]; **from *epi*: to (intens.), and *ekteinō*: to extend ▶ To stretch out** > Paul was reaching forward to {was straining toward} those things that were ahead (Phil. 3:13). ¶

[2] ***ephikneomai*** [verb: ἐφικνέομαι <2185>]; **from *epi*: to, and *hikneomai*: to come, to occur ▶ To come, to arrive at** > Paul spoke of reaching to the Corinthians (2 Cor. 10:13, 14). ¶

[3] ***kollaō*** [verb: κολλάω <2853>]; **from *kolla*: glue; lit.: to glue, to unite strongly ▶ To accumulate, to touch** > The sins of Babylon have reached {heaped up, piled up} to heaven (Rev. 18:5). All other refs.: CLEAVE <2853>, CLING <2853>, COMPANY (noun) <2853>, JOIN <2853>.

[4] ***pherō*** [verb: φέρω <5342>]; **lit.: to carry ▶ To advance, to bring** > After His resurrection, Jesus told Thomas to reach his finger, and to reach also his hand and put it into His side (John 20:27a, b). All other refs.: see entries in Lexicon at <5342>.

– [5] Matt. 8:3; 14:31; 26:51; Mark 1:41; Luke 5:13 → to reach out → to stretch out → STRETCH <1614> [6] Matt. 16:5 → COME <2064> [7] Luke 1:44 → COME <1096> [8] Luke 8:19 → to come at → COME <4940> [9] Luke 13:32 → to reach one's goal → to be perfected → PERFECT (verb) <5048> [10] Acts 16:4 → DETERMINE <2919> [11] Acts 17:27 → to reach after → to feel after → FEEL <5584> [12] Acts 27:12 → ATTAIN <2658> [13] Rom. 9:31 → to succeed in reaching → to come upon → COME <5348> [14] Rom. 16:19 → to become known → KNOWN <864> [15] 1 Cor. 14:36; Eph. 4:13 → ARRIVE <2658> [16] 2 Cor. 4:15 → to reach more → ABOUND <4121> [17] Eph. 1:10 → when the times reach their fulfillment → in the dispensation of the fullness of the times → DISPENSATION <3622> [18] Col. 2:2 → "reach" added in Engl. [19] Heb. 4:1 → to fail to reach → to come short → COME <5302> [20] Jas. 5:4 → ENTER <1525> [21] 2 Pet. 3:9 → COME <5562>.

READ – [1] ***anaginōskō*** [verb: ἀναγινώσκω <314>]; **from *ana*: again (intens.), and *ginōskō*: to know ▶ To look at a text in order to understand it** > Jesus used this verb in regard to the O.T. (Matt. 12:3, 5; 19:4; 21:16, 42; 22:31; Mark 2:25; 12:10, 26; Luke 6:3; 10:26 {reading} and to the great tribulation (Matt. 24:15 and Mark 13:14 {reader; lit.: he who reads}). Jesus stood up to read in the synagogue of Nazareth (Luke 4:16). Many of the Jews read the inscription on the cross of Jesus (John 19:20). The Ethiopian read the prophet Isaiah (Acts 8:28, 30a, b, 32). The prophets are read every Sabbath (Acts 13:27), as well as Moses (15:21). The letter of the apostles and the elders was read at Antioch (Acts 15:31). The governor read the letter concerning Paul (Acts 23:34). The Corinthians were Paul's letter known and read of all men (2 Cor. 3:2). When Moses is read, a veil lies on the heart of the children of Israel (2 Cor. 3:15). The Ephesians might read what Paul had already written concerning the mystery (Eph. 3:4). When the Colossians had read Paul's letter, they were to see that it was read also in the

church of the Laodiceans and they were to read the letter from Laodicea (Col. 4:16a–c). The letter to the Thessalonians was to be read to all the saints (1 Thes. 5:27). Blessed is he who reads and those who hear the words of the prophecy (Rev. 1:3). John wept much because no one was found worthy to open the book or to look into (i.e., read) it (Rev. 5:4 in some mss.). Other ref.: 2 Cor. 1:13 (to know well); see KNOW <314>. ¶
– 2 Mark 15:26 → WRITE <1924> 3 2 Cor. 3:14 → READING <320>.

READER – Matt. 24:15 and Mark 13:14 → lit.: he who reads → READ <314>.

READILY – 1 Acts 24:10 → more cheerfully → CHEERFULLY <2115a> 2 2 Cor. 11:4 → WELL (adv.) <2573> 3 2 Cor. 11:19 → GLADLY <2234>.

READINESS – 1 **readiness, readiness of mind: *prothumia*** [fem. noun: προθυμία <4288>]**; from *prothumos*: ready, willing, which is from *pro*: forward, and *thumos*: disposition, temperament ▶ Willingness, good predisposition; also transl.: eagerness** > The Christians of Berea received the word with all readiness of mind {with great eagerness} (Acts 17:11). As there was the readiness to be willing {eager willingness}, the Corinthians were now to complete what they had intended to do (2 Cor. 8:11). If the readiness {willing mind} is there, a man is accepted according to what he may have (2 Cor. 8:12). Paul knew and boasted in the readiness {forwardness of mind, eagerness to help} of the Corinthians (2 Cor. 9:2). Other ref.: 2 Cor. 8:19 (ready mind); see MIND (noun) <4288>. ¶
– 2 2 Cor. 7:11 → readiness to see justice done → VENGEANCE <1557> 3 2 Cor. 10:6 → in readiness → READY <2092> 4 Eph. 6:15 → PREPARATION <2091>.

READING – 1 ***anagnōsis*** [fem. noun: ἀνάγνωσις <320>]**; from *anaginōskō*: to read, which is from *ana*: intens., and *ginōskō*: to know, hence: to recognize, to read ▶ The act of grasping the sense of written words or of communicating them orally** > The reading of the law and the prophets was customary in the synagogue (Acts 13:15). Paul speaks of the reading of the Old Testament {when it is read} (2 Cor. 3:14). Timothy was to give himself to reading {the public reading of} the word of God (1 Tim. 4:13). ¶
– 2 Luke 10:26 → what is your reading → lit.: how do you read → READ <314>.

READY – 1 ***hetoimos*** [adj.: ἕτοιμος <2092>] ▶ **Thoroughly prepared; also transl.: accomplished, already done** > Paul spoke of things made ready to hand {ready to our hand} in regard to the glad tidings (2 Cor. 10:16). The word is also used in regard to a wedding feast (Matt. 22:4, 8), watching for the coming of the Son of Man (Matt. 24:44; Luke 12:40), wise virgins (Matt. 25:10), a large upper room that was furnished (Mark 14:15), a great supper (Luke 14:17), Peter (Luke 22:33), the time of the Jews (John 7:6 {opportune, right}), men who wanted to kill Paul (Acts 23:15, 21), the liberality (or: generous gift) of the Corinthians (2 Cor. 9:5), avenging all disobedience (2 Cor. 10:6 {in readiness}), every good work (Titus 3:1), salvation (1 Pet. 1:5), and answering for the Christians' hope (1 Pet. 3:15). ¶
2 ***hetoimōs*** [adv.: ἑτοίμως <2093>]**; from *hetoimos*: see 1 ▶ In a state of preparation (in view of accomplishing something)** > Paul was ready to die at Jerusalem for the name of Jesus (Acts 21:13). He was ready to come to the Corinthians (2 Cor. 12:14). Unbelievers will render account to Him who is ready to judge the living and the dead (1 Pet. 4:5). Other ref.: 2 Cor. 13:1 in some mss. ¶
3 **to make ready: *hetoimazō*** [verb: ἑτοιμάζω <2090>]**; from *hetoimos*: see 1 ▶ To prepare, in the sense of intrinsic fitness; also transl.: to make preparation** > This verb is used concerning the last Passover that Jesus would eat (Matt. 26:19; Mark 14:15, 16; Luke 22:8, 9, 12, 13). The master would say to his servant to make ready his supper (Luke 17:8). Other refs.: PREPARE <2090>.
4 **to be ready: *ephistēmi*** [verb: ἐφίστημι <2186>]**; from *epi*: near, upon, and *hi-***

***stēmi*: to stand ▶ To insist, to be pressing** > Timothy was to be ready {to be instant, to be prepared, to be urgent} in season and out of season (2 Tim. 4:2), in regard to preaching the word of God. All other refs.: see entries in Lexicon at <2186>.

[5] **to make ready: *paraskeuazō*** [verb: παρασκευάζω <3903>]; **from *para*: for, and *skeuazō*: to prepare, which is from *skeuē*: equipment, which is from *skeuos*: vessel, instrument▶ To prepare a meal** > While they made ready {were making preparations}, Peter fell into a trance (Acts 10:10). Other refs.: 1 Pet. 2:8 in some mss.; 1 Cor. 14:8; 2 Cor. 9:2, 3: see PREPARE <3903>. ¶

[6] **to keep, to have, to stand ready: *proskartereō*** [verb: προσκαρτερέω <4342>]; **from *pros*: to, and *kartereō*: to be strong, to endure, which is from *karteros*: strength ▶ To be available, to be reserved** > A small boat had to be kept ready for {wait on} Jesus (Mark 3:9). All other refs.: ATTEND <4342>, CONTINUE <4342>, PERSEVERING <4342>.

– [7] Mark 14:38 → WILLING <4289> [8] Luke 17:8 → to get oneself ready → GIRD <4024> [9] Acts 21:15 → to have the effects ready, to get ready → PACK <643> [10] 2 Cor. 1:17 → lit.: that there may be with me [11] 2 Cor. 8:19 → ready mind → MIND (noun) <4288> [12] 2 Cor. 9:4 → not ready → UNPREPARED <532> [13] 1 Tim. 6:18 → ready to distribute, ready to give → GENEROUS <2130> [14] 2 Pet. 1:12 in some mss. → to be ready → to be not negligent → NEGLIGENT <3195>.

READY (BE) – 1 Thes. 2:8 → PLEASED (BE) <2106>.

REAFFIRM – *kuroō* [verb: κυρόω <2964>]; **from *kuros*: authority, ratification ▶ To confirm, to assure, to ratify with authority** > Paul exhorted the Corinthians to reaffirm their love for the brother who had been the object of the discipline of the church (2 Cor. 2:8). Other ref.: Gal. 3:15; see CONFIRM <2964>. ¶

REAL – [1] ***alēthēs*** [adj.: ἀληθής <227>]; **from *a*: neg., and *lēthō*: form of *lanthanō*: to be hidden ▶ True, conform to reality** > Peter did not know that what was happening by the angel was real {true} (Acts 12:9). All other refs.: TRUE <227>.

– [2] Mark 11:32 → a real prophet → lit.: really a prophet → REALLY <3689> [3] John 6:55a, b → TRULY <230> [4] Acts 22:30 → real reason → CERTAINTY <804>.

REALITY – [1] 1 Cor. 2:13 → spiritual realities → spiritual things → SPIRITUAL <4152> [2] Heb. 10:1 → IMAGE <1504>.

REALIZE – [1] Mark 5:30; Acts 22:29 → KNOW <1921> [2] Luke 1:22; Acts 4:13; 2 Cor. 13:5 → RECOGNIZE <1921> [3] Luke 9:33; John 2:9a; 13:7a; 19:10; 20:14; 21:4; Acts 23:5; 1 Cor. 11:3; 1 Tim. 1:9 → KNOW <1492> [4] John 11:50 → CONSIDER <1260> [5] John 12:16 → REMEMBER <3415> [6] Acts 4:13; 10:34 → PERCEIVE <2638> [7] Acts 7:25a, b → UNDERSTAND <4920> [8] Acts 12:12 → CONSIDER <4894> [9] Rom. 2:4 → to not realize → to know not → KNOW <50> [10] 2 Cor. 10:11 → CONSIDER <3049> [11] Eph. 3:11 → ACCOMPLISH <4160> [12] 2 Tim. 3:1 → KNOW <1097> [13] Heb. 6:11 → what you hope for may be fully realized → to the full assurance of hope → ASSURANCE <4136>.

REALIZED (BE) – John 1:17 → lit.: to come (*ginomai*).

REALLY – [1] ***ontōs*** [adv.: ὄντως <3689>]; **from *on*: pres. ptcp. of *eimi*: to be ▶ In truth, in reality; also transl.: indeed, truly** > All held that John the Baptist was really a prophet (Mark 11:32). The Lord is really risen (Luke 24:34). Jesus said: "If the Son sets you free, you will really be free" (John 8:36). Timothy was to honor widows who were really widows (1 Tim. 5:3); she who is really a widow, and is left alone, trusts in God (v. 5). The church is to assist those who are really widows (1 Tim. 5:16). Paul speaks of laying hold of that which is really life (1 Tim. 6:19), certainly eternal life. All other refs.: CERTAINLY <3689>, INDEED <3689>, TRULY <3689>.

– [2] John 7:26, 40; 8:31; 1 Thes. 2:13 → TRULY <230> [3] Acts 12:9 → was doing was really happening → lit.: was happening was real → REAL <227>.

REALM – [1] Acts 2:27, 31 → realm of the dead → HADES <86> [2] Rom. 7:5; 8:8, 9a, b → in the realm of → lit.: in.

REALMS – Eph. 1:3, 20; 2:6; 3:10; 6:12 → heavenly realms → HEAVENLY <2032>.

REAP – [1] ***therizō*** [verb: θερίζω <2325>]; **from *theros*: hot season, summer, thus: harvest time, which is from *therō*: to heat ▶ To harvest >** This verb is used lit. in Matt. 6:26; 25:24, 26; Luke 12:24; 19:21, 22; Jas. 5:4 {harvester} (lit.: those who have reaped). In the figur. sense in John 4, it means to work in order to gain souls for God (v. 36a, b {reaper}, 37, 38). Paul spoke of reaping material things, after having sown spiritual things (1 Cor. 9:11). In 2 Cor. 9:6a, b, the verb is syn. with receiving a reward, i.e., a profit as the result of having shared one's material things. In Gal. 6:7, 8a, b, 9, the principle of doing that which is good, of sowing to the Spirit, leads to a rich harvest. In Rev. 14:15a, b, 16, to reap refers to the judgment of those who dwell on the earth. ¶

– [2] Rom. 1:13 → to reap some harvest → to obtain some fruit → OBTAIN <2192> [3] Jas. 3:18 → "reap" added in Engl. [4] Jas. 5:4a → to reap down → MOW <270>.

REAPER – [1] ***theristēs*** [masc. noun: θεριστής <2327>]; **from *therizō*: to reap, which is from *theros*: hot season, summer, which is from *therō*: to heat ▶ Person who harvests; also transl.: harvester, harvestman >** The word is used in the figur. sense in the parable of the wheat and the tares (Matt. 13:30); the reapers are angels who execute the judgment of God (v. 39). ¶

– [2] John 4:36a, b → lit.: who reaps → REAP <2325>.

REAR – John 2:20 → to raise up → RAISE <1453>.

REASON (noun) – [1] ***aitia*** [fem. noun: αἰτία <156>]; **from *aiteō*: to ask, or *aitios*: responsible ▶ Cause, motive >** Jesus asked a woman for what reason she had touched Him (Luke 8:47). Claudius Lysias wanted to know the reason {why} they accused Paul (Acts 23:28). The expr. "for this reason" is found in 2 Tim. 1:6, 12; Titus 1:13; Heb. 2:11. Other refs.: Acts 22:24; 28:20. All other refs.: ACCUSATION <156>, CASE <156>, CAUSE (noun) <156>, FAULT <156>.

[2] ***aition*** [neut. noun: αἴτιον <158>]; **from *aitios*: author, cause, source ▶ Motive, fault, what is worthy; also transl.: cause, guilt >** Pilate had found no reason for {no grounds for} the death of Jesus (Luke 23:22). The city clerk of Ephesus said there was no reason (*aition*) to give account (*logos*) for the disorderly gathering of the citizens of that city (Acts 19:40). Other refs.: Luke 23:4, 14; see FAULT <158>. ¶

[3] ***logos*** [masc. noun: λόγος <3056>] ▶ **a. Account, explanation >** No cause (*aition*) existed in reference to which the Ephesians could give a reason (*logos*) for their disorderly gathering (Acts 19:40). Christians are to be prepared to give an answer to everyone who asks them to give a reason for the hope that is in them (1 Pet. 3:15). **b. Matter, motive >** Peter asked for what reason {intent} he was sent for (Acts 10:29). Other refs.: WORD <3056>.

[4] **without reason: *alogos*** [adj.: ἄλογος <249>]; **from *a*: neg., and *logos*: reasoning, rationale ▶ Irrational, unreasonable; also transl.: brute, unreasoning >** Peter and Jude mention people who, like animal without reason, blaspheme about things they are ignorant of (2 Pet. 2:12 {brute, unreasoning}; Jude 10). Other ref.: Acts 25:27; see UNREASONABLE <249>. ¶

[5] **for this reason: *dia*** [prep.: διά <1223>] ***touto*** [pron.: τοῦτο <5124>] ▶ **Therefore, that is why >** Paul uses this expr. in Rom. 4:16 and Phm. 15. *

[6] **for this very reason; same: *autos*** [pron.: αὐτός <846>], **this: *touto*** [pron.: τοῦτο <5124>]; **lit.: as to even this ▶ With respect to this same thing >** Peter uses this expr. in 2 Pet. 1:5. *

– [7] Matt. 5:32 → CAUSE <3056> [8] Mark 12:28 → to reason together → DISPUTE (verb) <4802> [9] John 15:25 → without reason → without a cause → CAUSE <1432> [10] Acts 6:2 → DESIRABLE <701> [11] Acts 22:30 → real reason → CERTAINTY <804> [12] Acts 26:25 → SOBERNESS <4997> [13] Rom. 13:4; Col. 2:18 → for no reason, without reason → in vain → VAIN <1500> [14] Jas. 4:5 → without reason → in vain → VAIN <2761>.

REASON (verb) – [1] ***logizomai*** [verb: λογίζομαι <3049>]**; from *logos*: thought, word ▶ To reflect, to think** > Paul said that when he was a child, he reasoned as a child (1 Cor. 13:11). All other refs.: see entries in Lexicon at <3049>.

[2] ***dialogizomai*** [verb: διαλογίζομαι <1260>]**; from *dia*: intens., and *logizomai*: see [1] ▶ To consider, to reflect; also transl.: to argue, to cast, to discourse, to discuss, to dispute, to muse, to ponder, to talk, to wonder** > Jesus asked the scribes why they reasoned {were reasoning, thought} certain things in their hearts (Mark 2:8). On various occasions, the disciples of Jesus reasoned among themselves (Matt. 16:7, 8; 21:25; Mark 8:16, 17; 11:31 in some mss.), as likewise did the scribes (Mark 2:6, 8; 9:33), and also both the scribes and Pharisees (Luke 5:21, 22). Mary reasoned in her mind what the angel's salutation might be (Luke 1:29). The people reasoned concerning John the Baptist whether he might be the Christ (Luke 3:15). In a parable, a rich man reasoned concerning his crops (Luke 12:17); in another parable, husbandmen reasoned concerning the heir (20:14). Other ref.: John 11:50; see CONSIDER <1260>. ¶

[3] ***sullogizomai*** [verb: συλλογίζομαι <4817>]**; from *sun*: with, together, and *logizomai*: see [1] ▶ To consider together, to discuss** > The chief priests and the scribes with the elders reasoned among themselves concerning the baptism of John (Luke 20:5). ¶

[4] ***dialegomai*** [verb: διαλέγομαι <1256>]**; from *dia*: through, and *legō*: to speak ▶ To discourse, to discuss; also transl.: to dispute** > Paul reasoned in the synagogues in Thessalonica (Acts 17:2), Athens (17:17), Corinth (18:4), and Ephesus (18:19); he also reasoned in the school of Tyrannus (19:8, 9 {to have discussions}). He reasoned {discoursed} about righteousness, self-control and the judgment to come before Felix (Acts 24:25). All other refs.: DISCOURSE (verb) <1256>, DISPUTE (verb) <1256>, SPEAK <1256>.

[5] ***suzēteō*** [verb: συζητέω <4802>]**; from *sun*: together with, and *zēteō*: to seek ▶ To examine together, to discuss** > The two disciples who returned to Emmaus reasoned together (Luke 24:15). All other refs.: DISPUTE (verb) <4802>, QUESTION (verb) <4802>.

– [6] Heb. 11:19 → CONSIDER <3049>.

REASON (FOR THIS) – See BECAUSE <1360>.

REASONABLE – [1] Acts 26:25 → what I am saying is true and reasonable → lit.: I utter words of truth and soberness → SOBERNESS <4997> [2] Rom. 12:1 → INTELLIGENT <3050> [3] Jas. 3:17 → YIELDING <2138>.

REASONABLENESS – [1] Phil. 3:4a, b → "reason for" added twice in Engl. [2] Phil. 4:5 → GENTLENESS <1933>.

REASONING – [1] ***dialogismos*** [masc. noun: διαλογισμός <1261>]**; from *dialogizomai*: to reason, which is from *dia*: intens., and *logizomai*: to reason, to reflect, which is from *logos*: thought, word ▶ Reflection, consideration; also transl.: arguing, argument, dispute, disputing, dissension, doubting, imagination, speculation, thinking, thought** > Jesus knew the reasonings of the scribes and the Pharisees (Luke 5:22). A reasoning arose among the disciples of Jesus regarding who should be the greatest among them (Luke 9:46). Wicked men fell into folly in their reasonings (Rom. 1:21). We should receive him who is weak in the faith, not for the purpose of questions of reasoning {not to disputes over doubtful things, not to doubtful disputations, not for the purpose of passing judgment on his opinions, without passing judgment on disputable matters} (in the sense of: not criticizing the personal opinions of the weak person) (Rom. 14:1). The Lord knows the reasonings of the wise, that they are vain (1 Cor. 3:20). Paul exhorts to do all things without murmurings and reasonings (Phil. 2:14). Paul would that the men pray in every place, lifting up pious hands, without wrath or reasoning (1 Tim. 2:8). All other refs.: THOUGHT <1261>.

[2] ***logismos*** [masc. noun: λογισμός <3053>]; **from *logizomai*: to reason, to reflect, which is from *logos*: thought, word ▶ Pretentious rationale, device** > The weapons of the Christian are powerful according to God for overthrowing reasonings {arguments, imaginations, speculations} against God (2 Cor. 10:5). Other ref.: Rom. 2:15; see THOUGHT <3053>. ¶

– [3] John 3:25 → DISPUTE (noun) <2214> [4] Acts 28:29 → DISPUTE (noun) <2214> <4803>.

REASONING (BE) – Mark 2:8 → REASON (verb) <1260>.

REASSURE – 1 John 3:19 → ASSURE <3982>.

REBECCA – See REBEKAH <4479>.

REBEKAH – ***Rhebekka*** [fem. name: Ῥεβέκκα <4479>]: **attaching, fascinating (by beauty), in Heb.; see Gen. 24:15 ▶ Wife of Isaac; also transl.: Rebecca** > Rebekah gave birth to Jacob and Esau (Rom. 9:10; see vv. 11–13). ¶

REBEL (noun) – [1] Matt. 27:38, 44; Mark 15:27 → ROBBER <3027> [2] Mark 15:7 → FELLOW REBEL <4955> [3] 1 Tim. 1:9 → INSUBORDINATE <506>.

REBEL (verb) – [1] Rom. 13:2a → to rebel against → RESIST <498> [2] Rom. 13:2b, c → to rebel against → RESIST <436> [3] Heb. 3:16 → to rebel against → PROVOKE <3893>.

REBELLION – [1] Matt. 26:55; Mark 14:48; Luke 22:52; John 18:40 → one leading a rebellion, taking part in a rebellion → ROBBER <3027> [2] Mark 15:7; Luke 23:19, 25 → INSURRECTION <4714> [3] Luke 23:14 → to incite to rebellion → to turn away → TURN (verb) <654> [4] Acts 21:38 → to stir up a rebellion → to raise a sedition → SEDITION <387> [5] 2 Thes. 2:3 → APOSTASY <646> [6] Titus 1:6 → INSUBORDINATE <506> [7] Heb. 3:8, 15 → PROVOCATION <3894> [8] Jude 11 → CONTRADICTION <485>.

REBELLIOUS – 1 Tim. 1:9; Titus 1:10 → INSUBORDINATE <506>.

REBIRTH – Titus 3:5 → REGENERATION <3824>.

REBUILD – [1] ***anoikodomeō*** [verb: ἀνοικοδομέω <456>]; **from *ana*: again, and *oikodomeō*: to build, which is from *oikos*: house, and *demō*: to construct ▶ To edify again, to reconstruct** > According to Amos (see Amos 9:11, 12), the Lord would rebuild {would build again} the tabernacle of David and its ruins (Acts 15:16a, b). Other ref.: Jude 20 in some mss. ¶

– [2] Matt. 26:61; Gal. 2:18 → lit.: to build again → BUILD <3618>.

REBUKE (noun) – Phil. 2:15 → without rebuke → IRREPROACHABLE <298>.

REBUKE (verb) – [1] **to rebuke harshly: *embrimaomai*** [verb: ἐμβριμάομαι <1690>]; **from *en*: in (intens.), and *brimaomai*: to express anger ▶ To be angry against, to tell off** > Some rebuked harshly {criticized, murmured against, spoke very angrily at, scolded} the woman who had poured the perfume on the head of Jesus (Mark 14:5). Other refs.: MOVED (BE) <1690>, WARN <1690>.

[2] ***epitimaō*** [verb: ἐπιτιμάω <2008>]; **from *epi*: upon, and *timaō*: to evaluate, which is from *timē*: honor, price ▶ To charge, to reprimand, to reproach, to warn, to tell sternly** > Jesus rebuked the winds and the sea, and there was a great calm (Matt. 8:26;

Mark 4:39; Luke 8:24). He also rebuked Peter (Mark 8:33); He says to rebuke our brother who sins (Luke 17:3). Peter rebuked Jesus, who spoke of His death (Matt. 16:22; Mark 8:32). Jesus rebuked demons (Matt. 17:18; Mark 1:25; 9:25; Luke 4:35, 41; 9:42). He also rebuked (as one would do in speaking to a person) the fever of Peter's mother-in-law (Luke 4:39). The disciples rebuked those who brought little children to Jesus (Matt. 19:13; Mark 10:13; Luke 18:15). The crowd rebuked {warned, told sternly} the blind men who cried out to Jesus that they may be silent (Matt. 20:31); many rebuked Bartimaeus when he cried out to Jesus (Mark 10:48; Luke 18:39). The Lord rebuked James and John who wanted to destroy a village of Samaritans because they had not received them (Luke 9:55). Some of the Pharisees asked Jesus to rebuke His disciples (Luke 19:39). One of the malefactors who had been hanged on the cross rebuked the other one (Luke 23:40). Paul told Timothy to rebuke and encourage with great patience and instruction (2 Tim. 4:2). When disputing concerning the body of Moses, Michael the archangel told Satan: "The Lord rebuke you!" (Jude 9). All other refs.: CHARGE (verb) <2008>, WARN <2008>.

3 **to rebuke, to rebuke sharply, to rebuke harshly: *epiplēssō*** [verb: ἐπιπλήσσω <1969>]**; from *epi*: upon, and *plēssō*: to strike ▶ To blame, to reprimand** > Timothy was not to rebuke an elder sharply (1 Tim. 5:1). ¶

4 **lit.: to receive reproof; to receive: *echō*** [verb: ἔχω <2192>]**; reproof: *elenxis*** [fem. noun: ἔλεγξις <1649>] ¶**; from *elenchō*: to convict, to reprove ▶ To blame, to reprimand** > Balaam was rebuked for {had reproof of, received a rebuke for} his iniquity by a mute donkey (2 Pet. 2:16).

– 5 Matt. 11:20; Mark 16:14 → REPROACH (verb) <3679> 6 Luke 3:19; Titus 1:13; 2:15; Heb. 12:5; Rev. 3:19 → REPROVE <1651> 7 2 Cor. 2:6 → PUNISHMENT <2009> 8 1 Tim. 5:20; 2 Tim. 4:2 → CONVINCE <1651> 9 Titus 1:9 → REFUTE <1651>.

REBUKING – 2 Tim. 3:16 → REPROOF <1650>.

RECALL – 1 John 2:22; 2 Tim. 1:4; 2 Pet. 3:2 → REMEMBER <3415> 2 1 Thes. 2:9 → REMEMBER <3421> 3 1 Tim. 1:18 → "recalling" added in Engl. 4 Heb. 10:32 → REMIND <363> 5 2 Pet. 1:15 → MIND (CALL TO) <3420> <4160>.

RECEDE – ***apochōrizō*** [verb: ἀποχωρίζω <673>]**; from *apo*: from, and *chōrizō*: to separate ▶ To disjoin, to separate** > At the opening of the sixth seal, the sky receded {departed, was split apart, was removed} as when a scroll is rolled up (Rev. 6:14). Other ref.: Acts 15:39; see SEPARATE <673>. ¶

RECEIPT – Matt. 9:9; Mark 2:14; Luke 5:27 → receipt of custom → tax office → TAX (noun) <5058>.

RECEIVE – 1 ***lambanō*** [verb: λαμβάνω <2983>] **▶ To obtain, to accept what is offered** > Jesus said that every one who asks, receives (Matt. 7:8). He has given to as many as received Him the right to be children of God (John 1:12). Other refs.: Matt. 10:8, 41b, d; 13:20; 17:25; 19:29; 20:7, 9, 10a, b, 11; 21:22, 34; 25:16, 18, 20, 22, 24; Mark 4:16; 10:30; 11:24; 12:2, 40; Luke 11:10; 19:12, 15; 20:47; John 1:16; 3:11, 27, 32, 33; 4:36; 5:34, 41, 43a, b, 44; 6:7, 21; 7:23, 39; 10:18; 12:48; 13:20a–d, 30; 14:17; 16:24; 17:8; 20:22; Acts 1:8, 25; 2:33, 38; 3:5; 7:53; 8:15, 17, 19; 10:43, 47; 16:24; 17:9, 15; 19:2; 20:24, 35; 26:10, 18; Rom. 1:5; 4:11; 5:11, 17; 8:15a, b; 1 Cor. 2:12; 3:8, 14; 4:7a–c; 9:24, 25; 14:5; 2 Cor. 11:4, 8, 24; Gal. 3:2, 14; Phil. 3:12; Col. 4:10; Heb. 2:2; 4:16; 7:5, 8, 9; 9:15; 10:26; 11:8, 11, 13, 35; Jas. 1:7, 12; 3:1; 4:3; 5:7; 1 Pet. 4:10; 2 Pet. 1:17; 1 John 2:27; 3:22; 5:9; 2 John 4, 10; 3 John 7; Rev. 2:17, 27; 3:3; 4:11; 5:12; 14:9; 17:12a, b; 18:4; 19:20; 20:4. Other refs.: see entries in Lexicon at <2983>.

2 **to receive up: *analambanō*** [verb: ἀναλαμβάνω <353>]**; from *ana*: above, and *lambanō*: see 1 ▶ To raise, to exalt; also transl.: to take up** > The Lord was

received up into heaven (Mark 16:19; Acts 1:2, 11, 22). God (i.e., Jesus) was received up in glory (1 Tim. 3:16). The object that Peter saw was received up into {taken back to} heaven (Acts 10:16). All other refs.: BOARD (noun) <353>, TAKE <353>.

3 ***apolambanō*** [verb: ἀπολαμβάνω <618>]; **from *apo*: again, from, and *lambanō*: see 1 ► a. To welcome, to recover >** In Luke 15:27, the father received his son safe and well. **b. To obtain one from another; to receive fully >** The verb is used in Luke 6:34a, b; 16:25; 18:30; 23:41; Rom. 1:27; Gal. 4:5; Col. 3:24; 2 John 8; 3 John 8 {to support, to show hospitality}. Other ref.: Mark 7:33 (to take aside); see TAKE <618>. ¶

4 ***metalambanō*** [verb: μεταλαμβάνω <3335>]; **from *meta*: with, and *lambanō*: see 1 ► To obtain, to partake >** The ground that drinks the rain receives blessing from God (Heb. 6:7). All other refs.: FIND <3335>, PARTAKE <3335>, PARTICIPATE <3335>, TAKE <3335>.

5 ***paralambanō*** [verb: παραλαμβάνω <3880>]; **from *para*: from, and *lambanō*: see 1 ► To receive one from another; to receive something transmitted >** His own did not receive Jesus (John 1:11). The verb is used also in Mark 7:4; 1 Cor. 11:23; 15:1, 3; Gal. 1:9, 12; Phil. 4:9; Col. 2:6; 4:17; 1 Thes. 2:13; 4:1; 2 Thes. 3:6; Heb. 12:28. All other refs.: TAKE <3880>.

6 ***proslambanō*** [verb: προσλαμβάνω <4355>]; **from *pros*: to, and *lambanō*: see 1 ► To take into one's home (with the idea of kindness), to accept >** The natives received Paul and his companions (Acts 28:2); *prosanalambanō* in some mss. Other refs.: Rom. 14:1, 3; 15:7a, b; Phm. 12 (in some mss.), 17. All other refs.: TAKE <4355>.

7 ***hupolambanō*** [verb: ὑπολαμβάνω <5274>]; **from *hupo*: under, and *lambanō*: see 1 ► To take in order to carry higher >** Jesus was taken up and a cloud received {hid} Him (Acts 1:9). All other refs.: REPLY (verb) <5274>, SUPPOSE <5274>.

8 ***dechomai*** [verb: δέχομαι <1209>] **► To accept, to welcome >** The Thessalonians received the word of God as it is in truth, the word of God (1 Thes. 2:13b). The verb is also used in Matt. 10:14, 40a–d, 41a, c; 11:14; 18:5a, b; Mark 6:11; 9:37a–d; 10:15; Luke 8:13; 9:5, 11, 48a–d, 53; 10:8, 10; 16:4, 9; 18:17; 22:17; John 4:45; Acts 3:21; 7:38, 59; 8:14; 11:1; 17:11; 21:17; 22:5; 28:21; 1 Cor. 2:14; 2 Cor. 6:1; 7:15; 8:17; 11:4, 16; Gal. 4:14; Phil. 4:18; Col. 4:10; 1 Thes. 1:6; 2 Thes. 2:10; Heb. 11:31; Jas. 1:21. All other refs.: TAKE <1209>.

9 ***anadechomai*** [verb: ἀναδέχομαι <324>]; **from *ana*: intens., and *dechomai*: see 8 ► To welcome, to exercise hospitality, to receive as a responsibility >** Publius received Paul and his companions (Acts 28:7). Abraham had received to himself the promises of God (Heb. 11:17). ¶

10 ***apodechomai*** [verb: ἀποδέχομαι <588>]; **from *apo*: intens., and *dechomai*: see 8 ► To accept, to receive, to welcome >** The crowd gladly received {welcomed} Jesus (Luke 8:40). Those who had received the word were baptized (Acts 2:41). The verb is also found in Luke 9:11 in some mss.; Acts 15:4; 18:27; 28:30. Other ref.: Acts 24:3; see ACCEPT <588>. ¶

11 ***diadechomai*** [verb: διαδέχομαι <1237>]; **from *dia*: through, and *dechomai*: see 8 ► To receive through another, to inherit >** The Israelites had received the tent of the testimony (Acts 7:45). ¶

12 ***eisdechomai*** [verb: εἰσδέχομαι <1523>]; **from *eis*: into, and *dechomai*: see 8 ► To welcome (with kindness) >** The Lord receives those who separate themselves from evil (2 Cor. 6:17). ¶

13 ***epidechomai*** [verb: ἐπιδέχομαι <1926>]; **from *epi*: intens., and *dechomai*: see 8 ► a. To welcome, to accept, to accept the authority of >** Diotrephes did not receive John (3 John 9). **b. To extend hospitality, to welcome >** Diotrephes did not receive the brothers (3 John 10). ¶

14 ***paradechomai*** [verb: παραδέχομαι <3858>]; **from *para*: from, and *dechomai*: see 8 ► To accept, to appropriate, to approve >** This verb is used when Jesus spoke about receiving the word (Mark 4:20). Paul exhorted Timothy not to receive an accusation {to admit a charge} against an elder, unless there were witnesses (1 Tim.

5:19). The Lord scourges every son whom He receives (Heb. 12:6). Other refs.: Acts 15:4 in some mss.; 16:21; 22:18. ¶

15 ***prosdechomai*** [verb: προσδέχομαι <4327>]; **from *pros*: unto, and *dechomai*: see 8 ▶ To accept, to welcome** > Jesus received sinners (Luke 15:2). The Jews receive {accept, allow, cherish, have} hope toward God (Acts 24:15). Christians were to receive Phoebe in the Lord (Rom. 16:2) and Epaphroditus (Phil. 2:29). All other refs.: ACCEPT <4327>, LOOK (verb) <4327>, TAKE <4327>, WAIT (verb) <4327>.

16 ***hupodechomai*** [verb: ὑποδέχομαι <5264>]; **from *hupo*: under, and *dechomai*: see 8 ▶ To welcome, to take care, to receive with kindness** > Martha received Jesus into her house (Luke 10:38); Zaccheus also received Him (Luke 19:6). Other refs.: Acts 17:7; Jas. 2:25. ¶

17 ***komizō*** [verb: κομίζω <2865>]; **from *komeō*: to take care ▶ To recover, to withdraw (as from a bank)** > The Greek verb is used with regard to a bank investment (Matt. 25:27 {to get}). The Christian is to receive {to be recompensed for} the things done in the body (2 Cor. 5:10). Abraham received his son in a figure of resurrection (Heb. 11:19). Other refs.: Eph. 6:8 {to be rewarded}; Col. 3:25 {to be repaid}; Heb. 10:36; 11:39; 1 Pet. 1:9 {to obtain}; 5:4; 2 Pet. 2:13 {to be paid back}. Other ref.: Luke 7:37; see BRING <2865>. ¶

18 ***lanchanō*** [verb: λαγχάνω <2975>] **▶ To obtain by lot, to obtain by divine allocation** > Christians have received {have obtained} like precious faith as that of Peter (2 Pet. 1:1). In Acts 1:17, the expr. "to receive a part in" {to obtain a part, to receive a share, to share} is used to translate the Greek *lanchanō ton klēron*. Other refs.: Luke 1:9; John 19:24a (to fall by lot); see LOT[2] <2975>. ¶

19 ***chōreō*** [verb: χωρέω <5562>]; **from *chōra*: place; lit.: to make a place ▶ To accept, to agree to** > All could not receive the word of Jesus (Matt. 19:11, 12a, b). Paul asked the Corinthians to receive him (2 Cor. 7:2 {to open the heart, to make room}). All other refs.: see entries in Lexicon at <5562>.

20 **receiving up: *analēmpsis*** [fem. noun: ἀνάλημψις <354>]; **from *analambanō*: to receive up, which is from *ana*: up, and *lambanō*: to take, to receive; also spelled: *analēpsis* ▶ Ascension, rapture** > The time was come that Jesus should be received up {taken up} (lit.: the days of the receiving up of Him) (Luke 9:51). ¶

21 **acquisition: *peripoiēsis*** [fem. noun: περιποίησις <4047>]; **from *peripoieō*: to obtain, to purchase, which is from *peri*: around (denoting acquisition), and *poieō*: to make, to gain ▶ Possession, what is obtained** > God has appointed the Christians to receive {to obtain} (lit.: for the acquisition of) salvation through the Lord Jesus Christ (1 Thes. 5:9). All other refs.: OBTAINING <4047>, POSSESSION <4047>, SAVING <4047>.

– 22 Luke 12:47 → to receive lashes → to be beaten with stripes → BEAT <1194> 23 Luke 19:23 → COLLECT <4238> 24 Acts 21:40 → receiving the commander's permission → lit.: he having permitted him → PERMIT <2010> 25 Acts 27:3 → ENJOY <5177> 26 Rom. 3:25 → to be received by faith → lit.: through faith 27 Rom. 15:31 → to be received favorably → lit.: to be acceptable → BE <1096>, ACCEPTABLE <2144> 28 Phil. 4:18; Phm. 15 → POSSESS <568> 29 1 Tim. 1:13, 16 → to receive mercy → MERCY <1653> 30 1 Tim. 2:11 → to receive instruction → LEARN <3129> 31 1 Tim. 4:3 → RECEIVING <3336> 32 Heb. 6:15 → OBTAIN <2013> 33 Heb. 7:5 → to receive tithes → TITHE (noun and verb) <586> 34 Heb. 8:6 → OBTAIN <5177> 35 1 Pet. 1:18 → received by tradition from the fathers → FATHER <3970> 36 2 Pet. 1:11 → to be received → SUPPLY (verb) <2023>.

RECEIVING – 1 ***lēmpsis*** [fem. noun: λῆμψις <3028>]; **from *lambanō*: to obtain, to receive; also spelled: *lēpsis* ▶ Taking, act of accepting** > In the way of giving and receiving, only the church of Philippi had communicated anything to Paul (Phil. 4:15). ¶

[2] **receiving up: *analēmpsis*** [fem. noun: ἀνάλημψις <354>]; **from *ana*: above, and *lambanō*: see [1]; also spelled: *analēpsis* ▶ Lit.: the act of being taken to a higher place; ascension** > The time was come that Jesus should be received up {taken up} (lit.: the days of the receiving up of Him) (Luke 9:51). ¶
[3] ***metalēmpsis*** [fem. noun: μετάλημψις <3336>]; **from *metalambanō*: to partake, which is from *meta*: with, and *lambanō*: see [1]; also spelled: *metalēpsis* ▶ Act of partaking of something** > God has created foods for receiving {to be received} with thanksgiving (1 Tim. 4:3). ¶
– [4] Rom. 11:15 → ACCEPTANCE <4356>.

RECENT – 1 Tim. 3:6 → recent convert → NOVICE <3504>.

RECENTLY – [1] ***prosphatōs*** [adv.: προσφάτως <4373>]; **from *prosphatos*: new, recent (see Heb. 10:20) ▶ Newly, lately** > Aquilas and Priscilla had recently {just} come from Italy (Acts 18:2). ¶
– [2] Acts 21:38 → lit.: before these days.

RECEPTION – [1] Luke 5:29; 14:13 → FEAST (noun) <1403> [2] Rom. 11:15 → ACCEPTANCE <4356> [3] 1 Thes. 1:9 → ENTRY <1529>.

RECKLESS – [1] Luke 15:13 → prodigally → PRODIGAL <811> [2] 2 Tim. 3:4 → HEADSTRONG <4312> [3] 1 Pet. 4:4 → reckless, wild living → excess of dissipation → EXCESS <401>.

RECKON – [1] ***sunairō*** [verb: συναίρω <4868>]; **from *sun*: together, and *airō*: to bring ▶ To balance or settle accounts** > In a parable, the lord reckoned with his bondmen (Matt. 25:19). Other refs.: Matt. 18:23, 24; see to take account under ACCOUNT (noun) <4868>. ¶
– [2] Luke 22:37; Rom. 4:3, 4–6, 9, 10, 11, 22–24; 6:11; Gal. 3:6; Jas. 2:23 → COUNT <3049> [3] Acts 19:19 → to reckon up → CALCULATE <4860> [4] Rom. 3:28 → CONCLUDE[1] <3049> [5] Rom. 8:18, 36; 14:14; 2 Cor. 11:5 → CONSIDER <3049> [6] 2 Cor. 5:19 → IMPUTE <3049>.

RECKONING – Luke 16:2 → ACCOUNT (noun) <3056>.

RECLINE – [1] Matt. 8:11; 14:19; Luke 13:29 → to sit down → SIT <347> [2] Matt. 9:10; 26:20 → to recline, to recline at the table → TABLE[1] <345> [3] Mark 6:40; Luke 14:10; John 13:12 → to recline, to recline at the table → to sit down → SIT <377> [4] Luke 9:14, 15 → to sit down → SIT <2625> [5] Luke 17:7 → to lie at table → TABLE[1] <377> [6] John 21:20 → LEAN <377>.

RECOGNITION – [1] 1 Cor. 16:18 → to deserve, to give recognition → RECOGNIZE <1921> [2] 1 Pet. 2:17a → to give proper recognition → HONOR (verb) <5091>.

RECOGNIZE – [1] ***ginōskō*** [verb: γινώσκω <1097>] ▶ **To understand, to acknowledge** > The verb is used in regard to the act of acknowledging that Jesus was the Messiah (John 7:26 {to know, to conclude}), and to the grace that was given to Paul (Gal. 2:9 {to perceive}). The man speaking in Rom. 7:15 does not understand (or: recognize) {own, allow} that which he does, for it is not what he wills that he does, but, rather, he practices what he hates. All other refs.: see KNOW <1097>.
[2] ***epiginōskō*** [verb: ἐπιγινώσκω <1921>]; **from *epi*: upon, and *ginōskō*: see [1] ▶ To perceive, to discern, to distinguish among others; also transl.: to acknowledge, to know, to have knowledge, to own, to realize, to take note, to understand** > The verb is used in regard to persons: Jesus (Matt. 14:35; Mark 6:33, 54; Luke 24:16, 31; 2 Cor. 13:5), Elijah (Matt. 17:12), Zacharias (Luke 1:22), the voice of Peter (Acts 12:14), Paul and Timothy (2 Cor. 1:14), and other men (Matt. 7:16, 20; Acts 3:10; 4:13; 1 Cor. 16:18). It is also used in Acts 27:39; 1 Cor. 14:37; 2 Cor. 1:13a, b. All other refs.: KNOW <1921>, KNOWLEDGE <1921>.
– [3] Mark 10:42 → REGARD (verb) <1380> [4] Acts 13:27 → to not recognize → to

know not → KNOW <50> 5 1 Cor. 11:29 → DISCERN <1252> 6 1 Cor. 14:38a, b → to not recognize → to be ignorant → IGNORANT <50> 7 Gal. 2:7 → SEE <1492> 8 1 Thes. 5:12 → KNOW <1492>.

RECOGNIZED – ***phaneros*** [adj.: φανερός <5318>]; **from *phainō*: to shine, to become evident, which is from *phōs*: light ▶ Known, visible; also transl.: evident, manifest** > There must be sects that those who are approved may be recognized {may be shown} (1 Cor. 11:19). All other refs.: see entries in Lexicon at <5318>.

RECOLLECT – Luke 16:25 → REMEMBER <3415>.

RECOMMEND – Acts 14:26; 15:40 → COMMIT <3860>.

RECOMMENDATION – 1 2 Cor. 3:1a, b → letter of recommendation → EPISTLE OF COMMENDATION <1992> <4956> 2 2 Cor. 3:2 → "recommendation" added in Engl.

RECOMPENCE – 1 Luke 14:12 → RECOMPENSE (noun) <468> 2 Rom. 1:27 → PENALTY <489> 3 Rom. 11:9 → RETRIBUTION <468> 4 2 Cor. 6:13 → EXCHANGE (noun) <489> 5 Heb. 10:35 → recompence of reward → REWARD (noun) <3405>.

RECOMPENSE (noun) – 1 ***antapodoma*** [neut. noun: ἀνταπόδομα <468>]; **from *antapodidōmi*: to repay, which is from *anti*: in turn, and *apodidōmi*: to pay back, which is from *didōmi*: to give ▶ That which is offered in repayment** > The word is used in Luke 14:12; also transl.: recompence, repayment, to repay. Other ref.: Rom. 11:9; see RETRIBUTION <468>. ¶

– 2 Rom. 1:27 → PENALTY <489> 3 2 Cor. 6:13 → EXCHANGE <489> 4 Col. 3:24 → REWARD <469> 5 Heb. 10:35; 11:26 → REWARD <3405> 6 Rev. 11:18; 22:12 → REWARD <3408>.

RECOMPENSE (verb) – 1 ***antapodidōmi*** [verb: ἀνταποδίδωμι <467>]; **from *anti*: in turn, and *apodidōmi*: to pay back, to repay, which is from *apo*: from, and *didōmi*: to give ▶ To give in return** > The verb is used in Luke 14:14a, b. All other refs.: RENDER <467>.

– 2 2 Cor. 5:10 → to be recompensed → RECEIVE <2865> 3 Rev. 18:6a, b → GIVE <591>.

RECONCILE – 1 ***diallassomai*** [verb: διαλλάσσομαι <1259>]; **from *dia*: through, and *allassō*: to change ▶ To restore relations between persons in disagreement** > Jesus spoke of being reconciled to one's brother before offering one's gift (Matt. 5:24). ¶

2 ***katallassō*** [verb: καταλλάσσω <2644>]; **from *kata*: intens., and *allassō*: to change; lit.: to change mutually ▶ See 1.** > Christians have been reconciled to God through the death of His Son (Rom. 5:10a, b; 2 Cor. 5:18). Paul tells the woman who is separated from her husband to be reconciled to him (1 Cor. 7:11). God has reconciled Christians to Himself and they have the service of imploring unbelievers to be reconciled to God (2 Cor. 5:19, 20). Other ref.: Acts 12:22 in some mss. ¶

3 ***apokatallassō*** [verb: ἀποκαταλλάσσω <604>]; **from *apo*: from (intens.), and *katallassō*: see 2; lit.: to fully reconcile ▶ To fully restore relations between persons in disagreement** > The objective of the reconciliation of the things on the earth and the things in the heavens is to bring the entire present creation into conformity with the mind of God in the day of Christ's reign (Col. 1:20, 21 or 22). God has reconciled both the Jews and the nations by the death of His Son (Eph. 2:16). ¶

4 ***sunallassō*** [verb: συναλλάσσω <4871a>]; **from *sun*: together, and *allassō*: to change ▶ To persuade, to exhort** > Moses tried to reconcile in peace {to compel to peace, to set at one} his Israelite brothers (Acts 7:26); see 5. ¶

5 ***sunelaunō*** [verb: συνελαύνω <4900>]; **from *sun*: together, and *elaunō*: to drive ▶**

To persuade, to compel > Some mss. have this verb for Acts 7:26; see [4].
– [6] Luke 12:58 → to be reconciled → SETTLE <525>.

RECONCILIATION – [1] ***katallagē*** [fem. noun: καταλλαγή <2643>]; **from *katallassō*: to reconcile, which is from *kata*: intens., and *allassō*: to change; lit.: to change mutually ▶ Restoration of relations between persons in disagreement** > Christians have received the reconciliation through the Lord Jesus Christ (Rom. 5:11). God, from whom man has been separated since the fall, has reconciled the world to Himself (Rom. 11:15) by the death of His Son. Christians have the service of addressing the word of reconciliation to unbelievers (2 Cor. 5:18, 19). ¶
– [2] Heb. 2:17 → to make reconciliation → to make propitiation → PROPITIATION <2433>.

RECONCILING – See RECONCILE and RECONCILIATION.

RECORD – [1] Matt. 1:1 → BOOK <976> [2] John 1:19; 8:13, 14; 19:35b; 1 John 5:11; 3 John 12c → WITNESS (noun)[1] <3141> [3] John 1:34 → and bare record → and witnessed → WITNESS (verb) <3140> [4] Acts 20:26 → to take to record → TESTIFY <3143> [5] 1 Cor. 13:5 → to keep a record → IMPUTE <3049> [6] Col. 2:14 → HANDWRITING <5498>.

RECOUNT – Matt. 18:31 → TELL <1285>.

RECOVER – [1] Matt. 20:34; Mark 10:51, 52, Luke 18:41, 42, 43 → to recover one's sight → to see again → SEE <308> [2] John 4:51 → LIVE <2198> [3] 2 Tim. 2:26 → to awake up → AWAKE <366>.

RECOVERING – Luke 4:18 → recovering of sight → RECOVERY OF SIGHT <309>.

RECOVERY OF SIGHT – ***anablepsis*** [fem. noun: ἀνάβλεψις <309>]; **from *anablepō*: to see again, which is from *ana*: again (intens.), and *blepō*: to see ▶ Recovery of a blind person's vision** > Jesus had been sent to preach to the blind recovery of sight {recovering of sight, sight} (Luke 4:18). ¶

RED – [1] **red, fiery red: *purros*** [adj.: πυρρός <4450>]; **from *pur*: fire ▶ Flame-colored** > This is the color of the second horse seen by John in Patmos (Rev. 6:4) and of the great dragon (12:3). ¶
[2] **to be red: *purrazō*** [verb: πυρράζω <4449>]; **from *purros*: see [1] ▶ To turn red, to be fiery red in color** > The Pharisees and the Sadducees said there would be fair weather when the sky was red in the evening, and that there would be a storm when the sky was red in the morning (Matt. 16:2, 3). ¶

RED SEA – ***Eruthra Thalassa*** [fem. name: Ἐρυθρὰ Θάλασσα <2063>]; **from *eruthros*: red, and *thalassa*: sea ▶ Narrow sea of about 2,250 km (1,400 miles) between Africa and Arabia** > Moses led the Israelites in the Red Sea (Acts 7:36). By faith, they passed through the Red Sea as through dry land (Heb. 11:29). ¶

REDEEM – [1] ***exagorazō*** [verb: ἐξαγοράζω <1805>]; **from *ek*: from, and *agorazō*: to purchase; lit.: to seize, to capture, which is from *agora*: marketplace ▶ a. To buy out of the hands of someone, to liberate** > Christ has redeemed Christians out of the curse of the law (Gal. 3:13). God sent Him that He might redeem those under the law, that we might receive sonship (Gal. 4:5). **b. To take advantage of, to make the most of** > Christians are to redeem the time (or: opportunities) (Eph. 5:16; Col. 4:5). ¶
[2] ***lutroō*** [verb: λυτρόω <3084>]; **from *lutron*: ransom, which is from *luō*: to break, to unbind ▶ To liberate by paying a ransom, to deliver** > The disciples of Emmaus were hoping that Jesus was the one who was about to redeem Israel (Luke 24:21). Christ gave Himself for Christians, that He might redeem them from all lawlessness (Titus 2:14). They have been redeemed from their vain manner of life by

the precious blood of Christ (1 Pet. 1:18). Other ref.: Acts 28:19 in some mss. ¶
– [3] Luke 1:68 → REDEMPTION <3085> [4] Heb. 9:15 → that redeems → for redemption → REDEMPTION <629> [5] Rev. 5:9; 14:3 → BUY <59>.

REDEEMER – Acts 7:35 → DELIVERER <3086>.

REDEMPTION – [1] ***lutrōsis*** [fem. noun: λύτρωσις <3085>]; **from *lutroō*: to release after receipt of a ransom, which is from *lutron*: ransom, i.e., the price paid for the deliverance of someone, which is from *luō*: to loosen, to unbind ▶ Act of freeing after payment of a ransom, deliverance >** God has accomplished redemption for {has redeemed} His people (Luke 1:68). Anna spoke of the Lord to all those who looked for redemption in Jerusalem (Luke 2:38). Christ has obtained an eternal redemption (Heb. 9:12). ¶
[2] ***apolutrōsis*** [fem. noun: ἀπολύτρωσις <629>]; **from *apolutroō*: to let go after payment of a ransom, which is from *apo*: from, and *lutroō*: see [1] ▶ Repurchase at the price of a ransom, followed by deliverance >** During the great tribulation, the redemption of the Jews will draw near (Luke 21:28). The redemption of Christians, formerly slaves of sin, is eternal and has been obtained by the blood of Christ (Rom. 3:24; 1 Cor. 1:30; Eph. 1:7; Col. 1:14). The future day of redemption is related to the deliverance of the Christians' body at the Lord's coming (Rom. 8:23; Eph. 4:30), and to the inheritance already redeemed but not yet delivered from the enemy (Eph. 1:14). Christ paid the redemption {ransom} for the transgressions that were committed under the covenant of the law (Heb. 9:15). Other ref.: Heb. 11:35; see DELIVERANCE <629>. ¶

REDOUND – 2 Cor. 4:15 → ABOUND <4052>.

REED – ***kalamos*** [masc. noun: κάλαμος <2563>] **▶ Aquatic plant found in marshes or near rivers; its height may exceed 10 feet (3 meters); the stems are hollow and consequently fragile, and swayed easily by the wind >** As the disciples of John the Baptist went away, Jesus began to ask the crowds if they had gone out to the desert to see a reed shaken by the wind (Matt. 11:7; Luke 7:24). Jesus had not come to break a bruised reed, i.e., the nation of Israel under oppression (Matt. 12:20). To mock the Lord, a reed {staff} was put in His right hand in imitation of a royal scepter, and then He was beaten on the head with it (Matt. 27:29, 30; Mark 15:19). A sponge filled with vinegar was fixed on a reed {stick} and presented to the Lord on the cross (Matt. 27:48; Mark 15:36). In Rev. 11:1 and 21:15, 16, the reed {rod} is used symbolically as a measuring stick. Other refs.: 3 John 1:13; see PEN <2563>. ¶

REEF – Jude 12 → hidden reef → SPOT <4694>.

REFER – [1] Matt. 3:3 → SPEAK <4483> [2] Matt. 13:20, 22, 23 → to refer to → this is → BE <2076> [3] Luke 22:37 → that which refers to → CONCERNING <4012> [4] 1 Cor. 10:29 → SAY <3004>.

REFERENCE – Eph. 4:22a → in reference → CONCERNING <2596>.

REFINE – ***puroō*** [verb: πυρόω <4448>]; **from *pur*: fire ▶ To set on fire, to burn >** The feet of the Son of Man were like fine brass, as if refined {glowing, they burned, they had been caused to glow} in a furnace (Rev. 1:15). All other refs.: BURN <4448>, FIERY <4448>, FIRE <4448>, PURIFY <4448>.

REFLECT – [1] Acts 10:19 → THINK <1760> [2] 2 Cor. 3:18 → to behold as in a mirror → BEHOLD <2734> [3] 2 Tim. 2:7 → CONSIDER <3539>.

REFLECTION – 1 Cor. 13:12 → but a poor reflection → OBSCURELY <1722> <135>.

REFORM – Acts 24:2 → reforms → excellent measures → MEASURE (noun) <2735>.

REFORMATION – ***diorthōsis*** [fem. noun: διόρθωσις <1357>]; **from *diorthoō*: to correct, to modify ▶ Rectification, setting things right** > By His coming into the world and His expiatory sacrifice, Jesus Christ has restored things in perfect order; this is the time of reformation {new order} (Heb. 9:10). Gifts and sacrifices under the law were unable to perfect the conscience of him who worshipped; Christ has established a new order of things, having obtained an eternal redemption (see Heb. 9:9–12). ¶

REFRAIN – [1] ***pauō*** [verb: παύω <3973>] ▶ **To preserve, to keep** > He who would love life and see good days must refrain his tongue from evil (1 Pet. 3:10). All other refs.: CEASE <3973>.

– [2] Acts 5:38 → to refrain from → to keep away → KEEP (verb) <868> [3] 1 Cor. 7:38 → he who refrains from marriage → he who does not marry (other transl.: he who does not give his virgin daughter in marriage) → MARRY <1547> [4] 2 Cor. 1:23 → I refrained from coming again → lit.: I came no more [5] 2 Cor. 11:9a, b → to refrain from being a burden → to keep oneself from being a burden → BEWARE <5083> [6] 2 Cor. 12:6 → FORBEAR <5339>.

REFRESH – [1] ***anapauō*** [verb: ἀναπαύω <373>]; **from *ana*: again, and *pauō*: to cease ▶ To give rest, to tranquilize, to soothe** > Three brothers had refreshed the spirit of Paul and of the Corinthians (1 Cor. 16:18). The spirit of Titus had been refreshed by the Corinthians (2 Cor. 7:13). The bowels (or: hearts) of the saints were refreshed by Philemon (Phm. 7); Paul asked him to refresh his bowels (or: heart) in Christ (v. 20). All other refs.: REST (noun)[1] <373>, REST (verb) <373>.

[2] ***sunanapauō*** [verb: συναναπαύω <4875>]; **from *sun*: together, and *anapauō*: see [1] ▶ To rest with others, to enjoy recreation in the company of others** > Paul wanted to be refreshed with the Christians in Rome (Rom. 15:32). ¶

[3] ***anapsuchō*** [verb: ἀναψύχω <404>]; **from *ana*: again, and *psuchō*: to refresh ▶ To encourage, to comfort** > Onesiphorus had often refreshed Paul (2 Tim. 1:16). Other ref.: Rom. 15:32 in some mss. ¶

– [4] Acts 27:3 → ENJOY <5177> [5] Acts 27:3 → to refresh oneself → lit.: to receive care → CARE (noun) <1958> [6] 2 Pet. 1:13 → to refresh your memory → lit.: to stir you up (to wake you up) by putting you in remembrance → WAKE <1326>.

REFRESHED (BE) – Phil. 2:19 → to be encouraged → ENCOURAGE <2174>.

REFRESHING – ***anapsuxis*** [fem. noun: ἀνάψυξις <403>]; **from *anapsuchō*: to refresh, which is from *ana*: intens., and *psuchō*: to blow, to cool ▶ Freshness, coolness, rest** > Peter exhorted the men of Israel to repent so that times of refreshing might come (Acts 3:19 or 20), which corresponds to the return of the Lord to reign on earth. ¶

REFUGE – Heb. 6:18 → to flee for refuge → FLEE <2703>.

REFUSAL – Mark 16:14 → stubborn refusal → hardness of heart → HARDNESS <4641>.

REFUSE (noun) – ***peripsēma*** [neut. noun: περίψημα <4067>]; **from *peripsaō*: to scour all around, which is from *peri*: around, and *psaō*: to rub, to scour ▶ Waste, scum; also transl.: offscouring, dregs** > Paul and Apollos had become as the refuse of all things (1 Cor. 4:13). ¶

REFUSE (verb) – [1] ***atheteō*** [verb: ἀθετέω <114>]; **from *athetos*: not placed, which is from *a*: neg., and *tithēmi*: to set aside ▶ To disannul, to reject** > Herod did not want to refuse {reject, break his word with} the daughter of Herodias (Mark 6:26). All other refs.: REJECT <114>.

[2] ***arneomai*** [verb: ἀρνέομαι <720>] ▶ **To renounce, to reject, to not recognize** > The

Israelites refused {disowned} Moses (Acts 7:35). Moses refused to be called the son of Pharaoh's daughter (Heb. 11:24). All other refs.: DENY <720>.

[3] ***kōluō*** [verb: κωλύω <2967>]; **from *kolos*: truncated, and related to *kolouō*: to stop from doing something, to dissuade ▶ To prevent, to restrain** > No one could refuse {forbid} baptism to those {keep them from being baptized} who had received the Holy Spirit (Acts 10:47). All other refs.: FORBID <2967>, HINDER (verb) <2967>, RESTRAIN <2967>.

[4] ***paraiteomai*** [verb: παραιτέομαι <3868>]; **from *para*: aside, and *aiteō*: to ask ▶ To not consent, to repulse, to reject** > Paul did not refuse {deprecate, object to} dying (Acts 25:11). Timothy was to refuse {to decline} to inscribe younger widows on the list of those who were to receive assistance from the local church (1 Tim. 5:11). The verb is used in Heb. 12:25, in regard to refusing him who speaks. All other refs.: AVOID <3868>, BEG <3868>, EXCUSE (verb) <3868>.

– [5] Matt. 5:42 → to turn away → TURN (verb) <654> [6] Mark 16:11 → to refuse to believe → to not believe → BELIEVE <569> [7] Luke 21:15 → RESIST <436> [8] John 5:40 → lit.: to not want → WANT (verb) <2309> [9] Acts 14:2 → to refuse to believe → to believe not → UNBELIEVING <544> [10] Acts 18:15 → I refuse to be a judge of these matters → lit.: I do not want to be judge of these things [11] Acts 19:9 → to refuse to believe → DISBELIEVE <544> [12] 1 Cor. 16:11 → to refuse to accept → DESPISE <1848> [13] Heb. 11:35 → to not accept → ACCEPT <4327> [14] Rev. 2:21 in some mss. → she refuses to repent → lit.: she wants not to repent → WANT (verb) <2309> [15] Rev. 11:9 → lit.: to not let → LET <863>.

REFUSED – 1 Tim. 4:4 → REJECTED <579>.

REFUTE – [1] ***elenchō*** [verb: ἐλέγχω <1651>] ▶ **To reprimand, to convict** > An elder must be able to refute {to convince} gainsayers (Titus 1:9). All other refs.: CONVINCE <1651>, REPROVE <1651>.

[2] ***diakatelenchomai*** [verb: διακατελέγχομαι <1246>]; **from *dia*: (intens.), and *katelenchō*: to dispute, which is from *kata*: against, and *elenchō*: see [1] ▶ To completely dismiss the argument of others by demonstrating its falsity** > Apollos with great force refuted {convinced} the Jews publicly, showing by the Scriptures that Jesus was the Christ (Acts 18:28). ¶

– [3] Luke 21:15 → REPLY (verb) <471>.

REGAIN – Acts 9:19 → to get strength, to regain strength → STRENGTHEN <1765>.

REGARD (noun) – [1] **in regard, with regard: *en merei*; *en*** [prep.: ἐν <1722>], ***meros*** [neut. noun: μέρος <3313>]; **from *en*: in, and *meros*: part, portion ▶ In matter, concerning one particular thing among others** > No one was to judge the Corinthians in regard of {in respect of, regarding} the observance or nonobservance of a feast day (Col. 2:16). Other refs. (*meros*): see entries in Lexicon at <3313>.

– [2] Luke 1:48 → to have regard → to look upon → LOOK (verb) <1914> [3] Acts 8:11 → to have regard → to give heed → HEED (noun) <4337> [4] Acts 28:22 → with regard to → CONCERNING <4012> [5] Rom. 12:17; 2 Cor. 8:21 → to have regard for → PROVIDE <4306> [6] Phil. 2:29 → in high regard → in honor → HONOR (verb) <1784> [7] Col. 2:16 → in regard of → in respect of → RESPECT <1722> [8] 1 Thes. 5:13 → to hold in the highest regard → ESTEEM (verb) <2233> [9] 1 Pet. 1:17 → without regard of persons → without respect of persons → RESPECT OF PERSONS <678>.

REGARD (verb) – [1] ***blepō*** [verb: βλέπω <991>] ▶ **To see with the eyes, to direct the eyes toward** > Certain Jews recognized that Jesus did not regard the appearance of men (Matt. 22:16 and Mark 12:14 {to be partial, to pay attention}). Other refs.: SEE <991>.

[2] ***dokeō*** [verb: δοκέω <1380>] ▶ **To seem, to appear; also transl.: to account, to consider, to esteem, to recognize** > Jesus

spoke of those who are regarded as ruling over the nations (Mark 10:42). All other refs.: CONSIDER <1380>, REPUTATION <1380>, SEEM <1380>, SUPPOSE <1380>, THINK <1380>.
3 ***hēgeomai*** [verb: ἡγέομαι <2233>]; **from *agō*: to lead, from which: to lead one to think ▶ To consider, to view** > A brother who did not obey the word of Paul was not to be regarded {to be counted, to be esteemed} as an enemy (2 Thes. 3:15). All other refs.: see entries in Lexicon at <2233>.
4 ***skopeō*** [verb: σκοπέω <4648>]; **from *skopos*: goal on which to fix the eyes ▶ To consider, to have respect** > The Christian is not to regard {to look for} his own interests, but those of others also (Phil. 2:4). All other refs.: CONSIDER <4648>, EYES <4648>, WATCH <4648>.
– **5** Luke 1:48 → to look upon → LOOK (verb) <1914> **6** Luke 18:2, 4 → RESPECT (verb) <1788> **7** Acts 5:13 → to highly regard → to esteem highly → ESTEEM (verb) <3170> **8** Acts 19:27 → to regard as worthless → to count → DESPISE <3049> **9** Rom. 2:26; 9:8 → COUNT <3049> **10** Rom. 8:36; 14:14 → CONSIDER <3049> **11** Rom. 14:3, 10 → to regard with contempt → DESPISE <1848> **12** Rom. 14:5a, b → ESTEEM (verb) <2919> **13** Rom. 14:6 → THINK <5426> **14** 1 Cor. 4:1; 2 Cor. 10:2b; Phil. 3:13; 1 Pet. 5:12 → THINK <3049> **15** Phil. 2:30 → to not regard → VENTURE <3851> **16** Heb. 8:9 → to regard not → DISREGARD <272> **17** Heb. 12:5 → to regard lightly → DESPISE <3643>.

REGARDED – Luke 7:2 → highly regarded → DEAR <1784>.

REGARDING – Col. 2:16 → in regard → REGARD (noun) <1722> <3313>.

REGARDS (AS) – Rom. 11:28a, b → CONCERNING <2596>.

REGENERATION – ***palingenesia*** [fem. noun: παλιγγενεσία <3824>]; **from *palin*: anew, and *genesis*: generation ▶ Establishment of a new order of things in comparison to a former one** > God saved Christians through the washing of regeneration {rebirth} (Titus 3:5). In Matt. 19:28, the word "regeneration" {renewal of all things} is used in regard to the restoration of all things, during the future reign of Christ. ¶

REGIMENT – Acts 10:1; 27:1 → COHORT <4686>.

REGION – **1** ***klima*** [neut. noun: κλίμα <2824>]; **from *klinō*: to incline; from which: sloping zone of land ▶ Area, country, land** > Paul speaks of the regions of Achaia (2 Cor. 11:10). He also uses this word in Rom. 15:23 {part} and Gal. 1:21. ¶
2 ***meros*** [neut. noun: μέρος <3313>] ▶ **Part, province** > Having passed through the upper regions {coasts, country, districts, interior}, Paul came to Ephesus (Acts 19:1). Other refs.: see entries in Lexicon at <3313>.
3 ***horion*** [neut. noun: ὅριον <3725>]; **only in the plur.: *ta horia*; dimin. of *horos*: border, limit ▶ District, frontier; also transl.: area, border, coast, vicinity** > Capernaum is by the sea, in the regions of Zebulun and Naphtali (Matt. 4:13). A woman of Canaan, who came from the regions of Tyre and Sidon, cried out to Jesus (Matt. 15:22). Jesus came to the regions of Magadan (Matt. 15:39). He came to the region (lit.: regions) of Judea (Matt. 19:1; Mark 10:1). He departed from the region (lit.: regions) of Tyre and Sidon, and came to the Sea of Galilee, through the midst of the region (lit.: regions) of Decapolis (Mark 7:31a, b). The term is also used in regard to Bethlehem (Matt. 2:16), the country of the Gadarenes (Matt. 8:34; Mark 5:17), Tyre and Sidon (Mark 7:24 in some mss.), and Antioch (Acts 13:50). ¶
4 **region around, surrounding region: *perichōros*** [adj. used as noun: περίχωρος <4066>]; **from *peri*: around, and *chōra*: region, country ▶ Neighboring area; also transl.: country round, district round, district around, region round, surrounding district** > All the region around the Jordan went out to John the Baptist (Matt. 3:5; Luke 3:3). The fame of Jesus spread

throughout all the region around Galilee (Mark 1:28). The people from the whole surrounding region brought to Jesus those who were sick (Matt. 14:35; Mark 6:55). The whole multitude of the surrounding region of the Gadarenes asked Jesus to depart from them (Luke 8:37). Paul and Barnabas fled to the surrounding region of Lystra and Derbe, and they preached the gospel there (Acts 14:6). Other refs.: Luke 4:14, 37; 7:17; see COUNTRY <4066>. ¶
5 **region beyond: *huperekeina*** [adv.: ὑπερέκεινα <5238>]; **from *huper*: beyond, and *ekeinos*: that one; lit.: that which is beyond one ► Territory situated further >** Paul wanted to preach the gospel even to the regions beyond the Corinthians (2 Cor. 10:16). ¶
– 6 Matt. 4:16; 8:28; Mark 5:1; Luke 2:8; 3:1; 8:26; John 11:54; Acts 8:1; 13:49; 16:6; 18:23; 26:20 → COUNTRY <5561> 7 Matt. 9:26, 31 → LAND (noun) <1093> 8 Acts 16:3; 28:7 → PLACE (noun) <5117>.

REGISTER – ***apographō*** [verb: ἀπογράφω <583>]; **from *apo*: from, and *graphō*: to write; lit.: to copy ► a. To inscribe, to copy >** Christians have come to the general assembly and church of the firstborn who are registered {enregistered, enrolled, written} in heaven (Heb. 12:23). **b. To enter one's name on a list >** All went to be registered {inscribed, taxed}, including Joseph and Mary (Luke 2:1, 3, 5); see CENSUS <583>. ¶

REGISTRATION – Luke 2:2 → CENSUS <582>.

REGRET – 1 ***metamelomai*** [verb: μεταμέλομαι <3338>]; **from *meta*: denoting change, and *melō*: to be preoccupied, to repent ► Change of mind on a given subject >** Paul did not regret having grieved the Corinthians in his first letter, even if he had regretted it previously (2 Cor. 7:8a, b). All other refs.: MIND (noun) <3338>, REMORSE <3338>, REPENT <3338>.
2 **never to be regretted: *ametamelētos*** [adj.: ἀμεταμέλητος <278>]; **from *a*: neg., and *metamelomai*: see 1 ► Concerning which one has no inclination to change one's mind >** Repentance to salvation is never to be regretted; this was the effect produced by one of Paul's letters (2 Cor. 7:10). Other ref.: Rom. 11:29; see IRREVOCABLE <278>. ¶

REGULARLY – 1 Acts 5:12 → added in Engl. 2 Acts 10:2; Heb. 9:6 → ALWAYS <1275>.

REGULATION – 1 Luke 1:6; Heb. 9:1, 10 → ORDINANCE <1345> 2 Eph. 2:15; Col. 2:14 → ORDINANCE <1378> 3 Col. 2:20 → to subject to regulations → to subject to ordinances → ORDINANCE <1379> 4 Heb. 7:16, 18 → COMMANDMENT <1785>.

REHOBOAM – ***Rhoboam*** [masc. name: Ῥοβοάμ <4497>]**: who enlarges the people, in Heb. ► Son of Solomon (see 1 Kgs. 11:43; 14:21); also spelled: Roboam >** Rehoboam is mentioned in the genealogy of Jesus Christ (Matt. 1:7a, b). The kingdom of Israel was divided in two during his reign; only the tribes of Judah and Benjamin followed Rehoboam (see 1 Kgs. 12:16–24). The other ten tribes established Jeroboam king of Israel (see 1 Kgs. 12:20). ¶

REIGN (noun) – ***hēgemonia*** [fem. noun: ἡγεμονία <2231>]; **from *hēgemōn*: governor, sovereign ► Governmental administration >** John the Baptist preached during the reign {government} of Tiberius Caesar (Luke 3:1). ¶

REIGN (verb) – 1 ***basileuō*** [verb: βασιλεύω <936>]; **from *basileus*: king ► To exercise sovereign power >** The verb is used in regard to Jesus Christ (Luke 1:33; 19:14, 27; 1 Cor. 15:25; 1 Tim. 6:15: the king of those who reign; Rev. 11:15), Christians (Rom. 5:17b; 1 Cor. 4:8a, b {to become kings}; Rev. 5:10; 20:4, 6; 22:5), death (Rom. 5:14, 17a), sin (Rom. 5:21; 6:12), grace (Rom. 5:17b, 21), and Archelaus (Matt. 2:22). In the book of Revelation, the Lord God Almighty is seen as reigning

(Rev. 11:17; 19:6 {to take to oneself kingly power}). ¶

2 **to reign together, to reign with: *sumbasileuō*** [verb: συμβασιλεύω <4821>]**; from *sun*: together, with, and *basileuō*: see 1 ▶ To exercise power together** > The Greek verb describes the future reign of Christians with the Lord (1 Cor. 4:8c {to become kings}; 2 Tim. 2:12). ¶

– 3 Luke 22:53 → when darkness reigns → lit.: the power of darkness → AUTHORITY <1849> 4 Rom. 15:12 → to reign over → to rule over → RULE (verb) <757> 5 1 Tim. 6:15 → to have dominion → DOMINION <2961> 6 Rev. 17:18 → lit.: to have kingship → KINGSHIP <932>.

REIN – Jas. 1:26 → to keep a tight rein → BRIDLE (verb) <5468>.

REINS – ***nephros*** [masc. noun: νεφρός <3510>]**; used in the plur. ▶ Kidneys, the double organ of the body which purifies the blood; it symbolizes the inward life of man, fathomed by God** > The reins correspond to the sentiments, the thoughts, the will; the Lord searches the reins {minds} and hearts (Rev. 2:23; see Ps. 7:9; 26:2; Jer. 17:10). ¶

REJECT – 1 ***atheteō*** [verb: ἀθετέω <114>]**; from *athetos*: not placed, which is from *a*: neg., and *tithēmi*: to put ▶ To set aside, to annul, to cast off; also transl.: to despise, to disregard** > The Jews were rejecting the commandment of God in order to keep their tradition (Mark 7:9). The Pharisees and the lawyers rejected {rendered null} the counsel of God against themselves (Luke 7:30). He who rejected {despised} the disciples rejected Jesus and Him who had sent Him (Luke 10:16a–d). He who rejects Jesus will be judged later (John 12:48). God will reject {bring to nothing, frustrate} the understanding of the prudent (1 Cor. 1:19). Paul was not rejecting {frustrating, nullifying} the grace of God (Gal. 2:21). No man rejects {annuls, disannuls} a confirmed covenant (Gal. 3:15). He who rejects holiness rejects God, who has also given His Holy Spirit (1 Thes. 4:8a, b). Growing wanton against Christ, younger widows have cast off {abandoned, broken} their first faith (1 Tim. 5:12). If anyone rejected Moses's law, he died without mercy (Heb. 10:28). Jude speaks of dreamers who reject authority (Jude 8). Other ref.: Mark 6:26; see REFUSE (verb) <114>. ¶

2 ***apodokimazō*** [verb: ἀποδοκιμάζω <593>]**; from *apo*: from, and *dokimazō*: to examine, to prove; comp. *dokimos*: approved ▶ To cast aside after examination** > The verb is used in regard to Jesus Christ: rejected by men as the cornerstone (Matt. 21:42; Mark 12:10; Luke 20:17; 1 Pet. 2:4 and 7 {to cast away, to disallow}), by the elders (Mark 8:31; Luke 9:22), and by His generation (Luke 17:25). Esau was rejected (Heb. 12:17), having despised his birthright (see v. 16). ¶

3 ***apōtheō*** [verb: ἀπωθέω <683>]**; from *apo*: from, and *ōtheō*: to push ▶ To set aside, to refuse; also transl.: to push aside, to push away, to thrust away, to thrust from, to repudiate** > The Israelite who had wronged his neighbor thrust Moses away (Acts 7:27). The fathers of the Israelites would not be subject to Moses, but thrust him from them (Acts 7:39). The Jews rejected {put from them, repudiated, thrust from them} the word of God preached by Paul and Barnabas (Acts 13:46). God has not rejected His people Israel (Rom. 11:1, 2). Some had rejected {put away} a good conscience (1 Tim. 1:19). ¶

4 ***ekptuō*** [verb: ἐκπτύω <1609>]**; from *ek*: out, and *ptuō*: to spit; lit.: to spit out ▶ To reject with contempt, to have in horror** > The Galatians did not slight or reject {loathe, scorn} Paul's trial that was in his flesh (Gal. 4:14). ¶

– 5 Mark 9:12 → to be rejected → to be treated with contempt → CONTEMPT <1847> 6 Luke 6:22 → to cast out → CAST <1544> 7 John 3:36 → to not believe → BELIEVE <544> 8 Acts 4:11 → DESPISE <1848> 9 Acts 7:35 → REFUSE (verb) <720> 10 2 Cor. 4:2 → RENOUNCE <550> 11 1 Thes. 5:22 → to abstain from → ABSTAIN <567> 12 1 Tim. 4:4 → REJECTED <579> 13 1 Tim. 4:7; Titus 3:10 → AVOID <3868> 14 Titus 1:14;

Heb. 12:25 → to turn away → TURN (verb) <654>.

REJECTED – [1] ***apoblētos*** [verbal adj.: ἀπόβλητος <579>]; **from *apoballō*: to cast away, which is from *apo*: from, and *ballō*: to throw ▶ Set aside, thrown away >** No creature of God is to be rejected {refused} (1 Tim. 4:4). ¶
– [2] 2 Cor. 13:5; 2 Tim. 3:8; Heb. 6:8 → WORTHLESS <96>.

REJECTION – ***apobolē*** [fem. noun: ἀποβολή <580>]; **from *apo*: far from, and *ballō*: to throw ▶ Setting aside, casting away >** The rejection {casting away, being cast away} of Israel is the world's reconciliation (Rom. 11:15). Other ref.: Acts 27:22; see LOSS <580>. ¶

REJOICE – [1] ***agalliaō*** [verb: ἀγαλλιάω <21>]; **from *agan*: very much, and *hallomai*: to leap ▶ To rejoice greatly, to exult; also transl.: to be full of joy, to be filled with joy >** Mary's spirit rejoiced in God her Savior (Luke 1:47). Jesus rejoiced in spirit and praised the Father for having revealed things to little children (Luke 10:21). The jailer rejoiced with all his house (Acts 16:34). The Jews were willing for a season to rejoice in {to enjoy} the light of John the Baptist (John 5:35). Peter spoke of rejoicing greatly while being afflicted (1 Pet. 1:6) and of rejoicing in believing in Jesus Christ (v. 8). In Revelation, a great crowd rejoices (*chairō*) and exults (*agalliaō*) for the marriage of the Lamb is come (19:7); other transl.: to be glad and rejoice, to rejoice and be glad. All other refs.: EXULT <21>, EXULTATION <21>.
[2] ***euphrainō*** [verb: εὐφραίνω <2165>]; **from *euphrōn*: cheerful, which is from *eu*: well, and *phrēn*: mind ▶ To be glad, to exult >** The verb is used in regard to Israel (Rom. 15:10; Gal. 4:27) and the heavens (Rev. 12:12 {to be full of delight}; 18:20). David's heart rejoiced (Acts 2:26). The Israelites rejoiced in the golden calf that they had made (Acts 7:41 {to hold a celebration}). Paul uses this verb in 2 Cor. 2:2 {to gladden, to make glad}. Those who dwell upon the earth rejoice {gloat} over the death of the two prophets (Rev. 11:10). All other refs.: MERRY <2165>.
[3] ***chairō*** [verb: χαίρω <5463>] **▶ To be happy, to be full of joy; also transl.: to be glad, to have joy, to joy, to delight, to exult >** Jesus invites believers in Him to rejoice (Matt. 5:12; Luke 6:23; 10:20; John 14:28), as likewise did Paul (Rom. 12:12, 15a, b; 2 Cor. 13:11; Phil. 3:1; 4:4a, b; 1 Thes. 5:16) and Peter (1 Pet. 4:13a, b). A man who finds a lost sheep rejoices more over it than over the others that have not gone astray (Matt. 18:13). The shepherd lays his sheep on his own shoulders, rejoicing {joyfully} (Luke 15:5). Zaccheus received Jesus with joy {gladly, joyfully} (lit.: rejoicing) (Luke 19:6). Jesus rejoiced because His absence at the death of Lazarus gave His disciples the occasion to believe (John 11:15). Paul rejoiced concerning believers (Rom. 16:19; 1 Cor. 16:17; 2 Cor. 2:3; 7:7, 9, 13, 16; Col. 2:5; 1 Thes. 3:9), as did John likewise (2 John 4; 3 John 3). He told the Corinthians that those who rejoice should be as not rejoicing due to the difficult times (1 Cor. 7:30a, b), and that love does not rejoice in iniquity (1 Cor. 13:6). He was sorrowful, but always rejoicing (2 Cor. 6:10). Paul rejoiced in weakness (2 Cor. 13:9), in the preaching of the gospel (Phil. 1:18a, b), in the Lord (Phil. 4:10), and in sufferings (Col. 1:24). He rejoiced to be poured out as a drink offering on the sacrifice and service of the faith of the Philippians (Phil. 2:17); he encourages them to rejoice also (v. 18). The Philippians might rejoice on seeing Epaphroditus again (Phil. 2:28). We read about various people rejoicing: the wise men rejoiced when they saw the star (Matt. 2:10), the chief priests rejoiced at the prospect of seeing Jesus delivered up to them (Mark 14:11; Luke 22:5), many rejoiced at the birth of John the Baptist (Luke 1:14), the crowd rejoiced at all the glorious things that were done by Jesus (Luke 13:17), the father rejoiced over his son who was found (Luke 15:32), the multitude of the disciples rejoiced for the miracles of Jesus (Luke 19:37), Herod rejoiced to see Jesus (Luke 23:8), the friend of the bridegroom

rejoices because he hears the voice of the bridegroom (John 3:29), he who sows and he who reaps both rejoice (John 4:36), Abraham rejoiced that he had seen the day of Jesus (John 8:56), the world rejoiced at the departure of Jesus (John 16:20), the heart of the disciples rejoiced over Jesus at His resurrection (John 16:22), the disciples rejoiced when they saw Jesus risen from among the dead (John 20:20), Peter and John rejoiced to suffer for the name of Jesus (Acts 5:41), a eunuch rejoiced (Acts 8:39), Barnabas rejoiced seeing the grace of God at Antioch (Acts 11:23), those of the nations rejoiced over salvation (Acts 13:48), the Christians at Antioch rejoiced over the letter of the apostles (Acts 15:31), and those who dwell upon the earth rejoice over the death of the two prophets (Rev. 11:10). John heard a voice that told him to rejoice (Rev. 19:7). All other refs.: HAIL (verb) <5463>.
[4] **to rejoice with, to rejoice in common:** ***sunchairō*** [verb: συγχαίρω <4796>]; **from *sun*: together, and *chairō*: see [3] ▶ To be full of joy together with others, to share one's joy** > The shepherd who finds his lost sheep calls together the friends and neighbors to rejoice with him (Luke 15:6); the woman who finds the lost drachma assembles the friends and neighbors to rejoice with her (Luke 15:9). The neighbors and kinsfolk of Elizabeth rejoiced with her at the birth of her son (Luke 1:58). If one member of the body is glorified, all the members rejoice with it (1 Cor. 12:26). Love rejoices with the truth (1 Cor. 13:6). Paul rejoiced in common with the Philippians at the prospect of being poured out as a libation on the sacrifice and service of their faith (Phil. 2:17, 18). ¶
– [5] Phil. 2:16; Heb. 3:6 → to have something to boast → BOAST (verb) <2745>.

REJOICING – [1] Luke 15:5; 2 Cor. 6:10 → REJOICE <5463> [2] 1 Cor. 15:31; Jas. 4:16 → BOASTING <2746> [3] 2 Cor. 1:12; 1 Thes. 2:19 → reason to glorify → GLORIFY <2746> [4] 2 Cor. 1:14; Phil. 1:26 → BOAST (noun) <2745>.

REKINDLE – ***anazōpureō*** [verb: ἀναζωπυρέω <329>]; **from *ana*: again, and *zōpureō*: to revive a fire ▶ To revive, to enflame anew** > Paul put Timothy in mind to rekindle {to fan into flame, to kindle afresh, to stir up} the gift of the grace of God that was in him (2 Tim. 1:6). ¶

RELATE – [1] ***anangellō*** [verb: ἀναγγέλλω <312>]; **from *ana*: upon (intens.), and *angellō*: to bring news, a message ▶ To announce, to report, to tell** > Jesus told the demoniac who had been healed to go home to his own people and relate to them all that the Lord had done for him (Mark 5:19). Paul and Barnabas related {rehearsed, declared} all that God had done with them (Acts 14:27; 15:4). Titus had related to Paul the feelings of the Corinthians toward him (2 Cor. 7:7). All other refs.: see entries in Lexicon at <312>.
[2] ***apangellō*** [verb: ἀπαγγέλλω <518>]; ***apo*: from (intens.), and *angellō*: to bring news, a message ▶ To announce, to report, to tell** > Those who fed the swine related everything regarding the healing of the demoniacs (Matt. 8:33; Luke 8:34, 36). The apostles related to Jesus all that they had done (Mark 6:30). Some related to Jesus what had happened regarding the Galileans (Luke 13:1). A man related what an angel had said {had shown} to him regarding Peter (Acts 11:13). People related {declared, showed} what kind of reception Paul had by the Thessalonians (1 Thes. 1:9). All other refs.: DECLARE <518>, REPORT (verb) <518>, SHOW (verb) <518>, TELL <518>.
[3] ***diēgeomai*** [verb: διηγέομαι <1334>]; **from *dia*: through (intens.), and *hēgeomai*: to lead, to declare ▶ To speak in detail, to describe; also transl.: to tell, to report, to give an account, to show, to speak of** > The apostles related to Jesus all that they had done (Luke 9:10). Those who had seen what had taken place related what had happened to the demoniac and concerning the swine (Mark 5:16). After the transfiguration, Jesus charged His disciples that they should relate to no one what they had seen (Mark 9:9). He told the demoniac who had been healed to go to his house and relate all that the Lord had done for him (Luke 8:39). Isaiah asked who will relate the generation of the

Lord (Acts 8:33). Barnabas related to the apostles the conversion of Saul (Acts 9:27). Peter related how the Lord had brought him out of prison (Acts 12:17). Other ref.: Heb. 11:32; see TELL <1334>. ¶
4 ***ekdiēgeomai*** [verb: ἐκδιηγέομαι <1555>]; **from *ek*: out (intens.), and *diēgeomai*: see 3 ► To describe in detail; also transl.: to declare, to describe, to tell** > God was going to do a work that scoffers would not believe if one related {declared, described, told} it to them (Acts 13:41). Paul and Barnabas related the conversion of the nations (Acts 15:3). ¶
5 ***exēgeomai*** [verb: ἐξηγέομαι <1834>]; **from *ek*: out (intens.), and *hēgeomai*: to lead, to declare ► To reveal, to make known; also transl.: to declare, to describe, to explain, to report, to tell** > The disciples of Emmaus related what had happened on the way (Luke 24:35). Cornelius related all things concerning the visit of the angel (Acts 10:8). Barnabas and Paul related all the signs and wonders that God had wrought among the nations by them (Acts 15:12). Simeon related how God first visited the nations to take out of them a people for His name (Acts 15:14). Paul related one by one the things that God had wrought among the nations by his ministry (Acts 21:19). Other ref.: John 1:18; see DECLARE <1834>. ¶
– 6 Heb. 2:17; 5:1 → PERTAIN <4314>.

RELATED – Acts 19:25 → LIKE (adj., adv., noun) <5108>.

RELATION – 1 Luke 1:1 → ACCOUNT (noun) <1335> 2 Luke 2:44; Luke 21:16 → RELATIVE <4773> 3 Rom. 1:26, 27 → relations → USE (noun) <5540> 4 Rom. 7:3 → if she has sexual relations with another man → lit.: if she is (*ginomai*) to another man 5 1 Cor. 7:1 → for a man to have sexual relations with a woman → lit.: for a man to touch a woman → TOUCH <680> 6 1 Cor. 7:2 → "sexual relations with" added in Engl.

RELATIONSHIP – 1 Matt. 19:10 → CASE <156> 2 John 1:18 → in closest relationship with the Father → lit.: in the bosom of the Father 3 Phil. 2:5 → in your relationships with one another → lit.: among you.

RELATIVE – 1 ***oi par' autou; autos*** [pron.: αὐτός <846>]; **lit.: those near him ► Expr. that may designate parents, relatives, friends, neighbors; also transl.: family, people** > The relatives of Jesus went out to lay hold on Him (Mark 3:21).
2 ***sungenēs*** [adj. used as noun: συγγενής <4773>]; **from *sun*: with, together, and *genos*: family ► Person who is a member of the same family, related by blood; also transl.: countryman, kindred, kinsfolk, kinsman, people, relation** > Jesus warned His disciples that they would be betrayed even by relatives {kinsfolks, relations} (Luke 21:16). The word is also used in regard to the relatives of a prophet (Mark 6:4), the relatives of Elizabeth and her own relationship as a relative {cousin, kinswoman, kinsfolk} of Mary (Luke 1:36 {other mss.: *sungenis*}, 58), and the relatives {relations} of Joseph and Mary (Luke 2:44), the relatives of Cornelius (Acts 10:24), the relatives of Paul (Rom. 9:3; 16:7, 11, 21). Other refs.: Luke 14:12; John 18:26. ¶
– 3 1 Tim. 5:16 → "relatives who are" added in Engl.

RELATIVES – ***sungeneia*** [fem. noun: συγγένεια <4772>]; **from *sungenēs*: relative, which is from *sun*: with, together, and *genos*: family ► The whole group of people who are members of the same family, related by blood; also transl.: kinsfolk, kindred, people** > The word is used in regard to Zacharias (Luke 1:61), Abraham (Acts 7:3), and Jacob (Acts 7:14). ¶

RELAX – 1 Matt. 5:19 → ANNUL <3089> 2 Luke 12:19 → REST (verb) <373>.

RELEASE (noun) – 1 Luke 4:18a → LIBERTY <859> 2 Heb. 11:35 → DELIVERANCE <629>.

RELEASE (verb) – 1 ***apallassō*** [verb: ἀπαλλάσσω <525>]; **from *apo*: from, and *allassō*: to change ► To deliver, to set**

free; pass.: to be freed > Jesus has released {delivered, freed} those who through fear of death were all their lifetime subject to bondage (Heb. 2:15). Other refs.: Acts 19:12; Luke 12:58; see LEAVE (verb) <525>, SETTLE <525>. ¶

[2] ***katargeō*** [verb: καταργέω <2673>]; **from *kata*: down (intens.), and *argeō*: to be inactive, which is from *argos*: idle, useless, which is from *a*: neg., and *ergon*: work ▶ To free, to liberate >** If the husband dies, the woman is released {is clear, is loosed} from the law of her husband (Rom. 7:2); Christians have been delivered (or: released) from the law (v. 6). All other refs.: see entries in Lexicon at <2673>.

[3] ***luō*** [verb: λύω <3089>] **▶ To unbind, to free >** The captain released {loosed} Paul from his bonds (Acts 22:30). The order was given to release {loose} the four angels who were bound at the Euphrates (Rev. 9:14, 15). Satan must be released {loosed} for a little time from his prison at the end of the millennium (Rev. 20:3 {to set free}, 7). All other refs.: ANNUL <3089>, BREAK <3089>, DESTROY <3089>, DISSOLVE <3089>, LOOSE <3089>.

[4] ***apoluō*** [verb: ἀπολύω <630>]; **from *apo*: from, and *luō*: see [3] ▶ To unbind, to set at liberty; also transl.: to dismiss, to let go, to set free >** In a parable, the lord released {let go, loosed} his bondman and forgave him his debt (Matt. 18:27). The verb is used in the account of the liberation of Barabbas whom the crowd preferred to Jesus (Matt. 27:15, 17, 21, 26; Mark 15:6, 9, 11, 15; Luke 23:16–18, 20, 22, 25; John 18:39; 19:10, 12; Acts 3:13). Peter and John were released (Acts 4:21, 23). The apostles were released after having been beaten (Acts 5:40). Officers were sent to release Paul and Silas (Acts 16:35, 36). Jason and certain brothers were released after having been dragged before the magistrates (Acts 17:9). Paul might have been released, if he had not appealed to Caesar (Acts 26:32; 28:18). All other refs.: see entries in Lexicon at <630>.

– [5] Luke 4:18b → to release the oppressed → lit.: to send forth the oppressed in liberty → SEND <649>, LIBERTY <859> [6] Acts 3:14 → GRANT <5483> [7] Acts 24:26: the verb *luō* is added in some mss. [8] 1 Cor. 7:27 → LOOSE <3080> [9] Heb. 11:35 → to be released → lit.: release → DELIVERANCE <629> [10] Rev. 1:5 → WASH <3068>.

RELEASED – Rom. 7:3 → FREE (adj.) <1658>.

RELENT – [1] Matt. 21:32 → REPENT <3338> [2] Heb. 7:21 → to change one's mind → MIND (noun) <3338>.

RELIABLE – [1] John 8:26 → TRUE <227> [2] Heb. 2:2; 2 Pet. 1:19 → reliable, something completely reliable → FIRM <949>.

RELIEF – [1] Acts 11:29 → SERVICE <1248> [2] 2 Thes. 1:7 → REST (noun)[1] <425> [3] 1 Tim. 5:10, 16a, b → to impart relief → RELIEVE <1884>.

RELIEVE – ***eparkeō*** [verb: ἐπαρκέω <1884>]; **from *epi*: intens., and *arkeō*: to aid, to satisfy ▶ To aid, to help; also transl.: to assist, to impart relief >** Paul speaks of the widow who has relieved the afflicted (1 Tim. 5:10). A believing man or woman must relieve his widows, so the church may relieve those who are really widows (1 Tim. 5:16a, b). ¶

RELIEVED (BE) – 2 Cor. 8:13 → EASE <425>.

RELIGION – [1] ***deisidaimonia*** [fem. noun: δεισιδαιμονία <1175>]; **from *deisidaimōn*: fearing the gods, religious, which is from *deidō*: to fear, and *daimōn*: supernatural spirit ▶ System of religious worship, cult >** This word {system of worship; superstition} designates the Jewish religion in Acts 25:19. ¶

[2] ***thrēskeia*** [fem. noun: θρησκεία <2356>]; **from *thrēskeuō*: to worship God, which is from: *thrēskos*: religious ▶ System of religious worship in its practical and external aspect, Christian service >** This word designated the Jewish religion: Paul lived according to the strictest sect of his religion (Acts 26:5). It is transl. "worship"

{worshipping} concerning the cult of angels (Col. 2:18). One's religion is vain if the tongue is not bridled (Jas. 1:26). The pure and undefiled religion before God the Father is to visit orphans and widows in their affliction, and to keep oneself unspotted from the world. (Jas. 1:27). ¶
– 3 Gal. 1:13, 14 → Jews' religion → JUDAISM <2454> 4 Col. 2:23 → self-made religion → SELF-IMPOSED RELIGION <1479> 5 1 Tim. 5:4 → to put religion in practice → PIETY <2151>.

RELIGIOUS – 1 ***thrēskos*** [adj.: θρησκός <2357>] ▶ **Which concerns Christian service in its external expression** > If anyone thinks himself to be religious but deceives his heart, this man's religion is vain (Jas. 1:26). ¶
2 **very religious: *deisidaimonesteros*** [adj.: δεισιδαιμονέστερος <1174>]; **compar. of *deisidaimōn*: religious, from *deidō*: to fear, and *daimōn*: supernatural spirit ▶ Superstitious, devoting oneself to the cult of demons** > Paul told the men of Athens he perceived that they were very religious {given up to demon worship} in all things (Acts 17:22). ¶
– 3 Heb. 10:11 → to perform religious duties → MINISTER (verb) <3008>.

RELUCTANTLY – 2 Cor. 9:7 → GRIEVINGLY <3077>.

RELY – 1 Luke 11:22; 2 Cor. 1:9 → TRUST (verb) <3982> 2 Rom. 2:17 → REST (verb) <1879> 3 2 Cor. 1:12; Gal. 3:11 → added in Engl. 4 2 Cor. 8:4 → SERVICE <1248> 5 Gal. 3:9 → those who rely on faith → lit.: those of (*ek*) faith 6 Jude 8 → these people relying on their dreams → lit.: these dreaming ones → DREAMER <1797>.

REMAIN – 1 ***menō*** [verb: μένω <3306>] ▶ **To stay, to dwell, to continue; also transl.: to abide, to continue, to endure, to stand, to tarry** > The disciples of Emmaus constrained Jesus to remain with them, for it was toward evening, which He did (Luke 24:29a, b). Two disciples remained {spent the day} with Jesus (John 1:39). Paul remained and worked with Aquila and Priscilla (Acts 18:3). He remained with the brothers one day in Ptolemais (Acts 21:7). Each believer is encouraged to remain in the same calling (or: condition) in which he was called (1 Cor. 7:20, 24). Other refs.: Matt. 10:11; 11:23; 26:38; Mark 6:10; 14:34; Luke 1:56; 8:27 {to live}; 9:4; 10:7; 19:5; John 1:32, 33, 38, 39a, b; 2:12; 3:36; 4:40a, b; 5:38; 6:27, 56; 7:9; 8:35a, b; 9:41; 10:40; 11:6; 12:24, 34, 46; 14:10, 16, 17, 25 {to be present}; 15:4a–c, 5, 6, 7a, b, 9, 10 a, b, 11 in some mss., 16; 19:31; 21:22, 23; Acts 5:4a, b; 9:43; 16:15; 18:20; 21:8; 27:31, 41; 28:16, 30 (in some mss.); Rom. 9:11; 1 Cor. 3:14; 7:8, 11, 40; 13:13; 15:6; 2 Cor. 3:11, 14; 9:9; Phil. 1:25; 2 Tim. 2:13; 3:14; 4:20; Heb. 7:3, 24; 12:27; 13:1; 1 Pet. 1:25; 1 John 2:6, 10, 14, 17, 19, 24a–c, 27a, b, 28; 3:6, 9, 14, 15, 17, 24a, b; 4:12, 13, 15, 16a, b; 2 John 2, 9a, b; Rev. 17:10. All other refs.: AWAIT <3306>, CONTINUE <3306>, LASTING <3306>, STAY (verb) <3306>, TARRY <3306>.
2 ***diamenō*** [verb: διαμένω <1265>]; **from *dia*: *through* (intens.), and *menō*: see 1 ▶ To stay, to continue** > Paul acted to ensure the truth of the gospel might remain with the Galatians (Gal. 2:5). The Lord remains eternally (Heb. 1:11). Other refs.: Luke 1:22; 22:28 (see PERSEVERE <1265>); 2 Pet. 3:4 {to continue, to go on}. ¶
3 ***epimenō*** [verb: ἐπιμένω <1961>]; **from *epi*: at (intens.), and *menō*: see 1 ▶ To abide, to continue to live** > The verb is found in Acts 15:34 in some mss. All other refs.: CONTINUE <1961>, STAY (verb) <1961>, TARRY <1961>.
4 ***prosmenō*** [verb: προσμένω <4357>]; **from *pros*: with, and *menō*: see 1 ▶ To stay with, to continue with** > Paul still remained {tarried} a good while in Corinth (Acts 18:18). He had begged Titus to remain {to abide still, to stay} at Ephesus (1 Tim. 1:3). Other refs.: Matt. 15:32; Mark 8:2; Acts 11:23; 13:43 in some mss.; 1 Tim. 5:5: see CONTINUE <4357>. ¶
5 ***hupomenō*** [verb: ὑπομένω <5278>]; **from *hupo*: under, and *menō*: see 1 ▶ To stay behind, to linger behind** > Silas and Timothy remained {abode, stayed} in Berea

(Acts 17:14). All other refs.: ENDURE <5278>, LINGER <5278>, PATIENT <5278>, SUFFER <5278>.

6 ***leipō*** [verb: λείπω <3007>] ► **To leave** > Paul had left (*kataleipō*) Titus at Crete to set right the things that remained {that were lacking, wanting, left unfinished} (Titus 1:5), i.e., that remained unordered. All other refs.: LACK (verb) <3007>.

7 ***apoleipō*** [verb: ἀπολείπω <620>]; **from *apo*: from, and *leipō*: see 6 ► To be reserved, to be left** > It remains that some enter into the rest of God (Heb. 4:6). There remains a Sabbath rest to the people of God (Heb. 4:9). There no longer remains any sacrifice for sins for one who willfully sins after having received the knowledge of the truth (Heb. 10:26). Other refs.: 2 Tim. 4:13, 20; Jude 6; see LEAVE (verb) <620>. ¶

8 ***perileipō*** [verb: περιλείπω <4035>]; **from *peri*: intens., and *leipō*: see 6 ► To stay, to survive** > Christians who are alive and remain {are left} until the coming of the Lord will be caught up together with those believers who are asleep (1 Thes. 4:15, 17). ¶

9 **the things that remain: *loipos*** [adj. used as noun: λοιπός <3062>]; **from *leipō*: see 6 ► The portion left over** > The church in Sardis is told to strengthen the things that remain (Rev. 3:2). Other refs.: REST (noun)[2] <3062>.

10 ***perisseuō*** [verb: περισσεύω <4052>]; **from *perissos*: abundant, which is from *peri*: above, beyond ► To be left over, to exceed** > The disciples took up twelve baskets full of the fragments that remained of the multiplication of loaves (Matt. 14:20; 15:37; John 6:12, 13). Twelve baskets of fragments of what remained of the fragments after the multiplication of loaves were taken up (Luke 9:17). All other refs.: see entries in Lexicon at <4052>.

– 11 Matt. 2:13 → STAY (verb) <1510> 12 Luke 1:24 → to remain in seclusion → HIDE <4032> 13 Luke 21:37 → to stay at night → STAY (verb) <835> 14 Luke 24:49 → TARRY <2523> 15 John 3:22; 11:54; Acts 14:3, 28; 15:35; 16:12; 25:6 → STAY (verb) <1304> 16 John 6:22 → the crowd that remained → lit.: the crowd standing (*histēmi*) 17 John 11:20 → to remain seated → lit.: to sit 18 Acts 14:22; Heb. 8:9 → to remain true, to remain faithful → CONTINUE <1696> 19 Acts 18:11 → CONTINUE <2523> 20 Acts 19:22; 1 Cor. 16:6 → STAY (verb) <1907> 21 1 Tim. 5:25 → cannot remain hidden → lit.: cannot be hidden 22 Heb. 4:1 → LEAVE (verb) <2641> 23 Jas. 1:21 → all that remains → OVERFLOW (noun) <4050> 24 Rev. 14:4 → they remained virgins → lit.: they are virgins 25 Rev. 16:15 → to remain clothed → to keep one's garments → KEEP (verb) <5083>.

REMARK – ***epechō*** [verb: ἐπέχω <1907>]; **from *epi*: upon, and *echō*: to have, to hold ► To pay attention, to observe** > Jesus remarked {marked, noted, noticed} how guests in the house of a ruler were picking out the first places (Luke 14:7). All other refs.: ATTENTION <1907>, HEED (noun) <1907>, HOLD (verb) <1907>, STAY (verb) <1907>.

REMARKABLE – 1 Mark 6:2 → remarkable work → MIRACLE <1411> 2 Luke 5:26 → STRANGE <3861> 3 John 9:30 → MARVELOUS <2298>.

REMEMBER – 1 ***mimnēskō*** [verb: μιμνήσκω <3403>] ► **To recall to mind, to remind** > The alms of Cornelius had been remembered {had come in remembrance, were in remembrance} before God (Acts 10:31); some mss. have *mnaomai*. Someone said to God: "What is man that you remember him" (Heb. 2:6). We are to remember prisoners (Heb. 13:3). Other ref.: Rev. 16:19 (to come in remembrance); see REMEMBRANCE <3403>. ¶

2 ***anamimnēskō*** [verb: ἀναμιμνήσκω <363>]; **from *ana*: again, and *mimnēskō*: see 1 ► To call to mind again, to recall again** > Peter remembered {called to remembrance, was reminded of} the fig tree that Jesus had cursed (Mark 11:21). He remembered {called to mind} the word that he would deny Jesus (Mark 14:72). Other refs.: 1 Cor. 4:17; 2 Cor. 7:15; 2 Tim. 1:6; Heb. 10:32; see REMIND <363>. ¶

[3] ***hupomimnēskō*** [verb: ὑπομιμνήσκω <5279>]; **from *hupo*: under, and *mimnēskō*: see [1] ► To bring to remembrance, possibly after suggestion or warning** > Peter remembered the word that he would deny the Lord (Luke 22:61). Other refs.: John 14:26; 2 Tim. 2:14; Titus 3:1; 2 Pet. 1:12; Jude 5; 3 John 10; see REMIND <5279>. ¶

[4] ***mnaomai*** [verb: μνάομαι <3415>]; **comp. *mimnēskō*: to recall to one's mind ► To recall, to recollect** > Jesus said that if someone remembers his brother having something against him, he should be reconciled to him before offering his gift at the altar (Matt. 5:23). Peter remembered that Jesus had said he would deny Him (Matt. 26:75). The Lord has helped Israel in order to remember His mercy (Luke 1:54) and His holy covenant (v. 72). This verb is used concerning Abraham in Luke 16:25, as likewise the repentant malefactor on the cross (Luke 23:42). The angels said to the women who had come to the tomb that they ought to remember how Jesus had spoken to them when He was still in Galilee (Luke 24:6), and they remembered His words (v. 8). The disciples remembered passages of Scripture (John 2:17, 22; 12:16 {to realize}). Peter remembered the word of the Lord concerning baptism with the Holy Spirit (Acts 11:16). The Corinthians remembered Paul in all things (1 Cor. 11:2). Paul remembered Timothy's tears (2 Tim. 1:4). God would never remember any more the sins and iniquities of Israel (Heb. 8:12; 10:17). Peter wrote so that his readers might remember the words spoken beforehand by the holy prophets and the commandment of the Lord and Savior (2 Pet. 3:2). We ought to remember the words spoken beforehand by the apostles of the Lord (Jude 17). Other refs.: Matt. 27:63 {to call to mind}; Acts 10:31 (see [1]); Rev. 16:19 (to come in remembrance; see REMEMBRANCE <3403>). ¶

[5] ***mnēmoneuō*** [verb: μνημονεύω <3421>]; **from *mnēmōn*: who remembers, which is from *mimnēskō*: to recall to one's mind ► To keep in mind, to make mention, to recall** > Jesus said to remember the multiplication of bread (Matt. 16:9), Lot's wife (Luke 17:32), and His word concerning the servant and his master (John 15:20). He asked the disciples if they did not remember the miracle of the multiplication of the loaves of bread (Mark 8:18). He had spoken important things to His disciples so that they might remember them when the time should come (John 16:4). A woman who has given birth to a child remembers her anguish no more (John 16:21). Christians are to remember the words of the Lord regarding giving their possessions (Acts 20:35). This verb is used when Paul spoke with the elders of Ephesus regarding his warnings (Acts 20:31). He was to remember the poor (Gal. 2:10). He told the Ephesians to remember that they had formerly been without Christ (Eph. 2:11). He told the Colossians to remember his bonds (Col. 4:18). He told the Thessalonians to remember his labor and hardship (1 Thes. 2:9) and the things he had said to them (2 Thes. 2:5). He remembered their work of faith, labor of love, and patience of hope in the Lord (1 Thes. 1:3 {to bear in mind}). He told Timothy to remember Jesus Christ, raised from among the dead (2 Tim. 2:8). Christians are to remember their leaders (Heb. 13:7). The Lord tells the church of Ephesus to remember from where she has fallen (Rev. 2:5), and the church of Sardis how she has received and heard (3:3). God remembered the iniquities of Babylon (Rev. 18:5). Other refs.: Heb. 11:15 {to call to mind}; 11:22 (to make mention; see MENTION (noun) <3421>). ¶

– [6] Rom. 1:9; Eph. 1:16; Phm. 4 → to make mention → MENTION (noun) <3417> [7] 1 Cor. 1:16 → KNOW <1492> [8] 2 Cor. 7:15; Heb. 10:32 → REMIND <363> [9] 1 Thes. 3:6 → every time I remember → lit.: in all my remembrance → REMEMBRANCE <3417> [10] Jas. 5:20 → lit.: to let know → KNOW <1097> [11] 2 Pet. 1:15 → MIND (CALL TO) <3420> <4160>.

REMEMBRANCE – [1] ***anamnēsis*** [fem. noun: ἀνάμνησις <364>]; **from *anamimnēskō*: to remind, which is from *ana*: again, and *mimnēskō*: see [2] ► The act of**

recalling to mind, commemoration > At the institution of His supper, the Lord Jesus said to do as He did in remembrance of Him (Luke 22:19; 1 Cor. 11:24, 25). Other ref.: Heb. 10:3; see REMINDER <364>. ¶

[2] **to come in remembrance: *mimnēskō*** [verb: μιμνήσκω <3403>] ▶ **To recall to mind, to be mindful** > Great Babylon came in remembrance {was remembered} before God (Rev. 16:19); other mss. have *mnaomai*. Other refs.: Acts 10:31; Heb. 2:6; 13:3; see REMEMBER <3403>. ¶

[3] ***mneia*** [fem. noun: μνεία <3417>]; **from *mnaomai*: to recall; comp. *mimnēskō*: to recall to one's mind** ▶ **Memory, recollection** > Paul thanked God for his whole remembrance of the Philippians (Phil. 1:3). The Thessalonians always had a good remembrance of Paul (1 Thes. 3:6). All other refs.: MENTION (noun) <3417>.

[4] ***hupomnēsis*** [fem. noun: ὑπόμνησις <5280>]; **from *hupomimnēskō*: to recall to one's mind, which is from *hupo*: under, and *mimnēskō*: to recall, to remember** ▶ **Reminder, memory** > Peter accounted it right to stir up his readers by putting them in remembrance {refreshing their memory, reminding them, way of reminder} of certain things (2 Pet. 1:13). He had written two letters to stir up their pure mind in putting them in remembrance {by way of remembrance, by way of reminder, as reminders} of various things (3:1). Other ref.: 2 Tim. 1:5; see MIND (CALL TO) <5280>. ¶

– [5] Mark 11:21; 1 Cor. 4:17; 2 Tim. 1:6; Heb. 10:32 → to bring into, to put in, to call to remembrance → REMIND <363> [6] Luke 1:54 → in remembrance → lit.: to remember → REMEMBER <3415> [7] John 14:26; 2 Tim. 2:14; 2 Pet. 1:12; Jude 5; 3 John 10 → to bring to remembrance, to put in remembrance → REMIND <5279> [8] 1 Tim. 4:6 → to put in remembrance → to point out → POINT (verb) <5294> [9] 2 Pet. 1:15 → to have in remembrance → MIND (CALL TO) <3420> <4160>.

REMIND – [1] ***anamimnēskō*** [verb: ἀναμιμνήσκω <363>]; **from *ana*: again, and *mimnēskō*: to recall, to remember** ▶ **To cause to remember; also transl.: to call to mind, to put in mind, to put in remembrance, to bring into remembrance, to call to remembrance, to remember** > Timothy was to bring the Corinthians into remembrance of Paul's ways in Christ (1 Cor. 4:17). Titus remembered the obedience of all the Corinthians (2 Cor. 7:15). Paul reminded Timothy to rekindle the gift of grace that was in him (2 Tim. 1:6). The Hebrews were to remember {to recall} the earlier days in which they had been enlightened and had suffered (Heb. 10:32). Other refs.: Mark 11:21; 14:72; see REMEMBER <363>. ¶

[2] **to remind, to remind again: *epanamimnēskō*** [verb: ἐπαναμιμνήσκω <1878>]; **from *epi*: upon (intens.), and *anamimnēskō*: see [1]** ▶ **To cause someone to remember** > Paul wrote to his brothers to remind them again {by way of reminder} of some points (Rom. 15:15). ¶

[3] **to bring to remembrance, to put (someone) in remembrance, to remember: *hupomimnēskō*** [verb: ὑπομιμνήσκω <5279>]; **from *hupo*: under, and *mimnēskō*: see [1]** ▶ **To recall to mind, to call back in memory; also transl.: to call attention, to put in mind, to put in remembrance, to remember** > The Holy Spirit would remind the disciples of all the things that Jesus had said (John 14:26). Paul told Timothy to remind his hearers of certain things (2 Tim. 2:14). Titus was to remind Christians to be subject to rulers and authorities (Titus 3:1). Peter would be careful to put his readers always in remembrance of certain things (2 Pet. 1:12). Jude wanted to remind Christians of certain things (v. 5). John would bring to remembrance the works of Diotrephes (3 John 10). Other ref.: Luke 22:61; see REMEMBER <5279>. ¶

– [4] Mark 11:21 → to call to remembrance → REMEMBER <363> [5] 1 Cor. 15:1 → KNOW <1107> [6] 2 Cor. 10:7 → to remind oneself → to think again as to oneself → THINK <3049>, AGAIN <3825> [7] 2 Tim. 1:5 → MIND (CALL TO) <5280> <2983> [8] 2 Pet. 1:13 → by reminding → lit.: by remembrance → REMEMBRANCE <3420>.

REMINDER – [1] ***anamnēsis*** [fem. noun: ἀνάμνησις <364>]; **from *anamimnēskō*: to remind again, which is from *ana*: again, and *mimnēskō*: to remember, to remind ▶ Calling to mind, remembrance** > In the yearly sacrifices of the O.T., there was a reminder of sins (Heb. 10:3). Other refs.: Luke 22:19; 1 Cor. 11:24, 25; see REMEMBRANCE <364>. ¶
– [2] Rom. 15:15 → by way of reminder → to remind again → REMIND <1878> [3] 2 Pet. 1:13; 3:1 → by way of reminder → lit.: by reminder → REMEMBRANCE <5280> [4] 2 Pet. 1:15 → to have a reminder → MIND (CALL TO) <3420> <4160>.

REMISSION – [1] ***aphesis*** [fem. noun: ἄφεσις <859>]; **from *aphiēmi*: to send forth, to let go, which is from *apo*: from, and *hiēmi*: to send ▶ Forgiveness of sins, which necessitated the sacrifice of Christ on the cross where He bore our sins and was made sin for us** > The Greek word is used in the expr. "remission of sins" (Matt. 26:28; Mark 1:4; Luke 1:77; 3:3; 24:47; Acts 2:38; 5:31; 10:43; 13:38; 26:18; Col. 1:14; Heb. 10:18) and "forgiveness of offences" (or: remission of offences) (Eph. 1:7). Without blood-shedding, there is no remission (Heb. 9:22). Other ref.: Mark 3:29: see FORGIVENESS <859>; Luke 4:18a, b: see LIBERTY <859>. ¶
– [2] Rom. 3:25 → passing by, passing over → PASSING <3929>.

REMIT – [1] Luke 6:37a, b → FORGIVE <630> [2] Luke 11:4a, b; John 20:23 → FORGIVE <863> [3] Luke 23:7, 11 → to send back → SEND <375>.

REMNANT – [1] ***leimma*** [neut. noun: λεῖμμα <3005>]; **from *leipō*: to leave ▶ Smaller number of persons remaining from a larger group** > A remnant of Israel, embracing the Christian faith from the time of the apostles, is saved at this present time according to the election of grace (Rom. 11:5). ¶
[2] ***kataleimma*** [neut. noun: κατάλειμμα <2640>]; **from *kata*: intens., and *leimma*: see [1] ▶ A small remainder; see [1]** > The term designates a faithful residue in the midst of Israel that will be saved (Rom. 9:27, quoting Is. 10:22); other mss.: *hupoleimma*. ¶
[3] ***loipos*** [adj. used as noun: λοιπός <3062>]; **from *leipō*: to leave ▶ Small group of faithful believers in the midst of the people of Israel, whereas most have turned away from God** > Satan will make war against this remnant (Rev. 12:17). Other refs.: REST (noun)[2] <3062>.
[4] **the remnant: *oi kataloipoi*: plur. of *kataloipos*** [adj. used as plur. noun: κατάλοιπος <2645>]; **from *kataleipō*: to leave behind; lit.: those who remain, the rest ▶ A small group of faithful believers** > The remnant {residue, rest} of men will seek out the Lord and all the Gentiles who are called His name (Acts 15:17). ¶

REMORSE – **to feel, to be filled with, to be seized with remorse: *metamelomai*** [verb: μεταμέλομαι <3338>]; **from *meta*: concerning, and *melō*: to be preoccupied ▶ Agonizing regret, with a sense of a guilty conscience** > Judas was filled with remorse {repented himself, changed his mind} after having delivered Jesus up, and he hanged himself (Matt. 27:3). All other refs.: MIND (noun) <3338>, REGRET <3338>, REPENT <3338>.

REMOTE – [1] Matt. 14:15; Mark 6:35; Luke 9:12 → DESERTED <2048> [2] Matt. 15:33; Mark 8:4 → remote place → WILDERNESS <2047>.

REMOTEST – Acts 1:8 → remotest part → PART <2078>.

REMOVAL – [1] ***apothesis*** [fem. noun: ἀπόθεσις <595>]; **from *apotithēmi*: to put away, which is from *apo*: away, and *tithēmi*: to put ▶ The fact of leaving something behind** > Baptism is not the removal {putting away} of the filth of the flesh, but the answer of a good conscience toward God (1 Pet. 3:21). Peter knew he had to put off {put aside} his tent, referring to his body, shortly (lit.: The removal {laying

aside} of his tent was to take place shortly) (2 Pet. 1:14). ¶
– 2 Col. 2:11 → PUTTING OFF <555> 3 Heb. 12:27 → REMOVING <3331>.

REMOVE – 1 ***ekballō*** [verb: ἐκβάλλω <1544>]; **from *ek*: out, and *ballō*: to throw ▶ To remove, to extract; also transl.: to cast out, to pull out, to take out** > We must remove first the beam out of our own eye before removing the mote out of the eye of our brother (Matt. 7:4, 5a, b; Luke 6:42a–c). All other refs.: see entries in Lexicon at <1544>.
2 ***kineō*** [verb: κινέω <2795>]; **from *kiō*: to go ▶ To displace, to take away, to translocate** > The Lord told Ephesus to repent or He would remove her lamp (Rev. 2:5). Every mountain and every island were removed {were moved out} from their places (Rev. 6:14). All other refs.: DISTURB <2795>, MOVE <2795>, SHAKE <2795>.
3 ***methistēmi*** [verb: μεθίστημι <3179>]; **from *meta*: denoting change, and *histēmi*: to place ▶ a. To move from one place to another** > If someone were to have all faith, so as to remove {to move} mountains, but were not to have love, he would be nothing (1 Cor. 13:2: *methistanō*). **b. To lose one's job, to dismiss from an office** > The unjust steward in a parable feared being removed from {put out of} his stewardship (Luke 16:4). God removed Saul and made David the king (Acts 13:22). All other refs.: TRANSFER <3179>, TURN (verb) <3179>.
– 4 Matt. 3:11 → rather: to carry, to bear → BEAR <941> 5 Matt. 17:20a, b → MOVE <3327> 6 Mark 2:4 → UNCOVER <648> 7 Mark 7:35 → LOOSE <3089> 8 Mark 14:36; Luke 22:42 → to take away → TAKE <3911> 9 Luke 10:7 → PASS <3327> 10 John 7:3 → DEPART <3327> 11 John 11:39, 41; Eph. 4:31 → TAKE <142> 12 Acts 7:4 → MOVE <3351> 13 Acts 7:16 → to carry back → CARRY <3346> 14 Acts 7:43 → TRANSPORT <3351> 15 Rom. 11:26 → to turn away → TURN (verb) <654> 16 1 Cor. 5:2, 13 → to take away → TAKE <1808> 17 2 Cor. 3:11, 13, 14 → to do away → AWAY <2673> 18 2 Cor. 3:14 → not removed → UNLIFTED <343> 19 2 Cor. 3:16 → to take away → TAKE <4014> 20 Gal. 1:6 → CHANGE (verb) <3346> 21 Gal. 5:11 → CEASE <2673> 22 Rev. 6:14 → RECEDE <673>.

REMOVING – ***metathesis*** [fem. noun: μετάθεσις <3331>]; **from *metatithēmi*: to transfer, which is from *meta*: prep. indicating a change, and *tithēmi*: to put ▶ Change, taking away** > The expr. "yet once more" (Hag. 2:6) signifies the removing {removal} of what is shaken (Heb. 12:27). Other refs.: Heb. 7:12; 11:5; see CHANGE <3331>, TRANSLATION <3331>. ¶

REMPHAN – See ROMPHA <4481>.

REND – 1 **to rend off: *perirēgnumi*** [verb: περιρήγνυμι <4048>]; **from *peri*: around, and *rēgnumi*: to break, to tear; also spelled: *perirrēgnumi* ▶ To separate into parts with force; to tear, to rip off** > The magistrates rent off {stripped} the clothes of Paul and Silas and commanded them to be beaten with rods (Acts 16:22). ¶
– 2 Matt. 7:6 → TEAR (verb) <4486> 3 Matt. 26:65; Mark 14:63; Acts 14:14 → TEAR (verb) <1284> 4 Matt. 27:51; Mark 15:38; Luke 5:36; 23:45; John 19:24 → TEAR (verb) <4977> 5 Mark 9:26 → CONVULSE <4682> 6 John 21:11 → BREAK <4977>.

RENDER – 1 ***apodidōmi*** [verb: ἀποδίδωμι <591>]; **from *apo*: from, and *didōmi*: to give ▶ To fulfill an obligation; also transl.: to pay** > One must render to the Lord what he has sworn (Matt. 5:33). In a parable, vine-growers were to render the fruits in theirs seasons to the owner of the vineyard (Matt. 21:41). Other refs.: see entries in Lexicon at <591>.
2 ***antapodidōmi*** [verb: ἀνταποδίδωμι <467>]; **from *anti*: in place of, and *apodidōmi*: see 1 ▶ a. To give in return; also transl.: to pay back, to repay, to recompense** > Paul asks who has first given to the Lord and it will be rendered to him (Rom. 11:35). The Lord will render

vengeance (Rom. 12:19). What thanks could Paul render {render again} {How could he thank God enough in return} for the Thessalonians (1 Thes. 3:9). God will render tribulation to those who have caused Christians to suffer tribulation (2 Thes. 1:6). God will render vengeance (Heb. 10:30). **b. To acquit, to pay back; also transl.: to perform, to fulfill >** The Israelites were to render to the Lord what they had sworn (Matt. 5:33). Other refs.: Luke 14:14a, b; see RECOMPENSE (verb) <467>. ¶

[3] ***kathistēmi*** [verb: καθίστημι <2525>]; **from *kata*: down (intens.), and *histēmi*: to stand ▶ To make, to cause to be >** Various qualities, such as godliness and brotherly love, will render the Christian neither useless nor unfruitful (2 Pet. 1:8); other transl.: will keep from being ineffective and unproductive. All other refs.: APPOINT <2525>, CONDUCT (verb)[2] <2525>, MAKE <2525>.

– [4] Matt. 6:4, 6, 18 → REWARD <591> [5] John 16:2 → OFFER <4374> [6] Rev. 18:6a, b → GIVE <591>.

RENEW – [1] ***anakainizō*** [verb: ἀνακαινίζω <340>]; **from *ana*: again, and *kainizō*: to renew, which is from *kainos*: new ▶ To make new >** The author of the Epistle to the Hebrews speaks about the impossibility of apostates being renewed again {being brought back} to repentance (Heb. 6:6). ¶

[2] ***anakainoō*** [verb: ἀνακαινόω <341>]; **from *ana*: again, and *kainoō*: to make new, which is from *kainos*: new ▶ To make new again >** The inward man is renewed day by day (2 Cor. 4:16). The new (*neos*) man is renewed into full knowledge (Col. 3:10). ¶

[3] ***ananeoō*** [verb: ἀνανεόω <365>]; **from *ana*: again, and *neoō*: to renew, which is from *neos*: new, young ▶ To become a new person day after day >** The Christian is renewed {is being made new} in the spirit of his mind (Eph. 4:23). ¶

– [4] Phil. 4:10 → REVIVE <330>.

RENEWAL – [1] Matt. 19:28 → renewal of all things → REGENERATION <3824> [2] Rom. 12:2; Titus 3:5 → RENEWING <342>.

RENEWING – ***anakainōsis*** [fem. noun: ἀνακαίνωσις <342>]; **from *anakainoō*: to make new, which is from *ana*: again, and *kainoō*: to make new, which is from *kainos*: new ▶ The act of making new >** The Christian is called to be transformed by the renewing of his mind (Rom. 12:2). He is saved through the renewing {renewal} of the Holy Spirit (Titus 3:5). ¶

RENOUNCE – [1] ***apeipon*** [verb: ἀπεῖπον <550>]; **from *apo*: from, and *eipon*: I said; lit.: to speak out against ▶ To refuse entirely, to reject with aversion >** Paul had renounced the things hidden because of shame (2 Cor. 4:2). ¶

– [2] Luke 14:33 → FORSAKE <657> [3] Titus 2:12 → DENY <720> [4] Rev. 2:13 → to not renounce → lit.: to hold fast → FAST (HOLD) <2902>.

RENT (noun) – [1] Matt. 9:16; Mark 2:21 → TEAR (noun)[2] <4978> [2] Luke 5:36 → to make a rent → TEAR (verb) <4977>.

RENT (verb) – Matt. 21:33, 41; Mark 12:1; Luke 20:9 → to rent out → LEASE <1554>.

RENTED – Acts 28:30 → rented quarters → rented house → HOUSE <3410>.

REPAY – [1] ***apotinō*** [verb: ἀποτίνω <661>]; **from *apo*: again, and *tinō*: to pay a price ▶ To reimburse, to compensate >** If Onesimus owed something to Philemon, Paul would repay it {pay it back} for him (Phm. 19). ¶

[2] ***diploō*** [verb: διπλόω <1363>]; **from *diplous*: double, which is from *dis*: twice, and suffix *plous* denoting fold ▶ To render twice the quantity >** The angel said to repay {double the, give back the} double to Babylon the great according to her works (Rev. 18:6). ¶

– [3] Matt. 18:25, 26, 28–30, 34; Luke 7:42 → PAY (verb) <591> [4] Luke 6:34b → to be repaid in full → lit.: to receive the like → RECEIVE <618> [5] Luke 14:12 →

RECOMPENSE (noun) <468> 6 Luke 14:14a, b → RECOMPENSE (verb) <467> 7 Rom. 2:6 → RENDER <591> 8 Rom. 11:35; 12:19; 2 Thes. 1:6; Heb. 10:30 → RENDER <467> 9 Col. 3:25 → to be repaid → RECEIVE <2865> 10 1 Tim. 5:4 → lit.: to make a return → RETURN (noun) <287> 11 Rev. 22:12 → GIVE <591>.

REPAYMENT – 1 Matt. 18:25 → to make repayment → to make payment → PAYMENT <591> 2 Luke 6:34a → lit.: to receive → RECEIVE <618> 3 Luke 14:12 → RECOMPENSE (noun) <468>.

REPEAT – Heb. 10:1 → OFFER <4374>.

REPEATEDLY – Heb. 9:25, 26 → OFTEN <4178>.

REPENT – 1 ***metamelomai*** [verb: μεταμέλομαι <3338>]; **from *meta*: denoting a change, and *melō*: to be preoccupied ► To regret, with a sense of a guilty conscience and dread of consequences; also transl.: to change one's mind, to feel remorse, to relent** > The son of a man repented because he had not wanted to go work in the vineyard of his father, and afterwards he went to do so (Matt. 21:29); the Jews did not repent to believe John the Baptist (v. 32). All other refs.: MIND (noun) <3338>, REGRET <3338>, REMORSE <3338>.
2 ***metanoeō*** [verb: μετανοέω <3340>]; **from *meta*: denoting change, and *noeō*: to perceive, to think, which is from *nous*: mind, understanding ► To change one's manner of thinking and acting, to be converted** > In most cases in the N.T., it is a matter of repentance of sin. Jesus commanded and spoke of repenting (Matt. 3:2; 4:17; 11:20, 21; 12:41; Mark 1:15; 6:12; Luke 10:13; 11:32; 13:3, 5; 15:7, 10; 16:30; 17:3, 4). Peter said to repent (Acts 2:38; 3:19; 8:22), as likewise did Paul (26:20). God commands all men to repent (Acts 17:30). Many at Corinth had not repented of sins that they had practiced (2 Cor. 12:21). Ephesus is enjoined to repent (Rev. 2:5), as well as Pergamos (2:16), Jezebel in relation to Thyatira (2:21) and those who commit adultery with her (2:22), Sardis (3:3), and Laodicea (3:19). Following future divine punishments, men will not repent of their sins (Rev. 9:20, 21; 16:9, 11). ¶
– 3 Luke 15:7; 2 Cor. 7:9; Heb. 12:17 → lit.: repentance → REPENTANCE <3341>.

REPENTANCE – 1 ***metanoia*** [fem. noun: μετάνοια <3341>]; **from *metanoeō*: to repent, which is from *meta*: denoting change, and *noeō*: to perceive, to think, which is from *nous*: mind, understanding; lit.: change of mind ► Change of heart and mind, turning toward a better way; deep regret for a past action or course of action** > Repentance is toward God (Acts 20:21); it leads the sinner to pass the same judgment as God regarding his state of sin and the faults he has committed. The sinner is then able to turn toward God and implore His grace, and God grants him salvation in Christ. It is the goodness of God that leads the sinner to repentance (Rom. 2:4). God is not willing that any should perish, but that all should come to repentance (2 Pet. 3:9). The Jews were baptized by John with water for repentance (Matt. 3:11; Mark 1:4; Luke 3:3; Acts 13:24), in view of receiving Christ (Acts 19:4); they were to manifest their repentance by producing suitable fruits (Matt. 3:8; Luke 3:8). God gave repentance unto life to Israel and the nations (Acts 5:31; 11:18; 26:20). Paul's first letter had grieved the Corinthians, producing in them the effects of repentance; they had judged their bad behavior (2 Cor. 7:9, 10). Other refs.: Matt. 9:13; Mark 2:17; Luke 5:32; 15:7; 24:47; 2 Tim. 2:25; Heb. 6:1, 6; 12:17 {change of mind}. ¶
– 2 Rom. 11:29 → not subject to repentance, without repentance → IRREVOCABLE <278>.

REPETITION – **to use vain repetitions, to use meaningless repetitions: *battalogeō*** [verb: βατταλογέω <945>]; **poss. from *Battos*: a king of Cyrene known as a stammerer, and *logos*: word; also spelled: *battologeō* ► To use many words, to repeat continually** > Jesus taught to not use vain repetitions {to not keep on babbling} when praying (Matt. 6:7). Other ref.: Luke 11:2 in some mss. ¶

REPHAN – See ROMPHA <4481>.

REPLY (noun) – [1] Luke 10:30 → in reply → lit.: to reply → REPLY (verb) <5274> [2] Luke 14:6 → to make a reply → ANSWER (verb) <470> [3] Acts 4:14 → to say in reply → REPLY (verb) <471> [4] Rom. 11:4 → God's reply → lit.: divine answer → ANSWER (noun) <5538>.

REPLY (verb) – [1] **to reply against:** ***antapokrinomai*** [verb: ἀνταποκρίνομαι <470>]; **from *anti*: against, and *apokrinomai*: to reply, which is from *apo*: from, and *krinō*: to judge, to discern ▶ To contest, to argue** > Paul asks a man who he is to reply against {to answer again to, to answer back to, to talk back to} God (Rom. 9:20). Other ref.: Luke 14:6; see ANSWER (verb) <470>. ¶
[2] ***antepō*** [verb: ἀντέπω <471>]; **from *anti*: against, and *epō*: to speak, to say ▶ To contradict, to oppose, to refute; also transl.: to gainsay, to contradict** > Jesus told His disciples that their adversaries would not be able to reply to their wisdom (Luke 21:15). Beholding the man who had been healed, the Jews had nothing to reply {say, say against, say in reply} (Acts 4:14). ¶
[3] ***hupolambanō*** [verb: ὑπολαμβάνω <5274>]; **from *hupo*: below, and *lambanō*: to take, to receive ▶ To resume, to continue the conversation** > Jesus replied {answered, said} by a parable to a lawyer who wanted to know who was his neighbor (Luke 10:30). All other refs.: RECEIVE <5274>, SUPPOSE <5274>.
– [4] Matt. 2:5; Acts 21:39 → SPEAK <2036> [5] Matt. 16:16; 19:27; 20:13; John 7:46; 16:31; Acts 15:13; 25:4 → ANSWER (verb) <611> [6] John 4:21; 11:27 → SAY <3004>.

REPORT (noun) – [1] ***akoē*** [fem. noun: ἀκοή <189>]; **from *akouō*: to hear, to understand ▶ What is heard, what is understood** > Isaiah asks who has believed his report {message} (John 12:38; Rom. 10:16). The Thessalonians had received the word of the report that is of God by Paul (1 Thes. 2:13). All other refs.: EAR <189>, FAME <189>, HEARING <189>, RUMOR <189>.
[2] **bad report, evil report: *dusphēmia*** [fem. noun: δυσφημία <1426>]; **from *dus*: with difficulty, and *phēmē*: fame, news ▶ Bad reputation, evil speaking** > Paul uses this word in regard to himself in 2 Cor. 6:8. ¶
[3] **good report: *euphēmia*** [fem. noun: εὐφημία <2162>]; **from *euphēmos*: see [4] ▶ That which is favorable to say, good reputation** > Paul uses this word in regard to himself in 2 Cor. 6:8. ¶
[4] **of good report: *euphēmos*** [adj.: εὔφημος <2163>]; **from *eu*: well, and *phēmē*: fame, news ▶ Favorable, of good reputation** > Paul mentions things of good report {of good repute, admirable} in Phil. 4:8. ¶
[5] ***ēchos*** [masc. noun: ἦχος <2279>]; **lit.: sound, noise ▶ That which is heard regarding someone; also transl.: fame, news, rumour** > The report regarding Jesus went out into every place of Galilee (Luke 4:37). Other refs.: Acts 2:2; Heb. 12:19; see SOUND (noun) <2279>. ¶
[6] ***logos*** [masc. noun: λόγος <3056>]; **from *legō*: to speak ▶ That which is said, word** > The report {fame, news} concerning Jesus was spread abroad still more (Luke 5:15). Other refs.: WORD <3056>.
– [7] Matt. 9:26 → FAME <5345> [8] Mark 5:27 → to hear the report about → lit.: to hear about → HEAR <191> [9] Luke 4:14 → NEWS <5345> [10] Luke 7:17 → RUMOR <3056> [11] Acts 11:22 → TIDINGS <3056> [12] Acts 21:24 → in these reports → lit.: in these things of which they have been informed → INFORM <2727> [13] Acts 21:31 → TIDINGS <5334> [14] 1 Tim. 3:7 → WITNESS (noun)[1] <3141>.

REPORT (verb) – [1] ***anangellō*** [verb: ἀναγγέλλω <312>]; **from *ana*: upon (intens.), and *angellō*: to bring news, a message ▶ To announce, to communicate, to proclaim** > The news was reported {told} in the city and in the country concerning the herd of swine (Mark 5:14). The officers reported {told} the words of Paul to the magistrates (Acts 16:38). An unbeliever who is convicted by all may report {exclaim} that God is indeed among gathered Christians (1 Cor. 14:25). The things ministered by the prophets were now reported {had now been told} to the Christians scattered throughout various places (1 Pet. 1:12). All other refs.: see entries in Lexicon at <312>.

[2] ***apangellō*** [verb: ἀπαγγέλλω <518>]; **from *apo*: from (intens.), and *angellō*: see [1] ► To announce, to declare, to tell; also transl.: to show, to bring word, to bring back word, to exclaim, to relate, to say** > Herod wanted the wise men to report {bring word, bring back word} as soon as they found the child Jesus (Matt. 2:8). This verb is used concerning Jesus (Matt. 11:4; Luke 7:22), Peter (Acts 12:17), Paul (Acts 23:17; 1 Cor. 14:25), the chiliarch (Acts 23:19), those who were the leaders of the Jews (Acts 28:21). It is used also in regard to the disciples (Matt. 14:12; Luke 9:36; Acts 4:23), the disciples of John (Luke 7:18), Jews (Luke 8:20; 18:37), bondmen (Luke 14:21; John 4:51), women at the tomb of Jesus (Luke 24:9), Mary of Magdala (John 20:18; some mss. have *angellō*), guards (Matt. 28:11), officers (Acts 5:22), a man (Acts 5:25), Rhoda (Acts 12:14), the jailer (Acts 16:36), a centurion (Acts 22:26), and Paul's nephew (Acts 23:16). All other refs.: DECLARE <518>, RELATE <518>, SHOW (verb) <518>, TELL <518>.

[3] **to report slanderously: *blasphēmeō*** [verb: βλασφημέω <987>]; **from *blasphēmos*: blasphemer; which is poss. from *blaptō*: to harm, and *phēmē*: reputation ► To speak evil against someone, to make false accusations** > Paul was slanderously reported {injuriously charged} as saying to do evil that good may come (Rom. 3:8). All other refs.: see entries in Lexicon at <987>.

[4] ***mēnuō*** [verb: μηνύω <3377>] **► To declare, to say** > Anyone who knew where Jesus was had to report it {he should shew it, he should make it known}, that He might be seized (John 11:57). Other refs.: Luke 20:37; Acts 23:30; 1 Cor. 10:28; see SHOW (verb) <3377>. ¶

– [5] Matt. 18:31 → TELL <1285> [6] Matt. 28:15 → to be commonly reported → to be widely spread → SPREAD <1310> [7] Mark 2:1; 1 Cor. 5:1 → HEAR <191> [8] Luke 9:10 → RELATE <1334> [9] Luke 16:1 → ACCUSE <1225> [10] Acts 21:19 → RELATE <1834> [11] Acts 23:22 → REVEAL <1718> [12] Rom. 1:8 → PROCLAIM <2605> [13] 1 Cor. 1:11 → DECLARE <1213> [14] 1 Thes. 3:6 → "reported" added in Engl.

REPORTS – Matt. 14:1 → FAME <189>.

REPOSE (noun) – [1] Acts 7:49 → REST (noun)[1] <2663> [2] 2 Thes. 1:7 → REST (noun)[1] <425>.

REPOSE (verb) – Luke 12:19 → REST (verb) <373>.

REPRESENT – Acts 23:22 → REVEAL <1718>.

REPRESENTATION – [1] Acts 21:31 → TIDINGS <5334> [2] Acts 23:15 → to make a representation → SIGNIFY <1718> [3] Heb. 1:3 → exact representation → EXPRESSION <5481> [4] Heb. 8:5; 9:23 → COPY <5262>.

REPRESENTATIVE – 2 Cor. 8:23 → he who is sent → SENT <652>.

REPRIMAND – Luke 3:19 → REPROVE <1651>.

REPROACH (noun) – [1] ***loidoria*** [fem. noun: λοιδορία <3059>]; **from *loidoreō*: to revile, to reproach, which is from *loidoros*: reviler, one who insults ► Insult, railing** > Young widows are to give no occasion to the adversary for reproach {slander} (1 Tim. 5:14). Other refs.: 1 Pet. 3:9a, b; see REVILING <3059>. ¶

[2] ***oneidismos*** [masc. noun: ὀνειδισμός <3680>]; **from *oneidizō*: see [4] ► a. Defamation, reviling, insult** > As David wrote prophetically, the reproaches of those who reproached God fell upon Christ (Rom. 15:3; see Ps. 69:9). **b. Blame, disgrace** >

The overseer must have a good testimony from those without that he may not fall into reproach (1 Tim. 3:7). Believers in the Lord were made a spectacle by reproaches {insult} and afflictions (Heb. 10:33). Moses esteemed the reproach of Christ greater riches than the treasures of Egypt (Heb. 11:26). Christians are called to go forth to Jesus outside the camp, bearing His reproach (Heb. 13:13). ¶

3 ***oneidos*** [neut. noun: ὄνειδος <3681>] ▶ **Humiliation, disgrace** > The Lord took away the reproach of Elizabeth when He enabled her to conceive (Luke 1:25). ¶

4 **to suffer reproach: *oneidizō*** [verb: ὀνειδίζω <3679>]; **from *oneidos*: see 3 ▶ To be in disgrace, to be the object of criticism** > If we labor and suffer reproach {strive}, it is because we hope in a living God (1 Tim. 4:10); other mss. have *agōnizomai*: to fight, to struggle. All other refs.: INSULT (verb) <3679>, REPROACH (verb) <3679>, REVILE <3679>.

5 **above reproach, beyond reproach: *anenklētos*** [adj.: ἀνέγκλητος <410>]; **from *a*: neg., and *enkaleō*: to accuse, which is from *en*: in, and *kaleō*: to call ▶ Which cannot be blamed, with which one cannot find fault** > Christians are presented above reproach {free from accusation, irreproachable, unreproveable} before God (Col. 1:22). All other refs.: BLAMELESS <410>.

6 **above reproach: *anepilēmptos*** [adj.: ἀνεπίλημπτος <423>]; **from *a*: neg., and *epilambanō*: to catch, to seize, which is from *epi*: upon, and *lambanō*: to take ▶ Which one cannot blame, irreprehensible; also transl.: blameless, irreproachable, not open to blame** > The overseer must be above reproach (1 Tim. 3:2), as likewise widows (5:7). Timothy was to keep the commandment without reproach (1 Tim. 6:14). ¶

– 7 2 Cor. 11:21 → DISHONOR (noun) <819> 8 2 Cor. 12:10 → INSULT (noun) <5196> 9 Phil. 2:15 → above reproach → IRREPROACHABLE <298> 10 Titus 2:8 → beyond reproach → that cannot be condemned → CONDEMN <176>.

REPROACH (verb) – 1 ***oneidizō*** [verb: ὀνειδίζω <3679>]; **from *oneidos*: reproach ▶ To blame, to impute a fault; also transl.: to denounce, to rebuke, to upbraid** > Jesus began to reproach the cities in which He had performed most of His miracles (Matt. 11:20). After His resurrection, He reproached the eleven disciples with their unbelief and hardness of heart (Mark 16:14). As David wrote prophetically, the reproaches of those who reproached God fell upon Christ (Rom. 15:3; see Ps. 69:9). God gives to all freely and reproaches not those who ask Him for wisdom (Jas. 1:5 {without finding fault, without reproach}). All other refs.: INSULT (verb) <3679>, REPROACH (noun) <3679>, REVILE <3679>.

– 2 Luke 11:45 → INSULT (verb) <5195>.

REPROACHFULLY – 1 Tim. 5:14 → to speak reproachfully → lit.: for reproach → REPROACH (noun) <3059>.

REPROBATE – Rom. 1:28; 2 Cor. 13:5–7; 2 Tim. 3:8; Titus 1:16 → WORTHLESS <96>.

REPROOF – 1 ***elenchos*** [masc. noun: ἔλεγχος <1650>]; **from *elenchō*: to convict; lit.: conviction ▶ Refutation, proof** > All Scripture is given for reproof {rebuking} (2 Tim. 3:16); other mss.: *elegmos*: reproving. Other ref.: Heb. 11:1; see EVIDENCE <1650>. ¶

– 2 2 Pet. 2:16 → to have reproof → REBUKE (verb) <2192>.

REPROVE – ***elenchō*** [verb: ἐλέγχω <1651>] ▶ **To convince of error, to reprimand; also transl.: to expose, to rebuke** > Jesus said to reprove {to tell the fault to, to show the fault to} our brother who sins (Matt. 18:15). Herod was reproved by John the Baptist (Luke 3:19). He who does evil fears that his works may be reproved {shown to be as they are} (John 3:20). Christians are to reprove the works of darkness (Eph. 5:11); all things have their true character reproved by the light (v. 13). Paul exhorts Titus to reprove (Titus 1:13; 2:15). The

Christian is not to faint when he is reproved by the Lord (Heb. 12:5). The Lord reproves and disciplines all those He loves (Rev. 3:19). All other refs.: CONVINCE <1651>, REFUTE <1651>.

REPTILE – ***herpeton*** [neut. noun: ἑρπετόν <2062>]; **from *herpō*: to move slowly, to creep ▶ Animal which crawls, dragging itself along on its belly; also transl.: creeping thing, crawling creature** > In a trance, Peter saw a great sheet descending in which there were reptiles (Acts 10:12; 11:6). Men have changed the glory of God into the likeness of reptiles (Rom. 1:23). Every species of reptiles {serpents} is tamed (Jas. 3:7), but not the tongue (see v. 8). ¶

REPUDIATE – Acts 7:39 → REJECT <683>.

REPUTABLY – 1 Thes. 4:12 → PROPERLY <2156>.

REPUTATION – [1] **to be of reputation, to be of high reputation: *dokeō*** [verb: δοκέω <1380>]; **lit.: to think, to appear ▶ To be considered, to be respected; also transl.: to be conspicuous, to be influential** > Paul had communicated the gospel, which he preached among the Gentiles to those who were of reputation {who seemed to be leaders} in Jerusalem (Gal. 2:2). In Gal. 2:6a, b, the verb is used as a noun and is transl. "those who were of high reputation," "those who seemed to be something," "those who seemed to be somewhat," "those who seemed important," and "those who were conspicuous." James, Cephas, and John had the reputation {seemed, were reputed} to be pillars in the church of Jerusalem (Gal. 2:9). All other refs.: CONSIDER <1380>, REGARD (verb) <1380>, SEEM <1380>, SUPPOSE <1380>, THINK <1380>.

[2] **to make oneself of no reputation: *kenoō*** [verb: κενόω <2758>]; **from *kenos*: empty, void ▶ To empty, to reduce to nothing, to make of no effect** > Christ Jesus made Himself of no reputation {emptied Himself, made Himself nothing} by taking the form of a servant, He who was in the form of God (Phil. 2:7). All other refs.: VAIN <2758>, VOID <2758>.

– [3] Phil. 2:29 → in reputation → in honor → HONOR (noun) <1784>.

REPUTE (noun) – [1] Acts 6:3 → of good repute → lit.: being witnessed to → WITNESS (verb) <3140> [2] Phil. 4:8 → of good repute → of good report → REPORT (noun) <2163>.

REPUTE (verb) – Gal. 6:3 → THINK <1380>.

REPUTED – Gal. 2:9 → to be reputed → to be of reputation → REPUTATION <1380>.

REQUEST (noun) – [1] ***aitēma*** [neut. noun: αἴτημα <155>]; **from *aiteō*: to ask ▶ Petition, the act or instance of asking for something** > The Christian lets his requests be made known to God by prayer and supplication with thanksgiving (Phil. 4:6). Other refs.: 1 John 5:15; Luke 23:24; see PETITION (noun) <155>, REQUEST (verb) <155>. ¶

[2] **to make request: *deomai*** [verb: δέομαι <1189>]; **middle voice of *deō*: to lack, to need something ▶ To ask, to implore** > Paul was making request {beseeching, praying} that he would find a way by the will of God to come to the believers in Rome (Rom. 1:10). All other refs.: IMPLORE <1189>, PRAY <1189>, SUPPLICATE <1189>.

– [3] Luke 4:38; 7:36; John 12:21; Acts 23:20 → to make a request, with a request → ASK <2065> [4] Eph. 6:18a; 1 Tim. 2:1 → SUPPLICATION <1162>.

REQUEST (verb) – [1] **request: *aitēma*** [neut. noun: αἴτημα <155>]; **from *aiteō*: to request ▶ Petition, demand** > Pilate decided that it should be as the Jews requested {as they required, what they begged} (lit.: their request) (Luke 23:24), i.e., to crucify Jesus. Other refs.: 1 John 5:15; Phil. 4:6; see PETITION (noun) <155>, REQUEST (noun) <155>. ¶

– [2] Mark 15:6; Luke 23:25; 1 Cor. 1:22 → ASK <154> [3] Acts 24:4 → BESEECH <3870> [4] Acts 28:20 → CALL (verb) <3870> [5] 1 Thes. 4:1; 5:12; 2 Thes. 2:1 → ASK <2065>.

REQUIRE – [1] ***aiteō*** [verb: αἰτέω <154>] ▶ **To ask, to insist** > A judgment against Paul was required {desired} (Acts 25:15). All other refs.: ASK <154>.
[2] ***zēteō*** [verb: ζητέω <2212>] ▶ **To demand, to look for** > Much will be required {demanded} from everyone to whom much has been given (Luke 12:48). It is required in stewards that a man be found faithful (1 Cor. 4:2). All other refs.: INQUIRE <2212>, SEEK <2212>.
[3] ***ekzēteō*** [verb: ἐκζητέω <1567>]; **from *ek*: out (intens.), and *zēteō*: see [2] ▶ To demand insistently, to exact; also transl.: to charge, to hold responsible** > The verb is used in regard to the blood of the prophets, which will be required of the generation of the Lord's time (Luke 11:50, 51). Other refs.: Acts 15:17; Rom. 3:11; Heb. 11:6; 12:17; 1 Pet. 1:10; see SEEK <1567>. ¶
– [4] Luke 3:13 → ORDAIN <1299> [5] Luke 12:20 → DEMAND (verb) <523> [6] Luke 19:23 → COLLECT <4238> [7] Luke 23:24 → REQUEST (verb) <155> [8] Acts 15:5 → COMMAND (verb) <3853> [9] Rom. 3:27a, b; 1 Tim. 4:3 → added in Engl. [10] 1 Cor. 12:24 → do not require → have no need → NEED (noun) <5532>.

REQUIRED (BE) – Phm. 8 → FITTING (BE) <433>.

REQUIREMENT – [1] **requirement, just requirement, righteous requirement: *dikaiōma*** [neut. noun: δικαίωμα <1345>]; **from *dikaioō*: to justify, which is from *dikaios*: just ▶ Ordinance, prescription; also transl.: righteousness** > Paul spoke of the uncircumcision that keeps the requirements of the law (Rom. 2:26). God condemned sin in the flesh, in order that the righteous requirement of the law should be fulfilled in us (Rom. 8:4). All other refs.: JUSTIFICATION <1345>, ORDINANCE <1345>, RIGHTEOUS <1345>.
– [2] Acts 15:28 → NECESSARY <1876> [3] Acts 17:7 → ORDINANCE <1378>.

REQUITE – 1 Tim. 5:4 → lit.: to make a return → RETURN (noun) <287>.

RESA – See RHESA <4488>.

RESCUE – [1] Matt. 27:43; Luke 1:74; Rom. 7:24; 15:31; Col. 1:13; 1 Thes. 1:10; 2 Tim. 3:11; 4:18; 2 Pet. 2:7, 9 → DELIVER <4506> [2] Acts 7:10; 12:11; 23:27 → DELIVER <1807> [3] Acts 7:25 → lit.: to give salvation → SALVATION <4991> [4] Acts 26:17; Gal. 1:4 → to take out → TAKE <1807>.

RESEMBLE – [1] Luke 13:18 → LIKEN <3666> [2] Rom. 1:23 → images resembling → lit.: likeness of an image → LIKENESS <3667> [3] Rom. 9:29 → to be like → LIKE (adj., adv., noun) <3666> [4] Heb. 7:3 → to make like → LIKE (adj., adv., noun) <871>.

RESENTFUL – 2 Tim. 2:24 → not resentful → FORBEARING <420>.

RESENTFUL (BE) – 1 Cor. 13:5 → lit.: to impute evil → IMPUTE <3049>, EVIL <2556>.

RESERVE – [1] ***thēsaurizō*** [verb: θησαυρίζω <2343>]; **from *thēsauros*: treasure ▶ To set aside, to keep in store** > The present heavens and the earth are reserved {are kept} for fire by the word of God (2 Pet. 3:7). All other refs.: HEAP <2343>, LAY <2343>, STORE (verb) <2343>, TREASURE (verb) <2343>.
[2] ***kataleipō*** [verb: καταλείπω <2641>]; **from *kata*: intens., and *leipō*: to leave behind ▶ To preserve, to set aside** > God had told Elijah that He had reserved for {kept for, left to, reserved to} Himself seven thousand men who had not bowed the knee to Baal (Rom. 11:4). All other refs.: LEAVE (verb) <2641>.
[3] ***tēreō*** [verb: τηρέω <5083>]; **from *tēros*: warden, guard ▶ To guard; also transl.: to keep, to keep in custody, to hold, to hold over** > Paul had asked to be kept for

the decision of Augustus (Acts 25:21). The Lord knows how to reserve the unjust for the day of judgment (2 Pet. 2:9), to whom the gloom of darkness is reserved forever (2 Pet. 2:17; Jude 13). The Lord has reserved in eternal chains the angels who did not keep their own original state (Jude 6a, b). All other refs.: see entries in Lexicon at <5083>.

RESIDE – [1] 1 Pet. 1:1 → one who resides as alien → STRANGER <3927> [2] 1 John 3:15 → REMAIN <3306>.

RESIDENT – [1] Acts 2:9; 9:35; 19:10, 17 → lit.: one who resides → DWELL <2730> [2] Acts 21:12 → local resident → he who is from that place → PLACE (noun) <1786>.

RESIDUE – Acts 15:17 → REMNANT <2645>.

RESIST – [1] ***anthistēmi*** [verb: ἀνθίστημι <436>]; **from *anti*: against, and *histēmi*: to stand ▶ To not yield, to stand firm against; also transl.: to oppose, to withstand** > Jesus says not to resist the evil that anyone may inflict on us (Matt. 5:39). Opposers of believers in the Lord would not be able to reply or resist {resist or refuse, resist or contradict} the words (lit.: mouth) and wisdom that Jesus would give them (Luke 21:15). The Jews were not able to resist {to cope with, to stand up against} the wisdom of Stephen (Acts 6:10). Elymas opposed Barnabas and Saul (Acts 13:8). The verb is used in regard to resisting the will of God (Rom. 9:19) and the authority as the ordinance of God (13:2b, c {to rebel}). Paul withstood (or: resisted) Peter to his face (Gal. 2:11). The whole armor of God enables Christians to resist the artifices of the devil (Eph. 6:13 {to stand one's ground}; see v. 11). As Jannes and Jambres resisted Moses, so do others resist the truth (2 Tim. 3:8a, b). Christians are to resist the devil (1 Pet. 5:9); when they resist him, he will flee from them (Jas. 4:7). Other refs.: 2 Tim. 4:15; see WITHSTAND <436>. ¶

[2] ***antikathistēmi*** [verb: ἀντικαθίστημι <478>]; **from *anti*: against, and *kathistēmi*: to place, which is from *kata*: down, and *histēmi*: to stand ▶ To oppose, to stand firm against** > The Hebrews had not resisted to bloodshed in struggling against sin (Heb. 12:4). ¶

[3] ***antipiptō*** [verb: ἀντιπίπτω <496>]; **from *anti*: against, and *piptō*: to fall ▶ To oppose, to fight against** > Stephen reproached the Jews for always resisting the Holy Spirit (Acts 7:51). ¶

[4] ***antitassō*** [verb: ἀντιτάσσω <498>]; **from *anti*: against, and *tassō*: to arrange ▶ To oppose, to rise up against** > He who resists {sets himself in opposition to, rebels against} (*antitassō*) human authority resists (*anthistēmi*) the ordinance of God, and those who resist (*anthistēmi*) will bring a sentence of guilt upon themselves (Rom. 13:2a). God resists the proud (Jas. 4:6; 1 Pet. 5:5). Christians are still in this world, which is animated by the spirit which condemned and put Jesus to death; the righteous does not resist this evil spirit (Jas. 5:6). Other ref.: Acts 18:6; see OPPOSE <498>. ¶

RESOLUTELY – Luke 9:51 → to set resolutely → to set steadfastly → STEADFASTLY <4741>.

RESOLUTION – Acts 20:3 → opinion → PURPOSE (verb) <1106>.

RESOLVE (noun) – 2 Thes. 1:11 → resolve for good → good pleasure → PLEASURE <2107>.

RESOLVE (verb) – [1] ***bouleuō*** [verb: βουλεύω <1011>]; **from *boulē*: will ▶ To determine, to have the intention; also transl.: to be minded, to decide, to plan** > The crew on the ship that Paul had boarded had resolved to run the ship ashore (Acts 27:39). All other refs.: CONSIDER <1011>, CONSULT <1011>, PROPOSE <1011>.

– [2] Matt. 1:19 → PURPOSE (verb) <1014> [3] Luke 16:4 → KNOW <1097> [4] Acts 19:21 → PURPOSE (verb) <5087>.

RESORT – [1] Mark 14:53; Acts 16:13 → to come together → COME <4905> [2] John 18:2 → GATHER <4863>.

RESOUNDING – 1 Cor. 13:1 → sounding → SOUND (verb) <2278>.

RESPECT (noun) – 1 **in respect of: *en*** [prep.: ἐν <1722>] ▶ **About, concerning** > No one was to judge the Colossians in respect of {in regard of} various things (Col. 2:16). Other refs.: AMONG <1722>.

2 See RESPECT OF PERSONS.

– 3 Matt. 21:37; Mark 12:6; Heb. 12:9 → to have respect, to pay respect → RESPECT (verb) <1788> 4 Matt. 23:7; Mark 12:38; Luke 20:46 → to be greeted with respect → lit.: respectful greetings → GREETING <783> 5 Acts 5:34 → held in respect → HONORED <5093> 6 Acts 23:6; 24:21 → with respect → CONCERNING <4012> 7 Acts 25:13 → to pay respects → GREET <782> 8 Acts 28:10; 1 Tim. 6:1; 1 Pet. 3:7 → HONOR (noun) <5092> 9 Acts 28:22 → to have the (same) respect → THINK <5426> 10 Rom. 3:2 → MANNER <5158> 11 Rom. 12:16 → to have the same respect → lit.: to be of the same mind → MIND (noun) <5426> 12 Rom. 13:7a, b; 1 Pet. 2:18; 3:15 → FEAR (noun) <5401> 13 Col. 2:16 → in respect → in regard → REGARD (noun) <1722> <3313> 14 1 Thes. 4:12 → with the respect of → PROPERLY <2156> 15 1 Tim. 3:4; Titus 2:7 → GRAVITY <4587> 16 1 Tim. 3:8, 11; Titus 2:2 → worthy of respect → GRAVE <4586> 17 1 Tim. 6:2 → to show less respect → DESPISE <2706> 18 Heb. 11:26 → to have respect → LOOK (verb) <578> 19 Jas. 2:3 → to have respect → to look upon → LOOK (verb) <1914>.

RESPECT (verb) – 1 ***entrepō*** [verb: ἐντρέπω <1788>]; ***en*: toward, and *trepō*: to turn ▶ To consider with honor, to have regard for; also transl.: to care, to regard, to have respect, to pay respect, to reverence, to give reverence** > In one parable, the lord of the vineyard believed that the husbandmen might respect his son (Matt. 21:37; Mark 12:6; Luke 20:13). In another parable, a judge did not respect men (Luke 18:2, 4). We have respected our human fathers who disciplined us (Heb. 12:9). All other refs.: SHAME (verb) <1788>.

2 ***phobeō*** [verb: φοβέω <5399>]; **from *phobos*: fear ▶ To show consideration, esteem and honor** > The wife should respect {fear, reverence} her husband (Eph. 5:33). All other refs.: AFRAID <5399>.

– 3 Rom. 12:17 → to respect what is right → to provide things honest → PROVIDE <4306>.

RESPECT OF PERSONS – 1 ***prosōpolē(m)psia*** [fem. noun: προσωπολη(μ)ψία <4382>]; **from *prosōpon*: face, person, and *lambanō*: to take ▶ Favoritism, preference; also transl.: acceptance of persons, partiality** > With God, there is no respect of persons (Rom. 2:11; Eph. 6:9; Col. 3:25). As believers in the Lord Jesus, we should not show favoritism {personal favoritism} (Jas. 2:1). ¶

2 **to have respect of persons: *prosōpolē(m)pteō*** [verb: προσωπολη(μ)πτέω <4380>]; **from *prosōpon*: face, person, and *lambanō*: to take ▶ To act toward individuals with favoritism, not treating them equally** > If we have respect of persons {show partiality, show favoritism}, we sin (Jas. 2:9). ¶

3 **respecter of persons: *prosōpolē(m)ptēs*** [masc. noun: προσωπολή(μ)πτης <4381>]; **from *prosōpon*: face, person, and *lambanō*: to take ▶ Who acts with preference; who favors a person, sometimes to the prejudice of another one** > God is no respecter of persons {shows no partiality, does not show favoritism} (Acts 10:34). ¶

4 **without respect of persons: *aprosōpolē(m)ptōs*** [adv.: ἀπροσωπολή(μ)πτως <678>]; **from *a*: neg., *prosōpon*: face, person, and *lambanō*: to take ▶ Without favoritism, treating everyone equally, impartially** > God the Father judges each man's work without respect of persons {impartially, without partiality, without regard of persons} (1 Pet. 1:17). ¶

RESPECTABLE – ***kosmios*** [adj.: κόσμιος <2887>]; **from *kosmos*: order, harmonious arrangement ▶ Of good conduct, orderly** > The overseer must be respectable {decorous, of good behavior} (1 Tim. 3:2). Other ref.: 1 Tim. 2:9 (modest apparel); see APPAREL <2689> <2887>. ¶

RESPECTED – [1] Mark 15:43 → HONORABLE <2158> [2] Acts 5:34 → HONORED <5093>.

RESPECTER OF PERSONS – Acts 10:34 → RESPECT OF PERSONS <4381>.

RESPECTFUL – 1 Pet. 3:2 → FEAR (noun) <5401>.

RESPITE – Rev. 14:11 → REST (noun)[1] <372>.

RESPOND – [1] Luke 14:3; John 2:18; 3:3 → ANSWER (verb) <611> [2] Acts 16:14 → to give heed → HEED (noun) <4337>.

RESPONSE – [1] Rom. 11:4 → divine response → divine answer → ANSWER (noun) <5538> [2] Gal. 1:16 → "response" added in Engl. [3] 1 Pet. 3:21 → ANSWER (noun) <1906>.

RESPONSIBILITY – [1] Matt. 27:4, 24 → it is your responsibility → lit.: you see to it → SEE <3708> [2] Acts 6:3 → BUSINESS <5532> [3] Acts 6:3 → to turn the responsibility to → APPOINT <2525>.

RESPONSIBLE – Luke 11:50, 51 → to hold responsible → REQUIRE <1567>.

REST (noun)[1] – [1] ***anapausis*** [fem. noun: ἀνάπαυσις <372>]; **from *anapauō*: see [2] ▶ Cessation of all activity in order to refresh oneself >** With Jesus we find rest for our souls (Matt. 11:29). Jesus speaks of an unclean spirit seeking rest (Matt. 12:43; Luke 11:24). They will have no rest {respite} who will do homage to the beast and its image (Rev. 14:11). Other ref.: Rev. 4:8 (rest); see REST (verb) <372>. ¶

[2] **to give rest: *anapauō*** [verb: ἀναπαύω <373>]; **from *ana*: again, and *pauō*: to cease ▶ To cease all activity and refresh oneself >** Jesus gives rest to those who come to Him, who are weary and burdened (Matt. 11:28). All other refs.: REFRESH <373>, REST (verb) <373>.

[3] ***anesis*** [fem. noun: ἄνεσις <425>]; **from *aniēmi*: to undo, to loose, which is from *ana*: back, and *hiēmi*: to send ▶ Ease, liberty (e.g., from suffering and endurance) >** Paul had no rest for his spirit {no peace of mind}, because he had not found Titus (2 Cor. 2:13); when he came into Macedonia, his flesh had no rest, but he was afflicted in every way (7:5). God will give rest {relief, repose} to Christians at the revelation of the Lord Jesus from heaven (2 Thes. 1:7). All other refs.: EASE <425>, LIBERTY <425>.

[4] ***katapausis*** [fem. noun: κατάπαυσις <2663>]; **from *katapauō*: see [5] ▶ Act of stopping, of refraining from activities >** The word is used in regard to God: the place of His rest {place of His repose, His resting place} (Acts 7:49), and entrance into His rest (Heb. 3:11, 18; 4:1, 3, 5, 11). It is also used in regard to both God and man (Heb. 4:10). ¶

[5] **to give rest, to bring into rest: *katapauō*** [verb: καταπαύω <2664>]; **from *kata*: intens., and *pauō*: to cease ▶ To stop, to refrain from activities >** If Joshua had brought Israel into rest, God would not have spoken about another day (Heb. 4:8). All other refs.: REST (verb) <2664>, RESTRAIN <2664>.

[6] **rest, taking rest: *koimēsis*** [fem. noun: κοίμησις <2838>]; **from *koimaō*: to sleep, to die ▶ Repose, doziness >** The disciples thought that Jesus spoke of the rest of sleep {taking rest in sleep, of literal sleep, of natural sleep} when He spoke about Lazarus (John 11:13). ¶

– [7] Acts 9:31 → PEACE <1515> [8] Heb. 4:9 → SABBATH REST <4520> [9] 1 John 3:19 → to set at rest → ASSURE <3982>.

REST (noun)[2] – [1] ***loipos*** [adj. used as noun: λοιπός <3062>]; **from *leipō*: to leave ▶ Another thing, another person; what remains >** Jesus asked His disciples why they were careful about the rest {other matters} (Luke 12:26). Some made nothing of all the rest of men {of others} (Luke 18:9); the Pharisee in a parable said he was not like the rest of {other} men (v. 11). The rest of those who had been shipwrecked when sailing with Paul got to land on boards and other debris (Acts 27:44). The Christian should no longer walk as the rest {other} of the nations (Eph. 4:17). In a future day, the rest {remnant} will be slain with the sword of Him who will sit upon the horse (Rev. 19:21); the rest of the dead will not live until the end of the millennium (20:5). *

2 **for the rest: *loipon*** [adj. used as an adv.: λοιπόν <3063>]; **from *leipō*: to leave ▶ As for that which has not been mentioned, finally** > Paul uses this word repeatedly: 1 Cor. 1:16; 4:2 {further}; 7:29; 2 Cor. 13:11; Eph. 6:10; Phil. 3:1; 4:8; 1 Thes. 4:1; 2 Thes. 3:1. All other refs.: FINALLY <3063>, NOW <3063>.

3 ***epiloipos*** [adj. used as noun: ἐπίλοιπος <1954>]; **from *epi*: upon, and *loipos*: remaining, which is from *leipō*: to leave ▶ Which is still available** > The Christian should no longer live the rest of his time for lusts (1 Pet. 4:2). ¶

4 **that remained: *perisseuma*** [neut. noun: περίσσευμα <4051>]; **from *perisseuō*: to abound, which is from *perissos*: abundant, which is from *peri*: above, beyond ▶ Surplus, what is left over** > The disciples took up fragments that remained (lit.: over and above of fragments) of the multiplication of loaves (Mark 8:8). Other refs.: Matt. 12:34; Luke 6:45; 2 Cor. 8:14a, b; see ABUNDANCE <4051>. ¶

– 5 John 11:16 → the rest of the disciples → lit.: the fellow disciples → FELLOW DISCIPLE <4827> 6 Acts 15:17 → REMNANT <2645>.

REST (verb) – 1 ***anapauō*** [verb: ἀναπαύω <373>]; **from *ana*: again, and *pauō*: to cease ▶ To cease all activity and refresh oneself; also transl.: to get rest, to repose, to take rest, to take one's ease, to take life easy, to wait** > At Gethsemane, Jesus told His disciples to rest (Matt. 26:45; Mark 14:41). At their return from a mission (see Mark 6:7–13), the twelve apostles were invited by Jesus to come apart and rest a little (Mark 6:31). The rich man in the parable told his soul to rest (Luke 12:19). The Spirit of glory and of God rests upon those who are reproached in the name of Christ (1 Pet. 4:14; some mss. have 2). The souls of those who had been slain for the word of God and for the testimony were told to rest (Rev. 6:11). The dead who die in the Lord rest from their labors (Rev. 14:13). All other refs.: REFRESH <373>, REST (noun)[1] <373>.

2 ***epanapauō*** [verb: ἐπαναπαύω <1879>]; **from *epi*: upon, and *anapauō*: see 1 ▶ To rely on, to remain upon** > The peace of the seventy disciples was to rest on the sons of peace (Luke 10:6). Paul speaks of the Jew who rests (i.e., rests entirely) on the law (Rom. 2:17). ¶

3 ***katapauō*** [verb: καταπαύω <2664>]; **from *kata*: intens., and *pauō*: to cease ▶ To introduce a stable rest** > God rested from all His works on the seventh day (Heb. 4:4). He who has entered into the rest of God has also rested {ceased} from his own works (Heb. 4:10). All other refs.: REST (noun)[1] <2664>, RESTRAIN <2664>.

4 **rest: *anapausis*** [fem. noun: ἀνάπαυσις <372>]; **from *anapauō*: see 1 ▶ Interruption, pause** > The four living creatures do not rest {cease, stop} (lit.: have no rest) to say: "Holy, holy, holy, Lord God Almighty" (Rev. 4:8). Other refs.: Matt. 11:29; 12:43; Luke 11:24; Rev. 14:11; see REST (noun)[1] <372>. ¶

5 ***ō*** [verb: ὦ <5600>]; **subjunctive of *eimi*: to be ▶ To be** > The faith of Christians does not rest on {does not stand} (lit.: is not upon) men's wisdom, but on the power of God (1 Cor. 2:5).

6 ***episkēnoō*** [verb: ἐπισκηνόω <1981>]; **from *epi*: upon, and *skēnoō*: to pitch a tent, which is from *skēnē*: tent, habitation; lit.: to cover like a tent ▶ To stay, to remain, to cover** > Paul would rather boast in his infirmities, that the power of Christ might rest {dwell} on him (2 Cor. 12:9). ¶

7 ***hēsuchazō*** [verb: ἡσυχάζω <2270>]; **from *hēsuchos*: quiet, still ▶ To cease working, to rest** > The women who saw the body of Jesus placed in the tomb rested {remained quiet} on the Sabbath (Luke 23:56). All other refs.: QUIET <2270>, SILENT <2270>.

– 8 Matt. 2:9 → STAND (verb) <2476> 9 Matt. 3:16 → lit.: to come (*erchomai*) 10 Acts 2:3 → SIT <2523> 11 Acts 2:26 → DWELL <2681> 12 Rom. 4:16 → may rest on grace → lit.: by grace.

RESTING – Acts 7:49 → resting place → lit.: place of rest → REST (noun)[1] <2663>.

RESTLESS – Jas. 3:8 → UNRULY <183>.

RESTORATION – 1 2 Cor. 13:9 → PERFECTING <2676> 2 2 Cor. 13:11 → to strive for full restoration → PERFECTED (BE) <2675>.

RESTORE – 1 ***anorthoō*** [verb: ἀνορθόω <461>]; **from *ana*: again, up, and *orthoō*; to erect, which is from *orthos*: right, straight ▶ To build anew, to reconstruct >** God will rebuild and restore {set up} the tabernacle of David, which is fallen (Acts 15:16). Other refs.: Luke 13:13; Heb. 12:12; see STRAIGHT <461>, STRENGTHEN <461>. ¶

2 ***apokathistēmi*** [verb: ἀποκαθίστημι <600>]; **from *apo*: anew, and *kathistēmi*: to constitute, which is from *kata*: down, and *histēmi*: to stand ▶ a. To reconstitute, to re-establish, to heal >** A man's dried up hand was restored by Jesus (Matt. 12:13; Mark 3:5; Luke 6:10 in some mss.). Jesus said that Elijah will restore all things (Matt. 17:11; Mark 9:12: *apokatastanō* in some mss.). A blind man was restored by Jesus (Mark 8:25). The disciples of Jesus asked Him: "Will You at this time restore the kingdom to Israel?" (Acts 1:6). **b. To return to a previous place >** The author of the Epistle to the Hebrews wanted to be restored to his readers the sooner (Heb. 13:19). ¶

3 ***katartizō*** [verb: καταρτίζω <2675>]; **from *kata*: intens., and *artios*: fit, perfect ▶ To re-establish in a prior condition >** Spiritual brothers are to restore a man taken in some fault (Gal. 6:1). All other refs.: see entries in Lexicon at <2675>.

– 4 Luke 14:34 → to restore saltiness → SEASON (verb) <741> 5 Luke 22:32 → RETURN (verb) <1994> 6 2 Cor. 13:9 → to be fully restored → PERFECTING <2676> 7 Phm. 22 → GIVE <5483> 8 Heb. 6:6 → RENEW <340>.

RESTORING – ***apokatastasis*** [fem. noun: ἀποκατάστασις <605>]; **from *apokathistēmi*: to restore, which is from *apo*: anew, and *kathistēmi*: to constitute, which is from *kata*: down, and *histēmi*: to stand ▶ Reinstatement of a thing or person to its previous state >** The restoring of all things (Acts 3:21) is a time when Jesus Christ will reinstate all things according to the mind of God. ¶

RESTRAIN – 1 ***katapauō*** [verb: καταπαύω <2664>]; **from *kata*: down (intens.), and *pauō*: to cease ▶ To prevent, to stop >** Paul and Barnabas restrained with difficulty {kept with difficulty, had difficulty keeping} the multitudes from sacrificing to them (Acts 14:18). All other refs.: REST (noun)[1] <2664>, REST (verb) <2664>.

2 ***kōluō*** [verb: κωλύω <2967>]; **from *kolos*: truncated ▶ To prevent, to stop >** A beast of burden restrained {forbad} the folly of Balaam (2 Pet. 2:16). All other refs.: FORBID <2967>, HINDER (verb) <2967>, REFUSE (verb) <2967>.

3 ***stenochōreō*** [verb: στενοχωρέω <4729>]; **from *stenos*: narrow, and *chōra*: space ▶ To constrain, to withhold; also transl.: to restrict, to straiten >** Paul and Timothy were hard pressed on every side, yet not restrained {crushed, distressed} (2 Cor. 4:8). The Corinthians were not restrained by Paul, but they were restrained by their own affections (2 Cor. 6:12a, b). ¶

– 4 Luke 24:16 → HOLD (verb) <2902> 5 2 Thes. 2:6, 7 → KEEP (verb) <2722>.

RESTRAINT – 1 Cor. 7:35 → LEASH <1029>.

RESTRICT – 1 1 Cor. 7:35 → lit.: to put a leash → LEASH <1029>, PUT <1911> 2 2 Cor. 6:12a, b → RESTRAIN <4729>.

RESULT (noun) – 1 1 Cor. 9:1 → result of the work → WORK (noun) <2041> 2 1 Cor. 11:21 → "as a result" added in Engl. 3 1 Thes. 2:1 → without results →

in vain → VAIN <2756> [4] Heb. 13:7 → OUTCOME <1545> [5] 1 Pet. 1:9 → end result → END (noun) <5056>.

RESULT (verb) – [1] Luke 21:13 → to turn out → TURN (verb) <576> [2] 2 Cor. 9:11 → PRODUCE <2716>.

RESUME – John 13:12 → resumed His place → sat down again → SIT <377>, AGAIN <3825>.

RESURRECTION – [1] ***anastasis*** [fem. noun: ἀνάστασις <386>]; **from *anistēmi*: to stand up, which is from *ana*: again, and *histēmi*: to stand ▶ Return to life of a person who has died** > Jesus spoke about the resurrection (Matt. 22:30, 31; Luke 14:14; 20:35, 36), in particular the resurrection of life and the resurrection of judgment (John 5:29a, b). Martha knew that her brother Lazarus would rise again in the resurrection (John 11:24); Jesus told her that He Himself is the resurrection and the life (v. 25). The Sadducees said there was no resurrection (Matt. 22:23, 28; Mark 12:18, 23; Luke 20:27, 33; Acts 23:8), as did likewise some among the Corinthians (1 Cor. 15:12, 13); Hymenaeus and Philetus said that the resurrection had already taken place (2 Tim. 2:18). The resurrection of Jesus (Acts 1:22; 2:31; 4:33; 26:23; Rom. 6:5; Phil. 3:10; 1 Pet. 1:3; 3:21) constitutes one of the principal foundations of the Christian faith. The apostles preached the resurrection from among the dead, i.e., of Christians at the Lord's coming (Acts 4:2; 17:18), and spoke of the resurrection of the dead (Acts 17:32; 23:6; 24:21; 1 Cor. 15:42; Heb. 6:2; 11:35). There will be a resurrection of the just and of the unjust (Acts 24:15; Rev. 20:5, 6; see Rev. 20:13). Resurrection came by man, i.e., Jesus Christ (1 Cor. 15:21). Jesus is marked out (identified distinctly) Son of God by the resurrection of the dead (Rom. 1:4). The gospels relate that the Lord raised three dead people while on earth: a young girl (Matt. 9:18–26; Mark 5:35–43; Luke 8:40–56), an only son (Luke 7:11–17), and Lazarus (John 11:41–44). Other ref.: Luke 2:34; see RISING <386>. ¶

[2] ***egersis*** [fem. noun: ἔγερσις <1454>]; **from *egeirō*: to wake up ▶ See defin. in [1].** > After the resurrection {arising} of Jesus, risen saints appeared to many (Matt. 27:53). ¶

[3] ***exanastasis*** [fem. noun: ἐξανάστασις <1815>]; **from *ek*: out, and *anastasis*: resurrection ▶ Return to life of an O.T. believer or a Christian who has died** > Paul sought to arrive at the resurrection from among the dead (Phil. 3:11). ¶

RETAIN – [1] Luke 8:15; Phm. 13 → KEEP (verb) <2722> [2] John 20:23 → HOLD (verb) <2902>.

RETALIATE – 1 Pet. 2:23b → to revile again → REVILE <486>.

RETORT (noun)– Acts 7:29 → SAYING <3056>.

RETORT (verb) – [1] John 7:47 → ANSWER (verb) <611> [2] John 18:38 → SAY <3004>.

RETRIBUTION – [1] ***antapodoma*** [neut. noun: ἀνταπόδομα <468>]; **from *antapodidomi*: to repay, which is from *anti*: in place of, and *apodidōmi*: to render, which is from *apo*: from, and *didomi*: to give ▶ Punishment, recompense in the neg. sense** > The table of Israel was to become a retribution to them (Rom. 11:9). Other ref.: Luke 14:12; see RECOMPENSE (noun) <468>. ¶

[2] ***misthapodosia*** [fem. noun: μισθαποδοσία <3405>]; **from *misthapodotēs*: rewarder, which is from *misthos*: reward, salary, and *apodidōmi*: to give back, which is from *apo*: from, and *didōmi*: to give ▶ Punishment, reward in the neg. sense; also transl.: penalty** > Every transgression and disobedience received a just retribution (Heb. 2:2). Other refs.: Heb. 10:35; 11:26; see REWARD (noun) <3405>. ¶

– [3] 2 Thes. 1:8 → VENGEANCE <1557>.

RETURN (noun) – [1] ***amoibē*** [fem. noun: ἀμοιβή <287>]; **from *ameibō*: to change ▶ Repayment, requital** > The children of a

widow are to make a return to {to repay, to requite} their parents (1 Tim. 5:4). ¶
– 2 Matt. 16:26; Mark 8:37 → in return → in exchange → EXCHANGE (noun) <465> 3 Mark 2:1 → ENTER <1525> 4 Mark 6:30 → GATHER <4863> 5 Mark 7:31 → to go away → GO <1831> 6 Luke 6:35 → to hope in return, to expect in return → HOPE (verb) <560> 7 Luke 9:10 → on their return → having returned → RETURN (verb) <5290> 8 1 Thes. 3:9 → to thank in return → lit.: to render thanks in return → RENDER <467> 9 1 Pet. 2:23b → to revile in return → REVILE <486>.

RETURN (verb) – 1 ***anakamptō*** [verb: ἀνακάμπτω <344>]; **from *ana*: again, and *kamptō*: to fold, to bend ▶ To come back, to go back, to turn again** > The wise men had been warned not to return to Herod (Matt. 2:12). The peace of the disciples was to rest upon a house if a son of peace was there, but if not, it would return to them (Luke 10:6). Paul would return to those of Ephesus, if God wills (Acts 18:21). Other refs.: Heb. 11:15; 2 Pet. 2:21 in some mss. ¶
2 ***analuō*** [verb: ἀναλύω <360>]; **from *ana*: again, and *luō*: to loose, to release ▶ To come back** > The disciples were to be like men waiting for their master, whenever he may return from {he may leave} the wedding (Luke 12:36). Other refs.: Acts 16:26 in some mss.; Phil. 1:23; see DEPART <360>. ¶
3 ***ginomai*** [verb: γίνομαι <1096>] ▶ **To come** > Peter came to himself after having been delivered from the hand of Herod (Acts 12:11). Other refs.: see entries in Lexicon at <1096>.
4 ***epanerchomai*** [verb: ἐπανέρχομαι <1880>]; **from *epi*: unto, and *anerchomai*: to go up, which is from *ana*: up, and *erchomai*: to come, to go ▶ To come again** > When he would return, the Samaritan would repay the innkeeper whatever more he would spend for the wounded man (Luke 10:35). When he returned {On his arrival back again}, a nobleman commanded to call his servants (Luke 19:15). ¶
5 ***strephō*** [verb: στρέφω <4762>]; **from *trepō*: to bring back ▶ To send back, to bring back** > Filled with remorse, Judas returned {brought again, brought back} the thirty pieces of silver (Matt. 27:3). Some mss. have *apostrephō*: lit.: to return again. All other refs.: TURN (verb) <4762>.
6 ***anastrephō*** [verb: ἀναστρέφω <390>]; **from *ana*: again, and *strephō*: see 5 ▶ To go back** > The officers returned and reported that the apostles were no longer in the prison (Acts 5:22). Amos wrote that God would return and rebuild the tabernacle of David (Acts 15:16). Other ref.: Matt. 17:22 in some mss. All other refs.: CONDUCT (verb)[1] <390>, LIVE <390>, TREAT <390>.
7 ***apostrephō*** [verb: ἀποστρέφω <654>]; **from *apo*: again, from, and *strephō*: see 5 ▶ To replace; also transl.: to put, to put again, to put back** > Jesus told Peter to return his sword to its place (Matt. 26:52). Other ref.: Matt. 27:3; see 5. All other refs.: TURN (verb) <654>.
8 ***epistrephō*** [verb: ἐπιστρέφω <1994>]; **from *epi*: toward, and *strephō*: see 5 ▶ To come back, to bring back; also transl.: to turn** > The peace of the disciples was to return to them if the house was not worthy (Matt. 10:13). The unclean spirit says he will return to his house (Matt. 12:44). During the great tribulation, he who is in the field is not to return to get his clothes (Matt. 24:18; Mark 13:16). Jesus, turning round, saw the woman who had touched Him (Mark 5:30). Turning round, Jesus rebuked Peter, saying: Get away behind me (Mark 8:33). John the Baptist was to turn (i.e., cause to return) many of the sons of Israel to the Lord, hearts of fathers to children and disobedient ones to the thoughts of just men (Luke 1:16, 17). Jesus and His parents returned to Galilee (Luke 2:39 in some mss.). The spirit of the young girl returned (Luke 8:55). If a brother should sin, and should return in repentance to the one against whom he has sinned, he is to be forgiven (Luke 17:4). Peter, when once he had returned {had been converted, had turned again, had turned back, had been restored} to the Lord, was to strengthen his brothers (Luke 22:32). Paul wanted to return and visit the brothers (Acts 15:36). Peter, turning round, saw John following Jesus (John 21:20). Paul turned and said

to the spirit to come out of the possessed slave girl (Acts 16:18). The Galatians were in danger of returning to the elements of the law to which they had been in bondage (Gal. 4:9). The Christians of the dispersion had returned to the Shepherd of their souls (1 Pet. 2:25). The dog has returned to his own vomit (2 Pet. 2:22), image of people who have knowledge of the Lord and Savior Jesus Christ and who return to the defilement of the world. John turned back to see the voice that spoke with him, and having turned, he saw seven golden lamps (Rev. 1:12a, b). All other refs.: BRING <1994>, CONVERT (verb) <1994>, TURN (verb) <1994>.

9 ***hupostrephō*** [verb: ὑποστρέφω <5290>]; **from *hupo*: under, and *strephō*: see 5 ► To turn back, to go back >** After staying with Elizabeth for about three months, Mary returned to her home (Luke 1:56). The shepherds returned, glorifying God (Luke 2:20; some mss.: *epistrephō*). The parents of Jesus returned from Jerusalem (Luke 2:43), and then returned to Jerusalem (v. 45). Jesus returned from the Jordan (Luke 4:1); He returned to Galilee (v. 14). Those who had asked Jesus to heal the dying servant returned to the house (Luke 7:10). Jesus returned from the country of the Gaderenes (Luke 8:37). The man from whom demons had come out was to return to his own house and tell what great things God had done for him (Luke 8:39). The crowd welcomed Jesus when He returned (Luke 8:40). When the apostles had returned, they told Jesus all that they had done (Luke 9:10). The unclean spirit said he would return to his house (Luke 11:24). After the crucifixion of Jesus, the crowds returned (Luke 23:48), as likewise did the women who had accompanied Him (Luke 23:56). On the morning of the resurrection, the women returned and reported all that they had witnessed to the eleven (Luke 24:9). When Paul returned to Jerusalem, he became in a trance (Acts 22:17). Other refs.: Mark 14:40; Luke 24:33, 52; Acts 1:12; 8:25, 28; 12:25; 13:13, 34; 14:21; 20:3; 21:6; 23:32; Gal. 1:17. All other refs.: COME <5290>.

10 ***epanagō*** [verb: ἐπανάγω <1877>]; **from *epi*: upon, and *anagō*: to bring back, which is from *ana*: again, up, and *agō*: to go ► To come back >** As He returned {was on the way back} to the city, Jesus was hungry (Matt. 21:18). All other refs.: LAUNCH <1877>, PUT <1877>.

– **11** Matt. 2:12; 4:12 → DEPART <402> **12** John 13:12 → to return to one's place → to sit down → SIT <377> **13** Rom. 14:9 → to return to life → REVIVE <326>.

REU – ***Rhagau*** [masc. name: Ῥαγαύ <4466>]: **friend, in Heb.; Reu in Gen. 11:18, 20 ► Man of the O.T. >** Reu is mentioned in the genealogy of Jesus (Luke 3:35). ¶

REUBEN – ***Rhoubēn*** [masc. name: Ῥουβήν <4502>]: **see, a son!, in Heb.; see Gen. 29:32 ► One of the twelve sons of Jacob and the tribe descended from him >** Twelve thousand out of the tribe of Reuben will be sealed (Rev. 7:5). ¶

REVEAL – **1** ***apokaluptō*** [verb: ἀποκαλύπτω <601>]; **from *apo*: from, and *kaluptō*: to cover, to hide ► To disclose, to manifest, to unveil >** Jesus warned that there is nothing covered that will not be revealed (Matt. 10:26; Luke 12:2). The thoughts of many hearts were to be revealed at the coming of Jesus (Luke 2:35). Jesus praised His Father for having revealed things to little children (Matt. 11:25; Luke 10:21). It is the Son who reveals the Father (Matt. 11:27; Luke 10:22). The Father had revealed to Simon Bar-Jonah that Jesus was the Christ (Matt. 16:17). The day when the Son of Man will be revealed will be like the day when Sodom was destroyed (Luke 17:30). In relation to God, the following have been revealed: His arm (John 12:38), His righteousness (Rom. 1:17), His wrath (Rom. 1:18), His glory (Rom. 8:18; actually, it will be fully revealed in the future), the things that He has prepared for those who love Him (1 Cor. 2:10), His Son (Gal. 1:16), a different attitude (Phil. 3:15), salvation (1 Pet. 1:5), and the sufferings and the glories of Christ (1 Pet. 1:12). The fire of the judgment of God will reveal every man's work (1 Cor. 3:13). Before faith was

revealed, men were guarded under law (Gal. 3:23). The mystery of Christ has been revealed to His apostles and prophets by the Spirit (Eph. 3:5). Before the day of the Lord comes, the antichrist will be revealed (2 Thes. 2:3, 6, 8). Peter is a partaker of the glory that will be revealed (1 Pet. 5:1). Other refs.: 1 Cor. 14:30 {to make a revelation}. ¶
[2] ***emphanizō*** [verb: ἐμφανίζω <1718>]; **from *emphanēs*: manifest, known, which is from *en*: in, and *phainō*: to manifest, which is from *phōs*: light ▶ To make known, to unveil** > The chiliarch commanded Paul's nephew to tell no one he had revealed to him things concerning a plot to kill Paul (Acts 23:22 {to notify, to report, to represent, to show}). All other refs.: APPEAR <1718>, CHARGE (noun)[1] <1718>, MANIFEST (verb) <1718>, PLAINLY <1718>, SIGNIFY <1718>.
– [3] Mark 4:22; John 1:31; 2:11; 17:6; 9:3; 21:1a, b, 14; Rom. 3:21; 1 Cor. 4:5; 2 Cor. 7:12; Col. 1:26; 1 Tim. 3:16; 2 Tim. 1:10; 1 John 3:2a, b; Rev. 15:4 → MANIFEST (verb) <5319> [4] Luke 2:26 → to be revealed → WARN <5537> [5] Acts 26:16b → APPEAR <3708> [6] Rom. 2:5; 8:19; 1 Cor. 1:7; 2 Thes. 1:7; 1 Pet. 1:7, 13; 4:13 → to be revealed → REVELATION <602> [7] 1 Cor. 4:1 → "has revealed" added in Engl.

REVEALED – ***phaneros*** [adj.: φανερός <5318>]; **from *phainō*: to shine, to become evident, which is from *phōs*: light ▶ Known, visible** > Nothing is secret that will not be revealed {disclosed, evident, manifest} (Luke 8:17). The secrets of the heart of an unbeliever or of an uninformed person may be revealed {disclosed, laid bare, manifested} in a Christian meeting (1 Cor. 14:25). All other refs.: see entries in Lexicon at <5318>.

REVEALING – Rom. 8:19; 1 Cor. 1:7 → REVELATION <602>.

REVEL (noun) – ***kōmos*** [masc. noun: κῶμος <2970>]; **from *keimai*: to lie down, to lie stretched out ▶ Great feast, whence: excess, lasciviousness, debauchery accompanying an inebriated state; also transl.: carousal, carousing, orgy, reveling, revelling, revelry** > The Christian is called to behave in a becoming manner, not in revels {rioting} (Rom. 13:13). Revels are a work of the flesh (Gal. 5:21). Christians are to walk no longer in revels (1 Pet. 4:3). ¶

REVEL (verb) – [1] ***entruphaō*** [verb: ἐντρυφάω <1792>]; **from *en*: in, and *truphaō*: to live in indolence, in voluptuous pleasure ▶ To delight in some pleasure, to party** > Peter speaks of those reveling {carousing, revelling, rioting, sporting themselves} in their own deceits (2 Pet. 2:13). ¶
– [2] Acts 7:41 → REJOICE <2165> [3] 2 Pet. 2:13 → INDULGENCE <5172>.

REVELATION – [1] ***apokalupsis*** [fem. noun: ἀποκάλυψις <602>]; **from *apokaluptō*: to reveal, which is from *apo*: out of, and *kaluptō*: to cover, to hide ▶ Disclosure of that which was hidden; also transl.: appearance, appearing, manifestation, revealing** > The term is used in relation to the manifestation of Jesus Christ at His first coming (Luke 2:32) and at His second coming (1 Cor. 1:7 {coming}; 2 Thes. 1:7; 1 Pet. 1:7, 13; 4:13), to the righteous judgment of God (Rom. 2:5), and to the sons of God (Rom. 8:19). Paul mentions the revelation of the mystery that has now been made manifest (Rom. 16:25), the fact of speaking by revelation (1 Cor. 14:6, 26), the spirit of wisdom and of revelation (Eph. 1:17). The book of Revelation (or: Apocalypse) is the revelation of Jesus Christ that God gave to show the things that must soon take place (Rev. 1:1). Other refs.: 2 Cor. 12:1, 7; Gal. 1:12; 2:2; Eph. 3:3. ¶
[2] **to be, to make, to come a revelation: *apokaluptō*** [verb: ἀποκαλύπτω <601>]; **see [1] ▶ To manifest something formerly hidden** > If a revelation is made {anything is revealed} to another who is seated in the church, the first speaker must keep silent (1 Cor. 14:30). All other refs.: REVEAL <601>.

REVELING, REVELLING – Gal. 5:21; 1 Pet. 4:3 → REVEL (noun) <2970>.

REVELRY – [1] Rom. 13:13; 1 Pet. 4:3 → REVEL (noun) <2970> [2] 1 Cor. 10:7 → to indulge in revelry → PLAY <3815>.

REVENGE – [1] Rom. 12:19 → to take revenge → AVENGE <1556> [2] 2 Cor. 7:11 → VENGEANCE <1557> [3] 2 Cor. 10:6 → PUNISH <1556>.

REVENUE – Rom. 13:7a, b → CUSTOM <5056>.

REVERE – [1] 1 Pet. 3:15 → SANCTIFY <37> [2] Rev. 11:18 → FEAR (verb) <5399>.

REVERENCE (noun) – [1] ***eulabeia*** [fem. noun: εὐλάβεια <2124>]; **from *eulabēs*: devout, which is from *eu*: well, and *lambanō*: to take ► Piety, respect for God** > Christ was heard because of His piety {godly fear, reverent submission} (Heb. 5:7). It is by grace that Christians serve God acceptably, with reverence and godly fear (Heb. 12:28). ¶
– [2] Acts 10:25 → in reverence → lit.: and worshiped him → WORSHIP (verb) <4352> [3] Col. 3:22 → with reverence → lit.: fearing → FEAR (verb) <5399> [4] 1 Tim. 2:2; 3:4; Titus 2:7 → GRAVITY <4587> [5] Heb. 11:7 → in reverence → to be moved with fear → FEAR (noun) <2125> [6] Heb. 12:9 → to give reverence → RESPECT (verb) <1788> [7] 1 Pet. 2:18; 3:2 → FEAR (noun) <5401>.

REVERENCE (verb) – [1] Luke 20:13; Heb. 12:9 → RESPECT (verb) <1788> [2] Acts 17:23 → WORSHIP (verb) <2151> [3] Eph. 5:33 → RESPECT (verb) <5399> [4] Rev. 11:18 → FEAR (verb) <5399>.

REVERENT – [1] ***hieroprepēs*** [adj.: ἱεροπρεπής <2412>]; **from *hieros*: holy, sacred, and *prepō*: to be suitable ► Which is suitable to the saints, to what is holy** > Older women are to be reverent {as becometh holiness} in their behavior (Titus 2:3). ¶
– [2] 1 Tim. 3:8, 11; Titus 2:2 → GRAVE <4586> [3] Heb. 5:7 → reverent submission → PIETY <2124> [4] Heb. 11:7 → in reverent fear → to be moved with fear → FEAR (noun) <2125> [5] 1 Pet. 2:18 → reverent fear of God → lit.: in all fear → FEAR (noun) <5401>.

REVILE – [1] ***blasphēmeō*** [verb: βλασφημέω <987>]; **from *blasphēmos*: abusive, injurious, which poss. comes from *blaptō*: to injure, and *phēmē*: reputation ► To slander, to insult, to abuse; also transl.: to blaspheme, to deride, to heap abuse, to hurl abuse, to hurl insults, to malign, to rail, to slander, to speak evil, to speak injuriously, to speak insultingly, to speak railingly** > Those who passed by Jesus on the cross reviled Him (Matt. 27:39; Mark 15:29). One of the criminals spoke insultingly to Jesus (Luke 23:39). Titus was to remind people to speak evil of no one (Titus 3:2). Unbelievers speak evil of those who are converted (1 Pet. 4:4). Presumptuous men are not afraid to revile dignities (2 Pet. 2:10; also Jude 8), and what they do not know (Jude 10). Men revile the things they do not understand (2 Pet. 2:12). All other refs.: see entries in Lexicon at <987>.

[2] ***loidoreō*** [verb: λοιδορέω <3058>]; **from *loidoros*: one who insults ► To reproach, to insult; also transl.: to curse, to hurl insults, to insult, to rail** > The Pharisees reviled the blind man whom Jesus had healed (John 9:28). They asked Paul if he reviled the high priest (Acts 23:4). Being reviled, Paul blessed (1 Cor. 4:12). When Jesus was reviled, He reviled not again (1 Pet. 2:23a). ¶

[3] **to revile again, to revile in return: *antiloidoreō*** [verb: ἀντιλοιδορέω <486>]; **from *anti*: in return, and *loidoreō*: see [2] ► To insult in reply** > When Jesus was reviled, He reviled not again {did not retaliate} (1 Pet. 2:23b). ¶

[4] ***oneidizō*** [verb: ὀνειδίζω <3679>]; **from *oneidos*: blame, reproach ► To reproach, to insult** > Believers in the Lord are blessed when men revile them (Matt. 5:11). All other refs.: INSULT (verb) <3679>, REPROACH (noun) <3679>, REPROACH (verb) <3679>.

– [5] Matt. 15:4; Mark 7:10 → CURSE (verb) <2551> [6] 1 Pet. 3:16 → to falsely accuse → ACCUSE <1908>.

REVILER – [1] 1 Cor. 5:11 → ABUSIVE <3060> [2] 2 Tim. 3:2 → BLASPHEMER <989>.

REVILING – [1] ***blasphēmos*** [adj.: βλάσφημος <989>]; **poss. from *blaptō*: to injure, and *phēmē*: reputation ► Which is blasphemous, defaming, reproachful** > The angels do not bring a reviling {railing} accusation against dignities (2 Pet. 2:11). All other refs.: BLASPHEMER <989>, BLASPHEMOUS <989>.
[2] ***loidoria*** [fem. noun: λοιδορία <3059>]; **from *loidoreō*: to revile, to reproach, which is from *loidoros*: reviler, one who insults, i.e., one who uses abusive language, humiliates others ► Insult, malice, railing** > We should not render reviling for reviling (1 Pet. 3:9a, b). Other ref.: 1 Tim. 5:14; see REPROACH (noun) <3059>. ¶
– [3] 1 Tim. 6:4 → injurious word → INJURIOUS <988> [4] Jude 9 → reviling accusation → lit.: judgment of blasphemy → BLASPHEMY <988>.

REVIVE – [1] ***anazaō*** [verb: ἀναζάω <326>]; **from *ana*: again, and *zaō*: to live ► To live again, to return to life; also transl.: to become alive, to spring to life** > Paul speaks of sin that has revived (Rom. 7:9). Christ revived that He might rule over both dead and living (Rom. 14:9). All other refs.: LIFE <326>, LIVE <326>.
[2] ***anathallō*** [verb: ἀναθάλλω <330>]; **from *ana*: again, and *thallō*: to flourish ► To thrive again, to make effective again** > The Philippians had revived their thinking of Paul (Phil. 4:10 {to flourish, to renew}). ¶

REVOLT – [1] **to lead in revolt: *aphistēmi*** [verb: ἀφίστημι <868>]; **from *apo*: from, and *histēmi*: to stand ► To arouse, to stir up** > Judas the Galilean led a band of people in revolt (lit.: drew away people after him) (Acts 5:37). All other refs.: DEPART <868>, KEEP (verb) <868>.
– [2] Acts 21:38 → to stir up a revolt, to start a revolt → to raise a sedition → SEDITION <387>.

REVOLUTION – Luke 21:9 → TUMULT <181>.

REWARD (noun) – [1] ***antapodosis*** [fem. noun: ἀνταπόδοσις <469>]; **from *antapodidōmi*: to repay, to requite, which is from *anti*: in turn, and *apodidōmi*: to give, to pay, which is from *apo*: from, and *didōmi*: to give ► Recompense, compensation** > The Christian will receive of the Lord the reward of the inheritance (Col. 3:24). ¶
[2] ***misthos*** [masc. noun: μισθός <3408>]; **lit.: salary, wages ► a. Remuneration, recompense** > The faithful will receive a reward from God in the future (Matt. 5:12; 10:41a, b, 42; Mark 9:41; Luke 6:23, 35; 1 Cor. 3:8, 14; Rev. 11:18 {recompense}; 22:12). Other refs.: Matt. 5:46; 6:1, 2, 5, 16; Jude 11 {pay, profit}. **b. Retribution** > Peter speaks of the unrighteous who receive the reward {wages} (i.e., the punishment) of unrighteousness (2 Pet. 2:13). All other refs.: WAGES <3408>.
[3] ***misthapodosia*** [fem. noun: μισθαποδοσία <3405>]; **from *misthos*: see [2], and *apodidōmi*: see [1] ► Remuneration, recompense** > The confidence of Christians has a great reward {recompence of reward} (Heb. 10:35). Moses was looking to the reward (Heb. 11:26). Other ref.: Heb. 2:2; see RETRIBUTION <3405>. ¶
– [4] Luke 23:41 → due reward → things deserving → DESERVING <514> [5] Col. 2:18 → to beguile of the reward, to cheat of the reward → to defraud of the prize → DEFRAUD <2603>.

REWARD (verb) – [1] ***apodidōmi*** [verb: ἀποδίδωμι <591>]; **from *apo*: from, and *didōmi*: to give ► To give in return, to reimburse** > God the Father will reward {render} it to one who does alms in secret (Matt. 6:4), one who prays to Him (v. 6) and one who fasts without appearing to do so (v. 18). Other refs.: see entries in Lexicon at <591>.

– 2 2 Cor. 5:10 → to be rewarded → RECEIVE <2865> 3 Heb. 10:35 → to richly reward → lit.: to have a great reward → REWARD (noun) <3405> 4 Heb. 11:6 → lit.: to be a rewarder → REWARDER <3406> 5 2 John 8 → to reward fully → lit.: to receive full reward → WAGES <3408> 6 Rev. 18:6a, b → GIVE <591>.

REWARDER – ***misthapodotēs*** [masc. noun: μισθαποδότης <3406>]; **from *misthos*: remuneration, reward, and *apodidōmi*: to render, which is from *apo*: from, and *didōmi*: to give ▶ One who gives a salary, a recompense, or a reward** > God is the rewarder of those who seek Him out (Heb. 11:6). ¶

RHEGIUM – ***Rhēgion*** [neut. name: Ῥήγιον <4484>]: **breach ▶ Maritime city situated at the southwestern extremity of Italy** > Paul stayed in Rhegium for one day, during his fourth journey, when he was going to Rome as a prisoner (Acts 28:13). The city is now called Reggio and is the largest city of Calabria. ¶

RHESA – ***Rhēsa*** [masc. name: Ῥησά <4488>]: **Jehovah has healed; others: head ▶ Israelite man, son or descendant of Zerubbabel; also transl.: Resa** > Rhesa is mentioned in the genealogy of Jesus (Luke 3:27). ¶

RHODA – ***Rhodē*** [fem. name: Ῥόδη <4498>]: **rose ▶ Servant girl of Mary, the mother of John who was surnamed Mark** > Rhoda recognized Peter's voice, when he knocked at the door of the entry after having been miraculously delivered from prison (Acts 12:13; see vv. 14–16). ¶

RHODES – ***Rhodos*** [masc. name: Ῥόδος <4499>]: **rose ▶ Island of the Mediterranean Sea southwest of Asia Minor** > Rhodes is mentioned on the occasion of Paul's third journey (Acts 21:1). ¶

RICH – 1 ***liparos*** [adj.: λιπαρός <3045>]; **from *lipos*: fat ▶ Luxurious, refined** > All things that are rich {dainty, fair} and splendid {All riches and splendor, All delicacies and splendors} will have gone from Babylon (Rev. 18:14). ¶

2 ***plousios*** [adj. and adj. used as noun: πλούσιος <4145>]; **from *ploutos*: abundance, wealth ▶ Person who possesses goods in abundance** > A rich man will enter into the kingdom of God with difficulty (Matt. 19:23, 24; Mark 10:25; Luke 18:25). Joseph of Arimathea was a rich man (Matt. 27:57). Many who were rich cast much into the treasury of the temple (Mark 12:41; Luke 21:1). Jesus said woe to those who are rich, for they have their consolation (Luke 6:24). Rich men are mentioned in various parables: Luke 12:16; 16:1, 19, 21, 22. Jesus speaks of inviting the poor instead of rich neighbors (Luke 14:12). A certain ruler who was extremely rich {of great wealth} became very sorrowful when Jesus told him to distribute his goods to the poor (Luke 18:23). Zaccheus was rich {wealthy} (Luke 19:2). Jesus Christ, being rich, became poor (2 Cor. 8:9). God is rich in mercy (Eph. 2:4). Timothy was to charge those who are rich not to be conceited nor to trust in the uncertainty of riches (1 Tim. 6:17). James calls the rich man to glory in his humiliation (Jas. 1:10); the rich man will wither in his ways (v. 11); God has chosen the rich in faith (2:5); rich men oppress others (2:6) and they will weep for their miseries that will come upon them (5:1). Despite her material poverty, Smyrna was rich spiritually (Rev. 2:9). Laodicea says she is rich (Rev. 3:17). At the opening of the sixth seal, the rich men will hide themselves in caves (Rev. 6:15). The beast causes that they should give a mark to all, including the rich (Rev. 13:16). ¶

3 **to be rich, to become rich, to get rich, to abound in riches: *plouteō*** [verb: πλουτέω <4147>]; **from *ploutos*: abundance, wealth ▶ To possess goods in abundance, to become wealthy** > God has sent away the rich (lit.: the ones being rich) empty (Luke 1:53). He who lays up treasure for himself is not rich toward God (Luke 12:21). The same Lord of all is rich toward all who call on Him (Rom. 10:12). The Corinthians had already been enriched (1 Cor. 4:8). Jesus Christ became poor, that Christians might become

rich {be enriched} (2 Cor. 8:9). Those who desire to get rich fall into temptation (1 Tim. 6:9). Those who are rich in the present age are enjoined to be rich in good works (1 Tim. 6:18). Laodicea is advised to buy gold purified by fire so that she may be rich (Rev. 3:18). The merchants of the earth have become rich through the might of the luxury of Babylon the great (Rev. 18:3 {to grow rich, to wax rich}), as well as all who had ships in the sea (Rev. 18:19 {to make rich}). Merchants have become rich {have been made rich, have been enriched, gained their wealth} by Babylon (Rev. 18:15). Other ref.: Rev. 3:17; see WEALTHY <4147>. ¶
– [4] Mark 10:23; Luke 18:24 → one who has riches → RICHES <5536> [5] Rom. 11:17 → rich root → lit.: root and fatness → FATNESS <4096> [6] 2 Cor. 6:10; 9:11 → to make rich → ENRICH <4148> [7] 2 Cor. 8:2 → in rich generosity → lit.: in the riches of their generosity → RICHES <4149> [8] 2 Pet. 1:11 → you will receive a rich welcome → lit.: the entrance will be richly supplied to you → RICHLY <4146>.

RICHES – [1] ***ploutos*** [masc. noun: πλοῦτος <4149>] ▶ **Goods in abundance, wealth** > The deceitfulness of riches choke the word of God (Matt. 13:22; Mark 4:19; Luke 8:14). The term is related to the goodness of God (Rom. 2:4), His glory (Rom. 9:23; Eph. 3:16), the glory of His inheritance (Eph. 1:18), His riches in glory (Phil. 4:19), the riches of the glory of the mystery of the church (Col. 1:27), the riches of the full assurance of understanding of this mystery (Col. 2:2), as well as the riches of His grace (Eph. 1:7; 2:7). The fall of Israel is the riches of the Gentiles (Rom. 11:12). Paul marvels at the depth of the riches of the wisdom and knowledge of God (Rom. 11:33). The deep poverty of the churches of Macedonia had abounded in the riches of their liberality (2 Cor. 8:2). Grace had been given to Paul to announce the unsearchable riches of Christ (Eph. 3:8). Those who are rich in material goods are not to put their trust in the uncertainty of riches (1 Tim. 6:17). Moses esteemed the reproach of Christ greater riches than the treasures of Egypt (Heb. 11:26). For James, the riches of the rich have become corrupted (Jas. 5:2). The Lamb who has been slain is worthy to receive riches (Rev. 5:12). The great riches of Babylon has been made desolate (Rev. 18:17). ¶
[2] ***chrēmata*; plur. of *chrēma*** [neut. noun: χρῆμα <5536>]; **from *chraomai*: to use, to need** ▶ **Goods, wealth** > Jesus said it is hard for those who have riches {the rich} to enter the kingdom of God (Mark 10:23, 24 in some mss.; Luke 18:24); the expr. "to have riches" is also transl. "to be wealthy." Other refs.: Acts 4:37; 8:18, 20b; 24:26; see MONEY <5536>. ¶
– [3] Rev. 18:14 → RICH <3045>.

RICHLY – ***plousiōs*** [adv.: πλουσίως <4146>]; **from *plousios*: rich, wealthy** ▶ **Abundantly, in great quantity** > Paul wished that the word of Christ might dwell in the Colossians richly (Col. 3:16). God gives all things richly to enjoy (1 Tim. 6:17). He has richly {generously} poured out renewing by the Holy Spirit (Titus 3:6). Peter writes that the entrance into the everlasting kingdom will be richly provided (2 Pet. 1:11). ¶

RID – [1] Acts 21:36 → Get rid of him! → Take him away! → TAKE <142> [2] Col. 3:8 → to put off → PUT <659> [3] Jas. 1:21; 1 Pet. 2:1 → to cast away → CAST <659>.

RID (GET) – [1] Luke 22:2 → KILL <337> [2] 1 Cor. 5:7 → to purge out → PURGE <1571> [3] Gal. 4:30 → to cast out → CAST <1544>.

RIDE – [1] Matt. 21:5 → SIT <1910> [2] Luke 19:36 → GO <4198> [3] Acts 23:24 → for Paul to ride → lit.: having set Paul on → SET (verb) <1913> [4] Rev. 9:17 → to ride horses → to sit on horses → SIT <2521> [5] Rev. 17:7 → the beast she rides → lit.: the beast that carries her → BEAR <941>.

RIDICULE – [1] Matt. 9:24; Mark 5:40; Luke 8:53 → to laugh at → LAUGH <2606> [2] Luke 14:29 → MOCK <1702> [3] Luke 16:14 → MOCK <1592> [4] Luke

23:11 → to treat with contempt → CONTEMPT <1848>.

RIGHT (adj.) – [1] Matt. 20:15; 22:17; Mark 12:14; Luke 20:22 → to have the right, to be right → to be lawful → LAWFUL <1832> [2] Mark 7:27 → to be right → to be meet → MEET (adj.) <2076> <2570> [3] Mark 7:35; Luke 10:28 → PLAINLY <3723> [4] Luke 7:43; 20:21 → what is right → RIGHTLY <3723> [5] John 7:6 → READY <2092> [6] John 8:16 → TRUE <227> [7] John 18:23; Acts 28:25 → to say what is right → to speak well → WELL (adv.) <2573> [8] Acts 6:2 → DESIRABLE <701> [9] Acts 8:21; 13:10; 2 Pet. 2:15 → STRAIGHT <2117> [10] Rom. 3:4 → to prove right → JUSTIFY <1344> [11] Rom. 12:17; 2 Cor. 8:21 → HONEST <2570> [12] 1 Cor. 7:35 → a right way → COMELY <2158> [13] 1 Cor. 15:34 → as is right → JUSTLY <1346> [14] 2 Cor. 5:13 → to be in one's right mind → MIND (noun) <4993> [15] 2 Thes. 1:3 → FITTING <514> [16] 2 Thes. 3:13 → to do what is right → to do well → WELL <2569> [17] 2 Tim. 2:25 → to set right → CORRECT <3811> [18] Heb. 9:10 → setting things right → REFORMATION <1357> [19] 1 Pet. 2:14 → who does right → who does well → WELL <17> [20] 1 Pet. 3:6 → to do what is right → to do good → GOOD (adj. and noun) <15> [21] 1 Pet. 4:19 → doing what is right → well doing → DOING (WELL) <16>.

RIGHT (adj. and noun) – **right hand, right: *dexios*** [adj. and fem. noun: δεξιός <1188>]**; *dexter*, in Lat. ▶ On the side which is opposite the heart >** The Lord sat down at the right hand (lit.: at the right) of God (Mark 16:19). God has made Jesus to sit at His right hand (Matt. 22:44; Mark 12:36; Luke 20:42; Acts 2:34; Heb. 1:13). The Son of Man will be seen sitting at the right hand of the power of God (Matt. 26:64; Mark 14:62; Luke 22:69). Other refs. to Jesus standing or sitting at the right hand of God: Acts 7:55, 56; Rom. 8:34; Eph. 1:20; Col. 3:1; Heb. 1:3; 8:1; 10:12; 12:2; 1 Pet. 3:22. Other refs.: Matt. 5:29, 30, 39; 6:3; 20:21, 23; 25:33, 34; 27:29, 38; Mark 10:37, 40; 15:27; 16:5; Luke 1:11; 6:6; 22:50; 23:33; John 18:10; 21:6; Acts 2:25, 33; 3:7; 5:31; 2 Cor. 6:7; Gal. 2:9; Rev. 1:16, 17, 20; 2:1; 5:1, 7; 10:2, 5 in some mss.; 13:16. ¶

RIGHT (noun) – [1] ***exousia*** [fem. noun: ἐξουσία <1849>]**; from *exesti*: to be legal, which is from *ek*: out, and *eimi*: to be ▶ Authority, prerogative; also transl.: power, rightful claim >** Jesus has given the right to be children of God to those who believe in His name (John 1:12). Paul asked if he did not have a right to eat and drink (1 Cor. 9:4), if he did not have a right to take along a believing wife (v. 5), if it was only Barnabas and he himself who had no right to refrain from working {who must work for living} (v. 6). He also speaks of his right over the Corinthians to reap material things (1 Cor. 9:12a, b); he did not abuse his right {rights} in the gospel (v. 18). He did not exercise his right to be a burden to the Thessalonians (2 Thes. 3:9). Christians have an altar from which those who serve the tabernacle have no right to eat (Heb. 13:10). Rev. 22:14 speaks of those who have the right to the tree of life. All other refs.: AUTHORITY <1849>.

– [2] 1 Cor. 6:12a, b; 10:23a, b → I have the right to do anything → all things are lawful to me → LAWFUL <1832> [3] 1 Cor. 7:3 → to give conjugal rights → to give her due (lit.: what he owes); in some mss.: to give due good will → DUE <3784>, GOOD WILL <2133> [4] Gal. 4:5 → full rights of sons → ADOPTION <5206> [5] Eph. 5:9 → all that is right → all righteousness → RIGHTEOUSNESS <1343> [6] 1 Thes. 4:6 → to overstep the rights → to take advantage → ADVANTAGE <5233>.

RIGHTEOUS – [1] ***dikaios*** [adj. and adj. used as noun: δίκαιος <1342>]**; from *dikē*: justice, righteousness ▶ a. Quality of a person who is upright morally and in his actions; this word also applies to a thing >** This term is used to qualify Jesus (Luke 23:47), the Father (John 17:25), God (Rom. 3:26; 1 John 1:9; 2:29; 3:7b), the Lord (2 Tim. 4:8; Rev. 16:5), Joseph, the husband of Mary (Matt. 1:19), John the Baptist (Mark 6:20), Zacharias and Elisabeth (Luke 1:6), Simeon (Luke 2:25), Joseph of Arimathea (Luke 23:50), Cornelius (Acts 10:22), Abel (Heb. 11:4), and Lot (2 Pet. 2:7). Other refs.: Matt. 20:4, 7; 23:28, 35; Luke 12:57; 18:9; 20:20; John 5:30; 7:24; Acts 4:19; Rom. 2:13; 7:12; Eph. 6:1; Phil. 1:7; 4:8; Col. 4:1; 2 Thes. 1:5, 6; Titus 1:8; 2 Pet. 1:13; 2:8a, b; 1 John 3:7a, 12; Rev. 15:3; 16:7; 19:2; 22:11. **b. Person who is upright morally and because of his actions >** This term applies to the Lord Jesus, the supremely Righteous One (Matt. 27:19, 24; Acts 3:14; 7:52; 22:14; Jas. 5:6; 1 Pet. 3:18; 1 John 2:1). It also specifically characterizes two saints of the O.T.: Abel (Matt. 23:35) and Lot (2 Pet. 2:7). Those who are righteous because of their acts (Matt. 5:45; 9:13; Mark 2:17; Luke 5:32; Rom. 3:10; 5:7) are distinguished from those who are righteous morally, having been constituted righteous by God (Matt. 13:17, 43, 49; 25:37, 46; Luke 14:14; 15:7; Acts 24:15; Rom. 1:17; 5:19; Gal. 3:11; Heb. 10:38; 12:23; Jas. 5:16; 1 Pet. 3:12; 4:18). There are other passages (Matt. 10:41; 23:29; Luke 1:17; 1 Tim. 1:9) where this distinction is less evident. ¶

[2] **righteous judgment, requirement, act, decree: *dikaiōma*** [neut. noun: δικαίωμα <1345>]**; from *dikaioō*: to justify, which is from *dikaios*: righteous, which is from *dikē*: justice, righteousness ▶ Judicial decision, verdict; also transl.: ordinance, requirement, righteousness >** Wicked men have known the righteous judgment of God (Rom. 1:32). The righteous requirement of the law is fulfilled in the Christian (Rom. 8:4). The righteous acts of God have been revealed (Rev. 15:4). By Jesus Christ righteousness reigned toward all people for justification of life (Rom. 5:18). The fine linen is the righteousness of the saints (Rev. 19:8). All other refs.: JUSTIFICATION <1345>, ORDINANCE <1345>, REQUIREMENT <1345>.

– [3] Rom. 2:5 → righteous judgment → JUDGMENT <1341> [4] Rom. 2:13; 3:20; Jas. 2:21, 24, 25; Rev. 22:11b → to consider righteous, to declare righteous → JUSTIFY <1344> [5] 1 Thes. 2:10 → lit.: righteously → JUSTLY <1346> [6] Heb. 1:8 → righteous scepter → lit.: scepter of righteousness → RIGHTEOUSNESS <2118>.

RIGHTEOUSLY – 1 Cor. 15:34; 1 Thes. 2:10; Titus 2:12; 1 Pet. 2:23 → JUSTLY <1346>.

RIGHTEOUSNESS – [1] ***dikaiosunē*** [fem. noun: δικαιοσύνη <1343>]**; from *dikaios*: just, righteous, which is from *dikē*: justice, judgment ▶ Quality of that which is right, just >** The Epistle to the Romans completely develops the subject of righteousness and how man can be righteous before God. The righteousness of God (God acting in a manner consistent with Himself) presents a direct contrast to the unrighteousness of men (Rom. 1:17, see v. 18). The righteousness of God by faith in Jesus Christ is upon all those who believe (Rom. 3:22). Abraham believed God, and it was reckoned to him as righteousness; thus, the Christian's faith is counted to him as righteousness, quite apart from works (Rom. 4:3–5). Christ Jesus has been made righteousness (1 Cor. 1:30). Christ was made sin for us, that we might become the righteousness of God in Him (2 Cor. 5:21). (After Walter Scott.) All other refs.: Matt. 3:15; 5:6, 10, 20; 6:1 in some mss., 33; 21:32; Luke 1:75; John 16:8, 10; Acts 10:35; 13:10; 17:31; 24:25; Rom. 1:17; 3:5, 21, 22, 25, 26; 4:3, 5, 6, 9, 11, 13, 22; 5:17, 21; 6:13, 16, 18–20; 8:10; 9:28, 30, 31; 10:3–6, 10; 14:17; 1 Cor. 1:30; 2 Cor. 3:9; 5:21; 6:7, 14; 9:9, 10; 11:15; Gal. 2:21; 3:6, 21; 5:5; Eph. 4:24; 5:9; 6:14; Phil. 1:11; 3:6, 9; 1 Tim. 6:11; 2 Tim. 2:22; 3:16; 4:8; Titus 3:5; Heb. 1:9; 5:13; 7:2; 11:7, 33; 12:11; Jas. 1:20; 2:23; 3:18; 1 Pet. 2:24; 3:14; 2 Pet. 1:1; 2:5, 21; 3:13; 1 John 2:29; 3:7, 10; Rev. 19:11. ¶

[2] ***euthutēs*** [fem. noun: εὐθύτης <2118>]**; from *euthus*: straight, without deviation ▶ Moral rectitude, probity, integrity >** The scepter of the kingdom of the Son is a scepter of righteousness {righteous scepter, scepter of uprightness} (Heb. 1:8). ¶

– [3] Matt. 6:1 → acts of righteousness, righteousness → ALMS <1343> or <1654>

[4] Rom. 2:26; 8:4 → righteous requirement → REQUIREMENT <1345> [5] Rom. 5:18; 8:4; Rev. 15:4 → righteous judgment → RIGHTEOUS <1345> [6] 1 Cor. 15:34 → to awake to righteousness → to awake up righteously → JUSTLY <1346> [7] Rev. 22:11 → to practice righteousness → JUSTIFY <1344>.

RIGHTFUL – 1 Cor. 9:12 → rightful claim → RIGHT (noun) <1849>.

RIGHTLY – [1] ***orthōs*** [adv.: ὀρθῶς <3723>]; **from *orthos*: right ▶ In a right, just manner; also transl.: correctly** > Simon had judged rightly (Luke 7:43). Some said to Jesus that He taught rightly {what is right} (Luke 20:21). Other refs.: Mark 7:35; Luke 10:28; see PLAINLY <3723>. ¶
– [2] Acts 8:10 → "rightly" added in Engl. [3] 2 Thes. 1:3 → rightly so → as it is fitting → FITTING <514> [4] 2 Tim. 2:15 → to divide rightly → DIVIDE <3718> [5] Heb. 13:18 → to walk rightly → to conduct oneself well → CONDUCT (verb)[1] <390>, WELL <2573>.

RIGID – **to become rigid: *xērainō*** [verb: ξηραίνω <3583>]; **from *xēros*: dry ▶ To become stiff, to become withered** > The possessed son of a man was becoming rigid {was pining away, was stiffening out, was withering} (Mark 9:18). All other refs.: DRY (verb) <3583>, RIPE (BE) <3583>, WITHER <3583>, WITHERED <3583>.

RING (noun) – [1] ***daktulios*** [masc. noun: δακτύλιος <1146>]; **from *daktulos*: finger ▶ Small circle of metal, most often gold or silver, worn on the finger** > In the parable of the prodigal son, the father said to put a ring on the hand of his returned son (Luke 15:22). ¶
[2] **with a gold ring, with a golden ring: *chrusodaktulios*** [adj.: χρυσοδακτύλιος <5554>]; **from *chrusos*: gold, and *daktulios*: see [1] ▶ Who wears a ring made of gold** > James speaks of a man with a gold ring entering the church to whom respect is paid while a poor man is despised (Jas. 2:2). ¶

RING (verb) – 1 Thes. 1:8 → to ring out → to sound out → SOUND (verb) <1837>.

RINGLEADER – ***prōtostatēs*** [masc. noun: πρωτοστάτης <4414>]; **from *prōtos*: first, and *histēmi*: to stand ▶ In classical Greek, the word designates a high ranking officer; in the N.T., one who leads others, especially against established authority** > Paul was accused of being a ringleader {leader} of the sect of the Nazarenes (Acts 24:5). ¶

RIOT (noun) – [1] ***akatastasia*** [fem. noun: ἀκαταστασία <181>]; **from *akatastatos*: unstable, which is from *a*: neg., and *kathistēmi*: to establish, to settle, which is from *kata*: down, and *histēmi*: to stand ▶ Rebellion, uprising** > Paul had been in riots {tumults} (2 Cor. 6:5). Other refs.: 1 Cor. 14:33; 2 Cor. 12:20; Jas. 3:16; Luke 21:9; see CONFUSION <181>, TUMULT <181>. ¶
– [2] Matt. 26:5; 27:24; Mark 14:2 → TUMULT <2351> [3] Acts 17:5 → to start a riot → to set in an uproar → UPROAR <2350> [4] Acts 19:40; 24:5 → INSURRECTION <4714> [5] Acts 24:12 → to cause a riot → to raise up → RAISE <1999> <4160> [6] Titus 1:6; 1 Pet. 4:4 → DISSIPATION <810>.

RIOT (verb) – [1] 2 Pet. 2:13 → REVEL (verb) <1792> [2] 2 Pet. 2:13 → INDULGENCE <5172>.

RIOTING – [1] Acts 19:40 → INSURRECTION <4714> [2] Rom. 13:13 → REVEL (noun) <2970>.

RIOTOUS – Luke 15:13 → PRODIGAL <811>.

RIPE – Mark 4:29 → to be ripe → to be produced → PRODUCE <3860>.

RIPE (BE) – [1] ***xērainō*** [verb: ξηραίνω <3583>]; **from *xēros*: dry ▶ To be ready for harvesting** > One angel called out to another angel to reap, for the harvest of the earth was ripe {dried} (Rev. 14:15). All other refs.: DRY (verb) <3583>, RIGID <3583>, WITHER <3583>, WITHERED <3583>.

– [2] Rev. 14:18 → to be fully ripen → RIPENED (BE) <187>.

RIPENED (BE) – to be fully ripened: *akmazō* [verb: ἀκμάζω <187>]; **from *akmē*: point, summit ▶ To reach maturity** > An angel was ordered to harvest the grapes of the vine of the earth, for her grapes were fully ripened {were ripe} (Rev. 14:18). ¶

RISE (adj.) – [1] Luke 2:34 → RISING <386> [2] 1 Tim. 1:4 → to give rise → CAUSE (verb) <3930>.

RISE (verb) – [1] ***anatellō*** [verb: ἀνατέλλω <393>]; **from *ana*: up, upward, and *tellō*: to rise (for a star) ▶ To appear, to shine; also transl.: to come up** > The verb is used concerning the light (Matt. 4:16 {to spring up, to dawn}), the sun (Matt. 5:45; 13:6 {to be up}; Mark 4:6 {to arise, to be up}; 16:2 {after sunrise}; Jas. 1:11), a cloud (Luke 12:54 {to rise out}), and the morning star (2 Pet. 1:19 {to arise}). Other ref.: Heb. 7:14; see SPRING (verb) <393>. ¶

[2] **to rise up, to rise: *anistēmi*** [verb: ἀνίστημι <450>]; **from *ana*: above, and *histēmi*: to stand ▶ To arise, to oppose** > If Satan has risen up against himself, he cannot stand (Mark 3:26). Some rose up {arose, stood up} and bore false witness against Jesus (Mark 14:57). Judas the Galilean rose up {appeared} and drew away many people after him (Acts 5:37). Isaiah said that one will rise {arise} to reign over the Gentiles (Rom. 15:12). Other ref.: ARISE <450>, RAISE <450>.

[3] **to rise up: *epanistēmi*** [verb: ἐπανίστημι <1881>]; **from *epi*: upon, against, and *anistēmi*: see [2] ▶ To raise up, to oppose** > Jesus speaks of a time when children will rise up against parents (Matt. 10:21; Mark 13:12). ¶

[4] **to rise up: *exanistēmi*** [verb: ἐξανίστημι <1817>]; **from *ek*: intens., and *anistēmi*: see [2] ▶ To stand up (to speak), to intervene** > Believing Pharisees rose up saying it was necessary to circumcise the Gentiles (Acts 15:5). Other refs.: Mark 12:19; Luke 20:28 (to raise up); see RAISE <1817>. ¶

[5] **to rise up against: *katephistēmi*** [verb: κατεφίστημι <2721>]; **from *kata*: against (intens.), and *ephistēmi*: to come upon, which is from *epi*: upon, and *histēmi*: to stand ▶ To stand against, to oppose** > The Jews rose up {made insurrection with one accord, made a united attack} against Paul (Acts 18:12). ¶

[6] **to rise up together, to rise up too: *sunephistēmi*** [verb: συνεφίστημι <4911>]; **from *sun*: together, and *ephistēmi*: see [5] ▶ To join together in an attack, to assault jointly** > The crowd rose up together against Paul and Silas (Acts 16:22). ¶

[7] ***ginomai*** [verb: γίνομαι <1096>] **▶ To take place, to occur** > Pilate saw that a tumult was rising {was arising, was made, was starting} (Matt. 27:24). Other refs.: see entries in Lexicon at <1096>.

[8] **to rise, to rise up: *egeirō*** [verb: ἐγείρω <1453>] **▶ To stand against, to oppose; also transl.: to arise, to appear** > At the end, nation will rise against nation, and kingdom against kingdom (Matt. 24:7; Mark 13:8; Luke 21:10). Many false prophets will rise up and deceive many (Matt. 24:11); false christs and false prophets will rise (Matt. 24:24; Mark 13:22). All other refs.: ARISE <1453>, LIFT <1453>, RAISE <1453>, WAKE <1453>.

– [9] Matt. 2:2, 9 → when it rose → lit.: in the east → EAST <395> [10] Mark 10:50 in some mss. → to jump up → JUMP <375a> [11] Acts 4:26 → to rise up → to take one's stand → STAND <3936> [12] Eph. 2:21 → to rise to become → GROW <837> [13] Col. 2:12a; 3:1 → RAISE <4891> [14] Heb. 11:35 → to rise again to a better life → to obtain a better resurrection → OBTAIN <5177>, RESURRECTION <386> [15] Rev. 8:4; 11:7; 13:1; 14:11; 17:8; 19:3 → to rise up → GO UP <305>.

RISING – [1] ***anastasis*** [fem. noun: ἀνάστασις <386>]; **from *anistēmi*: to stand up, which is from *ana*: again, up, and *histēmi*: to stand ▶ Act of setting upright again** > Jesus was set for the fall and rising

up of {rising of} many in Israel (Luke 2:34). All other refs.: RESURRECTION <386>.
– [2] Matt. 8:11; Rev. 7:2; 16:12 → rising sun, rising of the sun → EAST <395> [3] Mark 16:2 → the rising of the sun → lit.: the sun having risen → RISE (verb) <393> [4] Luke 1:78 → rising sun → DAYSPRING FROM ON HIGH <395> <5311>.

RISK – [1] ***paradidōmi*** [verb: παραδίδωμι <3860>]; **from *para*: by the side, and *didōmi*: to give ▶ To put in danger, to put in peril** > Barnabas and Paul had risked {had given up, hazarded} their lives for the Lord Jesus Christ (Acts 15:26). All other refs.: see entries in Lexicon at <3860>.
[2] ***hupotithēmi*** [verb: ὑποτίθημι <5294>]; **from *hupo*: under, and *tithēmi*: to put ▶ To put in danger, to put in peril** > Prisca and Aquila had risked {had staked, had laid down} their own necks (sing. in Greek) for the life of Paul (Rom. 16:4). Other ref.: 1 Tim. 4:6; see POINT (verb) <5294>. ¶
– [3] Phil. 2:30 → VENTURE <3851>.

RITE – [1] Luke 2:22; Heb. 9:23 → "rites" added in Engl. [2] John 2:6 → for the Jewish rites of purification → lit.: according to the purifying of the Jews.

RITUAL DUTIES – Heb. 9:6 → ritual duties → SERVICE <2999>.

RIVALRY – [1] Gal. 5:20; Phil. 1:16 or 17; 2:3 → CONTENTION <2052> [2] Phil. 1:15 → STRIFE <2054>.

RIVER – [1] ***potamos*** [masc. noun: ποταμός <4215>]; **from *potazō*: to flow, which is from *potos*: drink (noun) ▶ Watercourse which is greater than a brook; also transl.: flood, riverside, stream, torrent, water** > The torrent could not shake the house built on the rock (Matt. 7:25; Luke 6:48), but it caused the house that was built on the sand to fall (Matt. 7:27; Luke 6:49). John baptized in the river Jordan (Mark 1:5). Rivers of living water will flow from the innermost being of one who believes in Jesus (John 7:38). Paul went out by the river where it was the custom for prayer to be made (Acts 16:13). He had been in perils of rivers (2 Cor. 11:26). A star fell on the third part of the rivers (Rev. 8:10). Four angels were bound at the great river Euphrates (Rev. 9:14). The serpent poured out of his mouth water, like a river, after the woman (Rev. 12:15a). The earth swallowed up the river (Rev. 12:16). The third angel poured out his bowl on the rivers (Rev. 16:4). The sixth angel poured out his bowl on the great river Euphrates (Rev. 16:12). John saw a river of water of life coming from the throne of God and of the Lamb (Rev. 22:1); the tree of life was in the middle of the street and on each side of the river (v. 2). ¶
[2] **carried away by a river: *potamophorētos*** [adj.: ποταμοφόρητος <4216>]; **from *potamos*: see [1], and *pherō*: to carry ▶ Roughly taken away by the water of a large stream of water; also transl.: carried away by a flood, swept away with the flood, swept away with the torrent** > The serpent poured out water like a river after the woman, that he might cause her to be carried away by a river (Rev. 12:15b). ¶

RIVERSIDE – Acts 16:13 → RIVER <4215>.

ROAD – [1] Matt. 7:13, 14; 20:17, 30; 21:8a, b, 19; Mark 8:27; 9:33, 34; 10:17, 32; 11:8a, b; Luke 3:5; 9:57; 10:4, 31; 14:23; 18:35; 19:36; 24:32, 35; Acts 8:26, 36; 9:17b, 27; et al. → WAY <3598> [2] Luke 19:37 → where the road goes down → DESCENT <2600> [3] Acts 19:1 → to take the road through → to pass through → PASS <1330>.

ROAR (noun) – [1] Luke 21:25 → to roar → ROARING <2278> [2] 2 Pet. 3:10 → with a roar → with a rushing noise → NOISE (noise) <4500> [3] Rev. 1:15 → VOICE <5456> [4] Rev. 10:3 → like the roar of a lion → lit.: as when a lion roars → ROAR (verb) <3455>.

ROAR (verb) – ***mukaomai*** [verb: μυκάομαι <3455>]; **comp. *muzō*: to grunt; *mugire*, in Lat.: to low, to bellow ▶ To cry out in the voice of an animal** > Another angel cried with a loud voice, as a lion roars (Rev. 10:3). ¶

ROARING – 1 **to roar: *ēcheō*** [verb: ἠχέω <2278>]; **from *ēchos*: sound ▶ To make a great, resounding noise** > The nations will be in perplexity at the roaring {roar} of the sea and rolling waves (Luke 21:25). Other ref.: 1 Cor. 13:1; see SOUND (verb) <2278>. ¶
2 **to roar: *ōruomai*** [verb: ὠρύομαι <5612>] **▶ To cry out as a lion after its prey** > The devil, like a roaring lion, prowls around Christians, seeking whom he may devour (1 Pet. 5:8). ¶

ROB – 1 ***sulaō*** [verb: συλάω <4813>]; **from *sulē*: spoils ▶ To spoil, to plunder** > Paul said he had robbed other churches, taking wages from them to minister to the Corinthians (2 Cor. 11:8). ¶
– 2 Matt. 12:29b; Mark 3:27b → PLUNDER (verb) <1283> 3 Mark 9:17 → robbed of his speech → DUMB <216> 4 Acts 19:27 → DESTROY <2507> 5 Acts 19:37 → they have neither robbed temples → lit.: they are not robbers of temples → robber of temples → TEMPLE <2417> 6 Rom. 2:22 → to rob temples → to commit sacrilege → SACRILEGE <2416> 7 1 Tim. 6:5 → DEPRIVE <650> 8 Titus 2:10 → PILFER <3557>.

ROBBER – 1 ***lēstēs*** [masc. noun: λῃστής <3027>]; **from *lēizomai*: to spoil, to plunder ▶ Brigand, outlaw, plunderer, thief using violence** > The temple had been made a den of thieves (Matt. 21:13; Mark 11:17; Luke 19:46). Jesus asked the multitudes if they had come out as against a robber {a thief, one leading a rebellion} (Matt. 26:55; Mark 14:48; Luke 22:52). Two robbers {thieves} were crucified with Jesus (Matt. 27:38; Mark 15:27); they were reviling Him (Matt. 27:44). A man who went down to Jericho fell into the hands of robbers (Luke 10:30, 36). He who does not enter the sheepfold by the door is a thief and a robber (John 10:1); all who came before Jesus were thieves and robbers (v. 8). Barabbas was a robber {had taken part in a rebellion} (John 18:40). Paul had been in perils of robbers {bandits} (2 Cor. 11:26). ¶
– 2 Luke 18:11 → RAPACIOUS <727> 3 Acts 19:37 → robber of churches, robber of temples → TEMPLE <2417>.

ROBBERY – 1 ***harpagē*** [fem. noun: ἁρπαγή <724>]; **from *harpazō*: to seize ▶ Action of seizing something by violence; that which is taken in this manner; also transl.: extortion, greed, plunder, rapine, ravening** > Jesus accused the scribes and Pharisees of being full of greed (Matt. 23:25; Luke 11:39). Other ref.: Heb. 10:34; see PLUNDERING <724>. ¶
2 ***harpagmos*** [masc. noun: ἁρπαγμός <725>]; **from *harpazō*: to seize by force, to snatch ▶ Object seized by force, something stolen** > Jesus did not esteem it robbery {an object of rapine, a thing to be grasped} to be equal with God (Phil. 2:6). ¶

ROBE (noun) – 1 **robe, long robe, flowing robe: *stolē*** [fem. noun: στολή <4749>]; **from *histēmi*: to stand, or *stellō*: to send ▶ Toga, long garment** > The scribes liked to walk about in long robes (Mark 12:38 {in long clothing}; Luke 20:46). In the tomb of Jesus, the women saw a young man clothed in a white robe (Mark 16:5). In a parable, the father had the best robe brought out to clothe his son (Luke 15:22). The believers in the Lord who had been put to death during the great tribulation were clothed in long white robes (Rev. 6:11; 7:9, 13, 14 (or 15). Blessed are those who wash their robes, that they may have right to the tree of life (Rev. 22:14). ¶
2 ***chlamus*** [fem. noun: χλαμύς <5511>] **▶ Chlamys, a short oblong mantle attached at the shoulder (worn by emperors, kings, military officers and other important people); a garment of dignity and office** > The soldiers of the governor put a scarlet robe {cloak} on Jesus (Matt. 27:28); after they had mocked Him, they stripped Him of it (v. 31). ¶
– 3 Matt. 26:65; John 19:2, 5 → CLOTHES <2440> 4 Luke 9:29 → CLOTHES <2441> 5 Luke 23:11; Acts 1:10 → CLOTHES <2066> 6 Acts 9:39 → TUNIC <5509>

7 Acts 12:21 → robes → APPAREL <2066> 8 Heb. 1:12 → CLOAK <4018> 9 Rev. 1:13 → to clothe with a robe → to clothe with a garment → GARMENT <1746>.

ROBE (verb) – Rev. 10:1 → CLOTHE <4016>.

ROBOAM – See REHOBOAM <4497>.

ROCK – 1 ***petra*** [fem. noun: πέτρα <4073>] ► **Mass of solid and immovable stone, in contrast to a detached stone (*petros*)** > Jesus compares one who acts on His words to a wise man who has built his house on the rock (Matt. 7:24, 25; Luke 6:48). He was going to build His church on the rock (Matt. 16:18), i.e., on Himself and on the testimony of Peter concerning His person (see v. 17). At the death of Jesus, the rocks were split (Matt. 27:51). The body of Jesus was placed in a new tomb that was hewn in the rock (Matt. 27:60; Mark 15:46). In the parable of the sower, seed fell on the rock (Luke 8:6); the ones on the rock represent those who receive the word with joy but who believe only for a time (v. 13). Isaiah speaks of a stumbling stone (*lithos*) and a rock (*petra*) of offence, image of Jesus Christ, laid in Zion (Rom. 9:33; 1 Pet. 2:8). The Israelites drank of a spiritual rock that followed them, and that rock was Christ (1 Cor. 10:4a, b). During the Apocalyptic judgments, men will hide themselves in the caves and in the rocks of the mountains (Rev. 6:15), saying to the mountains and to the rocks to fall on them (v. 16). ¶

2 **rocky place, rocky ground: *petrōdēs*** [adj. used as noun: πετρώδης <4075>]; **from *petra*: see 1, and *eidos*: appearance, form** ► **Stony, stony place** > In the parable of the sower, seed fell on rocky places (Matt. 13:5; Mark 4:5); those sown on the rocky places represent those who receive the word with joy but who endure only for a time (Matt. 13:20, see v. 21; Mark 4:16, see v. 17). ¶

3 **rocky place; place: *topos*** [masc. noun: τόπος <5117>]; **rocky, rough: *trachus*** [adj.: τραχύς <5138>] ► **Reef, ridge of rock or sand** > The sailors on board of Paul's ship were fearing lest they should run aground on the rocks (lit.: the rocky places) (Acts 27:29). Other ref. (*trachus*): Luke 3:5; see ROUGH <5138>. ¶ All other refs. (*topos*): COAST (noun) <5117>, OPPORTUNITY <5117>, PLACE (noun) <5117>.

4 **cut in the rock, hewn in the rock: *laxeutos*** [adj.: λαξευτός <2991>]; **from *laxeuō*; to cut in stone, which is from *las*: stone, and *xeō*: to scrape, to scratch** ► **To cut in a mass of solid stone** > Jesus was placed in a tomb hewn in the rock, where no one had ever been laid (Luke 23:53). ¶

ROCKY – 1 Luke 8:6, 13 → rocky ground → ROCK <4073> 2 Acts 27:29 → rocky place → ROCK <5117> <5138>.

ROD – 1 ***rhabdos*** [fem. noun: ῥάβδος <4464>] ► **Stick, staff for walking; also for inflicting a punishment** > Paul would rather not come to the Corinthians with a rod {whip} (1 Cor. 4:21). Aaron's rod {staff} that had sprouted was in the ark (Heb. 9:4). He who will overcome in Thyatira will rule the nations with an iron rod {scepter} (Rev. 2:27). A reed like a rod {measuring rod} was given to John to measure the temple of God (Rev. 11:1). The male Child (Christ) born by the woman (Israel) will shepherd all nations with an iron rod {scepter} (Rev. 12:5; 19:15). All other refs.: SCEPTER <4464>, STAFF <4464>.

2 **to beat, to beat with rods: *rhabdizō*** [verb: ῥαβδίζω <4463>]; **from *rhabdos*: see 1** ► **To hit with a stick, to birch; also transl.: to scourge** > The magistrates commanded to beat Paul and Silas with rods (Acts 16:22). Paul was beaten with rods three times (2 Cor. 11:25). ¶

– 3 Rev. 11:1; 21:15, 16 → REED <2563>.

ROLL – 1 **to roll up: *heilissō*** [verb: εἱλίσσω <1507>] ► **To put in the form of a cylinder by winding something over itself** > John saw the sky removed as a scroll rolled up {rolled together} (Rev. 6:14); some mss. have *helissō*. ¶

2 ***helissō*** [verb: ἑλίσσω <1667>] ► **To wrap round on itself, to fold up** > The

Lord will roll the heavens up like a garment (Heb. 1:12); some mss. have *heilissō*. ¶
3 **to roll, to roll around: *kuliō*** [verb: κυλίω <2947>] ▶ **To turn upon oneself** > Falling upon the earth, the child possessed by a spirit that made him mute rolled around {wallowed}, foaming at the mouth (Mark 9:20). ¶
4 **to roll away, to roll back: *apokuliō*** [verb: ἀποκυλίω <617>]; **from *apo*: from, and *kuliō*: see 3 ▶ To turn something over on itself in order to remove it** > The angel of the Lord came and rolled away the stone from the tomb of Jesus (Matt. 28:2). The women asked who would roll the stone away for them out of the entrance of the tomb of Jesus (Mark 16:3); when they looked, they saw that the stone had been rolled away (Mark 16:4: some mss. have *anakuliō*; Luke 24:2). ¶
5 **to roll against, to roll to: *proskuliō*** [verb: προσκυλίω <4351>]; **from *pros*: toward, and *kuliō*: see 3 ▶ To turn an object over on itself in order to move it up to a certain point** > Joseph rolled a great stone in front of the entrance of the tomb of Jesus (Matt. 27:60; Mark 15:46). ¶
6 **to roll up: *ptussō*** [verb: πτύσσω <4428>] ▶ **To fold up, to close** > Jesus rolled up the book of the prophet Isaiah (Luke 4:20). ¶
– 7 Acts 9:34 → roll up your mat → make your bed → BED <4766>.

ROLLING – 2 Pet. 2:22 → WALLOWING <2946>.

ROMAN – 1 ***Rhōmaios*** [masc. name: Ῥωμαῖος <4514>]; **from *Rhōmē*: Rome ▶ a. Inhabitant of the city of Rome** > On the day of Pentecost, visitors from Rome {Romans sojourning} heard the gospel in their own language in Jerusalem (Acts 2:10). **b. Citizen of the Roman Empire, enjoying the privileges which were reserved for this title** > At Philippi, Paul had made his Roman citizenship known and had been liberated (Acts 16:21, 37, 38). He had been delivered into the hands of the Romans by the Jews at Jerusalem (Acts 28:17); being a Roman citizen by birth, he escaped scourging (Acts 22:25–27, 29; 23:27; 25:16). He appealed to Caesar as a Roman citizen, to be judged before him (see Acts 25:10–12). The chief priests and Pharisees feared that the Romans would come and take away both their place and their nation, because they feared all would believe in Him as the political leader and king of the Jews, on account of His numerous miracles (John 11:48). ¶
2 ***Rhōmaikos*** [adj.: Ῥωμαϊκός <4513>]; **from *Rhōmaios*: see 1 ▶ In Roman (language), i.e., in Latin** > The inscription written over the cross of Jesus was written in Greek, Roman, and Hebrew letters (Luke 23:38). ¶

ROME – 1 ***Rhōmē*** [fem. name: Ῥώμη <4516>] ▶ **Rome was the capital of Italy and the Roman Empire** > At Corinth Paul met Aquila and Priscilla who had been obliged to leave Rome (Acts 18:2). He had wished to see Rome (Acts 19:21). The Lord, in a vision, had told him that he was to testify of the things concerning Him at Rome (Acts 23:11). He went to Rome as a prisoner during his fourth journey (Acts 28:14, 16). There, Onesiphorus sought and found him (2 Tim. 1:17). He wrote a letter to the Christians of Rome (Rom. 1:7), in which he said he was ready to preach the gospel to them (v. 15). ¶
– 2 Acts 2:10 → ROMAN <4514>.

ROMPHA – ***Rhemphan*** [masc. name: Ῥεμφάν <4481>]; **prob. a name of the god Saturn or Moloch (*Kiyyun*, in Heb.) ▶ Egyptian idol; also transl.: Remphan, Rephan** > Stephen reminds the Jews that the Israelites worshiped this idol in the desert (Acts 7:43). The emblem of this false god was a star (see Amos 5:25, 26). ¶

ROOF – 1 ***stegē*** [fem. noun: στέγη <4721>]; **from *stegō*: to cover ▶ Upper covering of a building** > A centurion told the Lord Jesus that he was not worthy that He should come under his roof (Matt. 8:8; Luke 7:6). Four men uncovered the roof of the place where Jesus was; and when they had broken through it, they lowered the

little bed on which a paralyzed man was lying (Mark 2:4). ¶
– [2] Matt. 10:27; 24:17; Mark 13:15; Luke 5:19; 12:3; 17:31; Acts 10:9 → HOUSETOP <1430>.

ROOM – [1] **upper room: *anōgeon*** [neut. noun: ἀνώγεον <508>]**; from *anō*: above, and *gē*: ground ▶ Upstairs room, portion of space within a building of two or more floors** > A man was to show the disciples a large upper room furnished and prepared to celebrate the Passover (Mark 14:15; Luke 22:12); other mss.: *anagaion*. ¶
[2] **room, inner room: *tameion*** [neut. noun: ταμεῖον <5009>]**; from *tamieuō*: to put in reserve ▶ Room inside, cabinet; also transl.: chamber, closet, inner chamber, secret chamber** > Jesus says to enter into our room to pray (Matt. 6:6). What has been spoken in the ear in the rooms will be proclaimed on the housetops (Luke 12:3). Some will say that the Christ is in the inner chambers (Matt. 24:26). Other ref.: Luke 12:24; see STOREHOUSE <5009>. ¶
[3] **upper room, upper chamber, upstairs room: *huperōon*** [neut. noun: ὑπερῷον <5253>]**; from *huperōos*: upper, which is from *huper*: above ▶ See [1].** > After the ascension of Jesus, the disciples went into an upper room (Acts 1:13). After her death, Dorcas was laid in an upper room (Acts 9:37); Peter was brought there (v. 39). There were many lamps in the upper room where Christians were gathered to listen to Paul (Acts 20:8); it was on the third floor (see v. 9). ¶
[4] **to be room: *chōreō*** [verb: χωρέω <5562>]**; from *chōra*: place ▶ To have space** > There was no longer any room in the house to listen to Jesus (Mark 2:2). All other refs.: see entries in Lexicon at <5562>.
– [5] Matt. 2:22 → in the room of → INSTEAD <473> [6] Matt. 9:24 → to make room → DEPART <402> [7] Matt. 23:6; Mark 12:39; Luke 14:7, 8; 20:46 → chief, highest, uppermost room → chief place → PLACE (noun) <4411> [8] Mark 14:14; Luke 22:11 → GUEST ROOM <2646> [9] Luke 2:7; 14:9b, 10, 22; Rom. 12:19; 15:23; 1 Cor. 14:16 → PLACE (noun) <5117> [10] John 14:2 → MANSION <3438> [11] Acts 25:23 → audience room → place of hearing → HEARING <201> [12] Acts 28:23; Phm. 22 → GUEST ROOM <3578> [13] Eph. 4:27 → OPPORTUNITY <5117>.

ROOST – Matt. 13:32; Mark 4:32; Luke 13:19 → NEST (verb) <2681>.

ROOSTER – [1] ***alektōr*** [masc. noun: ἀλέκτωρ <220>]**; comp. *alekō*: to defend, to protect ▶ Adult male of the chicken** > The word {cock, rooster} is found in the passages concerning the denial of Jesus by Peter (Matt. 26:34, 74, 75; Mark 14:30, 68, 72a, b; Luke 22:34, 60, 61; John 13:38; 18:27). ¶
[2] **crowing of the rooster: *alektorophōnia*** [fem. noun: ἀλεκτοροφωνία <219>]**; from *alektōr*: rooster, and *phōnē*: sound, voice ▶ At dawn, early in the morning** > The master of the house could come at the crowing of the rooster {cockcrow, cock-crowing, rooster crows} (Mark 13:35). ¶

ROOSTING-PLACE – Matt. 8:20; Luke 9:58 → NEST (noun) <2682>.

ROOT (noun) – [1] ***rhiza*** [fem. noun: ῥίζα <4491>]**; *radix*, in Lat. ▶ Part of a plant or tree that grows in the opposite direction from the stem or trunk and allows it to obtain nourishment** > The word is used in the natural sense in Matt. 3:10; 13:6, 21; Mark 4:6, 17; 11:20; Luke 3:9; 8:13. It is used in the sense of cause, of origin in regard to people (Rom. 11:16, 17, 18a, b), ancestors (Rom. 15:12; Rev. 5:5; 22:16), the love of money (1 Tim. 6:10), and bitterness (Heb. 12:15). ¶
– [2] Luke 17:6; Jude 12 → to pluck up, to pull up by the roots → UPROOT <1610>.

ROOT (verb) – [1] ***rhizoō*** [verb: ῥιζόω <4492>]**; from *rhiza*: root ▶ To establish, to start growing** > Paul prayed that the Ephesians would be rooted and grounded in love (Eph. 3:17). The Colossians were to walk in Christ Jesus rooted and built up in Him (Col. 2:7). ¶

– [2] Matt. 13:29; 15:13; Luke 17:6; Jude 12 → to root up → UPROOT <1610>.

ROPE – [1] Acts 27:17 → CABLE <996> [2] Acts 27:32 → CORD <4979> [3] Acts 27:40 → BAND (noun)[1] <2202>.

ROSTRUM – Acts 12:21 → THRONE <968>.

ROTTEN – to become rotten: *sēpō* [verb: σήπω <4595>] ▶ **To be corrupted, to perish** > Speaking to the rich, James told them that their wealth had become rotten (Jas. 5:2). ¶

ROUGH – [1] ***trachus*** [adj.: τραχύς <5138>] ▶ **Uneven, rugged, rocky** > John the Baptist, quoting Isaiah, said that the rough places were to become smooth ways (Luke 3:5). Other ref.: Acts 27:29 (rocky place); see ROCKY <5138>. ¶
– [2] John 6:18 → to become rough, to grow rough → ARISE <1326>.

ROUND – [1] **round about: *kuklō*** [adv.: κύκλῳ <2945>]**; from *kuklos*: circle; lit.: in circle** ▶ **Around, surrounding** > The disciples of Jesus told Him to send the people in the country round about {to the surrounding countryside} (Mark 6:36) and in the towns and country round about {to the surrounding villages and countryside} (Luke 9:12). From Jerusalem, and round about unto {all the way around to} Illyricum, Paul had fully preached the gospel of Christ (Rom. 15:19). All other refs.: AROUND <2945>, CIRCUIT <2945>.
[2] **round about: *perix*** [adv.: πέριξ <4038>]**; from *peri*: around** ▶ **Around, surrounding** > A multitude came out of the cities round about {around, in the vicinity of} Jerusalem bringing sick people to be healed by the apostles (Acts 5:16). ¶
– [3] Matt. 3:5; Luke 8:37 → region round, country round about, region that lies round about → region around, surrounding region → REGION <4066> [4] Matt. 14:35; Mark 6:55 → country round about, region round → country around, surrounding country → COUNTRY <4066> [5] Luke 19:43 → to compass round → SURROUND <4033> [6] John 10:24 → to come round about → SURROUND <2944> [7] Acts 25:7 → to stand round about → to stand about → STAND (verb) <4026> [8] Acts 28:13 → CIRCLE ROUND <4022> [9] Heb. 9:4 → round about → on all sides → SIDE <3840>.

ROUND UP – Acts 17:5 → to take aside → TAKE <4355>.

ROUSE – Acts 6:12 → to stir up → STIR (verb) <4787>.

ROUTE – Heb. 11:34 → to put to flight → FLIGHT <2827>.

ROW – ***elaunō*** [verb: ἐλαύνω <1643>] ▶ **To propel a boat by means of oars** > Jesus saw His disciples laboring in rowing (Mark 6:48). Having rowed three or four miles, the disciples saw Jesus walking on the sea (John 6:19). Other refs.: Luke 8:29; Jas. 3:4; 2 Pet. 2:17; see DRIVE <1643>. ¶

ROYAL – [1] ***basileios*** [adj.: βασίλειος <934>]**; from *basileus*: king** ▶ **Of the same nature as that of a king, suitable to a king** > Christians are a royal {kingly} priesthood (1 Pet. 2:9). Other ref.: Luke 7:25 in some mss. ¶
[2] ***basilikos*** [adj.: βασιλικός <937>]**; from *basileus*: king** ▶ **Which relates to a king, from a king** > Herod was clothed in royal apparel (Acts 12:21). He who fulfills the royal law of loving his neighbor as himself does well (Jas. 2:8). All other refs.: KING <937>, NOBLEMAN <937>.

ROYAL AUTHORITY – Rev. 17:17 → KINGSHIP <932>.

ROYAL POWER – Rev. 17:12 → KINGSHIP <932>.

RUB – ***psōchō*** [verb: ψώχω <5597>]**; from *psaō*: to touch lightly, to break into pieces, to grind** ▶ **To move back and forth with friction** > The disciples rubbed the heads of grain in their hands (Luke 6:1). ¶

RUBBISH – Phil. 3:8 → FILTH <4657>.

RUBY – Rev. 4:3 in some mss.; 21:20 → SARDIUS <4556>.

RUDDER – ***pēdalion*** [neut. noun: πηδάλιον <4079>]; **from *pēdon*: oar, blade of an oar ▶ Device for steering a ship** > The ropes that held the rudders were loosened (Acts 27:40). Ships are directed by a very small rudder (Jas. 3:4). ¶

RUDE – 1 1 Cor. 13:5 → to be rude → to behave unseemly → BEHAVE <807> 2 2 Cor. 11:6 → SIMPLE <2399>.

RUDELY – 1 Cor. 13:5 → to be rude → to behave uncomely → BEHAVE <807>.

RUDIMENT – Col. 2:8, 20 → ELEMENT <4747>.

RUE – ***pēganon*** [neut. noun: πήγανον <4076>] ▶ **Plant with heavily scented yellow flowers; it is used as an infusion, to season black olives and for medical purposes.** > The Pharisees paid tithes of rue, among other things, but neglected judgment and the love of God (Luke 11:42). ¶

RUFUS – ***Rhouphos*** [masc. name: Ῥοῦφος <4504>]: **red, redheaded; *rufus*, in Lat.: red ▶ Son of Simon of Cyrene** > Simon, the father of Rufus, carried the cross of Jesus (Mark 15:21). This is perhaps the same Rufus at Rome to whom Paul sends greetings (Rom. 16:13). ¶

RUIN (noun) – 1 ***katastrophē*** [fem. noun: καταστροφή <2692>]; **from *kata*: down, and *strephō*: to turn; in Engl.: catastrophe ▶ Destruction, overturning** > Disputes of words are profitable for nothing and lead to the ruin {subversion, subverting} of hearers (2 Tim. 2:14). Having reduced the cities of Sodom and Gomorrah to ashes, God condemned them to destruction {with an overthrow} (2 Pet. 2:6). ¶
2 ***olethros*** [masc. noun: ὄλεθρος <3639>]; **from *ollumi*: to destroy ▶ Destruction, death** > Those who desire to get rich fall into many unwise and hurtful lusts that plunge men into ruin (*olethros*) and destruction (*apōleia*) (1 Tim. 6:9). Other refs.: 1 Cor. 5:5; 1 Thes. 5:3; 2 Thes. 1:9; see DESTRUCTION <3639>. ¶
3 ***rhēgma*** [neut. noun: ῥῆγμα <4485>]; **from *rhēgnumi*: to break ▶ Fall, deterioration** > The ruin {breach, destruction} of the house built on the ground, without a foundation, was great (Luke 6:49). ¶
4 **to ruin: *kataskaptō*** [verb: κατασκάπτω <2679>]; **from *kata*: down, and *skaptō*: to dig; lit.: to dig beneath ▶ To undermine, to demolish** > The Lord will rebuild the ruins (lit.: the having been ruined) of the tabernacle of David (Acts 15:16). Other ref.: Rom. 11:3 (to dig down); see DIG <2679>. ¶
– 5 Rom. 3:16 → DESTRUCTION <4938> 6 Rev. 17:16; 18:17, 19 → to bring to ruin → to make desolate → DESOLATE <2049>.

RUIN (verb) – 1 Matt. 9:17; Mark 2:22; Luke 5:37 → LOSE <622> 2 Matt. 12:25; Luke 11:17 → to make desolate → DESOLATE <2049> 3 1 Cor. 8:11 → PERISH <622> 4 1 Cor. 15:33; 2 Cor. 7:2 → CORRUPT (verb) <5351> 5 Titus 1:11 → OVERTURN <396>.

RULE (noun) – 1 ***kanōn*** [masc. noun: κανών <2583>]; **from *kanē*: cane, straight reed; lit.: specifications, standard ▶ Instructions regarding required actions and tasks** > Paul boasted according to the measure of the rule {area of activity, field, sphere} that God had apportioned to him (2 Cor. 10:13, 15); he did not want to boast in another's rule {line of things, sphere, territory} (v. 16). Peace and mercy are in store for those who walk by the rule that the Christian is a new creation (Gal. 6:16). Other ref.: Phil. 3:16 in some mss. ¶
– 2 Matt. 15:9; Mark 7:7 → COMMANDMENT <1778> 3 Luke 20:20 → POWER[2] <746> 4 1 Cor. 7:17 → to lay down the rule → ORDAIN <1299> 5 1 Cor. 15:24; Eph. 1:21; 3:10; Col. 2:10 → PRINCIPALITY <746> 6 Col. 2:20 → to submit to rules → ORDINANCE <1379> 7 Col. 2:22; 1 Tim.

5:21 → "rules" added in Engl. [8] 2 Thes. 3:10 → to give the rule → COMMAND (verb) <3853> [9] 2 Tim. 2:5 → according to the rules → LAWFULLY <3545> [10] Heb. 13:17, 24 → one who has the rule → one who rules over → RULE (verb) <2233> [11] Rev. 17:18 → lit.: to have kingship → KINGSHIP <932>.

RULE (verb) – [1] **to rule over:** ***archō*** [verb: ἄρχω <757>]; **from *archē*: beginning ▶ To direct, to reign over** > Those who are esteemed to rule over the nations exercise lordship over them (Mark 10:42). There shall be one who arises to rule over the nations (Rom. 15:12). ¶

[2] ***brabeuō*** [verb: βραβεύω <1018>]; **from *brabeus*: arbitrator ▶ To reign, to dominate** > The peace of Christ is to rule {preside} in the hearts of Christians (Col. 3:15). ¶

[3] ***proistēmi*** [verb: προΐστημι <4291>]; **from *pro*: before, and *histēmi*: to stand ▶ To direct, to lead** > The overseer must rule his own house well (1 Tim. 3:4), otherwise he cannot take care of the church of God (v. 5). The deacons must rule their children and their own houses well (1 Tim. 3:12). The elders who rule {take the lead, direct the affairs of the church} well are to be esteemed worthy of double honor (1 Tim. 5:17). All other refs.: LEAD (verb) <4291>, MAINTAIN <4291>.

[4] **one who rules over: *hēgoumenos*, from: *hēgeomai*** [verb: ἡγέομαι <2233>]**: to rule ▶ One who guides, who commands; leader** > In the church, the "one who rules over" is an elder who cares for his brothers and sisters in the Lord by giving them direction. Christians should obey those who rule {have the rule} over them, for they watch for their souls (Heb. 13:17). Their faith, specifically the faith of those who have spoken the word of God, should be followed (Heb. 13:7). A special greeting is addressed to them at the end of this Epistle to the Hebrews (v. 24). The word is transl. "Ruler" {Governor} in Matt. 2:6 concerning Christ who will shepherd Israel. All other refs.: see entries in Lexicon at <2233>.

– [5] Matt. 2:6; Rev. 2:27; 12:5; 19:15 → SHEPHERD (verb) <4165> [6] Luke 22:25; Rom. 7:1; 14:9; 2 Cor. 1:24 → to have dominion → DOMINION <2961> [7] Rom. 6:6 → ruled by sin → lit.: of sin [8] 1 Cor. 4:8 → to share the rule → to reign with → REIGN (verb) <4821> [9] Col. 2:11 "ruled" added in Engl.

RULER – [1] ***archōn*** [masc. partic. of verb: ἄρχων <758>]; **ptcp. of *archō*: to rule, to command, which is from *archē*: beginning ▶ Person in a position of authority, chief; also transl.: authority, leader** > Jesus entered into the house of one of the rulers of the Pharisees (Luke 14:1). The rulers sneered at Jesus on the cross (Luke 23:35). Rulers are not a terror to good works (Rom. 13:3); the ruler (lit.: he) is God's minister (v. 4). The Greek term is transl. "magistrate" in Luke 12:58: Jesus speaks of going with one's adversary to the magistrate. Paul and Silas were dragged to the rulers {magistrates} (Acts 16:19). This word is used concerning Moses (Acts 7:27, 35a, b), Nicodemus, a ruler of the Jews {a member of the Jewish ruling council} (John 3:1), Jewish men (Luke 18:18; 23:13; 24:20; John 7:26, 48; 12:42; Acts 3:17; 4:5, 8, 26; 13:27; 14:5; 23:5), authorities of the synagogue (Matt. 9:18, 23; Luke 8:41), the authorities of this world (1 Cor. 2:6, 8 {prince}), and the authorities of the Gentiles {Matt. 20:25}. Jesus is the ruler {prince} of the kings of the earth (Rev. 1:5). All other refs.: MAGISTRATE <758>, PRINCE <758>.

[2] ***dunastēs*** [masc. noun: δυνάστης <1413>]; **from *dunamai*: to be capable ▶ Person in a position of authority, sovereign; also transl.: man of great authority, man in power** > God has put down rulers {the mighty} from their thrones (Luke 1:52). He is the blessed and only ruler {potentate, sovereign} (1 Tim. 6:15). Other ref.: Acts 8:27 (court official); see OFFICIAL <1413>. ¶

[3] ***hēgemōn*** [masc. noun: ἡγεμών <2232>]; **from *hēgeomai*: to lead, to administer ▶ One who is responsible for the administration** > Bethlehem is by no means least among the rulers {governors, leaders}

of Judah (Matt. 2:6). All other refs.: GOVERNOR <2232>.

4 ***kosmokratōr*** [masc. noun: κοσμοκράτωρ <2888>]; **from *kosmos*: world, and *krateō*: to hold, which is from *kratos*: might, power; lit.: sovereign of the world ► One who exercises authority on others >** Christians wrestle against the rulers {cosmic powers, universal lords, world forces} of the darkness of this age (Eph. 6:12). Those rulers are Satan and the fallen angels who are authorized by God to exercise their authority and influence on a world presently in moral darkness. ¶

5 **ruler of the city: *politarchēs*** [masc. noun: πολιτάρχης <4173>]; **from *polis*: city, and *archō*: to rule, to command, which is from *archē*: beginning ► Person in position of authority in a city >** Jason and some brothers were dragged before the rulers of the city {city authorities, city officials, politarchs} of Thessalonica (Acts 17:6, 8). ¶

– 6 Matt. 24:45, 47; 25:21, 23; Luke 12:42, 44 → to make, to make ruler → MAKE <2525> 7 Mark 5:22, 35, 36, 38; Luke 8:49; 13:14; Acts 13:15; 18:8, 17 → ruler of the synagogue → SYNAGOGUE <752> 8 Mark 10:42 → ruler over, as ruler over → lit.: to rule over → RULE (verb) <757> 9 Luke 12:11 → MAGISTRATE <746> 10 Rom. 8:38; Eph. 6:12; Col. 1:16; 2:15; Titus 3:1 → PRINCIPALITY <746> 11 Rom. 13:4 → rulers → lit.: he (sing.).

RULER OF THE FEAST – John 2:9a → FEAST (noun) <755>.

RULING – 1 John 3:1 → a member of the Jewish ruling council → lit.: a ruler of the Jews → RULER <758> 2 1 Cor. 6:4 → to ask for a ruling → to set to judge → JUDGE (verb) <2523>.

RUMOR – 1 ***akoē*** [fem. noun: ἀκοή <189>]; **from *akouō*: to hear ► Report, hearsay >** Before the great tribulation, wars and rumors {rumours} of war will be heard (Matt. 24:6; Mark 13:7). All other refs.: EAR <189>, FAME <189>, HEARING <189>, REPORT (noun) <189>.

2 ***logos*** [masc. noun: λόγος <3056>] ► **Word, news >** The rumor {report, rumour} of Jesus resurrecting a young man went throughout all Judea (Luke 7:17). Other refs.: WORD <3056>.

RUMOUR – 1 Matt. 24:6; Mark 13:7 → RUMOR <189> 2 Luke 4:14 → NEWS <5345> 3 Luke 4:37 → REPORT (noun) <2279> 4 Luke 7:17 → RUMOR <3056> 5 Acts 2:6 → SOUND (noun) <5456>.

RUN – 1 ***trechō*** [verb: τρέχω <5143>] ► **To move rapidly >** An individual ran and took a sponge filled with sour wine, and offered it to Jesus to drink on the cross (Matt. 27:48; Mark 15:36). Women ran to bring the disciples of Jesus word that He was risen (Matt. 28:8); Mary Magdalene ran and came to Simon Peter (John 20:2). A man with an unclean spirit ran toward Jesus (Mark 5:6). In a parable, the father ran toward his son who was coming back home (Luke 15:20). Peter ran to the tomb of Jesus (Luke 24:12); in John, we read that Peter and John were running together (John 20:4). Mercy is not of him who wills, nor of him who runs (in the sense of making efforts), but of God who shows mercy (Rom. 9:16). Among those who run in a race, only one receives the prize; Paul exhorts to run in such a way as to obtain it (1 Cor. 9:24a–c), and himself ran not with uncertainty (v. 26). He feared that he might run, or had run, in vain (Gal. 2:2a, b). The Galatians had run well (Gal. 5:7). By holding fast the word of life, the Thessalonians were testifying that Paul had not run in vain or labored in vain (Phil. 2:16). The Thessalonians were to pray for Paul that the word of the Lord might run {have free course, spread rapidly} (2 Thes. 3:1). Christians must run with perseverance the race that is set before them (Heb. 12:1). The sound of the wings of the locusts was like the sound of chariots with many horses running into {rushing to, into} the battle (Rev. 9:9). ¶

2 **to run in, to run back: *eistrechō*** [verb: εἰστρέχω <1532>]; **from *eis*: in, and *trechō*: see 1 ► To move rapidly inside >** When she recognized Peter's voice, Rhoda ran in

and announced that Peter stood before the gate (Acts 12:14). ¶

[3] **to run down:** ***katatrechō*** [verb: κατατρέχω <2701>]**; from *kata*: down, and *trechō*: see** [1] **▶ To go down, to descend rapidly** > The commander ran down to those seeking to kill Paul (Acts 21:32). ¶

[4] **to run about, through, throughout:** ***peritrechō*** [verb: περιτρέχω <4063>]**; from *peri*: around, and *trechō*: see** [1] **▶ To run around** > People ran through the whole country around, carrying to Jesus those who were sick (Mark 6:55). ¶

[5] **to run, to run to, to run up:** ***prostrechō*** [verb: προστρέχω <4370>]**; from *pros*: to, and *trechō*: see** [1] **▶ To run toward** > The people ran to greet Jesus (Mark 9:15); *proschairō* in some mss.: to be glad. A man ran up to Jesus and asked Him what to do to inherit eternal life (Mark 10:17). Philip ran up to the chariot of the Ethiopian (Acts 8:30). Other ref.: John 20:16 in some mss. ¶

[6] **to run ahead, to run before, to outrun:** ***protrechō*** [verb: προτρέχω <4390>]**; from *pro*: before, and *trechō*: see** [1] **▶ To run in front** > Zaccheus ran ahead and climbed up into a sycamore tree to see Jesus (Luke 19:4). John outran Peter and came to the tomb first (John 20:4). ¶

[7] **to run together, to run with:** ***suntrechō*** [verb: συντρέχω <4936>]**; from *sun*: together, and *trechō*: see** [1] **▶ To run with** > Many ran (lit.: ran together) on foot to the place where Jesus and His disciples were heading (Mark 6:33). All the people ran together {came running} (lit.: ran together) to Peter and John (Acts 3:11). Unbelievers think it strange that Christians do not run with them {do not plunge} in the same flood of dissipation (1 Pet. 4:4). ¶

[8] **to run together:** ***episuntrechō*** [verb: ἐπισυντρέχω <1998>]**; from *epi*: to, and *suntrechō*: see** [7] **▶ To come upon a scene or group by running together** > Jesus saw that the people came running together {was running, was rapidly gathering} to the scene (Mark 9:25). ¶

[9] **to run under:** ***hupotrechō*** [verb: ὑποτρέχω <5295>]**; from *hupo*: under, and *trechō*: see** [1] **▶ To pass under, to navigate under** > Paul's ship ran under the shelter of an island called Clauda (Acts 27:16). ¶

[10] **to run in:** ***eispēdaō*** [verb: εἰσπηδάω <1530>]**; from *eis*: toward, in, and *pēdaō*: to jump ▶ To rush** > Barnabas and Paul ran in {rushed in, rushed out} among the multitude (Acts 14:14; other mss.: *ekpēdaō*: to rush out). The jailer ran in {rushed in, sprang in} the prison (Acts 16:29). ¶

[11] **to run aground:** ***ekpiptō*** [verb: ἐκπίπτω <1601>]**; from *ek*: far from, and *piptō*: to fall ▶ a. To fall, to cast ashore** > It was necessary that Paul's ship be run aground {be cast ashore} on some island (Acts 27:26). **b. To be driven on reefs** > There was fear that Paul's ship would run aground on {fall upon, be cast on, be dashed against} the rocks (Acts 27:29). Other refs.: EFFECT (noun) <1601>, FAIL <1601>, FALL (verb) <1601>.

[12] **to run ashore, to run aground:** ***exōtheō*** [verb: ἐξωθέω <1856>]**; from *ek*: away from, and *ōtheō*: to push, to drive ▶ To run aground so as to immobilize** > It was planned to run {drive, thrust} ashore the ship of Paul onto a bay with a beach (Acts 27:39); in some mss.: *eksōzō*: to preserve. Other ref.: Acts 7:45 (to drive out); see DRIVE <1856>. ¶

[13] **to run aground:** ***epokellō*** [verb: ἐποκέλλω <2027>]**; from *epi*: intens., and *okellō*: to bring to land; also spelled: *epikellō* ▶ To bring, to drive to the shore** > Paul's ship was run aground (Acts 27:41). ¶

[14] **to run over:** ***huperekchunō*** [verb: ὑπερεκχύνω <5240>]**; from *huper*: above, and *ekcheō*: to pour, to spill, which is from *ek*: out, and *cheō*: to pour ▶ To overflow, to surpass the measure** > If we give, it will be given to us: a good measure running over (Luke 6:38). ¶

– [15] Matt. 6:32; Luke 12:30 → to run after → SEEK <1934> [16] Matt. 8:32; Mark 5:13; Luke 8:33; Acts 7:57; 19:29 → to run violently down, to run → RUSH <3729> [17] Matt. 8:33; Mark 5:14; Luke 8:34; John 10:5, 12, 13 → to run away, to run off → FLEE <5343> [18] Matt. 9:17; Mark 2:22; Luke 5:37 → to run out → POUR <1632> [19] Mark 14:52 → to run away → ESCAPE <5343> [20] Luke 5:11 → BRING <2609>

21 Luke 17:23 → to run after → FOLLOW <1377> 22 John 2:3 → to run out of → LACK (verb) <5302> 23 Acts 19:16 → to run out → FLEE <1628> 24 Acts 21:30 → the people ran together, from all directions → lit.: there was a concourse of the people → CONCOURSE <4890> 25 2 John 9 → to run ahead → TRANSGRESS <4254> 26 Jude 11 → to run greedily → to give oneself up → GIVE <1632>.

RUNNER – 1 Cor. 9:24 → lit.: one running → RUN <5143>.

RUSH – 1 ***hormaō*** [verb: ὁρμάω <3729>]; **from *hormē*: dash, attack ▶ To surge, to precipitate oneself, to throw oneself; also transl.: to run** > The herd of swine, into which the demons had entered, rushed down {ran violently down} the steep slope into the sea (Matt. 8:32; Mark 5:13; Luke 8:33). Those who had heard Stephen rushed {ran} at him (Acts 7:57). The Ephesians rushed into the theater (Acts 19:29). ¶
– 2 Acts 14:14; 16:29 → to rush in, to rush out → to run in → RUN <1530> 3 Acts 17:5 → ASSAULT <2186> 4 Acts 21:30 → the people rushed together → lit.: there was a concourse of the people → CONCOURSE <4890> 5 Acts 27:14 → to rush down → ARISE <906> 6 Jude 11 → to rush headlong into, to rush for profit into → to give oneself up → GIVE <1632> 7 Rev. 9:9 → RUN <5143>.

RUSHING – **to rush: *pherō*** [verb: φέρω <5342>]; **lit.: to carry ▶ To move with strength and speed** > At Pentecost, there came a sound, as of a rushing {blowing, impetuous} violent wind (Acts 2:2). Other refs.: see entries in Lexicon at <5342>.

RUST – 1 ***brōsis*** [fem. noun: βρῶσις <1035>]; **from *bibrōskō*: to eat; lit.: that which eats away ▶ Corrosion** > Moth and rust {vermin} destroy treasures on earth, but not treasures in heaven (Matt. 6:19, 20). All other refs.: EATING <1035>, FOOD <1035>, MEAL <1035>.
2 ***ios*** [masc. noun: ἰός <2447>]; ***hiēmi*: to send; lit.: something sent out, as rust formed on metals ▶ Result of the corrosion of metal in a humid environment** > The rust {canker, corrosion} of the gold and silver of the rich will be a witness against them (Jas. 5:3). Other refs.: Rom. 3:13; Jas. 3:8; see POISON (noun) <2447>. ¶

RUSTED (BE) – ***katioō*** [verb: κατιόω <2728>]; **from *kata*: intens., and *ios*: rust ▶ To be eaten away by rust, by corrosion** > The gold and silver of the rich have rusted {is eaten away, is cankered, are corroded} (Jas. 5:3). ¶

RUTH – ***Rhouth*** [fem. name: Ῥούθ <4503>]: **friend, in Heb. ▶ Moabite woman who married Boaz (or Booz) (see Ruth 1:4; 4:13)** > She is one of four women, in addition to Mary, mentioned in the genealogy of Jesus Christ (Matt. 1:5). ¶

RUTHLESS – Rom. 1:31 → UNMERCIFUL <415>.

S

SABACHTHANI – ***sabachthani*** [σαβαχθάνι <4518>] ▶ **Aram. term that means "you have forsaken me"** > On the cross, Jesus cried out with a loud voice: "*Eli, Eli,* (or *Eloi, Eloi*) *lama sabachthani*" (Matt. 27:46; Mark 15:34; see Ps. 22:2); these words mean: "My God, My God, why have You forsaken Me?" ¶

SABAOTH – ***Sabaōth*** [noun: Σαβαώθ <4519>]; **from the Heb. *tsaba*: crowd of people ▶ Multitude of people, troops assembled for combat; lit. in Heb.: of hosts** > The Lord of Sabaoth {Lord of Hosts, Lord Almighty} (Rom. 9:29; Jas. 5:4) is the Lord particularly of the armies of angels. ¶

SABBATH – [1] ***sabbaton*** [neut. noun: σάββατον <4521>]; **from the Heb. *shabbath*: rest ▶ Seventh and last day of the week, day of rest prescribed by the Lord for His people, in relation to the rest of God after creation (see Ex. 20:8–11; 31:17) and to redemption (see Deut. 5:12–15)** > The term is used frequently in the Gospels (e.g., Luke 4:16) and in Acts (e.g., 13:14); Col. 2:16 speaks of not being judged in respect to the observance of Sabbaths. For Christians, the Lord's Day, the first day of the week, has replaced the Sabbath. The Pharisees had introduced various prohibitions in relation to the Sabbath day, but Jesus told them that the Sabbath was made for man and not the contrary; Jesus is the Lord of the Sabbath (Matt. 12:8; Mark 2:28; Luke 6:5). *
[2] **day before the Sabbath: *prosabbaton*** [neut. noun: προσάββατον <4315>]; **from *pro*: before, and *sabbaton*: see [1] ▶ Eve of the Sabbath** > The Preparation day was the day before the Sabbath (Mark 15:42). ¶

SABBATH DAY'S JOURNEY – ***sabbatou hodos*; *sabbaton*** [neut. noun: σάββατον <4521>] ***hodos*** [fem. noun: ὁδός <3598>] ▶ **Measure of distance of approx. 3/4 of a mile (1,100 meters); the scribes allowed the Jews to travel only that distance on the day of the Sabbath** > After the ascension of the Lord, the apostles returned to Jerusalem from the mount of Olives, which is a Sabbath day's journey {walk} from Jerusalem (Acts 1:12). All other refs. (*hodos*): see WAY <3598>. ¶

SABBATH REST – ***sabbatismos*** [masc. noun: σαββατισμός <4520>]; **from *sabbatizō*: to observe the Sabbath, which is from *sabbaton*: Sabbath ▶ Cessation of activities on the Sabbath day** > There remains a Sabbath rest for the people of God (Heb. 4:9). This rest for the church corresponds to her introduction into the heavenly places. ¶

SABBATISM – Heb. 4:9 → SABBATH REST <4520>.

SACKCLOTH – ***sakkos*** [masc. noun: σάκκος <4526>]; **from the Heb. *sak*: cloth used for making sacks ▶ Rough clothing** > To express repentance, sackcloth was worn directly on the skin. The expr. "to repent in sackcloth and ashes" (Matt. 11:21; Luke 10:13) means to adopt an attitude of deep humiliation in repentance. John saw the sun becoming as hair sackcloth (Rev. 6:12). The two witnesses of Rev. 11:3 will prophesy, clothed in sackcloth as a mark of humility, during 1260 days. ¶

SACRED – [1] ***hieros*** [adj.: ἱερός <2413>] ▶ **Holy, consecrated to God** > Those who labor at sacred things (i.e., functions related to the service of the temple) partake of what is offered on the altar in the temple (1 Cor. 9:13). Other ref.: 2 Tim. 3:15; see HOLY (adj.) <2413>. ¶
[2] **as becomes sacred persons: *hieroprepēs*** [adj.: ἱεροπρεπής <2412>]; **from *hieros*: see [1], and *prepō*: to be appropriate, to be suitable ▶ As suits persons who are set apart, reverent** > The older women are to be in all their behavior as becomes sacred persons (Titus 2:3). ¶
– [3] Matt. 7:6; 1 Cor. 3:17; 2 Pet. 2:21 → that which is holy, holy → HOLY (adj.) <40> [4] Matt. 23:17, 19 → to make sacred → SANCTIFY <37>.

SACRED STONE – Acts 19:35 → "sacred stone" added in Engl.; others add "image."

SACRIFICE (noun) – [1] ***thusia*** [fem. noun: θυσία <2378>]; **from *thuō*: to sacrifice ▶ That which is slain as an offering to God or to an idol** > Sacrifices were offered under the law (Matt. 9:13; 12:7; Mark 9:49; 12:33; Luke 2:24; 13:1; Acts 7:42; 1 Cor. 10:18; Heb. 5:1; 7:27; 8:3; 9:9; 10:1, 11, 26). The Israelites brought a sacrifice to an idol (Acts 7:41), a golden calf that they had made. Christians are exhorted to present their bodies a living sacrifice to God (Rom. 12:1). Christ delivered Himself up as a sacrifice to God (Eph. 5:2). Paul was poured out as a drink offering on the sacrifice and service of faith of the Philippians (Phil. 2:17). That which the Philippians had sent to Paul was an acceptable sacrifice (Phil. 4:18). The sacrifice of Christ is better than those sacrifices offered under the law (Heb. 9:23). He was manifested once for the putting away of sin by the sacrifice of Himself (Heb. 9:26). God, not having desired sacrifice, prepared a body for His Son (Heb. 10:5, 8). Having offered one sacrifice for sins forever, Christ sat down at the right hand of God (Heb. 10:12). Abel offered a more excellent sacrifice than Cain (Heb. 11:4). Christians are exhorted to offer to God a sacrifice of praise (Heb. 13:15). God takes pleasure in sacrifices such as doing good (Heb. 13:16). Believers offer up spiritual sacrifices acceptable to God by Jesus Christ (1 Pet. 2:5). ¶

[2] **offered in sacrifice: *eidōlothuton*** [neut. noun: εἰδωλόθυτον <1494>]; **from *eidōlon*: idol, and *thuō*: to sacrifice ▶ What is presented to an idol as an offering** > Paul says not to eat something offered in sacrifice {offered to holy purposes, offered to idols, sacrificed to idols} (1 Cor. 10:28). Some mss. have *hierothutos*. All other refs.: IDOL <1494> SACRIFICE (verb) <1494>.

[3] Heb. 10:6, 8 → sacrifice for sin, sacrifices for sin → lit.: for sin (*peri hamartias*). Such sacrifices were offered in the O.T. to make atonement for sins committed (see Leviticus 4).

– [4] Acts 7:42 → slain beast → BEAST <4968> [5] Acts 14:13, 18; 1 Cor. 10:20a, b → to do sacrifice, to offer sacrifice → SACRIFICE (verb) <2380> [6] Acts 21:26; Heb. 10:10, 14, 18 → OFFERING <4376> [7] Heb. 13:11 → as a sacrifice for sin → lit.: concerning (*peri*) sins [8] 1 John 2:2; 4:10 → atoning sacrifice → PROPITIATION <2434>.

SACRIFICE (verb) – [1] ***thuō*** [verb: θύω <2380>] ▶ **To immolate, to kill as an offering to God or to demons; also transl.: to do sacrifice, to offer sacrifice, to slay** > The Jews sacrificed the Passover lamb (Mark 14:12; Luke 22:7). The priest of Zeus intended to sacrifice oxen in honor of Paul and Barnabas (Acts 14:13; *epithuō* in some mss.), as likewise did the crowds (v. 18). Christ, the Passover of Christians, has been sacrificed (1 Cor. 5:7). The things that the nations sacrifice, they sacrifice to demons and not to God (1 Cor. 10:20a, b). All other refs.: KILL <2380>.

[2] **sacrificed to idol, idols, a god: *eidōlothuton*** [neut. noun: εἰδωλόθυτον <1494>]; **from *eidōlon*: idol, and *thuō*: see [1] ▶ What one immolates, kills as as sacrificial victim in order to offer it to idols, i.e., to the demons behind these idols; also transl.: offered to idols** > The word is used by Paul (1 Cor. 8:1, 4, 7, 10; 10:19, 28 {other mss.: *ierothutos*}), Luke (Acts 15:29; 21:25) and John (Rev. 2:14, 20). ¶

– [3] Heb. 9:28 → OFFER <4374>.

SACRIFICE OF ATONEMENT – Rom. 3:25 → MERCY SEAT <2435>.

SACRIFICIAL – to carry on as a sacrificial service: *hierourgeō* [verb: ἱερουργέω <2418>]; **from *hierourgos*: sacrificing, which is from *hieron*: temple, and *ergon*: work ▶ To accomplish priestly functions; also transl.: to minister, to minister as a priest, with the priestly duty** > Paul carried on a sacrificial service symbolically in the gospel of God (Rom. 15:16), to present the redeemed from among the nations to Him as an offering. ¶

SACRIFICIAL FOOD – 1 Cor. 8:7 → added in Engl.

SACRIFICIAL OFFERING – [1] 1 Cor. 9:13 → to share in the sacrificial offerings → lit.: to partake of the altar → ALTAR <2379> [2] Phil. 2:17 → sacrifice and service → SACRIFICE (noun) <2378>.

SACRILEGE – to commit sacrilege: *hierosuleō* [verb: ἱεροσυλέω <2416>]; **from *hierosulos*: sacrilegious person, which is from *hieron*: temple, and *sulaō*: to spoil, to steal ▶ To despoil a temple, to steal its goods** > Paul asks those who abhor idols if they commit sacrilege {rob temples} (Rom. 2:22). ¶

SACRILEGIOUS – Acts 19:37 → lit.: robber of temples → TEMPLE <2417>.

SAD – [1] **to be sad: *lupeō*** [verb: λυπέω <3076>]; **from *lupē*: affliction, sorrow ▶ To be sorrowful; also transl.: to be grieved, to be grieving** > Having heard the word of Jesus, a young man went away sad (Matt. 19:22; Mark 10:22). All other refs.: SORROW (noun) <3076>, SORROW (verb) <3076>.

[2] **very sad: *perilupos*** [adj.: περίλυπος <4036>]; **from *peri*: about (intens.), and *lupē*: affliction, sorrow ▶ Very sorrowful, deeply chagrined** > Having heard the word of Jesus, a young man became very sad (Luke 18:23), which Jesus noticed (v. 24). All other refs.: SORROWFUL <4036>, SORRY <4036>.

[3] **sad countenance, sad: *skuthrōpos*** [adj.: σκυθρωπός <4659>]; **from *skuthros*: dark, sad, and *ōps*: eye, face, countenance ▶ Sad look on a person's face, showing sorrow, unhappiness** > The hypocrites have a sad countenance {are downcast in countenance, have a gloomy face, look somber} when they fast (Matt. 6:16) so that they will be noticed. The two disciples who were returning to Emmaus were sad {downcast} (Luke 24:17). ¶

[4] **to be sad: *stugnazō*** [verb: στυγνάζω <4768>]; **from *stugnos*: hateful, sad, which is from *stugos*: an object of horror, grief ▶ To be of a somber humor, to be afflicted** > A man who had observed various commandments was sad {disheartened} {The face of this man fell} at the word of Jesus to sell everything and follow Him (Mark 10:22). Other ref.: Matt. 16:3 (to be overcast); see OVERCAST <4768>. ¶

SADDUCEE – *Saddoukaios* [masc. noun: Σαδδουκαῖος <4523>]; **prob. from *Sadōk*: Sadoc (i.e., Zadok; see 1 Kgs. 2:35) ▶ Member of a Jewish sect; the Sadducees came from a political sect that promoted the Hellenization of Judaism, extolling the advantages of Greek life and culture** > The Sadducees and the Pharisees, firmly decried by John the Baptist, were strongly opposed to Jesus (Matt. 3:7; 16:1); Jesus said to be on guard against their leaven (Matt. 16:6) and their doctrine (vv. 11, 12). The Sadducees did not believe in the resurrection nor in the existence of angels and spirits (Matt. 22:23, 34; Mark 12:18; Luke 20:27; Acts 23:8). The Sadducees with the high priest threw the apostles into the public prison (Acts 5:17). They were opposed to Christians (Acts 4:1; 23:6, 7). ¶

SADOK – See ZADOK <4524>.

SAFE – [1] ***asphalēs*** [adj.: ἀσφαλής <804>]; **from *a*: neg., and *sphallō*: to throw down ▶ Providing certainty, contributing to security** > To write the same things was not irksome for Paul, and was safe {a safeguard} for the Philippians (Phil. 3:1). All other refs.: CERTAINTY <804>, SURE <804>.

– [2] Luke 11:21 → to be safe → lit.: to be in peace → PEACE <1515> [3] Acts 23:24; 27:44 → SAFELY <1295> [4] Rom. 15:31 → to be kept safe → to be delivered → DELIVER <4506>.

SAFEGUARD – Phil. 3:1 → SAFE <804>.

SAFELY – [1] **to bring safe, safely; to escape safely: *diasōzō*** [verb: διασῴζω <1295>]; **from *dia*: through (intens.), and *sōzō*: to deliver, to save, to protect ▶ To be preserved, to reach in security** > Paul was to be brought safely {safe} to Felix the governor (Acts 23:24). Those who had been shipwrecked while sailing with Paul all escaped safely {got safe, escaped all safe} to land (Acts 27:44). All other refs.: HEAL <1295>, SAVE (verb) <1295>.

[2] **to be safe and sound, to be safe and well: *hugiainō*** [verb: ὑγιαίνω <5198>]; **from *hu-***

***giēs*: healthy, sound ▶ To be healthy, to be physically well** > The father in the parable received his son safe and sound (lit.: being safe and sound) (Luke 15:27). All other refs.: HEALTH <5198>, SOUND (adj.) <5198>.
– 3 Mark 14:44; Acts 16:23 → SECURELY <806> 4 2 Tim. 4:18 → to bring safely → PRESERVE <4982>.

SAFETY – 1 ***asphaleia*** [fem. noun: ἀσφάλεια <803>]; **from *asphalēs*: firm, safe, which is from *a*: neg., and *sphallō*: to throw down ▶ Security, freedom from danger** > The officers found the prison shut with all safety {securely}, but they did not find the apostles inside (Acts 5:23). When they say "Peace and safety," then sudden destruction will come upon men, as labor pains upon a pregnant woman (1 Thes. 5:3). Other ref.: Luke 1:4; see CERTAINTY <803>. ¶
– 2 Acts 27:34 → SURVIVAL <4991> 3 Acts 27:44 → to reach in safety → to escape safely → SAFELY <1295>.

SAGE – Matt. 23:34 → wise man → WISE (noun) <4680>.

SAIL (noun) – 1 ***skeuos*** [neut. noun: σκεῦος <4632>] **▶ Ship's equipment used to harness the wind** > The sail was struck (The gear was lowered) on Paul's boat (Acts 27:17); other transl.: They let down the sea anchor, They lowered the sea anchor. All other refs.: ARTICLE <4632>, GOOD (adj. and noun) <4632>, VESSEL[1] <4632>.
2 **to set sail, to make sail: *anagō*** [verb: ἀνάγω <321>]; **from *ana*: up, and *agō*: to go ▶ To take to open water, to navigate; also transl.: to launch, to put to sea, to sail, to depart, to loose** > The verb is used in regard to Paul and his companions (Acts 27:2, 4; 28:11 {to depart}). Other refs.: Acts 27:12, 21. All other refs.: see entries in Lexicon at <321>.
– 3 Acts 18:18 → to set sail → SAIL (verb) <1602> 4 Acts 20:15 → to set sail → SAIL (verb) <636>.

SAIL (verb) – 1 **to sail, to sail away: *anagō*** [verb: ἀνάγω <321>]; **from *ana*: again, up, and *agō*: to lead ▶ To take to open water, to navigate; also transl.: to launch, to loose, to put out to sea, to set forth, to set sail** > Paul and his companions sailed away {loosed, put out to sea} from Troas (Acts 16:11). Paul sailed from Ephesus (Acts 18:21). On another occasion, he was about to sail to Syria (Acts 20:3). The verb is also used in Acts 13:13; 20:13; 21:1, 2. All other refs.: see entries in Lexicon at <321>.
2 ***pleō*** [verb: πλέω <4126>] **▶ To travel over water, to navigate** > As the disciples sailed, Jesus fell asleep (Luke 8:23). The ship Paul had boarded sailed to Syria (Acts 21:3). The centurion guarding Paul found a ship sailing to Italy (Acts 27:6). God had given Paul all those who sailed with him (Acts 27:24). Everyone who sails to any place {All who travel by ship, All the company in ships, Every passenger} will see the smoke of the burning of Babylon (Rev. 18:17). Other ref.: Acts 27:2. ¶
3 **to sail, to sail away: *apopleō*** [verb: ἀποπλέω <636>]; **from *apo*: from, and *pleō*: see 2 ▶ To depart by ship, to put out to sea** > The verb is used in Acts 13:4; 14:26; 20:15 {to set sail}; 27:1. ¶
4 **to sail across, over, through: *diapleō*** [verb: διαπλέω <1277>]; **from *dia*: through, and *pleō*: see 2 ▶ To navigate across** > Having sailed over the sea along the coast of Cilicia and Pamphylia, Paul and his companions came to Myra in Lycia (Acts 27:5). ¶
5 **to sail slowly: *braduploeō*** [verb: βραδυπλοέω <1020>]; **from *bradus*: slow, and *pleō*: see 2 ▶ To travel slowly on water** > The ship Paul had boarded sailed slowly {made slow headway} for many days (Acts 27:7a). ¶
6 **to sail, to sail away: *ekpleō*** [verb: ἐκπλέω <1602>]; **from *ek*: out, and *pleō*: see 2 ▶ To depart by ship, to put out to sea** > Paul and his companions sailed from Philippi to Troas (Acts 20:6). The verb is also used in Acts 15:39; 18:18. ¶
7 **to sail past, to sail by: *parapleō*** [verb: παραπλέω <3896>]; **from *para*: beside, and *pleō*: see 2 ▶ To navigate in front of (without stopping)** > Paul thought it desirable to sail past Ephesus (Acts 20:16). ¶

8 to sail under, to sail under the lee, to pass to the lee, to sail under the shelter: *hupopleō* [verb: ὑποπλέω <5284>]; **from *hupo*: under, and *pleō*: see 2 ▶ To follow a coastline protected from the wind, to travel along a coast** > The ship Paul had boarded sailed under the lee of Cyprus (Acts 27:4) and sailed under {sailed to the lee of} Crete (Acts 27:7b). ¶

9 to sail straight: *euthudromeō* [verb: εὐθυδρομέω <2113>]; **from *euthudromos*: running a straight course, which is from *euthus*: straight, and *dromos*: course ▶ To navigate in a direct line, to run a straight course** > The verb is used in regard to ships that Paul had boarded (Acts 16:11; 21:1). ¶

10 to sail close, to sail along: *paralegō* [verb: παραλέγω <3881>]; **from *para*: near, and *legō*: to lie ▶ To navigate near the coasts** > Paul's ship sailed close by Crete (Acts 27:13). Other refs.: Acts 27:8; see PASS <3881>. ¶

– 11 Luke 8:26 → ARRIVE <2668> 12 Acts 21:2 → to sail over → to pass over → PASS <1276> 13 Acts 28:13 → to sail, to sail around → CIRCLE ROUND <4022>.

SAILING – Acts 27:9 → NAVIGATION <4144>.

SAILOR – ***nautēs*** [masc. noun: ναύτης <3492>]; **from *naus*: ship ▶ Shipman, seaman** > The sailors on board Paul's ship sensed they were drawing near some land (Acts 27:27); they sought to escape from the ship (v. 30). The sailors stood at a distance when they saw the smoke of Babylon's burning (Rev. 18:17). ¶

SAINT – ***hagios*** [adj. used as noun: ἅγιος <40>]; **from *hagos*: religious respect, reverence toward God; same root as *hagnos*: pure ▶ The term used in the plur. means living people (as well as those who have died in faith) who have believed in the work of redemption accomplished by Jesus Christ; He Himself is the Holy One** > These people are sanctified (i.e., set apart) by this work, justified, and possess eternal life (see Rom. 6:22; 1 Cor. 6:11). Paul frequently addresses the saints in his letters to local churches and speaks of them (e.g., Rom. 1:7; 1 Cor. 1:2; 6:2; Phm. 5). Jesus Christ is the saint by excellence, or: "holy one" as the Greek word is usually transl. in reference to Him (Mark 1:24; Luke 4:34; John 6:69 in some mss.; Acts 3:14; 1 John 2:20; Rev. 3:7). The last verse of the Bible expresses the desire that the grace of the Lord Jesus Christ may be with all the saints (Rev. 22:21 in some mss.). Other refs.: see HOLY (adj.) <40>.

SAKE OF (FOR THE) – **1** ***dia*** [prep.: διά <1223>]; **lit.: because, for ▶ For the reason of, on account of** > Paul said he and others were fools for Christ's sake (1 Cor. 4:10), servants for Jesus's sake (2 Cor. 4:5), always delivered unto death for Jesus's sake (v. 11). The Thessalonians knew what manner of men Paul and others were among them for their sake (1 Thes. 1:5). Paul was enduring all things for the elect's sake (2 Tim. 2:10). Peter exhorts to submit ourselves to every ordinance of man for the Lord's sake (1 Pet. 2:13). *

2 ***heneken*** [adv.: ἕνεκεν <1752>]; **lit.: because ▶ For the reason of** > The Lord speaks about losing one's life for His sake (Matt. 10:39; 16:25; Mark 8:35; Luke 9:24). He speaks also of leaving one's house and family for His sake and the gospel's (Mark 10:29), for the sake of the kingdom of God (Luke 18:29), and for the sake of His name (Matt. 19:29). Paul speaks of those who are killed for the sake of God (Rom. 8:36). *

SALA – 1 Luke 3:32 → SALMON <4533> 2 Luke 3:35 → SHELAH <4527>.

SALAMIS – ***Salamis*** [fem. name: Σαλαμίς <4529>] **▶ City on the southeast of Cyprus** > During a first missionary journey, Barnabas and Paul announced the word of God in the synagogues of the Jews at Salamis (Acts 13:5). ¶

SALATHIEL – See SHEALTHIEL <4528>.

SALEM – ***Salēm*** [fem. name: Σαλήμ <4532>]: **peace, in Heb. ▶ This name**

refers to Jerusalem (see Ps. 76:2) > Melchizedek was king of Salem (Heb. 7:1, 2). ¶

SALIM – ***Saleim*** [fem. name: Σαλείμ <4530>]: **completed, in Aram.** ▶ **Place near Aenon** > John baptized in Aenon, near Salim (John 3:23). ¶

SALIVA – ***ptusma*** [neut. noun: πτύσμα <4427>]; **from *ptuō*; to spit** ▶ **Watery and viscid fluid expelled by the mouth** > Jesus spat on the ground and made mud with the saliva {spittle}; He anointed the eyes of the blind man with the mud (John 9:6). ¶

SALMON – ***Salmōn*** [masc. name: Σαλμών <4533>]: **investiture, in Heb.** ▶ **Man of the O.T., husband of Rahab and father of Boaz** > Salmon is mentioned in the genealogy of Jesus Christ (Matt. 1:4, 5; Luke 3:32). ¶

SALMONE – ***Salmōnē*** [fem. name: Σαλμώνη <4534>]: **clothing** ▶ **Promontory of eastern Crete** > Paul's ship sailed along the coast of Crete opposite Salmone during his fourth journey (Acts 27:7). ¶

SALOME – ***Salōmē*** [fem. name: Σαλώμη <4539>]: **peaceful, in Heb.** ▶ **One of the women who followed and served Jesus in Galilee** > Salome was present at the crucifixion (Mark 15:40). She bought aromatic spices to embalm the body of Jesus (Mark 16:1). ¶

SALT (adj.) – [1] ***halukos*** [adj.: ἁλυκός <252>]; **from *hals*: salt** ▶ **Tasting or containing salt** > Salt water cannot produce fresh water (Jas. 3:12). ¶
– [2] Jas. 3:11 → BITTER <4089>.

SALT (noun) – [1] ***halas*** [neut. noun: ἅλας <217>] ▶ **White crystalline substance that serves to season food and that was put on offerings to God** > Jesus says to His own that they are the salt of the earth, but if the salt has lost its savor, with what will it be salted? (Matt. 5:13a, b). He says that salt is good, but if the salt loses its flavor, with what will it be seasoned? (Mark 9:50a, b; Luke 14:34a, b); He adds that we are to have salt in ourselves, and to be at peace among ourselves (Mark 9:50). Paul says that the word of Christians should always be in a spirit of grace, seasoned with salt, so that they may know how they ought to answer each one (Col. 4:6). ¶
[2] ***hals*** [masc. noun: ἅλς <251>] ▶ **See [1].** > Everyone will be salted with fire, and every sacrifice will be salted with salt (Mark 9:49). ¶

SALT (verb) – ***halizō*** [verb: ἁλίζω <233>]; **from *hals*: salt** ▶ **To season with salt; other transl.: to make salty, to season** > Christians are the salt of the earth, but if the salt has lost its saltiness, with what will it be salted? (Matt. 5:13). Metaphorically, everyone will be salted with fire (Mark 9:49a), and every sacrifice will be salted with salt (v. 49b in some mss.). ¶

SALTINESS – [1] Matt. 5:13; Luke 14:34 → to lose its saltiness → to lose its flavor → LOSE <3471> [2] Mark 9:50 → to lose the saltiness → to become unsalty → UNSALTY <358>.

SALTLESS – Mark 9:50 → UNSALTY <358>.

SALTNESS – Mark 9:50 → to lose the saltiness → to become unsalty → UNSALTY <358>.

SALTY – [1] Matt. 5:13 → to make salty → SALT (verb) <233> [2] Mark 9:50; Luke 14:34 → to make salty again → SEASON (verb) <741>.

SALUTATION – Matt. 23:7; Mark 12:38; Luke 1:29, 41, 44; 11:43; 20:46; 1 Cor. 16:21; Col. 4:18; 2 Thes. 3:17 → GREETINGS <783>.

SALUTE – [1] Matt. 5:47; Mark 9:15; 15:18; Luke 1:40; 10:4; Acts 18:22; et al. → GREET <782> [2] Acts 21:19 → EMBRACE <782>.

SALVATION – [1] ***sōtēria*** [fem. noun: σωτηρία <4991>]; **from *sōtēr*: liberator, savior ▶ a. Eternal redemption of a sinful person, obtained by repentance and faith in the perfect sacrifice of Jesus Christ at the cross >** This so great salvation (Heb. 2:3) is the salvation of God (Rev. 7:10). Jesus Christ alone procures salvation (Acts 4:12); God has destined Christians to obtain salvation through Him (1 Thes. 5:9). Christ is the author of our salvation (Heb. 2:10) and the author of eternal salvation (5:9). God had chosen the Thessalonians from the beginning for salvation (2 Thes. 2:13). Salvation is of the Jews (John 4:22; 1 Pet. 1:10); the Lord sprang from this people; He was offered to them (Luke 1:77 {deliverance}; 19:9) as well as His salvation (Rom. 10:1). Salvation is also offered to the Gentiles (Acts 13:26, 47; 16:17; Rom. 11:11; 2 Tim. 2:10). Grace that brings salvation has appeared to all men (Titus 2:11 {*sōtērios*: see [3]}; 2 Cor. 6:2a, b). The gospel is the power of God to salvation to everyone who believes (Eph. 1:13; Rom. 1:16); with the mouth confession is made to salvation (Rom. 10:10). Salvation is seen as a present reality for Christians (Phil. 1:28; see 1 Cor. 1:18), the salvation of their souls (1 Pet. 1:9). In another aspect, salvation is ready to be revealed (1 Pet. 1:5), we will inherit it (Heb. 1:14), it is nearer than when we first believed (Rom. 13:11); this concerns future salvation when the bodies of Christians, in particular, will be transformed: Christ will appear for salvation to those who wait for Him (Heb. 9:28). At the present time, Christian salvation is continual deliverance from the servitude of sin (Phil. 2:12; 1 Pet. 2:3 in some mss.). Sorrow according to God works repentance leading to salvation (2 Cor. 7:10). Salvation may also designate a temporal deliverance (Phil. 1:19). The Christian is exhorted to take the helmet of salvation (1 Thes. 5:8). For the unbeliever, now is the day of salvation (2 Cor. 6:2). Paul's affliction was for the consolation and the salvation of the Corinthians (2 Cor. 1:6). The word of God is able to make a person wise to salvation through faith, which is in Christ Jesus (2 Tim. 3:15). The patience of the Lord is salvation, giving time before His return for more people to repent (2 Pet. 3:15). Jude reminds his readers of the common salvation that he shares with them (v. 3). The author of the Epistle to the Hebrews was persuaded of better things concerning his readers and things connected to salvation (Heb. 6:9). In Rev. 12:10 and 19:1, salvation is in relation to victory over Satan and Babylon. **b. Deliverance, liberation >** Zacharias speaks of a horn of salvation in the house of David (Luke 1:69), that they should be saved (lit.: a salvation) from their enemies (v. 71). Joseph's brothers did not understand that God would deliver them {would rescue them} (lit.: give them salvation) by Joseph (Acts 7:25). Other ref.: 1 Thes. 5:8; see [2]. All other refs.: SAVING <4991>, SURVIVAL <4991>.

[2] ***sōtērion*** [adj. used as noun: σωτήριον <4992>]; **from *sōter*: savior, liberator ▶ See a. in [1]. >** Salvation is of God (Luke 2:30; 3:6). Salvation is offered to the Gentiles (Acts 28:28). The Christian is exhorted to take the helmet of salvation (Eph. 6:17: *sōtērion*; 1 Thes. 5:8: *sōtēria*). ¶

[3] **that brings salvation: *sōtērios*** [adj.: σωτήριος <4992a>]; **from *sōter*: savior, liberator ▶ Which saves; see a. in [1]. >** The grace of God that brings {bringing, which carries with it} salvation has appeared to all men (Titus 2:11). ¶

– [4] 1 Tim. 4:16 → to ensure salvation → SAVE (verb) <4982>.

SALVE – Rev. 3:18 → salve, eye salve → EYESALVE <2854>.

SAMARIA – ***Samareia*** [fem. name: Σαμάρεια <4540>]: **watch-post, in Heb. ▶ Region of central Palestine >** Coming from the north, one must pass through Samaria to reach Jerusalem, which Jesus did (Luke 17:11), or to go to Galilee when coming from the south (John 4:4, 5, 7). Before His ascension, Jesus had told His disciples that they would be His witnesses in Samaria (Acts 1:8). Following persecution at Jerusalem, Christians were scattered throughout Samaria (Acts 8:1). Philip preached Christ there (Acts 8:5). Simon the magician was of Samaria, and received the word of God with others (Acts 8:9, 14); but he was a hypocrite (see v. 21). In the beginning, the churches of Samaria had peace, being edified and walking in the fear of the Lord; they increased through the Holy Spirit (Acts 9:31). Paul and Barnabas passed through Samaria on their way to Jerusalem (Acts 15:3). ¶

SAMARITAN – ***Samaritēs*** [masc. name: Σαμαρίτης <4541>]; ***Samaritis*** [fem. name: Σαμαρῖτις <4542>] in John 4:9 ▶ **Inhabitant of the district of Samaria, in central Palestine** > The Samaritans were not of pure Jewish race, and they practiced a mixed religion (see 2 Kgs. 17:24–41). In the beginning, Jesus did not send the twelve apostles to preach in the cities of the Samaritans, but rather among the Jews (Matt. 10:5; see v. 6). He rebuked James and John who wanted fire to consume a village of the Samaritans because they had not received Him (Luke 9:52; see vv. 52–56). The parable of the "Good Samaritan" (Luke 10:33; see vv. 30–37) illustrates the mercy of God toward the lost sinner. Jesus asked to drink of a Samaritan (*Samaritis*) woman at the well of Sychar (John 4:9) and taught her that God the Father seeks true worshipers. Many Samaritans believed on Jesus after the woman had spoken to them of the Lord, and He stayed there with them for two days (4:39, 40). The Jews called Jesus a Samaritan, a despised people in their eyes, and accused Him of having a demon (John 8:48). One of ten leprous men who had been healed by Jesus returned to Him, and he was a Samaritan (Luke 17:16). Peter and John preached the gospel to many villages of the Samaritans (Acts 8:25). ¶

SAME – [1] ***autos*** [pron.: αὐτός <846>] ▶ **Equal, corresponding in every aspect** > Members of the body (i.e., Christians) should have the same care {equal concern} for one another (1 Cor. 12:25). *

[2] ***isos*** [adj.: ἴσος <2470>] ▶ **Equal in quantity, quality, and dignity** > God has given the Holy Spirit to the Jews, and this same gift to the nations (Acts 11:17). All other refs.: AGREE <2470>, EQUAL <2470>, LIKE (adj., adv., noun) <2470>.

– [3] Jude 7 → LIKE (adj., adv., noun) <3664>.

SAMOS – ***Samos*** [fem. name: Σάμος <4544>]: **height** ▶ **Island of the Aegean Sea southwest of Asia Minor, near Ephesus** > Paul passed through Samos on his third missionary journey (Acts 20:15). ¶

SAMOTHRACE – ***Samothrakē*** [fem. name: Σαμοθρᾴκη <4543>]: **height of Thrace** ▶ **Island in the northeast part of the Aegean Sea** > Paul's ship sailed to Samothrace during the second missionary journey of the apostle (Acts 16:11). ¶

SAMSON – ***Sampsōn*** [masc. name: Σαμψών <4546>]: **like the sun, in Heb.** ▶ **One of the judges of the O.T.** > Samson delivered Israel from the yoke of the Philistines (see Judges 13–16). His great strength came from his Nazirite vow, according to which he was not to cut his hair, the secret of his strength. Samson is cited among O.T. men of faith (Heb. 11:32). ¶

SAMUEL – ***Samouēl*** [masc. name: Σαμουήλ <4545>]: **heard of God, God has answered, in Heb.** ▶ **One of the major prophets of the O.T.** > Peter speaks of Samuel in his preaching (Acts 3:24). The arrival of Samuel marked the end of the judges in Israel and the beginning of the kingship (Acts 13:20); he anointed Saul as king as well as David. Samuel is cited among O.T. men of faith (Heb. 11:32). ¶

SANCTIFICATION – Rom. 6:19, 22; 1 Cor. 1:30; 1 Thes. 4:3, 4, 7; 2 Thes. 2:13; Heb. 12:14; 1 Pet. 1:2 → HOLINESS <38>.

SANCTIFY – [1] ***hagiazō*** [verb: ἁγιάζω <37>]; **from *hagios*: holy, which is from *hagos*: religious respect, reverence toward God; same root as *hagnos*: pure** ▶ **To consecrate, to set apart for God; also transl.: to be holy, to hallow, to make holy, to make sacred** > Concerning his position before God, every Christian is sanctified

(Acts 20:32; 26:18; 1 Cor. 1:2; 6:11; Heb. 10:10, 14). He is set apart for God by the work of redemption and by the Holy Spirit who dwells in him. In Heb. 2:11a, b, both He who sanctifies (the Lord Jesus) and those who are sanctified (Christians) are all of one; that is to say, of the same lineage. Sanctification is also realized practically and progressively by the believer in the Lord (Rev. 22:11), by separation from evil (2 Tim. 2:21), and by God Himself (1 Thes. 5:23). Jesus asked the Father to sanctify those whom He had given to Him, and He sanctified Himself for them, so that they also might be sanctified by the truth (John 17:17, 19a, b). The blood of animals sanctified for the purifying of the flesh, under the law (Heb. 9:13); but Jesus has sanctified the people (i.e., Christians) by His own blood (Heb. 13:12). He has sanctified the church, purifying it by the washing of water by the word (Eph. 5:26). The Father has sanctified the Son (John 10:36); Christians are to sanctify Christ as Lord in their hearts (1 Pet. 3:15). Jesus prayed that the name of His Father might be sanctified (Matt. 6:9; Luke 11:2). The unbelieving husband or wife is sanctified by the believing spouse (1 Cor. 7:14a, b), sharing in Christian privileges. Other refs.: Matt. 23:17, 19; Rom. 15:16; 1 Tim. 4:5; Heb. 10:29; Jude 1 in some mss. ¶
– 2 1 Thes. 4:3 → that you should be sanctified → lit.: your sanctification → HOLINESS <38>.

SANCTIFYING – 2 Thes. 2:13; 1 Pet. 1:2 → sanctifying work → sanctification → HOLINESS <38>.

SANCTITY – 1 Tim. 2:15 → HOLINESS <38>.

SANCTUARY – 1 ***hagion*** [adj. used as noun: ἅγιον <39>]; **from *hagios*: holy, which is from *hagos*: religious respect, reverence toward God; same root as *hagnos*: pure ▶ Dwelling place of God on the earth in the O.T.** > The Lord had provided ordinances concerning the earthly sanctuary, that of the tabernacle in the wilderness (Heb. 9:1; see Exodus 25–31). This was a figure of the heavenly sanctuary into which Jesus, the high priest, has entered (see Heb. 9:24). Heb. 9:1–5 describes: in v. 1, the sanctuary (*hagion*) in the wilderness viewed as a whole, the court and the tabernacle; in v. 2 {Holy, Holy Place, sanctuary}, the contents of the Holy Place, the first part of the tabernacle (*hagia*); in v. 3 (Holy of Holies, Holiest of all, Most Holy Place); in v. 4, the contents of the Most Holy Place, or the Holy of Holies (*hagia hagiōn*). Christians presently have access in the heavenly places for entering into the Holy of Holies by the new and living way consecrated through the veil, i.e., the flesh of Jesus Christ (figur. represented by the veil of the Most Holy Place); see Heb. 10:19–21. Jesus is Minister of the sanctuary (Heb. 8:2). The Greek term is transl. "the Holiest" {the Most Holy Place} in Heb. 10:19: Christians have boldness to enter the Holiest by the blood of Jesus. The Greek term is also transl.: "the Holiest of All," "the Most Holy Place," "the holy place," and "the holy places" (Heb. 9:8, 12, 24, 25; 13:11). ¶
– 2 Matt. 23:35; Rev. 15:5, 6, 8a, b → TEMPLE <3485> 3 Luke 11:51 → HOUSE <3624>.

SAND – 1 ***ammos*** [fem. noun: ἄμμος <285>] ▶ **The entire aggregate of small mineral grains that cover the ground, especially of seashores and the desert** > He who does not put into practice the words of Jesus will be compared to a foolish man who built his house on the sand (Matt. 7:26), image of that which is unstable. Isaiah speaks of the number of the children of Israel being as the sand of the sea (Rom. 9:27). Those born of Abraham are as countless as the sand by the seashore (Heb. 11:12). John stood on the sand of the seashore and saw a beast rising out of the sea (Rev. 13:1). The number of the nations, Gog and Magog, assembled for war at the end of the millennium, will be as the sand of the seashore (Rev. 20:8). Other ref.: Rev. 12:17 in some mss. In Rom. 4:18, some mss. add *ammon*, apparently a form of *ammos*. ¶
2 **Syrtis Sands: *Surtis*** [fem. noun: Σύρτις <4950>]; **from *surō*: to draw ▶ Sandbanks, quicksands; the word is also**

transl.: Syrtis, Syrtis Sands, shallows of Syrtis, sandbar of Syrtis > The sailors of the ship that Paul had boarded feared running aground the shallows of Syrtis (Acts 27:17). See SYRTIS. ¶

SANDAL – [1] ***sandalion*** [neut. noun: σανδάλιον <4547>; **dimin. of *sandalon*: sole, sandal**] ► **Sole of wood or leather, protecting the sole of the foot and attached by straps >** When Jesus began to send the apostles to preach, He told them to wear sandals (Mark 6:9). The angel told Peter to gird himself and to bind on his sandals (Acts 12:8). ¶

[2] ***hupodēma*** [neut. noun: ὑπόδημα <5266>]; **from *hupodeō*: to bind under, which is from *hupo*: under, and *deō*: to attach, to bind ► Footwear whose sole is bound by straps; also transl.: shoe >** John the Baptist was not worthy to remove (or: to carry) the sandals of Jesus (Matt. 3:11) or to unloose the strap of His sandals (Mark 1:7; Luke 3:16; John 1:27; Acts 13:25). Jesus spoke of sandals in His instructions to those going forth to preach (Matt. 10:10; Luke 10:4; 22:35). Sandals were to be put on the feet of the prodigal son who had returned home (Luke 15:22). The Lord told Moses to take off the sandals from his feet (Acts 7:33). ¶

SANDBAR – [1] Acts 27:17 → sandbars of Syrtis → SAND <4950> [2] Acts 27:41 → lit.: a place where two seas meet → SEA <1337>.

SANHEDRIN – [1] ***sunedrion*** [neut. noun: συνέδριον <4892>]; **from *sun*: together, and *hezomai*: to sit; *hedra* is a seat, and *sunedros* is a member of an assembly ► Supreme judicial council of the Jewish nation, situated in Jerusalem; also transl.: council, court, supreme court >** It was composed of seventy members, chosen from among the chief priests and elders of the Jews; it was presided over by the high priest (Matt. 5:22; 10:17; 26:59; Mark 13:9; 14:55; 15:1; Luke 22:66; John 11:47; Acts 4:15; 5:21, 27, 34, 41; 6:12, 15; 22:30; 23:1, 6, 15, 20, 28; 24:20). The Sanhedrin did not have the authority to pronounce the death penalty; that was the prerogative of the Roman governor (see John 18:31). Originally, seventy men from among the elders of Israel had been chosen by Moses to assist in judicial matters (see Num. 11:16). ¶

– [2] Acts 5:35, 7:54 → "Sanhedrin" and "members of the Sanhedrin" added in Engl.

SAP – Rom. 11:17 → nourishing sap → lit.: root and fatness → FATNESS <4096>.

SAPPHIRA – ***Sapphira*** [fem. name: Σάπφιρα <4551>]: **beautiful, in Aram. ► Woman of the early church >** Sapphira was the wife of Ananias (Acts 5:1). Both of them lied to the Holy Spirit, which brought judgment on them; they died immediately (see Acts 5:1–11). ¶

SAPPHIRE – [1] ***sapphiros*** [fem. noun: σάπφιρος <4552>]; **from the Heb. *saphan*: to inscribe (perhaps as used for incising other objects); also spelled: *sappheiros* ► Very hard precious stone, mostly of blue color >** The second foundation of the wall of the heavenly Jerusalem is adorned with sapphire (Rev. 21:19). ¶

– [2] Rev. 9:17 → JACINTH <5191>.

SARAH – ***Sarra*** [fem. name: Σάρρα <4564>]: **princess, in Heb. ► Wife of Abraham >** Despite her advanced age and sterility (Rom. 4:19), God allowed her to have a son, Isaac (Rom. 9:9). Sarah's faith is mentioned: she counted God faithful to accomplish His promise and give her a son; thus she gave Abraham posterity (Heb. 11:11). Peter notes her obedience to her husband and the fact that she called him lord (1 Pet. 3:6). ¶

SARDINE – Rev. 4:3 → SARDIUS <4555>.

SARDIS – ***Sardeis*** [fem. name: Σάρδεις <4554>] ► **Principal city of Lydia in Asia Minor >** One of the seven letters of Revelation 2 and 3 is addressed to the church of Sardis (Rev. 1:11); the Lord reproaches her lack of vigilance and spiritual death (3:1, 4). ¶

SARDIUS – [1] ***sardinos*** [masc. noun: σάρδινος <4555>] ► **Precious stone found in the region of Sardis; it is a variety of chalcedony having a red color** > He who was seated on the throne was like a jasper and a sardius {sardine} stone in appearance (Rev. 4:3); some mss. have *sardios*. ¶
[2] ***sardios*** [masc. noun: σάρδιος <4556>] ► **Precious stone of red or reddish-yellow color** > Sardius {Carnelian} adorns the sixth foundation of the new Jerusalem (Rev. 21:20). Also Rev. 4:3 in some mss. ¶

SARDONYX – ***sardonux*** [fem. noun: σαρδόνυξ <4557>] ► **Precious stone, of various colors showing white or light brown stripes** > The fifth foundation of the wall of the heavenly Jerusalem is adorned with sardonyx (Rev. 21:20). ¶

SAREPTA – See ZAREPHATH <4558>.

SARON – See SHARON <4565>.

SARUCH – See SERUG <4562>.

SASH – Rev. 1:13; 15:6 → BELT <2223>.

SATAN – [1] ***Satanas*** [masc. name: Σατανᾶς <4567>]**: adversary, in Heb.** ► **The adversary of God, Christ, Christians, and humanity in general** > Satan tempted Jesus at the beginning of His public ministry (Mark 1:13); Jesus told him to depart (Matt. 4:10; Luke 4:8 in some mss.). In response to the accusation that He cast out demons by Beelzebul, Jesus answered that if that were the case, then Satan would be divided against himself (Matt. 12:26; Mark 3:23–26; Luke 11:18). Jesus rebuked Peter, telling Satan to get behind him, because of his thoughts (Matt. 16:23; Mark 8:33). It is Satan who takes away the word of God that has been sown (Mark 4:15). Jesus saw Satan falling out of Heaven (Luke 10:18). Satan had bound a woman with a spirit of infirmity (Luke 13:16). He entered into Judas Iscariot (Luke 22:3; John 13:27). He had asked to have the apostles to sift them (Luke 22:31). He had filled the heart of Ananias (Acts 5:3). Paul had been sent to the nations so that they might turn from the power of Satan to God (Acts 26:17, 18). The God of peace will soon bruise Satan under the feet of Christians (Rom. 16:20). Paul had judged to deliver a man who was guilty of sexual immorality to Satan (1 Cor. 5:5). Satan might tempt a couple because of their lack of self-control (1 Cor. 7:5). Forgiving others prevents Satan from getting an advantage against Christians (2 Cor. 2:11). He transforms himself into an angel of light (2 Cor. 11:14). He had twice hindered Paul from going to the Thessalonians (1 Thes. 2:18). The coming of the antichrist is according to the working of Satan (2 Thes. 2:9, 10). Paul had delivered Hymenaeus and Alexander to Satan (1 Tim. 1:20); he speaks of some who had turned aside after Satan (5:15). At Smyrna, those who claimed to be Jews were a synagogue of Satan (Rev. 2:9); believers in Pergamum were dwelling where the throne of Satan was, and Antipas had been put to death where Satan was dwelling (2:13); some at Thyatira had not known the depths of Satan (2:24); those of the synagogue of Satan who claim to be Jews will bow down before Philadelphia (3:9). The great dragon is he who is called the devil and Satan (Rev. 12:9). Satan will be bound for one thousand years (Rev. 20:2); then he will be released from his prison and will go out to deceive the nations (v. 7). Fire will come down from God out of heaven, and the devil will be cast into the lake of fire and brimstone where he will be tormented eternally (see Rev. 20:10). ¶
[2] ***Satan*** [masc. name: Σατάν <4566>]**: adversary, in Heb.** ► **See [1].** > A messenger of Satan had been given to Paul to torment him (2 Cor. 12:7). ¶

SATISFACTION – Col. 2:23 → INDULGENCE <4140>.

SATISFIED – [1] ***autarkēs*** [adj.: αὐτάρκης <842>]**; from *autos*: oneself, and *arkeō*: to be sufficient** ► **Contented, sufficient** > Paul had learned to be satisfied {to be content} in his circumstances (Phil. 4:11). ¶

[2] **to be satisfied:** ***arkeō*** [verb: ἀρκέω <714>]; ***arcere*, in Lat.: to contain, to retain ▶ To have one's needs fulfilled, to be happy; also transl.: to be content** > John the Baptist told soldiers to be satisfied with their wages (Luke 3:14). Christians should be satisfied with their present circumstances (Heb. 13:5). Not satisfied with babbling against John, Diotrephes did not himself receive the brothers (3 John 10). All other refs.: CONTENT (verb) <714>, ENOUGH <714>, SUFFICIENT <714>.

SATISFY – [1] Matt. 5:6; 14:20; 15:33, 37; Mark 6:42; 7:27; 8:4, 8; Luke 6:21; 9:17 → FILL (verb) <5526> [2] Matt. 28:14; Rom. 15:14; Gal. 1:10 → to satisfy, to seek to satisfy → PERSUADE <3982> [3] Mark 15:15 → CONTENT (verb) <4160> [4] Acts 14:17 → FILL (verb) <1705>.

SATISFYING – Col. 2:23 → INDULGENCE <4140>.

SAUL – [1] ***Saoul*** [masc. name: Σαούλ <4549>]: **asked, desired, in Heb. ▶ a. Hebrew name of the apostle Paul before his conversion** > This name is used when Jesus addresses him: "Saul, Saul! Why are you persecuting Me?" (Acts 9:4; 22:7; 26:14). Ananias also uses this name, addressing him as "Brother Saul" (Acts 9:17; 22:13). **b. First king whom God gave to His people Israel (see 1 Sam. 10:1)** > Saul reigned for forty years (Acts 13:21). David succeeded him. ¶
[2] ***Saulos*** [masc. name: Σαῦλος <4569>]: **asked, desired, in Heb. ▶ Greek name of the apostle Paul before his conversion** > Those who stoned Stephen laid their clothes at the feet of Saul (Acts 7:58); he consented to the death of Stephen (8:1). Saul ravaged the church (Acts 8:3). He was breathing out threats and slaughter against the disciples of the Lord (9:1), but the Lord stopped him on the road to Damascus (vv. 8, 11). He stayed with the disciples who were at Damascus (see Acts 9:19) and demonstrated to the Jews that Jesus was the Christ (v. 22). He learned of a plot of the Jews against himself (Acts 9:23, 24) and went to Jerusalem (v. 26). Later, Barnabas went to Tarsus to look for Saul and bring him to Antioch (Acts 11:25); Barnabas and Saul brought something for the relief of the brothers in Judea (v. 30). Later, they took along with them John who was surnamed Mark (Acts 12:25). Saul was among the prophets and teachers of the church of Antioch (Acts 13:1). The Holy Spirit set apart Barnabas and Saul for the Lord's work (v. 2). Sergius Paulus called them, desiring to hear the word of God (Acts 13:7, 9). ¶

SAVAGE – ***barus*** [adj.: βαρύς <926>] ▶ **Violent, oppressive** > Paul knew that after his departure savage {grievous} wolves, not sparing the flock, would come in among Christians (Acts 20:29). All other refs.: BURDENSOME <926>, HEAVY <926>, SERIOUS <926>, WEIGHTIER <926>.

SAVE (conj.) – ***ei mē*** [cond. expr.: εἰ μή <1508>]; **from *ei*: if, and *mē*: not ▶ Except, with the exclusion of** > No church communicated anything to Paul at the beginning, save {but} the Philippians (Phil. 4:15). *

SAVE (verb) – [1] ***sōzō*** [verb: σῴζω <4982>]; **from *sōs*: delivered, safe ▶** This verb is used in regard to: **a. deliverance from danger, suffering, death, etc.** > The witnesses told by what means the demon-possessed man had been saved {cured, healed, made well} (Luke 8:36). Jesus could have asked His Father to save Him from the hour of death (John 12:27). The Lord (some mss.: Jesus) saved {delivered} His people out of the land of Egypt (Jude 5). Other refs.: Matt. 8:25; Mark 13:20 {to survive}; Luke 23:35a, b; 1 Tim. 2:15 {preserved}), (Jas. 5:15 {to heal}); **b. spiritual and eternal salvation granted immediately by God to those who believe in the Lord Jesus Christ** > The word of the cross is God's power to those who are being saved (i.e., from eternal punishment) (1 Cor. 1:18). Other refs.: Acts 2:47; 16:31; Rom. 8:24; Eph. 2:5, 8; 1 Tim. 2:4; 2 Tim. 1:9; Titus 3:5; **c. human agent whom God uses to operate such a salvation** > Refs.: Rom. 11:14; 1 Cor. 7:16a, b; 9:22; 1 Tim. 4:16 {to ensure salvation};

d. present day experiences of the power of God to liberate from the slavery of sin > Refs.: Matt. 1:21; Rom. 5:10; 1 Cor. 15:2; Heb. 7:25; Jas. 1:21; 1 Pet. 3:21; **e. future deliverance of believers in the Lord at the second coming of Christ with His saints >** Ref.: Rom. 5:9; **f. deliverance of the nation of Israel at the second coming of Christ >** Ref.: Rom. 11:26; **g. deliverance of those who will stand firm to the end during the great tribulation >** Refs.: Matt. 10:22; Mark 13:13; **h. Christians who will lose their reward at the judgment seat of Christ, but who will not lose their salvation >** Refs.: 1 Cor. 3:15; 5:5. (After W. E. Vine.) Other refs.: Matt. 14:30; 16:25; 18:11; 19:25; 24:13, 22; 27:40, 42a, b, 49; Mark 3:4; 5:23; 8:35a, b; 10:26; 15:30, 31a, b; 16:16; Luke 6:9; 7:50; 8:12, 50; 9:24a, b, 56 in some mss.; 13:23; 17:33; 18:26; 19:10; 23:37, 39; John 3:17; 5:34; 10:9; 12:47; Acts 2:21, 40; 4:12; 11:14; 15:1, 11; 16:30, 31; 27:20, 31; Rom. 9:27; 10:9, 13; 1 Cor. 1:21; 10:33; 2 Cor. 2:15; 1 Thes. 2:16; 2 Thes. 2:10; 1 Tim. 1:15; 4:16; Heb. 5:7; Jas. 2:14; 4:12; 5:20; 1 Pet. 4:18; Jude 23. All other refs.: HEAL <4982>, PRESERVE <4982>.

[2] ***diasōzō*** [verb: διασῴζω <1295>]**; from *dia*: through, and *sōzō*: see [1] ► a. To heal >** The verb is used concerning a servant (Luke 7:3). **b. To preserve from danger >** The centurion wanted to save Paul (Acts 27:43 {to bring safely through, to spare the life}). Other refs.: Acts 28:1 {to escape, to bring safely}, 4 {to escape}; 1 Pet. 3:20. All other refs.: HEAL <1295>, SAFELY <1295>.

– [3] Matt. 6:13; 27:43; Luke 1:74; Rom. 15:31; 2 Pet. 2:7 → DELIVER <4506> [4] Luke 1:71; Acts 16:17; Rom. 10:10; Heb. 9:28 → SALVATION <4991> [5] Luke 17:33 → PURCHASE (verb) <4046> [6] 1 Cor. 16:2 → PROSPER <2137> [7] 1 Cor. 16:2 → to save up → to store up → STORE (verb) <2343> [8] 2 Cor. 12:14 → to save up → to lay up → LAY <2343> [9] Heb. 10:39 → and are saved → lit.: to the saving → SAVING <4047> [10] Heb. 11:7 → lit.: for the saving → SAVING <4991> [11] 2 Pet. 2:5 → PRESERVE <5442>.

SAVING – [1] ***peripoiēsis*** [fem. noun: περιποίησις <4047>]**; from *peripoieō*: to obtain, to purchase, which is from *peri*: around (denoting acquisition), and *poieō*: to make, to gain ► Acquisition, conservation >** The author of the Epistle to the Hebrews mentions those who believe to the saving {preserving} of the soul {and are saved} (Heb. 10:39). All other refs.: OBTAINING <4047>, POSSESSION <4047>, RECEIVE <4047>.

[2] ***sōtēria*** [fem. noun: σωτηρία <4991>]**; from *sōzō*: to save, to preserve ► Salvation, preservation >** By faith Noah prepared an ark for the saving of {to save} his household (Heb. 11:7). All other refs.: SALVATION <4991>, SURVIVAL <4991>.

– [3] Matt. 5:32 → saving for → except for → EXCEPT <3924>.

SAVIOR – ***Sōtēr*** [masc. name: Σωτήρ <4990>]**; from *sōzō*: to deliver, to save ► He who brings salvation, deliverance; liberator >** It is God who saves (Luke 1:47; 1 Tim. 1:1; 2:3; 4:10; Titus 1:3; 2:10; 3:4; Jude 25) and the Lord Jesus who saves (Luke 2:11; Acts 5:31; Phil. 3:20). Jesus Christ is the Savior of the world (John 4:42; 1 John 4:14), of Israel (Acts 13:23), and of the members of the church (Phil. 3:20; 2 Tim. 1:10). Jesus Christ is both God and Savior (Titus 2:13; 2 Pet. 1:1). Other refs.: Eph. 5:23; Titus 1:4; 3:6; 2 Pet. 1:11; 2:20; 3:2, 18. ¶

SAVOR – [1] 2 Cor. 2:14; 16a, b → ODOR <3744> [2] 2 Cor. 2:15; Phil. 4:18 → sweet savor → sweet odor → ODOR <2175>.

SAVOUR (noun) – [1] Matt. 5:13; Luke 14:34 → to lose its savour → to lose its flavor → LOSE <3471> [2] Eph. 5:2 → AROMA <3744>.

SAVOUR (verb) – Matt. 16:23; Mark 8:33 → MIND (verb) <5426>.

SAVOURLESS – Luke 14:34 → to become savourless → to lose its flavor → LOSE <3471>.

SAW – to saw asunder, to saw in two: *prizō* [verb: πρίζω <4249>] ▶ **To cut in two with a saw, a form of execution** > There were people of faith in the O.T. who were sawed in two (Heb. 11:37). ¶

SAY – [1] ***legō*** [verb: λέγω <3004>] ▶ **To ask, to talk, to communicate** > The verb describes a verbal communication (e.g., Matt. 1:20; Luke 2:13), an unexpressed thought (e.g., Matt. 3:9; Luke 3:8) or a written communication (e.g., Mark 15:28; Luke 1:63). It refers especially to the substance of what is said (e.g., John 8:26 {to speak}). Jesus said to the paralytic to arise (Mark 2:11). Other refs.: SPEAK <3004>.
[2] ***ereō*** [verb: ἐρέω <2046>] ▶ **To speak, to prescribe** > At the presentation of Jesus in the temple, Mary and Joseph offered a sacrifice according to what is said in the law (Luke 2:24). Other refs.: SPEAK <2046>.
[3] **to say before: *proeipon*** [verb: προεῖπον <4277>]; **form of *proeipō*, which is from *pro*: before, and *epō*: to tell** ▶ Ref.: Acts 1:16; Gal. 5:21; 1 Thes. 4:6. ¶
[4] **to say before, to say previously: *proereō*** [verb: προερέω <4280>]; **from *pro*: before, and *ereō*: see [2]** ▶ **To communicate in advance** > This verb is used concerning the prophetic word (Rom. 9:29; Jude 17 {to speak}), and the word of exhortation (Heb. 4:7b). *
[5] ***laleō*** [verb: λαλέω <2980>] ▶ **To tell, to speak** > This verb refers to words expressing what exists (e.g., John 8:26). Jesus was what he had been saying (John 8:25c). Other refs.: SPEAK <2980>.
[6] ***phaskō*** [verb: φάσκω <5335>]; **from *phēmi*: to say** ▶ **To declare, to affirm; also transl.: to claim** > Some Jews were saying {asserting, maintaining} that the things Tertullus spoke about concerning Paul were so (Acts 24:9). Paul said {affirmed, asserted} that Jesus was alive (Acts 25:19). Some said they were {were calling themselves} apostles and were not (Rev. 2:2). The verb is transl. "to profess" in Rom. 1:22: some professing to be wise became fools. ¶
[7] ***phēmi*** [verb: φημί <5346>]; **from *phaō*: to give light** ▶ **To bring to light by speech, i.e., to assert, to declare** > The verb is frequently used when one is citing the words of another (e.g., Matt. 13:29; 26:61). It is sometimes used in an impersonal way (e.g., 2 Cor. 10:10). Other refs.: AFFIRM <5346>.
[8] **that is, which is, that is to say: *toutesti*** [pron.: τουτέστι <5123>]; ***ho esti*** [pron. and verb: ὅ ἐστι <3603>] ▶ These words are found in Matt. 27:46; Mark 7:2, 11, 34; Acts 1:19; 19:4; Rom. 1:12 (*touto de estin*); 7:18; 9:8; 10:8; Heb. 2:14; 7:2, 5; 9:11; 10:20; 11:16; 13:15; Rev. 21:17. *
– [9] Matt. 2:5; John 3:12a, b; 12:38; 18:16; et al. → SPEAK <2036> [10] Matt. 14:19 → to say a blessing → BLESS <2127> [11] Mark 9:39 → to say something bad → to speak evil → EVIL (adv.) <2551> [12] Luke 4:36 → to say to → to speak to → SPEAK <4814> [13] Luke 9:61 → to say good-bye → to bid farewell → FAREWELL <657> [14] Luke 10:30 → REPLY (verb) <5274> [15] Luke 20:27 → DENY <483> [16] John 4:51; Acts 5:25; 22:26 → REPORT (verb) <518> [17] John 8:43 → what He was saying → His speech → SPEECH <2981> [18] Acts 4:14 → to say, to say, against, to say in reply → REPLY (verb) <471> [19] Acts 6:5 → what they said → SAYING <3056> [20] Acts 16:18 → COMMAND (verb) <3853> [21] Acts 21:40 → to say to → ADDRESS (verb) <4377> [22] Acts 22:28 → ANSWER (verb) <611> [23] 2 Cor. 2:5 → to say too much → OVERCHARGE <1912> [24] 1 Pet. 2:6 → CONTAIN <4023>.

SAYING – [1] ***logos*** [masc. noun: λόγος <3056>]; **from *legō*: to say, to speak** ▶ **Something spoken, word, discourse** > The phrase "Jesus has finished His sayings" is found in Matt. 7:28; 19:1; 26:1. Jesus was speaking this saying {matter, word} openly about His sufferings and death to come (Mark 8:32). He asked the disciples on the road to Emmaus what kind of saying {conversation, communication} they had with one another (Luke 24:17). The saying {teaching, statement} of Jesus was hard for many of his disciples (John 6:60). The saying {statement} of the twelve concerning the service pleased the whole multitude (Acts 6:5). Other refs.: WORD <3056>.

2 ***rhēma*** [neut. noun: ῥῆμα <4487>]; **from *rheō*: to speak ▶ Word, discourse** > The disciples did not understand the saying {statement} of Jesus concerning His future death and resurrection (Mark 9:32). Having concluded all His sayings, Jesus entered Capernaum (Luke 7:1). Other refs.: WORD <4487>.

– 3 John 4:35 → Don't you have a saying? → lit.: Do you not say? 4 John 4:42 → SPEECH <2981> 5 Acts 10:29 → without saying → without objection → OBJECTION <369> 6 Titus 1:13 → WITNESS (noun)[1] <3141>.

SCALE – 1 ***lepis*** [fem. noun: λεπίς <3013>]; **from *lepō*: to peal ▶ Sort of plaque or membrane** > Something like scales fell from the eyes of Paul, and he received his sight (Acts 9:18). ¶

– 2 Rev. 6:5 → pair of scales → BALANCE <2218>.

SCANDAL – Gal. 5:11 → STUMBLING BLOCK <4625>.

SCARCE – Acts 14:18; 27:7 → with difficulty → DIFFICULTY <3433>.

SCARCELY – 1 Luke 9:39 → with difficulty → DIFFICULTY <3425> 2 Acts 14:18; 27:16; Rom. 5:7 → with difficulty → DIFFICULTY <3433> 3 1 Pet. 4:18 → DIFFICULTLY <3433>.

SCARLET – ***kokkinos*** [adj.: κόκκινος <2847>]; **from *kokkos*: cochineal insect, grain (as the grain-shape of the eggs of the insect) ▶ Bright red color obtained from the cochineal** > A scarlet robe was put on Jesus before His crucifixion (Matt. 27:28). Moses took scarlet wool to sprinkle the book of the law and the people (Heb. 9:19). Scarlet symbolizes the greatness of this world; Babylon the great is arrayed in scarlet (Rev. 17:4; 18:12, 16). Babylon the great is sitting on a scarlet beast (Rev. 17:3). ¶

SCATTER – 1 ***dialuō*** [verb: διαλύω <1262>]; **from *dia*: through, and *luō*: to untie; lit.: to dissolve ▶ To disperse, to put to flight** > All who obeyed Theudas were scattered and came to nothing (Acts 5:36). Other ref.: Acts 27:41 in some mss. ¶

2 ***diaspeirō*** [verb: διασπείρω <1289>]; **from *dia*: through, and *speirō*: to sow ▶ To disseminate, to disperse** > Christians of the church in Jerusalem were scattered throughout the regions of Judea and Samaria (Acts 8:1, 4), at the time of Stephen's martyrdom (11:19). This verb suggests the positive effects of the scattering of Christians, resulting in sowing the word of God abroad. ¶

3 ***rhiptō*** [verb: ῥίπτω <4496>] **▶ To be thrown to the ground, to be dispirited** > Jesus was moved with compassion for the multitudes, because they were weary and scattered {cast away, downcast, helpless} (Matt. 9:36). All other refs.: CAST (verb) <4496>.

4 **to scatter, to scatter abroad: *skorpizō*** [verb: σκορπίζω <4650>] **▶ To disperse, to distribute** > He who does not gather with Jesus scatters (Matt. 12:30; Luke 11:23). The wolf scatters the sheep (John 10:12). The disciples would be scattered, and Jesus would be left alone (John 16:32). God has scattered abroad, He has given to the poor (2 Cor. 9:9). ¶

5 **to scatter, to scatter abroad: *diaskorpizō*** [verb: διασκορπίζω <1287>]; **from *dia*: through (intens.), and *skorpizō*: see 4 ▶ To disperse, to spread** > The lord in a parable gathered from where he had not scattered {strawed} (Matt. 25:24, 26). God has scattered the proud in the imagination of their hearts (Luke 1:51). Jesus would gather together in one the children of God scattered abroad (John 11:52). The sheep of the flock (the disciples of Jesus) would be scattered abroad when the Shepherd (Jesus) would be stricken (Matt. 26:31; Mark 14:27). All who obeyed Judas of Galilee were scattered abroad (Acts 5:37). Other refs.: Luke 15:13; 16:1; see WASTE (verb) <1287>. ¶

– 6 Matt. 21:44; Luke 20:18 → to scatter like dust → to grind to powder → POWDER <3039> 7 John 2:15 → to pour out → POUR <1632> 8 1 Cor. 10:5 → to lay low → LAY <2693> 9 Jas. 1:1 → to be scattered abroad → DISPERSION <1290>.

SCATTERED – John 7:35; Jas. 1:1; 1 Pet. 1:1 → the people who live scattered, scattered among the nations, scattered → DISPERSION <1290>.

SCENTED – Rev. 18:12 → scented wood → citron wood → CITRON <2367>.

SCEPTER – ***rhabdos*** [fem. noun: ῥάβδος <4464>]; **lit.: rod, staff ► Staff of commandment, symbol of supreme authority** > It is said about the Son, the Lord Jesus: Your throne, O God, is to the age of the age; and a scepter of uprightness is the scepter of Your kingdom (Heb. 1:8a, b). All other refs.: ROD <4464>, STAFF <4464>.

SCEVA – ***Skeuas*** [masc. name: Σκευᾶς <4630>]: **fitted ► Jewish high priest** > The seven sons of Sceva were exorcists (Acts 19:14). They attempted to cast out an evil spirit by calling on the name of the Lord Jesus, but the spirit attacked them; they fled naked and wounded (see Acts 19:13–18). ¶

SCHEME (noun) – [1] 2 Cor. 2:11 → DEVICE <3540> [2] Eph. 4:14 → deceitful schemes → DECEITFUL <4106> [3] Eph. 6:11 → WILE <3180>.

SCHEME (verb) – [1] Matt. 26:4 → CONSULT <4823> [2] Mark 14:1 → SEEK <2212>.

SCHEMING – Eph. 4:14 → PLOTTING <3180>.

SCHISM – 1 Cor. 12:25 → DIVISION <4978>.

SCHOOL – [1] ***scholē*** [fem. noun: σχολή <4981>]; **at first, the term meant leisure, then the activity practiced during leisure time, such as a debate or a course; *schola*, in Lat. ► Place where one learns** > Paul reasoned daily in the school {lecture hall} of Tyrannus (Acts 19:9). ¶
– [2] Gal. 5:20 → school of opinion → SECT <139>.

SCHOOLMASTER – Gal. 3:24, 25 → TUTOR <3807>.

SCIENCE – 1 Tim. 6:20 → KNOWLEDGE <1108>.

SCOFF – [1] Luke 16:14 → MOCK <1592> [2] Luke 23:35 → SNEER <1592>.

SCOFFER – [1] Acts 13:41 → DESPISER <2707> [2] 2 Pet. 3:3; Jude 18 → MOCKER <1703>.

SCOFFING – 2 Pet. 3:3 → MOCKING <1700a>.

SCOLD – Mark 14:5 → to rebuke harshly → REBUKE (verb) <1690>.

SCORCH – ***kaumatizō*** [verb: καυματίζω <2739>]; **from *kauma*: heat, burn ► To burn, to consume by heat** > Some seeds were scorched by the sun (Matt. 13:6: *kaumatoō* in some mss.; Mark 4:6). Power was given to the sun to scorch men with fire (Rev. 16:8), and they were scorched {were seared} with great heat (v. 9). ¶

SCORCHING – [1] Matt. 20:12; Luke 12:55; Jas. 1:11 → scorching heat → HEAT <2742> [2] Rev. 7:16 → scorching heat → HEAT <2738>.

SCORN – [1] Luke 6:22 → to cast out → CAST (verb) <1544> [2] 1 Cor. 6:4 → to esteem least → ESTEEM (verb) <1848> [3] Gal. 4:14 → REJECT <1609> [4] Heb. 12:2 → DESPISE <2706>.

SCORPION – ***skorpios*** [masc. noun: σκορπίος <4651>] **► Animal inhabiting hot countries, bearing a venomous stinger** > The sting of the scorpion is painful and may be fatal if treatment of the wound is neglected (Luke 10:19; 11:12; Rev. 9:3, 5, 10). ¶

SCOURGE (noun) – [1] ***phragellion*** [neut. noun: φραγέλλιον <5416>]; **from the Lat. *flagellum*: whip (used to flog slaves) ► Instrument formed of little cords used for**

striking; also transl.: whip > Jesus made a scourge and drove the sellers and money-changers out of the temple (John 2:15). ¶

– [2] Mark 5:29, 34 → AFFLICTION <3148>.

SCOURGE (verb) – [1] ***mastigoō*** [verb: μαστιγόω <3146>]; **from *mastix*: scourge ▶ To punish with a scourge, to beat with rods; also transl.: to flog** > Jesus warned His disciples that men would scourge them in their synagogues (Matt. 10:17); they would also scourge prophets, wise men, and scribes (Matt. 23:34). The nations would scourge the Son of Man (Matt. 20:19; Mark 10:34; Luke 18:33). Pilate had Jesus scourged (John 19:1). The Lord disciplines and scourges {chastens, chastises, punishes} every son whom He receives (Heb. 12:6). ¶

[2] ***mastizō*** [verb: μαστίζω <3147>]; **from *mastos*: chest, or *mastix*: scourge ▶ See [1].** > Paul asked the centurion if it was lawful for him to scourge a Roman citizen who had not been condemned (Acts 22:25). ¶

[3] ***phragelloō*** [verb: φραγελλόω <5417>]; **from the Lat. *flagellare*: to flagellate, or from the Greek *phragellion*: whip ▶ To strike with an instrument formed of strips of leather at the end of which sharp bits of bone or lead are attached; the blows tore the flesh of the back and chest; also transl.: to flog** > Pilate had Jesus scourged (Matt. 27:26; Mark 15:15). ¶

– [4] Acts 16:22; 2 Cor. 11:25 → to beat with rods → ROD <4463>.

SCOURGING – ***mastix*** [fem. noun: μάστιξ <3148>]; **comp. *maiomai*: to seek, to pursue with zeal ▶ Lit.: a whip, a scourge, from which: beating; flogging with a whip or another instrument** > The chiliarch ordered that Paul should be examined by scourging (Acts 22:24). O.T. people of faith had scourgings (Heb. 11:36). Other refs.: Mark 3:10; 5:29, 34; Luke 7:21; see AFFLICTION <3148>. ¶

SCREAM – Luke 9:39 → CRY (verb) <2896>.

SCRIBE – ***grammateus*** [masc. noun: γραμματεύς <1122>]; **from *gramma*: letter, written document, which is from *graphō*: to write ▶ The scribes studied the law and taught it to the Jewish people; also transl.: teacher of the law** > They even performed the function of jurists (see Ezra 7:6; Neh. 8:2, 13). They are often associated with the elders (e.g., Matt. 26:57), the Pharisees (e.g., Matt. 12:38), and the chief priests (e.g., Luke 20:1) in their hatred of Jesus. The Lord calls the scribes and Pharisees hypocrites and blind guides (Matt. 23:13–34). The term is used mainly in the Gospels. *

SCRIP – Matt. 10:10; Mark 6:8; Luke 9:3; 10:4; 22:35, 36 → BAG <4082>.

SCRIPTURE – [1] ***graphē*** [fem. noun: γραφή <1124>]; **from *graphō*: to write ▶ Document, text; also transl.: writing** > Paul speaks of the mystery that, by the prophetic Scriptures, was made known to all nations (Rom. 16:26). All Scripture is given by inspiration of God (2 Tim. 3:16). No prophecy of Scripture is of any private interpretation (2 Pet. 1:20). Some people were twisting things that Paul was writing about, as also the rest of the Scriptures (2 Pet. 3:16). The word is used to designate the writings of the O.T.: Matt. 21:42; 22:29; 26:54, 56; Mark 12:10, 24; 14:49; 15:28 (in some mss.); Luke 4:21; 24:27, 32, 45; John 2:22; 5:39; 7:38, 42; 10:35; 13:18; 17:12; 19:24, 28, 36, 37; 20:9; Acts 1:16; 8:32, 35; 17:2, 11; 18:24, 28; Rom. 1:2; 4:3; 9:17; 10:11; 11:2; 15:4; 1 Cor. 15:3, 4; Gal. 3:8, 22; 4:30; 1 Tim. 5:18; Jas. 2:8, 23; 4:5; 1 Pet. 2:6. ¶

– [2] Luke 22:37 → lit.: having been written → WRITE <1125> [3] 2 Tim. 3:15 → LETTER <1121>.

SCROLL – [1] ***kephalis*** [fem. noun: κεφαλίς <2777>]; **from *kephalē*: head ▶ Manuscript, such as was rolled on a knobbed rod** > It was written prophetically in the scroll {role, volume} of the book that Jesus would come to do the will of God (Heb. 10:7; see Ps. 40:7). ¶

– [2] Matt. 1:1; Acts 19:19 → BOOK <976> [3] Luke 4:17a, b, 20; 2 Tim. 4:13; Heb. 9:19; 10:7; Rev. 1:11; 5:1–5, 7–9; 6:14; 22:7, 9, 10, 18a, b, 19a, c → BOOK <975> [4] Rev. 10:2, 8–10 → BOOK <974>.

SCUM – [1] 1 Cor. 4:13 → FILTH <4027> [2] 1 Cor. 4:13 → REFUSE (noun) <4067>.

SCYTHIAN – ***Skuthēs*** [masc. name: Σκύθης <4658>] ▶ **Inhabitant of a region north of the Black Sea** > The name was used to designate a barbaric and uncultured person (Col. 3:11). ¶

SEA – [1] ***thalassa*** [fem. noun: θάλασσα <2281>] ▶ **Vast body of salty water; also transl.: lake, in some cases** > The word is used in regard to the Red Sea (Acts 7:36; 1 Cor. 10:1; Heb. 11:29), the sea of Galilee (e.g., Matt. 4:18; 15:29; Mark 6:47–49; John 6:1; 21:1), and the sea in a general sense (e.g., Luke 17:2, 6; Acts 4:24; Rom. 9:27; Rev. 16:3a, b; 18:17; 20:8, 13; 21:1). Jude compares wicked men to the raging waves of the sea (Jude 13). This word is also used to describe the agitated condition of the Gentiles (Rev. 13:1). Other refs.: Matt. 4:15; 8:24, 26, 27, 32; 13:1, 47; 14:24–26; 17:27; 18:6; 21:21; 23:15; Mark 1:16a, b; 2:13; 3:7; 4:1a–c, 39, 41; 5:1, 13a, b, 21; 7:31; 9:42; 11:23; Luke 21:25; John 6:16–19, 22, 25; 21:1, 7; Acts 10:6, 32; 14:15; 17:14; 27:30, 38, 40; 28:4; 1 Cor. 10:2; 2 Cor. 11:26; Heb. 11:12 {seashore}; Jas. 1:6; Rev. 4:6; 5:13; 7:1–3; 8:8a, b, 9; 10:2, 5, 6, 8; 12:12, 17 in some mss.; 14:7; 15:2; 18:19, 21. ¶

[2] **where two seas meet: *dithalassos*** [adj.: διθάλασσος <1337>]**; from *dis*: twice, and *thalassa*: see** [1] ▶ **With the sea on both sides** > The ship of Paul was ran aground in a place where two seas met (Acts 27:41); also transl.: the ship struck a sandbar and ran aground. ¶

[3] **by the sea, on the seaside, upon the sea coast, by the lake: *parathalassios*** [adj.: παραθαλάσσιος <3864>]**; from *para*: near, and *thalassa*: see** [1] ▶ **Beside the sea** > Jesus came and dwelt in Capernaum, which is by the sea of Galilee (Matt. 4:13). Other ref.: Luke 4:31 in some mss. ¶

[4] **creature of the sea, creature in the sea, sea animal, thing in the sea: *enalios*** [adj. used as noun: ἐνάλιος <1724>]**; from *en*: in, and *hals*: salt, sea; lit.: which is in the sea** ▶ **Marine animal** > Every kind of sea animals is tamed (Jas. 3:7), but no man can tame the tongue (see v. 8). ¶

[5] **sea, open sea: *pelagos*** [neut. noun: πέλαγος <3989>] ▶ **The high sea, the sea in its broad expanse; also transl.: waters** > The word is used in regard to the part of the Mediterranean that is off Cilicia and Pamphylia (Acts 27:5). Other ref.: Matt. 18:6; see DEPTH <3989>. ¶

[6] **sea: see** [1]**; of glass: *hualinos*** [adj.: ὑάλινος <5193>]**; from *huō*: to rain (with the notion of rain's transparency)** ▶ **Symbol of definitive, unchangeable purity, worthy of the glory of God** > In the O.T., the sea of brass (or: laver of bronze; see Ex. 30:17–21; 38:8) served for the purification of priests. In the N.T., the sea of glass represents the character of the heavenly saints in relation to the throne of the God of judgment (Rev. 4:6). In Rev. 15:2a, b, it is mixed with fire: those who will have the victory over the beast will pass through the fire of martyrdom. ¶

– [7] Matt. 12:40 → sea monster → WHALE <2785> [8] Acts 13:13; 16:11; 21:1 → to put out to sea → SAIL (verb) <321> [9] Acts 18:18 → to put out to sea → SAIL (verb) <1602> [10] Acts 27:2, 24 → to put out to sea → SAIL (verb) <4126> [11] Acts 27:12; 28:11 → SAIL <321> [12] 2 Cor. 11:25 → open sea → DEEP <1037>.

SEA COAST, SEACOAST – ***paralios*** [adj.: παράλιος <3882>]**; from *para*: near, and *hals*: sea, salt** ▶ **Maritime region, coastline** > A great multitude of people from the sea coast {coastal region, coast} of Tyre and Sidon came to hear Jesus and be healed (Luke 6:17). ¶

SEAFARING MAN – Rev. 18:17 → all seafaring men → lit.: all the company on the ships → COMPANY (noun) <3658>, SHIP <4143>.

SEAL (noun) – [1] ***sphragis*** [fem. noun: σφραγίς <4973>]; **comp. *phrassō*: to close up, to silence (by authenticating) ▶ Impressed mark, most frequently on a letter, allowing it to be stamped with a signet; the seal certifies the ownership of the document on which it is affixed** > Abraham received the sign of circumcision as seal (or: guarantee) of the righteousness of faith that he had while he was still in uncircumcision (Rom. 4:11). The Corinthians were the seal (or: proof) of the apostleship of Paul (1 Cor. 9:2). The seal of the firm foundation of God consists in the fact that the Lord knows those who are His and that everyone who pronounces the name of the Lord is to withdraw from iniquity (2 Tim. 2:19). Only the Lamb is worthy to open the book in the right hand of Him who is seated on the throne and to break the seven seals (Rev. 5:1, 2, 5, 9; 6:1, 3, 5, 7, 9, 12; 8:1). In the same book, the term corresponds to a distinct mark and certifies the ownership of him on whom it is affixed: certain men do not have the seal of God on their foreheads (Rev. 9:4) and an angel has the seal of the living God (7:2). ¶
– [2] Matt. 27:66; John 3:33; 6:27; Rom. 15:28; 2 Cor. 1:22; Eph. 1:13; Rev. 7:3; 20:3 → to mark with a seal, to put a seal, to set a seal, to set a seal of ownership, to set a seal of approval → SEAL (verb) <4972>.

SEAL (verb) – [1] ***sphragizō*** [verb: σφραγίζω <4972>]; **from *sphragis*: seal ▶ To affix a seal; to attest, to certify; also transl.: to make sure, to mark with a seal, to put a seal, to set a seal, to set a seal of approval, to set a seal of ownership** > The verb has the meaning of prohibiting access (Matt. 27:66: sealing the stone of a tomb), or of concealing the meaning (Rev. 10:4 and 22:10 {to seal up}). The apostle John sealed (i.e., solemnly declared) that God is true (John 3:33). The verb indicates a particular identification of Jesus by the Father (John 6:27) and of believers from among various tribes in a future day (Rev. 7:4, 5, 8); in Rev. 7:3, the servants of God are sealed on the forehead. Paul uses this verb in regard to a gift (Rom. 15:28). In 2 Cor. 1:22, we read that God has sealed Christians. In sealing them (Eph. 1:13), the Holy Spirit certifies that they belong to God; He has sealed them for the day of redemption (4:30). An angel will seal the abyss over Satan, that he should not any more deceive the nations (Rev. 20:3). Other ref.: 2 Cor. 11:10 in some mss. ¶
[2] ***katasphragizō*** [verb: κατασφραγίζω <2696>]; **from *kata*: intens., and *sphragizō*: see [1] ▶ Stronger term than the preceding one** > John saw a book sealed with seven seals (Rev. 5:1 {sealed up}). ¶
– [3] 2 Tim. 2:19 → lit.: to have the seal → SEAL (noun) <4973>.

SEAM – John 19:23 → without seam → SEAMLESS <729>.

SEAMLESS – ***arraphos*** [adj.: ἄρραφος <729>]; **from *a*: neg., and *rhaptō*: to sew; also spelled: *araphos* ▶ Not sewed together, but woven as a whole** > The tunic of Jesus was seamless {without seam}, woven from the top in one piece (John 19:23). ¶

SEAR – Rev. 16:9 → SCORCH <2739>.

SEARCH (noun) – [1] Matt. 2:8 → to make a careful search → SEARCH (verb) <1833> [2] Matt. 13:45 → in search → lit.: seeking → SEEK <2212> [3] Acts 12:19 → to make a thorough search → SEEK <1934> [4] 1 Pet. 1:10 → made careful searches and inquiries → sought out and searched out → to seek out → SEEK <1567>.

SEARCH (verb) – [1] ***anakrinō*** [verb: ἀνακρίνω <350>]; **from *ana*: intens., and *krinō*: to judge ▶ To examine carefully, to discern** > Christians in Berea searched {examined} the Scriptures daily (Acts 17:11). All other refs.: ASK <350>, DISCERN <350>, EXAMINE <350>, JUDGE (verb) <350>.
[2] ***exetazō*** [verb: ἐξετάζω <1833>]; **from *ek*: intens., and *etazō*: to examine ▶ To find out thoroughly, to question** > Herod told the wise men to go and search {search out} carefully {make a careful search} for the young child Jesus (Matt. 2:8). All other refs.: ASK <1833>, INQUIRE <1833>.

[3] ***ereunaō*** [verb: ἐρευνάω <2045>]; **from *ereō*: to ask; also spelled: *eraunaō* ▶ To examine, to investigate** > Jesus says to search {to study diligently} the Scriptures, for it is these that bear witness concerning Him (John 5:39). Nicodemus was told to search and see that no prophet had arisen out of Galilee (John 7:52). He who searches the hearts knows what the mind of the Spirit is, because He intercedes for the saints according to God (Rom. 8:27). The Spirit searches all things, even the depths of God (1 Cor. 2:10). The Son of God searches the minds and the hearts (Rev. 2:23). Other ref.: 1 Pet. 1:11; see SEEK <2037a>. ¶

[4] **to search carefully, diligently: *exereunaō*** [verb: ἐξερευνάω <1830>]; **from *ek*: intens., and *ereunaō*: see [3]; also spelled: *exeraunoō* ▶ To examine very carefully** > The prophets have inquired (*ekzēteō*) and searched carefully (*exereunaō*) {made careful search and inquiry, searched intently and with the greatest care} concerning the salvation of believers in the Lord under grace (1 Pet. 1:10). ¶

– [5] Matt. 2:13; 18:12; 26:16; Luke 2:48, 49; 4:42; 1 Cor. 1:22; et al. → SEEK <2212> [6] Mark 1:36 → to search for → to follow after → FOLLOW <2614> [7] Luke 2:44, 45 → SEEK <327> [8] Acts 12:19 → SEEK <1934> [9] 1 Pet. 1:10 → searched intently and with the greatest care → sought out and searched out → to seek out → SEEK <1567>.

SEASHORE – Heb. 11:12 → SEA <2281>.

SEASON (noun) – [1] **due season, convenient season, time, convenient time, due time, proper time, right time: *kairos*** [masc. noun: καιρός <2540>] ▶ **a. Specific time, expected period; also transl.: time, vintage-time, harvest time** > The term is used in regard to harvesting (Matt. 21:34, 41; Mark 11:13; 12:2; Luke 20:10; Acts 14:17). At a certain season, an angel stirred up the water of the pool of Bethesda (John 5:4). It was not for the apostles to know the times or the seasons {dates, epochs} that the Father had set for the restoration of the kingdom to Israel (Acts 1:7). The word is transl. "time" in Rom. 9:9. Paul did not need to write to the Thessalonians concerning the times and the seasons {epochs, dates} relative to the day of the Lord (1 Thes. 5:1). **b. Appropriate, convenient time** > Jesus speaks of a servant giving food in season to the household of his master (Matt. 24:45); Luke speaks of a faithful and wise steward who gives the measure of corn in season (Luke 12:42). Felix would call Paul when he had a convenient season {an opportunity} (Acts 24:25). Christ died for the ungodly in due time (Rom. 5:6). All other refs.: OCCASION <2540>, TIME <2540>.

[2] **in season: *eukairōs*** [adv.: εὐκαίρως <2122>]; **from *eukairos*: opportune time, which is from *eu*: well, and *kairos*: see [1] ▶ At an opportune moment, timely** > Paul told Timothy to preach the word, to be ready in season (*eukairōs*) and out of season (*akairōs*; see [3]) (2 Tim. 4:2). Other ref.: Mark 14:11; see CONVENIENTLY <2122>. ¶

[3] **out of season: *akairōs*** [adv.: ἀκαίρως <171>]; **from *a*: neg., and *kairos*: see [1] ▶ At an inopportune or disagreeable time** > Ref.: 2 Tim. 4:2 (see [2]). ¶

– [4] Luke 23:8 → long season → long time → TIME <2425> <5550> [5] John 5:35; 2 Cor. 7:8; Phm. 15 → TIME <5610> [6] Heb. 11:25 → for a season → for a time → TIME <4340>.

SEASON (verb) – [1] ***artuō*** [verb: ἀρτύω <741>]; **from which *artusis*: seasoning ▶ To prepare, to make ready; specifically: to make food more tasty by adding an ingredient such as salt; also transl.: to make salty again** > Jesus asks with what will the salt be seasoned {how can it be made salty again} if it becomes unsalty, tasteless (Mark 9:50; Luke 14:34). The word of the Christian should always be with grace, seasoned with salt (Col. 4:6). ¶

– [2] Matt. 5:13; Mark 9:49a, b → SALT (verb) <233>.

SEASONABLE – ***eukairos*** [adj.: εὔκαιρος <2121>]; **from *eu*: good, and *kairos*: occasion ▶ Appropriate, opportune, timely** > At the throne of grace, we find grace for seasonable help {to help in time of need} (Heb. 4:16). Other ref.: Mark 6:21; see OPPORTUNE <2121>. ¶

SEAT (noun) – 1 ***kathedra*** [fem. noun: καθέδρα <2515>]; **from *kathezomai*: to sit down, which is from *kata*: down, and *ezomai*: to sit ▶ Bench, chair** > Jesus overturned the seats of those who sold doves in the temple (Matt. 21:12; Mark 11:15). The scribes and the Pharisees had seated themselves in the seat of Moses (Matt. 23:2). ¶
2 **first seat: *prōtokathedria*** [fem. noun: πρωτοκαθεδρία <4410>]; **from *prōtos*: first, and *kathedra*: see 1 ▶ Chief seat, place of honor; also transl.: best seat, highest seat, most important seat, uppermost seat** > The scribes and the Pharisees loved the first seats in the synagogues (Matt. 23:6; Mark 12:39; Luke 11:43; 20:46). ¶
– 3 Luke 14:9 → PLACE (noun) <5117> 4 Acts 12:21 → elevated seat → THRONE <968> 5 Jas. 2:3 → in a good seat → in a good place → PLACE (noun) <2573>.

SEAT (verb) – See SIT.

SEATED (BE) – 1 Matt. 26:64; Rev. 4:2, 9, 10; 5:1, 7; 6:16; 17:1, 9, 15 → SIT <2521> 2 Heb. 12:2 → SIT <2523>.

SECLUSION – Luke 1:24 → to keep oneself in seclusion, to remain in seclusion → HIDE <4032>.

SECOND – 1 ***deuteros*** [adj.: δεύτερος <1208>]; **from *duo*: two ▶ That which immediately follows the first in order; also transl.: another, other** > Jesus spoke of the second greatest commandment, which is to love one's neighbor as oneself (Mark 12:31). The first man (Adam) came from the earth, the second Man (Jesus) came from heaven (1 Cor. 15:47). We are to reject a heretical man after a first and second admonition (Titus 3:10). The word is used in the expr. "second death" (Rev. 2:11; 20:6, 14; 21:8). Other refs.: Matt. 21:30; 22:26, 39; 26:42; Mark 12:21; Luke 12:38; 19:18; 20:30; John 4:54; Acts 12:10; 13:33; 2 Cor. 1:15; Heb. 8:7; 9:3, 7; 10:9; 2 Pet. 3:1; Rev. 4:7; 6:3a, b; 8:8; 11:14; 14:8 in some mss.; 16:3; 21:19. The word is also used as an adv. (*deuteron*) in 1 Cor. 12:28 {secondarily, secondly} and Jude 5 {afterward, in the second place, later, subsequently}. All other refs.: TIME <1208>.
– 2 Rev. 13:11 → lit.: another (*allos*) 3 Rev. 13:13 → "second beast" added in Engl.

SECONDARILY – 1 Cor. 12:28 → SECOND <1208>.

SECONDLY – 1 Cor. 12:28 → SECOND <1208>.

SECRET (adj. and noun) – 1 ***kruptos*** [adj. and adj. used as noun: κρυπτός <2927>]; **from *kruptō*: to hide ▶ Done without the knowledge of others, hidden, unseen** > Our charitable deed must be done in secret, and God the Father who sees in secret will reward us openly (Matt. 6:4a, b); the same is true of prayer (v. 6a, b) and fasting (v. 18a, b; other mss.: *kruphaios* or *kruphios*). There is nothing secret that will not be known (Matt. 10:26 {hid}; Mark 4:22; Luke 8:17; 12:2). No one does anything in secret when he himself seeks to be known in public (John 7:4). Jesus went up to the feast as in secret (John 7:10). He had spoken nothing in secret (John 18:20). Joseph of Arimathea was a disciple of Jesus, but a secret one {secretly} (John 19:38; lit.: being in secret: *kruptō*). God will judge the secrets of men by Jesus Christ according to the gospel of Paul (Rom. 2:16). The secrets of the heart of an unbeliever or of a simple person may be disclosed if he hears Christians prophesying (1 Cor. 14:25). Paul had renounced secret and shameful {disgraceful} things (2 Cor. 4:2). The term is transl. "inwardly" in Rom. 2:29. Other refs.: 1 Cor. 4:5 and 1 Pet. 3:4 (hidden); see HIDE <2927>. ¶
– 2 Matt. 13:11; Mark 4:11; Luke 8:10; 1 Cor. 2:7; 4:1; 2 Thes. 2:7 → secret, secret power → MYSTERY <3466> 3 Matt. 13:35 → to keep secret → HIDE <2928> 4 Matt. 24:26 → secret chamber → inner room → ROOM <5009> 5 Mark 7:24 → to keep one's presence secret → to be hidden

→ HIDDEN (BE) <2990> 6 Luke 11:33 → secret, secret place → PLACE (noun) <2926> 7 Rom. 16:25 → to keep secret → to keep silence → SILENCE (noun) <4601>.

SECRET (adv.) – **in secret: *kruphē*** [adv.: κρυφῇ <2931>]; **from *kruptō*; to hide ▶ Without the knowledge of others, in a hidden manner, not openly** > It is shameful to speak of the things that disobedient men do in secret (Eph. 5:12). ¶

SECRETLY – 1 ***lathra*** [adv.: λάθρᾳ <2977>]; **from *lanthanō*: to be hidden, to escape notice ▶ Without anyone knowing; also transl.: privily, quietly** > Joseph planned to send Mary away secretly (Matt. 1:19). Herod called the wise men secretly (Matt. 2:7). Martha secretly called Mary, her sister (John 11:28 [aside]; other mss.: have *siōpē*). The lictors wanted to put Paul and Silas out of prison secretly (Acts 16:37). Other ref.: Mark 5:33 in some mss. ¶
2 **secretly brought in: *pareisaktos*** [adj.: παρείσακτος <3920>]; **from *pareisagō*: see 3 ▶ Being brought in intrusively, in a surreptitious way** > False brothers had been secretly brought in {had infiltrated the ranks} to spy out Christian liberty (Gal. 2:4). ¶
3 **to secretly introduce, to secretly bring in: *pareisagō*** [verb: παρεισάγω <3919>]; **from *para*: beside, and *eisagō:* to introduce, which is from *eis*: in, and *agō*: to lead ▶ To bring in surreptitiously, by stealth** > False teachers will secretly introduce {will bring in by the bye} destructive heresies (2 Pet. 2:1). ¶
– 4 Matt. 26:4; Mark 14:1 → by subtlety → SUBTLETY <1388> 5 John 19:38 → lit.: being in secret → SECRET (adj. and noun) <2927> 6 Acts 6:11 → to secretly induce, to secretly persuade → SUBORN <5260>.

SECT – ***hairesis*** [fem. noun: αἵρεσις <139>]; **from *haireō*: to choose, to take; lit.: choice of a particular doctrine; from which: heresy ▶ A sect is characterized by the adherence of its members to a particular doctrine under the instigation and direction of a false teacher; also transl.: difference, division, faction, heresy, party, school of opinion** > In Acts, mention is made of the sects of the Sadducees (5:17), the Pharisees (15:5; 26:5), and the Nazarenes (24:5). Heresies are a work of the flesh (Gal. 5:20). The Jews called Christianity a sect, assimilated to a school of philosophy (Acts 24:14; 28:22). There must be factions among Christians to show which ones are approved of God (1 Cor. 11:19). Peter speaks of false teachers who will introduce destructive heresies (2 Pet. 2:1). ¶

SECTION – 1 Heb. 9:2 → "section" added in Engl. 2 Heb. 9:3, 6, 8 → second section, first section → lit.: a tabernacle, first tabernacle → TABERNACLE <4633>.

SECUNDUS – ***Sekoundos*** [masc. name: Σεκοῦνδος <4580>]; ***secundus*, in Lat.: second, happy, prosperous ▶ Christian Macedonian of Thessalonica** > Secundus accompanied Paul into Asia (Acts 20:4). ¶

SECURE (adj.) – 1 **to make secure: *asphalizō*** [verb: ἀσφαλίζω <805>]; **from *asphalēs*: sure, which is from *a*: neg., and *sphallō*: to defeat, to overthrow ▶ To keep close watch on, to keep in safe custody** > The tomb of Jesus was made secure {made sure, secured} (Matt. 27:64, 66). Other ref.: Acts 16:24; see FASTEN <805>. ¶
– 2 Acts 27:16 → making secure → SECURING <4031> 3 Heb. 6:19 → SURE <804> 4 2 Pet. 3:17 → secure position → STEADFASTNESS <4740>.

SECURE (verb) – 1 Matt. 27:64–66 → to make secure → SECURE (adj.) <805> 2 Matt. 28:14 → lit.: to keep out of trouble → TROUBLE (noun) <275> 3 Acts 12:20 → to secure the support → to win over → WIN <3982> 4 Acts 16:24 → FASTEN <805> 5 1 Cor. 9:15 → to secure provision → lit.: that it should be so done in my case 6 Heb. 9:12 → OBTAIN <2147>.

SECURELY – 1 ***asphalōs*** [adv.: ἀσφαλῶς <806>]; **from *asphalēs*: firm, safe, which is**

from *a*: neg., and *sphallō*: to bring down, to overthrow ▶ Firmly, taking security measures > Judas said to lead Jesus away securely {safely, under guard} (Mark 14:44). The jailer was commanded to keep Paul and Silas securely {carefully} (Acts 16:23). Other ref.: Acts 2:36; see ASSUREDLY <806>. ¶
– [2] Acts 5:23 → lit.: with all safety → SAFETY <803>.

SECURING – ***perikratēs*** [adj.: περικρατής <4031>]; **from *peri*: around, and *krateō*: to dominate, to hold fast, which is from *kratos*: strength ▶ Having full power or mastery over something >** The term is used in the expr. "securing with difficulty" {coming by, getting under control, making oneself master, making secure} in Acts 27:16. ¶

SECURITY – [1] ***hikanon*; noun from *hikanos*** [adj.: ἱκανός <2425>]**: sufficient, which is from *hikneomai*: to come, to occur ▶ Sufficient guarantee, pledge >** In Acts 17:9, it is likely that rulers of the city received a guarantee {security, bond}, poss. a sum of money, from Jason that Paul would leave and not return to Thessalonica (see Acts 17:10; 1 Thes. 2:18). Other refs.: see entries in Lexicon at <2425>.
– [2] Acts 5:23; 1 Thes. 5:3 → SAFETY <803>.

SEDITION – [1] **to raise a sedition: *anastatoō*** [verb: ἀναστατόω <387>]; **from *anastatos*: involved in a riot or revolt, which is from *anistēmi*: to stand up, which is from *ana*: up, and *histēmi*: to stand ▶ To organize an uprising, a rebellion >** An Egyptian had raised a sedition {had made an uproar, had stirred up a rebellion, had stirred up a revolt, started a revolt} (Acts 21:38). Other refs.: Acts 17:6; Gal. 5:12; see TURN (verb) <387>, TROUBLE (verb) <387>. ¶
– [2] Luke 23:19, 25; Acts 19:40; 24:5 → INSURRECTION <4714> [3] Gal. 5:20 → DIVISION <1370>.

SEDUCE – [1] Mark 13:22 → DECEIVE <635> [2] 2 Pet. 2:14 → ENTICE <1185> [3] 1 John 2:26; Rev. 2:20 → STRAY <4105>.

SEDUCING – 1 Tim. 4:1 → DECEIVER <4108>.

SEE – [1] ***blepō*** [verb: βλέπω <991>] **▶ a. To direct the eyes toward; to understand; this verb puts emphasis on the person who sees >** The verb is used in regard to physical vision (e.g., Matt. 11:4) and mental perception (e.g., Matt. 13:13a, b, 14a, b). God the Father sees in secret (Matt. 6:4, 6, 18). The Son sees what the Father does (John 5:19). **b. To pay attention, to consider carefully; also transl.: to take heed, to watch, to watch out >** Jesus said to see that no one mislead His own, for many will come in His name (Matt. 24:4; Mark 13:5; Luke 21:8). He says to take heed to what we hear (Mark 4:24), and how we hear (Luke 8:18). He tells His disciples to take heed to themselves in regard to the times of the end (Mark 13:9). He says to take heed, watch, and pray in regard to the coming of the Son of Man in glory (Mark 13:33). Paul told the Jews of Antioch to see that they not fall into unbelief (Acts 13:40). The Corinthians were to see that their liberty should not become a stumbling block to the weak (1 Cor. 8:9). He who thinks he is standing is to take heed that he does not fall (1 Cor. 10:12). The Galatians were to see that they be not consumed by one another (Gal. 5:15). The Ephesians were to see that they walk carefully (Eph. 5:15). The Philippians were to see to dogs, evil workers, and the concision (Phil. 3:2a–c). The Colossians were to see that no one lead them away as a prey through philosophy and vain deceit (Col. 2:8). Archippus was to take heed to the service that he had received in the Lord (Col. 4:17). The Hebrews were to see that there be not in anyone of them a wicked heart of unbelief (Heb. 3:12); they were to see that they refuse not Him who speaks (12:25). John tells his readers to see to themselves that they do not lose what they have accomplished (2 John 8). **c. To make sure, to take care >** The Corinthians were to see to it that Timothy should have nothing to fear when he was with them (1 Cor. 16:10). *
[2] ***anablepō*** [verb: ἀναβλέπω <308>]; **from *ana*: again (intens.), and *blepō*: see [1] ▶**

To view for the first time or anew; also transl.: to receive sight, to regain sight, to have the sight restored > Thanks to Jesus, the blind saw (Matt. 11:5; 20:34; Mark 10:51, 52; Luke 7:22; 18:41–43; John 9:11; 15a, 18a, b). Saul saw, thanks to Ananias, after having lost his vision on the road to Damascus (Acts 9:12, 17, 18; 22:13). All other refs.: LOOK (verb) <308>.

3 ***emblepō*** [verb: ἐμβλέπω <1689>]; **from *en*: in, on, and *blepō*: see 1 ▶ To fix one's gaze on** > The blind man who had been healed by Jesus saw all things clearly (Mark 8:25). Paul could not see because of the glory of the light that had appeared to him (Acts 22:11). All other refs.: see LOOK (verb) <1689>.

4 ***horaō*** [verb: ὁράω <3708>] ▶ **a. To look at, to consider; this verb puts emphasis on the object that is seen** > Concerning the thirty pieces of silver, Judas was to see to it (Matt. 27:4). Pilate told the Jewish people to see to it concerning the blood of Jesus (Matt. 27:24). The verb is used in regard to physical vision (e.g., John 6:36) and discernment (e.g., Matt. 9:4). It is used in regard to Christ who has seen the Father (John 6:46b) and what He has seen with His Father (8:38a). **b. To take care, to be careful, to take heed** > The leper healed by Jesus was to see that he told no one (Matt. 8:4; Mark 1:44). Two blind men healed by Jesus were to see that no one knew it (Matt. 9:30). Jesus said to see that one despise not a little child (Matt. 18:10). He says to see that one is not disturbed when hearing of wars and rumors of wars (Matt. 24:6). The Thessalonians were to see {to make sure} that no one render to any man evil for evil (1 Thes. 5:15). Moses was to see that he made all things according to the pattern that had been shown to him on the mountain when he was about to make the tabernacle (Heb. 8:5). Other refs.: APPEAR <3708>, BEWARE <3708>, LOOK (verb) <3708>.

5 ***apeidon*** [verb: ἀπεῖδον <542>]; **from the verb: *aphoraō*** [verb: ἀφοράω <872>]; **from *apo*: from (intens.), and *horaō*: see 4 ▶ To see clearly** > Paul uses this verb in regard to his affairs in Phil. 2:23. Other ref.: Heb. 12:2 (to fix the eyes); see FIX <872>. ¶

6 **to see clearly: *kathoraō*** [verb: καθοράω <2529>]; **from *kata*: down (intens.), and *horaō*: see 4 ▶ To become visible** > The invisible attributes of God are clearly seen {are perceived}, being understood by the things that are made (Rom. 1:20). ¶

7 **to see again: *palin*** [adv.: πάλιν <3825>] ***horaō*** [verb: ὁράω <3708>]; **lit.: to see once more ▶ To look in on once more, to visit and company with anew** > Jesus would see His disciples again and their heart would rejoice (John 16:22). The Philippians would rejoice on seeing Epaphroditus again (Phil. 2:28).

8 ***theaomai*** [verb: θεάομαι <2300>]; **from *thaomai*: to wonder ▶ To look closely at, to contemplate** > Women saw {beheld, observed} where the body of Jesus was placed (Luke 23:55). John saw the glory of the Word, the glory as of the only begotten of the Father (John 1:14). John the Baptist saw the Spirit descending like a dove and remaining on Jesus (John 1:32). This verb puts emphasis on the person who sees. Other refs.: LOOK (verb) <2300>.

9 ***theōreō*** [verb: θεωρέω <2334>]; **from *theōros*: spectator, which is from *theaomai*: see 8 ▶ To contemplate, to watch; also transl.: to behold, to look, to observe; this verb puts emphasis on the person who sees** > Women came to see the tomb of Jesus on the first day of the week (Matt. 28:1). The unclean spirits fell down before Jesus when they saw Him (Mark 3:11). Jesus saw how the crowd was casting money into the treasury (Mark 12:41). He spoke of the temple that some were seeing (Luke 21:6). Many women saw the crucifixion of Jesus from afar off (Matt. 27:55; Mark 15:40). Women saw the tomb where Jesus was put (Mark 15:47). The people beheld (or: saw) Jesus crucified (Luke 23:35). Many believed in the name of Jesus when they saw the miracles that He did (John 2:23). Everyone who sees {looks to} the Son and believes in Him has eternal life (John 6:40). Great fear fell on those who saw the two prophets who had returned to life (Rev. 11:11); their enemies saw {beheld, looked on} them ascending to heaven in a cloud (v. 12). Other refs.: CONSIDER <2334>.

[10] ***phainō*** [verb: φαίνω <5316>]; **from *phōs*: light ► To manifest, to become conspicuous** > Jesus speaks of hypocrites who pray so that they may be seen by men (Matt. 6:5). All other refs.: APPEAR <5316>.

(Preceding entries: after W. E. Vine.)

[11] ***eidon*** [verb: εἶδον <1492>]; **form of *horaō*; see [4] ► To see clearly, to distinguish** > Israel could behold, but not see {perceive} (Matt. 13:14; Mark 4:12; Acts 28:26). In a parable, the king saw {beheld, noticed} a man who did not have on a wedding garment (Matt. 22:11). When he saw Jesus, a man possessed by demons fell down before Him (Luke 8:28). A servant girl saw Peter warming himself (Mark 14:67, 69). *

[12] **to see before, to see previously: *prooraō*** [verb: προοράω <4308>]; **from *pro*: before, and *horaō*: see [4] ► To have seen on a previous occasion** > Trophimus was seen before with Paul (Acts 21:29). Other ref.: Acts 2:25; see FORESEE <4308>. ¶

[13] **to see to it: *optomai*** [verb: ὀπτομαι <3700>] ► **To look after, to attend to** > In matters of religious differences with Paul, the Jews were to see to it {look after it, look to it, settle the matter} themselves (Acts 18:15). – [14] Matt. 6:28 → CONSIDER <2648> [15] Matt. 7:3; Luke 6:41 → LOOK (verb) <991> [16] Matt. 7:5; Luke 6:42 → to see clearly → CLEARLY <1227> [17] Matt. 15:17 → UNDERSTAND <3539> [18] Matt. 17:9 → what you have seen → lit.: the vision → VISION <3705> [19] Mark 7:18; 8:17 → PERCEIVE <3539> [20] Mark 8:33 → LOOK (verb) <1492> [21] Luke 11:35 → WATCH (verb) <4648> [22] Luke 20:23 → to see through → PERCEIVE <2657> [23] John 3:21; 9:3 → to be clearly seen, to see plainly → MANIFEST (verb) <5319> [24] John 16:19 → KNOW <1097> [25] John 16:30a → KNOW <1492> [26] Acts 2:31 → to see before, to see what was ahead, to see what was to come → FORESEE <4275> [27] Acts 3:16 → as you can see → lit.: in the presence of all → PRESENCE <561> [28] Acts 10:40 → to be seen → to become manifest → MANIFEST (adj.) <1717> [29] Acts 26:16b → you will see → I will appear to you → APPEAR <3700> [30] Acts 27:39 → DISCOVER <2657> [31] Rom. 1:28 → to see fit → LIKE (verb) <1381> [32] 1 Cor. 1:26 → CONSIDER <991> [33] 1 Cor. 3:10 → to take heed → HEED (noun) <991> [34] 1 Cor. 4:7 → to see anything different → to make a distinction → DISTINCTION <1252> [35] 1 Cor. 10:18 → BEHOLD (verb) <991> [36] 2 Cor. 3:13 → BEHOLD (verb) <816> [37] 2 Cor. 4:4 → SHINE <826> [38] 2 Cor. 5:12 → what is seen → APPEARANCE <4383> [39] Gal. 1:18 → to make acquaintance → ACQUAINTANCE <2477> [40] Eph. 3:9 → to make to see → to bring to light → LIGHT (noun) <5461> [41] 1 Tim. 4:15 → seen → EVIDENT <5318> [42] Heb. 12:15 → to see to it → WATCH (verb) <1983> [43] 1 Pet. 2:12; 3:2 → WITNESS (verb) <2029> [44] 2 Pet. 1:9 → to be unable to see afar off → SHORTSIGHTED (BE) <3467> [45] 2 Pet. 2:8 what he saw → lit.: seeing → SEEING <990>.

SEED – [1] ***sperma*** [neut. noun: σπέρμα <4690>]; **from *speirō*: to sow ► a. Grain or kernel containing the germ of a future plant** > Jesus spoke about the good seed in a parable (Matt. 13:24, 27, 37, 38). God has given to each of the seeds its own body (1 Cor. 15:38). The seed of God remains in the Christian (1 John 3:9). Other refs.: Matt. 13:32; Mark 4:31; 2 Cor. 9:10a. **b. Descendant, offspring, progeny; also transl.: children, posterity** > The term is used in relation to Abraham (Luke 1:55; Acts 3:25; Rom. 4:13, 16, 18; 9:7a, b, 8; 11:1; 2 Cor. 11:22; Gal. 3:16a–c, 19, 29; Heb. 2:16; 11:18), David (John 7:42 {family}; Acts 13:23; Rom. 1:3; 2 Tim. 2:8), and Israel (Rom. 9:29; Rev. 12:17 {children}). According to levirate law (see Deut. 25:5–10), if anyone died, not having children, his brother was to marry his wife and raise up seed to his brother (Matt. 22:24, 25 {issue}; Mark 12:19–22; Luke 20:28). The Jews said they were Abraham's seed (John 8:33), which Jesus acknowledged (v. 37). God promised Abraham to give a land to him and to his seed (Acts 7:5). This same seed of Abraham sojourned in a strange land where they were enslaved and mistreated (Acts 7:6); their sojourn lasted 215 years in Egypt, but the total duration of the oppression of the seed of Abraham was 400 years and began with the birth of Isaac. Sarah received strength for the conception of seed (Heb. 11:11). ¶

2 ***spora*** [fem. noun: σπορά <4701>]; **from *speirō*: to sow ▶ Lit.: the act of sowing; the spiritual seed is the word of God** > Christians are born again, not of corruptible seed, but of incorruptible one, by the living and enduring word of God (1 Pet. 1:23). ¶

3 ***sporos*** [masc. noun: σπόρος <4703>]; **from *speirō*: to sow ▶ Seeding, seed used in planting** > This term is used in a parable about the kingdom of God (Mark 4:26, 27; Luke 8:5, 11). Other ref.: 2 Cor. 9:10b {sowing}. ¶

– 4 Matt. 13:4, 19b, 20, 22, 23; Mark 4:4; Luke 8:5b → to receive the seed, to scatter the seed → SOW (verb) <4687>
5 Matt. 13:5 → other seeds → lit.: others → OTHER <243>.

SEEING – ***blemma*** [neut. noun: βλέμμα <990>]; **from *blepō*: to see ▶ Act of seeing or object seen** > Oppressed by the filthy conduct of the people in Sodom and Gomorrah, through seeing and hearing, the righteous Lot was tormenting his soul day after day (2 Pet. 2:8). ¶

SEEK – 1 ***zēteō*** [verb: ζητέω <2212>] ▶ **a. To try to discover, to find; also transl.: to go about, to look for, to search** > Herod would seek the child Jesus (Matt. 2:13). Jesus says to seek first the kingdom of God (Matt. 6:33). He says also to seek and we will find, for he who seeks finds (Matt. 7:7, 8; Luke 11:9, 10). The kingdom of heaven is like a merchant seeking beautiful pearls (Matt. 13:45). The angel knew that the women were seeking Jesus who had been crucified (Matt. 28:5; Mark 16:6); the angels asked the women why they were seeking the living (Jesus) among the dead (Luke 24:5). All were seeking Jesus (Mark 1:37); later His mother and His brothers were seeking Him (3:32). To His parents who were seeking Him, when He was twelve years old, Jesus said that He had to be about His Father's business (Luke 2:48, 49). The Son of Man has come to seek and to save that which was lost (Luke 19:10). The Father seeks true worshippers who worship Him in spirit and in truth (John 4:23). The people were seeking Jesus in Capernaum (John 6:24, 26); the Jews sought Him at the feast (7:11; also 11:56). Jesus said that He would be sought (John 7:34, 36; 8:21; 13:33). He asked those who came to arrest Him whom they were seeking (John 18:4, 7, 8). He asked Mary whom she was seeking (John 20:15). Ananias was to seek {enquire for, inquire for} Saul (Acts 9:11). Three men were seeking Peter (Acts 10:19, 21). Elymas was seeking someone to lead him by the hand (Acts 13:11). The Jews were seeking Paul and Silas (Acts 17:5). God wants men to seek Him (Acts 17:27). He was found by those who did not seek Him (Rom. 10:20). If one is bound to a wife, he should not seek to be loosed; if he is loosed from a wife, he should not seek a wife (1 Cor. 7:27a, b). Onesiphorus had sought Paul very diligently (2 Tim. 1:17). The devil seeks whom he may devour (1 Pet. 5:8). **b. To carefully, diligently look for a person or an object; also transl.: to search, to look** > The crowds sought Jesus (Luke 4:42). Jesus told His disciples they were not to seek {to set their heart on} what they should eat or drink (Luke 12:29), but that they were to seek the kingdom of their Father (v. 31). The chief priests, the scribes, and the chief of the people sought to destroy Jesus (Luke 19:47). The Greeks seek wisdom (1 Cor. 1:22). The Christian is to seek peace and pursue it (1 Pet. 3:11). Other refs.: Matt. 2:20; 12:43, 46, 47 {to desire}; 18:12; 21:46; 26:16, 59 {to keep trying to obtain}; Mark 8:11; 11:18; 12:12; 14:1, 11, 55 {to keep trying to obtain}; Luke 2:44, 45 (in some mss.); 5:18; 6:19; 9:9 {to desire}; 11:16 {to demand, to keep seeking}, 24, 54 (in some mss.); 12:48; 13:6, 7, 24; 15:8; 17:33; 19:3; 20:19; 22:2, 6; John 1:38; 4:27; 5:16 (in some mss.), 18, 30, 44; 7:1, 4, 18a, b, 19, 20, 25, 30; 8:37, 40, 50a, b; 10:39; 11:8; 16:19; 19:12 {to make efforts}; Acts 13:8; 16:10 {to endeavor}; 21:31; 27:30; Rom. 2:7; 10:3; 11:3; 1 Cor. 4:2; 10:24, 33; 13:5; 14:12; 2 Cor. 12:14; 13:3; Gal. 1:10;

2:17; Phil. 2:21; Col. 3:1; 1 Thes. 2:6; Heb. 8:7; Rev. 9:6. ¶

2 ***anazēteō*** [verb: ἀναζητέω <327>]; **from *ana*: again (intens.), and *zēteō*: see 1 ▶ To make an effort to discover, to seek diligently** > The parents of Jesus were seeking {looking for} Him (Luke 2:44). Not having found Jesus, his parents returned to Jerusalem seeking {looking for} Him (Luke 2:45). Barnabas departed to Tarsus to seek Saul (Acts 11:25). ¶

3 **to seek; to seek after, diligently, out: *ekzēteō*** [verb: ἐκζητέω <1567>]; **from *ek*: out (intens.), and *zēteō*: see 1 ▶ To look for diligently, to search earnestly** > James, quoting Amos, spoke of the residue of men who might seek out the Lord (Acts 15:17). Paul says that there is no one who seeks God (Rom. 3:11). God is a rewarder of those who seek Him out (Heb. 11:6). Esau sought the blessing earnestly with tears (Heb. 12:17). The prophets sought out (*ekzēteō*) and searched out (*exeraunaō*) {enquired and searched diligently, inquired and searched carefully, made careful searches and inquiries, searched intently and with the greatest care} concerning the salvation destined for believers in the Lord under grace (1 Pet. 1:10). Other refs.: Luke 11:50, 51; see REQUIRE <1567>. ¶

4 **to seek; to seek after, diligently, eagerly, for: *epizēteō*** [verb: ἐπιζητέω <1934>]; **from *epi*: intens., and *zēteō*: see 1 ▶ To look for, to search diligently; also transl.: to ask, to crave, to desire, to run after** > The nations seek after various things, such as food and clothing (Matt. 6:32; Luke 12:30). The generation of the Lord sought after a sign from Him (Matt. 12:39; 16:4; Mark 8:12; Luke 11:29). Herod had sought {had searched, had a thorough search made} for Peter (Acts 12:19). Sergius Paulus sought {desired, wanted} to hear the word of God (Acts 13:7). What Israel seeks for, that he has not obtained (Rom. 11:7). Paul sought fruit abounding to the account of the Philippians (Phil. 4:17). O.T. people of faith confessed that they were strangers and sojourners on the earth, showing clearly that they were seeking a country of their own (Heb. 11:14). They were seeking the lasting city to come (Heb. 13:14). In Acts 19:39, the verb is transl. "to inquire" {to enquire, to have an inquiry, to want something beyond}. ¶

5 ***epicheireō*** [verb: ἐπιχειρέω <2021>]; **from *epi*: upon, and *cheir*: hand ▶ Lit.: to put the hand to, from which: to attempt, to try** > The Hellenists sought {went about} to put Paul to death (Acts 9:29). Other refs.: Luke 1:1; Acts 19:13 (to take in hand); see TAKE <2021>. ¶

6 ***eraunaō*** [verb: ἐραυνάω <2037a>] ▶ **To search, to examine, to scrutinize** > The prophets were seeking {were trying to find out} what time and what manner of circumstances the Spirit of Christ pointed out, testifying of the sufferings and the glories of Christ (1 Pet. 1:11); some mss. have *ereunaō*. ¶

– 7 Acts 6:3 → to look out → LOOK (verb) <1980> 8 Acts 10:17 → to seek out → to make inquiry → INQUIRY <1331> 9 Acts 21:4 → FIND <429> 10 Acts 25:11 → to seek to escape → REFUSE (verb) <3868> 11 Rom. 12:13 → to seek to show hospitality → to be given to hospitality → GIVE <1377> 12 Gal. 1:10 → to seek to satisfy → PERSUADE <3982> 13 1 Thes. 5:15 → PURSUE <1377> 14 Heb. 11:16 → DESIRE (verb) <3713>.

SEEM – ***dokeō*** [verb: δοκέω <1380>] ▶ **To think, to appear, to consider** > If any man among the Corinthians seemed {thought, thought himself} to be wise in this world, he had to become a fool, that he might become wise (1 Cor. 3:18), i.e., to give up the wisdom of this world. The members of the body that seem to be weaker are necessary (1 Cor. 12:22). Paul did not want to seem as if he were frightening the Corinthians by his letters (2 Cor. 10:9). Someone might seem to have failed of the promise to enter into God's rest (Heb. 4:1). Other refs.: Luke 8:18; 1 Cor. 11:16 {to think}. All other refs.: CONSIDER <1380>, REGARD (verb) <1380>, REPUTATION <1380>, SUPPOSE <1380>, THINK <1380>.

SEEMLY – 1 1 Cor. 7:35 → what is seemly → that which is comely → COMELY

<2158> [2] 1 Cor. 12:24 → PRESENTABLE <2158>.

SEEN (BE) – [1] Matt. 6:16, 18 → APPEAR <5316> [2] Rev. 3:18 → to be made manifest → MANIFEST (verb) <5319>.

SEINE – Matt. 13:47 → DRAGNET <4522>.

SEIZE – [1] ***harpazō*** [verb: ἁρπάζω <726>] ► **a. To seize by force, to snatch** > The violent seize on {take by force, lay hold of} the kingdom of the heavens (Matt. 11:12). In the parable of the sower, the wicked one comes and seizes {catches away, snatches away} what was sown in the heart (Matt. 13:19). The wolf seizes {attacks, catches, snatches} the sheep (John 10:12). No one will seize {pluck, snatch} His sheep out of the hand of the Lord Jesus (John 10:28); no one can seize {snatch, pluck} them out of the hand of His Father (v. 29). **b. To catch up, to take away (in view of being introduced in heaven)** > Paul was caught up (or: seized) to the third heaven (2 Cor. 12:2), into paradise (v. 4). At the Lord's coming, living Christians will be caught up (or: seized) together with the believers who have fallen asleep in the Lord (i.e., who have died) to meet Him in the air (1 Thes. 4:17). All other refs.: CATCH (verb) <726>, PULL <726>, TAKE <726>.

[2] ***sunarpazō*** [verb: συναρπάζω <4884>]; **from *sun*: together (intens.), and *harpazō*: see [1] ► To grab, to take by force and keep a firm hold on** > An unclean spirit had seized {had caught} a Gadarene man (Luke 8:29). All other refs.: CATCH (verb) <4884>.

[3] ***epipiptō*** [verb: ἐπιπίπτω <1968>]; **from *epi*: upon, and *piptō*: to fall ► To fall upon, to grip, to take possession** > Fear seized Zacharias (Luke 1:12). Those dwelling at Ephesus were seized with fear (Acts 19:17). All other refs.: FALL (verb) <1968>.

[4] ***krateō*** [verb: κρατέω <2902>]; **from *kratos*: strength ► To lay hands on someone, to lay hold, to retain; also transl.: to arrest, to hold fast, to take** > A servant seized {grabbed} and throttled another servant who owed him one hundred denarii (Matt. 18:28). The chief priests and the Pharisees thought to seize Jesus (Matt. 21:46; 26:4; Mark 3:21 {to take charge, to take custody}; 12:12; 14:1). In a parable, servants were seized and killed (Matt. 22:6). Judas gave a sign to seize Jesus (Matt. 26:48; Mark 14:44), which was done (Matt. 26:50, 57; Mark 14:46); Jesus said they could have seized Him previously in the temple (Matt. 26:55; Mark 14:49). Women clasped (or: seized) the feet of Jesus and worshipped Him (Matt. 28:9). A young man who followed Jesus was seized (Mark 14:51). Paul was seized (Acts 24:6). Believers in the Lord have fled for refuge to take hold of (or: seize) the hope set before them (Heb. 6:18). An angel seized the dragon (Rev. 20:2). All other refs.: FAST (HOLD) <2902>, GAIN (verb) <2902>, HOLD (verb) <2902>, KEEP (verb) <2902>, TAKE <2902>.

[5] ***lambanō*** [verb: λαμβάνω <2983>] ► **To overcome, to hold** > Astonishment (or: Amazement) seized {struck} all the Jews, and they glorified God after Jesus had healed the paralyzed man (Luke 5:26); similarly, fear seized {came on, filled, gripped} them all when He resurrected a young man (7:16). At the supplication of a man, Jesus healed his son whom a spirit had seized (Luke 9:39). Sin, seizing opportunity by the commandment, produced in the man of Romans 7 every lust (v. 8), and deceived him (v. 11). Other refs.: see entries in Lexicon at <2983>.

[6] ***epilambanō*** [verb: ἐπιλαμβάνω <1949>]; **from *epi*: upon, and *lambanō*: see [5] ► To lay hands on, to lay hold of, to take hold of, to appropriate** > Paul and Silas were seized {caught}, and dragged before the magistrates (Acts 16:19); Paul was seized on other occasions (Acts 21:30, 33 {to arrest, to take}). The Jews laid hold on {turned on} Sosthenes and beat him before the judgment-seat (Acts 18:17). Paul told Timothy to lay hold of eternal life (1 Tim. 6:12); we are to lay hold of what is really life (v. 19). All other refs.: CATCH (verb) <1949>, TAKE <1949>.

7 ***katalambanō*** [verb: καταλαμβάνω <2638>]; **from *kata*: intens., and *lambanō*: see 5 ▶ To take over, to take possession >** A dumb spirit seized {took} the son of a man and threw him to the ground (Mark 9:18). All other refs.: see entries in Lexicon at <2638>.

8 ***sullambanō*** [verb: συλλαμβάνω <4815>]; **from *sun*: together (intens.), and *lambanō*: see 5 ▶ To apprehend (in a hostile sense), to arrest as a prisoner >** Jesus was seized {arrested, laid hold on, took} (Luke 22:54; John 18:12). Paul was seized by the Jews (Acts 23:27). All other refs.: CONCEIVE <4815>, HELP (verb) <4815>, TAKE <4815>.

9 ***periechō*** [verb: περιέχω <4023>]; **from *peri*: about, and *echō*: to hold, to possess; lit.: to encompass, to surround ▶ To take possession >** Amazement had seized {had laid hold on} Peter and all those who were with him (Luke 5:9). All other refs.: see: AFTER <4023>, CONTAIN <4023>.

10 ***sunechō*** [verb: συνέχω <4912>]; **from *sun*: together (intens.), and *echō*: to hold, to possess; lit.: to hold completely, to hold together ▶ To take completely >** The whole multitude of the Gadarenes were seized {were possessed, were taken, were overcome} with great fear (Luke 8:37). All other refs.: see entries in Lexicon at <4912>.

11 ***piazō*** [verb: πιάζω <4084>]; **lit.: to press ▶ To take, to capture forcefully, firmly >** The ethnarch under the king Aretas wanted to seize {to apprehend, to arrest} Paul (2 Cor. 11:32). The beast was seized in Rev. 19:20. All other refs.: TAKE <4084>.

– 12 Matt. 21:35; Mark 12:3; Rev. 3:11 → TAKE <2983> 13 Matt. 21:38 → POSSESS <2722> 14 Matt. 26:50; Mark 14:46; Luke 21:12 → LAY <1911> 15 Mark 16:8 → GRIP <2192> 16 Luke 17:34, 36 → TAKE <3880> 17 Luke 22:53 → to try to seize → to stretch out → STRETCH <1614> 18 Acts 4:3 → lit.: to lay hands on someone → HAND (noun) <5495> 19 Acts 28:3 → FASTEN <2510> 20 1 Cor. 10:13 → OVERTAKE <2983>.

SEIZURE – 1 Matt. 4:24; 17:15 → one who has seizure → to be epileptic → EPILEPTIC <4583> 2 Heb. 10:34 → PLUNDERING <724>.

SELECT – 1 Acts 6:3 → to look out → LOOK (verb) <1980> 2 Acts 15:22, 25 → CHOOSE <1586> 3 Heb. 5:1 → TAKE <2983>.

SELEUCIA – ***Seleukeia*** [fem. name: Σελεύκεια <4581>] **▶ City of Syria near Antioch and port of the Mediterranean Sea >** Paul and Barnabas, leaving Antioch, went down to Seleucia and returned to Antioch at the end of their first missionary journey (Acts 13:4; see 14:26). ¶

SELF-ABASEMENT – Col. 2:18, 23 → HUMILITY <5012>.

SELF-CONDEMNED – Titus 3:11 → condemned of oneself → CONDEMN <843>.

SELF-CONTROL (adj.) – **without self-control: *akratēs*** [adj.: ἀκρατής <193>]; **from *a*: neg., and *kratos*: strength, power ▶ Which lacks self-restraint, self-possession >** In the last times, men will be without self-control {incontinent, of unsubdued passions} (2 Tim. 3:3). ¶

SELF-CONTROL (noun) – 1 ***enkrateia*** [fem. noun: ἐγκράτεια <1466>]; **from *enkratēs*: temperate, self-controlled, which is from: *en*: in, and *kratos*: power, strength ▶ Restraint of one's desires, moderation; also transl.: temperance >** Paul reasoned concerning righteousness, self-control, and judgment to come (Acts 24:25). Self-control is part of the fruit of the Spirit (Gal. 5:23). Peter says to add self-control to knowledge and perseverance to self-control (2 Pet. 1:6a, b). ¶

2 **lack of self-control: *akrasia*** [fem. noun: ἀκρασία <192>]; **from *akratēs*: incontinent, which is from *a*: neg., and *kratos*: strength, power ▶ Absence of self-restraint, disorderly conduct >** A couple can deprive one another, following a mutual agreement to reserve time for prayer; but the spouses are to come together again so that Satan does not tempt them on account of

a possible lack of self-control {incontinency} (1 Cor. 7:5). Other ref.: Matt. 23:25; see SELF-INDULGENCE <192>. ¶
– 3 1 Cor. 7:9; 9:25 → to have self-control, to exercise self-control → to have control over oneself → CONTROL (noun) <1467> 4 1 Tim. 2:9, 15 → MODERATION <4997> 5 2 Tim. 1:7 → sound mind → MIND (noun) <4995>.

SELF-CONTROLLED – 1 **to be self-controlled: *sōphroneō*** [verb: σωφρονέω <4993>]; **from *sōphrōn*: sober-minded, which is from *sōos*: sound, and *phrēn*: mind, understanding ▶ To exercise self-control, to be of sound mind; also transl.: to be discreet, to be sensible, to be serious, to be sober, to be sober-minded >** Titus exhorts the younger men to be self-controlled (Titus 2:6). Peter exhorts his readers to be self-controlled (1 Pet. 4:7). All other refs.: JUDGMENT <4993>, MIND (noun) <4993>, THINK <4993>.
– 2 1 Thes. 5:6, 8; 1 Pet. 1:13 → to be self-controlled → to be sober → SOBER <3525> 3 1 Tim. 3:2; Titus 1:8; 2:2, 5 → DISCREET <4998> 4 Titus 1:8 → TEMPERATE <1468> 5 Titus 2:12 → SOBERLY <4996> 6 1 Pet. 4:7 → to be self-controlled → WATCH (verb) <3525>.

SELF-DISCIPLINE – 2 Tim. 1:7 → sound mind → MIND (noun) <4995>.

SELF-IMPOSED RELIGION – ***ethelothrēskia*** [fem. noun: ἐθελοθρησκία <1479>]; **from *thelō*: to want, to choose, and *thrēskeuō*: to worship God, which is from: *thrēskos*: religious; also spelled: *ethelothrēskeia* ▶ Worship by one's own will, and not according to the mind of God or imposed from outside >** Religious ordinances of men have an appearance of wisdom in self-imposed religion {self-made religion, voluntary worship, will worship, self-imposed worship} and false humility, but are of no value against the indulgence of the flesh (Col. 2:23). ¶

SELF-IMPOSED WORSHIP – Col. 2:23 → SELF-IMPOSED RELIGION <1479>.

SELF-INDULGENCE – 1 ***akrasia*** [fem. noun: ἀκρασία <192>]; **from *akratēs*: who lacks self-control, which is from *a*: neg., and *kratos*: strength, power; lit.: without strength, without power ▶ Lack of self-control, disorderly conduct >** The cup and the plate of the scribes and Pharisees were full of self-indulgence {excess, intemperance} (Matt. 23:25). Other ref.: 1 Cor. 7:5 (lack of self-control); see SELF-CONTROL (noun) <192>. ¶
2 **to live in self-indulgence: *spatalaō*** [verb: σπαταλάω <4684>]; **from *spatalē*: life of luxury ▶ To lead a life of luxury, pleasure >** James speaks of those who live in self-indulgence (Jas. 5:5 {to be wanton, to lead a life of wanton pleasure, to indulge oneself}). Other ref.: 1 Tim. 5:6 (to live in pleasure); see PLEASURE <4684>. ¶

SELF-INDULGENT – 1 Tim. 5:6 → to be self-indulgent → to live in pleasure → PLEASURE <4684>.

SELF-INTEREST – Matt. 27:18; Mark 15:10 → ENVY (noun) <5355>.

SELF-RESTRAINT – 1 Tim. 2:15 → MODERATION <4997>.

SELF-SEEKING – **dispute: *eritheia*** [fem. noun: ἐριθεία <2052>]; **from *erithos*: a hireling ▶ Strife, self-interest >** God will render indignation and wrath to those who are self-seeking {those who are contentious, those who are selfishly ambitious} (lit.: those of self-seeking) (Rom. 2:8). All other refs.: CONTENTION <2052>, STRIFE <2052>.

SELF-WILLED – ***authadēs*** [adj.: αὐθάδης <829>]; **from *autos*: oneself, and *hēdomai*: to please ▶ One who seeks to please himself, has his own ideas fixed in his mind, is arrogant >** The overseer must not be self-willed {headstrong, overbearing} (Titus 1:7). Peter mentions those walking according to the flesh who are self-willed {arrogant} (2 Pet. 2:10). ¶

SELFISH – Jas. 3:14, 16 → selfish ambition → STRIFE <2052>.

SELFISH AMBITION – Phil. 1:16 or 17; 2:3 → CONTENTION <2052>.

SELFISHLY – Rom. 2:8 → one who is selfishly ambitious → SELF-SEEKING <2052>.

SELFISHNESS – Phil. 2:3 → CONTENTION <2052>.

SELL – [1] ***apodidōmi*** [verb: ἀποδίδωμι <591>]; **from *apo*: from, and *didōmi*: to give ▶ To give up for money** > The patriarchs, consumed by their envy of Joseph, sold him to be led away into Egypt (Acts 7:9). For a single meal, Esau sold his birthright (Heb. 12:16). Other refs.: see entries in Lexicon at <591>.
[2] ***piprasko*** [verb: πιπράσκω <4097>]; **from *peraō*: to traffic, which is from *peran*: beyond, particularly beyond the sea ▶ To provide goods in exchange for money, to engage in commerce** > A merchant sold all that he had in order to buy one pearl of great value (Matt. 13:46). Because of his inability to pay his debt, a servant found himself in danger of being sold by his master, as well as his family and everything that he had (Matt. 18:25). The perfume poured on Jesus could have been sold for a high price (Matt. 26:9; Mark 14:5; John 12:5). The first Christians sold their possessions and goods (Acts 2:45; 4:34b). Ananias and Sapphira had lied about the land that they had sold (Acts 5:4). The man of Romans 7 realizes that he is sold into bondage to sin (v. 14). ¶
[3] ***pōleō*** [verb: πωλέω <4453>] **▶ See defin. of [2].** > Jesus found in the temple those who were selling {the sellers of} oxen, sheep, and doves (John 2:14). The verb is also used in regard to sparrows (Matt. 10:29; Luke 12:6), all that a man has (Matt. 13:44), what a young man possessed (Matt. 19:21; Mark 10:21; Luke 18:22), doves and other animals in the temple (Matt. 21:12a, b; Mark 11:15a, b; Luke 19:45; John 2:16), oil (Matt. 25:9), the possessions of the little flock (Luke 12:33), commerce in the days of Lot (Luke 17:28), one's coat (Luke 22:36), lands and houses of the early Christians (Acts 4:34a), land belonging to Barnabas (Acts 4:37), a possession belonging to Ananias and Sapphira (Acts 5:1), anything in the meat market (1 Cor. 10:25), and commerce as governed by the mark of the beast (Rev. 13:17). ¶
– [4] Luke 10:35 → GIVE <591>.

SELLER – [1] John 2:14 → lit.: one who sells → SELL <4453> [2] Acts 16:14 → seller of purple → PURPLE (noun) <4211>.

SEM – See SHEM <4590>.

SEMEI – See SEMEIN <4584>.

SEMEIN – ***Semein*** [masc. name: Σεμεΐν <4584>]: **renowned, in Heb.; also spelled: *Semei* ▶ Man of the O.T.; also transl.: Semei** > Semein is mentioned in the genealogy of Jesus (Luke 3:26). ¶

SENATE – ***gerousia*** [fem. noun: γερουσία <1087>]; **from *gerōn*: old man ▶ Assembly of elders among the Jews, prob. constituting the Council in Jerusalem** > The high priest called the Council together, even all the senate {the elderhood, the elders, the full assembly of the elders} of the sons of Israel, against the apostles (Acts 5:21). ¶

SEND – [1] **to send; to send away, back, forth, off: *apostellō*** [verb: ἀποστέλλω <649>]; **from *apo*: from, and *stellō*: to send ▶ To cause to go; this verb usually suggests a more official or authoritative sending** > Jesus was sent by His Father (Matt. 10:40; 15:24; Mark 9:37; Luke 4:43; 9:48; John 3:17, 34; 5:36, 38; 6:29, 57; 7:29; 8:42; 10:36; 11:42; 17:3 {*apopempō* in some mss.}, 8, 18a, 21, 23, 25; 20:21a; Acts 3:26; 1 John 4:9, 10, 14); the Holy Spirit was sent down from heaven (1 Pet. 1:12). Jesus sent the blind man whom He had healed to his house (Mark 8:26). He had come to send forth those who are oppressed (Luke 4:18 {to release, to set free, to set at liberty}). In a parable, the husbandmen beat a bondman and sent him away empty to his master (Mark 12:3). The verb is also used in reference to prophets (Matt. 23:37; Luke 13:34), Gabriel (Luke 1:19, 26), John the Baptist (Luke 7:27; John 1:6; 3:28), the salvation of God (Acts 28:28), evangelists (Rom. 10:15), other angels (Heb. 1:14), and the seven spirits of God (Rev. 5:6). Jesus sent His disciples (e.g., Matt. 10:5, 16; 21:1); He will send His angels (Matt. 13:41; 24:31; Mark 13:27). Other refs.: Matt. 2:16; 8:31 (some mss.: *aperchomai*) {to go away}; 11:10; 14:35; 20:2; 21:3, 34, 36, 37; 22:3, 4, 16; 23:34; 27:19; Mark 1:2; 3:14, 31; 4:29 {to put in}; 5:10; 6:7, 17, 27; 11:1, 3; 12:2, 4–6, 13; 14:13; Luke 4:18; 7:3, 20; 9:2, 52; 10:1, 3, 16; 11:49; 14:17, 32; 19:14 (*empempō* in some mss.), 29, 32; 20:10, 20; 22:8, 35; 24:49; John 1:19, 24; 4:38; 5:33; 7:32; 9:7; 11:3; 17:18b; 18:24; Acts 3:20; 5:21; 7:14, 34, 35; 8:14; 9:17, 38; 10:8, 17, 20, 21, 36; 11:11, 13, 30; 13:15, 26; 15:27, 33 in some mss.; 16:35, 36; 19:22; 26:17; 1 Cor. 1:17; 2 Cor. 12:17; 2 Tim. 4:12; Rev. 1:1; 22:6. ¶

2 **to send, to send away, to send forth: *exapostellō*** [verb: ἐξαποστέλλω <1821>]; **from *ek*: away, and *apostellō*: see 1 ► To cause to go far, to dispatch far away** > God has sent the rich away empty (Luke 1:53). In a parable, the husbandmen beat a bondman and sent him away empty (Luke 20:10, 11). The brothers sent away Paul as a result of Jews stirring up the crowds at Berea (Acts 17:14). God has sent forth His Son into the world (Gal. 4:4), and the Spirit of His Son into the hearts of Christians (v. 6). The Lord had sent His angel to deliver Peter (Acts 12:11). Paul would be sent to the Gentiles afar off (Acts 22:21). Other refs.: Acts 7:12; 9:30; 11:22; 13:26. ¶

3 **to send with: *sunapostellō*** [verb: συναποστέλλω <4882>]; **from *sun*: together, and *apostellō*: see 1 ► To cause to go with** > Paul had sent a brother with Titus (2 Cor. 12:18). ¶

4 ***pempō*** [verb: πέμπω <3992>] **► a. To cause to go; this verb is more general than *apostellō* and emphasizes the destination or arrival** > Elijah was sent only to a woman who was a widow in Zarephath (Luke 4:26). Governors are sent by the Lord to punish evildoers (1 Pet. 2:14). He who receives whomever Jesus sends receives Him, and he who receives Jesus receives Him (i.e., the Father) who sent Him (John 13:20a, b). Other refs.: Matt. 2:8; 11:2; 14:10; 22:7; Mark 5:12; Luke 7:6, 10, 19; 15:15; 16:24, 27; 20:11–13; John 1:22, 33; 4:34; 5:23, 24, 30, 37; 6:38–40, 44; 7:16, 18, 28, 33; 8:16, 18, 26, 29; 9:4; 12:44, 45, 49; 13:16; 14:24, 26; 15:21, 26; 16:5, 7; 20:21; Acts 10:5, 32, 33; 11:29; 15:22, 25; 19:31; 20:17; 23:30; 25:21, 25, 27; Rom. 8:3; 1 Cor. 4:17; 16:3; 2 Cor. 9:3; Eph. 6:22; Phil. 2:19, 23, 25, 28; Col. 4:8; 1 Thes. 3:2, 5; 2 Thes. 2:11; Titus 3:12; Rev. 1:11; 11:10; 14:15 and 18 {to thrust}; 22:16. **b. To transmit** > The Philippians had sent once and again for the necessities of Paul (Phil. 4:16), prob. a monetary gift. ¶

5 ***anapempō*** [verb: ἀναπέμπω <375>]; **from *ana*: again, and *pempō*: see 4 ► To send back to someone of importance, to an authority** > Pilate sent Jesus to Herod (Luke 23:7), and Herod sent Him back to Pilate (v. 11). Pilate had sent back {remitted} the accusers of Jesus to Herod (Luke 23:15). Paul had sent Onesimus back to Philemon (Phm. 12). Other refs. in some mss.: Acts 25:21; 26:32. ¶

6 **to send forth, out, away: *ekpempō*** [verb: ἐκπέμπω <1599>]; **from *ek*: out, and *pempō*: see 4 ► To cause to go far** > Barnabas and Saul were sent out {sent forth, sent on their way} by the Holy Spirit (Acts 13:4). Other ref.: Acts 17:10 {to send away}. ¶

7 **to send for: *metapempō*** [verb: μεταπέμπω <3343>]; **from *meta*: after, and *pempō*: see 4 ► To ask to come** > Cornelius had sent for Peter (Acts 10:29a, b). Felix sent for Paul (Acts 24:24). The verb is also used in Acts 10:5, 22; 11:13; 20:1 in some mss.; 24:26; 25:3. ¶

8 **to send with: *sumpempō*** [verb: συμπέμπω <4842>]; **from *sun*: together, and *pempō*: see 4 ► To cause to go with** > Paul had sent with Titus a brother praised in the gospel (2 Cor. 8:18, 22). ¶

9 **to send away, to send off: *apoluō*** [verb: ἀπολύω <630>]; **from *apo*: from, and *luō*: to loose ► To let go, to dismiss** > The verb is used when Jesus sent away the crowds who heard Him (Matt. 14:15, 22, 23; 15:32,

39; Mark 6:36, 45; 8:3, 9; Luke 9:12). The disciples asked Jesus to send away the woman who cried after them (Matt. 15:23). Jesus sent away a man out of whom demons had gone (Luke 8:38). He healed and sent away a man whose body was abnormally swollen with fluid (Luke 14:4). The brothers in Antioch sent Paul and Barnabas away {let them go} (Acts 13:3). The chiliarch dismissed {let depart} the young man who had divulged to him a plot against Paul (Acts 23:22). Other refs.: Acts 15:30, 33. All other refs.: see entries in Lexicon at <630>.

10 to send away: *apotassō* [verb: ἀποτάσσω <657>]; **from *apo*: from, and *tassō*: to determine, to place in order ▶ To let go, to dismiss** > Jesus sent away {bid farewell to, left} His disciples and departed to the mountain to pray (Mark 6:46). All other refs.: FAREWELL <657>, FORSAKE <657>, LEAVE (noun) <657>.

11 to send away: *aphiēmi* [verb: ἀφίημι <863>]; **from *apo*: from, and *hiēmi*: to send ▶ To dismiss, to let go from oneself; also transl.: to leave** > Jesus sent the multitude away {left the multitude} and went into the house (Matt. 13:36). Having sent away the crowd, the disciples of Jesus took Him in a ship (Mark 4:36). All other refs.: see entries in Lexicon at <863>.

12 to send forth, to send out: *bruō* [verb: βρύω <1032>] **▶ To flow out, to gush forth** > James asks if a fountain sends forth {pours forth} sweet and bitter at the same opening (Jas. 3:11), i.e., if fresh and salt water flow from the same spring. ¶

13 to send out, to send forth: *ekballō* [verb: ἐκβάλλω <1544>]; **from *ek*: out of, and *ballō*: to throw ▶ To compel to depart with irresistible force, to dispatch** > The disciples were to supplicate the Lord that He would send forth workmen into His harvest (Matt. 9:38; Luke 10:2). The Spirit sent out {drove out, impelled to go} Jesus into the wilderness (Mark 1:12). Jesus sent away a leper who had been cleansed (Mark 1:43). Stephen was sent out of the city (Acts 7:58 {to cast, to drag, to drive}). All other refs.: see entries in Lexicon at <1544>.

– 14 Matt. 4:19 → to send you out to fish → lit.: to make you fishers → FISHER <231> 15 Matt. 10:34a, b → PUT <906> 16 Matt. 26:53 → to put at the disposal → DISPOSAL <3936> 17 John 13:16a; 2 Cor. 8:23; Phil. 2:25 → SENT <652> 18 Acts 7:4 → MOVE <3351> 19 Acts 7:14; 20:17; 24:25 → to send for → CALL (verb) <3333> 20 Acts 15:3 → to send on the way → WAY <4311> 21 Acts 21:25 → to send a letter → WRITE <1989>.

SENSE (noun) – 1 ***aisthētērion*** [neut. noun: αἰσθητήριον <145>]; **from *aisthanomai*: to perceive ▶ Faculty of discerning, spiritual judgment** > Full-grown people (i.e., Christians with spiritual maturity), on account of practice, have their senses exercised for discerning both good and evil (Heb. 5:14). ¶

– 2 1 Cor. 12:17 → sense of hearing → lit.: hearing → HEARING <189> 3 1 Cor. 15:34 → to come back to one's senses → lit.: to awake righteously → AWAKE (verb) <1594>, JUSTLY <1346> 4 2 Tim. 2:26 → to come to one's senses → lit.: to awake up → AWAKE (verb) <366>.

SENSE (verb) – Acts 27:27 → SUPPOSE <5282>.

SENSELESS – 1 ***apaideutos*** [adj.: ἀπαίδευτος <521>]; **from *a*: neg., and *paideuō*: to teach, to correct, which is from *pais*: child ▶ Which reflects ignorance, stupid; also transl.: ignorant, unlearned** > Timothy was to avoid foolish (*mōros*) and senseless (*apaideutos*) questions (2 Tim. 2:23). ¶

– 2 Luke 24:25; Gal. 3:1, 3; 1 Tim. 6:9 → FOOLISH <453> 3 Acts 25:27 → UNREASONABLE <249> 4 1 Pet. 2:15 → FOOLISH <878>.

SENSIBLE – 1 Matt. 24:45; Luke 12:42 → PRUDENT <5429> 2 Mark 5:15; Luke 8:35 → to be sensible → to be in one's right mind → MIND (noun) <4993> 3 1 Cor. 10:15 → INTELLIGENT <5429> 4 Titus 1:8; 2:2, 5 → DISCREET <4998> 5 Titus 2:6 → to be sensible → to be self-controlled → SELF-CONTROLLED <4993>.

SENSIBLY – Titus 2:12 → SOBERLY <4996>.

SENSITIVITY – Eph. 4:19 → to lose all sensitivity → to cast off all feeling → FEELING <524>.

SENSUAL – [1] ***psuchikos*** [adj.: ψυχικός <5591>]; **from *psuchē*: soul ► Dictated by natural instincts, governed by the soul, and therefore lacking in moral restraint >** Bitter envying and strife are earthy, sensual {natural, unspiritual}, and devilish (Jas. 3:15). Other refs.: 1 Cor. 2:14; 15:44a, b, 46; Jude 19; see NATURAL <5591>. ¶
– [2] 1 Tim. 5:11 → to feel sensual desire → to wax wanton → WANTON <2691> [3] 2 Pet. 2:7 → LEWDNESS <766> [4] 2 Pet. 2:18 → of the flesh → FLESH <4561>.

SENSUALITY – [1] Mark 7:22; Rom. 13:13; 2 Cor. 12:21; Gal. 5:19; Eph. 4:19; 1 Pet. 4:3; 2 Pet. 2:18; Jude 4 → LEWDNESS <766> [2] 2 Pet. 2:2 → dissolute way → DISSOLUTE <766> <684> [3] Rev. 18:3 → LUXURY <4764>.

SENSUOUS – Col. 2:18 → of the flesh → FLESH <4561>.

SENSUOUSLY – Rev. 18:7, 9 → to live sensuously → to live luxuriously → LUXURIOUSLY <4763>.

SENT – [1] **to send: *apostellō*** [verb: ἀποστέλλω <649>]; **from *apo*: from, and *stellō*: to set, to send ► To cause to go >** Siloam means "Sent" (*Apestalmenos*) (John 9:7). All other refs.: SEND <649>.
[2] **he who is sent: *apostolos*** [masc. noun: ἀπόστολος <652>]; **from *apostellō*: see [1] ► One who is bidden to go, apostle; also transl.: messenger, representative >** He who is sent {A messenger} (*apostolos*) is not greater than he who has sent (*pempō*) him (John 13:16a). Paul's brothers in the Lord were sent by the churches (2 Cor. 8:23). Epaphroditus was the messenger of (lit.: the one who was sent by) the Philippians to minister to Paul's need (Phil. 2:25). All other refs.: APOSTLE <652>.
[3] **to send: *pempō*** [verb: πέμπω <3992>] **► To bid to go >** See [2] for this verb in John 13:16b.

SENTENCE – [1] ***apokrima*** [neut. noun: ἀπόκριμα <610>]; **from *apokrinomai*: to answer, which is from *apo*: from, and *krinō*: to discern, to judge ► Judicial decision, condemnation >** Paul had in himself the sentence of death (2 Cor. 1:9). ¶
[2] **to decide: *krinō*** [verb: κρίνω <2919>] **► To be of the opinion, to judge >** In Acts 15:19, the expr. "my sentence {judgment} is" is lit.: "I decide {judge}." All other refs.: see entries in Lexicon at <2919>.
[3] **to give sentence, to pronounce sentence: *epikrinō*** [verb: ἐπικρίνω <1948>]; **from *epi*: upon, and *krinō*: see [2] ► To decide, to decree >** Pilate gave sentence {adjudged, decided} that what the crowd begged in regard to Jesus should take place (Luke 23:24). ¶
– [4] Luke 24:20; Rev. 17:1 → JUDGMENT <2917> [5] Acts 25:15 → sentence of condemnation → JUDGMENT <1349>.

SENTENCED – [1] Matt. 23:33 → to escape being sentenced → lit.: to escape the judgment → JUDGMENT <2920> [2] 1 Cor. 4:9 → sentenced to death → condemned to death → DEATH <1935>.

SENTRY – Acts 12:6, 19 → GUARD (noun) <5441>.

SEPARATE – [1] ***chōrizō*** [verb: χωρίζω <5563>]; **from *chōris*: apart, without ► To leave, to depart; also transl.: to put asunder, to set apart >** This verb has the sense of severing relations with one's spouse in Matt. 19:6; Mark 10:9; 1 Cor. 7:10, 11. In Phm. 15, it corresponds to a separation after a departure. It is used in regard to the position of Christ in resurrection: the high priest separated from sinners (Heb. 7:26). It has the sense of interrupting union: nothing will be able to separate the Christian from the love of Christ or from the love of God (Rom. 8:35, 39). All other refs.: DEPART <5563>, LEAVE (verb) <5563>.

[2] ***apochōrizō*** [verb: ἀποχωρίζω <673>]; **from *apo*: from, and *chōrizō*: see [1] ▶ To leave, to withdraw** > Paul and Barnabas separated {departed asunder, parted} from one another {parted company} following a difference of opinion regarding the possibility of taking Mark with them (Acts 15:39). Other ref.: Rev. 6:1; see RECEDE <673>. ¶

[3] **to separate oneself: *apodiorizō*** [verb: ἀποδιορίζω <592>]; **from *apo*: from, *dia*: through, and *horizō*: to limit, to determine ▶ To set oneself apart by establishing limits, to distance oneself** > Mockers, not having the Spirit, separate themselves {cause divisions, divide} (Jude 19). ¶

[4] ***aporphanizō*** [verb: ἀπορφανίζω <642>]; **from *apo*: from, and *orphanos*: orphan ▶ To deprive of someone's presence** > Paul had been separated {had been taken away, had been torn away} from his Thessalonian brothers for a short time (1 Thes. 2:17). ¶

[5] ***aphorizō*** [verb: ἀφορίζω <873>]; **from *apo*: from, and *horizō*: to determine, to limit ▶ a. To establish limits; also transl.: to divide, to hold oneself aloof, to take away, to take out, to take with oneself, to sever, to withdraw** > The verb is used in regard to divine judgment on men (Matt. 13:49; 25:32) and of the withdrawal of Christians from among unbelievers (Acts 19:9; 2 Cor. 6:17). Peter was guilty of separating himself from Christians of the Gentiles (Gal. 2:12). **b. To designate for a function, a specific purpose; also transl.: to set apart** > Paul had been separated for the gospel of God (Rom. 1:1). It had pleased God to separate him from his mother's womb (Gal. 1:15). The Holy Spirit said to separate Barnabas and Saul for the work to which He had called them (Acts 13:2). Other ref.: Luke 6:22; see EXCLUDE <873>. ¶

[6] ***diistēmi*** [verb: διΐστημι <1339>]; **from *dia*: indicating separation, and *histēmi*: to stand; lit.: to withdraw oneself ▶ To leave, to set apart, to pass** > As He was blessing His disciples, the Lord was separated {parted} from them, and was carried up into heaven (Luke 24:51). Other refs.: Luke 22:59; Acts 27:28 (to go a little farther; see FARTHER <1339>). ¶

– [7] Luke 6:22 → EXCLUDE <873> [8] Acts 13:13 → DEPART <672>.

SEPARATED (BE) – Eph. 4:18 → ALIENATED (BE) <526>.

SEPARATION – ***phragmos*** [masc. noun: φραγμός <5418>]; **from *phrassō*: to stop, to shut ▶ Upright structure, such as a fence, which divides, protects** > Jesus has broken down the middle wall of separation {middle wall of partition, middle wall of enclosure, the barrier of the dividing wall} between the Jews and the Gentiles (Eph. 2:14). Other refs.: Matt. 21:33; Mark 12:1; Luke 14:23; see HEDGE (noun) <5418>. ¶

SEPULCHRE – [1] Matt. 23:27, 29a; 27:61, 64, 66; 28:1; Rom. 3:13 → TOMB <5028> [2] Matt. 23:29; 27:60b; Mark 15:46a, b; 16:2, 3, 5, 8; Luke 11:44, 47, 48; 23:55; 24:2, 9, 12, 22, 24; John 19:41, 42; 20:1a, b; 2–4, 6, 8, 11a, b; Acts 13:29 → TOMB <3419> [3] Luke 23:53; 24:1; Acts 7:16; Rev. 11:9 → TOMB <3418>.

SEQUENCE – Acts 11:4 → in orderly sequence → in order → ORDER (noun) <2517>.

SERAPHIM – In Heb.: *seraph* (lit.: burning) ▶ Angels proclaiming the holiness and glory of God > The sole mention of these angels is found in the O.T. (Is. 6:2, 6). Comp.: CHERUBIM <5502>.

SERGIUS PAULUS – ***Sergios*** [masc. name: Σέργιος <4588>] ***Paulos*** [masc. name: Παῦλος <3972>] **▶ Proconsul of Cyprus** > Sergius Paulus called for Barnabas and Saul that he might hear the word of God (Acts 13:7). After having seen what had happened to Elymas the sorcerer, he believed, having been astonished at the doctrine of the Lord (see Acts 13:8–12). ¶

SERIOUS – [1] ***barus*** [adj.: βαρύς <926>]; **lit.: heavy ▶ Grave, severe; also transl.: weighty** > The Jews brought many and serious charges against Paul (Acts 25:7). They said that Paul's letters were weighty

and strong (2 Cor. 10:10). All other refs.: BURDENSOME <926>, HEAVY <926>, SAVAGE <926>, WEIGHTIER <926>.
– [2] 1 Pet. 4:7 → to be serious → to be self-controlled → SELF-CONTROLLED <4993>.

SERIOUSNESS – Titus 2:7 → DIGNITY <4587>.

SERJEANT – Acts 16:35, 38 → OFFICER <4465>.

SERPENT – ***ophis*** [masc. noun: ὄφις <3789>] ► **Prudent and cunning reptile, many species of which have good to excellent eyesight; also transl.: snake** > Jesus says to be prudent like serpents (Matt. 10:16). Moses lifted up the bronze serpent in the desert (John 3:14) in order to heal those bitten by serpents who then looked on the bronze serpent (1 Cor. 10:9; see Num. 21:9). The devil is so called (Rev. 12:9, 14, 15; 20:2), for it is he, the ancient serpent, who deceived Eve by his craftiness in the garden of Eden (2 Cor. 11:3). The term is also used elsewhere in the lit. sense (Matt. 7:10; Mark 16:18; Luke 10:19; 11:11) and as a metaphor (Matt. 23:33; Rev. 9:19). ¶

SERUCH – See SERUG <4562>.

SERUG – ***Sarouch*** [masc. name: Σαρούχ <4562>]**: branch, in Heb.** ► **Man of the O.T.; also transl.: Saruch, Seruch** > Serug is mentioned in the genealogy of Jesus (Luke 3:35). He was the ancestor of Abraham (see Gen. 11:20–23). ¶

SERVANT – [1] ***diakonos*** [masc. and fem. noun: διάκονος <1249>] ► **Person who accomplishes a service, with emphasis on his work; also transl.: attendant, deacon, minister, ministering servant** > The Greek term designates one who has received a service from the Lord (John 12:26; 1 Cor. 3:5; 2 Cor. 6:4; Eph. 3:7; 6:21; Phil. 1:1; Col. 1:7, 23, 25; 4:7; 1 Thes. 3:2 in some mss.; 1 Tim. 3:8, 12; 4:6). The ruler is God's servant to do good to Christians, as well as God's servant to bring wrath on one doing evil (Rom. 13:4a, b). Jesus Christ became a servant of the circumcision (Rom. 15:8). Phoebe was a servant of the church at Cenchrea (Rom. 16:1 {minister}). The term designates in a general way a person who serves another of higher rank (Matt. 20:26; 22:13; 23:11; Mark 9:35; 10:43; John 2:5, 9). All other refs.: MINISTER (noun) <1249>.
[2] ***doulos*** [masc. noun: δοῦλος <1401>] ► **Slave or bondservant, i.e., a person dominated by another one through birth, purchase, conquest; household servant, with emphasis on the relationship to his master** > The word is used with this meaning of being a slave, a servant possessed by his master (e.g., Matt. 8:9; Eph. 6:8). Among believers in the Lord, whoever desires to be first should be a servant for the others (Matt. 20:27; Mark 10:44). Simeon presented himself as a servant of God (Luke 2:29). God would pour out of His Spirit on His bondmen and on His bondwomen {handmaiden, maidservants} (Acts 2:18); other transl.: my servants {bondslaves}, both men and women. Christ has taken the form of a servant {bondservant} (Phil. 2:7). Before their conversion, Christians were slaves of sin (Rom. 6:17, 20); whoever commits sin is a slave of sin (John 8:34). *
[3] **servant, ministering servant: *therapōn*** [masc. noun: θεράπων <2324>]**; from which *therapeuō*: to serve, to heal** ► **Person who attends to service, with emphasis on the freedom of the service, dignity of the office, and personal relationship to the one served** > Moses was faithful in all his house, as a ministering servant (Heb. 3:5). ¶
[4] **hired servant: *misthios*** [adj. used as noun: μίσθιος <3407>]**; from *misthos*: reward, salary** ► **Person who works for a salary, worker; also transl.: hired man** > The prodigal son, in a distant land, remembered the hired servants of his father who had bread in abundance (Luke 15:17); he was prepared to ask his father to treat him like one of his hired servants (v. 19). Other ref.: Luke 15:21 in some mss. ¶
[5] **household servant, servant: *oiketēs*** [masc. noun: οἰκέτης <3610>]**; from *oikos*: house** ► **Domestic, often a slave; with**

emphasis on the privileged place in the family household > No servant can serve two masters (Luke 16:13). Cornelius sent two of his household servants to Joppa (Acts 10:7). We cannot judge another's servant (Rom. 14:4). Servants must be submissive to their masters with all fear (1 Pet. 2:18). ¶

6 ***pais*** [masc. and fem. noun: παῖς <3816>]; **lit.: child ▶ Lit.: boy, young man; with emphasis on a personal relationship with the master** > The term sometimes designates an attendant, one who renders service, and even a slave (Matt. 8:6, 8, 13; 14:2; Luke 7:7; 12:45 {male slave, manservant}; 15:26). It is applied to Jesus (Matt. 12:18; Acts 3:13 and 26 {Son}; 4:27 and 30 {Child}), to Israel (Luke 1:54), and to David (Luke 1:69; Acts 4:25). All other refs.: BOY <3816>, CHILD <3816>, DAUGHTER <3816>, SON <3816>.

7 ***hupēretēs*** [masc. noun: ὑπηρέτης <5257>]; **from *hupo*: under, and *ēretēs*: rower ▶ Minister, attendant having a special service, emphasizing assistance to his superior** > This term applies to John called Mark (Acts 13:5 {assistant, helper}), Paul in particular (Acts 26:16), and Paul and Sosthenes (1 Cor. 4:1). In John 18:36, the servants of the Lord are prob. angels. All other refs.: ATTENDANT <5257>, MINISTER (noun) <5257>, OFFICER <5257>.

– 8 Matt. 26:71 → another servant girl → lit.: another 9 Mark 1:20 → he who serves for wages → hired servant → WAGES <3411> 10 Luke 1:38, 48; Acts 2:18 → HANDMAID <1399> 11 Luke 12:36; 2 Tim. 3:17 → lit.: man → MAN <444> 12 Luke 22:26 → like the servant → lit.: as one who serves → SERVE <1247> 13 John 18:16 → servant girl who kept watch, servant girl on duty → DOORKEEPER <2377> 14 Acts 2:18 → servant ... woman → BONDWOMAN <1399> 15 Acts 12:20 → personal servant → CHAMBERLAIN <2846> 16 Rom. 6:18, 22; 1 Cor. 9:19; 2 Pet. 2:19 → to become servant, to make oneself servant, to be the servant → to bring into bondage → BONDAGE <1402> 17 Rom. 6:19a, b → SLAVE (noun) <1400> 18 Rom. 13:6; Heb. 1:7 → MINISTER (noun) <3011>.

SERVANT GIRL – ***paidiskē*** [fem. noun: παιδίσκη <3814>]; **dimin. of *pais*: girl ▶ Young maid, one who accomplishes a service; also transl.: bondmaid, bondwoman, damsel, female servant, female slave, girl, maid, maid servant, slave girl, slave woman** > A servant-girl said to Peter that he had been with Jesus (Matt. 26:69; Mark 14:66; 69; Luke 22:56; John 18:17). His master delaying to come, a bondman might begin to beat the other male and female servants (Luke 12:45). Rhoda was a servant girl (Acts 12:13). A slave girl had a spirit of divination (Acts 16:16). Abraham had two sons, the one of a bondwoman, the other of the freewoman (Gal. 4:22, 23); he cast out the bondwoman and the son of the bondwoman (v. 30a, b); Christians are not children of the bondwoman, but of the free woman (v. 31). ¶

SERVANTS – Luke 12:42 → HOUSEHOLD <2322>.

SERVE – 1 ***diakoneō*** [verb: διακονέω <1247>]; **from *diakonos*: servant, deacon ▶ To assume the responsibility of a service, or ministry, in response to needs, emphasizing the work to be done; it involves directly helping others; also transl.: to care for the needs, to help, to minister, to take care, to wait on** > Angels came and ministered to {attended} Jesus (Matt. 4:11; Mark 1:13). The Son of Man did not come to be served, but to serve and to give His life a ransom for many (Matt. 20:28a, b; Mark 10:45a, b). Jesus was in the midst of His disciples as the One who serves (Luke 22:27b). Mary left Martha to serve alone {to do the work by herself, to do all the serving alone} (Luke 10:40); it is said that Martha served in John 12:2. When he comes, the master will gird himself and serve his servants (Luke 12:37). Peter's mother-in-law served Jesus and His disciples (Matt. 8:15; Mark 1:31; Luke 4:39). Many women had followed Jesus from Galilee ministering to Him {caring for His needs} (Matt. 27:55).

The Hebrew Christians had ministered to the saints and were still ministering (Heb. 6:10a, b). It was not right that the twelve should serve tables (Acts 6:2). Timothy and Erastus ministered to Paul (Acts 19:22). Paul went to Jerusalem, serving the saints (Rom. 15:25). Timothy knew best how Onesiphorus ministered at Ephesus (2 Tim. 1:18 {to help, to render service, to render services}). Those who have served {have served as deacon} well obtain for themselves a good standing (1 Tim. 3:13). The leader is to be as he who serves (Luke 22:26). If anyone serves Jesus, he is to follow Him; and where He is, there will also His servant be; if anyone serves Him, him will the Father honor (John 12:26a, b). If anyone serves, he is to do it as of the strength that God supplies (1 Pet. 4:11). Deacons must first be proved before serving as deacons, being found blameless (1 Tim. 3:10). Other refs.: Matt. 25:44; Mark 15:41; Luke 17:8; 22:27a; Phm. 13. All other refs.: ADMINISTER <1247>, MINISTER (verb) <1247>.

2 **service: *diakonia*** [fem. noun: διακονία <1248>]; **from *diakonos*: servant ▶ Ministry, occupation in response to the needs of others emphasizing the work to be done; it involves directly helping others >** Paul had spoiled other churches, taking wages to serve (lit.: for the service of) the Corinthians (2 Cor. 11:8). Angels are ministering spirits sent out to serve {to render service} (lit.: for service) on account of those who will inherit salvation (Heb. 1:14). All other refs.: ADMINISTRATION <1248>, MINISTRY <1248>, SERVICE <1248>.

3 ***douleuō*** [verb: δουλεύω <1398>]; **from *doulos*: slave ▶ To do the service of a slave, to submit oneself to a master emphasizing the relationship to the master or lord; also transl.: to be slave >** No one can serve two masters (Matt. 6:24a, b; Luke 16:13a, b). Paul had served the Lord with all lowliness (Acts 20:19). Christians are to no longer serve sin (Rom. 6:6); they serve in newness of spirit (7:6). Paul served the law of God (Rom. 7:25). God had said that Esau, the older, would serve Jacob, the younger (Rom. 9:12). We are to serve the Lord (Rom. 12:11). He who serves Christ in regard to the kingdom of God is pleasing to God and approved by men (Rom. 14:18). Brothers are to serve one another in love (Gal. 5:13). Servants are to serve joyfully (Eph. 6:7). Timothy had served with Paul in the gospel (Phil. 2:22). The Colossians served the Lord Christ (Col. 3:24). The Thessalonians had turned to God from idols, to serve the living and true God (1 Thes. 1:9). Before their conversion, the Christians were serving {were enslaved by} various lusts and pleasures (Titus 3:3). Other refs.: Luke 15:29 {to slave}; Rom. 16:18; 1 Tim. 6:2. All other refs.: BONDAGE <1398>, SERVICE <1398>.

4 ***therapeuō*** [verb: θεραπεύω <2323>]; **from *therapon*: servant ▶ To render service >** God is not served {worshipped} by men's hands (Acts 17:25). All other refs.: HEAL <2323>.

5 ***latreuō*** [verb: λατρεύω <3000>]; **from *latris*: hired person ▶ To accomplish a service; to worship >** One is to serve God alone (Matt. 4:10; Luke 4:8). God had granted Israel that they should serve Him without fear (Luke 1:74). Anna served God night and day with fastings and prayers (Luke 2:37). Israel was to go forth out of Egypt and serve God (Acts 7:7). God delivered Israel up to serve the host of heaven (Acts 7:42). Paul served the God of his fathers (Acts 24:14; 2 Tim. 1:3); he served God (Acts 27:23). The twelve tribes served God earnestly (Acts 26:7). Paul served God in his spirit in the gospel of His Son (Rom. 1:9). Men have honored and served the creature more than Him who had created it (Rom. 1:25). Those who offer gifts according to the law serve the representation and shadow of heavenly things (Heb. 8:5). The blood of Christ purifies our conscience from dead works to serve the living God (Heb. 9:14). Believers in the Lord are to have grace, by which they are to serve God acceptably with reverence and godly fear (Heb. 12:28). They have an altar from which those who serve {minister at} the tabernacle have no right to eat (Heb. 13:10). Those who will come out of the great tribulation will serve God day and night in His temple (Rev. 7:15). The

servants of the Lamb will serve Him (Rev. 22:3). Other refs.: Phil. 3:3; Heb. 9:9; 10:2; see WORSHIP (verb) <3000>. ¶

6 ***paredreuō*** [verb: παρεδρεύω <3917a>]; **from *para*: near, and *hedra*: seat ▶ To attend assiduously to service, to wait beside** > Some mss. have this verb in 1 Cor. 9:13; see 7. ¶

7 ***prosedreuō*** [verb: προσεδρεύω <4332>]; **from *prosedros*: one siting by, which is from *pros*: to, and *hedra*: seat ▶ To attend assiduously to service, to wait near** > Those who serve at {attend at, attend to, wait at} the altar have their share from the altar (1 Cor. 9:13). Certain mss. have *paredreuō*; see 6. ¶

8 ***tithēmi*** [verb: τίθημι <5087>] ▶ **To put, to bring out** > Every man serves the good wine first (John 2:10). All other refs.: see entries in Lexicon at <5087>.

– 9 Mark 8:6a, b, 7 → SET (verb) <3908> 10 Acts 13:36 → MINISTER (verb) <5256> 11 Rom. 3:5 → to serve to show → COMMEND <4921> 12 1 Cor. 7:35 → DEVOTION <2137a> 13 2 Thes. 2:9 → "that serve" added in Engl. 14 Heb. 8:2 → who serves → MINISTER (noun) <3011> 15 Jude 7 → to set forth → SET (verb) <4295> 16 Jude 12 → FEED <4165>.

SERVICE – 1 ***diakonia*** [fem. noun: διακονία <1248>]; **from *diakonos*: servant ▶ Ministry, occupation in response to the needs of others; also transl.: administration, help, ministering, ministration, mission, preparations, relief, serving, support, task, work** > Martha was distracted with much service {preparations, serving} (Luke 10:40). Judas had received the same service as the other apostles (Acts 1:17) and had fallen from it (v. 25); Matthias replaced Judas (see v. 26). The widows of the Hellenists were overlooked in the daily service (Acts 6:1 {distribution, distribution of food, serving of food}). The apostles devoted themselves to prayer and the ministry of the word (Acts 6:4). The disciples, each according to his means, determined to send something for the relief of the brothers living in Judea (Acts 11:29). Barnabas and Saul, having fulfilled their service, returned to Jerusalem (Acts 12:25). Paul wanted to finish the ministry (or: service) that he had received of the Lord Jesus (Acts 20:24). He related the things that God had done among the nations by his ministry (Acts 21:19). If we have a gift of service, we are to be occupied in service (Rom. 12:7a, b {to serve}). Paul speaks of service to the saints (Rom. 15:31: *dōrophoria,* gift-bringing, in some mss.; 1 Cor. 16:15; 2 Cor. 6:3; 8:4; 9:1, 13; Eph. 4:12). There are distinctions of service, but the same Lord (1 Cor. 12:5). God has reconciled Christians to Himself by Christ, and has given to them the ministry of reconciliation (2 Cor. 5:18). Archippus was to take heed to the ministry that he had received in the Lord, that he might fulfill it (Col. 4:17). Christ Jesus strengthened Paul, having counted him faithful and having appointed him to His service (1 Tim. 1:12). Timothy was to fulfill his ministry (2 Tim. 4:5). Mark was helpful to Paul for the service (2 Tim. 4:11). The Son of God knows the service of those of Thyatira (Rev. 2:19). All other refs.: ADMINISTRATION <1248>, MINISTRY <1248>, SERVE <1248>.

2 **service, good and ready service: *euergesia*** [fem. noun: εὐεργεσία <2108>]; **from *euergetēs*: benefactor, which is from *eu*: well, and *ergon*: work ▶ Service well performed; also transl.: benefit** > Those who have believing masters are not to despise them because they are brothers, but rather are to serve them all the more because those who profit by their service are faithful and beloved (1 Tim. 6:2). Other ref.: Acts 4:9; see DEED <2108>. ¶

3 ***latreia*** [fem. noun: λατρεία <2999>]; **from *latreuō*: to serve for a salary, to worship, which is from *latris*: one hired ▶ Worship rendered to God, with emphasis on sacrifice; also transl.: divine worship, ministry, worship** > Everyone who would kill the disciples of Jesus would think to render service to God (John 16:2). The service of God pertains to the Israelites (Rom. 9:4). Presenting their bodies a living sacrifice, holy, acceptable to God, constitutes the reasonable service of Christians (Rom. 12:1). The first covenant had ordinances of divine service and the earthly sanctuary

(Heb. 9:1). The priests entered constantly into the first tabernacle, accomplishing the service {ritual duties} (Heb. 9:6). ¶
4 ***leitourgia*** [fem. noun: λειτουργία <3009>]; **from *leitourgos*: public servant, which is from *laos*: people, and *ergon*: work ▶ Ministry for the benefit of Christians and to the glory of God, with emphasis on its official and public nature** > In 2 Cor. 9:12, the ministry of the service mentioned is the carrying of the Corinthians' offerings to other believers. Even if Paul was poured out as a drink offering on the sacrifice and service of the faith of the Philippians, he was glad and rejoiced in common with them all (Phil. 2:17). Epaphroditus had exposed his life, in order that he might fill up what lacked in the service of the Philippians toward Paul (Phil. 2:30 {help}). Moses sprinkled with blood both the tabernacle and all the vessels of service (Heb. 9:21 {ministry, ceremony}). Other refs.: Luke 1:23; Heb. 8:6; see MINISTRY <3009>. ¶
5 **to do service, to render service, to serve: *douleuō*** [verb: δουλεύω <1398>]; **from *doulos*: servant, slave ▶ To be in a position of servitude or slavery and to act accordingly** > Christians should do service with goodwill, as to the Lord, and not to men (Eph. 6:7). All other refs.: BONDAGE <1398>, SERVE <1398>.
– 6 Luke 12:35, 37 → to be dressed for service → lit.: to have the loins girded → GIRD <4024> 7 Rom. 15:25; 2 Tim. 1:18 → in the service; to render service, to render services → lit.: to serve → SERVE <1247> 8 Rom. 15:27; Heb. 10:11 → MINISTER (verb) <3008> 9 1 Cor. 3:9 → "service" added in Engl. 10 1 Cor. 9:13 → those employed in temple service → lit.: those ministering about holy things → MINISTER (verb) <2038> 11 2 Cor. 10:13 → sphere of service → measure of rule → RULE (noun) <2583> 12 Col. 3:22 → external service → EYESERVICE <3787> 13 1 Thes. 3:2 → in God's service → servant of God → SERVANT <1249> 14 2 Tim. 2:4 → to be a soldier in active service → to engage in warfare → WARFARE <4758> 15 Heb. 7:13 → to be attached to the service → to give attendance → ATTENDANCE <4337> 16 Heb. 9:9 → to perform the service, to do the service → WORSHIP (verb) <3000> 17 Heb. 12:28 → to offer a service → SERVE <3000>.

SERVICEABLE – 2 Tim. 2:21; 4:11; Phm. 11 → USEFUL <2173>.

SERVING – 1 Luke 10:40 → to do the serving → SERVE <1247> 2 Luke 10:40 → SERVICE <1248>.

SET (adj.) – 1 ***taktos*** [adj.: τακτός <5002>]; **from *tassō*: to organize, to arrange ▶ Fixed, stated** > On a set {the appointed} day, Herod delivered an address (Acts 12:21). ¶
– 2 Acts 2:23 → DETERMINED <3724> 3 Gal. 4:2 → date set → time appointed → TIME <4287> 4 Gal. 4:4 → set time → fullness of the time → FULLNESS <4138>.

SET (verb) – 1 ***apodeiknumi*** [verb: ἀποδείκνυμι <584>]; **from *apo*: far from, and *deiknumi*: to show ▶ To expose, to present** > God had set the apostles for the last, as appointed to death (1 Cor. 4:9). All other refs.: APPROVE <584>, PROVE <584>, SHOW (verb) <584>.
2 ***histēmi*** [verb: ἵστημι <2476>]; **same as *stare*, in Lat.: to stand ▶ a. To put, to place, to have to stand (in front)** > The devil set Jesus up on the edge of the temple (Matt. 4:5; Luke 4:9). Jesus set a little child in the midst of the disciples (Matt. 18:2; Mark 9:36; also Luke 9:47). A woman taken in adultery was set before Jesus (John 8:3). The apostles were set {stood, were made to appear} before the Sanhedrin (Acts 5:27). Seven disciples were set before {were brought before, were presented to} the apostles (Acts 6:6). False witnesses were set {were put forward, were produced} against Stephen (Acts 6:13). Paul was set before the Sanhedrin (Acts 22:30). God is able to set {to present} Christians blameless before His glory (Jude 24). **b. To stand, to appear (for judgment)** > The Son of Man will set {put} the sheep on His right hand and the goats on His left hand (Matt. 25:33). Peter and John were set {were placed} in the midst of

{were brought before} the Jewish rulers and elders (Acts 4:7). Other refs.: STAND (verb) <2476>.

3 ***anakeimai*** [verb: ἀνάκειμαι <345>]; **from *ana*: behind (intens.), and *keimai*: to lie ▶ To lie down (to eat), to sit >** The disciples distributed the loaves to those who were set down {seated} after Jesus had given thanks (John 6:11). All other refs.: LIE (verb)[1] <345>, TABLE[1] <345>.

4 **to set before, to set forth: *prokeimai*** [verb: πρόκειμαι <4295>]; **from *pro*: before, and *keimai*: to be placed, to lie ▶ To place in front of, to destine >** Believers in the Lord must run with endurance the race that is set {marked out} before them (Heb. 12:1). For the joy set before Him, Jesus endured the cross (Heb. 12:2). Believers in the Lord have fled for refuge to lay hold on the hope set before {offered to} them (Heb. 6:18). Sodom and Gomorrah, and the cities around them, are set forth {are exhibited, serve} as an example, undergoing the judgment of eternal fire (Jude 7). Other ref.: 2 Cor. 8:12; see FIRST <4295>. ¶

5 ***dichazō*** [verb: διχάζω <1369>]; **from *dicha*: separately, which is from *dis*: twice ▶ To separate, to bring division >** Jesus came to set {turn} one member of a family against another in the same family (Matt. 10:35). ¶

6 ***dunō*** [verb: δύνω <1416>]; **lit.: to sink, to go down ▶ To disappear behind the horizon >** This verb is used concerning the sun (Mark 1:32; Luke 4:40). ¶

7 ***epibibazō*** [verb: ἐπιβιβάζω <1913>]; **from *epi*: upon, and *bibazō*: to cause to go ▶ To cause to mount an animal for riding, to put someone on an animal >** This verb is used in regard to Jesus (Luke 19:35), a wounded man (Luke 10:34), and Paul (Acts 23:24). ¶

8 **to set right, to set in order: *epidiorthoō*** [verb: ἐπιδιορθόω <1930>]; **from *epi*: above, and *diorthoō*: to correct, which is from *dia*: intens., and *orthos*: straight, right ▶ To finalize ordering >** Titus was to set right (or: set in order) {straighten out} what remained unordered at Crete (Titus 1:5). ¶

9 **to set on: *epikathizō*** [verb: ἐπικαθίζω <1940>]; **from *epi*: upon, and *kathizō*: to install, to set ▶ To sit on >** They set Jesus {Jesus sat} on the donkey and the colt (Matt. 21:7). ¶

10 **to set forward: *propempō*** [verb: προπέμπω <4311>]; **from *pro*: before, and *pempō*: to send, to lead ▶ To accompany, to escort a visitor >** Paul uses this verb in regard to himself (Rom. 15:24; 1 Cor. 16:6; 2 Cor. 1:16) and to Timothy (1 Cor. 16:11). John uses the verb in regard to brothers who visited Gaius (3 John 6). All other refs.: ACCOMPANY <4311>, JOURNEY (noun) <4311>, WAY <4311>.

11 ***tithēmi*** [verb: τίθημι <5087>] **▶ To put, to establish; also transl.: to arrange, to appoint, to lay, to make, to place >** The sick were laid in the marketplaces that Jesus might touch them (Mark 6:56). Pilate wrote a title and put it on {fastened it to} the cross of Jesus (John 19:19). God has set the members, each one of them, in the body, according as it has pleased Him (1 Cor. 12:18), and He has set some in the church with various gifts (v. 28). Other refs.: Mark 4:21 and Luke 8:16 in some mss.; John 2:10 {to serve}; Acts 13:47; 20:28; 27:12; Rom. 4:17. All other refs.: see entries in Lexicon at <5087>.

12 **to set, to set on, to set upon: *epitithēmi*** [verb: ἐπιτίθημι <2007>]; **from *epi*: on, and *tithēmi*: see 11 ▶ To put, to place on >** The written accusation of Jesus was set up over His head (Matt. 27:37). A lamp should be set {put} on a lampstand (Mark 4:21 in some mss.). One who lights a lamp sets it on a lampstand (Luke 8:16 in some mss.). All other refs.: see entries in Lexicon at <2007>.

13 **to set before: *paratithēmi*** [verb: παρατίθημι <3908>]; **from *para*: next to, and *tithēmi*: to put; lit.: to place before ▶ To offer, to present; also transl.: to put forth, to serve, to tell >** Jesus set parables before His listeners (Matt. 13:24, 31). The disciples were to eat what was set {was placed} before them (Luke 10:8); it is the same for Christians in general (1 Cor. 10:27 {to put before}). A man had nothing to set before his friend on a journey who had come to him (Luke 11:6). The jailer set the table

{laid a table, set food, set a meal} before Paul and Silas (Acts 16:34). Other refs.: Mark 6:41; 8:6a, b, 7; Luke 9:16. All other refs.: COMMIT <3908>, LAY <3908>.

14 **to set around: *peritithēmi*** [verb: περιτίθημι <4060>]**; from *peri*: around, and *tithēmi*: to put ▶ To encircle** > A landowner planted a vineyard and set a hedge around it {hedged it round about, made a fence round it, put a wall around it, set a hedge about it} (Matt. 21:33; Mark 12:1). All other refs.: BESTOW <4060>, PUT <4060>.

15 **to set forth: *protithēmi*** [verb: προτίθημι <4388>]**; from *pro*: before, forward, and *tithēmi*: to put ▶ To place, to dispose, to destine** > God has set forth {has displayed publicly, presented} Christ Jesus as a propitiation, through faith in His blood (Rom. 3:25). Other refs.: Rom. 1:13; Eph. 1:9; see PURPOSE (verb) <4388>. ¶

– **16** Matt. 5:1; Eph. 1:20; Heb. 1:3; 8:1; 12:2; Rev. 3:21b → to set, to set down → SIT <2523> **17** Matt. 5:14 → SITUATE <2749> **18** Matt. 5:19 → to set aside → ANNUL <3089> **19** Matt. 14:8 → PROMPT <4264> **20** Matt. 22:7 → to set on fire → BURN <1714> **21** Matt. 24:45; 25:21, 23; Luke 12:42, 44; Jas. 3:6 → to set, to set ruler, to set over → to make, to make ruler → MAKE <2525> **22** Mark 7:9; 1 Cor. 1:19; Gal. 2:21; 3:15; Heb. 10:28 → to set aside → REJECT <114> **23** Mark 9:12 → to be set at nought → to be treated with contempt → CONTEMPT <1847> **24** Luke 2:34 → to be set → LAY <2749> **25** Luke 7:8 → PLACE (verb) <5021> **26** Luke 8:22 → to set out, to set off from shore → LAUNCH <321> **27** Luke 9:6; Acts 21:5 → to set out → GO <1831> **28** Luke 14:31; Acts 20:1 → to set out → DEPART <4198> **29** Luke 16:26 → to set in place → FIX <4741> **30** Luke 19:43 → to set up a barricade → to build around → BUILD <4016> **31** Luke 22:55 → to set down together → to sit down together → SIT <4776> **32** Luke 23:11 → to set at nought → to treat with contempt → CONTEMPT <1848> **33** John 2:6; Rev. 4:2 → STAND (verb) <2749> **34** John 10:35 → to set aside → BREAK <3089> **35** John 13:12 → to set down → to sit down → SIT <377> **36** Acts 4:11; Rom. 14:10 → to set at nought → DESPISE <1848> **37** Acts 4:26 → to set oneself → to take one's stand → STAND (noun) <3936> **38** Acts 7:5 → GROUND <968> **39** Acts 7:21 → to set out → EXPOSED <1570> **40** Acts 7:26 → to set at one → RECONCILE <4900> **41** Acts 11:4 → to set forth → EXPLAIN <1620> **42** Acts 13:2; Rom. 1:1; Gal. 1:15 → to set apart → SEPARATE <873> **43** Acts 13:9 → to set the eyes → to fix the eyes → FIX <816> **44** Acts 15:16 → to set up → RESTORE <461> **45** Acts 17:31 → APPOINT <2476> **46** Acts 18:18 → to set sail → SAIL (verb) <1602> **47** Acts 19:27 → to be set → FALL (verb) <2064> **48** Acts 20:18 → to set foot → COME <1910> **49** Acts 21:2 → to set forth → SAIL (verb) <321> **50** Acts 28:2 → to come upon → COME <2186> **51** Acts 28:10 → to set sail → DEPART <321> **52** Acts 28:18 → to set at liberty → RELEASE (verb) <630> **53** Acts 28:23; Rom. 13:1 → to set, to set up → APPOINT <5021> **54** Rom. 7:24 → to set free → DELIVER <4506> **55** 1 Cor. 6:4 → to set to judge → to appoint to judge → JUDGE (verb) <2523> **56** 2 Cor. 4:2 → by setting forth plainly → lit.: by manifestation of → MANIFESTATION <5321> **57** 2 Cor. 10:5 → to set itself up → EXALT <1869> **58** Gal. 2:2 → to set before → to lay before → LAY <394> **59** Gal. 3:1 → to evidently set forth → PORTRAY <4270> **60** Gal. 3:17 → to set aside → to make of no effect → EFFECT (noun) <208> **61** Gal. 5:17 → to set one's desire → LUST (verb) <1937> **62** Eph. 2:15 → to set aside → ABOLISH <2673> **63** Eph. 4:26 → to set upon → to go down → GO <1931> **64** Phil. 1:17; 1 Thes. 3:3 → APPOINT <2749> **65** Phil. 4:15 → to set out → DEPART <1831> **66** Col. 2:14 → to set aside → to take out of the way → TAKE <142> **67** 1 Tim. 4:10; 5:5 → to have one's hope set, to set one's hope → HOPE (verb) <1679> **68** 2 Tim. 2:21 → to set apart → SANCTIFY <37> **69** 2 Tim. 2:25 → to set right → CORRECT <3811> **70** Titus 2:7 → SHOW (verb) <3930> **71** Heb. 2:7 → APPOINT <2525> **72** Heb.

4:7 → DETERMINE <3724> 73 Heb. 8:2 → to set up → ERECT (verb) <4078> 74 Heb. 9:2 → to set up → MAKE <2680> 75 Heb. 10:9 → to set aside → to take away → TAKE <337> 76 Heb. 13:23 → to set at liberty, to set free → FREE <630> 77 1 Pet. 2:9 → to set forth → to show forth → SHOW (verb) <1804> 78 2 Pet. 3:12 → to set on fire → FIRE <4448> 79 Rev. 3:8 → GIVE <1325>.

SETH – ***Sēth*** [masc. name: Σήθ <4589>]: **compensation, in Heb.** ► **Third son of Adam** > Seth is mentioned in the genealogy of Jesus (Luke 3:38). See Gen. 4:25. ¶

SETTER FORTH – Acts 17:18 → PROCLAIMER <2604>.

SETTING – 1 Matt. 8:11 → setting of the (sun) → WEST <1424> 2 Heb. 7:18 → setting aside → putting away → PUTTING <115> 3 Heb. 9:10 → setting things right → REFORMATION <1357>.

SETTLE – 1 ***apallassō*** [verb: ἀπαλλάσσω <525>]; **from *apo*: from, and *allassō*: to change** ► **To deliver, to free; to be reconciled** > Jesus says to settle with {be delivered from} an adversary while going to a magistrate (Luke 12:58). Other refs.: Acts 19:12; Heb. 2:15; see LEAVE (verb) <525>, RELEASE (verb) <525>. ¶

2 ***epiluō*** [verb: ἐπιλύω <1956>]; **from *epi*: upon (intens.), and *luō*: to loose** ► **To decide, to determine** > Matters would be settled in a legal assembly in Ephesus (Acts 19:39}. Other ref.: Mark 4:34; see EXPLAIN <1956>. ¶

3 ***themelioō*** [verb: θεμελιόω <2311>]; **from *themelios*: belonging to a foundation** ► **To establish on a solid foundation** > God will settle {establish, ground, make steadfast} the Christians who have suffered a little while (1 Pet. 5:10). All other refs.: FOUND <2311>.

– 4 Matt. 4:13; Rev. 14:6 → DWELL <2730> 5 Matt. 5:25 → to settle matters → AGREE <2132> 6 Matt. 18:23, 24 → to settle accounts → ACCOUNT (noun) <4868> 7 Luke 21:14 → LAY <5087> 8 Acts 18:11 → CONTINUE <2523> 9 Acts 18:15 → to settle the matter → to see to it → SEE <3700> 10 Acts 19:39 → DETERMINE <1956> 11 1 Cor. 6:5 → to settle a dispute → JUDGE (verb) <1252> 12 1 Cor. 7:37 → to settle the matter → lit.: to stand (*histēmi*) firm (*hedraios*) 13 2 Thes. 3:12 → to settle down → lit.: to work in quietness → QUIETNESS <2271>, WORK (verb) <2038>.

SETTLED – Col. 1:23 → FIRM <1476>.

SEVEN – ***hepta*** [card. num.: ἑπτά <2033>] ► This number is used regarding wicked spirits (Matt. 12:45; Luke 11:26), loaves of bread (Matt. 15:34, 36; 16:10; Mark 8:5, 6, 20a), baskets full of bread (Matt. 15:37; Mark 8:8, 20b), brothers (Matt. 22:25, 28; Mark 12:20, 22, 23; Luke 20:29, 31, 33), a seventh brother (Matt. 22:26; lit.: unto the seven), demons (Mark 16:9; Luke 8:2), years (Luke 2:36), men (Acts 6:3), nations (Acts 13:19), the sons of Sceva (Acts 19:14), days (Acts 20:6; 21:4, 27; 28:14; Heb. 11:30), Christians (Acts 21:8), churches (Rev. 1:4a, 11, 20d, f), the Spirits of God (Rev. 1:4b; 3:1a; 4:5b; 5:6c), lamps (Rev. 1:12, 13, 20b, e; 2:1b; 4:5a), stars (Rev. 1:16, 20a, c; 2:1a; 3:1b), seals (Rev. 5:1, 5; 6:1), horns (Rev. 5:6a), eyes (Rev. 5:6b), angels (Rev. 8:2a, 6a; 15:1a, 6a, 7a, 8b; 16:1a; 17:1a; 21:9a), trumpets (Rev. 8:2b, 6b), thunders (Rev. 10:3, 4a, b), heads (Rev. 12:3a; 13:1; 17:3, 7, 9a), diadems (Rev. 12:3b), plagues (Rev. 15:1b, 6b, 8a; 21:9c), bowls (Rev. 15:7b; 16:1b; 17:1b; 21:9b), mountains (Rev. 17:9b), and kings (Rev. 17:10, 11). Other refs.: Matt. 22:26; Rev. 11:13; see SEVENTH <2033>, SEVEN THOUSAND <2033> <5505>. ¶

SEVEN THOUSAND – 1 ***heptakischilioi*** [card. num.: ἑπτακισχίλιοι <2035>]; **from *heptakis*: seven times, and *chilioi*: one thousand** ► This number is used regarding men who have not bowed the knee to Baal (Rom. 11:4). ¶

2 ***hepta*** **(seven)** [card. num.: ἑπτά <2033>] ***chilias*** **(thousand)** [fem. noun: χιλιάς <5505>]; **from *chilioi*: thousand** ► This

number is used regarding names of men who were killed in an earthquake (Rev. 11:13). ¶

SEVENTH – [1] **seven:** ***hepta*** [card. num.: ἑπτά <2033>] ▶ This number is used regarding a brother (Matt. 22:26; lit.: unto the seven). All other refs.: SEVEN <2033>.
[2] ***hebdomos*** [ord. num.: ἕβδομος <1442>]; **from** ***hepta*****: seven** ▶ This number is used in regard to an hour (John 4:52), a day (Heb. 4:4a, b), a man (Jude 14), a seal (Rev. 8:1), an angel (Rev. 10:7; 11:15; 16:17), and a precious stone (Rev. 21:20). ¶

SEVENTY – ***hebdomēkonta*** [card. num.: ἑβδομήκοντα <1440>]; **from** ***hepta*****: seven** ▶ This number is used regarding disciples appointed by Jesus (Luke 10:1, 17; some mss. have seventy-two) and horsemen (Acts 23:23). ¶

SEVENTY-FIVE – **seventy:** ***hebdomēkonta*** [card. num.: ἑβδομήκοντα <1440>], **five:** ***pente*** [card. num.: πέντε <4002>] ▶ This number is used regarding Jacob and his family (Acts 7:14 {threescore and fifteen}). ¶

SEVENTY-TWO – Rev. 21:17 → seventy-two yards → lit.: one hundred forty-four cubits.

SEVER – [1] Matt. 13:49 → SEPARATE <873> [2] Gal. 5:4 → to make of no effect → EFFECT (noun) <2673>.

SEVERALLY – 1 Cor. 12:11 → PRIVATELY <2398>.

SEVERE – [1] **severer:** ***perissoteros*** [adj.: περισσότερος <4055>]; **compar. of** ***perissos*****: abundant, which is from** ***peri*****: above, beyond** ▶ **Exceeding a certain measure, more important** > Those who devour the houses of widows, and as a pretext make long prayers, will receive a severer judgment (Mark 12:40; Luke 20:47). Other refs.: EXCESSIVE <4055>, GREAT <4055>, MORE <4055>.
[2] **severer:** ***cheirōn*** [adj.: χείρων <5501>]; **compar. of** ***kakos*****: bad, evil** ▶ **Worse, more grievous** > He who has trodden underfoot the Son of God will be judged worthy of severer punishment (Heb. 10:29 {sorer}). Other refs.: WORSE <5501>.
– [3] Luke 12:47 → to receive a severe beating → lit.: to be beaten with many (stripes) → MANY <4183> [4] Luke 15:14 → STRONG <2478> [5] Luke 19:21, 22 → HARSH <840> [6] Acts 20:19 → severe testing → TRIAL <3986> [7] 2 Cor. 2:5 → to be severe → OVERCHARGE <1912> [8] 2 Cor. 13:10 → to have to be severe → lit.: to deal severely → SEVERITY <664> [9] Col. 2:23 → severe treatment → NEGLECT (noun) <857> [10] Rev. 11:19 → GREAT <3173>.

SEVERELY – [1] ***apotomōs*** [adv.: ἀποτόμως <664>]; **from** ***apotemnō*****: to cut off, which is from** ***apo*****: off, and** ***temnō*****: to cut** ▶ **Abruptly, sharply** > Titus was to severely rebuke the Cretans, that they might be sound in the faith (Titus 1:13). Other ref.: 2 Cor. 13:10 (severely); see SEVERITY <664>. ¶
[2] ***kakōs*** [adv.: κακῶς <2560>]; **from** ***kakos*****: bad, evil** ▶ **Painfully, terribly** > The daughter of a woman of Canaan was severely {cruelly, grievously, miserably} demon-possessed (Matt. 15:22). The son of a man was epileptic and was suffering severely {greatly, sore vexed, sorely} {was very ill} (Matt. 17:15). All other refs.: MISERABLY <2560>, SICK (adv.) <2560>.
– [3] Mark 12:40; Luke 20:47 → to punish more severely → lit.: to receive a severer judgment → SEVERE <4055> [4] Acts 16:23 → they had been severely flogged → lit.: many stripes were laid upon them → MANY <4183> [5] 2 Cor. 2:5 → to put it severely → OVERCHARGE <1912> [6] 2 Cor. 11:23 → more severely → to excess → EXCESS <5234> [7] Heb. 10:29 → more severely → severer → SEVERE <5501>.

SEVERITY – [1] ***apotomia*** [fem. noun: ἀποτομία <663>]; **from** ***apotemnō*****: to cut off, which is from** ***apo*****: from, and** ***temnō*****: to cut** ▶ **Rigor, sharp character, sternness** > Paul says to consider the goodness and the severity of God; severity on them who have fallen and the goodness of God toward him who continues in this goodness (Rom. 11:22a, b). ¶

2 **severely:** ***apotomōs*** [adv.: ἀποτόμως <664>]; **from *apotemnō*: see 1 ▶ Sharply, with rigor** > Paul did not want to use severity {have to be harsh, use sharpness} (lit.: to deal severely) with the Corinthians (2 Cor. 13:10). Other ref.: Titus 1:13; see SEVERELY <664>. ¶

– 3 Col. 2:23 → NEGLECT (noun) <857>.

SEW – 1 ***epiraptō*** [verb: ἐπιράπτω <1976>]; **from *epi*: upon, and *rhaptō*: to sew; also spelled: *epirraptō* ▶ To stitch on with thread** > No one sews a patch of new cloth on an old garment (Mark 2:21). ¶

– 2 Matt. 9:16; Luke 5:36 → PUT <1911>.

SEX – 1 Cor. 6:9 → men who have sex with men → HOMOSEXUAL <733>.

SEXUAL – 1 Matt. 5:32; 19:9; John 8:41; 1 Cor. 5:1a, b; 7:2; Rev. 2:14; et al. → sexual immorality → FORNICATION <4202>, <4203> 2 Rom. 1:26 → "sexual" added in Engl. 3 Rom. 7:3 → if she has sexual relations with another man → lit.: if she is (*ginomai*) to another man 4 Rom. 13:13 → sexual promiscuity, sexual immorality → LEWDNESS <2845> 5 1 Cor. 7:1 → for a man to have sexual relations with a woman → lit.: for a man to touch a woman → TOUCH <680> 6 1 Cor. 7:2 → "sexual relations with" added in Engl. 7 Jude 7 → to give oneself up to sexual immorality → to give oneself over to fornication → FORNICATION <1608>.

SEXUALLY – 1 Cor. 5:9–11; 6:9; Eph. 5:5; 1 Tim. 1:10; Heb. 12:16; 13:4; Rev. 21:8; 22:15 → immoral people, sexually immoral people → FORNICATOR <4205>.

SHABBY – Jas. 2:2 → DIRTY <4508>.

SHACKLE – ***pedē*** [fem. noun: πέδη <3976>]; **comp. *pous*: foot ▶ Restraint, bond attached to the feet; also transl.: fetter** > A possessed man had often been bound with shackles {fetters} and chains (Mark 5:4a; Luke 8:29; he had pulled the chains apart and broken the shackles {irons} in pieces (Mark 5:4b). ¶

SHADE – Mark 4:32 → SHADOW (noun) <4639>.

SHADOW (noun) – 1 ***skia*** [fem. noun: σκιά <4639>] ▶ **Somber zone created by an opaque body which blocks the light** > Light has sprung up to those sitting in the shadow of death (Matt. 4:16; Luke 1:79). The birds of heaven can roost under the shadow {shade} of a grain of mustard seed that has grown up disproportionately (Mark 4:32). The multitudes hoped that at least the shadow of Peter might overshadow one of the sick (Acts 5:15). Paul speaks of various things under the law, which are a shadow of things to come (Col. 2:17). Earthly priests serve the representation and shadow of heavenly things (Heb. 8:5). The law had a shadow of the coming good things (Heb. 10:1). ¶

2 ***aposkiasma*** [neut. noun: ἀποσκίασμα <644>]; **from *apo*: from, and *skiazō*: to cast a shadow, which is from *skia*: see 1 ▶ Shadow of one object on another object, obscuration** > There is no variation or shadow of turning with the Father of lights (Jas. 1:17). ¶

SHADOW (verb) – ***kataskiazō*** [verb: κατασκιάζω <2683>]; **from *kata*: intens., and *skiazō*: to cast a shadow, which is from *skia*: shadow ▶ To cover with one's shadow** > The cherubim of glory shadowed {overshadowed} the mercy-seat above the ark (Heb. 9:5). ¶

SHAFT – Rev. 9:1, 2a–c → shaft of the bottomless pit, shaft → WELL (noun) <5421>.

SHAKE – 1 **to shake off:** ***apotinassō*** [verb: ἀποτινάσσω <660>]; **from *apo*: from, and *tinassō*: to agitate, to stir ▶ To agitate in order to cause to fall** > Having shaken off the viper into the fire, Paul suffered no harm (Acts 28:5). Other ref.: Luke 9:5; see SHAKE OFF <660>. ¶

[2] ***kineō*** [verb: κινέω <2795>]; **from *kiō*: to go ► To wag, to agitate** > Those who passed by reviled Jesus, shaking their heads (Matt. 27:39; Mark 15:29). All other refs.: DISTURB <2795>, MOVE <2795>, REMOVE <2795>.

[3] ***sainō*** [verb: σαίνω <4525>]; **lit.: to move ► To disturb, to trouble** > The Thessalonians were not to be shaken {moved, unsettled} by their afflictions (1 Thes. 3:3); *siainomai* in some mss.: to be disgruntled. ¶

[4] **to shake, to shake together: *saleuō*** [verb: σαλεύω <4531>]; **from *salos*: agitation, wave ► To move, to agitate well** > Jesus asked the multitudes concerning John if they had gone out to see a reed shaken {moved about, swayed} by the wind (Matt. 11:7; Luke 7:24). After the tribulation, the powers of the heavens will be shaken (Matt. 24:29; Mark 13:25; Luke 21:26). Jesus says to give, and it will be given to us; good measure, pressed down, and shaken together, and running over, will be given into our bosom (Luke 6:38). The house founded on the rock was not shaken (Luke 6:48). The Lord was at the right hand of David that he might not be shaken (Acts 2:25). The place where the disciples were assembled together was shaken (Acts 4:31). The foundations of the prison where Paul and Silas were kept prisoners were shaken (Acts 16:26). The Thessalonians were not to be shaken {become unsettled} rapidly in mind as if the day of Christ had come (2 Thes. 2:2). The voice of God once shook the earth (Heb. 12:26a). Things that can be shaken, i.e., created things, will be removed, so that what cannot be shaken may remain (Heb. 12:27a, b). Other ref.: Acts 17:13 (to stir up); see STIR (verb) <4531>. ¶

[5] ***seiō*** [verb: σείω <4579>] ► **a. To be physically agitated as a result of great fear, to tremble** > The guards of the tomb of Jesus shook and became as dead men (Matt. 28:4). **b. To be agitated as the result of an earthquake, to quake** > When Jesus yielded up His spirit, the earth shook (Matt. 27:51). God will shake (*saleuō*) not only the earth, but He will shake (*seiō*) also the heaven (Heb. 12:26). **c. To move, to agitate violently** > John saw the stars of heaven falling upon the earth as the late figs of a fig tree shaken by a great wind (Rev. 6:13). Other ref.: Matt. 21:10 (to be moved); see MOVE <4579>. ¶

[6] See SHAKE OFF for "to shake off the dust."

– [7] Mark 1:26 → to shake violently → CONVULSE <4682>.

SHAKE OFF – [1] ***apomassō*** [verb: ἀπομάσσω <631>]; **from *apo*: from, and *massō*: to handle, to touch ► In the case of the dust clinging to the feet or the clothes, to wipe it off; it constituted, on the part of those sent by the Lord, a testimony against those who refused their message.** > This verb is used in Luke 10:11; other transl.: to wipe off. ¶

[2] ***apotinassō*** [verb: ἀποτινάσσω <660>]; **from *apo*: from, and *tinassō*: to jostle ► See [1]; to agitate in order to make fall** > This verb is used in Luke 9:5. Other ref.: Acts 28:5; see SHAKE <660>. ¶

[3] ***ektinassō*** [verb: ἐκτινάσσω <1621>]; **from *ek*: from, and *tinassō*: to shake, to stir ► To agitate brusquely in order to remove** > This verb is used for feet (Matt. 10:14; Mark 6:11; Acts 13:51) and clothes (Acts 18:6). ¶

SHAKEN – which cannot be shaken: *asaleutos* [adj.: ἀσάλευτος <761>]; **from *a*: neg., and *saleuō*: to agitate, to disturb ► Immobile, stable** > Christians receive a kingdom that cannot be shaken {that cannot be moved} (Heb. 12:28). Other ref.: Acts 27:41; see IMMOVABLE <761>. ¶

SHALLOW – [1] Matt. 13:5; Mark 4:5 → the soil was shallow → there was no depth of soil → DEPTH <899> [2] Acts 27:17 → shallows of Syrtis → SAND <4950>.

SHAMBLES – ***makellon*** [neut. noun: μάκελλον <3111>]; ***macellum*, in Lat.: market ► Market where meat is sold, butcher shop** > Paul says to eat whatever is sold in the shambles {meat market} (1 Cor. 10:25). ¶

SHAME (noun) – [1] ***aischunē*** [fem. noun: αἰσχύνη <152>]; **from *aischos*: disfigure-**

ment, baseness, disgrace ▶ a. What causes disgrace and dishonor, producing a sense of guilt > Paul had entirely rejected the hidden things of shame {dishonesty} (2 Cor. 4:2). **b. Humiliation, dishonor** > A guest at a wedding might be obliged to take with shame the last place (Luke 14:9). The glory of some is in their shame (Phil. 3:19). Jesus endured the cross, having despised the shame (Heb. 12:2). The shame of the nakedness {shameful nakedness} of Laodicea ought not to be revealed (Rev. 3:18). **c. Dishonoring, disgraceful conduct or thing** > Jude speaks of wicked men foaming out their own shame (Jude 13; lit.: shames). ¶

[2] ***aschēmosunē*** [fem. noun: ἀσχημοσύνη <808>]; **from *aschēmōn*: deformed, inappropriate, indecent, which is from *a*: neg., and *schēma*: appearance ▶ Disgrace, indecency; also transl.: indecent acts, shameful acts, what is shameful, that which is unseemly** > The practice of homosexuality by men is called shame (Rom. 1:27). The shame of him who watches and keeps his garments will not be seen (Rev. 16:15 {to shamefully expose}). ¶

[3] ***entropē*** [fem. noun: ἐντροπή <1791>]; **from *entrepō*: to withdraw, which comes from *en*: in, and *trepō*: to turn ▶ Return upon oneself, humiliation, dishonor emphasizing a wholesome attitude leading to a change of behavior** > Paul said certain things to the Corinthians to put them to shame (1 Cor. 6:5). He also spoke to them as a matter of shame (15:34). ¶

[4] **to put to shame: *kataischunō*** [verb: καταισχύνω <2617>]; **from *kata*: intens., and *aischunō*: to be ashamed, which is from *aischos*: shame ▶ To dishonor, to humiliate; also transl.: to confound, to shame** > All who opposed Jesus were put to shame {were ashamed} (Luke 13:17). God has chosen the foolish things of the world that He may put to shame the wise, and the weak things that He may put to shame the strong things (1 Cor. 1:27a, b). Paul asked the Corinthians if they put to shame those who had nothing (1 Cor. 11:22). All other refs.: ASHAMED <2617>, ASHAMED (BE) <2617>, DISHONOR (verb) <2617>.

– [5] Matt. 1:19 → to put to shame → to make a public example → EXAMPLE <3856> [6] Luke 16:3; 2 Cor. 10:8; Phil. 1:20; 1 Pet. 4:16 → to be put to shame, to shrink away in shame → to be ashamed → ASHAMED <153> [7] Acts 5:41 → to suffer shame → DISHONORED (BE) <818> [8] 1 Cor. 11:6; 14:35; Eph. 5:12 → a shame → lit.: shameful → SHAMEFUL <149> [9] 1 Cor. 11:14; 2 Cor. 11:21 → DISHONOR (noun) <819> [10] Col. 2:15 → to put to an open shame → to make a spectacle in public → SPECTACLE <1165> [11] 2 Thes. 3:14; Titus 2:8 → to put to shame → SHAME (verb) <1788> [12] 2 Tim. 1:12 → to be a cause for shame → ASHAMED (BE) <1870> [13] Heb. 6:6 → to put to open shame → to make a show → SHOW (noun) <3856>.

SHAME (verb) – [1] ***entrepō*** [verb: ἐντρέπω <1788>]; **from *en*: in, and *trepō*: to turn ▶ To return on oneself; to experience a feeling of humiliation emphasizing a wholesome attitude leading to a change of behavior; also transl.: to be ashamed, to put to shame** > Paul did not write certain things to the Corinthians to shame {to chide} them, but to warn them (1 Cor. 4:14). A brother would be ashamed of himself {would be put to shame} if Christians did not associate with him (2 Thes. 3:14). Having nothing evil to say about Paul, he who opposed would be ashamed (Titus 2:8). All other refs.: RESPECT (verb) <1788>.

– [2] 1 Cor. 1:27a, b; 11:22 → to put to shame → SHAME (noun) <2617>.

SHAMEFACEDNESS – 1 Tim. 2:9 → MODESTY <127>.

SHAMEFUL – [1] ***aischron*** [adj. and adj. used as noun: αἰσχρόν <149>]; **neut. of *aischros*: inappropriate, dishonorable ▶ Inappropriate, unseemly; also transl.: disgraceful, improper** > If it was shameful {a shame, a disgrace} for a woman to have her hair cut off or to be shaved, she should have had her head covered (1 Cor. 11:6). It is shameful {improper, disgraceful} for a woman to speak in the church (1 Cor.

14:35). It is shameful to even speak of some things that are done in secret (Eph. 5:12). For *aischros*, see DISHONEST <150>. ¶

2 **shameful acts, what is shameful: *aschēmosunē*** [fem. noun: ἀσχημοσύνη <808>]; **from *aschēmōn*: improper, inappropriate, which is from *a*: neg., and *schēma*: appearance ► Immodesty, infamy; also transl.: indecent acts** > Men committed with other men shameful acts (Rom. 1:27). The term is also transl. "shame" in Rev. 16:15. ¶

3 **shame: *atimia*** [fem. noun: ἀτιμία <819>]; **from *atimos*: without honor, which is from *a*: neg., and *timē*: honor ► Dishonor, disgrace** > God has given wicked men up to shameful {degrading, vile} (lit.: of shame) passions (Rom. 1:26). All other refs.: DISHONOR (noun) <819>.

– 4 2 Cor. 4:2 → secret and shameful ways → lit.: hidden things of shame → SHAME (noun) <152> 5 Titus 1:11 → DISHONEST <150> 6 1 Pet. 5:2 → for shameful gain → GAIN (noun) <147> 7 2 Pet. 2:2 → shameful way → dissolute way → DISSOLUTE <766> <684> 8 Rev. 3:18 → shameful nakedness → lit.: the shame of nakedness 9 Rev. 21:27 → what is shameful → ABOMINATION <946>.

SHAMEFULLY – 1 **to treat shamefully: *atimazō*** [verb: ἀτιμάζω <818>]; **from *atimos*: without honor, which is from *a*: neg., and *timē*: honor ► To despise, to judge unworthy** > In a parable, a servant was treated shamefully by vine-growers (Luke 20:11 {to cast insult upon, to entreat shamefully}). All other refs.: DISHONOR (verb) <818>, DISHONORED (BE) <818>, INSULT (noun) <818>.

– 2 Matt. 22:6; Luke 18:32; 1 Thes. 2:2 → to treat shamefully → MISTREAT <5195> 3 Rev. 16:15 → be shamefully exposed → lit.: the shame will not be seen → SHAME (noun) <808>.

SHAMELESS – 1 Luke 11:8 → shameless audacity → PERSISTENCE <335> 2 Rom. 1:27 → shameless acts → shameful acts → SHAMEFUL <808>.

SHAMELESSNESS – Luke 11:8 → PERSISTENCE <335>.

SHAPE – 1 Luke 3:22; John 5:37 → FORM (noun) <1491> 2 Rev. 9:7 → LIKENESS <3667>.

SHAPED – Acts 17:29 → something shaped → graven form → FORM (noun) <5480>.

SHARE (noun) – 1 John 13:8 → PART (noun) <3313> 2 1 Cor. 9:13 → to have one's share → PARTAKE <4829> 3 2 Tim. 2:6 → PARTAKE <3335> 4 Heb. 12:10 → PARTICIPATE <3335> 5 1 Pet. 4:13 → to have share in → PARTICIPATE <2841>.

SHARE (verb) – 1 **to share in, to share with: *sunkoinōneō*** [verb: συγκοινωνέω <4790>]; **from *sun*: with, together and *koinōneō*: to share, which is from *koinōnos*: associate, participant, which is from *koinos*: common ► To participate, to take part** > The Philippians had done well to share in {to communicate with} the afflictions of Paul (Phil. 4:14). All other refs.: FELLOWSHIP <4790>, PARTICIPATE <4790>.

2 **ready to share, willing to share: *koinōnikos*** [adj.: κοινωνικός <2843>]; **from *koinōnos*: see 1 ► Generous, liberal in affording joint use of one's possessions to others** > Christians who are rich in this present world should be willing to share {willing to communicate} what they have (1 Tim. 6:18). ¶

3 **share: *meris*** [fem. noun: μερίς <3310>]; **from *meros*: part, which is from *meiromai*: to receive as an allotment ► Assigned part, portion** > God has made Christians fit to share the inheritance of the saints (lit.: has made them fit for the share) of the inheritance of the saints (Col. 1:12). All other refs.: PART (noun) <3310>, PARTAKER <3310>.

– 4 Luke 3:11; Eph. 4:28 → GIVE <3330> 5 Luke 22:17; Acts 2:45 → DIVIDE <1266> 6 John 13:18 → EAT <5176> 7 Acts 1:17 → lit.: to receive a share (or: part) → PART (noun) <2819>, RECEIVE <2975> 8 Acts

2:44; 4:32; Jude 3 → COMMON <2839> **9** Rom. 4:16 → the verb is added en Engl. **10** Rom. 11:17; 1 Cor. 9:23; Phil. 1:7 → to be, to become partaker → PARTAKER <4791> **11** Rom. 12:13 → DISTRIBUTE <2841> **12** Rom. 15:27; Gal. 6:6; 1 Tim. 5:22; Heb. 2:14; 1 Pet. 4:13; 2 John 11 → to share, to share responsibility → PARTICIPATE <2841> **13** Rom. 15:27 → MINISTER (verb) <3008> **14** 1 Cor. 4:8 → to share the rule → to reign with → REIGN (verb) <4821> **15** 1 Cor. 9:10, 12; 10:17; Heb. 2:14 → PARTAKE <3348> **16** 1 Cor. 9:13 → PARTAKE <4829> **17** 2 Cor. 1:5 → we share abundantly in the sufferings → lit.: the sufferings abound in us → ABOUND <4052> **18** 2 Cor. 6:15 → "does share" added in Engl. **19** Phil. 3:10 → to share His sufferings → fellowship of His sufferings → FELLOWSHIP <2842> **20** Phil. 4:15 → COMMUNICATE[1] <2841> **21** 1 Thes. 2:8 → IMPART <3330> **22** 2 Thes. 2:14 → that they may share → lit.: for the obtaining → OBTAINING <4047> **23** Phm. 6 → which we share → lit.: in you (*en humin*) in some mss., in us (*en hēmin*) in other mss. **24** Heb. 3:1; 6:4 → who share in, who have shared in → lit.: partakers of → PARTAKER <3353> **25** Heb. 3:14 → to become companions → PARTNER <3353> **26** Heb. 4:2 → MIX <4786> **27** Heb. 13:16 → sharing of goods → COMMUNICATE[1] <2842> **28** Rev. 20:6 → lit.: to have part → HAVE <2192>, PART (noun) <3313>.

SHARER – **1** 1 Cor. 10:18, 20; Heb. 10:33 → PARTAKER <2844> **2** Eph. 3:6 → sharer together → PARTAKER <4830>.

SHARING – ***koinōnia*** [fem. noun: κοινωνία <2842>]; **from *koinōneō*: to share, which is from *koinōnos*: associate, participant, which is from *koinos*: common ► Contribution, gift jointly imparted** > God was glorified through the liberal sharing {communicating, contribution, distribution} of the Corinthians for the saints (2 Cor. 9:13). All other refs.: COMMUNICATE[1] <2842>, CONTRIBUTION <2842>, DISPENSATION <2842>, FELLOWSHIP <2842>.

SHARON – ***Sarōn*** [masc. name: Σάρων <4565>]**: plain, in Heb. ► District of Samaria north of Joppa, near the Mediterranean Sea; also transl.: Saron** > Those who lived in Sharon saw that Aeneas, who had been paralyzed, was healed; they turned to the Lord (Acts 9:35). ¶

SHARP – ***oxus*** [adj.: ὀξύς <3691>] **► Piercing, cutting** > A sharp two-edged sword went out of the mouth of the Son of Man (Rev. 1:16). He is seen the same way when addressing Pergamum (Rev. 2:12). An angel like the Son of Man had a sharp sickle in his hand (Rev. 14:14), as likewise did another angel (vv. 17, 18a, b). With the sharp sword, He will smite the nations (Rev. 19:15). Other ref.: Rom. 3:15; see SWIFT <3691>. ¶

SHARPER – ***tomōteros*** [adj.: τομώτερος <5114>]**; from *temnō*: to cut ► More cutting, finer edged** > The word of God is sharper than any two-edged sword (Heb. 4:12). ¶

SHARPLY – **1** Matt. 9:30; Mark 1:43 → to charge sharply → to warn sternly → WARN <1690> **2** Acts 23:9 → to contend sharply → STRIVE <1264> **3** Titus 1:13 → SEVERELY <664>.

SHARPNESS – 2 Cor. 13:10 → SEVERITY <664>.

SHATTER – **1** Mark 5:4 → to break in pieces → PIECE <4937> **2** Luke 9:39 → BRUISE <4937>.

SHAVE – ***xuraō*** [verb: ξυράω <3587>]**; from *xuron*: razor, comp. *xuō*: to scratch, to make smooth ► To cut off hair close to the skin using a razor** > Four men had made a vow to have their heads shaved (Acts 21:24). Paul speaks of shame for a woman having her hair shaved (1 Cor. 11:5); if it is disgraceful for her to be shaved, she is to be covered when she prays or prophesies (v. 6). ¶

SHEALTIEL – ***Salathiēl*** [masc. name: Σαλαθιήλ <4528>]**: I asked God, in Heb. ▶ Man of the O.T. (Shealtiel, son of Jeconiah: 1 Chr. 3:17); also transl.: Salathiel** > Shealtiel is mentioned in the two genealogies of Jesus Christ (Matt. 1:12a, b; Luke 3:27). ¶

SHEAR – ***keirō*** [verb: κείρω <2751>] ▶ **a. To shave off fleece** > The Ethiopian was reading this passage of Scripture: He was led like a sheep to slaughter; and as a lamb is silent before him who shears him, so He did not open His mouth (Acts 8:32). **b. To remove the hair by using scissors or clippers to cut or clip close to the skin** > Paul had his head shorn {hair cut off} in Cenchrea following a vow (Acts 18:18). If a woman is not covered when praying or prophesying, Paul said she should also be shorn {have her hair cut off}; he adds that if it is disgraceful for a woman to be shorn {have her hair cut off} or shaved, let her be covered (1 Cor. 11:6a, b). ¶

SHEARER – Acts 8:32 → lit.: he who shears → SHEAR <2751>.

SHEATH – ***thēkē*** [fem. noun: θήκη <2336>]**; from *tithēmi*: to put ▶ Case in which to put a sword** > Jesus told Peter to put the sword into the sheath (John 18:11). ¶

SHECHEM – ***Suchem*** [fem. name: Συχέμ <4966>]**: shoulder, in Heb.; also spelled: Sychem ▶ Man of the O.T.** > Abraham had bought a tomb from Shechem and his brothers, sons of Hamor (Acts 7:16a, b). Shechem dishonored Dinah, Jacob's daughter; Simeon and Levi, two of Jacob's sons, avenged her by killing Shechem and his father Hamor as well as all their male fellow citizens (see Gen. 34:1–31). ¶

SHED – [1] Matt. 23:35; 26:28; Mark 14:24; Luke 11:50; 22:20; Acts 2:33; 22:20; Rom. 3:15; 5:5; Titus 3:6; Rev. 16:6 → to shed, to shed abroad, to shed forth → to pour out → POUR <1632> [2] Heb. 12:4 → to the point of shedding blood → lit.: to blood → BLOOD <129> [3] Rev. 6:13 → THROW (verb) <906>.

SHEDDING – Rom. 3:25 → the shedding of His blood → lit.: in His blood.

SHEDDING OF BLOOD – ***haimatekchusia*** [fem. noun: αἱματεκχυσία <130>]**; from *haima*: blood, and *ekcheō*: to shed, which is from *ek*: out, and *cheō*: to pour ▶ Giving, pouring out of blood** > Without shedding of blood, there is no remission (Heb. 9:22). ¶

SHEEP – [1] ***probaton*** [neut. noun: πρόβατον <4263>]**; from *probainō*: to walk forward or in front, which is from *pro*: before, and *bainō*: to go ▶ Domesticated bovid ruminant** > The word is used with its natural meaning (Matt. 12:11, 12; 18:12; 25:32; Luke 15:4, 6; John 2:14, 15; Rev. 18:13). It is also used figur.: the lost sheep of Israel (Matt. 9:36; 10:6; 15:24; Mark 6:34), the disciples of Jesus (Matt. 10:16; 26:31; Mark 14:27), the believers in the Lord among the Gentiles (Matt. 25:33), those who belong to the good Shepherd (John 10:1, 2, 3a, b, 7, 8, 11, 12a–c, 13, 15, 16, 26, 27), Jesus who was led as a sheep to the slaughter (Acts 8:32), Paul and his companions (Rom. 8:36), and Christians before their conversion (1 Pet. 2:25). Jesus is the good shepherd who gives His life for the sheep (John 10:11), the great Shepherd of the sheep (Heb. 13:20); He is also the Chief Shepherd (see 1 Pet. 5:4). Jesus told Peter to tend His sheep (John 21:16), to feed them (v. 17); *probation* in some mss.: most likely a term evoking affection. False prophets come in sheep's clothing (Matt. 7:15). ¶

[2] **Sheep Gate: *Probatikē*** [adj. used as noun: Προβατική <4262>]**; from *probaton*: see [1]; lit.: concerning sheep ▶ Name of a door in Jerusalem** > The pool of Bethesda was by the Sheep Gate {sheep market} (John 5:2). ¶

[3] **to feed the sheep: *poimainō*** [verb: ποιμαίνω <4165>]**; from *poimēn*: shepherd ▶ To ensure the sheep have enough food,**

to watch over and tend them > Jesus told Simon Peter to feed {shepherd, tend, take care of} His sheep (John 21:16). All other refs.: SHEPHERD (verb) <4165>.
– [4] Heb. 11:37 → skins of sheep → SHEEPSKIN <3374>.

SHEEPFOLD – John 10:1 → lit.: fold of the sheep → FOLD (noun) <833>.

SHEEPSKIN – ***mēlōtē*** [fem. noun: μηλωτή <3374>]; **from *mēlon*: sheep or goat ▶ Skin, fleece of sheep >** O.T. people of faith wandered about in sheepskins and goatskins (Heb. 11:37). ¶

SHEET – [1] ***othonē*** [fem. noun: ὀθόνη <3607>] ▶ **Cloth, most likely of linen >** Peter saw an object like a great sheet being let down from heaven by its four corners, and it came down to earth (Acts 10:11; 11:5). ¶
– [2] Mark 14:51, 52 → linen sheet → LINEN <4616> [3] Acts 10:16 → lit.: object → VESSEL[1] <4632>.

SHELAH – ***Sala*** [masc. name: Σαλά <4527>]: **sprout, in Heb. ▶ Man of the O.T.; also transl.: Sala >** Shelah is mentioned in the genealogy of Jesus (Luke 3:35). ¶

SHELTER (noun) – Matt. 17:4; Mark 9:5; Luke 9:33 → TENT <4633>.

SHELTER (verb) – Rev. 7:15 → to shelter with one's presence → lit.: to spread one's tent → TENT <4637>.

SHEM – ***Sēm*** [masc. name: Σήμ <4590>]: **name, renown, in Heb. ▶ One of Noah's sons; also transl.: Sem >** Shem is mentioned in the genealogy of Jesus (Luke 3:36). Shem and his brother Japheth showed respect to their father who had become drunk after the flood; Noah blessed them (see Gen. 9:20–27). ¶

SHEPHERD (noun) – [1] ***poimēn*** [masc. noun: ποιμήν <4166>] ▶ **a. Person who takes care of sheep >** The term is found in Matt. 9:36; 25:32; Mark 6:34; Luke 2:8, 15, 18, 20; John 10:2. Figur., Jesus is the shepherd of the sheep, i.e., of the believers in the Lord (Matt. 26:31; Mark 14:27; John 10:16; 1 Pet. 2:25). He is the good Shepherd (John 10:11a, b, 14), in opposition to the hireling who is not the shepherd (v. 12). **b. One who watches out for the welfare of souls >** The Lord Jesus is the great Shepherd of the sheep (Heb. 13:20). He has given some shepherds {pastors} for the perfecting of the saints (Eph. 4:11). Some translators add the word in Jude 12. ¶
[2] **Chief Shepherd: *Archipoimēn*** [masc. noun: Ἀρχιποίμην <750>]; **from *archē*: chief, and *poimēn*: see [1] ▶ The Chief Shepherd, Jesus Christ Himself >** The elders who shepherd the flock of God well will receive the unfading crown of glory when the Chief Shepherd is manifested (1 Pet. 5:4). ¶
– [3] Acts 20:28; 1 Pet. 5:2; Rev. 7:17 → to be shepherd → SHEPHERD (verb) <4165>.

SHEPHERD (verb) – [1] ***poimainō*** [verb: ποιμαίνω <4165>]; **from *poimēn*: shepherd ▶ a. In a lit. sense: to guide, guard, and otherwise take care of the flock, as well as lead it to nourishment; also transl.: to feed, to tend, to look after >** The verb is used in Luke 17:7; 1 Cor. 9:7 {to herd}. **b. In a spiritual sense: to act as a shepherd taking care of souls, i.e., ensuring they have good food, guiding them in the right way, and taking care of those who are weak and sick; this verb also means to rule, to govern; also transl.: to feed, to tend, to look after, to rule, to be shepherd >** A leader was to go forth out of Bethlehem who would shepherd Israel (Matt. 2:6). Jesus told Peter to shepherd His sheep (John 21:16). The Holy Spirit had set the elders of Ephesus as overseers to shepherd the church of God (Acts 20:28). Peter exhorts the elders to shepherd the flock of God that is among them (1 Pet. 5:2). The one in Thyatira who overcomes will shepherd the nations with a rod of iron (Rev. 2:27). The Lamb will shepherd those who come out of the great tribulation (Rev. 7:17). A male son (the Lord Jesus) will shepherd all the nations

with a rod of iron (Rev. 12:5; 19:15). Other ref.: Jude 12; see FEED <4165>. ¶
– [2] John 21:16 → to feed the sheep → SHEEP <4165>.

SHEW (noun) – [1] Gal. 6:12 → to make a fair shew → to make a good showing → SHOWING <2146> [2] Col. 2:23 → APPEARANCE <3056>.

SHEW (verb) – [1] archaic form of "to show" → SHOW (verb) [2] John 11:57 → REPORT (verb) <3377> [3] John 21:1a, b, 14; Rom. 1:19b → MANIFEST (verb) <5319> [4] Acts 7:26 → APPEAR <3700> [5] Acts 23:22 → REVEAL <1718>.

SHEWBREAD – Matt. 12:4; Mark 2:26; Luke 6:4; Heb. 9:2 → EXPOSITION OF THE LOAVES <4286>.

SHEWING – Luke 1:80 → MANIFESTATION <323>.

SHIELD (noun) – ***thureos*** [masc. noun: θυρεός <2375>]; **from *thura*: door ► Originally, a stone to close the entry of a cavern; later, a defensive arm to protect warriors, and sufficiently large to protect them completely; made of leather, it was often soaked in water before battle in order to quench flaming enemy projectiles** > The Christian should take the shield of faith to quench all the fiery darts of the wicked one (Eph. 6:16). ¶

SHIELD (verb) – 1 Pet. 1:5 → GUARD (verb) <5432>.

SHIFT – Col. 1:23 → MOVE <3334>.

SHIFTING – Jas. 1:17 → shifting shadow, shifting shadows → lit.: shadow of turning → TURNING <5157>.

SHINE – [1] ***astraptō*** [verb: ἀστράπτω <797>]; **comp. *astēr*: star ► To illuminate, to sparkle** > In His day, the Son of Man will be as the lightning shines {flashes} (*astraptō*), which lightens {lights} (*lampō*: see [4]) from one end under heaven to the other (Luke 17:24). Other ref.: Luke 24:4 (to shine); see SHINING <797>. ¶
[2] **to shine around: *periastraptō*** [verb: περιαστράπτω <4015>]; **from *peri*: around, and *astraptō*: see [1] ► To illuminate like the flash of lightning all around** > A light shone around {flashed around} Paul from heaven (Acts 9:3; 22:6). ¶
[3] ***augazō*** [verb: αὐγάζω <826>]; **from *augē*: dawn ► To give light, to irradiate; to dawn on** > The god of this age has blinded the minds of unbelievers, so the light of the gospel of the glory of Christ cannot shine on them (2 Cor. 4:4; *kataugazō* in some mss.); other transl.: so they cannot see the light of the gospel of the glory of Christ. ¶
[4] ***lampō*** [verb: λάμπω <2989>] **► To emit light flash, to radiate brilliancy, to lighten** > The lamp shines {gives light} to all who are in the house (Matt. 5:15); we should let our light shine before men (v. 16). On the mountain, the face of Jesus shone like the sun (Matt. 17:2). For the use of the verb in Luke 17:24, see [1]. A light shone in Peter's prison (Acts 12:7; *epilampō* in some mss.). God had said that the light shines out of darkness; His light has shone in the hearts of Christians (2 Cor. 4:6a, b). ¶
[5] **to shine, to shine forth: *eklampō*** [verb: ἐκλάμπω <1584>]; **from *ek*: out (intens.), and *lampō*: see [4] ► To gleam brightly, to glow** > The righteous will shine forth like the sun in the kingdom of their Father (Matt. 13:43). ¶
[6] **to shine around, to shine all around, to shine round about: *perilampō*** [verb: περιλάμπω <4034>]; **from *peri*: around, and *lampō*: see [4] ► To envelop with light, to illuminate around** > The glory of the Lord shone around the shepherds (Luke 2:9). A light above the brightness of the sun was shining from heaven around Paul and those who were journeying with him on the road to Damascus (Acts 26:13 {to blaze around}). ¶
[7] ***phainō*** [verb: φαίνω <5316>]; **from *phōs*: light ► To give light, to illuminate** > The light (i.e., The Lord Jesus) shines {appears} in the darkness (John 1:5). Christians are to shine {to appear} as lights in the world (Phil. 2:15). The prophetic word is like a

light shining in a dark place (2 Pet. 1:19). The true light already shines (1 John 2:8). The face of the Son of Man was like the sun shining in its strength (Rev. 1:16). The light of a lamp will shine no more at all in Babylon (Rev. 18:23). The new Jerusalem has no need of the sun or of the moon to shine upon it (Rev. 21:23). All other refs.: APPEAR <5316>.

– [8] Luke 1:79 → to shine on, upon → to give light → LIGHT (noun) <2014> [9] Eph. 5:14 → to shine on, upon → to give light → LIGHT (noun) <2017> [10] Rev. 4:3 → that shone like an emerald → lit.: like in appearance to an emerald → VISION <3706> [11] Rev. 22:5 → to shine upon → to give light, to bring life → LIGHT (noun) <5461>.

SHINING – [1] **bright shining:** ***astrapē*** [fem. noun: ἀστραπή <796>] ▶ **Bright, glowing light** > The bright shining {brightness, light, rays} of a lamp gives light (Luke 11:36). Other refs.: Matt. 24:27; 28:3; Luke 10:18; 17:24; Rev. 4:5; 8:5; 11:19; 16:18; see LIGHTNING <796>. ¶

[2] **to shine:** ***astraptō*** [verb: ἀστράπτω <797>]; **comp.** ***aster*****: star** ▶ **To glow, to dazzle** > At the tomb of Jesus, two men stood by the women in shining garments {dazzling garments, clothes that gleamed like lightning} (Luke 24:4). Other ref.: Luke 17:24; see SHINE <797>. ¶

[3] **to shine:** ***stilbō*** [verb: στίλβω <4744>] ▶ **To gleam, to glitter, to glisten** > At the transfiguration, the garments of Jesus became shining {dazzling, radiant} (Mark 9:3). ¶

[4] **to shine:** ***phainō*** [verb: φαίνω <5316>]; **from** ***phōs*****: light** ▶ **To gleam, to become radiant** > John the Baptist was the burning and shining lamp {a lamp that burned and gave light} (John 5:35). All other refs.: APPEAR <5316>.

– [5] Luke 1:79 → to shine on → to give light → LIGHT (noun) <2014> [6] Luke 11:36 → to shine on → to give light → LIGHT (noun) <5461> [7] Luke 23:45 → to stop shining → DARKEN <4654> [8] Acts 10:30 → BRIGHT <2986> [9] Eph. 5:14 → to shine on → to give light → LIGHT (noun) <2017> [10] Rev. 21:11 → LIGHT (noun) <5458>.

SHIP – [1] ***ploion*** [neut. noun: πλοῖον <4143>]; **from** ***pleō*****: to sail, to navigate** ▶ **Vessel for traveling on water, including small fishing boats and larger seafaring sailboats or galleys** > The term "ship" {boat} is frequently used in the four Gospels: Matt. 4:21, 22; 8:23, 24; 9:1; 13:2; 14:13, 22, 24, 29, 32, 33; 15:39; Mark 1:19, 20; 4:1, 36a, 37; 5:2, 18, 21; 6:32, 45, 47, 51, 54; 8:10, 13, 14; Luke 5:2, 3a, b, 7a, b, 11; 8:22, 37; John 6:17, 19, 21a, b, 22b in some mss., 24; 21:3, 6, as well as in the book of Acts (20:13, 38; 21:2, 3, 6; 27:2, 6, 10, 15, 17, 19, 22, 30, 31, 37–39, 44; 28:11). James speaks of ships that are turned about by a very small rudder (Jas. 3:4). In the book of Revelation, the word prob. refers, according to the context, to some sort of modern floating construction (Rev. 8:9; 18:17 in some mss., 19). ¶

[2] **small ship, little ship, boat:** ***ploiarion*** [neut. noun: πλοιάριον <4142>]; **dimin. of** [1] ▶ **Smaller version of the previous term** > It is found in Mark 3:9; 4:36b; John 6:22a, b in some mss., 23; 21:8. ¶

[3] ***naus*** [fem. noun: ναῦς <3491>]; ***navis*****, in Lat.** ▶ **Boat, vessel of any (often large) size** > The ship that Paul had boarded was run aground (Acts 27:41). ¶

– [4] Acts 27:11 → owner of the ship → SHIPOWNER <3490> [5] Acts 27:18 → to lighten the ship → LIGHTEN <1546> [6] Rev. 18:17 → to travel by ship, the company in ship → SAIL (verb) <4126>.

SHIPMAN – Acts 27:27, 30 → SAILOR <3492>.

SHIPMASTER – Rev. 18:17 → PILOT <2942>.

SHIPOWNER – ***nauklēros*** [masc. noun: ναύκληρος <3490>]; **from** ***naus*****: ship, and** ***klēros*****: portion, possession** ▶ **Owner of a sailing vessel or a boat** > The centurion believed rather the helmsman and the shipowner {owner of the ship, captain of the ship} than what was said by Paul (Acts 27:11). ¶

SHIPWRECK – to suffer shipwreck, to be shipwrecked, to make shipwreck: *nauageō* [verb: ναυαγέω <3489>]; **from *nauagos*: shipwrecked person, which is from *naus*: ship, and *agnumi*: to break ▶ a. Loss of a ship as the result of a storm or navigational accident** > Paul had suffered shipwreck three times (2 Cor. 11:25). **b. To experience moral ruin** > Having put away faith and a good conscience, some have shipwrecked as to faith (1 Tim. 1:19). ¶

SHIRT – Matt. 5:40; 10:10; Mark 6:9; Luke 3:11; 6:29; 9:3 → TUNIC <5509>.

SHIVER – Rev. 2:27 → to break to shivers → BREAK <4937>.

SHOD – ***hupodeō*** [verb: ὑποδέω <5265>]; **from *hupo*: under, and *deō*: to tie ▶ To wear on the feet** > The twelve were to be shod with {to wear} sandals when Jesus sent them to preach (Mark 6:9). Peter was to have shod {bind on, put on, tie on} his sandals (Acts 12:8). Christians must have their feet shod {fitted} with the preparation of the gospel of peace (Eph. 6:15). ¶

SHOE – [1] Matt. 3:11; 10:10; Mark 1:7; Luke 3:16; 10:4; 15:22; 22:35; John 1:27; Acts 7:33; 13:25 → SANDAL <5266> [2] Eph. 6:15 → to put on as shoes → SHOD <5265>.

SHOOT (noun) – Rom. 11:17 → wild olive shoot → wild olive tree → OLIVE TREE <1636>.

SHOOT (verb) – [1] ***katatoxeuō*** [verb: κατατοξεύω <2700>]; **from *kata*: against, and *toxeuō*: to shoot an arrow, which is from *toxon*: bow ▶ To shoot down with an arrow or dart; also transl.: to thrust through** > This verb is found in some mss. in Heb. 12:20 concerning a beast touching a mountain. ¶

– [2] Matt. 13:26 → to shoot up → SPROUT <985> [3] Luke 21:30 → to shoot forth → SPROUT <4261>.

SHORE – [1] ***aigialos*** [masc. noun: αἰγιαλός <123>]; **from *aissō*: to rush, and *als*: sea ▶ Coast of a sea or a lake, beach** > The crowd stood on the shore, listening to Jesus speaking from a ship (Matt. 13:2). Jesus compares the kingdom of the heavens to a dragnet full of fish that is pulled up on the shore (Matt. 13:48). After His resurrection, Jesus stood on the shore (John 21:4). Paul and the disciples of Tyre knelt down on the shore and prayed (Acts 21:5). Other refs.: Acts 27:39, 40 (see [4]); see BEACH <123>. ¶

[2] ***cheilos*** [neut. noun: χεῖλος <5491>]; **lit.: lip ▶ Coast of the sea** > There have been born of Abraham as many as the countless sand that is by the sea shore (Heb. 11:12). All other refs.: Matt. 15:8; Mark 7:6; Rom. 3:13; 1 Cor. 14:21; Heb. 13:15; 1 Pet. 3:10; see LIP <5491>. ¶

[3] **to draw to, to make, to moor to the shore: *prosormizō*** [verb: προσορμίζω <4358>]; **from *pros*: to, and *hormizō*: to anchor, to moor ▶ To draw to the shore, to accost** > Jesus and His disciples drew to the shore {anchored} in the land of Gennesaret (Mark 6:53). ¶

[4] **to make for the shore: *katechō eis ton aigialon*; *katechō*** [verb: κατέχω <2722>]; **from *kata*: intens., and *echō*: to have, to hold; *aigialos*: see [1] ▶ To sail toward a specific place** > The boat on which Paul journeyed made for the shore {headed for the beach, made for the beach, made for the strand}, i.e., it was made run aground (Acts 27:40). All other refs. (*katechō*): see entries in Lexicon at <2722>.

– [5] Luke 5:11 → EARTH <1093> [6] Luke 8:22 → to set off from shore → LAUNCH <321>.

SHORN – 1 Cor. 11:6a, b → SHEAR <2751>.

SHORT – [1] **to cut short: *suntemnō*** [verb: συντέμνω <4932>]; **from *sun*: together (intens.), and *temnō*: to cut ▶ To reduce by cutting** > In relation to Israel, the Lord

will finish the work {carry out His sentence with speed} and cut it short in righteousness (Rom. 9:28). ¶
2 **to be short: *sustellō*** [verb: συστέλλω <4958>]; **from *sun*: together, and *stellō*: to send, to draw; i.e., to draw together or shrink ▶ To be reduced, to be contracted** > The time before the return of the Lord is short {has been shortened, has grown very short, is straitened} (1 Cor. 7:29). Other ref.: Acts 5:6 (to wrap up); see WRAP <4958>. ¶
– 3 Matt. 24:22; Mark 13:20 → to cut short → SHORTEN <2856> 4 Luke 19:3 → LITTLE <3398> 5 Acts 26:28 → in a short time → ALMOST <1722> <3641> 6 Rom. 3:23; Heb. 4:1 → to come short, to fall short → COME <5302> 7 1 Cor. 1:7; Heb. 12:15 → to come short, to fall short → LACK (verb) <5302> 8 1 Cor. 11:6 → to cut short → SHEAR <2751> 9 2 Cor. 8:15 → to be short → to have lack → LACK (noun) <1641>.

SHORTEN – 1 ***koloboō*** [verb: κολοβόω <2856>]; **from *kolobos*: truncated ▶ To cut short, to reduce the duration** > Unless the days of the great tribulation were shortened by the Lord, no flesh would be saved (Matt. 24:22; Mark 13:20). ¶
– 2 1 Cor. 7:29 → to be short → SHORT <4958>.

SHORTLY – 1 ***eutheōs*** [adv.: εὐθέως <2112>]; **from *euthus*: straight ▶ Soon, in a little while** > John was hoping to see Gaius shortly (3 John 14). All other refs.: IMMEDIATELY <2212>.
2 ***tacheōs*** [adv.: ταχέως <5030>]; **from *tachus*: rapid, prompt ▶ Promptly, quickly; also transl.: soon, very soon** > Paul would come to the Corinthians shortly (1 Cor. 4:19). He was trusting to send Timothy shortly to the Philippians (Phil. 2:19), and that himself would come shortly (v. 24). He asked Timothy to come to him shortly (2 Tim. 4:9). All other refs.: HASTILY <5030>, QUICKLY <5030>.
3 ***tachinos*** [adj.: ταχινός <5031>]; **from *tachus*: fast; lit.: quick ▶ Imminent, coming soon** > Peter knew that the putting off of his tent would shortly {soon, speedily} take place {would be imminent} (2 Pet. 1:14). Other ref.: 2 Pet. 2:1; see SWIFT <5031>. ¶
4 ***tachion*** [adv.: τάχιον <5032>]; **neuter of *tachiōn*, which is the comp. of *tachus*: rapid, prompt ▶ Fairly quickly, within a brief time frame** > Paul was hoping to come to Timothy shortly {before long, more quickly, soon} (1 Tim. 3:14; some mss.: *en tachei*). The author of the Epistle to the Hebrews would see them if Timothy came shortly {soon} (Heb. 13:23). All other refs.: FASTER <5032>, QUICKLY <5032>, SOONER <5032>.
5 ***en tachei*; *en*** [prep.: ἐν <1722>] ***tachos*** [neut. noun: τάχος <5034>]; **from *tachos*: speed; lit.: in haste ▶ Promptly, soon, hastily** > Festus would depart shortly for Caesarea (Acts 25:4). The God of peace will bruise Satan under the feet of the Christians shortly (Rom. 16:20). The last book of the Bible shows the things that must shortly take place (Rev. 1:1; 22:6). Other refs. (*tachos*): QUICKLY <5034>, SPEEDILY <5034>.
– 6 Matt. 14:25 → shortly before dawn → lit.: in the fourth watch of the night → WATCH (noun) <5438>.

SHORTSIGHTED (BE) – ***muōpazō*** [verb: μυωπάζω <3467>]; **from *muōps*: shortsighted, which is from *muō*: to shut, to blink, and *ōps*: eye ▶ To be unable to see clearly, to be nearsighted** > Peter uses this verb in his second epistle concerning someone who lacks faith, virtue, and other qualities (2 Pet. 1:9). ¶

SHOULDER – ***ōmos*** [masc. noun: ὦμος <5606>]; ***humerus*, in Lat. ▶ Upper part of the arm; it suggests strength and security** > The scribes and the Pharisees were binding burdens heavy and hard to bear on the shoulders of men (Matt. 23:4). The shepherd lays his lost sheep on his own shoulders, rejoicing (Luke 15:5). ¶

SHOUT (noun) – 1 ***keleusma*** [neut. noun: κέλευσμα <2752>]; **from *keleuō*: to give an order ▶ Signal, order to gather people** > The Lord Himself will descend from heaven with a shout {an assembling shout, a loud command}, with the voice of an archangel,

and with the trumpet of God to gather the Christians at the Lord's coming (1 Thes. 4:16). ¶
– [2] Matt. 25:6 → CRY (noun) <2906> [3] Luke 23:23a, b → VOICE <5456> [4] Acts 12:22 → to give a shout → SHOUT (verb) <2019>.

SHOUT (verb) – [1] ***boaō*** [verb: βοάω <994>]; **from *boē*: cry ▶ To express oneself with a loud voice, e.g., to manifest one's feelings** > Isaiah has written concerning Jerusalem to break forth and shout {cry, cry aloud} (Gal. 4:27). All other refs.: CRY (verb) <994>.

[2] **to shout, to shout against: *epiphōneō*** [verb: ἐπιφωνέω <2019>]; **from *epi*: upon, against, and *phōneō*: to call ▶ To raise the voice against someone or in acclamation** > The people shouted {cried, kept on calling out}, saying to crucify Jesus (Luke 23:21). The people kept shouting {cried out; gave a shout, saying} that the voice of Herod was the voice of a god (Acts 12:22). The commander wanted to know why the Jews were shouting against {crying against} Paul (Acts 22:24; *kataphōneō* in some mss.). Other ref.: Acts 21:34 in some mss. ¶
– [3] Matt. 8:29; 15:23; 20:30, 31; 21:9, 15; 27:23; Mark 5:7; 10:47, 48; 11:9; 15:13, 14; Luke 4:41; 18:39; John 12:13; 19:12; Acts 14:14; 16:17; 19:28, 32, 34; 21:28, 36; 23:6; 24:21; Rev. 10:3a, b; 18:2 → CRY (verb) <2896> [4] Luke 9:38 → CRY (verb) <310> [5] John 18:40; 19:6, 15 → CRY (verb) <2905> [6] Acts 14:11 → to raise the voice → RAISE <1869> [7] Acts 16:28 → CRY (verb) <5455> [8] Acts 25:24 → CRY (verb) <1916> [9] Luke 23:18 → to cry out → CRY (verb) <349>.

SHOW (noun) – [1] **to make a show: *paradeigmatizō*** [verb: παραδειγματίζω <3856>]; **from *para*: alongside, and *deigmatizō*: to make an example, to make a spectacle, which is from *deigma*: thing shown, example ▶ To expose to public shame, to ignominy** > Those who merely profess to be Christians make a show of {hold up to contempt, put to open shame, subject to public disgrace} the Son of God (Heb. 6:6). Other ref.: Matt. 1:19 (to make a public example); see EXAMPLE <3856>. ¶
– [2] Col. 2:15 → to make a show → to make a spectacle → SPECTACLE <1165>.

SHOW (verb) – [1] ***anangellō*** [verb: ἀναγγέλλω <312>]; **from *ana*: upon (intens.), and *angellō*: to bring news, a message ▶ To announce, to communicate** > The Holy Spirit would show {tell} the things to come and show {declare, make known} those concerning Christ (John 16:13–15). All other refs.: see entries in Lexicon at <312>.

[2] ***apangellō*** [verb: ἀπαγγέλλω <518>]; **from *apo*: from, and *angellō*: to bring news, a message ▶ To declare, to publish, to preach; also transl.: to announce, to proclaim, to report, to show forth** > Jesus would show justice to the Gentiles (Matt. 12:18). Paul showed to many that they should repent, turn to God, and do the work of repentance (Acts 26:20). John was showing the eternal life, which was with the Father, and had been manifested (1 John 1:2); he was showing what he had seen and heard (v. 3). All other refs.: DECLARE <518>, RELATE <518>, REPORT (verb) <518>, TELL <518>.

[3] **to show forth: *exangellō*** [verb: ἐξαγγέλλω <1804>]; **from *ek*: out, and *angellō*: to bring news, a message ▶ To announce, to publish, to manifest** > Christians should show forth {declare, proclaim, set forth} the praises of Him who has called them out of darkness into His marvelous light (1 Pet. 2:9). ¶

[4] ***deiknumi*** [verb: δείκνυμι <1166>] ▶ **To expose to sight, to reveal** > Jesus told the healed leper to show himself to the priest (Matt. 8:4). Other refs.: Matt. 4:8; 16:21; Mark 1:44; 14:15; Luke 4:5; 5:14; 20:24 in some mss.; 22:12; John 2:18; 5:20a, b; 14:8, 9; 20:20; Acts 7:3; 10:28; 1 Cor. 12:31; 1 Tim. 6:15 {to manifest}; Heb. 8:5; Jas. 2:18a, b; 3:13; Rev. 1:1; 4:1; 17:1; 21:9, 10; 22:1, 6, 8. ¶

[5] ***anadeiknumi*** [verb: ἀναδείκνυμι <322>]; **from *ana*: intens., and *deiknumi*: see [4] ▶ To designate, to declare** > The Lord was asked to show which of two disciples He had

chosen to replace Judas (Acts 1:24). Other ref.: Luke 10:1; see APPOINT <322>. ¶

6 **to show oneself: *apodeiknumi*** [verb: ἀποδείκνυμι <584>]; **from *apo*: before (intens.), and *deiknumi*: see 4 ► To designate oneself, to proclaim oneself** > The man of sin will show {proclaim, display} himself to be God (2 Thes. 2:4). All other refs.: APPROVE <584>, PROVE <584>, SET (verb) <584>.

7 ***endeiknumi*** [verb: ἐνδείκνυμι <1731>]; **from *en*: in, and *deiknumi*: see 4 ► To display, to demonstrate** > The Gentiles show the work of the law written in their hearts (Rom. 2:15). Other refs.: Rom. 9:17, 22; 2 Cor. 8:24; Eph. 2:7; 1 Tim. 1:16; 2 Tim. 4:14 {to do}; Titus 2:10; 3:2; Heb. 6:10, 11. ¶

8 ***epideiknumi*** [verb: ἐπιδείκνυμι <1925>]; **from *epi*: intens., and *deiknumi*: see 4 ► a. To exhibit, to indicate** > Jesus was asked to show a sign from heaven (Matt. 16:1). Other refs.: Matt. 22:19; 24:1 {to call the attention, to point out}; Luke 17:14; 20:24 in some mss.; 24:40; Acts 9:39; Heb. 6:17 {to make very clear}. **b. To demonstrate, to prove** > Apollos was showing from the Scriptures that Jesus is the Christ (Acts 18:28). ¶

9 ***hupodeiknumi*** [verb: ὑποδείκνυμι <5263>]; **from *hupo*: under and *deiknumi*: see 4 ► To make known, to teach** > Jesus showed Paul how many things he must suffer for His name's sake (Acts 9:16). Matt. 3:7 and Luke 3:7: see WARN <5263>. Other refs.: Luke 6:47; 12:5 {to forewarn, to warn}; Acts 20:35. ¶

10 ***dēloō*** [verb: δηλόω <1213>]; **from *dēlos*: clear, manifest ► To indicate, to manifest** > Jesus had shown {made clear to, manifested to} Peter that the moment to put off his tent, referring to his body, was approaching shortly (2 Pet. 1:14). All other refs.: DECLARE <1213>, INDICATE <1213>.

11 ***didōmi*** [verb: δίδωμι <1325>] **► To give, to present** > False christs and false prophets will show {perform} signs and wonders (Matt. 24:24; Mark 13:22). Other ref.: Acts 2:19 {to grant}. Other refs.: GIVE <1325>.

12 ***mēnuō*** [verb: μηνύω <3377>] **► To warn, to reveal, to make known something hidden** > Moses showed that the dead are raised (Luke 20:37). Claudius was told (or: was shown) {was informed, received information} how the Jews lay in wait for Paul (Acts 23:30). Someone might show {inform, point out, tell} a Christian that the food of a dinner had been offered to idols (1 Cor. 10:28). Other ref.: John 11:57; see REPORT (verb) <3377>. ¶

13 ***parechō*** [verb: παρέχω <3930>]; **from *para*: near, and *echō*: to have ► a. To present** > Titus was to show himself to be {to afford himself as, to set himself} a model of good works (Titus 2:7). **b. To exhibit, to manifest** > The natives showed unusual kindness toward Paul and his companions (Acts 28:2). All other refs.: see entries in Lexicon at <3930>.

14 ***poieō*** [verb: ποιέω <4160>]; **lit.: to do ► To act, to behave** > Mary said that God had shown {had wrought} strength {had done mighty deeds, had performed mighty deeds} with His arm (Luke 1:51). Other refs.: see entries in Lexicon at <4160>.

15 ***sēmainō*** [verb: σημαίνω <4591>]; **from *sēma*: sign; lit.: to give a sign ► To declare, to indicate** > Agabus showed {predicted, signified} by the Spirit that there was going to be a great famine (Acts 11:28). Other refs.: John 12:33; 18:32; 21:19; Acts 25:27; Rev. 1:1; see SIGNIFY <4591>. ¶

16 ***phaneroō*** [verb: φανερόω <5319>]; **from *phaneros*: manifest, visible ► To manifest, to expose to view** > Jesus was told to show {manifest} Himself to the world (John 7:4). All other refs.: APPEAR <5319>, MANIFEST (verb) <5319>.

– 17 Matt. 14:2; Mark 6:14 → to show forth → WORK (verb) <1754> 18 Mark 12:40; Luke 20:47 → PRETEXT <4392> 19 Mark 14:70 → AGREE <3662> 20 Luke 1:58 → to show great → MAGNIFY <3170> 21 Luke 8:39 → RELATE <1334> 22 John 3:20 → to show to be as what it is → REPROVE <1651> 23 John 14:21, 22 → MANIFEST (verb) <1718> 24 Acts 1:3; 2 Tim. 2:15 → PRESENT (verb) <3936> 25 Acts 3:18; 7:52 → to show before → to announce beforehand → ANNOUNCE

<4293> 26 Acts 10:40; Rom. 10:20 → to show openly → MANIFEST (adj.) <1717> 27 Acts 14:17 → to show kindness → to do good → GOOD (adj. and noun) <15> 28 Acts 23:22 → REVEAL <1718> 29 Acts 24:27 → ACQUIRE <2698> 30 Acts 26:16b → APPEAR <3708> 31 Acts 26:23; 1 Cor. 11:26 → PREACH <2605> 32 Acts 28:7 → to show generous hospitality → lit.: to lodge courteously → LODGE <3579>, COURTEOUSLY <5390> 33 Rom. 2:4; 1 Tim. 6:2 → to show contempt, to show less respect → DESPISE <2706> 34 Rom. 3:5; 5:8 → to serve to show → COMMEND <4921> 35 Rom. 3:25, 26 → DEMONSTRATE <1732> 36 Rom. 12:10 → "showing" added in Engl. 37 Rom. 12:13 → to seek to show hospitality → to be given to hospitality → GIVE <1377> 38 Rom. 14:10 → to show contempt → DESPISE <1848> 39 1 Cor. 11:19 → RECOGNIZED <5318> 40 2 Cor. 2:7 → to show grace → FORGIVE <5483> 41 Gal. 2:6 → God does not show favoritism → lit.: God does not accept the face of man 42 Heb. 11:14 → to show, to show clearly → to declare plainly → PLAINLY <1718> 43 Heb. 12:28 → to show gratitude → lit.: to have (*echō*) grace 44 Jas. 2:4 → to show partiality → PARTIALITY <1252> 45 Jas. 2:20 → to want to be shown → lit.: to want to know → KNOW <1097> 46 1 Pet. 3:7 → GIVE <632> 47 1 Pet. 4:9 → to show hospitality → to be hospitable → HOSPITABLE <5382> 48 Jude 16 → to show favoritism → lit.: to have men's persons in admiration → ADMIRATION <2296>.

SHOWBREAD – Matt. 12:4; Mark 2:26; Luke 6:4; Heb. 9:2 → EXPOSITION OF THE LOAVES <4286>.

SHOWER – *ombros* [masc. noun: ὄμβρος <3655>]; ***imber*, in Lat. ▶ Abundant rain, downpour** > One may predict a shower {it is going to rain} when a cloud rises out of the west (Luke 12:54). ¶

SHOWING – 1 to make a good showing: *euprosōpeō* [verb: εὐπροσωπέω <2146>]; **from *euprosōpos*: good looking, which is from *eu*: well, and *prosōpon*: aspect, appearance, which is from *pro*: toward, and *ōps*: eye ▶ To have a nice appearance, to make oneself look good** > Those desiring to make a good showing {to have a fair appearance, to make a fair shew} in the flesh {to make a good impression outwardly} were constraining the Galatians to be circumcised (Gal. 6:12). ¶

– 2 2 Cor. 10:2 → showing boldness → to be bold → BOLD <5111>.

SHREWD – Matt. 10:16; Luke 16:8 → PRUDENT <5429>.

SHREWDLY – 1 Luke 16:8 → PRUDENTLY <5430> 2 Acts 7:19 → to deal shrewdly → DEAL <2686>.

SHREWDNESS – Luke 16:8 → for his shrewdness → PRUDENTLY <5430>.

SHRIEK (noun) – 1 Mark 1:26 → with a shriek → lit.: crying out → CRY (verb) <2896> 2 Acts 8:7 → with shrieks → lit.: crying with a loud voice → CRY (verb) <994>.

SHRIEK (verb) – Mark 9:26 → CRY (verb) <2896>.

SHRINE – Acts 17:23 → object of worship → WORSHIP <4574>.

SHRINK – *hupostellō* [verb: ὑποστέλλω <5288>]; **from *hupo*: under, and *stellō*: to send, to draw ▶ To avoid, to draw back, to shirk (e.g., from the responsibility)** > Paul did not shrink {hesitate, shun} from announcing all the counsel of God to the Ephesians (Acts 20:27). Other refs.: Acts 20:20 (to keep back); Gal. 2:12; Heb. 10:38; see KEEP (verb) <5288>, WITHDRAW <5288>. ¶

SHRIVELED – 1 Matt. 12:10; Luke 6:6, 8 → WITHERED <3584> 2 Mark 3:1, 3 → WITHERED <3583>.

SHROUD – Matt. 27:59; Mark 15:46a, b; Luke 23:53 → linen shroud → LINEN, LINEN CLOTH <4616>.

SHUDDER – ***phrissō*** [verb: φρίσσω <5425>]; **from *phrix*: trembling, shivering ▶ To tremble, to fear greatly** > The demons shudder (Jas. 2:19), because they know their fate. ¶

SHUN – 1 ***periistēmi*** [verb: περιΐστημι <4026>]; **from *peri*: about, and *histēmi*: to stand ▶ To avoid, to flee** > Timothy had to shun profane and vain babblings (2 Tim. 2:16). Titus had to shun foolish disputes and other unprofitable and useless things (Titus 3:9). Other refs.: John 11:42 and Acts 25:7 {to stand around}; see STAND (verb) <4026>. ¶
– 2 Acts 20:27 → SHRINK <5288>.

SHUT – 1 **to shut up: *kleiō*** [verb: κλείω <2808>]; **comp. *kleis*: key ▶ To close, to lock up** > This verb is used with doors (Matt. 6:6; 25:10; Luke 11:7; John 20:19, 26; Acts 21:30; Rev. 3:8), the kingdom of the heavens (Matt. 23:13), heaven (Luke 4:25; Rev. 11:6), a prison (Acts 5:23), bowels (1 John 3:17), and a gate (Rev. 21:25). Other refs.: Rev. 3:7a, b; 20:3. ¶
2 ***apokleiō*** [verb: ἀποκλείω <608>]; **from *apo*: from, and *kleiō*: see 1 ▶ To close (with the thought that it is impossible to enter thereafter)** > The master of the house will shut the door (Luke 13:25), an image of the impossibility of being saved once the door of grace has been closed. ¶
3 **to shut up: *katakleiō*** [verb: κατακλείω <2623>]; **from *kata*: intens., and *kleiō*: see 1 ▶ To confine; also transl.: to lock** > Herod shut up John in prison (Luke 3:20). Paul had shut up {had put} in prisons many of the saints (Acts 26:10). ¶
4 **to shut up: *sunkleiō*** [verb: συγκλείω <4788>]; **from *sun*: together, and *kleiō*: see 1 ▶ To enclose together** > God has shut up together all men in unbelief (or: disobedience}, in order that He might show mercy to all (Rom. 11:32 {to bind, to commit, to conclude}). Scripture has shut up all things under sin (Gal. 3:22 {to conclude, to confine, to declare}); under the law, men were shut up to the gift of the promise of salvation, according to the principle of faith (v. 23 {to keep, to lock}). Other ref.: Luke 5:6; see CATCH (verb) <4788>. ¶
– 5 2 Cor. 4:8 → to be entirely shut up → to be in despair → DESPAIR <1820> 6 Gal. 4:17 → to shut out → EXCLUDE <1576> 7 Heb. 11:33 → STOP <5420>.

SICK (adj. and noun) – 1 ***arrōstos*** [adj. and adj. used as noun: ἄρρωστος <732>]; **from *a*: neg., and *rhōnnumi*: to strengthen; lit.: which is not strong ▶ Infirm, invalid** > Jesus healed the sick {those who were sick; *arrōsteō*: to be sick} of a large crowd (Matt. 14:14). In His own country, Jesus laid His hands on a few sick people and healed them (Mark 6:5). The twelve disciples anointed with oil many sick people and healed them (Mark 6:13). Those who have believed will lay hands on the sick, and they will recover (Mark 16:18). Many were weak (*asthenēs*) and sick (*arrōstos*) {infirm, sickly} among the Corinthians (1 Cor. 11:30), for they had failed to judge themselves (see v. 28, 31). ¶
2 ***asthenēs*** [adj. and adj. used as noun: ἀσθενής <772>]; **from *a*: neg., and *sthenos*: strength, physical vigor; lit.: without strength ▶ Weak, ill** > Jesus sent His disciples to heal the sick (Luke 10:9). When He comes in His glory, Jesus will speak of having been sick (Matt. 25:39, 43, 44), i.e., by identifying Himself with His disciples. Peter and John had done a good deed to a sick man (Acts 4:9 {helpless, impotent, infirm, lame}); this man was lame (see 3:1–11). The sick were brought to be healed by Peter (Acts 5:15, 16). For the use of the word in 1 Cor. 11:30, see 1. All other refs.: POWERLESS <772>, WEAK <772>, WEAKNESS <772>.
3 **to be sick: *astheneō*** [verb: ἀσθενέω <770>]; **from *asthenēs*: see 2 ▶ To be weak, to be ill; often transl.: the sick, lit.: the being sick** > The disciples of Jesus were to heal the sick (Matt. 10:8; Luke 9:2 {to perform healing}). When He comes in His glory, Jesus will say that He had been sick {had been ill} and that He had been visited (i.e., by identifying Himself with His disciples) (Matt. 25:36). People begged

Jesus to let the sick {infirm} touch Him (Mark 6:56); they brought the sick to Him (Luke 4:40). There was a multitude of sick {disabled people, impotent folk} at the pool of Bethesda (John 5:3). The sick were healed by Paul (Acts 19:12). All other refs.: SICK (adv.) <770>, WEAK <770>.

– [4] Luke 4:38 → to be sick with → to suffer from → SUFFER <4912> [5] Acts 28:9 → those who were sick → those who had sicknesses → SICKNESS <769>.

SICK (adv.) – [1] ***kakōs*** [adv.: κακῶς <2560>]**; from *kakos*: bad ▶ The opposite of well, in a state of illness; also transl.: diseased, ill** > Sick (lit.: Having it badly, Being ill, i.e., the ailing) people were brought to Jesus, and He healed them (Matt. 4:24; 8:16; 14:35; Mark 6:55). Those who are sick need the physician (Matt. 9:12; Mark 2:17; Luke 5:31). The Greek word is also transl. "evil": Jesus told the officer that if He had spoken evil {spoken wrongly, said something wrong}, the officer should bear witness of the evil (John 18:23a). One should not speak evil {evilly} of the ruler of the Jews (Acts 23:5). In Jas. 4:3, the Greek word is transl. "amiss" {evilly, with wrong motives}: some ask God amiss (lit.: badly). See [4]. All other refs.: MISERABLY <2560>, SEVERELY <2560>.

[2] **to be sick, to fall sick: *astheneō*** [verb: ἀσθενέω <770>]**; from *a*: neg., and *sthenos*: strength ▶ To be weak, to lack strength; also transl.: to be ill** > The sick {impotent, infirm, invalid} man (lit.: He who was sick) answered the Lord that he had no man to put him into the pool (John 5:7). It was Mary who anointed the feet of Jesus, whose brother Lazarus was sick (John 11:2). The verb is also used regarding the servant of a centurion who had been sick (Luke 7:10 in some mss.), a nobleman's son (John 4:46), those whom Jesus healed (John 6:2 {diseased}), Lazarus (John 11:1, 3, 6), Dorcas (Acts 9:37), Epaphroditus (Phil. 2:26, 27), Trophimus (2 Tim. 4:20), and a member of the church (Jas. 5:14). All other refs.: SICK (adj. and noun) <770>, WEAK <770>.

[3] **to be sick: *kamnō*** [verb: κάμνω <2577>] **▶ To be downcast, to be worn out, to be exhausted** > The prayer of faith will heal the one who is sick, and the Lord will raise up such a Christian (Jas. 5:15). Other ref.: Heb. 12:3 (to become weary); see WEARY (adj.) <2577>. ¶

[4] **to be sick; lit.: to have badly; to have: *echō*** [verb: ἔχω <2192>] **badly: *kakōs*** [adv.: κακῶς <2560>] **▶ To be physically ill, to be suffering** > The expr. is used regarding the servant of a centurion (Luke 7:2) and others (Mark 1:32, 34). Other refs. (*kakōs*): see [1].

– [5] Acts 28:8 → to be sick → LAY <2621> [6] 1 Tim. 6:4 → to be sick → OBSESSED (BE) <3552>.

SICKBED – Rev. 2:22 → BED <2825>.

SICKLE – ***drepanon*** [neut. noun: δρέπανον <1407>]**; from *drepō*: to gather, to pluck, to cut off ▶ Sharp cutting tool used by harvesters and grape pickers >** When fruit is produced, immediately one puts the sickle to it (Mark 4:29). John saw someone like the Son of Man with a sharp sickle in His hand (Rev. 14:14); He was told to put in His sickle and reap (v. 15); He put His sickle on the earth, and the earth was reaped (v. 16). Another angel came out, also having a sharp sickle (Rev. 14:17); he was told to put in his sharp sickle and gather the clusters of grapes from the vine of the earth (v. 18a, b), which he did (v. 19). ¶

SICKLY – 1 Cor. 11:30 → SICK (adj. and noun) <732>.

SICKNESS – [1] ***astheneia*** [fem. noun: ἀσθένεια <769>]**; from *asthenēs*: weak, sick, which is from *a*: neg., and *sthenos*: strength ▶ Weakness, failing health** > Jesus declared that the sickness of Lazarus was not unto death (John 11:4). Those who had sicknesses {diseases} {Those of the sick} in the island of Malta came and were healed (Acts 28:9). All other refs.: ILLNESS <769>, INFIRMITY <769>, WEAKNESS <769>.

[2] ***nosos*** [fem. noun: νόσος <3554>] **▶ Serious or chronic health problem; also**

transl.: disease, infirmity > Jesus healed all kinds of sickness (Matt. 4:23, 24; 9:35; Mark 1:34; Luke 4:40; 6:17 or 18; 7:21). On earth, Jesus bore the sicknesses of His people (Matt. 8:17; see Is. 53:4). He gave His disciples power to heal all kinds of sickness (Matt. 10:1; Mark 3:15; Luke 9:1). God healed diseases {illnesses} by the hands of Paul (Acts 19:12). ¶

SIDE – [1] ***pleura*** [fem. noun: πλευρά <4125>] ▶ **Side of the body** > A soldier pierced the side of Jesus with a spear (John 19:34). Jesus showed His disciples His hands and His side (John 20:20). Thomas wanted to put his hand into the side of Jesus (John 20:25); Jesus told him to put his hand into His side (v. 27). An angel struck Peter on the side and raised him up (Acts 12:7). Other ref.: Matt. 27:49 in some mss. ¶

[2] **to pass by on the other side: *antiparerchomai*** [verb: ἀντιπαρέρχομαι <492>]; **from *anti*: against, and *parerchomai*: to pass by, which is from *para*: near, *erchomai*: to go, to come** ▶ **To take another road** > A priest passed by (came by) on the other side to avoid a man half dead on the road (Luke 10:31), and a Levite as well (v. 32). ¶

[3] **right, right side, right-hand side: *dexios*** [adj.: δεξιός <1188>]; ***dexter*, in Lat.** ▶ **The side opposite to the heart** > An angel of the Lord appeared to Zacharias on the right side of the altar of incense (Luke 1:11). At the tomb of Jesus, the women saw a young man sitting on the right side (Mark 16:5). Jesus told the disciples to cast the net on the right side of the ship (John 21:6). All other refs.: RIGHT[1] <1188>.

[4] **on either side, on each side: *enteuthen*** [adv.: ἐντεῦθεν <1782>] ***kai*** [conj.: καί <2532>] ***ekeithen*** [adv.: ἐκεῖθεν <1564>] ▶ **On both sides** > The tree of life was in the middle of the street of the heavenly Jerusalem, on either side of the river (Rev. 22:2). *

[5] **one on either side, one on each side: *enteuthen*** [adv.: ἐντεῦθεν <1782>] ***kai*** [conj.: καί <2532>] ***enteuthen*** [adv.: ἐντεῦθεν <1782>]; **lit.: here and there** ▶ **On one side and on the other** > Two criminals were crucified with Jesus, one on either side (John 19:18). *

[6] **on every side, on all sides: *pantothen*** [adv.: πάντοθεν <3840>]; **from *pas*: all** ▶ **From everywhere, completely** > Jerusalem would be closed in on every side (Luke 19:43). The Greek word is transl. "from every direction {quarter}," "from everywhere" in Mark 1:45 (some mss.: *pantachothen*). The ark of the covenant was covered on all sides with gold {round about with gold, gold-covered} (Heb. 9:4). ¶

[7] ***peran*** [adv.: πέραν <4008>]; **from *pera*: beyond, which comes from *peirō*: to pierce** ▶ **On the other side, beyond** > Jesus commanded to cross to the other side (Matt. 8:18; Mark 4:35; Luke 8:22). Jesus came to the other side (Matt. 8:28; Mark 5:1, 21; 8:13). He constrained His disciples to go before Him to the other side (Matt. 14:22; Mark 6:45). The disciples came to the other side (Matt. 16:5). *

– [8] Luke 16:22, 23; John 1:18 → BOSOM <2859> [9] John 6:1, 22, 25 → on the other side → OVER <4008> [10] Phil. 1:27a, b → to strive side by side → to strive together → STRIVE <4866> [11] Rev. 5:1 → on both sides → lit.: inside and on the back → BACK <3693>.

SIDON – [1] ***Sidōn*** [fem. name: Σιδών <4605>]: **fishing, in Heb.** ▶ **Phoenician port city on the Mediterranean Sea** > Jesus referred to Tyre and Sidon in relation to the incredulity of the cities of Galilee (Matt. 11:21, 22; Luke 10:13, 14). He withdrew to the region of Tyre and Sidon during His travels (Matt. 15:21; Mark 7:24, 31); many people of this region came to Him at the beginning (Mark 3:8; Luke 6:17). Paul passed through Sidon on his journey to Rome (Acts 27:3). ¶

[2] **of Sidon: *Sidōnios*** [adj.: Σιδώνιος <4606>]; **see** [1] ▶ **Region of Sidon** > Zarephath is in the land of Sidon {of Sidonia} (Luke 4:26). Herod was highly displeased with the people of Sidon, but the reason is not given (Acts 12:20). Jezebel was the daughter of Ethbaal, king of the Sidonians (see 1 Kgs. 16:31). ¶

SIFT – ***siniazō*** [verb: σινιάζω <4617>]; **from *sinion*: instrument for sifting, e.g., sieve or winnowing van ▶ To pass objects through an instrument with constricted openings to sort them** > Satan had asked for the disciples in order to sift them like wheat (Luke 22:31), i.e., to submit them to temptations and tribulations. ¶

SIGH (noun) – Mark 7:34 → with a deep sigh → lit.: he sighed → GROAN (verb) <4727>.

SIGH (verb) – 1 Mark 7:34 → GROAN (verb) <4727> 2 Mark 8:12 → to sigh deeply → GROAN (verb) <389>.

SIGHT (noun) – 1 ***eidos*** [neut. noun: εἶδος <1491>]; **from *eidō*: to see ▶ What is seen, what is visible** > Paul walked by faith, not by sight (2 Cor. 5:7). All other refs.: FASHION (noun) <1491>, FORM (noun) <1491>.
– 2 Matt. 11:5; 20:34; Mark 10:51, 52; Luke 7:22; 18:41, 42; John 9:11, 15a, 18a, b; Acts 9:12, 17, 18; 22:13 → to have the sight restored, to receive sight, to regain sight → SEE <308> 3 Mark 2:12 → in the presence of → PRESENCE <1715> 4 Luke 2:31; Gal. 1:22 → FACE (noun) <4383> 5 Luke 4:18 → RECOVERY OF SIGHT <309> 6 Luke 21:11 → fearful sight → FEARFUL <5400> 7 Luke 23:48 → SPECTACLE <2335> 8 John 3:21 → in the sight of God → lit.: in God 9 John 7:24 → APPEARANCE <3799> 10 Acts 1:9 → EYE <3788> 11 Acts 7:31 → VISION <3705> 12 Acts 21:3 → to come in sight → SIGHT (verb) <398> 13 Rom. 11:25; 12:16 → wise in one's own sight → WISE (adj.) <5429> 14 2 Cor. 2:10 → PERSON <4383> 15 Heb. 12:21 → lit.: the thing appearing → APPEAR <5324> 16 Rev. 4:3 → VISION <3706>.

SIGHT (verb) – ***anaphainō*** [verb: ἀναφαίνω <398>]; **from *ana*: above (intens.), and *phainō*: to shine, to come to view, which is from *phōs*: light ▶ To appear visibly, to render visible; to experience an appearing** > When those on Paul's ship had sighted {had come in sight of, had discovered} Cyprus, they sailed to Syria (Acts 21:3). Other ref.: Luke 19:11; see MANIFEST (verb) <398>. ¶

SIGN – 1 ***sēmeion*** [neut. noun: σημεῖον <4592>] ▶ **a. Work or deed whose cause is of a supernatural character; also transl.: miraculous sign** > Jesus was pressured to justify His position and His word by signs, but He said He would show only the sign of the prophet Jonah (Matt. 12:38, 39a–c; 16:1, 4a–c; Mark 8:11, 12a, b; Luke 11:16, 29a–c, 30). False christs and false prophets, warns Jesus, will give great signs (Matt. 24:24; Mark 13:22). Herod hoped to see some sign done by Jesus (Luke 23:8). Jesus did the beginning of His signs in Cana of Galilee (John 2:11). He reproached the nobleman of refusing to believe unless he saw signs and wonders (John 4:48). People said Jesus was doing many signs (John 11:47). Although Jesus had done many signs, people did not believe in Him (John 12:37). God showed His approval of Jesus by the signs that He did by Him (Acts 2:22). The Gospels and the book of Acts record many signs done by Jesus and His apostles (e.g., Acts 4:16). Signs accompanied the preaching of the disciples (Mark 16:20) and that of Paul (2 Cor. 12:12a, b), and were to accompany those who believe (Mark 16:17). The man of sin, according to the working of Satan, will show signs to them who perish (2 Thes. 2:9). By signs, God bore witness to those who had heard the Lord (Heb. 2:4). Other refs. where the word is transl. "sign" or "miracle": John 2:18, 23; 3:2; 4:54; 6:2, 14, 26, 30; 7:31; 9:16; 10:41; 12:18; 20:30; Acts 2:43; 4:22, 30; 5:12; 6:8; 7:36; 8:6, 13; 14:3; 15:12; Rom. 15:19; 1 Cor. 1:22; Rev. 13:13 {wonder}, 14; 16:14; 19:20. **b. Indication of something yet to come** > The Jews did not know how to discern the signs of the times (Matt. 16:3). The disciples asked Jesus what would be the sign of His coming and of the completion of the age (Matt. 24:3; Mark 13:4; Luke 21:7); He said there will be great signs from heaven (Luke 21:11, 25). The sign of the Son of Man will appear in heaven (Matt. 24:30). God will give signs before the coming of the day of the Lord (Acts 2:19). **c. Testimony** > Jesus was set for a sign that would be spoken against (Luke 2:34). Tongues are for a sign to unbelievers; but prophecy to those who believe (1 Cor. 14:22). **d. Mark, indication** > Judas gave a sign {signal} by which to recognize Jesus (Matt. 26:48). An angel gave a sign concerning the birth of Jesus (Luke 2:12). Abraham received the sign of circumcision as the seal of the righteousness of faith (Rom. 4:11). The salutation of Paul was in his own hand, which was the sign {mark, sign of genuineness} (in the sense of: proof) in every one of his letters (2 Thes. 3:17). **e. Extraordinary thing, prodigy** > On three occasions John saw a sign in heaven (Rev. 12:1, 3; 15:1). ¶

[2] ***sussēmon*** [neut. noun: σύσσημον <4953>]; **from *sun*: together, and *sēma*: sign ▶ Agreed upon signal** > Judas had given a sign {signal, token} by which to recognize Jesus (Mark 14:44). ¶

[3] **to make a sign: *kataseiō*** [verb: κατασείω <2678>]; **from *kata*: down, and *seiō*: to move, to shake ▶ To wave the hand in order to attract attention; also transl.: to beckon, to motion** > Having returned to his own company, Peter made a sign with his hand to be silent (Acts 12:17). Paul made a sign with the hand to indicate that he wished to speak (Acts 13:16; 21:40). Alexander did the same in order to make a defense (Acts 19:33). ¶

[4] **to make a sign: *neuō*** [verb: νεύω <3506>] **▶ To give an indication, to signify by nodding; also transl.: to beckon, to gesture, to motion, to nod** > The verb is used in regard to Simon Peter (John 13:24) and to a governor (Acts 24:10). ¶

[5] **to make signs: *dianeuō*** [verb: διανεύω <1269>]; **from *dia*: intens., and *neuō*: see [4] ▶ To express oneself by means of gestures; also transl.: to beckon** > Zacharias, who had become mute after seeing a vision, made signs (Luke 1:22). ¶

[6] **to make signs: *enneuō*** [verb: ἐννεύω <1770>]; **from *en*: in, and *neuō*: see [4] ▶ To communicate with the head or eyes** > Neighbors and relatives made signs to Zacharias as to what he might wish his son to be called (Luke 1:62). ¶

– [7] Luke 17:20 → with signs to be observed → with observation → OBSERVATION <3326> <3907> [8] John 19:20 → TITLE <5102> [9] Acts 28:11 → FIGUREHEAD <3902> [10] Phil. 1:28 → PROOF <1732>.

SIGNAL (noun) – [1] Matt. 26:48 → SIGN <4592> [2] Mark 14:44 → SIGN <4953>.

SIGNAL (verb) – ***kataneuō*** [verb: κατανεύω <2656>]; **from *kata*: down (intens.), and *neuō*: to make a sign ▶ To indicate by a gesture, e.g., a nod of the head** > Simon and his companions signaled {beckoned to} those who were in the other ship to come and help them (Luke 5:7). ¶

SIGNIFICANCE – without significance: *aphōnos* [adj.: ἄφωνος <880>]; **from *a*: neg., and *phōnē*: sound; lit.: without voice ▶ Without a distinct sound, without meaning** > None of the languages in the world is without significance {without meaning, without signification, of undistinguishable sound} (1 Cor. 14:10); some mss. have *amorphos* (without form), but this is questionable. Other refs.: Acts 8:32; 1 Cor. 12:2; 2 Pet. 2:16; see DUMB <880>. ¶

SIGNIFICANT – Phil. 2:3 → IMPORTANT <5242>.

SIGNIFICATION – 1 Cor. 14:10 → without signification → without significance → SIGNIFICANCE <880>.

SIGNIFY – [1] ***diangellō*** [verb: διαγγέλλω <1229>]; **from *dia*: through, and *angellō*: to bring news, to tell ▶ To declare, to announce** > Paul signified the accomplishment {announced the expiration, gave notice} of the days of purification (Acts 21:26). Other refs.: Luke 9:60; Rom. 9:17; see PREACH <1229>, DECLARE <1229>. ¶

[2] ***emphanizō*** [verb: ἐμφανίζω <1718>]; **from *emphanēs*: manifest, known, which is from *en*: in, and *phainō*: to make appear, which is from *phōs*: light ▶ To propose, to**

request > The council had to signify {make a representation to, notify, petition, suggest to} the chief captain to bring down Paul to them (Acts 23:15). All other refs.: APPEAR <1718>, CHARGE (noun)[1] <1718>, MANIFEST (verb) <1718>, PLAINLY <1718>, REVEAL <1718>.

3 ***sēmainō*** [verb: σημαίνω <4591>]; **from *sēma*: mark, sign ▶ To communicate, to make known; also transl.: to specify** > Jesus signified by what death He would die (John 12:33; 18:32; 21:19). One ought to signify the charges against a prisoner (Acts 25:27). God signified the revelation of Jesus Christ by sending His angel to John (Rev. 1:1). Other ref.: Acts 11:28; see SHOW (verb) <4591>. ¶

– 4 Heb. 9:8; 12:27; 1 Pet. 1:11 → INDICATE <1213>.

SILAS – ***Silas*** [masc. name: Σιλᾶς <4609>]; **dimin. of Silvanus ▶ Christian man of Jerusalem** > Silas was chosen by the church of Jerusalem to accompany Paul and Barnabas in order to communicate to Christians of Antioch the decisions taken about questions concerning Jewish law (Acts 15:22, 27, 32; v. 34 in some mss.). A little later, he accompanied Paul in order to strengthen the churches of Syria and Cilicia (v. 40). Silas and Paul were miraculously freed from the prison at Philippi (Acts 16:19, 25, 29). Silas also accompanied Paul to Thessalonica and Berea (Acts 17:4, 10, 14, 15). He stayed at Thessalonica, and then met Paul at Corinth (Acts 18:5). See SILVANUS. ¶

SILENCE (noun) – 1 ***hēsuchia*** [fem. noun: ἡσυχία <2271>]; **from *hēsuchos*: calm ▶ Calm, tranquility** > The people kept the more silence when they heard Paul speak in Hebrew (Acts 22:2 {quiet, silent}). The woman is to learn in silence (1 Tim. 2:11 {quietly, in quietness}, 12 {quiet, quietly, in quietness, silent}). Other ref.: 2 Thes. 3:12; see QUIETNESS <2271>. ¶

2 ***sigē*** [fem. noun: σιγή <4602>] **▶ Absence of sound, the fact of keeping quiet** > A great silence {hush} was made among the people, and Paul was able to address them (Acts 21:40). When the seventh seal was opened, there was silence in heaven about half an hour (Rev. 8:1). ¶

3 **to keep silence: *sigaō*** [verb: σιγάω <4601>]; **from *sigē*: see 2 ▶ To be hidden, to not be manifested; also transl.: to keep hidden, to keep secret** > Paul speaks of the mystery (the church of the living God) concerning which silence had been kept for long ages past (Rom. 16:25). Other refs.: SILENT <4601>.

4 **to put to silence: *phimoō*** [verb: φιμόω <5392>]; **from *phimos*: muzzle; lit.: to muzzle ▶ To cause to be speechless** > Jesus had put to silence {silenced} the Sadducees (Matt. 22:34). By doing good, the Christians put to silence {silence} the ignorance of foolish men (1 Pet. 2:15). All other refs.: see MUZZLE <5392>, QUIET (adj.) <5392>, SPEECHLESS <5392>.

SILENCE (verb) – 1 Matt. 22:34; 1 Pet. 2:15 → to put to silence → SILENCE (noun) <5392> 2 Rom. 3:19; 2 Cor. 11:10 → STOP <5420> 3 Titus 1:11 → to stop the mouth → MOUTH (noun) <1993>.

SILENT – 1 **to be, to become, to fall, to keep, to remain silent: *hēsuchazō*** [verb: ἡσυχάζω <2270>]; **from *hēsuchos*: calm, quiet ▶ To hold one's peace, to say nothing** > The doctors of the law and the Pharisees were silent after hearing Jesus ask if it was lawful to heal on the Sabbath (Luke 14:4). People of the circumcision became silent and glorified God upon learning that He had also granted repentance to life to the nations (Acts 11:18 {to quiet down, to have no further objections}). When Paul would not be persuaded not to go up to Jerusalem, his companions were silent (Acts 21:14 {to cease, to give up}). All other refs.: QUIET (adj.) <2270>, REST (verb) <2270>.

2 **to be, to become, to keep, to remain silent, to fall silent: *sigaō*** [verb: σιγάω <4601>]; **from *sigē*: silence ▶ To remain quiet; also transl.: to be quiet, to hold one's peace, to keep quiet, to keep silence, to stop** > On the mountain, the disciples kept silent (Luke 9:36 {to keep close, to keep to oneself}). Astonished at the answer of Jesus about whether or not to pay taxes to

Caesar, the chief priests and the scribes were silent (Luke 20:26). Peter made a sign with his hand to those who were gathered in the house of Mary, the mother of Mark, to be silent (Acts 12:17). All the multitude kept silent and listened to Barnabas and Paul (Acts 15:12); and after they had become silent, then James spoke (v. 13 {to stop speaking, to finish}). If there is no interpreter, let him who speaks with a tongue be silent in the church (1 Cor. 14:28). If there is a revelation made to another brother who is seated in the church, he who has been speaking is to be silent (1 Cor. 14:30). Women are to be silent in the churches (1 Cor. 14:34). Other ref.: Rom. 16:25 (to keep silence); see SILENCE (noun) <4601>. ¶

3 **to be, to become, to keep silent: *siōpaō*** [verb: σιωπάω <4623>]; **from *siōpē*: silence ▶ To keep quiet, to remain mute; also transl.: to be quiet, to be still, to hold one's peace, to keep one's peace** > Jesus was silent (Matt. 26:63; Mark 14:61). Those who were in the synagogue were silent, without answering Jesus (Mark 3:4). Jesus told the sea to be still {to be mute} (Mark 4:39). The disciples remained silent (Mark 9:34). Zacharias was to be silent and unable to speak because he had not believed the words of the angel Gabriel (Luke 1:20). Jesus said that if the disciples were to be silent, the stones would cry out (Luke 19:40). The Lord told Paul to speak and not to be silent (Acts 18:9). Many rebuked Bartimaeus that he might be silent (Mark 10:48; Luke 18:39). Other ref.: Matt. 20:31. ¶

– 4 Acts 8:32 → DUMB <880> 5 Acts 21:40 → SILENCE (noun) <4602> 6 Acts 22:2; 1 Tim. 2:12 → SILENCE (noun) <2271>.

SILENT (BE) – Mark 1:25; Luke 4:35 → to be quiet → QUIET (adj.) <5392>.

SILK – **of silk: *sērikos*** [adj.: σηρικός <4596>]; **from *Sēres*: tribe of India, from whom silk (*sēr*) was obtained; also spelled: *sirikos* ▶ Glossy thread produced by the silkworm** > Babylon bought merchandise of silk from the merchants of the earth (Rev. 18:12). ¶

SILL – Acts 20:9 → window sill → WINDOW <2376>.

SILLY – 1 Eph. 5:4 → silly talk → foolish talk → FOOLISH <3473> 2 1 Tim. 4:7 → old wives' → OLD <1126>.

SILLY WOMAN – **gullible, silly, weak, weak-willed woman: *gunaikarion*** [neut. noun: γυναικάριον <1133>]; **dimin. of *gunē*: woman ▶ Foolish, immature person** > Paul speaks of those who lead captive silly women loaded down with sins (2 Tim. 3:6); such people are never able to come to the knowledge of the truth (see v. 7). ¶

SILOAM – ***Silōam*** [masc. name: Σιλωάμ <4611>]: **sent ▶ Pool of water at Jerusalem, fed by the spring of Gihon (see 2 Chr. 32:3, 4; Neh. 3:15; Is. 8:6)** > A tower in Siloam fell on eighteen people and killed them (Luke 13:4). Jesus sent a man who was blind from birth to wash himself to Siloam, and he returned seeing (John 9:7, 11). ¶

SILVANUS – ***Silouanos*** [masc. name: Σιλουανός <4610>]; **from *silva*: forest, in Lat. ▶ Christian man of Jerusalem** > Paul reminded the Corinthians that he, Silvanus, and Timothy had preached among them the Son of God, Jesus Christ (2 Cor. 1:19; see vv. 20, 21). Paul, Silvanus, and Timothy addressed his greetings to the church of Thessalonica (1 Thes. 1:1; 2 Thes. 1:1). Peter wrote his first letter by Silvanus, prob. the same believer (1 Pet. 5:12). See SILAS <4609>. ¶

SILVER – 1 ***arguros*** [masc. noun: ἄργυρος <696>]; **from *argos*: bright, shining ▶ Precious metal following gold in the scale of values** > The word is used by Jesus (Matt. 10:9), Paul (Acts 17:29; 1 Cor. 3:12), James (Jas. 5:3), and an angel (Rev. 18:12). ¶

2 **silver, of silver: *argureos*** [adj.: ἀργύρεος <693>]; **from *arguros*: see 1; also spelled: *argurous* ▶ Which is made in silver** > Demetrius made silver temples of the goddess Diana (Acts 19:24). In a great house (i.e., Christendom), there are vessels of silver

(2 Tim. 2:20). In the future, men will still be worshipping idols of silver (Rev. 9:20). ¶ [3] **money, silver, silver coin, piece of silver:** ***argurion*** [neut. noun: ἀργύριον <694>]; **from *arguros*: see [1] ▶ Coins of silver used to buy or sell >** The word is used in Matt. 25:18, 27; 26:15; 27:3, 5, 6, 9; 28:12, 15; Mark 14:11; Luke 9:3; 19:15, 23; 22:5; Acts 3:6; 7:16; 8:20a; 19:19; 20:33; 1 Pet. 1:18. ¶ – [4] Matt. 18:28 → silver coins → lit.: denarii → DENARIUS <1220> [5] Luke 15:8a, b, 9 → silver coin, piece of silver → COIN <1406> [6] Acts 19:24 → silver beater → SILVERSMITH <695>.

SILVERSMITH – ***argurokopos*** [masc. noun: ἀργυροκόπος <695>]; **from *arguros*: silver, and *koptō*: to beat repeatedly ▶ One who works with silver >** Demetrius was a silversmith {silver beater} making silver shrines of the goddess Diana (Acts 19:24). ¶

SIMEON – ***Sumeōn*** [masc. name: Συμεών <4826>]: **hearing, in Heb.; see Gen. 29:33 ▶ a. Son of Jacob and name of one of the twelve tribes descended from him >** Twelve thousand out of the tribe of Simeon will be sealed (Rev. 7:7). **b. Just and devout man living at Jerusalem >** He took the little child Jesus in his arms; he praised God and blessed the parents of Jesus (Luke 2:25, 34). **c. Other form of the name of Simon Peter >** James uses this name (Acts 15:14) as does Peter himself (2 Pet. 1:1). **d. Man of the O.T. >** This Simeon is mentioned in the genealogy of Jesus (Luke 3:30). **e. Christian man of Antioch >** See NIGER <3526>. ¶

SIMILAR – [1] Acts 19:25 → LIKE (adj., adv., noun) <5108> [2] Jude 7 → LIKE (adj., adv., noun) <3664>.

SIMILITUDE – [1] Rom. 5:14 → LIKENESS <3667> [2] Heb. 7:15 → LIKENESS <3665> [3] Jas. 3:9 → LIKENESS <3669>.

SIMON – ***Simōn*** [masc. name: Σίμων <4613>]: **hearing, in Heb. ▶ a. One of the twelve apostles called Peter >** Andrew had spoken to his brother Simon Peter about Jesus (John 1:41, 42); he brought him to Jesus who called him Cephas (v. 43). Jesus saw him and told him to come after Him (Matt. 4:18; see vv. 19, 20; Mark 1:16; see vv. 17, 18). Simon is listed first among the names of the twelve apostles (Matt. 10:2; Mark 3:16; Luke 6:14; 22:31a, b; John 21:2). He said that Jesus was the Christ, the Son of the living God (Matt. 16:16, 17), and that He had the words of eternal life (John 6:68). Jesus healed Simon's mother-in-law (Mark 1:29, 30; see v. 31; Luke 4:38; see v. 39; 5:3–10). Simon Peter cut off the right ear of the high priest's servant with his sword (John 18:10). He denied Jesus (John 18:15, 25); Jesus later restored His disciple (John 21:15–17). Other refs.: Matt. 17:24, 25, 27; Mark 1:36; 14:37; John 6:8, 9; 13:6, 9, 24, 36; 20:2, 6; 21:3, 7, 11; Acts 10:5, 18; 11:13. See P ETER <4074>. **b. Another of the twelve apostles >** Simon the Zealot, or Canaanite, was one of the twelve apostles (Matt. 10:4; Mark 3:18; Luke 6:15; Acts 1:13). **c. Man of Cyrene >** This Simon was constrained to bear the cross of Jesus (Matt. 27:32; Mark 15:21; Luke 23:26). **d. Man who was a Pharisee >** Simon the Pharisee received Jesus to eat at his table (Luke 7:40, 43, 44). **e. Man who was a magician >** Simon the magician believed in the name of Jesus Christ and was baptized. But he offered the apostles money that he might obtain the power to give the Holy Spirit by the laying on of hands. Peter severely rebuked him because of his iniquity (Acts 8:9, 13, 18, 24). **f. Man who was a tanner >** A certain Simon, a tanner, received Peter in his home at Joppa for several days (Acts 9:43; 10:6, 17, 32). **g. One of the brothers of Jesus >** This Simon is mentioned in Matt. 13:55; Mark 6:3. **h. Leprous man >** Jesus went to his house in Bethany, and a woman poured a perfume of great price on His head (Matt. 26:6; Mark 14:3). **i. Father of Judas Iscariot >** This Simon is mentioned in John 6:71; 12:4; 13:2, 26. ¶

SIMPLE – [1] ***akakos*** [adj. used as noun: ἄκακος <172>]; **from *a*: neg., and *kakos*: bad, wicked ▶ Person who is innocent, without malice >** Paul speaks of those who deceive the hearts of the simple {naive, unsuspecting} (Rom. 16:18). Other ref.: Heb. 7:26; see INNOCENT <172>. ¶

2 ***idiōtēs*** [masc. noun: ἰδιώτης <2399>]; **from *idios*: one's own ▶ Common person, person lacking professional knowledge** > He who speaks in the church is to take the simple {one who does not understand, ungifted, uninformed, unlearned} into account (1 Cor. 14:16, 23, 24). Paul considered himself to be a simple {not trained, rude, unskilled, untrained} person in regard to speech (2 Cor. 11:6). Other ref.: Acts 4:13; see UNINSTRUCTED <2399>. ¶

– 3 Luke 11:34 → SINGLE <573> 4 Rom. 16:19; Phil. 2:15 → INNOCENT <185> 5 Phil. 2:15 → PURE <185> 6 Jas. 5:12 → "simple" added in Engl.

SIMPLICITY – 1 ***haplotēs*** [fem. noun: ἁπλότης <572>]; **from *haplous*: simple, single ▶ Sincerity, generosity** > He who contributes to the needs of others is to do it with simplicity {with liberality, generously} (Rom. 12:8). Paul had conducted himself with simplicity {holiness} and sincerity before God (2 Cor. 1:12). He feared that the thoughts of the Corinthians might be corrupted from simplicity as to the Christ (2 Cor. 11:3). Servants are to obey their masters in simplicity {singleness} of heart (Eph. 6:5; Col. 3:22). Other refs.: 2 Cor. 8:2; 9:11, 13; see LIBERALITY <572>. ¶

2 ***aphelotēs*** [fem. noun: ἀφελότης <858>]; **same as *apheleia*: simplicity in the lifestyle, which is from *aphelēs*: not rugged, which is from *a*: neg., and *phelleus*: stony ground, i.e., smooth ▶ Without complication or exaggeration** > The early Christians received their food with gladness and simplicity {sincerity, singleness} of heart (Acts 2:46). ¶

SIMPLY – Acts 8:16; Gal. 6:12; 1 Thes. 1:5 → ONLY <3440>.

SIN (noun) – 1 ***hamartia*** [fem. noun: ἁμαρτία <266>]; **from *hamartanō*: to miss the mark, to go astray, hence: to commit a fault, to sin ▶ a. The principle of moral evil transmitted to all men from the disobedience of Adam; also generic manifestation of that principle** > Sin had affected the devil before the creation of man (1 John 3:8). It is characterized by insubordination to the will of God and His word, and leads to a lawless, unbridled walk (1 John 3:4a, b); it is made binding by death, which is its wages (Rom. 5:12a, b; 6:23). Before conversion, people are seen as being dead in their offences and sins (Eph. 2:1). God, having sent His own Son, in the likeness of flesh of sin, and for sin, has condemned sin in the flesh (Rom. 8:3a–c). Christ died for our sins (1 Cor. 15:3), i.e., for all the manifestations of the principle of evil, which is sin. Jesus Christ committed no sin (1 Pet. 2:22); He did not know sin (2 Cor. 5:21); there is no sin in Him (1 John 3:5). The word is found more than forty times in the Epistle to the Romans alone. **b. Offense constituted by disobeying the will and the word of God** > Paul asks the Corinthians if he had committed sin {an offence} in humbling himself (2 Cor. 11:7). *

2 ***hamartēma*** [neut. noun: ἁμάρτημα <265>]; **from *hamartanō*: see 1 ▶ Act of disobedience to the will of God** > The word is used in Mark 3:28; 4:12; Rom. 3:25; 1 Cor. 6:18. ¶

3 **who is without sin: *anamartētos*** [adj. used as noun: ἀναμάρτητος <361>]; **from *a*: neg., and *hamartanō*: see 1 ▶ Person who has never committed sin, who is without fault** > He who was without sin was to throw the first stone at the adulterous woman (John 8:7). ¶

– 4 Matt. 5:29, 30; 18:6, 8, 9; 1 Cor. 8:13a, b; 2 Cor. 11:29 → to cause to sin, to fall into sin, to lead into sin → lit.: to be offended → OFFEND <4624> 5 Matt. 13:41; 18:7; Luke 17:1 → thing that causes sin, thing that causes people to sin → STUMBLING BLOCK <4625> 6 Acts 8:23; Rom. 6:13 → INIQUITY <93> 7 Acts 13:39 → from every sin → lit.: from all things 8 Rom. 4:25; 2 Cor. 5:19; Gal. 6:1; Eph. 1:7; 2:5; Col. 2:13a, b; Jas. 5:16 → TRANSGRESSION <3900> 9 1 Cor. 14:24; Heb. 9:22 → "of sin," "of sins" added in Engl. 10 2 Thes. 2:3 → some mss. have "lawlessness" → LAWLESSNESS <458> 11 1 Tim. 5:22 → free from sin → PURE

<53> [12] Heb. 9:7 → sin committed in ignorance → IGNORANCE <51> [13] Heb. 9:15 → TRANSGRESSION <3847>.

SIN (verb) – [1] ***hamartanō*** [verb: ἁμαρτάνω <264>]; **lit.: to miss the mark ▶ To disobey the will of God, thus offending Him by such transgression >** We are to reprove our brother who sins against us (Matt. 18:15; Luke 17:3, 4). Judas had sinned by delivering up Jesus (Matt. 27:4). Jesus told a man whom He had healed to sin no more (John 5:14); likewise, a woman (8:11). The prodigal son had sinned against heaven and before his father (Luke 15:18, 21). As many as have sinned without law will perish also without law; and as many as have sinned under law will be judged by the law (Rom. 2:12a, b). All have sinned and come short of the glory of God (Rom. 3:23; also Rom. 5:12). He who commits sexual immorality sins against his own body (1 Cor. 6:18). If someone sins against the brothers, he sins against Christ (1 Cor. 8:12a, b). Paul says to be angry and not sin (Eph. 4:26). God did not spare the angels who had sinned (2 Pet. 2:4). If anyone sin, we have an advocate with the Father, Jesus Christ (1 John 2:1). From the beginning the devil sins (1 John 3:8). Everyone begotten of God does not sin (1 John 5:18), i.e., his new nature is incapable of sinning; he cannot sin (1 John 3:9); the old nature of Christians still remain with them. Other refs.: Matt. 18:21; John 9:2, 3; Acts 25:8 {to offend, to commit offense}; Rom. 5:14, 16; 6:15; 1 Cor. 7:28a, b, 36; 15:34; 1 Tim. 5:20; Titus 3:11; Heb. 3:17; 10:26; 1 John 1:10; 3:6a, b; 1 John 5:16 (see SIN TO DEATH). Other ref.: 1 Pet. 2:20 (to sin); see FAULT <264>. ¶
[2] **to sin before, earlier, in the past, already: *proamartanō*** [verb: προαμαρτάνω <4258>]; **from *pro*: before, and *hamartanō*: see [1] ▶ To sin previously, in the past >** Paul addressed those who had sinned before (2 Cor. 12:21; 13:2). ¶
– [3] Mark 9:42, 43, 45, 47; Luke 17:2 → lit.: to be offended → OFFEND <4624> [4] Luke 17:1 → temptation to sin → STUMBLING BLOCK <4625> [5] John 8:34 → lit.: to practice sin → PRACTICE (verb) <4160> <266> [6] Heb. 4:15; 1 John 3:4 → SIN (noun) <266> [7] Jas. 2:9 → lit.: to commit sin → COMMIT <2038> [8] Jas. 5:15 → lit.: to commit sin → COMMIT <4160>.

SIN TO DEATH – ***hamartia pros thanaton*; sin: *hamartia*** [fem. noun: ἁμαρτία <266>]; **death: *thanatos*** [masc. noun: θάνατος <2288>] **▶ Very serious sin committed by a believer in particular conditions intensifying his responsibility >** This sin (1 John 5:16) is such that God intervenes with an extreme form of discipline, removing a believer from the earth by death; v. 17 speaks of a sin that does not lead to death. We find two examples of sin leading to death in the N.T.: Ananias and Sapphira who lied to the Holy Spirit (see Acts 5:1–11), and believers at Corinth who were taking part in the Lord's Supper in an unworthy manner (see 1 Cor. 11:30). Divine punishment of this sort does not affect the believer's salvation, for we are saved by grace; it is rather related to the government of God, which reproves a public dishonor committed by a believer. Other refs. (*hamartia*): SIN <266>. Other refs. (*thanatos*): DEATH <2288>.

SINA – Acts 7:30, 38 → SINAI <4614>.

SINAI – ***Sina*** [neut. name: Σινᾶ <4614>] **▶ Mountain in Arabia, where Moses received the law of God (see Ex. 19:20); also transl.: Sina >** The covenant of Mount Sinai inaugurated the dispensation (or period) of the law for Israel, the earthly people of God. An angel (the Lord Himself) appeared in the wilderness of Mount Sinai (Acts 7:30, 38). In contrast, Jerusalem above represents the covenant of grace introduced by Jesus Christ (Gal. 4:24, 25; see v. 26). ¶

SINCE INDEED, SINCE NOW – ***epeiper*** [conj.: ἐπείπερ <1897>]; **from *epei*: upon, and *per*: truly, a particle of abundance or emphasis ▶** The word is used by Paul (Rom. 3:30). ¶ ‡

SINCERE – [1] ***anupokritos*** [adj.: ἀνυπόκριτος <505>]; **from *a*: neg., and *hu-***

***pokrinomai*: to pretend, which is from *hupo*: under, and *krinō*: to judge ▶ Without dissimulation, without hypocrisy; also transl.: genuine, unfeigned** > Love proceeds out of a pure heart, a good conscience, and sincere faith (1 Tim. 1:5). Paul called to remembrance the sincere faith that was in Timothy (2 Tim. 1:5). All other refs.: see without hypocrisy under HYPOCRISY <505>.
– 2 Luke 20:20 → RIGHTEOUS <1342> 3 Acts 2:46 → lit.: sincerity of → SIMPLICITY <858> 4 2 Cor. 11:3; Eph. 6:5 → lit.: sincerity → SIMPLICITY <572> 5 Phil. 1:10; 2 Pet. 3:1 → PURE <1506> 6 1 Tim. 3:8 → not double-tongued → DOUBLE-TONGUED <1351> 7 Heb. 10:22 → TRUE <228> 8 1 Pet. 2:2 → PURE <97>.

SINCERELY – 1 ***gnēsiōs*** [adv.: γνησίως <1104>]; **from *gnēsios*: legitimate ▶ Truly, genuinely** > Timothy sincerely cared for the welfare of the Philippians (Phil. 2:20 {naturally, with genuine feeling, with genuine interest}). ¶
– 2 Phil. 1:17 → PURELY <55>.

SINCERITY – 1 ***gnēsios*** [adj. used as noun: γνήσιος <1103>]; **from *genos*: born ▶ Truth, authenticity** > Paul spoke to prove the sincerity {genuineness} of the Corinthians' love (2 Cor. 8:8). Other refs.: Phil. 4:3; 1 Tim. 1:2; Titus 1:4; see TRUE <1103>. ¶
2 ***eilikrineia*** [fem. noun: εἰλικρίνεια <1505>]; **from *eilikrinēs*: pure, sincere; which is from *heilē*: shining of the sun, and *krinō*: to judge ▶ Purity, freedom from hypocrisy** > Christians celebrate the feast with unleavened bread of sincerity and truth (1 Cor. 5:8). Paul had conducted himself in simplicity and sincerity before God (2 Cor. 1:12). He spoke with sincerity in Christ (2 Cor. 2:17). ¶
– 3 Acts 2:46 → SIMPLICITY <858>.

SINEW – Col. 2:19 → BOND[1] <4886>.

SINFUL – 1 ***hamartōlos*** [adj.: ἁμαρτωλός <268>]; **from *hamartanō*: to miss the mark, to go astray, hence: to commit a fault ▶ Possessing the sinful nature and committing sins** > The Lord called His generation adulterous and sinful (Mark 8:38). Simon Peter acknowledged that he was a sinful man (Luke 5:8). If Jesus had been a sinful man, He could not have performed signs such as opening the eyes of a blind man (John 9:16). By the disobedience of Adam, men have been constituted sinners (Rom. 5:19). Sin has become exceeding sinful by the introduction of the law (Rom. 7:13). All other refs.: SINNER <268>.
– 2 Rom. 7:7 → is the law sinful? → lit.: the law is a sin? → SIN (noun) <266> 3 1 Pet. 2:11 → CARNAL <4559> 4 2 Pet. 1:4; 3:3; Jude 16 → sinful desires → LUST (noun) <1939>.

SING – 1 ***adō*** [verb: ᾄδω <103>] **▶ To make musical sounds with the voice** > Paul invites Christians to sing in their heart to the Lord (Eph. 5:19), and with grace (Col. 3:16). John saw the elders singing a new song (Rev. 5:9), as well as the one hundred and forty-four thousand (14:3); those who will have the victory over the beast will sing the song of Moses (15:3). ¶
2 ***psallō*** [verb: ψάλλω <5567>]; **from *psaō*: to touch lightly ▶ To play a stringed instrument, to sing praises to God** > Paul referred to a Psalm where it is written that David would sing {sing hymns} to the name of God (Rom. 15:9, quoting Ps. 18:49). Christians are exhorted to make melody {to make music} (or: to sing) with their heart to the Lord (Eph. 5:19). Paul would sing with the spirit, and with the understanding also (1 Cor. 14:15a, b). If anyone is happy, this person should sing psalms (Jas. 5:13). ¶
3 **to sing a hymn, to sing praise: *humneō*** [verb: ὑμνέω <5214>]; **from *humnos*: hymn ▶ To address a song of praise to God** > After His last meal, before being betrayed, Jesus sang a hymn with His disciples (Matt. 26:30; Mark 14:26). Other refs.: Acts 16:25; Heb. 2:12 (to sing praises); see PRAISE (noun) <5214>. ¶
– 4 Matt. 11:17; Luke 7:32 → to sing a dirge → MOURN <2354>.

SINGLE – 1 ***haplous*** [adj.: ἁπλοῦς <573>] ► **Which is in good condition; also transl.: clear, good, simple** > If the eye is simple, the whole body will be full of light (Matt. 6:22; Luke 11:34). ¶
– 2 1 Cor. 7:8 → "single" added in Engl. 3 1 Cor. 10:8, 12:19; Rev. 18:8, 10, 17, 19 → lit.: one.

SINGLENESS – 1 Acts 2:46 → SIMPLICITY <858> 2 Eph. 6:5; Col. 3:22 → SIMPLICITY <572>.

SINK (noun) – 1 Pet. 4:4 → EXCESS <401>.

SINK (verb) – 1 ***buthizō*** [verb: βυθίζω <1036>]; **from *buthos*: depth** ► **To drop beneath the surface of water** > The boats of the apostles were sinking (Luke 5:7). Other ref.: 1 Tim. 6:9; see PLUNGE <1036>. ¶
2 ***katapontizō*** [verb: καταποντίζω <2670>]; **from *kata*: down, and *pontizō*: to sink, which is from *pontos*: sea** ► **To drop beneath the surface of water, to plunge into the sea** > Having walked on the water, Peter began to sink (Matt. 14:30). It is better to be sunk {to drown} in the depths of the sea than to offend one of the little ones who believes in Jesus (Matt. 18:6). ¶
– 3 Acts 20:9 → FALL (verb) <2702>.

SINNER – 1 ***hamartōlos*** [adj. and adj. used as noun: ἁμαρτωλός <268>]; **from *hamartanō*: to miss the mark, to go astray, hence: to commit a fault** ► **One who possesses the sinful nature and commits sins; this is the natural state of every man and woman** > Jesus ate with those who were publicly known as sinners; moreover He had come to call sinners to repentance (Matt. 9:10, 11, 13; Mark 2:15–17; Luke 5:30, 32 {sinful ones}; 15:2). People reproached Him for being a friend of tax collectors and sinners (Matt. 11:19; Luke 7:34), and they accused Him of being a sinner (or: sinful) Himself (John 9:24, 25). Jesus said He was delivered up into the hands of sinners (Matt. 26:45; Mark 14:41; Luke 24:7). There is joy in heaven for one repenting sinner (Luke 15:7, 10). If Jesus had been a sinner, He could not have performed signs such as opening the eyes of a blind man (John 9:16). The word sometimes designates those who are not Jews (Rom. 3:7; Gal. 2:15). Christ has died for us, we being still sinners (Rom. 5:8). By the disobedience of Adam, men have been constituted sinners (Rom. 5:19). The Lord was separated from sinners (Heb. 7:26) on account of His nature, which is exempt from sin, and therefore incapable of sinning; but He came into the world to save sinners (1 Tim. 1:15). Other refs.: Luke 5:8; 6:32–34; 7:37, 39; 13:2; 15:1; 18:13; 19:7 {sinful man}; John 9:31; Rom. 7:13; Gal. 2:17; 1 Tim. 1:9 {sinful}; Heb. 12:3; Jas. 4:8; 5:20; 1 Pet. 4:18; Jude 15. ¶
2 ***opheiletēs*** [masc. noun: ὀφειλέτης <3781>]; **from *opheilō*: to owe** ► **One who owes something, one who is guilty** > The eighteen, who were killed when the tower in Siloam fell on them, were not worse sinners {worse culprits, worse debtors, more guilty) than all other men in Jerusalem (Luke 13:4). All other refs.: DEBTOR <3781>, OWE <3781>.
– 3 Rom. 5:14 → whose sinning → who had not sinned → SIN (verb) <264> 4 1 Tim. 2:14 → became a sinner → lit.: fell into transgression → TRANSGRESSION <3847>.

SION – See ZION <4622>.

SIR – 1 Matt. 21:30; 25:11a, b; 27:63; Luke 19:25; Acts 16:30; Rev. 7:14; et al. → LORD (noun) <2962> 2 Luke 13:8 → MASTER (noun) <2962> 3 Acts 27:10 → sirs → lit.: men → MAN <435>.

SISTER – 1 ***adelphē*** [fem. noun: ἀδελφή <79>]; **from *a*: connective particle, and *delphus*: uterus, womb** ► **a. Daughter of the same mother** > The term is used to designate the sisters of Jesus (Matt. 13:56; Mark 6:3), the members of a family (Matt. 19:29; Mark 10:29, 30; Luke 14:26; 1 Tim. 5:2), Mary and Martha, sisters of Lazarus (Luke 10:39, 40; John 11:1, 3, 5, 28, 39), Mary, the sister of the mother of Jesus (John 19:25), the sister of Paul (Acts 23:16), the sister of Nereus, and a Christian at Rome

(Rom. 16:15). **b. Female Christian; the term thus designates a spiritual relation in Christ, marking the unity of the family of God** > The word is used in Matt. 12:50; Mark 3:35; Rom. 16:1; 1 Cor. 7:15 {believing woman}; 9:5 {believing (wife)}; Phm. 2 (some mss.: beloved); Jas. 2:15; 2 John 13. ¶

– [2] Matt. 5:22a, b, 23; 18:15, 21, 35; 25:40; Luke 14:12; 17:3; 18:29; 21:16; et al. → the word does not appear in Greek mss.

SIT – [1] ***kathēmai*** [verb: κάθημαι <2521>]; **from *kata*: down (intens.), and *hēmai*: to sit ▶ To be on a seat; also transl.: to be seated** > Jesus sits at God's right hand until His enemies are made His footstool (Matt. 22:44; Mark 12:36; Luke 20:42; Acts 2:34; Heb. 1:13). Other refs.: Luke 21:35; see DWELL <2521>. All other refs.: Matt. 4:16a, b; 9:9; 11:16; 13:1, 2; 15:29; 20:30; 23:22; 24:3; 26:58, 64, 69; 27:19 {to set down}, 36, 61; 28:2; Mark 2:6, 14; 3:32, 34; 4:1; 5:15; 10:46; 13:3; 14:62; 16:5; Luke 1:79; 5:17, 27; 7:32; 8:35; 10:13; 18:35; 22:55, 56, 69; John 2:14; 6:3; 9:8; 12:15; Acts 2:2; 3:10; 8:28; 14:8; 20:9; 23:3; 1 Cor. 14:30; Col. 3:1; Jas. 2:3a, b; Rev. 4:2–4, 9, 10; 5:1, 7, 13; 6:2, 4, 5, 8, 16; 7:10, 15; 9:17; 11:16; 14:14–16; 17:1, 3, 9, 15; 18:7; 19:4, 11, 18, 19, 21; 20:11; 21:5. ¶

[2] **to sit with: *sunkathēmai*** [verb: συγκάθημαι <4775>]; **from *sun*: together, and *kathēmai*: see [1] ▶ To sit in company of someone** > Following Jesus at a distance, Peter sat with the servants (Mark 14:54). Those who sat with the king rose up after having heard Paul speaking for his defense (Acts 26:30). ¶

[3] **to sit, to sit down, to sit over: *kathizō*** [verb: καθίζω <2523>]; **from *kata*: down (intens.), and *hizō*: to sit, to cause to sit ▶ a. To install oneself; also transl.: to set, to set down** > Jesus sat down on the right hand of the majesty on high (Heb. 1:3; 8:1; 10:12). Other refs.: Luke 24:29; Acts 18:11; 1 Cor. 6:4 (to appoint to judge), see CONTINUE <2523>, JUDGE (verb) <2523>. All other refs.: Matt. 5:1; 13:48; 19:28a, b; 20:21, 23; 23:2; 25:31; 26:36; Mark 9:35; 10:37, 40; 11:2, 7; 12:41; 14:32; 16:19; Luke 4:20; 5:3; 14:28, 31; 16:6; 19:30; 22:30; John 8:2; 12:14; 19:13; Acts 2:30; 8:31; 12:21; 13:14; 16:13; 25:6, 17; 1 Cor. 10:7; Eph. 1:20; 2 Thes. 2:4; Heb. 12:2; Rev. 3:21a, b; 20:4. **b. To rest, to be placed** > Parted tongues, as of fire, sat upon each one of those who were gathered at Pentecost (Acts 2:3). ¶

[4] **to sit up: *anakathizō*** [verb: ἀνακαθίζω <339>]; **from *ana*: up, and *kathizō*: see [3] ▶ To straighten oneself up and sit** > Jesus raised a dead man who sat up (Luke 7:15). Seeing Peter, Tabitha sat up (Acts 9:40). ¶

[5] **to sit together, to sit down together: *sunkathizō*** [verb: συγκαθίζω <4776>]; **from *sun*: together, and *kathizō*: see [3] ▶ To sit in company of someone** > Those who took Jesus sat {were set} down together (Luke 22:55); *perikathizō* in some mss. God has made the Christians sit together in {seated with} Christ Jesus in the heavenlies (Eph. 2:6). ¶

[6] ***kathezomai*** [verb: καθέζομαι <2516>]; **from *kata*: down (intens.), and *hizō*: to sit ▶ To be on a seat** > Jesus's parents found Him sitting in the midst of the teachers (Luke 2:46). Jesus sat on Jacob's well (John 4:6). Mary of Bethany was sitting in the house (John 11:20). Jesus was sitting daily, teaching in the temple (Matt. 26:55). Mary Magdalene saw two angels sitting where the body of Jesus had lain (John 20:12). All who sat in the council saw the face of Stephen as the face of an angel (Acts 6:15). ¶

[7] ***parakathezomai*** [verb: παρακαθέζομαι <3869>]; **from *para*: near, and *kathezomai*: see [6] ▶ To sit beside** > Having sat down at the feet of Jesus, Mary of Bethany was listening to His word (Luke 10:39; other mss.: *parakathizō*). ¶

[8] **to sit down: *anaklinō*** [verb: ἀνακλίνω <347>]; **from *ana*: backward (intens.), and *klinō*: to lean, to bend ▶ To lie down at table, to recline** > Jesus speaks of people who will sit down {take their places} in the kingdom of heaven (Matt. 8:11; Luke 13:29 {in the kingdom of God}). Jesus commanded the multitude to sit down on the grass (Matt. 14:19; Mark 6:39), which they did (Luke 9:15). All other refs.: LAY <347>, TABLE[1] <347>.

[9] to sit down: *kataklinō* [verb: κατακλίνω <2625>]; **from *kata*: down, and *klinō*: to lean, to bend ▶ To make to lie to eat, to recline** > Jesus made the five thousand men to sit down by groups of fifty (Luke 9:14, 15). Other ref.: Luke 24:30; see "to be at table" under TABLE[1] <2625>. ¶

[10] to sit down: *anapiptō* [verb: ἀναπίπτω <377>]; **from *ana*: backward (intens.), and *piptō*: to fall ▶ To lie down for a meal (according to the Eastern manner of taking one's place at the table); also transl.: to recline** > At an occasion, Jesus commanded to the multitude to sit down {lie down} on the ground (Matt. 15:35; Mark 8:6). The one who is invited to a meal must go and sit down in {put himself down in, take} the lowest place (Luke 14:10). Jesus made five thousand men to sit down (John 6:10a, b); they sat down by hundreds and by fifties (Mark 6:40). Jesus sat down {was set down, reclined at the table, returned to his place} again after having washed the feet of His disciples (John 13:12). All other refs.: LEAN <377>, TABLE[1] <377>.

[11] to sit at table: *katakeimai* [verb: κατάκειμαι <2621>]; **from *kata*: down, and *keimai*: to lie ▶ To eat at a table** > Paul speaks of a Christian sitting at table {dining, eating, sitting at meat} in an idol's temple (1 Cor. 8:10). All other refs.: BEDRIDDEN (BE) <2621>, LAY <2621>, LIE (verb)[1] <2621>, TABLE[1] <2621>.

[12] *epibainō* [verb: ἐπιβαίνω <1910>]; **from *epi*: upon, and *bainō*: to go ▶ To mount an animal** > Jesus sat {was mounted, was riding} on a colt, the foal of a donkey (Matt. 21:5). All other refs.: BOARD <1910>, COME <1910>.

– [13] Matt. 9:10; 26:20; et al. → to sit, to sit down → to be at the table → TABLE[1] <345> [14] Matt. 21:7 → SET (verb) <1940> [15] John 6:11 → SET (verb) <345>.

SITUATE – *keimai* [verb: κεῖμαι <2749>] **▶ To establish, to set** > Believers in the Lord are the light of the world: a city situated on a mountain cannot be hidden (Matt. 5:14). Other refs.: APPOINT <2749>, LAID OUT (BE) <2749>, LAY <2749>, LIE (verb)[1] <2749>, STAND (verb) <2749>.

SITUATION – [1] Matt. 19:10 → CASE <156> [2] 1 Cor. 7:20 → CALLING <2821>.

SIX – *hex* [card. num.: ἕξ <1803>] ▶ This number is used in regard to days (Matt. 17:1; Mark 9:2; Luke 13:14; John 12:1), months (Luke 4:25; Acts 18:11; Jas. 5:17), vessels (John 2:6), brothers (Acts 11:12), and wings (Rev. 4:8). ¶

SIX HUNDRED AND SIXTY-SIX – [1] six hundred: *hexakosioi* [card. num.: ἑξακόσιοι <1812>], **sixty: *hexēkonta*** [card. num.: ἑξήκοντα <1835>], **six: *hex*** [card. num.: ἕξ <1803>] ▶ The number 666 is used in regard to the beast (Rev. 13:18). Some mss. have χξς for this number, corresponding to the letters *chi*, *xi*, and *stigma*, the *chi* standing for 600, the *xi* for 60, and the *stigma* for 6. ¶

[2] *chi xi stigma* [χξς <5516>] ▶ See [1]. Note that *stigma* is not used to spell any N.T. Greek words. ¶

SIXTH – *hektos* [ord. num.: ἕκτος <1623>]; **from *hex*: six** ▶ This number is used in regard to an hour (Matt. 20:5; 27:45; Mark 15:33; Luke 23:44; John 4:6; 19:14; Acts 10:9), a month (Luke 1:26, 36), a seal (Rev. 6:12), an angel (Rev. 9:13, 14; 16:12), and a foundation of the holy city (Rev. 21:20). ¶

SIXTY – [1] *hexēkonta* [card. num.: ἑξήκοντα <1835>]; **from *hex*: six** ▶ This number is used in regard to fruit (Matt. 13:8, 23; Mark 4:8, 20), stadia (Luke 24:13; one stadion was about 600 feet or 183 meters), and years (1 Tim. 5:9 {threescore}). ¶

– [2] Matt. 13:33 → sixty pounds → lit.: three measures → THREE <5140> [3] Luke 13:21 → sixty pounds → lit.: three measures → MEASURE (noun) <4568>.

SIZEABLE – Luke 7:12 → LARGE <2425>.

SKIFF – Acts 27:16, 30, 32 → BOAT <4627>.

SKILL – Acts 17:29 → IMAGINATION <1761>.

SKILLED – 1 Cor. 3:10 → WISE (adj.) <4680>.

SKIN – [1] ***derma*** [neut. noun: δέρμα <1192>]; **from *derō*: to remove the skin ▶ The covering of an animal body** > O.T. believer went about in goatskins (lit.: skins of goat) (Heb. 11:37). ¶
– [2] Matt. 9:17; Mark 2:22; Luke 5:37, 38 → WINESKIN <779> [3] Mark 1:6 → of skin → LEATHER <1193> [4] Acts 19:12 → i.e., the surface of the body → BODY <5559> [5] Heb. 11:37 → skins of sheep → SHEEPSKIN <3374>.

SKULL – ***Kranion*** [neut. name: Κρανίον <2898>]; **comp. *kara*: head ▶ Rock near Jerusalem having the form of a skull; in Aram.: *Golgotha*; in Lat.: *Cranium*** > Jesus was crucified between two criminals at the Place of the Skull, which is called Golgotha (Matt. 27:33; Mark 15:22; Luke 23:33; John 19:17). ¶

SKY – [1] Matt. 16:3; et al. → HEAVEN <3772> [2] Acts 19:35 → the sacred stone that fell from the sky → lit.: that (i.e., the stone or the statue) fallen from the sky → FALL (verb) <1356> [3] Phil. 2:15 → like stars in the sky → like lights in the world → WORLD <2889> [4] Rev. 9:2 → AIR <109>.

SLACK – 2 Pet. 3:9 → to be slack → DELAY (verb) <1019>.

SLAIN – Acts 7:42 → slain beast → BEAST <4968>.

SLANDER (noun) – [1] Matt. 12:31; 15:19; Mark 3:28; 7:22; Eph. 4:31; Col. 3:8; Jude 9 → injurious language → BLASPHEMY <988> [2] Mark 3:28; 1 Tim. 6:4 → injurious speech, injurious words → INJURIOUS <988> [3] 2 Cor. 6:8 → bad report, evil report → REPORT (noun) <1426> [4] 2 Cor. 12:20; 1 Pet. 2:1 → BACKBITING <2636> [5] 1 Tim. 5:14 → REPROACH (noun) <3059> [6] Jude 10 → REVILE <987> [7] Rev. 2:9 → RAILING <988>.

SLANDER (verb) – [1] Rom. 2:24; 1 Tim. 6:1 → BLASPHEME <987> [2] 1 Cor. 4:13 → DEFAME <987> [3] 1 Cor. 10:30 → to speak evil → EVIL (adv.) <987> [4] Titus 3:2; Jude 10 → REVILE <987> [5] Jas. 4:11a; 1 Pet. 2:12; 3:16 → to speak against → SPEAK <2635>.

SLANDERER – [1] Rom. 1:30 → BACKBITER <2637> [2] 1 Cor. 5:11 → ABUSIVE <3060> [3] 1 Tim. 3:11; 2 Tim. 3:3; Titus 2:3 → false accuser → ACCUSER <1228>.

SLANDEROUS – 2 Tim. 3:3 → false accuser → ACCUSER <1228>.

SLANDEROUSLY – Rom. 3:8 → to report slanderously → REPORT (verb) <987>.

SLAP (noun) – **slap in the face: *rhapisma*** [neut. noun: ῥάπισμα <4475>]; **from *rhapizō*: to strike with the hand ▶ Blow with the flat of the hand** > The officers struck (lit.: received) Jesus with slaps in the face (Mark 14:65). Other refs.: John 18:22; 19:3; see BLOW <4475>. ¶

SLAP (verb) – [1] ***rhapizō*** [verb: ῥαπίζω <4474>]; **from *rhapis*: rod; primary meaning: to strike with a rod ▶ To hit the face with the palm of the hand; also transl.: to smite, to strike** > If someone slaps on the right cheek, one is to turn to him the other cheek (Matt. 5:39). Some slapped Jesus (Matt. 26:67). ¶
– [2] Luke 6:29 → STRIKE <5180> [3] John 18:22; 19:3 → to give a slap → GIVE <1325>, SLAP (noun) <4475> [4] 2 Cor. 11:20 → BEAT <1194>.

SLAUGHTER (noun) – [1] ***kopē*** [fem. noun: κοπή <2871>]; **from *koptō*: to cut down, to smite, to slay ▶ Carnage, defeat** > Melchizedek met Abraham returning from the slaughter of {smiting} the kings and blessed him (Heb. 7:1). ¶
[2] ***sphagē*** [fem. noun: σφαγή <4967>]; **from *sphazō*: to kill, to cut the throat ▶ Killing of an animal, butchering** > Jesus was led as a sheep to the slaughter (Acts 8:32). Paul quotes a verse from the O.T.: "For your

sake, we are put to death all day long; we are accounted as sheep for the slaughter" (Rom. 8:36; see Ps. 44:22). The rich have nourished their hearts as in a day of slaughter (Jas. 5:5). ¶

– 3 Acts 9:1 → MURDER (noun) <5408>.

SLAUGHTER (verb) – 1 Matt. 22:4 → KILL <2380> 2 Luke 19:27 → KILL <2695> 3 Rom. 8:36 → to be slaughtered → lit.: for the slaughter → SLAUGHTER (noun) <4967> 4 Rev. 18:24 → SLAY <4969>.

SLAUGHTERED – Acts 7:42 → slaughtered animal → slain beast → BEAST <4968>.

SLAVE (noun) – 1 ***doulon*** [masc. noun: δοῦλον <1400>]**; acc. of *doulos*: slave ► Bondservant, household servant; also transl.: bondage, slavery** > Paul establishes a contrast for Christians between formerly yielding their members as slaves {servants} of uncleanness and presently yielding them as slaves {servants} of righteousness (Rom. 6:19a, b). ¶

2 See SERVANT <1401> <3610>.

– 3 Luke 12:45; John 18:17; Acts 16:16; Gal. 4:22, 23, 30a, b, 31 → slave girl, slave woman → SERVANT GIRL <3814> 4 John 8:33; Acts 7:7; Gal. 4:8, 9 → BONDAGE <1398> 5 Rom. 6:6; 16:18 → to be a slave → SERVE <1398> 6 Rom. 6:18, 22; 1 Cor. 9:19; Titus 2:3; 2 Pet. 2:19 → to become a slave, to make oneself a slave, to be the slave → to bring into bondage → BONDAGE <1402> 7 Rom. 8:15; Gal. 4:24 → that makes one a slave, to be a slave → lit.: slavery → BONDAGE <1397> 8 1 Cor. 9:27 → to make his slave → to bring into subjection → SUBJECTION <1396> 9 2 Cor. 11:20; Gal. 2:4 → to make slaves → to bring into bondage → BONDAGE <2615> 10 1 Tim. 6:2 → "of the slaves" added in Engl. 11 Rev. 18:13 → BODY <4983>.

SLAVE (verb) – Luke 15:29 → SERVE <1398>.

SLAVE TRADER – 1 Tim. 1:10 → KIDNAPPER <405>.

SLAVERY – 1 Rom. 6:19a, b → SLAVE (noun) <1400> 2 Rom. 8:15, 21; Gal. 4:24; 5:1; Heb. 2:15 → BONDAGE <1397> 3 Gal. 2:4 → BONDAGE <2615> 4 Gal. 4:3 → to be in slavery → to bring into bondage → BONDAGE <1402> 5 Gal. 4:25 → to be in slavery → to be in bondage → BONDAGE <1398>.

SLAY – 1 ***sphazō*** [verb: σφάζω <4969>] ► **To put to death, to slaughter, to offer a victim in sacrifice** > The Lord Jesus is represented as the Lamb who was slain (Rev. 5:6, 9, 12; 13:8). John also saw under the altar the souls of those who had been slain for the word of God (Rev. 6:9). He saw one of the heads of the beast as if it had been slain {had been mortally wounded} (lit.: had been slaughtered to death) (Rev. 13:3). Babylon is responsible for the blood of people slain {slaughtered} on the earth (Rev. 18:24). All other refs.: KILL <4969>, MURDER (verb) <4969>.

2 **death: *phonos*** [masc. noun: φόνος <5408>]**; from *phenō*: to kill ► Murder, slaughter** > O.T. people of faith were slain with the sword (lit.: were put to death with the sword) (Heb. 11:37). Other refs.: DEATH <5408>, MURDER (noun) <5408>.

– 3 Matt. 2:16; Acts 5:33, 36; 9:29; 10:39; 12:2; 13:28; 22:20 → KILL <337> 4 Matt. 22:6; Luke 9:22; John 5:18; Acts 7:52; Rom. 7:11; Eph. 2:16; Rev. 2:13 6:8; 9:15; 11:13; 13:10a, b, 15; 19:21 → KILL <615> 5 Matt. 23:31, 35 → KILL <5407> 6 Mark 14:12 → SACRIFICE (verb) <2380> 7 Acts 2:23 (to put to death) → DEATH <337> 8 Acts 5:30 → MURDER (verb) <1315> 9 Acts 10:13; 11:7 → KILL <2380> 10 2 Thes. 2:8 → CONSUME <355> 11 Heb. 7:8 → lit.: to die by murder of sword → DIE <599>.

SLEEP (noun) – 1 ***hupnos*** [masc. noun: ὕπνος <5258>] ► **State of a person who is not awake, dormant** > The term is used in regard to Joseph (Matt. 1:24), Peter and those who were with him (Luke 9:32),

Eutychus (Acts 20:9a, b), and Christians in a spiritual sense (Rom. 13:11 {slumber}). People thought that Jesus had spoken of natural sleep, whereas He had spoken of the death of Lazarus (John 11:13). ¶

2 **awaking from, awaking out of, being awakened out of, roused out of sleep: *exupnos*** [adj.: ἔξυπνος <1853>]; **from *ek*: out, and *hupnos*: see 1 ▶ Awake, not sleeping anymore** > Awaking from sleep {Waking up}, the jailer saw the prison doors open (Acts 16:27). ¶

– 3 John 11:11 → to awake out of sleep → WAKE UP <1852> 4 2 Cor. 11:27 → without sleep → SLEEPLESSNESS <70>.

SLEEP (verb) – 1 **to fall asleep: *aphupnoō*** [verb: ἀφυπνόω <879>]; **from *apo*: intens., and *hupnoō*: to fall asleep, which is from *hupnos*: sleep ▶ To fall in a state of physical sleep** > Jesus fell asleep in the boat (Luke 8:23). ¶

2 **to be asleep, to sleep, to fall asleep: *katheudō*** [verb: καθεύδω <2518>]; **from *kata*: down, and *heudō*: to sleep ▶ a. To be in or to enter a state of physical sleep** > The verb is used about Jesus (Matt. 8:24; Mark 4:38), His disciples (Matt. 26:40, 43, 45; Mark 14:37a, b, 40, 41; Luke 22:46), men in parables (Matt. 13:25; Mark 4:27), the ten virgins in a parable (Matt. 25:5), and men in general (1 Thes. 5:7a, b). **b. To be in or to enter a state of spiritual sleep** > The verb is used about the disciples of Jesus (Mark 13:36), men in general (Eph. 5:14), and Christians (1 Thes. 5:6). **c. Term describing the physical death of the Christian** > At the coming of Christ, some Christians will be awake, others will sleep, but all will live together with Him (1 Thes. 5:10). **d. To be in a state of physical (but not spiritual or eternal) death** > The verb is used about the daughter of a ruler, where the Lord said she had not died (*apothnēskō*) but slept (*katheudō*) (Matt. 9:24; Mark 5:39; Luke 8:52). ¶

3 **to sleep, to fall asleep: *koimaō*** [verb: κοιμάω <2837>]; **from *keimai*: to lie, to lie down ▶ a. To be in a state of physical sleep** > The verb is used about the guards at the tomb of Jesus (Matt. 28:13), the disciples of Jesus (Luke 22:45), Lazarus (John 11:12), and Peter (Acts 12:6). **b. Verb describing the physical death of the Christian** > Many Christians among the Corinthians were sleeping (1 Cor. 11:30). Paul did not want the Thessalonians to be ignorant concerning those who had fallen asleep (1 Thes. 4:13). The verb is also used in the case of saints who had died before Jesus and were raised when Jesus yielded up His spirit (Matt. 27:52), Lazarus (John 11:11), Stephen (Acts 7:60), David (Acts 13:36), a Christian husband (1 Cor. 7:39 {to be dead, to die}), Christians in Corinth (1 Cor. 15:6), Christians in general (1 Cor. 15:18, 20; 1 Thes. 4:14, 15), and the fathers among the Israelites, e.g., Abraham, Jacob (2 Pet. 3:4). The Christians will not all sleep (i.e., be dead) before the coming of the Lord (1 Cor. 15:51). ¶

SLEEPER – Eph. 5:14 → lit.: he who sleeps → SLEEP (verb) <2518>.

SLEEPING – 1 1 Cor. 5:1 → to be sleeping with → lit: to have 2 2 Pet. 2:3 → to be sleeping → SLUMBER (verb) <3573>.

SLEEPLESS – 2 Cor. 6:5; 11:27 → sleepless nights → SLEEPLESSNESS <70>.

SLEEPLESSNESS – ***agrupnia*** [fem. noun: ἀγρυπνία <70>]; **from *agrupnos*: who does not sleep, which is from *agreō*: to chase, and *hupnos*: sleep ▶ Time when one does not sleep; also transl.: sleepless nights, watchings, without sleep** > Paul uses this term in relation to his hours of insomnia, perhaps in prison (2 Cor. 6:5; 11:27). ¶

SLEIGHT – 1 Eph. 4:14 → TRICKERY <2940> 2 Eph. 4:14 → CUNNING <3834>.

SLIDE – John 5:13 → to slide away → WITHDRAW <1593>.

SLIP – 1 Luke 5:16 → to slip away → WITHDRAW <5298> 2 John 5:13 → to slip away → WITHDRAW <1593> 3 2 Cor. 11:33 → ESCAPE <1628> 4 Gal.

2:4 → to slip in → to be secretly brought in → SECRETLY <3920> 5 Heb. 2:1 → to slip away → to drift away → DRIFT <3901>.

SLOPE – Matt. 8:32; Mark 5:13; Luke 8:33 → steep slope → steep place → PLACE (noun) <2911>.

SLOTHFUL – 1 ***oknēros*** [adj.: ὀκνηρός <3636>]; **from *okneō*: to delay, or *oknos*: hesitation ▶ Indolent, idle** > In a parable, a lord accused his bondman of being wicked and slothful {lazy} (Matt. 25:26). As regard diligent zealousness, Christians ought not to be slothful {lagging, lacking} (Rom. 12:11). Other ref.: Phil. 3:1; see TEDIOUS <3636>. ¶
– 2 Heb. 6:12 → SLUGGISH <3576>.

SLOW – 1 ***bradus*** [adj.: βραδύς <1021>] ▶ **Not quick to understand or to act** > The disciples of Emmaus were slow of heart to believe in all that the prophets had said (Luke 24:25). Every man should be slow to speak, slow to wrath (Jas. 1:19a, b). ¶
– 2 Titus 1:12 → LAZY <692> 3 Heb. 5:11 → SLUGGISH <3576> 4 2 Pet. 3:9 → to be slow → DELAY (verb) <1019>.

SLOWLY – Acts 27:7 → to sail slowly → SAIL (verb) <1020>.

SLUGGISH – ***nōthros*** [adj.: νωθρός <3576>] ▶ **Slow, apathetic** > The author of the Epistle to the Hebrews did not want his readers to be sluggish {slothful, lazy}, but rather that they might show diligence to the full assurance of hope to the end (Heb. 6:12); they had become sluggish {dull, slow} in hearing (5:11). ¶

SLUMBER (noun) – Rom. 13:11 → SLEEP (noun) <5258>.

SLUMBER (verb) – 1 ***nustazō*** [verb: νυστάζω <3573>]; **from *neuō*: to nod; lit.: to let the head fall ▶ a. To become sleepy, somnolent; also transl.: to be asleep, to be sleeping** > In the parable, while the bridegroom tarried, all the virgins slumbered {got drowsy, became drowsy, grew heavy} and slept (Matt. 25:5). **b. To delay** > The destruction of false teachers does not slumber (2 Pet. 2:3). ¶
– 2 Luke 9:32 → to be very sleepy → to be overcome with sleep → SLEEP (noun) <5258>.

SLY WAY – Matt. 26:4; Mark 14:1 → SUBTLETY <1388>.

SMALL, SMALLEST – 1 Matt. 13:32; Mark 4:31; Luke 19:3; Acts 8:10; 26:22; Jas. 3:5a; Rev. 11:18; 13:16; 19:5, 18; 20:12 → LITTLE <3398> 2 Luke 12:26; 1 Cor. 6:2; Jas. 3:4 → as small as that, smallest, very small → LEAST <1646> 3 Jas. 3:5b → LITTLE <3641>.

SMELL – 1 1 Cor. 12:17 → sense of smell → SMELLING <3750> 2 2 Cor. 2:16a → ODOR <3744> 3 Phil. 4:18 → sweet smell → sweet odor → ODOR <2175>.

SMELLING – ***osphrēsis*** [fem. noun: ὄσφρησις <3750>]; **from *osphrainomai*: to smell ▶ Sense which permits perceiving odors** > Paul asks where the smelling {sense of smell} would be if the whole body were hearing (1 Cor. 12:17). ¶

SMITE – 1 Matt. 5:39 → SLAP (verb) <4474> 2 Matt. 24:49 → BEAT <5180> 3 Matt. 26:31, 51; Mark 14:27; Luke 22:49, 50; Acts 7:24; 12:7, 23; Rev. 11:6; 19:15 → to strike, to strike down → STRIKE <3960> 4 Matt. 26:51 → to smite off → to cut off → CUT <851> 5 Matt. 26:68; Mark 14:47; Luke 22:64; John 18:10 → STRIKE <3817> 6 Luke 6:29; 18:13; 23:48; Acts 23:2, 3a, b → STRIKE <5180> 7 Luke 22:63; John 18:23; 2 Cor. 11:20 → BEAT <1194> 8 John 19:3 → to smite with the hands → to give a blow on the face → BLOW (noun) <4475> 9 Rev. 8:12 → STRIKE <4141>.

SMITER – 1 Tim. 1:9 → smiter of father, smiter of mother → murderer of father, murderer of mother → MURDERER <3964> <3389>.

SMITH – 2 Tim. 4:14 → COPPERSMITH <5471>.

SMITING – Heb. 7:1 → SLAUGHTER (noun) <2871>.

SMOKE – ***kapnos*** [masc. noun: καπνός <2586>] ► **Gaseous product resulting from the combustion of material** > This term appears in Acts 2:19 and a dozen times in Revelation (8:4; 9:2a–c, 3, 17, 18; 14:11; 15:8; 18:9, 18; 19:3). ¶

SMOKING – **to smoke:** ***tuphō*** [verb: τύφω <5188>] ► **To rise up in smoke, to undergo slow combustion** > Jesus would not quench a smoking flax {smoldering wick} (Matt. 12:20). ¶

SMOLDERING – Matt. 12:20 → SMOKING <5188>.

SMOOTH – [1] ***leios*** [adj.: λεῖος <3006>] ► **Leveled, of an equal plane** > The rough ways will become smooth ways (Luke 3:5; see Is. 40:4). ¶
[2] **smooth word, smooth talk:** ***chrēstologia*** [fem. noun: χρηστολογία <5542>]; **from** ***chrēstos*****: good, fine, and** ***logos*****: word** ► **Nice word, sugary language** > Those who cause divisions and offenses by smooth words {good words, smooth} and flattering speech deceive the hearts of the simple (Rom. 16:18). ¶

SMYRNA – [1] ***Smurna*** [fem. name: Σμύρνα <4667>]**: myrrh** ► **City of western Asia Minor, north of Ephesus** > One of the seven letters of the book of Revelation is addressed to Smyrna (Rev. 1:11; 2:8 in some mss.). ¶
[2] **of Smyrna:** ***Smurnaios*** [adj.: Σμυρναῖος <4668>]; **from** ***Smurna*****: see** [1] ► **Which is of Smyrna** > The Lord addresses the church of Smyrna (Rev. 2:8 in other mss.). He recognizes her tribulation and poverty, and He warns that she will suffer yet more (see 2:9, 10). ¶

SNAKE – [1] Matt. 7:10; 10:16; 23:33; Mark 16:18; Luke 10:19; 11:11; John 3:14; 1 Cor. 10:9; Rev. 9:19 → SERPENT <3789> [2] Acts 28:4, 5 → BEAST <2342>.

SNARE – [1] ***pagis*** [fem. noun: παγίς <3803>]; **from** ***pēgnumi*****: to set up, to fix** ► **Mechanism used for trapping; devious means for causing a difficulty; also transl.: trap** > The kingdom of God will come as a snare on all those who dwell on the face of the whole earth (Luke 21:34 or 35). David says to let the table of the Jews become a snare to them (Rom. 11:9). The expr. "snare of the devil" is used in 1 Tim. 3:7 and 2 Tim. 2:26 to describe the seduction of Satan. Those who desire to be rich fall into a snare (1 Tim. 6:9). ¶
– [2] Matt. 5:29, 30; 18:9; Mark 9:42, 43, 45, 47; Luke 7:23; 17:2 → to be a snare, to serve as a snare → OFFEND <4624> [3] 1 Cor. 7:35 → LEASH <1029> [4] Rev. 2:14 → STUMBLING BLOCK <4625>.

SNATCH – [1] Matt. 13:19; John 10:12, 28, 29 → to snatch away, to snatch → SEIZE <726> [2] Acts 8:39; Rev. 12:5 → to snatch away, to snatch up → to catch away, to catch up → CATCH (verb) <726> [3] Acts 24:7 → to take out → TAKE <520> [4] Jude 23 → to snatch out → to pull out → PULL <726>.

SNEAK – Gal. 2:4 → to sneak in → to come in surreptitiously → SURREPTITIOUSLY <3922>.

SNEER – [1] ***ekmuktērizō*** [verb: ἐκμυκτηρίζω <1592>]; **from** ***ek*****: of (intens.), and** ***muktērizō*****: to mock, which is from** ***muktēr*****: nose, nostril** ► **To mock at** > The rulers sneered at {derided} Jesus (Luke 23:35). Other ref.: Luke 16:14; see MOCK <1592>. ¶
– [2] Acts 17:32 → MOCK <5512>.

SNOW – ***chiōn*** [fem. noun: χιών <5510>] ► **Frozen water that falls from the sky in light, white flakes** > The clothes of Jesus became white as the snow at His transfiguration (Mark 9:3 in some mss.). The angel sitting on the stone at the tomb of Jesus had clothing white as snow (Matt. 28:3). In the vision of John at Patmos, the Son of Man had hair white like white wool, as snow (Rev. 1:14). ¶

SNUFF – Matt. 12:20 → to snuff out → QUENCH <4570>.

SO! – Mark 15:29 → HA! <3758>.

SO AS – Matt. 24:24 → THAT <5620>.

SO FAR – Rom. 1:13 → HITHERTO <1204>.

SO THAT – 1 ***hina*** [conj.: ἵνα <2443>] ▶ **That, so that, for the purpose of** >Also used to indicate the cause for, or on account of which anything is done. Can be transl.: to the end that, in order that it might [or may] be. It may also be used simply to indicate a happening, event or result of anything, or that in which the action terminates. The Greek word can be transl.: so that it was (is, or will be). ‡
2 ***hopōs*** [adv.: ὅπως <3704>] ▶ **In order that, for this reason** > This word is used in Matt. 2:8, 23; 5:16, 45; 6:4, 18; 8:17; 13:35; 26:59 {to}; Luke 2:35; 16:26; Acts 8:24; 9:2; 15:17; 20:16 {because}; Rom. 3:4; 1 Cor. 1:29; 2 Thes. 1:12; Phm. 6; Heb. 2:9; 9:15; Jas. 5:16; it is transl. by various words and exprs. *
3 ***hōs*** [adv.: ὡς <5613>] ▶ **Used as a conjunction of purpose: in order that, if only** > Paul made no account of his life, so that he might finish his course (Acts 20:24). *
4 ***hōste*** [conj.: ὥστε <5620>] ▶ **Insomuch that, therefore** > This Greek word is used in Matt. 8:24, 28; 12:22; 13:2, 32; 15:31; 23:31; 27:14; Mark 1:45; 2:28; 3:10; 4:1, 32; 9:26; 15:5; Acts 1:19; 5:15; 15:39; Rom. 7:6; 2 Cor. 5:16, 17; Phil. 1:13; 1 Thes. 1:8; 2 Thes. 1:4; 2:4; Heb. 13:6; 1 Pet. 1:21; it is transl. by various words and exprs. Other refs.: THAT <5620>.
– 5 Matt. 4:6; 5:25; Luke 4:11; 12:58; 21:34; Heb. 2:1 → LEST <3379> 6 1 Cor. 9:27; 2 Cor. 2:7 → LEST <3381>.

SO TO SPEAK – **word: *epos*** [neut. noun: ἔπος <2031>]; **from *epō*: to speak** ▶ The expr. "so to speak" is lit. "as to say a word" in Heb. 7:9. ¶

SOAK – John 19:29 → FILL (verb) <4130>.

SOBER – 1 **to be sober: *nēphō*** [verb: νήφω <3525>] ▶ **To not be under the influence of a substance that excites; to be calm and concentrated** > Christians are to be sober {to be self-controlled} (1 Thes. 5:6, 8). Timothy was to be sober {to watch, to be watchful, to keep one's head} in all things (2 Tim. 4:5). Peter exhorts to be sober (1 Pet. 1:13 {to keep sober, to be self-controlled, to be vigilant}). Other refs.: 1 Pet. 4:7; 5:8. ¶
– 2 Acts 26:25 → sober truth → lit.: truth and soberness → SOBERNESS <4997> 3 2 Cor. 5:13 → to be sober → to be of sound mind → MIND (noun) <4993> 4 1 Tim. 3:2; Titus 1:8 → DISCREET <4998> 5 1 Tim. 3:2, 11; Titus 2:2 → TEMPERATE <3524> 6 Titus 2:6; 1 Pet. 4:7 → to be sober → to be self-controlled → SELF-CONTROLLED <4993>.

SOBER-MINDED – 1 1 Cor. 15:34 → to become sober-minded → lit.: to awake righteously → AWAKE (verb) <1594>, JUSTLY <1346> 2 1 Tim. 3:2; Titus 1:8 → DISCREET <4998> 3 1 Tim. 3:2, 11; Titus 2:2 → TEMPERATE <3524> 4 Titus 2:6 → to be sober-minded → to be self-controlled → SELF-CONTROLLED <4993> 5 1 Pet. 1:13, 5:8 → to be sober-minded → to be sober → SOBER <3525> 6 1 Pet. 4:7 → to be sober-minded → WATCH (verb) <3525>.

SOBERLY – 1 ***sōphronōs*** [adv.: σωφρόνως <4996>]; **from *sōphrōn*: sober-minded, which is from *sōos*: sound, and *phrēn*: mind, understanding** ▶ **With self-control, moderately** > The grace of God teaches Christians to live soberly {self-controlled, sensibly}, justly, and piously in the present age (Titus 2:12). ¶
– 2 Rom. 12:3 → lit.: so as to have sound judgment → JUDGMENT <4993>.

SOBERNESS – ***sōphrosunē*** [fem. noun: σωφροσύνη <4997>]; **from *sōphron*: of a**

sound mind, temperate, which is from *sōs*: healthy, and *phrēn*: spirit, reason ▶ Sound mind, wisdom > Paul uttered words of truth and soberness {truth and reason, sober truth} before Festus (Acts 26:25). Other refs.: 1 Tim. 2:9, 15; see MODERATION <4997>. ¶

SOBRIETY – 1 Tim. 2:9, 15 → MODERATION <4997>.

SODOM – ***Sodoma*** [neut. plur. name: Σόδομα <4670>]**: burning, in Heb. ▶ City of the plain of the Jordan River; see GOMORRAH** <1116> > Lot went out from Sodom to escape divine punishment (Luke 17:29), being urged by two angels (see Gen. 19:15, 16). The Lord recalls that, in the Day of Judgment, the lot of Sodom will be more bearable than that of Capernaum (Matt. 11:23, 24; Luke 10:12). Jerusalem, the sinful city guilty of having crucified the Lord, and which will yet persecute His witnesses, is called spiritually Sodom (Rev. 11:8). Other refs.: Matt. 10:15; Rom. 9:29; 2 Pet. 2:6; Jude 7. ¶

SODOMITE – 1 Cor. 6:9; 1 Tim. 1:10 → HOMOSEXUAL <733>.

SOFT – Matt. 11:8a, b; Luke 7:25 → DELICATE <3120>.

SOIL – Rev. 3:4 → DEFILE <3435>.

SOJOURN (noun) – Acts 13:17; 1 Pet. 1:17 → STAY (noun) <3940>.

SOJOURN (verb) – [1] Luke 24:18 → VISIT (verb) <3939> [2] John 11:54 → STAY (verb) <1304> [3] Acts 17:21 → STAY (verb) <1927> [4] Heb. 11:9a → DWELL <3939>.

SOJOURNER – [1] ***parepidēmos*** [adj. and adj. used as noun: παρεπίδημος <3927>]**; from *para*: near, and *epidēmos*: stranger, which is from *epi*: among, and *dēmos*: people ▶ Pilgrim, one who resides in a strange place temporarily, near a strange people** > The believers of Hebrews 11 confessed that they were strangers and sojourners {exiles, pilgrims, strangers} on the earth (v. 13). Peter exhorts the Christians of the dispersion as strangers and sojourners {pilgrims, strangers} (1 Pet. 2:11). Other ref.: 1 Pet. 1:1; see STRANGER <3927>. ¶

– [2] Acts 7:29 → DWELLER <3941> [3] 1 Pet. 2:11 → FOREIGNER <3941>.

SOJOURNING – 1 Pet. 1:17 → STAY <3940>.

SOLDIER – [1] ***stratiōtēs*** [masc. noun: στρατιώτης <4757>]**; from *stratia*: army ▶ Person enlisted in an army, trained to go to war** > The soldiers of the governor took Jesus to the Praetorium (Matt. 27:27; Mark 15:16). The soldiers were paid to say that the disciples had stolen the body of Jesus (Matt. 28:12). The soldiers mocked Jesus (Luke 23:36). The soldiers twisted together a crown of thorns and put it on the head of Jesus (John 19:2). When they had crucified Jesus, the soldiers took His clothes and made four parts, one part for each soldier (John 19:23a, b, 24). The soldiers did not break the legs of Jesus (John 19:32; see v. 33), but one of the soldiers pierced His side with a spear (v. 34). Cornelius called one of his soldiers to go to Joppa and bring Peter (Acts 10:7). Peter was delivered to four squads of four soldiers each to guard him (Acts 12:4). Paul was allowed to stay by himself with a soldier who guarded him (Acts 28:16). Timothy was to take his share in suffering as a good soldier, figur. speaking of Jesus Christ (2 Tim. 2:3). Other refs.: Matt. 8:9; Luke 7:8; Acts 12:6, 18; 21:32a, b, 35; 23:23, 31; 27:31, 32, 42. ¶

– [2] Matt. 27:65 → guard of soldiers → GUARD (noun) <2892> [3] Luke 3:14; 1 Cor. 9:7; 2 Tim. 2:4 → soldier, to serve as a soldier → lit.: to go to war → WAR (noun) <4754> [4] Luke 23:11; Acts 23:10, 27 → soldiers → TROOPS <4753> [5] Luke 23:26 → lit.: they [6] Phil. 2:25; Phm. 2 → fellow soldier <4961> [7] 2 Tim. 2:4 → to serve as a soldier, to be a soldier in active service → to engage in warfare → WARFARE <4758>.

SOLEMNLY – Acts 2:40; 10:42; 1 Thes. 4:6 → to solemnly warn, to solemnly testify → TESTIFY <1263>.

SOLID – ***stereos*** [adj.: στερεός <4731>] ▶ **Firm, unshakeable, substantial** > The solid foundation of God stands in that the Lord knows those who are His (2 Tim. 2:19). The Hebrew Christians had need of milk and not of solid {strong} food (Heb. 5:12); solid {strong} food belongs to full-grown men, who have their senses exercised to discern good and evil (v. 14). Other ref.: 1 Pet. 5:9; see FIRM <4731>. ¶

SOLITARY – Matt. 14:13; Mark 1:35; 6:32; Luke 4:42 → DESERTED <2048>.

SOLOMON – ***Solomōn*** [masc. name: Σολομών <4672>]**: peaceful, in Heb.** ▶ **Son of David and king of Israel** > Solomon is mentioned in the genealogy of Jesus Christ (Matt. 1:6, 7). He was renowned for his glory (Matt. 6:29; Luke 12:27) and his wisdom (Matt. 12:42a, b; Luke 11:31a, b). He built the temple of God at Jerusalem (Acts 7:47). A porch of this temple bore the name of Solomon in the times of the Lord (John 10:23; Acts 3:11; 5:12). ¶

SOMBER – Matt. 6:16 → sad countenance → SAD <4659>.

SOMEHOW – 1 ***pōs*** [particle: πώς <4458>] ▶ **By any means** > Paul sought somehow to provoke to jealousy his own people and save some of the Jews (Rom. 11:14). Other refs.: HOW <4458>.
– 2 Gal. 4:11 → LEST <3381>.

SOMEONE GREAT – ***tis megas; megas*** [adj.: μέγας <3173>] ▶ **A great figure, personage** > Simon the magician claimed that he was someone great {some great one} (Acts 8:9). All other refs. (*megas*): GREAT <3173>.

SOMETIME(S) – Eph. 2:2, 3, 11, 13; 5:8; Col. 1:21; 3:7; Titus 3:3; 1 Pet. 3:20 → in time(s) past → PAST <4218>.

SOMEWHERE ELSE – ***allachou*** [adv.: ἀλλαχοῦ <237a>] ▶ **To another place, elsewhere** > Jesus wanted to go somewhere else to preach (Mark 1:38). ¶

SON – 1 ***huios*** [masc. noun: υἱός <5207>] ▶ **Person of masculine gender, considered in relation to father or mother** > This term signifies the relationship of a descendant with a parent (e.g., John 9:19, 20; Gal. 4:30a–c). It is used in the N.T. to designate a. a male descendant (Gal. 4:30), b. a legitimate descendant in contrast to an illegitimate one (Heb. 12:8), c. descendants, without reference to gender (Rom. 9:27), d. friends present at a wedding (Matt. 9:15), e. those who enjoy certain privileges (Acts 3:25), f. those who do wrong (Matt. 23:31; Gal. 3:7), g. those who give evidence of a wicked character (Acts 13:10; Eph. 2:2) or a good character (Luke 6:35; Acts 4:36; Rom. 8:14), h. the destiny corresponding to a wicked character (Matt. 23:15; John 17:12; 2 Thes. 2:3) or a good character (Luke 20:36a, b), i. the dignity of the relationship with God into which the Holy Spirit introduces Christians (Rom. 8:19; Gal. 3:26). (After Walter Scott.) See SON (Son of God). *
2 ***pais*** [masc. noun: παῖς <3816>]**; lit.: child** ▶ **Lit.: boy, young man** > The son of a royal official was living again (John 4:51). All other refs.: BOY <3816>, CHILD <3816>, DAUGHTER <3816>, SERVANT <3816>.
– 3 Matt. 9:2; 21:28a, b; Mark 2:5; Luke 2:48; 16:25; 1 Cor. 4:17; Phil. 2:22; 1 Tim. 1:2, 18; 2 Tim. 1:2; 2:1; Titus 1:4; Phm. 10; et al. → CHILD <5043> 4 Gal. 4:5 → full rights of sons → ADOPTION <5206> 5 Col. 1:15 → "son" added in Engl.

SON (Son of God) – ***Huios*** [masc. name: Υἱός <5207>] ▶ **Name of the Lord Jesus** > The Lord Jesus is the Son of God (e.g., Matt. 16:16; John 1:34; Gal. 2:20) and the Son of Man (Matt. 8:20; John 3:13). He is the Son of the Father (1 John 1:3; 2 John 3). He is the Son of David (Matt. 9:27) and the Son of the Most High (Mark 5:7; Luke 1:32). He who has the Son of God has life; he who does not have the Son of God does not have life (1 John 5:12a, b).

SON OF DAY – ***huios hēmeras*; son: *huios*** [masc. noun: υἱός <5207>]; **day: *hēmera*** [fem. noun: ἡμέρα <2250>] ► **Christian morally characterized by the light of the word of God** > Sons of day {Children of day} are not of the night nor of darkness (1 Thes. 5:5). ¶

SON OF HELL – ***huios geennēs*; son: *huios*** [masc. noun: υἱός <5207>]; **hell: *geenna*** [fem. noun: γέεννα <1067>]; **see HELL ► Person who is morally characterized by the sphere of eternal torment** > The scribes and the Pharisees made a convert twice as much a son of hell {child of hell} as they were (Matt. 23:15). ¶

SON OF LIGHT – ***huios tou phōtos*; son: *huios*** [masc. noun: υἱός <5207>]; **light: *phōs*** [neut. noun: φῶς <5457>] ► **Christian morally characterized by the light of the word of God** > In Luke 16:8, the sons of this world are more shrewd than the sons of light. It is by believing in Jesus, the light, that we become sons of light {children of light} (John 12:36). The Christians of Thessalonica were all sons of light and sons of the day (1 Thes. 5:5). ¶ All other refs. (*phōs*): see FIRE <5457>, LIGHT (noun) <5457>.

SON OF PERDITION – ***huios tēs apōleias*; son: *huios*** [masc. noun: υἱός <5207>]; **perdition: *apōleia*** [fem. noun: ἀπώλεια <684>]; **from *apollumi*: to completely destroy, which is from *apo*: intens., and *ollumi*: to destroy ► One who is doomed to eternal perdition** > In John 17:12, the expr. refers to Judas, one of the twelve apostles, who betrayed Jesus. It is one of the names of the antichrist in 2 Thes. 2:3. ¶ All other refs. (*apōleia*): see DESTRUCTION <684>, PERISH <684>, WASTE (noun) <684>.

SON OF THE BRIDECHAMBER – ***huios tou numphōnos*; son: *huios*** [masc. noun: υἱός <5207>]; **bridechamber: *numphōn*** [masc. noun: νυμφών <3567>] **¶; from *numphē*: bride ► Companion of him who is getting married; also transl.: friend, attendant, guest of the bridegroom, child of the bridechamber** > In using this expr., Jesus likens His disciples to such companions (Matt. 9:15; Mark 2:19; Luke 5:34). He is speaking figur. of Himself as the bridegroom in relation to Israel. ¶

SON OF THIS AGE, SON OF THIS WORLD – ***huios tou aiōnos*; son: *huios*** [masc. noun: υἱός <5207>]; **age, world: *aiōn*** [masc. noun: αἰών <165>] ► **Exprs. describing those who belong to this world and who are not saved** > The sons of this world are more shrewd than the sons of light (Luke 16:8). They marry and are given in marriage (Luke 20:34). ¶

SONG – [1] *ōdē* [fem. noun: ᾠδή <5603>]; **from *adō*: to sing ► Piece of music composed for singing; in the N.T., more specifically, a song to praise God and Christ** > Christians are invited to speak to one another and admonish themselves with psalms, hymns, and spiritual songs (Eph. 5:19; Col. 3:16). In the last book of the Bible, a new song is sung (Rev. 5:9; 14:3a, b), as well as the song of Moses and the song of the Lamb (15:3a, b). ¶
– [2] Eph. 5:19 → songs from the Spirit → spiritual songs → SONG <5603>, SPIRITUAL <4152>.

SONSHIP – Rom. 8:15, 23; 9:4; Eph. 1:5 → adoption to sonship → ADOPTION <5206>.

SOON – [1] Mark 5:36; 11:2 → as soon → IMMEDIATELY <2112> <2117> [2] Mark 9:39 → soon afterward → LIGHTLY <5035> [3] Acts 17:15 → as soon as possible → as quickly as possible → QUICKLY <5033> [4] Acts 25:4; Rom. 16:20; Rev. 1:1; 22:6 → SHORTLY <1722> <5034> [5] 1 Cor. 4:19; Phil. 2:19, 24; 2 Tim. 4:9 → SHORTLY <5030> [6] Gal. 1:6; 2 Thes. 2:2 → QUICKLY <5030> [7] 1 Tim. 3:14; Heb. 13:23 → SHORTLY <5032> [8] Heb. 13:19 → SOONER <5032> [9] 2 Pet. 1:14 →

SHORTLY <5031> [10] 3 John 14 → SHORTLY <2112> [11] Rev. 2:16; 3:11; 11:14; 22:7, 20 → QUICKLY <5035>.

SOONER – ***tachion*** [adv.: τάχιον <5032>]; **neuter of *tachiōn*, which is the compar. of *tachus*: rapid, prompt ▶ More quickly, more rapidly, soon** > The author of the Epistle to the Hebrew believers asked them to pray for him so that he might the more quickly be restored to them (Heb. 13:19). All other refs.: FASTER <5032>, QUICKLY <5032>, SHORTLY <5032>.

SOOTHSAYING – Acts 16:16 → PROPHESY <3132>.

SOP – John 13:26a, b, 27, 30 → piece of bread → PIECE <5596>.

SOPATER – ***Sōpatros*** [masc. name: Σώπατρος <4986>]: **safe father ▶ Christian man of Berea, son of Pyrrhus** > Sopater accompanied Paul to Asia (Acts 20:4). ¶

SORCERER – [1] ***magos*** [masc. noun: μάγος <3097>] **▶ Individual who pretends to be invested with supernatural powers, magician** > During their first voyage, Paul and Barnabas sailed to Cyprus where they found a sorcerer named Bar-Jesus who sought to turn the proconsul away from the faith; but this sorcerer was struck blind (Acts 13:6, 8). Other refs.: Matt. 2:1, 7, 16a, b; see WISE MAN <3097>. ¶

[2] ***pharmakeus*** [masc. noun: φαρμακεύς <5332>]; **from *pharmakeuō*: to administer a drug ▶ Individual who uses poisons, drugs** > Some mss. have this word in Rev. 21:8. ¶

[3] ***pharmakos*** [masc. noun: φάρμακος <5333>]; **from *pharmakon*: drug, potion ▶ See [2].** > Sorcerers {Those who practice magic arts} will have their part in the lake that burns with fire (Rev. 21:8; 22:15). ¶

SORCERY – [1] ***mageia*** [fem. noun: μαγεία <3095>]; **from *magos*: wise man, magician ▶ Occult practice by which one pretends to produce, by the use of supernatural means, surprising and marvelous effects** > It calls upon, sometimes through incantations, occult, hence diabolical powers. Simon had astonished the people of Samaria with his sorceries {magic, magic arts} (Acts 8:11). ¶

[2] **to practice sorcery, to use sorcery: *mageuō*** [verb: μαγεύω <3096>]; **from *magos*: wise man, magician ▶ To practice magic; see defin. of [1].** > Simon practiced sorcery {used magic arts, practiced magic} and astonished the people of Samaria (Acts 8:9). ¶

[3] ***pharmakeia*** [fem. noun: φαρμακεία <5331>]; **from *pharmakon*: drug (to cure or to poison), potion ▶ Witchcraft which calls on the use of drugs** > Sorcery {Witchcraft} is one of the works of the flesh (Gal. 5:20). In Rev. 9:21, men did not repent of their sorceries {magic arts, witchcrafts}; *pharmakon* in some mss. In Rev. 18:23, the nations were deceived by the sorcery {magic spell} of Babylon. ¶

– [4] Acts 19:19 → MAGIC <4021>.

SORDID – [1] 1 Tim. 3:8; Titus 1:7 → fond of sordid gain → greedy for money → GREEDY <146> [2] Titus 1:11 → DISHONEST <150>.

SORE – [1] ***helkos*** [neut. noun: ἕλκος <1668>] **▶ Ulcer, wound (especially a fester)** > The dogs licked the sores of Lazarus (Luke 16:21). An evil and painful sore came upon the men who had the mark of the beast and on those who worshipped his image (Rev. 16:2); they blasphemed the God of heaven, because of their pains and their sores, and did not repent of their deeds (v. 11). ¶

[2] **to be full of sores, to be covered with sores: *helkoō*** [verb: ἑλκόω <1669>]; **from *helkos*: see [1] ▶ To be entirely covered with ulcers** > A poor man named Lazarus, full of sores, was laid at the gateway of a rich man (Luke 16:20). ¶

– [3] Matt. 17:15 → sore vexed → SEVERELY <2560> [4] Mark 6:51 → sore beyond measure → exceedingly beyond measure → EXCEEDINGLY <3029> <1537> <4053> [5] Mark 9:6 → sore afraid → greatly afraid → AFRAID <1630> 6 Mark 14:33 → to be sore amazed → to be troubled → TROUBLED <1568>.

SORELY – Matt. 17:15 → SEVERELY <2560>.

SORER – Heb. 10:29 → severer → SEVERE <5501>.

SORROW (noun) – 1 ***lupē*** [fem. noun: λύπη <3077>] ▶ **Affliction, grief; also transl.: heaviness, pain** > The disciples were sleeping from sorrow (Luke 22:45). Sorrow had filled their heart (John 16:6, 22), but their sorrow would be turned into joy (v. 20). When she gives birth to a child, a woman has sorrow (John 16:21). Paul had great sorrow and continual grief in his heart (Rom. 9:2). He did not want to return to the Corinthians in sorrow (2 Cor. 2:1). He did not want to have sorrow from those from whom he ought to have joy (2 Cor. 2:3). The Corinthians were to forgive the one among them who had repented, lest he should be overcome by excessive sorrow (2 Cor. 2:7). Sorrow that is according to God produces repentance to salvation never to be regretted, but the sorrow of the world produces death (2 Cor. 7:10a, b). God had mercy on Paul that he might not have sorrow upon sorrow (Phil. 2:27a, b). No discipline, for the present, seems to be a matter of joy, but of sorrow (Heb. 12:11). This is acceptable, if one, for the sake of conscience toward God, endures sorrows, suffering unjustly (1 Pet. 2:19). Other ref.: 2 Cor. 9:7; see GRIEVINGLY <3077>. ¶

2 ***odunē*** [fem. noun: ὀδύνη <3601>]; **from which *odunaō*: to pain** ▶ **Pain, affliction** > Paul had a continual sorrow {grief, pain} in his heart for his Jewish brothers (Rom. 9:2). Because of their love for money, some have pierced themselves through with many sorrows {griefs} (1 Tim. 6:10). ¶

3 **to cause sorrow: *lupeō*** [verb: λυπέω <3076>]; **from *lupē*: see** 1 ▶ **To sadden or to be saddened, to grieve another or be grieved; also transl.: to be sorrowful, to cause grief** > The disciples would be sorrowful (John 16:20). If anyone had caused sorrow at Corinth, he had caused sorrow not to Paul, but to all of the Corinthians (2 Cor. 2:5a, b). All other refs.: SAD <3076>, SORROW (verb) <3076>.

– 4 Matt. 24:8; Mark 13:8 → PAIN (noun) <5604> 5 Mark 14:34 → overwhelmed with sorrow → exceedingly sorrowful → SORROWFUL <4036> 6 2 Cor. 7:7 → deep sorrow → MOURNING <3602> 7 Rev. 18:7a, b; 21:4 → MOURNING <3997>.

SORROW (verb) – 1 **to sorrow, to be sorrowful, to be sorry, to cause sorrow, to make sorry, to grieve, to cause to grieve, to be grieved, to be in heaviness: *lupeō*** [verb: λυπέω <3076>]; **from *lupē*: sadness, affliction** ▶ **To sadden, to afflict; pass.: to be saddened** > Jesus began to be sorrowful (Matt. 26:37). The Christians should not grieve the Holy Spirit of God (Eph. 4:30). The Thessalonians were not to sorrow concerning those who had fallen asleep (1 Thes. 4:13). The verb is used also about a king (Matt. 14:9), the disciples (Matt. 17:23; 26:22; Mark 14:19), servants (Matt. 18:31), Peter (John 21:17), a brother in Christ (Rom. 14:15 {to be distressed}), Christians (2 Cor. 2:2a, b, 4; 7:8a, b, 9a–c, 11; 1 Pet. 1:6), and Paul (2 Cor. 2:5a, b; 6:10). All other refs.: SAD <3076>, SORROW (noun) <3076>.

– 2 Acts 20:38 → GRIEVE <3600>.

SORROWFUL – 1 **exceeding, exceedingly, very sorrowful: *perilupos*** [adj.: περίλυπος <4036>]; **from *peri*: about (intens.), and *lupē*: affliction, grief** ▶ **Very saddened, severely grieved; also transl.: deeply grieved, full of grief, overwhelmed with sorrow** > The soul of the Lord Jesus was exceedingly sorrowful, to the point of death (Matt. 26:38; Mark 14:34). All other refs.: SAD <4036>, SORRY <4036>.

2 **to be less sorrowful: *alupoteros*** [adj.: ἀλυπότερος <253>]; **compar. of *alupos*: sad, which is from *a*: neg., and *lupē*: affliction, grief** ▶ **Less saddened, less grieved** > Paul had sent Epaphroditus to the Philippians, so that seeing him again the Philippians might rejoice, and that Paul

might be less sorrowful {be less concerned, be less anxious, have less anxiety} (Phil. 2:28). ¶

– 3 Matt. 19:22; Mark 10:22 → to be sorrowful → to be sad → SAD <3076> 4 Matt. 26:37; 2 Cor. 6:10; et al. → to be sorrowful → SORROW (verb) <3076> 5 John 16:20 → to be sorrowful → to cause sorrow → SORROW (noun) <3076> 6 Acts 20:38 → to be sorrowful → GRIEVE <3600> 7 Heb. 12:11 → lit.: of sorrow → SORROW (noun) <3077>.

SORROWING – Luke 2:48 → to be distressed → DISTRESSED <3600>.

SORRY – 1 **very sorry:** ***perilupos*** [adj.: περίλυπος <4036>]**; from *peri*: excessively, and *lupē*: sadness, sorrow ▶ Much afflicted, greatly saddened** > Herod was very sorry {exceeding sorry, exceedingly sorry, greatly distressed} when the daughter of Herodias asked him for the head of John the Baptist (Mark 6:26). All other refs.: SAD <4036>, SORROWFUL <4036>.

– 2 Matt. 17:23; et al. → to be sorry, to make sorry → SORROW (verb) <3076>.

SORT (noun) – 1 Acts 17:5 → of the baser sort → from the market place → MARKETPLACE <60> 2 1 Cor. 14:10 → KIND (noun) <1085> 3 3 John 6 → after a godly sort → in a manner worthy of God → WORTHY <516>.

SORT (verb) – Matt. 13:48 → GATHER <4816>.

SOSIPATER – ***Sōsipatros*** [masc. name: Σωσίπατρος <4989>]**: preserved father ▶ Relative of Paul** > Sosipater joined his greetings to those of Paul to the Christians of Rome (Rom. 16:21). ¶

SOSTHENES – ***Sōsthenēs*** [masc. name: Σωσθένης <4988>]**: of sound strength; *sōs*: sound, and *sthenos*: strength ▶ Ruler of the synagogue of Corinth** > Sosthenes was beaten before the judgment seat of Gallio (Acts 18:17). Paul associated himself with Sosthenes, the brother, in his First Epistle to the Corinthians (1 Cor. 1:1). ¶

SOUL – 1 ***psuchē*** [fem. noun: ψυχή <5590>]**; from *psuchō*: to breathe, to blow ▶ a. One of the three components of a person, the seat of emotions; the soul and the spirit constitute the immaterial part of a human being** > The soul designates the natural life in us (e.g., Acts 20:10). The word is often transl. "life" (e.g., John 10:15: Jesus laid down His life for the sheep). There are two views concerning this word. As explained by S. Zodhiathes, "Dichotomists view man as consisting of two parts (or substances), material and immaterial, with spirit and soul denoting the immaterial and bearing only a functional and not a metaphysical difference. Trichotomists also view man as consisting of two parts (or substances), but with spirit and soul representing in some contexts a real subdivision of the immaterial." The latter view is adopted here. The spirit, the body, and the soul constitute the person (1 Thes. 5:23). The spirit and the soul are the immaterial and invisible element of the person (e.g., Matt. 10:28a, b). It is the seat of emotions and feelings (Luke 1:46); the spirit is rather the one of intelligence and conscience. The word can designate living persons (Acts 2:41, 43; Rom. 2:9; et al.) or deceased persons who live separated from their bodies (Rev. 6:9; 20:4). The spirit is the principle of life given by God to men; the soul is the life that results from it in the individual (see Gen. 2:7); the body is the material organism animated by the spirit. It is not easy to differentiate between the spirit and the soul (Heb. 4:12); they are similar in their nature and activities. **b. Person** > There were in all 276 souls in the ship that Paul had taken (Acts 27:37). Eight souls were saved into the ark through water (1 Pet. 3:20). Other refs.: Matt. 11:29; 12:18; 16:25, 26a, b; 20:28; 22:37; 26:38; Mark 3:4; 8:35–37; 12:30, 33; 14:34; Luke 2:35; 6:9; 10:27; 12:19a, b, 20, 23; 14:26; 17:33; 21:19; John 10:11, 17, 24; 12:25, 27; 13:37, 38; 15:13; Acts 2:27, 31; 3:23; 4:32; 7:14; 14:2, 22; 15:24, 26; 20:14; 27:10, 22; Rom. 11:3; 13:1; 16:4; 1 Cor. 15:45; 2 Cor. 1:23;

12:15; Eph. 6:6; Phil. 1:27; 2:30; 1 Thes. 2:8; Heb. 6:19; 10:38, 39; 12:3; 13:17; Jas. 1:21; 5:20; 1 Pet. 1:9, 22; 2:11, 25; 4:19; 2 Pet. 2:8, 14; 3 John 2; Rev. 18:13, 14. All other refs.: LIFE <5590>.

2 **joined in soul: *sumpsuchos*** [adj.: σύμψυχος <4861>]**; from *sun*: together, and *psuchē*: soul ▶ Being in agreement, being in harmony; also transl.: being of one accord, being one in spirit, united in spirit** > Paul told the Philippians to be joined in soul (Phil. 2:2). ¶

SOUND (adj.) – 1 ***hugiēs*** [adj.: ὑγιής <5199>] **▶ Healthy; according to the truth, therefore: wise** > Jesus restored the withered hand of a man just as sound {to normal, whole} as the other (Matt. 12:13). Titus was to demonstrate sound word {soundness} in teaching (Titus 2:8). Other refs.: Matt. 15:31; Mark 3:5 {whole} in some mss.; 5:34; Luke 6:10 {whole} in some mss.; John 5:4, 6, 9, 11, 14, 15; 7:23. All other refs.: HEALTH <5199>.

2 **lit.: to be sound: *hugiainō*** [verb: ὑγιαίνω <5198>]**; from *hugiēs*: see 1 ▶ To be healthy, to be in health; to be pure (e.g., in relation to Christian doctrine)** > The law is good for those opposed to sound doctrine (1 Tim. 1:10). He who teaches must consent to sound words, those of the Lord Jesus Christ (1 Tim. 6:3). Timothy was to have a pattern of sound words that he had heard from Paul (2 Tim. 1:13). Paul speaks of a time when men will not endure sound teaching (2 Tim. 4:3). The overseer must be able to exhort by sound teaching (Titus 1:9). The Cretans were to be rebuked so that they might be sound in the faith (Titus 1:13). Titus was to speak the things that become sound doctrine (Titus 2:1). Older men are to be sound in the faith (Titus 2:2). All other refs.: HEALTH <5198>, SAFELY <5198>.

SOUND (noun) – 1 ***ēchos*** [masc. noun: ἦχος <2279>] **▶ What is heard, resounding noise** > At Pentecost, there came suddenly a sound {noise}, as of a violent impetuous blowing (Acts 2:2). The Hebrew Christians had not come to the sound {blast} of a trumpet (Heb. 12:19). Other ref.: Luke 4:37; see REPORT <2279>. ¶

2 ***phthongos*** [masc. noun: φθόγγος <5353>]**; from *phtengomai*: to emit a sound ▶ Musical sound, note** > Inanimate things, such as a flute or harp, must produce a distinction in the sounds {tones} so that one may recognize them (1 Cor. 14:7b). Other ref.: Rom. 10:18; see VOICE <5353>. ¶

3 ***phōnē*** [fem. noun: φωνή <5456>]**; from *phaō*: to shine, in the sense that the voice clarifies the thoughts ▶ Noise, voice, rumor** > One hears the sound of the wind (John 3:8). The sound of what had happened at Pentecost had spread (Acts 2:6). Paul speaks of inanimate things that produce a sound (1 Cor. 14:7a). One cannot prepare for battle if the trumpet makes an uncertain sound (1 Cor. 14:8). The sound of the wings of the locusts was as the sound of chariots with many horses (Rev. 9:9a, b {thundering}). The sound of a millstone will not be heard in the new Jerusalem (Rev. 18:22). All other refs.: VOICE <5456>.

– 4 1 Cor. 14:10 → of undistinguishable sound → without significance → SIGNIFICANCE <880> 5 2 Cor. 5:13 → to be of sound mind → MIND (noun) <4993> 6 1 Thes. 4:16 → "with the sound of the trumpet"; lit.: "with the trumpet."

SOUND (verb) – 1 ***ēcheō*** [verb: ἠχέω <2278>]**; from *ēchos*: sound ▶ To produce a loud noise** > If Paul had spoken with the tongues of men and of angels, but without having love, he would have become as sounding brass {noisy gong, resounding gong} (1 Cor. 13:1). Other ref.: Luke 21:25 (to roar); see ROARING <2278>. ¶

2 **to sound out, to sound forth: *exēcheō*** [verb: ἐξηχέω <1837>]**; from *ek*: out, forth, and *ēcheō*: see 1 ▶ To fill with a noise, to resound** > The word of the Lord had sounded out {had rang out} from the Thessalonians in every place (1 Thes. 1:8). ¶

– 3 Luke 1:44 → COME <1096> 4 Acts 27:28a, b → to take sounding → SOUNDING <1001> 5 Rev. 8:6–8, 10, 12, 13; 9:1, 13; 10:7; 11:15 → to sound a trumpet → TRUMPET <4537> 6 Rev. 10:3, 4 → the seven thunders sounded →

lit.: the seven thunders spoke their voices → VOICE <5456>.

SOUNDING – to take a sounding: *bolizō* [verb: βολίζω <1001>]; **from *bolis*: that which is thrown, e.g., mariners' plummet ▶ To drop a sinker held by a line to measure the depth of water >** The verb is used in Acts 27:28a, b. ¶

SOUNDNESS – [1] complete, perfect soundness: *holoklēria* [fem. noun: ὁλοκληρία <3647>]; **from *holoklēros*: entire, perfect, which is from *holos*: complete, full, and *klēros*: lot, part ▶ Full vigor, perfect health >** Faith in the name of Jesus had given to a lame man the complete soundness {complete healing, perfect health} (i.e., of all his members) (Acts 3:16). ¶
– [2] Titus 2:8 → lit.: sound word → SOUND (adj.) <5199>.

SOUR – Rev. 10:9, 10 → to turn sour → to make bitter → BITTER <4087>.

SOURCE – [1] Heb. 2:11 → all have one source → lit.: all of one [2] Heb. 5:9 → AUTHOR <159>.

SOUTH – [1] *mesēmbria* [fem. noun: μεσημβρία <3314>]; **from *mesos*: middle, and *hēmera*: day ▶ Hour corresponding to the middle of the day, or the southern direction, the direction directly opposite to the north >** An angel of the Lord told Philip to go toward the south {southward} (Acts 8:26); it is also possible that Philip was told to go at noon. Other ref.: Acts 22:6; see NOON <3314>. ¶
[2] **south, south wind: *notos*** [masc. noun: νότος <3558>] **▶ The south is the direction directly opposite to the north >** A queen of the south will rise up in judgment with the generation of Jesus and will condemn that generation (Matt. 12:42; Luke 11:31). There will be people who come from the south who will sit down in the kingdom of God (Luke 13:29). The new Jerusalem has three gates on the south (Rev. 21:13). The term also designates the south wind (Luke 12:55; Acts 27:13; 28:13). ¶

SOUTHWARD – Acts 8:26 → SOUTH <3314>.

SOUTHWEST – *lips* [masc. noun: λίψ <3047>] **▶ Direction situated between the south and the west >** Phoenix was a harbor in Crete facing both the southwest and the northwest where Paul spent the winter (Acts 27:12). ¶

SOVEREIGN – [1] *Dunastēs* [masc. name: Δυνάστης <1413>]; **from *dunamai*: to be able ▶ Powerful person, who rules; also transl.: Potentate, Ruler >** This name is used in regard to God in 1 Tim. 6:15: the blessed and only Sovereign. ¶
– [2] Acts 4:24; Rev. 6:10 → Sovereign Lord, Sovereign Ruler → LORD (noun) <1203> [3] 2 Pet. 2:1; Jude 4 → sovereign Lord, Sovereign → MASTER (noun) <1203>.

SOW (noun) – ***hus*** [fem. noun: ὗς <5300>]; ***sus*, in Lat. ▶ Hog, swine >** The washed sow returns to wallowing in the mud (2 Pet. 2:22). ¶

SOW (verb) – **[1] *speirō*** [verb: σπείρω <4687>] **▶ a. To scatter seed on the ground, to plant >** The birds of heaven neither sow, nor reap, nor gather into granaries, and God the heavenly Father feeds them (Matt. 6:26; Luke 12:24). Jesus speaks of sowing in His parables (Matt. 13:3, 4, 19a, b, 20, 22–25 (v. 25: *epispeirō* in some mss.), 27, 31, 37, 39; 25:24, 26; Mark 4:3, 4, 14, 15a, b, 16, 18, 20, 31, 32; Luke 8:5a, b; 12:24; 19:21, 22). He who sows and he who reaps rejoice together (John 4:36); it is written regarding the word of God that one sows and another reaps (v. 37). **b. To bury the body of a believer >** Paul uses this term in 1 Cor. 15 regarding the death of Christians (vv. 36, 37a, b, 42, 43a, b, 44). **c. To share one's goods >** He who sows sparingly will also reap sparingly, and he who sows bountifully will also reap bountifully (2 Cor. 9:6a, b). Paul had sown spiritual things for the Corinthians (1 Cor. 9:11). **d. To occupy one's time >** Whatever a man sows, that he will also reap (Gal. 6:7); he who sows to his own flesh will reap corruption from the

flesh; but he who sows to the Spirit, from the Spirit will reap eternal life (v. 8a, b). The fruit of righteousness, in peace, is sown for them who make peace (Jas. 3:18). Other refs.: Matt. 13:18 (lit.: he who sows); 2 Cor. 9:10 (lit.: the one sowing). ¶
– 2 Luke 13:19 → to throw seed → THROW (verb) <906>.

SOWER – 1 **to sow:** ***speirō*** [verb: σπείρω <4687>] ▶ **To scatter seed on the ground** > This verb is often transl. "sower" (lit. "the sowing one") in Matt. 13:3, 18; Mark 4:3, 14; Luke 8:5). Paul tells the Corinthians that He who supplies seed to the sower (lit.: the one sowing) and bread for eating will supply and multiply their sowing, and increase the fruits of their righteousness (2 Cor. 9:10). All other refs.: SOW (verb) <4687>.
– 2 John 4:36 → the sower → lit.: he who sows → SOW (verb) <4687>.

SOWING – 2 Cor. 9:10 → SEED <4703>.

SPAIN – ***Spania*** [fem. name: Σπανία <4681>] ▶ **Country of southwestern Europe** > Paul wanted to go to Spain (Rom. 15:24, 28). We may suppose that he arrived there because in around A.D. 96 Clement of Rome wrote that Paul had reached the limits of the West. ¶

SPAN – Matt. 6:27 → to add a single hour to his span of life → lit.: to add one cubit to his stature → STATURE <2244>.

SPARE – 1 ***pheidomai*** [verb: φείδομαι <5339>] ▶ **To save, to treat with mercy** > God did not spare His own Son, but delivered Him up for us all (Rom. 8:32). After Paul's departure, grievous wolves would not spare the flock (Acts 20:29). Paul was sparing the Corinthians (1 Cor. 7:28; 2 Cor. 1:23); he would not spare those who had sinned if he came back (2 Cor. 13:2). God did not spare the angels who sinned, nor the ancient world (2 Pet. 2:4, 5). If God did not spare the natural branches (unbelievers in Israel), He might not spare high-minded Christians (Rom. 11:21a, b). Other ref.: 2 Cor. 12:6; see FORBEAR <5339>. ¶
– 2 Luke 15:17 → to have enough and to spare, to spare, to have to spare → to have in abundance → ABUNDANCE <4052> 3 Acts 27:21 → to not incur → INCUR <2770> 4 Acts 27:43 → to spare the life → SAVE (verb) <1295>.

SPARINGLY – ***pheidomenōs*** [adv.: φειδομένως <5340>]; **from *pheidomai*: to spare** ▶ **Scantily, meagerly** > He who sows sparingly will also reap sparingly (2 Cor. 9:6a, b). ¶

SPARROW – ***strouthion*** [neut. noun: στρουθίον <4765>]; **dimin. of *strouthos*: sparrow; lit.: little sparrow** ▶ **Sparrows (or more precisely: passerines) are an order of birds which includes the common sparrow, the blackbird, the swallow; they are small and very common in populated places** > Jesus used the example of the sparrows, which are sold very cheaply, and which do not die without God knowing it; we have nothing to fear for we are worth more than many sparrows (Matt. 10:29, 31; Luke 12:6, 7). ¶

SPEAK – 1 ***anangellō*** [verb: ἀναγγέλλω <312>]; **from *ana*: upon (intens.), and *angellō*: to bring news, a message** ▶ **To announce, to communicate; also transl.: to have news** > Those to whom the gospel was not spoken of {announced, told} will see salvation (Rom. 15:21). All other refs.: see entries in Lexicon at <312>.
2 ***legō*** [verb: λέγω <3004>] ▶ **To say, to confirm, to communicate** > The verb is used in regard to Jesus (Matt. 9:30; 21:45; Mark 1:42 in some mss.; John 2:21; 6:71; 8:27; 11:13b; 13:18, 22, 24; Acts 1:3), the disciples (Mark 1:30; Acts 13:15a, b), Moses and Elijah (Luke 9:31), Paul (Acts 24:10; 26:1; Rom. 3:5; 6:19; 11:13; 1 Cor. 6:5; 10:15; 2 Cor. 6:13; 8:8; 11:21; Gal. 3:15; Eph. 5:32), and the Scripture (Jas. 4:5). Other refs.: Mark 14:71; Luke 21:5; Rom. 10:6; 1 Cor. 1:10; 9:10; Phil. 4:11; Heb. 9:5. *
3 **to speak against: *antilegō*** [verb: ἀντιλέγω <483>]; **from *anti*: against, and *legō*: see** 2 ▶ **To contradict, to refuse to obey, to**

oppose > Jesus would be a sign that would be spoken against (Luke 2:34). In regard to Jesus, the Jews said everyone making himself a king speaks against Caesar (John 19:12). The Jews spoke against {talked abusively against} what Paul was saying, speaking against, and blaspheming (Acts 13:45a, b). The Jews spoke against {objected} the mind of the Romans to let Paul go (Acts 28:19). The Jews were saying that Christianity was a sect spoken against {talked against} everywhere (Acts 28:22). Concerning Israel as a people, the word is transl. "gainsaying" {contrary, obstinate, opposing} in Rom. 10:21. The overseer must be able to convince the gainsayers {those who oppose} (lit.: those speaking against) (Titus 1:9). All other refs.: ANSWER (verb) <483>, DENY <483>.

4 **to speak, to speak unto: *dialegō*** [verb: διαλέγω <1256>], **from *dia*: one with the other, and *legō*: see 2 ▶ To say, to talk, to discuss** > At Troas, Paul spoke {discoursed, preached} to the disciples on the first day of the week (Acts 20:7). Christians who are rebuked by the Lord should not forget the exhortation that speaks {is addressed} to them as to sons to not despise His chastening or be discouraged (Heb. 12:5). All other refs. (*dialegomai*): see DISCOURSE (verb) <1256>, DISPUTE (verb) <1256>, REASON (verb) <1256>.

5 **to speak ill, to speak evil: *kakologeō*** [verb: κακολογέω <2551>]; **from *kakologos*: evil-speaking, which is from *kakos*: bad, wicked, and *legō*: see 2 ▶ To say bad things, to revile** > One who does a miracle in the name of Jesus is not able soon after to speak ill {to say anything bad} of Him (Mark 9:39). All other refs.: CURSE (verb) <2551>.

6 ***epō*** [verb: ἔπω <2036>]: **form of *legō*: see 2 ▶ To talk, to say** > The mother of the sons of Zebedee said to Jesus to speak {command, speak the word, grant} that her sons might sit at His side in His kingdom (Matt. 20:21). Whoever will have spoken a word against the Son of Man, it will be forgiven him, but whoever will speak against the Holy Spirit, it will not be forgiven him (Matt. 12:32a, b). God spoke to Moses (Mark 12:26). Other refs.: Matt. 2:5 {to tell, to say, to reply}; 12:48; 17:13; 22:1; Luke 14:3; 20:2; John 3:12a, b; 12:38; 18:16. *

7 ***laleō*** [verb: λαλέω <2980>] ▶ **a. To pronounce articulate sounds, to say** > The scribes and the Pharisees accused Jesus of speaking blasphemies (Luke 5:21). When the devil speaks a lie, he speaks from his own nature (John 8:44a, b). Men falsely accused Stephen of having spoken blasphemous words against Moses and God (Acts 6:11), and against the holy place and the law (v. 13). While Peter was yet speaking words regarding Jesus, the Holy Spirit fell upon all those who were hearing the word (Acts 10:44). He who speaks with a tongue in spirit speaks mysteries (1 Cor. 14:2). Paul desired to speak five words with his intelligence, that he might instruct others, rather than ten thousand words in a tongue (1 Cor. 14:19). God has spoken formerly to the fathers in the prophets (Heb. 1:1); at the end of these days, He has spoken to us in the person of the Son (v. 2). The word that was spoken by angels was firm (Heb. 2:2). The mouth of murmurers speaks swelling words (Jude 16). Every commandment had been spoken {had been proclaimed} by Moses to the people (Heb. 9:19). He who will love life and see good days is to cause his lips to speak no deceit (1 Pet. 3:10). Ungodly sinners have spoken hard things against the Lord (Jude 15). John was to seal the things that the seven thunders had spoken, and not to write them (Rev. 10:4). The first beast spoke {uttered} great things and blasphemies (Rev. 13:5). The verb is often used in regard to the Lord Jesus (Matt. 12:46a; 13:10, 13; 14:27; 23:1; 26:47; 28:18; Mark 2:7; 4:34; 5:35; 6:50; 14:43; 16:19; Luke 5:4; 8:49; 9:11; 11:37; 22:47; 24:6, 32; John 3:34; 4:26, 27a, b; 7:17, 26, 46; 8:12; 9:37; 12:49a, b; 14:30; 15:22; 16:25a, 29; 18:20, 23; 19:10; Acts 9:27a; 22:9; 26:14; 2 Cor. 13:3; Rev. 1:12), God (Luke 1:55; John 9:29; Acts 3:21; 7:6; 1 Cor. 14:21; Heb. 4:8), and the Spirit (Matt. 10:20b; John 16:13a, b; Acts 28:25). It is also used in regard to dumb men (Matt. 9:33; 12:22; 15:31; Mark 7:35, 37; Luke 11:14), disciples or apostles (Matt. 10:19a, b, 20a {speakers; lit.: the ones speaking}; Mark 13:11a–c {speakers; lit.:

the one(s) speaking}; Acts 2:4, 7; 4:1, 17, 20; 5:40; 10:32; 11:15; 2 John 12; 3 John 14), the mouth (Matt. 12:34b; Luke 6:45), the mother and the brothers of Jesus (Matt. 12:46b, 47), Peter (Matt. 17:5; Luke 22:60), demons (Mark 1:34; Luke 4:41), angels (Luke 1:19; Acts 7:38; 8:26; 10:7; Rev. 17:1; 21:9, 15), Zacharias (Luke 1:20, 22, 64), Anna (Luke 2:38), a dead young man who had been brought back to life (Luke 7:15), John the Baptist (John 1:37), he who has his origin in the earth (John 3:31), Satan (John 8:44a, b), a blind man (John 9:21), Isaiah (John 12:41), Stephen (Acts 6:10), Paul (Acts 9:29; 14:1, 9; 16:13; 17:19; 18:9; 21:39; 26:26; Rom. 7:1; 1 Cor. 2:6, 7, 13; 3:1; 13:1, 11; 2 Cor. 2:17; 11:23; 12:19; Eph. 6:20; Col. 4:4; 1 Thes. 2:4, 16; 2 Pet. 3:16), Christians (Acts 11:20; 19:6), Apollos (Acts 18:25; *apolaleō* in some mss.), Abel (Heb. 11:4), the blood of sprinkling (Heb. 12:24), the prophets (Jas. 5:10; 2 Pet. 1:21), the image of the first Beast (Rev. 13:15), and the second Beast (Rev. 13:11). Other refs.: Matt. 26:13; Mark 14:9; 16:17; Luke 2:20; 12:3; John 7:13, 18; 12:29; Acts 2:6; 3:24; 10:46; 22:10 {to tell}; 23:9; 1 Cor. 12:3, 30; 14:2a, b, 3, 4, 5a, b, 6a, b, 9a, b, 11a, b, 13, 18, 23, 27–29, 34, 35, 39; 2 Cor. 4:13a, b; Eph. 4:25; Heb. 2:5; 6:9; 12:25; Jas. 1:19; 2:12; 1 Pet. 4:11; 1 John 4:5; Rev. 4:1; 10:4, 8. **b. To announce, to preach, to proclaim, to declare, to tell** > Jesus spoke the word (Mark 4:33). The verb is also used concerning the preaching of the gospel by the apostles and the disciples (Acts 2:11; 4:29, 31; 5:20; 13:46; 16:32; Phil. 1:14; Col. 4:3; 1 Thes. 2:2; Heb. 2:3; 13:7). Titus had to speak {teach} the things that become sound doctrine (Titus 2:1, 15). After Paul's departing, men would arise, speaking perverse things (Acts 20:30). Paul was saying (*legō*) none other things than those that the prophets and Moses did say (*laleō*) should come (Acts 26:22). **c. To talk, to converse** > Christians should speak to one another in psalms, hymns, and spiritual songs (Eph. 5:19). *

8 to speak against, maliciously, evil: *katalaleō* [verb: καταλαλέω <2635>]; **from *kata*: against, and *laleō*: see 7 ▶ To speak against someone, to slander** > Brothers are not to speak against one another (Jas. 4:11a {to slander}, b, c). Unbelievers may speak against {accuse} Christians as those who do evil (1 Pet. 2:12; 3:16 {to defame}). ¶

9 to speak to, to speak with: *proslaleō* [verb: προσλαλέω <4354>]; **from *pros*: to, and *laleō*: see 7 ▶ To talk to** > Paul and Barnabas, speaking to {talking with} the Jews and proselytes, persuaded them to continue in the grace of God (Acts 13:43). Paul had called the leaders of the Jews in Rome to speak to them (Acts 28:20). ¶

10 to speak to, to speak with: *sullaleō* [verb: συλλαλέω <4814>]; **from *sun*: with, together, and *laleō*: see 7 ▶ To converse with someone; also transl.: to say, to commune, to confer, to discuss, to talk with** > Moses and Elijah talked with Jesus (Matt. 17:3; Mark 9:4; Luke 9:30). The people of Galilee spoke to one another about Jesus (Luke 4:36). Judas spoke to the chief priest and captains as to how he should deliver Jesus (Luke 22:4). Other ref.: Acts 25:12; see CONFER <4814>. ¶

11 to speak out: *anaphōneō* [verb: ἀναφωνέω <400>]; **from *ana*: intens., and *phōneō*: to talk, to call ▶ To raise the voice** > Elizabeth spoke out {cried out, exclaimed} with a loud voice and said that Mary and the fruit of her womb were blessed (Luke 1:42). ¶

12 *prosphōneō* [verb: προσφωνέω <4377>]: **from *pros*: to, and *phōneō*: to talk, to call ▶ To call out to (someone)** > Pilate called out {addressed, appealed} again to the crowd, wishing to release Jesus (Luke 23:20). All other refs.: ADDRESS (verb) <4377>, CALL (verb) <4377>.

13 to make to speak, to provoke to speak: *apostomatizō* [verb: ἀποστοματίζω <653>]; **from *apo*: out of, and *stoma*: mouth ▶ To speak from memory (in classical Greek); to force (someone) to answer** > The scribes and the Pharisees made (in the sense of: provoked) Jesus to speak of many things (Luke 11:53); "to make to speak of many things" is also transl.: to question on many subjects, to besiege with questions. ¶

14 to speak injuriously: *blasphēmeō* [verb: βλασφημέω <987>]; **from *blasphēmos*: blas-**

phemer; which is poss. from *blaptō*: to harm, and *phēmē*: reputation ▶ To pronounce blasphemies regarding God > Whoever will speak injuriously {will blaspheme} against the Holy Spirit is guilty of an eternal sin, and he will not be forgiven (Mark 3:29; Luke 12:10). All other refs.: see entries in Lexicon at <987>.

15 ***rheō*** [verb: ῥέω <4483>] **▶ To name, to mention >** Isaiah spoke of {referred to} John the Baptist (Matt. 3:3). Daniel spoke of the abomination of desolation (Matt. 24:15). *

16 ***ereō*** [verb: ἐρέω <2046>] **▶ To say >** Jesus spoke of the death of Lazarus (John 11:13a). Whoever will speak (*ereō*) a word against the Son of Man it will be forgiven him; but to him who speaks injuriously (*blasphēmeō*) against the Holy Spirit it will not be forgiven (Luke 12:10). Other ref.: Acts 8:24. *

17 ***prostithēmi*** [verb: προστίθημι <4369>]**: from *pros*: to, and *tithēmi*: to set, to place ▶ Lit.: to add >** The Israelites begged that no further word be spoken {addressed} to them (Heb. 12:19). All other refs.: ADD <4369>.

18 ***phthengomai*** [verb: φθέγγομαι <5350>] **▶ To make a clear sound, to talk >** Peter and John were charged not to speak at all in the name of Jesus (Acts 4:18). A dumb donkey speaking with a man's voice restrained the folly of Balaam (2 Pet. 2:16). Peter made mention of those who speak {mouth} great swelling words of vanity (2 Pet. 2:18). ¶

19 **to speak forth to: *apophthengomai*** [verb: ἀποφθέγγομαι <669>]**; from *apo*: forth, and *phthengomai*: see 18 ▶ To express oneself, to proclaim (by divine inspiration) >** Peter spoke forth to the men of Judea (Acts 2:14). Other refs.: Acts 2:24 (to utter); 26:25; see UTTERANCE <669>, UTTER (verb) <669>. ¶

20 **who cannot speak right, who speaks with difficulty: *mogilalos*** [adj.: μογιλάλος <3424>]**; from *mogis*: hardly, with difficulty, and *laleō*: see 7 ▶ Experiencing difficulty in pronouncing articulate sounds >** A deaf man who could not speak right was brought to Jesus (Mark 7:32); also transl.: who has an impediment in his speech, who can hardly talk. ¶

21 See TONGUE <2980> for speaking in tongues.

– 22 Matt. 17:25 → to speak first → ANTICIPATE <4399> 23 Mark 2:2; Acts 8:25; 11:19, 20; 13:42; 14:25; 16:6 → PREACH <2980> 24 Mark 14:5c → to speak very angrily at → to rebuke harshly → REBUKE (verb) <1690> 25 Luke 1:22 → unable to speak → DUMB <2974> 26 Luke 6:11 → DISCUSS <1255> 27 Luke 12:11 → ANSWER (verb) <626> 28 Acts 1:16 in some mss.; 1 Thes. 4:6; 2 Pet. 3:2 → to speak before, to speak long ago → to tell before → TELL <4302> 29 Acts 8:33 → to speak of → RELATE <1334> 30 Acts 9:27–29; 13:46 → to grow bold → BOLD <3955> 31 Acts 19:36 → which cannot be spoken against → UNDENIABLE <368> 32 Acts 21:37 → KNOW <1097> 33 Acts 26:24 → to speak for oneself → to make one's defense → DEFENSE <626> 34 Acts 26:31 → TALK (verb) <2980> 35 Rom. 1:8 → to speak of → PROCLAIM <2605> 36 Rom. 4:6 → DECLARE <3004> 37 1 Cor. 14:9 → GIVE <1325> 38 2 Cor. 7:4; 2 Thes. 2:2, 15 → added in Engl. 39 2 Cor. 12:4 → UTTER (verb) <2980> 40 Eph. 6:19 → whenever I speak → lit.: in the opening of my mouth → OPENING <457>, MOUTH (noun) <4750> 41 Titus 3:8 → to speak confidently → AFFIRM <1226> 42 Heb. 11:22 → to make mention → MENTION (noun) <3421> 43 Heb. 12:25 → to utter the oracles → ORACLE <5537> 44 1 Pet. 3:16 → to speak maliciously against → to falsely accuse → ACCUSE <1908>.

SPEAKER – 1 Matt. 10:20a; Mark 13:11c → lit.: the one speaking → SPEAK <2980> 2 2 Cor. 11:6 → not a trained speaker → lit.: a simple person in speech → SPEECH <3056> 3 Titus 1:10 → vain speaker → idle talker → TALKER <3151>.

SPEAKING – 1 **much speaking: *polulogia*** [fem. noun: πολυλογία <4180>]**; from *polus*: much, and *logos*: word, speech ▶ Many words >** Some Gentiles suppose that they will be heard through much speaking

{because of their many words} (Matt. 6:7). Other ref.: Luke 11:2 in some mss. ¶
– 2 2 Cor. 11:6 → SPEECH <3056> 3 2 Cor. 12:20; 1 Pet. 2:1 → evil speaking → BACKBITING <2636>.

SPEAR – ***lonchē*** [fem. noun: λόγχη <3057>] ▶ **An offensive weapon made of a long pole and an iron point** > A soldier pierced the side of Jesus with a spear (John 19:34). Other ref.: Matt. 27:49 in some mss. ¶

SPEARMAN – ***dexiolabos*** [masc. noun: δεξιολάβος <1187>]; **from *dexios*: the right (hand), and *lambanō*: to hold ▶ Soldier armed most likely with a lance** > Two hundred spearmen {light-armed footmen} accompanied Paul to Caesarea (Acts 23:23). ¶

SPECIAL – 1 Acts 19:11 → lit.: non the being ordinary → to be ordinary → ORDINARY <5177> 2 Rom. 9:21; 2 Tim. 2:20, 21; 1 Pet. 1:7 → for special purposes → lit.: to honor → HONOR (noun) <5092> 3 Titus 2:14 → PECULIAR <4041> 4 1 Pet. 2:9 → own special → POSSESSION <4047>.

SPECIALLY – Acts 20:38; 25:26; Gal. 6:10; Phil. 4:22; et al. → ESPECIALLY <3122>.

SPECIES – Jas. 3:7a, b → KIND (noun) <5449>.

SPECIFY – Acts 25:27 → SIGNIFY <4591>.

SPECK – **speck, speck of sawdust: *karphos*** [neut. noun: κάρφος <2595>]; **from *karphō*: to dry, to wither ▶ Wisp of straw, small splinter of wood** > In the Lord's teaching, the speck in the eye of our brother is a minor fault of which we take notice, while failing to see the much greater faults in our own life (Matt. 7:3–5; Luke 6:41, 42a, b). ¶

SPECTACLE – 1 ***theatron*** [neut. noun: θέατρον <2302>]; **from *theaomai*: to behold ▶ What is presented to people observing, public show** > Paul thought that God had set forth the apostles, the last on the scene, as men appointed to death; for they had been made a spectacle to the world, to angels, and to men (1 Cor. 4:9). Other refs.: Acts 19:29, 31; see THEATER <2302>. ¶
2 **to make a spectacle, to make a public spectacle: *theatrizō*** [verb: θεατρίζω <2301>]; **from *theatron*: see 1 ▶ To expose to view; to scorn** > The Hebrew Christians had been made a spectacle {had been made a gazingstock, had been publicly exposed} both in reproaches and afflictions (Heb. 10:33). ¶
3 ***theōria*** [fem. noun: θεωρία <2335>]; **from *theōreō*: to behold ▶ Events which unfold before people, public show** > All the crowds who had come together for the spectacle {sight} of the crucifixion of Jesus, having seen the things that had taken place, returned, beating their breasts (Luke 23:48). ¶
4 **to make a spectacle: *deigmatizō*** [verb: δειγματίζω <1165>]; **from *deigma*: thing shown, example, which is from *deiknuō*: to show ▶ To make an example, to expose** > Having spoiled principalities and powers, Christ made a public spectacle {made a display, made a show} of them publicly (Col. 2:15). Other ref.: Matt. 1:19 (to make an example); see EXAMPLE <1165>. ¶

SPECULATION – 1 Rom. 1:21 → REASONING <1261> 2 2 Cor. 10:5 → REASONING <3053> 3 1 Tim. 1:4 → controversial speculation → DISPUTE (noun) <2214> 4 2 Tim. 2:23 → STRIFE <3163>.

SPEECH – 1 ***lalia*** [fem. noun: λαλιά <2981>]; **from *laleō*: to talk ▶ Dialect, pronunciation; saying, discourse** > The speech of Peter {The way he talked, His accent} betrayed him (Matt. 26:73). Jesus asked why the Pharisees did not understand His speech {His language, what He was saying} (John 8:43). The Jews believed no longer because of what the woman had said (lit.: her speech), but because they had themselves heard Jesus (John 4:42). Other ref.: Mark 14:70 in some mss. ¶

2 ***logos*** [masc. noun: λόγος <3056>]; **from *legō*: to tell, to utter ▶ Word, discourse >** Paul was a simple person in speech {was not a trained speaker}, but not in knowledge (2 Cor. 11:6). Other refs.: see entries in Lexicon at <3056>.

3 **fair speeches: *eulogia*** [fem. noun: εὐλογία <2129>]; **from *eulogeō*: to bless, which is from *eu*: well, good, and *logos*: word ▶ Insincere or excessive words to flatter or praise >** Those who cause divisions deceive the hearts of the unsuspecting by good words and fair speeches {flattering speech, flattery} (Rom. 16:18); *euglōttia* in some mss.: smooth talk. All other refs.: BLESSING <2129>, BOUNTIFULLY <2129>, GIFT <2129>.

– 4 Mark 9:17 → robbed of his speech → DUMB <216> 5 John 10:6; 16:25a, b, 29 → figure of speech, figurative speech → ALLEGORY <3942> 6 Col. 2:4 → persuasive speech → persuasive word → WORD <4086> 7 2 Pet. 2:16 → without speech → DUMB <880> 8 1 John 3:18 → TONGUE <1100>.

SPEECHLESS – 1 ***enneos*** [adj.: ἐννεός <1769>]; **also spelled: *eneos* ▶ Incapable of speaking, stupefied >** The men who traveled with Paul stood speechless (Acts 9:7). ¶

2 **to be speechless: *phimoō*** [verb: φιμόω <5392>]; **from *phimos*: muzzle; lit.: to muzzle ▶ To reduce to silence >** A man who was asked about his wedding garment, and did not have one, was speechless (Matt. 22:12). All other refs.: see MUZZLE <5392>, QUIET (adj.) <5392>, SILENCE (noun) <5392>.

– 3 Mark 7:37 → DUMB <216> 4 Luke 1:22 → DUMB <2974> 5 2 Pet. 2:16 → DUMB <880>.

SPEED (noun) – 1 Acts 17:15 → with all speed → as quickly as possible → QUICKLY <5033> 2 Rom. 9:28 → to carry with speed → to cut short → SHORT <4932> 3 2 John 10, 11 → to bid God speed → HAIL (verb) <5463>.

SPEED (verb) – 1 2 Thes. 3:1 → to speed ahead → RUN <5143> 2 2 Pet. 3:12 → HASTEN <4692>.

SPEEDILY – 1 ***en tachei***; ***en*** [prep.: ἐν <1722>] ***tachos*** [neut. noun: τάχος <5034>]; **from *tachos*: speed; lit.: in haste ▶ Promptly, rapidly, hastily >** The Lord will avenge His own elect speedily {quickly} (Luke 18:8). Other refs.: QUICKLY <5034>, SHORTLY <5034>.
– 2 2 Pet. 1:14 → SHORTLY <5031>.

SPELL – Rev. 18:23 → magic spell → SORCERY <5331>.

SPEND – 1 ***dapanaō*** [verb: δαπανάω <1159>]; **from *dapanē*: cost, expense ▶ a. To pay the cost, the expense >** The woman who had a hemorrhage for twelve years had spent everything she had and was no better (Mark 5:26). After the prodigal son had spent all he had, a severe famine arose in the land where he was (Luke 15:14). Paul would most gladly spend for the souls of the Corinthians (2 Cor. 12:15a). **b. To waste, to squander >** James' readers did not receive because they asked so they could spend {consume} it in their own pleasures (Jas. 4:3). Other ref.: Acts 21:24 (to pay the expenses); see EXPENSE <1159>. ¶

2 **to be spent, to be utterly spent: *ekdapanaō*** [verb: ἐκδαπανάω <1550>]; **from *ek*: intens., and *dapanaō*: see 1 ▶ To devote oneself completely >** Paul would be utterly spent {would be expended} for the souls of the Corinthians (2 Cor. 12:15b). ¶

3 **to spend more: *prosdapanaō*** [verb: προσδαπανάω <4325>]; **from *pros*: moreover, and *dapanaō*: see 1 ▶ To pay the extra costs >** In the parable, whatever the innkeeper would spend more {expend more} {his extra expense} for the wounded man would be repaid by the Samaritan (Luke 10:35). ¶

4 ***parerchomai*** [verb: παρέρχομαι <3928>]; **from *para*: near, and *erchomai*: to go, to come ▶ To accomplish already >** Peter speaks about the sufficient time spent {past} by Christians doing the will of the Gentiles (1 Pet. 4:3). All other refs.: COME <3928>,

GO <3928>, PASS <3928>, TRANSGRESS <3928>.

[5] ***prosanaliskō*** [verb: προσαναλίσκω <4321>]; **from *pros*: beside (i.e., in addition), and *analiskō*: to consume, which is from *ana*: away and *aliskō*: to take ▶ To pay much, to disburse much** > The woman having a hemorrhage had spent all her living on physicians (Luke 8:43); other mss.: *prosanaloō*. ¶

[6] **to be far spent: *proekopsa*; aorist of *prokoptō*** [verb: προκόπτω <4298>]; ***prokoptō*: to advance, to progress, which is from *pro*: forward, and *koptō*: to strike, to impel ▶ To be advanced** > The (moral) night of this world is far spent {is almost gone, is nearly over}, and the day (of the coming of the Lord) is at hand (Rom. 13:12). All other refs.: GROW <4298>, INCREASE (verb) <4298>, PROCEED <4298>.

[7] **to spend time: *eukaireō*** [verb: εὐκαιρέω <2119>]; **from *eukairos*: timely, convenient, which is from *eu*: well, and *kairos*: time, opportune time ▶ To occupy one's time** > The people of Athens spent their time telling and hearing the news (Acts 17:21). Other refs.: Mark 6:31 (to have time); 1 Cor. 16:12 (to have opportunity); see TIME <2119>, OPPORTUNITY <2119>. ¶

[8] **to spend time: *chronotribeō*** [verb: χρονοτριβέω <5551>]; **from *chronos*: time, and *tribō*: to rub, to wear away ▶ To lose one's time, to linger (behind)** > Paul did not want to spend time in Asia (Acts 20:16). ¶

– [9] Mark 6:35 → far spent → PASS <4183> [10] Mark 6:37 → BUY <59> [11] Luke 2:43 → to spend the full number → FULFILL <5048> [12] Luke 21:37 → to spend the night → to stay at night → STAY (verb) <835> [13] Luke 24:29 → to be far spent → to wear away → WEAR <2827> [14] John 1:39 → to spend the day → REMAIN <3306> [15] John 3:22; Acts 12:19; 14:3, 28; 20:6; 25:6, 14 → to spend (time) → STAY (verb) <1304> [16] Acts 27:9 → ELAPSE <1230> [17] Acts 28:14; 1 Cor. 16:7, 8 → STAY (verb) <1961> [18] 2 Cor. 11:25; Jas. 4:13 → PASS <4160> [19] Rev. 12:15, 16 → CAST (verb) <906>.

SPHERE – 2 Cor. 10:13, 15, 16 → RULE (noun) <2583>.

SPICE – [1] ***arōma*** [neut. noun: ἄρωμα <759>] ▶ **Prob. aromatic spices or a mixture of myrrh and aloes; also transl.: aromatic spice, sweet spice** > Nicodemus and Joseph of Arimathea bound the body of Jesus in linen with the spices (John 19:40). Later, women bought sweet spices to anoint the body of Jesus (Mark 16:1; Luke 23:56; 24:1). ¶

[2] ***amōmon*** [neut. noun: ἄμωμον <298a>]; **from *a*: neg. and *mōmos*: blemish; *amomum*, in Lat. ▶ Poss. an Indian spice plant** > The merchants of the earth will weep over the fall of Babylon who will no longer buy from them various products, cinnamon and spice among others (Rev. 18:13 in some mss.). ¶

SPIKENARD – Mark 14:3; John 12:3 → NARD <3487>.

SPILL – [1] Matt. 9:17; Mark 2:22; Luke 5:37 → to pour out → POUR <1632> [2] Acts 1:18 → to spill out → to gush out → GUSH <1632a>.

SPIN – ***nēthō*** [verb: νήθω <3514>] ▶ **To transform fiber into yarn or thread** > The lilies of the field neither toil nor spin (Matt. 6:28 {other mss.: *xainō*}; Luke 12:27). ¶

SPIRIT – [1] ***pneuma*** [neut. noun: πνεῦμα <4151>]; **from *pneō*: to breathe ▶ Immaterial part of a person where the intellectual and moral power resides; it is the principle of life in the human being** > It is difficult to differentiate the spirit and the soul, but the word of God recognizes the distinction (Heb. 4:12). This invisible and immaterial part of the person leaves the body at the time of death (Luke 8:55). Jesus committed His spirit into the hands of His Father (Matt. 27:50; Luke 23:46; John 19:30). The word is used to designate God the Holy Spirit (e.g., Matt. 4:1; Luke

4:18); see HOLY SPIRIT <40> <4151>. It also designates demons (e.g., Matt. 8:16) and angels (e.g., Heb. 1:14). Other refs.: BREATH <4151>, WIND (noun) <4151>. *

– [2] Matt. 14:26; Mark 6:49 → GHOST <5326> [3] Acts 19:13 → driving out evil spirits → EXORCIST <1845> [4] 1 Cor. 2:14 → man without the Spirit → lit.: natural man → NATURAL <5591> [5] 1 Cor. 2:15; 12:1; 14:1, 37; Col. 1:9; 3:16 → SPIRITUAL <4152> [6] Eph. 5:9 in some mss. → LIGHT (noun) <5457> [7] Phil. 2:2 → being one in spirit, united in spirit → joined in soul → SOUL <4861> [8] Phil. 2:20 → of kindred spirit → LIKEMINDED <2473> [9] Col. 2:8 → elemental spirits → ELEMENT <4747> [10] 2 Thes. 2:8 → BREATH <4151> [11] 1 Pet. 4:7 → to be of sober spirit → WATCH (verb) <3525>.

SPIRIT-TAUGHT – 1 Cor. 2:13 → Spirit-taught words → spiritual means → SPIRITUAL <4152>.

SPIRITUAL – [1] ***pneumatikos*** [adj.: πνευματικός <4152>]; **from *pneuma*: spirit ► a. Related to God Himself** > The spiritual rock that followed the Israelites was Christ Himself (1 Cor. 10:4b). **b. Relative to the spirit or soul in communion with God** > Paul wished to impart some spiritual gift (Rom. 1:11). He communicated spiritual things by spiritual means (lit.: by spirituals) (1 Cor. 2:13a, b). **c. Which has its source in God and which God gives** > The law is spiritual (Rom. 7:14). The nations have participated in the spiritual blessings of Israel (Rom. 15:27). Paul had sown spiritual things among the Corinthians (1 Cor. 9:11). The Israelites had all eaten the same spiritual food and drunk the same spiritual drink (1 Cor. 10:3, 4a). Christians are to earnestly desire spiritual gifts (1 Cor. 14:1). The God and Father of Christians has blessed them with every spiritual blessing in the heavenlies in Christ (Eph. 1:3). Paul prayed that the Colossians might be filled with the knowledge of the will of God, in all wisdom and spiritual understanding (Col. 1:9). **d. State of one who is full of and governed by the Spirit of God** > He who is spiritual discerns all things (1 Cor. 2:15). Paul had not been able to speak to the Corinthians as to spiritual men (1 Cor. 3:1). Someone at Corinth might think himself to be a prophet or spiritual (1 Cor. 14:37). Spiritual brothers are to restore in a spirit of meekness a brother who has been overtaken in a fault (Gal. 6:1). **e. State of the body of the resurrected Christian** > The body of the Christian is sown a natural body, it is raised a spiritual body (1 Cor. 15:44a, b); that which is spiritual did not come first, but that which is natural, then that which is spiritual (v. 46a, b). **f. Which is inspired by God, His person, and His actions** > Christians speak to one another in spiritual songs (Eph. 5:19; Col. 3:16). **g. What characterizes the church of Christians on earth and what they offer to God** > As living stones, Christians are being built up as a spiritual house to offer up spiritual sacrifices, acceptable to God through Jesus Christ (1 Pet. 2:5a, b). Other refs.: Rom. 15:27 (see [2]); 1 Cor. 9:11 (see [2]); 12:1 (see GIFT <4152>); Eph. 6:12 (spiritual force, spiritual power). ¶

[2] **spiritual *things*: *ta pneumatika*; plur. of *pneumatikos*: see [1]; lit.: the spirituals ► Matters concerning the spiritual component, the highest one, of the person** > The Gentiles have participated in the spiritual things {spiritual blessings} of the saints in Jerusalem (Rom. 15:27). Paul had sown spiritual things {spiritual seed} for the Corinthians (1 Cor. 9:11).

– [3] Rom. 12:1 → INTELLIGENT <3050> [4] 1 Pet. 2:2 → INTELLECTUAL <3050>.

SPIRITUALLY – ***pneumatikōs*** [adv.: πνευματικῶς <4153>]; **from *pneumatikos*: spiritual, which is from *pneuma*: spirit ► a. Related to what the Holy Spirit produces among men** > The things that are of the Spirit of God are spiritually discerned (1 Cor. 2:14). **b. Symbolically, mystically** > Jerusalem is called spiritually Sodom and Egypt (Rev. 11:8). Other ref.: 1 Cor. 2:13 in some mss. ¶

SPIT – [1] ***ptuō*** [verb: πτύω <4429>] ► **To expel saliva from the mouth** > Jesus spat and touched the tongue of a deaf man (Mark 7:33). He spat on the eyes of a blind man (Mark 8:23). He spat on the ground and made clay with His saliva; He anointed the eyes of the blind man with the clay (John 9:6). ¶

[2] ***emptuō*** [verb: ἐμπτύω <1716>]; **from *en*: in, upon, and *ptuō*: to spit.; lit.: to spit upon ► See defin. of [1].** > Men spat in the face of Jesus and upon Him (Matt. 26:67; 27:30; Mark 14:65; 15:19). Jesus Himself had said that He would be spit upon (Mark 10:34; Luke 18:32). ¶

– [3] Rev. 3:16 → VOMIT (verb) <1692>.

SPITEFULLY – [1] Matt. 22:6; 1 Thes. 2:2 → to treat spitefully, to entreat spitefully → MISTREAT <5195> [2] Luke 18:32 → to entreat spitefully → INSULT (verb) <5195>.

SPITTLE – John 9:6 → SALIVA <4427>.

SPLENDID – [1] Luke 7:25 → gorgeous → GORGEOUSLY <1741> [2] Luke 23:11; Jas. 2:2, 3; Rev. 18:14 → BRIGHT <2986>.

SPLENDIDLY – Luke 7:25 → GORGEOUSLY <1741>.

SPLENDOR, SPLENDOUR – [1] Luke 16:19 → in splendor, in splendour → SUMPTUOUSLY <2988> [2] Eph. 5:27 → in splendor → GLORIOUS <1741> [3] 2 Thes. 2:8 → APPEARING <2015> [4] Rev. 18:14 → BRIGHT <2986>.

SPLIT – [1] ***schizō*** [verb: σχίζω <4977>] ► **To open, to divide** > At the death of Jesus, the rocks were split {were rent} (Matt. 27:51). Jesus came up out of the Jordan and saw the heavens opening (Mark 1:10 {to part, to part asunder, to tear open}). All other refs.: BREAK <4977>, DIVIDE <4977>, TEAR (verb) <4977>.

– [2] Rev. 6:14 → to split apart → RECEDE <673> [3] Rev. 16:19 → DIVIDE <1096>.

SPOIL – [1] Matt. 6:19, 20 → DESTROY <853> [2] Matt. 12:29a, b; Mark 3:27a, b → PLUNDER (verb) <1283> [3] John 6:27 → PERISH <622> [4] 2 Cor. 11:8 → ROB <4813> [5] Col. 2:8 → to lead away as a prey → PREY <4812> [6] Col. 2:15 → DISARM <554> [7] 1 Pet. 1:4 → that can never spoil → UNDEFILED <283>.

SPOILING – Heb. 10:34 → PLUNDERING <724>.

SPOILS – [1] ***akrothinion*** [neut. noun: ἀκροθίνιον <205>]; **from *akron*: upper part, and *this*: heap, pile; lit.: best part of the spoils ► Plunder taken from the enemy after the victory** > Abraham gave a tenth of the spoils {choicest spoils} to Melchizedek after the slaughter of the kings (Heb. 7:4). ¶

[2] ***skulon*** [neut. noun: σκῦλον <4661>]; **from *skullō*: to tear ► In the plur.: weaponry and objects of value taken from the enemy** > He who overcomes the strong man divides his spoils {plunder} (Luke 11:22). ¶

SPOKESMAN – Acts 24:1 → ORATOR <4489>.

SPONGE – ***spongos*** [masc. noun: σπόγγος <4699>] ► **Light and porous substance which facilitates the absorption of a liquid** > A sponge {spunge} was filled with sour wine and offered to Jesus to drink (Matt. 27:48; Mark 15:36; John 19:29). ¶

SPORT – 2 Pet. 2:13 → to sport oneself → REVEL (verb) <1792>.

SPOT – [1] ***spilas*** [fem. noun: σπιλάς <4694>] ► **Reef, person who causes others to make shipwreck** > Jude speaks of those who are spots {blemishes, hidden reefs} in the love-feasts of Christians, feasting together with them without fear (Jude 12). ¶

[2] ***spilos*** [masc. noun: σπίλος <4696>] ► **Defilement, moral defect** > Jesus will present the church to Himself, glorious, having no spot {stain}, or wrinkle, or any such thing (Eph. 5:27). Peter speaks of unrigh-

teous men who are spots {blots, stains} and blemishes (2 Pet. 2:13). ¶

3 **without spot: *aspilos*** [adj.: ἄσπιλος <784>]; **from *a*: neg., and *spilos*: see 2 ▶ Immaculate, without defect; also transl.: spotless, without stain** > Timothy was to keep the commandment to take hold of eternal life without spot, irreprehensible, until the appearing of the Lord Jesus Christ (1 Tim. 6:14). Christians have been redeemed from their vain conduct by the precious blood of Christ, as of a lamb without blemish and without spot (1 Pet. 1:19). Christians should be diligent to be found by the Lord in peace, without spot and blameless (2 Pet. 3:14). Other ref.: Jas. 1:27; see UNSPOTTED <784>. ¶

4 **without spot: *amōmos*** [adj.: ἄμωμος <299>]; **from *a*: neg., and *mōmos*: criticism, reprimand ▶ Without defect, irreprehensible; also transl.: spotless, without blemish, unblemished** > The blood of Christ, who by the Eternal Spirit offered Himself without spot to God, purifies the conscience of Christians from dead works, so that we may serve the living God (Heb. 9:14). All other refs.: BLAMELESS <299>, BLEMISH <299>.

– 5 Jude 23 → DEFILE <4695>.

SPOTLESS – 1 1 Tim. 6:14; 1 Pet. 1:19; 2 Pet. 3:14 → without spot → SPOT <784> 2 Heb. 9:14 → without spot → SPOT <299>.

SPREAD – 1 ***aperchomai*** [verb: ἀπέρχομαι <565>]; **from *apo*: from, and *erchomai*: to come, to go ▶ To reach, to attain** > The fame of Jesus spread throughout {went out into, went throughout} the whole of Syria (Matt. 4:24). All other refs.: see entries in Lexicon at <565>.

2 **to spread, to spread abroad: *dierchomai*** [verb: διέρχομαι <1330>]; **from *dia*: through, and *erchomai*: to come, to go ▶ To extend, to go out** > The report concerning Jesus was spread abroad {went abroad, went around} still more (Luke 5:15). All other refs.: COME <1330>, GO <1330>, PASS <1330>, PIERCE <1330>.

3 ***exerchomai*** [verb: ἐξέρχομαι <1831>]; **from *ek*: from, and *erchomai*: to come, to go; lit.: to go out of a place ▶ To propagate, to become known; also transl.: to go abroad, to go out, etc.** > The fame of the resurrection of a young girl by Jesus spread to all the land (Matt. 9:26), as likewise the report of the resurrection of a young man spread in all Judaea (Luke 7:17). The fame of Jesus spread into the whole region of Galilee (Mark 1:28; Luke 4:14). The word that the apostle John would not die spread {spread abroad} among the brothers (John 21:23). The faith of the Thessalonians toward God had spread (1 Thes. 1:8). All other refs.: COME <1831>, DEPART <1831>, ESCAPE <1831>, GO <1831>, STEP (verb) <1831>.

4 ***dianemō*** [verb: διανέμω <1268>]; **from *dia*: denoting dispersion, and *nemō*: to share, to distribute ▶ To divulge, to circulate** > The Jews did not want the report to be further spread of the miracle that had been worked by Peter at Jerusalem (Acts 4:17). ¶

5 **to spread through: *diapherō*** [verb: διαφέρω <1308>]; **from *dia*: through, and *pherō*: to bear ▶ To publish, to proclaim** > The word of the Lord was spread through {carried through, published throughout} the whole country where Paul and Barnabas were found (Acts 13:49). All other refs.: see entries in Lexicon at <1308>.

6 **to spread; to spread abroad, throughout, widely: *diaphēmizō*** [verb: διαφημίζω <1310>]; **from *dia*: denoting dispersion, and *phēmizō*: to affirm, to say ▶ To make known, to proclaim** > The story that His disciples had stolen the body of Jesus had been widely spread {was current, was commonly reported, had been widely circulated} among the Jews (Matt. 28:15); other mss.: *phēmizō*. The leper who was healed by Jesus began to spread abroad {blaze abroad} the matter (Mark 1:45). Other ref.: Matt. 9:31 (to spread the news); see NEWS <1310>. ¶

7 ***ekporeuomai*** [verb: ἐκπορεύομαι <1607>]; **from *ek*: out, and *poreuomai*: to go, to proceed ▶ To circulate, to propagate** > The report concerning Jesus spread

{went out} into every locality in the surrounding region after He had cast a demon out of a man (Luke 4:37). All other refs.: DEPART <1607>, GO <1607>, PROCEED <1607>.
8 ***strōnnuō*** [verb: στρωννύω <4766>] ▶ **To distribute over a large area, to lay out** > The crowd spread {strew} their clothes and branches on the road taken by Jesus (Matt. 21:8; Mark 11:8); Luke uses *hupostrōnnuō*: see **9**. Other ref.: Acts 9:34 (to make one's bed); see BED <4766>. ¶
9 ***hupostrōnnuō*** [verb: ὑποστρωννύω <5291>]; **from *hupo*: under, and *strōnnuō*: see 8** ▶ **To strew, to lay on the ground** > Many spread their clothes on the road where Jesus was passing (Luke 19:36); Matthew and Mark use *strōnnuō*: see **8**. ¶
– **10** Luke 2:17 → to make widely known → KNOW <1107> or <1232> **11** Acts 2:6 → OCCUR <1096> **12** Acts 6:7; 19:20 → GROW <837> **13** Acts 11:19 → spreading the word → speaking the word → SPEAK <2980> **14** Acts 12:24 → MULTIPLY <4129> **15** 2 Cor. 2:14 → to spread the fragrance → to manifest the aroma → MANIFEST (verb) <5319> **16** 2 Cor. 4:15 → to spread the more, having spread → ABOUND <4121> **17** 2 Thes. 3:1 → to spread rapidly → RUN <5143> **18** 2 Tim. 2:17 → to spread as gangrene → lit.: to have pasture as gangrene → GANGRENE <1044>, PASTURE <3542> **19** 3 John 10 → to spread malicious nonsense about → to prate against with malicious words → PRATE <5396>.

SPREAD ABROAD – Mark 6:14 → PUBLIC <5318>.

SPREADING – 2 Cor. 4:15 → ABOUND <4121>.

SPRING (noun) – **1** John 4:14; Jas. 3:11; 2 Pet. 2:17; Rev. 7:17; 8:10; 14:7; 16:4; 21:6 → FOUNTAIN <4077> **2** Jas. 3:11 → OPENING <3692>.

SPRING (verb) – **1** **to spring up: *hallomai*** [verb: ἅλλομαι <242>] ▶ **To gush out** > The water that Jesus gives someone is in him a fountain of water springing up {welling up} into eternal life (John 4:14). Other refs.: Acts 3:8b; 14:10; see LEAP <242>. ¶
2 ***anatellō*** [verb: ἀνατέλλω <393>]; **from *ana*: up, and *tellō*: to rise** ▶ **To come forth, to arise; also transl.: to descend** > The Lord sprang out of Judah (Heb. 7:14). All other refs.: RISE (verb) <393>.
3 **to spring up: *exanatellō*** [verb: ἐξανατέλλω <1816>]; **from *ek*: out, and *anatellō*: to rise, which is from *ana*: up, and *tellō*: to rise** ▶ **To come out the ground, to grow** > The verb is used concerning seed that was sowed (Matt. 13:5; Mark 4:5). ¶
4 **to spring up: *phuō*** [verb: φύω <5453>] ▶ **To grow, to germinate** > The verb is used concerning seed that was sowed (Luke 8:6, 8); also transl.: to come up. A root of bitterness springing up {growing up} could cause trouble for the Christian (Heb. 12:15). ¶
5 **to spring up with: *sumphuō*** [verb: συμφύω <4855>]; **from *sun*: together, and *phuō*: see 4** ▶ **To grow up with** > The verb is used concerning thorns (Luke 8:7). ¶
– **6** Matt. 4:16 → to spring up → RISE (verb) <393> **7** Matt. 13:7; Mark 4:8 → to spring up → GO UP <305> **8** Matt. 13:26 → to spring up → TO SPROUT <985> **9** Mark 10:50 → to spring up → ARISE <450> **10** Acts 16:29 → to spring in → to run in → RUN <1530> **11** Acts 28:13 → to spring up → BLOW (verb) <1920> **12** Rom. 7:9 → to spring to life → REVIVE <326> **13** 1 Tim. 3:16 → "from which springs true" added in Engl. **14** Jas. 3:11 → to send forth → SEND <1032> **15** Jas. 5:18 → to bring forth → PRODUCE <985>.

SPRINKLE – **1** ***rhantizō*** [verb: ῥαντίζω <4472>]; **from *rhainō*: to sprinkle** ▶ **a. To scatter with a liquid; see SPRINKLING <4378>** > This verb is used concerning the blood of animals in Heb. 9:13, 19, 21 (e.g., in the O.T., Ex. 24:6, 8; 29:16, 21). **b. To cleanse by aspersion, sprinkling; to free from all defilement** > Christians have hearts that are sprinkled (in the sense of: purified by aspersion) from a guilty conscience (Heb. 10:22). ¶

– [2] Heb. 11:28 → he sprinkled the blood → he kept the sprinkling of blood → SPRINKLING <4378>.

SPRINKLED – Heb. 12:24; 1 Pet. 1:2 → SPRINKLING <4473>.

SPRINKLING – [1] ***proschusis*** [fem. noun: πρόσχυσις <4378>]; **from *proscheō*: to pour upon, which is from *pros*: upon, and *chuō*: to pour ▶ Action of scattering a liquid (blood or water for purification), in order to attribute its value to a person or an object** > Through faith, Moses kept the Passover and the sprinkling of blood (Heb. 11:28). ¶
[2] ***rhantismos*** [masc. noun: ῥαντισμός <4473>]; **from *rhantizō*: to sprinkle ▶ See defin. of [1].** > The term "sprinkling" {sprinkled; lit.: of sprinkling} is used figur. of Jesus's blood in Heb. 12:24 and 1 Pet. 1:2. ¶

SPROUT – [1] ***blastanō*** [verb: βλαστάνω <985>]; **from *blastos*: young shoot ▶ To grow, to germinate** > The grain of wheat sprouted {shot up, sprang up} and produced a crop (Matt. 13:26). The kingdom of God is like a seed that sprouts and grows, one does not know how (Mark 4:27). All other refs.: BUD <985>, PRODUCE <985>.
[2] ***proballō*** [verb: προβάλλω <4261>]; **from *pro*: forward, and *ballō*: to throw ▶ To bud, to grow, to produce fruit; also transl.: to put forth leaves, to shoot forth, to sprout leaves** > When the trees already sprout, already the summer is near (Luke 21:30). Other ref.: Acts 19:33 (to push forward); see PUSH <4261>. ¶

SPUE – Rev. 3:16 → VOMIT (verb) <1692>.

SPUNGE – Matt. 27:48; Mark 15:36; John 19:29 → SPONGE <4699>.

SPUR – Heb. 10:24 → PROVOKE <3948>.

SPURN – [1] Luke 6:22 → to cast out → CAST (verb) <1544> [2] Heb. 10:29 → to tread underfoot → TREAD <2662>.

SPY (noun) – [1] ***enkathetos*** [adj. used as noun: ἐγκάθετος <1455>]; **from *en*: in, and *katatithēmi*: to put down, which is from *kata*: down, and *tithēmi*: to put; lit.: to put in a secret place to watch ▶ Secret agent** > The chief priests and the scribes sent forth spies {suborned persons} that they might take hold of Jesus's words (Luke 20:20). ¶
[2] ***kataskopos*** [masc. noun: κατάσκοπος <2685>]; ***kata*: down (intens.), and *skopos*: goal, which is from *skeptomai*: to look about ▶ Person responsible to collect information secretly** > Rahab had received the spies in peace in Jericho (Heb. 11:31). Other ref.: Jas. 2:25 in some mss. ¶
– [3] Jas. 2:25 → MESSENGER <32>.

SPY (verb) – **to spy out: *kataskopeō*** [verb: κατασκοπέω <2684>]; **from *kata*: down, and *skopeō*: to pay attention to ▶ To watch closely, to observe secretly** > False brothers were spying out the liberty that the Christians had in Christ Jesus (Gal. 2:4). ¶

SQUAD – Acts 12:4 → QUATERNION <5069>.

SQUALL – Luke 8:23 → STORM <2978>.

SQUANDER – [1] Luke 15:13 → WASTE (verb) <1287> [2] Luke 15:30 → DEVOUR <2719>.

SQUARE – Rev. 21:16 → as a square, like a square → FOURSQUARE <5068>.

STABILITY – [1] Col. 2:5 → STEADFASTNESS <4733> [2] 2 Pet. 3:17 → STEADFASTNESS <4740>.

STABLE – Col. 1:23 → founded → FOUND <2311>.

STABLISH – See ESTABLISH.

STACHYS – ***Stachus*** [masc. name: Στάχυς <4720>]: **ear of corn ▶ Christian man of Rome** > Paul sends greetings to Stachys (Rom. 16:9). ¶

STADIA – Luke 24:13; John 6:19; 11:18; Rev. 14:20; 21:16 → plur. of stadion → STADION <4712>.

STADION – ***stadion*** [neut. noun: στάδιον <4712>]; **from *histēmi*: to stand ▶ Measure of distance of about 600 feet (183 meters); also transl.: furlong, mile >** Emmaus was about 60 stadia (i.e., about seven miles or 11 kilometers) from Jerusalem (Luke 24:13). Other refs.: Matt. 14:24; John 6:19; 11:18; Rev. 14:20; 21:16. Other ref.: 1 Cor. 9:24; see RACE[2] <4712>. ¶

STAFF – 1 ***rhabdos*** [fem. noun: ῥάβδος <4464>] **▶ Stick, staff for walking; also for inflicting a punishment >** Jesus's disciples were to go preaching without taking a staff {stave} for the journey (Matt. 10:10; Luke 9:3). Later He would allow them to take a staff (Mark 6:8). When he was dying, Jacob worshipped, leaning on the top of his staff (Heb. 11:21). All other refs.: ROD <4464>, SCEPTER <4464>.
– 2 Matt. 27:29, 30, 48; Mark 15:19, 36 → REED <2563>.

STAIN (noun) – 1 Eph. 5:27; 2 Pet. 2:13 → SPOT <4696> 2 1 Tim. 6:14 → without stain → without spot → SPOT <784>.

STAIN (verb) – Jas. 3:6; Jude 23 → DEFILE <4695>.

STAIR – ***anabathmos*** [masc. noun: ἀναβαθμός <304>]; **from *anabainō*: to go up, which is from *ana*: up, and *bainō*: to go; lit.: a means to go up ▶ Step of a stairway >** In Acts 21:35, 40, the stairs {steps} were most likely leading from the palace of Antonia to the temple. ¶

STAKE – 1 Rom. 16:4 → RISK <5294> 2 2 Cor. 1:23 → I call God as my witness — and I stake my life on it → I call God to witness on my soul → SOUL <5590>.

STALK – Mark 4:28 → GRASS <5528>.

STALL – Luke 13:15 → MANGER <5336>.

STANCH – Luke 8:44 → STOP <2476>.

STAND (noun) – 1 **to take one's stand: *paristēmi*** [verb: παρίστημι <3936>]; **from *para*: beside, near, and *histēmi*: to stand ▶ To be present, to present oneself >** David has said that the kings of the earth took their stand, and the rulers were assembled against the Lord and against His Christ (Acts 4:26). Other refs.: see entries in Lexicon at <3936>.
– 2 Matt. 5:15; Mark 4:21; Luke 8:16; 11:33 → LAMPSTAND <3087> 3 Acts 2:14 → to take one's stand → STAND (verb) <2476> 4 Col. 2:18 → to take a stand on → to intrude into → INTRUDE <1687>.

STAND (verb) – 1 **to stand, to stand still, to stand up: *histēmi*** [verb: ἵστημι <2476>]; **same as *stare*, in Lat. ▶ a. To be on one's feet in a vertical position, to remain upright >** The hypocrites loved to pray standing in the synagogues and on the street corners (Matt. 6:5). Peter was standing up {taking his stand} with the eleven (Acts 2:14). Healed by Peter, the lame man stood {jumped to his feet} and walked (Acts 3:8). Stephen saw Jesus standing at the right hand of God (Acts 7:55, 56). A man appeared to Paul in a vision, standing and pleading with him to come over and help them in Macedonia (Acts 16:9). Having obtained help from God, Paul stood {continued} and witnessed concerning Christ (Acts 26:22). If one stands {stands fast} by faith, he should not be haughty but fear (Rom. 11:20). The servant of another will be made to stand {to be held up}, for God is able to make him stand (Rom. 14:4b, c). He who thinks he stands should take heed lest he falls (1 Cor. 10:12). The Corinthians were standing by faith (2 Cor. 1:24). Epaphras was praying that the Colossians might stand perfect and complete in all the will of God (Col. 4:12). The solid foundation of the Lord stands: The Lord knows those who are His, and let everyone who names the name of Christ depart from iniquity (2 Tim. 2:19). Every priest stood ministering daily in Israel (Heb. 10:11). The poor man might have been told to stand rather than to sit in the synagogue

(Jas. 2:3). John saw four angels standing at the four corners of the world (Rev. 7:1); he also saw an angel standing at the altar (8:3). Those who had the victory over the beast were standing on the sea of glass (Rev. 15:2). **b. To stop and remain in one place, to come to a halt** > The star stood over where the little child Jesus was (Matt. 2:9). Jesus stood still {stopped} and called blind men (Matt. 20:32; Mark 10:49; Luke 18:40). Jesus stood in the plain (Luke 6:17). Those who carried the dead young man stood still {came to a halt} (Luke 7:14). Ten lepers stood at a distance (Luke 17:12). The friend of the bridegroom stands {waits} (i.e., to help) and hears the bridegroom (John 3:29). The Ethiopian commanded the chariot to stand still {stop} so that he could be baptized (Acts 8:38). The men who traveled with Paul stood speechless (Acts 9:7). **c. To appear (for judgment)** > Paul was standing and being judged for the hope of the promise made by God to the Israelites (Acts 26:6). **d. To place, to establish** > The abomination of desolation will be standing in the holy place (Matt. 24:15; Mark 13:14). **e. To maintain oneself, to subsist** > Every city or house divided against itself will not stand (Matt. 12:25; Mark 3:25); it will be the same for a kingdom (Mark 3:24). If Satan is divided against himself, neither he nor his kingdom will subsist (Matt. 12:26; Mark 3:26; Luke 11:18). The question is raised: Who will be able to stand before the wrath of the Lamb, when the great day of His wrath will come? (Rev. 6:17). **f. To station oneself in an upright position with stability** > The devil has not stood in {abode not in, did not hold} the truth (John 8:44). **g. To station oneself against, to station oneself firmly** > The whole armor of God enables Christians to stand against the wiles of the devil (Eph. 6:11), to withstand, and, having accomplished all things, to stand (v. 13); we are to stand therefore (v. 14). Other refs.: Matt. 16:28; Mark 9:1; Luke 9:27; Acts 4:14. Other refs.: see entries in Lexicon at <2476>.

2 to stand; to stand before, by, next: *ephistēmi* [verb: ἐφίστημι <2186>]**; from *epi*: upon, and *histēmi*: see 1 ► To appear, to come upon** > An angel of the Lord stood before the shepherds (Luke 2:9). Two men stood by the women at the tomb of Jesus (Luke 24:4). Jesus stood over {bent over} Peter's mother-in-law and rebuked her fever (Luke 4:39). Other refs.: Acts 10:17 {to stop}; 11:11; 22:13; 23:11. All other refs.: ASSAULT (verb) <2186>, COME <2186>, FALL (verb) <2186>, HAND (noun) <2186>, READY <2186>.

3 to stand by, before, beside, near: *paristēmi* [verb: παρίστημι <3936>]**; from *para*: near, and *histēmi*: see 1 ► a. To be near, to appear** > Two men in white clothing stood beside the disciples who had witnessed the ascension of Jesus (Acts 1:10). **b. To stand before (e.g., a judge)** > Paul had to stand before {be brought before} Caesar (Acts 27:24). We will all stand before {be placed before} the judgment seat of God (Rom. 14:10). **c. To be present, to stand nearby** > A certain one of those who stood by Jesus, struck the bondman of the high priest (Mark 14:47). The word is also used in Mark 14:70; 15:35; Luke 19:24; Acts 9:39; 23:4; 27:23. Other refs.: see entries in Lexicon at <3936>.

4 to stand by, about, around: *periistēmi* [verb: περιΐστημι <4026>]**; from *peri*: around, and *histēmi*: see 1 ► To stand around, to encircle** > People were standing around when Jesus spoke to His Father at the tomb of Lazarus (John 11:42). The Jews stood about {stood round about} the tribunal and laid many complaints against Paul (Acts 25:7). Other refs.: 2 Tim. 2:16; Titus 3:9; see SHUN <4026>. ¶

5 *sunistēmi* [verb: συνίστημι <4921>]**; from *sun*: together, and *histēmi*: to set, to stand ► To be with** > Ref. Luke 9:32. All other refs.: COMMEND <4921>, MAKE <4921>, PROVE <4921>, SUBSIST <4921>.

6 *keimai* [verb: κεῖμαι <2749>] **► To be placed, to be set** > Stone water-vessels stood for the purification of the Jews (John 2:6). John saw a throne standing in the heaven (Rev. 4:2). Other refs.: APPOINT <2749>, LAID OUT (BE) <2749>, LAY <2749>, LIE (verb)[1] <2749>, SITUATE <2749>.

7 **to stand, to stand fast, to stand firm:** ***stēkō*** [verb: στήκω <4739>]; **from *histēmi*: see 1 ▶ a. To stand straight up** > Whenever we stand praying, we should forgive him whom we have something against (Mark 11:25). A servant stands or falls to his own master (Rom. 14:4a). **b. To remain firm, to persevere** > Paul exhorts the Philippians to stand firm in the Lord (Phil. 4:1). He tells the Thessalonians to stand firm and hold the instructions that they were taught (2 Thes. 2:15). All other refs.: FIRM <4739>.

– 8 Matt. 4:5; 18:2; Mark 9:36; Luke 4:9; 9:47; John 8:3; Acts 5:27; Jude 24 → to stand, to have to stand, to make stand → SET (verb) <2476> 9 Matt. 10:22; 24:13; Mark 13:13; Heb. 10:32 → to stand firm, to stand one's ground → ENDURE <5278> 10 Matt. 12:41; Mark 14:60; Luke 4:16; 10:25; 11:32; Acts 1:15; 5:34; 10:26; 11:28; 13:16; 14:10; 26:30; et al. → to stand up → ARISE <450> 11 Matt. 18:16 → to stand upon → ESTABLISH <2476> 12 Mark 3:3; Luke 6:8b → to stand forth → ARISE <1453> 13 Mark 13:9 → to bring before → BRING <2476> 14 Luke 21:28 → to stand up → to look up → LOOK (verb) <352> 15 Luke 22:28 → to stand by → PERSEVERE <1265> 16 John 8:7, 10 → to stand up → to straighten oneself up → STRAIGHTEN <352> 17 Acts 6:10 → to stand up against → RESIST <436> 18 Acts 7:5 → GROUND <968> 19 Acts 8:36 → to stand in the way → HINDER (verb) <2967> 20 Acts 11:17 → to stand in one's way → FORBID <2967> 21 Acts 14:20 → to stand around → SURROUND <2944> 22 Acts 15:5 → to stand up → to rise up → RISE (verb) <1817> 23 Rom. 9:11 → REMAIN <3306> 24 1 Cor. 2:5 → REST (verb) <5600> 25 1 Cor. 10:13 → to stand up under → ENDURE <5297> 26 1 Cor. 15:30 → to stand in jeopardy → JEOPARDY <2793> 27 1 Tim. 5:20 → may stand in fear → lit.: may have (*echō*) fear 28 2 Tim. 4:16 → to come together → COME <4836> 29 Heb. 9:8 → to be standing → lit.: to have its standing → STANDING <4714> 30 Heb. 10:33 → to stand side by side → to become partakers → PARTAKER <2844> 31 Jas. 5:8 → to stand firm → lit.: to establish the hearts → ESTABLISH <4741> 32 1 Pet. 2:6 → CONTAIN <4023>.

STANDARD – 1 Matt. 7:2; Mark 4:24; Luke 6:38 → standard of measure → MEASURE (noun) <3358> 2 John 8:15 → by human standards → lit.: according to the flesh 3 Rom. 6:17 → FORM (noun) <5179> 4 2 Tim. 1:13 → PATTERN <5296>.

STANDING – 1 ***bathmos*** [masc. noun: βαθμός <898>]; **from *bainō*: to walk; lit.: step, stair ▶ Position, rank** > The expr. "to obtain a good standing {a high standing, an excellent standing, a good degree}" (1 Tim. 3:13) means "to attain a good position," particularly in the Christian ministry. ¶

2 ***stasis*** [fem. noun: στάσις <4714>]; **from *histēmi*: to stand ▶ Position** > The first tabernacle had yet its standing {was standing} (Heb. 9:8). All other refs.: DISSENSION <4714>, INSURRECTION <4714>, TUMULT <4714>.

– 3 Acts 13:50; 17:12 → of high standing → PROMINENT <2158> 4 Acts 21:16 → of long standing → OLD <744> 5 1 Cor. 6:4 → those who have no standing → those who are least esteemed → ESTEEM (verb) <1848>.

STANDPOINT – Rom. 11:28a, b → from the standpoint → CONCERNING <2596>.

STAR – 1 ***astēr*** [masc. noun: ἀστήρ <792>]; ***stella*, in Lat. ▶ Celestial body visible in the sky at night** > The wise men saw the star of Jesus (Matt. 2:2, 7, 9, 10). During the great tribulation, the stars will fall from heaven (Matt. 24:29; Mark 13:25; Rev. 6:13). The glory of the stars differs from one to another (1 Cor. 15:41a–c). Jude speaks of evil men who are like wandering stars (Jude 13). Other refs.: Rev. 1:16, 20a, b; 2:1, 28; 3:1; 8:10–12; 9:1; 12:1, 4; 22:16. ¶

2 ***astron*** [neut. noun: ἄστρον <798>] **▶ See defin. of 1; also used for a constellation of several stars** > During the great tribulation, there will be signs in the stars (Luke 21:25). The Israelites took up the star of their god

Remphan (Acts 7:43). No stars appeared for many days during the storm that Paul went through (Acts 27:20). From Abraham and Sara were born people as many as the stars of heaven (Heb. 11:12). ¶
3 2 Pet. 1:19; Rev. 2:28; 22:16 → See MORNING STAR.
– 4 Acts 7:42 → the sun, moon, and stars → lit.: the host of heaven → HOST[1] <4756>, HEAVEN <3772> 5 Phil. 2:15 → LIGHT <5458>.

STARE – 1 John 13:22 → LOOK (verb) <991> 2 Acts 3:12; 10:4 → to fix the eyes → FIX <816>.

START – 1 Matt. 23:32 → to complete what one's ancestors started → to fill up the measure of one's fathers → MEASURE (noun) <3358> 2 Matt. 27:24 → RISE (verb) <1096> 3 Mark 10:50 in some mss. → to start up → to jump up → JUMP <375a> 4 Luke 9:46 → ARISE <1525> 5 Luke 23:19 → to take place → PLACE (noun) <1096> 6 2 Cor. 8:6, 10 → BEGIN <4278>.

STARTLE – 1 Luke 1:12 → TROUBLE (verb) <5015> 2 Luke 24:37 → TERRIFY <4422>.

STARVE – Luke 15:17 → PERISH <622>.

STATE – 1 **original state: *archē*** [fem. noun: ἀρχή <746>] ▶ **Conditions at the beginning, commencement** > The angels who had not kept their original state {own domain, proper domain, first estate, positions of authority} are kept in eternal chains for the judgment of the great day (Jude 6; see 2 Pet. 2:4 and Gen. 6:1, 2). All other refs.: BEGINNING <746>, CORNER <746>, MAGISTRATE <746>, POWER[2] <746>, PRINCIPALITY <746>.
2 **last state: *eschatos*** [adj. used as noun: ἔσχατος <2078>] ▶ **Final condition** > The last state of a man possessed by many wicked spirits is worse than his first when he was possessed by only one of them (Matt. 12:45; Luke 11:26). If a Christian is again entangled in the defilements of the world, his last state {end, latter end} is worse than before his conversion (2 Pet. 2:20). All other refs.: END (noun) <2078>, LAST (adv. and noun) <2078>, PART (noun) <2078>.
– 3 Luke 1:48; Phil. 3:21 → lowly state, humble state → HUMILIATION <5014> 4 Phil. 2:19 → AFFAIR <3588> <4012>.

STATEMENT – 1 Mark 7:29 → WORD <3056> 2 Mark 9:32 → SAYING <4487> 3 Mark 14:56 → WITNESS (noun)[1] <3141> 4 John 6:60; Acts 6:5 → SAYING <3056> 5 Acts 24:21 → VOICE <5456> 6 2 Cor. 4:2 → open statement → MANIFESTATION <5321>.

STATER – ***statēr*** [masc. noun: στατήρ <4715>]; **from *histēmi*: to stand** ▶ **Piece of money worth two didrachmas** > Peter would find a stater in the mouth of a fish (Matt. 17:27), which would pay the temple tax of a *didrachmon* for two persons; see TAX (noun) <1323>. ¶

STATURE – ***hēlikia*** [fem. noun: ἡλικία <2244>]; **from *hēlikos*: how tall or small, or from *hēlix*: of the same age** ▶ **Height, size** > No one by taking careful thought can add one cubit to his stature (Matt. 6:27 {growth, height}; Luke 12:25). Jesus increased in wisdom and in stature, and in favor with God and man (Luke 2:52). Zaccheus was little in stature {a short man} (Luke 19:3). Gifts in the church are for edification until all Christians arrive at the unity of the faith and of the knowledge of the Son of God, at the state of a mature man, at the measure of the stature (in the moral, spiritual sense) of the fullness of Christ (Eph. 4:13). Other refs.: John 9:21, 23; Heb. 14:11; see AGE <2244>. ¶

STATUTE – Luke 1:6 → ORDINANCE <1345>.

STAVE – 1 ***xulon*** [neut. noun: ξύλον <3586>]; **from *xuō*: to scrape, to plane; lit.: wood** ▶ **Club, stick of wood** > A great multitude with swords and staves {clubs, sticks} came with Judas to take Jesus (Matt. 26:47, 55; Mark 14:43, 48; Luke 22:52).

All other refs.: STOCKS <3586>, TREE <3586>, WOOD <3586>.
– 2 Matt. 10:10; Luke 9:3 → STAFF <4464>.

STAY (noun) – ***paroikia*** [fem. noun: παροικία <3940>]; **from *paroikos*: sojourner, which is from *para*: near, and *oikos*: house ► Period of time during which a person resides at a foreign place (e.g., a country)** > God exalted the people of Israel during their stay {during their sojourn, when they dwelt as strangers} in the land of Egypt (Acts 13:17). We ought to pass the time of our stay {sojourn, sojourning} on earth in fear (1 Pet. 1:17). ¶

STAY (verb) – 1 ***diatribō*** [verb: διατρίβω <1304>]; **from *dia*: through (intens.), and *tribō*: to rub, to wear, whence: to pass the time ► To spend time in a place, to remain for a while; also transl.: to abide, to continue, to remain, to sojourn, to tarry** > The verb is used in regard to Jesus and His disciples (John 3:22; 11:54), Peter (Acts 12:19 or 20), Paul and Barnabas (Acts 14:3, 28; 15:35), Paul and other companions (Acts 16:12; 20:6), Festus (Acts 25:6), and Agrippa and Bernice (Acts 25:14). ¶
2 ***eimi*** [verb: εἰμί <1510>] ► **To be** > Joseph was to stay {remain} in Egypt until the angel told him to leave (Matt. 2:13).
3 ***epechō*** [verb: ἐπέχω <1907>]; **from *epi*: upon, and *echō*: to have, to hold ► To remain at a place** > Paul stayed {remained} in Asia for a time (Acts 19:22). All other refs.: ATTENTION <1907>, HEED (noun) <1907>, HOLD (verb) <1907>, REMARK <1907>.
4 ***epidēmeō*** [verb: ἐπιδημέω <1927>]; **from *epi*: among, and *dēmos*: people ► To reside as a foreigner among another people; also transl.: to be, to live, to sojourn, to visit** > There were Romans staying in Jerusalem (Acts 2:10). All the Athenians and the strangers staying in Athens spent their time in nothing else than to tell and to hear something new (Acts 17:21). Other ref.: Acts 18:27 in some mss. ¶
5 ***katoikeō*** [verb: κατοικέω <2730>]; **from *kata*: intens., and *oikeō*: to dwell, which is from *oikos*: house ► To live in a place, to reside** > Devout Jews from every nation were staying in {living in, dwelling at} Jerusalem (Acts 2:5). All other refs.: DWELL <2730>.
6 ***menō*** [verb: μένω <3306>] ► **To dwell, to reside** > Jesus entered in to stay {to tarry} with two disciples on the evening of His resurrection (Luke 24:29). All other refs.: AWAIT <3306>, CONTINUE <3306>, LASTING <3306>, REMAIN <3306>, TARRY <3306>.
7 ***epimenō*** [verb: ἐπιμένω <1961>]; **from *epi*: in, at, and *menō*: see 6 ► To continue in, to remain; also transl.: to abide, to tarry, to spend** > The brothers from Puteoli invited Paul to stay {spend} with them seven days (Acts 28:14). Other refs.: Acts 10:48; 21:4; 28:12; 1 Cor. 16:7, 8; Gal. 1:18; Phil. 1:24. All other refs.: CONTINUE <1961>, REMAIN <1961>, TARRY <1961>.
8 ***katamenō*** [verb: καταμένω <2650>]; **from *kata*: intens., and *menō*: see 6 ► To stay frequently** > Peter and the other apostles were staying {abiding} in an upper room (Acts 1:13). Other ref.: 1 Cor. 16:6 in some mss. ¶
9 ***paramenō*** [verb: παραμένω <3887>]; **from *para*: beside, and *menō*: see 6 ► To remain nearby, to stay close** > Paul thought perhaps to stay {to abide, to remain} with the Corinthians (1 Cor. 16:6). Other refs.: Phil. 1:25; Heb. 7:23; Jas. 1:25; see CONTINUE <3887>. ¶
10 ***sustrephō*** [verb: συστρέφω <4962>]; **from *sun*: together, and *trephō*: to turn ► To come together, to gather together** > The verb is used in regard to Jesus and His disciples (Matt. 17:22 in some mss.). Other ref.: Acts 28:3; see GATHER <4962>. ¶
11 **to stay at night: *aulizomai*** [verb: αὐλίζομαι <835>]; **from *aulē*: enclosure, sheepfold ► To lodge at night, to remain at night** > At night, Jesus went out and stayed {abode, remained, spent the night} (lit.: stayed at night) on the mount called Olivet (Luke 21:37). Other ref.: Matt. 21:17 (to pass the night); see NIGHT <835>. ¶
– 12 Matt. 15:32; Mark 8:2 → CONTINUE <4357> 13 Matt. 24:43; Mark 13:34, 35, 37 → to stay awake → WATCH (verb) <1127> 14 Matt. 24:48; Luke 1:21 → to

stay, to stay away → DELAY (verb) <5549> 15 Luke 2:43 → to stay behind → to linger behind → LINGER <5278> 16 Luke 4:42 → to keep back → KEEP (verb) <2722> 17 Luke 22:28 → those who have stayed with me → those who have persevered with me → PERSEVERE <1265> 18 Luke 24:49 → TARRY <2523> 19 John 20:10 → where they were staying → lit.: their own (homes) 20 Acts 1:4 → while staying with them → being assembled with them → ASSEMBLE <4871> 21 Acts 5:38 → to stay away → to keep away → KEEP (verb) <868> 22 Acts 8:29 → to stay near → JOIN <2853> 23 Acts 10:6, 18, 32; 21:16 → LODGE <3579> 24 Acts 17:14 → REMAIN <5278> 25 Acts 18:11 → CONTINUE <2523> 26 Acts 18:18; 1 Tim. 1:3 → REMAIN <4357> 27 Jude 6 → KEEP (verb) <5083>.

STEADFAST – 1 Acts 11:23 → steadfast purpose → lit.: purpose of heart <4286> <2588> 2 1 Cor. 7:37; 15:58; Col. 1:23 → FIRM <1476> 3 2 Cor. 1:7; Heb. 2:2; 3:14; 6:19 → FIRM <949> 4 1 Pet. 5:9 → FIRM <4731> 5 Jas. 1:12; 5:11 → to remain steadfast → ENDURE <5278> 6 1 Pet. 5:10 → to make steadfast → SETTLE <2311>.

STEADFASTLY – 1 **to set steadfastly:** ***stērizō*** [verb: στηρίζω <4741>]; **comp. *stereos*: solid, stable ▶ To fix in a certain direction with determination** > Jesus steadfastly set His face to go to {resolutely set out for, was determined to go to} Jerusalem (Luke 9:51). All other refs.: ESTABLISH <4741>, FIX <4741>, STRENGTHEN <4741>.

– 2 Acts 3:4 → to look steadfastly → to fasten the eyes → FASTEN <816> 3 Acts 6:15; 7:55; 2 Cor. 3:13 → to look steadfastly → LOOK (verb) <816> 4 Col. 4:2 → to continue steadfastly → CONTINUE <4342>.

STEADFASTNESS – 1 ***stereōma*** [neut. noun: στερέωμα <4733>]; **from *stereoō*: to confirm, to strengthen, which is from *stereos*: firm, solid ▶ Stability, strength; also transl.: firmness** > Paul rejoiced at the steadfastness of the faith of the Colossians in Christ (Col. 2:5). ¶

2 ***stērigmos*** [masc. noun: στηριγμός <4740>]; **from *stērizō*: to establish, to make stable; comp. *stereos*: solid, stable ▶ Solidity, stability, constancy (in mind and faith)** > Christians are to take care so that they do not fall from their own steadfastness, being led away by the error of lawless people (or: those who are wicked) (2 Pet. 3:17). ¶

– 3 Col. 1:11; 1 Thes. 1:3; 2 Thes. 1:4; 3:5; 1 Tim. 6:11; 2 Tim. 3:10; Titus 2:2; Jas. 1:3, 4; 5:11; 2 Pet. 1:6a, b → PATIENCE <5281> 4 1 Pet. 1:13 → with perfect steadfastness → COMPLETELY <5049>.

STEADILY – 2 Cor. 3:7, 13 → to look steadily at → BEHOLD (verb) <816>.

STEAL – 1 ***kleptō*** [verb: κλέπτω <2813>]; ***clepere*, in Lat. ▶ To take another's property without permission, to commit theft** > Jesus says to not lay up treasures on earth where thieves break in and steal, but in heaven (Matt. 6:19, 20). The commandment orders to not steal (Matt. 19:18; Mark 10:19; Luke 18:20; Rom. 13:9). The chief priests and Pharisees were afraid that the disciples of Jesus would steal His body (Matt. 27:64); the soldiers were to say that His disciples had come at night and had stolen Him away while they slept (28:13). The thief of the sheep comes only to steal, kill, and destroy, but Jesus has come that they may have life and may have it abundantly (John 10:10). Paul asks one preaching that a man should not steal if he preaches against stealing (Rom. 2:21a, b). One who was stealing before his conversion should steal no longer (Eph. 4:28a, b). ¶

– 2 Titus 2:10 → PILFER <3557>.

STEALTH – 1 Matt. 26:4; Mark 14:1 → SUBTLETY <1388> 2 Gal. 2:4 → to come in by stealth → to come in surreptitiously → SURREPTITIOUSLY <3922>.

STEDFAST – See STEADFAST.

STEDFASTNESS – See STEADFASTNESS.

STEEP – Matt. 8:32; Mark 5:13; Luke 8:33 → steep bank, steep slope → steep place → PLACE (noun) <2911>.

STEEPED (BE) – John 9:34 → to be steeped in sin at birth → lit.: to be completely born in sins → BORN (BE) <1080>, COMPLETELY <3650>.

STEER – Jas. 3:4 → DIRECT <2116>.

STEERSMAN – Acts 27:11; Rev. 18:17 → PILOT <2942>.

STENCH – to be a stench: *ozō* [verb: ὄζω <3605>] ▶ **To give an odor, as at the decomposition of a body** > Martha told the Lord about Lazarus that there was a stench already {there was a bad odor, he was stinking} (John 11:39). ¶

STEP (noun) – 1 ***ichnos*** [neut. noun: ἴχνος <2487>]; **from *hikneomai*: to go, to come** ▶ **Footstep, trace; to follow in the steps of another is to imitate his conduct** > Paul speaks of those who walk in the steps of the faith of Abraham (Rom. 4:12). Titus and Paul had walked in the same steps {course} (2 Cor. 12:18). Christ has suffered for us, leaving us a model, that we should follow in His steps (1 Pet. 2:21). ¶

– 2 Acts 21:35, 40 → STAIR <304> 3 Gal. 2:14 → their conduct was not in step → lit.: they did not walk straightforwardly → STRAIGHTFORWARD <3716> 4 Gal. 5:25 → to keep in step → to walk orderly → WALK <4748>.

STEP (verb) – 1 **to step in: *embainō*** [verb: ἐμβαίνω <1684>]; **from *en*: in, and *bainō*: to go** ▶ **To enter, to penetrate** > Whoever first stepped in {went in} the water of Bethesda was made well (John 5:4). All other refs.: ENTER <1684>, GET <1684>.

2 **to step out: *exerchomai*** [verb: ἐξέρχομαι <1831>]; **from *ek*: out, and *erchomai*: to come** ▶ **To come out, to disembark** > Jesus stepped out on {came out onto, got out on, went forth to} the land of the Gadarenes (Luke 8:27). All other refs.: COME <1831>, DEPART <1831>, ESCAPE <1831>, GO <1831>, SPREAD <1831>.

3 **to step down: *katabainō*** [verb: καταβαίνω <2597>]; **from *kata*: down, and *bainō*: to go** ▶ **To go down, to descend** > The verb is used concerning a sick man at the pool of Bethesda (John 5:7). All other refs.: COME <2597>, DESCEND <2597>, FALL (verb) <2597>, GO <2597>.

– 4 Mark 3:3 → to step forward → ARISE <1453> 5 Luke 12:1 → TREAD <2662> 6 Acts 23:19 → to step aside → DEPART <402>.

STEPHANAS – ***Stephanas*** [masc. name: Στεφανᾶς <4734>]: **crown (*stephanos*)** ▶ **Christian man of Corinth** > Paul baptized the house of Stephanas (1 Cor. 1:16). Stephanas and his household were among the first converts of Achaia and had devoted themselves to the service of the saints (1 Cor. 16:15). Paul had rejoiced at the coming of Stephanas (1 Cor. 16:17). ¶

STEPHEN – ***Stephanos*** [masc. name: Στέφανος <4736>]: **crown (*stephanos*)** ▶ **First Christian martyr** > Stephen was full of faith and of the Holy Spirit, of grace and power (Acts 6:5, 8). He was chosen with others by the apostles to serve tables (see Acts 6:2–6). Men from the synagogue disputed with him (Acts 6:9). He was stoned (Acts 7:59) and devout men carried his body to burial (8:2); then persecution occurred and brought about the dispersion of Christians (11:19). At his martyrdom, he saw the heavens opened and the Son of Man, the Lord Jesus, standing at the right hand of God (see Acts 7:55, 56). Paul was present at the martyrdom of Stephen and kept the clothes of those who killed him (Acts 22:20). ¶

STERN – ***prumna*** [fem. noun: πρύμνα <4403>]; **from *prumnos*: at the end, furthest to the rear, which is from *peras*: extremity, end** ▶ **Rear portion of a ship, back part** > The Lord slept on a cushion in the stern {hinder part} of a ship (Mark 4:38). The sailors on board Paul's ship cast four anchors out of the stern (Acts 27:29); the stern was broken by the force of the waves (v. 41). ¶

STERNLY – [1] Matt. 9:30; Mark 1:43 → to warn sternly → WARN <1690> [2] Matt. 20:31; Mark 10:48; Luke 18:39 → to tell sternly → REBUKE (verb) <2008>.

STERNNESS – Rom. 11:22a, b → SEVERITY <663>.

STEWARD – [1] ***epitropos*** [masc. noun: ἐπίτροπος <2012>]; **from *epitrepō*: to permit, which is from *epi*: to, and *trepō*: to turn ▶ Administrator of someone's goods** > Chuza was Herod's steward {manager of Herod's household} (Luke 8:3). In Matt. 20:8, the steward {foreman} had the responsibility of paying the workmen of the lord of the vineyard. Other ref.: Gal. 4:2; see GUARDIAN <2012>. ¶

[2] ***oikonomos*** [masc. noun: οἰκονόμος <3623>]; **from *oikos*: house, and *nemō*: to distribute, to manage ▶ a. Administrator, manager, distributor; also transl.: one who is entrusted** > The two qualities desired in a steward are to be faithful and prudent (Luke 12:42). Jesus told the story of an unjust steward (Luke 16:1, 3, 8). Paul was a steward of the mysteries of God (1 Cor. 4:1); it is required in stewards {those given a trust} that one be found faithful (v. 2). An overseer must be blameless, as a steward of God (Titus 1:7). As Christians have received a gift, they must minister it to one another as good stewards of the various grace of God (1 Pet. 4:10). **b. Curator, one who looks after a minor** > An heir, as long as he is a child, is under guardians and stewards {governors, managers, trustees} until the time appointed by the father (Gal. 4:2). Other ref.: Rom. 16:23; see CHAMBERLAIN <3623>. ¶

[3] **to be a steward: *oikonomeō*** [verb: οἰκονομέω <3621>]; **from *oikonomos*: see [2] ▶ To manage, to assume a responsibility** > The unfaithful steward could not be steward {be a manager} any longer; he had to give account of his stewardship (Luke 16:2). ¶

– [4] Rom. 16:23 → CHAMBERLAIN <3623>.

STEWARDSHIP – [1] ***oikonomia*** [fem. noun: οἰκονομία <3622>]; **from *oikonomeō*: to be a manager, which is from *oikonomos*: steward, which is from *oikos*: house, and *nemō*: to distribute, to manage ▶ Conduct or supervision of a house or goods entrusted, administration; also transl.: management, job** > A steward had to give an account of his stewardship (Luke 16:2–4). All other refs.: DISPENSATION <3622>.

– [2] 1 Tim. 1:4 → stewardship from God → godly edifying → EDIFYING <3622>.

STICK (noun) – [1] ***phruganon*** [neut. noun: φρύγανον <5434>]; **from *phrugō*: to burn ▶ Dry branch, brushwood** > Paul gathered a bundle of sticks and laid them on the fire (Acts 28:3). ¶

– [2] Matt. 26:47, 55; Mark 14:43, 48; Luke 22:52 → STAVE <3586> [3] Matt. 27:48; Mark 15:36 → REED <2563>.

STICK (verb) – [1] **to stick fast: *ereidō*** [verb: ἐρείδω <2043>] **▶ To push in, to drive in** > The prow of the ship stuck fast and remained immovable (Acts 27:41). ¶

– [2] Luke 10:11 → CLEAVE <2853>.

STIFF-NECKED, STIFFNECKED – ***sklērotrachēlos*** [adj.: σκληροτράχηλος <4644>]; **from *sklēros*: hard, unyielding, and *trachēlos*: throat, neck ▶ Stubborn, obstinate** > Term used metaphorically to designate those who were resisting the Holy Spirit at the time of Stephen (Acts 7:51). ¶

STIFFEN – Mark 9:18 → to stiffen out → to become rigid → RIGID <3583>.

STILL (adj.) – Mark 4:39 → to be still → to be silent → SILENT <4623>.

STILL (adv.) – [1] ***akmēn*** [adv.: ἀκμήν <188>]; **from *akmē*: point of time ▶ Yet, as previously, even now** > Jesus asked his disciples if they were still without intelligence (Matt. 15:16). ¶

– [2] 1 Cor. 15:6 → HITHERTO <737>.

STILL (verb) – 1 Cor. 13:8 → CEASE <3973>.

STIMULATE – [1] ***erethizō*** [verb: ἐρεθίζω <2042>]; **from *erethō*: to trouble, to stir, to anger ▶ To excite, to provoke >** The zeal of the Corinthians had stimulated {provoked, stirred, stirred up} the mass of the brothers (2 Cor. 9:2). Other ref.: Col. 3:21; see PROVOKE <2042>. ¶

– [2] Heb. 10:24 → provoking → PROVOKE <3948> [3] 2 Pet. 3:1 → to wake up → WAKE <1326>.

STING (noun) – ***kentron*** [neut. noun: κέντρον <2759>]; **from *kenteō*: to sting, to stimulate ▶ Object which pricks or wounds, tormenting in a painful way; goad >** Paul heard a voice saying it was hard for him to kick against the stings {goads, pricks} (Acts 26:14). Hosea asks where is the sting of death (1 Cor. 15:55); Paul says that the sting of death is sin (v. 56). The locusts had tails like scorpions, and stings (Rev. 9:10). ¶

STING (verb) – Rev. 9:5 → STRIKE <3817>.

STINGER – Rev. 9:10 → STING <2759>.

STINK – John 11:39 → to be a stench → STENCH <3605>.

STIR (noun) – Acts 12:18; 19:23 → DISTURBANCE <5017>.

STIR (verb) – [1] **to stir up: *anaseiō*** [verb: ἀνασείω <383>]; **from *ana*: up (intens.), and *seiō*: to stir, to disturb ▶ To excite, to agitate >** The chief priests stirred up {moved} the crowd to have Pilate release Barabbas instead of Jesus (Mark 15:11). Jesus was accused of stirring up the people (Luke 23:5). ¶

[2] **to stir up: *epegeirō*** [verb: ἐπεγείρω <1892>]; **from *epi*: upon (intens.), and *egeirō*: to awake, to raise ▶ To stimulate, to excite >** The unbelieving Jews stirred up the minds of the nations against the brothers (Acts 14:2). Other refs.: Acts 13:50; see RAISE <1892>. ¶

[3] ***epipherō*** [verb: ἐπιφέρω <2018>]; **from *epi*: upon, and *pherō*: to carry ▶ To add, to inflict; also transl.: to arouse, to cause >** Some thought to arouse tribulation for Paul's bonds (Phil. 1:16 or 17). All other refs.: BRING <2018>, INFLICT <2018>.

[4] **to stir up: *saleuō*** [verb: σαλεύω <4531>]; **from *salos*: agitation, wave ▶ To shake, to agitate >** The Jews of Thessalonica stirred up the crowds in Berea (Acts 17:13). All other refs.: SHAKE <4531>.

[5] **to stir up: *sunkineō*** [verb: συγκινέω <4787>]; **from *sun*: together (intens.), and *kineō*: to move ▶ To excite, to provoke (to sedition) >** The people were stirred against Stephen (Acts 6:12 {to rouse}). ¶

[6] **to stir up: *suncheō*** [verb: συγχέω <4797>]; **from *sun*: together, and *cheō*: to pour; lit.: to pour together ▶ To excite, to provoke an uproar, to cause confusion >** The Jews from Asia stirred up the whole crowd against Paul (Acts 21:27 {to set in a tumult}). Other refs.: Acts 19:32 {to be in confusion}; 21:31 {to be in confusion, to be in uproar}. All other refs.: CONFOUND <4797>, CONFUSED (BE) <4797>, UPROAR <4797>.

– [7] Matt. 21:10 → to be stirred → to be moved → MOVE <4579> [8] John 5:4, 7; Acts 17:8 → TROUBLE (verb) <5015> [9] John 6:18 → ARISE <1326> [10] Acts 13:50 → to stir up → EXCITE <3951> [11] Acts 17:16 → to painfully excite → EXCITE <3947> [12] Acts 21:30 → to stir up → DISTURB <2795> [13] Acts 21:38 → to stir up a rebellion → to raise a sedition → SEDITION <387> [14] Acts 24:5 → to stir up → MOVE <2795> [15] Acts 24:12 → to stir up → to raise up → RAISE <1999> <4160> [16] 2 Cor. 9:2 → to stir up → STIMULATE <2042> [17] 2 Tim. 1:6 → to stir up → REKINDLE <329> [18] Heb. 10:24 → stirring up → provoking → PROVOKE <3948> [19] 2 Pet. 1:13 → to stir up → to wake up → WAKE <1326>.

STIRRING UP – John 5:4 → TROUBLING <5016>.

STOCK – Acts 13:26 → RACE[1] <1085>.

STOCKS – ***xulon*** [neut. noun: ξύλον <3586>]; **from *xuō*: to scrape, to plane; lit.: wood ▶ Wood instrument in which were inserted the feet of prisoners** > The feet of Paul and Silas were fastened in the stocks (Acts 16:24). All other refs.: STAVE <3586>, TREE <3586>, WOOD <3586>.

STOIC – ***Stoikos*** [adj. and adj. used as noun: Στοϊκός <4770>] ▶ **For the Stoic philosophers, happiness lay in virtue and in indifference regarding that which affects one's person.** > Some of the Epicurean and Stoic {Stoick} philosophers conversed with Paul at Athens (Acts 17:18). ¶

STOMACH – [1] ***koilia*** [fem. noun: κοιλία <2836>]; **from *koilos*: hollow ▶ Digestive tract** > The prodigal son longed to fill his stomach with the pods that the swine were eating (Luke 15:16 in some mss.). Foods are for the stomach {belly} and the stomach for the foods (1 Cor. 6:13a, b). All other refs.: WOMB <2836>.

[2] ***stomachos*** [masc. noun: στόμαχος <4751>]; **from *stoma*: mouth, opening ▶ Organ for digestion** > The word has its usual meaning in 1 Tim. 5:23 where Paul advises Timothy to use a little wine on account of his stomach. ¶

[3] **to fill one's stomach: *chortazō*** [verb: χορτάζω <5526>]; **from *chortos*: grass, hay ▶ To satisfy hunger with food; to fill the stomach** > The prodigal son longed to fill his belly with the pods that the swine were eating (Luke 15:16); in some mss.: <1072>. All other refs.: FILL (verb) <5526>.

STONE (noun) – [1] ***lithos*** [masc. noun: λίθος <3037>] ▶ **Solid mineral material, derived from a rock** > God is able from stones to raise up children to Abraham (Matt. 3:9; Luke 3:8). Satan wanted Jesus to speak that stones might become bread (Matt. 4:3; Luke 4:3). The angels would have borne Jesus on their hands lest He strike His foot against a stone (Matt. 4:6; Luke 4:11). A father will not give a stone to a son who asks him for a loaf of bread (Matt. 7:9; Luke 11:11). Christ is the stone that was rejected (Matt. 21:42a; Mark 12:10a; Luke 20:17a; 1 Pet. 2:7a) and set at naught (Acts 4:11a). But He is a living stone (1 Pet. 2:4) and Christians are also living stones (v. 5). Not a stone will be left upon a stone after the destruction of the temple (Matt. 24:2a, b; Mark 13:1, 2a, b; Luke 21:5, 6a, b) and the city (Luke 19:44a, b). Jesus withdrew from His disciples about a stone's throw (Luke 22:41). Joseph of Arimathea rolled a great stone to the door of the tomb of Jesus (Matt. 27:60; Mark 15:46); the Jews sealed the stone (Matt. 27:66). An angel of the Lord rolled away this stone (Matt. 28:2; Mark 16:3, 4; Luke 24:2; John 20:1). There was a stone lying upon the tomb of Lazarus (John 11:38, 39, 41). Other refs.: Matt. 21:44; Mark 5:5; Luke 19:40; 20:18; John 8:7, 59; 10:31; Acts 17:29; 1 Cor. 3:12; 2 Cor. 3:7; Rev. 4:3; 17:4; 18:12, 16, 21; 21:11a, b, 19. The word is used in the expr. "millstone" (Mark 9:42). ¶

[2] **stone, of stone: *lithinos*** [adj.: λίθινος <3035>]; **from *lithos*: see [1] ▶ Made of stone** > There were six stone water-vessels at the marriage in Cana (John 2:6). Other refs.: 2 Cor. 3:3; Rev. 9:20. ¶

[3] ***psēphos*** [fem. noun: ψῆφος <5586>]; **from *psaō*: to rub, to touch the surface ▶ Relatively small piece of rock; they were used to vote (black to condemn, white to dismiss or to approve)** > The one who overcomes in Pergamum will receive a white stone and a new name will be written on the stone (Rev. 2:17a, b). This alludes to a custom according to which a host gave to a special guest who was appreciated a white stone with a name or a message written on it; it expresses the Lord's personal appreciation of those who overcome in that church. Other ref.: Acts 26:10; see VOICE <5586>. ¶

[4] See CORNER STONE.

– [5] Luke 23:53 → cut in stone → cut in the rock → ROCK <2991> [6] Acts 19:35 → "sacred stone" added in Engl. [7] 2 Cor. 11:25 → to pelt with stones → STONE (verb) <3034>.

STONE (verb) – [1] ***lithazō*** [verb: λιθάζω <3034>]; **from *lithos*: a stone ▶ To put**

a person or animal to death by throwing stones at them > O.T. people of faith were stoned by their persecutors (Heb. 11:37). The Jews wanted to stone Jesus (John 10:31–33; 11:8). Paul was stoned once (Acts 14:19; 2 Cor. 11:25). Other ref.: Acts 5:26. ¶

2 ***katalithazō*** [verb: καταλιθάζω <2642>]; ***kata*: intens., and *lithazō*: to stone ▶ See defin. of 1.** > The chief priests and the scribes feared all the people would stone them on account of their answer to the question raised by Jesus (Luke 20:6). ¶

3 ***lithoboleō*** [verb: λιθοβολέω <3036>]; **from *lithos*: a stone, and *ballō*: to throw ▶ See defin. of 1.** > This was the method prescribed by God for putting the wicked to death (see Lev. 20:2, 27; Deut. 21:18–21; Josh. 7:25). In a parable, Jesus spoke of the vinedressers (the Jews) who stone the servants (the prophets) of the landowner (God) (Matt. 21:35). He accused Jerusalem of stoning those who were sent to her (Matt. 23:37; Luke 13:34). Stephen was stoned to death (Acts 7:58, 59). When the law was given, any beast that touched Mount Sinai was to be stoned to death (Heb. 12:20; see Ex. 19:12, 13). Other refs.: Mark 12:4 in some mss.; John 8:5; Acts 14:5. ¶

STONING – Heb. 11:37 → to be put to death by stoning → to be stoned → STONE (verb) <3034>.

STONY – Matt. 13:5, 20; Mark 4:5, 16 → stony ground, stony place → rocky place, rocky ground → ROCKY <4075>.

STOOP – 1 **to stoop down: *kuptō*** [verb: κύπτω <2955>] **▶ To bend forward, to humble oneself** > John the Baptist said he was not worthy to stoop down and loose the sandal strap of Jesus (Mark 1:7). Jesus stooped down {bent down} and wrote on the ground with His finger (John 8:6; other mss.: *katakuptō*); He stooped down again after having responded to the scribes and Pharisees (v. 8; other mss.: *katakuptō*). ¶

2 **to stoop, to stoop down: *parakuptō*** [verb: παρακύπτω <3879>]; **from *para*: near, and *kuptō*: see 1 ▶ To bend forward to look, to bend over** > Stooping down at the tomb of Jesus, John saw the linen clothes lying (John 20:5); Peter also (Luke 24:12). Mary stooped down and saw two angels sitting where the body of Jesus had lain (John 20:11). Other refs.: Jas. 1:25 and 1 Pet. 1:12 (to look into); see LOOK (verb) <3879>. ¶

STOP – 1 ***histēmi*** [verb: ἵστημι <2476>]; **lit.: to cause to stand still ▶ To cease, to be stayed** > The hemorrhage of the woman stopped {stanched} after she had touched Jesus (Luke 8:44). Other refs.: see entries in Lexicon at <2476>.

2 ***sunechō*** [verb: συνέχω <4912>]; **from *sun*: together, and *echō*: to have, to keep; lit.: to hold together, to hold tight ▶ To shut, to close** > The adversaries of Stephen stopped {covered, held} their ears and ran at him with one accord (Acts 7:57). Other refs.: see entries in Lexicon at <4912>.

3 ***phrassō*** [verb: φράσσω <5420>]; **from which *phragmos*: fence ▶ To block, to hinder, to reduce to silence; also transl.: to close, to silence, to shut** > Whatever things the law says, it speaks to those who are under the law, that every mouth may be stopped (Rom. 3:19). O.T. people of faith stopped the mouths of lions (Heb. 11:33). As the truth of Christ was in Paul, his boasting of not being a burden in any way would not be stopped in the regions of Achaia (2 Cor. 11:10). ¶

– 4 Matt. 14:32; Mark 6:51 → FALL (verb) <2869> 5 Mark 5:29 → to dry up → DRY (verb) <3583> 6 Mark 9:38, 39; Luke 6:29; 9:49, 50; 3 John 10 → to stop, to tell to stop, to try to stop → FORBID <2967> 7 Luke 5:4; 8:24; Acts 5:42; 6:13; 20:31; 21:32; Eph. 1:16; Col. 1:9; Heb. 10:2 → CEASE <3973> 8 Luke 7:45 → CEASE <1257> 9 Luke 22:51 → ALLOW <1439> 10 Luke 23:45 → to stop shining → DARKEN <4654> 11 Acts 5:39 → DESTROY <2647> 12 Acts 10:17 → STAND (verb) <2186> 13 Acts 15:13; 1 Cor. 14:30 → to stop speaking, to stop → to be silent → SILENT <4601> 14 1 Cor. 12:15, 16 → would not stop being → lit.: is not 15 Eph. 6:9 → to give up → GIVE <447> 16 1 Thes. 2:18 → HINDER (verb)

<1465> 17 Titus 1:11 → to stop the mouth → MOUTH (noun) <1993> 18 2 Pet. 2:14 → that cannot cease → CEASE <180> 19 Rev. 4:8 → rest → REST (verb) <372>.

STORE (noun) – 2 Tim. 4:8 → to be in store → to lay up → LAY <606>.

STORE (verb) – 1 ***thēsaurizō*** [verb: θησαυρίζω <2343>]; **from *thēsauros*: treasure ▶ To save, to reserve** > Every first day of the week, each Christian should put something aside, storing up {laying up, saving it up} as he may have prospered for the collection (1 Cor. 16:2). All other refs.: HEAP <2343>, LAY <2343>, RESERVE <2343>, TREASURE (verb) <2343>.
– 2 Matt. 6:26; Luke 12:17, 18 → to store away, to store → GATHER <4863> 3 Matt. 12:35a, b; Luke 6:45 → stored up in him → lit.: his treasure → TREASURE (noun) <2344> 4 Col. 1:5 → to store up → to lay up → LAY <606> 5 1 Tim. 6:19 → to store up → to lay up in store → LAY <597>.

STOREHOUSE – ***tameion*** [neut. noun: ταμεῖον <5009>]; **from *tamieuō*: to collect in one place ▶ Place to put aside food** > The ravens have neither storehouse {storeroom} or barn, and yet God feeds them (Luke 12:24). Other refs.: Matt. 6:6; 24:26; Luke 12:3; see ROOM <5009>. ¶

STOREROOM – 1 Matt. 13:52 → out of his storeroom new treasures as well as old → lit.: out of his treasure things new and old → TREASURE (noun) <2344> 2 Luke 12:24 → STOREHOUSE <5009>.

STORM – 1 ***thuella*** [fem. noun: θύελλα <2366>]; **from *thuō*: to rush furiously ▶ Sudden squall, turbulent cyclone** > The Hebrew Christians had not come to gloom and storm {tempest} (Heb. 12:18). ¶
2 ***lailaps*** [fem. noun: λαῖλαψ <2978>] ▶ **Whirlwind, tempest characterized by darkness, wild gusts of wind and heavy rain** > A violent storm of wind {gale of wind, squall, windstorm} arose, and the waves beat into the boat where Jesus and His disciples were found (Mark 4:37). A sudden storm {fierce gale, sudden squall} of wind came down on the lake (Luke 8:23). Peter speaks of the unrighteous who are springs without water and clouds driven by a storm (2 Pet. 2:17). ¶
3 ***seismos*** [masc. noun: σεισμός <4578>]; **from *seiō*: to agitate, to shake ▶ Perturbation of the air, gale, tempest** > A great storm arose on the sea, so that the boat, in which were Jesus and His disciples, was covered by the waves (Matt. 8:24). All other refs.: EARTHQUAKE <4578>.
4 ***cheimōn*** [masc. noun: χειμών <5494>]; **from *cheima*: bad weather, winter ▶ Rainy weather, characteristic of winter; tempest** > They say there will be a storm {there will be foul weather, it will be stormy} when the sky is red and overcast in the morning (Matt. 16:3). A great storm {tempest} beat on Paul and the passengers who were in the boat (Acts 27:20). Other refs.: Matt. 24:20; Mark 13:18; John 10:22; 2 Tim. 4:21; see WINTER (noun) <5494>. ¶
– 5 Matt. 8:24 → EARTHQUAKE <4578> 6 Acts 27:18 → to take a violent battering from the storm → to be tossed with a tempest → TEMPEST <5492>.

STORM-TOSSED (BE) – Acts 27:18 → to be tossed with a tempest → TEMPEST <5492>.

STORMY – Matt. 16:3 → lit.: storm → STORM <5494>.

STORY[1] – **third story: *tristegon*** [neut. noun: τρίστεγον <5152>]; **from *treis*: three, and *stegē*: roof ▶ Third floor of a habitation** > Eutychus fell down from the third story as Paul continued speaking (Acts 20:9). ¶

STORY[2] – 1 Acts 11:4 → told them the whole story → told them in order → ORDER (noun) <2517> 2 2 Pet. 1:16 → FABLE <3454>.

STOUTLY – Luke 22:59 → to stoutly maintain → to confidently affirm → AFFIRM <1340>.

STRAIGHT – [1] ***euthus*** [adj.: εὐθύς <2117>] ▶ **a. Without deviation, having the same direction** > Isaiah said to make straight the paths of the Lord (Matt. 3:3; Mark 1:3; Luke 3:4). He also said that the crooked places will be made straight (Luke 3:5). **b. Name of a street** > Ananias had to go to the street called Straight (*eutheia*) (Acts 9:11). **c. Which is morally right, which is according to God** > The heart of Simon, who had practiced sorcery, was not straight {right, upright} in the sight of God (Acts 8:21). Elymas the sorcerer was perverting the straight {right} ways of the Lord (Acts 13:10). Peter speaks of those who have forsaken the straight {right} way and gone astray (2 Pet. 2:15). All other refs.: IMMEDIATELY <2117>.
[2] ***orthos*** [adj.: ὀρθός <3717>] ▶ **a. In a vertical position** > Paul said to the man who was a cripple to stand up straight {upright} on his feet (Acts 14:10). **b. Without deviation** > Christians must make straight {level} paths for their feet (Heb. 12:13). ¶
[3] **to make straight: *anorthoō*** [verb: ἀνορθόω <461>]; **from *ana*: again, up, and *orthoō*: to erect, which is from *orthos*: see [2]** ▶ **To make upright** > A woman bent over for eighteen years was made straight {made erect, straightened up} the instant Jesus laid His hands on her (Luke 13:13). Other refs.: Acts 15:16; Heb. 12:12; see RESTORE <461>, STRENGTHEN <461>. ¶
[4] **to make straight: *euthunō*** [verb: εὐθύνω <2116>]; **from *euthus*: see [1]** ▶ **To make without deviation** > Isaiah said to make straight the path of the Lord (John 1:23). Other ref.: Jas. 3:4; see DIRECT <2116>. ¶
– [5] John 20:6 → to go straight → ENTER <1525> [6] Acts 3:4 → to look straight → to fasten the eyes → FASTEN <816> [7] Acts 17:23 → to look carefully at → BEHOLD (verb) <333> [8] 2 Tim. 2:15 → to cut in a straight line → to divide rightly → DIVIDE <3718>.

STRAIGHTEN – [1] **to straighten oneself up: *anakuptō*** [verb: ἀνακύπτω <352>]; **from *ana*: again, up (sense of reversal), and *kuptō*: to lean forward** ▶ **To stand up straight again** > After having stooped down and having written with His finger on the ground, Jesus straightened Himself up {lifted Himself up, raised Himself up} and addressed the accusers of the adulterous woman (John 8:7, 10). All other refs.: LIFT <352>, LOOK (verb) <352>.
– [2] Luke 13:13 → to straighten up → to make straight → STRAIGHT <461> [3] Titus 1:5 → to straighten out → SET (verb) <1930>.

STRAIGHTFORWARD, STRAIGHTFORWARDLY – **to walk straightforwardly: *orthopodeō*** [verb: ὀρθοποδέω <3716>]; **from *orthopous*: standing upright, which is from *orthos*: straight, and *pous*: foot** ▶ **To behave without deviation, according to one thing** > Peter and other Jews did not walk straightforwardly about {were not straightforward about, did not walk uprightly about, were not acting in line with} the truth of the gospel, so Paul had to rebuke Peter (Gal. 2:14). ¶

STRAIGHTWAY – [1] Matt. 4:20; 14:22, 27; et al. → IMMEDIATELY <2112> [2] Luke 8:55; 19:11 → IMMEDIATELY <3916> [3] Matt. 3:16; John 13:32 → IMMEDIATELY <2117>.

STRAIN – [1] ***diulizō*** [verb: διϋλίζω <1368>]; **from *dia*: intens., and *hulizō*: to filter** ▶ **To filter completely** > Jesus told the scribes and Pharisees they were blind guides who strained out a gnat and swallowed a camel (Matt. 23:24). ¶
– [2] Mark 6:48 → TORMENT (verb) <928> [3] Phil. 3:13 → REACH <1901>.

STRAIT – [1] Matt. 7:13, 14; Luke 13:24 → NARROW <4728> [2] 2 Cor. 6:4; 12:10 → DISTRESS <4730> [3] Phil. 1:23 → to be in a strait → PRESS <4912>.

STRAITEN – [1] 1 Cor. 7:29 → to be straitened → to be short → SHORT <4958> [2] 2 Cor. 4:8; 6:12a, b → RESTRAIN <4729>.

STRAITENED (BE) – ***thlibō*** [verb: θλίβω <2346>] ▶ **To be enclosed within a**

restricted space, to be narrow > The way that leads to eternal life is straitened (Matt. 7:14). All other refs.: AFFLICTED (BE) <2346>.

STRAITEST – Acts 26:5 → most straitest → STRICTEST <196>.

STRAITLY – 1 Luke 9:21 → to straitly charge → to earnestly charge → CHARGE (verb) <2008> 2 Acts 5:28 → to straitly command → COMMAND (verb) <3853>.

STRAND – 1 Acts 27:39, 40 → BEACH <123> 2 Acts 27:40 → to make for the strand → to make for the shore → SHORE <2722> <1519> <123>.

STRANGE – 1 ***paradoxos*** [adj.: παράδοξος <3861>]; **from *para*: beyond, and *doxa*: opinion ▶ Surprising, extraordinary** > The witnesses of the healing of a man who was paralyzed said they had seen strange {remarkable} things (Luke 5:26). ¶
2 **strange thing: *xenos*** [adj.: ξένος <3581>] ▶ **Something extraordinary** > Peter told the Christians of the dispersion to not think strange (*xenizō*; see 3) the fire of persecution, as if a strange thing (*xenos*) was happening to them (1 Pet. 4:12). All other refs.: FOREIGN <3581>, HOST[2] <3581>, STRANGER <3581>.
3 **to think strange, to bring strange things: *xenizō*** [verb: ξενίζω <3579>]; **from *xenos*: stranger, foreigner ▶ a. To speak about novel or surprising matters** > Paul had brought some strange things to the ears of the philosophers in Athens (Acts 17:20). **b. To find surprising, to be surprised** > Unbelievers think it strange that Christians do not run with them in the same flood of dissipation (1 Pet. 4:4). Other ref.: 1 Pet. 4:12; see 2. All other refs.: LODGE <3579>.
– 4 Acts 7:6; Heb. 11:9 → FOREIGN <245> 5 Acts 10:28 → strange race → one of another nation → NATION <246> 6 Acts 26:11 → FOREIGN <1854> 7 1 Cor. 14:21 → OTHER <2087>.

STRANGER – 1 ***allotrios*** [adj. used as noun: ἀλλότριος <245>]; **from *allos*: other ▶ Someone else, unknown person** > The sheep will by no means follow a stranger; they do not know the voice of strangers (John 10:5a, b). Other refs.: Matt. 17:25 and 26 {other}; Heb. 9:25 {of another, of others, that is not his own}; 11:34 {alien, foreign}. All other refs.: ANOTHER <245>, FOREIGN <245>.
2 ***xenos*** [adj. used as noun: ξένος <3581>] ▶ **Person who comes from somewhere else, foreigner** > Jesus spoke about taking in a stranger (Matt. 25:35, 38, 43, 44). With Judas's money, the chief priests bought a field to bury strangers in (Matt. 27:7). Other refs.: Acts 17:21, Eph. 2:12, 19; Heb. 11:13; 3 John 5. All other refs.: FOREIGN <3581>, HOST[2] <3581>, STRANGE <3581>.
3 **to lodge strangers: *xenodocheō*** [verb: ξενοδοχέω <3580>]; **from *xenodochos*: receptive to strangers, which is from *xenos*: see 2, and *dechomai*: to receive; lit.: to receive strangers ▶ To practice hospitality** > One of the qualities of a widow to be helped by the church was that she had lodged strangers {exercised hospitality, shown hospitality to strangers} (1 Tim. 5:10). ¶
4 ***parepidēmos*** [masc. noun: παρεπίδημος <3927>]; **from *para*: near, and *epidēmos*: stranger, which is from *epi*: upon, and *dēmos*: people ▶ Who lives as a stranger in a place, temporary resident** > Peter addressed the Christians who were strangers {pilgrims, sojourners, strangers in the world, those who reside as aliens} among the nations (1 Pet. 1:1). Other refs.: Heb. 11:13; 1 Pet. 2:11; see SOJOURNER <3927>. ¶
– 5 Luke 17:18 → FOREIGNER <241> 6 Luke 24:18 → to be a stranger → VISIT (verb) <3939> 7 Acts 2:10 → lit.: ones staying → STAY (verb) <1927> 8 Acts 7:29 → DWELLER <3941> 9 Acts 13:17; 1 Pet. 1:17 → when they dwelt as strangers; to live lives as strangers → lit.: during their stay; to pass the time of stay → STAY (noun) <3940> 10 1 Cor. 14:21 → OTHER <2087> 11 Heb. 13:2 → to entertain strangers → HOSPITALITY <5381> 12 1 Pet. 2:11 → FOREIGNER <3941>.

STRANGLED – ***pniktos*** [adj.: πνικτός <4156>]; **from *pnigō*: to choke, which is from *pneō*: to breathe ▶ Meat of animals killed by strangulation, without the blood being shed** > Christians were to abstain from what is strangled (Acts 15:20, 29; 21:25). ¶

STRAP – ***himas*** [masc. noun: ἱμάς <2438>] ▶ **Narrow strip of leather** > John the Baptist was not worthy to loose the sandal strap {latchet, thong} of Jesus (Mark 1:7; Luke 3:16; John 1:27). Paul was bound with straps {thongs} {was stretched out} to be scourged (Acts 22:25). ¶

STRATEGIC – Mark 6:21 → OPPORTUNE <2121>.

STRAW (noun) – 1 Cor. 3:12 → STUBBLE <2562>.

STRAW (verb) – Matt. 25:24, 26 → SCATTER <1287>.

STRAY – 1 ***astocheō*** [verb: ἀστοχέω <795>]; **from *astochos*: one who misses his goal, which is from *a*: neg., and *stochos*: goal; lit.: to miss the goal ▶ To fail, to move away; also transl.: to err, to go astray, to miss, to miss the mark, to swerve, to wander away** > Some had strayed from a pure heart, a good conscience, and a sincere faith (1 Tim. 1:6); others have strayed concerning the faith (6:21). Hymenaeus and Philetus had strayed concerning the truth (2 Tim. 2:18). ¶
2 ***planaō*** [verb: πλανάω <4105>]; **from *planē*: wandering ▶ a. To go off the right path, to wander off; also transl.: to go astray, to lead astray, to be deceived, to err, to seduce; to wander in error, away, off** > If a man has one hundred sheep, and one of them goes astray, he will leave the ninety-nine to seek the one that is straying (Matt. 18:12a, b, 13). The Israelites always went astray in their heart (Heb. 3:10). **b. To deceive, to seduce** > Christians were once deceived (Titus 3:3). James tells his beloved brothers not to be deceived (Jas. 1:16), and speaks of turning back anyone among them wandering from the truth (5:19). Some have forsaken the right way and gone astray, following the way of Balaam (2 Pet. 2:15). John had written concerning those who were deceiving his readers (1 John 2:26); no one should deceive them (3:7). Jezebel seduces {misleads} the servants of the Son of God into sexual immorality and eating of idol sacrifices (Rev. 2:20). The nations were deceived by Babylon the great (Rev. 18:23). Satan will go out to deceive the nations (Rev. 20:8, 10). All other refs.: ASTRAY <4105>, DECEIVE <4105>, MISTAKEN (BE) <4105>, WANDER <4105>.
3 ***apoplanaō*** [verb: ἀποπλανάω <635>]; **from *apo*: from, and *planaō*: see 2 ▶ To move far away, to be seduced** > For the love of money, some have strayed {erred, wandered, wandered away} from the faith in their greediness (1 Tim. 6:10). Other ref.: Mark 13:22; see DECEIVE <635>. ¶
– 4 1 Tim. 5:15 → to turn aside → TURN (verb) <1624>.

STRAYING – 1 Pet. 2:25 → to go astray → ASTRAY <4105>.

STREAM – 1 ***potamos*** [masc. noun: ποταμός <4215>]; **from *potazō*: to flow, which is from *potos*: beverage, which is from *pinō*: to drink ▶ Impetuous watercourse, river** > The streams {floods} came against the house that was built on the rock and against another house that was not (Matt. 7:25, 27). All other refs.: RIVER <4215>.
– 2 Luke 6:48, 49; John 7:38 → RIVER <4215>.

STREET – 1 ***plateia*** [fem. noun: πλατεῖα <4113>]; **from *platus*: broad ▶ Place, road** > Hypocrites love to pray standing in the corners of the streets (Matt. 6:5). No one heard the voice of Jesus in the streets when He withdrew from a certain place (Matt. 12:19). When they were not received in a city, the disciples were to go out into its street and shake its dust off their feet against the inhabitants of that city (Luke 10:10). Workers of iniquity will say that the Lord had taught in their streets (Luke 13:26). The master of the house sent his servant into the streets to bring in the poor, the crippled, the blind, and the lame (Luke 14:21). The sick were brought out into the streets so that Peter might heal them (Acts 5:15). The dead bodies of the two witnesses will lie in the street of the great city (Rev. 11:8). The street of the heavenly Jerusalem was of pure gold (Rev. 21:21); in the middle of the street was the tree of life (Rev. 22:2). ¶

2 ***rhumē*** [fem. noun: ῥύμη <4505>] ▶ **Alley, lane** > Hypocrites sound a trumpet before themselves in the streets when they give to the poor (Matt. 6:2). Saul of Tarsus was in the house of Judas located on the street called Straight (Acts 9:11). The angel and Peter went down one street, and immediately the angel left him (Acts 12:10). Other ref.: Luke 14:21; see LANE <4505>. ¶

– 3 Matt. 22:9 → street corner → THOROUGHFARE <1327> 4 Mark 6:56 → MARKETPLACE <58> 5 Mark 11:4 → place where two ways meet → PLACE (noun) <296>.

STRENGTH – 1 ***dunamis*** [fem. noun: δύναμις <1411>]; **from *dunamai*: to be able** ▶ **Might, power** > Paul had been excessively pressed, beyond his strength {ability to endure} (2 Cor. 1:8). Christians are strengthened with all power according to the strength of the glory of God (Col. 1:11). Sarah received strength {ability} to found a posterity (Heb. 11:11). O.T. people of faith quenched the power {fury, violence} of fire (Heb. 11:34). The angel of the church of Philadelphia has a little strength (Rev. 3:8). The face of the Son of Man was like the sun shining in its strength {brilliance, full strength, power} (Rev. 1:16). All other refs.: ABILITY <1411>, MEANING <1411>, MIRACLE <1411>, POWER[1] <1411>, POWER[3] <1411>.

2 ***ischus*** [fem. noun: ἰσχύς <2479>]; **comp. *ixus*: hip** ▶ **Ability, power; also transl.: might** > Jesus says to love God with all one's strength (Mark 12:30, 33; Luke 10:27). The power of God is exercised toward Christians according to the operation of the might of His strength (Eph. 1:19). The Christian is to strengthen himself in the Lord and in the might of His strength (Eph. 6:10). God gives the strength to serve Him (1 Pet. 4:11). The Lamb is worthy to receive strength (Rev. 5:12). Strength is ascribed to our God (Rev. 7:12). Other refs.: 2 Thes. 1:9; 2 Pet. 2:11. ¶

3 ***kratos*** [neut. noun: κράτος <2904>] ▶ **Might, power** > God has shown strength {has done mighty deeds} with His arm (Luke 1:51). All other refs.: MIGHT <2904>.

4 **full strength: *akratos*** [adj.: ἄκρατος <194>]; **from *a*: neg., and *kerranumi*: to mix** ▶ **Pure, undiluted** > The wine of the wrath of God will be poured out full strength {unmixed, without mixture} into the cup of His anger (Rev. 14:10). ¶

5 **without strength: *adunatos*** [adj.: ἀδύνατος <102>]; **from *a*: neg., and *dunatos*: capable, possible** ▶ **Incapable of doing something, weak** > In Acts 14:8, a man without strength {who had no strength, impotent} had never walked; Paul healed him (see v. 9, 10). All other refs.: IMPOSSIBLE <102>.

– 6 Mark 5:4 → to have strength → to be able → ABLE <2480> 7 Luke 21:36 → to have strength → to count worthy → WORTHY <2661> 8 Acts 3:7 → to receive strength → to become strong → STRONG <4732> 9 Acts 9:19 → to get strength, to regain strength → STRENGTHEN <1765> 10 Acts 9:22; Rom. 4:20; Phil. 4:13; 1 Tim. 1:12; 2 Tim. 4:17 → to increase in strength, to give strength → STRENGTHEN <1743> 11 Acts 27:34 → to give strength → lit.: to be for survival → SURVIVAL <4991> 12 Rom. 5:6 → without strength → POWERLESS <772> 13 Rom. 15:1 → without strength → WEAK <102> 14 Eph. 3:18 → to have strength → to be able, to be fully able → ABLE <1840> 15 Heb. 9:17 → to be of strength → PREVAIL <2480> 16 Heb. 11:34 → to turn to strength → to become strong → STRONG <1743> 17 Jude 8 → on the strength of their dreams → lit.: dreaming ones → DREAMER <1797>.

STRENGTHEN – 1 ***dunamoō*** [verb: δυναμόω <1412>]; **from *dunamis*: strength, power, which is from *dunamai*: to be**

able ► To make strong, to become mighty > Believers are strengthened with all power (Col. 1:11). Some mss. have Eph. 6:10; Heb. 11:34. ¶
[2] ***endunamoō*** [verb: ἐνδυναμόω <1743>]; **from *en*: in, and *dunamoō*: see [1] ► To be powerful, to increase in strength, to be strong** > Paul increased all the more in strength (Acts 9:22). He could do all things in Christ who strengthened him (Phil. 4:13). The Lord had strengthened him (1 Tim. 1:12; 2 Tim. 4:17). Timothy was to be strong in the grace that is in Christ Jesus (2 Tim. 2:1). Abraham was strengthened in faith (Rom. 4:20). The Christians in Ephesus were to be strong in the Lord (Eph. 6:10). Other ref.: Heb. 11:34 (to be made strong); see STRONG (adj.) <1743>. ¶
[3] ***enischuō*** [verb: ἐνισχύω <1765>]; **from *en*: intens., and *ischuō*: to be strong, to be able ► To increase the strength** > An angel appeared to Jesus, strengthening Him (Luke 22:43). Having eaten, Paul was strengthened {got strength, regained his strength} (Acts 9:19). Other ref.: Acts 19:20 in some mss. ¶
[4] ***krataioō*** [verb: κραταιόω <2901>]; **from *krataios*: strong, powerful, which is from *kratos*: strength, power ► To increase in strength; also transl.: to become strong, to be strong** > The child Jesus was strengthened in spirit (Luke 1:80); He became strong, being filled with wisdom (2:40). Paul told the Corinthians to be strong (1 Cor. 16:13). He prayed that God might grant the Ephesians to be strengthened with power by His Spirit (Eph. 3:16). ¶
[5] ***anorthoō*** [verb: ἀνορθόω <461>]; **from *ana*: again, up, and *orthoō*: to erect, which is from *orthos*: right, straight ► To erect again, to establish** > Heb. 12:12 exhorts to strengthen {lift up} the hands that hang down and the failing knees. Other refs.: Luke 13:13; Acts 15:16; see STRAIGHT <461>, RESTORE <461>. ¶
[6] ***sthenoō*** [verb: σθενόω <4599>]; **from *sthenos*: strength ► To make strong** > The God of all grace shall strengthen Christians (1 Pet. 5:10). ¶
[7] ***stērizō*** [verb: στηρίζω <4741>]; **comp. *stereos*: solid, stable ► To establish, to fortify** > When once Peter had been restored, he was to strengthen {to confirm} his brothers (Luke 22:32). Sardis was to strengthen the things that remain (Rev. 3:2). All other refs.: ESTABLISH <4741>, FIX <4741>, STEADFASTLY <4741>.
[8] ***epistērizō*** [verb: ἐπιστηρίζω <1991>]; **from *epi*: upon (intens.), and *stērizō*: see [7] ► To establish, to affirm; also transl.: to confirm** > Paul and Barnabas strengthened the souls of the disciples (Acts 14:22). Judas and Silas strengthened the brothers (Acts 15:32). Paul strengthened the churches of Syria and Cilicia (Acts 15:41). He strengthened all the disciples of Galatia and Phrygia (Acts 18:23). Other ref.: Acts 11:2 in some mss. ¶
– [9] Acts 3:16 → to make strong → STRONG <4732> [10] Acts 9:31 → EDIFY <3618> [11] Acts 16:5 → ESTABLISH <4732> [12] 1 Cor. 8:10 → EMBOLDENED (BE) <3618> [13] Col. 2:7; Heb. 13:9 → ESTABLISH <950>.

STRENGTHENED (BE) – Acts 3:7 → to become strong → STRONG <4732>.

STRENGTHENING – 1 Cor. 14:3, 26; 2 Cor. 12:19 → EDIFICATION <3619>.

STRENUOUSLY – Col. 1:29 → to strenuously contend → to labor, fighting → LABOR (verb) <2872>, FIGHT (verb) <75>.

STRESS – Titus 3:8 → AFFIRM <1226>.

STRETCH – [1] **to stretch out: *ekpetannumi*** [verb: ἐκπετάννυμι <1600>]; **from *ek*: far from, and *pettanumi*: to stretch out, to spread out ► To extend (as holding out the hands in supplication)** > God had stretched out {stretched forth, held out} His hands to Israel all day long (Rom. 10:21). ¶
[2] **to stretch out, to stretch forth: *ekteinō*** [verb: ἐκτείνω <1614>]; **from *ek*: out, and *teinō*: to stretch ► To stretch a member in all its length; also transl.: to reach, to reach out** > Jesus stretched out {put forth, put out} His hand and touched a leper (Matt. 8:3; Mark 1:41; Luke 5:13). He said to the man who had a withered hand to stretch it out (Matt. 12:13a, b; Mark 3:5a,

b; Luke 6:10). He stretched out His hand toward {pointed to} His disciples (Matt. 12:49) and Peter (14:31). Peter stretched out his hand and drew his sword (Matt. 26:51). The Jews had not stretched forth their hands against {did not lay hands on, did not try to seize} Jesus in the temple (Luke 22:53). When Peter would be old, he would stretch out his hands and another would gird him (John 21:18). Peter asked the Lord to stretch out {extend} His hand to heal (Acts 4:30). Paul stretched out {motioned with} his hand and answered for himself (Acts 26:1). Other ref.: Acts 27:30 (to carry out); see CARRY <1614>. ¶

– [3] Acts 12:1 → to stretch forth, to stretch out → LAY <1911> [4] Acts 22:25 → to stretch forward, to stretch out → lit.: to be bound with straps → STRAP <2438>, BIND <4385> [5] 2 Cor. 10:14 → to stretch oneself beyond measure → OVEREXTEND <5239> [6] Phil. 3:13 → to stretch out → REACH <1901>.

STRETCHER – Luke 5:19, 24 → little bed → BED <2826>.

STREW – [1] Matt. 21:8; Mark 11:8 → SPREAD <4766> [2] Luke 19:36 → SPREAD <5291> [3] 1 Cor. 10:5 → to lay low → LAY <2693>.

STRICKEN – Luke 1:7, 18 → to be well stricken → to be well advance → ADVANCE <4260>.

STRICT – [1] **stricter: *meizōn*** [adj.: μείζων <3187>]; **compar. of *megas*: great ▶ Greater** > James tells his brothers not to be many teachers, knowing that they will receive a stricter judgment (Jas. 3:1). All other refs.: GREAT <3187>, GREAT (adj. expressing the majesty of God) <3187>.

– [2] Acts 5:28 → to give strict orders → lit.: to strictly enjoin → charge → STRICTLY <3852> [3] Acts 22:3 → according to the strict manner → according to strictness → STRICTNESS <195>.

STRICTEST – ***akribestatos*** [adj.: ἀκριβέστατος <196>]; **superl. of *akribēs*: exact, conscientious ▶ Most exact, most precise** > Paul had lived a Pharisee according to the strictest {the most straitest} sect of his religion (Acts 26:5). ¶

STRICTLY – [1] **charge: *parangelia*** [fem. noun: παραγγελία <3852>]; **from *parangellō*: to command, which is from *para*: near, and *angellō*: to announce ▶ Commandment, order** > The council had strictly {straitly} (lit.: by a charge) enjoined {had given strict orders to} the apostles not to teach in the name of Jesus (Acts 5:28). Other refs.: Acts 16:24; 1 Thes. 4:2; 1 Tim. 1:5, 18; see CHARGE (noun)[2] <3852>. ¶

– [2] Matt. 16:20 → to strictly charge → COMMAND (verb) <1291> [3] Mark 1:43 → to warn strictly → WARN <1690> [4] Mark 3:12 → EARNESTLY <4183> [5] Acts 22:3 → STRICTNESS <195> [6] Acts 23:14 → to strictly bind oneself → to put oneself under a curse → CURSE <332> [7] Jas. 3:1 → to judge more strictly → lit.: to receive a stricter judgment → STRICT <3187>.

STRICTNESS – [1] ***akribeia*** [fem. noun: ἀκρίβεια <195>]; **from *akribēs*: accurate, conscientious ▶ Precision, exactitude** > Paul had been brought up according to the strictness {to the exactness, to the perfect manner, strictly} of {was thoroughly trained in} the law of his fathers (Acts 22:3). ¶

– [2] Jas. 3:1 → to be judged with greater strictness → lit.: to receive greater judgment.

STRIFE – [1] ***eritheia*** [fem. noun: ἐριθεία <2052>]; **from *eritheuō*: to work for hire, i.e., seeking one's own interest ▶ Spirit of faction, contention** > Strife {Self-seeking, Selfish ambition} is not suitable for Christian conduct (Jas. 3:14, 16). All other refs.: CONTENTION <2052>, SELF-SEEKING <2052>.

[2] ***eris*** [fem. noun: ἔρις <2054>] **▶ Discord, dispute, dissension; also transl.: contention, debate, quarreling, variance** > Unrighteous men are full of strife (Rom. 1:29). Christians are not to walk in strife (Rom. 13:13). There was strife among the Corinthians (1 Cor. 3:3); Paul feared that

later strifes might still be found among them (2 Cor. 12:20). Strifes are among the works of the flesh (Gal. 5:20); they arise out of sickness about questions and disputes of words (1 Tim. 6:4). Some were preaching Christ from envy and strife (Phil. 1:15). Other refs.: 1 Cor. 1:11; Titus 3:9; see CONTENTION <2054>. ¶

3 ***machē*** [fem. noun: μάχη <3163>]; **from *machomai*: to fight ▶ Contention, quarrel, fight** > Foolish and ignorant speculations (or: controversies) generate strife (2 Tim. 2:23). All other refs.: FIGHTING <3163>, STRIVING <3163>.

4 ***philoneikia*** [fem. noun: φιλονεικία <5379>]; **from *philoneikos*: contentious, which is from *philos*: friend, and *neikos*: conflict ▶ Dispute, quarrel** > There was a strife among the apostles, as to which of them should be considered the greatest (Luke 22:24). ¶

– 5 1 Tim. 6:4 → strife of words → argument over words → ARGUMENT <3055> 6 Heb. 6:16 → DISPUTE (noun) <485>.

STRIKE – 1 ***epitithēmi*** [verb: ἐπιτίθημι <2007>]; **from *epi*: upon, and *tithēmi*: to put ▶ To put on, to impose** > Paul and Silas were struck with many blows (Acts 16:23); other transl.: many stripes were laid upon them, they were severely flogged. All other refs.: see entries in Lexicon at <2007>.

2 ***paiō*** [verb: παίω <3817>]; ***pavire*, in Lat.: to strike ▶ To beat, to hit; also transl.: to smite** > Jesus was asked to prophesy who had struck Him (Matt. 26:68; Luke 22:64). Peter struck the servant of the high priest (Mark 14:47; John 18:10). A scorpion causes torment when it strikes {stings} a man (Rev. 9:5). ¶

3 **to strike, to strike down: *patassō*** [verb: πατάσσω <3960>]; **from *patagos*: clashing, sharp noise ▶ To deliver a blow, to inflict a wound (perhaps mortal); also transl.: to smite** > God would strike the Shepherd (Jesus), and the sheep of the flock would be scattered (Matt. 26:31; Mark 14:27). Those who were around Jesus wanted to strike with the sword (Luke 22:49). Peter struck the servant of the high priest (Matt. 26:51; Luke 22:50). Moses struck down the Egyptian (Acts 7:24). An angel struck Peter on the side (Acts 12:7). An angel of the Lord struck Herod (Acts 12:23). The two witnesses have the power to strike the earth with all sorts of plagues (Rev. 11:6). He who is seated on the white horse will strike the nations with His sword (Rev. 19:15). ¶

4 ***piptō*** [verb: πίπτω <4098>] **▶ To fall** > The sun shall not at all strike {beat down on, light on} those of the great tribulation (Rev. 7:16). All other refs.: FALL (verb) <4098>, PERISH <4098>.

5 ***plēssō*** [verb: πλήσσω <4141>]; **comp. *plēgē*: plague, major calamity ▶ To beat, to afflict with calamity** > The third part of the sun was struck (Rev. 8:12). ¶

6 ***proskoptō*** [verb: προσκόπτω <4350>]; **from *pros*: against, and *koptō*: to strike ▶ To hit, to dash; also transl.: to stumble** > The angels would bear the Lord Jesus up on their hands so that He would not strike {dash} His foot against a stone (Matt. 4:6; Luke 4:11). Israel has stumbled over the stumbling stone (Rom. 9:32). Disobedient people stumble at the word (1 Pet. 2:8). All other refs.: BEAT <4350>, STUMBLE <4350>.

7 ***tuptō*** [verb: τύπτω <5180>] **▶ To beat, to deliver blows; also transl.: to hit, to slap, to smite** > Jesus was struck on the head with a reed (Matt. 27:30; Mark 15:19). If someone strikes one cheek, one is to offer also the other cheek (Luke 6:29). The tax collector was beating his breast (Luke 18:13). The crowds returned, beating their breasts (Luke 23:48). Ananias commanded to strike Paul on the mouth (Acts 23:2); Paul told him that God would strike him, for he had ordered Paul to be stricken contrary to the law (v. 3a, b). Other ref.: Luke 22:64 in some mss. All other refs.: BEAT <5180>, WOUND (verb) <5180>.

– 8 Matt. 5:39 → SLAP (verb) <4474> 9 Mark 12:4 → to strike on the head → to wound in the head → WOUND (verb) <2775> 10 Mark 14:65 → to strike with the fists → to beat with the fists → BEAT <2852> 11 Mark 14:65 → to strike with the palms of their hands → lit.: to receive (*lambanō*) with slaps in the face (*rapisma*) → SLAP (noun) <4475> 12 Luke 5:26 →

SEIZE <2983> [13] Luke 6:48, 49 → to break upon → BREAK <4366> [14] John 18:22; 19:3 → to strike, to strike with the hands, to strike with the palm of the hand, to strike in the face → to give a blow on the face → BLOW (noun) <4475> [15] John 18:23; 2 Cor. 11:20 → BEAT <1194> [16] Acts 7:11 → COME <2064> [17] Acts 27:14 → lit.: to fall (*ballō*) [18] Acts 27:41 → FALL (verb) <4045> [19] 1 Cor. 9:27 → to strike a blow to the body → to discipline the body → DISCIPLINE (verb) <5299> [20] 1 Tim. 1:9 → those who strike their fathers and mothers → FATHER <3964>, MOTHER <3389>.

STRIKER – ***plēktēs*** [masc. noun: πλήκτης <4131>]; **from *plēssō*: to hit, to strike ▶ One who is given to fighting, who is aggressive** > An overseer must not be a striker {pugnacious, violent} (1 Tim. 3:3; Titus 1:7). ¶

STRING – Mark 7:35 → CHAIN (noun) <1199>.

STRIP (noun) – [1] John 11:44 → strips of linen → GRAVECLOTHES <2750> [2] John 19:40 → strip of linen → LINEN, LINEN CLOTH <3608>.

STRIP (verb) – [1] Matt. 27:28, 31; Mark 15:20; Luke 10:30 → to take off, to take off the clothing → TAKE <1562> [2] Acts 16:22 → to rend off → REND <4048>.

STRIPE – [1] ***mōlōps*** [masc. noun: μώλωψ <3468>]; **from *molops*: battle, and *ōps*: eye, face ▶ Mark on the skin resulting from an inflicted wound** > In 1 Pet. 2:24, Christians are healed by the stripes {wounds} of Jesus Christ, which refer to the divine judgment that He endured on the cross in their place. ¶

[2] ***plēgē*** [fem. noun: πληγή <4127>]; **from *plēssō*: to hit ▶ Wound, bruise** > After many stripes {blows} were laid on them {After they had been severely flogged}, Paul and Silas were thrown into prison (Acts 16:23). Paul had been in stripes {beaten, in beatings} (2 Cor. 6:5; 11:23 {to flog}). Other ref.: Luke 12:48 {flogging}. All other refs.: PLAGUE <4127>, WOUND (verb) <4127>.

STRIPPED – John 21:7 → NAKED <1131>.

STRIVE – [1] ***agōnizomai*** [verb: ἀγωνίζομαι <75>]; **from *agōn*: struggle, conflict, which is from *agō*: to lead ▶ To exert a great effort, to fight** > Jesus said to strive {strive with earnestness, make every effort} to enter through the narrow gate to obtain salvation (Luke 13:24). Other refs.: John 18:36; 1 Cor. 9:25; Col. 1:29; 4:12; 1 Tim. 6:12; 2 Tim. 4:7; see FIGHT (verb) <75>. ¶

[2] **to strive against: *antagōnizomai*** [verb: ἀνταγωνίζομαι <464>]; **from *anti*: against, and *agōnizomai*: see [1] ▶ To fight against** > The Hebrews had not yet resisted to bloodshed, striving {wrestling, in their struggle} against sin (Heb. 12:4). ¶

[3] **to strive together: *sunagōnizomai*** [verb: συναγωνίζομαι <4865>]; **from *sun*: together, and *agōnizomai*: see [1] ▶ To fight with** > Paul was beseeching the brothers in Rome to strive together with him {join him in his struggle} in prayers to God for him (Rom. 15:30). ¶

[4] **to strive, to strive for masteries: *athleō*** [verb: ἀθλέω <118>]; **from *athlos*: competitive game ▶ To fight, in the sense of participating to public games; also transl.: to compete (in athletics, as an athlete), to contend** > If a man strives for masteries, he is not crowned, except he strives lawfully (2 Tim. 2:5a, b). ¶

[5] **to strive together: *sunathleō*** [verb: συναθλέω <4866>]; **from *sun*: together, and *athleō*: see [4] ▶ To fight together** > Paul wanted to hear that the Philippians were striving together {laboring together in the same conflict, contending as one man} for the faith of the gospel with one mind (Phil. 1:27). He urges a companion to help women who have strived together {contended, labored} with him {shared his struggle} in the gospel (Phil. 4:3). ¶

[6] ***erizō*** [verb: ἐρίζω <2051>]; **from *eris*: dispute ▶ To dispute, to contest** > Isaiah

said that the Lord would not strive {quarrel} (Matt. 12:19). ¶

7 ***machomai*** [verb: μάχομαι <3164>] ► **To argue, to fight** > The servant of the Lord must not strive {contend, quarrel, be quarrelsome} (2 Tim. 2:24). The word is transl. "to fight" in Jas. 4:2: those who fight and war {quarrel and fight}, yet they do not have because they do not ask. Other refs.: John 6:52; Acts 7:26; see QUARREL (verb) <3164>, FIGHT (verb) <3164>. ¶

8 ***diamachomai*** [verb: διαμάχομαι <1264>]; **from *dia*: intens., and *machomai*: see 7 ► To dispute vigorously, to contend** > Further to what Paul had said, the scribes of the Pharisees' party strove {argued heatedly, argued vigorously, protested} (Acts 23:9). ¶

9 **to strive about words: *logomacheō*** [verb: λογομαχέω <3054>]; **from *logomachos*: disputing about words, which is from *logos*: word, and *machē*: fight ► To have quarrelsome exchange about words** > Christians should not strive about {have disputes of, wrangle about, quarrel about} words (2 Tim. 2:14). ¶

10 ***philotimeomai*** [verb: φιλοτιμέομαι <5389>]; **from *philotimos*: fond of honor, ambitious, which is from *philos*: friend, and *timē*: honor ► To make an effort, to aim (motivated by love of honor)** > Paul was striving {was aspiring, was making it his aim, had the ambition} to preach the gospel where Christ had not been named (Rom. 15:20). All other refs.: LABOR (verb) <5389>, STUDY <5389>.

– 11 Luke 12:58 → to make every effort → EFFORT <2039> 12 Acts 24:16 → EXERCISE (verb) <778> 13 1 Cor. 14:12 → SEEK <2212> 14 2 Cor. 13:11 → to strive for full restoration → PERFECTED (BE) <2675> 15 Gal. 1:10 → to strive to please → PERSUADE <3982> 16 1 Thes. 5:15; Heb. 12:14 → to strive to do, to strive for → PURSUE <1377> 17 1 Tim. 4:10 → to suffer reproach → REPROACH (noun) <3679> 18 Heb. 4:11 → LABOR (verb) <4704>.

STRIVING – 1 ***machē*** [fem. noun: μάχη <3163>]; **from *machomai*: to fight ► Controversy, quarrel** > Titus was to avoid strivings {contentions, disputes} about the law (Titus 3:9). All other refs.: FIGHTING <3163>, STRIFE <3163>.

– 2 1 Thes. 2:2 → earnest striving → CONFLICT <73>.

STROKE – Matt. 5:18; Luke 16:17 → TITTLE <2762>.

STRONG (adj.) – 1 ***dunatos*** [adj.: δυνατός <1415>]; **from *dunamai*: to be able ► Having strength of soul, moral power** > When he was weak, Paul was strong {powerful} (2 Cor. 12:10). All other refs.: see entries in Lexicon at <1415>.

2 ***ischuros*** [adj.: ἰσχυρός <2478>]; **from *ischuō*: see 5 ► Powerful, vigorous; also transl.: mighty** > Seeing that the wind was strong {boisterous}, Peter was afraid (Matt. 14:30). God has chosen the weak things of the world, that He may put to shame the strong things (1 Cor. 1:27). Paul said he was weak, but that the Corinthians were strong (1 Cor. 4:10). He asks if we are stronger than the Lord (1 Cor. 10:22). They said that Paul's letters were strong {forceful} (2 Cor. 10:10). Christ offered up both prayers and supplications with strong {fervent, loud, vehement} crying and tears to the One able to save Him from death, and He was heard because of His piety (Heb. 5:7). There is strong encouragement for those who have fled to refuge to lay hold on the hope set before them (Heb. 6:18). O.T. people of faith became mighty {valiant} in war (Heb. 11:34). John wrote to the young men because they were strong (1 John 2:14). An angel cried with a strong {loud} voice concerning the fall of Babylon (Rev. 18:2). Babylon is called the strong city (Rev. 18:10). John heard a voice, as a voice of strong peals of thunder (Rev. 19:6). Other ref.: Luke 15:14 {severe, violent}; 11:22 (see 3). All other refs.: GREAT <2478>, MAN <2478>, MIGHTY (adj.) <2478>.

3 **stronger: *ischuroteros*** [adj.: ἰσχυρότερος <2478>]; **compar. of 2 ► Of greater physical strength** > A stronger man is able to overcome a strong man who guards his own house (Luke 11:22). The weakness of God is stronger than men (1 Cor. 1:25).

[4] **to be made strong, to become strong:** ***endunamoō*** [verb: ἐνδυναμόω <1743>]; **from *en*: in, and *dunamoō*: to strengthen, which is from *dunamis*: strength ▶ To be fortified, to become vigorous** > O.T. people of faith became strong out of weakness (Heb. 11:34 {to turn to strength}). All other refs.: STRENGTHEN <1743>.

[5] **to be strong enough:** ***ischuō*** [verb: ἰσχύω <2480>]; **from *ischus*: ability, power ▶ To be more powerful, to prevail** > The dragon was not strong enough to resist against Michael and his angels (Rev. 12:8). All other refs.: see entries in Lexicon at <2480>.

[6] **to be made strong, to become strong:** ***stereoō*** [verb: στερεόω <4732>]; **from *stereos*: firm, steadfast ▶ To be strengthened, to become firm** > The feet and the ankle bones of a lame man who was healed by Peter were made strong {received strength, were strengthened} (Acts 3:7). Faith in the name of Jesus had made the lame man strong (Acts 3:16). Other ref.: Acts 16:5; see ESTABLISH <4732>. ¶

– [7] Luke 1:80; 2:40; 1 Cor. 16:13 → to be strong, to become strong, to wax strong → STRENGTHEN <2901> [8] Rom. 1:11; 1 Pet. 5:10 → to make strong → ESTABLISH <4741> [9] 1 Cor. 1:8 → to keep strong → CONFIRM <950> [10] 1 Cor. 7:36 → if the passions are too strong → who has passed the flower of age → AGE <5230> [11] 2 Thes. 2:11 → strong delusion → DELUSION <4106> [12] Heb. 5:12, 14 → SOLID <4731> [13] Jas. 3:4 → VIOLENT (adj.) <4642> [14] 1 Pet. 5:10 → to make strong → STRENGTHEN <4599>.

STRONG (noun) – **one who is strong, the strong:** ***dunatos*** [adj. used as noun: δυνατός <1415>]; **from *dunamai*: to be capable ▶ One who has moral strength** > Those who are strong are to bear the infirmities of the weak (Rom. 15:1). The strong {mighty} will hide themselves when the sixth seal is opened (Rev. 6:15). All other refs.: see entries in Lexicon at <1415>.

STRONG (BE) – ***krataioō*** [verb: κραταιόω <2901>]; **from *krataios*: strong, powerful ▶ To strengthen oneself** > Paul exhorts the Corinthians to be strong (1 Cor. 16:13). Other refs.: Luke 1:80; 2:40; Eph. 3:16; see STRENGTHEN <2901>. ¶

STRONGHOLD – 2 Cor. 10:4 → FORTRESS <3794>.

STRUCK DOWN (BE) – 2 Cor. 4:9 → to be cast down → CAST (verb) <2598>.

STRUCTURE – Eph. 2:21 → BUILDING <3619>.

STRUGGLE (noun) – [1] ***palē*** [fem. noun: πάλη <3823>]; **from *pallō*: to shake, to strike ▶ Hand to hand combat, wrestling** > The struggle of the Christian is {The Christian wrestles} against spiritual powers of wickedness (Eph. 6:12), i.e., the fallen angels. ¶

– [2] Rom. 15:30 → to join in a struggle → to strive together → STRIVE <4865> [3] Phil. 1:30; Col. 2:1 → CONFLICT <73> [4] Phil. 4:3 → to share one's struggle → to strive together → STRIVE <4866> [5] Heb. 12:4 → in their struggle → lit.: struggling, striving → to strive against → STRIVE <464>.

STRUGGLE (verb) – Col. 1:29; 4:12 → FIGHT (verb) <75>.

STUBBLE – ***kalamē*** [fem. noun: καλάμη <2562>]; **comp. *kalamos*: reed ▶ Short stumps of corn or grain left standing after the harvest; it was used as a lesser material for thatching roofs** > In 1 Cor. 3:12 stubble {straw} represents worthless work that will be burned. ¶

STUBBORN – [1] Mark 3:5 → HARDNESS <4457> [2] Mark 16:14 → stubborn refusal → hardness of heart → HARDNESS <4641>.

STUBBORN (BE) – Acts 19:9 → to become stubborn → lit.: to be hardened → HARDEN <4645>.

STUBBORNNESS – Rom. 2:5 → HARDNESS <4643>.

STUDENT – Matt. 10:24 → DISCIPLE <3101>.

STUDY – [1] ***philotimeomai*** [verb: φιλοτιμέομαι <5389>]; **from *philotimos*: fond of honor, ambitious, which is from *philos*: friend, and *timē*: honor ► To be zealous, to make it a point of honor** > The Thessalonians were to study {aspire, seek earnestly, make it their ambition} to be quiet and mind their own affairs and work with their hands (1 Thes. 4:11). All other refs.: LABOR (verb) <5389>, STRIVE <5389>.
– [2] John 5:39 → to study diligently → SEARCH (verb) <2045> [3] John 7:15 → LEARN <3129> [4] Acts 22:3 → EDUCATE <3811> [5] 2 Tim. 2:15 → to be diligent → DILIGENT <4704>.

STUFF – Luke 17:31 → GOOD (adj. and noun) <4632>.

STUMBLE – [1] ***proskoptō*** [verb: προσκόπτω <4350>]; **from *pros*: against, and *koptō*: to strike ► To trip against an obstacle, to fall** > If anyone walks in the day, he does not stumble (John 11:9); but if he walks in the night, he stumbles (v. 10). It is good to do nothing by which our brother stumbles (Rom. 14:21). All other refs.: BEAT <4350>, STRIKE <4350>.
[2] **not giving occasion to stumble, not causing to stumble: *aproskopos*** [adj.: ἀπρόσκοπος <677>]; **from *a*: neg., and *proskoptō*: see [1] ► Not causing harm to another that may lead to fall** > Paul warned the Corinthians to not be of those giving occasion to stumble {giving no offense}, whether to Jews, or Greeks, or the church of God (lit.: be of those who give them no occasion to stumble) (1 Cor. 10:32). Other refs.: Acts 24:1; Phil. 1:10 (without offense); see OFFENSE <677>. ¶
[3] ***ptaiō*** [verb: πταίω <4417>]; **akin to *piptō*: to fall ► To fall, to sin** > Whoever shall stumble in just one point of the law is guilty of breaking all of it (Jas. 2:10). We all stumble in many ways (Jas. 3:2a). He who does not stumble in words is a perfect man (Jas. 3:2b {to be at fault}). Using diligence to make their calling and election sure, Christians shall never stumble (2 Pet. 1:10). The Jews have stumbled (Rom. 11:11). ¶
[4] **from stumbling, without stumbling: *aptaistos*** [adj.: ἄπταιστος <679>]; **from *a*: neg., and *ptaiō*: see [3] ► Without tripping, without doing wrong** > God is able to keep Christians from stumbling {falling} (Jude 24). ¶
– [5] Matt. 5:29, 30; 11:6; 13:21; 18:6, 8; 26:31, 33; Mark 4:17; 9:42, 43, 45, 47; 14:27, 29; Luke 7:23; 17:2; John 6:61; 16:1; Rom. 14:21; 1 Cor. 8:13a, b; 2 Cor. 11:29 → to cause to stumble, to stumble → OFFEND <4624> [6] Matt. 18:7; Luke 17:1; 1 John 2:10 → things that cause people to stumble, cause for stumbling, occasion of stumbling → STUMBLING BLOCK <4625> [7] Rom. 14:20 → while stumbling, that causes someone else to stumble → OFFENSE <4348> [8] 1 Pet. 2:8 → stone that causes to stumble → STUMBLING BLOCK <4348>.

STUMBLING – Rom. 14:20 → OFFENSE <4348>.

STUMBLING BLOCK – [1] ***proskomma*** [neut. noun: πρόσκομμα <4348>]; **from *proskoptō*: to trip, which is from *pros*: against, and *koptō*: to strike ► Obstacle against which one falls carelessly; that which causes harm to another and may lead to a fall** > Jesus Christ, a precious corner stone, is a stone (*lithos*) of stumbling (*proskomma*) for unbelieving Jews (Rom. 9:32, 33) and the disobedient (1 Pet. 2:8 {stone that causes to stumble}). We ought not to put a stumbling block before our brother (Rom. 14:13). The Christian is to take care that his liberty does not become a stumbling block for the weak (1 Cor. 8:9). Other ref.: Rom. 14:20; see OFFENSE <4348>. ¶
[2] ***proskopē*** [fem. noun: προσκοπή <4349>]; **from *proskoptō*: see [1] ► Scandal, occasion of falling** > Christians are to put no stumbling block {to give no cause for offense} in anyone's way (2 Cor. 6:3). ¶

3 ***skandalon*** [neut. noun: σκάνδαλον <4625>]; **lit.: hook to trigger a trap ▶ Occasion, means of falling or stumbling for another; also transl.: obstacle, occasion of stumbling, occasion to fall, cause to fall, fall-trap, hindrance, offence, offense, scandal, thing that causes sin, thing that offends >** The term is used in the figur. sense in regard to unbelievers (Matt. 13:41), Satan (Matt. 16:23), and those who say they are believers in the Lord (Luke 17:1). The stumbling block of the cross would have been done away if Paul had still preached circumcision (Gal. 5:11). Balaam taught Balak to put a stumbling block before {to entice} Israel (Rev. 2:14), i.e., at his suggestion the daughters of Moab led the sons of Israel to sin (see Num. 25:1–3). Rom. 9:33; 1 Pet. 2:8: see OFFENSE <4625>. Other refs.: Matt. 18:7a–c; Rom. 11:9; 14:13; 16:17; 1 Cor. 1:23; 1 John 2:10. ¶

STUPID – 2 Tim. 2:23 → SENSELESS <521>.

STUPOR – 1 ***katanuxis*** [fem. noun: κατάνυξις <2659>]; **from *katanussō*: to prick, to pierce, which is from *kata*: intens., and *nussō*: to prick, to pierce, to stun ▶ Deep sleep, numbness >** In Rom. 11:8, the spirit of stupor {slumber} that God has given to Israel corresponds to a moral torpor to prevent their discernment. ¶
– 2 1 Cor. 15:34 → to wake up from one's drunken stupor → AWAKE <1594>.

SUBDUE – 1 Mark 5:4 → TAME <1150> 2 1 Cor. 15:28; Phil. 3:21 → SUBJECT (verb) <5293> 3 Heb. 11:33 → CONQUER <2610> 4 2 Pet. 2:19, 20 → OVERCOME <2274>.

SUBJECT (noun)[1] – 1 **subject, subject to: *enochos*** [adj.: ἔνοχος <1777>]; **from *enechō*: to hold, to keep something to oneself, which is from *en*: in, and *echō*: to have, to hold ▶ a. In danger of suffering punishment for a misdeed; also transl.: in danger of, liable to, guilty to, answerable to >** Whoever will kill will be subject to {in danger of, liable to} the judgment (Matt. 5:21); everyone who is lightly angry with his brother or call him "stupid" will be subject to {in danger of, guilty to go before} the judgment (v. 22a, b); whoever will say "fool" will be subject to the penalty of hell fire (v. 22c). Whoever will speak injuriously against the Holy Spirit lies under the guilt {is guilty, is in danger} of an everlasting sin (Mark 3:29). **b. Under the domination of, controlled by >** Jesus has delivered those who through fear of death were subject {were held} to bondage all their lifetime (Heb. 2:15). All other refs.: DESERVING <1777>, GUILTY <1777>.

2 **to be subject: *hupotassō*** [verb: ὑποτάσσω <5293>]; **from *hupo*: under, and *tassō*: to arrange in order ▶ To be obedient; also transl.: to be in subjection, to be subjected, to be submissive, to obey, to submit >** Jesus was subject to His parents (Luke 2:51). It is necessary to be subject to the authorities on account of conscience (Rom. 13:5). Christians are to be subject to one another in the fear of Christ (Eph. 5:21). Wives are to be subject to their own husbands (Eph. 5:22; Titus 2:5; 1 Pet. 3:1, 5), as the church is subject to Christ (Eph. 5:24) and as is fitting in the Lord (Col. 3:18). Titus was to exhort servants to be subject to their own masters (Titus 2:9); he was to remind Christians to be subject to rulers and authorities (3:1). We are to be subject to the Father of spirits (Heb. 12:9). Christians are to submit themselves to every human institution for the Lord's sake (1 Pet. 2:13). Servants are to be subject to their own masters (1 Pet. 2:18). Angels, authorities, and powers are being subjected {are being made subject} to the Lord Jesus (1 Pet. 3:22). Young people are to be subject to those who are older (1 Pet. 5:5). All other refs.: SUBJECT (verb) <5293>.
– 3 Acts 7:39 → OBEDIENT <5255> 4 Rom. 7:24; 8:10 → "subject" added in Engl. 5 1 Cor. 9:21 → legitimately subject → LAWFUL <1772> 6 Gal. 5:1 → to be subject to → ENTANGLED (BE) <1758> 7 Titus 3:1 → to be subject → OBEY <3980>.

SUBJECT (noun)[2] – Luke 19:14 → CITIZEN <4177>.

SUBJECT (verb) – 1 **to subject, to make subject, to be subject, to put under, to put in subjection:** ***hupotassō*** [verb: ὑποτάσσω <5293>]; **from** ***hupo*****: under, and** ***tassō*****: to arrange in order ▶ a. To place under the authority of someone; also transl.: to place under, to submit** > The devils were subjected to the seventy disciples (Luke 10:17, 20). The creation was subjected to vanity because of Him who subjected it in hope that the creation itself will be liberated (Rom. 8:20a, b). The spirits of the prophets are subject to the prophets (1 Cor. 14:32). The women are to keep silent in the churches; they are to subject themselves (1 Cor. 14:34). God has put all things under the feet of Christ (1 Cor. 15:27a–c; Eph. 1:22; Heb. 2:8a, b, d); Heb. 2:8c {not put under}: see 2. When all things will be subjected to Him {subdued, brought under subjection, made subject}, then will the Son also Himself be subjected {made subject} to God who subjected all things to Him (1 Cor. 15:28a–c). The Lord Jesus Christ is able to subject {subdue, bring under control} even all things to Himself (Phil. 3:21). God has not put in subjection {subjected} the world to come to angels (Heb. 2:5), but to Jesus; however, we do not see yet all things subjected to Him (v. 8). **b. To obey, to submit; also transl.: to be subject, to be in subjection** > The mind of the flesh is not subject to the law of God (Rom. 8:7). The Jews did not subject themselves to the righteousness of God (Rom. 10:3). Every soul is to be subject to governing authorities (Rom. 13:1). Paul exhorted the Corinthians to be subject to men such as Stephanas and to every one joined in the work and laboring (1 Cor. 16:16). James says to subject oneself to God, for He gives grace to the humble (Jas. 4:7). All other refs.: SUBJECT (noun)[1] <5293>.

2 **not subject, not put under:** ***anupotaktos*** [adj.: ἀνυπότακτος <506>]; **from** ***a*****: neg., and** ***hupotassō*****: see** 1 **▶ Who is not placed under the authority, who is not submitted** > God has left nothing that is not put under {unsubject to} Jesus (Heb. 2:8c). Other refs.: 1 Tim. 1:9; Titus 1:6, 10; see INSUBORDINATE <506>. ¶

3 **to be subject:** ***perikeimai*** [verb: περίκειμαι <4029>]; **from** ***peri*****: around, and** ***keimai*****: to put ▶ To be surrounded** > Every high priest is himself subject to {is beset with, is clothed with, is compassed with} weakness (Heb. 5:2). All other refs.: BIND <4029>, HANG <4029>, SURROUND <4029>.

– 4 Acts 13:34 → so that He will never be subject to decay → lit.: no more being about to return to corruption 5 Col. 2:20 → to subject to ordinances → ORDINANCE <1379> 6 Heb. 6:6 → to subject to public disgrace → to make a show → SHOW (noun) <3856>.

SUBJECT (BE) – See SUBJECT (verb).

SUBJECTED (BE) – 1 Matt. 11:12 → to be subjected to violence → VIOLENCE <971> 2 Eph. 5:24; 1 Pet. 3:22 → to be subjected → to be subject → SUBJECT <5293>.

SUBJECTION – 1 **to bring into subjection:** ***doulagōgeō*** [verb: δουλαγωγέω <1396>]; **from:** ***doulos*****: servant, slave, and** ***agō*****: to lead ▶ To treat like a slave, to submit, to keep under control** > Concerning his body, Paul was bringing it into subjection {was leading it captive, was making his body his slave} (1 Cor. 9:27). ¶

– 2 Luke 2:51; Rom. 13:5; Heb. 12:9; 1 Pet. 2:13; 3:1, 5 → to be in subjection, to continue in subjection → to be subject → SUBJECT (noun)[1] <5293> 3 Rom. 13:1; 1 Cor. 14:34; 16:16; 1 Cor. 15:27a–c, 28a–c; Eph. 1:22; Heb. 2:5, 8a–c → to be, continue, put in subjection → to be subject → SUBJECT (verb) <5293> 4 Gal. 2:5; 1 Tim. 2:11; 3:4 → SUBMISSION <5292>.

SUBMISSION – 1 ***hupotagē*** [fem. noun: ὑποταγή <5292>]; **from** ***hupotassō*****: to submit, which is from** ***hupo*****: under, and** ***tassō*****: to arrange in order ▶ Obedience, subjection** > The Corinthians professed obedience to the gospel of Christ (2 Cor.

9:13). Paul had not yielded in submission to false brothers (Gal. 2:5). A woman is to learn in silence with all submission (1 Tim. 2:11 {submissiveness}). The overseer must have his children in submission {control, subjection} with all dignity (1 Tim. 3:4). ¶

– [2] 1 Cor. 14:34 → to be submissive, to be in submission → SUBJECT (verb) <5293> [3] Heb. 5:7 → submission, reverent submission → REVERENCE (noun) <2124> [4] 1 Pet. 3:22 → in submission → lit.: having been subjected → to be subject → SUBJECT (noun)[1] <5293>.

SUBMISSIVE – [1] Luke 2:51; Titus 2:5, 9; 1 Pet. 2:18; 3:1, 5, 22 → to be submissive → to be subject → SUBJECT (noun)[1] <5293> [2] 1 Tim. 3:4 → to keep submissive → to have in submission → SUBMISSION <5292> [3] Heb. 13:17 → to be submissive → SUBMIT <5226> [4] Jas. 3:17 → YIELDING <2138>.

SUBMISSIVENESS – 1 Tim. 2:11 → SUBMISSION <5292>.

SUBMIT – [1] ***hupeikō*** [verb: ὑπείκω <5226>]; **from *hupo*: under, and *eikō*: to yield ▶ To yield, to be submissive** > Christians are to obey their leaders and be submissive (Heb. 13:17). ¶

– [2] Luke 10:17, 20; Rom. 8:7; 10:3; 13:1, 5; 1 Cor. 16:16; Jas. 4:7 → to be subject → SUBJECT (verb) <5293> [3] Gal. 2:2 → to lay before → LAY <394> [4] Gal. 5:1 → ENTANGLED (BE) <1758> [5] Eph. 5:21, 22; Col. 3:18; Heb. 12:9; 1 Pet. 2:13, 18; 3:1, 5, 22 → to be subject → SUBJECT (noun)[1] <5293> [6] Col. 2:20 → to submit to decrees, to rules → to subject to ordinances → ORDINANCE <1379>.

SUBORN – ***hupoballō*** [verb: ὑποβάλλω <5260>]; **from *hupo*: under, and *ballō*: to throw, to place ▶ To persuade (to do something evil), to corrupt; also transl.: to secretly induce, to secretly persuade** > Men were suborned to say that Stephen had spoken blasphemous words against Moses and against God (Acts 6:11). ¶

SUBORNED – Luke 20:20 → suborned person → SPY (noun) <1455>.

SUBSEQUENT – 1 Pet. 1:11 → subsequent glories → lit.: glories after these.

SUBSEQUENTLY – Jude 5 → SECOND <1208>.

SUBSIDE – Luke 8:24 → CEASE <3973>.

SUBSIST – [1] **to subsist, to subsist together: *sunistēmi*** [verb: συνίστημι <4921>]; **from *sun*: together, and *histēmi*: to stand ▶ To maintain together, to remain together** > Jesus is before all things, and all things subsist together by Him (Col. 1:17 {to consist, to hold together}). Men are willingly ignorant that, by the word of God, the heavens existed of old, and an earth subsisting {formed, standing} out of the water and in the water (2 Pet. 3:5). All other refs.: COMMEND <4921>, MAKE <4921>, PROVE <4921>, STAND (verb) <4921>.

– [2] Matt. 12:25, 26; Mark 3:24–26; Luke 11:18 → STAND (verb) <2476>.

SUBSISTENCE – 2 Pet. 3:5 → to have its subsistence → to subsist together → SUBSIST <4921>.

SUBSTANCE – [1] ***huparchonta*** [pres. ptcp. neut. plur.: ὑπάρχοντα <5224>]; **from *huparchō*: to begin, to exist, which is from *hupo*: under, and *archō*: to begin, which is from *archē*: beginning ▶ Means of existing, possession, resource** > Many women provided for Jesus from their substance {own means, private means} (Luke 8:3). All other refs.: GOOD (adj. and noun) <5224>, POSSESSIONS <5224>.

[2] ***hupostasis*** [fem. noun: ὑπόστασις <5287>]; **from *huphistēmi*: to place under, which is from *hupo*: under, and *histēmi*: to put; lit.: what one puts underneath, foundation ▶ a. Firm conviction, guarantee** > Faith is the substance {the assurance, the substantiating, being sure} of things hoped for (Heb. 11:1). **b. Essential nature, reality; also transl.: being, nature,**

person > Jesus is the exact representation of the substance of God (Heb. 1:3). All other refs.: CONFIDENCE <5287>.

– [3] Luke 15:13 → GOOD (adj. and noun) <3776> [4] Luke 15:30; 1 John 3:17 → LIVING (noun) <979> [5] Heb. 10:34 → GOOD (adj. and noun) <5223>.

SUBSTANTIATING – Heb. 11:1 → SUBSTANCE <5287>.

SUBSTITUTION – The term is not found as such in the Bible; nevertheless, it well describes the act by which Jesus Christ, the only righteous One, took the place of sinful man on the cross. Not only did He bear the sins of many (see Heb. 9:28; 1 Pet. 2:24), and die for our sins (see 1 Cor. 15:3), but God made Him "sin" and condemned sin in the flesh, so that all who believe in Him might become God's righteousness in Him (see Rom. 8:3; 2 Cor. 5:21).

SUBTILTY – [1] Matt. 26:4 → SUBTLETY <1388> [2] 2 Cor. 11:3 → CRAFTINESS <3834>.

SUBTLETY – ***dolos*** [masc. noun: δόλος <1388>]; ***dolus*, in Lat.: trick, ruse, bad faith ▶ Deceit, fraud, guile; also transl.: attempt to deceive, subtilty, trickery** > The chief priests and the elders took counsel together that they might take Jesus by subtlety and kill Him (Matt. 26:4; Mark 14:1). Paul's exhortation to the Thessalonians was not of error (*apatē*) nor in guile (*dolos*) (1 Thes. 2:3). Paul told the Corinthians he caught them by trickery (2 Cor. 12:16). All other refs.: DECEIT <1388>.

SUBVERSION – 2 Tim. 2:14 → RUIN (noun) <2692>.

SUBVERT – [1] ***anaskeuazō*** [verb: ἀνασκευάζω <384>]; **from *ana*: back (in the sense of reversal), and *skeuazō*: to prepare, which is from *skeuē*: equipment, which is from *skeuos*: vessel, instrument ▶ To distress, to trouble, to reverse what has been accomplished** > Some had subverted {unsettled, upset} the souls of the Christians in Antioch (Acts 15:24). ¶

– [2] Luke 23:2 → PERVERT (verb) <1294> [3] Titus 1:11 → OVERTURN <396>.

SUBVERTING – 2 Tim. 2:14 → RUIN (noun) <2692>.

SUCCEED – [1] Matt. 23:15 → when you have succeeded → lit.: when he becomes (*ginomai*) so [2] Acts 24:27 → to be succeeded → lit.: to receive a successor → SUCCESSOR <1240> [3] Rom. 1:10 → to have a prosperous journey → JOURNEY (noun) <2137> [4] Rom. 9:31 → to succeed in reaching → to come upon → COME <5348>.

SUCCESSIVELY – ***kathexēs*** [adv.: καθεξῆς <2517>]; **from *kata*: according to, and *hexēs*: after ▶ In order, consecutively** > Paul passed successively {from place to place, in order} through the region of Galatia and Phrygia, strengthening all the disciples (Acts 18:23). All other refs.: ORDER (noun) <2517>.

SUCCESSOR – ***diadochos*** [masc. noun: διάδοχος <1240>]; **from *diadechomai*: to receive by succession, which is from *dia*: through, and *dechomai*: to receive ▶ Person who replaces another** > Felix had Porcius Festus as his successor (Acts 24:27). ¶

SUCCOUR – 2 Cor. 6:2; Heb. 2:18 → HELP (verb) <997>.

SUCCOURER – Rom. 16:2 → HELPER <4368>.

SUCH – Acts 19:25; 21:25; Eph. 5:27 → LIKE (adj., adv., noun) <5108>.

SUCK (GIVE) – Matt. 24:19; Mark 13:17; Luke 11:27; 21:23; 23:29 → NURSE (verb) <2337>.

SUCKLING – Matt. 21:16 → nursing baby → NURSE (verb) <2337>.

SUDDEN – 1 Thes. 5:3 → SUDDENLY <160>.

SUDDENLY – [1] ***aiphnidios*** [adj. or adv.: αἰφνίδιος <160>]; **from *aiphnēs*: unexpected, abrupt, unforeseen ▶ In an unexpected, unforeseen manner, abruptly >** The Day of the Lord to establish His reign could come upon certain people suddenly {suddenly [αἰφνίδιος] like a trap [παγίς], unawares, unexpectedly} (Luke 21:34). When they say "Peace and safety," destruction will come suddenly {sudden destruction will come} upon people (1 Thes. 5:3). ¶

[2] ***aphnō*** [adv.: ἄφνω <869>] **▶ Unexpectedly, which cannot be foreseen immediately >** At Pentecost, suddenly there came a sound from heaven, as of a violent impetuous wind (Acts 2:2). Suddenly, there was a great earthquake and the doors of Paul's prison were opened (Acts 16:26). The people expected that Paul would have fallen down suddenly dead (Acts 28:6). ¶

[3] ***exaiphnēs*** [adv.: ἐξαίφνης <1810>]; **from *ek*: out, and *aiphnēs*: suddenly ▶ Immediately, unexpectedly (a strengthened form) >** In a parable, the master of the house might come suddenly (Mark 13:36). On the occasion of the birth of Jesus, suddenly there was with the angel who was with the shepherds a multitude of the heavenly host (Luke 2:13). A spirit seized a man's only son, and suddenly he cried out (Luke 9:39). A light shone suddenly from heaven around Paul when he came near Damascus (Acts 9:3; 22:6). ¶

[4] ***exapina*** [adv.: ἐξάπινα <1819>] **▶ Immediately, unexpectedly >** Suddenly, Peter, James, and John saw no one anymore, but only Jesus (Mark 9:8). ¶

– [5] 1 Tim. 5:22 → HASTILY <5030>.

SUE – ***krinō*** [verb: κρίνω <2919>]; **lit.: to make a distinction, to distinguish, to judge ▶ To prosecute; to go to court >** Jesus said to leave our cloak to him who would sue {go to law with, sue at the law} us and take our tunic (Matt. 5:40). All other refs.: see entries in Lexicon at <2919>.

SUFFER – [1] ***paschō*** [verb: πάσχω <3958>] **▶ To endure evil, to be afflicted >** The verb is used in regard to the sufferings of Christ (Matt. 16:21; 17:12; Mark 8:31; 9:12; Luke 9:22; 17:25; 22:15; 24:26, 46; Acts 1:3; 3:18; 17:3; Heb. 2:18; 5:8; 9:26; 13:12; 1 Pet. 2:21, 23; 3:18 {to die}; 4:1a, b), a lunatic (Matt. 17:15 {to be vexed, to be ill}), the wife of Pilate (Matt. 27:19), a woman who had a flow of blood (Mark 5:26 {to endure}), the Galileans (Luke 13:2), Paul (Acts 9:16; 28:5 {to feel}; 2 Cor. 1:6; 2 Tim. 1:12), Christians (1 Cor. 12:26a; 1 Pet. 2:19, 20; 3:14, 17; 4:15, 19; 5:10), the Galatians (Gal. 3:4), the Philippians (Phil. 1:29), the Thessalonians (1 Thes. 2:14; 2 Thes. 1:5), and Smyrna (Rev. 2:10). ¶

[2] **to suffer already, before, previously: *propaschō*** [verb: προπάσχω <4310>]; **from *pro*: before, and *paschō*: see [1] ▶ To endure evil, to be afflicted previously >** Paul had suffered before at Philippi (1 Thes. 2:2). ¶

[3] **to suffer with: *sumpaschō*** [verb: συμπάσχω <4841>]; **from *sun*: together, and *paschō*: see [1] ▶ To endure evil, to be afflicted with others >** Christians suffer with {share in the sufferings of} Christ, that they may also be glorified with Him (Rom. 8:17). If one Christian suffers, all Christians suffer with him (1 Cor. 12:26b). ¶

[4] ***anechō*** [verb: ἀνέχω <430>]; **from *ana*: in, and *echō*: to hold ▶ To bear, to endure, to put up with; also transl.: to forbear, to show tolerance, to sustain, to tolerate >** Three evangelists use this verb when Jesus was addressing His generation (Matt. 17:17; Mark 9:19; Luke 9:41). This verb is used when Gallio was addressing the Jews (Acts 18:14). Paul suffered persecution (1 Cor. 4:12). He desired that the Corinthians would bear with him and bear with his folly (2 Cor. 11:1a, b). The Corinthians might well bear with a different gospel (2 Cor. 11:4). They suffered fools (2 Cor. 11:19) and they suffered it if anyone beat them on the face (v. 20). The Ephesians were to bear with one another in love (Eph. 4:2). The Colossians were to bear with one another and forgive one another (Col. 3:13). The Thessalonians were enduring persecutions and tribulations (2 Thes. 1:4). Paul warned

Timothy of a time when men will not endure sound teaching (2 Tim. 4:3). The Hebrews were exhorted to bear the word of exhortation (Heb. 13:22). ¶

5 ***sunechō*** [verb: συνέχω <4912>]; **from *sun*: together, and *echō*: to have, to hold ▶ To be afflicted, to be oppressed (by an illness)** > The mother-in-law of Peter was suffering from {was taken with, was sick with} a high fever (Luke 4:38). The father of Publius was suffering from fever and dysentery (Acts 28:8). All other refs.: see entries in Lexicon at <4912>.

6 ***hupomenō*** [verb: ὑπομένω <5278>]; **from *hupo*: under, and *menō*: to remain ▶ To endure, to persevere** > If we suffer with Christ Jesus, we will also reign together with Him (2 Tim. 2:12). All other refs.: ENDURE <5278>, LINGER <5278>, PATIENT <5278>, REMAIN <5278>.

7 **to suffer; to suffer evil, hardship, trouble: *kakopatheō*** [verb: κακοπαθέω <2553>]; **from *kakos*: bad, evil, and *pathos*: passion, which is from *paschō*: to suffer ▶ To endure pain, difficulty** > Paul was suffering trouble as an evildoer, even to the point of chains (2 Tim. 2:9). Timothy was to suffer {bear evils, endure afflictions, endure hardship} (2 Tim. 2:3; 4:5). He who is suffering {is afflicted, is in trouble} should pray (Jas. 5:13). ¶

8 **subject to suffering: *pathētos*** [adj.: παθητός <3805>]; **from *pathos*: affliction ▶ Exposed to suffering, liable to suffer** > The prophets and Moses said that Christ should suffer (lit.: was subject to suffering) (Acts 26:23). ¶

9 **to suffer long: *makrothumeō*** [verb: μακροθυμέω <3114>]; **from *makrothumos*: long-suffering, which is from *makros*: long, and *thumos*: heart, the seat of feelings ▶ To endure contradictions, to persevere in difficult circumstances** > Love suffers long {has long patience, is patient} (1 Cor. 13:4). All other refs.: PATIENCE <3114>, PATIENT <3114>.

– **10** Matt. 3:15a, b; 13:30; 19:14; 23:13; Mark 1:34; 5:19, 37; 7:12, 27; 10:14; 11:16; Luke 8:51; 9:60; 12:39; 18:16; John 12:7; Rev. 11:9 → LET <863> **11** Matt. 8:6 → TORMENT (verb) <928> **12** Matt. 8:21, 31; 19:8; Mark 10:4; Luke 8:32; 9:59; Acts 21:39; 27:3; 28:16; 1 Tim. 2:12 → PERMIT <2010> **13** Matt. 9:20 → to suffer from a discharge of blood → to have a flow of blood → FLOW (noun) <131> **14** Matt. 11:12 → to suffer violence → VIOLENCE <971> **15** Matt. 15:22 → to suffer from demon-possession → to be possessed by a demon → DEMON <1139> **16** Matt. 24:43; Luke 4:41; 22:51; Acts 16:7; 19:30; 28:4; 1 Cor. 10:13; Rev. 2:20 → ALLOW <1439> **17** Luke 16:24, 25 → TORMENT (verb) <3600> **18** Acts 2:27; 13:35 → LET <1325> **19** Acts 5:41 → to suffer shame, to suffer disgrace → DISHONORED (BE) <818> **20** Acts 13:18 → to suffer the manners → to endure the conduct → ENDURE <5159> **21** Acts 27:7 → to permit to proceed → PROCEED <4330> **22** 1 Cor. 9:12 → BEAR (verb) <4722> **23** 2 Cor. 2:3 → to suffer pain → lit.: to have sorrow → SORROW (noun) <3077> **24** 2 Cor. 11:25; 1 Tim. 1:19 → to suffer shipwreck → SHIPWRECK <3489> **25** Col. 1:24; Heb. 2:9, 10 → in what was suffered, because He suffered death → lit.: in sufferings, because of the suffering of death → SUFFERING <3804> **26** 2 Thes. 1:9 → ENDURE <5099> **27** 2 Tim. 1:8 → to suffer evil along → to join in suffering → SUFFERING <4777> **28** Heb. 7:23 → to not suffer → FORBID <2967> **29** Heb. 10:34 → to suffer along with → SYMPATHIZE <4834> **30** Heb. 11:36 → lit.: to receive trial → TRIAL <3984> **31** Heb. 13:3 → to suffer adversity → TORMENTED (BE) <2558> **32** Jude 7 → UNDERGO <5254> **33** Rev. 2:22 → to suffer intensely → lit.: with great tribulation → TRIBULATION <2347>.

SUFFERING – **1** ***pathēma*** [neut. noun: πάθημα <3804>]; **from *paschō*: to suffer ▶ Affliction, difficulty, grief, trouble** > Paul reckoned that the sufferings of the present time are not worthy to be compared with the coming glory to be revealed to Christians (Rom. 8:18). The sufferings of Christ abounded toward Paul (2 Cor. 1:5). The Corinthians endured the same sufferings that Paul also suffered (2 Cor. 1:6); as they were partakers of the sufferings, so also they were partakers of the encouragement (v. 7). Paul wanted to know Jesus and the fellowship of His sufferings (Phil. 3:10). He rejoiced in sufferings for the Colossians (Col. 1:24). Timothy was thoroughly acquainted with the sufferings of Paul (2 Tim. 3:11). Jesus knew the suffering of death (Heb. 2:9). God had perfected the Lord Jesus through sufferings (Heb. 2:10). The Hebrew Christians endured much conflict of sufferings (Heb. 10:32). The Spirit of Christ that was in the prophets testified beforehand of the sufferings of Christ and the glories that should follow (1 Pet. 1:11). We may rejoice inasmuch as we have share in the sufferings of Christ (1 Pet. 4:13). Peter had been a witness of the sufferings of Christ (1 Pet. 5:1). For Christians, the same sufferings coming from Satan are accomplished in their brothers who are in the world (1 Pet. 5:9). Other refs.: Rom. 7:5; Gal. 5:24; see PASSION <3804>. ¶

2 ***kakopatheia*** [fem. noun: κακοπάθεια <2552>]; **from *kakopatheō*: to suffer evil, which is from *kakos*: evil, and *pathos*: passion ▶ Affliction, difficulty** > We are to take the prophets who have spoken in the name of the Lord as an example of suffering and patience (Jas. 5:10). ¶

3 **to join in suffering, to share in the sufferings: *sunkakopatheō*** [verb: συγκακοπαθέω <4777>]; **from *sun*: together, and *kakopateō*: see 2 ▶ To endure the same afflictions, to suffer with; also transl.: to be partaker of the afflictions, to suffer evil along** > Timothy was to share with Paul in the sufferings for the gospel (2 Tim. 1:8). Other ref.: 2 Tim. 2:3 in some mss. ¶

– 4 Matt. 8:6 → in terrible suffering → lit.: suffering terribly → TORMENT (verb) <928> 5 Mark 1:32, 34 → SICK (adv.) <2192> <2560> 6 Mark 5:29, 34 → AFFLICTION <3148> 7 Luke 14:2 → suffering from abnormal swelling of the body → DROPSICAL <5203> 8 Acts 1:3; Phil. 1:29; 1 Thes. 2:14 → suffering, to endure suffering; lit.: to suffer → SUFFER <3958> 9 Acts 7:11 → TROUBLE (noun) <2347> 10 Rom. 5:3a, b; Eph. 3:13; 1 Thes. 1:6; Rev. 1:9 → TRIBULATION <2347> 11 Rom. 8:17 → to share in the sufferings of → to suffer with → SUFFER <4841> 12 2 Tim. 2:3 → to take one's share in suffering → to endure hardship → HARDSHIP <2553>.

SUFFICE – 1 Matt. 25:9 → to be enough → ENOUGH <714> 2 John 14:8; 2 Cor. 12:9 → to be sufficient → SUFFICIENT <714> 3 1 Pet. 4:3 → lit.: to be sufficient → SUFFICIENT <713>.

SUFFICIENCY – 1 **all-sufficiency: *autarkeia*** [fem. noun: αὐτάρκεια <841>]; **from *autarkēs*: content with one's lot, which is from *autos*: himself, and *arkeō*: to suffice ▶ That which concerns the necessities of life, all that one needs, self-sufficiency** > Having always all-sufficiency in everything, the Corinthians could abound in every good work (2 Cor. 9:8). Other ref.: 1 Tim. 6:6; see CONTENTMENT <841>. ¶

2 ***hikanotēs*** [fem. noun: ἱκανότης <2426>]; **from *hikanos*: sufficient, capable ▶ Ability, aptitude** > The sufficiency {adequacy, competence, competency} of Paul was from God (2 Cor. 3:5). ¶

SUFFICIENT – 1 ***arketos*** [adj.: ἀρκετός <713>]; **from *arkeō*: see 2 ▶ Which is enough, which is adequate** > Sufficient to the day is its own evil (Matt. 6:34). It is sufficient for the disciple that he should become as his master (Matt. 10:25). Peter says that the time past may be sufficient for Christians to have carried out the will of the nations (1 Pet. 4:3). ¶

2 **to be sufficient: *arkeō*** [verb: ἀρκέω <714>]; ***arcere*, in Lat.: to contain, to retain ▶ To be satisfactory, to be enough, to be a source of contentment** > Loaves for two hundred denarii would not have been sufficient {been enough} to feed the crowd (John 6:7). It would be sufficient for {be enough for, suffice} Philip that Jesus should show him the Father (John 14:8). The Lord had said to Paul that His grace was sufficient for {sufficed} him, for His strength was made perfect in weakness (2 Cor. 12:9). All other refs.: CONTENT (verb) <714>, ENOUGH <714>, SATISFIED <714>.

3 ***hikanos*** [adj.: ἱκανός <2425>]; **from *hikneomai*: to come, to occur ▶ a. Adequate, enough** > The chief priests and elders gave sufficient money to the soldiers (Matt. 28:12). Paul said that the punishment inflicted by the majority was sufficient for a brother in Corinth (2 Cor. 2:6). **b. Who is qualified, up to the demands of a role** > Paul asks: "Who is sufficient for {adequate for, equal to} these things?" after having spoken of the apostles as being a sweet odor of Christ for God in the saved and in those who perish (2 Cor. 2:16). Other refs.: see entries in Lexicon at <2425>.
– 4 2 Cor. 3:5 → ABLE <2425> 5 2 Cor. 3:6 → to make sufficient → to make competent → COMPETENT <2427>.

SUGGEST – Acts 23:15 → SIGNIFY <1718>.

SUIT (noun) – 1 **to prosecute one's suit: *krinō*** [verb: κρίνω <2919>] ▶ **To bring a litigation before a court** > It is shameful for a Christian to prosecute his suit {to go to law, to go for judgment} before unbelievers (1 Cor. 6:1, 6). All other refs.: see entries in Lexicon at <2919>.
– 2 1 Cor. 6:7 → LAWSUIT <2917>.

SUIT (verb) – Luke 5:36 → AGREE <4856>.

SUITABLE – 1 **not suitable: *aneuthetos*** [adj.: ἀνεύθετος <428>]; **from *a*: neg., and *euthetos*: fit, which is from *eu*: well, and *tithēmi*: to put, to set ▶ Inappropriate, not convenient** > The harbor of Fair Havens was not suitable {not commodious, ill adapted} for wintering (Acts 27:12). ¶
– 2 1 Cor. 16:4 → MEET (adj.) <514>.

SULFER – See SULFUR <2303>.

SULFUR – 1 ***theion*** [neut. noun: θεῖον <2303>] ▶ **Originally: fire from heaven (as flashing lightning, which leaves a sulfurous odor), from which: chemical element of a yellow color; also transl.: brimstone** > On the day that Lot went out from Sodom, it rained fire and sulfur from heaven (Luke 17:29). John saw horse riders having breastplates of fiery red, hyacinth blue, and sulfur yellow (*theiōdēs*), and the heads of the horses were like the heads of lions; and out of their mouths came fire, smoke, and sulfur (*theion*) (Rev. 9:17b). The third part of men was killed by the fire, smoke, and sulfur (Rev. 9:18). If anyone worship the beast and receive his mark, he will be tormented with burning sulfur (Rev. 14:10). The beast and the false prophet will be cast alive into the lake of fire that burns with sulfur (Rev. 19:20), as also the devil (Rev. 20:10). The fearful, the unbelieving, those who make themselves abominable, murderers, fornicators, sorcerers, idolaters, and all liars will have their part in the lake that burns with fire and sulfur, which is the second death (Rev. 21:8). ¶
2 **as sulfur: *theiōdēs*** [adj.: θειώδης <2306>]; **from *theion*: see 1 ▶ Characterized by sulfur** > The word is used in Rev. 9:17a {of brimstone; yellow as sulfur}. ¶

SULPHER – See SULFUR <2303>.

SULPHUR – See SULFUR <2303>.

SUM – 1 ***kephalaion*** [neut. noun: κεφάλαιον <2774>]; **from *kephalaios*: of the head, principal, which is from *kephalē*: head ▶ a. Amount of money** > The commander had bought his citizenship for a great sum {price} (Acts 22:28). **b. Main point, summary** > The sum of what the author of the Epistle to the Hebrews says is that we have a High Priest who has sat down on the right hand of the throne of the Majesty in the heavens (Heb. 8:1). ¶
– 2 Matt. 26:9 → large sum → lit.: much (*polus*) 3 Acts 7:16 → sum of money → lit.: price of silver → PRICE (noun) <5092>.

SUM UP – 1 ***anakephalaioō*** [verb: ἀνακεφαλαιόω <346>]; **from *ana*: again (intens.), and *kephalaioō*: to recapitulate, which is from *kephalē*: head ▶ To recapitulate, to resume briefly** > Love for one's neighbor sums up {comprehends} various commandments (Rom. 13:9). Other

ref.: Eph. 1:10 (to gather together); see GATHER <346>. ¶
– 2 1 Pet. 3:8 → FINALLY <1161> <5056>.

SUMMARY – Heb. 8:1 → SUM <2774>.

SUMMER – ***theros*** [neut. noun: θέρος <2330>]; **from *therō*: to heat ▶ Hottest season of the year in Israel** > One knows that summer is near when leaves are growing on the fig tree (Matt. 24:32; Mark 13:28; Luke 21:30). ¶

SUMMON – 1 Matt. 2:7 → CALL (verb) <2564> 2 Matt. 10:1; 18:32; Mark 3:13; 6:7; 8:34; 15:44; Luke 7:19; 15:26; 16:5; Acts 6:2; 13:7 → CALL (verb) <4341> 3 Luke 23:13 → CALL (verb) <4779> 4 Acts 7:14; 24:25 → CALL (verb) <3333>.

SUMPTUOUSLY – 1 ***lamprōs*** [adv.: λαμπρῶς <2988>]; **from *lampros*: bright ▶ Magnificently, with spendor, luxuriously** > A rich man lived sumptuously {in luxury, in splendor, in splendour} every day (Luke 16:19). ¶
– 2 Luke 16:19 → to fare sumptuously → to be merry → MERRY <2165>.

SUN – 1 ***hēlios*** [masc. noun: ἥλιος <2246>] ▶ **Star which illuminates and warms the earth** > God the Father makes His sun rise on the evil and the good (Matt. 5:45). The righteous will shine forth as the sun in the kingdom of their Father (Matt. 13:43). Jesus was transfigured and His face shone like the sun (Matt. 17:2). We are not to let the sun set on our anger (Eph. 4:26). Other refs.: Matt. 13:6; 24:29; Mark 1:32; 4:6; 13:24; 16:2; Luke 4:40; 21:25; 23:45; Acts 2:20; 13:11; 26:13; 27:20; 1 Cor. 15:41; Jas. 1:11; Rev. 1:16; 6:12; 7:2 {east, lit.: rising of the sun}; 7:16; 8:12; 9:2; 10:1; 12:1; 16:8, 12 {east, lit.: rising of the sun}; 19:17; 21:23; 22:5. ¶
– 2 Matt. 8:11; Rev. 16:12 → rising sun, rising of the sun → EAST <395> 3 Luke 1:78 → rising sun → DAYSPRING FROM ON HIGH <395> <5311> 4 Acts 7:42 → the sun, moon, and stars → lit.: the host of heaven → HOST[1] <4756>, HEAVEN <3772>.

SUN OF RIGHTEOUSNESS – Expr. found in the O.T. (Mal. 4:2) that characterizes the Lord at His coming to judge and to reign. Prophetically, the Sun of righteousness appears after the Morning Star. They are both figures of the Lord Jesus Christ.

SUNDER – Luke 12:46 → to cut in sunder → to cut in two → CUT <1371>.

SUNDOWN – Mark 1:32 → EVENING <3798>.

SUNRISE – 1 Mark 16:2 → RISE (verb) <393> 2 Luke 1:78 → the sunrise from on high → DAYSPRING FROM ON HIGH <395> <5311>.

SUNRISING – Rev. 7:2 → EAST <395>.

SUNSET – Mark 1:32; Luke 4:40 → lit.: to set → SET (verb) <1416>.

SUP – ***deipneō*** [verb: δειπνέω <1172>]; **from *deipnon*: evening meal ▶ To take the evening meal, suggesting a time of fellowship** > This verb is found in Luke 17:8; 22:20 and 1 Cor. 11:25: Jesus took the cup after having supped. If anyone hears His voice and opens the door to Him, Jesus will come in to him and sup {dine, eat} with him, and he with Jesus (Rev. 3:20). Other ref.: Matt. 20:28 in some mss. ¶

SUPER – 2 Cor. 11:5; 12:11 → in surpassing degree → SURPASSING <5244a>; in some mss.: <5228> <3029>.

SUPERFLUITY – Jas. 1:21 → OVERFLOW (noun) <4050>.

SUPERFLUOUS – ***perissos*** [adj.: περισσός <4053>]; **from *peri*: above, beyond ▶ Not necessary, useless** > It was superfluous {There was no need} for Paul to write to the Corinthians concerning the service to the saints (2 Cor. 9:1). Other refs.: Matt.

5:37, 47; Mark 14:31; Eph. 3:20; 1 Thes. 3:10; 5:13. All other refs.: ABUNDANTLY <4053>, ADVANTAGE (noun) <4053>.

SUPERIOR – [1] Rom. 2:18 → what is superior → excellent thing → EXCELLENT <1308> [2] Rom. 11:18a, b → to consider oneself superior → GLORIFY <2620> [3] 1 Cor. 4:7 → who regards you as superior → lit.: who makes a distinction of you → DISTINCTION <1252> [4] Heb. 1:4; 8:6 → more excellent → EXCELLENT <1313> [5] Heb. 1:4; 7:7; 8:6a, b → BETTER <2909>.

SUPERIORITY – [1] Rom. 3:1 → ADVANTAGE (noun) <4053> [2] 1 Cor. 2:1 → EXCELLENCE <5247>.

SUPERSCRIPTION – Matt. 22:20; Mark 12:16; 15:26; Luke 20:24; 23:38 → INSCRIPTION <1923>.

SUPERSTITION – Acts 25:19 → RELIGION <1175>.

SUPERSTITIOUS – Acts 17:22 → RELIGIOUS <1174>.

SUPERVISION – Gal. 3:25 → TUTOR <3807>.

SUPPER – [1] ***deipnon*** [neut. noun: δεῖπνον <1173>] ▶ **a. Evening meal, banquet, feast** > The scribes and the Pharisees loved the first places at suppers (Matt. 23:6; Mark 12:39; Luke 20:46). Herod made a supper for people of importance when the daughter of Herodias asked him for the head of John the Baptist (Mark 6:21). Jesus uses the expr. "a dinner or a supper" (other transl.: a luncheon or a dinner) in regard to the man who had invited Him (Luke 14:12). In a parable, He mentions that a man made a great supper (Luke 14:16: *deipnos* in some mss., 17, 24 {banquet, dinner}). At Bethany a supper was made for Jesus (John 12:2 {dinner}). John speaks of the last supper of the Lord with His disciples before He suffered (John 13:2 {evening meal}, 4 {meal}; 21:20). Paul uses this term in 1 Cor. 11:21. An angel told all the birds to gather themselves together for the great supper of God (Rev. 19:17: *deipnos* in some mss.). **b. Lord's supper** > The Lord's supper (1 Cor. 11:20) is the memorial instituted by the Lord Jesus the night He was betrayed. In Israel, it was customary to break the bread and to drink the cup of consolation for a deceased person (see Jer. 16:7). The bread symbolizes the unity of the church, the body of Christ; the broken bread speaks of the body of Jesus in which He suffered on the cross. The cup reminds the Christians of the blood of Christ, shed to purify them from all sins and to introduce them into a realm of heavenly blessings. The Lord's desire is that this memorial in remembrance of Him be perpetuated until His return. Read 1 Cor. 10:14–22 and 11:20–34. In the beginning, it appears that the custom for Christians was to break bread on the first day of the week (see Acts 20:7). **c. Supper of the Lamb** > Blessed are those who are called to the marriage supper of the Lamb (Rev. 19:9: *deipnos* in some mss.). ¶

– [2] Luke 17:8; 22:20; 1 Cor. 11:25 → prepare my supper, after supper → lit.: something for me to take my supper, after having taken the supper → SUP <1172>.

SUPPLEMENT – 2 Pet. 1:5 → ADD <2023>.

SUPPLICATE – ***deomai*** [verb: δέομαι <1189>]; **middle voice of *deō*: to lack, to need something ▶ To ask, to beseech, to pray; also transl.: to beg, to implore, to make an appeal** > Jesus says to supplicate the Lord of the harvest, that He may send out workmen into His harvest (Matt. 9:38; Luke 10:2). A leper implored Jesus (Luke 5:12), as did likewise a demoniac (Luke 8:28, 38) and a man regarding his son who was possessed by an unclean spirit (Luke 9:38, 40). The verb is also used in regard to Simon the magician (Acts 8:22, 24) and Paul (2 Cor. 5:20; 10:2). All other refs.: IMPLORE <1189>, PRAY <1189>, REQUEST (noun) <1189>.

SUPPLICATION – 1 ***deēsis*** [fem. noun: δέησις <1162>]; **from *deomai*: to make known a particular need, which is the middle voice of *deō*: to lack, to need something ▶ Request, prayer; also transl.: entreaty, petition** > Paul exhorts to pray at all seasons, with all prayer and supplication in the Spirit, and to watch to this end with all perseverance and supplication for all the saints (Eph. 6:18a, b). He exhorts above all things that supplications, prayers, intercessions, and thanksgivings be made for all men (1 Tim. 2:1). The fervent supplication of the righteous man can accomplish much (Jas. 5:16). The eyes of the Lord are on the righteous, and His ears are toward their supplications (1 Pet. 3:12). The term is also used in regard to Zacharias (Luke 1:13), Paul (Rom. 10:1; Phil. 1:4a, b; 2 Tim. 1:3), the Corinthians (2 Cor. 1:11), the Macedonians (2 Cor. 9:14), the Philippians (Phil. 1:19; 4:6), and a true widow (1 Tim. 5:5). Other ref.: Acts 1:14 in some mss. All other refs.: PRAYER <1162>.

2 ***hiketēria*** [fem. noun: ἱκετηρία <2428>]; **from *hiketēs*: suppliant ▶ Humble and earnest prayer** > In the days of His flesh, Jesus offered up both prayers (*deēsis*) and supplications (*hiketēria*) {supplications and entreaties, prayers and petitions}, with strong cries and tears, to Him who was able to save Him out of death, and He was heard because of His piety (Heb. 5:7). ¶

SUPPLY (noun) – ***epichorēgia*** [fem. noun: ἐπιχορηγία <2024>]; **from *epichorēgeō*: to supply abundantly, which is from *epi*: intens., and *chorēgeō*: see SUPPLY** (verb) <5524 > Every Christian is a member of the church and connected to other Christians, as in a body, by every joint of supply and contributes to the growth of the whole (Eph. 4:16). Other ref.: Phil. 1:19; see HELP <2024>. ¶

SUPPLY (verb) – 1 ***epitithēmi*** [verb: ἐπιτίθημι <2007>]; **from *epi*: upon, and *tithēmi*: to place, to put ▶ To provide, to give** > At Paul's departure, the inhabitants of Malta supplied {furnished, laded, provided, made presents to} him as well as to the passengers of the ship with the supplies they needed (Acts 28:10). All other refs.: see entries in Lexicon at <2007>.

2 ***katartizō*** [verb: καταρτίζω <2675>]; **from *kata*: with (intens.), and *artios*: complete ▶ To complete, to fill out, to perfect** > Paul prayed night and day most earnestly, that he might see the face of the Thessalonians and supply what was lacking in their faith (1 Thes. 3:10). All other refs.: see entries in Lexicon at <2675>.

3 ***plēroō*** [verb: πληρόω <4137>]; **lit.: to make full ▶ To satisfy, to meet** > Paul's God would supply all the needs of the Philippians according to His riches in glory by Christ Jesus (Phil. 4:19). All other refs.: see entries in Lexicon at <4137>.

4 ***anaplēroō*** [verb: ἀναπληρόω <378>]; **from *ana*: up (intens.), and *plēroō*: see 3; lit.: to make very full, to supply abundantly ▶ To fulfill entirely, to complete what was lacking** > The arrival of three brothers supplied what had been lacking on the part of the Corinthians (1 Cor. 16:17). Epaphroditus had supplied {filled up, made up for} the lack of the Philippians' service toward Paul (Phil. 2:30). All other refs.: FILL (verb) <378>, FULFILL <378>.

5 **to supply, to fully supply: *prosanaplēroō*** [verb: προσαναπληρόω <4322>]; **from *pros*: beside (in addition to), and *anaplēroō*: see 4 ▶ To provide what is needed** > The administration of the service of bringing the gift from the Corinthians was supplying {was filling up the measure, was fully supplying} the need of other saints (2 Cor. 9:12). Brothers who came from Macedonia supplied the needs of Paul (2 Cor. 11:9). ¶

6 ***chorēgeō*** [verb: χορηγέω <5524>]; **from *chorēgos*: one who directed an ancient chorus at his personal expense, which is from *choros*: chorus, and *hēgeomai*: to lead ▶ To provide, to give** > He who supplies {ministers} (*epichorēgeō*: see 7) seed to the sower will also supply (*chorēgeō*) and multiply Christians' seed for sowing (2 Cor. 9:10b). He who serves is to do so according to the strength that God supplies {gives, provides} (1 Pet. 4:11). ¶

7 ***epichorēgeō*** [verb: ἐπιχορηγέω <2023>]; **from *epi*: intens., and *chorēgeō*: see 6 ▶ To provide abundantly** > For this verb in 2 Cor. 9:10a, see 6. He who supplies {gives, ministers, provides} the Spirit does so on the principle of the hearing of faith (Gal. 3:5). The entrance into the eternal kingdom will be supplied {abundantly supplied, ministered, richly furnished} to those who are more diligent to make their call and election sure (2 Pet. 1:11). All other refs.: ADD <2013>, NOURISH <2023>.

– 8 Acts 12:20 → to supply with food → NOURISH <5142> 9 Acts 20:34 → PROVIDE <5256> 10 Eph. 4:16 → every joint supplies → lit.: every joint of supply → SUPPLY (noun) <2024> 11 1 Tim. 6:17 → GIVE <3930>.

SUPPORT (noun) – 1 Matt. 10:10 → FOOD <5160> 2 Luke 8:3 → to contribute to the support → MINISTER (verb) <1247> 3 Acts 12:20 → to secure the support → to win over → WIN <3982> 4 Acts 20:35 → to come in aid → HELP (verb) <482> 5 Acts 27:17 → they used supports → they used supporting cables → CABLE <996> 6 2 Cor. 8:4 → SERVICE <1248> 7 2 Cor. 11:8 → WAGES <3800> 8 1 Tim. 3:15 → FOUNDATION <1477>.

SUPPORT (verb) – 1 ***antechō*** [verb: ἀντέχω <472>]; **from *anti*: in front, and *echō*: to have, to keep ▶ To help, to sustain** > Christians must support {uphold} the weak (1 Thes. 5:14). All other refs.: FAST (HOLD) <472>, HOLD (verb) <472>.

– 2 Luke 8:3 → MINISTER (verb) <1247> 3 Rom. 11:18 → BEAR (verb) <941> 4 Col. 2:19 → NOURISH <2023> 5 2 Tim. 4:16 → to come to the support → to come together → COME <4836> 6 3 John 8 → RECEIVE <618>.

SUPPORTING – 1 Acts 27:17 → supporting cable → CABLE <996> 2 Eph. 4:16 → every supporting ligament → lit.: every ligament of supply → SUPPLY (noun) <2024>.

SUPPOSE – 1 ***dokeō*** [verb: δοκέω <1380>] **▶ To think, to believe** > Seeing Jesus walking on the sea, His disciples supposed it was a ghost (Mark 6:49). Seeing Jesus risen, His disciples supposed they had seen a spirit (Luke 24:37). Jesus asked some if they supposed that the Galileans who had suffered were worse sinners than all others (Luke 13:2), or if they supposed that others on whom a tower fell were worse sinners than all others in Jerusalem (v. 4). All other refs.: CONSIDER <1380>, REGARD (verb) <1380>, REPUTATION <1380>, SEEM <1380>, THINK <1380>.

2 ***nomizō*** [verb: νομίζω <3543>]; **from *nomos*: law ▶ To think, to believe, to consider** > In a parable, those who were hired first supposed that {expected} they would receive more (Matt. 20:10). The parents of Jesus were supposing Him to have been in the company that journeyed together (Luke 2:44). Jesus was, as was supposed {supposedly}, the son of Joseph (Luke 3:23). Moses supposed that his brothers would have understood that God would deliver them by his hand (Acts 7:25). The Jews stoned Paul and dragged him out of the city, supposing him to have died (Acts 14:19). The jailer was supposing the prisoners had escaped (Acts 16:27). The Jews supposed {assumed} that Paul had brought Trophimus into the temple (Acts 21:29). Paul supposed that it is good for a man to remain as he was, matrimonially speaking, before his conversion (1 Cor. 7:26). A man may suppose he is behaving improperly toward his virgin (1 Cor. 7:36). Men of corrupted minds suppose {hold} that godliness is a means of gain (1 Tim. 6:5). All other refs.: CUSTOM[1] <3543>, THINK <3543>.

3 ***oiomai*** [verb: οἴομαι <3633>] **▶ To think, to believe** > Some were preaching Christ from selfish ambition, supposing to arouse tribulations for Paul's bonds (Phil. 1:16 or 17). Other refs.: John 21:25; Jas. 1:7; see THINK <3633>. ¶

4 ***hupolambanō*** [verb: ὑπολαμβάνω <5274>]; **from *hupo*: under, and *lambanō*: to take, to receive ▶ To think, to believe, to presume** > Simon supposed that the

one who was forgiven more would love his master more (Luke 7:43). Some supposed that those speaking other tongues were drunk (Acts 2:15). All other refs.: RECEIVE <5274>, REPLY (verb) <5274>.
[5] ***huponoeō*** [verb: ὑπονοέω <5282>]; **from *hupo*: under, and *noeō*: to think, which is from *nous*: mind, understanding ▶ To suspect, to assume, to presume** > John the Baptist asked the people whom they supposed {thought} he was (Acts 13:25). The sailors supposed {deemed, sensed, surmised} that they were approaching some land (Acts 27:27). Other ref.: Acts 25:18; see EXPECT <5282>. ¶
– [6] Luke 11:7 → "suppose" added in Engl. [7] Rom. 2:3; 1 Pet. 5:12 → THINK <3049> [8] 2 Cor. 11:5 → CONSIDER <3049> [9] Phil. 2:25; Heb. 10:29 → CONSIDER <2233>.

SUPPOSEDLY – Luke 3:23 → as was supposed → SUPPOSE <3543>.

SUPPRESS – Rom. 1:18 → POSSESS <2722>.

SUPREMACY – Col. 1:18 → to have the supremacy → to have the first place → PLACE (noun) <4409>.

SUPREME – 1 Pet. 2:13 → AUTHORITY <5242>.

SUPREMELY – 2 Cor. 1:12 → ABUNDANTLY <4056>.

SURE – [1] ***asphalēs*** [adj.: ἀσφαλής <804>]; **from *a*: neg., and *sphallō*: to throw down ▶ Which inspires confidence, certain; also transl.: firm, secure** > Christians have a hope set before them as an anchor of the soul, both sure and steadfast, entering within the veil where Jesus is as forerunner for them (Heb. 6:19). All other refs.: CERTAINTY <804>, SAFE <804>.
[2] ***bebaios*** [adj.: βέβαιος <949>]; **from *bainō*: to walk; lit.: on which one can walk ▶ Solid, firm, certain** > The promise made to Abraham and to his seed is sure {guaranteed} on the principle of faith, by grace (Rom. 4:16). Christians should use diligence to make their calling and election sure (2 Pet. 1:10). All other refs.: FIRM <949>, VALID <949>.
[3] ***pistos*** [adj.: πιστός <4103>]; **from *peithō*: to persuade, to convince ▶ Faithful, which can be trusted** > God said that He would give the sure mercies of David (Acts 13:34). Other refs.: BELIEVING <4103>, FAITHFUL <4103>.
– [4] Matt. 24:43a; Luke 10:11; 12:39a; John 6:69; Gal. 3:7; Eph. 5:5; 1 John 2:29 → to be sure → KNOW <1097> [5] Matt. 27:64–66 → to make sure → to make secure → SECURE (adj.) <805> [6] Luke 12:39a; John 16:30a; Rom. 2:2; 15:29; Titus 3:11 → to be sure → KNOW <1492> [7] Luke 17:1 → certain things are sure to come → it is impossible that certain things do not come → IMPOSSIBLE <418> [8] Acts 12:11 → for sure → SURELY <230> [9] Rom. 2:19; Phil. 1:6; Heb. 13:18 → CONFIDENT <3982> [10] Rom. 8:38; 2 Tim. 1:5; Heb. 6:9 → to be sure, to feel sure → to be persuaded → PERSUADE <3982> [11] Rom. 15:28 → to make sure → SEAL (verb) <4972> [12] 2 Cor. 1:15 → I was sure → in this confidence → CONFIDENCE <4006> [13] 2 Cor. 2:3 → to feel sure → to have confidence → CONFIDENCE <3982> [14] 1 Thes. 5:15 → to make sure → SEE <3708> [15] Heb. 6:11 → much assurance → ASSURANCE <4136> [16] Heb. 6:16 → to make matter sure → lit.: for confirmation → CONFIRMATION <951> [17] Heb. 11:1 → being sure → SUBSTANCE <5287> [18] Heb. 11:1 → being sure → EVIDENCE <1650>.

SURELY – [1] ***alēthōs*** [adv.: ἀληθῶς <230>]; **from *alēthēs*: true, which is from *a*: neg., and *lēthō*: form of *lanthanō*: to be hidden ▶ Verily, certainly** > Peter was told that he was surely {truly} one of those who had been with Jesus (Matt. 26:73; Mark 14:70). The word is transl. "for sure" {certainly, for certain, of a surety, without a doubt} in Acts 12:11. All other refs.: TRULY <230>.
[2] ***ē*** [particle: ἦ <2229>] ▶ **Particle of affirmation meaning truly, assuredly, cer-**

tainly > In the NT, only in the connection *ē mēn*, another particle of affirmation, the usual intens. form of oaths meaning most certainly, most surely (Heb. 6:14 quoted from Gen. 22:17). ¶ ‡

3 ***mēn*** [particle: μήν <3375>] ▶ **Verily, assuredly** > Surely, in blessing, God would bless Abraham and his descendants (Heb. 6:14). ¶

4 ***pantōs*** [adv.: πάντως <3843>]; **from *pas*: all** ▶ **Certainly, without doubt** > Jesus said that they would surely {no doubt} say to Him a physician should heal himself (Luke 4:23). Other refs.: ALTOGETHER <3843>, DOUBT (adv.) <3843>.

– 5 Matt. 15:4 → must surely die → lit.: must die the death 6 Luke 1:1 → to believe most surely → BELIEVE <4135> 7 Luke 11:8 → "surely" added in Engl. 8 Luke 20:16 → Surely not! → lit.: May this not become (*ginomai*) 9 Luke 23:47 → CERTAINLY <3689> 10 Rom. 10:18 → surely, yes surely → yes verily → VERILY <3304>.

SURETY – 1 Acts 12:11 → of a surety → SURELY <230> 2 Heb. 7:22 → GUARANTOR <1450>.

SURF – Acts 27:41 → lit.: the waves → WAVE <2949>.

SURFACE – 2 Cor. 10:7 → on the surface of things → after the outward appearance → PRESENCE <4383>.

SURFEITING – Luke 21:34 → CAROUSING <2897>.

SURMISE – Acts 27:27 → SUPPOSE <5282>.

SURMISING – 1 Tim. 6:4 → SUSPICION <5283>.

SURNAME (noun) – 1 Matt. 10:3 in some mss.; Acts 10:5, 32; 11:13; 12:12, 25 → the surname was → SURNAME (verb) <1941> 2 Acts 15:37 → whose surname was → CALL (verb) <2564>.

SURNAME (verb) – ***epikaleō*** [verb: ἐπικαλέω <1941>]; **from *epi*: upon, and *kaleō*: to call** ▶ **To give another name** > Lebbaeus was surnamed Thaddaeus (Matt. 10:3). Judas was surnamed {called} Iscariot (Luke 22:3). Joseph, who was called Barsabbas, was surnamed Justus (Acts 1:23). The apostles had surnamed Joseph (or: Joses), Barnabas (Acts 4:36). Simon was surnamed Peter (Acts 10:5, 18, 32; 11:13). John was surnamed Mark (Acts 12:12, 25). Other refs.: Acts 15:22 and 25:21 in some mss. All other refs.: APPEAL <1941>, CALL (verb) <1941>, INVOKE <1941>, PRAY <1941>.

SURPASS – 1 ***perisseuō*** [verb: περισσεύω <4052>]; **from *perissos*: abundant, which is from *peri*: above, beyond** ▶ **To exceed, to go beyond** > Jesus said to people that unless their righteousness surpassed that of the scribes and Pharisees, they would in no wise enter into the kingdom of the heavens (Matt. 5:20). All other refs.: see entries in Lexicon at <4052>.

2 ***huperballō*** [verb: ὑπερβάλλω <5235>]; **from *huper*: above, beyond, and *ballō*: to throw** ▶ **To exceed in excellence** > Paul speaks of the surpassing {exceeding, incomparable} greatness of the power of God toward Christians (Eph. 1:19). The love of Christ surpasses all understanding (Eph. 3:19). All other refs.: EXCEEDING <5235>, EXCEL <5235>, SURPASSING <5235>.

3 ***huperechō*** [verb: ὑπερέχω <5242>]; **from *huper*: above, and *echō*: to have** ▶ **To be superior, to be better** > The peace of God surpasses {passes} all understanding (Phil. 4:7). All other refs.: AUTHORITY <5242>, EXCELLENCE <5242>, GOVERNING <5242>, IMPORTANT <5242>.

– 4 John 1:15, 30 → has surpassed me → lit.: has been before me.

SURPASSING – 1 **in surpassing degree: *huperlian*** [prep. and adv.: ὑπερλίαν <5244a>]; **from *huper*: over, above, beyond, and *lian*: excessively** ▶ **Preeminent** > Paul was nothing behind those who were in surpassing degree {the very chiefest, most eminent, super-} apostles (2 Cor. 11:5; 12:11). ¶

2 **to surpass: *huperballō*** [verb: ὑπερβάλλω <5235>]; **from *huper*: beyond, and *ballō*: to throw ▶ Overabounding, which excels** > God will show the surpassing {exceeding, incomparable} riches (lit.: the riches that surpass) of His grace in kindness toward Christians (Eph. 2:7). All other refs.: EXCEEDING <5235>, EXCEL <5235>, SURPASS <5235>.

– 3 1 Cor. 12:31; 2 Cor. 4:7 → surpassing excellence, surpassing greatness → EXCELLENCE <5236> 4 2 Cor. 4:17 → in surpassing measure → MEASURE (noun) <5236> 5 2 Cor. 12:7 → surpassing greatness → GREATNESS <5236> 6 Phil. 3:8 → surpassing greatness, surpassing value → EXCELLENCE <5242>.

SURPASSINGLY – 2 Cor. 12:7 → surpassingly great → GREATNESS <5236>.

SURPASSINGNESS – 2 Cor. 4:7 → EXCELLENCE <5236>.

SURPLUS – 1 **from the verb "to abound": *perisseuō*** [verb: περισσεύω <4052>]; **from *peri*: around, beyond ▶ What one has in excess** > All had put in out of their surplus {abundance, wealth} into the treasury of the temple, except one poor widow (Mark 12:44; Luke 21:4). All other refs.: see entries in Lexicon at <4052>.

– 2 Luke 12:18 → my surplus goods → lit.: all my wheat and my goods.

SURPRISE (noun) – 2 Cor. 11:15 → it is no surprise → lit.: it is not a great thing → GREAT <3173>.

SURPRISE (verb) – 1 Thes. 5:4 → CATCH (verb) <2638>.

SURPRISED (BE) – 1 Luke 11:38; John 3:7 → MARVEL (verb) <2296> 2 1 Pet. 4:12 → to think strange → STRANGE <3579>.

SURREPTITIOUSLY – 1 **to come in surreptitiously: *pareiserchomai*** [verb: παρεισέρχομαι <3922>]; **from *para*: beside, and *eiserchomai*: to enter, which is from *eis*: in, and *erchomai*: to come; also transl.: to come in privily, to come in by stealth, to sneak in, to infiltrate the ranks ▶ To creep in, to work one's way in secretly** > False brothers had come in surreptitiously to spy out the liberty that Christians had in Christ Jesus (Gal. 2:4). Other ref.: Rom. 5:20 (to come in); see COME <3922>. ¶

– 2 Gal. 2:4 → brought in surreptitiously → secretly brought in → SECRETLY <3920>.

SURROUND – 1 ***kukloō*** [verb: κυκλόω <2944>]; **from *kuklos*: circle ▶ To encompass, to enclose** > Jerusalem would be seen surrounded {compassed, encompassed} by armies (Luke 21:20). The Jews surrounded {came round about, gathered around} Jesus (John 10:24). Gog and Magog will surround {compass} the camp of the saints and the beloved city (Rev. 20:9); some mss. have *kukleuō* [verb: κυκλεύω <2942a>]. The disciples surrounded {encircled, gathered around, stood around} Paul who had been stoned (Acts 14:20). Other ref.: Heb. 11:30; see ENCIRCLE <2944>. ¶

2 ***perikukloō*** [verb: περικυκλόω <4033>]; **from *peri*: around, and *kukloō*: see 1 ▶ To encircle, to enclose** > The enemies of Israel would surround it (*perikukloō*) {close it round, compass it round} and close it in (*sunechō*) on every side (Luke 19:43). ¶

3 ***perikeimai*** [verb: περίκειμαι <4029>]; **from *peri*: around, and *keimai*: to lie ▶ To encircle, to encompass** > Christians are surrounded {compassed} by a great cloud of witnesses of the truth of life by faith (Heb. 12:1). All other refs.: BIND <4029>, HANG <4029>, SUBJECT (verb) <4029>.

– 4 Luke 8:45 → to close in → CLOSE (verb) <4912>.

SURROUNDING – 1 Matt. 14:35; Mark 6:55; Luke 4:14, 37; 7:17 → surrounding region, district, area → COUNTRY <4066> 2 Mark 6:36; Luke 9:12 → round about → ROUND <2945> 3 Luke 8:37; Acts 14:6 → surrounding region → REGION <4066> 4 Acts 5:16 → round about →

ROUND <4038> [5] Jude 7 → ABOUT <4012> <846>.

SURVIVAL – ***sōtēria*** [fem. noun: σωτηρία <4991>]; **from *sōtēr*: deliverer ▶ Salvation, preservation** > Paul was urging the passengers on the boat to take some food for their survival {for their health, for their safety, to survive} (Acts 27:34). All other refs.: SALVATION <4991>, SAVING <4991>.

SURVIVE – Mark 13:20 → SAVE (verb) <4982>.

SUSANNA – ***Sousanna*** [fem. name: Σουσάννα <4677>]: **lily ▶ Christian woman of the N.T.** > Susanna assisted Jesus out of her own means (Luke 8:3). ¶

SUSPECT – [1] Acts 27:27 → SUPPOSE <5282> [2] 2 Cor. 10:2 → THINK <3049>.

SUSPENSE – [1] **to hold in suspense, to keep in suspense: *airō*** [verb: αἴρω <142>] **▶ To make (someone) wait, to hold in uncertainty** > The Jews asked Jesus how long He would keep their soul in suspense, as to whether He was indeed the Christ (John 10:24). All other refs.: see entries in Lexicon at <142>.
– [2] Acts 27:33 → to be in constant suspense → TARRY <4328>.

SUSPICION – ***huponoia*** [fem. noun: ὑπόνοια <5283>]; **from *huponoeō*: to suspect, which is from *hupo*: under, and *noeō*: to think, which is from *nous*: mind, understanding ▶ Distrust, doubt** > Evil suspicions {surmisings} arise from an unhealthy interest in questions and disputes about words (1 Tim. 6:4). ¶

SUSTAIN – [1] 1 Cor. 1:8 → CONFIRM <950> [2] 1 Thes. 5:14 → SUPPORT (verb) <472> [3] 2 Thes. 1:4 → SUFFER <430> [4] Heb. 1:3 → UPHOLD <5342>.

SUSTENANCE – [1] ***chortasma*** [neut. noun: χόρτασμα <5527>]; **from *chortazō*: to satisfy with food ▶ Nourishment for people, or for herds or flocks** > The Israelites found no sustenance {food} in the land of Egypt and Canaan during a famine (Acts 7:11). ¶
– [2] 1 Tim. 6:8 → FOOD <1305>.

SWADDLING – Luke 2:7, 12 → to wrap in swaddling cloths → WRAP <4683>.

SWALLOW – [1] **to swallow up: *katapinō*** [verb: καταπίνω <2666>]; **from *kata*: down (intens.), and *pinō*: to drink ▶ a. To drink down** > Jesus criticized the scribes and the Pharisees for straining out a gnat and swallowing a camel (Matt. 23:24). **b. To be overwhelmed, to be engulfed** > The man under the discipline of the church in Corinth could be swallowed up with excessive grief if he was not forgiven and comforted (2 Cor. 2:7). **c. To be absorbed, to be engulfed** > Death will be swallowed up in victory (1 Cor. 15:54). Paul wished to be clothed with his heavenly dwelling, so that mortality might be swallowed up by life (2 Cor. 5:4). The earth swallowed up the flood that the dragon had cast out of his mouth (Rev. 12:16). Other refs.: Heb. 11:29; 1 Pet. 5:8; see DROWN <2666>, DEVOUR <2666>. ¶
– [2] Heb. 11:29 → to swallow up → DROWN <2666>.

SWAMP – [1] Mark 4:37 → FILL (verb) <1072> [2] Luke 8:23 → FILL (verb) <4845>.

SWAMPED (BE) – Matt. 8:24 → COVER <2572>.

SWATH – [1] Mark 15:46 → WRAP <1750> [2] Acts 5:6 → to swath up → to wrap up → WRAP <4958>.

SWAY – [1] Matt. 11:7; Luke 7:24 → SHAKE <4531> [2] 2 Tim. 3:6 → LEAD (verb) <71>.

SWAYED (BE) – Matt. 22:16; Mark 12:14 → CARE <3199>.

SWEAR – [1] ***omnuō*** [verb: ὀμνύω <3660>] **▶ To affirm, to promise with an oath** > Jesus spoke on various occasions of swearing and not swearing (Matt. 5:34 and 36 {to make, swear, take an oath}; 23:16a, b, 18a, b, 20a, b, 21a, b, 22a, b). Peter began to curse and to swear (Matt. 26:74; Mark 14:71). Herod swore (Mark 6:23). God swore {promised} to Abraham with an oath (Luke 1:73). He had sworn {had promised} also with an oath to David (Acts 2:30). He swore by Himself (Heb. 6:13a, b). The Holy Spirit swore in His wrath that some would not enter into God's rest (Heb. 3:11, 18; 4:3). Men swear by someone greater than themselves (Heb. 6:16). The Lord has sworn in regard to the priesthood of Melchizedek and will not repent (Heb. 7:21). James tells his brothers not to swear (Jas. 5:12). An angel swore by Him who lives to the age of ages (Rev. 10:6). Other ref.: Acts 7:17; see PROMISE (verb) <3660>. ¶

– [2] Matt. 5:33 → what you have sworn → lit.: your oath → OATH <3727> [3] Mark 5:7 → ADJURE <3726>.

SWEAT – ***hidrōs*** [masc. noun: ἱδρώς <2402>] ► **Perspiration** > Being in agony, Jesus prayed more intently, and His sweat became as great drops of blood falling down to the ground (Luke 22:44). ¶

SWEEP – [1] ***saroō*** [verb: σαρόω <4563>]; **from *saros*: broom** ► **To clean with a broom** > The unclean spirit finds his house swept {swept clean} (Matt. 12:44; Luke 11:25). The woman who lost a piece of silver sweeps the house and seeks carefully for it (Luke 15:8). ¶

– [2] Matt. 8:24 → to sweep over → COVER <2572> [3] Matt. 24:39 → to sweep away → to take away → TAKE <142> [4] Acts 27:14 → to sweep down → ARISE <906> [5] Jude 12 → swept along → carried about → CARRY <4064> [6] Rev. 12:4 → to sweep, to sweep away → DRAW <4951>.

SWEET – [1] ***glukus*** [adj.: γλυκύς <1099>] ► **Having a taste like sugar** > The little book was sweet as honey in John's mouth, as the angel had told him (Rev. 10:9, 10). Other refs.: Jas. 3:11, 12; see FRESH <1099>. ¶

– [2] Mark 16:1; Luke 23:56; 24:1 → sweet spice → SPICE <759> [3] 2 Cor. 2:14 → sweet aroma → ODOR <3744> [4] 2 Cor. 2:15; Eph. 5:2; Phil. 4:18 → sweet odor, sweet smell, sweet-smelling → sweet odor → ODOR <2175>.

SWEET-SMELLING – Eph. 5:2 → sweet odor → ODOR <2175>.

SWELL – **to swell up: *pimprēmi*** [verb: πίμπρημι <4092>]; **poss. from *prēthō*: to burn** ► **To become larger further to infection or burning** > After a viper fastened on Paul's hand, the natives of Malta were expecting that he would swell up or suddenly fall dead (Acts 28:6); *empiprēmi* in some mss. ¶

SWELLING – [1] Luke 14:2 → suffering from abnormal swelling of the body → DROPSICAL <5203> [2] 2 Cor. 12:20 → PUFFING UP <5450> [3] 2 Pet. 2:18; Jude 16 → swelling word → WORD <5246>.

SWERVE – 1 Tim. 1:6; 6:21; 2 Tim. 2:18 → STRAY <795>.

SWIFT – [1] ***oxus*** [adj.: ὀξύς <3691>] ► **Rapid, eager** > Paul spoke of those whose feet are swift to shed blood (Rom. 3:15). Other refs.: Rev. 1:16; 2:12; 14:14, 17, 18a, b; 19:15; see SHARP <3691>. ¶

[2] ***tachus*** [adj.: ταχύς <5036>] ► **Rapid, keen, quick** > Every man is to be swift to hear (Jas. 1:19). ¶

[3] ***tachinos*** [adj.: ταχινός <5031>]; **from *tachus*: see [2]** ► **Rapid, sudden** > False teachers will bring upon themselves swift destruction (2 Pet. 2:1). Other ref.: 2 Pet. 1:14; see IMMINENT <5031>. ¶

SWIM – [1] ***kolumbaō*** [verb: κολυμβάω <2860>]; **from *kolumbos*: diving bird** ► **To propel oneself in water using one's members** > Those who were able to swim were to jump first into the sea (Acts 27:43). ¶

[2] **to swim off, away: *ekkolumbaō*** [verb: ἐκκολυμβάω <1579>]; **from *ek*: out, and *kolumbaō*: see [1]** ► **To escape by swimming** > The soldiers feared lest a pris-

oner should swim off and escape (Acts 27:42). ¶

SWINDLER – Luke 18:11; 1 Cor. 5:10, 11; 6:10 → RAPACIOUS <727>.

SWINE – ***choiros*** [neut. noun: χοῖρος <5519>] ► **Pig, hog** > This voracious animal does not refuse to eat garbage; it symbolizes impurity. Indeed, according to Lev. 11:7, it was forbidden to eat the meat of swine: this animal was impure, for even though it has cloven hoofs and feet completely split open, nevertheless it does not chew the cud. Jesus allowed demons to go into a herd of swine, which then rushed down a steep slope into the sea (Matt. 8:30, 31, 32a, b; Mark 5:11–14, 16; Luke 8:32, 33). He commands His own not to throw their pearls (the precious truths of the word of God) before the swine (those who are unable to appreciate them) (Matt. 7:6). The younger son in the parable was sent to feed swine (Luke 15:15); they were eating husks (v. 16). ¶

SWING – Rev. 14:16, 19 → PUT <906>.

SWOLLEN – 2 Tim. 3:4 → to become swollen with conceit → to be puffed up → PUFF UP <5187>.

SWORD – 1 ***machaira*** [fem. noun: μάχαιρα <3162>]**; poss. from *machomai*: to fight** ► **Short sword, dagger** > Peter drew his sword and smote the servant of the high priest (Matt. 26:51, 52a, b; Mark 14:47; Luke 22:49; John 18:10, 11). The sword will not separate Christians from the love of Christ (Rom. 8:35). The jailer drew his sword and was about to kill himself (Acts 16:27). The Christian must take the sword of the Spirit (Eph. 6:17). The word of God is sharper than any two-edged sword (Heb. 4:12). Other refs.: Matt. 10:34; 26:47, 55; Mark 14:43, 48; Luke 21:24; 22:36, 38, 52; Acts 12:2; Rom. 13:4; Heb. 11:34, 37; Rev. 6:4; 13:10a, b, 14. ¶
2 ***rhomphaia*** [fem. noun: ῥομφαία <4501>] ► **Longer and wider sword than the preceding one** > Out of the mouth of the Son of Man went a sharp two-edged sword (Rev. 1:16; 2:12, 16; 19:15). Power was given to him who sat on the pale horse to kill with the sword (Rev. 6:8). In Luke 2:35, it speaks figur. of anguish for the soul of Mary, the mother of Jesus. Other ref.: Rev. 19:21. ¶

SYCAMINE TREE – ***sukaminos*** [fem. noun: συκάμινος <4807>]**; from *sukon*: fig** ► **Black tree producing edible fruit and measuring between 20 and 30 feet (6 and 9 meters)** > Jesus said if someone had faith as a grain of mustard seed, he would say to a sycamine tree {mulberry tree} to be rooted up and to be planted in the sea, and it would have obeyed him (Luke 17:6). The city of Haifa in Israel was called Sycaminopolis, after the name of this tree. ¶

SYCAMORE – ***sukomorea*** [fem. noun: συκομορέα <4809>]**; from *sukon*: fig, and *moron*: berry** ► **Tall fig tree having a thick trunk and leaves which are downy on the underside; the fruit is edible; also transl.: sycomore** > Zaccheus climbed up into a sycamore to see Jesus who was passing by (Luke 19:4). ¶

SYCHAR – ***Suchar*** [fem. name: Συχάρ <4965>]**; site of Shechem: shoulder, in Heb.; see Gen. 12:6; 33:18; Judg. 9:1** ► **City of Samaria** > Jesus came to Sychar and met a woman at Jacob's well; He offered her living water (John 4:5); read vv. 1–30. ¶

SYCHEM – See SHECHEM <4562>.

SYCOMORE – See SYCAMORE <4809>.

SYMBOL – Heb. 9:9 → FIGURE <3850>.

SYMBOLIC – 1 Gal. 4:24 → to be symbolic → to be an allegory → ALLEGORY <238> 2 Heb. 9:9 → lit.: a symbol → FIGURE <3850>.

SYMBOLICALLY – Rev. 11:8 → lit.: spiritually → SPIRITUALLY <4153>.

SYMBOLIZE – 1 Pet. 3:21 → to be the figure → FIGURE <499>.

SYMPATHETIC – ***sumpathēs*** [adj.: συμπαθής <4835>]; **from *sun*: together, and *pathos*: suffering ▶ Having compassion, capable of sharing the feelings of another** > Peter exhorts Christians to be sympathetic (1 Pet. 3:8). ¶

SYMPATHISING – 1 Pet. 3:8 → SYMPATHETIC <4835>.

SYMPATHIZE – ***sumpatheō*** [verb: συμπαθέω <4834>]; **from *sumpathēs*: sympathizing, which is from *sun*: together, and *pathos*: suffering ▶ To be capable of sharing the feelings of another, to have compassion** > Christians do not have a high priest who cannot sympathize {be touched} with their weaknesses, but One (i.e., Jesus) who has been tempted in all things as they are, yet without sin (Heb. 4:15). The Hebrew Christians had sympathized with prisoners and had accepted with joy the spoiling of their goods (Heb. 10:34). ¶

SYMPATHY – [1] Phil. 2:1 → MERCY <3628> [2] Heb. 10:34 → to show sympathy → SYMPATHIZE <4834> [3] 1 Pet. 3:8 → having sympathy → SYMPATHETIC <4835>.

SYNAGOGUE – [1] ***sunagōgē*** [fem. noun: συναγωγή <4864>]; **from *sunagō:* to assemble, which is from *sun*: together, and *agō*: to lead ▶ Religious assembly of the Jews** > The term is found, for example, in Acts 9:2; 13:14, 43 {congregation}; 14:1. The synagogue was identified with the place where it was convened; meetings were held mainly on the Sabbath day (Mark 1:21; Luke 4:16). Jesus, Paul, Barnabas, and Apollos preached in the synagogues (e.g., Matt. 4:23; Acts 9:20; 13:5). The expr. "synagogue of Satan" is used regarding religious groups professing affiliation to Judaism or Christianity, but which are, in reality, under the influence of Satan. Such groups oppose the faithful who are represented by two churches: Smyrna and Philadelphia (Rev. 2:9; 3:9), against whom no reproach is made. Other refs.: Matt. 6:2, 5; 9:35; 10:17; 12:9; 13:54; 23:6, 34; Mark 1:23, 29, 39; 3:1; 6:2; 12:39; 13:9; Luke 4:15, 20, 28, 33, 38, 44; 6:6; 7:5; 8:41; 11:43; 12:11; 13:10; 20:46; 21:12; John 6:59; 18:20; Acts 6:9; 15:21; 17:1, 10, 17; 18:4, 7, 19, 26; 19:8; 22:19; 24:12; 26:11; Jas. 2:2. ¶

[2] **ruler of the synagogue: *archisunagōgos*** [masc. noun: ἀρχισυνάγωγος <752>]; **from *archō*: to begin, to command, which is from *archē*: beginning, ruling, and *sunagōgē*: synagogue, which is from *sunagō*: to lead together ▶ Person in authority in a synagogue; also transl.: leader, chief ruler of the synagogue** > Crispus was the ruler of the synagogue (Acts 18:8), as well as Sosthenes (18:17). Other refs.: Mark 5:22, 35, 36, 38; Luke 8:49; 13:14; Acts 13:15. ¶

– [3] Matt. 9:23 → leader of the synagogue → ruler of the synagogue → RULER <758> [4] John 9:22; 12:42; 16:2 → excommunicated from the synagogue → EXCOMMUNICATED <656>.

SYNTYCHE – ***Suntuchē*** [fem. name: Συντύχη <4941>]**: fortunate ▶ Christian woman of Philippi** > Paul urges Euodia and Syntyche to be of the same mind in the Lord (Phil. 4:2); they had contended along with Paul in the gospel (see v. 3). ¶

SYRACUSE – ***Surakousai*** [fem. plur. name: Συράκουσαι <4946>] **▶ Capital of Sicily, in the southeastern part of the island** > Paul's ship, sailing to Rome, stayed in Syracuse for three days (Acts 28:12). ¶

SYRIA – ***Suria*** [fem. name: Συρία <4947>] **▶ Region north of Palestine** > During the census, at the birth of Jesus, Quirinius was governor of Syria (Luke 2:2). The fame of Jesus at the beginning of His ministry went throughout all Syria (Matt. 4:24). In the book of Acts, we read that Paul and Barnabas strengthened the brothers in Syria (15:23, 41; 18:18). Paul journeyed in this region (Acts 20:3; 21:3; Gal. 1:21). ¶

SYRIAN – ***Suros*** [masc. name: Σύρος <4948>] ► **Inhabitant of Syria** > Naaman, the leper, was Syrian (Luke 4:27). ¶

SYRIAN PHOENICIA – Mark 7:26 → in Syrian Phoenicia → see SYROPHOENICIAN <4949>.

SYROPHOENICIAN – ***Surophoinikissa*** [fem. name: Συροφοινίκισσα <4949>] ► **Phoenician woman who was a native of Phoenicia in Syria; also transl.: Syrophenician** > Jesus healed a demon-possessed daughter at the request of her mother, a Greek woman, Syrophoenician by race {born in Syrian Phoenicia} (Mark 7:26). ¶

SYRTIS – ***Surtis*** [fem. name: Σύρτις <4950>]; **from *surō*: to draw** ► **Region of northern Africa (coasts of Cyrenaica and Tripolitania)** > Its sandbanks were feared by the crew of Paul's ship during his journey to Rome (Acts 27:17). See SAND <4950>. ¶

SYSTEM OF WORSHIP – Acts 25:19 → RELIGION <1175>.

T

TABERNACLE – [1] ***skēnē*** [fem. noun: σκηνή <4633>] ▶ **a. Term designating the tent constructed to be God's habitation in the desert among the Israelites** > Moses made the tabernacle according to the pattern that God had shown to him on the mountain (Heb. 8:5). The tabernacle (or tent of meeting, tabernacle of meeting) consisted of a holy place, in which was found a table with the showbread, a lampstand, and an altar where incense was burned; on the other side of the veil was located the Most Holy Place, or Holy of holies, with the ark of the covenant. Only the high priest could enter into the Most Holy Place once a year, with the blood of a sacrifice and with incense: see Leviticus 16. The presence of God was made visible above the tabernacle, by a cloud during the day and by a pillar of fire during the night. In front of the tabernacle there was an altar for offering sacrifices and a laver of bronze used for the purification of the priests. The court of the tabernacle was surrounded by an enclosure of curtains of fine linen. The term "tabernacle" is used in Heb. 9:1 (in some mss.), 2, 3, 6, 8, 21; 13:10. The tabernacle is called the tabernacle of testimony in Acts 7:44 {tent of the testimony, tabernacle of witness} and Rev. 15:5 {tabernacle of witness, tabernacle of testimony}. See SANCTUARY. **b. Dwelling** > The expr. "eternal tabernacles" has the meaning of "eternal dwellings" in Luke 16:9 {everlasting habitations, everlasting home}. **c. Habitation or tent of Moloch, a pagan god** > The house of Israel was guilty of having carried the tabernacle {tent} of Moloch (Acts 7:43). **d. Other refs.:** Acts 7:46; 15:16. **e. Heavenly habitation** > Elsewhere the tabernacle corresponds to the heavenly places (Heb. 8:2; 9:11; Rev. 15:5). All other refs.: DWELLING PLACE <4633>, TENT <4633>.

[2] ***skēnōma*** [neut. noun: σκήνωμα <4638>]; **from *skēnoō*: to pitch a tent, which is from *skēnos*: tent** ▶ **Tent considered as the habitation of God or as the body of the Christian** > David asked to find a tabernacle {dwelling, dwelling place} for God (Acts 7:46). Other refs.: 2 Pet. 1:13, 14; see TENT <4638>. ¶

– [3] 2 Cor. 5:1, 4 → TENT <4636> [4] Rev. 7:15 → to spread one's tabernacle → to spread one's tent → TENT <4637>.

TABERNACLES (FEAST OF) – ***Skēnopēgia*** [fem. noun: Σκηνοπηγία <4634>]; **from *skēnē*: tent, habitation, and *pēgnumi*: to fix, to pitch** ▶ **Seventh and last annual feast in Israel, celebrated for seven days starting from the fifteenth day of the seventh month (our month of October), at the end of the harvest; also transl.: Feast of Booths, Festival of Tabernacles** > The Jews, in the time of the Lord, still celebrated the Feast of Tabernacles (John 7:2; see v. 37). This feast reminded them that their fathers had lived in tents after their departure from Egypt, before entering into the promised land. On the eighth day of this feast, there was a holy convocation of the people before the Lord. See Lev. 23:39–44; Deut. 16:13; Zech. 14:16, 18, 19. ¶

TABITHA – ***Tabitha*** [fem. name: Ταβιθά <5000>]: **gazelle, in Aram.** ▶ **Name of a woman who was a disciple** > Tabitha is named in Acts 9:36, 40. See DORCAS <1393>. ¶

TABLE[1] – [1] ***trapeza*** [fem. noun: τράπεζα <5132>]; **from *tetra*: four, and *peza*: foot** ▶ **Piece of furniture on which food is placed, from which (lit. and figur.): all that is provided on the table; also: the stand of one who changes money** > The term is used in relation to crumbs that fall (Matt. 15:27; Mark 7:28; Luke 16:21), money changers in the temple (Matt. 21:12; Mark 11:15; John 2:15), the hand of Judas (Luke 22:21), the table of Jesus in His kingdom (Luke 22:30), the service of the twelve apostles (Acts 6:2), the table of the wicked (Rom. 11:9), and the table in the Holy Place of the tabernacle (Heb. 9:2). The jailer laid a table after having been baptized (Acts 16:34). The Christian cannot partake of the Lord's table and the table of demons (1 Cor. 10:21a, b). Other ref.: Luke 19:23; see BANK[1] <5132>. ¶

[2] **to be, to lie, to lie down, to recline, to sit at the table: *anakeimai*** [verb: ἀνάκειμαι <345>]; **from *ana*: intens., and *keimai*: to lie down, to recline; this verb is used to designate people who are at table (*anakeimenos*)** ▶ **To recline (to eat), to have dinner; guest (lit.: one being at table)** >

Jesus lay at table in the house of Matthew (Matt. 9:10) and in the house of Simon the leper (Matt. 26:7). A woman, who was a sinner, knew that Jesus was reclining at the table (Luke 7:37 {to eat}). Jesus lay down at table {sat down} with the twelve (Matt. 26:20); they lay at table and were eating (Mark 14:18). He appeared to the eleven apostles as they lay at table (Mark 16:14). The wedding hall was filled with guests {dinner guests} (lit.: those at table) (Matt. 22:10); the king went in to see the guests {dinner guests} (v. 11). He who is at table is greater than he who serves, but Jesus served (Luke 22:27a, b). One of the disciples, whom Jesus loved, was at table with Him, in His bosom (John 13:23); the other disciples were also at the table (v. 28). All other refs.: LIE (verb)[1] <345>, SET (verb) <345>.

3 to be, to lie, to recline, to sit at the table: *katakeimai* [verb: κατάκειμαι <2621>]; **from *kata*: down, and *keimai*: to lie down, to recline ▶ To recline at a table to eat; also transl.: to dine, to eat, to have dinner** > Jesus lay at table in the house of Levi (Mark 2:15; Luke 5:29). He lay at table in the house of Simon the leper (Mark 14:3). Paul speaks of a Christian sitting at table in an idol's temple (1 Cor. 8:10). All other refs.: BEDRIDDEN (BE) <2621>, LAY <2621>, LIE (verb)[1] <2621>, SIT <2621>.

4 to be, to lie, to sit at table with: *sunanakeimai* [verb: συνανάκειμαι <4873>]; **from *sun*: together, and *anakeimai*: see 2; one who is at table with others, guest: *sunanakeimenos* ▶ To recline together to eat, to dine with others** > Many publicans and sinners came and lay at table with Jesus and His disciples in the house of Matthew (Matt. 9:10; Mark 2:15). Herod had made oaths before those who were at table with him (Matt. 14:9; Mark 6:22, 26). Those who were with Jesus at table asked who He was who had the power to forgive sins (Luke 7:49). Lazarus was at table with Jesus (John 12:2). Other refs.: Luke 14:10, 15. ¶

5 to sit, to take one's place, to recline at the table: *anaklinō* [verb: ἀνακλίνω <347>]; **from *ana*: backward, and *klinō*: to incline ▶ To stretch out, to lie down to eat** > Jesus took His place at table in the house of a Pharisee (Luke 7:36). He says that the servants of a master are blessed when he shall come and find them watching; he will gird himself and make them recline at table, and coming up, will serve them (Luke 12:37). All other refs.: LAY <347>, SIT <347>.

6 to be at table, to lay oneself down at table: *kataklinō* [verb: κατακλίνω <2625>]; **from *kata*: down, and *klinō*: to incline ▶ To stretch out, to lie down to eat** > Jesus tells guests not to lay themselves down in the first place at table when they are invited by someone to a wedding (Luke 14:8). Jesus was at table with His apostles (Luke 24:30). Other refs.: Luke 9:14, 15; see "to sit down" under SIT <2625>. ¶

7 to place oneself, to recline again, to lie down at the table: *anapiptō* [verb: ἀναπίπτω <377>]; **from *ana*: backward, and *piptō*: to fall ▶ To lean back, to lie down for a meal** > Jesus entered into the house of a Pharisee and placed Himself at table (Luke 11:37). When the hour was come, Jesus placed Himself at table with the twelve apostles (Luke 22:14). He reclined at the table again after having washed their feet (John 13:12). Other ref.: Luke 17:7. All other refs.: LEAN <377>, SIT <377>.

– 8 Mark 7:4 → BED <2825> 9 John 21:20 → SUPPER <1173> 10 2 Cor. 3:3a, b; Heb. 9:4 → TABLET <4109>.

TABLE[2] – 1 ***plax*** [fem. noun: πλάξ <4109>] **▶ Flat piece of wood or stone on which one can write; also transl.: tablet; *planum*, in Lat.: flat surface** > The Corinthians were manifested as being a letter of Christ, ministered by Paul, written, not with ink, but by the Spirit of the living God, not on stone tables, but on fleshy tables of the heart (2 Cor. 3:3a, b). The tables of the covenant were kept in the ark of the covenant (Heb. 9:4). ¶

– 2 Luke 1:63 → writing table → TABLET <4093>.

TABLET – 1 ***pinakidion*** [neut. noun: πινακίδιον <4093>]; **dimin. of *pinax*: plate ▶ Small board covered with a layer of**

wax placed horizontally for writing > Having asked for a tablet {writing table, writing tablet}, Zacharias wrote that the name of his son was John (Luke 1:63). ¶
– [2] 2 Cor. 3:3a, b; Heb. 9:4 → TABLE[2] <4109>.

TACKLE – Acts 27:19 → TACKLING <4631>.

TACKLING – ***skeuē*** [fem. noun: σκευή <4631>]; **from *skeuos*: instrument ▶ Equipment necessary on a sailboat** > Paul and other passengers on board of a ship cast out its tackling {tackle, furniture} (Acts 27:19). ¶

TAIL – ***oura*** [fem. noun: οὐρά <3769>]; **comp. *orros*: coccyx, tailbone ▶ Extension of the vertebral column of many animals** > In Rev. 9:10a, b, the locusts have tails like scorpions; the tails of the horses are like serpents (v. 19a, b). The dragon's tail casts the third part of the stars of the heaven to the earth (Rev. 12:4). ¶

TAKE – [1] ***lambanō*** [verb: λαμβάνω <2983>] ▶ **To seize, to accept, to receive; also transl.: to catch, to get** > The verb is used in regard to Jesus (Matt. 27:59; John 18:31; 19:1, 6; Phil. 2:7). It is also used in regard to infirmities (Matt. 8:17), our cross (Matt. 10:38), a grain of mustard seed (Matt. 13:31; Luke 13:19), leaven (Matt. 13:33; Luke 13:21), loaves of bread (Matt. 14:19; 15:26, 36; 16:5, 7, 8; 26:26a, b; Mark 6:41; 7:27; 8:6, 14; 14:22a, b; Luke 6:4; 9:16; 22:19; 24:30; John 6:11; 21:13; Acts 27:35; 1 Cor. 11:23), a piece of money (Matt. 17:27b), bondmen (Matt. 21:35; Mark 12:3), the son of a householder (Matt. 21:39), torches (Matt. 25:1, 3), a cup (Matt. 26:27; Mark 14:23; Luke 22:17b), a sword (Matt. 26:52 {to draw}), pieces of silver (Matt. 27:6 {to pick up}, 9), water (Matt. 27:24), a sponge (Matt. 27:48), money (Matt. 28:15), a little child (Mark 9:36a), a heir (Mark 12:8), a widow {to marry} (Mark 12:19–21; Luke 20:28, 29, 31), wine mixed with myrrh (Mark 15:23), fish (Luke 5:5), a honeycomb (Luke 24:43), ointment (John 12:3), branches of palms (John 12:13), a linen towel (John 13:4), what is of Jesus (John 16:14, 15), a band of soldiers (John 18:3), Mary (John 19:27), vinegar (John 19:30), the charge of overseership (Acts 1:20), Paul (Acts 9:25), Timothy (Acts 16:3), courage (Acts 28:15), our goods (2 Cor. 11:20), guile (2 Cor. 12:16), a high priest (Heb. 5:1 {to select}), blood (Heb. 9:19), an example (Jas. 5:10), a crown (Rev. 3:11), a book (Rev. 5:7–9), a golden censer (Rev. 8:5), a little book (Rev. 10:8–10), great power (Rev. 11:17), the mark of the name of the beast (Rev. 14:11), and the water of life (Rev. 22:17). *
[2] **to take, to take out: *lambanō*** [verb: λαμβάνω <2983>]: **see [1]; again, up: *palin*** [adv.: πάλιν <3825>] ▶ **a. To take another time** > Jesus laid down His life in that He might take it again (John 10:17); He had authority to take it again (v. 18). He took {put on} His clothes after He had washed the feet of His disciples (John 13:12). **b. To withdraw, to choose** > God visited the nations to take a people for His name (Acts 15:14). **c. To seize, to appropriate to oneself** > We must surrender our cloak to one who would take away our body coat (Matt. 5:40). No man takes the honor to himself of being high priest, but he who is called by God (Heb. 5:4). It was given to a horseman to take peace from the earth (Rev. 6:4). Other refs.: see [1].
[3] **to take, to take up, to take along: *analambanō*** [verb: ἀναλαμβάνω <353>]; **from *ana*: up, and *lambanō*: see [1] ▶ a. To seize, to carry off (with the intention of using)** > The verb is used in regard to the armor of God (Eph. 6:13 {to take up, to put on}) and the shield of faith (v. 16). **b. To bring along with oneself** > The verb is used in regard to Mark (2 Tim. 4:11 {to get, to pick up}) and Paul (Acts 20:14; 23:31). **c. To raise, to transport** > The verb {to lift up} is used in regard to the idols Moloch and Remphan (Acts 7:43). All other refs.: BOARD (noun) <353>, RECEIVE <353>.
[4] **to take aside, to take away: *apolambanō*** [verb: ἀπολαμβάνω <618>]; **from *apo*: from, and *lambanō*: see [1] ▶ To take out with oneself** > Jesus took a deaf

man, who spoke with difficulty, away from the crowd (Mark 7:33). All other refs.: RECEIVE <618>.

5 to take, to take hold: *epilambanō* [verb: ἐπιλαμβάνω <1949>]; **from *epi*: on, upon, over and *lambanō*: see 1 ► To seize >** The verb is used in regard to Peter (Matt. 14:31 {to catch}), a blind man (Mark 8:23), a little child (Luke 9:47), a man suffering from an abnormal swelling of his body (Luke 14:4), Paul (Acts 9:27; 17:19), Paul's nephew (Acts 23:19), angels and the seed of Abraham {to give aid, to give help} (Heb. 2:16a, b), and the Israelites (Heb. 8:9). All other refs.: CATCH (verb) <1949>, SEIZE <1949>.

6 *metalambanō* [verb: μεταλαμβάνω <3335>]; **from *meta*: with, and *lambanō*: see 1 ► To share (food), to partake, to eat >** The verb is used in regard to the food of the early Christians (Acts 2:46 {to receive}). Other refs.: Acts 27:33, 34 (*proslambanō* in some mss.). All other refs.: FIND <3335>, PARTAKE <3335>, PARTICIPATE <3335>, RECEIVE <3335>.

7 to take, to take along, to take with: *paralambanō* [verb: παραλαμβάνω <3880>]; **from *para*: beside, with, and *lambanō*: see 1 ► To take with oneself, alongside, to seize >** This verb is used in regard to Jesus (Matt. 4:5, 8; 27:27; Mark 4:36; John 19:16). It is also used in regard to Mary and the infant Jesus (Matt. 1:20; 2:13, 14, 20, 21), Mary (Matt. 1:24), wicked spirits (Matt. 12:45; Luke 11:26), three disciples (Matt. 17:1; Mark 9:2 {to lead, to bring}; 14:33; Luke 9:28), people (Matt. 18:16; Acts 21:24), the twelve (Matt. 20:17; Mark 10:32; Luke 9:10; 18:31), a man in a field (Matt. 24:40; Luke 17:36), a woman grinding (Matt. 24:41; Luke 17:35), Peter and the two sons of Zebedee (Matt. 26:37), the parents of a young girl who had died (Mark 5:40), a person on a bed (Luke 17:34), believers in the Lord (John 14:3 {to receive}), Mark (Acts 15:39), Paul and Barnabas (Acts 16:33), men (Acts 21:26), soldiers and centurions (Acts 21:32), and Paul (Acts 23:18). All other refs.: RECEIVE <3880>.

8 to take ahead, before, first: *prolambanō* [verb: προλαμβάνω <4301>]; **from *pro*: before, and *lambanō*: see 1 ► To seize in advance >** The verb is used in 1 Cor. 11:21. All other refs.: CATCH (verb) <4301>, COME <4301>.

9 to take to (oneself), along, aside: *proslambanō* [verb: προσλαμβάνω <4355>]; **from *pros*: to, aside, and *lambanō*: see 1 ► a. To draw to oneself >** The verb is used in regard to Jesus (Matt. 16:22; Mark 8:32), wicked men (Acts 17:5 {to round up}), and Apollos (Acts 18:26 {to invite}). **b. To take (food) >** Paul encouraged all the passengers to take {partake of} food {to eat} (Acts 27:33), which they did (v. 36), following his exhortation. All other refs.: RECEIVE <4355>.

10 *sullambanō* [verb: συλλαμβάνω <4815>]; **from *sun* (intens.): with, and *lambanō*: to take ► To seize (in a hostile sense), to make (someone) a prisoner; also transl.: to arrest, to capture, to catch >** The verb is used in regard to Jesus (Matt. 26:55; Mark 14:48; Acts 1:16), Peter (Acts 12:3), Paul (Acts 26:21), and fish (Luke 5:9). All other refs.: CONCEIVE <4815>, HELP (verb) <4815>, SEIZE <4815>.

11 to take with, to take along with: *sumparalambanō* [verb: συμπαραλαμβάνω <4838>]; **from *sun*: together, and *paralambanō*: see 7 ► To bring along >** Barnabas and Saul took with them John, whose surname was Mark (Acts 12:25). Barnabas proposed to take with him John, called Mark (Acts 15:37), but Paul refused (v. 38). Paul had taken Titus with himself (Gal. 2:1). ¶

12 to take up, to take upstairs: *anagō* [verb: ἀνάγω <321>]; **from *ana*: up, and *agō*: to take, to bring ► To lead up, to bring >** The devil took Jesus up on a high mountain (Luke 4:5). They took up Peter to an upper room (Acts 9:39). All other refs.: see entries in Lexicon at <321>.

13 to take out: *apagō* [verb: ἀπάγω <520>]; **from *apo*: from, and *agō*: to lead, to take ► To take along, to take (somebody) away (somewhere) >** Lysias had taken out {had snatched} Paul of the hands of the Jews (Acts 24:7 in some mss.). All other refs.: BRING <520>, CARRY <520>, DEATH <520>, LEAD (verb) <520>.

14 **to take along: *periagō*** [verb: περιάγω <4013>]; **from *peri*: about, and *agō*: to take, to bring ▶ To lead about with oneself >** The other apostles, the brothers of the Lord and Cephas took along {led about} a sister as a wife (1 Cor. 9:5). All other refs.: GO <4913>.

15 **to take; to take away, along, up: *airō*** [verb: αἴρω <142>] ▶ **a. To take upon oneself; to remove >** This verb is used in regard to those who do not receive the word of Jesus (Matt. 13:12; Mark 4:25; Luke 8:18) and to His service (Matt. 25:29; Luke 19:26). The disciples took away the body of John the Baptist (Matt. 14:12; Mark 6:29). Jesus spoke of telling a mountain to be taken up and cast into the sea (Matt. 21:21; Mark 11:23). The kingdom of God was to be taken away from the Jewish nation (Matt. 21:43). The man who did not have on a wedding garment was taken away and cast into outer darkness (Matt. 22:13). When he sees the abomination of desolation, he who is on the housetop must not go down to take {get} anything out of his house (Matt. 24:17; Mark 13:15; Luke 17:31). He who is in the field must not go back to take up {get} his clothes (Matt. 24:18; Mark 13:16). The flood took away all the people of Noah's time (Matt. 24:39). A master said to take the talent from a bondman (Matt. 25:28); Luke speaks of a mina taken from a bondman (Luke 19:24). Jesus told a man to follow Him after having taken up the cross (Mark 10:21 in some mss.). Jesus tells us to surrender our tunic to him who would take away our garment (Luke 6:29, 30). The devil takes away the word from the heart of those who hear it (Luke 8:12). Jesus took away the full armor of Satan (Luke 11:22). The lawyers had taken away the key of knowledge (Luke 11:52). The crowd cried out to take away Jesus and crucify Him (Luke 23:18; John 19:15a, b); the crowd cried to take away Paul (Acts 21:36; 22:22). John saw the Lamb of God who takes away the sin of the world (John 1:29). Jesus said to take the doves away from the temple (John 2:16). No one took the life of Jesus from Him (John 10:18). The stone was taken away {removed} from the tomb of Lazarus (John 11:39, 41). The Jews feared that the Romans would take away both their place of worship and their nation (John 11:48). The Father takes away every branch in Jesus not bearing fruit (John 15:2). No one would take their joy from the disciples (John 16:22). Jesus did not demand that God should take His own out of the world (John 17:15). The Jews demanded of Pilate that the bodies of the two robbers might be taken away (John 19:31). Joseph of Arimathea took away the body of Jesus (John 19:38a, b). Mary of Magdala saw the stone taken away from the tomb (John 20:1). Mary of Magdala believed that the body of Jesus had been taken away (John 20:2, 13). She wanted to take away the body of Jesus (John 20:15). The judgment of Jesus was taken away, and His life taken from the earth (Acts 8:33a, b). Certain evil behaviors and attitudes were to be taken away {put away, removed} from among the Ephesians (Eph. 4:31). God effaced the handwriting in ordinances that stood out against us and He took it also out of the way, having nailed it to the cross (Col. 2:14). Jesus was manifested that He might take away our sins (1 John 3:5). An angel took up a stone and threw it into the sea (Rev. 18:21). **b. To raise, to carry, to transport; also transl.: to pick up >** The verb is used in regard to a bed (Matt. 9:6; Mark 2:9, 11, 12; Luke 5:24, 25; John 5:8–12), the yoke of the Lord (Matt. 11:29), one's cross (Matt. 16:24; Mark 8:34; Luke 9:23), a fish (Matt. 17:27a), that which is one's own (Matt. 20:14), the clothes of Jesus (Mark 15:24 {to get}), serpents (Mark 16:18), a purse (Luke 22:36), stones (John 8:59), a belt (Acts 21:11), and members of Christ (1 Cor. 6:15). Other refs.: Mark 6:8; Luke 9:3; 19:21, 22 {to collect}. **c. To seize, to remove >** In the parable of the sower, Satan comes and takes away the word that was sown in the heart (Mark 4:15). All other refs.: see entries in Lexicon at <142>.

16 **to take away: *apairō*** [verb: ἀπαίρω <522>]; **from *apo*: from, and *airō*: see** **15** ▶ **To remove >** The bridegroom will be taken away from the attendants of the bridegroom (Matt. 9:15; Mark 2:20; Luke 5:35). Other ref.: Acts 1:9 in some mss. ¶

17 **to take away:** ***exairō*** [verb: ἐξαίρω <1808>]; **from** ***ek*****: out, and** ***airō*****: see** **15** ▶ **To take away from a place; also transl.: to remove, to put away, to put out** > He who had committed an evil act was to be taken away out of the midst of the Corinthians (1 Cor. 5:2); Paul instructed them to take away {expel} the wicked person from among themselves (v. 13). ¶

18 **to take up:** ***epairō*** [verb: ἐπαίρω <1869>]; **from** ***epi*****: upon, and** ***airō*****: see** **15** ▶ **To elevate, to go up** > Jesus was taken up {lifted up} while His disciples were looking (Acts 1:9). All other refs.: EXALT <1869>, LIFT <1869>, RAISE <1869>.

19 **to take, to take away, to take up:** ***anaireō*** [verb: ἀναιρέω <337>]; **from** ***ana*****: up (intens.), and** ***haireō*****: to appropriate, to choose** ▶ **a. To remove, to carry, to lift up; used of acknowledging or adopting as one's child** > Pharaoh's daughter took Moses and brought him up as her son (Acts 7:21). **b. To suppress, to set aside** > Jesus took away the first manner of worship that He might establish the second (Heb. 10:9). All other refs.: DEATH <337>, KILL <337>.

20 **to take, to take away:** ***aphaireō*** [verb: ἀφαιρέω <851>]; **from** ***apo*****: from, and** ***haireō*****: to appropriate, to choose** ▶ **To remove** > The Lord took away the reproach of Elizabeth (Luke 1:25). The good part would not be taken from Mary (Luke 10:42). A lord took the stewardship away from his steward (Luke 16:3). God will take away the sins of Israel (Rom. 11:27). The blood of bulls and goats is incapable of taking away sins (Heb. 10:4). If anyone takes from the words of the book of this prophecy, God will take away his part from the tree of life and out of the holy city (Rev. 22:19a, b). All other refs.: CUT <851>.

21 **to take out:** ***exaireō*** [verb: ἐξαιρέω <1807>]; **from** ***ek*****: out, and** ***haireō*****: to take** ▶ **To remove, to pluck out; also transl.: to deliver, to rescue** > Paul had been taken out from among the Jewish people, as well as the nations, to whom he was sent to open their eyes (Acts 26:17). Jesus Christ has taken Christians out of the present evil world, according to the will of God (Gal. 1:4). All other refs.: DELIVER <1807>, PLUCK <1807>.

22 **to take down:** ***kathaireō*** [verb: καθαιρέω <2507>]; **from** ***kata*****: down, and** ***haireō*****: to appropriate, to choose** ▶ **To make go down, to make descend** > At the cross someone said to see if Elijah would come to take Jesus down (Mark 15:36). Jesus was taken down from the cross (Mark 15:46; Luke 23:53; Acts 13:29). All other refs.: DESTROY <2507>, PULL <2507>, PUT <2507>.

23 **to take away, to take up:** ***periaireō*** [verb: περιαιρέω <4014>]; **from** ***peri*****: around, and** ***haireō*****: to appropriate, to choose** ▶ **To remove** > All hope of being saved was taken away from {was given up by, was gradually abandoned by} Paul and the passengers on the ship (Acts 27:20). When Israel will turn to the Lord, the veil will be taken away (2 Cor. 3:16). The sacrifices (from the O.T.) can never take away sins (Heb. 10:11). All other refs.: LOOSE <4014>.

24 **to take by force:** ***harpazō*** [verb: ἁρπάζω <726>] ▶ **To seize, to take forcefully** > Jesus knew that the people intended to take Him by force to make Him king (John 6:15). Paul was taken by force from among the Jews (Acts 23:10). All other refs.: CATCH (verb) <726>, PULL <726>, SEIZE <726>.

25 **to take up:** ***bastazō*** [verb: βαστάζω <941>]; **from** ***basis*****: base (of the foot; with the notion of carrying something away)** ▶ **To pick up** > The Jews took up stones to stone Jesus (John 10:31). All other refs.: BEAR (verb) <941>.

26 **to take place:** ***ginomai*** [verb: γίνομαι <1096>] ▶ **To become, to happen** > Refs.: Luke 1:20; 21:32; Acts 4:28. Other refs.: see entries in Lexicon at <1096>.

27 ***didōmi*** [verb: δίδωμι <1325>]; **lit.: to give** ▶ **To manifest, to employ to a certain end** > The Lord Jesus and the angels of His power will take vengeance on those who do not know God (2 Thes. 1:8). Other refs.: GIVE <1325>.

28 **to take off; to take off the clothing, the garment:** ***ekduō*** [verb: ἐκδύω <1562>]; **from** ***ek*****: out, and** ***duō*****: to go** ▶ **To remove, to undress** > The soldiers took off the garment of {stripped} Jesus (Matt. 27:28), His cloak also (v. 31). They took the purple robe off Jesus (Mark 15:20). In a parable, thieves took off the clothing of a man {stripped a man of his clothing} and wounded him (Luke 10:30). The Greek verb is transl. "to be unclothed" in 2 Cor. 5:4: Paul did not wish to be unclothed, but further clothed, that mortality might be swallowed up by life. ¶

29 **to take in hand, to take upon oneself: *epicheireō*** [verb: ἐπιχειρέω <2021>]; **from *epi*: upon, and *cheir*: hand ▶ To assume the responsibility, to try** > Many had taken in hand to set in order a narrative of those things concerning the life of Jesus (Luke 1:1). Some Jewish exorcists took in hand {attempted, tried} to call the name of the Lord over those who had evil spirits (Acts 19:13). Other ref.: Acts 9:29; see SEEK <2021>. ¶

30 ***katechō*** [verb: κατέχω <2722>]; **from *kata*: intens., and *echō*: to have ▶ To hold, to occupy** > The verb is used regarding the last place at a wedding (Luke 14:9). All other refs.: see entries in Lexicon at <2722>.

31 ***sunechō*** [verb: συνέχω <4912>]; **from *sun*: together, and *echō*: to have ▶ To hold tight, to be afflicted** > Sick people taken with {suffering} various diseases and pains were brought to Jesus (Matt. 4:24). All other refs.: see entries in Lexicon at <4912>.

32 **to take, to take away, to take up: *metatithēmi*** [verb: μετατίθημι <3346>]; **from *meta*: prep. indicating change of place or condition, and *tithēmi*: to put, to place ▶ To move from one place to another one** > By faith, Enoch was taken up {was translated}, and was not found because God had taken him up {translated him} (Heb. 11:5a, b). All other refs.: CARRY <3346>, CHANGE (verb) <3346>, TURN (verb) <3346>.

33 ***prosdechomai*** [verb: προσδέχομαι <4327>]; **from *pros*: to, and *dechomai*: to accept, to receive ▶ To endure without protest, to consent, to accept** > The Hebrews took {accepted} with joy the spoiling of their goods, knowing they had a better and enduring possession (Heb. 10:34). All other refs.: ACCEPT <4327>, LOOK (verb) <4327>, RECEIVE <4327>, WAIT (verb) <4327>.

34 **to take out: *ekballō*** [verb: ἐκβάλλω <1544>]; **from *ek*: out, and *ballō*: to throw ▶ To bring out** > The good Samaritan took out two denarii and gave them to the innkeeper (Luke 10:35). All other refs.: see entries in Lexicon at <1544>.

35 ***dechomai*** [verb: δέχομαι <1209>] **▶ To accept, to receive** > The verb is used in regard to the little child Jesus (Luke 2:28), a writing (Luke 16:6, 7), a cup that the Lord took on the night He was delivered (Luke 22:17a), and the helmet of salvation (Eph. 6:17 {to have}). All other refs.: RECEIVE <1209>.

36 ***drassomai*** [verb: δράσσομαι <1405>] **▶ To grasp with the hand, to seize (by a snare)** > God takes {catches} the wise in their craftiness (1 Cor. 3:19). ¶

37 **to take, to take hold, to lay hold: *krateō*** [verb: κρατέω <2902>]; **from *kratos*: power, strength ▶ a. To seize, to hold firmly** > Jesus took the hand of Peter's mother-in-law (Mark 1:31). The verb is used in regard to the hand of a child (Matt. 9:25; Mark 5:41; Luke 8:54), a sheep that has fallen into a ditch (Matt. 12:11), and a possessed child (Mark 9:27). **b. To take hold of someone in order to turn him over to an authority; also transl.: to arrest, to seize** > The verb is used in regard to John the Baptist (Matt. 14:3; Mark 6:17). All other refs.: FAST (HOLD) <2902>, GAIN (verb) <2902>, HOLD (verb) <2902>, KEEP (verb) <2902>, SEIZE <2902>.

38 **to take, to take hold of: *piazō*** [verb: πιάζω <4084>]; **from *piezō*: to press ▶ To seize hold of, to capture, to catch** > The verb is used in regard to Jesus (John 7:30, 32, 44; 8:20; 10:39; 11:57), fish (John 21:3, 10), a lame man (Acts 3:7), Peter (Acts 12:4), and the beast (Rev. 19:20). Other ref.: 2 Cor. 11:32; see SEIZE <4084>. ¶

39 **to take away: *parapherō*** [verb: παραφέρω <3911>]; **from *para*: beyond, and *pherō*: to carry ▶ To remove, to avert** > Jesus asked His Father to take away the cup of suffering from Him (Mark 14:36; Luke 22:42). Other refs.: Heb. 13:9; Jude 12 in some mss. ¶

– 40 Matt. 9:2, 22; 14:27; Mark 6:50; 10:49; Luke 8:48; John 16:33; Acts 23:11 → to take courage → COURAGE <2293> 41 Matt. 10:9 → to take along → PROVIDE <2932> 42 Matt. 13:49; Acts 19:9 → to take away, to take out, to take with oneself → SEPARATE <873> 43 Matt. 15:39; John 6:24 → to take shipping → to get into → GET <1684> 44 Matt. 16:9, 10 → to take up → to pick up → PICK <2983> 45 Matt. 17:1; Mark 9:2 → to take up → to lead up → LEAD (verb) <399> 46 Matt. 18:4 → to take the lowly position → HUMBLE (verb) <5013> 47 Matt. 18:28 → to take by the throat → THROAT <4155> 48 Matt. 25:35, 38, 43 → to take in → INVITE <4863> 49 Matt. 26:39, 42 → PASS <3928> 50 Mark 9:18 → SEIZE <2638> 51 Mark 15:23; Luke 1:15 → DRINK (verb) <4095> 52 Luke 3:13 → COLLECT <4238> 53 Luke 4:9; John 18:28 → LEAD (verb) <71> 54 Luke 5:18, 19 → to take in → to bring in → BRING <1533> 55 Luke 5:18; John 2:8a, b → BRING <5342> 56 Luke 9:39; Rom. 7:8, 11 → SEIZE <2983> 57 Luke 9:51 → to be taken up → to be received up → receiving up → RECEIVE <354> 58 Luke 10:34; Acts 22:5 → BRING <71> 59 Luke 12:15 → to take care → BEWARE <3708> 60 Luke 22:54; Acts 21:37; 22:24 in some mss. → BRING <1521> 61 Luke 24:51 → to take up → to carry up → CARRY <399> 62 John 8:3, 4 → CATCH (verb) <2638> 63 John 11:13 → taking rest → REST (verb) <2838> 64 John 11:44, Acts 7:33 → to take off the grave clothes, to take off → LOOSE <3089> 65 John 21:7 → to take off → to be naked → NAKED <1131> 66 John 21:16 → to take care → SHEPHERD (verb) <4165> 67 Acts 1:9 → i.e., to take in order to carry higher → RECEIVE <5274> 68 Acts 5:40 → AGREE <3982> 69 Acts 7:45 → when they took the land from the nations → lit.: when they entered into possession of the nations → POSSESSION <2697> 70 Acts 9:30 → to take down → to bring down → BRING <2609> 71 Acts 10:26 → to take up → to raise up → RAISE <1453> 72 Acts 11:2 → to take issue → CONTEND <1252> 73 Acts 16:37, 39 → to take out of prison → to lead out of prison → LEAD (verb) <1806> 74 Acts 19:12 in some mss. → BRING <667> 75 Acts 20:1 → to take one's leave → EMBRACE <782> 76 Acts 20:10 → to take in one's arms → EMBRACE <4843> 77 Acts 21:6 → to take (ship) → BOARD (verb) <1910> 78 Acts 21:15 → to take one's carriages → PACK <643> 79 Acts 24:16 → to take pains → to exercise oneself → EXERCISE (verb) <778> 80 Rom. 3:5 → INFLICT <2018> 81 Rom. 4:8 → to take into account → COUNT <3049> 82 Rom. 9:6 → to take no effect → EFFECT (noun) <1601> 83 Rom. 13:14 → to take forethought → to make provision → MAKE <4160> 84 1 Cor. 10:6 → to take place → PLACE (noun) <1096> 85 1 Cor. 10:13 → OVERTAKE <2983> 86 2 Cor. 7:2; 12:17, 18 → to take advantage → CHEAT <4122> 87 2 Cor. 8:20 → to take precaution → AVOID <4724> 88 2 Cor. 12:8 → to take it away from me → lit.: that it might depart from me → DEPART <868> 89 Gal. 1:16 → to take counsel → CONFER <4323> 90 Eph. 4:8 → to take many captives → to lead captivity captive → CAPTIVE (adj.) <162> 91 Col. 3:9 → to take off → DISARM <554> 92 1 Thes. 2:17 → to take away → SEPARATE <642> 93 1 Tim. 6:7 → to take out → to carry out → CARRY <1627> 94 2 Tim. 2:26 → to take, to take captive → CATCH (verb) <2221> 95 Heb. 6:1 → to take forward → to go on → GO <5342> 96 Heb. 7:5 → to take tithe → TITHE (noun and verb) <586> 97 Heb. 9:28 → to take away → BEAR (verb) <399> 98 Heb. 11:5 → to take away → TRANSLATION <3331> 99 1 Pet. 2:20a, b → to take it patiently → ENDURE <5278> 100 2 Pet. 2:12 → CAPTURE (noun) <259> 101 Rev. 14:15, 18 → to thrust in → THRUST <3992>.

TALE – 1 **idle tale:** ***lēros*** [masc. noun: λῆρος <3026>] ► **Foolish talk, invented story** > The words of the women returning from the tomb of Jesus seemed like idle tales {nonsense} to the apostles (Luke 24:11). ¶

– 2 2 Pet. 1:16 → FABLE <3454>.

TALENT – [1] ***talanton*** [neut. noun: τάλαντον <5007>]; **from *tlaō*: to bear; lit.: scale of a balance ▶ Unit of weight, also used as a denomination for money; it is estimated that the talent was worth at least one thousand dollars** > The man in a parable owed 10,000 talents (Matt. 18:24); it was impossible for him to repay this fabulous sum that constituted his debt. The parable of the talents (Matt. 25:15, 16a, b, 20a–d, 22a–c, 24, 25, 28a, b) illustrates the abilities entrusted to the servants of the Lord; they must give an account of the use they have made of these abilities. ¶
[2] **the weight of a talent, as the weight of a talent: *talantiaios*** [adj.: ταλαντιαῖος <5006>]; **from *talanton*: see [1] ▶ Which weighs one talent** > Hail about the weight of a talent {about one hundred pounds each} (Rev. 16:21; see 8:7) symbolizes a sudden and terrifying judgment, of heavenly origin. ¶

TALITHA KOUMI – **young girl: *talitha*** [fem. noun: ταλιθά <5008>]; **lit.: the fresh (fem.); to arise: *koumi*** [verb: κοῦμι <2891>] ▶ **Aram. words which mean "young girl" and "arise"; also transl.: *talitha cumi, talitha koum, talitha kum*** > Jesus said to a young girl who was dead (Mark 5:41): "*Talitha koumi,*" i.e., "Young girl, arise." ¶

TALK (noun) – [1] Rom. 16:18 → smooth talk → SMOOTH <5542> [2] 1 Cor. 4:19 → WORD <3056> [3] Eph. 5:4 → foolish talk, silly talk → FOOLISH <3473> [4] Col. 3:8 → obscene talk → filthy language → FILTHY <148> [5] 1 Tim. 1:6 → idle talk, meaningless talk → vain discourse → VAIN <3150> [6] Titus 1:10 → people full of meaningless talk → idle talkers → TALKER <3151> [7] 1 Pet. 2:15 → ignorant talk → IGNORANCE <56> [8] 1 John 3:18 → TONGUE <1100>.

TALK (verb) – [1] ***laleō*** [verb: λαλέω <2980>] ▶ **To speak, to discuss** > Agrippa and others talked among themselves concerning Paul (Acts 26:31). Other refs.: SPEAK <2980>.
[2] ***homileō*** [verb: ὁμιλέω <3656>]; **from *homilos*: company, crowd, which is from *homos*: similar, and *ilē*: crowd ▶ To discuss; also transl.: to commune, to converse, to speak** > The disciples of Emmaus were talking together about all the things that had happened in Jerusalem (Luke 24:14, 15). Paul talked a long while in the upper room at Troas (Acts 20:11). Felix talked with Paul (Acts 24:26). ¶
[3] **to talk with: *sunomileō*** [verb: συνομιλέω <4926>]; **from *sun*: together, and *homileō*: see [2] ▶ To talk together, to converse** > Peter was talking with Cornelius (Acts 10:27). Other ref.: 1 Pet. 3:7 in some mss. ¶
– [4] Matt. 9:32 → who could not talk → DUMB <2974> [5] Matt. 16:8; Mark 8:17; Luke 20:14 → REASON (verb) <1260> [6] Matt. 17:3; Mark 9:4; Luke 4:36; 9:30 → to talk, to talk with → to speak with → SPEAK TO <4814> [7] Matt. 26:73 → the way you talk → your speech → SPEECH <2981> [8] Mark 1:45; 7:36 → PROCLAIM <2784> [9] Mark 7:32 → who can hardly talk → who cannot speak right → SPEAK <3424> [10] Mark 12:13 → WORD <3056> [11] Luke 1:65 → to talk about → DISCUSS <1255> [12] Acts 13:43; 28:20 → to talk with → to speak to → SPEAK <4354> [13] Acts 13:45a; 28:22 → to talk abusively against, to talk against → to speak against → SPEAK <483> [14] Acts 20:7 → SPEAK <1256> [15] Acts 20:7 → to keep on talking → lit.: to continue one's message → MESSAGE <3056> [16] Acts 20:9 → DISCOURSE (verb) <1256> [17] Acts 20:9 → to talk still longer → lit.: to talk for longer (*epi pleion*) [18] Acts 24:25 → REASON (verb) <1256> [19] Rom. 9:20 → to talk back to → to reply against → REPLY (verb) <470> [20] 1 Tim. 5:13 → who talk nonsense → TATTLER <5397> [21] Titus 2:9 → to talk back → to answer back → ANSWER (verb) <483> [22] 3 John 10 → to talk wicked nonsense → to prate with malicious words → PRATE <5396>.

TALKER – [1] **idle talker: *mataiologos*** [adj. used as noun: ματαιολόγος <3151>]; **from *mataios*: without profit, vain, and *legō*: to speak ▶ Person who speaks much, but**

whose words are not worthwhile or relevant > Paul wrote to Titus that there were many disorderly idle talkers {empty, vain, mere talkers; vain speakers} and deceivers of people's minds (Titus 1:10). ¶
– [2] 1 Tim. 3:11 → malicious talker → false accuser → ACCUSER <1228>.

TALKING – Eph. 5:4 → foolish talking → FOOLISH <3473>.

TAMAR – ***Thamar*** [fem. name: Θαμάρ <2283>]: **palm tree, in Heb.** ▶ **Wife successively of two sons of Judah, Er and Onan** > Tamar is one of four women, in addition to Mary, mentioned in the genealogy of Jesus Christ (Matt. 1:3). ¶

TAME – ***damazō*** [verb: δαμάζω <1150>] ▶ **To overcome, to control** > No one could tame {subdue} the man with an unclean spirit (Mark 5:4). Animals are tamed and have been tamed by men, but no man can tame the tongue (Jas. 3:7a, b, 8). ¶

TAMPER – 2 Cor. 4:2 → to tamper with → FALSIFY <1389>.

TANNER – ***burseus*** [masc. noun: βυρσεύς <1038>]; **from *bursa*: skin of an animal** ▶ **Workman who makes leather from hides** > Peter stayed with Simon, a tanner (Acts 9:43; 10:6, 32). ¶

TARE – Luke 9:42 → past tense of "to tear" → CONVULSE <4952>.

TARES – Matt. 13:25–27, 29, 30, 36, 38, 40 → DARNEL <2215>.

TARRY – [1] ***menō*** [verb: μένω <3306>] ▶ **To stay, to remain** > Many brothers tarried {waited} for Paul at Troas (Acts 20:5). Paul tarried at Trogyllium (Acts 20:15 in some mss.). All other refs.: AWAIT <3306>, CONTINUE <3306>, LASTING <3306>, REMAIN <3306>, STAY (verb) <3306>.
[2] ***epimenō*** [verb: ἐπιμένω <1961>]; **from *epi*: upon, and *menō*: see [1]** ▶ **To stay, to remain** > Paul tarried {was} many days in the house of Philip the evangelist (Acts 21:10). All other refs.: CONTINUE <1961>, REMAIN <1961>, STAY (verb) <1961>.
[3] ***kathizō*** [verb: καθίζω <2523>]; **from *kata*: down, and *hizō*: to sit; lit.: to sit down** ▶ **To stay, to remain at the same place** > The disciples were to tarry in Jerusalem until they were clothed with power from on high (Luke 24:49). All other refs.: CONTINUE <2523>, JUDGE (verb) <2523>, SIT <2523>.
[4] ***prosdokaō*** [verb: προσδοκάω <4328>]; **from *pros*: to, and *dokaō*: to expect, to look for, from which *prodokia*: expectation** ▶ **To be waiting for, to expect something to happen** > The passengers aboard Paul's ship had been tarrying {waiting, constantly watching, watching in expectation, in constant suspense} fourteen days and continued without food (Acts 27:33). All other refs.: EXPECT <4328>, EXPECTATION <4328>, LOOK (verb) <4328>, WAIT (verb) <4328>.
– [5] Matt. 25:5; Luke 1:21; Heb. 10:37 → DELAY (verb) <5549> [6] Luke 2:43 → to tarry behind → to linger behind → LINGER <5278> [7] John 3:22; Acts 25:6 → STAY (verb) <1304> [8] Acts 18:18 → REMAIN <4357> [9] Acts 22:16 → DELAY (verb) <3195> [10] 1 Cor. 11:33 → to wait for → WAIT (verb) <1551> [11] 1 Tim. 3:15 → DELAY (verb) <1019>.

TARSUS – [1] ***Tarsos*** [fem. name: Ταρσός <5019>]; **maybe: flat basket** ▶ **Capital of Cilicia in Asia Minor** > Paul was born in Tarsus (Acts 22:3). The brothers sent him away to Tarsus after his conversion (Acts 9:30). Barnabas went away to Tarsus to seek out Paul and brought him to Antioch (Acts 11:25). ¶
[2] **of Tarsus: *Tarseus*** [masc. name: Ταρσεύς <5018>] ▶ **Inhabitant of Tarsus** > Saul, who would become the apostle Paul, was a native of Tarsus (Acts 9:11); he was a Jew, of Tarsus (21:39). ¶

TASK – [1] Mark 13:34 → WORK (noun) <2041> [2] Acts 6:3 → BUSINESS <5532> [3] Acts 20:24 → SERVICE <1248>.

TASSEL – Matt. 23:5 → FRINGE <2899>.

TASTE (noun) – Matt. 5:13; Luke 14:34 → to lose its taste → to lose its flavor → LOSE <3471>.

TASTE (verb) – ***geuō*** [verb: γεύω <1089>] ▶ **a. To appreciate the flavor, to eat or drink** > Jesus tasted the vinegar mingled with gall and would not drink it (Matt. 27:34). None of the men who had been invited were to taste of their host's supper (Luke 14:24). The master of the banquet tasted the water that had become wine (John 2:9). Certain Jews had put themselves under an oath to taste nothing until they had killed Paul (Acts 23:14). Certain people say not to handle and not to taste (Col. 2:21). **b. To go through, to experience** > Certain disciples would not taste death before seeing the Son of Man coming in His kingdom (Matt. 16:28; Mark 9:1; Luke 9:27). If anyone keeps the word of the Lord, he shall never taste (eternal) death (John 8:52). Jesus tasted death for everyone (Heb. 2:9). Some have tasted the heavenly gift (Heb. 6:4) and the good word of God (v. 5). Peter speaks of tasting that the Lord is good (1 Pet. 2:3). Other refs.: Acts 10:10; 20:11; see EAT <1089>. ¶

TASTELESS – Matt. 5:13; Luke 14:34 → to become tasteless → to lose its flavor → LOSE <3471>.

TATTLER – ***phluaros*** [adj.: φλύαρος <5397>]; **from *phluō*: to overflow, to talk foolishly or too much ▶ Prattler, one who repeats rumors, who chats vainly** > Young widows supported by the church were in danger of being idle and tattlers {gossips, gossipers} (1 Tim. 5:13). ¶

TAUGHT – [1] ***didaktos*** [verbal adj.: διδακτός <1318>]; **from *didaskō*: to teach ▶ Instructed, receiving knowledge** > Isaiah has written that all will be taught of God (John 6:45). Paul was not speaking in words taught by human wisdom, but taught by the Holy Spirit (1 Cor. 2:13a, b). ¶
[2] **taught by God, taught of God: *theodidaktos*** [adj.: θεοδίδακτος <2312>]; **from *Theos*: God, and *didaktos*: see [1] ▶ Instructed by God** > The Thessalonians were taught by God to love one another (1 Thes. 4:9). ¶
– [3] Rom. 15:4 → taught in the Scriptures → lit.: of the Scriptures.

TAUGHT (BE) – John 7:15 → LEARN <3129>.

TAX (noun) – [1] ***didrachmon*** [neut. noun: δίδραχμον <1323>]; **from *dis*: twice, and *drachmē*: drachma ▶ Personal tax paid by a Jewish adult for the maintenance and the service of the temple** > The didrachma, or double drachma, was about equivalent to two Roman denarii; see DENARIUS <1220>. Jesus made a miracle in order to pay this personal tax {tribute, two-drachma tax} (Matt. 17:24a, b; see vv. 25–27). ¶
[2] **tax office, tax booth, tax collector's booth, receipt of taxes: *telōnion*** [neut. noun: τελώνιον <5058>]; **from *telōnēs*: tax collector, which is from *telos*: tax, and *ōneomai*: to buy, or *ōnos*: amount of money, price ▶ Business place of a tax collector; also transl.: receipt of taxes, receipt of custom** > Matthew was sitting at the tax office when Jesus told him to follow Him (Matt. 9:9; Mark 2:14; Luke 5:27). ¶
– [3] Matt. 17:25; 22:17, 19; Mark 12:14 → tax, taxes → TRIBUTE <2778> [4] Luke 19:2 → chief tax collector, chief tax-gatherer → PUBLICAN <754> [5] Luke 20:22; 23:2; Rom. 13:6, 7a, b → tax, taxes → TRIBUTE <5411>.

TAX (verb) – [1] Luke 2:1 → to make a census → CENSUS <583> [2] Luke 2:3, 5 → REGISTER <583>.

TAX COLLECTOR – [1] ***telōnēs*** [masc. noun: τελώνης <5057>]; **from *telos*: tax, and *oneomai*: to buy ▶ Jewish collector of public revenue operating on behalf of the Romans in a specified district; also transl.: publican, tax-gatherer** > The people hated the tax collectors, especially since some took advantage to enrich themselves (Luke 3:12; see v. 13). Matthew (or: Levi), one of the twelve apostles, was a tax collector (Matt. 10:3; Luke 5:27). Other refs.: Matt. 5:46,

47; 9:10, 11; 11:19; 18:17; 21:31, 32; Mark 2:15, 16; Luke 5:29, 30; 7:29, 34; 15:1; 18:10, 11, 13. ¶

[2] **chief tax collector: *architelōnēs*** [masc. noun: ἀρχιτελώνης <754>]; **from *archē*: chief, and *telōnēs*: see [1]; also transl.: chief among the publicans, chief tax-gatherer ▶ Person in charge of those responsible to collect taxes** > Zaccheus was a chief tax collector (Luke 19:2). ¶

TAX-GATHERER – See TAX COLLECTOR <5057>.

TEACH – [1] ***didaskō*** [verb: διδάσκω <1321>]; **from *daō*: to know, to teach; *discere*, in Lat.: to learn ▶ To share knowledge so that a person may learn** > Paul tells the Ephesians that they had been taught in the Christ according to the truth that is in Jesus (Eph. 4:21). Faithful men are to be competent to teach others (2 Tim. 2:2). The verb is also used concerning Jesus (Matt. 4:23; 5:2; 7:29; 9:35; 11:1; 13:54; 21:23; 22:16; 26:55; 28:20; Mark 1:21, 22; 2:13; 4:1, 2; 6:2, 6, 34; 8:31; 9:31; 10:1; 11:17; 12:14, 35; 14:49; Luke 4:15, 31; 5:3, 17; 6:6; 11:1a; 13:10, 22, 26; 19:47; 20:1, 21a, b; 21:37; 23:5; John 6:59; 7:14, 28, 35; 8:2, 20; 18:20; Acts 1:1), the Holy Spirit (Luke 12:12; John 14:26), the Father (John 8:28), John the Baptist (Luke 11:1b), the apostles (Mark 6:30; Acts 4:2, 18; 5:21, 25, 28, 42), Paul (Acts 18:11; 20:20; 21:21, 28; 28:31; 1 Cor. 4:17; Col. 1:28; 3:16), Paul and Barnabas (Acts 11:26; 15:35), Apollos (Acts 18:25), Timothy (1 Tim. 4:11; 6:2), the Pharisees (Matt. 15:9; Mark 7:7), a Jew (Rom. 2:21a, b), a man who had been blind (John 9:34), the Colossians (Col. 2:7), the Thessalonians (2 Thes. 2:15), the Hebrews (Heb. 5:12), the one who teaches in the church (Rom. 12:7), the woman (1 Tim. 2:12), Balaam (Rev. 2:14), Jezebel (Rev. 2:20), and nature (1 Cor. 11:14). Other refs.: Matt. 5:19a, b; 28:15; Acts 15:1; Gal. 1:12; Titus 1:11; Heb. 8:11; 1 John 2:27a–c. ¶

[2] **able to teach: *didaktikos*** [adj.: διδακτικός <1317>]; **from *didaskō*: see [1] ▶ Capable of transmitting knowledge** > An overseer must be able to teach {apt to teach} (1 Tim. 3:2), as well as a servant of the Lord (2 Tim. 2:24). ¶

[3] ***katēcheō*** [verb: κατηχέω <2727>]; **from *kata*: intens., and *ēcheō*: to resonate, which is from *ēchos*: sound ▶ To share knowledge orally, to inform; also transl.: to instruct** > Luke had written his Gospel so that Theophilus might know the certainty of the things he had been taught (Luke 1:4). Apollos was instructed in the way of the Lord (Acts 18:25). Paul speaks of a Jew who is instructed by the law (Rom. 2:18). He would rather speak five words with his intelligence in order to instruct others than ten thousand words in tongues (1 Cor. 14:19). He who is taught {receives instruction in} the word of God should share in all good things with him who teaches {his instructor} (Gal. 6:6a, b). Other refs.: Acts 21:21, 24 (to be informed); see INFORM <2727>. ¶

[4] ***paideuō*** [verb: παιδεύω <3811>]; **from *pais*: child ▶ To provide knowledge and guidance, to instruct** > The grace of God teaches us how to live in this present age (Titus 2:12). All other refs.: CHASTEN <3811>, CORRECT <3811>, EDUCATE <3811>, LEARN <3811>.

– [5] Matt. 28:19; Acts 14:21 → to make a disciple → DISCIPLE <3100> [6] Mark 12:38 → DOCTRINE <1322> [7] John 6:45; 1 Cor. 2:13a, b → TAUGHT <1318> [8] Acts 6:14 → DELIVER <3860> [9] Acts 16:21 → PREACH <2605> [10] Acts 22:3 → EDUCATE <3811> [11] Rom. 15:4 → to teach us → lit.: for our teaching → INSTRUCTION <1319> [12] Rom. 16:17 → which you have been taught → which you have learned → LEARN <3129> [13] 1 Thes. 4:9 → taught by God → TAUGHT <2312> [14] 1 Tim. 4:1 → things taught → DOCTRINE <1319> [15] 1 Tim. 6:3 → to teach otherwise → to teach other doctrines → DOCTRINE <2085> [16] Titus 2:1, 15 → SPEAK <2980> [17] Titus 2:3 → teaching what is right, good → lit.: teacher of what is right → TEACHER <2567> [18] Titus 2:4 → ADMONISH <4994>.

TEACHER – [1] ***didaskalos*** [masc. noun: διδάσκαλος <1320>]; **from *didaskō*: to**

teach, to instruct, which is from *daō*: to know, to teach; *discere*, in Lat.: to learn ▶ Person who helps another to learn; more specifically in the N.T., one who teaches the commandments of God and the responsibilities of man; also transl.: master > Christ is the only Teacher of the believers in Him; they should not be called teachers, for one is their Teacher (Matt. 23:8, 10; some mss.: *kathēgētēs*). The term is used in regard to the Lord Jesus (Matt. 8:19; 9:11; 10:24, 25a; 12:38; 17:24; 19:16; 22:16, 24, 36; 26:18; Mark 4:38; 5:35; 9:17, 38; 10:17, 20, 35; 12:14, 19, 32; 13:1; 14:14; Luke 6:40a, b; 7:40; 8:49; 9:38; 10:25; 11:45; 12:13; 18:18; 19:39; 20:21, 28, 39; 21:7; 22:11; John 1:38; 8:4; 11:28; 13:13, 14; 20:16), John the Baptist (Luke 3:12), and a Jewish teacher (Rom. 2:20). There were teachers {doctors} in Israel (Luke 2:46), Nicodemus in particular (John 3:10). He recognized that Jesus was a teacher come from God (John 3:2). There were teachers in the church of Antioch (Acts 13:1). In the epistles, mention is made of Christians having received a spiritual gift as teachers of the word of God (1 Cor. 12:28, 29; Eph. 4:11; Jas. 3:1). Paul had been appointed a teacher of the Gentiles (1 Tim. 2:7; 2 Tim. 1:11). The Hebrews should have been teachers (Heb. 5:12), i.e., advanced in the knowledge of the word of God. Paul speaks of a time when men will heap up for themselves teachers (2 Tim. 4:3). ¶

2 **teacher of good things, of what is right: *kalodidaskalos*** [adj.: καλοδιδάσκαλος <2567>]; **from *kalos*: good, and *didaskalos*: see 1 ▶ Person who helps another learn good things** > The older women should be teachers of good things {teaching what is right, teaching what is good} (Titus 2:3). ¶

3 ***kathēgētēs*** [masc. noun: καθηγητής <2519>]; **from *kathēgeomai*: to lead, which is from *kata*: in front, before, and *hēgeomai*: to lead, to give direction ▶ Guide, conductor, instructor; in the N.T., the word also means: leader** > This word is found in Matt. 23:10a, b; also Matt. 23:8 in certain mss. ¶

– 4 Matt. 12:38; 26:57; Luke 20:1; et al. → teacher of the law → SCRIBE <1122> 5 Luke 5:17; Acts 5:34; 1 Tim. 1:7 → TEACHER OF THE LAW <3547> 6 2 Tim. 3:8 → "teachers" added in Engl.

TEACHER OF THE LAW – *nomodidaskalos* [masc. noun: νομοδιδάσκαλος <3547>]; **from *nomos*: law, and *didaskalos*: see TEACHER 1 ▶ Scribe specialized in the teaching of the law, and Scriptures in general; also transl.: doctor of the law** > Pharisees and teachers of the law had come to listen to Jesus (Luke 5:17). Gamaliel was a teacher of the law (Acts 5:34). Paul speaks of those wanting to be teachers of the law (1 Tim. 1:7). See SCRIBE <1122>. ¶

TEACHING – 1 Matt. 7:28; 16:12; 22:33; Mark 1:22, 27; 4:2; 11:18; 12:38; Luke 4:32; John 7:16; 18:19; Acts 2:42; 5:28; 13:12; 17:19; Rom. 6:17; 16:17; 1 Cor. 14:6, 26; 2 Tim. 4:2; Titus 1:9; Heb. 13:9; 2 John 9, 10; Rev. 2:14, 15, 24 → DOCTRINE <1322> 2 Matt. 15:3, 6; Mark 7:13; 1 Cor. 11:2; Col. 2:8; 2 Thes. 2:15; 3:6 → traditional teaching → TRADITION <3862> 3 Matt. 15:9; Mark 7:7; Rom. 12:7; Eph. 4:14; Col. 2:22; 1 Tim. 1:10; 4:1, 6, 13, 16; 5:17; 6:1; 2 Tim. 3:10, 16; 4:3; Titus 1:9; 2:1, 7, 10 → DOCTRINE <1319> 4 Luke 10:39 → WORD <3056> 5 John 6:60 → SAYING <3056> 6 2 Thes. 2:2 → "by the teaching asserting" added in Engl.

TEAR (noun)[1] – ***dakruon*** [neut. noun: δάκρυον <1144>]; **from which *dakruō*: to weep ▶ Liquid which is secreted by the lachrymal glands and moistens the eyes** > The term is used referring to the Lord Jesus (Heb. 5:7). It is also used referring to the father of a possessed child (Mark 9:24), a woman who washed the feet of Jesus with her tears (Luke 7:38, 44), Paul (Acts 20:19, 31; 2 Cor. 2:4), Timothy (2 Tim. 1:4), and Esau (Heb. 12:17). God will wipe all tears from the eyes of those who come out of the great tribulation (Rev. 7:17), and from the eyes of men when He will dwell among them (21:4). ¶

TEAR (noun)[2] – 1 ***schisma*** [neut. noun: σχίσμα <4978>]; **from *schizō*: to split, to divide ▶ Rip, rent** > A tear is made worse if a patch of unshrunk cloth is put on an old garment and the patch pulls away from the garment (Matt. 9:16; Mark 2:21). Other refs.: John 7:43; 9:16; 10:19; 1 Cor. 1:10; 11:18; 12:25; see DIVISION <4978>. ¶
– 2 Luke 5:36 → to make a tear → TEAR (verb) <4977>.

TEAR (verb) – 1 **to tear apart, to tear asunder: *diaspaō*** [verb: διασπάω <1288>]; **from *dia*: separately, and *spaō*: to draw, to pull ▶ To draw apart, to tear to pieces** > A possessed man tore apart {plucked asunder, pulled apart} the chains with which he had been bound (Mark 5:4). Other ref.: Acts 23:10 (to tear to pieces); see PIECE <1288>. ¶
2 ***rhēgnumi*** [verb: ῥήγνυμι <4486>] ▶ **To agitate violently, to throw down, to lacerate; also transl.: to throw down to the ground, to slam to the ground** > The swine might turn and tear to pieces {rend} those casting their pearls before them (Matt. 7:6). A dumb spirit was taking the son of a man and tearing him {dashing him to the ground, throwing him down, throwing him to the ground} (Mark 9:18). A demon tore (lit.: threw down) a man's son (Luke 9:42). All other refs.: BREAK <4486>, BURST <4486>.
3 ***diarrēgnumi*** [verb: διαρρήγνυμι <1284>]; **from *dia*: through, and *rhēgnumi*: see 2; lit.: to tear in two ▶ To rip apart by pulling on two sides; also transl.: to rend** > The high priest tore his clothes after Jesus had declared He was the Son of God (Matt. 26:65; Mark 14:63). Barnabas and Paul tore their clothes, having heard the priest of Zeus wanted to sacrifice oxen in their honor and crown them (Acts 14:14). Other ref.: Luke 5:6; see BREAK <1284>. ¶
4 ***schizō*** [verb: σχίζω <4977>] ▶ **To split, to divide; also transl.: to rend** > When Jesus yielded up His spirit, the veil of the temple was torn in two, from top to bottom (Matt. 27:51; Mark 15:38; Luke 23:45). By putting a new piece of garment on an old one, the old tears the new {the new makes a tear, a rent} (Luke 5:36). The soldiers agreed not to tear the tunic of Jesus, but to cast lots for it (John 19:24). All other refs.: BREAK <4977>, DIVIDE <4977>, SPLIT <4977>.
– 5 Matt. 5:29; 18:9 → PLUCK <1807> 6 Matt. 9:16; Mark 2:21 → to pull away → PULL <142> 7 Matt. 24:2; Mark 13:2; Luke 21:6 → to tear down → to throw down → THROW (verb) <2647> 8 Mark 1:26; 9:20, 26; Luke 9:39 → CONVULSE <4682> – 9 Mark 9:47 → PLUCK <1544> 10 Luke 12:18 → to tear down → to pull down → PULL <2507> 11 Luke 19:44 → to tear down → to lay even with the ground → GROUND (noun)[1] <1474> 12 Acts 16:22 → to rend off → REND <4048> 13 Acts 21:1 → to tear away → to get away → GET <645> 14 Acts 22:23 → CAST (verb) <4495> 15 Rom. 11:3 → to tear down → to dig down → DIG <2679> 16 Rom. 14:20; 2 Cor. 5:1; Gal. 2:18 → to tear down → DESTROY <2647> 17 2 Cor. 13:10 → tearing down → DESTRUCTION <2506> 18 Gal. 4:15 → to tear out → to pluck out → PLUCK <1846> 19 Phil. 1:23 → PRESS <4912> 20 Phil. 3:18 → with tears → lit.: weeping → WEEP <2799> 21 1 Thes. 2:17 → to tear away → SEPARATE <642>.

TEARING – 2 Cor. 10:8 → tearing down → DESTRUCTION <2506>.

TEDIOUS – ***oknēros*** [adj.: ὀκνηρός <3636>]; **from *okneō*: to delay, or *oknos*: hesitation ▶ Wearisome, tiring** > To write the same things to the Philippians was not tedious {not grievous, not irksome, no trouble} for Paul (Phil. 3:1). Other refs.: Matt. 25:26; Rom. 12:11; see SLOTHFUL <3636>. ¶

TEDIOUS (BE) – ***enkoptō*** [verb: ἐγκόπτω <1465>]; **from *en*: in, and *koptō*: to hit repeatedly, to stop abruptly ▶ To intrude (on the time of someone), to importune** > Tertullus did not want to be any further tedious to {to detain, to weary} Felix (Acts 24:4). Other refs.: Rom. 15:22; 1 Thes. 2:18; 1 Pet. 3:7; Gal. 5:7; see HINDER (verb) <1465>. ¶

TELL – [1] ***anangellō*** [verb: ἀναγγέλλω <312>]; **from *ana*: upon (intens.), and *angellō*: to bring news, a message ▶ To announce, to communicate, to make known; also transl.: to declare, to disclose** > The Messiah would tell {explain} all things (John 4:25). A man told the Jews that Jesus had made him well (John 5:15). Many who had believed came confessing and telling {showing, openly confessing} their deeds (Acts 19:18). All other refs.: see entries in Lexicon at <312>.

[2] ***apangellō*** [verb: ἀπαγγέλλω <518>]; **from *apo*: from (intens.), and *angellō*: to bring news, a message ▶ To *declare*, to publish, to preach; also transl.: to bring word, to take word, to report** > The verb is used concerning the resurrection of Jesus (Matt. 28:8–10; Mark 16:10, 13). Judas and Silas were to tell {confirm} the same things to Antioch as Paul and Barnabas (Acts 15:27). Other ref.: Luke 8:20. All other refs.: DECLARE <518>, RELATE <518>, REPORT (verb) <518>, SHOW (verb) <518>.

[3] ***diasapheō*** [verb: διασαφέω <1285>]; **from *dia*: intens., and *sapheō*: to manifest, which is from *saphēs*: clear ▶ To declare, to explain** > In a parable, servants told {recounted to, reported to} their master about the behavior of a wicked servant (Matt. 18:31). Other refs.: Matt. 13:36; Acts 10:25 in some mss. ¶

[4] ***diēgeomai*** [verb: διηγέομαι <1334>]; **from *dia*: through (intens.), and *hēgeomai*: to relate, to describe ▶ To speak in detail, to describe** > The time would have failed the author of the Epistle to the Hebrews to tell of various O.T. people of faith (Heb. 11:32). All other refs.: RELATE <1334>.

[5] ***eklaleō*** [verb: ἐκλαλέω <1583>]; **from *ek*: out, and *laleō*: to speak ▶ To say, to divulge** > The commander instructed the nephew of Paul to tell {utter to} no one what he had revealed to him (Acts 23:22). ¶

[6] ***epo*** [verb: ἔπω <2036>]: **form of *legō*** [verb: λέγω <3004>] **▶ To talk, to say** > The woman who had been healed by Jesus told Him all the truth (Mark 5:33). Other refs.: SPEAK <3004>.

[7] **to tell before, beforehand, in time past, ahead of time; to foretell: *prolegō*** [verb: προλέγω <4302>]; **from *pro*: before, and *legō*: to say ▶ To declare in advance, to warn, to forewarn; to speak before** > Paul was telling beforehand, as he had told in time past, of evil things practiced by some who would not inherit the kingdom of God (Gal. 5:21a, b). He had told before {told already, forewarned} and testified certain things (1 Thes. 4:6). The verb is transl. "to speak before" {to foretell, to speak long ago} (Acts 1:16). Other refs.: Matt. 24:25; Mark 13:23; 2 Cor. 13:2; 1 Thes. 3:4; 2 Pet. 3:2. ¶

– [8] Matt. 7:23 → to tell plainly → DECLARE <3670> [9] Matt. 13:24, 31 → to set before → SET (verb) <3908> [10] Matt. 14:28; 15:35 → COMMAND (verb) <2753> [11] Matt. 20:31; Mark 10:48; Luke 18:39 → to tell sternly → REBUKE (verb) <2008> [12] Matt. 22:3a → to tell to come → INVITE <2564> [13] Matt. 28:16 → to tell to go → APPOINT <5021> [14] Mark 5:20; Luke 8:39 → PROCLAIM <2784> [15] Mark 8:6 → COMMAND (verb) <3853> [16] Mark 11:6; 13:34 → COMMAND (verb) <1781> [17] Mark 11:33; Luke 20:7; John 3:8; 8:14b; 16:18; 2 Cor. 12:2b, c; Eph. 6:21a → KNOW <1492> [18] Luke 8:55; 17:9, 10 → COMMAND (verb) <1299> [19] Luke 24:35; Acts 10:8; 15:12; 21:19 → RELATE <1834> [20] Acts 5:20; 22:10; 1 Thes. 2:2 → SPEAK <2980> [21] Acts 7:13 → KNOWN (MAKE) <319> [22] Acts 8:34 → please tell me → lit.: I ask you → PRAY <1189> [23] Acts 10:22 → to be told → to be divinely warned → WARN <5537> [24] Acts 11:4 → EXPLAIN <1620> [25] Acts 11:19, 20 → PREACH <2980> [26] Acts 13:41; 15:3 → RELATE <1555> [27] Acts 16:17 → PREACH <2605> [28] Acts 21:21, 24 → to be told → to be informed → INFORM <2727> [29] 1 Cor. 10:28 → SHOW (verb) <3377> [30] 1 Cor. 12:3; Phil. 1:22; Col. 4:7 → KNOW <1107> [31] 1 Cor. 15:50 → SAY <5346> [32] 1 Cor. 16:1 → to tell to do → ORDAIN <1299> [33] 2 Cor. 12:4 → cannot be told → INEXPRESSIBLE <731> [34] 2 Cor. 12:4 → UTTER (verb) <2980> [35] Col. 1:8 → DECLARE <1213> [36] Col. 4:9 → INFORM <1107>.

TEMPER (noun) – 2 Cor. 12:20 → angry temper → WRATH <2372>.

TEMPER (verb) – 1 Cor. 12:24 → to temper together → COMPOSE <4786>.

TEMPERANCE – Acts 24:25; Gal. 5:23; 2 Pet. 1:6a, b → SELF-CONTROL (noun) <1466>.

TEMPERATE – [1] ***enkratēs*** [adj.: ἐγκρατής <1468>]; **from *en*: in, and *kratos*: power, strength ► Continent, self-restrained** > The overseer must be temperate {self-controlled} (Titus 1:8). ¶
[2] ***nēphalios*** [adj.: νηφάλιος <3524>]; **from *nēphō*: to be sober, to refrain from the abuse of wine ► Sober-minded, wise; also transl.: sober, vigilant** > The overseer must be temperate (1 Tim. 3:2), as likewise believing women (1 Tim. 3:11), older men (Titus 2:2). ¶
– [3] 1 Cor. 9:25 → to be temperate → to have control over oneself → CONTROL (noun) <1467> [4] Titus 2:2 → DISCREET <4998>.

TEMPEST – [1] **to be tossed with a tempest: *cheimazō*** [verb: χειμάζω <5492>]; **from *cheima*: bad weather, winter ► To be shaken by a storm** > Paul and the passengers on the boat were being exceedingly tossed with a tempest {were storm-tossed, were tempest-tossed, took a violent battering from the storm} (Acts 27:18). ¶
– [2] Matt. 8:24 → STORM <4578> [3] Acts 27:20 → STORM <5494> [4] Heb. 12:18 → STORM <2366> [5] 2 Pet. 2:17 → STORM <2978>.

TEMPEST-TOSSED (BE) – Acts 27:18 → to be tossed with a tempest → TEMPEST <5492>.

TEMPESTUOUS – ***tuphōnikos*** [adj.: τυφωνικός <5189>]; **from *tuphōn*: hurricane, typhoon ► Like a whirlwind, a hurricane** > A tempestuous wind {violent wind, hurricane, wind of hurricane force}, called Euroclydon, descended violently on the island of Crete (Acts 27:14). ¶

TEMPLE – [1] ***hieron*** [neut. noun: ἱερόν <2411>]; **from *hieros*: holy, sacred ► Building where worship is rendered; courts and sacred building considered as a whole** > Worship in this place may be rendered to God (e.g., Matt. 21:12a, b) or to a pagan divinity (e.g., the temple of Diana in Acts 19:24; see [2]). The temple of God at Jerusalem included the Holy Place wherein was found the table of consecrated bread, the candlestick, and the altar of incense; in the Most Holy Place was found the ark covered by the mercy seat (until the day of the destruction of Solomon's temple; it no longer appears after the rebuilding of the temple). Solomon's temple was destroyed by Nebuchadnezzar, King of Babylon. Rebuilt under Ezra by the order of Cyrus, King of Persia, it was razed by Antiochus. Restored by Judas Maccabee in the year 164 B.C., then enlarged by Herod the Great, it was destroyed once again by the Romans. In all ages, the temple remains the sole and unique physical house of God on earth. Other refs.: Matt. 4:5; 12:5, 6; 21:14, 15, 23; 24:1; 26:55; Mark 11:11, 15, 16, 27; 12:35; 13:1, 3; 14:49; Luke 2:27, 37, 46; 4:9; 18:10; 19:45, 47; 20:1; 21:5, 37, 38; 22:52, 53; 24:53; John 2:14, 15; 5:14; 7:14, 28; 8:2, 20, 59; 10:23; 11:56; 18:20; Acts 2:46; 3:1, 2a, b, 3, 8, 10; 4:1; 5:20, 21, 24, 25, 42; 19:27; 21:26–30; 22:17; 24:6, 12, 18; 25:8; 26:21; 1 Cor. 9:13. ¶
[2] ***naos*** [masc. noun: ναός <3485>]; **from *naiō*: to dwell ► Sanctuary itself within the precinct of the temple grounds, i.e., the holy place where the priests might enter; this holy place also includes the most holy place where the high priest alone might enter once a year** > Jesus speaks of His body as the temple of God (John 2:19, 21). Christians are the temple of God (1 Cor. 3:16), the temple of the Holy Spirit, who dwells in them (1 Cor. 6:19). The temple of God is holy (1 Cor. 3:17b); God shall destroy anyone who corrupts it (v. 17a). The church is the temple of the living God (2 Cor. 6:16b), a holy temple in the Lord (Eph. 2:21). The antichrist shall sit down in the temple of God (2 Thes. 2:4). The term is also used to designate the dwelling of false

gods (Acts 17:24; 19:24). Other refs.: Matt. 23:16a, b, 17, 21, 35; 26:61; 27:5, 40, 51; Mark 14:58; 15:29, 38; Luke 1:9, 21, 22; 23:45; John 2:20; Acts 7:48; 2 Cor. 6:16a; Rev. 3:12; 7:15; 11:1, 2, 19a, b; 14:15, 17; 15:5, 6, 8a, b; 16:1, 17; 21:22a, b. ¶

3 **robber of temples: *hierosulos*** [adj. used as noun: ἱερόσυλος <2417>]; **from *hieron*: temple, and *sulaō*: to spoil, to steal ▶ One who steals the goods of a temple, a sacrilegious person** > The city clerk told the Ephesians that Paul and his companions were not robbers of temples {robbers of churches, temple-plunderers} (Acts 19:37). ¶

– 4 Luke 11:51 → HOUSE <3624> 5 John 11:48 → lit.: place 6 Acts 19:35 → temple guardian, temple keeper, guardian of the temple → GUARDIAN <3511> 7 Rom. 2:22 → to rob temples → to commit sacrilege → SACRILEGE <2416> 8 1 Cor. 9:13 → those employed in temple service → lit.: those ministering about holy things → MINISTER (verb) <2038>.

TEMPLE GUARD – John 7:32, 45 → OFFICER <5257>.

TEMPLE-PLUNDERER – Acts 19:37 → robber of temples → TEMPLE <2417>.

TEMPORAL – 2 Cor. 4:18 → for a time → TIME <4340>.

TEMPORARY – Matt. 13:21; Mark 4:17; 2 Cor. 4:18; Heb. 11:25 → for a time → TIME <4340>.

TEMPT – 1 ***peirazō*** [verb: πειράζω <3985>]; **from *peira*: attempt, trial ▶ To inflict a time of trial, to test, to try** > Jesus was tempted by Satan (Matt. 4:1; Mark 1:13; Luke 4:2). Paul says not to tempt (*ekpeirazō*; see 2) the Christ as some tempted Him (*peirazō*) and were killed by serpents (1 Cor. 10:9). Jesus asked certain Jews why they were tempting Him as to whether or not to pay taxes to Caesar (Matt. 22:18; Mark 12:15 or 16; Luke 20:23). Ananias and Sapphira had agreed together to tempt the Spirit of the Lord (Acts 5:9). It would have been tempting God to impose the ordinances of the law on new Christians (Acts 15:10). Satan might tempt spouses because of their lack of self-control (1 Cor. 7:5). God is faithful, who will not allow Christians to be tempted beyond what we can bear, but with the temptation He will also provide a way out, so that we may stand up under it (1 Cor. 10:13). The Christian should watch himself lest he should be tempted, being overtaken by some fault (Gal. 6:1). Paul feared that the tempter might have tempted the Thessalonians (1 Thes. 3:5). O.T. people of faith were tempted (Heb. 11:37). In that He Himself suffered, being tempted, Christ is able to help those who are being tempted (Heb. 2:18a, b). As High Priest, He is able to sympathize with the infirmities of the Christians, having been tempted in all things as we are, sin apart (Heb. 4:15). The Israelites tempted God, by trying Him, and saw His works for forty years (Heb. 3:9). No one being tempted should say that he is being tempted of God (Jas. 1:13a, b); God cannot be tempted (*apeirastos*: 1:13c; see 3) by evil, and He Himself tempts no one (v. 13d). But every one is tempted, being drawn away and enticed by his own lust (Jas. 1:14). All other refs.: EXAMINE <3985>, TEMPTER <3985>, TEST (noun and verb) <3985>, TRY[1] <3985>.

2 ***ekpeirazō*** [verb: ἐκπειράζω <1598>]; **from *ek*: intens., and *peirazō*: to tempt, to test, which is from *peira*: attempt, trial ▶ See 1.** > The Lord said it was written, You shall not tempt {put to the test} the Lord your God (Matt. 4:7; Luke 4:12). Paul says not to tempt {to test, to try} (*ekpeirazō*) the Christ as some tempted Him (*peirazō*) and were killed by serpents (1 Cor. 10:9). Other ref.: Luke 10:25 → TEST (noun and verb) <1598>. ¶

3 **not tempted: *apeirastos*** [adj.: ἀπείραστος <551>]; **from *a*: neg. neg., and *peirazō*: see 1 ▶ Not affected by the temptation of sin, incapable of being tempted by evil** > God cannot be tempted (lit.: God is not tempted, untempted} by evil (Jas. 1:13c). ¶

– 4 1 Cor. 10:13b → but when you are tempted → lit.: but with the temptation → TEMPTATION <3986>.

TEMPTATION – [1] ***peirasmos*** [masc. noun: πειρασμός <3986>]; **from *peirazō*: to tempt, to test, which is from *peira*: attempt, trial ▶ Test, trial >** The Jews were to pray God that they might not be led into temptation (Matt. 6:13; Luke 11:4); in fact, the injunctions of Jesus in Matthew 5 and 6 are particularly addressed to the disciples (see Matt. 5:1, 2). Jesus told His disciples to pray that they might not enter into temptation (Matt. 26:41; Mark 14:38; Luke 22:40, 46). Having finished every temptation {all this tempting}, the devil withdrew from Jesus (Luke 4:13). Jesus spoke of those who fall away in time of temptation {testing} (Luke 8:13). His disciples stood by Jesus in His temptations (Luke 22:28). No temptation overtakes a Christian except what is common to man, but with the temptation God will also provide a way out so that the Christian may stand up under it (1 Cor. 10:13a, b). The Galatians had not rejected with contempt the temptation {illness} of Paul (Gal. 4:14). Those who desire to become rich fall into temptation (1 Tim. 6:9). The Israelites had experienced the day of temptation {testing} in the desert (Heb. 3:8). The Christian is to consider it pure joy when he faces temptations of various kinds (Jas. 1:2); blessed is the man who endures temptation (v. 12). He is grieved for a short while by various temptations (1 Pet. 1:6); the Lord knows how to deliver godly persons out of temptation (2 Pet. 2:9). God will keep the Christians of Philadelphia out of the hour of trial that will come upon the whole world Rev. 3:10. Other refs.: Acts 20:19; Rev. 3:10; see TRIAL <3986>. ¶
– [2] Matt. 18:7a–c; Luke 17:1 → temptation to sin → STUMBLING BLOCK <4625> [3] 1 Cor. 7:2 → "the temptation to" added in Engl.

TEMPTED – Jas. 1:13c → cannot be tempted → lit.: is not tempted, is untempted → not tempted → TEMPT <551>.

TEMPTER – **to tempt: *peirazō*** [verb: πειράζω <3985>]; **from *peira*: attempt, trial ▶ To examine, to test >** The devil is the tempter (lit.: the one who tempts). After Jesus had fasted forty days, the tempter came up to Him (Matt. 4:3). Paul feared that his work among the Thessalonians might have been rendered useless because of the tempter (1 Thes. 3:5). All other refs.: EXAMINE <3985>, TEMPT <3985>, TEST (noun and verb) <3985>, TRY[1] <3985>.

TEMPTING – Luke 4:13; Heb. 3:8 → TEMPTATION <3986>.

TEN – ***deka*** [card. num.: δέκα <1176>] ▶ This number is used in regard to disciples (Matt. 20:24; Mark 10:41), virgins (Matt. 25:1), talents (Matt. 25:28, silver coins (Luke 15:8), lepers (Luke 17:12, 17), minas {pounds} (Luke 19:13, 16, 24, 25), servants (Luke 19:13), cities (Luke 19:17), days (Acts 25:6; Rev. 2:10), horns (Rev. 12:3; 13:1; 17:3, 7, 12, 16), crowns (Rev. 13:1), and kings (Rev. 17:12). ¶

TEN THOUSAND – [1] ***deka* (ten)** [card. num.: δέκα <1176>] ***chilias* (thousand)** [fem. noun: χιλιάς <5505>] ▶ This number is used in regard to warriors (Luke 14:31). ¶ [2] ***murioi*; plur. of *murios*** [adj.: μυρίος <3463>] ▶ This number is used in regard to talents (Matt. 18:24), instructors in Christ (1 Cor. 4:15), and words in a tongue (1 Cor. 14:19). ¶
– [3] Rev. 5:11; 9:16 → MYRIAD <3461>.

TENANT – Matt. 21:33–35, 38, 40, 41; Mark 12:1, 2, 7, 9; Luke 20:9; 10a, b, 14, 16 → VINEDRESSER <1092>.

TEND – [1] Matt. 8:33; Mark 5:14; Luke 8:34; John 21:15, 17 → FEED <1006> [2] Luke 17:7; John 21:16; 1 Cor. 9:7 → SHEPHERD (verb) <4165> [3] John 21:16 → to tend the sheep → to feed the sheep → SHEEP <4165>.

TENDER – [1] ***hapalos*** [adj.: ἁπαλός <527>] ▶ **Full of sap, soft >** When the fig tree's branch is tender and produces leaves, we know that summer is near (Matt. 24:32; Mark 13:28). ¶
– [2] Luke 1:78; Col. 3:12 → ENTRAILS <4698> [3] Jas. 5:11 → of tender mercy →

MERCIFUL <3629> [4] Jas. 5:11 → full of tender compassion → very compassionate → COMPASSIONATE <4184>.

TENDER-HEARTED – ***eusplanchnos*** [adj.: εὔσπλαγχνος <2155>]; **from *eu*: well, and *splanchnon*: bowel, compassion ▶ Showing compassion, sympathy; also transl.: compassionate** > Paul exhorts Christians to be tender-hearted (Eph. 4:32). Peter also exhorts them to be tenderhearted {kindhearted, pitiful} (1 Pet. 3:8). ¶

TENDERLY – 1 Thes. 2:7 → to tenderly care → CHERISH <2282>.

TENDERNESS – ***splanchnon*** [neut. noun: σπλάγχνον <4698>]; **comp. *splēn*: spleen; lit.: bowel ▶ Affection, kindness** > Paul speaks of the tenderness {affection} and compassion found in Christ (Phil. 2:1). All other refs.: AFFECTION <4698>, ENTRAILS <4698>.

TENT – [1] ***skēnē*** [fem. noun: σκηνή <4633>] ▶ **Portable shelter used particularly by nomads; also transl.: shelter, tabernacle** > Peter wanted to make three tents on the mountain of transfiguration (Matt. 17:4; Mark 9:5; Luke 9:33). Abraham lived in tents with Isaac and Jacob (Heb. 11:9). All other refs.: DWELLING PLACE <4633>, TABERNACLE <4633>.
[2] ***skēnos*** [neut. noun: σκῆνος <4636>] ▶ **Dwelling, equivalent of [1]** > The body of the Christian is compared to a tent that he lays down at his death (2 Cor. 5:1, 4). ¶
[3] ***skēnōma*** [neut. noun: σκήνωμα <4638>]; **from *skēnoō*: see [4] ▶ Equivalent of [1].** > Peter compares his body to a tent {earthly dwelling} that he would lay down at his death (2 Pet. 1:13, 14). Other ref.: Acts 7:46; see TABERNACLE <4638>. ¶
[4] **to spread one's tent: *skēnoō*** [verb: σκηνόω <4637>]; **from *skēnos*: tent, dwelling ▶ To dwell, to reside** > He who sits on the throne will spread His tent over {will spread His tabernacle over, will dwell among} the saints who come out of the great tribulation (Rev. 7:15). All other refs.: DWELL <4637>.
– [5] 2 Cor. 5:2 → "tent" added in Engl.

TENTH – [1] ***dekatos*** [adj.: δέκατος <1182>]; **from *deka*: ten ▶** This word is used in regard to an hour (John 1:39), a part of a city (Rev. 11:13), and one of the foundations of the wall of the heavenly Jerusalem (Rev. 21:20). Other ref.: Acts 19:9 in some mss. ¶
– [2] Matt. 23:23; Luke 11:42; 18:12; Heb. 7:2, 4, 5, 6, 8, 9 → tenth, tenth part, tenth portion, to collect a tenth, to give a tenth → TITHE (noun and verb) <1181>, <1183>, <586>.

TENTMAKER – ***skēnopoios*** [masc. noun: σκηνοποιός <4635>]; **from *skēnē*: tent, and *poieō*: to make ▶ One who fabricates tents** > Aquila and Priscilla were tentmakers by trade, as well as the apostle Paul (Acts 18:3). ¶

TERAH – ***Thara*** [masc. name: Θάρα <2291>]: **loiterer, in Heb.; see Terah in Gen. 11:24–26 ▶ Father of Abraham; also transl.: Thara** > Terah took Abraham and Lot to go to the land of Canaan. He died in Haran. Terah is mentioned in the genealogy of Jesus (Luke 3:34). ¶

TERM – [1] Matt. 5:25 → to come to terms → AGREE <2132> [2] 2 Cor. 11:12 → same terms → lit.: even as (*kathōs*) [3] Heb. 6:16 → END (noun) <4009>.

TERRESTRIAL – 1 Cor. 15:40a, b → EARTHLY <1919>.

TERRIBLE – [1] 2 Tim. 3:1 → DIFFICULT <5467> [2] Heb. 12:21 → FEARFUL <5398>.

TERRIBLY – [1] ***deinōs*** [adv.: δεινῶς <1171>]; **from *deinos*: terrible, which inspires fear ▶ Horribly, sorely** > The servant of a centurion was suffering terribly {dreadfully, fearfully, grievously} (Matt. 8:6). The word is transl. "vehemently" {fiercely, urgently} in Luke 11:53: the scribes and the Pharisees began to press Jesus vehemently, i.e., in a very hostile way. ¶

– [2] Matt. 15:22; 17:15 → SEVERELY <2560> [3] Mark 9:26 → MUCH <4183>.

TERRIFIED – [1] Matt. 17:6, 7; 27:54; Mark 4:41; 6:50; John 6:19 → to be terrified → FEAR (verb) <5399> [2] Mark 9:6 → greatly afraid → AFRAID <1630> [3] Luke 24:5; Rev. 11:13 → AFRAID <1719> [4] Phil. 1:28 → TERRIFY <4426> [5] Rev. 18:10, 15 → lit.: because of the fear → FEAR (noun) <5401>.

TERRIFY – [1] ***ekphobeō*** [verb: ἐκφοβέω <1629>]; **from *ek*: intens., and *phobeō*: to fear; lit.: to frighten away ▶ To frighten much, to fill with terror** > Paul did not want to terrify the Corinthians by his letters (2 Cor. 10:9). ¶
[2] ***ptoeō*** [verb: πτοέω <4422>] ▶ **To fear much, to be scared; also transl.: to frighten** > Jesus says not to be terrified when hearing of wars and tumults (Luke 21:9). The disciples were terrified (*ptoeō*) and frightened (*emphobos*) when Jesus appeared to them after He had risen (Luke 24:37); other mss. have *throeō*: see "to be troubled" under TROUBLE (verb) <2360>. ¶
[3] ***pturō*** [verb: πτύρω <4426>] ▶ **In pass.: to be scared, to dread** > The Philippians were not to be terrified {be alarmed, be frightened} by their adversaries (Phil. 1:28). ¶
– [4] Matt. 14:26; Mark 6:50 → TROUBLE (verb) <5015>.

TERRIFYING – Heb. 10:27, 31; 12:21 → FEARFUL <5398>.

TERRITORY – [1] Matt. 4:13 → REGION <3725> [2] 2 Cor. 10:16 → RULE (noun) <2583>.

TERROR – [1] Luke 21:11 → fearful event → FEARFUL <5400> [2] Luke 21:26; Rom. 13:3; 1 Pet. 3:14; Rev. 11:11 → FEAR (noun) <5401> [3] Acts 10:4 → in terror → AFRAID <1719> [4] 1 Pet. 3:6 → FEAR (noun) <4423>.

TERRORIST – Acts 21:38 → MURDERER <4607>.

TERTIUS – ***Tertios*** [masc. name: Τέρτιος <5060>]: **third, in Lat. ▶ Christian man to whom Paul dictated his letter to the Christians of Rome** > Tertius greets them in the Lord (Rom. 16:22). ¶

TERTULLUS – ***Tertullos*** [masc. name: Τέρτυλλος <5061>]; **dimin. of Tertius: third, in Lat. ▶ Roman orator** > The Jews appealed to Tertullus to accuse Paul before the governor Felix (Acts 24:1, 2). ¶

TEST (noun and verb) – [1] **test: *dokimē*** [fem. noun: δοκιμή <1382>]; **to test: *dokimazō*** [verb: δοκιμάζω <1381>]; **from *dokimos*: approved, tested; comp. *dechomai*: to accept, to receive ▶ a. A test is what acts upon a person to demonstrate the reality of certain qualities; also transl.: proof, trial, to prove, to examine, to try** > These qualities may be obedience (2 Cor. 2:9), liberality (2 Cor. 8:2 {ordeal}), sincerity of love (2 Cor. 8:8), diligence (2 Cor. 8:22), faith (2 Cor. 13:5; Phil. 2:22 {proven character}), hearts (1 Thes. 2:4), and personal life (1 Tim. 3:10). The Christian must test himself before remembering the Lord (1 Cor. 11:28); he must prove his own work (Gal. 6:4); he must test all things (1 Thes. 5:21); he must test the spirits of the prophets (1 John 4:1). He must find out {try to learn} (lit.: test, discern) what is acceptable to the Lord (Eph. 5:10). The fire will test each one's works, of what sort it is (1 Cor. 3:13), at the tribunal of Christ so the works will be approved or disapproved. **b. To try** > A man was going to test the oxen he had bought and asked to be excused from the great supper (Luke 14:19). Other refs.: Heb. 3:9; see [2]; 1 Pet. 1:7. All other refs. (*dokimē*): see EXPERIENCE (noun) <1382>, PROOF <1382>. All other refs. (*dokimazō*): see APPROVE <1381>, DISCERN <1381>, LIKE (verb) <1381>.
[2] **to test: *peirazō*** [verb: πειράζω <3985>]; **from *peira*: experience, trial ▶ To tempt; to prove, to examine; also transl.: to try, to put to the test** > On many occasions, Jesus was tested by demands and questions from the Pharisees and the Sadducees; they were seeking to find fault in him (Matt. 16:1;

19:3; 22:35; Mark 8:11; 10:2; Luke 11:16; John 8:6). The Israelites tried {tempted, tested} (*peirazō*) God by testing (*dokimazō*) Him in the desert (Heb. 3:9). When he was tested, Abraham offered up Isaac (Heb. 11:17). Jesus tested the faith of Philip (John 6:6). Ephesus had tested those who said they were apostles (Rev. 2:2). Some in Smyrna would be tested by being thrown into prison (Rev. 2:10). All other refs.: EXAMINE <3985>, TEMPT <3985>, TEMPTER <3985>, TRY[1] <3985>.

[3] **to test, to put to the test: *ekpeirazō*** [verb: ἐκπειράζω <1598>]**; from *ek*: intens., and *peirazō*: see** [2] **▶ To tempt, to prove** > A certain lawyer tested Jesus (Luke 10:25). Other refs.: Matt. 4:7; Luke 4:12; 1 Cor. 10:9 → TEMPT <1598>. ¶

– [4] Acts 20:19; 1 Pet. 4:12 → TRIAL <3986> [5] Rom. 16:10; 2 Cor. 13:7; Jas. 1:12 → to stand the test → lit.: to be approved → APPROVE <1384> [6] 2 Cor. 13:5–7 → you fail the test → lit.: you are worthless → WORTHLESS <96>.

TESTAMENT – ***diathēkē*** [fem. noun: διαθήκη <1242>]**; from *diatithēmi*: to place in a particular order, which is from *dia*: intens., and *tithēmi*: to place, to set ▶ Last wishes of a person, disposition in view of the death of a person** > A testament {covenant, will} is not valid unless the death of the testator occurs (Heb. 9:16, 17). All other refs.: COVENANT (noun) <1242>.

TESTATOR – ***diathemenos*; from *diatithemai*** [verb: διατίθεμαι <1303>]**: to arrange, to dispose, which is from *dia*: intens., and *tithēmi*: to place; lit.: one who disposes ▶ One who makes a testament, expressing his last will** > Where there is a testament, the death of the testator must of necessity come in (Heb. 9:16); a testament never takes effect while the testator is alive (v. 17). All other refs.: APPOINT <1303>, MAKE <1303>.

TESTIFY – [1] ***martureō*** [verb: μαρτυρέω <3140>]**; from *martus*: witness, a person bearing witness ▶ To report on that which one had seen or heard, to declare something** > John had seen and testified that the Father has sent the Son as Savior of the world (1 John 4:14). Other ref.: Acts 22:5. All other refs.: WITNESS (noun)[1] <3140>, WITNESS (noun)[2] <3140>, WITNESS (verb) <3140>.

[2] ***epimartureō*** [verb: ἐπιμαρτυρέω <1957>]**; from *epi*: upon (intens.), and *martureō*: see** [1] **▶ To attest, to affirm** > Peter testifies that the grace in which the Christians stand is the true grace of God (1 Pet. 5:12). ¶

[3] **to testify against: *katamartureō*** [verb: καταμαρτυρέω <2649>]**; from *kata*: against, and *martureō*: see** [1] **▶ To assert something against someone, to accuse; also transl.: to bear witness against, to bring against, to bring testimony against, to witness against** > Jesus answered nothing to those who testified against Him (Matt. 26:62; 27:13; Mark 14:60; 15:4). ¶

[4] ***marturomai*** [verb: μαρτύρομαι <3143>]**; from *martus*: see** [1] **▶ To solemnly declare before someone; to affirm, to attest** > Paul testified to the elders of Ephesus that he was innocent from the blood of all (Acts 20:26 {to declare, to take to record, to witness}). Paul testified {declared, witnessed} again to every man who is circumcised that he is a debtor to do the whole law (i.e., he has to obey the whole law) (Gal. 5:3). Paul testified in the Lord that the Ephesians should no longer walk as the rest of the nations walk, in the vanity of their minds (Eph. 4:17 {to affirm, to insist}). ¶

[5] **to testify, to testify solemnly: *diamarturomai*** [verb: διαμαρτύρομαι <1263>]**; from *dia*: intens., and *marturomai*: see** [4] **▶ a. To warn, to bear witness solemnly; to confirm; also transl.: to solemnly warn** > The rich man in hell wanted Abraham to testify to his brothers that they might not come to that place of torment (Luke 16:28). Peter testified and exhorted the people to be saved from their perverse generation (Acts 2:40). Peter and John testified in Samaria (Acts 8:25). Paul testified to the Jews that Jesus was the Christ (Acts 18:5). The Holy Spirit testified that bonds and tribulations awaited Paul (Acts 20:23 {to warn, to witness}). Paul had received the service of

the Lord Jesus to testify of the gospel of the grace of God (Acts 20:24). As Paul had testified (*diamarturomai*) the things concerning Jesus at Jerusalem, so he would bear witness (*martureō*) at Rome (Acts 23:11). He testified at Rome of the kingdom of God (Acts 28:23). Other ref.: Heb. 2:6. **b. To attest, to affirm** > Jesus had commanded to testify that it is He who was appointed of God to be Judge of the living and the dead (Acts 10:42). Paul had solemnly testified of {had declared} repentance toward God and faith in the Lord Jesus Christ (Acts 20:21). He testified {solemnly warned} that the Lord is the avenger of sinful conduct, such as a man defrauding his brother (1 Thes. 4:6). All other refs.: CHARGE (verb) <1263>.

6 **to testify before, to testify beforehand: *promarturomai*** [verb: προμαρτύρομαι <4303>]**; from *pro*: before, and *marturomai*: see 4 ► To affirm beforehand, to predict** > The Spirit of Christ, which was in the prophets, testified before of the sufferings which belonged to Christ and the glories that would follow (1 Pet. 1:11). ¶

– 7 Matt. 24:14; 2 Cor. 1:12; 1 Tim. 2:6; 2 Tim. 1:8; Heb. 3:5; Jas. 5:3 → WITNESS (noun)[1] <3142> 8 Mark 14:56 → to testify falsely → to bear false witness → WITNESS (noun)[1] <5576> 9 Acts 2:40 → to solemnly testify → EXHORT <3870> 10 Rom. 8:16; 9:1; Rev. 22:18 → to bear witness → WITNESS (noun)[1] <4828> 11 Heb. 2:4 → to bear witness with → WITNESS (noun)[1] <4901>.

TESTIMONY – 1 **false testimony: *pseudomarturia*** [fem. noun: ψευδομαρτυρία <5577>]**; from *pseudēs*: false, and *marturia*: testimony, which is from *martus*: witness ► Untrue report or declaration of what one has seen or heard** > False testimony and other evils come forth out of the heart (Matt. 15:19 {false witness, false witnessings}). The leaders sought false testimony {false witness} against Jesus (Matt. 26:59). ¶

– 2 Matt. 8:4; 10:18; 24:14; Mark 1:44; 6:11; Luke 5:14; 9:5; 21:13; Acts 7:44; 1 Cor. 1:6; 2:1; 2 Thes. 1:10; 1 Tim. 2:6; Heb. 3:5; Rev. 15:5 → WITNESS (noun)[1] <3142> 3 Matt. 26:62; 27:13; Mark 14:60 → to bring testimony against → to testify against → TESTIFY <2649> 4 Mark 14:55, 56, 59; Luke 22:71; John 1:19; 3:11b, 32b, 33; 5:31b, 32b, 34, 36a; 8:13, 14, 17; 19:35b; 21:24b; Acts 22:18; 1 Tim. 3:7; Titus 1:13; 1 John 5:9a–c, 10a, b, 11; 3 John 12c; Rev. 1:2b, 9; 6:9; 11:7; 12:11, 17; 19:10a, b; 20:4 → WITNESS (noun)[1] <3141> 5 Mark 14:56, 57 → to give false testimony → to bear false witness → WITNESS (noun)[1] <5576> 6 Acts 14:17 → without testimony → without witness → WITNESS (noun)[1] <267> 7 1 Tim. 6:13 → who in His testimony made the good confession → lit.: the One having witnessed the good confession → WITNESS (verb) <3140>.

TESTING – 1 ***dokimasia*** [fem. noun: δοκιμασία <1381a>]**; from *dokimazō*: to test, which is from *dokimos*: approved; comp. *dechomai*: to accept, to receive ► Evaluation to determine if something is according to expectation** > The Israelites tried God by a testing in the desert (Heb. 3:9 in some mss.). ¶

2 ***dokimion*** [neut. noun: δοκίμιον <1383>]**; from *dokimos*: see 1 ► What acts upon a person to demonstrate the reality of something; the word was used concerning metals that were without alloy** > The testing {proving, trying} of the faith of Christians produces patience (Jas. 1:3). Peter speaks of the testing {genuineness, proof, proving, trial, greater worth} of their faith, which is more precious than gold (1 Pet. 1:7). ¶

– 3 Luke 8:13; Heb. 3:8; Rev. 3:10 → TEMPTATION <3986> 4 Acts 20:19; 1 Pet. 4:12; Rev. 3:10 → TRIAL <3986> 5 Rom. 12:2 → to discern by testing → DISCERN <1381>.

TETRARCH – 1 ***tetrarchēs*** [masc. noun: τετράρχης <5076>]**; from *tetra*: four, and *archō*: to rule, which is from *archē*: beginning, authority, rule; also spelled: *tetraarchēs* ► Governor of the fourth part of a country; this title also designated a governor subordinated to an ethnarch or**

a king > Herod was a tetrarch (Matt. 14:1; Luke 3:19; 9:7; Acts 13:1). ¶

[2] **to rule as tetrarch:** ***tetrarcheō*** [verb: τετραρχέω <5075>]; **from** ***tetrarchēs*: see** [1] ▶ **Who rules as tetrarch; also spelled:** ***tetraarcheō*** > Luke mentions the names of three tetrarchs (lit.: who rule as tetrarchs): Herod, Philip, and Lysanias (Luke 3:1a–c). ¶

THADDAEUS – ***Thaddaios*** [masc. name: Θαδδαῖος <2280>] ▶ **One of the twelve apostles of Jesus** > Thaddaeus was the surname of Lebbaeus and was the brother of James (Matt. 10:3). This is prob. Jude, author of the epistle of the same name (Mark 3:18; see Acts 1:13). ¶

THAN – ***ēper*** [adv.: ἤπερ <2260>]; **from** ***ē*: or, and** ***per*:** **truly (intens.)** ▶ Ref.: John 12:43. ¶ ‡

THANK (noun) – Luke 6:32–34 → CREDIT <5485>.

THANK (verb) – [1] ***exomologeō*** [verb: ἐξομολογέω <1843>]; **from** ***ek*:** **out, and** ***homologeō*:** **to agree, to acknowledge, which is from** ***homologos*:** **assenting, which is from** ***homos*:** **same, and** ***legō*:** **to say** ▶ **To acknowledge with praise, to celebrate** > Jesus said: I thank {praise} you, Father (Matt. 11:25; Luke 10:21). All other refs.: CONFESS <1843>, PROMISE (verb) <1843>.

– [2] Luke 18:11; John 11:41; Acts 28:15; Rom. 1:8; 7:25; et al. → to give thanks → THANKS <2168> [3] 2 Tim. 1:3 → to be thankful → THANKFUL <5485> <2192>.

THANKFUL – [1] ***eucharistos*** [adj.: εὐχάριστος <2170>]; **from** ***eu*:** **well, and** ***charizomai*:** **to grant, to give, which is from** ***charis*:** **grace, which is from** ***chairō*:** **to rejoice** ▶ **Acknowledging, expressing one's appreciation for what is done on one's behalf** > Paul exhorted the Colossians to be thankful (Col. 3:15). ¶

[2] **to be thankful; lit.: to give grace; grace:** ***charis*** [fem. noun: χάρις <5485>]; **to give:** ***echō*** [verb: ἔχω <2192>] ▶ **To express one's appreciation, to thank** > Paul was thankful to God as he had remembrance of Timothy (2 Tim. 1:3). Other refs.: see entries in Lexicon at <5485>.

THANKFULNESS – [1] ***eucharistia*** [fem. noun: εὐχαριστία <2169>]; **from** ***eucharistos*:** **grateful, which is from** ***eu*:** **well, and** ***charizomai*:** **to grant, to give, which is from** ***charis*:** **grace, which is from** ***chairō*:** **to rejoice** ▶ **Gratitude, thanksgiving** > Tertullus received the measures executed by Felix in regard to Israel with all thankfulness (Acts 24:3). All other refs.: THANKSGIVING <2169>.

– [2] Phm. 7 → JOY (noun) <5485>.

THANKS – [1] **to give thanks:** ***anthomologeomai*** [verb: ἀνθομολογέομαι <437>]; **from** ***anti*:** **in turn, and** ***homologeō*:** **to acknowledge, which is from** ***homologos*:** **assenting, which is from** ***homos*:** **same, and** ***legō*:** **to say; lit.: to acknowledge in turn** ▶ **To respond in praise, to celebrate in praise with thanksgivings** > Anna the prophetess gave thanks {gave praise} to the Lord in the temple (Luke 2:38). ¶

[2] **to give thanks:** ***eucharisteō*** [verb: εὐχαριστέω <2168>]; **from** ***eucharistos*:** **grateful, which is from** ***eu*:** **well, and** ***charizomai*:** **to give, which is from** ***charis*:** **grace, which is from** ***chairō*:** **to rejoice**▶ **To express gratitude** > This verb is used in regard to the Lord Jesus (Matt. 15:36; 26:27; Mark 8:6; 14:23; Luke 22:17, 19; John 6:11, 23; 11:41; 1 Cor. 11:24), a Pharisee (Luke 18:11), and a leper healed by Jesus (Luke 17:16). It is used by Paul in his epistles (Rom. 1:8, 21; 7:25; 14:6; 16:4; 1 Cor. 1:4, 14; 10:30; 14:17, 18; 2 Cor. 1:11; Eph. 1:16; 5:20; Phil. 1:3; Col. 1:3; 3:17; 1 Thes. 1:2; 2:13; 5:18; 2 Thes. 1:3; 2:13; Phm. 4). Other refs.: Acts 27:35; 28:15; Col. 1:12; Rev. 11:17. ¶

– [3] Matt. 14:19; 26:26; Mark 6:41; 8:7; 14:22; Luke 9:16; 24:30; 1 Cor. 10:16 → BLESS <2127> [4] 1 Cor. 14:16; 2 Cor. 4:15; et al. → giving of thanks → THANKSGIVING <2169> [5] Heb. 13:15 → CONFESS <3670>.

THANKSGIVING – 1 ***eucharistia*** [fem. noun: εὐχαριστία <2169>]; **from *eucharistos*: thankful, which is from *eu*: well, and *charizomai*: to give freely, which is from *charis*: grace, which is from *chairō*: to rejoice ► Prayer of gratitude; also transl.: giving of thanks** > Paul speaks of saying amen at someone's thanksgiving (1 Cor. 14:16). Grace causes thanksgiving to abound to the glory of God (2 Cor. 4:15). Paul's service produced thanksgiving to God (2 Cor. 9:11, 12). Thanksgiving is becoming for the saints (Eph. 5:4). Thanksgiving can accompany the prayers and supplications of Christians (Phil. 4:6; Col. 4:2) and the walk of faith (Col. 2:7). Paul rendered thanksgiving to God for the Thessalonians (1 Thes. 3:9). He exhorted them to make thanksgivings for all men (1 Tim. 2:1). God has created foods to be taken with thanksgiving (1 Tim. 4:3, 4). The living creatures shall give thanksgiving to Him who is seated on the throne (Rev. 4:9; 7:12). Other ref.: Acts 24:3; see THANKFULNESS <2169>. ¶
– 2 1 Cor. 10:16 → BLESSING <2129>.

THANKWORTHY – 1 Pet. 2:19 → grace → ACCEPTABLE <5485>.

THARA – Luke 3:34 → TERAH <2291>.

THAT – 1 ***hoti*** [conj.: ὅτι <3754>] ► Refs.: John 3:19; Rom. 2:3; 2 Cor. 5:14; Rev. 2:4, 6. *
2 ***hōste*** [conj.: ὥστε <5620>] ► **So as to, with the design that** > The word is found in Matt. 24:24 {to, so as}; Luke 4:29 {in order to, so that} in some mss.; 1 Cor. 13:2 {so that, so as}. *

THAT ONE THERE – ***ekeínos*** [pron.: ἐκεῖνος <1565>]; **from *ekei*: there** ► This pron. usually refers to the person or the thing more remote or absent. * ‡

THEATER – ***theatron*** [neut. noun: θέατρον <2302>]; **from *theaomai*: to behold ► Public building used for theatrical performances, public speeches, public meetings; theaters were open air structures** > The theater at Ephesus (Acts 19:29, 31) could accommodate up to 24,500 spectators. Other ref.: 1 Cor. 4:9; see SPECTACLE <2302>. ¶

THEATRE – See THEATER <2302>.

THEE, THOU – ***se*** [sing. pron.: σέ <4571>] ► Archaic form of "you." *

THEFT – 1 ***klemma*** [neut. noun: κλέμμα <2809>]; **from *kleptō*: to steal (by fraud and in secret) ► The act of stealing, larceny** > In a time yet future, men will not repent of their thefts (Rev. 9:21). Other ref.: Mark 7:22 in some mss. ¶
2 ***klopē*** [fem. noun: κλοπή <2829>]; **from *kleptō*: to steal ► The act of taking something from another without his consent** > Thefts come out of the heart of man (Matt. 15:19; Mark 7:21 or 22). ¶

THEN – 1 ***eita*** [adv.: εἶτα <1534>]; **from *ei*: if, and *mē*: not, and *ti*: some ► Adv. of time or order** > Refs.: Mark 4:17, 28 (*eiten* in some mss.); 8:25; Luke 8:12; John 13:5; 19:27; 20:27; 1 Cor. 2:28; 15:5, 7, 24; 1 Tim. 2:13; 3:10; Heb. 12:9; Jas. 1:15. ¶ ‡
2 ***oukoun*** [adv.: οὐκοῦν <3766>]; **from *ouk*: no, not, and *oun*: certainly** ► Ref.: John 18:37. ¶
3 ***oun*** [conj.: οὖν <3767>] ► Also transl.: accordingly, thereupon, now, certainly. Refs.: Luke 6:9; John 12:1, 9; 18:11, 16; 19:29; 21:5; Rom. 11:1, 11; 15:17. *
4 ***tote*** [adv.: τότε <5119>]. *
5 See THEREUPON <1899>.

THEOPHILUS – ***Theophilos*** [masc. name: Θεόφιλος <2321>]: **friend of God ► Man to whom Luke addresses his Gospel and the book of Acts** > Luke calls him "most excellent Theophilus" in his Gospel (Luke 1:3). He simply calls him by his name in the Acts (Acts 1:1). ¶

THERE – 1 ***ekei*** [adv.: ἐκεῖ <1563>] ► **At that place** > If Paul was to journey to Spain, he hoped to be helped by the Christians in Rome on his way there {thither, thitherward} (Rom. 15:24). *

2 ***ekeíse*** [adv.: ἐκεῖσε <1566>]; **from *ekei*: there, and *sea*: suffix denoting at a place ▶ To that place >** Refs.: Acts 21:3; 22:5. ¶ ‡
3 See HERE <847>.

THERE IS – ***eni*** [verb: ἔνι <1762>]; **contraction of *enesti*: there is ▶** Refs.: Gal. 3:28; Col. 3:11; Jas. 1:17. ¶ ‡

THEREFORE – 1 ***toinun*** [particle: τοίνυν <5106>] ▶ Refs.: Luke 20:25; 1 Cor. 9:26; Heb. 13:13; Jas. 2:24. ¶
2 See WHEREFORE <1352>.
– 3 Rom. 4:16; Phm. 15 → for this reason → REASON (noun) <1223> <5124>.

THEREUPON – ***epeita*** [adv.: ἔπειτα <1899>]; **from *epi*: upon, and *eita*: then, a particle of abundance or emphasis ▶ Adv. of time and order; also transl.: afterwards, next, then >** Refs.: Mark 7:5; Luke 16:7; John 11:7; 1 Cor. 12:28; 15:6, 7, 23, 46; Gal. 1:18, 21; 2:1; 1 Thes. 4:17; Heb. 7:2, 27; Jas. 3:17; 4:14. ¶ ‡

THESE – ***toutois*** [pron.: τούτοις <5125>]. *

THESE ONES – ***tautais*** [pron.: ταύταις <5025>]. *

THESE PERSONS – ***toutous*** [pron.: τούτους <5128>]. *

THESE THINGS – 1 ***tauta*** [pron.: ταῦτα <5023>]. *
2 ***tauta*** [ταὐτά <5024>] ▶ Refs.: Luke 6:23, 26; 17:30; 1 Thes. 2:14. ¶

THESSALONIAN – ***Thessalonikeus*** [masc. name: Θεσσαλονικεύς <2331>] **▶ Inhabitant of the city of Thessalonica in Macedonia; also transl.: from Thessalonica >** Two Thessalonians, Aristarchus and Secundus, accompanied Paul to Asia (Acts 20:4). Aristarchus was a Macedonian of Thessalonica (Acts 27:2). Paul addresses two letters to the Christians of the church of Thessalonica (1 Thes. 1:1; 2 Thes. 1:1). ¶

THESSALONICA – 1 ***Thessalonikē*** [fem. name: Θεσσαλονίκη <2332>] **▶ City in northern Greece, which was the most populous at the time of the apostle Paul; it was named in honor of Thessalonica, the sister of Alexander the Great >** It was one of the starting points for preaching the gospel in Europe (Acts 17:1, 11, 13). The Philippians had sent a gift to Paul during his stay at Thessalonica (Phil. 4:16). At the end of his life, Paul would say that Demas had abandoned him and had gone to Thessalonica (2 Tim. 4:10). Paul wrote two letters to the Thessalonians (see 1 Thes. 1:1; 2 Thes. 1:1). ¶
– 2 Acts 20:4; 27:2 → from Thessalonica → THESSALONIAN <2331>.

THEUDAS – ***Theudas*** [masc. name: Θευδᾶς <2333>]: **thanksgiving ▶ Israelite man >** Theudas stirred up four hundred men in order to achieve his ambitions; he was slain, and those who followed him were dispersed (Acts 5:36). ¶

THICK, THICKLY – Luke 11:29 → to gather thick together → GATHER <1865>.

THIEF – 1 ***kleptēs*** [masc. noun: κλέπτης <2812>]; **from *kleptō*: to steal ▶ One who commits theft, who steals >** Thieves dig through and steal treasures on earth (Matt. 6:19), but not in heaven (Matt. 6:20; Luke 12:33). If the owner of the house had known at what time of night the thief was coming, he would have kept watch (Matt. 24:43; Luke 12:39). Jesus speaks of the thief of the sheep in John 10:1, 8, 10. Judas was a thief (John 12:6). Thieves will not inherit the kingdom of God (1 Cor. 6:10). The day of the Lord shall come as a thief (1 Thes. 5:2: thief in the night; 2 Pet. 3:10; Rev. 16:15); Christians are not in darkness, that this day should surprise them like a thief (1 Thes. 5:4). No Christian is to suffer as a thief (1 Pet. 4:15). If Sardis should fail to watch, the Lord will come upon her as a thief (Rev. 3:3). ¶
– 2 Matt. 21:13; 26:55; 27:38, 44; Mark 11:17; 14:48; 15:27; Luke 10:30, 36; 19:46; 22:52 → ROBBER <3027> 3 Eph. 4:28 → he who has been stealing → STEAL <2813>.

THIGH – ***mēros*** [masc. noun: μηρός <3382>] ▶ **Part of the leg between the knee and the hip** > He who was sitting on the white horse had a name written on his thigh: King of kings and Lord of lords (Rev. 19:16). ¶

THINE – ***sos*** [sing. pron.: σός <4674>]; **from *su*: thou, you** ▶ Archaic form of "your," "yours." Refs.: Matt. 7:3, 22; 13:27. *

THING – **1** ***pragma*** [neut. noun: πρᾶγμα <4229>]; **from *prassō*: to do, to execute ▶ Matter, action** > The thing {deed} Ananias wanted to do was equivalent to lying to God (Acts 5:4). All other refs.: BUSINESS <4229>, MATTER <4229>, WORK (noun) <4229>.

– **2** Matt. 7:18a; Luke 1:53; 16:25; Gal. 6:6; Eph. 6:8; Phm. 6; Heb. 9:11; 10:1 → good thing → GOOD (adj. and noun) <18> **3** Luke 12:15; Acts 4:32 → things one possesses → GOOD (adj. and noun) <5224> **4** Acts 10:16 → lit.: object → VESSEL[1] <4632> **5** Rom. 15:27; 1 Cor. 9:11 → spiritual things → SPIRITUAL <4152> **6** 1 Cor. 9:11 → carnal things, material things → CARNAL <4559> **7** 2 Cor. 10:5 → high thing, lofty thing → HEIGHT <5313> **8** 2 Cor. 12:4 → unspeakable things; (lit.: unspeakable words) → WORD <4487> **9** Gal. 4:18b → good thing → GOOD (adj. and noun) <2570> **10** Heb. 4:13 → creation → CREATURE <2937> **11** Jas. 3:7 → thing in the sea → SEA <1724>.

THING COMMITTED – ***parakatathēkē*** [fem. noun: παρακαταθήκη <3872>]; **from *para*: near, and *katatithēmi*: to deposit, which is from *kata*: down, and *tithēmi*: to put ▶ What is entrusted to someone; also transl.: entrusted deposit, entrusted treasure, what has been entrusted, what was committed to the trust** > Paul exhorts Timothy by the Holy Spirit to keep that good thing committed to him (1 Tim. 6:20; 2 Tim. 1:14 in some mss.), i.e., the teaching he had transmitted to him. ¶

THINGS WITHIN – ***tá enonta*; lit.: things which are within; to be within: *eneimi*** [verb.: ἔνειμι <1751>]; **from *en*: in, and *eimi*: to be ▶ Things which are in the human heart** > Ref.: Luke 11:41. ¶ ‡

THINK – **1** **to think it good, well, wise: *axioō*** [verb: ἀξιόω <515>]; **from *axios*: worthy ▶ To consider appropriate, suitable** > Paul thought it not well to take {insisted not to take, kept insisting not to take} Mark with himself and Barnabas (Acts 15:38). All other refs.: DESIRE (verb) <515>, WORTHY <515>.

2 ***dokeō*** [verb: δοκέω <1380>] ▶ **a. To believe, to consider, to suppose; describes judging subjectively based on reflection on facts in relation to oneself; also transl.: to be the opinion, to seem** > This verb is used when Jesus was questioning Simon (Matt. 17:25), the disciples (18:12), the chief priests and the elders of the people (21:28), the Pharisees (22:42), and a doctor of the law (Luke 10:36). It is also used by the Pharisees when they sent people to question Jesus (Matt. 22:17), the high priest in addressing the scribes and elders assembled against Jesus (Matt. 26:66), those seeking Jesus in speaking among themselves (John 11:56), as well as the Athenian philosophers concerning that which Paul announced as doctrine (Acts 17:18). The Jews thought they had eternal life in the Scriptures (John 5:39). Peter thought he was seeing a vision when the angel made him leave the prison (Acts 12:9). We find the Greek verb, transl. by the expr. "it seemed good," applied to the apostles, the elders, and the church at Jerusalem (Acts 15:25 {to agree}; as likewise in Acts 15:22 {to decide, to please}), to all the latter in association with the Holy Spirit (Acts 15:28), as well as to Luke (Luke 1:3 {to seem fitting}). The verb is also used concerning the remarks presented by Festus before Agrippa (Acts 25:27). Paul thought he also had the Spirit of God (1 Cor. 7:40). He who thinks he stands should take heed lest he fall (1 Cor. 10:12). We bestow greater honor on those members of the body that we think {esteem, deem} to be less honorable (1 Cor. 12:23). No chastening, at the time, seems to be a matter of joy, but of grief; yet afterwards, it yields the peaceful fruit of righteousness to those exercised by it (Heb. 12:11). **b. To seem good, to consider best >** Those who are of the nations think they will be heard because of their many words (Matt. 6:7). If anyone else thought {had a mind that} he could have confidence in the flesh, Paul could do so far more (Phil. 3:4). Human fathers disciplined for a short time, as they thought best (Heb. 12:10). **c. To realize, to allege; also transl.: to consider, to expect, to suppose >** The verb is used in relation to Jesus (Matt. 3:9; 24:44; 26:53; Luke 12:40, 51; 17:9 {to judge, to trow}; John 5:45; 11:13), Paul (Acts 26:9 {to be convinced}; 1 Cor. 4:9 {to seem}; 8:2; 14:37; 2 Cor. 11:16; 12:19; Gal. 6:3 {to repute}; Heb. 10:29), and James (Jas. 1:26; 4:5). It is also used in regard to the disciples (Luke 19:11; John 13:29; 16:2). Other refs.: John 20:15; Acts 27:13. All other refs.: CONSIDER <1380>, REGARD (verb) <1380>, REPUTATION <1380>, SEEM <1380>, SUPPOSE <1380>.

3 **to think good, to think best: *eudokeō*** [verb: εὐδοκέω <2106>]; **from *eu*: well, and *dokeō*: see 2 ► To judge good, to be ready >** Macedonia and Achaia had thought good {had been well pleased} to make a contribution for the poor among the saints in Jerusalem (Rom. 15:26). Paul had thought good to be left alone in Athens (1 Thes. 3:1). All other refs.: PLEASED (BE) <2106>.

4 ***enthumeomai*** [verb: ἐνθυμέομαι <1760>]; **from *en*: in, and *thumos*: intimate thoughts, heart ► To meditate, to reflect; also transl.: to consider, to ponder >** Joseph thought about the things that concerned Mary (Matt. 1:20). Jesus asked some scribes why they were thinking {entertaining} evil things in their hearts after He had forgiven the sins of a paralytic (Matt. 9:4). Peter thought about the vision (Acts 10:19). ¶

5 ***epiballō*** [verb: ἐπιβάλλω <1911>]; **from *epi*: upon, and *ballō*: to throw; lit.: to throw (one's spirit) on ► To reflect, to ponder; also transl.: to break down, to rush out, to begin >** When he thought about the fact he had denied the Lord, Peter wept (Mark 14:72). All other refs.: BEAT <1911>, FALL (verb) <1911>, LAY <1911>, PUT <1911>.

6 ***hēgeomai*** [verb: ἡγέομαι <2233>]; **from *agō*: to lead ► To consider, to believe; denotes judging objectively, deliberately, and carefully based on consideration of facts >** Paul thought {counted} himself happy to answer for himself before Agrippa (Acts 26:2). Other refs.: 2 Cor. 9:5; 2 Pet. 1:13 {to account}. All other refs.: see entries in Lexicon at <2233>.

7 ***logizomai*** [verb: λογίζομαι <3049>]; **from *logos*: word, intelligence ► To esteem, to judge; also transl.: to account, to consider, to count, to regard, to suppose; this verb relates to reality and fact, as distinguished from supposition or opinion >** Paul used this verb (Rom. 2:3; 1 Cor. 4:1; 2 Cor. 3:5; 10:2a {to expect, to intend, to propose}, b, 7; Phil. 3:13) and Peter (1 Pet. 5:12). All other refs.: see entries in Lexicon at <3049>.

8 ***noeō*** [verb: νοέω <3539>]; **from *nous*: mind, understanding ► To perceive with the spirit, to comprehend >** God is able to do far above all that we ask or think {imagine} (Eph. 3:20). All other refs.: CONSIDER <3539>, PERCEIVE <3539>, UNDERSTAND <3539>.

9 ***nomizō*** [verb: νομίζω <3543>]; **from *nomos*: law, manner of behavior, custom ► To consider, to suppose; denotes judging objectively based on consideration of facts >** This verb is used in relation to Jesus (Matt. 5:17; 10:34), Peter (Acts 8:20), and Paul (Acts 17:29). All other refs.: CUSTOM[1] <3543>, SUPPOSE <3543>.

10 ***oiomai*** [verb: οἴομαι <3633>] **► To suppose, to believe; describes judging subjectively based on feelings when viewing facts in relation to oneself >** The apostle John used this verb (John 21:25), as did James (Jas. 1:7). Other ref.: Phil. 1:16 or 17; see SUPPOSE <3633>. ¶

11 ***phainō*** [verb: φαίνω <5316>]; **from *phōs*: light ► To appear, to think according to the judgment or opinion of someone >** This verb is used in regard to the high priest in Mark 14:64 and to the women who returned from the tomb of Jesus (Luke 24:11). All other refs.: APPEAR <5316>.

[12] ***phroneō*** [verb and verb used as noun: φρονέω <5426>]; **from *phrēn*: mind, understanding ▶ a. To exercise the understanding or the mind** > Every one should think so as to be wise (Rom. 12:3). The Corinthians were to learn not to think above {to exceed, to go beyond} what is written (1 Cor. 4:6). The Philippians had revived their thinking of {care of, care for, concern for} Paul, though surely they did think of him (Phil. 4:10a, b). Other refs.: 1 Cor. 13:11 {to understand, to feel}; Phil. 1:7 {to feel}; 2:2 {to think one thing}. **b. To have an understanding, to have an opinion; also transl.: to be one's views, to be of the (same) mind, to be like-minded, to have the attitude** > Paul was asked what he thought concerning Christianity (Acts 28:22). We should have the same mind (or: view) one for another; not minding high things, but associating with the humble (Rom. 12:16 {to have the same respect}). Paul prayed that the God of patience and encouragement might give the Christians at Rome to be of the same mind {a spirit of unity} according to Christ Jesus (Rom. 15:5). He told the Corinthians to be of one mind among themselves (2 Cor. 13:11). He also uses this verb with the Galatians (Gal. 5:10) and the Philippians (Phil. 3:15a, b, 16). The verb is transl. "to observe," "to regard" in Rom. 14:6. All other refs.: MIND (noun) <5426>, MIND (verb) <5426>.

[13] **to think so as to be wise, soberly, as to have sound judgment, with sober judgment: *sōphroneō*** [verb: σωφρονέω <4993>]; **from *sōphrōn*: sober-minded, which is from *sōs*: sober, and *phroneō*: see [12] ▶ To think with sound judgment and moderation** > The Romans were to think so as to be wise (Rom. 12:3). All other refs.: JUDGMENT <4993>, MIND (noun) <4993>, SELF-CONTROLLED <4993>.

[14] **to think highly: *huperphroneō*** [verb: ὑπερφρονέω <5252>]; **from *huper*: above, and *phroneō*: see [12] ▶ To be pretentious, to have an exaggerated opinion of oneself** > Paul said not to think highly {to have high thoughts} of oneself (Rom. 12:3). ¶

– [15] Mark 2:6, 8; Luke 5:21, 22; 12:17 → REASON (verb) <1260> [16] Luke 5:22; 6:8; 9:47 → what they were thinking → lit.: their thoughts → THOUGHT <1261> [17] Luke 16:15 → highly thought → highly esteemed → ESTEEMED <5308> [18] Luke 18:2, 4 → nor cared what people thought → lit.: and not respecting man → RESPECT (verb) <1788> [19] Acts 5:4 → PURPOSE (verb) <5087> [20] Acts 13:25 → SUPPOSE <5282> [21] Rom. 1:28 → to think good, to think worthwhile → LIKE (verb) <1381> [22] Rom. 2:4 → to think lightly → DESPISE <2706> [23] Rom. 13:14 → to think about how to gratify → to make provision → MAKE <4160>, PROVISION <4307> [24] 1 Cor. 1:26 → CONSIDER <991> [25] 1 Cor. 14:20a → stop thinking like children → lit.: be not children in your thinking → UNDERSTANDING <5424> [26] 1 Tim. 3:7 → to be well thought of → to have a good witness → WITNESS (noun)[1] <3141> [27] Heb. 7:4 → CONSIDER <2334> [28] 1 Pet. 4:4, 12 → to think strange → STRANGE <3579>.

THINKING – [1] Rom. 1:21 → REASONING <1261> [2] 1 Cor. 14:20a, b → UNDERSTANDING <5424> [3] 2 Pet. 3:1 → MIND (noun) <1271>.

THIRD – [1] **third, third part: *tritos*** [ord. num.: τρίτος <5154>]; **from *treis*: three ▶** This number is used in regard to a day (Matt. 16:21; 17:23; 20:19; 27:64; Mark 9:31; 10:34; Luke 9:22; 13:32; 18:33; 24:7, 21, 46; John 2:1; Acts 10:40; 27:19; 1 Cor. 15:4), an hour (Matt. 20:3; Mark 15:25; Acts 2:15; 23:23), a brother of a man who had died (Matt. 22:26; Mark 12:21; Luke 20:31), the watch (Luke 12:38), a servant (Luke 20:12), heaven (2 Cor. 12:2), a living creature (Rev. 4:7; 6:5), a seal (Rev. 6:5), angels (Rev. 8:10; 14:9; 16:4), a woe (Rev. 11:14), and a foundation of the holy city (Rev. 21:19). It is also used in Revelation concerning the earth (8:7), trees (8:7), the sea (8:8), creatures (8:9), ships (8:9), rivers (8:10), waters (8:11), length of day (8:12), luminaries (8:12), the moon (8:12), stars (8:12; 12:4), the sun (8:12), and men (9:15,

18). Other refs.: Matt. 26:44; Mark 14:41; Luke 23:22; John 21:14, 17a, b; 2 Cor. 12:14; 13:1; see "third time" under TIME <5154>. ¶

– [2] Acts 20:9 → third story → STORY <5152>.

THIRST (noun) – ***dipsos*** [neut. noun: δίψος <1373>]**; same as *dipsa*: thirst ▶ Need to drink water or another liquid >** Paul had been in hunger and thirst (2 Cor. 11:27). ¶

THIRST (verb) – ***dipsaō*** [verb: διψάω <1372>]**; from *dipsa*: thirst; also transl.: to be thirsty ▶ a. To need to drink >** The verb is used in the natural sense in Matt. 25:35, 37, 42, 44; John 4:13, 15; 19:28; Rom. 12:20; 1 Cor. 4:11; Rev. 7:16. **b. To feel a spiritual need >** Jesus says blessed are those who hunger and thirst after righteousness (Matt. 5:6). Whoever will drink of the water that Jesus will give him will never thirst for ever (John 4:14); he who believes in Him will never thirst (John 6:35). Jesus invites anyone who thirsts to come to Him and drink (John 7:37); to him who thirsts {is athirst} Jesus will give of the fountain of living water freely (Rev. 21:6). He who thirsts {is athirst} and whoever wishes is to take of the water of life freely (Rev. 22:17). ¶

THIRSTY – Matt. 25:35, 37, 42, 44; John 4:13–15; 6:35; 7:37; 19:28; Rom. 12:20; 1 Cor. 4:11; Rev. 21:6 → to be thirsty → THIRST (verb) <1372>.

THIRTY – ***triakonta*** [card. num.: τριάκοντα <5144>] ▶ This number is used in regard to fruit (Matt. 13:8, 23; Mark 4:8, 20), pieces of silver (Matt. 26:15; 27:3, 9), the age of Jesus (Luke 3:23), and stadia (John 6:19: twenty-five or thirty stadia is equivalent to approx. three or four miles). ¶

THIRTY-EIGHT – thirty: *triakonta* [card. num.: τριάκοντα <5144>]**, eight: *oktō*** [card. num.: ὀκτώ <3638>] ▶ A certain man had been ill for thirty-eight years (John 5:5). ¶

THIRTY-NINE – 2 Cor. 11:24 → lit.: forty minus one → FORTY <5062>.

THIS – ***touton*** [pron.: τοῦτον <5126>]. *

THIS, THAT – [1] ***hode*** [pron.: ὅδε <3592>]**; from *ho*: the, as a pron., and *de*: this, that ▶** This, that, such a one. It refers to the person or thing that was last mentioned (Luke 10:39; 16:25). It introduces what follows (Acts 15:23; 21:11; Rev. 2:1, 8, 12, 18; 3:1, 7, 14). Used instead of an adv. for here, there (Jas. 4:13). ¶ ‡

[2] ***houtos*** [pron.: οὗτος <3778>] ▶ Refs.: Luke 1:32; 2:25; John 1:2; 3:2; 6:71; Acts 10:36; Rom. 14:18. *

[3] ***tautē*** [pron.: ταύτῃ <5026>]. *

THISTLE – Matt. 7:16; Heb. 6:8 → BRIAR <5146>.

THITHER – Rom. 15:24 → THERE <1563>.

THITHERWARD – Rom. 15:24 → THERE <1563>.

THOMAS – ***Thōmas*** [masc. name: Θωμᾶς <2381>]**: twin, in Aram. ▶ One of the twelve apostles of Jesus Christ >** The Greek name of Thomas was Didymus or Twin (John 11:16; 20:24; 21:2). He said he was ready to die with Jesus (John 11:16), but he did not understand that Jesus would suffer and die (John 14:5). He was not with the other disciples when Jesus appeared to them on the evening of the resurrection, and he refused to believe that Jesus was risen (John 20:24). The following first day of the week, Jesus appeared again to His disciples, and Thomas was with them (John 20:26); Jesus reproached him for his unbelief (v. 27); then Thomas believed and exclaimed "My Lord and my God" (v. 28). Later he went fishing with Peter, and Jesus again manifested Himself to him and the other disciples (John 21:2, see vv. 3, 4). Other refs.: Matt. 10:3; Mark 3:18; Luke 6:15; Acts 1:13. ¶

THONG – Mark 1:7; Luke 3:16; John 1:27; Acts 22:25 → STRAP <2438>.

THORN – [1] **thorn:** ***akantha*** [fem. noun: ἄκανθα <173>]; **of thorns:** ***akanthinos*** [adj.: ἀκάνθινος <174>]; **from *akē*: point ▶ Bush with sharp, pointed spines on its flexible branches; the sharp, prickly, pointed spines growing on such a bush** > A great number of plants in Israel have thorns. The crown of thorns of the Lord was wreathed with twisted thorns from a bush that is plentiful on the hills around Jerusalem (Matt. 27:29; Mark 15:17; John 19:2); this plant is very flexible, and it was cruelly used for this purpose. Jesus came out, wearing the crown of thorns (John 19:5); He was thus being ridiculed since Roman emperors were wearing crowns. In a parable, some seed fell among thorns (Matt. 13:7a, b, 22; Mark 4:7a, b, 18; Luke 8:7a, b, 14). Figs are not gathered from thorns (Luke 6:44), or grapes from thorns {thornbushes} (Matt. 7:16). The earth bearing thorns and briers is rejected, because it is a sign of curse (Heb. 6:8). ¶
[2] ***skolops*** [masc. noun: σκόλοψ <4647>] ▶ **Object with a sharp point which pierces like a thorn or a stake; something that keeps troubling or irritating** > The thorn in the flesh given to the apostle Paul (2 Cor. 12:7) was a painful bodily infirmity; he had pleaded with the Lord three times that it might depart from him, but the Lord did not permit it, so that His strength would be made perfect in weakness (see v. 8, 9). ¶
– [3] Acts 7:30, 35 → thorn bush → BUSH <942>.

THORNBUSH – Matt. 7:16 → THORN <173>.

THOROUGH – Acts 23:15 → more thorough → more accurately → ACCURATELY <197>.

THOROUGHFARE – ***diexodos*** [fem. noun: διέξοδος <1327>]; **from *dia*: through, and *exodos*: exit ▶ Crossroads or the place where a street crosses the boundary of a city and leads to open country** > In a parable, the king sent his servants into the thoroughfares of the highways {into the highways, to the main highways, to the street corners} to invite people to the wedding of his son (Matt. 22:9). ¶

THOROUGHLY – [1] Matt. 3:12; Luke 3:17 → to thoroughly purge, clean out, clear → PURGE <1245> [2] Acts 22:3 → STRICTNESS <195> [3] Acts 23:20 → more thoroughly → more accurately → ACCURATELY <197>.

THOUGH – [1] ***kaiper*** [conj.: καίπερ <2539>]; **from *kai*: and, though, and *per*: very** ▶ Refs.: Phil. 3:4; Heb. 5:8; 7:5; 12:17; 2 Pet. 1:12; Rev. 17:8. ¶ ‡
– [2] John 4:2 → ALTHOUGH <2544> [3] Rom. 9:6 → YET <1161>.

THOUGH INDEED – See THOUGH <2539>.

THOUGHT – [1] ***dialogismos*** [masc. noun: διαλογισμός <1261>]; **from *dialogizomai*: to reason, which is from *dia*: intens., and *logizomai*: to reason, to take into account, which is from *logos*: thought, word ▶ Reflection, reasoning** > Out of the heart come forth evil thoughts (Matt. 15:19; Mark 7:21). The thoughts were to be revealed from many hearts (Luke 2:35). Jesus knew the thoughts of men {what they were thinking} (Luke 5:22; 6:8; 9:47; 24:38 {doubts}). James speaks of becoming judges with evil thoughts {motives} (Jas. 2:4). All other refs.: REASONING <1261>.
[2] ***logismos*** [masc. noun: λογισμός <3053>]; **from *logizomai*: see [1] ▶ Reasoning, decision following an evaluation** > The thoughts of those of the nations accuse or else excuse themselves between themselves (Rom. 2:15). Other ref.: 2 Cor. 10:5; see REASONING <3053>. ¶
[3] ***noēma*** [neut. noun: νόημα <3540>]; **from *noeō*: to perceive, to understand, which is from *nous*: mind, understanding ▶ Mental perception, intelligence; also transl.: mind** > The god of this world (Satan) has blinded the thoughts of the unbelieving (2 Cor. 4:4). Paul led captive every thought into the obedience of Christ (2 Cor. 10:5). He feared lest the thoughts of the Corinthians should be corrupted from simplicity as

to the Christ (2 Cor. 11:3). The peace of God will guard the Christians' hearts and minds (or: thoughts) in Christ Jesus (Phil. 4:7). Other refs.: 2 Cor. 2:11; 3:14; see DEVICE <3540>, MIND (noun) <3540>. ¶
4 ***dianoēma*** [neut. noun: διανόημα <1270>]; **from *dia*: through (denotes separation), and *noēma*: see 3 ▶ Reflection, machination** > Jesus knew the thoughts of those who sought from Him a sign out of heaven (Luke 11:17). Other ref.: Luke 3:16 in some mss. ¶
5 ***enthumēsis*** [fem. noun: ἐνθύμησις <1761>]; **from *en*: in, and *thumos*: disposition of soul, intent ▶ Reasoning, reflection** > Jesus saw the thoughts of people (Matt. 9:4). He knew their thoughts (Matt. 12:25). The word of God discerns the thoughts and intentions of the heart (Heb. 4:12). Other ref.: Acts 17:29; see IMAGINATION <1761>. ¶
6 ***epinoia*** [fem. noun: ἐπίνοια <1963>]; **from *epinoeō*: to think, which is from *epi*: upon (intens.), and *noeō*: to consider, which is from *nous*: mind, understanding ▶ Project, goal, plot, stratagem** > Simon the magician was to supplicate the Lord that the thought {intention} of his heart might be forgiven him (Acts 8:22). ¶
7 ***phronēsis*** [fem. noun: φρόνησις <5428>]; **from *phroneō*: to think, which is from *phrēn*: mind, understanding ▶ Practical wisdom, prudence** > John the Baptist was to turn the disobedient to the thoughts of the just (Luke 1:17). Other ref.: Eph. 1:8; see INTELLIGENCE <5428>. ¶
– 8 Matt. 6:25, 27, 28, 31; Luke 12:11, 22, 25, 26 → to take thought → WORRY (verb) <3309> 9 Mark 13:11 → to take thought beforehand → to worry beforehand → WORRY (verb) <4305> 10 Luke 1:51; Eph. 2:3 → UNDERSTANDING <1271> 11 Rom. 12:3 → to have high thoughts → to think highly → THINK <5252> 12 Rom. 12:17 → to give thought to do what is honorable → to provide things honest → PROVIDE <4306> 13 1 Cor. 1:10 → JUDGMENT <1106>.

THOUSAND – 1 ***chilias*** [fem. noun: χιλιάς <5505>]; **from *chilioi*: see 2 ▶ Number of approximately 1,000** > The number of angels around the throne was thousands of thousands (Rev. 5:11). One hundred forty-four thousand stood with the Lamb (Rev. 14:1); they sang a new song (v. 3). ¶
2 ***chilioi*** [num. adj.: χίλιοι <5507>] **▶ The number 1,000** >This number is used in regard to years (2 Pet. 3:8a, b; Rev. 20:2–7). ¶
– 3 Luke 12:1; Acts 21:20 → INNUMERABLE <3461> 4 Heb. 12:22; Jude 14; Rev. 5:11a, b; 9:16a, b → ten thousands, many thousands; thousands upon thousands → MYRIAD <3461> 5 Rev. 7:5–8; 21:16 → TWELVE THOUSAND <1427> <5505>.

THOUSAND SIX HUNDRED – thousand: *chilioi* [card. num.: χίλιοι <5507>] **six hundred: *hexakosioi*** [card. num.: ἑξακόσιοι <1812>] ▶ This number is used in regard to distance (Rev. 14:20). ¶

THOUSAND TWO HUNDRED AND SIXTY – thousand: *chilioi* [card. num.: χίλιοι <5507>] **two hundred: *diakosioi*** [card. num.: διακόσιοι <1250>] **sixty: *hexēkonta*** [card. num.: ἑξήκοντα <1835>] ▶ This number {one thousand two hundred and three score} is used in relation to the days of prophecy (Rev. 11:3; 12:6). ¶

THOUSAND TWO HUNDRED AND THREE SCORE – Rev. 11:3, 12:6 → THOUSAND TWO HUNDRED AND SIXTY <5507> <1250> <1835>.

THREAT – 1 ***apeilē*** [fem. noun: ἀπειλή <547>]; **from *apeileō*: to threaten, to defend something ▶ Hostile or angry speech; also transl.: threatening** > Peter and John were severely threatened {warned} (lit.: they were threatened with threat) to speak no more in the name of Jesus (Acts 4:17). When Peter and John went to their own company, they asked the Lord to look upon the threats {threatening} of unbelievers (Acts 4:29). Saul was still breathing threats and murder against the disciples of the Lord (Acts 9:1). Masters should give

up threatening (lit.: the threat of) their bondservants (Eph. 6:9). ¶
– [2] Luke 3:14 → to extort by threat → OPPRESS <1286> [3] Acts 4:21 → after further threats → to further threaten → THREATEN <4324> [4] 1 Pet. 2:23 → to utter threats, to make threats → THREATEN <546> [5] 1 Pet. 3:14 → FEAR (noun) <5401>.

THREATEN – [1] ***apeileō*** [verb: ἀπειλέω <546>] ▶ **To adopt an hostile attitude, to become angry; to warn with an impending punishment** > Peter and John were severely threatened {were warned} (lit.: threatened with threats) to speak in the name of Jesus to no man (Acts 4:17). When Jesus suffered, He did not threaten {uttered no threats, made no threats} (1 Pet. 2:23). ¶
[2] **to further threaten: *prosapeileō*** [verb: προσαπειλέω <4324>]; **from *pros*: in addition to, and *apeileō*: see [1] ▶ To menace additionally, to prohibit something yet further** > Peter and John were let go after they had been further threatened {after further threats} (Acts 4:21). ¶

THREATENING – [1] Matt. 16:3 → to be threatening → to be overcast → OVERCAST <4768> [2] Acts 4:29; 9:1; Eph. 6:9 → THREAT <547>.

THREE – [1] ***treis*** [card. num.: τρεῖς <5140>] ▶ This number is used in regard to days (Matt. 12:40a, c; 15:32; 26:61; 27:40, 63; Mark 8:2, 31; 14:58; 15:29; Luke 2:46; John 2:19, 20; Acts 9:9; 25:1; 28:7, 12, 17; Rev. 11:9, 11), nights (Matt. 12:40b, d), measures of flour (Matt. 13:33; Luke 13:21), shelters (in the sense of tents) (Matt. 17:4; Mark 9:5; Luke 9:33), witnesses (Matt. 18:16; 2 Cor. 13:1; 1 Tim. 5:19; Heb. 10:28), believers in the Lord (Matt. 18:20), months (Luke 1:56; Acts 7:20; 19:8; 20:3; 28:11), years (Luke 4:25; 13:7; Gal. 1:18; Jas. 5:17), men (Luke 10:36; Acts 10:19; 11:11), loaves of bread (Luke 11:5), members of a household (Luke 12:52a, b), liquid measures (John 2:6), hours (Acts 5:7), Sabbath days (Acts 17:2), things that remain (1 Cor. 13:13), those who speak in tongues (1 Cor. 14:27), prophets (1 Cor. 14:29), those who bear witness (1 John 5:7, 8), measures of barley (Rev. 6:6), angels (Rev. 8:13), plagues (Rev. 9:18), unclean spirits (Rev. 16:13), parts (Rev. 16:19), and gates (Rev. 21:13a–d). ¶
– [2] Matt. 20:5; 27:45, 46; Mark 15:33, 34; Luke 23:44 → three in the afternoon → lit.: the ninth hour → NINTH <1766> [3] Acts 20:31 → three years old → YEAR <5148>.

THREE HUNDRED – ***triakosioi*** [card. num.: τριακόσιοι <5145>]; **from *treis*: three, and *hekaton*: hundred** ▶ This number is used in regard to denarii (Mark 14:5; John 12:5). ¶

THREE INNS – ***Treis Tabernai*** [fem. plur. name: Τρεῖς Ταβέρναι <4999>]; ***taberna*, in Lat.: inn ▶ Name of a place south of Rome** > Brothers from Three Inns came to meet Paul; seeing them, Paul gave thanks to God and took courage (Acts 28:15). ¶

THREE THOUSAND – ***trischilioi*** [card. num.: τρισχίλιοι <5153>]; **from *tris*: three times, and *chilioi*: thousand** ▶ Three thousand souls were added to the church at the preaching of Peter after Pentecost (Acts 2:41). ¶

THREESCORE – [1] Acts 7:14 → threescore and fifteen → SEVENTY-FIVE <1440> <4002> [2] Acts 23:23 → threescore and ten → SEVENTY <1440> [3] 1 Tim. 5:9 → SIXTY <1835>.

THRESH – 1 Cor. 9:9, 10; 1 Tim. 5:18 → TREAD <248>.

THRESHING FLOOR – ***halōn*** [fem. noun: ἅλων <257>]; **from which *halōneomai*: to beat the grain ▶ Surface where the grain was beaten and lying on it >** He who would come after John the Baptist would thoroughly clear His threshing floor, and gather the wheat into His barn (Matt. 3:12; Luke 3:17). ¶

THRICE – Matt. 26:34, 75; Mark 14:30, 72; et al. → three times → TIME <5151>.

THROAT – 1 ***larunx*** [masc. noun: λάρυγξ <2995>] ▶ **Larynx, the organ of the voice** > The throat of wicked men is an open tomb (Rom. 3:13). ¶
2 **to take by the throat: *pnigō*** [verb: πνίγω <4155>]; **comp. *pneō*: to breathe** ▶ **To strangle, to choke** > A servant was taking by the throat {was throttling} a fellow servant who owed him something (Matt. 18:28). Other ref.: Mark 5:13; see DROWN <4155>. ¶

THROES – Matt. 24:8; Mark 13:8 → pain, labor pain → PAIN (noun) <5604>.

THRONE – 1 ***bēma*** [neut. noun: βῆμα <968>]; **from *bainō*: to go, to walk; lit.: step** ▶ **Tribune, elevated platform for a speaker; poss. the chair of a ruler** > Herod sat on a throne {an elevated seat, a rostrum} and made a public oration (Acts 12:21). All other refs.: GROUND (noun)[1] <968>, JUDGMENT SEAT <968>.
2 ***thronos*** [masc. noun: θρόνος <2362>]; **from *thraō*: to sit** ▶ **Seat, often raised, on which a person of authority sits** > The term is used in regard to God (Matt. 5:34; 23:22; Acts 7:49; Heb. 12:2; Rev. 1:4; 3:21b (the Father); Rev. 5:1, 6, 7, 11, 13; 6:16; 7:9, 10, 11a, b, 15a, b; 8:3; 12:5; 14:3; 16:17; 19:4, 5), the Lord Jesus (Matt. 19:28a; 25:31; Heb. 1:8; Rev. 3:21a; 4:2a, b, 3, 4a, 5a, b, 6a–c, 9, 10a, b; 7:17; 20:11 (see GREAT WHITE THRONE); 21:5), God and the Lamb (Rev. 22:1, 3), the twelve tribes of Israel (Matt. 19:28b), David (Luke 1:32; Acts 2:30), the apostles (Luke 22:30), twenty-four elders (Rev. 4:4a, b; 11:16), rulers (Luke 1:52), grace (Heb. 4:16), the Majesty (Heb. 8:1), Satan (Rev. 2:13; 13:2), and the beast (Rev. 16:10). Other refs.: Col. 1:16; Rev. 20:4. ¶

THRONG (noun) – Mark 12:37 → great throng → large crowd → CROWD <3793>.

THRONG (verb) – 1 ***sumpnigō*** [verb: συμπνίγω <4846>]; **from *sun*: together (intens.), and *pnigō*: to choke** ▶ **To press upon in a crowd nearly to the point of suffocation** > The crowds thronged {pressed against} Jesus (Luke 8:42). Other refs.: Matt. 13:22; Mark 4:7, 19; Luke 8:14; see CHOKE <4846>. ¶
– 2 Mark 3:9 → → PRESS <2346> 3 Mark 5:24, 31 → PRESS <4918> 4 Luke 8:45 → PRESS <598> 5 Luke 8:45 → to close in → CLOSE (verb) <4912> 6 Luke 11:29 → to gather thick together → GATHER <1865>.

THROTTLE – Matt. 18:28 → to take by the throat → THROAT <4155>.

THROUGH – 1 Matt. 10:23 → to go through → FINISH <5055> 2 Rev. 8:13 → AMONG <1722>.

THROUGH AND THROUGH – 1 Thes. 5:23 → COMPLETELY <3651>.

THROW (noun) – ***bolē*** [fem. noun: βολή <1000>]; **from *ballō*: to throw** ▶ **Casting, in relation to distance** > Jesus was withdrawn about a stone's throw {cast} from His disciples (Luke 22:41). ¶

THROW (verb) – 1 ***ballō*** [verb: βάλλω <906>] ▶ **To cast, to drop, to hurl** > This verb is used in regard to fire (Matt. 3:10; 7:19; Mark 9:22; Luke 3:9; 12:49; Rev. 8:5), the pinnacle of the temple (Matt. 4:6; Luke 4:9), a net (Matt. 4:18; Mark 1:16: some mss. have *amphiballō*; John 21:6), salt (Matt. 5:13; 13:48; Luke 14:35; John 15:6a), prison (Matt. 5:25; 18:30; Luke 12:58; 23:19, 25; John 3:24; Acts 16:23, 24, 37; Rev. 2:10), the right eye (Matt. 5:29a, 30a; 18:8a, 9a), hell (Matt. 5:29b, 30b; 18:8b, 9b; Mark 9:45, 47; Rev. 19:20; 20:10, 14, 15), an oven (Matt. 6:30; Luke 12:28), the furnace of fire (Matt. 13:42, 50), pearls (Matt. 7:6), the sea (Matt. 13:47; 21:21; Mark 9:42; 11:23; John 21:7; Rev. 8:8; 18:21a), dogs (Matt. 15:26; Mark 7:27), a hook (Matt. 17:27), the earth (Mark 4:26; Rev. 8:7; 12:4), the treasury (Mark 12:41a, b, 42, 43; Luke 21:1–3, 4a, b), a garden (Luke 13:19), a pool (John 5:7), stones (John 8:7, 59), lots (John 19:24b), a snare (Rev. 2:14), a bed and great tribulation (Rev. 2:22), crowns (Rev. 4:10), figs (Rev. 6:13), grapes (Rev. 14:19), dust (Rev. 18:19), Babylon (Rev.

18:21b), and the abyss (Rev. 20:3). All other refs.: see entries in Lexicon at <906>.

2 **to throw aside, to throw away: *apoballō*** [verb: ἀποβάλλω <577>]**; from *apo*: away, and *ballō*: see** 1 ▶ **To cast away, to get rid of** > The blind man threw away his garment (Mark 10:50). Other ref.: Heb. 10:35 (to cast away); see CAST (verb) <577>. ¶

3 **to throw out: *ekballō*** [verb: ἐκβάλλω <1544>]**; from *ek*: out of, and *ballō*: see** 1 ▶ **To push away, to expel, to reject; also transl.: to cast out, to drive out** > This verb is used in regard to outer darkness (Matt. 8:12; 22:13; 25:30; Luke 13:28; John 12:31), a vineyard (Matt. 21:39; Mark 12:8; Luke 20:12, 15), and wheat (Acts 27:38). All other refs.: see entries in Lexicon at <1544>.

4 ***emballō*** [verb: ἐμβάλλω <1685>]**; from *en*: in, and *ballō*: see** 1 ▶ **To cast into** > God has the authority to cast into hell (*gehenna*) (Luke 12:5). ¶

5 **to throw down: *kataluō*** [verb: καταλύω <2647>]**; from *kata*: intens., and *luō*: to loose** ▶ **To destroy, to demolish; also transl.: to tear down** > This verb is used in regard to the stones of the temple (Matt. 24:2; Mark 13:2; Luke 21:6). All other refs.: DESTROY <2647>, LODGE <2647>.

6 **to throw down: *katakrēmnizō*** [verb: κατακρημνίζω <2630>]**; from *kata*: down (intens.), and *krēmnos*: precipice** ▶ **To project from a high place** > The people in the synagogue got up and led Jesus up to the brow of a mountain, so that they might throw Him down {cast Him down} the precipice (Luke 4:29). ¶

– 7 Matt. 27:5; Luke 4:35; 17:2; Acts 27:19 → to throw away, down, etc. → to cast down → CAST (verb) <4496> 8 Mark 1:26; 9:20, 26; Luke 9:39 → to throw into convulsions → CONVULSE <4682> 9 Mark 9:18; Luke 9:42 → to throw down, to throw to the ground → TEAR (verb) <4486> 10 Mark 11:7 → PUT <1911> 11 Mark 14:51 → to throw around → WEAR <4016> 12 Luke 17:16 → FALL (verb) <4098> 13 Luke 19:35 → CAST (verb) <1977> 14 Luke 19:43 → to throw a bank → to build around → BUILD <4016> 15 Acts 7:19 → forcing them to throw out → lit.: by making them exposed → EXPOSED <1570> 16 Acts 19:31 → to throw oneself → to adventure oneself → ADVENTURE <1325> <1438> 17 Acts 20:10 → FALL (verb) <1968> 18 Acts 22:23 → CAST (verb) <4495> 19 Rom. 13:12 → to throw off → to cast away → CAST (verb) <659> 20 Gal. 5:12 → to throw into confusion → TROUBLE (verb) <387> 21 Rev. 12:10 → to throw down → to cast down → CAST (verb) <2598>.

THRUST – 1 **to thrust in: *pempō*** [verb: πέμπω <3992>] ▶ **To cause to go, to dispatch; to strike** > An angel cried to him who sat on the cloud to thrust in {put in, send, take} his sickle (Rev. 14:15, 18). All other refs.: SEND <3992>.

– 2 Luke 4:29; Acts 16:37 → to thrust out → CAST OUT <1544> 3 Luke 5:3 → to thrust out → to put out → PUT <1877> 4 John 20:25a, b, 27; Rev. 14:16, 19 → PUT <906> 5 Acts 7:27, 39; 13:46 → REJECT <683> 6 Acts 27:39 → RUN <1856> 7 Heb. 12:20 → to thrust through → SHOOT (verb) <2700>.

THUNDER (noun) – ***brontē*** [fem. noun: βροντή <1027>]**; from *bremō*: to roar** ▶ **Noise which accompanies lightning** > Jesus surnamed James and John Boanerges, which means "Sons of Thunder" (Mark 3:17). The term is transl. by "it thundered" (lit.: to become thunder) in John 12:29. It is used ten times in the book of Revelation (4:5; 6:1; 8:5; 10:3, 4a, b; 11:19; 14:2; 16:18; 19:6). ¶

THUNDER (verb) – John 12:29 → it had thundered → lit.: the thunder became (*ginomai*); see THUNDER (noun) <1027>.

THUNDERING – 1 Rev. 4:5; 8:5; 11:19; 16:18; 19:6 → THUNDER (noun) <1027> 2 Rev. 9:9b → SOUND (noun) <5456>.

THUS – ***houtō*, *houtōs*** [adv.: οὕτω, οὕτως <3779>] ▶ Refs.: Luke 11:30; John 3:14; 2 Cor. 1:5; 1 Thes. 2:4. *

THWART – [1] 1 Cor. 1:19 → REJECT <114> [2] 1 Thes. 2:18 → HINDER (verb) <1465>.

THY – ***soi*** [sing. pron.: σοί <4671>] ▶ Archaic form of "your." *

THYATIRA – ***Thuateira*** [neut. name: Θυάτειρα <2363>] ▶ **City of Lydia in Asia Minor** > Lydia was a seller of purple, of the city of Thyatira (Acts 16:14). One of the seven letters in the book of Revelation is addressed to the church of Thyatira (Rev. 1:11). The Lord recognizes her works, her love, her faith, her service, and her patience; but He reproaches her for tolerating the woman Jezebel who calls herself a prophetess (Rev. 2:18, 24; see v. 20). ¶

THYINE – Rev. 18:12 → CITRON <2367>.

TIBERIAS – ***Tiberias*** [fem. name: Τιβεριάς <5085>]: **from the name of Tiberius, Roman emperor** ▶ **a. Other name of the Sea of Galilee** > Jesus went to the other side of the Sea of Tiberias (John 6:1). Risen, He manifested Himself to His disciples at the Sea of Tiberias (John 21:1). **b. City southwest of the Sea of Tiberias** > Little boats had come from Tiberias to Jesus (John 6:23). ¶

TIBERIUS – ***Tiberios*** [masc. name: Τιβέριος <5086>]: **which relates to the Tiber, the main river of Rome** ▶ **Second emperor of Rome, known as Tiberius Caesar** > During the reign of Tiberius Caesar, the word of God came to John who preached the baptism of repentance (Luke 3:1). ¶

TICKLED – 2 Tim. 4:3 → ITCHING <2833>.

TIDINGS – [1] ***logos*** [masc. noun: λόγος <3056>] ▶ **Word, news, report** > The tidings concerning the conversions in Antioch came to the ears of the church in Jerusalem (Acts 11:22). Other refs.: WORD <3056>.
[2] ***phasis*** [fem. noun: φάσις <5334>]; **from *phēmi*: to say** ▶ **Rumor, news** > Tidings {report, representation} came to the chief captain that all Jerusalem was in an uproar (Acts 21:31). ¶
[3] Glad tidings → see GOSPEL <2098>.
– [4] Luke 1:19; 2:10; Acts 13:32 → to announce good tidings, to bring good tidings, to bring glad tidings, to show glad tidings → PREACH <2097> [5] 1 Thes. 3:6 → to bring good tidings → BRING <2097>.

TIE – [1] ***deō*** [verb: δέω <1210>] ▶ **To attach, to bind** > Jesus told His disciples they would find a donkey tied and a colt with her (Matt. 21:2; Mark 11:2, 4; Luke 19:30). All other refs.: BIND <1210>.
– [2] Matt. 23:4 → BIND <1195> [3] Mark 9:42; Luke 17:2 → to tie around → to hang around → HANG <4029> [4] John 13:4 → GIRD <1241> [5] Acts 12:8 → to tie on → SHOD <5265>.

TILE – ***keramos*** [masc. noun: κέραμος <2766>]; **from *kerannumi*: to mix** ▶ **Slab of clay used to cover a building** > Some men went up on the housetop and let down a paralytic through the tiles {tiling}, with his little bed, into the middle of the crowd, before Jesus (Luke 5:19). ¶

TILING – Luke 5:19 → TILE <2766>.

TILL – Heb. 6:7 → CULTIVATE <1090>.

TIMAEUS – ***Timaios*** [masc. name: Τιμαῖος <5090>]: **honorable, from *timē*: honor, respect** ▶ **Father of Bartimaeus** > Jesus healed the blind man Bartimaeus, the son of Timaeus (Mark 10:46). ¶

TIME – [1] ***kairos*** [masc. noun: καιρός <2540>] ▶ **Definite temporal period; also transl.: moment, opportunity, right time, season** > The term is used in regard to Jesus Christ (Matt. 11:25; 12:1; 26:18 {appointed time}; John 7:6a, 8; Rom. 5:6; Eph. 1:10; 1 Tim. 2:6) and His return (Acts 3:19; 1 Cor. 4:5; 1 Pet. 1:5), God (Rom. 3:26; Titus 1:3). It is also used in regard to demon-possessed men (Matt. 8:29), the harvest (Matt. 13:30), Herod Antipas and

Herod Agrippa I (Matt. 14:1; Acts 12:1), signs (Matt. 16:3), repentance (Mark 1:15), reward for one who has left things or people for the Lord's sake (Mark 10:30; Luke 18:30), tribulation (Mark 13:33; Luke 21:8, 36), the angel's words to Zacharias (Luke 1:20), the devil (Luke 4:13), those who receive the word but who have no root (Luke 8:13a, b), hypocrites (Luke 12:56), Jerusalem (insensitive to the presence of Jesus: Luke 19:44; trampled under foot by the nations: 21:24), the Jews (John 7:6b), Moses (Acts 7:20), blinded Elymas (Acts 13:11), the sufferings of the Christian (Rom. 8:18), the period of grace (Rom. 11:5; 13:11; 1 Cor. 7:29; Heb. 9:9, 10), abstinence on the part of a couple for the purpose of prayer (1 Cor. 7:5), Christians before their conversion (Eph. 2:12), the end of the period of grace (1 Tim. 4:1; 2 Tim. 3:1; 4:3), and Paul (2 Tim. 4:6). We are not to be weary in doing good, for in due time we shall reap if we do not faint (Gal. 6:9). In Rev. 12:14a–c, the term signifies a year. Other refs.: Luke 13:1; Acts 17:26; 19:23; Rom. 12:11 in some mss.; 2 Cor. 6:2a, b; 8:14; Gal. 4:10; Eph. 6:18; 1 Thes. 2:17 (lit.: a time of hour); 2 Thes. 2:6; 1 Tim. 6:15; Heb. 11:11, 15; 1 Pet. 1:11; 4:17; 5:6; Rev. 1:3; 11:18; 12:12; 22:10. All other refs.: OCCASION <2540>, SEASON (noun) <2540>.

[2] **for a time:** ***proskairos*** [adj.: πρόσκαιρος <4340>]; **from** ***pros*****: for, and** ***kairos*****: see** [1] ► **Temporary, for a season; also transl.: for a short time, for a while, passing, temporal, temporary** > The term is used in regard to one who has been sown on rocky places (Matt. 13:21; Mark 4:17). The things that are seen are for a time, but those that are not seen are eternal (2 Cor. 4:18). Moses chose to suffer affliction along with the people of God, rather than to enjoy the pleasure of sin for a short time (Heb. 11:25). ¶

[3] **to have time:** ***eukaireō*** [verb: εὐκαιρέω <2119>]; **from** ***eukairos*****: favorable, convenient, which is from** ***eu*****: well, and** ***kairos*****: see** [1] ► **To have the opportunity** > The disciples did not even have time {have leisure, have a chance} to eat (Mark 6:31). Other refs.: Acts 17:21 (to spend time); 1 Cor. 16:12 (to have opportunity); see SPEND <2119>, OPPORTUNITY <2119>. ¶

[4] ***chronos*** [masc. noun: χρόνος <5550>] ► **Period of time, more or less long** > The term is used in regard to Jesus (John 7:33; 12:35; Acts 1:21; 1 Pet. 1:20), the star that the wise men saw (Matt. 2:7, 16), a child possessed by a dumb spirit (Mark 9:21), Elizabeth (Luke 1:57), Judas and Silas (Acts 15:33), Paul (Acts 18:23; 19:22; 20:18; 1 Cor. 16:7), our stay on earth (1 Pet. 1:17; 4:2), the period before conversion (1 Pet. 4:3), the day of the Lord (1 Thes. 5:1), the kingdom (Acts 1:6, 7; 3:21a), and eternity (Rom. 16:25; 2 Tim. 1:9; Titus 1:2). God, having overlooked the times of ignorance, now commands all men to repent (Acts 17:30). Other refs.: Matt. 25:19; Mark 2:19; Luke 4:5; 8:27, 29; 18:4; 20:9; John 5:6; 14:9; Acts 7:17, 23; 8:11; 13:18; 14:3, 28; 18:20; 27:9; Rom. 7:1; 1 Cor. 7:39; Gal. 4:1, 4; Heb. 4:7; 5:12; 11:32; Jude 18; Rev. 2:21; 6:11; 10:6; 20:3. ¶

[5] ***hēmera*** [fem. noun: ἡμέρα <2250>] ► **This term may describe an undetermined temporal period, such as a day** > At the time of the martyrdom of Stephen, there was a great persecution against the church in Jerusalem (Acts 8:1). Other refs.: AGE <2250>, DAY <2250>, YEAR <2250>.

[6] **long time:** ***hikanos chronos*** [adj.: ἱκανός <2425>] [masc. noun: χρόνος <5550>] ► **Extended duration** > The expr. is employed regarding a man who leased his vineyard and went into a far country (Luke 20:9), Herod who desired to see Jesus (Luke 23:8 {long season}), Simon the magician (Acts 8:11), as well as Paul and Barnabas (Acts 14:3 {considerable time}). Other refs. (*hikanos*): see entries in Lexicon at <2425>.

[7] **long time, great length of time:** ***polus*** [adj.: πολύς <4183>] ***chronos*** [masc. noun: χρόνος <5550>] ► **Much time** > The expr. is used in regard to the lord of servants (Matt. 25:19) and an infirm man (John 5:6).

[8] **time appointed:** ***prothesmia*** [fem. noun: προθεσμία <4287>]; **from** ***pro*****: before, and** ***thesmos*****: custom, which is from** ***tithēmi*****: to put, to designate** ► **Determined date,**

deadline > As long as the heir is a child, he is under guardians and stewards until the time appointed {period fixed, date set, time set} by the father (Gal. 4:2). ¶

9 ***hōra*** [fem. noun: ὥρα <5610>]; ***hora*, in Lat.** ▶ **Temporal period of undetermined, but short duration, hour; a while, a little while, a season** > The term is used in regard to John the Baptist (John 5:35), the Corinthians (2 Cor. 7:8), and Onesimus (Phm. 15). All other refs.: HOUR <5610>.

10 **at the same time: *hama*** [adv. and prep.: ἅμα <260>] ▶ **On the same occasion, meanwhile; also transl.: also, too** > The Greek word is used in Acts 24:26; 27:40; Col. 4:3; 1 Tim. 5:13; Phm. 22; See also Matt. 13:29; 20:1; Rom. 3:12; 1 Thes. 4:17; 5:10. ¶

11 **for a short time: *brachus*** [adj. used as adv.: βραχύς <1024>] ▶ **For an instant, for a short while** > The term is used in Acts 5:34 in regard to the apostles whom Gamaliel commanded to be put out of the Sanhedrin. Other refs. (various transl.): Luke 22:58; John 6:7; Acts 27:28; Heb. 2:7, 9; 13:22. ¶

12 **at any time: *hekastote*** [adv.: ἑκάστοτε <1539>]; **from *hekastos*: each, every one** ▶ **On each occasion, always** > Peter would make every effort to see that after his departure Christians would be able to remember his teachings at any time (2 Pet. 1:15). ¶

13 **for a long time, now of a long time: *ekpalai*** [adv.: ἔκπαλαι <1597>]; **from *ek*: from, and *palai*: long ago** ▶ **Since an extended period of time; also transl.: of old, from long, as long** > The term is used in regard to false teachers among Christians (2 Pet. 2:3). Other ref.: 2 Pet. 3:5 (long ago); see LONG (adj.) <1597>. ¶

14 **time to come: *mellon*; from *mellō*** [verb: μέλλω <3195>] ▶ **Future** > Those who are ready to give are storing up for themselves a good foundation for the time to come {coming age} (1 Tim. 6:19).

15 **second time: *deuteros*** [adj.: δεύτερος <1208>]; **from *duo*: two** ▶ **On a second occasion** > This term is used in Matt. 26:42; Mark 14:72; John 3:4; 9:24; 21:16; Acts 7:13; 10:15; 11:9; 2 Cor. 13:2; Heb. 9:28; Rev. 19:3. All other refs.: SECOND <1208>.

16 **three times: *tris*** [adv.: τρίς <5151>]; **from *tria*: neut. of *treis*: three** ▶ **On three occasions** > This term is used in Matt. 26:34, 75; Mark 14:30, 72; Luke 22:34, 61; John 13:38; Acts 10:16; 11:10; 2 Cor. 11:25a, b; 12:8. ¶

17 **third time: *tritos*** [ord. num.: τρίτος <5154>]; **from *treis*: three** ▶ **On a third occasion** > This term is used in Matt. 26:44; Mark 14:41; Luke 23:22; John 21:14, 17a, b; 2 Cor. 12:14; 13:1. All other refs.: THIRD <5154>.

18 **five times: *pentakis*** [adv.: πεντάκις <3999>]; **from *pente*: five** ▶ **On five occasions** > This term is used in 2 Cor. 11:24. ¶

19 **seven times: *heptakis*** [adv.: ἑπτάκις <2034>]; **from *hepta*: seven** ▶ **On seven occasions** > This term is used in Matt. 18:21, 22; Luke 17:4a, b. In Matt. 18:22, one also reads in Greek "until seventy times seven." ¶

20 **seventy times: *hebdomēkontakis*** [adv.: ἑβδομηκοντάκις <1441>]; **from *hebdomēkonta*: seventy** ▶ **On seventy occasions** > This term is used in Matt. 18:22. ¶

21 **hundred times: *hekatontaplasiōn*** [adj.: ἑκατονταπλασίων <1542>]; **from *hekaton*: one hundred, and *plasiōn*: suffix indicating a numeral termination** ▶ **Centuple, hundredfold** > This term is used in Matt. 19:29; Mark 10:30; Luke 8:8. Other ref.: Luke 18:30 in some mss. ¶

– 22 Mark 14:11 → at an opportune time → CONVENIENTLY <2122> 23 Mark 15:44 → for some time → long ago → LONG (adj.) <3819> 24 Luke 1:3 → for some time past → lit.: from the beginning 25 Luke 8:27 → for a long time, long time → *chronō hikanō* <5550> <2425> 26 Luke 8:29 → often times → lit.: many times (*pollois chronois*) <4183> <5550> 27 Luke 18:1; 2 Cor. 5:6; 9:8; Gal. 4:18; Eph. 5:20 → at all times → ALWAYS <3842> 28 John 2:13; 11:55 → almost time → NEAR (adv.) <1451> 29 John 14:9 → so long a time, so long → *tosoutō chronō* 30 Acts 7:12 → the first time → lit.: first → FIRST <4412> 31 Acts 14:28 → long time → lit.: a time not little (*chronon ouk oligon*) 32 Acts 15:21 → of old time → OLD <744> 33 Acts 18:20 → longer time → lit.: over a longer time (*epi pleiona chronon*) 34 Acts 21:26 → at which time an offering should be made → lit.: until that (*eōs ou*) an offering should be made 35 Acts 26:5 → for a long time → from the beginning → BEGINNING <509> 36 Acts 26:28 → in a short time → ALMOST <1722> <3641> 37 Rom. 9:10 → "at the same time" added in Engl. 38 1 Cor. 15:8 → born out of due time → BORN <1626> 39 Heb. 1:1 → in time past → PAST <3819> 40 Heb. 4:7 → after such a long time, after so long a time → lit.: after all this time (*meta tosouton chronon*) 41 Heb. 4:16 → in time of need → SEASONABLE <2121> 42 Heb. 10:12, 14 → for all time → CONTINUALLY <1519> <1336> 43 Heb. 10:13 → from that time → FINALLY <3063> 44 Heb. 11:11 → beyond the proper time of life → AGE <2244> 45 Heb. 12:11 → at the time → lit.: for the being present → PRESENT <3918> 46 1 Pet. 3:5 → in former times, in the old time → FORMERLY <4218> 47 Rev. 10:6 → DELAY (noun) <5550>.

TIMES (AT MANY) – at many, various, sundry times: *polumerōs* [adv.: πολυμερῶς <4181>]**; from *polus*: many, and *meros*: part ▶ At numerous occasions, often** > God has spoken at various times {in many parts, in many portions} and in many ways long ago to Israel by the prophets (Heb. 1:1). ¶

TIMID – 1 Matt. 8:26; Mark 4:40 → FEARFUL <1169> 2 2 Cor. 10:1 → LOWLY <5011> 3 1 Thes. 5:14 → FAINT-HEARTED <3642> 4 2 Tim. 1:7 → does not make us timid → not of fear → FEAR (noun) <1167>.

TIMIDITY – 2 Tim. 1:7 → FEAR (noun) <1167>.

TIMON – *Timōn* [masc. name: Τίμων <5096>]**: who honors; from *timē*: honor, respect ▶ Christian man of the N.T.** > Timon was one of seven Christian men chosen to be occupied with service in the church of Jerusalem (Acts 6:5). ¶

TIMOTHY – *Timotheos* [masc. name: Τιμόθεος <5095>]**: who honors God; from *timē*: honor, respect, and *Theos*: God ▶ Christian man of the N.T. to whom Paul addresses two letters** > Timothy was a disciple from Derbe who had a good testimony of the brothers; he was the son of a believing Jewish woman and a Greek father (Acts 16:1). Paul took him for the ministry. Timothy remained with Silas at Berea (17:14, 15) and met Paul at Corinth (18:5). He ministered to Paul (19:22) and accompanied him to Asia (20:4). Paul associates Timothy with himself when he addresses his letters to various Christian gatherings (2 Cor. 1:1; Phil. 1:1; Col. 1:1; 1 Thes. 1:1; 3:2, 6; 2 Thes. 1:1; Phm. 1). He speaks of him as his fellow worker (Rom. 16:21) and his child in the faith (1 Cor. 4:17; 1 Tim. 1:2, 18; 2 Tim. 1:2). He bears witness to the zeal of Timothy; the latter worked the work of the Lord, as Paul did (1 Cor. 16:10). The two of them and Silvanus had preached the Son of God among the Corinthians (2 Cor. 1:19). Paul hoped to send him to the Philippians so that he might know how they were getting on (Phil. 2:19). He urged Timothy to keep that which had been committed to him (1 Tim. 6:20). Paul wrote two letters to Timothy (1 Tim. 1:2; 2 Tim. 1:2). Timothy was imprisoned, then released (Heb. 13:23). ¶

TINKLING – 1 Cor. 13:1 → CLANGING <214>.

TIP – Luke 16:24 → END (noun) <206>.

TIRE – 2 Thes. 3:13 → to become weary, to be weary → WEARY <1573> under <1457a>.

TIRED (BE) – 1 Matt. 9:36 → to be weary → WEARY (adj.) <1590> 2 John 4:6 → to be weary → WEARY (adj.) <2872>.

TITHE (noun and verb) – 1 **tenth, tenth part, tenth portion: *dekatē*** [fem. noun:

δεκάτη <1181>]; **to receive tithe, to tithe, to give a tenth:** ***dekatoō*** [verb: δεκατόω <1183>]; **from** ***deka*****: ten ▶ Tenth part of an income; to give this part >** The tithe was given to the Lord under the law (e.g., the tithe of the seed of the land, the fruit of the tree, the herd of the flock), and it was holy (see Lev. 27:30–32). Tithing was practiced before the law: Abraham gave a tenth part of all to Melchizedek (Heb. 7:2, 4, 6, 8, 9a, b). ¶
2 **to tithe; to pay, take, give tithes; to give a tenth:** ***apodekatoō*** [verb: ἀποδεκατόω <586>]; **from** ***apo*****: from, and** ***dekatoō*****: see** 1 **▶ To give the tenth part of one's income >** The scribes and the Pharisees were paying tithe of mint, anise, and cumin (Matt. 23:23; Luke 11:42; other mss.: *apodekateuō*). In a parable, a Pharisee gave tithes of all he acquired (Luke 18:12). The sons of Levi received tithes {collect a tenth} from the people (Heb. 7:5). ¶

TITLE – ***titlos*** [masc. noun: τίτλος <5102>]; **from the Lat.** ***titulus*** **▶ Inscription, sign >** Pilate wrote a title {notice} and put it on the cross (John 19:19); many of the Jews read this title (v. 20). ¶

TITTLE – ***keraia*** [fem. noun: κεραία <2762>]; **from** ***keras*****: horn ▶ Accent or small stroke distinguishing one Heb. letter from another >** One tittle {stroke, stroke of a pen} will by no means pass from the law until all is fulfilled (Matt. 5:18; Luke 16:17). ¶

TITUS – ***Titos*** [masc. name: Τίτος <5103>] **▶ Christian man of the N.T. to whom Paul addresses a letter >** Fellow worker of Paul (2 Cor. 8:23), who speaks of him as his brother (2 Cor. 2:13), his true child according to their common faith (Titus 1:4). Paul had been encouraged and gladdened by his coming, when he brought him news of the Corinthians (2 Cor. 7:6, 13). Titus had accompanied Paul to Jerusalem at the beginning, when the latter communicated to the believing Jews the gospel that he preached to the nations; Titus was not compelled to be circumcised according the Jewish custom (Gal. 2:1, 3). At the end of Paul's life, Titus went to Dalmatia (2 Tim. 4:10). Other refs.: 2 Cor. 7:14; 8:6, 16; 12:18. Other ref.: Acts 18:7, surname of a certain Justus, in some mss; also spelled *Titios* in Greek. ¶

TO – 1 **to, unto:** ***eis*** [prep.: εἰς <1519>] **▶ Inside, among >** This prep. is found in Acts 26:17. *
2 ***pros*** [prep.: πρός <4314>] **▶ Toward >** This prep. is also transl. "among," "toward," "unto," "with." For example, John 7:35; 1 Cor. 16:10; Phil. 1:26; 1 Thes. 2:1. *
– 3 Matt. 24:24 → THAT <5620> 4 Matt. 26:59 → SO THAT <3704>.

TO DAY – See DAY <4594>.

TO THEE, THOU, THINE OWN – ***soi*** [sing. pron.: σοί <4671>] ▶ Archaic form of "to you," "you," "your own," "your." *

TO US – ***hēmin*** [pron.: ἡμῖν <2254>] ▶ Personal pron. dative plur. of *ego*: I. * ‡

TODAY – See DAY <4594>.

TOGETHER – 1 ***homou*** [adv.: ὁμοῦ <3674>]; **from** ***homos*****: like, similar ▶** Used of place (John 21:2); of time (John 4:36; 20:4). ¶ ‡
– 2 Acts 1:14; 2:46; 4:24; 5:12; 12:20; 15:25; Rom. 15:6 → with one accord → ACCORD <3661> 3 Rom. 1:12 → to be comforted together → to be encouraged together → COMFORT (verb) <4837> 4 2 Cor. 1:11 → to help together → HELP (verb) <4943>.

TOGETHER, TOGETHER WITH – ***sun*** [prep.: σύν <4862>]. *

TOIL (noun) – 1 ***mochthos*** [masc. noun: μόχθος <3449>]; **comp.** ***mogis*****: with effort, with difficulty,** ***mogos*****: labor ▶ Work requiring a painful effort; also transl.: painfulness, travail >** Paul uses this term to describe his service for the Lord (2 Cor. 11:27; 1 Thes. 2:9; 2 Thes. 3:8). ¶

– [2] 1 Cor. 15:58; 1 Thes. 2:9; 2 Thes. 3:8; Rev. 2:2 → LABOR <2873>.

TOIL (verb) – [1] Matt. 6:28; Luke 12:27; 1 Cor. 4:12; Phil. 2:16; 1 Tim. 4:10; et al. → LABOR (verb) <2872> [2] 2 Cor. 11:27; 2 Thes. 3:8 → lit., a noun → TOIL (noun) <3449>.

TOKEN – [1] Mark 14:44 → SIGN <4953> [2] Phil. 1:28 → evident token → PROOF <1732> [3] 2 Thes. 1:5 → manifest token → manifest evidence → EVIDENCE <1730>.

TOLERABLE – more tolerable: *anektoteros* [adj.: ἀνεκτότερος <414>]; **compar. of *anektos*: tolerable; from *anechō*: to bear, which is from *ana*: in, and *echō*: to have, to hold ▶ More bearable, less rigorous** > The term is used regarding the fate of Sodom and Gomorrah (Matt. 10:15; 11:24; Luke 10:12) and that of Tyre and Sidon (Matt. 11:22; Mark 6:11 in some mss.; Luke 10:14). ¶

TOLERANCE – [1] Rom. 2:4 → FORBEARANCE <463> [2] Eph. 4:2 → to show tolerance → SUFFER <430>.

TOLERATE – [1] 1 Cor. 5:1 → verb added in Engl. [2] 2 Cor. 11:16 → RECEIVE <1209> [3] 2 Cor. 11:19, 20 → SUFFER <430> [4] Rev. 2:2 → BEAR (verb) <941> [5] Rev. 2:20 → ALLOW <1439>.

TOLL – Matt. 17:25 → CUSTOM[2] <5056>.

TOMB – [1] ***mnēma*** [neut. noun: μνῆμα <3418>]; **from *mnaomai*: to remember; comp. *mimnēskō*: to recall to one's mind ▶ Grave, sepulchre** > A man possessed by an unclean spirit was continually in the tombs (Mark 5:5; Luke 8:27). The term is used in regard to the tomb of Jesus (Luke 23:53; 24:1), David (Acts 2:29 {monument}), and Abraham (7:16). Other ref.: Mark 16:2 in some mss.; Rev. 11:9 {burial}. ¶

[2] ***mnēmeion*** [neut. noun: μνημεῖον <3419>]; **from *mnaomai*: see [1] ▶ Grave, sepulchre; among the Hebrews, in general a cave closed by a door or a stone** > Two demoniacs came out of the tombs and met Jesus (Matt. 8:28). The scribes and the Pharisees adorned the tombs of the just (Matt. 23:29b). The tombs were opened when Jesus died (Matt. 27:52); saints went out of the tombs after His resurrection (v. 53). Joseph of Arimathea laid the body of Jesus in a new tomb that he had hewn in the rock and rolled a great stone to its door (Matt. 27:60a, b). A man possessed by an unclean spirit had his dwelling in the tombs (Mark 5:2, 3). The disciples of John the Baptist laid his body in a tomb (Mark 6:29). The Pharisees were like tombs that are not seen; and the men walking over them do not know it (Luke 11:44). The doctors of the law built the tombs of the prophets (Luke 11:47, 48). Lazarus had already been in the tomb four days (John 11:17); Mary went to the tomb to weep there (11:31), and Jesus went there also (11:38) and called Lazarus out of the tomb (12:17). Other refs. regarding the tomb of Jesus: Matt. 28:8; Mark 15:46a, b; 16:2 in most mss., 3, 5, 8; Luke 23:55; 24:2, 9, 12, 22, 24; John 19:41, 42; 20:1a, b, 2–4, 6, 8, 11a, b; Acts 13:29. The hour is coming in which all who are in the tombs will hear the voice of the Son of God (John 5:28). ¶

[3] ***taphos*** [masc. noun: τάφος <5028>]; **from *thaptō*: to bury, to lay in the grave ▶ Grave, tomb** > Jesus called the scribes and Pharisees whitewashed tombs (Matt. 23:27). The scribes and the Pharisees built the tombs of the prophets (Matt. 23:29). Mary Magdalene and the other Mary sat opposite the tomb of Jesus (Matt. 27:61). Other refs. in regard to the tomb of Jesus: Matt. 27:64, 66; 28:1. Other ref.: Rom. 3:13. ¶

TOMORROW – ***aurion*** [adv.: αὔριον <839>] **▶ The day after today; also transl.: next day** > God clothes the grass of the field that is thrown into the oven the next day (Matt. 6:30; Luke 12:28). Jesus said to not worry about tomorrow, for tomorrow will worry about its own things (Matt. 6:34a, b). He sent Pharisees to tell Herod He was performing cures today and tomorrow (Luke 13:32); He had to journey today, tomorrow, and the third day (v. 33). The Jews wanted

Paul to come down to the council tomorrow (Acts 23:20). Festus told Agrippa he would hear Paul tomorrow (Acts 25:22). Men say to eat and drink, for tomorrow they die (1 Cor. 15:32). To those who make plans for tomorrow, James says they do not know what will happen tomorrow (Jas. 4:13, 14). Other refs.: Luke 10:35; Acts 4:3, 5; 23:15 in some mss. ¶

TONE – [1] 1 Cor. 14:7b → SOUND (noun) <5353> [2] Gal. 4:20 → VOICE <5456>.

TONGUE – [1] ***glōssa*** [fem. noun: γλῶσσα <1100>] ▶ **a. The organ of speech found in the mouth >** James, in particular, warns against all the evil the tongue may cause (Jas. 1:26; 3:5, 6, 8). Other refs.: Mark 7:33, 35; Luke 1:64; 16:24; Acts 2:3, 26; Rom. 3:13; 14:11; Phil. 2:11; 1 Pet. 3:10; 1 John 3:18; Rev. 16:10. **b. A particular language spoken by a group of people >** Jesus redeemed saints by His blood out of every tongue (Rev. 5:9). A multitude of diverse tongues (i.e., people with various languages) stood before the throne of the Lamb (Rev. 7:9; 10:11). Other refs.: Rev. 11:9; 13:7; 14:6; 17:15. **c. The gift of tongues consists in speaking another language without having learned it >** In Acts, those who spoke in tongues announced the wonderful works of God and were understood by their listeners in their own languages (Acts 2:4, 11; 10:46; 19:6). The Lord had said that this would be a sign that would accompany those who believed (Mark 16:17). Paul deals with this gift in addressing the Corinthians (1 Cor. 12:10, 28, 30; 13:1); the gift of tongues was to cease (13:8). In 1 Corinthians 14, the disorder generated by speaking in tongues in the local church prompted Paul to give instructions for the exercise of this gift: three at the most were to speak, each in turn, and an interpreter was to give the meaning; tongues were a sign for unbelievers and not for Christians (vv. 2, 4, 5a, b, 6, 9, 13, 14, 18, 19, 21–23, 26, 27, 39). ¶
[2] **other tongue, strange tongue: *heteroglōssos*** [adj.: ἑτερόγλωσσος <2084>]**; from *heteros*: another, and *glōssa*: see [1]** ▶ **Different language >** The Lord would speak to Israel by people of other tongues (1 Cor. 14:21). ¶
[3] ***dialektos*** [fem. noun: διάλεκτος <1258>]**; from *dialegomai*: to deliberate (by reflection or discussion)** ▶ **The whole body of words in use in a particular community; also transl.: language, dialect >** Paul spoke to the Jews in the Heb. tongue (Acts 21:40; 22:2). The Lord spoke to Paul in the same Heb. tongue on the road to Damascus (Acts 26:14). Other refs.: Acts 1:19; 2:6, 8; see LANGUAGE <1258>. ¶
– [4] Acts 1:19; 2:8 → LANGUAGE <1258>.

TOOTH – ***odous*** [masc. noun: ὀδούς <3599>] ▶ **Hard, bone-like structure in the mouth used for biting and chewing >** Jews had heard that it was said: An eye for an eye and a tooth for a tooth (Matt. 5:38a, b). In the outer darkness, the furnace of fire, there will be weeping, wailing, and gnashing of teeth (Matt. 8:12; 13:42, 50; 22:13; 24:51; 25:30; Luke 13:28). The son of a man who had a mute spirit was gnashing his teeth (Mark 9:18). The Jews were gnashing at Stephen with their teeth (Acts 7:54). In John's vision, the teeth of the locusts were like those of lions (Rev. 9:8). ¶

TOP – [1] **from the top: *anōthen*** [adv.: ἄνωθεν <509>]**; from *anō*: above, and suffix *then*: from** ▶ **From the highest part >** The veil of the temple was torn in two, from the top to the bottom (Matt. 27:51; Mark 15:38). The tunic of Jesus was woven in one piece from the top to the bottom (John 19:23). All other refs.: ABOVE <509>, AGAIN <509>, BEGINNING <509>, FIRST <509>.
– [2] Heb. 11:21 → END <206>.

TOPAZ – ***topazion*** [neut. noun: τοπάζιον <5116>] ▶ **Transparent yellow precious stone >** The ninth foundation of the wall of the heavenly Jerusalem is adorned with topaz (Rev. 21:20). ¶

TORCH – [1] ***lampas*** [fem. noun: λαμπάς <2985>]**; from *lampō*: to light up, to shine** ▶ **Lamp that is fed with oil >** Judas came with lanterns, torches, and weapons

to arrest Jesus (John 18:3). A great star fell from heaven, burning like a torch {lamp} (Rev. 8:10). Other refs.: Matt. 25:1, 3, 4, 7, 8; Acts 20:8; Rev. 4:5; see LAMP <2985>. ¶
– 2 John 18:3 → LANTERN <5322>.

TORMENT (noun) – 1 ***basanismos*** [masc. noun: βασανισμός <929>]; **from *basanizō*: to afflict, to torture ▶ Torture, pain inflicted** > The term is used in regard to divine judgments in Rev. 9:5a {agony}, b; 14:11; 18:7, 10, 15. ¶
2 ***basanos*** [fem. noun: βάσανος <931>]; **primary meaning: touchstone for testing gold or silver; also: instrument of torture used to force someone to tell the truth ▶ a. Torture, atrocious pain** > Hades was a place of torment for the wicked rich man (Luke 16:23, 28). **b. Suffering resulting from illness** > Jesus healed people who were afflicted with various torments {pains, severe pains} (Matt. 4:24). ¶
3 ***kolasis*** [fem. noun: κόλασις <2851>]; **from *kolazō*: to punish ▶ Punishment, chastisement** > Jesus speaks of those who shall go away into eternal punishment and of the righteous who will go into eternal life (Matt. 25:46). Fear involves torment (1 John 4:18). ¶
– 4 Rev. 11:10 → to be a torment → TORMENT (verb) <928>.

TORMENT (verb) – 1 ***basanizō*** [verb: βασανίζω <928>]; **from *basanos*: suffering, torture ▶ To be put to the test, to suffer; also transl.: to strain, to torture, to vex** > A paralyzed servant was tormented {was suffering} terribly (Matt. 8:6). People possessed by demons asked Jesus not to torment them (Matt. 8:29; Mark 5:7; Luke 8:28). Jesus saw His disciples straining {laboring} at rowing {making headway painfully} (Mark 6:48). Seeing and hearing the inhabitants of Sodom and Gomorrah, Lot tormented his righteous soul day after day because of their lawless deeds (2 Pet. 2:8). The men who did not have the seal of God on their foreheads were tormented for five months (Rev. 9:5). Two prophets will torment those who dwell on the earth after the resurrection of believers in the Lord (Rev. 11:10). Anyone who worships the beast and receives his mark will be tormented with fire and brimstone (Rev. 14:10). The devil, the beast, and the false prophet will be tormented, day and night, forever and ever in the lake of fire and brimstone (Rev. 20:10). Other refs.: Matt. 14:24; Rev. 12:2 (to be in pain); see TOSS <928>, PAIN (noun) <928>. ¶
2 ***odunaō*** [verb: ὀδυνάω <3600>]; **from *odunē*: sorrow, suffering, distress ▶ To be in anguish, to be grievously distressed** > The rich man was tormented {was suffering, was in agony} in the flame (Luke 16:24, 25). All other refs.: DISTRESSED <3600>, GRIEVE <3600>.
3 ***ochleō*** [verb: ὀχλέω <3791>]; **from *ochlos*: crowd, multitude ▶ To afflict, to trouble; also transl.: to beset, to vex** > Jesus healed those who were tormented by unclean spirits (Luke 6:18; other mss.: *enochleō*), as likewise did Peter (Acts 5:16). ¶
– 4 2 Cor. 12:7 → BEAT <2852> 5 Rev. 9:10 → INJURE <91>.

TORMENTED (BE) – ***kakoucheō*** [verb: κακουχέω <2558>]; **from *kakos*: bad, evil, and *echō*: to have, to hold ▶ To oppress, also transl.: to be evil treated, mistreated, ill-treated** > O.T. people of faith were tormented (Heb. 11:37). We ought to remember those who are evil treated {are suffering adversity} (Heb. 13:3). ¶

TORMENTOR – See TORTURER <930>.

TORRENT – 1 ***cheimarros*** [masc. noun: χείμαρρος <5493>]; **from *cheima*: bad weather, and *rheō*: to flow ▶ Watercourse which flows only in winter or when it is swollen by rain; also transl.: brook, ravine, valley** > Jesus went out with His disciples beyond the torrent of the Kidron, where there was a garden (John 18:1). ¶
– 2 Luke 6:48, 49 → RIVER <4215> 3 Rev. 12:15b → swept away with the torrent → carried away by a river → RIVER <4216>.

TORTURE (noun) – Rev. 18:7 → TORMENT (noun) <929>.

TORTURE (verb) – 1 Matt. 8:29; Mark 5:7; Luke 8:28; Rev. 9:5 → TORMENT (verb) <928> 2 Matt. 18:34 → to be tortured → lit.: to the torturers → TORTURER <930>.

TORTURED (BE) – ***tumpanizō*** [verb: τυμπανίζω <5178>]; **from *tumpanon*: instrument of torture in the form of a drum on which a criminal was bound and beaten to death, which is poss. from *tuptō*: to strike, to beat ▶ To inflict punishment with the tympanum** > O.T. people of faith were tortured, not having accepted deliverance, that they may obtain a better resurrection (Heb. 11:35). ¶

TORTURER – ***basanistēs*** [masc. noun: βασανιστής <930>]; **from *basanizō*: to agitate, to torture, which is from *basanos*: torture, interrogation ▶ Individual inflicting severe pains to obtain information or force confession** > In Matt. 18:34, the master delivers his wicked servant to the torturers {tormentors}. ¶

TOSS – 1 ***basanizō*** [verb: βασανίζω <928>]; **from *basanos*: suffering, torture ▶ To shake, to agitate** > Jesus and His disciples were in a boat tossed {battered, buffeted} by the waves (Matt. 14:24). All other refs.: PAIN <928>, TORMENT (verb) <928>.

2 ***kludōnizomai*** [verb: κλυδωνίζομαι <2831>]; **from *kludōn*: wave ▶ To make go one way and the other as an object rocked by the waves** > The exercise of the gifts allows Christians to be no longer children, tossed and carried about by every wind of doctrine (Eph. 4:14). ¶

3 ***rhipizō*** [verb: ῥιπίζω <4494>]; **from *rhipis*: fan; lit.: to make a breeze, to agitate ▶ To sway, to raise** > The one who doubts is like a wave of the sea driven and tossed by the wind (Jas. 1:6). ¶

– 4 Acts 22:23 → CAST (verb) <906> 5 Acts 27:18 → to be tossed with a tempest → TEMPEST <5492>.

TOUCH – 1 ***haptomai*** [verb: ἅπτομαι <680>]; **from *haptō*: to attach, to connect ▶ To place the hand on a person, an object** > Jesus touched a leper (Matt. 8:3; Mark 1:41; Luke 5:13), Peter's mother-in-law (Matt. 8:15), blind men (Matt. 9:29; 20:34; Mark 8:22), Peter, James, and John (Matt. 17:7), a deaf man who spoke with difficulty (Mark 7:33), little children (Mark 10:13; Luke 18:15), a coffin (Luke 7:14), and Malchus (Luke 22:51). Jesus was touched by a woman who had been suffering from a hemorrhage (Matt. 9:20, 21; Mark 5:27, 28, 30, 31; Luke 8:44, 45a, b, 46, 47), people who were sick (Matt. 14:36a, b; Mark 6:56a, b), as many as had diseases (Mark 3:10), an entire crowd (Luke 6:19), and a woman who was a sinner (Luke 7:39). In resurrection, Jesus told Mary of Magdala not to touch Him (John 20:17). It is good for a man not to touch a woman (1 Cor. 7:1). The Christian is not to touch that which is impure (2 Cor. 6:17). The one who has been born of God keeps himself, and the wicked one does not touch him (1 John 5:18 {to harm}). Other ref.: Col. 2:21, see 2. ¶

2 ***thinganō*** [verb: θιγγάνω <2345>]; **form of *thigō*: to handle, to manipulate ▶ a. To do violence** > By faith, Moses celebrated the Passover, that the destroyer of the firstborn might not touch the Israelites (Heb. 11:28). **b. To come into contact** > The verb is used in regard to Mount Sinai: if a beast should touch the mountain, it will be stoned (Heb. 12:20). **c. To manipulate** > Some were establishing ordinances to not handle (*haptomai*), to not taste, to not touch (*thinganō*) (Col. 2:21); some transl. inverse "to handle" and "to touch."¶

3 ***katagō*** [verb: κατάγω <2609>]; **from *kata*: down (intens.), and *agō*: to lead ▶ To land, to arrive** > Paul's ship touched {put in} at Sidon (Acts 27:3). All other refs.: BRING <2609>, LAND (verb) <2609>.

4 ***prospsauō*** [verb: προσψαύω <4379>]; **from *pros*: near, and *psauō*: to touch lightly ▶ To barely allow the hand to come in contact with a person or thing** > The doctors of the law weighed men down with burdens hard to bear, but they themselves did not touch those burdens with even one of their fingers (Luke 11:46). ¶

5 ***psēlaphaō*** [verb: ψηλαφάω <5584>]; **from *psaō*: to touch lightly ▶ To feel with**

the fingers, to handle > In resurrection, Jesus told His disciples to touch Him (Luke 24:39). The verb is used in regard to the mountain of Sinai (Heb. 12:18). John speaks of that which his hands have touched concerning the word of life (1 John 1:1). Other ref.: Acts 17:27 (to feel after); see FEEL <5584>. ¶
– [6] Acts 19:12 → lit.: from his body → BODY <5559> [7] Acts 20:15 → touched at Samos → arrived at Samos → ARRIVE <3846>.

TOUCHED (BE) – Heb. 4:15 → SYMPATHIZE <4834>.

TOUCHING – Rom. 11:28b → CONCERNING <2596>.

TOW – John 21:8 → DRAG <4951>.

TOWEL – [1] ***lention*** [neut. noun: λέντιον <3012>]; ***linteum*, in Lat.: linen cloth ▶ Linen cloth, apron worn by servants to carry out their work ▶** Jesus girded Himself with a towel {linen towel} (John 13:4); He used it to wipe the feet of His disciples (v. 5). ¶
– [2] Luke 19:20 → HANDKERCHIEF <4676>.

TOWER – ***purgos*** [masc. noun: πύργος <4444>]; **comp. Pergamum: citadel ▶ Fortified structure more or less elevated** > The term is used in regard to the watchtower of a vineyard (Matt. 21:33; Mark 12:1; Luke 14:28) and the tower in Siloam that fell (Luke 13:4). ¶

TOWN – [1] ***kōmē*** [fem. noun: κώμη <2968>]; **from *keimai*: to lie outstretched ▶ Village, small town** > Pharisees and doctors of the law had come out of every town of Galilee and Judea, and from Jerusalem to listen to Jesus (Luke 5:17). The Christ comes from the town of Bethlehem (John 7:42). Jesus healed a blind man from the town of Bethsaida (Mark 8:23, 26a, b). All other refs.: VILLAGE <2968>.
[2] ***kōmopolis*** [fem. noun: κωμόπολις <2969>]; **from *kōmē*: see [1], and *polis*: city ▶ Important village** > Jesus wanted to go in the next towns, that He might preach there also (Mark 1:38). ¶
– [3] Matt. 5:14; 10:23; 11:20; Luke 2:11; John 11:54; Jas. 4:13 → CITY <4172> [4] Matt. 13:57; Mark 6:4 → his own town → COUNTRY <3968>.

TOWN CLERK – ***grammateus*** [masc. noun: γραμματεύς <1122>]; **from *gramma*: letter, written document, which is from *graphō*: to write ▶ Scribe, public writer, secretary in the service of the city with a certain political influence** > The town clerk {city clerk} of Ephesus quieted the crowd (Acts 19:35). Other refs.: SCRIBE <1122>.

TRACE – Heb. 7:6 → to trace the genealogy, the descent → to have genealogy → GENEALOGY <1075>.

TRACHONITUS – ***Trachōnitis*** [fem. name: Τραχωνῖτις <5139>]: **rough or rugged; from *trachus*: rough ▶ Region northeast of Palestine** > Philip was tetrarch of the region of Trachonitus (Luke 3:1). ¶

TRACING – Rom. 11:33 → beyond tracing out → UNTRACEABLE <421>.

TRADE (noun) – [1] **of the same trade: *homotechnos*** [adj.: ὁμότεχνος <3673>]; **from *homos*: same, and *technē*: trade, skill ▶ Of the same occupation** > Because they were of the same trade {same craft}, i.e., tentmaking, Paul stayed with Aquila and Priscilla (Acts 18:3). ¶
– [2] John 2:16 → BUSINESS <1712> [3] Acts 18:3; Rev. 18:22 → OCCUPATION <5078> [4] Acts 19:25 → in related trades, of similar trades → lit.: concerning such things: *peri ta toiauta* [5] Acts 19:27 → PART (noun) <3313> [6] 2 Cor. 2:17 → to make a trade → PEDDLE <2585>.

TRADE (verb) – [1] ***ergazomai*** [verb: ἐργάζομαι <2038>]; **from *ergon*: work ▶ a. To fructify, to labor, to produce** > He who had received five talents went and traded with them {put his money to work, trafficked}, and gained five other talents (Matt. 25:16).

b. To work, to do business > Those who trade {exercise their calling, make their living, earn their living} on the sea stood far off from burning Babylon (Rev. 18:17). All other refs.: see entries in Lexicon at <2038>.

– [2] Luke 19:13 → to do business → BUSINESS <4231> [3] Jas. 4:13 → EXPLOIT <1710>.

TRADITION – [1] ***paradosis*** [fem. noun: παράδοσις <3862>]; **from *paradidōmi*: to bring, to deliver, which is from *para*: over to, and *didōmi*: to give ▶ Teaching, doctrine that which is passed on; also transl.: direction, instruction, ordinance** > The scribes and the Pharisees asked Jesus if His disciples transgressed the tradition of the ancients by not washing their hands before eating bread (Matt. 15:2; Mark 7:3, 5); but He asked them why they transgressed the commandment of God in regard to honoring one's parents on account of their tradition (Matt. 15:3). They had invalidated the commandment of God by their tradition (Matt. 15:6; Mark 7:8, 9, 13). The doctrine of God was delivered by the apostles (1 Cor. 11:2; 2 Thes. 2:15; 3:6). Paul was more zealous than many of his contemporaries for the traditions of his fathers (Gal. 1:14). The Colossians were not to be cheated through philosophy and empty deceit according to the tradition of men (Col. 2:8). ¶

– [2] Mark 7:4 → other traditions → lit.: other things [3] 1 Pet. 1:18 → received by tradition from the fathers → FATHER <3970>.

TRAFFIC – James 4:13 → EXPLOIT <1710>.

TRAFFICK – Matt. 25:16 → TRADE (verb) <2038>.

TRAIL – 1 Tim. 5:24 → to trail behind → to follow after → FOLLOW <1872>.

TRAIN (noun) – Eph. 4:8 → He led captive in His train → lit.: He led captivity captive → CAPTIVITY <161>.

TRAIN (verb) – [1] Matt. 13:52 → to be trained → to become a disciple → DISCIPLE <3100> [2] 1 Tim. 4:6 → NOURISH <1789> [3] 1 Tim. 4:7; Heb. 5:14; 12:11; 2 Pet. 2:14 → EXERCISE (verb) <1128> [4] Titus 2:12 → TEACH <3811>.

TRAINED – [1] Luke 6:40 → to be perfectly trained, to be fully trained → to be perfect → PERFECT (adj.) <2675> [2] 2 Cor. 11:6 → not trained → SIMPLE <2399>.

TRAINING – [1] ***paideia*** [fem. noun: παιδεία <3809>]; **from *paideuō*: to raise, to educate a child, which is from *pais*: child ▶ Way of raising a child, which includes education, instruction, and discipline** > Fathers must bring up their children in the training {discipline, nurture} and admonition of the Lord (Eph. 6:4). All Scripture is divinely inspired and profitable for training in righteousness (2 Tim. 3:16). The word is transl. "chastening" {discipline} in Heb. 12: the Christian should consider as profitable the discipline of God dealing as a father toward a son (vv. 5, 7, 8, 11). ¶

– [2] 1 Cor. 9:25 → to go into strict training → to exercise self-control in all things → CONTROL (noun) <1467> [3] 1 Tim. 4:8 → EXERCISE (noun) <1129>.

TRAITOR – ***prodotēs*** [masc. noun: προδότης <4273>]; **from *prodidōmi*: to give before, which is from *pro*: before, and *didōmi*: to give ▶ One who is guilty of betrayal, i.e., of breaching trust, of delivering someone up** > Judas Iscariot became a traitor (Luke 6:16 {betrayer}). The Jews became traitors {betrayers, deliverers up} and murderers of the Just One (Acts 7:52). In the last days men shall be traitors (2 Tim. 3:4 {treacherous}). ¶

TRAMPLE – [1] ***pateō*** [verb: πατέω <3961>]; **from *patos*: path ▶ To move forward by setting the foot down upon, to step on** > Jesus gave to the seventy disciples the power to trample {tread} on serpents and scorpions (Luke 10:19). Other refs.: Luke

21:24; Rev. 11:2; 14:20; 19:15; see TREAD <3961>. ¶
– [2] Matt. 5:13; 7:6; Luke 8:5; 12:1; Heb. 10:29 → TREAD <2662>.

TRANCE – Acts 10:10; 11:5; 22:17 → ECSTASY <1611>.

TRANQUIL – [1] 1 Tim. 2:2 → QUIET (adj.) <2263> [2] 1 Tim. 2:2 → QUIET (adj.) <2272>.

TRANSFER – [1] ***methistēmi*** [verb: μεθίστημι <3179>]; **from *meta*: indicating change, and *histhēmi*: to stand ▶ To move from one place to another; other transl.: to bring, to convey, to translate** > God the Father has delivered us from the authority of darkness, and has transferred us into the kingdom of the Son of His love (Col. 1:13). All other refs.: REMOVE <3179>, TURN (verb) <3179>.
– [2] 1 Cor. 4:6 → to transfer, to transfer in its application → APPLY <3345>.

TRANSFIGURE – ***metamorphoō*** [verb: μεταμορφόω <3339>]; **from *meta*: indicating change, and *morphoō*: to form, which is from *morphē*: form, shape ▶ To transform the appearance, referring to a change which is related to the inward reality** > Jesus was transfigured before three of His disciples on a high mountain: His face shone like the sun, and His clothes became white as snow, as white as the light (Matt. 17:2; Mark 9:2). The Greek verb is also transl. by "to transform": the Christian is called to be transformed by the renewing of his mind (Rom. 12:2), and he is transformed {changed} by contemplating the glory of the Lord (2 Cor. 3:18). ¶

TRANSFORM – [1] ***metaschēmatizō*** [verb: μετασχηματίζω <3345>]; **from *meta*: indicating change, and *schēmatizō*: to form, which is from *schēma*: figure; lit.: to transfigure ▶ a. To take another form, to disguise oneself, referring to a superficial, outward change which does not correspond to inner reality** > Satan is able to transform himself into an angel of light in order to deceive; false apostles and deceitful workers also transform themselves as servants of righteousness in order to seduce (2 Cor. 11:13–15 {to disguise, to masquerade}). **b. To change the form (from a transient condition)** > At His coming, the Lord will transform {will change} the bodies of Christians into conformity to His glorious body (Phil. 3:21). Other ref.: 1 Cor. 4:6; see APPLY <3345>. ¶
– [2] Rom. 12:2; 2 Cor. 3:18 → TRANSFIGURE <3339>.

TRANSGRESS – [1] ***parabainō*** [verb: παραβαίνω <3845>]; **from *para*: beside, and *bainō*: to go ▶ To contravene, to violate; also transl.: to break** > The scribes and the Pharisees asked Jesus why His disciples transgressed the tradition of the elders by not washing their hands before eating bread (Matt. 15:2); but He asked them why they transgressed the commandment of God to honor one's parents by their tradition (v. 3). Other refs.: 2 John 9 in some mss. Other ref.: Acts 1:25 (to fall by transgression); see FALL (verb) <3845>. ¶
[2] ***parerchomai*** [verb: παρέρχομαι <3928>]; **from *para*: against, beside, and *erchomai*: to go ▶ To neglect, to disobey** > The older son in the parable of Luke 15 had never transgressed the commandment of his father (v. 29). All other refs.: COME <3928>, GO <3928>, PASS <3928>, SPEND <3928>.
[3] ***proagō*** [verb: προάγω <4254>]; **from *pro*: before, and *agō*: to go ▶ To go (forward), to lead** > Whoever transgresses {goes too far, runs ahead} and does not abide in the doctrine of Christ does not have God (2 John 9); in some mss.: *parabainō* <3845>: to transgress, to disobey. All other refs.: see entries in Lexicon at <4254>.
– [4] Rom. 2:27 → lit.: transgressor → TRANSGRESSOR <3848> [5] 1 Thes. 4:6 → to take advantage → ADVANTAGE (noun) <5233>.

TRANSGRESSING – Acts 1:25 → to fall transgressing → to fall by transgression → FALL (verb) <3845>.

TRANSGRESSION – [1] ***parabasis*** [fem. noun: παράβασις <3847>]; **from *parabainō*: to transgress, which is from *para*: against, and *bainō*: to go, to walk ▶ Contravention, non-compliance, violation** > The term is used in regard to the Mosaic law (Rom. 2:23 {breaking}; 4:15; Heb. 9:15 {sin}) and disobedience to a divine commandment, as in the case of Adam and Eve (Rom. 5:14 {breaking a command, offense}; 1 Tim. 2:14). The law was added because of transgressions (Gal. 3:19). Every transgression and disobedience received a just punishment (Heb. 2:2). ¶

[2] ***paraptōma*** [neut. noun: παράπτωμα <3900>]; **from *parapiptō*: to fall beside, which is from *para*: beside, and *piptō*: to fall ▶ Error with the idea of a fall, sin; also transl.: fault, offense, trespass** > If we forgive or not men their transgressions, God the Father will forgive or not forgive our transgressions (Matt. 6:14, 15a, b; Mark 11:25, 26). Jesus was delivered for our transgressions (Rom. 4:25). In Romans 5, the transgression corresponds to the sin of Adam and Eve; the transgressions are those of their descendants (vv. 15a, b, 16–18, 20). God in Christ does not count against the world their trespasses (2 Cor. 5:19). A man who is caught in some fault (or: offence) is to be restored by his brothers in a spirit of meekness (Gal. 6:1). In Jesus we have the forgiveness of sins (Eph. 1:7). Before their conversion, Christians were dead in their transgressions (Eph. 2:1, 5; Col. 2:13a). God has forgiven Christians all their transgressions (Col. 2:13b). Christians are to confess their sins to one another (Jas. 5:16). Other refs.: Rom. 11:11, 12; see FALL (noun) <3900>. ¶

– [3] Acts 1:25 → to fall by transgression → FALL (verb) <3845> [4] Rom. 4:7; 1 John 3:4a, b → transgression, transgression of the law → INIQUITY <458> [5] 2 Pet. 2:16 → INIQUITY <3892>.

TRANSGRESSOR – [1] ***parabatēs*** [masc. noun: παραβάτης <3848>]; **from *parabainō*: to transgress, which is from *para*: against, and *bainō*: to go, to walk ▶ One who contravenes to the law; also transl.: breaker, lawbreaker** > The term describes one who breaks the law of God given by Moses (Rom. 2:25, 27; Gal. 2:18; Jas. 2:9, 11). ¶

– [2] Mark 15:28; Luke 22:37 → LAWLESS (noun) <459> [3] 1 Tim. 2:14 → became a transgressor → lit.: fell into transgression → TRANSGRESSION <3847>.

TRANSIENT – 2 Cor. 4:18 → for a time → TIME <4340>.

TRANSITORY – 2 Cor. 3:7, 11 → to pass away, to do away → AWAY <2673>.

TRANSLATE – [1] ***hermēneuō*** [verb: ἑρμηνεύω <2059>] **▶ To explain; also transl.: to interpret** > Interpreted, Rabbi signifies: Teacher (John 1:38 in some mss.; other mss. have [2]). Cephas signifies: Peter (or: a stone) (John 1:42). Siloam is translated {means}: Sent (John 9:7). Melchizedek is interpreted: King of righteousness (Heb. 7:2). Other ref.: Luke 24:27 in some mss. ¶

[2] ***methermēneuō*** [verb: μεθερμηνεύω <3177>]; **from *meta*: particle which indicates change, and *hermēneuō*: see [1] ▶ To interpret from one language into another, to mean; also transl.: to interpret** > Immanuel is interpreted: God with us (Matt. 1:23). "*Talitha koumi*" is interpreted: "Little girl, I say to you, get up!" (Mark 5:41). Golgotha is interpreted: Place of a Skull (Mark 15:22). "*Eloi, Eloi, lama sabachthani*" is interpreted: "My God, My God, why have You forsaken Me?" (Mark 15:34). Interpreted, Rabbi signifies: Teacher (John 1:38). The Messiah is interpreted: Christ (John 1:41). Barnabas is interpreted: Son of Encouragement (Acts 4:36). The name of Elymas by interpretation (or: being translated) was: magician (Acts 13:8). ¶

– [3] Acts 9:36 → INTERPRET <1329> [4] Col. 1:13 → TRANSFER <3179> [5] Heb. 11:5a, b → to take up → TAKE <3346>.

TRANSLATION – ***metathesis*** [fem. noun: μετάθεσις <3331>]; **from *metatithēmi*: to transfer, which is from *meta*: prep. indicating a change, and *tithēmi*: to put ▶ Action of removing from one place and**

bringing into another > Enoch was taken away so that he did not see death, having received the testimony that he pleased God before he was taken away {before his being taken} (lit.: before his translation) (Heb. 11:5). The translation of Enoch is a figure of the translation of the Christians who will be caught up to meet the Lord (see 1 Thes. 4:17). Other refs.: Heb. 7:12; 12:27; see CHANGE <3331>, REMOVING <3331>. ¶

TRANSPARENT – ***diaphanēs*** [adj.: διαφανής <1307>]; **from *diaphainō*: to shine through, which is from *dia*: through, and *phainō*: to shine, which is from *phōs*: light; other mss.: *diaugēs* ► Translucent, which one may see through >** The street of the new Jerusalem was pure gold, like transparent glass (Rev. 21:21). ¶

TRANSPORT – 1 ***metoikizō*** [verb: μετοικίζω <3351>]; **from *meta*: indicating change, and *oikizō*: to cause to dwell, which is from *oikos*: house ► To transfer, to deport >** God had told the Israelites that He would transport them beyond Babylon (Acts 7:43 {to carry away, to remove, to send into exile}). Other ref.: Acts 7:4; see MOVE <3351>. ¶
– 2 Matt. 17:20a, b → MOVE <3327>.

TRAP (noun) – 1 ***thēra*** [fem. noun: θήρα <2339>]; **from *thēr*: wild animal, game ► Mechanism used for trapping, gin >** The word is used in Rom. 11:9 in regard to Israel. ¶
– 2 John 8:6 → to use as a trap → TEST (noun and verb) <3985> 3 Rom. 11:9; 1 Tim. 3:7; 6:9; 2 Tim. 2:26 → SNARE <3803>.

TRAP (verb) – 1 Matt. 22:15 → ENTANGLE <3802> 2 Matt. 22:18; Mark 12:15 → to try to trap → TEMPT <3985> 3 Mark 12:3; Luke 20:26 → CATCH (verb) <1949>.

TRAVAIL (noun) – 1 John 16:21 → to be in travail → to give birth → BIRTH <5088> 2 Gal. 4:27; Rev. 12:2 → to be in travail → to be in labor → LABOR (noun) <5605> 3 1 Thes. 2:9; 2 Thes. 3:8 → TOIL (noun) <3449> 4 1 Thes. 5:3 → PAIN (noun) <5604>.

TRAVAIL (verb) – Gal. 4:19, 27; Rev. 12:2 → to travail in birth, to travail → to be in labor → LABOR (verb) <5605>.

TRAVEL – 1 ***poreuomai*** [verb: πορεύομαι <4198>]; **from *poros*: passage ► To go from one place to another >** Jesus was not received because He was traveling toward (lit.: His face was going to) Jerusalem (Luke 9:53); other transl.: His face was turned as going to, His face was set for the journey to, His face was as though He would go to, He was heading for. All other refs.: DEPART <4198>, FOLLOW <4198>, GO <4198>, WALK <4198>.
2 **to travel with: *sunodeuō*** [verb: συνοδεύω <4922>]; **from *sun*: together, and *odeuō*: to travel, which is from *hodos*: road, journey ► To journey with >** The men who were traveling with Saul heard the voice, but saw no one (Acts 9:7). ¶
– 3 Matt. 25:14 → to travel to a far country → COUNTRY <589> 4 Luke 2:44 → GO <2064> 5 Luke 8:1 → to travel about → to go through → GO <1353> 6 Luke 10:33 → JOURNEY (verb) <3593> 7 Luke 14:25 → to travel with → to go along with → GO <4848> 8 Luke 17:11; Acts 13:6, 14; 15:3; 16:6; 18:23; 20:2 → to travel, to travel through → to pass through → PASS <1330> 9 Acts 8:40; 11:19 → to go over → GO <1330> 10 Acts 13:31 → to come up → COME <4872> 11 Acts 17:1 → to travel through → to pass through → PASS <1353> 12 Acts 19:29; 2 Cor. 8:19 → to travel with → lit.: as a travel companion → FELLOW TRAVELER <4898> 13 Rev. 18:17 in some mss. → to travel by ship → SAIL (verb) <4126>.

TRAVELING – Acts 19:29 → traveling companion → FELLOW TRAVELER <4898>.

TRAVELLER – Acts 19:29; 2 Cor. 8:19 → FELLOW TRAVELER <4898>.

TRAWL-NET – See NET.

TREACHEROUS – 2 Tim. 3:4 → TRAITOR <4273>.

TREAD – **1 to tread out the grain, to tread out the corn: *aloaō*** [verb: ἀλοάω <248>]; **comp. *alōē*: threshing floor ▶ Action of an ox trampling heads of wheat, in order to separate the grain of wheat from its chaff; also transl.: to thresh** > The law said not to muzzle the ox that is treading out grain (1 Cor. 9:9; 1 Tim. 5:18), an image of the servant of God; for he who treads out the grain is to do so in hope of partaking of it (1 Cor. 9:10). ¶
2 to tread, to tread down, to tread underfoot: *pateō* [verb: πατέω <3961>]; **from *patos*: path ▶ To trample (e.g., grapes), to bring (people) into subjection** > Jesus warned that Jerusalem would be trodden under the foot {trampled underfoot} by the Gentiles (Luke 21:24), which took place at its destruction in the year A.D. 70; the Gentiles will again tread the holy city under foot in the future (Rev. 11:2). The grapes of the vine are trodden to make wine; Rev. 14:20 symbolizes the judgment of apostasy on the earth, and Rev. 19:15 the destruction of enemies (see Is. 63:1–6). Other ref.: Luke 10:19; see TRAMPLE <3961>. ¶
3 to tread, to tread underfoot: *katapateō* [verb: καταπατέω <2662>]; **from *kata*: intens., and *pateō*: see 2 ▶ a. To trample, to step** > Salt that has lost its flavor (has become tasteless) is good for nothing, except to be trampled underfoot (Matt. 5:13). In Matt. 7:6, that which is holy and pearls are trampled under feet; in Luke 8:5, it is seed that is trodden under foot. Being gathered together to hear Jesus, the myriads of the crowd trod one on another (Luke 12:1). **b. To despise** > The one who had trodden underfoot the Son of God shall be judged worthy of more severe punishment (Heb. 10:29). ¶

TREASURE (noun) – **1 *thēsauros*** [masc. noun: θησαυρός <2344>]; **from *tithēmi*: to put, to deposit ▶ Precious possession** > The wise men offered the gifts out of their treasures to Jesus (Matt. 2:11). Jesus says not to store up treasures on earth (Matt. 6:19), but to store up treasures in heaven (v. 20), for where our treasure is, there our heart will be also (Matt. 6:21; Luke 12:34). The good man, out of the good treasure, brings forth good things, and the evil man, out of the evil treasure, brings forth evil things (Matt. 12:35a, b; Luke 6:45). Jesus compares the kingdom of heaven to a treasure hidden in a field (Matt. 13:44). Every scribe instructed concerning the kingdom of heaven is like an owner of a house who brings out of his treasure things new and old (Matt. 13:52). Jesus told a young man, if he wanted to be perfect, to go and sell all that he had and give to the poor and he would have treasure in heaven; and to come and follow Him (Matt. 19:21; Mark 10:21; Luke 18:22). Jesus says to make ourselves an unfailing treasure in heaven (Luke 12:33). Paul speaks of the treasure that we have in earthen vessels (2 Cor. 4:7). All the treasures of wisdom and knowledge are hidden in the mystery of God (Col. 2:3). Moses considered the reproach of Christ greater riches than the treasures of Egypt (Heb. 11:26). ¶
2 *gaza* [fem. noun: γάζα <1047>] **▶ Persian term which signifies: royal treasure, riches** > The Ethiopian who was converted was a court official who had charge of all the treasure of his queen (Acts 8:27). ¶
3 treasury, temple treasury: *gazophulakion* [neut. noun: γαζοφυλάκιον <1049>]; **from *gaza*: see 2, and *phulakē*: act of watching, guarding, which is from *phulassō*: to keep ▶ Place where the offerings of the temple were deposited** > Jesus, having sat down opposite the treasury of the temple, saw how the crowd (and the rich in particular) cast money into the treasury (Mark 12:41a, b; Luke 21:1). A poor widow had cast more into the treasury than all the others (Mark 12:43). Jesus spoke words in the treasury, teaching in the temple (John 8:20). ¶
4 treasury, temple treasury: *korbanas* [masc. noun: κορβανᾶς <2878a>]; **from a Heb. term which means: offering ▶ Treasure room of the temple where one**

brought one's offerings > The chief priests did not allow the pieces of silver from the betrayal of Judas to be put into the treasury (Matt. 27:6). ¶
– 5 2 Tim. 1:14 → entrusted treasure → THING COMMITTED <3872> 6 Jas. 5:3 → to heap up treasure together → HEAP <2343>.

TREASURE (verb) – 1 **to treasure up: *thēsaurizō*** [verb: θησαυρίζω <2343>]**; from *thēsauros*: treasure, which is from *tithēmi*: to put, to set ▶ To gather, to put in a reserve** > The man who judges others treasures up {stores up} for himself wrath (Rom. 2:5). All other refs.: HEAP <2343>, LAY <2343>, RESERVE <2343>, STORE (verb) <2343>.
– 2 Luke 2:51 → KEEP (verb) <1301>.

TREASURER – Rom. 16:23 → CHAMBERLAIN <3623>.

TREASURY – See TREASURE.

TREAT – 1 ***anastrephō*** [verb: ἀναστρέφω <390>]**; from *ana*: again, and *strephō*: to turn ▶ In the pass., to receive a particular treatment, to be abused** > There were Hebrew believers in the Lord who had been made a spectacle both in reproaches and afflictions; others were associated with those who had been so treated (Heb. 10:33 {to pass through, to be used}). All other refs.: CONDUCT (verb)[1] <390>, LIVE <390>, RETURN (verb) <390>.
2 ***chraomai*** [verb: χράομαι <5530>]**; from *chraō*: to lend or to provide what is needed ▶ To behave toward** > Julius, treating {entreating} Paul kindly, allowed him to go to his friends (Acts 27:3). All other refs.: USE (verb) <5530>.
– 3 Matt. 22:6; Luke 18:32; 1 Thes. 2:2 → to treat spitefully, shamefully, ill → MISTREAT <5195> 4 Mark 9:12 → to be treated with contempt → CONTEMPT <1847> 5 Mark 12:4 in some mss. → to treat shamefully → to insult → INSULT (noun) <818> 6 Luke 15:19 → to treat as → to make as → MAKE <4160> 7 Luke 18:9 → to treat with contempt → CONTEMPT <1848> 8 Rom. 14:3, 10; 1 Cor. 16:11 Gal. 4:14; 1 Thes. 5:20 → to treat with contempt → DESPISE <1848> 9 1 Cor. 4:11 → to treat brutally, to treat harshly, to treat roughly → BEAT <2852> 10 1 Cor. 12:23 → BESTOW <4060> 11 2 Cor. 6:8 → "we are treated" added in Engl. 12 Col. 4:1 → to treat justly and fairly → to give what is just and fair → GIVE <3930> 13 Heb. 12:7 → DEAL <4374> 14 1 Pet. 3:7 → GIVE <632>.

TREATED – Heb. 11:37; 13:3 → to be evil treated, to be ill-treated → TORMENTED (BE) <2558>.

TREATISE – Acts 1:1 → ACCOUNT (noun) <3056>.

TREATMENT – 1 Acts 7:34 → ill treatment → OPPRESSION <2561> 2 Col. 2:23 → harsh treatment, severe treatment → NEGLECT (noun) <857>.

TREE – 1 ***dendron*** [neut. noun: δένδρον <1186>] **▶ Tall woody plant with branches** > Jesus says that the axe is laid to the root of the trees and every tree that does not produce good fruit is cut down and thrown into the fire (Matt. 3:10a, b; 7:17a, b, 18a, b, 19; 12:33a–c; Luke 3:9a, b; 6:43a, b, 44). In a parable, a grain of mustard becomes a tree (Matt. 13:32; Luke 13:19). The man who had been blind was seeing men like trees, walking (Mark 8:24). Branches from the trees were cut down and spread on the road before Jesus (Matt. 21:8; Mark 11:8). Jesus told a parable using the fig tree (*sukē*) and all the trees (*dendron*) (Luke 21:29). Jude compares evil persons to late autumn trees without fruit (Jude 12). Trees are also mentioned in the book of Revelation (7:1, 3; 8:7; 9:4). ¶
2 ***xulon*** [neut. noun: ξύλον <3586>]**; from *xuō*: to scrape, to plane ▶ a. The wooden cross on which Jesus was crucified; also transl.: cross** > The word is used in Acts 5:30; 10:39; 13:29; 1 Pet. 2:24. It is written that everyone who hangs on a tree is cursed (Gal. 3:13). **b. Term designating Christ** > He is named the "green tree" {wood}, spir-

itually alive and unjustly condemned, in contrast to Israel, "the dry" (Luke 23:31). **c. Tree of life** > The tree of life (Rev. 2:7; 22:2a, b, 14, 19 in some mss.) will provide eternal enjoyment of the fruits of divine life of which Christ is the source. All other refs.: STAVE <3586>, STOCKS <3586>, WOOD <3586>.

TREMBLE – [1] ***tremō*** [verb: τρέμω <5141>]; **from *treō*: to dread, to tremble ▶ To be physically agitated because one is afraid** > Healed by Jesus, a woman was fearing and trembling (Mark 5:33; Luke 8:47). Peter speaks of those who do not tremble {do not fear, are not afraid} when they revile angelic dignitaries (2 Pet. 2:10). Other ref.: Acts 9:6 in some mss. ¶
– [2] Matt. 28:4 → SHAKE <4579> [3] Mark 16:8 → lit.: trembling (noun) → TREMBLING <5156> [4] Acts 7:32; 16:29; Heb. 12:21 → full of trembling → TREMBLING <1790> [5] Acts 24:25 → AFRAID <1719> [6] Rom. 11:20 → to be afraid → AFRAID <5399> [7] Jas. 2:19 → SHUDDER <5425>.

TREMBLING – [1] ***tromos*** [masc. noun: τρόμος <5156>]; **from *tremō*: to tremble ▶ Physical agitation produced by fear, tremor** > Trembling and astonishment had gripped the women at the tomb of Jesus (Mark 16:8). Paul had been among the Corinthians in weakness, fear, and much trembling (1 Cor. 2:3). The Corinthians had received Titus with fear and trembling (2 Cor. 7:15). Servants are to obey their masters according to the flesh with fear and trembling (Eph. 6:5). The Philippians were to work out their own salvation with fear and trembling (Phil. 2:12). ¶

[2] **trembling, full of trembling: *entromos*** [adj.: ἔντρομος <1790>]; **from *en*: in, and *tromos*: see [1] ▶ Thoroughly frightened, terrified, shaken with fear** > Moses trembled and (lit.: Having become full of trembling, Moses) did not dare look when God spoke to him (Acts 7:32; Heb. 12:21: *ektromos* in some mss.). The jailer fell down trembling before Paul and Silas whom God had just delivered (Acts 16:29). Other ref.: Luke 8:47 in some mss. ¶

TRENCH – Luke 19:43 → EMBANKMENT <5482>.

TRESPASS – [1] Matt. 6:14, 15a, b; Mark 11:25, 26; Rom. 4:25; 5:15–18, 20; 2 Cor. 5:19; Gal. 6:1; Eph. 1:7; 2:1, 5; Col. 2:13a, b; Jas. 5:16 → TRANSGRESSION <3900> [2] Rom. 5:16 → "trespass" added in Engl. [3] Rom. 11:11, 12 → FALL (noun) <3900>.

TRESSING – 1 Pet. 3:3 → BRAIDING <1708>.

TRIAL – [1] ***peirasmos*** [masc. noun: πειρασμός <3986>]; **from *peirazō*: to try, to tempt ▶ Temptation, difficulty; also transl.: testing** > Paul had served the Lord in Asia with many tears and trials (Acts 20:19). The fire of persecution had taken place among Christians for their trial (1 Pet. 4:12). Blessed is the man who endures trial (Jas. 1:12). The Lord promises Philadelphia to keep her from (lit.: out of) the hour of trial that will come upon the whole world (Rev. 3:10). All other refs.: TEMPTATION <3986>.

[2] ***peira*** [fem. noun: πεῖρα <3984>]; **from *peirō*: to pierce ▶ a. Attempt** > The Egyptians made trial {attempted, assayed, tried} to pass through the Red Sea (Heb. 11:29). **b. Temptation, difficulty** > O.T. people of faith had trial of {experienced, faced} mockings and scourgings (Heb. 11:36). ¶
– [3] Acts 4:9 → to be on trial → EXAMINE <350> [4] Acts 16:37 → without a trial → UNCONDEMNED <178> [5] 2 Cor. 8:2 → TEST (noun and verb) <1382> <1381> [6] 1 Thes. 3:3; 2 Thes. 1:4 → TRIBULATION <2347> [7] Heb. 11:29 → attempt → ATTEMPT <3984> [8] 1 Pet. 1:7 → TESTING <1383> [9] 1 Pet. 4:12 → fiery trial, painful trial → FIERY <4451>.

TRIBE – [1] ***phulē*** [fem. noun: φυλή <5443>]; **from *phulon*: race, clan, which is from *phuō*: to engender, to grow ▶ Company of people assembled from the same kindred; also transl.: kindred, na-**

tion, people > a. Those of the earth in general. All the tribes of the earth shall mourn, and they shall see the Son of Man coming on the clouds of heaven with power and great glory (Matt. 24:30; Rev. 1:7). Jesus has redeemed to God with His blood from every tribe, tongues, people, and nation (Rev. 5:9). John saw a great crowd that no one could number, out of every nation, and all tribes, peoples, and tongues, standing before the throne and before the Lamb (Rev. 7:9). Those from the peoples, tribes, tongues, and nations shall see the dead bodies of the two witnesses for three and one half days (Rev. 11:9). Authority was given to the beast over every tribe, people, tongue, and nation (Rev. 13:7). John saw an angel flying in the midheaven, having the eternal gospel to preach to those settled on the earth, and to every nation, tribe, tongue, and people (Rev. 14:6). **b. Israelites (all twelve tribes descended from the patriarch Jacob, who was also named Israel) and later the Jews (two tribes, Judah and Benjamin, descended from Jacob).** The Son of Man will judge the twelve tribes of Israel (Matt. 19:28), as likewise will do His apostles (Luke 22:30). The prophetess Anna was of the tribe of Asher (Luke 2:36). King Saul was of the tribe of Benjamin (Acts 13:21), as was likewise the apostle Paul (Rom. 11:1; Phil. 3:5). The Lord did not belong to the tribe of Levi (Heb. 7:13), but He descended from the tribe of Judah (Heb. 7:14; Rev. 5:5). James writes to the twelve tribes, which are dispersed abroad (Jas. 1:1). John heard the number of those who had been sealed, one hundred forty-four thousand, sealed out of all the tribes of the sons of Israel (Rev. 7:4–8 [12x]). The heavenly Jerusalem had twelve gates, and at the gates twelve angels, and names written on them, which are the names of the twelve tribes of the sons of Israel (Rev. 21:12). ¶

[2] **twelve tribes: *dōdekaphulon*** [neut. noun: δωδεκάφυλον <1429>]; **from *dōdeka*: twelve, and *phulē*: see [1] ▶ This noun makes reference to the twelve tribes of Israel as a whole >** Paul speaks of the hope of the promise to which the twelve tribes hope to arrive (Acts 26:7). ¶

– [3] Phil. 3:5 → RACE[1] <1085>.

TRIBULATION – [1] ***thlipsis*** [fem. noun: θλῖψις <2347>]; **from *thlibō*: to compress, to oppress ▶ Physical or moral trial provoking great suffering; also transl.: affliction, distress, hardship, persecution, suffering, trial, trouble >** Jesus warns believers in Him that they have tribulation in the world, but He has overcome the world (John 16:33). We must enter the kingdom of God with much tribulation {many hardships} (Acts 14:22). Paul boasted in tribulations, knowing that tribulation produces perseverance (Rom. 5:3a, b; 12:12; 2 Cor. 6:4); the Christians' momentary and light affliction is producing for us an eternal weight of glory (2 Cor. 4:17). God the Father comforted Paul in all his tribulation that he might be able to comfort those who were in any tribulation (2 Cor. 1:4a, b). Paul was exceeding joyful in all his tribulation (2 Cor. 7:4). He was asking that the Ephesians do not lose heart at his tribulations for them (Eph. 3:13). The Thessalonians had received the word of God accompanied by much tribulation (1 Thes. 1:6). See GREAT TRIBULATION. Other refs.: Matt. 13:21; 24:21, 29; Mark 4:17; 13:19, 24; Acts 11:19; 20:23; Rom. 2:9; 8:35; 2 Cor. 8:2; Phil. 1:16 or 17; 1 Thes. 3:3, 7; 2 Thes. 1:4, 6; Rev. 1:9; 2:9, 10, 22; 7:14. All other refs.: AFFLICTION <2347>, ANGUISH <2347>, DISTRESS <2347>, TROUBLE (noun) <2347>.

– [2] 2 Cor. 1:6; 4:8 → to be in tribulation, to suffer tribulation → to be afflicted → AFFLICTED (BE) <2346>.

TRIBUNAL – [1] Acts 18:12, 16, 17; 25:6, 10, 17 → JUDGMENT SEAT <968> [2] Jas. 2:6 → JUDGMENT SEAT <2922>.

TRIBUNE – Acts 21:31–33, 37; 22:24, 26–29; 23:10, 15, 17–19, 22; 24:22; 25:23 → tribune, military tribune → CAPTAIN <5506>.

TRIBUTE – [1] ***kēnsos*** [masc. noun: κῆνσος <2778>]; **from Lat. *census*: census, counting of people ▶ Personal or property tax; also transl.: tax, taxes, poll-**

tax > The term is used in Matt. 17:25; 22:17, 19; Mark 12:14 (*epikephalaion* in some mss.). ¶

2 ***phoros*** [masc. noun: φόρος <5411>]; **from *pherō*: to bring ▶ Tax imposed upon people annually; also transl.: tax, taxes** > The Jews had to pay a tribute to Caesar (Luke 20:22; 23:2). The Christians in Rome had to pay tribute to authorities (Rom. 13:6, 7a, b). ¶

– 3 Matt. 17:24a, b → TAX (noun) <1323>.

TRICK – 1 Matt. 2:16 → MOCK <1702> 2 1 Thes. 2:3 → nor are we trying to trick you → lit.: nor in guile → SUBTLETY <1388>.

TRICKERY – 1 ***kubeia*** [fem. noun: κυβεία <2940>]; **from *kubos*: dice; sometimes a dice player cheated, hence the term *kubeia* ▶ Deception, fraud** > Christ has given gifts for the perfecting of the saints, in order that we may no longer be little children, tossed here and there and carried about by every wind of doctrine and by the trickery {sleight, cunning} and craftiness of men (Eph. 4:14). ¶

– 2 Matt. 26:4; Mark 14:1; 2 Cor. 12:16 → SUBTLETY <1388> 3 Luke 20:23 → DECEIT <3834> 4 Acts 13:10 → FRAUD <4468> 5 2 Cor. 12:16 → DECEIT <1388> 6 Eph. 4:14 → CUNNING <3834>.

TRIM – ***kosmeō*** [verb: κοσμέω <2885>]; **from *kosmos*: order, world ▶ To arrange, to put in good order** > In the parable, all the virgins trimmed their lamps (Matt. 25:7). All other refs.: ADORN <2885>.

TRIUMPH (noun and verb) – **to cause to triumph, to lead in triumph, to lead in triumphal procession: *thriambeuō*** [verb: θριαμβεύω <2358>]; **from *thriambos*: triumph ▶ To conquer, to conduct a victorious procession, during which associates share in a display of the glory won by their leader and conquered foes are publicly presented in a display of their defeat** > Paul gave thanks to God who always leads Christians in triumph in Christ (2 Cor. 2:14). Christ has disarmed rulers and authorities and made a public display of them, leading them in triumph by the cross (Col. 2:15). ¶

TRIUMPH (verb) – Rev. 5:5; 12:11; 17:14 → to triumph over → OVERCOME <3528>.

TRIUMPHAL – 2 Cor. 2:14 → to lead in triumphal procession → TRIUMPH (noun and verb) <2358>.

TRIVIAL – 1 Cor. 6:2 → LEAST <1646>.

TROAS – ***Trōas*** [fem. name: Τρῳάς <5174>] ▶ **Region of northwestern Asia Minor** > Paul came to Troas during his second missionary journey (Acts 16:8, 11). During his third journey, he stayed there seven days (Acts 20:5, 6; 2 Cor. 2:12). He had left a cloak there (2 Tim. 4:13). ¶

TROGYLLIUM – ***Trōgullion*** [neut. name: Τρωγύλλιον <5175>] ▶ **City of western Asia Minor, southwest of Ephesus** > Paul stayed in Trogyllium during his third missionary journey (Acts 20:15 in some mss.). ¶

TROOP – 1 Acts 21:31 → COHORT <4686> 2 Rev. 9:16 → ARMY <4753> 3 Rev. 9:16 → HORSEMAN <2461>.

TROOPS – ***strateuma*** [neut. noun: στράτευμα <4753>]; **from *strateuomai*: to serve as a soldier, which is from *stratos*: camp, army ▶ Army, company of soldiers assembled for battle and of variable size; also transl.: armies, forces, men of war, soldiers** > A king sent his troops to destroy the murderers of his servants (Matt. 22:7). Herod, with his troops, having treated Jesus with contempt and having mocked Him, dressed Him in a gorgeous robe and sent Him back to Pilate (Luke 23:11). The chiliarch commanded the troops to take Paul away and to bring him into the barracks (Acts 23:10, 27). Other refs.: Rev. 9:16; 19:14, 19; see ARMY <4753>. ¶

TROPHIMUS – ***Trophimos*** [masc. name: Τρόφιμος <5161>]: **adopted child; from *trophē*: nourishment ▶ Christian man originally from Ephesus** > Trophimus accompanied Paul with other brothers in Asia (Acts 20:4). At the end of this journey, he was with Paul in Jerusalem (Acts 21:29). Paul was obliged to leave him sick at Miletus (2 Tim. 4:20). ¶

TROUBLE (noun) – 1 ***thlipsis*** [fem. noun: θλῖψις <2347>]; **from *thlibō*: to compress, to oppress ▶ Oppression, suffering, tribulation; also transl.: affliction, distress** > In the time of Joseph, a famine and great trouble came over all the lands of Egypt and Canaan (Acts 7:11). Those who marry will have trouble in the flesh (1 Cor. 7:28). Paul would not have his brothers in Corinth to be ignorant of the trouble {hardships} he experienced in Asia (2 Cor. 1:8). All other refs.: AFFLICTION <2347>, ANGUISH <2347>, DISTRESS <2347>, TRIBULATION <2347>.

2 ***kakia*** [fem. noun: κακία <2549>]; **from *kakos*: bad ▶ Wickedness, evil** > Sufficient to the day is its own trouble (Matt. 6:34). All other refs.: MALICE <2549>, WICKEDNESS <2549>.

3 ***kopos*** [masc. noun: κόπος <2873>]; **from *koptō*: to cut, to strike ▶ Displeasure, annoyance** > A man could say to his friend asking for three loaves of bread to not bother {disturb, trouble} him (lit.: to not cause (*parechō*) him trouble) (Luke 11:7). No one was to cause trouble to Paul, for he bore in his body the marks of the Lord Jesus (Gal. 6:17). All other refs.: LABOR (noun) <2873>, TROUBLE (verb) <2873>.

4 ***tarachē*** [fem. noun: ταραχή <5016>]; **from *tarassō*: to disturb, to stir ▶ Agitation, tumult, upheaval** > Jesus speaks of a time when there will be famines and troubles (Mark 13:8 in some mss.). Other ref.: John 5:4; see TROUBLING <5016>. ¶

5 **out of trouble: *amerimnos*** [adj.: ἀμέριμνος <275>]; **from *a*: neg., and *merimna*: anxiety, care ▶ Without cause to worry or to be anxious; also transl.: from all anxiety** > Soldiers were to be kept out of trouble if they would be caught after lying concerning the resurrection of the body of the Lord (Matt. 28:14). Other ref.: 1 Cor. 7:32 (free from concern); see CONCERN (noun) <275>. ¶

– 6 Acts 17:6 → to cause trouble → to turn upside down → TURN (verb) <387> 7 Phil. 3:1 → TEDIOUS <3636> 8 1 Tim. 5:10 → those in trouble → lit.: the afflicted → AFFLICTED (BE) <2346> 9 2 Tim. 2:9; Jas. 5:13 → to suffer trouble, to be in trouble → SUFFER <2553> 10 Heb. 12:15 → to cause trouble → TROUBLE (verb) <1776>.

TROUBLE (verb) – 1 ***anastatoō*** [verb: ἀναστατόω <387>]; **from *anastatos*: ruined entirely ▶ To shatter, to upset** > Paul would have wished that those who were troubling {who were throwing into confusion, agitators of} the Galatians would cut themselves off (Gal. 5:12). Other refs.: Acts 17:6; 21:38 (to raise a sedition); see TURN TO <387>, SEDITION <387>. ¶

2 ***enochleō*** [verb: ἐνοχλέω <1776>]; **from *en*: in, and *ochleō*: to disturb, to upset, which is from *ochlos*: crowd ▶ To disturb, to excite** > Jesus healed those who were tormented by unclean spirits (Luke 6:18; other mss.: *ochleō*). A root of bitterness, springing up, might trouble {cause trouble to} Christians (Heb. 12:15). ¶

3 ***parenochleō*** [verb: παρενοχλέω <3926>]; **from *para*: beside, and *enochleō*: see 2 ▶ To disturb, to create additional trouble** > James judged not to trouble {make it difficult for} those from the nations who turned to God (Acts 15:19). ¶

4 **to be troubled: *throeō*** [verb: θροέω <2360>]; **from *throos*: sound of a voice, murmur of a crowd ▶ To be alarmed, to be frightened due to a sudden clamor or a sense of unrest** > Jesus told His disciples to see to it that they be not troubled when they should hear of wars and of rumors of wars (Matt. 24:6; Mark 13:7). The Thessalonians were not to be troubled, as though the day of the Lord had already come (2 Thes. 2:2). ¶

5 **to cause trouble: *parechō*** [verb: παρέχω <3930>]; **from *para*: near, and *echō*: to have ▶ To provoke, to disturb** > No one was to trouble (lit.: to cause trouble to) Paul,

for he bore in his body the marks of the Lord Jesus (Gal. 6:17). See [11] and entries in Lexicon at <3930>.

[6] ***skullō*** [verb: σκύλλω <4660>] ▶ **To bother, to harass > To take pains, to bother >** Some reproached the ruler of the synagogue whose daughter had died of troubling Jesus further (Mark 5:35; Luke 8:49). The centurion sent to tell Jesus not to trouble Himself, for he did not consider himself worthy that Jesus should enter under his roof (Luke 7:6). ¶

[7] ***tarassō*** [verb: ταράσσω <5015>] ▶ **a. To disturb, to worry, to be upset; also transl.: to frighten, to startle, to stir, to terrify, to throw into confusion, to throw into turmoil >** King Herod was troubled in regard to the birth of Jesus (Matt. 2:3). Seeing Jesus walking on the sea, the disciples were troubled (Matt. 14:26; Mark 6:50). Zacharias was troubled when he saw the angel of the Lord (Luke 1:12). Jesus asked the disciples why they were troubled (Luke 24:38). Jesus said to His disciples: "Do not let your heart be troubled" (John 14:1, 27). Some had troubled those of Antioch by their words (Acts 15:24). The crowd and the city authorities of Thessalonica were troubled, when they heard that there was another king, Jesus (Acts 17:8). There were some people who troubled the Galatians, and who wanted to distort the gospel of Christ (Gal. 1:7; 5:10). Peter says that even if we should suffer for the sake of righteousness, we are blessed; he also says not to fear what others fear and to not be troubled (1 Pet. 3:14). Other ref.: Acts 17:13 {to stir}. **b. To affect, to shake >** When Jesus saw Mary, the sister of Lazarus, weeping and the Jews who had come with her also weeping, He was deeply moved in His spirit and was troubled (John 11:33). The soul of the Lord Jesus was troubled (John 12:27); He was troubled in His spirit (13:21). **c. To agitate, to stir >** An angel troubled the water of the pool of Bethesda (John 5:4 in some mss., 7). ¶

[8] ***diatarassō*** [verb: διαταράσσω <1298>]; **from *dia*: through (intens.), and *tarassō*: see [7] ▶ To be wholly disturbed, to be greatly concerned >** Mary was troubled {was perplexed, was troubled greatly} at the word of the angel (Luke 1:29). ¶

[9] **to trouble exceedingly, to trouble utterly: *ektarassō*** [verb: ἐκταράσσω <1613>]; **from *ek*: out (intens.), and *tarassō*: see [7] ▶ To agitate, to disturb greatly; also transl.: to throw into confusion, to throw in an uproar >** Certain men accused Paul and Silas of utterly troubling the city of Philippi (Acts 16:20). ¶

[10] **to be troubled: *turbazō*** [verb: τυρβάζω <5182>]; **from *turbē*: crowd, tumult ▶ To be disturbed, to be anxious >** Martha was worried and troubled {bothered, upset} about many things (Luke 10:41; other mss.: *thorubazō*). ¶

[11] **to give trouble, to cause trouble: *parechen kopon*; to give: *parechō*** [verb: παρέχω <3930>]; **from *para*: near, and *echō*: to have; trouble: *kopos*** [masc. noun: κόπος <2873>]; **from *koptō*: to cut, to strike ▶ a. To importune, to irritate; also transl.: to annoy, to bother >** In a parable, a widow was troubling {was annoying, was bothering} (lit.: was giving trouble to) a judge to obtain justice (Luke 18:5). **b. To give displeasure, to cause sorrow >** The disciples had troubled (lit.: given trouble to) the woman who had poured her perfume on the head of Jesus (Matt. 26:10; Mark 14:6). See [5]. All other refs. (*kopos*): see LABOR (noun) <2873>, TROUBLE (noun) <2873>.

– [12] Luke 6:18 → TORMENT (verb) <3791> [13] Acts 15:24 → SUBVERT <384> [14] Acts 18:17 → to trouble oneself → CARE <3199> [15] 2 Cor. 4:8; 2 Thes. 1:6, 7 → to be troubled → AFFLICTED (BE) <2346>.

TROUBLED – [1] **to be troubled: *ekthambeō*** [verb: ἐκθαμβέω <1568>]; **from *ekthambos*: astonished, which is from *ek*: out (intens.), and *thambos*: astonishment, amazement ▶ To be terrified >** In Gethsemane, Jesus began to be troubled {be amazed, be sore amazed} and deeply distressed (Mark 14:33). Other refs.: Mark 9:15; 16:5, 6; see ALARM (verb) <1568>. ¶

– [2] Mark 14:33 → to be troubled → to be full of heaviness → HEAVINESS <85> [3] Acts 16:18 → to become troubled → to be grieved → GRIEVE <1278> 4 1 Cor. 7:21 → to be troubled → CARE <3199> 5 2 Cor. 7:5 → to be troubled → AFFLICTED (BE) <2346>.

TROUBLEMAKER – Acts 24:5 → PEST <3061>.

TROUBLING – ***tarachē*** [fem. noun: ταραχή <5016>]; **from *tarassō*: to disturb, to stir ▶ Agitation, stirring up** > After the troubling {disturbance} of the water by the angel, the first person to step in was made well of his disease (John 5:4 in some mss.). Other ref.: Mark 13:8; see TROUBLE (noun) <5016>. ¶

TROW – Luke 17:9 → THINK <1380>.

TRUCEBREAKER – 2 Tim. 3:3 → IMPLACABLE <786>.

TRUE – 1 ***alēthēs*** [adj.: ἀληθής <227>]; **from *a*: neg., and *lēthō*, a form of *lanthanō*: to be hidden ▶ Real, sincere, one who cannot lie; also transl.: right, truly, truthful, valid** > People acknowledged that Jesus was true (Matt. 22:16; Mark 12:14). God is true (John 3:33). The Father is true {reliable} (John 8:26). What the woman at the well of Sychar said about her matrimonial state was true (John 4:18). The testimony of Jesus is true (John 8:14), as likewise is His judgment (v. 16). Paul uses this term in 2 Cor. 6:8 {genuine} about himself; Peter uses it in 2 Pet. 2:22 concerning a proverb. The grace in which Christians stand is the true grace of God (1 Pet. 5:12). The testimony of John concerning Demetrius was true (3 John 12). Ref.: Acts 12:9; see REAL <227>. Other refs.: John 5:31, 32; 7:18; 8:13, 17; 10:41; 19:35b; 21:24; Rom. 3:4; Phil. 4:8; Titus 1:13; 1 John 2:8a, 27. ¶

2 ***alēthinos*** [adj.: ἀληθινός <228>]; **from *alēthēs*: see 1 ▶ Which corresponds perfectly to something else, real, sincere** > Jesus asks who will entrust the true riches to those who have not been faithful in the unrighteous riches (i.e., the riches of this world) (Luke 16:11). Jesus is the true light (John 1:9). The Father gives the true bread that comes from heaven (John 6:32). The Father who sent Jesus is true (John 7:28). Jesus is the true vine (John 15:1). The true worshippers shall worship the Father in spirit and in truth (John 4:23). Eternal life is to know the Father as the only true God and Jesus Christ, whom He has sent (John 17:3). The witness of John concerning the crucifixion of Jesus is true (John 19:35a). The Thessalonians had turned to God from idols, to serve the living and true God (1 Thes. 1:9). Christians are to draw near to God with a true heart (Heb. 10:22). We know Him who is true, the Lord Jesus, we are in Him who is true, and He is the true God and eternal life (1 John 5:20a–c). Jesus is also called true in Rev. 3:7, 14; 6:10; 19:11; righteous and true are His ways (15:3) and His judgments (16:7; 19:2). Other refs.: John 4:37; Heb. 8:2; 9:24; 1 John 2:8b, Rev. 19:9; 21:5; 22:6. ¶

3 ***gnēsios*** [adj.: γνήσιος <1103>]; **from *genos*: born ▶ Primary meaning: legitimate; other meaning: consistent with reality, genuine** > Paul uses this term in regard to a companion (Phil. 4:3 {loyal}). Timothy was the true child of Paul in the faith (1 Tim. 1:2), as was also Titus according to the common faith (Titus 1:4). Other ref.: 2 Cor. 8:8; see SINCERITY <1103>. ¶

– 4 Luke 24:34 → it is true → REALLY <3689> 5 John 1:47; John 6:55a, b → TRULY <230> 6 John 3:21; Eph. 5:9; Col. 1:5 → what is true, all that is true, true message → word of truth, all truth → TRUTH <225> 7 Acts 14:22 → to remain true → CONTINUE <1696> 8 Rom. 11:20 → that is true → lit.: well! → WELL (adv.) <2573> 9 Rom. 12:1 → true and proper → INTELLIGENT <3050> 10 1 Cor. 15:15 → if it is true → if in fact → FACT <1512> 11 2 Cor. 12:12 → TRULY <3303> 12 Phil. 3:16 → to hold true → to walk by the same; to walk by the same rule in some mss. → RULE (noun) <2583> 13 1 Tim. 3:1 → FAITHFUL <4103> 14 1 Tim. 3:16 → "true" added in Engl.

TRULY – 1 ***alēthōs*** [adv.: ἀληθῶς <230>]; **from *alēthēs*: real, true, which is from *a*: neg., and *lēthō*, a form of *lanthanō*:**

to be hidden ▶ Really, certainly; also transl.: actually, indeed, surely, truth, of truth, truthfully, verily > The centurion said that Jesus was truly the Son of God (Matt. 27:54; Mark 15:39). It was said of Jesus that He was truly {of truth} the Son of God (Matt. 14:33), the Savior of the world (John 4:42), and the prophet (John 6:14; 7:40). This term is used concerning Jesus speaking of seeing the kingdom of God (Luke 9:27), establishing a servant over his master's household (12:44), and a poor widow (21:3). The flesh of Jesus is truly (or: of a truth) food, and His blood is truly drink (John 6:55a, b); other mss. have *alēthēs*: real, true. Nathanael was truly an Israelite {indeed, true} (John 1:47). Some people asked if the leaders of the Jews had truly {indeed} recognized that Jesus was the Christ (John 7:26). Jesus therefore said to the Jews who believed in Him, that if they persevered in His word, they were truly {indeed} His disciples (John 8:31). His disciples had known truly {surely, with certainty} that He had come out from the Father (John 17:8). The word of Paul's preaching was truly the word of God (1 Thes. 2:13). Whoever keeps the word of the Lord Jesus, in him the love of God is truly perfected (1 John 2:5). Other refs.: Matt. 26:73; Mark 14:70; Acts 12:11; see SURELY <230>. ¶

[2] ***dē*** [adv.: δή <1211>] ▶ Used as a particle giving to a sentence an expression of certainty and reality in opposition to mere opinion or conjecture meaning: indeed, then, now. Used as an affirmative meaning of: truly, in truth, really (Matt. 13:23; 2 Cor. 12:1 in the sense of doubtless). With the meaning of: exhorting, by all means (Luke 2:15; Acts 15:36); with the meaning of: inference or conclusion, therefore (1 Cor. 6:20). This, however, includes the meaning of affirmation and wish giving it the meaning of: therefore truly, therefore by all means. ¶ ‡

[3] ***men*** [conj.: μέν <3303>] ▶ **Verily, certainly** > Truly {Indeed} the signs of an apostle {The signs of a true apostle} were accomplished among the Corinthians (2 Cor. 12:12). *

[4] ***ontōs*** [adv.: ὄντως <3689>]; **from *on*: pres. ptcp. of "to be" ▶ Really, in truth; also transl.: certainly, indeed, of a truth, really, truly** > The term is used in 1 Cor. 14:25 in regard to the presence of God among believers. All other refs.: CERTAINLY <3689>, INDEED <3689>, REALLY <3689>.

[5] See WHEREFORE <1355>.

– [6] Matt. 5:18, 26; 18:18, 19 in some mss.; Mark 11:23; Luke 12:37; et al. → VERILY <281> [7] Matt. 26:73; Mark 14:70 → SURELY <230> [8] Luke 20:21; John 16:7; Acts 10:34; Col. 1:6 → TRUTH <225> [9] John 4:18 → TRUE <227>.

TRUMP – 1 Cor. 15:52a; 1 Thes. 4:16 → TRUMPET <4536>.

TRUMPET – [1] ***salpinx*** [fem. noun: σάλπιγξ <4536>] ▶ **Wind instrument which produces a blasting sound; also transl.: bugle, trump** > The sound of the trumpet accompanies divine interventions. After the great tribulation, the elect shall be assembled with a great sound of trumpet (lit.: with the great trumpet) (Matt. 24:31). The trumpet calling to battle should not give an unclear sound (1 Cor. 14:8). At the coming of the Lord, the last trumpet, the trumpet of God will sound, and Christians will be resurrected or changed, and assembled to go to meet Him in the clouds (1 Cor. 15:52a; 1 Thes. 4:16). Hebrew Christians had not come to the sound of a trumpet (Heb. 12:19). John heard a great voice, as of a trumpet (Rev. 1:10; 4:1). Trumpets precede divine judgments in Rev. 8:2, 6a, 13; 9:14. In Israel, the feast of trumpets was celebrated in the seventh month (see Num. 29:1; Ps. 81:3): this speaks of a future day when God Himself will invite His people Israel to remember Him; Israel will be assembled again in her land to receive her Messiah. ¶

[2] **to sound a trumpet: *salpizō*** [verb: σαλπίζω <4537>]; **from *salpinx*: see [1] ▶ To produce a sound with a trumpet** > He who gives to the poor is not to sound a trumpet before himself (Matt. 6:2). At the resurrection of Christians, the trumpet will sound, and the dead shall be resurrected

incorruptible, and we shall be changed (1 Cor. 15:52b). In the book of Revelation, seven angels sound seven trumpets to announce a divine judgment (8:6–8, 10, 12, 13; 9:1, 13; 10:7; 11:15). ¶

TRUMPETER – ***salpistēs*** [masc. noun: σαλπιστής <4538>]; **from *salpizō*: to sound a trumpet, which is from *salpinx*: trumpet ▶ One who produces a sound with a trumpet** > The sound of trumpeters will never be heard in Babylon, the great city, again (Rev. 18:22). ¶

TRUST (noun) – [1] Luke 16:11; 1 Thes. 2:4 → COMMIT <4100> [2] 1 Cor. 4:2 → one given a trust → STEWARD <3623> [3] 1 Cor. 9:17 → DISPENSATION <3622> [4] 2 Cor. 1:9; Heb. 2:13 → to have one's trust, to put one's trust → TRUST (verb) <3982> [5] 2 Cor. 3:4 → CONFIDENCE <4006> [6] Phil. 3:4 → to have one's trust → to have confidence → CONFIDENCE <3982> [7] 1 Tim. 6:20 → what is committed to the trust → COMMIT <3866> or, in other mss., THING COMMITTED <3872>.

TRUST (verb) – [1] ***elpizō*** [verb: ἐλπίζω <1679>]; **from *elpis*: hope, trust ▶ To have confidence, to have hope** > Those who are rich must not trust in {fix their hope on, put their hope in} uncertain riches, but in the living God who gives us richly all things to enjoy (1 Tim. 6:17). All other refs.: HOPE (verb) <1679>.

[2] **to first trust: *proelpizō*** [verb: προελπίζω <4276>]; **from *pro*: before, and *elpizō*: see [1] ▶ To hope in advance, to expect in advance** > Paul speaks of those who first trusted {pre-trusted, were the first to hope} in Christ (Eph. 1:12). ¶

[3] ***peithō*** [verb: πείθω <3982>] **▶ To have inward confidence, to depend on, to be persuaded, with the implication of outward obedience; also transl.: to be confident, to rely** > Jesus trusted in God (Matt. 27:43; also Heb. 2:13 {to put one's trust}). The strong man trusted in his armor (Luke 11:22). It is hard for those who trust in riches {those who are wealthy} to enter the kingdom of God (Mark 10:24 in some mss.). Jesus spoke a parable to some who trusted in themselves (Luke 18:9). Paul did not trust {have his trust} in himself, but in God (2 Cor. 1:9). He speaks of a man trusting {convinced} in himself that he is of Christ (2 Cor. 10:7). He trusted in the Lord that he would visit the Philippians shortly (Phil. 2:24). He might trust {put confidence} in the flesh more than anyone else (Phil. 3:4). All other refs.: see entries in Lexicon at <3982>.

– [4] Luke 16:11 → to trust with → COMMIT <4100> [5] Phil. 3:4 → CONFIDENCE <4006> [6] Titus 2:10 → they can be fully trusted → lit.: all good faithfulness → FAITHFULNESS <4102>.

TRUSTEE – Gal. 4:2 → STEWARD <3623>.

TRUSTWORTHY – [1] John 8:26 → TRUE <227> [2] 1 Tim. 1:12, 15; 3:1; 4:9; 2 Tim. 2:11; Titus 3:8; Rev. 21:5; 22:6 → FAITHFUL <4103>.

TRUTH – [1] ***alētheia*** [fem. noun: ἀλήθεια <225>]; **from *alēthēs*: real, true, which is from *a*: neg., and *lēthō*, a form of *lanthanō*: to be hidden ▶ Conformity to reality, indisputable fact** > Jesus taught according to the truth (Matt. 22:16; Mark 12:14, 32; Luke 20:21). Healed by Jesus, a woman told Him the whole truth (Mark 5:33). In truth, there were many widows in Israel in the days of Elijah (Luke 4:25). The Word (Jesus) dwelt among men, full of grace and truth (John 1:14). Grace and truth came (sing. in Greek) by Jesus Christ (John 1:17). He who practices truth comes to the light (John 3:21). The true worshippers worship the Father in spirit and in truth (John 4:23, 24). John the Baptist testified to the truth (John 5:33). Jesus told the Jews who had believed in Him that they would know the truth and that the truth would set them free (John 8:32a, b). Jesus spoke the truth (John 8:40, 45, 46; 16:7). He is the way, the truth, and the life (John 14:6). The Holy Spirit is called the Spirit of truth (John 14:17; 15:26; 16:13a; 1 John 5:6); He leads into all the truth (John 16:13b). Jesus asked the Father to sanctify His disciples by the truth, His word being the truth (John 17:17a, b, 19). Jesus came into the world to testify to the truth; whoever is of the truth hears His voice (John 18:37a, b). Pilate said to Jesus: "What is truth?" (John 18:38). The devil has not persevered in the truth, for there is no truth in him (John 8:44a, b). Paul spoke according to the truth (Acts 26:25; Rom. 9:1; 2 Cor. 7:14a, b); the truth of Christ was in him (2 Cor. 11:10). Christians celebrate the feast with the unleavened bread of sincerity and truth (1 Cor. 5:8). Love rejoices with the truth (1 Cor. 13:6). The truth is in Jesus (Eph. 4:21). Christians are to speak the truth each one with his neighbor (Eph. 4:25). The church of the living God is the pillar and foundation of the truth (1 Tim. 3:15). Other refs.: Luke 22:59; Acts 4:27; 10:34; Rom. 1:18, 25; 2:2, 8, 20; 3:7; 15:8; 2 Cor. 4:2; 6:7; 12:6; 13:8a, b; Gal. 2:5, 14; 3:1 (in some mss.); 5:7; Eph. 1:13; 4:24; 5:9; 6:14; Phil. 1:18; Col. 1:5, 6; 2 Thes. 2:10, 12, 13; 1 Tim. 2:4, 7a, b; 4:3; 6:5; 2 Tim. 2:15, 18, 25; 3:7, 8; 4:4; Titus 1:1, 14; Heb. 10:26; Jas. 1:18; 3:14; 5:19; 1 Pet. 1:22; 2 Pet. 1:12; 2:2; 1 John 1:6, 8; 2:4, 21a, b; 3:18, 19; 4:6; 2 John 1a, b, 2–4; 3 John 1, 3a, b, 4, 8, 12. ¶

[2] **to hold the truth, to speak the truth:** ***alētheuō*** [verb: ἀληθεύω <226>]; **from *alēthēs*: see [1] ▶ To speak in accordance with reality** > Paul spoke the truth to the Galatians (Gal. 4:16). Christians should speak the truth in love (Eph. 4:15). ¶

– [3] Matt. 5:18, 26; Mark 11:23; Luke 12:37; et al. → I tell you the truth → VERILY <281> [4] Matt. 14:33; Luke 9:27; 12:44; 21:3; John 6:55a, b; 6:14; 7:40; 17:8; 1 Thes. 2:13 → in truth, of truth, of a truth → TRULY <230> [5] Luke 1:4 → exact truth → CERTAINTY <803> [6] John 7:18; 19:35b; 1 John 2:27 → a man of truth, truth → TRUE <227> [7] John 9:24 → "by telling the truth" added in Engl. [8] Acts 21:34 → CERTAINTY <804> [9] Acts 24:8 → to learn the truth → to take knowledge → KNOWLEDGE <1921> [10] 1 Cor. 14:25 → of a truth → TRULY <3689> [11] 1 Tim. 3:9 → deep truths → MYSTERY <3466> [12] Heb. 5:12 → ELEMENT <4747>.

TRUTHFUL – Matt. 22:16; Mark 12:14; John 3:33 → TRUE <227>.

TRUTHFULLY – [1] Matt. 22:16 → in truth → TRUTH <225> [2] Luke 9:27; 21:3 → truth, of a truth → TRULY <230>.

TRUTHFULNESS – Rom. 15:8 → to show God's truthfulness → lit.: for the truth of God → TRUTH <225>.

TRY[1] – [1] ***peirazō*** [verb: πειράζω <3985>]; **from *peira*: attempt, effort ▶ To make an effort, to attempt** > Saul tried {assayed, essayed} to join the disciples in Jerusalem (Acts 9:26). He and his companions tried {assayed} to go into Bithynia (Acts 16:7). He was accused of having tried to desecrate the temple (Acts 24:6). All other refs.: EXAMINE <3985>, TEMPT <3985>, TEMPTER <3985>, TEST (noun and verb) <3985>.

[2] ***peiraō*** [verb: πειράω <3987>]; **from *peira*: effort, attempt ▶ To make an effort, to attempt** > The Jews had tried {went about} to kill Paul (Acts 26:21). Other ref.: Acts 9:26 in some mss. ¶

– [3] Mark 9:38; Luke 9:49 → to try to hinder → lit.: to hinder → FORBID <2967> [4] Luke 5:18; 6:19; 9:9; 19:3, 47; 20:19; Acts 27:30 → SEEK <2212> [5] Luke 12:58 → to try hard → to make every effort → EFFORT <1325> [6] Luke 14:19; 1 Cor. 3:13; 1 Thes. 2:4; 1 John 4:1 → TEST (noun and verb) <1382> <1381> [7] Luke 22:53 → to try to seize → to stretch out → STRETCH <1614> [8] Acts 9:29 → SEEK <2021> [9] Acts 19:13 → to take in hand → TAKE <2021> [10] Acts 25:9, 20 → to be tried → to be judged → JUDGE (verb) <2919> [11] Acts 26:11 → to try to force → CONSTRAIN <315> [12] 1 Cor. 6:2 → incompetent to try trivial cases → lit.: unworthy of small judgments [13] 1 Thes. 5:15 → PURSUE <1377> [14] 2 Tim. 2:4 → "tries to" added in Engl. [15] Heb. 5:11 → you no longer try to understand → you have become sluggish in hearing → SLUGGISH <3576>, HEARING <189> [16] Heb. 11:29 → attempt → ATTEMPT <3984> [17] Jas. 1:12 → approved → APPROVE <1384>.

TRY[2] – Rev. 3:18 → PURIFY <4448>.

TRYING – Jas. 1:3 → TESTING <1383>.

TRYPHAENA – ***Truphaina*** [fem. name: Τρύφαινα <5170>]**: refined; from *truphē*: luxury ▶ Christian woman of Rome; also spelled Tryphena** > Paul sends greetings to Tryphaena who labored in the Lord (Rom. 16:12). She and Tryphosa were perhaps twin sisters. ¶

TRYPHENA – Rom. 16:12 → TRYPHAENA <5170>.

TRYPHOSA – ***Truphōsa*** [fem. name: Τρυφῶσα <5173>]**: delicate; from *truphaō*: to be delicate ▶ Christian woman of Rome** > Paul sends greetings to Tryphosa who labored in the Lord, as well as her sister Tryphaena (Rom. 16:12). ¶

TUMULT – 1 ***thorubos*** [masc. noun: θόρυβος <2351>] **▶ Noise, uproar; also transl.: commotion, disturbance, riot** > Jesus saw the tumult in the house of the ruler of the synagogue (Mark 5:38). The chief priests and the elders of the people did not want to put Jesus to death during the feast, that there be not a tumult among the people (Matt. 26:5; Mark 14:2). A tumult was rising in regard to Jesus when the people wanted Him to be crucified (Matt. 27:24). Other refs.: Acts 20:1; 21:34; 24:18.¶
2 **to make a tumult: *thorubeō*** [verb: θορυβέω <2350>]**; from *thorubos*: see 1 ▶ To make a great noise; also transl.: to make an ado, to make a commotion** > Jesus asked the people in the house of the ruler of the synagogue why they were making a tumult (Mark 5:39). All other refs.: NOISE (noun) <2350>, UPROAR <2350>.
3 ***stasis*** [fem. noun: στάσις <4714>]**; from *histēmi*: to stand ▶ Insurrection, riot** > A great tumult {dispute, dissension} arose in regard to Paul (Acts 23:10). All other refs.: DISSENSION <4714>, INSURRECTION <4714>, STANDING <4714>.
4 ***akatastasia*** [fem. noun: ἀκαταστασία <181>]**; from *akatastatos*: unstable, which is from *a*: neg., and *kathistēmi*: to settle, which is from *kata*: down, and *histēmi*: to stand ▶ Instability, uprising; also transl.: commotion, disturbance, revolution** > Jesus told His disciples not to be terrified when they would hear of wars and tumults (Luke 21:9). Other refs.: 1 Cor. 14:33; 2 Cor. 12:20; Jas. 3:16; see CONFUSION <181>. Other ref.: 2 Cor. 6:5; see RIOT (noun) <181>. ¶
– 5 Acts 17:6 → to set in tumult → to turn upside down → TURN (verb) <387> 6 Acts 21:27 → to set in a tumult → to stir up → STIR (verb) <4797> 7 Acts 21:31 → to be in tumult → to be in an uproar → UPROAR <4797> 8 2 Cor. 6:5 → RIOT (noun) <181>.

TUMULTUOUS – 1 Acts 19:32 → to be tumultuous → CONFUSED (BE) <4797> 2 Acts 24:12 → to make a tumultuous gathering → to raise up → RAISE <1999> <4160>.

TUNIC – ***chitōn*** [masc. noun: χιτών <5509>]**; from the Heb. *kethoneth*: shirt ▶ Coat, garment** > Jesus says that if anyone wants to go to law against someone and take away his tunic, one should leave him one's coat as well (Matt. 5:40); Luke inverts the garments (Luke 6:29). Jesus says that he who had two tunics is to give one to him who has none (Luke 3:11). He told His disciples not to take two tunics for the journey (Matt. 10:10; Mark 6:9; Luke 9:3). The soldiers took the tunic of Jesus; it was seamless, woven of one piece from the top to the bottom (John 19:23a, b). The widows showed Peter the tunics {body-coats, robes} that Dorcas had made (Acts 9:39). Other refs.: Mark 14:63; Jude 23; see CLOTHES <5509>. ¶

TURMOIL – Acts 17:8 → to throw into turmoil → TROUBLE (verb) <5015>.

TURN (noun) – 1 Cor. 15:23 → RANK (noun) <5001>.

TURN (verb) – 1 **to turn upside down: *anastatoō*** [verb: ἀναστατόω <387>]**; from *anastatos*: ruined completely, which is**

from *anistēmi*: to stand up; from *ana*: above, again, and *histēmi*: to stand ▶ To trouble, to upset > Jason and other brothers were accused to have turned upside down {set in tumult, upset, caused trouble all over} the world (Acts 17:6). Other refs.: Acts 21:38 (to raise a sedition); Gal. 5:12; see SEDITION <387>, TROUBLE (verb) <387>. ¶

2 to turn, to turn out: *apobainō* [verb: ἀποβαίνω <576>]**; from *apo*: from, and *bainō*: to go ▶ To give occasion, to result; also transl.: to lead >** The things that would be inflicted on the disciples would turn out for them for a testimony (Luke 21:13). What had happened to Paul would turn out to his deliverance (Phil. 1:19). Other refs.: Luke 5:2; John 21:9; see GO <576>, COME <576>. ¶

3 to turn away: *apotrepō* [verb: ἀποτρέπω <665>]**; from *apo*: from, and *trepō*: to turn ▶ To go away, to avoid >** Timothy was to turn away from {avoid, have nothing to do with} those who had a form of piety, but were denying its power (2 Tim. 3:5). ¶

4 to turn, to turn aside, to turn away: *ektrepō* [verb: ἐκτρέπω <1624>]**; from *ek*: from, and *trepō*: to turn ▶ To go away, to draw aside, to part >** Some have turned aside to vain discourse (1 Tim. 1:6). Some younger women had turned aside after Satan (1 Tim. 5:15). Paul speaks of a time when men will turn away (*apostrepō*) their ear from the truth and will turn aside (*ektrepō*) to myths (2 Tim. 4:4). All other refs.: AVOID <1624>, DISLOCATE <1624>.

5 *metatithēmi* [verb: μετατίθημι <3346>]; **from *meta*: prep. indicating a change, and *tithēmi*: to put ▶ To change, to transform >** Certain ungodly persons have turned the grace of God into dissoluteness (Jude 4). All other refs.: CARRY <3346>, CHANGE (verb) <3346>, TAKE <3346>.

6 to turn oneself; to turn about, around, back, round, etc.: *strephō* [verb: στρέφω <4762>] **▶ a. To turn oneself, to look behind, to look away >** The swine might turn around and rend those who cast their pearls before them (Matt. 7:6). Jesus having turned saw the woman who had touched Him (Matt. 9:22; some mss.: *epistrephō*). He turned around and told Peter to get away behind Him (Matt. 16:23). Jesus turned to the crowd (Luke 7:9), as well as to the woman who had washed His feet with tears (Luke 7:44), His disciples (Luke 9:55; 10:23), crowds (Luke 14:25), Peter (Luke 22:61), the women of Jerusalem (Luke 23:28). Having turned, Jesus saw two disciples following Him (John 1:38). Mary Magdalene turned herself back and saw Jesus (John 20:14). Mary, turning round, said to Jesus: Rabboni (John 20:16). Paul and Barnabas turned to the Gentiles (Acts 13:46). The fathers of the Israelites would not be subject to Moses, but thrust him from them and in their hearts turned back to Egypt (Acts 7:39). God turned away and delivered the Israelites up to serve the host of heaven (Acts 7:42). **b. To present, to tender >** Jesus taught to turn also the other cheek to him who strikes on one cheek (Matt. 5:39). **c. To change completely, to transform >** The two witnesses will have the power to turn waters into blood (Rev. 11:6). Other refs.: Matt. 18:3; 27:3 in some mss.; see CONVERT (verb) <4762>, RETURN (verb) <4762>. ¶

7 to turn, to turn away: *apostrephō* [verb: ἀποστρέφω <654>]**; from *apo*: from, and *strephō*: see 6 ▶ To go away, to turn one's back, to divert >** Jesus says to not turn away from one who wants to borrow from us (Matt. 5:42). He was accused of turning away {inciting to rebellion, perverting, misleading} the people (Luke 23:14). God has sent Jesus first to the Jews to turn away every one of them from their wickedness (Acts 3:26). The Deliverer will turn away {banish, remove} ungodliness from Jacob (Rom. 11:26). All those in Asia had turned away from {had deserted} Paul (2 Tim. 1:15). Paul says that there will be men who will turn their ear away from the truth (2 Tim. 4:4). The Cretans were not to pay attention to commandments of men turning away from {rejecting} the truth (Titus 1:14). Those who turn away from Him who speaks from heaven will not escape judgment (Heb. 12:25). Other refs.: Matt. 26:52; 27:3; see RETURN (verb) <654>. ¶

8 **to turn away: *diastrephō*** [verb: διαστρέφω <1294>]; **from *dia*: denotes separation, and *strephō*: see 6 ▶ To put aside, to pervert** > Elymas was seeking to turn away the proconsul Sergius Paulus from the faith (Acts 13:8). All other refs.: PERVERT (verb) <1294>, PERVERTED (BE) <1294>.

9 ***epistrephō*** [verb: ἐπιστρέφω <1994>]; **from *epi*: to, and *strephō*: see 6 ▶ a. To convert; see CONVERSION** <1995> > Those who lived at Lydda and Sharon turned to the Lord (Acts 9:35). A great number believed and turned to the Lord (Acts 11:21). Paul and Barnabas exhorted those of Lystra to turn to the living God (Acts 14:15). James judged not to trouble those from the nations who turned to God (Acts 15:19), with the exception that they were to abstain from certain things (see v. 20). Paul was to be sent to the nations so that they might turn from darkness to light (Acts 26:18), which also he did (v. 20). When Israel will turn to the Lord, the veil will be taken away (2 Cor. 3:16). The Thessalonians had turned to God from idols (1 Thes. 1:9). **b. To look** > Peter turned to the body of Tabitha (Acts 9:40). **c. To go away, to turn one's back** > It would have been better to not have known the way of righteousness, than to turn from the holy commandment (2 Pet. 2:21). **d. To return** > During the great tribulation, the one who is in the field must not turn back (Luke 17:31). All other refs.: BRING <1994>, CONVERT (verb) <1994>, RETURN (verb) <1994>.

10 ***metastrephō*** [verb: μεταστρέφω <3344>]; **from *meta*: prep. indicating a change, and *strephō*: see 6 ▶ To transform into something of an opposite or different character** > In the last days, the sun will be turned {be changed} into darkness (Acts 2:20). James wanted the laughter of sinners to be turned {be changed} to mourning, and their joy to heaviness (Jas. 4:9); *metatrepō* in some mss. Other ref.: Gal. 1:7; see PERVERT (verb) <3344>.¶

11 **to become: *ginomai*** [verb: γίνομαι <1096>] **▶ To be changed, to be transformed** > The grief of the disciples would be turned to (lit.: would become) joy (John 16:20). Other refs.: see entries in Lexicon at <1096>.

12 **to turn, to turn aside, to turn away: *ekklinō*** [verb: ἐκκλίνω <1578>]; **from *ek*: out, and *klinō*: to incline, to lean ▶ To go away, to avoid** > Paul speaks of those who have turned away {gone out of the way} from God (Rom. 3:12). He who would love life and see good days should turn away from {avoid, eschew} evil and do good (1 Pet. 3:11). Other ref.: Rom. 16:17; see AVOID <1578>. ¶

13 **to turn away: *methistēmi*** [verb: μεθίστημι <3179>]; **from *meta*: prep. indicating a change of position, and *histēmi*: to stand ▶ To move, to take away** > Paul was accused of having persuaded and turned away {led astray} many people from the false gods in Asia (Acts 19:26). All other refs.: REMOVE <3179>, TRANSFER <3179>.

14 ***metagō*** [verb: μετάγω <3329>]; **from *meta*: indicates a change of direction, and *agō*: to lead ▶ To lead here and there, to direct** > We turn horses by putting bits in their mouths (Jas. 3:3). Ships are turned {are steered} by a very small rudder (Jas. 3:4). ¶

– 15 Matt. 2:22 → to turn aside → DEPART <402> 16 Matt. 10:35 → SET (verb) <1369> 17 Matt. 24:10 → to turn away → OFFEND <4624> 18 Luke 6:20 → to turn one's gaze → to lift one's eyes → LIFT <1869> 19 Luke 6:29 → OFFER <3930> 20 Luke 10:6 → to turn again → RETURN (verb) <344> 21 Luke 16:2 → to turn in → GIVE <591> 22 Luke 17:15 → to turn back → RETURN (verb) <5290> 23 John 2:16 → MAKE <4160> 24 John 6:66 → DEPART <565> 25 John 13:18 → has turned against me → lit.: has lifted up his heel against me 26 Acts 1:25 → to turn aside → to fall by transgression → FALL (verb) <3845> 27 Acts 18:17 → to turn on → SEIZE <1949> 28 Acts 21:21 → to turn away → lit.: apostasy → APOSTASY <646> 29 Acts 26:24 → DRIVE <4062> 30 2 Cor. 2:7 → "turn to" added in Engl. 31 Phil. 1:12 → to turn out → COME <2064> 32 2 Tim. 2:19; Heb. 3:12 → to turn away → DEPART <868> 33 Heb. 8:9 → to turn away → DISREGARD <272>

[34] Jas. 3:4 → to turn about → DIRECT <2116>.

TURNING – ***tropē*** [fem. noun: τροπή <5157>]; **from *trepō*: to turn ▶ Change, revolution** > There is no variation or shadow of turning {shifting shadow, shifting shadows} with the Father of lights (Jas. 1:17). ¶

TURQUOISE – Rev. 21:20 → CHRYSOPRASE, CHRYSOPRASUS <5556>.

TURTLEDOVE – ***trugōn*** [fem. noun: τρυγών <5167>]; **from *truzō*: to coo, to murmur ▶ Wild dove, smaller than a pigeon** > The sacrifice of a pair of turtledoves was prescribed by the law, so the poor might bring an offering according to their means. This is what the parents of Jesus offered at the occasion of His presentation at the temple (Luke 2:24). ¶

TUTOR – [1] ***paidagōgos*** [masc. noun: παιδαγωγός <3807>]; **from *pais*: child, and *agogos*: leader, which is from *agō*: to lead; lit.: pedagogue ▶ Teacher, conductor** > The law was a tutor {schoolmaster} up {was put in charge to lead us} to Christ (Gal. 3:24, 25 {supervision}). Other ref.: 1 Cor. 4:15; see INSTRUCTOR <3807>. ¶
– [2] Gal. 4:2 → GUARDIAN <2012>.

TWELFTH – ***dōdekatos*** [adj.: δωδέκατος <1428>]; **from *dōdeka*: twelve, which is from *duo*: two, and *deka*: ten ▶** This number refers to one of the foundations of the wall of the city in Rev. 21:20. ¶

TWELVE – [1] ***dōdeka*** [card. num.: δώδεκα <1427>]; **from *duo*: two, and *deka*: ten ▶** This number is used in regard to years (Matt. 9:20; Mark 5:25, 42; Luke 2:42; 8:42, 43), apostles (Matt. 10:1, 2, 5; 11:1; 20:17; 26:14, 20, 47; Mark 3:14; 4:10; 6:7; 9:35; 10:32; 11:11; 14:10, 17, 20, 43; Luke 6:13; 8:1; 9:1, 12; 18:31; 22:3, 47; John 6:67, 70, 71; 20:24; Acts 6:2; 1 Cor. 15:5; Rev. 21:14), baskets (Matt. 14:20; Mark 6:43; 8:19; Luke 9:17; John 6:13), thrones (Matt. 19:28), tribes (Matt. 19:28; Luke 22:30; Jas. 1:1; Rev. 21:12), legions of angels (Matt. 26:53), hours (John 11:9), patriarchs (Acts 7:8), stars (Rev. 12:1), angels (Rev. 21:12), gates (Rev. 21:12, 21), foundations (Rev. 21:14), names (Rev. 21:14), pearls (Rev. 21:21), and fruits (Rev. 22:2). ¶
[2] ***dekaduo*** [card. num.: δεκαδύο <1177>]; **from *deka*: ten, and *duo*: two; less usual form of [1] ▶** This number is used in regard to men (Acts 19:7) and days (Acts 24:11). ¶

TWELVE THOUSAND – **twelve: *dōdeka*** [card. num.: δώδεκα <1427>]; **from *duo*: two, and *deka*: ten; thousand: *chilias*** [card. num.: χιλιάς <5505>] ▶ This number is used in regard to sealed persons in Israel (twelve times in Rev. 7:5–8) and furlongs (Rev. 21:16). ¶

TWENTY – ***eikosi*** [card. num.: εἴκοσι <1501>] ▶ This number is used in regard to fathoms (Acts 27:28); 20 fathoms is equivalent to 120 feet (36.5 meters). ¶

TWENTY-FIVE – **twenty: *eikosi*** [card. num.: εἴκοσι <1501>] **five: *pente*** [card. num.: πέντε <4002>] ▶ This number is used in regard to stadia (John 6:19); 25 or 30 stadia is equivalent to 3 or 4 miles. ¶

TWENTY-FOUR – **lit.: twenty and four; twenty: *eikosi*** [card. num.: εἴκοσι <1501>] **four: *tessares*** [card. num.: τέσσαρες <5064>] ▶ This number is used in regard to elders (Rev. 4:4b, 10; 5:8; 11:16; 19:4a) and thrones (4:4a). ¶

TWENTY THOUSAND – **twenty: *eikosi*** [card. num.: εἴκοσι <1501>] **thousand: *chilias*** [card. num.: χιλιάς <5505>] ▶ This number is used in regard to men (Luke 14:31). ¶

TWENTY-THREE THOUSAND – **twenty: *eikosi*** [card. num.: εἴκοσι <1501>] **three: *treis*** [card. num.: τρεῖς <5140>] **thousand: *chilias*** [fem. noun: χιλιάς <5505>] ▶ This number is used in regard to fallen men in Israel (1 Cor. 10:8). ¶

TWICE – [1] ***dis*** [adv.: δίς <1364>] ▶ **Two times** > This term is used in Mark 14:30,

72; Luke 18:12; Phil. 4:16; 1 Thes. 2:18; Jude 12 {doubly}. ¶
2 **twice as much: *diplous*** [adj.: διπλοῦς <1362>] ▶ **Doubly** > This word is used in Matt. 23:15 {twofold more}. Other refs.: 1 Tim. 5:17, Rev. 18:6a, b; see DOUBLE (adj.) <1362>. ¶
– 3 2 Cor. 1:15 → to receive twice → to receive a second → SECOND <1208>.

TWILIGHT – Luke 23:54 → the Sabbath twilight was coming on → lit.: the Sabbath began to dawn → DAWN (verb) <2020>.

TWIN – See DIDYMUS <1324>.

TWIN BROTHERS – ***Dioskouroi*** [plur. masc. name: Διόσκουροι <1359>]; **sons of Zeus** ▶ **Name of two demigods of the Greeks and Romans, Castor and Pollux; actually, they were both sons of Jupiter (or Zeus for the Greeks) but of different mothers according to mythology; also transl.: Castor and Pollux, Dioscuri** > The Alexandrian ship on which Paul set sail had "the Twin Brothers" for the ensign on its prow (Acts 28:11). They were supposed to protect vessels from shipwrecks. ¶

TWINKLING – ***rhipē*** [fem. noun: ῥιπή <4493>]; **from *rhiptō*: to throw, to scatter** ▶ **Quick movement like the winking of the eye** > In a moment, in the twinkling of an eye, at the last trumpet, the Christians will be changed at the resurrection (1 Cor. 15:52); *rhopē* in some mss. ¶

TWIST – 1 **to twist, to twist together: *plekō*** [verb: πλέκω <4120>] ▶ **To interlace together; also transl.: to plait, to weave** > Having twisted together a crown of thorns, the soldiers put it on the head of Jesus (Matt. 27:29; Mark 15:17; John 19:2). ¶
– 2 2 Pet. 3:16 → DISTORT <4761>.

TWISTED (BE) – Matt. 17:17; Luke 9:41; Acts 20:30; Phil. 2:15 → PERVERTED (BE) <1294>.

TWO – 1 ***duo*** [card. num.: δύο <1417>] ▶ This number is used in regard to brothers (Matt. 4:18, 21; 20:24), miles (Matt. 5:41), masters (Matt. 6:24; Luke 16:13), demon-possessed men (Matt. 8:28), blind men (Matt. 9:27; 20:30), tunics (Matt. 10:10; Mark 6:9; Luke 3:11; 9:3), sparrows (Matt. 10:29), fish (Matt. 14:17, 19; Mark 6:38, 41a, b; Luke 9:13, 16; John 6:9), hands (Matt. 18:8; Mark 9:43), feet (Matt. 18:8; Mark 9:45), eyes (Matt. 18:9; Mark 9:47), people (Matt. 18:16; Luke 17:34, 36), witnesses (Matt. 18:16; 2 Cor. 13:1; 1 Tim. 5:19; Heb. 10:28; Rev. 11:3), believers in the Lord (Matt. 18:19, 20), a man joined to a woman (Matt. 19:5, 6; Mark 10:8a, b; 1 Cor. 6:16; Eph. 5:31), sons (Matt. 20:21; 26:37; Luke 15:11; Acts 7:29; Gal. 4:22), disciples (Matt. 21:1; Mark 11:1; 14:13; 16:12; Luke 7:19; 10:1 (lit.: by two); 19:29; 24:13; John 1:35, 37, 40; 20:4 (both); 21:2; Acts 1:23, 24; 19:22), children (Matt. 21:28, 31), commandments (Matt. 22:40), men (Matt. 24:40; Luke 9:30, 32; 18:10; 24:4 (actually: angels); John 8:17; Acts 1:10; 9:38), women (Matt. 24:41; Luke 17:35), talents (Matt. 25:15, 17a, b, 22a–c), days (Matt. 26:2; Mark 14:1; John 4:40, 43; 11:6), false witnesses (Matt. 26:60), Jesus and Barabbas (Matt. 27:21), robbers or criminals (Matt. 27:38; Mark 15:27; Luke 23:32; John 19:18), the torn veil of the temple (Matt. 27:51; Mark 15:38), apostles (Mark 6:7 {two by two}), mites (Mark 12:42; Luke 21:2), pigeons (Luke 2:24), boats (Luke 5:2), debtors (Luke 7:41), denarii (Luke 10:35), copper coins (Luke 12:6), individuals in one house (Luke 12:52a, b), swords (Luke 22:38), measures (John 2:6; lit.: two or three measures), angels (John 20:12), servants (Acts 10:7), chains (Acts 12:6; 21:33), soldiers (Acts 12:6), years (Acts 19:10), hours (Acts 19:34), centurions (Acts 23:23), those who speak in a tongue (1 Cor. 14:27), prophets (1 Cor. 14:29; Rev. 11:10), covenants (Gal. 4:24), circumcision and uncircumcision (Eph. 2:15), the possibility of living and dying (Phil. 1:23), immutable things (Heb. 6:18), woes (Rev. 9:12), number (Rev. 9:16; lit.: two myriads of myriad), lampstands (Rev. 11:4), olive trees (Rev. 11:4), wings (Rev. 12:14), horns

(Rev. 13:11), and the beast and the false prophet (Rev. 19:20). ¶
– [2] Matt. 2:16 → two years old → YEAR <1332> [3] Luke 23:45 → in two → in the midst → MIDST <3319> [4] Eph. 2:14 → BOTH <297> [5] 2 Tim. 3:9 → "two men" added in Engl.

TWO-DRACHMA – See TAX (noun) <1323>.

TWO-EDGED – ***distomos*** [adj.: δίστομος <1366>]; **from *dis*: two, and *stoma*: edge ▶ With two cutting edges; also transl.: double-edged** > The word of God is living and active, and more penetrating than any two-edged sword (Heb. 4:12). The Son of Man has a two-edged sword coming out of His mouth (Rev. 1:16; 2:12; 19:15 in some mss.). ¶

TWO HUNDRED – ***diakosioi*** [card. num.: διακόσιοι <1250>]; **from *dis*: twice, and *hekaton*: hundred ▶** This number is used in regard to denarii (Mark 6:37; John 6:7), cubits (John 21:8), soldiers (Acts 23:23), and spearmen (Acts 23:23). ¶

TWO HUNDRED AND SEVENTY-SIX – two hundred: *diakosioi* [card. num.: διακόσιοι <1250>]; **from *dis*: twice, and *hekaton*: hundred; seventy: *hebdomēkonta*** [card. num.: ἑβδομήκοντα <1440>]; **six: *hex*** [card. num.: ἕξ <1803>] **▶** This was the number of passengers aboard Paul's ship (Acts 27:37). ¶

TWO THOUSAND – ***dischilioi*** [card. num.: δισχίλιοι <1367>]; **from *dis*: twice, and *chilioi*: thousand ▶** This number is used in regard to swine (Mark 5:13). ¶

TWOFOLD – Matt. 23:15 → twofold more → twice as much → TWICE <1362>.

TYCHICUS – ***Tuchikos*** [masc. name: Τυχικός <5190>]: **fortuitous; close to *tunchanō*: to obtain ▶ Christian man of Asia** > Tychicus accompanied Paul with other brothers in Asia (Acts 20:4). Paul charged this beloved brother and faithful servant in the Lord to bring his letters to the Ephesians (Eph. 6:21) and to the Colossians (Col. 4:7). He sent Tychicus to Ephesus (2 Tim. 4:12), and proposed to send him to Titus (Titus 3:12). ¶

TYPE – [1] ***tupos*** [masc. noun: τύπος <5179>]; **from *tuptō*: to strike, as in using a stamp ▶ Figure, representation of a reality; also transl.: example, form, idol, image, pattern** > The Israelites had made themselves forms of foreign gods (Acts 7:43). The types of the O.T. have their actual correspondence in the teaching of the N.T. (1 Cor. 10:6, 11: *tupikōs* in some mss., i.e., serving for admonition). For example, Adam is a type of Christ, the second man (Rom. 5:14). All other refs.: FORM (noun) <5179>, MARK (noun) <5179>, PATTERN <5179>.
– [2] Heb. 11:19 → as a type → in a figure → PARABLE <3850>.

TYRANNUS – ***Turannos*** [masc. name: Τύραννος <5181>]: **ruler, tyrant ▶ Man of Ephesus** > Paul reasoned daily in the school (or: lecture hall) of Tyrannus for two years (Acts 19:9). ¶

TYRE – [1] ***Turos*** [fem. name: Τύρος <5184>]: **rock, in Heb. ▶ Port city of Phoenicia on the Mediterranean Sea, south of Sidon** > Paul's ship landed at Tyre on his return from his third missionary journey; he stayed there for seven days (Acts 21:3, 7). All other refs.: see SIDON <4605>.
– [2] Acts 12:20 → people of Tyre → TYRIAN <5183>.

TYRIAN – ***Turios*** [masc. name: Τύριος <5183>]: **rock ▶ Inhabitant of Tyre** > Herod was very displeased with the Tyrians (people of Tyre), without Luke mentioning the reason for this (Acts 12:20). ¶

U

UN- – See DIS- <1418>.

UNAFRAID – Rom. 13:3 → to be unafraid → lit.: to not be afraid → to be afraid → AFRAID <5399>.

UNALTERABLE – Heb. 2:2 → FIRM <949>.

UNAPPARENT – Heb. 4:13 → not manifest → MANIFEST (adj.) <852>.

UNAPPEASABLE – 2 Tim. 3:3 → IMPLACABLE <786>.

UNAPPROACHABLE – ***aprositos*** [adj.: ἀπρόσιτος <676>]**; from *a*: neg., and *proseimi*: to approach, which is from *pros*: toward, and *eimi*: to be, to go ▶ Which one cannot reach, inaccessible >** God dwells in unapproachable light {in the light which that no man can approach} (1 Tim. 6:16). ¶

UNAPPROVED – 2 Cor. 13:7 → WORTHLESS <96>.

UNASHAMED – 1 John 2:28 → to be unashamed → lit.: to not be ashamed → ASHAMED (BE) <153>.

UNAWARE – [1] Matt. 24:39; Luke 2:43; 24:18 → to be unaware → to know not → KNOW <1097> [2] Luke 11:44 → to be unaware → to know not → KNOW <1492> [3] Rom. 1:13; 1 Cor. 10:1; 12:1; 2 Cor. 1:8; 2:11 → to be unaware → to be ignorant → IGNORANT <50>.

UNAWARES – [1] Gal. 2:4 → unawares brought in → secretly brought in → SECRETLY <3920> [2] Heb. 13:2 → lit.: without knowing it → to not know → KNOW <2990>.

UNBECOMINGLY – 1 Cor. 7:36; 13:5 → to act unbecomingly → to behave uncomely → BEHAVE <807>.

UNBELIEF – [1] ***apistia*** [fem. noun: ἀπιστία <570>]**; from *apistos*: faithless, unfaithful, which is from *a*: neg., and *pistos*: believing, faithful ▶ Lack of confidence, lack of faith; also transl.: little faith, littleness of faith, unfaithfulness >** Jesus did not do many miracles because of the unbelief of the Jews (Matt. 13:58; Mark 6:6). He reproached His disciples for their unbelief (Matt. 17:20 {other mss.: *oligopistia*: small faith}; Mark 16:14). The father of a possessed child asked Jesus to help his unbelief (Mark 9:24). The unbelief of those who have not believed does not nullify the faithfulness of God (Rom. 3:3). Abraham did not hesitate through unbelief at the promise of God to have a son (Rom. 4:20). Other refs.: Rom. 11:20, 23; 1 Tim. 1:13; Heb. 3:12 {unbelieving heart; lit.: heart of unbelief}, 19. ¶
– [2] Acts 19:9 → to continue in unbelief → DISBELIEVE <544> [3] Rom. 11:30, 32; Heb. 4:6, 11 → DISOBEDIENCE <543>.

UNBELIEVER – [1] ***apistos*** [adj. used as noun: ἄπιστος <571>]**; from *a*: neg., and *pistos*: believing, faithful ▶ Person without faith, incredulous individual >** In a parable, the manager who had acted badly would be appointed his portion with the unbelievers (Luke 12:46). All other refs.: INCREDIBLE <571>, UNBELIEVING <571>.
– [2] Rom. 15:31 → lit.: one who does not believe → BELIEVE <544>.

UNBELIEVING – [1] ***apistos*** [adj. and adj. used as noun: ἄπιστος <571>]**; from *a*: neg., and *pistos*: believing, faithful ▶ Who does not believe, unfaithful; also transl.: doubting, faithless, infidel, unbeliever, who is not a Christian >** The unbelieving does not put his trust in God and His word. Consequently, he does not have a relationship with God. Jesus used this term to designate His contemporaries (Matt. 17:17; Mark 9:19; Luke 9:41). He told Thomas not to be unbelieving, but believing (John 20:27). Paul speaks several times of the unbelievers in contrast to the believers: he enjoins Christians to not be unequally yoked together with unbelievers (2 Cor. 6:14). The portion of the unbelieving will be in the lake of fire (Rev. 21:8). Other refs.: 1 Cor. 6:6; 7:12, 13, 14a, b, 15; 10:27; 14:22a, b, 23, 24; 2 Cor. 4:4; 6:15; 1 Tim. 5:8; Titus

1:15. Other refs.: Luke 12:46; Acts 26:8; see UNBELIEVER <571>, INCREDIBLE <571>. ¶

2 **to believe not: *apeitheō*** [verb: ἀπειθέω <544>]; **from *apeithēs*: disobedient, which is from *a*: neg., and *peithō*: to believe, to have confidence ► To not have confidence >** The Jews who did not believe {who disbelieved, who refused to believe, unbelieving} stirred up the Gentiles against the brothers (Acts 14:2). Rahab did not perish with those who did not believe {the unbelieving, those who were disobedient} (Heb. 11:31). All other refs.: BELIEVE <544>, DISBELIEVE <544>, DISOBEDIENT <544>, OBEY <544>.

– 3 Heb. 3:12 → unbelieving heart → lit.: heart of unbelief → UNBELIEF <570>.

UNBIND – 1 John 11:44 → LOOSE <3089> 2 Acts 22:30 → lit.: to release; in some mss.: to release from chains → RELEASE (verb) <3089>, CHAIN <1189>.

UNBLAMABLE, UNBLAMEABLE – 1 Col. 1:22 → BLAMELESS <299> 2 1 Thes. 3:13 → BLAMELESS <273>.

UNBLAMEABLY – 1 Thes. 2:10; 5:23 → BLAMELESSLY <274>.

UNBLEMISHED – 1 Heb. 9:14 → without spot → SPOT <299> 2 1 Pet. 1:19 → without blemish → BLEMISH <299>.

UNCEASING – 1 ***ektenēs*** [adj.: ἐκτενής <1618>]; **from *ekteinō*: to stretch out, to extend, which is from *ek*: out of, and *teinō*: to reach, to stretch ► Urgent, fervent >** The church made unceasing {constant, earnest, without ceasing} prayer to God for Peter (Acts 12:5); other mss. have *ektenōs*: see 2. Other ref.: 1 Pet. 4:8; see FERVENT <1618>. ¶

2 **unceasingly: *ektenōs*** [adv.: ἐκτενῶς <1619>]; **from *ekteinō*: see 1 ► Earnestly, fervently >** The church prayed fervently to God for Peter (Acts 12:5). Other ref.: 1 Pet. 1:22; see FERVENTLY <1619>. ¶

– 3 Rom. 9:2 → UNINTERRUPTED <88>.

UNCEASINGLY – Rom. 1:9; 1 Thes. 1:3; 2:13; 5:17 → CEASING (WITHOUT) <89>.

UNCERTAIN – 1 ***adēlos*** [adj.: ἄδηλος <82>]; **from *a*: neg., and *dēlos*: manifest, evident ► Confused, not clear >** Paul asks if the trumpet makes an uncertain {indistinct} sound, who will prepare himself for war (1 Cor. 14:8). Other ref.: Luke 11:44 (which appear not); see APPEAR <82>. ¶

2 **to be uncertain: *aporeō*** [verb: ἀπορέω <639>]; **from *aporos*: without means, without resources, which is from *a*: neg., and *poros*: way, means ► To be in doubt, to not know what to do >** Festus was uncertain {doubted, was at a loss} how to go about an inquiry into some questions concerning Paul (Acts 25:20). Other refs.: John 13:22; 2 Cor. 4:8; Gal. 4:20; see PERPLEXED (BE) <639>. ¶

– 3 1 Tim. 6:17 → uncertain riches → lit.: uncertainty of riches → UNCERTAINTY <83>.

UNCERTAINLY – ***adēlōs*** [adv.: ἀδήλως <84>]; **from *adēlos*: uncertain, which is from *a*: neg., and *dēlos*: manifest, evident ► Without knowing for sure the issue >** Paul was not running as uncertainly {as not without aim, with uncertainty, aimlessly} (1 Cor. 9:26). ¶

UNCERTAINTY – 1 ***adēlotēs*** [fem. noun: ἀδηλότης <83>]; **from *adēlos*: uncertain, which is from *a*: neg., and *dēlos*: manifest, evident ► Insecurity, fragility >** Those who are rich are not to put their confidence in the uncertainty of riches {in uncertain riches} (1 Tim. 6:17). ¶

– 2 1 Cor. 9:36 → with uncertainty → UNCERTAINLY <84>.

UNCHANGEABLE – 1 ***ametathetos*** [adj.: ἀμετάθετος <276>]; **from *a*: neg., and *metatithēmi*: to change, which is from *meta*: indicates change, and *tithēmi*: to put ► Which cannot change, unalterable >** The two unchangeable {immutable} things (Heb. 6:18) correspond to the promise of God to Abraham and His oath (see v. 13).

This term is used as a noun in Heb. 6:17: God was willing to show more abundantly to the heirs of the promise the unchangeableness {immutability, unchanging nature} of His purpose. ¶

2 ***aparabatos*** [adj.: ἀπαράβατος <531>]; **from *a*: neg., and *parabainō*: to transgress, which is from *para*: against, and *bainō*: to go, to walk ▶ That which one cannot entrust to another or transmit, permanent** > Because He continues forever, Jesus has a priesthood that is unchangeable {holds His priesthood permanently} (Heb. 7:24). ¶

UNCHANGEABLENESS – Heb. 6:17 → UNCHANGEABLE <276>.

UNCHANGING – Heb. 6:17 → unchanging nature → UNCHANGEABLE <276>.

UNCHASTITY – Matt. 5:32 → FORNICATION <4202>, <4203>.

UNCIRCUMCISED – 1 ***aperitmētos*** [adj.: ἀπερίτμητος <564>]; **from *a*: neg., and *peritemnō*: to circumcise, which is from *peri*: around, and *temnō*: to cut ▶ Term used as a metaphor to signify alienation from God** > Stephen spoke to the Jews as to people uncircumcised in heart and ears, in the sense that they were disobedient to the word of God (Acts 7:51). ¶

2 **to become uncircumcised: *epispaō*** [verb: ἐπισπάω <1986>]; **from *epi*: upon, and *spaō*: to draw ▶ To hide one's circumcision** > He who is called being circumcised is not to remove the marks of uncircumcision (1 Cor. 7:18). ¶

– 3 Acts 11:3; Rom. 2:25; Gal. 2:7; et al. → lit.: uncircumcision → UNCIRCUMCISION <203>.

UNCIRCUMCISION – ***akrobustia*** [fem. noun: ἀκροβυστία <203>]; **from *akron*: extremity, and *buō*: to cover; this word designates the foreskin ▶ State of a man who has not been circumcised; the word is often transl. "uncircumcised"** > This term is used in its lit. sense in Acts 11:3 (lit.: having uncircumcision); Rom. 2:25, 26a, b, 27; 4:9, 10a, b, 11a, b, 12; 1 Cor. 7:18, 19; Gal. 5:6; 6:15; Col. 2:13; 3:11). The nations are called "uncircumcision" by the Jews (Rom. 3:30; Eph. 2:11). The gospel of the uncircumcision had been entrusted to Paul (Gal. 2:7), i.e., he was responsible for preaching the gospel to the nations. ¶

UNCLEAN – 1 ***akathartos*** [adj.: ἀκάθαρτος <169>]; **from *a*: neg., and *kathairō*: to cleanse, which is from *katharos*: pure, clean ▶ a. Which is not holy, not separated** > Children would be unclean if an unbelieving spouse was not sanctified in the believing spouse (1 Cor. 7:14). The Lord says not to touch what is unclean (2 Cor. 6:17). No unclean {impure} person has an inheritance in the kingdom of Christ and of God (Eph. 5:5). **b. Impure, soiled** > This term is often used to describe spirits, i.e., fallen angels (Matt. 10:1; 12:43; Mark 1:23, 26, 27; 3:11, 30; 5:2, 8, 13; 6:7; 7:25; 9:25; Luke 4:33, 36; 6:18; 8:29; 9:42; 11:24; Acts 5:16; 8:7; Rev. 16:13). Babylon is the habitation of every unclean spirit and every unclean bird (Rev. 18:2a, b). Peter had never eaten anything unclean (Acts 10:14; 11:8). He was to call no man common or unclean (Acts 10:28). ¶

2 **unclean thing: *akathartēs*** [fem. noun: ἀκαθάρτης <168>]; **from *akathartos*: see 1 ▶ Defilement, impurity** > The great prostitute had in her hand a cup full of abominations and the unclean things {abominable things, filthiness} of her sexual immorality (Rev. 17:4). ¶

3 ***koinos*** [adj.: κοινός <2839>]; **lit.: common ▶ Defiled, impure** > Some disciples ate bread with unclean, i.e., unwashed, hands (Mark 7:2). Paul was persuaded in the Lord Jesus that nothing is unclean (or: defiled) of itself, except to him who reckons anything to be unclean (or: defiled), to that man it is unclean (Rom. 14:14a–c). All other refs.: COMMON <2839>.

– 4 Matt. 7:5 → UNWASHED, UNWASHEN <449> 5 Matt. 15:11a, b, 18, 20a, b; Mark 7:15a, b, 18, 20, 23; Heb. 9:13; Rev. 21:27 → to be unclean, to make unclean → DEFILE <2840> 6 Matt. 23:27

→ UNCLEANNESS <167> 7 Mark 7:5 → IMPURE <449>.

UNCLEANNESS – 1 ***akatharsia*** [fem. noun: ἀκαθαρσία <167>]; **from *akathartos*: unclean, which is from *a*: neg., and *kathairō*: to cleanse, which is from *katharos*: pure, clean ▶ Dirtiness; defilement, moral impurity** > The scribes and the Pharisees were like whitewashed tombs, which outwardly look beautiful, but inside are full of all uncleanness {everything unclean} (Matt. 23:27). God has given men over to uncleanness (Rom. 1:24). Before their conversion, the Romans had yielded their members in bondage to uncleanness (Rom. 6:19). Many at Corinth had not repented of their uncleanness (2 Cor. 12:21). Uncleanness is one of the works of the flesh (Gal. 5:19). Men have practiced all uncleanness with greediness (Eph. 4:19). No uncleanness is to be named among Christians (Eph. 5:3). Christians are to consider their members as dead to uncleanness (Col. 3:5). Paul's exhortation was not on the principle of uncleanness {impure motives} (1 Thes. 2:3). God has not called us to uncleanness {to be impure} (1 Thes. 4:7). ¶
2 ***miasmos*** [masc. noun: μιασμός <3394>]; **from *miainō*: to defile ▶ Defilement, contamination** > The Lord knows how to keep the unrighteous to the day of judgment, especially those who follow after the flesh in the lust of uncleanness {in its corrupt desires, in the lust of defiling passion} (2 Pet. 2:10). ¶
– 3 John 18:28 → to avoid ceremonial uncleanness → to be defiled → DEFILE <3392>.

UNCLOTHED (BE) –2 Cor. 5:4 → to take off the clothing → TAKE <1562>.

UNCOMELY – 1 1 Cor. 7:36 → to behave uncomely → BEHAVE <807> 2 1 Cor. 12:23 → UNPRESENTABLE <809>.

UNCONDEMNED – ***akatakritos*** [adj.: ἀκατάκριτος <178>]; **from *a*: neg., and *katakrinō*: to blame, to condemn; from *kata*: against, and *krinō*: to judge; lit.: without being judged against ▶ Against whom a sentence is not pronounced** > Paul had been beaten publicly, but was uncondemned {without a trial} (Acts 16:37). A centurion wanted to scourge him who was a Roman and uncondemned {not found guilty} (Acts 22:25). ¶

UNCORRUPTEDNESS – Titus 2:7 → INCORRUPTIBILITY <861>.

UNCORRUPTNESS – Titus 2:7 → INCORRUPTIBILITY <861>.

UNCOVER – ***apostegazō*** [verb: ἀποστεγάζω <648>]; **from *apo*: from, and *stegazō*: to cover, which is from *stegē*: roof ▶ To open, to remove the roof** > Some men brought a paralytic and uncovered {removed, made an opening in} the roof where Jesus was (Mark 2:4). ¶

UNCOVERED – 1 ***akatakaluptos*** [adj.: ἀκατακάλυπτος <177>]; **from *a*: neg., and *katakaluptō*: to cover; from *kata*: intens., and *kaluptō*: to cover ▶ Not veiled, not concealed** > Every woman who prays or prophesies with her head uncovered dishonors her head (1 Cor. 11:5); Paul asks if it is proper for a woman to pray to God uncovered (v. 13). ¶
– 2 Heb. 4:13 → NAKED <1131>.

UNCTION – ***chrisma*** [neut. noun: χρῖσμα <5545>]; **from *chriō*: to anoint ▶ Preparation of oil and aromatic herbs; the word applies to the Holy Spirit; also transl.: anointing** > Christians have received the unction from the Holy One (1 John 2:20); this unction abides in them and teaches them all things (v. 27a, b). ¶

UNDEFILED – ***amiantos*** [adj.: ἀμίαντος <283>]; **from *a*: neg., and *miainō*: to contaminate, to defile; lit.: without defilement ▶ Faultless, pure, without contamination** > Such a high priest (the Lord Jesus) became us, holy, harmless, undefiled, separated from sinners, and exalted higher than the heavens (Heb. 7:26). The marriage bed is to be undefiled (Heb. 13:4), i.e., free from illicit relationships. Christians have been born again to an undefiled inheritance (1 Pet. 1:4 {that can never spoil}). Pure and undefiled religion before God and the Father is to visit orphans and widows in their affliction, and to keep oneself without spot from the world (Jas. 1:27). ¶

UNDENIABLE – ***anantirrētos*** [adj.: ἀναντίρρητος <368>]; **from *a*: neg., *anti*: against, and *ereō*: to speak; lit.: that cannot be spoken against ▶ Which cannot be challenged, indisputable; also transl.: which cannot be denied, which cannot be spoken against** > It was undeniable that Ephesus was consecrated as the guardian of the temple of Diana (Acts 19:36). ¶

UNDER – 1 ***hupo*** [prep.: ὑπό <5259>]. *
– 2 1 Tim. 5:9 → LESSER <1640>.

UNDERAGE – Gal. 4:1, 3 → CHILD <3516>.

UNDERFOOT – Matt. 7:6 → to trample underfoot → to trample under their feet → FOOT[1] <4228>.

UNDERGIRD – ***hupozōnnumi*** [verb: ὑποζώννυμι <5269>]; **from *hupo*: under, and *zōnnumi*: to gird ▶ To tie with a cable passed underneath** > During the storm, the men undergirded {frapped} the ship with ropes {they passed ropes under it} (Acts 27:17). ¶

UNDERGO – 1 ***hupechō*** [verb: ὑπέχω <5254>]; **from *hupo*: under, and *echō*: to have, to hold ▶ To incur, to suffer** > Sodom, Gomorrah, and the cities around them, having gone after strange flesh, undergo the judgment of eternal fire (Jude 7). ¶
– 2 1 Pet. 5:9 → ACCOMPLISH <2005>.

UNDERHANDED – 2 Cor. 4:2 → of shame → SHAME <152>.

UNDERMINE – 2 Cor. 11:12 → to undermine the claim → to cut off the opportunity → CUT <1581>.

UNDERNEATH – ***hupokatō*** [adv.: ὑποκάτω <5270>]; **from *hupo*: under, and *katō*: down ▶** Refs.: Mark 6:11; 7:28; Luke 8:16; John 1:50; Heb. 2:8; Rev. 5:3, 13; 6:9; 12:1. ¶

UNDERSTAND – 1 ***ginōskō*** [verb: γινώσκω <1097>] ▶ **To know, to grasp the meaning based on personal experience** > Jesus asked the Jews why they did not understand His speech {His language was not clear to them} (John 8:43). The disciples did not understand the illustration of the good shepherd (John 10:6). They did not understand why Jesus sat on a donkey to enter in Jerusalem (John 12:16). Philip asked the Ethiopian if he understood what he was reading (Acts 8:30). All other refs.: KNOW <1097>.

2 ***epistamai*** [verb: ἐπίσταμαι <1987>]; **from *epi*: upon, and *histēmi*: to stand ▶ To have knowledge, to grasp the meaning based on nearness to the thing known** > Peter was pretending to neither know nor understand what the servant was saying (Mark 14:68). All other refs.: KNOW <1987>.

3 ***noeō*** [verb: νοέω <3539>]; **from *nous*: mind, understanding ▶ To grasp by the intelligence, to think; also transl.: to apprehend, to perceive** > From the creation of the world, the invisible things of God, i.e., His eternal power and divinity, are perceived, being understood {being apprehended} by the things that are made (Rom. 1:20). Paul told the Ephesians they could understand his intelligence in the mystery of Christ (Eph. 3:4). Whoever reads about the abomination of desolation must understand (Matt. 24:15; Mark 13:14). God has hardened the hearts of those from Israel that they might not understand with their hearts (John 12:40). By faith we understand that the worlds were formed by the word of God (Heb. 11:3). Other refs.: Matt. 15:17 {to see}; 16:9, 11; 1 Tim. 1:7 {to know}. All other refs.: CONSIDER <3539>, PERCEIVE <3539>, THINK <3539>.

4 ***suniēmi*** [verb: συνίημι <4920>]; **from *sun*: together, and *hiēmi*: to send; primarily: to put (thoughts) together ▶ To**

perceive mentally, to comprehend using insight based on information perceived through the senses > Jesus spoke in parables so that the people would not understand (Matt. 13:13; Mark 4:12; Luke 8:10); this way, a prophecy of Isaiah was being fulfilled (Matt. 13:14, 15; Acts 28:26, 27). One person may not understand the parable of the kingdom (Matt. 13:19), another one may understand it (v. 23). Jesus asked His disciples if they had understood the things concerning the parables (Matt. 13:51). He said to the crowd to understand that what comes out of the mouth defiles the man (Matt. 15:10, see v. 11; Mark 7:14, see v. 15). The disciples understood that Jesus was telling them to beware of the doctrine of the Pharisees and the Sadducees (Matt. 16:12). They had not understood {had not gained insight, had not considered} through the miracle of the loaves (Mark 6:52). They understood that He spoke to them of John the Baptist (Matt. 17:13). Jesus asked His disciples if they did not understand (Mark 8:17, 21). Jesus's parents did not understand what He was telling them (Luke 2:50). His disciples understood none of the sufferings that Jesus would suffer (Luke 18:34). Moses supposed that his brothers would understand {would realize} that God would deliver them by his hand, but they did not (Acts 7:25a, b). The natural man does not seek or understand God (Rom. 3:11). Those who have not heard will understand (Rom. 15:21). Paul speaks of some who, comparing themselves among themselves, are without understanding {are not intelligent, are without understanding} (2 Cor. 10:12). Christians must understand what is the will of the Lord (Eph. 5:17). Other ref.: Luke 24:45; see COMPREHEND <4920>. ¶

5 **to understand not: *agnoeō*** [verb: ἀγνοέω <50>]; **from *a*: neg., and *noeō*: see 3 ▶ To perceive not, to not be able to grasp with the intelligence** > The disciples did not understand that Jesus had to suffer (Mark 9:32; Luke 9:45). All other refs.: IGNORANT <50>, KNOW <50>, UNKNOWN <50>.

6 **hard to understand: *dusnoētos*** [adj.: δυσνόητος <1425>]; **from *dus*: with difficulty, and *noētos*: understood, which is from *noeō*: see 3 ▶ Difficult to grasp with the intelligence** > Paul spoke of some things hard to understand (2 Pet. 3:16). ¶

7 ***punthanomai*** [verb: πυνθάνομαι <4441>] **▶ To learn, to find out** > The governor understood that Paul was from Cilicia (Acts 23:34). All other refs.: ASK <4441>.

– 8 Mark 4:13a; Luke 12:39a; John 13:7a; 16:18; Rom. 13:11; 1 Cor. 2:12 (*eidō*); 11:3; 14:16; 1 Tim. 1:9; Jude 10 (*oida*) → KNOW <1492> 9 John 1:5 → COMPREHEND <2638> 10 John 11:50 → CONSIDER <1260> 11 Acts 4:13; 10:34 → PERCEIVE <2638> 12 Acts 19:13 → to take in hand → TAKE <2021> 13 1 Cor. 12:3 → KNOW <1107> 14 1 Cor. 13:11 → THINK <5426> 15 1 Cor. 14:9 → easy to understand → INTELLIGIBLE <2154> 16 1 Cor. 14:16, 23, 24 → one who does not understand → SIMPLE <2399> 17 2 Cor. 1:13a, b, 14 → RECOGNIZE <1921> 18 2 Cor. 10:11 → CONSIDER <3049> 19 Col. 1:6 → KNOW <1921> 20 Heb. 5:11 → you no longer try to understand → you have become sluggish in hearing → SLUGGISH <3576>, HEARING <189> 21 2 Pet. 3:9 → COUNT <2233>.

UNDERSTANDING – 1 ***dianoia*** [fem. noun: διάνοια <1271>]; **from *dia*: through, and *nous*: spirit ▶ Ability to think, comprehension** > Jesus said to love God with all one's heart, with all one's soul, and with all one's understanding {mind} (Matt. 22:37; Mark 12:30; Luke 10:27). God has scattered haughty ones in the thought {thoughts, inmost thoughts, imagination} (or: understanding) of their heart (Luke 1:51). Other ref.: Eph. 2:3 {thought, mind}. All other refs.: MIND (noun) <1271>.

2 ***epistēmōn*** [adj.: ἐπιστήμων <1990>]; **from *epistamai*: to grasp with the intelligence, to know, which is from *epi*: upon, and *histēmi*: to stand ▶ Who possesses knowledge, especially of an expert** > James asks who is wise and understanding {endued with knowledge} among his readers (Jas. 3:13). ¶

3 ***nous*** [masc. noun: νοῦς <3563>] ► **Seat of perception and mental comprehension, as well as of judgment and determination to act; also transl.: mind** > This term is found in Luke 24:45; 1 Cor. 14:14, 15a, b, 19; Phil. 4:7; Rev. 13:18. All other refs.: MIND (noun) <3563>.

4 ***sunesis*** [fem. noun: σύνεσις <4907>]; **from *suniēmi*: to understand, which is from *sun*: together, and *hiēmi*: to send, to put ► Critical ability of grasping the bearing of things with the intelligence; also transl.: cleverness, insight, intelligence, knowledge** > A scribe acknowledged before Jesus that a divine commandment enjoined to love one's God with all one's understanding (Mark 12:33). The teachers in the temple were astonished at the understanding and answers of Jesus at the age of twelve years (Luke 2:47). God will bring to nothing the understanding (*sunesis*) of the understanding ones (*sunetos*) (1 Cor. 1:19). Paul speaks of his intelligence in the mystery of the Christ (Eph. 3:4); he also speaks of the full assurance of understanding (Col. 2:2). He prayed that the Colossians might be filled with the full knowledge of the will of God, in all wisdom and spiritual understanding (Col. 1:9). He told Timothy that the Lord would give him understanding in all things (2 Tim. 2:7). ¶

5 ***sunetos*** [adj.: συνετός <4908>]; **from *suniēmi*: see 4 ► Intelligent, discerning, insightful; also transl.: learned, prudent** > God the Father has hidden things from the wise and understanding (Matt. 11:25; Luke 10:21). The proconsul Sergius Paulus was an intelligent man (Acts 13:7). God will bring to nothing the understanding (*sunesis*) of the understanding ones (*sunetos*) (1 Cor. 1:19). ¶

6 **without understanding, lacking in understanding, etc.: *asunetos*** [adj.: ἀσύνετος <801>]; **from *a*: neg., and *suniēmi*: see 4 ► Incapacity of grasping with the intelligence, of discerning; also transl.: foolish, undiscerning, unintelligent, without intelligence** > Jesus asked His disciples if they were yet without understanding concerning a parable (Matt. 15:16; Mark 7:18). Paul speaks of men whose heart is without understanding (Rom. 1:21) and who are void of understanding (v. 31). God has provoked Israel to anger through a nation without understanding (Rom. 10:19). ¶

7 ***phrēn*** [fem. noun: φρήν <5424>] ► **Intelligence; also transl.: mind, thinking** > Christians must not be children in their understanding, but mature in their understanding (1 Cor. 14:20a, b). ¶

– 8 Luke 1:3 → to have understanding → INVESTIGATE <3877> 9 2 Cor. 10:12 → to be without understanding → to not understand → UNDERSTAND <4920> 10 Eph. 1:8 → INTELLIGENCE <5428> 11 Col. 2:2; Phm. 6 → KNOWLEDGE <1922> 12 1 Pet. 3:7 → KNOWLEDGE <1108>.

UNDERTAKE – Luke 1:1 → to take in hand → HAND (noun) <2021>.

UNDERTAKING – Acts 5:38 → WORK (noun) <2041>.

UNDISCERNING – Rom. 1:31 → without understanding → UNDERSTANDING <801>.

UNDISCIPLINED – 1 2 Thes. 3:7 → to act in an undisciplined manner → to be disorderly → DISORDERLY <812> 2 2 Thes. 3:11 → undisciplined life → DISORDERLY <814>.

UNDISTINGUISHABLE – 1 Cor. 14:10 → of undistinguishable sound → without significance → SIGNIFICANCE <880>.

UNDISTRACTED – 1 Cor. 7:35 → without distraction → DISTRACTION <563>.

UNDISTURBED – Luke 11:21 → to be undisturbed → lit.: to be in peace → PEACE <1515>.

UNDIVIDED – 1 Cor. 7:35 → in undivided devotion → without distraction → DISTRACTION <563>.

UNDO – 1 John 3:8 → DESTROY <3089>.

UNDOUBTEDLY – [1] Acts 28:4 → no doubt → DOUBT (adv.) <3843> [2] 1 Cor. 14:10 → it may be → PERHAPS <5177>.

UNDYING – Eph. 6:24 → undying love → lit.: love in incorruptibility → INCORRUPTIBILITY <861>.

UNEDUCATED – ***agrammatos*** [adj.: ἀγράμματος <62>]; **from *a*: neg., and *gramma*: what is written, which is from *graphō*: to write ▶ Whoever does not know how to read or write, or who is uninstructed in a particular area of knowledge** > Peter and John were uneducated {unlearned, unlettered, unschooled} and ordinary men at the beginning of book of Acts (4:13). Some suggest that they were illiterate, others that they were not versed in the teaching of Judaic schools. ¶

UNESTABLISHED – 2 Pet. 2:14 → UNSTABLE <793>.

UNFADING – [1] ***amarantinos*** [adj.: ἀμαράντινος <262>]; **comp. *amarantos*: see [2]: and, suffix *inos*, referring to the substance of which something is made ▶ Which remains perpetually, incorruptible; also transl.: that does not fade away** > The elders shall receive the unfading crown of glory (1 Pet. 5:4). ¶

[2] ***amarantos*** [adj.: ἀμάραντος <263>]; **from *a*: neg., and *marainō*: to fade, to wither ▶ Which remains forever, incorruptible** > Christians have been regenerated to obtain an unfading inheritance (1 Pet. 1:4 {that does not fade}). ¶

– [3] 1 Pet. 3:4 → INCORRUPTIBLE <862>.

UNFAIR – Matt. 20:13 → to be unfair → to do wrong → WRONG (verb) <91>.

UNFAITHFUL – [1] Luke 12:46 → the unfaithful → the unbelievers → UNBELIEVER <571> [2] Rom. 3:3; 2 Tim. 2:13 → to be unfaithful → to not believe → BELIEVE <569>.

UNFAITHFULNESS – Rom. 3:3 → UNBELIEF <570>.

UNFASTEN – Acts 16:26 → LOOSE <447>.

UNFATHOMABLE – [1] Rom. 11:33 → UNTRACEABLE <421> [2] Eph. 3:8 → UNSEARCHABLE <421>.

UNFEIGNED – [1] Rom. 12:9; 2 Cor. 6:6; 1 Tim. 1:5; 2 Tim. 1:5; Jas. 3:17; 1 Pet. 1:22 → without hypocrisy → HYPOCRISY <505> [2] 1 Tim. 1:5; 2 Tim. 1:5 → SINCERE <505>.

UNFINISHED – Rev. 3:2 → found unfinished → lit.: not found completed → COMPLETE (verb) <4137>.

UNFIT – Titus 1:16 → WORTHLESS <96>.

UNFOLD – Acts 18:26 → EXPLAIN <1620>.

UNFORGIVING – Rom. 1:31; 2 Tim. 3:3 → IMPLACABLE <786>.

UNFRUITFUL – ***akarpos*** [adj.: ἄκαρπος <175>]; **from *a*: neg., and *karpos*: fruit ▶ Without fruit, barren, without result** > Christians are to have no fellowship with the unfruitful {fruitless} works of darkness (Eph. 5:11). Faith, virtue, knowledge, and other qualities in Christians make them to be neither idle nor unfruitful in the knowledge of the Lord (2 Pet. 1:8). Other refs.: Matt. 13:22; Mark 4:19; 1 Cor. 14:14; Titus 3:14; Jude 12 → without fruit → FRUIT <175>. ¶

UNGIFTED – 1 Cor. 14:16, 23, 24 → SIMPLE <2399>.

UNGODLINESS – [1] ***asebeia*** [fem. noun: ἀσέβεια <763>]; **from *asebēs*: ungodly, wicked, which is from *a*: neg., and *sebomai*: to worship, to honor ▶ Wickedness, contempt of God and His word; also transl.: godlessness, impiety** > The

wrath of God is revealed against all ungodliness (Rom. 1:18). The deliverer, i.e., the Messiah, will remove ungodliness from Jacob (the nation of Israel) (Rom. 11:26). Those who engage in profane and vain babblings will advance to greater ungodliness (2 Tim. 2:16). The Christian is to deny ungodliness (Titus 2:12). Jude speaks of deeds of ungodliness (v. 15) and lusts of ungodlinesses (v. 18). ¶
– [2] Jude 15 → to commit in ungodliness → to commit in an ungodly way → UNGODLY <764>.

UNGODLY – [1] ***asebēs*** [adj. and adj. used as noun: ἀσεβής <765>]**; from *a*: neg., and *sebomai*: to worship, to honor ► Who despises God and His word by acting against His will; also transl.: impious** > The ungodly who believes can be justified (Rom. 4:5); Christ died for the ungodly (5:6). The law is for the ungodly (1 Tim. 1:9). The judgment of God is reserved for the ungodly {godless man} (1 Pet. 4:18). God brought the flood on the world of the ungodly (2 Pet. 2:5). Peter speaks of the destruction of ungodly men (2 Pet. 3:7). Ungodly people have turned the grace of God into dissoluteness (Jude 4, 15). ¶
[2] **to live ungodly, to commit in an ungodly way: *asebeō*** [verb: ἀσεβέω <764>]**; from *asebēs*: see [1] ► To conduct oneself in contempt of God and His word, in opposition to His will** > The condemnation of the inhabitants of Sodom and Gomorrah serves as an example for those who afterwards would live an ungodly life (2 Pet. 2:6). Jude speaks of ungodly workers and the works of ungodliness which they have committed in an ungodly way {have wrought ungodlily, have committed in their ungodliness} (Jude 15). ¶
– [3] 1 Cor. 6:1 → UNJUST (noun) <94> [4] 2 Tim. 2:16; Jude 15, 18 → lit.: of ungodliness → UNGODLINESS <763> [5] Jude 8 → on the strength of their dreams these ungodly people → lit.: these dreaming ones → DREAMER <1797>.

UNGRATEFUL – Luke 6:35; 2 Tim. 3:2 → UNTHANKFUL <884>.

UNGUENT – Rev. 18:13 → OINTMENT <3464>.

UNHALLOWED – 1 Pet. 4:3 → ABOMINABLE <111>.

UNHEALTHY – [1] Matt. 6:23; Luke 11:34 → EVIL (adj.) <4190> [2] 1 Tim. 6:4 → to have an unhealthy interest → OBSESSED (BE) <3552>.

UNHEARD – John 9:32 → it has been unheard → lit.: it has not been heard → HEAR <191>.

UNHINDERED, UNHINDEREDLY – Acts 28:31 → no one forbidding → FORBID <209>.

UNHOLY – [1] ***anosios*** [adj.: ἀνόσιος <462>]**; from *a*: neg., and *hosios*: consecrated, holy ► Ungodly, wicked** > The law is for the unholy (1 Tim. 1:9). In the last days, men will be unholy {profane} (2 Tim. 3:2). ¶
– [2] Acts 10:14, 28; 11:8; Heb. 10:29 → COMMON <2839> [3] Acts 10:15; 11:9 → to consider unholy → to call common → COMMON <2840> [4] Heb. 12:16 → PROFANE (adj. and noun) <952>.

UNIMPEACHABLE – 1 Cor. 1:8 → without charge → BLAMELESS <410>.

UNIMPRESSIVE – 2 Cor. 10:10 → WEAK <772>.

UNINFORMED – [1] Rom. 11:25; 1 Cor. 12:1; 2 Cor. 1:8; 1 Thes. 4:13 → to be uniformed → to be ignorant → IGNORANT <50> [2] 1 Cor. 14:16, 23, 24 → SIMPLE <2399>.

UNINSTRUCTED – ***idiōtēs*** [masc. noun: ἰδιώτης <2399>]**; from *idios*: which relates to oneself ► Ordinary person, without formal training in contrast to the religious leaders** > The rulers of the people and the elders of Israel perceived that Peter and John were unlettered and uninstructed {uneducated and untrained, unlearned and ignorant, unschooled and ordinary} men (Acts 4:13). Other refs.: 1 Cor. 14:16, 23, 24; 2 Cor. 11:6; see SIMPLE <2399>. ¶

UNINTELLIGENT – [1] Mark 7:18 → without understanding → UNDERSTANDING <801> [2] Rom. 1:14 → FOOLISH <453>.

UNINTENTIONAL – Heb. 9:7 → in ignorance → IGNORANCE <51>.

UNINTERRUPTED – ***adialeiptos*** [adj.: ἀδιάλειπτος <88>]; **from *a*: neg., and *dialeipō*: to interrupt, which is from *dia*: through, and *leipō*: to leave ▶ Unceasing, constant** > Paul had great grief and uninterrupted {continual, unceasing} pain in his heart concerning the Israelites (Rom. 9:2). Other ref.: 2 Tim. 1:3; see CEASING (WITHOUT) <88>. ¶

UNION – Matt. 1:25 → KNOW <1097>.

UNITE – [1] **to unite, to unite together: *sumbibazō*** [verb: συμβιβάζω <4822>]; **from *sun*: together, and *bibazō*: to cause to come ▶ To assemble, to join together** > Paul desired that the hearts of believers might be encouraged, being united together in love, and have all the riches of the full assurance of understanding and the full knowledge of the mystery of God (Col. 2:2). The church, like a body, having nourishment ministered and united together by the joints and ligaments, grows with a growth that is from God (Col. 2:19 {to knit together, to hold together}). All other refs.: CONCLUDE[1] <4822>, INSTRUCT <4822>, KNIT <4822>, PROVE <4822>.

– [2] Matt. 19:5; Mark 10:7; Eph. 5:31 → JOIN <4347> [3] 1 Cor. 1:10 → to perfectly unite → PERFECTLY <2675> [4] 1 Cor. 6:16, 17 → JOIN <2853> [5] Eph. 1:10 → to gather together → GATHER <346> [6] Heb. 4:2 → to mix with → MIX <4786>.

UNITED – [1] Acts 18:12 → to make a united attack → lit.: to rise against with one accord → ACCORD <3661> [2] Rom. 6:5 → united, united together → lit.: same plant → IDENTIFIED <4854>.

UNITY – [1] ***henotēs*** [fem. noun: ἑνότης <1775>]; **from *henos*: of one ▶ Oneness, unanimity** > Christians are to be diligent to preserve the unity of the Spirit in the bond of peace (Eph. 4:3). The spiritual gifts have been given until we all attain to the unity of the faith and of the knowledge of the Son of God (Eph. 4:13). ¶

– [2] John 17:23 → to bring to complete unity → PERFECT (verb) <5048> [3] Rom. 15:5 → a spirit of unity → to be of the (same mind) → THINK <5426> [4] Eph. 1:10 → to bring unity → to gather together → GATHER <346> [5] Col. 3:14 → PERFECTION <5047> [6] 1 Pet. 3:8 → having unity of mind → MIND (noun) <3675>.

UNIVERSAL – Eph. 6:12 → universal lord → RULER <2888>.

UNIVERSALLY – [1] See ALL <537>.
– [2] 1 Cor. 5:1 → ACTUALLY <3654>.

UNIVERSE – [1] Eph. 4:10 → the whole universe → lit.: all things (*ta panta*) [2] Heb. 1:2; 11:3 → WORLD <165> [3] Heb. 1:3 → He upholds the universe → lit.: upholding all things.

UNJUST (adj.) – [1] **injustice: *adikia*** [fem. noun: ἀδικία <93>]; **from *adikos*: unrighteous, which is from *a*: neg., and *dikē*: justice ▶ Unrighteousness, unfairness** > The Lord speaks in a parable of an unjust judge (lit.: a judge of injustice) (Luke 18:6). All other refs.: INIQUITY <93>, UNRIGHTEOUSNESS <93>, WRONG (noun) <93>.

– [2] Luke 16:10a, b; 18:11; Rom. 3:5; Heb. 6:10 → UNRIGHTEOUS (adj. and noun) <94> [3] 1 Pet. 2:18 → HARSH <4646> [4] 1 Pet. 2:19 → unjust suffering → lit.: to suffer unjustly → UNJUSTLY <95> [5] Rev. 22:11a, b → to be unjust → to do wrong → WRONG (noun) <91>.

UNJUST (noun) – ***adikos*** [adj. used as noun: ἄδικος <94>]; **from *a*: neg., and *dikē*: justice ▶ One who acts contrary to justice, to what is right; also transl.: ungodly, unrighteous, wicked, wrongdoer** > God the Father sends His rain on the just and on the unjust (Matt. 5:45). There will be a resurrection, both of the just and of the unjust (Acts 24:15). Would any Christian dare to go to law before the unjust (1 Cor. 6:1)? The unrighteous (or: The unjust) shall not inherit the kingdom of God (1 Cor. 6:9). Christ has suffered once for sins, the just for the unjust (1 Pet. 3:18). The Lord knows how to reserve the unjust for the day of judgment (2 Pet. 2:9). All other refs.: UNRIGHTEOUS (adj. and noun) <94>.

UNJUSTLY – [1] ***adikōs*** [adv.: ἀδίκως <95>]; **from *adikos*: unjust, which is from *a*: neg., and *dikē*: justice ▶ In a manner contrary to justice, unfairly** > A Christian may suffer unjustly {wrongfully} (1 Pet. 2:19). ¶
– [2] Acts 7:24 → to treat unjustly → to suffer wrong → WRONG (noun) <91> [3] 3 John 10 → to unjustly accuse → PRATE <5396>.

UNKNOWN – [1] ***agnōstos*** [adj.: ἄγνωστος <57>]; **from *a*: neg., and *gnōstos*: known ▶ Which one does not know, which does not make itself known** > Paul had found at Athens an altar to the unknown God (Acts 17:23). ¶
[2] **to be unknown: *agnoeō*** [verb: ἀγνοέω <50>]; **from *a*: neg., and *noeō*: to conceive, to think, which is from *nous*: mind, understanding ▶ To be a stranger, to be unacquainted with** > Paul was unknown, yet well known (2 Cor. 6:9). He was unknown personally to the churches of Judea (Gal. 1:22). All other refs.: IGNORANT <50>, KNOW <50>, UNDERSTAND <50>.

UNLADE – See UNLOAD <670>.

UNLAWFUL – [1] ***athemitos*** [adj.: ἀθέμιτος <111>]; **from *a*: neg., and *themistos*: lawful, permitted, or *themis*: law ▶ Which is not allowed, illegal** > It was unlawful {against the law} for a Jew to be joined or come to a person of another nation (Acts 10:28). Other ref.: 1 Pet. 4:3; see ABOMINABLE <111>. ¶
– [2] Matt. 12:2; Mark 2:24; Luke 6:2; Acts 16:21 → lit.: not lawful → LAWFUL <1832> [3] 2 Pet. 2:8 → LAWLESS (adj.) <459>.

UNLEARNED – [1] Acts 4:13 → UNEDUCATED <62> [2] 1 Cor. 14:16, 23, 24 → SIMPLE <2399> [3] 2 Tim. 2:23 → SENSELESS <521> [4] 2 Pet. 3:16 → UNTAUGHT <261>.

UNLEAVENED – ***azumos*** [adj.: ἄζυμος <106>]; **from *a*: neg., and *zumē*: leaven ▶ Without leaven, yeast; leaven, in Scripture, is always a figure of evil** > See UNLEAVENED BREAD <106>.

UNLEAVENED BREAD – ***azumos*** [adj. used as noun: ἄζυμος <106>]; **from *a*: neg., and *zumē*: leaven ▶ Bread without yeast** > Leaven, in Scripture, is always a figure of evil. Only unleavened bread might be offered to the Lord in the O.T. (see Ex. 29:2, 23–25; Num. 6:15; see also Jug. 6:19–21); this bread was then given as food to the priests (Lev. 8:26, 31; 10:12). These offerings prefigured Jesus Christ as the sinless man. There is one remarkable exception: the two wave-loaves baked with leaven, which were to be offered at Pentecost (Lev. 23:15–17), represent the church (Jews and Gentiles according to Eph. 2:11–18; Gal. 3:28), i.e., worshippers whose imperfections are recognized; but these two loaves are not burned on the altar for a sweet odor (comp. Lev. 2:11, 12), and a sin-offering is mentioned immediately afterwards (23:19). Unleavened bread was served as food at certain meals (Gen. 19:3; Ex. 12:8; 2 Kgs. 23:9). The feast of unleavened bread was celebrated for a period of seven days, commencing on the first day after the Passover (Ex. 12:15; 13:6; Lev. 23:6; Deut. 16:3, 8; Matt. 26:17; Mark 14:1, 12; Luke 22:1, 7; Acts 12:3; 20:6). Paul makes a practical application to every aspect of the Christian's life; the Christian, washed from his sins in the blood of the Lamb, puts away the leaven of evil in his life, a life that is now consecrated to the Lord (1 Cor. 5:8; see v. 7). ¶

UNLESS PERHAPS – See EXCEPT <1509>.

UNLETTERED – Acts 4:13 → UNEDUCATED <62>.

UNLIFTED – to lift: *anakaluptō* [verb: ἀνακαλύπτω <343>]; **from *ana*: back again, and *kaluptō*: to cover, to hide ▶ To discover, to unveil** > The veil of Moses remains unlifted {unremoved, untaken away, not removed} (lit.: not lifted) in the reading of the Old Testament (2 Cor. 3:14). Other ref.: 2 Cor. 3:18; see UNVEIL <343>. ¶

UNLOAD – *apophortizomai* [verb: ἀποφορτίζομαι <670>]; **from *apo*: away from, and *phortizō*: to load ▶ To remove, to disembark merchandise** > Paul's ship was to unload {discharge, unlade} its cargo at Tyre (Acts 21:3). ¶

UNLOOSE – Mark 1:7; Luke 3:16; John 1:27 → LOOSE <3089>.

UNLOVING – Rom. 1:31; 2 Tim. 3:3 → without natural affection → AFFECTION <794>.

UNMARRIED – [1] ***agamos*** [adj. and adj. used as noun: ἄγαμος <22>]; **from *a*: neg., and *gamos*: marriage ▶ One who is not joined with another person as spouses** > Paul recommends to the unmarried that it is good for them to remain unmarried as he was, to care for the things of the Lord, how to please Him (1 Cor. 7:8, 11, 32, 34). ¶
– [2] 1 Cor. 7:27 → to be unmarried → lit.: to be loosed from a wife → LOOSE <3089>.

UNMERCIFUL – *aneleēmōn* [adj.: ἀνελεήμων <415>]; **from *a*: neg., and *eleēmōn*: merciful, which is from *eleos*: mercy ▶ Without compassion for the misery of others** > Paul speaks of unbelievers who are unmerciful {ruthless} (Rom. 1:31). Other ref.: Titus 1:9 in some mss. ¶

UNMIXED – Rev. 14:10 → full strength → STRENGTH <194>.

UNMOVEABLE – [1] Acts 27:41 → IMMOVABLE <761> [2] 1 Cor. 15:58 → IMMOVABLE <277>.

UNMOVED – Acts 27:41 → IMMOVABLE <761>.

UNNATURAL – [1] Rom. 1:26 → contrary to nature → NATURE <5449> [2] Jude 7 → unnatural desire → lit.: other flesh → ANOTHER <2087>.

UNNOTICED – Luke 8:47 → to go unnoticed → to be hidden → HIDDEN (BE) <2990>.

UNOCCUPIED – to be unoccupied: *scholazō* [verb: σχολάζω <4980>]; **from *scholē*: leisure ▶ To be empty, vacant** > The unclean spirit finds his house empty (lit.: being empty) (Matt. 12:44). Other ref.: 1 Cor. 7:5 (to devote oneself); see DEVOTE <4980>. ¶

UNPOPULATED – Mark 1:45 → DESERTED <2048>.

UNPREPARED – *aparaskeuastos* [adj.: ἀπαρασκεύαστος <532>]; **from *a*: neg., and *paraskeuazō*: to be prepared, which is from *para*: beside, and *skeuazō*: to prepare, which is from *skeuē*: equipment, which is from *skeuos*: vessel, instrument ▶ Not ready** > Paul used this word in regard to the Corinthians who were supposed to make a gift for the needs of the saints (2 Cor. 9:4). ¶

UNPRESENTABLE – *aschēmōn* [adj.: ἀσχήμων <809>]; **from *a*: neg., and *schēma*: shape, aspect ▶ Which is not decent, immodest** > The unpresentable {uncomely, unseemly} parts of our body have greater modesty (i.e., we treat them more decently) (1 Cor. 12:23). ¶

UNPRINCIPLED MAN – 2 Pet. 2:7; 3:17 → LAWLESS MAN <113>.

UNPRODUCTIVE – 2 Pet. 1:8 → UNFRUITFUL <175>.

UNPROFITABLE – [1] ***alusitelēs*** [adj.: ἀλυσιτελής <255>]; **from *a*: neg., and *lusitelēs*: paying what is due, profitable, which is from *luō*: to loose, and *telos*: tax ▶ Netting no gain, useless >** It would be unprofitable {of no advantage} for Christians if their leaders were to carry out their service without joy (Heb. 13:17). ¶
[2] ***anōphelēs*** [adj. and adj. used as noun: ἀνωφελής <512>]; **from *a*: neg., and *ōpheleō*: to benefit, which is from *ōphelos*: benefit, utility ▶ a. Without profit, without benefit >** Foolish questions, genealogies, strifes, and contentions about the law are unprofitable and worthless (Titus 3:9). **b. Unprofitableness, uselessness >** The commandment is set aside because of its weakness and unprofitableness {because it is weak and useless} (Heb. 7:18). ¶
[3] ***achrēstos*** [adj.: ἄχρηστος <890>]; **from *a*: neg., and *chrēstos*: profitable, useful, which is from *chraomai*: to use ▶ Of no profit, useless >** Onesimus had formerly been unprofitable {unserviceable} to his master Philemon (Phm. 11). ¶
[4] **to become unprofitable: *achreioō*** [verb: ἀχρειόω <889>]; **from *achreios*: unworthy, which is from *a*: neg., and *chreia*: necessity, utility ▶ To be of no profit, to be worthless; also transl.: to become useless >** God affirms that all men have together become unprofitable (Rom. 3:12). ¶
– [5] Matt. 25:30 → WORTHLESS <888> [6] Luke 17:10 → UNWORTHY <888>.

UNPROFITABLENESS – Heb. 7:18 → UNPROFITABLE <512>.

UNPUNISHED – Rom. 3:25 → to leave unpunished → lit.: passing by → PASSING <3929>.

UNQUENCHABLE – ***asbestos*** [adj.: ἄσβεστος <762>]; **from *a*: neg., and *sbennumi*: to extinguish ▶ Which one cannot extinguish >** The Lord uses this term in regard to the fire of hell (Mark 9:43, 45; see also Matt. 3:12; Luke 3:17). ¶

UNQUESTIONING – ***adiakritos*** [adj.: ἀδιάκριτος <87>]; **from *a*: neg., and *diakrinō*: to judge, which is from *dia*: denotes separation in two, and *krinō*: to judge ▶ Without distinction, without prior bias >** The wisdom from above is unquestioning {impartial, unwavering, without partiality}, according to one translator's note: uncontentious (Jas. 3:17). ¶

UNREASONABLE – [1] ***alogos*** [adj.: ἄλογος <249>]; **from *a*: neg., and *logos*: reason ▶ Illogical, senseless >** It seemed to Festus unreasonable {absurd} to send Paul, a prisoner, without specifying the charges against him (Acts 25:27). Other refs.: 2 Pet. 2:12 and Jude 10 (without reason); see REASON <249>. ¶
– [2] 2 Thes. 3:2 → BAD <824> [3] 1 Pet. 2:18 → HARSH <4646>.

UNREASONING – 2 Pet. 2:12; Jude 10 → without reason → REASON (noun) <249>.

UNREBUKABLE – 1 Tim. 6:14 → above reproach → REPROACH (noun) <423>.

UNREMOVED – 2 Cor. 3:14 → to lift → UNLIFTED <343>.

UNREPENTANT – ***ametanoētos*** [adj.: ἀμετανόητος <279>]; **from *a*: neg., and *metanoeō*: to repent, which is from *meta*: denoting change, and *noeō*: to perceive, to think, which is from *nous*: mind, understanding ▶ Characteristic of a person in whom one does not observe a change of heart and mind to turn to a better way >** He whose heart is unrepentant {impenitent} treasures up for himself wrath, in the day of wrath and revelation of the righteous judgment of God (Rom. 2:5). ¶

UNREPROVEABLE – Col. 1:22 → above reproach → REPROACH (noun) <410>.

UNRIGHTEOUS (adj. and noun) – [1] ***adikos*** [adj. and adj. used as noun: ἄδικος <94>]; **from *a*: neg., and *dikē*: justice ▶ Which acts contrary to justice, to what is right; also transl.: dishonest, evildoer, unjust** > He who is unrighteous in what is least is unrighteous also in much (Luke 16:10a, b). One must be faithful in unrighteous {worldly} wealth (Luke 16:11). A Pharisee claimed he was not unjust (or: unrighteous) like the rest of men (Luke 18:11). Paul asks if God is unrighteous if He inflicts His wrath (Rom. 3:5). God is not unrighteous to forget those who serve the saints (Heb. 6:10). All other refs.: UNJUST (noun) <94>.
– [2] Luke 16:8, 9; 2 Thes. 2:10 → unrighteous deception → UNRIGHTEOUSNESS <93>.

UNRIGHTEOUSLY – Rev. 22:11a, b → to do unrighteously → to do wrong → WRONG (noun) <91>.

UNRIGHTEOUSNESS – [1] ***adikia*** [fem. noun: ἀδικία <93>]; **from *adikos*: unjust, which is from *a*: neg., and *dikē*: justice ▶ What is contrary to justice, dishonesty; also transl.: evil, iniquity, injustice, unrighteous deception, wickedness** > In a parable, the master praised the unrighteous {dishonest, unjust} manager (lit.: the manager of unrighteousness) (Luke 16:8). Jesus says to make friends with wealth of unrighteousness {unrighteous mammon, worldly wealth} (Luke 16:9). There is no unrighteousness {nothing false} in the Son who seeks the glory of the Father who has sent Him (John 7:18). Men are filled with all unrighteousness (Rom. 1:29). Our unrighteousness demonstrates the righteousness of God (Rom. 3:5). Paul asks rhetorically if there is unrighteousness with God (Rom. 9:14). Love does not rejoice in unrighteousness (1 Cor. 13:6). The coming of the antichrist will be in all deceit of unrighteousness (2 Thes. 2:10). Those who have taken pleasure in unrighteousness will be judged (2 Thes. 2:12). God will be merciful to the unrighteousnesses of His people (Heb. 8:12). All other refs.: INIQUITY <93>, UNJUST (adj.) <93>, WRONG (noun) <93>.
– [2] Heb. 1:9 → INIQUITY <458> [3] Rev. 18:5 → INIQUITY <92>.

UNROLL – Luke 4:17 → OPEN (verb) <380>.

UNRULY – [1] ***akatastatos*** [adj.: ἀκατάστατος <182>]; **from *a*: neg., and *kathistēmi*: to set in order, which is from *kata*: intens., and *histēmi*: to set, to place ▶ Unstable, fluctuating, unsteady** > The tongue is an unruly {restless, unsettled} evil, full of deadly poison (Jas. 3:8 in some mss.). Other ref.: Jas. 1:8; see UNSTABLE <182>. ¶
[2] ***akataschetos*** [adj.: ἀκατάσχετος <183>]; **from *a*: neg., and *katechō*: to restrain, which is from *kata*: intens., and *echō*: to have ▶ That cannot be controlled, restrained; disorderly** > The tongue is an unsettled {restless} evil, full of deadly poison (Jas. 3:8 in some mss.). ¶
[3] ***ataktos*** [adj.: ἄτακτος <813>]; **from *a*: neg., and *tassō*: to set in order ▶ Person living in a disorderly way, unsubordinated** > The Thessalonians had to warn those who were unruly {disorderly, idle} (1 Thes. 5:14). ¶
– [4] 2 Thes. 3:6 → unruly life → DISORDERLY <814> [5] Titus 1:6, 10 → INSUBORDINATE <506>.

UNSALTY – ***analos*** [adj.: ἄναλος <358>]; **from *a*: neg., and *hals*: salt; lit.: without salt ▶ Desalted, without flavor** > Jesus speaks of salt that becomes unsalty {saltless} (Mark 9:50); also transl.: to lose the flavor, the saltiness, the saltness. ¶

UNSCHOOLED – Acts 4:13 → UNEDUCATED <62>.

UNSEARCHABLE – [1] ***anexereunētos*** [adj.: ἀνεξερεύνητος <419>]; **from *a*: neg., and *exereunaō*: to look into, to search with care, which is from *ek*: intens., and *ereunaō*: to examine, to search; other spelling: *anexeraunētos* ▶ Which one cannot examine, impenetrable** > The judgments of God are unsearchable (Rom. 11:33). ¶

2 ***anexichniastos*** [adj.: ἀνεξιχνίαστος <421>]; **from *a*: neg., *ek*: out of, and *exichniazō*: to explore, to trace out, which is from *ichnos*: imprint; lit.: whose trace one cannot find ► Impenetrable, incomprehensible** > Paul announced the unsearchable {boundless, unfathomable} riches of Christ (Eph. 3:8). Other ref.: Rom. 11:33; see UNTRACEABLE <421>. ¶

UNSEEMLY – 1 Rom. 1:27 → that which is unseemly → SHAME (noun) <808> 2 Rom. 1:28 → FITTING (BE) <2520> 3 1 Cor. 12:23 → UNPRESENTABLE <809> 4 1 Cor. 13:5 → to behave unseemly → BEHAVE <807>.

UNSEEN – 1 Matt. 6:18a → SECRET (adj. and noun) <2927> 2 Heb. 11:7 → not yet seen → SEE <991> 3 Heb. 11:27 → INVISIBLE <517>.

UNSERVICEABLE – Phm. 11 → UNPROFITABLE <890>.

UNSETTLE – 1 Acts 15:24 → SUBVERT <384> 2 Gal. 5:12 → TROUBLE (verb) <387> 3 1 Thes. 3:3 → SHAKE <4525> 4 2 Thes. 2:2 → SHAKE <4531>.

UNSETTLED – Jas. 3:8 → UNRULY <183>.

UNSHAKEN – 2 Cor. 1:7 → FIRM <949>.

UNSHRUNK – Matt. 9:16; Mark 2:21a → NEW <46>.

UNSKILFUL – Heb. 5:13 → not accustomed → UNSKILLED <552>.

UNSKILLED – 1 ***apeiros*** [adj.: ἄπειρος <552>]; **from *a*: neg., and *peira*: experience ► Without experience, i.e., without knowledge acquired by long practice** > Whoever uses milk, i.e., only the rudiments of Scriptures, is unskilled {not accustomed, being still an infant, unskilful}, in the word of God (Heb. 5:13). ¶
– 2 2 Cor. 11:6 → SIMPLE <2399>.

UNSPEAKABLE – 1 2 Cor. 9:15 → INDESCRIBABLE <411> 2 2 Cor. 12:4 → INEXPRESSIBLE <731> 3 1 Pet. 1:8 → INEXPRESSIBLE <412>.

UNSPIRITUAL – 1 Rom. 7:14 → CARNAL <4559> 2 Jas. 3:15 → SENSUAL <5591>.

UNSPOTTED – ***aspilos*** [adj.: ἄσπιλος <784>]; **from *a*: neg., and *spilos*: spot ► Unsmirched, without smudge, without spot** > Pure (*katharos*) religion is to visit orphans and widows in their affliction, and to keep oneself unspotted (*aspilos*) from {unstained from, from being polluted by} the world (Jas. 1:27). Other refs. (without spot): 1 Tim. 6:14; 1 Pet. 1:19; 2 Pet. 3:14; see SPOT <784>. ¶

UNSTABLE – 1 ***akatastatos*** [adj.: ἀκατάστατος <182>]; **from *a*: neg., and *kathistēmi*: to firmly establish, which is from *kata*: down, and *histēmi*: to stand ► Unsettled, vacillating** > The man who asks the Lord (for wisdom in particular) doubting is an unstable man in all his ways (Jas. 1:8). Other ref.: Jas. 3:8 in some mss.; see UNRULY <182>. ¶

2 ***astēriktos*** [adj.: ἀστήρικτος <793>]: **from *a*: neg., and *stērizō*: to establish, to strengthen, comp. *stereos*: solid, stable ► Not established, not firm** > Evil persons were enticing unstable {unestablished, unsteady} souls (2 Pet. 2:14). Ignorant and unstable {ill-established} people were distorting the writings of Paul (2 Pet. 3:16). ¶

UNSTAINED – 1 1 Tim. 6:14 → without spot → SPOT <784> 2 Heb. 7:26 → UNDEFILED <283> 3 Jas. 1:27 → UNSPOTTED <784>.

UNSTEADY – 2 Pet. 2:14 → UNSTABLE <793>.

UNSUBJECT – Heb. 2:8c → not put under, not subject → SUBJECT (verb) <506>.

UNSUITABLE – Acts 27:12 → not suitable → SUITABLE <428>.

UNSUSPECTING – Rom. 16:18 → SIMPLE <172>.

UNSWERVINGLY – Heb. 10:23 → without wavering → WAVERING <186>.

UNTAKEN AWAY – 2 Cor. 3:14 → to lift → UNLIFTED <343>.

UNTAUGHT – ***amathēs*** [adj.: ἀμαθής <261>]; **from *a*: neg., and *manthanō*: to learn, to teach ▶ Without instruction; also transl.: ignorant, unlearned** > Untaught and unstable people distorted things that Paul had written (2 Pet. 3:16). ¶

UNTHANKFUL – ***acharistos*** [adj.: ἀχάριστος <884>]; **from *a*: neg., and *charizomai*: to grant as a favor, which is from *charis*: grace, which is from *chairō*: to rejoice ▶ Who does not show gratitude; also transl.: ungrateful** > God is good to unthankful and evil men (Luke 6:35). In the last days, men will be unthankful (2 Tim. 3:2). ¶

UNTIE – [1] Matt. 21:2; Mark 1:7; 11:2, 4, 5; Luke 3:16; 13:15; 19:30, 31, 33a, b; John 1:27; Acts 13:25 → LOOSE <3089> [2] Acts 27:40 → LOOSE <4014>.

UNTIL – [1] ***heōs*** [adv.: ἕως <2193>] ▶ Adv. of time and place. Refs.: Matt. 2:13; 5:18, 26; 10:11; 12:20; Mark 9:1; 12:36; Luke 9:27; 13:35; 21:32; 1 Cor. 4:5; Jas. 5:7. * ‡

[2] ***mechri, mechris*** [adv.: μέχρι, μέχρις <3360>] ▶ Refs.: Matt. 11:23; 13:30; Heb. 3:6, 14; 9:10. *

– [3] Luke 22:34 → BEFORE <4250>.

UNTIMELY – 1 Cor. 15:8 → untimely born → BORN <1626>.

UNTO – [1] Acts 26:17 → TO <1519> [2] 1 Thes. 2:1 → TO <4314>.

UNTOWARD – Acts 2:40 → PERVERSE <4646>.

UNTRACEABLE – ***anexichniastos*** [adj.: ἀνεξιχνίαστος <421>]; **from *a*: neg., *ek*: out of, and *exichniazō*: to explore, to trace out, which is from *ichnos*: imprint; lit.: whose trace one cannot find ▶ Impenetrable, incomprehensible** > The ways of God are untraceable {beyond tracing out, past finding out, unfathomable} (Rom. 11:33). Other ref.: Eph. 3:8; see UNSEARCHABLE <421>. ¶

UNTRAINED – [1] Acts 4:13 → UNINSTRUCTED <2399> [2] 2 Cor. 11:6 → SIMPLE <2399>.

UNTRUSTWORTHY – Rom. 1:31 → FAITHLESS <802>.

UNUSUAL – [1] ***atopos*** [adj.: ἄτοπος <824>]; **from *a*: neg., and *topos*: place ▶ Abnormal, unfortunate; the word is used as a medical term for anything out of place, i.e., deadly** > People of Malta saw nothing unusual {no harm} happen to Paul as a result of a viper bite (Acts 28:6). All other refs.: BAD <824>.

– [2] Acts 19:11 → lit.: not the being ordinary → to be ordinary → ORDINARY <5177> [3] Acts 28:2 → no common → to be common → COMMON <5177>.

UNVEIL – ***anakaluptō*** [verb: ἀνακαλύπτω <343>]; **from *ana*: again, and *kaluptō*: to cover, to hide ▶ To uncover; metaphorically, to remove anything that might obscure or hinder perception** > Those who behold the glory of the Lord with unveiled {open} face are transformed into the same image from glory to glory (2 Cor. 3:18). Other ref.: 2 Cor. 3:14 (to lift); see UNLIFTED <343>. ¶

UNWASHED – ***aniptos*** [adj.: ἄνιπτος <449>]; **from *a*: neg., and *niptō*: to wash ▶ Not cleansed** > Eating with unwashed hands does not defile a man (Matt. 15:20). Some of Jesus's disciples were eating bread with unwashed hands (Mark 7:2, 5 {unclean, unwashen}); for Matt. 7:5, some mss. have *koinos* (common). ¶

UNWASHEN – Mark 7:5 → IMPURE <449>.

UNWAVERING – [1] Heb. 10:23 → without wavering → WAVERING <186> [2] Jas. 3:17 → UNQUESTIONING <87>.

UNWHOLESOME – Eph. 4:29 → CORRUPT (adj.) <4550>.

UNWILLING – [1] Matt. 1:19; 15:32; John 5:40 → lit.: not wanting → WANT (verb) <2309> [2] 2 Thes. 3:10 → to be unwilling → lit.: to not desire → DESIRE (verb) <2309>.

UNWISE – [1] Rom. 1:14; 1 Tim. 6:9 → FOOLISH <453> [2] Eph. 5:17 → FOOLISH <878>.

UNWITTINGLY – Heb. 13:2 → lit.: without knowing it → to not know → KNOW <2990>.

UNWORTHILY – ***anaxiōs*** [adv.: ἀναξίως <371>]**; from *anaxios*: unworthy, which is from *a*: neg., and *axios*: worthy ▶ In an unbecoming manner, without reverence >** To eat the bread and drink the cup of the Lord unworthily {in an unworthy manner}, when taking part in the Lord's supper (1 Cor. 11:27, 29 in some mss.), is to fail to recognize the full symbolic value of the emblems representing the body and the blood of the Lord Jesus Christ who offered Himself up at the cross. ¶

UNWORTHY – [1] **worthy: *axios*** [adj.: ἄξιος <514>] **▶ Deserving, of inherent merit >** In rejecting the word of God, the Jews judged themselves unworthy (lit.: not worthy) of eternal life (Acts 13:46). Other refs.: DESERVING <514>, FITTING <514>, MEET (adj.) <514>, WORTHY <514>.
[2] ***anaxios*** [adj.: ἀνάξιος <370>]**; from *a*: neg., and *axios*: see [1] ▶ Incapable, incompetent >** Paul asked the Corinthians if they were unworthy {not competent} to judge the smallest matters (1 Cor. 6:2). ¶
[3] ***achreios*** [adj.: ἀχρεῖος <888>]**; from *a*: neg., and *chreia*: necessity, utility; lit.: not indispensable ▶ Undeserving, unprofitable >** The servants of the Lord can say that they are unworthy servants (Luke 17:10). Other ref.: Matt. 25:30; see WORTHLESS <888>. ¶
– [4] 1 Cor. 11:27 → in an unworthy manner → UNWORTHILY <371> [5] 1 Cor. 15:9 → not worthy → WORTHY <2425>.

UPBRAID – Matt. 11:20; Mark 16:14; Jas. 1:5 → REPROACH (verb) <3679>.

UPBUILDING – Rom. 14:19; 1 Cor. 14:3; 2 Cor. 12:19 → EDIFICATION <3619>.

UPHOLD – [1] ***pherō*** [verb: φέρω <5342>] **▶ To carry, to sustain >** Jesus upholds all things by the word of His power (Heb. 1:3). All other refs.: see entries in Lexicon at <5342>.
– [2] Rom. 3:31 → ESTABLISH <2476> [3] Rom. 14:4 → he will be upheld → he will be made to stand → STAND (verb) <2476> [4] 1 Thes. 5:14 → SUPPORT (verb) <472>.

UPLIFTED – ***hupsēlos*** [adj.: ὑψηλός <5308>]**; from *hupsos*: height ▶ Raised, set higher >** God brought out the Israelites from Egypt with an uplifted {a high} arm {with mighty power} (Acts 13:17). All other refs.: ESTEEMED <5308>, HIGH (adj.) <5308>.

UPON – ***ana*** [prep.: ἀνά <303>] **▶** a. In the N.T., it forms a periphrasis (a longer phrasing in place of a possible shorter and plainer form of expression) for an adv. (e.g., *ana meros*: part), by turns, alternately (1 Cor. 14:27); *ana meson*: in the midst of, through the midst of, between. It is spoken of place (Matt. 13:25; Mark 7:31; Rev. 7:17) and of persons (1 Cor. 6:5). In Matt. 20:9, 10: *ana dēnarion*: "to each a dinar." b. With numerical words it marks distribution (Mark 6:40; Luke 9:3, 14; 10:1; John 2:6; Rev. 4:8; see Is. 6:2). In Rev. 21:21, "each one of the gates." c. It is also used in composition with other words: *ana* denotes up or upward, as *anabaínō*: I go up. It means back or again, equal to the Engl. prefix re-, implying repetition, increase, intensity, as *anakainízō*: to renew; *anachōréō*: to depart; *anaginōskō*: to know again, to read.* ‡

UPPER – 1 ***anōterikos*** [adj.: ἀνωτερικός <510>]; **from *anōteros*: higher, upper ► Higher, more elevated** > After having passed through the upper regions {the interior}, Paul came to Ephesus (Acts 19:1). ¶
– 2 Mark 14:15; Luke 22:12 → upper room → ROOM <508> 3 Acts 1:13; 9:37, 39; 20:8 → upper room, upper chamber → ROOM <5253>.

UPRIGHT – 1 Acts 8:21 → STRAIGHT <2117> 2 Acts 10:22 → RIGHTEOUS <1342> 3 Acts 14:10 → STRAIGHT <3717> 4 Titus 2:12 → lit.: uprightly → JUSTLY <1346>.

UPRIGHTLY – 1 Gal. 2:14 → to walk uprightly → to be straightforward → STRAIGHTFORWARD <3716> 2 1 Thes. 2:10 → JUSTLY <1346>.

UPRIGHTNESS – Heb. 1:8 → RIGHTEOUSNESS <2118>.

UPRISING – 1 Mark 15:7 → INSURRECTION <4714> 2 Luke 21:9 → TUMULT <181> 3 John 18:40 → one taking part in an uprising → ROBBER <3027>.

UPROAR – 1 **to set in an uproar: *thorubeō*** [verb: θορυβέω <2350>]; **from *thorubos*: tumult ► To provoke agitation, to sow confusion, to be disturbed, troubled in mind; also transl.: to set in confusion, to start a riot, to be troubled, to be alarmed** > The Jews started a riot {set in an uproar} in all the city of Thessalonica and sought Paul and Silas (Acts 17:5). Paul told Christians not to be troubled, for Eutychus was alive (Acts 20:10). All other refs.: NOISE (noun) <2350>, TUMULT <2350>.
2 **to be in an uproar: *suncheō*** [verb: συγχέω <4797>]; **from *sun*: together, and *cheō*: to pour ► To be confused, to be agitated** > All Jerusalem was in an uproar {was in tumult, was in confusion} while Paul was being beaten (Acts 21:31; see v. 32). All other refs.: CONFOUND <4797>, CONFUSED (BE) <4797>, STIR (verb) <4797>.
– 3 Matt. 26:5; 27:54; Mark 14:2; Acts 20:1; 21:34; 24:18 → TUMULT <2351> 4 Acts 16:20 → to throw in an uproar → to trouble exceedingly → TROUBLE (verb) <1613> 5 Acts 19:29 → the city was in an uproar → lit.: the city was filled with confusion → FILL (verb) <4130>, CONFUSION <4799> 6 Acts 19:40 → INSURRECTION <4714> 7 Acts 21:38 → to make an uproar → to raise a sedition → SEDITION <387> 8 Acts 23:9 → CRY (noun) <2906>.

UPROOT – ***ekrizoō*** [verb: ἐκριζόω <1610>]; **from *ek*: out, and *riza*: root ► To pull out by the roots; also transl.: to root up, to pluck by the roots, to pull up** > In a parable, a householder warned his servants not to uproot the wheat with the tares (Matt. 13:29). Every plant that the Father has not planted will be uprooted (Matt. 15:13). If they had faith as a mustard seed, the apostles could say to a mulberry tree to be uprooted {pulled up, plucked by the roots} and be planted in the sea (Luke 17:6). Jude speaks of evil men who are like late autumn trees uprooted (Jude 12). ¶

UPSET (adj.) – Luke 10:41 → to be upset → to be troubled → TROUBLE (verb) <5182>.

UPSET (verb) – 1 Acts 15:24 → SUBVERT <384> 2 Acts 17:6 → to turn upside down → TURN (verb) <387> 3 2 Tim. 2:18 → OVERTURN <396>.

UPSTAIRS – Mark 14:15; Luke 22:12 → room upstairs → upper room → ROOM <508>.

UPWARD – Phil. 3:14 → HIGH (adv.) <507>.

URBANUS – ***Ourbanos*** [masc. name: Οὐρβανός <3773>]: **polite, refined, in Lat. ► Paul's fellow-worker at Rome >** Paul sends greetings to Urbanus (Rom. 16:9). ¶

URGE – [1] Matt. 15:23; John 4:31, 40; Phil. 4:3; 1 Thes. 4:1; 5:12 → ASK <2065> [2] Luke 11:53 → PRESS <1758> [3] Luke 24:29; Acts 16:15 → to urge, to urge strongly → CONSTRAIN <3849> [4] Acts 13:43 → PERSUADE <3982> [5] Acts 16:9, 15; 19:31; 25:2; 1 Cor. 16:12; 2 Cor. 9:5; 12:18; 1 Tim. 1:3; Heb. 13:19 → BESEECH <3870> [6] Acts 21:12; 1 Cor. 4:16; Phil. 4:2a, b → PLEAD <3870> [7] Acts 27:22 → EXHORT <3867> [8] Acts 27:33, 34; Rom. 12:1; 15:30; 16:17; 1 Cor. 16:15; 2 Cor. 2:8; 6:1; 8:6; 10:1; Eph. 4:1; 1 Thes. 4:1, 10; 5:14; 2 Thes. 3:12; 1 Tim. 2:1; 6:2; Titus 2:6; Heb. 13:22; 1 Pet. 2:11; Jude 3 → EXHORT <3870> [9] 1 Tim. 6:13 → ENJOIN <3853> [10] Titus 2:4 → ADMONISH <4994>.

URGENCY – 2 Cor. 8:4 → ENTREATY <3874>.

URGENT – [1] Luke 23:5 → to be urgent → to be insistent → INSISTENT <2001> [2] Luke 23:23 → to be urgent → to be insistent → INSISTENT <1945> [3] 2 Tim. 4:2 → to be urgent → to be ready → READY <2186> [4] Titus 3:14 → NECESSARY <316>.

URGENTLY – [1] Luke 11:53 → VEHEMENTLY <1171> [2] 2 Cor. 8:4 → lit.: with much entreaty → ENTREATY <3874>.

URGING – 2 Cor. 8:4 → ENTREATY <3874>.

URIAH – ***Ourias*** [masc. name: Οὐρίας <3774>]: **Jehovah is my light, in Heb. ► Man of the O.T. >** The wife of Uriah, Bathsheba, was the mother of Solomon (Matt. 1:6). David had Uriah killed and took Bathsheba as his wife (see 2 Sam. 11:14–17; 12:9). ¶

URN – Heb. 9:4 → POT <4713>.

US – ***hēmōn*** [pron.: ἡμῶν <2257>] ► Personal pron. plur. of *ego*: I. * ‡

USE (noun) – [1] ***chrēsis*** [fem. noun: χρῆσις <5540>]; **from *chraomai*: to use, which is from *chraō*: to lend ► Act of having sexual relations; also transl.: function, relations >** Women changed the natural use into that which is against nature (Rom. 1:26). Likewise also the men, leaving the natural use of the woman, were inflamed in their lust toward one another (Rom. 1:27). ¶

[2] ***apochrēsis*** [fem. noun: ἀπόχρησις <671>]; **from *apochraomai*: to use completely, which is from *apo*: from, and *chraomai*: see [1] ► Full consumption >** Paul speaks of things that are destined to perish with use {using} (Col. 2:22). ¶

– [3] Luke 14:35 → of use → FIT (adj.) <2111> [4] Rom. 9:21 → common use → DISHONOR (noun) <819> [5] 1 Cor. 9:12, 15 → to make use → USE (verb) <5530> [6] Eph. 4:29 → NEED (noun) <5532> [7] Eph. 5:16; Col. 4:5 → to make the best use → REDEEM <1805> [8] 2 Tim. 2:20, 21 → "use" added in Engl. [9] Heb. 5:14 → HABIT <1838> [10] Jas. 2:14, 16 → PROFIT (noun) <3786>.

USE (verb) – [1] **to use despitefully, to use spitefully: *epēreazō*** [verb: ἐπηρεάζω <1908>]; **from *epēreia*: unrestrained abuse or insult, threat, which is from *epi*: against, and *areia*: insult, threat ► To despise, to mistreat >** Jesus said to pray for those who use us despitefully (Matt. 5:44 in some mss.; Luke 6:28). Other ref.: 1 Pet. 3:16 (to falsely accuse); see ACCUSE <1908>. ¶

[2] **to use up: *katargeō*** [verb: καταργέω <2673>]; **from *kata*: intens., and *argeō*: to be inactive ► To leave (something) unproductive; also transl.: to cumber, to render useless >** A fig tree was using up the ground (Luke 13:7). All other refs.: see entries in Lexicon at <2673>.

[3] ***metechō*** [verb: μετέχω <3348>]; **from *meta*: with, and *echō*: to have ► To partake, to share >** Whoever uses {lives on}

milk is unskilled in the word of righteousness (Heb. 5:13). All other refs.: PARTAKE <3348>, PERTAIN <3348>.
4 ***prassō*** [verb: πράσσω <4238>] ► **To practice, to give oneself to** > Many Ephesians who used {had practiced} magic burned their books (Acts 19:19). Other refs.: COLLECT <4238>, CONTRARY <4238>, DO <4238>, KEEP (verb) <4238>.
5 ***chraomai*** [verb: χράομαι <5530>]; **from *chraō*: to lend ► To avail oneself of something, to make the most of** > Cables were used to undergird the ship of Paul (Acts 27:17). A slave is not to be concerned if he is called being a slave, however, if he has the opportunity to become free, he is encouraged to use that opportunity {to do that, to do so} (1 Cor. 7:21). Christians who use (*chraomai*) the world are not to dispose of it as their own (*katachraomai*; see 6) (1 Cor. 7:31). Paul had not used the right to reap carnal things from the Corinthians (1 Cor. 9:12, 15). He uses the exprs. "to use lightness" (2 Cor. 1:17), "to use great boldness" (3:12), and "to use severity" (13:10). The law is good, if one uses it lawfully (1 Tim. 1:8). Paul told Timothy to use a little wine, because of his stomach and his frequent illnesses (1 Tim. 5:23). Other ref.: Acts 27:3; see TREAT <5530>. ¶
6 **to make use, to make full use: *katachraomai*** [verb: καταχράομαι <2710>]; **from *kata*: against (intens.), and *chraomai*: see 5 ► To abuse, to utilize fully** > This verb {to dispose, to engross, to make full use, to misuse} is found in 1 Cor. 7:31; see 5; *parachraomai* in other mss. In preaching the gospel, Paul made it free to others, so as not to make full use {to abuse} of his right in the gospel (1 Cor. 9:18). ¶
– 7 Matt. 7:2; Mark 4:24; Luke 6:38 → to use (a measure) → MEASURE (verb) <3354> 8 Matt. 15:5 → what might have been used → lit.: whatever you would be profited → PROFIT (verb) <5623> 9 Acts 14:5 → to use despitefully, to use ill → MISTREAT <5195> 10 Acts 14:8 → who could not use → without strength → STRENGTH <102> 11 Rom. 3:13 → they use their tongues to deceive → lit.: with their tongues they deceive 12 2 Cor. 2:14 → God uses us → lit.: God through (*dia*) us 13 Phil. 2:6 → something to be used to His own advantage → ROBBERY <725> 14 Col. 2:22 → as they are used → with use → USE (noun) <671> 15 Heb. 9:21 → everything used → lit.: all the vessels → VESSEL[1] <4632> 16 Heb. 10:33 → to be used → to be treated → TREAT <390> 17 2 Pet. 1:5 → GIVE <3923>.

USEFUL – 1 ***euthetos*** [adj.: εὔθετος <2111>]; **from *eu*: well, and *tithēmi*: to set ► Fitting, suitable** > The earth produces useful {meet} herbs for those by whom it is cultivated (Heb. 6:7). Other refs.: Luke 9:62; 14:35; see FIT (adj.) <2111>. ¶
2 ***euchrēstos*** [verb: εὔχρηστος <2173>]; **from *eu*: well, and *chrēstos*: profitable, useful ► Which one may easily employ, suitable; also transl.: helpful, meet, profitable, serviceable** > If one purifies himself from vessels to dishonor, he shall be a vessel useful {meet, serviceable} to the Master (2 Tim. 2:21). Mark was useful {very useful} to Paul for service (2 Tim. 4:11). Onesimus was now useful to Philemon and to Paul (Phm. 11). ¶
– 3 Eph. 4:28 → GOOD (adj.) <18> 4 2 Tim. 3:16 → PROFITABLE <5624>.

USELESS – 1 Matt. 25:30 → WORTHLESS <888> 2 Luke 13:7 → to render useless → USE (verb) <2673> 3 Luke 14:35 → it is useless for either → lit.: it is fit for neither → FIT <2111> 4 Acts 14:15; 1 Cor. 3:20; Titus 3:9; Jas. 1:26 → VAIN <3152> 5 Rom. 3:12 → to become useless → to become unprofitable → UNPROFITABLE <889> 6 1 Cor. 15:14a, b; 1 Thes. 3:5 → VAIN <2756> 7 1 Tim. 6:5 in some mss. → useless wrangling → WRANGLING <1275a> 8 2 Tim. 2:14 → PROFITABLE <5539> 9 Phm. 11 → UNPROFITABLE <890> 10 Heb. 7:18 → UNPROFITABLE <512> 11 2 Pet. 1:8 → IDLE <692>.

USELESSNESS – Heb. 7:18 → UNPROFITABLE <512>.

USING – Col. 2:22 → USE (noun) <671>.

USUAL – Luke 22:39 → as usual → as the custom → CUSTOM <1485>.

USUALLY – Mark 15:8 → ALWAYS <104>.

USURP – 1 Tim. 2:12 → to usurp authority → AUTHORITY <831>.

USURY – Matt. 25:27; Luke 19:23 → INTEREST[1] <5110>.

UTENSIL – Mark 7:4 → brazen utensil → BRAZEN VESSEL <5473>.

UTMOST – 2 Tim. 4:21 → to do one's utmost → to make every effort → EFFORT <4704>.

UTTER (adj.) – [1] John 9:34 → born in utter sin → completely born in sin → COMPLETELY <3650> [2] 1 Cor. 6:7 → UTTERLY <3654> [3] 2 Pet. 2:17; Jude 13 → utter darkness → lit.: blackness of darkness → BLACKNESS <2217>.

UTTER (verb) – [1] ***apophthengomai*** [verb: ἀποφθέγγομαι <669>]; **from *apo*: from, and *phthengomai*: to speak ▶ To express, to proclaim (under divine inspiration) >** Paul uttered {spoke, spoke forth} words of truth and soberness (Acts 26:25). Other refs.: Acts 2:4; 2:14 (to speak forth); see UTTERANCE <669>, SPEAK <669>. ¶
[2] ***aphiēmi*** [verb: ἀφίημι <863>]; **from *apo*: from, and *hiēmi*: to send ▶ To emit, to let out; also transl.: to cry, to cry out >** Having uttered a loud cry, Jesus expired (Mark 15:37). All other refs.: see entries in Lexicon at <863>.
[3] ***ereugomai*** [verb: ἐρεύγομαι <2044>] **▶ To declare openly, to announce >** According to a prophecy, Jesus uttered things hidden from the world's foundation (Matt. 13:35). ¶
[4] ***laleō*** [verb: λαλέω <2980>] **▶ To say, to disclose >** Paul was caught up into paradise and heard unspeakable things that man is not allowed to utter {speak, tell} (2 Cor. 12:4). Other refs.: SPEAK <2980>.
[5] **which cannot be uttered: *alalētos*** [adj.: ἀλάλητος <215>]; **from *a*: neg., and *laleō*:** see [4] **▶ Which one cannot express, put into words >** The Spirit makes intercession with groanings that cannot be uttered {too deep for words} (Rom. 8:26). ¶
– [6] Matt. 5:11 → SAY <2036> [7] Matt. 26:65; Mark 3:28 → BLASPHEME <987> [8] Acts 2:16 → SPEAK <2046> [9] Acts 23:22 → TELL <1583> [10] 1 Cor. 14:9 → GIVE <1325> [11] 2 Cor. 1:20 → that is why it is through Him that we utter our Amen to God → lit.: and in Him the Amen to God through us [12] Heb. 5:11 → hard to be uttered → hard to explain → HARD <1421> [13] Heb. 12:25 → to utter the oracles → ORACLE <5537> [14] 2 Pet. 1:17, 18 → COME <5342> [15] Rev. 13:6 → to utter → lit.: to open the mouth → OPEN (verb) <455>, MOUTH (noun) <4750>.

UTTERANCE – [1] **to utter: *apophthengomai*** [verb: ἀποφθέγγομαι <669>]; **from *apo*: from, and *phthengomai*: to speak ▶ To pronounce words, to express oneself >** At Pentecost, Christians began to speak with other tongues, as the Spirit gave them utterance {gave them to speak forth, enabled them} (lit.: gave them to utter) (Acts 2:4). Other refs.: Acts 2:14 (to speak forth); 26:25; see SPEAK <669>, UTTER (verb) <669>. ¶
– [2] 1 Cor. 12:8a, b → WORD <3056> [3] 1 Pet. 4:11 → ORACLE <3051>.

UTTERLY – [1] ***holōs*** [adv.: ὅλως <3654>]; **from *holos*: whole, all ▶ Entirely, completely >** It was utterly a fault {altogether a fault, an utter failure} for the Corinthians to have suits among themselves (1 Cor. 6:7). All other refs.: ACTUALLY <3654>, ALL <3654>.
– [2] Mark 7:37 → above measure → MEASURE (noun) <5249> [3] Acts 3:23 → to utterly destroy → DESTROY <1842> [4] Rom. 7:13; 2 Cor. 1:8 → EXCEEDINGLY <5236>.

UTTERMOST – [1] **to the uttermost: *eis to pantelēs*; *pantelēs*** [adj.: παντελής <3838>]; **from *pas*: all, and *telos*: end; lit.: until the completion ▶ To the highest degree >** Jesus is able to save to the uttermost

{completely, forever} those who come to God through Him (Heb. 7:25). This expr. is transl. "at all" in Luke 13:11: A woman was bent together and could not lift her head up at all {in no way, in no wise, wholly}. ¶
– 2 Matt. 5:26 → LAST (adv. and noun) <2078> 3 Mark 13:27a, b → uttermost part → END (noun) <206> 4 Acts 1:8 → uttermost part → PART (noun) <2078> 5 Acts 24:22 → to know the uttermost → to make a decision → DECISION <1231>.

UZZIAH – ***Ozias*** [masc. name: Ὀζίας <3604>]**: might of Jehovah, in Heb. ▶ King of Judah, also called Azariah (see 2 Kgs. 15:1, 2; 2 Chr. 26:1, 3)** > Uzziah is mentioned in the genealogy of Jesus Christ (Matt. 1:8, 9). ¶

 V 

VACILLATE – 2 Cor. 1:17 → lit.: to use lightness → LIGHTNESS <1644>.

VAIL – 2 Cor. 3:13–16 → VEIL (noun) <2571>.

VAIN – 1 **vain: *kenos*** [adj.: κενός <2756>]; **in vain: *eis kenon* ▶ Empty, without effect, without value; also transl.: foolish, futile, hollow, useless** > David asks why the peoples have imagined vain things (Acts 4:25). The grace of God toward Paul had not been vain (1 Cor. 15:10). Paul says that if Christ has not been raised, his preaching is vain, and the faith of the Corinthians is also vain (1 Cor. 15:14a, b). The toil of Christians is not in vain in the Lord (1 Cor. 15:58). Paul exhorted the Corinthians that they might not have received the grace of God in vain (2 Cor. 6:1). He feared that he might be running or have run in vain (Gal. 2:2). No one was to deceive the Philippians with vain words (Eph. 5:6). The Philippians were to hold fast the word of life, so that Paul would have reason to glory in the day of Christ that he had not run in vain or labored in vain (Phil. 2:16a, b). The Colossians were to see that no one should take them captive through philosophy and vain deception (Col. 2:8). Paul's coming to the Thessalonians had not been in vain {a failure} (1 Thes. 2:1), but he feared that the tempter might have tempted them, and that his labor might have been in vain {have come to nothing} (3:5). James speaks to a vain man, telling him that faith without works is useless (Jas. 2:20). Other refs.: Mark 12:3; Luke 1:53; 20:10, 11; see EMPTY-HANDED <2756>. ¶

2 **in vain: *kenōs*** [adv.: κενῶς <2761>]; **from *kenos*: empty, vain ▶ To no purpose, without reason, for nothing** > James asks those to whom he writes if they think that Scripture speaks in vain (Jas. 4:5). ¶

3 **to make vain: *kenoō*** [verb: κενόω <2758>]; **from *kenos*: see 1 ▶ a. To make empty, to render useless** > If those who are of the law are heirs, faith is made vain and the promise made of no effect (Rom. 4:14 {to make void, to be of no value}). Christ had not sent Paul to baptize, but to preach the gospel, not with wisdom of speech, that the cross of Christ might not be made vain (1 Cor. 1:17 {to be empty of power, to make of no effect, to make void}). **b. To show that something has no foundation** > Paul did not want his boasting in the Corinthians, i.e., in regard to their willingness to serve the saints, to be in vain {be made void, be empty, prove hollow} (2 Cor. 9:3). All other refs.: REPUTATION <2758>, VOID <2758>.

4 **vain glory: *kenodoxia*** [fem. noun: κενοδοξία <2754>]; **from *kenodoxos*: self-conceited, boastful without reason, which is from *kenos*: see 1, and *doxa*: glory ▶ Conceit, desire for praise, empty glorification; also transl.: empty conceit, vain conceit** > Nothing is to be done in the spirit of strife or vain glory (Phil. 2:3). ¶

5 ***mataios*** [adj.: μάταιος <3152>]; **from *matēn*: in vain ▶ Useless, without result; also transl.: aimless, empty, futile, worthless** > Paul asked the men of Lystra to turn from vain things {vanities} to the living God (Acts 14:15). The Lord knows the reasonings of the wise, that they are vain (1 Cor. 3:20). If Christ had not been raised, the faith of the Corinthians was vain (1 Cor. 15:17). Titus was to avoid foolish questions, genealogies, strifes, and disputes about the law, for they are unprofitable and vain (Titus 3:9). If anyone does not bridle his tongue, the religion of this man is vain (Jas. 1:26). Christians have not been redeemed from their vain way of life by corruptible things (1 Pet. 1:18). ¶

6 **to become vain: *mataioō*** [verb: ματαιόω <3154>]; **from *mataios*: see 5 ▶ To become foolish, worthless** > Men became vain {became futile, fell into folly} in their thoughts (Rom. 1:21). ¶

7 **vain discourse, vain jangling: *mataiologia*** [fem. noun: ματαιολογία <3150>]; **from *mataiologos*: vain talker, which is from *mataios*: see 5, and *legō*: to talk ▶ Futile conversation, babbling; also transl.: fruitless conversation, idle talk, meaningless talk** > Some people at Ephesus had turned aside to vain talk (1 Tim. 1:6). ¶

8 **in vain: *eikē*** [adv.: εἰκῇ <1500>] ▶ **Aimlessly, without purpose; also transl.: for nothing, vainly** > The ruler does not bear the sword in vain (Rom. 13:4). Paul speaks to the Corinthians of having believed in vain (1 Cor. 15:2). He asks the Galatians if they had suffered so many things in vain, if

indeed it was in vain (Gal. 3:4a, b); he feared that he had perhaps labored in vain for them (4:11). The mind of the flesh inflates with pride in vain {without cause, with idle notions} (Col. 2:18). Other ref.: Matt. 5:22 (without cause); see CAUSE <1500>. ¶
[9] ***matēn*** [adv.: μάτην <3155>]; **from *matē*: something vain, futile ▶ Falsely, with no purpose** > Isaiah wrote that Israel worshipped God in vain, teaching as doctrines the commandments of men (Matt. 15:9; Mark 7:7). ¶
– [10] Matt. 6:7 → to use vain repetitions → REPETITION <945> [11] Gal. 2:21 → in vain → FREELY <1432> [12] 1 Tim. 6:20; 2 Tim. 2:16 → vain babbling → idle babbling → BABBLING <2757> [13] Titus 1:10 → vain speaker, vain talker → idle talker → TALKER <3151>.

VAIN-GLORIOUS – Gal. 5:26 → CONCEITED <2755>.

VAINLY – Col. 2:18 → in vain → VAIN <1500>.

VALIANT – Heb. 11:34 → STRONG <2478>.

VALID – [1] ***bebaios*** [adj.: βέβαιος <949>]; **from *bainō*: to go ▶ Applicable, which has strength** > A testament is valid {in force, of force} only when men are dead (Heb. 9:17). All other refs.: FIRM <949>, SURE <949>.
– [2] John 5:31, 32; 8:13, 14, 17 → TRUE <227>.

VALLEY – [1] ***pharanx*** [fem. noun: φάραγξ <5327>] ▶ **Gorge, ravine** > Isaiah says that every valley will be filled when the Lord returns (Luke 3:5). ¶
– [2] John 18:1 → TORRENT <5493>.

VALUABLE – [1] Matt. 6:26; 12:12; Luke 12:24 → to be more valuable → to be of more value → VALUE (noun) <1308> [2] Jas. 5:7 → PRECIOUS <5093>.

VALUE (noun) – [1] **to be of more value: *diapherō*** [verb: διαφέρω <1308>]; **from *dia*: beyond, through, and *pherō*: to carry ▶ To be better, more important, more excellent, more valuable; to be worth more, much more** > The children of the heavenly Father are of more value than the birds (Matt. 6:26; Luke 12:24). We are of more value than many sparrows (Matt. 10:31; Luke 12:7). A man is of more value than a sheep (Matt. 12:12). All other refs.: see entries in Lexicon at <1308>.
[2] **to have value: *ischuō*** [verb: ἰσχύω <2480>]; **from *ischus*: ability, strength ▶ To avail, to be effective; also transl.: to have force, to mean something** > In Christ Jesus, neither circumcision nor uncircumcision has any value, but faith working through love (Gal. 5:6). All other refs.: see entries in Lexicon at <2480>.
[3] **to have value, to be of value: *ōpheleō*** [verb: ὠφελέω <5623>]; **from *ophelos*: gain, advantage ▶ To be beneficial, advantageous** > Circumcision has value for him who keeps the law (Rom. 2:25 {to profit, to be profitable}). All other refs.: HELPED (BE) <5623>, PREVAIL <5623>, PROFIT (verb) <5623>.
– [4] Matt. 13:46 → of great value → of great price → PRICE (noun) <4186> [5] Matt. 27:9; Acts 19:19; 1 Pet. 2:7 → value, precious value → PRICE (noun) <5092> [6] Acts 20:24 → of any value → lit.: of nothing account → ACCOUNT (noun) <3056> [7] Rom. 3:1 → PROFIT (noun) <5622> [8] Rom. 4:14 → to be of no value → to make vain → VAIN <2758> [9] Phil. 3:8 → surpassing value → EXCELLENCE <5242> [10] Col. 2:23 → HONOR (noun) <5092> [11] 1 Tim. 4:8a, b → to be of value, to have value → lit.: to be profitable → PROFITABLE <5624> [12] 2 Tim. 2:14 → of no value → profitable for nothing → PROFITABLE <5539>.

VALUE (verb) – [1] Matt. 27:9a, b → PRICE (verb) <5091> [2] Phil. 2:3 → ESTEEM (verb) <2233>.

VALUED – [1] Luke 7:2 → highly valued → DEAR <1784> [2] Luke 16:15 → highly valued → highly esteemed → ESTEEMED <5308>.

VANISH – [1] **to vanish away:** ***aphanizō*** [verb: ἀφανίζω <853>]; **from** ***aphanēs*****: hidden, not apparent, which is from** ***a*****: neg., and** ***phainō*****: to appear, which is from** ***phōs*****: light ▶ To disappear from sight, to become invisible; lit.: to be made unseen** > Our life is only a vapor that appears for a little time and then vanishes away (Jas. 4:14). All other refs.: DESTROY <853>, DISFIGURE <853>, PERISH <853>.
[2] **disappearance:** ***aphanismos*** [masc. noun: ἀφανισμός <854>]; **from** ***aphanizō*****: see** [1] **▶ Cessation of being seen or existing; figur.: abrogation** > What is becoming obsolete and growing old is ready to vanish away {will soon disappear, is ready to disappear, is near disappearing} (lit.: is near of disappearance) (Heb. 8:13). ¶
– [3] Luke 24:31 → DISAPPEAR <855> [4] Rev. 6:14 → RECEDE <673> [5] Rev. 18:14 → PERISH <565>.

VANITY – [1] ***mataiotēs*** [fem. noun: ματαιότης <3153>]; **from** ***mataios*****: vain, without value ▶ Emptiness, futility; also transl.: frustration** > The creation was subjected to vanity (Rom. 8:20). The Christians at Ephesus were not to walk as the rest of the nations walk, in the vanity of their mind (Eph. 4:17). Peter denounces those who speak out arrogant words of vanity (2 Pet. 2:18). ¶
– [2] Acts 14:15 → lit.: vain things → VAIN <3152>.

VAPOR – ***atmis*** [fem. noun: ἀτμίς <822>] **▶ a. Emanation, mist** > In the last days, God will show wonders, including a vapor {billows} of smoke (Acts 2:19). **b. Substance produced by the evaporation of a liquid (such as water)** > Our life is but a vapor {mist} appearing for a little while and then disappearing (Jas. 4:14). ¶

VAPOUR – See VAPOR <822>.

VARIABLENESS – Jas. 1:17 → VARIATION <3883>.

VARIANCE – Gal. 5:20 → STRIFE <2054>.

VARIATION – ***parallagē*** [fem. noun: παραλλαγή <3883>]; **from** ***paralassō*****: to alternate, which is from** ***para*****: denoting transition, and** ***allattō*****: to change ▶ Change, variableness** > There is no variation or shadow of turning with the Father of lights (Jas. 1:17). ¶

VARIED – [1] Heb. 13:9 → VARIOUS <4164> [2] 1 Pet. 4:10 → MANIFOLD <4164>.

VARIETY – [1] 1 Cor. 12:4–6 → DIVERSITY <1243> [2] 1 Cor. 12:28 → KIND (noun) <1085>.

VARIOUS – [1] ***diaphoros*** [adj.: διάφορος <1313>]; **from** ***diapherō*****: to be different, which is from** ***dia*****: through, and** ***pherō*****: to bear ▶ Diverse, different** > Under the law, the religious service included various {divers} washings (Heb. 9:10). All other refs.: DIFFERING <1313>, EXCELLENT <1313>.
[2] **in various:** ***kata*** [prep.: κατά <2596>] **▶ Diverse, different** > During the great tribulation, there will be famines, pestilences, and earthquakes in various {divers} places (Matt. 24:7; Mark 13:8; Luke 21:11). Other refs.: CONCERNING <2596>.
[3] ***poikilos*** [adj.: ποικίλος <4164>] **▶ Different, of all kinds; also transl.: divers, of many kinds** > Sick people afflicted with various diseases and pains were brought to Jesus (Matt. 4:24; Mark 1:34; Luke 4:40). Some are led away by various lusts (2 Tim. 3:6). Before their conversion, Christians were enslaved to various lusts and pleasures (Titus 3:3). God has been bearing witness by various miracles (Heb. 2:4). Christians must not be carried away by various {varied} and strange doctrines (Heb. 13:9). Christians should count it all joy when they fall into various trials (Jas. 1:2). They are grieved now for a while by various {manifold} trials (1 Pet. 1:6). Other ref.: 1 Pet. 4:10; see MANIFOLD <4164>. ¶
– [4] Heb. 1:1 → in various ways → WAY <4187>.

VAT – Mark 12:1 → WINEVAT <5276>.

VAUNT – 1 Cor. 13:4 → BOAST (verb) <4068>.

VAUNTING – Jas. 4:16 → ARROGANCE <212>.

VEGETABLE – Rom. 14:2 → garden plant → PLANT (noun) <3001>.

VEGETATION – ***botanē*** [fem. noun: βοτάνη <1008>]; **from *boskō*: to feed, to graze ▶ Herbage (for grazing), grass >** The earth produces useful vegetation {crop, herbs} (Heb. 6:7). ¶

VEHEMENT – [1] 2 Cor. 7:11 → vehement desire → ardent desire → DESIRE (noun) <1972> [2] Heb. 5:7 → STRONG <2478>.

VEHEMENTLY – [1] ***deinōs*** [adv.: δεινῶς <1171>]; **from *deinos*: terrible, vehement ▶ Fiercely, with violence >** The scribes and the Pharisees began to oppose Jesus vehemently {urgently} (Luke 11:53). Other ref.: Matt. 8:6 {dreadfully, fearfully, grievously, terribly}. ¶
[2] **more vehemently: *ek*** [prep.: ἐκ <1537>] ***perissōs*** [adv.: περισσῶς <4057>] **▶ With greater force, with greater insistence >** Peter spoke more vehemently {insistently}, saying he would never deny Jesus (Mark 14:31); some mss. have one word: *ekperissōs*. All other refs. (*perissōs*): EXCEEDINGLY <4057>, MORE <4057>.
– [3] Luke 23:10 → VIGOROUSLY <2159>.

VEIL (noun) – [1] ***kalumma*** [neut. noun: κάλυμμα <2571>]; **from *kaluptō*: to cover ▶ Piece of material to conceal the face, covering >** Moses wore a veil on account of the radiance of his face; this veil is not taken away for those who remain under the old covenant (2 Cor. 3:13–16 {vail}). ¶
[2] ***katapetasma*** [neut. noun: καταπέτασμα <2665>]; **from *katapetannuni*: to expand, to spread, which is from *kata*: down, and *petannumi*: to spread ▶ Curtain >** The veil of the temple was torn in two from the top to the bottom (Matt. 27:51; Mark 15:38; Luke 23:45). The veil of the tabernacle separated the Holy Place from the Most Holy Place (Heb. 6:19; 9:3); this veil is a figure of the flesh of the crucified Lord; through this veil, we have access into the presence of God (10:20). ¶
[3] ***peribolaion*** [neut. noun: περιβόλαιον <4018>]; **from *periballō*: to cast around, which is from *peri*: around, and *ballō*: to cast, to put; lit.: covering used to wrap oneself around ▶ Covering for the head >** Hair is given to the woman as a veil {covering} (1 Cor. 11:15). Other ref.: Heb. 1:12; see CLOAK <4018>. ¶

VEIL (verb) – ***kaluptō*** [verb: καλύπτω <2572>] **▶ To cover over, to hide >** If the gospel of Paul was veiled, it was veiled in those who are perishing (2 Cor. 4:3a, b). All other refs.: COVER <2572>.

VENERATION – 2 Thes. 2:4 → object of veneration → object of worship → WORSHIP (noun) <4574>.

VENGEANCE – [1] ***ekdikēsis*** [fem. noun: ἐκδίκησις <1557>]; **from *ekdikeō*: to execute justice, which is from *ek*: from, out, and *dikē*: justice ▶ Retribution, revenge, fact of obtaining justice following a wrong done >** Jesus speaks of the days of vengeance {avenging, punishment} to come during the great tribulation (Luke 21:22). Moses took vengeance for {avenged} the oppressed Israelite, by striking down the Egyptian (Acts 7:24). Vengeance belongs to the Lord (Rom. 12:19; Heb. 10:30). Godly sorrow had produced vengeance {avenging of wrong, readiness to see justice done, vindication} among the Corinthians (2 Cor. 7:11). The angels of the Lord Jesus will take vengeance on {will punish} those who do not know God and do not obey the gospel of the Lord Jesus Christ (2 Thes. 1:8). All other refs.: JUSTICE <1557>, PUNISHMENT <1557>.
– [2] Acts 28:4; see JUSTICE <1349> [3] Rom. 3:5 → WRATH <3709> [4] Jude 7 → JUDGMENT <1349>.

VENOM – Rom. 3:13 → POISON (noun) <2447>.

VENTURE – 1 There are two different Greek words for the verb in Phil. 2:30. Some mss. have *paraboleuomai* and other mss. have *parabouleuomai*. **a. *paraboleuomai*** [verb: παραβολεύομαι <3849a>]**; from *para*: aside, and *ballō*: to throw ▶ To take a risk, to put in danger** > Epaphroditus had ventured (risked) his life for the Philippians (Phil. 2:30). ¶ **b. *parabouleuomai*** [verb: παραβουλεύομαι <3851>]**; from *para*: aside, and *bouleuō*: to consult ▶ To disregard, to ignore** > Epaphroditus had not regarded his life for the Philippians (Phil. 2:30). ¶
– 2 Mark 12:34; John 21:12; Acts 7:32; Rom. 15:18 → DARE <5111> 3 Acts 19:31 → ADVENTURE <1325> <1438>.

VERDICT – John 3:19 → JUDGMENT <2920>.

VERILY – 1 ***amēn*** [adv.: ἀμήν <281>]**; word transliterated from the Heb. ▶ Certainly, truly; also transl.: assuredly, truly, I tell you the truth** > This word is used in passages where Jesus spoke of the accomplishment of the law (Matt. 5:18), rewards and punishments (Matt. 5:26; 6:2, 5, 16; 10:42; 24:47; 25:40, 45; Mark 9:41; 10:29; Luke 12:37; 18:29), a centurion (Matt. 8:10), the portion of Sodom and Gomorrah (Matt. 10:15), things to come upon Israel (Matt. 10:23; 23:36; 24:2, 34; Mark 13:30; Luke 21:32), John the Baptist (Matt. 11:11), what His contemporaries saw (Matt. 13:17), the Son of Man coming in His kingdom (Matt. 16:28; Mark 9:1), having faith (Matt. 17:20; 21:21; Mark 11:23), being converted (Matt. 18:3, 13; 19:23), whatever believers in the Lord bind on earth (Matt. 18:18), anything about which two believers in the Lord on earth agree (Matt. 18:19 in some mss.), what awaits the apostles in the glory (Matt. 19:28), tax collectors and prostitutes in the kingdom of God (Matt. 21:31), the foolish virgins (Matt. 25:12), a woman who poured perfume on Him (Matt. 26:13; Mark 14:9), Judas (Matt. 26:21; Mark 14:18; John 13:21a, b), Peter (Matt. 26:34; John 13:38a, b; 21:18a, b), the forgiveness of sins (Mark 3:28), a sign (Mark 8:12), receiving the kingdom (Mark 10:15; Luke 18:17), a poor widow who had cast into the treasury (Mark 12:43), drinking of the fruit of the vine (Mark 14:25), Peter who told Jesus that he would not be scandalized to the point of denying Him (Mark 14:30), a prophet in his own country (Luke 4:24), the repentant malefactor on the cross (Luke 23:43), the heavens opened and the Son of Man (John 1:51a, b), being born anew (John 3:3a, b, 5a, b), His testimony (John 3:11a, b), what He does as the Son of God (John 5:19a, b), he who hears His word (John 5:24a, b), hearing His voice (John 5:25a, b), those who seek Him (John 6:26a, b), the bread from heaven (John 6:32a, b), he who believes in Him (John 6:47a, b; 14:12a, b), eating His flesh and drinking His blood (John 6:53), practicing sin (John 8:34a, b), keeping His word (John 8:51a, b), His existence before Abraham (John 8:58), he who does not enter in by the door to the sheepfold (John 10:1a, b), the fact that He is the door of the sheep (John 10:7a, b), the grain of wheat (John 12:24a, b), the position of a servant and one who is sent (John 13:16a, b), he who receives whomever He sends (John 13:20a, b), the grief of His disciples (John 16:20a, b), and asking the Father in His name (John 16:23a, b). All other refs.: AMEN <281>.

2 ***gar*** [particle: γάρ <1063>] **▶ In effect, indeed, for** > Refs.: Acts 16:37, Gal. 2:6. *

3 ***dēpou*** [adv.: δήπου <1222>]**; from *dē*: certainly, and *pou*: in a certain way ▶ Assuredly, without doubt** > For verily {indeed}, God took the seed of Abraham to raise a Savior, Jesus (Heb. 2:16). ¶

4 **yes verily: *menounge*** [particle: μενοῦνγε <3304>]**; from *men*: verily, *oun*: really, and *ge*: intens. ▶ Without any doubt** > All Jews have not obeyed the gospel, but yes verily {yes indeed, yes surely, of course} the sound of those preaching went into all the earth, so that effectively they have heard the word of God (Rom. 10:18). Other refs.: Luke 11:28; Rom. 9:20; Phil. 3:8. ¶

– 5 Luke 12:44; 21:3; 1 John 2:5 → TRULY <230> 6 Gal. 3:21 → INDEED <3689>.

VERMIN – Matt. 6:19, 20 → RUST <1035>.

VERY – [1] ***lian*** [adv.: λίαν <3029>] ▶ **Extremely, excessively, greatly** > Herod became very enraged when he saw that he had been deceived by the wise men (Matt. 2:16). The devil took Jesus to a very high mountain (Matt. 4:8). The governor wondered exceedingly (or: was very amazed) that Jesus did not answer him (Matt. 27:14). The women came to the tomb of Jesus very early in the morning (Mark 16:2). Herod was very glad when he saw Jesus (Luke 23:8). Alexander was very opposed to Paul's words (2 Tim. 4:15). John was very glad to have found some of the children of the chosen lady walking in the truth (2 John 4). He was very glad when brothers came and testified to the truth of Gaius (3 John 3). Other refs.: Mark 1:35; 6:51; 2 Cor. 11:5; 12:11. All other refs.: EXCEEDINGLY <3029>.
– [2] Matt. 18:31; Luke 18:23 → GREATLY <4970> [3] John 1:51; 3:3, 5; et al. → very truly → lit.: truly, truly <281> <281>.

VERY GREAT – ***pampolus*** [adj.: πάμπολυς <3827>]; **from *pas*: all, and *polus*: many** ▶ **Extremely large** > A very great {A large} crowd gathered around Jesus (Mark 8:1). ¶

VERY LITTLE – 1 Cor. 4:3 → VERY SMALL <1646>.

VERY SMALL – ***elachistos*** [adj.: ἐλάχιστος <1646>]; **superl. of *mikros*: small, little (the compar. of *mikros* is *elassōn*: smaller)** ▶ **Exceedingly little, the least** > It was the very smallest matter for Paul to be judged by the Corinthian (1 Cor. 4:3 {very little}). All other refs.: LEAST <1646>.

VERY WELL – [1] ***kallion*** [adv.: καλλίον <2566>]; **compar. of *kalos*: good, used as a superl.** ▶ **Better, certainly** > Festus knew very well that Paul had done no wrong against the Jews (Acts 25:10). ¶
– [2] 1 Thes. 5:2 → PERFECTLY <199>.

VESSEL[1] – [1] ***angeion*** [neut. noun: ἀγγεῖον <30>]; **dimin. of *angos*: pail, basket** ▶ **Vase, container** > It may be used to contain fish (Matt. 13:48 {basket}) and oil for lamps (25:4 {flask, jar}). ¶

[2] ***xestēs*** [masc. noun: ξέστης <3582>]; ***sextarius*, in Lat.: a measure of capacity** ▶ **Pitcher containing a small measure of liquid, approx. a cup** > The washing of vessels {pots, pitchers} was part of the tradition of the Pharisees (Mark 7:4, 8 in some mss.). ¶

[3] ***skeuos*** [neut. noun: σκεῦος <4632>] ▶ **a. Object, item** > Jesus would not allow anyone to carry any vessel {merchandise, package, wares} through the temple (Mark 11:16). No one, after having lighted a lamp, covers it with a vessel (Luke 8:16 {container, jar, clay jar}). Peter saw the heaven opened, and a certain vessel {an object, something} descending like a great sheet bound by four corners (Acts 10:11, 16; 11:5). Moses sprinkled the tabernacle and all the vessels of service with blood (Heb. 9:21). **b. Receptacle** > Near the cross there was a vessel {jar} full of vinegar (John 19:29). The potter has power over the clay from the same lump to make one vessel {some pottery} for honor and another for dishonor (Rom. 9:21). He who overcomes in Thyatira will rule the nations with a rod of iron; as vessels of pottery they will be broken to pieces (Rev. 2:27). **c. Instrument** > Paul was a chosen vessel to the Lord, to bear His name before nations, kings, and the sons of Israel (Acts 9:15). **d. Body, person; the body was considered by the Greeks as a vessel** > God has endured with much patience vessels {objects} of wrath fitted for destruction (Rom. 9:22); He has made known the riches of His glory on vessels {objects} of mercy that He had prepared beforehand for glory (v. 23). We have this treasure of the knowledge of the glory of God in earthen vessels {jars of clay} (2 Cor. 4:7). Every Christian is to know how to possess his own vessel in sanctification and honor (1 Thes. 4:4). In a large house, there are not only vessels {articles} of gold and of silver (2 Tim. 2:20); if someone purifies himself from vessels for dishonor, he will be a vessel {an instrument} for honor, sanctified, useful to the Master, prepared for every good work (2 Tim. 2:21). Husbands are to live with their wives in an understanding way, as with a weaker vessel {someone weaker, weaker partner} (i.e., having regard to their

more delicate feminine nature) (1 Pet. 3:7). All other refs.: ARTICLE <4632>, GOOD (adj. and noun) <4632>, SAIL (noun) <4632>.

– [4] Mark 7:4 → copper vessel, brazen vessel → BRAZEN VESSEL <5473>.

VESSEL[2] – Acts 27:41 → SHIP <3491>.

VESTIBULE – Mark 14:68 → PORCH <4259>.

VESTURE – [1] John 19:24 → CLOTHING <2441> [2] Heb. 1:12 → CLOAK <4018>.

VEX – [1] Luke 6:18; Acts 5:16 → TORMENT (verb) <3791> [2] 2 Pet. 2:8 → TORMENT (verb) <928>.

VEXED (BE) – [1] ***kataponeō*** [verb: καταπονέω <2669>]**; from *kata*: down (intens.), and *poneō*: to labor, which is from *ponos*: pain, tiredness ► To suffer morally greatly, to be overwhelmed** > Lot was vexed {was distressed, was oppressed} with the filthy conduct of the wicked (2 Pet. 2:7). Other ref.: Acts 7:24; see OPPRESSED (BE) <2669>. ¶

– [2] Matt. 15:22 → to be vexed with a devil → to be demon-possessed → DEMON <1139> [3] Matt. 17:15 → SUFFER <3958>.

VIAL – [1] Matt. 26:7; Mark 14:3a, b; Luke 7:37 → alabaster vial → alabaster box → ALABASTER <211> [2] Rev. 5:8; 15:7; 16:1–4, 8, 10, 12, 17; 17:1; 21:9 → BOWL <5357>.

VICINITY – [1] Matt. 2:16; 15:22, 39; Mark 7:31a → REGION <3725> [2] Mark 7:24 in some mss. → BORDER <3725> [3] Mark 7:31 → COAST (noun) <3725> [4] Acts 5:16 → round about → ROUND <4038>.

VICTIM – [1] Matt. 5:32 → to make someone the victim of adultery → lit.: to make someone commit adultery → ADULTERY <3429> [2] Acts 7:42 → slain beast → BEAST <4968>.

VICTOR – Rev. 2:10 → victor's crown → CROWN (noun) <4735>.

VICTORIOUS (BE) – [1] Rev. 2:7, 11, 17, 26; 3:5, 12, 21a, b; 21:7 → OVERCOME <3528> [2] Rev. 15:2 → to gain the victory → VICTORY <3528>.

VICTORY – [1] ***nikē*** [fem. noun: νίκη <3529>] ► **Success, triumph** > The Christian's faith is the victory that has overcome the world (1 John 5:4). ¶

[2] ***nikos*** [neut. noun: νῖκος <3534>]**; form of *nikē*: see [1] ► Success, triumph** > Jesus will lead justice to victory (Matt. 12:20). Death will be swallowed up in victory (1 Cor. 15:54); it will then no longer have any victory (v. 55). God gives Christians the victory through the Lord Jesus Christ (1 Cor. 15:57). ¶

[3] **to gain, to get, to have the victory: *nikaō*** [verb: νικάω <3528>]**; from *nikē*: see [1] ► To overcome, to be victorious** > Those who had gained the victory stood upon the glass sea (Rev. 15:2). All other refs.: OVERCOME <3528>.

VICTUALS – [1] Matt. 14:15 → FOOD <1033> [2] Luke 9:12 → FOOD <1979>.

VIEW (noun) – [1] Mark 2:12 in some mss. → in full view of → in the presence of → PRESENCE <1715> [2] Acts 28:22; Gal. 5:10; Phil. 3:15 → to be of one's views, to adopt a view, to take a view → THINK <5426> [3] Jas. 1:25 → to fix one's view → to look into → LOOK (verb) <3879>.

VIEW (verb) – Luke 18:9 → to view with contempt → CONTEMPT <1848>.

VIGILANT – [1] 1 Cor. 16:13; Col. 4:2; 1 Pet. 5:8 → to be vigilant → WATCH (verb) <1127> [2] 1 Tim. 3:2, 11 → TEMPERATE <3524> [3] 1 Pet. 5:8 → to be vigilant → to be sober → SOBER <3525>.

VIGOROUSLY – ***eutonōs*** [adv.: εὐτόνως <2159>]**; from *eu*: well (intens.), and *teinō*: to stretch ► With energy, with great force; also transl.: mightily, powerfully,**

vehemently > The chief priests and the scribes were accusing Jesus vehemently (Luke 23:10). Apollos refuted the Jews vigorously (Acts 18:28). ¶

VILE – [1] Rom. 1:26 → SHAMEFUL <819> [2] Phil. 3:21 → HUMILIATION <5014> [3] Col. 3:8 → vile language → filthy language → FILTHY <148> [4] Jas. 2:2 → DIRTY <4508> [5] Jas. 3:16 → EVIL (adj.) <5337> [6] Rev. 21:8 → ABOMINABLE <948a> [7] Rev. 22:11a, b → to be vile → to be filthy → FILTHY <4510>.

VILLAGE – ***kōmē*** [fem. noun: κώμη <2968>]; **from *keimai*: to lie outstretched ▶ Agglomeration of dwellings in a rural area** > Jesus went through all the cities and villages, teaching, preaching, and healing (Matt. 9:35; Mark 6:6, 56; 8:27; Luke 8:1; 9:56; 10:38; 13:22; 17:12). He drew near and walked along with two disciples who were going to a village called Emmaus (Luke 24:13, 28). Lazarus lived in the village of Bethany with his two sisters (John 11:1, 30). Peter and John preached the gospel in many villages of the Samaritans (Acts 8:25). Other refs.: Matt. 10:11; 14:15; 21:2; Mark 6:36; 11:2; Luke 9:6, 12, 52; 19:30. All other refs.: TOWN <2968>.

VILLAINY – Acts 13:10 → FRAUD <4468>.

VINDICATE – Matt. 11:19; Luke 7:35; 1 Tim. 3:16 → JUSTIFY <1344>.

VINDICATION – [1] 2 Cor. 7:11 → EXCUSING <627> [2] 2 Cor. 7:11 → VENGEANCE <1557>.

VINE – ***ampelos*** [fem. noun: ἄμπελος <288>] **▶ Woody climbing plant producing clusters of grapes; the vine is cultivated only for its fruit** > The Lord will drink of the fruit of the vine in the kingdom of His Father (Matt. 26:29; Mark 14:25; Luke 22:18). In John 15:1, the vine (i.e.: in this context, specifically the foot or main stem of the vine) is an image of the Lord; the branches represent those who belong to Him (vv. 4, 5). James uses the example of a vine that cannot produce figs to demonstrate the necessity of a Christian walk consistent with the position of the Christian (3:12). The vine of the earth (Rev. 14:18, 19) represents apostate Jews and Gentiles, upon whom the Lord will execute His judgment. ¶

VINE-GROWER – Matt. 21:33–35, 38, 40, 41; Mark 12:1, 2, 7, 9; Luke 20:9, 10a, b, 14, 16; John 15:1 → VINEDRESSER <1092>.

VINEDRESSER – [1] ***geōrgos*** [masc. noun: γεωργός <1092>]; **from *gē*: earth, and *ergon*: work ▶ Person who cultivates the soil, wine grower; also transl.: vine-grower, farmer, husbandman, tenant** > Jesus told a parable about a landowner who leased his vineyard to vinedressers (Matt. 21:33–35, 38, 40, 41; Mark 12:1, 2, 7, 9; Luke 20:9, 10a, b, 14, 16). Jesus is the true vine, and His Father is the vinedresser {gardener} (John 15:1). Other refs.: 2 Tim. 2:6; Jas. 5:7; see FARMER <1092>. ¶
– [2] Luke 13:7 → dresser of the vineyard → VINEYARD <289>.

VINEGAR – ***oxos*** [neut. noun: ὄξος <3690>]; **from *oxus*: sharp ▶ Sour wine used as drink in the Roman army; also transl.: sour wine, wine** > At the crucifixion, the soldiers offered the Lord a mixture of vinegar and gall to alleviate His sufferings, but having tasted it, He would not drink it (Matt. 27:34). Later, Jesus received the vinegar that they presented to Him on a sponge (Matt. 27:48; Mark 15:36; Luke 23:36; John 19:29, 30), that the Scripture might be fulfilled (see Ps. 69:21; John 19:28). ¶

VINEYARD – [1] ***ampelōn*** [masc. noun: ἀμπελών <290>]; **from *ampelos*: vine ▶ Field or area planted with vines** > Jesus told a parable about workers hired to work in the vineyard of a landowner (Matt. 20:1, 2, 4, 7, 8), and another about a fig tree planted in a vineyard (Luke 13:6). Two parables of the vineyard (Matt. 21:28, 33, 39–41; Mark 12:1, 2, 8, 9a, b; Luke 13:6; 20:9, 10, 13, 15a, b, 16) illustrate Israel (comp.

Is. 5:7) who did not obey and did not want to receive the prophets (the servants) or the Lord Jesus (the beloved Son). He who plants a vineyard eats of its fruit (1 Cor. 9:7). ¶

2 **dresser of the vineyard, keeper of the vineyard, vineyard-keeper, man who takes care of the vineyard: *ampelourgos*** [masc. noun: ἀμπελουργός <289>]; **from *ampelos*: vine, and *ergon*: work ▶ Person who cultivates a vineyard and produces wine** > The term is used in Luke 13:7 where someone who had a fig tree planted in a vineyard asked the keeper of the vineyard {vinedresser} to cut it down because it did not produce fruit. ¶

VINTAGE – Luke 6:44 → GATHER <5166>.

VIOLATE – 1 John 5:18; 7:23 → BREAK <3089> 2 Acts 23:3 → to violate the law → to break the law → CONTRARY <3891>.

VIOLATION – 1 Acts 23:3 → in violation of the law → to break the law → CONTRARY <3891> 2 Rom. 4:15; Heb. 2:2 → TRANSGRESSION <3847>.

VIOLENCE – 1 ***bia*** [fem. noun: βία <970>] ▶ **Use of force; force, virulence** > The apostles were brought, without violence, before the Sanhedrin (Acts 5:26). Paul was carried by the soldiers because of the violence of the mob (Acts 21:35). Tertullus reported that the chiliarch had taken Paul away from the hands of the Jews with great violence (Acts 24:7). The stern of the ship that Paul had boarded was broken by the violence {pounding} of the waves (Acts 27:41). ¶

2 **to suffer violence, to take by violence, to strive violently to go in: *biazō*** [verb: βιάζω <971>]; **from *bia*: see 1 ▶ To use force in order to achieve one's end** > Jesus speaks of the kingdom of the heavens that is taken by violence {has been forcefully advancing} (*biazō*), and of the violent men (*biastēs*) taking it by force (Matt. 11:12). Every one strives violently to go in the kingdom of God (Luke 16:16 {to force one's way, to press into}). This pressing to enter the kingdom of heavens is necessary given the difficulties and opposition to such an endeavor. ¶

3 ***hormēma*** [neut. noun: ὅρμημα <3731>]; **from *hormaō*: to run violently, which is from *hormē*: attack, impulsion ▶ The expr. "with violence" means: impetuously, suddenly** > Babylon will be thrown down with violence like a great millstone into the sea (Rev. 18:21). ¶

– 4 Luke 3:14 → to do violence → OPPRESS <1286> 5 Heb. 11:34 → STRENGTH <1411>.

VIOLENT (adj.) – 1 ***biaios*** [adj.: βίαιος <972>]; **from *bia*: strength, violence ▶ Mighty, very strong** > On the day of Pentecost, suddenly there came a sound out of heaven, like the blowing of a violent, impetuous wind, and it filled the whole house where the disciples were sitting (Acts 2:2). ¶

2 ***sklēros*** [adj.: σκληρός <4642>]; **from *skellō*: to harden, to dry up ▶ Impetuous, harsh, severe; also transl.: fierce, strong** > Ships, which are so great and driven by violent winds, are steered here and there by a very small rudder (Jas. 3:4). All other refs.: HARD <4642>.

3 ***chalepos*** [adj.: χαλεπός <5467>] ▶ **Difficult to approach, fierce; also transl.: dangerous** > The two demon-possessed men who met Jesus were extremely violent (Matt. 8:28). Other ref.: 2 Tim. 3:1; see DIFFICULT <5467>. ¶

– 4 Matt. 11:12 → violent men → lit.: the violent → VIOLENT (noun) <973> 5 Luke 15:14 → STRONG <2478> 6 Acts 12:1 → to lay violent hands → lit.: to lay hands to oppress → OPPRESS <2559> 7 Acts 27:14 → TEMPESTUOUS <5189> 8 Acts 27:18 → VIOLENTLY <4971> 9 Rom. 1:30; 1 Tim. 1:13 → violent aggressor, violent man → insolent man → INSOLENT <5197> 10 1 Tim. 3:3; Titus 1:7 → STRIKER <4131>.

VIOLENT (noun) – ***biastēs*** [masc. noun: βιαστής <973>]; **from *biazō*: to suffer violence, which is from *bia*: strength, violence ▶ Person who uses force, who is energetic** > Jesus speaks of the kingdom of the heavens that is taken by violence, and the violent {forceful men, violent men} take it by force (Matt. 11:12). See VIOLENCE <971>. ¶

VIOLENTLY – [1] ***sphodrōs*** [adv.: σφοδρῶς <4971>]; **from *sphodros*: strong, violent ▶ Excessively, strongly** > The ship Paul had boarded was violently {exceedingly} beaten by the storm (Acts 27:18). ¶

– [2] Mark 1:26 → to shake violently → CONVULSE <4682> [3] Luke 23:10 → VIGOROUSLY <2159> [4] Gal. 1:13 → beyond measure → MEASURE (noun) <5236>.

VIPER – [1] ***echidna*** [fem. noun: ἔχιδνα <2191>] ▶ **Venomous serpent** > John the Baptist called the Pharisees and Sadducees who came to be baptized a brood of vipers (Matt. 3:7; Luke 3:7). Jesus also used this expr. in regard to the leaders of Israel (Matt. 12:34; 23:33). At the island of Malta, a viper fastened itself on Paul's hand, but he suffered no harm (Acts 28:3; comp. Mark 16:18 <3789>). ¶

– [2] Rom. 3:13 → ASP <785>.

VIRGIN – [1] ***parthenos*** [adj. used as noun: παρθένος <3933>] ▶ **Person who has never had sexual relations** > Mary was a virgin engaged to Joseph (Luke 1:27a, b). The virgin was to be with child and give birth to a son (Matt. 1:23). Jesus told the parable of the ten virgins (Matt. 25:1, 7, 11). Philip had four daughters, virgins, who prophesied (Acts 21:9). Concerning virgins, Paul had received no commandment from the Lord (1 Cor. 7:25). If a virgin marries, she has not sinned (1 Cor. 7:28). Paul makes a difference between the married woman and the virgin in regard to being occupied with the things of the Lord (1 Cor. 7:34). If someone thinks that he is behaving improperly in regard to his virgin daughter, he should let her marry (1 Cor. 7:36); he who stands firm in his heart to keep his own virgin daughter does well (v. 37). Paul had promised the Corinthians to one husband, that he might present them to Christ as a pure virgin (2 Cor. 11:2). Those who follow the Lamb are virgins (Rev. 14:4). Other ref.: 1 Cor. 7:38 in some mss. ¶

– [2] Luke 1:34 → I am a virgin → lit.: I do not know a man → KNOW <1097> [3] Luke 2:36 → from when she was a virgin → from her virginity → VIRGINITY <3932>.

VIRGINITY – [1] ***parthenia*** [fem. noun: παρθενία <3932>]; **from *parthenos*: virgin ▶ Condition of a person who has never had sexual relations** > Anna had lived with a husband seven years from her virginity {after her marriage} (Luke 2:36). ¶

– [2] 1 Cor. 7:36, 37 → VIRGIN <3933>.

VIRTUE – ***aretē*** [fem. noun: ἀρετή <703>]; **from *areskō*: to give satisfaction, to please ▶ Excellency, moral preeminence; also transl.: excellence, moral excellence, goodness, praise** > The things that have some virtue in them are to occupy our thoughts (Phil. 4:8). Christians are to proclaim the excellencies (or: virtues) of Him who has called them out of darkness into His wonderful light (1 Pet. 2:9). He has called them by glory and virtue (2 Pet. 1:3). Christians are to add virtue to their faith, and knowledge to virtue (2 Pet. 1:5a, b). ¶

VISIBLE – [1] ***horatos*** [adj.: ὁρατός <3707>]; **from *horaō*: to see ▶ What one can see, apparent to sight** > By the Lord Jesus were created all things: the things that are in the heavens and the things that are on the earth, the visible and the invisible, whether thrones, dominions, rulers, or authorities; all things were created by Him and for Him (Col. 1:16). ¶

– [2] Matt. 24:27 → to be visible → APPEAR <5316> [3] Acts 10:40 → MANIFEST (adj.) <1717> [4] Eph. 5:13a, b → to become visible → MANIFEST (verb) <5319>.

VISION – [1] ***optasia*** [fem. noun: ὀπτασία <3701>]; **from *optanomai*: to appear ▶ Unexpected or sudden sight, apparition** > Zacharias had seen a vision in the temple (Luke 1:22). The women at the tomb of Jesus said that they had seen a vision of angels saying that He was alive (Luke 24:23). Paul was not disobedient to the heavenly vision

(Acts 26:19). He could have come to visions and revelations of the Lord (2 Cor. 12:1). ¶
2 ***horama*** [neut. noun: ὅραμα <3705>]; **from *horaō*: to see, to perceive ▶ Apparition, manifestation of something invisible which becomes visible** > Jesus charged His disciples to tell no one the vision {what they had seen} on the mountain of the transfiguration (Matt. 17:9). Moses wondered at the vision {sight} of the burning bush (Acts 7:31). The Lord spoke to Ananias in a vision (Acts 9:10). Paul had seen Ananias in a vision (Acts 9:12). Cornelius distinctly saw an angel of God in a vision (Acts 10:3). Peter had a vision (Acts 10:17, 19; 11:5). On another occasion, he believed he had seen a vision, but that what the angel had done was real (Acts 12:9). Paul had a vision in the night of a Macedonian man beseeching him to come over to Macedonia and help them (Acts 16:9, 10). The Lord appeared to Paul in a vision in the night (Acts 18:9). ¶
3 ***horasis*** [fem. noun: ὅρασις <3706>]; **from *horaō*: to see, to perceive ▶ Appearance sent by God, sight presented to the mind** > In the last days young men shall see visions (Acts 2:17). The rainbow around the throne was like an emerald in appearance {sight} (Rev. 4:3). John saw the horses in a vision (Rev. 9:17). ¶

VISIT (noun) – 1 Acts 7:12 → on their first visit → lit.: first → FIRST <4412> 2 2 Cor. 2:1 → to make a visit → COME <2064> 3 2 Cor. 13:2 → "visit" added in Engl.

VISIT (verb) – 1 ***episkeptomai*** [verb: ἐπισκέπτομαι <1980>]; **from *epi*: upon, and *skeptomai*: to look ▶ To go see someone in order to help him or her; also transl.: to come, to come to help, to look after, to look upon** > Jesus speaks of those who will have visited Him (Matt. 25:36), and of those who shall not have visited Him (v. 43). The God of Israel has visited and redeemed His people (Luke 1:68; 7:16); the rising sun from on high has visited them (Luke 1:78). It came into the heart of Moses to visit his brothers, the sons of Israel (Acts 7:23). God first visited the nations to take out a people for His name (Acts 15:14 {to concern oneself, to show concern}). Paul wanted to return and visit the brothers (Acts 15:36). God visited the son of man (Heb. 2:6 {to care, to be concerned, to take care}). Pure and undefiled religion before God the Father is to visit the orphans and the widows in their affliction (Jas. 1:27). Other ref.: Acts 6:3 (to look out); see LOOK (verb) <1980>. ¶
2 ***paroikeō*** [verb: παροικέω <3939>]; **from *para*: beside, near, and *oikeō*: to dwell, which is from *oikos*: house ▶ To be a stranger, to stay at a place for a short time; also transl.: to sojourn, to be a visitor** > This verb is used when Cleopas addressed Jesus after He had risen (Luke 24:18). Other ref.: Heb. 11:9a; see DWELL <3939>. ¶
– 3 Acts 10:28 → to go to → GO <4334> 4 Acts 16:40; 28:8 → they visited Lydia, Paul visited the father of Publius → they entered the house of Lydia, Paul entered in to the father of Publius → ENTER <1525> 5 Acts 17:21 → STAY (verb) <1927> 6 Rom. 15:23; 1 Cor. 16:5, 12 → COME <2064> 7 2 Cor. 1:16 → to go over → GO <1330> 8 2 Cor. 9:5 → to visit in advance → GO <4281> 9 Gal. 1:18 → to make acquaintance → ACQUAINTANCE <2477> 10 1 Thes. 2:1 → ENTRY <1529> 11 1 Pet. 2:12 → the day He visits us → lit.: the day of visitation → VISITATION <1984>.

VISITATION – ***episkopē*** [fem. noun: ἐπισκοπή <1984>]; **from *episkopeō*: to look after, which is from *epi*: upon, and *skopeō*: to watch, to give attention, which is from *skopos*: goal, mark ▶ Intervention of God, whether in grace or in judgment** > The Lord Jesus had visited Israel in grace; this nation had not known the time of her visitation (Luke 19:44; see 1:68, 78). On the day of the visitation of God, those who do not repent will be obliged to acknowledge that the good works of Christians whom they had slandered had been done to the glory of God (1 Pet. 2:12; see Is. 26:21). Other refs.: Acts 1:20; 1 Tim. 3:1; see OFFICE <1984>, OVERSIGHT <1984>. ¶

VISITOR – 1 Luke 24:18 → to be a visitor → VISIT (verb) <3939> 2 Acts 2:10 → lit.: ones staying → STAY (verb) <1927>.

VOCATION – Eph. 4:1 → CALLING <2821>.

VOICE – 1 ***phōnē*** [fem. noun: φωνή <5456>]; **from *phaō*: to shine, in the sense that the voice clarifies the thoughts ▶ Vocal noise, sound (divine, human, angelic)** > A voice was heard in Rama (Matt. 2:18). The Father's voice was heard when Jesus submitted Himself to the baptism of John (Matt. 3:17; Mark 1:11; Luke 3:22), when He was transfigured on the mountain (Matt. 17:5; Mark 9:7; Luke 9:35, 36; 2 Pet. 1:17, 18), and when He spoke to the crowd who had come to the feast (John 12:28, 30). Isaiah had prophesied that no one would hear the voice of God's chosen servant, His beloved Son, in the streets (Matt. 12:19). On the cross, Jesus cried out with a loud voice (Matt. 27:46; Mark 15:34), as likewise when He committed His spirit into the hands of His Father (Matt. 27:50; Luke 23:46). He cried out with a loud voice and expired (Mark 15:37). The people were insistent, demanding with loud voices that Jesus be crucified; the voices of these men and of the chief priests prevailed (Luke 23:23a, b). The Lord had said that the hour had come when the dead would hear His voice and live (John 5:25), and that the hour would come when those who are in the graves will hear His voice (v. 28) and come out. Jesus told those who sought to kill Him that they had not heard the Father's voice (John 5:37). The sheep hear the voice of the good shepherd (John 10:3, 27), because they know it (10:4). Other sheep that are not of the fold of Israel were to hear it also (John 10:16). Jesus cried with a loud voice, and Lazarus came out of the tomb (John 11:43). Jesus told Pilate that everyone who is of the truth hears His voice (John 18:37). Stephen recalled that Moses heard the voice of the God of Abraham, Isaac, and Jacob (Acts 7:31). On the road to Damascus, the Lord stopped Saul and caused him to hear His voice from heaven (Acts 9:4; 22:7; 26:14). Those who accompanied him heard the sound of the voice (Acts 9:7), but not the voice of Him who spoke thus to Paul (22:9). A voice was addressed to Peter telling him to get up, kill, and eat (Acts 10:13; 11:7); then a voice spoke to him again a second time, telling him not to consider impure what God has purified (10:15; 11:9). Ananias told Paul that the God of their fathers had chosen him to hear the voice of His mouth (Acts 22:14). Paul cried out a voice {a statement, a thing, i.e., a sentence} before the council (Acts 24:21). Paul desired to be present with the Galatians and to change his voice {tone} (Gal. 4:20). The Lord Himself, with the voice of an archangel, will catch up believers in Him together in the clouds to meet Him in the air (1 Thes. 4:16). "Today," says the Holy Spirit, "if you will hear His voice, do not harden your hearts" (Heb. 3:7, 15; 4:7). The voice of God once shook the earth (Heb. 12:26). An angel, who had power over fire, cried with a loud voice (Rev. 14:18); other mss. have *kraugē*. The term is also used in regard to other people and spirits: those in Ramah (Matt. 2:18), John the Baptist (Matt. 3:3; Mark 1:3; Luke 3:4; John 1:23), evil spirits (Mark 1:26; 5:7; Luke 4:33; 8:28; Acts 8:7), Elizabeth (Luke 1:42, 44), a woman in the time of Jesus (Luke 11:27), leprous men (Luke 17:13), an individual leper (Luke 17:15), the multitude of the disciples (Luke 19:37), the bridegroom (John 3:29), strangers (John 10:5), Peter (Acts 2:14; 12:14), the apostles (Acts 4:24), those who stoned Stephen (Acts 7:57), Stephen (Acts 7:60), Herod (Acts 12:22), the prophets (Acts 13:27), Paul (Acts 14:10; 16:28), crowds (Acts 14:11), the inhabitants of Ephesus (Acts 19:34), Jews (Acts 22:22), and Festus (Acts 26:24). It is even used in regard to a beast of burden (2 Pet. 2:16). The term is found also in the book of Revelation in regard to the Lord (1:10, 12, 15a, b; 3:20; 4:1, 5; 5:2, 11, 12; 6:1, 6, 7, 10; 7:2, 10; 8:5, 13; 10:3, 4, 7, 8; 11:12, 15, 19; 12:10; 14:2, 7, 9, 13, 15; 16:1, 17, 18; 18:2, 4, 23; 19:1, 5, 6, 17; 21:3). Other refs.: Matt. 24:31 and Luke 17:13 in some mss.; 1 Cor. 14:10, 11; Heb. 12:19. All other refs.: SOUND (noun) <5456>.

2 ***phthongos*** [masc. noun: φθόγγος <5353>]; **from *phthengomai*: to utter a sound ▶ Musical sound, either vocal or instrumental** > The term is used in Rom.

10:18. Other ref.: 1 Cor. 14:7b; see SOUND (noun) <5353>. ¶

[3] ***psēphos*** [fem. noun: ψῆφος <5586>]; **from *psaō*: to touch lightly ► Lit.: stone which was used for voting, i.e., for expressing agreement or not; also transl.: vote >** Before his conversion, Paul gave his voice {cast his vote} against the saints when they were being put to death (Acts 26:10). Other refs.: Rev. 2:17a, b; see STONE (noun) <5586>. ¶

– [4] John 7:37 → to say in a loud voice → to cry out → CRY (verb) <2896>.

VOID – [1] **to make void: *kenoō*** [verb: κενόω <2758>]; **from *kenos*: empty, void ► To make empty, to reduce to nothing >** It was better for Paul to die, than that any man should make void {make vain, deprive him of} his boast (1 Cor. 9:15). All other refs.: REPUTATION <2758>, VAIN <2758>.

– [2] Matt. 5:17a, b → to make void → DESTROY <2647> [3] Matt. 15:6; Mark 7:13 → to make void → to make of no effect → EFFECT (noun) <208> [4] Luke 16:17 → to become void → FALL (verb) <4098> [5] Rom. 3:31; Gal. 3:17 → EFFECT (noun) <2673>.

VOLUNTARILY – [1] ***hekousios*** [adj.: ἑκούσιος <1595>]; **from *hekōn*: voluntarily; lit.: voluntary ► Willingly, without obligation >** The expr. "that it might be voluntary" {of free will, of willingness, not forced} translates *kata hekousion* in Phm. 14. ¶

[2] ***hekousiōs*** [adv.: ἑκουσίως <1596>]; **from *hekousios*: see [1] ► Deliberately, willingly >** If we sin willingly after receiving the knowledge of the truth, there no longer remains any sacrifice for sins (Heb. 10:26). The elders are to shepherd the flock of God voluntarily (1 Pet. 5:2). ¶

[3] ***hekōn*** [adj. used as adv.: ἑκών <1635>] ► **Of one's own accord, willingly >** If Paul preached the gospel voluntarily, he had a reward (1 Cor. 9:17). Other ref.: Rom. 8:20; see WILLINGLY <1635>. ¶

– [4] 1 Cor. 9:17 → not voluntarily → against one's will → WILL (noun)[1] <210> [5] 1 Pet. 5:2 → WILLINGLY <4290>.

VOLUNTARY – Phm. 14 → VOLUNTARILY <1595>.

VOMIT (noun) – ***exerama*** [neut. noun: ἐξέραμα <1829>]; **from *exeraō*: to vomit out, which is from *ek*: out, and *eraō*: to spew ► That which is thrown out of the mouth from the stomach >** The dog returns to its own vomit (2 Pet. 2:22). ¶

VOMIT (verb) – ***emeō*** [verb: ἐμέω <1692>] ► **To expel through the mouth what is in the stomach, to disgorge >** Because the angel of the church in Laodicea is lukewarm, and neither cold nor hot, the Lord will vomit him out of His mouth (Rev. 3:16). ¶

VOTE – Acts 26:10 → VOICE <5586>.

VOTIVE – Luke 21:5 → votive gift → OFFERING <334>.

VOW (noun) – [1] ***euchē*** [fem. noun: εὐχή <2171>]; **from *euchomai*: to wish, to pray ► Commitment, pledge made before God to fulfill a promise >** The vow of a Nazirite was practiced among the Israelites (see Numbers 6), as a sign of separation and consecration to the Lord. Because he had taken a vow, Paul had shaved his head in Cenchrea (Acts 18:18). Similarly, four men at Jerusalem had taken a vow (Acts 21:23), and were also to shave their heads (see v. 24). Other ref.: Jas. 5:15; see PRAYER <2171>. ¶

– [2] Matt. 5:33 → to make false vows → FORSWEAR <1964>, OATH <3727>.

VOW (verb) – Mark 6:23 → SWEAR <3660>.

VOYAGE – [1] Acts 16:11 → to make a direct voyage → to sail straight → SAIL (verb) <2113> [2] Acts 21:7; 27:9, 10 → NAVIGATION <4144>.

VULTURE – Matt. 24:28; Luke 17:37 → EAGLE <105>.

WAG – Matt. 27:39; Mark 15:29 → SHAKE <2795>.

WAGE (noun) – [1] Rom. 4:4 → WAGES <3408> [2] 1 Cor. 3:8 → REWARD (noun) <3408>.

WAGE (verb) – [1] Rom. 7:23 → to wage war → WAR (verb) <497> [2] 2 Cor. 10:3; 1 Tim. 1:18 → waging war → WAR (verb) <4754> [3] Rev. 12:7a, b; 13:4; 17:14; 19:11 → to wage war → FIGHT (verb) <4170> [4] Rev. 12:17; 13:7; 19:19 → to wage war → to make war → MAKE <4160>.

WAGES – [1] ***misthos*** [masc. noun: μισθός <3408>] ▶ **a. What is due for work, pay; also transl.: hire, reward** > The workman is worthy of his wages (Luke 10:7; 1 Tim. 5:18). The term is used in regard to workmen in a vineyard (Matt. 20:8), he who reaps (John 4:36), and laborers who have harvested the fields of the rich (Jas. 5:4). **b. Punishment, compensation for wickedness** > Judas purchased a field with the reward (or: wages) of his iniquity (Acts 1:18 {price}). **c. Recompense, reward** > To him who works, the wages are reckoned as something due (Rom. 4:4). If Paul preached the gospel voluntarily, he had a reward (1 Cor. 9:17); his reward was that when he preached the gospel, he made the gospel costless to others (v. 18). Balaam loved the reward (or: "wages") of unrighteousness (2 Pet. 2:15). John wanted to receive full wages for what he had accomplished (2 John 8). All other refs.: REWARD (noun) <3408>.

[2] **he who serve for wages: *misthōtos*** [masc. noun: μισθωτός <3411>]; **from *misthoō*: to hire, which is from *misthos*: see [1] ▶ a. Person who works for a salary, employee** > Answering the call of Jesus, James and John left their father Zebedee in the ship with the hired servants {hired men} (or: those serving for wages) and went away after Him (Mark 1:20). **b. Person who works for a salary, mercenary; also transl.: hired hand, hireling** > He who serves for wages sees the wolf coming, leaves the sheep, and flees (John 10:12); he who serves for wages flees because he serves for wages and does not care about the sheep (v. 13a, b in some mss.). ¶

[3] **wage: *opsōnion*** [neut. noun: ὀψώνιον <3800>]; **from *opson*: food, and *ōneomai*: to buy ▶ a. Lit.: soldier's allowance, from which: salary** > John the Baptist told the soldiers to be content with their wages (Luke 3:14). Paul had received wages {support} from other churches so that he might serve the Corinthians (2 Cor. 11:8). **b. What is reaped, result** > The wages of sin is death (Rom. 6:23). Other ref.: 1 Cor. 9:7; see EXPENSE <3800>. ¶

– [4] John 6:7 → half a year's wages → lit.: two hundred denarii → DENARIUS <1220>.

WAIL – [1] ***alalazō*** [verb: ἀλαλάζω <214>]; **from *alalē*: war cry ▶ To shout, to lament, to groan** > People were weeping and wailing greatly because of the death of the daughter of the ruler of the synagogue (Mark 5:38). Other ref.: 1 Cor. 13:1; see CLANGING <214>. ¶

– [2] Matt. 9:23 → the noisy crowd wailing → lit.: the crowd making a noise → NOISE (noun) <2350> [3] Matt. 11:17; Rev. 1:7 → LAMENT <2875> [4] Mark 5:39; Luke 8:52; Jas. 4:9 → WEEP <2799> [5] Luke 23:27 → LAMENT <2354> [6] Jas. 5:1 → HOWL <3649> [7] Rev. 18:15, 19 → MOURN <3996>.

WAILING – Matt. 13:42, 50 → WEEPING <2805>.

WAIST – John 13:4, 5 → to wrap around the waist → GIRD <1241>.

WAIT (noun) – [1] Acts 23:21 → to lie in wait → WAIT (verb) <4327> [2] Acts 25:3 → AMBUSH <1747>.

WAIT (verb) – [1] **to wait for: *anamenō*** [verb: ἀναμένω <362>]; **from *ana*: intens., and *menō*: to stay, to wait ▶ To wait patiently** > The Thessalonians were waiting for {were awaiting} the Son of God from heaven (1 Thes. 1:10). ¶

[2] **to wait for: *perimenō*** [verb: περιμένω <4037>]; **from *peri*: about, and *menō*: to stay, to wait ▶ To remain in one place until an event happens** > The apostles were to wait for {await} the promise of the Father (Acts 1:4), i.e., the baptism with the Holy Spirit. Other ref.: Acts 10:24 in some mss. ¶

3 to wait for: ***ekdechomai*** [verb: ἐκδέχομαι <1551>]; **from** ***ek*****: from, and** ***dechomai*****: to receive ► To hope for, to await; also transl.: to expect, to look, to tarry** > Paul waited for Silas and Timothy in Athens (Acts 17:16). The Corinthians were to wait for another when they came to eat (1 Cor. 11:33). Paul was waiting for {looking for} Timothy with the brothers (1 Cor. 16:11). Jesus is waiting until His enemies are made the footstool of His feet (Heb. 10:13). Abraham waited for {was looking forward to} the city that has foundations (Heb. 11:10). The farmer waits for the precious fruit of the earth (Jas. 5:7). Other ref.: John 5:3 in some mss. ¶

4 to wait eagerly, to wait: ***apekdechomai*** [verb: ἀπεκδέχομαι <553>]; **from** ***apo*****: intens., and** ***ekdechomai*****: see 3 ► To await keenly, with great expectation; also transl.: to await, to look for, to expect** > The earnest expectation of the creation waits for the manifestation of the sons of God (Rom. 8:19). Christians wait for the adoption, the redemption of their body (Rom. 8:23); they wait for it with patience (v. 25). They wait for the coming of the Lord Jesus Christ (1 Cor. 1:7), the hope of righteousness (Gal. 5:5), the Savior, the Lord Jesus Christ (Phil. 3:20), and Christ at His second coming (Heb. 9:28). The long suffering of God waited in the days of Noah (1 Pet. 3:20; some mss.: *ekdechomai*). ¶

5 to wait for: ***prosdechomai*** [verb: προσδέχομαι <4327>]; **from** ***pros*****: to, and** ***dechomai*****: to receive, to welcome ► To expect, to remain in anticipation of; also transl.: to await, to lie in wait, to look for** > Simeon was waiting for the consolation of Israel (Luke 2:25). Believers in the Lord should be like men waiting for their master, when he will return from the wedding (Luke 12:36). Joseph of Arimathea was waiting for the kingdom of God (Mark 15:43; Luke 23:51). There were Jews waiting for the chief captain to bring down Paul to the council (Acts 23:21). All other refs.: ACCEPT <4327>, LOOK (verb) <4327>, RECEIVE <4327>, TAKE <4327>.

6 to wait for: ***prosdokaō*** [verb: προσδοκάω <4328>]; **from** ***pros*****: for, and** ***dokaō*****: to expect, to look for, from which** ***prosdokia*****: expectation ► To look for, to expect** > The people were waiting for {were awaiting} Zacharias to come out of the temple (Luke 1:21). All the people were waiting for Jesus (Luke 8:40). Cornelius was waiting for {was looking for} the brothers of Joppa (Acts 10:24). All other refs.: EXPECT <4328>, EXPECTATION <4328>, LOOK (verb) <4328>, TARRY <4328>.

– 7 Matt. 8:15; Mark 1:31; Luke 4:39; 12:37; 17:8; Acts 6:2 → to wait on → SERVE <1247> 8 Mark 3:9 → to wait on → to keep ready for → READY <4342> 9 John 3:29 → STAND (verb) <2476> 10 Acts 10:7 → to wait on continually → to continue with → CONTINUE <4342> 11 Acts 20:3, 19; 23:30 → to lay in wait, lying in wait → PLOT <1917> 12 Acts 20:5 → TARRY <3306> 13 Acts 22:16 → DELAY (verb) <3195> 14 1 Cor. 7:35 in some mss. → to wait on → DEVOTION <2137a> 15 1 Cor. 9:13 → to wait at → SERVE <4332> 16 Rev. 6:11 → REST (verb) <373>.

WAIT! – Matt. 27:49 → Let be! → LET <863>.

WAITING – 2 Thes. 3:5 → patient waiting → PATIENCE <5281>.

WAIVER – Jas. 1:6a, b → DOUBT (verb) <1252>.

WAKE – **1 to wake up:** ***egeirō*** [verb: ἐγείρω <1453>] **► To rise from sleep, to get up; also transl.: to awake, to arise, to raise** > Joseph, having wakened from his sleep, did as the angel had commanded him in the dream (Matt. 1:24 in some mss.). The disciples woke Jesus in the storm (Matt. 8:25; Mark 4:38 in some mss.). The Father raises the dead and gives them life (John 5:21). An angel woke up Peter in the prison (Acts 12:7). It is already the hour for us to wake up from sleep (Rom. 13:11). Isaiah tells the sleeper to wake up (Eph. 5:14). All other refs.: ARISE <1453>, LIFT <1453>, RAISE <1453>, RISE (verb) <1453>.

2 to wake, to wake up: *diegeirō* [verb: διεγείρω <1326>]**; from *dia*: intens., and *egeirō*: see 1; lit.: to wake up completely ▶ To rouse from sleep, to become alert; also transl.: to awake, to stir up, to stimulate** > Waking up, Jesus rebuked the wind (Mark 4:39). The disciples woke up Jesus in the storm (Luke 8:24). Peter accounted it right to stir up his readers (2 Pet. 1:13); he stirred up their pure minds (3:1). Some mss. have *diegeirō* in Matt. 1:24 and Mark 4:38 rather than *egeirō* (see 1). Other ref.: John 6:18; see ARISE <1326>. ¶

3 to wake up: *exupnizō* [verb: ἐξυπνίζω <1852>]**; from *exupnos*: awakened, which is from *ek*: out, and *hupnos*: sleep ▶ To cause to come out of sleep** > Jesus was going to wake up {awake out of sleep} Lazarus (John 11:11), i.e., from the sleep of death. ¶

– 4 Acts 16:27 → to wake up → awaking from sleep → SLEEP (noun) <1853> 5 1 Cor. 15:34 → to wake up from one's drunken stupor → AWAKE (verb) <1594> 6 1 Thes. 5:10; Rev. 3:3 → to wake, to wake up → WATCH (verb) <1127> 7 Rev. 3:2 → to wake up → to be watchful → WATCHFUL <1127>.

WALK – **1 *peripateō*** [verb: περιπατέω <4043>]**; from *peri*: around, here and there, and *pateō*: to walk; used especially of walking individually ▶ a. To come and go, to move at large; also transl.: to live** > The verb is used in regard to the Lord Jesus (Matt. 4:18; 14:25, 26; Mark 1:16 {to go along}; 6:48, 49; 11:27; John 1:36 {to pass by}; 6:19; 7:1 {to go around}; 10:23; 11:54 {to move about}; 1 John 2:6b; Rev. 2:1), Peter (Matt. 14:29; John 21:18 {to go}), Paul (2 Cor. 10:2, 3; 12:18 {to conduct, to act}), the disciples (Mark 7:5; John 12:35a), the scribes (Mark 12:38; Luke 20:46), a paralytic (Matt. 9:5; Mark 2:9; Luke 5:23; John 5:8, 9, 11, 12), lame men (Matt. 11:5; 15:31; Luke 7:22), a young girl (Mark 5:42), men (Mark 8:24; Luke 11:44), the disciples travelling to Emmaus (Mark 16:12; Luke 24:17), many disciples (John 6:66 {to follow}), he who follows Jesus (John 8:12), one who walks in the day (John 11:9) or in the night (John 11:10), one who walks in darkness (John 12:35b), a lame beggar (Acts 3:6, 8a, b, 9, 12), a crippled man without strength (Acts 14:8, 10), Christians (Rom. 6:4; 8:4; 13:13 {to behave}; 14:15 {to act}; 1 Cor. 7:17 {to retain the place}; 2 Cor. 4:2; 5:7; Gal. 5:16; Eph. 2:2, 10 {to do}; 4:1, 17a; 5:2, 8, 15; Phil. 3:17; Col. 1:10; 2:6; 3:7; 4:5 {to conduct, to act}; 1 Thes. 2:12; 4:1; 1 John 1:6, 7; 2:6a; 2 John 6a, b), the Corinthians (1 Cor. 3:3 {to behave, to act}), certain Thessalonians who were walking in a disorderly manner {leading a disorderly life, idle} (2 Thes. 3:11), the rest of the Gentiles (Eph. 4:17b), enemies of the cross of Christ (Phil. 3:18), a brother who was walking in a disorderly manner {leading an unruly life} (2 Thes. 3:6), those who have been carried away with strange doctrines (Heb. 13:9 {where the Greek word is transl. "to be occupied": i.e., those who have been occupied, lit.: "those having walked" in these strange doctrines have not been profited by them}), he who hates his brother (1 John 2:11), the children of a believing lady (2 John 4), Gaius (3 John 3), the spiritual children of John (3 John 4), believers in Sardis (Rev. 3:4), idols that cannot walk (Rev. 9:20), he who watches (Rev. 16:15 {to go}), and the nations (Rev. 21:24). **b. To circulate, to tread around with a suspect or hostile intention** > The devil, as a roaring lion, walks about {prowls around} Christians, seeking whom he may devour (1 Pet. 5:8). Some mss. have this verb in Rom. 8:1 ("who walk not after the flesh, but after the Spirit"), but the best mss. do not have this phrase. Other ref.: Acts 21:21; see LIVE <4043>. ¶

2 to walk among: *emperipateō* [verb: ἐμπεριπατέω <1704>]**; from *en*: in, among, and *peripateō*: see 1 ▶ To circulate in the midst of** > God has promised to walk among Christians (2 Cor. 6:16). ¶

3 *poreuomai* [verb: πορεύομαι <4198>]**; from *poros*: passage ▶ To travel, to behave; also transl.: to follow, to go, to pursue, to live** > The verb is used in reference to Zacharias and Elizabeth (Luke 1:6 {to observe}), the Lord Jesus (Luke 13:33 {to journey}), the churches (Acts 9:31), the nations (Acts 14:16), Christians before their conversion (1 Pet. 4:3), scoffers (2 Pet. 3:3), wicked, ungodly men (Jude 11 {to take the way}, 16, 18). All other refs.: DEPART <4198>, FOLLOW <4198>, GO <4198>, TRAVEL <4198>.

4 **to walk, to walk orderly: *stoicheō*** [verb: στοιχέω <4748>]**; from *stoichos*: row, rank; lit.: to march in rank ▶ To conduct oneself, to live; used especially of walking in relation to others** > This verb is used in regard to Paul (Acts 21:24), to those who are not Jews but who walk {follow} in the steps of the faith of Abraham (Rom. 4:12), and to Christians (Gal. 5:25 {to keep in step}; 6:16; Phil. 3:16 {to live}). ¶

– 5 Matt. 12:43; Luke 11:24; Acts 17:23 → GO <1330> 6 Matt. 15:29 → COME <2064> 7 Mark 2:14 → to walk along → to pass on → PASS <3855> 8 Luke 24:15 → to walk along → to go along with → GO <4848> 9 Acts 23:1 → LIVE <4176> 10 Gal. 2:14 → to walk uprightly → to be straightforward → STRAIGHTFORWARD <3716> 11 Heb. 13:18 → to walk rightly → to conduct oneself well → CONDUCT (verb)[1] <390>, WELL (adv.) <2573> 12 2 Pet. 2:18 → LIVE <390>.

WALL – 1 ***teichos*** [neut. noun: τεῖχος <5038>] **▶ Masonry (ramparts, masonry enclosure) raised up around a city to protect it** > The disciples let Paul down by the wall (Acts 9:25; 2 Cor. 11:33). By faith the walls of Jericho fell down (Heb. 11:30). The word is also used in regard to the new Jerusalem (Rev. 21:12, 14, 15, 17–19). ¶

2 **middle wall: *mesotoichon*** [neut. noun: μεσότοιχον <3320>]**; from *mesos*: middle, and *toichos*: wall of a house ▶ Expr. used in a figur. sense to describe the law of commandments which separated the Jews from the Gentiles** > Christ has broken down the middle wall of separation {barrier [*phragmos*] of the dividing wall [*mesotoichon*]; lit.: the dividing wall of the barrier} (Eph. 2:14) by introducing grace. ¶

– 3 Matt. 21:33; Mark 12:1 → HEDGE (noun) <5418>.

WALLOW – 1 Mark 9:20 → to roll around → ROLL <2947> 2 2 Pet. 2:22 → returns to wallow → returns to her wallowing → WALLOWING <2946>.

WALLOWING – ***kulisma*** [neut. noun: κύλισμα <2946>]**; from *kuliō*: to roll oneself ▶ Result of rolling about** > The washed sow has returned to her wallowing in the mud (2 Pet. 2:22); other spelling: *kulismos*, which means the act of rolling about. ¶

WANDER – 1 **to wander about: *perierchomai*** [verb: περιέρχομαι <4022>]**; from *peri*: around, and *erchomai*: to go ▶ To go about, to go around** > Younger widows learn to be idle, wandering about from house to house (1 Tim. 5:13). O.T. people of faith wandered about in sheepskins and goatskins, afflicted and tormented (Heb. 11:37). Other refs.: Acts 19:13 (to go here and there); 28:13; see ITINERANT <4022>, CIRCLE AROUND <4022>. ¶

2 ***planaō*** [verb: πλανάω <4105>]**; from *planē*: error, delusion ▶ To go about without fixed destination** > O.T. people of faith wandered in deserts and mountains (Heb. 11:38). All other refs.: ASTRAY <4105>, DECEIVE <4105>, MISTAKEN (BE) <4105>, STRAY <4105>.

– 3 1 Tim. 1:6; 6:21; 2 Tim. 2:18 → to wander, to wander away → STRAY <795> 4 1 Tim. 6:10 → to wander, to wander away → STRAY <635> 5 2 Tim. 4:4 → to wander off into → to turn aside to → TURN (verb) <1624>.

WANDERING – 1 ***planētēs*** [masc. noun: πλανήτης <4107>]**; from *planaō*; to wander, which is from *planē*: error, delusion ▶ One who moves about aimlessly, drifts away, turns astray** > Jude speaks of evil men, most likely false teachers, who are wandering stars (v. 13). ¶

– 2 Jas. 5:20 → his wandering → lit.: error of his way → ERROR <4106>, WAY <3598>.

WANT (noun) – 1 **person in want: *endeēs*** [adj.: ἐνδεής <1729>]**; from *endeō*: to be**

in want, which is from *en*: in, and *deō*: to lack, to have need of ▶ Indigent person, needy person > In the beginning of the church, there was no person in want {any that lacked, anyone who lacked} among the Christians (Acts 4:34). ¶

2 **to be in want: *hustereō*** [verb: ὑστερέω <5302>]**; from *husteros*: which comes behind, last ▶ To be poverty-stricken, indigent; also transl.: to be in need** > The prodigal son began to be in want (Luke 15:14). Other refs.: 2 Cor. 11:9; Heb. 11:37 {to be destitute}. All other refs.: COME <5302>, INFERIOR <5302>, LACK (verb) <5302>, PRIVATION <5302>, WORSE <5302>.

– 3 Mark 12:44 → POVERTY <5304> 4 Acts 20:34; 28:10; Phil. 2:25 → NEED (noun) <5532> 5 2 Cor. 8:14a, b; 9:12 → what is lacking → LACK (noun) <5303> 6 Phil. 4:11 → PRIVATION <5304>.

WANT (verb) – 1 ***boulomai*** [verb: βούλομαι <1014>] **▶ To desire, to intend** > Jude wanted {desired, willed} to remind his readers of certain things in his letter (Jude 5). Other refs.: ADVISE <1014>, PLEASE <1014>, PURPOSE (verb) <1014>, WILL (verb) <1014>.

2 ***thelō*** [verb: θέλω <2309>] **▶ To have the desire, the intention; also transl.: to desire, to be desirous, to wish, would have, to be willing** > Joseph did not want {was unwilling} to expose Mary publicly (Matt. 1:19). The scribes and the Pharisees wanted to see a sign from Jesus (Matt. 12:38). Herod wanted to kill John the Baptist (Matt. 14:5), as did also Herodias (Mark 6:19). Paul wanted the Christians to be wise in what is good and simple concerning evil (Rom. 16:19). The Christian does not want to be unclothed, but further clothed with his heavenly dwelling (2 Cor. 5:4). Esau wanted to inherit the blessing (Heb. 12:17). The author of the Epistle to the Hebrews wanted in all things to live honorably (Heb. 13:18). Other ref.: Rev. 2:21 in some mss. Other refs.: see entries in Lexicon at <2309>.

– 3 Matt. 9:6 → I want you to know → lit.: that you may know → KNOW <1492> 4 Luke 11:8 → to have need → NEED (noun) <5535> 5 John 2:3 → LACK (verb) <5302> 6 Acts 5:33 → CONSULT <1011> 7 Acts 13:7 → SEEK <1934> 8 Acts 15:37; 2 Cor. 1:17 → PROPOSE <1011> 9 Acts 28:22 → DESIRE (verb) <515> 10 1 Cor. 4:8 → to have what one wants → to be filled → FILL (verb) <2880> 11 2 Cor. 1:16 → "I wanted" added in Engl. 12 Titus 1:5 → REMAIN <3007> 13 Heb. 6:11 → DESIRE (verb) <1937> 14 1 Pet. 4:3 → what the Gentiles want to do → lit.: the will of the Gentiles → WILL (noun)[1] <2307>.

WANTING (BE) – Titus 3:13; Jas. 1:4 → LACK (verb) <3007>.

WANTON – 1 **to wax wanton: *katastrēniaō*** [verb: καταστρηνιάω <2691>]**; from *kata*: against, and *strēniaō*: to live in luxury or in dissolution, which is from *strēnos*: luxury, voluptuousness ▶ To be overcome by sensual desires** > Paul speaks of younger widows waxing wanton {growing wanton, feeling sensual desires} against Christ (1 Tim. 5:11). ¶

– 2 Jas. 5:5 → to be wanton, to lead a life of wanton pleasure → to live in self-indulgence → SELF-INDULGENCE <4684>.

WANTONNESS – Rom. 13:13; 2 Pet. 2:18 → LEWDNESS <766>.

WAR (noun) – 1 ***polemos*** [masc. noun: πόλεμος <4171>] **▶ Armed conflict between two or more groups, referring to prolonged hostilities; from which: dispute** > Jesus tells His disciples that they will hear of wars and rumors of wars (Matt. 24:6a, b; Mark 13:7a, b; Luke 21:9: of wars and tumults). He speaks of a king going to war against another king (Luke 14:31). James asks what causes wars and conflicts among Christians (Jas. 4:1). The beast shall make war against the two witnesses (Rev. 11:7). The dragon will make war against the rest of the offspring of the woman (Rev. 12:17). It was given to the beast to make war against the saints (Rev. 13:7). All other refs.: BATTLE (noun) <4171>, FIGHT (noun) <4171>.

2 **to go to war, to wage war, to war: *strateuomai*** [verb: στρατεύομαι <4754>]; **from *stratos*: army ▶ To make war, to fight in an armed conflict** > Soldiers (lit.: Those going to war) questioned John the Baptist (Luke 3:14). No one goes to war at his own expense (1 Cor. 9:7). No man who wars entangles himself with the affairs of this life (2 Tim. 2:4). Fleshly lusts wage war against the soul (1 Pet. 2:11). All other refs.: WAR (verb) <4754>.

– 3 Luke 23:11 → men of war → TROOPS <4753> 4 Rom. 7:23 → to wage war → to war against → WAR (verb) <497> 5 Rev. 2:16; 12:7a, b; 13:4; 17:14; 19:11 → to make war, to wage war, to go to war → FIGHT (verb) <4170>.

WAR (verb) – 1 ***polemeō*** [verb: πολεμέω <4170>]; **from *polemos*: war, armed conflict ▶ To quarrel, to struggle** > James speaks of those who fight (*machomai*, implying a particular conflict) and war (*polemeō*, implying prolonged conflict) (Jas. 4:2). Other refs.: Rev. 2:16; 12:7a, b; 13:4; 17:14; 19:11; see FIGHT (verb) <4170>. ¶

2 ***strateuomai*** [verb: στρατεύομαι <4754>]; **from *stratos*: army ▶ To make war, to fight, to combat** > Paul did not war {wage war} according to the flesh (2 Cor. 10:3). He wanted Timothy to war {wage} the good warfare {fight the good fight} (1 Tim. 1:18). Wars come from the lusts that war {wage war, battle} in our members (Jas. 4:1). All other refs.: WAR (noun) <4754>.

3 **to war in opposition: *antistrateuomai*** [verb: ἀντιστρατεύομαι <497>]; **from *anti*: against, and *strateuomai*: see 2 ▶ To fight against** > The man in Romans 7 sees in his members another law warring in opposition to {waging war against} the law of his mind (v. 23). ¶

– 4 2 Tim. 2:4 → to engage in warfare → WARFARE <4758>.

WARD – Acts 4:3 → PRISON <5084>.

WARE – 1 Mark 11:16 → VESSEL[1] <4632> 2 Acts 14:6 → to be ware → to be aware → AWARE <4894>.

WARES – Rev. 18:15 → "wares" added in Engl.

WARFARE – 1 ***strateia*** [fem. noun: στρατεία <4752>]; **from *strateuomai*: to lead an army, which is from *stratos*: army ▶ Combat; term used in the case of spiritual conflicts** > The weapons of warfare of the Christian are not of the flesh (2 Cor. 10:4). Timothy was to fight a good warfare {battle, fight} (1 Tim. 1:18). ¶

2 **to engage in warfare: *stratologeō*** [verb: στρατολογέω <4758>]; **from *stratos*: army, and *legō*: to choose ▶ To enlist in an army as a soldier** > No one engaged in warfare {No one that warreth, No one serving as a soldier, No soldier in active service} entangles himself with the affairs of this life (2 Tim. 2:4). ¶

WARM (adj.) – Jas. 2:16 → to keep warm → WARM (verb) <2328>.

WARM (verb) – ***thermainō*** [verb: θερμαίνω <2328>]; **from *thermos*: warm, which is from *therō*: to heat ▶ To expose oneself to a source of heat** > Peter was warming himself at the fire (Mark 14:54; John 18:25), and a servant girl saw him (Mark 14:67); there were also servants and officers warming themselves with Peter (John 18:18a, b). It does not profit a Christian to tell a brother or a sister to be warmed {keep warm} if we do not give them the things they need (Jas. 2:16). ¶

WARMLY – 1 Acts 21:17 → WARMLY <780> 2 1 Cor. 16:19 → HEARTILY <4183>.

WARN – 1 **to warn sternly, to warn strictly: *embrimaomai*** [verb: ἐμβριμάομαι <1690>]; **from *en*: in (intens.), and *brimaomai*: to express anger ▶ To caution, to admonish seriously; also transl.: to charge sharply** > Jesus sternly warned the two blind men (Matt. 9:30). He sternly warned the leper whom He had healed, sending him away (Mark 1:43). Other refs.: MOVED (BE) <1690>, REBUKE (verb) <1690>.

[2] ***epitimaō*** [verb: ἐπιτιμάω <2008>]; **from *epi*: against, and *timaō*: to evaluate, which is from *timē*: honor, price ▶ To admonish, to expressly prohibit; also transl.: to charge, to charge strictly** > Jesus warned not to make Him known (Matt. 12:16), that no one should be told about Him (Mark 8:30). He sternly warned {earnestly warned, straitly charged, rebuked much, gave strict orders to} the unclean spirits that they should not make Him known (Mark 3:12). All other refs.: CHARGE (verb) <2008>, REBUKE (verb) <2008>.

[3] ***noutheteō*** [verb: νουθετέω <3560>]; **from *nous*: mind, intelligence, and *tithēmi*: to put, to set ▶ To remind, to admonish** > Paul did not cease to warn every one of the Ephesians (Acts 20:31). He wrote to the Corinthians to warn them as his beloved children (1 Cor. 4:14). The Thessalonians were to warn the disorderly (1 Thes. 5:14). Other refs.: Rom. 15:14; Col. 1:28; 3:16; 1 Thes. 5:12; 2 Thes. 3:15; see ADMONISH <3560>. ¶

[4] ***hupodeiknumi*** [verb: ὑποδείκνυμι <5263>]; **from *hupo*: under, and *deiknumi*: to reveal ▶ To show, to teach; also transl.: to forewarn** > John asked the Pharisees and Sadducees who had warned them to flee from the wrath to come (Matt. 3:7). He asked the same question to the multitudes who came out to be baptized (Luke 3:7). Other refs.: Luke 6:47; 12:5; Acts 9:16; 20:35 see SHOW (verb) <5263>. ¶

[5] **to be divinely warned (instructed), to be warned of (by, from) God, to be warned: *chrēmatizō*** [verb: χρηματίζω <5537>]; **from *chrēma*: matter, business ▶ To be instructed, to receive a communication by a divine revelation; also transl.: to be admonished, to be revealed** > The wise men were warned by God in a dream that they should not return to Herod (Matt. 2:12). Joseph was warned of God in a dream to go to Galilee (Matt. 2:22). It had been revealed {had been divinely communicated} to Simeon that he would not see death before he had seen the Lord's Christ (Luke 2:26). Cornelius was warned from God {divinely directed, told} to send for Peter (Acts 10:22). Moses was warned {admonished, oracularly told} by God to build the tabernacle according to the model (Heb. 8:5). Noah was warned by God of things that were not seen yet (Heb. 11:7). All other refs.: CALL (verb) <5537>, ORACLE <5537>.

– [6] Matt. 16:20; Mark 8:15 → COMMAND (verb) <1291> [7] Luke 9:21 → to strictly warn → COMMAND (verb) <3853> [8] Luke 16:28; Acts 2:40; 20:23; 1 Thes. 4:6 → to warn, to solemnly warn → TESTIFY <1263> [9] Acts 4:17 → lit.: to threaten with threat → THREAT <547>, THREATEN <546> [10] Acts 27:9 → ADMONISH <3867> [11] 2 Cor. 13:2a → to say before → SAY <4280> [12] 2 Cor. 13:2b; Gal. 5:21 → to tell before → TELL <4302> [13] 2 Tim. 2:14 → to charge solemnly → CHARGE (verb) <1263> [14] Titus 3:10 → lit.: warning → ADMONITION <3559> [15] Rev. 22:18 → to bear witness → WITNESS <4828>.

WARNING – [1] Mark 1:43 → with a strong warning → lit.: warning strongly → WARN <1690> [2] Luke 10:11 → as a warning to you → lit.: against you, for you [3] Acts 13:51 → as a warning to them → lit.: against them [4] Acts 23:22 → with this warning → lit.: commanding → COMMAND (verb) <3853> [5] 1 Cor. 10:11; Titus 3:10 → ADMONITION <3559> [6] 1 Tim. 5:20 → to take warning → lit.: to have fear → FEAR (noun) <5401>.

WARPED – Phil. 2:15 → CROOKED <4646>.

WARPED (BE) – Titus 3:11 → PERVERTED (BE) <1612>.

WAS (I) – [1] ***ēmēn*** [verb: ἤμην <2252> ▶ Imperfect of *eimi*: I am.

[2] ***ēn*** [verb: ἦν <2258> ▶ Imperfect of *eimi*: I am.

WASH – [1] ***louō*** [verb: λούω <3068>] ▶ **To bathe, i.e., to cleanse the whole body with water; the verb is used of living beings and sometimes of one who has died** > He who is washed {who has had a bath} (*louō*) needs only to wash (*niptō*) his feet (John 13:10a). Dorcas was washed after her death (Acts

9:37). The jailer washed the stripes of Paul and Silas (Acts 16:33). The Christian can draw near to Jesus, having his body washed with pure water (Heb. 10:22). The sow that was washed returns to wallowing in the mire (2 Pet. 2:22). Jesus has washed {has released, has freed} Christians from their sins in His blood (Rev. 1:5). ¶

2 **to wash, to wash away:** ***apolouō*** [verb: ἀπολούω <628>]; **from *apo*: from, and *louō*: to bathe ► To cleanse from, to cleanse away** > Ananias had told Saul to have his sins washed away (Acts 22:16). The Corinthians had been washed (1 Cor. 6:11) from their sins. ¶

3 ***baptizō*** [verb: βαπτίζω <907>]; **from *baptō*: to dip, to immerse ► To purify with much water, to perform ablutions** > When they return from the marketplace, the Jews do not eat unless they wash {cleanse themselves} (Mark 7:4a). Jesus had not first washed {had not ceremonially washed} before dinner (Luke 11:38). All other refs.: BAPTISM <907>.

4 ***brechō*** [verb: βρέχω <1026>] **► To make wet, to moisten** > A woman who was a sinner washed {wet} the feet of Jesus with her tears (Luke 7:38, 44). All other refs.: FALL (verb) <1026>, RAIN (noun) <1026>, RAIN (verb) <1026>.

5 ***niptō*** [verb: νίπτω <3538>] **► To cleanse a part of the body (especially the hands, the feet, and the face)** > Jesus says to wash the face when fasting (Matt. 6:17). His disciples were not washing their hands when they were eating bread (Matt. 15:2). All the Jews wash their hands carefully {give their hands a ceremonial washing} before they eat (Mark 7:3). At the order of Jesus, a blind man went and washed himself in the pool of Siloam (John 9:7a, b, 11a, b, 15). Jesus washed the feet of His disciples (John 13:5, 12); initially Simon Peter did not want Jesus to wash his feet (vv. 6, 8a), but it was necessary for Jesus to do this (v. 8b). He who is washed (*louō*) has only to wash (*niptō*) his feet (John 13:10b). Since the Lord had washed the feet of His disciples, they ought also to wash one another's feet (John 13:14a, b). A widow was to be put on the list if she had washed the saints' feet (1 Tim. 5:10). ¶

6 ***aponiptō*** [verb: ἀπονίπτω <633>]; **from *apo*: from, and *niptō*: to wash ► See 5.** > Pilate washed his hands in front of the crowd (Matt. 27:24). ¶

7 ***plunō*** [verb: πλύνω <4150>] **► To cleanse; always used of inanimate objects** > Fishermen were washing their nets (Luke 5:2); some mss. have *apoplunō* (see 8). Those coming out of the great tribulation have washed their robes and made them white in the blood of the Lamb (Rev. 7:14). Blessed are those who wash their robes that they may have the right to the tree of life (Rev. 22:14 in some mss.). ¶

8 ***apoplunō*** [verb: ἀποπλύνω <637>]; **from *apo*: from, and *plunō*: see 7 ► To cleanse** > Ref.: Luke 5:2; see 7. ¶

– 9 Jas. 4:8 → CLEANSE <2511>.

WASHING – 1 ***baptismos*** [masc. noun: βαπτισμός <909>]; **from *baptizō*: to purify with much water, which is from *baptō*: to dip, to immerse ► Purification with water** > The Jews hold the tradition of the washing of cups and other objects (Mark 7:4b, 8 in some mss.). Other refs.: Heb. 6:2; 9:10; see BAPTISM <909>. ¶

2 ***loutron*** [neut. noun: λουτρόν <3067>]; **from *louō*: to bathe (the whole body), to cleanse by means of a liquid ► Act of bathing** > Christ sanctified the church and cleansed her with the washing of water by the word (Eph. 5:26). God saved us through the washing of regeneration (Titus 3:5). ¶

– 3 Mark 7:3 → WASH <3538> 4 John 2:6; 3:25 → ceremonial washing → PURIFICATION <2512>.

WASTE (noun) – 1 ***apōleia*** [fem. noun: ἀπώλεια <684>]; **from *apollumi*: to destroy fully, which is from *apo*: intens., and *ollumi*: to destroy ► Ruinous expense, squandering** > The disciples considered the ointment poured out on the head of Jesus as waste (Matt. 26:8; Mark 14:4). All other refs.: DESTRUCTION <684>, PERISH <684>, SON OF PERDITION <684>.

– 2 Matt. 12:25; Luke 11:17; Rev. 18:17, 19 → to lay waste → to make desolate → DESOLATE <2049>.

WASTE (verb) – 1 ***diaskorpizō*** [verb: διασκορπίζω <1287>]; **from *dia*: through (intens.), and *skorpizō*: to scatter ▶ To squander, to use up** > The younger son in the parable wasted {dissipated, squandered} his possessions with prodigal living (Luke 15:13). The steward of a rich man was accused of wasting the goods of his master (Luke 16:1). Other refs.: Matt. 25:24, 26; 26:31; Mark 14:27; Luke 1:51; John 11:52; Acts 5:37; see SCATTER <1287>. ¶
– 2 Mark 14:4 → lit.: to make a waste → WASTE (noun) <684> 3 John 6:12 → LOSE <622> 4 2 Cor. 4:16 → to waste away → PERISH <1311>.

WATCH (noun) – 1 ***phulakē*** [fem. noun: φυλακή <5438>]; **from *phulassō*: to keep, to watch > Division of the night into a period of hours** > For the Israelites, there were three watches: from sunset to 10 pm, from 10 pm to 2 am, and from 2 am to sunrise. Under Roman rule, there were four watches sometimes referred to in these terms: evening, midnight, cock-crow, and morning. The word is used in Matt. 14:25; 24:43 {hour, time}; Mark 6:48; Luke 2:8; 12:38. All other refs.: GUARD (noun) <5438>, HOLD (noun) <5438>, PRISON <5438>.
– 2 Matt. 24:42, 43; 25:13; 26:40; Mark 13:34, 35; 14:37 → to keep watch → WATCH (verb) <1127> 3 Matt. 27:36, 54 → to keep watch → WATCH (verb) <5083> 4 Matt. 27:65, 66; 28:11 → GUARD (noun) <2892> 5 Luke 20:20; Acts 9:24 → to keep a close watch → WATCH (verb) <3906> 6 Luke 21:36; Heb. 13:17 → to be on the watch, to keep watch → WATCH (verb) <69> 7 John 18:16 → servant girl who kept watch → DOORKEEPER <2377> 8 Acts 20:28 → to keep watch → BEWARE <4337> 9 Gal. 6:1 → to keep watch → WATCH (verb) <4648> 10 1 Tim. 4:16 → to keep a close watch → to take heed → HEED (noun) <1907> 11 1 Pet. 5:2 → to watch over → to exercise oversight → OVERSIGHT <1983>.

WATCH (verb) – 1 ***agrupneō*** [verb: ἀγρυπνέω <69>]; **from *agrupnos*: who does not sleep, watchful, which is from *agreuō*: to chase, and *hupnos*: sleep ▶ To stay awake, to stay attentive; also transl.: to be alert, to be on the alert, to be on the watch, to be watchful, to keep on the alert, to keep watch** > Jesus says to take heed, watch, and pray (Mark 13:33; Luke 21:36). Christians are to pray with all prayer and supplication, at all times, in the Spirit, and watch to this end with all perseverance and supplications for all the saints (Eph. 6:18). Christian leaders watch over the souls of those entrusted to them (Heb. 13:17). ¶
2 ***grēgoreō*** [verb: γρηγορέω <1127>]; **from *egeirō*: to arise ▶ To not sleep, to sustain one's attention, to be on one's guard; also transl.: to be alert, to be on the alert, to keep alert, to be awake, to stay awake, to stay on the alert, to be vigilant, to keep watch, to be watching, to wake, to wake up** > Jesus says to watch, for we do not know at what hour He will come (Matt. 24:42; 25:13; Mark 13:35, 37). If the master of the house had known at what hour the thief was coming, he would have watched (Matt. 24:43; Luke 12:39). Jesus told His disciples to watch with Him (Matt. 26:38; Mark 14:34), but they were not able to watch one hour with Him (Matt. 26:40), Simon Peter in particular (Mark 14:37). He told them to watch and pray that they might not enter into temptation (Matt. 26:41; Mark 14:38). A man commanded the doorkeeper to watch (Mark 13:34). Blessed are those servants whom the master, when he comes, shall find watching (Luke 12:37). Paul told the elders of Ephesus to watch (Acts 20:31), and the Corinthians to watch and stand firm in the faith (1 Cor. 16:13). The apostle says to persevere in prayer, watching in the same with thanksgiving (Col. 4:2). Christians are to watch and be sober (1 Thes. 5:6; 1 Pet. 5:8). The church in Sardis is exhorted to watch (Rev. 3:3). Other refs.: 1 Thes. 5:10; Rev. 16:15. Other ref.: Rev. 3:2 (to be watchful); see WATCHFUL <1127>. ¶
3 ***nēphō*** [verb: νήφω <3525>]; **lit.: to be sober, to be unintoxicated ▶ To stay alert, to remain concentrated** > Christians are to be sober (*sōphroneō*) and watch (*nēphō*) {to be sober and watchful, to be of sound

judgment and sober spirit, to be clear minded and self-controlled} for the purpose of prayer (1 Pet. 4:7). All other refs.: to be sober under SOBER <3525>.

4 ***skopeō*** [verb: σκοπέω <4648>]; **from *skopos*: goal ▶ To examine, to attentively see >** Jesus says to watch that the light in the body be not darkness (Luke 11:35). The Galatians were to watch {to look to} themselves (Gal. 6:1) so that they also would not be tempted. All other refs.: CONSIDER <4648>, EYES <4648>, REGARD (verb) <4648>.

5 ***episkopeō*** [verb: ἐπισκοπέω <1983>]; **from *epi*: upon, and *skopeō*: see 4 ▶ To look carefully, to give attention; also transl.: to look diligently, to see to it >** We are to watch that no one lacks the grace of God (Heb. 12:15). Other ref.: 1 Pet. 5:2 (to exercise oversight); see OVERSIGHT <1983>. ¶

6 ***tēreō*** [verb: τηρέω <5083>]; **from *tēros*: warden, guard ▶ To keep an eye on, to guard attentively, as having in present possession; also transl.: to keep guard, to keep watch, to watch >** The soldiers watched Jesus (Matt. 27:36, 54). All other refs.: see entries in Lexicon at <5083>.

7 **to watch, to watch closely: *paratēreō*** [verb: παρατηρέω <3906>]; **from *para*: near, and *tēreō*: see 6 ▶ To observe carefully to see what will happen; also transl.: to keep a close watch >** The Pharisees watched Jesus to see if He would heal on the Sabbath (Mark 3:2; Luke 6:7). They watched Him on the Sabbath, as He went into the house of one of the rulers of the Pharisees to eat bread (Luke 14:1). They watched Jesus that they might take hold of Him (Luke 20:20).The Jews were watching the gates day and night that they might kill Paul (Acts 9:24). The verb is also transl. "to observe": the Galatians were observing days and months and seasons and years (Gal. 4:10); the middle voice of the verb suggests the observances of the Galatians were marked by self interest. ¶

– 8 Matt. 7:15; Luke 17:3; 21:34 → to watch out → to take heed → HEED (noun) <4337> 9 Matt. 24:4; Mark 4:24; et al. → to watch, to watch out → to see, to see to it → SEE <991> 10 Matt. 27:55; Mark 12:41; 15:40; Luke 23:35 → SEE <2334> 11 Mark 8:15 → to watch out → BEWARE <3708> 12 Mark 12:38 → to watch out → BEWARE <991> 13 Luke 12:15 → GUARD (verb) <5442> 14 Luke 23:49 → LOOK (verb) <3708> 15 Acts 27:33 → to constantly watch, to watch in expectation → TARRY <4328> 16 1 Tim. 4:16 → to watch closely → to take heed → HEED (noun) <1907>.

WATCHFUL – 1 **to be watchful: *grēgoreō*** [verb: γρηγορέω <1127>]; **from *egeirō*: to arise ▶ To refrain from sleeping, to be vigilant, to pay attention >** Sardis is told to be watchful {to wake up} and strengthen the things that remain (Rev. 3:2). All other refs.: WATCH (verb) <1127>.

– 2 Eph. 6:18 → to be watchful → WATCH (verb) <69> 3 2 Tim. 4:5 → to be watchful → to be sober → SOBER <3525> 4 1 Pet. 4:7 → to be watchful → WATCH (verb) <3525>.

WATCHING – 2 Cor. 6:5; 11:27 → watchings → SLEEPLESSNESS <70>.

WATCHTOWER – Matt. 21:33; Mark 12:1 → TOWER <4444>.

WATER (noun) – 1 ***hudōr*** [neut. noun: ὕδωρ <5204>]; **from *huō*: to rain ▶ The most familiar colorless and odorless liquid occurring in nature >** In Cana, Jesus had made wine out of water (John 2:7, 9a, b). To a woman who had come to draw water, Jesus offered living water (John 4:7, 10, 11, 13, 14a–c, 15). Out of the heart of one who believes in Jesus will flow rivers of living water (John 7:38). Blood and water came out of the pierced side of Jesus (John 19:34). Philip baptized the eunuch in water (Acts 8:36a, b, 38, 39). The bodies of Christians are washed with pure water (Heb. 10:22); it is the effect of the word of God (Eph. 5:26). Noah and his family were saved through water (1 Pet. 3:20), while the world that existed then was flooded with water (2 Pet. 3:6). John heard a voice as the sound of many waters (Rev. 1:15), a voice from heaven like the voice of many waters (14:2), and the voice of a great multitude as the sound of many waters (19:6). Whoever desires can take the water of life freely (Rev. 22:17). Other refs.: Matt. 3:11, 16; 8:32; 14:28, 29; 17:15; 27:24; Mark 1:8, 10; 9:22, 41; 14:13; Luke 3:16; 7:44; 8:25; 16:24; 22:10; John 1:26, 31, 33; 3:5, 23; 5:3, 4a, b, 7; 13:5; Acts 1:5; 10:47; 11:16; Heb. 9:19; Jas. 3:12; 2 Pet. 3:5; 1 John 5:6a–c, 8; Rev. 7:17; 8:10, 11a, b; 11:6; 12:15; 14:7; 16:4, 5, 12; 17:1, 15; 21:6; 22:1. ¶

[2] **without water:** ***anudros*** [adj.: ἄνυδρος <504>]; **from *a*: neg., and *hudōr*: see [1] ▶ Dry >** Peter speaks of men who are springs without water (2 Pet. 2:17). Jude speaks of men who are clouds without water {without rain} (Jude 12). Other refs.: Matt. 12:43; Luke 11:24; see DRY (noun) <504>. ¶

– [3] Luke 5:2 → water edge → LAKE <3041> [4] Luke 13:15 → to be given water → to give to drink → DRINK (verb) <4222> [5] John 4:28 → water jar → WATERPOT <5201> [6] 2 Cor. 11:26 → RIVER <4215> [7] 1 Tim. 5:23 → to drink water only → DRINK (verb) <5202>.

WATER (verb) – ***potizō*** [verb: ποτίζω <4222>]; **from *poton*: drink ▶ To pour a liquid, often to promote growth >** Figur., Paul had planted and Apollos had watered in Corinth (1 Cor. 3:6); but neither he who plants is anything, neither he who waters, but it is God who gives the increase (v. 7); he who plants and he who waters are one (v. 8). All other refs.: DRINK (verb) <4222>.

WATER POT – ***hudria*** [fem. noun: ὑδρία <5201>]; **from *hudōr*: water ▶ Vessel to hold water, jar; also transl.: water jar, water-vessel >** At Cana, Jesus said to fill the six stone water pots (John 2:6, 7); each one could contain two or three measures of about 40 liters (twenty to thirty gallons). After her encounter with Jesus, the woman at the well of Sychar left her water pot {water jar, waterpot} and went into the city (John 4:28). ¶

WATER-VESSEL – John 2:6, 7 → WATER POT <5201>.

WATERER – 1 Cor. 3:7, 8 → lit.: the one who waters → WATER (verb) <4222>.

WATERLESS – [1] Matt. 12:43; Luke 11:24; Jude 12 → DRY <504> [2] 2 Pet. 2:17 → without water → WATER (verb) <504>.

WATERPOT – John 4:28 → WATER POT <5201>.

WATERS – Acts 27:5 → SEA <3989>.

WAVE – [1] ***kludōn*** [masc. noun: κλύδων <2830>]; **from *kluzō*: to precipitate ▶ Great swell, surging billow of great size and extent, agitated surge >** Jesus rebuked the wind and the surging waves {the raging of the water} (lit.: the wave of the water) (Luke 8:24). He who doubts is like a wave of the sea (Jas. 1:6). ¶

[2] ***kuma*** [neut. noun: κῦμα <2949>]; **from *kuō*: to be pregnant, to be expanded ▶ Billow of water, large surging swell on a lake or sea occurring in uninterrupted successions >** Jesus slept in the ship covered by the waves (Matt. 8:24; Mark 4:37). The ship boarded by the disciples was in the middle of the sea, tossed by the waves (Matt. 14:24). The stern of the ship boarded by Paul was being broken by the violence of the waves {the pounding of the surf} (Acts 27:41). Jude speaks of men who are like raging waves of the sea, foaming out their own shame (Jude 13). ¶

[3] ***salos*** [masc. noun: σάλος <4535>]; **from which *saleuō*: to shake, to agitate ▶ Agitated tossing, especially rolling swell of a rough sea >** The nations will be in perplexity before the roaring of the sea and waves (Luke 21:25). ¶

WAVER – ***diakrinō*** [verb: διακρίνω <1252>]; **from *dia*: through, and *krinō*: to separate, to judge ▶ To doubt, to hesitate, to be divided in one's own mind >** Abraham did not waver at the promise of God through unbelief (Rom. 4:20). All other refs.: see entries in Lexicon at <1252>.

WAVERING – **without wavering: *aklinēs*** [adj.: ἀκλινής <186>]; **from *a*: neg., and**

***klinō*: to tilt, to bend ▶ Without bending, firm, stable** > Christians must hold fast the profession of their hope without wavering {unwavering, unswervingly} (Heb. 10:23). ¶

WAX – [1] Matt. 13:15; Acts 28:27 → to wax gross → to grow dull → DULL <3975> [2] Acts 13:46 → to wax bold → to grow bold → BOLD <3955> [3] Phil. 1:14 → to wax confident → to be confident → CONFIDENT <3982> [4] 1 Tim. 5:11 → to wax wanton → WANTON <2691> [5] 2 Tim. 3:13 → GROW <4298>.

WAY – [1] ***hodos*** [fem. noun: ὁδός <3598>] **▶ a. Road, path; also transl.: highway, journey** > Broad is the way {road} that leads to destruction (Matt. 7:13) and straitened is the way that leads to life (v. 14). A great multitude spread their garment in the way of Jesus, and others spread branches in His way (Matt. 21:8a, b; Mark 11:8a, b; Luke 19:36). As Jesus went forth into the way, a man ran up to Him and fell on his knees before Him (Mark 10:17). John the Baptist was to prepare the ways of the Lord (Luke 1:76). The rough ways (lit.: The rough) will become smooth ways (Luke 3:5). In a parable, the master told the servant to go out into the ways and hedges and to compel the people to come to his supper (Luke 14:23). The disciples did not understand the way Jesus was going (John 14:4, 5); He is the way, the truth, and the life (v. 6). Jesus had appeared to Paul in the way (Acts 9:17b; 27). Some wanted to kill Paul on the way (Acts 25:3). Paul saw in the way a light from heaven (Acts 26:13). Christians have boldness to enter into the holiest by a new and living way (Heb. 10:20); the way into the holiest had not been manifested at the time of the first tabernacle (9:8). He who converts a sinner from the error of his way will save a soul from death (Jas. 5:20). Some men have forsaken the right way, having followed the way of Balaam (2 Pet. 2:15a, b). Some men have gone in the way of Cain (Jude 11). Other refs.: Matt. 2:12; 3:3; 4:15; 5:25; 8:28; 10:5, 10; 11:10; 13:4, 19; 15:32; 20:17, 30; 21:19; 22:9, 10; Mark 1:2, 3; 2:23; 4:4, 15; 6:8; 8:3, 27; 9:33, 34; 10:32, 46, 52; Luke 1:79; 2:44; 3:4; 7:27; 8:5, 12; 9:3, 57; 10:4, 31; 12:58; 18:35; 24:32, 35; John 1:23; Acts 2:28; 8:26, 36, 39; 1 Cor. 12:31; 1 Thes. 3:11; Jas. 2:25. **b. Manner of conduct** > John the Baptist had come in the way of righteousness (Matt. 21:32). Jesus taught the way of God in truth (Matt. 22:16; Mark 12:14; Luke 20:21). The term designates early Christianity as a new doctrine (Acts 9:2; 19:9, 23; 22:4; 24:14, 22). Elymas perverted the right ways of the Lord (Acts 13:10). In the past generations God had allowed all the nations to walk in their own ways (Acts 14:16). Paul announced the way of salvation (Acts 16:17). Apollos was instructed in the way of the Lord (Acts 18:25); Aquila and Priscilla explained to him the way of God more exactly (Acts 18:26). Ruin and misery are in the ways of wicked men (Rom. 3:16); they have not known the way of peace (v. 17). The ways of God are unfathomable (Rom. 11:33). Timothy was to remind the Corinthians of Paul's ways in Christ (1 Cor. 4:17). The Holy Spirit says that the Israelites had not known His ways (Heb. 3:10). He who doubts is a double-minded man, unstable in all his ways (Jas. 1:8). Peter speaks of the way of truth (2 Pet. 2:2) and the way of righteousness (v. 21). The ways of the Lord God Almighty are righteous and true (Rev. 15:3). The way of the kings of the east will be prepared (Rev. 16:12). Other refs.: Luke 11:6; Acts 1:12; see JOURNEY (noun) <3598>, SABBATH DAY'S JOURNEY <4521> <3598>. ¶

[2] **some other way: *allachothen*** [adv.: ἀλλαχόθεν <237>]**; from *allos*: other, and suffix *then*: from a place ▶ By another place** > The thief climbs up some other way {elsewhere} to enter into the sheepfold (John 10:1). ¶

[3] **way out, way to escape: *ekbasis*** [fem. noun: ἔκβασις <1545>]**; from *ekbainō*: to go outside, which is from *ek*: out, outside, and *bainō*: to go ▶ Way out, solution** > With the temptation, God will also provide the way to escape {make the issue} (1 Cor. 10:13). Other ref.: Heb. 13:7; see OUTCOME <1545>. ¶

[4] **what way, any way, a way: *poios*** [pron.: ποῖος <4169>]**; comp. *pos*: what,**

and *hoios*: in such a manner ▶ In what manner, how > The men did not find what way to bring the paralyzed man into the house (Luke 5:19). *

5 **in various ways: *polutropōs*** [adv.: πολυτρόπως <4187>]; **from *polus*: many, and *tropos*: manner ▶ In many manners >** God at various occasions and in various ways {in divers manners} spoke in time past to the fathers by the prophets (Heb. 1:1). ¶

6 **to bring, to send, to set on the way: *propempō*** [verb: προπέμπω <4311>]; **from *pro*: before, and *pempō*: to send ▶ To accompany, to go with, to provide (for a journey) >** The church brought Paul and Barnabas on their way (Acts 15:3). The disciples and their families brought Paul and his companions on their way {accompanied them, escorted them} (Acts 21:5). All other refs.: ACCOMPANY <4311>, JOURNEY (noun) <4311>, SET (verb) <4311>.

– 7 Matt. 14:24 → a long way from land → lit.: in the middle of the sea → SEA <2281> 8 Matt. 21:18 → to be on the way back → RETURN (verb) <1877> 9 Matt. 27:41; Mark 4:16; 15:31; Rom. 1:27; Jas. 2:25; 1 Pet. 3:1, 7; 5:5 → in the same way, in a similar way → in like manner → MANNER <3668> 10 Mark 11:4 → place where two ways met → PLACE (noun) <296> 11 Luke 13:11 → in no way → to the uttermost → UTTERMOST <3838> 12 Luke 13:22 → to proceed on the way, to make way → way → JOURNEY (verb) <4197> 13 Luke 14:32 → a great way off, a long way off → FAR <4206> 14 Luke 15:13 → a long way off → FAR <3117> 15 John 4:6 → the way he had come → his journey → JOURNEY (noun) <3597> 16 John 7:1 → looking for a way to kill Him → lit.: seeking to kill Him → SEEK <2212> 17 Acts 1:11; 15:11; Rom. 3:2; Phil. 1:18; 2 Thes. 3:16; Jude 7 → MANNER <5158> 18 Acts 3:26 → wicked ways → WICKEDNESS <4189> 19 Acts 5:41 → to go one's way → DEPART <4198> 20 Acts 9:3; 21:5 → to go one's way → GO <4198> 21 Acts 10:9 → to be on one's way → → to go on one's journey → JOURNEY <3596> 22 Acts 10:47 → to stand in the way → REFUSE (verb) <2967> 23 Acts 11:19 → to make one's way → to go over → GO <1330> 24 Acts 24:3 → every way → EVERYWHERE <3837> 25 Acts 28:10 → HONOR (noun) <5092> 26 Rom. 1:10 → to find a way, that the way may be opened → that he may have a prosperous journey → to have a prosperous journey → JOURNEY (noun) <2137> 27 Rom. 3:12 → to go out of the way → to turn aside → TURN (verb) <1578> 28 Rom. 9:31 → "as the way" added in Engl. 29 1 Cor. 6:4 → those whose way of life is scorned → those who are least esteemed → ESTEEM (verb) <1848> 30 1 Cor. 7:35 → a right way → that which is comely → COMELY <2158> 31 1 Cor. 16:7 → on the way, by the way → PASSING <3844> <3938> 32 Eph. 2:2 → ways → COURSE <165> 33 Eph. 5:2 → "the way of" added in Engl. 34 2 Thes. 2:10 → all the ways that wickedness deceives → lit.: all deceitfulness → DECEITFULNESS <539> 35 2 Tim. 3:10 → way of life → LIFE <72> 36 Titus 2:3 → the way one lives → BEHAVIOR <2688> 37 Heb. 5:2 → to be out of the way → to go astray → ASTRAY <4105> 38 Heb. 9:21 → in the same way → LIKEWISE <3668> 39 Heb. 11:34 → to make to give way → to put to flight → FLIGHT <2827> 40 Heb. 12:13 → to turn out of the way → DISLOCATE <1624> 41 Jas. 1:11 → PURSUIT <4197> 42 1 Pet. 1:18 → way of life → CONDUCT (noun) <391> 43 Jude 11 → to take the way → WALK <4198>.

WAY OF THINKING – 1 Pet. 4:1 → MIND (noun) <1771>.

WAYSIDE – Matt. 21:19 → by the wayside → in the way → WAY <3598>.

WAYWARD – Heb. 5:2 → ASTRAY <4105>.

WE – ***hēmeis*** [plur. pron.: ἡμεῖς <2249>] ▶ To be distinguished from *humeís*, you. * ‡

WEAK – 1 ***adunatos*** [adj. used as noun: ἀδύνατος <102>]; **from *a*: neg., and *dunatos*: powerful, strong ▶ Who is unable, powerless >** The strong are to bear the weaknesses of the weak {those without strength} (Rom. 15:1). All other refs.: IMPOSSIBLE <102>.

[2] ***asthenēs*** [adj.: ἀσθενής <772>]; **from *a*: neg., and *sthenos*: strength, physical vigor; lit.: without strength, powerless ▶ Powerless, without vigor, helpless >** The flesh is weak (Matt. 26:41; Mark 14:38). God has chosen the weak things that He may put to shame the strong things (1 Cor. 1:27). Paul was weak (1 Cor. 4:10). He speaks of a weak conscience that is defiled (1 Cor. 8:7, 10). He had become to the weak as weak, in order that he might gain the weak (1 Cor. 9:22a–c). Many were weak (*asthenēs*) and sick (*arrōstos*) among the Corinthians (1 Cor. 11:30), for they failed to judge themselves (see vv. 28, 31). The members of the body that seem to be weaker {feeble} are necessary (1 Cor. 12:22). Some said that Paul's personal presence was weak {unimpressive} (2 Cor. 10:10). The Galatians were not to return to weak and miserable principles (Gal. 4:9). Paul exhorts the Thessalonians to help the weak (1 Thes. 5:14). Husbands are to dwell with their wives as with a weaker vessel (1 Pet. 3:7), i.e., more delicate. All other refs.: POWERLESS <772>, SICK (adj. and noun) <772>, WEAKNESS <772>.

[3] **to be weak: *astheneō*** [verb: ἀσθενέω <770>]; **from *asthenēs*: see [2] ▶ To be powerless, without vigor, helpless; also used as an adj., e.g., the weak one >** We are to help the weak (lit.: those who are weak) (Acts 20:35). Abraham was not weak {was not weakening} in faith (Rom. 4:19). The law was weak {was weakened} through the flesh (Rom. 8:3). Paul speaks of one who is weak in the faith (Rom. 14:1, 2, 21; 1 Cor. 8:11) and whose conscience is weak (1 Cor. 8:12). Christian liberty is not to become a stumbling block for the weak (lit.: those who are weak) (1 Cor. 8:9). The Corinthians might have thought that Paul had been weak (2 Cor. 11:21), but he could be weak for one who was weak (2 Cor. 11:29a, b). When he was weak, then he was strong (2 Cor. 12:10). Christ is not weak toward us (2 Cor. 13:3); we are weak in Him (v. 4). Paul rejoiced when he was weak and the Corinthians were strong (2 Cor. 13:9). All other refs.: SICK (adj. and noun) <770>, SICK (adv.) <770>.

– [4] Heb. 7:28 → who are weak → lit.: who have weakness → WEAKNESS <769> [5] Heb. 12:12 → weak hands → hands that hang down → HANG <3886> or <3935> [6] Heb. 12:12 → weak knees → paralyzed knees → PARALYZED (BE) <3886>.

WEAK-WILLED WOMAN – 2 Tim. 3:6 → SILLY WOMAN <1133>.

WEAK WOMAN – 2 Tim. 3:6 → SILLY WOMAN <1133>.

WEAKEN – Rom. 4:19; 8:3 → lit.: to be weak → WEAK (adj. and noun) <770>.

WEAKNESS – [1] ***astheneia*** [fem. noun: ἀσθένεια <769>]; **from *asthenēs*: see [3] ▶ Helplessness, infirmity, fragility; also transl.: bodily illness, disease, illness, physical infirmity, sickness >** Jesus healed people of many weaknesses (Luke 5:15; 8:2; 13:11, 12). The Spirit helps in the weakness of the Christian (Rom. 8:26), and the Lord sympathizes with his weaknesses (Heb. 4:15). Paul speaks of the weakness of the flesh (Rom. 6:19 {human limitations}; Gal. 4:13) and of his infirmity (2 Cor. 11:30; 12:5, 9a, b, 10). He had been among the Corinthians in weakness (1 Cor. 2:3). The body of the Christian is sown in weakness, but it will be raised in power (1 Cor. 15:43). There were O.T. people of faith who from weakness were made strong (Heb. 11:34). The high priest himself was clothed with infirmity, on account of which he was required to offer a sacrifice for his sins (Heb. 5:2, see v. 3; 7:28). Christ was crucified in weakness, but He lives by the power of God (2 Cor. 13:4). All other refs.: ILLNESS <769>, INFIRMITY <769>, SICKNESS <769>.

[2] ***asthenēma*** [neut. noun: ἀσθένημα <771>]; **from *astheneō*: to be weak, to lack strength, which is from *asthenēs*: see [3] ▶ Infirmity, scruple of conscience >** Christians are to help each other by bearing the weaknesses of those without strength (Rom. 15:1 {failing}). ¶

[3] ***asthenēs*** [adj. used as noun: ἀσθενής <772>]; **from *a*: neg., and *sthenos*: strength, physical vigor; lit.: without strength ▶ Powerless, without vigor, helpless** > The weakness of God is stronger than men (1 Cor. 1:25). The former commandment has been set aside because of its weakness (Heb. 7:18). All other refs.: POWERLESS <772>, SICK (adj. and noun) <772>, WEAK <772>.

WEALTH – [1] ***euporia*** [fem. noun: εὐπορία <2142>]; **from *euporeō*: to have plenty of every thing, which is from *euporos*: having plenty, prosperous, which is from *eu*: well, and *poros*: financial resource ▶ Affluence, abundance** > The wealth {well-living, prosperity, good income} of the craftsmen in Ephesus came from the making of silver shrines of Diana (Acts 19:25). ¶
[2] ***timiotēs*** [fem. noun: τιμιότης <5094>]; **from *timios*: of great price, highly valued ▶ Abundance of goods, opulence; also transl.: wealth** > Those who had ships on the sea were enriched through the wealth of Great Babylon (Rev. 18:19). ¶
– [3] Matt. 6:24; Luke 16:9, 11, 13 → MAMMON <3126> [4] Matt. 13:22; Mark 4:19; Rom. 11:12; 2 Cor. 8:2; Col. 2:2; 1 Tim. 6:17; Heb. 11:26; Jas. 5:2; Rev. 5:12; 18:17 → RICHES <4149> [5] Matt. 19:22; Mark 10:22 → POSSESSION <2933> [6] Matt. 25:14 → goods → GOOD (adj. and noun) <5224> [7] Mark 10:23; Luke 18:24 → RICHES <5536> [8] Mark 12:44; Luke 21:4 → SURPLUS <4052> [9] Luke 15:12, 30 → LIVING (noun) <979> [10] Luke 15:13 → GOOD (adj. and noun) <3776> [11] Luke 18:23 → of great wealth → extremely rich → RICH <4145> [12] Jas. 5:3 → to hoard wealth → to heap up treasure together → HEAP <2343> [13] Rev. 3:17 → to acquire wealth → to become wealthy → WEALTHY <4147> [14] Rev. 18:15 → to gain one's wealth → to become rich → RICH <4147>.

WEALTHY – [1] **to become wealthy: *plouteō*** [verb: πλουτέω <4147>]; **from *ploutos*: wealth ▶ To become rich, affluent** > Laodicea says that she is rich and has become wealthy {has grown rich, has increased with goods, has acquired wealth} (Rev. 3:17). All other refs.: to be rich under RICH <4147>.
– [2] Mark 10:23; Luke 18:24 → RICHES <5536> [3] Mark 10:24 → to be wealthy → lit.: to trust in riches → TRUST (verb) <3982> [4] Luke 18:23; 19:2 → RICH <4145>.

WEAPON – ***hoplon*** [neut. noun: ὅπλον <3696>] ▶ **Instrument of warfare (used only in the plur.); also transl.: arms** > Judas came to Jesus with weapons (John 18:3). Christians must put on the armor (lit.: the weapons) of light (Rom. 13:12). As a minister of God, Paul was holding the weapons {armor} of righteousness on the right hand and on the left (2 Cor. 6:7). The weapons of the warfare of Christians are not carnal, but mighty in God (2 Cor. 10:4). Other ref.: Rom. 6:13a, b; see INSTRUMENT <3696>. ¶

WEAR – [1] ***endiduskō*** [verb: ἐνδιδύσκω <1737>]; **lengthened form of *enduō*: to clothe in a garment, which is from *en*: in, and *duō*: to put on ▶ To clothe oneself, to wear** > A demoniac wore {put on} no clothes (Luke 8:27 in some mss.). Other refs.: Mark 15:17 in some mss.; Luke 16:19; see CLOTHE <1737>. ¶
[2] **to wear away: *klinō*** [verb: κλίνω <2827>] ▶ **To decline** > The day began to wear away and {Late in the afternoon} the apostles said to Jesus to send the multitude away (Luke 9:12). The verb is transl. "to be far spent," "to be nearly over," "to be almost over" in Luke 24:29. All other refs.: BOW (verb) <2827>, FLIGHT <2827>, LAY <2827>.
[3] ***periballō*** [verb: περιβάλλω <4016>]; **from *peri*: around, and *ballō*: to throw ▶ To put on, to clothe oneself** > A young man followed Jesus, wearing {having casted about} a linen sheet over his naked body (Mark 14:51 {to throw around}). All other refs.: BUILD <4016>, CLOTHE <4016>, WRAP <4016>.
[4] ***phoreō*** [verb: φορέω <5409>]; **form of *pherō*: to carry, to bring ▶ To be clothed, to carry; also transl.: to bear** > The verb

is used in regard to delicate things (Matt. 11:8), the crown of thorns (John 19:5), the sword (Rom. 13:4), the image of the one made of dust and the image of the heavenly One (1 Cor. 15:49a, b), and fine clothes (Jas. 2:3). ¶

– 5 Matt. 3:4 → lit.: to have (*echō*) 6 Matt. 6:25; 22:11; Luke 12:22; Acts 12:21 → CLOTHE <1746> 7 Mark 6:9 → SHOD <5265> 8 Mark 14:51 → wearing nothing → NAKED <1131> 9 Luke 12:33; Heb. 1:11; 8:13 → to wear out → to grow old → OLD <3822> 10 Luke 18:5 → to wear out → to completely harass → HARASS <5299> 11 Acts 28:20 → to be bound with → BIND <4029> 12 1 Cor. 11:14 → to wear long hair → HAIR <2863> 13 1 Pet. 3:3 → PUTTING ON <1745> 14 Rev. 15:6 → to be girded → GIRD <4024>.

WEARING – 1 1 Pet. 3:3 → putting on → PUTTING <1745> 2 1 Pet. 3:3 → wearing, wearing of → lit.: ornament of → ORNAMENT <4025>.

WEARY (adj.) – 1 **to become, to grow, to be weary: *enkakeō*** [verb: ἐγκακέω <1457a>]**; from *en*: in (intens.), and *kakos*: bad ▶ Lit.: to behave badly in, from which: to lack courage, to give in to evil** > The Galatians were not to grow weary {lose heart, faint} while doing good (Gal. 6:9), as also the Thessalonians {to tire} (2 Thes. 3:13); other mss. have *ekkakeō* <1573>: to be completely dispirited, to be exhausted. Other ref.: Eph. 3:13 (to loose heart); see HEART <1573>. ¶

2 **to be weary: *ekluō*** [verb: ἐκλύω <1590>]**; from *ek*: out (intens.), and *luō*: to loose ▶ To be loosened, to be unharnessed; whence: to be weakened, to be tired** > Jesus was moved with compassion for the multitudes because they were weary {distressed, fainted, harassed, tired} and scattered (Matt. 9:36 in some mss.); better mss. have *skullō* <4660>: to be vexed, troubled. All other refs.: DISCOURAGED <1590>, FAINT <1590>, HEART <1590>.

3 **to become, to grow weary: *kamnō*** [verb: κάμνω <2577>] **▶ To become tired, to be overwhelmed** > Christians are to consider the example of Jesus, so that they may not become weary and discouraged in their souls (Heb. 12:3). Other ref.: Jas. 5:15 (to be sick); see SICK (adv.) <2577>. ¶

4 **to be weary, to grow weary: *kopiaō*** [verb: κοπιάω <2872>]**; from *kopos*: difficult labor ▶ To be tired, to work hard** > Jesus tells all who are weary {who labor} and heavily burdened to come to Him and He will give them rest (Matt. 11:28). He was weary {was wearied, was tired} from His journey (John 4:6). The church of Ephesus had labored and had not grown weary {had not fainted} (Rev. 2:3). All other refs.: LABOR (verb) <2872>.

– 5 Acts 24:4 → TEDIOUS (BE) <1465>.

WEARY (verb) – Luke 18:5 → to completely harass → HARASS <5299>.

WEATHER – 1 **fair weather, fine weather: *eudia*** [fem. noun: εὐδία <2105>]**; from *eudios*: fair weather, which is from *eu*: well, and *Dios* (*Zeus*): the supreme divinity of the Greeks ▶ Pleasant atmospheric condition** > The Pharisees and the Sadducees were saying that it would be fair weather the next day, for the sky was red (Matt. 16:2). ¶

– 2 Matt. 16:3 → foul weather → STORM <5494> 3 Luke 12:55 → hot weather → HEAT <2742>.

WEAVE – Matt. 27:29 → to twist together → TWIST <4120>.

WEDDING – 1 **wedding, wedding banquet, wedding feast: *gamos*** [masc. noun: γάμος <1062>] **▶ Meal and celebration which accompanies a marriage; marriage** > Jesus told a parable about a king who made a wedding feast for his son (Matt. 22:2–4, 8–10); a man was not clothed with a wedding garment (vv. 11, 12); lit.: garment of wedding. He spoke of a wedding feast in the parable of the ten virgins (Matt. 25:10). Jesus was invited to a wedding in Cana of Galilee (John 2:1, 2). The marriage of the Lamb, which illustrates the union of Christ with the church, is described in Rev. 19:7, 9. Other refs.: see MARRIAGE <1062>.

– [2] Matt. 9:15; Mark 2:19; Luke 5:34 → wedding guest → lit.: son of the bridechamber → BRIDECHAMBER <3567>.

WEED OUT – Matt. 13:41 → GATHER <4816>.

WEEDS – Matt. 13:25–27, 29, 30, 36, 38, 40 → DARNEL <2215>.

WEEK – [1] ***sabbaton*** [neut. noun: σάββατον <4521>]; **from the Heb. *shabbath*: cessation of activities, rest ▶ Period of seven days** > Very early on the first day of the week, Mary of Magdala and the other Mary came to see the tomb of Jesus (Matt. 28:1; Mark 16:2; Luke 24:1; John 20:1). Jesus rose on the first day of the week (Mark 16:9). He manifested Himself to His disciples on the evening of the first day of the week (John 20:19). A Pharisee fasted twice a week (Luke 18:12). On the first day of the week Paul was assembled with other Christians to break bread (Acts 20:7). On the first day of every week, the Corinthians were to set aside a sum of money at home in view of an eventual collection for the work of the Lord (1 Cor. 16:2). Other refs.: see SABBATH <4521>.
– [2] Acts 28:14 → lit.: seven days → DAY <2033>.

WEEP – [1] ***dakruō*** [verb: δακρύω <1145>]; **from *dakruon*: tear ▶ To shed tears (without accompanying them with audible moaning, wailing)** > Jesus wept on the occasion of the death of Lazarus (John 11:35). ¶
[2] ***klaiō*** [verb: κλαίω <2799>] **▶ To shed tears, to lament audibly; also transl.: to cry, to wail, to bewail, to mourn** > The word is used in regard to Jesus (Luke 19:41). It is also used in regard to Rachel (Matt. 2:18), Peter (Matt. 26:75; Mark 14:72; Luke 22:62), a widow (Luke 7:13), children (Luke 7:32), a woman who was a sinner (Luke 7:38), the daughters of Jerusalem (Luke 23:28a, b), Mary (John 11:31, 33a; 20:11a, b, 13, 15), the Jews with her (John 11:33b), widows (Acts 9:39), the companions of Paul (Acts 21:13), Paul (Phil. 3:18 {with tears}), the rich (Jas. 5:1), John (Rev. 5:4, 5), the merchants of the earth (Rev. 18:11, 15), the kings of the earth (Rev. 18:9), and all who exercise their calling on the sea (Rev. 18:19). Other refs.: Mark 5:38, 39; 16:10; Luke 6:21, 25; 8:52; John 16:20; Rom. 12:15a, b; 1 Cor. 7:30a, b; Jas. 4:9. ¶
[3] **weeping: *klauthmos*** [masc. noun: κλαυθμός <2805>]; **from *klaiō*: to weep, to lament aloud ▶ Wailing, lamentation** > The Greek word is used in regard to the elders at Ephesus (Acts 20:37): they all wept freely (lit.: there was much weeping of all). Other refs.: Matt. 2:18; 8:12; 13:42, 50; 22:13; 24:51; 25:30; Luke 13:28; see WEEPING <2805>. ¶

WEEPING – ***klauthmos*** [masc. noun: κλαυθμός <2805>]; **from *klaiō*: to weep, to lament aloud ▶ Lamentation, loud crying** > Weeping had been heard in Rama (Matt. 2:18). The word is used in the expr. "the weeping and the gnashing of teeth" in regard to the outer darkness (Matt. 8:12; 22:13; 25:30), the furnace of fire (Matt. 13:42, 50 {wailing}), the portion with the hypocrites (Matt. 24:51), and being cast out (Luke 13:28). Other ref.: Acts 20:37; see WEEP <2805>. ¶

WEIGH – [1] **to raise nearer: *airō*** [verb: αἴρω <142>]; **nearer: *asson*** [verb: ἆσσον <788>] **▶ To take up, to lift** > The expr. is used in Acts 27:13: to weigh the anchor (lit.: to raise nearer); the word "anchor" is implied. The verb is also transl. "to loose," "to put out to sea." All other refs. (*airō*): see entries in Lexicon at <142>.
– [2] Matt. 26:15 → to weigh out → to count out → COUNT <2476> [3] Luke 11:46 → to weigh down → LOAD (verb) <5412> [4] Luke 21:34 → to be weighed down → OVERCHARGED (BE) <925> [5] 1 Cor. 4:4 → to weigh carefully → JUDGE (verb) <350> [6] 2 Tim. 3:6 → to weigh down → to load down → LOAD (verb) <4987> [7] Rev. 16:21 → weighing about one hundred pounds → lit.: as the size of a talent → TALENT <5006>.

WEIGHT – [1] ***baros*** [neut. noun: βάρος <922>] ► **Load, burden (but not arduous); in the sense of: value** > The Christians' momentary and light affliction works for them in surpassing measure an eternal weight of glory (2 Cor. 4:17). All other refs.: BURDEN (noun) <922>.

[2] ***onkos*** [masc. noun: ὄγκος <3591>] ► **Burden, load in the sense of bulk, mass; therefore indicating it may be troublesome** > Christians are to lay aside every weight {every encumbrance, everything that hinders} and sin that so easily entangles them (Heb. 12:1). ¶

WEIGHTIER – ***barus*** [adj.: βαρύς <926>] ► **Serious, more important** > The scribes and the Pharisees had neglected the weightier matters of the law (Matt. 23:23). All other refs.: BURDENSOME <926>, HEAVY <926>, SAVAGE <926>, SERIOUS <926>.

WEIGHTY – 2 Cor. 10:10 → SERIOUS <926>.

WELCOME (adj. and noun) – [1] Luke 4:24; Acts 10:35 → ACCEPTED <1184> [2] Heb. 11:31 → to give a friendly welcome to → RECEIVE <1209> [3] 2 Pet. 1:11 → ENTRY <1529>.

WELCOME (verb) – [1] Matt. 10:40a–d, 41a, b → RECEIVE <1209> [2] Matt. 25:35, 38, 43 → INVITE <4863> [3] Luke 8:40; Acts 15:4; 18:27; 28:30 → RECEIVE <588> [4] Luke 10:38; 19:6 → RECEIVE <5264> [5] Luke 15:2; Rom. 16:2; Phil. 2:29 → RECEIVE <4327> [6] Acts 28:2; Rom. 14:1, 3; 15:7a, b; Phm. 17 → RECEIVE <4355> [7] Acts 28:7 → RECEIVE <324> [8] 2 Cor. 6:17 → RECEIVE <1523> [9] Heb. 11:13 → GREET <782> [10] Heb. 11:31 → lit.: to receive in peace → PEACE <1515> [11] 2 John 10, 11 → HAIL (verb) <5463> [12] 3 John 9, 10 → RECEIVE <1926>.

WELFARE – 1 Tim. 6:2 → masters … are devoted to the welfare of their slaves → note: some understand that this kindness is not of the masters, but of the slaves accomplishing a better service → SERVICE <2108>.

WELL (adv.) – [1] ***kalōs*** [adv.: καλῶς <2573>]; **adv. from *kalos*: beautiful, nice** ► **With goodness, honesty** > It is lawful to do well {good} on the Sabbath (Matt. 12:12). Other refs.: Luke 6:26, 27 {good}; 1 Tim. 5:17; Heb. 13:18. Other refs.: COMMENDABLY <2573>, PLACE (noun) <2573>.

[2] **very well: *beltiōn*** [adj. used as adv.: βελτίων <957>] ► **Compar. of *agathos*: good, i.e., better, best** > Timothy knew very well (better than anyone else) in how many ways Onesiphorus ministered at Ephesus (2 Tim. 1:18). ¶

[3] **who does well: *agathopoios*** [adj.: ἀγαθοποιός <17>]; **from *agathos*: good, and *poieō*: to do, to make** ► **One who does good things** > The governors are sent for the praise of those who do well {who do good, who do right} (1 Pet. 2:14). ¶

[4] **to do well: *kalopoieō*** [verb: καλοποιέω <2569>]; **from *kalos*: good, and *poieō*: to do** ► **To do what is honest and good** > The Thessalonians were not to be weary in well doing {doing good, well-doing, doing what is right} (2 Thes. 3:13). ¶

– [5] Matt. 9:12; Mark 2:17 → to be well → to be healthy → HEALTHY <2480> [6] Matt. 15:26 → to be well → to be meet → MEET (adj.) <2076> <2570> [7] Matt. 15:31; Mark 5:34; John 5:4, 6; et al. → SOUND (adj.) <5199> [8] Luke 5:31; 7:10; 3 John 2 → to be well, to go well → to be in health, to be in good health → HEALTH <5198> [9] Luke 8:50 → SAVE (verb) <4982> [10] Gal. 4:17 → COMMENDABLY <2573> [11] Gal. 6:9 → GOOD (adj. and noun) <2570> [12] 1 Pet. 2:15, 20; 3:6, 17 → to do well → GOOD (adj. and noun) <15> [13] 1 Pet. 4:19 → well doing → DOING <16>.

WELL (noun) – [1] ***phrear*** [neut. noun: φρέαρ <5421>] ► **Hole dug in the ground to reach a layer of water and to draw water out from it** > Jesus spoke of a donkey or an ox falling into a well on the Sabbath day (Luke 14:5). He met a woman at a well of the city of Sychar; this well dated back to the time of Jacob (John 4:11, 12). In Rev. 9:1, 2a–c, the Greek word is transl. "pit" {shaft}: the pit of the abyss refers to an opening overlooking the abyss. ¶

– [2] John 4:6a, b, 14; 2 Pet. 2:17 → FOUNTAIN <4077> [3] Acts 4:10 → in good health → HEALTH <5199> [4] 1 Tim. 1:18 → to fight the battle well → to war the good warfare → GOOD (adj.) <2570>.

WELL-DOING – Rom. 2:7 → lit.: good work → WORK <2041>, GOOD <18>.

WELL DONE – ***euge*** [adv.: εὖγε <2103a>]; **from *eu*: well, and *ge*: intens. ▶ Interj. of satisfaction** > A nobleman said to his servant: Well done!, because he had been faithful in a very little thing (Luke 19:17 in some mss.). ¶

WELL-KNOWN – Matt. 27:16 → NOTORIOUS <1978>.

WELL-LIVING – Acts 19:25 → WEALTH <2142>.

WELL PLEASING – [1] ***euarestos*** [adj.: εὐάρεστος <2101>]; **from *eu*: well, and *arestos*: pleasing, or *areskō*: to please ▶ Fully agreeable; also transl.: agreeable, pleasing** > The gift received by Paul was a sacrifice well pleasing to God (Phil. 4:18). It is well pleasing unto {it pleases} the Lord for children to obey their parents (Col. 3:20). The author of the Epistle to the Hebrews wishes that God may work in Christians that which is well pleasing in His sight (Heb. 13:21). All other refs.: ACCEPTABLE <2101>.

[2] **good pleasure: *eudokia*** [fem. noun: εὐδοκία <2107>]; **from *eudokeō*: to please, which is from *eu*: well, and *dokeō*: to think, to appear ▶ Benevolence, gracious purpose** > It has been well-pleasing (lit.: the good pleasure) for the Father to reveal hidden things to infants (Matt. 11:26; Luke 10:21). All other refs.: DESIRE <2107>, PLEASURE <2107>, WILL (noun)[1] <2107>.

WELL UP – [1] John 4:14 → to spring up → SPRING (verb) <242> [2] 2 Cor. 8:2 → ABOUND <4052>.

WELLBELOVED – Mark 12:6; Rom. 16:5; 3 John 1 → BELOVED <27>.

WEST – ***dusmē*** [fem. noun: δυσμή <1424>]; **from *dunō*: to sink, to set (as the sun) ▶ Direction to the left of one facing north, one of the four cardinal points, opposite direction from the east; region where the sun sets** > The word is used in Matt. 24:27; Luke 12:54; 13:29; Rev. 21:13. In Matt. 8:11, the Greek word is also transl.: setting (sun). ¶

WET – Luke 7:38, 44 → WASH <1026>.

WHALE – ***kētos*** [neut. noun: κῆτος <2785>]; ***cetus*, in Lat. ▶ Huge sea fish most likely, rather than a whale** > Jonas was three days and three nights in the belly of the whale {great fish, huge fish, sea monster} (Matt. 12:40), which prefigured the Lord who would remain for that period of time in death before His resurrection. ¶

WHAT? – ***potapos*** [adj.: ποταπός <4217>] ▶ Refs.: Matt. 8:27; Mark 13:1; Luke 1:29; 7:39; 2 Pet. 3:11; 1 John 3:1. ¶

WHATEVER – ***dēpote*** [adv.: δήποτε <1221>]; **from *dē*: truly, and *pote*: ever ▶ Also transl.: whatsoever** > The word is found in John 5:4. ¶ ‡

WHATEVER PLACE – Mark 6:10 → WHEREVER <3699>.

WHATSOEVER – John 5:4 → WHATEVER <1221>.

WHEAT – [1] ***sitos*** [masc. noun: σῖτος <4621>] **▶ Cereal such as corn or grain** > This term is used lit. in Acts 27:38; Rev. 6:6. Wheat typifies true believers in the Lord (Matt. 3:12; 13:25, 29, 30; Luke 3:17). When the mature grain is produced, a man immediately puts his sickle to it because the harvest has come (Mark 4:28; see v. 29). In a parable, a man owed one hundred measures of wheat (Luke 16:7). The excessive cost of one denarius for a measure of wheat or three measures of barley refers to a time of scarcity in Rev. 6:6. Babylon buys various goods, including wheat (Rev. 18:13). All other refs.: CORN <4621>, GRAIN OF WHEAT <4621>.

– 2 Matt. 13:26 → BLADE <5528>.

WHEN – 1 ***hopote*** [particle: ὁπότε <3698>]; **from *hote*: when** ▶ At what time, of what actually took place at a certain time. Ref.: Luke 6:3. ¶ ‡

2 ***hotan*** [conj.: ὅταν <3752>]; **from *hote*: when, and *an*: prep. denoting a supposition, wish, possibility, or uncertainty** ▶ Refs.: Matt. 15:2; Luke 11:21; John 16:21; 2 Cor. 13:9. * ‡

3 ***hote*** [conj.: ὅτε <3753>]; **from *pote*: at what time, and *tote*: then** ▶ Refs.: Matt. 21:1; Mark 11:1; John 17:12; Jude 9. * ‡

WHEN, WHENEVER – ***hēnika*** [adv.: ἡνίκα <2259>] ▶ **Adv. of time** > Refs.: 2 Cor. 3:15, 16. ¶ ‡

WHENEVER – 1 ***epan*** [conj.: ἐπάν <1875>]; **from *epei*: because, since, and *an*: if** ▶ **As soon as** > Refs.: Matt. 2:8; Luke 11:22, 34. ¶ ‡

– 2 Mark 6:10; 9:18 → WHEREVER <3699>.

WHERE – 1 ***hopou*** [adv.: ὅπου <3699>]; **from *pou*: where** ▶ Refs.: Matt. 6:19–21; Mark 9:44; Luke 12:33; John 1:28; Rev. 12:6, 14; 17:9. * ‡

2 ***hothen*** [pron.: ὅθεν <3606>]; **from *hos*: who, which, and suffix *then*: denoting from or at a place** ▶ It is used of place (Matt. 12:44; 25:24, 26; Luke 11:24; Acts 14:26; Heb. 11:19). Other refs.: Matt. 14:7; Acts 26:19; 28:13 (where); Heb. 2:17; 3:1; 7:25; 8:3; 9:18; 1 John 2:18. ¶ ‡

3 ***hou*** [adv.: οὗ <3757>] ▶ Refs.: Matt. 18:20; Luke 4:16; Rom. 5:20. *

4 ***pou*** [pron.: ποῦ <4226>] ▶ Ref.: Matt. 2:2, 4; Heb. 11:8. *

WHEREFORE – 1 ***dio*** [conj.: διό <1352>]; **from *dia*: for, and *ho*: which** ▶ **Also transl.: for which, therefore** > Refs.: Matt. 27:8, 14; Luke 1:35; 7:7; Heb. 3:7. * ‡

2 ***dioper*** [conj.: διόπερ <1355>]; **from *dio*: therefore, and *per*: intens.** ▶ **Also transl.: truly, wherefore by all means, or especially** > Refs.: 1 Cor. 8:13; 10:14; 14:13. ¶ ‡

3 ***hinati*** [interrog. expr.: ἱνατί <2444>]; **from *hina*: so that, and *ti*: what, to what end** ▶ Refs.: Matt. 9:4; 27:46; Luke 13:7; Acts 4:25; 7:26; 1 Cor. 10:29. ¶ ‡

WHEREFORE? – ***diati*** [adv.: διατί <1302>]; **from *dia*: on account of, and *ti*: what, which** ▶ **Also transl.: on what account?, why?** > Refs.: Matt. 9:11, 14; 15:3; 17:19; 21:25; Mark 11:31; Luke 5:30, 33; 19:31; 20:5; 24:38; John 8:43, 46; 12:5; 13:37; Rom. 9:32; 1 Cor. 6:7; 2 Cor. 11:11; Rev. 17:7. In the above instances the two words *dia* and *ti* are separated. In some mss., they are joined together as one word: Matt. 13:10; 15:2; Mark 2:18; 7:5; Luke 19:23; John 7:45; Acts 5:3. ¶ ‡

WHERESOEVER – Mark 6:10; 9:18 → WHEREVER <3699>.

WHEREVER – ***hopou*** [adv.: ὅπου <3699>]; **from *pou*: anywhere, at whichever spot** ▶ **In any place** > Jesus used this word in Mark 6:10 {whatever place, wheresoever, what place soever, whenever}, as did the father of a possessed son (Mark 9:18). *

WHETHER – 1 ***eite*** [conj.: εἴτε <1535>]; **from *ei*: if, and *te*: and** ▶ **This word is most often used to set items in contrast or opposition to one another; also transl.: and if.** > Refs.: Rom. 12:6–8; 1 Cor. 3:22; 8:5; 12:26; 13:8; 15:11; 2 Cor. 1:6; 12:2, 3; 1 Thes. 5:10; 1 Pet. 2:13, 14. * ‡

2 ***poteron*** [pron.: πότερον <4220>] ▶ Ref.: John 7:17. ¶

WHETHER ANYONE IS – ***mē tis, mētis*** [interrog. pron.: μή τις, μήτις <3387>]; **from *mē*: denoting a question, and *tis*: anyone** ▶ Refs.: John 4:33; 7:48; 21:5; 2 Cor. 12:18. ¶ ‡

WHICH (FOR) – See WHEREFORE <1352>.

WHILE – [1] ***hotou*** [adv.: ὅτου <3755>] ▶ Refs.: Matt. 5:25; Luke 13:8; 15:8; 22:16, 18; John 9:18. ¶
– [2] Matt. 13:21 → for a while → for a time → TIME <4340> [3] Mark 15:44; Luke 10:13 → any while, a great while ago → long ago → LONG (adj.) <3819> [4] John 5:35; 2 Cor. 7:8; Phm. 15 → while, little while → TIME <5610> [5] Acts 15:7 → a good while ago → OLD <744> [6] Acts 18:18 → a good while → lit.: a considerable number of days (*hēmeras hikanas*) [7] Acts 20:11 → a long while → lit.: over enough (time) (*eph' hikanon*) [8] Acts 28:6 → a great while → lit.: much (*polu*) [9] Phil. 1:22 → this is for me worth the while → lit.: this to me (is the) fruit (*karpos*) of labor (*ergon*) [10] Phm. 22 → for a short while → for a short time → TIME <260> [11] Heb. 3:13 → while → syn.: as long as (*achris*).

WHIP – [1] John 2:15 → SCOURGE (noun) <5416> [2] Acts 22:25 → for the whips → with the straps → STRAP <2438> [3] 1 Cor. 4:21 → ROD <4464>.

WHISPER – John 7:32 → MURMUR <1111>.

WHISPERER – ***psithuristēs*** [masc. noun: ψιθυριστής <5588>]; **from *psithurizō*: to whisper, which is from *psithuros*: who whispers, who speaks ill ▶ Person who speaks against another one, who slanders secretly** > Paul mentions men who are whisperers {gossips} (Rom. 1:29). ¶

WHISPERING – [1] ***psithurismos*** [masc. noun: ψιθυρισμός <5587>]; **from *psithurizō*: to murmur softly, which is from *psithuros*: who whispers, who speaks ill ▶ The act of speaking against someone without their knowledge, denigration** > Paul feared whisperings {gossip} among the Corinthians (2 Cor. 12:20). ¶
– [2] John 7:12 → MURMURING <1112>.

WHITE (adj.) – [1] ***leukos*** [adj.: λευκός <3022>] ▶ **Well known color which results from the synthesis of the other colors** > Jesus's clothes became white as the light (Matt. 17:2; Luke 9:29); Mark says they became exceedingly white, like snow (Mark 9:3). The clothing of the angel was white as snow (Matt. 28:3; Mark 16:5). The fields are already white for harvest (John 4:35). Mary Magdalene saw two angels in white (John 20:12). The word is used to describe hair (Matt. 5:36), the head and hair of the Son of Man (Rev. 1:14), wool (Rev. 1:14), clothes (Acts 1:10; Rev. 3:4, 5, 18; 4:4; 6:11; 7:9, 13; 19:14), horses (Rev. 6:2; 19:11, 14), a cloud (Rev. 14:14), a stone (Rev. 2:17), and the great white throne that John saw (Rev. 20:11). ¶
– [2] Rev. 7:14 → to make white → WHITE (verb) <3021> [3] Rev. 15:6; 19:8 → BRIGHT <2986>.

WHITE (verb) – [1] ***koniaō*** [verb: κονιάω <2867>]; **from *konia*: dust, lime ▶ To make white by covering with a coat of lime; also transl.: to whitewash** > Scribes and Pharisees were like whited tombs (Matt. 23:27). Paul called the high priest a whited wall (Acts 23:3). ¶
[2] ***leukainō*** [verb: λευκαίνω <3021>]; **from *leukos*: white ▶ To make white or whiter** > At His transfiguration, the clothes of Jesus became white as snow, such as no launderer on earth can whiten {bleach} them (Mark 9:3). The saints of the great tribulation have made their robes white in the blood of the Lamb (Rev. 7:14). ¶

WHITED WALL – Acts 23:3 → WHITEWASHED WALL <5109> <2867>.

WHITEN – See WHITE (verb) <2867>.

WHITEWASH – Matt. 23:27; Acts 23:3 → WHITE (verb) <2867>.

WHITEWASHED WALL – **wall: *toichos*** [masc. noun: τοῖχος <5109>]; **to whitewash: *koniaō*** [verb: κονιάω <2867>]; **from *konia*: dust, lime ▶ This expr. refers to tombs whose walls had been whitened by lime on**

the outside, but which contained bones on the inside > Paul accused the high priest of being a whited wall (Acts 23:3), figur. of being a hypocrite. Other ref. (to whitewash): Matt. 23:27; see WHITE (verb) <2867>. ¶

WHO?, WHICH?, WHAT? – ***tis*** [pron.: τίς <5101>]. *

WHOLE – [1] ***holos*** [adj.: ὅλος <3650>] ▶ **Complete, completely; also transl.: all** > The word is used in relation to the body (Matt. 6:22, 23; Luke 11:34, 36; 1 Cor. 12:17), the world (Matt. 16:26; 26:13; Mark 8:36; 14:9; Luke 9:25; Rom. 1:8; 1 John 2:2; 5:19), the law (Matt. 22:40), a city (Mark 1:33), a man (John 7:23), the nation of Israel (John 11:50), a year (Acts 11:26), Asia (Acts 19:27), two years (Acts 28:30), the lump (1 Cor. 5:6; Gal. 5:9), a church (1 Cor. 14:23), Achaia (2 Cor. 1:1), households (Titus 1:11), the body of horses (Jas. 3:3), the habitable world (Rev. 3:10; 12:9; 13:3; 16:14), and the moon (Rev. 6:12 in some mss.). Other ref.: John 9:34; see COMPLETELY <3650>. *

[2] ***holoklēros*** [adj.: ὁλόκληρος <3648>]; **from *holos*: see [1], and *klēros*: lot, part ▶ Complete, entire, intact** > The whole spirit, soul, and body of the Christian must be preserved blameless at the coming of our Lord Jesus Christ (1 Thes. 5:23). Other ref.: Jas. 1:4; see ENTIRE <3648>. ¶

– [3] Matt. 9:12; Mark 2:17 → to be whole → to be healthy → HEALTHY <2480> [4] Mark 3:5; Luke 6:10; John 5:4, 6; et al.; Titus 2:8 → SOUND (adj.) <5199> [5] Luke 5:31; 7:10 → to be whole → to be in health, to be in good health → HEALTH <5198> [6] Acts 4:10 → in good health → HEALTH <5199> [7] Rom. 13:10 → FULFILLMENT <4138>.

WHOLE (THE) – See ALL <537>.

WHOLEHEARTEDLY – Eph. 6:7 → GOOD WILL <2133>.

WHOLESOME – 2 Pet. 3:1 → PURE <1506>.

WHOLLY – [1] Luke 13:11 → to the uttermost → UTTERMOST <3838> [2] John 9:34 → COMPLETELY <3650> [3] 1 Thes. 5:23 → COMPLETELY <3651>.

WHOLLY AS – ***hōsper*** [adv.: ὥσπερ <5618>]; **from *hōs*: as, and *per*: much ▶ Also transl.: just as, exactly like** > This word is used only in comparisons. a. It introduces a comparison followed by a corresponding clause with *houtōs*: thus, or the like (Matt. 12:40; 13:40; 24:27, 37; Luke 17:24; John 5:21, 26; Rom. 5:19, 21; 6:4, 19; 11:30; 1 Cor. 11:12; 15:22; 16:1; 2 Cor. 1:7; Gal. 4:29; Eph. 5:24; Jas. 2:26). Once with *hoútōs* omitted as inconsequential (Matt. 25:14), and in Rom. 5:12 suspended by a parenthetic clause (see Rom. 5:18). In 2 Cor. 8:7 used with *kaí*: and. b. Generally and without *hoútōs*: thus, corresponding (Matt. 5:48; 6:2, 5, 7, 16; 20:28; 25:32; Luke 18:11; Acts 2:2; 3:17; 11:15; 2 Cor. 9:5; 1 Thes. 5:3; Heb. 4:10; 7:27; 9:25; Rev. 10:3). In Matt. 18:17 it should be transl. "just as." c. After a hypothetical proposition, as asserting or confirming its truth and reality, meaning as indeed (1 Cor. 8:5). ¶ ‡

WHOM, WHOMSOEVER – ***hosper*** [pron.: ὅσπερ <3746>]; **from *hos*: he who, and *per*: intens.** ▶ Ref.: Mark 15:6, meaning the very one they demanded. ¶ ‡

WHORE – Rev. 17:1, 15, 16; 19:2 → PROSTITUTE <4204>.

WHOREMONGER – Eph. 5:5; 1 Tim. 1:10; Heb. 13:4; Rev. 21:8; 22:15 → FORNICATOR <4205>.

WHY? – See WHEREFORE? <1302>.

WICK – Matt. 12:20 → FLAX <3043>.

WICKED (adj.) – [1] **more wicked: *ponēroteros*** [adj.: πονηρότερος <4191>]; **compar. of *ponēros*: wicked, malicious ▶ Worse, more evil** > The word is used in regard to spirits (Matt. 12:45a; Luke 11:26). ¶

– 2 Matt. 5:11 → wicked thing → EVIL (noun) <4190> 3 Matt. 12:45b; 16:4; 18:32; 25:26; Luke 19:22; Acts 18:14; Col. 1:21; 2 Thes. 3:2 → EVIL (adj.) <4190> 4 Matt. 24:48 → EVIL (adj.) <2556> 5 John 3:20 → wicked things → EVIL (adj.) <5337> 6 Acts 2:23 → LAWLESS (adj.) <459> 7 2 Thes. 2:10 → all wicked deception → DECEITFULNESS <539> 8 2 Thes. 3:2 → BAD <824> 9 2 Pet. 2:7; 3:17 → LAWLESS MAN <113>.

WICKED (noun) – 1 ***kakos*** [adj. used as noun: κακός <2556>] ► **Bad, evil, wretched** > The word is used in regard to vinedressers (Matt. 21:41). All other refs.: EVIL (adj.) <2556>, EVIL (noun) <2556>, HARM (noun) <2556>.

2 ***ponēros*** [adj. used as noun: πονηρός <4190>] ► **Bad, evil person** > The Greek word is also transl. "evil" and "wicked." God makes His sun rise on the evil and the good (Matt. 5:45). The word is also used regarding Satan (Matt. 13:19, 38; Eph. 6:16; 2 Thes. 3:3; 1 John 2:13, 14; 3:12; 5:18, 19), men (Matt. 13:49; Luke 6:35), and a man of Corinth (1 Cor. 5:13). All other refs.: EVIL (adj.) <4190>, EVIL (noun) <4190>.

– 3 Acts 3:26 → wicked ways → WICKEDNESS <4189> 4 Acts 24:15 → UNJUST (noun) <94> 5 2 Thes. 2:8 → LAWLESS (noun) <459>.

WICKEDNESS – 1 ***kakia*** [fem. noun: κακία <2549>]; **from *kakos*: bad, evil** ► **Will to do that which is evil** > Simon the magician ought to have repented himself of his wickedness (Acts 8:22). Liberty is not to be used as a cloak of wickedness {evil, malice, maliciousness, vice} (1 Pet. 2:16). All other refs.: MALICE <2549>, TROUBLE <2549>.

2 ***ponēria*** [fem. noun: πονηρία <4189>]; **from *ponēros*: evil, malicious** ► **Iniquity, depravity, active expression of a will to do evil** > Wickednesses come {Malice comes} out of the heart of men (Mark 7:22). Jesus knew the wickedness {malice, evil intent} of certain Pharisees and Herodians who sought to ensnare Him in His words (Matt. 22:18). The Pharisees were full of wickedness (Luke 11:39). God sent Jesus to turn the Jews away from their wickedness {iniquities, wicked ways} (Acts 3:26). Men were filled with wickedness (Rom. 1:29). Christians celebrate the feast, not with the leaven of wickedness, but with the unleavened bread of sincerity and truth (1 Cor. 5:8). The warfare of Christians is against spiritual powers of wickedness {evil} (Eph. 6:12). ¶

– 3 Matt. 23:28; 24:12; Rom. 6:19; 2 Cor. 6:14; Titus 2:14 → INIQUITY <458> 4 Acts 1:18; Rom. 1:18a, b; 2 Tim. 2:19; Heb. 8:12; 2 Pet. 2:15 → INIQUITY <93> 5 Acts 25:5 → improper → FAULT <824> 6 2 Thes. 2:10, 12; Heb. 8:12 → UNRIGHTEOUSNESS <93> 7 2 Pet. 2:16 → INIQUITY <3892>.

WIDE – 1 ***platus*** [adj.: πλατύς <4116>] ► **Large, broad** > The gate that leads to destruction is wide (Matt. 7:13). ¶

– 2 Eph. 3:18; Rev. 21:16a, b → lit.: width → BREADTH <4114>.

WIDELY – 1 Luke 2:17 → to make widely known → KNOW <1107> <1232> 2 Acts 19:20 → to spread widely → lit.: to increase with might → MIGHT <2904>.

WIDEN – 2 Cor. 6:13 → EXPAND <4115>.

WIDOW – ***chēra*** [fem. noun: χήρα <5503>] ► **Woman whose husband has died** > Scribes devoured the houses of widows (Matt. 23:14 in some mss.; Mark 12:40; Luke 20:47). Jesus noticed a poor widow who had cast two mites into the treasury of the temple (Mark 12:42, 43; Luke 21:2, 3). Anna was a widow of about eighty-four years (Luke 2:37). There were many widows in Israel in the days of Elijah (Luke 4:25), but he was sent to a widow at Sarepta (v. 26). A dead man was carried out, the only son of a widow (Luke 7:12). A widow wanted to be avenged of her adversary (Luke 18:3, 5). The widows of the Hellenists were neglected in the daily service (Acts 6:1). The widows stood beside Peter, weeping over the death of Dorcas (Acts 9:39, 41). It is good for the unmarried and widows to remain unmarried, as Paul was (1 Cor. 7:8). Paul speaks much about widows to Timothy (1 Tim. 5:3a, b, 4, 5, 9, 11, 16a, b). Pure and undefiled religion before God the Father is to visit orphans and widows in their affliction, to keep oneself pure from the world (Jas. 1:27). Babylon says that she is not a widow (Rev. 18:7). ¶

WIDTH – Eph. 3:18; Rev. 21:16a, b → BREADTH <4114>.

WIFE – [1] Matt. 8:14; 10:35; Mark 1:30; Luke 4:38; 12:53 → wife's mother → MOTHER <3994> [2] 1 Cor. 11:3, 5, 6a, b, 10, 13; Eph. 5:33a, b; Rev. 21:9; et al. → WOMAN <1135> [3] 1 Tim. 4:7 → old wives' → OLD <1126>.

WILD – [1] ***agrios*** [adj.: ἄγριος <66>]**; from *agros*: field ▶ Which comes from fields or woods** > John fed on locusts and wild honey (Matt. 3:4; Mark 1:6). Other ref.: Jude 13; see RAGING <66>. ¶
– [2] Mark 1:13 → wild beast, wild animal → BEAST <2342> [3] Luke 12:27 → wild flower → LILY <2918> [4] Luke 15:13 → prodigally → PRODIGAL <811> [5] 1 Cor. 15:32 → to fight wild beasts → BEAST <2341> [6] Titus 1:6 → being wild → DISSIPATION <810>.

WILD LIVING – 1 Pet. 4:4 → DISSIPATION <810>.

WILDERNESS – [1] ***erēmia*** [fem. noun: ἐρημία <2047>]**; from *erēmos*: see [2] ▶ Uninhabited and uncultivated region; also transl.: desert** > The disciples asked where they could get enough bread in the wilderness {remote place} to feed a great multitude (Matt. 15:33; Mark 8:4). Paul had been in perils in the wilderness {country} (2 Cor. 11:26). O.T. people of faith have wandered in deserts and mountains (Heb. 11:38). ¶
[2] ***erēmos*** [adj. and adj. used as noun: ἔρημος <2048>] **▶ See [1]; also transl.: desert, desert place, desolate place** > John the Baptist was the voice of One crying in the wilderness (Matt. 3:3; Mark 1:3; Luke 3:4; John 1:23); he was in the deserts {wilderness} until the day of his manifestation to Israel (Luke 1:80); he baptized in the wilderness (Mark 1:4) and he preached in the wilderness of Judea (Matt. 3:1). Jesus was led up by the Holy Spirit into the wilderness (Matt. 4:1; Mark 1:12; Luke 4:1); He was in the wilderness forty days (Mark 1:13). He withdrew into the wilderness {desert} and prayed (Luke 5:16). As Moses lifted up the serpent in the wilderness, even so the Son of Man had to be lifted up (John 3:14). God put up with the ways of Israel in the wilderness (Acts 13:18). In Rev. 12:6, the woman fled into the wilderness; she was given two wings of a great eagle so she might fly into the wilderness (v. 14). Other refs.: Matt. 11:7; 24:26; Luke 3:2; 7:24; 8:29; 15:4; John 6:31, 49; 11:54; Acts 7:30, 36, 38, 42, 44; 21:38; 1 Cor. 10:5; Heb. 3:8, 17; Rev. 17:3. All other refs.: DESERTED <2048>, DESOLATE <2048>.

WILE – ***methodeia*** [fem. noun: μεθοδεία <3180>]**; from *methodeuō*: to work by method, which is from *meta*: prep. indicating change, and *hodos*: way, road ▶ Craftiness, subterfuge; also transl.: artifice, scheme** > The Christian must put on the whole armor of God to stand against the wiles of the devil (Eph. 6:11). Other ref.: Eph. 4:14; see PLOTTING <3180>. ¶

WILL (noun)[1] – [1] ***thelēma*** [neut. noun: θέλημα <2307>]**; from *thelō*: to want, to will ▶ Objectively: what has been determined; subjectively: the abstract act of choice, decision** > The term is used in regard to God the Father (Matt. 6:10; 7:21; 12:50; 18:14; 26:42; Mark 3:35; Luke 11:2 in some mss.; John 4:34; 5:30b; 6:38b, 39, 40; 7:17; 9:31; Gal. 1:4; Eph. 1:5, 9, 11; Heb. 10:7, 9, 10, 36; 13:21) and the Lord Jesus or God (Luke 22:42; John 5:30a; 6:38a; Acts 13:22; 21:14; 22:14; Rom. 1:10; 2:18; 12:2; 15:32; 1 Cor. 1:1; 2 Cor. 1:1; 8:5; Eph. 1:1; 5:17; 6:6; Col. 1:1, 9; 4:12; 1 Thes. 4:3; 5:18; 2 Tim. 1:1; 1 Pet. 2:15; 3:17; 4:2, 19; 1 John 2:17; 5:14; Rev. 4:11). It is also used in regard to the father of two sons (Matt. 21:31), the master of a servant

(Luke 12:47a, b), Jews (Luke 23:25), the flesh (John 1:13a; Eph. 2:3), man (John 1:13b; 2 Pet. 1:21), an unmarried man (1 Cor. 7:37), Apollos (1 Cor. 16:12), God (the remote antecedent, not Satan) (2 Tim. 2:26), and the Gentiles (1 Pet. 4:3). ¶

[2] ***thelēsis*** [fem. noun: θέλησις <2308>]; **from *thelō*: to want, to will ▶ Good pleasure, desire** > God bore witness with the disciples of the Lord by signs, wonders, various miracles, and gifts of the Holy Spirit, according to His own will (Heb. 2:4). ¶

[3] **against one's will: *akōn*** [adj.: ἄκων <210>]; **from *a*: neg. part, and *ekōn*: of one's own will ▶ Unwillingly, contrary to one's liking** > If Paul preached the gospel against his will {not voluntarily}, he had been entrusted with a stewardship (1 Cor. 9:17). ¶

[4] **good will: *eudokia*** [fem. noun: εὐδοκία <2107>]; **from *eudokeō*: to please, which is from *eu*: well, and *dokeō*: to think, to appear ▶ Graciousness, kind intention** > Some preached Christ from good will (Phil. 1:15). All other refs.: DESIRE (noun) <2107>, PLEASURE <2107>, WELL PLEASING <2107>.

[5] ***boulēma*** [neut. noun: βούλημα <1013>]; **from *boulomai*: to want ▶ Goal, intention, determination** > The term is used in regard to God in Rom. 9:19 {purpose}. Other ref.: Acts 27:43; see PURPOSE (noun) <1013>. ¶

– [6] Luke 7:30; Acts 13:36 → COUNSEL (noun) <1012> [7] John 7:17; Rom. 9:16 → if anyone's will is to do; human will → lit.: if anyone will do, lit.: of the one willing → WILL (verb) <2309> [8] John 8:44 → your will is → lit.: you want → WANT (verb) <2309> [9] Rom. 7:18; Phil. 2:13 → WILLING <2309> [10] Rom. 8:20 → of its will → WILLINGLY <1635> [11] Col. 2:23 → voluntary worship, will worship → SELF-IMPOSED RELIGION <1479> [12] Phm. 14 → of free will → VOLUNTARY <1595> [13] Heb. 9:16, 17 → TESTAMENT <1242> [14] Rev. 17:17a, b → MIND (noun) <1106>.

WILL (noun)[2] – Heb. 9:16, 17 → COVENANT <1242>.

WILL (verb) – [1] ***boulomai*** [verb: βούλομαι <1014>] ▶ **To have as deliberated purpose; to desire** > No one knows the Father, except the Son, and he to whom the Son wills to reveal Him (Matt. 11:27; Luke 10:22). Jesus asked the Father if He would remove the cup from Him (Luke 22:42). The Lord is not willing that any should perish, but that all should come to repentance (2 Pet. 3:9). Other refs.: ADVISE <1014>, PLEASE <1014>, PURPOSE (verb) <1014>, WANT (verb) <1014>.

[2] ***thelō*** [verb: θέλω <2309>] ▶ **To have the intention, to be resolved, to be determined, with emphasis on the spontaneous impulse** > God shows mercy to whom He will, and whom He will He hardens (Rom. 9:18a, b). He has placed the members in the body just as He willed (1 Cor. 12:18). He will have all men to be saved and to come to the knowledge of the truth (1 Tim. 2:4). The verb is also used elsewhere in regard to God or the Lord Jesus: Matt. 8:2, 3; 15:32 17:4; 23:37; 26:17, 39; 27:34; Mark 1:40, 41; 3:13; 6:48; 7:24; 9:30; 14:12, 36; Luke 5:12, 13; 9:54; 12:49; 13:34a; 22:9; John 1:43; 5:21; 7:1; 17:24; 21:22, 23; Acts 18:21b; Rom. 9:22; 1 Cor. 4:19b; 15:38; Col. 1:27; Heb. 10:5, 8; Jas. 4:15a. Other refs.: see entries in Lexicon at <2309>.

[3] **to be willing: *suneudokeō*** [verb: συνευδοκέω <4909>]; **from *sun*: together, and *eudokeō*: to take pleasure, to be well pleased, which is from *eu*: well, and *dokeō*: to think, to appear ▶ To agree, to consent** > Paul speaks of a brother whose unbelieving wife is willing to live with him (1 Cor. 7:12) and of a woman who has an unbelieving husband who is willing to live with her (v. 13). All other refs.: APPROVE <4909>, CONSENT (verb) <4909>.

WILLFUL – 2 Pet. 2:10 → SELF-WILLED <829>.

WILLFULLNESS – 2 Pet. 3:5 → through their own willfulness → WILLFULLY <2309>.

WILLFULLY – [1] **to want: *thelō*** [verb: θέλω <2309>] ▶ **To intend, to wish, to**

be determined > Some willfully {through their own willfulness, willingly} forget (lit.: forget, them wanting) this that by the word of God the heavens existed long ago and the earth was formed out of water and in the water (2 Pet. 3:5). Other refs.: see entries in Lexicon at <2309>.
– 2 Heb. 10:26 → VOLUNTARILY <1596>.

WILLING – 1 **to will:** ***thelō*** [verb used as noun: θέλω <2309>] ▶ **Intent, resolution** > The willing {The desire, To will} of doing good was present with the man of Romans 7, but the doing of the good was not (v. 18). It is God who works in the Christian both the willing and the doing {to will and to act}, according to His good pleasure (Phil. 2:13). Other refs.: see entries in Lexicon at <2309>.
2 ***prothumos*** [adj.: πρόθυμος <4289>]; **from *pro*: before, and *thumos*: passion** ▶ **Well disposed, full of good will** > The spirit is willing {ready}, but the flesh is weak (Matt. 26:41; Mark 14:38). Other ref.: Rom. 1:15 (desire); see PART (noun) <4289>. ¶
– 3 2 Cor. 8:3 → willing of one's own accord, willing of oneself, freely willing → of one's own accord → ACCORD (noun) <830> 4 2 Cor. 9:5 → willing gift → generous gift → GIFT <2129>.

WILLING (BE) – 1 John 6:21 → WILLINGLY <2309> 2 1 Thes. 2:8 → to be well pleased → PLEASE (BE) <2106> 3 1 Thes. 3:1 → to think good → THINK <2106> 4 1 Pet. 5:2 → because you are willing → lit.: but willingly → WILLINGLY <4290>.

WILLINGLY – 1 ***hekōn*** [adj. used as adv.: ἑκών <1635>] ▶ **Of one's own choice, voluntarily** > The creation has been made subject to vanity, not willingly {by its own choice, of its will} (Rom. 8:20). Other ref.: 1 Cor. 9:17; see VOLUNTARILY <1635>. ¶
2 ***prothumōs*** [adv.: προθύμως <4290>]; **from *prothumos*: ready, which is from *pro*: before, and *thumos*: passion** ▶ **Voluntarily, earnestly** > The elders are to shepherd the flock of God willingly (1 Pet. 5:2). ¶
3 **to be willing:** ***thelō*** [verb: θέλω <2309>] ▶ **To have the intention, to want** > The disciples willingly received (lit.: were willing to receive) Jesus into their boat (John 6:21). Other refs.: see entries in Lexicon at <2309>.
– 4 Phm. 14 → of willingness → VOLUNTARY <1595> 5 Heb. 10:26; 1 Pet. 5:2 → VOLUNTARILY <1596>.

WILLINGNESS – 1 2 Cor. 8:11, 12; 9:2 → READINESS <4288> 2 Phm. 14 → of willingness → VOLUNTARY <1595>.

WIN – 1 **to win over:** ***peithō*** [verb: πείθω <3982>] ▶ **To obtain the support, to gain the approval** > The Tyrians and the Sidonians had won over {gained, made a friend of, secured the support of} Blastus, the king's chamberlain (Acts 12:20). Jews came from Antioch and Iconium, and having won over {persuaded} the crowds, they stoned Paul (Acts 14:19; *episeiō* in some mss.: to incite). All other refs.: see entries in Lexicon at <3982>.
– 2 Matt. 18:15; 1 Cor. 9:19, 20a, b, 21, 22; Phil. 3:8; 1 Pet. 3:1 → GAIN (verb) <2770> 3 Luke 21:19 → to win your lives → to possess your souls → POSSESS <2932> 4 Acts 14:21 → to win disciples → DISCIPLE <3100> 5 1 Cor. 9:24 → OBTAIN <2638> 6 2 Tim. 2:5 → to win the prize → CROWN (verb) <4737> 7 2 John 8 → to win a full reward → to receive a full reward → RECEIVE <618>.

WIND (noun) – 1 ***anemos*** [masc. noun: ἄνεμος <417>] ▶ **Current of air which may be more or less violent** > In a parable, the winds blew and slammed against a house (Matt. 7:25, 27). Jesus rebuked the winds and the sea, and they obeyed Him (Matt. 8:26, 27; Mark 4:39a, b, 41; Luke 8:23–25). He compared John the Baptist to a reed shaken by the wind (Matt. 11:7; Luke 7:24). The Son of Man will send His angels to gather His elect from the four winds (i.e., from the four cardinal points) (Matt. 24:31; Mark 13:27). Christians are to no longer be, in the figur. sense, little children, tossed and carried about by every wind of doctrine in the trickery of men (Eph. 4:14). Other refs.: Matt. 14:24, 30, 32; Mark 4:37; 6:48, 51; John 6:18; Acts 27:4, 7, 14, 15; Jas. 3:4; Jude 12; Rev. 6:13; 7:1. ¶

[2] **to blow by the wind, to drive by the wind: *anemizō*** [verb: ἀνεμίζω <416>]; **from *anemos*: see [1] ► To carry away, to push by the wind** > He who doubts as he prays is like a wave of the sea, driven by the wind and tossed about (Jas. 1:6). ¶

[3] ***pneuma*** [neut. noun: πνεῦμα <4151>]; **from *pneō*: to breathe ► Movement of the air; used of pleasant and measured movement** > The Lord Jesus compares the activity of the Holy Spirit to produce new birth to that of the wind blowing where it wishes (John 3:8). Other refs.: BREATH <4151>, SPIRIT <4151>.

[4] ***pnoē*** [fem. noun: πνοή <4157>]; **from *pneō*: to blow, to breathe ► Blowing, breath** > At Pentecost, there suddenly came a sound from heaven, as of a violent impetuous wind {blowing}, and it filled the entire house where the believers in the Lord were sitting (Acts 2:2). In Acts 27:40, some mss. have lit. "to the blowing" (*tē pneousē*), i.e., the blowing wind; other mss. have *pnoē*, i.e., the wind. Other ref.: Acts 17:25; see BREATH <4157>. ¶

[5] **south wind: *notos*** [masc. noun: νότος <3558>] **► Wind which blows from the south** > Heat is associated with the south wind (Luke 12:55). Other refs.: Acts 27:13; 28:13. All other refs.: SOUTH <3558>.

WIND (verb) – [1] John 19:40 → BIND <1210> [2] Acts 5:6 → to wind up → to wrap up → WRAP <4958>.

WINDOW – [1] ***thuris*** [fem. noun: θυρίς <2376>]; **dimin. of *thura*: door ► Opening in a wall to allow air and light to penetrate** > Sitting at the window {window-opening, window sill}, Eutychus fell down from the third story (Acts 20:9). Paul was let down in a basket through a window in the wall (2 Cor. 11:33). ¶

– [2] 1 Cor. 13:12 → MIRROR <2072>.

WINDSTORM – Mark 4:37 → lit. storm of wind → STORM <2978>.

WINE – [1] ***oinos*** [masc. noun: οἶνος <3631>] **► Fermented juice of grapes >** Jesus teaches that one cannot put new wine in old wineskins (Matt. 9:17a–c; Mark 2:22a–d; Luke 5:37a, b, 38). At Golgotha, they gave Jesus wine with myrrh to drink (Mark 15:23). John the Baptist was to drink no wine or liquor (Luke 1:15; 7:33). The Samaritan poured oil and wine on the injuries of the man covered with wounds (Luke 10:34). Jesus transformed water into wine at the wedding of Cana (John 2:3a, b, 9, 10a, b; 4:46). Paul teaches to abstain from wine if another Christian is offended (Rom. 14:21); on the other hand, he recommended that Timothy use a little wine because of his stomach (1 Tim. 5:23). The Christian is not to be drunk with wine (Eph. 5:18). The overseers and the deacons of the church are to be careful not to indulge in much wine (1 Tim. 3:8), as likewise elderly women (Titus 2:3). He who sat on the black horse was not to damage the oil and the wine (Rev. 6:6). In the book of Revelation, mention is made of the wine of the sexual immorality of Babylon (14:8; 17:2; 18:3) and the cup of the wine of the wrath of God (14:10; 16:19; 19:15). No one will buy wine from the merchants of the earth after the fall of Babylon (Rev. 18:13). ¶

[2] **new wine, sweet wine: *gleukos*** [neut. noun: γλεῦκος <1098>]; **from *glukus*: sweet ► Intoxicating wine that has undergone fermentation for some time** > At Pentecost, people mocked the disciples, saying that they were full of new wine (Acts 2:13); other transl.: they have had too much wine. ¶

– [3] Matt. 27:34, 48; Mark 15:36; Luke 23:36; John 19:29, 30 → sour wine, wine → VINEGAR <3690> [4] Acts 2:15 → to be full of wine → to be drunk → DRUNK (BE) <3184> [5] 1 Tim. 3:3; Titus 1:7 → given to wine → GIVE <3943> [6] 1 Pet. 4:3 → excess of wine → DRUNKENNESS <3632>.

WINE-DRINKER, WINE-DRINKING – [1] Matt. 11:19; Luke 7:34 → WINEBIBBER <3630> [2] 1 Pet. 4:3 → DRINKING <4224> [3] 1 Pet. 4:3 → DRUNKENNESS <3632>.

WINEBIBBER – ***oinopotēs*** [masc. noun: οἰνοπότης <3630>]; **from *oinos*: wine, and *potēs*: drinker, which is from *pinō*: to drink ▶ Drinker of wine, drunkard** > People were saying the Son of Man was a glutton and a winebibber {wine-drinking, wine-drinker man} (Matt. 11:19; Luke 7:34). ¶

WINEFAT – Mark 12:1 → WINEVAT <5276>.

WINEPRESS – ***lēnos*** [fem. noun: ληνός <3025>] ▶ **Place where grapes were pressed under a turning millstone or crushed underfoot** > Jesus told the parable of a man who dug a winepress (Matt. 21:33). The word also occurs in Rev. 14:19, 20a, b; 19:15: this winepress of the wrath of God or of the fury of the wrath of God makes reference to the execution of the judgment of God on the wicked before the millennium. ¶

WINESKIN – ***askos*** [masc. noun: ἀσκός <779>]; **comp. *skeuos*: vessel ▶ Container used to transport and store liquids, wine in this case; it was made of animal skin** > New wine could cause wineskins {skins, bottles} to burst due to the effect of fermentation (Matt. 9:17a–d; Mark 2:22a–d; Luke 5:37a–c, 38). The new wine (i.e., the wine of the current year) corresponds to a new order of things, the teaching of grace, presented by the Lord, that could not be received by those who remained under the principle of the law and old religious forms. ¶

WINEVAT – ***hupolēnion*** [neut. noun: ὑπολήνιον <5276>]; **from *hupo*: under, and *lēnos*: winepress ▶ Receptacle placed under the winepress which is destined to receive the juice of the grapes** > A man dug a wine-vat {winefat, vat, pit} (Mark 12:1). ¶

WING – ***pterux*** [fem. noun: πτέρυξ <4420>]; **from *pteron*: feather ▶ One of the two forelimbs of a bird allowing it to fly** > Jesus would have gathered the children of Jerusalem as a hen gathers her chicks under her wings (Matt. 23:37; Luke 13:34). In John's vision, the four living creatures had each six wings (Rev. 4:8); the sound of the wings of the locusts was as the sound of chariots of many horses (9:9), and the two wings of a great eagle were given to the woman to fly into the wilderness (12:14). ¶

WINK – Acts 17:30 → OVERLOOK <5237>.

WINNOWING FAN – ***ptuon*** [neut. noun: πτύον <4425>]; **from *ptuō*: to spit ▶ Sort of basket which is flat at the front, used to toss beaten grain in the air, so that the wind may carry away the chaff and thus separate it from the kernel of wheat; possibly a shovel to throw grain against the wind; also transl.: fan, winnowing fork** > In Matt. 3:12 and Luke 3:17, winnowing symbolizes the exercise of the judgment of God by Christ. ¶

WINNOWING FORK – Matt. 3:12; Luke 3:17 → WINNOWING FAN <4425>.

WINTER (noun) – [1] ***cheimōn*** [masc. noun: χειμών <5494>]; **from *cheima*: bad weather, winter ▶ Coldest season of the year in Israel** > Jesus told the Jews to pray that their flight might not happen in winter (Matt. 24:20; Mark 13:18). The Feast of the Dedication was celebrated in winter (John 10:22). Paul told Timothy to make every effort to come before winter (2 Tim. 4:21). Other refs.: Matt. 16:3; Acts 27:20; see STORM <5494>. ¶
– [2] Acts 27:12; 28:11; 1 Cor. 16:6; Titus 3:12 → to spend the winter → WINTER (verb) <3914>.

WINTER (verb) – [1] ***paracheimazō*** [verb: παραχειμάζω <3914>]; **from *para*: at, and *cheimazō*: to be tossed by the storm, which is from *cheima*: bad weather, winter ▶ To remain in a place during the cold season, to spend the winter** > The passengers on the ship that Paul had boarded wanted to winter at Phoenix (Acts 27:12). Paul sailed in a ship that had wintered in the island of Malta (Acts 28:11). Paul thought of wintering at

Corinth (1 Cor. 16:6). He had decided to winter at Nicopolis (Titus 3:12). ¶
– [2] Acts 27:12 → to winter in → lit.: for wintering → WINTERING <3915>.

WINTER FRUIT – Rev. 6:13 → unseasonable fig → FIG <3653>.

WINTERING–***paracheimasia*** [fem. noun: παραχειμασία <3915>]; **from *paracheimazō*: to spend the winter, which is from *para*: at, and *cheimazō*: to spend the winter, which is from *cheima*: bad weather, winter ▶ Action of spending winter in a place** > Fair Havens was not suitable for wintering (Acts 27:12). ¶

WIPE – [1] ***ekmassō*** [verb: ἐκμάσσω <1591>]; **from *ek*: intens., and *massō*: to handle, to wipe ▶ To dry what is wet** > A woman who was a sinner washed the feet of Jesus with her tears and wiped them with the hair of her head (Luke 7:38, 44). Mary of Bethany anointed the feet of Jesus with oil of spikenard and wiped His feet with her hair (John 12:3; 11:2). Jesus wiped {dried} the feet of His disciples with a towel (John 13:5). ¶
[2] ***exaleiphō*** [verb: ἐξαλείφω <1813>]; **from *ek*: out of, and *aleiphō*: to anoint ▶ To dry what is wet** > God will wipe away every tear from the eyes of those who come out of the great tribulation (Rev. 7:17), and from the eyes of men when He will dwell among them (21:4). Other refs.: Acts 3:19; Col. 2:14; Rev. 3:5; see BLOT (verb) <1813>. ¶
– [3] Luke 10:11 → to wipe off → SHAKE OFF <631>.

WISDOM – [1] ***sophia*** [fem. noun: σοφία <4678>]; **from *sophos*: wise ▶ Deep understanding of things with the skill of practical application; sound judgment, natural and moral insight** > The term is used to qualify: **a. God:** The wisdom of God said: "I will send them prophets and apostles" (Luke 11:49). Paul marvels at the wisdom of God (Rom. 11:33). In the wisdom of God, the world through its wisdom has not known God (1 Cor. 1:21a). Paul spoke the wisdom of God in a mystery (1 Cor. 2:7). The manifold wisdom of God is now made known in heaven through the church (Eph. 3:10). Jealousy and strife are not the wisdom that descends from above (Jas. 3:15). The wisdom from above is first pure (Jas. 3:17). In the doxology of Rev. 7:12, God receives wisdom. **b. Jesus Christ:** Many asked what was this wisdom given to Jesus (Matt. 13:54; Mark 6:2). Jesus grew, being filled with wisdom (Luke 2:40); He grew in wisdom and stature (v. 52). Christ is the wisdom of God (1 Cor. 1:24). Christ Jesus has been made to us wisdom from God (1 Cor. 1:30). In the doxology of Rev. 5:12, the Lamb receives wisdom. **c. Believers:** The Queen of Sheba heard the wisdom of Solomon (Matt. 12:42; Luke 11:31). Jesus would give His disciples a wisdom that all their adversaries would not be able to reply to or resist (Luke 21:15). The disciples were to choose seven men from among themselves, full of wisdom (Acts 6:3), to settle a matter. Those who disputed with Stephen were not able to resist his wisdom (Acts 6:10). God gave Joseph favor and wisdom in the presence of Pharaoh (Acts 7:10). In the church, to one is given, by the Spirit, the word of wisdom (1 Cor. 12:8). The grace of God has abounded in all wisdom toward Christians (Eph. 1:8). Paul prayed that God the Father would give the Ephesians the spirit of wisdom (Eph. 1:17) and that the Colossians might be filled with the full knowledge of the will of God in all wisdom (Col. 1:9). Paul taught every man in all wisdom (Col. 1:28). All the treasures of wisdom and knowledge are hidden in the mystery of God (Col. 2:3). Paul prayed that the word of Christ might dwell in the Colossians in all wisdom (Col. 3:16); he exhorted them to walk in wisdom toward those without (Col. 4:5). James exhorts one who lacks wisdom to ask of God (Jas. 1:5). By good behavior, the Christian shows his works in the meekness of wisdom (Jas. 3:13). Paul wrote according to the wisdom that had been given to him (2 Pet. 3:15). There is wisdom related to the understanding of the name and number of the beast (Rev. 13:18) and to the vision of Babylon the Great (17:9). **d. The natural man:** Moses was instructed in all the wisdom of the Egyptians (Acts 7:22). Christ had not sent Paul to preach the gospel with wisdom {cleverness} of word (1 Cor. 1:17). God will destroy the wisdom of the wise (1 Cor. 1:19). He has made foolish the wisdom of the world (1 Cor. 1:20); the wisdom of the world is foolishness before God (1 Cor. 3:19). The world, by wisdom, has not known God (1 Cor. 1:21b). The Greeks seek after wisdom (1 Cor. 1:22). Paul had not gone to the Corinthians with excellence of word or of wisdom (1 Cor. 2:1); his word and his preaching had not been in persuasive words of human wisdom (1 Cor. 2:4 {not with wise and persuasive words}). The faith of the Corinthians was not to rest on the wisdom of men (1 Cor. 2:5). He spoke wisdom among the mature, but not the wisdom of this age (1 Cor. 2:6a, b). He did not speak in words taught by human wisdom (1 Cor. 2:13). He had not conducted himself with fleshly wisdom (2 Cor. 1:12). Human ordinances have an appearance of wisdom (Col. 2:23). Other ref.: 1 Cor. 1:21b. **e. Wisdom personified:** Wisdom is justified by her children (Matt. 11:19; Luke 7:35). ¶

– 2 2 Tim. 3:15 → to give wisdom → to make wise → WISE <4679>.

WISE (adj.) – 1 ***sophos*** [adj.: σοφός <4680>] ▶ **Capable of seeing things clearly, of understanding them; having sound judgment, as well as natural and moral insight** > Professing themselves to be wise, men became fools and changed the glory of God into an image of man and of animals (Rom. 1:22). God only is wise (Rom. 16:27; Jude 25 in some mss.). The foolishness of God is wiser (*sophōteros*) than men (1 Cor. 1:25). God has put wise men to shame (1 Cor. 1:27). Paul wanted Christians to be wise as to that which is good (Rom. 16:19). He had been a wise {an expert} master builder (1 Cor. 3:10). If anyone among the Corinthians thought himself to be wise in this age, Paul advised him to become foolish, that he might become wise (1 Cor. 3:18a, b), for the wisdom of this world is foolishness with God (see v. 19). There was no wise man among the Corinthians who was able to decide between his brothers (1 Cor. 6:5). Christians are to see that they walk carefully, as being wise (Eph. 5:15). James asks his readers who is wise and understanding (Jas. 3:13). All other refs.: WISE (noun) <4680>.

2 **to make wise: *sophizō*** [verb: σοφίζω <4679>]; **from *sophos*: see** 1 ▶ **To communicate wisdom, the ability to see and understand things clearly** > The Holy Scriptures were able to make Timothy wise for salvation through the faith that is in Christ Jesus (2 Tim. 3:15). Other ref.: 2 Pet. 1:16; see DEVISED <4679>. ¶

3 ***phronimos*** [adj.: φρόνιμος <5429>]; **from *phroneō*: to think, which is from *phrēn*: mind, understanding** ▶ **Capable of discerning, prudent** > The Christians at Rome were not to be wise in their own eyes {wise in their own sight} (Rom. 11:25; 12:16). The Corinthians were wise in Christ (1 Cor. 4:10); they put up with fools, being wise themselves (2 Cor. 11:19). All other refs.: INTELLIGENT <5429>, PRUDENT <5429>.

– 4 1 Cor. 2:4 → with wise and persuasive words → lit.: in persuasive words of human wisdom → WISDOM <4678> 5 1 Cor. 6:5 → wise enough → to be able → ABLE <1410> 6 2 Tim. 1:7 → wise discretion → sound mind → MIND (noun) <4995>.

WISE (noun) – 1 **wise, wise man: *sophos*** [adj. used as noun: σοφός <4680>] ▶ **Who sees and understands things clearly, who has sound judgment and discernment** > Jesus praised His Father for having hidden certain things from the wise and intelligent (Matt. 11:25; Luke 10:21). He sent wise men to the scribes and Pharisees (Matt. 23:34). God will destroy the wisdom of the wise (1 Cor. 1:19); He catches the wise in their craftiness (3:19) and He knows the reasonings of the wise (3:20). Paul asks where is the wise (1 Cor. 1:20 {wise man}). There were not many wise according to the flesh among the Corinthians (1 Cor. 1:26). Paul was a debtor both to the wise and the foolish (Rom. 1:14). All other refs.: WISE (adj.) <4680>.

2 **unwise: *asophos*** [adj.: ἄσοφος <781>]; **from *a*: neg., and *sophos*: wise** ▶ **Who**

lacks wisdom, i.e., who does not see things accurately and have sound judgment; also transl.: fool, unwise man > Believers are not to walk as unwise (Eph. 5:15). ¶
– 3 Matt. 7:24; 10:16; 24:45; 25:2, 4, 8, 9; Luke 12:42; 16:8 → PRUDENT <5429> 4 Rom. 12:3 → so as to be wise → so as to have sound judgment → JUDGMENT <4993>.

WISE (IN NO) – 1 ***oudamōs*** [adv.: οὐδαμῶς <3760>]; **from *oudeis*: not even one, nothing ▶ In no way, by no means** > Bethlehem was in no wise the least among the rulers of Judah (Matt. 2:6). ¶
– 2 Luke 13:11 → to the uttermost → UTTERMOST <3838>.

WISE MAN – ***magos*** [masc. noun: μάγος <3097>] ▶ **Member of a caste of priests and astrologers** > This is the name given to the learned men of sound judgment who came from the East to worship the young Child (Matt. 2:1, 7, 16a, b). These wise men {magi}, whose number and names are not mentioned, offered their gifts of gold, frankincense, and myrrh. Other Acts 13:6, 8; see SORCERER <3097>. ¶

WISELY – 1 Mark 12:34 → INTELLIGENTLY <3562> 2 Luke 16:8 → PRUDENTLY <5430>.

WISH – 1 ***euchomai*** [verb: εὔχομαι <2172>] ▶ **To desire, to pray, to want** > The sailors wished for the day to come (Acts 27:29). Paul had wished to be accursed from Christ for his brothers, his kinsmen according to the flesh (Rom. 9:3). John wished that in all things Gaius should prosper and be in good health, even as his soul prospered (3 John 2). Other refs.: Acts 26:29; 2 Cor. 13:7, 9; Jas. 5:16; see PRAY <2172>. ¶
2 ***thelō*** [verb: θέλω <2309>] ▶ **To desire, to want** > There were Greeks who wished to {would, would like to} see Jesus (John 12:21). Pilate was wishing {was willing, was desirous} to release Jesus (Luke 23:20). Paul wished {would, would like} that all in Corinth spoke in tongues (1 Cor. 14:5). Other refs.: see entries in Lexicon at <2309>.
– 3 Acts 18:27 → PURPOSE (verb) <1014> 4 Acts 19:30; 27:43; 28:18 → WANT (verb) <1014> 5 Jas. 2:16 → go, I wish you well → lit.: go in peace → PEACE <1515>.

WIST – Mark 9:6; 14:40; Luke 2:49; John 5:13; Acts 12:9; 23:5 → past tense of "to wit," archaic form of "to know" → KNOW <1492>.

WIT – 2 Cor. 8:1 → to make known → KNOW <1107>.

WITCHCRAFT – Gal. 5:20; Rev. 9:21 → SORCERY <5331>.

WITH – ***meta*** [prep.: μετά <3326>] ▶ Its primary meaning is mid, amid, in the midst, among, implying accompaniment. *

WITHDRAW – 1 ***apospaō*** [verb: ἀποσπάω <645>]; **from *apo*: from, and *spaō*: to draw ▶ To go at some distance** > In Gethsemane, Jesus withdrew from His disciples about a stone's throw (Luke 22:41). All other refs.: DRAW <645>, GET <645>.
2 ***ekneuō*** [verb: ἐκνεύω <1593>]; **from *ek*: out, and *neuō*: to move ▶ To leave quietly, to withdraw privately, to disappear** > Jesus withdrew {conveyed Himself away, slided away, slipped away} after having healed a man who had an infirmity for thirty-eight years (John 5:13). ¶
3 ***metairō*** [verb: μεταίρω <3332>]; **from *meta*: particle indicating change, and *airō*: to move from a place ▶ To depart, to leave, to retire** > The verb is used in regard to Jesus (Matt. 19:1). Other ref.: Matt. 13:53; see DEPART <3332>. ¶
4 ***stellō*** [verb: στέλλω <4724>] ▶ **To avoid** > Paul was avoiding {taking precaution} that no one should blame him concerning the gift he was administering (2 Cor. 8:20). He exhorted the Thessalonians to withdraw {to keep away} from every brother who walks disorderly (2 Thes. 3:6). ¶
5 ***hupochōreō*** [verb: ὑποχωρέω <5298>]; **from *hupo*: under, and *chōreō*: to go ▶ To leave secretly, to depart unnoticed** >

Jesus withdrew Himself in the desert (Luke 5:16 {to slip away}). He withdrew apart {went aside privately} into a desert place of Bethsaida (Luke 9:10). ¶

6 ***hupostellō*** [verb: ὑποστέλλω <5288>]; **from *hupo*: under, and *stellō*: to send, to draw, to withdraw ► To retire due to timidity and failure to assert the truth, to draw back** > Cephas withdrew and separated himself from those of the nations (Gal. 2:12). If anyone draws back {shrinks back}, the soul of God takes no pleasure in him (Heb. 10:38); the author of that epistle says not to be of those who draw back (lit.: who are of desertion; see DESERTION <5289>) to perdition (v. 39). Other refs.: Acts 20:20 (to keep back), 27; see KEEP (verb) <5288>, SHRINK <5288>. ¶

– 7 Matt. 4:12; 9:24; 12:15; 14:13; 15:21; Mark 3:7; John 6:15; Acts 26:31 → DEPART <402> 8 John 6:66 → lit.: to go away back → DEPART <565> 9 Acts 5:38 → to keep away → KEEP (verb) <868> 10 Acts 15:38; 19:9; 22:29; 2 Tim. 2:19 → DEPART <868> 11 Acts 19:9 → SEPARATE <873>.

WITHER – 1 ***marainō*** [verb: μαραίνω <3133>]; **lit.: to consume, to extinguish ► To fade away, from which: to end miserably** > The rich shall wither in his pursuits (Jas. 1:11b). ¶

2 **to wither, to wither away: *xērainō*** [verb: ξηραίνω <3583>]; **from *xēros*: dry ► To dry up, to desiccate** > The fig tree that Jesus had cursed had withered away (Matt. 21:20; Mark 11:21). All other refs.: DRY (verb) <3583>, RIGID <3583>, RIPE (BE) <3583>, WITHERED <3583>.

– 3 Jude 12 → trees whose fruit withereth → lit.: trees of late autumn without fruit → AUTUMNAL <5352>.

WITHERED – 1 **to wither: *xērainō*** [verb: ξηραίνω <3583>]; **from *xēros*: dry ► To be dry, to be paralyzed** > A man had a withered {shriveled} hand (Mark 3:1, 3), and Jesus healed him. All other refs.: DRY (verb) <3583>, RIGID <3583>, RIPE (BE) <3583>, WITHER <3583>.

2 ***xēros*** [adj.: ξηρός <3584>] ► **Deprived of natural circulation, paralyzed** > Jesus healed a man who had a withered {shriveled} hand (Matt. 12:10; Luke 6:6, 8). Withered people lay near the pool of Bethesda (John 5:3). All other refs.: DRY (noun) <3584>, LAND (noun) <3584>.

WITHHOLD – 1 Luke 6:29 → FORBID <2967> 2 John 20:23a, b → to withhold → lit.: to hold; i.e., to hold or retain sins → HOLD (verb) <2902> 3 Acts 10:47 → REFUSE (verb) <2967> 4 2 Cor. 6:12a, b → RESTRAIN <4729> 5 Jas. 5:4 → to wrongfully keep back → KEEP (verb) <650>.

WITHIN – 1 ***entos*** [adv.: ἐντός <1787>]; **from *en*: in ► Inside, among** > This word is used in Matt. 23:26 {inside}; Luke 17:21. ¶

– 2 Heb. 6:19 → INNER <2082>.

WITHIN (FROM) – ***esōthen*** [adv.: ἔσωθεν <2081>]; **from *esō*: within, and suffix *then*: from a place** ► Refs.: Matt. 7:15; 23:25, 27, 28; Mark 7:21, 23; Luke 11:7, 39, 40; 2 Cor. 4:16; 7:5; Rev. 4:8; 5:1; 11:2. ¶ ‡

WITHOUT – 1 ***aneu*** [adv.: ἄνευ <427>] ► **Not with** > A sparrow will not fall to the ground without God the Father, i.e., apart from His will (Matt. 10:29). Some husbands may be won without a word by the behavior of their wife (1 Pet. 3:1). Christians should be hospitable to one another without murmuring (1 Pet. 4:9). Other ref.: Mark 13:2 in some mss. ¶

2 ***ater*** [adv.: ἄτερ <817>] ► **Not with, not having** > The word is found in Luke 22:35. It is transl. "in the absence of" in Luke 22:6. ¶ ‡

3 ***parektos*** [adv.: παρεκτός <3924>]; **from *para*: near, and *ektos*: at the exterior; lit.: from outside ► Out of the ordinary, exceptional, outward** > Besides those things that were without {everything else, external things, other things}, Paul was pressed by his solicitude for all the churches (2 Cor. 11:28). Other refs.: Matt. 5:32; Acts 26:29; see EXCEPT <3924>. ¶

– [4] Mark 7:15; Rev. 11:2 → OUTWARD <1855> [5] John 15:5 → apart from → APART <5565>.

WITHSTAND – [1] ***anthistēmi*** [verb: ἀνθίστημι <436>]; **from *anti*: against, and *histēmi*: to stand ► To rise up against, to resist, to oppose >** Alexander greatly withstood the words of Paul (2 Tim. 4:15). All other refs.: RESIST <436>.
– [2] Luke 21:15 → REPLY (verb) <471> [3] Acts 11:17 → FORBID <2967> [4] Rev. 6:17 → STAND (verb) <2476>.

WITNESS (noun)[1] – [1] ***marturia*** [fem. noun: μαρτυρία <3141>]; **from *martureō*: see [3] ► Report of a person concerning what he has seen or heard, declaration; also transl.: record, report, testimony >** John the Baptist bore witness concerning Jesus (John 1:7a, 19; 5:32b, 36a). No one received the witness of Jesus (John 3:11b, 32b). He who had received the testimony of Jesus has set his seal that God is true (John 3:33). If Jesus bore witness concerning Himself, His witness was not true (John 5:31b); He knew that if another should bear witness (*martureō*) of Him, his witness (*marturia*) would be true (John 5:32b). Jesus did not receive witness from man (John 5:34). He had a witness greater than that of John (John 5:36a). Even if the Pharisees maintained the contrary, the witness that Jesus bore concerning Himself was true (John 8:13b, 14b). According to the law, the testimony of two men is true (John 8:17). The witness of John regarding Jesus was true (John 19:35b; 21:24b). The Greek word is used in regard to Paul (Acts 22:18 {testimony}). The overseer must have a good testimony from those without (1 Tim. 3:7). John was exiled to Patmos for the testimony of Jesus Christ (Rev. 1:9). Other refs.: Mark 14:55 {evidence}, 56 {statement}, 59; Luke 22:71; Titus 1:13; 1 John 5:9a–c, 10a, b, 11; 3 John 12c; Rev. 1:2b; 6:9; 11:7; 12:11, 17; 19:10a, b; 20:4. ¶

[2] ***marturion*** [neut. noun: μαρτύριον <3142>]; **from *martureō*: see [3] ► Evidence which is given, proof; also transl.: testimony >** With great power the apostles gave witness of the resurrection of the Lord Jesus (Acts 4:33). The Israelites had the tabernacle of the testimony in the desert (Acts 7:44). The testimony of Christ had been confirmed in the Corinthians (1 Cor. 1:6); Paul had announced the testimony of God to them (2:1). Timothy was not to be ashamed of the testimony of the Lord (2 Tim. 1:8). Other refs.: Matt. 8:4; 10:18; 24:14; Mark 1:44; 6:11; 13:9; Luke 5:14; 9:5; 21:13; 2 Cor. 1:12; 2 Thes. 1:10; 1 Tim. 2:6; Heb. 3:5; Jas. 5:3; Rev. 15:5. ¶

[3] **to bear witness: *martureō*** [verb: μαρτυρέω <3140>]; **from *martus*: witness ► To testify, to declare what one has seen or heard >** John bears witness and declares the eternal life that was with the Father (1 John 1:2). All other refs.: TESTIFY <3140>, WITNESS (noun)[2] <3140>, WITNESS (verb) <3140>.

[4] **to bear witness: *summartureō*** [verb: συμμαρτυρέω <4828>]; **from *sun*: together, and *martureō*: see [3] ► To add testimony; also transl.: to confirm, to testify with >** Those of the nations show the work of the law written in their hearts, their conscience also bearing witness (Rom. 2:15). The Spirit Himself bears witness with the spirit of Christians, that they are children of God (Rom. 8:16). Paul's conscience bore witness with him in the Holy Spirit (Rom. 9:1). Other ref.: Rev. 22:18 {to warn} in some mss. ¶

[5] **to bear witness with: *sunepimartureō*** [verb: συνεπιμαρτυρέω <4901>]; **from *sun*: together, *epi*: upon, and *martureō*: see [3] ► To join together to attest to something >** God bore witness with those who announced the word, both by signs and wonders, and various miracles and distributions of the Holy Spirit, according to His will (Heb. 2:4). ¶

[6] **to bear false witness, to give false witness: *pseudomartureō*** [verb: ψευδομαρτυρέω <5576>]; **from *pseudēs*: false, and *martureō*: see [3] ► To give testimony which is not true, to perjure; also transl.: to give false testimony, to testify falsely >** Jesus says not to bear false witness (Matt. 19:18; Mark 10:19; Luke 18:20). Many bore false witness against Jesus, but their testimony

did not agree (Mark 14:56); certain people bore false witness against Jesus (v. 57). ¶

7 **without witness:** ***amarturos*** [adj.: ἀμάρτυρος <267>]; **from *a*: neg., and *martus*: witness ▶ Without testimony, without attestation** > God did not leave Himself without witness, in that He did good and gave rain from heaven and fruitful seasons (Acts 14:17). ¶

– 8 Matt. 15:19; 26:59 → false witness → false testimony → TESTIMONY <5577> 9 Mark 15:4 → to bear witness against → to testify against → TESTIFY <2649> 10 Acts 2:22 → to bear witness → APPROVE <584>.

WITNESS (noun)² – 1 ***martus*** [masc. or fem. noun: μάρτυς <3144>] **▶ Person who can affirm that he has seen or heard a certain thing** > The term is used in regard to God (Rom. 1:9; 2 Cor. 1:23; Phil. 1:8; 1 Thes. 2:5, 10) and Jesus Christ (Rev. 1:5; 3:14). It is also used in regard to the disciples of Jesus (Luke 24:48; Acts 1:8, 22; 2:32; 3:15; 5:32; 10:39, 41; 13:31), Paul (Acts 22:15; 26:16), Stephen (Acts 22:20; *protomartus* in some mss.: first witness, first martyr), the Thessalonians (1 Thes. 2:10), two or three who are to be present in the event of an accusation against an elder (1 Tim. 5:19), those before whom Timothy had confessed the good confession (1 Tim. 6:12), those in whose presence Timothy had heard the words of Paul (2 Tim. 2:2), those who surrounded the author of the Epistle to the Hebrews (Heb. 12:1), Peter (1 Pet. 5:1), Antipas (Rev. 2:13), those who will prophesy during the great tribulation (Rev. 11:3), and the witnesses of Jesus (Rev. 17:6). By the mouth of two or three witnesses every matter shall be established (Matt. 18:16; 2 Cor. 13:1; Heb. 10:28). The high priest said he had no further need of witnesses against Jesus (Matt. 26:65; Mark 14:63). False witnesses were presented against Stephen (Acts 6:13; 7:58). ¶

2 **false witness:** ***pseudomartus*** [masc. noun: ψευδόμαρτυς <5575>]; **from *pseudēs*: false, and *martus*: see 1; also spelled; *pseudomartur* ▶ Person who lies when presented as a witness** > False witnesses came forward against Jesus (Matt. 26:60a, b). Other ref.: 1 Cor. 15:15. ¶

3 **to be witness:** ***martureō*** [verb: μαρτυρέω <3140>]; **from *martus*: see 1 ▶ To report what one has seen or heard, to declare something** > The scribes and the Pharisees were witnesses against themselves that they were the sons of those who had killed the prophets (Matt. 23:31 {to bear witness, to testify against}). All other refs.: TESTIFY <3140>, WITNESS (noun)¹ <3140>, WITNESS (verb) <3140>.

– 4 Mark 13:9 → as witnesses → lit.: as a witness, as a testimony → WITNESS¹ <3142> 5 John 8:17 → two witnesses → lit.: two men 6 Acts 2:40 → to bear witness → TESTIFY <1263>.

WITNESS (verb) – 1 ***epopteuō*** [verb: ἐποπτεύω <2029>]; **from *epoptēs*: eye witness, which is from *epi*: upon, and *horaō*: to see ▶ To observe attentively, to contemplate; also transl.: to observe, to behold, to see** > The Gentiles witness the good works of Christians (1 Pet. 2:12). Having witnessed the behavior of their wives, unbelieving husbands may be gained without the word (1 Pet. 3:2). ¶

2 ***martureō*** [verb: μαρτυρέω <3140>]; **from *martus*: witness, a person bearing witness ▶ To report on what one has seen or heard, to declare something, to have an honorable report, to substantiate by word or deed; also transl.: to bear witness, to testify** > John the Baptist came to witness concerning the light (John 1:7b, 8, 15); he has borne witness to the truth (John 5:33). His disciples bore witness that he had said he was not the Christ, but that he had been sent before Him (John 3:28). Jesus had no need that anyone should testify concerning man (John 2:25). He said that we bear witness of that which we have seen (John 3:11a). Having come out of heaven, He testified of what He had seen and heard (John 3:32a). Many Samaritans believed on Jesus because of the Samaritan woman who had borne witness (John 4:39). Jesus bore witness that a prophet has no honor in his own country (John 4:44). If He bore witness concerning Himself, His witness was

not true (John 5:31a); another bore witness concerning Him, and He knew that the witness that He bore concerning Himself was true (John 5:32a). The works that Jesus did bore witness concerning Him, that the Father had sent Him (John 5:36b); the Father who had sent Him had borne witness concerning Him (v. 37). The Scriptures bore witness concerning Jesus (John 5:39), as likewise did all the prophets (Acts 10:43). Jesus bore witness concerning the world, that its works are evil (John 7:7). Even if the Pharisees maintained the contrary, the witness that Jesus bore concerning Himself was true (John 8:13a, 14a). Jesus bore witness concerning Himself, and the Father also bore witness concerning Jesus (John 8:18a, b). The works that Jesus did bore witness concerning Him (John 10:25). The crowd bore Him witness (John 12:17). Jesus testified in regard to Judas (John 13:21). The Holy Spirit would bear witness concerning Jesus (John 15:26), as also did His disciples (v. 27). He had come to bear witness to the truth (John 18:37). John bore witness of Jesus (John 19:35a; 21:24a). The whole nation of the Jews had borne witness to Cornelius (Acts 10:22). God bore witness concerning David (Acts 13:22). The Lord gave witness to the word of His grace by the miracles that He did by the hands of Paul and Barnabas (Acts 14:3). God bore witness to the nations {was borne witness to} (Acts 15:8). Timothy had a good reputation of the brothers (Acts 16:2); Ananias had a good testimony (Acts 22:12). It was necessary that Paul should bear witness at Rome (Acts 23:11b). He had witnessed concerning Jesus (Acts 26:22), and concerning God that He had raised the Christ (1 Cor. 15:15). A widow to whom witness was borne concerning her good works {having a reputation for her good works} was to be put on the list for the care of the church (1 Tim. 5:10). Jesus has witnessed the good confession before Pontius Pilate (1 Tim. 6:13); see CONFESSION <3671>. By his sacrifice, Abel obtained witness of being righteous, God bearing testimony to his gifts (Heb. 11:4a, b). Enoch obtained the witness that he had pleased God (Heb. 11:5). Other refs.: Luke 4:22; 11:48; John 1:32, 34; 3:26; 18:23; Acts 6:3; 26:5; Rom. 3:21; 10:2; 2 Cor. 8:3; Gal. 4:15; Col. 4:13; 1 Thes. 2:11; Heb. 7:8, 17; 10:15; 11:2, 39; 1 John 1:2; 5:6–10; 3 John 3, 6, 12a, b; Rev. 1:2a; 22:16, 20. All other refs.: TESTIFY <3140>, WITNESS (noun)[1] <3140>, WITNESS (noun)[2] <3140>.

– **3** Matt. 24:14; 1 Tim. 2:6 → lit.: to give witness → WITNESS (noun)[1] <3142> **4** Matt. 26:62; 27:13; Mark 14:60; 15:4 → to witness against → to testify against → TESTIFY <2649> **5** Acts 20:26; Gal. 5:3 → TESTIFY <3143> **6** Acts 23:11; 28:23 → to witness, to witness solemnly → TESTIFY <1263>.

WITNESSING – Matt. 15:19 → false witnessing → false testimony → TESTIMONY <5577>.

WOE! – ***ouai*** [interj.: οὐαί <3759>] ► **a. Interj. denoting pain or displeasure, used mainly to denounce or imprecate doom** > The Lord uses this word to denounce Chorazin and Bethsaida (Matt. 11:21a, b; Luke 10:13a, b), the world and that man by whom the offense comes (Matt. 18:7a, b), the scribes and Pharisees (Matt. 23:13, 15, 16, 23, 25, 27, 29), the Pharisees (Luke 11:42–44), the lawyers (Luke 11:46, 47, 52), Judas (Matt. 26:24; Mark 14:21; Luke 22:22), the rich (Luke 6:24), those who are full and those who laugh now (Luke 6:25a, b), those of whom all men speak well (Luke 6:26), and him through whom offenses come (Luke 17:1). Paul said: "woe is me if I do not preach the gospel" (1 Cor. 9:16). Jude uses this word also (Jude 11). An eagle (some mss.: angel) says with a loud voice "woe" to those who live on the earth (Rev. 8:13a–c). A loud voice says: Woe to the inhabitants of the earth and the sea (lit.: Woe to the earth and the sea) (Rev. 12:12). This word is used when the Lord pitied women who will be pregnant during the great tribulation (Matt. 24:19; Mark 13:17; Luke 21:23). The word is used as a noun in Rev. 9:12a, b and 11:14a, b. **b. An exclamation of grief** > This interj. is used six times in regard to Babylon the great (Rev. 18:10a, b, 16a, b, 19a, b). ¶

WOLF – ***lukos*** [masc. noun: λύκος <3074>] ▶ **Wild carnivorous mammal which resembles a dog; also used figur.** > False prophets are compared to ravenous wolves (Matt. 7:15). Jesus sent out His disciples like sheep in the midst of wolves (Matt. 10:16; Luke 10:3). The wolf seeks to catch and scatter the sheep (John 10:12a, b). After Paul's departure, savage wolves that would not spare the flock would attack the church (Acts 20:29). ¶

WOMAN – 1 ***gunē*** [fem. noun: γυνή <1135>] ▶ **Person of the feminine gender, female spouse; a term of respect or affection when used in direct address** > Jesus addressed a woman of Canaan and His mother as "woman" (Matt. 15:28; John 2:4). God sent His Son, born of a woman (Gal. 4:4). Each one is to love his woman (or: wife) as himself, and the woman (or: wife) is to respect her husband (Eph. 5:33a, b). The church is the bride, the wife (or: woman) of the Lamb (Rev. 21:9). *

2 ***thēleia*** [adj. used as noun: θήλεια <2337a>]; **fem. of *thēlus*: of the feminine gender** ▶ **Female, which belongs to the feminine gender** > This term is used in Rom. 1:26, 27. ¶

– 3 1 Tim. 4:7 → fit only for woman → old wives' → OLD <1126> 4 1 Tim. 5:2 → elder woman → ELDER <4245> 5 Titus 2:3 → AGED WOMAN <4247> 6 1 Pet. 3:7 → FEMALE <1134>.

WOMB – 1 ***gastēr*** [fem. noun: γαστήρ <1064>] ▶ **Uterus** > The Greek term is used in regard to Mary in Luke 1:31. All other refs.: CHILD <1064>, GLUTTON <1064>.

2 ***koilia*** [fem. noun: κοιλία <2836>]; **from *koilos*: hollow** ▶ **Interior of the human body where the vital organs are found; most often: matrix of the woman; also transl.: belly, stomach** > Nicodemus asked: How can a man enter a second time into the womb of his mother and be born? (John 3:4). The Greek term is also used in regard to mothers (Matt. 19:12; Luke 23:29), Elizabeth (Luke 1:15, 41, 44), Mary (Luke 1:42; 2:21; 11:27), and the mother of Paul (Gal. 1:15). Elsewhere, the Greek word is used in regard to a huge fish (Matt. 12:40). He who believes in Jesus, rivers of living water shall flow out of his belly {heart, innermost being} (John 7:38). Paul speaks of those who serve their own belly {appetites} (Rom. 16:18), whose god is the belly (Phil. 3:19). The little book would fill John's belly with bitterness (Rev. 10:9), which came to pass (v. 10). Other refs.: Matt. 15:17 {belly}; Mark 7:19 {belly}; Luke 15:16 in some mss.; Acts 3:2; 14:8. Other refs.: 1 Cor. 6:13a, b; see STOMACH <2836>. ¶

3 ***mētra*** [fem. noun: μήτρα <3388>]; **from *mētēr*: mother** ▶ **Common name for a woman's uterus, matrix; used also of a uterus that had been closed** > Every male who opens the womb, i.e., every firstborn male, will be called holy to the Lord according to the law of the O.T. (Luke 2:23). Abraham did not consider the deadness of Sarah's womb, but believed God (Rom. 4:19). ¶

WONDER (adj. and noun) – 1 ***thaumastos*** [adj.: θαυμαστός <2298>]; **from *thaumazō*: to wonder, to be astonished, which is from *thauma*: admiration, astonishment** ▶ **Strange, unusual** > It is no wonder {no marvel, not wonderful} that false apostles, deceitful workers, transform themselves into apostles of Christ, for Satan himself transforms himself into an angel of light (2 Cor. 11:14); other mss. have *thauma*: an object of wonder, of admiration. Other refs.: Matt. 21:42; Mark 12:11; John 9:30; 1 Pet. 2:9; Rev. 15:1, 3; see MARVELOUS <2298>. ¶

2 ***teras*** [neut. noun: τέρας <5059>] ▶ **Something strange and marvelous, extraordinary phenomenon appealing to the imagination; usually in the plur. and often found in the expr. "signs and wonders"** > False christs and false prophets showed wonders {miracles} (Matt. 24:24; Mark 13:22). Jesus spoke of signs and wonders for those who will not believe (John 4:48). God will show wonders (Acts 2:19).

Jesus was approved by God by miracles and wonders (Acts 2:22). The apostles did many wonders and signs (Acts 2:43; 4:30; 5:12). Stephen wrought wonders and great signs (Acts 6:8). Moses wrought wonders and signs (Acts 7:36). The Lord gave signs and wonders to be done by the hands of Paul and Barnabas (Acts 14:3; 15:12; also Rom. 15:19 {miracle}; 2 Cor. 12:12). The antichrist will show wonders of falsehood (2 Thes. 2:9). God bore witness by signs and wonders by those who had heard Jesus (Heb. 2:4). ¶
– 3 Matt. 7:22 → MIRACLE <1411> 4 Matt. 21:15 → wonderful work → WONDERFUL <2297> 5 Mark 9:15 → to be overwhelmed with wonder → AMAZED (BE) <1568> 6 Acts 2:11 → wonderful work → WONDERFUL <3167> 7 Rev. 13:3 → to fill with wonder → WONDER (verb) <2296> 8 Rev. 13:13 → SIGN <4592> 9 Rev. 17:6 → AMAZEMENT <2295>.

WONDER (verb) – 1 ***thaumazō*** [verb: θαυμάζω <2296>]; **from *thauma*: object of surprise, of astonishment ▶ To be amazed, to be astonished, to marvel** > In John's vision, the whole world wondered and followed the beast (Rev. 13:3). John wondered with great wonder (Rev. 17:6). Other refs.: Matt. 8:27; 15:31; 21:20; 22:22; 27:14; Mark 5:20; 12:17; 15:44; Luke 1:21, 63; 2:18, 33; 4:22; 7:9; 8:25; 9:43; 11:14, 38; 20:26; 24:12, 41; John 3:7; 4:27; 5:20, 28; 7:15, 21; Acts 2:7; 4:13; 7:31; 13:41; Gal. 1:6; 2 Thes. 1:10; 1 John 3:13; Rev. 17:7, 8. All other refs.: ADMIRATION <2296>, ADMIRE <2296>, MARVEL (verb) <2296>.
– 2 Luke 1:29; 3:15 → REASON (verb) <1260> 3 Luke 24:4; Acts 5:24; 10:17 → PERPLEXED (BE) <1280> 4 Rev. 17:6 → to wonder greatly → to marvel with amazement → AMAZEMENT <2295>.

WONDERFUL – 1 **wonderful works: *ta megaleia*; wonderful: *megaleios*** [adj. used as noun: μεγαλεῖος <3167>]; **from *megas*: great ▶ Great deeds, great things; used in regard to God's glory and power** > The Mighty one had done to Mary great things (Luke 1:49). People from various dialects were hearing the apostles speaking the wonderful works {great things, mighty deeds, wonders} of God (Acts 2:11). ¶
2 **wonderful thing: *thaumasios*** [adj. used as noun: θαυμάσιος <2297>]; **from *thaumazō*: to admire, which is from *thauma*: admiration ▶ Admirable, astonishing, extraordinary (thing)** > The scribes were indignant when they saw the wonderful things {the wonders} that Jesus did and the children crying out in the temple (Matt. 21:15). ¶
– 3 Matt. 7:22 → wonderful work → MIRACLE <1411> 4 Matt. 21:42; Mark 12:11; John 9:30; 2 Cor. 11:14; 1 Pet. 2:9; Rev. 15:1, 3 → MARVELOUS <2298> 5 2 Cor. 11:14 → WONDER (adj. and noun) <2298>.

WONDERING – Acts 3:11 → greatly wondering → greatly amazed → AMAZED <1569>.

WONT (BE) – 1 Mark 10:1 → ACCUSTOMED (BE) <1486> 2 Luke 22:39 → CUSTOM <1485> 3 Acts 16:13 → to be wont to be made → to be the custom → CUSTOM <3543>.

WOOD – 1 ***xulon*** [neut. noun: ξύλον <3586>]; **from *xuō*: to scrape, to plane ▶ Material from the trunk or main branches of a tree used to build or fabricate an object** > The word is used in 1 Cor. 3:12 and Rev. 18:12. All other refs.: STAVE <3586>, STOCKS <3586>, TREE <3586>.
2 **of wood: *xulinos*** [adj.: ξύλινος <3585>]; **from *xulon*: see 1 ▶ Made of wood; also transl.: wooden** > The word is used in 2 Tim. 2:20; Rev. 9:20. ¶
– 3 Jas. 3:5 → FOREST <5208>.

WOODEN – 2 Tim. 2:20; Rev. 9:20 → of wood → WOOD <3585>.

WOOL – ***erion*** [neut. noun: ἔριον <2053>] ▶ **Fleece of a sheep or some other animal (e.g., goat)** > The term is used in Heb. 9:19 {scarlet wool} and Rev. 1:14 {white wool}. ¶

WORD – 1 ***logos*** [masc. noun: λόγος <3056>] ▶ **The expression of thought, not the mere name of an object** > The term describes a conception or idea (e.g., Luke 7:7; 1 Cor. 14:19), and is used in regard to God (e.g., John 15:25; Rom. 9:9; Gal. 5:14; Heb. 4:12) and to Christ (e.g., Matt. 24:35; John 2:22; 4:41; 14:23; 15:20). The expr. "the word of the Lord," i.e., the revealed will of God, (very frequently found in the O.T.), is used of direct revelation given by Christ (1 Thes. 4:15) and of the gospel (Acts 8:25; 13:49; 15:35, 36; 16:32; 19:10; 1 Thes. 1:8; 2 Thes. 3:1). In this respect, the word is the message from the Lord, delivered with His authority and made effective by His power (Acts 10:36). The term is also used in regard to the good tidings in the following verses: Acts 13:26; 14:3; 15:7; 1 Cor. 1:18; 2 Cor. 2:17; 4:2; 5:19; 6:7; Eph. 1:13; Phil. 2:16; Col. 1:5; Heb. 5:13. Sometimes the term describes the totality of the declarations of God (e.g., Mark 7:13; John 10:35; Gal. 6:6; Rev. 1:2, 9). It is also used in regard to a discourse or to instructions (e.g., Acts 2:40; 1 Cor. 2:13; 12:8; 2 Cor. 1:18; 1 Thes. 1:5; 2 Thes. 2:15; Heb. 6:1) and doctrine (e.g., Matt. 13:20; Col. 3:16; 1 Tim. 4:6; 2 Tim. 1:13; Titus 1:9; 1 John 2:7. The Word is a name of the Son of God: In the beginning was the Word, and the Word was with God, and the Word was God (John 1:1); the Word became flesh, and dwelled among us (v. 14). (After W. E. Vine). Jesus answered the woman of Canaan not one word (Matt. 15:23). No one was able to answer Jesus a word (Matt. 22:46). The brothers among the Gentiles had been troubled with the words of some from among the brothers in Jerusalem (Acts 15:24); Judas and Silas exhorted the former with many words {a lengthy message} (v. 32). People listened to Paul until the word "Gentiles" (Acts 22:22). The Corinthians were to speak words easy to understand (1 Cor. 14:9). Other refs.: see entries in Lexicon at <3056>.

2 ***rhēma*** [neut. noun: ῥῆμα <4487>]**; from *rheō*: to speak** ▶ **That which is spoken, what is expressed in speech or in writing** > The Greek term is used (collectively) in the sing. to describe something that is said (e.g., Matt. 12:36; 2 Cor. 12:4 {unspeakable things; lit.: unspeakable words}; Heb. 12:19a). In the plur., it describes a discourse (e.g., John 3:34; 8:20; Acts 2:14; 6:11, 13; 13:42; 26:25; Rom. 10:18; 2 Pet. 3:2; Jude 17). It is used of the glad tidings (Acts 11:14; Rom. 10:8a, b, 17, 18; 1 Pet. 1:25a, b), a statement or instruction (e.g., Matt. 26:75; Luke 1:38; Acts 11:16), and a powerful statement of God (Heb. 11:3). (After W. E. Vine.) Jesus answered Pilate not one word (Matt. 27:14). While Peter was still speaking the words (*rēma*) about the work accomplished by the Lord Jesus, the Holy Spirit fell upon all those who heard the word (*logos*) (Acts 10:44a). By the mouth of two or three witnesses every word {fact, matter} will be established (2 Cor. 13:1). No word {nothing} from God will ever fail (Luke 1:37). *

3 **persuasive word: *pithanologia*** [fem. noun: πιθανολογία <4086>]**; from *pitanologos*: speaking persuasively, which is from *pithanos*: persuasive, plausible, and *logos*: see** 1 ▶ **Such words are aimed at convincing by arguments, rather than by demonstration** > The Colossians were not to be deceived by persuasive words {enticing words, persuasive speech, persuasive arguments, fine-sounding arguments} (Col. 2:4). ¶

4 **a few words: *suntomōs*** [adv.: συντόμως <4935>]**; from *suntemnō*: to cut short, to shorten** ▶ **Briefly, concisely** > Tertullus prayed the governor to hear a few words from him (Acts 24:4). ¶

5 **boastful, swelling word: *huperonkos*** [adj. used as noun: ὑπέρογκος <5246>]**; from *huper*: above, and *onkos*: weight** ▶ **Boastful, insolent word or speech** > Peter and Jude wrote about those speaking great swelling words {highflown words, arrogant words, arrogantly} {those boasting about themselves} (2 Pet. 2:18; Jude 16). ¶

– 6 Matt. 2:8; 14:12; 28:11; Luke 7:18, 22; 14:21; John 4:51; 20:18 → to bring word, to bring back word → REPORT (verb) <518> 7 Matt. 27:19 → to send word → to send, saying → SAY <3004> 8 Matt. 28:8–10; Mark 16:10, 13 → to bring word, to take word → TELL <518>

9 Acts 7:38; Rom. 3:2; Heb. 5:12; 1 Pet. 4:11 → ORACLE <3051> 10 Acts 21:31 → TIDINGS <5334> 11 Rom. 9:28 → WORK <3056> 12 Rom. 16:18 → good word, smooth word → SMOOTH <5542> 13 Eph. 3:3 → in few words → lit.: in brief (*en oligō*) 14 1 Tim. 6:4 → argument over words, strife of words → ARGUMENT <3055> 15 2 Tim. 2:14 → to strive about words → STRIVE <3054> 16 Heb. 4:7 in some mss. → in the words already quoted → lit.: He has previously said → SAY <4280> 17 Heb. 13:22b: in few words → lit.: in brief (*dia bracheōn*) 18 1 Pet. 2:2 → of the word → INTELLECTUAL <3050>.

WORDLESS – Rom. 8:26 → which cannot be uttered → UTTER (verb) <215>.

WORK (noun) – 1 ***ergon*** [neut. noun: ἔργον <2041>]**; from *ergō*: to work ▶ Action, task, result of working; also transl.: deed** > This word is used in regard to the Lord Jesus Christ (Matt. 11:2; Luke 24:19; John 7:3, 21; 10:25, 32a, b, 33, 38; 14:10–12; 15:24; 1 Cor. 15:58; 16:10; Heb. 1:10; Rev. 15:3), God the Father (John 4:34; 5:20, 36a, b; 9:4; 10:37; 17:4), God (John 6:28, 29; 9:3; Acts 13:41a, b; Rom. 14:20; Eph. 2:10; Phil. 1:6; Heb. 2:7; 4:3, 4), and the Holy Spirit (Acts 13:2; Heb. 3:9). The Lord is like a man who has given to each one his work (Mark 13:34). It is also used in regard to believers in the Lord (Matt. 5:16; John 3:21; 2 Cor. 9:8; Gal. 6:4; Col. 1:10; 3:17; 1 Tim. 2:10; 5:10a, b, 25; 6:18; 2 Tim. 1:9; Titus 2:14; 3:1, 8, 14; Heb. 4:10; 6:10; 10:24; 13:21; Jas. 1:25; 3:13; 1 Pet. 2:12; Rev. 14:13; 22:12), the scribes and the Pharisees (Matt. 23:3, 5), a woman (Matt. 26:10; Mark 14:6), the Israelites (Luke 11:48; Acts 7:41), men in general (John 3:19, 20; Rom. 2:6, 7, 15; 13:3; Col. 1:21; Titus 1:16a, b; Heb. 9:14; 1 Pet. 1:17; Rev. 20:12, 13), the world (John 7:7), Abraham, (John 8:39), Satan (John 8:41; 1 John 3:8), Peter (Acts 5:38), Dorcas (Acts 9:36), Paul (Acts 14:26; 15:38; Rom. 15:18; 2 Tim. 4:18), repentance (Acts 26:20; Heb. 6:1), the law (Rom. 3:20, 27, 28; Gal. 2:16a–c; 3:2, 5, 10), justification (Rom. 4:2, 6; Jas. 2:21, 24, 25), the principle of works (Rom. 9:11, 32; 11:6; Eph. 2:9; Titus 3:5), darkness (Rom. 13:12; Eph. 5:11), the Christian's works (i.e., his works) to be tried by fire (1 Cor. 3:13a, b, 14, 15), the Corinthians (1 Cor. 9:1), the ministers of Satan (2 Cor. 11:15), the flesh (Gal. 5:19), the ministry (Eph. 4:12; Phil. 2:30; 1 Thes. 5:13; 1 Tim. 3:1; 2 Tim. 2:21; 3:17; 4:5), faith (1 Thes. 1:3; 2 Thes. 1:11; 2:17; Jas. 2:14, 17, 18a–c, 20, 22a, b, 26), Alexander (2 Tim. 4:14), Titus (Titus 2:7), patience (Jas. 1:4), the earth (2 Pet. 3:10), Cain (1 John 3:12), one who does not bring the doctrine of Christ (2 John 11), Diotrephes (3 John 10), the ungodly (Jude 15), men who did not repent (Rev. 9:20; 16:11), and Babylon (Rev. 18:6). The word is often used in the letters John wrote to the seven churches (Rev. 2:2, 5, 6, 19a, b, 22, 23, 26; 3:1, 2, 8, 15). Other refs. in some mss.: Acts 15:18; Rev. 2:9, 13. Other refs.: Acts 7:22; 1 Cor. 5:2; 2 Cor. 10:11; 2 Pet. 2:8; see DEED <2041>, ACTION <2041>. ¶

2 ***logos*** [masc. noun: λόγος <3056>] ▶ **Matter, subject** > Isaiah cried out concerning a work {word, matter} that the Lord will finish and cut short (Rom. 9:28). Other refs.: WORD <3056>.

3 ***pragma*** [neut. noun: πρᾶγμα <4229>]**; from *prassō*: to accomplish, to execute ▶ Accomplished matter, action** > Where we have envying and strife, there is confusion and every evil work {thing} (Jas. 3:16). All other refs.: BUSINESS <4229>, MATTER <4229>, THING <4229>.

4 ***praxis*** [fem. noun: πρᾶξις <4234>]**; from *prassō*: see 3 ▶ Action, conduct, behavior viewed as incomplete, in progress; the sum of one's doings** > The Son of Man will reward each according to his works {his deeds, his doings, what he has done} (Matt. 16:27). All other refs.: DEED <4234>, FUNCTION (noun) <4234>.

– 5 Matt. 7:22; 11:20, 21, 23; 13:54, 58; 14:2; Mark 6:2, 5, 14; 9:39; Luke 10:13; 19:37; Acts 2:22 → mighty work, wonderful work → MIRACLE <1411> 6 Matt. 14:2; Mark 6:14; Rom. 7:5; 1 Cor. 12:6; 2 Thes. 2:7 → to be at work → WORK (verb) <1754> 7 Matt. 25:16 → to put to work →

TRADE (verb) <2038> **8** Luke 13:14; John 6:30; 9:4; 2 Thes. 3:12 → to do work, to do the work → lit.: to work, to work the works → WORK (verb) <2038> **9** Acts 2:11 → wonderful work → WONDERFUL <3167> **10** Acts 13:25 → COURSE <1408> **11** Acts 19:25 → BUSINESS <2039> **12** Acts 27:16 → with much work → with difficulty → DIFFICULTY <3433> **13** Rom. 7:23 → at work → lit.: existing → EXIST <1510> **14** Rom. 15:17 → in my work → lit.: in the things **15** Rom. 16:23 → director of public works → CHAMBERLAIN <3623> **16** 1 Cor. 16:16 → to join, to help in the work → WORK (verb) <4903> **17** 2 Cor. 6:5; 10:15; Rev. 2:2 → hard work, work → LABOR (noun) <2873> **18** 2 Cor. 8:10 → "this work" added in Engl. **19** Col. 4:17 → SERVICE <1248> **20** 1 Tim. 1:4 → DISPENSATION <3622> **21** Titus 2:5 → diligent in home work → DILIGENT <3626>.

WORK (verb) – **1** ***energeō*** [verb: ἐνεργέω <1754>]; **from *energēs*: operative, active, which is from *en*: in, and *ergon*: work ▶ To act, to produce an effect; also transl.: to operate >** The verb is used in regard to the works of power that displayed their force {were at work, were showing themselves forth} in Jesus, whom Herod believed to be John the Baptist risen from the dead (Matt. 14:2); Mark 6:14 {to show forth}). When the Christians were in the flesh, the motions of sins did work in their members (Rom. 7:5). The same God works all things in all, in relation to spiritual gifts (1 Cor. 12:6); the same Spirit works these things (v. 11). The salvation of the Corinthians was worked {was effectual, was effective} in the endurance of the same sufferings that Paul also suffered (2 Cor. 1:6). Death worked in Paul, but life in the Corinthians (2 Cor. 4:12). He who worked {wrought effectually, effectively} in Peter for the apostleship of the circumcision worked {was mighty, wrought effectively} also in Paul toward the Gentiles (Gal. 2:8a, b). God worked miracles among the Galatians (Gal. 3:5). He works all things according to the counsel of His own will (Eph. 1:11). He worked according to the working of the might of His strength in Christ in raising Him from among the dead (Eph. 1:20). A spirit now works in the sons of disobedience (Eph. 2:2). The power of God works in Christians (Eph. 3:20). God works in Christians both to will and to work {the willing and the working} (Phil. 2:13a, b). Paul combated according to the working of God that worked in him in power (Col. 1:29). God's word worked {effectually, effectively worked} in the Thessalonians who believed (1 Thes. 2:13). The mystery of lawlessness already works {is already at work} (2 Thes. 2:7). Other refs.: Gal. 5:6; Jas. 5:16 (to act); see WORKING (verb) <1754>, EFFECTIVE <1754>. ¶

2 ***ergazomai*** [verb: ἐργάζομαι <2038>]; **from *ergon*: work ▶ To perform an activity, to undertake a task, to devote sustained effort; also transl.: to labor >** A man sent his son to work in his vineyard (Matt. 21:28). According to the ruler of the synagogue, one should not work on the Sabbath, and Jesus should not have healed on that day (Luke 13:14). Jesus and His Father work (John 5:17a, b). Jesus said to work for the food that endures to eternal life (John 6:27). The crowd asked Jesus what they should do that they might work the works of God (John 6:28). The crowd asked Jesus what work He would perform (lit.: to what worked He) that they might believe Him (John 6:30). The night is coming when no one can work (John 9:4). Paul worked with Aquila and Priscilla (Acts 18:3 {to have wrought}). He worked with his own hands (1 Cor. 4:12). He asked if it were he alone and Barnabas who had no right to refrain from working (1 Cor. 9:6). He had preached the gospel to the Thessalonians, working night and day so as not to be a burden to any of them (1 Thes. 2:9; 2 Thes. 3:8); he exhorted them to work with their own hands (1 Thes. 4:11). He had enjoined this, that if anyone was unwilling to work, neither should he eat (2 Thes. 3:10); he had learned that some were not working at all, but were busy-bodies (v. 11 {to be busy}), whom he exhorted to work quietly {to settle down} (v. 12). John did not want to lose what he had worked for {accomplished, wrought}

(2 John 8). Other refs.: Rom. 4:4, 5. All other refs.: see entries in Lexicon at <2038>.

3 ***katergazomai*** [verb: κατεργάζομαι <2716>]; **from *kata*: intens., and *ergazomai*: see 2 ► a. To accomplish, to produce as result >** Sin has worked {has effected, has produced} death through what is good (the law) (Rom. 7:13). The momentary and light affliction of Christians works {produces, is achieving} for them in surpassing measure an eternal weight of glory (2 Cor. 4:17). Grief according to God works {brings, produces} repentance to salvation, but the grief of the world works {brings, produces} death (2 Cor. 7:10a, b). The signs of an apostle were worked {accomplished, done, performed, wrought} among the Corinthians (2 Cor. 12:12). **b. To produce, to bring to a successful conclusion through performing an activity >** Paul tells the Philippians to work out their own salvation with fear and trembling (Phil. 2:12). All other refs.: see entries in Lexicon at <2716>.

4 **to work together, to work with: *sunergeō*** [verb: συνεργέω <4903>]; **from *sunergos*: fellow worker, which is from *sun*: together, and *ergon*: work ► To act together for a purpose, to contribute to a goal, to collaborate >** After His ascension, the Lord was working with His disciples (Mark 16:20). We know that all things work together for good to those who love God (other mss.: that in all things God works for the good of those who love Him), to those who are called according to His purpose (Rom. 8:28). The Corinthians were to submit to everyone who worked {helped in the work, was joined in the work} and labored with Paul (1 Cor. 16:16). Working together {As workers together, As fellow-workmen}, Paul and Timothy were pleading with the Corinthians not to receive the grace of God in vain (2 Cor. 6:1). The faith of Abraham worked with {wrought with} his works (Jas. 2:22). ¶

5 ***poieō*** [verb: ποιέω <4160>] ► **To produce, to accomplish >** The men who were hired last worked only one hour in the vineyard (Matt. 20:12). Other refs.: see entries in Lexicon at <4160>.

– 6 Matt. 13:33; Luke 13:21; 1 Cor. 5:6; Gal. 5:9 → to work through → LEAVEN (verb) <2220> 7 Matt. 20:1 → man to work → WORKMAN <2040> 8 Luke 5:5; John 4:38; Acts 20:35; Rom. 16:6; 1 Cor. 4:12; 15:10; et al. → to work, to work hard → LABOR (verb) <2872> 9 John 7:4 → lit.: to do (*poieō*) 10 2 Cor. 1:24; 3 John 8 → to work with, together → FELLOW WORKER <4904> 11 2 Cor. 11:12 → to work on the same terms → lit.: to be found even as → FIND <2147> 12 2 Cor. 11:23 → I have worked much harder → lit.: I have been in labors more abundantly → LABOR (noun) <2873> 13 Eph. 4:16 → PRODUCE <4160> 14 Eph. 4:19 → WORKING (noun) <2039> 15 Col. 4:13 → he is working hard → lit.: he has a great work → ZEAL <2205> 16 2 Thes. 2:9 → WORKING (noun) <1753> 17 Titus 2:5 → working at home → diligent in home work → DILIGENT <3626>.

WORKER – 1 Matt. 7:23 → lit.: one who practices → PRACTICE (verb) <2038> 2 Matt. 9:37, 38; 10:10; 20:1, 2, 8; Luke 10:2a, b, 7; 13:27; Acts 19:25; 2 Cor. 11:13; Phil. 3:2; 1 Tim. 5:18; 2 Tim. 2:15; Jas. 5:4 → WORKMAN <2040> 3 Matt. 20:14 → lit.: to this last 4 Rom. 16:3, 9, 21; 2 Cor. 1:24; 8:23; Phil. 2:25; 4:3; Col. 4:11 → worker, worker with → FELLOW WORKER <4904> 5 1 Cor. 3:9 → fellow worker → LABORER TOGETHER <4904> 6 2 Cor. 6:1 → worker together → to work together → WORK (verb) <4903> 7 Titus 2:5 → worker at home → diligent in home work → DILIGENT <3626>.

WORKFELLOW – Rom. 16:21 → FELLOW WORKER <4904>.

WORKING (noun) – 1 ***energeia*** [fem. noun: ἐνέργεια <1753>]; **from *energēs*: operative, active, which is from *en*: in, and *ergon*: work ► Power, energy >** Paul speaks of the working of the might of the strength of God (Eph. 1:19) and the working of His power (3:7). The working in its measure of each believing member works for itself the increase of the body, i.e., the church (Eph.

4:16). Jesus Christ has the working {exertion} of the power to subdue all things to Himself (Phil. 3:21). Paul combated according to the working of Christ that worked in him (Col. 1:29); in 2:12, he speaks of the working {operation} of God who raised Christ from among the dead. The coming of the antichrist is according to the working {activity, work} of Satan (2 Thes. 2:9). Other ref.: 2 Thes. 2:11 (strong delusion); see DELUSION <1753>. ¶

2 ***ergasia*** [fem. noun: ἐργασία <2039>]; **from *ergazomai*: to toil, to work, which is from *ergon*: work ► Act of devoting oneself to something, realization, practice** > Paul spoke of those of the nations who have given themselves up to lasciviousness, to work {to indulge in} (lit.: in view of the working of) all uncleanness with greediness (Eph. 4:19). All other refs.: BUSINESS <2039>, EFFORT <2039>, GAIN (noun) <2039>.

– 3 1 Cor. 12:6, 10 → OPERATION <1755> 4 Phil. 2:13 → WORK (verb) <1754> 5 2 Thes. 2:11 → working of error → strong delusion → DELUSION <4106>.

WORKING (verb) – **to work: *energeō*** [verb: ἐνεργέω <1754>]; **from *energēs*: operative, active, which is from *en*: in, and *ergon*: work ► Acting, producing an effect** > In Christ Jesus, there is faith working {expressing itself} (lit.: which works) through love (Gal. 5:6). All other refs.: WORK (verb) <1754>.

WORKMAN – 1 ***ergatēs*** [masc. noun: ἐργάτης <2040>]; **from *ergazomai*: to work, which is from *ergon*: work, workmanship ► One who accomplishes a task; also transl.: worker, laborer, labourer** > Jesus said the harvest is great, but the workmen are few (Matt. 9:37; Luke 10:2a). He said to supplicate the Lord of the harvest that He may send out workmen into His harvest (Matt. 9:38; Luke 10:2b). The workman is worthy of his food (Matt. 10:10) and his hire (Luke 10:7; 1 Tim. 5:18). In a parable, a householder hired workmen for his vineyard (Matt. 20:1, 2, 8). Demetrius gathered together workmen {workers} of occupations like his own (Acts 19:25). We find the exprs. "worker of iniquity" {evildoer} (Luke 13:27), "deceitful workman" {deceitful worker} (2 Cor. 11:13), and "evil workman" {evil worker, man who does evil} (Phil. 3:2). Timothy was to be a workman who had not to be ashamed (2 Tim. 2:15). James speaks of the wages of workmen (Jas. 5:4). ¶

– 2 Rev. 18:22 → CRAFTSMAN <5079>.

WORKMANSHIP – 1 ***poiēma*** [neut. noun: ποίημα <4161>]; **from *poieō*: to make, to do ► Something that is made, created; a work of God as creator** > The Greek word is transl. "the things that are made," i.e., God the Creator's works, in Rom. 1:20. Christians are the workmanship of God (Eph. 2:10). ¶

– 2 1 Cor. 9:1 → WORK (noun) <2041>.

WORLD – 1 ***aiōn*** [masc. noun: αἰών <165>] **► Primary meaning: era, age; the worlds (referring to the universe)** > God made the worlds through His Son (Heb. 1:2). By faith we understand that the worlds were framed {created, formed, prepared} by the word of God (Heb. 11:3). Other refs.: AGE <165>, COURSE <165>, FOREVER <165>, TROUBLE (noun) <165>.

2 ***kosmos*** [masc. noun: κόσμος <2889>]; **prob. from *komeō*: to take care of; primary meaning: order, arrangement, ornament ► a. The earth on which we live** > Matt. 13:35; John 21:25; Acts 17:24; Rom. 1:20; 1 Tim. 6:7; Heb. 4:3; 9:26. **b. The earth in contrast to the heavens** > Rom. 4:13; 1 John 3:17. **c. The human race** > Matt. 5:14; John 1:9, 10a–c; 3:16, 17a–c, 19; 4:42; the word is often used in Romans, 1 Corinthians, and 1 John. **d. The Gentiles, as distinguished from the Jews** > Rom. 11:12, 15. **e. The present condition of man as a stranger and enemy of God** > John 7:7; 8:23; 14:30; 1 Cor. 2:12; Gal. 4:3; 6:14; Col. 2:8; Jas. 1:27; 1 John 4:5a–c; 5:19. **f. Temporal possessions considered as a whole** > Matt. 16:26; 1 Cor. 7:31a. **g. The expression of magnitude and variety (i.e., in the case of the tongue)** > Jas. 3:6. (After W. E. Vine.) * Other ref.: 1 Pet. 3:3; see ADORNMENT <2889>.

[3] ***oikoumenē*** [fem. noun: οἰκουμένη <3625>]; **from *oikeō*: to live, to reside ▶ Inhabited world, inhabited earth** > The gospel of the kingdom shall be preached in the whole habitable world (Matt. 24:14). God will judge the habitable earth in righteousness, by the Man whom He has appointed for this (Acts 17:31); this Man is the Lord Jesus whom He has raised from among the dead. Other refs.: Luke 2:1; 4:5; 21:26; Acts 11:28; 17:6; 19:27; 24:5; Rom. 10:18; Heb. 1:6; 2:5; Rev. 3:10; 12:9; 16:14. ¶

– [4] Matt. 19:28 → new world → REGENERATION <3824> [5] Rom. 16:25 → since the world began → since eternal times → ETERNAL <166>, TIME <5550> [6] 2 Cor. 10:4 → of the world → CARNAL <4559> [7] Gal. 4:9 → "of the world" added in Engl. [8] Eph. 6:12 → world force → RULER <2888>.

WORLDLY – [1] ***kosmikos*** [adj.: κοσμικός <2886>]; **from *kosmos*: world ▶ Characterizing those of the world, men in general, their manner of being and behavior; earthly** > The grace of God teaches us to deny impiety and worldly lusts (Titus 2:12). Other ref.: Heb. 9:1; see EARTHLY <2886>. ¶

– [2] Luke 16:9 → UNRIGHTEOUSNESS <93> [3] Luke 16:11 → UNRIGHTEOUS (adj. and noun) <94> [4] 1 Cor. 1:26; 7:28 → according to worldly standards, worldly troubles → according to flesh, troubles in the flesh → FLESH <4561> [5] 1 Cor. 3:1, 3a, b; 2 Cor. 1:12 → CARNAL <4559> [6] 1 Cor. 7:33, 34 → of the world → WORLD <2889> [7] 1 Tim. 4:7; 6:20; 2 Tim. 2:16 → PROFANE (adj. and noun) <952> [8] Heb. 9:1 → EARTHLY <2886> [9] Jude 19 → NATURAL <5591>.

WORLDLY-MINDED – Jude 19 → NATURAL <5591>.

WORM (noun) – [1] ***skōlēx*** [masc. noun: σκώληξ <4663>] ▶ **Invertebrate animal which sometimes feeds on cadavers** > In hell, the worm does not die and the fire is not quenched (Mark 9:44, 46, 48). ¶

[2] **eaten by worms: *skōlēkobrōtos*** [adj.: σκωληκόβρωτος <4662>]; **from *skolēx*: worm, and *bibrōskō*: to eat ▶ Devoured by worms, which are small, elongated soft-bodied creatures** > Eaten by worms, Herod Agrippa I expired (Acts 12:23). ¶

WORM (verb) – 2 Tim. 3:6 → to worm into → to creep into → CREEP <1744>.

WORMWOOD – ***apsinthos*** [fem. noun: ἄψινθος <894>] ▶ **Bitter aromatic plant; also: absinthe, the noxious spirit extracted from this plant** > The reference to a star named "Wormwood" and to the third of the waters becoming wormwood (Rev. 8:11a, b) suggests, according to the O.T., bitterness (see Lam. 3:15) and unrighteousness (see Amos 5:7; 6:12) that poison the moral life of men and lead them to a spiritual death. It is a terrible judgment of God on the rebellious nations (see APOSTASY) before the reign of Christ during the millennium. ¶

WORRY (noun) – Matt. 13:22; Mark 4:19; Luke 8:14; 21:34 → CARE (noun) <3308>.

WORRY (verb) – [1] ***merimnaō*** [verb: μεριμνάω <3309>]; **from *merimna*: anxiety, care ▶ To be anxious, to be concerned; also transl.: to care, to be careful, to take thought** > Jesus says not to worry about our life, what we will eat and what we will drink, nor for our body, what we will put on (Matt. 6:25, 31; Luke 12:22). No one can add one cubit to his stature by worrying (Matt. 6:27; Luke 12:25). We are not to worry about clothing (Matt. 6:28). Jesus says not to worry about tomorrow, for tomorrow will worry about itself; sufficient to the day is its own evil (Matt. 6:34a, b). When they are arrested, believers are not to worry how or what they will speak (Matt. 10:19; Luke 12:11). Martha was worried and troubled about many things (Luke 10:41). Other ref.: Luke 12:26. All other refs.: ANXIOUS (BE) <3309>, CARE <3309>, CARE <3309>.

[2] **to worry beforehand: *promerimnaō*** [verb: προμεριμνάω <4305>]; **from *pro*: before, and *merimnaō*: see [1] ▶ To be anxious beforehand, to be preoccupied;**

also transl.: to be careful beforehand, to take thought beforehand > When they are arrested, believers in the Lord are not to worry beforehand as to what they are to say (Mark 13:11). ¶
– 3 Mark 13:11 → to worry beforehand → PREMEDITATE <3191> 4 Luke 12:29 → to be in anxiety → ANXIETY <3349> 5 Luke 21:14 → to worry beforehand → to meditate beforehand → MEDITATE <4304> 6 1 Cor. 7:21 → CARE <3199> 7 1 Cor. 7:36 → to be worried → SUPPOSE <3543>.

WORSE – 1 ***hēssōn*** [adj. used as noun and as adv.: ἥσσων <2276>] ► **Something of much less value, inferior; detrimentally** > The Corinthians were coming together not for the better but for the worse (*eis to ēssōn*) (1 Cor. 11:17), i.e., for their detriment. The word is transl. "the less" in 2 Cor. 12:15. ¶
2 ***cheirōn*** [adj.: χείρων <5501>]; **from *cherēs*, serves as compar. to *kakos*: bad** ► **Bad, evil, or corrupt in a greater degree** > The word is used in Matt. 9:16 and Mark 2:21 in regard to a tear in a garment. Other refs.: SEVERE <5501>.
3 **to the worse: *eis to cheiron*; *cheirōn*** [adj.: χείρων <5501>]; **see** 2 ► **Expr. describing decline, deterioration** > A woman who had suffered many things had grown worse (lit.: to the worse) (Mark. 5:26).
4 **to be the worse: *hustereō*** [verb: ὑστερέω <5302>]; **from *husteros*: which come after, last** ► **To fall short** > Ref.: 1 Cor. 8:8. All other refs.: COME <5302>, INFERIOR <5302>, LACK (verb) <5302>, PRIVATION <5302>, WANT (noun) <5302>.
– 5 John 2:10 → LESSER <1640>.

WORSHIP (noun) – 1 **object of worship: *sebasma*** [neut. noun: σέβασμα <4574>]; **from *sebazomai*: to venerate** ► **Religious object, sacred monument** > Paul had considered the objects of worship {the devotions, the shrines} of the Athenians (Acts 17:23). The man of sin opposes and exalts himself above all that is called God or object of worship {object of veneration, that is worshipped} (2 Thes. 2:4). ¶
– 2 Acts 17:22 → given up to demon worship → very religious → RELIGIOUS <1174> 3 Acts 25:19 → system of worship → RELIGION <1175> 4 Col. 2:18 → RELIGION <2356> 5 Col. 2:23 → will worship → SELF-IMPOSED RELIGION <1479> 6 Heb. 9:1 → divine worship, worship → divine service → SERVICE <2999> 7 Heb. 9:21 → SERVICE <3009> 8 Heb. 11:21 → to bow in worship → WORSHIP (verb) <4352>.

WORSHIP (verb) – 1 ***eusebeō*** [verb: εὐσεβέω <2151>]; **from *eusebēs*: godly, respectful, which is from *eu*: well, and *sebomai*: see** 5 ► **To adore, to venerate** > Paul proclaimed the One whom the Athenians worshiped {reverenced} without knowing Him (Acts 17:23). Other ref.: 1 Tim. 5:4 (to show piety); see PIETY <2151>. ¶
2 ***latreuō*** [verb: λατρεύω <3000>]; **from *latris*: servant (male or female)** ► **To serve God, to bring Him homage and glory** > Those who worship God in the Spirit are the true circumcision (Phil. 3:3), i.e., the spiritual one separated from the world. The verb is used in relation to the Israelites in the desert {to perform, to do the service} (Heb. 9:9) and the worshippers (lit.: those worshipping) under the law (Heb. 10:2). All other refs.: SERVE <3000>.
3 ***proskuneō*** [verb: προσκυνέω <4352>]; **from *pros*: before, and *kuneō*: to kiss (to show respect or homage)** ► **To adore, to do homage; this verb is used in regard to God and men; also transl.: to bow before, to bow down, to do homage, to fall on one's knees, to kneel down, to prostrate oneself** > The wise men had come to worship Jesus (Matt. 2:2, 11); Herod said he wanted to worship Him (v. 8). Satan wanted Jesus to worship him (Matt. 4:9; Luke 4:7); Jesus replied: It is written you shall worship the Lord and serve Him only (Matt. 4:10; Luke 4:8). A leper worshiped Jesus, asking Him to cleanse him (Matt. 8:2); a demoniac also worshiped Jesus (Mark 5:6). A synagogue ruler worshiped Jesus (Matt. 9:18), as did likewise the disciples in the ship with Him (Matt. 14:33), a blind man whom He

had healed (John 9:38), a woman whose daughter was tormented by a demon (Matt. 15:25), the mother of the sons of Zebedee (Matt. 20:20), the soldiers who mocked Him (Mark 15:19), Mary Magdalene and the other Mary (Matt. 28:9), and the eleven disciples (Matt. 28:17; Luke 24:52). In a parable, a servant prostrated himself before his master (Matt. 18:26). When Jesus met the woman at the well of Sychar, the verb is used many times (John 4:20a, b, 21, 22a, b, 23a, b, 24a, b). There were Greeks who came up to worship at the feast in Jerusalem (John 12:20); also, on other occasions, a man of Ethiopia (Acts 8:27) and Paul (Acts 24:11). The Israelites did homage to Moloch and Remphan (Acts 7:43). Cornelius worshiped Peter, but Peter made him rise (Acts 10:25). Paul speaks of an unbeliever who will worship God if Christians prophesy (1 Cor. 14:25). All the angels of God are to worship the Son (Heb. 1:6). Jacob, when he was dying, worshipped (Heb. 11:21). Those of the synagogue of Satan will worship before the feet of the church of Philadelphia (Rev. 3:9). The twenty-four elders will do homage to Him who sits upon the throne (Rev. 4:10). The elders worshiped Him who sits on the throne and the Lamb (Rev. 5:14). The twenty-four elders worshiped God (Rev. 11:16), as did likewise the elders and the four living creatures (19:4) and the angels (Rev. 7:11). Men worshiped demons and various idols (Rev. 9:20). In Rev. 11:1, there are those who worship {the worshippers} in the temple of God. The whole earth will worship the dragon (Rev. 13:4a) and the beast or his image (Rev. 13:4b, 8, 12; 14:9, 11; 16:2; 19:20); but some will not worship the beast (Rev. 13:15; 20:4). An angel will proclaim to worship God (Rev. 14:7). All the nations will come and worship before the Lord (Rev. 15:4). John wanted to worship the angel whose voice he heard (Rev. 19:10a; 22:8), but the angel told him to worship God (19:10b; 22:9). ¶

[4] ***sebazomai*** [verb: σεβάζομαι <4573>]; **from *sebas*: religious awe, which is from *sebomai*: see [5] ► To venerate religiously, to adore** > Men worshiped {honored} and served the creature rather than Him who had created it (Rom. 1:25). ¶

[5] ***sebomai*** [verb: σέβομαι <4576>] ► **To adore, to honor, to venerate, to be a worshiper; also transl. by an adj.: devout, God-fearing, religious** > The scribes and the Pharisees worshiped God in vain (Matt. 15:9; Mark 7:7). Many Jews and worshipping proselytes followed Paul and Barnabas (Acts 13:43). The Jews stirred up women who were devout (lit.: worshipping) and of high standing, and raised a persecution against Paul and Barnabas (Acts 13:50). Lydia worshipped God (Acts 16:14). A great multitude of Greeks worshipped God (Acts 17:4). Paul reasoned with those who worshipped in the synagogue of Athens (Acts 17:17). Justus worshipped God (Acts 18:7). The Jews said that Paul persuaded men to worship God contrary to the law (Acts 18:13). Demetrius said that the whole of Asia and the world worshipped the great goddess Diana (Acts 19:27). ¶

– [6] Acts 13:2 → MINISTER (verb) <3008> [7] Acts 13:16 → FEAR (verb) <5399> [8] Acts 17:25 → SERVE <2323> [9] Rom. 9:4; 12:1; Heb. 9:1, 6 → SERVICE <2999> [10] 2 Thes. 2:4 → that is worshipped → lit.: that is an object of worship → WORSHIP (noun) <4574> [11] 1 Tim. 2:10 → to profess to worship God → lit.: to profess godliness → GODLINESS <2317>.

WORSHIPPER – [1] ***proskunētēs*** [masc. noun: προσκυνητής <4353>]; **from *proskuneō*: to adore, to do homage, which is from *pros*: to, and *kuneō*: to kiss; lit.: one who bows low in reverence ► Person who gives homage, who adores** > The true worshippers worship the Father in spirit and truth (John 4:23). ¶

– [2] John 9:31 → a worshipper of God → lit.: God-fearing → GOD-FEARING <2318> [3] Acts 13:50; 16:14; 17:17; 18:7 → to be a worshipper → WORSHIP (verb) <4576> [4] Acts 19:35 → temple guardian → GUARDIAN <3511> [5] Heb. 9:9; 10:2 → lit.: one who worships → WORSHIP (verb) <3000> [6] Rev. 11:1; 14:11 → lit.: one who worships, those who worship → WORSHIP (verb) <4352>.

WORSHIPPING – [1] Acts 13:43, 50 → WORSHIP (verb) <4576> [2] Col. 2:18 → RELIGION <2356>.

WORTH (adj.) – [1] Matt. 10:10; Rom. 8:18 → WORTHY <514> [2] 1 Pet. 1:7 → of greater worth → much more precious → PRECIOUS <5093> [3] 1 Pet. 3:4 → of great worth → of great price → PRICE (noun) <4185>.

WORTH (noun) – [1] Phil. 3:8 → surpassing worth → EXCELLENCE <5242> [2] 1 Pet. 1:7 → greater worth → TESTING <1383>.

WORTH (BE) – Matt. 6:26; 10:31; Luke 12:7 → to be worth more, much more → to be of more value → VALUE <1308>.

WORTHILY – Rom. 16:2; Phil. 1:27; Col. 1:10 → in a manner worthy → WORTHY <516>.

WORTHLESS – [1] ***adokimos*** [adj.: ἀδόκιμος <96>]; **from *a*: neg., and *dokimos*: approved, tested; comp. *dechomai*: to accept, to receive ▶ Set aside, rejected; also transl.: debased, depraved, disqualified, reprobate, unapproved, unfit** > The word originally applied to metals (see Jer. 6:29, 30). God has given up men inflamed in their lust to a depraved mind (Rom. 1:28). Ground that brings forth thorns and briars is worthless {rejected} (Heb. 6:8), as likewise is one professing to be a Christian who is in fact lifeless (2 Cor. 13:5). The word is also used in regard to Christian service (1 Cor. 9:27), faith (2 Cor. 13:5–7; 2 Tim. 3:8), and good works (Titus 1:16). ¶

[2] ***achreios*** [adj.: ἀχρεῖος <888>]; **from *a*: neg., and *chreia*: necessity, utility ▶ Which is not useful, which is profitless** > In a parable, the worthless {unprofitable, useless} servant was thrown out into the outer darkness (Matt. 25:30). Other ref.: Luke 17:10; see UNWORTHY <888>. ¶

– [3] Acts 14:15; Titus 3:9; Jas. 1:26 → VAIN <3152> [4] Acts 19:27 → to regard as worthless → to count → DESPISE <3049> [5] Rom. 3:12 → to become worthless → to become unprofitable → UNPROFITABLE <889> [6] Rom. 4:14 → to be worthless → to make of no effect → EFFECT (noun) <2673> [7] Gal. 4:9 → BEGGARLY <4434>.

WORTHWHILE – Rom. 1:28 → to think worthwhile → LIKE (verb) <1381>.

WORTHY – [1] ***axios*** [adj.: ἄξιος <514>]; **from *agō*: to weigh; lit.: to bring down by its weight, hence: which has value ▶ Deserving, suitable, appropriate; also transl.: to deserve, deserving, worth** > Jesus tells the Pharisees and Sadducees to bear fruit worthy of {meet for, in keeping with} repentance (Matt. 3:8; Luke 3:8). A worker is worthy of his food or wages (Matt. 10:10; Luke 10:7; 1 Tim. 5:18). The disciples were to inquire who was worthy in a town for them to stay there (Matt. 10:11; 13a, b). He who loves a member of his family more than Jesus is not worthy of Him (Matt. 10:37a, b), and he who does not take his cross and follow after Him (v. 38). Those who were invited to the wedding were not worthy (Matt. 22:8). John the Baptist was not worthy to loose the sandal strap of Jesus (John 1:27; Acts 13:25). The leaders of the Jews said the centurion was worthy that Jesus should heal his servant (Luke 7:4). The prodigal son was no longer worthy to be called the son of his father (Luke 15:19, 21). Nothing worthy of death had been done by Jesus (Luke 23:15). Paul had committed nothing worthy of death (Acts 25:11, 25; 26:31). He speaks of those worthy of death because they practice evil things (Rom. 1:32). The sufferings of the present time are not worthy to be compared with the glory that will be revealed to Christians (Rom. 8:18). The coming of Christ Jesus to save sinners is a faithful saying and worthy of all acceptance (1 Tim. 1:15), as is also the fact that we have the promise of the life that now is and of that which is to come (4:9; see v. 8). Bondservants had to count their own masters worthy of all honor (1 Tim. 6:1). The world was not worthy of those who were persecuted because of their faith (Heb. 11:38). Some in Sardis will be worthy to walk with the Lord in white garments (Rev. 3:4).

The Lord is worthy to receive glory, honor, and power (Rev. 4:11). No one was worthy to open the scroll and to loose its seals (Rev. 5:2, 4), but the Lamb (v. 9); He is worthy to receive the praise (v. 12). Those who have shed the blood of saints and prophets are worthy to have been given blood to drink {it is their just due, they deserve it} (Rev. 16:6). Other refs.: DESERVING <514>, FITTING <514>, MEET (adj.) <514>, UNWORTHY <514>.

[2] **to consider, to count, to be, to be found, to think worthy: *axioō*** [verb: ἀξιόω <515>]**; from *axios*: see** [1] **▶ To believe that one is deserving >** The centurion did not count himself worthy to come to Jesus (Luke 7:7). Paul was praying God that He would count worthy of His calling the Christians in Thessalonica (2 Thes. 1:11). The elders who take the lead must be counted worthy of a double honor (1 Tim. 5:17). Jesus has been counted worthy of more glory than Moses (Heb. 3:3). One who has trampled the Son of God under foot will be thought worthy of {will deserve} a much worse punishment (Heb. 10:29). All other refs.: DESIRE (verb) <515>, THINK <515>.

[3] **to count, to consider, to account worthy: *kataxioō*** [verb: καταξιόω <2661>]**; from *kata*: intens., and *axioō*: see** [2] **▶ To believe that one is very much deserving, meritorious >** There will be those counted worthy to attain the resurrection (Luke 20:35). The Jews had to pray to be counted worthy {to have strength, to be able} to escape the things about to come to pass (Luke 21:36 in some mss.; the most authentic mss. have *katischuō*: to prevail, to be able). The disciples rejoiced that they were counted worthy to suffer shame for the name of Jesus (Acts 5:41). The Thessalonians were to be counted worthy of the kingdom of God (2 Thes. 1:5). ¶

[4] **worthy, in a manner worthy, in a way worthy: *axiōs*** [adv.: ἀξίως <516>]**; from *axios*: see** [1] **▶ In a fitting, suitable manner; also transl.: worthily >** Christians in Rome were to receive Phoebe in a manner worthy of {as becometh, worthily of} saints (Rom. 16:2). Christians are to walk worthy of the calling with which they are called (Eph. 4:1), of the Lord to fully please him (Col. 1:10), and of God who calls them into His own kingdom and glory (1 Thes. 2:12). Their conduct must be worthy of the gospel of Christ (Phil. 1:27). Gaius was to send forward on their journey brothers and strangers in a manner worthy of God {after a godly sort} (3 John 6). ¶

[5] ***hikanos*** [adj.: ἱκανός <2425>]**; from *hikneomai*: to come, to occur ▶ Sufficient, deserving; also transl.: fit >** John the Baptist was not worthy to bear the sandals of Jesus (Matt. 3:11) and to untie His sandal strap (Mark 1:7; Luke 3:16). The centurion said he was not worthy {did not deserve} that Jesus should come under his roof (Matt. 8:8; Luke 7:6). Paul was not worthy {was not meet, did not deserve} to be called an apostle (1 Cor. 15:9). Other refs.: see entries in Lexicon at <2425>.

[6] ***kalos*** [adj.: καλός <2570>] **▶ Beautiful, agreeable, honorable >** James speaks of those blaspheming the worthy {excellent, fair, noble} name of Jesus (Jas. 2:7). Other refs.: see entries in Lexicon at <2570>.

[7] **to be worthy: *parechō*** [verb: παρέχω <3930>]**; from *para*: near, and *echō*: to have, to hold ▶ To deserve >** The elders of the Jews said the centurion was worthy that Jesus should heal his servant (Luke 7:4). All other refs.: see entries in Lexicon at <3930>.

– [8] Matt. 26:66; Mark 14:64 → DESERVING <1777> [9] Acts 24:2 → very worthy deeds → excellent measures → MEASURE (noun) <2735> [10] Acts 28:18 → there was nothing worthy of death → lit.: there was no cause → CAUSE (noun) <156> [11] 1 Tim. 3:4 → in a manner worthy of full respect → with all gravity → DIGNITY <4587>.

WOT – [1] Acts 3:17; 7:40; Rom. 11:2 → indic. pres. of "to wit," archaic form of "to know" → KNOW <1492> [2] Phil. 1:22 → KNOW <1107>.

WOUND (noun) – [1] ***trauma*** [neut. noun: τραῦμα <5134>]**; from *titrōskō*: to hurt, to wound ▶ Injury to the body resulting from a cut or blow >** The Samaritan in the parable bandaged the wounds of a man who

had been beaten and left half dead (Luke 10:34). ¶
– [2] 1 Pet. 2:24 → STRIPE <3468> [3] Rev. 13:3, 12, 14 → PLAGUE <4127> [4] Rev. 13:3 → it had a fatal wound → lit.: it had been slain to death → SLAY <4969>.

WOUND (verb) – [1] ***traumatizō*** [verb: τραυματίζω <5135>]; **from *trauma*: wound, which is from *titrōskō*: to hurt, to wound ▶ To injure, to hurt the body** > In a parable, a slave sent by his master to receive the fruit of the vineyard was wounded by the vine dressers (Luke 20:12). The seven sons of Sceva were wounded {given a beating} by the evil spirit (Acts 19:16). ¶
[2] ***tuptō*** [verb: τύπτω <5180>]; **lit.: to inflict a blow ▶ To offend** > The Corinthians were sinning against Christ by sinning against the brothers and wounding their weak conscience (1 Cor. 8:12). All other refs.: BEAT <5180>, STRIKE <5180>.
[3] **to cover: *epitithēmi*** [verb: ἐπιτίθημι <2007>]; **from *epi*: upon, and *tithēmi*: to put ▶ To inflict, to give** > Thieves wounded {beat} (lit.: covered with wounds, inflicted wounds; wound: see [4]) a man going down from Jerusalem to Jericho (Luke 10:30). All other refs.: see entries in Lexicon at <2007>.
[4] **wound: *plēgē*** [fem. noun: πληγή <4127>]; **from *plēssō*: to smite ▶ Blow, bruise** > Luke 10:30; See [3]. All other refs.: PLAGUE <4127>, STRIPE <4127>.
– [5] Mark 12:4 → to wound in the head → HEAD → <2775> [6] Rev. 9:19 → INJURE <91> [7] Rev. 13:3 → SLAY <4969>.

WOVEN – ***huphantos*** [adj.: ὑφαντός <5307>]; **from *huphainō*: to weave ▶ Made entirely by interweaving threads** > The tunic of Jesus was woven from the top in one piece (John 19:23). The verb *huphainō* (to weave) is added in some mss. in Luke 12:27. ¶

WRANGLE – 2 Tim. 2:14 → to wrangle about words → to strive about words → STRIVE <3054>.

WRANGLING – [1] **useless wrangling: *diaparatribē*** [fem. noun: διαπαρατριβή <1275a>]; **from *dia*: through., *para*: near, and *tribō*: to wear, which suggest the wearing effect of disputes ▶ Constant quarrel, altercation** > Disputes and arguments over words are followed by useless wranglings {constant frictions, constant quarrellings, perverse disputing} (1 Tim. 6:5); some mss. have *paradiatribē*; see [2]. ¶
[2] **useless wrangling: *paradiatribē*** [fem. noun: παραδιατριβή <3859>]; **from *para*: beside, and *diaparatribē*: see [1] ▶ Constant quarrel, altercation** > The word is used in 1 Tim. 6:5 in some mss.; see [1]. ¶

WRAP – [1] ***eneileō*** [verb: ἐνειλέω <1750>]; **from *en*: in, and *eilō*: to roll ▶ To cover all around** > Joseph wrapped {swathed} the body of Jesus in the linen (Mark 15:46). ¶
[2] ***entulissō*** [verb: ἐντυλίσσω <1794>]; **from *en*: in, and *tulissō*: to roll, to wrap ▶ To cover, to envelop** > Joseph wrapped the body of Jesus in a clean linen cloth he had bought (Matt. 27:59; Luke 23:53). Other ref.: John 20:7 (to fold up); see FOLD (verb) <1794>. ¶
[3] **to wrap around: *periballō*** [verb: περιβάλλω <4016>]; **from *peri*: around, and *ballō*: to throw ▶ To envelop, to put on; also transl.: to cast about** > The angel told Peter to wrap around himself his cloak and follow him (Acts 12:8). All other refs.: BUILD <4016>, CLOTHE <4016>, WEAR <4016>.
[4] ***perideō*** [verb: περιδέω <4019>]; **from *peri*: around, and *deō*: to fasten, to tie ▶ To cover** > The face of Lazarus was wrapped {bound about} with a cloth (John 11:44). ¶
[5] **to wrap in cloths, in swaddling clothes: *sparganoō*** [verb: σπαργανόω <4683>]; **from *sparganon*: band ▶ To swathe** > Mary wrapped her firstborn Son in swaddling cloths {clothes} (Luke 2:7, 12). ¶
[6] **to wrap up: *sustellō*** [verb: συστέλλω <4958>]; **from *sun*: together, and *stellō*: to contract, to shrink ▶ To cover, to envelop** > The young men wrapped up {swathed up, wound up} the body of Ananias, and buried him (Acts 5:6). Other ref.: 1 Cor. 7:29 (to be short); see SHORT <4958>. ¶

– [7] John 11:44; 19:40 → BIND <1210> [8] John 13:4, 5; 21:7 → to wrap around the waist, around oneself → GIRD <1241> [9] John 20:7 → that had been wrapped around → that was (*eimi* <1510>) around.

WRAPPING – Luke 24:12; John 19:40; 20:5–7 → linen wrappings → LINEN, LINEN CLOTH <3608>.

WRAPPINGS – John 11:44 → GRAVE-CLOTHES <2750>.

WRATH – [1] ***orgē*** [fem. noun: ὀργή <3709>] ▶ **a. Violent, intense anger as a settled disposition; also transl.: anger** > The law brings wrath (Rom. 4:15). Christians must not avenge themselves, but rather give place to wrath, for vengeance belongs to the Lord (Rom. 12:19). A person in authority is God's minister to execute wrath on him who practices evil (Rom. 13:4); therefore, we must be subject, not only because of wrath {punishment}, but also for conscience's sake (v. 5). Christians were children of wrath before their conversion, just as the unbelievers (Eph. 2:3). All wrath was to be put away from the Ephesians (Eph. 4:31); Colossians were to put aside wrath (Col. 3:8). Paul desired that the men pray everywhere, lifting up holy hands, without wrath or reasoning (1 Tim. 2:8). Christians should be slow to wrath {to become angry} (Jas. 1:19); the wrath of man does not produce the righteousness of God (v. 20). **b. Wrath of God** > This wrath expresses the horror that God has of evil. All the unbelievers are under that wrath of God, and God will retribute evil (Matt. 3:7; Luke 3:7; 21:23; Rom. 2:8; 3:5 {vengeance}; 9:22a, b; Eph. 5:6; Col. 3:6; 1 Thes. 2:16; Heb. 4:3; Rev. 14:10; 16:19; 19:15). In Mark 3:5, Jesus looked around with anger (lit.: wrath) at those who were in the synagogue. The wrath of God abides on him who does not believe (or: obey) the Son (John 3:36). The wrath of God is revealed now against all ungodliness and unrighteousness (Rom. 1:18). The Lord is "slow to anger" (see Ex. 34:6), but once the day of grace will be ended, there will be the "day of wrath and revelation of the righteous judgment of God" (Rom. 2:5a, b; Rev. 6:17). Jesus delivers Christians from the wrath to come (Rom. 5:9; 1 Thes. 1:10; 5:9). The Holy Spirit swore in His wrath against Israel (Heb. 3:11). In Rev. 6:16, we read about the wrath of the Lamb. This day is the day of the wrath to come (Rev. 11:18). ¶

[2] ***thumos*** [masc. noun: θυμός <2372>]; **from *thuō*: to move impetuously ▶ Sudden burst of indignation, burning furor; also transl.: anger, rage** > All those in the synagogue were filled with wrath {were furious} against Jesus (Luke 4:28). The Ephesians were full of wrath {were furious} after having heard Demetrius (Acts 19:28). Paul feared that there would be wraths {outbursts of wrath, outbursts of anger, angry tempers} among the Corinthians (2 Cor. 12:20); wrath is among the works of the flesh (Gal. 5:20 {outburst of anger, fits of rage}). All wrath must be removed from the Christians (Eph. 4:31; Col. 3:8). Moses did not fear the wrath of the king (Heb. 11:27). In the book of Revelation, we find the wrath {fury} of God against the inhabitants of the earth (14:19; 15:1, 7; 16:1). All other refs.: FURY <2372>, INDIGNATION <2372>.

[3] ***parorgismos*** [masc. noun: παροργισμός <3950>]; **from *parorgizō*: to provoke to wrath, which is from *para*: beside (intens.), and *orgē*: anger, wrath ▶ Exasperation, irritation** > The believer is not to let the sun set on his wrath {anger} (Eph. 4:26). ¶

– [4] Acts 5:17 → JEALOUSY <2205> [5] Rev. 11:18 → to be full of wrath → ENRAGED (BE) <3710>.

WREATH – [1] Acts 14:13 → GARLAND <4725> [2] 1 Cor. 9:25 → CROWN (noun) <4735>.

WRENCH – Mark 5:4 → to tear apart → TEAR (verb) <1288>.

WREST – 2 Pet. 3:16 → TWIST <4761>.

WRESTLE – [1] Eph. 6:12 → STRUGGLE <3823> [2] Col. 4:12 → FIGHT (verb) <75> [3] Heb. 12:4 → STRIVE <464>.

WRETCH – Matt. 21:41 → WICKED (noun) <2556>.

WRETCHED (adj.) – [1] ***talaipōros*** [adj.: ταλαίπωρος <5005>]; **from *tlaō*: to suffer, to endure, and *pēros*: crippled ▶ Inspiring pity on account of suffering, moral distress; miserable** > Paul uses this word in regard to the man who seeks to please God, but who practices the evil that he does not wish to do (Rom. 7:24). The Lord tells the angel of the church of Laodicea that he is wretched (lit.: the wretched one) (Rev. 3:17). ¶
– [2] Matt. 21:41 → to a wretched end → MISERABLY <2560> [3] Matt. 21:41 → to bring to a wretched end → PERISH <622> [4] Jas. 4:9 → to be wretched → LAMENT <5003>.

WRETCHED (noun) – Matt. 21:41 → WICKED (noun) <2556>.

WRINKLE – ***rhutis*** [fem. noun: ῥυτίς <4512>]; **from *rhuō*: to contract ▶ Fold in the skin due in particular to advancing age** > Christ will present the church to Himself glorious, having no spot, or wrinkle, or any such thing (Eph. 5:27). ¶

WRITE – [1] ***graphō*** [verb: γράφω <1125>]; **lit.: to engrave ▶ To inscribe letters or other symbols on a surface** > Jesus often used the verb "it is written": Matt. 4:4, 7, 10; 11:10; 21:13; 26:24, 31; Mark 1:2; 7:6; 9:12, 13; 11:17; 14:21, 27; Luke 4:4, 8; 7:27; 10:26; 19:46; 20:17; 22:37; 24:46; John 6:45; 8:17; 15:25. This verb is also used by Paul (Rom. 1:17; 2:24; 3:4, 10; 4:17, 23; 8:36; 9:13, 33; 10:5 {to describe}, 15; 11:8, 26; 12:19; 14:11; 15:3, 9, 21; 1 Cor. 1:19, 31; 2:9; 3:19; 4:6; 9:9, 10; 10:7; 14:21; 15:45; 2 Cor. 4:13; 8:15; 9:9; Gal. 3:10, 13; 4:22, 27; Heb. 10:7) and by others (Matt. 2:5; 4:6; Luke 2:23; 3:4; 4:10, 17; John 2:17; 6:31; 10:34; 12:14; 19:20; 20:30; 21:25a, b; Acts 1:20; 7:42; 13:33; 15:15; 23:5; 1 Pet. 1:16). Other refs. for the verb *graphō*: Matt. 27:37; Mark 10:4, 5; 12:19; Luke 1:3, 63; 10:20; 16:6, 7; 18:31; 20:28; 21:22; 23:38 in some mss.; 24:44; John 1:45; 5:46; 8:6 and 8 (*katagraphō* in some mss.); 12:16; 19:19–22; 20:31; 21:24; Acts 13:29; 15:23; 18:27; 23:25; 24:14; 25:26a, b; Rom. 15:4b, 15; 16:22; 1 Cor. 4:14; 5:9, 11; 7:1; 9:15; 10:11; 14:37; 15:54; 2 Cor. 1:13; 2:3, 4, 9; 7:12; 9:1; 13:2 in some mss., 10; Gal. 1:20; 6:11; Phil. 3:1; 1 Thes. 4:9; 5:1; 2 Thes. 3:17; 1 Tim. 3:14; Phm. 19, 21; 1 Pet. 5:12; 2 Pet. 3:1, 15; 1 John 1:4; 2:1, 7, 8, 12, 13a–c, 14a, b, 21, 26; 5:13; 2 John 5, 12; 3 John 9, 13a, b; Jude 3a, b; Rev. 1:3, 11, 19; 2:1, 8, 12, 17, 18; 3:1, 7, 12, 14; 5:1; 10:4a, b; 13:8; 14:1, 13; 17:5, 8; 19:9, 12, 16; 20:12, 15; 21:5, 27; 22:18, 19. ¶
[2] ***engraphō*** [verb: ἐγγράφω <1449>]; **from *en*: in, and *graphō*: see [1] ▶ To inscribe, to engrave** > The Corinthians were the epistle of Paul written in his heart (2 Cor. 3:2), an epistle of Christ written by the Spirit of the living God (v. 3). Other ref.: Luke 10:20 in some mss. ¶
[3] ***epigraphō*** [verb: ἐπιγράφω <1924>]; **from *epi*: upon, and *graphō*: see [1] ▶ To write upon, to inscribe** > The inscription of Jesus's accusation was written {read} above him: The King of the Jews (Mark 15:26). Other refs.: Heb. 8:10; 10:16; Rev. 21:12. Other ref.: Acts 17:23; see INSCRIBE <1924>. ¶
[4] **to write already, to write before: *prographō*** [verb: προγράφω <4270>]; **from *pro*: before, and *graphō*: see [1] ▶ To write previously** > Whatever things were written before {written aforetime, in earlier times} (*prographō*) were written (*graphō*) for our learning (Rom. 15:4a). Paul had already written {written afore} briefly concerning the mystery made known to him (Eph. 3:3). Other refs.: Gal. 3:1; Jude 4; see PORTRAY <4270>, MARK (verb) <4270>. ¶
[5] **written: *graptos*** [adj.: γραπτός <1123>]; **from *graphō*: see [1] ▶ Which has been inscribed to communicate a message** > The Gentiles show the work of the law written in their hearts (Rom. 2:15). ¶
[6] ***epistellō*** [verb: ἐπιστέλλω <1989>]; **from *epi*: to, and *stellō*: to send ▶ To transmit**

a message > The author of the Epistle to the Hebrews had written to them in few words (Heb. 13:22). Other refs.: Acts 15:20; 21:25.

– [7] John 5:47 → what he wrote → lit.: his writings → WRITING <1121> [8] Acts 1:1 → MAKE <4160> [9] Rom. 2:27; 2 Cor. 3:7 → LETTER <1121> [10] 1 Cor. 6:16 → it is written → lit.: He says → SAY <5346> [11] Col. 2:14 → written code → HANDWRITING <5498> [12] Heb. 12:23 → REGISTER <583> [13] Rev. 22:7 → "written" added in Engl.

WRITING – [1] ***gramma*** [neut. noun: γράμμα <1121>]; **from *graphō*: to write ▶ Letter, what is written** > If the Jews did not believe the writings of Moses {what Moses wrote}, they would not believe the words of Jesus (John 5:47). All other refs.: BILL <1121>, LEARNING <1121>, LETTER <1121>.

– [2] Matt. 19:7 → CERTIFICATE <975> [3] Matt. 26:56; Rom. 16:26 → SCRIPTURE <1124> [4] Luke 16:6, 7 → BILL <1121> [5] 2 Tim. 3:15 → LETTER <1121>.

WRITTEN – [1] Mark 15:26; Luke 23:38 → written notice → INSCRIPTION <1923> [2] Rom. 2:27, 29; 7:6 → written code → LETTER <1121>.

WRONG (adj.) – ***atopos*** [adj.: ἄτοπος <824>]; **from *a*: neg., and *topos*: place; lit.: out of place ▶ Bad, deplorable, untoward** > In the confession of a thief on the cross, Jesus had done nothing wrong {amiss} (Luke 23:41). All other refs.: BAD <824>.

WRONG (noun) – [1] ***adikēma*** [neut. noun: ἀδίκημα <92>]; **from *adikeō*: see [3] ▶ Criminal act, offense** > If it had been a matter of some wrong {misdemeanor, wrongdoing}, it would have been reasonable for Gallio to have put up with the Jews (Acts 18:14). Paul asked that his accusers might say what wrong {crime, evil, misdeed, wrongdoing} they had found in him (Acts 24:20). Other ref.: Rev. 18:5; see INIQUITY <92>. ¶

[2] ***adikia*** [fem. noun: ἀδικία <93>]; **from *adikos*: unjust, which is from *a*: neg., and *dikē*: justice ▶ Fault, injustice** > Paul asked the Corinthians to forgive him the wrong {injury} of not having become a burden to them (2 Cor. 12:13). All other refs.: INIQUITY <93>, UNJUST (adj.) <93>, UNRIGHTEOUSNESS <93>.

[3] **to do wrong: *adikeō*** [verb: ἀδικέω <91>]; **from *adikos*: unjust ▶ To act unjustly, to injure; in the pass.: to suffer injustice; also transl.: to be an offender, to be a wrongdoer, to be unfair, to suffer wrong, to hurt, to mistreat, to wrong, to do unrighteously, to be unjust** > The landowner did not do wrong to a laborer (Matt. 20:13). Moses saw an Israelite suffering wrong (Acts 7:24 {to mistreat, to treat unjustly, to wrong}). Two Israelites were hurting one another (Acts 7:26, 27). Paul had done no wrong to the Jews (Acts 25:10, 11). The Corinthians should have suffered wrong (1 Cor. 6:7), but they were doing wrong (v. 8). Paul had wronged no one (2 Cor. 7:2). The Galatians had not at all wronged Paul (Gal. 4:12). He who does a wrong will receive the wrong he has done (Col. 3:25a, b). If Onesimus wronged Philemon in any way, Philemon was to charge it to Paul's account (Phm. 18). The angel told John to let him who is doing wrong continue doing wrong (Rev. 22:11a, b). Other refs.: 2 Cor. 7:12a, b. All other refs.: HURT (verb) <91>, INJURE <91>.

– [4] Matt. 22:29; Mark 12:27 → to be wrong → MISTAKEN (BE) <4105> [5] John 16:8 → to prove to be in the wrong → CONVINCE <1651> [6] John 18:23b; Acts 23:9; Rom. 13:10; 1 Cor. 13:5; 2 Cor. 13:7 → EVIL (noun) <2556> [7] 1 Cor. 13:5 → to take into account a wrong suffered, to keep record of wrongs → to be quickly provoked → PROVOKE <3947> [8] Gal. 2:11 → in the wrong → CONDEMN <2607> [9] Heb. 8:7 → nothing wrong → BLAMELESS <273> [10] 1 Pet. 2:12, 14 → doing wrong → EVILDOER <2555> [11] 1 Pet. 2:20 → doing wrong → to sin → FAULT <264> [12] 1 Pet. 3:17 → to do what is wrong → to do evil → EVIL (adv.) <2554>.

WRONG (verb) – 1 ***pleonekteō*** [verb: πλεονεκτέω <4122>]; **from *pleion*: more, and *echō*: to have ▶ To covet, to take advantage** > No one is to wrong his brother in coveting his wife (1 Thes. 4:6). All other refs.: ADVANTAGE (noun) <4122>, CHEAT <4122>.

– 2 Matt. 20:13; Acts 7:26, 27; 1 Cor. 6:7, 8; 2 Cor. 7:2a; Phm. 18 → to be wronged, to wrong → to suffer wrong, to do wrong → WRONG (noun) <91>.

WRONGDOER – 1 Acts 25:11; 2 Cor. 7:12a → to be a wrongdoer → to do wrong → WRONG (verb) <91> 2 1 Cor. 6:9 → UNJUST (noun) <94> 3 Col. 3:25 → he that does a wrong → WRONG (noun) <91>.

WRONGDOING – 1 Acts 18:14; 24:20 → WRONG (noun) <92> 2 1 Cor. 13:6 → UNRIGHTEOUSNESS <93> 3 2 Pet. 2:13, 15; 1 John 5:17 → INIQUITY <93> 4 2 Pet. 2:16 → INIQUITY <3892>.

WRONGFULLY – 1 Jas. 5:4 → to wrongfully keep back → KEEP (verb) <650> 2 1 Pet. 2:19 → UNJUSTLY <95>.

WRONGLY – John 18:23a; Jas. 4:3 → SICK (adv.) <2560>.

WROTH (BE) – 1 Matt. 2:16 → to be angry → ANGRY <2373> 2 Matt. 18:34 → to be angry → ANGRY <3710> 3 Matt. 22:7; Rev. 12:17 → ENRAGED (BE) <3710> 4 Heb. 3:10, 17 → to be wroth → to be angry → ANGRY <4360>.

WROUGHT (HAVE) – 1 ***ergazomai*** [verb: ἐργάζομαι <2038>]; **from *ergon*: work; this verb is the past tense and past ptcp. of "to work" ▶ To accomplish, to produce** > Through faith, O.T. believers wrought {administered, performed acts of, worked} righteousness (Heb. 11:33). All other refs.: see entries in Lexicon at <2038>.

– 2 Matt. 20:12 → WORK (verb) <4160> 3 Mark 6:2 → DO <1096> 4 Mark 6:14; 2 Cor. 1:6; Gal. 2:8a, b; Eph. 1:20; et al. → WORK (verb) <1754> 5 Acts 19:25 → those who wrought → WORKMAN <2040> 6 1 Cor. 5:4 → COMMIT <2716> 7 2 Cor. 12:12 → WORK (verb) <2716> 8 Jas. 2:22 → WORK (verb) <4903>.

Y

YARD[1] – [1] John 21:8; Rev. 21:17 → CUBIT <4083> [2] Rev. 21:17 → seventy-two yards → lit.: one hundred and forty-four cubits.

YARD[2] – Luke 22:55 → COURTYARD <833>.

YEA – Rom. 3:31 → RATHER <235>.

YEAR – [1] ***eniautos*** [masc. noun: ἐνιαυτός <1763>] ▶ **Period of time corresponding to a duration of twelve lunar months (approx. 354 days)** > Jesus was sent to proclaim the acceptable year of the Lord (Luke 4:19). Paul and Barnabas assembled themselves for a whole year with the church in Antioch (Acts 11:26). Paul continued in Corinth a year and six months (Acts 18:11). The high priest entered the second part of the tabernacle alone once a year (Heb. 9:7). Elijah prayed earnestly, and it did not rain for three years and six months (Jas. 5:17). Other refs.: John 11:49, 51; 18:13; Gal. 4:10; Heb. 9:25; 10:1, 3; Jas. 4:13; Rev. 9:15. ¶

[2] ***etos*** [neut. noun: ἔτος <2094>] ▶ **Division of time in units corresponding to twelve lunar months; used for dating** > Jesus healed a woman who had a flow of blood for twelve years (Matt. 9:20; Mark 5:25; Luke 8:43), and a woman who had a spirit of infirmity eighteen years (Luke 13:11, 16). He resurrected and made to walk a young girl of the age of twelve years old who had died (Mark 5:42; Luke 8:42). When He was twelve years old, Jesus went up with His parents to Jerusalem (Luke 2:42). He began His public ministry at about thirty years of age (Luke 3:23). He healed a man who had an infirmity thirty-eight years (John 5:5). Other refs.: Luke 2:36, 37, 41; 3:1; 4:25; 12:19; 13:7, 8; 15:29; John 2:20; 8:57; Acts 4:22; 7:6, 30, 36, 42; 9:33; 13:20, 21; 19:10; 24:10, 17; Rom. 15:23; 2 Cor. 12:2; Gal. 1:18; 2:1; 3:17; 1 Tim. 5:9; Heb. 1:12; 3:9, 17; 2 Pet. 3:8a, b; Rev. 20:2–7. ¶

[3] **two years: *dietia*** [fem. noun: διετία <1333>]; **from *dietēs*: see** [4] ▶ **Duration of two years** > Porcius Festus succeeded Felix after two years (Acts 24:27). Paul dwelt two whole years in his own rented house in Rome (Acts 28:30). ¶

[4] **two years old: *dietēs*** [adj.: διετής <1332>]; **from *dis*: twice, and *etos*: year** ▶ **Of the age of two years** > Herod slew all the children from two years old and under (Matt. 2:16). ¶

[5] **three years: *trietia*** [fem. noun: τριετία <5148>]; **from *treis*: three, and *etos*: year** ▶ **Duration of three years** > During three years, Paul did not cease to warn the Ephesians (Acts 20:31). Other ref.: Acts 20:18 in some mss. ¶

[6] **forty years old: *tesserakontaetēs*** [adj.: τεσσερακονταετής <5063>]; **from *tessarakonta*: forty, and *etos*: year** ▶ **Of a duration or age of forty years** > It came into Moses's heart to visit his brothers when he was forty years old (Acts 7:23). God put up with the ways of Israel in the desert for a time of about forty years (Acts 13:18). ¶

[7] **hundred years old: *hekatontaetēs*** [adj.: ἑκατονταετής <1541>]; **from *hekaton*: hundred, and *etos*: year** ▶ **Centenarian** > Abraham was about one hundred years old when God promised him a son (Rom. 4:19). ¶

[8] ***hēmera*** [fem. noun: ἡμέρα <2250>] ▶ **Day** > Zacharias and Elisabeth were both advanced in years (lit.: in their days) (Luke 1:7, 18). Other refs.: AGE <2250>, DAY <2250>, TIME <2250>.

[9] **a year ago, last year: *perusi*** [adv.: πέρυσι <4070>]; **from *peras*: beyond** ▶ **The previous year** > The Christians in Achaia were ready a year ago to contribute to the service of the saints (2 Cor. 8:10; 9:2). ¶

[10] ***chronos*** [masc. noun: χρόνος <5550>] ▶ **Time** > When he was full forty years old (lit.: As the time of forty years was being accomplished for him), it came into Moses's heart to visit his brothers, the children of Israel (Acts 7:23). All other refs.: TIME <5550>.

– [11] Rom. 9:9 → "next year" added in Engl. [12] 1 Cor. 7:36 → who is getting along in years → who has passed the flower of age → AGE <5230>.

YEARN – [1] ***epipotheō*** [verb: ἐπιποθέω <1971>]; **from *epi*: intens., and *potheō*: to desire something far away** ▶ **To desire**

earnestly, to long > The Spirit who dwells in the Christians yearns jealously {jealously desires, lusts to envy, envies intensely} (Jas. 4:5). All other refs.: DESIRE (verb) <1971>, LONG (verb) <1971>.
– [2] 1 Thes. 2:8 → to yearn over → to be affectionately desirous → AFFECTIONATELY <2442>.

YEAST – [1] See LEAVEN <2219>.
– [2] 1 Cor. 5:7 → without yeast → UNLEAVENED <106> [3] 1 Cor. 5:8 → without yeast → UNLEAVENED BREAD <106>.

YELL – Acts 7:57 → CRY (verb) <2896>.

YES – [1] ***nai*** [adv.: ναί <3483>] ▶ **Certainly, assuredly** > Yes, God is also the God of the Gentiles (Rom. 3:29). *
– [2] Rom. 10:18 → yes verily, yes indeed → VERILY <3304>.

YESTERDAY – ***chthes*** [adv.: χθές <5504>]; **also spelled: *echtes*** ▶ **Day which precedes today** > Jesus Christ is the same yesterday and today and eternally (Heb. 13:8). Other refs.: John 4:52; Acts 7:28. Other ref.: Acts 16:35 in some mss. ¶

YET – [1] ***alla*** [particle: ἀλλά <235>] ▶ **All the same, but, for to be sure** > Though He was crucified in weakness, yet Christ lives by God's power (2 Cor. 13:4). Other refs.: Mark 14:29 and 2 Cor. 11:6. *
[2] ***ge*** [particle: γε <1065>] ▶ **Truly, without doubt** > Refs.: Luke 11:8; 18:5 {at any rate}; 1 Cor. 9:2. *
[3] ***de*** [particle: δέ <1161>] ▶ **But, nevertheless** > Refs.: Matt. 6:29; Luke 12:27; Rom. 9:6 {though}; 1 Cor. 7:28; Heb. 12:11. *
[4] ***mentoi*** [conj.: μέντοι <3305>] ▶ **But, however** > Refs.: John 20:5; Jude 8. *
[5] ***pō*** [particle: πω <4452>] ▶ Used only in composition.
– [6] Rom. 8:37 → RATHER <235>.

YIELD – [1] ***peithō*** [verb: πείθω <3982>]; **lit.: to persuade, to believe** ▶ **To consent, to agree** > The commander was told by Paul's nephew not to yield to {listen to, be persuaded by, give in to} the Jews who wanted to bring Paul down to the council so they could kill him on the way (Acts 23:21). All other refs.: see entries in Lexicon at <3982>.
– [2] Matt. 13:8 → to bring forth → PRODUCE <1325> [3] Matt. 13:23; Luke 8:8 → PRODUCE <4160> [4] Rom. 6:13a, b, 16, 19a, b → PRESENT (verb) <3936> [5] 1 Cor. 7:4a, b → "yields it to" added twice in Engl. [6] Gal. 2:5 → to give place → PLACE (noun) <1502> [7] Heb. 6:8 → to bring forth → BRING <1627> [8] Jas. 3:17 → willing to yield → YIELDING <2138>.

YIELDING – ***eupeithēs*** [adj.: εὐπειθής <2138>]; **from *eu*: well, and *peithō*: to obey, to persuade; lit.: ready to obey, compliant** ▶ **Readily inclined to comply, from which: accommodating, conciliatory** > Wisdom from above is yielding {easy to be intreated, reasonable, submissive, willing to yield} (Jas. 3:17). ¶

YOKE – [1] ***zeugos*** [neut. noun: ζεῦγος <2201>]; **from *zeugnumi*: to join** ▶ **Pair** > A man had bought five yoke of oxen (Luke 14:19). Other ref.: Luke 2:24; see PAIR <2201>. ¶
[2] ***zugos*** [masc. noun: ζυγός <2218>]; **from *zeugnumi*: to join** ▶ **Piece of wood used for harnessing draft animals** > The yoke speaks figur. of subjection, constraint (1 Tim. 6:1). But it also evokes the authority of the Lord over the believer in Him, authority that is easy to bear (Matt. 11:29, 30). The law of the O.T. was a yoke of bondage for the Israelites; the Lord has set the Christians free from it (Acts 15:10; Gal. 5:1). Other ref.: Rev. 6:5; see BALANCE <2218>. ¶

YOKED (BE) – **to be yoked, to be diversely (unequally) yoked: *heterozugeō*** [verb: ἑτεροζυγέω <2086>]; **from *heteros*: other, strange, and *zugos*: yoke** ▶ **To form a discordant, improper association** > In marrying an unbeliever, the Christian is unequally yoked (2 Cor. 6:14 {to be bound together}); comp. Lev. 19:19 and Deut. 22:10. ¶

YOKEFELLOW – ***suzugos*** [adj. used as noun: σύζυγος <4805>]; **from *suzeugnumi*: to join together, which is from *sun*: together, and *zugos*: yoke ▶ Collaborator, associate in the work of the Lord** > Paul addresses such a yokefellow {companion, comrade, fellow worker} in Phil. 4:3 without naming him. ¶

YOU (plur.) – [1] ***humas*** [pron.: ὑμᾶς <5209>]. * [2] ***humeis*** [pron.: ὑμεῖς <5210>]. *

YOU (OF, FROM, CONCERNING) (plur.) – ***humōn*** [pron.: ὑμῶν <5216>]. *

YOU (UNTO, WITH, BY) (plur.) – ***humin*** [pron.: ὑμῖν <5213>]. *

YOU, THOU (sing.) – ***su*** [pron.: σύ <4771>]. *

YOUNG – [1] **young: *neos*** [adj. and adj. used as noun: νέος <3501>]; **younger: *neōteros*** [adj.: νέωτερος <3501>]; **compar. from *neos* ▶ Youthful person; person less advanced in years** > The younger of two sons asked his father to give him his share of the inheritance (Luke 15:12), and he went away into a country a long way off (v. 13). The greater among the apostles was to be as the younger (Luke 22:26). When he was young (lit.: younger), Peter girded himself (John 21:18). The young men (lit.: The younger) carried Ananias out (Acts 5:6). Timothy was to exhort the younger women as sisters (1 Tim. 5:2). He was to refuse younger widows who wanted to be supported by the church (1 Tim. 5:11). Paul wanted the younger widows (lit.: the younger) to marry (1 Tim. 5:14). The young women (lit.: The young) were to be instructed to love their husbands and their children (Titus 2:4). Titus was to exhort the younger men (lit.: the younger) to be sober-minded (Titus 2:6). All other refs.: NEW <3501>, YOUNGER <3501>.

[2] **young man: *neanias*** [masc. noun: νεανίας <3494>]; **from *neos*: young, new ▶ Male of a youthful age** > Saul was a young man at the time of the martyrdom of Stephen (Acts 7:58). Eutychus was a young man (Acts 20:9). The centurion was to bring the young man, Paul's nephew, to the chiliarch (Acts 23:17), which he did (v. 18); the chiliarch dismissed him after having listened to him (v. 22). ¶

[3] **young man: *neaniskos*** [masc. noun: νεανίσκος <3495>]; **dimin. of *neanias*: see [2] ▶ Male of a youthful age** > A young man told Jesus that he had kept all the things He had said (Matt. 19:20), but he went away sad after Jesus had added one thing (v. 22). A certain young man followed Jesus (Mark 14:51). The women saw a young man sitting in the tomb of Jesus (Mark 16:5). Jesus told a young man to wake up (Luke 7:14). In the last days, young men will see visions (Acts 2:17). The young men carried Sapphira out (Acts 5:10). John writes to the young men because they have overcome the wicked one (1 John 2:13), and because they are strong and the word of God abides in them and they have overcome the wicked one (v. 14). ¶

[4] ***neossos*** [masc. noun: νεοσσός <3502>]; **from *neos*: young, new; also spelled: *nossos* ▶ Young creature (e.g., bird)** > The parents of Jesus came to offer a sacrifice of a pair of turtle doves or two young pigeons (Luke 2:24). ¶

– [5] Luke 15:29 → young goat → GOAT <2056> [6] Acts 7:19 → young child → BABE <1025> [7] Acts 21:12 → boy, child, young man → BOY <3816> [8] 1 Thes. 2:7 in some mss. → like young children → CHILD <3516>.

YOUNGER – [1] ***elassōn*** [adj. used as noun: ἐλάσσων <1640>]; **compar. of *mikros*: small, little ▶ Less in age, not as important** > The greater (Esau) is to serve the younger {less} (Jacob) (Rom. 9:12). Other refs.: John 2:10; 1 Tim. 5:9; Heb. 7:7; see LESSER <1640>. ¶

[2] **younger, younger man: *neōteros*** [adj. used as noun: νέωτερος <3501>]; **compar. of *neos*: young ▶ Person who is more youthful** > Timothy was to exhort younger men as brothers (1 Tim. 5:1). The younger are to be subject to their elders (1 Pet. 5:5). All other refs.: YOUNG <3501>.

– [3] Mark 15:40 → LESS <3398>.

YOUR, YOURS (plur.) – ***humeteros*** [pron.: ὑμέτερος <5212>]. *

YOUTH – [1] ***neotēs*** [fem. noun: νεότης <3503>]; **from *neos*: young, new ▶ Period between childhood and adulthood; youthful age** > A man had kept all the commandments from his youth {since he was a boy} (Mark 10:20; Luke 18:21). All the Jews in Jerusalem knew Paul's manner of life from his youth (Acts 26:4). No one was to despise the youth of Timothy (1 Tim. 4:12). Other ref.: Matt. 19:20 in some mss. ¶

– [2] Luke 7:14 → young man → YOUNG <3495> [3] Acts 20:9; 23:17, 18, 22 → young man → YOUNG <3494> [4] Acts 20:12 → BOY <3816> [5] 2 Tim. 2:22 → of youth → YOUTHFUL <3512>.

YOUTHFUL – ***neōterikos*** [adj.: νεωτερικός <3512>]; **from *neoteros*, compar. of *neos*: new ▶ Which characterizes the period between childhood and adulthood** > Timothy was to flee youthful lusts (2 Tim. 2:22 {of youth}). ¶

Z

ZABULON – See ZEBULUN <2194>.

ZACCHAEUS – See ZACCHEUS <2195>.

ZACCHEUS – ***Zakchaios*** [masc. name: Ζακχαῖος <2195>]**: pure, in Heb. ▶ Man of the N.T.; also spelled: Zacchaeus** > Zaccheus was a chief tax collector and he was rich (Luke 19:2). He climbed up into a sycamore tree to see Jesus. Jesus told him to come down for He must stay in his house (Luke 19:5); Zaccheus received Jesus with joy in his house (see v. 6). Zaccheus told the Lord that he was giving the half of his goods to the poor, and that if he had taken anything by false accusation, he would restore four times the amount (Luke 19:8). Jesus told him: "Today salvation is come to this house" (see Luke 19:9). ¶

ZACHARIAS – ***Zacharias*** [masc. name: Ζαχαρίας <2197>]**: Jehovah remembers, in Heb.; also transl.: Zechariah ▶ a. Priest of the O.T.** > Zechariah was stoned in the court of the temple (Matt. 23:35; Luke 11:51; see 2 Chr. 24:20–22) at the order of king Joash. **b. Priest of the N.T.** > This Zacharias was a priest of the order of Abijah (Luke 1:5), and father of John the Baptist. An angel appeared to him to tell him that his wife Elizabeth would bear a son and told him to call his name John (Luke 1:12, 13). The neighbors and relatives of Zacharias wanted to call his son after his own name (Luke 1:59), which Zacharias opposed. He was mute until after the birth of John (Luke 1:18, 21, see vv. 20, 22); after having recovered speech, he was filled with the Holy Spirit and prophesied (v. 67, see v. 64). Mary, the mother of Jesus, came to visit her cousin Elizabeth, the wife of Zacharias, when they were each expecting a child (Luke 1:40). The word of God came to John, the son of Zacharias, in the wilderness (Luke 3:2). ¶

ZADOK – ***Sadōk*** [masc. name: Σαδώκ <4524>]**: just, in Heb. ▶ Man of the O.T.** > Zadok is mentioned in the genealogy of Jesus Christ (Matt. 1:14a, b). ¶

ZARA – See ZERAH <2196>.

ZAREPHATH – ***Sarepta*** [neut. plur. name: Σάρεπτα <4558>]**: smelting house, in Heb. ▶ City of Phoenicia between Tyre and Sidon on the coast of the Mediterranean Sea; also transl.: Sarepta** > Jesus recalled that it was to a widow of Zarephath that Elijah had been sent during a great famine (Luke 4:26; see 1 Kgs. 17:9). ¶

ZEAL – 1 ***zēlos*** [masc. noun: ζῆλος <2205>]**; from *zeō*: to be hot, to be fervent ▶ Ardor, fervor for a cause** > The zeal for the house of God devoured the Lord Jesus (John 2:17). Paul testified that the Jews had zeal for God, but not according to knowledge (Rom. 10:2); as to zeal, he had persecuted the church (Phil. 3:6). The fact that they had sorrowed according to God had produced zeal among the Corinthians (2 Cor. 7:11 {concern}). The zeal of the Corinthians had stirred up most of the brothers (2 Cor. 9:2 {enthusiasm}). Epaphras had a great zeal for the Colossians and other Christians (Col. 4:13); other mss. have *kopos* {concern, work}. All other refs.: ENVY <2205>, HEAT <2205>, JEALOUSY <2205>, MIND <2205>.

2 ***spoudē*** [fem. noun: σπουδή <4710>]**; from *speudō*: to hasten ▶ Diligence, eagerness; also transl.: care, concern, earnest care, earnestness** > The term is used in 2 Cor. 7:12; 8:16. All other refs.: DILIGENCE <4710>, HASTE (noun) <4710>, ZEALOUSNESS <4710>.

– 3 Gal. 4:17 → to have zeal → lit.: to be zealous → ZEALOUS <2206>.

ZEALOT – 1 ***Zēlōtēs*** [masc. name: Ζηλωτής <2208>]**: zealous ▶ Member of an extremist faction of the Pharisees, very zealous for the law and tradition; surname of Simon, one of the twelve apostles** > The name Zealot is used in Luke 6:15; Acts 1:13. See SIMON (b). The Zealots were Jewish militants who hated the Roman occupiers and who fought them fiercely. ¶

– 2 Matt. 10:4; Mark 3:18 → CANANITE <2581>.

ZEALOUS – 1 ***zēlōtēs*** [masc. noun used as an adj.: ζηλωτής <2207>]**; from *zēloō*: see 2 ▶ a. Person who shows ardent enthusiasm for a cause, fanatic** > Many thousands of Jews were zealous for the law (Acts 21:20). Paul was zealous for God (Acts 22:3). Jesus Christ has redeemed Christians from all iniquity and purified for Himself a people for His own possession, zealous for {eager to do} good works (Titus 2:14). Paul was exceedingly zealous of the traditions of his fathers before his conversion (Gal. 1:14). **b. Ambitious** > The Corinthians were zealous of {eager to have} spiritual gifts (1 Cor. 14:12). **c.** Other ref.: 1 Pet. 3:13 in some mss.; see IMITATOR <3402>. ¶

2 **to be zealous: *zēloō*** [verb: ζηλόω <2206>]; **from *zēlos*: zeal, which is from *zeō*: to be hot, to be fervent ▶ To show ardent enthusiasm for a cause** > Laodicea is told to be zealous {to be earnest} and repent (Rev. 3:19). Other refs.: Gal. 4:17a, b, 18. All other refs.: COVET <2206>, DESIRE (verb) <2206>, ENVY (verb) <2206>, JEALOUS <2206>.

3 ***spoudaios*** [adj.: σπουδαῖος <4705>]; **from *spoudē*: eagerness, zeal ▶ Earnest, diligent** > Paul had often tested a certain brother and found him zealous {of diligent zeal} (2 Cor. 8:22). ¶

4 **diligently zealous, more zealous: *spoudaioteros*** [adj.: σπουδαιότερος <4707>]; **compar. of *spoudaios*: see 3 ▶ Very earnest, diligent; also transl.: more diligent, more forward, with much enthusiasm** > The term is used in regard to Titus (2 Cor. 8:17) and a certain brother (2 Cor. 8:22). ¶

– 5 2 Cor. 5:9 → to be zealous → LABOR (verb) <5389> 6 1 Pet. 3:13 → IMITATOR <3402>.

ZEALOUSLY – 1 Mark 7:36 → lit.: so much the more 2 2 Tim. 1:17 → very zealously → very diligently → DILIGENTLY <4706>.

ZEALOUSNESS – diligent zealousness: *spoudē* [fem. noun: σπουδή <4710>]; **from *speudō*: to hasten, to act with diligence ▶ Diligence, eagerness in pursuing something** > Christians should not be slothful in diligent zealousness {diligence, business, zeal} (Rom. 12:11). All other refs.: DILIGENCE <4710>, HASTE (noun) <4710>, ZEAL <4710>.

ZEBEDEE – *Zebedaios* [masc. name: Ζεβεδαῖος <2199>]: **gift of Jehovah ▶ Father of James and John, two of the Lord's disciples** > Zebedee was a fisherman (Matt. 4:21a, b, see v. 22; 10:2; 20:20, see v. 21; 26:37; 27:56; Mark 1:19, 20; 3:17; 10:35, see vv. 36–38; Luke 5:10; John 21:2). ¶

ZEBULUN – *Zaboulōn* [masc. name: Ζαβουλών <2194>]: **habitation, in Heb.; see Gen. 30:20 ▶ Son of Jacob and name of one of the twelve tribes descended from him** > Capernaum is in the borders of Zebulun and Naphtali (Matt. 4:13, 15). Jesus began to preach repentance there (see Matt. 4:16, 17). Twelve thousand out of the tribe of Zebulun will be sealed (Rev. 7:8). ¶

ZECHARIAH – See ZACHARIAS <2197>.

ZELOTES – Luke 6:15; Acts 1:13 → ZEALOT <2208>.

ZENAS – *Zēnas* [masc. name: Ζηνᾶς <2211>] **▶ Jewish doctor of the law** > Paul urges Titus to diligently bring Zenas, the lawyer, on his journey (Titus 3:13). ¶

ZERAH – *Zara* [masc. name: Ζάρα <2196>]: **dawn, in Heb.; Zerah or Zarah in Gen. 38:30 ▶ Man of the O.T., son of Judah and Tamar** > Zerah is mentioned in the genealogy of Jesus Christ, although he was not part of the line of descent (Matt. 1:3). ¶

ZERUBBABEL – *Zorobabel* [masc. name: Ζοροβαβέλ <2216>]: **begotten in Babylon, in Heb. ▶ Descendant of David; also transl.: Zorobabel** > Zerubbabel was governor of Judah at the return from captivity (See Ezra 2:2; Hag. 1:1; 2:21, 23). His name is mentioned in the genealogy of Jesus Christ (Matt. 1:12, 13; Luke 3:27). ¶

ZEUS – *Zeus* [masc. name: Ζεύς <2203>] **▶ Supreme divinity of the Greeks, identified as Jupiter among the Romans; also transl.: Jupiter** > After Paul had healed a lame man at Lystra, the crowds called Barnabas by the name of Zeus and Paul by the name of Hermes (Acts 14:12, 13). ¶

ZION – ***Siōn*** [fem. name: Σιών <4622>]: **sunny, in Heb. ▶ One of the hills of Jerusalem (see Ps. 48:2; 78:68, 69); Zion also designated the city of Jerusalem (see 1 Kgs. 8:1)** > Zion symbolizes the future messianic reign on earth (Matt. 21:5; John 12:15; Rom. 9:33; 11:26). Mount Zion represents the heavenly Jerusalem, i.e., the blessing of believers in the Lord under grace (Heb. 12:22; 1 Pet. 2:6; Rev. 14:1). ¶

ZOROBABEL – See ZERUBBABEL <2216>.

Part II

Greek-English Lexicon

Greek-English Lexicon

A

<1> ἄλφα ***alpha*** [ALPHA] 4x
<2> Ἀαρών ***Aarōn*** [AARON] 5x
<3> Ἀβαδδών ***Abaddōn*** [ABADDON] 1x
<4> ἀβαρής ***abarēs*** [not burdensome: BURDENSOME 2] 1x
<5> Ἀββά ***Abba*** [ABBA] 3x
<6> Ἄβελ ***Abel*** [ABEL] 4x
<7> Ἀβιά ***Abia*** [ABIA] 2x
<8> Ἀβιαθάρ ***Abiathar*** [ABIATHAR] 1x
<9> Ἀβιληνή ***Abilēnē*** [ABILENE] 1x
<10> Ἀβιούδ ***Abioud*** [ABIHUD] 2x
<11> Ἀβραάμ ***Abraam*** [ABRAHAM] 73x
<12> ἄβυσσος ***abussos*** [abyss: BOTTOMLESS] 9x
<13> Ἄγαβος ***Hagabos*** [AGABUS] 2x
<14> ἀγαθοεργέω ***agathoergeō*** [to do good: GOOD (adj. and noun) 8] 2x
<15> ἀγαθοποιέω ***agathopoieō*** [to do good: GOOD (adj. and noun) 9] 11x
<16> ἀγαθοποιΐα ***agathopoiia*** [well doing: DOING 1] 1x
<17> ἀγαθοποιός ***agathopoios*** [who does well: WELL (adv.) 3] 1x
<18> ἀγαθός ***agathos*** [good: GOOD (adj.) 1, good, good thing: GOOD (adj. and noun) 1] 107x
<19> ἀγαθωσύνη ***agathōsunē*** [GOODNESS 1] 4x
<20> ἀγαλλίασις ***agalliasis*** [GLADNESS 1, JOY (noun) 1] 5x
<21> ἀγαλλιάω ***agalliaō*** [EXULT 1, to exult: EXULTATION 1, REJOICE 1] 11x
<22> ἄγαμος ***agamos*** [UNMARRIED 1] 4x
<23> ἀγανακτέω ***aganakteō*** [to be indignant: INDIGNANT 1] 7x
<24> ἀγανάκτησις ***aganaktēsis*** [INDIGNATION 1] 1x
<25> ἀγαπάω ***agapaō*** [BELOVED 2, LOVE (verb) 1] 143x
<26> ἀγάπη ***agapē*** [LOVE (noun) 1, LOVE FEASTS] 116x
<27> ἀγαπητός ***agapētos*** [BELOVED 1, DEAR 1] 62x
<28> Ἀγάρ ***Hagar*** [AGAR] 2x
<29> ἀγγαρεύω ***angareuō*** [COMPEL 1] 3x
<30> ἀγγεῖον ***angeion*** [VESSEL[1] 1] 2x
<31> ἀγγελία ***angelia*** [MESSAGE 1] 2x
<32> ἄγγελος ***angelos*** [ANGEL 1, MESSENGER 1] 177x
<33> ἄγε ***age*** [COME NOW] 2x
<34> ἀγέλη ***agelē*** [HERD 1] 7x
<35> ἀγενεαλόγητος ***agenealogētos*** [without genealogy: GENEALOGY 4] 1x
<36> ἀγενής ***agenēs*** [BASE (adj.) 1] 1x
<37> ἁγιάζω ***hagiazō*** [SANCTIFY 1] 28x
<38> ἁγιασμός ***hagiasmos*** [HOLINESS 1] 10x
<39> ἅγιον ***hagion*** [SANCTUARY 1] 11x
<40> ἅγιος ***hagios*** [HOLY (adj.) 1, that which is holy: HOLY (adj.) 2, HOLY ONE, HOLY THING, HOLY SPIRIT, SAINT] 233x
<41> ἁγιότης ***hagiotēs*** [HOLINESS 2] 1x
<42> ἁγιωσύνη ***hagiōsunē*** [HOLINESS 3] 3x
<43> ἀγκάλη ***ankalē*** [ARM (noun)[1] 1] 1x
<44> ἄγκιστρον ***ankistron*** [HOOK] 1x
<45> ἄγκυρα ***ankura*** [ANCHOR (noun) 1] 4x
<46> ἄγναφος ***agnaphos*** [NEW 1] 2x
<47> ἁγνεία ***hagneia*** [PURITY 1] 2x

<48> ἁγνίζω ***hagnizō*** [PURIFY 1] 7x
<49> ἁγνισμός ***hagnismos*** [PURIFICATION 1] 1x
<50> ἀγνοέω ***agnoeō*** [to be ignorant: IGNORANT 1, to know not: KNOW 10, to understand not: UNDERSTAND 5, to be unknown: UNKNOWN 2] 22x
<51> ἀγνόημα ***agnoēma*** [sin committed in ignorance: IGNORANCE 1] 1x
<52> ἄγνοια ***agnoia*** [IGNORANCE 2] 4x
<53> ἁγνός ***hagnos*** [CHASTE, PURE 1] 8x
<54> ἁγνότης ***hagnotēs*** [PURITY 2] 1x
<55> ἁγνῶς ***hagnōs*** [PURELY] 1x
<56> ἀγνωσία ***agnōsia*** [IGNORANCE 3] 2x
<57> ἄγνωστος ***agnōstos*** [UNKNOWN 1] 1x
<58> ἀγορά ***agora*** [MARKETPLACE 1] 11x
<59> ἀγοράζω ***agorazō*** [BUY 1] 31x
<60> ἀγοραῖος ***agoraios*** [COURT 1, from the marketplace: MARKETPLACE 2] 2x
<61> ἄγρα ***agra*** [CATCH (noun)] 2x
<62> ἀγράμματος ***agrammatos*** [UNEDUCATED] 1x
<63> ἀγραυλέω ***agrauleō*** [to stay out in the fields: FIELD 2] 1x
<64> ἀγρεύω ***agreuō*** [CATCH (verb) 1] 1x
<65> ἀγριέλαιος ***agrielaios*** [wild olive tree: OLIVE TREE 2] 2x
<66> ἄγριος ***agrios*** [RAGING 1, WILD 1] 3x
<67> Ἀγρίππας ***Agrippas*** [AGRIPPA] 12x
<68> ἀγρός ***agros*** [COUNTRY 1, FIELD 1, FIELD OF BLOOD, LAND (noun) 1] 36x
<69> ἀγρυπνέω ***agrupneō*** [WATCH (verb) 1] 4x
<70> ἀγρυπνία ***agrupnia*** [SLEEPLESSNESS] 2x
<71> ἄγω ***agō*** [BRING 1, GO 1, LEAD (verb) 1] 67x
<72> ἀγωγή ***agōgē*** [manner of life: LIFE 1] 1x
<73> ἀγών ***agōn*** [CONFLICT 1, FIGHT (noun) 1, RACE[2] 1] 6x
<74> ἀγωνία ***agōnia*** [AGONY 1] 1x
<75> ἀγωνίζομαι ***agōnizomai*** [FIGHT (verb) 1, STRIVE 1] 7x
<76> Ἀδάμ ***Adam*** [ADAM] 9x
<77> ἀδάπανος ***adapanos*** [COSTLESS] 1x
<78> Ἀδδί ***Addi*** [ADDI] 1x
<79> ἀδελφή ***adelphē*** [SISTER 1] 25x
<80> ἀδελφός ***adelphos*** [BROTHER] 343x
<81> ἀδελφότης ***adelphotēs*** [BROTHERHOOD] 2x
<82> ἄδηλος ***adēlos*** [which appear not: APPEAR 8, UNCERTAIN 1] 2x
<83> ἀδηλότης ***adēlotēs*** [UNCERTAINTY 1] 1x
<84> ἀδήλως ***adēlōs*** [UNCERTAINLY] 1x
<85> ἀδημονέω ***adēmoneō*** [to be full of heaviness: HEAVINESS 1, to be very heavy: HEAVY 4] 3x
<86> ᾅδης ***hadēs*** [HADES] 11x
<87> ἀδιάκριτος ***adiakritos*** [UNQUESTIONING] 1x
<88> ἀδιάλειπτος ***adialeiptos*** [CEASING (WITHOUT) 1, UNINTERRUPTED] 2x
<89> ἀδιαλείπτως ***adialeiptōs*** [CEASING (WITHOUT) 2] 5x
<90> ἀδιαφθορία ***adiaphthoria*** [INCORRUPTIBILITY 2] 1x
<91> ἀδικέω ***adikeō*** [HURT 1, INJURE 1, to do wrong: WRONG (noun) 3] 27x
<92> ἀδίκημα ***adikēma*** [INIQUITY 1, WRONG (noun) 1] 3x
<93> ἀδικία ***adikia*** [INIQUITY 2, injustice: UNJUST (adj.) 1, UNRIGHTEOUSNESS 1, WRONG (noun) 2] 25x
<94> ἄδικος ***adikos*** [UNJUST (noun), UNRIGHTEOUS (adj. and noun) 1] 12x
<95> ἀδίκως ***adikōs*** [UNJUSTLY 1] 1x
<96> ἀδόκιμος ***adokimos*** [WORTHLESS 1] 8x
<97> ἄδολος ***adolos*** [PURE 2] 1x
<98> Ἀδραμυττηνός ***Adramuttēnos*** [ADRAMYTTIUM] 1x
<99> Ἀδρίας ***Adrias*** [ADRIATIC SEA] 1x

<100> ἁδρότης ***hadrotēs*** [ABUNDANCE 1] 1x
<101> ἀδυνατέω ***adunateō*** [to be impossible: IMPOSSIBLE 2] 2x
<102> ἀδύνατος ***adunatos*** [IMPOSSIBLE 1, without strength: STRENGTH 5, WEAK 1] 10x
<103> ᾄδω ***adō*** [SING 1] 5x
<104> ἀεί ***aei*** [ALWAYS 1] 8x
<105> ἀετός ***aetos*** [EAGLE] 5x
<106> ἄζυμος ***azumos*** [UNLEAVENED, UNLEAVENED BREAD] 9x
<107> Ἀζώρ ***Azōr*** [AZOR] 2x
<108> Ἄζωτος ***Azōtos*** [AZOTUS] 1x
<109> ἀήρ ***aēr*** [AIR 1] 7x
<110> ἀθανασία ***athanasia*** [IMMORTALITY 1] 3x
<111> ἀθέμιτος ***athemitos*** [ABOMINABLE 1, UNLAWFUL 1] 2x
<112> ἄθεος ***atheos*** [GOD (WITHOUT)] 1x
<113> ἄθεσμος ***athesmos*** [LAWLESS MAN] 2x
<114> ἀθετέω ***atheteō*** [REFUSE (verb) 1, REJECT 1] 16x
<115> ἀθέτησις ***athetēsis*** [putting away: PUTTING 1] 2x
<116> Ἀθῆναι ***Athēnai*** [ATHENS] 4x
<117> Ἀθηναῖος ***Athēnaios*** [ATHENIAN] 2x
<118> ἀθλέω ***athleō*** [STRIVE 4] 2x
<119> ἄθλησις ***athlēsis*** [FIGHT (noun) 2] 1x
<120> ἀθυμέω ***athumeō*** [to become discouraged: DISCOURAGED 1] 1x
<121> ἀθῷος ***athōos*** [INNOCENT 1] 2x
<122> αἴγειος ***aigeios*** [of a goat: GOAT 4] 1x
<123> αἰγιαλός ***aigialos*** [BEACH 1, SHORE 1] 6x
<124> Αἰγύπτιος ***Aiguptios*** [EGYPTIAN] 5x
<125> Αἴγυπτος ***Aiguptos*** [EGYPT] 25x
<126> ἀΐδιος ***aidios*** [ETERNAL 1] 2x
<127> αἰδώς ***aidōs*** [MODESTY] 2x
<128> Αἰθίοψ ***Aithiops*** [ETHIOPIAN] 1x
<129> αἷμα ***haima*** [BLOOD 1, FIELD OF BLOOD] 97x
<130> αἱματεκχυσία ***haimatekchusia*** [SHEDDING OF BLOOD] 1x
<131> αἱμορροέω ***haimorroeō*** [to have a flow of blood: FLOW (noun) 3] 1x
<132> Αἰνέας ***Aineas*** [AENEAS] 2x
<133> αἴνεσις ***ainesis*** [PRAISE (noun) 1] 1x
<134> αἰνέω ***aineō*** [PRAISE (verb) 1] 9x
<135> αἴνιγμα ***ainigma*** [in enigma, in obscure saying: OBSCURELY] 1x
<136> αἶνος ***ainos*** [PRAISE (noun) 2] 2x
<137> Αἰνών ***Ainōn*** [AENON] 1x
<138> αἱρέω ***haireō*** [CHOOSE 1] 3x
<139> αἵρεσις ***hairesis*** [SECT] 9x
<140> αἱρετίζω ***hairetizō*** [CHOOSE 2] 1x
<141> αἱρετικός ***hairetikos*** [HERETICAL] 1x
<142> αἴρω ***airō*** [BEAR (verb) 1, to take on board: BOARD (noun) 2, to lift, to lift up: LIFT 1, to pick up: PICK 1, to pull away: PULL 1, to hold in suspense: SUSPENSE 1, TAKE 15, to raise nearer: WEIGH 1] 101x
<143> αἰσθάνομαι ***aisthanomai*** [PERCEIVE 1] 1x
<144> αἴσθησις ***aisthēsis*** [DISCERNMENT 1] 1x
<145> αἰσθητήριον ***aisthētērion*** [SENSE (noun) 1] 1x
<146> αἰσχροκερδής ***aischrokerdēs*** [greedy for money: GREEDY 1] 2x
<147> αἰσχροκερδῶς ***aischrokerdōs*** [for dishonest gain: GAIN (noun) 3] 1x
<148> αἰσχρολογία ***aischrologia*** [filthy language: FILTHY 1] 1x
<149> αἰσχρόν ***aischron*** [SHAMEFUL 1] 3x
<150> αἰσχρός ***aischros*** [DISHONEST 1] 1x
<151> αἰσχρότης ***aischrotēs*** [FILTHINESS 1] 1x
<152> αἰσχύνη ***aischunē*** [SHAME (noun) 1] 6x

<153> αἰσχύνω ***aischunō*** [ASHAMED (BE) 1] 5x

<154> αἰτέω ***aiteō*** [ASK 1, REQUIRE 1] 70x

<155> αἴτημα ***aitēma*** [PETITION (noun) 1, REQUEST (noun) 1, request (noun): REQUEST (verb) 1] 3x

<156> αἰτία ***aitia*** [ACCUSATION 1, CASE 1, CAUSE (noun) 1, FAULT 1, REASON (noun) 1] 20x

<157> αἰτίαμα ***aitiama*** [CHARGE (noun)[1] 1] 1x

<158> αἴτιον ***aition*** [FAULT 2, REASON (noun) 2] 4x

<159> αἴτιος ***aitios*** [AUTHOR 1] 1x

<159a> αἰτίωμα ***aitiōma*** [CHARGE (noun)[1] 1] 1x

<160> αἰφνίδιος ***aiphnidios*** [SUDDENLY 1] 2x

<161> αἰχμαλωσία ***aichmalōsia*** [CAPTIVITY 1] 3x

<162> αἰχμαλωτεύω ***aichmalōteuō*** [to lead captive: CAPTIVE (adj.) 1] 2x

<163> αἰχμαλωτίζω ***aichmalōtizō*** [to lead captive: CAPTIVE (adj.) 2] 4x

<164> αἰχμάλωτος ***aichmalōtos*** [CAPTIVE (noun) 1] 1x

<165> αἰών ***aiōn*** [AGE 1, COURSE 1, EVER AGAIN, unto the age: FOREVER 1, FOREVER 3, SON OF THIS AGE, SON OF THIS WORLD, WORLD 1] 133x

<166> αἰώνιος ***aiōnios*** [AGE 1, ETERNAL 2, LIFE ETERNAL] 71x

<167> ἀκαθαρσία ***akatharsia*** [UNCLEANNESS 1] 10x

<168> ἀκαθάρτης ***akathartēs*** [unclean thing: UNCLEAN 2] 1x

<169> ἀκάθαρτος ***akathartos*** [UNCLEAN 1] 30x

<170> ἀκαιρέομαι ***akaireomai*** [to lack opportunity: OPPORTUNITY 2] 1x

<171> ἀκαίρως ***akairōs*** [out of season: SEASON (noun) 3] 1x

<172> ἄκακος ***akakos*** [INNOCENT 2, SIMPLE 1] 2x

<173> ἄκανθα ***akantha*** [THORN 1] 14x

<174> ἀκάνθινος ***akanthinos*** [of thorns: THORN 1] 2x

<175> ἄκαρπος ***akarpos*** [without fruit: FRUIT 2, UNFRUITFUL] 7x

<176> ἀκατάγνωστος ***akatagnōstos*** [that cannot be condemned: CONDEMN 2] 1x

<177> ἀκατακάλυπτος ***akatakaluptos*** [UNCOVERED 1] 2x

<178> ἀκατάκριτος ***akatakritos*** [UNCONDEMNED] 2x

<179> ἀκατάλυτος ***akatalutos*** [INDESTRUCTIBLE] 1x

<180> ἀκατάπαυστος ***akatapaustos*** [who cannot cease, who cease not: CEASE 4] 1x

<181> ἀκαταστασία ***akatastasia*** [CONFUSION 1, RIOT (noun) 1, TUMULT 4] 5x

<182> ἀκατάστατος ***akatastatos*** [UNRULY 1, UNSTABLE 1] 2x

<183> ἀκατάσχετος ***akataschetos*** [UNRULY 2] 1x

<184> Ἀκελδαμά ***Hakeldama*** [ACELDAMA] 1x

<185> ἀκέραιος ***akeraios*** [INNOCENT 3, PURE 3] 3x

<186> ἀκλινής ***aklinēs*** [without wavering: WAVERING] 1x

<187> ἀκμάζω ***akmazō*** [to be fully ripened: RIPENED (BE)] 1x

<188> ἀκμήν ***akmēn*** [STILL (adv.) 1] 1x

<189> ἀκοή ***akoē*** [EAR 3, FAME 1, HEARING 1, REPORT (noun) 1, RUMOR 1] 24x

<190> ἀκολουθέω ***akoloutheō*** [FOLLOW 1] 90x

<191> ἀκούω ***akouō*** [HEAR 1, to hear: HEARER 2] 431x

<192> ἀκρασία ***akrasia*** [lack of self-control: SELF-CONTROL (noun) 2, SELF-INDULGENCE 1] 2x

<193> ἀκρατής ***akratēs*** [without self-control: SELF-CONTROL (adj.)] 1x

<194> ἄκρατος ***akratos*** [full strength: STRENGTH 4] 1x

<195> ἀκρίβεια ***akribeia*** [STRICTNESS 1] 1x

<196> ἀκριβέστατος ***akribestatos*** [STRICTEST] 1x

<197> ἀκριβέστερον ***akribesteron*** [more accurately: ACCURATELY 2] 4x

<198> ἀκριβόω ***akriboō*** [DETERMINE 1] 2x

<199> ἀκριβῶς ***akribōs*** [ACCURATELY 1, CAREFULLY 1, PERFECTLY 1] 5x

<200> ἀκρίς ***akris*** [LOCUST] 4x

<201> ἀκροατήριον ***akroatērion*** [place of hearing: HEARING 2] 1x

<202> ἀκροατής ***akroatēs*** [HEARER 1] 4x

<203> ἀκροβυστία ***akrobustia*** [UNCIRCUMCISION] 20x
<204> ἀκρογωνιαῖος ***akrogōniaios*** [CHIEF CORNERSTONE 1, CORNER STONE 2] 2x
<205> ἀκροθίνιον ***akrothinion*** [SPOILS 1] 1x
<206> ἄκρον ***akron*** [END (noun) 1] 6x
<207> Ἀκύλας ***Akulas*** [AQUILAS] 6x
<208> ἀκυρόω ***akuroō*** [to make of no effect: EFFECT (noun) 1] 3x
<209> ἀκωλύτως ***akōlutōs*** [no one forbidding: FORBID 3] 1x
<210> ἄκων ***akōn*** [against one's will: WILL (noun)[1] 3] 1x
<211> ἀλάβαστρον ***alabastron*** [alabaster box: ALABASTER] 4x
<212> ἀλαζονεία ***alazoneia*** [ARROGANCE 1, PRIDE 1] 2x
<213> ἀλαζών ***alazōn*** [BOASTER 1] 2x
<214> ἀλαλάζω ***alalazō*** [to clang: CLANGING, WAIL 1] 2x
<215> ἀλάλητος ***alalētos*** [which cannot be uttered: UTTER (verb) 5] 1x
<216> ἄλαλος ***alalos*** [DUMB 1] 3x
<217> ἅλας ***halas*** [SALT (noun) 1] 8x
<218> ἀλείφω ***aleiphō*** [ANOINT 1] 9x
<219> ἀλεκτοροφωνία ***alektorophōnia*** [crowing of the rooster: ROOSTER 2] 1x
<220> ἀλέκτωρ ***alektōr*** [ROOSTER 1] 12x
<221> Ἀλεξανδρεύς ***Alexandreus*** [ALEXANDRIAN 1] 2x
<222> Ἀλεξανδρῖνος ***Alexandrinos*** [ALEXANDRIAN 2] 2x
<223> Ἀλέξανδρος ***Alexandros*** [ALEXANDER] 6x
<224> ἄλευρον ***aleuron*** [FLOUR 1] 2x
<225> ἀλήθεια ***alētheia*** [TRUTH 1] 109x
<226> ἀληθεύω ***alētheuō*** [to hold the truth, to speak the truth: TRUTH 2] 2x
<227> ἀληθής ***alēthēs*** [REAL 1, TRUE 1] 25x
<228> ἀληθινός ***alēthinos*** [TRUE 2] 27x
<229> ἀλήθω ***alēthō*** [GRIND 1] 2x
<230> ἀληθῶς ***alēthōs*** [SURELY 1, TRULY 1] 20x
<231> ἁλιεύς ***halieus*** [FISHER] 5x
<232> ἁλιεύω ***halieuō*** [FISH (verb) 1] 1x
<233> ἁλίζω ***halizō*** [SALT (verb)] 3x
<234> ἀλίσγημα ***alisgēma*** [food polluted, thing polluted: POLLUTED 1] 1x
<235> ἀλλά ***alla*** [BUT 1, RATHER 1, YET 1] 632x
<236> ἀλλάσσω ***allassō*** [CHANGE (verb) 1] 6x
<237> ἀλλαχόθεν ***allachothen*** [some other way: WAY 2] 1x
<237a> ἀλλαχοῦ ***allachou*** [SOMEWHERE ELSE] 1x
<238> ἀλληγορέω ***allēgoreō*** [to be an allegory: ALLEGORY 2] 1x
<239> ἀλληλουϊά ***hallēlouia*** [ALLELUIA] 4x
<240> ἀλλήλων ***allēlōn*** [ONE ANOTHER] 100x
<241> ἀλλογενής ***allogenēs*** [FOREIGNER 1] 1x
<242> ἅλλομαι ***hallomai*** [LEAP 1, to spring up: SPRING (verb) 1] 3x
<243> ἄλλος ***allos*** [OTHER 1] 155x
<244> ἀλλοτριεπίσκοπος ***allotriepiskopos*** [busybody in other people's matters: BUSYBODY 3] 1x
<245> ἀλλότριος ***allotrios*** [another, another man: ANOTHER 1, FOREIGN 1, STRANGER 1] 14x
<246> ἀλλόφυλος ***allophulos*** [one of another nation: NATION 5] 1x
<247> ἄλλως ***allōs*** [OTHERWISE 1] 1x
<248> ἀλοάω ***aloaō*** [to tread out the grain, to tread out the corn: TREAD 1] 3x
<249> ἄλογος ***alogos*** [without reason: REASON (noun) 4, UNREASONABLE 1] 3x
<250> ἀλόη ***aloē*** [ALOES] 1x
<251> ἅλς ***hals*** [SALT (noun) 2] 1x
<252> ἁλυκός ***halukos*** [SALT (adj.) 1] 1x
<253> ἀλυπότερος ***alupoteros*** [to be less sorrowful: SORROWFUL 2] 1x
<254> ἅλυσις ***halusis*** [CHAIN (noun) 1] 11x

<255> ἀλυσιτελής ***alusitelēs*** [UNPROFITABLE 1] 1x
<256> Ἀλφαῖος ***Halphaios*** [ALPHAEUS] 5x
<257> ἅλων ***halōn*** [THRESHING FLOOR] 2x
<258> ἀλώπηξ ***alōpēx*** [FOX] 3x
<259> ἅλωσις ***halōsis*** [CAPTURE (noun)] 1x
<260> ἅμα ***hama*** [at the same time: TIME 10] 10x
<261> ἀμαθής ***amathēs*** [UNTAUGHT] 1x
<262> ἀμαράντινος ***amarantinos*** [UNFADING 1] 1x
<263> ἀμάραντος ***amarantos*** [UNFADING 2] 1x
<264> ἁμαρτάνω ***hamartanō*** [to sin: FAULT 6, SIN (verb) 1] 43x
<265> ἁμάρτημα ***hamartēma*** [SIN (noun) 2] 4x
<266> ἁμαρτία ***hamartia*** [SIN (noun) 1, SIN TO DEATH] 173x
<267> ἀμάρτυρος ***amarturos*** [without witness: WITNESS (noun)[1] 7] 1x
<268> ἁμαρτωλός ***hamartōlos*** [SINFUL 1, SINNER 1] 47x
<269> ἄμαχος ***amachos*** [not quarrelsome: QUARRELSOME 1] 2x
<270> ἀμάω ***amaō*** [MOW] 1x
<271> ἀμέθυστος ***amethustos*** [AMETHYST] 1x
<272> ἀμελέω ***ameleō*** [DISREGARD 1, to make light: LIGHT (adj.) 2, to be negligent: NEGLIGENT 1] 5x
<273> ἄμεμπτος ***amemptos*** [BLAMELESS 1] 5x
<274> ἀμέμπτως ***amemptōs*** [BLAMELESSLY 1] 2x
<275> ἀμέριμνος ***amerimnos*** [free from concern: CONCERN (noun) 2, out of trouble: TROUBLE (noun) 5] 2x
<276> ἀμετάθετος ***ametathetos*** [UNCHANGEABLE 1] 2x
<277> ἀμετακίνητος ***ametakinētos*** [IMMOVABLE 1] 1x
<278> ἀμεταμέλητος ***ametamelētos*** [IRREVOCABLE, never to be regretted: REGRET 2] 2x
<279> ἀμετανόητος ***ametanoētos*** [UNREPENTANT] 1x
<280> ἄμετρος ***ametros*** [beyond, out of, without measure: MEASURE (noun) 9] 2x
<281> Ἀμήν ***Amēn*** and ἀμήν ***amēn*** [AMEN 1, AMEN 2, VERILY 1] 129x
<282> ἀμήτωρ ***amētōr*** [without mother: MOTHER 3] 1x
<283> ἀμίαντος ***amiantos*** [UNDEFILED] 4x
<284> Ἀμιναδάβ ***Aminadab*** [AMINADAB] 3x
<285> ἄμμος ***ammos*** [SAND 1] 6x
<286> ἀμνός ***amnos*** [LAMB 1] 4x
<287> ἀμοιβή ***amoibē*** [RETURN (noun) 1] 1x
<288> ἄμπελος ***ampelos*** [VINE] 9x
<289> ἀμπελουργός ***ampelourgos*** [keeper of the vineyard: VINEYARD 2] 1x
<290> ἀμπελών ***ampelōn*** [VINEYARD 1] 24x
<291> Ἀμπλίας ***Amplias*** [AMPLIAS] 1x
<292> ἀμύνω ***amunō*** [DEFEND 1] 1x
<293> ἀμφίβληστρον ***amphiblēstron*** [NET 1] 2x
<294> ἀμφιέννυμι ***amphiennumi*** [CLOTHE 4] 4x
<295> Ἀμφίπολις ***Amphipolis*** [AMPHIPOLIS] 1x
<296> ἄμφοδον ***amphodon*** [place where two ways meet: PLACE (noun) 5] 1x
<297> ἀμφότερος ***amphoteros*** [BOTH] 14x
<298> ἀμώμητος ***amōmētos*** [IRREPROACHABLE 1] 2x
<298a> ἄμωμον ***amōmon*** [SPICE 2] 1x
<299> ἄμωμος ***amōmos*** [BLAMELESS 2, without blemish: BLEMISH 2, without spot: SPOT 4] 7x
<300> Ἀμών ***Amōn*** [AMON] 2x
<301> Ἀμώς ***Amōs*** [AMOS 1] 1x
<302> ἄν ***an*** [PERHAPS 1] 171x
<303> ἀνά ***ana*** [UPON] 13x
<304> ἀναβαθμός ***anabathmos*** [STAIR] 2x
<305> ἀναβαίνω ***anabainō*** [COME 17, GO 17] 82x

<306> ἀναβάλλω ***anaballō*** [ADJOURN] 1x

<307> ἀναβιβάζω ***anabibazō*** [to draw, to draw up: DRAW 1] 1x

<308> ἀναβλέπω ***anablepō*** [to look up: LOOK (verb) 3, SEE 2] 25x

<309> ἀνάβλεψις ***anablepsis*** [RECOVERY OF SIGHT] 1x

<310> ἀναβοάω ***anaboaō*** [to cry, to cry aloud, to cry out: CRY (verb) 2] 3x

<311> ἀναβολή ***anabolē*** [DELAY (noun) 1] 1x

<312> ἀναγγέλλω ***anangellō*** [ANNOUNCE 1, DECLARE 1, RELATE 1, REPORT (verb) 1, SHOW (verb) 1, SPEAK 1, TELL 1] 18x

<313> ἀναγεννάω ***anagennaō*** [BORN AGAIN (BE) 2] 2x

<314> ἀναγινώσκω ***anaginōskō*** [to know well: KNOW 2, READ 1] 32x

<315> ἀναγκάζω ***anankazō*** [CONSTRAIN 1] 9x

<316> ἀναγκαῖος ***anankaios*** [CLOSE (adj. and adv.) 1, NECESSARY 1] 8x

<317> ἀναγκαστῶς ***anankastōs*** [by constraint: CONSTRAINT 1] 1x

<318> ἀνάγκη ***anankē*** [DISTRESS 1, need: MUST 2, necessity: NECESSARY 3, NECESSITY 1] 18x

<319> ἀναγνωρίζω ***anagnōrizō*** [to make known: KNOWN 3] 1x

<320> ἀνάγνωσις ***anagnōsis*** [READING 1] 3x

<321> ἀνάγω ***anagō*** [to bring, to bring up: BRING 2, DEPART 1, to launch forth: LAUNCH 1, to lead, to lead up: LEAD (verb) 2, OFFER 1, to set sail, to make sail: SAIL (noun) 2, to sail, to sail away: SAIL (verb) 1, to take up, to take upstairs: TAKE 12] 23x

<322> ἀναδείκνυμι ***anadeiknumi*** [APPOINT 1, SHOW (verb) 5] 2x

<323> ἀνάδειξις ***anadeixis*** [MANIFESTATION 1] 1x

<324> ἀναδέχομαι ***anadechomai*** [RECEIVE 9] 2x

<325> ἀναδίδωμι ***anadidōmi*** [DELIVER 1] 1x

<326> ἀναζάω ***anazaō*** [to come to life, to come to life again: LIFE 9, to live again: LIVE 2, REVIVE 1] 5x

<327> ἀναζητέω ***anazēteō*** [SEEK 2] 3x

<328> ἀναζώννυμι ***anazōnnumi*** [to gird up: GIRD 2] 1x

<329> ἀναζωπυρέω ***anazōpureō*** [REKINDLE] 1x

<330> ἀναθάλλω ***anathallō*** [REVIVE 2] 1x

<331> ἀνάθεμα ***anathema*** [curse: ACCURSED 1] 6x

<332> ἀναθεματίζω ***anathematizō*** [to invoke, to put, to bind oneself under a curse, an oath: CURSE (noun) 3, CURSE (verb) 1] 4x

<333> ἀναθεωρέω ***anatheōreō*** [BEHOLD (verb) 1, CONSIDER 5] 2x

<334> ἀνάθημα ***anathēma*** [consecrated offering: OFFERING 1] 1x

<335> ἀναίδεια ***anaideia*** [PERSISTENCE 1] 1x

<336> ἀναίρεσις ***anairesis*** [DEATH 2] 2x

<337> ἀναιρέω ***anaireō*** [to put to death: DEATH 6, KILL 1, to take, to take away, to take up: TAKE 19] 24x

<338> ἀναίτιος ***anaitios*** [BLAMELESS 3, GUILTLESS 1] 2x

<339> ἀνακαθίζω ***anakathizō*** [to sit up: SIT 4] 2x

<340> ἀνακαινίζω ***anakainizō*** [RENEW 1] 1x

<341> ἀνακαινόω ***anakainoō*** [RENEW 2] 2x

<342> ἀνακαίνωσις ***anakainōsis*** [RENEWING] 2x

<343> ἀνακαλύπτω ***anakaluptō*** [to unlift: UNLIFTED, UNVEIL] 2x

<344> ἀνακάμπτω ***anakamptō*** [RETURN (verb) 1] 4x

<345> ἀνάκειμαι ***anakeimai*** [LIE (verb)[1] 2, SET (verb) 3, to be, to lie, to lie down, to recline, to sit at the table: TABLE[1] 2] 14x

<346> ἀνακεφαλαιόω ***anakephalaioō*** [to gather together, to gather together in one: GATHER 9, SUM UP 1] 2x

<347> ἀνακλίνω ***anaklinō*** [LAY 12, to sit down: SIT 8, to sit, to take one's place, to recline at the table: TABLE[1] 5] 8x

<348> ἀνακόπτω ***anakoptō*** [HINDER (verb) 1] 1x

<349> ἀνακράζω ***anakrazō*** [to cry out: CRY (verb) 5] 5x

<350> ἀνακρίνω ***anakrinō*** [to ask questions: ASK 3, DISCERN 1, EXAMINE 1, JUDGE (verb) 2, SEARCH (verb) 1] 16x

<351> ἀνάκρισις ***anakrisis*** [INVESTIGATION] 1x

<352> ἀνακύπτω ***anakuptō*** [to lift up: LIFT 3, to look up: LOOK (verb) 16, to straighten oneself up: STRAIGHTEN 1] 4x

<353> ἀναλαμβάνω ***analambanō*** [to take on board: BOARD (noun) 3, to receive up: RECEIVE 2, to take, to take up, to take along: TAKE 3] 13x

<354> ἀνάλημψις ***analēmpsis*** [receiving up: RECEIVE 20] or [receiving up: RECEIVING 2] 1x

<355> ἀναλίσκω ***analiskō*** [CONSUME 1] 3x

<356> ἀναλογία ***analogia*** [PROPORTION] 1x

<357> ἀναλογίζομαι ***analogizomai*** [CONSIDER 11] 1x

<358> ἄναλος ***analos*** [UNSALTY] 1x

<359> ἀνάλυσις ***analusis*** [DEPARTURE 1] 1x

<360> ἀναλύω ***analuō*** [DEPART 2, RETURN (verb) 2] 2x

<361> ἀναμάρτητος ***anamartētos*** [who is without sin: SIN (noun) 3] 1x

<362> ἀναμένω ***anamenō*** [to wait for: WAIT (verb) 1] 1x

<363> ἀναμιμνήσκω ***anamimnēskō*** [REMEMBER 2, REMIND 1] 6x

<364> ἀνάμνησις ***anamnēsis*** [REMEMBRANCE 1, REMINDER 1] 4x

<365> ἀνανεόω ***ananeoō*** [RENEW 3] 1x

<366> ἀνανήφω ***ananēphō*** [AWAKE (verb) 1] 1x

<367> Ἀνανίας ***Hananias*** [ANANIAS] 10x

<368> ἀναντίρρητος ***anantirrētos*** [UNDENIABLE] 1x

<369> ἀναντιρρήτως ***anantirrētōs*** [without objection, without raising any objection: OBJECTION 1] 1x

<370> ἀνάξιος ***anaxios*** [UNWORTHY 2] 1x

<371> ἀναξίως ***anaxiōs*** [UNWORTHILY] 2x

<372> ἀνάπαυσις ***anapausis*** [REST (noun)[1] 1, rest: REST (verb) 4] 5x

<373> ἀναπαύω ***anapauō*** [REFRESH 1, to give rest: REST (noun)[1] 2, REST (verb) 1] 12x

<374> ἀναπείθω ***anapeithō*** [PERSUADE 2] 1x

<375> ἀναπέμπω ***anapempō*** [SEND 5] 6x

<375a> ἀναπηδάω ***anapēdaō*** [to jump up: JUMP 1] 1x

<376> ἀνάπηρος ***anapēros*** [MAIMED 1] 2x

<377> ἀναπίπτω ***anapiptō*** [to lean, to lean back: LEAN, to sit down: SIT 10, to place oneself, to recline again, to lie down at the table: TABLE[1] 7] 12x

<378> ἀναπληρόω ***anaplēroō*** [to fill, to fill up: FILL (verb) 3, FULFILL 6, SUPPLY (verb) 4] 6x

<379> ἀναπολόγητος ***anapologētos*** [INEXCUSABLE] 2x

<380> ἀναπτύσσω ***anaptussō*** [OPEN (verb) 1] 1x

<381> ἀνάπτω ***anaptō*** [KINDLE 1] 3x

<382> ἀναρίθμητος ***anarithmētos*** [INNUMERABLE 1] 1x

<383> ἀνασείω ***anaseiō*** [to stir up: STIR (verb) 1] 2x

<384> ἀνασκευάζω ***anaskeuazō*** [SUBVERT 1] 1x

<385> ἀνασπάω ***anaspaō*** [to pull out, to pull up: PULL 2] 2x

<386> ἀνάστασις ***anastasis*** [RESURRECTION 1, RISING 1] 42x

<387> ἀναστατόω ***anastatoō*** [to raise a sedition: SEDITION 1, TROUBLE (verb) 1, to turn upside down: TURN (verb) 1] 3x

<388> ἀνασταυρόω ***anastauroō*** [to crucify again: CRUCIFY 2] 1x

<389> ἀναστενάζω ***anastenazō*** [GROAN (verb) 2] 1x

<390> ἀναστρέφω ***anastrephō*** [CONDUCT (verb)[1] 1, LIVE 4, RETURN (verb) 6, TREAT 1] 10x

<391> ἀναστροφή ***anastrophē*** [CONDUCT (noun) 1, manner of life, way of life: LIFE 2] 13x

<392> ἀνατάσσομαι ***anatassomai*** [to draw up: DRAW 7] 1x

<393> ἀνατέλλω ***anatellō*** [RISE (verb) 1, SPRING (verb) 2] 9x

<394> ἀνατίθημι ***anatithēmi*** [to lay before: LAY 2] 2x

<395> ἀνατολή ***anatolē*** [DAYSPRING FROM ON HIGH, EAST 1] 10x

<396> ἀνατρέπω ***anatrepō*** [OVERTURN 1] 3x

<397> ἀνατρέφω ***anatrephō*** [to bring up: BRING 19, NOURISH 3] 4x

<398> ἀναφαίνω ***anaphainō*** [MANIFEST (verb) 1, SIGHT (verb)] 2x

<399> ἀναφέρω ***anapherō*** [BEAR (verb) 2, to carry up: CARRY 5, to lead up: LEAD (verb) 10, to offer, to offer up: OFFER 2] 9x
<400> ἀναφωνέω ***anaphōneō*** [to speak out: SPEAK 11] 1x
<401> ἀνάχυσις ***anachusis*** [EXCESS 1] 1x
<402> ἀναχωρέω ***anachōreō*** [DEPART 4] 14x
<403> ἀνάψυξις ***anapsuxis*** [REFRESHING] 1x
<404> ἀναψύχω ***anapsuchō*** [REFRESH 3] 1x
<405> ἀνδραποδιστής ***andrapodistēs*** [KIDNAPPER] 1x
<406> Ἀνδρέας ***Andreas*** [ANDREW] 13x
<407> ἀνδρίζω ***andrizō*** [to act like a man: MAN 3] 1x
<408> Ἀνδρόνικος ***Andronikos*** [ANDRONICUS] 1x
<409> ἀνδροφόνος ***androphonos*** [MURDERER 1] 1x
<410> ἀνέγκλητος ***anenklētos*** [BLAMELESS 4, above reproach, beyond reproach: REPROACH (noun) 5] 5x
<411> ἀνεκδιήγητος ***anekdiēgētos*** [INDESCRIBABLE] 1x
<412> ἀνεκλάλητος ***aneklalētos*** [INEXPRESSIBLE 1] 1x
<413> ἀνέκλειπτος ***anekleiptos*** [unfailing, that does not fail: FAIL 2] 1x
<414> ἀνεκτότερος ***anektoteros*** [more tolerable: TOLERABLE] 6x
<415> ἀνελεήμων ***aneleēmōn*** [UNMERCIFUL] 1x
<416> ἀνεμίζω ***anemizō*** [to blow by the wind, to drive by the wind: WIND (noun) 2] 1x
<417> ἄνεμος ***anemos*** [WIND (noun) 1] 30x
<418> ἀνένδεκτος ***anendektos*** [IMPOSSIBLE 3] 1x
<419> ἀνεξερεύνητος ***anexereunētos*** [UNSEARCHABLE 1] 1x
<420> ἀνεξίκακος ***anexikakos*** [FORBEARING 1] 1x
<421> ἀνεξιχνίαστος ***anexichniastos*** [UNSEARCHABLE 2, UNTRACEABLE] 2x
<422> ἀνεπαίσχυντος ***anepaischuntos*** [who does not need to be ashamed: ASHAMED 2] 1x
<423> ἀνεπίλημπτος ***anepilēmptos*** [above reproach: REPROACH (noun) 6] 3x
<424> ἀνέρχομαι ***anerchomai*** [to go up: GO 7] 3x
<425> ἄνεσις ***anesis*** [EASE 1, LIBERTY 1, REST (noun)[1] 3] 5x
<426> ἀνετάζω ***anetazō*** [EXAMINE 2] 2x
<427> ἄνευ ***aneu*** [WITHOUT 1] 3x
<428> ἀνεύθετος ***aneuthetos*** [not suitable: SUITABLE 1] 1x
<429> ἀνευρίσκω ***aneuriskō*** [to find, to find out: FIND 2] 2x
<430> ἀνέχω ***anechō*** [SUFFER 4] 15x
<431> ἀνεψιός ***anepsios*** [COUSIN 1] 1x
<432> ἄνηθον ***anēthon*** [ANISE] 1x
<433> ἀνήκω ***anēkō*** [FITTING (BE) 1] 3x
<434> ἀνήμερος ***anēmeros*** [BRUTAL] 1x
<435> ἀνήρ ***anēr*** [HUSBAND 1, MAN 1] 216x
<436> ἀνθίστημι ***anthistēmi*** [RESIST 1, WITHSTAND 1] 14x
<437> ἀνθομολογέομαι ***anthomologeomai*** [to give thanks: THANKS 1] 1x
<438> ἄνθος ***anthos*** [FLOWER 1] 4x
<439> ἀνθρακιά ***anthrakia*** [fire of coals: COAL 2] 2x
<440> ἄνθραξ ***anthrax*** [COAL 1] 1x
<441> ἀνθρωπάρεσκος ***anthrōpareskos*** [MEN-PLEASER] 2x
<442> ἀνθρώπινος ***anthrōpinos*** [human, in human terms: HUMAN 1] 7x
<443> ἀνθρωποκτόνος ***anthrōpoktonos*** [MURDERER 2] 3x
<444> ἄνθρωπος ***anthrōpos*** [MAN 2, inner man, inward man, MAN 5, MAN OF GOD] 553x
<445> ἀνθυπατεύω ***anthupateuō*** [to be proconsul: PROCONSUL 2] 1x
<446> ἀνθύπατος ***anthupatos*** [PROCONSUL 1] 4x
<447> ἀνίημι ***aniēmi*** [GIVE 8, LEAVE (verb) 1, LOOSE 1] 4x
<448> ἀνέλεος ***aneleos*** [without mercy: MERCY 4] 1x
<449> ἄνιπτος ***aniptos*** [IMPURE 1, UNWASHED] 3x
<450> ἀνίστημι ***anistēmi*** [ARISE 1, to raise up: RAISE 5, to rise up, to rise: RISE (verb) 2] 108x
<451> Ἄννα ***Hanna*** [ANNA] 1x

<452> Ἄννας ***Hannas*** [ANNAS] 4x

<453> ἀνόητος ***anoētos*** [FOOLISH 1] 6x

<454> ἄνοια ***anoia*** [MADNESS 1] 2x

<455> ἀνοίγω ***anoigō*** [OPEN (verb) 2] 77x

<456> ἀνοικοδομέω ***anoikodomeō*** [REBUILD 1] 2x

<457> ἄνοιξις ***anoixis*** [OPENING 1] 1x

<458> ἀνομία ***anomia*** [INIQUITY 3, LAWLESSNESS] 18x

<459> ἄνομος ***anomos*** [he who is without law, he who does not have the law: LAW 3, LAWLESS (adj.) 1, LAWLESS (noun)] 10x

<460> ἀνόμως ***anomōs*** [without the law, apart from the law: LAW 4] 2x

<461> ἀνορθόω ***anorthoō*** [RESTORE 1, to make straight: STRAIGHT 3, STRENGTHEN 5] 3x

<462> ἀνόσιος ***anosios*** [UNHOLY 1] 2x

<463> ἀνοχή ***anochē*** [FORBEARANCE 1] 2x

<464> ἀνταγωνίζομαι ***antagōnizomai*** [to strive against: STRIVE 2] 1x

<465> ἀντάλλαγμα ***antallagma*** [in exchange: EXCHANGE (noun) 2] 2x

<466> ἀνταναπληρόω ***antanaplēroō*** [to fill up: FILL (verb) 4] 1x

<467> ἀνταποδίδωμι ***antapodidōmi*** [RECOMPENSE (verb) 1, RENDER 2] 8x

<468> ἀνταπόδομα ***antapodoma*** [RECOMPENSE (noun) 1, RETRIBUTION 1] 2x

<469> ἀνταπόδοσις ***antapodosis*** [REWARD (noun) 1] 1x

<470> ἀνταποκρίνομαι ***antapokrinomai*** [ANSWER (verb) 3, to reply against: REPLY (verb) 1] 2x

<471> ἀντέπω ***antepō*** [REPLY (verb) 2] 2x

<472> ἀντέχω ***antechō*** [FAST (HOLD) 1, HOLD (verb) 2, SUPPORT (verb) 1] 4x

<473> ἀντί ***anti*** [INSTEAD 1] 22x

<474> ἀντιβάλλω ***antiballō*** [EXCHANGE 1] 1x

<475> ἀντιδιατίθημι ***antidiatithēmi*** [OPPOSE 1] 1x

<476> ἀντίδικος ***antidikos*** [ADVERSARY 1] 5x

<477> ἀντίθεσις ***antithesis*** [OPPOSITION 1] 1x

<478> ἀντικαθίστημι ***antikathistēmi*** [RESIST 2] 1x

<479> ἀντικαλέω ***antikaleō*** [to invite back, to invite in return: INVITE 2] 1x

<480> ἀντίκειμαι ***antikeimai*** [to be the adversary: ADVERSARY 3, OPPOSE 2] 8x

<481> ἄντικρυς ***antikrus*** [OPPOSITE 1] 1x

<482> ἀντιλαμβάνω ***antilambanō*** [HELP (verb) 2, PROFIT (verb) 1] 3x

<483> ἀντιλέγω ***antilegō*** [to answer back: ANSWER (verb) 1, DENY 3, to speak against: SPEAK 3] 10x

<484> ἀντίλημψις ***antilēmpsis*** [HELP (noun) 1] 1x

<485> ἀντιλογία ***antilogia*** [CONTRADICTION 1, DISPUTE (noun) 1] 4x

<486> ἀντιλοιδορέω ***antiloidoreō*** [to revile again, to revile in return: REVILE 3] 1x

<487> ἀντίλυτρον ***antilutron*** [RANSOM (noun) 2] 1x

<488> ἀντιμετρέω ***antimetreō*** [to measure; to measure again, back, in return: MEASURE (verb) 2] 2x

<489> ἀντιμισθία ***antimisthia*** [EXCHANGE (noun) 1, PENALTY 1] 2x

<490> Ἀντιόχεια ***Antiocheia*** [ANTIOCH 1] 18x

<491> Ἀντιοχεύς ***Antiocheus*** [ANTIOCH 2] 1x

<492> ἀντιπαρέρχομαι ***antiparerchomai*** [to pass by on the other side: SIDE 2] 2x

<493> Ἀντιπᾶς ***Antipas*** [ANTIPAS] 1x

<494> Ἀντιπατρίς ***Antipatris*** [ANTIPATRIS] 1x

<495> ἀντιπέραν ***antiperan*** [OPPOSITE 2] 1x

<496> ἀντιπίπτω ***antipiptō*** [RESIST 3] 1x

<497> ἀντιστρατεύομαι ***antistrateuomai*** [to war in opposition: WAR (verb) 3] 1x

<498> ἀντιτάσσω ***antitassō*** [OPPOSE 3, RESIST 4] 5x

<499> ἀντίτυπον ***antitupon*** [COPY 1, FIGURE 1] 2x

<500> ἀντίχριστος ***antichristos*** [ANTICHRIST] 5x

<501> ἀντλέω ***antleō*** [DRAW 13] 4x

<502> ἄντλημα ***antlēma*** [vessel: DRAW 15] 1x
<503> ἀντοφθαλμέω ***antophthalmeō*** [to head into: HEAD (verb) 1] 1x
<504> ἄνυδρος ***anudros*** [DRY (noun) 1, without water: WATER (noun) 2] 4x
<505> ἀνυπόκριτος ***anupokritos*** [without hypocrisy: HYPOCRISY 2, SINCERE 1] 6x
<506> ἀνυπότακτος ***anupotaktos*** [INSUBORDINATE, not subject, not put under: SUBJECT (verb) 2] 4x
<507> ἄνω ***anō*** [HIGH (adv.), HIGH (ON)] 9x
<508> ἀνώγεον ***anōgeon*** [upper room: ROOM 1] 2x
<509> ἄνωθεν ***anōthen*** [ABOVE 1, AGAIN 1, from the beginning: BEGINNING 3, from the very first: FIRST 6, from the top: TOP 1] 13x
<510> ἀνωτερικός ***anōterikos*** [UPPER 1] 1x
<511> ἀνώτερον ***anōteron*** [HIGHER 1] 2x
<512> ἀνωφελής ***anōphelēs*** [unprofitable, unprofitableness: UNPROFITABLE 2] 2x
<513> ἀξίνη ***axinē*** [AXE] 2x
<514> ἄξιος ***axios*** [DESERVING 1, FITTING 1, MEET (adj.) 1, worthy: UNWORTHY 1, WORTHY 1] 41x
<515> ἀξιόω ***axioō*** [DESIRE (verb) 1, to think it good: THINK 1, to consider worthy: WORTHY 2] 7x
<516> ἀξίως ***axiōs*** [worthy, in a manner worthy: WORTHY 4] 6x
<517> ἀόρατος ***aoratos*** [INVISIBLE] 5x
<518> ἀπαγγέλλω ***apangellō*** [DECLARE 2, RELATE 2, REPORT (verb) 2, SHOW (verb) 2, TELL 2] 45x
<519> ἀπάγχω ***apanchō*** [HANG 1] 1x
<520> ἀπάγω ***apagō*** [BRING 3, to carry away: CARRY 1, to put to death: DEATH 7, to lead, to lead away: LEAD (verb) 3, to take out: TAKE 13] 16x
<521> ἀπαίδευτος ***apaideutos*** [SENSELESS 1] 1x
<522> ἀπαίρω ***apairō*** [to take away: TAKE 16] 3x
<523> ἀπαιτέω ***apaiteō*** [to demand, to demand back: DEMAND (verb) 1] 2x
<524> ἀπαλγέω ***apalgeō*** [to cast off all feeling: FEELING 1] 1x
<525> ἀπαλλάσσω ***apallassō*** [LEAVE (verb) 3, RELEASE (verb) 1, SETTLE 1] 3x
<526> ἀπαλλοτριόω ***apallotrioō*** [ALIENATED (BE) 1] 3x
<527> ἁπαλός ***hapalos*** [TENDER 1] 2x
<528> ἀπαντάω ***apantaō*** [MEET (verb) 1] 7x
<529> ἀπάντησις ***apantēsis*** [meeting: MEET (verb) 5] 4x
<530> ἅπαξ ***hapax*** [ONCE 1] 15x
<531> ἀπαράβατος ***aparabatos*** [UNCHANGEABLE 2] 1x
<532> ἀπαρασκεύαστος ***aparaskeuastos*** [UNPREPARED] 1x
<533> ἀπαρνέομαι ***aparneomai*** [to deny, to deny oneself: DENY 2] 13x
<534> ἀπάρτι ***aparti*** [HEREAFTER 1] 2x
<535> ἀπαρτισμός ***apartismos*** [completion: FINISH 8] 1x
<536> ἀπαρχή ***aparchē*** [FIRSTFRUITS 1] 9x
<537> ἅπας ***hapas*** [ALL 3] 34x
<537a> ἀπασπάζομαι ***apaspazomai*** [EMBRACE 1] 1x
<538> ἀπατάω ***apataō*** [DECEIVE 1] 3x
<539> ἀπάτη ***apatē*** [DECEIT 1, DECEITFULNESS] 7x
<540> ἀπάτωρ ***apatōr*** [without father: FATHER 2] 1x
<541> ἀπαύγασμα ***apaugasma*** [RADIANCE 1] 1x
<542> ἀπεῖδον ***apeidon*** [SEE 5] 1x
<543> ἀπείθεια ***apeitheia*** [DISOBEDIENCE 1] 7x
<544> ἀπειθέω ***apeitheō*** [to not believe: BELIEVE 3, DISBELIEVE 1, to disobey, to be disobedient: DISOBEDIENT 2, to obey not: OBEY 4, to believe not: UNBELIEVING 2] 16x
<545> ἀπειθής ***apeithēs*** [DISOBEDIENT 1] 6x
<546> ἀπειλέω ***apeileō*** [THREATEN 1] 2x
<547> ἀπειλή ***apeilē*** [THREAT 1] 4x

<548> ἄπειμι ***apeimi*** [ABSENT (BE) 1] 7x
<549> ἄπειμι ***apeimi*** [to go to, to go into: GO 28] 1x
<550> ἀπεῖπον ***apeipon*** [RENOUNCE 1] 1x
<551> ἀπείραστος ***apeirastos*** [not tempted: TEMPT 3] 1x
<552> ἄπειρος ***apeiros*** [UNSKILLED 1] 1x
<553> ἀπεκδέχομαι ***apekdechomai*** [to wait eagerly, to wait: WAIT (verb) 4] 8x
<554> ἀπεκδύομαι ***apekduomai*** [DISARM] 2x
<555> ἀπέκδυσις ***apekdusis*** [putting off: PUTTING 2] 1x
<556> ἀπελαύνω ***apelaunō*** [DRIVE 2] 1x
<557> ἀπελεγμός ***apelegmos*** [DISREPUTE 1] 1x
<558> ἀπελεύθερος ***apeleutheros*** [FREEDMAN] 1x
<559> Ἀπελλῆς ***Apellēs*** [APELLES] 1x
<560> ἀπελπίζω ***apelpizō*** [to hope in return: HOPE (verb) 2] 1x
<561> ἀπέναντι ***apenanti*** [to do contrary, to act contrary: CONTRARY 6, in the presence of: PRESENCE 3] 6x
<562> ἀπέραντος ***aperantos*** [ENDLESS 1] 1x
<563> ἀπερισπάστως ***aperispastōs*** [without distraction: DISTRACTION] 1x
<564> ἀπερίτμητος ***aperitmētos*** [UNCIRCUMCISED 1] 1x
<565> ἀπέρχομαι ***aperchomai*** [to draw back: BACK (adv.) 3, DEPART 7, to go away, to go back: GO 8, LEAVE (verb) 4, to pass, to pass away: PASS 1, PERISH 3, SPREAD 1] 117x
<566> ἀπέχει ***apechei*** [it is enough: ENOUGH 2] 1x
<567> ἀπέχομαι ***apechomai*** [ABSTAIN 1] 6x
<568> ἀπέχω ***apechō*** [to be far: FAR 4, HAVE 2, POSSESS 2] 19x
<569> ἀπιστέω ***apisteō*** [to not believe: BELIEVE 2, to be faithless: FAITHLESS 2] 8x
<570> ἀπιστία ***apistia*** [UNBELIEF 1] 12x
<571> ἄπιστος ***apistos*** [INCREDIBLE, UNBELIEVER 1, UNBELIEVING 1] 23x
<572> ἁπλότης ***haplotēs*** [LIBERALITY 1, SIMPLICITY 1] 8x
<573> ἁπλοῦς ***haplous*** [SINGLE 1] 2x
<574> ἁπλῶς ***haplōs*** [LIBERALLY] 1x
<575> ἀπό ***apo*** [from, from among: AMONG 1, AWAY 2, at a distance: DISTANCE 1] 648x
<576> ἀποβαίνω ***apobainō*** [COME 18, GO 18, to turn, to turn out: TURN (verb) 2] 4x
<577> ἀποβάλλω ***apoballō*** [to cast away: CAST (verb) 2, to throw aside, to throw away: THROW (verb) 2] 2x
<578> ἀποβλέπω ***apoblepō*** [LOOK (verb) 4] 1x
<579> ἀπόβλητος ***apoblētos*** [REJECTED 1] 1x
<580> ἀποβολή ***apobolē*** [LOSS 1, REJECTION] 2x
<581> ἀπογενόμενος ***apogenomenos*** [having died: DIE 4] 1x
<582> ἀπογραφή ***apographē*** [CENSUS 1] 2x
<583> ἀπογράφω ***apographō*** [to make a census, to take a census: CENSUS 2, REGISTER] 4x
<584> ἀποδείκνυμι ***apodeiknumi*** [APPROVE 1, PROVE 1, SET (verb) 1, to show oneself: SHOW (verb) 6] 4x
<585> ἀπόδειξις ***apodeixis*** [DEMONSTRATION 1] 1x
<586> ἀποδεκατόω ***apodekatoō*** [to tithe; to pay, take, give tithes; to give a tenth: TITHE (noun and verb) 2] 4x
<587> ἀπόδεκτος ***apodektos*** [ACCEPTABLE 2] 2x
<588> ἀποδέχομαι ***apodechomai*** [ACCEPT 1, RECEIVE 10] 7x
<589> ἀποδημέω ***apodēmeō*** [to go to a far country, to go on a journey: COUNTRY 2] 6x
<590> ἀπόδημος ***apodēmos*** [away on a journey, taking a far journey: JOURNEY (noun) 6] 1x
<591> ἀποδίδωμι ***apodidōmi*** [GIVE 2, PAY (verb) 1, to make payment: PAYMENT 1, RENDER 1, REWARD (verb) 1, SELL 1] 48x
<592> ἀποδιορίζω ***apodiorizō*** [to separate oneself: SEPARATE 3] 1x
<593> ἀποδοκιμάζω ***apodokimazō*** [REJECT 2] 9x
<594> ἀποδοχή ***apodochē*** [ACCEPTATION] 2x
<595> ἀπόθεσις ***apothesis*** [REMOVAL 1] 2x
<596> ἀποθήκη ***apothēkē*** [BARN] 6x

<597> ἀποθησαυρίζω ***apothēsaurizō*** [to lay by, to lay up in store: LAY 15] 1x

<598> ἀποθλίβω ***apothlibō*** [PRESS 5] 1x

<599> ἀποθνήσκω ***apothnēskō*** [to be dead, to die: DEAD 5, to die, to be dead: DIE 1, to die: DYING 2] 112x

<600> ἀποκαθίστημι ***apokathistēmi*** [RESTORE 2] 8x

<601> ἀποκαλύπτω ***apokaluptō*** [REVEAL 1, to be, to make, to come a revelation: REVELATION 2] 26x

<602> ἀποκάλυψις ***apokalupsis*** [REVELATION 1] 18x

<603> ἀποκαραδοκία ***apokaradokia*** [earnest expectation: EXPECTATION 1] 2x

<604> ἀποκαταλλάσσω ***apokatallassō*** [RECONCILE 3] 3x

<605> ἀποκατάστασις ***apokatastasis*** [RESTORING] 1x

<606> ἀπόκειμαι ***apokeimai*** [APPOINT 5, to lay up: LAY 8, to keep put away: PUT 5] 4x

<607> ἀποκεφαλίζω ***apokephalizō*** [BEHEAD 1] 4x

<608> ἀποκλείω ***apokleiō*** [SHUT 2] 1x

<609> ἀποκόπτω ***apokoptō*** [to cut off, to cut away, to cut oneself off: CUT 3] 6x

<610> ἀπόκριμα ***apokrima*** [SENTENCE 1] 1x

<611> ἀποκρίνομαι ***apokrinomai*** [ANSWER (verb) 2] 234x

<612> ἀπόκρισις ***apokrisis*** [ANSWER (noun) 1] 4x

<613> ἀποκρύπτω ***apokruptō*** [HIDE 2] 6x

<614> ἀπόκρυφος ***apokruphos*** [hid, hidden: HIDE 6] 3x

<615> ἀποκτείνω ***apokteinō*** [KILL 2] 74x

<616> ἀποκυέω ***apokueō*** [to bring forth: BRING 23] 2x

<617> ἀποκυλίω ***apokuliō*** [to roll away, to roll back: ROLL 4] 4x

<618> ἀπολαμβάνω ***apolambanō*** [RECEIVE 3, to take aside, to take away: TAKE 4] 11x

<619> ἀπόλαυσις ***apolausis*** [enjoyment: ENJOY 3] or [PLEASURE 1] 2x

<620> ἀπολείπω ***apoleipō*** [LEAVE (verb) 5, REMAIN 7] 6x

<621> ἀπολείχω ***apoleichō*** [LICK 2] 1x

<622> ἀπόλλυμι ***apollumi*** [DESTROY 1, LOSE 1, PERISH 1] 90x

<623> Ἀπολλύων ***Apolluōn*** [APOLLYON] 1x

<624> Ἀπολλωνία ***Apollōnia*** [APOLLONIA] 1x

<625> Ἀπολλῶς ***Apollōs*** [APOLLOS] 10x

<626> ἀπολογέομαι ***apologeomai*** [ANSWER (verb) 4, to defend oneself: DEFEND 2, to make one's defense, to answer for one's defense: DEFENSE 2, to excuse oneself: EXCUSE (verb) 1] 10x

<627> ἀπολογία ***apologia*** [ANSWER (noun) 2, defense: ANSWER (verb) 6, DEFENSE 1, EXCUSING] 8x

<628> ἀπολούω ***apolouō*** [to wash, to wash away: WASH 2] 2x

<629> ἀπολύτρωσις ***apolutrōsis*** [DELIVERANCE 1, REDEMPTION 2] 10x

<630> ἀπολύω ***apoluō*** [to depart, to let depart: DEPART 3, DISMISS 1, DIVORCE (verb) 1, FORGIVE 1, to set free: FREE (adj.) 3, LOOSE 3, RELEASE (verb) 4, to send away, to send off: SEND 9] 66x

<631> ἀπομάσσω ***apomassō*** [SHAKE OFF 1] 1x

<632> ἀπονέμω ***aponemō*** [GIVE 9] 1x

<633> ἀπονίπτω ***aponiptō*** [WASH 6] 1x

<634> ἀποπίπτω ***apopiptō*** [to fall from: FALL (verb) 2] 1x

<635> ἀποπλανάω ***apoplanaō*** [DECEIVE 6, STRAY 3] 2x

<636> ἀποπλέω ***apopleō*** [to sail, to sail away: SAIL (verb) 3] 4x

<637> ἀποπλύνω ***apoplunō*** [WASH 8] 1x

<638> ἀποπνίγω ***apopnigō*** [CHOKE 1] 3x

<639> ἀπορέω ***aporeō*** [PERPLEXED (BE) 1, to be uncertain: UNCERTAIN 2] 4x

<640> ἀπορία ***aporia*** [PERPLEXITY 1] 1x

<641> ἀπορρίπτω ***aporriptō*** [CAST (verb) 9] 1x

<642> ἀπορφανίζω ***aporphanizō*** [SEPARATE 4] 1x

<643> ἀποσκευάζω ***aposkeuazō*** [PACK 1] 1x

<644> ἀποσκίασμα ***aposkiasma*** [SHADOW (noun) 2] 1x

<645> ἀποσπάω ***apospaō*** [to draw, to draw away: DRAW 4, to get, to get away: GET 1, WITHDRAW 1] 4x

<646> ἀποστασία ***apostasia*** [APOSTASY] 2x

<647> ἀποστάσιον ***apostasion*** [DIVORCE (noun) 1] 3x

<648> ἀποστεγάζω ***apostegazō*** [UNCOVER] 1x

<649> ἀποστέλλω ***apostellō*** [to put in: PUT 11, to send; to send away, back, forth, off: SEND 1, to send: SENT 1] 132x

<650> ἀποστερέω ***apostereō*** [DEFRAUD 1, DEPRIVE 1, to wrongfully keep back, to keep back by fraud: KEEP (verb) 1] 6x

<651> ἀποστολή ***apostolē*** [APOSTLESHIP] 4x

<652> ἀπόστολος ***apostolos*** [APOSTLE, he who is sent: SENT 2] 80x

<653> ἀποστοματίζω ***apostomatizō*** [to make to speak, to provoke to speak: SPEAK 13] 1x

<654> ἀποστρέφω ***apostrephō*** [RETURN (verb) 7, to turn, to turn away: TURN (verb) 7] 10x

<655> ἀποστυγέω ***apostugeō*** [ABHOR 1] 1x

<656> ἀποσυνάγωγος ***aposunagōgos*** [excommunicated from the synagogue: EXCOMMUNICATED] 3x

<657> ἀποτάσσω ***apotassō*** [to bid farewell: FAREWELL 1, FORSAKE 1, to take leave: LEAVE (noun) 1, to send away: SEND 10] 6x

<658> ἀποτελέω ***apoteleō*** [FINISH 2] 2x

<659> ἀποτίθημι ***apotithēmi*** [to cast away, to cast off: CAST (verb) 6, to lay aside, to lay down: LAY 3, to put, to put off, to put away: PUT 2] 9x

<660> ἀποτινάσσω ***apotinassō*** [to shake off: SHAKE 1, SHAKE OFF 2] 2x

<661> ἀποτίνω ***apotinō*** [REPAY 1] 1x

<662> ἀποτολμάω ***apotolmaō*** [to be very bold: BOLD 4] 1x

<663> ἀποτομία ***apotomia*** [SEVERITY 1] 2x

<664> ἀποτόμως ***apotomōs*** [SEVERELY 1, severely: SEVERITY 2] 2x

<665> ἀποτρέπω ***apotrepō*** [to turn away: TURN (verb) 3] 1x

<666> ἀπουσία ***apousia*** [ABSENCE 1] 1x

<667> ἀποφέρω ***apopherō*** [BRING 11, to carry, to carry away: CARRY 6, to lead away: LEAD (verb) 11] 6x

<668> ἀποφεύγω ***apopheugō*** [ESCAPE 2] 3x

<669> ἀποφθέγγομαι ***apophthengomai*** [to speak forth to: SPEAK 19, UTTER (verb) 1, to utter: UTTERANCE 1] 3x

<670> ἀποφορτίζομαι ***apophortizomai*** [UNLOAD] 1x

<671> ἀπόχρησις ***apochrēsis*** [USE (noun) 2] 1x

<672> ἀποχωρέω ***apochōreō*** [DEPART 5] 3x

<673> ἀποχωρίζω ***apochōrizō*** [RECEDE, SEPARATE 2] 2x

<674> ἀποψύχω ***apopsuchō*** [to have one's heart fail: HEART 3] 1x

<675> Ἀππιου Φόρον ***Appiou Phoron*** [MARKET OF APPIUS] 1x

<676> ἀπρόσιτος ***aprositos*** [UNAPPROACHABLE] 1x

<677> ἀπρόσκοπος ***aproskopos*** [without offense: OFFENSE 2, not giving occasion to stumble, not causing to stumble: STUMBLE 2] 3x

<678> ἀπροσωπολή(μ)πτως ***aprosōpolē(m)ptōs*** [without respect of persons: RESPECT OF PERSONS 4] 1x

<679> ἄπταιστος ***aptaistos*** [from stumbling, without stumbling: STUMBLE 4] 1x

<680> ἅπτομαι ***haptomai*** [TOUCH 1] 36x

<681> ἅπτω ***haptō*** [LIGHT (verb) 1] 4x

<682> Ἀπφία ***Apphia*** [APPHIA] 1x

<683> ἀπωθέω ***apōtheō*** [REJECT 3] 6x

<684> ἀπώλεια ***apōleia*** [DESTRUCTION 1, destruction: PERISH 8, SON OF PERDITION, WASTE (noun) 1] 18x

<685> ἀρά ***ara*** [CURSING 1] 1x

<686> ἄρα ***ara*** [ELSE 3, PERHAPS 2] 49x

<687> ἆρα ***ara*** [NEVERTHELESS 1] 3x

<688> Ἀραβία ***Arabia*** [ARABIA] 2x

<689> Ἀράμ ***Aram*** [ARAM] 3x
<690> Ἄραψ ***Araps*** [ARAB] 1x
<691> ἀργέω ***argeō*** [IDLE (BE) 1] 1x
<692> ἀργός ***argos*** [IDLE 1, LAZY 1] 8x
<693> ἀργύρεος ***argureos*** [silver, of silver: SILVER 2] 3x
<694> ἀργύριον ***argurion*** [money, silver, silver coin, piece of silver: SILVER 3] 20x
<695> ἀργυροκόπος ***argurokopos*** [SILVERSMITH] 1x
<696> ἄργυρος ***arguros*** [SILVER 1] 5x
<697> Ἄρειος Πάγος ***Areios Pagos*** [AREOPAGUS] 2x
<698> Ἀρεοπαγίτης ***Areopagitēs*** [AREOPAGITE] 1x
<699> ἀρεσκεία ***areskeia*** [all pleasing, all well-pleasing: PLEASE 2] 1x
<700> ἀρέσκω ***areskō*** [PLEASE 1] 17x
<701> ἀρεστός ***arestos*** [DESIRABLE 1, PLEASING 1] 4x
<702> Ἀρέτας ***Aretas*** [ARETAS] 1x
<703> ἀρετή ***aretē*** [VIRTUE] 5x
<704> ἀρήν ***arēn*** [LAMB 2] 1x
<705> ἀριθμέω ***arithmeō*** [NUMBER (verb) 1] 3x
<706> ἀριθμός ***arithmos*** [NUMBER (noun) 1] 18x
<707> Ἀριμαθαία ***Arimathaia*** [ARIMATHEA] 4x
<708> Ἀρίσταρχος ***Aristarchos*** [ARISTARCHUS] 5x
<709> ἀριστάω ***aristaō*** [DINE 1] 3x
<710> ἀριστερός ***aristeros*** [left, left hand, the left: LEFT 1] 4x
<711> Ἀριστόβουλος ***Aristoboulos*** [ARISTOBULUS] 1x
<712> ἄριστον ***ariston*** [DINNER 1] 3x
<713> ἀρκετός ***arketos*** [SUFFICIENT 1] 3x
<714> ἀρκέω ***arkeō*** [CONTENT (verb) 1, to be enough: ENOUGH 3, to be satisfied: SATISFIED 2, to be sufficient: SUFFICIENT 2] 8x
<715> ἄρκτος ***arktos*** [BEAR (noun)] 1x
<716> ἅρμα ***harma*** [CHARIOT 1] 4x
<717> Ἁρμαγεδών ***Harmagedōn*** [ARMAGEDDON] 1x
<718> ἁρμόζω ***harmozō*** [PROMISE (verb) 1] 1x
<719> ἁρμός ***harmos*** [JOINT 1] 1x
<720> ἀρνέομαι ***arneomai*** [DENY 1, REFUSE (verb) 2] 33x
<721> Ἀρνίον ***Arnion*** [LAMB (name)] and ἀρνίον ***arnion*** [LAMB (noun) 3] 30x
<722> ἀροτριάω ***arotriaō*** [PLOW (verb)] 3x
<723> ἄροτρον ***arotron*** [PLOW (noun)] 1x
<724> ἁρπαγή ***harpagē*** [PLUNDERING, ROBBERY 1] 3x
<725> ἁρπαγμός ***harpagmos*** [ROBBERY 2] 1x
<726> ἁρπάζω ***harpazō*** [to catch away, to catch up: CATCH (verb) 2, to pull out: PULL 3, SEIZE 1, to take by force: TAKE 24] 14x
<727> ἅρπαξ ***harpax*** [RAPACIOUS] 5x
<728> ἀρραβών ***arrabōn*** [EARNEST (noun)] 3x
<729> ἄρραφος ***arraphos*** [SEAMLESS] 1x
<730> ἄρρην or ἄρσην ***arrēn*** or ***arsēn*** [MALE (noun) 1] 9x
<731> ἄρρητος ***arrētos*** [INEXPRESSIBLE 2] 1x
<732> ἄρρωστος ***arrōstos*** [SICK (adj. and noun) 1] 5x
<733> ἀρσενοκοίτης ***arsenokoitēs*** [HOMOSEXUAL 1] 2x
<734> Ἀρτεμᾶς ***Artemas*** [ARTEMAS] 1x
<735> Ἄρτεμις ***Artemis*** [DIANA] 5x
<736> ἀρτέμων ***artemōn*** [MAINSAIL] 1x
<737> ἄρτι ***arti*** [HITHERTO 1, now, from now on, hereafter: NOW 4] 36x
<738> ἀρτιγέννητος ***artigennētos*** [NEWBORN] 1x
<739> ἄρτιος ***artios*** [COMPLETE (adj.) 1] 1x
<740> ἄρτος ***artos*** [BREAD 1, BREAK BREAD, EXPOSITION OF THE LOAVES] 97x
<741> ἀρτύω ***artuō*** [SEASON (verb) 1] 3x

<742> Ἀρφαξάδ ***Arphaxad*** [ARPHAXAD] 1x

<743> ἀρχάγγελος ***archangelos*** [ARCHANGEL] 2x

<744> ἀρχαῖος ***archaios*** [ANCIENT 1, OLD 1] 11x

<745> Ἀρχέλαος ***Archelaos*** [ARCHELAUS] 1x

<746> ἀρχή ***archē*** [BEGINNING 1, BEGINNING 2, CORNER 2, MAGISTRATE 1, POWER[2] 1, PRINCIPALITY, original state: STATE 1] 55x

<747> ἀρχηγός ***archēgos*** [AUTHOR 2, CAPTAIN 1, PRINCE 1] 4x

<748> ἀρχιερατικός ***archieratikos*** [HIGH-PRIESTLY] 1x

<749> ἀρχιερεύς ***archiereus*** [HIGH PRIEST 1, chief priest: PRIEST 2, high priest: PRIESTHOOD 4] 122x

<750> Ἀρχιποίμην ***Archipoimēn*** [SHEPHERD (noun) 2] 1x

<751> Ἄρχιππος ***Archippos*** [ARCHIPPUS] 2x

<752> ἀρχισυνάγωγος ***archisunagōgos*** [ruler of the synagogue: SYNAGOGUE 2] 9x

<753> ἀρχιτέκτων ***architektōn*** [MASTER BUILDER] 1x

<754> ἀρχιτελώνης ***architelōnēs*** [chief among the publicans: PUBLICAN 1] or [chief tax collector: TAX COLLECTOR 2] 1x

<755> ἀρχιτρίκλινος ***architriklinos*** [governor of the feast, master of the feast: FEAST (noun) 4] 3x

<756> ἄρχομαι ***archomai*** [BEGIN 1] 82x

<757> ἄρχω ***archō*** [to rule over: RULE (verb) 1] 2x

<758> ἄρχων ***archōn*** [MAGISTRATE 2, PRINCE 2, RULER 1] 37x

<759> ἄρωμα ***arōma*** [SPICE 1] 4x

<760> Ἀσά ***Asa*** [ASA] 2x

<761> ἀσάλευτος ***asaleutos*** [IMMOVABLE 2, which cannot be shaken: SHAKEN] 2x

<762> ἄσβεστος ***asbestos*** [UNQUENCHABLE] 4x

<763> ἀσέβεια ***asebeia*** [UNGODLINESS 1] 6x

<764> ἀσεβέω ***asebeō*** [to live ungodly, to commit in an ungodly way: UNGODLY 2] 2x

<765> ἀσεβής ***asebēs*** [UNGODLY 1] 8x

<766> ἀσέλγεια ***aselgeia*** [dissolute way: DISSOLUTE, LEWDNESS 1] 10x

<767> ἄσημος ***asēmos*** [INSIGNIFICANT] 1x

<768> Ἀσήρ ***Asēr*** [ASHER] 2x

<769> ἀσθένεια ***astheneia*** [ILLNESS 1, INFIRMITY 1, SICKNESS 1, WEAKNESS 1] 24x

<770> ἀσθενέω ***astheneō*** [to be sick: SICK (adj. and noun) 3, to be sick, to fall sick: SICK (adv.) 2, to be weak: WEAK 3] 36x

<771> ἀσθένημα ***asthenēma*** [WEAKNESS 2] 1x

<772> ἀσθενής ***asthenēs*** [POWERLESS 1, SICK (adj. and noun) 2, WEAK 2, WEAKNESS 3] 26x

<773> Ἀσία ***Asia*** [ASIA 1] 20x

<774> Ἀσιανός ***Asianos*** [ASIAN 1] 1x

<775> Ἀσιάρχης ***Asiarchēs*** [ASIARCH] 1x

<776> ἀσιτία ***asitia*** [ABSTINENCE 1] 1x

<777> ἄσιτος ***asitos*** [without taking food: FOOD 8] 1x

<778> ἀσκέω ***askeō*** [EXERCISE (verb) 1] 1x

<779> ἀσκός ***askos*** [WINESKIN] 12x

<780> ἀσμένως ***asmenōs*** [GLADLY 1] 2x

<781> ἄσοφος ***asophos*** [unwise: WISE (noun) 2] 1x

<782> ἀσπάζομαι ***aspazomai*** [EMBRACE 1, GREET 1] 59x

<783> ἀσπασμός ***aspasmos*** [greetings, respectful greetings: GREETINGS 1] 10x

<784> ἄσπιλος ***aspilos*** [without spot: SPOT 3, UNSPOTTED] 4x

<785> ἀσπίς ***aspis*** [ASP] 1x

<786> ἄσπονδος ***aspondos*** [IMPLACABLE 1] 2x

<787> ἀσσάριον ***assarion*** [PENNY 1] 2x

<788> ἆσσον ***asson*** [nearer: WEIGH 1] 1x

<789> Ἄσσος ***Assos*** [ASSOS] 2x

<790> ἀστατέω ***astateō*** [to be homeless: HOMELESS] 1x

<791> ἀστεῖος ***asteios*** [BEAUTIFUL 1, well pleasing to God: PLEASING 2] 2x

<792> ἀστήρ ***astēr*** [MORNING STAR 1, MORNING STAR 2, STAR 1] 24x

<793> ἀστήρικτος ***astēriktos*** [UNSTABLE 2] 2x

<794> ἄστοργος ***astorgos*** [without natural affection: AFFECTION 3] 2x

<795> ἀστοχέω ***astocheō*** [STRAY 1] 3x

<796> ἀστραπή ***astrapē*** [LIGHTNING 1, bright shining: SHINING 1] 9x

<797> ἀστράπτω ***astraptō*** [SHINE 1, to shine: SHINING 2] 2x

<798> ἄστρον ***astron*** [STAR 2] 4x

<799> Ἀσύγκριτος ***Asunkritos*** [ASYNCRITUS] 1x

<800> ἀσύμφωνος ***asumphōnos*** [who does not agree: AGREE 7] 1x

<801> ἀσύνετος ***asunetos*** [without understanding, lacking in understanding: UNDERSTANDING 6] 5x

<802> ἀσύνθετος ***asunthetos*** [FAITHLESS 1] 1x

<803> ἀσφάλεια ***asphaleia*** [CERTAINTY 1, SAFETY 1] 3x

<804> ἀσφαλής ***asphalēs*** [CERTAINTY 2, SAFE 1, SURE 1] 5x

<805> ἀσφαλίζω ***asphalizō*** [FASTEN 1, to make secure: SECURE (adj.) 1] 4x

<806> ἀσφαλῶς ***asphalōs*** [ASSUREDLY 1, SECURELY 1] 3x

<807> ἀσχημονέω ***aschēmoneō*** [to behave uncomely, unseemly: BEHAVE 2] 2x

<808> ἀσχημοσύνη ***aschēmosunē*** [SHAME (noun) 2] or [shameful acts, what is shameful: SHAMEFUL 2] 2x

<809> ἀσχήμων ***aschēmōn*** [UNPRESENTABLE] 1x

<810> ἀσωτία ***asōtia*** [DISSIPATION 1] 3x

<811> ἀσώτως ***asōtōs*** [prodigally: PRODIGAL] 1x

<812> ἀτακτέω ***atakteō*** [to be disorderly: DISORDERLY 2] 1x

<813> ἄτακτος ***ataktos*** [UNRULY 3] 1x

<814> ἀτάκτως ***ataktōs*** [DISORDERLY 1] 2x

<815> ἄτεκνος ***ateknos*** [childless, without children: CHILD 9] 3x

<816> ἀτενίζω ***atenizō*** [to behold earnestly, steadfastly: BEHOLD (verb) 2, to fasten, to fasten the eyes: FASTEN 2, to fix the eyes, to fix one's gaze: FIX 1, to look intently, steadfastly, steadily, up, upon: LOOK (verb) 1] 14x

<817> ἄτερ ***ater*** [WITHOUT 2] 2x

<818> ἀτιμάζω ***atimazō*** [DISHONOR (verb) 1, DISHONORED (BE), to insult: INSULT (noun) 2, to treat shamefully: SHAMEFULLY 1] 7x

<819> ἀτιμία ***atimia*** [DISHONOR (noun) 1, shame: SHAMEFUL 3] 7x

<820> ἄτιμος ***atimos*** [DISHONORED, without honor: HONOR (noun) 4, less honorable: HONORABLE 3] 4x

<821> ἀτιμόω ***atimoō*** [to insult: INSULT (noun) 3] 1x

<822> ἀτμίς ***atmis*** [VAPOR] 2x

<823> ἄτομος ***atomos*** [MOMENT 1] 1x

<824> ἄτοπος ***atopos*** [BAD 1, improper: FAULT 7, UNUSUAL 1, WRONG (adj.)] 4x

<825> Ἀττάλεια ***Attaleia*** [ATTALIA] 1x

<826> αὐγάζω ***augazō*** [SHINE 3] 1x

<827> αὐγή ***augē*** [BREAK OF DAY] 1x

<828> Αὔγουστος ***Augoustos*** [AUGUSTUS 1] 1x

<829> αὐθάδης ***authadēs*** [SELF-WILLED] 2x

<830> αὐθαίρετος ***authairetos*** [of one's own accord, willing of one's own accord: ACCORD (noun) 1] 2x

<831> αὐθεντέω ***authenteō*** [to usurp authority: AUTHORITY 6] 1x

<832> αὐλέω ***auleō*** [to play the flute: FLUTE 2] 3x

<833> αὐλή ***aulē*** [COURT 2, COURTYARD, FOLD (noun), PALACE 1] 12x

<834> αὐλητής ***aulētēs*** [FLUTE PLAYER] 2x

<835> αὐλίζομαι ***aulizomai*** [to pass the night, to spend the night: NIGHT 2, to stay at night: STAY (verb) 11] 2x

<836> αὐλός ***aulos*** [FLUTE 1] 1x

<837> αὐξάνω ***auxanō*** [GROW 1, to give the increase: INCREASE (noun) 2, INCREASE (verb) 1] 25x

<838> αὔξησις ***auxēsis*** [INCREASE (noun) 1] 2x

<839> αὔριον ***aurion*** [TOMORROW] 14x

<840> αὐστηρός ***austēros*** [HARSH 1] 2x

<841> αὐτάρκεια ***autarkeia*** [CONTENTMENT, all-sufficiency: SUFFICIENCY 1] 2x

<842> αὐτάρκης ***autarkēs*** [SATISFIED 1] 1x

<843> αὐτοκατάκριτος ***autokatakritos*** [self-condemned: CONDEMN 5] 1x

<844> αὐτόματος ***automatos*** [of itself: ITSELF] 2x

<845> αὐτόπτης ***autoptēs*** [EYEWITNESS 1] 1x

<846> αὐτός ***autos*** [about them, around them: ABOUT 2, OWN (adj. and pron.) 1, for this very reason: REASON (noun) 6, RELATIVE 1, SAME 1] 5,000x +

<847> αὐτοῦ ***autou*** [HERE 1] 4x

<848> αὑτοῦ ***hautou*** [HIMSELF] 6x

<849> αὐτόχειρ ***autocheir*** [with their own hands: OWN HANDS] 1x

<850> αὐχμηρός ***auchmēros*** [OBSCURE (adj.)] 1x

<851> ἀφαιρέω ***aphaireō*** [to cut off: CUT 1, to take, to take away: TAKE 20] 10x

<852> ἀφανής ***aphanēs*** [not manifest: MANIFEST (adj.) 5] 1x

<853> ἀφανίζω ***aphanizō*** [DESTROY 2, to disfigure the face: DISFIGURE, PERISH 4, to vanish away: VANISH 1] 5x

<854> ἀφανισμός ***aphanismos*** [disappearance: VANISH 2] 1x

<855> ἄφαντος ***aphantos*** [invisible: DISAPPEAR 1] 1x

<856> ἀφεδρών ***aphedrōn*** [DRAUGHT 1] 2x

<857> ἀφειδία ***apheidia*** [NEGLECT (noun)] 1x

<858> ἀφελότης ***aphelotēs*** [SIMPLICITY 2] 1x

<859> ἄφεσις ***aphesis*** [FORGIVENESS, LIBERTY 2, REMISSION 1] 17x

<860> ἁφή ***haphē*** [JOINT 2] 2x

<861> ἀφθαρσία ***aphtharsia*** [INCORRUPTIBILITY 1] 8x

<862> ἄφθαρτος ***aphthartos*** [INCORRUPTIBLE 1] 7x

<863> ἀφίημι ***aphiēmi*** [DIVORCE (verb) 2, FORGIVE 2, FORSAKE 2, to lay aside: LAY 13, LEAVE (verb) 2, LET 1, to send away: SEND 11, UTTER (verb) 2] 146x

<864> ἀφικνέομαι ***aphikneomai*** [to become known: KNOWN 4] 1x

<865> ἀφιλάγαθος ***aphilagathos*** [despiser of good, of those who are good: DESPISER 2] 1x

<866> ἀφιλάργυρος ***aphilarguros*** [without covetousness: COVETOUSNESS 2, not greedy for money, not greedy of filthy lucre: GREEDY 2] 2x

<867> ἄφιξις ***aphixis*** [DEPARTURE 2] 1x

<868> ἀφίστημι ***aphistēmi*** [DEPART 9, to keep away: KEEP (verb) 10, to lead in revolt: REVOLT 1] 14x

<869> ἄφνω ***aphnō*** [SUDDENLY 2] 3x

<870> ἀφόβως ***aphobōs*** [without fear: FEAR (noun) 3] 4x

<871> ἀφομοιόω ***aphomoioō*** [to make like: LIKE (adj., adv., noun) 4] 1x

<872> ἀφοράω ***aphoraō*** [to fix the eyes: FIX 2, SEE 5] 2x

<873> ἀφορίζω ***aphorizō*** [EXCLUDE 1, SEPARATE 5] 9x

<874> ἀφορμή ***aphormē*** [OCCASION 1] 7x

<875> ἀφρίζω ***aphrizō*** [FOAM (verb) 1] 2x

<876> ἀφρός ***aphros*** [foam (noun): FOAM (verb) 3] 1x

<877> ἀφροσύνη ***aphrosunē*** [FOOLISHNESS 1] 4x

<878> ἄφρων ***aphrōn*** [FOOL 1, FOOLISH 2] 11x

<879> ἀφυπνόω ***aphupnoō*** [to fall asleep: SLEEP (verb) 1] 1x

<880> ἄφωνος ***aphōnos*** [DUMB 2, without significance: SIGNIFICANCE] 4x

<881> Ἀχάζ ***Achaz*** [AHAZ] 2x

<882> Ἀχαΐα ***Achaia*** [ACHAIA] 11x

<883> Ἀχαϊκός ***Achaikos*** [ACHAICUS] 1x

<884> ἀχάριστος ***acharistos*** [UNTHANKFUL] 2x

<885> Ἀχίμ ***Achim*** [ACHIM] 2x

<886> ἀχειροποίητος ***acheiropoiētos*** [made without hands, not made with hands: HAND (noun) 3] 3x

<887> ἀχλύς ***achlus*** [MIST 1] 1x

<888> ἀχρεῖος ***achreios*** [UNWORTHY 3, WORTHLESS 2] 2x

<889> ἀχρειόω ***achreioō*** [to become unprofitable: UNPROFITABLE 4] 1x

<890> ἄχρηστος ***achrēstos*** [UNPROFITABLE 3] 1x

<891> ἄχρι ***achri*** [until the end, unto the end: END (noun) 5] 50x

<892> ἄχυρον ***achuron*** [CHAFF] 2x

<893> ἀψευδής ***apseudēs*** [who cannot lie, that cannot lie: LIE (verb)[2] 2] 1x

<894> Ἄψινθος, ἄψινθος ***Apsinthos, apsinthos*** [WORMWOOD] 2x

<895> ἄψυχος ***apsuchos*** [LIFELESS] 1x

B

<896> Βάαλ ***Baal*** [BAAL] 1x

<897> Βαβυλών ***Babulōn*** [BABYLON] 12x

<898> βαθμός ***bathmos*** [STANDING 1] 1x

<899> βάθος ***bathos*** [DEEP (noun) 1, DEPTH 1] 9x

<900> βαθύνω ***bathunō*** [to dig, to dig deep: DIG 1] 1x

<901> βαθύς ***bathus*** [DEEP (adj.) 1] 3x

<902> βαΐον ***baion*** [BRANCH 1] 1x

<903> Βαλαάμ ***Balaam*** [BALAAM] 3x

<904> Βαλάκ ***Balak*** [BALAK] 1x

<905> βαλλάντιον ***ballantion*** [PURSE 1] 4x

<906> βάλλω ***ballō*** [ARISE 2, CAST (verb) 1, to cast out: CAST (verb) 4, IMPOSE 1, LIE (verb)[1] 4, POUR 1, PUT 6, THROW (verb) 1] 122x

<907> βαπτίζω ***baptizō*** [to baptize: BAPTISM 1, WASH 3] 77x

<908> βάπτισμα ***baptisma*** [BAPTISM 1] 19x

<909> βαπτισμός ***baptismos*** [BAPTISM 2, WASHING 1] 4x

<910> βαπτιστής ***baptistēs*** [BAPTIST 1] 14x

<911> βάπτω ***baptō*** [DIP 1] 3x

<912> Βαραββᾶς ***Barabbas*** [BARABBAS] 11x

<913> Βαράκ ***Barak*** [BARAK] 1x

<914> Βαραχίας ***Barachias*** [BARACHIAS] 1x

<915> βάρβαρος ***barbaros*** [BARBARIAN] 6x

<916> βαρέω ***bareō*** [BURDEN (verb) 1, to be heavy: HEAVY 2] 6x

<917> βαρέως ***bareōs*** [HARD 1] 2x

<918> Βαρθολομαῖος ***Bartholomaios*** [BARTHOLOMEW] 4x

<919> Βαριησοῦς ***Bariēsous*** [BAR-JESUS] 1x

<920> Βαριωνᾶς ***Bariōnas*** [BARJONAS] 1x

<921> Βαρναβᾶς ***Barnabas*** [BARNABAS] 28x

<922> βάρος ***baros*** [BURDEN (noun) 1, WEIGHT 1] 6x

<923> Βαρσαββᾶς ***Barsabbas*** [BARSABBAS] 2x

<924> Βαρτιμαῖος ***Bartimaios*** [BARTIMAEUS] 1x

<925> βαρύνω ***barunō*** [OVERCHARGED (BE)] 1x

<926> βαρύς ***barus*** [BURDENSOME 1, HEAVY 1, SAVAGE, SERIOUS 1, WEIGHTIER] 6x

<927> βαρύτιμος ***barutimos*** [very precious: PRECIOUS 1] or [very precious: PRICE (noun) 2] 1x

<928> βασανίζω ***basanizō*** [to be in pain: PAIN (noun) 3, TORMENT (verb) 1, TOSS 1] 12x

<929> βασανισμός ***basanismos*** [TORMENT (noun) 1] 6x

<930> βασανιστής ***basanistēs*** [TORTURER] 1x

<931> βάσανος ***basanos*** [TORMENT (noun) 2] 3x

<932> βασιλεία ***basileia*** [KINGDOM 1, KINGDOM OF GOD, KINGDOM OF HEAVEN, KINGSHIP] 162x

<933> βασίλειον ***basileion*** [court of kings: KING 2] 1x

<934> βασίλειος ***basileios*** [ROYAL 1] 1x

<935> βασιλεύς ***basileus*** [KING 1] 115x

<936> βασιλεύω ***basileuō*** [REIGN (verb) 1] 21x

<937> βασιλικός ***basilikos*** [king's: KING 3, NOBLEMAN 1, ROYAL 2] 5x

<938> βασίλισσα ***basilissa*** [QUEEN] 4x

<939> βάσις ***basis*** [FOOT[1] 2] 1x

<940> βασκαίνω ***baskainō*** [BEWITCH 1] 1x

<941> βαστάζω ***bastazō*** [BEAR (verb) 3, to carry away: CARRY 11, to take up: TAKE 25] 27x

<942> βάτος ***batos*** (fem.) [BUSH] 5x

<943> βάτος ***batos*** (masc.) [MEASURE (noun) 1] 1x

<944> βάτραχος ***batrachos*** [FROG] 1x

<945> βατταλογέω ***battalogeō*** [to use vain repetitions, to use meaningless repetitions: REPETITION] 1x

<946> βδέλυγμα ***bdelugma*** [ABOMINATION] 6x

<947> βδελυκτός ***bdeluktos*** [ABOMINABLE 2] 1x

<948> βδελύσσομαι ***bdelussomai*** [ABHOR 2, ABOMINABLE 3] 2x

<949> βέβαιος ***bebaios*** [FIRM 1, SURE 2, VALID 1] 9x

<950> βεβαιόω ***bebaioō*** [CONFIRM 1, ESTABLISH 1] 8x

<951> βεβαίωσις ***bebaiōsis*** [CONFIRMATION] 2x

<952> βέβηλος ***bebēlos*** [PROFANE (adj. and noun) 1] 5x

<953> βεβηλόω ***bebēloō*** [PROFANE (verb) 1] 2x

<954> Βεελζεβούλ ***Beelzeboul*** [BEELZEBUL] 7x

<955> Βελίαλ ***Belial*** or Βελιάρ ***Beliar*** [BELIAL] 1x

<956> βέλος ***belos*** [DART 1] 1x

<957> βελτίων ***beltiōn*** [very well: WELL (adv.) 2] 1x

<958> Βενιαμίν ***Beniamin*** [BENJAMIN] 4x

<959> Βερνίκη ***Bernikē*** [BERNICE] 3x

<960> Βέροια ***Beroia*** [BEREA 1] 2x

<961> Βεροιαῖος ***Beroiaios*** [BEREA 2] 1x

<962> Βηθαβαρά ***Bēthabara*** [BETHANY 2] 1x

<963> Βηθανία ***Bēthania*** [BETHANY 1] 12x

<964> Βηθεσδά ***Bēthesda*** [BETHESDA] 1x

<965> Βηθλέεμ ***Bēthleem*** [BETHLEHEM] 8x

<966> Βηθσαϊδά ***Bēthsaida*** [BETHSAIDA] 7x

<967> Βηθφαγή ***Bēthphagē*** [BETHPHAGE] 3x

<968> βῆμα ***bēma*** [GROUND (noun)[1] 1, JUDGMENT SEAT 1, THRONE 1] 12x

<969> βήρυλλος ***bērullos*** [BERYL] 1x

<970> βία ***bia*** [VIOLENCE 1] 4x

<971> βιάζω ***biazō*** [to suffer violence, to take by violence, to strive violently to go in: VIOLENCE 2] 2x

<972> βίαιος ***biaios*** [VIOLENT (adj.) 1] 1x

<973> βιαστής ***biastēs*** [VIOLENT (noun)] 1x

<974> βιβλαρίδιον ***biblaridion*** [little book: BOOK 3] 4x

<975> βιβλίον ***biblion*** [BOOK 2, CERTIFICATE 1] 34x

<976> βίβλος ***biblos*** [BOOK 1] 10x

<977> βιβρώσκω ***bibrōskō*** [EAT 1] 1x

<978> Βιθυνία ***Bithunia*** [BITHYNIA] 2x

<979> βίος ***bios*** [LIFE 3, LIVELIHOOD, LIVING (noun) 1] 11x

<980> βιόω ***bioō*** [LIVE 5] 1x

<981> βίωσις ***biōsis*** [manner of life: LIFE 4] 1x

<982> βιωτικός ***biōtikos*** [*biōtika*: things that pertain to this life, things of this life, matters of this life: LIFE 5] 3x

<983> βλαβερός ***blaberos*** [HARMFUL 1] 1x

<984> βλάπτω ***blaptō*** [HURT 2, INJURE 2] 2x

<985> βλαστάνω ***blastanō*** [BUD 1, PRODUCE 1, SPROUT 1] 4x

<986> Βλάστος ***Blastos*** [BLASTUS] 1x

<987> βλασφημέω ***blasphēmeō*** [BLASPHEME 1, to blaspheme: BLASPHEMER 2, DEFAME 1, to speak evil: EVIL (adv.) 1, INJURE 3, to report slanderously: REPORT (verb) 3, REVILE 1, to speak injuriously: SPEAK 14] 34x
<988> βλασφημία ***blasphēmia*** [BLASPHEMY 1, injurious speech, injurious word: INJURIOUS 1, RAILING 1] 18x
<989> βλάσφημος ***blasphēmos*** [BLASPHEMER 1, BLASPHEMOUS 1, REVILING 1] 5x
<990> βλέμμα ***blemma*** [SEEING] 1x
<991> βλέπω ***blepō*** [BEHOLD (verb) 3, BEWARE 1, CONSIDER 1, FACE (verb) 1, to take heed: HEED (noun) 1, LOOK (verb) 2, REGARD (verb) 1, SEE 1] 133x
<992> βλητέος ***blēteos*** [which must be put: PUT 8] 2x
<993> Βοανηργές ***Boanērges*** [BOANERGES] 1x
<994> βοάω ***boaō*** [to cry, to cry out: CRY (verb) 1, SHOUT (verb) 1] 11x
<995> βοή ***boē*** [CRY (noun) 1] 1x
<996> βοήθεια ***boētheia*** [CABLE, HELP (noun) 2] 2x
<997> βοηθέω ***boētheō*** [HELP (verb) 1] 8x
<998> βοηθός ***boēthos*** [HELPER 1] 1x
<999> βόθυνος ***bothunos*** [PIT 1] 3x
<1000> βολή ***bolē*** [THROW (noun)] 1x
<1001> βολίζω ***bolizō*** [to take sounding: SOUNDING] 2x
<1002> βολίς ***bolis*** [DART 2] 1x
<1003> Βοόζ ***Booz*** [BOAZ] 3x
<1004> βόρβορος ***borboros*** [MIRE] 1x
<1005> βορρᾶς ***borras*** [NORTH] 2x
<1006> βόσκω ***boskō*** [FEED 1] 9x
<1007> Βοσόρ ***Bosor*** [BEOR] 1x
<1008> βοτάνη ***botanē*** [VEGETATION] 1x
<1009> βότρυς ***botrus*** [CLUSTER] 1x
<1010> βουλευτής ***bouleutēs*** [COUNSELLOR, COUNSELOR 1] 2x
<1011> βουλεύω ***bouleuō*** [CONSIDER 2, CONSULT 1, PROPOSE 1, RESOLVE (verb) 1] 6x
<1012> βουλή ***boulē*** [advice: ADVISE 1, COUNSEL (noun) 1, PLAN (noun) 1] 12x
<1013> βούλημα ***boulēma*** [PURPOSE (noun) 1, WILL (noun)[1] 5] 2x
<1014> βούλομαι ***boulomai*** [ADVISE 1, PLEASE 4, PURPOSE (verb) 1, WANT (verb) 1, WILL (verb) 1] 37x
<1015> βουνός ***bounos*** [HILL 1] 2x
<1016> βοῦς ***bous*** [OX 1] 8x
<1017> βραβεῖον ***brabeion*** [PRIZE 1] 2x
<1018> βραβεύω ***brabeuō*** [RULE (verb) 2] 1x
<1019> βραδύνω ***bradunō*** [DELAY (verb) 1] 2x
<1020> βραδυπλοέω ***braduploeō*** [to sail slowly: SAIL (verb) 5] 1x
<1021> βραδύς ***bradus*** [SLOW 1] 3x
<1022> βραδύτης ***bradutēs*** [DELAY (verb) 2] 1x
<1023> βραχίων ***brachiōn*** [ARM (noun)[1] 3] 3x
<1024> βραχύς ***brachus*** [for a short time: TIME 11] 7x
<1025> βρέφος ***brephos*** [BABE 1, child: CHILDHOOD 1] 8x
<1026> βρέχω ***brechō*** [FALL (verb) 13, to send rain: RAIN (noun) 2, RAIN (verb) 1, WASH 4] 7x
<1027> βροντή ***brontē*** [THUNDER (noun)] 12x
<1028> βροχή ***brochē*** [RAIN (noun) 1] 2x
<1029> βρόχος ***brochos*** [LEASH] 1x
<1030> βρυγμός ***brugmos*** [GNASHING] 7x
<1031> βρύχω ***bruchō*** [GNASH 2] 1x
<1032> βρύω ***bruō*** [to send forth, to send out: SEND 12] 1x
<1033> βρῶμα ***brōma*** [food, solid food: FOOD 1] 17x
<1034> βρώσιμος ***brōsimos*** [FOOD 3] 1x
<1035> βρῶσις ***brōsis*** [EATING 1, FOOD 2, MEAL 1, RUST 1] 11x

<1036> βυθίζω ***buthizō*** [PLUNGE 1, SINK (verb) 1] 2x
<1037> βυθός ***buthos*** [DEEP (noun) 2] 1x
<1038> βυρσεύς ***burseus*** [TANNER] 3x
<1039> βύσσινος ***bussinos*** [with fine linen, in fine linen: FINE LINEN] 5x
<1040> βύσσος ***bussos*** [FINE LINEN] 1x
<1041> βωμός ***bōmos*** [ALTAR 1] 1x

Γ

<1042> Γαββαθᾶ ***Gabbatha*** [GABBATHA] 1x
<1043> Γαβριήλ ***Gabriēl*** [GABRIEL] 2x
<1044> γάγγραινα ***gangraina*** [GANGRENE] 1x
<1045> Γάδ ***Gad*** [GAD] 1x
<1046> Γαδαρηνός ***Gadarēnos*** [GADARENE] 2x
<1047> γάζα ***gaza*** [TREASURE (noun) 2] 1x
<1048> Γάζα ***Gaza*** [GAZA] 1x
<1049> γαζοφυλάκιον ***gazophulakion*** [treasury, temple treasury: TREASURE (noun) 3] 5x
<1050> Γάϊος ***Gaios*** [GAIUS] 5x
<1051> γάλα ***gala*** [MILK] 5x
<1052> Γαλάτης ***Galatēs*** [GALATIAN 1] 1x
<1053> Γαλατία ***Galatia*** [GALATIA 1] 4x
<1054> Γαλατικός ***Galatikos*** [GALATIA 2] 2x
<1055> γαλήνη ***galēnē*** [CALM (adj. and noun) 1] 3x
<1056> Γαλιλαία ***Galilaia*** [GALILEE] 61x
<1057> Γαλιλαῖος ***Galilaios*** [GALILEAN] 11x
<1058> Γαλλίων ***Galliōn*** [GALLIO] 3x
<1059> Γαμαλιήλ ***Gamaliēl*** [GAMALIEL] 2x
<1060> γαμέω ***gameō*** [MARRY 1] 29x
<1061> γαμίσκω ***gamiskō*** [to give in marriage: MARRIAGE 2] 1x
<1062> γάμος ***gamos*** [MARRIAGE 1, wedding, wedding banquet, wedding feast: WEDDING 1] 16x
<1063> γάρ ***gar*** [NOW 1, VERILY 2] 1,041x
<1064> γαστήρ ***gastēr*** [with child: CHILD 11, GLUTTON 1, WOMB 1] 9x
<1065> γε ***ge*** [YET 2] 25x
<1066> Γεδεών ***Gedeōn*** [GIDEON] 1x
<1067> γέεννα ***geenna*** [HELL 1, SON OF HELL] 12x
<1068> Γεθσημανί ***Gethsēmani*** [GETHSEMANE] 2x
<1069> γείτων ***geitōn*** [NEIGHBOR 1] 4x
<1070> γελάω ***gelaō*** [LAUGH 1] 2x
<1071> γέλως ***gelōs*** [LAUGHTER] 1x
<1072> γεμίζω ***gemizō*** [FILL (verb) 1] 9x
<1073> γέμω ***gemō*** [to be full: FULL 5] 11x
<1074> γενεά ***genea*** [GENERATION 1] 42x
<1075> γενεαλογέω ***genealogeō*** [to have a genealogy: GENEALOGY 2] 1x
<1076> γενεαλογία ***genealogia*** [GENEALOGY 1] 2x
<1077> γενέσια ***genesia*** [BIRTHDAY] 2x
<1078> γένεσις ***genesis*** [GENEALOGY 3, nature: NATURAL 3, NATURE 3] 4x
<1079> γενετή ***genetē*** [BIRTH 1] 1x
<1079a> γένημα ***genēma*** [FRUIT 4, GRAIN 1] 5x
<1080> γεννάω ***gennaō*** [BEAR (verb) 4, BEGET 1, to have by birth: BIRTH 4, to beget: BORN (BE) 1, to beget: BORN AGAIN (BE) 1, to bring forth: BRING 24, CONCEIVE 1, GENERATE] 97x
<1081> γέννημα ***gennēma*** [BROOD 1] 4x
<1082> Γεννησαρέτ ***Gennēsaret*** [GENNESARET] 3x

<1083> γέννησις ***gennēsis*** [BIRTH 2] 2x
<1084> γεννητός ***gennētos*** [BORN 1] 2x
<1085> γένος ***genos*** [BIRTH 3, COUNTRYMAN 1, FAMILY 1, KIND (noun) 1, NATION 1, OFFSPRING 1, RACE[1] 1] 20x
<1086> Γερασηνός ***Gerasēnos*** [GERASENE] 3x
<1087> γερουσία ***gerousia*** [SENATE] 1x
<1088> γέρων ***gerōn*** [OLD 2] 1x
<1089> γεύω ***geuō*** [EAT 2, TASTE (verb)] 15x
<1090> γεωργέω ***geōrgeō*** [CULTIVATE] 1x
<1091> γεώργιον ***geōrgion*** [FIELD 3] 1x
<1092> γεωργός ***geōrgos*** [FARMER, VINEDRESSER 1] 18x
<1093> γῆ ***gē*** [EARTH 1, LAND (noun) 2] 250x
<1094> γῆρας ***gēras*** [OLD AGE 1] 1x
<1095> γηράσκω ***gēraskō*** [to be old, to grow old: OLD 7] 2x
<1096> γίνομαι ***ginomai*** [ARISE 3, BE 3, BECOME 1, BEFALL (verb) 1, BEGIN 4, BEHAVE 1, BORN (BE) 2, to bring near: BRING 25, to come, to come to pass, to come upon, to come on, to come to be: COME 1, CONTINUE 7, DIVIDE 5, DO 1, to draw near, to draw nigh: DRAW 11, FORBID 1, FULFILL 4, HAPPEN 1, KEEP (verb) 5, LIVE 6, MAKE 2, OCCUR 1, PERFORM 1, to take place: PLACE (noun) 9, RETURN (verb) 3, RISE (verb) 7, to take place: TAKE 26, to become: TURN (verb) 11] 683x
<1097> γινώσκω ***ginōskō*** [KNOW 1, RECOGNIZE 1, UNDERSTAND 1] 222x
<1098> γλεῦκος ***gleukos*** [new wine, sweet wine: WINE 2] 1x
<1099> γλυκύς ***glukus*** [FRESH, SWEET 1] 4x
<1100> γλῶσσα ***glōssa*** [TONGUE 1] 50x
<1101> γλωσσόκομον ***glōssokomon*** [BAG 1] 2x
<1102> γναφεύς ***gnapheus*** [LAUNDERER] 1x
<1103> γνήσιος ***gnēsios*** [SINCERITY 1, TRUE 3] 4x
<1104> γνησίως ***gnēsiōs*** [SINCERELY 1] 1x
<1105> γνόφος ***gnophos*** [OBSCURITY] 1x
<1106> γνώμη ***gnōmē*** [ADVICE 1, JUDGMENT 1, MIND (noun) 1, OPINION 1, opinion: PURPOSE (verb) 5] 9x
<1107> γνωρίζω ***gnōrizō*** [INFORM 1, to know, to make known: KNOW 5] 25x
<1108> γνῶσις ***gnōsis*** [KNOWLEDGE 1] 29x
<1109> γνώστης ***gnōstēs*** [EXPERT 1] 1x
<1110> γνωστός ***gnōstos*** [ACQUAINTANCE 1, EVIDENT 1, KNOWN 1] 15x
<1111> γογγύζω ***gonguzō*** [MURMUR 1] 8x
<1112> γογγυσμός ***gongusmos*** [MURMURING] 4x
<1113> γογγυστής ***gongustēs*** [MURMURER] 1x
<1114> γόης ***goēs*** [IMPOSTOR 1] 1x
<1115> Γολγοθᾶ ***Golgotha*** [GOLGOTHA] 3x
<1116> Γόμορρα ***Gomorra*** [GOMORRAH] 5x
<1117> γόμος ***gomos*** [BURDEN (noun) 4, MERCHANDISE 1] 3x
<1118> γονεύς ***goneus*** [PARENT 1] 20x
<1119> γόνυ ***gonu*** [KNEE 1] 12x
<1120> γονυπετέω ***gonupeteō*** [to kneel down, to fall on the knees, to bow the knee: KNEE 2] 4x
<1121> γράμμα ***gramma*** [BILL 1, LEARNING 1, LETTER 1, WRITING 1] 14x
<1122> γραμματεύς ***grammateus*** [SCRIBE, TOWN CLERK] 63x
<1123> γραπτός ***graptos*** [written: WRITE 5] 1x
<1124> γραφή ***graphē*** [SCRIPTURE 1] 51x
<1125> γράφω ***graphō*** [WRITE 1] 191x
<1126> γραώδης ***graōdēs*** [old wives': OLD 6] 1x
<1127> γρηγορέω ***grēgoreō*** [WATCH (verb) 2, to be watchful: WATCHFUL 1] 23x
<1128> γυμνάζω ***gumnazō*** [EXERCISE (verb) 2] 4x
<1129> γυμνασία ***gumnasia*** [EXERCISE (noun)] 1x
<1130> γυμνητεύω ***gumnēteuō*** [to be naked: NAKED 2] 1x

<1131> γυμνός ***gumnos*** [BARE 1, NAKED 1] 15x
<1132> γυμνότης ***gumnotēs*** [NAKEDNESS 1] 3x
<1133> γυναικάριον ***gunaikarion*** [SILLY WOMAN] 1x
<1134> γυναικεῖος ***gunaikeios*** [FEMALE 1] 1x
<1135> γυνή ***gunē*** [WOMAN 1] 219x
<1136> Γώγ ***Gōg*** [GOG] 1x
<1137> γωνία ***gōnia*** [CHIEF CORNERSTONE 2, CORNER 1, CORNER STONE 1] 9x

Δ

<1138> Δαυίδ ***Dauid*** [DAVID] 58x
<1139> δαιμονίζομαι ***daimonizomai*** [to be possessed by a demon: DEMON 3] 13x
<1140> δαιμόνιον ***daimonion*** [DEMON 1, GOD (other god) 1] 63x
<1141> δαιμονιώδης ***daimoniōdēs*** [DEMONIC 1] 1x
<1142> δαίμων ***daimōn*** [DEMON 2] 5x
<1143> δάκνω ***daknō*** [BITE] 1x
<1144> δάκρυον ***dakruon*** [TEAR (noun)[1]] 11x
<1145> δακρύω ***dakruō*** [WEEP 1] 1x
<1146> δακτύλιος ***daktulios*** [RING (noun) 1] 1x
<1147> δάκτυλος ***daktulos*** [FINGER] 8x
<1148> Δαλμανουθά ***Dalmanoutha*** [DALMANUTHA] 1x
<1149> Δαλματία ***Dalmatia*** [DALMATIA] 1x
<1150> δαμάζω ***damazō*** [TAME] 4x
<1151> δάμαλις ***damalis*** [HEIFER] 1x
<1152> Δάμαρις ***Damaris*** [DAMARIS] 1x
<1153> Δαμασκηνός ***Damaskēnos*** [DAMASCENE] 1x
<1154> Δαμασκός ***Damaskos*** [DAMASCUS] 15x
<1155> δανείζω ***daneizō*** [BORROW, LEND 1] 4x
<1156> δάνειον ***daneion*** [DEBT 1] 1x
<1157> δανειστής ***daneistēs*** [CREDITOR] 1x
<1158> Δανιήλ ***Daniēl*** [DANIEL] 1x
<1159> δαπανάω ***dapanaō*** [to pay the expenses: EXPENSE 2, SPEND 1] 5x
<1160> δαπάνη ***dapanē*** [COST 1] 1x
<1161> δέ ***de*** [BUT 2, FINALLY 2, last of all: LAST (adv. and noun) 3, YET 3] 2,800x +
<1162> δέησις ***deēsis*** [PRAYER 1, SUPPLICATION 1] 19x
<1163> δεῖ ***dei*** [MUST 1, it is needed: NEEDED 1, OUGHT 1, it ought: OUGHT 2] 101x
<1164> δεῖγμα ***deigma*** [EXAMPLE 1] 1x
<1165> δειγματίζω ***deigmatizō*** [to make an example: EXAMPLE 3, to make a spectacle: SPECTACLE 4] 2x
<1166> δείκνυμι ***deiknumi*** [SHOW (verb) 4] 31x
<1167> δειλία ***deilia*** [FEAR (noun) 4] 1x
<1168> δειλιάω ***deiliaō*** [to be afraid: AFRAID 4] 1x
<1169> δειλός ***deilos*** [FEARFUL 1] 3x
<1170> δεῖνα ***deina*** [a certain man: MAN 4] 1x
<1171> δεινῶς ***deinōs*** [TERRIBLY 1] or [VEHEMENTLY 1] 2x
<1172> δειπνέω ***deipneō*** [SUP] 4x
<1173> δεῖπνον ***deipnon*** [SUPPER 1] 16x
<1174> δεισιδαιμονέστερος ***deisidaimonesteros*** [very religious: RELIGIOUS 2] 1x
<1175> δεισιδαιμονία ***deisidaimonia*** [RELIGION 1] 1x
<1176> δέκα ***deka*** [EIGHTEEN, TEN, TEN THOUSAND 1] 27x
<1177> δεκαδύο ***dekaduo*** [TWELVE 2] 2x
<1178> δεκαπέντε ***dekapente*** [FIFTEEN] 3x
<1179> Δεκάπολις ***Dekapolis*** [DECAPOLIS] 3x
<1180> δεκατέσσαρες ***dekatessares*** [FOURTEEN] 5x

<1181> δεκάτη ***dekatē*** [tenth, tenth part, tenth portion: TITHE (noun and verb) 1] 4x

<1182> δέκατος ***dekatos*** [TENTH 1] 3x

<1183> δεκατόω ***dekatoō*** [to receive tithe, to tithe, to give a tenth: TITHE (noun and verb) 1] 2x

<1184> δεκτός ***dektos*** [ACCEPTABLE 1, ACCEPTED 1] 5x

<1185> δελεάζω ***deleazō*** [ENTICE 1] 3x

<1186> δένδρον ***dendron*** [TREE 1] 26x

<1187> δεξιολάβος ***dexiolabos*** [SPEARMAN] 1x

<1188> δεξιός ***dexios*** [to give the right hand of fellowship; right: FELLOWSHIP 3, right, right hand: RIGHT (adj. and noun), right, right side, right-hand side: SIDE 3] 54x

<1189> δέομαι ***deomai*** [IMPLORE 1, PRAY 1, to make request: REQUEST (noun) 2, SUPPLICATE] 22x

<1189a> δέος ***deos*** [godly fear: FEAR (noun) 5] 1x

<1190> Δερβαῖος ***Derbaios*** [DERBE 2] 1x

<1191> Δέρβη ***Derbē*** [DERBE 1] 3x

<1192> δέρμα ***derma*** [SKIN 1] 1x

<1193> δερμάτινος ***dermatinos*** [LEATHER] 2x

<1194> δέρω ***derō*** [BEAT 1] 15x

<1195> δεσμεύω ***desmeuō*** [BIND 1] 3x

<1196> δεσμέω ***desmeō*** [BIND 1] 1x

<1197> δέσμη ***desmē*** [BUNDLE 1] 1x

<1198> δέσμιος ***desmios*** [PRISONER 1] 17x

<1199> δεσμός ***desmos*** [CHAIN (noun) 2] 20x

<1200> δεσμοφύλαξ ***desmophulax*** [JAILER] 3x

<1201> δεσμωτήριον ***desmōtērion*** [PRISON 1] 4x

<1202> δεσμώτης ***desmōtēs*** [PRISONER 2] 2x

<1203> δεσπότης ***despotēs*** [MASTER (noun) 1] and Δεσπότης ***Despotēs*** [LORD (noun) 2] 10x

<1204> δεῦρο ***deuro*** [PRESENT TIME 1] 9x

<1205> δεῦτε ***deute*** [HERE 2] 13x

<1206> δευτεραῖος ***deuteraios*** [next day, second day, day later: DAY 2] 1x

<1207> δευτερόπρωτος ***deuteroprōtos*** [second-first, second after the first: FIRST 4] 1x

<1208> δεύτερος ***deuteros*** [SECOND 1, second time: TIME 15] 43x

<1209> δέχομαι ***dechomai*** [RECEIVE 8, TAKE 35] 56x

<1210> δέω ***deō*** [BIND 2, CHAIN (verb) 1, TIE 1] 43x

<1211> δή ***dē*** [TRULY 2] 5x

<1212> δῆλος ***dēlos*** [EVIDENT 2, MANIFEST (adj.) 1] 4x

<1213> δηλόω ***dēloō*** [DECLARE 4, INDICATE 1, SHOW (verb) 10] 7x

<1214> Δημᾶς ***Dēmas*** [DEMAS] 3x

<1215> δημηγορέω ***dēmēgoreō*** [to make a public oration, to make an oration, to give an oration: ORATION] 1x

<1216> Δημήτριος ***Dēmētrios*** [DEMETRIUS] 3x

<1217> δημιουργός ***dēmiourgos*** [MAKER] 1x

<1218> δῆμος ***dēmos*** [PEOPLE 1] 4x

<1219> δημοσία, δημόσιος ***dēmosia, dēmosios*** [PUBLICLY 1, PUBLIC 1] 4x

<1220> δηνάριον ***dēnarion*** [DENARIUS] 16x

<1221> δήποτε ***dēpote*** [WHATEVER] 1x

<1222> δήπου ***dēpou*** [VERILY 3] 1x

<1223> διά ***dia*** [ALWAYS 2, BRIEFLY 1, for this reason: REASON (noun) 5, SAKE OF (FOR THE) 1] 670x

<1224> διαβαίνω ***diabainō*** [to pass, to pass through: PASS 4] 3x

<1225> διαβάλλω ***diaballō*** [ACCUSE 1] 1x

<1226> διαβεβαιόομαι ***diabebaioomai*** [to affirm; to affirm constantly, confidently, strenuously: AFFIRM 1] 2x

<1227> διαβλέπω ***diablepō*** [to see clearly: CLEARLY 3] 3x

<1228> διάβολος ***diabolos*** [false accuser: ACCUSER 2, DEVIL 1] 37x

<1229> διαγγέλλω ***diangellō*** [DECLARE 3, PREACH 1, SIGNIFY 1] 3x

<1230> διαγίνομαι ***diaginomai*** [ELAPSE 1, to be past: PAST 1] 3x

<1231> διαγινώσκω ***diaginōskō*** [to make a decision: DECISION 2, DETERMINE 2] 2x

<1232> διαγνωρίζω ***diagnōrizō*** [to make known, to make widely known: KNOW 6] 1x

<1233> διάγνωσις ***diagnōsis*** [DECISION 1] 1x

<1234> διαγογγύζω ***diagonguzō*** [MURMUR 2] 2x

<1235> διαγρηγορέω ***diagrēgoreō*** [to be fully awake: AWAKE (BE)] 1x

<1236> διάγω ***diagō*** [LEAD (verb) 4, LIVE 7] 2x

<1237> διαδέχομαι ***diadechomai*** [RECEIVE 11] 1x

<1238> διάδημα ***diadēma*** [CROWN (noun) 1] 3x

<1239> διαδίδωμι ***diadidōmi*** [DISTRIBUTE 1, DIVIDE 1, GIVE 3] 5x

<1240> διάδοχος ***diadochos*** [SUCCESSOR] 1x

<1241> διαζώννυμι ***diazōnnumi*** [GIRD 3] 3x

<1242> διαθήκη ***diathēkē*** [COVENANT (noun), TESTAMENT] 33x

<1243> διαίρεσις ***diairesis*** [DIVERSITY 1] 3x

<1244> διαιρέω ***diaireō*** [DISTRIBUTE 2, DIVIDE 2] 2x

<1245> διακαθαρίζω ***diakatharizō*** [to thoroughly purge: PURGE 1] 2x

<1246> διακατελέγχομαι ***diakatelenchomai*** [REFUTE 2] 1x

<1247> διακονέω ***diakoneō*** [ADMINISTER 1, MINISTER (verb) 1, SERVE 1] 37x

<1248> διακονία ***diakonia*** [ADMINISTRATION 1, MINISTRY 1, service: SERVE 2, SERVICE 1] 34x

<1249> διάκονος ***diakonos*** [MINISTER (noun) 1, SERVANT 1] 29x

<1250> διακόσιοι ***diakosioi*** [THOUSAND TWO HUNDRED AND SIXTY, TWO HUNDRED, TWO HUNDRED AND SEVENTY-SIX] 8x

<1251> διακούω ***diakouō*** [to hear fully: HEAR 2] 1x

<1252> διακρίνω ***diakrinō*** [CONTEND 1, DISCERN 2, to make a distinction, to make to differ: DISTINCTION 2, DOUBT (verb) 1, JUDGE (verb) 3, to show partiality: PARTIALITY 2, WAVER] 19x

<1253> διάκρισις ***diakrisis*** [DISCERNING 1, DISPUTE (noun) 2] 3x

<1254> διακωλύω ***diakōluō*** [PREVENT 1] 1x

<1255> διαλαλέω ***dialaleō*** [DISCUSS 1] 2x

<1256> διαλέγω ***dialegō*** [to speak, to speak unto: SPEAK 4] 2x

<1256> διαλέγομαι ***dialegomai*** [DISCOURSE (verb), DISPUTE (verb) 1, REASON (verb) 4] 13x

<1257> διαλείπω ***dialeipō*** [CEASE 1] 1x

<1258> διάλεκτος ***dialektos*** [LANGUAGE 1, TONGUE 3] 6x

<1259> διαλλάσσομαι ***diallassomai*** [RECONCILE 1] 1x

<1260> διαλογίζομαι ***dialogizomai*** [CONSIDER 12, REASON (verb) 2] 17x

<1261> διαλογισμός ***dialogismos*** [REASONING 1, THOUGHT 1] 14x

<1262> διαλύω ***dialuō*** [SCATTER 1] 1x

<1263> διαμαρτύρομαι ***diamarturomai*** [to charge, to charge solemnly: CHARGE (verb) 1, to testify, to testify solemnly: TESTIFY 5] 15x

<1264> διαμάχομαι ***diamachomai*** [STRIVE 8] 1x

<1265> διαμένω ***diamenō*** [PERSEVERE 1, REMAIN 2] 5x

<1266> διαμερίζω ***diamerizō*** [DIVIDE 4] 11x

<1267> διαμερισμός ***diamerismos*** [DIVISION 2] 1x

<1268> διανέμω ***dianemō*** [SPREAD 4] 1x

<1269> διανεύω ***dianeuō*** [to make signs: SIGN 5] 1x

<1270> διανόημα ***dianoēma*** [THOUGHT 4] 1x

<1271> διάνοια ***dianoia*** [MIND (noun) 2, UNDERSTANDING 1] 12x

<1272> διανοίγω ***dianoigō*** [EXPLAIN 1, OPEN (verb) 3] 8x

<1273> διανυκτερεύω ***dianuktereuō*** [to spend the night, to continue all night: NIGHT 3] 1x

<1274> διανύω ***dianuō*** [FINISH 7] 1x

<1275> διαπαντός ***diapantos*** [ALWAYS 3, CONTINUALLY 1] 7x

<1275a> διαπαρατριβή ***diaparatribē*** [useless wrangling: WRANGLING 1] 1x

<1276> διαπεράω ***diaperaō*** [to cross over: CROSS (verb) 1, to pass, to pass over: PASS 6] 6x

<1277> διαπλέω ***diapleō*** [to sail across, over, through: SAIL (verb) 4] 1x

<1278> διαπονέω ***diaponeō*** [DISTURBED (BE), GRIEVE 1] 2x

<1279> διαπορεύομαι ***diaporeuomai*** [to go through, to go by: GO 24, PASS 10] 5x

<1280> διαπορέω ***diaporeō*** [PERPLEXED (BE) 2] 5x

<1281> διαπραγματεύομαι ***diapragmateuomai*** [to gain, to gain by trading: GAIN (verb) 1] 1x

<1282> διαπρίω ***diapriō*** [to be furious: FURIOUS 1] 2x

<1283> διαρπάζω ***diarpazō*** [PLUNDER (verb)] 4x

<1284> διαρρήγνυμι ***diarrēgnumi*** [BREAK 8, TEAR (verb) 3] 4x

<1284> διαρρήσσω ***diarrēssō*** [BREAK 9] 1x

<1285> διασαφέω ***diasapheō*** [TELL 3] 1x

<1286> διασείω ***diaseiō*** [OPPRESS 1] 1x

<1287> διασκορπίζω ***diaskorpizō*** [to scatter, to scatter abroad: SCATTER 5, WASTE (verb) 1] 9x

<1288> διασπάω ***diaspaō*** [to tear to pieces, to pull to pieces: PIECE 5, to tear apart, to tear asunder: TEAR (verb) 1] 2x

<1289> διασπείρω ***diaspeirō*** [SCATTER 2] 3x

<1290> διασπορά ***diaspora*** [DISPERSION] 3x

<1291> διαστέλλω ***diastellō*** [COMMAND (verb) 4, to give a commandment: COMMANDMENT 5] 8x

<1292> διάστημα ***diastēma*** [INTERVAL 1] 1x

<1293> διαστολή ***diastolē*** [DIFFERENCE 1, DISTINCTION 1] 3x

<1294> διαστρέφω ***diastrephō*** [PERVERT (verb) 1, PERVERTED (BE) 1, to turn away: TURN (verb) 8] 7x

<1295> διασῴζω ***diasōzō*** [to completely heal: HEAL 4, to bring safe, safely; to escape safely: PRESERVE 4, SAVE (verb) 2] 8x

<1296> διαταγή ***diatagē*** [DISPOSITION 1, ORDINANCE 1] 2x

<1297> διάταγμα ***diatagma*** [ORDINANCE 2] 1x

<1298> διαταράσσω ***diatarassō*** [TROUBLE (verb) 8] 1x

<1299> διατάσσω ***diatassō*** [COMMAND (verb) 1, ORDAIN 1, to set in order: ORDER (noun) 3] 16x

<1300> διατελέω ***diateleō*** [GO 5] 1x

<1301> διατηρέω ***diatēreō*** [BEWARE 3, KEEP (verb) 3] 2x

<1302> διατί ***diati*** [WHEREFORE?] 27x

<1303> διατίθεμαι ***diatithemai*** [APPOINT 9, MAKE 1, one who disposes: TESTATOR] 7x

<1304> διατρίβω ***diatribō*** [STAY (verb) 1] 9x

<1305> διατροφή ***diatrophē*** [FOOD 7] 1x

<1306> διαυγάζω ***diaugazō*** [DAWN (verb) 1] 1x

<1307> διαφανής ***diaphanēs*** [TRANSPARENT] 1x

<1308> διαφέρω ***diapherō*** [CARRY 7, DIFFER 1, to make a difference: DIFFERENCE 2, to be driven about, across, up and down: DRIVEN (BE), the more excellent things: EXCELLENT 2, to spread through: SPREAD 5, to be of more value: VALUE (noun) 1] 13x

<1309> διαφεύγω ***diapheugō*** [ESCAPE 3] 1x

<1310> διαφημίζω ***diaphēmizō*** [to spread the news: NEWS 2, to spread; to spread abroad, throughout, widely: SPREAD 6] 3x

<1311> διαφθείρω ***diaphtheirō*** [CORRUPT (verb) 2, DESTROY 9, PERISH 5] 6x

<1312> διαφθορά ***diaphthora*** [CORRUPTION 2] 6x

<1313> διάφορος ***diaphoros*** [DIFFERING, more excellent: EXCELLENT 3, VARIOUS 1] 4x

<1314> διαφυλάσσω ***diaphulassō*** [GUARD (verb) 2] 1x

<1315> διαχειρίζω ***diacheirizō*** [KILL 3, MURDER (verb) 1] 2x

<1316> διαχωρίζω ***diachōrizō*** [DEPART 16] 1x

<1317> διδακτικός ***didaktikos*** [able to teach: TEACH 2] 2x

<1318> διδακτός ***didaktos*** [TAUGHT 1] 3x

<1319> διδασκαλία ***didaskalia*** [DOCTRINE 1, INSTRUCTION 1] 21x

<1320> διδάσκαλος ***didaskalos*** [TEACHER 1] 59x

<1321> διδάσκω ***didaskō*** [TEACH 1] 97x

<1322> διδαχή ***didachē*** [DOCTRINE 2] 30x

<1323> δίδραχμον ***didrachmon*** [TAX (noun) 1] 2x

<1324> Δίδυμος ***Didumos*** [DIDYMUS] 3x

<1325> δίδωμι ***didōmi*** [to adventure oneself: ADVENTURE, BESTOW 1, DRAW 14, to make every effort, to make an effort: EFFORT 1, to give the right hand of fellowship: FELLOWSHIP 3, GIVE 1, GRANT 1, LET 3, MINISTER (verb) 2, OFFER 5, PRODUCE 2, SHOW (verb) 11, TAKE 27] 415x

<1326> διεγείρω ***diegeirō*** [ARISE 5, WAKE 2] 7x

<1327> διέξοδος ***diexodos*** [THOROUGHFARE] 1x

<1328> διερμηνευτής ***diermēneutēs*** [INTERPRETER] 1x

<1329> διερμηνεύω ***diermēneuō*** [EXPLAIN 2, INTERPRET 1] 6x

<1330> διέρχομαι ***dierchomai*** [COME 5, to go; to go around, over, etc.: GO 5, to pass, to pass through: PASS 2, PIERCE 1, to spread abroad: SPREAD 2] 43x

<1331> διερωτάω ***dierōtaō*** [to make inquiry: INQUIRY 2] 1x

<1332> διετής ***dietēs*** [two years old: YEAR 4] 1x

<1333> διετία ***dietia*** [two years: YEAR 3] 2x

<1334> διηγέομαι ***diēgeomai*** [RELATE 3, TELL 4] 8x

<1335> διήγησις ***diēgēsis*** [ACCOUNT (noun) 3] 1x

<1336> διηνεκής ***diēnekēs*** [CONTINUALLY 2] 4x

<1337> διθάλασσος ***dithalassos*** [where two seas meet: SEA 2] 1x

<1338> διϊκνέομαι ***diikneomai*** [PIERCE 2] 1x

<1339> διΐστημι ***diistēmi*** [to go a little farther: FARTHER 2, SEPARATE 6] 3x

<1340> διϊσχυρίζομαι ***diischurizomai*** [to confidently affirm, to constantly affirm: AFFIRM 2] 2x

<1341> δικαιοκρισία ***dikaiokrisia*** [righteous judgment: JUDGMENT 2] 1x

<1342> δίκαιος ***dikaios*** [RIGHTEOUS 1] 80x

<1343> δικαιοσύνη ***dikaiosunē*** [ALMS 1, RIGHTEOUSNESS 1] 92x

<1344> δικαιόω ***dikaioō*** [JUSTIFY 1] 41x

<1345> δικαίωμα ***dikaiōma*** [JUSTIFICATION 1, ORDINANCE 3, requirement, just requirement, righteous requirement: REQUIREMENT 1, righteous judgment, requirement, act, decree: RIGHTEOUS 2] 10x

<1346> δικαίως ***dikaiōs*** [JUSTLY 1] 5x

<1347> δικαίωσις ***dikaiōsis*** [JUSTIFICATION 2] 2x

<1348> δικαστής ***dikastēs*** [JUDGE (noun) 1] 3x

<1349> Δίκη ***Dikē*** [JUSTICE (name)] and δίκη ***dikē*** [JUDGMENT 3, PUNISHMENT 1] 4x

<1350> δίκτυον ***diktuon*** [NET 2] 12x

<1351> δίλογος ***dilogos*** [DOUBLE-TONGUED] 1x

<1352> διό ***dio*** [WHEREFORE 1] 53x

<1353> διοδεύω ***diodeuō*** [to go through, throughout, around: GO 31, to pass through: PASS 7] 2x

<1354> Διονύσιος ***Dionusios*** [DIONYSIUS] 1x

<1355> διόπερ ***dioper*** [WHEREFORE 2] 3x

<1356> διοπετής ***diopetēs*** [fallen down from heaven: FALL (verb) 10] 1x

<1357> διόρθωσις ***diorthōsis*** [REFORMATION] 1x

<1358> διορύσσω ***diorussō*** [to break in, into, through: BREAK 1] 4x

<1359> Διόσκουροι ***Dioskouroi*** [TWIN BROTHERS] 1x

<1360> διότι ***dioti*** [BECAUSE 1] 21x

<1361> Διοτρέφης ***Diotrephēs*** [DIOTREPHES] 1x

<1362> διπλοῦς ***diplous*** [DOUBLE (adj.) 1, twice as much: TWICE 2] 4x

<1363> διπλόω ***diploō*** [REPAY 2] 1x

<1364> δίς ***dis*** [TWICE 1] 6x

<1365> διστάζω ***distazō*** [DOUBT (verb) 2] 2x

<1366> δίστομος ***distomos*** [TWO-EDGED] 4x

<1367> δισχίλιοι ***dischilioi*** [TWO THOUSAND] 1x

<1368> διϋλίζω ***diulizō*** [STRAIN 1] 1x

<1369> διχάζω ***dichazō*** [SET (verb) 5] 1x

<1370> διχοστασία ***dichostasia*** [DIVISION 3] 3x

<1371> διχοτομέω ***dichotomeō*** [to cut in two: CUT 6] 2x

<1372> διψάω ***dipsaō*** [THIRST (verb)] 16x

<1373> δίψος ***dipsos*** [THIRST (noun)] 1x

<1374> δίψυχος ***dipsuchos*** [DOUBLE-MINDED] 2x

<1375> διωγμός ***diōgmos*** [PERSECUTION 1] 10x

<1376> διώκτης ***diōktēs*** [PERSECUTOR 1] 1x

<1377> διώκω ***diōkō*** [FOLLOW 7, GIVE 10, PERSECUTE 1, PRESS 1, PURSUE 1] 45x

<1378> δόγμα ***dogma*** [DECREE (noun) 1, ORDINANCE 4] 5x

<1379> δογματίζω ***dogmatizō*** [to subject to ordinances, to submit to rules: ORDINANCE 5] 1x

<1380> δοκέω ***dokeō*** [CONSIDER 3, REGARD (verb) 2, to be of reputation, to be of high reputation: REPUTATION 1, SEEM, SUPPOSE 1, THINK 2] 62x

<1381> δοκιμάζω ***dokimazō*** [APPROVE 2, DISCERN 3, LIKE (verb) 1, TEST (noun and verb) 1] 21x

<1381a> δοκιμασία ***dokimasia*** [TESTING 1] 1x

<1382> δοκιμή ***dokimē*** [EXPERIENCE 1, PROOF 1, TEST (noun and verb) 1] 7x

<1383> δοκίμιον ***dokimion*** [TESTING 2] 2x

<1384> δόκιμος ***dokimos*** [approved: APPROVE 3] 7x

<1385> δοκός ***dokos*** [BEAM] 6x

<1386> δόλιος ***dolios*** [DECEITFUL 1] 1x

<1387> δολιόω ***dolioō*** [to practice deceit, to use deceit: DECEIT 3] 1x

<1388> δόλος ***dolos*** [DECEIT 2, SUBTLETY] 12x

<1389> δολόω ***doloō*** [FALSIFY] 1x

<1390> δόμα ***doma*** [GIFT 1] 4x

<1391> δόξα ***doxa*** [DIGNITARY, GLORY (noun) 1] 167x

<1392> δοξάζω ***doxazō*** [GLORIFY 1, to glorify: GLORIOUS 2] 62x

<1393> Δορκάς ***Dorkas*** [DORCAS] 2x

<1394> δόσις ***dosis*** [GIVING 1] 2x

<1395> δότης ***dotēs*** [GIVER] 1x

<1396> δουλαγωγέω ***doulagōgeō*** [to bring into subjection: SUBJECTION 1] 1x

<1397> δουλεία ***douleia*** [BONDAGE 1] 5x

<1398> δουλεύω ***douleuō*** [to be in bondage, to be under bondage: BONDAGE 2, SERVE 3, to do service, to render service, to serve: SERVICE 5] 25x

<1399> δούλη ***doulē*** [BONDWOMAN 1, HANDMAID] 3x

<1400> δοῦλον ***doulon*** [SLAVE (noun) 1] 2x

<1401> δοῦλος ***doulos*** [SERVANT 2] 126x

<1402> δουλόω ***douloō*** [to bring into bondage: BONDAGE 3] 8x

<1403> δοχή ***dochē*** [FEAST (noun) 1] 2x

<1404> δράκων ***drakōn*** [DRAGON] 13x

<1405> δράσσομαι ***drassomai*** [TAKE 36] 1x

<1406> δραχμή ***drachmē*** [coin, silver coin: COIN 1] 3x

<1407> δρέπανον ***drepanon*** [SICKLE] 8x

<1408> δρόμος ***dromos*** [COURSE 2] 3x

<1409> Δρούσιλλα ***Drousilla*** [DRUSILLA] 1x

<1410> δύναμαι ***dunamai*** [to be able: ABLE 2, to be possible: POSSIBLE 2] 210x

<1411> δύναμις ***dunamis*** [ABILITY 1, MEANING 1, MIRACLE 1, POWER[1] 1, POWER[3] 1, STRENGTH 1] 119x

<1412> δυναμόω ***dunamoō*** [STRENGTHEN 1] 1x

<1413> Δυνάστης ***Dunastēs*** [SOVEREIGN 1] and δυνάστης ***dunastēs*** [court official, important official: OFFICIAL 1, man in power: POWER[2] 2, RULER 2] 4x

<1414> δυνατέω ***dunateō*** [to be powerful: POWERFUL 2] 1x

<1415> δυνατός ***dunatos*** [ABLE 1, of authority, who has authority: AUTHORITY 4, MIGHTY (adj.) 1, POSSIBLE 1, POWER[1] 2, POWERFUL 1, STRONG (adj.) 1, one who is strong, the strong: STRONG (noun)] 35x

<1416> δύνω ***dunō*** [SET (verb) 6] 2x

<1417> δύο ***duo*** [FORTY-TWO, TWO 1] 137x
<1418> δυσ- ***dus-*** [DIS-]
<1419> δυσβάστακτος ***dusbastaktos*** [hard to bear: HARD 4] 2x
<1420> δυσεντερία ***dusenteria*** [DYSENTERY] 1x
<1421> δυσερμήνευτος ***dusermēneutos*** [hard to explain: HARD 5] 1x
<1422> δύσκολος ***duskolos*** [HARD 2] 1x
<1423> δυσκόλως ***duskolōs*** [HARD 3] 3x
<1424> δυσμή ***dusmē*** [WEST] 5x
<1425> δυσνόητος ***dusnoētos*** [hard to understand: UNDERSTAND 6] 1x
<1425a> δυσφημέω ***dusphēmeō*** [DEFAME 1] 1x
<1426> δυσφημία ***dusphēmia*** [bad report, evil report: REPORT (noun) 2] 1x
<1427> δώδεκα ***dōdeka*** [TWELVE 1, TWELVE THOUSAND] 75x
<1428> δωδέκατος ***dōdekatos*** [TWELFTH] 1x
<1429> δωδεκάφυλον ***dōdekaphulon*** [twelve tribes: TRIBE 2] 1x
<1430> δῶμα ***dōma*** [HOUSETOP] 7x
<1431> δωρεά ***dōrea*** [GIFT 2] 11x
<1432> δωρεάν ***dōrean*** [without a cause: CAUSE 5, FREELY 1] 9x
<1433> δωρέομαι ***dōreomai*** [GIVE 11] 3x
<1434> δώρημα ***dōrēma*** [GIFT 3] 2x
<1435> δῶρον ***dōron*** [GIFT 4] 19x

E

<1436> ἔα ***ea*** [EH!] 2x
<1437> ἐάν ***ean*** [IF 1] 333x
<1438> ἑαυτοῦ ***heautou*** [to adventure oneself: ADVENTURE, OWN (adj. and pron.) 2] 319x
<1439> ἐάω ***eaō*** [ALLOW 1] 13x
<1440> ἑβδομήκοντα ***hebdomēkonta*** [SEVENTY, SEVENTY-FIVE, TWO HUNDRED AND SEVENTY-SIX] 5x
<1441> ἑβδομηκοντάκις ***hebdomēkontakis*** [seventy times: TIME 20] 1x
<1442> ἕβδομος ***hebdomos*** [SEVENTH 2] 9x
<1443> Ἔβερ ***Eber*** [HEBER] 1x
<1444> Ἑβραϊκός ***Hebraikos*** [HEBREW 2] 1x
<1445> Ἑβραῖος ***Hebraios*** [HEBREW 1] 4x
<1446> Ἑβραΐς ***Hebrais*** [HEBREW 3] 3x
<1447> Ἑβραϊστί ***Hebraisti*** [in Hebrew: HEBREW 4] 7x
<1448> ἐγγίζω ***engizō*** [to come into the neighborhood: COME 22, to draw near, to draw nigh: DRAW 6, to be at hand: HAND (noun) 5, to be near, to be nigh, to draw near, to draw nigh: NEAR (adv.) 2, to come into the neighborhood: NEIGHBORHOOD] 42x
<1449> ἐγγράφω ***engraphō*** [WRITE 2] 2x
<1450> ἔγγυος ***enguos*** [GUARANTOR] 1x
<1451> ἐγγύς ***engus*** [to bring near: BRING 25, to draw near, to draw nigh: DRAW 11, NEAR (adv.) 1] 31x
<1452> ἐγγύτερον ***enguteron*** [NEARER 1] 1x
<1453> ἐγείρω ***egeirō*** [ARISE 4, to lift up: LIFT 4, to raise up, to rise, to arise: RAISE 1, to rise, to rise up: RISE (verb) 8, to wake up: WAKE 1] 144x
<1454> ἔγερσις ***egersis*** [RESURRECTION 2] 1x
<1455> ἐγκάθετος ***enkathetos*** [SPY (noun) 1] 1x
<1456> ἐγκαίνια ***enkainia*** [FEAST OF DEDICATION] 1x
<1457> ἐγκαινίζω ***enkainizō*** [CONSECRATE 1, INAUGURATE] 2x
<1457a> ἐγκακέω ***enkakeō*** [to lose heart: HEART 4, to lose heart: HEART 5, to become, to grow, to be weary: WEARY (adj.) 1] 3x
<1458> ἐγκαλέω ***enkaleō*** [to bring an accusation: ACCUSATION 3, ACCUSE 2, to call in question: CALL (verb) 2] 7x
<1459> ἐγκαταλείπω ***enkataleipō*** [FORSAKE 3, LEAVE (verb) 7] 9x

<1460> ἐγκατοικέω ***enkatoikeō*** [DWELL 4] 1x
<1461> ἐγκεντρίζω ***enkentrizō*** [GRAFT] 6x
<1462> ἔγκλημα ***enklēma*** [CHARGE (noun)[1] 2, CRIME 1] 2x
<1463> ἐγκομβόομαι ***enkomboomai*** [to clothe with: CLOTHE 6] 1x
<1464> ἐγκοπή ***enkopē*** [HINDRANCE 1] 1x
<1465> ἐγκόπτω ***enkoptō*** [HINDER (verb) 2, TEDIOUS (BE)] 5x
<1466> ἐγκράτεια ***enkrateia*** [SELF-CONTROL (noun) 1] 4x
<1467> ἐγκρατεύομαι ***enkrateuomai*** [to exercise self-control, to have control over oneself: CONTROL (noun) 1] 2x
<1468> ἐγκρατής ***enkratēs*** [TEMPERATE 1] 1x
<1469> ἐγκρίνω ***enkrinō*** [CLASS] 1x
<1470> ἐγκρύπτω ***enkruptō*** [HIDE 3] 2x
<1471> ἔγκυος ***enkuos*** [with child: CHILD 12] 1x
<1472> ἐγχρίω ***enchriō*** [ANOINT 4] 1x
<1473> ἐγώ ***egō*** [ME 1] 2,600x +
<1474> ἐδαφίζω ***edaphizō*** [to lay even with the ground, to level to the ground, to dash to the ground: GROUND (noun)[1] 3] 1x
<1475> ἔδαφος ***edaphos*** [GROUND (noun)[1] 2] 1x
<1476> ἑδραῖος ***hedraios*** [FIRM 2] 3x
<1477> ἑδραίωμα ***hedraiōma*** [FOUNDATION 1] 1x
<1478> Ἑζεκίας ***Ezekias*** [HEZEKIAH] 2x
<1479> ἐθελοθρησκία ***ethelothrēskia*** [SELF-IMPOSED RELIGION] 1x
<1480> ἐθίζω ***ethizō*** [to be customary: CUSTOM[1] 2] 1x
<1481> ἐθνάρχης ***ethnarchēs*** [GOVERNOR 1] 1x
<1482> ἐθνικός ***ethnikos*** [one who is of the nations, one of the nations: NATION 3] 2x
<1483> ἐθνικῶς ***ethnikōs*** [as the nations: NATION 4] 1x
<1484> ἔθνος ***ethnos*** [NATION 2, PEOPLE 2] 163x
<1485> ἔθος ***ethos*** [CUSTOM[1] 1] 13x
<1486> ἔθω ***ethō*** [ACCUSTOMED (BE) 1] 4x
<1487> εἰ ***ei*** [IF 2] 389x
<1488> εἶ ***ei*** [ARE (YOU) 1] 92x
<1489> εἴ γε ***ei ge*** [IF INDEED] 5x
<1490> εἰ δὲ μή ***ei de mē*** [ELSE 1] 15x
<1491> εἶδος ***eidos*** [FASHION (noun) 1, FORM (noun) 1, SIGHT (noun) 1] 5x
<1492> εἴδω ***eidō*** [BEHOLD (verb) 4, KNOW 7, to have knowledge: KNOWLEDGE 4, to look at: LOOK (verb) 10]
<1492> εἶδον ***eidon*** [SEE 11]
<1492> οἶδα ***oida*** [KNOW 8]
<1493> εἰδωλεῖον ***eidōleion*** [idol's temple: IDOL 2] 1x
<1494> εἰδωλόθυτον ***eidōlothuton*** [thing sacrificed to the idol, thing offered to idols, etc.: IDOL 3, offered in sacrifice: SACRIFICE (noun) 2, sacrificed to idol, idols, a god: SACRIFICE (verb) 2] 10x
<1495> εἰδωλολατρεία ***eidōlolatreia*** [IDOLATRY 1] 4x
<1496> εἰδωλολάτρης ***eidōlolatrēs*** [IDOLATER] 7x
<1497> εἴδωλον ***eidōlon*** [IDOL 1] 11x
<1498> εἴην ***eiēn*** [MIGHT BE] 12x
<1499> εἰ καί ***ei kai*** [IF ALSO] 18x
<1500> εἰκῇ ***eikē*** [without cause, without a cause: CAUSE 6, in vain: VAIN 8] 7x
<1501> εἴκοσι ***eikosi*** [HUNDRED AND TWENTY, TWENTY, TWENTY-FIVE, TWENTY THOUSAND, TWENTY-FOUR, TWENTY-THREE THOUSAND] 11x
<1502> εἴκω ***eikō*** [to give place: PLACE (noun) 10] 1x
<1503> εἴκω ***eikō*** [to be like: LIKE (adj., adv., noun) 9] 2x
<1504> εἰκών ***eikōn*** [IMAGE 1] 23x
<1505> εἰλικρίνεια ***eilikrineia*** [SINCERITY 2] 3x
<1506> εἰλικρινής ***eilikrinēs*** [PURE 4] 2x

<1507> εἱλίσσω ***heilissō*** [to roll up: ROLL 1] 1x

<1508> εἰ μή ***ei mē*** [SAVE]

<1509> εἰ μή τι ***ei mē ti*** [EXCEPT 4] 3x

<1510> εἰμί ***eimi*** [BE 1, EXIST 1, REST (verb) 5, STAY (verb) 2] 2,472x

<1511> εἶναι ***einai*** [BE 2] 126x

<1512> εἴπερ ***eiper*** [if in fact: FACT 1] 6x

<1513> εἴ πως ***ei pōs*** [IF POSSIBLY] 4x

<1514> εἰρηνεύω ***eirēneuō*** [to be in, to be at, to have, to live at, to live in peace: PEACE 2] 4x

<1515> εἰρήνη ***eirēnē*** [PEACE 1] 92x

<1516> εἰρηνικός ***eirēnikos*** [PEACEFUL 1] 2x

<1517> εἰρηνοποιέω ***eirēnopoieō*** [to make peace: PEACE 3] 1x

<1518> εἰρηνοποιός ***eirēnopoios*** [PEACEMAKER 1] 1x

<1519> εἰς ***eis*** [CONTINUALLY 2, LIGHT (noun) 9, NAME (noun) 2, PERPETUALLY 1, TO 1] 1,865x

<1520> εἷς ***heis*** [ONE] 375x

<1521> εἰσάγω ***eisagō*** [to bring, to bring in, into: BRING 4, LEAD (verb) 5] 11x

<1522> εἰσακούω ***eisakouō*** [HEAR 3] 5x

<1523> εἰσδέχομαι ***eisdechomai*** [RECEIVE 12] 1x

<1524> εἴσειμι ***eiseimi*** [to go in, to go into: GO 29] 4x

<1525> εἰσέρχομαι ***eiserchomai*** [ARISE 6, to come, to come in: COME 6, ENTER 1, to go out into: GO 10] 194x

<1526> εἰσί ***eisi*** [AM (I)] 163x

<1527> εἷς καθ' εἷς ***heis kath' heis*** [ONE BY ONE] 2x

<1528> εἰσκαλέω ***eiskaleō*** [to invite in: INVITE 3] 1x

<1529> εἴσοδος ***eisodos*** [ENTRY 1] 5x

<1530> εἰσπηδάω ***eispēdaō*** [to run in: RUN 10] 2x

<1531> εἰσπορεύομαι ***eisporeuomai*** [COME 14, ENTER 3] 17x

<1532> εἰστρέχω ***eistrechō*** [to run in, to run back: RUN 2] 1x

<1533> εἰσφέρω ***eispherō*** [to bring in: BRING 12, CARRY 8, LEAD (verb) 12] 7x

<1534> εἶτα ***eita*** [THEN 1] 15x

<1535> εἴτε ***eite*** [WHETHER 1] 29x

<1536> εἴ τις ***ei tis*** [IF ANY, IF SOMEONE] 79x

<1537> ἐκ ***ek*** [FROM, through means of, by the means of: MEANS 3, more vehemently: VEHEMENTLY 2] 915x

<1538> ἕκαστος ***hekastos*** [EACH] 82x

<1539> ἑκάστοτε ***hekastote*** [at any time: TIME 12] 1x

<1540> ἑκατόν ***hekaton*** [HUNDRED 1, HUNDRED AND FIFTY-THREE, HUNDRED AND FORTY-FOUR, HUNDRED AND FORTY-FOUR THOUSAND, HUNDRED AND TWENTY] 17x

<1541> ἑκατονταετής ***hekatontaetēs*** [hundred years old: YEAR 7] 1x

<1542> ἑκατονταπλασίων ***hekatontaplasiōn*** [HUNDREDFOLD 1, hundred times: TIME 21] 3x

<1543> ἑκατοντάρχης, ἑκατόνταρχος ***hekatontarchēs, hekatontarchos*** [CENTURION 1] 20x

<1544> ἐκβάλλω ***ekballō*** [to bring, to bring forth, to bring out: BRING 26, to cast out: CAST (verb) 3, ELIMINATE 1, to pluck out: PLUCK 1, REMOVE 1, to send out, to send forth: SEND 13, to take out: TAKE 34, to throw out: THROW (verb) 3] 81x

<1545> ἔκβασις ***ekbasis*** [way out, way to escape: OUTCOME 1, WAY 3] 2x

<1546> ἐκβολή ***ekbolē*** [to lighten the ship: LIGHTEN 2] 1x

<1547> ἐκγαμίζω ***ekgamizō*** [to give in marriage: MARRIAGE 4, MARRY 2] 5x

<1548> ἐκγαμίσκω ***ekgamiskō*** [to give in marriage: MARRIAGE 3] 2x

<1549> ἔκγονος ***ekgonos*** [GRANDCHILD] 1x

<1550> ἐκδαπανάω ***ekdapanaō*** [to be spent, to be utterly spent: SPEND 2] 1x

<1551> ἐκδέχομαι ***ekdechomai*** [to wait for: WAIT (verb) 3] 7x

<1552> ἔκδηλος ***ekdēlos*** [manifest, completely manifest: MANIFEST (adj.) 4] 1x

<1553> ἐκδημέω ***ekdēmeō*** [ABSENT (BE) 2] 3x

<1554> ἐκδίδωμι ***ekdidōmi*** [LEASE] 4x

<1555> ἐκδιηγέομαι ***ekdiēgeomai*** [RELATE 4] 2x

<1556> ἐκδικέω ***ekdikeō*** [AVENGE 1, to give justice, to see that one gets justice: JUSTICE 2, PUNISH 1] 6x

<1557> ἐκδίκησις ***ekdikēsis*** [JUSTICE (noun) 1, PUNISHMENT 2, VENGEANCE 1] 9x

<1558> ἔκδικος ***ekdikos*** [AVENGER] 2x

<1559> ἐκδιώκω ***ekdiōkō*** [PERSECUTE 2] 2x

<1560> ἔκδοτος ***ekdotos*** [being delivered, delivered up: DELIVER 7] 1x

<1561> ἐκδοχή ***ekdochē*** [EXPECTATION 4] 1x

<1562> ἐκδύω ***ekduō*** [to take off; to take off the clothing, the garment: TAKE 28] 5x

<1563> ἐκεῖ ***ekei*** [THERE 1] 97x

<1564> ἐκεῖθεν ***ekeithen*** [on either side, on each side: SIDE 4] 27x

<1565> ἐκεῖνος ***ekeinos*** [THAT ONE THERE] 249x

<1566> ἐκεῖσε ***ekeise*** [THERE 2] 2x

<1567> ἐκζητέω ***ekzēteō*** [REQUIRE 3, to seek; to seek after, diligently, out: SEEK 3] 7x

<1567a> ἐκζήτησις ***ekzētēsis*** [DISPUTE 3] 1x

<1568> ἐκθαμβέω ***ekthambeō*** [ALARM (verb) 1, AMAZED (BE) 4, to be troubled: TROUBLED 1] 4x

<1569> ἔκθαμβος ***ekthambos*** [greatly amazed: AMAZED] 1x

<1570> ἔκθετος ***ekthetos*** [EXPOSED] 1x

<1571> ἐκκαθαίρω ***ekkathairō*** [to purge out: PURGE 2, PURIFY 3] 2x

<1572> ἐκκαίω ***ekkaiō*** [BURN 2] 1x

<1573> ἐκκακέω ***ekkakeō*** [to lose heart: HEART 5, to be completely dispirited, to be exhausted: WEARY (adj.) 1] 3x

<1574> ἐκκεντέω ***ekkenteō*** [PIERCE 3] 2x

<1575> ἐκκλάω ***ekklaō*** [to break off: BREAK 3] 3x

<1576> ἐκκλείω ***ekkleiō*** [EXCLUDE 2] 2x

<1577> ἐκκλησία ***ekklēsia*** [CHURCH 1] 114x

<1578> ἐκκλίνω ***ekklinō*** [AVOID 1, to turn, to turn aside, to turn away: TURN (verb) 12] 3x

<1579> ἐκκολυμβάω ***ekkolumbaō*** [to swim off, away: SWIM 2] 1x

<1580> ἐκκομίζω ***ekkomizō*** [to carry out: CARRY 12] 1x

<1581> ἐκκόπτω ***ekkoptō*** [to cut, to cut down, to cut off, to cut out: CUT 4] 11x

<1582> ἐκκρεμάννυμι ***ekkremannumi*** [to hang on: HANG 3] 1x

<1583> ἐκλαλέω ***eklaleō*** [TELL 5] 1x

<1584> ἐκλάμπω ***eklampō*** [to shine, to shine forth: SHINE 5] 1x

<1585> ἐκλανθάνομαι ***eklanthanomai*** [FORGET 1] 1x

<1586> ἐκλέγω ***eklegō*** [CHOOSE 3] 20x

<1587> ἐκλείπω ***ekleipō*** [FAIL 1] 3x

<1588> ἐκλεκτός ***eklektos*** [chosen: CHOOSE 4, ELECT 1] 23x

<1589> ἐκλογή ***eklogē*** [ELECTION] 7x

<1590> ἐκλύω ***ekluō*** [to be discouraged: DISCOURAGED 2, FAINT 1, to lose heart: HEART 6, to be weary: WEARY (adj.) 2] 6x

<1591> ἐκμάσσω ***ekmassō*** [WIPE 1] 5x

<1592> ἐκμυκτηρίζω ***ekmuktērizō*** [MOCK 3, SNEER 1] 2x

<1593> ἐκνεύω ***ekneuō*** [WITHDRAW 2] 1x

<1594> ἐκνήφω ***eknēphō*** [AWAKE (verb) 2] 1x

<1595> ἑκούσιος ***hekousios*** [voluntary: VOLUNTARILY 1] 1x

<1596> ἑκουσίως ***hekousiōs*** [VOLUNTARILY 2] 2x

<1597> ἔκπαλαι ***ekpalai*** [long ago: LONG (adj.) 5, for a long time, now of a long time: TIME 13] 2x

<1598> ἐκπειράζω ***ekpeirazō*** [TEMPT 2, to test, to put to the test: TEST (noun and verb) 3] 4x

<1599> ἐκπέμπω ***ekpempō*** [to send forth, out, away: SEND 6] 2x

<1600> ἐκπετάννυμι ***ekpetannumi*** [to stretch out: STRETCH 1] 1x

<1601> ἐκπίπτω ***ekpiptō*** [to take no effect: EFFECT (noun) 2, FAIL 3, to fall; to fall away, down, off: FALL (verb) 4, to run aground: RUN 11] 10x

<1602> ἐκπλέω ***ekpleō*** [to sail, to sail away: SAIL (verb) 6] 3x

<1603> ἐκπληρόω ***ekplēroō*** [FULFILL 7] 1x

<1604> ἐκπλήρωσις ***ekplērōsis*** [ACCOMPLISHMENT 1] 1x

<1605> ἐκπλήσσω ***ekplēssō*** [AMAZED (BE) 2, ASTONISHED (BE) 1] 13x

<1606> ἐκπνέω ***ekpneō*** [EXPIRE 1] 3x

<1607> ἐκπορεύομαι ***ekporeuomai*** [DEPART 14, to go out, to go forth: GO 25, PROCEED 1, SPREAD 7] 33x

<1608> ἐκπορνεύω ***ekporneuō*** [to give oneself over to fornication: FORNICATION 2] 1x

<1609> ἐκπτύω ***ekptuō*** [REJECT 4] 1x

<1610> ἐκριζόω ***ekrizoō*** [UPROOT] 4x

<1611> ἔκστασις ***ekstasis*** [AMAZEMENT 1, ASTONISHMENT 1, ECSTASY] 7x

<1612> ἐκστρέφω ***ekstrephō*** [PERVERTED (BE) 2] 1x

<1613> ἐκταράσσω ***ektarassō*** [to trouble exceedingly, to trouble utterly: TROUBLE (verb) 9] 1x

<1614> ἐκτείνω ***ekteinō*** [to carry out: CARRY 3, to stretch out, to stretch forth: STRETCH 2] 16x

<1615> ἐκτελέω ***ekteleō*** [FINISH 3] 2x

<1616> ἐκτένεια ***ekteneia*** [earnestness: EARNESTLY 1] 1x

<1617> ἐκτενέστερον ***ektenesteron*** [more earnestly: EARNESTLY 2] 1x

<1618> ἐκτενής ***ektenēs*** [FERVENT 1, UNCEASING 1] 2x

<1619> ἐκτενῶς ***ektenōs*** [FERVENTLY 1, unceasingly: UNCEASING 2] 2x

<1620> ἐκτίθημι ***ektithēmi*** [EXPLAIN 3, EXPOSE 1] 4x

<1621> ἐκτινάσσω ***ektinassō*** [SHAKE OFF 3] 4x

<1622> ἐκτός ***ektos*** [EXCEPT 1] 8x

<1623> ἕκτος ***hektos*** [SIXTH] 14x

<1624> ἐκτρέπω ***ektrepō*** [AVOID 2, DISLOCATE, to turn, to turn aside, to turn away: TURN (verb) 4] 5x

<1625> ἐκτρέφω ***ektrephō*** [to bring up: BRING 20, NOURISH 4] 2x

<1626> ἔκτρωμα ***ektrōma*** [born out of due time, untimely born, one abnormally born: BORN 2] 1x

<1627> ἐκφέρω ***ekpherō*** [to bring out, to bring forth: BRING 13, to carry out, to carry forth: CARRY 9] 7x

<1628> ἐκφεύγω ***ekpheugō*** [ESCAPE 4, FLEE 2] 8x

<1629> ἐκφοβέω ***ekphobeō*** [TERRIFY 1] 1x

<1630> ἔκφοβος ***ekphobos*** [exceedingly afraid, greatly afraid: AFRAID 1] 2x

<1631> ἐκφύω ***ekphuō*** [PRODUCE 3] 2x

<1632> ἐκχέω ***ekcheō*** [to give oneself up: GIVE 12, to pour out: POUR 2] 24x

<1632a> ἐκχύνω ***ekchunō*** [to gush out: GUSH, to pour out: POUR 2] 4x

<1633> ἐκχωρέω ***ekchōreō*** [DEPART 6] 1x

<1634> ἐκψύχω ***ekpsuchō*** [EXPIRE 2] 3x

<1635> ἑκών ***hekōn*** [VOLUNTARILY 3, WILLINGLY 1] 2x

<1636> ἐλαία ***elaia*** [MOUNT OF OLIVES 1, OLIVE, OLIVE TREE 1] 15x

<1637> ἔλαιον ***elaion*** [OIL 1] 11x

<1638> ἐλαιών ***elaiōn*** [MOUNT OF OLIVES 2] 1x

<1639> Ἐλαμίτης ***Elamitēs*** [ELAMITE] 1x

<1640> ἐλάσσων ***elassōn*** [LESSER, YOUNGER 1] 4x

<1641> ἐλαττονέω ***elattoneō*** [to have lack: LACK (noun) 2] 1x

<1642> ἐλαττόω ***elattoō*** [DECREASE, to make lower: LOWER (adj.) 2] 3x

<1643> ἐλαύνω ***elaunō*** [DRIVE 1, ROW] 5x

<1644> ἐλαφρία ***elaphria*** [LIGHTNESS] 1x

<1645> ἐλαφρός ***elaphros*** [LIGHT (adj.) 1] 2x

<1646> ἐλάχιστος ***elachistos*** [LEAST 1, VERY SMALL] 13x

<1647> ἐλαχιστότερος ***elachistoteros*** [the very least, less than the least: LEAST 2] 1x

<1648> Ἐλεάζαρ ***Eleazar*** [ELEAZAR] 2x

<1649> ἔλεγξις ***elenxis*** [to receive reproof: REBUKE (verb) 4] 1x

<1650> ἔλεγχος ***elenchos*** [EVIDENCE 1, REPROOF 1] 2x

<1651> ἐλέγχω ***elenchō*** [CONVINCE 1, REFUTE 1, REPROVE] 17x

<1652> ἐλεεινός ***eleeinos*** [MISERABLE 1] 2x
<1653> ἐλεέω ***eleeō*** [to have compassion: COMPASSION 1, to be object of, to enjoy, to find, to have, to obtain, to receive, to show mercy: MERCY 2] 30x
<1654> ἐλεημοσύνη ***eleēmosunē*** [alms, alms-deeds: ALMS 2] 13x
<1655> ἐλεήμων ***eleēmōn*** [MERCIFUL 1] 2x
<1656> ἔλεος ***eleos*** [MERCY 1] 27x
<1657> ἐλευθερία ***eleutheria*** [LIBERTY 3] 11x
<1658> ἐλεύθερος ***eleutheros*** [FREE (adj.) 1] 23x
<1659> ἐλευθερόω ***eleutheroō*** [to set free, to make free, to free: FREE (adj.) 2] 7x
<1660> ἔλευσις ***eleusis*** [COMING 1] 1x
<1661> ἐλεφάντινος ***elephantinos*** [in ivory: IVORY] 1x
<1662> Ἐλιακίμ ***Eliakim*** [ELIAKIM] 3x
<1663> Ἐλιέζερ ***Eliezer*** [ELIEZER] 1x
<1664> Ἐλιούδ ***Elioud*** [ELIUD] 2x
<1665> Ἐλισάβετ ***Elisabet*** [ELIZABETH] 9x
<1666> Ἐλισαῖος ***Elisaios*** [ELISHA] 1x
<1667> ἑλίσσω ***helissō*** [ROLL 2] 1x
<1668> ἕλκος ***helkos*** [SORE 1] 3x
<1669> ἑλκόω ***helkoō*** [to be full of sores, to be covered with sores: SORE 2] 1x
<1670> ἑλκύω, ἕλκω ***helkuō, helkō*** [DRAG 1, DRAW 5] 8x
<1671> Ἑλλάς ***Hellas*** [GREECE] 1x
<1672> Ἕλλην ***Hellēn*** [GREEK 1] 26x
<1673> Ἑλληνικός ***Hellēnikos*** [GREEK 2] 2x
<1674> Ἑλληνίς ***Hellēnis*** [GREEK 1] 2x
<1675> Ἑλληνιστής ***Hellēnistēs*** [HELLENISTIC JEW] 3x
<1676> Ἑλληνιστί ***Hellēnisti*** [GREEK 3] 2x
<1677> ἐλλογέω ***ellogeō*** [IMPUTE 2] 2x
<1678> Ἐλμαδάμ ***Elmadam*** [ELMADAM] 1x
<1679> ἐλπίζω ***elpizō*** [to have hope: HOPE (noun) 2, HOPE (verb) 1, TRUST (verb) 1] 32x
<1680> ἐλπίς ***elpis*** [HOPE (noun) 1] 53x
<1681> Ἐλύμας ***Elumas*** [ELYMAS] 1x
<1682> Ἐλωΐ ***Elōi*** [ELOI] 2x
<1683> ἐμαυτοῦ ***emautou*** [MYSELF 1] 37x
<1684> ἐμβαίνω ***embainō*** [ENTER 4, to get into: GET 2, to step in: STEP (verb) 1] 18x
<1685> ἐμβάλλω ***emballō*** [THROW (verb) 4] 1x
<1686> ἐμβάπτω ***embaptō*** [DIP 2] 3x
<1687> ἐμβατεύω ***embateuō*** [to intrude into: INTRUDE 1] 1x
<1688> ἐμβιβάζω ***embibazō*** [to put on board: PUT 14] 1x
<1689> ἐμβλέπω ***emblepō*** [to look at, into, on, upon, closely: LOOK (verb) 6, SEE 3] 12x
<1690> ἐμβριμάομαι ***embrimaomai*** [to be deeply moved: MOVED (BE), to rebuke harshly: REBUKE (verb) 1, to warn sternly, to warn strictly: WARN 1] 5x
<1691> ἐμέ ***eme*** [MYSELF 2] 88x
<1692> ἐμέω ***emeō*** [VOMIT (verb)] 1x
<1693> ἐμμαίνομαι ***emmainomai*** [to be exceedingly furious: FURIOUS 2] 1x
<1694> Ἐμμανουήλ ***Emmanouēl*** [IMMANUEL] 1x
<1695> Ἐμμαοῦς ***Emmaous*** [EMMAUS] 1x
<1696> ἐμμένω ***emmenō*** [CONTINUE 2] 4x
<1697> Ἐμμώρ ***Hemmōr*** [HAMOR] 1x
<1698> ἐμοί ***emoi*** [MINE 1] 190x
<1699> ἐμός ***emos*** [MINE 2] 389x
<1700> ἐμοῦ ***emou*** [MINE 3] 109x
<1700a> ἐμπαιγμονή ***empaigmonē*** [MOCKING 2] 1x
<1701> ἐμπαιγμός ***empaigmos*** [MOCKING 1] 1x
<1702> ἐμπαίζω ***empaizō*** [MOCK 1] 14x
<1703> ἐμπαίκτης ***empaiktēs*** [MOCKER] 2x

<1704> ἐμπεριπατέω ***emperipateō*** [walk among: WALK 2] 1x
<1705> ἐμπίπλημι ***empiplēmi*** [ENJOY 1, FILL (verb) 8] 5x
<1706> ἐμπίπτω ***empiptō*** [to fall into: FALL (verb) 4] 7x
<1707> ἐμπλέκω ***emplekō*** [to entangle with, to entangle in: ENTANGLE 1] 2x
<1708> ἐμπλοκή ***emplokē*** [BRAIDING] 1x
<1709> ἐμπνέω ***empneō*** [to breathe, to breathe out: BREATHE 1] 1x
<1710> ἐμπορεύομαι ***emporeuomai*** [EXPLOIT 1] 2x
<1711> ἐμπορία ***emporia*** [BUSINESS 1] 1x
<1712> ἐμπόριον ***emporion*** [BUSINESS 2] 1x
<1713> ἔμπορος ***emporos*** [MERCHANT] 5x
<1714> ἐμπρήθω ***emprēthō*** [BURN 5] 1x
<1715> ἔμπροσθεν ***emprosthen*** [in the presence of: PRESENCE 4] 48x
<1716> ἐμπτύω ***emptuō*** [SPIT 2] 6x
<1717> ἐμφανής ***emphanēs*** [MANIFEST (adj.) 3] 2x
<1718> ἐμφανίζω ***emphanizō*** [APPEAR 2, to bring charges, to present charges: CHARGE (noun)[1] 3, MANIFEST (verb) 3, to declare plainly: PLAINLY 3, REVEAL 2, SIGNIFY 2] 10x
<1719> ἔμφοβος ***emphobos*** [AFRAID 2, FRIGHTENED 1] 6x
<1720> ἐμφυσάω ***emphusaō*** [to breathe on: BREATHE 2] 1x
<1721> ἔμφυτος ***emphutos*** [IMPLANTED] 1x
<1722> ἐν ***en*** [ALMOST 1, AMONG 2, with child: CHILD 11, MEANTIME 1, in enigma: OBSCURELY, in passing: PASSING 2, QUICKLY 4, REGARD (noun) 1, in respect of: RESPECT 1, SHORTLY 5, SPEEDILY 1] 2,800x +
<1723> ἐναγκαλίζομαι ***enankalizomai*** [to take in one's arms: ARM (noun)[1] 2] 2x
<1724> ἐνάλιος ***enalios*** [creature of the sea, creature in the sea, sea animal, thing in the sea: SEA 4] 1x
<1725> ἔναντι ***enanti*** [BEFORE 1] 1x
<1726> ἐναντίον ***enantion*** [BEFORE 2] 5x
<1727> ἐναντίος ***enantios*** [CONTRARY 1, he who is opposed: OPPOSED 1] 8x
<1728> ἐνάρχομαι ***enarchomai*** [to begin in: BEGIN 2] 2x
<1729> ἐνδεής ***endeēs*** [person in want: WANT (noun) 1] 1x
<1730> ἔνδειγμα ***endeigma*** [manifest evidence: EVIDENCE 2] 1x
<1731> ἐνδείκνυμι ***endeiknumi*** [SHOW (verb) 7] 11x
<1732> ἔνδειξις ***endeixis*** [DEMONSTRATE 1, PROOF 2] 4x
<1733> ἕνδεκα ***hendeka*** [ELEVEN] 6x
<1734> ἑνδέκατος ***hendekatos*** [ELEVENTH] 3x
<1735> ἐνδέχομαι ***endechomai*** [it must be, it can be: BE 4] 1x
<1736> ἐνδημέω ***endēmeō*** [PRESENT (BE) 1] 3x
<1737> ἐνδιδύσκω ***endiduskō*** [CLOTHE 2, WEAR 1] 3x
<1738> ἔνδικος ***endikos*** [JUST (adj.) 1] 2x
<1739> ἐνδώμησις ***endōmēsis*** [BUILDING 1] 1x
<1740> ἐνδοξάζω ***endoxazō*** [GLORIFY 2] 2x
<1741> ἔνδοξος ***endoxos*** [GLORIOUS 1, gorgeous: GORGEOUSLY, HONORED 1] 4x
<1742> ἔνδυμα ***enduma*** [CLOTHES 1, CLOTHING 1, GARMENT 1] 8x
<1743> ἐνδυναμόω ***endunamoō*** [STRENGTHEN 2, to be made strong, to become strong: STRONG (adj.) 4] 8x
<1744> ἐνδύνω ***endunō*** [to creep into: CREEP] 1x
<1745> ἔνδυσις ***endusis*** [putting on: PUTTING 3] 1x
<1746> ἐνδύω ***enduō*** [CLOTHE 1, to clothe with a garment: GARMENT 3, to put on: PUT 12] 29x
<1747> ἐνέδρα ***enedra*** [AMBUSH 1] 1x
<1748> ἐνεδρεύω ***enedreuō*** [to wait in ambush: AMBUSH 2] 2x
<1749> ἔνεδρον ***enedron*** [AMBUSH 3] 1x
<1750> ἐνειλέω ***eneileō*** [WRAP 1] 1x
<1751> ἔνειμι ***eneimi*** [THINGS WITHIN] 1x

<1752> ἕνεκεν ***heneken*** [SAKE OF (FOR THE) 2] 24x

<1753> ἐνέργεια ***energeia*** [strong delusion: DELUSION, WORKING (noun) 1] 8x

<1754> ἐνεργέω ***energeō*** [to act: EFFECTIVE 2, WORK (verb) 1, to work: WORKING (verb)] 21x

<1755> ἐνέργημα ***energēma*** [OPERATION 1] 2x

<1756> ἐνεργής ***energēs*** [EFFECTIVE 1, OPERATIVE] 3x

<1757> ἐνευλογέω ***eneulogeō*** [BLESS 2] 2x

<1758> ἐνέχω ***enechō*** [ENTANGLED (BE), to hold a grudge, to nurse a grudge: GRUDGE (noun), PRESS 2] 3x

<1759> ἐνθάδε ***enthade*** [HERE 3] 8x

<1760> ἐνθυμέομαι ***enthumeomai*** [THINK 4] 3x

<1761> ἐνθύμησις ***enthumēsis*** [IMAGINATION 1, THOUGHT 5] 4x

<1762> ἔνι ***eni*** [THERE IS] 3x

<1763> ἐνιαυτός ***eniautos*** [YEAR 1] 14x

<1764> ἐνίστημι ***enistēmi*** [COME 24, PRESENT (BE) 2] 7x

<1765> ἐνισχύω ***enischuō*** [STRENGTHEN 3] 2x

<1766> ἔνατος ***ennatos*** [NINTH] 10x

<1767> ἐννέα ***ennea*** [NINE 1] 1x

<1768> ἐννενηκονταεννέα ***ennenēkontaennea*** [NINETY AND NINE] 4x

<1769> ἐννεός ***enneos*** [SPEECHLESS 1] 1x

<1770> ἐννεύω ***enneuō*** [to make signs: SIGN 6] 1x

<1771> ἔννοια ***ennoia*** [INTENT 1, MIND (noun) 3] 2x

<1772> ἔννομος ***ennomos*** [LAWFUL 1] 2x

<1773> ἔννυχον ***ennuchon*** [very early in the morning: MORNING 3] 1x

<1774> ἐνοικέω ***enoikeō*** [DWELL 2] 5x

<1774a> ἐνορκίζω ***enorkizō*** [ADJURE 1] 1x

<1775> ἑνότης ***henotēs*** [UNITY 1] 2x

<1776> ἐνοχλέω ***enochleō*** [TROUBLE (verb) 2] 2x

<1777> ἔνοχος ***enochos*** [DESERVING 2, GUILTY 1, subject, subject to: SUBJECT (noun)[1] 1] 10x

<1778> ἔνταλμα ***entalma*** [COMMANDMENT 1] 3x

<1779> ἐνταφιάζω ***entaphiazō*** [to bury: BURIAL 3, BURY 3] 2x

<1780> ἐνταφιασμός ***entaphiasmos*** [BURIAL 1] 2x

<1781> ἐντέλλομαί ***entellomai*** [CHARGE (noun)[2] 2; COMMAND (verb) 5] 17x

<1782> ἐντεῦθεν ***enteuthen*** [on either side, on each side: SIDE 4, one on either side, one on each side: SIDE 5] 10x

<1783> ἔντευξις ***enteuxis*** [INTERCESSION 1] or [PRAYER 2] 2x

<1784> ἔντιμος ***entimos*** [DEAR 2, in honor: HONOR (noun) 5, one more honorable: HONORABLE 2, PRECIOUS 1] 5x

<1785> ἐντολή ***entolē*** [COMMAND (noun) 1, COMMANDMENT 2] 67x

<1786> ἐντόπιος ***entopios*** [he who is from that place: PLACE (noun) 12] 1x

<1787> ἐντός ***entos*** [WITHIN 1] 2x

<1788> ἐντρέπω ***entrepō*** [RESPECT (verb) 1, SHAME (verb) 1] 9x

<1789> ἐντρέφω ***entrephō*** [NOURISH 5] 1x

<1790> ἔντρομος ***entromos*** [trembling, full of trembling: TREMBLING 2] 3x

<1791> ἐντροπή ***entropē*** [SHAME (noun) 3] 2x

<1792> ἐντρυφάω ***entruphaō*** [REVEL (verb) 1] 1x

<1793> ἐντυγχάνω ***entunchanō*** [INTERCEDE 1, PETITION (verb) 1, PLEAD 1] 5x

<1794> ἐντυλίσσω ***entulissō*** [FOLD (verb) 1, WRAP 2] 3x

<1795> ἐντυπόω ***entupoō*** [ENGRAVE] 1x

<1796> ἐνυβρίζω ***enubrizō*** [INSULT (verb) 2] 1x

<1797> ἐνυπνιάζω ***enupniazō*** [DREAM (verb), to dream: DREAMER] 2x

<1798> ἐνύπνιον ***enupnion*** [DREAM (noun) 1] 1x

<1799> ἐνώπιον ***enōpion*** [in the presence: PRESENCE 5] 92x

<1800> Ἐνώς ***Enōs*** [ENOSH] 1x

<1801> ἐνωτίζομαι ***enōtizomai*** [HEED (noun) 4] 1x
<1802> Ἑνώχ ***Henōch*** [ENOCH] 3x
<1803> ἕξ ***hex*** [FORTY-SIX, SIX, SIX HUNDRED AND SIXTY-SIX 1, TWO HUNDRED AND SEVENTY-SIX] 13x
<1804> ἐξαγγέλλω ***exangellō*** [to show forth: SHOW (verb) 3] 1x
<1805> ἐξαγοράζω ***exagorazō*** [REDEEM 1] 4x
<1806> ἐξάγω ***exagō*** [to bring out, to bring forth: BRING 5, to lead out: LEAD (verb) 6] 13x
<1807> ἐξαιρέω ***exaireō*** [to deliver out, to deliver: DELIVER 4, to pluck out: PLUCK 2, to take out: TAKE 21] 8x
<1808> ἐξαίρω ***exairō*** [TAKE 17] 2x
<1809> ἐξαιτέω ***exaiteō*** [to ask for: ASK 2] 1x
<1810> ἐξαίφνης ***exaiphnēs*** [SUDDENLY 3] 5x
<1811> ἐξακολουθέω ***exakoloutheō*** [FOLLOW 2] 3x
<1812> ἑξακόσιοι ***hexakosioi*** [SIX HUNDRED AND SIXTY-SIX 1, THOUSAND SIX HUNDRED] 2x
<1813> ἐξαλείφω ***exaleiphō*** [to blot out: BLOT (verb), WIPE 2] 5x
<1814> ἐξάλλομαι ***exallomai*** [to leap up: LEAP 2] 1x
<1815> ἐξανάστασις ***exanastasis*** [RESURRECTION 3] 1x
<1816> ἐξανατέλλω ***exanatellō*** [to spring up: SPRING (verb) 3] 2x
<1817> ἐξανίστημι ***exanistēmi*** [to raise up: RAISE 6, to rise up: RISE (verb) 4] 3x
<1818> ἐξαπατάω ***exapataō*** [DECEIVE 2] 6x
<1819> ἐξάπινα ***exapina*** [SUDDENLY 4] 1x
<1820> ἐξαπορέομαι ***exaporeomai*** [to be in despair: DESPAIR] 2x
<1821> ἐξαποστέλλω ***exapostellō*** [to send, to send away, to send forth: SEND 2] 12x
<1822> ἐξαρτίζω ***exartizō*** [ACCOMPLISH 1] 2x
<1823> ἐξαστράπτω ***exastraptō*** [to become glistening: GLISTENING] 1x
<1824> ἐξαυτῆς ***exautēs*** [IMMEDIATELY 2, at once: ONCE 3] 6x
<1825> ἐξεγείρω ***exegeirō*** [to raise, to raise up: RAISE 2] 2x
<1826> ἔξειμι ***exeimi*** [DEPART 10, GET 3, to go out: GO 30] 4x
<1827> ἐξελέγχω ***exelenchō*** [CONVINCE 2] 1x
<1828> ἐξέλκω ***exelkō*** [to draw away: DRAW 8] 1x
<1829> ἐξέραμα ***exerama*** [VOMIT (noun)] 1x
<1830> ἐξερευνάω ***exereunaō*** [to search carefully, diligently: SEARCH (verb) 4] 1x
<1831> ἐξέρχομαι ***exerchomai*** [to come, to come forth, to come out: COME 8, DEPART 8, ESCAPE 5, to go; to go away, to go out, to go forth, to go forward, to leave, etc.: GO 11, SPREAD 3, to step out: STEP (verb) 2] 218x
<1832> ἔξεστι ***exesti*** [to be lawful: LAWFUL 2] 32x
<1833> ἐξετάζω ***exetazō*** [ASK 4, INQUIRE 1, SEARCH (verb) 2] 3x
<1834> ἐξηγέομαι ***exēgeomai*** [DECLARE 5, RELATE 5] 6x
<1835> ἑξήκοντα ***hexēkonta*** [SIX HUNDRED AND SIXTY-SIX 1, SIXTY 1, THOUSAND TWO HUNDRED AND SIXTY] 8x
<1836> ἑξῆς ***hexēs*** [AFTERWARD 1] 5x
<1837> ἐξηχέω ***exēcheō*** [to sound out, to sound forth: SOUND (verb) 2] 1x
<1838> ἕξις ***hexis*** [HABIT 1] 1x
<1839> ἐξίστημι ***existēmi*** [AMAZED (BE) 1, to astonish, to be astonished: ASTONISHED (BE) 2, to be out of one's mind: MIND (noun) 13] 17x
<1840> ἐξισχύω ***exischuō*** [to be able, to be fully able: ABLE 5] 1x
<1841> ἔξοδος ***exodos*** [DECEASE (noun), DEPARTURE 3] 3x
<1842> ἐξολεθρεύω ***exolethreuō*** [DESTROY 5] 1x
<1843> ἐξομολογέω ***exomologeō*** [CONFESS 2, PROMISE (verb) 6, THANK (verb) 1] 11x
<1844> ἐξορκίζω ***exorkizō*** [ADJURE 2] 1x
<1845> ἐξορκιστής ***exorkistēs*** [EXORCIST] 1x
<1846> ἐξορύσσω ***exorussō*** [DIG 3, to pluck out: PLUCK 3] 2x
<1847> ἐξουδενέω ***exoudeneō*** [to be treated with contempt: CONTEMPT 1] 1x
<1848> ἐξουθενέω ***exoutheneō*** [to treat with contempt, to view with contempt: CONTEMPT 2,

to treat with contempt: CONTEMPTIBLE, DESPISE 1, to esteem least: ESTEEM (verb) 2] 11x

<1849> ἐξουσία ***exousia*** [AUTHORITY 1, JURISDICTION 1, LIBERTY 4, RIGHT (noun)[2] 1] 102x

<1850> ἐξουσιάζω ***exousiazō*** [to exercise authority, to have authority: AUTHORITY 2, to bring under the power: POWER[2] 3] 4x

<1851> ἐξοχή ***exochē*** [prominent: PROMINENT 3] 1x

<1852> ἐξυπνίζω ***exupnizō*** [to wake up: WAKE 3] 1x

<1853> ἔξυπνος ***exupnos*** [awaking from, awaking out of, being awakened out of, roused out of sleep: SLEEP (noun) 2] 1x

<1854> ἔξω ***exō*** [to cast out: CAST (verb) 4, FOREIGN 2, OUTWARD 1] 63x

<1855> ἔξωθεν ***exōthen*** [OUTWARD 2] 13x

<1856> ἐξωθέω ***exōtheō*** [to drive out: DRIVE 3, to run ashore, to run aground: RUN 12] 2x

<1857> ἐξώτερος ***exōteros*** [OUTER 1] 3x

<1858> ἑορτάζω ***heortazō*** [to celebrate the feast: FEAST (noun) 3] 1x

<1859> ἑορτή ***heortē*** [FEAST (noun) 2] 26x

<1860> ἐπαγγελία ***epangelia*** [PROMISE (noun) 1] 52x

<1861> ἐπαγγέλλω ***epangellō*** [to make profession: PROFESSION 1, to make a promise: PROMISE (noun) 3, PROMISE (verb) 2] 15x

<1862> ἐπάγγελμα ***epangelma*** [PROMISE (noun) 2] 2x

<1863> ἐπάγω ***epagō*** [to bring upon, to bring in upon: BRING 6] 3x

<1864> ἐπαγωνίζομαι ***epagōnizomai*** [to contend, to contend earnestly: CONTEND 2] 1x

<1865> ἐπαθροίζω ***epathroizō*** [to gather together: GATHER 3] 1x

<1866> Ἐπαίνετος ***Epainetos*** [EPAENETUS] 1x

<1867> ἐπαινέω ***epaineō*** [PRAISE (verb) 2] 5x

<1868> ἔπαινος ***epainos*** [PRAISE (noun) 3] 11x

<1869> ἐπαίρω ***epairō*** [EXALT 1, LIFT 2, RAISE 7, to take up: TAKE 18] 19x

<1870> ἐπαισχύνομαι ***epaischunomai*** [ASHAMED (BE) 2] 11x

<1871> ἐπαιτέω ***epaiteō*** [BEG 1] 2x

<1872> ἐπακολουθέω ***epakoloutheō*** [to follow diligently: DILIGENTLY 1, to follow; to follow after, in, later: FOLLOW 3] 4x

<1873> ἐπακούω ***epakouō*** [LISTEN 1] 1x

<1874> ἐπακροάομαι ***epakroaomai*** [LISTEN 2] 1x

<1875> ἐπάν ***epan*** [WHENEVER 1] 3x

<1876> ἐπάναγκες ***epanankes*** [NECESSARY 2] 1x

<1877> ἐπανάγω ***epanagō*** [to launch out: LAUNCH 2, to put out: PUT 13, RETURN (verb) 10] 3x

<1878> ἐπαναμιμνῄσκω ***epanamimnēskō*** [to remind, to remind again: REMIND 2] 1x

<1879> ἐπαναπαύω ***epanapauō*** [REST (verb) 2] 2x

<1880> ἐπανέρχομαι ***epanerchomai*** [RETURN (verb) 4] 2x

<1881> ἐπανίστημι ***epanistēmi*** [to rise up: RISE (verb) 3] 2x

<1882> ἐπανόρθωσις ***epanorthōsis*** [CORRECTION] 1x

<1883> ἐπάνω ***epanō*** [ABOVE 2] 18x

<1884> ἐπαρκέω ***eparkeō*** [HELP (verb) 5] or [RELIEVE] 3x

<1885> ἐπαρχεία ***eparcheia*** [PROVINCE 1] 2x

<1886> ἔπαυλις ***epaulis*** [DWELLING PLACE (noun) 1] 1x

<1887> ἐπαύριον ***epaurion*** [next day, following day: DAY 3] 17x

<1888> ἐπαυτοφώρῳ ***epautophōrō*** [in the very act: ACT (noun) 1] 1x

<1889> Ἐπαφρᾶς ***Epaphras*** [EPAPHRAS] 3x

<1890> ἐπαφρίζω ***epaphrizō*** [to foam up: FOAM (verb) 2] 1x

<1891> Ἐπαφρόδιτος ***Epaphroditos*** [EPAPHRODITUS] 2x

<1892> ἐπεγείρω ***epegeirō*** [to raise, to raise up: RAISE 3, to stir up: STIR (verb) 2] 2x

<1893> ἐπεί ***epei*** [ELSE 2, ELSE 3] 26x

<1894> ἐπειδή ***epeidē*** [AS INDEED, AS NOW] 11x

<1895> ἐπειδήπερ ***epeidēper*** [FORASMUCH 1] 1x

<1896> ἐπεῖδον ***epeidon*** [to look upon, on, with favor; to show one's favor: LOOK (verb) 11] 2x

<1897> ἐπείπερ ***epeiper*** [SINCE INDEED, SINCE NOW] 1x

<1898> ἐπεισαγωγή ***epeisagōgē*** [INTRODUCTION 1] 1x

<1899> ἔπειτα ***epeita*** [THEREUPON] 16x

<1900> ἐπέκεινα ***epekeina*** [BEYOND 1] 1x

<1901> ἐπεκτείνω ***epekteinō*** [REACH (verb) 1] 1x

<1902> ἐπενδύομαι ***ependuomai*** [to put on: CLOTHE 3] 2x

<1903> ἐπενδύτης ***ependutēs*** [OVERCOAT] 1x

<1904> ἐπέρχομαι ***eperchomai*** [ATTACK (verb) 1, to come, to come on, to come upon: COME 9] 10x

<1905> ἐπερωτάω ***eperōtaō*** [ASK 6] 58x

<1906> ἐπερώτημα ***eperōtēma*** [ANSWER (noun) 3] 1x

<1907> ἐπέχω ***epechō*** [to give attention: ATTENTION 1, to take heed, to give heed: HEED (noun) 2, to hold forth, fast, out: HOLD (verb) 3, REMARK, STAY (verb) 3] 5x

<1908> ἐπηρεάζω ***epēreazō*** [ACCUSE 4, USE (verb) 1] 3x

<1909> ἐπί ***epi*** [on the basis of: BASIS 1, as long as: LONG (adj.) 6, on the occasion of: OCCASION 3] 890x

<1910> ἐπιβαίνω ***epibainō*** [BOARD (verb), COME 19, SIT 12] 6x

<1911> ἐπιβάλλω ***epiballō*** [BEAT 2, FALL (verb) 14, LAY 16, PUT 7, THINK 5] 18x

<1912> ἐπιβαρέω ***epibareō*** [to be a burden: BURDEN (noun) 2, OVERCHARGE] 3x

<1913> ἐπιβιβάζω ***epibibazō*** [SET (verb) 7] 3x

<1914> ἐπιβλέπω ***epiblepō*** [to look upon: LOOK (verb) 6] 3x

<1915> ἐπίβλημα ***epiblēma*** [PIECE 1] 4x

<1916> ἐπιβοάω ***epiboaō*** [to cry, to cry out: CRY (verb) 3] 1x

<1917> ἐπιβουλή ***epiboulē*** [PLOT (noun) 1] 4x

<1918> ἐπιγαμβρεύω ***epigambreuō*** [MARRY 3] 1x

<1919> ἐπίγειος ***epigeios*** [EARTHLY 1] 7x

<1920> ἐπιγίνομαι ***epiginomai*** [BLOW (verb) 1] 1x

<1921> ἐπιγινώσκω ***epiginōskō*** [KNOW 3, to take knowledge: KNOWLEDGE 3, RECOGNIZE 2] 44x

<1922> ἐπίγνωσις ***epignōsis*** [KNOWLEDGE 2] 20x

<1923> ἐπιγραφή ***epigraphē*** [INSCRIPTION 1] 5x

<1924> ἐπιγράφω ***epigraphō*** [INSCRIBE 1, WRITE 3] 5x

<1925> ἐπιδείκνυμι ***epideiknumi*** [SHOW (verb) 8] 9x

<1926> ἐπιδέχομαι ***epidechomai*** [RECEIVE 13] 2x

<1927> ἐπιδημέω ***epidēmeō*** [STAY (verb) 4] 2x

<1928> ἐπιδιατάσσομαι ***epidiatassomai*** [ADD 1] 1x

<1929> ἐπιδίδωμι ***epididōmi*** [DELIVER 2, to let drive, to drive along: DRIVE 4, GIVE 4] 9x

<1930> ἐπιδιορθόω ***epidiorthoō*** [to set right, to set in order: SET (verb) 8] 1x

<1931> ἐπιδύω ***epiduō*** [to go down: GO 32] 1x

<1932> ἐπιείκεια ***epieikeia*** [COURTESY, GENTLENESS 1] 2x

<1933> ἐπιεικής ***epieikēs*** [GENTLE 1, GENTLENESS 2] 5x

<1934> ἐπιζητέω ***epizēteō*** [to seek; to seek after, diligently, eagerly, for: SEEK 4] 13x

<1935> ἐπιθανάτιος ***epithanatios*** [condemned to death, condemned to die: DEATH 5] 1x

<1936> ἐπίθεσις ***epithesis*** [LAYING ON OF HANDS] 4x

<1937> ἐπιθυμέω ***epithumeō*** [COVET 1, DESIRE (verb) 2, LUST (verb) 1] 16x

<1938> ἐπιθυμητής ***epithumētēs*** [one who lusts: LUST (verb) 2] 1x

<1939> ἐπιθυμία ***epithumia*** [DESIRE (noun) 1, LUST (noun) 1] 38x

<1940> ἐπικαθίζω ***epikathizō*** [to set on: SET (verb) 9] 1x

<1941> ἐπικαλέω ***epikaleō*** [APPEAL 1, CALL (verb) 3, INVOKE 1, PRAY 2, SURNAME (verb)] 30x

<1942> ἐπικάλυμμα ***epikalumma*** [COVERING 1] 1x

<1943> ἐπικαλύπτω ***epikaluptō*** [COVER 2] 1x

<1944> ἐπικατάρατος ***epikataratos*** [CURSED 1] 3x

<1945> ἐπίκειμαι ***epikeimai*** [BEAT 3, IMPOSE 2, to be insistent: INSISTENT, to lay, to lay on:

LAY 9, to press around, on, etc.: PRESS 7] 7x
<1946> Ἐπικούρειος ***Epikoureios*** [EPICUREAN] 1x
<1947> ἐπικουρία ***epikouria*** [HELP (noun) 3] 1x
<1948> ἐπικρίνω ***epikrinō*** [to give sentence, to pronounce sentence: SENTENCE 3] 1x
<1949> ἐπιλαμβάνω ***epilambanō*** [CATCH (verb) 4, SEIZE 6, to take, to take hold: TAKE 5] 19x
<1950> ἐπιλανθάνω ***epilanthanō*** [FORGET 2] 8x
<1951> ἐπιλέγω ***epilegō*** [CALL (verb) 9, CHOOSE 5] 2x
<1952> ἐπιλείπω ***epileipō*** [FAIL 3] 1x
<1952a> ἐπιλείχω ***epileichō*** [LICK 1] 1x
<1953> ἐπιλησμονή ***epilēsmonē*** [forgetfulness: FORGETFUL 1] 1x
<1954> ἐπίλοιπος ***epiloipos*** [REST (noun)[2] 3] 1x
<1955> ἐπίλυσις ***epilusis*** [INTERPRETATION 1] 1x
<1956> ἐπιλύω ***epiluō*** [DETERMINE 3, EXPLAIN 4, SETTLE 2] 2x
<1957> ἐπιμαρτυρέω ***epimartureō*** [TESTIFY 2] 1x
<1958> ἐπιμέλεια ***epimeleia*** [CARE (noun) 1] 1x
<1959> ἐπιμελέομαι ***epimeleomai*** [to take care of: CARE (noun) 2] 3x
<1960> ἐπιμελῶς ***epimelōs*** [CAREFULLY 2] 1x
<1961> ἐπιμένω ***epimenō*** [CONTINUE 3, REMAIN 3, STAY (verb) 7, TARRY 2] 18x
<1962> ἐπινεύω ***epineuō*** [CONSENT (verb) 1] 1x
<1963> ἐπίνοια ***epinoia*** [THOUGHT 6] 1x
<1964> ἐπιορκέω ***epiorkeō*** [FORSWEAR] 1x
<1965> ἐπίορκος ***epiorkos*** [PERJURER] 1x
<1966> ἐπιοῦσα ***epiousa*** [next day, day following: DAY 4, FOLLOWING 1] 5x
<1967> ἐπιούσιος ***epiousios*** [DAILY 1] 2x
<1968> ἐπιπίπτω ***epipiptō*** [FALL (verb) 5, SEIZE 3] 12x
<1969> ἐπιπλήσσω ***epiplēssō*** [to rebuke, to rebuke sharply, to rebuke harshly: REBUKE (verb) 3] 1x
<1970> ἐπιπνίγω ***epipnigō*** [CHOKE 2] 1x
<1971> ἐπιποθέω ***epipotheō*** [to desire; to desire earnestly, ardently, greatly, much: DESIRE (verb) 3, LONG (verb) 1, YEARN 1] 9x
<1972> ἐπιπόθησις ***epipothēsis*** [ardent desire: DESIRE (noun) 2] 2x
<1973> ἐπιπόθητος ***epipothētos*** [longed for: LONGED] 1x
<1974> ἐπιποθία ***epipothia*** [great desire: DESIRE (noun) 3] 1x
<1975> ἐπιπορεύομαι ***epiporeuomai*** [COME 15] 1x
<1976> ἐπιράπτω ***epiraptō*** [SEW 1] 1x
<1977> ἐπιρίπτω ***epiriptō*** [CAST (verb) 10] 2x
<1978> ἐπίσημος ***episēmos*** [of note: NOTE (noun) 1, NOTORIOUS] 2x
<1979> ἐπισιτισμός ***episitismos*** [FOOD 4] 1x
<1980> ἐπισκέπτομαι ***episkeptomai*** [to look out: LOOK (verb) 8, VISIT (verb) 1] 11x
<1980a> ἐπισκευάζομαι ***episkeuazomai*** [PACK 2] 1x
<1981> ἐπισκηνόω ***episkēnoō*** [REST (verb) 6] 1x
<1982> ἐπισκιάζω ***episkiazō*** [OVERSHADOW 1] 5x
<1983> ἐπισκοπέω ***episkopeō*** [to exercise oversight, to take the oversight: OVERSIGHT 2, WATCH (verb) 5] 2x
<1984> ἐπισκοπή ***episkopē*** [OFFICE 1, OVERSIGHT 1, VISITATION] 4x
<1985> ἐπίσκοπος ***episkopos*** [OVERSEER 1] 5x
<1986> ἐπισπάω ***epispaō*** [to become uncircumcised: UNCIRCUMCISED 2] 1x
<1987> ἐπίσταμαι ***epistamai*** [KNOW 13, UNDERSTAND 2] 14x
<1987a> ἐπίστασις ***epistasis*** [PREOCCUPATION 1] 1x
<1988> ἐπιστάτης ***epistatēs*** [MASTER (noun) 2] 7x
<1989> ἐπιστέλλω ***epistellō*** [WRITE 6] 3x
<1990> ἐπιστήμων ***epistēmōn*** [UNDERSTANDING 2] 1x
<1991> ἐπιστηρίζω ***epistērizō*** [STRENGTHEN 8] 4x
<1992> ἐπιστολή ***epistolē*** [EPISTLE 1, EPISTLE OF COMMENDATION, LETTER 2] 24x
<1993> ἐπιστομίζω ***epistomizō*** [to stop the mouth: MOUTH (noun) 2] 1x

<1994> ἐπιστρέφω ***epistrephō*** [to bring back: BRING 27, CONVERT (verb) 2, RETURN (verb) 8, TURN (verb) 9] 36x

<1995> ἐπιστροφή ***epistrophē*** [CONVERSION] 1x

<1996> ἐπισυνάγω ***episunagō*** [to gather, to gather together: GATHER 2] 8x

<1997> ἐπισυναγωγή ***episunagōgē*** [ASSEMBLING 1] 2x

<1998> ἐπισυντρέχω ***episuntrechō*** [to run together: RUN 8] 1x

<1999> ἐπισύστασις ***episustasis*** [PREOCCUPATION 2, to raise up: RAISE 8] 2x

<2000> ἐπισφαλής ***episphalēs*** [DANGEROUS 1] 1x

<2001> ἐπισχύω ***epischuō*** [INSIST 1] 1x

<2002> ἐπισωρεύω ***episōreuō*** [HEAP 2] 1x

<2003> ἐπιταγή ***epitagē*** [AUTHORITY 5, COMMANDMENT 3] 7x

<2004> ἐπιτάσσω ***epitassō*** [COMMAND (verb) 2] 10x

<2005> ἐπιτελέω ***epiteleō*** [ACCOMPLISH 6, DO 2, FINISH 4, MAKE 7, to make perfect: PERFECT (adj.) 2, PERFECT (verb) 1, PERFORM 3] 10x

<2006> ἐπιτήδειος ***epitēdeios*** [NEEDFUL 1] 1x

<2007> ἐπιτίθημι ***epitithēmi*** [ADD 2, GIVE 13, to lay on: LAY 4, to lay upon: LAYING ON OF HANDS, PLACE (verb) 2, PUT 3, to set, to set on, to set upon: SET (verb) 12, STRIKE 1, SUPPLY (verb) 1, to cover: WOUND (verb) 3] 39x

<2008> ἐπιτιμάω ***epitimaō*** [to earnestly charge: CHARGE (verb) 2, REBUKE (verb) 2, WARN 2] 29x

<2009> ἐπιτιμία ***epitimia*** [PUNISHMENT 3] 1x

<2010> ἐπιτρέπω ***epitrepō*** [PERMIT 1] 19x

<2011> ἐπιτροπή ***epitropē*** [COMMISSION 1] 1x

<2012> ἐπίτροπος ***epitropos*** [GUARDIAN 1, STEWARD 1] 3x

<2013> ἐπιτυγχάνω ***epitunchanō*** [OBTAIN 6] 5x

<2014> ἐπιφαίνω ***epiphainō*** [APPEAR 3, to give light: LIGHT (noun) 6] 4x

<2015> ἐπιφάνεια ***epiphaneia*** [APPEARING 1] 6x

<2016> ἐπιφανής ***epiphanēs*** [AWESOME] 1x

<2017> ἐπιφαύσκω ***epiphauskō*** [to give light: LIGHT (noun) 7] 1x

<2018> ἐπιφέρω ***epipherō*** [BRING 14, INFLICT 1, STIR (verb) 3] 3x

<2019> ἐπιφωνέω ***epiphōneō*** [to shout, to shout against: SHOUT (verb) 2] 3x

<2020> ἐπιφώσκω ***epiphōskō*** [to begin to dawn: DAWN (verb) 2] 2x

<2021> ἐπιχειρέω ***epicheireō*** [to take in hand: HAND (noun) 4, SEEK 5, to take in hand, to take upon oneself: TAKE 29] 3x

<2022> ἐπιχέω ***epicheō*** [POUR 3] 1x

<2023> ἐπιχορηγέω ***epichorēgeō*** [ADD 3, NOURISH 1, SUPPLY (verb) 7] 5x

<2024> ἐπιχορηγία ***epichorēgia*** [HELP (noun) 4, SUPPLY (noun)] 2x

<2025> ἐπιχρίω ***epichriō*** [ANOINT 5] 2x

<2026> ἐποικοδομέω ***epoikodomeō*** [to build up, to build upon: BUILD 3] 8x

<2027> ἐποκέλλω ***epokellō*** [to run aground: RUN 13] 1x

<2028> ἐπονομάζω ***eponomazō*** [NAME (verb) 3] 1x

<2029> ἐποπτεύω ***epopteuō*** [WITNESS (verb) 1] 2x

<2030> ἐπόπτης ***epoptēs*** [EYEWITNESS 2] 1x

<2031> ἔπος ***epos*** [word: SO TO SPEAK] 1x

<2032> ἐπουράνιος ***epouranios*** [HEAVENLY 2] 20x

<2033> ἑπτά ***hepta*** [SEVEN, SEVEN THOUSAND 2, seven: SEVENTH 1] 88x

<2034> ἑπτάκις ***heptakis*** [seven times: TIME 19] 4x

<2035> ἑπτακισχίλιοι ***heptakischilioi*** [SEVEN THOUSAND 1] 1x

<2036> ἔπω ***epō*** [COMMAND (verb) 6, SPEAK 6, TELL 6]

<2037> Ἔραστος ***Erastos*** [ERASTUS] 3x

<2037a> ἐραυνάω ***eraunaō*** [SEEK 6] 1x

<2038> ἐργάζομαι ***ergazomai*** [COMMIT 1, DO 3, MINISTER (verb) 3, PRACTICE (verb) 1, TRADE (verb) 1, WORK (verb) 2, WROUGHT (HAVE) 1] 41x

<2039> ἐργασία ***ergasia*** [BUSINESS 3, EFFORT 1, GAIN (noun) 1, WORKING (noun) 2] 6x

<2040> ἐργάτης ***ergatēs*** [WORKMAN 1] 16x

<2041> ἔργον ***ergon*** [ACTION 1, DEED 1, WORK (noun) 1] 169x
<2042> ἐρεθίζω ***erethizō*** [PROVOKE 1, STIMULATE 1] 2x
<2043> ἐρείδω ***ereidō*** [to stick fast: STICK (verb) 1] 1x
<2044> ἐρεύγομαι ***ereugomai*** [UTTER (verb) 3] 1x
<2045> ἐρευνάω ***ereunaō*** [SEARCH (verb) 3, SEEK 6] 6x
<2046> ἐρέω ***ereō*** [SAY 2, SPEAK 16] 70x
<2047> ἐρημία ***erēmia*** [WILDERNESS 1] 4x
<2048> ἔρημος ***erēmos*** [DESERTED, DESOLATE 1, WILDERNESS 2] 48x
<2049> ἐρημόω ***erēmoō*** [to make desolate, to bring to desolation, to bring to ruin, to change in desolation: DESOLATE 2] 5x
<2050> ἐρήμωσις ***erēmōsis*** [DESOLATION 1] 3x
<2051> ἐρίζω ***erizō*** [STRIVE 6] 1x
<2052> ἐριθεία ***eritheia*** [CONTENTION 1, dispute: SELF-SEEKING, STRIFE 1] 7x
<2053> ἔριον ***erion*** [WOOL] 2x
<2054> ἔρις ***eris*** [CONTENTION 2, STRIFE 2] 9x
<2055> ἐρίφιον ***eriphion*** [GOAT 2] 1x
<2056> ἔριφος ***eriphos*** [GOAT 1] 2x
<2057> Ἑρμᾶς ***Hermas*** [HERMAS] 1x
<2058> ἑρμηνεία ***hermēneia*** [INTERPRETATION 2] 2x
<2059> ἑρμηνεύω ***hermēneuō*** [TRANSLATE 1] 3x
<2060> Ἑρμῆς ***Hermēs*** [HERMES] 2x
<2061> Ἑρμογένης ***Hermogenēs*** [HERMOGENES] 1x
<2062> ἑρπετόν ***herpeton*** [REPTILE] 4x
<2063> Ἐρυθρὰ Θάλασσα ***Eruthra Thalassa*** [RED SEA] 2x
<2064> ἔρχομαι ***erchomai*** [COME 4, FALL (verb) 15, GO 6, GROW 4] 641x
<2065> ἐρωτάω ***erōtaō*** [ASK 5] 63x
<2066> ἐσθής ***esthēs*** [APPAREL 1, CLOTHES 2] 8x
<2067> ἔσθησις ***esthēsis*** [CLOTHES 3] 1x
<2068> ἐσθίω ***esthiō*** [DEVOUR 1, EAT 3] 158x
<2069> Ἑσλί ***Hesli*** [HESLI] 1x
<2070> ἐσμέν ***esmen*** [ARE (WE)] 53x
<2071> ἔσομαι ***esomai*** [I shall be: BE 5]
<2072> ἔσοπτρον ***esoptron*** [MIRROR 1] 2x
<2073> ἑσπέρα ***hespera*** [EVENING 1] 3x
<2074> Ἑσρώμ ***Hesrōm*** [HEZRON] 3x
<2074a> ἔσται ***estai*** [it shall be: BE 6]
<2075> ἐστέ ***este*** [ARE (YOU) 2] 92x
<2076> ἐστί ***esti*** [he (she, it) is: BE 7, it is meet: MEET (adj.) 3] 2,472x
<2077> ἔστω ***estō*** [BE THOU 1] 16x
<2078> ἔσχατος ***eschatos*** [END (noun) 3, LAST (adv. and noun) 1, uttermost part, remotest part: PART (noun) 4, last state: STATE 2] 52x
<2079> ἐσχάτως ***eschatōs*** [at extremity: EXTREMITY 2] 1x
<2080> ἔσω ***esō*** [INTO, inner man, inward man: MAN 5] 9x
<2081> ἔσωθεν ***esōthen*** [WITHIN (FROM)] 14x
<2082> ἐσώτερος ***esōteros*** [INNER 1] 2x
<2083> ἑταῖρος ***hetairos*** [COMPANION 1, FRIEND 1] 4x
<2084> ἑτερόγλωσσος ***heteroglōssos*** [other tongue, strange tongue: TONGUE 2] 1x
<2085> ἑτεροδιδασκαλέω ***heterodidaskaleō*** [to teach other, strange, false doctrines: DOCTRINE 3] 2x
<2086> ἑτεροζυγέω ***heterozugeō*** [YOKED (BE)] 1x
<2087> ἕτερος ***heteros*** [ANOTHER 2, DIFFERENT 1, OTHER 2] 98x
<2088> ἑτέρως ***heterōs*** [OTHERWISE 2] 1x
<2089> ἔτι ***eti*** [MORE 1] 93x
<2090> ἑτοιμάζω ***hetoimazō*** [PREPARE 1, to make ready: READY 3] 40x
<2091> ἑτοιμασία ***hetoimasia*** [PREPARATION 1] 1x

<2092> ἕτοιμος ***hetoimos*** [READY 1] 17x

<2093> ἑτοίμως ***hetoimōs*** [READY 2] 3x

<2094> ἔτος ***etos*** [YEAR 2] 49x

<2095> εὖ ***eu*** [to do good: GOOD (adv.) 1] 6x

<2096> Εὕα ***Eua*** [EVE] 2x

<2097> εὐαγγελίζω ***euangelizō*** [to bring good news, to bring good tidings: BRING 28, to preach, to preach the gospel, to preach the glad tidings, to preach the good news: PREACH 3] 54x

<2098> εὐαγγέλιον ***euangelion*** [GOSPEL 1] 76x

<2099> εὐαγγελιστής ***euangelistēs*** [EVANGELIST] 3x

<2100> εὐαρεστέω ***euaresteō*** [PLEASE 3, PLEASED (BE) 1] 3x

<2101> εὐάρεστος ***euarestos*** [ACCEPTABLE 4, well-pleasing: PLEASING 3, WELL PLEASING 1] 9x

<2102> εὐαρέστως ***euarestōs*** [ACCEPTABLY] 1x

<2103> Εὔβουλος ***Euboulos*** [EUBULUS] 1x

<2103a> εὖγε ***euge*** [WELL DONE] 1x

<2104> εὐγενής ***eugenēs*** [NOBLE 1] 3x

<2105> εὐδία ***eudia*** [fair weather, fine weather: WEATHER 1] 1x

<2106> εὐδοκέω ***eudokeō*** [PLEASED (BE) 2, to think good, to think best: THINK 3] 21x

<2107> εὐδοκία ***eudokia*** [DESIRE (noun) 4, good pleasure: PLEASURE 2, good pleasure: WELL PLEASING 2, good will: WILL (noun)[1] 4] 9x

<2108> εὐεργεσία ***euergesia*** [good deed: DEED 2, service, good and ready service: SERVICE 2] 2x

<2109> εὐεργετέω ***euergeteō*** [to do good: GOOD (adj. and noun) 10] 1x

<2110> εὐεργέτης ***euergetēs*** [BENEFACTOR 1] 1x

<2111> εὔθετος ***euthetos*** [FIT (adj.) 1, USEFUL 1] 3x

<2112> εὐθέως ***eutheōs*** [IMMEDIATELY 1, SHORTLY 1] 36x

<2113> εὐθυδρομέω ***euthudromeō*** [to sail straight: SAIL (verb) 9] 2x

<2114> εὐθυμέω ***euthumeō*** [to be happy: HAPPY 2, to take heart: HEART 7] 3x

<2115> εὔθυμος ***euthumos*** [encouraged: ENCOURAGE 3] 1x

<2115a> εὐθύμως ***euthumōs*** [cheerfully, more cheerfully: CHEERFULLY 1] 1x

<2116> εὐθύνω ***euthunō*** [DIRECT 1, to make straight: STRAIGHT 4] 2x

<2117> εὐθύς ***euthus*** [IMMEDIATELY 1, STRAIGHT 1] 59x

<2118> εὐθύτης ***euthutēs*** [RIGHTEOUSNESS 2] 1x

<2119> εὐκαιρέω ***eukaireō*** [to have opportunity: OPPORTUNITY 3, to spend time: SPEND 7, to have time: TIME 3] 3x

<2120> εὐκαιρία ***eukairia*** [OPPORTUNITY 1] 2x

<2121> εὔκαιρος ***eukairos*** [OPPORTUNE 1, SEASONABLE] 2x

<2122> εὐκαίρως ***eukairōs*** [CONVENIENTLY, in season: SEASON (noun) 2] 2x

<2123> εὔκοπος ***eukopos*** [EASIER] 7x

<2124> εὐλάβεια ***eulabeia*** [PIETY 1] or [REVERENCE (noun) 1] 2x

<2125> εὐλαβέομαι ***eulabeomai*** [to be moved with fear: FEAR (noun) 6] 1x

<2126> εὐλαβής ***eulabēs*** [DEVOUT 1] 4x

<2127> εὐλογέω ***eulogeō*** [BLESS 1, PRAISE (verb) 3] 41x

<2128> Εὐλογητός ***Eulogētos*** [BLESSED ONE] 8x

<2129> εὐλογία ***eulogia*** [BLESSING 1, blessing: BOUNTIFULLY, generous gift: GIFT 5, fair speeches: SPEECH 3] 16x

<2130> εὐμετάδοτος ***eumetadotos*** [GENEROUS 1] 1x

<2131> Εὐνίκη ***Eunikē*** [EUNICE] 1x

<2132> εὐνοέω ***eunoeō*** [AGREE 1] 1x

<2133> εὔνοια ***eunoia*** [GOOD WILL 1] 2x

<2134> εὐνουχίζω ***eunouchizō*** [to make eunuch: EUNUCH] 2x

<2135> εὐνοῦχος ***eunouchos*** [EUNUCH] 8x

<2136> Εὐοδία ***Euodia*** [EUODIA] 1x

<2137> εὐοδόω ***euodoō*** [to have a prosperous journey: JOURNEY (noun) 4, PROSPER 1] 4x

<2137a> εὐπάρεδρος ***euparedros*** [DEVOTION 1] 1x

<2138> εὐπειθής ***eupeithēs*** [YIELDING] 1x

<2139> εὐπερίστατος ***euperistatos*** [which ensnares so easily: ENSNARE 1] 1x

<2140> εὐποιΐα ***eupoiia*** [GOOD (adj. and noun) 2] 1x

<2141> εὐπορέομαι ***euporeomai*** [to have means: MEANS 1] 1x

<2142> εὐπορία ***euporia*** [WEALTH 1] 1x

<2143> εὐπρέπεια ***euprepeia*** [GRACE 2] 1x

<2144> εὐπρόσδεκτος ***euprosdektos*** [ACCEPTABLE 3] 5x

<2145> εὐπρόσεδρος ***euprosedros*** [DEVOTION 2] 1x

<2146> εὐπροσωπέω ***euprosōpeō*** [to make a good showing: SHOWING 1] 1x

<2147> εὑρίσκω ***heuriskō*** [FIND 1, OBTAIN 1] 176x

<2148> Εὐροκλύδων ***Eurokludōn*** [EUROCLYDON] 1x

<2149> εὐρύχωρος ***euruchōros*** [BROAD 1] 1x

<2150> εὐσέβεια ***eusebeia*** [GODLINESS 1] 15x

<2151> εὐσεβέω ***eusebeō*** [to be pious, to show piety, to practice piety, to put religion in practice: PIETY 2, WORSHIP (verb) 1] 2x

<2152> εὐσεβής ***eusebēs*** [DEVOUT 2] 4x

<2153> εὐσεβῶς ***eusebōs*** [GODLY 1] 2x

<2154> εὔσημος ***eusēmos*** [INTELLIGIBLE 1] 1x

<2155> εὔσπλαγχνος ***eusplanchnos*** [TENDER-HEARTED] 2x

<2156> εὐσχημόνως ***euschēmonōs*** [DECENTLY, HONESTLY 1, PROPERLY 1] 3x

<2157> εὐσχημοσύνη ***euschēmosunē*** [HONOR (noun) 1] 1x

<2158> εὐσχήμων ***euschēmōn*** [that which is comely: COMELY 1, HONORABLE 1, PRESENTABLE, PROMINENT 1] 5x

<2159> εὐτόνως ***eutonōs*** [VIGOROUSLY] 2x

<2160> εὐτραπελία ***eutrapelia*** [JESTING] 1x

<2161> Εὔτυχος ***Eutuchos*** [EUTYCHUS] 1x

<2162> εὐφημία ***euphēmia*** [good report: REPORT (noun) 3] 1x

<2163> εὔφημος ***euphēmos*** [of good report: REPORT (noun) 4] 1x

<2164> εὐφορέω ***euphoreō*** [to bring forth abundantly, plentifully: BRING 29] 1x

<2165> εὐφραίνω ***euphrainō*** [to be merry, to make merry: MERRY 1, REJOICE 2] 14x

<2166> Εὐφράτης ***Euphratēs*** [EUPHRATES] 2x

<2167> εὐφροσύνη ***euphrosunē*** [JOY (noun) 2] 2x

<2168> εὐχαριστέω ***eucharisteō*** [to give thanks: THANKS 2] 38x

<2169> εὐχαριστία ***eucharistia*** [THANKFULNESS 1, THANKSGIVING 1] 15x

<2170> εὐχάριστος ***eucharistos*** [THANKFUL 1] 1x

<2171> εὐχή ***euchē*** [PRAYER 3, VOW (noun) 1] 3x

<2172> εὔχομαι ***euchomai*** [PRAY 3, WISH 1] 7x

<2173> εὔχρηστος ***euchrēstos*** [USEFUL 2] 3x

<2174> εὐψυχέω ***eupsucheō*** [to be encouraged: ENCOURAGE 4] 1x

<2175> εὐωδία ***euōdia*** [sweet odor: ODOR 2] 3x

<2176> εὐώνυμος ***euōnumos*** [left, the left, on the left hand: LEFT 2] 9x

<2177> ἐφάλλομαι ***ephallomai*** [LEAP 3] 1x

<2178> ἐφάπαξ ***ephapax*** [once for all, at once: ONCE 2] 5x

<2179> Ἐφεσῖνος ***Ephesinos*** [EPHESIAN 2] 1x

<2180> Ἐφέσιος ***Ephesios*** [EPHESIAN 1] 4x

<2181> Ἔφεσος ***Ephesos*** [EPHESUS] 16x

<2182> ἐφευρετής ***epheuretēs*** [INVENTOR] 1x

<2183> ἐφημερία ***ephēmeria*** [COURSE 3] 2x

<2184> ἐφήμερος ***ephēmeros*** [DAILY 2] 1x

<2185> ἐφικνέομαι ***ephikneomai*** [REACH (verb) 2] 2x

<2186> ἐφίστημι ***ephistēmi*** [ASSAULT (verb), to come on, there, up, upon: COME 25, to come upon, to come up to: FALL (verb) 16, to be at hand: HAND (noun) 6, to be ready: READY 4, to stand; to stand before, by, next: STAND (verb) 2] 21x

<2187> Ἐφραίμ ***Ephraim*** [EPHRAIM] 1x

<2188> εφφαθα ***ephphatha*** [EPHPHATHA] 1x

<2189> ἔχθρα ***echthra*** [ENMITY] 6x
<2190> ἐχθρός ***echthros*** [ENEMY 1] 32x
<2191> ἔχιδνα ***echidna*** [VIPER 1] 5x
<2192> ἔχω ***echō*** [CONCEIVE 4, COUNT 1, DO 4, GRIP 1, HAVE 1, OBTAIN 2, POSSESS 1, to receive reproof: REBUKE (verb) 4, to be sick: SICK (adv.) 4, to be thankful: THANKFUL 2] 706x
<2193> ἕως ***heōs*** [UNTIL 1] 193x

Z

<2194> Ζαβουλών ***Zaboulōn*** [ZEBULUN] 3x
<2195> Ζακχαῖος ***Zakchaios*** [ZACCHEUS] 3x
<2196> Ζάρα ***Zara*** [ZERAH] 1x
<2197> Ζαχαρίας ***Zacharias*** [ZACHARIAS] 11x
<2198> ζάω ***zaō*** [to come to life: LIFE 8, LIVE 1, to live: LIVING (adj.) 1, to live: LIVING (noun) 2] 140x
<2199> Ζεβεδαῖος ***Zebedaios*** [ZEBEDEE] 12x
<2200> ζεστός ***zestos*** [HOT 1] 3x
<2201> ζεῦγος ***zeugos*** [PAIR 1, YOKE 1] 2x
<2202> ζευκτηρία ***zeuktēria*** [BAND (noun)[1] 1] 1x
<2203> Ζεύς ***Zeus*** [ZEUS] 2x
<2204> ζέω ***zeō*** [to be fervent: FERVENT 2] 2x
<2205> ζῆλος ***zēlos*** [ENVY (noun) 2, HEAT 1, JEALOUSY 1, fervent mind: MIND (noun) 6, ZEAL 1] 17x
<2206> ζηλόω ***zēloō*** [COVET 2, to desire; to desire earnestly, eagerly: DESIRE (verb) 4, ENVY (verb) 1, to be jealous, to become jealous, to be stirred up to jealousy: JEALOUS 1, to be zealous: ZEALOUS 2] 11x
<2207> ζηλωτής ***zēlōtēs*** [ZEALOUS 1] 5x
<2208> Ζηλωτής ***Zēlōtēs*** [ZEALOT] 2x
<2209> ζημία ***zēmia*** [LOSS 2] 4x
<2210> ζημιόω ***zēmioō*** [FORFEIT, LOSS 3] 6x
<2211> Ζηνᾶς ***Zēnas*** [ZENAS] 1x
<2212> ζητέω ***zēteō*** [INQUIRE 2, REQUIRE 2, SEEK 1] 117x
<2213> ζήτημα ***zētēma*** [QUESTION (noun) 1] 5x
<2214> ζήτησις ***zētēsis*** [DISPUTE (noun) 3, INQUIRY 1, QUESTION (noun) 2] 7x
<2215> ζιζάνιον ***zizanion*** [DARNEL] 8x
<2216> Ζοροβαβέλ ***Zorobabel*** [ZERUBBABEL] 3x
<2217> ζόφος ***zophos*** [BLACKNESS 1, DARKNESS 1] 5x
<2218> ζυγός ***zugos*** [BALANCE, YOKE 2] 6x
<2219> ζύμη ***zumē*** [LEAVEN (noun)] 13x
<2220> ζυμόω ***zumoō*** [LEAVEN (verb)] 4x
<2221> ζωγρέω ***zōgreō*** [CATCH (verb) 7] 2x
<2222> ζωή ***zōē*** [LIFE 6, LIFE ETERNAL] 135x
<2223> ζώνη ***zōnē*** [BELT] 8x
<2224> ζώννυμι ***zōnnumi*** [GIRD 1] 3x
<2225> ζῳογονέω ***zōogoneō*** [LIVE 8] or [PRESERVE 1] 3x
<2226> ζῷον ***zōon*** [BEAST 1] 23x
<2227> ζῳοποιέω ***zōopoieō*** [to make alive: ALIVE 1, to come to life, to give life: LIFE 10] 11x

H

<2228> ἤ ***ē*** [OR] 384x
<2229> ἦ ***ē*** [SURELY 2] 1x
<2230> ἡγεμονεύω ***hēgemoneuō*** [to be the governor: GOVERNOR 3] 2x

<2231> ἡγεμονία ***hēgemonia*** [REIGN (noun)] 1x
<2232> ἡγεμών ***hēgemōn*** [GOVERNOR 2, RULER 3] 21x
<2233> ἡγέομαι ***hēgeomai*** [to be the chief: CHIEF 2, CONSIDER 6, COUNT 2, ESTEEM (verb) 1, to govern: GOVERNOR 4, JUDGE (verb) 4, LEADER 1, to lead: LEADING 1, REGARD (verb) 3, one who rules over: RULE (verb) 4, THINK 6] 28x
<2234> ἡδέως ***hēdeōs*** [GLADLY 2] 3x
<2235> ἤδη ***ēdē*** [at last: LAST (adv. and noun) 4] 59x
<2236> ἥδιστα ***hēdista*** [all the more gladly, most gladly, very gladly: GLADLY 3] 2x
<2237> ἡδονή ***hēdonē*** [PLEASURE 3] 5x
<2238> ἡδύοσμον ***hēduosmon*** [MINT] 2x
<2239> ἦθος ***ēthos*** [HABIT 2] 1x
<2240> ἥκω ***hēkō*** [COME 29] 26x
<2241> Ἠλί ***Ēli*** [ELI] 2x
<2242> Ἡλί ***Hēli*** [ELI] 1x
<2243> Ἠλίας ***Ēlias*** [ELIJAH] 30x
<2244> ἡλικία ***hēlikia*** [AGE 2, STATURE] 8x
<2245> ἡλίκος ***hēlikos*** [HOW GREAT] 2x
<2246> ἥλιος ***hēlios*** [SUN 1] 32x
<2247> ἧλος ***hēlos*** [NAIL (noun)] 2x
<2248> ἡμᾶς ***hēmas*** [OUR] 8x
<2249> ἡμεῖς ***hēmeis*** [WE] 717x
<2250> ἡμέρα ***hēmera*** [AGE 3, DAY 1, DAY OF THE LORD, SON OF DAY, TIME 5, YEAR 8] 390x
<2251> ἡμέτερος ***hēmeteros*** [MY OWN] 9x
<2252> ἤμην ***ēmēn*** [WAS (I) 1] 16x
<2253> ἡμιθανής ***hēmithanēs*** [half dead: DEAD 3] 1x
<2254> ἡμῖν ***hēmin*** [TO US] 177x
<2255> ἥμισυ ***hēmisu*** [HALF 1] 5x
<2256> ἡμιώριον ***hēmiōrion*** [half an hour: HOUR 2] 1x
<2257> ἡμῶν ***hēmōn*** [US] 410x
<2258> ἦν ***ēn*** [WAS (I) 2] 189x
<2259> ἡνίκα ***hēnika*** [WHEN, WHENEVER] 2x
<2260> ἤπερ ***ēper*** [THAN] 1x
<2261> ἤπιος ***ēpios*** [GENTLE 2] 2x
<2262> Ἤρ ***Ēr*** [ER] 1x
<2263> ἤρεμος ***ēremos*** [QUIET (adj.) 1] 1x
<2264> Ἡρῴδης ***Hērōdēs*** [HEROD] 43x
<2265> Ἡρῳδιανοί ***Hērōdianoi*** [HERODIANS] 3x
<2266> Ἡρῳδιάς ***Hērōdias*** [HERODIAS] 6x
<2267> Ἡρῳδίων ***Hērōdiōn*** [HERODION] 1x
<2268> Ἠσαΐας ***Ēsaias*** [ISAIAH] 22x
<2269> Ἠσαῦ ***Ēsau*** [ESAU] 3x
<2270> ἡσυχάζω ***hēsuchazō*** [to be quiet, to lead a quiet life: QUIET (adj.) 3, REST (verb) 7, to be, to become, to fall, to keep, to remain silent: SILENT 1] 5x
<2271> ἡσυχία ***hēsuchia*** [QUIETNESS 1, SILENCE (noun) 1] 4x
<2272> ἡσύχιος ***hēsuchios*** [QUIET (adj.) 2] 2x
<2273> ἤτοι ***ētoi*** [EITHER] 1x
<2274> ἡττάομαι ***hēttaomai*** [to be inferior: INFERIOR 1, OVERCOME 2] 3x
<2275> ἥττημα ***hēttēma*** [FAILURE 1, FAULT 3] 2x
<2276> ἥσσων ***hēssōn*** [WORSE 1] 2x
<2277> ἤτω ***ētō*** [LET BE] 2x
<2278> ἠχέω ***ēcheō*** [to roar: ROARING 1, SOUND (verb) 1] 2x
<2279> ἦχος ***ēchos*** [REPORT (noun) 5, SOUND (noun)] 3x

Θ

<2280> Θαδδαῖος ***Thaddaios*** [THADDAEUS] 2x

<2281> θάλασσα ***thalassa*** [SEA 1] 93x

<2282> θάλπω ***thalpō*** [CHERISH 1] 2x

<2283> Θαμάρ ***Thamar*** [TAMAR] 1x

<2284> θαμβέω ***thambeō*** [AMAZED (BE) 3] 4x

<2285> θάμβος ***thambos*** [amazement, wonder: AMAZED (BE) 5, ASTONISHMENT 2] 3x

<2286> θανάσιμος ***thanasimos*** [DEADLY 1]1x

<2287> θανατηφόρος ***thanatēphoros*** [DEADLY 2] 1x

<2288> θάνατος ***thanatos*** [death: DEADLY 3, DEATH 1, SIN TO DEATH] 120x

<2289> θανατόω ***thanatoō*** [to put to death, to deliver to death: DEATH 8, KILL 6] 11x

<2290> θάπτω ***thaptō*** [BURY 1] 11x

<2291> Θάρα ***Thara*** [TERAH] 1x

<2292> θαρρέω ***tharreō*** [to be bold, to have confidence: BOLD 1, to have confidence: BOLDLY 2, to be confident, to have confidence: CONFIDENT 1] 6x

<2293> θαρσέω ***tharseō*** [to take courage: COURAGE 2] 7x

<2294> θάρσος ***tharsos*** [COURAGE 1] 1x

<2295> θαῦμα ***thauma*** [AMAZEMENT 2] 2x

<2296> θαυμάζω ***thaumazō*** [to have in admiration: ADMIRATION 1, ADMIRE, MARVEL (verb) 1, WONDER (verb) 1] 43x

<2297> θαυμάσιος ***thaumasios*** [wonderful thing: WONDERFUL 2] 1x

<2298> θαυμαστός ***thaumastos*** [MARVELOUS, WONDER (adj. and noun) 1] 7x

<2299> θεά ***thea*** [GODDESS 1] 3x

<2300> θεάομαι ***theaomai*** [to look upon, to look at: LOOK (verb) 14, SEE 8] 22x

<2301> θεατρίζω ***theatrizō*** [to make a spectacle, to make a public spectacle: SPECTACLE 2] 1x

<2302> θέατρον ***theatron*** [SPECTACLE 1, THEATER] 3x

<2303> θεῖον ***theion*** [SULFUR 1] 7x

<2304> θεῖος ***theios*** [DIVINE 1] 3x

<2305> θειότης ***theiotēs*** [GODHEAD 1] 1x

<2306> θειώδης ***theiōdēs*** [as sulfur: SULFUR 2] 1x

<2307> θέλημα ***thelēma*** [WILL (noun)[1] 1] 62x

<2308> θέλησις ***thelēsis*** [WILL (noun)[1] 2] 1x

<2309> θέλω ***thelō*** [DESIRE (verb) 5, LIKE (verb) 2, WANT (verb) 2, WILL (verb) 2, to want: WILLFULLY 1, to will: WILLING 1, to be willing: WILLINGLY 3, WISH 2] 211x

<2310> θεμέλιος ***themelios*** [FOUNDATION 3] 16x

<2311> θεμελιόω ***themelioō*** [FOUND 1, SETTLE 3] 6x

<2312> θεοδίδακτος ***theodidaktos*** [taught by God, taught of God: TAUGHT 2] 1x

<2313> θεομαχέω ***theomacheō*** [to fight against God: FIGHT (verb) 3] 1x

<2314> θεομάχος ***theomachos*** [fighter against God: FIGHTER] 1x

<2315> θεόπνευστος ***theopneustos*** [DIVINELY INSPIRED] 1x

<2316> Θεός ***Theos*** [GOD, KINGDOM OF GOD, MAN OF GOD, well pleasing to God: PLEASING 2] 1,333x

<2316> θεός ***theos*** [GOD (other god) 2]

<2317> θεοσέβεια ***theosebeia*** [GODLINESS 2] 1x

<2318> θεοσεβής ***theosebēs*** [GOD-FEARING 1] 1x

<2319> θεοστυγής ***theostugēs*** [hater of God: HATER 1] 1x

<2320> θεότης ***theotēs*** [GODHEAD 2] 1x

<2321> Θεόφιλος ***Theophilos*** [THEOPHILUS] 2x

<2322> θεραπεία ***therapeia*** [HEALING 1, HOUSEHOLD 1] 4x

<2323> θεραπεύω ***therapeuō*** [HEAL 1, SERVE 4] 43x

<2324> θεράπων ***therapōn*** [servant, ministering servant: SERVANT 3] 1x

<2325> θερίζω ***therizō*** [REAP 1] 21x

<2326> θερισμός ***therismos*** [HARVEST (noun) 1] 13x

<2327> θεριστής ***theristēs*** [REAPER 1] 2x

<2328> θερμαίνω ***thermainō*** [WARM (verb)] 6x
<2329> θέρμη ***thermē*** [HEAT 2] 1x
<2330> θέρος ***theros*** [SUMMER] 3x
<2331> Θεσσαλονικεύς ***Thessalonikeus*** [THESSALONIAN] 4x
<2332> Θεσσαλονίκη ***Thessalonikē*** [THESSALONICA 1] 5x
<2333> Θευδᾶς ***Theudas*** [THEUDAS] 1x
<2334> θεωρέω ***theōreō*** [CONSIDER 4, SEE 9] 58x
<2335> θεωρία ***theōria*** [SPECTACLE 3] 1x
<2336> θήκη ***thēkē*** [SHEATH] 1x
<2337> θηλάζω ***thēlazō*** [to nurse, to nurse babies: NURSE (verb) 1] 6x
<2337a> θήλεια ***thēleia*** [WOMAN 2] 2x
<2338> θῆλυς ***thēlus*** [FEMALE 2] 5x
<2339> θήρα ***thēra*** [TRAP (noun) 1] 1x
<2340> θηρεύω ***thēreuō*** [CATCH (verb) 9] 1x
<2341> θηριομαχέω ***thēriomacheō*** [to fight with beasts, to fight wild beasts: BEAST 5] 1x
<2342> θηρίον ***thērion*** [beast, wild beast: BEAST 2] 45x
<2343> θησαυρίζω ***thēsaurizō*** [to heap up treasure together: HEAP 3, to lay up: LAY 15, RESERVE 1, STORE (verb) 1, to treasure up: TREASURE (verb) 1] 8x
<2344> θησαυρός ***thēsauros*** [TREASURE (noun) 1] 17x
<2345> θιγγάνω ***thinganō*** [TOUCH 2] 3x
<2346> θλίβω ***thlibō*** [AFFLICTED (BE) 1, PRESS 4, STRAITENED (BE)] 10x
<2347> θλῖψις ***thlipsis*** [AFFLICTION 1, ANGUISH 1, DISTRESS 2, GREAT TRIBULATION, TRIBULATION 1, TROUBLE (noun) 1] 45x
<2348> θνήσκω ***thnēskō*** [to be dead: DEAD 4] 14x
<2349> θνητός ***thnētos*** [MORTAL 1] 6x
<2350> θορυβέω ***thorubeō*** [to make a noise: NOISE (noun) 2, to make a tumult: TUMULT 2, to set in an uproar: UPROAR 1] 4x
<2351> θόρυβος ***thorubos*** [TUMULT 1] 7x
<2352> θραύω ***thrauō*** [OPPRESSED (BE) 2] 1x
<2353> θρέμμα ***thremma*** [CATTLE 1] 1x
<2354> θρηνέω ***thrēneō*** [LAMENT 2, MOURN 1] 4x
<2355> θρῆνος ***thrēnos*** [LAMENTATION 2] 1x
<2356> θρησκεία ***thrēskeia*** [RELIGION 2] 4x
<2357> θρησκός ***thrēskos*** [RELIGIOUS 1] 1x
<2358> θριαμβεύω ***thriambeuō*** [to cause to triumph, to lead in triumph, to lead in triumphal procession: TRIUMPH (noun and verb)] 2x
<2359> θρίξ ***thrix*** [HAIR 1] 15x
<2360> θροέω ***throeō*** [to be troubled: TROUBLE (verb) 4] 3x
<2361> θρόμβος ***thrombos*** [DROP (noun)] 1x
<2362> θρόνος ***thronos*** [GREAT WHITE THRONE, THRONE 2] 62x
<2363> Θυάτειρα ***Thuateira*** [THYATIRA] 4x
<2364> θυγάτηρ ***thugatēr*** [DAUGHTER 1] 29x
<2365> θυγάτριον ***thugatrion*** [young daughter, little daughter: DAUGHTER 2] 2x
<2366> θύελλα ***thuella*** [STORM 1] 1x
<2367> θύϊνος ***thuinos*** [CITRON] 1x
<2368> θυμίαμα ***thumiama*** [INCENSE 1] 6x
<2369> θυμιατήριον ***thumiatērion*** [CENSER 1] 1x
<2370> θυμιάω ***thumiaō*** [to burn incense: INCENSE 2] 1x
<2371> θυμομαχέω ***thumomacheō*** [to be very angry: ANGRY 3] 1x
<2372> θυμός ***thumos*** [FURY 1, INDIGNATION 2, WRATH 2] 18x
<2373> θυμόω ***thumoō*** [to be angry: ANGRY 4] 1x
<2374> θύρα ***thura*** [DOOR 1] 39x
<2375> θυρεός ***thureos*** [SHIELD (noun)] 1x
<2376> θυρίς ***thuris*** [WINDOW 1] 2x
<2377> θυρωρός ***thurōros*** [DOORKEEPER] 4x

<2378> θυσία ***thusia*** [SACRIFICE (noun) 1] 29x

<2379> θυσιαστήριον ***thusiastērion*** [ALTAR 2] 24x

<2380> θύω ***thuō*** [KILL 7, SACRIFICE (verb) 1] 14x

<2381> Θωμᾶς ***Thōmas*** [THOMAS] 12x

<2382> θώραξ ***thōrax*** [BREASTPLATE] 5x

I

<2383> Ἰάϊρος ***Iairos*** [JAIRUS] 2x

<2384> Ἰακώβ ***Iakōb*** [JACOB] 26x

<2385> Ἰάκωβος ***Iakōbos*** [JAMES] 42x

<2386> ἴαμα ***iama*** [HEALING 2] 3x

<2387> Ἰαμβρῆς ***Iambrēs*** [JAMBRES] 1x

<2388> Ἰαννά ***Ianna*** [JANNAI] 1x

<2389> Ἰάννης ***Iannēs*** [JANNES] 1x

<2390> ἰάομαι ***iaomai*** [HEAL 2] 26x

<2391> Ἰάρεδ ***Iared*** [JARED] 1x

<2392> ἴασις ***iasis*** [CURE (noun), HEALING 3] 3x

<2393> ἴασπις ***iaspis*** [JASPER] 4x

<2394> Ἰάσων ***Iasōn*** [JASON] 5x

<2395> ἰατρός ***iatros*** [PHYSICIAN] 7x

<2396> ἴδε ***ide*** [BEHOLD (interj.)] 34x

<2397> ἰδέα ***idea*** [COUNTENANCE 1] 1x

<2398> ἴδιος ***idios*** [his own nature: NATURE 4, OWN (adj. and pron.) 3, PRIVATELY 1, PRIVATELY 2] 113x

<2399> ἰδιώτης ***idiōtēs*** [SIMPLE 2, UNINSTRUCTED] 5x

<2400> ἰδού ***idou*** [LO AND BEHOLD!] 200x

<2401> Ἰδουμαία ***Idoumaia*** [IDUMEA] 1x

<2402> ἱδρώς ***hidrōs*** [SWEAT] 1x

<2403> Ἰεζάβελ ***Iezabel*** [JEZEBEL] 1x

<2404> Ἱεράπολις ***Hierapolis*** [HIERAPOLIS] 1x

<2405> ἱερατεία ***hierateia*** [PRIESTHOOD 1] 2x

<2406> ἱεράτευμα ***hierateuma*** [PRIESTHOOD 2] 2x

<2407> ἱερατεύω ***hierateuō*** [to execute the priest's office, to fulfill priestly service, to serve as priest, to perform priestly service: PRIEST 3] 1x

<2408> Ἱερεμίας ***Ieremias*** [JEREMIAH] 3x

<2409> ἱερεύς ***hiereus*** [PRIEST 1] 31x

<2410> Ἱεριχώ ***Ierichō*** [JERICHO] 7x

<2411> ἱερόν ***hieron*** [TEMPLE 1] 72x

<2412> ἱεροπρεπής ***hieroprepēs*** [REVERENT 1] or [as become sacred persons: SACRED 2] 1x

<2413> ἱερός ***hieros*** [HOLY (adj.) 3, SACRED 1] 2x

<2414> Ἱεροσόλυμα ***Hierosoluma*** [JERUSALEM 1] 59x

<2415> Ἱεροσολυμίτης ***Hierosolumitēs*** [JERUSALEM 2] 2x

<2416> ἱεροσυλέω ***hierosuleō*** [to commit sacrilege: SACRILEGE] 1x

<2417> ἱερόσυλος ***hierosulos*** [robber of temples: TEMPLE 3] 1x

<2418> ἱερουργέω ***hierourgeō*** [to carry on as a sacrificial service: SACRIFICIAL] 1x

<2419> Ἱερουσαλήμ ***Ierousalēm*** [JERUSALEM 1] 83x

<2420> ἱερωσύνη ***hierōsunē*** [PRIESTHOOD 3] 4x

<2421> Ἰεσσαί ***Iessai*** [JESSE] 5x

<2422> Ἰεφθάε ***Iephthae*** [JEPHTHAH] 1x

<2423> Ἰεχονίας ***Iechonias*** [JECONIAH] 2x

<2424> Ἰησοῦς ***Iēsous*** [JESUS, JOSHUA] 949x

<2425> ἱκανός ***hikanos*** [ABLE 3, CONTENT (verb) 2, ENOUGH 1, GREAT 5, LARGE 1, LONG (adj.) 1, many, good many: MANY 1, SECURITY 1, SUFFICIENT 3, long time: TIME 6, WORTHY 5] 41x

<2426> ἱκανότης ***hikanotēs*** [SUFFICIENCY 2] 1x

<2427> ἱκανόω ***hikanoō*** [to make competent: COMPETENT 1, to make meet: MEET (adj.) 2] 2x

<2428> ἱκετηρία ***hiketēria*** [SUPPLICATION 2] 1x

<2429> ἰκμάς ***ikmas*** [MOISTURE] 1x

<2430> Ἰκόνιον ***Ikonion*** [ICONIUM] 6x

<2431> ἱλαρός ***hilaros*** [CHEERFUL 1] 1x

<2432> ἱλαρότης ***hilarotēs*** [CHEERFULNESS] 1x

<2433> ἱλάσκομαι ***hilaskomai*** [to be merciful: MERCIFUL 3, to make propitiation: PROPITIATION 2] 2x

<2434> ἱλασμός ***hilasmos*** [PROPITIATION 1] 2x

<2435> ἱλαστήριον ***hilastērion*** [MERCY SEAT] 2x

<2436> ἵλεως ***hileōs*** [FAVORABLE 1, MERCIFUL 2] 2x

<2437> Ἰλλυρικόν ***Illurikon*** [ILLYRICUM] 1x

<2438> ἱμάς ***himas*** [STRAP] 4x

<2439> ἱματίζω ***himatizō*** [CLOTHE 5] 2x

<2440> ἱμάτιον ***himation*** [CLOAK 1, CLOTHES 4, GARMENT 2] 60x

<2441> ἱματισμός ***himatismos*** [CLOTHES 5, CLOTHING 2] 5x

<2442> ἱμείρομαι ***himeiromai*** [to be affectionately desirous: AFFECTIONATELY] 1x

<2443> ἵνα ***hina*** [SO THAT] 663x

<2444> ἱνατί ***hinati*** [WHEREFORE 3] 6x

<2445> Ἰόππη ***Ioppē*** [JOPPA] 10x

<2446> Ἰορδάνης ***Iordanēs*** [JORDAN] 15x

<2447> ἰός ***ios*** [POISON (noun), RUST 2] 3x

<2448> Ἰούδα ***Iouda*** [JUDAH 1] 1x

<2449> Ἰουδαία ***Ioudaia*** [JUDEA 1] 45x

<2450> ἰουδαΐζω ***ioudaizō*** [JUDAIZE] 1x

<2451> Ἰουδαϊκός ***Ioudaikos*** [JEWISH 1] 1x

<2452> Ἰουδαϊκῶς ***Ioudaikōs*** [JEW 2] 1x

<2453> Ἰουδαῖος ***Ioudaios*** [JEW 1] 195x

<2454> Ἰουδαϊσμός ***Ioudaismos*** [JUDAISM] 2x

<2455> Ἰούδας ***Ioudas*** [JUDAH 2, JUDAS] 45x

<2456> Ἰουλία ***Ioulia*** [JULIA] 1x

<2457> Ἰούλιος ***Ioulios*** [JULIUS] 2x

<2458> Ἰουνιᾶς ***Iounias*** [JUNIAS] 1x

<2459> Ἰοῦστος ***Ioustos*** [JUSTUS] 3x

<2460> ἱππεύς ***hippeus*** [HORSEMAN 1] 2x

<2461> ἱππικόν ***hippikon*** [HORSEMAN 2] 1x

<2462> ἵππος ***hippos*** [HORSE 1] 17x

<2463> ἶρις ***iris*** [RAINBOW] 2x

<2464> Ἰσαάκ ***Isaak*** [ISAAC] 20x

<2465> ἰσάγγελος ***isangelos*** [equal unto angels, like angels: ANGEL 2] 1x

<2466> Ἰσαχάρ ***Isachar*** [ISSACHAR] 1x

<2467> ἴσημι ***isēmi*** [KNOW 12] 2x

<2468> ἴσθι ***isthi*** [BE THOU 2] 5x

<2469> Ἰσκαριώθης ***Iskariōthēs*** [ISCARIOT] 11x

<2470> ἴσος ***isos*** [to not agree: AGREE 6, EQUAL 1, the like: LIKE (adj., adv., noun) 1, SAME 2] 8x

<2471> ἰσότης ***isotēs*** [EQUALITY 1, what is fair: FAIR 1] 3x

<2472> ἰσότιμος ***isotimos*** [like precious, as precious: PRECIOUS 2] 1x

<2473> ἰσόψυχος ***isopsuchos*** [LIKEMINDED 1] 1x

<2474> Ἰσραήλ ***Israēl*** [ISRAEL] 69x

<2475> Ἰσραηλίτης ***Israēlitēs*** [ISRAELITE] 9x

<2476> ἵστημι ***histēmi*** [APPOINT 2, to bring before: BRING 30, CHARGE (verb) 3, to count out: COUNT 5, ESTABLISH 2, SET (verb) 2, to stand, to stand still, to stand up: STAND (verb) 1, STOP 1] 154x

<2477> ἱστορέω ***historeō*** [to make acquaintance: ACQUAINTANCE 2] 1x
<2478> ἰσχυρός ***ischuros*** [GREAT 6, strong man: MAN 6, MIGHTY (adj.) 2, STRONG (adj.) 2] 29x
<2478> ἰσχυρότερος ***ischuroteros*** [stronger: STRONG (adj.) 3] 2x
<2479> ἰσχύς ***ischus*** [STRENGTH 2] 10x
<2480> ἰσχύω ***ischuō*** [to be able: ABLE 4, to be good: GOOD (adj. and noun) 11, to be healthy: HEALTHY 1, OVERPOWER 1, PREVAIL 1, to be strong enough: STRONG (adj.) 5, to be of value: VALUE (noun) 2] 29x
<2481> ἴσως ***isōs*** [PERHAPS 3] 1x
<2482> Ἰταλία ***Italia*** [ITALY] 4x
<2483> Ἰταλικός ***Italikos*** [ITALIAN] 1x
<2484> Ἰτουραία ***Itouraia*** [ITURAEA] 1x
<2485> ἰχθύδιον ***ichthudion*** [small fish, little fish: FISH 2] 2x
<2486> ἰχθύς ***ichthus*** [FISH 1] 20x
<2487> ἴχνος ***ichnos*** [STEP (noun) 1] 3x
<2488> Ἰωαθάμ ***Iōatham*** [JOTHAM] 2x
<2489> Ἰωάννα ***Iōanna*** [JOANNA] 2x
<2490> Ἰωαννᾶς ***Iōannas*** [JOANAN] 1x
<2491> Ἰωάννης ***Iōannēs*** [JOHN] 135x
<2492> Ἰώβ ***Iōb*** [JOB (name)] 1x
<2493> Ἰωήλ ***Iōēl*** [JOEL] 1x
<2494> Ἰωνάμ ***Iōnam*** [JONAM] 1x
<2495> Ἰωνᾶς ***Iōnas*** [JONAH] 11x
<2496> Ἰωράμ ***Iōram*** [JORAM] 2x
<2497> Ἰωρείμ ***Iōreim*** [JOREIM] 1x
<2498> Ἰωσαφάτ ***Iōsaphat*** [JEHOSHAPHAT] 2x
<2499> Ἰωσή ***Iōsē*** [JOSHUA] 1x
<2500> Ἰωσῆς ***Iōsēs*** [JOSES 1] 6x
<2501> Ἰωσήφ ***Iōsēph*** [JOSEPH] 35x
<2502> Ἰωσίας ***Iōsias*** [JOSIAH] 2x
<2503> ἰῶτα ***iōta*** [IOTA] 1x

K

<2504> κἀγώ ***kagō*** [I ALSO] 76x
<2505> καθά ***katha*** [ACCORDING AS 1] 1x
<2506> καθαίρεσις ***kathairesis*** [DESTRUCTION 2] 3x
<2507> καθαιρέω ***kathaireō*** [DESTROY 3, to pull down: PULL 4, to put down: PUT 9, to take down: TAKE 22] 9x
<2508> καθαίρω ***kathairō*** [PRUNE, PURIFY 2] 2x
<2509> καθάπερ ***kathaper*** [AS, EVEN AS, AS WELL AS] 13x
<2510> καθάπτω ***kathaptō*** [FASTEN 3] 1x
<2511> καθαρίζω ***katharizō*** [CLEANSE 1, PURIFY 4] 31x
<2512> καθαρισμός ***katharismos*** [PURIFICATION 2] 7x
<2513> καθαρός ***katharos*** [CLEAN (adj.) 1, PURE 5] 27x
<2514> καθαρότης ***katharotēs*** [PURITY 3] 1x
<2515> καθέδρα ***kathedra*** [SEAT (noun) 1] 3x
<2516> καθέζομαι ***kathezomai*** [SIT 6] 6x
<2517> καθεξῆς ***kathexēs*** [in order, in consecutive order: ORDER (noun) 2, SUCCESSIVELY] 5x
<2518> καθεύδω ***katheudō*** [to be asleep, to sleep, to fall asleep: SLEEP (verb) 2] 22x
<2519> καθηγητής ***kathēgētēs*** [TEACHER 3] 2x
<2520> καθήκω ***kathēkō*** [FITTING (BE) 2] 2x
<2521> κάθημαι ***kathēmai*** [DWELL 8, SIT 1] 91x

<2522> καθημερινός ***kathēmerinos*** [DAILY 3] 1x

<2523> καθίζω ***kathizō*** [CONTINUE 8, to appoint to judge: JUDGE (verb) 5, to sit, to sit down, to sit over: SIT 3, TARRY 3] 46x

<2524> καθίημι ***kathiēmi*** [to let down: LET 2] 4x

<2525> καθίστημι ***kathistēmi*** [APPOINT 3, CONDUCT (verb)[2], to make, to make ruler, to make oneself: MAKE 9, RENDER 3] 21x

<2526> καθό ***katho*** [according, according to what: ACCORDING 2] 3x

<2527> καθόλου ***katholou*** [AT ALL] 1x

<2528> καθοπλίζω ***kathoplizō*** [to be armed, to be fully armed: ARMED] 1x

<2529> καθοράω ***kathoraō*** [to see clearly: SEE 6] 1x

<2530> καθότι ***kathoti*** [ACCORDING AS 2, FORASMUCH 2] 5x

<2531> καθώς ***kathōs*** [ACCORDING AS 3] 182x

<2532> καί ***kai*** [AND] 9,000x +

<2533> Καϊάφας ***Kaiaphas*** [CAIAPHAS] 9x

<2534> καί γε ***kai ge*** [INDEED 1] 2x

<2535> Κάϊν ***Kain*** [CAIN] 3x

<2536> Καϊνάν ***Kainan*** [CAINAN] 2x

<2537> καινός ***kainos*** [NEW 2, NEW CREATION] 44x

<2538> καινότης ***kainotēs*** [NEWNESS] 2x

<2539> καίπερ ***kaiper*** [THOUGH, THOUGH INDEED 1] 6x

<2540> καιρός ***kairos*** [OCCASION 2, due season, convenient season, time, convenient time, due time, proper time, right time: SEASON (noun) 1, TIME 1] 85x

<2541> Καῖσαρ ***Kaisar*** [CAESAR] 29x

<2542> Καισάρεια ***Kaisareia*** [CAESAREA, CAESAREA PHILIPPI] 17x

<2543> καίτοι ***kaitoi*** [NEVERTHELESS 2] 1x

<2544> καίτοιγε ***kaitoige*** [ALTHOUGH] 3x

<2545> καίω ***kaiō*** [BURN 1, LIGHT (verb) 2] 12x

<2546> κἀκεῖ ***kakei*** [AND THERE] 11x

<2547> κἀκεῖθεν ***kakeithen*** [AND FROM THERE, AND FROM THAT TIME] 9x

<2548> κἀκεῖνος ***kakeinos*** [AND HE, AND SHE, AND IT] 22x

<2549> κακία ***kakia*** [MALICE 1, TROUBLE (noun) 2, WICKEDNESS 1] 11x

<2550> κακοήθεια ***kakoētheia*** [EVIL-MINDEDNESS] 1x

<2551> κακολογέω ***kakologeō*** [CURSE (verb) 3, to speak evil: EVIL (adv.) 2, to speak ill, to speak evil: SPEAK 5] 4x

<2552> κακοπάθεια ***kakopatheia*** [SUFFERING 2] 1x

<2553> κακοπαθέω ***kakopatheō*** [to endure hardship, to suffer hardship: HARDSHIP 1, to suffer; to suffer evil, hardship, trouble: SUFFER 7] 4x

<2554> κακοποιέω ***kakopoieō*** [to do evil: EVIL (adv.) 3] 4x

<2555> κακοποιός ***kakopoios*** [EVILDOER 1] 5x

<2556> κακός ***kakos*** [EVIL (adj.) 1, EVIL (noun) 1, HARM (noun) 1 (*kakon*), WICKED (noun) 1] 50x

<2557> κακοῦργος ***kakourgos*** [CRIMINAL 1] 4x

<2558> κακουχέω ***kakoucheō*** [TORMENTED (BE)] 2x

<2559> κακόω ***kakoō*** [HURT 3, OPPRESS 2, POISON (verb) 1] 6x

<2560> κακῶς ***kakōs*** [MISERABLY, SEVERELY 2, SICK (adv.) 1, SICK (adv.) 4] 16x

<2561> κάκωσις ***kakōsis*** [OPPRESSION] 1x

<2562> καλάμη ***kalamē*** [STUBBLE] 1x

<2563> κάλαμος ***kalamos*** [PEN[1], REED] 12x

<2564> καλέω ***kaleō*** [CALL (verb) 1, INVITE 1] 146x

<2565> καλλιέλαιος ***kallielaios*** [good olive tree: OLIVE TREE 3] 1x

<2566> καλλίον ***kallion*** [VERY WELL 1] 1x

<2567> καλοδιδάσκαλος ***kalodidaskalos*** [teacher of good things, of what is right: TEACHER 2] 1x

<2568> Καλοὶ Λιμένες ***Kaloi Limenes*** [FAIR HAVENS] 1x

<2569> καλοποιέω ***kalopoieō*** [to do well: WELL (adv.) 4] 1x

<2570> καλός ***kalos*** [BEAUTIFUL 2, BETTER 1, GOOD (adj.) 2, GOOD (adj. and noun) 3, HONEST 1, it is meet: MEET (adj.) 3, WORTHY 6] 101x

<2571> κάλυμμα ***kalumma*** [VEIL (noun) 1] 4x

<2572> καλύπτω ***kaluptō*** [COVER 1, VEIL (verb)] 8x

<2573> καλῶς ***kalōs*** [COMMENDABLY, in a good place: PLACE (noun) 6, WELL (adv.) 1] 37x

<2574> κάμηλος ***kamēlos*** [CAMEL] 6x

<2575> κάμινος ***kaminos*** [FURNACE 1] 4x

<2576> καμμύω ***kammuō*** [CLOSE (verb) 1] 2x

<2577> κάμνω ***kamnō*** [to be sick: SICK (adv.) 3, to become, to grow weary: WEARY (adj.) 3] 2x

<2578> κάμπτω ***kamptō*** [BOW (verb) 1] 4x

<2579> κἄν ***kan*** [IF (AND, ALSO)] 17x

<2580> Κανά ***Kana*** [CANA] 4x

<2581> Καναναῖος, Κανανίτης ***Kananaios, Kananitēs*** [CANANITE] 2x

<2582> Κανδάκη ***Kandakē*** [CANDACE] 1x

<2583> κανών ***kanōn*** [RULE (noun) 1] 5x

<2584> Καπερναούμ, Καφαρναούμ ***Kapernaoum, Kapharnaoum*** [CAPERNAUM] 16x

<2585> καπηλεύω ***kapēleuō*** [PEDDLE] 1x

<2586> καπνός ***kapnos*** [SMOKE] 13x

<2587> Καππαδοκία ***Kappadokia*** [CAPPADOCIA] 2x

<2588> καρδία ***kardia*** [HEART 1] 158x

<2589> καρδιογνώστης ***kardiognōstēs*** [who knows the hearts: HEART 2] 2x

<2590> καρπός ***karpos*** [FRUIT 1] 66x

<2591> Κάρπος ***Karpos*** [CARPUS] 1x

<2592> καρποφορέω ***karpophoreō*** [to bear fruit, to bring forth fruit: FRUIT 3] 8x

<2593> καρποφόρος ***karpophoros*** [FRUITFUL 1] 1x

<2594> καρτερέω ***kartereō*** [PERSEVERE 2] 1x

<2595> κάρφος ***karphos*** [speck, speck of sawdust: SPECK] 6x

<2596> κατά ***kata*** [ACCORDING 1, ALONG, CONCERNING 1, EXCEEDINGLY 6, PRIVATELY 2, in various: VARIOUS 2] 472x

<2597> καταβαίνω ***katabainō*** [to come down: COME 20, DESCEND 1, to fall, to fall down: FALL (verb) 11, to go down: GO 19, to step down: STEP (verb) 3] 81x

<2598> καταβάλλω ***kataballō*** [to cast down, to cast out: CAST (verb) 5, LAY 17] 3x

<2599> καταβαρέω ***katabareō*** [BURDEN (verb) 2, to be heavy: HEAVY 3] 2x

<2600> κατάβασις ***katabasis*** [DESCENT 1] 1x

<2601> καταβιβάζω ***katabibazō*** [DESCEND 2] 2x

<2602> καταβολή ***katabolē*** [conception: CONCEIVE 3, FOUNDATION 2] 11x

<2603> καταβραβεύω ***katabrabeuō*** [to defraud of the prize: DEFRAUD 2] 1x

<2604> καταγγελεύς ***katangeleus*** [PROCLAIMER] 1x

<2605> καταγγέλλω ***katangellō*** [PREACH 2, PROCLAIM 1] 17x

<2606> καταγελάω ***katagelaō*** [to laugh at, to laugh to scorn: LAUGH 2] 3x

<2607> καταγινώσκω ***kataginōskō*** [CONDEMN 1] 3x

<2608> κατάγνυμι ***katagnumi*** [BREAK 5] 4x

<2609> κατάγω ***katagō*** [to bring, to bring down: BRING 7, LAND (verb) 1, TOUCH 3] 9x

<2610> καταγωνίζομαι ***katagōnizomai*** [CONQUER 1] 1x

<2611> καταδέω ***katadeō*** [to bind up: BIND 3] 1x

<2612> κατάδηλος ***katadēlos*** [EVIDENT 3] 1x

<2613> καταδικάζω ***katadikazō*** [CONDEMN 3] 5x

<2614> καταδιώκω ***katadiōkō*** [to follow after: FOLLOW 8] 1x

<2615> καταδουλόω ***katadouloō*** [to bring into bondage: BONDAGE 4] 2x

<2616> καταδυναστεύω ***katadunasteuō*** [OPPRESS 3] 2x

<2617> καταισχύνω ***kataischunō*** [to make ashamed: ASHAMED 1, ASHAMED (BE) 3, DISHONOR (verb) 2, to put to shame: SHAME (noun) 4] 13x

<2618> κατακαίω ***katakaiō*** [BURN 3] 13x

<2619> κατακαλύπτω ***katakaluptō*** [COVER 3] 3x

<2620> κατακαυχάομαι ***katakauchaomai*** [GLORIFY 5] 4x

<2621> κατάκειμαι ***katakeimai*** [to be lying: BEDRIDDEN (BE), LAY 10, LIE (verb)[1] 3, to sit at table: SIT 11, to be, to lie, to recline, to sit at the table: TABLE[1] 3] 12x

<2622> κατακλάω ***kataklaō*** [BREAK 4] 2x

<2623> κατακλείω ***katakleiō*** [to shut up: SHUT 3] 2x

<2624> κατακληροδοτέω ***kataklērodoteō*** [to give as an inheritance: INHERITANCE 3] 1x

<2624a> κατακληρονομέω ***kataklēronomeō*** [to give as an inheritance: INHERITANCE 4] 1x

<2625> κατακλίνω ***kataklinō*** [to sit down: SIT 9, to be at table, to lay oneself down at table: TABLE[1] 6] 4x

<2626> κατακλύζω ***katakluzō*** [DELUGE] 1x

<2627> κατακλυσμός ***kataklusmos*** [FLOOD (noun) 1] 4x

<2628> κατακολουθέω ***katakoloutheō*** [to come along with, to come with: COME 30, FOLLOW 4] 2x

<2629> κατακόπτω ***katakoptō*** [CUT 5] 1x

<2630> κατακρημνίζω ***katakrēmnizō*** [to throw down: THROW (verb) 6] 1x

<2631> κατάκριμα ***katakrima*** [CONDEMNATION 1] 3x

<2632> κατακρίνω ***katakrinō*** [CONDEMN 4, JUDGE (verb) 6] 19x

<2633> κατάκρισις ***katakrisis*** [CONDEMNATION 2] 2x

<2634> κατακυριεύω ***katakurieuō*** [to lord over, to be lord of: LORD (verb) 1, OVERPOWER 2] 4x

<2635> καταλαλέω ***katalaleō*** [to speak against, maliciously, evil: SPEAK 8] 5x

<2636> καταλαλιά ***katalalia*** [BACKBITING] 2x

<2637> κατάλαλος ***katalalos*** [BACKBITER] 1x

<2638> καταλαμβάνω ***katalambanō*** [ATTAIN 1, CATCH (verb) 5, COMPREHEND 1, FIND 3, to lay hold, to take hold: HOLD (noun) 2, OBTAIN 3, OVERTAKE 2, PERCEIVE 2, SEIZE 7] 15x

<2639> καταλέγω ***katalegō*** [to put on the list: LIST (noun)] 1x

<2640> κατάλειμμα ***kataleimma*** [REMNANT 2] 1x

<2641> καταλείπω ***kataleipō*** [LEAVE (verb) 6, RESERVE 2] 25x

<2642> καταλιθάζω ***katalithazō*** [STONE (verb) 2] 1x

<2643> καταλλαγή ***katallagē*** [RECONCILIATION 1] 4x

<2644> καταλλάσσω ***katallassō*** [RECONCILE 2] 6x

<2645> κατάλοιπος ***kataloipos*** [the remnant: REMNANT 4] 1x

<2646> κατάλυμα ***kataluma*** [GUEST ROOM 1, INN 1] 3x

<2647> καταλύω ***kataluō*** [DESTROY 11, LODGE 1, to throw down: THROW (verb) 5] 17x

<2648> καταμανθάνω ***katamanthanō*** [CONSIDER 7] 1x

<2649> καταμαρτυρέω ***katamartureō*** [to testify against: TESTIFY 3] 4x

<2650> καταμένω ***katamenō*** [STAY (verb) 8] 1x

<2651> καταμόνας ***katamonas*** [ALONE 2] 2x

<2652> κατανάθεμα ***katanathema*** [CURSE (noun) 1] 1x

<2653> καταθεματίζω ***katathematizō*** [CURSE (verb) 2] 1x

<2654> καταναλίσκω ***katanaliskō*** [to consume: CONSUMING] 1x

<2655> καταναρκάω ***katanarkaō*** [to be burdensome: BURDENSOME 3] 3x

<2656> κατανεύω ***kataneuō*** [SIGNAL (verb)] 1x

<2657> κατανοέω ***katanoeō*** [CONSIDER 9, DISCOVER 1, PERCEIVE 4] 14x

<2658> καταντάω ***katantaō*** [ARRIVE 1, ATTAIN 2, COME 31] 13x

<2659> κατάνυξις ***katanuxis*** [STUPOR 1] 1x

<2660> κατανύσσω ***katanussō*** [PRICK 1] 1x

<2661> καταξιόω ***kataxioō*** [to count, to consider, to account worthy: WORTHY 3] 4x

<2662> καταπατέω ***katapateō*** [to tread, to tread underfoot: TREAD 3] 5x

<2663> κατάπαυσις ***katapausis*** [REST (noun)[1] 4] 8x

<2664> καταπαύω ***katapauō*** [to give rest, to bring into rest: REST (noun)[1] 5, REST (verb) 3, RESTRAIN 1] 4x

<2665> καταπέτασμα ***katapetasma*** [VEIL (noun) 2] 6x

<2666> καταπίνω ***katapinō*** [DEVOUR 3, DROWN 1, to swallow up: SWALLOW 1] 7x

<2667> καταπίπτω ***katapiptō*** [to fall down: FALL (verb) 6] 3x

<2668> καταπλέω ***katapleō*** [ARRIVE 2] 1x
<2669> καταπονέω ***kataponeō*** [OPPRESSED (BE) 1, VEXED (BE) 1] 2x
<2670> καταποντίζω ***katapontizō*** [to be sunk in the depth of the sea, to sink: DEPTH 2, SINK (verb) 2] 2x
<2671> κατάρα ***katara*** [CURSE (noun) 2] 6x
<2672> καταράομαι ***kataraomai*** [CURSE (verb) 4, to curse: CURSED 2] 6x
<2673> καταργέω ***katargeō*** [ABOLISH 1, to do away: AWAY 1, CEASE 2, to come to nothing: COME 32, DESTROY 4, to make of no effect, to make without effect, to become of no effect: EFFECT (noun) 3, to render powerless: POWERLESS 2, to put away, to put behind: PUT 10, RELEASE (verb) 2, to use up: USE (verb) 2] 27x
<2674> καταριθμέω ***katarithmeō*** [NUMBER (verb) 2] 1x
<2675> καταρτίζω ***katartizō*** [MEND, to be perfect, to make perfect: PERFECT (adj.) 3, PERFECT (verb) 2, PERFECTED (BE), to perfectly unite, to perfectly join: PERFECTLY 2, PREPARE 3, to prepare: PREPARED 1, RESTORE 3, SUPPLY (verb) 2] 13x
<2676> κατάρτισις ***katartisis*** [PERFECTING 1] 1x
<2677> καταρτισμός ***katartismos*** [PERFECTING 2] 1x
<2678> κατασείω ***kataseiō*** [to make a sign: SIGN 3] 4x
<2679> κατασκάπτω ***kataskaptō*** [to dig down: DIG 5, to ruin: RUIN (noun) 4] 2x
<2680> κατασκευάζω ***kataskeuazō*** [BUILD 1, MAKE 3, PREPARE 4] 11x
<2681> κατασκηνόω ***kataskēnoō*** [DWELL 10, NEST (verb)] 4x
<2682> κατασκήνωσις ***kataskēnōsis*** [NEST (noun) 1] 2x
<2683> κατασκιάζω ***kataskiazō*** [SHADOW (verb)] 1x
<2684> κατασκοπέω ***kataskopeō*** [to spy out: SPY (verb)] 1x
<2685> κατάσκοπος ***kataskopos*** [SPY (noun) 2] 1x
<2686> κατασοφίζομαι ***katasophizomai*** [to deal treacherously: DEAL 1] 1x
<2687> καταστέλλω ***katastellō*** [APPEASE 1] or [to be calm, to keep calm: CALM (adj. and noun) 2] 2x
<2688> κατάστημα ***katastēma*** [BEHAVIOR 1] 1x
<2689> καταστολή ***katastolē*** [APPAREL 2] 1x
<2690> καταστρέφω ***katastrephō*** [OVERTURN 2] 2x
<2691> καταστρηνιάω ***katastrēniaō*** [to wax wanton: WANTON 1] 1x
<2692> καταστροφή ***katastrophē*** [RUIN (noun) 1] 2x
<2693> καταστρώννυμι ***katastrōnnumi*** [to lay low: LAY 18] 1x
<2694> κατασύρω ***katasurō*** [DRAG 3] 1x
<2695> κατασφάζω ***katasphazō*** [KILL 5] 1x
<2696> κατασφραγίζω ***katasphragizō*** [SEAL (verb) 2] 1x
<2697> κατάσχεσις ***kataschesis*** [POSSESSION 1] 2x
<2698> κατατίθημι ***katatithēmi*** [ACQUIRE 1, LAY 5] 3x
<2699> κατατομή ***katatomē*** [CONCISION] 1x
<2700> κατατοξεύω ***katatoxeuō*** [SHOOT (verb) 1] 1x
<2701> κατατρέχω ***katatrechō*** [to run down: RUN 3] 1x
<2702> καταφέρω ***katapherō*** [CAST (verb) 11, FALL (verb) 17] 4x
<2703> καταφεύγω ***katapheugō*** [to flee, to flee for refuge: FLEE 3] 2x
<2704> καταφθείρω ***kataphtheirō*** [CORRUPT (verb) 3, PERISH 6] 2x
<2705> καταφιλέω ***kataphileō*** [KISS (verb) 2] 6x
<2706> καταφρονέω ***kataphroneō*** [DESPISE 2] 9x
<2707> καταφρονητής ***kataphronētēs*** [DESPISER 1] 1x
<2708> καταχέω ***katacheō*** [POUR 4] 2x
<2709> καταχθόνιος ***katachthonios*** [under the earth: EARTH 2] 1x
<2710> καταχράομαι ***katachraomai*** [to make use, to make full use: USE (verb) 6] 2x
<2711> καταψύχω ***katapsuchō*** [COOL] 1x
<2712> κατείδωλος ***kateidōlos*** [full of idols: IDOL 4] 1x
<2713> κατέναντι ***katenanti*** [OPPOSITE 3] 5x
<2714> κατενώπιον ***katenōpion*** [PRESENCE OF (IN THE VERY)] 5x

<2715> κατεξουσιάζω ***katexousiazō*** [to exercise authority: AUTHORITY 3] 2x

<2716> κατεργάζομαι ***katergazomai*** [ACCOMPLISH 2, COMMIT 2, DO 4, MAKE 4, PREPARE 6, PRODUCE 4, WORK (verb) 3] 22x

<2717> Omitted in Strong's Dictionary

<2718> κατέρχομαι ***katerchomai*** [to come, to come down: COME 10, DESCEND 3, to go, to go down, to depart: GO 12, LAND (verb) 2] 16x

<2719> κατεσθίω ***katesthiō*** [DEVOUR 2] 15x

<2720> κατευθύνω ***kateuthunō*** [DIRECT 2, GUIDE (verb) 1] 3x

<2721> κατεφίστημι ***katephistēmi*** [to rise up against: RISE (verb) 5] 1x

<2722> κατέχω ***katechō*** [FAST (HOLD) 2, HAVE 3, to hold, to hold firmly: HOLD (verb) 4, to keep, to keep back: KEEP (verb) 6, POSSESS 3, to make for the shore: SHORE 4, TAKE 30] 17x

<2723> κατηγορέω ***katēgoreō*** [ACCUSE 3] 23x

<2724> κατηγορία ***katēgoria*** [ACCUSATION 2, ACCUSE 6] 4x

<2725> κατήγορος ***katēgoros*** [ACCUSER 1] 7x

<2726> κατήφεια ***katēpheia*** [GLOOM 1] 1x

<2727> κατηχέω ***katēcheō*** [to be informed: INFORM 2, TEACH 3] 8x

<2728> κατιόω ***katioō*** [RUSTED (BE)] 1x

<2729> κατισχύω ***katischuō*** [to prevail, to prevail against: PREVAIL 2] 2x

<2730> κατοικέω ***katoikeō*** [DWELL 3, STAY (verb) 5] 44x

<2731> κατοίκησις ***katoikēsis*** [DWELLING 1] 1x

<2732> κατοικητήριον ***katoikētērion*** [DWELLING PLACE 2] 2x

<2733> κατοικία ***katoikia*** [HABITATION 1] 1x

<2734> κατοπτρίζω ***katoptrizō*** [BEHOLD (verb) 5] 1x

<2735> κατόρθωμα ***katorthōma*** [excellent measures: MEASURE (noun) 6] 1x

<2736> κάτω, κάτωτέρω ***katō, katōterō*** [DOWNWARDS] 11x

<2737> κατώτερος ***katōteros*** [LOWER (adj.) 1] 1x

<2738> καῦμα ***kauma*** [HEAT 3] 2x

<2739> καυματίζω ***kaumatizō*** [SCORCH] 4x

<2740> καῦσις ***kausis*** [burning: BURN 4] 1x

<2741> καυσόω ***kausoō*** [to burn with fervent heat, to be destroyed with intense heat, to be destroyed by fire: HEAT 5] 2x

<2742> καύσων ***kausōn*** [burning heat, scorching heat, heat: HEAT 4] 3x

<2743> καυτηριάζω ***kautēriazō*** [to sear with a hot (or: branding) iron: IRON 3] 1x

<2744> καυχάομαι ***kauchaomai*** [GLORIFY 4] 38x

<2745> καύχημα ***kauchēma*** [BOAST (noun) 1, BOASTING 1, something to boast: GLORIFY 6] 11x

<2746> καύχησις ***kauchēsis*** [BOASTING 2, reason to glorify: GLORIFY 7] 11x

<2747> Κεγχρεαί ***Kenchreai*** [CENCHREA] 2x

<2748> Κεδρών ***Kedrōn*** [KIDRON] 1x

<2749> κεῖμαι ***keimai*** [APPOINT 4, LAID OUT (BE), LAY 7, LIE (verb)[1] 1, SITUATE, STAND (verb) 6] 24x

<2750> κειρία ***keiria*** [GRAVECLOTHES] 1x

<2751> κείρω ***keirō*** [SHEAR] 4x

<2752> κέλευσμα ***keleusma*** [SHOUT (noun) 1] 1x

<2753> κελεύω ***keleuō*** [COMMAND (verb) 7] 27x

<2754> κενοδοξία ***kenodoxia*** [vain glory: VAIN 4] 1x

<2755> κενόδοξος ***kenodoxos*** [CONCEITED 1] 1x

<2756> κενός ***kenos*** [EMPTY-HANDED, VAIN 1] 18x

<2757> κενοφωνία ***kenophōnia*** [idle babbling: BABBLING] 2x

<2758> κενόω ***kenoō*** [to make oneself of no reputation: REPUTATION 2, to make vain: VAIN 3, to make void: VOID 1] 5x

<2759> κέντρον ***kentron*** [STING (noun)] 4x

<2760> κεντυρίων ***kenturiōn*** [CENTURION 2] 3x

<2761> κενῶς ***kenōs*** [in vain: VAIN 2] 1x

<2762> κεραία ***keraia*** [TITTLE] 2x
<2763> κεραμεύς ***kerameus*** [POTTER 1] 3x
<2764> κεραμικός ***keramikos*** [of pottery: POTTERY 1] 1x
<2765> κεράμιον ***keramion*** [PITCHER 1] 2x
<2766> κέραμος ***keramos*** [TILE] 1x
<2767> κεράννυμι ***kerannumi*** [MIX 1, to pour out: POUR 5] 3x
<2768> κέρας ***keras*** [HORN] 11x
<2769> κεράτιον ***keration*** [HUSK] 1x
<2770> κερδαίνω ***kerdainō*** [GAIN (verb) 2, INCUR 1, MAKE 5] 17x
<2771> κέρδος ***kerdos*** [GAIN (noun) 2] 3x
<2772> κέρμα ***kerma*** [MONEY 1] 1x
<2773> κερματιστής ***kermatistēs*** [MONEYCHANGER 2] 1x
<2774> κεφάλαιον ***kephalaion*** [SUM 1] 2x
<2775> κεφαλαιόω ***kephalaioō*** [to strike on the head, to wound in the head: HEAD (noun) 2] 1x
<2776> κεφαλή ***kephalē*** [CHIEF CORNERSTONE 2, CORNER STONE 1, HEAD (noun) 1] 75x
<2777> κεφαλίς ***kephalis*** [SCROLL 1] 1x
<2778> κῆνσος ***kēnsos*** [TRIBUTE 1] 4x
<2779> κῆπος ***kēpos*** [GARDEN] 5x
<2780> κηπουρός ***kēpouros*** [GARDENER 1] 1x
<2781> κηρίον ***kērion*** [COMB] 1x
<2782> κήρυγμα ***kērugma*** [PREACHING 1] 8x
<2783> κῆρυξ ***kērux*** [HERALD] 3x
<2784> κηρύσσω ***kērussō*** [PREACH 5, PROCLAIM 2, PUBLISH 1] 61x
<2785> κῆτος ***kētos*** [WHALE] 1x
<2786> Κηφᾶς ***Kēphas*** [CEPHAS] 9x
<2787> κιβωτός ***kibōtos*** [ARK] 6x
<2788> κιθάρα ***kithara*** [HARP (noun) 1] 4x
<2789> κιθαρίζω ***kitharizō*** [to play the harp, to play on the harp: HARP (noun) 2] 2x
<2790> κιθαρῳδός ***kitharōdos*** [HARPIST] 2x
<2791> Κιλικία ***Kilikia*** [CILICIA] 8x
<2792> κινάμωμον ***kinamōmon*** [CINNAMON] 1x
<2793> κινδυνεύω ***kinduneuō*** [to be in danger, to be in great danger: DANGER 2, to stand in jeopardy: JEOPARDY] 4x
<2794> κίνδυνος ***kindunos*** [DANGER 1] 2x
<2795> κινέω ***kineō*** [DISTURB 1, MOVE 1, REMOVE 2, SHAKE 2] 8x
<2796> κίνησις ***kinēsis*** [MOVING] 1x
<2797> Κίς ***Kis*** [KISH] 1x
<2798> κλάδος ***klados*** [BRANCH 2] 11x
<2799> κλαίω ***klaiō*** [WEEP 2] 39x
<2800> κλάσις ***klasis*** [BREAKING 1] 2x
<2801> κλάσμα ***klasma*** [FRAGMENT] 9x
<2802> Κλαύδα ***Klauda*** [CLAUDA] 1x
<2803> Κλαυδία ***Klaudia*** [CLAUDIA] 1x
<2804> Κλαύδιος ***Klaudios*** [CLAUDIUS] 3x
<2805> κλαυθμός ***klauthmos*** [weeping: WEEP 3, WEEPING] 9x
<2806> κλάω ***klaō*** [BREAK 2, BREAK BREAD] 14x
<2807> κλείς ***kleis*** [KEY] 6x
<2808> κλείω ***kleiō*** [to shut up: SHUT 1] 16x
<2809> κλέμμα ***klemma*** [THEFT 1] 1x
<2810> Κλεοπᾶς ***Kleopas*** [CLEOPAS] 1x
<2811> κλέος ***kleos*** [GLORY (noun) 2] 1x
<2812> κλέπτης ***kleptēs*** [THIEF 1] 16x
<2813> κλέπτω ***kleptō*** [STEAL 1] 13x
<2814> κλῆμα ***klēma*** [BRANCH 3] 4x

<2815> Κλήμης ***Klēmēs*** [CLEMENT] 1x

<2816> κληρονομέω ***klēronomeō*** [INHERIT] 18x

<2817> κληρονομία ***klēronomia*** [INHERITANCE 1] 14x

<2818> κληρονόμος ***klēronomos*** [HEIR 1] 15x

<2819> κλῆρος ***klēros*** [one who is entrusted to the charge (of another): ENTRUST 3, INHERITANCE 2, LOT (noun) 1, PART (noun) 1] 11x

<2820> κληρόω ***klēroō*** [to obtain an inheritance: INHERITANCE 5] 1x

<2821> κλῆσις ***klēsis*** [CALLING 1] 11x

<2822> κλητός ***klētos*** [CALLED 1] 11x

<2823> κλίβανος ***klibanos*** [OVEN] 2x

<2824> κλίμα ***klima*** [REGION 1] 3x

<2824a> κλινάριον ***klinarion*** [little bed: BED 2] 1x

<2825> κλίνη ***klinē*** [BED 1] 9x

<2826> κλινίδιον ***klinidion*** [little bed: BED 3] 2x

<2827> κλίνω ***klinō*** [to bow, to bow down: BOW (verb) 3, to put to flight, to turn to flight: FLIGHT 2, LAY 11, to wear away: WEAR 2] 7x

<2828> κλισία ***klisia*** [COMPANY (noun) 1] 1x

<2829> κλοπή ***klopē*** [THEFT 2] 2x

<2830> κλύδων ***kludōn*** [WAVE 1] 2x

<2831> κλυδωνίζομαι ***kludōnizomai*** [TOSS 2] 1x

<2832> Κλωπᾶς ***Klōpas*** [CLOPAS] 1x

<2833> κνήθω ***knēthō*** [ITCHING] 1x

<2834> Κνίδος ***Knidos*** [CNIDUS] 1x

<2835> κοδράντης ***kodrantēs*** [QUADRANS] 2x

<2836> κοιλία ***koilia*** [STOMACH 1, WOMB 2] 22x

<2837> κοιμάω ***koimaō*** [to sleep, to fall asleep: SLEEP (verb) 3] 18x

<2838> κοίμησις ***koimēsis*** [rest, taking rest: REST (noun)[1] 6] 1x

<2839> κοινός ***koinos*** [COMMON 1, UNCLEAN 3] 12x

<2840> κοινόω ***koinoō*** [to call common, to make common: COMMON 2, DEFILE 1] 15x

<2841> κοινωνέω ***koinōneō*** [COMMUNICATE[1] 1, DISTRIBUTE 3, PARTICIPATE 1] 8x

<2842> κοινωνία ***koinōnia*** [sharing of good: COMMUNICATE[1] 2, CONTRIBUTION 1, fellowship: DISPENSATION 2, FELLOWSHIP 1, to give the right hand of fellowship: FELLOWSHIP 3, SHARING] 19x

<2843> κοινωνικός ***koinōnikos*** [ready to share, willing to share: SHARE (verb) 2] 1x

<2844> κοινωνός ***koinōnos*** [PARTAKER 1, PARTNER 1] 10x

<2845> κοίτη ***koitē*** [BED 4, LEWDNESS 2] 4x

<2846> κοιτών ***koitōn*** [CHAMBERLAIN 2] 1x

<2847> κόκκινος ***kokkinos*** [SCARLET] 6x

<2848> κόκκος ***kokkos*** [GRAIN OF MUSTARD, GRAIN OF WHEAT] 8x

<2849> κολάζω ***kolazō*** [PUNISH 2] 2x

<2850> κολακεία ***kolakeia*** [flattery: FLATTERING] 1x

<2851> κόλασις ***kolasis*** [TORMENT (noun) 3] 2x

<2852> κολαφίζω ***kolaphizō*** [to beat, to beat with the fists: BEAT 4] 5x

<2853> κολλάω ***kollaō*** [CLEAVE 1, CLING 1, to keep company: COMPANY (noun) 4, to join, to join oneself: JOIN 1, REACH (verb) 3] 11x

<2854> κολλούριον ***kollourion*** [EYESALVE] 1x

<2855> κολλυβιστής ***kollubistēs*** [changer, money changer, money-changer: MONEYCHANGER 1] 3x

<2856> κολοβόω ***koloboō*** [SHORTEN 1] 2x

<2857> Κολοσσαί ***Kolossai*** [COLOSSAE] 1x

<2858> Κολασσαεύς ***Kolassaeus*** [COLOSSIAN] 1x

<2859> κόλπος ***kolpos*** [BAY, BOSOM 1] 6x

<2860> κολυμβάω ***kolumbaō*** [SWIM 1] 1x

<2861> κολυμβήθρα ***kolumbēthra*** [POOL] 5x

<2862> κολωνία ***kolōnia*** [COLONY] 1x

<2863> κομάω ***komaō*** [to have long hair, to wear long hair: HAIR 4] 2x

<2864> κόμη ***komē*** [HAIR 3] 1x

<2865> κομίζω ***komizō*** [BRING 31, RECEIVE 17] 11x

<2866> κομψότερον ***kompsoteron*** [BETTER 4] 1x

<2867> κονιάω ***koniaō*** [WHITE (verb) 1, WHITEWASHED WALL] 2x

<2868> κονιορτός ***koniortos*** [DUST 1] 5x

<2869> κοπάζω ***kopazō*** [FALL (verb) 18] 3x

<2870> κοπετός ***kopetos*** [LAMENTATION 1] 1x

<2871> κοπή ***kopē*** [SLAUGHTER (noun) 1] 1x

<2872> κοπιάω ***kopiaō*** [LABOR (verb) 1, to be weary, to grow weary: WEARY (adj.) 4] 23x

<2873> κόπος ***kopos*** [LABOR (noun) 1, TROUBLE (noun) 3, to give trouble: TROUBLE (verb) 11] 18x

<2874> κοπρία ***kopria*** [DUNG (noun) 1] 2x

<2874a> κοπρίον ***koprion*** [DUNG 1] 1x

<2875> κόπτω ***koptō*** [to cut, to cut down: CUT 2, LAMENT 1, MOURN 2] 8x

<2876> κόραξ ***korax*** [RAVEN] 1x

<2877> κοράσιον ***korasion*** [girl, little girl: DAUGHTER 3] 8x

<2878> κορβᾶν ***korban*** [CORBAN] 1x

<2878a> κορβανᾶς ***korbanas*** [treasury, temple treasury: TREASURE (noun) 4] 1x

<2879> Κόρε ***Kore*** [KORAH] 1x

<2880> κορέννυμι ***korennumi*** [EAT 7, FILL (verb) 6] 2x

<2881> Κορίνθιος ***Korinthios*** [CORINTHIAN] 2x

<2882> Κόρινθος ***Korinthos*** [CORINTH] 6x

<2883> Κορνήλιος ***Kornēlios*** [CORNELIUS] 10x

<2884> κόρος ***koros*** [MEASURE (noun) 2] 1x

<2885> κοσμέω ***kosmeō*** [ADORN, TRIM] 10x

<2886> κοσμικός ***kosmikos*** [EARTHLY 2, WORLDLY 1] 2x

<2887> κόσμιος ***kosmios*** [modest apparel: APPAREL 2, RESPECTABLE] 2x

<2888> κοσμοκράτωρ ***kosmokratōr*** [RULER 4] 1x

<2889> κόσμος ***kosmos*** [ADORNMENT, WORLD 2] 186x

<2890> Κούαρτος ***Kouartos*** [QUARTUS] 1x

<2891> κοῦμι ***koumi*** [young girl: TALITHA KOUMI] 1x

<2892> κουστωδία ***koustōdia*** [GUARD (noun) 1] 3x

<2893> κουφίζω ***kouphizō*** [LIGHTEN 1] 1x

<2894> κόφινος ***kophinos*** [BASKET 1] 6x

<2895> κράβαττος ***krabattos*** [BED 5, COUCH] 12x

<2896> κράζω ***krazō*** [to cry, to cry out: CRY (verb) 4] 55x

<2897> κραιπάλη ***kraipalē*** [CAROUSING 1] 1x

<2898> Κρανίον ***Kranion*** [SKULL] 4x

<2899> κράσπεδον ***kraspedon*** [FRINGE] 5x

<2900> κραταιός ***krataios*** [MIGHTY (adj.) 3] 1x

<2901> κραταιόω ***krataioō*** [STRENGTHEN 4, STRONG (BE)] 4x

<2902> κρατέω ***krateō*** [FAST (HOLD) 3, GAIN (verb) 3, HOLD (verb) 1, KEEP (verb) 11, SEIZE 4, to take, to take hold, to lay hold: TAKE 37] 47x

<2903> κράτιστος ***kratistos*** [more excellent: EXCELLENT 4] 4x

<2904> κράτος ***kratos*** [MIGHT 1, POWER[3] 2, STRENGTH 3] 12x

<2905> κραυγάζω ***kraugazō*** [to cry, to cry out: CRY (verb) 6] 7x

<2906> κραυγή ***kraugē*** [CLAMOR, CRY (noun) 2] 6x

<2907> κρέας ***kreas*** [FLESH 2] 2x

<2908> κρεῖσσον ***kreisson*** [BETTER 2] 8x

<2909> κρείσσων ***kreissōn*** [BETTER 3] 12x

<2910> κρεμάννυμι ***kremannumi*** [HANG 2] 7x

<2911> κρημνός ***krēmnos*** [steep place: PLACE (noun) 7] 3x

<2912> Κρής ***Krēs*** [CRETAN] 2x

<2913> Κρήσκης ***Krēskēs*** [CRESCENS] 1x

<2914> Κρήτη ***Krētē*** [CRETE] 5x

<2915> κριθή ***krithē*** [BARLEY (noun)] 1x

<2916> κρίθινος ***krithinos*** [BARLEY (adj.)] 2x

<2917> κρίμα ***krima*** [CAUSE 2, FAULT 4, JUDGMENT 4, LAWSUIT] 27x

<2918> κρίνον ***krinon*** [LILY] 2x

<2919> κρίνω ***krinō*** [DECIDE 1, DETERMINE 4, ESTEEM (verb) 3, JUDGE (verb) 1, to be judged: JUDGMENT 6, to decide: SENTENCE 2, SUE, to prosecute one's suit: SUIT (noun) 1] 114x

<2920> κρίσις ***krisis*** [JUDGMENT 4] 47x

<2921> Κρίσπος ***Krispos*** [CRISPUS] 2x

<2922> κριτήριον ***kritērion*** [JUDGMENT 5, JUDGMENT SEAT 2] 3x

<2923> κριτής ***kritēs*** [JUDGE (noun) 2] 18x

<2924> κριτικός ***kritikos*** [DISCERNER] 1x

<2925> κρούω ***krouō*** [KNOCK] 9x

<2926> κρύπτη ***kruptē*** [secret place: PLACE (noun) 8] 1x

<2927> κρυπτός ***kruptos*** [hidden: HIDE 7, SECRET (adj. and noun) 1] 19x

<2928> κρύπτω ***kruptō*** [HIDE 1] 15x

<2929> κρυσταλλίζω ***krustallizō*** [to be clear as crystal: CRYSTAL 2] 1x

<2930> κρύσταλλος ***krustallos*** [CRYSTAL 1] 2x

<2931> κρυφῇ ***kruphē*** [in secret: SECRET (adv.)] 1x

<2932> κτάομαι ***ktaomai*** [OBTAIN 4, POSSESS 4, to provide oneself with: PROVIDE 1, PURCHASE (verb) 1] 7x

<2933> κτῆμα ***ktēma*** [POSSESSION 2] 4x

<2934> κτῆνος ***ktēnos*** [BEAST 3, CATTLE 2, MOUNT (noun)[1]] 4x

<2935> κτήτωρ ***ktētōr*** [OWNER 1] 1x

<2936> κτίζω ***ktizō*** [CREATE 1] 15x

<2937> κτίσις ***ktisis*** [CREATION 1, CREATURE 1, INSTITUTION, NEW CREATION] 19x

<2938> κτίσμα ***ktisma*** [CREATURE 2] 4x

<2939> κτίστης ***ktistēs*** [CREATOR 1] 1x

<2940> κυβεία ***kubeia*** [TRICKERY 1] 1x

<2941> κυβέρνησις ***kubernēsis*** [ADMINISTRATION 2] 1x

<2942> κυβερνήτης ***kubernētēs*** [PILOT] 2x

<2942a> κυκλεύω ***kukleuō*** [SURROUND 1] 1x

<2943> κυκλόθεν ***kuklothen*** [AROUND 1] 4x

<2944> κυκλόω ***kukloō*** [ENCIRCLE 1, SURROUND 1] 5x

<2945> κύκλῳ ***kuklō*** [AROUND 2, in a circuit: CIRCUIT 1, round about: ROUND 1] 8x

<2946> κύλισμα ***kulisma*** [WALLOWING] 1x

<2947> κυλίω ***kuliō*** [to roll, to roll around: ROLL 3] 1x

<2948> κυλλός ***kullos*** [MAIMED 2] 4x

<2949> κῦμα ***kuma*** [WAVE 2] 5x

<2950> κύμβαλον ***kumbalon*** [CYMBAL] 1x

<2951> κύμινον ***kuminon*** [CUMIN] 1x

<2952> κυνάριον ***kunarion*** [dog, little dog: DOG 2] 4x

<2953> Κύπριος ***Kuprios*** [CYPRIAN] 3x

<2954> Κύπρος ***Kupros*** [CYPRUS] 5x

<2955> κύπτω ***kuptō*** [to stoop down: STOOP 1] 3x

<2956> Κυρηναῖος ***Kurēnaios*** [CYRENIAN] 6x

<2957> Κυρήνη ***Kurēnē*** [CYRENE] 1x

<2958> Κυρήνιος ***Kurēnios*** [QUIRINIUS] 1x

<2959> κυρία ***kuria*** [LADY] 2x

<2960> κυριακός ***kuriakos*** [Lord's: LORD (noun) 3] 2x

<2961> κυριεύω ***kurieuō*** [to have dominion: DOMINION 2] 7x

<2962> κύριος ***kurios*** [DAY OF THE LORD, LORD (noun) 1, MASTER (noun) 3] 729x

<2963> κυριότης ***kuriotēs*** [DOMINION 1] 4x

<2964> κυρόω ***kuroō*** [CONFIRM 2, REAFFIRM] 2x

<2965> κύων ***kuōn*** [DOG 1] 5x
<2966> κῶλον ***kōlon*** [CORPSE 1] 1x
<2967> κωλύω ***kōluō*** [FORBID 2, HINDER (verb) 3, REFUSE (verb) 3, RESTRAIN 2] 23x
<2968> κώμη ***kōmē*** [TOWN 1, VILLAGE] 28x
<2969> κωμόπολις ***kōmopolis*** [TOWN 2] 1x
<2970> κῶμος ***kōmos*** [REVEL (noun)] 3x
<2971> κώνωψ ***kōnōps*** [GNAT] 1x
<2972> Κῶς ***Kōs*** [COS] 1x
<2973> Κωσάμ ***Kōsam*** [COSAM] 1x
<2974> κωφός ***kōphos*** [DEAF, DUMB 3] 14x

Λ

<2975> λαγχάνω ***lanchanō*** [to fall by lot, to cast lots, to choose by lot, to decide by lot: LOT^{2} 2, RECEIVE 18] 4x
<2976> Λάζαρος ***Lazaros*** [LAZARUS] 15x
<2977> λάθρᾳ ***lathra*** [SECRETLY 1] 4x
<2978> λαῖλαψ ***lailaps*** [STORM 2] 3x
<2979> λακτίζω ***laktizō*** [KICK] 2x
<2980> λαλέω ***laleō*** [PREACH 6, SAY 5, SPEAK 7, TALK (verb) 1, UTTER (verb) 4] 296x
<2981> λαλιά ***lalia*** [SPEECH 1] 3x
<2982> λαμά ***lama*** [LAMA] 2x
<2983> λαμβάνω ***lambanō*** [BRING 32, COLLECT 1, to call to mind: MIND (CALL TO) 2, OVERTAKE 1, to pick up: PICK 2, RECEIVE 1, SEIZE 5, TAKE 1, to take, to take out: TAKE 2] 262x
<2984> Λάμεχ ***Lamech*** [LAMECH] 1x
<2985> λαμπάς ***lampas*** [LAMP 1, TORCH 1] 9x
<2986> λαμπρός ***lampros*** [BRIGHT 1] 9x
<2987> λαμπρότης ***lamprotēs*** [BRIGHTNESS 1] 1x
<2988> λαμπρῶς ***lamprōs*** [SUMPTUOUSLY 1] 1x
<2989> λάμπω ***lampō*** [SHINE 4] 7x
<2990> λανθάνω ***lanthanō*** [HIDDEN (BE), to know not: KNOW 11] 6x
<2991> λαξευτός ***laxeutos*** [cut in the rock, hewn in the rock: ROCK 4] 1x
<2992> λαός ***laos*** [PEOPLE 3] 142x
<2993> Λαοδίκεια ***Laodikeia*** [LAODICEA] 6x
<2994> Λαοδικεύς ***Laodikeus*** [LAODICEAN] 1x
<2995> λάρυγξ ***larunx*** [THROAT 1] 1x
<2996> Λασαία ***Lasaia*** [LASEA] 1x
<2997> λάσχω ***laschō*** [BURST 1] 1x
<2998> λατομέω ***latomeō*** [to hew, to hew out: HEW 1] 2x
<2999> λατρεία ***latreia*** [SERVICE 3] 5x
<3000> λατρεύω ***latreuō*** [SERVE 5, WORSHIP (verb) 2] 21x
<3001> λάχανον ***lachanon*** [garden plant: PLANT (noun) 2] 4x
<3002> Λεββαῖος ***Lebbaios*** [LEBBAEUS] 1x
<3003> Λεγιών ***Legiōn*** [LEGION] and λεγιών ***legiōn*** [LEGION] 4x
<3004> λέγω ***legō*** [ASK 7, CALL (verb) 8, DECLARE 6, NAME (verb) 1, SAY 1, SPEAK 2, TELL 6] 2,369x
<3005> λεῖμμα ***leimma*** [REMNANT 1] 1x
<3006> λεῖος ***leios*** [SMOOTH 1] 1x
<3007> λείπω ***leipō*** [LACK (verb) 2, REMAIN 6] 6x
<3008> λειτουργέω ***leitourgeō*** [MINISTER (verb) 4] 3x
<3009> λειτουργία ***leitourgia*** [MINISTRY 2, SERVICE 4] 6x
<3010> λειτουργικός ***leitourgikos*** [MINISTERING 1] 1x
<3011> λειτουργός ***leitourgos*** [MINISTER (noun) 2] 5x

<3012> λέντιον ***lention*** [TOWEL 1] 2x
<3013> λεπίς ***lepis*** [SCALE 1] 1x
<3014> λέπρα ***lepra*** [LEPROSY 1] 4x
<3015> λεπρός ***lepros*** [LEPER] 9x
<3016> λεπτόν ***lepton*** [MITE] 3x
<3017> Λευί ***Leui*** [LEVI (men of the O.T.)] 5x
<3018> Λευίς ***Leuis*** [LEVI (man of the N.T.)] 3x
<3019> Λευίτης ***Leuitēs*** [LEVITE] 3x
<3020> Λευιτικός ***Leuitikos*** [LEVITICAL] 1x
<3021> λευκαίνω ***leukainō*** [WHITE (verb) 2] 2x
<3022> λευκός ***leukos*** [GREAT WHITE THRONE, WHITE (adj.) 1] 25x
<3023> λέων ***leōn*** [LION] 9x
<3024> λήθη ***lēthē*** [forgetfulness: FORGET 3] 1x
<3025> ληνός ***lēnos*** [WINEPRESS] 5x
<3026> λῆρος ***lēros*** [idle tale: TALE 1] 1x
<3027> λῃστής ***lēstēs*** [ROBBER 1] 15x
<3028> λῆμψις ***lēmpsis*** [RECEIVING 1] 1x
<3029> λίαν ***lian*** [EXCEEDINGLY 1, exceedingly beyond measure: EXCEEDINGLY 5, VERY 1] 12x
<3030> λίβανος ***libanos*** [FRANKINCENSE] 2x
<3031> λιβανωτός ***libanōtos*** [CENSER 2] 2x
<3032> Λιβερτῖνος ***Libertinos*** [FREEDMAN] 1x
<3033> Λιβύη ***Libuē*** [LIBYA] 1x
<3034> λιθάζω ***lithazō*** [STONE (verb) 1] 8x
<3035> λίθινος ***lithinos*** [stone, of stone: STONE (noun) 2] 3x
<3036> λιθοβολέω ***lithoboleō*** [STONE (verb) 3] 9x
<3037> λίθος ***lithos*** [CORNER STONE 2, STONE (noun) 1] 57x
<3038> λιθόστρωτος ***lithostrōtos*** [PAVEMENT] 1x
<3039> λικμάω ***likmaō*** [to grind to powder: POWDER] 2x
<3040> λιμήν ***limēn*** [HARBOR] 3x
<3041> λίμνη ***limnē*** [LAKE 1] 10x
<3042> λιμός ***limos*** [FAMINE, HUNGER (noun) 1] 12x
<3043> λίνον ***linon*** [FLAX, LINEN, LINEN CLOTH 1] 2x
<3044> Λίνος ***Linos*** [LINUS] 1x
<3045> λιπαρός ***liparos*** [RICH 1] 1x
<3046> λίτρα ***litra*** [POUND 1] 2x
<3047> λίψ ***lips*** [SOUTHWEST] 1x
<3047a> λογεία ***logeia*** [COLLECTION] or
<3048> λογία ***logia*** [COLLECTION] 2x
<3049> λογίζομαι ***logizomai*** [CONCLUDE[1] 1, CONSIDER 10, COUNT 3, to count for nothing: DESPISE 3, IMPUTE 1, MEDITATE 1, REASON (verb) 1, THINK 7] 40x
<3050> λογικός ***logikos*** [INTELLECTUAL, INTELLIGENT 1] 2x
<3051> λόγιον ***logion*** [ORACLE 1] 4x
<3052> λόγιος ***logios*** [ELOQUENT 1] 1x
<3053> λογισμός ***logismos*** [REASONING 2, THOUGHT 2] 2x
<3054> λογομαχέω ***logomacheō*** [to strive about words: STRIVE 9] 1x
<3055> λογομαχία ***logomachia*** [argument over words: ARGUMENT 1] 1x
<3056> λόγος ***logos*** [ACCOUNT (noun) 1, APPEARANCE 1, CAUSE 3, MATTER 2, MESSAGE 2, word: MOUTH (noun) 3, REASON (noun) 3, REPORT (noun) 6, RUMOR 2, SAYING 1, SPEECH 2, TIDINGS 1, WORD 1, WORK (noun) 2] 333x
<3057> λόγχη ***lonchē*** [SPEAR] 1x
<3058> λοιδορέω ***loidoreō*** [REVILE 2] 4x
<3059> λοιδορία ***loidoria*** [REPROACH (noun) 1, REVILING 2] 3x
<3060> λοίδορος ***loidoros*** [ABUSIVE 1] 2x
<3061> λοιμός ***loimos*** [PEST, PESTILENCE 1] 3x

<3062> λοιπός ***loipos*** [the things that remain: REMAIN 9, REMNANT 3, REST (noun)[2] 1] 54x
<3063> λοιπόν ***loipon*** [FINALLY 1, NOW 5, for the rest: REST (noun)[2] 2] 14x
<3064> λοιποῦ ***loipou*** [HENCEFORTH 1] 1x
<3065> Λουκᾶς ***Loukas*** [LUKE] 3x
<3066> Λούκιος ***Loukios*** [LUCIUS] 2x
<3067> λουτρόν ***loutron*** [WASHING 2] 2x
<3068> λούω ***louō*** [WASH 1] 6x
<3069> Λύδδα ***Ludda*** [LYDDA] 3x
<3070> Λυδία ***Ludia*** [LYDIA] 2x
<3071> Λυκαονία ***Lukaonia*** [LYCAONIA] 1x
<3072> Λυκαονιστί ***Lukaonisti*** [LYCAONIAN] 1x
<3073> Λυκία ***Lukia*** [LYCIA] 1x
<3074> λύκος ***lukos*** [WOLF] 6x
<3075> λυμαίνομαι ***lumainomai*** [RAVAGE 1] 1x
<3076> λυπέω ***lupeō*** [to be sad: SAD 1, to cause sorrow: SORROW (noun) 3, to sorrow, to be sorrowful, to be sorry, to cause sorrow, to make sorry, to grieve, to cause to grieve, to be grieved, to be in heaviness: SORROW (verb) 1] 26x
<3077> λύπη ***lupē*** [grief: GRIEVINGLY, SORROW (noun) 1] 16x
<3078> Λυσανίας ***Lusanias*** [LYSANIAS] 1x
<3079> Λυσίας ***Lusias*** [LYSIAS] 3x
<3080> λύσις ***lusis*** [loosening: LOOSE 5] 1x
<3081> λυσιτελέω ***lusiteleō*** [to be better: BETTER 6] 1x
<3082> Λύστρα ***Lustra*** [LYSTRA] 6x
<3083> λύτρον ***lutron*** [RANSOM (noun) 1] 2x
<3084> λυτρόω ***lutroō*** [REDEEM 2] 3x
<3085> λύτρωσις ***lutrōsis*** [REDEMPTION 1] 3x
<3086> λυτρωτής ***lutrōtēs*** [DELIVERER 1] 1x
<3087> λυχνία ***luchnia*** [LAMPSTAND] 12x
<3088> λύχνος ***luchnos*** [LAMP 2] 14x
<3089> λύω ***luō*** [ANNUL 1, BREAK 6, DESTROY 10, DISSOLVE 1, LOOSE 2, RELEASE (verb) 3] 42x
<3090> Λωΐς ***Lōis*** [LOIS] 1x
<3091> Λώτ ***Lōt*** [LOT (name)] 4x

M

<3092> Μάαθ ***Maath*** [MAATH] 1x
<3092a> Μαγαδάν ***Magadan*** [MAGADAN] 1x
<3093> Μαγδαλά ***Magdala*** [MAGDALA 1] 1x
<3094> Μαγδαληνή ***Magdalēnē*** [MAGDALA 2] 12x
<3095> μαγεία ***mageia*** [SORCERY 1] 1x
<3096> μαγεύω ***mageuō*** [to practice sorcery, to use sorcery: SORCERY 2] 1x
<3097> μάγος ***magos*** [SORCERER 1, WISE MAN] 6x
<3098> Μαγώγ ***Magōg*** [MAGOG] 1x
<3099> Μαδιάμ ***Madiam*** [MIDIAN] 1x
<3100> μαθητεύω ***mathēteuō*** [to become a disciple, to be a disciple, to make a disciple, to be discipled, to win disciples, to instruct, to teach: DISCIPLE 3] 4x
<3101> μαθητής ***mathētēs*** [DISCIPLE 1] 261x
<3102> μαθήτρια ***mathētria*** [DISCIPLE 2] 1x
<3103> Μαθουσάλα ***Mathousala*** [METHUSELAH] 1x
<3104> Μαϊνάν ***Mainan*** [MENNA] 1x
<3105> μαίνομαι ***mainomai*** [to be mad: MAD 1, to be out of one's mind: MIND (noun) 15] 5x
<3106> μακαρίζω ***makarizō*** [to call blessed, to count blessed: BLESSED 3] 2x
<3107> μακάριος ***makarios*** [BLESSED 2, HAPPY 1] 50x

<3108> μακαρισμός ***makarismos*** [BLESSEDNESS] 3x
<3109> Μακεδονία ***Makedonia*** [MACEDONIA] 2x
<3110> Μακεδών ***Makedōn*** [MACEDONIAN] 5x
<3111> μάκελλον ***makellon*** [SHAMBLES] 1x
<3112> μακράν ***makran*** [FAR 2] 10x
<3113> μακρόθεν ***makrothen*** [at a distance: DISTANCE 1] 14x
<3114> μακροθυμέω ***makrothumeō*** [to have patience: PATIENCE 2, to be patient: PATIENT 1, to suffer long: SUFFER 9] 10x
<3115> μακροθυμία ***makrothumia*** [LONGSUFFERING 1, PATIENCE 1] 14x
<3116> μακροθύμως ***makrothumōs*** [PATIENTLY 1] 1x
<3117> μακρός ***makros*** [FAR 1, LONG (adj.) 2] 5x
<3118> μακροχρόνιος ***makrochronios*** [living long, long-lived: LIFE 11] or [living a long time: LIVE 12] 1x
<3119> μαλακία ***malakia*** [DISEASE 1] 3x
<3120> μαλακός ***malakos*** [DELICATE, HOMOSEXUAL 2] 4x
<3121> Μαλελεήλ ***Maleleēl*** [MAHALALEEL] 1x
<3122> μάλιστα ***malista*** [ESPECIALLY 1] 12x
<3123> μᾶλλον ***mallon*** [ESPECIALLY 2, more, the more, more so, more than ever, more and more, even more: MORE 2, rather than: RATHER 2] 80x
<3124> Μάλχος ***Malchos*** [MALCHUS] 1x
<3125> μάμμη ***mammē*** [GRANDMOTHER] 1x
<3126> μαμωνᾶς ***mamōnas*** [MAMMON] 4x
<3127> Μαναήν ***Manaēn*** [MANAEN] 1x
<3128> Μανασσῆς ***Manassēs*** [MANASSEH] 3x
<3129> μανθάνω ***manthanō*** [LEARN 1] 24x
<3130> μανία ***mania*** [MADNESS 2] 1x
<3131> μάννα ***manna*** [MANNA] 5x
<3132> μαντεύομαι ***manteuomai*** [PROPHESY 1] 1x
<3133> μαραίνω ***marainō*** [WITHER 1] 1x
<3134> μαράνα θά ***marana tha*** [MARANATHA] 1x
<3135> μαργαρίτης ***margaritēs*** [PEARL] 9x
<3136> Μάρθα ***Martha*** [MARTHA] 13x
<3137> Μαρία, Μαρίαμ ***Maria, Mariam*** [MARY] 54x
<3138> Μᾶρκος ***Markos*** [MARK (name)] 8x
<3139> μάρμαρος ***marmaros*** [MARBLE] 1x
<3140> μαρτυρέω ***martureō*** [TESTIFY 1, to bear witness: WITNESS (noun)[1] 3, to be witness: WITNESS (noun)[2] 3, WITNESS (verb) 2] 76x
<3141> μαρτυρία ***marturia*** [WITNESS (noun)[1] 1] 39x
<3142> μαρτύριον ***marturion*** [WITNESS (noun)[1] 2] 20x
<3143> μαρτύρομαι ***marturomai*** [TESTIFY 4] 3x
<3144> μάρτυς ***martus*** [WITNESS (noun)[2] 1] 35x
<3145> μασάομαι ***masaomai*** [GNAW] 1x
<3146> μαστιγόω ***mastigoō*** [SCOURGE (verb) 1] 7x
<3147> μαστίζω ***mastizō*** [SCOURGE (verb) 2] 1x
<3148> μάστιξ ***mastix*** [AFFLICTION 2, SCOURGING] 6x
<3149> μαστός ***mastos*** [BREAST 1] 3x
<3150> ματαιολογία ***mataiologia*** [vain discourse, vain jangling: VAIN 7] 1x
<3151> ματαιολόγος ***mataiologos*** [idle talker: TALKER 1] 1x
<3152> μάταιος ***mataios*** [VAIN 5] 6x
<3153> ματαιότης ***mataiotēs*** [VANITY 1] 3x
<3154> ματαιόω ***mataioō*** [to become vain: VAIN 6] 1x
<3155> μάτην ***matēn*** [VAIN 9] 2x
<3156> Ματθαῖος ***Matthaios*** [MATTHEW] 5x
<3157> Ματθάν ***Matthan*** [MATTHAN] 2x
<3158> Ματθάτ ***Matthat*** [MATTHAT] 2x

<3159> Ματθίας ***Matthias*** [MATTHIAS] 1x
<3160> Ματταθά ***Mattatha*** [MATTATHA] 1x
<3161> Ματταθίας ***Mattathias*** [MATTATHIAS] 2x
<3162> μάχαιρα ***machaira*** [SWORD 1] 28x
<3163> μάχη ***machē*** [FIGHTING, STRIFE 3, STRIVING 1] 4x
<3164> μάχομαι ***machomai*** [FIGHT (verb) 2, QUARREL (verb) 1, STRIVE 7] 4x
<3165> μέ ***me*** [ME 2] 301x
<3166> μεγαλαυχέω ***megalaucheō*** [to boast great things: BOAST (verb) 1] 1x
<3167> μεγαλεῖος ***megaleios*** [wonderful works: WONDERFUL 1] 2x
<3168> μεγαλειότης ***megaleiotēs*** [GREATNESS 1, MAJESTY 1] 3x
<3169> μεγαλοπρεπής ***megaloprepēs*** [EXCELLENT 1] 1x
<3170> μεγαλύνω ***megalunō*** [ENLARGE 1, to esteem highly: ESTEEM (verb) 4, MAGNIFY] 8x
<3171> μεγάλως ***megalōs*** [GREATLY 1] 1x
<3172> μεγαλωσύνη ***megalōsunē*** [MAJESTY 2] 3x
<3173> μέγας ***megas*** [GREAT 1, GREAT (adj. expressing the majesty of God) 1, GREAT (noun), LOUD 1, GREAT TRIBULATION, GREAT WHITE THRONE, SOMEONE GREAT] 243x
<3174> μέγεθος ***megethos*** [GREATNESS 2] 1x
<3175> μεγιστάνες ***megistanes*** [LORD (noun) 4] 3x
<3176> μέγιστος ***megistos*** [greatest: GREAT 4] 1x
<3177> μεθερμηνεύω ***methermēneuō*** [TRANSLATE 2] 8x
<3178> μέθη ***methē*** [DRUNKENNESS 1] 3x
<3179> μεθίστημι ***methistēmi*** [REMOVE 3, TRANSFER 1, to turn away: TURN (verb) 13] 5x
<3180> μεθοδεία ***methodeia*** [PLOTTING 1, WILE] 2x
<3181> μεθόριος ***methorios*** [BORDER 2] 1x
<3182> μεθύσκω ***methuskō*** [to be drunk, to get drunk: DRUNK 2] 3x
<3183> μέθυσος ***methusos*** [DRUNKARD 1] 2x
<3184> μεθύω ***methuō*** [to drink well, to have too much to drink: DRINK (verb) 5, to be drunk, to get drunk, to be made drunk: DRUNK (BE) 1] 7x
<3185> μεῖζον ***meizon*** [the more: MORE 3] 1x
<3186> μειζότερος ***meizoteros*** [greater: GREAT 3] 1x
<3187> μείζων ***meizōn*** [greater, greatest: GREAT 2, greater: GREAT (adj. expressing the majesty of God) 2, stricter: STRICT 1] 48x
<3188> μέλαν ***melan*** [INK] 3x
<3189> μέλας ***melas*** [BLACK 1] 3x
<3190> Μελεᾶς ***Meleas*** [MELEA] 1x
<3191> μελετάω ***meletaō*** [MEDITATE 2, OCCUPY 1, PREMEDITATE] 3x
<3192> μέλι ***meli*** [HONEY] 4x
<3193> μελίσσιος ***melissios*** [HONEYCOMB] 1x
<3194> Μελίτη ***Melitē*** [MALTA] 1x
<3195> μέλλω ***mellō*** [COME 33, DELAY (verb) 2, INTEND 1, to not be negligent: NEGLIGENT 2, time to come: TIME 14] 113x
<3196> μέλος ***melos*** [MEMBER 1] 33x
<3197> Μελχί ***Melchi*** [MELCHI] 2x
<3198> Μελχισέδεκ ***Melchisedek*** [MELCHIZEDEK 1] 8x
<3199> μέλω ***melō*** [CARE 1, OCCUPY 2] 10x
<3200> μεμβράνα ***membrana*** [PARCHMENT] 1x
<3201> μέμφομαι ***memphomai*** [to find fault: FAULT 5] 3x
<3202> μεμψίμοιρος ***mempsimoiros*** [COMPLAINER] 1x
<3203> to <3302> Omitted in Strong's Dictionary
<3303> μέν ***men*** [TRULY 3] 179x
<3304> μενοῦνγε ***menounge*** [yes, verily: VERILY 4] 4x
<3305> μέντοι ***mentoi*** [YET 4] 8x
<3306> μένω ***menō*** [AWAIT 1, CONTINUE 1, to last: LASTING, REMAIN 1, STAY (verb) 6, TARRY 1] 118x

<3307> μερίζω ***merizō*** [there is a difference: DIFFERENCE 3, DISTRIBUTE 4, DIVIDE 3, GIVE 14] 14x

<3308> μέριμνα ***merimna*** [CARE (noun) 3, CONCERN (noun) 1] 6x

<3309> μεριμνάω ***merimnaō*** [ANXIOUS (BE) 1, to have care: CARE (noun) 4, CARE 2, WORRY (verb) 1] 19x

<3310> μερίς ***meris*** [PART (noun) 2, share: PARTAKER 5, share: SHARE (verb) 3] 5x

<3311> μερισμός ***merismos*** [DIVISION 1, GIFT 6] 2x

<3312> μεριστής ***meristēs*** [DIVIDER] 1x

<3313> μέρος ***meros*** [DETAIL 1, PART (noun) 3, in particular: PARTICULAR 1, PARTY 1, PIECE 2, in regard, with regard: REGARD (noun) 1, REGION 2] 42x

<3314> μεσημβρία ***mesēmbria*** [NOON 1, SOUTH 1] 2x

<3315> μεσιτεύω ***mesiteuō*** [INTERVENE 1] 1x

<3316> μεσίτης ***mesitēs*** [MEDIATOR] 6x

<3317> μεσονύκτιον ***mesonuktion*** [MIDNIGHT 1] 4x

<3318> Μεσοποταμία ***Mesopotamia*** [MESOPOTAMIA] 2x

<3319> μέσος ***mesos*** [MIDDAY, in the midst, into the midst: MIDST 1] 55x

<3320> μεσότοιχον ***mesotoichon*** [middle wall: WALL 2] 1x

<3321> μεσουράνημα ***mesouranēma*** [midst of heaven: HEAVEN 3] 3x

<3322> μεσόω ***mesoō*** [to be the middle: MIDDLE 1] 1x

<3323> Μεσσίας ***Messias*** [MESSIAH] 2x

<3324> μεστός ***mestos*** [FULL 3] 8x

<3325> μεστόω ***mestoō*** [to be full: FULL 4] 1x

<3326> μετά ***meta*** [WITH] 472x

<3327> μεταβαίνω ***metabainō*** [DEPART 11, MOVE 3, PASS 5] 12x

<3328> μεταβάλλω ***metaballō*** [to change one's mind: MIND (noun) 17] 1x

<3329> μετάγω ***metagō*** [TURN (verb) 14] 2x

<3330> μεταδίδωμι ***metadidōmi*** [GIVE 5, IMPART 1] 5x

<3331> μετάθεσις ***metathesis*** [CHANGE (noun) 1, REMOVING, TRANSLATION] 3x

<3332> μεταίρω ***metairō*** [DEPART 12, WITHDRAW 3] 2x

<3333> μετακαλέω ***metakaleō*** [CALL (verb) 4] 4x

<3334> μετακινέω ***metakineō*** [to move, to move away: MOVE 2] 1x

<3335> μεταλαμβάνω ***metalambanō*** [FIND 4, PARTAKE 1, PARTICIPATE 3, RECEIVE 4, TAKE 6] 6x

<3336> μετάλημψις ***metalēmpsis*** [RECEIVING 3] 1x

<3337> μεταλλάσσω ***metallassō*** [CHANGE (verb) 2] 2x

<3338> μεταμέλομαι ***metamelomai*** [to change one's mind: MIND (noun) 16, REGRET 1, to feel, to be filled with, to be seized with remorse: REMORSE, REPENT 1] 6x

<3339> μεταμορφόω ***metamorphoō*** [TRANSFIGURE] 4x

<3340> μετανοέω ***metanoeō*** [REPENT 2] 32x

<3341> μετάνοια ***metanoia*** [REPENTANCE 1] 24x

<3342> μεταξύ ***metaxu*** [MEANWHILE, NEXT 1] 9x

<3343> μεταπέμπω ***metapempō*** [to send for: SEND 7] 9x

<3344> μεταστρέφω ***metastrephō*** [PERVERT (verb) 2, TURN (verb) 10] 3x

<3345> μετασχηματίζω ***metaschēmatizō*** [to apply, to figuratively apply: APPLY 1, TRANSFORM 1] 5x

<3346> μετατίθημι ***metatithēmi*** [to carry back, to carry over: CARRY 14, CHANGE (verb) 3, to take, to take away, to take up: TAKE 32, TURN (verb) 5] 6x

<3347> μετέπειτα ***metepeita*** [AFTERWARD 2] 1x

<3348> μετέχω ***metechō*** [PARTAKE 2, PERTAIN 1, USE (verb) 3] 8x

<3349> μετεωρίζω ***meteōrizō*** [to be in anxiety: ANXIETY 1] 1x

<3350> μετοικεσία ***metoikesia*** [DEPORTATION] 4x

<3351> μετοικίζω ***metoikizō*** [MOVE 4, TRANSPORT 1] 2x

<3352> μετοχή ***metochē*** [PARTICIPATION 1] 1x

<3353> μέτοχος ***metochos*** [PARTAKER 3, PARTNER 2] 6x

<3354> μετρέω ***metreō*** [MEASURE (verb) 1] 11x

<3355> μετρητής ***metrētēs*** [MEASURE (noun) 3] 1x

<3356> μετριοπαθέω ***metriopatheō*** [to have compassion: COMPASSION 2] 1x

<3357> μετρίως ***metriōs*** [MODERATELY] 1x

<3358> μέτρον ***metron*** [MEASURE (noun) 4] 12x

<3359> μέτωπον ***metōpon*** [FOREHEAD] 8x

<3360> μέχρι, μέχρις ***mechri, mechris*** [UNTIL 2] 17x

<3361> μή ***mē*** [NOT 1] 1,042x

<3362> ἐὰν μή ***ean mē*** [but by: BY 2]

<3363> ἵνα μή ***hina mē*** [LEST 3] 97x

<3364> οὐ μή ***ou mē*** [by no means: MEANS 2, NEVER 1] 94x

<3365> μηδαμῶς ***mēdamōs*** [BY NO MEANS] 2x

<3366> μηδέ ***mēde*** [NEITHER 1] 55x

<3367> μηδείς ***mēdeis*** [NO ONE 2] 90x

<3368> μηδέποτε ***mēdepote*** [NEVER 2] 1x

<3369> μηδέπω ***mēdepō*** [NOT YET 1] 1x

<3370> Μῆδος ***Mēdos*** [MEDE] 1x

<3371> μηκέτι ***mēketi*** [EVER AGAIN, never more, (no one) any more: NEVER 3, from now on: NOW 6] 22x

<3372> μῆκος ***mēkos*** [LENGTH 1] 3x

<3373> μηκύνω ***mēkunō*** [GROW 5] 1x

<3374> μηλωτή ***mēlōtē*** [SHEEPSKIN] 1x

<3375> μήν ***mēn*** [SURELY 3] 1x

<3376> μήν ***mēn*** [MONTH 1] 18x

<3377> μηνύω ***mēnuō*** [REPORT (verb) 4, SHOW (verb) 12] 4x

<3378> μὴ ου ***mē ou*** [HAS NOT?] 5x

<3379> μήποτε ***mēpote*** [LEST 1, PERHAPS 4] 25x

<3380> μήπω ***mēpō*** [NOT YET 2] 2x

<3381> μήπως ***mēpōs*** [LEST 2] 11x

<3382> μηρός ***mēros*** [THIGH] 1x

<3383> μήτε ***mēte*** [NOT EVEN, AND NOT, ALSO NOT, NEITHER] 18x

<3384> μήτηρ ***mētēr*** [MOTHER 1] 84x

<3385> μήτι ***mēti*** [NOT AT ALL] 14x

<3386> μήτιγε ***mētige*** [HOW MUCH MORE] 1x

<3387> μή τις ***mē tis*** [WHETHER ANYONE IS] 4x

<3388> μήτρα ***mētra*** [WOMB 3] 2x

<3389> μητραλῴας ***mētralōas*** [murderer of mother, smiter of mother, who kills his mother: MOTHER 2] 1x

<3390> μητρόπολις ***mētropolis*** [METROPOLIS] 1x

<3391> μία ***mia*** [FIRST 5]

<3392> μιαίνω ***miainō*** [DEFILE 2] 5x

<3393> μίασμα ***miasma*** [DEFILEMENT 1] 1x

<3394> μιασμός ***miasmos*** [UNCLEANNESS 2] 1x

<3395> μίγμα ***migma*** [MIXTURE 1] 1x

<3396> μίγνυμι ***mignumi*** [MINGLE 1] 4x

<3397> μικρόν ***mikron*** [LITTLE (A)] 10x

<3398> μικρός ***mikros*** [LESS 1, LITTLE 1] 46x

<3398a> μικρότερος ***mikroteros*** [LEAST 3] 2x

<3399> Μίλητος ***Milētos*** [MILETUS] 3x

<3400> μίλιον ***milion*** [MILE 1] 1x

<3401> μιμέομαι ***mimeomai*** [IMITATE 1] 4x

<3402> μιμητής ***mimētēs*** [IMITATOR 1] 7x

<3403> μιμνήσκω ***mimnēskō*** [REMEMBER 1, to come in remembrance: REMEMBRANCE 2] 4x

<3404> μισέω ***miseō*** [HATE 1, HATED (BE)] 42x

<3405> μισθαποδοσία ***misthapodosia*** [RETRIBUTION 2, REWARD (noun) 3] 3x

<3406> μισθαποδότης ***misthapodotēs*** [REWARDER] 1x
<3407> μίσθιος ***misthios*** [hired servant: SERVANT 4] 2x
<3408> μισθός ***misthos*** [REWARD (noun) 2, WAGES 1] 29x
<3409> μισθόω ***misthoō*** [HIRE (verb) 1] 2x
<3410> μίσθωμα ***misthōma*** [rented house: HOUSE 3] 1x
<3411> μισθωτός ***misthōtos*** [he who serve for wages: WAGES 2] 4x
<3412> Μιτυλήνη ***Mitulēnē*** [MITYLENE] 1x
<3413> Μιχαήλ ***Michaēl*** [MICHAEL] 2x
<3414> μνᾶ ***mna*** [MINA] 9x
<3415> μνάομαι ***mnaomai*** [REMEMBER 4] 21x
<3416> Μνάσων ***Mnasōn*** [MNASON] 1x
<3417> μνεία ***mneia*** [MENTION (noun) 1, REMEMBRANCE 3] 7x
<3418> μνῆμα ***mnēma*** [TOMB 1] 7x
<3419> μνημεῖον ***mnēmeion*** [TOMB 2] 42x
<3420> μνήμη ***mnēmē*** [MIND (CALL TO) 1] 1x
<3421> μνημονεύω ***mnēmoneuō*** [to make mention: MENTION (noun) 2, REMEMBER 5] 21x
<3422> μνημόσυνον ***mnēmosunon*** [MEMORIAL] 3x
<3423> μνηστεύω ***mnēsteuō*** [to be pledged to be married: MARRIED (BE)] 3x
<3424> μογιλάλος ***mogilalos*** [who cannot speak right, who speaks with difficulty: SPEAK 20] 1x
<3425> μόγις ***mogis*** [with difficulty: DIFFICULTY 1] 1x
<3426> μόδιος ***modios*** [BUSHEL 1] 3x
<3427> μοι ***moi*** [ME 3] 240x
<3428> μοιχαλίς ***moichalis*** [ADULTEROUS (adj.)] 7x
<3429> μοιχάω ***moichaō*** [to commit adultery: ADULTERY 2] 4x
<3430> μοιχεία ***moicheia*** [ADULTERY 1] 4x
<3431> μοιχεύω ***moicheuō*** [ADULTERY 2] 15x
<3432> μοιχός ***moichos*** [ADULTERER] 5x
<3433> μόλις ***molis*** [with difficulty: DIFFICULTY 2] 6x
<3434> Μολόχ ***Moloch*** [MOLOCH] 1x
<3435> μολύνω ***molunō*** [DEFILE 3] 3x
<3436> μολυσμός ***molusmos*** [DEFILEMENT 2] 1x
<3437> μομφή ***momphē*** [COMPLAINT 1] 1x
<3438> μονή ***monē*** [MANSION] 2x
<3439> μονογενής ***monogenēs*** [ONLY BEGOTTEN] 9x
<3440> μόνον ***monon*** [ONLY 1] 66x
<3441> μόνος ***monos*** [ALONE 1, ONLY 2] 44x
<3442> μονόφθαλμος ***monophthalmos*** [with one eye: EYE 3] 2x
<3443> μονόω ***monoō*** [to be desolate: DESOLATE 3] 1x
<3444> μορφή ***morphē*** [FORM (noun) 2] 3x
<3445> μορφόω ***morphoō*** [FORM (verb) 1] 1x
<3446> μόρφωσις ***morphōsis*** [FORM (noun) 3] 2x
<3447> μοσχοποιέω ***moschopoieō*** [to make a calf: CALF 2] 1x
<3448> μόσχος ***moschos*** [CALF 1] 6x
<3449> μόχθος ***mochthos*** [TOIL (noun) 1] 3x
<3450> μου ***mou*** [MINE 4] 587x
<3451> μουσικός ***mousikos*** [MUSICIAN] 1x
<3452> μυελός ***muelos*** [MARROW] 1x
<3453> μυέω ***mueō*** [LEARN 2] 1x
<3454> μῦθος ***muthos*** [FABLE] 5x
<3455> μυκάομαι ***mukaomai*** [ROAR (verb)] 1x
<3456> μυκτηρίζω ***muktērizō*** [MOCK 2] 1x
<3457> μυλικός ***mulikos*** [of a mill: MILLSTONE 2] 1x
<3458> μύλος ***mulos*** [MILLSTONE 1] 4x
<3459> μύλων ***mulōn*** [MILL 1] 1x
<3460> Μύρα ***Mura*** [MYRA] 1x

<3461> μυριάς ***murias*** [FIFTY THOUSAND, INNUMERABLE 2, MYRIAD] 9x
<3462> μυρίζω ***murizō*** [ANOINT 2] 1x
<3463> μυρίος ***murios*** [TEN THOUSAND 2] 3x
<3464> μύρον ***muron*** [OINTMENT 1] 14x
<3465> Μυσία ***Musia*** [MYSIA] 2x
<3466> μυστήριον ***mustērion*** [MYSTERY] 27x
<3467> μυωπάζω ***muōpazō*** [SHORTSIGHTED (BE)] 1x
<3468> μώλωψ ***mōlōps*** [STRIPE 1] 1x
<3469> μωμάομαι ***mōmaomai*** [BLAME (verb) 1] 2x
<3470> μῶμος ***mōmos*** [BLEMISH 1] 1x
<3471> μωραίνω ***mōrainō*** [to become fool: FOOL 3, to make foolish: FOOLISH 5, to lose its flavor: LOSE 2] 4x
<3472> μωρία ***mōria*** [FOOLISHNESS 2] 5x
<3473> μωρολογία ***mōrologia*** [foolish talk, foolish talking: FOOLISH 4] 1x
<3474> μωρός ***mōros*** [FOOL 2, FOOLISH 3, FOOLISHNESS 3] 13x
<3475> Μωσεύς ***Mōseus*** [MOSES] 80x

N

<3476> Ναασσών ***Naassōn*** [NAHSHON] 3x
<3477> Ναγγαί ***Nangai*** [NAGGAI] 1x
<3478> Ναζαρέτ, Ναζαρέθ ***Nazaret, Nazareth*** [NAZARETH 1] 10x
<3479> Ναζαρηνός ***Nazarēnos*** [NAZARENE] 6x
<3480> Ναζωραῖος ***Nazōraios*** [NAZARENE] 13x
<3481> Ναθάν ***Nathan*** [NATHAN] 1x
<3482> Ναθαναήλ ***Nathanaēl*** [NATHANAEL] 6x
<3483> ναί ***nai*** [YES 1] 31x
<3484> Ναΐν ***Nain*** [NAIN] 1x
<3485> ναός ***naos*** [TEMPLE 2] 46x
<3486> Ναούμ ***Naoum*** [NAHUM] 1x
<3487> νάρδος ***nardos*** [NARD] 2x
<3488> Νάρκισσος ***Narkissos*** [NARCISSUS] 1x
<3489> ναυαγέω ***nauageō*** [to suffer shipwreck, to be shipwrecked, to make shipwreck: SHIPWRECK] 2x
<3490> ναύκληρος ***nauklēros*** [SHIPOWNER] 1x
<3491> ναῦς ***naus*** [SHIP 3] 1x
<3492> ναύτης ***nautēs*** [SAILOR] 3x
<3493> Ναχώρ ***Nachōr*** [NAHOR] 1x
<3494> νεανίας ***neanias*** [young man: YOUNG 2] 5x
<3495> νεανίσκος ***neaniskos*** [young man: YOUNG 3] 9x
<3496> Νεάπολις ***Neapolis*** [NEAPOLIS] 1x
<3497> Ναιμάν ***Naiman*** [NAAMAN] 1x
<3498> νεκρός ***nekros*** [DEAD 1] 128x
<3499> νεκρόω ***nekroō*** [dead, as good as dead: DEAD 2, to put to death: DEATH 9] 3x
<3499> νενεκρωμένος ***nenekrōmenos*** [dead, as good as dead: DEAD 2] 3x
<3500> νέκρωσις ***nekrōsis*** [DEADNESS, DYING 1] 2x
<3500a> νεομηνία ***neomēnia*** [new moon: MOON 2] 1x
<3501> νέος ***neos*** [NEW 3, YOUNG 1, YOUNGER 2] 24x
<3501> νέωτερος ***neōteros*** [YOUNG 1, younger, younger man: YOUNGER 2]
<3502> νεοσσός ***neossos*** [YOUNG 4] 1x
<3503> νεότης ***neotēs*** [YOUTH] 5x
<3504> νεόφυτος ***neophutos*** [NOVICE] 1x
<3505> Νέρων ***Nerōn*** [NERO] 1x
<3506> νεύω ***neuō*** [to make a sign: SIGN 4] 2x

<3507> νεφέλη ***nephelē*** [CLOUD 1, MIST 2] 26x
<3508> Νεφθαλίμ ***Nephthalim*** [NAPHTALI] 3x
<3509> νέφος ***nephos*** [CLOUD 2] 1x
<3510> νεφρός ***nephros*** [REINS] 1x
<3511> νεωκόρος ***neōkoros*** [GUARDIAN 2] 1x
<3512> νεωτερικός ***neōterikos*** [YOUTHFUL] 1x
<3513> νή ***nē*** [AFFIRM (I)] 1x
<3514> νήθω ***nēthō*** [SPIN] 2x
<3515> νηπιάζω ***nēpiazō*** [to be children: CHILD 2] 1x
<3516> νήπιος ***nēpios*** [BABE 2, CHILD 1] 14x
<3517> Νηρεύς ***Nēreus*** [NEREUS] 1x
<3518> Νηρί ***Nēri*** [NERI] 1x
<3519> νησίον ***nēsion*** [ISLAND 2] 1x
<3520> νῆσος ***nēsos*** [ISLAND 1] 9x
<3521> νηστεία ***nēsteia*** [FAST, FASTING, FAST] 8x
<3522> νηστεύω ***nēsteuō*** [FAST, FASTING, FAST] 21x
<3523> νῆστις ***nēstis*** [HUNGRY 1] 2x
<3524> νηφάλιος ***nēphalios*** [TEMPERATE 2] 3x
<3525> νήφω ***nēphō*** [to be sober: SOBER 1, WATCH (verb) 3] 6x
<3526> Νίγερ ***Niger*** [NIGER] 1x
<3527> Νικάνωρ ***Nikanōr*** [NICANOR] 1x
<3528> νικάω ***nikaō*** [OVERCOME 1, to gain, to get, to have the victory: VICTORY 3] 28x
<3529> νίκη ***nikē*** [VICTORY 1] 1x
<3530> Νικόδημος ***Nikodēmos*** [NICODEMUS] 5x
<3531> Νικολαΐτης ***Nikolaitēs*** [NICOLAITAN] 2x
<3532> Νικόλαος ***Nikolaos*** [NICOLAS] 1x
<3533> Νικόπολις ***Nikopolis*** [NICOPOLIS] 1x
<3534> νῖκος ***nikos*** [VICTORY 2] 4x
<3535> Νινευή ***Nineuē*** [NINEVEH 1] 1x
<3536> Νινευΐτης ***Nineuitēs*** [NINEVITE] 3x
<3537> νιπτήρ ***niptēr*** [BASIN] 1x
<3538> νίπτω ***niptō*** [WASH 5] 17x
<3539> νοέω ***noeō*** [CONSIDER 8, PERCEIVE 3, THINK 8, UNDERSTAND 3] 14x
<3540> νόημα ***noēma*** [DEVICE 1, MIND (noun) 4, THOUGHT 3] 6x
<3541> νόθος ***nothos*** [ILLEGITIMATE 1] 1x
<3542> νομή ***nomē*** [PASTURE 1] 2x
<3543> νομίζω ***nomizō*** [to be the custom: CUSTOM[1] 4, SUPPOSE 2, THINK 9] 15x
<3544> νομικός ***nomikos*** [about the law: LAW 5, LAWYER 1] 9x
<3545> νομίμως ***nomimōs*** [LAWFULLY] 2x
<3546> νόμισμα ***nomisma*** [MONEY 2] 1x
<3547> νομοδιδάσκαλος ***nomodidaskalos*** [TEACHER OF THE LAW] 3x
<3548> νομοθεσία ***nomothesia*** [giving of the law: GIVING 2] 1x
<3549> νομοθετέω ***nomotheteō*** [ESTABLISH 3, to receive the law, to have the law given: LAW 2] 2x
<3550> νομοθέτης ***nomothetēs*** [LAWGIVER] 1x
<3551> νόμος ***nomos*** [LAW 1] 195x
<3552> νοσέω ***noseō*** [OBSESSED (BE) 1] 1x
<3553> νόσημα ***nosēma*** [DISEASE 2] 1x
<3554> νόσος ***nosos*** [SICKNESS 2] 12x
<3555> νοσσιά ***nossia*** [BROOD 2] 1x
<3556> νοσσίον ***nossion*** [CHICKEN] 1x
<3557> νοσφίζω ***nosphizō*** [to keep back, to keep for oneself: KEEP (verb) 12] or [PILFER 1] 3x
<3558> νότος ***notos*** [south, south wind: SOUTH 2, south wind: WIND(noun) 5] 7x
<3559> νουθεσία ***nouthesia*** [ADMONITION] 3x
<3560> νουθετέω ***noutheteō*** [ADMONISH 1, WARN 3] 8x

<3561> νουμηνία ***noumēnia*** [new moon: MOON 2] 1x
<3562> νουνεχῶς ***nounechōs*** [INTELLIGENTLY] 1x
<3563> νοῦς ***nous*** [MIND (noun) 5, UNDERSTANDING 3] 24x
<3564> Νυμφᾶς ***Numphas*** [NYMPHAS] 1x
<3565> νύμφη ***numphē*** [BRIDE] 8x
<3566> νυμφίος ***numphios*** [BRIDEGROOM 1] 15x
<3567> νυμφών ***numphōn*** [BRIDECHAMBER, SON OF THE BRIDECHAMBER] 3x
<3568> νῦν ***nun*** [NOW 2, present, for the present: PRESENT 7, PRESENT TIME 2] 138x
<3569> τανῦν ***tanun*** [BUT NOW] 5x
<3570> νυνί ***nuni*** [NOW 3] 21x
<3571> νύξ ***nux*** [NIGHT 1] 62x
<3572> νύσσω ***nussō*** [PIERCE 4] 1x
<3573> νυστάζω ***nustazō*** [SLUMBER (verb) 1] 2x
<3574> νυχθήμερον ***nuchthēmeron*** [a night and day, a night and a day: DAY 5] 1x
<3575> Νῶε ***Nōe*** [NOAH] 8x
<3576> νωθρός ***nōthros*** [SLUGGISH] 2x
<3577> νῶτος ***nōtos*** [BACK (noun)] 1x

Ξ

<3578> ξενία ***xenia*** [GUEST ROOM 2] 2x
<3579> ξενίζω ***xenizō*** [LODGE 2, to think strange, to bring strange things: STRANGE 3] 10x
<3580> ξενοδοχέω ***xenodocheō*** [to lodge strangers: STRANGER 3] 1x
<3581> ξένος ***xenos*** [FOREIGN 3, HOST[2] 1, strange thing: STRANGE 2, STRANGER 2] 14x
<3582> ξέστης ***xestēs*** [VESSEL[1] 2] 2x
<3583> ξηραίνω ***xērainō*** [to dry up: DRY (verb) 1, to become rigid: RIGID, RIPE (BE) 1, to wither, to wither away: WITHER 2, to wither: WITHERED 1] 15x
<3584> ξηρός ***xēros*** [DRY (noun) 2, dry land, dry: LAND (noun) 5, WITHERED 2] 8x
<3585> ξύλινος ***xulinos*** [of wood: WOOD 2] 2x
<3586> ξύλον ***xulon*** [STAVE 1, STOCKS, TREE 2, WOOD 1] 19x
<3587> ξυράω ***xuraō*** [SHAVE] 3x

Ο

<3588> ὁ ***ho*** [AFFAIR 2, BUSINESS 7, CASE 2, CAUSE 4]
<3589> ὀγδοήκοντα ***ogdoēkonta*** [EIGHTY, EIGHTY-FOUR] 2x
<3590> ὄγδοος ***ogdoos*** [EIGHTH 1] 5x
<3591> ὄγκος ***onkos*** [WEIGHT 2] 1x
<3592> ὅδε ***hode*** [THIS, THAT 1] 12x
<3593> ὁδεύω ***hodeuō*** [JOURNEY (verb) 1] 1x
<3594> ὁδηγέω ***hodēgeō*** [LEAD (verb) 8] 5x
<3595> ὁδηγός ***hodēgos*** [GUIDE (noun) 1] 5x
<3596> ὁδοιπορέω ***hodoiporeō*** [to go on one's journey: JOURNEY (noun) 3] 1x
<3597> ὁδοιπορία ***hodoiporia*** [JOURNEY (noun) 2] 2x
<3598> ὁδός ***hodos*** [JOURNEY (noun) 1, SABBATH DAY'S JOURNEY, WAY 1] 101x
<3599> ὀδούς ***odous*** [TOOTH] 12x
<3600> ὀδυνάω ***odunaō*** [to be distressed: DISTRESSED 1, GRIEVE 2, TORMENT (verb) 2] 4x
<3601> ὀδύνη ***odunē*** [SORROW (noun) 2] 2x
<3602> ὀδυρμός ***odurmos*** [MOURNING 1] 2x
<3603> ὅ ἐστι ***ho esti*** [that is, which is, that is to say: SAY 8]
<3604> Ὀζίας ***Ozias*** [UZZIAH] 2x
<3605> ὄζω ***ozō*** [to be a stench: STENCH] 1x
<3606> ὅθεν ***hothen*** [WHERE 2] 15x
<3607> ὀθόνη ***othonē*** [SHEET 1] 2x

<3608> ὀθόνιον ***othonion*** [LINEN, LINEN CLOTH 2] 5x
<3609> οἰκεῖος ***oikeios*** [of the household: HOUSEHOLD 3] 3x
<3609a> οἰκετεία ***oiketeia*** [HOUSEHOLD 4] 1x
<3610> οἰκέτης ***oiketēs*** [household servant, servant: SERVANT 5] 4x
<3611> οἰκέω ***oikeō*** [DWELL 1] 9x
<3612> οἴκημα ***oikēma*** [PRISON 2] 1x
<3613> οἰκητήριον ***oikētērion*** [HABITATION 2] 2x
<3614> οἰκία ***oikia*** [HOUSE 1] 95x
<3615> οἰκιακός ***oikiakos*** [one of the household: HOUSEHOLD 2] 2x
<3616> οἰκοδεσποτέω ***oikodespoteō*** [MANAGE 1] 1x
<3617> οἰκοδεσπότης ***oikodespotēs*** [master of the house: MASTER (noun) 4] 12x
<3618> οἰκοδομέω ***oikodomeō*** [BUILD 2, EDIFY 1, EMBOLDENED (BE)] 40x
<3619> οἰκοδομή ***oikodomē*** [BUILDING 2, EDIFICATION 1] 18x
<3620> οἰκοδομία ***oikodomia*** [EDIFYING 2] 1x
<3621> οἰκονομέω ***oikonomeō*** [to be a steward: STEWARD 3] 1x
<3622> οἰκονομία ***oikonomia*** [DISPENSATION 1, EDIFYING 1, STEWARDSHIP 1] 9x
<3623> οἰκονόμος ***oikonomos*** [CHAMBERLAIN 1, STEWARD 2] 10x
<3624> οἶκος ***oikos*** [HOUSE 2] 114x
<3625> οἰκουμένη ***oikoumenē*** [WORLD 3] 15x
<3626> οἰκουργός ***oikourgos*** [busy at home, worker at home, diligent in home work, keeper at home, homemaker: HOME 1] 1x
<3627> οἰκτείρω ***oikteirō*** [to have compassion: COMPASSION 3] 2x
<3628> οἰκτιρμός ***oiktirmos*** [MERCY 3] 5x
<3629> οἰκτίρμων ***oiktirmōn*** [MERCIFUL 4] 3x
<3630> οἰνοπότης ***oinopotēs*** [WINEBIBBER] 2x
<3631> οἶνος ***oinos*** [WINE 1] 33x
<3632> οἰνοφλυγία ***oinophlugia*** [DRUNKENNESS 2] 1x
<3633> οἴομαι ***oiomai*** [SUPPOSE 3, THINK 10] 3x
<3634> οἷος ***hoios*** [OF WHAT KIND] 12x
<3635> ὀκνέω ***okneō*** [DELAY (verb) 3] 1x
<3636> ὀκνηρός ***oknēros*** [SLOTHFUL 1, TEDIOUS] 3x
<3637> ὀκταήμερος ***oktaēmeros*** [eight day: EIGHTH 2] 1x
<3638> ὀκτώ ***oktō*** [EIGHT, EIGHTEEN, THIRTY-EIGHT] 9x
<3639> ὄλεθρος ***olethros*** [DESTRUCTION 3, RUIN (noun) 2] 4x
<3640> ὀλιγόπιστος ***oligopistos*** [of little faith: FAITH 2] 5x
<3641> ὀλίγος ***oligos*** [ALMOST 1, BRIEFLY 1, FEW 1, not a few: FEW 2, LITTLE 2, not short: LONG (adj.) 3] 40x
<3642> ὀλιγόψυχος ***oligopsuchos*** [FAINTHEARTED 1] 1x
<3643> ὀλιγωρέω ***oligōreō*** [DESPISE 4] 1x
<3643a> ὀλίγως ***oligōs*** [JUST (adv.)] 1x
<3644> ὀλοθρευτής ***olothreutēs*** [DESTROYER 1] 1x
<3645> ὀλοθρεύω ***olothreuō*** [he who destroys: DESTROY 6] 1x
<3646> ὁλοκαύτωμα ***holokautōma*** [BURNT OFFERING] 3x
<3647> ὁλοκληρία ***holoklēria*** [complete, perfect soundness: SOUNDNESS 1] 1x
<3648> ὁλόκληρος ***holoklēros*** [ENTIRE 1, WHOLE 2] 2x
<3649> ὀλολύζω ***ololuzō*** [HOWL] 1x
<3650> ὅλος ***holos*** [COMPLETELY 1, WHOLE 1] 109x
<3651> ὁλοτελής ***holotelēs*** [COMPLETELY 2] 1x
<3652> Ὀλυμπᾶς ***Olumpas*** [OLYMPAS] 1x
<3653> ὄλυνθος ***olunthos*** [unseasonable fig: FIG 2] 1x
<3654> ὅλως ***holōs*** [ACTUALLY 1, at all: ALL 1, UTTERLY 1] 4x
<3655> ὄμβρος ***ombros*** [SHOWER] 1x
<3656> ὁμιλέω ***homileō*** [TALK (verb) 2] 4x
<3657> ὁμιλία ***homilia*** [COMMUNICATION 1] 1x
<3658> ὅμιλος ***homilos*** [COMPANY (noun) 2] 1x

<3658a> ὁμίχλη ***homichlē*** [MIST 3] 1x

<3659> ὄμμα ***omma*** [EYE 2] 2x

<3660> ὀμνύω ***omnuō*** [PROMISE (verb) 4, SWEAR 1] 27x

<3661> ὁμοθυμαδόν ***homothumadon*** [with one accord: ACCORD 2] 11x

<3662> ὁμοιάζω ***homoiazō*** [AGREE 2] 1x

<3663> ὁμοιοπαθής ***homoiopathēs*** [of like passions: PASSION 3] 2x

<3664> ὅμοιος ***homoios*** [LIKE (adj., adv., noun) 2] 46x

<3665> ὁμοιότης ***homoiotēs*** [LIKENESS 3] 2x

<3666> ὁμοιόω ***homoioō*** [to be like, to become like, to make like: LIKE (adj., adv., noun) 3, LIKEN] 15x

<3667> ὁμοίωμα ***homoiōma*** [LIKENESS 1] 6x

<3668> ὁμοίως ***homoiōs*** [LIKEWISE 1, in like manner: MANNER 1] 30x

<3669> ὁμοίωσις ***homoiōsis*** [LIKENESS 2] 1x

<3670> ὁμολογέω ***homologeō*** [CONFESS 1, to make confession: CONFESSION 2, DECLARE 7, PROFESS 1, PROMISE (verb) 5] 24x

<3671> ὁμολογία ***homologia*** [CONFESSION 1] 6x

<3672> ὁμολογουμένως ***homologoumenōs*** [without controversy: CONTROVERSY 1] 1x

<3673> ὁμότεχνος ***homotechnos*** [of the same trade: TRADE (noun) 1] 1x

<3674> ὁμοῦ ***homou*** [TOGETHER 1] 3x

<3675> ὁμόφρων ***homophrōn*** [of one mind: MIND (noun) 14] 1x

<3676> ὅμως ***homōs*** [NEVERTHELESS 3] 3x

<3677> ὄναρ ***onar*** [DREAM (noun) 2] 6x

<3678> ὀνάριον ***onarion*** [young donkey: DONKEY 2] 1x

<3679> ὀνειδίζω ***oneidizō*** [INSULT (verb) 3, to suffer reproach: REPROACH (noun) 4, REPROACH (verb) 1, REVILE 4] 10x

<3680> ὀνειδισμός ***oneidismos*** [REPROACH (noun) 2] 5x

<3681> ὄνειδος ***oneidos*** [REPROACH (noun) 3] 1x

<3682> Ὀνήσιμος ***Onēsimos*** [ONESIMUS] 2x

<3683> Ὀνησίφορος ***Onēsiphoros*** [ONESIPHORUS] 2x

<3684> ὀνικός ***onikos*** [of a donkey: DONKEY 3] 3x

<3685> ὀνίνημι ***oninēmi*** [BENEFIT 1] 1x

<3686> ὄνομα ***onoma*** [NAME (noun) 1, in the name of: NAME (noun) 2] 231x

<3687> ὀνομάζω ***onomazō*** [to call, to call over, to call upon: CALL (verb) 10, NAME (verb) 2] 9x

<3688> ὄνος ***onos*** [DONKEY 1] 6x

<3689> ὄντως ***ontōs*** [CERTAINLY 1, INDEED 2, REALLY 1, TRULY 4] 10x

<3690> ὄξος ***oxos*** [VINEGAR] 6x

<3691> ὀξύς ***oxus*** [SHARP, SWIFT 1] 8x

<3692> ὀπή ***opē*** [HOLE 1, OPENING 2] 2x

<3693> ὄπισθεν ***opisthen*** [back, on the back: BACK (adv. and noun) 1, behind, from behind: BEHIND 2] 7x

<3694> ὀπίσω ***opisō*** [BACK (adv. and noun) 2, to draw back: BACK (adv. and noun) 3, BEHIND 1] 35x

<3695> ὁπλίζω ***hoplizō*** [ARM (verb)] 1x

<3696> ὅπλον ***hoplon*** [INSTRUMENT 1, WEAPON] 6x

<3697> ὁποῖος ***hopoios*** [OF WHAT KIND, OF WHAT SORT] 5x

<3698> ὁπότε ***hopote*** [WHEN 1] 1x

<3699> ὅπου ***hopou*** [WHERE 1, WHEREVER] 82x

<3700> ὀπτάνομαι ***optanomai*** and ὄπτομαι ***optomai*** [APPEAR 5, APPEAR 6, APPEAR 7, to see to it: SEE 13] 57x

<3701> ὀπτασία ***optasia*** [VISION 1] 4x

<3702> ὀπτός ***optos*** [BROILED] 1x

<3703> ὀπώρα ***opōra*** [FRUIT 5] 1x

<3704> ὅπως ***hopōs*** [SO THAT 2] 55x

<3705> ὅραμα ***horama*** [VISION 2] 12x

<3706> ὅρασις ***horasis*** [VISION 3] 3x

<3707> ὁρατός ***horatos*** [VISIBLE 1] 1x
<3708> ὁράω ***horaō*** [APPEAR 6, BEWARE 4, LOOK (verb) 9, SEE 4, to see again: SEE 7] 454x
<3709> ὀργή ***orgē*** [WRATH 1] 36x
<3710> ὀργίζω ***orgizō*** [to be angry, to become angry: ANGRY 2, ENRAGED (BE) 1] 8x
<3711> ὀργίλος ***orgilos*** [soon angry: ANGRY 1] 1x
<3712> ὀργυιά ***orguia*** [FATHOM] 2x
<3713> ὀρέγω ***oregō*** [COVET 3, DESIRE (verb) 6] 3x
<3714> ὀρεινός ***oreinos*** [hill country: HILL 2] 2x
<3715> ὄρεξις ***orexis*** [LUST (noun) 2] 1x
<3716> ὀρθοποδέω ***orthopodeō*** [STRAIGHTFORWARD, STRAIGHTFORWARDLY] 1x
<3717> ὀρθός ***orthos*** [STRAIGHT 2] 2x
<3718> ὀρθοτομέω ***orthotomeō*** [to divide rightly: DIVIDE 6] 1x
<3719> ὀρθρίζω ***orthrizō*** [to come early in the morning: MORNING 2] 1x
<3720> ὀρθρινός ***orthrinos*** [MORNING STAR 1] 1x
<3721> ὄρθριος ***orthrios*** [early, very early: EARLY 1] 1x
<3722> ὄρθρος ***orthros*** [morning, early in the morning: MORNING 1] 3x
<3723> ὀρθῶς ***orthōs*** [PLAINLY 1, RIGHTLY 1] 4x
<3724> ὁρίζω ***horizō*** [DETERMINE 5, to determine: DETERMINED, ORDAIN 4] 8x
<3725> ὅριον ***horion*** [BORDER 1, COAST (noun) 1, REGION 3] 12x
<3726> ὁρκίζω ***horkizō*** [ADJURE 1] 3x
<3727> ὅρκος ***horkos*** [OATH 1] 10x
<3728> ὁρκωμοσία ***horkōmosia*** [OATH 2] 4x
<3729> ὁρμάω ***hormaō*** [RUSH 1] 5x
<3730> ὁρμή ***hormē*** [ATTEMPT (noun) 1, INCLINATION] 2x
<3731> ὅρμημα ***hormēma*** [VIOLENCE 3] 1x
<3732> ὄρνεον ***orneon*** [BIRD 1] 3x
<3733> ὄρνις ***ornis*** [HEN] 2x
<3734> ὁροθεσία ***horothesia*** [BOUNDARY] 1x
<3735> ὄρος ***oros*** [MOUNT (noun)[2], MOUNT OF OLIVES 1, MOUNT OF OLIVES 2, MOUNTAIN] 65x
<3736> ὀρύσσω ***orussō*** [DIG 2] 3x
<3737> ὀρφανός ***orphanos*** [ORPHAN (noun)] 2x
<3738> ὀρχέομαι ***orcheomai*** [DANCE] 4x
<3739> ὅσ ***hos*** [MEANTIME]
<3740> ὁσάκις ***hosakis*** [OFTEN 1] 3x
<3741> ὅσιος ***hosios*** [DEVOUT 3, HOLY (adj.) 4, HOLY (noun) 1] 8x
<3742> ὁσιότης ***hosiotēs*** [HOLINESS 4] 2x
<3743> ὁσίως ***hosiōs*** [DEVOUTLY] 1x
<3744> ὀσμή ***osmē*** [AROMA 1, ODOR 1] 6x
<3745> ὅσος ***hosos*** [as long as: LONG (adj.) 6] 120x
<3746> ὅσπερ ***hosper*** [WHOM, WHOMSOEVER] 1x
<3747> ὀστέον ***osteon*** [BONE 1] 5x
<3748> ὅστις ***hostis*** [ANYONE] 154x
<3749> ὀστράκινος ***ostrakinos*** [EARTHEN 1] 2x
<3750> ὄσφρησις ***osphrēsis*** [SMELLING] 1x
<3751> ὀσφύς ***osphus*** [LOINS] 8x
<3752> ὅταν ***hotan*** [WHEN 2] 123x
<3753> ὅτε ***hote*** [WHEN 3] 103x
<3754> ὅτι ***hoti*** [BECAUSE 2, THAT 1] 1,296x
<3755> ὅτου ***hotou*** [WHILE 1] 6x
<3756> οὐκ ***ouk*** [to not agree: AGREE 6, not a few: FEW 2, not short: LONG (adj.) 3] 1,700x +
<3757> οὗ ***hou*** [WHERE 3] 41x
<3758> οὐά ***oua*** [HA!] 1x
<3759> οὐαί ***ouai*** [WOE!] 46x
<3760> οὐδαμῶς ***oudamōs*** [WISE (IN NO) 1] 1x

<3761> οὐδέ ***oude*** [NOT 2] 134x

<3762> οὐδείς ***oudeis*** [NO ONE 1] 235x

<3763> οὐδέποτε ***oudepote*** [NEVER 4] 16x

<3764> οὐδέπω ***oudepō*** [NEVER 5] 5x

<3765> οὐκέτι ***ouketi*** [NO MORE] 46x

<3766> οὐκοῦν ***oukoun*** [THEN 2] 1x

<3767> οὖν ***oun*** [THEN 3] 526x

<3768> οὔπω ***oupō*** [NOT YET, NOT EVEN YET] 26x

<3769> οὐρά ***oura*** [TAIL] 5x

<3770> οὐράνιος ***ouranios*** [HEAVENLY 1] 7x

<3771> οὐρανόθεν ***ouranothen*** [from heaven: HEAVEN 2] 2x

<3772> οὐρανός ***ouranos*** [HEAVEN 1, KINGDOM OF HEAVEN] 277x

<3773> Οὐρβανός ***Ourbanos*** [URBANUS] 1x

<3774> Οὐρίας ***Ourias*** [URIAH] 1x

<3775> οὖς ***ous*** [EAR 1] 36x

<3776> οὐσία ***ousia*** [goods: GOOD (adj. and noun) 4] 2x

<3777> οὔτε ***oute*** [NEITHER 2] 87x

<3778> οὗτος ***houtos*** [THIS, THAT 2] 356x

<3779> οὕτω, οὕτως ***houtō, houtōs*** [THUS] 212x

<3780> οὐχί ***ouchi*** [BY NO MEANS ALL] 56x

<3781> ὀφειλέτης ***opheiletēs*** [DEBTOR 1, one who owes: OWE 3, SINNER 2] 7x

<3782> ὀφειλή ***opheilē*** [DEBT 2, DUE 1] 2x

<3783> ὀφείλημα ***opheilēma*** [DEBT 3] 2x

<3784> ὀφείλω ***opheilō*** [to owe: DEBT 4, to be a debtor: DEBTOR 3, to owe: DUE 2, INDEBTED (BE), OUGHT 3, OWE 1] 35x

<3785> ὄφελον ***ophelon*** [OH THAT!, WOULD THAT!] 4x

<3786> ὄφελος ***ophelos*** [PROFIT (noun) 1] 3x

<3787> ὀφθαλμοδουλεία ***ophthalmodouleia*** [EYESERVICE] 2x

<3788> ὀφθαλμός ***ophthalmos*** [EYE 1] 100x

<3789> ὄφις ***ophis*** [SERPENT] 14x

<3790> ὀφρῦς ***ophrus*** [BROW] 1x

<3791> ὀχλέω ***ochleō*** [TORMENT (verb) 3] 2x

<3792> ὀχλοποιέω ***ochlopoieō*** [to gather a mob, a company, a crowd: GATHER 5] 1x

<3793> ὄχλος ***ochlos*** [CROWD (noun) 1, MULTITUDE 1] 175x

<3794> ὀχύρωμα ***ochurōma*** [FORTRESS 2] 1x

<3795> ὀψάριον ***opsarion*** [fish, small fish: FISH 3] 5x

<3796> ὀψέ ***opse*** [evening, in the evening: EVENING 2, late on: LATE 1] 3x

<3797> ὄψιμος ***opsimos*** [late rain, latter rain: RAIN (noun) 4] 1x

<3798> ὄψιος ***opsios*** [EVENING 3] 15x

<3799> ὄψις ***opsis*** [APPEARANCE 2, FACE (noun) 1] 3x

<3800> ὀψώνιον ***opsōnion*** [EXPENSE 1, wage: WAGES 3] 4x

<3801> ὁ ὢν καὶ ὁ ἦν καὶ ὁ ἐρχόμενος ***ho ōn kai ho ēn kai ho erchomenos*** [HE WHO IS, AND WAS, AND IS COMING] 4x

Π

<3802> παγιδεύω ***pagideuō*** [ENTANGLE 2] 1x

<3803> παγίς ***pagis*** [SNARE 1] 5x

<3804> πάθημα ***pathēma*** [PASSION 2, SUFFERING 1] 16x

<3805> παθητός ***pathētos*** [subject to suffering: SUFFER 8] 1x

<3806> πάθος ***pathos*** [inordinate affection: AFFECTION 2, PASSION 1] 3x

<3807> παιδαγωγός ***paidagōgos*** [INSTRUCTOR 1, TUTOR 1] 3x

<3808> παιδάριον ***paidarion*** [BOY 2, CHILD 5] 2x

<3809> παιδεία ***paideia*** [TRAINING 1] 6x

<3810> παιδευτής ***paideutēs*** [who corrects: CORRECT 2, INSTRUCTOR 2] 2x
<3811> παιδεύω ***paideuō*** [CHASTEN 1, CORRECT 1, EDUCATE, LEARN 3, TEACH 4] 13x
<3812> παιδιόθεν ***paidiothen*** [from childhood: CHILDHOOD 2] 1x
<3813> παιδίον ***paidion*** [child, little child, young child: CHILD 4] 52x
<3814> παιδίσκη ***paidiskē*** [SERVANT GIRL] 13x
<3815> παίζω ***paizō*** [PLAY 1] 1x
<3816> παῖς ***pais*** [BOY 1, CHILD 3, DAUGHTER 4, SERVANT 6, SON 2] 24x
<3817> παίω ***paiō*** [STRIKE 2] 5x
<3818> Πακατιανή ***Pakatianē*** [PACATIANA] 1x
<3819> πάλαι ***palai*** [long ago: LONG (adj.) 4, OLD 3, in time past, in the past: PAST 4] 6x
<3820> παλαιός ***palaios*** [OLD 4] 19x
<3821> παλαιότης ***palaiotēs*** [OLD AGE 2] 1x
<3822> παλαιόω ***palaioō*** [to grow old, to make old: OLD 5] 4x
<3823> πάλη ***palē*** [STRUGGLE (noun) 1] 1x
<3824> παλιγγενεσία ***palingenesia*** [REGENERATION] 2x
<3825> πάλιν ***palin*** [AGAIN 2, to see again: SEE 7, to take again, to take out again: TAKE 2] 140x
<3826> παμπληθεί ***pamplēthei*** [ALL TOGETHER] 1x
<3827> πάμπολυς ***pampolus*** [VERY GREAT] 1x
<3828> Παμφυλία ***Pamphulia*** [PAMPHYLIA] 5x
<3829> πανδοχεῖον ***pandocheion*** [INN 2] 1x
<3830> πανδοχεύς ***pandocheus*** [INNKEEPER] 1x
<3831> πανήγυρις ***panēguris*** [ASSEMBLY 1] 1x
<3832> πανοικεί ***panoikei*** [with all the household: HOUSEHOLD 5] 1x
<3833> πανοπλία ***panoplia*** [armor, whole armor, full armor: ARMOR 1] 3x
<3834> πανουργία ***panourgia*** [CRAFTINESS, CUNNING 1, DECEIT 4] 5x
<3835> πανοῦργος ***panourgos*** [CRAFTY 1] 1x
<3836> πανταχόθεν ***pantachothen*** [FROM EVERYWHERE] 1x
<3837> πανταχοῦ ***pantachou*** [EVERYWHERE 1] 7x
<3838> παντελής ***pantelēs*** [to the uttermost: UTTERMOST 1] 2x
<3839> πάντῃ ***pantē*** [IN EVERY WAY, IN ALL THINGS] 1x
<3840> πάντοθεν ***pantothen*** [on every side, on all sides: SIDE 6] 3x
<3841> Παντοκράτωρ ***Pantokratōr*** [ALMIGHTY 1] 10x
<3842> πάντοτε ***pantote*** [ALWAYS 4] 41x
<3843> πάντως ***pantōs*** [ALTOGETHER 1, no doubt: DOUBT (adv.) 1, SURELY 4] 9x
<3844> παρά ***para*** [BY 1, CONTRARY 4] 198x
<3845> παραβαίνω ***parabainō*** [to fall by transgression: FALL (verb) 12, TRANSGRESS 1] 4x
<3846> παραβάλλω ***paraballō*** [ARRIVE 3, COMPARE 1] 2x
<3847> παράβασις ***parabasis*** [TRANSGRESSION 1] 7x
<3848> παραβάτης ***parabatēs*** [TRANSGRESSOR 1] 5x
<3849> παραβιάζομαι ***parabiazomai*** [CONSTRAIN 2] 2x
<3849a> παραβολεύομαι ***paraboleuomai*** [VENTURE 1] 1x
<3850> παραβολή ***parabolē*** [FIGURE 2, PARABLE 1] 50x
<3851> παραβουλεύομαι ***parabouleuomai*** [VENTURE 1] 1x
<3852> παραγγελία ***parangelia*** [CHARGE (noun)[2] 1, COMMANDMENT 4, charge: STRICTLY 1] 5x
<3853> παραγγέλλω ***parangellō*** [COMMAND (verb) 8, ENJOIN 1, PRESCRIBE] 32x
<3854> παραγίνομαι ***paraginomai*** [COME 2, GO 33] 37x
<3855> παράγω ***paragō*** [to pass; to pass away, by, forth, on: PASS 8] 10x
<3856> παραδειγματίζω ***paradeigmatizō*** [to make a public example: EXAMPLE 4, to make a show: SHOW (noun) 1] 2x
<3857> παράδεισος ***paradeisos*** [PARADISE 1] 3x
<3858> παραδέχομαι ***paradechomai*** [RECEIVE 14] 5x
<3859> παραδιατριβή ***paradiatribē*** [useless wrangling: WRANGLING 2] 1x
<3860> παραδίδωμι ***paradidōmi*** [BETRAY 1, COMMIT 3, to deliver, to deliver up:

DELIVER 3, ENTRUST 2, to give over: GIVE 6, INSTRUCT 1, PRODUCE 5, RISK 1] 119x

<3861> παράδοξος ***paradoxos*** [STRANGE 1] 1x

<3862> παράδοσις ***paradosis*** [TRADITION 1] 13x

<3863> παραζηλόω ***parazēloō*** [to arouse the jealousy of, to move to jealousy, to provoke to jealousy: JEALOUSY 2] 4x

<3864> παραθαλάσσιος ***parathalassios*** [by the sea, on the seaside, upon the sea coast, by the lake: SEA 3] 1x

<3865> παραθεωρέω ***paratheōreō*** [OVERLOOK 1] 1x

<3866> παραθήκη ***parathēkē*** [what is committed, what is committed to the trust: COMMIT 8] 3x

<3867> παραινέω ***paraineō*** [ADMONISH 2, EXHORT 1] 2x

<3868> παραιτέομαι ***paraiteomai*** [AVOID 3, BEG 2, EXCUSE (verb) 2, REFUSE (verb) 4] 12x

<3869> παρακαθέζομαι ***parakathezomai*** [SIT 7] 1x

<3870> παρακαλέω ***parakaleō*** [BEG 3, BESEECH 1, to call for: CALL (verb) 5, to be encouraged together, mutually: ENCOURAGE 1, EXHORT 2, to exhort: EXHORTATION 2, to plead with: PLEAD 2] 109x

<3871> παρακαλύπτω ***parakaluptō*** [HIDE 5] 1x

<3872> παρακαταθήκη ***parakatathēkē*** [THING COMMITTED] 2x

<3873> παράκειμαι ***parakeimai*** [PRESENT (BE) 5] 2x

<3874> παράκλησις ***paraklēsis*** [CONSOLATION 1, ENTREATY 1, EXHORTATION 1] 29x

<3875> Παράκλητος ***Paraklētos*** [ADVOCATE (noun)] 5x

<3876> παρακοή ***parakoē*** [DISOBEDIENCE 2] 3x

<3877> παρακολουθέω ***parakoloutheō*** [to follow, to follow carefully, to follow closely: FOLLOW 5, INVESTIGATE 1] 4x

<3878> παρακούω ***parakouō*** [HEAR 4] 3x

<3879> παρακύπτω ***parakuptō*** [to look into: LOOK (verb) 16, to stoop, to stoop down: STOOP 2] 5x

<3880> παραλαμβάνω ***paralambanō*** [RECEIVE 5, to take, to take along, to take with: TAKE 7] 49x

<3881> παραλέγω ***paralegō*** [PASS 9, to sail close, to sail along: SAIL (verb) 10] 2x

<3882> παράλιος ***paralios*** [SEA COAST, SEACOAST] 1x

<3883> παραλλαγή ***parallagē*** [VARIATION] 1x

<3884> παραλογίζομαι ***paralogizomai*** [DECEIVE 4] 2x

<3885> παραλυτικός ***paralutikos*** [PARALYTIC] 9x

<3886> παραλύω ***paraluō*** [HANG 4, PARALYZED (BE)] 5x

<3887> παραμένω ***parameno*** [CONTINUE 4, STAY (verb) 9] 4x

<3888> παραμυθέομαι ***paramutheomai*** [COMFORT (verb) 1] 4x

<3889> παραμυθία ***paramuthia*** [COMFORT (noun) 1] 1x

<3890> παραμύθιον ***paramuthion*** [CONSOLATION 2] 1x

<3891> παρανομέω ***paranomeō*** [to break the law: CONTRARY 5] 1x

<3892> παρανομία ***paranomia*** [INIQUITY 4] 1x

<3893> παραπικραίνω ***parapikrainō*** [PROVOKE 2] 1x

<3894> παραπικρασμός ***parapikrasmos*** [PROVOCATION] 2x

<3895> παραπίπτω ***parapiptō*** [to fall away: FALL (verb) 7] 1x

<3896> παραπλέω ***parapleō*** [to sail past, to sail by: SAIL (verb) 7] 1x

<3897> παραπλήσιον ***paraplēsion*** [CLOSE (adj. and adv.) 2] 1x

<3898> παραπλησίως ***paraplēsiōs*** [in like manner: LIKEWISE 2] 1x

<3899> παραπορεύομαι ***paraporeuomai*** [to pass through, to pass by: PASS 11] 5x

<3900> παράπτωμα ***paraptōma*** [FALL (noun) 1, TRANSGRESSION 2] 22x

<3901> παραρρέω ***pararreō*** [to drift away: DRIFT 1] 1x

<3902> παράσημος ***parasēmos*** [FIGUREHEAD] 1x

<3903> παρασκευάζω ***paraskeuazō*** [PREPARE 5, to make ready: READY 5] 4x

<3904> Παρασκευή ***Paraskeuē*** [PREPARATION DAY] 6x

<3905> παρατείνω ***parateinō*** [PROLONG] 1x

<3906> παρατηρέω ***paratēreō*** [OBSERVE 2, to watch, to watch closely: WATCH (verb) 7] 6x
<3907> παρατήρησις ***paratērēsis*** [with observation, with careful observation: OBSERVATION] 1x
<3908> παρατίθημι ***paratithēmi*** [COMMIT 4, to lay down: LAY 6, to set before: SET (verb) 13] 19x
<3909> παρατυγχάνω ***paratunchanō*** [MEET (verb) 6] 1x
<3910> παραυτίκα ***parautika*** [for a moment: MOMENT 3] 1x
<3911> παραφέρω ***parapherō*** [to take away: TAKE 39] 2x
<3912> παραφρονέω ***paraphroneō*** [to be out of one's mind: MIND (noun) 11] 1x
<3913> παραφρονία ***paraphronia*** [MADNESS 3] 1x
<3914> παραχειμάζω ***paracheimazō*** [WINTER (verb) 1] 4x
<3915> παραχειμασία ***paracheimasia*** [WINTERING] 1x
<3916> παραχρῆμα ***parachrēma*** [IMMEDIATELY 3] 18x
<3917> πάρδαλις ***pardalis*** [LEOPARD] 1x
<3917a> παρεδρεύω ***paredreuō*** [SERVE 6] 1x
<3918> πάρειμι ***pareimi*** [COME 26, PRESENT (BE) 3] 24x
<3919> παρεισάγω ***pareisagō*** [to secretly introduce, to secretly bring in: SECRETLY 3] 1x
<3920> παρείσακτος ***pareisaktos*** [secretly brought in: SECRETLY 2] 1x
<3921> παρεισδύω ***pareisduō*** [to get in unnoticed: GET 4] 1x
<3922> παρεισέρχομαι ***pareiserchomai*** [to come in: COME 7, to come in surreptitiously: SURREPTITIOUSLY 1] 2x
<3923> παρεισφέρω ***pareispherō*** [GIVE 15] 1x
<3924> παρεκτός ***parektos*** [except, except for: EXCEPT 2, WITHOUT 3] 3x
<3925> παρεμβολή ***parembolē*** [ARMY 1, CAMP 1, FORTRESS 1] 10x
<3926> παρενοχλέω ***parenochleō*** [TROUBLE (verb) 3] 1x
<3927> παρεπίδημος ***parepidēmos*** [SOJOURNER 1, STRANGER 4] 3x
<3928> παρέρχομαι ***parerchomai*** [COME 11, GO 13, to pass; to pass over, by: PASS 3, SPEND 4, TRANSGRESS 2] 29x
<3929> πάρεσις ***paresis*** [passing by, passing over: PASSING 1] 1x
<3930> παρέχω ***parechō*** [BRING 33, CAUSE (verb) 1, GIVE 16, OFFER 3, SHOW (verb) 13, to cause trouble: TROUBLE (verb) 5, to give trouble: TROUBLE (verb) 11, to be worthy: WORTHY 7] 16x
<3931> παρηγορία ***parēgoria*** [COMFORT (noun) 2] 1x
<3932> παρθενία ***parthenia*** [VIRGINITY 1] 1x
<3933> παρθένος ***parthenos*** [VIRGIN 1] 15x
<3934> Πάρθος ***Parthos*** [PARTHIAN] 1x
<3935> παρίημι ***pariēmi*** [to hang down: HANG 5] 2x
<3936> παρίστημι ***paristēmi*** [ASSIST 1, COME 34, COMMEND 1, to put at the disposal: DISPOSAL 1, PRESENT (verb) 1, PROVE 2, PROVIDE 2, to take one's stand: STAND (noun) 1, to stand by, before, beside, near: STAND (verb) 3] 41x
<3937> Παρμενᾶς ***Parmenas*** [PARMENAS] 1x
<3938> πάροδος ***parodos*** [in passing: PASSING 2] 1x
<3939> παροικέω ***paroikeō*** [DWELL 5, VISIT (verb) 2] 2x
<3940> παροικία ***paroikia*** [STAY (noun)] 2x
<3941> πάροικος ***paroikos*** [DWELLER 1, FOREIGNER 2] 4x
<3942> παροιμία ***paroimia*** [ALLEGORY 1, PROVERB 1] 5x
<3943> πάροινος ***paroinos*** [given to wine: GIVE 19] 2x
<3944> παροίχομαι ***paroichomai*** [to pass: PAST 3] 1x
<3945> παρομοιάζω ***paromoiazō*** [to be like: LIKE (adj., adv., noun) 6] 1x
<3946> παρόμοιος ***paromoios*** [LIKE (adj., adv., noun) 5] 2x
<3947> παροξύνω ***paroxunō*** [to be painfully excited: EXCITE 1, to be quickly (easily) provoked: PROVOKE 3] 2x
<3948> παροξυσμός ***paroxusmos*** [DISAGREEMENT 1, PROVOKE 4] 2x
<3949> παροργίζω ***parorgizō*** [ANGER (verb), PROVOKE 5] 2x
<3950> παροργισμός ***parorgismos*** [WRATH 3] 1x

<3951> παροτρύνω ***parotrunō*** [EXCITE 2] 1x

<3952> παρουσία ***parousia*** [COMING 2, PRESENCE 1] 24x

<3953> παροψίς ***paropsis*** [DISH 1] 2x

<3954> παρρησία ***parrēsia*** [boldness: BOLDLY 2, BOLDNESS 1, CONFIDENCE 1, OPENLY 1, PUBLIC 2] 31x

<3955> παρρησιάζομαι ***parrēsiazomai*** [to grow bold: BOLD 2, to speak boldly: BOLDLY 3] 9x

<3956> πᾶς ***pas*** [ALL 2, ALWAYS 2] 1,243x

<3957> Πάσχα ***Pascha*** [PASSOVER] 29x

<3958> πάσχω ***paschō*** [SUFFER 1] 42x

<3959> Πάταρα ***Patara*** [PATARA] 1x

<3960> πατάσσω ***patassō*** [to strike, to strike down: STRIKE 3] 10x

<3961> πατέω ***pateō*** [TRAMPLE 1, to tread, to tread down, to tread underfoot:TREAD 2] 5x

<3962> πατήρ ***patēr*** [FATHER 1, PARENT 3] 415x

<3963> Πάτμος ***Patmos*** [PATMOS] 1x

<3964> πατρολῴας ***patrolōas*** [murderer of father: FATHER 3] 1x

<3965> πατριά ***patria*** [FAMILY 2] 3x

<3966> πατριάρχης ***patriarchēs*** [PATRIARCH] 4x

<3967> πατρικός ***patrikos*** [of one's fathers: FATHER 4] 1x

<3968> πατρίς ***patris*** [COUNTRY 3] 8x

<3969> Πατροβᾶς ***Patrobas*** [PATROBAS] 1x

<3970> πατροπαράδοτος ***patroparadotos*** [received by tradition from the fathers: FATHER 6] 1x

<3971> πατρῷος ***patrōos*** [of the fathers: FATHER 5] 3x

<3972> Παῦλος ***Paulos*** [PAUL, SERGIUS PAULUS] 158x

<3973> παύω ***pauō*** [CEASE 3, REFRAIN 1] 15x

<3974> Πάφος ***Paphos*** [PAPHOS] 2x

<3975> παχύνω ***pachunō*** [to become dull, to grow dull: DULL 1] 2x

<3976> πέδη ***pedē*** [SHACKLE] 3x

<3977> πεδινός ***pedinos*** [LEVEL (adj.) 1] 1x

<3978> πεζεύω ***pezeuō*** [to go on foot: FOOT[1] 5] 1x

<3979> πεζῇ ***pezē*** [on foot: FOOT[1] 4] 2x

<3980> πειθαρχέω ***peitharcheō*** [LISTEN 3, to be obedient: OBEDIENT 2, OBEY 3] 4x

<3981> πειθός ***peithos*** [PERSUASIVE 1] 1x

<3982> πείθω ***peithō*** [AGREE 3, ASSURE 1, to have confidence, to put confidence, to be confident: CONFIDENCE 4, to be confident, to become confident: CONFIDENT 2, OBEY 2, PERSUADE 1, PERSUADED (BE) 1, TRUST (verb) 3, to win over: WIN 1, YIELD 1] 52x

<3983> πεινάω ***peinaō*** [to be hungry, to become hungry: HUNGRY 3] 23x

<3984> πεῖρα ***peira*** [ATTEMPT (verb) 1, TRIAL 2] 2x

<3985> πειράζω ***peirazō*** [EXAMINE 3, TEMPT 1, to tempt: TEMPTER, to test: TEST (noun and verb) 2, TRY[1] 1] 38x

<3986> πειρασμός ***peirasmos*** [TEMPTATION 1, TRIAL 1] 21x

<3987> πειράω ***peiraō*** [TRY[1] 2] 2x

<3988> πεισμονή ***peismonē*** [PERSUASION] 1x

<3989> πέλαγος ***pelagos*** [to be sunk in the depth of the sea: DEPTH 2, sea, open sea: SEA 5] 2x

<3990> πελεκίζω ***pelekizō*** [BEHEAD 2] 1x

<3991> πέμπτος ***pemptos*** [FIFTH] 4x

<3992> πέμπω ***pempō*** [SEND 4, to send: SENT 3, to thrust in: THRUST 1] 79x

<3993> πένης ***penēs*** [POOR (noun) 1] 1x

<3994> πενθερά ***penthera*** [wife's mother, mother in law, mother-in-law: MOTHER 4] 6x

<3995> πενθερός ***pentheros*** [FATHER-IN-LAW] 1x

<3996> πενθέω ***pentheō*** [BEWAIL 1, MOURN 3] 10x

<3997> πένθος ***penthos*** [MOURNING 2] 5x

<3998> πενιχρός ***penichros*** [POOR (adj.) 1] 1x

<3999> πεντάκις ***pentakis*** [five times: TIME 18] 1x

<4000> πεντακισχίλιοι ***pentakischilioi*** [FIVE THOUSAND 1] 6x

<4001> πεντακόσιοι ***pentakosioi*** [FIVE HUNDRED] 2x

<4002> πέντε ***pente*** [FIFTY THOUSAND, FIVE 1, SEVENTY-FIVE, TWENTY-FIVE] 34x

<4003> πεντεκαιδέκατος ***pentekaidekatos*** [FIFTEENTH] 1x

<4004> πεντήκοντα ***pentēkonta*** [FIFTY, FOUR HUNDRED AND FIFTY, HUNDRED AND FIFTY-THREE] 7x

<4005> Πεντηκοστή ***Pentēkostē*** [PENTECOST] 3x

<4006> πεποίθησις ***pepoithēsis*** [CONFIDENCE 2] 6x

<4007> περ ***per*** [IF 3] 3x

<4007a> περαιτέρω ***peraiterō*** [FURTHER (adv.) 1] 1x

<4008> πέραν ***peran*** [OVER 1, SIDE 7] 23x

<4009> πέρας ***peras*** [END (noun) 2, EXTREMITY 1, uttermost part: PART (noun) 5] 4x

<4010> Πέργαμος ***Pergamos*** [PERGAMUM] 2x

<4011> Πέργη ***Pergē*** [PERGA] 3x

<4012> περί ***peri*** [about them, around them: ABOUT 2, CONCERNING 2] 330x

<4013> περιάγω ***periagō*** [to go, to go about, to go around, etc.: GO 3, to take along: TAKE 14] 6x

<4014> περιαιρέω ***periaireō*** [LOOSE 4, to take away, to take up: TAKE 23] 4x

<4014a> περιάπτω ***periaptō*** [KINDLE 2] 1x

<4015> περιαστράπτω ***periastraptō*** [to shine around: SHINE 2] 2x

<4016> περιβάλλω ***periballō*** [to build around: BUILD 5, CLOTHE 7, WEAR 3, to wrap around: WRAP 3] 23x

<4017> περιβλέπω ***periblepō*** [to look around, round upon, etc.: LOOK (verb) 7] 7x

<4018> περιβόλαιον ***peribolaion*** [CLOAK 2, VEIL (noun) 3] 2x

<4019> περιδέω ***perideō*** [WRAP 4] 1x

<4020> περιεργάζομαι ***periergazomai*** [to be a busybody, to act like a busybody: BUSYBODY 1] 1x

<4021> περίεργος ***periergos*** [BUSYBODY 2, MAGIC 1] 2x

<4022> περιέρχομαι ***perierchomai*** [CIRCLE ROUND, to go here and there, about, around, from place to place: ITINERANT, to wander about: WANDER 1] 4x

<4023> περιέχω ***periechō*** [to contain: AFTER 1, CONTAIN 1, SEIZE 9] 3x

<4024> περιζώννυμι ***perizōnnumi*** [to gird, to gird about: GIRD 4] 7x

<4025> περίθεσις ***perithesis*** [ORNAMENT 1] 1x

<4026> περιΐστημι ***periistēmi*** [SHUN 1, to stand by, about, around: STAND (verb) 4] 4x

<4027> περικάθαρμα ***perikatharma*** [FILTH 1] 1x

<4028> περικαλύπτω ***perikaluptō*** [COVER 4] 3x

<4029> περίκειμαι ***perikeimai*** [to be bound with: BIND 5, to hang about, to hang around: HANG 6, to be subject: SUBJECT (verb) 3, SURROUND 3] 5x

<4030> περικεφαλαία ***perikephalaia*** [HELMET] 2x

<4031> περικρατής ***perikratēs*** [SECURING] 1x

<4032> περικρύπτω ***perikruptō*** [HIDE 4] 1x

<4033> περικυκλόω ***perikukloō*** [SURROUND 2] 1x

<4034> περιλάμπω ***perilampō*** [to shine around, to shine all around, to shine round about: SHINE 6] 2x

<4035> περιλείπω ***perileipō*** [REMAIN 8] 2x

<4036> περίλυπος ***perilupos*** [very sad: SAD 2, exceeding, exceedingly, very sorrowful: SORROWFUL 1, very sorry: SORRY 1] 5x

<4037> περιμένω ***perimenō*** [to wait for: WAIT (verb) 2] 1x

<4038> πέριξ ***perix*** [round about: ROUND 2] 1x

<4039> περιοικέω ***perioikeō*** [to dwell around: DWELL 6] 1x

<4040> περίοικος ***perioikos*** [NEIGHBOR 2] 1x

<4041> περιούσιος ***periousios*** [PECULIAR] 1x

<4042> περιοχή ***periochē*** [PASSAGE 1] 1x

<4043> περιπατέω ***peripateō*** [LIVE 9, WALK 1] 95x

<4044> περιπείρω ***peripeirō*** [PIERCE 5] 1x

<4045> περιπίπτω ***peripiptō*** [to fall among, to fall into, to fall into the hands: FALL (verb) 8] 3x

<4046> περιποιέω ***peripoieō*** [PURCHASE (verb) 2] 2x
<4047> περιποίησις ***peripoiēsis*** [OBTAINING, acquired possession, own possession: POSSESSION 3, acquisition: RECEIVE 21, SAVING 1] 5x
<4048> περιρήγνυμι ***perirēgnumi*** [to rend off: REND 1] 1x
<4049> περισπάω ***perispaō*** [DISTRACTED (BE)] 1x
<4050> περισσεία ***perisseia*** [ABUNDANCE 2, overabundance: ABUNDANTLY 1, OVERFLOW (noun) 1] 4x
<4051> περίσσευμα ***perisseuma*** [ABUNDANCE 3, that remained: REST (noun)[2] 4] 5x
<4052> περισσεύω ***perisseuō*** [ABOUND 1, to be in abundance, to consist in the abundance, to have abundance, to have in abundance: ABUNDANCE 4, EXCEED 1, EXCEL 1, INCREASE (verb) 2, REMAIN 10, SURPASS 1, SURPLUS 1] 39x
<4053> περισσός ***perissos*** [ABUNDANTLY 2, ADVANTAGE (noun) 1, exceedingly beyond measure: EXCEEDINGLY 5, HIGHLY (VERY), SUPERFLUOUS] 6x
<4054> περισσότερον ***perissoteron*** [more abundantly: ABUNDANTLY 3] 4x
<4055> περισσότερος ***perissoteros*** [EXCESSIVE, greater: GREAT 7, MORE 8, severer: SEVERE 1] 16x
<4056> περισσοτέρως ***perissoterōs*** [exceedingly abundant, more abundant: ABUNDANT 1, very abundantly: ABUNDANTLY 4, EXCEEDINGLY 3, the more, all the more: MORE 4] 12x
<4057> περισσῶς ***perissōs*** [EXCEEDINGLY 2, more than ever: MORE 5, more vehemently: VEHEMENTLY 2] 4x
<4058> περιστερά ***peristera*** [DOVE] 10x
<4059> περιτέμνω ***peritemnō*** [CIRCUMCISE 1] 18x
<4060> περιτίθημι ***peritithēmi*** [BESTOW 2, to put on: PUT 4, to set around: SET (verb) 14] 8x
<4061> περιτομή ***peritomē*** [CIRCUMCISION 1] 36x
<4062> περιτρέπω ***peritrepō*** [DRIVE 5] 1x
<4063> περιτρέχω ***peritrechō*** [to run about, through, throughout: RUN 4] 1x
<4064> περιφέρω ***peripherō*** [to bear about: BEAR (verb) 5, to carry, to carry about, away, along: CARRY 10] 5x
<4065> περιφρονέω ***periphroneō*** [DESPISE 5] 1x
<4066> περίχωρος ***perichōros*** [country around, surrounding country: COUNTRY 5, region around, surrounding region: REGION 4] 10x
<4067> περίψημα ***peripsēma*** [REFUSE (noun)] 1x
<4068> περπερεύομαι ***perpereuomai*** [BOAST (verb) 2] 1x
<4069> Περσίς ***Persis*** [PERSIS] 1x
<4070> πέρυσι ***perusi*** [a year ago, last year: YEAR 9] 2x
<4071> πετεινόν ***peteinon*** [BIRD 2] 14x
<4072> πέτομαι ***petomai*** [FLY] 5x
<4073> πέτρα ***petra*** [ROCK 1] 15x
<4074> Πέτρος ***Petros*** [PETER] 154x
<4075> πετρώδης ***petrōdēs*** [rocky place, rocky ground: ROCK 2] 4x
<4076> πήγανον ***pēganon*** [RUE] 1x
<4077> πηγή ***pēgē*** [FLOW (noun) 1, FOUNTAIN] 12x
<4078> πήγνυμι ***pēgnumi*** [ERECT (verb) 1] 1x
<4079> πηδάλιον ***pēdalion*** [RUDDER] 2x
<4080> πηλίκος ***pēlikos*** [how great: GREAT 8, what large: LARGE 2] 2x
<4081> πηλός ***pēlos*** [CLAY 1] 6x
<4082> πήρα ***pēra*** [BAG 2] 6x
<4083> πῆχυς ***pēchus*** [CUBIT] 4x
<4084> πιάζω ***piazō*** [SEIZE 11, to take, to take hold of: TAKE 38] 12x
<4085> πιέζω ***piezō*** [to press down: PRESS 8] 1x
<4086> πιθανολογία ***pithanologia*** [persuasive word: WORD 3] 1x
<4087> πικραίνω ***pikrainō*** [to be bitter, to make bitter: BITTER 2] 4x
<4088> πικρία ***pikria*** [BITTERNESS] 4x
<4089> πικρός ***pikros*** [BITTER 1] 2x

<4090> πικρῶς ***pikrōs*** [BITTERLY] 2x
<4091> Πιλᾶτος ***Pilatos*** [PONTIUS PILATE] 55x
<4091a> πίμπλημι; see <4130>.
<4092> πίμπρημι ***pimprēmi*** [to swell up: SWELL] 1x
<4093> πινακίδιον ***pinakidion*** [TABLET 1] 1x
<4094> πίναξ ***pinax*** [DISH 2] 5x
<4095> πίνω ***pinō*** [DRINK (verb) 1] 73x
<4096> πιότης ***piotēs*** [FATNESS] 1x
<4097> πιπράσκω ***pipraskō*** [SELL 2] 9x
<4098> πίπτω ***piptō*** [to fall, to fall down: FALL (verb) 1, PERISH 7, STRIKE 4] 90x
<4099> Πισιδία ***Pisidia*** [PISIDIA] 2x
<4100> πιστεύω ***pisteuō*** [BELIEVE 1, to believe: BELIEVER 1, COMMIT 5, ENTRUST 1] 241x
<4101> πιστικός ***pistikos*** [PURE 6] 2x
<4102> πίστις ***pistis*** [ASSURANCE 1, faith: BELIEVE 4, FAITH 1, FAITHFULNESS] 243x
<4102a> πιστὸν ***piston*** [FAITHFULLY] 1x
<4103> πιστός ***pistos*** [BELIEVING 1, FAITHFUL 1, SURE 3] 66x
<4104> πιστόω ***pistoō*** [ASSURED (BE) 1] 1x
<4105> πλανάω ***planaō*** [to go astray: ASTRAY 1, DECEIVE 5, MISTAKEN (BE), STRAY 2, WANDER 2] 39x
<4106> πλάνη ***planē*** [deceit: DECEITFUL 2, DECEPTION 1, strong delusion: DELUSION, ERROR 1] 10x
<4107> πλανήτης ***planētēs*** [WANDERING] 1x
<4108> πλάνος ***planos*** [DECEIVER 1] 5x
<4109> πλάξ ***plax*** [TABLE[2] 1] 3x
<4110> πλάσμα ***plasma*** [thing molded: MOLDED] 1x
<4111> πλάσσω ***plassō*** [FORM (verb) 2] 2x
<4112> πλαστός ***plastos*** [FEIGNED] 1x
<4113> πλατεῖα ***plateia*** [STREET 1] 9x
<4114> πλάτος ***platos*** [BREADTH] 4x
<4115> πλατύνω ***platunō*** [EXPAND 1] 3x
<4116> πλατύς ***platus*** [WIDE 1] 1x
<4117> πλέγμα ***plegma*** [BRAIDED HAIR] 1x
<4118> πλεῖστος ***pleistos*** [GREAT 10, MOST 1] 3x
<4119> πλεῖον ***pleion*** [MORE 6] and πλείων ***pleiōn*** [more excellent: EXCELLENT 5, greater: GREAT 9, MORE 7] 55x
<4120> πλέκω ***plekō*** [to twist, to twist together: TWIST 1] 3x
<4121> πλεονάζω ***pleonazō*** [ABOUND 3, to have something over: OVER 2] 9x
<4122> πλεονεκτέω ***pleonekteō*** [to take advantage: ADVANTAGE (noun) 2, CHEAT 1, WRONG (verb) 1] 5x
<4123> πλεονέκτης ***pleonektēs*** [COVETOUS (noun)] 4x
<4124> πλεονεξία ***pleonexia*** [COVETOUSNESS 1, GREEDINESS 1] 10x
<4125> πλευρά ***pleura*** [SIDE 1] 5x
<4126> πλέω ***pleō*** [SAIL (verb) 2] 6x
<4127> πληγή ***plēgē*** [PLAGUE 1, STRIPE 2, wound: WOUND (verb) 4] 22x
<4128> πλῆθος ***plēthos*** [MULTITUDE 2, QUANTITY 1] 32x
<4129> πληθύνω ***plēthunō*** [ABOUND 4, MULTIPLY] 12x
<4130> πίμπλημι ***pimplēmi*** and πλήθω ***plēthō*** [ACCOMPLISH 3, to come, to come fully: COME 35, FILL (verb) 7, FILL (verb) 9] 24x
<4131> πλήκτης ***plēktēs*** [STRIKER] 2x
<4132> πλήμμυρα ***plēmmura*** [FLOOD (noun) 2] 1x
<4133> πλήν ***plēn*** [BUT 3, EXCEPT 3, NEVERTHELESS 4, ONLY 3] 31x
<4134> πλήρης ***plērēs*** [FULL 1] 17x
<4135> πληροφορέω ***plērophoreō*** [to believe most surely: BELIEVE 5, to be complete: COMPLETE (adj.) 2, to be fully persuaded: PERSUADE 3, to preach fully: PREACH 7,

to make full proof: PROOF 4] 6x

<4136> πληροφορία ***plērophoria*** [full assurance, much assurance: ASSURANCE 2] 4x

<4137> πληρόω ***plēroō*** [COMPLETE (verb) 1, CONCLUDE[2], to fill up: FILL (verb) 2, FILLED (BE) 1, FULFILL 5, PASS 12, to be past: PAST 2, to preach fully: PREACH 8, SUPPLY (verb) 3] 86x

<4138> πλήρωμα ***plērōma*** [FULFILLMENT 1, filling: FULL 2, FULLNESS, PATCH 1, PIECE 3] 17x

<4139> πλησίον ***plēsion*** [NEIGHBOR 3] 17x

<4140> πλησμονή ***plēsmonē*** [INDULGENCE 1] 1x

<4141> πλήσσω ***plēssō*** [STRIKE 5] 1x

<4142> πλοιάριον ***ploiarion*** [small ship, little ship, boat: SHIP 2] 5x

<4143> πλοῖον ***ploion*** [SHIP 1] 67x

<4144> πλόος ***ploos*** [NAVIGATION] 3x

<4145> πλούσιος ***plousios*** [RICH 2] 28x

<4146> πλουσίως ***plousiōs*** [RICHLY] 4x

<4147> πλουτέω ***plouteō*** [to be rich, to become rich, to get rich, to abound in riches: RICH 3, to become wealthy: WEALTHY 1] 12x

<4148> πλουτίζω ***ploutizō*** [ENRICH 1] 3x

<4149> πλοῦτος ***ploutos*** [RICHES 1] 21x

<4150> πλύνω ***plunō*** [WASH 7] 3x

<4151> πνεῦμα ***pneuma*** [BREATH 1, HOLY SPIRIT, SPIRIT 1, WIND (noun) 3] 383x

<4152> πνευματικός ***pneumatikos*** [GIFT 9, SPIRITUAL 1] 26x

<4153> πνευματικῶς ***pneumatikōs*** [SPIRITUALLY] 2x

<4154> πνέω ***pneō*** [BLOW (verb) 2] 7x

<4155> πνίγω ***pnigō*** [DROWN 2, to take by the throat: THROAT 2] 2x

<4156> πνικτός ***pniktos*** [STRANGLED] 3x

<4157> πνοή ***pnoē*** [BREATH 2, WIND (noun) 4] 3x

<4158> ποδήρης ***podērēs*** [reaching to the feet, down to the feet: FOOT[1] 3] 1x

<4159> πόθεν ***pothen*** [FROM WERE] 28x

<4160> ποιέω ***poieō*** [ACCOMPLISH 4, APPOINT 6, BEAR (verb) 6, CAUSE (verb) 2, COMMIT 6, CONTENT (verb) 2, CONTINUE 9, DO 5, EARN 1, EXECUTE 1, EXERCISE (verb) 3, FULFILL 8, GOOD (adv.) 1, JOURNEY (verb) 3, KEEP (verb) 7, to lighten the ship: LIGHTEN 2, MAKE 6, MIND (CALL TO) 1, PASS 13, PERFORM 4, to put in practice: PRACTICE (noun) 1, PRACTICE (verb) 2, PRODUCE 7, to make an uprising: RAISE 8, SHOW (verb) 14, WORK (verb) 5] 568x

<4161> ποίημα ***poiēma*** [WORKMANSHIP 1] 2x

<4162> ποίησις ***poiēsis*** [DOING 2] 1x

<4163> ποιητής ***poiētēs*** [DOER 1, POET] 6x

<4164> ποικίλος ***poikilos*** [MANIFOLD 1, VARIOUS 3] 10x

<4165> ποιμαίνω ***poimainō*** [FEED 2, to feed the sheep: SHEEP 3, SHEPHERD (verb) 1] 11x

<4166> ποιμήν ***poimēn*** [SHEPHERD (noun) 1] 18x

<4167> ποίμνη ***poimnē*** [FLOCK 1] 5x

<4168> ποίμνιον ***poimnion*** [FLOCK 2] 5x

<4169> ποῖος ***poios*** [what way, any way, a way: WAY 4] 34x

<4170> πολεμέω ***polemeō*** [FIGHT (verb) 4, WAR (verb) 1] 7x

<4171> πόλεμος ***polemos*** [BATTLE (noun) 1, FIGHT (noun) 3, WAR (noun) 1] 18x

<4172> πόλις ***polis*** [CITY 1] 162x

<4173> πολιτάρχης ***politarchēs*** [ruler of the city: RULER 5] 2x

<4174> πολιτεία ***politeia*** [CITIZENSHIP 1] 2x

<4175> πολίτευμα ***politeuma*** [CITIZENSHIP 2] 1x

<4176> πολιτεύω ***politeuō*** [LIVE 10] 2x

<4177> πολίτης ***politēs*** [CITIZEN] 4x

<4178> πολλάκις ***pollakis*** [OFTEN 2] 19x

<4179> πολλαπλασίων ***pollaplasiōn*** [MANY TIMES MORE] 1x

<4180> πολυλογία ***polulogia*** [much speaking: SPEAKING 1] 1x

<4181> πολυμερῶς ***polumerōs*** [at many, various, sundry times: TIMES (AT MANY)] 1x
<4182> πολυποίκιλος ***polupoikilos*** [MANIFOLD 2] 1x
<4183> πολύς ***polus*** [EARNESTLY 3, GREAT 11, HEARTILY, MANY 2, MUCH 1, far past, far spent: PASS 14, long time, great length of time: TIME 7] 358x
<4184> πολύσπλαγχνος ***polusplanchnos*** [very compassionate: COMPASSIONATE 1] 1x
<4185> πολυτελής ***polutelēs*** [COSTLY 1, of great price: PRICE (noun) 3] 3x
<4186> πολύτιμος ***polutimos*** [of great price: PRICE (noun) 4] 2x
<4187> πολυτρόπως ***polutropōs*** [in various ways: WAY 5] 1x
<4188> πόμα ***poma*** [DRINK (noun) 1] 2x
<4189> πονηρία ***ponēria*** [WICKEDNESS 2] 7x
<4190> πονηρός ***ponēros*** [EVIL (adj.) 2, EVIL (noun) 2, WICKED (noun) 2] 78x
<4191> πονηρότερος ***ponēroteros*** [more wicked: WICKED (adj.) 1] 2x
<4192> πόνος ***ponos*** [PAIN (noun) 1] 3x
<4193> Ποντικός ***Pontikos*** [PONTUS 2] 1x
<4194> Πόντιος ***Pontios*** [PONTIUS PILATE] 4x
<4195> Πόντος ***Pontos*** [PONTUS 1] 2x
<4196> Πόπλιος ***Poplios*** [PUBLIUS] 2x
<4197> πορεία ***poreia*** [way: JOURNEY (verb) 2, PURSUIT 1] 2x
<4198> πορεύομαι ***poreuomai*** [DEPART 13, FOLLOW 10, GO 23, TRAVEL 1, WALK 3] 153x
<4199> πορθέω ***portheō*** [DESTROY 12] 3x
<4200> πορισμός ***porismos*** [gain, means of gain, means to financial gain: GAIN (noun) 4] 2x
<4201> Πόρκιος ***Porkios*** [PORCIUS] 1x
<4202> πορνεία ***porneia*** [FORNICATION 1] 25x
<4203> πορνεύω ***porneuō*** [to commit fornication: FORNICATION 1] 8x
<4204> πόρνη ***pornē*** [PROSTITUTE 1] 12x
<4205> πόρνος ***pornos*** [FORNICATOR] 10x
<4206> πόρρω ***porrō*** [FAR 3] 3x
<4207> πόρρωθεν ***porrōthen*** [AFAR OFF 1] 2x
<4208> πορρώτερον ***porrōteron*** [FARTHER 1] 1x
<4209> πορφύρα ***porphura*** [PURPLE (noun) 1] 5x
<4210> πορφυροῦς ***porphurous*** [PURPLE (adj.)] 3x
<4211> πορφυρόπωλις ***porphuropōlis*** [seller of purple, dealer in purple: PURPLE (noun) 2] 1x
<4212> ποσάκις ***posakis*** [how often: OFTEN 3] 3x
<4213> πόσις ***posis*** [DRINK (noun) 2] 3x
<4214> πόσος ***posos*** [HOW GREAT?, HOW MUCH MORE?] 27x
<4215> ποταμός ***potamos*** [RIVER 1, STREAM 1] 16x
<4216> ποταμοφόρητος ***potamophorētos*** [carried away by a river: RIVER 2] 1x
<4217> ποταπός ***potapos*** [WHAT?] 6x
<4218> ποτέ ***pote*** [AFORETIME, FORMERLY 1, in time(s) past: PAST 5] 29x
<4219> πότε ***pote*** [HOW LONG?] 19x
<4220> πότερον ***poteron*** [WHETHER 2] 1x
<4221> ποτήριον ***potērion*** [CUP] 31x
<4222> ποτίζω ***potizō*** [to drink, to give to drink: DRINK (verb) 3, WATER (verb)] 15x
<4223> Ποτίολοι ***Potioloi*** [PUTEOLI] 1x
<4224> πότος ***potos*** [DRINKING 1] 1x
<4225> πού ***pou*** [ABOUT 1] 3x
<4226> ποῦ ***pou*** [WHERE 4] 47x
<4227> Πούδης ***Poudēs*** [PUDENS] 1x
<4228> πούς ***pous*** [FOOT[1] 1] 93x
<4229> πρᾶγμα ***pragma*** [BUSINESS 4, MATTER 1, THING 1, WORK (noun) 3] 11x
<4230> πραγματεία ***pragmateia*** [AFFAIR 1] 1x
<4231> πραγματεύομαι ***pragmateuomai*** [to do business, to engage in business: BUSINESS 5] 1x
<4232> πραιτώριον ***praitōrion*** [PRAETORIUM] 8x
<4233> πράκτωρ ***praktōr*** [OFFICER 1] 2x
<4234> πρᾶξις ***praxis*** [DEED 3, FUNCTION (noun) 1, WORK (noun) 4] 6x

<4235> πρᾶος ***praos*** [GENTLE 3] 1x
<4236> πραότης ***praotēs*** [GENTLENESS 3] 9x
<4237> πρασιά ***prasia*** [rank: GROUP 1] 2x
<4238> πράσσω ***prassō*** [COLLECT 2, to do contrary, to act contrary: CONTRARY 6, DO 6, KEEP (verb) 8, USE (verb) 4] 39x
<4239> πραΰς ***praus*** [GENTLE 4, MEEK 1] 4x
<4240> πραΰτης ***prautēs*** [MEEKNESS 1] 3x
<4241> πρέπω ***prepō*** [to be comely: COMELY 2, FITTING (BE) 3, to be proper: PROPER 1] 7x
<4242> πρεσβεία ***presbeia*** [DELEGATION] 2x
<4243> πρεσβεύω ***presbeuō*** [AMBASSADOR (BE)] 2x
<4244> πρεσβυτέριον ***presbuterion*** [council of elders, elderhood: ELDER 2] 3x
<4245> πρεσβύτερος ***presbuteros*** [ELDER 1, ELDEST, OLD MAN 1] 66x
<4246> πρεσβύτης ***presbutēs*** [OLD MAN 2] 3x
<4247> πρεσβῦτις ***presbutis*** [AGED WOMAN] 1x
<4248> πρηνής ***prēnēs*** [HEADLONG 1] 1x
<4249> πρίζω ***prizō*** [to saw asunder, to saw in two: SAW] 1x
<4250> πρίν ***prin*** [BEFORE 5] 13x
<4251> Πρίσκα ***Priska*** [PRISCA, PRISCILLA] and
<4252> Πρίσκιλλα ***Priskilla*** [PRISCA, PRISCILLA] 6x
<4253> πρό ***pro*** [BEFORE 3] 48x
<4254> προάγω ***proagō*** [to go ahead: AHEAD 1, to bring out, forth, before, etc.: BRING 8, to enter before, to go before: ENTER 5, to go before: FORMER 3, to go before, ahead of: GO 2, to make previously: PREVIOUSLY 1, TRANSGRESS 3] 20x
<4255> προαιρέω ***proaireō*** [PURPOSE (verb) 2] 1x
<4256> προαιτιάομαι ***proaitiaomai*** [to prove before: PROVE 3] 1x
<4257> προακούω ***proakouō*** [to hear already, before, previously: HEAR 5] 1x
<4258> προαμαρτάνω ***proamartanō*** [SIN (verb) 2] 2x
<4259> προαύλιον ***proaulion*** [PORCH 1] 1x
<4260> προβαίνω ***probainō*** [to be well advanced: ADVANCE 1, to go on: GO 20] 5x
<4261> προβάλλω ***proballō*** [to push forward: PUSH 1, SPROUT 2] 2x
<4262> Προβατική ***Probatikē*** [SHEEP 2] 1x
<4263> πρόβατον ***probaton*** [SHEEP 1] 40x
<4264> προβιβάζω ***probibazō*** [to draw out: DRAW 2, PROMPT 1] 2x
<4265> προβλέπω ***problepō*** [FORESEE 1] 1x
<4266> προγίνομαι ***proginomai*** [to commit previously, to commit beforehand: COMMIT 7] 1x
<4267> προγινώσκω ***proginōskō*** [FOREKNOW, to know; to know already, before, beforehand, etc.: KNOW 4] 5x
<4268> πρόγνωσις ***prognōsis*** [FOREKNOWLEDGE] 2x
<4269> πρόγονος ***progonos*** [FOREFATHER 1, PARENT 2] 2x
<4270> προγράφω ***prographō*** [to mark out beforehand: MARK (verb) 2, to portray, to portray clearly, to portray publicly: PORTRAY, to write already, to write before: WRITE 4] 4x
<4271> πρόδηλος ***prodēlos*** [clearly evident, quite evident: CLEARLY 2, EVIDENT 4] 3x
<4272> προδίδωμι ***prodidōmi*** [to give first: GIVE 7] 1x
<4273> προδότης ***prodotēs*** [BETRAYER 1, TRAITOR] 3x
<4274> πρόδρομος ***prodromos*** [FORERUNNER] 1x
<4275> προεῖδον ***proeidon*** [FORESEE 2] 2x
<4276> προελπίζω ***proelpizō*** [to first trust: TRUST (verb) 2] 1x
<4277> προεῖπον ***proeipon*** [to say before: SAY 3] 3x
<4278> προενάρχομαι ***proenarchomai*** [BEGIN 3] 2x
<4279> προεπαγγέλλω ***proepangellō*** [to previously promise: NOTICE (verb) 1, to promise beforehand, before, afore: PROMISE (verb) 3] 2x
<4280> προερέω ***proereō*** [to say before, to say previously: SAY 4]
<4281> προέρχομαι ***proerchomai*** [to go farther, ahead, before, forward, on, through: GO 14, PRECEDE 1] 9x
<4282> προετοιμάζω ***proetoimazō*** [to prepare afore, before, beforehand, in advance: PREPARE 2] 2x

<4283> προευαγγελίζομαι ***proeuangelizomai*** [to preach the gospel before: PREACH 4] 1x

<4284> προέχω ***proechō*** [to be better: BETTER 7] 1x

<4285> προηγέομαι ***proēgeomai*** [to give preference: PREFERENCE] 1x

<4286> πρόθεσις ***prothesis*** [EXPOSITION OF THE LOAVES, PURPOSE (noun) 2] 12x

<4287> προθεσμία ***prothesmia*** [time appointed: TIME 8] 1x

<4288> προθυμία ***prothumia*** [ready mind: MIND (noun) 7, readiness, readiness of mind: READINESS 1] 5x

<4289> πρόθυμος ***prothumos*** [desire: PART (noun) 6, WILLING 2] 3x

<4290> προθύμως ***prothumōs*** [WILLINGLY 2] 1x

<4291> προΐστημι ***proistēmi*** [LEAD (verb) 13, MAINTAIN 1, RULE (verb) 3] 8x

<4292> προκαλέω ***prokaleō*** [to provoke one another: PROVOKE 6] 1x

<4293> προκαταγγέλλω ***prokatangellō*** [to announce beforehand, to announce previously: ANNOUNCE 2, FORETELL 1, to notice before: NOTICE (verb) 1] 4x

<4294> προκαταρτίζω ***prokatartizō*** [to make up beforehand: MAKE 11] 1x

<4295> πρόκειμαι ***prokeimai*** [to be the first: FIRST 7, to set before, to set forth: SET (verb) 4] 5x

<4296> προκηρύσσω ***prokērussō*** [to proclaim before: PROCLAIM 3] 2x

<4297> προκοπή ***prokopē*** [FURTHERANCE, PROGRESS 1] 3x

<4298> προκόπτω ***prokoptō*** [GROW 6, INCREASE (verb) 3, to proceed further: PROCEED 2, to be far spent: SPEND 6] 6x

<4299> πρόκριμα ***prokrima*** [PREJUDICE] 1x

<4300> προκυρόω ***prokuroō*** [to confirm before, to confirm beforehand: CONFIRM 3] 1x

<4301> προλαμβάνω ***prolambanō*** [CATCH (verb) 6, to come aforehand, to come beforehand, to have beforehand: COME 36, to take ahead, before, first: TAKE 8] 3x

<4302> προλέγω ***prolegō*** [to tell before, beforehand, in time past, ahead of time; to foretell: TELL 7] 9x

<4303> προμαρτύρομαι ***promarturomai*** [to testify before, to testify beforehand: TESTIFY 6] 1x

<4304> προμελετάω ***promeletaō*** [to meditate beforehand: MEDITATE 3] 1x

<4305> προμεριμνάω ***promerimnaō*** [to worry beforehand: WORRY (verb) 2] 1x

<4306> προνοέω ***pronoeō*** [PROVIDE 3] 3x

<4307> πρόνοια ***pronoia*** [FORETHOUGHT, PROVISION 1] 2x

<4308> προοράω ***prooraō*** [FORESEE 3, to see before, to see previously: SEE 12] 2x

<4309> προορίζω ***proorizō*** [to determine before: DETERMINE 6, PREDESTINE] 6x

<4310> προπάσχω ***propaschō*** [to suffer already, before, previously: SUFFER 2] 1x

<4311> προπέμπω ***propempō*** [ACCOMPANY 1, to bring on one's journey: JOURNEY (noun) 5, to set forward: SET (verb) 10, to bring, to send, to set on the way: WAY 6] 9x

<4312> προπετής ***propetēs*** [HEADSTRONG 1, RASH 1] 2x

<4313> προπορεύομαι ***proporeuomai*** [to go before: GO 26] 2x

<4314> πρός ***pros*** [PERTAIN 2, TO 2] 701x

<4315> προσάββατον ***prosabbaton*** [day before the Sabbath: SABBATH 2] 1x

<4316> προσαγορεύω ***prosagoreuō*** [DESIGNATE 1] 1x

<4317> προσάγω ***prosagō*** [BRING 9, to draw near: DRAW 9] 4x

<4318> προσαγωγή ***prosagōgē*** [ACCESS] 3x

<4319> προσαιτέω ***prosaiteō*** [BEG 4, to beg: BEGGAR 1] 3x

<4320> προσαναβαίνω ***prosanabainō*** [to go up: GO 21] 1x

<4321> προσαναλίσκω ***prosanaliskō*** [SPEND 5] 1x

<4322> προσαναπληρόω ***prosanaplēroō*** [to supply, to fully supply: SUPPLY (verb) 5] 2x

<4323> προσανατίθημι ***prosanatithēmi*** [ADD 4, CONFER 3] 2x

<4324> προσαπειλέω ***prosapeileō*** [to further threaten: THREATEN 2] 1x

<4325> προσδαπανάω ***prosdapanaō*** [to spend more: SPEND 3] 1x

<4326> προσδέομαι ***prosdeomai*** [NEED (verb) 1] 1x

<4327> προσδέχομαι ***prosdechomai*** [ACCEPT 2, to look for: LOOK (verb) 12, RECEIVE 15, TAKE 33, to wait for: WAIT (verb) 5] 14x

<4328> προσδοκάω ***prosdokaō*** [EXPECT 1, to be in expectation: EXPECTATION 3, to look for, to look when, to look forward: LOOK (verb) 13, TARRY 4, to wait for: WAIT (verb) 6] 16x

<4329> προσδοκία ***prosdokia*** [EXPECTATION 2] 2x
<4330> προσεάω ***proseaō*** [to permit to proceed, to permit to go: PROCEED 3] 1x
<4331> προσεγγίζω ***prosengizō*** [to come near, to come nigh, to get near, to get to: COME 23] 1x
<4332> προσεδρεύω ***prosedreuō*** [SERVE 7] 1x
<4333> προσεργάζομαι ***prosergazomai*** [PRODUCE 6] 1x
<4334> προσέρχομαι ***proserchomai*** [COME 12, CONSENT (verb) 2, to draw near: DRAW 10, to go to, to go unto, to go near: GO 15] 86x
<4335> προσευχή ***proseuchē*** [with prayer: EARNESTLY 5, PRAYER 4] 36x
<4336> προσεύχομαι ***proseuchomai*** [PRAY 4, to make a prayer, to offer a prayer, to be praying, to pray: PRAYER 5] 85x
<4337> προσέχω ***prosechō*** [to give attendance: ATTENDANCE, BEWARE 5, to be given to: GIVE 17, to give heed, to give earnest heed, to heed, to take heed: HEED (noun) 3] 24x
<4338> προσηλόω ***prosēloō*** [NAIL (verb) 1] 1x
<4339> προσήλυτος ***prosēlutos*** [PROSELYTE] 4x
<4340> πρόσκαιρος ***proskairos*** [for a time: TIME 2] 4x
<4341> προσκαλέω ***proskaleō*** [to call, to call unto, to call to: CALL (verb) 6] 30x
<4342> προσκαρτερέω ***proskartereō*** [to attend continually: ATTEND 1, CONTINUE 10, to persevere: PERSEVERING 1, to keep, to have, to stand ready: READY 6] 10x
<4343> προσκαρτέρησις ***proskarterēsis*** [PERSEVERANCE 1] 1x
<4344> προσκεφάλαιον ***proskephalaion*** [CUSHION] 1x
<4345> προσκληρόω ***prosklēroō*** [to join oneself to: JOIN 3] 1x
<4346> πρόσκλισις ***prosklisis*** [PARTIALITY 1] 1x
<4347> προσκολλάω ***proskollaō*** [JOIN 2] 4x
<4348> πρόσκομμα ***proskomma*** [OFFENSE 1, STUMBLING BLOCK 1] 6x
<4349> προσκοπή ***proskopē*** [STUMBLING BLOCK 2] 1x
<4350> προσκόπτω ***proskoptō*** [to beat upon, to beat against: BEAT 5, STRIKE 6, STUMBLE 1] 8x
<4351> προσκυλίω ***proskuliō*** [to roll against, to roll to: ROLL 5] 2x
<4352> προσκυνέω ***proskuneō*** [WORSHIP (verb) 3] 60x
<4353> προσκυνητής ***proskunētēs*** [WORSHIPPER 1] 1x
<4354> προσλαλέω ***proslaleō*** [to speak to, to speak with: SPEAK 9] 2x
<4355> προσλαμβάνω ***proslambanō*** [RECEIVE 6, to take to (oneself), along, aside: TAKE 9] 12x
<4356> πρόσληψις ***proslēpsis*** [ACCEPTANCE 1] 1x
<4357> προσμένω ***prosmenō*** [CONTINUE 6, REMAIN 4] 7x
<4358> προσορμίζω ***prosormizō*** [to draw to, to make, to moor to the shore: SHORE 3] 1x
<4359> προσοφείλω ***prosopheilō*** [OWE 2] 1x
<4360> προσοχθίζω ***prosochthizō*** [to be angry: ANGRY 5] 2x
<4361> πρόσπεινος ***prospeinos*** [HUNGRY 2] 1x
<4362> προσπήγνυμι ***prospēgnumi*** [CRUCIFY 4] 1x
<4363> προσπίπτω ***prospiptō*** [to beat upon: BEAT 6, to fall down before, to fall at the feet (or knees): FALL (verb) 9] 8x
<4364> προσποιέω ***prospoieō*** [to act as if: ACT (verb) 1] 1x
<4365> προσπορεύομαι ***prosporeuomai*** [to come to: COME 16] 1x
<4366> προσρήγνυμι ***prosrēgnumi*** [to break upon: BREAK 10] 2x
<4367> προστάσσω ***prostassō*** [COMMAND (verb) 3, ORDAIN 2] 7x
<4368> προστάτις ***prostatis*** [HELPER 2] 1x
<4369> προστίθημι ***prostithēmi*** [ADD 5, INCREASE (verb) 4, to proceed, to proceed further: PROCEED 4, SPEAK 17] 18x
<4370> προστρέχω ***prostrechō*** [to run, to run to, to run up: RUN 5] 3x
<4371> προσφάγιον ***prosphagion*** [FOOD 5] 1x
<4372> πρόσφατος ***prosphatos*** [NEW 4] 1x
<4373> προσφάτως ***prosphatōs*** [RECENTLY 1] 1x
<4374> προσφέρω ***prospherō*** [BRING 15, to deal with: DEAL 2, to offer, to offer up: OFFER 4] 47x
<4375> προσφιλής ***prosphilēs*** [LOVELY 1] 1x

<4376> προσφορά ***prosphora*** [OFFERING 2] 9x
<4377> προσφωνέω ***prosphōneō*** [ADDRESS (verb) 1, CALL (verb) 12, SPEAK 12] 7x
<4378> πρόσχυσις ***proschusis*** [SPRINKLING 1] 1x
<4379> προσψαύω ***prospsauō*** [TOUCH 4] 1x
<4380> προσωπολη(μ)πτέω ***prosōpolē(m)pteō*** [to have respect of persons: RESPECT OF PERSONS 2] 1x
<4381> προσωπολή(μ)πτης ***prosōpolē(m)ptēs*** [respecter of persons: RESPECT OF PERSONS 3] 1x
<4382> προσωπολη(μ)ψία ***prosōpolē(m)psia*** [RESPECT OF PERSONS 1] 4x
<4383> πρόσωπον ***prosōpon*** [APPEARANCE 3, FACE (noun) 2, PERSON 1, PRESENCE 2] 76x
<4384> προτάσσω ***protassō*** [ORDAIN 3] 1x
<4385> προτείνω ***proteinō*** [BIND 6] 1x
<4386> πρότερον ***proteron*** [BEFORE 4, EARLIER 1, first, at first, at the first, first of all, the first time: FIRST 1, FORMER 1] 10x
<4387> πρότερος ***proteros*** [FORMER 2] 1x
<4388> προτίθημι ***protithēmi*** [PURPOSE (verb) 4, to set forth: SET (verb) 15] 3x
<4389> προτρέπω ***protrepō*** [ENCOURAGE 5, EXHORT 3] 1x
<4390> προτρέχω ***protrechō*** [to run ahead, to run before, to outrun: RUN 6] 2x
<4391> προϋπάρχω ***prouparchō*** [to be before: BEFORE 6] 2x
<4392> πρόφασις ***prophasis*** [PRETEXT] 7x
<4393> προφέρω ***propherō*** [to bring, to bring forth: BRING 16] 2x
<4394> προφητεία ***prophēteia*** [PROPHECY 1] 19x
<4395> προφητεύω ***prophēteuō*** [PROPHESY 2] 28x
<4396> προφήτης ***prophētēs*** [PROPHET 1] 144x
<4397> προφητικός ***prophētikos*** [PROPHETIC 1] 2x
<4398> προφῆτις ***prophētis*** [PROPHETESS] 2x
<4399> προφθάνω ***prophthanō*** [ANTICIPATE 1] 1x
<4400> προχειρίζομαι ***procheirizomai*** [CHOOSE 6, FOREORDAIN 1] 3x
<4400> προχειρίζω ***procheirizō*** [MAKE 12] 1x
<4401> προχειροτονέω ***procheirotoneō*** [to choose before, to choose beforehand: CHOOSE 7] 1x
<4402> Πρόχορος ***Prochoros*** [PROCHORUS] 1x
<4403> πρύμνα ***prumna*** [STERN] 3x
<4404> πρωΐ ***prōi*** [early in the morning, in the morning, early, from morning: MORNING 4] 10x
<4405> πρωΐα ***prōia*** [MORNING 5] 4x
<4406> πρώϊμος ***prōimos*** [EARLY 2] 1x
<4407> πρωϊνός ***prōinos*** [MORNING STAR 2] 1x
<4408> πρῷρα ***prōra*** [PROW] 2x
<4409> πρωτεύω ***prōteuō*** [to have the first place: PLACE (noun) 11] 1x
<4410> πρωτοκαθεδρία ***prōtokathedria*** [first seat: SEAT (noun) 2] 4x
<4411> πρωτοκλισία ***prōtoklisia*** [chief place, place of honor, best place, first place: PLACE (noun) 2] 5x
<4412> πρῶτον ***prōton*** [first, at first: FIRST 2] 60x
<4413> πρῶτος ***prōtos*** [BEST 1, CHIEF 1, FIRST 3, PROMINENT 2] 95x
<4414> πρωτοστάτης ***prōtostatēs*** [RINGLEADER] 1x
<4415> πρωτοτόκια ***prōtotokia*** [BIRTHRIGHT] 1x
<4416> πρωτότοκος ***prōtotokos*** [FIRSTBORN] 8x
<4417> πταίω ***ptaiō*** [STUMBLE 3] 5x
<4418> πτέρνα ***pterna*** [HEEL] 1x
<4419> πτερύγιον ***pterugion*** [PINNACLE] 2x
<4420> πτέρυξ ***pterux*** [WING] 5x
<4421> πτηνόν ***ptēnon*** [BIRD 3] 1x
<4422> πτοέω ***ptoeō*** [TERRIFY 2] 2x
<4423> πτόησις ***ptoēsis*** [FEAR (noun) 1] 1x
<4424> Πτολεμαΐς ***Ptolemais*** [PTOLEMAIS] 1x

<4425> πτύον ***ptuon*** [WINNOWING FAN] 2x
<4426> πτύρω ***pturō*** [TERRIFY 3] 1x
<4427> πτύσμα ***ptusma*** [SALIVA] 1x
<4428> πτύσσω ***ptussō*** [to roll up: ROLL 6] 1x
<4429> πτύω ***ptuō*** [SPIT 1] 3x
<4430> πτῶμα ***ptōma*** [CORPSE 2] 5x
<4431> πτῶσις ***ptōsis*** [FALL (noun) 2] 2x
<4432> πτωχεία ***ptōcheia*** [POVERTY 1] 3x
<4433> πτωχεύω ***ptōcheuō*** [to become poor: POOR (adj.) 3] 1x
<4434> πτωχός ***ptōchos*** [BEGGARLY, POOR (adj.) 2, POOR (noun) 2] 34x
<4435> πυγμή ***pugmē*** [fist: CAREFULLY 3] 1x
<4436> Πύθων ***Puthōn*** [PYTHON] 1x
<4437> πυκνός ***puknos*** [FREQUENT 1, OFTEN 4] 3x
<4438> πυκτεύω ***pukteuō*** [FIGHT (verb) 5] 1x
<4439> πύλη ***pulē*** [GATE 1] 11x
<4440> πυλών ***pulōn*** [GATE 2, GATEWAY 1] 18x
<4441> πυνθάνομαι ***punthanomai*** [ASK 8, INQUIRE 3, UNDERSTAND 7] 12x
<4442> πῦρ ***pur*** [FIRE 1] 71x
<4443> πυρά ***pura*** [FIRE 2] 2x
<4444> πύργος ***purgos*** [TOWER] 4x
<4445> πυρέσσω ***puressō*** [to be in a fever, with a fever; to be sick in a fever, with a fever: FEVER 2] 2x
<4446> πυρετός ***puretos*** [FEVER 1] 6x
<4447> πύρινος ***purinos*** [of fire, the color of fire, fiery red: FIRE 4] 1x
<4448> πυρόω ***puroō*** [BURN 6, to inflame: FIERY 2, to be on fire: FIRE 3, PURIFY 5, REFINE] 6x
<4449> πυρράζω ***purrazō*** [to be red: RED 2] 2x
<4450> πυρρός ***purros*** [red, fiery red: RED 1] 2x
<4450a> Πύρρος ***Purros*** [PYRRHUS] 1x
<4451> πύρωσις ***purōsis*** [BURNING 1, fiery trial, fiery ordeal: FIERY 1] 3x
<4452> πω ***pō*** [YET 5]
<4453> πωλέω ***pōleō*** [SELL 3] 22x
<4454> πῶλος ***pōlos*** [COLT] 12x
<4455> πώποτε ***pōpote*** [ANY TIME (AT)] 6x
<4456> πωρόω ***pōroō*** [HARDEN 1] 5x
<4457> πώρωσις ***pōrōsis*** [HARDNESS 1] 3x
<4458> πώς ***pōs*** [HOW 1, SOMEHOW 1] 15x
<4459> πῶς ***pōs*** [HOW 2] 103x

Ρ

<4460> Ῥαάβ ***Rhaab*** [RAHAB 1] 2x
<4461> Ῥαββί ***Rhabbi*** [RABBI 1] 16x
<4462> Ῥαββουνί ***Rhabbouni*** [RABBONI] 2x
<4463> ῥαβδίζω ***rhabdizō*** [to beat, to beat with rods: ROD 2] 2x
<4464> ῥάβδος ***rhabdos*** [ROD 1, SCEPTER, STAFF 1] 12x
<4465> ῥαβδοῦχος ***rhabdouchos*** [OFFICER 2] 2x
<4466> Ῥαγαύ ***Rhagau*** [REU] 1x
<4467> ῥᾳδιούργημα ***rhadiourgēma*** [CRIME 2] 1x
<4468> ῥᾳδιουργία ***rhadiourgia*** [FRAUD 1] 1x
<4469> ῥακά ***rhaka*** [RACA] 1x
<4470> ῥάκος ***rhakos*** [CLOTH 1] 2x
<4471> Ῥαμά ***Rhama*** [RAMAH] 1x
<4472> ῥαντίζω ***rhantizō*** [SPRINKLE 1] 4x

<4473> ῥαντισμός ***rhantismos*** [SPRINKLING 2] 2x

<4474> ῥαπίζω ***rhapizō*** [SLAP (verb) 1] 2x

<4475> ῥάπισμα ***rhapisma*** [BLOW (noun) 1, slap in the face: SLAP (noun)] 3x

<4476> ῥαφίς ***rhaphis*** [NEEDLE] 3x

<4477> Ῥαχάβ ***Rhachab*** [RAHAB 2] 1x

<4478> Ῥαχήλ ***Rhachēl*** [RACHEL] 1x

<4479> Ῥεβέκκα ***Rhebekka*** [REBEKAH] 1x

<4480> ῥέδη ***rhedē*** [CHARIOT 2] 1x

<4481> Ῥεμφάν ***Rhemphan*** [ROMPHA] 1x

<4482> ῥέω ***rheō*** [FLOW (verb) 1] 1x

<4483> ῥέω ***rheō*** [SPEAK 15]

<4484> Ῥήγιον ***Rhēgion*** [RHEGIUM] 1x

<4485> ῥῆγμα ***rhēgma*** [RUIN (noun) 3] 1x

<4486> ῥήγνυμι ***rhēgnumi*** [to break forth: BREAK 7, BURST 2, TEAR (verb) 2] 7x

<4487> ῥῆμα ***rhēma*** [SAYING 2, WORD 2] 68x

<4488> Ῥησά ***Rhēsa*** [RHESA] 1x

<4489> ῥήτωρ ***rhētōr*** [ORATOR] 1x

<4490> ῥητῶς ***rhētōs*** [EXPRESSLY] 1x

<4491> ῥίζα ***rhiza*** [ROOT(noun) 1] 17x

<4492> ῥιζόω ***rhizoō*** [ROOT (verb) 1] 2x

<4493> ῥιπή ***rhipē*** [TWINKLING] 1x

<4494> ῥιπίζω ***rhipizō*** [TOSS 3] 1x

<4495> ῥιπτέω ***rhipteō*** [CAST (verb) 7] 1x

<4496> ῥίπτω ***rhiptō*** [to cast, to cast down, to cast up, to cast out: CAST (verb) 8, SCATTER 3] 7x

<4497> Ῥοβοάμ ***Rhoboam*** [REHOBOAM] 2x

<4498> Ῥόδη ***Rhodē*** [RHODA] 1x

<4499> Ῥόδος ***Rhodos*** [RHODES] 1x

<4500> ῥοιζηδόν ***rhoizēdon*** [with a rushing noise: NOISE (noun) 1] 1x

<4501> ῥομφαία ***rhomphaia*** [SWORD 2] 7x

<4502> Ῥουβήν ***Rhoubēn*** [REUBEN] 1x

<4503> Ῥούθ ***Rhouth*** [RUTH] 1x

<4504> Ῥοῦφος ***Rhouphos*** [RUFUS] 2x

<4505> ῥύμη ***rhumē*** [LANE 1, STREET 2] 4x

<4506> ῥύομαι ***rhuomai*** [DELIVER 5, to deliver: DELIVERER 2] 17x

<4506a> ῥυπαίνω ***rhupainō*** [to be filthy, to make oneself filthy: FILTHY 2] 1x

<4507> ῥυπαρία ***rhuparia*** [FILTHINESS 2] 1x

<4508> ῥυπαρός ***rhuparos*** [DIRTY] 2x

<4509> ῥύπος ***rhupos*** [FILTH 2] 1x

<4510> ῥυπόω ***rhupoō*** [to be filthy, to make oneself filthy: FILTHY 2] 1x

<4511> ῥύσις ***rhusis*** [FLOW (noun) 2] 3x

<4512> ῥυτίς ***rhutis*** [WRINKLE] 1x

<4513> Ῥωμαϊκός ***Rhōmaikos*** [ROMAN 2] 1x

<4514> Ῥωμαῖος ***Rhōmaios*** [ROMAN 1] 12x

<4515> Ῥωμαϊστί ***Rhōmaisti*** [in Latin: LATIN] 1x

<4516> Ῥώμη ***Rhōmē*** [ROME 1] 8x

<4517> ῥώννυμι ***rhōnnumi*** [to farewell: FAREWELL 2] 2x

Σ

<4518> σαβαχθάνι ***sabachthani*** [SABACHTHANI] 2x

<4519> Σαβαώθ ***Sabaōth*** [SABAOTH] 2x

<4520> σαββατισμός ***sabbatismos*** [SABBATH REST] 1x

<4521> σάββατον ***sabbaton*** [SABBATH 1, SABBATH DAY'S JOURNEY, WEEK 1] 68x

<4522> σαγήνη ***sagēnē*** [DRAGNET] 1x
<4523> Σαδδουκαῖος ***Saddoukaios*** [SADDUCEE] 14x
<4524> Σαδώκ ***Sadōk*** [ZADOK] 2x
<4525> σαίνω ***sainō*** [SHAKE 3] 1x
<4526> σάκκος ***sakkos*** [SACKCLOTH] 4x
<4527> Σαλά ***Sala*** [SHELAH] 1x
<4528> Σαλαθιήλ ***Salathiēl*** [SHEALTIEL] 3x
<4529> Σαλαμίς ***Salamis*** [SALAMIS] 1x
<4530> Σαλείμ ***Saleim*** [SALIM] 1x
<4531> σαλεύω ***saleuō*** [to shake, to shake together: SHAKE 4, to stir: STIR (verb) 4] 15x
<4532> Σαλήμ ***Salēm*** [SALEM] 2x
<4533> Σαλμών ***Salmōn*** [SALMON] 3x
<4534> Σαλμώνη ***Salmōnē*** [SALMONE] 1x
<4535> σάλος ***salos*** [WAVE 3] 1x
<4536> σάλπιγξ ***salpinx*** [TRUMPET 1] 11x
<4537> σαλπίζω ***salpizō*** [to sound a trumpet: TRUMPET 2] 12x
<4538> σαλπιστής ***salpistēs*** [TRUMPETER] 1x
<4539> Σαλώμη ***Salōmē*** [SALOME] 2x
<4540> Σαμάρεια ***Samareia*** [SAMARIA] 11x
<4541> Σαμαρίτης ***Samaritēs*** [SAMARITAN] 8x
<4542> Σαμαρῖτις ***Samaritis*** [SAMARITAN] 1x
<4543> Σαμοθρᾴκη ***Samothrakē*** [SAMOTHRACE] 1x
<4544> Σάμος ***Samos*** [SAMOS] 1x
<4545> Σαμουήλ ***Samouēl*** [SAMUEL] 3x
<4546> Σαμψών ***Sampsōn*** [SAMSON] 1x
<4547> σανδάλιον ***sandalion*** [SANDAL 1] 2x
<4548> σανίς ***sanis*** [BOARD (noun) 1] 1x
<4549> Σαούλ ***Saoul*** [SAUL 1] 6x
<4550> σαπρός ***sapros*** [BAD 2, CORRUPT (adj.) 1] 8x
<4551> Σάπφιρα ***Sapphira*** [SAPPHIRA] 1x
<4552> σάπφιρος ***sapphiros*** [SAPPHIRE 1] 1x
<4553> σαργάνη ***sarganē*** [BASKET 3] 1x
<4554> Σάρδεις ***Sardeis*** [SARDIS] 3x
<4555> σάρδινος ***sardinos*** [SARDIUS 1] 1x
<4556> σάρδιος ***sardios*** [SARDIUS 2] 2x
<4557> σαρδόνυξ ***sardonux*** [SARDONYX] 1x
<4558> Σάρεπτα ***Sarepta*** [ZAREPHATH] 1x
<4559> σαρκικός ***sarkikos*** [CARNAL 1, carnal things: CARNAL 2] 11x
<4560> σάρκινος ***sarkinos*** [FLESHLY] 1x
<4561> σάρξ ***sarx*** [FLESH 1] 147x
<4562> Σαρούχ ***Sarouch*** [SERUG] 1x
<4563> σαρόω ***saroō*** [SWEEP 1] 3x
<4564> Σάρρα ***Sarra*** [SARAH] 4x
<4565> Σάρων ***Sarōn*** [SHARON] 1x
<4566> Σατάν ***Satan*** [SATAN 2] 1x
<4567> Σατανᾶς ***Satanas*** [SATAN 1] 36x
<4568> σάτον ***saton*** [MEASURE (noun) 5] 2x
<4569> Σαῦλος ***Saulos*** [SAUL 2] 17x
<4570> σβέννυμι ***sbennumi*** [QUENCH 1] 8x
<4571> σέ ***se*** [THEE, THOU] 197x
<4572> σεαυτοῦ ***seautou*** [OF THYSELF] 40x
<4573> σεβάζομαι ***sebazomai*** [WORSHIP (verb) 4] 1x
<4574> σέβασμα ***sebasma*** [object of worship: WORSHIP (noun) 1] 2x
<4575> Σεβαστός ***Sebastos*** [AUGUSTUS 2] 3x
<4576> σέβομαι ***sebomai*** [WORSHIP (verb) 5] 10x

<4577> σειρά ***seira*** [CHAIN (noun) 3] 1x
<4578> σεισμός ***seismos*** [EARTHQUAKE, STORM 3] 14x
<4579> σείω ***seiō*** [to be moved: MOVE 5, SHAKE 5] 5x
<4580> Σεκοῦνδος ***Sekoundos*** [SECUNDUS] 1x
<4581> Σελεύκεια ***Seleukeia*** [SELEUCIA] 1x
<4582> σελήνη ***selēnē*** [MOON 1] 9x
<4583> σεληνιάζομαι ***selēniazomai*** [to be epileptic: EPILEPTIC] 2x
<4584> Σεμεΐν ***Semein*** [SEMEIN] 1x
<4585> σεμίδαλις ***semidalis*** [fine flour: FLOUR 2] 1x
<4586> σεμνός ***semnos*** [GRAVE, NOBLE 2] 4x
<4587> σεμνότης ***semnotēs*** [DIGNITY 1] or [GRAVITY] 3x
<4588> Σέργιος Παῦλος ***Sergios Paulos*** [SERGIUS PAULUS] 1x
<4589> Σήθ ***Sēth*** [SETH] 1x
<4590> Σήμ ***Sēm*** [SHEM] 1x
<4591> σημαίνω ***sēmainō*** [SHOW (verb) 15, SIGNIFY 3] 6x
<4592> σημεῖον ***sēmeion*** [MIRACLE 2, SIGN 1] 77x
<4593> σημειόω ***sēmeioō*** [MARK (verb) 1] 1x
<4594> σήμερον ***sēmeron*** [this day, to day, today: DAY 6] 41x
<4595> σήπω ***sēpō*** [to become rotten: ROTTEN] 1x
<4596> σηρικός ***sērikos*** [of silk: SILK] 1x
<4597> σής ***sēs*** [MOTH] 3x
<4598> σητόβρωτος ***sētobrōtos*** [MOTH-EATEN] 1x
<4599> σθενόω ***sthenoō*** [STRENGTHEN 6] 1x
<4600> σιαγών ***siagōn*** [CHEEK] 2x
<4601> σιγάω ***sigaō*** [to keep silence: SILENCE (noun) 3, to be, to become, to keep, to remain silent, to fall silent: SILENT 2] 9x
<4602> σιγή ***sigē*** [SILENCE (noun) 2] 2x
<4603> σιδήρεος, σιδηροῦς ***sidēreos, sidērous*** [iron, of iron: IRON 2] 5x
<4604> σίδηρος ***sidēros*** [IRON 1] 1x
<4605> Σιδών ***Sidōn*** [SIDON 1] 10x
<4606> Σιδώνιος ***Sidōnios*** [SIDON 2] 2x
<4607> σικάριος ***sikarios*** [MURDERER 3] 1x
<4608> σίκερα ***sikera*** [strong drink: DRINK (noun) 3] 1x
<4609> Σιλᾶς ***Silas*** [SILAS] 13x
<4610> Σιλουανός ***Silouanos*** [SILVANUS] 4x
<4611> Σιλωάμ ***Silōam*** [SILOAM] 3x
<4612> σιμικίνθιον ***simikinthion*** [APRON] 1x
<4613> Σίμων ***Simōn*** [SIMON] 75x
<4614> Σινᾶ ***Sina*** [SINAI] 4x
<4615> σίναπι ***sinapi*** [GRAIN OF MUSTARD] 5x
<4616> σινδών ***sindōn*** [LINEN, LINEN CLOTH 3] 6x
<4617> σινιάζω ***siniazō*** [SIFT] 1x
<4618> σιτευτός ***siteutos*** [FATTENED 1] 3x
<4619> σιτιστός ***sitistos*** [FATLING] 1x
<4620> σιτομέτριον ***sitometrion*** [MEASURE OF CORN] 1x
<4621> σῖτος ***sitos*** [CORN 1, GRAIN OF WHEAT, WHEAT 1] 14x
<4622> Σιών ***Siōn*** [ZION] 7x
<4623> σιωπάω ***siōpaō*** [to be, to become, to keep silent: SILENT 3] 11x
<4624> σκανδαλίζω ***skandalizō*** [OFFEND 1] 29x
<4625> σκάνδαλον ***skandalon*** [OFFENSE 3, STUMBLING BLOCK 3] 15x
<4626> σκάπτω ***skaptō*** [to dig, to dig around, to dig about: DIG 4] 3x
<4627> σκάφη ***skaphē*** [BOAT 1] 3x
<4628> σκέλος ***skelos*** [LEG] 3x
<4629> σκέπασμα ***skepasma*** [CLOTHING 3] 1x
<4630> Σκευᾶς ***Skeuas*** [SCEVA] 1x

<4631> σκευή ***skeuē*** [TACKLING] 1x

<4632> σκεῦος ***skeuos*** [ARTICLE, GOOD (adj. and noun) 5, SAIL (noun) 1, VESSEL[1] 3] 23x

<4633> σκηνή ***skēnē*** [DWELLING PLACE 3, TABERNACLE 1, TENT 1] 20x

<4634> Σκηνοπηγία ***Skēnopēgia*** [TABERNACLES (FEAST OF)] 1x

<4635> σκηνοποιός ***skēnopoios*** [TENTMAKER] 1x

<4636> σκῆνος ***skēnos*** [TENT 2] 2x

<4637> σκηνόω ***skēnoō*** [DWELL 9, to spread one's tent: TENT 4] 5x

<4638> σκήνωμα ***skēnōma*** [TABERNACLE 2, TENT 3] 3x

<4639> σκιά ***skia*** [SHADOW (noun) 1] 7x

<4640> σκιρτάω ***skirtaō*** [to leap for joy: JOY (noun) 5, LEAP 4] 3x

<4641> σκληροκαρδία ***sklērokardia*** [hardness of heart, hardheartedness: HARDNESS 2] 3x

<4642> σκληρός ***sklēros*** [HARD 6, VIOLENT (adj.) 2] 5x

<4643> σκληρότης ***sklērotēs*** [HARDNESS 3] 1x

<4644> σκληροτράχηλος ***sklērotrachēlos*** [STIFFNECKED, STIFF-NECKED] 1x

<4645> σκληρύνω ***sklērunō*** [HARDEN 2] 6x

<4646> σκολιός ***skolios*** [CROOKED 1, HARSH 2, PERVERSE 1] 4x

<4647> σκόλοψ ***skolops*** [THORN 2] 1x

<4648> σκοπέω ***skopeō*** [CONSIDER 13, to fix the eyes: EYES 1, REGARD (verb) 4, WATCH (verb) 4] 6x

<4649> σκοπός ***skopos*** [MARK (noun) 1] 1x

<4650> σκορπίζω ***skorpizō*** [to scatter, to scatter abroad: SCATTER 4] 5x

<4651> σκορπίος ***skorpios*** [SCORPION] 5x

<4652> σκοτεινός ***skoteinos*** [full of darkness: DARKNESS 3] 3x

<4653> σκοτία ***skotia*** [DARKNESS 2] 16x

<4654> σκοτίζω ***skotizō*** [DARKEN 1] 8x

<4655> σκότος ***skotos*** [DARKNESS 2] 31x

<4656> σκοτόω ***skotoō*** [DARKEN 2] 3x

<4657> σκύβαλον ***skubalon*** [FILTH 3] 1x

<4658> Σκύθης ***Skuthēs*** [SCYTHIAN] 1x

<4659> σκυθρωπός ***skuthrōpos*** [sad countenance, sad: SAD 3] 2x

<4660> σκύλλω ***skullō*** [TROUBLE (verb) 6] 3x

<4661> σκῦλον ***skulon*** [SPOILS 2] 1x

<4662> σκωληκόβρωτος ***skōlēkobrōtos*** [eaten by worms: WORM (noun) 2] 1x

<4663> σκώληξ ***skōlēx*** [WORM (noun) 1] 3x

<4664> σμαράγδινος ***smaragdinos*** [of an emerald: EMERALD 2] 1x

<4665> σμάραγδος ***smaragdos*** [EMERALD 1] 1x

<4666> σμύρνα ***smurna*** [MYRRH 1] 2x

<4667> Σμύρνα ***Smurna*** [SMYRNA 1] 1x

<4668> Σμυρναῖος ***Smurnaios*** [of Smyrna: SMYRNA 2] 1x

<4669> σμυρνίζω ***smurnizō*** [to mingle with myrrh: MINGLE 2] 1x

<4670> Σόδομα ***Sodoma*** [SODOM] 9x

<4671> σοί ***soi*** [TO THEE] 221x

<4672> Σολομών ***Solomōn*** [SOLOMON] 12x

<4673> σορός ***soros*** [BIER] 1x

<4674> σός ***sos*** [THINE] 27x

<4675> σοῦ ***sou*** [OF THEE, THY, THINE]

<4676> σουδάριον ***soudarion*** [cloth, burial cloth, face cloth: CLOTH 2, HANDKERCHIEF 1] 4x

<4677> Σουσάννα ***Sousanna*** [SUSANNA] 1x

<4678> σοφία ***sophia*** [WISDOM 1] 51x

<4679> σοφίζω ***sophizō*** [to be cleverly devised, to be cunningly devised: DEVISED, to make wise: WISE (adj.) 2] 2x

<4680> σοφός ***sophos*** [WISE (adj.) 1, wise, wise man: WISE (noun) 1] 21x

<4681> Σπανία ***Spania*** [SPAIN] 2x

<4682> σπαράσσω ***sparassō*** [CONVULSE 1] 3x

<4683> σπαργανόω ***sparganoō*** [to wrap in cloths, in swaddling clothes: WRAP 5] 2x

<4684> σπαταλάω ***spatalaō*** [to live in pleasure: PLEASURE 5, to live in self-indulgence: SELF-INDULGENCE 2] 2x

<4685> σπάω ***spaō*** [DRAW 3] 2x

<4686> σπεῖρα ***speira*** [COHORT] 7x

<4687> σπείρω ***speirō*** [SOW (verb) 1, to sow: SOWER 1] 50x

<4688> σπεκουλάτωρ ***spekoulatōr*** [GUARD (noun) 2] 1x

<4689> σπένδω ***spendō*** [to be poured out as a drink offering, as a libation: DRINK OFFERING] 2x

<4690> σπέρμα ***sperma*** [SEED 1] 44x

<4691> σπερμολόγος ***spermologos*** [BABBLER] 1x

<4692> σπεύδω ***speudō*** [to come with haste, to make haste: HASTE (noun) 2, HASTEN] 6x

<4693> σπήλαιον ***spēlaion*** [CAVE 1, DEN 1] 6x

<4694> σπιλάς ***spilas*** [SPOT 1] 1x

<4695> σπιλόω ***spiloō*** [DEFILE 4] 2x

<4696> σπίλος ***spilos*** [SPOT 2] 2x

<4697> σπλαγχνίζομαι ***splanchnizomai*** [to have, to feel, to be moved with compassion: COMPASSION 4] 12x

<4698> σπλάγχνον ***splanchnon*** [affection, inward affection: AFFECTION 1, ENTRAILS, TENDERNESS] 11x

<4699> σπόγγος ***spongos*** [SPONGE] 3x

<4700> σποδός ***spodos*** [ASH 1] 3x

<4701> σπορά ***spora*** [SEED 2] 1x

<4702> σπόριμος ***sporimos*** [corn, cornfield: CORN 2] 3x

<4703> σπόρος ***sporos*** [SEED 3] 5x

<4704> σπουδάζω ***spoudazō*** [to be diligent: DILIGENT 1, to make every effort: EFFORT 2, ENDEAVOR (verb) 1, LABOR (verb) 3] 11x

<4705> σπουδαῖος ***spoudaios*** [ZEALOUS 3] 1x

<4706> σπουδαιότερον ***spoudaioteron*** [very diligently: DILIGENTLY 2] 1x

<4707> σπουδαιότερος ***spoudaioteros*** [diligently zealous, more zealous: ZEALOUS 4] 2x

<4708> σπουδαιοτέρως ***spoudaioterōs*** [the more eagerly: EAGERLY 1] 1x

<4709> σπουδαίως ***spoudaiōs*** [DILIGENTLY 3, EARNESTLY 4] 2x

<4710> σπουδή ***spoudē*** [DILIGENCE 1, HASTE (noun) 1, ZEAL 2, diligent zealousness: ZEALOUSNESS] 12x

<4711> σπυρίς ***spuris*** [BASKET 2] 5x

<4712> στάδιον ***stadion*** [RACE^{2} 2, STADION] 7x

<4713> στάμνος ***stamnos*** [POT 1] 1x

<4714> στάσις ***stasis*** [DISSENSION 1, INSURRECTION 1, STANDING 2, TUMULT 3] 9x

<4715> στατήρ ***statēr*** [STATER] 1x

<4716> σταυρός ***stauros*** [CROSS (noun) 1] 27x

<4717> σταυρόω ***stauroō*** [CRUCIFY 1] 46x

<4718> σταφυλή ***staphulē*** [GRAPE] 3x

<4719> στάχυς ***stachus*** [head of grain, head: GRAIN 2] 5x

<4720> Στάχυς ***Stachus*** [STACHYS] 1x

<4721> στέγη ***stegē*** [ROOF 1] 3x

<4722> στέγω ***stegō*** [BEAR (verb) 7] 4x

<4723> στεῖρος ***steiros*** [BARREN 1] 4x

<4724> στέλλω ***stellō*** [AVOID 4] or [WITHDRAW 4] 2x

<4725> στέμμα ***stemma*** [GARLAND 1] 1x

<4726> στεναγμός ***stenagmos*** [GROANING] 2x

<4727> στενάζω ***stenazō*** [COMPLAIN 1, GROAN (verb) 1] 6x

<4728> στενός ***stenos*** [NARROW] 3x

<4729> στενοχωρέω ***stenochōreō*** [RESTRAIN 3] 3x

<4730> στενοχωρία ***stenochōria*** [ANGUISH 2, DISTRESS 3] 4x

<4731> στερεός ***stereos*** [FIRM 3, SOLID] 4x

<4732> στερεόω ***stereoō*** [ESTABLISH 4, to be made strong, to become strong: STRONG (adj.) 6] 3x

<4733> στερέωμα ***stereōma*** [STEADFASTNESS 1] 1x

<4734> Στεφανᾶς ***Stephanas*** [STEPHANAS] 3x

<4735> στέφανος ***stephanos*** [CROWN (noun) 2] 18x

<4736> Στέφανος ***Stephanos*** [STEPHEN] 7x

<4737> στεφανόω ***stephanoō*** [CROWN (verb)] 3x

<4738> στῆθος ***stēthos*** [BREAST 2] 5x

<4739> στήκω ***stēkō*** [to stand firm: FIRM 4, to stand, to stand fast, to stand firm: STAND (verb) 7] 8x

<4740> στηριγμός ***stērigmos*** [STEADFASTNESS 2] 2x

<4741> στηρίζω ***stērizō*** [ESTABLISH 5, FIX 3, to set steadfastly: STEADFASTLY 1, STRENGTHEN 7] 13x

<4741a> στιβάς ***stibas*** [BRANCH 4] 1x

<4742> στίγμα ***stigma*** [MARK (noun) 2] 1x

<4743> στιγμή ***stigmē*** [MOMENT 2] 1x

<4744> στίλβω ***stilbō*** [to shine: SHINING 3] 1x

<4745> στοά ***stoa*** [PORCH 2] 4x

<4746> στοιβάς ***stoibas*** [BRANCH 4] 1x

<4747> στοιχεῖον ***stoicheion*** [ELEMENT] 7x

<4748> στοιχέω ***stoicheō*** [to walk, to walk orderly: WALK 4] 5x

<4749> στολή ***stolē*** [robe, long robe, flowing robe: ROBE (noun) 1] 9x

<4750> στόμα ***stoma*** [EDGE 1, MOUTH (noun) 1] 78x

<4751> στόμαχος ***stomachos*** [STOMACH 2] 1x

<4752> στρατεία ***strateia*** [WARFARE 1] 2x

<4753> στράτευμα ***strateuma*** [ARMY 2, TROOPS] 7x

<4754> στρατεύομαι ***strateuomai*** [to go to war, to wage war, to war: WAR (noun) 2, WAR (verb) 2] 7x

<4755> στρατηγός ***stratēgos*** [CAPTAIN 2, MAGISTRATE 3] 10x

<4756> στρατιά ***stratia*** [HOST[1] 1] 2x

<4757> στρατιώτης ***stratiōtēs*** [SOLDIER 1] 26x

<4758> στρατολογέω ***stratologeō*** [to engage in warfare: WARFARE 2] 1x

<4759> στρατοπεδάρχης ***stratopedarchēs*** [PRAETORIAN PREFECT] 1x

<4760> στρατόπεδον ***stratopedon*** [ARMY 3] 1x

<4761> στρεβλόω ***strebloō*** [DISTORT 1] 1x

<4762> στρέφω ***strephō*** [CONVERT (verb) 1, RETURN (verb) 5, to turn oneself; to turn about, around, back, round, etc.: TURN (verb) 6] 19x

<4763> στρηνιάω ***strēniaō*** [to live luxuriously: LUXURIOUSLY 1] 2x

<4764> στρῆνος ***strēnos*** [LUXURY 1] 1x

<4765> στρουθίον ***strouthion*** [SPARROW] 4x

<4766> στρώννυμι ***strōnnumi*** [FURNISH 1] 2x

<4766> στρωννύω ***strōnnuō*** [to make one's bed: BED 6, SPREAD 8] 3x

<4767> στυγητός ***stugētos*** [HATEFUL 1] 1x

<4768> στυγνάζω ***stugnazō*** [to be overcast: OVERCAST, to be sad: SAD 4] 2x

<4769> στῦλος ***stulos*** [PILLAR] 4x

<4770> Στοϊκός ***Stoikos*** [STOIC] 1x

<4771> σύ ***su*** [YOU, THOU] 178x

<4772> συγγένεια ***sungeneia*** [RELATIVES] 3x

<4773> συγγενής ***sungenēs*** [RELATIVE 2] 12x

<4774> συγγνώμη ***sungnōmē*** [CONCESSION] 1x

<4775> συγκάθημαι ***sunkathēmai*** [to sit with: SIT 2] 2x

<4776> συγκαθίζω ***sunkathizō*** [to sit together, to sit down together: SIT 5] 2x

<4777> συγκακοπαθέω ***sunkakopatheō*** [to join in suffering, to share in the sufferings: SUFFERING 3] 2x

<4778> συγκακουχέομαι ***sunkakoucheomai*** [to suffer affliction with: AFFLICTION 3] 1x

<4779> συγκαλέω ***sunkaleō*** [to call together: CALL (verb) 7] 8x

<4780> συγκαλύπτω ***sunkaluptō*** [COVER 5] 1x

<4781> συγκάμπτω ***sunkamptō*** [to bow down: BOW (verb) 2] 1x

<4782> συγκαταβαίνω ***sunkatabainō*** [to go down with: GO 22] 1x

<4783> συγκατάθεσις ***sunkatathesis*** [AGREEMENT 1] 1x

<4784> συγκατατίθεμαι ***sunkatatithemai*** [CONSENT (verb) 3] 1x

<4785> συγκαταψηφίζω ***sunkatapsēphizō*** [NUMBER (verb) 3] 1x

<4786> συγκεράννυμι ***sunkerannumi*** [COMPOSE 1, to mix with: MIX 2] 2x

<4787> συγκινέω ***sunkineō*** [to stir up: STIR (verb) 5] 1x

<4788> συγκλείω ***sunkleiō*** [CATCH (verb) 8, to shut up: SHUT 4] 4x

<4789> συγκληρονόμος ***sunklēronomos*** [heir together: HEIR 2, JOINT HEIR] 4x

<4790> συγκοινωνέω ***sunkoinōneō*** [to have fellowship with: FELLOWSHIP 2, PARTICIPATE 2, to share in, to share with: SHARE (verb) 1] 3x

<4791> συγκοινωνός ***sunkoinōnos*** [COMPANION 2, PARTAKER 2] 4x

<4792> συγκομίζω ***sunkomizō*** [to carry to one's burial: CARRY 13] 1x

<4793> συγκρίνω ***sunkrinō*** [COMPARE 2] 3x

<4794> συγκύπτω ***sunkuptō*** [to bend over: BEND 1] 1x

<4795> συγκυρία ***sunkuria*** [CHANCE (noun) 1] 1x

<4796> συγχαίρω ***sunchairō*** [to rejoice with, to rejoice in common: REJOICE 4] 7x

<4797> συγχέω ***suncheō*** [CONFOUND 1, CONFUSED (BE), to stir up: STIR (verb) 6, to be in an uproar: UPROAR 2] 5x

<4798> συγχράομαι ***sunchraomai*** [to have dealings: DEALINGS 1] 1x

<4799> σύγχυσις ***sunchusis*** [CONFUSION 2] 1x

<4800> συζάω ***suzaō*** [to live together, to live with: LIVE 3] 3x

<4801> συζεύγνυμι ***suzeugnumi*** [to join together: JOIN 4] 2x

<4802> συζητέω ***suzēteō*** [to dispute, to dispute with, to dispute against: DISPUTE (verb) 2, to question together: QUESTION (verb) 1, REASON (verb) 5] 10x

<4803> συζήτησις ***suzētēsis*** [DISPUTE 3] 3x

<4804> συζητητής ***suzētētēs*** [DISPUTER] 1x

<4805> σύζυγος ***suzugos*** [YOKEFELLOW] 1x

<4806> συζωοποιέω ***suzōopoieō*** [to make alive with: ALIVE 2] 2x

<4807> συκάμινος ***sukaminos*** [SYCAMINE TREE] 1x

<4808> συκῆ ***sukē*** [FIG TREE] 16x

<4809> συκομορέα ***sukomorea*** [SYCAMORE] 1x

<4810> σῦκον ***sukon*** [FIG 1] 4x

<4811> συκοφαντέω ***sukophanteō*** [to accuse falsely: ACCUSE 5] 2x

<4812> συλαγωγέω ***sulagōgeō*** [to lead away as a prey: PREY 1] 1x

<4813> συλάω ***sulaō*** [ROB 1] 1x

<4814> συλλαλέω ***sullaleō*** [CONFER 1, to speak to, to speak with: SPEAK 10] 6x

<4815> συλλαμβάνω ***sullambanō*** [CONCEIVE 2, HELP (verb) 3, SEIZE 8, TAKE 10] 16x

<4816> συλλέγω ***sullegō*** [GATHER 7] 8x

<4817> συλλογίζομαι ***sullogizomai*** [REASON (verb) 3] 1x

<4818> συλλυπέω ***sullupeō*** [to be grieved: GRIEVE 3] 1x

<4819> συμβαίνω ***sumbainō*** [HAPPEN 2] 8x

<4820> συμβάλλω ***sumballō*** [CONFER 2, HELP (verb) 6, to meet, to meet with: MEET (verb) 4, PONDER 1] 6x

<4821> συμβασιλεύω ***sumbasileuō*** [to reign together, to reign with: REIGN (verb) 2] 2x

<4822> συμβιβάζω ***sumbibazō*** [CONCLUDE[1] 2, INSTRUCT 2, to knit together: KNIT 1, PROVE 4, to unite, to unite together: UNITE 1] 7x

<4823> συμβουλεύω ***sumbouleuō*** [CONSULT 2, to take counsel together: COUNSEL (noun) 3, COUNSEL (verb) 1] 5x

<4824> συμβούλιον ***sumboulion*** [COUNCIL 1, COUNSEL (noun) 2] 8x

<4825> σύμβουλος ***sumboulos*** [COUNSELLOR, COUNSELOR 2] 1x

<4826> Συμεών ***Sumeōn*** [SIMEON] 7x

<4827> συμμαθητής ***summathētēs*** [FELLOW DISCIPLE] 1x

<4828> συμμαρτυρέω ***summartureō*** [to bear witness: WITNESS (noun)[1] 4] 4x
<4829> συμμερίζω ***summerizō*** [PARTAKE 3] 1x
<4830> συμμέτοχος ***summetochos*** [PARTAKER 4] 2x
<4831> συμμιμητής ***summimētēs*** [imitator together: IMITATOR 2] 1x
<4831a> συμμορφίζω ***summorphizō*** [to be conformed: CONFORM 2] 1x
<4832> σύμμορφος ***summorphos*** [CONFORMED 1] 2x
<4833> συμμορφόω ***summorphoō*** [to be conformed: CONFORM 2] 1x
<4834> συμπαθέω ***sumpatheō*** [SYMPATHIZE] 2x
<4835> συμπαθής ***sumpathēs*** [SYMPATHETIC] 1x
<4836> συμπαραγίνομαι ***sumparaginomai*** [COME 3] 2x
<4837> συμπαρακαλέω ***sumparakaleō*** [to be encouraged together, mutually: ENCOURAGE 2] 1x
<4838> συμπαραλαμβάνω ***sumparalambanō*** [to take with, to take along with: TAKE 11] 4x
<4839> συμπαραμένω ***sumparamenō*** [to continue with: CONTINUE 5] 1x
<4840> συμπάρειμι ***sumpareimi*** [PRESENT (BE) 4] 1x
<4841> συμπάσχω ***sumpaschō*** [to suffer with: SUFFER 3] 2x
<4842> συμπέμπω ***sumpempō*** [to send with: SEND 8] 2x
<4843> συμπεριλαμβάνω ***sumperilambanō*** [EMBRACE 2] 1x
<4844> συμπίνω ***sumpinō*** [DRINK (verb) 2] 1x
<4845> συμπληρόω ***sumplēroō*** [to fully come, to come, to fill: COME 37, FILL (verb) 5] 3x
<4846> συμπνίγω ***sumpnigō*** [CHOKE 3, THRONG (verb) 1] 5x
<4847> συμπολίτης ***sumpolitēs*** [FELLOW CITIZEN 1] 1x
<4848> συμπορεύομαι ***sumporeuomai*** [GATHER 10, to go along with: GO 27] 4x
<4849> συμπόσιον ***sumposion*** [GROUP 2] 2x
<4850> συμπρεσβύτερος ***sumpresbuteros*** [elder with: ELDER 3] 1x
<4851> συμφέρω ***sumpherō*** [to bring together: BRING 17, profit, of profit: PROFIT (noun) 3, to be profitable: PROFIT (noun) 4, to be profitable: PROFITABLE 2, what is profitable: PROFITABLE 3] 15x
<4852> σύμφημι ***sumphēmi*** [CONSENT (verb) 4] 1x
<4852a> σύμφορον ***sumphoron*** [PROFIT (noun) 5] 2x
<4853> συμφυλέτης ***sumphuletēs*** [COUNTRYMAN 2] 1x
<4854> σύμφυτος ***sumphutos*** [IDENTIFIED] 1x
<4855> συμφύω ***sumphuō*** [to spring up with: SPRING (verb) 5] 1x
<4856> συμφωνέω ***sumphōneō*** [AGREE 4] 6x
<4857> συμφώνησις ***sumphōnēsis*** [CONCORD] 1x
<4858> συμφωνία ***sumphōnia*** [MUSIC 1] 1x
<4859> σύμφωνος ***sumphōnos*** [CONSENT (noun) 1] 1x
<4860> συμψηφίζω ***sumpsēphizō*** [CALCULATE 1] 1x
<4861> σύμψυχος ***sumpsuchos*** [joined in soul: SOUL 2] 1x
<4862> σύν ***sun*** [TOGETHER, TOGETHER WITH] 128x
<4863> συνάγω ***sunagō*** [to gather, to gather together, etc.: GATHER 1, INVITE 4, LEAD (verb) 7] 60x
<4864> συναγωγή ***sunagōgē*** [SYNAGOGUE 1] 56x
<4865> συναγωνίζομαι ***sunagōnizomai*** [to strive together: STRIVE 3] 1x
<4866> συναθλέω ***sunathleō*** [to strive together: STRIVE 5] 2x
<4867> συναθροίζω ***sunathroizō*** [to gather together: GATHER 4] 3x
<4868> συναίρω ***sunairō*** [to take account, to settle accounts: ACCOUNT (noun) 2, RECKON 1] 3x
<4869> συναιχμάλωτος ***sunaichmalōtos*** [FELLOW PRISONER] 3x
<4870> συνακολουθέω ***sunakoloutheō*** [FOLLOW 6] 3x
<4871> συναλίζω ***sunalizō*** [to be assembled together: ASSEMBLE 1] 1x
<4871a> συναλλάσσω ***sunallassō*** [RECONCILE 4] 1x
<4872> συναναβαίνω ***sunanabainō*** [to come up: COME 21] 2x
<4873> συνανάκειμαι ***sunanakeimai*** [to be, to lie, to sit at table with: TABLE[1] 4] 9x
<4874> συναναμίγνυμι ***sunanamignumi*** [to keep company, to have company:

COMPANY (noun) 5] 3x

<4875> συναναπαύω ***sunanapauō*** [REFRESH 2] 1x

<4876> συναντάω ***sunantaō*** [BEFALL 2, MEET (verb) 2] 6x

<4877> συνάντησις ***sunantēsis*** [meeting: MEET (verb) 7] 1x

<4878> συναντιλαμβάνω ***sunantilambanō*** [HELP (verb) 4] 2x

<4879> συναπάγω ***sunapagō*** [ASSOCIATE (verb) 1, to carry away with, by: CARRY 2] 3x

<4880> συναποθνήσκω ***sunapothnēskō*** [to die with, to die together: DIE 2] 3x

<4881> συναπόλλυμι ***sunapollumi*** [to perish with: PERISH 2] 1x

<4882> συναποστέλλω ***sunapostellō*** [to send with: SEND 3] 1x

<4883> συναρμολογέω ***sunarmologeō*** [to fit together: FIT (verb) 1] 2x

<4884> συναρπάζω ***sunarpazō*** [CATCH (verb) 3, SEIZE 2] 4x

<4885> συναυξάνω ***sunauxanō*** [to grow together: GROW 2] 1x

<4886> σύνδεσμος ***sundesmos*** [BOND[1] 1] 4x

<4887> συνδέω ***sundeō*** [to bind with: BIND 4] 1x

<4888> συνδοξάζω ***sundoxazō*** [to be glorified with: GLORIFY 3] 1x

<4889> σύνδουλος ***sundoulos*** [FELLOW SERVANT] 10x

<4890> συνδρομή ***sundromē*** [CONCOURSE 1] 1x

<4891> συνεγείρω ***sunegeirō*** [to raise up together, to raise with: RAISE 4] 3x

<4892> συνέδριον ***sunedrion*** [SANHEDRIN 1] 22x

<4893> συνείδησις ***suneidēsis*** [CONSCIENCE 1] 29x

<4894> συνείδω ***suneidō*** [to be aware, to become aware: AWARE 1, to be conscious: CONSCIOUS 1, CONSIDER 14, KNOW 9, to be privy: PRIVY] 4x

<4895> σύνειμι ***suneimi*** [BE WITH] 2x

<4896> σύνειμι ***suneimi*** [to gather, to gather together: GATHER 6] 1x

<4897> συνεισέρχομαι ***suneiserchomai*** [to enter with: ENTER 2] 2x

<4898> συνέκδημος ***sunekdēmos*** [FELLOW TRAVELER] 2x

<4899> συνεκλεκτός ***suneklektos*** [elected together: ELECT 2] 1x

<4900> συνελαύνω ***sunelaunō*** [RECONCILE 5] 1x

<4901> συνεπιμαρτυρέω ***sunepimartureō*** [to bear witness with: WITNESS (noun)[1] 5] 1x

<4902> συνέπομαι ***sunepomai*** [ACCOMPANY 2] 1x

<4903> συνεργέω ***sunergeō*** [to work together, to work with: WORK (verb) 4] 5x

<4904> συνεργός ***sunergos*** [FELLOW WORKER, LABORER TOGETHER] 13x

<4905> συνέρχομαι ***sunerchomai*** [ACCOMPANY 3, COME 13, FOLLOW 9, to go with, to go along: GO 16] 30x

<4906> συνεσθίω ***sunesthiō*** [to eat with: EAT 4] 5x

<4907> σύνεσις ***sunesis*** [UNDERSTANDING 4] 7x

<4908> συνετός ***sunetos*** [UNDERSTANDING 5] 4x

<4909> συνευδοκέω ***suneudokeō*** [APPROVE 4, CONSENT (verb) 5, to be willing: WILL (verb) 3] 6x

<4910> συνευωχέω ***suneuōcheō*** [to feast with, to feast together with: FEAST (verb) 1] 2x

<4911> συνεφίστημι ***sunephistēmi*** [to rise up together, to rise up too: RISE (verb) 6] 1x

<4912> συνέχω ***sunechō*** [to close in: CLOSE (verb) 2, COMPEL 2, to be distressed: DISTRESSED 2, HOLD (verb) 5, PRESS 3, SEIZE 10, STOP 2, SUFFER 5, TAKE 31] 12x

<4913> συνήδομαι ***sunēdomai*** [DELIGHT (verb) 1] 1x

<4914> συνήθεια ***sunētheia*** [CUSTOM[1] 3] 3x

<4915> συνηλικιώτης ***sunēlikiōtēs*** [EQUAL 2] 1x

<4916> συνθάπτω ***sunthaptō*** [to bury with: BURY 2] 2x

<4917> συνθλάω ***sunthlaō*** [BREAK 11] 2x

<4918> συνθλίβω ***sunthlibō*** [PRESS 6] 2x

<4919> συνθρύπτω ***sunthruptō*** [BREAK 12] 1x

<4920> συνίημι ***suniēmi*** [COMPREHEND 2, UNDERSTAND 4] 26x

<4921> συνίστημι ***sunistēmi*** [COMMEND 2, MAKE 10, PROVE 5, STAND (verb) 5, to subsist, to subsist together: SUBSIST 1] 16x

<4922> συνοδεύω ***sunodeuō*** [to travel with: TRAVEL 2] 1x
<4923> συνοδία ***sunodia*** [COMPANY (noun) 3] 1x
<4924> συνοικέω ***sunoikeō*** [to dwell with: DWELL 7] 1x
<4925> συνοικοδομέω ***sunoikodomeō*** [to build together: BUILD 4] 1x
<4926> συνομιλέω ***sunomileō*** [to talk with: TALK (verb) 3] 1x
<4927> συνομορέω ***sunomoreō*** [to be adjoined to: ADJOINED (BE)] 1x
<4928> συνοχή ***sunochē*** [ANGUISH 3, DISTRESS 4] 2x
<4929> συντάσσω ***suntassō*** [DIRECT 3] 2x
<4930> συντέλεια ***sunteleia*** [END (noun) 6] 6x
<4931> συντελέω ***sunteleō*** [END (verb) 1, FINISH 5, FULFILL 2, MAKE 8] 7x
<4932> συντέμνω ***suntemnō*** [to cut short: SHORT 1] 1x
<4933> συντηρέω ***suntēreō*** [KEEP (verb) 4, PRESERVE 3] 4x
<4934> συντίθημι ***suntithēmi*** [AGREE 5, to join in pressing a matter, an attack, an accusation: JOIN 5] 4x
<4935> συντόμως ***suntomōs*** [a few words: WORD 4] 1x
<4936> συντρέχω ***suntrechō*** [to run together, to run with: RUN 7] 3x
<4937> συντρίβω ***suntribō*** [to break, to break in pieces, to break to pieces, to break to shivers, to dash to pieces: BREAK 13, BRUISE 1, to break in pieces: PIECE 6] 8x
<4938> σύντριμμα ***suntrimma*** [DESTRUCTION 4] 1x
<4939> σύντροφος ***suntrophos*** [brought up with: BRING 22] 1x
<4940> συντυγχάνω ***suntunchanō*** [to come at: COME 38] 1x
<4941> Συντύχη ***Suntuchē*** [SYNTYCHE] 1x
<4942> συνυποκρίνομαι ***sunupokrinomai*** [to play the hypocrite with: HYPOCRITE 2] 1x
<4943> συνυπουργέω ***sunupourgeō*** [to help, to help together: HELP (verb) 7] 1x
<4944> συνωδίνω ***sunōdinō*** [to suffer the pains of childbirth, to travail in pain, to labor with birth pangs: PAIN (noun) 4] 1x
<4945> συνωμοσία ***sunōmosia*** [CONSPIRACY 1] 1x
<4946> Συράκουσαι ***Surakousai*** [SYRACUSE] 1x
<4947> Συρία ***Suria*** [SYRIA] 8x
<4948> Σύρος ***Suros*** [SYRIAN] 1x
<4949> Συροφοινίκισσα ***Surophoinikissa*** [SYROPHOENICIAN] 1x
<4950> Σύρτις ***Surtis*** [Syrtis Sands: SAND 2] or [SYRTIS] 1x
<4951> σύρω ***surō*** [DRAG 2, DRAW 12] 5x
<4952> συσπαράσσω ***susparassō*** [CONVULSE 2] 2x
<4953> σύσσημον ***sussēmon*** [SIGN 2] 1x
<4954> σύσσωμος ***sussōmos*** [same body: BODY 2] 1x
<4955> συστασιαστής ***sustasiastēs*** [FELLOW REBEL] 1x
<4956> συστατικός ***sustatikos*** [EPISTLE OF COMMENDATION] 1x
<4957> συσταυρόω ***sustauroō*** [to crucify with: CRUCIFY 3] 5x
<4958> συστέλλω ***sustellō*** [to be short: SHORT 2, to wrap up: WRAP 6] 2x
<4959> συστενάζω ***sustenazō*** [to groan together: GROAN (verb) 3] 1x
<4960> συστοιχέω ***sustoicheō*** [CORRESPOND 1] 1x
<4961> συστρατιώτης ***sustratiōtēs*** [FELLOW SOLDIER] 2x
<4962> συστρέφω ***sustrephō*** [GATHER 11, STAY (verb) 10] 2x
<4963> συστροφή ***sustrophē*** [CONCOURSE 2, CONSPIRACY 2] 2x
<4964> συσχηματίζω ***suschēmatizō*** [CONFORM 1] 2x
<4965> Συχάρ ***Suchar*** [SYCHAR] 1x
<4966> Συχέμ ***Suchem*** [SHECHEM] 2x
<4967> σφαγή ***sphagē*** [SLAUGHTER (noun) 2] 3x
<4968> σφάγιον ***sphagion*** [slain beast: BEAST 4] 1x
<4969> σφάζω ***sphazō*** [KILL 4, MURDER (verb) 3, SLAY 1] 10x
<4970> σφόδρα ***sphodra*** [EXCEEDINGLY 7, GREATLY 2] 11x
<4971> σφοδρῶς ***sphodrōs*** [VIOLENTLY 1] 1x
<4972> σφραγίζω ***sphragizō*** [SEAL (verb) 1] 15x
<4973> σφραγίς ***sphragis*** [SEAL (noun) 1] 16x

<4974> σφυρόν ***sphuron*** [ANKLE] 1x

<4975> σχεδόν ***schedon*** [ALMOST 2] 3x

<4976> σχῆμα ***schēma*** [APPEARANCE 4] 2x

<4977> σχίζω ***schizō*** [BREAK 14, DIVIDE 7, SPLIT 1, TEAR (verb) 4] 9x

<4978> σχίσμα ***schisma*** [DIVISION 4, TEAR (noun)[2] 1] 8x

<4979> σχοινίον ***schoinion*** [CORD] 2x

<4980> σχολάζω ***scholazō*** [to devote oneself: DEVOTE 1, to be unoccupied: UNOCCUPIED] 2x

<4981> σχολή ***scholē*** [SCHOOL 1] 1x

<4982> σῴζω ***sōzō*** [HEAL 3, PRESERVE 4, SAVE (verb) 1] 106x

<4983> σῶμα ***sōma*** [BODY 1] 142x

<4984> σωματικός ***sōmatikos*** [BODILY (adj.) 1] 2x

<4985> σωματικῶς ***sōmatikōs*** [BODILY (adv.) 1] 1x

<4986> Σώπατρος ***Sōpatros*** [SOPATER] 1x

<4987> σωρεύω ***sōreuō*** [HEAP 1, to load down: LOAD (verb) 2] 2x

<4988> Σωσθένης ***Sōsthenēs*** [SOSTHENES] 2x

<4989> Σωσίπατρος ***Sōsipatros*** [SOSIPATER] 1x

<4990> Σωτήρ ***Sōtēr*** [SAVIOR] 24x

<4991> σωτηρία ***sōtēria*** [SALVATION 1, SAVING 2, SURVIVAL] 46x

<4992> σωτήριον ***sōtērion*** [SALVATION 2] 4x

<4992a> σωτήριος ***sōtērios*** [that brings salvation: SALVATION 3] 1x

<4993> σωφρονέω ***sōphroneō*** [to have sound judgment, to have sober judgment: JUDGMENT 7, to be of sound mind, to be in one's right mind: MIND (noun) 12, to be self-controlled: SELF-CONTROLLED 1, to think so as to be wise, soberly, as to have sound judgment, with sober judgment: THINK 13] 6x

<4994> σωφρονίζω ***sōphronizō*** [ADMONISH 3] 1x

<4995> σωφρονισμός ***sōphronismos*** [MIND (noun) 8] 1x

<4996> σωφρόνως ***sōphronōs*** [SOBERLY 1] 1x

<4997> σωφροσύνη ***sōphrosunē*** [MODERATION 1, SOBERNESS] 3x

<4998> σώφρων ***sōphrōn*** [DISCREET 1] 4x

T

<4999> Τρεῖς Ταβέρναι ***Treis Tabernai*** [THREE INNS] 1x

<5000> Ταβιθά ***Tabitha*** [TABITHA] 2x

<5001> τάγμα ***tagma*** [RANK (noun) 1] 1x

<5002> τακτός ***taktos*** [SET (adj.) 1] 1x

<5003> ταλαιπωρέω ***talaipōreō*** [LAMENT 3] 1x

<5004> ταλαιπωρία ***talaipōria*** [MISERY] 2x

<5005> ταλαίπωρος ***talaipōros*** [WRETCHED (adj.) 1] 2x

<5006> ταλαντιαῖος ***talantiaios*** [the weight of a talent, as the weight of a talent: TALENT 2] 1x

<5007> τάλαντον ***talanton*** [TALENT 1] 15x

<5008> ταλιθά ***talitha*** [young girl: TALITHA KOUMI] 1x

<5009> ταμεῖον ***tameion*** [room, inner room: ROOM 2, STOREHOUSE] 4x

<5010> τάξις ***taxis*** [ORDER (noun) 1] 10x

<5011> ταπεινός ***tapeinos*** [CAST DOWN, HUMAN 1, HUMBLE (adj.) 1, LOWLY 1] 8x

<5012> ταπεινοφροσύνη ***tapeinophrosunē*** [humility, humility of mind: HUMILITY 1] 7x

<5012a> ταπεινόφρων ***tapeinophrōn*** [humble, humble minded, humble in spirit: HUMBLE (adj.) 3] 1x

<5013> ταπεινόω ***tapeinoō*** [ABASE, HUMBLE (verb), to bring low, to make low: LOW 1] 14x

<5014> ταπείνωσις ***tapeinōsis*** [humble state, lowly state: HUMBLE (adj.) 2, HUMILIATION] 4x

<5015> ταράσσω ***tarassō*** [TROUBLE (verb) 7] 17x

<5016> ταραχή ***tarachē*** [TROUBLE (noun) 4, TROUBLING] 2x

<5017> τάραχος ***tarachos*** [DISTURBANCE 1] 2x

<5018> Ταρσεύς ***Tarseus*** [of Tarsus: TARSUS 2] 2x

<5019> Ταρσός ***Tarsos*** [TARSUS 1] 3x

<5020> ταρταρόω ***tartaroō*** [to cast to hell, to cast down to hell: HELL 2] 1x

<5021> τάσσω ***tassō*** [APPOINT 7, DETERMINE 7, to devote oneself: DEVOTE 2, PLACE (verb) 1] 8x

<5022> ταῦρος ***tauros*** [BULL] 4x

<5023> ταῦτα ***tauta*** [THESE THINGS 1] 247x

<5024> ταὐτά ***tauta*** [THESE THINGS 2] 4x

<5025> ταύταις ***tautais*** [THESE ONES] 21x

<5026> ταύτῃ ***tautē*** [THIS, THAT 3] 122x

<5027> ταφή ***taphē*** [burial place: BURIAL 2] 1x

<5028> τάφος ***taphos*** [TOMB 3] 7x

<5029> τάχα ***tacha*** [PERHAPS 5] 2x

<5030> ταχέως ***tacheōs*** [HASTILY, QUICKLY 1, SHORTLY 2] 10x

<5031> ταχινός ***tachinos*** [IMMINENT, SHORTLY 3, SWIFT 3] 2x

<5032> τάχιον ***tachion*** [FASTER, QUICKLY 2, SHORTLY 4, SOONER] 5x

<5033> τάχιστα ***tachista*** [as quickly as possible: QUICKLY 3] 1x

<5034> τάχος ***tachos*** [QUICKLY 4, SHORTLY 5, SPEEDILY 1] 7x

<5035> ταχύ ***tachu*** [LIGHTLY 1, QUICKLY 5] 12x

<5036> ταχύς ***tachus*** [SWIFT 2] 1x

<5037> τέ ***te*** [AND] 215x

<5038> τεῖχος ***teichos*** [WALL 1] 9x

<5039> τεκμήριον ***tekmērion*** [infallible proof, convincing proof: PROOF 3] 1x

<5040> τεκνίον ***teknion*** [child, little child: CHILD 10] 9x

<5041> τεκνογονέω ***teknogoneō*** [to bear, to have children: CHILD 7] 1x

<5042> τεκνογονία ***teknogonia*** [CHILDBEARING 1] 1x

<5043> τέκνον ***teknon*** [CHILD 6] 99x

<5044> τεκνοτροφέω ***teknotropheō*** [to bring up children: BRING 21] 1x

<5045> τέκτων ***tektōn*** [CARPENTER] 2x

<5046> τέλειος ***teleios*** [mature, mature man: MATURE 1, PERFECT (adj.) 1] 19x

<5047> τελειότης ***teleiotēs*** [PERFECTION 1] 2x

<5048> τελειόω ***teleioō*** [FINISH 6, FULFILL 3, to make perfect: PERFECT (adj.) 4, to perfect, to make perfect, to be perfected: PERFECT (verb) 3] 23x

<5049> τελείως ***teleiōs*** [COMPLETELY 3] 1x

<5050> τελείωσις ***teleiōsis*** [PERFECTION 2, PERFORMANCE 1] 2x

<5051> τελειωτής ***teleiōtēs*** [FINISHER] 1x

<5052> τελεσφορέω ***telesphoreō*** [to bring fruit to maturity, to bring fruit to perfection: FRUIT 6] 1x

<5053> τελευτάω ***teleutaō*** [to be dead, to die: DEAD 6, DIE 3] 12x

<5054> τελευτή ***teleutē*** [DEATH 3] 1x

<5055> τελέω ***teleō*** [ACCOMPLISH 5, COMPLETE (verb) 2, EXPIRE 3, FINISH 1, FULFILL 1, PAY (verb) 2, PERFORM 2] 28x

<5056> τέλος ***telos*** [CUSTOM[2] 1, END (noun) 4, until the end, unto the end: END (noun) 5, FINALLY 2, PERPETUALLY 1] 40x

<5057> τελώνης ***telōnēs*** [TAX COLLECTOR 1] 21x

<5058> τελώνιον ***telōnion*** [tax office, tax booth, tax collector's booth, receipt of taxes: TAX (noun) 2] 3x

<5059> τέρας ***teras*** [WONDER (adj. and noun) 2] 16x

<5060> Τέρτιος ***Tertios*** [TERTIUS] 1x

<5061> Τέρτυλλος ***Tertullos*** [TERTULLUS] 2x

<5062> τεσσαράκοντα ***tessarakonta*** [FORTY 1, FORTY-SIX, FORTY-TWO, HUNDRED AND FORTY-FOUR THOUSAND] 22x

<5063> τεσσερακονταετής ***tesserakontaetēs*** [forty years old: YEAR 6] 2x

<5064> τέσσαρες ***tessares*** [EIGHTY-FOUR, FOUR 1, HUNDRED AND FORTY-FOUR,

TWENTY-FOUR] 41x
<5065> τεσσαρεσκαιδέκατος ***tessareskaidekatos*** [FOURTEENTH] 2x
<5066> τεταρταῖος ***tetartaios*** [four days: FOUR 2] 1x
<5067> τέταρτος ***tetartos*** [fourth: FOUR 3, FOURTH] 10x
<5068> τετράγωνος ***tetragōnos*** [FOURSQUARE] 1x
<5069> τετράδιον ***tetradion*** [QUATERNION] 1x
<5070> τετρακισχίλιοι ***tetrakischilioi*** [FOUR THOUSAND] 5x
<5071> τετρακόσιοι ***tetrakosioi*** [FOUR HUNDRED, FOUR HUNDRED AND FIFTY, FOUR HUNDRED AND THIRTY] 4x
<5072> τετράμηνος ***tetramēnos*** [four months: MONTH 2] 1x
<5073> τετραπλοῦς ***tetraplous*** [FOURFOLD] 1x
<5074> τετράπους ***tetrapous*** [QUADRUPED] 3x
<5075> τετραρχέω ***tetrarcheō*** [to rule as tetrarch: TETRARCH 2] 3x
<5076> τετράρχης ***tetrarchēs*** [TETRARCH 1] 4x
<5077> τεφρόω ***tephroō*** [to reduce, to burn to ashes: ASH 2] 1x
<5078> τέχνη ***technē*** [ART 1, OCCUPATION 1] 3x
<5079> τεχνίτης ***technitēs*** [BUILDER 1, CRAFTSMAN] 4x
<5080> τήκω ***tēkō*** [MELT 1] 1x
<5081> τηλαυγῶς ***tēlaugōs*** [CLEARLY 1] 1x
<5082> τηλικοῦτος ***tēlikoutos*** [so great: GREAT 12] 4x
<5083> τηρέω ***tēreō*** [BEWARE 2, to guard: GUARD (noun) 5, KEEP (verb) 2, OBSERVE 1, PRESERVE 2, RESERVE 3, WATCH (verb) 6] 70x
<5084> τήρησις ***tērēsis*** [KEEPING 1, PRISON 3] 3x
<5085> Τιβεριάς ***Tiberias*** [TIBERIAS] 3x
<5086> Τιβέριος ***Tiberios*** [TIBERIUS] 1x
<5087> τίθημι ***tithēmi*** [APPOINT 8, FIX 4, LAY 1, LET 4, OFFER 6, PURPOSE (verb) 3, PUT 1, SERVE 8, SET (verb) 11] 100x
<5088> τίκτω ***tiktō*** [to give birth: BIRTH 5, BORN (BE) 3, to bring forth: BRING 34, DELIVERED (BE) 1, PRODUCE 8] 19x
<5089> τίλλω ***tillō*** [PLUCK 4] 3x
<5090> Τιμαῖος ***Timaios*** [TIMAEUS] 1x
<5091> τιμάω ***timaō*** [HONOR (verb) 1, PRICE (verb)] 21x
<5092> τιμή ***timē*** [HONOR (noun) 2, PRICE (noun) 1] 43x
<5093> τίμιος ***timios*** [in honor: HONOR (noun) 3, HONORED 2, PRECIOUS 3] 13x
<5094> τιμιότης ***timiotēs*** [WEALTH 2] 1x
<5095> Τιμόθεος ***Timotheos*** [TIMOTHY] 24x
<5096> Τίμων ***Timōn*** [TIMON] 1x
<5097> τιμωρέω ***timōreō*** [PUNISH 3] 2x
<5098> τιμωρία ***timōria*** [PUNISHMENT 4] 1x
<5099> τίνω ***tinō*** [ENDURE 1] or [PAY (verb) 3] 1x
<5100> τὶς ***tis*** [CERTAIN 1] 448x
<5101> τίς ***tis*** [WHO?, WHICH?, WHAT?] 537x
<5102> τίτλος ***titlos*** [TITLE] 2x
<5103> Τίτος ***Titos*** [TITUS] 12x
<5104> τοι ***toi*** [CONSEQUENTLY 1]
<5105> τοιγαροῦν ***toigaroun*** [CONSEQUENTLY 2] 2x
<5106> τοίνυν ***toinun*** [THEREFORE 1] 4x
<5107> τοιόσδε ***toiosde*** [OF THIS KIND, SUCH] 1x
<5108> τοιοῦτος ***toioutos*** [LIKE, THE LIKE: LIKE (ADJ., ADV., NOUN) 7] 53x
<5109> τοῖχος ***toichos*** [WHITEWASHED WALL] 1x
<5110> τόκος ***tokos*** [INTEREST 1] 2x
<5111> τολμάω ***tolmaō*** [to be bold: BOLD 3, to go boldly: BOLDLY 4, DARE] 16x
<5112> τολμηρότερον ***tolmēroteron*** [more, quite, very boldly: BOLDLY 5] 1x
<5113> τολμητής ***tolmētēs*** [PRESUMPTUOUS] 1x
<5114> τομώτερος ***tomōteros*** [SHARPER] 1x

<5115> τόξον ***toxon*** [BOW (noun) 1] 1x

<5116> τοπάζιον ***topazion*** [TOPAZ] 1x

<5117> τόπος ***topos*** [COAST (noun) 2, OPPORTUNITY 4, PLACE (noun) 1, rocky place: ROCK 3] 94x

<5118> τοσοῦτος ***tosoutos*** [so great: GREAT 13, so much: MUCH 2] 19x

<5119> τότε ***tote*** [THEN 4] 160x

<5120> τοῦ ***tou*** [OF ITS]

<5121> τοὐναντίον ***tounantion*** [on the contrary: CONTRARY 2] 3x

<5122> τοὔνομα ***tounoma*** [the name: NAMED 1] 1x

<5123> τουτέστι ***toutesti*** [that is, which is, that is to say: SAY 8]

<5124> τοῦτο ***touto*** [for this reason: REASON (noun) 5, for this very reason: REASON (noun) 6]

<5125> τούτοις ***toutois*** [THESE] 19x

<5126> τοῦτον ***touton*** [THIS] 64x

<5127> τούτου ***toutou*** [OF THIS PERSON, OF THIS THING] 77x

<5128> τούτους ***toutous*** [these persons] 27x

<5129> τούτῳ ***toutō*** [BY THIS PERSON, BY THIS THING] 89x

<5130> τούτων ***toutōn*** [OF THESE PERSONS, OF THESE THINGS] 69x

<5131> τράγος ***tragos*** [GOAT 3] 4x

<5132> τράπεζα ***trapeza*** [BANK, TABLE[1] 1] 15x

<5133> τραπεζίτης ***trapezitēs*** [EXCHANGER] 1x

<5134> τραῦμα ***trauma*** [WOUND (noun) 1] 1x

<5135> τραυματίζω ***traumatizō*** [WOUND (verb) 1] 2x

<5136> τραχηλίζω ***trachēlizō*** [OPEN (verb) 4] 1x

<5137> τράχηλος ***trachēlos*** [NECK] 7x

<5138> τραχύς ***trachus*** [rocky place: ROCK 3, ROUGH 1] 2x

<5139> Τραχωνῖτις ***Trachōnitis*** [TRACHONITUS] 1x

<5140> τρεῖς ***treis*** [HUNDRED AND FIFTY-THREE, THREE 1, TWENTY-THREE THOUSAND] 68x

<5141> τρέμω ***tremō*** [TREMBLE 1] 4x

<5142> τρέφω ***trephō*** [to bring up: BRING 18, NOURISH 2] 8x

<5143> τρέχω ***trechō*** [RUN 1] 20x

<5144> τριάκοντα ***triakonta*** [FOUR HUNDRED AND THIRTY, THIRTY, THIRTY-EIGHT] 11x

<5145> τριακόσιοι ***triakosioi*** [THREE HUNDRED] 2x

<5146> τρίβολος ***tribolos*** [BRIAR 1] 2x

<5147> τρίβος ***tribos*** [PATH 1] 3x

<5148> τριετία ***trietia*** [three years: YEAR 5] 1x

<5149> τρίζω ***trizō*** [GNASH 1] 1x

<5150> τρίμηνον ***trimēnon*** [three months: MONTH 3] 1x

<5151> τρίς ***tris*** [three times: TIME 16] 12x

<5152> τρίστεγον ***tristegon*** [third story: STORY[1]] 1x

<5153> τρισχίλιοι ***trischilioi*** [THREE THOUSAND] 1x

<5154> τρίτος ***tritos*** [third, third part: THIRD 1, third time: TIME 17] 56x

<5155> τρίχινος ***trichinos*** [made of hair: HAIR 2] 1x

<5156> τρόμος ***tromos*** [TREMBLING 1] 5x

<5157> τροπή ***tropē*** [TURNING] 1x

<5158> τρόπος ***tropos*** [CONDUCT (noun) 2, MANNER 2] 13x

<5159> τροποφορέω ***tropophoreō*** [to endure the conduct: ENDURE 5] 1x

<5160> τροφή ***trophē*** [FOOD 6] 16x

<5161> Τρόφιμος ***Trophimos*** [TROPHIMUS] 3x

<5162> τροφός ***trophos*** [NURSE (noun)] 1x

<5162a> τροφοφορέω ***trophophoreō*** [to endure the conduct: ENDURE 5] 1x

<5163> τροχιά ***trochia*** [PATH 2] 1x

<5164> τροχός ***trochos*** [COURSE 4] 1x

<5165> τρύβλιον ***trublion*** [DISH 3] 2x

<5166> τρυγάω ***trugaō*** [GATHER 8] 3x

<5167> τρυγών ***trugōn*** [TURTLEDOVE] 1x

<5168> τρυμαλιά ***trumalia*** [HOLE 2] 2x

<5169> τρύπημα ***trupēma*** [HOLE 3] 1x

<5170> Τρύφαινα ***Truphaina*** [TRYPHAENA] 1x

<5171> τρυφάω ***truphaō*** [to live in pleasure: PLEASURE 4] 1x

<5172> τρυφή ***truphē*** [INDULGENCE 2, LUXURY 2] 2x

<5173> Τρυφῶσα ***Truphōsa*** [TRYPHOSA] 1x

<5174> Τρῳάς ***Trōas*** [TROAS] 6x

<5175> Τρωγύλλιον ***Trōgullion*** [TROGYLLIUM] 1x

<5176> τρώγω ***trōgō*** [EAT 6] 6x

<5177> τυγχάνω ***tunchanō*** [ATTAIN 3, to be common: COMMON 3, ENJOY 2, OBTAIN 5, to be ordinary: ORDINARY 1, it may be that: PERHAPS 6, it may be: PERHAPS 7] 12x

<5178> τυμπανίζω ***tumpanizō*** [TORTURED (BE)] 1x

<5179> τύπος ***tupos*** [FORM (noun) 4, MARK (noun) 3, PATTERN 1, TYPE 1] 15x

<5180> τύπτω ***tuptō*** [BEAT 7, STRIKE 7, WOUND (verb) 2] 13x

<5181> Τύραννος ***Turannos*** [TYRANNUS] 1x

<5182> τυρβάζω ***turbazō*** [to be troubled: TROUBLE (verb) 10] 1x

<5183> Τύριος ***Turios*** [TYRIAN] 1x

<5184> Τύρος ***Turos*** [TYRE 1] 11x

<5185> τυφλός ***tuphlos*** [BLIND (adj.), BLIND (noun)] 50x

<5186> τυφλόω ***tuphloō*** [BLIND (verb) 1] 3x

<5187> τυφόω ***tuphoō*** [PUFF UP 2] 3x

<5188> τύφω ***tuphō*** [to smoke: SMOKING] 1x

<5189> τυφωνικός ***tuphōnikos*** [TEMPESTUOUS] 1x

<5190> Τυχικός ***Tuchikos*** [TYCHICUS] 5x

Y

<5191> ὑακίνθινος ***huakinthinos*** [of jacinth: JACINTH 2] 1x

<5192> ὑάκινθος ***huakinthos*** [JACINTH 1] 1x

<5193> ὑάλινος ***hualinos*** [sea of glass: SEA 6] 3x

<5194> ὕαλος ***hualos*** [GLASS 1] 2x

<5195> ὑβρίζω ***hubrizō*** [INSULT (verb) 1, MISTREAT 1] 5x

<5196> ὕβρις ***hubris*** [DISASTER, HARM (noun) 2, INSULT (noun) 1] 3x

<5197> ὑβριστής ***hubristēs*** [insolent man: INSOLENT] 2x

<5198> ὑγιαίνω ***hugiainō*** [to be in health, in good health, in sound health: HEALTH 2, to be safe and sound, to be safe and well: SAFELY 2, to be safe: SOUND (adj.) 2] 12x

<5199> ὑγιής ***hugiēs*** [in good health: HEALTH 1, SOUND (adj.) 1] 14x

<5200> ὑγρός ***hugros*** [GREEN 1] 1x

<5201> ὑδρία ***hudria*** [WATER POT] 3x

<5202> ὑδροποτέω ***hudropoteō*** [to drink water only: DRINK (verb) 4] 1x

<5203> ὑδρωπικός ***hudrōpikos*** [DROPSICAL] 1x

<5204> ὕδωρ ***hudōr*** [WATER (noun) 1] 76x

<5205> ὑετός ***huetos*** [RAIN (noun) 3] 6x

<5206> υἱοθεσία ***huiothesia*** [ADOPTION] 5x

<5207> υἱός ***huios*** [FOAL, SON 1, SON OF DAY, SON OF HELL, SON OF LIGHT, SON OF PERDITION, SON OF THE BRIDECHAMBER, SON OF THIS AGE, SON OF THIS WORLD] 381x

<5207> Υἱός ***Huios*** [SON (Son of God)]

<5208> ὕλη ***hulē*** [FOREST] 1x

<5209> ὑμᾶς ***humas*** [YOU (plur.) 1] 437x

<5210> ὑμεῖς ***humeis*** [YOU (plur.) 2] 242x

<5211> Ὑμέναιος ***Humenaios*** [HYMENAEUS] 2x

<5212> ὑμέτερος ***humeteros*** [YOUR, YOURS (plur.)] 11x
<5213> ὑμῖν ***humin*** [YOU (UNTO, WITH, BY) (plur.)] 624x
<5214> ὑμνέω ***humneō*** [to sing praises: PRAISE (noun) 4, to sing a hymn, to sing praise: SING 3] 4x
<5215> ὕμνος ***humnos*** [HYMN 1] 2x
<5216> ὑμῶν ***humōn*** [YOU (OF, FROM, CONCERNING) (plur.)] 581x
<5217> ὑπάγω ***hupagō*** [to go, to go away: GO 4] 80x
<5218> ὑπακοή ***hupakoē*** [OBEDIENCE 1] 15x
<5219> ὑπακούω ***hupakouō*** [ANSWER (verb) 5, OBEY 1] 21x
<5220> ὕπανδρος ***hupandros*** [who has a husband: HUSBAND 2] 1x
<5221> ὑπαντάω ***hupantaō*** [MEET (verb) 3] 7x
<5222> ὑπάντησις ***hupantēsis*** [meeting: MEET (verb) 8] 2x
<5223> ὕπαρξις ***huparxis*** [GOOD (adj. and noun) 6] 2x
<5224> ὑπάρχοντα ***huparchonta*** [goods: GOOD (adj. and noun) 7, POSSESSIONS, SUBSTANCE 1] 14x
<5225> ὑπάρχω ***huparchō*** [BE 8, BELONG 1, EXIST 2, HAVE 4, LIVE 11] 60x
<5226> ὑπείκω ***hupeikō*** [SUBMIT 1] 1x
<5227> ὑπεναντίος ***hupenantios*** [ADVERSARY 2, CONTRARY 3] 2x
<5228> ὑπέρ ***huper*** [HIGHLY (VERY)]
<5229> ὑπεραίρω ***huperairō*** [to exalt above measure, to exalt: EXALT 2] 3x
<5230> ὑπέρακμος ***huperakmos*** [who has passed the flower of age: AGE 4] 1x
<5231> ὑπεράνω ***huperanō*** [ABOVE (UP, HIGH, FAR)] 3x
<5232> ὑπεραυξάνω ***huperauxanō*** [to grow exceedingly, to grow more and more: GROW 3] 1x
<5233> ὑπερβαίνω ***huperbainō*** [to take advantage: ADVANTAGE (noun) 3] 1x
<5234> ὑπερβαλλόντως ***huperballontōs*** [to excess: EXCESS 2] 1x
<5235> ὑπερβάλλω ***huperballō*** [to exceed: EXCEEDING 1, EXCEL 2, SURPASS 2, to surpass: SURPASSING 2] 5x
<5236> ὑπερβολή ***huperbolē*** [EXCEEDINGLY 6, excellence, surpassing excellence: EXCELLENCE 1, exceeding greatness, surpassing greatness, surpassingly great: GREATNESS 3, beyond measure, in surpassing measure: MEASURE (noun) 7] 7x
<5237> ὑπεροράω ***huperoraō*** [OVERLOOK 2] 1x
<5238> ὑπερέκεινα ***huperekeina*** [region beyond: REGION 5] 1x
<5238a> ὑπερεκπερισσοῦ ***huperekperissou*** [exceeding, exceedingly, far more abundantly: ABUNDANTLY 5, EXCEEDINGLY 4] 3x
<5239> ὑπερεκτείνω ***huperekteinō*** [OVEREXTEND] 1x
<5240> ὑπερεκχύνω ***huperekchunō*** [to run over: RUN 14] 1x
<5241> ὑπερεντυγχάνω ***huperentunchanō*** [INTERCEDE 2] 1x
<5242> ὑπερέχω ***huperechō*** [in authority: AUTHORITY 7, EXCELLENCE 2, GOVERNING, more important: IMPORTANT 1, SURPASS 3] 5x
<5243> ὑπερηφανία ***huperēphania*** [PRIDE 2] 1x
<5244> ὑπερήφανος ***huperēphanos*** [PROUD (adj.) 1, PROUD (noun)] 5x
<5244a> ὑπερλίαν ***huperlian*** [in surpassing degree: SURPASSING 1] 2x
<5245> ὑπερνικάω ***hupernikaō*** [to be more than conqueror: CONQUEROR 1] 1x
<5246> ὑπέρογκος ***huperonkos*** [boastful, swelling word: WORD 5] 2x
<5247> ὑπεροχή ***huperochē*** [AUTHORITY 8, EXCELLENCE 3] 2x
<5248> ὑπερπερισσεύω ***huperperisseuō*** [to abound much more, to abound all the more: ABOUND 2] 2x
<5249> ὑπερπερισσῶς ***huperperissōs*** [above measure, beyond measure: MEASURE (noun) 8] 1x
<5250> ὑπερπλεονάζω ***huperpleonazō*** [to be more than abundant, to be exceeding abundant, to be exceedingly abundant: ABUNDANT 2] 1x
<5251> ὑπερυψόω ***huperupsoō*** [to highly exalt: EXALT 4] 1x
<5252> ὑπερφρονέω ***huperphroneō*** [to think highly: THINK 14] 1x
<5253> ὑπερῷον ***huperōon*** [upper room, upper chamber, upstairs room: ROOM 3] 4x
<5254> ὑπέχω ***hupechō*** [UNDERGO 1] 1x
<5255> ὑπήκοος ***hupēkoos*** [OBEDIENT 1] 3x

<5256> ὑπηρετέω ***hupēreteō*** [MINISTER (verb) 5, PROVIDE 4] 3x
<5257> ὑπηρέτης ***hupēretēs*** [ATTENDANT 1, MINISTER (noun) 3, OFFICER 3, SERVANT 7] 20x
<5258> ὕπνος ***hupnos*** [SLEEP (noun) 1] 6x
<5259> ὑπό ***hupo*** [UNDER 1] 212x
<5260> ὑποβάλλω ***hupoballō*** [SUBORN] 1x
<5261> ὑπογραμμός ***hupogrammos*** [EXAMPLE 5] 1x
<5262> ὑπόδειγμα ***hupodeigma*** [COPY 2, EXAMPLE 2] 6x
<5263> ὑποδείκνυμι ***hupodeiknumi*** [SHOW (verb) 9, WARN 4] 6x
<5264> ὑποδέχομαι ***hupodechomai*** [RECEIVE 16] 4x
<5265> ὑποδέω ***hupodeō*** [SHOD] 3x
<5266> ὑπόδημα ***hupodēma*** [SANDAL 2] 10x
<5267> ὑπόδικος ***hupodikos*** [GUILTY 2] 1x
<5268> ὑποζύγιον ***hupozugion*** [DONKEY 4] 2x
<5269> ὑποζώννυμι ***hupozōnnumi*** [UNDERGIRD] 1x
<5270> ὑποκάτω ***hupokatō*** [UNDERNEATH] 9x
<5271> ὑποκρίνομαι ***hupokrinomai*** [PRETEND 1] 1x
<5272> ὑπόκρισις ***hupokrisis*** [HYPOCRISY 1] 6x
<5273> ὑποκριτής ***hupokritēs*** [HYPOCRITE 1] 19x
<5274> ὑπολαμβάνω ***hupolambanō*** [RECEIVE 7, REPLY (verb) 3, SUPPOSE 4] 4x
<5275> ὑπολείπω ***hupoleipō*** [LEAVE (verb) 8] 1x
<5276> ὑπολήνιον ***hupolēnion*** [WINEVAT] 1x
<5277> ὑπολιμπάνω ***hupolimpanō*** [LEAVE (verb) 9] 1x
<5278> ὑπομένω ***hupomenō*** [ENDURE 2, to linger behind: LINGER 1, to be patient: PATIENT 2, REMAIN 5, SUFFER 6] 17x
<5279> ὑπομιμνήσκω ***hupomimnēskō*** [to bring to remembrance, to put (someone) in remembrance, to remember: REMEMBER 3, REMIND 3] 7x
<5280> ὑπόμνησις ***hupomnēsis*** [mind: MIND (CALL TO) 2, REMEMBRANCE 4] 3x
<5281> ὑπομονή ***hupomonē*** [ENDURANCE 1, PATIENCE 3, PATIENT CONTINUANCE] 32x
<5282> ὑπονοέω ***huponoeō*** [EXPECT 2, SUPPOSE 5] 3x
<5283> ὑπόνοια ***huponoia*** [SUSPICION] 1x
<5284> ὑποπλέω ***hupopleō*** [to sail under, to sail under the lee, to pass to the lee, to sail under the shelter: SAIL (verb) 8] 2x
<5285> ὑποπνέω ***hupopneō*** [to blow gently, to blow softly: BLOW (verb) 3] 1x
<5286> ὑποπόδιον ***hupopodion*** [FOOTSTOOL] 9x
<5287> ὑπόστασις ***hupostasis*** [CONFIDENCE 3, SUBSTANCE 2] 5x
<5288> ὑποστέλλω ***hupostellō*** [to keep back: KEEP (verb) 13, SHRINK, WITHDRAW 6] 4x
<5289> ὑποστολή ***hupostolē*** [DESERTION] 1x
<5290> ὑποστρέφω ***hupostrephō*** [COME 27, RETURN (verb) 9] 35x
<5291> ὑποστρωννύω ***hupostrōnnuō*** [SPREAD 9] 1x
<5292> ὑποταγή ***hupotagē*** [SUBMISSION 1] 4x
<5293> ὑποτάσσω ***hupotassō*** [to be subject: SUBJECT (noun)[1] 2, to subject, to make subject, to be subject, to put under, to put in subjection: SUBJECT (verb) 1] 38x
<5294> ὑποτίθημι ***hupotithēmi*** [to point out: POINT (verb) 1, RISK 2] 2x
<5295> ὑποτρέχω ***hupotrechō*** [to run under: RUN 9] 1x
<5296> ὑποτύπωσις ***hupotupōsis*** [EXAMPLE 6, PATTERN 2] 2x
<5297> ὑποφέρω ***hupopherō*** [ENDURE 4] 3x
<5298> ὑποχωρέω ***hupochōreō*** [WITHDRAW 5] 2x
<5299> ὑπωπιάζω ***hupōpiazō*** [DISCIPLINE (verb) 1, to completely harass: HARASS 1] 2x
<5300> ὗς ***hus*** [SOW (noun)] 1x
<5301> ὕσσωπος ***hussōpos*** [HYSSOP] 2x
<5302> ὑστερέω ***hustereō*** [to come short: COME 39, to be inferior: INFERIOR 2, LACK (verb) 1, to suffer privation: PRIVATION 2, to be in want: WANT (noun) 2, to be the worse: WORSE 4] 16x

<5303> ὑστέρημα ***husterēma*** [what is lacking: LACK (noun) 1, NEED (noun) 3] 9x
<5304> ὑστέρησις ***husterēsis*** [POVERTY 2, PRIVATION 1] 2x
<5305> ὕστερον ***husteron*** [AFTERWARD 3, at the last: LAST (adv. and noun) 2, last of all, at last: LAST (adv. and noun) 3] 12x
<5306> ὕστερος ***husteros*** [LATTER 1] 1x
<5307> ὑφαντός ***huphantos*** [WOVEN] 1x
<5308> ὑψηλός ***hupsēlos*** [highly esteemed: ESTEEMED, HIGH (adj.) 1, UPLIFTED] 11x
<5309> ὑψηλοφρονέω ***hupsēlophroneō*** [to be conceited: CONCEITED 2] 2x
<5310> Ὕψιστος ***Hupsistos*** [MOST HIGH] and ὕψιστος ***hupsistos*** [highest, most high: HIGH (adj.) 2, HIGHEST] 13x
<5311> ὕψος ***hupsos*** [DAYSPRING FROM ON HIGH, EXALTATION, HEIGHT 1, HIGH (noun)] 6x
<5312> ὑψόω ***hupsoō*** [EXALT 3, to lift up: LIFT 5] 20x
<5313> ὕψωμα ***hupsōma*** [HEIGHT 2] 2x

Φ

<5314> φάγος ***phagos*** [GLUTTON 2] 2x
<5315> φάγω ***phagō*** [EAT 5] 95x
<5316> φαίνω ***phainō*** [APPEAR 1, SEE 10, SHINE 7, to shine: SHINING 4, THINK 11] 31x
<5317> Φάλεκ ***Phalek*** [PHALEK] 1x
<5318> φανερός ***phaneros*** [CLEAR (adj.) 1, EVIDENT 5, KNOWN 2, to light: LIGHT (noun) 9, MANIFEST (adj.) 2, open: OPENLY 2, OUTWARD 3, PUBLIC 3, RECOGNIZED, REVEALED] 18x
<5319> φανερόω ***phaneroō*** [APPEAR 4, MANIFEST (verb) 2, SHOW (verb) 16] 40x
<5320> φανερῶς ***phanerōs*** [OPENLY 3, PLAINLY 2] 3x
<5321> φανέρωσις ***phanerōsis*** [MANIFESTATION 2] 2x
<5322> φανός ***phanos*** [LANTERN] 1x
<5323> Φανουήλ ***Phanouēl*** [PHANUEL] 1x
<5324> φαντάζω ***phantazō*** [APPEAR 7] 1x
<5325> φαντασία ***phantasia*** [POMP] 1x
<5326> φάντασμα ***phantasma*** [GHOST 1] 2x
<5327> φάραγξ ***pharanx*** [VALLEY 1] 1x
<5328> Φαραώ ***Pharaō*** [PHARAOH] 5x
<5329> Φαρές ***Phares*** [PHARES] 3x
<5330> Φαρισαῖος ***Pharisaios*** [PHARISEE] 100x
<5331> φαρμακεία ***pharmakeia*** [SORCERY 3] 3x
<5332> φαρμακεύς ***pharmakeus*** [SORCERER 2] 1x
<5333> φάρμακος ***pharmakos*** [SORCERER 3] 2x
<5334> φάσις ***phasis*** [TIDINGS 2] 1x
<5335> φάσκω ***phaskō*** [SAY 6] 4x
<5336> φάτνη ***phatnē*** [MANGER] 4x
<5337> φαῦλος ***phaulos*** [EVIL (adj.) 3, EVIL (noun) 3] 6x
<5338> φέγγος ***phengos*** [LIGHT (noun) 5] 3x
<5339> φείδομαι ***pheidomai*** [FORBEAR 1, SPARE 1] 10x
<5340> φειδομένως ***pheidomenōs*** [SPARINGLY] 2x
<5341> φελόνης, φαιλόνης ***phelonēs, phailonēs*** [CLOAK 3] 1x
<5342> φέρω ***pherō*** [to bring, to bring against, to bring forth: BRING 10, CARRY 4, COME 40, DRIVE 6, ENDURE 3, to go on, to go forth: GO 34, LEAD (verb) 9, MOVE 6, REACH (verb) 4, to rush: RUSHING, UPHOLD 1] 66x
<5343> φεύγω ***pheugō*** [ESCAPE 1, FLEE 1] 30x
<5344> Φῆλιξ ***Phēlix*** [FELIX] 9x
<5345> φήμη ***phēmē*** [FAME 2, NEWS 1] 2x
<5346> φημί ***phēmi*** [AFFIRM 3, SAY 7] 66x
<5347> Φῆστος ***Phēstos*** [FESTUS] 13x

<5348> φθάνω ***phthanō*** [COME 28, PRECEDE 2] 7x

<5349> φθαρτός ***phthartos*** [CORRUPTIBLE 1] 6x

<5350> φθέγγομαι ***phthengomai*** [SPEAK 18] 3x

<5351> φθείρω ***phtheirō*** [CORRUPT (verb) 1, DESTROY 7] 8x

<5352> φθινοπωρινός ***phthinopōrinos*** [AUTUMNAL] 1x

<5353> φθόγγος ***phthongos*** [SOUND (noun) 2, VOICE 2] 2x

<5354> φθονέω ***phthoneō*** [ENVY (verb) 2] 1x

<5355> φθόνος ***phthonos*** [ENVY (noun) 1] 9x

<5356> φθορά ***phthora*** [CORRUPTION 1, destruction: DESTROY 8, destruction: PERISH 9] 8x

<5357> φιάλη ***phialē*** [BOWL 1] 12x

<5358> φιλάγαθος ***philagathos*** [lover of what is good, lover of goodness, loving what is good, lover of good men: LOVER 1] 1x

<5359> Φιλαδέλφεια ***Philadelpheia*** [PHILADELPHIA] 2x

<5360> φιλαδελφία ***philadelphia*** [love of the brothers, love of the brethren, brotherly love: LOVE (noun) 2] 6x

<5361> φιλάδελφος ***philadelphos*** [brotherly, full of brotherly love: BROTHERLY 1] 1x

<5362> φίλανδρος ***philandros*** [loving one's husband: HUSBAND 3] 1x

<5363> φιλανθρωπία ***philanthrōpia*** [KINDNESS 1, love, love toward man, love to man: LOVE (noun) 3] 2x

<5364> φιλανθρώπως ***philanthrōpōs*** [KINDLY] 1x

<5365> φιλαργυρία ***philarguria*** [love of money: LOVE (noun) 4] 1x

<5366> φιλάργυρος ***philarguros*** [COVETOUS (adj.) 1] 2x

<5367> φίλαυτος ***philautos*** [lover of self: LOVER 2] 1x

<5368> φιλέω ***phileō*** [KISS (verb) 1, LOVE (verb) 2] 24x

<5369> φιλήδονος ***philēdonos*** [lover of pleasure: LOVER 3] 1x

<5370> φίλημα ***philēma*** [KISS (noun)] 7x

<5371> Φιλήμων ***Philēmōn*** [PHILEMON] 1x

<5372> Φίλητος ***Philētos*** [PHILETUS] 1x

<5373> φιλία ***philia*** [FRIENDSHIP 1] 1x

<5374> Φιλιππήσιος ***Philippēsios*** [PHILIPPIAN] 1x

<5375> Φίλιπποι ***Philippoi*** [PHILIPPI] 4x

<5376> Φίλιππος ***Philippos*** [CAESAREA PHILIPPI, PHILIP] 37x

<5377> φιλόθεος ***philotheos*** [lover of God: LOVER 4] 1x

<5378> Φιλόλογος ***Philologos*** [PHILOLOGUS] 1x

<5379> φιλονεικία ***philoneikia*** [STRIFE 4] 1x

<5380> φιλόνεικος ***philoneikos*** [CONTENTIOUS 1] 1x

<5381> φιλοξενία ***philoxenia*** [HOSPITALITY 1] 2x

<5382> φιλόξενος ***philoxenos*** [HOSPITABLE] 3x

<5383> φιλοπρωτεύω ***philoprōteuō*** [to love to have the preeminence: PREEMINENCE 1] 1x

<5384> φίλος ***philos*** [FRIEND 2] 29x

<5385> φιλοσοφία ***philosophia*** [PHILOSOPHY] 1x

<5386> φιλόσοφος ***philosophos*** [PHILOSOPHER 1] 1x

<5387> φιλόστοργος ***philostorgos*** [kindly affectionate: AFFECTIONATE] 1x

<5388> φιλότεκνος ***philoteknos*** [loving one's children: CHILD 8] 1x

<5389> φιλοτιμέομαι ***philotimeomai*** [LABOR (verb) 4, STRIVE 10, STUDY 1] 3x

<5390> φιλοφρόνως ***philophronōs*** [COURTEOUSLY 1] 1x

<5391> φιλόφρων ***philophrōn*** [COURTEOUS] 1x

<5392> φιμόω ***phimoō*** [MUZZLE, to be quiet: QUIET (adj.) 4, to put to silence: SILENCE (noun) 4, to be speechless: SPEECHLESS 2] 8x

<5393> Φλέγων ***Phlegōn*** [PHLEGON] 1x

<5394> φλογίζω ***phlogizō*** [to set fire, to set on fire: FIRE 6] 2x

<5395> φλόξ ***phlox*** [FLAME 1] 7x

<5396> φλυαρέω ***phluareō*** [PRATE] 1x

<5397> φλύαρος ***phluaros*** [TATTLER] 1x

<5398> φοβερός ***phoberos*** [FEARFUL 2] 3x
<5399> φοβέω ***phobeō*** [to be afraid, to fear: AFRAID 3, FEAR (verb) 1, RESPECT (verb) 2] 95x
<5400> φόβητρον ***phobētron*** [fearful event, fearful sight: FEARFUL 3] 1x
<5401> φόβος ***phobos*** [FEAR (noun) 2] 47x
<5402> Φοίβη ***Phoibē*** [PHOEBE] 1x
<5403> Φοινίκη ***Phoinikē*** [PHOENICIA] 3x
<5404> φοῖνιξ ***phoinix*** [PALM, PALM TREE] 2x
<5405> Φοίνιξ or Φοῖνιξ ***Phoinix*** [PHOENIX] 1x
<5406> φονεύς ***phoneus*** [MURDERER 4] 7x
<5407> φονεύω ***phoneuō*** [KILL 8, MURDER (verb) 2] 12x
<5408> φόνος ***phonos*** [DEATH 4, MURDER (noun) 1, death: SLAY 2] 10x
<5409> φορέω ***phoreō*** [WEAR 4] 6x
<5410> Φόρον ***Phoron*** [MARKET OF APPIUS] 1x
<5411> φόρος ***phoros*** [TRIBUTE 2] 5x
<5412> φορτίζω ***phortizō*** [to be heavy laden, to load: LOAD (verb) 1] 2x
<5413> φορτίον ***phortion*** [BURDEN (noun) 3] 5x
<5414> φόρτος ***phortos*** [LADING] 1x
<5415> Φορτουνάτος ***Phortounatos*** [FORTUNATUS] 1x
<5416> φραγέλλιον ***phragellion*** [SCOURGE (noun) 1] 1x
<5417> φραγελλόω ***phragelloō*** [SCOURGE (verb) 3] 2x
<5418> φραγμός ***phragmos*** [HEDGE (noun), SEPARATION] 4x
<5419> φράζω ***phrazō*** [EXPOUND 1] 2x
<5420> φράσσω ***phrassō*** [STOP 3] 3x
<5421> φρέαρ ***phrear*** [WELL (noun) 1] 7x
<5422> φρεναπατάω ***phrenapataō*** [DECEIVE 3] 1x
<5423> φρεναπάτης ***phrenapatēs*** [DECEIVER 2] 1x
<5424> φρήν ***phrēn*** [UNDERSTANDING 7] 2x
<5425> φρίσσω ***phrissō*** [SHUDDER] 1x
<5426> φρονέω ***phroneō*** [to be of the mind, to set the mind, to have the mind: MIND (noun) 10, MIND (verb) 1, THINK 12] 26x
<5427> φρόνημα ***phronēma*** [MIND (noun) 9] 4x
<5428> φρόνησις ***phronēsis*** [INTELLIGENCE 1, THOUGHT 7] 2x
<5429> φρόνιμος ***phronimos*** [INTELLIGENT 2, PRUDENT 1, WISE (adj.) 3] 14x
<5430> φρονίμως ***phronimōs*** [PRUDENTLY] 1x
<5431> φροντίζω ***phrontizō*** [to be careful: CAREFUL 1] 1x
<5432> φρουρέω ***phroureō*** [GUARD (verb) 3] 4x
<5433> φρυάσσω ***phruassō*** [RAGE (verb) 1] 1x
<5434> φρύγανον ***phruganon*** [STICK (noun) 1] 1x
<5435> Φρυγία ***Phrugia*** [PHRYGIA] 3x
<5436> Φύγελος ***Phugelos*** [PHYGELUS] 1x
<5437> φυγή ***phugē*** [FLIGHT 1] 2x
<5438> φυλακή ***phulakē*** [GUARD (noun) 4, HOLD (noun) 1, PRISON 4, WATCH (noun) 1] 47x
<5439> φυλακίζω ***phulakizō*** [IMPRISON 1] 1x
<5440> φυλακτήριον ***phulaktērion*** [PHYLACTERY] 1x
<5441> φύλαξ ***phulax*** [GUARD (noun) 3] 3x
<5442> φυλάσσω ***phulassō*** [to be on one's guard: GUARD (noun) 6, GUARD (verb) 1, KEEP (verb) 9, PRESERVE 5] 31x
<5443> φυλή ***phulē*** [TRIBE 1] 31x
<5444> φύλλον ***phullon*** [LEAF 1] 6x
<5445> φύραμα ***phurama*** [LUMP] 5x
<5446> φυσικός ***phusikos*** [NATURAL 1] 3x
<5447> φυσικῶς ***phusikōs*** [by mere nature: NATURE 2] 1x
<5448> φυσιόω ***phusioō*** [PUFF UP 1] 7x
<5449> φύσις ***phusis*** [KIND (noun) 2, NATURE 1] 14x

<5450> φυσίωσις ***phusiōsis*** [PUFFING UP] 1x
<5451> φυτεία ***phuteia*** [PLANT (plant) 1] 1x
<5452> φυτεύω ***phuteuō*** [PLANT (verb) 1] 11x
<5453> φύω ***phuō*** [to spring up: SPRING (verb) 4] 3x
<5454> φωλεός ***phōleos*** [HOLE 4] 2x
<5455> φωνέω ***phōneō*** [CALL (verb) 11, CROW, to cry, to cry out: CRY (verb) 7] 43x
<5456> φωνή ***phōnē*** [SOUND (noun) 3, VOICE 1] 139x
<5457> φῶς ***phōs*** [FIRE 5, LIGHT (noun) 1, SON OF LIGHT] 73x
<5458> φωστήρ ***phōstēr*** [LIGHT (noun) 2] 2x
<5459> φωσφόρος ***phōsphoros*** [MORNING STAR 3] 1x
<5460> φωτεινός ***phōteinos*** [BRIGHT 2, light, full of light: LIGHT (noun) 3] 5x
<5461> φωτίζω ***phōtizō*** [ENLIGHTEN, ILLUMINATE 1, LIGHT (noun) 8] 11x
<5462> φωτισμός ***phōtismos*** [LIGHT (noun) 4] 2x

X

<5463> χαίρω ***chairō*** [HAIL (verb), REJOICE 3] 74x
<5464> χάλαζα ***chalaza*** [HAIL (noun)] 4x
<5465> χαλάω ***chalaō*** [to let down: LET 5] 7x
<5466> Χαλδαῖος ***Chaldaios*** [CHALDEAN] 1x
<5467> χαλεπός ***chalepos*** [DIFFICULT 1, VIOLENT (adj.) 3] 2x
<5468> χαλιναγωγέω ***chalinagōgeō*** [BRIDLE (verb)] 2x
<5469> χαλινός ***chalinos*** [BIT] 2x
<5470> χάλκεος ***chalkeos*** [of brass: BRASS 2] 1x
<5471> χαλκεύς ***chalkeus*** [COPPERSMITH] 1x
<5472> χαλκηδών ***chalkēdōn*** [CHALCEDONY] 1x
<5473> χαλκίον ***chalkion*** [BRAZEN VESSEL] 1x
<5474> χαλκολίβανον ***chalkolibanon*** [fine brass: BRASS 3] 2x
<5475> χαλκός ***chalkos*** [BRASS 1, MONEY 3] 5x
<5476> χαμαί ***chamai*** [on the ground, to the ground: GROUND (noun)[1] 4] 2x
<5477> Χανάαν ***Chanaan*** [CANAAN] 2x
<5478> Χαναναῖος ***Chananaios*** [CANAANITE 1] 1x
<5479> χαρά ***chara*** [JOY (noun) 3] 57x
<5480> χάραγμα ***charagma*** [graven form: FORM (noun) 5, MARK (noun) 4] 9x
<5481> χαρακτήρ ***charaktēr*** [EXPRESSION] 1x
<5482> χάραξ ***charax*** [EMBANKMENT] 1x
<5483> χαρίζομαι ***charizomai*** [DELIVER 6, FORGIVE 3, to freely give, to graciously give, to give: GIVE 18, GRANT 2] 23x
<5484> χάριν ***charin*** [on account of what: ACCOUNT (noun) 4] 9x
<5485> χάρις ***charis*** [grace: ACCEPTABLE 5, CREDIT (noun) 1, FAVOR (noun) 1, GIFT 7, GRACE 1, JOY (noun) 4, to give grace: THANKFUL 2] 156x
<5486> χάρισμα ***charisma*** [gift, free gift, spiritual gift: GIFT 8] 17x
<5487> χαριτόω ***charitoō*** [to make accepted: ACCEPTED 2, FAVOR (verb)] 2x
<5488> Χαρράν ***Charran*** [HARRAN] 2x
<5489> χάρτης ***chartēs*** [PAPER] 1x
<5490> χάσμα ***chasma*** [CHASM] 1x
<5491> χεῖλος ***cheilos*** [LIP, SHORE 2] 7x
<5492> χειμάζω ***cheimazō*** [to be tossed with a tempest: TEMPEST 1] 1x
<5493> χείμαρρος ***cheimarros*** [TORRENT 1] 1x
<5494> χειμών ***cheimōn*** [STORM 4, WINTER (noun) 1] 6x
<5495> χείρ ***cheir*** [HAND (noun) 1, LAYING ON OF HANDS] 177x
<5496> χειραγωγέω ***cheiragōgeō*** [to lead by the hand: LEAD (verb) 14] 2x
<5497> χειραγωγός ***cheiragōgos*** [someone who leads by the hand: LEAD (verb) 15] 1x
<5498> χειρόγραφον ***cheirographon*** [HANDWRITING] 1x

<5499> χειροποίητος ***cheiropoiētos*** [made with, made by, built by hands: HAND (noun) 2] 6x
<5500> χειροτονέω ***cheirotoneō*** [ORDAIN 5] 2x
<5501> χείρων ***cheirōn*** [severer: SEVERE 2, WORSE 2, to the worse: WORSE 3] 11x
<5502> χερουβίμ ***cheroubim*** [CHERUBIM] 1x
<5503> χήρα ***chēra*** [WIDOW] 27x
<5504> χθές, ἐχθές ***chthes, echtes*** [YESTERDAY] 3x
<5505> χιλιάς ***chilias*** [FIVE THOUSAND 2, HUNDRED AND FORTY-FOUR THOUSAND, SEVEN THOUSAND 2, TEN THOUSAND 1, THOUSAND 1, TWELVE THOUSAND, TWENTY THOUSAND, TWENTY THREE THOUSAND] 23x
<5506> χιλίαρχος ***chiliarchos*** [captain, chief captain, high captain, chiliarch, commander, military commander, high officer: CAPTAIN 3] 21x
<5507> χίλιοι ***chilioi*** [THOUSAND 2, THOUSAND SIX HUNDRED, THOUSAND TWO HUNDRED AND SIXTY] 10x
<5508> Χίος ***Chios*** [CHIOS] 1x
<5509> χιτών ***chitōn*** [CLOTHES 6, TUNIC] 11x
<5510> χιών ***chiōn*** [SNOW] 3x
<5511> χλαμύς ***chlamus*** [ROBE (noun) 2] 2x
<5512> χλευάζω ***chleuazō*** [MOCK 4] 2x
<5513> χλιαρός ***chliaros*** [LUKEWARM] 1x
<5514> Χλόη ***Chloē*** [CHLOE] 1x
<5515> χλωρός ***chlōros*** [GREEN 2, PALE] 4x
<5516> χ ξ ς ***chi xi stigma*** [SIX HUNDRED AND SIXTY SIX 2] 1x
<5517> χοϊκός ***choikos*** [EARTHY] 4x
<5518> χοῖνιξ ***choinix*** [QUART] 2x
<5519> χοῖρος ***choiros*** [SWINE] 14x
<5520> χολάω ***cholaō*** [to be angry: ANGRY 6] 1x
<5521> χολή ***cholē*** [GALL] 2x
<5522> χοῦς ***chous*** [DUST 2] 2x
<5523> Χοραζίν ***Chorazin*** [CHORAZIN] 2x
<5524> χορηγέω ***chorēgeō*** [SUPPLY (verb) 6] 2x
<5525> χορός ***choros*** [DANCING] 1x
<5526> χορτάζω ***chortazō*** [FILL (verb) 10, to fill one's stomach: STOMACH 3] 16x
<5527> χόρτασμα ***chortasma*** [SUSTENANCE 1] 1x
<5528> χόρτος ***chortos*** [BLADE, GRASS, HAY] 15x
<5529> Χουζᾶς ***Chouzas*** [CHUZA] 1x
<5530> χράομαι ***chraomai*** [TREAT 2, USE (verb) 5] 11x
<5531> χράω ***chraō*** [LEND 2] 1x
<5532> χρεία ***chreia*** [BUSINESS 6, NECESSITY 2, NEED (noun) 1] 49x
<5533> χρεωφειλέτης ***chreōpheiletēs*** [DEBTOR 2] 2x
<5534> χρή ***chrē*** [OUGHT 4] 1x
<5535> χρῄζω ***chrēzō*** [to have need, to need: NEED (noun) 2] 5x
<5536> χρῆμα ***chrēma*** [MONEY 4, RICHES 2] 7x
<5537> χρηματίζω ***chrēmatizō*** [CALL (verb) 13, to utter the oracles: ORACLE 2, to be divinely warned (instructed), to be warned of (by, from) God, to be warned: WARN 5] 9x
<5538> χρηματισμός ***chrēmatismos*** [divine answer, answer of God: ANSWER (noun) 4] 1x
<5539> χρήσιμος ***chrēsimos*** [PROFITABLE 4] 1x
<5540> χρῆσις ***chrēsis*** [USE (noun) 1] 2x
<5541> χρηστεύομαι ***chrēsteuomai*** [to be kind: KIND (adj.) 1] 1x
<5542> χρηστολογία ***chrēstologia*** [smooth word, smooth talk: SMOOTH 2] 1x
<5543> χρηστόν ***chrēston*** [GOODNESS 2]
<5543> χρηστός ***chrēstos*** [BETTER 5, EASY 1, GOOD (adj.) 3] 7x
<5544> χρηστότης ***chrēstotēs*** [GENTLENESS 4, GOODNESS 3, KINDNESS 2] 10x
<5545> χρῖσμα ***chrisma*** [UNCTION] 3x
<5546> Χριστιανός ***Christianos*** [CHRISTIAN] 3x
<5547> Χριστός ***Christos*** [CHRIST] 541x

<5548> χρίω *chriō* [ANOINT 3] 5x
<5549> χρονίζω *chronizō* [DELAY (verb) 4] 5x
<5550> χρόνος *chronos* [DELAY (noun) 3, as long as: LONG (adj.) 6, TIME 4, long time: TIME 6, long time, great length of time: TIME 7, YEAR 10] 54x
<5551> χρονοτριβέω *chronotribeō* [to spend time: SPEND 8] 1x
<5552> χρυσέος *chruseos* [GOLDEN 1] 18x
<5553> χρυσίον *chrusion* [GOLD (noun) 2] 9x
<5554> χρυσοδακτύλιος *chrusodaktulios* [with a gold ring, with a golden ring: RING (noun) 2] 1x
<5555> χρυσόλιθος *chrusolithos* [CHRYSOLITE, CHRYSOLYTE] 1x
<5556> χρυσόπρασος *chrusoprasos* [CHRYSOPRASE, CHRYSOPRASUS] 1x
<5557> χρυσός *chrusos* [GOLD (noun) 1] 13x
<5558> χρυσόω *chrusoō* [to have ornaments: ORNAMENT 2] 2x
<5559> χρώς *chrōs* [BODY 3] 1x
<5560> χωλός *chōlos* [LAME 1] 14x
<5561> χώρα *chōra* [COUNTRY 4, FIELD 4, LAND (noun) 3] 28x
<5562> χωρέω *chōreō* [COME 41, CONTAIN 2, to go into: GO 35, HOLD (verb) 6, to have a place: PLACE (noun) 4, RECEIVE 19, to be room: ROOM 4] 9x
<5563> χωρίζω *chōrizō* [DEPART 15, LEAVE (verb) 10, SEPARATE 1] 13x
<5564> χωρίον *chōrion* [FIELD 5, FIELD OF BLOOD, parcel of ground, plot of ground: GROUND (noun)[1] 5, LAND (noun) 4, PLACE (noun) 3] 10x
<5565> χωρίς *chōris* [APART 1, BESIDES] 41x
<5566> χῶρος *chōros* [NORTHWEST] 1x

Ψ

<5567> ψάλλω *psallō* [SING 2] 5x
<5568> ψαλμός *psalmos* [PSALM 1] 7x
<5569> ψευδάδελφος *pseudadelphos* [false brother: FALSE 2] 2x
<5570> ψευδαπόστολος *pseudapostolos* [false apostle: FALSE 3] 1x
<5571> ψευδής *pseudēs* [FALSE 1, LIAR (adj. and noun) 1] 3x
<5572> ψευδοδιδάσκαλος *pseudodidaskalos* [false teacher: FALSE 4] 1x
<5573> ψευδολόγος *pseudologos* [one speaking lies, liar: LIE (noun) 2] 1x
<5574> ψεύδομαι *pseudomai* [LIE (verb)[2] 1] 12x
<5575> ψευδόμαρτυς *pseudomartus* [false witness: WITNESS (noun)[2] 2] 3x
<5576> ψευδομαρτυρέω *pseudomartureō* [to bear false witness, to give false witness: WITNESS (noun)[1] 6] 5x
<5577> ψευδομαρτυρία *pseudomarturia* [false testimony: TESTIMONY 1] 2x
<5578> ψευδοπροφήτης *pseudoprophētēs* [false prophet: FALSE 5] 11x
<5579> ψεῦδος *pseudos* [LIE (noun) 1] 9x
<5580> ψευδόχριστος *pseudochristos* [false Christ: FALSE 6] 2x
<5581> ψευδώνυμος *pseudōnumos* [FALSELY NAMED] 1x
<5582> ψεῦσμα *pseusma* [LIE (noun) 3] 1x
<5583> ψεύστης *pseustēs* [LIAR (noun) 1] 10x
<5584> ψηλαφάω *psēlaphaō* [to feel after: FEEL 1, TOUCH 5] 4x
<5585> ψηφίζω *psēphizō* [COUNT 4] 2x
<5586> ψῆφος *psēphos* [STONE (noun) 3, VOICE 3] 3x
<5587> ψιθυρισμός *psithurismos* [WHISPERING 1] 1x
<5588> ψιθυριστής *psithuristēs* [WHISPERER] 1x
<5589> ψιχίον *psichion* [CRUMB] 3x
<5590> ψυχή *psuchē* [LIFE 7, SOUL 1] 103x
<5591> ψυχικός *psuchikos* [natural, natural man: NATURAL 2, SENSUAL 1] 6x
<5592> ψῦχος *psuchos* [COLD 1] 3x
<5593> ψυχρός *psuchros* [COLD 2] 4x

<5594> ψύχω ***psuchō*** [to grow cold, to wax cold: COLD 3] 1x
<5595> ψωμίζω ***psōmizō*** [to feed, to bestow to feed, to give to feed, to give: FEED 3] 2x
<5596> ψωμίον ***psōmion*** [piece of bread, piece: PIECE 4] 4x
<5597> ψώχω ***psōchō*** [RUB] 1x

Ω

<5598> Ω ***Ō*** [OMEGA] 4x
<5599> ὦ ***ō*** [O!, OH!] 16x
<5600> ὦ ***ō*** [MAY, MIGHT, REST (verb) 5] 66x
<5601> Ὠβήδ ***Ōbēd*** [OBED] 3x
<5602> ὧδε ***hōde*** [HITHER] 60x
<5603> ᾠδή ***ōdē*** [SONG] 7x
<5604> ὠδίν ***ōdin*** [pain, labor pain: PAIN (noun) 2] 4x
<5605> ὠδίνω ***ōdinō*** [to be in labor, to have labor pains: LABOR (noun) 2, LABOR (verb) 2] 3x
<5606> ὦμος ***ōmos*** [SHOULDER] 2x
<5607> ὤν ***ōn*** [BEING] 154x
<5608> ὠνέομαι ***ōneomai*** [BUY 2] 1x
<5609> ᾠόν ***ōon*** [EGG] 1x
<5610> ὥρα ***hōra*** [HOUR 1, TIME 9] 106x
<5611> ὡραῖος ***hōraios*** [BEAUTIFUL 3] 4x
<5612> ὠρύομαι ***ōruomai*** [to roar: ROARING 2] 1x
<5613> ὡς ***hōs*** [ABOUT 3, LIKE (adj., adv., noun) 8, SO THAT 3] 504x
<5614> Ὡσαννά ***Hōsanna*** [HOSANNA] 6x
<5615> ὡσαύτως ***hōsautōs*** [LIKEWISE 3] 17x
<5616> ὡσεί ***hōsei*** [ABOUT 4] 34x
<5617> Ὡσηέ ***Hōsēe*** [HOSEA] 1x
<5618> ὥσπερ ***hōsper*** [WHOLLY AS] 42x
<5619> ὡσπερεί ***hōsperei*** [AS IT WERE] 1x
<5620> ὥστε ***hōste*** [SO THAT 4, THAT 2] 83x
<5620a> ὠτάρίον ***ōtarion*** [EAR 2] 2x
<5621> ὠτίον ***ōtion*** [EAR 2] 6x
<5622> ὠφέλεια ***ōpheleia*** [PROFIT (noun) 2] 2x
<5623> ὠφελέω ***ōpheleō*** [HELPED (BE), PREVAIL 3, PROFIT (verb) 2, to have value, to be of value: VALUE (noun) 3] 15x
<5624> ὠφέλιμος ***ōphelimos*** [PROFITABLE 1] 4x

Bibliography

Bailly, Anatole. *Dictionnaire Grec-Français.* Reprint, Paris (France): Hachette, 2000.

BibleGateway.com at http://www.biblegateway.com.

BibleStudyTools.com. *The New Testament Greek Lexicon* at http://www.searchgodsword.org/lex/grk.

Carrez, Maurice. *Nouveau Testament Interlinéaire Grec/Français.* Société biblique française, 1993.

Carrez, Maurice and François Morel. *Dictionnaire Grec-Français du Nouveau Testament.* Genève (Suisse) / Villiers-le-Bel (France): Labor et Fides / Société biblique française, 4ème édition revue et corrigée, 1998.

Cochrane, Jack. *Dictionnaire Grec-Français du Nouveau Testament.* Sherbrooke, Québec (Canada): Distributions évangéliques du Québec Inc., 2006.

Danker, Frederick William with Kathryn Krug. *The Concise Greek-English Lexicon of the New Testament.* Chicago and London: The University of Chicago Press, 2009.

Darby, John Nelson. *The "Holy Scriptures," a New Translation from the Original Languages.* Reprint, Kingston-on-Thames, Surrey (England): Stow Hill Bible and Tract Depot, 1970.

Easton, Matthew George. *Illustrated Bible Dictionary.* Nashville, Tennessee (U.S.A.): Thomas Nelson Publishers, 1897.

Éditions Bibles et Traités Chrétiens. *Concordance de la Bible.* Vevey (Suisse): Éditions Bibles et Traités Chrétiens, 1984.

Friberg, Barbara and Timothy Friberg, eds. *Analytical Greek New Testament.* Reprint, Grand Rapids, Michigan: Baker Book House, 1986.

Georgin, Ch. *Dictionnaire Grec-Français.* Paris (France): Librairie A. Hatier, 1959.

Green, Rev. Thomas Sheldon. *Greek-English Lexicon to the New Testament.* Reprint, London (Great Britain): Samuel Bagster and Sons Limited, 1972.

Green, Sr., Jay P. *The Interlinear Greek-English New Testament (Volume IV of The Interlinear Hebrew-Greek-English Bible).* Reprint, Lafayette, Indiana (U.S.A.): Sovereign Grace Publishers, 2000.

Hitchcock, Roswell D. and A. J. Johnson. *Hitchcock's Bible Names Dictionary* (1869) at BibleStudyTools.com.

Holy Bible — New American Standard. Nashville, Tennessee (U.S.A.): Holman Bible Publishers, 1977.

Ingelaere, Jean-Claude, Pierre Maraval, and Pierre Prigent. *Dictionnaire Grec-Français du Nouveau Testament.* Société biblique française, Alliance biblique universelle, 2000.

Liddell, Henry George and Robert Scott. *A Greek-English Lexicon.* Reprint, New York: Harper and Brothers, 1859.

Mounce, William D. (General Editor), D. Matthew Smith (Associate Editor), and Miles V. Van Pelt (Associate Editor). *Mounce's Complete Expository Dictionary of Old and New Testament Words.* Grand Rapids, Michigan (U.S.A.): Zondervan, 2006.

Nestle, Eberhard and Alfred Marshall. *The Interlinear Greek-English New Testament.* Reprint, Grand Rapids, Michigan (U.S.A.): Zondervan Publishing House, 1982.

Nestle-Aland. *Novum Testamentum Graece.* Stuttgart (Germany): Deutsche Bibelgesellschaft, Gesamtherstellung Biblia-Druck, 1898 and 1993.

Newberry, Thomas. *The Englishman's Greek New Testament (with an Interlinear Literal Translation).* Reprint, Grand Rapids, Michigan (U.S.A.): Zondervan Publishing House, 1974.

Newberry, Thomas. *The Newberry Reference Bible.* Reprint, Grand Rapids, Michigan (U.S.A.): Kregel Publications, 1973.

Pigeon, E. Richard. *Dictionnaire du Nouveau Testament.* Valence (France): Bibles et Publications Chrétiennes, 2008.

________. *Petit Dictionnaire du Nouveau Testament.* Gatineau, Québec (Canada): Le Messager Chrétien, 1994.

Rienecker, Fritz. *Linguistic Key to the Greek New Testament.* Edited by Cleon L. Rogers, Jr. Grand Rapids, Michigan (U.S.A.): The Zondervan Corporation, 1980.

Scofield, Cyrus I. *The Scofield Reference Bible.* Copyright renewed, New York, New York (U.S.A.): Oxford University Press, 1945.

Scott, Walter. *Handbook of the New Testament.* Reprint, Charlotte, North Carolina (U.S.A.): Books for Christians, 1977.

Smith, William. *Smith's Bible Dictionary, from A Dictionary of the Bible.* Boston, Massachusetts (U.S.A.): Little, Brown and Company, 1884.

Strong, James. *Strong's Exhaustive Concordance.* Nashville, Tennessee (U.S.A.): Crusade Bible Publishers, Inc.

Thayer, Joseph H. *Thayer's Greek-English Lexicon of the New Testament.* Reprint, Peabody, Massachusetts (U.S.A.): Hendrickson Publishers, 2007.

The Holy Bible — English Standard Version. Wheaton, Illinois (U.S.A.): Crossway, 2002.

The Holy Bible — King James Version. Toronto, Ontario (Canada): Canadian Bible Society, 1981.

The Holy Bible — New International Version. Grand Rapids, Michigan (U.S.A.): Zondervan, 1984, 2011.

The Holy Bible — New King James Version. Nashville, Tennessee (U.S.A.): Thomas Nelson Bibles, 1982.

Trench, Richard C. and Paul Kegan. *Synonyms of the New Testament.* London (Great Britain): Trench, Trübner & Co. Ltd., 1915.

Vine, W. E. *Vine's Expository Dictionary of New Testament Words.* McLean, Virginia (U.S.A.): MacDonald Publishing Company.

Wigram, George V. *The Englishman's Greek Concordance.* Reprint, Grand Rapids, Michigan (U.S.A.): Baker Book House, 1985.

Willis, G. Christopher. *A Few Hid Treasures Found in the Greek New Testament.* Reprint, Kowloon, Hong Kong: Christian Book Room, 1976.

Young, Robert. *Young's Literal Translation.* Grand Rapids Michigan (U.S.A.): scanned from a reprint of the 1898 edition as published by Baker Book House.

Zodhiates, Spiros (Executive Editor), Warren Baker (Managing Editor), Rev. George Hadjiantoniou (Associate Editor), and Mark Oshman (Associate Editor). *The Complete Word Study New Testament.* Chattanooga, Tennessee (U.S.A.): AMG Publishers, 1991.

Zodhiates, Spiros (General Editor), Warren Baker (Managing Editor), and Rev. George Hadjiantoniou (Associate Editor). *The Complete Word Study Dictionary: New Testament.* Chattanooga, Tennessee (U.S.A.): AMG Publishers, 1993.

About the Author

Richard Pigeon has been active for more than 35 years in the life of his local church in Gatineau, Quebec, teaching the Word of God. Richard and his wife, Géraldine, have hosted young people meetings in their home and participated in home Bible studies. He has written articles for Christian magazines and is the co-founder of *L'Étoile du Matin*, which he coedited for many years. He has also participated to Christian conferences, and made presentations in Canada and abroad.

Richard and his wife have been married since 1972; they have three married sons and seven grandchildren. Richard has a Ph.D. in Education from the University of Ottawa. He has spent his professional career in the fields of teaching and adult learning and development.

As a tentmaker, he has authored a dictionary in French of about one thousand New Testament words (also translated in Spanish) and commentaries in French on the epistles to the Thessalonians (also translated in Italian). He is the author of the comprehensive *Dictionnaire du Nouveau Testament* published in France by Éditions Bibles et Publications Chrétiennes in 2008. During the last six years, this work was translated and adapted into English, becoming *AMG's Comprehensive Dictionary of New Testament Words.*

Israel in the Time of Jesus
Extent of Herod's kingdom
Herodian fortress city
Decapolis city (time of Herod)
Other city
ABILENE
Abila
ITUREA
Abana R.
Sidon
Damascus
SYRIA
Mt. Hermon
Pharpar R.
Leontes R.
Tyre
PHOENICIA
Caesarea-Philippi
GAULANITIS
TRACHONITIS
Raphana
L. Hula
J. Jarmuk
Hazor
GALILEE
TETRARCHY OF PHILIP
Ptolemais (Acco)
Chorazin
Capernaum
Bethsaida
Gennesaret
Gergesa
Mt. Carmel
Sea of Galilee
Magdala
Cana
Kishon R.
Tiberias
Hippos
BATANEA
Mediterranean Sea
Yarmuk R.
AURANITIS
Nazareth
Mt. Tabor
Abila
Gadara
Nain
Dor
Bethany beyond Jordan
Megiddo
Caesarea (Strato's Tower)
Scythopolis
Pella
Dion
SAMARIA
DECAPOLIS
Salim?
Sebaste (Samaria)
Gerasa
Jordan R.
Mt. Ebal
Amathus
Mt. Gerizim
Sychar
Jabbok R.
Me Jarkon
Antipatris (Aphek)
Alexandrium
Joppa
PEREA
Philadelphia (Amman)
(SEMI-INDEPENDENT MUNICIPALITY)
Jamnia
Jericho
Cyprus
Esbus (Heshbon)
Azotus (Ashdod)
Emmaus
Mt. Olivet
Jerusalem
Bethany
Medeba
Hyrcania
Bethlehem
Ashkelon
JUDEA
Herodium
Machaerus
Hebron
Adora
Gaza
Dead Sea
Arnon R.
Masada
IDUMEA
Arad
Besor Br.
Beersheba
Malatha
NABATEA
0 10 20 30 miles
0 10 20 30 kilometers
Zered Br.
© GeoNova Publishing, Inc.